SEVENTH EDITION

# THE KOVELS'
# COMPLETE
# ANTIQUES PRICE LIST

**BOOKS BY RALPH AND TERRY KOVEL**

The Complete Antiques Price List

Know Your Antiques

American Country Furniture 1780–1875

Dictionary of Marks — Pottery and Porcelain

The Official Bottle Price List

SEVENTH EDITION

# THE KOVELS'
# COMPLETE
# ANTIQUES PRICE LIST

A guide to the 1974-1975 market
for professionals, dealers, and collectors

**by Ralph and Terry Kovel**
*ILLUSTRATED*

Crown Publishers, Inc., New York

# INTRODUCTION

The stock market may have hit new lows for the year, but antique prices have continued to rise in the United States. The inflationary pressures on the dollar, plus the eagerness of foreign buyers, have sent the prices of modern art and jewels to all-time highs. These same pressures have affected the eighteenth- and nineteenth-century-antiques market. English and continental silver of the seventeenth, eighteenth, and nineteenth centuries has risen faster than any other category. Only part of this rise is because of the rising cost of raw silver. Museum-quality American furniture has also advanced, setting several new records for high prices. Cut glass of the American brilliant period (1880) has renewed interest, and prices continue to rise. Bicentennial items have already started their predictable price rise. This will probably continue through 1976.

The nostalgia craze is continuing, and the everyday items that would have been ignored a few years ago are now bringing good money. Any memorabilia from the Beatles, Walt Disney, or celebrity items such as Shirley Temple, Hopalong Cassidy, and the Lone Ranger have renewed interest. Toys from the 1940s, especially the celluloid toys from Japan, are now selling well. Nineteenth-century toys and mechanical banks still continue to rise in price.

The prints from the 1920s have continued to interest new collectors. Louis Icart, Wallace Nutting, and Maxfield Parrish pictures are part of the new demand. Prices of early prints such as Currier and Ives, Kellogg, Prang, and Kurz and Allison are rising. Rare bottles, unusual lithographed containers, and exceptional advertising items have gained in price. Even rare postcards have seen some movement.

The newest and most active collector's area seems to be in

the late glass of the United States. Fenton, Cambridge, Heisey, McKee, Fostoria, Pairpoint, Handel, and other factories are being seriously collected and their prices reflect the growing interest. Depression glass collecting is becoming more organized as more information becomes available.

# GUIDE TO USE

There are just a few simple rules to follow in using this book. Each listing is arranged in the following manner: CATEGORY (such as pressed glass, silver, or furniture); OBJECT (such as vase, spoon, table); DESCRIPTION (which includes as much information as possible about size, age, color, and pattern). All items are presumed perfect unless otherwise noted. Leaf through the book and examine the various category headings. Most of them are exactly as one would expect.

Several special categories were formed to make a more sensible listing of items possible. "Fire" includes andirons, fire-fighting equipment, fireplace equipment, and related pieces. "Household," "kitchen," and "tool" include the various special equipment. It seems impossible to expect the casual collector to know the proper name for each variety of tool, such as an "adze" or a "trephine," so we have lumped them in the special categories.

This book has several idiosyncrasies of style that must be noted before it can be used properly. The prices are compiled by computer, and the machine has dictated several strange rules. Everything in the book is listed alphabetically according to the IBM alphabetic system. This means that words such as "dr." are alphabetized as "D-R," not as "D-O-C-T-O-R." Another peculiarity of the machine alphabetizing is that all numerals come after all letters, thus 2 comes after z. A quick glance at a listing will make this clear, as the alphabetizing is consistent throughout the book.

We have made several editorial decisions that affect the use of the book. A bowl is a bowl and not a dish unless it is a special type of dish such as a saucedish. A butter dish is a "butter" and a celery dish a "celery." A salt dish is called a "salt" to differentiate it from a saltshaker. A toothpick holder is called a "toothpick." It is always a "sugar and creamer," never a "creamer and sugar."

There are many new categories again this year. The most important of these are Moriaga, McKee, Walt Disney, Beatles, Hampshire pottery, and Dorchester pottery. The list of Hummel figures is much more complete. More marks have been added and more paragraph headings are included to help identify the antiques.

Several categories such as "milk glass" and "bottles" include special reference numbers. These numbers refer the reader to the most widely known books about the category. When these numbers appear, the name of the special book is given in the paragraph heading. All of these numbers take the form "B-22, C-103," and so forth. The letter is the author's initial; the number refers to a picture in the author's book.

All black and white pictures in KOVELS' COMPLETE ANTIQUES PRICE LIST are of antiques sold during the past year. The prices are as reported by the seller. Each piece pictured is listed with the word *illus.* as part of the description. Pictures are placed as close to the price listing as is possible. Color pictures are all from the Shelburne Museum collection, and no prices are given for these antiques.

All prices listed in this book were recorded from antique shows, sales, flea markets, and auctions between June 1973 and June 1974. The prices have been taken from sales in all parts of the country, and variations are sometimes due to the geographic differences in pricing. Antiques of top quality tend to be most expensive near the town where they originated because the local collectors are informed about them. Bottles and advertising items seem higher priced in the West. We have tried to be accurate in all of the prices reported, but we cannot be responsible for any errors that may have occurred. We welcome any suggestions for future editions of this book, but cannot answer letters asking for advice or appraisals.

## AN IMPORTANT ANNOUNCEMENT TO COLLECTORS AND DEALERS

Each year, THE KOVELS' COMPLETE ANTIQUES PRICE LIST is completely rewritten. Every entry and every picture is new because of the rapidly changing antiques market. The only way so complete a revision can be accomplished is by using a computer, making it possible to publish the bound book two months after the last price is received.

Yet many price changes occur between editions of THE KOVELS' COMPLETE ANTIQUES PRICE LIST. Important sales produce new record prices each day. Inflation, the changing price of silver and gold, and the international demand for some types of antiques influence sales in the United States.

The curious collector will want to keep up with developments from month to month rather than from year to year. Therefore, we call your attention to a new service to provide price information almost instantaneously: "Ralph and Terry Kovel on Antiques" a nationally distributed illustrated newsletter, published monthly.

This new monthly newsletter covers prices, special interest antiques, what to buy now, how to save and make money on antiques, forums and classes to attend, refinishing and first aid for your possessions, marks, decorating and displaying antiques, book reviews and other pertinent antique news.

Additional information about the newsletter and a complimentary copy are available from the authors at P.O. Box 957, Des Moines, Iowa 50304.

# PICTURE ACKNOWLEDGMENTS

A. B. Kane Antiques

Elaine Cameron

Carriage House Antiques

Coachman Antiques

Covered Bridge Antiques

Stan Ekenas

Forster Antiques

Gerald Grady

Grandma's Drawers

Jeannie's Antiques

Lewallen Antiques

Maple Valley Antiques

Mary Jane's Dolls

Sandra Osborn

Rural Retreat Antiques

Jean Stephens

Whetstones Antiques

# COLOR PICTURES

All of the color pictures that we have used in this book depict items from the collection of the Shelburne Museum, Shelburne, Vermont. Thirty-five buildings located on forty-five acres of green Vermont land house the Shelburne collections. The museum was founded in 1947 by Electra Havemeyer Webb and her husband J. Watson Webb. The family is still interested in helping the museum grow and flourish. The special interest of the founders can be seen in Mrs. Webb's doll collection, the carriage collection of Mr. Webb's father and mother, and the memorial building that houses part of the contents of the Webb apartment in New York City.

Collectors will find special interest exhibits that will delight different members of the family. The tool collection is extensive, well displayed, and labeled. The carriage collection includes fire equipment, wagons, sleighs, coaches, and many other types of vehicles. Dolls, toys, bandboxes, wallpaper, quilts, coverlets, rugs, folk art, carvings, and decoys are shown in fine collections. Never to be overlooked is the spectacular *Ticonderoga*, a side-wheel steamer. There are a covered bridge, period houses, stores, and offices. The crafts are "working," and you can see blacksmithing, weaving, a working sawmill, and even a live bee exhibit.

The Shelburne Museum is an ongoing collection. The buildings and items date from the seventeenth century to the twentieth century. It is not from a restricted period of past time but rather a collection of many types of art, antiques, tools, and architecture that interested the Webb family.

Take your family to the Shelburne Museum and find something of interest for all ages. It requires at least two days for even a partial look at the exhibits, longer if you wish to study a special interest collection.

The cover picture is a view of the dining room of the Prentis House, built in 1733 in Hadley, Massachusetts. It is the oldest building at the Shelburne Museum. The dining room is furnished with period pieces, including the pilgrim oak and pine court cupboard, bannister back chairs, and a collection of English delft.

Our special thanks to Mr. Sterling Emerson, museum director, for his help, time, and information about the museum. Another thank-you to Nancy Muller and the Shelburne Museum staff.

# DEDICATION

*Students of antiques know that to use a book wisely you must read the introductory material.*

*If you read this page, you are a true scholar, and we dedicate this book to you.*

*Also to Lee & Kim.*

SEVENTH EDITION

# THE KOVELS'
# COMPLETE
# ANTIQUES PRICE LIST

*ABC plates, or children's alphabet plates, were popular from 1780 to 1860. The letters on the plate were meant as teaching aids for the children who were learning to read. The plates were made of pottery, porcelain, metal, or glass.*

| | |
|---|---|
| ABC, Bowl, Little Bopeep, Straight Sided | 30.00 |
| ABC, Bowl, Pekingese Dog Looking In Mirror On Cream, Crown Potterie | 25.00 |
| ABC, Creamer, Blue Letters & Alternating Animals On White, German | 10.00 |
| ABC, Cup & Saucer, Rooster & Hens, Full Alphabet In Relief, German | 24.00 |
| ABC, Cup, Illustrating K & L, Black Transfer With Overglaze, 2 1/2 In.High | 30.00 |
| ABC, Fork, Alphabet On Back, Girl On Front | 3.00 |
| ABC, Mug, Alphabet Impressed Between 2 Christmas Scenes, Glass, Bark Handle | 32.50 |
| ABC, Plate, Alphabet & Numbers 0-9, Silver Plate, 8 In. | 22.00 |
| ABC, Plate, Alphabet Border, Jack & Jill Scene, 8 In. | 15.00 |
| ABC, Plate, Boys Sitting On Elephant, Barnum & Co. On Blanket, 6 In. | 46.00 |
| ABC, Plate, Cat's Head Center, W.Adams | 28.50 |
| ABC, Plate, Child's, Baseball Transfer Scene, Staffordshire, C.1870 | 34.00 |
| ABC, Plate, Christmas Scene, 4 Children, Snowman, Tree, & Flowers | 17.50 |
| ABC, Plate, Clockface Center, Clear Pressed Glass | 24.00 |
| ABC, Plate, Clockface Center, Months & Days Border, Clear Pressed Glass | 38.00 |
| ABC, Plate, Dog & Tree Center | 32.00 |
| ABC, Plate, Dog Center, Glass, 6 1/4 In. | 25.00 |
| ABC, Plate, Elephant & Howdah, Clear Glass, 6 In. | 35.00 |
| ABC, Plate, Elephant, Flag | 32.00 |
| ABC, Plate, Emma, Amber | 25.00 |
| ABC, Plate, Emma, Blue Pressed Glass, 6 1/4 In. | 45.00 |
| ABC, Plate, Feeding, Child's, Aluminum, 7 1/2 In. | 15.00 |
| ABC, Plate, Franklin Proverb, Black Transfer, Meakin, 6 In. | 40.00 |
| ABC, Plate, Garfield, Frosted Center, Clear Pressed Glass, 6 In. | 45.00 |
| ABC, Plate, Glass, Sunflower Center, Beaded Rim, Bryce-Higbee, 1800s, 6 In. | 25.00 |
| ABC, Plate, Helping Little Brother, Raised Border | 21.00 |
| ABC, Plate, Hey Diddle Diddle, Clear | 26.00 |
| ABC, Plate, Hunting Scene, Embossed Alphabet, Staffordshire | 22.50 |
| ABC, Plate, Maxim, "Handle Your Tools, Etc.," C.1790, 5 In. | 44.50 |
| ABC, Plate, N.Currier Lithographer, Black & White, Piecrust Edge, Adams | 26.00 |
| ABC, Plate, Our Baby In Script, German, Porcelain | 19.00 |
| ABC, Plate, Pewter, Reed & Barton, 7 In. | 30.00 |
| ABC, Plate, Pink Transfer Print On White | 22.00 |
| ABC, Plate, President Garfield, Brown Transfer, Raised Letters, 7 1/2 In. | 70.00 |
| ABC, Plate, Pressed Glass, Barley, Star Center | 20.00 |
| ABC, Plate, Pretty Poll Hold Down Your Head & You'll Get, Etc., 6 In. | 24.00 |
| ABC, Plate, Running Rabbit | 35.00 |
| ABC, Plate, Scalloped, 6 In. | 19.50 |
| ABC, Plate, Silver Over Tin, 7 3/4 In. | 22.50 |
| ABC, Plate, Stork Center, Marigold | 35.00 |
| ABC, Plate, Sunbonnet Boy & Girl With Doll Carriage, We Three | 32.50 |
| ABC, Plate, Transfer Printed, Baseball Players, C.1850, 7 1/8 In. | 90.00 |
| ABC, Plate, Two Children Flying Kites On Castle Grounds, Meakin, 6 In. | 20.00 |
| ABC, Plate, Two Kittens Dancing, Deaf Hand Signals | 26.50 |
| ABC, Plate, Who Killed Cock Robin, Tin | 28.00 |

*Adams china was made by William Adams and Sons of Staffordshire, England. The firm was founded in 1769 and is still working.*

| | |
|---|---|
| Adams, Bowl, Flow Blue, Fairy Villas, Gold, 8 3/4 In. | 8.00 |
| Adams, Bowl, Soup, Caledonia, Red, 10 3/4 In. | 35.00 |
| Adams, Bowl, Vegetable, Caledonia, Black Transfer, 11 X 9 In. | 45.00 |
| Adams, Bowl, Vegetable, Caledonia, Purple, 10 In. | 38.00 |
| Adams, Cachepot, Signed J.C.M., Tunstall, England, 5 1/4 X 5 1/2 In. | 60.00 |
| Adams, Cup & Saucer, Handleless, Flowers | 10.00 |
| Adams, Cup & Saucer, Handleless, Red Rose, Plain Rim | 60.00 |
| Adams, Cup & Saucer, Tonquin, Handleless | 38.50 |
| Adams, Cup, Handleless, Birdcage, Dark Blue | 20.00 |
| Adams, Eggcup, Hand-Painted Florals, Pair | 11.00 |
| Adams, Jar, Cookie, Jasperware, White Classical Figures On Blue, C.1896 | 95.00 |
| Adams, Jar, Marmalade, Jasperware, Blue & White, C.1900, 4 1/2 In.High | 46.00 |
| Adams, Pitcher, Applied U.S.Seal On Dark Blue, Wedgwood Imitation | 49.00 |
| Adams, Pitcher, Blue & White, 11 In.High | 85.00 |

| | |
|---|---|
| Adams, Pitcher, White, Ironstone, 6 Sided, Ribbed, 1 Cup Size | 5.00 |
| Adams, Pitcher, White, Ironstone, 6 Sided, Ribbed, 1 3/4 Cup Size | 6.00 |
| Adams, Pitcher, White, Ironstone, 6 Sided, Ribbed, 6 1/2 Cup Size | 12.00 |
| Adams, Plate, Adams Pattern, 9 1/4 In. | 40.00 |
| Adams, Plate, Andalusia, Deep Pink, 10 In. | 24.00 |
| Adams, Plate, Andalusia, Rose Pink, 8 In. | 26.50 |
| Adams, Plate, Caledonia, Purple, 9 1/4 In. | 35.00 |
| Adams, Plate, Christmas Eve At Mr.Wardles, 9 3/4 In. | 37.50 |
| Adams, Plate, Columbia, Blue, Staffordshire, 7 3/4 In. | 13.00 |
| Adams, Plate, Columbia, Blue, Staffordshire, 8 1/2 In. | 15.00 |
| Adams, Plate, Columbus, Sepia, 10 3/4 In. | 35.00 |
| Adams, Plate, Dessert, Chinese Bird, England, 6 In. | 3.00 |
| Adams, Plate, Dr.Syntax Stopped By Highwaymen, Silver Luster Border, 8 In. | 30.00 |
| Adams, Plate, Jeddo, Black & White, 9 1/4 In. | 14.50 |
| Adams, Plate, Jeddo, Sepia, 9 1/2 In. | 16.00 |
| Adams, Plate, Lorraine, Brown & White, 7 3/4 In. | 5.00 |
| Adams, Plate, Monte Video, Conn., Pink, 6 3/4 In. | 21.00 |
| Adams, Plate, Mormon Temple, Blue, 10 In. | 14.75 |
| Adams, Plate, Mr.Micawber Delivers Some Valedictory Remarks, 9 3/4 In. | 37.50 |
| Adams, Plate, Near Conway, New Hampshire, Deep Pink, 9 In. | 58.00 |
| Adams, Plate, Palestine, Deep Pink, 8 1/2 In. | 25.00 |
| Adams, Plate, Palestine, Pink, 9 1/2 In. | 22.00 |
| Adams, Plate, Palestine, Violet Color, 9 In. | 20.00 |
| Adams, Plate, Rural Scene, Blue, Flower Border, 10 In. | 25.00 |
| Adams, Plate, Shannondale Springs, Va., Pink, 8 In. | 40.00 |
| Adams, Plate, Soup, English Rural Scene, Dark Blue, 8 7/8 In. | 45.00 |
| Adams, Plate, Soup, Palestine, Pink | 26.00 |
| Adams, Plate, The House Of The Seven Gables, 6 In. | 3.75 |
| Adams, Plate, View From Conway, N.H., Pink, 9 1/4 In. | 58.00 |
| Adams, Plate, View Near Conway, New Hampshire, Pink, 9 In. | 42.00 |
| Adams, Plate, Yankee Doodle, Spirit Of '76, Floral Swag Rim, 10 1/4 In. | 15.00 |
| Adams, Platter, Currier & Ives, The Old Farm House, Transfer, 14 In. | 20.00 |
| Adams, Platter, Jedburgh Abbey, Roxburghshire, Deep Blue, 17 In. | 145.00 |
| Adams, Platter, Jeddo, Ironstone, 18 X 14 In. | 40.00 |
| Adams, Sauceboat, Country Estate Scene, Blue, 7 1/4 In. | 45.00 |
| Adams, Sugar & Creamer, Cries Of London, Tunstall, England | 22.00 |
| Adams, Tankard, Jasperware, Blue, Canadian Coat Of Arms, Oak Leaf, 5 1/4 In. | 42.50 |
| Adams, Vase, White Classic Cameo On Dark Blue Ground, 6 In. | 42.50 |

*Agata glass was made by Joseph Locke of the New England Glass Company of Cambridge, Massachusetts, after 1885. A metallic stain was applied to New England Peachblow and the mottled design characteristic of agata appeared.*

| | |
|---|---|
| Agata, Bowl, Ruffled Top, Acid Spots, 5 1/2 In. | 300.00 |
| Agata, Toothpick | 425.00 |
| Agata, Tumbler, Acid Spotting, 3 3/4 In., Pair | 745.00 |
| Agata, Tumbler, Gold Tracery, Blue Black Oil Spots | 650.00 |
| Agata, Vase, Lily, Mottled, 8 In. | 750.00 To 900.00 |
| Agate, Coffeepot, Tan & White, Copper Bottom, Tin Lid, Black Wood Handle | 15.00 |
| Agate, Creamer, Japanese Signature, Glazed Inside Only, 3 In. | 15.00 |
| Agate, Snuffbox, Hinged, Brass Bound, Wood Grain Finish, 2 1/4 X 1 1/2 In. | 40.00 |
| Agate, Toothpick, Square Top | 425.00 |
| Agate, Vase, Gold, Cabachon Sapphires, Cartier, 2 1/8 In. | *Illus* 600.00 |
| Agateware, Figurine, Cat, C.1740, 4 3/4 In.High | *Illus* 400.00 |

*AKRO AGATES*

*Akro agate glass was made in Clarksburg, West Virginia, from 1932 to 1951. Before that time the firm made children's glass marbles. Most of the glass is marked with a crow flying through the letter A.*

| | |
|---|---|
| Akro Agate, Ashtray, Shell, Blue Green Marbleized, 3 3/4 In. | 3.00 |
| Akro Agate, Ashtray, Shell, Green, White, & Orange Marbleized, 3 3/4 In. | 3.00 |
| Akro Agate, Ashtray, Shell, Orange & White Marbleized, 3 3/4 In. | 3.00 |
| Akro Agate, Ashtray, Shell, Orange Slag | 3.50 |
| Akro Agate, Dishes, Child's, Green, 7 Piece | 18.00 |
| Akro Agate, Dishes, Child's, Open Handles, Pastel Colors, 11 Piece | 15.00 |
| Akro Agate, Flowerpot, Orange Marbleized, 2 1/4 In.High | 3.00 |

| | |
|---|---|
| Akro Agate, Flowerpot, Pink Marbleized, 2 1/4 In.High | 3.00 |
| Akro Agate, Flowerpot, Raised Design, Yellow, 3 In. | 8.00 |
| Akro Agate, Jar, Powder, Blue, Scottie Standing On Cover, Marked A In Crow | 27.50 |
| Akro Agate, Jar, Powder, Colonial Lady | 34.00 |
| Akro Agate, Jar, Powder, Covered, Orange Slag, Mexicali | 18.00 |
| Akro Agate, Match Holder, Cornucopia Shape, Green Marbleized | 8.00 |
| Akro Agate, Planter, Green | 6.00 |
| Akro Agate, Planter, Oblong, Green & White | 6.00 |
| Akro Agate, Planter, Raised Floral, Green & White, 5 1/2 X 3 X 2 In. | 12.00 |
| Akro Agate, Planter, Raised Floral, Orange & White, 5 1/2 X 3 X 2 In. | 12.00 |
| Akro Agate, Shade, Lamp, Green, 3 In.Square | 11.00 |
| Akro Agate, Teaset, Childrens, 7 Piece | 14.00 |
| Akro Agate, Vase, White, Lily Design, 4 1/2 In.High | 10.00 |
| Alabaster, Box, Cigar, Hinged, 4 1/2 In.High | 12.00 |
| Alabaster, Box, Powder, Pink, Round | 5.50 |
| Alabaster, Box, Powder, Yellow & Pink, Square | 5.50 |
| Alabaster, Urn, Satyrs & Bacchantes, C.1825, 13 1/8 In.High, Pair | 250.00 |
| Albertine, Jar, Cracker, Signed, Paper Label | 300.00 |
| Albertine, Jar, Cracker, Yellow Pansies Outlined In Gold & White, Silver | 395.00 |

*Albums were popular in Victorian times to hold the myriad pictures and
cutouts favored by the collectors. All sorts of scrapbooks and albums can
still be found.*

| | |
|---|---|
| Album, Classics Illustrated, Leather, 12 Classics From 1942 & 1953 | 38.00 |
| Album, North Wales Views, Leatherette, C.1850 | 4.00 |
| Album, Photograph, see Photography, Album | |
| Album, Picture, Leather, Brass Bound, Lincoln, Washington, Tom Thumb, Etc. | 25.00 |
| Album, Picture, Musical, 2 Tune, 12 X 12 X 3 In. | 65.00 |
| Album, Postcard, Greetings, Scenes, 1900s, 177 Cards | 20.00 |
| Album, Postcard, Inlaid Mother-Of-Pearl On Black Lacquer, Silver Border | 75.00 |
| Album, Postcard, Nebraska, Iowa, & Missouri, 1907-1915, 93 Cards | 20.00 |
| Album, Postcard, Patriotic Motif, C.1909 | 60.00 |
| Album, Postcard, Sussex County, 1900s | 3.00 |
| Album, Postcard, 1900s, 96 Cards | 8.00 |
| Album, World Cruise Of Empress Of Australia, 1927-28, 390 Pictures & Cards | 35.00 |

*Alexandrite glass was first made by Thomas Webb & Sons at the beginning
of the 20th century. It is a transparent glass shading from pale yellow to
rose to blue. Stevens & Williams later produced Alexandrite glassware by
plating a transparent yellow body with rose and blue glass.*

| | |
|---|---|
| Alexandrite, Bowl & Underplate, Finger, Blue Green Purple At Fluted Rims | 2250.00 |
| Alexandrite, Toothpick, Scalloped Top | 850.00 |
| Alexandrite, Vase, Bud, Blue To Fuchsia To Citron, 6 Petal Top, Paneled | 700.00 |
| Almanac, see Paper, Almanac | |

*Amber glass is the name of any glassware with the proper yellow-brown shade.
It was a popular color after the Civil War.*

| | |
|---|---|
| Amber Glass, Basket, Applied Amber Handle, 4 In. High | 12.50 |
| Amber Glass, Bottle, Applied Crimped Handle, Quart | 40.00 |

Agate, Vase, Gold,
Cabachon Sapphires,
Cartier, 2 1/8 In.
*(See Page 2)*

Agateware, Figurine,
Cat, C.1740,
4 3/4 In.High
*(See Page 2)*

| | |
|---|---|
| Amber Glass, Bowl, Oval, 2 Panel, Low Base, 7 X 5 1/2 In. | 33.50 |
| Amber Glass, Box, Enameled Flowers On Hinged Lid, 1 3/4 In. Diameter | 25.00 |
| Amber Glass, Box, Hinged, Enamel Vines On Lid, Signed, 2 1/4 In. Diameter | 25.00 |
| Amber Glass, Candlestick, Low, Pair | 9.00 |
| Amber Glass, Card Case, Satchel, Marked Sowerby, 1877 | 20.00 |
| Amber Glass, Compote, Finecut & 6 Floral Plaques, 8 1/2 In.Diameter | 17.00 |
| Amber Glass, Cruet, Applied Rope Handle, Sapphire Blue Stopper, Gold Floral | 110.00 |
| Amber Glass, Cruet, Blue Handle, Stopper & Flowers, Green Leaves, Iridescent | 45.00 |
| Amber Glass, Cruet, Bulbous, Inverted Thumbprint, Stopper | 150.00 |
| Amber Glass, Cruet, Clear Applied Handle, Cut Stopper, Cut Square Base | 75.00 |
| Amber Glass, Decanter, Cut To Clear, 18 In.High, Pair | 200.00 |
| Amber Glass, Decanter, Horn, Brass Base, Gold, Rust, & Green Berries & Vines | 97.50 |
| Amber Glass, Decanter, Ribbed Mushroom Blown Stopper, Ribbed Base, 12 In. | 58.00 |
| Amber Glass, Dish, Hen Cover, Nest Base, Head Turned, 2 1/2 In.Long | 15.00 |
| Amber Glass, Figurine, Hen, White Head, 5 In. | 76.50 |
| Amber Glass, Glass, Pilsner, Berry Prunts, Enamel Flowers, German Verse | 35.00 |
| Amber Glass, Goblet, Mary Gregory Type, Deer, Blue Base | 35.00 |
| Amber Glass, Hat, Cube | 20.00 |
| Amber Glass, Hat, Daisy & Button, Miniature | 17.00 |
| Amber Glass, Hat, Military | 38.00 |
| Amber Glass, Holder, Cigar, Sterling Overlay | 19.50 |
| Amber Glass, Holder, Curtain, Wall Screw, Design, 2 1/2 In. | 10.00 |
| Amber Glass, Humidor, Cigar, Mercantile, Patent Jan. 1895 | 17.50 |
| Amber Glass, Inkwell, Hinge Lid, Enamel | 42.50 |
| Amber Glass, Jar, Covered, Opalescent Stripe, 8 1/4 In.High | 35.00 |
| Amber Glass, Match Holder, Boot Shape | 32.00 |
| Amber Glass, Match Holder, Hanging, Boot, Striker | 16.50 |
| Amber Glass, Mug, Child's, Butterflies | 27.50 |
| Amber Glass, Pitcher, Inverted Thumbprint, Clear Reeded Handle, C.1880 | 55.00 |
| Amber Glass, Pitcher, Toby Shape, 8 In. | 30.00 |
| Amber Glass, Plaque, Lincoln Log | 125.00 |
| Amber Glass, Plate, Cake, Anniversary | 5.00 |
| Amber Glass, Plate, Cake, Engraved, 1/2 In.Gold Border, 8 In. | 3.98 |
| Amber Glass, Plate, Cake, 22K Gold Etched Border, Center Handle | 12.50 |
| Amber Glass, Plate, Salad, 22K Gold Etched Border, 8 In. | 2.65 |
| Amber Glass, Prism, U Drop, 3 1/4 In., Set Of 13 | 4.50 |
| Amber Glass, Salt & Pepper, Hobnail, Silver Plated Tops | 10.00 |
| Amber Glass, Salt, Octagonal, Angel Blowing Bubble In Relief, 2 1/2 In. | 15.00 |
| Amber Glass, Salt, Scalloped, Handled, Pedestal | 2.65 |
| Amber Glass, Salt, Wheelbarrow | 25.00 |
| Amber Glass, Shoe, Fiddle Shape Base, Bouquet Holder, Herman Tappan, 1886 | 37.50 |
| Amber Glass, Slipper, Cane Pattern | 17.50 |
| Amber Glass, Slipper, Cats' Heads Across Top, 5 3/4 In.Long | 15.00 |
| Amber Glass, Slipper, High Shoe, Marked Bouquet Holder | 24.00 |
| Amber Glass, Slipper, 5 In.Long | 10.00 |
| Amber Glass, Spittoon, Lady's, Spittoon Shape Pontil, 4 1/4 In.High | 95.00 |
| Amber Glass, Toothpick, Cherubs Holding Barrel | 20.00 |
| Amber Glass, Toothpick, Embossed Monkeys | 3.50 |
| Amber Glass, Toothpick, Ribbed, Hat Shape | 8.50 |
| Amber Glass, Toothpick, Saddle & Barrel | 22.00 |
| Amber Glass, Toothpick, Two Roosters | 37.50 |
| Amber Glass, Tray, Serving, Pierced Handles, Etched & Frosted Flower Trim | 30.00 |
| Amber Glass, Tumbler, Hobnail | 14.00 |
| Amber Glass, Tumbler, Lemonade, Blue Twisted Handle, Polished Pontil | 12.00 |
| Amber Glass, Vase, Jack-In-The-Pulpit, Amber To Green, 14 In.High | 55.00 |
| Amber Glass, Vase, 2 Hook Handles At Top, 2 Raised Dancing Girls, 9 In. | 45.00 |
| Amber Glass, Wine, Diamond-Quilted, Disc In Stem | 25.00 |
| Amber Glass, Wine, Rhine, Gold Decoration | 20.00 |
| Amber, Elephant, Cherry, Molded, 8 In.Long | 210.00 |
| Amber, Figurine, Elephant, Cherry, Teakwood Stand, 4 In. High | 145.00 |

*Amberina is a two-toned glassware made from 1883 to about 1900. It was patented by Joseph Locke of the New England Glass Company. The glass shades from red to amber.*

**Amberina, see also Baccarat, Bluerina, Plated Amberina**

| | |
|---|---|
| Amberina, Basket, Hobnail, Berry Prunts, Gold Floral, Amber Feet & Handle | 1450.00 |

Amberina, Basket, Wicker Handle, 11 X 4 1/2 X 5 In. ................................................................ 115.00
Amberina, Bowl, Boat Shape, 10 In. .................................................................................... 110.00
Amberina, Bowl, Finger, Inverted Thumbprint ................................................. 90.00 To 95.00
Amberina, Bowl, Finger, Ruffled Edge ................................................................................ 160.00
Amberina, Bowl, Inverted Thumbprint, Amber To Cranberry, 14 In.Diameter ................. 125.00
Amberina, Bowl, Punch, Clear Reeded Finial, Ovoid, Inverted Thumbprint ..................... 500.00
Amberina, Bowl, Scalloped Top, Open Rose, 10 In.Diameter ........................................... 95.00
Amberina, Butter, Covered, 7 In. Diameter ........................................................................ 125.00
Amberina, Castor, Pickle, Inverted Thumbprint, Enameled, Silver Plate Holder ............... 230.00
Amberina, Celery, Diamond-Quilted, Scalloped Square Top, 6 In. .................................... 225.00
Amberina, Celery, Diamond-Quilted, Square Scalloped Top, 6 1/4 In.High ....................... 210.00
Amberina, Celery, Elongated Thumbprint, Scalloped Top, 5 In. ...................................... 72.50
Amberina, Celery, Inverted Thumbprint ............................................................................. 125.00
Amberina, Celery, New England, Corset Shape, Inverted Thumbprint, Crimped ............... 275.00
Amberina, Creamer, Diamond-Quilted, Tankard Shape, Applied Amber Handle ............... 500.00
Amberina, Creamer, Individual, Inverted Thumbprint, Clear Reeded Handle ................... 125.00
Amberina, Creamer, Inverted Melon Ribbed, Applied Amber Handle, 5 1/4 In. ............... 150.00
Amberina, Creamer, New England, Inverted Thumbprint, Amber Ribbed Handle ............... 150.00
Amberina, Cruet, Applied Amber Handle ............................................................................ 220.00
Amberina, Cruet, Diamond Thumbprint At Bottom, Deep Color, 6 1/2 In.High ............... 500.00
Amberina, Cruet, Dimpled Sides, Amber Handle & Stopper, 8 In.High ............................. 175.00
Amberina, Cup, Punch, Diamond-Quilted, Paneled, Applied Amber Reeded Handle ......... 115.00
Amberina, Cup, Punch, Inverted Thumbprint ..................................................................... 65.00
Amberina, Cup, Punch, Thumbprint ................................................................................... 30.00
Amberina, Cup, Punch, Thumbprint, Engraved Ivan Malcon 1888 ................................... 42.00
Amberina, Decanter, Green Shading To Ruby At Top, Enameled Floral, Stopper ............... 750.00
Amberina, Dish, Candy, Inverted Thumbprint, Clear To Pink To Green, 8 In. ................... 125.00
Amberina, Epergne, Single Lily, Silver Holder Marked England, No.875036 ................... 52.50
Amberina, Ice Cream Set, Daisy & Button, Square Plates, 7 Piece .................................. 850.00
Amberina, Lamp, Applied Amber Feet & Leaves Spread Upwards, 4 1/2 In. ................... 175.00
Amberina, Lamp, Buttercup Shade, Miniature ................................................................... 195.00
Amberina, Mug, Inverted Thumbprint, 2 3/4 In. ............................................................... 30.00
Amberina, Mug, Swirl ....................................................................................................... 65.00
Amberina, Nappy, Leaf Shape, Reeded Amber Handle, 6 1/2 In.Diameter ...................... 250.00
Amberina, Parfait, Mt.Washington, Optic, Applied Amber Reeded Handle, 5 In. ............... 166.00
Amberina, Pitcher, Applied High Amber Handle ................................................................ 235.00
Amberina, Pitcher, Blown Pontil, 8 In. .............................................................................. 150.00
Amberina, Pitcher, Coin Spot, Amber Handle, Square Mouth, 8 In. .................................. 65.00
Amberina, Pitcher, Inverted Thumbprint, Tricorner Top, Amber Reeded Handle ............... 135.00
Amberina, Pitcher, Milk, Thumbprint, Applied Amber Handle, 6 In.High ......................... 160.00
Amberina, Pitcher, Swirled, Bulbous Body, Fuchsia Handle, 5 In.High ........................... 135.00
Amberina, Pitcher, Swirled, Strap Handle, 8 In. ............................................................... 165.00
Amberina, Pitcher, Thumbprint, Square Top, Bulbous, 7 In. ............................................ 100.00
Amberina, Pitcher, Water, Almond Thumbprint, Amber Handle, 9 In.High ....................... 195.00
Amberina, Pitcher, Water, New England, Inverted Thumbprint, Amber Handle ............... 265.00
Amberina, Rose Bowl, Diamond-Quilted, Flaring, 5 In.Diameter ................. 160.00 To 395.00
Amberina, Saltshaker, Diamond-Quilted ........................................................................... 65.00
Amberina, Sauce, Daisy & Button, Diamond Shape, Footed, Sandwich, Flint ................... 42.00
Amberina, Sauce, Daisy & Button, Square, 4 1/4 In. ....................................................... 65.00
Amberina, Sauce, Pressed Daisy & Button, Square, Hobbs-Brockunier ........................... 85.00
Amberina, Sauce, Sandwich, Daisy In Diamond, Footed, Square, Scalloped Top ............. 85.00
Amberina, Shade, Gas, New England, Venetain Diamond, 5 X 7 In. ................................ 185.00
Amberina, Shade, Light, Acid Etched Floral, 4 1/4 In.High .............................................. 95.00
Amberina, Spooner, New England, Corset Shape, Inverted Thumbprint, 4 1/2 In. ........... 215.00
Amberina, Sugar & Creamer, Signed Libbey, Footed, Fuchsia Halfway Down ............... 2500.00
Amberina, Syrup, Hobnail, Silver Plated Top & Handle, 6 In.High .................................. 525.00
Amberina, Tankard, Enameled ........................................................................................... 165.00
Amberina, Tieback, 3 In.Shanks, Pair ............................................................................... 40.00
Amberina, Tomahawk, Indian Chief Embossed On Blade, 7 In. ....................................... 40.00
Amberina, Toothpick, Daisy & Button, Footed .................................................................. 350.00
Amberina, Toothpick, Daisy & Button, 3 In. High ............................................................. 120.00
Amberina, Toothpick, New England, Daisy & Button, 3 Footed ....................................... 145.00
Amberina, Toothpick, Sandwich ....................................................................................... 125.00
Amberina, Toothpick, Venetian Diamond, Square Top, Fuchsia To Amber ..................... 150.00
Amberina, Toothpick, Venetian Diamond, Tricorner, Deep Fuchsia ................................ 225.00
Amberina, Toothpick, Venetian Diamond, Tricorner, Fuchsia .......................................... 145.00

| | |
|---|---|
| Amberina, Tray, Daisy & Button, 15 X 9 In. | 350.00 |
| Amberina, Tray, Thumbprint, 10 1/2 In. | 200.00 |
| Amberina, Tumbler, Baby Thumbprint | 30.00 |
| Amberina, Tumbler, Diamond-Quilted | 60.00 To 95.00 |
| Amberina, Tumbler, Diamond-Quilted, Deep Color Halfway Down | 95.00 |
| Amberina, Tumbler, Expanded Diamond | 95.00 |
| Amberina, Tumbler, Expanded Diamond, Deep Color | 150.00 |
| Amberina, Tumbler, Inverted Baby Thumbprint | 40.00 |
| Amberina, Tumbler, Inverted Baby Thumbprint, Amber To Cranberry, 4 In. | 82.00 |
| Amberina, Tumbler, Inverted Thumbprint, Fuchsia To Amber | 55.00 To 75.00 |
| Amberina, Tumbler, Juice | 25.00 |
| Amberina, Tumbler, Lemonade, Dark Amber Handle, 5 In.High | 125.00 |
| Amberina, Tumbler, New England, Diamond-Quilted | 85.00 |
| Amberina, Tumbler, New England, Inverted Thumbprint | 88.00 |
| Amberina, Tumbler, New England, Swirls, Polished Pontil | 95.00 |
| Amberina, Tumbler, New England, Thumbprint | 88.00 |
| Amberina, Tumbler, New England, Venetian Diamond | 60.00 To 95.00 |
| Amberina, Tumbler, Western | 40.00 |
| Amberina, Tumbler, Wildflower | 45.00 |
| Amberina, Vase, Crimped Top, Swirled, Blown In The Mold, 9 In., Pair | 137.50 |
| Amberina, Vase, Cylindrical, Slender Neck, 9 In.High | 150.00 |
| Amberina, Vase, Frosted Silenium, Small Size | 100.00 |
| Amberina, Vase, Libbey, No.3013 | 350.00 |
| Amberina, Vase, Lily, New England, Ribbed, 12 1/2 In.High | 235.00 |
| Amberina, Vase, Lily, Ribbed, 3 Pour Top, Ground Pontil, 8 In.High | 225.00 |
| Amberina, Vase, Ribbed, Ruffled Top, Twisted Amber Filigree, 11 1/2 In. | 160.00 |
| Amberina, Water Set, Fuchsia, Swirl Ribbed, 7 Piece | 750.00 |
| Amberina, Water Set, Western Expanded Diamond, 4 Piece | 375.00 |
| Amberina, Wine, Conical, Footed, 4 1/2 In.High | 175.00 |
| Amberina, Wine, Inverted Thumbprint, Stemmed | 120.00 |
| Amberina, Wine, Thumbprint, 5 In.High | 30.00 |
| Amelung Type, Pitcher, Milk, Amber, Applied Colored Glass Decoration | 135.00 |

*American Encaustic Tiling Co. of Zanesville, Ohio, worked from 1879
to 1935. Decorative glazed, embossed, and faience tiles were made.*

| | |
|---|---|
| American Encaustic Tiling Co., Ashtray, Art Deco Frog, Matte Green | 36.00 |
| American Encaustic Tiling Co., Inkwell, Double, Pink Gloss Glaze | 35.00 |
| American Encaustic Tiling Co., Tile, Fireplace, Pink, 6 X 18 In. *Illus* | 70.00 |
| American Encaustic Tiling Co., Tile, Girl On Skis, Bird, and Boat, Vellum, glaze 4 X 4 In. | 15.00 |
| American Encaustic Tiling Co., Tile, Hand-Painted Flowers, signed Hoffman, 6 X 6 In. | 35.00 |
| American Encaustic Tiling Co., Tile, Hand-Painted Trees, Road, House, 6 X 6 In. | 25.00 |
| American Encaustic Tiling Co., Tile, Vase With Bird On Brown, 6 In. | 12.50 |

*Amethyst glass is any of the many glasswares made in the proper dark purple
shade. It was a color popular after the Civil War.*

| | |
|---|---|
| Amethyst Glass, Bowl & Underplate, Finger, Lutz Type, Threaded | 41.75 |
| Amethyst Glass, Bowl, Fluted, Tinted, 11 1/2 In.Diameter | 20.00 |
| Amethyst Glass, Bowl, Fluted, 11 1/2 In. | 20.00 |
| Amethyst Glass, Bowl, Fruit, Low Pedestal, 10 In. | 15.00 |
| Amethyst Glass, Bowl, Pairpoint Type, Flanged, 12 In. | 19.00 |
| Amethyst Glass, Bowl, 8 In.Square | 12.75 |
| Amethyst Glass, Box, Enamel Violets On Hinged Lid, 2 In. Diameter | 45.00 |
| Amethyst Glass, Box, Enamel Wild Flowers On Hinged Lid, 2 1/2 In. Diameter | 40.00 |
| Amethyst Glass, Candlestick, Bulbous Stem | 15.00 |
| Amethyst Glass, Cruet, Wine, White Enameled Floral & Leaves, Blown | 67.50 |
| Amethyst Glass, Decanter & Goblet, Stopper, Footed Goblet, Pittsburgh | 300.00 |
| Amethyst Glass, Decanter, Bell Shape, Gold Decoration, Deep Color, 9 In. | 32.00 |
| Amethyst Glass, Decanter, Silver Deposit, Gondola, Dancers, Trees, Stopper | 65.00 |
| Amethyst Glass, Gum Stand, Teaberry, Signed | 25.00 |
| Amethyst Glass, Hat, Blown, 3 1/2 In.High | 34.00 |
| Amethyst Glass, Holder, Pen & Inkwell, Scalloped, Ovoid Shape | 15.00 |
| Amethyst Glass, Mug, Applied Handle, 4 Molded Rings, 3 3/4 In. High | 22.00 |
| Amethyst Glass, Mug, Pattern Of Tiny Circles, Pontil Mark | 6.50 |
| Amethyst Glass, Pitcher, Water, Clear Handle | 36.00 |
| Amethyst Glass, Rose Bowl, Flint | 25.00 |
| Amethyst Glass, Salt Dip, Intaglio, Reclining Nude | 20.00 |

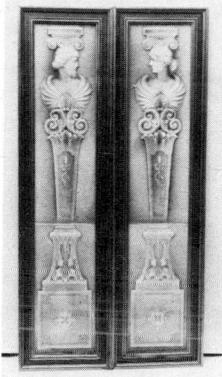

American Encaustic
Tiling Co., Tile,
Fireplace, Pink
*(See Page 6)*

Art Deco, Bowl, Enamel,
Faure, C.1930,
10 In.Diameter

| | |
|---|---:|
| Amethyst Glass, Salt, Master | 14.00 |
| Amethyst Glass, Sugar & Creamer, Ribbed, Elongated, Miniature | 10.00 |
| Amethyst Glass, Sugar, Covered, Strutting Peacock | 45.00 |
| Amethyst Glass, Tieback, Flint, Pewter Post, 4 3/8 In.Diameter | 20.00 |
| Amethyst Glass, Tumbler, Blown, Gold & White Enamel, Pinprick On Gold Rim | 17.50 |
| Amethyst Glass, Tumbler, S Repeat | 37.50 |
| Amethyst Glass, Tumbler, Straight Sided | 22.00 |
| Amethyst Glass, Tumbler, White Enamel Decoration | 15.00 |
| Amethyst Glass, Vase, Enameled Pink & Green Floral, 6 Sided Top, Gold Trim | 65.00 |
| Amethyst Glass, Vase, Footed, Gold Trim, 5 In.High | 8.00 |
| Amethyst Glass, Vase, Presentation, Dated 1916, Etched, 6 In., Pair | 20.00 |
| Amethyst Glass, Vase, Silver Overlay, Bulbous, Floral Band, 9 In. | 22.50 |
| Amethyst Glass, Vase, Squatty, Satin Finish, Gun Metal, Red, & Gold Trim | 25.00 |
| Amethyst Glass, Vase, Urn Shape, Scalloped Top, White Enamel, Gold Trim, Dark | 27.50 |
| Amethyst Glass, Witch's Ball, Blown | 60.00 |
| Amphora, see Teplitz | |
| Andiron, many related fireplace items, see, Fire | |
| Apothecary jar, see Bottle, Apothecary | |
| Apple Peeler, see Kitchen, Peeler, Apple | |
| Arc-En-Ceil, Vase, Gold & Puple, 8 1/2 In.High | 100.00 |

*Art Deco, or Art Moderne, is a style started at the Paris Exposition
of 1925. All types of furniture and decorative arts, jewelry, bookbindings, and
even games, were designed in this style.*

| | |
|---|---:|
| Art Deco, Ashtray, Marble, Bronze & Ivory Mandolin Player Sits On Edge | 225.00 |
| Art Deco, Ashtray, Octagonal, Girl Smoking Cigarette, Butterfly Mark | 16.00 |
| Art Deco, Atomizer, Steel Base, Black Geometric Design, 5 In.High | 9.00 |
| Art Deco, Bag, Mesh, Green, Silver & Enamel Frame, Whiting & Davis | 30.00 |
| Art Deco, Bag, Mesh, Green, Violet, & Orange, Sawtooth Border, Whiting & Davis | 35.00 |
| Art Deco, Bookend, Expandable, Pair | 30.00 |
| Art Deco, Bookend, Nude Figure, White Metal, Silver Finish, 5 In.High, Pair | 35.00 |
| Art Deco, Bottle, Frosted, Cork, Female Nude Holding Urn, 14 1/ In.High | 24.00 |
| Art Deco, Bowl, Enamel, Faure, C.1930, 10 In.Diameter  *Illus* | 350.00 |
| Art Deco, Box, Cigarette, Ashtray, Gold Enamel & Jade  *Illus* | 475.00 |
| Art Deco, Brush & Mirror, Black On Metal | 10.00 |
| Art Deco, Buckle, Belt, Clear & Frosted, Double Teardrop, 2 1/4 In.Square | 16.00 |
| Art Deco, Buckle, Ladies, Bronze, Enamel Decoration, 2 1/2 X 1 In. | 18.00 |
| Art Deco, Card, Tally | .15 |
| Art Deco, Dresser Set, Black Geometrics On Brush, 2 Piece | 15.00 |
| Art Deco, Dresser Set, Green Frosted Glass, Triangular, 3 Piece | 27.50 |
| Art Deco, Figurine, Cat, Bronze Finish On Metal, 6 1/2 X 4 In. | 24.00 |
| Art Deco, Figurine, Nude Balancing 3 Balls On Extended Arms & Leg, 9 In. | 55.00 |
| Art Deco, Figurine, Nude, Frosted Glass, Signed Etling, France, 8 In.High | 105.00 |
| Art Deco, Figurine, Porcelain, Society Girl With Dog On Leash, 6 In.High | 9.00 |
| Art Deco, Figurine, Sexy Elongated Lady With 2 Wolfhounds, Chalkware | 37.00 |
| Art Deco, Flask, Whiskey, Lady's, 4 Shot Capacity | 85.00 |
| Art Deco, Flower Frog, Dancing Nude, Marked Germany, 7 1/2 In.High | 20.00 |

Art Deco, Lighter,
Gold & Enamel,
Cartier, C.1935

Art Deco, Box,
Cigarette, Ashtray,
Gold Enamel & Jade
*(See Page 7)*

Art Deco, **Frame,** Silver & Enamel, Onyx Base, Malachite Borders, 11 1/2 In. .............................. 500.00
Art Deco, **Holder,** Pin, Amethyst, Engraved, Brass Holder, 3 Tray, Emeralds ......................... 38.00
Art Deco, **Lamp,** Dancing Girl, Metal, Frosted Shade ............................................. 25.00
Art Deco, **Lamp,** Silhouette, Nude Figure, Frosted Glass, Frankart, 1928 ......................... 45.00
Art Deco, **Lighter,** Gold & Enamel, Cartier, C.1935 ....................................... *Illus* 425.00
Art Deco, **Purse,** Silver, Enamel & Jewels, C.1925, 8 3/4 In.Long ............................. 375.00
Art Deco, **Smoking Set,** Sterling Design On Bronze, Divided Box, 5 Piece ...................... 30.00
Art Deco, **Spoon & Fork,** Salad Serving, Crystal, Faceted Ruby Prisms .......................... 35.00
Art Deco, **Vase,** Blue, Black, & Beige ....................................................... 25.00
Art Deco, **Vase,** Cased, Purple Threading & Berries On Calcite Type, 8 In. ....................... 25.00
Art Deco, **Vase,** Czechoslovakia, White, Painted Woman's Head Center, 8 In. ...................... 18.00
Art Deco, **Vase,** Fan, Flesh Nude On Chocolate, 2 Panel, R Mark, 9 In. .......................... 68.00
Art Deco, **Vase,** Pottery, Sepia On Beige, Signed L.M.Chantrier, 1934, 10 In. .................... 75.00
Art Deco, **Vase,** Yellow Leaves On Purple, Shamrock Shape Metal Collar, 5 In. ................... 20.00
Art Deco, **Walking Stick,** Gold Filled, T Shape, Engraved Name ................................. 38.50
Art Deco, **Wine,** Crystal And Black Satin Stripes, 2 1/2 In.High, Set Of 6 ....................... 50.00

     *Art glass means any of the many forms of glassware made during the late
nineteenth century or early twentieth century. These wares were expensive and
made in limited production. Art glass is not the typical commercial glassware
that was made in large quantities, and most of the art glass was produced by
hand methods.*
  **Art Glass, see also Schneider, Nash**
  **Art Glass, see also spearate headings such as Burmese, etc.**

Art Glass, **Barrel,** Biscuit, Threaded, Iridescent ................................................ 87.50
Art Glass, **Basket,** Blue & White ........................................................... 49.00
Art Glass, **Basket,** Blue, Mica Flakes, Thorn Handle ......................................... 65.00
Art Glass, **Basket,** Cased & Blown, Milk White, Twisted Crystal Handle ........................ 60.00
Art Glass, **Basket,** Cased, Clear Crystal Ribbon Around Rim, White & Pink ..................... 38.00
Art Glass, **Basket,** Ruffled Crimped Top, White, Light Green Handle & Lining .................. 35.00
Art Glass, **Basket,** White To Cranberry, Mica Flakes, Thorn Handle ............................ 75.00
Art Glass, **Bowl Vase,** Fluted, 3 Applied Prunts, Iridescent, Pontil, 3 In.High ................. 49.00
Art Glass, **Bowl,** Bride's, Crimped, Pleated, Overlay, Applied Crystal Rim ..................... 43.00
Art Glass, **Bowl,** Finger, Blue, Green Crimped Threaded Top, Polished Pontil .................. 25.00
Art Glass, **Bowl,** Finger, Threaded, Blue ................................................... 22.00
Art Glass, **Bowl,** Green, Ruffled Opalescent Edge, 8 In. ..................................... 21.00
Art Glass, **Bowl,** Pink, Overshot, Inverted Lip, 7 1/2 In.High ............................... 12.00
Art Glass, **Bowl,** Spittoon Shape, Green Iridescent, Scalloped, 7 1/2 In. .................... 50.00
Art Glass, **Bowl,** Stretched, Iridescent Blue, 6 1/2 In. ..................................... 13.00
Art Glass, **Box,** Hinged, Frosted, Enameled Violets & Leaves, 5 In.Diameter .................. 67.50
Art Glass, **Box,** Powder, Lime Green Knob, Round, Clear Overshot ............................ 21.50
Art Glass, **Burner,** Perfume, Cased, Footed, Electrified, Orange, Black, & White .............. 84.00
Art Glass, **Compote,** White Frosted, Blue Overlay Edge, Silver Plate Base .................... 52.00
Art Glass, **Creamer,** Emerald Optic, Beaded Enamel Bands, Applied Handle ................... 18.00
Art Glass, **Cruet,** Clear Blown Stopper ..................................................... 65.00
Art Glass, **Cruet,** Vinegar, Blue, Pink, Amber & Blue Stopper, Amber Handle ................. 75.00

Art Glass, Decanter, Russian, Triple Overlay, Cut Floral, C.1750, 20 In. ............................................. 375.00
Art Glass, Epergne, Clear To Blue Opalescent, 2 Vases, 2 Canes, 16 In. .......................................... 135.00
Art Glass, Epergne, Clear To Cranberry Bowl, 3 Lilies, Center Trumpet ........................................... 295.00
Art Glass, Epergne, Victorian, 3 Lily, Emerald Green, Filigree Decorations ...................................... 100.00
Art Glass, Epergne, 3 Lily, Light Green Opalescent, Dark Green Rigaree ......................................... 195.00
Art Glass, Epergne, 4 Lily, Pink Overlay ................................................................................................. 169.50
Art Glass, Epergne, 4 Trumpets, On Beveled Mirror, Canary & Clear, 14 In. ................................... 160.00
Art Glass, Figurine, Elephant, Metallic Luster, Dimpled, 7 In. ..................................... 495.00 To 650.00
Art Glass, Goblet, Overlay, Crimson To Clear, Thumbprint, 6 Sided Stem ...................................... 110.00
Art Glass, Inkwell, Brass Hinged Lid, 3 1/2 In.Base .......................................................................... 135.00
Art Glass, Lampshade, Web Effect, Iridescent, Yellow Green Coloring, 5 In. .................................... 45.00
Art Glass, Lemonade Set, Expanded Diamond, Amber Handle, Footed, 7 Piece ............................. 125.00
Art Glass, Nappy, Amber Threading Ending In Swirls, Applied Rigaree ............................................... 95.00
Art Glass, Night-Light, Robj, France, Egg Shape Orange Globe, Iron Base ....................................... 95.00
Art Glass, Perfume, Iridescent Green, Enameled Flowers, Gilded Plunger Top ................................. 30.00
Art Glass, Pitcher, Amber, Applied Aqua Handle, 10 In.High .............................................................. 47.50
Art Glass, Pitcher, Blue, Overshot, Amber Handle, Bulbous, 7 1/2 In. ................................................ 75.00
Art Glass, Pitcher, Clear, Overshot, Reeded Handle, 5 In.High .......................................................... 45.00
Art Glass, Pitcher, Diamond-Quilted, Emerald Green To White, Enamel Floral ................................. 45.00
Art Glass, Pitcher, Frosted, Applied Clear Reeded Handle, Gold & Enamel ...................................... 45.00
Art Glass, Pitcher, Lime Green, Frosted Clear Handle, Satin Finish .................................................. 135.00
Art Glass, Pitcher, Opal Swirl, Ruffled Top, Applied Handle ............................................................... 75.00
Art Glass, Pitcher, Overshot, Ground Pontil, Applied Handle .............................................................. 32.00
Art Glass, Pitcher, Water, Blue, Enameled Daisies, Applied Handle, Pleated ..................................... 50.00
Art Glass, Rose Bowl, Jade Green, Clear To Opalescent, Gold Enamel Floral ................................... 65.00
Art Glass, Rose Bowl, Mottled Canary, Enameled Floral, Scalloped Top ........................................... 50.00
Art Glass, Rose Bowl, Overlay, Rose Floral & Amber Leaves On Shiny Custard .............................. 150.00
Art Glass, Shade, Frosted, Topaz Allover Design ................................................................................ 15.00
Art Glass, Shade, Gold & Silver Snakeskin Tortoise On Gold Iridescent ........................................... 51.00
Art Glass, Shade, White Frosted, Puffed-Out Flowers, Pink & Green Inside ...................................... 14.00
Art Glass, Slipper, Harem, Clear, Gold Traces, Turned Up Toe, Cuban Heel ...................................... 22.00
Art Glass, Sugar & Creamer, Amber Overlay & Handles, White Lining, Pitts. .................................... 25.00
Art Glass, Sugar, Covered, Swirled Rib, Clear To Opalescent ............................................................ 30.00
Art Glass, Syrup, Azure Color Swirl, White Enamel Flecks ................................................................ 55.00
Art Glass, Tankard, Green, Enameled Flowers & Gold, Applied Handle, 13 In. .................................. 39.00
Art Glass, Toothpick, Opaque Green, Patent Date Label ................................................................... 675.00
Art Glass, Tumble-Up, Opalescent Stripes On Pink, 7 In.High ........................................................... 19.50
Art Glass, Tumbler, Blue & White Enamel Flowers On Green ............................................................. 15.00
Art Glass, Tumbler, Blue Opalescent Swirl ......................................................................................... 24.00
Art Glass, Tumbler, New England, Gold Edging, Green Opaque ........................................................ 575.00
Art Glass, Vase, Blue Green, Enameled Lilies Of The Valley, 4 In.Wide ............................................. 35.00
Art Glass, Vase, Blue Opalescent Diagonal Stripes, Ruffled Top, 4 In.High ...................................... 42.00
Art Glass, Vase, Bud, Clear To Ruby, Gold Enamel, South Jersey ..................................................... 35.00
Art Glass, Vase, Cased, White Leaves & Bluebirds On Rose, 7 1/4 In. .............................................. 40.00
Art Glass, Vase, Fan, Jade Green, Opaque, 7 1/2 In. ........................................................................ 14.00
Art Glass, Vase, Green Swirled, Opalescent, 15 In.High .................................................................... 45.00
Art Glass, Vase, Hyacinth, Aqua, Inverted Trumpet Base, Threading, 7 1/2 In. ................................. 21.50
Art Glass, Vase, Ming Blue, Opaque Flared Top, 6 In. ....................................................................... 15.00
Art Glass, Vase, Overlay, White To Emerald Green, 7 3/4 In.High, Pair ........................................... 350.00
Art Glass, Vase, Peacock Blue, Integral Gold Flecks & Air Traps, 14 In.High .................................... 69.00
Art Glass, Vase, Stick Neck, Bulbous, Pink Cased, Silver Mica Flecks, 6 In. ..................................... 45.00
Art Glass, Vase, Swirled Base, Relief Diamonds, Bulbous, Clear, 4 1/2 In. ....................................... 12.00
Art Glass, Water Set, Blue, Opalescent Inverted Thumbprint, Enamel, 6 Piece .............................. 175.00

*Art Nouveau, a style characterized by free-flowing organic design, reached
its zenith between 1895 and 1905. The style encompassed all decorative and
functional arts from architecture to furniture and posters.*
Art Nouveau, see also Glass, Furniture, etc.
Art Nouveau, see also Royal Dux, Schneider, Faberge
Art Nouveau, Blotter, Roller, Raised Design, Sterling Silver ................................................................. 8.50
Art Nouveau, Bookend, Grecian Lady, Copper On White Metal, Morani, 1914, Pair ......................... 27.50
Art Nouveau, Bookend, Lily Pads & Cattails, Metal, 5 In.High, Pair ................................................... 10.00
Art Nouveau, Bookend, Mermaid, Pair ............................................................................................... 37.00
Art Nouveau, Box, Jewel, Footed, Raised Flowers, Silver Plate, 6 1/2 In. ......................................... 30.00
Art Nouveau, Buckle, Belt, Parcel Gilt, Chrysanthemums & Leafage ................................................ 20.00
Art Nouveau, Bust, Lady, Bronze, Signed Gouli Meddor, Trumpet Base, 8 In. ............................... 175.00

Art Nouveau, Candlestick, Girl Holding Tulip Bud, Austria, Pair ..................... 75.00
Art Nouveau, Clock Set, Mantel, Brass, Cutouts, Embossed, Tulips, 3 Piece ................ 300.00
Art Nouveau, Cocktail Glass, Gilt Rooster & Rim, Crystal, 5 1/2 In.High ............... 10.00
Art Nouveau, Comb, Mustache, Silver, Drinking Scene ..................... 15.00
Art Nouveau, Dresser Set, Sterling Silver Handles, 5 Piece ..................... 32.50
Art Nouveau, Dresser Set, Woman 3 Ornate Roses, Silver Plate, 3 Piece ................ 19.00
Art Nouveau, Figurine, Confidence, Signed Grisard, Silver Plate, Pedestal ........ 95.00
Art Nouveau, Figurine, Nude, Gray Cast Metal, 21 In.High ..................... 35.00
Art Nouveau, Frame, Easel, Brassed Iron, Painted Flowers, 10 In.High .............. 24.00
Art Nouveau, Frame, Picture, Silver, Enamel, Flowers, 6 X 6 In. ..................... 275.00
Art Nouveau, Holder, Book, Bronze Lady's Head & Flowers At Each End ............... 22.00
Art Nouveau, Jar, Candy, White Metal Frame & Lid, Cobalt Insert, 8 1/2 In. ........... 39.50
Art Nouveau, Jardiniere, Pottery, Blue To Dark Brown, Scrolled Handle ............. 130.00
Art Nouveau, Lamp, Peacock In Garden, Cast Metal, Toledo, Ohio ............... 49.00
Art Nouveau, Lamp, 2 Nudes Holding Golden Amber Shade, Pair, 18 1/2 In.High ............ 250.00
Art Nouveau, Looking Glass, Silver Plate, Advertisement For Minn.Firm ............. 8.50
Art Nouveau, Magnifying Glass, Lady's, Raised Pearl Floral, Gold Filled ........... 10.00
Art Nouveau, Mirror, Pocket, Pen & Ink Designs Of Ladies, 2 In. ..................... 1.00
Art Nouveau, Mirror, Silver Bronze Metal, Woman & Flowers, 12 In.High ............ 32.50
Art Nouveau, Paperclip, Bronze, Woman's Head Within Magnolia ................. 18.00
Art Nouveau, Plaque, Bronze & Wood, Four Season, Set Of 4, 16 3/4 In.Long ............ 275.00
Art Nouveau, Plaque, Bust Of Woman Smelling Daisy, Ceramic, Luneville, 5 In. ........ 30.00
Art Nouveau, Print, Alphonse Mucha, Salome, 1897, 10 X 14 In., Signed ............ 250.00
Art Nouveau, Shade, Light, Turquoise Blue, Satin Finish, 4 In. ..................... 21.00
Art Nouveau, Spoon, Figural Cupid Handle, Sterling ..................... 6.50
Art Nouveau, Tazza, Bronze Clad, Embossed, 8 In. ..................... 55.00
Art Nouveau, Tray, Bronze, Girl Looking At The Sun, Maxim, 7 1/2 X 4 In. ........... 80.00
Art Nouveau, Vase, Bronze & Sterling, Blooming Iris & Leafage, 11 In.High ........ 80.00
Art Nouveau, Vase, Silver Overlay, Emerald Green Glass, 10 In.High ............... 125.00
Art Nouveau, Vase, Twisted, Thumbprint, Blue Green To Violet, 5 In. ............... 65.00
Art Nouveau, Watch Holder, Bronzed White Metal, Cockatoo With Hook In Beak ........ 35.00

# AURENE

*Aurene glass was made by Frederick Carder of New York about 1904. It is an iridescent gold glass, usually marked Aurene or Steuben.*

Aurene, see also Steuben
Aurene, Candlestick, Gold, Mirror Finish, Signed ..................... 250.00
Aurene, Candlestick, Gold, Twisted Stem, Signed, 8 In., Pair ............... 295.00
Aurene, Centerpiece, Blue, Removable Insert ..................... 485.00
Aurene, Champagne, Gold, Swirled Top, Signed Steuben ............... 125.00
Aurene, Cologne, Amphora Shape, Peacock Blue Iridescent, Stopper, 2 1/2 In. ........ 450.00
Aurene, Compote, Iridescent Gold With Purple & Blue Highlights, Signed ............ 250.00
Aurene, Goblet, Gold, Twisted Stem, Signed ..................... 150.00
Aurene, Liqueur Set, Gold, Round Tray, Signed, 7 Piece ..................... 775.00
Aurene, Perfume, Gold, Melon Ribbed, Long Stem Stopper ............... 325.00
Aurene, Perfume, Iridescent, Signed, 4 1/4 In. ..................... 275.00
Aurene, Perfume, Signed, No.3294, Blue ..................... 265.00
Aurene, Planter, Gold, 4 Legs, Signed Steuben ..................... 275.00
Aurene, Rose Bowl, Blue Highlights, Signed, 3 In.High ..................... 175.00
Aurene, Saltshaker, Blue, Signed ..................... 165.00
Aurene, Shade, Gold, Red & Green Iridescence, 4 1/2 In. ..................... 30.00
Aurene, Shade, Gold, Red & Green Iridescence, 7 1/2 In. ..................... 30.00
Aurene, Shade, Gold, Signed Steuben ..................... 45.00
Aurene, Sherbet & Underplate, Gold, Twisted Stem, Signed ............... 195.00
Aurene, Sugar & Creamer, Gold, Signed Steuben ..................... 550.00
Aurene, Toothpick, Gold, Barrel Shape ..................... 40.00
Aurene, Tumble-Up Set, Blue, Handled Pitcher, Signed, 2 Piece ............... 675.00
Aurene, Vase, Cabinet, Blue, Miniature, Signed ..................... 345.00
Aurene, Vase, Fan, Blue, White Uneven Lines & Hearts, 8 In.High ............... 750.00
Aurene, Vase, Gold Iridescent Hook Feathers On White, Signed, 3 1/4 In. ........ 650.00
Aurene, Vase, Gold, Pink Highlights, Signed, 7 In. High ..................... 270.00
Aurene, Vase, Gold, Signed, 8 1/2 In.High ..................... 185.00
Aurene, Vase, Miniature, Pale Blue, Silver & Gold Iridescence, 5 In.High ........ 125.00
Aurene, Vase, Stick, Blue, Signed & Numbered, 8 1/4 In.High ............... 125.00
Aurene, Wine, Gold, Twisted Stem, 4 1/2 In. ..................... 125.00
    Austria, see Royal Dux, Kauffmann, Porcelain

*Auto parts and accessories are collectors' items today.*

| | |
|---|---:|
| Auto, **Bulb,** For Horn, Rubber, Large Size | 15.00 |
| Auto, **Carburetor,** Ford, C.1941, 6 Cylinder | 12.00 |
| Auto, **Carburetor,** Model T Ford | 15.00 |
| Auto, **Clock,** Waltham, 8 Day | 22.50 |
| Auto, **Coil,** Model T Ford | 2.50 |
| Auto, **Cover,** Tire, Side Mount, Chrome | 30.00 |
| Auto, **Drum Puller,** Chevrolet, 1924-26 | 14.00 |
| Auto, **Flower Holder,** Crystal, C.1900 | 15.00 |
| Auto, **Foot Warmer,** Model T, The Clark Heater Co. | 30.00 |
| Auto, **Gauge,** Balloon Tire, Schrader's | 3.00 |
| Auto, **Gauge,** Tire, Ballone, Dated 1923, Metal, Leather Case | 8.00 |
| Auto, **Gearshift Knob,** Lady's Picture | 2.00 |
| Auto, **Headlamp,** M.Hall Lamp Co., Detroit, Model No.199, Brass, Pair | 125.00 |
| Auto, **Headlight,** Whippett, Chrome, 1930, Pair | 8.00 |
| Auto, **Hood Ornament,** Chrysler | 6.50 |
| Auto, **Hood Ornament,** Greyhound, Mounted On Wooden Base, 9 1/2 In.Long | 15.00 |
| Auto, **Hood Ornament,** Swan, Raised Wings, Chrome Plated, 6 In. High | 10.00 |
| Auto, **Horn,** Brass, Brackets For Mounting, Rubber Bulb, Patent Jan.1909 | 65.00 |
| Auto, **Horn,** Brass, Bugle Type, Rubber Bulb, Peacock | 20.00 |
| Auto, **Horn,** Brass, Flexible Cable, Rubber Bulb, 56 In.Long | 65.00 |
| Auto, **Horn,** Motovox, Ornate | 12.50 |
| Auto, **Horn,** Taxi, Brass, 9 In.Round | 4.00 |
| Auto, **Horn,** Taxi, Brass, 18 In.Round | 6.00 |
| Auto, **Hub Cap,** Chevrolet, For Wooden Spoke Wheels | 10.00 |
| Auto, **Hub Cap,** Hupmobile, For Wooden Spoke Wheels | 10.00 |
| Auto, **Hub Cap,** Overland, For Wooden Spoke Wheels | 10.00 |
| Auto, **Hub Cap,** Whippet, For Wooden Spoke Wheels | 10.00 |
| Auto, **Hub Cap,** Willys Knight, For Wooden Spoke Wheels | 10.00 |
| Auto, **Jack,** Iron | 2.50 |
| Auto, **Knob,** Gearshift, Constance Bennett Under Glass | 7.50 |
| Auto, **Lamp Kit,** Eveready Mazda | 2.50 |
| Auto, **Lamp,** Driving, Dietz, Union, Kerosene, Brass Trim, Bail Handle, 1897 | 35.00 |
| Auto, **Lamp,** Ford, Brass & Iron, Ino W.Brown Mfg.Co., Model 110, Columbus, O. | 58.00 |
| Auto, **Lamp,** Model T, Brass, License Bracket, C.1912 | 40.00 |
| Auto, **License Plate,** Arizona, 1934, Solid Copper | 20.00 |
| Auto, **License Plate,** New Hampshire, 1914 | 15.00 |
| Auto, **License Plate,** 1915, Porcelain | 12.00 |
| Auto, **License Plate,** 1930, Enamel | 8.00 |
| Auto, **Light,** Carbon | 3.50 |
| Auto, **Light,** Cowl, C.1920, Pair | 15.00 |
| Auto, **Light,** Grip-Lite, Emergency Parking | 4.95 |
| Auto, **Light,** Side, Model T Ford, Iron, Red Glass | 1.00 |
| Auto, **Light,** Side, Nickel Plated, Pair | 29.50 |
| Auto, **Light,** Solar 1005, Brass, Red & Clear Lenses, Dated 6-08-09 | 85.00 |
| Auto, **Light,** Stop, Word Stop On Lens | 6.00 |
| Auto, **Light,** Tail, Chevrolet, 1937, Left Side | 10.00 |
| Auto, **Meter,** Motor, Boyce, Universal | 20.00 |
| Auto, **Oil Stick,** Model T Ford | 1.50 |
| Auto, **Oilcan,** Ford, Script | 4.00 |
| Auto, **Pump,** Brass | 15.00 |
| Auto, **Pump,** Running Board, Inland | 22.00 |
| Auto, **Radiator Cap,** Dog Bone, Brass, Boyce Motometer | 18.50 |
| Auto, **Radiator Cap,** Knight's Head In Armor | 6.00 |
| Auto, **Radiator Cap,** Model T Ford, Metal Eagle, Wings Attached | 12.50 |
| Auto, **Radiator Cap,** Studebaker, Patent 1913 | 25.00 |
| Auto, **Radiator Ornament,** Mack, Bulldog | 7.50 |
| Auto, **Radiator,** Maxwell, Shell & Emblem | 125.00 |
| Auto, **Ring,** Key, Ford, Celluloid, Chain | 11.00 |
| Auto, **Running Board,** Ford, 1939, Left Side | 35.00 |
| Auto, **Sign,** Packard, Chromed, Script, 8 1/2 In. | 10.00 |
| Auto, **Speedometer,** Model A Ford, Oval | 7.50 |
| Auto, **Spotlight,** Model T Ford | 9.50 |
| Auto, **Taillight Assembly,** Ford, 1937, Pair | 20.00 |
| Auto, **Tire Gauge,** Schrader Universal | 2.75 |
| Auto, **Valve Seater,** For Model T Ford, Brass & Iron | 6.95 |

Auto, Vase, Carnival Glass, Tree Of Life, Marigold, Pair ............................................. 16.00
Auto, Vase, Chartreuse Glass, Bracket ......................................................................... 12.50
Auto, Vase, Clear, Curved Shape, 10 In. ...................................................................... 14.00
Auto, Vase, Cut Glass, Engraved, Bracket, Pair ........................................................... 35.00
Auto, Vase, Electric Car, Cut Glass, Hobstar & Fan, Aluminum Bracket ....................... 50.00
Auto, Vase, Grapevines, Grapes, & Leaves, 10 In.High, Pair ........................................ 30.00
Auto, Vase, Rolls Royce, Etched Crystal, Pair .............................................................. 14.00
Auto, Vase, Vaseline Glass, Ornate, Pair ....................................... 50.00 To 65.00
Auto, Water Pump, Ford, 1949 .................................................................................... 7.00
Auto, Whistle, Explosion .............................................................................................. 12.50
Auto, Wrench, Nash, Open End ..................................................................................... 2.00
  Avon, see Bottle, Avon
Baby Carriage, Wicker, Wire Wheels ........................................................................ 195.00

*Baccarat glass was made in France by La Compagnie des Cristalleries*
*de Baccarat, located about 150 miles from Paris. The factory was started*
*in 1765. The firm went bankrupt and began operating about 1822. Famous cane*
*and millefiori paperweights were made there during the 1860-1880 period. The*
*firm is still working near Paris making paperweights and glasswares.*

Baccarat, Atomizer, Amberina Swirl, 5 1/2 In.High ...................................................... 30.00
Baccarat, Bonbon, Swirl, Short Pedestal, Shallow, 5 1/2 In., Pair ................................. 25.00
Baccarat, Bottle, Dresser, Amberina, Swirled, 5 1/2 In.High ....................................... 34.50
Baccarat, Bottle, Swirled, Ruby To Clear, 5 In. ........................................................... 22.00
Baccarat, Bottle, Swirled, Ruby To Clear, 5 1/2 In. ..................................................... 24.00
Baccarat, Bottle, Swirled, Ruby To Clear, 6 1/4 In. ..................................................... 24.00
Baccarat, Bottle, Swirled, Ruby To Clear, 7 In. ........................................................... 30.00
Baccarat, Bowl, Covered, Frosted Turtle, Marked, 3 1/4 X 5 1/2 X 2 1/4 In. ............... 52.50
Baccarat, Bowl, Pedestal, Green, Swirl, Signed, 4 In. High ......................................... 38.00
Baccarat, Box, Covered, Round, Amberina Swirls, Signed, 2 1/4 In.High ..................... 25.00
Baccarat, Candelabra, Clear Swirl, 2-Light, Pair ........................................................ 250.00
Baccarat, Candlestick, Bobeche & Prisms, 10 In.High, Pair ....................................... 120.00
Baccarat, Candlestick, Cut Prisms, Bobeche, 10 In.High, Pair .................................. 120.00
Baccarat, Candlestick, Diamond Point, Signed, 9 In.High, Pair ................................. 150.00
Baccarat, Candlestick, Paperweight Type, 4 Ball, Changeable Colors, 3 Mold ............. 10.50
Baccarat, Cologne, Amberina Swirl, Stopper, 5 3/4 In.High ......................................... 25.00
Baccarat, Cologne, Clear Swirl, Enameled Floral & Leaf, 7 In.High ............................. 25.00
Baccarat, Cologne, Hobnail, Clear, Signed .................................................................. 20.00
Baccarat, Cologne, Pink, Lacy, 5 In. ........................................................................... 12.50
Baccarat, Cologne, Pink, Lacy, 6 In. ........................................................................... 15.00
Baccarat, Cologne, Rose Tiente With Pattern, Stopper ................................................. 8.50
Baccarat, Compote, Amber Diamonds On Clear, 9 1/2 In.High ................................. 120.00
Baccarat, Compote, Covered, Amber Birds & Vines On Frosted, 4 X 5 In. .................. 925.00
Baccarat, Compote, Scalloped Rim, Diamond Point Base, Lacy, C.1840 ................... 250.00
Baccarat, Cruet, Clear, 9 1/4 In.High, Pair ................................................................. 36.00
Baccarat, Cruet, Clear, 9 3/4 In.High .......................................................................... 18.00
Baccarat, Cruet, Footed, Clear, Gold Enamel, 10 In.High ............................................ 40.00
Baccarat, Decanter, Crystal, Round, Bulbous Stopper, 13 1/4 In. ............................... 32.00
Baccarat, Dish, Dresser, Covered, Oval, Cranberry Floral On Frosted & Clear ............. 75.00
Baccarat, Dish, Dresser, Oval, Cranberry Floral On Frosted & Clear, Cameo ............... 50.00
Baccarat, Dish, Dresser, Oval, Cranberry Floral On Frosted & Clear, Long ................... 85.00
Baccarat, Dish, Metal Toothbrush Holder, Amberina, Swirled, Signed .......................... 32.00
Baccarat, Dish, Olive, Amberina, Swirl & Diamond Point, Pewter Fork Post ................. 35.00
Baccarat, Dish, Olive, Melon Ribbed, Scalloped Top, Salmon Shading, Signed ............ 68.00
Baccarat, Inkwell, Clear Swirl, Silver Art Nouveau Lid ................................................. 39.00
Baccarat, Jar, Amber Flashed Panels & Buttons, Clear, 2 5/8 In.High .......................... 22.00
Baccarat, Jar, Pin, Cranberry Floral On Frosted & Clear, Cameo, Acid Cut .................. 25.00
Baccarat, Paperweight, Apple .................................................................................... 250.00
Baccarat, Paperweight, Butterfly, Blue & White Canes, 24 Point Star Base ................ 850.00
Baccarat, Paperweight, Closed Concentric, Coral, Green, Blue & White Canes .......... 150.00
Baccarat, Paperweight, Closed Millefiori, Dated 1847, 2 3/16 In. .............................. 525.00
Baccarat, Paperweight, Colored Concentric Circles Of Canes .................................... 140.00
Baccarat, Paperweight, Concentric Canes, Red, Green, Pink, White, & Apricot .......... 170.00
Baccarat, Paperweight, Concentric Millefiori, 2 1/2 In. ................................................ 90.00
Baccarat, Paperweight, Dahlia .................................................................................. 200.00
Baccarat, Paperweight, Double Overlay, 3 1/8 In. ........................................ *Illus* 2000.00
Baccarat, Paperweight, Filigree, Special ...................................................................... 90.00

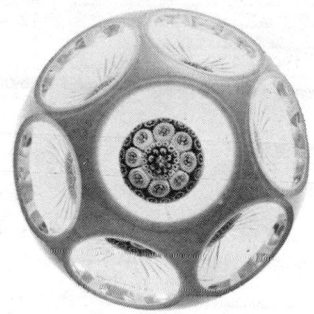

Baccarat, Paperweight, Double Overlay, 3 1/8 In.
*(See Page 12)*

| | |
|---|---|
| Baccarat, Paperweight, Gridel Elephant | 150.00 |
| Baccarat, Paperweight, Gridel Horse | 150.00 |
| Baccarat, Paperweight, Gridel Rooster, 1971 | 145.00 |
| Baccarat, Paperweight, Gridel Squirrel | 150.00 |
| Baccarat, Paperweight, Huntsman, Faceted, Blue Ground, 3 1/2 In. | 1200.00 |
| Baccarat, Paperweight, Intaglio Winged Assyrian Bull On Crystal Block | 400.00 |
| Baccarat, Paperweight, Millefiori, Special | 170.00 |
| Baccarat, Paperweight, Multicane Mushroom, Latticinio & Blue Spiral Ring | 550.00 |
| Baccarat, Paperweight, Mushroom, Overlay | 225.00 |
| Baccarat, Paperweight, Mushroom, 2 5/8 In. | 200.00 |
| Baccarat, Paperweight, Pansy, Nine Leaves, 1 Bud, 2 3/4 In.Diameter | 600.00 |
| Baccarat, Paperweight, Pear | 250.00 |
| Baccarat, Paperweight, Red & Black Coiled Snake On Blue & Yellow | 300.00 |
| Baccarat, Paperweight, Rooster, Gridel Silhouettes | 150.00 |
| Baccarat, Paperweight, Ruby Flash, Seven Windows, 2 1/2 In. | 700.00 |
| Baccarat, Paperweight, Salamander | 350.00 |
| Baccarat, Paperweight, Signs Of The Zodiac In Canes On Carpet | 140.00 |
| Baccarat, Paperweight, Snake | 300.00 |
| Baccarat, Paperweight, Sulfide, Adlai Stevenson | 62.50 |
| Baccarat, Paperweight, Sulfide, Andrew Jackson | 47.50 |
| Baccarat, Paperweight, Sulfide, Eleanor Roosevelt | 47.50 To 55.00 |
| Baccarat, Paperweight, Sulfide, Harry S.Truman | 55.00 |
| Baccarat, Paperweight, Sulfide, Herbert Hoover | 62.50 To 85.00 |
| Baccarat, Paperweight, Sulfide, James Monroe | 62.50 To 90.00 |
| Baccarat, Paperweight, Sulfide, John F.Kennedy, 1963 | 195.00 |
| Baccarat, Paperweight, Sulfide, John F.Kennedy, 1963, Signed A.David | 500.00 |
| Baccarat, Paperweight, Sulfide, Pope John XXIII | 120.00 |
| Baccarat, Paperweight, Sulfide, Pope Pius XII | 120.00 |
| Baccarat, Paperweight, Sulfide, Theodore Roosevelt | 85.00 To 95.00 |
| Baccarat, Paperweight, Sulfide, Will Rogers | 110.00 To 120.00 |
| Baccarat, Paperweight, Sulfide, Woodrow Wilson | 50.00 |
| Baccarat, Paperweight, Winged Assyrian Bull, Crystal Block, 5 Pounds | 400.00 |
| Baccarat, Paperweight, Zodiac, 12 Signs, Millefiori | 120.00 |
| Baccarat, Perfume, Amberina Swirl, 5 1/2 In. | 24.00 |
| Baccarat, Perfume, Bulbous, Swirled, Hinged Sterling Silver Cover | 28.00 |
| Baccarat, Perfume, Clear To Amberina Swirls, Amberina Swirl Stopper | 25.00 |
| Baccarat, Perfume, Cranberry Floral On Frosted & Clear, Cameo, Acid Cut | 75.00 |
| Baccarat, Perfume, Faceted Crystal, Enameled Fish & Insects, 5 1/2 In. | 70.00 |
| Baccarat, Perfume, Paneled Leaf, Amberina, 5 1/2 In.High | 35.00 |
| Baccarat, Perfume, Stopper, Signed, 5 3/4 In. | 17.50 |
| Baccarat, Pitcher, Crystal, Pontil, 12 In. High | 50.00 |
| Baccarat, Plate, Cake, Clear, Diamond Point, Embossed Signature | 75.00 |
| Baccarat, Plate, Lacy Sandwich Type, Signed, 7 1/2 In. | 65.00 |
| Baccarat, Plate, Rubena Swirl, Scalloped, 5 1/4 In. | 14.00 |
| Baccarat, Plate, Toddy, Lacy, Pale Chartreuse, McKearin 137-7, 4 5/8 In. | 60.00 |
| Baccarat, Relish, Melon Ribbed, Clear To Salmon, Scalloped Top, Signed | 48.00 |
| Baccarat, Relish, Rubina Coloring, Signed, 9 1/2 In.Long | 46.00 |
| Baccarat, Ring Tree, Amber Swirls, Unsigned | 16.50 |
| Baccarat, Tray, Dresser, Amberina, Round, Swirl, 11 1/4 In.Diameter | 55.00 |

Baccarat, Tumble-Up, Swirl, Clear To Ruby, Signed ........................................ 85.00
Baccarat, Tumbler, Rubena Swirl, Signed ........................................ 12.50
Baccarat, Vase, Cut Crystal, Honeycomb, 3 1/2 In.High, Signed ........................ 14.75
Baccarat, Vase, Opalescent, Enamel, Gold Serpent, Red Ladybug, 1900s, 9 In. ............ 425.00
Baccarat, Wine, Yellow Bowl, Clear Twisted Stem, Signed ......................... 25.00
   Bag, Beaded, see Beaded Bag

   *The Whiting numbers refer to the book 'Old Iron Still Banks' by*
   *Hubert B.Whiting.*
Bank, A & P Eight O'clock Coffee, Tin, Rectangular, 1 1/2 X 2 X 4 In. ............... 10.00
Bank, A & P Red Circle Coffee, Tin, 4 In.High ....................................... 4.50
Bank, American Eagle, Ceramic, "Emigrant Savings, " 7 1/4 In. ...................... 4.00
Bank, Apple, Red, Chalkware, 3 In. Diameter ....................................... 10.00
Bank, Atlas, Jar ..................................................................... 4.00
Bank, Atlas, Jar, Amber ............................................................. 5.00
Bank, Aunt Jemima, Iron ............................................................. 18.00
Bank, Baby's Shoe, Blue Plastic, "Jumping Jacks" ................................... 2.00
Bank, Building, Embossed Equitable Loan & Savings, Dayton, O., Iron ................ 45.00
Bank, Building, 4 Slots, Metal, Patent 1918 ........................................ 45.00
Bank, Barrel, Glass ................................................................. 10.00
Bank, Barrel, The Morris Plan Co.Of R.I., Chrome Over Brass ........................ 4.95
Bank, Barrel, Wooden, American Slicer, Key ......................................... 15.00
Bank, Baseball, "Reds, " Camphor Glass, Slotted Base ............................... 14.00
Bank, Battleship Oregon, Iron, Small ............................................... 92.00
Bank, Bear & Beehive, Cast Iron, Wh-169 ............................................ 75.00
Bank, Bear, On Haunches & 2 Feet, Cast Iron ........................................ 50.00
Bank, Bear, Standing, Cast Iron .................................................... 15.00
Bank, Bear, Upright, Brass, 6 In.High .............................................. 40.00
Bank, Bears & Beehive, Wh-169 ............................................. 60.00 To 65.00
Bank, Beehive, Sterling Silver, Wooden Base ........................................ 18.00
Bank, Benjamin Franklin, Metal, Wh-313 ............................................. 4.95
Bank, Billiken, Cast Iron, Patent Number ........................................... 28.00
Bank, Billiken, Good Luck, Iron, Wh-50 ............................................. 24.75
Bank, Bird Dog, Wh-107 ...................................................... 26.00 To 32.00
Bank, Blackpool Tower, English ..................................................... 45.00
Bank, Bokar Coffee, Tin, 4 1/4 In.High ............................................. 3.95
Bank, Book, "Book Of Thrift, "valley National, Arizona, Patent 1923 ................ 5.95
Bank, Book, Berkshire Savings, Pittsfield, Mass., Leather Bound ..................... 6.00
Bank, Book, Crosley Radio, Brass, Leather Bound .................................... 12.50
Bank, Book, Marked G.M.Frigidaire, Green, "A Quarter A Day" Metal .................. 5.95
Bank, Book, Mickey Mouse, Walt Disney .............................................. 32.00
Bank, Book, Mother Hubbard, Lithographed, Tin, Chein, 4 X 3 In. .................... 6.50
Bank, Book, Scrappy ................................................................ 22.00
Bank, Book, Springfield Institute, Mass., Leather Bound ............................ 6.00
Bank, Book, Three Pigs, Walt Disney ................................................ 24.00
Bank, Book, World's Fair, 1939 New York ..................................... 6.50 To 15.00
Bank, Bottle, Figural, Bear, Clear, 4 3/4 In. ...................................... 3.00
Bank, Bottle, Lincoln, Clear, Lincoln Foods, 9 In. ................................. 5.00
Bank, Brick, Save With Standard Oil, Glass ......................................... 17.00
Bank, Bronzed Baby Shoes, Key, 5 In.Long ........................................... 6.50
Bank, Buccaneer With Pipe, Doulton Type, Porcelain, 14 In.High ..................... 37.50
Bank, Buddy, Shape Of World War I Doughboy Hat, "Camp McClellan" ................... 5.50
Bank, Buffalo, Cast Iron, Wh-208 ........................................... 28.00 To 40.00
Bank, Building, Birds, 6 Sided, Wh-320 ............................................. 45.00
Bank, Building, Dime Slot, Iron & Nickel, 3 1/2 X 2 1/4 In. ........................ 25.00
Bank, Building, Flower Panels, 6 Sided, Fancy Finial ............................... 50.00
Bank, Building, Marked City Bank, 2 Story, Iron .................................... 27.50
Bank, Building, Roof Slants & Extends, Porch, 2 Stories, Chimney, Iron, 4 In. ...... 25.00
Bank, Building, 4 Pillars On Top, 9 Stories, Iron, 4 1/2 X 2 1/2 In. ............... 25.00
Bank, Building, 4 Towers, Cast Iron, 5 1/2 In.High ................................. 20.00
Bank, Building, 6 Sided, Birds Of Paradise On Sides, Cast Iron, 6 1/2 In. .......... 50.00
Bank, Bulldog, Sitting, Collar, Iron, 4 1/2 X 4 In. ................................ 25.00
Bank, Buster Brown & Tige, Iron .................................................... 53.00
Bank, Camel With Pack, Wh-256 ...................................................... 65.00
Bank, Cash Register, Tin, Chein .................................................... 2.50
Bank, Cat, Penny, Cast Iron ........................................................ 5.00

| | |
|---|---:|
| Bank, Cat, Sitting, Iron | 14.00 |
| Bank, Charlestown Savings, 100th Anniversary, 1854-1954, Metal, Patent 1917 | 2.95 |
| Bank, Chauffeur Driven 1900 Vintage Limousine, Blue & White | 32.00 |
| Bank, Chest Of Drawers, Saving's, Redware, Yellow Rosettes In Corners | 100.00 |
| Bank, Chevrolet, 1949, Tin | 6.50 |
| Bank, Child's Safe, Picture Of Battleship, Red, Green, & White, Tin | 16.70 |
| Bank, Clock, Wh-224 | 33.00 |
| Bank, Clown, Cast Iron, Gilded, 6 1/4 In.High | 40.00 |
| Bank, Clown, Cast Iron, Wh-29 | 37.00 |
| Bank, Clown, Glass | 2.95 |
| Bank, Clown, Tin, Chein | 12.50 To 15.00 |
| Bank, Cocker Spaniel, Taffy Coloring, Porcelain, 9 In.High | 18.00 |
| Bank, Coin Deposit, Iron | 12.00 |
| Bank, Cottage, Staffordshire, Decorated, 6 3/4 In. | 15.00 To 25.00 |
| Bank, Cottage, Staffordshire, Salmon Color, C.1850 ............................ *Illus* | 80.00 |

Bank, Cottage, Staffordshire, Salmon Color, C.1850

| | |
|---|---:|
| Bank, Court Jester, Coin Slot On Top Of Head, Porcelain | 20.00 |
| Bank, Cow, Iron | 100.00 |
| Bank, Daily Dime Register, Jackie Robinson, Lithographed, Tin | 11.00 |
| Bank, Daily Dime Register, Statue Of Liberty | 4.00 |
| Bank, Daily Dime Register, United Nations | 4.00 |
| Bank, Derche Combination Clock & Alarm, Patent March, 1889 | 55.00 |
| Bank, Davy Crockett, Pony Express, Canvas, Lock & Key | 4.00 |
| Bank, Deer With Antlers, Iron, Painted, Wh-195 | 25.00 |
| Bank, Door, Cast Iron, Large Size, Wh-196 | 95.00 |
| Bank, Dime & Cent Register, Cast Iron, Patent 1891 | 20.00 |
| Bank, Dime Register, Chein, Tin, 2 In. | 4.00 To 10.00 |
| Bank, Dime Register, Luckey | 8.00 |
| Bank, Dime Register, New York World's Fair, 1964 | 2.75 To 5.00 |
| Bank, Dime Register, Popeye, 1929 | 14.50 |
| Bank, Dime Savings, Porcelain, Penholder, Paper Clip, & Band Holder | 11.00 |
| Bank, Dog With Bee, Iron, Painted, Wh-338 | 29.00 |
| Bank, Dog, Seated, Pug, Cast Iron, Wh-111 | 50.00 |
| Bank, Dog's Head, Porcelain, C.1880, 2 In.High | 25.00 |
| Bank, Donkey With Saddle, Cast Iron, Gilt | 45.00 |
| Bank, Donkey, Cast Iron, Wh-198 | 18.00 To 42.00 |
| Bank, Drum, Design Pressed In Sides, Tin, 3 1/4 In.High | 5.00 |
| Bank, Drum, Round Trap Door, Key, No Wording, Tin, Chein, 3 In.Diameter | 8.00 |
| Bank, Drum, Round Trap Door, Key, Wording, Tin, Chein, 3 In.Diameter | 8.00 |
| Bank, Duck, Standing, Iron | 24.50 |
| Bank, Dutch Shoe, Wooden, Tin Closure, Hand-Painted Scene | 4.00 |
| Bank, Eagle, Outstretched Wings, Cast Iron, Gold Gilt, 6 In. | 75.00 |
| Bank, Electrolux Refrigerator | 20.00 |
| Bank, Elephant, Cast Iron, Wh-68 | 30.00 |
| Bank, Elephant, Cast Iron, 4 Wheels, 1 1/8 In.Diameter, Wh-75 | 75.00 |
| Bank, Elephant, Glass | 4.00 |
| Bank, Elephant, Tin, Chein | 15.00 |

| | |
|---|---|
| Bank, Embossed Pittsburgh Paints, Glass | 4.00 |
| Bank, Fidelity Security, Cast Iron | 50.00 |
| Bank, Fido, iron, Black & White Paint, Wh-337 | 26.00 |
| Bank, General Douglas MacArthur Picture In Glass Dome, Cardboard | 10.50 |
| Bank, Glass, Embossed Advertising, 2 1/2 X 2 1/2 X 2 In. | 4.00 |
| Bank, Globe, Eagle Finial, Enterprise Mfg.Co., Phila., Cast Iron | 32.00 |
| Bank, Globe, Tin, Chein | 3.50 To 6.00 |
| Bank, Golliwog | 65.00 |
| Bank, Happy Days, Round Money Trap Bottom, Tin, Chein, 3 3/4 In.High | 8.00 |
| Bank, Happy Days, Square Money Trap Bottom, Tin, Chein, 3 3/4 In.High | 8.00 |
| Bank, Hat, Amos & Andy | 9.00 |
| Bank, Home Thrift Corp., Chicago, Tin, Slot Bottom, 2 1/2 In.High | 15.00 |
| Bank, Home, Decorated, Tin | 60.00 |
| Bank, Horse, Black Beauty, Cast Iron, Wh-82 | 35.00 To 42.00 |
| Bank, Horse, Prancing, Cast Iron, Wh-77 | 42.00 |
| Bank, Horse, Rearing, Cast Iron, Wh-78 | 40.00 |
| Bank, Horse's Head & Horseshoe, Cast Iron | 30.00 |
| Bank, Horseshoe, Buster Brown & Tige, Iron | 36.00 |
| Bank, House, Iron, 3 In.High, Wh-356 | 18.75 |
| Bank, House, Pittsburgh Paints, Glass | 27.00 |
| Bank, House, Wooden, Paper Windows, 3 In. | 2.00 |
| Bank, Humpty-Dumpty, Egg Man On Wall, Brass | 24.00 |
| Bank, Independence Hall, Cast Iron, Wh-447 | 110.00 |
| Bank, Indian, Iron | 100.00 |
| Bank, Indian's Head, "The National Shawmut Bank Of Boston, " Metal | 4.95 |
| Bank, Iron, Black, Tan, & Red Paint, Wh-82 | 30.00 |
| Bank, Jug, Pottery | 2.50 |
| Bank, Kendall Motor Oil, Metal | 4.50 |
| Bank, Kitten, Cast Iron, Wh-335 | 35.00 |
| Bank, Lamb, Iron, Beige Paint, Wh-191 | 30.00 |
| Bank, Lamb, Wh-181 | 27.00 |
| Bank, Liberty Bell, "1926, Sesquicentennial, 1776," Iron, Wh-281 | 14.75 |
| Bank, Liberty Bell, Bank Hawaii, Key, Metal | 6.50 |
| Bank, Liberty Bell, Embossed "Proclaim Liberty Throughout The Land, "iron | 30.00 |
| Bank, Liberty Bell, Glass, Marigold, 200th Year Centennial | 3.00 |
| Bank, Lincoln's Log Cabin, Porcelain, Van Dyk Teas | 12.75 |
| Bank, Lion On Tub, Iron, 4 1/4 In.High | 25.00 |
| Bank, Lion On Wheels, Cast Iron, Wh-95 | 110.00 |
| Bank, Lion, Cast Iron, Gold Paint, 5 In. | 14.00 |
| Bank, Lion, Cast Iron, Wh-89 | 20.00 To 35.00 |
| Bank, Lion, Wh-91 | 20.00 |
| Bank, Little Gem, Pocket, Steel, Marked Little Gem, N.Y. & Chicago, 1891 | 10.00 |
| Bank, Little Red Schoolhouse, Milk Glass | 27.50 |
| Bank, Little Victorian Girl Leaning On Pocketbook, Porcelain | 45.00 |
| Bank, Log Cabin Syrup Bottle, Clear | 35.00 |
| Bank, Log Cabin, Milk Glass | 27.50 |
| Bank, Lord Nelson, Toby Mug Type, Porcelain, 10 1/4 In.High | 32.00 |
| Bank, Lucky Joe, Glass | 4.00 |
| Bank, Luncheonette, Battery Operated | 12.00 |
| Bank, Mailbox, Cast Iron, Wh-122 | 35.00 |
| Bank, Mailbox, Iron, Wh-124 | 38.00 |
| Bank, Mailbox, Red Top, Blue Bottom, Iron | 14.00 |
| Bank, Majestic Radio | 22.50 |
| Bank, Mammy, Cast Iron, Wh-22 | 30.00 |
| Bank, Mammy, Iron, Red Dress, White Apron, Blue & White Polka Dot Scarf | 30.00 |
| Bank, Man With Nodding Head Holding High Hat, Carved Wood, 10 1/2 In. High | 110.00 |
| Bank, Man, Plastic, Hair, Germany, U.S.Zone | 25.00 |
| Bank, Marx Budget, Red, Tin | 2.00 |

*Mechanical banks were first made about 1870. Any bank with moving parts is considered mechanical, although those most collected are the metal banks made before World War I. Reproductions are being made.*

| | |
|---|---|
| Bank, Mechanical, Always Did Spise A Mule, Iron, 6 In. *Illus* | 250.00 |
| Bank, Mechanical, Artillery, Cast Iron, Bronze Finish | 290.00 |
| Bank, Mechanical, Billy Grin, Painted | 400.00 |
| Bank, Mechanical, Boy Scout, Cast Iron | 900.00 |

| | |
|---|---|
| Bank, Mechanical, Bull & Bear, Brass | 1250.00 |
| Bank, Mechanical, Bulldog, Dog Swallows Coin | 150.00 |
| Bank, Mechanical, Chief Big Moon | 275.00 |
| Bank, Mechanical, Chimpanzee | 800.00 |
| Bank, Mechanical, Creedmore | 120.00 To 235.00 |
| Bank, Mechanical, Darktown Battery | 230.00 To 350.00 |
| Bank, Mechanical, Darktown Battery, Brass Pattern | 450.00 |
| Bank, Mechanical, Dinah, Iron | 145.00 To 225.00 |
| Bank, Mechanical, Dog Charges Boy, Bronze Finish | 400.00 |
| Bank, Mechanical, Eagle & Eaglets | 225.00 |
| Bank, Mechanical, Elephant With Howdah, Iron | 130.00 |
| Bank, Mechanical, Elephant, Cast Iron, Hubley | 60.00 |
| Bank, Mechanical, Elephant, Jumbo, Meyers No.84 | 120.00 |
| Bank, Mechanical, Elephant, Painted, 3 Stars, Cast Iron | 190.00 |
| Bank, Mechanical, Elephant, 3 Star, Brass | 80.00 |
| Bank, Mechanical, Fortune Teller | 175.00 |
| Bank, Mechanical, French's Automotive, Cast Iron | 900.00 |
| Bank, Mechanical, Frog On Lattice, Painted | 100.00 |
| Bank, Mechanical, Globe Savings Fund | 375.00 |
| Bank, Mechanical, Hall's Excelsior, Monkey Cashier, Label | 160.00 |
| Bank, Mechanical, Hand-Carved Money Box On Wooden Base, 10 1/4 In. | 1050.00 |
| Bank, Mechanical, Hippo, Windup, Tin, 6 In. | 5.75 To 12.00 |
| Bank, Mechanical, Humpty-Dumpty, Clown, 8 1/2 In.  *Illus* | 175.00 |
| Bank, Mechanical, Indian Shooting Bear, Cast Iron | 225.00 |
| Bank, Mechanical, Johah & The Whale, Cast Iron | 350.00 |
| Bank, Mechanical, Jolly Nigger, Butterfly Tie | 100.00 |
| Bank, Mechanical, Jolly Nigger, Cast Iron, J.E. Stevens Co. | 70.00 |
| Bank, Mechanical, Jolly Nigger, Shepard | 40.00 |
| Bank, Mechanical, Jolly Nigger, Starkey, Aluminum | 65.00 To 76.00 |
| Bank, Mechanical, Lilliput, Painted | 110.00 |
| Bank, Mechanical, Lion & Monkey | 175.00 |
| Bank, Mechanical, Little Joe, Iron | 90.00 To 125.00 |
| Bank, Mechanical, Magic | 260.00 |
| Bank, Mechanical, Monkey & Coconut, Painted | 600.00 |
| Bank, Mechanical, Monkey With Organ, Iron | 75.00 |
| Bank, Mechanical, Monkey With Organ, Tips Hat, Tin, Chein | 35.00 |
| Bank, Mechanical, Owl With Turned Head, Painted, Patent Date 1875 | 125.00 |
| Bank, Mechanical, Owl, Slot In Book, Cast Iron, Painted | 250.00 |
| Bank, Mechanical, Owl, Slot In Head | 280.00 |
| Bank, Mechanical, Paddy & His Pig | 425.00 |
| Bank, Mechanical, Punch & Judy, Painted | 350.00 |
| Bank, Mechanical, Rabbit In Cabbage Patch, Cast Iron | 250.00 |
| Bank, Mechanical, Rooster, Iron | 55.00 |
| Bank, Mechanical, Sambo, Wiggles Ears, Aluminum | 300.00 |
| Bank, Mechanical, Santa Claus, C.1889 | 75.00 To 100.00 |
| Bank, Mechanical, Snapping Bulldog, Savings, Patent 1878 | 1050.00 |
| Bank, Mechanical, Speaking Dog, Iron, 7 1/2 In.  *Illus* | 225.00 |

Bank, Mechanical, Always Did Spise A Mule, Iron, 6 In.
*(See Page 16)*

Bank, Mechanical, Speaking Dog,
Iron, 7 1/2 In.

Bank, Mechanical, Humpty-Dumpty, Clown, 8 1/2 In.
*(See Page 17)*

| | |
|---|---|
| Bank, Mechanical, Stump Speaker, Cast Iron | 425.00 |
| Bank, Mechanical, Tabby | 110.00 |
| Bank, Mechanical, Tammany, Iron | 80.00 To 140.00 |
| Bank, Mechanical, Tammany, Square Receptacle | 90.00 |
| Bank, Mechanical, Teddy & The Bear, Cast Iron | 125.00 To 310.00 |
| Bank, Mechanical, The Forty-Niner, Made Over Cigar Cutter | 375.00 |
| Bank, Mechanical, The Mortar, Cast Iron, Square Fort | 750.00 |
| Bank, Mechanical, Trick Pony | 400.00 |
| Bank, Mechanical, Uncle Sam, Cast Iron | 170.00 To 475.00 |
| Bank, Mechanical, Uncle Tom, Lapels, 1 Star, Brass Base, Painted | 95.00 |
| Bank, Mechanical, Wild West | 24.00 |
| Bank, Mechanical, William Tell | 235.00 |
| Bank, Mechanical, Wireless | 200.00 |
| Bank, Mechanical, World's Fair, Painted | 170.00 |
| Bank, Mickey Mouse Club | 7.00 |
| Bank, Mickey Mouse, English Pie Cut Eyes, Tin | 18.00 |
| Bank, Model T 1927 Ford Sedan Shape, Metal, Key | 7.75 |
| Bank, Money Chest, Pottery, "Replica 1st Money Chest, 1834, Bowery Savings" | 4.00 |
| Bank, Monkey, Tin, Chein | 12.50 |
| Bank, Mr.Peanut, Plastic, 8 In. | 8.00 |
| Bank, Mule, Saddled, Cast Iron | 29.00 |
| Bank, Mutt & Jeff, Cast Iron, Gold Gilt On Black, Wh-13 | 55.00 To 75.00 |
| Bank, Oilcan, Atlantic Premium Motor Oil, Tin, 2 7/8 In. High | 4.75 |
| Bank, Old Man Seated In Chair, Fez Hat, Turkish Pipe, Staffordshire Type | 35.00 |
| Bank, Oval Shape, "Plymouth County Trust Co., " Nickel On Brass, 1913 | 7.75 |
| Bank, Oval, Merchants Co-Op Bank, Boston, Chrome Over Brass | 7.75 |
| Bank, Owl On Stump, "Be Wise-Save Money, " Wh-204 | 63.00 |
| Bank, Pail, Tin, Penny, "A Penny Saved, Etc." | 5.00 |
| Bank, Penny, Blown Glass, Blue | 7.50 |
| Bank, Penny, Pyramid Shape, Penny Goes Through Series Of Slots, Cast Iron | 600.00 |
| Bank, Pewter, Handwrought, Hinge & Clasp, Star At Each Side Of Slot | 25.00 |
| Bank, Pig, Brown Mottled Pottery, 6 X 3 1/2 In. | 25.00 |
| Bank, Pig, Carnival Glass, Marigold, 4 In. | 3.00 |
| Bank, Pig, Iron, Wh-179 | 28.00 |
| Bank, Pig, Iron, Wh-181 | 26.00 |
| Bank, Pig, Razorback, Pottery, 14 In. Long | 5.00 |
| Bank, Pig, Risque, Twist Tail, Cast Iron | 270.00 |
| Bank, Pig, Sitting, Cast Iron, Wh-179 | 30.00 |
| Bank, Pig, Standing, Pottery | 2.50 |
| Bank, Pig, White, Small | 20.00 |
| Bank, Pink Pig Inside, Green | 25.00 |
| Bank, Poodle, Seated, Redware, C.1850, 6 3/4 In. | 250.00 |
| Bank, Pottery, Coach | 2.50 |
| Bank, Pottery, Grapes | 2.50 |
| Bank, Presto, Cast Iron, Wh-26 | 15.00 To 20.00 |
| Bank, Puppy & Bee, Wh-338 | 20.00 |
| Bank, Puppy, Iron, Wh-337 | 32.00 |

Bank, Purse Shape, Porcelain, Raised Flowers, "pin Money" .......... 5.00
Bank, Radio Shape, Cast Iron, Embossed Radio Bank .......... 25.00
Bank, Radio, Glass .......... 10.00
Bank, Radio, Kenton Toys, Ohio, Painted, 4 In.Wide, 2 1/2 In.Long .......... 12.75
Bank, Raised Indian's Head In Center, Savings Bank In Raised Letters, Tin .......... 5.95
Bank, Randolph Savings Bank, Ma., Patent 1917 & 1926, Metal, Round .......... 2.95
Bank, Red Brick, Tin, Marx .......... 12.00
Bank, Refrigerator, Metal, 2 X 4 In. .......... 14.00
Bank, Register, Uncle Sam, Metal, Red, 3 Coin .......... 10.00
Bank, Replica Of Instamatic Kodak, Plastic .......... 4.00
Bank, Rooster, Cast Iron, Gold Gilt, 4 3/4 In.High, Wh-187 .......... 50.00
Bank, Roy Rogers, Savings, Horseshoe Lock, Key, Lithographed, Tin .......... 9.50
Bank, Rustic Log Cabin, Wooden, Hand-Carved, Painted, 9 X 6 1/4 In. .......... 8.00
Bank, Safe, Cast Iron, Gilded Filigree, 4 Footed, Marked 1896 .......... 20.00
Bank, Safe, Coin Deposit Band, Combination Lock, Iron, 5 1/8 In. High .......... 18.75
Bank, Safe, Coin Deposit, Combination Lock, Iron, 5 1/8 In.High .......... 18.75
Bank, Safe, Columbus, Combination Lock, Iron, 5 3/8 In.High .......... 18.75
Bank, Safe, Combination, Iron & Steel, Kenton, 4 In. .......... 25.00
Bank, Safe, Deposit, Ideal, Combination Lock, Iron, Patent Applied For .......... 22.00
Bank, Safe, Double Combination, Cast Iron, Dated '81 & '87, 6 In High .......... 49.00
Bank, Safe, Henry Chart Mfg.Co., Mich., Patent May 2, 1885, Cast Iron, Painted .......... 75.00
Bank, Safe, Iron, Patent 1896, 3 1/2 In. .......... 12.50
Bank, Safe, Iron, Wh-4 .......... 50.00
Bank, Safe, J.E.Stevens' Key Lock, Dated 1897, Iron .......... 20.00
Bank, Safe, Key, Iron, 3 3/4 In.High .......... 12.75
Bank, Safe, Marked Sport, Sporting Scenes, Iron, Patent 1882 .......... 19.75
Bank, Safe, Openwork Design, Iron, 3 1/4 In.High .......... 12.75
Bank, Safe, Openwork Design, Patent 1896, Key, Iron, 3 3/8 In.High .......... 14.75
Bank, Safe, Security Safe Deposit, Gold Trim, Black, Brass Lock, 1887 .......... 58.00
Bank, Safe, State, Combination Lock, Iron, 4 1/8 In.High .......... 16.75
Bank, Sailor, Cast Iron, C.World War I, 5 1/2 In. .......... 30.00
Bank, Sailor, Cast Iron, Gold Gilt, Wh-16 .......... 60.00
Bank, Save & Smile Money Box .......... 75.00
Bank, Savings Deposit, Combination Lock, Kenton Brand .......... 10.00
Bank, Savings, 10 Cents, Tin, Red, Gold Trim, Slot In Back, 3 X 2 X 5/8 In. .......... 10.00
Bank, Scottie Dog, White Metal .......... 2.50 To 10.00
Bank, Security Safe Deposit, Cast Iron .......... 19.00
Bank, Security, 5 Coin, Tin, Painted .......... 20.00
Bank, Sharecropper, Cast Iron, Wh-18 .......... 40.00
Bank, Shell, Cast Iron, 8 In.High .......... 50.00
Bank, Six Sided Stove .......... 50.00
Bank, Six Sided Stove, Flower Finial .......... 60.00
Bank, Skyscraper, Iron .......... 12.00
Bank, Sleeping Bulldog On Top, White Porcelain, 1 1/2 X 2 In. .......... 5.50
Bank, Speaking Dog, Savings, Wooden Box, Dovetailed .......... 80.00
Bank, St.Bernard Dog With Pack, Iron, Painted, 5 3/4 X 4 3/4 In. .......... 25.00
Bank, Standing Bear, Patent Applied For On Back .......... 35.00
Bank, Standing Bear, Wh-329 .......... 18.00
Bank, State Bank, Cupola, 6 In. .......... 45.00
Bank, Tally Ho .......... 60.00
Bank, The Late Duke Wellington, Toby Mug Type, Porcelain, 7 1/2 In.High .......... 25.00
Bank, Tin, "watch Me Grow" .......... 45.00
Bank, Top Hat, Iron, "pass Around The Hat" .......... 22.50
Bank, Tower, Cast Iron, Wh-437 .......... 125.00
Bank, Transvaal Money Box, Squatty Man, High Hat, Brass .......... 36.00
Bank, Turkey, Cast Iron .......... 45.00 To 50.00
Bank, Two Faced Woman, Cast Iron, Wh-44 .......... 75.00
Bank, U.S.Mail, Green, Slot Top, "letters, " 4 Legs, Cast Iron, 3 3/4 In.High .......... 18.00
Bank, U.S.Mail, Wh-127 .......... 18.00
Bank, U.S.Mailbox, Cast Iron, Green Paint, 3 3/4 In. High .......... 16.00
Bank, U.S.Mailbox, Movable Slot, 4 In. .......... 30.00
Bank, Uncle Sam, "time To Save Bank, " Cutout Of Uncle Sam, Wooden Base .......... 5.50
Bank, Westminster Abbey, Cast Iron, Wh-170 .......... 75.00
Bank, Williamsburg Savings, Porcelain, Clock & Domed Tower, Penholder .......... 8.50
Bank, Windmill, Sterling Silver, 5 In. High .......... 80.00
Bank, Woman, 2 Faced, Cast Iron, Gold Trim, 4 In.High .......... 60.00

| | |
|---|---|
| Bank, Woolworth Building, Iron, 8 In. | 25.00 |
| Bank, World Globe, Ohio Art, Tin, "As You Save, So You Prosper" | 5.00 |
| Bank, Yorkshire Terrier, Begging, Chalkware, Red & Black On White, 12 In. | 20.00 |
| Bank, Young Negro | 50.00 |
| Barometer, Angle Tube, Mahogany, Scottish, C.1750, Molliner, 35 In.High | 775.00 |
| Barometer, Banjo, Rosewood, Cavel, C.1825, 38 1/4 In.High | 140.00 |
| Barometer, Brass & Copper, Stick, James Green, N.Y., C.1850, 41 1/2 In. | 400.00 |
| Barometer, Directoire, Carved Gilt Wood, Ormolu Case, 34 1/2 In.High | 325.00 |
| Barometer, Mantel, Oak, Hand-Carved, Victorian | 85.00 |
| Barometer, Oak Case, Arched Top, Shell Base, Enamel Lettering, C.1890 | 75.00 |
| Barometer, Passement Au Louvre, Louis XVI Style, Ormolu, Sevres, C.1890 | 1100.00 |
| Barometer, Simmon's, Portable | 185.00 |

Barr, see Worcester

*Basalt is a black stoneware made by mixing iron and oxides into a basic clay. It is very hard and can be finished on a lathe. Wedgwood developed his famous black basalt in 1769, which was an improvement on a similar ware made in Staffordshire, England, as early as 1740. Basalt is still being made in England and on the Continent.*

| | |
|---|---|
| Basalt, Coffeepot, Black, Greek Figures, Acanthus Leaf Trim, 10 1/2 In.High | 275.00 |
| Batman, Key Ring, On Card, Picture Of Batman & Robin | 1.00 |
| Batman, Mug, Milk Glass | 3.00 |

*Battersea enamels are enamels painted on copper and made in the Battersea District of London from about 1750 to 1756. Many similar enamels are mistakenly called Battersea.*

| | |
|---|---|
| Battersea, Box, Floral Lid, "Lay Hold On Time While In Your Prime, " 2 In. | 168.00 |
| Battersea, Box, Hinged, Oval, Blue | 130.00 |
| Battersea, Box, Patch, Oval, Motto On Top, Green Enamel Base, C.1750 | 175.00 |
| Battersea, Box, Serpentine Front, Floral On Yellow | 145.00 |
| Battersea, Knob, Mirror, Medieval Scene, Pair | 125.00 |

*Bavaria was a district where many types of pottery and porcelain were made for centuries. The words Bavaria, Germany, appeared after 1871.*

Bavarian, see also Rosenthal

| | |
|---|---|
| Bavarian, Bowl, Carmer, 8 1/2 X 1 3/4 In. | 12.50 |
| Bavarian, Bowl, Cherries, Leaves & Sky, Scalloped Gold Rim, 9 In. | 16.00 |
| Bavarian, Bowl, Lattice Sides, Floral, Gold Trim, 10 In. | 20.00 |
| Bavarian, Bowl, Oval, Pink & Green Leaves, Hutschenreuther Selb, 10 In. | 10.00 |
| Bavarian, Box, Collar & Cuffs, Collar Shape, Floral, Gold Trim, 2 1/2 In. | 18.00 |
| Bavarian, Box, Trinket, Finger Roll Shape, Roses, Signed W.Wilson | 12.00 |
| Bavarian, Cake Set, Hand-Painted Forget-Me-Nots, 5 Piece | 50.00 |
| Bavarian, Celery, Mother-Of-Pearl Center, Fruit Basket Center, C.1900, 11 In. | 8.00 |
| Bavarian, Celery, Pink Roses, Gold Edge & Center, Pierced Handles | 9.50 |
| Bavarian, Celery, Pink Roses, Pale Blue Border, 12 1/2 X 5 In. | 15.00 |
| Bavarian, Celery, Purple & Yellow Violets On White, Z.S.& Co. | 12.00 |
| Bavarian, Chocolate Pot, Maple Leaves, Daisies & Blueberries On Cream | 52.50 |
| Bavarian, Chocolate Pot, Roses & Medallion On White, 9 1/2 In.High | 9.00 |
| Bavarian, Chocolate Set, Bank Of Wild Roses On Cream, 11 Piece | 60.00 |
| Bavarian, Creamer, Hand-Painted Roses On White | 6.50 |
| Bavarian, Cup & Saucer, Bouillon, Gold Fleur-De-Lis & Band On White | 9.50 |
| Bavarian, Cup & Saucer, Demitasse, Alka, Brown, Gold Design | 7.00 |
| Bavarian, Cup & Saucer, Demitasse, Fuchsia & White, Floral, Gold Trim | 9.50 |
| Bavarian, Cup & Saucer, Gold Band, White & Pink Floral, Yellow Band | 12.00 |
| Bavarian, Cup & Saucer, Purple With Roses, Thomas | 12.00 |
| Bavarian, Dish, Bone, Gold, Scalloped Edge, Floral, Mitterteich, Bavaria | 3.50 |
| Bavarian, Group, Two Ducks At Water Trough, 1 1/4 In.High | 4.50 |
| Bavarian, Hatpin Holder, Pine & Pinecones On Blue & White, Coin Gold Top | 20.00 |
| Bavarian, Jar & Underplate, Jam, Covered, Roses & Gold On Pink & Green | 55.00 |
| Bavarian, Jar, Biscuit, Squatty, Pink, Yellow, & White Roses On White, Gold | 29.50 |
| Bavarian, Match Holder, Pocket, Saucer Base, Boats Scene, Signed Waldez | 18.00 |
| Bavarian, Muffineer, Purple Pansies & Green On Pastel | 20.00 |
| Bavarian, Pipe, Ram's Head | 30.00 |
| Bavarian, Plate, Autumn Leaves & Acorns, Scalloped, Signed Alberti, 8 In. | 11.00 |
| Bavarian, Plate, Black & Cream, Gold & Floral, Curved Corners, 8 In.Square | 12.50 |
| Bavarian, Plate, Bread, Open Handles, "Give Us This Day, " Floral, 9 3/4 In. | 22.00 |
| Bavarian, Plate, Cake, Gold Handles & Trim, Yellow Roses, 10 In. | 16.00 |

Bavarian, Plate, Cake, Open Iris & Bud With Leaves Center, Cobalt Border ........................ 27.00
Bavarian, Plate, Cake, Open Iris Center, Cobalt Border ........................ 22.00
Bavarian, Plate, Cake, Pierced, Floral & Gold On Mottled Green, Schumann ........................ 27.50
Bavarian, Plate, Cake, Purple & White Grapes, Pierced Handles, Louise, 11 In. ........................ 30.00
Bavarian, Plate, Cake, Red, Yellow, & Pink Roses, Raised Scrolls, 9 1/2 In. ........................ 26.00
Bavarian, Plate, Chop, Hand-Painted Lavendar & Gold Mums ........................ 35.00
Bavarian, Plate, Colorado Columbine, Artist-Signed, J.& C.Louise, 8 1/2 In. ........................ 14.50
Bavarian, Plate, Giant Yellow Roses, Green Leaves, Gilt Edge, 8 1/2 In. ........................ 16.00
Bavarian, Plate, Gleaners, Green Border, Gold Scrolls, 10 In. ........................ 60.00
Bavarian, Plate, Gold Band On White, 7 3/4 In. ........................ 3.00
Bavarian, Plate, Hand-Painted Fruits & Nuts, Signed Thomas, 9 In. ........................ 15.00
Bavarian, Plate, Man & Woman Harvesting, 6 In. ........................ 8.00
Bavarian, Plate, Portrait, Lady & Cherub, Pink & Gold Border, 9 In. ........................ 12.50
Bavarian, Plate, Two Turkeys, 7 1/2 In. ........................ 12.75
Bavarian, Platter, Game, Deer & Doe In Water, Gold Border, Signed R.K.Beck ........................ 33.00
Bavarian, Platter, Purple & Yellow Pansies On Blue, Gold Trim, 11 1/2 In. ........................ 15.00
Bavarian, Relish, Cosmos, 2 Handled, Gold, Hutschenreuther, 8 3/4 In. ........................ 10.50
Bavarian, Relish, Hand Painted Donatello, Signed, 10 In.Long ........................ 8.50
Bavarian, Relish, Oval, Pink Roses, Scalloped Gold Edge, Malmaison, 9 In. ........................ 16.00
Bavarian, Relish, Oval, 6 Pink Roses With Green On White, Pierced Ends ........................ 9.50
Bavarian, Salt, Individual, White, Wide Gold Band, 3 Gold Ball Feet ........................ 4.00
Bavarian, Saltshaker, Hand-Painted Forget-Me-Nots, Z.S.& C.Bavaria ........................ 12.00
Bavarian, Sauce, Blue Forget-Me-Nots On Pale Blue, 2 Handled, 10 In.Long ........................ 12.00
Bavarian, Sauce, Hand-Painted Cherries, Signed M Kemp, 5 In. ........................ 6.00
Bavarian, Saucer, Yellow Leaves Border, Blue Bows, Mitterteich, Bavaria ........................ 2.00
Bavarian, Tea Set, Butterflies, 3 Piece ........................ 30.00
Bavarian, Tea Set, Pink Roses & Leaf Decoration, 3 Piece ........................ 45.00
Bavarian, Teapot & Underplate, Individual, Poppies, Gold, Schlegelmilch ........................ 45.00
Bavarian, Teapot, Individual, Floral, Luster, Marked Bavaria ........................ 10.00
Bavarian, Tile, Tea, Gold I Script Center, Pink Roses Border ........................ 7.00
Bavarian, Tile, Tea, Pink, Red, & Yellow Roses Center, Pink Luster Border ........................ 8.00
Bavarian, Tile, Tea, Red Roses Center, Mottled Pink, Red, & Yellow Border ........................ 8.00
Bavarian, Urn, Covered, Lady's Portrait On Sides, Handled, Gold Trim, 10 In. ........................ 425.00
    Bayonet, see Weapon, Bayonet
Beaded Bag, Black & Silver Sequins, Chain Handle, Clasp ........................ 3.95
Beaded Bag, Black, Coin Size ........................ 6.00
Beaded Bag, Black, Silverlike Chain & Frame ........................ 6.50
Beaded Bag, Carnival Glasslike Beads, Gray Silver ........................ 16.50
Beaded Bag, Carved Ivory Top ........................ 75.00
Beaded Bag, Child's, Gold Mesh, Whiting & Davis ........................ 16.50
Beaded Bag, Diamond Pattern Iridescent Beads, Gilt Filigree Frame, Fringe ........................ 16.00
Beaded Bag, Flowers, Drawstring ........................ 6.50
Beaded Bag, Gray, Silver & Gold ........................ 15.00
Beaded Bag, Iridescent Beads In Diamond Pattern, Fringe, Gilt Frame ........................ 16.00
Beaded Bag, Multicolor Beads In Scroll & Floral Design, Fringe ........................ 16.00
Beaded Bag, Multicolor Floral Beading On White, Fringed Bottom ........................ 10.00
Beaded Bag, Multicolored Beads, Bronze, Fringed ........................ 20.00
Beaded Bag, Scroll & Floral Multicolor Beads, Gilt Filigree Frame, Fringe ........................ 16.00
Beaded Bag, Shades Of White, Bead Handle ........................ 7.50
    Beam, see Bottle, Beam
Beatles, Bag, Zipper, 1964 ........................ 5.00
Beatles, Doll, George Harrison, Inflatable ........................ 5.00
Beatles, Doll, Paul, Vinyl, Saran Hair, Guitar, 1964, 4 1/2 In. Tall ........................ 5.00
Beatles, Doll, Ringo ........................ 20.00
Beatles, Pail, Lunch, Yellow Submarine ........................ 10.00
Beck, Game Set, Flying Ducks, Standing Birds, Scalloped Platter, 5 Piece ........................ 69.00
Beck, Plate, Ear Of Corn, Signed, 9 In. ........................ 18.50
Beck, Plate, Fish, Gold Scalloped Edge, Dresden, Semiporcelain, 9 1/2 In. ........................ 16.00
Beck, Plate, Two Deer In Stream, Woods, 12 1/2 In. ........................ 37.50
Beck, Platter, Fish, New Jersey China Pottery Co., Artist-Signed ........................ 15.00
Beck, Platter, Fish, Snapping At Lure, Signed, 13 1/2 In. ........................ 35.00
Beck, Platter, Fish, 16 In. ........................ 32.00

 *Beehive, Austria, or Beehive, Vienna, china includes all the many types of decorated porcelain marked with the famous beehive mark. The mark has been used since the eighteenth century.*

Beehive, Bowl, Square, Hand-Painted Classical Scenes, 9 1/2 In., Pair ............................................ 200.00
Beehive, Box, Dome Cover, Square, Girl & Cupid, Signed Herr, 2 1/2 In. ............................ 25.00
Beehive, Compote, Rouge, Cobalt, & Gold, Beehive Mark ............................................ 26.50
Beehive, Creamer, Hand-Painted, 3 Footed, Miniature .................................................. 28.00
Beehive, Cup & Saucer, Demitasse, Diagonal Swirl Ribbed, Pink Chrysanthemum ...................... 25.00
Beehive, Cup & Saucer, Empire Style, Fox Hunt Scene ............................................ 110.00
Beehive, Cup & Saucer, Hunting Scene, Wearing Red Coats, Empire Style ........................... 110.00
Beehive, Figurine, Cat, White, Preening, Augarten, Austria, 5 1/2 2n. .............................. 27.50
Beehive, Plate, Man & Lady, Cat Edge, Rose & Gold Floral, 7 1/2 In. .............................. 14.00
Beehive, Plate, Portrait, Brownette With Lyre, Gold Rim, 9 7/8 In. ................................... 79.00
Beehive, Plate, Portrait, Girl & Name Constance, Blue & Gold, 9 1/2 In. ........................... 52.00
Beehive, Plate, Portrait, Lady With Artist's Palette, Gold Rim, 9 7/8 In. ............................ 79.00
Beehive, Plate, Portrait, Lady, Gold & Mahogany Border, 9 1/2 In. .................................. 75.00
Beehive, Plate, Red & Gold, 9 3/4 In. ..............................................................*Illus* 65.00

Beehive, Plate, Red & Gold, 9 3/4 In.

Beehive, Plate, Vignettes, Royal Vienna, 7 In. .................................................. 14.50
Beehive, Urn, Covered, Rococo Scroll Handled, Footed, Pierced, Applique, 7 In. ................ 65.00
Beehive, Urn, Double Handled, Classical Figures On Maroon, Gold, Beading ..................... 45.00

*Bells have been made of china, glass, or metal. All types are collected.*
Bell, Amber Glass, Crystal Corset Shape Handle, Crystal Clapper, 10 In. ....................... 95.00
Bell, Blown Glass, Blue, White Rim, Diamond-Quilted, Clear Handle, 9 3/4 In. .................. 80.00
Bell, Blown Glass, Dark Green, 6 In. ............................................................ 6.00
Bell, Bohemian Glass, Ruby, Vintage, Clear Handle .............................................. 17.00
Bell, Brass, Altar, Embossed Swan, Lion, Owl, & Angel, Latin Words, 2 In. ...................... 15.00
Bell, Brass, Apostle, Openwork, Names, Embossed Birds & Animals, 4 3/4 In. ................... 45.00
Bell, Brass, Clapper, Marked M, C.1870, 3 3/4 In.High ........................................ 9.75
Bell, Brass, Cluster Of 3 That Strike One Another ............................................ 6.50
Bell, Brass, Colonial Lady .................................................................... 16.50
Bell, Brass, Country Store, Circular Spring Attachment For Door, 2 1/2 In. ..................... 15.00
Bell, Brass, Cow, Handmade ................................................... 12.00 To 15.00
Bell, Brass, Cow, Leather Handle, 4 In. ........................................................ 5.00
Bell, Brass, Cow, Leather Handle, 5 In. ........................................................ 9.00
Bell, Brass, Cow, Stamped 1878 ............................................................... 75.00
Bell, Brass, Cow, Swiss, Musical, Reeded Chiantel Fondeur, 1878 ............................. 22.00
Bell, Brass, Cow, 4 1/2 In.High ............................................................... 10.00
Bell, Brass, Cow, 5 1/2 In. ................................................................... 9.00
Bell, Brass, Dickens' Fat Boy Figural Handle ................................................. 22.00
Bell, Brass, Dinner, Embossed Fishtail Handle ............................................... 12.50
Bell, Brass, Disciple, Marked Luxembourg, 5 1/2 X 4 In. ...................................... 40.00
Bell, Brass, Door, Spring, Spider Shape, Conical, 3 In. Diameter ............................. 10.00
Bell, Brass, Dutch Boy ...................................................... 16.50 To 20.00
Bell, Brass, Dutch Girl Carrying Umbrella & Basket, 3 3/4 In.High ............................ 14.00
Bell, Brass, Dutch Girl, 2 1/8 In.High ......................................................... 10.00
Bell, Brass, Figural Schoolhouse, 7 In.High ................................................... 24.00
Bell, Brass, Figural, Girl Carrying Water Pitcher, 4 In.High ................................... 16.00
Bell, Brass, Figural, Mary, Queen Of Scots ................................................... 12.00

| | |
|---|---|
| Bell, Brass, Flatbuckle Shape Handle, Flared At Base, 3 1/2 In.High | 8.50 |
| Bell, Brass, From Ahriens Fox Fire Engine, 1918 | 22.50 |
| Bell, Brass, Hand, Beehive Shape, 3 5/8 In. High | 4.75 |
| Bell, Brass, Hand, Handle Is Figure Of Dutch Boy, 7 In.High | 15.00 |
| Bell, Brass, Hand, 9 In.High, 4 1/2 In.At Base | 26.00 |
| Bell, Brass, Harness, 3 In.Diameter | 15.00 |
| Bell, Brass, Horse Saddle, Nickel Plated, 2 Inside Of Frame, 3 Finials | 25.00 |
| Bell, Brass, Horse Shaft, Nickel Plated, 4 Graduated On Metal Strap | 15.00 |
| Bell, Brass, Horseshoe Shape Hanger Device, 6 In.Diameter | 27.50 |
| Bell, Brass, Lady In Ruffled Skirt, 4 3/4 In.High | 29.50 |
| Bell, Brass, Lady, Bow Headdress, Laced Bodice, Ypres On Back, 3 In.High | 27.00 |
| Bell, Brass, Marked China, Phoenix Birds Form Arch, 4 X 10 X 10 In. | 42.50 |
| Bell, Brass, Miss Muffet | 17.50 |
| Bell, Brass, Monkey Shape | 20.00 |
| Bell, Brass, Nickel Plated, Spain, Horse, 12 1 1/2 In. On Leather Strap | 19.50 |
| Bell, Brass, Oval, 3 On Strap | 12.50 |
| Bell, Brass, Plantation, 7 1/2 In. | 30.00 |
| Bell, Brass, Push Down, 3 Legged Table Form, Opera Glasses & Book On Table | 125.00 |
| Bell, Brass, Queen Elizabeth, Hands At Side, 2 1/4 In. | 18.50 |
| Bell, Brass, Rearing Horse, China | 8.00 |
| Bell, Brass, School, Dunkard Family | 19.50 |
| Bell, Brass, School, Hand, Embossed Floral Design, Dated 1878, 3 1/4 In. | 7.00 |
| Bell, Brass, School, Hand, Embossed Floral Design, Dated 1878, 4 In. | 9.00 |
| Bell, Brass, School, Hand, Embossed Floral Design, Dated 1878, 5 In. | 10.00 |
| Bell, Brass, School, Turned Wood Brass Tipped Handle, 10 In. High | 38.00 |
| Bell, Brass, Schoolteacher's, Hand, Wooden Handle, 8 In. High | 20.00 |
| Bell, Brass, Schoolteacher's, Hand, Wooden Handle, 9 1/4 In. High | 22.75 |
| Bell, Brass, Schoolteacher's, Hand, 6 3/8 In. High | 15.00 |
| Bell, Brass, Schoolteacher's, Hand, 8 1/4 In. High | 20.00 |
| Bell, Brass, Shaft, Musical, Chime, Pair On 10 1/2 In.Shaft | 12.50 |
| Bell, Brass, Shaft, Musical, Set Of 3 On Leather Strap | 15.00 |
| Bell, Brass, Sheep, Clapper | 3.75 |
| Bell, Brass, Ship's, Brunswick, Ga., Mount On Side, 1898 | 155.00 |
| Bell, Brass, Ship's, U.S.N., 1898, Eagle Finial, Mounting Arm, 11 1/2 In. | 175.00 |
| Bell, Brass, Silver Plated, Ornate Handle, 4 In. | 16.50 |
| Bell, Brass, Sleigh, Buckeye, Top Slot, Riveted, 36 On 89 In.Strap, 1 1/4 In. | 85.00 |
| Bell, Brass, Sleigh, Cotter Keys, Rivets, 31 Graduated On 92 In.Strap | 200.00 |
| Bell, Brass, Sleigh, Open, 15 Graduated On 58 In.Strap | 20.00 |
| Bell, Brass, Sleigh, Riveted Top Slot, 30 On 90 In Strap, 1 1/4 In.Diameter | 50.00 |
| Bell, Brass, Sleigh, Riveted, Rim In Center, 29 On 83 In.Strap, 1 1/4 In | 40.00 |
| Bell, Brass, Sleigh, Riveted, Slotted Both Ways, C.1876, 36 On 78 In.Strap | 75.00 |
| Bell, Brass, Sleigh, 29 1 1/4 In. On Leather Strap | 85.00 |
| Bell, Brass, Sleigh, 6 Graduated On Leather Strap, 3 To 2 1/4 In. | 65.00 |
| Bell, Brass, Stylized Owl, Wind, 4 1/2 In.High | 4.00 |
| Bell, Brass, Town Crier's, 10 In.High | 47.50 |
| Bell, Brass, Tulip Shape, Brass Finial, Wooden Handle, 8 In. | 32.50 |
| Bell, Brass, U.S.N., 14 Pounds | 42.50 |
| Bell, Brass, Victorian Lady | 18.00 |
| Bell, Brass, Walnut Handle, 10 1/2 In. | 25.00 |
| Bell, Brass, Wooden Handle, 5 1/4 In. | 15.00 |
| Bell, Brass, Wooden Handle, 6 1/2 In.High | 10.00 |
| Bell, Brass, 4 Graduated On Metal Strap | 28.00 |
| Bell, Bristol Type Milk Glass, Smoke, Ruffled Skirt Edged In Cobalt | 28.00 |
| Bell, Bronze, Church, Single Tier, Iron Clapper, C.1850, 12 1/4 In.High | 175.00 |
| Bell, Bronze, Church, Vanduzen Bell Co., Cincinnati, Ohio, 36 In. | 1290.00 |
| Bell, Bronze, Engraved A D 1880, Embossed Designs, 13 1/2 In.High | 225.00 |
| Bell, Bronze, Handle Attached With Claw & Ball Foot, Filigree | 25.00 |
| Bell, Bronze, Standing Bull, French, 5 X 5 In. | 45.00 |
| Bell, Bronze, Wooden Handle, C.1850, 11 In.High | 48.00 |
| Bell, Carnival Glass, Marigold | 18.50 |
| Bell, Cast Iron, Mule, Scalloped Leather Strap | 135.00 |
| Bell, Cast Iron, Open, 12 In.On Double Leather Strap, Scalloped | 135.00 |
| Bell, Cast Iron, Sheep, 4 In. | 10.00 |
| Bell, Cathedral, Dated 1852 | 1000.00 |
| Bell, Copper & Pewter, 2 1/2 In. | 15.00 |
| Bell, Cow, Dutch, Handmade | 47.50 |

| | |
|---|---|
| Bell, Cow, New England, 5 In.High | 4.95 |
| Bell, Cow, New England, 9 In.High | 4.75 |
| Bell, Cranberry Glass, Clear Glass Handle, 12 In.High | 110.00 |
| Bell, Cranberry Glass, Smoke, Ribbed, Brass Hanging Ring, 3 1/4 In.High | 14.50 |
| Bell, Cut Glass, Hobstar, Crosshatching, & Fan In Miter & Pinwheel Frame | 97.50 |
| Bell, Figural, Pilgrim Lady, Boot Clappers, 2 In. | 15.00 |
| Bell, Glass, Carlsbad, Twisted Stem, Blue Handle, Clear Base, 7 1/2 In. | 8.00 |
| Bell, Glass, Carlsbad, Twisted Stem, Clear Handle, Blue Base, 6 1/2 In. | 8.00 |
| Bell, Glass, Carlsbad, Twisted Stem, Green Handle, Clear Base, 9 In. | 8.00 |
| Bell, Glass, Opalescent, Smoke, Cobalt Trim, Brass Fixture, 4 3/4 In. | 25.00 |
| Bell, Glass, Smoke, Clear With Cranberry Stripes, 3 1/2 In.High | 15.00 |
| Bell, Glass, Smoke, Opalescent, Applied Hanger, 9 3/4 In. | 25.00 |
| Bell, Glass, Smoke, Opalescent, Cranberry Trim, Brass Fixture, 4 1/2 In. | 25.00 |
| Bell, Iron, Cow, Italian, Clapper, 4 3/4 In.High | 14.00 |
| Bell, Iron, Cow, Italian, Clapper, 5 3/4 In.High | 17.00 |
| Bell, Iron, Cow, Ornate, French, Dated 8-15-02, 7 X 7 In. | 45.00 |
| Bell, Iron, Cow, Spanish, Wooden Clapper, 5 In. | 4.50 |
| Bell, Iron, Cow, Spanish, Wooden Clapper, 7 In. | 6.00 |
| Bell, Iron, Cow, Spanish, Wooden Clapper, 9 In. | 7.50 |
| Bell, Iron, Cow, Spanish, Wooden Clapper, 11 In. | 8.75 |
| Bell, Iron, Cow, Spanish, Wooden Clapper, 16 In. | 12.50 |
| Bell, Iron, Goat, Wooden Yoke, 14 In. | 10.00 |
| Bell, Iron, Goat, Wooden Yoke, 22 In. | 14.00 |
| Bell, Iron, Italian, Clapper, C.1880, 4 3/4 In.High | 14.00 |
| Bell, Iron, Italian, Clapper, C.1880, 5 3/4 In.High | 17.00 |
| Bell, Iron, Sargent, Kentucky, 5 In. | 12.00 |
| Bell, Iron, School Yard, Gray Paint, South Carolina, 1885 | 135.00 |
| Bell, Iron, Sheep, Small Size | 5.50 |
| Bell, Iron, Sheep, X Shape Clapper, Leather Straps, 5 In. High | 5.50 |
| Bell, Iron, 2 Clappers, 4 On Iron Strap, Pair | 11.50 |
| Bell, Mechanical, Turtle, Push Tail Or Head | 70.00 |
| Bell, Milk Glass, Smoke | 8.50 |
| Bell, Milk Glass, Smoke, For Hanging Lamp, 10-Point Ruffled Edge | 25.00 |
| Bell, Milk Glass, Soot, Fluted Opening, C.1870, 4 1/2 In. | 20.00 |
| Bell, Milk Glass, Soot, Fluted Opening, C.1870, 7 In. | 20.00 |
| Bell, Nailsea Glass, Pink Body, White & Pink Loops, Fluted Handle | 190.00 |
| Bell, Nickel Plate, Sleigh, Brass Hames & Bands, 4 Graduated On 48 In.Strap | 50.00 |
| Bell, Nickel Plate, Sleigh, Brass Hames, Cotter Keys, 1 On A Side | 25.00 |
| Bell, Nickel Plate, Sleigh, Brass Hames, Cotter Keys, 2 Each Side, Graduated | 35.00 |
| Bell, Nickel Plate, Sleigh, Brass Hames, Cotter Keys, 2 On A Side, 2 1/2 In. | 35.00 |
| Bell, Nickel Plate, Sleigh, 30 On 7 Foot Strap, 1 1/2 In.Diameter | 20.00 |
| Bell, Porcelain Woman Handle, Clay Clapper, Marked Mexican, 3 1/4 In.High | 4.00 |
| Bell, Porcelain, Dinner, Handmade, Pink Latticework, Floral, Gilding | 5.00 |
| Bell, Porcelain, Flared Shirt, Woman, Flowers, White & Gold, Japan | 6.50 |
| Bell, Porcelain, Green Luster, Pink Roses | 12.00 |
| Bell, Ruby Glass, 12 In. | 48.00 |
| Bell, Ship's, Brass, 8 In.Diameter | 32.00 |
| Bell, Silver, Faberge, Gilded, Enamel, Moonstone Push, Aarne, C.1900 | 1300.00 |
| Bell, Silver, Rooster Handle | 35.00 |
| Bell, Silver, Russian, Gilded, Champleve Enamel, Kuzmitchev, C.1900, 4 In. | 750.00 |
| Bell, Sleigh, 92 Inch Strap, 23 Bells From Size 8 To 1 | 100.00 |
| Bell, Sterling Silver, Figural, Woman In Long Dress, Peru, 3 In. | 50.00 |
| Bell, Tankard, Pansy & Gold Decoration On White To Blue, Findlay, Ohio | 37.50 |
| Belle Ware, Box, Hinged, Blue Floral On Blue & White, 4 1/2 In. | 175.00 |
| Belle Ware, Box, Hinged, Forget-Me-Nots, Blue Satin Lined | 195.00 |
| Belle Ware, Box, White Lilies & Allover Green Lattice Design On Frosted | 145.00 |

*Belleek china was made in Ireland, other European countries, and the United States. The glaze is creamy yellow and appears wet. The first Belleek was made in 1857.*

**Belleek, see also Lenox**

| | |
|---|---|
| Belleek, Ashtray, Lattice, Green Mark, 4 1/2 In.Wide | 7.50 |
| Belleek, Ashtray, Thorn, Green Mark, 4 In.Square At Base | 7.50 |
| Belleek, Ashtray, Thorn, Square, Green Mark, 4 In. | 12.00 |
| Belleek, Basket, Flowered, Black Mark, 5 In. Diameter | 180.00 |
| Belleek, Basket, Flowers & Leaves, 2nd Black Mark, 6 1/2 X 6 1/2 In. | 200.00 |
| Belleek, Basket, Heart, Irish, 4 X 2 In. | 45.00 |

| | |
|---|---|
| Belleek, Basket, Heart, Marked Belleek, R, Green Mark, 6 1/2 In. | 85.00 |
| Belleek, Basket, Ornamented, 3 Strand Weave, 3 Lobed, Irish | 160.00 |
| Belleek, Basket, Purse Shape, Applied Flowers, 2nd Black Mark | 90.00 |
| Belleek, Basket, Spill, Raised Flowers, Green Mark | 45.00 |
| Belleek, Biscuit Barrel, Sawtooth Pattern Squares & Green Octagons | 120.00 |
| Belleek, Bowl, Covered, 3 Oriental Women Carrying Flowers, Willet, 5 1/2 In. | 135.00 |
| Belleek, Bowl, Grasses, Raised Design, 2nd Black Mark, 4 In.Diameter | 110.00 |
| Belleek, Bowl, Handled, White, Willet, 7 In. Diameter | 48.00 |
| Belleek, Bowl, Oval, Fluted, Black Mark, 3 3/4 X 5 3/4 In. | 24.00 |
| Belleek, Bowl, Punch, Lizard Handles, Ivory, Willet, 13 In. Diameter | 100.00 |
| Belleek, Bowl, Quilted, Sawtooth Rim, 2nd Black Mark, 3 5/8 In.High | 47.50 |
| Belleek, Bowl, Slop, Neptune, Shell Shape, 2nd Black Mark, 5 1/2 In.Diameter | 110.00 |
| Belleek, Bowl, White, Pink & Gold Trim, 2nd Black Mark, 5 1/4 In. Long | 36.00 |
| Belleek, Box, Covered, Rectangular, Grapes & Head Of Bacchus, Black Mark | 125.00 |
| Belleek, Box, Hand-Painted, Lenox, Palette Mark, 3 1/2 X 2 1/2 X 1 1/4 In. | 10.00 |
| Belleek, Box, Twisted Gold Leaf Finial, Gold Scrolls & Trim, 1889 | 16.00 |
| Belleek, Cake Set, Black Mark, 7 Piece | 250.00 |
| Belleek, Coffeepot, Limpet, Green Mark | 34.00 |
| Belleek, Coffeepot, Limpet, Yellow Luster Trim, Green Mark | 34.00 |
| Belleek, Compote, Band Of Roses On White, Gold Stem & Base, Willet | 42.00 |
| Belleek, Compote, Shell, 3 Dolphins On Base, Belleek Co., Fermanagh | 250.00 |
| Belleek, Cornucopia, Leans Against A Rock, Seashells, 3 1/4 In.High | 40.00 |
| Belleek, Creamer, Celtic, Gold Trim, 2nd Black Mark | 55.00 |
| Belleek, Creamer, Ivy, Yellow Trim, Green Mark, Large Size | 28.50 |
| Belleek, Creamer, Neptune, Green Mark | 17.00 |
| Belleek, Creamer, No.735 | 20.00 |
| Belleek, Creamer, Shell, Black Hound & Harp Mark | 25.00 |
| Belleek, Creamer, Shell, Miniature, Irish, 1st Mark, 3 In.High | 35.00 |
| Belleek, Creamer, Snail, Black Mark, 3 1/2 In.High | 30.00 |
| Belleek, Creamer, Swan Shape, 2nd Black Mark, 4 1/4 In.Long | 85.00 |
| Belleek, Creamer, Swan, Yellow Luster Trim, Small Size, Green Mark | 13.00 |
| Belleek, Creamer, Swan, 2nd Black Mark, 4 1/2 In.High | 85.00 |
| Belleek, Creamer, Toy, Shamrock, 1st Green Mark | 18.00 |
| Belleek, Creamer, Toy, Shell, 2nd Black Mark | 32.50 |
| Belleek, Creamer, Tridacna Pattern, Pink Trim, Gold Edge, Black Mark | 50.00 |
| Belleek, Creamer, Tulip Blossoms, Black Mark, 3 In.High | 22.00 |
| Belleek, Cup & Saucer, Coin Gold Bands & Handle, Ivory, Palette Mark | 22.00 |
| Belleek, Cup & Saucer, Demitasse, Hexagons, Green Trim, 2nd Black Mark | 35.00 |
| Belleek, Cup & Saucer, Demitasse, Hexagons, Pink Trim, 2nd Black Mark | 35.00 |
| Belleek, Cup & Saucer, Demitasse, Lily, 2nd Black Mark | 25.00 |
| Belleek, Cup & Saucer, Demitasse, Melon Ribbed, Gold On Ivory, Marked CAC | 48.00 |
| Belleek, Cup & Saucer, Demitasse, Neptune, Green Trim, 2nd Black Mark | 35.00 |
| Belleek, Cup & Saucer, Demitasse, Pink Trim, Ott & Brewer | 62.00 |
| Belleek, Cup & Saucer, Demitasse, Shamrock, Green Mark | 15.00 |
| Belleek, Cup & Saucer, Echinus, White, 1st Black Mark | 45.00 |
| Belleek, Cup & Saucer, Erne, Black Mark | 29.00 |
| Belleek, Cup & Saucer, Floral, Gold Gilt Handle, American | 28.00 |
| Belleek, Cup & Saucer, Green Edge & Handle, 2nd Black Mark | 28.00 |
| Belleek, Cup & Saucer, Harp, Shamrock, 2nd Black Mark | 30.00 |
| Belleek, Cup & Saucer, Heart Shape, Raised Gold Leaf, Footed Cup, Willet | 28.00 |
| Belleek, Cup & Saucer, Limpet, Yellow Luster Trim, Green Mark | 19.00 |
| Belleek, Cup & Saucer, Neptune Pattern, Green Trim, Black Mark | 30.00 |
| Belleek, Cup & Saucer, Neptune, Green Border, 2nd Black Mark | 48.00 |
| Belleek, Cup & Saucer, Neptune, Green Trim, Black Mark | 30.00 |
| Belleek, Cup & Saucer, Octagonal, Green, Ruffled & Crimped Edges, Black Mark | 110.00 |
| Belleek, Cup & Saucer, Princeton Emblem, Gold On Ivory, 2 Handled, Willet | 30.00 |
| Belleek, Cup & Saucer, Shamrocks, Basket Weave, 2nd Black Mark | 22.00 To 27.50 |
| Belleek, Cup & Saucer, Shell-Shaped, Small Shell Feet, Black Mark | 38.00 |
| Belleek, Cup & Saucer, Thistle, Pink Border, 2nd Black Mark | 48.00 |
| Belleek, Cup & Saucer, Tridacna Pattern, Pink Trim, Black Mark | 30.00 |
| Belleek, Cup & Saucer, White, Square Pedestal Base Cut, Willet | 25.00 |
| Belleek, Cup & Saucer, White, Thistle, 1st Black Mark | 45.00 |
| Belleek, Cup, Chocolate, White, Scrolled Fish Handle, Willet | 32.50 |
| Belleek, Cup, Demitasse, Limpet, Green Mark | 6.50 |
| Belleek, Dish, Heart Shape, Green Mark, 6 In. | 27.50 |
| Belleek, Dish, Heart Shape, Pink Tinted Rim, Black Mark, 5 1/4 X 1 1/2 In. | 32.50 |

Belleek, Dish, Maple Leaf Shape, Cream To Green, 2nd Black Mark .................................. 20.00
Belleek, Dish, Maple Leaf Shape, Cream To Pink, Green Mark .................................... 12.00
Belleek, Dish, Sweet, Sycamore Leaf, 2nd Green Mark ........................................ 18.50
Belleek, Dish, Sweetmeat, Maple Leaf, 6 In.Diameter ........................................ 25.00
Belleek, Eggcup, Limpet, Green Mark ...................................................... 6.00
Belleek, Ewer, Green In Grooves, Flowers, Handle, & Inner Lip, 2nd Black Mark ................ 112.50
Belleek, Figurine, Madonna, 19 In.High .................................................... 350.00
Belleek, Figurine, Pig, Green Mark ................................................ 13.00 To 19.00
Belleek, Figurine, Piglet, Yellow Luster Trim, Green Mark ................................... 15.00
Belleek, Figurine, Terrier, Green Mark .................................................... 9.00
Belleek, Figurine, Wolfhound On Cushion, Green Mark ........................................ 35.00
Belleek, Flower Holder, Sea Horse, Yellow Trim, Black Mark ................................. 75.00
Belleek, Flowerpot, Diamond, Plain, Black Mark ............................................ 75.00
Belleek, Flowerpot, Swirled Sides, Fluted Edges, Green Mark, 3 1/2 In. ...................... 14.00
Belleek, Font, Cherub, Black Mark ........................................................ 100.00
Belleek, Hatpin Holder, Flower Center, Willet ............................................. 27.50
Belleek, Horn Of Plenty, Horse's Head, Black Mark ......................................... 90.00
Belleek, Insert, Demitasse, Silver Plate, Saucer & Holder, Willet ......................... 25.00
Belleek, Jar, Cracker, Covered, Cartoon Panels Of Town Clerk & Drunk, Willet .............. 45.00
Belleek, Jar, Honey, Covered, Shamrock, Green Mark ........................................ 18.00
Belleek, Jar, Honey, Gold Honey Bees On Knob & Body, Palette Mark L ....................... 40.00
Belleek, Jar, Marmalade, Shamrock, Green Mark ............................................. 32.50
Belleek, Jug, Milk, Shamrock, 3rd Black Mark ............................................. 32.50
Belleek, Jug, Spill, Typha, Green Mark, 7 In. ............................................ 12.00
Belleek, Kettle, 3 Legged, Black Mark, 2 1/2 In.High ..................................... 28.00
Belleek, Mug, Ears Of Corn, Tan To Yellow ................................................ 75.00
Belleek, Mug, Fruit & Fraternity Emblem, Gold Edge, Lenox ................................. 20.00
Belleek, Mug, Peacocks, Trees, Gold Trim, Handle, Lenox, 7 1/4 In.High .................... 37.50
Belleek, Mug, Scenic, Water, Trees, Palette Mark L, 7 1/2 In. ............................. 55.00
Belleek, Mug, Shamrock, Green Mark ....................................................... 25.00
Belleek, Mug, Shamrock, 2nd Black Mark ................................................... 33.00
Belleek, Pitcher, Cider, Apples & Leaves On Green, Marked Palette, CAC .................... 65.00
Belleek, Pitcher, Cider, Cherries & Foliage, Squat, Willet ............................... 65.00
Belleek, Pitcher, Cider, Hand-Painted Apples, Marked ..................................... 14.00
Belleek, Pitcher, Satin Finish, Pink Flowers, Gold Leaves, Bearded Man Spout ............. 45.00
Belleek, Pitcher, White, Ayr, Coat Of Arms, 2nd Black Mark, 3 1/2 In. .................... 48.00
Belleek, Plate, Bread, Gold Trim, 3rd Black Mark, 9 1/2 In.Diameter ...................... 85.00
Belleek, Plate, Bread, Limpet, Black Mark ................................................ 50.00
Belleek, Plate, Bread, Shamrock, 3rd Black Mark .......................................... 45.00
Belleek, Plate, Cake, Harp, Hound, Tower, Green Mark, 10 In. ............................. 40.00
Belleek, Plate, Cake, Hexagonal, Black Mark .............................................. 115.00
Belleek, Plate, Cake, Shamrocks, Basket Weave, 2 Handles, Black Mark, 9 In. .............. 45.00
Belleek, Plate, Cake, Shell & Coral, Handled, Green Mark ................................. 22.00
Belleek, Plate, Dessert, Shamrocks, 3rd Black Mark, 6 1/2 In. ............................ 8.00
Belleek, Plate, Dessert, Tridacna Pattern, Gold Edge, Black Mark, 6 In. .................. 12.00
Belleek, Plate, Dinner, Yellow Border, Flower Center, Coxan .............................. 22.50
Belleek, Plate, Open Weave, Raspberry Trim, 1st Black Mark, 9 1/4 In. .................... 47.50
Belleek, Plate, Scalloped Shell, White, Green Trim, 2nd Black Mark, 8 In. ................ 35.00
Belleek, Plate, Shaded Green Rim, Pink Edge, 5 1/2 In. ........................... 35.00 To 55.00
Belleek, Plate, Shamrock, 1st Green Mark, 6 1/2 In. ...................................... 11.00
Belleek, Plate, Shamrock, 2nd Black Mark, 7 In. .......................................... 20.00
Belleek, Plate, Shamrocks, Basket Weave, Black Mark, 8 In. ............................... 25.00
Belleek, Plate, Tea, Black Hound & Harp Mark, 6 1/2 In. .................................. 10.00
Belleek, Plate, Tea, Limpet, 3rd Mark, 5 1/2 In. ........................................ 8.00
Belleek, Plate, Tridacna, Green Mark, 7 In. .............................................. 7.00
Belleek, Pot, Honey, Lid, Hand-Painted Floral & Bees, 3 Legs, Black Mark ................. 150.00
Belleek, Pot, Irish, Gold Rim, 1st Black Mark ............................................ 35.00
Belleek, Pot, Irish, Shamrock, 2nd Black Mark, 3 1/4 In. High ............................ 42.00
Belleek, Salt, Diamond Shape, Fine Rib, 2nd Black Mark ................................... 12.00
Belleek, Salt, Gold Edging, Willets ...................................................... 8.00
Belleek, Salt, Gold, Lenox, 1 1/2 In.Across .............................................. 3.00
Belleek, Salt, Green Shamrocks, Green Mark ............................................... 6.00
Belleek, Salt, Hand-Painted Flowers 3 Gold Feet, Lenox, Set Of 6 ......................... 6.00
Belleek, Salt, Hand-Painted, Footed ...................................................... 6.25
Belleek, Salt, Hand-Painted, Gold Decoration, Marked, Set Of 8 ........................... 20.00
Belleek, Salt, New Shell, Green Mark ..................................................... 7.00

Belleek, Salt, Ruffled Edge, Red Mark, 1 1/2 In.Across .................................................. 6.00
Belleek, Salt, Shell With Green Shamrocks, Oval, Black Mark, 3 1/2 In. ..................... 14.00
Belleek, Salt, Shell, Twig Legs, Green Mark ...................................................................... 5.50
Belleek, Salt, Swan, Green Mark ........................................................................................ 14.00
Belleek, Salt, Violets, Pink Roses, Green, Gold Rims, Willet ..................................... 6.50
Belleek, Snack Set, Limpet Cob, 3rd Black Mark, 2 Piece ........................................... 82.50
Belleek, Spill, Green Trim, 2nd Black Mark, 3 1/2 In.High ......................................... 60.00
Belleek, Spill, Rock, Black Mark, 5 1/2 In. High ........................................................... 55.00
Belleek, Spill, Rock, Green Mark, 3 1/2 In.High ........................................................... 10.00
Belleek, Spill, Rock, 3rd Black Mark, 5 1/2 In.High ..................................................... 60.00
Belleek, Spoon Rest, Cresting Waves Design, 1st Black Mark, 4 In.Long ................ 65.00
Belleek, Stein, Hand-Painted Purple Berries, C.A.C., 6 In. ........................................ 45.00
Belleek, Sugar & Creamer, Cover, Green Celtic Design, 3rd Black Mark .................. 80.00
Belleek, Sugar & Creamer, Harp, Hound, Tower, Green Mark ..................................... 50.00
Belleek, Sugar & Creamer, Harp, Shamrock, 2nd Black Mark ..................................... 45.00
Belleek, Sugar & Creamer, Harp, Shamrock, 3rd Black Mark ..................................... 45.00
Belleek, Sugar & Creamer, Hexagon, Yellow Trim, Large, Black Mark ..................... 65.00
Belleek, Sugar & Creamer, Irish Pot, 2nd Black Mark .................................................. 45.00
Belleek, Sugar & Creamer, Kettle Shape, Green Mark .................................................. 17.50
Belleek, Sugar & Creamer, Lily, Yellow Trim, 3rd Black Mark .................................. 42.50
Belleek, Sugar & Creamer, Lotus, 3rd Black Mark ........................................................ 38.00
Belleek, Sugar & Creamer, Mask, 3rd Black Mark ........................................................ 55.00
Belleek, Sugar & Creamer, Ribbon, Irish, 2nd Mark ..................................................... 50.00
Belleek, Sugar & Creamer, Ribbon, 3rd Black Mark ..................................................... 45.00
Belleek, Sugar & Creamer, Shamrock, Black Mark, Pair .............................................. 35.00
Belleek, Sugar & Creamer, Shamrock, 2nd Black Mark ................................................ 50.00
Belleek, Sugar & Creamer, Shamrocks, Basket Weave, Twig Handles, Green Mark .... 35.00
Belleek, Sugar & Creamer, Shell ......................................................................................... 50.00
Belleek, Sugar & Creamer, Toy Shell, Yellow Trim, Black Mark ............................... 60.00
Belleek, Sugar & Creamer, Tridacna, 2nd Black Mark, 3 1/4 In.High ...................... 70.00
Belleek, Sugar & Creamer, Yellow Ribbon Garland, Green Harp & Hound Mark ...... 40.00
Belleek, Sugar, Green Edge & Handle, 2nd Black Mark ............................................... 20.00
Belleek, Sugar, Ivy, Black Mark ......................................................................................... 16.00
Belleek, Sugar, Shamrocks On Basket Weave, Black Mark ........................................... 22.50
Belleek, Sugar, Shell & Seaweed, Ivory, Yellow Inside, 2nd Black Mark .................. 32.50
Belleek, Sugar, Snail, Black Mark ...................................................................................... 30.00
Belleek, Swan, Willet, 4 1/2 In. Long ................................................................................. 65.00
Belleek, Tankard, Gold Decoration On Ivory, Initial R, Willet, 15 In. .................... 125.00
Belleek, Tea Set, Black Mark, 8 Piece ............................................................................... 750.00
Belleek, Tea Set, Gold Trim & Finials, Trenton, N.J., 1894-1896, 3 Piece ............... 225.00
Belleek, Tea Set, Hexagonal, Pink Trim, 2nd Black Mark, 8 Piece ............................ 185.00
Belleek, Tea Set, Neptune, Green Trim, Black Mark, 7 Piece ...................................... 235.00
Belleek, Tea Set, Shamrock, Basket Weave, 3rd Black Mark, 3 Piece ....................... 85.00
Belleek, Tea Set, Shamrock, Green Mark, 5 Piece ......................................................... 33.00
Belleek, Tea Set, Shell, Black Hound & Harp Mark, 20 Piece ..................................... 350.00
Belleek, Tea Set, Tridacna Pattern, Black Mark, 3 Piece ............................................. 175.00
Belleek, Teacup & Saucer, Lily, 2nd Black Mark ........................................................... 25.00
Belleek, Teacup & Saucer, Shamrock, Green Mark ......................................................... 18.00
Belleek, Teacup & Saucer, Tridacna, Pink Trim, Black Mark ..................................... 38.50
Belleek, Teacup, Black Hound & Harp Mark .................................................................. 6.50
Belleek, Teakettle, Shamrock, Basket Weave, Handle Over Top, 2nd Black Mark .... 95.00
Belleek, Teakettle, Shamrock, Handle, Green Mark ....................................................... 44.00
Belleek, Teapot, Harp, Shamrock, 2nd Black Mark .............................. 75.00 To 85.00
Belleek, Teapot, Hexagonal, Green Trim, Gold Gilt, 2nd Black Mark ...................... 85.00
Belleek, Teapot, Hexagonal, Pink Trim, 2nd Black Mark ............................................ 85.00
Belleek, Teapot, Limpet, Yellow Trim, 3rd Black Mark .............................................. 110.00
Belleek, Teapot, Neptune, Pink Trim, 2nd Black Mark, 4 1/2 In.High ...................... 140.00
Belleek, Teapot, Neptune, Shell Feet & Finial, 2nd Black Mark, 5 In. ...................... 160.00
Belleek, Teapot, Neptune, 2nd Black Mark ...................................................................... 85.00
Belleek, Teapot, Shamrock, Brown Handle & Finial, 2nd Black Mark, 4 In. .......... 125.00
Belleek, Teapot, Shamrock, Green Mark ........................................................................... 33.00
Belleek, Teapot, Shamrock, 2nd Black Mark ................................................................... 52.00
Belleek, Teapot, Shamrocks On Basket Weave, Brown On Handle, 2nd Black Mark .... 95.00
Belleek, Teapot, Shamrocks, 3rd Black Mark, 7 In.High .............................................. 65.00
Belleek, Teapot, Tridacna, Yellow Luster Trim, Green Mark ...................................... 38.00
Belleek, Teapot, Tridacna, 1st Black Mark ...................................................................... 90.00

Belleek, Teapot, Twelve Orientals With Parasols, Gold, Black, & White, Willet ............................. 49.00
Belleek, Toby Mug, George Washington, Morris & Gallimore, 1896 ......................................... 195.00
Belleek, Tray, Bowl Type, Round, Gold Trim, Willet, 5 1/2 In.Diameter ..................................... 28.00
Belleek, Tray, Grasses, Luster On Wheat Heads, 1st Black Mark, 12 X 15 In. ............................ 115.00
Belleek, Tray, Oblong, Coxon, 12 In. ........................................................................................ 22.00
Belleek, Tray, Shamrocks, Basket Weave, Black Mark, 13 1/2 X 6 1/4 In. ................................ 55.00
Belleek, Tray, Swirled, Pink Turned Up Edge, 2nd Black Mark, 17 X 14 In. .............................. 135.00
Belleek, Tub, Shamrock Decoration On White, 3rd Black Mark, 2 In.High ................................. 22.00
Belleek, Vase, Aberdeen, Applied Work, Black Mark, 6 In.High .............................................. 85.00
Belleek, Vase, Aberdeen, Black Mark, 9 In. High .............................................................. 195.00
Belleek, Vase, Aberdeen, Cream, Applied Floral, Green Mark, C.1949, 6 In. ............................ 35.00
Belleek, Vase, Aberdeen, Flowers, Black Mark B, 5 3/4 In.High ............................................ 150.00
Belleek, Vase, Aberdeen, Green Mark, 6 In.High ................................................................ 43.00
Belleek, Vase, Bud, Fan, Pink Trim, 2nd Black Mark, 5 3/4 In. ............................................... 85.00
Belleek, Vase, Conical, Lozenge Pattern, Yellow Lined, 2nd Black Mark, 6 In. ........................ 105.00
Belleek, Vase, Gold Grapes On Black, Willet, 12 In.High ...................................................... 180.00
Belleek, Vase, Nile, Yellow Luster Trim, Green Mark, 13 1/2 In.High ....................................... 55.00
Belleek, Vase, Pink & Yellow Roses On Green, Willet, 11 1/2 In. ............................................ 85.00
Belleek, Vase, Prince Arthur, Green Mark, 10 1/4 In.High ..................................................... 78.00
Belleek, Vase, Scenic, Japanese Lady In Kimona & Obi, Ott & Brewer, 10 In. ......................... 45.00
Belleek, Vase, Shamrock, Tree Trunk, 3 Openings, Greem Mark, 6 In.High .............................. 26.00
Belleek, Vase, Spill, Shamrock, Black Mark, 5 1/2 In.High .................................................... 50.00
Belleek, Vase, Sunflower, Yellow Luster Trim, 2nd Black Mark, 7 In. ....................................... 80.00
Belleek, Vase, Tree, Shamrocks, Black Mark, Hound, Harp, & Tower, 6 1/2 In. ........................ 42.50
Belleek, Vase, White Enameled Flowers, Palette Mark L, 10 In.High ...................................... 32.00

Bennington ware was the product of two factories working in Bennington,
Vermont. Both firms were out of business by 1896. The wares include the
brown and yellow mottled pottery, Parian, scroddled ware, stoneware, graniteware,
yellowware, and Staffordshire-like vases.

Bennington, see also Rockingham
Bennington Type, Base, 7 In. High .............................................................................. 15.00
Bennington Type, Bowl, Deep, 7 1/4 X 2 In. ................................................................... 36.00
Bennington Type, Creamer, Cow, Plinth Base, C.1840 ...................................................... 55.00
Bennington Type, Creamer, Gold Trim ......................................................................... 22.50
Bennington Type, Creamer, 5 1/4 In.High ..................................................................... 30.00
Bennington Type, Cuspidor ....................................................................................... 35.00
Bennington Type, Jug, Brown & Yellow, Tulips, Rockingham, 10 In.High ............................... 58.00
Bennington Type, Mug, Pressed In Center, 3 1/2 In.Diameter ............................................. 25.00
Bennington Type, Pitcher, Batter, Strap Handle, Brown To Cream, Rockingham ..................... 38.00
Bennington Type, Plate, Pie, 12 In. ............................................................................. 60.00
Bennington Type, Saucer, Brown, White Hunt Scenes ..................................................... 70.00
Bennington Type, Teapot, Gold Trim, 9 1/2 In.High ......................................................... 65.00
Bennington Type, Toby Mug, Looks Like Benjamin Franklin, Large Size ................................ 45.00
Bennington, Bottle, Coachman, C.1850, 9 7/8 In.High ............................................. Illus 325.00
Bennington, Bottle, Coachman, C.1850, 10 3/4 In.High ........................................... Illus 500.00
Bennington, Box, Trinket, Parian ................................................................................ 33.00
Bennington, Coffeepot, C.1850, 12 3/4 In. High .................................................... Illus 850.00
Bennington, Crock, Basket Of Flowers, J.& E.Norton, Bennington, Vt.4 Gallon ...................... 375.00
Bennington, Crock, Flower, Stoneware, 2 Gallon ............................................................ 45.00
Bennington, Cuspidor, Brown & Yellow ........................................................................ 30.00
Bennington, Cuspidor, Lady's, Brown & Yellow .............................................................. 25.00
Bennington, Cuspidor, Leaf Design, Brown Glaze ........................................................... 45.00
Bennington, Cuspidor, Signed .................................................................................... 85.00
Bennington, Dish, Soap, 1 Piece, 8 1/2 X 6 In. .............................................................. 22.00
Bennington, Doorknob, Brown & Tan, Pair .................................................................... 20.00
Bennington, Figurine, Cat, Sitting, Brown Stripes On Yellow, 7 In. ...................................... 50.00
Bennington, Figurine, Man & Lady, Parian, C.1847, Pair ......................................... Illus 300.00
Bennington, Figurine, Poodle, C.1850, 9 3/4 In.Long, Pair ...................................... Illus 950.00
Bennington, Flask, Book, C.1850, 10 3/4 In.High .................................................. Illus 375.00
Bennington, Flask, Book, C.1850, 8 In.High ........................................................ Illus 250.00
Bennington, Flask, Book, Two Quart, 7 3/4 In.High ............................................... Illus 225.00
Bennington, Flask, Coachman .................................................................................... 300.00
Bennington, Flask, Rockingham Glaze, C.1850, 6 In.High ....................................... Illus 225.00
Bennington, Inkwell, 3 1/4 In.High .............................................................................. 200.00
Bennington, Jug, Blue Floral Decoration, Signed Norton ................................................... 75.00

Bennington, Coffeepot, C.1850,
12 3/4 In. High
*(See Page 28)*

Bennington, Figurine, Man & Lady,
Parian, C.1847, Pair
*(See Page 28)*

Bennington, Flask, Book,
C.1850, 8 In.High
*(See Page 28)*

Bennington, Flask, Book,
Two Quart, 7 3/4 In.High
*(See Page 28)*

Bennington, Flask, Book,
C.1850, 10 3/4 In.High
*(See Page 28)*

Bennington, Flask, Rockingham Glaze,
C.1850, 6 In.High
*(See Page 28)*

Bennington, Bottle,
Coachman, C.1850,
10 3/4 In.High
*(See Page 28)*

Bennington, Bottle,
Coachman, C.1850,
9 7/8 In.High
*(See Page 28)*

Bennington, Pitcher,
Blue & White,
C.1852, 10 3/4 In.

Bennington, Pitcher,
Charter Oak,
Blue & White, C.1852

Bennington, Pitcher,
Brown & White, C.1852, 7 5/8 In.

Bennington, Pitcher,
C.1850,
7 1/2 In.High

Bennington, Sugar,
Covered, C.1850

Bennington, Vase,
Tulip, C.1850, 9 3/4 In.High

Bennington, Figurine, Poodle,
C.1850, 9 3/4 In.Long, Pair
*(See Page 28)*

| | | |
|---|---|---|
| **Bennington, Jug,** Cobalt Floral, Marked Norton Bennington, Vt., 3 Gallon | | 75.00 |
| **Bennington, Jug,** Cobalt Flower & L.P.Norton, Bennington, Vt., 12 In. | | 65.00 |
| **Bennington, Jug,** Imprint Of A Mask, Daisylike Flower Under Mask | | 100.00 |
| **Bennington, Mold,** Round, 9 In. | | 3.00 |
| **Bennington, Pitcher,** Blue & White, C.1852, 10 3/4 In. | *Illus* | 325.00 |
| **Bennington, Pitcher,** Brown & White, C.1852, 7 5/8 In. | *Illus* | 750.00 |
| **Bennington, Pitcher,** C.1850, 7 1/2 In.High | *Illus* | 425.00 |
| **Bennington, Pitcher,** Charter Oak, Blue & White, C.1852 | *Illus* | 325.00 |
| **Bennington, Pitcher,** Hound Handle, Eagle Under Spout, Birds & Animals | | 95.00 |
| **Bennington, Pitcher,** Marked U.S.Pottery | | 185.00 |
| **Bennington, Pitcher,** Water, Profile Of James Garfield In Relief, Tan, 10 In. | | 115.00 |
| **Bennington, Pitcher,** Water, Salt Glaze, Raised Grapes, Leaves, Deer, & Dog | | 150.00 |
| **Bennington, Pitcher,** Water, Salt Glaze, Raised Men Playing Cards & Grapes | | 125.00 |
| **Bennington, Plate,** Pie, 9 In. | | 17.50 |
| **Bennington, Platter,** Fish Shape, Signed, Dated 1807, 17 1/2 X 8 In. | | 95.00 |
| **Bennington, Saltbox,** Hanging, Brown & Yellow, Peacock, Fountains, Pillars | | 85.00 |
| **Bennington, Sugar,** Covered, C.1850 | *Illus* | 350.00 |
| **Bennington, Syrup,** Parian, Ribbon Mark, Signed | | 125.00 |
| **Bennington, Teapot,** Raised Pattern, Dark Brown Glaze | | 45.00 |
| **Bennington, Vase,** Tulip, C.1850, 9 3/4 In.High | *Illus* | 300.00 |

*Berlin, a German porcelain factory, was started in 1751 by Wilhelm Kaspar Wegely. In 1763 the factory was taken over by Frederick the Great and became the Royal Berlin Porcelain Manufactory. It is still in operation today.*

| | |
|---|---:|
| Berlin, Cup & Saucer, Coffee, Cartouches, Floral, Gilt Scrolls, C.1790 | 180.00 |
| Berlin, Figurine, Goatherd, Standing Before Tree Stump, 8 3/4 In. | 225.00 |
| Berlin, Jardiniere, Columnar Feet, Floral, Gilt Scrolls, C.1800, Pair | 325.00 |
| Berlin, Plaque, 16th Century Lady, 19th Century, 9 1/4 In. High | 1700.00 |
| Berlin, Plate, Soup, Military Symbols & Animals On Oxblood | 100.00 |
| Berlin, Platter, Oval, Bouquets & Floral Sprigs, C.1820, 11 In. | 50.00 |
| Berlin, Sucrier, Puce Floral Finial, Yellow, Gilt Vines, Figures, C.1765 | 375.00 |
| Berlin, Tea Caddy, Covered, Fruit & Flowers, C.1760, 5 1/4 In. High | 175.00 |
| Berlin, Urn, Ovoid, Covered, Loop Handles, Landscape Medallions, C.1850, Pair | 275.00 |
| Berlin, Vaso, Potpourri, Covered, Bouquets & Sprigs, C.1760, 6 In.High | 525.00 |
| Bicycle, Boneshaker | 1250.00 |
| Bicycle, Gas, Patent 1899 | 15.00 |

*Bing & Grondahl is a famous Danish factory making fine porcelains from 1853 to the present. Their Christmas plates are especially well known.*

**Bing & Grondahl, see also Collector, Plate**

| | |
|---|---:|
| Bing & Grondahl, Brooch, Viking Ship & Denmark In Underglaze Blue | 5.00 |
| Bing & Grondahl, Condiment Set, Leaf Shape Tray, Blue & White, 4 Piece | 65.00 |
| Bing & Grondahl, Group, Pair Of Monkeys, Picking Lice, 5 In.High | 55.00 |
| Bing & Grondahl, Tea & Coffee Set, Sea Gulls, Blue, Snail Finials, 4 Piece | 130.00 |
| Bing & Grondahl, Vase, Ship Scene, 10 1/2 In. | 135.00 |

*Bisque is an unglazed baked porcelain. Finished bisque has a slightly sandy texture with a dull finish. Some of it may be decorated with various colors. Bisque gained favor during the late Victorian era when thousands of bisque figurines were made.*

| | |
|---|---:|
| Bisque, Bottle, Figural, Skeleton Sitting On Barrel, Glass Eyes, 9 In. | 125.00 |
| Bisque, Bust, Child, Soft Colors, Pair | 250.00 |
| Bisque, Bust, Girl & Boy, German, 10 1/2 In., Pair | 125.00 |
| Bisque, Bust, Napoleon I, Young General, C.1890, 10 1/4 In. | 75.00 |
| Bisque, Candelabra, German, Boy & Girl, Crystal Prisms, Pair | 450.00 |
| Bisque, Dish, Hen Cover, Brown Nest Base, 4 In.Long | 30.00 |
| Bisque, Doll, Potty, German | 15.00 |
| Bisque, Egg, Black Child Emerging, 2 In. | 18.00 |
| Bisque, Figurine, Andy Gump, 2 In.High | 12.00 |
| Bisque, Figurine, Angel With Tambourine, Occupied Japan | 14.50 |
| Bisque, Figurine, Boy, Baseball, Hat, & Bat, C.1900, 2 1/4 In. | 3.00 |
| Bisque, Figurine, Boy, Pink Base, Gold Trim, Green Anchor Mark, 10 In. | 75.00 |
| Bisque, Figurine, Cat, German, Pink Blanket, Blue Ribbon, C.1900, 4 In. | 25.00 |
| Bisque, Figurine, Charlie Chaplin, Marked Germany, 5 In. | 35.00 |
| Bisque, Figurine, Child, Sitting By Basket, Pink & Gold, 3 1/2 In., Pair | 39.00 |
| Bisque, Figurine, Cow, Sheep, Stoke-On-Trent | 155.00 |
| Bisque, Figurine, Dog, Dark Brown Splotches Of Glaze, Tooled Features, 7 In. | 35.00 |
| Bisque, Figurine, Dwarf, Sneezy, Walt Disney | 8.00 |
| Bisque, Figurine, Girl Standing By Horse Drawn Cart, 6 1/2 In.High | 40.00 |
| Bisque, Figurine, Indian Chief, Multicolored, 12 In.Tall | 100.00 |
| Bisque, Figurine, Indian, Standing & Sitting, 1 1/4 In., Pair | 9.00 |
| Bisque, Figurine, Lady, Art Nouveau | 25.00 |
| Bisque, Figurine, Lady, Pastel Blue, Pink, & Yellow, Gold Trim, Pair | 125.00 |
| Bisque, Figurine, Lady, Square Base, 12 1/2 In. | 50.00 |
| Bisque, Figurine, Maggie & Jiggs, 3 1/2 In.High, Pair | 65.00 |
| Bisque, Figurine, Mama Bear, 4 In.High | 10.00 |
| Bisque, Figurine, Man & Woman Sitting In Chair, C.1750, 8 1/2 In. High, Pair | 195.00 |
| Bisque, Figurine, Man, Marked Germany, Standing In Open Gate, Grape Arbor | 27.50 |
| Bisque, Figurine, Negro Boy Riding An Alligator, 3 In. | 32.50 |
| Bisque, Figurine, Papa Bear, 5 In.High | 10.00 |
| Bisque, Figurine, Pink, Green, 5 1/2 In. *Illus* | 14.00 |
| Bisque, Figurine, Potty Babies, Double, 3 X 3 1/2 In. | 25.00 |
| Bisque, Figurine, Potty Girl In Blue | 12.50 |
| Bisque, Figurine, Pug Dog, Blue Ribbon Around Neck, 3 In.High | 40.00 |
| Bisque, Figurine, Rebecca At The Well, 8 1/2 In.High | 50.00 |
| Bisque, Figurine, Seated Indian, Headdress, Ear Of Corn, 1 1/2 In.High | 8.00 |

Bisque, Figurine, Pink, Green, 5 1/2 In.
*(See Page 31)*

| | |
|---|---:|
| Bisque, Figurine, Snow White | 12.00 |
| Bisque, Figurine, Swan & 8 Babies, White, Open Tops, 9 Pieces | 45.00 |
| Bisque, Figurine, Wirehaired Terrier, German, Mother & 3 Pups, Set Of 4 | 12.50 |
| Bisque, Figurine, Young Boy, Standing Next To Vase, Applied Flowers, 6 In. | 34.00 |
| Bisque, Group, Baby & Dog Sitting In Tub, Marked H In Triangle | 95.00 |
| Bisque, Group, Two Girls Feeding Pigeons Beside Garden Urn, Enameled, 14 In. | 75.00 |
| Bisque, Group, Two Pigs, Walt Disney, 2 1/2 In.High | 8.00 |
| Bisque, Hatpin Holder, Art Nouveau Lady, Real Hair, Cloth Hat | 65.00 |
| Bisque, Hatpin Holder, Clown Hat Shape, Colored | 35.00 |
| Bisque, Match Holder, Boy Rabbit Hunting, Bunny Peeking Out, Striker | 30.00 |
| Bisque, Match Holder, Full Figure Of A Man, 6 In.High | 45.00 |
| Bisque, Match Holder, Rosy Cheeked Boy In Blue Apron, Pink Nightcap On End | 18.50 |
| Bisque, Nodder, Boy & Girl, Incised Germany, 3 In.Tall, Pair | 22.00 |
| Bisque, Outhouse, Negro Child Inside, Mother Waiting Outside | 5.00 |
| Bisque, Planter, Boy & Girl On Green Log, White Doves, 5 1/4 In.High, Pair | 35.00 |
| Bisque, Salt & Pepper, Form Of Seated Indian, 3 In.High | 4.75 |
| Bisque, Shoe, Lady's, Cupid Delivering Letter To An Elf Painting, 6 1/2 In. | 17.00 |
| Bisque, Shoe, Victorian, Pale Green, Orange Bow, 2 Lovebirds On Toe | 28.00 |
| Bisque, Toothbrush Holder, Three Little Pigs | 11.00 To 14.00 |
| Bisque, Toothpick, Crocodile Coming Out Of Egg | 18.50 |
| Bisque, Toothpick, German, Clown With Ice Cream Cone Next To Drum | 35.00 |
| Bisque, Toothpick, Rabbit | 4.00 |
| Bisque, Vase, Girl Holding Cornucopia, Pink Luster Lining, Pair, 8 In. | 50.00 |
| Bisque, Vase, Girl In Front Of Garden Gate, Soft Colors, 6 In. | 27.50 |

*Black amethyst glass appears black until it is held to the light, then a dark purple can be seen. It was made in many factories from 1860 to the present time.*

| | |
|---|---:|
| Black Amethyst, Basket, Bushel, Northwood | 30.00 |
| Black Amethyst, Boot, Spur | 30.00 |
| Black Amethyst, Bowl, Fruit, Eight Fluted, 12 In. Diameter | 22.50 |
| Black Amethyst, Candlestick, Blown, Controlled Bubble, 12 In.High, Pair | 135.00 |
| Black Amethyst, Candlesticks, 4 In,High | 7.00 |
| Black Amethyst, Cologne, Blown Stopper, Floral & Bird, Gilt, 9 1/2 In. | 50.00 |
| Black Amethyst, Dish, Candy, Covered | 12.00 |
| Black Amethyst, Muffineer | 10.00 |
| Black Amethyst, Plate, S Border, 5 In.Square | 14.00 |
| Black Amethyst, Rose Bowl, Crimped Top, 3 1/4 In. | 22.00 |
| Black Amethyst, Sugar & Creamer On A Tray, Pyramid | 14.00 |
| Black Amethyst, Tray, Dresser | 14.00 |
| Black Amethyst, Tray, Pin, Rectangular | 5.00 |
| Black Amethyst, Vase, Bud, Ruffled Top, 8 In.High | 12.00 |
| Black Amethyst, Vase, Etched Birds & Flowers, 8 1/2 In. | 27.50 |
| Black Amethyst, Vase, Flower Swags, Pedestaled, Square Base, 8 In. | 38.00 |
| Black Amethyst, Vase, Hand Blown, Rough Pontil, 11 1/2 In., Pair | 45.00 |
| Black Amethyst, Vase, Painted Flowers, 9 In. | 9.00 |
| Black Amethyst, Vase, Swan, Silver Deposit On Bill & Top Edge, 8 1/2 In. | 45.00 |

| | |
|---|---|
| Bloor Derby, Figurine, Peacock, On Stump, C.1825, 7 In. | 130.00 |
| Bloor Derby, Ring Tree, White & Gold On Blue, C.1825 | 25.00 |
| Bloor Derby, Sugar, Covered, Sevres Style, Fruit, Floral, Insects, C.1835 | 140.00 |

*Blown glass was formed by forcing air through a rod into molten glass. Early glass and some forms of art glass were hand blown. Other types of glass were molded or pressed. The McKearin numbers refer to the book "American Glass" by George and Helen McKearin.*

| | |
|---|---|
| Blown Glass, Basket, Miniature, Cased, Lined Yellow, Silver Frame & Handle | 68.00 |
| Blown Glass, Beaker, Mourning, Engraved, Coat Of Arms, Greenish, C.1780, Pair | 310.00 |
| Blown Glass, Bottle, Hollow Handle, Applied Ring, Decoration, & Feet, Pair | 30.00 |
| Blown Glass, Bottle, Snuff, Olive Green | 70.00 |
| Blown Glass, Bottle, Toilet, Etched Grape & Leaf, Blown Stopper, Ruby | 45.00 |
| Blown Glass, Bottle, Water, Bulbous, Polished Pontil, Clear, 8 1/2 In.High | 15.00 |
| Blown Glass, Bowl & Underplate, Finger, Raised Red Stripes | 45.00 |
| Blown Glass, Bowl, Finger, Apple Green | 35.00 |
| Blown Glass, Bowl, Finger, Dark Turquoise | 24.50 |
| Blown Glass, Bowl, Flint, Straight Sides, Folded Rim, C.1750, 1 3/4 In. High | 32.00 |
| Blown Glass, Bowl, Folded Rim, Rough Pontil, 6 1/2 In.Diameter | 25.00 |
| Blown Glass, Bowl, McKearin G III-6, 3 Mold, Folded Rim, Flint, 5 In. | 80.00 |
| Blown Glass, Bowl, Pittsburgh, Folded Rim, Deep, 4 1/2 In. Diameter | 15.00 |
| Blown Glass, Bowl, Punch, Covered, Free Blown, Art Nouveau, Painted Poppies | 65.00 |
| Blown Glass, Bowl, Ruby To Amber, Free-Blown, Ruffled, 7 In. High | 15.00 |
| Blown Glass, Box, Powder, Hinged, Green, Enameled Floral, Brass Mountings | 45.00 |
| Blown Glass, Breast Pump, Blown Loop For Hanging, 3 1/2 In.Diameter | 6.75 |
| Blown Glass, Breast Pump, Dated 1870 | 10.75 |
| Blown Glass, Candlestick, Sausagelike Stem, Knopped, Folded Lip, Clear, Pair | 50.00 |
| Blown Glass, Celery, Engraved | 45.00 |
| Blown Glass, Celery, Engraved, Cut Stem & Foot, Flint | 15.00 |
| Blown Glass, Champagne, Frills, Cotton Twist Stem, C.1750, 8 1/2 In.High | 45.00 |
| Blown Glass, Cocktail Set, Coaching Scene, Hand-Painted, 7 Piece | 90.00 |
| Blown Glass, Cologne, Boot Shape, Lace & Tie Front, Clear, Cork Stopper | 25.00 |
| Blown Glass, Compote, Flint, Free-Blown, Applied Stem, Folded Rim, 7 In. | 100.00 |
| Blown Glass, Compote, Pittsburgh, Pillar Mold, 11 In. Diameter | 105.00 |
| Blown Glass, Cordial, Lime Soda, Flint, Applied Stem & Foot, Round Pontil | 16.00 |
| Blown Glass, Cordial, McKearin G III-12, Three Mold, Clear | 300.00 |
| Blown Glass, Creamer, Cobalt, Midwestern, Applied Handle & Foot, 4 3/4 In. | 180.00 |
| Blown Glass, Creamer, Pittsburgh, Clear Threading, Applied Hollow Handle | 85.00 |
| Blown Glass, Creamer, Pittsburgh, 12 Ribs, Applied Handle, 6 In. High | 55.00 |
| Blown Glass, Cruet, Blue, Paneled, Applied Amber Handle, Amber Stopper | 39.00 |
| Blown Glass, Cruet, Engraved Floral, Vines, Bird, & Bee On Cut Panels, 6 In. | 22.50 |
| Blown Glass, Cruet, Gold Trim At Base & Rim, Blue & Pink Floral, Green | 85.00 |
| Blown Glass, Cruet, Midwestern, 15 Panels, Applied Handle & Foot, 9 1/4 In. | 55.00 |
| Blown Glass, Cruet, Olive Green, Clover Lip, Gold Bands, Apple Blossoms | 50.00 |
| Blown Glass, Cruet, Pale Green, Pink Enamel Floral, Gilt, Faceted Stopper | 49.50 |
| Blown Glass, Cruet, Pittsburgh, 16 Ribs, Applied Handle, Pewter Cap | 70.00 |
| Blown Glass, Cruet, Double S Pattern, Raisin Amethyst, 7 1/2 In.High | 150.00 |
| Blown Glass, Cruet, 24 Ribs, Applied Crimped Handle, 12 Rib Stopper, 9 In. | 27.50 |
| Blown Glass, Cup & Saucer, Applied Coin Gold, Floral Drape, Applied Handle | 12.00 |
| Blown Glass, Decanter, Blown Stopper, Dark Blue, 12 In.High | 45.00 |
| Blown Glass, Decanter, Captain's Type, Almond Thumbprint, Green | 26.50 |
| Blown Glass, Decanter, Clear, 3 Applied Neck Rings | 21.00 |
| Blown Glass, Decanter, Diamond Point, 3 Mold, Quart | 75.00 |
| Blown Glass, Decanter, Faceted Stopper, Engraved Daisies, Clear, 11 1/2 In. | 45.00 |
| Blown Glass, Decanter, Flint, Pillar Mold, 8 Rib, Applied Stem & Foot, 10 In. | 65.00 |
| Blown Glass, Decanter, Free-Blown, Folded Lip, Rough Pontil, Flint, 1/2 Pint | 35.00 |
| Blown Glass, Decanter, Green, Clover Lip, White Lilies Of The Valley, 11 In. | 30.00 |
| Blown Glass, Decanter, McKearin G II-18, 3 Mold, Rigaree Rings, Quart | 90.00 |
| Blown Glass, Decanter, McKearin G Ii-18, Flint, Applied Double Rings, Pair | 175.00 |
| Blown Glass, Decanter, McKearin G 2-7, 3 Mold, Stopper, Green, Pint | 250.00 |
| Blown Glass, Decanter, Molded, McKearin G III-5, 3 Rings, Quart | 100.00 |
| Blown Glass, Decanter, Riverboat, Flint, 2 Rib Pillar Mold, Neck Ring, Quart | 65.00 |
| Blown Glass, Decanter, Sunburst, 3 Mold, Stopper, Pint | 85.00 |
| Blown Glass, Decanter, Three Mold, Stopper, 5 Quart, McKearin G III-5 | 95.00 |
| Blown Glass, Decanter, Whiskey, Pressed Cut Glasslike Pattern | 45.00 |
| Blown Glass, Decanter, 3 Mold, Diamond Point, Quart | 75.00 |

Blown Glass, Decanter, 3 Mold, Lacy Stopper, McKearin G II-22, 8 1/2 In. ............................ 75.00
Blown Glass, Doorstop, Paperweight Type, Bubbles, Colored, 6 In.Diameter .................... 250.00
Blown Glass, Egg, Nesting ................................................................................................ 2.50
Blown Glass, Flip, Cut Almond Punty With Crow's-Foot Flutes, 9 In. High ...................... 49.50
Blown Glass, Flip, Flint, 3 Mold, McKearin G I-6 .............................................................. 85.00
Blown Glass, Flytrap, Clear, 3 Applied Feet ...................................................................... 35.00
Blown Glass, Funnel, Ribbed, 8 3/4 In. High ...................................................................... 15.00
Blown Glass, Garniture Set, Flint, Engraved Floral & Vine, C.1890, 3 Piece .................... 89.00
Blown Glass, Goblet, Flint, Wine Bowl, Amber Overlay, Engraved Hunt Scene ................ 23.00
Blown Glass, Goblet, Lime Soda, Cone, Applied Foot, Flint .............................................. 15.00
Blown Glass, Hat, Free-Blown, Cobalt, Turned Down Brim, C.1850, 4 1/2 In. .................... 55.00
Blown Glass, Hat, McKearin G III-5, Folded Brim, Flint .................................................... 100.00
Blown Glass, Hat, Stippled Border On Brim, Clear, 5 In.High .......................................... 32.00
Blown Glass, Ink, Cone, Open Pontil, 8 Sided, Amber ...................................................... 85.00
Blown Glass, Inkwell, A.W.Brinkerhoff, 1872, 12 Paneled Base, Folded Top .................. 15.00
Blown Glass, Inkwell, Aqua, Circular, 1 Flat Side, 2 3/4 In. .............................................. 2.00
Blown Glass, Inkwell, Aqua, 8 Panels, Pyramid, 2 1/2 In. .................................................. 10.00
Blown Glass, Inkwell, Aqua, 12 Panels, Pyramid Shape, Opalescent, 2 3/4 In. ................ 25.00
Blown Glass, Inkwell, Green, 8 Panels, Pyramid, 2 1/2 In. ................................................ 10.00
Blown Glass, Inkwell, McKearin G II-2, Olive Brown, Coventry, 3 Mold ............................ 85.00
Blown Glass, Inkwell, McKearin G II-18, Coventry, Amber, 2 3/4 In. ................................ 450.00
Blown Glass, Inkwell, Southern Mexico, School Desk, Cobalt, 1 3/4 In.High .................... 1.50
Blown Glass, Jar, Mustard, Flint ........................................................................................ 30.00
Blown Glass, Knife Rest, Blue, Swirled Posts, Triangular Shape Ends ............................ 15.00
Blown Glass, Ladle, Hollow, 15 1/2 In.Long ...................................................................... 12.00
Blown Glass, Lemonade Set, Pointed Hobnail, Amber, Rough Pontil, 7 Piece .................. 125.00
Blown Glass, Liqueur Set, Applied Blue Twisted Handle, Amber, 8 Piece ........................ 95.00
Blown Glass, Liqueur Set, Frosted, Enameled, Stemmed Glasses, 3 Piece ...................... 20.00
Blown Glass, Mortar & Pestle, Photography Work, Blue Mortar, Clear Pestle .................. 22.50
Blown Glass, Muffineer, Applied Circular Foot, Pewter Top, Flint .................................... 55.00
Blown Glass, Muffineer, Cobalt, Bar & Waffle, 3 Mold ...................................................... 77.50
Blown Glass, Mug, Flint, Applied Handle, Enamel Decoration, McKearin G I-6 ................ 55.00
Blown Glass, Mug, McKearin G I-6, 3 Mold, Enamel Decoration ...................................... 52.00
Blown Glass, Mug, Pear Shape, Applied Handle, Free Form, Maria In Gold, 1750 ............ 25.00
Blown Glass, Mug, Ruby Stained, Etched Flower Clusters, Motto, Gold, Pair .................. 35.00
Blown Glass, Pan, Amber, Folded Rim, 12 1/2 In. Diameter .............................................. 275.00
Blown Glass, Pan, Aqua, Folded Rim, 10 Diamond, 5 1/4 In. Diameter ............................ 475.00
Blown Glass, Pan, Aqua, Folded Rim, 12 In. Diameter ...................................................... 90.00
Blown Glass, Pan, Eastern, Bottle Glass, Folded Rim, Light Green, 6 In. ........................ 55.00
Blown Glass, Pan, Eastern, Dark Aqua, Folded Over Rim, 5 In. High .............................. 25.00
Blown Glass, Pan, Folded Rim, 6 In. Diameter .................................................................. 20.00
Blown Glass, Pan, Golden Amber, Folded Over Rim, 9 In. Diameter ................................ 90.00
Blown Glass, Pan, Mantua, Ohio, Amber, 7 1/2 In. Diameter ............................................ 175.00
Blown Glass, Pan, Mantua, Ohio, Amethyst, Folded Rim, 8 1/4 In. Diameter .................. 350.00
Blown Glass, Pan, Milk, Aqua, Folded Rim, 9 5/8 In. Diameter ........................................ 85.00
Blown Glass, Pan, Milk, Light Green, New York State ...................................................... 185.00
Blown Glass, Pan, Ohio, Golden Amber, Broken Swirl, 5 1/2 In. Diameter ...................... 900.00
Blown Glass, Pan, Pittsburgh, Applied Cobalt Rim, 4 7/8 In. Diameter ............................ 105.00
Blown Glass, Pan, Zanesville, Reddish Amber, Folded Rim, 7 1/2 In. Diameter .............. 300.00
Blown Glass, Pilsner, Cut, Wheat Pattern .......................................................................... 2.00
Blown Glass, Pitcher, Applied Hollow Handle, Tooled Lines At Lip .................................. 200.00
Blown Glass, Pitcher, Blue, Large Size .............................................................................. 5.98
Blown Glass, Pitcher, Green, Pontil, 8 In. .......................................................................... 15.00
Blown Glass, Pitcher, Midwestern, Applied Hollow Handle, 8 In. .................................... 70.00
Blown Glass, Pitcher, Midwestern, Green, Broken Swirl, 16 Ribs, 6 In. .......................... 200.00
Blown Glass, Pitcher, Midwestern, Green, Broken Swirl, 32 Ribs, Pint ............................ 200.00
Blown Glass, Pitcher, Midwestern, Olive, Broken Swirl, 16 Ribs, 6 1/2 In. ...................... 225.00
Blown Glass, Pitcher, Milk, Amber, Hand Threading, Rough Pontil .................................. 95.00
Blown Glass, Pitcher, Milk, Blue, Hand Blown, 5 In.High .................................................. 2.95
Blown Glass, Pitcher, Milk, South Jersey Type, Amber, Applied Threading ...................... 95.00
Blown Glass, Pitcher, New Hampshire, Olive Green, Applied Handle & Base .................... 275.00
Blown Glass, Pitcher, Pittsburgh, Amethyst, Pillar Mold, Swirled, 8 Ribs ...................... 1400.00
Blown Glass, Pitcher, Pittsburgh, Cobalt, Hollow Handle, Tooled Rim, 8 In. .................. 450.00
Blown Glass, Pitcher, South Jersey, Aqua, Applied Foot & Grooved Handle .................... 245.00
Blown Glass, Pitcher, Water, Applied Handle, 5 Tooled Rings, Flint, C.1840 .................... 155.00
Blown Glass, Pitcher, Water, Bulbous, Applied Handle, Hand-Painted Floral .................... 29.50

Blown Glass, Pitcher, Water, Clear, Applied Crimped Handle, Pittsburgh .................... 150.00
Blown Glass, Pitcher, Water, Coin Spot, Clear & Opalescent, Flared Top .................... 75.00
Blown Glass, Plate, Latticinio, Multicolored Canes & Spirals, 5 In. ......................... 18.00
Blown Glass, Plate, McKearin G I-5, 3 Mold, 6 In. ........................................ 45.00
Blown Glass, Plate, Narrow Swirl, Blue, Clear Cased, White Stripe, 5 1/2 In. ............... 38.00
Blown Glass, Pot, Mustard, McKearin G I-15, Covered, Molded, Rough Pontil ................. 45.00
Blown Glass, Rose Bowl, Applied Coin Gold Decoration, Ground Pontil ...................... 37.50
Blown Glass, Rose Bowl, Crimped Top, Mauve, Gold Decoration, 4 In.High .................. 20.00
Blown Glass, Rose Bowl, Hobnail, Blown In Mold, Clear, 6 In.Diameter ..................... 20.00
Blown Glass, Rose Bowl, Hobnail, Clear, Blown In Mold ................................... 25.00
Blown Glass, Rose Bowl, Ribbed, Wavy Top, Opalescent, 3 5/8 In.High ..................... 62.50
Blown Glass, Salt & Pepper, Engraved Design, Star Holes In Sterling Tops ................. 65.00
Blown Glass, Salt, Cobalt, 3 Mold, 1 3/4 In. ............................................ 28.00
Blown Glass, Salt, Double Ogee, Ogival Pattern, Footed, 2 1/2 In. ....................... 45.00
Blown Glass, Salt, Hat Shape, Cane For Pepper .......................................... 5.00
Blown Glass, Salt, Master, Clambroth, Paneled, Checkered Base, 4 1/2 In. ................. 10.00
Blown Glass, Salt, Master, Cobalt Blue, Ogival Pattern, Footed, 2 7/8 In. ................. 150.00
Blown Glass, Salt, Master, Cobalt, Patterned, 2 5/8 In. .................................. 235.00
Blown Glass, Salt, Master, 16 Ribs, Double Ogee, Applied Foot, 2 3/4 In. ................. 35.00
Blown Glass, Salt, Monot Stumpf, Pantin, France, Gold & Pink Stripes ..................... 47.50
Blown Glass, Shade, Hurricane Lamp, Turned Over Rim, 14 In., Pair ........................ 130.00
Blown Glass, Spittoon, Aqua, Folded Over Rim, 3 In. High ................................ 35.00
Blown Glass, Spooner, Hat Shape, Free Form, Paneled Sides, Rayed Base, Flint ............. 32.50
Blown Glass, Stein, Threaded Base, Pewter Top, 10 In. ................................... 55.00
Blown Glass, Sugar & Creamer, Blue, Hand Blown ........................................ 3.95
Blown Glass, Swan, Crystal, 9 X 9 In. ................................................... 40.00
Blown Glass, Syrup, Applied Handle, Rose Color Overlay, Pewter Lift & Spout .............. 65.00
Blown Glass, Syrup, Lincoln Drape, Applied Handle, Pewter Top ........................... 89.50
Blown Glass, Syrup, Sunk Honeycomb ................................................... 18.00
Blown Glass, Syrup, Teepee ............................................................ 18.00
Blown Glass, Tankard, Amber, Hand-Painted Stag & White Foliage, Pewter Lid .............. 225.00
Blown Glass, Tankard, Blue, Applied Blue Handle, Floral Decal ........................... 78.50
Blown Glass, Tankard, Blue, Applied Loop Handle & Flowers, 10 1/2 In.High ............... 75.50
Blown Glass, Tumbler, Clear, 6 In.High ................................................. 85.00
Blown Glass, Tumbler, Cobalt, Pittsburgh, 6 Panels, 3 1/8 In. ................. 40 00 To 45.00
Blown Glass, Tumbler, Dark Amber, South Jersey ....................................... 97.00
Blown Glass, Tumbler, Golden Amber, Swirled Rib, 4 In. ................................ 30.00
Blown Glass, Tumbler, Ohio, Yellow Amber, Broken Swirl, 20 Ribs, 4 3/4 In. ............. 850.00
Blown Glass, Tumbler, Whiskey, Amethyst, Pittsburgh, 6 Panels, 2 5/8 In. ............... 50.00
Blown Glass, Tumbler, Whiskey, Amethyst, Pittsburgh, 8 Panels, 2 3/8 In. ............... 45.00
Blown Glass, Tumbler, Whiskey, Apple Green, Pittsburgh, 8 Panels, 2 5/8 In. ............. 80.00
Blown Glass, Tumbler, Whiskey, Cobalt, 8 Panels, 2 1/4 In. ............................. 20.00
Blown Glass, Tumbler, Whiskey, Fiery Opalescent, 7 Panels, 2 1/4 In. ................... 65.00
Blown Glass, Tumbler, Whiskey, Golden Amber, Pittsburgh, 6 Panels, 2 3/4 In. ........... 95.00
Blown Glass, Tumbler, Whiskey, Light Amber, Pittsburgh, 6 Panels, 2 5/8 In. ............. 55.00
Blown Glass, Tumbler, Whiskey, Sapphire Blue, Pittsburgh, 6 Panels, 2 3/4 In. ........... 45.00
Blown Glass, Tumbler, Yellow Green Tint, Pillar Mold, 8 Ribs, 4 1/4 In. ................. 50.00
Blown Glass, Urinal .................................................................... 75.00
Blown Glass, Vase, Blue, Straight Sides, Enamel Jester, 6 1/2 In. ....................... 37.50
Blown Glass, Vase, Bud, Pale Green, Bull's-Eyes, Pinched, Center Hole, 3 Holes .......... 37.50
Blown Glass, Vase, Bulb, Blue, Hyacinth ............................................... 25.00
Blown Glass, Vase, Covered, Pale Green, 6 X 4 In. ..................................... 3.98
Blown Glass, Vase, Flint, 16 Expanded Swirled Ribs, Applied Stem, 9 In. ................. 50.00
Blown Glass, Vase, Free Form, Air Traps, Cerulean Blue, 12 X 5 In. ..................... 89.00
Blown Glass, Vase, Greenish Aqua, 2 Handled, 8 In. High ............................... 15.00
Blown Glass, Vase, Midwestern, Aqua, 20 Ribs, Flared & Threaded Top, 7 In. ............. 200.00
Blown Glass, Vase, New Hampshire, Dark Olive Green, 5 In. ............................. 105.00
Blown Glass, Vase, Pittsburgh, Pink Loops, White Casing, Ruffled Top, 10 In. ........... 100.00
Blown Glass, Vase, South Jersey, Aqua, White Loops, 11 In. ............................ 65.00
Blown Glass, Vase, Swirl Design, Pale Green, 8 1/2 X 6 In. ............................. 3.98
Blown Glass, Vase, Swirl, Blue, 2 Applied Handles, 3 1/2 In.High ....................... 7.00
Blown Glass, Water Set, Hobnail, Footed Tumblers, 7 Piece ............................. 87.00
Blown Glass, Wine, Applied Folded Foot, Flint ......................................... 30.00
Blown Glass, Wine, Cone, 26 Ribs, Folded Foot, Molded Pattern, Flint ................... 30.00
Blown Glass, Wine, Cut, Polished Pontil ............................................... 25.00
Blown Glass, Wine, Engraved Vintage Bowl, Air Twist Stem, 5 1/2 In. ................... 45.00

| | |
|---|---:|
| Blown Glass, Wine, Etched Grapes & Leaves, 4 3/4 In.High | 24.50 |
| Blown Glass, Wine, Flint | 16.00 |
| Blown Glass, Wine, McKearin G II-19, 3 Mold | 90.00 |
| Blown Glass, Wine, Ruby & Clear Air Twist Stem, C.1750 | 50.00 |
| Blown Glass, Witch's Ball, Green Glass, 4 Crystal Legs, 10 In.High | 50.00 |
| Blown Glass, Witch's Ball, Olive Green, 3 In. | 15.00 |
| Blown Glass, Witch's Ball, Opalescent Loopings, Aqua, 4 In.Diameter | 50.00 |
| Blown Glass, Witch's Ball, White Loopings, Clear, 5 3/4 In.Diameter | 40.00 |

Blue Amberina, see Bluerina
Blue Glass, see Cobalt Blue
Blue Onion, see Onion

*Blue Willow pattern has been made in England since 1780. The pattern
has been copied by factories in many countries, including Germany, Japan, and
the United States. It is still being made. Willow was named for a
pattern that pictures a bridge, birds, willow trees, and a Chinese landscape.*

| | |
|---|---:|
| Blue Willow, Bowl, Ridgway, 5 1/2 In., Pair | 10.00 |
| Blue Willow, Bowl, Vegetable, Covered, Square, 7 In.High | 29.00 |
| Blue Willow, Bowl, Vegetable, Ridgway, 9 1/2 In. | 22.50 |
| Blue Willow, Butter Pat, Allerton | 2.85 |
| Blue Willow, Butter, Buffalo Pottery, 1911, 8 In.Diameter | 55.00 |
| Blue Willow, Butter, Covered, Strainer | 24.00 |
| Blue Willow, Creamer, Miniature | 5.00 |
| Blue Willow, Cup & Saucer, Doll's, C.1850, Set Of 12 | 26.00 |
| Blue Willow, Cup, Scenes, 5 1/2 In.Diameter | 10.00 |
| Blue Willow, Gravy Boat, Ridgway | 15.00 |
| Blue Willow, Nest Of Platters, W.A.& Sons, England, 11 1/2 X 17 In., 4 | 72.50 |
| Blue Willow, Pitcher, Buffalo Pottery, 1907, 5 In.High | 25.00 |
| Blue Willow, Pitcher, Buffalo Pottery, 2 Pints, 14 Ozs. | 30.00 |
| Blue Willow, Pitcher, Milk, Buffalo Pottery, 1909, Quart | 25.00 |
| Blue Willow, Plate, Buffalo Pottery, 1916, 10 In. | 7.00 |
| Blue Willow, Plate, Cake | 44.00 |
| Blue Willow, Plate, Child's, Divided, Set Of 8 | 24.00 |
| Blue Willow, Plate, Dessert, Marked Patent Ironstone China, C.1835 | 18.00 |
| Blue Willow, Plate, Impressed Ashworth, 10 1/4 In. | 29.00 |
| Blue Willow, Plate, Ironstone, 10 In. | 28.50 |
| Blue Willow, Plate, Royal Worcester, 9 In. | 18.00 |
| Blue Willow, Plate, Toddy, Soft Paste, C.1800, 5 1/2 In. | 12.00 |
| Blue Willow, Plate, Turned Rim, English, Ironstone, 9 In. | 38.00 |
| Blue Willow, Platter, Buffalo Pottery, 1909, 14 In. | 25.00 |
| Blue Willow, Platter, England | 4.00 |
| Blue Willow, Platter, Ironstone, 16 X 13 In. | 29.00 |
| Blue Willow, Platter, Ridgway, 11 X 14 In. | 27.50 |
| Blue Willow, Platter, Ridgway, 12 1/2 In. | 25.00 |
| Blue Willow, Platter, Staffordshire, C.1850, 15 X 12 In. | 25.00 |
| Blue Willow, Platter, Stone China, Staffordshire, C.1850, 9 1/4 X 11 3/4 In. | 18.00 |
| Blue Willow, Platter, T.& B. Godwin, 11 1/2 X 9 1/4 In. | 16.00 |
| Blue Willow, Platter, Wedgwood, England, 11 X 9 In. | 20.00 |
| Blue Willow, Platter, Well & Tree, Underskirt, 21 X 16 1/2 In. | 65.00 |
| Blue Willow, Platter, 15 1/2 X 12 1/4 X 1 1/4 In. | 28.00 |
| Blue Willow, Relish, Buffalo Pottery, Pinched Sides, 8 1/4 In.Long | 22.00 |
| Blue Willow, Sauce, Buffalo Pottery, 1911, 5 In.Diameter | 8.00 |
| Blue Willow, Sauce, Meakin | 4.00 |
| Blue Willow, Saucer, Buffalo Pottery | 1.25 |
| Blue Willow, Sugar, Buffalo Pottery, 1911 | 22.00 |
| Blue Willow, Sugar, Covered, 2 Handled, Ridgway, England | 18.00 |
| Blue Willow, Tea Set, Child's, C.1935, 33 Piece | 22.00 |
| Blue Willow, Tea Set, Child's, Japanese, 22 Piece | 20.00 |
| Blue Willow, Tea Set, Child's, Occupied Japan, 9 Piece | 37.50 |
| Blue Willow, Tea Set, Child's, Open Handles Cake Plate, Japan, 1930, 22 Piece | 32.00 |
| Blue Willow, Teapot, Four Cup, Sadler, Made In England | 15.50 |
| Blue Willow, Trembleuse & Saucer, Soup, Covered, 2 Handled, C.1840 | 50.00 |
| Blue Willow, Washstand Set, Marked 8 In Blue On Bottom, 2 Piece | 45.00 |
| Blue Willow, Washstand Set, Wedgwood, 2 Piece | 165.00 |

*Bluerina is a type of art glass which shades from light blue to ruby. It is
often called blue amberina.*

Bluerina, Bowl, Ruffled, Diamond-Quilted, Mold Blown, 7 In.Diameter .............. 55.00

*Bohemian glass is an ornate, overlay, or flashed glass made during the Victorian era. It has been reproduced in Bohemia, which is now a part of Czechoslovakia. Glass made from 1875 to 1900 is preferred by collectors.*

| | |
|---|---|
| Bohemian Glass, Bottle & Glass, Bedside, Red | 27.50 |
| Bohemian Glass, Bottle, Grape Pattern, Stopper, 16 In.High, Pair | 120.00 |
| Bohemian Glass, Bottle, Red & Clear, 14 1/2 In.High, Pair | 100.00 |
| Bohemian Glass, Bottle, Ruby, Etched, Blown, Stopper, 9 In., Pair | 54.00 |
| Bohemian Glass, Bottle, Scent, Cut Grapes & Etched Leaves, Red Overlay | 137.50 |
| Bohemian Glass, Bottle, Water, Amber, Deer & Dog, Applied Ring At Base | 55.00 |
| Bohemian Glass, Bowl, Amber Cut To Clear, 5 1/2 In.High | 95.00 |
| Bohemian Glass, Bowl, Finger, Red, Etched Grape | 32.50 |
| Bohemian Glass, Bowl, Ruby, 8 X 3 1/2 In. | 49.00 |
| Bohemian Glass, Carafe & Tumbler, Ruby, Clear Vintage, 2 Rings Around Neck | 35.00 |
| Bohemian Glass, Carafe & Tumbler, Ruby, Frosted Vintage | 35.00 |
| Bohemian Glass, Cornucopia, Cranberry, Butterfly On Marble Base, Gilt | 100.00 |
| Bohemian Glass, Cruot, Cranberry, Bubble Swirl, Applied Clear Handle | 25.00 |
| Bohemian Glass, Cruet, Wine, Cranberry | 8.00 |
| Bohemian Glass, Decanter, Gold Detail, Steeple Stopper, 18 In. | 175.00 |
| Bohemian Glass, Decanter, Ruby Flashed, Engraved & Cut, Polished Stopper | 75.00 |
| Bohemian Glass, Decanter, Ruby, Etched Vintage, Hollow Stopper, 11 1/4 In. | 70.00 |
| Bohemian Glass, Goblet, Overlay, Amber Swags, Engraved Floral, C.1835 | 95.00 |
| Bohemian Glass, Goblet, Red, Painted Medallion, Enamel Floral, Scalloped | 35.00 |
| Bohemian Glass, Goblet, Ruby, Etched Lady & Gentleman In Boat, Swans | 45.00 |
| Bohemian Glass, Liqueur Set, Ruby Flashed, Floral & Leaf Engraving, 7 Piece | 95.00 |
| Bohemian Glass, Perfume, Red Designs, Gold Trim, 5 In.High | 375.00 |
| Bohemian Glass, Pokal, Covered, Ruby To Clear, Deer & Pine Tree, 9 In. | 45.00 |
| Bohemian Glass, Tumbler, Overlay, Blue, Clear Quatrefoil, Gold Trim, C.1835 | 75.00 |
| Bohemian Glass, Tumbler, Ribbed, Formally Dressed Girl On Porcelain Insert | 150.00 |
| Bohemian Glass, Tumbler, Ribbed, Girl In Riding Clothes Porcelain Insert | 150.00 |
| Bohemian Glass, Urn, Spear Finial, Cranberry & Camphor, Birds & Flowers | 65.00 |
| Bohemian Glass, Vase, Covered, Blue Flash, Woodland Scene, 14 In.High, Pair | 325.00 |
| Bohemian Glass, Vase, Red, Bird Design, 13 1/2 In.High | 35.00 |
| Bohemian Glass, Vase, Red, Birds, 6 In., Pair | 48.00 |
| Bohemian Glass, Vase, Red, Engraved Deer & Woodland Scene, 10 In., Pair | 125.00 |
| Bohemian Glass, Vase, Ruby Flashed, Castle & Birds, Footed, Flared, 8 In. | 45.00 |
| Bohemian Glass, Vase, Ruby, Cut & Etched, 12 1/2 In. | 30.00 |
| Bohemian Glass, Wine, Ruby, Etched Vintage | 25.00 |
| Bohemian Glass, Wine, Ruby, Etching At Top Edge, Pontil | 22.00 |
| Book, Almanac, Ayer's American, 1867 | 3.00 |
| Book, Almanac, Bradley, Colored Indian Cover, 1913 To 1915, Each | 2.50 |
| Book, Almanac, Brandeth, 1885 | 3.00 |
| Book, Almanac, Christian, 1855 | 2.25 |
| Book, Almanac, Crusade Temperance, 1875 | 4.50 |
| Book, Almanac, Farmers', 1878 To 1911, Each | 1.00 |
| Book, Almanac, Tucker Cultivator, 1846 | 3.00 |
| Book, Better Little Book, Convoy Patrol, 1942 | 3.50 |
| Book, Better Little Book, Nevada | 3.50 |
| Book, Better Little Book, U.S.Coast Guard, 1942 | 3.50 |
| Book, Big Little Book, Dick Tracy | 8.00 |
| Book, Big Little Book, Flash Gordon Red Sword Invaders | 18.00 |
| Book, Big Little Book, John Carter Of Marks, 1940 | 25.00 |
| Book, Big Little Book, Mickey Mouse & The Bat Bandit | 3.50 |
| Book, Big Little Book, Mickey Mouse The Mail Pilot | 17.00 |
| Book, Big Little Book, The Lone Ranger & His Horse Silver, 1935 | 30.00 |
| Book, Comic, Captain Marvel, Jr., Master Comics | 7.50 |
| Book, Comic, Superman No.3, Comic Fair | 50.00 |
| Book, Jack The Giant Killer, 1896, 6 Color Plates | 6.50 |

    Boston & Sandwich Co., see Sandwich, Fireglow, Lutz

*Bottle collecting has become a major American hobby. There are several general categories of bottles such as historic flasks, bitters, household, figural and others.*

Bottle, Apothecary, Aralia Rac On Gold & Red Glass Label, 8 3/4 In.High .............. 25.00

| | |
|---|---|
| Bottle, Apothecary, Bulbous, 12 In.High | 27.50 |
| Bottle, Apothecary, Cotton's Fine Bay Rum On Gold & Red Glass Label, 9 In. | 20.00 |
| Bottle, Apothecary, Fl.Ext.Verat.Vir.On Gold & Red Glass Label, 7 1/2 In. | 22.50 |
| Bottle, Apothecary, Free-Blown, C.1840, Jet Black, 8 In. | 40.00 |
| Bottle, Apothecary, Gossipium On Gold & Red Glass Label, 8 3/4 In.High | 25.00 |
| Bottle, Apothecary, Imbedded Gold Label Outlined In Red, Cobalt Blue, Pair | 35.00 |
| Bottle, Apothecary, Ol.Tiglii On Gold & Red Glass Label, 7 1/2 In.High | 22.50 |
| Bottle, Apothecary, Pull Stopper, San Francisco, Amber, 10 1/2 In. | 17.50 |
| Bottle, Apothecary, Red Smalts On Gold & Red Glass Label, 8 3/4 In.High | 25.00 |
| Bottle, Apothecary, Small Mouth, Thumbprint Stopper, Glass Label, 9 1/2 In. | 17.50 |
| Bottle, Apothecary, Square, Flat Top Stopper, Amber, 6 1/2 In. | 8.50 |
| Bottle, Apothecary, Square, Flat Top Stopper, Glass Label, Amber, 8 In. | 15.00 |
| Bottle, Apothecary, Statue Of Liberty, Spread Winged American Eagle, Clear | 125.00 |
| Bottle, Apothecary, T.C.W.Co., U.S.A., Finger Pull Stopper, Amber, 10 In. | 15.00 |
| Bottle, Apothecary, Thumbprint Stopper, Glass Label, C.1850, 1/2 Gallon | 55.00 |
| Bottle, Apothecary, Thumbprint Stopper, Glass Label, R.Zingib, 1/2 Gallon | 42.50 |
| Bottle, Apothecary, Thumbprint Stopper, Glass Label, Tr.Arnicae, 1/2 Gallon | 42.50 |
| Bottle, Apothecary, Tinct. Zingib, J. On Gold & Red Glass Label, 7 1/2 In. | 22.50 |
| Bottle, Apothecary, Wide Mouth, Flat Top Stopper, Glass Label, 9 1/2 In. | 25.00 |
| Bottle, Apothecary, Wide Mouth, Pull Stopper, San Francisco, Amber, 8 In. | 27.50 |
| Bottle, Apothecary, Wide Mouth, Thumbprint Stopper, Glass Label, 9 In. | 17.50 |
| Bottle, Art Deco, Delraux Enameled Glass, Flattened Stopper, C.1930, 10 In. | 80.00 |

*Avon started in 1886 as the California Perfume Company. It was not until 1929 that the name Avon was used. In 1939 it became the Avon Products, Inc. Each year Avon sells many figural bottles filled with cosmetic products. Ceramic, plastic, and glass bottles are made in limited editions.*

| | |
|---|---|
| Bottle, Avon, Bath Urn, 1963, Milk Glass | 7.50 |
| Bottle, Avon, Bucking Bronco, Copper Cowboy, Amber, Boxed | 5.00 |
| Bottle, Avon, C.P.C. Smoker's Tooth Powder | 65.00 |
| Bottle, Avon, C.P.C. Tooth Tablets, 1906, Contents | 55.00 |
| Bottle, Avon, Cotillion Powder Sachet, 1937, Full | 13.00 |
| Bottle, Avon, Gavel | 10.00 |
| Bottle, Avon, Nearness Body Powder, 1956, Full | 8.00 |
| Bottle, Avon, Nearness Powder Sachet, 1956, Full | 6.00 |
| Bottle, Avon, Persian Wood Cologne Mist, 1956, Label | 12.00 |
| Bottle, Avon, Snail, 1968, Full & Boxed | 5.50 |
| Bottle, Avon, Snoopy, Milk Glass, Label | 2.50 |
| Bottle, Avon, Stein, 1965, Silver | 5.00 |
| Bottle, Avon, 54 Hair Lotion, 1953, 1 Oz. | 14.00 |
| Bottle, Barber, Clambroth, Bay Rum | 12.00 |
| Bottle, Barber, Cranberry Casing, White Opalescent Overlay, 6 Sided Base | 85.00 |
| Bottle, Barber, Gold Incised Lettering Bitters & Absinthe, Amethyst, Pair | 60.00 |
| Bottle, Barber, Honeycomb, 3 Petal Flowers, Pewter Shaker Top, Clear, 6 In. | 30.00 |
| Bottle, Barber, Oriental Type, Pair | 215.00 |
| Bottle, Barber, Purple, Enameled Flowers, Gold Trim | 60.00 |
| Bottle, Barber, Sapphire, Ribbed Palm Interior | 60.00 |
| Bottle, Barber, Squared, Spanish Lace, Cranberry With Opalescence | 115.00 |

*Beam bottles are made to hold Kentucky Straight Bourbon made by the James B.Beam Distilling Company. The Beam series of ceramic bottles began in 1953.*

| | |
|---|---|
| Bottle, Beam, Antioch, 1972 | 3.95 |
| Bottle, Beam, Antique Trader, 1968, 11th Anniversary | 6.00 |
| Bottle, Beam, Bass, 1973, Mint 400 | 9.00 |
| Bottle, Beam, Bing Crosby, 1970, National Pro American | 6.00 |
| Bottle, Beam, Bowling Pin, Gold, 1965 | 3.00 |
| Bottle, Beam, Boxer, 1964 | 12.95 |
| Bottle, Beam, Cameo, 1956, Blue | 3.95 |
| Bottle, Beam, Centennial, St.Louis, 1964 | 27.00 |
| Bottle, Beam, Centennial, St.Louis, 1967 | 18.00 |
| Bottle, Beam, Cherub, 1972, Salmon | 3.95 |
| Bottle, Beam, Cheyenne Centennial, 1972 | 3.95 |
| Bottle, Beam, China Jug, 1972, Turquoise | 3.95 |
| Bottle, Beam, Churchill Downs, 1972, Pink Roses | 3.95 |
| Bottle, Beam, Cleopatra, 1956, Rust | 3.95 |

| | |
|---|---|
| Bottle, Beam, Cocktail Shaker, 1956 | 3.95 |
| Bottle, Beam, Coffee Warmer, 1969, Pyrex | 3.95 |
| Bottle, Beam, Collector's Edition IV | 2.00 |
| Bottle, Beam, Convention, 1973 | 25.00 |
| Bottle, Beam, Crystal, 1956, Clear | 3.95 |
| Bottle, Beam, Crystal, 1956, Emerald | 3.95 |
| Bottle, Beam, Crystal, 1956, Marbleized | 3.95 |
| Bottle, Beam, Customer Specialty, Harold's Club, V.I.P., 1967, Case | 49.00 |
| Bottle, Beam, Customer Specialty, Harold's Club, V.I.P., 1973 | 35.00 |
| Bottle, Beam, Delft, 1956, Blue | 3.95 |
| Bottle, Beam, Desert Classic, 1974 | 16.50 |
| Bottle, Beam, Desert Valley, 1973, Case | 12.00 |
| Bottle, Beam, Donkey, Football, 1972 | 11.00 |
| Bottle, Beam, Duck, 1956 | 3.95 |
| Bottle, Beam, Elephant, Football, 1972 | 11.00 |
| Bottle, Beam, Executive, Charisma, 1970 | 12.00 |
| Bottle, Beam, Executive, Sovereign, 1969 | 11.00 |
| Bottle, Beam, Executive, 1955 | 219.50 |
| Bottle, Beam, Executive, 1956 | 120.00 To 125.00 |
| Bottle, Beam, Executive, 1957 | 84.00 |
| Bottle, Beam, Executive, 1959 | 70.00 |
| Bottle, Beam, Executive, 1960 | 135.00 |
| Bottle, Beam, Executive, 1961 | 74.00 |
| Bottle, Beam, Executive, 1962 | 45.00 To 53.00 |
| Bottle, Beam, Executive, 1963 | 45.00 |
| Bottle, Beam, Executive, 1964 | 55.00 |
| Bottle, Beam, Executive, 1965 | 74.00 |
| Bottle, Beam, Executive, 1966 | 32.00 |
| Bottle, Beam, Executive, 1967 | 15.00 To 19.00 |
| Bottle, Beam, Executive, 1968 | 8.00 To 10.00 |
| Bottle, Beam, Executive, 1969 | 8.00 To 10.00 |
| Bottle, Beam, Executive, 1970 | 8.00 To 10.00 |
| Bottle, Beam, Executive, 1972, Case | 12.00 To 16.00 |
| Bottle, Beam, Germany, 1970 | 8.00 |
| Bottle, Beam, Germany, 1973 | 9.95 |
| Bottle, Beam, Goose, 1956 | 3.95 |
| Bottle, Beam, Grecian, 1956 | 3.95 |
| Bottle, Beam, Hamm's Beer Bear, 1973, Large Size | 9.95 |
| Bottle, Beam, Hamm's Beer Mug, Oktoberfest, 1973 | 5.95 |
| Bottle, Beam, Hansel & Gretel, 1969 | 3.95 |
| Bottle, Beam, Harold's Club, 1958, Man In A Barrel | 225.00 |
| Bottle, Beam, Harry Hoffman, 1969 | 3.95 |
| Bottle, Beam, Hawaiian Open, 1974 | 8.50 |
| Bottle, Beam, Indiana, 1970, Imperial Session | 6.00 |
| Bottle, Beam, Indianapolis 500, 1970, 54th Anniversary | 6.00 |
| Bottle, Beam, Jade, 1956 | 3.95 |
| Bottle, Beam, Las Vegas, 1969 | 3.95 |
| Bottle, Beam, London Bridge, 1969 | 3.95 |
| Bottle, Beam, Maine, 1972 | 3.95 |
| Bottle, Beam, Mr.Richards, 1972 | 3.95 |
| Bottle, Beam, Mt.Rushmore, 1956 | 3.95 |
| Bottle, Beam, Olympia Beam Cannon, 1956 | 3.95 |
| Bottle, Beam, Olympian, 1956 | 3.95 |
| Bottle, Beam, Olympic | 8.50 |
| Bottle, Beam, Ponderosa, 1969 | 18.00 |
| Bottle, Beam, Ponderosa, 1972 | 3.95 |
| Bottle, Beam, Poodle, Gray, 1970 | 6.00 |
| Bottle, Beam, Portula Trek, 1972 | 3.95 |
| Bottle, Beam, Preakness, Pimlico, 1970, 100th Anniversary | 8.00 |
| Bottle, Beam, Preakness, 1972 | 3.95 |
| Bottle, Beam, Redheaded Woodpecker, 1969 | 9.00 |
| Bottle, Beam, Redwood Map, 1967 | 10.00 |
| Bottle, Beam, Redwood, 1972 | 3.95 |
| Bottle, Beam, Royal Crystal, 1956 | 3.95 |
| Bottle, Beam, Royal Emperor, 1969 | 3.95 |
| Bottle, Beam, Shriners, 1970 | 3.95 |

Bottle, Beam, Slot Machine, 1968, Gray ............................................................... 9.00
Bottle, Beam, State, Alaska Star, 1958 ............................................................... 80.00
Bottle, Beam, State, Alaska Star, 1959 ............................................................... 80.00
Bottle, Beam, State, Alaska Star, 1963 ............................................................... 75.00
Bottle, Beam, State, Alaska Star, 1964 ............................................................... 75.00
Bottle, Beam, State, Hawaii, 1959 ...................................................................... 55.00
Bottle, Beam, Tombstone, 1970 .......................................................................... 5.00
Bottle, Beam, Trophy, Doe, 1963 ........................................................................ 35.00
Bottle, Beam, Trophy, Fox, Green, 1965 ............................................................ 45.00
Bottle, Beam, Trophy, Horse, Black, 1962 ......................................................... 26.00
Bottle, Beam, Trophy, Pheasant, 1961 ............................................................... 18.00
Bottle, Beam, Trophy, Pheasant, 1966 ............................................................... 16.00
Bottle, Beam, Trophy, Pheasant, 1967 ............................................................... 16.00
Bottle, Beam, V.I.P., 1970, Case ........................................................................ 65.00
Bottle, Beam, V.I.P., 1971, Case ........................................................................ 75.00
Bottle, Beam, West Virginia, Centennial, 1963 ................................................ 150.00
Bottle, Beam, Yosemite, 1967 ............................................................................ 6.00
Bottle, Beam, Yosemite, 1972 ............................................................................ 3.95
Bottle, Beer, Ashland Brewing Co., Ashland, Wis. ........................................... .75
Bottle, Beer, Ruby Glass ................................................................................... 3.00
Bottle, Beer, Schlitz, Ruby Red ......................................................................... 7.00
Bottle, Bitters, Atwood's Jaundice, 12 Sides, Aqua, 6 In.High ............. 4.75 To 7.50
Bottle, Bitters, Bitters In Silver On Side, Metal Shaker Top, Clear, 6 In. ......... 18.00
Bottle, Bitters, Burdock's Blood, Buffalo, N.Y., Embossed, Amethyst .............. 18.00
Bottle, Bitters, Burdock's Blood, Toronto, Ont., Embossed, Aqua .................... 15.00
Bottle, Bitters, Caldwell's Herb, The Great Tonic, 3 Sided, Amber, 12 3/4 In. ... 175.00
Bottle, Bitters, Doyle's Hop, 1872, Embossed Lips, Amber, 9 1/2 In. .............. 30.00
Bottle, Bitters, Doyle's Hop, 1879, Square, Amber, 9 1/2 In. ........................... 15.00
Bottle, Bitters, Dr.Boyce's Tonic, Embossed, Light Citron ................................ 35.00
Bottle, Bitters, Dr.Boyce's Tonic, Waterbury, Vt., Embossed, Aqua ................. 35.00
Bottle, Bitters, Dr.C.W.Roback's Stomach, Barrel, Light Amber, 9 1/4 In. ........ 110.00
Bottle, Bitters, Dr.Carey's Original Mandrake, Elmira, N.Y., Embossed, Aqua .... 33.00
Bottle, Bitters, Dr.Harter's, St.Louis, Embossed, Light Red Amber, 3 3/4 In. ..... 27.00
Bottle, Bitters, Dr.Hoofland's, Blown In The Mold ............................................ 35.00
Bottle, Bitters, Dr.Hoofland's, Philadelphia, Embossed, Etched, Aqua, 8 In. ..... 30.00
Bottle, Bitters, Dr.Hoofland's, Philadelphia, Embossed, Etched, 7 In.High ....... 17.00
Bottle, Bitters, Dr.Langley's, Embossed, Aqua, W-206F ................................... 20.00
Bottle, Bitters, Dr.Langley's, 99 Union St., Boston, Aqua ................................ 27.00
Bottle, Bitters, Drake's, 4 Log, Amber .............................................................. 50.00
Bottle, Bitters, Electric, Amber, Pint ................................................................. 16.00
Bottle, Bitters, Fish, W.H.Ware, Amber, 11 1/2 In. ........................... 40.00 To 100.00
Bottle, Bitters, Goff's Herd, Camden, N.J., Embossed, Aqua, 7 1/2 In. ........... 22.00
Bottle, Bitters, H.H.Warner & Co., Tippecanoe, Amber, 8 3/4 In. ................... 52.50
Bottle, Bitters, Holtzermann's Patent Stomach, Log Cabin, Amber, 9 3/4 In. .... 145.00
Bottle, Bitters, Indian Restorative, Lowell, Mass., Aqua .................................. 38.00
Bottle, Bitters, King Solomon, Amber ............................................................... 75.00
Bottle, Bitters, Mishler's Herb, Embossed, Amber ........................................... 35.00
Bottle, Bitters, N.K.Brown, Iron & Quinine, Burlington, Vt., Embossed, Aqua ... 40.00
Bottle, Bitters, Paine's Celery Compound, Amber, 10 In.High .......................... 25.00
Bottle, Bitters, Poor Man's Family, Embossed, Aqua ....................................... 20.00
Bottle, Bitters, Ramsey's Trinidad, Embossed, Dark Green ............................. 40.00
Bottle, Bitters, St.Drake's 1860 Plantation, Cabin, Dark Amber, 9 3/4 In. ....... 100.00
Bottle, Bitters, St.Drake's 1860 Plantation, Cabin, Light Amber, 10 1/4 In. ..... 45.00
Bottle, Bitters, Star Anchor, Portsmouth Ohio, Embossed, Amber ................... 80.00
Bottle, Bitters, Tippecanoe, Amber ................................................................... 75.00
Bottle, Bitters, White Enamel Bitters, Pewter Cap & Rim, Red, 6 In. ............... 24.00
Bottle, Bitters, Wood's Tonic Wine, Cincinnati, Ohio, Aqua, 9 1/4 In. ............. 75.00
Bottle, Bitters, Yerba Buena, Flask, Amber ...................................................... 75.00

*The McKearin numbers refer to the book "American Glass" by George
and Helen McKearin.*

Bottle, Blown, Block On Stilts, Threaded Top, 5 1/2 In.High ............................ 15.00
Bottle, Blown, Chestnut, 25 Swirled Ribs, Aqua, 4 5/8 In. .............................. 65.00
Bottle, Blown, Cylindrical, Tapering Neck, Deep Amber, 9 3/4 In. ................... 65.00
Bottle, Blown, Globular, Applied Handle, 32 Vertical Ribs, Aqua, 7 In. ........... 150.00
Bottle, Blown, Globular, Blue Green, 11 3/4 In. ............................................... 35.00

| | |
|---|---:|
| Bottle, Blown, Globular, Flanged Lip, Deep Aqua, 6 1/2 In. | 35.00 |
| Bottle, Blown, Globular, 24 Swirled Ribs, Aqua, 7 1/4 In. | 65.00 |
| Bottle, Blown, Globular, 25 Swirled Ribs, Aqua, 8 1/2 In. | 75.00 |
| Bottle, Blown, McKearin G III-16, 2 Mold, Olive Green, 7 1/2 In. | 325.00 |
| Bottle, Blown, McKearin G VIII-2, Sunburst, Green, Pint, 8 1/4 In. | 450.00 |
| Bottle, Blown, McKearin G VIII-17, Coventry, Sunburst, Olive, 1/2 Pint | 375.00 |
| Bottle, Blown, Olive Green, Gallon, 1790-1810 | 35.00 |
| Bottle, Blown, Taper Shape, C.1818, Translucent Blue, 15 1/2 In.High | 85.00 |
| Bottle, Blown, 24 Swirled Ribs, Flaring Lip, Aqua, 6 5/8 In. | 55.00 |
| Bottle, Calabash, Eagle & Banner, Iron Pontil, Green, 9 In. | 135.00 |
| Bottle, Calabash, Hunter & Fisherman, Aqua, 9 1/2 In. | 45.00 |
| Bottle, Calabash, Jenny Lind & Fisherville Glass Works, Aqua, 9 In. | 40.00 |
| Bottle, Calabash, Jenny Lind & Glass House, Fisherville, Green, 9 1/2 In. | 310.00 |
| Bottle, Calabash, Jenny Lind & Glass House, Ravenna, Aqua, 10 In. | 135.00 |
| Bottle, Calabash, McKearin G I-107, Jenny Lind & Fisherville, Aqua, 10 In. | 55.00 |
| Bottle, Calabash, McKearin G I-99, Jenny Lind & Huffsey, Aqua, 10 1/2 In. | 65.00 |
| Bottle, Calabash, Sheaf Of Rye & Star, Applied Handle, Amber, 9 In. | 340.00 |
| Bottle, Calabash, Tree In Foliage & Sheaf Of Rye, Rake, & Fork, Aqua, 9 In. | 25.00 |
| Bottle, Calabash, Union & Clasped Hands & Eagle & 2 Banners, Amber, 9 In. | 100.00 |
| Bottle, Calabash, Union, Clasped Hands, & Masonic & Eagle, Aqua, 9 In. | 36.00 |
| Bottle, Case, Blown, Cut Decoration, 9 3/4 In. | 20.00 |
| Bottle, Case, Free-Blown, Rough Pontil, Gold Trim | 25.00 |
| Bottle, Case, Square, Blown, Half Post, Gold Leaf, Ball Stopper, C.1750 | 23.00 |
| Bottle, Coca-Cola, see Coca-Cola, Bottle | |
| Bottle, Cologne, Crackle, Depression Glass | 6.00 |
| Bottle, Cologne, French Poodle, Sapphire Blue, 8 In.High | 25.00 To 30.00 |
| Bottle, Decanter, Blown & Cut, Three Ring | 39.00 |
| Bottle, Decanter, Bulbous, Thumbprint, Applied Clear Reeded Handle, Emerald | 40.00 |
| Bottle, Decanter, Captain's Shape, Fluted Neck, Clear | 18.00 |
| Bottle, Decanter, Clear Applied Handle, White Enamel, Green, 9 1/2 In., Pair | 65.00 |
| Bottle, Decanter, Cut Panels, Lacy Stopper, 3 Ring, 10 In., Pair | 40.00 |
| Bottle, Decanter, Etched Grapes, Cut Panels, Plume Stopper, Ruby Flashed | 50.00 |
| Bottle, Decanter, Etched Stars On Side | 20.00 |
| Bottle, Decanter, Etched, Initial W.Stopper, Polished Pontil, 10 3/4 In. | 15.00 |
| Bottle, Decanter, Flattened Sides, Acid Cut Back Birds & Poppies, Clear | 52.00 |
| Bottle, Decanter, Green, 10 In.High | 5.98 |
| Bottle, Decanter, King's Gate, Caernarvon Castle | 5.00 |
| Bottle, Decanter, McKearin G II-10, Pint | 57.00 |
| Bottle, Decanter, McKearin G III-12, Three Mold, Clear, Miniature | 125.00 |
| Bottle, Decanter, McKearin G V-8, Baroque Shell & Ribbing, Quart | 88.00 |
| Bottle, Decanter, Ohio Riverboat, 8 Rib, Polished Pontil, Clear, Quart | 65.00 |
| Bottle, Decanter, Pressed Glass, Bull's Eye Variant, Flint, Quart | 70.00 |
| Bottle, Decanter, White & Gold Enamel, 1 Handle, Green | 35.00 |
| Bottle, Decanter, Wine, Embossed In Silver, Glass, Stopper | 25.00 |
| Bottle, Demijohn, Blown, Black 31 Painted On Gold, Olive Amber, 13 In. | 55.00 |
| Bottle, Demijohn, Blown, 21 On Gold Paper, Olive, 14 In. | 65.00 |
| Bottle, Demijohn, 2 Part Mold Blown, Painted Harbor Scene, Olive, 13 1/2 In. | 35.00 |
| Bottle, Dresser, Etched Floral, Amber & Clear | 45.00 |
| Bottle, Dresser, Paneled Flutes, Mushroom Stopper, Cranberry, 7 In., Pair | 75.00 |
| Bottle, Dresser, Pressed & Cut, Strawberry Diamond, Star Base, 8 In. | 21.50 |
| Bottle, Drug, Brown Bros. Chemist's, Glasgow, Scotland, 9 In. | 6.00 |
| Bottle, Drug, Conical, Pale Aqua, 5 1/8 In.High | 3.00 |
| Bottle, Drug, Emil Cermak, Omaha, Neb., 5 In. | 1.00 |
| Bottle, Drug, R.E.Sellers, Pittsburgh, Aqua, 4 3/4 In.High | 20.00 |
| Bottle, Drug, South Carolina Dispensary, Amber, C.1800 | 22.50 |
| Bottle, Drug, 12 Sided, Flat Lip, Pale Aqua, 2 1/2 In.High | 5.00 |
| Bottle, Error, Warner's Safe Rheumatic Cure, Backwards S In U.S.A., Amber | 55.00 |
| Bottle, Ezra Brooks, Grizzly Bear, 1968 | 9.00 |
| Bottle, Figural, Barrel, Lancaster, N.Y.& Glass Works, Dark Amber, 9 1/2 In. | 192.00 |
| Bottle, Figural, Carry Nation | 10.00 |
| Bottle, Figural, Cherub Holding Medallion, Blown In The Mold | 35.00 |
| Bottle, Figural, Chestnut, Blown, Dark Green, 7 1/4 In.High | 68.00 |
| Bottle, Figural, Chestnut, Blown, Ludlow Type, C.1850, Olive Amber, 7 In. | 48.00 |
| Bottle, Figural, Chestnut, Blown, 4 In. | 55.00 |
| Bottle, Figural, Chestnut, Domed Bottom, Collared Lip, Deep Amber, Quart | 50.00 |
| Bottle, Figural, Chestnut, Flattened, Applied Handle, Deep Red Amber, 7 In. | 25.00 |

Bottle, Figural, Chestnut, Free-Blown, Sheared Lip, C.1750, Olive Green ..................... 55.00
Bottle, Figural, Chestnut, Green, 3/4 Pint ................................................ 40.00
Bottle, Figural, Chestnut, Green, 9 1/4 In. .............................................. 88.00
Bottle, Figural, Christmas Tree, Star Stopper, Blown In The Mold ..................... 125.00
Bottle, Figural, Cigar, Amber ............................................................. 20.00
Bottle, Figural, Cigar, Marshall ......................................................... 35.00
Bottle, Figural, Claw Egg, Blown In The Mold ........................................... 28.00
Bottle, Figural, Dog, 10 In. .............................................................. 5.00
Bottle, Figural, Ear Of Corn, Blown, Light Amber, 9 1/2 In. ........................... 80.00
Bottle, Figural, Eiffel Tower, 14 In. .................................................... 20.00
Bottle, Figural, Elephant, Old Sol, Clorox .............................................. 25.00
Bottle, Figural, Fat Nude ................................................................ 35.00
Bottle, Figural, Fish, Cod Liver Oil, Amber ............................................. 15.00
Bottle, Figural, Fish, Flared Top, Green ................................................ 10.00
Bottle, Figural, Fish, Screw Cap, 8 3/4 In. ............................................. 28.50
Bottle, Figural, Flapper ................................................................. 15.00
Bottle, Figural, General Electric Refrigerator, Embossed, 1930s, Green ............... 10.00
Bottle, Figural, George Washington, Clear, 9 1/2 In.High ............................... 6.95
Bottle, Figural, George Washington, 1732-1932 .......................................... 18.00
Bottle, Figural, Golfer Caddy, 12 In.High ............................................... 35.00
Bottle, Figural, Hand Holding Dagger .................................................... 15.00
Bottle, Figural, Hausdoktor, Military Coat, Blue, 6 1/2 In.High ....................... 37.25
Bottle, Figural, Husted Santa, Blown In The Mold ....................................... 55.00
Bottle, Figural, Joan Of Arc On Horseback, 10 In.High .................................. 18.00
Bottle, Figural, Lemon, 'paul Mangiet Will Hand You One, ' 4 In.High ................. 15.00
Bottle, Figural, Mermaid ................................................................. 15.00
Bottle, Figural, Moses, Poland Water, Blown In The Mold ................................ 75.00
Bottle, Figural, Moses, Screw Cap, Green, 10 In. ........................................ 2.95
Bottle, Figural, Mr.Pickwick, 9 In.High .......................................... 6.95 To 10.00
Bottle, Figural, Penguin, 11 In.High .................................................... 10.00
Bottle, Figural, Pig, Blown, Green, 10 1/2 In. .......................................... 40.00
Bottle, Figural, Pretzel, Porcelain, 5 1/4 In.High ..................................... 35.00
Bottle, Figural, Pumpkin, Leaf & Fruit Design Center, Dated 1870, 5 1/4 In. .......... 14.00
Bottle, Figural, Quahog, Screw Cap ...................................................... 18.00
Bottle, Figural, Refrigerator, Wishing Well Patent, 1932, Embossed, Green ............ 7.00
Bottle, Figural, Scallop, Screw Cap ..................................................... 18.00
Bottle, Figural, Shamrock, Swirled Rib, Applied Handle, Dark Blue, 6 In. ............. 35.00
Bottle, Figural, Shrouded Finger Wagging Skeleton, "spirits, " China, 8 In. .......... 75.00
Bottle, Figural, Slipper, 5 3/4 In. ..................................................... 22.00
Bottle, Figural, Spanish Lady, Lace Mantilla, Compania Hollandesa, 12 In. ............ 55.00
Bottle, Figural, Tippecanoe .............................................................. 72.00
Bottle, Figural, Tippecanoe, N.Y., Log Shape, Mushroom Collar, Amber, 9 In. .......... 65.00
Bottle, Figural, Violin, Fleur-De-Lis, Aqua, 1/2 Pint, 6 In. .......................... 30.00
Bottle, Figural, Violin, Iron Pontil, Aqua, 1/2 Pint, 5 3/4 In. ....................... 40.00
Bottle, Figural, Violin, Scrolled, Aqua-Green, 1/2 Pint, 6 1/4 In. .................... 22.50
Bottle, Figural, Violin, Scrolled, Aqua, Pint, 7 In. .......................... 2K.00 To 30.00
Bottle, Figural, Violin, Scrolled, Aqua, Quart, 8 3/4 In. ............................. 35.00
Bottle, Figural, Violin, Scrolled, Aqua, 1/2 Pint ..................................... 25.00
Bottle, Figural, Violin, Scrolled, Gunmetal Blue, Pint, 5 3/4 In. .................... 505.00
Bottle, Figural, Violin, Scrolled, Iron Pontil, Aqua, Quart, 7 1/4 In. ............... 35.00
Bottle, Figural, Violin, Scrolled, McKearin G IX-1, Aqua, Pint, 7 In. ................ 35.00
Bottle, Figural, Violin, Scrolled, Yellow Green, Pint, 6 In. ......................... 380.00
Bottle, Figural, Washington Bust, Whiskey, Blown In The Mold, Cobalt ................. 25.00
Bottle, Figural, Washington Standing .................................................... 10.00
Bottle, Figural, Woman's High Laced Shoe & Stockinged Leg, C.1880 .................... 35.00

*The McKearin numbers refer to the book "American Glass" by George*
*and Helen McKearin.*
Bottle, Flask, Baltimore Glass Works & Phoenix & Resurgam, Aqua, Pint ................ 50.00
Bottle, Flask, Blown, Ribbed, Flanged Lip, 6 1/2 In. .................................. 25.00
Bottle, Flask, Chestnut, Blown, 21 Swirled Ribs, Gray Blue, 6 1/2 In. ................ 25.00
Bottle, Flask, Chestnut, Blown, 4 1/2 In. ............................................. 20.00
Bottle, Flask, Chestnut, Bulbous, 14 Vertical Ribs, Sapphire Blue, 5 1/2 In. ........ 450.00
Bottle, Flask, Chestnut, 19 Swirled Ribs, Amethystine, 4 1/2 In. .................... 195.00
Bottle, Flask, Clasped Hands & Eagle & Banner, Aqua, 1/2 Pint, 6 1/4 In. ............ 12.00
Bottle, Flask, Cornucopia & Basket Of Flowers, Olive Green, 1/2 Pint ................. 95.00

| | |
|---|---:|
| Bottle, Flask, Cornucopia & Urn, Olive Green, 1/2 Pint, 5 1/4 In. | 45.00 |
| Bottle, Flask, Double Eagle & Cunningham, Pittsburgh In Oval, Aqua, Pint | 30.00 |
| Bottle, Flask, Double Eagle & Oval, Amber, Pint | 65.00 |
| Bottle, Flask, Double Eagle, Amber, Pint | 50.00 |
| Bottle, Flask, Double Eagle, Aqua, Pint, 7 1/4 In. | 20.00 |
| Bottle, Flask, Double Eagle, Light Amber, 7 In. | 810.00 |
| Bottle, Flask, Double Eagle, Olive Amber, 1/2 Pint | 45.00 To 75.00 |
| Bottle, Flask, Double Eagle, Olive Green, 2 Quart | 105.00 |
| Bottle, Flask, Double Eagle, Pittsburgh, Pa. In Oval, Aqua, Quart, 9 In. | 35.00 |
| Bottle, Flask, Double Eagle, Pittsburgh, Pa., Yellow Green, Pint | 80.00 |
| Bottle, Flask, Double Eagle, Stoddard, Rough Pontil, Amber, 1/2 Pint | 95.00 |
| Bottle, Flask, Double Sheaf Of Wheat & Westford Glass Co., Amber, 1/2 Pint | 55.00 |
| Bottle, Flask, Double Sheaf Of Wheat & Westford Glass Co., Dark Amber, Pint | 60.00 |
| Bottle, Flask, Double Union & Clasped Hands, Aqua, Quart | 35.00 |
| Bottle, Flask, Eagle & Clasped Hands, Aqua, 1/2 Pint, 6 1/4 In. | 20.00 |
| Bottle, Flask, Eagle & Credo & For Pike's Peak, Aqua, 1/2 Pint | 40.00 |
| Bottle, Flask, Eagle & For Pike's Peak, Aqua, 1/2 Pint | 30.00 |
| Bottle, Flask, Eagle & Oval & Eagle & Pittsburgh, Pa., Green, Pint | 80.00 |
| Bottle, Flask, Eagle & Pittsburgh, Pa In Oval & Eagle & Oval, Green, Quart | 75.00 |
| Bottle, Flask, Eagle & Stars & Ravenna Glass Co. & Anchor, Aqua, Pint | 90.00 |
| Bottle, Flask, Eagle & 13 Stars & Ravenna Glass Co. & Anchor, Amber, Pint | 250.00 |
| Bottle, Flask, Eagle Medallion, Louisville, Ky.Glass Works, Ribbed, Aqua, Pint | 140.00 |
| Bottle, Flask, Eagle With Granite Glass Co.& Stoddard, Amber, Pint | 195.00 |
| Bottle, Flask, Eagle, Liberty, & Willington Glass Co., Dark Amber, Pint | 125.00 |
| Bottle, Flask, Flint Glass & Pewter, C.1860 | 18.00 |
| Bottle, Flask, For Pike's Peak & Eagle & Credo, Aqua, Pint | 25.00 |
| Bottle, Flask, For Pike's Peak & Eagle With Banner, Aqua, Pint | 15.00 |
| Bottle, Flask, For Pike's Peak & Eagle, Applied Lip Ring, Aqua, Pint | 60.00 |
| Bottle, Flask, French, Blown, Molded Ribs, Diamond & Daisy, 7 1/4 In. | 20.00 |
| Bottle, Flask, Hunter & Running Dogs, Olive Yellow, Pint | 320.00 |
| Bottle, Flask, Isabella Glass Works & Anchor & Glass House, Aqua, Quart | 55.00 |
| Bottle, Flask, Jenny Lind, Fisherville Glass Works, Light Green, Quart | 85.00 |
| Bottle, Flask, Klondike, Gold Nugget, Screw Cap Marked Klondyk | 125.00 |
| Bottle, Flask, L.G.Co., Whittled Base, Amber, Pink | 20.00 |
| Bottle, Flask, Lady On Bicycle & A & DHC In Oval & Eagle, Aqua, Pint | 80.00 |
| Bottle, Flask, Lady's, Cut Glass, 1/2 Pint | 75.00 |
| Bottle, Flask, Leather Top, Pewter Bottom & Cap, M.V.Olry's Patent, 1866 | 8.95 |
| Bottle, Flask, McKearin G I-2, Washington & Eagle, Light Green, Pint | 235.00 |
| Bottle, Flask, McKearin G I-6, Washington & Eagle, Amethyst, Pint | 800.00 |
| Bottle, Flask, McKearin G I-10, Washington & Eagle & 15 Pearls, Aqua, Pint | 310.00 |
| Bottle, Flask, McKearin G I-24, Washington & Taylor, Aqua, Pint | 80.00 |
| Bottle, Flask, McKearin G I-25, Washington & Clay, Bridgeton, Aqua, Quart | 50.00 |
| Bottle, Flask, McKearin G I-37, Washington & Taylor, Sage Green, Quart | 150.00 |
| Bottle, Flask, McKearin G I-51, Washington & Taylor, Yellow Green, Quart | 310.00 |
| Bottle, Flask, McKearin G I-66, Jackson & Eagle & J.R., Amethyst, Pint | 1200.00 |
| Bottle, Flask, McKearin G I-71, Taylor & Major Ringgold, Pale Aqua, Pint | 40.00 |
| Bottle, Flask, McKearin G I-97, Double Franklin, Aqua, Quart | 150.00 |
| Bottle, Flask, McKearin G I-107, Jenny Lind, Calabash, Aqua, Quart Plus | 40.00 |
| Bottle, Flask, McKearin G I-111, Kossuth, Bridgeton & Sloop, Aqua, Pint | 115.00 |
| Bottle, Flask, McKearin G II-11, Eagle & Cornucopia, Aqua, 1/2 Pint | 80.00 |
| Bottle, Flask, McKearin G II-11, Eagle & Cornucopia, Green, 1/2 Pint | 150.00 |
| Bottle, Flask, McKearin G II-11, Eagle & Inverted Cornucopia, 1/2 Pint | 300.00 |
| Bottle, Flask, McKearin G II-12, Eagle & Cornucopia, Aqua, 1/2 Pint | 265.00 |
| Bottle, Flask, McKearin G II-16, Eagle & Cornucopia, Aqua, 1/2 Pint | 20.00 |
| Bottle, Flask, McKearin G II-26, Double Eagle, Dark Blue Green, Quart | 80.00 |
| Bottle, Flask, McKearin G II-41, Eagle & Tree, Aqua, 6 1/2 In. | 105.00 |
| Bottle, Flask, McKearin G II-47, Eagle & Tree, Light Aqua, Quart | 250.00 |
| Bottle, Flask, McKearin G II-48, Eagle & Coffin & Hay, Aqua, Quart | 160.00 |
| Bottle, Flask, McKearin G II-49, Eagle & Stag, Hammonton, Aqua, 1/2 Pint | 205.00 |
| Bottle, Flask, McKearin G II-53, Eagle & Our Country, Aqua, 6 1/2 In. | 85.00 |
| Bottle, Flask, McKearin G II-60, Eagle & Liberty Tree, Aqua, 1/2 Pint | 250.00 |
| Bottle, Flask, McKearin G II-60, Eagle & Liberty Tree, Green, 1/2 Pint | 270.00 |
| Bottle, Flask, McKearin G II-63, Eagle & Willington, Olive, 1/2 Pint | 75.00 |
| Bottle, Flask, McKearin G II-63, Liberty Eagle & Willington, Olive, Pint | 150.00 |
| Bottle, Flask, McKearin G II-71, Double Eagle, Olive Green, 1/2 Pint | 160.00 |
| Bottle, Flask, McKearin G II-71, Eagle & Coventry, Olive Amber, Pint | 190.00 |

Bottle, Flask, McKearin G II-72, Eagle & Cornucopia, Golden Amber, Pint ................................ 60.00
Bottle, Flask, McKearin G II-73, Eagle & Cornucopia, Olive, Pint ........................................... 55.00
Bottle, Flask, McKearin G II-73, Eagle & Cornucopia, Olive, 6 3/4 In. ..................................... 65.00
Bottle, Flask, McKearin G II-74, Eagle, Shield & Cornucopia, Green, Pint ................................ 70.00
Bottle, Flask, McKearin G III-10, Cornucopia, Golden Amber, 1/2 Pint ...................................... 60.00
Bottle, Flask, McKearin G III-10, Cornucopia, Olive Amber, 1/2 Pint ........................................ 50.00
Bottle, Flask, McKearin G III-12, Cornucopia & Urn, Amber, 1/2 Pint ........................................ 45.00
Bottle, Flask, McKearin G III-14, Cornucopia & Urn, Green, 1/2 Pint ........................................ 65.00
Bottle, Flask, McKearin G III-16, Cornucopia & Urn, Blue, Pint .............................................. 725.00
Bottle, Flask, McKearin G IV-1, Masonic & Eagle, Blue Green, 7 1/2 In. .................................. 280.00
Bottle, Flask, McKearin G IV-11, Masonic, Aqua, 7 In. .......................................................... 350.00
Bottle, Flask, McKearin G IV-14, Masonic & Eagle, Blue Green, 5 3/4 In. ................................. 320.00
Bottle, Flask, McKearin G IV-32, Shepherd & Masonic, Aqua, 6 1/2 In. ................................... 190.00
Bottle, Flask, McKearin G IV-34, Masonic & Ship Franklin, Aqua, Pint ..................................... 180.00
Bottle, Flask, McKearin G V-4, Success To The Railroad, Olive, 6 1/2 In. ................................. 190.00
Bottle, Flask, McKearin G V-10, Railroad Lowell & Eagle, Olive, 5 1/2 In. ................................ 240.00
Bottle, Flask, McKearin G VIII-10, Keene, Sunburst, Olive, 1/2 Pint ........................................ 475.00
Bottle, Flask, McKearin G VIII-16, Sunburst, Olive, 1/2 Pint, 6 In. .......................................... 435.00
Bottle, Flask, McKearin G VIII-29, Double Sunburst, Blue Green, 3/4 Pint ................................ 250.00
Bottle, Flask, McKearin G X-1, Stag & Weeping Willow, Aqua, Pint ........................................ 145.00
Bottle, Flask, McKearin G X-17, Tree In Circle, Aquamarine, 6 3/4 In. ..................................... 375.00
Bottle, Flask, Midwestern, 18 Swirled Ribs, Aqua, 7 In. ........................................................ 55.00
Bottle, Flask, Midwestern, 18 Swirled Ribs, Light Green, 6 1/4 In. .......................................... 35.00
Bottle, Flask, Midwestern, 25 Swirled Ribs, Blue Green, 7 1/4 In. .......................................... 85.00
Bottle, Flask, Ohio, Broken Swirl, 20 Ribs, Yellow Green, Pint, 7 In. ...................................... 200.00
Bottle, Flask, Ohio, 16 Swirled Ribs, Amber, Pint, 6 3/4 In. .................................................. 200.00
Bottle, Flask, Ohio, 16 Swirled Ribs, Amethystine Tint, Pint, 6 In. .......................................... 65.00
Bottle, Flask, Ohio, 18 Swirled Ribs, Yellow Green, Pint, 6 1/4 In. ......................................... 175.00
Bottle, Flask, Ohio, 24 Swirled Ribs, 16 Vertical Ribs, Light Green, Pint ................................. 160.00
Bottle, Flask, Pink Loopings On Opaque White, Pint .......................................................... 50.00
Bottle, Flask, Pitkin, Broken Swirl Bottom, 32 Ribs, Olive, Pint ............................................. 175.00
Bottle, Flask, Pitkin, Connecticut, Broken Swirl, 36 Ribs, Olive, 5 3/8 In. ................................ 190.00
Bottle, Flask, Pitkin, Eastern, Broken Swirl, 36 Ribs, Yellow Olive, 6 1/2 In. ........................... 150.00
Bottle, Flask, Pitkin, Eastern, 32 Swirled Ribs, Olive, Pint, 7 In. ........................................... 185.00
Bottle, Flask, Pitkin, Midwestern, Broken Swirl, 20 Ribs, Yellow Green, 5 In. .......................... 750.00
Bottle, Flask, Pitkin, Midwestern, Broken Swirl, 32 Ribs, Olive, 5 In. ..................................... 200.00
Bottle, Flask, Pitkin, Midwestern, Broken Swirl, 36 Ribs, Yellow Olive, 5 In. ........................... 180.00
Bottle, Flask, Pitkin, New England, Blown, Applied Handle, Amber, 7 3/4 In. ............................ 70.00
Bottle, Flask, Pitkin, New England, Broken Swirl, 24 Ribs, Olive, 5 1/4 In. ............................... 195.00
Bottle, Flask, Pitkin, New England, 36 Ribs Swirled To Right, Olive Green ............................... 230.00
Bottle, Flask, Pitkin, Pennsylvania, Broken Swirl, 36 Ribs, Olive, Pint .................................... 200.00
Bottle, Flask, Pitkin, Swirled, Olive Yellow To Amber, 5 1/4 In. ............................................. 205.00
Bottle, Flask, Pumpkin Seed, 4 3/4 In. .............................................................................. 1.75
Bottle, Flask, Railroad Pig, C.1880, 7 In.Long ...................................................... *Illus* 900.00
Bottle, Flask, Ravenna Glass Works & Anchor & Star, Yellow Green, Pint .............................. 145.00
Bottle, Flask, Ravenna Glass Works, Aqua, Pint, 7 3/4 In. ................................................... 75.00
Bottle, Flask, Ravenna Traveler's Companion, Applied Neck Ring, Aqua, Quart ...................... 85.00
Bottle, Flask, Ribbed Sides, Drapery & Star Molding, Cobalt, 7 In. ....................................... 45.00
Bottle, Flask, Saddle, Persian, Free-Blown, Open Pontil, Emerald Green ............................... 13.50
Bottle, Flask, Scroll, Iron Pontil, Blue Aqua, Quart ........................................................... 45.00
Bottle, Flask, Scroll, McKearin G IX-11, Blue Green, Pint .................................................... 100.00
Bottle, Flask, Scroll, McKearin G IX-34, Aqua, 1/2 Pint ...................................................... 75.00

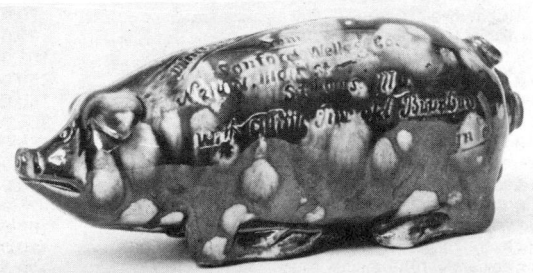

Bottle, Flask, Railroad Pig,
C.1880, 7 In.Long

**Bottle, Flask**, Sheaf Of Rye, Scythe, & Rake & Westford, Yellow, 1/2 Pint ............... 70.00
**Bottle, Flask**, Soldier Riding Horse & Dog, Aqua, Quart ................................................. 32.00
**Bottle, Flask**, Stiegel Type, Ribbed, Enamel Polychrome Lady & Flower, 6 In. ............. 35.00
**Bottle, Flask**, Success To The Railroad, Clear Deep Olive Green, Pint ......................... 190.00
**Bottle, Flask**, Taylor & Dyottville Glass Works, Light Blue, Quart .............................. 145.00
**Bottle, Flask**, Traveler's Companion & Ravenna Glass Co., Aqua, Pint ........................ 65.00
**Bottle, Flask**, Traveling, Blown, 18 Vertical Ribs, Green, 8 3/4 In. ............................ 32.50
**Bottle, Flask**, Traveling, Cobalt Blue, 8 1/4 In. ........................................................ 25.00
**Bottle, Flask**, Traveling, 18 Ribs, Light Green, 5 3/4 In. ............................................ 65.00
**Bottle, Flask**, Union & Clasped Hands & Cannon, Aqua, Pint, 7 1/2 In. ...................... 35.00
**Bottle, Flask**, Union & Clasped Hands & Eagle & 2 Banners, Aqua, Quart .................. 35.00
**Bottle, Flask**, Union & Clasped Hands In Shield & Eagle, Amber, 1/2 Pint ................. 55.00
**Bottle, Flask**, Union & Eagle & Banner, Aqua, 1/2 Pint, 6 In. ................................... 17.50
**Bottle, Flask**, Union & Eagle, L.F.& Co., Pittsburgh, Pa., Aqua, 7 1/2 In. .................. 30.00
**Bottle, Flask**, Union & Eagle, Pittsburgh, Pa. In Oval, Aqua, Pint .............................. 45.00
**Bottle, Flask**, Union & Eagle, Ring At Neck, Aqua, 1/2 Pint ...................................... 45.00
**Bottle, Flask**, Union, Oval, Banded, Embossed Anchor, Amber, Pint .......................... 16.00
**Bottle, Flask**, Violin, Scrolled, Blue Green, Pint, 7 1/4 In. ........................................ 50.00
**Bottle, Flask**, Whiskey, Cut Glass, Sterling Silver Top .............................................. 68.00
**Bottle, Flask**, White Loopings On Clear, Pint ........................................................... 30.00
**Bottle, Flask**, Zanesville City Glass Works, Aqua, Pint .............................................. 42.50
**Bottle, Flask**, Zanesville, Broken Swirl, 24 Ribs, Honey Amber, 7 In. ........................ 550.00
**Bottle, Flask**, Zanesville, Grandfather's, Broken Swirl, 24 Ribs, Amber, 8 In. ............. 900.00
**Bottle, Flask**, Zanesville, Melon Ribbed, Amber, Quart ............................................. 800.00
**Bottle, Flask**, Zanesville, Vertical Ribbing, Deep Reddish Amber, 1/2 Pint ................. 200.00
**Bottle, Flask**, Zanesville, 24 Vertical Ribs, Yellow Green, 7 1/4 In. ........................... 220.00
**Bottle, Flask**, 16 Vertical Ribs, Half Post Neck, 7 1/4 In. .......................................... 45.00
**Bottle, Food**, Eskay's Albumenizer, Patent 1893, Tin Cap, Amber, 7 1/4 In. ............... 5.95
**Bottle, Food**, Golden Tree Brand Syrup, Copyright 1904, Clear, 8 1/4 In. .................. 3.95
**Bottle, Food**, Missouri Ozark Made Country Sorghum, Cottage, Brown ...................... 5.00
**Bottle, Food**, Prune Juice, Green, Large Size ........................................................... 3.98
**Bottle, Food**, Valentine's Meat Juice, Blown, Amber, 3 1/8 In. .................................. 17.50
**Bottle, Fruit Jar**, Atlas E-Z Seal, Aqua, 1/2 Pint ........................................ 1.50 To 4.00
**Bottle, Fruit Jar**, Atlas Good Luck, 1/2 Pint ........................................................... 6.00
**Bottle, Fruit Jar**, Atlas H-A Mason, 1/2 Pint .......................................................... 3.00
**Bottle, Fruit Jar**, Atlas Mason, Clear, 10 X 4 1/2 In. ............................................... 5.98
**Bottle, Fruit Jar**, Atlas Wholefruit, Embossed ........................................................ 1.15
**Bottle, Fruit Jar**, B.B.Wilcox, Quart ..................................................................... 35.00
**Bottle, Fruit Jar**, Ball Ideal, Blue Green, 1/2 Pint .................................................. 12.00
**Bottle, Fruit Jar**, Ball Ideal, 1/2 Pint ................................................................... 1.50
**Bottle, Fruit Jar**, Ball Ideal, 1/3 Pint ................................................................... 1.50
**Bottle, Fruit Jar**, Ball Ideal, 1908, 1/2 Pint ........................................................... 2.00
**Bottle, Fruit Jar**, Ball Perfect Mason, Saltshaker, Miniature ...................................... 4.50
**Bottle, Fruit Jar**, Ball, Dated July 14, 1908, Aqua, Quart .......................................... 6.50
**Bottle, Fruit Jar**, Banner, Press Down Lid, Stain, Quart ............................................ 45.00
**Bottle, Fruit Jar**, Blown In Whittled Mold, Sealing Wax Lip, Aqua, 10 In. ................... 265.00
**Bottle, Fruit Jar**, Blown, Folded Over Rim, Iron Top, Quart, 6 3/8 In. ........................ 75.00
**Bottle, Fruit Jar**, Crockery Jug, Blue Writing, 7 1/2 In.High ...................................... 25.00
**Bottle, Fruit Jar**, Crown, Midget .......................................................................... 7.50
**Bottle, Fruit Jar**, Eagle, Aqua, 1/2 Gallon ............................................................. 45.00
**Bottle, Fruit Jar**, Eureka, 1/2 Pint ....................................................................... 12.00
**Bottle, Fruit Jar**, Glass Top, Pint ......................................................................... 1.50
**Bottle, Fruit Jar**, Glass Top, Quart ....................................................................... 1.50
**Bottle, Fruit Jar**, Johnson & Johnson, Amber, 1/2 Pint ............................................ 12.00
**Bottle, Fruit Jar**, Kerr Mason, 1/2 Pint ................................................................. 1.00
**Bottle, Fruit Jar**, King, Oval, 1/2 Pint ................................................................... 18.00
**Bottle, Fruit Jar**, Lightning, Aqua, Pint ................................................................. 1.00
**Bottle, Fruit Jar**, Lightning, Aqua, Quart ............................................................... 1.00
**Bottle, Fruit Jar**, Lightning, Aqua, 1/2 Gallon ........................................................ 2.50
**Bottle, Fruit Jar**, Lightning, Clear, Pint ................................................................. 1.00
**Bottle, Fruit Jar**, Lightning, Clear, Quart ............................................................... 1.00
**Bottle, Fruit Jar**, Lightning, Clear, 1/2 Gallon ........................................................ 2.50
**Bottle, Fruit Jar**, Lightning, On Base, Aqua, 1/2 Pint ................................... 3.00 To 5.00
**Bottle, Fruit Jar**, Lightning, Putnam, Aqua, Pint ..................................................... 10.00
**Bottle, Fruit Jar**, Lightning, 4 3/4 In.High ............................................................. 38.00
**Bottle, Fruit Jar**, Mason's Cross, Patent Nov.30th, 1858, Amber, Quart ..................... 35.00

| | |
|---|---|
| Bottle, Fruit Jar, Mason's III, 1858, Aqua, Midget | 20.00 |
| Bottle, Fruit Jar, Mason's Improved, The, Amber, 1/2 Gallon | 48.00 |
| Bottle, Fruit Jar, Mason's No.2, Quart | 5.00 |
| Bottle, Fruit Jar, Mason's No.4, Quart | 5.00 |
| Bottle, Fruit Jar, Mason's Patent 1858, Aqua, Pint | 3.00 |
| Bottle, Fruit Jar, Mason's Patent 1858, Aqua, Quart | 2.00 |
| Bottle, Fruit Jar, Mason's Patent 1858, Aqua, 1/2 Gallon | 2.00 |
| Bottle, Fruit Jar, Mason's Patent 1858, Snowflake Back, Zinc Lid, Midget | 40.00 |
| Bottle, Fruit Jar, Mason's Patent 1858, Snowflake On Back, Blue, Quart | 20.00 |
| Bottle, Fruit Jar, Mason's Patent, Nov.30th, 1858, Aqua, Quart | 5.00 |
| Bottle, Fruit Jar, Mason's 1858, Whittled, Bubbles, Vaseline, Pint | 90.00 |
| Bottle, Fruit Jar, Mason's, Patent Nov.30, 1858, Zinc Top, Aqua, Quart | 5.00 |
| Bottle, Fruit Jar, Mason's, 1858, 1/2 Gallon | 4.50 |
| Bottle, Fruit Jar, McDonald, Glass Lid, Quart | 5.00 |
| Bottle, Fruit Jar, Millville Atmospheric, Aqua, 1/2 Pint | 55.00 |
| Bottle, Fruit Jar, Moore's Patent, Dec.3, 1861, Aqua, 1 1/2 Quart | 45.00 |
| Bottle, Fruit Jar, Moore's, Patent Dec.3rd, 1861, Aqua, Quart | 22.50 |
| Bottle, Fruit Jar, Old Judge, Embossed Owl | 1.15 |
| Bottle, Fruit Jar, Perfection, Mar.29, 1887, Blue | 35.00 |
| Bottle, Fruit Jar, Pine Deluxe, Clear Glass Lid, Pint | 2.25 |
| Bottle, Fruit Jar, Pine Deluxe, Clear Glass Lid, Quart | 2.25 |
| Bottle, Fruit Jar, Queen, Kant Krack Lid, 1/2 Pint | 6.00 |
| Bottle, Fruit Jar, Queen, Side Clamps, 1/2 Pint | 6.00 |
| Bottle, Fruit Jar, Queen, 1/2 Pint | 4.00 |
| Bottle, Fruit Jar, Quick Seal In Circle, Aqua, Quart | 3.50 |
| Bottle, Fruit Jar, Safety Valve, Greek Key, Carrying Handle, Aqua, 1/2 Gallon | 25.00 |
| Bottle, Fruit Jar, Safety Valve, 1/4 Pint | 20.00 |
| Bottle, Fruit Jar, Safety Valve, 1/2 Pint | 11.00 |
| Bottle, Fruit Jar, Sanford, July 10, 1900, Clear, Quart | 15.00 |
| Bottle, Fruit Jar, Smalley, On Base, Side Clamps, 1/2 Pint | 5.00 |
| Bottle, Fruit Jar, Star Mason, Quart | 2.00 |
| Bottle, Fruit Jar, Stoneware, Gray Glaze, Wavy Red & Green Band, 8 3/4 In. | 35.00 |
| Bottle, Fruit Jar, Sun, Monier Closure, Pint | 25.00 |
| Bottle, Fruit Jar, Unembossed, 1/2 Pint | 1.00 |
| Bottle, Fruit Jar, Victory, On Lid, Side Clamps, 1/2 Pint | 6.00 |
| Bottle, Fruit Jar, Wan-Eta Cocoa, Amber, 1/2 Pint | 8.00 |
| Bottle, Fruit Jar, Wax Seal, Stoneware, Brown | 4.00 |
| Bottle, Fruit Jar, Wear's, 1/2 Pint | 6.00 |
| Bottle, Gemel, Blown, 8 1/2 In. | 17.50 |
| Bottle, Gemel, Opaque White Lips, Pink & White Loopings On Clear, 9 1/2 In. | 70.00 |
| Bottle, Gin, Blown, Amber, 9 1/4 In. | 45.00 |
| Bottle, Gin, Blown, Olive Amber, Pair | 75.00 |
| Bottle, Gin, Square, Tall, Olive Green | 17.00 |
| Bottle, Hand Blown, Amber, 4 1/4 In.High | 6.00 |
| Bottle, Household, Elisha Waters Liquid Mirror Blacking, N.Y., Olive, 6 In. | 75.00 |
| Bottle, Ink, Aqua, 2 Ozs. | 5.00 |
| Bottle, Ink, Bell Shape, Light Green | 36.00 |
| Bottle, Ink, Boat Shape, Green | 32.00 |
| Bottle, Ink, Cabin, Green | 17.00 |
| Bottle, Ink, Carter's Cathedral, Cobalt, Quart | 40.00 |
| Bottle, Ink, Carter's, Cathedral, Medium Cobalt, Pint | 55.00 |
| Bottle, Ink, Carter's, Cathedral, Pouring Spout, Label, Cobalt, Quart | 45.00 |
| Bottle, Ink, Carter's, Impressed On Bottom & Base, Cobalt, 9 3/4 In. | 45.00 |
| Bottle, Ink, Carter's, Ma & Pa Carter, Pair | 50.00 To 60.00 |
| Bottle, Ink, Carter's, Metal Collar, Cobalt, 8 1/4 In. | 20.00 |
| Bottle, Ink, China, Paperweight, Mushroom Type, Multicolor Spatter On Red | 125.00 |
| Bottle, Ink, Cone, Aqua, 2 1/2 In.High | 2.75 |
| Bottle, Ink, Coventry, Geometric | 85.00 |
| Bottle, Ink, F.W.Styles, Springfield, Vt., Pair | 14.00 |
| Bottle, Ink, Harrison's Columbian, Pontil, Pint | 53.50 |
| Bottle, Ink, Josiah Jonson's Japan Writing Fluid, Lighthouse, Pottery | 100.00 |
| Bottle, Ink, Porcelain, Hinged Brass Collar, Floral On Black, C.1860, 3 In. | 35.00 |
| Bottle, Ink, Traveling, Figural, Brown Leather Covered Shoe, Glass Bottle | 60.00 |
| Bottle, Ink, Turtle, Ground Lip, Blown In The Mold, Aqua | 16.00 |
| Bottle, Ink, Waterman's, Rubber Bulb Dropper Top | 10.00 |
| Bottle, Jar, Blown, Cylindrical, Aqua, 5 1/8 In. | 6.00 |

| | |
|---|---|
| Bottle, Jar, Candletender, Beaded Cross On Side, 3 X 7 3/4 In. | 2.50 |
| Bottle, Jar, Powder, Imitation Cut Pattern, Metal Top | 6.00 |
| Bottle, Jar, Snuff, Blown, Aqua, 5 3/4 In. | 15.00 |
| Bottle, Liqueur, A.Bauer, Pineapple Rock & Rye, Sun Colored Amethyst, 10 In. | 15.00 |
| Bottle, Liqueur, Benedictine, Wax Seal On Side, Dark Green | 5.98 |
| Bottle, Liqueur, Bols, Ballerina | 8.00 |
| Bottle, Liqueur, Bulbous, Blown Teardrop Stopper, Gold & Forget-Me-Nots | 18.00 |
| Bottle, Ludlow, Globular, Olive, 8 1/4 In. | 75.00 |
| Bottle, Mantua, Club Shape, 16 Vertical & 16 Swirled Ribs, Aqua, 8 In. | 45.00 |
| Bottle, McConnell Club, 1973 | 50.00 |
| Bottle, Medicine, Acker's English Remedy, Cobalt Blue, 5 1/2 In.High | 10.00 |
| Bottle, Medicine, Alvas Brazilian Specific Co., Star Shape, Aqua, 9 1/2 In. | 7.50 |
| Bottle, Medicine, Antique Brand Alcoholic Stimulant, Brass Label, Amber | 9.50 |
| Bottle, Medicine, B.Fosgate's Anodyne Cordial, Light Aqua, 4 3/4 In.High | 15.00 |
| Bottle, Medicine, Bell & Tossler-Prevost, A Paris, Blue Green, 7 1/2 In. | 35.00 |
| Bottle, Medicine, Blown, Flat, Aqua, 4 In. | 12.50 |
| Bottle, Medicine, Blown, Green, 4 1/4 In. | 6.00 |
| Bottle, Medicine, Blown, 6 Panels, Light Yellow Green Tint, 4 3/4 In. | 5.00 |
| Bottle, Medicine, Brant's Indian Pulmonary Balsam, M.T.Wallace, Green, 7 In. | 25.00 |
| Bottle, Medicine, Compound A.Diuretic, Remedies Co., Label, 12 1/2 Ozs. | 15.00 |
| Bottle, Medicine, DeWitt's Eye Bath, Eyecup, Contents | 8.50 |
| Bottle, Medicine, Dr.C.W.Roback's Scandinavian Blood Purifier, Aqua, 8 In. | 17.50 |
| Bottle, Medicine, Dr.Cumming's Vegetine, Oval, Aqua, 9 3/4 In High | 3.95 |
| Bottle, Medicine, Dr.Haynes' Arabian Balsam, R.I., 12 Sided, Aqua, 4 1/2 In. | 2.75 |
| Bottle, Medicine, Dr.Kennedy's Medical Discovery, Aqua, 8 3/4 In. | 32.00 |
| Bottle, Medicine, Dr.M.M.Fenner's Kidney & Backache Remedy, 1872, Amber | 20.00 |
| Bottle, Medicine, Dr.McMunn's Flixir Of Opium, Round, Aqua, 4 1/2 In.High | 3.75 |
| Bottle, Medicine, Foley's Kidney & Bladder Cure, Blown In The Mold, Amber | 13.50 |
| Bottle, Medicine, Forni's Magolo, P.Fahrney, M.D., Cough Syrup, 5 1/2 In. | 3.50 |
| Bottle, Medicine, Genuine Sanford's Ginger, 1876, Rectangular, Aqua | 3.75 |
| Bottle, Medicine, Gold Dandruff Cure, Blown In The Mold, Clear | 10.00 |
| Bottle, Medicine, Healy & Bigelow Indian Squaw, Dug | 10.00 |
| Bottle, Medicine, Kidney & Liver Remedy, Light Olive Green, 16 Ozs. | 75.00 |
| Bottle, Medicine, Kilmer's Swamp Root | 7.00 |
| Bottle, Medicine, L.Q.C.Wishart's Pine Tree Tar Cordial, Green, 9 1/2 In. | 50.00 |
| Bottle, Medicine, Langenbach Dysentery Cure, Blown In The Mold, Labels | 12.00 |
| Bottle, Medicine, Miller's Genuine Arabian Balsam, R.I., 12 Sided, Aqua | 2.75 |
| Bottle, Medicine, Mitchell's Eye Salve, Pale Aqua, 1 7/8 In.High | 17.00 |
| Bottle, Medicine, Modex, Nerve & Health Beverage, Patent 1901, Clear | 4.75 |
| Bottle, Medicine, Mrs.Winslow's Soothing Syrup, Light Aqua, 5 In.High | 5.00 |
| Bottle, Medicine, Musterole, Cleveland, Embossed, Milk Glass | 2.00 |
| Bottle, Medicine, Oriental, Tear Shape, Label & Contents, 1 1/2 In. | 7.50 |
| Bottle, Medicine, Red Amber, 9 1/2 In. | 7.50 |
| Bottle, Medicine, Robt.E.Seller's Vermifuge, Stain, Aqua, 4 3/8 In.High | 5.00 |
| Bottle, Medicine, Rohrer's Expectoral Wild Cherry Tonic, Amber, 10 1/2 In | 125.00 |
| Bottle, Medicine, Safe Cure Co., Label, Sample Size | 8.00 To 12.00 |
| Bottle, Medicine, Shiloh Consumption Cure, Blown In The Mold | 4.50 |
| Bottle, Medicine, Smelling Salts, Metal Screw Cap, Green Stopper, Green | 6.00 |
| Bottle, Medicine, The Cup That Cures, Old Man With Flowing Beard, Clear | 9.50 |
| Bottle, Medicine, Turlington's Balsam, The King's Patent, Aqua, 2 1/2 In. | 20.00 |
| Bottle, Medicine, Vapo-Cresolene Co., Patent 1894, Square, Aqua, 5 1/4 In. | 3.75 |
| Bottle, Medicine, Warner's & Co. Ingluvin Powder, Label & Contents, 1 Oz. | 12.00 |
| Bottle, Medicine, Warner's Diabetes Remedy, Label, Contents, 16 Ozs. | 40.00 |
| Bottle, Medicine, Warner's Safe Kidney & Liver Cure, Amber | 10.00 To 15.00 |
| Bottle, Medicine, Warner's Safe Remedies Co., Dug, Abm, Light Amber | 14.00 |
| Bottle, Medicine, William Radam's Microbe Killer, Embossed, Amber | 70.00 |
| Bottle, Medicine, Wyeth, Dose Cap, Cobalt Blue | 32.00 |
| Bottle, Milk, Amber, Quart | 3.00 |
| Bottle, Milk, Baby Face, Impressed | 10.00 |
| Bottle, Milk, Borden's, Whipper, Dated 1915, Pint | 10.00 |
| Bottle, Milk, Brookfield, Baby Face, Cream Top, 1/2 Pint | 6.00 |
| Bottle, Milk, Cast Iron, Pint | 30.00 |
| Bottle, Milk, Dairlee, Double Baby Face, Cream Top, Quart | 6.00 |
| Bottle, Milk, Hood's Cream, Painted White Inside, 1/2 Pint | 1.98 |
| Bottle, Milk, Metal Closure, Lock, 1/2 Pint | 6.00 |
| Bottle, Milk, Missouri Pacific Railroad, Embossed, Quart | 3.00 |

Bottle, Milk, Missouri Pacific Railroad, Embossed, 1/2 Pint ....................... 2.00
Bottle, Milk, Twin City Dairy, Hurley, Wis., Pint ....................................... .50
Bottle, Milk, Upton's Farm, Bridgewater, Mass., Baby's Head Top, Clear, Pint ........ 2.75
Bottle, Mr.Pickwick, Clear, 9 In.High .................................................. 6.95
Bottle, Nursing, Embossed Kittens ...................................................... 7.00
Bottle, Nursing, Flat, Molded, 'The Graduated Nursing Bottle,' C.1870 .................. 25.00
Bottle, Nursing, Madame Lang's Perfected, Embossed, Nipple & Stopper .................. 15.00
Bottle, Nursing, May's Sterile, Blown In The Mold ..................................... 10.00
Bottle, Nursing, Welfare, Twins, Nipple Openings Both Ends ............................ 23.00
Bottle, Nursing, 12 Diamond, Light Blue Green, 6 1/2 In. .............................. 55.00
Bottle, Ohio, Flattened Globular, 24 Swirled Ribs, Aqua, 8 3/4 In. ................... 60.00
Bottle, Oil, Bear Oil, Blown, Aqua, 2 3/4 In. ........................................ 17.50
Bottle, Pepper Sauce, Emerald Green, 8 In. ........................................... 7.50
Bottle, Pepper Sauce, Gothic Arches & Windows, Blue Green, 8 3/4 In. ................. 25.00
Bottle, Pepper Sauce, Hexagonal, "Pat.App.For S & P, " Green Swirl, 8 In. ............ 22.50
Bottle, Pepsi, Amber ................................................................. 11.00
Bottle, Pepsi, Green ................................................................. 5.00
Bottle, Perfume & Snuff, Ruby Glass, Sterling Caps, S.Mordan, 4 3/4 In. .............. 92.00
Bottle, Perfume, Agate, Gold Top & Chain, C.1820 .................................... 225.00
Bottle, Perfume, Atomizer, DeVilbiss, Deep Pink, Signed ............................. 20.00
Bottle, Perfume, Atomizer, DeVilbiss, Gold Overlay, Opaque Rose, 6 1/2 In. .......... 12.00
Bottle, Perfume, Atomizer, DeVilbiss, Opalescent, 6 1/2 In. ......................... 8.00
Bottle, Perfume, Bell Shape, Gilt Striping, Ground Pontil, Opaque Jade Green ........ 36.50
Bottle, Perfume, Beveled, Stopper, Tortoiseshell Holder, 3 1/2 In.High .............. 12.00
Bottle, Perfume, Blown, Aqua, 16 Ribs, Applied Handle, 4 1/8 In. .................... 22.50
Bottle, Perfume, Blown, Ribbed, 2 5/8 In. ........................................... 15.00
Bottle, Perfume, Brass Screw Cap, Stopper, Miniature, Amethyst, 2 3/4 In. ........... 6.00
Bottle, Perfume, Bulbous, Light Green Opaque, Gold & Blue Stopper ................... 18.50
Bottle, Perfume, Crystal, Double, Silver Gilt Trim, Coral Beads, C.1867 ............. 275.00
Bottle, Perfume, Cut Smoky Crystal, 4 In.High ....................................... 10.00
Bottle, Perfume, Figural, High Boot, Clear, 3 1/2 In. ............................... 15.00
Bottle, Perfume, Flat Flame Design, Ground Stopper, 3 In. ........................... 5.00
Bottle, Perfume, French Transfer Print On Cover, Jules Hauel, Phila., 1830 .......... 75.00
Bottle, Perfume, Germany, Miniature, Clear, Painted, Cat, 2 In.High ................. 9.00
Bottle, Perfume, Gilt Jacket With Blue Stones ....................................... 5.00
Bottle, Perfume, Glass Boot, Cover .................................................. 15.00
Bottle, Perfume, Green Overlay, Cut White To Green, Pedestal, Hand-Painted .......... 65.00
Bottle, Perfume, Hand Blown, Bubble Glass, 10 In. ................................... 7.50
Bottle, Perfume, Hand-Painted Dog, Miniature ........................................ 7.50
Bottle, Perfume, Hexagonal, Cut Amethyst, Dark To Clear ............................. 50.00
Bottle, Perfume, Lithyalin, Reddish Browns, 4 3/4 In.High ........................... 245.00
Bottle, Perfume, Marble Glass, Eggerman Type, Oriental Carvings ..................... 125.00
Bottle, Perfume, Moon Mullins, 2 In. ................................................ 15.00
Bottle, Perfume, Narrow, Glass Flowers On Stopper ................................... 15.00
Bottle, Perfume, New England Glass Co., Clear ....................................... 45.00
Bottle, Perfume, Openwork Sterling Chrysanthemums, Emerald Green ................... 135.00
Bottle, Perfume, Overlay, Blue & Clear, Embossed Silver Screw Cap, 2 3/4 In. ....... 175.00
Bottle, Perfume, Overlay, Royal Blue & White Cut To Clear, Gold Tracery ............ 65.00
Bottle, Perfume, Palmer, Cork ....................................................... 2.50
Bottle, Perfume, Pencil Shape, Blue & Gold Stripes On Clear ......................... 15.00
Bottle, Perfume, Pressed Glass, Designs, Atomizer, Dated 1890, 7 1/4 In. ............ 16.00
Bottle, Perfume, Purse, Etched Flower On Clear, Silver Plate Stopper ................ 9.50
Bottle, Perfume, Purse, Silver, Crystal Flacon Inside, W.Comyns, 1901 ............... 98.00
Bottle, Perfume, Rose Color, Flowers, White Frosted Intaglio Stopper ................ 13.50
Bottle, Perfume, Silver Overlay, Masonic Inscription, 1858-1908, Clear .............. 14.50
Bottle, Perfume, Silver Overlay, 3 1/2 In.High ...................................... 15.00
Bottle, Perfume, Silver, Pink, Green, & Orange Enameled Flowers & Crabs ............. 40.00
Bottle, Perfume, Square, Intaglio Flowers ........................................... 12.00
Bottle, Perfume, Sterling Inlay On Green Glass ...................................... 24.00
Bottle, Perfume, Sterling Overlay, Iris Decoration, Round Bottom, 5 In.High ......... 95.00
Bottle, Perfume, Sterling Overlay, Lily Design, Alvin, 5 3/4 In. .................... 55.00
Bottle, Perfume, Sterling Overlay, Poppies, 4 1/2 In. ............................... 30.00
Bottle, Perfume, Sterling Silver Overlay Of Chrysanthemums, Initials, Green ......... 150.00
Bottle, Perfume, Sterling Silver Scroll On Glass, Medium Size ....................... 20.00
Bottle, Perfume, Swirl Cut, Pewter Dispenser Cap, McIlhenny, New Iberia ............. 5.00
Bottle, Perfume, Teardrop Shape, Paneled, Sterling Cap, 3 1/2 In. ................... 24.00

| | |
|---|---|
| Bottle, Perfume, Tortoiseshell Glass | 38.00 |
| Bottle, Perfume, Vial, Bird's Egg, Porcelain, Sterling Cap, 1885, 2 1/2 In. | 58.00 |
| Bottle, Perfume, Vial, Chinese, Glass, Gold Paint | 8.00 |
| Bottle, Perfume, 12 Panels, Stopper, Amethyst To Clear, 7 In.High | 23.00 |
| Bottle, Pickle, Bunker Hill, Whittled, 5 1/4 In. | 10.00 |
| Bottle, Pickle, Cathedral, Deep Aqua | 18.00 |
| Bottle, Pickle, Gothic Arch, Rolled Collar, Hollow Ring, Aqua, 12 1/2 In. | 40.00 |
| Bottle, Planter's Peanuts, Signed Leap Year 1940 | 22.00 |
| Bottle, Poison, "Not To Be Taken, " Cobalt | 6.50 |
| Bottle, Poison, Carbolic Acid, Coffin, Embossed, Cobalt, 1/2 Oz. | 8.00 |
| Bottle, Poison, Diamond Shape, Amber, 2 3/4 In.High | 2.95 |
| Bottle, Poison, Gift German, 6 Panel, Skull & Crossbones, Blown, Pint | 15.00 |
| Bottle, Poison, Square, Ribbed Panels, Glass Stopper, Dark Cobalt, 8 Ozs. | 20.00 |
| Bottle, Saratoga Type, Whitney Glass Works, N.J., Monogram, Dug, Green, Pint | 27.50 |
| Bottle, Saratoga, Embossed Lavator, Lime Green, Quart | 17.50 |
| Bottle, Sarsaparilla, Apothecary, Aqua, Cork | 5.00 |
| Bottle, Sarsaparilla, Dr.Townsend's, N.Y., Bulge In Side, Green, 9 1/4 In. | 50.00 |
| Bottle, Sarsaparilla, Foley's, Label, Contents, Aqua | 25.00 |
| Bottle, Sarsaparilla, Hood's | 7.00 |
| Bottle, Sarsaparilla, Log Cabin, Rochester, N.Y., Flat Back, Amber, 9 In. | 60.00 |
| Bottle, Scent, Cranberry, Aventurine, 12 Sided, Silver Top Marked C.M. | 85.00 |
| Bottle, Scent, Elongated Egg Shape, Pewter, Cobalt Blue Glass, 2 In.Long | 18.00 |
| Bottle, Scent, Faceted, 2 Compartments, Engraved Silver Lid Each End, Red | 50.00 |
| Bottle, Scent, French, Allover Gold Tracery, Etched Greek Key, Clear, Pair | 40.00 |
| Bottle, Scent, Gold & Enamel Mounts, English, C.1750, 2 In.High | 800.00 |
| Bottle, Scent, Marcel Redon, Floral & Gold On Cream | 18.00 |
| Bottle, Scent, Sandwich, McKearin 241-31, Amethyst To Cobalt, Pewter Top | 55.00 |
| Bottle, Scent, Silver Overlay, Stopper, 3 1/2 In. | 22.50 |
| Bottle, Slug Plate Shoulder, J.L.Leavitt, Boston, Olive Amber, 8 1/4 In. | 30.00 |
| Bottle, Snuff, Agate, Spider, Chinese | 300.00 |
| Bottle, Snuff, Best Virginia, Scotch Snuff, Sweetser Bros., Boston, 2 1/4 In. | 38.00 |
| Bottle, Snuff, Blown, Flared Lip, Square, Dark Olive Amber, 3 3/4 In. | 12.50 |
| Bottle, Snuff, Carved Jadite, Turquoise & Coral In Silver Gilt Stopper | 335.00 |
| Bottle, Snuff, Chinese, Black Koro Design On Clambroth, 3 In.High | 65.00 |
| Bottle, Snuff, Chinese, Iron Red Foo Dogs On Both Sides, 3 In.High | 75.00 |
| Bottle, Snuff, Enameled People Fishing & Man In Pagoda On White | 100.00 |
| Bottle, Snuff, Flat Cylindrical, Chinese, Florals & Insects On White Opaque | 85.00 |
| Bottle, Snuff, Green Crackled, Green Stone Top, C.1850 | 48.00 |
| Bottle, Snuff, Ivory, Carved Tao T'uh Masks, C.1850 | 80.00 |
| Bottle, Snuff, Ivory, Seated Frog Under Lily Pad | 125.00 |
| Bottle, Snuff, Lady's, Hinged Brass Lid With Chain, Blue, Gold Design, Round | 35.00 |
| Bottle, Snuff, Lapis Lazuli, Carved Birds, Malachite Stopper | 95.00 |
| Bottle, Snuff, Mei Ping Shape, Mother-Of-Pearl Landscape, Lacquer, 2 In. | 95.00 |
| Bottle, Snuff, Ovoid, Lacquer Burquate, Mother-Of-Pearl Floral, 2 In. | 95.00 |
| Bottle, Snuff, Pebble Shape, Chinese, Matrix On 1 Side, Near White, 3 In.High | 125.00 |
| Bottle, Snuff, Porcelain, Hourglass Shape, Green Jade Cap, Ivory Spoon | 18.00 |
| Bottle, Snuff, Porcelain, Jade Stopper | 20.00 |
| Bottle, Snuff, Red Overlay, Clear & Frosted, Ivory Spoon, Inside Painted | 25.00 |
| Bottle, Soda, Donald Duck Cola | 5.00 |
| Bottle, Soda, Dr.Pepper, Embossed | 1.25 |
| Bottle, Soda, Knickerbocker, Saratoga, Carpenter & Cobb, Blue Green, Pint | 130.00 |
| Bottle, Soda, Moxie, Clear Picture Of Man, Red Paint | 3.00 |
| Bottle, Soda, Pepsi Cola, Cap & Label, 2 1/2 In.High | 4.50 |
| Bottle, Souvenir, World's Fair, 1939 | 7.00 |
| Bottle, Spice, Chinese, Underglaze Blue Decoration, Calligraphy, C.1750 | 95.00 |
| Bottle, Stiegel Type, Broken Swirl, 18 Ribs, Deep Amethyst, 7 1/4 In. | 625.00 |
| Bottle, Vinegar, F.C.P. Piegaro, Molded, Green, 8 1/2 In. | 5.00 |
| Bottle, Vinegar, McKearin G I-7, Type 4, Three Mold, Sandwich, Cobalt Blue | 170.00 |
| Bottle, Vinegar, White House, Embossed, Gallon | 10.95 |
| Bottle, Water, Empire Spring Co., Saratoga, N.Y., Embossed, Emerald, Quart | 33.00 |
| Bottle, Water, Gleason & Cole Mineral, Pittsburgh, Blue, 7 3/4 In. | 175.00 |
| Bottle, Water, Mold Blown & Cut | 22.00 |
| Bottle, Water, Moses' Poland, Clear, Pint | 9.50 |
| Bottle, Water, Moses' Poland, Stopper Top, Amber, Quart | 17.00 |
| Bottle, Wheaton Commemorative, Christmas, 1973, Ruby | 6.00 |
| Bottle, Wheaton Commemorative, Humphrey & Muskie, 1968 | 3.50 |

Bottle, Wheaton Commemorative, McGovern & Shriver, 1972 ......................... 5.00
Bottle, Wheaton Commemorative, Nixon & Agnew, 1968 ........................... 5.00
Bottle, Wheaton Commemorative, Nixon & Agnew, 1972 ........................... 5.00
Bottle, Whiskey, Booz, 2 Story House, Beveled Roof, Amethyst, Quart ............... 1100.00
Bottle, Whiskey, C.Oppel & Co., Olive Green, 8 1/2 In. ........................ 7.50
Bottle, Whiskey, D.H.Chambers, Pittsburgh, Pa. On Base, Whittled, Amber, Fifth ...... 13.75
Bottle, Whiskey, Duffy's Malt ............................................ 3.95
Bottle, Whiskey, Duffy's Malt, Miniature ................................... 35.00
Bottle, Whiskey, Golden Wedding, Carnival Glass, Marigold, Pint ................. 10.00
Bottle, Whiskey, I.W.Harper, Wicker Basket .................................. 18.50
Bottle, Whiskey, Iron Pontil, Olive, 9 1/4 In. ............................... 40.00
Bottle, Whiskey, J.A.Gilka, Berlin, Schutzen Str.No.9, Red Amber, 9 3/4 In. ........ 5.00
Bottle, Whiskey, Jesse Moore American Pure Rye, Amber, Pint .................... 3.95
Bottle, Whiskey, Jug, Sailboat Inside, Miniature, 3/4 In. ...................... 6.50
Bottle, Whiskey, K.T.K. Porcelain, 7 3/4 In. ................................ 75.00
Bottle, Whiskey, Kit Carson, Wood, Pollard & Co., Boston, Clear, Pint ........... 4.75
Bottle, Whiskey, Meredith's Diamond Club, Signed K.T.& K., 4 3/4 In. ............ 60.00
Bottle, Whiskey, Mold Blown, Massachusetts Pattern, 3 1/2 X 11 In. .............. 25.00
Bottle, Whiskey, Old Fitzgerald, Flagship, Decanter .......................... 4.00
Bottle, Whiskey, Old Mr.Boston, Wooden Ship Inside, C.1941, Quart .............. 35.00
Bottle, Whiskey, Paul Jones, Louisville, Ky., Seal On Shoulder, Amber, 9 In. ...... 5.00
Bottle, Whiskey, Peru Brewery One Quart, Blown, Amber, 9 3/4 In. ............... 15.00
Bottle, Whiskey, Sterling Overlay ......................................... 95.00
Bottle, Whiskey, Strickland's, Flask, Aqua .................................. 50.00
Bottle, Whiskey, The Campus Gossler Bros., N.Y., Handle, Amber, 9 1/4 In. ........ 40.00
Bottle, Whiskey, Van Arsdell Sour Mash, Mercer Co., Ky., Dark Amber, 10 In. ...... 5.00
Bottle, Wine, W.H.Clark In Raised Print, Flat Flask, Light Green, 5 1/4 In. ....... 60.00
Bottle, Zanesville, Blown, Globular, Blue Green, 10 In. ....................... 90.00
Bottle, Zanesville, Chestnut, 10 Diamond, Amber, 4 3/4 In. ..................... 600.00
Bottle, Zanesville, Chestnut, 10 Diamond, Citron, 5 In. ....................... 1400.00
Bottle, Zanesville, Chestnut, 24 Ribs, Golden Amber, 5 In. ..................... 250.00
Bottle, Zanesville, Club Shape, Broken Swirl, 24 Ribs, Sapphire, 7 3/4 In. ....... 1200.00
Bottle, Zanesville, Club Shape, 24 Swirled Ribs, Aqua, 8 1/2 In. ............... 55.00
Bottle, Zanesville, Globular, Aqua, 8 1/2 In. ............................... 55.00
Bottle, Zanesville, Globular, Broken Swirl, 24 Ribs, Golden Amber, 7 3/4 In. ...... 2500.00
Bottle, Zanesville, Globular, 24 Swirled Ribs, Amber, 7 In. .................... 250.00
Bottle, Zanesville, Globular, 24 Swirled Ribs, Aqua, 8 1/4 In. ......... 70.00 To 100.00
Bottle, Zanesville, Globular, 24 Swirled Ribs, Aqua, 8 1/4 In. ................. 140.00
Bottle, Zanesville, Globular, 24 Swirled Ribs, Citron, 7 1/2 In. ............... 1000.00
Bottle, Zanesville, Globular, 24 Swirled Ribs, Golden Amber, 8 In. .............. 350.00
Bottle, Zanesville, Globular, 24 Swirled Ribs, Light Blue, 7 1/2 In. ............ 150.00
Bottle, Zanesville, Globular, 24 Swirled Ribs, Red Amber, 2 Quart, 9 1/2 In. ..... 425.00
Bottle, Zanesville, Shepherd & Eagle, Neck Lip, Dark Amber, 6 1/2 In. ........... 450.00
Bottle, Zanesville, Swirled, Domed Bottom, Aqua, Quart ....................... 60.00
Bow, Dish, Sweetmeat, Triple Shell, White, C.1750, 7 1/2 In. .................. 200.00
Bow, Figurine, Neptune, On Dolphin, C.1755, 7 1/4 In.High .................... 200.00
Bow, Figurine, Potted Flowering Trees, C.1760, 6 3/4 In.High, Pair ............. 230.00
Bow, Flowering Tree, Potted, Mask Handles, Scrollwork, C.1755, Pair ............ 280.00
Bow, Group, Bocage Fountain, Boy & Girl, Scroll Feet, C.1765, 7 3/8 In. ......... 450.00
Bow, Sauceboat, Flattened Leaf Shape, Scroll Handle, Floral, Insects, C.1760 ..... 125.00

*Boxes of all kinds are collected. They were made of thin strips of inlaid wood, metal, tortoiseshell, embroidery, or other material.*

Box, see also Ivory, Box, Porcelain, Box, Store, Box, Tin, Box
Box, see also various porcelain categories
Box, Battersea, see Battersea, Box
Box, Tea Caddy, see also Furniture, Tea Caddy, Pewter, Tea Caddy,
Silver, Sterling, Tea Caddy, Tin, Tea Caddy, and various porcelain
categories

Box, Art Deco, Metal ................................................... 12.00
Box, Art Nouveau Silver Cover, Engraved Crystal ............................ 9.00
Box, Ballot, Fraternal, Wooden, Drawer, Handle, Hole In Back ................. 45.00
Box, Bark, Oval, Finger Lapped, Embossed Deer & Men ........................ 25.00
Box, Battersea Type, Pate A La Rose On Hinged Lid, Footed, Roses On White ..... 22.00
Box, Bible, Oak, Chip Carved, Wrought Iron Strap Hinges & Lock, 1705 ......... 385.00
Box, Birchbark, Hinged Lid, Oval, Embossed Man Fishing ...................... 25.00

| | |
|---|---:|
| Box, Bird On Hinged Lid, Egg Shape, China, Signed | 65.00 |
| Box, Black Lacquer, Mother-Of-Pearl Inlay | 125.00 |
| Box, Book Shape, Mahogany, Multicolored Wood Inlay, 10 X 7 1/2 X 4 In. | 20.00 |
| Box, Book Shape, Wooden, Gilt Decoration On Green, 1 Drawer, 13 X 10 1/2 In. | 40.00 |
| Box, Bride's, Pine, Floral, Swans & Children On Top, 18 In. Long | 180.00 |
| Box, Bride's, Wooden, Red & Black Tulip Decoration, 6 1/2 X 4 X 2 In. | 175.00 |
| Box, Camphorwood, Carved Oriental Figures & Trees, 9 3/4 X 6 1/4 In. | 48.50 |
| Box, Candle, Double, Hand-Hewn, Dovetailed | 68.00 |
| Box, Cardboard, Covered With Paper, Seashells, & Lacquer, 3 1/4 X 2 In. | 5.00 |
| Box, Casket, Agate & Gilt Metal, Beveled Panels, Ball Feet, C.1890 | 190.00 |
| Box, Casket, Jewel, Victorian, Raised Leaves & Cones, 4 Footed, 5 1/2 In.High | 9.75 |
| Box, Cheese, Wooden, Printing On Lid, 18 In.Diameter | 17.00 |
| Box, Chinese Lacquer, Gold & Red On Black, 4 Dragon Feet, C.1750 | 295.00 |
| Box, Chinese Lacquer, Gold Trim | 18.00 |
| Box, Chinese, Rosewood, Greek Key Design In Silver Inlay, 5 1/4 X 3 3/4 In. | 35.00 |
| Box, Chinese, Wooden, Silk, Appliques Design In 'forbidden Stitch' | 8.00 |
| Box, Cigar, Resembles Desk, Grooved Drawers, Dovetailed | 95.00 |
| Box, Cigarette, Ebony, Oriental | 15.00 |
| Box, Cigarette, Eggshell, Lacquer, Hinged, 2 Sharks, Marcat, C.1930 | 175.00 |
| Box, Cigarette, Gilt Metal & Enamel, Panels Of Filigree, 3 3/4 In.Long | 125.00 |
| Box, Cigarette, Hinged Top, Elephant Shape, 3 Compartments, Wooden | 37.00 |
| Box, Cigarette, Onyx, Silver Mounts, Asprey, C.1910, Medallion, 6 In.Long | 250.00 |
| Box, Cigarette, Silver Gilt & Enamel, German, Oriental Decoration, 4 1/2 In | 200.00 |
| Box, Clown & Harlequin Bank, Wooden, Dovetailed, J.E.Stevens Co. | 250.00 |
| Box, Collar, Deer's Head On Top & Front | 15.00 |
| Box, Conch Shell, 3 In. | 35.00 |
| Box, Covered, Black Chinese Lacquer, 2 Raised Tinted Bone Samurai | 85.00 |
| Box, Cricket, Gourd Grown In Terra-Cotta Mold, Ivory, Carved, Ch'ein Lung | 225.00 |
| Box, Crystal, Daisies On Cover, Monroe Decorated, Heimschmied Swirl Pattern | 225.00 |
| Box, Document, Painted, Decorated, Brass Bail Handle, Domed, Pa., C.1810 | 325.00 |
| Box, Document, Pine, Wm.C.Frysinger Inside Of Lid, Brass Handle | 45.00 |
| Box, Egg Shape, Olivewood, Carved, Openwork, Unscrews In Center, 2 1/2 In. | 12.50 |
| Box, Eggshell, Lacquer, Marcat, France, C.1930, 5 1/2 In. *Illus* | 100.00 |
| Box, Flint, Round, Candle Top | 185.00 |
| Box, Food, Covered, Wooden, Lunch Box Type | 25.00 |
| Box, For Shoot The Chute Bank, Wooden | 75.00 |
| Box, Glass, Enamel Dragonfly & Water Lily On Hinged Lid, Blue, 2 1/4 In. | 40.00 |
| Box, Glass, Enamel Floral On Hinged Lid, Sapphire Blue, 2 In. Diameter | 45.00 |
| Box, Glass, Hinged, Enamel Daisies On Lid, Yellow Green, 2 In. Diameter | 25.00 |
| Box, Glass, White Enamel Star Design On Hinged Lid, Yellow Green, 2 In. | 35.00 |
| Box, Glove, Hinged, Celluloid, Indian Chief In Full Headdress | 27.50 |
| Box, Glove, Mission, Burned Wood Design, Gibson Girl Type, 9 3/4 In.Long | 30.00 |
| Box, Glove, Red Velvet | 10.00 |
| Box, Gold Gilt Metal, Embossed, Lining | 8.50 |
| Box, Hand-Painted Seascape & Schooners, Round, 7 1/2 In.Diameter | 30.00 |
| Box, Heart Shape, Victorian, Metal, Ivory Enamel, Cupids, Pink Hearts, Swans | 29.50 |
| Box, Hinged, Trunk Shape, Painted Oval Scene Of U.S.Capitol, Wooden | 12.50 |
| Box, Horn, Gilt Scratch Carved Dragon On Lid, Oval, 3 1/2 X 2 1/2 In. | 28.00 |
| Box, Horn, Silver Shield On Cover, Oval | 24.00 |
| Box, Inlaid Rosewood, C.1850, 7 1/2 X 10 1/2 X 5 In. | 32.00 |
| Box, Jewel, Casket, Victorian, Gold Finish, Raised Roses, 4 Footed, 2 1/2 In. | 4.95 |
| Box, Jewel, Chinese, Enameled, Flowers, Brass Stand | 30.00 |
| Box, Jewel, Decoupage, Hinged, 2 Doors & 2 Drawers, Ivory Knobs, English, 1840 | 85.00 |
| Box, Jewel, Gilt Metal, Footed, Lined, 4 1/2 X 3 In. | 8.50 |
| Box, Jewel, Hinged Lid, Copper & Brass, Carved Boar Hunt | 65.00 |
| Box, Jewel, Hinged, Gilded Brass, Floral Relief, 24K Gold Plate | 25.00 |
| Box, Jewel, Hinged, Glass, Brass Bound, Footed, Satin Lining, 2 1/2 In.High | 19.00 |
| Box, Jewel, Hinged, Gold Over Bronze, Fairy Tale Scenes, Signed B & W | 88.00 |
| Box, Jewel, Hinged, Heart Shape, Gold Over Bronze, 3 Footed, Relief Floral | 25.00 |
| Box, Jewel, Pink Onyx, Gold Metal Rims | 14.50 |
| Box, Jewel, Raised Rose On Lid & Sides, Victorian, Footed, Lined | 15.00 |
| Box, Jewel, Repousse Angels & Floral Urns, Marked E O B & S, 7 1/4 In. | 35.00 |
| Box, Jewel, Silver Color, Lined | 8.00 |
| Box, Jewel, Victorian, Gilt, Embossed Rose | 8.00 |
| Box, Jewel, Victorian, Metal, Embossed Flowers, Enameled | 7.00 |
| Box, Jewelry, Acid Cut Back, Pink Roses & Blue Forget-Me-Nots On Gold | 35.00 |

Box, Eggshell, Lacquer, Marcat, France,
C.1930, 5 1/2 in.
(See Page 51)

Box, Trinket, Painted Wood, C.1810, 7 1/4 In.High
(See Page 53)

Box, Wall, Pine, Painted,
American, C.1820, 16 In. High
(See Page 53)

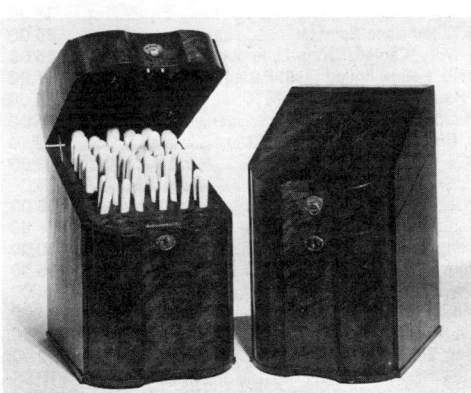

Box, Knife, Inlaid Mahogany, Connelly, Phila., 1800s. Pair
(See Page 53)

Box, Pipe, Pine, Connecticut, C.1775, 17 1/2 In.High
(See Page 53)

Box, Work, Inlaid Mahogany, C.1850, 14 In. Long
(See Page 53)

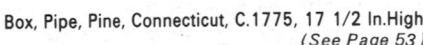

Box, Jewelry, Black Leatherette, Silver Plate Lock, Hinges, & Corners .................................. 7.50
Box, Knife, Burl Grain, Painted Decoration, Black Trim ................................................ 35.00
Box, Knife, Inlaid Mahogany, Connelly, Phila., 1800s, Pair ................................ *Illus* 2200.00
Box, Knife, Mahogany, Inlaid Shell Medallions & Star, Slant Top, Pair ........................ 500.00
Box, Knife, Walnut, Carved Winglike Handle ................................................................ 75.00
Box, Knife, Wooden, Handles, 11 X 7 X 1/2 In. .............................................................. 15.00
Box, Knife, Wooden, Two Compartments, Center Handle ............................................ 12.75
Box, Lacquer, Red, Gold Bird Design, 5 X 3 In. ............................................................ 8.50
Box, Lapis Lazuli, Chinese, Oval Shape, Carved, C.1900, 1 1/2 In. ............................ 75.00
Box, Leather, Book Shape, Hand-Tooled, 3 1/2 X 6 X 2 In. ........................................ 12.50
Box, Made In Russia, Covered, Wooden, Round, Red, Black, & Gold Decoration ............ 15.00
Box, Money Chest, Flat Top, Handle On Top, Key, 5 1/2 X 4 X 3 In. ............................ 12.00
Box, Neckties, Celluloid Cover, Woven Grass On Wood Frame, Floral ............................ 7.50
Box, Nephrite, Gold & Enamel, Cartier, Zigzag Design, 2 In.Long .............................. 375.00
Box, New York Hudson Valley On Lid, Bird, Dog, & Flowerbasket On Black ................ 210.00
Box, Oriental, Round, Mutton Fat Jade Medallion, Gold Brocade, 5 In. ........................ 45.00
Box, Pen, Rectangular, Wood In 4 Different Colors, Double Construction, 1850 ............ 18.00
Box, Pennsylvania Dutch, Dome Top, Floral On Brown, Iron Lock & Hinges ................ 275.00
Box, Pennsylvania Dutch, Dome Top, Tulips, Birds, Iron Hinges & Lock, 11 In. ............ 325.00
Box, Pine, Dovetailed, Red & Black Graining, 20 X 9 X 10 1/2 In. .............................. 55.00
Box, Pine, Hinged, Sponge Decoration, Mustard Color, 3 Compartments, C.1850 ........ 25.00
Box, Pine, Hinged, Yellow, Dovetailed, Ball Feet, Keyhole, 12 X 7 X 4 In. .................. 49.00
Box, Pine, Lithograph Of U.S.Capitol On Lid, Painted To Resemble Maple .................. 20.00
Box, Pipe & Cigar, Celluloid, Hunting Scene, Cigar Holder & Match Safe ...................... 35.00
Box, Pipe, Pine, Connecticut, C.1775, 17 1/2 In.High ........................................ *Illus* 1400.00
Box, Poplar, Dome Top, Blue Wallpaper, Tin Hinges & Clasp, 7 1/2 In.Long ................ 55.00
Box, Poplar, Yellow & Red On Lid, Bird On Black, 14 X 8 3/4 X 8 In. ........................ 175.00
Box, Powder, Covered, Green Glass, Etched Flowers, Octagonal .................................... 7.50
Box, Powder, Embossed Lovebirds On Lid, Clear Glass, Painted, Lavender, Green ............ 10.00
Box, Primitive House On Lid & Sides, 4 X 3 1/2 X 6 1/2 In. ...................................... 125.00
Box, Ring, Art Nouveau, Embossed Floral, 4 Footed ...................................................... 5.00
Box, Ring, Beveled Glass Top, Heart Shape, Footed, Red Velvet Lining .......................... 18.00
Box, Saffron, Acorn Finial, Turned Foot, 8 1/2 In. High ................................................ 75.00
Box, Sailor's Ditty, Hinged, Hand-Carved Wood, Scenes, Brass .................................... 65.00
Box, Shaker Type, Marked Mount Washington Inside Cover, Wooden, Round .................. 8.00
Box, Silver, Moss Agate Top & Bottom, Oval, 1 3/4 In. ................................................ 55.00
Box, Snuff, Louis XV, Three Color Gold, Paris, 1771, 3 1/2 In.Long ........................ 8750.00
Box, Spice, Levi Beal On Lid, Natural Light Wood, 6 1/8 X 4 1/2 In. .......................... 15.00
Box, Spice, Sprague On Lift Off Lid, Handmade, Oval, Wooden, Blue Paint .................. 15.00
Box, Stamp, Austria, Blue Floral, 2 1/2 X 3 1/2 In. ...................................................... 10.00
Box, Swiss, Gold & Enamel, Peasant Children & Animals, C.1810, 3 1/2 In.Long .......... 4400.00
Box, Trinket, Covered, Denmark, Round, Gray & Wine .................................................. 6.00
Box, Trinket, Embossed Flowers & Cutouts On Cover, Footed, Cream Color .................. 4.50
Box, Trinket, Figural Lady, Hoopskirt Forms Base, Pink Luster Base .......................... 20.00
Box, Trinket, Hen, Rooster, & 3 Chicks Before A Gate ................................................ 45.00
Box, Trinket, Hinged Lid, Tree Trunk Shape, Hand-Painted Flowers, 3 In.High .............. 10.00
Box, Trinket, India, Camphorwood, Brass, Enameled Blue & Red Peafowl ...................... 25.00
Box, Trinket, Painted Wood, C.1810, 7 1/4 In.High .............................................. *Illus* 300.00
Box, Trinket, Painted Wood, Gothic Cottage, C.1810, 7 1/4 In.High .......................... 300.00
Box, Victorian, Enameled Apple Blossoms On Hinged Top, Blue, 3 1/2 In. .................... 45.00
Box, Wall, Pine, Painted, American, C.1820, 16 In. High ...................................... *Illus* 275.00
Box, Wooden, Covered, Acorn Shape, 5 In.Diameter ...................................................... 7.00
Box, Wooden, Wooden Hinges & Carved Thumbpieces, Made In Soviet Union ................ 45.00
Box, Work, Inlaid Mahogany, C.1850, 14 In. Long .............................................. *Illus* 325.00
Box, Writing, Black Lacquer, Gilt, Mother-Of-Pearl Medallion On Lid .......................... 25.00

*Brass has been used for decorative pieces and useful tablewares since ancient
times. It is an alloy of copper, zinc, and other metals.*
**Brass, see also Bell, Bronze, Miniature, Tool, Trivet, etc.**
Brass, Ashtray, Art Nouveau Girl With Draped Dress .................................................... 22.50
Brass, Ashtray, Art Nouveau Robed Girl With Feather Fan, 6 In. .................................. 15.00
Brass, Ashtray, Embossed Cat's Face, Stones For Eyes, 3 3/4 In. Diameter .................. 22.00
Brass, Ashtray, Marked China, Floral Design, 4 5/8 In.Across ...................................... 2.75
Brass, Ashtray, Marked China, Flowers & Scrolls, 3 3/4 In.Diameter, Set Of 4 .............. 6.95
Brass, Ashtray, Signed China, Donkey, Saddlebags Are Trays, 4 In. High ...................... 17.50
Brass, Astrolabe, Arabic, Engraving, 4 Interchangeable Discs, Handmade ...................... 175.00

Brass, **Astrolabe**, Arabic, Miniature, Mideast, Handmade ............................................................. 79.50
Brass, **Banner Holder**, Eagle, Wings Spread, Chinese, C.1850, 28 1/2 In. .................................... 150.00
Brass, **Bed Warmer**, Child's, Embossed Colonial Design On Lid ................................................... 165.00
Brass, **Bed Warmer**, Iron Handle ...................................................................................................... 35.00
Brass, **Belt Plate**, British Cross, Brigade Major Meemuch, Engraved, C.1810 ............................. 110.00
Brass, **Bill Clip**, Egyptian Woman's Head, Large Eyes .................................................................... 8.50
Brass, **Bill Clip**, Wall, Marked L.E.Co. ............................................................................................. 2.95
Brass, **Binnacle** ................................................................................................................................. 75.00
Brass, **Bookend**, Boxing Bears, Pair ................................................................................................. 15.00
Brass, **Bookend**, Elephant, C.1920, Pair ......................................................................................... 10.00
Brass, **Bookend**, Indian Slumped In Saddle, 6 In.High, Pair .......................................................... 18.00
Brass, **Bookrack**, Stretch, Camels .................................................................................................... 35.00
Brass, **Bottle Opener**, Revere .......................................................................................................... 10.50
Brass, **Bowl**, Barber's Bleeding, Copper Rim, Loop For Hanging, 12 In. ....................................... 59.50
Brass, **Bowl**, Korea, 12 Chinese Years Animals, 4 1/8 In. .............................................................. 7.00
Brass, **Bowl**, Marked China, Dragon Design, 10 In.Diameter ......................................................... 9.75
Brass, **Bowl**, Mixing, 11 In. ............................................................................................................... 30.00
Brass, **Bowl**, Oval, Ruffled Flange, Embossed & Engraved, 9 In. ................................................... 8.00
Brass, **Bowl**, Raised Roses, 9 In. ...................................................................................................... 6.00
Brass, **Box**, Cigarette, Embossed Buddha, Cedar Lined .................................................................. 8.50
Brass, **Box**, Eiland Marken, Enamel Dutch Girl & Boy On Cover, 1 1/4 In. .................................... 55.00
Brass, **Box**, Flint, English, Candle Inside Lid, Square ..................................................................... 145.00
Brass, **Box**, Hinged, Copper Decoration, Birds, Branches ............................................................... 10.00
Brass, **Box**, Jewel, China, New York World's Fair ........................................................................... 15.00
Brass, **Box**, Marked China, Enamel Dragon, Sky, & Ocean ............................................................ 20.00
Brass, **Box**, Stamp, China, Hinged, Enameled Pagodas, 4 Feet, Handle, 3 X 1 In. ...................... 15.00
Brass, **Box**, Turtle Shape, Hinged Shell, Victorian, 5 In.Long ....................................................... 15.00
Brass, **Brasier**, Copper Bottom, 2 Brass Handles, C.1860, 16 In.Diameter .................................. 65.00
Brass, **Brasier**, Round, Copper Bottom, 2 Brass Handles, C.1880, 16 In. ..................................... 65.00
Brass, **Brazier**, Pinched Sides, 3 Scrolled Supports, Vase & Ring Handle, 1750 .......................... 175.00
Brass, **Bridle Rosette**, U.S. ............................................................................................................... 4.00
Brass, **Bucket**, Sugar, American, 5 Gallon ....................................................................................... 59.00
Brass, **Buckle**, Harness Strap, Heart Decoration, Pair .................................................................... 14.00
Brass, **Calculator**, "The Millionaire, " Dated 1895, 25 In. Long .................................................... 150.00
Brass, **Calipers**, French Artillery, Opens To 13 In., 17th Century .................................................. 325.00
Brass, **Candelabra**, Chinese, 7-Arm, Arms Turn, 11 In.High, Pair .................................................. 40.00
Brass, **Candelabra**, 3-Arm, 11 In., Pair ........................................................................................... 45.00
Brass, **Candelabrum**, Mid-Victorian, Grape Clusters, Marble Base, 3-Arm .................................. 48.00
Brass, **Candleholder**, Amber Glass In Sides, 9 In.High .................................................................... 30.00
Brass, **Candleholder**, Bradley & Hubbard, Saucer, Foo Dog Handles, 4 In., Pair ......................... 35.00
Brass, **Candleholder**, C.1700 ........................................................................................................... 160.00
Brass, **Candleholder**, Colored Jewels, Openwork, Handled, 4 In.High ......................................... 35.00
Brass, **Candleholder**, Cutout Handle, Footed Base, 8 In.High, Pair ............................................... 25.00
Brass, **Candleholder**, Marked China, Wall, Engraved, Arm Extends 6 In. ..................................... 8.50
Brass, **Candleholder**, Marked China, 3-Light, Burnished, Lacquered ........................................... 18.00
Brass, **Candleholder**, Miniature, Heart Shape, Saucer Base, Footed, Beaded Rim ...................... 8.00
Brass, **Candleholder**, Miniature, Square Base, Footed, C.1850, 4 In.High, Pair ........................... 22.00
Brass, **Candleholder**, Oval Boat Shape, Ring Handle, Hanging Loop, C.1850 ............................... 25.00
Brass, **Candleholder**, Piano, Bracket .............................................................................................. 25.00
Brass, **Candleholder**, Push-Up, C.1850, 10 In.High, Pair ............................................................... 55.00
Brass, **Candleholder**, Saucer Base, 6 1/2 In.Diameter Base .......................................................... 14.00
Brass, **Candleholder**, Square Base, Dragons' Heads Center, 6 1/2 In., Pair ................................. 45.00
Brass, **Candleholder**, 7-Arm, 16 1/2 In.High .................................................................................. 25.00
Brass, **Candlesnuffer**, Chinese, Man With Hat Figural ................................................................... 8.50
Brass, **Candlesnuffer**, Eagle's Head Shape, C.1865, 2 1/4 In. ....................................................... 38.00
Brass, **Candlesnuffer**, Scissors Shape, Side Holder For Trimmings .............................................. 28.00
Brass, **Candlesnuffer**, Scissors Shape, 3 Footed, Box Top ............................................................ 11.75
Brass, **Candlestick**, Adjustable Push-Up, Deep Drip Pan At Top, 11 In. ........................................ 45.00
Brass, **Candlestick**, Barley Twist, 10 In., Pair ................................................................................. 60.00
Brass, **Candlestick**, Beehive, Push-Up, Diamond Knop, C.1850, 10 In., Pair ................................ 55.00
Brass, **Candlestick**, Beehive, Push-Up, 6 In., Pair .......................................................................... 35.00
Brass, **Candlestick**, Beehive, Push-Up, 7 In.High ........................................................................... 12.75
Brass, **Candlestick**, Bulbous, 2 5/8 In.High, Pair ........................................................................... 8.50
Brass, **Candlestick**, C.1750, 9 1/4 In., Pair ..................................................................... *Illus* 150.00
Brass, **Candlestick**, Center Push-Up, Square Base, 6 1/4 In.High .................................................. 11.75
Brass, **Candlestick**, Center Push-Up, 5 In.Diameter At Base, 11 1/2 In.High ................................ 29.75

Brass, Candlestick,
C.1750, 9 1/4 In.,
Pair
*(See Page 54)*

Brass, Door Knocker,
Birmingham,
England, C.1800

| | |
|---|---:|
| Brass, Candlestick, China, Hexagonal Base, Incised Fish Scale & Floral, Pair | 38.00 |
| Brass, Candlestick, Columnar, Push-Up, Domed Petal Form Base, C.1750, Pair | 225.00 |
| Brass, Candlestick, England, Picket, Footed Base, C.1750, 27 In.High, Pair | 2100.00 |
| Brass, Candlestick, Etched Hurricane Shade, Pair | 59.00 |
| Brass, Candlestick, Hand Engraved On Base, Marked China, 4 In.High, Pair | 15.00 |
| Brass, Candlestick, Hexagonal Flared Panels, Pairpoint, 8 In., Pair | 25.00 |
| Brass, Candlestick, Indian Cobra Figural, Lacquered, 6 In.High, Pair | 22.00 |
| Brass, Candlestick, Miniature, Square Footed Base, 4 In.High, Pair | 22.00 |
| Brass, Candlestick, Miniature, 2 1/4 In.High, Pair | 15.00 |
| Brass, Candlestick, Push-Up, Bulbous, 9 1/2 In.High, Pair | 60.00 |
| Brass, Candlestick, Push-Up, Chippendale Period, Pair | 48.50 |
| Brass, Candlestick, Push-Up, Oval Saucer Base, Handle, 4 Regulator Notched | 35.00 |
| Brass, Candlestick, Relief Of Leaves & Designs At Base, 12 3/4 In.High | 35.00 |
| Brass, Candlestick, Ring Thumb Rest Handle, Saucer Type, Snuffer, Embossed | 22.00 |
| Brass, Candlestick, Russian, C.1650, 11 In.High, Pair | 69.00 |
| Brass, Candlestick, Saucer Base, Push-Up, 9 In.High | 27.50 |
| Brass, Candlestick, Saucer Type, Center Push-Up, Ring Handle, 5 In.Diameter | 20.00 |
| Brass, Candlestick, Spool Design, Push-Up, 10 1/4 In.High, Pair | 85.00 |
| Brass, Candlestick, Square Base, 3 5/8 In.High, Pair | 12.00 |
| Brass, Casket, Jewel, Engraved, Great War, 1914-1919, 4 Squared Feet | 85.00 |
| Brass, Chamberstick, Art Nouveau, Lily Pad Base, Floral Handle & Top | 28.00 |
| Brass, Chamberstick, Marked China, Ring Handle, Pair | 9.75 |
| Brass, Chopstick, Oriental, C.1825, 16 In.Long, Pair | 49.50 |
| Brass, Cigar Cutter, Dinner Table Model, Victorian, Bottle Shape, 5 In. | 18.00 |
| Brass, Cigar Cutter, Pig, 2 X 3 In. | 25.00 |
| Brass, Cigar Cutter, Wine Bottle With Twisted Cap Shape | 30.00 |
| Brass, Coffee Server, Turkish, Engraved | 14.00 |
| Brass, Collar, Bulldog, Spikes & Other Decoration On Leather | 7.75 |
| Brass, Compass, German, Closed Face, 1 3/4 In. | 18.00 |
| Brass, Compass, Singer's Patent, Night, Round, Black & White Dial | 54.50 |
| Brass, Compote, Marked China, Burnished, Lacquered, 7 In.Diameter | 17.00 |
| Brass, Container, Finial On Top, Pressed Glass 3 Part Dish Inside, C.1903 | 10.50 |
| Brass, Cup, Cyclist's, Collapsible, Raised Design, Nickel Plated, 1897 | 4.95 |
| Brass, Dipper, Forged Iron Handle | 12.50 |
| Brass, Door Knocker, Birmingham, England, C.1800 ... *Illus* | 450.00 |
| Brass, Door Knocker, Bust Of Shakespeare, 4 In.High | 12.00 |
| Brass, Door Knocker, Eagle | 2.25 |
| Brass, Door Knocker, Lion's Head Shape, Ring In Mouth, Dated 1880 | 37.50 |
| Brass, Door Knocker, Lion's Head, C.1800, 7 In.Long | 40.00 |
| Brass, Doorknob & Lock With Plate, Pair | 20.00 |
| Brass, Figurine, Angel, Screw Hole On Head, C.1820, 4 1/2 In.High | 37.00 |
| Brass, Figurine, Camel, 3 In. | 45.00 |
| Brass, Figurine, Deer, Austrian, Stands On Hind Legs, Oval Base, 3 3/4 In. | 37.50 |
| Brass, Figurine, Negro Baby On Donkey, Painted, 1 3/4 In. | 18.00 |
| Brass, Figurine, Neptune, Hole In Stomach, Holding Trident, C.1860, 2 3/4 In. | 80.00 |
| Brass, Font, Holy Water, Standing, Cranberry Insert, 9 In. | 15.00 |

| | |
|---|---|
| **Brass, Foot Warmer,** French, Alcohol Fuel, Bail Handle, 8 X 6 1/4 X 2 1/4 In. | 50.00 |
| **Brass, Fork,** Forged Iron Handle | 12.50 |
| **Brass, Fork,** Toasting, Extends To 21 1/2 In. | 12.00 |
| **Brass, Fork,** Toasting, Fireside, Ship Handle | 7.00 |
| **Brass, Frame,** Easel Type, Woman, Floral, Trees, 8 X 11 In. | 22.50 |
| **Brass, Frame,** Ornate, Jeweled, 5 1/2 X 9 In. | 18.00 |
| **Brass, Funnel,** Round, Long Spout, Copper Ribs, 9 1/2 In. | 36.00 |
| **Brass, Gong,** Dinner, Chinese Pagoda Gate Shape, Hammer, Marked China | 6.95 |
| **Brass, Hammer,** Chinese, Clawhead, Miniature, Incising On Handle, 5 1/3 In. | 7.50 |
| **Brass, Hand Warmer,** Chinese, Openwork On Top, 4 3/4 X 4 In. | 45.00 |
| **Brass, Hatpin,** Indian Chief In Full Headdress, Stone Insert | 18.00 |
| **Brass, Heraldry,** House Of Savoy, King Humbert I, Italy, C.1886, Wood Base | 45.00 |
| **Brass, Holder,** Umbrella | 16.00 |
| **Brass, Hook,** Ceiling, Dolphin Shape, Screw-In Type, 11 In. | 3.75 |
| **Brass, Hook,** Hall Tree, Fancy | 4.00 |
| **Brass, Hook,** Wall Bracket, Back Plate, Patent 1898, Extends 8 In.From Wall | 3.95 |
| **Brass, Hook,** Wall Bracket, Screw-In Type, Extends 8 In. From Wall | 2.50 |
| **Brass, Incense Burner,** Chinese, Foo Dog On Top, C.1874 | 185.00 |
| **Brass, Incense Burner,** Chinese, Soapstone, Jade Decoration On Hinged Lid | 45.00 |
| **Brass, Incense Burner,** Japanese, Basket Shape, Bombe Type Panels, Carved | 85.00 |
| **Brass, Incense Burner,** Persian, Bird Shape, C.1850 | 15.00 |
| **Brass, Ink Drier,** For Sand, Cylindrical, Holes On Top, C.1850, 2 In. High | 34.00 |
| **Brass, Ink Drier,** For Sand, Removable Cover, C.1850, 3 In. High | 39.00 |
| **Brass, Inkstand,** Amethyst Glass Wells, Loop Handles, Fruit Finials | 75.00 |
| **Brass, Inkstand,** Art Deco, Single Well, Pen Tray In Front, 11 In.Long | 38.00 |
| **Brass, Inkstand,** Art Nouveau, Lilies & Designs, Hinged, Open Handles, 8 In. | 35.00 |
| **Brass, Inkstand,** Marked B & H, Footed, Handled, 2 Diamond Point Wells | 65.00 |
| **Brass, Inkwell,** Dog Sitting On Hassock Smoking Pipe, Glass Liner | 22.50 |
| **Brass, Inkwell,** Face Of Devil, Glass Insert | 30.00 |
| **Brass, Inkwell,** Hinged Lid, Footed, Violets & 2 Children Kissing In Relief | 45.00 |
| **Brass, Inkwell,** Owl, Birds, Grapes, & Branches, Ruffled Glass Well | 8.95 |
| **Brass, Inkwell,** Pierced Flowers, Vines, & Animals' Faces, Footed | 75.00 |
| **Brass, Jardiniere,** Copper Coat Of Arms & Trim On 3 Paw Feet, C.1860 | 148.00 |
| **Brass, Jardiniere,** Lion's Head Handles, 10 1/2 X 9 1/2 In. | 20.00 |
| **Brass, Jardiniere,** Russian, Lions' Masks Handles, Paw Feet, C.1850, 8 1/2 In. | 175.00 |
| **Brass, Kettle,** American Made, 12 In. | 67.50 |
| **Brass, Kettle,** Ansonia Brass Works, Spun, Dated 1851, 11 In. | 85.00 |
| **Brass, Kettle,** Bail, 10 In.Diameter | 27.50 |
| **Brass, Kettle,** Engraved Design, 2 Brass Handles, Perforated Insert | 35.00 |
| **Brass, Kettle,** Hayden's Ansonia, 12/16/1851, 9 1/2 In. | 37.00 |
| **Brass, Kettle,** Iron Bail Handle, 8 1/2 In. Diameter | 19.95 |
| **Brass, Kettle,** Jam, Cast Iron Handle, 14 In.Diameter | 35.00 |
| **Brass, Key,** City Of Lowell, 4 In. | 4.50 |
| **Brass, Key,** 5 1/4 In.Long | 7.00 |
| **Brass, Key,** 6 1/2 In.Long | 5.00 |
| **Brass, Key,** 6 3/4 In.Long | 15.00 |
| **Brass, Knocker,** Door, Tiger Mask, Ring In Mouth, 3 1/2 In. Diameter | 17.50 |
| **Brass, Ladle,** Cast Iron Handle, Hook For Hanging, 19 In.Long | 35.00 |
| **Brass, Ladle,** Cast Iron.Handle, Rattail End, 14 In.Long | 35.00 |
| **Brass, Ladle,** Cast Iron Handle, Rattail End, 20 In.Long | 35.00 |
| **Brass, Ladle,** Richard Lee, Sr. & Jr., Shank Riveted To Bowl, Pierced, C.1795 | 300.00 |
| **Brass, Letter Opener,** Art Nouveau, Head Of Dante | 32.00 |
| **Brass, Letter Opener,** Bohemia, Flow Blue China Handle | 6.00 |
| **Brass, Letter Opener,** Clarence A.O'Brien Registered Patent Attorney | 2.95 |
| **Brass, Letter Opener,** Dagger Shape, 3 Masks Of Theatre & 2 Faces | 25.00 |
| **Brass, Letter Opener,** Design Of Old Norse Ship At Top, 7 In.Long | 2.95 |
| **Brass, Letter Opener,** L.D.M.Dillon, Steam Boiler Works, Fitchburg, Mass. | 3.95 |
| **Brass, Letter Opener,** "Lord, Where There Is Sadness Let Me Sow Joy" | 2.75 |
| **Brass, Letter Opener,** "Maine Casket Co., Inc., The House Of Quality, " 8 In. | 2.95 |
| **Brass, Letter Opener,** Peacock Handle, Embossed Feathers On Blade | 8.50 |
| **Brass, Letter Opener,** Raised Design Of Gardener With Shovel | 5.95 |
| **Brass, Letter Opener,** Scrolls, 8 1/2 In. Long | 2.75 |
| **Brass, Letter Slot,** For Door | 17.50 |
| **Brass, Lock & Key,** Bohannan | 10.00 |
| **Brass, Lock,** Marked L.Slatcher, Pat.Dec.13, 1865, Newark, N.J. | 4.95 |
| **Brass, Match Holder,** Holders Like Broken Eggshells, Hammered, Round | 12.50 |

| | |
|---|---:|
| Brass, Match Holder, Two Eggshells On Hammered Plaque | 8.00 |
| Brass, Match Holder, Wall, Dead Game, 2 Compartments | 50.00 |
| Brass, Match Safe, Bryant & May Ltd., 2 X 7 In. | 5.00 |
| Brass, Match Safe, Pig Holding Bundle Of Gold, Washurst Farms | 70.00 |
| Brass, Match Safe, Pocket, Gold Finish | 3.95 |
| Brass, Match Safe, Raised Roses & Butterflies | 14.00 |
| Brass, Matchbox Holder, French Rooster Trampling German Soldier | 3.95 |
| Brass, Matchbox, Engraved Lighthouse & Ship Scene On Hinged Lid, C.1750 | 95.00 |
| Brass, Microscope, Y Base, Mounted On Black Cast Iron, Lens & Mirror | 45.00 |
| Brass, Mold, Bullet, 4 1/4 In.Long | 9.00 |
| Brass, Mortar & Pestle, Cast, Miniature, 1 1/8 In. Mortar | 10.00 |
| Brass, Mortar & Pestle, Dated 1750, 2 3/4 In.High Mortar | 68.00 |
| Brass, Mortar & Pestle, Dated 1870 | 30.00 |
| Brass, Mortar & Pestle, E.F.Caldwell Co., New York City | 47.50 |
| Brass, Mortar & Pestle, Round, Ball Type Handle, 3 1/2 In. High | 30.00 |
| Brass, Mortar & Pestle, Side Handles, 4 In.Diameter | 30.00 |
| Brass, Mortar & Pestle, 2 In.High | 10.00 |
| Brass, Mortar & Pestle, 3 1/2 In.High | 30.00 |
| Brass, Mortar & Pestle, 4 In.Diameter, 3 In.High | 30.00 |
| Brass, Mortar & Pestle, 4 1/2 In High | 67.50 |
| Brass, Nutcracker, Incised China, Alligator, 7 3/4 In. | 9.00 |
| Brass, Nutcracker, Ornate, Cherubs | 10.00 |
| Brass, Ornament, Art Nouveau Bearded Man With Mustache, 5 In.High | 35.00 |
| Brass, Padlock & Key, Marked Climax | 5.25 |
| Brass, Padlock, American Eagle, 'russell-Irwin-New Britain, Conn.-1898' | 47.50 |
| Brass, Padlock, Hinged Escutcheon Cover | 75.00 |
| Brass, Padlock, Russell, Irwin, New Britian, Patent Nov.8, 1898, Eagle | 47.50 |
| Brass, Pail, American Brass Kettle Mfg.Co., Spun, Iron Handle, 11 In. | 40.00 |
| Brass, Pan, Warming, Chased Florals, Handle, 9 1/2 In. | 135.00 |
| Brass, Pan, 2 Copper Handles, 12 X 7 In. | 14.50 |
| Brass, Paper Clip, Desk, Figural, Owl, 4 In. | 28.50 |
| Brass, Paper Clip, Eagle, U.S.Shield, Stars, Stripes, E Pluribus Unum | 27.00 |
| Brass, Paper Clip, Shape Of Man's Pipe, Wooden Base, 6 In. | 20.00 |
| Brass, Pencil, Purse, Engraved, Extension, Gem End | 8.00 |
| Brass, Pipe Holder, Figural, Scottie Dog | 8.00 |
| Brass, Plate, Door, 3 X 9 In. | 1.65 |
| Brass, Plate, White House, 1800s, Flowers In Relief Around Rim, 4 1/4 In. | 18.00 |
| Brass, Police Siren, 14 Inch Chain, C.1880 | 8.50 |
| Brass, Pot, 3 Hand-Forged Wrought Iron Legs, 15 In Handle | 45.00 |
| Brass, Rack, Cordial Cups, Place For 2 Bottles | 38.00 |
| Brass, Rack, Key, Wall, Dutch, 9 X 13 1/2 In. | 20.00 |
| Brass, Ruler, Dog, 6 In.Long | 5.00 |
| Brass, Samovar, Indented Hearts, Square Footed Base, Iran, 17 In.High | 100.00 |
| Brass, Sconce, Candle, Wall, C.1850, Pair | 95.00 |
| Brass, Sconce, Wall, Openwork Finial, Domed Back Plate, Scrolled, C 1750, Pair | 500.00 |
| Brass, Scoop, Flour, Hardwood Grained Handle, C.1850, 16 In. | 30.00 |
| Brass, Shelf, Book, Bulldogs On Each Side, 22 In.Wide | 16.50 |
| Brass, Skimmer, Forged Iron Handle | 12.50 |
| Brass, Slipper, Scuff, Engraved To Simulate Brocade Fabric, Bows, Pair | 18.00 |
| Brass, Spittoon, Copper Bottom, 2 Ornate Brass Handles, C.1850, 16 In. | 65.00 |
| Brass, Spittoon, 1 Piece, 7 1/2 In.Diameter | 12.00 |
| Brass, Spoon & Fork, Hand-Painted Porcelain Handles, Halga, Paris, Set Of 12 | 75.00 |
| Brass, Spoon, Man's Head Shape | 4.00 |
| Brass, Spur, Chain Mail, Pair | 7.50 |
| Brass, Stand, Umbrella, Embossed, Shape Of Closed Umbrella, 34 In.High | 200.00 |
| Brass, Sugar, Basket Shape, Filigree, Cranberry Glass Insert | 48.00 |
| Brass, Syrup, Marked Villedieu Manche, Tin Lined, Squatty Base | 12.50 |
| Brass, Tamper, Pipe, Dickens' Dandy, Full Figure, C.1850, 2 1/4 In.High | 38.00 |
| Brass, Tamper, Pipe, George III Cutout Bust, C.1800, 2 3/4 In.High | 40.00 |
| Brass, Tamper, Pipe, Naval Officer's Bust, C.1800, 2 3/4 In.High | 40.00 |
| Brass, Tea Warmer, Four Lithophane Panels, Round, Handle, Burner | 85.00 |
| Brass, Teapot, Amber Glass Handle | 56.00 |
| Brass, Teapot, Miniature, 1 1/2 In.High | 22.00 |
| Brass, Telescope, C.1890, Extends To 23 Inches | 110.00 |
| Brass, Telescope, Leather Covering, Extends To 48 In. | 80.00 |
| Brass, Telescope, Pocket, Leather Covering, Opens To 14 In. | 32.50 |

| | |
|---|---|
| Brass, Tieback, Convex Center Bull's-Eye, Raised Floral, C.1850, Pair | 12.50 |
| Brass, Tieback, Floral Design, 3 3/4 In.Diameter, Pair | 17.50 |
| Brass, Tieback, Green Sailing Ship, 2 3/4 In., Pair | 19.50 |
| Brass, Tieback, Leaf Design, 5 In.Diameter, Pair | 24.50 |
| Brass, Tieback, Rosette Center, C.1850, 2 In.Diameter, Pair | 12.50 |
| Brass, Tray, China, Reclining Maiden Center, Etched Dragon, 11 In.Diameter | 12.00 |
| Brass, Tray, Marionnet, Branch Rim, Root Handles, C.1900, 18 In. Long | 80.00 |
| Brass, Tray, Patent 1885, 12 3/4 In.Diameter | 9.75 |
| Brass, Tray, Pen, 12 In.Long | 4.95 |
| Brass, Tray, Pin, Marked China, Etched Design, 3 In. | 8.00 |
| Brass, Tray, Russian, 2 Handled, 25 1/2 X 15 1/2 In. | 35.00 |
| Brass, Tray, Russian, 8 3/8 In.Diameter | 10.75 |
| Brass, Tray, Scale, 12 1/2 X 7 1/4 In. | 15.00 |
| Brass, Tumbler, Russian, Signed, 3 3/4 In. | 18.00 |
| Brass, Vase, Bulbous, Flared Lip, Engraved, 8 In.High | 12.00 |
| Brass, Vase, India, Red & Black Decoration, 9 In.High | 15.00 |
| Brass, Vase, Marked China, 3 Enameled Flowers On Base, 6 In. High | 3.95 |
| Brass, Vase, Ornate Handles, Footed, Dated 1845, 6 3/4 In.High, Pair | 75.00 |
| Brass, Vase, Trumpet, Hammered, 14 In.High | 60.00 |
| Brass, Watch Stand, Marked C.I.Ochs, Maker, Milton, Mass., 2 5/8 In.High | 3.95 |
| Brass, Whistle, Steam Engine, From Threshing Machine | 39.50 |

*Brides' baskets of glass were usually one-of-a-kind novelties made in
American and European glass factories. They were especially popular about
1880 when the decorated basket was often given as a wedding gift. Cut-glass
baskets were popular after 1890. All brides' baskets lost favor about 1905.*

| | |
|---|---|
| Bride's Basket, Applied Amber Band On Cream, Rose Interior, Silver Holder | 150.00 |
| Bride's Basket, Blue, Fluted, Benedict Plated Footed Frame, Open Handle | 200.00 |
| Bride's Basket, Butterscotch, Hand-Painted Flowers | 85.00 |
| Bride's Basket, Cased Apricot Fluted Bowl, Footed Silver Plate Frame | 150.00 |
| Bride's Basket, Cased, White & Raspberry, Enameled, Fluted & Ruffled | 95.00 |
| Bride's Basket, Cranberry Glass, Ruffled, White Overlay, Enamel, Silver | 150.00 |
| Bride's Basket, Cranberry Overlay, Coin Dot | 45.00 |
| Bride's Basket, Fluted Edge, Blue, Silver Frame, 10 1/2 In. | 70.00 |
| Bride's Basket, Green, Colorado Pattern, Silver Plated Holder | 165.00 |
| Bride's Basket, Green, Ruffled Rim, Signed Star, Dated 1850, 6 1/2 In. | 42.00 |
| Bride's Basket, Lime Green, Opalescent, Ruffled, 11 1/2 In. | 20.00 |
| Bride's Basket, Miniature, Green To Opalescent, Ruffled, Silver Plate Frame | 75.00 |
| Bride's Basket, Miniature, White Loops On Clear, Vaseline Ruffles, Holder | 26.00 |
| Bride's Basket, Orange, Black Wrought Iron Cutout Frame, Twisted Handle | 165.00 |
| Bride's Basket, Pink To White, Mica Flakes, Clear Cased, Silver Holder | 60.00 |
| Bride's Basket, Pink To White, White Casing, Silver Frame | 85.00 |
| Bride's Basket, Pink, Ruffled, Fern Decoration, Silver Plate Holder | 125.00 |
| Bride's Basket, Pink, White Casing, Ruffled, Silver Handled Holder | 145.00 |
| Bride's Basket, Pressed Square Flowers, 12 X 11 1/2 In. | 29.00 |
| Bride's Basket, Ruffled, White To Ruby To Clear, Silver Plate Frame, 11 In. | 55.00 |
| Bride's Basket, Square, Aqua Interior, White Overlay, Vaseline Handle | 185.00 |
| Bride's Basket, White, Ruffled Clear Edge, Rose Interior, 13 In.Diameter | 50.00 |
| Bride's Bowl, Deep Rose & Amber Edges, Cream Lining, Crimped, 10 1/2 In. | 55.00 |
| Bride's Bowl, White Casing, Gilt Trimmed Blown Beaded Edge, Polychrome | 50.00 |
| Bridle, Rosette, Brass, U.S.A. | 4.00 |
| Bridle, Rosette, Crest Of Prince Of Italy, Embossed Gilt Lead | 10.00 |
| Bridle, Rosette, Horses' Heads Under Glass, Pair | 5.00 |
| Bridle, Rosette, Initial N Under Glass | 3.50 |

*Bristol glass was made in Bristol, England, after the 1700s. The
Bristol glass most often seen today is a Victorian, lightweight opaque glass
that is often blue. Some of the glass was decorated with enamels.*

| | |
|---|---|
| Bristol, Barrel, Biscuit, Blue, Birds, Acorn Finial On Silver Plated Lid | 75.00 |
| Bristol, Bottle, Toilet, Frosty White, Matching Stopper, 8 1/2 In.High | 15.00 |
| Bristol, Bowl, Finger, Emerald Green, Polished Pontil, Pair | 100.00 |
| Bristol, Champagne, Blue Green, 4 In.High, Pair | 21.00 |
| Bristol, Cologne, White, Bulbous Base, Thumbprint Stopper, 7 In., Pair | 35.00 |
| Bristol, Dish, Sweetmeat, Dark Pink, Enamel & Gold, Silver Plate Frame | 100.00 |
| Bristol, Epergne, Pink, Decorated | 100.00 |
| Bristol, Epergne, Pink, Silver Holder | 79.00 |

Bristol, Figurine, Winter, Boy With Black Hat, Carrying Bakset Of Game .................... 200.00
Bristol, Jar, Brass Cover, Sea Captain With Cap & Pipe ................................ 65.00
Bristol, Lamp Base, Hand-Painted Bird ................................................ 65.00
Bristol, Lamp, Oil, Mantel, Mary Gregory Boy & Girl, Pair ............................ 300.00
Bristol, Lampshade, White, Student ................................................... 10.00
Bristol, Perfume, Blown, Frosted, Painting, 9 3/4 In.High ............................ 18.50
Bristol, Plate, Lobed, Center Bouquet, Pink Tulip, C.1780, 9 In. ..................... 160.00
Bristol, Rolling Pin, English, Decorated With Figures & Inscription .................. 75.00
Bristol, Salt & Pepper, Light Green, Leaf Palm, 2 3/4 In.High ........................ 25.00
Bristol, Tumbler, Brown Leaf Sprays & Silver Luster Seed Pods On Caramel ............. 45.00
Bristol, Tumbler, Hand-Painted Pink Tulip ............................................ 22.50
Bristol, Vase, Blue, Fan With Enameled Floral, 6 3/4 In. High ........................ 27.50
Bristol, Vase, Blue, Urn Shape, Enamel Flowers, 9 1/2 In. ............................ 25.00
Bristol, Vase, Brown Top, Cream Base, Enameled Flowers, 6 In.High, Pair .............. 35.00
Bristol, Vase, Brown, Enameled, 7 In. ................................................ 15.00
Bristol, Vase, Bud, Smoke, Apple Blossom Decoration, 4 In.High, Pair ................. 16.50
Bristol, Vase, Caramel, Bird With Flowers, 10 In. .................................... 18.00
Bristol, Vase, Chocolate, Enameled Stork & Floral, 9 1/4 In.High ..................... 35.00
Bristol, Vase, Clambroth, Painted Flowers, 15 In. .................................... 15.00
Bristol, Vase, Cream, Hand-Painted Purple & Yellow Pansies, 16 1/2 In.High ........... 78.00
Bristol, Vase, Dancing Boy & Girl, 10 1/2 In.High .................................... 35.00
Bristol, Vase, Dark Green Ground, Hand-Painted Flowers, 17 1/2 In.High, Pair ......... 168.00
Bristol, Vase, Dark To Light Green Top, Colonial Lady, 10 1/2 In., Pair .............. 50.00
Bristol, Vase, Enamel Bird, Berries, & Flowers On Gray, 12 1/2 In.High ............... 21.00
Bristol, Vase, Enamel Scrolls, Cherubs Playing, 6 1/2 In., Pair ...................... 95.00
Bristol, Vase, Fireglow, Fluted Rim, 7 In.High ....................................... 65.00
Bristol, Vase, Footed, Pink Satin, Gold & Silver Decoration, 10 In.High .............. 58.00
Bristol, Vase, Gold & Green Leaf, 10 In.High ......................................... 20.00
Bristol, Vase, Gold Decoration On White, 6 3/4 In.High ............................... 15.00
Bristol, Vase, Hand-Painted Stork Scene, Cylinder Shape, 6 In.High ................... 11.00
Bristol, Vase, Pink On White Cased, Fluted Neck, Birds & Flowers, 5 In. High ......... 55.00
Bristol, Vase, Pink, Covered, Hand-Painted Floral, 12 In.High ........................ 20.00
Bristol, Vase, Pink, Jeweled, Hand-Painted Scrolls & Floral, 7 1/4 In. ............... 110.00
Bristol, Vase, Smoky, 4 In. .......................................................... 15.00
Bristol, Vase, Trumpet, Blue, Enameled Floral, Held By Bronzed Cherub, 14 In. ........ 28.00
Bristol, Vase, White Flowers, Gold Leaves & Branches, Ruffled, 11 3/4 In. ............ 39.50
Bristol, Vase, White Frosted, Flowers, Crimped Top, 10 In. ........................... 25.00
Bristol, Vase, White, Floral Design, Blue Crimped Top, 8 In. ......................... 25.00
Bristol, Vase, White, Slim, Enameled Tropical Scene, C.1850, 13 3/4 In. .............. 75.00

*Signed bronze figurines by known artists are listed separately at the end of
the bronze section.*

Bronze, Ashtray, Art Nouveau Figure, 7 1/2 In.Long ................................... 23.00
Bronze, Blotter, Roll Type, World Globe .............................................. 15.00
Bronze, Bookend, Architectural, Pair ................................................. 19.50
Bronze, Bookend, Art Deco, Bust Of Lady, 8 In.High, Pair ............................. 50.00
Bronze, Bookend, Charging Elephants, Young, C.1920, Pair, 5 3/4 In.High .............. 750.00
Bronze, Bookend, Eagle On Marble Base, 8 1/4 In.High, Pair ........................... 125.00
Bronze, Bookend, Indian, Pair ........................................................ 35.00
Bronze, Bookend, Men Pushing, Isidore Konti, C.1925, Pair ............................ 325.00
Bronze, Bookend, Owl, Pair ........................................................... 45.00
Bronze, Bookend, Shell, Art Nouveau Nudes Gazing At Frog, 9 1/2 In., Pair ............ 50.00
Bronze, Bookend, The Thinker, 8 1/2 In.High, Pair .................................... 65.00
Bronze, Bottle Opener, Sea Horse ..................................................... 7.00
Bronze, Bowl, Chinese, Dogs' Heads Form Loop Handles, Geometrics, 8 In. .............. 85.00
Bronze, Box, Covered, Bas Relief Classical Figures In Gilt Finish, 8 In. ............. 225.00
Bronze, Box, Figural, Temple Of Diana, Lift-Off Lid, Marble Base, 9 In. .............. 40.00
Bronze, Box, Hinged Turtle, 4 1/4 In.Long ............................................ 62.00
Bronze, Brush & Mirror, Lavender Enamel, Miniature Paintings On Ivory ................ 325.00
Bronze, Bust, Boy, Toothpick In Mouth, Sighed T.Jensen ............................... 51.00
Bronze, Bust, Lady With Tricorn Hat, Onyx Base, 5 In.High ............................ 45.00
Bronze, Bust, Napoleon, 4 In. ........................................................ 75.00
Bronze, Bust, Woman, Signed Bulio, Octagonal Onyx Base, 20 X 12 In. .................. 420.00
Bronze, Candelabra, Russian, Gilt, Malachite, 4-Arm, C.1850, 15 3/4 In., Pair ........ 1300.00
Bronze, Candelabra, 2-Arm, Red Enamel, Footed, 10 X 8 In., Pair ...................... 350.00
Bronze, Candleholder, Chinese Pricket, 20 In. ........................................ 225.00

| | |
|---|---|
| Bronze, Candlestick, Russian, Lathe Turned, Maker's Mark, 8 1/2 In.High | 33.00 |
| Bronze, Dish, Candy, Art Nouveau, 3 Section Glass Liner, Silver Crest | 18.00 |
| Bronze, Doorknob, Ram's Horn Shape, From Coach Of Governor Of Mass., C.1836 | 18.00 |
| Bronze, Ewer, Children Form Handle, Ram's Head, Onyx Base, 13 X 8 In., Pair | 425.00 |
| Bronze Figurines, see also Bronze Figurine listing at end of this list | |
| Bronze, Figurine, Baby Chick, Signed Geschutz, Austrian, 2 In. | 30.00 |
| Bronze, Figurine, Boy Holding Jewel Chest, Ivory Face & Head, Marble Base | 300.00 |
| Bronze, Figurine, Boy Scout, 6 In. | 75.00 |
| Bronze, Figurine, Buddha, Siam, 6 1/2 In. | 53.00 |
| Bronze, Figurine, Butterfly, On Marble Cube, Dore, 3 In.High | 38.00 |
| Bronze, Figurine, Cat, Vienna, Striped Gray, Hunched Back | 24.00 |
| Bronze, Figurine, Dancer, Ivory Inlaid, C.1900, 19 In.High | 300.00 |
| Bronze, Figurine, Dancer, Pixie Costume, Ivory Face & Hands, Marble Base | 135.00 |
| Bronze, Figurine, Dancing Faun, Composition Base, 22 1/2 In.High | 200.00 |
| Bronze, Figurine, Daniel Webster, 28 1/4 In.High | 700.00 |
| Bronze, Figurine, Dante, Seated, 10 3/4 In.High | 175.00 |
| Bronze, Figurine, Discus Thrower, Sand Cast, 5 In. | 56.00 |
| Bronze, Figurine, Dog, Shepherd, Sitting | 105.00 |
| Bronze, Figurine, Dog, Viennese, Lying, Polychrome, Memo Holder, Wood Base | 80.00 |
| Bronze, Figurine, Dying Slave, French, C.1880, 17 In.High | 100.00 |
| Bronze, Figurine, Ewe, England, Dark Gray, 1 3/8 In. X 1 3/4 In. | 15.00 |
| Bronze, Figurine, Farm Worker Holding Scythe, 2 Step Marble Base | 30.00 |
| Bronze, Figurine, Farmer Boy Carrying Butter Bucket, Marble Plinth | 90.00 |
| Bronze, Figurine, Fish & Woman, Erotic, 8 In. | 110.00 |
| Bronze, Figurine, George Washington, Holding Spyglass, Hat, 22 In. High | 300.00 |
| Bronze, Figurine, Gladiator Preparing For Battle, 23 In.High | 600.00 |
| Bronze, Figurine, Hen, Austrian, Polychromed, 1 1/2 X 1 3/4 In. | 25.00 |
| Bronze, Figurine, Hunting Hound, Viennese, White & Brown Polychrome, 12 In. | 295.00 |
| Bronze, Figurine, Kate Greenaway Type Barefoot Boy, Marble Base, 6 In. | 85.00 |
| Bronze, Figurine, King Arthur, Movable Visor, 14 1/4 In.High | 450.00 |
| Bronze, Figurine, Little Boy With Dog, Marble Base, 7 In.High | 250.00 |
| Bronze, Figurine, Magpie, Vienna, Miniature, 1 In.High | 21.00 |
| Bronze, Figurine, Man Holding Smelting Pot In Long Tongs, Marble Base | 195.00 |
| Bronze, Figurine, Man On Marble Base, Art Nouveau, Polychrome, 18 In.High | 350.00 |
| Bronze, Figurine, Man Standing Playing Mandolin, Dated, 1891, 22 In.High | 400.00 |
| Bronze, Figurine, Man With Disc, 10 In.High | 165.00 |
| Bronze, Figurine, Mercury, 7 Children In Roman Scene, 24 X 10, Dark Patina | 275.00 |
| Bronze, Figurine, Nude Gladiator Pulling Chain, Marble Base, 9 In. | 48.00 |
| Bronze, Figurine, Nude Indian Girl, Sitting Position, 6 In.High | 35.00 |
| Bronze, Figurine, Nymph, Standing, Holding Shell, 14 3/4 In. | 60.00 |
| Bronze, Figurine, Panther Of India, Rockwork Base, 1898, 10 1/2 In.Long | 300.00 |
| Bronze, Figurine, Puritan, 17th Century Costume, 31 In.High | 3750.00 |
| Bronze, Figurine, Rebecca At The Well, 14 In.High | 99.00 |
| Bronze, Figurine, Red Cardinal, Vienna, 5 1/2 In.High | 150.00 |
| Bronze, Figurine, Ruler As Hermes, Standing, Marble Base, 30 7/8 In. | 350.00 |
| Bronze, Figurine, Seated Dog, 4 In. | 75.00 |
| Bronze, Figurine, Seminude Man Holding Reins Of Morley Horse, Oval Vase | 65.00 |
| Bronze, Figurine, Sitting Terrier, 2 1/2 In.High | 48.00 |
| Bronze, Figurine, Spaniel, Reclining, Head Alert, 8 X 4 In. | 55.00 |
| Bronze, Figurine, Sparrow, Vienna Type, Decorated, 1 X 3/4 In. | 18.00 |
| Bronze, Figurine, Stag, Bronze & Wooden Base, 8 In.High | 75.00 |
| Bronze, Figurine, Stag, Vienna, Red, 3 In.High | 75.00 |
| Bronze, Figurine, Standing Dog, 4 In. | 85.00 |
| Bronze, Figurine, Tiger & Alligator, Chinese, 18 In.Long, Marked | 350.00 |
| Bronze, Figurine, 4 Sided Bacchanalian Heads, Pedestal Base, 17 X 9 In. | 145.00 |
| Bronze, Group, Angel Giving Blessing To Knight In Full Armor, 14 In. | 475.00 |
| Bronze, Group, Birds, Wooden Base, 4 1/2 In.High | 135.00 |
| Bronze, Group, Diana, Silvered, C.1915, 29 1/2 In.Long | 325.00 |
| Bronze, Group, Doe & Stag Playing | 150.00 |
| Bronze, Group, Equestrian, George Washington, 24 1/2 In.High | 850.00 |
| Bronze, Group, Gaggle Of Geese, 6 Geese, 4 1/4 In.Long | 80.00 |
| Bronze, Group, Three Children Playing Ring Around The Rosy | 175.00 |
| Bronze, Group, Three Dogs, Austrian, Polychromed, 2 X 1 1/2 In. | 40.00 |
| Bronze, Group, 2 Satyrs Cavorting Before A Tree, Silvered, 6 3/4 In.High | 600.00 |
| Bronze, Incense Burner, Chinese, Figural, 3 Toed Dragon, Symbols | 50.00 |
| Bronze, Incense Burner, Chinese, Rosewood Stand | 60.00 |

Bronze, Incense Burner, Foo Dog Finial, Reticulated Cover, 3 Dragons, Footed .............. 100.00
Bronze, Incense Burner, Gargoyle, Hinged Top, 3 X 4 In. .......................... 85.00
Bronze, Incense Burner, Japanese, Bird With Head Under Wing, 6 In.High .............. 75.00
Bronze, Incense Burner, Nippon, 3 Sided, Turtles On Sides, 3 Footed .................. 19.75
Bronze, Incense Burner, Phoenix, Eagles, Crouchant Kirin Finial, C.1850 .............. 225.00
Bronze, Inkstand, Animals, Scrollwork, Figure Of Christ & Angels, 8 In.High .......... 40.00
Bronze, Inkstand, Legs, 2 Wells With Hinged Cover, Ornate ........................... 85.00
Bronze, Inkwell & Letter Opener, 2 Bears On Rock Formation, F.Gornik ................ 295.00
Bronze, Inkwell, Girl, Figure With Violin, 2 Crystal Wells, Signed Cigale ............ 400.00
Bronze, Inkwell, Hinged Cover, Relief Cherubs Kissing, Glass Well, Footed ........... 28.00
Bronze, Inkwell, Sphinx With Nude Girl Seated At Foot, Flowing Hair ................. 115.00
Bronze, Inkwell, Tereszezuk, Hinged, Semiclothed Maiden, C.1890, 9 In. .............. 130.00
Bronze, Inkwell, Viennese, Bird On Nest, 2 1/2 X 3 In. .............................. 135.00
Bronze, Inkwell, World Globe, Ship Finial .......................................... 22.00
Bronze, Match Holder, Vienna, Monkey, Brass Coloring & Patina, 4 1/2 In. ............ 145.00
Bronze, Match Safe, Eros & Grapes, Signed Camberworth, English, C.1825 .............. 150.00
Bronze, Mirror, Japanese, Handle, Buddhist Design, C.1750, 12 In. ................... 75.00
Bronze, Mirror, Shaving, Figural ................................................... 17.50
Bronze, Mirror, Standing, Art Nouveau, Woman In Bas Relief, 12 In.High .............. 125.00
Bronze, Pen Wiper, Quill, Donkey, Signed Geschutz .................................. 100.00
Bronze, Plaque, Abraham Lincoln, Signed Gudebrod, 8 X 11 In. ....................... 65.00
Bronze, Plaque, Art Nouveau Winged Nude On Leaf, A.Vilbert, 12 1/2 In. .............. 350.00
Bronze, Plaque, Bust Of Young Boy Facing Right, Gold Edged, Miniature ............... 45.00
Bronze, Plaque, Diana, The Huntress & Dog, 16 X 12 In. ............................. 169.00
Bronze, Plaque, Indian Chief, Seltice, Olin L.Warner, 1891, 7 1/2 In.Diameter ....... 850.00
Bronze, Plaque, Lincoln, With Malice Toward None, Gudebrod, 1914, 12 In. ............ 80.00
Bronze, Plaque, Lincoln, Signed Leo Nock, 1914, Framed, 6 1/2 In. ................... 135.00
Bronze, Plaque, W.W.I Nurse, Edith Cavell, 5 X 7 In. ............................... 24.00
Bronze, Seal, Art Deco Monkey, 4 1/2 In.High ....................................... 65.00
Bronze, Seal, Standing Figure Of Napoleon, C.1845, 2 1/2 In. ....................... 55.00
Bronze, Statue, Maiden, Nude, Torch Lights, C.1893, Oak Base, 56 In.High ............ 1650.00
Bronze, Tamper, Pipe, Woman's Leg, C.1800, 3 In. Long .............................. 40.00
Bronze, Tray, Card, Tortoise & Crane With Snake Forming Handle Of Shell ............. 135.00
Bronze, Tray, J.Zomere, Art Nouveau Nude Floating On Waves, 11 3/4 In.Long .......... 185.00
Bronze, Urn, Chinese, Tiger, Dragon, & Phoenix, Saber Tooth Tiger Handles ........... 165.00
Bronze, Urn, Covered, Dead Game, Mene, C.1850, 14 1/2 In.High, Pair ................. 1400.00
Bronze, Urn, Japanese, Fowl, Dragon & Floral, Mask Handles, C.1890, 43 In. .......... 200.00
Bronze, Vase, Four Heads Of Bacchus In Relief, 14 In.High .......................... 145.00
Bronze, Vase, Ikebana, 3 Parts, Japanese, C.1850, 18 3/4 In., Pair ................. 500.00
Bronze, Vase, Japanese, C.1875, 4 Ft.High ............................. *Illus* 500.00
Bronze, Vase, Oriental, Embossed Bat, 9 1/4 In.High ................................ 165.00
Bronze, Vase, Oriental, Pear Shape, Stylized Leaf Designs, 9 In., Pair .............. 175.00
Bronze, Vase, Oriental, Relief Leaf, Square Foot, Scalloped Rim, 9 In., Pair ........ 150.00
Bronze, Vase, Sterling Overlay, Signed & Numbered, Dated 1912, 10 1/4 In. ........... 89.00
*Bronze Figurines and Groups*
Bronze, A.A.Weinman, Nude Golfer Swinging At A Ball, 17 1/2 In.High ................. 595.00
Bronze, Alonzo, Dancer On Tambourine, 1 Naked Ivory Bust, 12 In.High ................ 350.00
Bronze, Anfrie, French Soldier With Sword By Side, 24 In.High ...................... 595.00
Bronze, Antoine Bofill, Fisher Boy, Nude, Loincloth, Standing, C.1920, 18 In. ....... 525.00
Bronze, Arion, Mother Hen With 4 Chicks, Basket On Ground, 3 In.High ................ 250.00
Bronze, Barbedienne-Fondeur, Dying Gaul Nude, 16 In.Wide ........................... 350.00
Bronze, Barye, African Elephant Charging, C.1875, 7 1/2 In. ....................... 800.00
Bronze, Barye, African Elephant Charging, C.1890, 4 1/4 In. ....................... 225.00
Bronze, Barye, Elephant Running, C.1890, 13 In. ................................... 450.00
Bronze, Barye, Elephant, 22 In. High ............................................... 1500.00
Bronze, Barye, Indian Elephant, Wrestling Tree Stump, C.1890, 7 In. ................ 300.00
Bronze, Barye, Ostrich, Standing, C.1890, 8 1/2 In. ............................... 275.00
Bronze, Barye, Panther Of India, Reclining, C.1901, 7 5/8 In. ..................... 150.00
Bronze, Barye, Panther Of India, Reclining, 1901, 10 5/8 In. ...................... 250.00
Bronze, Barye, Seated Rabbit, Ears Lowered, C.1850, 2 3/8 In. ..................... 350.00
Bronze, Barye, Stag, Doe, & Fawn, C.1875, 8 1/4 In. ...................... *Illus* 800.00
Bronze, Barye, Walking Pheasant, C.1875, 8 1/2 In. ................................ 500.00
Bronze, Beckmann, Greyhound, Reclining, 1912, 29 1/2 In. .......................... 650.00
Bronze, Bofill, Man With Dead Wolf Over Shoulder, C.1850, Spanish, 9 X 8 In. ....... 325.00
Bronze, Boisseau, Amour Enchaine, Cupid, Unhappy, C.1890, 23 3/8 In. ............... 425.00
Bronze, Boisseau, Young Mandolin Player Sitting, C.1650, 22 3/4 In.High ............ 625.00

Bronze, Vase, Japanese,
C.1875, 4 Ft.High
(See Page 61)

Bronze, Chiparus, Clown,
Painted, Marble, 29 1/4 In.
(See Page 63)

Bronze, Chiparus, The Starfish Lady,
Gilt, Enamel, 14 In.
(See Page 63)

Bronze, Bonheur, Mare & Foal, Marble Base
(See Page 63)

Bronze, Bonheur, Grazing Ewe,
C.1822, 8 1/2 In.
(See Page 63)

Bronze, Barye, Stag, Doe, & Fawn, C.1875, 8 1/4 In.
(See Page 61)

Bronze, Gerome,
Equestrian Group Of Caesar, 17 In.Long
(See Page 63)

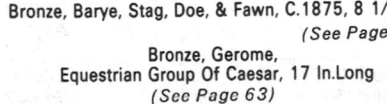

Bronze, Bonheur, Grazing Ewe, C.1822, 8 1/2 In. ............ *Illus* 525.00
Bronze, Bonheur, Lioness With Cubs, Stalking Prey, C.1827, 18 7/8 In. ............ 550.00
Bronze, Bonheur, Mare & Foal, Marble Base ............ *Illus* 2700.00
Bronze, Bouret, Seated Classic Woman, Signed, 9 1/2 X 11 In. ............ 310.00
Bronze, Boyle, The Stone Age In America, Indian Squaw, Child, Bear, C.1890 ............ 1000.00
Bronze, C.Masson, Panther Crouched On Stony Hill, 7 1/4 In.Long ............ 275.00
Bronze, Carpeaux, Bust Of A Bacchante & Roses, 24 3/4 In. ............ 1500.00
Bronze, Carpeaux, Cupid Disarmed, Venus, C.1827, 30 1/2 In. ............ 3100.00
Bronze, Cecioni, Enfante En Coq, Signed Adriano Cecioni, 21 1/2 X 12 In. ............ 750.00
Bronze, Chiparus, Clown, Painted, Marble, 29 1/4 In. ............ *Illus* 1000.00
Bronze, Chiparus, Dancing Girl, Ivory, C.1925, 22 In.High ............ 2200.00
Bronze, Chiparus, Dancing Girl, Ivory, Marble Ball, 18 In. ............ 600.00
Bronze, Chiparus, The Starfish Lady, Gilt, Enamel, 14 In. ............ *Illus* 1650.00
Bronze, Chiparus, Young Boy & Accordion, Polychrome, Ivory, 9 In. ............ 350.00
Bronze, Cholovna, Cossack & Son On Horseback, 11 1/2 In.High ............ 750.00
Bronze, Christophe, Heron, Seated, Head Tucked Into Ruff, C.1890, 8 7/8 In. ............ 200.00
Bronze, Clesinger, Bull, 1869, 11 1/2 In High ............ 1200.00
Bronze, Clesinger, 2 Bulls Fighting, One Goring The Other, C.1890, 55 In. ............ 2800.00
Bronze, Coustou, Rearing Horse & Semidraped Male Figure At Side, 23 In. ............ 650.00
Bronze, Coustou, Rearing Horse & Seminude Male Holding Reins, 13 X 11 In. ............ 350.00
Bronze, Crouzat, Satyr & Squirrel, C.1920, 24 1/4 In. ............ 350.00
Bronze, D'Aste, Girl With Cabbages, Signed J.D'Aste, 11 1/2 X 6 In. ............ 350.00
Bronze, Dalou, Woman Reading, C.1880, 21 1/2 In.High ............ 1500.00
Bronze, Descomps, Bacchante & Infant, C.1900, 27 1/2 In.Long ............ 400.00
Bronze, Devrier, Dancing Girl, Nude, C.1920, 17 In. ............ 20.00
Bronze, DuBois, Masked Pirate Drawing His Sword, 24 In.High ............ 575.00
Bronze, Duret, Dancing Neapolitan Boy, C.1804, 17 1/4 In. ............ 400.00
Bronze, Falguiere, Diana, Gilt, C.1890, 18 3/8 In. ............ 325.00
Bronze, Falguiere, Nude Standing Girl, 15 1/8 In. ............ 250.00
Bronze, Fanny Marc, Adam & Eve Driven From Eden, Dated 1906, 9 In.High ............ 225.00
Bronze, Fiot, Seagull In Flight, Wave Shape Base, Susse Fres., Paris, C.1850 ............ 650.00
Bronze, Fratin, Bull, Striding Forward, C.1890, 8 1/2 In. ............ 300.00
Bronze, Fratin, Mare & Foal, C.1890, 16 1/4 In. ............ 950.00
Bronze, Fratin, Reclining & Dead Hare, C.1890, 5 1/2 In. ............ 160.00
Bronze, Frischmuth, Nude At Fountain, Signed Harriet Frischmuth, 20 In. ............ 1500.00
Bronze, Gaudez, Joan Of Arc Riding Horse, 15 In.High ............ 475.00
Bronze, Gerome, Equestrian Group Of Caesar, 17 In.Long ............ *Illus* 2100.00
Bronze, Granger, Dutch Maiden, Silvered, Ivory, 1877, 11 1/4 In. ............ 325.00
Bronze, Gratchev, Equestrian Group, Man In Sleigh, Horse, C.1890, 9 5/8 In. ............ 550.00
Bronze, Gratchev, Pointing Cossack With Rifle On Horseback, 9 In. High ............ 1300.00
Bronze, Harvey, Stag, Fourteen Point Antler, 1904, 16 3/4 In.High ............ 600.00
Bronze, Houdon, Bust Of Robert Fulton, 29 In. ............ 1000.00
Bronze, Houdon, Bust Of Young Woman, Ormolu Stand, C.1890, 9 1/2 In. ............ 200.00
Bronze, Hudelet, Nude Boy, Kneeling, Rolling Dice, C.1849, 5 3/4 In. ............ 150.00
Bronze, Hukia, Young Farmer Standing Barefooted, 15 In.High ............ 260.00
Bronze, Jacques, Hand Of Madame Delphine Say, 1885, 8 In.Long ............ 150.00
Bronze, Jennewein, Cupid On A Gazelle, C.1890, 27 In. High ............ 3150.00
Bronze, Jensen, Pheasant, 12 X 19 In. ............ 115.00
Bronze, Joire, German Shepherd, Attentive, C.1862, 11 3/8 In. ............ 350.00
Bronze, Kauba, Indian Chief On Horse, Scout Kneeling, 4 3/4 In.High ............ 925.00
Bronze, Keck, Gladiator & Spear, 13 In.High ............ 185.00
Bronze, Kley, Cupid Holding Urn, Pair ............ 345.00
Bronze, Koiselalckz, Worker With Tool Chest, Marble Base, 7 In.High ............ 150.00
Bronze, La Porte, Cavaliere, Signed Emile La Porte, 21 X 10 In. ............ 450.00
Bronze, Lanceray, Equestrian Group, Cossack Warrior & Horses, C.1890, 22 In. ............ 4250.00
Bronze, Lanceray, Equestrian Group, Tartar Man & Horses, C.1890, 17 X 25 In. ............ 3750.00
Bronze, Lassaunt, Soldier In Full Dress, Signed C.Anfrie, C.1850, 18 X 7 In. ............ 475.00
Bronze, Le Faguays, Diana, Tunic, C.1920, 26 1/2 In. ............ 275.00
Bronze, Le Verrier, Lamb, Signed, 2 X 2 In. ............ 50.00
Bronze, Lequesne, Pan Piping, Nude, Grape Leaves Garland, C.1815, 44 In. ............ 1150.00
Bronze, Levasseur, Young Girl, Standing, Marble Base, C.1853, 11 3/4 In. ............ 125.00
Bronze, Machoult Fils, Seated Woman Holding Child, 11 In.High ............ 210.00
Bronze, Marc, Adam & Eve Driven From Eden, 9 In.High ............ 200.00
Bronze, Marioton, Hermes & Formation Of Caduceus, Tiffany, C.1890, 32 In. ............ 375.00
Bronze, Marioton, Peasant Girl, Standing, Tambourine, C.1844, 17 3/4 In. ............ 250.00

| | |
|---|---:|
| Bronze, Martel, Pigeon, Stylized, 10 3/4 In.High | 1000.00 |
| Bronze, Masson, Lion, 9 In.Wide | 200.00 |
| Bronze, Melchiore, Baby With Peaked Cap, 6 In.High | 150.00 |
| Bronze, Mene, Cheval A La Barriere, C.1860, 10 5/8 In. | 500.00 |
| Bronze, Mene, Cheval A La Barriere, Spirited Stallion, C.1810, 16 5/8 In. | 900.00 |
| Bronze, Mene, Dog, Signed, C.1860 | 500.00 |
| Bronze, Mene, Fox, Standing, Alert, Among Leaves & Twigs, C.1810, 6 1/2 In. | 400.00 |
| Bronze, Mene, Goat, One Hoof Up, 5 In.Long | 150.00 |
| Bronze, Mene, Horse, Signed, Dated 1846, 16 In.Long | 875.00 |
| Bronze, Mene, Pheasant, Signed Verde, 7 1/2 In.Long | 245.00 |
| Bronze, Mene, Pheasant, 7 In.Long | 295.00 |
| Bronze, Mene, Rabbit, Signed, Miniature | 225.00 |
| Bronze, Mene, Stag Watching Doe, 7 1/2 In.Long | 375.00 |
| Bronze, Mene, Stallion Ibrahim, C.1810, 8 3/4 In. | 450.00 |
| Bronze, Mene, Two Deer, Signed, 5 In.Long | 425.00 |
| Bronze, Mene, Two Foxes Standing Over Their Kill, 10 In.Long | 1200.00 |
| Bronze, Mene, 2 Whippets At Play, Crouching & Standing, C.1810, 8 3/4 In. | 650.00 |
| Bronze, Mercie, David With Head Of Goliath, C.1845, 17 5/8 In. | 775.00 |
| Bronze, Mercie, David, Nude, Foot On Head Of Goliath, C.1890, 27 3/4 In. | 550.00 |
| Bronze, Meunier, Miner, Standing, Hard Hat, Pick, C.1831, 20 1/4 In. | 350.00 |
| Bronze, Minne, Bust Of Man, C.1890, 23 1/2 In. | 325.00 |
| Bronze, Moigniez, Bird Feeding Fledglings, C.1890, 22 1/8 In. | 750.00 |
| Bronze, Moigniez, Setter, Rabbit Hiding Under Leaves, 10 In. Long | 650.00 |
| Bronze, Moigniez, Setter, 14 3/4 In.Long | 350.00 |
| Bronze, Moingniez, Two Grouse, Eating Tall Stalk Of Wheat, Pecking, 9 In. | 600.00 |
| Bronze, Moreau, Allegorical Group, Le Char De L'aurore, C.1890, 33 1/2 In. | 1900.00 |
| Bronze, Moreau, Le Reveil, A Young Lady Figure, C.1890, 28 In. | 650.00 |
| Bronze, Morlon, Maiden & A Kid, Nude, Seated, C.1920, 31 3/8 In. | 250.00 |
| Bronze, Moselsio, Airedale, Dated 1928, 3 In. | 58.00 |
| Bronze, Nisini, Roma, Dancing Faun, Arms Extended, 19 In. High | 100.00 |
| Bronze, Oge, Full Female Figure, Signed Pierre Oge, 22 X 9 In. | 475.00 |
| Bronze, Ouilloncarrere, Circus Performer, Nude, C.1919, 18 1/2 In. | 275.00 |
| Bronze, Peyrol, Lion, Signed H.Peyrol, 12 In.Long | 225.00 |
| Bronze, Poertzel, Golfer, Silvered, Ivory, C.1876, 10 In. _Illus_ | 700.00 |
| Bronze, Pouret, Fleeing Woman, Signed, 19 X 7 In. | 325.00 |
| Bronze, Preiss, Champagne Lady, Ivory, C.1925, 16 1/4 In.High | 700.00 |
| Bronze, Preiss, Turbaned Dancing Woman, Polychromed, C.1883, 15 In. | 1500.00 |
| Bronze, Rieder, Dancer, Seminude, Black Marble Base, C.1910, 11 3/8 In.High | 150.00 |
| Bronze, Rudolph, Ballerina, Marble Base, 8 In. | 105.00 |
| Bronze, Salkowski, Goat, Marble Base, 5 In.High | 110.00 |
| Bronze, Schmidt-Hofer, Hunter & Hawk, C.1920, 15 In. | 120.00 |
| Bronze, Seifert, Icarus, Nude, Green & Black Marble Socle, C.1890, 13 In. | 100.00 |
| Bronze, Stammen, Nude Girl, Standing, C.1886, 24 In. | 150.00 |
| Bronze, Suriakov, Bust, Czar Nicholas I, 1855, 6 1/2 In. High | 250.00 |
| Bronze, Thomas, Lion, Signed P.Thomas, 14 X 8 X 4 In. | 475.00 |
| Bronze, Thomas, Lion, Signed P.Thomas, 15 1/2 X 4 In. | 550.00 |
| Bronze, Thomas, Stalking Lion, 14 1/2 X 8 1/2 X 4 In. | 595.00 |
| Bronze, Tourgueneff, Dog, 14 1/2 In.Long | 550.00 |
| Bronze, Valton, The Wounded Lioness, 11 In.Long | 325.00 |
| Bronze, Van Pelt, Salome, Signed Marse Van Pelt, 13 X 7 In. | 345.00 |
| Bronze, Verbanck, Walking Girl, Flowing Hair, C.1916, 19 In. | 250.00 |
| Bronze, Von Stuck, Equestrian Group Of Amazons, C.1897, 25 1/2 In.High | 1200.00 |
| Bronze, Vriens, Dancing Girl On Left Foot, C.1929, 16 3/4 In. | 175.00 |
| Bronze, Woertz, Nude Maiden Sitting On Rocks, Foot In Wave, C.1896, 14 In. | 200.00 |
| Bronze, Wolff, Equestrian Group, C.1890, 9 In. Long _Illus_ | 1000.00 |
| Bronze, Zack, Dancing Instructor, Young Girl, 16 1/4 In. | 200.00 |
| Bronze, Zristaboro, Boy Scout, Signed, 8 X 12 In. | 750.00 |
| Brownie, Book, Brownies & Other Stories, Palmer Cox | 13.00 |
| Brownie, Book, Brownies, Palmer Cox, 1st Edition | 35.00 |
| Brownie, Book, Fun For Tiny Tots, Palmer Cox | 11.00 |
| Brownie, Book, Funny Animals, Palmer Cox | 8.00 |
| Brownie, Book, Juvenile Budget, Palmer Cox | 8.00 |
| Brownie, Book, Mirth & Melody, Palmer Cox | 8.00 |
| Brownie, Book, Queer People With Wings & Stings, Palmer Cox, 1891 | 12.00 |
| Brownie, Booklet, Bee Soap, Palmer Cox | 10.00 |
| Brownie, Booklet, Rhyme & Reason, Palmer Cox, O.N.T. | 7.00 |

Bronze, Poertzel, Golfer,
Silvered, Ivory, C.1876, 10 In.
*(See Page 64)*

Bronze, Wolff, Equestrian Group,
C.1890, 9 In. Long
*(See Page 64)*

| | |
|---|---:|
| Brownie, Bowl, Palmer Cox, 6 In. | 10.00 |
| Brownie, Calendar, Signed Palmer Cox, 1898, Action Brownies, 2 Month | 22.50 |
| Brownie, Candlestick, Irishman, 7 1/2 In. | 55.00 |
| Brownie, Cup & Saucer, Child's, Brownies & Dog | 14.50 |
| Brownie, Cup, Signed Palmer Cox | 9.00 |
| Brownie, Dish, Cracker & Jelly, Glass, Gold Dancing Pixies, 2 Piece, 10 In. | 22.00 |
| Brownie, Figurine, Cast Metal Brownie, Brownie Baking Co., 5 In.High | 22.50 |
| Brownie, Handkerchief, Palmer Cox, 5 Brownies, Patent 1893 | 25.00 |
| Brownie, Jar, Powder, Covered, Palmer Cox, Hand-Painted Limoges Blank, 1894 | 48.00 |
| Brownie, Knife & Fork, Child's | 10.00 |
| Brownie, Music Sheet, Frisky Frolics, Palmer Cox, 11 X 14 In. | 13.00 |
| Brownie, Plate, Cake, Glass, Center Handle, Gold Dancing Pixies, 10 In. | 22.00 |
| Brownie, Plate, Palmer Cox, Scalloped, 6 In. | 22.00 |
| Brownie, Stickpin, Chinaman | 10.00 |
| Brownie, Tile, Tea, Palmer Cox, 6 1/4 In. | 24.00 |
| Buck Rogers, Glasses, Space, Official | 15.00 |

*Buffalo pottery was made in Buffalo, New York, after 1902. The company was established by the Larkin Company, famous manufacturers of soap. The wares are marked with a picture of a buffalo and the date of manufacture. Deldare ware is the most famous pottery made at the factory. It is a khaki-colored transfer-decorated ware.*

**Buffalo Pottery, see also Blue Willow**

| | |
|---|---:|
| Buffalo Pottery, Bowl, Child's, Feeding, Campbell Kids, Grace Drayton | 23.00 |
| Buffalo Pottery, Bowl, Vegetable, Covered, Round, White, Gold Band, 8 In. | 15.00 |
| Buffalo Pottery, Deldare, Bowl, Cereal, The Start, 6 In. | 75.00 |
| Buffalo Pottery, Deldare, Bowl, Cereal, Ye Olden Days, 6 In. | 75.00 |
| Buffalo Pottery, Deldare, Bowl, Dated 1908, 9 In. | 210.00 |
| Buffalo Pottery, Deldare, Bowl, Fruit, Fallowfield Hunt, The Death, 7 In. | 175.00 |
| Buffalo Pottery, Deldare, Bowl, Fruit, 9 Fruits | 200.00 |
| Buffalo Pottery, Deldare, Bowl, Salad, Village Life, Signed Newman, 8 In. | 235.00 |
| Buffalo Pottery, Deldare, Creamer, Village Life, Signed P.M. | 95.00 |
| Buffalo Pottery, Deldare, Cup & Saucer, Ye Olden Days, 1909 | 90.00 |
| Buffalo Pottery, Deldare, Cup, Olden Days | 90.00 |
| Buffalo Pottery, Deldare, Humidor, Sailor | 350.00 |
| Buffalo Pottery, Deldare, Mug, At Ye Lion Inn | 115.00 |
| Buffalo Pottery, Deldare, Mug, Fallowfield Hunt, 4 1/2 In. | 65.00 |
| Buffalo Pottery, Deldare, Mug, Inn, 4 1/4 In.High | 140.00 |
| Buffalo Pottery, Deldare, Mug, Ye Lion Inn, 3 In. | 125.00 |
| Buffalo Pottery, Deldare, Mug, 2 1/2 In.High | 175.00 |
| Buffalo Pottery, Deldare, Pitcher, Returned With A Curtsey, Octagonal | 100.00 |
| Buffalo Pottery, Deldare, Pitcher, Their Manner Of Telling Stories, 6 In. | 150.00 |
| Buffalo Pottery, Deldare, Pitcher, To Demand My Annual Rent, Octagonal | 290.00 |
| Buffalo Pottery, Deldare, Pitcher, To Demand My Annual Rent, 8 In. | 200.00 |
| Buffalo Pottery, Deldare, Pitcher, To Spare An Old Broken Soldier, 7 In. | 165.00 |
| Buffalo Pottery, Deldare, Pitcher, Water, Welcomed Me, Demand For Rent, 1908 | 175.00 |

Buffalo Pottery, Deldare, Pitcher, With A Cane Superior Air, 9 In. ...................... 225.00
Buffalo Pottery, Deldare, Pitcher, Ye Olden Times, Signed M.Vogt, 1908, 6 In. ........................ 225.00
Buffalo Pottery, Deldare, Plaque, At Ye Lion Inn, 12 In. ...................... 175.00
Buffalo Pottery, Deldare, Plate, At Ye Lion Inn, 6 1/4 In. ...................... 70.00
Buffalo Pottery, Deldare, Plate, Bread & Butter, 6 1/4 In. ...................... 72.50
Buffalo Pottery, Deldare, Plate, Breaking Cover, 7 1/4 In. ...................... 85.00
Buffalo Pottery, Deldare, Plate, Chop, Dr.Syntax Sells Grizzle, M.Gerhardt ...................... 540.00
Buffalo Pottery, Deldare, Plate, Dr.Syntax, Garden Trio, Emerald, 10 In. ...................... 375.00
Buffalo Pottery, Deldare, Plate, Evening At Ye Lion Inn, Pierced, 13 In. ...................... 185.00
Buffalo Pottery, Deldare, Plate, Fallowfield Hunt, The Death, 8 1/2 In. ...................... 150.00
Buffalo Pottery, Deldare, Plate, Village, 7 1/4 In. ...................... 70.00
Buffalo Pottery, Deldare, Plate, Ye Olden Times, 1909, 10 In. ...................... 100.00
Buffalo Pottery, Deldare, Plate, Ye Town Crier, 8 1/4 In. ...................... 75.00 To 90.00
Buffalo Pottery, Deldare, Saltshaker, Art Nouveau, Emerald, 3 In.High ...................... 150.00
Buffalo Pottery, Deldare, Sugar & Creamer, Cover, Ye Village Life ...................... 185.00
Buffalo Pottery, Deldare, Sugar, Covered, Village Life, Signed Stiller ...................... 100.00
Buffalo Pottery, Deldare, Teapot, Village Life ...................... 165.00
Buffalo Pottery, Deldare, Teapot, Village Life In Olden Days, Artist-Signed ...................... 175.00
Buffalo Pottery, Deldare, Tile, Tea, Traveling In Ye Olden Days, 6 In. ...................... 125.00
Buffalo Pottery, Deldare, Tray, Minuet ...................... 225.00
Buffalo Pottery, Deldare, Tray, Tea, Dr.Syntax, Rural Sports, Emerald, Foster ...................... 445.00
Buffalo Pottery, Dish, Feeding, Campbell Kids, Signed Drayton ...................... 15.00 To 35.00
Buffalo Pottery, Gravy Boat, White, Gold Band ...................... 10.00
Buffalo Pottery, Jug, Cinderella, 6 3/4 In.High ...................... 145.00
Buffalo Pottery, Jug, George Washington, 6 1/2 In. ...................... 150.00 To 175.00
Buffalo Pottery, Mug, Calumet Club, 1913 ...................... 55.00
Buffalo Pottery, Mug, Saturn Buffalo Club, 1914 ...................... 55.00
Buffalo Pottery, Pitcher, Cinderella ...................... 175.00
Buffalo Pottery, Pitcher, Deer Hunt, Dated 1906.6 1/2 In. ...................... 200.00
Buffalo Pottery, Pitcher, Dutch ...................... 150.00
Buffalo Pottery, Pitcher, George Washington, Bulbous ...................... 150.00 To 185.00
Buffalo Pottery, Pitcher, Geranium, Multicolor, Dated 1906, 5 In. High ...................... 75.00
Buffalo Pottery, Pitcher, Landing Of Roger Williams, Dated 1907 ...................... 180.00
Buffalo Pottery, Pitcher, Milk, Oriental Scene, Cobalt Spout, 1907 ...................... 25.00
Buffalo Pottery, Pitcher, Stag & Hounds ...................... 150.00
Buffalo Pottery, Pitcher, The Fox Hunt ...................... Illus 125.00

Buffalo Pottery, Pitcher, The Fox Hunt

Buffalo Pottery, Pitcher, Willow Oak, 7 In. ...................... 25.00
Buffalo Pottery, Plate, Child's, This Is The House That Jack Built ...................... 15.00
Buffalo Pottery, Plate, Christmas, 1952 ...................... 25.00
Buffalo Pottery, Plate, Christmas, 1953 ...................... 25.00
Buffalo Pottery, Plate, Christmas, 1956 ...................... 25.00
Buffalo Pottery, Plate, Christmas, 1958 ...................... 25.00
Buffalo Pottery, Plate, Christmas, 1959 ...................... 25.00
Buffalo Pottery, Plate, Colorado Ware, House In Autumn Landscape, 5 1/2 In. ...................... 6.65
Buffalo Pottery, Plate, Game, Deer Scene, 9 In. ...................... 20.00

| | |
|---|---|
| Buffalo Pottery, Plate, Game, Moose Scene, 9 In. | 20.00 |
| Buffalo Pottery, Plate, Jumping Fish On Green Border, Signed Beck, 9 In. | 18.00 |
| Buffalo Pottery, Plate, McKinley Monument, 7 In. | 50.00 |
| Buffalo Pottery, Plate, Mount Vernon, 10 In. | 22.50 |
| Buffalo Pottery, Plate, Souvenir, Mt.Vernon, Blue & White, 10 In.Diameter | 11.95 |
| Buffalo Pottery, Plate, The Gunner, 1907, 9 In. | 50.00 |
| Buffalo Pottery, Plate, U.S.Capitol, Green Blue, 10 In. | 22.00 |
| Buffalo Pottery, Plate, Wild Ducks, Scalloped Border, 9 In. | 35.00 |
| Buffalo Pottery, Platter, Buffalo Hunt, Oval | 135.00 |
| Buffalo Pottery, Platter, Game, Deer Scene, Round, 13 In. | 55.00 |
| Buffalo Pottery, Teapot, Tea Ball, Argyle, Dated 1914 | 36.00 |

*Burmese glass was developed by Frederick Shirley at the Mt.Washington
Glass Works in New Bedford, Massachusetts, in 1885. It is a two-tone
glass, shading from peach to yellow. Some have a pattern mold design. A few
Burmese pieces were decorated with pictures or applied glass flowers of
colored Burmese glass.*

| | |
|---|---|
| Burmese, Bowl & Underplate, Finger, Mt.Washington, Acid Finish | 300.00 |
| Burmese, Bowl, Finger, Diamond-Quilted, Turned-In Scalloped Top, 2 1/8 In. | 300.00 |
| Burmese, Bowl, Finger, Ruffled, Candy Ribbon Edge | 150.00 |
| Burmese, Creamer, Applied Handle, 3 1/2 In. | 225.00 |
| Burmese, Creamer, Applied Lemon Yellow Handle, Salmon To Deep Lemon Yellow | 495.00 |
| Burmese, Creamer, Mt.Washington, Applied Yellow Handle & Ruffled Rim | 450.00 |
| Burmese, Creamer, Mt.Washington, Tomato, Ribbed, Raised Yellow & White Mums | 220.00 |
| Burmese, Cruet, Maple Leaf, Fenton | 50.00 |
| Burmese, Cruet, Mt.Washington, Acid Finish | 500.00 |
| Burmese, Cruet, Mt Washington, Ribbed | 550.00 |
| Burmese, Cuspidor, Lady's, Decorated | 495.00 |
| Burmese, Dish, Sweetmeat, Pairpoint, Bryden | 60.00 |
| Burmese, Epergne, 3 Connecting Pieces, Ruffled Single Top, 10 1/2 In.High | 495.00 |
| Burmese, Jar, Cracker, Albertine Acorns & Leaves, Silver Lid, Bail, & Handle | 350.00 |
| Burmese, Lamp, Fairy | 450.00 |
| Burmese, Lamp, Fairy, Base Marked S.Clarke's Trade Fairy | 175.00 |
| Burmese, Lamp, Fairy, Clarke Base, 4 In.High | 225.00 |
| Burmese, Lamp, Fairy, Hat With Folded Up Brim Shape, Decorated | 1250.00 |
| Burmese, Lamp, Fairy, Pink To Yellow, Pattern Glass Base, C.1885, 10 In. High | 235.00 |
| Burmese, Lamp, Gilt Metal Base, Domical Shade, 2 Flower Holders, 24 In. | 600.00 |
| Burmese, Lamp, Oil, Queen's Design Umbrella Shade, Dark Base, Signed, 23 In. | 1995.00 |
| Burmese, Lamp, Oil, Shade, Decorated, Signed, 23 In. High | 1995.00 |
| Burmese, Muffineer, Egg Shape, Blue Enameled Floral | 175.00 To 185.00 |
| Burmese, Pitcher, Applied Shell-Like Amber Handle, Fluted Top, 6 In. High | 80.00 |
| Burmese, Pitcher, Hexagonal Top, Miniature, 3 In.High | 375.00 |
| Burmese, Pitcher, Water, Mt.Washington, Applied Yellow Handle, 2 Quart | 765.00 |
| Burmese, Pitcher, 3 Footed, Miniature, 3 In.High | 375.00 |
| Burmese, Plate, Mt.Washington, Enameled Chrysanthemums, 11 3/4 In. | 750.00 |
| Burmese, Rose Bowl, Acid Finish, Scalloped Rim Edged In Yellow, 2 1/2 In. | 265.00 |
| Burmese, Rose Bowl, Enamel Leaves, Miniature | 180.00 |
| Burmese, Rose Bowl, Mt.Washington, Hobnail, Applied Yellow Rigaree | 465.00 |
| Burmese, Rose Bowl, Refired To Yellow At Crimped Top, Enamel Leaves | 200.00 |
| Burmese, Salt & Pepper | 150.00 |
| Burmese, Sauce, Fancy Edge | 150.00 |
| Burmese, Shade, Mt.Washington, Umbrella, Gold Encrusted Yellow Sunflower | 325.00 |
| Burmese, Toothpick, Mt.Washington | 150.00 |
| Burmese, Toothpick, Mt.Washington, Tricorner, Venetian Diamond, 2 In. | 325.00 |
| Burmese, Toothpick, Tricorner | 225.00 |
| Burmese, Toothpick, Tricorner, Venetian Diamond, Shiny | 245.00 |
| Burmese, Toothpick, Tricornered, Diamond-Quilted, Glossy Finish, 2 In.High | 250.00 |
| Burmese, Toothpick, Tricornered, Hand-Decorated Florals, Satin Finish, 2 In. | 300.00 |
| Burmese, Tumbler, Diamond-Quilted, Glossy | 395.00 |
| Burmese, Tumbler, Juice, Footed, Decorated | 495.00 |
| Burmese, Tumbler, Mt.Washington | 225.00 |
| Burmese, Tumbler, Mt.Washington, Acid Finish, Salmon Pink | 185.00 |
| Burmese, Tumbler, Whiskey, Diamond-Quilted | 210.00 |
| Burmese, Tumbler, Whiskey, Mt.Washington, Diamond-Quilted, Raspberry Trim | 285.00 |
| Burmese, Vase, Bulbous, Square Top, Pink To Yellow, 3 In.High | 250.00 |
| Burmese, Vase, Diamond-Quilted, Pinched Neck, Ruffled Rim, C.1890, 6 In. | 125.00 |

| | |
|---|---:|
| Burmese, Vase, Enameled Glass, Frieze Of Blossoms, Blue & Brown, 12 1/2 In. | 150.00 |
| Burmese, Vase, Flared, Decorated, 3 In.High | 195.00 |
| Burmese, Vase, Gourd Shaped, Mt.Washington, 8 In.High | 310.00 |
| Burmese, Vase, Lily Shape, 6 1/2 In.High | 350.00 |
| Burmese, Vase, Lily, Acid Finish, 10 In. High | 300.00 |
| Burmese, Vase, Mt.Washington, Enameled Flowers, 3 In.High | 250.00 |
| Burmese, Vase, Mt.Washington, Glossy, Rigaree, 3 In.High | 200.00 |
| Burmese, Vase, Mt.Washington, Lily, 12 In. High | 150.00 |
| Burmese, Vase, Mt.Washington, Reheated Rim, Matte Finish, 7 3/4 In.High | 265.00 |
| Burmese, Vase, Mt.Washington, Square Neck, Enameled Flowers, 3 In.High | 250.00 |
| Burmese, Vase, Pink To Lemon, 2 Handled, 6 1/2 In.High | 475.00 |
| Burmese, Vase, Welsh Decorated, 5 Petal Top, 3 In. High | 395.00 |
| Burmese, Vase, 4 1/2 In.High | 160.00 |
| Burmese, Webb, see Webb Burmese | |
| Buster Brown, Book, Coloring | 5.50 |
| Buster Brown, Boot, Boy's, Paratrooper, C.1940, Size 6, Pair | 10.00 |
| Buster Brown, Cup, Tige Balancing Teapot On Nose, Buster & Girl | 15.00 |
| Buster Brown, Pencil, Buster & Tige, Metal | 8.00 |
| Buster Brown, Perfume, Frosted Glass, Buster In Black Hat, 3 1/2 In. | 12.00 |
| Buster Brown, Periscope | 6.00 |
| Buster Brown, Plate, Buster & Tige, Marked Austria | 22.00 |
| Buster Brown, Plate, Hot, Pouring Tea For Tige, 6 1/2 In. | 45.00 |
| Buster Brown, Plate, Serving Tea, Porcelain, R.S.Austria, 7 1/2 In. | 27.00 |
| Buster Brown, Plate, Tige Balancing Teapot On Nose, Buster & Girl, 6 In. | 15.00 |
| Buster Brown, Postcard, Buster & Tige | 5.00 |
| Buster Brown, Ring, Club, 1957 | .50 |
| Buster Brown, Tumbler, Tige Pulling At Buster's Stocking | 22.00 |
| Buster Brown, Whistle, Buster & Tige | 8.00 |
| Buster Brown, Yo-Yo | 14.00 |
| Buttermilk Glass, see Custard Glass | |

*Buttons have been known throughout the centuries, and there are millions of styles. Only a few of the most common types are listed for comparison.*

| | |
|---|---:|
| Button, Black Glass, Silver Luster, 10 | 3.50 |
| Button, Brass & Pewter, Bird, 1/2 In. | 3.00 |
| Button, Brass, Angel Carrying Flowers In Relief, 2 1/4 In. | 10.00 |
| Button, Brass, Art Nouveau Girl's Head, 4 Amber Brilliants On Rim | 10.00 |
| Button, Brass, Boy Scout, Set Of 2 | 2.50 |
| Button, Brass, Bridled Horse's Head In Relief, 1 5/8 In. | 10.00 |
| Button, Brass, Conductor, Set Of 6 | 5.00 |
| Button, Brass, Embossed Cranes, Reeds, & Lily Pads, 1 In., Set Of 5 | 12.50 |
| Button, Brass, Horses | 625.00 |
| Button, Brass, Pierrot & Pierrette, 11 1/2 In. | 3.00 |
| Button, Collar, National Guard, World War I, Round | 2.00 |
| Button, George Washington, Inaugural | 245.00 |
| Button, Gilt Color, Sailboat, 1/2 In., Set Of 6 | 10.00 |
| Button, Gilt, Spool Of Thread Shape | 19.00 |
| Button, Goldies, Black Glass, Small Size, 10 | 3.75 |
| Button, Ivory, Carved Animal, Sporting, 3/4 In., Set Of 6 | 50.00 |
| Button, Metal, Art Nouveau Edge, Cupid With Arrow, Black & Gold, 1 1/2 In. | 5.00 |
| Button, Metal, Girl With Bonnet | 4.00 |
| Button, Paperweight, Handblown | 3.00 |
| Button, Pewter, Marked US, War Of 1812 | 10.00 |
| Button, Satsuma, Flowered, 1 1/2 In. | 15.00 |
| Button, Satsuma, Flowered, 1 7/8 In. | 20.00 |
| Button, Satsuma, Houses & Trees, 1 In.Diameter | 4.00 |
| Button, Wedgwood, Jasperware, Center Perforation, C.1800, 1 In. | 30.00 |
| Button, Wedgwood, Jasperware, Daisy, Pair | 50.00 |
| Button, Wedgwood, Jasperware, No Perforation, C.1800, 1/2 In. | 15.00 |
| Button, Wedgwood, Jasperware, Single Center Perforation, C.1800, 1/2 In. | 15.00 |

Buttonhook, see Silver Plate, Buttonhook, Silver, Sterling,
Buttonhook, Store, Buttonhook
Calcite, see Steuben

*Calendar plates were very popular in the United States from 1906 to 1929. Since then plates have been made every year. A calendar, the name of a store, a picture of flowers, a girl, or a scene was featured on the plate.*

Calendar Plate, 1908, C.B.McMillan, Frankfort Springs, Pa., Cottage Scene ............... 25.00
Calendar Plate, 1908, Five Fruits, Merry Christmas In Gold, 9 1/4 In. ............... 19.50
Calendar Plate, 1908, Pink Roses & Portrait Of Lady, Embossed Rim, 9 In. ............... 25.00
Calendar Plate, 1909, Christmas, Iowa, Holly, Apples, & Nuts, 8 1/2 In. ............... 15.00
Calendar Plate, 1909, Melon & Chinquapins, Advertising, 9 1/4 In. ............... 22.00
Calendar Plate, 1909, Moths & 4 Seasons Scenes ............... 17.00
Calendar Plate, 1909, Mountain & Lake Scene, 8 In. ............... 18.00
Calendar Plate, 1909, Octagonal, Dutch Children On Bench, Dog, Flowers ............... 22.50
Calendar Plate, 1909, Red Rose, H.Wilson Maxwell, Mt.Union, Pa. ............... 25.00
Calendar Plate, 1909, Uneven Edge, Covered Bridge, Old Mill ............... 39.50
Calendar Plate, 1909, W.F.Youngblood, Toyah, Tex., Chinquapins & Melon ............... 22.00
Calendar Plate, 1909, Woman Driving Auto, Joseph Newchurch, La. ............... 28.00
Calendar Plate, 1910, Angel Center ............... 16.00
Calendar Plate, 1910, Betsy Ross Making Flag, Advertising, 9 1/2 In. ............... 28.00
Calendar Plate, 1910, Black & White Terrier, Begging ............... 16.00
Calendar Plate, 1910, Cherubs Ringing In New Year, Norwich, O. ............... 25.00
Calendar Plate, 1910, Christy Type Girl Center, Floral, Irregular Edge ............... 20.00
Calendar Plate, 1910, Dresden Art, Tin, Portrait Minerva ............... 26.00
Calendar Plate, 1910, Florals, Tulips, 9 In. ............... 27.50
Calendar Plate, 1910, Happy New Year, Cherubs ............... 10.00
Calendar Plate, 1910, Holly Berries, Dresden, 7 1/2 In. ............... 14.50
Calendar Plate, 1910, Horseshoe & Hunting Scene ............... 13.50
Calendar Plate, 1910, Niagara Falls ............... 15.00
Calendar Plate, 1910, The Big Cash Store, Watertown, Wis., Betsy Ross Scene ............... 28.00
Calendar Plate, 1910, Violets, 7 In. ............... 15.00
Calendar Plate, 1911-1912, Spangle, Washington, Farm Scene ............... 18.00
Calendar Plate, 1911, Ducks ............... 13.00
Calendar Plate, 1911, Gen.Furn.Co., Chicago, World Time On 21 Clocks ............... 25.00
Calendar Plate, 1911, Rabbits Center, Three Rivers, Michigan ............... 25.00
Calendar Plate, 1911, South Dakota, Hunter & Dog After Quail, 7 1/2 In. ............... 17.00
Calendar Plate, 1911, Vintage Auto With 2 Couples, 8 In. ............... 18.00
Calendar Plate, 1912, Clocks With Time Around The World, 10 In. ............... 18.00
Calendar Plate, 1912, Horseshoe Calendars, Floral, Lion, Gold, 7 1/4 In. ............... 15.00
Calendar Plate, 1913, Old Fashioned Airplane, Cobalt & Gold Border ............... 20.00
Calendar Plate, 1913, Silverton, Oregon, Horseshoe & Spring Scene ............... 15.00
Calendar Plate, 1914, Betsy Ross Making The 1st Flag, 8 1/4 In. ............... 19.50
Calendar Plate, 1914, II.Boducker, Havana, III., Pink Roses In Basket ............... 22.50
Calendar Plate, 1915, Black Boy Eating Watermelon, 8 1/2 In. ............... 35.00
Calendar Plate, 1917, Bluebird In Flight
Calendar Plate, 1917, War Scene, Aircraft & Battleships, 9 1/2 In. ............... 30.00
Calendar Plate, 1920, Allied Flags, Dove Of Peace, Victory ............... 16.00
Calendar Plate, 1920, The Great World War, 7 1/4 In. ............... 25.00
Calendar Plate, 1921, Peace Center, 8 In. ............... 30.00
Calendar Plate, 1931, Blue Pastoral Scene With Cows ............... 32.00
Calendar Plate, 1953, Ben Gordon, Jewelery, Homer Laughlin ............... 3.00
Calendar Plate, 1957, Gold Scroll & Calendar ............... 6.00
Calendar Plate, 1959, Young & Rubicam, 4 In. ............... 2.50
Calendar Plate, 1960, Gold Scroll & Calendar ............... 5.50
Calendar Plate, 1961, Gold Scroll & Calendar ............... 5.00
Calendar Plate, 1962, Zodiac, "God Bless This House, " 9 In. ............... 10.00
Calendar Plate, 1963, Gold Scroll & Calendar ............... 5.00
Calendar Plate, 1965, Gold Scroll & Calendar ............... 5.00
Calendar Plate, 1965, Green Calendar & Scenes ............... 6.00
Calendar Plate, 1965, Maroon Calendar & Scenes ............... 6.00
Calendar Plate, 1966, American Eagle & U.S.A.In Gold On White, 10 1/4 In. ............... 3.00
Calendar Plate, 1967, Gold Scrolls ............... 5.00
Calendar Plate, 1972, Currier & Ives Scenes, Calendar & Zodiac In Brown ............... 5.00
Calendar Tile, 1898, King's Chapel Boston, Hanging, Wedgwood ............... 40.00
California Art Company, Tile, Embossed Pictorial Design, 3 5/8 In.Square ............... 10.00

*Cambridge art pottery was made in Cambridge, Ohio, from about 1895 until World War I. The factory made brown glazed decorated wares marked with a variety of marks including an acorn, the name Cambridge, the name Oakwood, or the name Terrhea.*

CAMBRIDGE

**Cambridge Pottery, Cup,** Custard, Guernsey Ware ............... 10.00

Cambridge Pottery, Ewer, Formed Like Candleholder, High Brown Glaze, Floral ......................... 67.00
Cambridge Pottery, Vase, Floral Decoration, Squat Shape ............................................. 125.00
Cambridge Pottery, Vase, Terrhea, 10 In.High .................................................... 210.00
Cambridge Tile Company, Tile, Floral Decoration, 6 In.Square, Signed ......................... 12.00

 *The Cambridge Glass Company made pressed glass in Cambridge, Ohio. It was marked with a C in a triangle about 1902. The words "near-cut" were used after 1906.*

Cambridge, Ashtray, Amber, Marked, 2 1/2 In. ................................................... 3.00
Cambridge, Ashtray, Four Lips, Crown Tuscan, 7 In.Diameter ................................ 12.00
Cambridge, Basket, Crown Tuscan, 2 Handled, Gold Trim, 5 In. ............................. 25.00
Cambridge, Basket, Teardrop, Fluted Rim, Cobalt Handle, 10 X 10 In. .................... 30.00
Cambridge, Basket, 2 Handled, Crown Tuscan, 3 In.High .................................... 20.00
Cambridge, Bonbon, Rosepoint, 2 Handled, 8 1/2 In. ....................................... 18.00
Cambridge, Bottle, Apple Green, Figural, Dog, 7 3/4 In. .................................... 37.50
Cambridge, Bouillon Set, Amber, Marked, 12 Piece ........................................ 33.00
Cambridge, Bowl, Amethyst, Square, 6 In. ................................................... 9.00
Cambridge, Bowl, Azurite, 6 In.Diameter ..................................................... 12.00
Cambridge, Bowl, Blue, Caprice, Shallow, 13 1/2 In. ....................................... 18.00
Cambridge, Bowl, Caprice, Oblong, Footed, 12 In. .......................................... 6.00
Cambridge, Bowl, Center, Amberina, Flaring, Signed C In Triangle, 9 In. .................. 150.00
Cambridge, Bowl, Center, Petal Edge, Footed, Crown Tuscan, 12 In.Wide .................. 80.00
Cambridge, Bowl, Centerpiece, Bashful Maiden, 2 Frogs, 8 1/2 In.High ................... 38.00
Cambridge, Bowl, Centerpiece, Ruffled Edge, Beaded Feet, Signed, 11 In. ................ 18.00
Cambridge, Bowl, Cobalt, 2 Handled Cutout Farber Holder, 4 3/4 In. ..................... 22.00
Cambridge, Bowl, Console, Caprice, Moonlight, 12 1/2 In.Diameter ....................... 18.00
Cambridge, Bowl, Console, Flying Nude Lady, Crown Tuscan ............................... 110.00
Cambridge, Bowl, Crimped, 4 Toed, Crown Tuscan, 8 In. .................................. 55.00
Cambridge, Bowl, Crystal, Canterbury, 9 In. ................................................ 7.00
Cambridge, Bowl, Crystal, Ram's Head, Etched, Gold Encrusted, 12 In. .................... 100.00
Cambridge, Bowl, Fruit, Flying Nude, Enameled Roses & Gold, Crown Tuscan .............. 185.00
Cambridge, Bowl, Fruit, Shell Shape, Scalloped, Footed, Clear ............................ 35.00
Cambridge, Bowl, Hand-Painted Roses, Gold Trim, 3 Toed, Crown Tuscan, 11 In. ......... 65.00
Cambridge, Bowl, Ivy, Amethyst, Clear Stem & Base, 8 3/4 In.High ....................... 38.00
Cambridge, Bowl, Opaque, Jade, Stand, 6 1/2 In. .......................................... 20.00
Cambridge, Bowl, Paneled Oak, Crown Tuscan, 7 3/4 In. .................................. 12.50
Cambridge, Bowl, Pink, Tricornered Hat, Footed, Signed, 10 In. Diameter ................. 15.00
Cambridge, Bowl, Rosepoint, 2 Handled, Footed, 8 In. ..................................... 9.00
Cambridge, Bowl, Shell, Oval, 4 Footed, Crown Tuscan, 6 In.Long ........................ 48.00
Cambridge, Bowl, Square, 4 Footed, Crown Tuscan, 12 In. ................................ 40.00
Cambridge, Box, Candy, Covered, Seashell, Footed, Crown Tuscan ....................... 27.50
Cambridge, Box, Candy, Crown Tuscan ..................................................... 25.00
Cambridge, Box, Cigarette, Caprice ......................................................... 20.00
Cambridge, Box, Vanity, Covered, Amber, 9 In.Long ...................................... 19.50
Cambridge, Bucket, Ice, Carmen Red, Heirloom ........................................... 27.00
Cambridge, Bucket, Ice, Green, Tulips, Signed ............................................. 23.00
Cambridge, Bucket, Ice, Peachblow Color, Paneled, Metal Handle, Marked C .............. 13.50
Cambridge, Butter Pat, Pink, Rose Decoration, Footed, Crown Tuscan ................... 14.00
Cambridge, Candleholder, Crystal, Calla Lily ............................................... 10.00
Cambridge, Candleholder, Engraved Radiant Rose, 4 In. High, Pair ....................... 12.00
Cambridge, Candleholder, Green, Calla Lily, 6 1/2 In. High, Pair .......................... 32.00
Cambridge, Candleholder, Moonlight Blue, Star, 4 In., Pair ................................ 8.00
Cambridge, Candleholder, Moonlight, Double, Pair ........................................ 25.00
Cambridge, Candlestick, Alpine, Caprice .................................................... 9.00
Cambridge, Candlestick, Apple Green, Dolphin, 9 1/2 In., Pair ............................ 75.00
Cambridge, Candlestick, Cathay Lady Figure, Virginia B.Evans, 9 In. ..................... 60.00
Cambridge, Candlestick, Crystal, Dolphin, 2-Light, Pair .................................... 25.00
Cambridge, Candlestick, Dolphin, 9 1/2 In. ................................................ 30.00
Cambridge, Candlestick, Elaine, 2 Hole ..................................................... 28.00
Cambridge, Candlestick, Experimental, Tomato, 9 In.High, Pair ........................... 150.00
Cambridge, Candlestick, Green, Calla Lily, Pair ............................................ 30.00
Cambridge, Candlestick, Helio, Doric ....................................................... 45.00
Cambridge, Candlestick, Wildflower, Pair ................................................... 30.00
Cambridge, Celery, Crystal, Etched, Oval, Signed, 9 1/2 In. ............................... 5.75
Cambridge, Celery, Vaseline, Flat, Signed .................................................. 10.00
Cambridge, Champagne, Rosepoint .......................................................... 10.00

| | |
|---|---:|
| Cambridge, Cocktail Glass, Black, Nude Lady, Clear Foot & Bowl, 6 1/2 In. | 20.00 |
| Cambridge, Cocktail Set, Crystal, Mt.Vernon, 8 Piece | 65.00 |
| Cambridge, Cocktail Set, Tulip Shape Cocktails, Amber Lined, Farber, 8 Piece | 57.00 |
| Cambridge, Cologne, Carnival Glass, Dark | 225.00 |
| Cambridge, Compote, Amber Bowl, Metal Stem & Base, 5 1/2 In.Diameter | 20.00 |
| Cambridge, Compote, Amber, 10 Sided, Footed, 2 In.High | 10.00 |
| Cambridge, Compote, Amethyst, Nude, Farber, 8 In. | 40.00 |
| Cambridge, Compote, Jade, Signed, 8 In.High | 55.00 |
| Cambridge, Compote, Jade, Tall Stem, 12 In.Diameter | 65.00 |
| Cambridge, Compote, Nude Lady, Dark Blue Top, Clear Nude, 8 In. | 55.00 |
| Cambridge, Compote, Shell, Crown Tuscan | 45.00 To 60.00 |
| Cambridge, Compote, Tomato, 4 In.High | 22.00 |
| Cambridge, Console Set, Ebony, Ram's Head Bowl, Doric Candlesticks, 3 Piece | 225.00 |
| Cambridge, Console Set, Green, Etched Peacocks, 3 Piece | 45.00 |
| Cambridge, Console Set, Heliotrope, Ram's Head, Doric Candlesticks, 3 Piece | 365.00 |
| Cambridge, Console Set, Jade, Ram's Head | 345.00 |
| Cambridge, Console Set, Jade, 3 Piece | 85.00 |
| Cambridge, Console Set, Rubina, 8 In. Candlesticks | 215.00 |
| Cambridge, Console Set, Tomato Glass, 10 In.Bowl, 3 Piece | 165.00 |
| Cambridge, Cornucopia, Shell Foot, Crown Tuscan, 9 3/4 In., Pair | 95.00 |
| Cambridge, Creamer, Blue, Miniature | 8.00 |
| Cambridge, Creamer, Chantilly, Sterling Foot | 15.00 |
| Cambridge, Creamer, Child's, Dark Blue, Colonial | 12.50 |
| Cambridge, Cup & Saucer, Blue, Caprice | 6.50 To 7.00 |
| Cambridge, Cup & Saucer, Coffee, Cobalt, Ruby, Black, & Purple, Set Of 4 | 25.00 |
| Cambridge, Cup & Saucer, Green, Paneled | 5.00 |
| Cambridge, Cup, Apple Green, Carmen | 3.00 |
| Cambridge, Cup, Apple Green, Decagon | 3.00 |
| Cambridge, Cup, Punch, Swan, Crystal | 16.00 |
| Cambridge, Decanter, Cordial, Amethyst, Footed, Farber Bros. Lacy Holder | 35.00 |
| Cambridge, Decanter, Nautilus | 21.00 |
| Cambridge, Dish, Candy, Chicken Cover, Clear, 5 1/2 In.High | 28.50 |
| Cambridge, Dish, Candy, Covered, Crystal Blue, Caprice, Pearl Glaze | 35.00 |
| Cambridge, Dish, Candy, Purple Roses Top, Gold On Base, Crown Tuscan | 50.00 |
| Cambridge, Dish, Candy, Turkey Cover, Clear, 7 In.High | 30.00 |
| Cambridge, Dish, Candy, 3 Compartments, Crown Tuscan | 50.00 |
| Cambridge, Dish, Cobalt Blue, Divided, Scalloped Edge, Oblong | 45.00 |
| Cambridge, Dish, Nut, Green, 4 Footed | 14.00 |
| Cambridge, Dish, Seafood, Crown Tuscan | 31.00 |
| Cambridge, Dish, Swan, Pink & Frosted, Crooked Neck, 7 In. | 22.50 |
| Cambridge, Figurine, Bear | 6.00 |
| Cambridge, Figurine, Pouter Pigeon, Crystal | 13.00 |
| Cambridge, Figurine, Sea Gull | 26.00 |
| Cambridge, Figurine, Swan, Clear, Marked, 4 1/2 In. | 20.00 |
| Cambridge, Flower Holder, Figure, Gold, 9 In. | 22.00 |
| Cambridge, Flower Holder, Crystal, Nude With Long Hair & Scarf, 11 In. | 25.00 |
| Cambridge, Flower Holder, Crystal, Sea Gull, 11 In. | 15.00 To 25.00 |
| Cambridge, Flower Holder, Light Green, Girl Figure, 8 1/2 In. | 25.00 |
| Cambridge, Flower Holder, Pink, Girl Figure, 8 1/2 In. | 25.00 |
| Cambridge, Flower Holder, Seashell, Hand Decorated Roses, Crown Tuscan | 85.00 |
| Cambridge, Goblet, Chantilly, 6 1/2 In. | 12.00 |
| Cambridge, Goblet, Clear Cup, Black Square Base & Stem | 13.50 |
| Cambridge, Goblet, Cocktail, Black Nude Stem | 25.00 |
| Cambridge, Goblet, Corinth | 6.00 |
| Cambridge, Goblet, Crystal Line 3121, Rosepoint, 12 Ozs. | 1.50 |
| Cambridge, Goblet, Etched Elk, Dog, & Trees On King's Crown Bands | 65.00 |
| Cambridge, Goblet, Rosepoint Stem, 12 Oz. | 10.00 |
| Cambridge, Ivy Ball, Amethyst, Melon Ribbed, Clear Ring Stem, 8 1/2 In. | 32.50 |
| Cambridge, Ivy Ball, Amethyst, Ribbed Optic Crystal Foot, 8 1/2 In. | 17.00 |
| Cambridge, Ivy Ball, Cobalt, Crystal Foot, 6 In. | 18.00 |
| Cambridge, Ivy Ball, Crown Tuscan | 60.00 |
| Cambridge, Ivy Ball, Green, Honeycomb, Knob Stem | 18.00 |
| Cambridge, Ivy Ball, Nude Lady, Crown Tuscan, 9 1/2 In. | 150.00 |
| Cambridge, Jar, Candy, Covered, Jade | 55.00 |
| Cambridge, Jar, Marmalade, Covered, Royal Blue, Farber Holder | 12.50 |
| Cambridge, Jug, Water, Emerald Green, Crystal Handle, Ball Shape, 80 Ozs. | 22.50 |

Cambridge, Mug, Rounded Panels, 15 Point Star Base, Marked, 3 1/2 In. ...................................... 10.00
Cambridge, Pencil Holder, Amethyst, Dog, Crown Tuscan ...................................... 15.00
Cambridge, Pitcher, Milk, Prize, Signed ...................................... 15.00
Cambridge, Pitcher, Water, Crystal, Tally-Ho, C In Triangle, 1/2 Gallon ...................................... 18.50
Cambridge, Plate, Apple Green, Carmen, 6 1/4 In. ...................................... 1.50
Cambridge, Plate, Apple Green, Carmen, 7 In. ...................................... 1.75
Cambridge, Plate, Apple Green, Carmen, 8 In. ...................................... 2.00
Cambridge, Plate, Apple Green, Decagon, 8 In. ...................................... 2.50
Cambridge, Plate, Cake, Cleo, Ring Handle ...................................... 9.00
Cambridge, Plate, Carmen, Ground Bottom, 8 In. ...................................... 7.00
Cambridge, Plate, Crystal, Caprice, 6 1/4 In. ...................................... 2.75
Cambridge, Plate, Dinner, Green, Scalloped Amethyst Edge, 10 1/2 In. ...................................... 8.00
Cambridge, Plate, Light Blue, Decagon, 8 In. ...................................... 3.00
Cambridge, Plate, Pink, Square, 8 1/4 In. ...................................... 6.00
Cambridge, Plate, Seashell, Crown Tuscan, 5 In. ...................................... 27.50
Cambridge, Plate, Seashell, Decorated, Crown Tuscan, 7 In. ...................................... 35.00
Cambridge, Plate, Serving, Azurite, Gold Encrusted Band, Center Handle ...................................... 36.00
Cambridge, Relish, Covered, Divided, Crown Tuscan ...................................... 67.50
Cambridge, Relish, Covered, Rose Point, Gold Encrusted, 3 Compartments ...................................... 48.00
Cambridge, Relish, Emerald Green, 3 Handled, 3 Sections, Signed ...................................... 12.00
Cambridge, Relish, Romance, Flanged Rim, 8 1/4 X 4 5/8 In. ...................................... 15.00
Cambridge, Salt & Pepper, Amber, Farber ...................................... 10.00
Cambridge, Salt & Pepper, Amethyst, Farber Holders, Jug Type, Pair ...................................... 15.00
Cambridge, Salt & Pepper, Cobalt, Farber ...................................... 7.95
Cambridge, Salt, Crystal, Swan, Signed ...................................... 10.00
Cambridge, Salt, Master, Green, Swan ...................................... 12.00
Cambridge, Salt, Pale Green, Swan, Signed, 3 1/2 In. Long ...................................... 12.00
Cambridge, Salt, Square, Sterling Spoon, Crown Tuscan ...................................... 20.00
Cambridge, Sauce, Inverted Thistle, Near Cut, Signed ...................................... 15.00
Cambridge, Saucer, Apple Green, Carmen ...................................... 1.50
Cambridge, Saucer, Apple Green, Decagon ...................................... 1.75
Cambridge, Saucer, Pistachio, Acid Finish, 6 1/4 In. ...................................... 7.00
Cambridge, Shell, Rose In Center, Gold Flecks, 3 Footed, Crown Tuscan ...................................... 20.00
Cambridge, Shell, Shell Finial, Pedestal, Gold Trim, Crown Tuscan, 6 In. ...................................... 75.00
Cambridge, Sherbet, Chantilly, 5 In. ...................................... 12.00
Cambridge, Sherbet, Chantilly, 6 In. ...................................... 12.00
Cambridge, Sherbet, Crystal Line 3121, Rose Point ...................................... 1.95
Cambridge, Sherbet, Dolphin Stem, Crown Tuscan ...................................... 38.00
Cambridge, Shoe, Lady's, Blue, Kitten Peeking Over Edge ...................................... 28.00
Cambridge, Smoking Set, Caprice, Footed Dolphins, Crown Tuscan, 5 Piece ...................................... 58.00
Cambridge, Smoking Set, Crystal, Seashell Box, Dolphin Feet, 5 Piece ...................................... 15.00
Cambridge, Spooner, Child's, Dark Blue, Colonial ...................................... 11.50
Cambridge, Sugar & Creamer, Blue, Caprice ...................................... 12.00
Cambridge, Sugar & Creamer, Cover, Emerald, Farber Bros. Chrome Holder, Tray ...................................... 28.00
Cambridge, Sugar & Creamer, Green, Signed ...................................... 18.00
Cambridge, Swan, Crown Tuscan, 3 1/2 In. ...................................... 22.50
Cambridge, Swan, Ebony, Signed ...................................... 55.00
Cambridge, Swan, Green, Marked, 3 In.Long ...................................... 18.00
Cambridge, Swan, Green, Signed, 3 1/2 In. ...................................... 20.00
Cambridge, Swan, Pink, Signed, 5 In. ...................................... 24.50
Cambridge, Swan, Pink, Signed, 7 In. ...................................... 30.00
Cambridge, Swan, Signed, 7 In. ...................................... 28.50
Cambridge, Swan, Sterling Over Glass, Crown Tuscan ...................................... 50.00
Cambridge, Swan, 10 1/2 In. ...................................... 38.50
Cambridge, Tray, Sandwich, Rose Point, Handled ...................................... 28.00
Cambridge, Tray, Torte, Blue, Caprice, Footed, 13 3/4 In. ...................................... 15.00
Cambridge, Tumbler, Amber, Georgian, 9 In. ...................................... 10.00
Cambridge, Tumbler, Etched Wide Optic Top, Cobalt Foot, 4 In. ...................................... 9.00
Cambridge, Tumbler, Etched Wide Optic Top, Cobalt Foot, 5 In. ...................................... 12.00
Cambridge, Tumbler, Inverted Thistle, Marked Near Cut ...................................... 10.00
Cambridge, Vase, Amethyst, Clear Openwork Foot, Flared Top, 10 In., Pair ...................................... 35.00
Cambridge, Vase, Bud, Cobalt Blue, Clear Foot, 8 In. ...................................... 7.00
Cambridge, Vase, Carmen Red, Footed, 11 In. ...................................... 35.00
Cambridge, Vase, Crystal, Cascade, Paper Label, 9 In. ...................................... 15.00
Cambridge, Vase, Helio, Gold Trim, 10 1/4 In.High ...................................... 25.00
Cambridge, Vase, Ivory, 5 1/2 In.High ...................................... 22.00

Cambridge, Vase, Ivy, Clear Lady Base, Amber Bowl, 10 In.High ............................................ 25.00
Cambridge, Vase, Primrose, Bulbous, 6 In. ............................................................................... 27.50
Cambridge, Vase, Ring Stem, Crown Tuscan, 12 In. ............................................................... 48.00
Cambridge, Vase, Tomato, 10 In. High .................................................................................... 85.00
Cambridge, Wine, Caprice .......................................................................................................... 5.00
Cambridge, Wine, Cobalt Top, Stemmed ................................................................................ 25.00
Cambridge, Wine, Lynnbrook ..................................................................................................... 4.25
Cambridge, Wine, Nude ............................................................................................................ 15.00
Cambridge, Wine, Pink, Gold Bands, Set Of 6 ....................................................................... 18.50

*Cameo glass was made in layers in much the same manner as a cameo in jewelry.*
*Part of the top layer of glass was cut away to reveal a different colored*
*glass beneath. The most famous cameo glass was made during the nineteenth*
*century.*

Cameo, see also De Vez, Daum Nancy, Galle, Le Verre Francais,
Richard, Webb
Cameo, Bowl, Amethyst, Acid Cut Back Flowers & Leaves, 7 1/2 In.High ....................... 1200.00
Cameo, Box, Crab On Cover, Rust, White, & Brown, Signed Nancy ..................................... 280.00
Cameo, Box, Jewel, Round, Acid Cut Back, Gold, Enameled Flowers ................................... 40.00
Cameo, Cologne, Blue To White To Clear, Silver Fittings, 4 3/4 In. ...................................... 40.00
Cameo, Cuspidor, Lady's, English, Band Of Carved Pink Floral On White .......................... 550.00
Cameo, Dish, Sweetmeat, Covered, English, Blue, Cut Flowers .......................................... 950.00
Cameo, Goblet, White To Clear, 5 In., Pair .............................................................................. 50.00
Cameo, Jar, Cracker, Florentine, Gold Plated Lid, White Enamel On Red .......................... 165.00
Cameo, Liqueur, Burnt Orange On Frosted, Crystal Stem, Vessiere, Nancy ...................... 125.00
Cameo, Liqueur, Green On Frosted, Crystal Stem, Vessiere, Nancy .................................... 125.00
Cameo, Perfume, English, White, Pink, & White ................................................................... 400.00
Cameo, Pitcher, Acid Finish, Dark Fall Colors, Signed G.De Feure, 7 In.High ................... 350.00
Cameo, Rose Bowl, Chipped Ice Ground, Enamel, Gilt Violets, St.Denis, 4 In. ................. 165.00
Cameo, Rose Bowl, English, White Ground, Three Color Layers, 3 In.Wide ...................... 595.00
Cameo, Salt, English, Pond Lilies On Citron ........................................................................... 325.00
Cameo, Tumbler, Florentine, White Enamel On Red .............................................................. 85.00
Cameo, Vase, Acid Cut Back Black Floral Sprays On White, 9 1/2 In.High ........................ 875.00
Cameo, Vase, Acid Cut Back Green Flying Horses On Black, 10 1/2 In.High .................... 3800.00
Cameo, Vase, Amethyst Vines & Tendrils, Belgian, 4 1/2 X 7 1/4 In. ................................... 80.00
Cameo, Vase, Bar, Baluster, Yellow & Brown On Pink & Yellow, 1900s, 4 1/2 In. .......... 125.00
Cameo, Vase, Blueberries On Lemon, Signed Crois Mare, 14 In.High ................................. 145.00
Cameo, Vase, Bud, Brown Floral Cut To Orange, Signed BR, 4 1/2 In.High ...................... 105.00
Cameo, Vase, Burgun & Schverer, Marquetry De Verre, Blossoms, C.1895, 9 In. ......... 1300.00
Cameo, Vase, Casale, Orange & Brown Flowers & Vine On Frosted, 12 In. ...................... 300.00
Cameo, Vase, Dark Blue Berries On Lemon, Signed Crois Mare, 14 In.High ..................... 185.00
Cameo, Vase, English, Blue, Heavy Cut, 5 In.High ................................................................ 750.00
Cameo, Vase, English, Butterfly & Trailing Leaves On Deep Pink, 11 1/2 In. ................. 1195.00
Cameo, Vase, English, Cobalt & White Grapes On Vine, 3 Layers, 13 In.High ................. 875.00
Cameo, Vase, English, Floral Spray & Butterfly On Rose Color, 10 In.High ...................... 795.00
Cameo, Vase, Gold Color, Enamel Foliage & Birds, Signed Lune, 7 1/2 In. ........................ 95.00
Cameo, Vase, Grecian Figures, Deep Amethyst, Signed G.De Feure, 5 1/2 In. .................. 97.50
Cameo, Vase, Pink Acid Cut Back, Bulbous, Iridescent, Ground Pontil, 8 In. ................... 100.00
    Cameo, Webb, see Webb
    Campaign, see Political Campaign
Campbell Kids, Spoon, Figural, Boy ........................................................................................... 3.25
Campbell Kids, Spoon, Figural, Girl ........................................................................................... 3.25
Campbell Soup Kids, Spoon & Fork, Child's, Engraved, Wm.Rogers Silver Plate ............. 12.00

*Camphor glass is a cloudy white glass that has been blown or pressed. It*
*was made by many factories in the Midwest during the mid-nineteenth century.*

Camphor Glass, Ale Glass .......................................................................................................... 5.00
Camphor Glass, Basket, Basket Weave, 2 Compartments .................................................... 15.00
Camphor Glass, Bowl, Footed, Green & White Enameling, 7 3/4 In. ................................... 10.00
Camphor Glass, Bowl, Melon Ribbed, Sterling Fruit Inside, 9 1/2 In.Diameter ................. 40.00
Camphor Glass, Box, Covered, Elephants, Elephant Finial, 5 In.Diameter ......................... 12.50
Camphor Glass, Box, Covered, Heart Shape, 6 1/2 In. .......................................................... 22.50
Camphor Glass, Box, Powder, Figural, Woman On Cover, Pink ............................................ 18.00
Camphor Glass, Compote, Green, Enameled Design, 7 In. .................................................... 15.00
Camphor Glass, Dish, Elephant Cover, Green, 6 1/2 In. ........................................................ 35.00
Camphor Glass, Dish, Hen Cover, Nest Base, 7 In. ............................................................... 55.00

Candelabra, Ormolu, C.1825,
20 1/4 In.High, Pair

Candlestick, Bell Metal, C.1650, 5 1/2 In., Pair

| | |
|---|---|
| Camphor Glass, Epergne, White | 75.00 |
| Camphor Glass, Jar, Covered, Grapes & Leaves, Standard, 6 In. | 11.00 |
| Camphor Glass, Knife Rest, Frosted Duck | 20.00 |
| Camphor Glass, Knife Rest, Satin Baby's Head Each End | 20.00 |
| Camphor Glass, Muffineer, Bulbous, Clear Etched & Engraved Floral, White | 48.00 |
| Camphor Glass, Muffineer, Satin Finish, Etched & Engraved, Clear Floral | 48.00 |
| Camphor Glass, Perfume, Bulbous, Hand-Painted Pansies & Dragonfly, White | 35.00 |
| Camphor Glass, Salt, Master, Duck, Blue | 22.00 |
| Camphor Glass, Salt, Swan, Pastel Blue Green, 2 1/2 In. Long | 25.00 |
| Camphor Glass, Sherbet, Iris & Herringbone | 5.00 |
| Camphor Glass, Slipper, Cuban Heel, 5 X 1 1/2 In. | 15.00 |
| Camphor Glass, Tray, Shell Pattern, 8 X 6 In. | 8.00 |
| Camphor Glass, Vase, Flowers, Leaves, Butterfly, Enamel Flowers, 10 In.High | 40.00 |
| Camphor Glass, Water Set, Tumble-Up & Jar, Hand-Painted Decoration, 2 Piece | 12.00 |
| Canary Glass, see Vaseline Glass | |
| Candelabra, Bronze, 3-Light, Floriform Sockets, 13 In.High, C.1850, Pair | 50.00 |
| Candelabra, Charles X Style, Ormolu & Bronze, Female, 4-Arm, 28 1/2 In., Pair | 500.00 |
| Candelabra, Cut Glass, Regency Style, Three Arms, 25 In.High, Pair | 275.00 |
| Candelabra, Empire Style, Bronze & Gilt Metal, 6-Arm, C.1890, 26 In., Pair | 400.00 |
| Candelabra, Louis XV Style, Cut Glass & Gilt Metal, 5-Arm, C.1890, Pair | 175.00 |
| Candelabra, Louis XV Style, Ormolu, S-Shape Supports, 30 In., Pair | 850.00 |
| Candelabra, Napoleon III, Ormolu & Sang De Boeuf, C.1890, 26 In., Pair | 150.00 |
| Candelabra, Ormolu, C.1825, 20 1/4 In.High, Pair *Illus* | 900.00 |
| Candelabra, Rock Crystal, Three Light, Form Of Vase, Branches, 29 1/2 In. | 650.00 |
| Candelabra, Victorian, Ormolu, Pierced Nozzle, 3-Arm, C.1850, 12 1/2 In., Pair | 550.00 |
| Candelabrum, Ornate Fire Gilt, Prisms, Stepped Marble Base, 3-Arm, 19 In. | 55.00 |
| Candleholder, see also Brass, Candlestick, Pewter, Porcelain, Pressed Glass, Sandwich Glass, Silver Plate, Silver, Sterling, Vaseline Glass, Wooden, various porcelain categories | |
| Candleholder, Birdcage, Square Base, 7 1/2 In. | 175.00 |
| Candleholder, Black & Gold Base, Cream & Gold Top, Pickard & R.S., Pair | 25.00 |
| Candleholder, Cornflower On Base, Knob Center, 3-Branch, Low, Pair | 16.00 |
| Candleholder, Flower Shape, Ruby To Amber, 3 Applied Feet, Pair | 15.00 |
| Candleholder, Girandole Type, Romeo & Juliet, Marble Bases, C.1840, Pair | 85.00 |
| Candleholder, Spiral, Adjustable, Wooden Base, 8 In. | 145.00 |
| Candleholder, Walnut, Ball Feet, Wired, 11 In., Pair | 18.50 |
| Candleholder, Wrought Iron, Rushlight, Penny Feet, Cabriole Legs, 15 In. | 225.00 |
| Candlestick, see also Brass, Candleholder, Pewter, Porcelain, Pressed Glass, Sandwich Glass, Silver Plate, Silver, Sterling, Vaseline Glass, Wooden, various porcelain categories | |
| Candlestick, Bell Metal, C.1650, 5 1/2 In., Pair *Illus* | 475.00 |
| Candlestick, Bell Metal, Elongated Socket, Columnar, C.1790, 12 In., Pair | 200.00 |
| Candlestick, Birdcage, Turned Wooden Base, C.1750, 9 In.High | 145.00 |

Candlestick, Brass, Ring Turned, Continental, C.1750, 10 In.High, Pair .................... 250.00
Candlestick, Britannia, Removable Bobeche, Signed W In Star & Web, Pair ............. 65.00
Candlestick, Bronze Over Glass, Swirl Pattern, 9 In.High, Pair ............................... 18.00
Candlestick, Chamber, Gilt Metal, Enamel & Mosaic, Foliage Flower Heads ............. 225.00
Candlestick, Crucifix, Clear Glass, 9 1/4 In. ............................................................ 10.00
Candlestick, Cut Glass, Victorian, Drip Pan, Baluster Standard, 16 1/2 In. .............. 30.00
Candlestick, Dolphin, Glass, 9 1/4 In.High ............................................................. 22.00
Candlestick, Dolphin, Stemmed, Shell & Ribbed Base & Holder, Pair ..................... 35.00
Candlestick, Glass, Flint, Hexagonal Base & Font, Pewter Socket, Amethyst ........... 300.00
Candlestick, Glass, Flint, Hexagonal, Light Yellow Green, 9 5/8 In.High ................. 300.00
Candlestick, Glass, Flint, Hexagonal, Pale Honey Amber, 9 5/8 In.High ................. 175.00
Candlestick, Glass, Heavy Socket, Opaque Blue & White, 9 3/4 In.High, Pair .......... 450.00
Candlestick, Glass, Midwestern, Dolphin, Canary Yellow, 6 3/4 In.High .................. 200.00
Candlestick, Glass, Midwestern, Hexagon Stem, Round Foot, Pewter Inset, Clear ...... 25.00
Candlestick, Hog Scraper, Push-Up, Chair Hook, C.1750, 6 In.High ....................... 32.00
Candlestick, Jenkins, Clear, Lacy, Stippled Sunflower & Scroll Base, Pair .............. 25.00
Candlestick, Louis XVI Style, Ormolu & Silvered Metal, Swans, C.1890, Pair .......... 175.00
Candlestick, Ormolu, Louis XVI Style, Vase Form Nozzle, C.1890, Pair ................... 130.00
Candlestick, Pricket, Silvered Metal, Continental, C.1790, 33 1/2 In. ...................... 258.50
Candlestick, Sheffield Type, Telescopic, Ornate Trim, 7 1/4 In.High, Pair ............... 87.50
Candlestick, Spiral, Round Wooden Base, Lip & Lift ............................................... 120.00
Candlestick, Table, Gilt Metal, Engraved Crests, Corinthian Column, 11 In. ............ 37.50
Candlestick, Tiffany Style, Bronze, Pierced Cup, Green Glass Extrusions ................. 170.00
Candlestick, Venetian Style, Green, Swans, 11 1/2 In.High, Pair ........................... 395.00
Candlestick, Wall, White Metal, Marked B.A.Bte.S.G.Paris, C.1890 ....................... 15.00
Candlestick, Wax Jack, Silver Gadrooned Edge ..................................................... 190.00
Candlestick, White Porcelain, White Bisque George & Martha, 14 In., Pair ............. 325.00

*Candy containers, especially those made of glass, were popular during the late
Victorian era.*

Candy Container, Airplane ................................................................................. 14.00
Candy Container, Airplane, Spirit Of Good Will, Pilot ............................................ 36.00
Candy Container, Alarm Clock ........................................................................... 1.00
Candy Container, Army Tank .............................................................................. 10.50
Candy Container, Baby Carriage, Tin Top Slides Back ........................................... 19.00
Candy Container, Barrel .................................................................................... 3.00
Candy Container, Baseball ................................................................................. 15.00
Candy Container, Bell, Red Cross, 2 1/4 In. ........................................................ 6.00
Candy Container, Boot, Large Size ...................................................................... 5.00
Candy Container, Boot, Santa's, 2 1/2 In. ........................................................... 6.00
Candy Container, Boot, Small Size ...................................................................... 3.00
Candy Container, Bulldog .................................................................................. 20.00
Candy Container, Chamberstick .......................................................................... 5.50
Candy Container, Charlie Chaplin ....................................................................... 34.00
Candy Container, Chicken On A Nest, 5 In.Long ................................................... 8.00
Candy Container, Chicken On Nest, Marked Millstein, 4 1/2 In. ............................. 9.00
Candy Container, Chicken, Large Size ................................................................. 6.00
Candy Container, Clown Dog ............................................................................. 4.25
Candy Container, Cruiser ................................................................................... 10.50
Candy Container, Dog, Brass Top, 5 In. ............................................................... 12.50
Candy Container, Dog, Scottie ........................................................................... 5.00
Candy Container, Dog, Scottie, Standing ............................................................. 12.50
Candy Container, Dog, Sitting ............................................................................ 6.00
Candy Container, Ducks, Swimming .................................................................... 25.00
Candy Container, Felix ...................................................................................... 135.00
Candy Container, Fire Engine, Penny Candy ........................................................ 25.00
Candy Container, Fire Truck, Dept.1 ................................................................... 9.50
Candy Container, Hat, Military ........................................................................... 9.00
Candy Container, Hen On Nest, Bottom Opening, 5 In. .......................................... 12.50
Candy Container, Horn ...................................................................................... 22.00
Candy Container, Horse Pulling Cart, Clear .............................................. 7.50 To 12.50
Candy Container, Hound Dog, Screw Top, 2 1/2 In.High ........................................ 4.00
Candy Container, Iron Horse Train ...................................................................... 12.00
Candy Container, Jack O'lantern ......................................................................... 23.00
Candy Container, Lamp, Miniature ...................................................................... 10.00
Candy Container, Lantern, Black Tin Top ................................................. 10.00 To 18.00

| | |
|---|---|
| Candy Container, Lantern, Clear, Tin Top & Bottom, Handle .............................................. | 4.75 |
| Candy Container, Lantern, Flint Globe | 20.00 |
| Candy Container, Lantern, Green & Red Metal Lid, T.H.Stough, Jeanette, Pa. .............. | 12.00 |
| Candy Container, Lantern, Tin Top, Bottom, & Bail Handle ...................................... | 4.75 To 9.00 |
| Candy Container, Liberty Bell, Pale Green | 18.50 |
| Candy Container, Lighthouse, 5 1/2 In. | 10.00 |
| Candy Container, Locomotive, Victory Glass Company ................................................ | 12.00 |
| Candy Container, Locomotive, 5 In. | 6.00 To 10.00 |
| Candy Container, Midget Washer ............................................................................ | 23.00 |
| Candy Container, Moon Mullins ............................................................................ | 32.00 |
| Candy Container, Motorboat, Clear ........................................................................ | 4.95 |
| Candy Container, Mug, Child's | 4.50 |
| Candy Container, Mug, Drum ................................................................................ | 19.00 |
| Candy Container, Mule Pulling Barrel | 27.00 |
| Candy Container, Nursing Bottle, Nipple, 3 In.High .................................................. | 4.00 |
| Candy Container, Nursing Bottle, Wooden Nipple | 15.00 |
| Candy Container, Opera Glasses | 65.00 |
| Candy Container, Owl, Camphor Glass .................................................................... | 18.00 |
| Candy Container, Pistol, Amber | 20.00 |
| Candy Container, Pistol, Clear, 7 1/2 In. .............................................................. | 9.00 To 12.00 |
| Candy Container, Queen Elizabeth | 8.00 |
| Candy Container, Rabbit Family .............................................................................. | 27.50 |
| Candy Container, Rabbit, Sitting, Marked Millstein .................................................. | 6.00 To 9.00 |
| Candy Container, Rabbit, Sitting, 6 1/2 In. | 20.00 |
| Candy Container, Railroad Engine, Covered, Clear, 6 In.Long | 89.50 |
| Candy Container, Revolver, Checkered Grip, Tin Cap, 8 In.Long .............................. | 35.00 |
| Candy Container, Revolver, Round Butt, Tin Cover, 6 1/2 In. | 10.00 |
| Candy Container, Sadiron ...................................................................................... | 20.00 |
| Candy Container, Santa Claus At Chimney, Closure .................................................. | 27.50 |
| Candy Container, Santa Claus, Screw Closure ...................................................... | 28.00 |
| Candy Container, Santa Climbing Down Chimney, Bank ............................................ | 35.00 |
| Candy Container, Scottie Dog, 4 In. ...................................................................... | 8.00 To 18.00 |
| Candy Container, Sedan With 6 Vents, Yellow Paint ................................................ | 40.00 |
| Candy Container, Spark Plug, Painted .................................................................... | 38.00 |
| Candy Container, Speedboat ................................................................................ | 6.00 To 9.00 |
| Candy Container, Suitcase .................................................................................... | 12.00 To 17.00 |
| Candy Container, Suitcase, Decal Victorian Ladies & Man, Milk Glass ...................... | 35.00 |
| Candy Container, Telephone, Metal Receiver Over Screw Top, 1 3/4 In.High .............. | 4.00 |
| Candy Container, Twins On Anchor ...................................................................... | 12.75 To 18.00 |
| Candy Container, Uncle Sam ................................................................................ | 150.00 |
| Candy Container, Volkswagen | 25.00 |
| Candy Container, Washtub, Mary Louise Stanley .................................................... | 4.50 |
| Candy Container, Willys Jeep, Driver, J.H.Millstein Co. ............................................ | 12.50 |
| Candy Container, Windmill, Tin Bottom & Windmill Arms, 4 3/4 In.High .................... | 10.00 |
| Cane Handle, Silver, Enamel, & Rubies, Head Of Dog, C.1900, 2 3/4 In. .................. | 500.00 |
| Cane, Bird's Head Handle, Knotty Wood ................................................................ | 15.00 |
| Cane, Blown, Yellow, White, & Pink Stripes In Clear, 37 3/4 In. .............................. | 27.50 |
| Cane, Ebony, 14 K Gold Handle, Carved Flowers & Scrolls ...................................... | 50.00 |
| Cane, Gearshift Knob, Wooden | 12.00 |
| Cane, Head, Gold Plated | 9.00 |
| Cane, Shinglehouse, Pa., Glass Factory, Aqua, Twisted Handle, 37 In. ...................... | 35.00 |
| Cane, Swagger Stick, English, Ebony, Carved Hound's Head, Silver Tip .................... | 25.00 |
| Cane, Swagger Stick, Leather Bound, Brass Tip & Head, 34 In. ................................ | 15.00 |
| Cane, Sword, Carved ............................................................................................ | 45.00 |

*Canton china is a blue-and-white ware made near Canton, China, from about 1785 to 1895. It has hand-decorated Chinese scenes.*

| | | |
|---|---|---|
| Canton, Bowl, Blue & White, Deep, C.1850, 14 In. | *Illus* | 175.00 |
| Canton, Bowl, Serving, Blue & White, Willow, C.1850 ............................ | *Illus* | 120.00 |
| Canton, Bowl, Vegetable, Blue & White, Willow, C.1850 ........................ | *Illus* | 375.00 |
| Canton, Bowl, Vegetable, Covered, Blue & White, Landscape Panel, C.1850 ...... | | 150.00 |
| Canton, Dish, Gravy, Blue & White ...................................................... | | 95.00 |
| Canton, Dish, Hot Water, Octagonal, Blue ............................................ | | 125.00 |
| Canton, Dish, Shrimp, Orange Peel Finish ............................................ | | 225.00 |
| Canton, Drain, Blue & White, Oval, 13 1/8 In. ...................................... | | 125.00 |
| Canton, Jar, Ginger, 6 1/4 In.High ...................................................... | | 65.00 |

Canton, Teacup & Saucer.
Blue & White, Willow, C.1850

Canton, Bowl, Blue & White,
Deep, C.1850, 14 In.
*(See Page 76)*

Canton, Bowl, Vegetable,
Blue & White, Willow, C.1850
*(See Page 76)*

Canton, Bowl,
Serving, Blue & White,
Willow, C.1850
*(See Page 76)*

Canton, Platter, Blue & White,
C.1850, 14 1/4 In.

| | |
|---|---:|
| **Canton, Knife Rest,** Fish Shape | 12.00 |
| **Canton, Plate,** Blue & White, C.1850, 7 1/2 In. | 11.30 |
| **Canton, Plate,** C.1830, 7 1/2 In. | 48.00 |
| **Canton, Plate,** Chop, Full Figure, 14 In. | 145.00 |
| **Canton, Plate,** 6 In. | 22.00 |
| **Canton, Plate,** 9 In. | 40.00 |
| **Canton, Platter,** Blue & White, C.1850, 14 1/4 In.   *Illus* | 125.00 |
| **Canton, Platter,** Blue & White, Clipped Corners, 15 1/4 X 18 1/2 In. | 225.00 |
| **Canton, Platter,** Blue & White, Rectangular, Clipped Corners, 19 In. | 225.00 |
| **Canton, Platter,** Hot Water, Beefsteak, Blue | 175.00 |
| **Canton, Platter,** Orange Peel Bottom, 19 X 16 In. | 148.00 |
| **Canton, Platter,** Oval, Blue & White, 15 In. | 95.00 |
| **Canton, Platter,** Oval, Well And Tree, Landscape Scenes, C.1820, 19 In.Long | 225.00 |
| **Canton, Platter,** Rectangular, Blue & White, Clipped Corners, 15 X 18 3/4 In. | 225.00 |
| **Canton, Sugar & Creamer,** Cover, Blue & White, Willow, C.1850 | 200.00 |
| **Canton, Teacup & Saucer,** Blue & White, Willow, C.1850   *Illus* | 37.50 |
| **Canton, Tray,** Blue & White, C.1850, 8 In. Long | 120.00 |
| **Canton, Tureen & Stand,** Covered, Blue & White, Oval, Willow, C.1850 | 325.00 |
| **Canton, Vase,** Dark Blue, Enamel Floral & Butterflies, 9 In. | 120.00 |
| **Canton, Washbasin,** Blue, 18 1/2 In.Diameter | 365.00 |

*Capo-Di-Monte porcelain was first made in Naples, Italy, from 1743 to 1759. The factory moved near Madrid, Spain, and reopened in 1771 and worked to 1834. Since that time the Doccia factory of Italy acquired the molds and style, even using the N and crown mark, which was made famous by the factory.*

| | |
|---|---:|
| **Capo-Di-Monte, Bowl,** Barber's, Shell Shaped, Eagle & Foliage, C.1880, 17 In. | 250.00 |
| **Capo-Di-Monte, Box,** Brass Catch & Rim, Oval, Cupid Scenes, Crown & N Mark | 195.00 |
| **Capo-Di-Monte, Box,** Cigar, Covered, Square, Figures, Gilt, Crown & N Mark | 400.00 |
| **Capo-Di-Monte, Box,** Hinged, Children At Play, Gold Trim, Brass Bound, Signed | 145.00 |
| **Capo-Di-Monte, Box,** Jewel, Hinged, Oval, 4 X 5 1/2 X 2 1/2 In. | 110.00 |

Capo-Di-Monte, Box, Oval, Scenes, Crown & N Mark, 1 3/4 In.High ......................... 235.00
Capo-Di-Monte, Box, Ring, Covered, Crown & N Mark, 3 In. Diameter ..................... 20.00
Capo-Di-Monte, Cup & Saucer, Coffee, Country Views, Gilt Rims, C.1750 ............... 2000.00
Capo-Di-Monte, Cup & Saucer, Griffin Handle, Maidens & Cherubs, Gold Lined ......... 25.00
Capo-Di-Monte, Figurine, Greek Goddess Holding Laurel Wreath, 7 In.High ............. 95.00
Capo-Di-Monte, Figurine, Nude Child Tumbling On Pillow, White, Gold ................... 125.00
Capo-Di-Monte, Group, Pastoral ............................................................................ 235.00
Capo-Di-Monte, Jardiniere, Hunting Scenes & Nude Children Playing, 6 In. ........... 225.00
Capo-Di-Monte, Lamp, Silk Shade, 28 1/2 In.High, Pair ........................................ 188.00
Capo-Di-Monte, Plaque, Adam & Eve, Holy Family, C.1890, 8 X 6 1/2 In., Pair ......... 600.00
Capo-Di-Monte, Plaque, Cupid & Venus, C.1890, 7 1/4 X 5 1/8 In. .......................... 200.00
Capo-Di-Monte, Plaque, The Transfiguration, C.1890, 19 1/2 X 10 3/4 In. ............... 400.00
Capo-Di-Monte, Plate, Armorial, Cherub Border, C.1830, 9 In. ............................... 75.00
Capo-Di-Monte, Plate, Gold "Au Roi De Rome-Naples 1811," 10 3/4 In. ................. 125.00
Capo-Di-Monte, Tankard, C.1850, 8 3/8 In.High ........................................ *Illus* 400.00
Capo-Di-Monte, Tea Set, 14 Piece ........................................................................ 1200.00
Capo-Di-Monte, Teapot, Relief Nude Women, Coral Handle, Animal Spout ............. 185.00
Capo-Di-Monte, Vase, Muses & Warriors Marching, 8 In.High, Pair ....................... 400.00
Captain Midnight, Badge, Flight Patrol ................................................................. 12.50
Captain Midnight, Decoder ................................................................................... 30.00
Captain Midnight, Mug ......................................................................................... 15.00
   Caramel Slag, see Chocolate Glass
   Card, see also Postcard
Card, Advertising, Black Duck Shooting, Currier & Ives ....................................... 25.00
Card, Advertising, Cigarette, Kinney Bors., Derby Winners, Set Of 22 .................... 12.00
Card, Advertising, Getting A Hoist, Currier & Ives .............................................. 20.00
Card, Advertising, Hason Cigarette, Indian, Set Of 12 .......................................... 10.00
Card, Advertising, The Sports Who Lost Their Tin, Currier & Ives ......................... 25.00
Card, Fortune Telling, Military, World War I ........................................................ 16.00
Card, Fortune Telling, Zodiac, Ingalls, Miniature, 30 ............................................ 3.00
Card, Greeting, Christmas, Hold To The Light ..................................................... 8.00
Card, Greeting, Christmas, Tots, Nister ............................................................... 3.00
Card, Greeting, Easter, Cord Outlined Maltese Cross Of Flying Doves .................. 8.00
Card, Greeting, Easter, Tuck, Tinsled Cross, Booklet ........................................... 1.50
Card, Greeting, Valentine, Buster Brown & Tige, Signed Outcault ........................ 7.50
Card, Greeting, Valentine, Lacy, Decoupage On Pink Satin, Child, C.1885 ............. 9.00
Card, Greeting, Valentine, Pink & White Victorian Lamp Shade, Die Cut Girl ........ 12.00
Card, Greeting, Valentine, Prang, Copyright 1882, 9 X 12 1/2 In. ......................... 12.00
Card, Greeting, Valentine, Prang-Signed Church Print, Cherubs In Birdbath, Fringed ... 12.50
Card, Greeting, Valentine, Rose O'Neill ............................................................... 3.50
Card, Greeting, Valentine, Three Layers, Girl, Die Cut ......................................... 8.00
Card, Greeting, Valentine, Tuck, Art Nouveau, Topless Angel, Easel Back ............. 8.50
Card, Greeting, Valentine, Victorian, Heart Shape Pillow, Die Cuts, Multilayer ...... 12.50
Card, Greeting, Valentine, Victorian, Stand-Up, Die Cuts, 3 Layer, 6 X 9 X 2 1/2 In. ... 8.00
Card, Greeting, Valentine, Victorian, Stand-Up, Pillow, Die Cuts, 14 In. Square ..... 12.50
Card, Greeting, World War II, Envelope ............................................................... .50

Capo-Di-Monte, Tankard, C.1850, 8 3/8 In.High

Card, Playing, Anti-Religious ............................................................................ 65.00
Card, Playing, Austrian, Piatnik, C.1925, Miniature, 52 ................................. 6.00
Card, Playing, Belgian, French Line, Miniature, 52 ........................................ 3.00
Card, Playing, Belgian, Renovation 2000, Bierman, Miniature, 52 .............. 5.75
Card, Playing, Danish, Pinup, Handa, Miniature, 52 ...................................... 2.00
Card, Playing, Dutch, Geometric Design, Miniature, 52 ................................. 1.00
Card, Playing, English, Blue Star Line, Waddington, Miniature, 52 ............. 3.70
Card, Playing, French, Dated 1917, 52 ........................................................... 15.00
Card, Playing, French, Old French Courts, Miniature, 52 .............................. 6.90
Card, Playing, German, A.S.S., Miniature, 32 ................................................. 2.00
Card, Playing, German, Simultane, Sonia Delaunay, 1958, Miniature, 52 .... 3.00
Card, Playing, German, Stadtische Theater, My Fair Lady, 1967, 50 ........... 4.40
Card, Playing, German, Swiss Costumes, Dondorf, Miniature, 52 ................ 6.70
Card, Playing, German, Transformation, Fromann, C.1870, Miniature, 52 .... 135.00
Card, Playing, Indonesian, Money, Miniature, 60 ........................................... 2.30
Card, Playing, Irish, Emerald Isle, Ormond Printing Co., Miniature, 52 ...... 1.25
Card, Playing, Japanese, Edwards, Nintendo, Miniature, Man & Wife Embracing .... 14.00
Card, Playing, Japanese, Young Men, Nintendo, 1967, 52 ........................... 6.00
Card, Playing, Kem, Western Casino ................................................................ 5.50
Card, Playing, Russian, 150th Anniversary Of M.F.R., 1967, Miniature, 52 .... 20.00
Card, Playing, Snow White & The Seven Dwarfs, Walt Disney, Miniature .... 8.50
Card, Playing, Southern Pacific Railroad, C.1915, Ogden & Shasta Routes .... 25.00
Card, Playing, Spanish, Bullfighter, Antonio Casero, Miniature, 48 ............. 2.35
Card, Playing, Stock Market Bulls & Bears .................................................... 10.00
Card, Playing, U.S.A., American Airlines, U.S.P.C., Miniature, 52 ............... 1.75
Card, Playing, U.S.A., British War Relief Society, E.E.Fairchild, 1939, 52 .... 2.50
    Carder, see Steuben, Aurene

*Carlsbad, Germany, is a mark found on china made by several factories in*
*Germany. Most of the pieces available today were made after 1891.*
Carlsbad, Bowl, Floriform, Fuchsia Petals, 4 Twig & Leaf Legs, 5 In. ......... 45.00
Carlsbad, Bowl, Salad, Gold Lobster, Center, Scalloped Edge, Gold, Enamel .... 38.00
Carlsbad, Butter Pat, Hand-Painted Floral ...................................................... 4.00
Carlsbad, Creamer, Apple Blossoms & Goldfinch, Medallions, Gold Handle .... 50.00
Carlsbad, Dish, Bone, Pink Bell Shape Blossoms, Gold Edge ...................... 4.50
Carlsbad, Dish, Candy, Dark Red Iris & Gold Leaves, Cutoff Corners, Square .... 8.00
Carlsbad, Fish Set, Flowers & Gold, Various Fish, Hand-Painted, 12 Piece .... 295.00
Carlsbad, Fish Set, Transfer Trout, 13 Piece ................................................. 125.00
Carlsbad, Jar & Underplate, Jam, Covered, Gold Handles, Violets On White .... 30.00
Carlsbad, Jar, Cracker, Gold Outlined Florals ............................................... 22.00
Carlsbad, Match Holder, Hand-Painted Florals, Striker Inside Cover, Oval .... 15.00
Carlsbad, Pitcher, Gold Floral On Cream, Pronged Handle, 8 In. ................. 30.00
Carlsbad, Pitcher, Gold Leaves In Raised Design On Satin Finish ............... 15.00
Carlsbad, Plate, Benson, Minnesota Street Scene, 7 In. .............................. 8.00
Carlsbad, Plate, Napoleon's Portrait, Gold & Green Decoration, 6 In. ........ 28.50
Carlsbad, Plate, Oyster, Green & Gold Floral, Set Of 10 .............................. 125.00
Carlsbad, Plate, Reclining Female & Cupid, C.1900, 10 1/2 In. ................... 85.00
Carlsbad, Plate, Scenic Center, Green & Gold Border, 8 In. ........................ 18.00
Carlsbad, Plate, Swirl Molded, Multicolor Floral, Marx & Gutherz, 8 In. .... 7.00
Carlsbad, Plate, White, Gold Trim, Ornate, Signed, 8 In. ............................. 9.00
Carlsbad, Tray, Pin, Rectangular, Couple Center, Blue Green Border ......... 25.00
Carlsbad, Tureen, Soup, Pink & Blue Wild Flowers On White, Oblong ....... 38.00
Carlton, Pitcher, Hot Water, Floral, Cream, Silver Plate Lid, Stoke-On-Trent .... 38.00
Carnelian, Tray, Pin, Oval, Carved, Pedestal, 3 X 2 5/16 In. ....................... 65.00

*Carnival, or taffeta, glass was an inexpensive, pressed, iridescent glass made*
*from about 1900 to 1920. Carnival glass is currently being reproduced. Over*
*200 different patterns are known.*
    Carnival Glass, see also Northwood
Carnival Glass, Banana Boat, Cherry, Amethyst ............................................ 128.00
Carnival Glass, Banana Boat, Footed, Wreath Of Cherries, Purple ............. 75.00
Carnival Glass, Banana Boat, Grape & Cable, Amethyst ............................... 215.00
Carnival Glass, Banana Boat, Grape & Cable, Marigold ................................ 95.00
Carnival Glass, Banana Boat, Grape & Cable, Purple, 4 Footed, 12 1/4 In.Long .... 265.00
Carnival Glass, Base, Punch Bowl, Fashion, Clambroth ............................... 35.00
Carnival Glass, Base, Punch Bowl, Memphis, Ice Green, Marked N ............ 62.00
Carnival Glass, Base, Punch Bowl, Wreath Of Roses, Purple, 4 1/4 In. ..... 35.00

| | |
|---|---|
| Carnival Glass, Basket, Basket Weave, Marigold, Small Size | 40.00 |
| Carnival Glass, Basket, Basket Weave, Red, Double Lattice Edge | 98.00 |
| Carnival Glass, Basket, Beaded, Marigold | 21.00 |
| Carnival Glass, Basket, Bushel, Green, Marked N | 55.00 |
| Carnival Glass, Basket, Fenton, Marigold | 14.00 |
| Carnival Glass, Basket, Fenton's Basket, Red | 62.50 |
| Carnival Glass, Basket, Imperial Grape, Marigold, 2 Handled, 9 In. | 30.00 |
| Carnival Glass, Basket, Lacy Edge, Blue, Butterscotch, Iridescent, Fenton | 22.00 |
| Carnival Glass, Basket, Miller's Furniture, Marigold, Open Edge, Marked N | 45.00 |
| Carnival Glass, Berry Set, Crackle, Marigold, Scalloped Rim, 8 Piece | 35.00 |
| Carnival Glass, Berry Set, Crackle, Marigold, 5 Piece | 30.00 |
| Carnival Glass, Berry Set, Diamond Panel, Marigold, 5 Piece | 15.00 |
| Carnival Glass, Berry Set, Fluted Panels, Purple, 7 Piece | 155.00 |
| Carnival Glass, Berry Set, Grape & Cable With Thumbprint, Purple, N, 7 Piece | 200.00 |
| Carnival Glass, Berry Set, Grape & Cable, Green, 6 Piece | 200.00 |
| Carnival Glass, Berry Set, Jeweled Heart, Peach, Flower & Fan In, 8 Piece | 395.00 |
| Carnival Glass, Bonbon, Basket Weave, Cobalt, Berries Inside | 25.00 |
| Carnival Glass, Bonbon, Basket Weave, Cobalt, Footed, Fruit & Floral Inside | 55.00 |
| Carnival Glass, Bonbon, Beaded Cable, Green, Footed, 7 1/2 In. | 32.00 |
| Carnival Glass, Bonbon, Finecut & Roses, White, Footed, Fanciful Inside | 60.00 |
| Carnival Glass, Bonbon, Floral & Wheat, Cobalt, Gold | 60.00 |
| Carnival Glass, Bonbon, Orange Tree, Marigold, Small Size | 15.00 |
| Carnival Glass, Bonbon, Peacock At Urn, Marigold, 6 In.High | 29.00 |
| Carnival Glass, Bonbon, Question Marks, Amethyst, 2 Handles, Pedestal | 22.50 |
| Carnival Glass, Bonbon, Question Marks, Peach & Opalescent, Stem & Handles | 29.00 |
| Carnival Glass, Bonbon, Stippled Rays, Green | 15.00 |
| Carnival Glass, Bonbon, Stippled Rays, Purple | 22.00 |
| Carnival Glass, Bonbon, Strawberry, Purple, Signed Northwood | 30.00 |
| Carnival Glass, Bonbon, Swan, Pink | 28.00 |
| Carnival Glass, Bonbon, Three Fruits, Blue, Footed, 2 Handles | 37.50 |
| Carnival Glass, Bonbon, Three Fruits, Purple, Stemmed, 2 Handles, 7 1/2 In. | 48.00 |
| Carnival Glass, Bonbon, Wreath Of Roses, Green, Stemmed, 2 Handled | 37.00 |
| Carnival Glass, Bottle, Corn, Green | 125.00 |
| Carnival Glass, Bottle, Golden Wedding, Marigold | 10.00 |
| Carnival Glass, Bottle, Water, Imperial Grape, Marigold | 49.00 |
| Carnival Glass, Bowl & Base, Punch, Fashion, Marigold | 48.00 |
| Carnival Glass, Bowl & Base, Punch, Grape & Cable, Purple | 295.00 To 395.00 |
| Carnival Glass, Bowl & Base, Punch, Orange Tree, Marigold | 70.00 To 145.00 |
| Carnival Glass, Bowl, Acorn, Dark Green, 8 In. | 45.00 |
| Carnival Glass, Bowl, Acorn, Green, Serrated Rim, 7 1/2 In. | 36.00 |
| Carnival Glass, Bowl, Acorn, Marigold, 7 1/2 In.Diameter | 37.00 |
| Carnival Glass, Bowl, Acorns & Leaves, Cobalt, Scalloped Rim, 6 1/2 In. | 22.50 |
| Carnival Glass, Bowl, Autumn Acorns, Blue, 7 1/2 In.Across | 45.00 |
| Carnival Glass, Bowl, Banana, Grape & Cable, Purple | 225.00 |
| Carnival Glass, Bowl, Banana, Two Fruits, Marigold, Ornate Edge, 13 X 10 In. | 189.00 |
| Carnival Glass, Bowl, Basket Weave, Purple, Latticework, 4 In. | 35.00 |
| Carnival Glass, Bowl, Battenburg, Marigold, 8 In. | 25.00 To 28.00 |
| Carnival Glass, Bowl, Berry, Acorn Burr, Purple, Marked N | 125.00 |
| Carnival Glass, Bowl, Berry, Banded Daisy, Marigold | 12.00 |
| Carnival Glass, Bowl, Berry, Bark, Marigold, 4 1/4 In. | 2.95 |
| Carnival Glass, Bowl, Berry, Bouquet & Lattice, Marigold, 5 In. | 1.95 |
| Carnival Glass, Bowl, Berry, Diamond Band, Marigold | 18.00 |
| Carnival Glass, Bowl, Berry, Feathered Serpent, Marigold, 5 1/4 In. | 11.00 |
| Carnival Glass, Bowl, Berry, Feathered Serpent, Marigold, 8 7/8 In. | 25.00 |
| Carnival Glass, Bowl, Berry, Flute, Purple, Small Size | 20.00 |
| Carnival Glass, Bowl, Berry, Grape & Cable, Purple, Marked N, 5 In. | 30.00 |
| Carnival Glass, Bowl, Berry, Panther, Marigold | 85.00 |
| Carnival Glass, Bowl, Berry, Peach, White, Gold Trim, Northwood, 9 1/2 In. | 145.00 |
| Carnival Glass, Bowl, Berry, Peacock At Fountain, Blue, Small Size, Marked N | 40.00 |
| Carnival Glass, Bowl, Berry, Peacock Tail, Amethyst | 18.00 |
| Carnival Glass, Bowl, Berry, Peacock Tail, Purple, Small Size | 18.00 |
| Carnival Glass, Bowl, Berry, Split Diamond, Marigold | 15.00 |
| Carnival Glass, Bowl, Berry, Three Fruits, Purple, N Mark, Small Size | 20.00 |
| Carnival Glass, Bowl, Berry, Vintage, Green | 11.00 |
| Carnival Glass, Bowl, Berry, Windmill, Orange, 7 In. | 23.50 |
| Carnival Glass, Bowl, Berry, Zipper, Marigold | 18.00 |

| | |
|---|---|
| Carnival Glass, Bowl, Blackberry, Amethyst, Millersburg, 9 In. | 35.00 |
| Carnival Glass, Bowl, Blackberry, Purple, Low, 6 In. | 35.00 |
| Carnival Glass, Bowl, Butterfly & Berry, Blue, 3 Ball & Claw Feet, 4 In.High | 138.00 |
| Carnival Glass, Bowl, Butterfly & Berry, Blue, 3 Footed, 9 1/2 In. | 80.00 |
| Carnival Glass, Bowl, Center, Flute, Marigold, 10 In. | 22.50 |
| Carnival Glass, Bowl, Center, Waffle Block, Marigold, Square, Serrated Edge | 35.00 |
| Carnival Glass, Bowl, Cereal, Bouquet & Lattice, Marigold | 1.95 |
| Carnival Glass, Bowl, Cereal, Kittens, Marigold, 3 1/2 In. | 60.00 |
| Carnival Glass, Bowl, Cherry Wreath, Purple, 12 1/2 X 9 1/4 In. | 125.00 |
| Carnival Glass, Bowl, Chrysanthemum, Marigold, Footed, 11 In. | 65.00 |
| Carnival Glass, Bowl, Coin Dot, Green, Piecrust Edge, 9 In. | 30.00 |
| Carnival Glass, Bowl, Coin Dot, Marigold, Ruffled, Low, 7 1/2 In. | 28.00 |
| Carnival Glass, Bowl, Coin Dot, Purple, 9 In. | 27.50 |
| Carnival Glass, Bowl, Coin Spot, Amethyst, Pleated Ruffled Top, 9 X 3 In. | 38.00 |
| Carnival Glass, Bowl, Comet, Amethyst, Ruffled, 8 In. | 40.00 |
| Carnival Glass, Bowl, Comet, Amethyst, 8 1/2 In. | 38.00 |
| Carnival Glass, Bowl, Comet, Green & Amber, Ruffled, Frilled, 8 1/2 In. | 47.00 |
| Carnival Glass, Bowl, Cosmos, Marigold, Ruffled, 9 In. | 25.00 |
| Carnival Glass, Bowl, Daisy, Marigold, Ruffled, 6 1/2 In. | 18.00 |
| Carnival Glass, Bowl, Diamond Panel, Marigold, 8 In. | 9.00 |
| Carnival Glass, Bowl, Diamond Point & Dutton, Marigold, 7 1/2 In. | 18.50 |
| Carnival Glass, Bowl, Diamond Point In Long Ovals, Marigold, 8 In. | 18.50 |
| Carnival Glass, Bowl, Diamond Ring, Smoky, Deep, 8 In. | 45.00 |
| Carnival Glass, Bowl, Dolphin, Marigold, 8 X 4 1/2 In. | 80.00 |
| Carnival Glass, Bowl, Dragon & Lotus, Blue, 9 In. | 50.00 |
| Carnival Glass, Bowl, Dragon & Lotus, Cobalt, Ruffled Edge, 7 In. | 55.00 |
| Carnival Glass, Bowl, Dragon & Lotus, Green, 9 In. | 38.00 |
| Carnival Glass, Bowl, Dragon & Lotus, Marigold, Ruffled, 9 In. | 30.00 To 50.00 |
| Carnival Glass, Bowl, Dragon & Lotus, Marigold, 8 In. | 50.00 |
| Carnival Glass, Bowl, Dragon & Lotus, Purple, 8 In. | 55.00 |
| Carnival Glass, Bowl, Dutch Windmill, Marigold, 7 In. | 22.00 |
| Carnival Glass, Bowl, Embossed Grape, Marigold, 6 1/2 In. | 15.00 |
| Carnival Glass, Bowl, Embossed Grape, Marigold, 8 1/2 In. | 17.50 |
| Carnival Glass, Bowl, Fishscale & Beads, Marigold, Fluted, 6 In. | 15.00 |
| Carnival Glass, Bowl, Flowering Almond, Marigold, 6 1/2 In. | 12.00 |
| Carnival Glass, Bowl, Flute, Marigold, Embossed Grape Interior, 8 3/4 In. | 20.00 |
| Carnival Glass, Bowl, Fruit, Hattie, Purple, 8 In. | 50.00 |
| Carnival Glass, Bowl, Fruits & Flower, Purple, 9 In. | 40.00 |
| Carnival Glass, Bowl, Good Luck, Amethyst, 9 In.Diameter | 110.00 |
| Carnival Glass, Bowl, Good Luck, Aqua Opalescent | 295.00 |
| Carnival Glass, Bowl, Good Luck, Blue | 95.00 |
| Carnival Glass, Bowl, Good Luck, Blue, Ruffled | 110.00 |
| Carnival Glass, Bowl, Good Luck, Marigold | 80.00 To 95.00 |
| Carnival Glass, Bowl, Good Luck, Purple | 125.00 To 175.00 |
| Carnival Glass, Bowl, Grape & Cable, Dark Green, Signed Northwood, 8 1/2 In. | 62.50 |
| Carnival Glass, Bowl, Grape & Cable, Green, Ruffled, Footed, 8 In. | 45.00 |
| Carnival Glass, Bowl, Grape & Cable, Ice Green, Stippled, Flared, N, 9 In. | 85.00 |
| Carnival Glass, Bowl, Grape & Cable, Marigold, Footed, Deep, 7 In. | 28.75 |
| Carnival Glass, Bowl, Grape & Cable, Marigold, Shallow, 7 In. | 23.50 |
| Carnival Glass, Bowl, Grape & Cable, Purple, Footed | 35.00 To 38.00 |
| Carnival Glass, Bowl, Grape & Cable, Purple, Ruffled, Footed, 8 In. | 50.00 |
| Carnival Glass, Bowl, Grape & Cable, Purple, Signed Northwood, 9 1/4 In. | 62.50 |
| Carnival Glass, Bowl, Grape, Amethyst, Ruffled, Signed Northwood, 9 In. | 47.00 |
| Carnival Glass, Bowl, Grape, Marigold, Fenton, 6 1/4 In. | 16.00 |
| Carnival Glass, Bowl, Grape, Marigold, Panther Inside, 7 1/2 In.Diameter | 39.50 |
| Carnival Glass, Bowl, Grape, Purple, Fluted, 8 In. | 3.00 |
| Carnival Glass, Bowl, Grape, Purple, 6 In. | 75.00 |
| Carnival Glass, Bowl, Headdress, Purple, Serrated Rim, 7 1/2 In. | 32.00 |
| Carnival Glass, Bowl, Hearts & Flowers, Marigold, Fluted, 9 In. | 48.50 |
| Carnival Glass, Bowl, Heavy Grape, Green, Ruffled, Fenton, 7 In.Diameter | 32.50 |
| Carnival Glass, Bowl, Heavy Grape, Purple, 7 In. | 65.00 |
| Carnival Glass, Bowl, Hobstar, Marigold, 10 3/4 In. | 42.00 To 65.00 |
| Carnival Glass, Bowl, Holly Swirl, Purple, Ruffled, 4 In. | 35.00 |
| Carnival Glass, Bowl, Holly, Cobalt, Ruffled, 8 1/2 In. | 29.00 |
| Carnival Glass, Bowl, Holly, Green, Footed, 9 In. | 90.00 |
| Carnival Glass, Bowl, Holly, Purple, 8 1/4 In. | 29.75 |

Carnival Glass, Bowl, Holly, White, 9 In. ......... 45.00
Carnival Glass, Bowl, Horses' Heads Medallion, Marigold, Ruffled, 7 1/2 In. ......... 65.00
Carnival Glass, Bowl, Ice Cream, Hanging Cherry, Aqua, Millersburg ......... 75.00
Carnival Glass, Bowl, Ice Cream, Peacock At The Urn, White ......... 195.00
Carnival Glass, Bowl, Ice Cream, Peacock, Frosty White, Marked N, 11 In. ......... 150.00
Carnival Glass, Bowl, Ice Cream, Persian Garden, White, Low, 11 1/2 In. ......... 155.00
Carnival Glass, Bowl, Imitation Cut Glass, Marigold, Ruffled Edge, 8 In. ......... 10.00
Carnival Glass, Bowl, Imperial Grape, Green, 7 In. ......... 27.50
Carnival Glass, Bowl, Imperial Grape, Marigold, 7 In. ......... 12.00
Carnival Glass, Bowl, Imperial Jewels, Red, Paneled, 11 1/2 In.Across ......... 125.00
Carnival Glass, Bowl, Isaac Benesch & Sons, Amethyst, Ruffled, 8 In. ......... 120.00
Carnival Glass, Bowl, Leaf & Thistle, Marigold, 3 Tree Limb Feet, 6 In. ......... 22.50
Carnival Glass, Bowl, Leaf Chain, White, Fluted, 7 1/4 In. ......... 55.00
Carnival Glass, Bowl, Lotus & Grape, Green, 8 3/4 In. ......... 45.00
Carnival Glass, Bowl, Magpie, Marigold, Reg.Mark, 9 1/2 In. ......... 70.00
Carnival Glass, Bowl, Nut, Grape Delight, Purple, 6 Footed ......... 45.00
Carnival Glass, Bowl, Open Rose, Marigold, 8 1/2 In. ......... 23.00 To 32.50
Carnival Glass, Bowl, Orange Tree, Blue, Fluted, 8 3/4 In. ......... 45.00
Carnival Glass, Bowl, Orange Tree, Marigold, 6 1/2 In. ......... 21.00
Carnival Glass, Bowl, Orange, Grape & Cable, Marigold, Persian Medallion ......... 100.00
Carnival Glass, Bowl, Orange, Grape & Cable, Purple ......... 175.00
Carnival Glass, Bowl, Orange, Orange Tree, Marigold, Footed ......... 85.00
Carnival Glass, Bowl, Paneled, Marigold, Pedestal, 5 3/4 In. ......... 18.00
Carnival Glass, Bowl, Peacock & Grape, Amethyst, 3 Footed, 8 In. ......... 95.00
Carnival Glass, Bowl, Peacock & Grape, Blue, 9 In. ......... 45.00
Carnival Glass, Bowl, Peacock & Grape, Dark Blue, 8 1/2 In.Diameter ......... 30.00
Carnival Glass, Bowl, Peacock At Urn, Blue, 9 In. ......... 69.00
Carnival Glass, Bowl, Peacock At Urn, Marigold, 8 1/2 In. ......... 45.00
Carnival Glass, Bowl, Peacock Feather, Green, 7 In. ......... 14.50 To 22.00
Carnival Glass, Bowl, Peacock Tail, Green, 6 X 5 1/4 In. ......... 35.00
Carnival Glass, Bowl, Peacock's-Eye, Purple, 7 1/2 In. ......... 24.50
Carnival Glass, Bowl, Persian Medallion, Green, Ruffled, 6 In. ......... 40.00
Carnival Glass, Bowl, Pinwheel, Marigold, Crimped In Rim, Shallow, 6 In. ......... 9.75
Carnival Glass, Bowl, Pods & Posies, Purple, 10 1/2 In. ......... 60.00
Carnival Glass, Bowl, Poinsettia, Footed, 9 In. ......... 115.00
Carnival Glass, Bowl, Poinsettia, Ice Blue, Footed, Shallow, 9 In. ......... 130.00
Carnival Glass, Bowl, Poppies, Blue, Ruffled, Signed N, 9 In. ......... 44.00
Carnival Glass, Bowl, Primrose, Green, Ruffled, 10 In. ......... 50.00
Carnival Glass, Bowl, Punch, Grape & Cable, Purple, Base, Northwood ......... 550.00
Carnival Glass, Bowl, Punch, Imperial Grape, Marigold, 12 In. ......... 175.00
Carnival Glass, Bowl, Rainbow, Marigold, 7 1/2 In. ......... 12.00
Carnival Glass, Bowl, Raindrops, Purple, Dome Footed, 9 In. ......... 35.00
Carnival Glass, Bowl, Rays, Green, 9 In. ......... 16.50
Carnival Glass, Bowl, Rays, Peach, 9 1/4 In. ......... 17.00
Carnival Glass, Bowl, Ribbon & Rags, Marigold, 9 In. ......... 45.00
Carnival Glass, Bowl, Ruffle, Blue ......... 30.00 To 35.00
Carnival Glass, Bowl, Ruffle, Marigold ......... 15.00
Carnival Glass, Bowl, Ruffle, Purple ......... 30.00
Carnival Glass, Bowl, Sailboat, Marigold, 6 1/2 In. ......... 21.00
Carnival Glass, Bowl, Sailing Ship, Orange, Pedestal, 6 In. ......... 28.50
Carnival Glass, Bowl, Shell, Green, 7 1/2 In. ......... 22.00
Carnival Glass, Bowl, Stag & Holly, Cobalt, Footed, 11 In. ......... 95.00
Carnival Glass, Bowl, Stag & Holly, Green, Ruffled Top, Footed, 8 In. ......... 65.00
Carnival Glass, Bowl, Stag & Holly, Marigold, Flat, 10 In. ......... 65.00
Carnival Glass, Bowl, Stag & Holly, Marigold, Footed, 7 1/4 In. ......... 65.00 To 75.00
Carnival Glass, Bowl, Stag & Holly, Marigold, Footed, 11 In. ......... 75.00
Carnival Glass, Bowl, Star Of David, Amethyst, 9 In. ......... 65.00
Carnival Glass, Bowl, Stippled Coin Dot, Amethyst, 6 In. ......... 20.00
Carnival Glass, Bowl, Stippled Coin Dot, Green, 7 In. ......... 18.00
Carnival Glass, Bowl, Stippled Flowers, Peach, 8 In. ......... 28.00 To 32.00
Carnival Glass, Bowl, Stippled Rays, Amethyst, 6 In. ......... 15.00
Carnival Glass, Bowl, Stippled Rays, Purple, Marked N, 8 1/2 In. ......... 35.00
Carnival Glass, Bowl, Stork In Rushes, Red, 4 1/2 In. ......... 110.00
Carnival Glass, Bowl, Thistle, Green, Ribbon Candy Edge, 8 In. ......... 35.00
Carnival Glass, Bowl, Three Fruits, Amethyst, Marked N, 7 In.Across ......... 75.00
Carnival Glass, Bowl, Three Fruits, Dark Amber, Signed Northwood, 9 In. ......... 62.50

Carnival Glass, Bowl, Twins, Marigold, 9 In. .................................................................................. 27.00
Carnival Glass, Bowl, Vegetable, Bouquet & Lattice, Marigold, 10 1/2 In.Long ................. 3.95
Carnival Glass, Bowl, Vintage Grape, Amethyst, Fluted, 7 In. ........................................... 22.50
Carnival Glass, Bowl, Vintage, Amethyst, 3 Footed, 7 1/2 In. ............................................ 22.50
Carnival Glass, Bowl, Vintage, Cobalt Blue, Piecrust Edge, 8 In. ...................................... 25.00
Carnival Glass, Bowl, Vintage, Green, 8 3/4 In. ................................................................. 25.00
Carnival Glass, Bowl, Vintage, Marigold, Shallow, 9 1/2 In. ............................................. 32.00
Carnival Glass, Bowl, Waffle Block, Marigold, Square, 8 In. ............................................. 22.50
Carnival Glass, Bowl, Wild Daisy & Lotus, Amethyst, 3 Feet, Fenton, 9 1/2 In. ............... 35.00
Carnival Glass, Bowl, Windflower, Marigold, 8 In. ........................................ 13.00 To 25.00
Carnival Glass, Bowl, Windmill, Marigold, Footed, 9 In.Across ........................................ 40.00
Carnival Glass, Bowl, Windmill, Marigold, Oval, 9 In. ....................................................... 22.00
Carnival Glass, Bowl, Windmill, Purple, Ruffled Rim, 8 In. ............................................... 52.50
Carnival Glass, Bride's Basket, Diamond Block, White, Scalloped, Frame ..................... 350.00
Carnival Glass, Butter, Cherry, Marigold, Domed Cover ................................................. 85.00
Carnival Glass, Butter, Dahlia, Marigold ............................................................................. 40.00
Carnival Glass, Butter, Grape & Cable, Purple ........................................ 170.00 To 200.00
Carnival Glass, Butter, Luster Rose, Marigold, Covered ................................................... 35.00
Carnival Glass, Butter, Pear Shape, Marigold, Covered .................................................... 28.00
Carnival Glass, Butter, Split Diamond, Marigold, Covered ............................................... 25.00
Carnival Glass, Cake Stand, Peacock & Grape, Marigold ................................................. 38.00
Carnival Glass, Candleholder, Crackle, Marigold, Pair ..................................................... 35.00
Carnival Glass, Candlestick, Band At Base & Top, Apple Green, Pair .............................. 25.00
Carnival Glass, Candlestick, Florentine, Purple, 11 In.High, Pair ..................................... 90.00
Carnival Glass, Candlestick, Imperial Jewels, Ice Blue, Gold, Pair ................................... 50.00
Carnival Glass, Candlestick, Lydia, Marigold, Pair ........................................................... 25.00
Carnival Glass, Candlestick, Meandering Vine, Orange, Pair ............................................ 25.00
Carnival Glass, Candlestick, Round, Light Green, 9 1/2 In., Pair ...................................... 22.50
Carnival Glass, Candlestick, Wide Panel, Marigold, 6 1/2 In.High, Pair ........................... 45.00
Carnival Glass, Candlestick, 6 Sided, Marigold, 8 1/2 In., Pair ........................................ 14.50
Carnival Glass, Cologne, Grape & Cable, Purple ............................................................. 210.00
Carnival Glass, Compote, Basket Weave, Purple, Raspberry Interior, N, 8 In. ................. 65.00
Carnival Glass, Compote, Basket Weave, Purple, Swirled Stem, 5 1/2 In.High ............... 38.00
Carnival Glass, Compote, Bird & Flowers, Purple ............................................................. 34.00
Carnival Glass, Compote, Blackberry, Green, Stemmed ................................................... 30.00
Carnival Glass, Compote, Blackberry, Green, Stemmed, Signed Northwood ................... 48.00
Carnival Glass, Compote, Coin Spot, Peach, Opalescent ................................................. 29.00
Carnival Glass, Compote, Fruits & Flowers, Aqua Opalescent, 2 Handled ..................... 120.00
Carnival Glass, Compote, Geometric, Marigold, Peacock's-Eye Inside, 8 In. ................... 17.50
Carnival Glass, Compote, Hearts & Flowers, Aqua Opalescent ...................................... 105.00
Carnival Glass, Compote, Hearts & Flowers, White, Ruffled ............................................. 48.00
Carnival Glass, Compote, Iris, Green, Pedestal, Ruffled Top ............................................ 34.00
Carnival Glass, Compote, Jelly, Holly & Berry, Blue, 6 In. ................................................ 22.00
Carnival Glass, Compote, Jelly, Holly, Blue, 4 1/2 In. ...................................................... 20.00
Carnival Glass, Compote, Jelly, Stippled Oak Leaf & Acorn, Green, 4 1/2 In. ................. 35.00
Carnival Glass, Compote, Mikado, Marigold, 10 In.Diameter .......................................... 73.00
Carnival Glass, Compote, Rays, Marigold, Rainbow Iridescence, 6 In. ............................ 20.00
Carnival Glass, Compote, Rose, Purple, Stemmed, 5 In. .................................................. 35.00
Carnival Glass, Compote, Three Fruits, Purple ................................................................. 42.00
Carnival Glass, Compote, Three Fruits, Purple, Side Handles .......................................... 57.50
Carnival Glass, Compote, Thumbprint, Marigold ........................................ 18.00 To 24.00
Carnival Glass, Creamer, Grape & Cable With Thumbprint, Purple, Marked N ............... 135.00
Carnival Glass, Creamer, Grape With Gothic Arches, Clear, Gold Trim ........................... 20.00
Carnival Glass, Creamer, Hobstar & File, Marigold .......................................................... 20.00
Carnival Glass, Creamer, Inverted Strawberry, Marigold ................................................. 35.00
Carnival Glass, Creamer, Long Thumbprint, Marigold ...................................................... 11.00
Carnival Glass, Creamer, Luster With Clear ....................................................................... 7.00
Carnival Glass, Creamer, Maple Leaf, Purple ................................................................... 47.50
Carnival Glass, Creamer, Peacock At Fountain, Purple ..................................................... 85.00
Carnival Glass, Creamer, Singing Bird, Green ................................................................... 65.00
Carnival Glass, Creamer, Stippled Rib, Marigold, Pedestal .............................................. 12.00
Carnival Glass, Cruet, Buzz Star, Green ......................................................................... 210.00
Carnival Glass, Cup & Saucer, Imperial Grape, Marigold ................................................. 35.00
Carnival Glass, Cup, Custard, Orange Peel, Amethyst ...................................................... 23.00
Carnival Glass, Cup, Kittens, Marigold ............................................................................. 55.00
Carnival Glass, Cup, Loving, Orange Tree, Cobalt, Peacock's Tail Inside ....................... 145.00

Carnival Glass, Cup, Loving, Orange Tree, Marigold ............................................................ 85.00
Carnival Glass, Cup, Loving, Orange Tree, Purple ............................................................. 125.00
Carnival Glass, Cup, Punch, Acorn Burr, Marigold ............................................................ 27.50
Carnival Glass, Cup, Punch, Broken Arches, Purple ........................................................ 24.00
Carnival Glass, Cup, Punch, Colonial, Green ................................................................. 13.00
Carnival Glass, Cup, Punch, Fashion, Marigold ...................................................... 8.00 To 12.00
Carnival Glass, Cup, Punch, Grape & Cable, Green ........................................................ 18.00
Carnival Glass, Cup, Punch, Grape & Cable, Marigold ..................................................... 16.00
Carnival Glass, Cup, Punch, Grape & Cable, Purple ............................................. 22.50 To 30.00
Carnival Glass, Cup, Punch, Grape, Marigold ................................................................ 10.00
Carnival Glass, Cup, Punch, Memphis, Amethyst, Marked N ............................................. 37.50
Carnival Glass, Cup, Punch, Memphis, Ice Blue ............................................................ 45.00
Carnival Glass, Cup, Punch, Memphis, Marigold, Signed N ..................................... 12.00 To 14.50
Carnival Glass, Cup, Punch, Memphis, Purple .............................................................. 27.00
Carnival Glass, Cup, Punch, Orange Peel, Marigold ...................................................... 12.00
Carnival Glass, Cup, Punch, Orange Tree, Marigold ................................................ 8.00 To 20.00
Carnival Glass, Cup, Punch, Peacock At Fountain, Purple ............................................... 15.00
Carnival Glass, Cup, Punch, S Repeat, Amber ............................................................. 25.00
Carnival Glass, Cup, Punch, S Repeat, Amethyst .......................................................... 25.00
Carnival Glass, Cup, Punch, Stork & Rushes, Amethyst .......................................... 12.50 To 16.00
Carnival Glass, Cup, Punch, Stork & Rushes, Marigold ........................................... 12.50 To 18.00
Carnival Glass, Cup, Punch, Stork & Rushes, Purple ..................................................... 24.00
Carnival Glass, Cup, Punch, Vintage, Blue, Luster Rose Inside ......................................... 12.50
Carnival Glass, Cup, Punch, Vintage, Marigold ............................................................. 7.00
Carnival Glass, Cup, Punch, Wreaths Of Roses, Green ................................................... 18.50
Carnival Glass, Decanter, Golden Harvest, Marigold ............................................. 35.00 To 90.00
Carnival Glass, Decanter, Honeycomb, Marigold ........................................................... 6.00
Carnival Glass, Decanter, Whiskey, Grape & Cable, Purple ............................................. 850.00
Carnival Glass, Dish, Basket Weave, Marigold, Hat Shape ............................................... 15.00
Carnival Glass, Dish, Candy, Butterfly, Green, 2 Handled ............................................... 60.00
Carnival Glass, Dish, Candy, Crackle, Marigold, Covered ................................................ 13.00
Carnival Glass, Dish, Candy, Honeycomb & Chain, Marigold ..................................... 17.00 To 19.00
Carnival Glass, Dish, Candy, Peacock Feather, Marigold ................................................. 17.00
Carnival Glass, Dish, Candy, Persian Medallion, Blue, 2 Handled ...................................... 35.00
Carnival Glass, Dish, Candy, Pulled Loop, Deep Marigold, 6 In. ....................................... 20.00
Carnival Glass, Dish, Candy, Pulled Loop, Light Marigold, 6 In. ....................................... 20.00
Carnival Glass, Dish, Candy, Rays, Marigold, 2 Handled ................................................. 14.00
Carnival Glass, Dish, Candy, Thistle, Green, Ribbon Edge, 8 In. Diameter ........................... 35.00
Carnival Glass, Dish, Jelly, Basket Weave, Marigold, Loganberries Inside ............................. 14.50
Carnival Glass, Dish, Jelly, Berries & Leaves, Marigold, 6 In. .......................................... 12.00
Carnival Glass, Dish, Jelly, Rays, Green, Footed, 6 In. .................................................. 19.50
Carnival Glass, Dish, Jelly, Stippled Rays, Purple, Footed, 6 In. ....................................... 22.50
Carnival Glass, Dish, Nut, Vintage Grape, Amethyst, 3 Footed ......................................... 37.50
Carnival Glass, Dish, Nut, Vintage, Blue, 3 Footed ...................................................... 45.00
Carnival Glass, Dish, Pickle, Pansy, Marigold .............................................................. 22.50
Carnival Glass, Dish, Sundae, Tulip Shape, Green, Signed N ............................................ 18.00
Carnival Glass, Epergne, Fishnet, Peach .................................................................. 150.00
Carnival Glass, Epergne, Fishnet, Purple .................................................................. 215.00
Carnival Glass, Epergne, Vintage, Blue .................................................................... 115.00
Carnival Glass, Epergne, Wishbone, Purple ............................................................... 240.00
Carnival Glass, Epergne, 5 Marigold Lilies ................................................................ 225.00
Carnival Glass, Fernery, Luster Rose, Green, 3 Feet, 4 In.High ....................................... 150.00
Carnival Glass, Fernery, Open Rose, Marigold, 3 Legs, 7 1/2 In. ...................................... 35.00
Carnival Glass, Fernery, Vintage, Purple, Iridescent, Footed, 6 1/2 In. ............................... 65.00
Carnival Glass, Frog, Marigold, 4 In. ....................................................................... 10.00
Carnival Glass, Globe, Drapery, Peach, Opalescent ...................................................... 29.50
Carnival Glass, Globe, Ski Star, Marigold, Hexagonal, 4 1/2 In.Diameter, Pair ....................... 37.00
Carnival Glass, Goblet, Buttermilk, Iris, Marigold ......................................................... 35.00
Carnival Glass, Goblet, Imperial Grape, Marigold .......................................................... 26.00
Carnival Glass, Hat, Basket Weave, Red, Blackberry Inside, Open Lattice Edge ...................... 120.00
Carnival Glass, Hat, Basket Weave, Red, Lattice Edge, One Edge Turned Up .......................... 135.00
Carnival Glass, Hat, Holly, Amethyst ....................................................................... 25.00
Carnival Glass, Hat, Holly, Aqua Base, Butterscotch Top ................................................ 25.00
Carnival Glass, Hat, Holly, Red ............................................................................. 115.00
Carnival Glass, Hat, Stork & Rushes, Marigold ............................................................ 18.50
Carnival Glass, Hat, Waffle Band, Green, Marked N ...................................................... 20.00

Carnival Glass, Hatpin Holder, Grape & Cable, Green ............................................................ 135.00
Carnival Glass, Hatpin Holder, Grape & Cable, Marigold ................................... 100.00 To 115.00
Carnival Glass, Hatpin Holder, Grape & Cable, Purple ........................................................ 145.00
Carnival Glass, Hatpin Holder, Orange Tree, Marigold ............................... 75.00 To 90.00
Carnival Glass, Hatpin, Belle, Purple, Steel Pin ................................................................ 18.00
Carnival Glass, Hatpin, Cattails, Purple, Steel Pin ............................................................ 16.00
Carnival Glass, Hatpin, Hearts In Maltese Cross, Purple, Steel Pin ................................ 16.00
Carnival Glass, Hatpin, Lattice, Purple, Steel Pin .............................................................. 15.00
Carnival Glass, Hatpin, Plums, Purple, Steel Pin .............................................................. 15.00
Carnival Glass, Hatpin, Rooster, Purple .............................................................................. 21.00
Carnival Glass, Hatpin, Scarab, Purple ................................................................................ 10.00
Carnival Glass, Hatpin, Scarab, Top O' The Walk, Amethyst ............................................ 15.00
Carnival Glass, Hatpin, Scarab, Top O' The Walk, Red .................................................... 30.00
Carnival Glass, Hatpin, Top O' The Morning, Blue ............................................................ 10.00
Carnival Glass, Hatpin, Top O' The Morning, Green .......................................................... 10.00
Carnival Glass, Hatpin, Top O' The Morning, Purple ........................................ 10.00 To 22.00
Carnival Glass, Hatpin, 3 Bumblebees, Purple, Steel Pin ................................................ 25.00
Carnival Glass, Jar, Pickle, Swirl, Smoke .......................................................................... 18.00
Carnival Glass, Jar, Powder, Duck, Marigold ...................................................................... 18.00
Carnival Glass, Jar, Powder, Milady, Marigold .................................................................... 43.00
Carnival Glass, Jar, Powder, Orange Tree, Blue ................................................................ 49.00
Carnival Glass, Jar, Powder, Scottie .................................................................................... 6.00
Carnival Glass, Jar, Powder, Vintage, Marigold, Covered ................................................ 35.00
Carnival Glass, Jar, Rose Petal, Purple .............................................................................. 175.00
Carnival Glass, Lampshade, Light Holder, Marigold .......................................................... 15.00
Carnival Glass, Lampshade, Star, Marigold, Pair .............................................................. 39.50
Carnival Glass, Mug, Beaded Shell, Amethyst .................................................................... 35.00
Carnival Glass, Mug, Beaded Shell, Purple ........................................................................ 55.00
Carnival Glass, Mug, Heron, Purple .................................................................................... 140.00
Carnival Glass, Mug, Orange Tree, Blue ................................................ 24.00 To 30.00
Carnival Glass, Mug, Orange Tree, Green .......................................................................... 35.00
Carnival Glass, Mug, Orange Tree, Marigold ...................................................................... 21.00
Carnival Glass, Mug, Orange Tree, Marigold ........................................ 13.00 To 25.00
Carnival Glass, Mug, Orange Tree, Purple, 3 1/2 In. High ................................................ 42.00
Carnival Glass, Mug, Singing Bird, Marigold, Marked N .................................................. 30.00
Carnival Glass, Mug, Singing Bird, Purple, Signed N ...................................................... 48.00
Carnival Glass, Mug, Stork & Rushes, Marigold ................................................................ 15.00
Carnival Glass, Nappy, Bird & Cherries, Blue, Handled, Turned Up Sides ...................... 35.00
Carnival Glass, Nappy, Butterflies, Amethyst, 2 Handled .................................................. 20.00
Carnival Glass, Nappy, Grape & Cable, Light Marigold ...................................................... 55.00
Carnival Glass, Nappy, Grape & Cable, Purple, 2 Handled, Bronze Tone ...................... 80.00
Carnival Glass, Nappy, Leaf Rays, Marigold, Pale Coloring, Handled .............................. 15.00
Carnival Glass, Nappy, Leaf, Marigold, Opalescent, Handled .......................................... 23.00
Carnival Glass, Nappy, Louisa, Marigold ............................................................................ 25.00
Carnival Glass, Nappy, Pansy Spray, Amethyst, Handled ................................................ 25.00
Carnival Glass, Nappy, Persian Medallion, True Red, 2 Handled .................................... 210.00
Carnival Glass, Nappy, Water Lily, Marigold, 2 Handled .................................................... 15.00
Carnival Glass, Paperweight, Welch, Purple ...................................................................... 50.00
Carnival Glass, Parfait, Colonial, Marigold, 5 In. High ...................................................... 18.00
Carnival Glass, Parfait, Frosted Block, Clambroth, Pink & Blue Highlights ...................... 18.00
Carnival Glass, Perfume, DeVilbiss, Marigold, Signed ...................................................... 20.00
Carnival Glass, Pitcher, Apple Tree, Marigold .................................................................... 165.00
Carnival Glass, Pitcher, Buttermilk, Swirl, Marigold .......................................................... 75.00
Carnival Glass, Pitcher, Grape With Gothic Arch, Marigold .............................................. 110.00
Carnival Glass, Pitcher, Iris & Herringbone, Marigold ...................................................... 8.00
Carnival Glass, Pitcher, Lemonade, Wide Panel, Marigold .............................................. 30.00
Carnival Glass, Pitcher, Milk, Imperial Grape, White, 6 1/4 In. ........................................ 100.00
Carnival Glass, Pitcher, Milk, Poinsettia, Marigold ............................................................ 35.00
Carnival Glass, Pitcher, Milk, Star Medallion, Marigold .............................. 20.00 To 25.00
Carnival Glass, Pitcher, Milk, Studs, Light Amber Marigold .............................................. 25.00
Carnival Glass, Pitcher, Oriental Poppy, Marigold ............................................................ 175.00
Carnival Glass, Pitcher, Pansy Spray, Green .................................................................... 29.50
Carnival Glass, Pitcher, Peacock At Fountain, Blue .......................................................... 275.00
Carnival Glass, Pitcher, Raspberry, Dark Marigold ............................................................ 150.00
Carnival Glass, Pitcher, Singing Birds, Purple .................................................................. 195.00
Carnival Glass, Pitcher, Sunflower & Wheat, Red Amber, 1 1/2 Quarts .......................... 175.00

Carnival Glass, Pitcher, Tiger Lily, Marigold ............................................ 135.00
Carnival Glass, Pitcher, Water, Acorn Burr, Purple ............................................ 295.00
Carnival Glass, Pitcher, Water, Diamond Lace, Purple ............................................ 210.00
Carnival Glass, Pitcher, Water, Double Star, Green ............................................ 250.00
Carnival Glass, Pitcher, Water, Floral & Grape, Blue ............................................ 180.00
Carnival Glass, Pitcher, Water, Frosted Ribbon, Light Amber Marigold ............................................ 35.00
Carnival Glass, Pitcher, Water, Grape & Cable, Green ............................ 215.00 To 240.00
Carnival Glass, Pitcher, Water, Grape & Cable, Marigold ............................................ 145.00
Carnival Glass, Pitcher, Water, Heavy Iris, Marigold ............................................ 195.00
Carnival Glass, Pitcher, Water, Imperial Grape, Marigold ............................................ 55.00
Carnival Glass, Pitcher, Water, Luster & Clear, Marigold ............................................ 95.00
Carnival Glass, Pitcher, Water, Paneled Dandelion, Marigold ............................................ 285.00
Carnival Glass, Pitcher, Water, Tiger Lily, Green ............................................ 200.00
Carnival Glass, Pitcher, Water, Tree Bark, Marigold ............................................ 17.00
Carnival Glass, Plate, Acanthus, Marigold, 10 In. ............................................ 150.00
Carnival Glass, Plate, Apple Blossom Twigs, Purple, 9 In. ............................................ 145.00
Carnival Glass, Plate, Basket Weave, Green, Signed N, 9 In. ............................................ 75.00
Carnival Glass, Plate, Bread, Bouquet & Lattice, Marigold, 6 1/4 In. ............................................ 1.95
Carnival Glass, Plate, Cake, Iris & Herringbone, Marigold, 12 In. ............................................ 15.00
Carnival Glass, Plate, Chop, Heavy Grape, Green ............................................ 30.00
Carnival Glass, Plate, Chop, Oval & Round, Marigold, 10 3/4 In. ............................................ 85.00
Carnival Glass, Plate, Embossed Scrolls, Green, Marigold Overla ............................ 69.00 To 85.00
Carnival Glass, Plate, Fanciful, Purple, 9 In. ............................................ 115.00
Carnival Glass, Plate, Fishscale & Beads, Peach, Opalescent, Deep, 7 In. ............................................ 28.00
Carnival Glass, Plate, Good Luck, Purple, 8 3/4 In. ............................................ 175.00
Carnival Glass, Plate, Grape & Cable, Purple, N Mark, 9 In. ............................................ 90.00
Carnival Glass, Plate, Heavy Grape, Green, 8 In. ............................................ 70.00
Carnival Glass, Plate, Horses' Heads Medallion, Marigold, 8 In. ............................................ 75.00
Carnival Glass, Plate, Illinois Soldiers And Sailors ............................................ 750.00
Carnival Glass, Plate, Imperial Grapes, Marigold, 9 In. ............................ 29.00 To 32.00
Carnival Glass, Plate, Jewels, Sapphire Blue, 9 In. ............................................ 12.00
Carnival Glass, Plate, Kittens, Marigold, 4 1/4 In. ............................................ 45.00
Carnival Glass, Plate, Orange Tree, Clambroth, 9 In. ............................................ 45.00
Carnival Glass, Plate, Peacock On Fence, Blue, 9 In. ............................................ 165.00
Carnival Glass, Plate, Peacock On Fence, Cobalt Blue, 9 In. ............................................ 125.00
Carnival Glass, Plate, Peacock On Fence, Ice Green, Marked N ............................................ 140.00
Carnival Glass, Plate, Persian Medallion, Purple, 6 In. ............................................ 24.00
Carnival Glass, Plate, Ribbon Tie, Blue, Ruffled, 9 In. ............................................ 85.00
Carnival Glass, Plate, Stippled Rays, Marigold, 7 In. ............................................ 23.50
Carnival Glass, Plate, Strawberry, Green, 9 In. ............................................ 80.00
Carnival Glass, Plate, Strawberry, Marigold, Signed N, 9 In. ............................................ 85.00
Carnival Glass, Plate, Strawberry, Purple, 9 In. ............................................ 85.00
Carnival Glass, Plate, Three Fruits, Purple, 9 1/2 In. ............................................ *Illus* 125.00
Carnival Glass, Plate, Tree Of Life, Marigold, 8 In. ............................................ 60.00
Carnival Glass, Plate, Vintage Grape, Green, 7 1/2 In. ............................................ 65.00
Carnival Glass, Plate, Vintage Grape, Marigold, 7 In. ............................................ 28.00

Carnival Glass, Plate, Three Fruits, Purple, 9 1/2 In.

| | |
|---|---|
| Carnival Glass, Plate, Wide Panel, Clambroth, 10 In. | 15.00 |
| Carnival Glass, Plate, Windflower, Blue, 9 In. | 135.00 |
| Carnival Glass, Punch Set, Fashion, Marigold, 7 Piece | 125.00 |
| Carnival Glass, Punch Set, Grape & Cable, Purple, Signed N, 12 Piece | 1000.00 |
| Carnival Glass, Punch Set, Grape & Cable, Purple, 10 Piece | 475.00 |
| Carnival Glass, Punch Set, Hobstars, Marigold, 7 Piece | 129.00 |
| Carnival Glass, Punch Set, Imperial Grape, Marigold, 14 Piece | 140.00 |
| Carnival Glass, Punch Set, Memphis, Marigold, Marked N, 9 Piece | 285.00 |
| Carnival Glass, Punch Set, Orange Tree, Blue, 8 Piece | 300.00 |
| Carnival Glass, Punch Set, Orange Tree, Marigold, 13 Piece | 165.00 |
| Carnival Glass, Punch Set, Stork & Rushes, Marigold, 7 Piece | 125.00 |
| Carnival Glass, Relish, Pansy, Amber, Round | 14.00 |
| Carnival Glass, Relish, Pansy, Marigold | 22.50 |
| Carnival Glass, Relish, Star And File, Marigold | 16.50 |
| Carnival Glass, Rose Bowl, Daisy & Plume, Marigold, Stemmed | 25.00 |
| Carnival Glass, Rose Bowl, Drapery, Aqua Opalescent, Northwood | 11.00 |
| Carnival Glass, Rose Bowl, Drapery, Aqua Opalescent, Northwood | 110.00 |
| Carnival Glass, Rose Bowl, Finecut & Roses, Ice Blue | 65.00 |
| Carnival Glass, Rose Bowl, Finecut & Roses, Purple | 55.00 |
| Carnival Glass, Rose Bowl, Garland, Blue | 65.00 |
| Carnival Glass, Rose Bowl, Garland, Marigold | 55.00 |
| Carnival Glass, Rose Bowl, Grape Delight, Blue | 65.00 |
| Carnival Glass, Rose Bowl, Grape Delight, White | 75.00 |
| Carnival Glass, Rose Bowl, Hobnail Swirl, Purple, Millersburg | 385.00 |
| Carnival Glass, Rose Bowl, Hobnail, Marigold | 75.00 |
| Carnival Glass, Rose Bowl, Horses' Heads, Marigold | 85.00 |
| Carnival Glass, Rose Bowl, Leaf & Beads, Amethyst | 55.00 |
| Carnival Glass, Rose Bowl, Leaf & Beads, Aqua Opalescent, N Mark | 95.00 |
| Carnival Glass, Rose Bowl, Leaf & Beads, Green, Footed, Marked N | 50.00 |
| Carnival Glass, Rose Bowl, Leaf & Beads, Orange, 3 Footed | 42.00 |
| Carnival Glass, Rose Bowl, Leaf & Beads, Purple, Marked N | 65.00 |
| Carnival Glass, Rose Bowl, Louisa, Green | 49.00 |
| Carnival Glass, Rose Bowl, Luster Rose, Marigold, 6 In. | 16.50 |
| Carnival Glass, Rose Bowl, Opalescent Leaf & Bead, Aqua | 118.00 |
| Carnival Glass, Rose Bowl, Open Rose, Marigold | 35.00 |
| Carnival Glass, Rose Bowl, Swirl Hobnail, Marigold | 90.00 |
| Carnival Glass, Rose Bowl, Wild Rose, Green, Open Heart Edges, 3 Footed, N | 35.00 |
| Carnival Glass, Rose Bowl, Wreath Of Roses, Marigold | 25.00 |
| Carnival Glass, Salt & Pepper, Spider Web, Smoky | 150.00 |
| Carnival Glass, Salt, Master, Swan, Pastel Green | 35.00 |
| Carnival Glass, Salt, Swan, Grape Cable, Green | 18.00 |
| Carnival Glass, Salt, Swan, Ice Green | 18.50 |
| Carnival Glass, Sauce, Acorn Burrs, Green | 25.00 |
| Carnival Glass, Sauce, Butterfly & Berry, Marigold, Footed | 12.50 |
| Carnival Glass, Sauce, Fan, Purple, Footed, Marked N | 59.00 |
| Carnival Glass, Sauce, Fentonia, Blue, Claw Footed, 5 In. | 25.00 |
| Carnival Glass, Sauce, Grape & Cable, Green | 25.00 |
| Carnival Glass, Sauce, Grape & Thumbprint, Green, N, 5 In.Diameter | 22.50 |
| Carnival Glass, Sauce, Heavy Grape, Marigold | 14.00 |
| Carnival Glass, Sauce, Heavy Grape, Purple, 5 In. | 18.00 |
| Carnival Glass, Sauce, Maple Leaf, Blue, Footed, Northwood | 22.50 |
| Carnival Glass, Sauce, Orange Tree, Marigold, Footed, 4 In. | 12.00 |
| Carnival Glass, Sauce, Panther & Butterfly & Berries, Marigold, Claw Feet | 26.00 |
| Carnival Glass, Sauce, Peacock At Fountain, Purple | 30.00 |
| Carnival Glass, Sauce, Peacock, Purple, Millersburg | 22.00 |
| Carnival Glass, Sauce, Stork & Rushes, Purple | 24.00 |
| Carnival Glass, Sauce, Windmill, Marigold | 10.50 |
| Carnival Glass, Saucer, Kitten, Marigold, Fluted | 55.00 |
| Carnival Glass, Server, Vintage, Clambroth | 15.00 |
| Carnival Glass, Shade, Astral, Marigold | 25.00 |
| Carnival Glass, Shade, Drapery, Peach, Scalloped, 5 1/2 In.Long | 45.00 |
| Carnival Glass, Sherbet & Underplate, Swirl, Marigold | 5.00 |
| Carnival Glass, Sherbet, Bouquet & Lattice, Marigold | 1.98 To 2.50 |
| Carnival Glass, Sherbet, Bouquet & Lattice, Marigold, Footed | 1.95 |
| Carnival Glass, Sherbet, Cane, Marigold | 7.00 |
| Carnival Glass, Sherbet, Orange Tree, Blue | 26.00 |

Carnival Glass, Sherbet, Stretch, White, Stemmed ................................................. 17.00
Carnival Glass, Spittoon, Lady's, Hobnail Swirl, Purple, Millersburg ................... 395.00
Carnival Glass, Spooner, Butterfly & Berry, Blue ................................................... 47.00
Carnival Glass, Spooner, Cherry, Green, Marked N ............................................... 60.00
Carnival Glass, Spooner, Grape With Gothic Arches, Clear, Gold Trim ................. 18.00
Carnival Glass, Spooner, Grape With Gothic Arches, Marigold ............................. 38.50
Carnival Glass, Spooner, Kittens, Marigold ........................................................... 65.00
Carnival Glass, Spooner, Peacock At Fountain, Marigold ...................................... 30.00
Carnival Glass, Spooner, Peacock At Fountain, Purple .......................................... 75.00
Carnival Glass, Sugar & Creamer, Breakfast, Orange Tree, Blue .......................... 35.00
Carnival Glass, Sugar & Creamer, Flute & Diamond Point Band, Green, N ........... 25.00
Carnival Glass, Sugar & Creamer, Grape & Gothic Arches, Green, Cover, Gold, N ...... 43.00
Carnival Glass, Sugar & Creamer, Long Thumbprint, Marigold ............................. 35.00
Carnival Glass, Sugar & Creamer, Paneled Apple, Marigold ................................. 30.00
Carnival Glass, Sugar & Creamer, Pansy, Marigold .............................................. 19.00
Carnival Glass, Sugar & Creamer, Royal Lace, Cobalt Blue .................................. 32.00
Carnival Glass, Sugar & Creamer, Shell & Jewel, Marigold .................................. 60.00
Carnival Glass, Sugar & Creamer, Stippled Pansies, Marigold ............................. 30.00
Carnival Glass, Sugar & Creamer, Stippled Rays, Marigold .................................. 22.00
Carnival Glass, Sugar, Butterfly & Berry, Marigold, Covered ............................... 65.00
Carnival Glass, Sugar, Grape & Cable, Purple, Covered ..................................... 175.00
Carnival Glass, Sugar, Grape With Gothic Arches, Clear, Covered, Gold Trim ...... 30.00
Carnival Glass, Sugar, Grape With Gothic Arches, Marigold, Covered ................. 40.00
Carnival Glass, Sugar, Shell & Jewel, Green, Covered .......................................... 49.00
Carnival Glass, Sugar, Strutting Peacock, Purple, Covered .................................. 59.00
Carnival Glass, Swan, Blue ..................................................................................... 35.00
Carnival Glass, Swan, Blue Pastel .......................................................................... 22.00
Carnival Glass, Table Set, Luster Rose, Marigold, 4 Piece ................................. 150.00
Carnival Glass, Table Set, Quartered Block, Marigold, 3 Piece ............................. 95.00
Carnival Glass, Tankard Tumbler, Grape & Cable, Marigold ................................. 55.00
Carnival Glass, Tankard, Blackberry Block, Green .............................................. 500.00
Carnival Glass, Tankard, Daisy & Lattice, Marigold ........................................... 125.00
Carnival Glass, Tankard, Grape Arbor, Marigold .................................................. 17.50
Carnival Glass, Tankard, Tree Bark, Marigold ....................................................... 30.00
Carnival Glass, Three Flowers & Leaves, Peach, Ruffled Edge, 7 In. ................... 20.00
Carnival Glass, Toothpick, Cherry Wreath, Pastel Blue ........................................ 85.00
Carnival Glass, Toothpick, Flute Purple ................................................ 50.00 To 85.00
Carnival Glass, Toothpick, Fluted, Green .............................................................. 47.50
Carnival Glass, Toothpick, Fluted, Green, Star Base ............................................. 60.00
Carnival Glass, Toothpick, S Repeat, Amethyst ..................................................... 85.00
Carnival Glass, Toothpick, Swan, Green, Figural, 3 Swans .................................... 6.00
Carnival Glass, Town Pump & Trough, Blue Opalescent, Signed Northwood ....... 185.00
Carnival Glass, Tray, Balloon, Marigold, Footed, 5 In. ........................................... 9.00
Carnival Glass, Tray, Dresser, Grape & Cable, Green .......................................... 200.00
Carnival Glass, Tray, Dresser, Grape & Cable, Purple ........................................ 210.00
Carnival Glass, Tray, Dresser, Imperial Pansy, True Amber ................................. 90.00
Carnival Glass, Tumbler, Acorn Burr, Green, Marked N ........................................ 65.00
Carnival Glass, Tumbler, Acorn Burr, Marigold ..................................................... 29.00
Carnival Glass, Tumbler, Acorn Burr, Purple, Signed Northwood .......................... 40.00
Carnival Glass, Tumbler, Apple Tree, Blue ........................................... 32.50 To 35.00
Carnival Glass, Tumbler, Apple Tree, Marigold ..................................................... 20.00
Carnival Glass, Tumbler, Beaded Shell, Purple ..................................................... 55.00
Carnival Glass, Tumbler, Berry & Butterfly, Blue .................................................. 22.50
Carnival Glass, Tumbler, Blueberry, Blue .............................................................. 55.00
Carnival Glass, Tumbler, Bouquet, Marigold ......................................................... 25.00
Carnival Glass, Tumbler, Butterfly & Berry, Cobalt ............................................... 35.00
Carnival Glass, Tumbler, Butterfly & Berry, Marigold ........................................... 15.00
Carnival Glass, Tumbler, Butterfly & Fern, Amethyst ............................................ 24.00
Carnival Glass, Tumbler, Cactus, White ................................................................. 15.00
Carnival Glass, Tumbler, Cattail & Lily, Marigold ................................................. 10.00
Carnival Glass, Tumbler, Concave Diamonds, Pastel Blue .................................... 24.00
Carnival Glass, Tumbler, Daisy & Lattice, Marigold .............................................. 16.00
Carnival Glass, Tumbler, Dandelion, Marigold ...................................................... 22.50
Carnival Glass, Tumbler, Dandelion, Purple, Marked N ........................................ 22.00
Carnival Glass, Tumbler, Diamond Lace, Purple .................................................... 39.00
Carnival Glass, Tumbler, Double Star, Green ........................................................ 35.00

Carnival Glass, Tumbler, Drapery, White Opalescent, Signed N ............................................. 14.00
Carnival Glass, Tumbler, Enameled Cherries, Blue .......................................................... 12.50
Carnival Glass, Tumbler, Enameled Cherries, Cobalt ....................................................... 25.00
Carnival Glass, Tumbler, Enameled Flowers, Marigold ....................................................... 7.35
Carnival Glass, Tumbler, Fashion, Marigold ..................................................................... 14.00
Carnival Glass, Tumbler, Floral & Grape, Blue .............................................. 22.00 To 27.00
Carnival Glass, Tumbler, Floral & Grape, Marigold ........................................................ 12.50
Carnival Glass, Tumbler, Floral & Grape, Purple ........................................................... 22.50
Carnival Glass, Tumbler, Fluffy Peacock, Amethyst ........................................................ 50.00
Carnival Glass, Tumbler, Flute, Purple ............................................................................ 75.00
Carnival Glass, Tumbler, Frosted Ribbon, Light Marigold .............................................. 10.00
Carnival Glass, Tumbler, God & Home, Purple ............................................................. 200.00
Carnival Glass, Tumbler, Grape & Cable With Thumbprint, Blue, N .............................. 22.00
Carnival Glass, Tumbler, Grape & Cable With Thumbprint, Purple, Signed N ................ 25.00
Carnival Glass, Tumbler, Grape & Cable, Marigold ....................................... 15.00 To 19.00
Carnival Glass, Tumbler, Grape & Cable, Marigold, Signed N ..................................... 15.00
Carnival Glass, Tumbler, Grape & Cable, Peacock Blue, Signed N ............................... 16.00
Carnival Glass, Tumbler, Grape & Gothic Arches, Blue ............................................... 30.00
Carnival Glass, Tumbler, Grape & Gothic Arches, Green ............................................. 30.00
Carnival Glass, Tumbler, Grape & Gothic Arches, Marigold .......................... 15.00 To 30.00
Carnival Glass, Tumbler, Grape & Lattice, Marigold ..................................................... 15.00
Carnival Glass, Tumbler, Grape Arbor, Marigold ........................................................... 27.50
Carnival Glass, Tumbler, Grape, Orange, Northwood ................................................... 12.50
Carnival Glass, Tumbler, Grapevine & Lattice, Purple .................................................. 45.00
Carnival Glass, Tumbler, Hand-Painted Cherries, Blue, Fenton ................................... 15.00
Carnival Glass, Tumbler, Imperial Grape, Marigold ...................................................... 13.50
Carnival Glass, Tumbler, Lattice & Grape, Marigold ..................................................... 25.00
Carnival Glass, Tumbler, Maple Leaf, Purple ................................................................ 35.00
Carnival Glass, Tumbler, Milady, Blue ........................................................................... 32.50
Carnival Glass, Tumbler, Octagon, Marigold ................................................................. 15.00
Carnival Glass, Tumbler, Orange Tree, Orange, Handled .............................................. 13.50
Carnival Glass, Tumbler, Orange Tree, Reddish Marigold, 4 Footed ............................ 22.50
Carnival Glass, Tumbler, Oriental Poppy, Green, Gold Trim, Northwood ..................... 20.00
Carnival Glass, Tumbler, Oriental Poppy, Marigold ....................................... 30.00 To 35.00
Carnival Glass, Tumbler, Oriental Poppy, Marigold, N .................................................. 32.50
Carnival Glass, Tumbler, Oriental Poppy, Purple ........................................................... 50.00
Carnival Glass, Tumbler, Oriental Poppy, Purple, Silver Iridescence ............................ 20.00
Carnival Glass, Tumbler, Paneled Dandelion, Green ..................................................... 37.50
Carnival Glass, Tumbler, Peach, Blue ............................................................................ 60.00
Carnival Glass, Tumbler, Peach, Green, Gold, N ........................................................... 18.00
Carnival Glass, Tumbler, Peacock At Fountain, Blue ..................................................... 30.00
Carnival Glass, Tumbler, Peacock At Fountain, Marigold ............................... 20.00 To 30.00
Carnival Glass, Tumbler, Poppy, Blue, Marked N ........................................................... 32.00
Carnival Glass, Tumbler, Raspberry, Marigold, Marked N ............................................. 25.00
Carnival Glass, Tumbler, Rose, Mulberry, Iridescent ..................................................... 16.50
Carnival Glass, Tumbler, Singing Bird, Green, Northwood ............................ 27.50 To 40.00
Carnival Glass, Tumbler, Singing Bird, Marigold ........................................................... 22.00
Carnival Glass, Tumbler, Singing Bird, Purple ............................................................... 40.00
Carnival Glass, Tumbler, Stork & Rushes, Blue ............................................................ 22.50
Carnival Glass, Tumbler, Stork & Rushes, Marigold ..................................................... 18.50
Carnival Glass, Tumbler, Swirl, Green, Marked N ......................................................... 45.00
Carnival Glass, Tumbler, Ten Mums, Blue ..................................................................... 35.00
Carnival Glass, Tumbler, Tiger Lily, Marigold ............................................................... 18.00
Carnival Glass, Tumbler, Vineyard, Marigold ................................................................ 25.00
Carnival Glass, Tumbler, Vintage, Marigold .................................................. 10.00 To 15.00
Carnival Glass, Tumbler, Windmill, Marigold ................................................................ 10.00
Carnival Glass, Vase, Corinth, Green, 12 Ribs, 8 1/2 In.High ....................................... 20.00
Carnival Glass, Vase, Diamond & Rib, Green, 10 In. High ............................................ 12.50
Carnival Glass, Vase, Diamond Point, Green, Signed N, 10 In.High ............................. 23.00
Carnival Glass, Vase, Drapery, Ice Green, Signed N, 7 3/4 In.High .............................. 55.00
Carnival Glass, Vase, Fan, Imperial Jewels, Green, 5 1/2 In.High ................................ 22.00
Carnival Glass, Vase, Fine Rib, Purple, Ornate Top, 10 3/4 In.High ............................. 24.00
Carnival Glass, Vase, Holly, Marigold, Hat Shape ........................................ 11.00 To 18.50
Carnival Glass, Vase, Iris & Herringbone, Marigold, Flared Top, 9 In. ......................... 9.75
Carnival Glass, Vase, Iris, Marigold, 9 In. ..................................................................... 14.50
Carnival Glass, Vase, Jack-In-The-Pulpit, Marigold, 6 In. ............................................. 22.50

Carnival Glass, Vase, Lined Lattice, White, 9 1/2 In. ....................................................... 20.00
Carnival Glass, Vase, Mary Ann, Marigold ........................................... 40.00 To 50.00
Carnival Glass, Vase, Maryland, Purple & Bronze, 18 1/2 In.High ........................ 145.00
Carnival Glass, Vase, Opalescent, White, 9 In. ............................................ 30.00
Carnival Glass, Vase, People's, Blue ........................................................ 8100.00
Carnival Glass, Vase, Ribbed, Amethyst, Fluted Top, Northwood, 10 1/2 In. .......... 25.00
Carnival Glass, Vase, Ribbed, True Red, 9 1/2 In. ....................................... 100.00
Carnival Glass, Vase, Ripple, Marigold ...................................... 11.00 To 18.00
Carnival Glass, Vase, Ripple, Purple, Wide Mouth, 8 In. High ......................... 16.50
Carnival Glass, Vase, Ruffle, Marigold, 11 In. High ...................................... 30.00
Carnival Glass, Vase, Rustic, Purple ......................................... 27.00 To 49.00
Carnival Glass, Vase, Thin Rib, Blue, Marked N.10 1/2 In.X 4 In. ..................... 45.00
Carnival Glass, Vase, Thin Rib, Cobalt, Ruffled Top, 17 In. ............................ 50.00
Carnival Glass, Vase, Tree Bark, Marigold, 7 1/2 In.High ............................... 4.95
Carnival Glass, Vase, Tree Of Life, Marigold, 7 1/2 In. ................................. 12.50
Carnival Glass, Vase, Tree Trunk, Green, Scalloped Rim, Marked N, 8 In. ............ 15.00
Carnival Glass, Vase, Tree Trunk, Purple, Scalloped Rim, Marked N, 11 In. .......... 30.00
Carnival Glass, Vase, Twig, Purple, 4 1/2 In. ............................................. 345.00
Carnival Glass, Vase, Wall, Bird & Grapes, Marigold ................................... 35.00
Carnival Glass, Water Set, Acorn Burr, Marigold, Marked N, 7 Piece .................. 400.00
Carnival Glass, Water Set, Butterfly & Plume, Green, 5 Piece .......................... 400.00
Carnival Glass, Water Set, Crackle, Marigold, 7 Piece .................................. 45.00
Carnival Glass, Water Set, Daisy, Blue, Enameled, Marked N, 3 Piece ................ 110.00
Carnival Glass, Water Set, Dandelion, Green, Northwood, 7 Piece .................... 1250.00
Carnival Glass, Water Set, Diamond & Lace, Purple, 7 Piece ........................... 475.00
Carnival Glass, Water Set, Double Star, Green, 7 Piece ................................. 475.00
Carnival Glass, Water Set, Grape & Cable, Green, 7 Piece .............................. 525.00
Carnival Glass, Water Set, Grape & Cable, Marigold, 5 Piece .......................... 245.00
Carnival Glass, Water Set, Grape & Cable, Marigold, 6 Piece .......................... 325.00
Carnival Glass, Water Set, Grape & Cable, Purple, 7 Piece ............................. 450.00
Carnival Glass, Water Set, Grape Arbor, Marigold, 7 Piece ............................. 400.00
Carnival Glass, Water Set, Heavy Iris, Marigold, 7 Piece ............................... 600.00
Carnival Glass, Water Set, Iris & Herringbone, Marigold, Footed, 7 Piece ............ 45.00
Carnival Glass, Water Set, Maple Leaf, Marigold, 5 Piece .............................. 210.00
Carnival Glass, Water Set, Octagon, Marigold, 7 Piece .................................. 250.00
Carnival Glass, Water Set, Paneled Dandelion, Green, 7 Piece ......................... 650.00
Carnival Glass, Water Set, Peacock At Fountain, Blue, 7 Piece ......................... 450.00
Carnival Glass, Water Set, Peacock At Fountain, Purple, 7 Piece ...................... 495.00
Carnival Glass, Water Set, Raspberry, Green, Marked N, 7 Piece ...................... 395.00
Carnival Glass, Water Set, Singing Bird, Green, 7 Piece ................................ 550.00
Carnival Glass, Water Set, Tree Back, Marigold, 7 Piece ............................... 50.00
Carnival Glass, Water Set, Tree Bark, Marigold, 9 Piece ............................... 30.00
Carnival Glass, Water Set, Tree Of Life, Marigold, 3 Piece ............................. 27.50
Carnival Glass, Water Set, Vineyard, Purple, 7 Piece ................................... 450.00
Carnival Glass, Whimsy, Horse Medallion, Blue ......................................... 120.00
Carnival Glass, Wine Set, Sunburst, Marigold, 3 Piece ................................. 85.00
Carnival Glass, Wine Set, Wine & Roses, Marigold, 6 Piece ........................... 400.00
Carnival Glass, Wine, Imperial Grape, Green ............................... 18.00 To 22.50
Carnival Glass, Wine, Imperial Grape, Marigold ......................................... 6.50
Carnival Glass, Wine, Orange Tree, Marigold ............................................ 16.00
Carnival Glass, Wine, Sailboat, Marigold, Stemmed ................................... 18.00
Carnival Glass, Wine, Vintage Grape, Amethyst ......................................... 20.00
Carnival Glass, Wine, Vintage, Marigold .................................................. 15.00
Carousel, Bear, Carved Wood, White Painted Saddle, C.1850, 20 In. ................ 300.00
Carousel, Figure, Dancing Female, Carved & Painted, 1800s, 39 In.High ........... 1100.00
Carousel, Horse, Carved & Painted Wood, Hair Tail, C.1890, 4 Ft.2 In. .............. 275.00
Carousel, Horse, Hand-Carved, Jewel Eyes, Large ..................................... 2500.00
Carousel, Horse, Parker, Hand-Carved, Wooden, Hair Tail ............................ 250.00
Carousel, Horse, Wood, Polychrome, 38 X 62 In. ............................. Illus 500.00
Carousel, Horse, Wooden, Daniel Muller, C.1890, 46 In. ...................... Illus 1200.00

*Cased glass is made with one thin layer of glass over another layer or layers*
*of colored glass. Many types of art glass were cased. Cased glass is*
*usually a well-made piece by a reputable factory.*

Cased Glass, Bowl, Pink To Blue, Ruffled, 7 1/2 In. ..................................... 30.00
Cased Glass, Dish, Bride's, Cranberry, Ruffled, Enamel Floral, 10 1/4 In. ........... 275.00

Cased Glass, Mug, Triple Overlay, Blue, White, & Clear, 5 In. ........................................ 300.00
Cased Glass, Tumbler, Triple Overlay, Pink, White, & Clear, 4 3/4 In. ........................ 200.00
Cased Glass, Vase, Blue Overlay, Enameled Floral, White Lining, 5 In. ..................... 20.00
Cased Glass, Vase, White With Yellow, 9 1/4 In. ................................................... 12.50
Cased Glass, Wine Set, Overlay, White To Cranberry, Gold Edged, 5 Piece .............. 200.00
   Cash Register, see Store, Cash Register

*Castor sets have been known as early as 1705. Most of those that have been found today date from Victorian times. A castor set usually consists of a silver-plated frame that holds three to seven condiment bottles. The pickle castor was a single glass jar about six inches high and held in a silver frame. A cover and tongs were kept with the jar. They were popular from 1890 to 1900.*

Castor Set, Two Bottles, Blown, Square, Reed & Barton Handled Holder ................. 33.00
Castor Set, Three Bottles, Child's, Twisted Wire Frame ...................................... 30.00
Castor Set, Three Bottles, Daisy & Button, Glass Frame With Toothpick Top ........... 57.50
Castor Set, Three Bottles, New England Glass, Silver Plate Frame, 1870 ................ 45.00
Castor Set, Three Bottles, Star & Punty Type, Stand ......................................... 35.00
Castor Set, Four Bottles, Cut Glass, Pewter Holder Marked PA & S ....................... 110.00
Castor Set, Four Bottles, Etched Thumbprint, Oval Silver Plate Holder .................. 45.00
Castor Set, Four Bottles, King's Crown, Pressed Glass ....................................... 65.00
Castor Set, Four Bottles, Mustard Spoon, Silver Plate Stand ............................... 65.00
Castor Set, Four Bottles, Pewter Stand & Tops, American .................................. 65.00
Castor Set, Four Bottles, Pink Overlay, Puffed, Center Handle ............................ 90.00
Castor Set, Four Bottles, 3 Mold, Eben Smith Pewter Frame .............................. 150.00
Castor Set, Five Bottles, Clear Grape Etched Bottles, Silver Plate Frame .............. 55.00
Castor Set, Five Bottles, Pewter, C.1850, 8 3/4 In. ...............................................*Illus* 50.00

Castor, Pickle, Cupid & Psyche Glass, Silver Plate, 7 In
*(See Page 92)*

Carousel Horse, Wooden, Daniel Muller, C.1890, 46 In. *(See Page 90)*

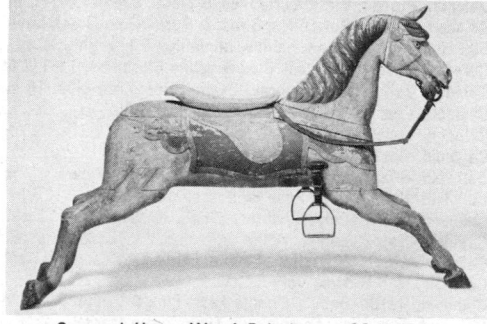

Carousel, Horse, Wood, Polychrome, 38 X 62 In.
*(See Page 90)*

Castor Set, Five Bottles, Pewter, C.1850, 8 3/4 In.

| | |
|---|---|
| Castor Set, Five Bottles, Three Mold, Trask Pewter Stand | 200.00 |
| Castor Set, Five Bottles, Twisted Wire | 36.00 |
| Castor Set, Six Bottles, Blown, Rectangular Stand, Flint | 120.00 |
| Castor Set, Six Bottles, Cut & Etched, Wilcox Plate Revolving Frame | 98.00 |
| Castor Set, Six Bottles, Etched, 3 Silver Tops & Holder, 3 Glass Stoppers | 100.00 |
| Castor Set, Six Bottles, Pressed Glass, Silver Plate Tops & Frame | 80.00 |
| Castor Set, Six Bottles, Silver Plate Frame With Grapes & Vines | 175.00 |
| Castor, Condiment, Barrel Shape Bottles, Inverted Thumbprint, Silver Plate | 45.00 |
| Castor, Condiment, Cambridge, Pink, Center Handled Tray, Signed | 15.00 |
| **Castor, Pickle, see also Amberina, Castor, Pickle** | |
| Castor, Pickle, Amber, Quilted, Silver Tongs & Holder | 95.00 |
| Castor, Pickle, Clear Insert, Block & Bull's-Eye Type, Silver Frame & Tongs | 60.00 |
| Castor, Pickle, Clear Insert, Leaf Design, Silver Plate Holder & Tongs | 47.50 |
| Castor, Pickle, Cranberry Glass, Thumbprint, Enameled, Tongs | 135.00 |
| Castor, Pickle, Cranberry Inverted Thumbprint Insert, Enameled, Tongs | 135.00 |
| Castor, Pickle, Cranberry, Owl & Fan Finial | 100.00 |
| Castor, Pickle, Cupid & Psyche Glass, Silver Plate, 7 In *Illus* | 42.00 |
| Castor, Pickle, Cupid & Venus Insert, Silver Frame & Tongs | 47.50 |
| Castor, Pickle, Daisy, Clear, Silver Plate Frame & Tongs | 52.00 |
| Castor, Pickle, Frosted Stork Double Insert, Silver Plate Frame & Tongs | 180.00 |
| Castor, Pickle, Little River | 39.00 |
| Castor, Pickle, Pattern Glass Insert, Silver Tongs & Frame | 30.00 |
| Castor, Pickle, Pomona Insert, Cornflower, 2nd Grind, Silver Holder & Lid | 235.00 |
| Castor, Pickle, Pressed Glass, Actress, Frame | 120.00 |
| Castor, Pickle, Pressed Glass, Silver Plate Rim, Lid, Bail, & Spoon | 25.00 |
| Castor, Pickle, Pressed, Flower & Quill, Silver Plate Frame & Tongs | 55.00 |
| Castor, Pickle, Rubena, Hobnail, Meriden Handled Holder | 225.00 |
| Castor, Pickle, Vaseline Swirl Ribbed, Enamel Asters, Silver Frame & Tongs | 180.00 |
| **Catalogue, see Paper, Catalogue** | |
| Caughley, Jug, Mask, Blue & White, Parrot & Fruit, C.1780, 5 1/2 In.High | 175.00 |

*Cauldon is an English pottery factory working after 1905.*

**Cauldon, see also Indian Tree**

| | |
|---|---|
| Cauldon, Cup, Cream Soup, 2 Handled, Pink Rose, Pink & Gold, C.1905 | 5.60 |
| Cauldon, Plate, Service, Apple Green Border, Flowers, Marked | 10.00 |
| Cauldon, Platter, Turkey, C.1900 | 65.00 |

*Celadon is a Chinese porcelain having a velvet-textured green-gray glaze.*
*Japanese and Korean factories also made a celadon-colored glaze.*

| | |
|---|---|
| Celadon, Bottle, Oil, Korean, Hidden Design, Celadon Coloring, 2 1/2 In.High | 100.00 |
| Celadon, Bowl, Covered, 2 Handled, 3 In.High | 195.00 |
| Celadon, Bowl, Sung, 2 Swimming Fish, 8 In. | 360.00 |
| Celadon, Cup & Saucer, Floral, Large Size | 11.50 |
| Celadon, Dish, Shrimp, Handle, 10 1/2 In.Diameter | 325.00 |
| Celadon, Plate, Bird, Butterflies, & Flowers, 7 3/8 In. | 25.00 |
| Celadon, Plate, Enamel Decoration, 9 3/4 In. | 90.00 |
| Celadon, Plate, 8 1/2 In. | 20.00 |
| Celadon, Platter, Birds, Butterflies, & Floral, Greek Key, 14 In. Diameter | 275.00 |
| Celadon, Platter, Butterflies, Birds, & Floral, Gold Greek Key Center, 14 In. | 250.00 |
| Celadon, Teapot, Straw Handle, Miniature, 3 In.High | 12.50 |
| Celadon, Vase, Cylindrical, Blue & White Blossoms, 11 1/2 In.High | 35.00 |
| Celadon, Vase, Raised Figural Design, Underglaze Blue, 18 In.High | 125.00 |
| Celadon, Vase, Stick, Bulbous Bottom, 7 1/2 In. | 20.00 |
| Celadon, Vase, 11 In.High | 35.00 |
| Celluloid, Bookmark, Ivory | 1.00 |
| Celluloid, Box, Collar, Woman's Head Framed In Flowers, 7 In.Diameter | 13.00 |
| Celluloid, Box, Trinket, Rose Embossed, Ivory Color, 6 X 3 In. | 12.00 |
| Celluloid, Hair Receiver, Ivory | 2.00 |
| Celluloid, Hair Receiver, White | 2.50 |
| Celluloid, Mirror & Stand, Shaving, Folding | 5.00 |
| Celluloid, Nail Buffer, Ivory | 1.00 |
| Celluloid, Rattle, Baby's, Double Face, Pink & White, 5 1/2 In. | 4.00 |
| Celluloid, Tea Cosy, Kewpie Doll Type, Turtle Mark | 8.50 |
| Celluloid, Toilet, Lady's, In Case, 7 Piece | 22.50 |
| Celluloid, Whistle, Bluebird On Stump, Relief Floral & Knots On Stump, Blue | 20.00 |

*Chalkware is really plaster of Paris decorated with watercolors. The* pieces were molded from known Staffordshire and other porcelain models and painted and sold as inexpensive decorations. Most of this type of chalkware was made from about 1820 to 1870.

| | |
|---|---|
| **Chalkware, Bookend**, Pictures Of F.D.Roosevelt & 48 Star Flag, Pair | 7.50 |
| **Chalkware, Bust**, Felix Mendelssohn-Bartholdy, 24 In. | 175.00 |
| **Chalkware, Bust**, Small Boy, Signed David, Copy 1900, By S.J.Eddy, 11 In. | 85.00 |
| **Chalkware, Church**, 19th Century, 28 In.High ........................... *Illus* | 800.00 |
| **Chalkware, Figurine**, Cat, Yellow, Red, & Black Paint, 16 In. | 500.00 |
| **Chalkware, Figurine**, Cherry Boy, Painted, 10 In. | 55.00 |
| **Chalkware, Figurine**, Dog, Reclining, Red, Yellow, & Black Paint, 2 1/2 In. | 15.00 |
| **Chalkware, Figurine**, Dog, Seated, Black, Red, & Dark Brown, 8 In. | 55.00 |
| **Chalkware, Figurine**, Dog, Seated, Brown Red & Yellow, Varnished, 8 In. | 85.00 |
| **Chalkware, Figurine**, Dog, Seated, Cream, Brown, & Orange Paint, 8 1/4 In. | 15.00 |
| **Chalkware, Figurine**, Dog, Seated, Red, Yellow & Black Paint, 8 1/2 In. | 20.00 |
| **Chalkware, Figurine**, Dog, Seated, Red, Yellow Green, & Black, Tooled, 5 1/4 In. | 25.00 |
| **Chalkware, Figurine**, Dog, Seated, Yellow, Black, & Ocher, 7 1/2 In. | 35.00 |
| **Chalkware, Figurine**, Dog, Seated, Yellow, Red, Black, & Green | 45.00 |
| **Chalkware, Figurine**, Dog, Standing, Signed A.K., Red & Black On White, 5 In. | 40.00 |
| **Chalkware, Figurine**, Dove, Green, Yellow & Red Paint, 11 In. | 65.00 |
| **Chalkware, Figurine**, German Shepherd Dog, Sitting, White, 5 In., Pair | 5.00 |
| **Chalkware, Figurine**, Kneeling Figure, Yellow, Black, Green, & Red, Paint, 3 In. | 15.00 |
| **Chalkware, Figurine**, Lion, Inscribed Bayre, 15 In. | 20.00 |
| **Chalkware, Figurine**, Lion, Reclining, Red & Black Paint, 2 In. | 25.00 |
| **Chalkware, Figurine**, Little Girl In Old-Fashioned Dress & Bonnet, Sitting | 25.00 |
| **Chalkware, Figurine**, Parrot, Dark Green & Yellow, Varnished, 7 1/2 In. | 115.00 |
| **Chalkware, Figurine**, Parrot, Perched On Orb, C.1850, 8 1/2 In. | 425.00 |
| **Chalkware, Figurine**, Pluto | 3.50 |
| **Chalkware, Figurine**, Poodle, Standing, Yellow, Red, & Black, Tooled, 8 In. | 85.00 |
| **Chalkware, Figurine**, Rabbit, Easter, Brown, Blue, & Yellow Paint, 6 In. | 40.00 |
| **Chalkware, Figurine**, Rooster, Strutting, Circular Base, 1800s, 22 X 14 In. | 375.00 |
| **Chalkware, Figurine**, Santa Claus, 7 In. | 9.00 |
| **Chalkware, Figurine**, Sheep, Soft Colors, 7 3/4 In. | 20.00 |
| **Chalkware, Figurine**, Shepherd, Polychrome, 1800s, 15 In.High | 75.00 |
| **Chalkware, Figurine**, Spaniel, Staffordshire Type, Black, Red Collar, Pair | 150.00 |
| **Chalkware, Figurine**, Squirrel, 19th Century, 6 3/4 In. ........................... *Illus* | 200.00 |
| **Chalkware, Garniture**, Yellow, Red, & Light Green, 10 In. | 185.00 |
| **Chalkware, Group**, Three Classical Dancing Girls, 10 In. | 10.00 |
| **Chalkware, Lamp**, Drunken Tramp, Wife With Rolling Pin, C.1920, Pair | 52.00 |
| **Chalkware, Match Holder**, Dog Leaning Nonchalantly On A Tub, 4 1/2 In. | 12.00 |
| **Chalkware, Twine Holder**, Black Boy, Large | 10.00 |
| **Chalkware, Watch Holder**, Woman & Man, Polychrome & Yellow Varnish, 13 In. | 55.00 |
| **Champleve, Vase**, Floral & Leaves On Apple Green, Dark Blue, & Dark Red | 75.00 |
| **Chantilly, Dish**, Sweetmeat, Silver Shape, C.1725, 8 1/8 In.Long | 200.00 |
| **Chantilly, Plate**, Basketwork Rim, Floral Decoration, C.1760, 9 1/8 In. | 140.00 |
| **Chantilly, Pot**, Kakiemon, Squirrel & Gourd Vine, C.1725, 3 1/8 In.High | 250.00 |

Chalkware, Church,
19th Century, 28 In.High

Chalkware, Figurine, Squirrel,
19th Century, 6 3/4 In.

Chantilly, Vase, Potpourri,
Tin Glazed, C.1725, 6 In.High
*(See Page 94)*

| | |
|---|---|
| Chantilly, Vase, Potpourri, Tin Glazed, C.1725, 6 In.High .................................... *Illus* | 375.00 |
| Charlie McCarthy, Book, A Day With Charlie McCarthy ................................. | 8.50 |
| Charlie McCarthy, Book, Paint ............................................................. | 17.00 |
| Charlie McCarthy, Cutouts, Cardboard, 4 Dolls, Clothes ............................. | 15.00 |
| Charlie McCarthy, Doll, Dressed, 20 In.Tall .......................................... | 42.50 |
| Charlie McCarthy, Doll, String Operated Mouth, 21 In. .............................. | 50.00 |
| Charlie McCarthy, Doll, Vinyl Head, Stuffed Body, Marked Juro, 1968, 29 In. ...... | 12.00 |
| Charlie McCarthy, Spoon, Silver Plate ................................................ | 9.00 |
| Charlie McCarthy, Statue, Plaster, Painted, 16 In.High ............................. | 13.00 |
| Charlie McCarthy, Teaspoon ........................................................... | 6.00 |
| Charlie McCarthy, Toy, Tin, Windup ................................................... | 20.00 |
| Chelsea Derby, Bowl, Square, Claret Border, Bouquets, C.1775, 8 5/8 In., Pair ...... | 200.00 |
| Chelsea Derby, Figurine, Four Seasons, C.1775, Set Of 4 .................... *Illus* | 1350.00 |
| Chelsea Derby, Figurine, Mars, Standing, C.1775, 7 1/2 In. ........................ | 200.00 |
| Chelsea Derby, Group, Allegorical Figure Of Autumn, C.1770, 8 In.High ............ | 275.00 |

*Chelsea grape pattern was made before 1840. A small bunch of grapes in a raised design, colored with purple or blue luster, is on the border of the white plate. Most of the pieces are unmarked. The pattern is sometimes called Aynsley or Grandmother.*

| | |
|---|---|
| Chelsea Grape, Cup Plate, Luster ..................................................... | 16.50 |
| Chelsea Grape, Plate, Cake, Molded Handles, Luster, 9 X 10 In. .................. | 20.00 |
| Chelsea Grape, Plate, Luster, 7 In. ................................................... | 20.00 |
| Chelsea Grape, Saucer, Blue .......................................................... | 5.00 |
| Chelsea Grape, Sugar, Covered, Large Size ......................................... | 40.00 |

*Chelsea porcelain was made in the Chelsea area of London from about 1745 to 1784. Recent copies of this work have been made from the original molds.*

| | |
|---|---|
| Chelsea, Bowl, Octagonal, Kakiemon Decoration, Raised Anchor, 6 1/4 In.Wide ...... | 600.00 |
| Chelsea, Candelabrum, Young Man In Lavender Coat, Bocage, C.1775, 9 3/4 In. ...... | 300.00 |
| Chelsea, Candlestick, Figural, Cupid & Aphrodite, Ares, C.1775, 11 In., Pair ........ | 250.00 |
| Chelsea, Dish, Peony, Puce Center, Sepia Petals, Stalk Handle, Red Anchor .......... | 400.00 |
| Chelsea, Dish, Peony, Red Anchor, 8 7/8 In.Long ............................ *Illus* | 600.00 |
| Chelsea, Dish, Silver Shape, Rococo Thumbpiece, Bouquets, Red Anchor, Pair ...... | 900.00 |
| Chelsea, Dish, Vine Leaf, Green, Puce Veins, Stalks Handle, Red Anchor, Pair ...... | 550.00 |
| Chelsea, Figurine, Boy, Autumn, Gold Anchor Mark, 3 1/2 In.High ................. | 45.00 |
| Chelsea, Figurine, Farm Boy, Gold Anchor, 3 In.High ............................... | 65.00 |
| Chelsea, Fob, Seal, Bust Of Woman, Gold Mounted, "tout A Vous, " C.1790 .......... | 250.00 |
| Chelsea, Garniture, Gold Anchor Period ................................... *Illus* | 650.00 |
| Chelsea, Plate, Fluted, Green Birds On Sprigs, Insects, Gold Anchor, 9 In. ........ | 35.00 |
| Chelsea, Plate, Sprig, Handled, Anchor Mark, C.1750, 9 1/2 In. ................... | 15.00 |
| Chelsea, Platter, Imari Pattern, 14 X 11 1/2 In. ................................... | 68.00 |
| Chelsea, Sauceboat, Leaf Form, Red & Blue Flowers, Red Anchor Period ........... | 325.00 |
| Chelsea, Toby Mug, Sitting Man, Gold Anchor Mark, 5 In.High ..................... | 90.00 |
| Chelsea, Tureen, Covered, Cauliflower, Red Anchor Period, 4 5/8 In. Long ......... | 800.00 |
| Chelsea, Vase, Rococo, Mythological & Animal Design, Gold Anchor, 14 1/2 In. ...... | 1100.00 |

*Chinese export porcelain is all the many kinds of porcelain made in China for export to America and Europe in the 18th and 19th centuries. Included in the category are Nanking, Canton, Chinese Lowestoft, Armorial, Jesuit, and other types of the ware.*

**Chinese Export, see also Canton, Celadon, Nanking**

| | |
|---|---|
| Chinese Export, Basin, Blue & White, Lotus Plants, C.1820, 16 In.Diameter ......... | 90.00 |
| Chinese Export, Basin, Famille Rose, Lady Reading, C.1850, 11 1/2 In. ............. | 225.00 |
| Chinese Export, Basin, Famille Rose, Millefleurs, C.1850, 10 1/2 In. .............. | 300.00 |
| Chinese Export, Basin, 4 Puce Camaieu Landscape Medallions, C.1780 .............. | 250.00 |
| Chinese Export, Bottle, Scent, Decorated ........................................... | 15.50 |
| Chinese Export, Bottle, Snuff, Blue Floral, Green Jade Stopper ................... | 38.00 |
| Chinese Export, Bowl & Saucer, Bouillon, Sepia Eagle, Gilt Floral, C.1790 ......... | 425.00 |
| Chinese Export, Bowl & Spoon, Rice, Blue & Red On White ....................... | 10.00 |
| Chinese Export, Bowl, Armorial, Famille Rose, C.1746, 11 3/8 In. ................. | 800.00 |
| Chinese Export, Bowl, Armorial, C.1760, 4 1/2 In. ......................... *Illus* | 275.00 |
| Chinese Export, Bowl, Covered, Foliage On Yellow, 7 1/2 In. ..................... | 120.00 |
| Chinese Export, Bowl, Fish, Famille Rose, Lotus Blossoms, 16 In.High ............ | 1400.00 |
| Chinese Export, Bowl, Fish, Globular, 2 Pairs Kissing Fish On White, 16 In. ...... | 1400.00 |
| Chinese Export, Bowl, Fitzhugh, Blue, Pagodas, Figures, C.1780, 8 1/4 In. ........ | 175.00 |
| Chinese Export, Bowl, Flared Lip, Three Color, San-Sai, C.1850, 6 3/4 In. ......... | 75.00 |
| Chinese Export, Bowl, Flared, 3 Colors, San-Sai, 6 X 3 In. ........................ | 75.00 |

Chelsea Derby, Figurine,
Four Seasons, C.1775, Set Of 4
*(See Page 94)*

Chelsea, Garniture, Gold Anchor Period
*(See Page 94)*

Chinese Export, Teabowl & Saucer,
Armorial, C.1740
*(See Page 98)*

Chinese Export, Bowl,
Armorial, C.1760, 4 1/2 In.
*(See Page 94)*

Chinese Export, Cup & Saucer,
Armorial, C.1765
*(See Page 96)*

Chelsea, Dish, Peony, Red Anchor,
8 7/8 In.Long
*(See Page 94)*

Chinese Export, Charger,
Famille Rose, C.1750, 13 3/4 In
*(See Page 96)*

Chinese Export, Bowl, Mandarin Palette, Figures, Fluted, C.1780, 7 7/8 In. ............................... 350.00
Chinese Export, Bowl, Meat, Covered, Animal's Head Handles, C.1760, Pair ......................... 1500.00
Chinese Export, Bowl, Oriental Figures, C.1780, 10 1/2 In.Diameter ................................. 300.00
Chinese Export, Bowl, Oval, Mandarin Palette, Lady, Lobed, C.1780, 8 1/8 In. ..................... 175.00
Chinese Export, Bowl, Punch, Famille Rose, Continuous Scene, C.1800, 20 In. ..................... 1600.00
Chinese Export, Bowl, Punch, Famille Rose, Figures & Birds Panels, C.1820 ......................... 300.00
Chinese Export, Bowl, Punch, Famille Rose, Panels, Figures, Floral, Birds, 1820 ................... 500.00
Chinese Export, Bowl, Punch, Famille Rose, Peacock On Rock, C.1730, 15 In. ..................... 1600.00
Chinese Export, Bowl, Punch, Figures Taking Tea, C.1780, 12 1/4 In. ............................... 950.00
Chinese Export, Bowl, Serving, Covered, Famille Rose, Lozenge Shape, C.1820 ................... 300.00
Chinese Export, Bowl, Serving, Fitzhugh, Green, Oval, Everted Rim, C.1820 ......................... 450.00
Chinese Export, Bowl, Shipping, Ship Decoration, Sailor's Farewell, 9 1/8 In ..................... 300.00
Chinese Export, Bowl, Small Bouquets, Diaper Bands Rim, C.1790, 11 In. ........................... 625.00
Chinese Export, Bowl, Vegetable, Covered, Oval Medallions, Blue, Gilt, C.1790 ................... 525.00
Chinese Export, Bowl, Vegetable, Fitzhugh, Green, Rectangular, C.1820, Pair ....................... 450.00
Chinese Export, Box, Silver, Rectangular, Dragon Chased, W.H., C.1880, 6 In. ..................... 100.00
Chinese Export, Can & Saucer, Coffee, Carousing Figures, Sepia, C.1780 ........................... 170.00
Chinese Export, Charger, Blue & White, Bouquets In Medallion, C.1750, 16 In. ..................... 225.00
Chinese Export, Charger, Famille Rose, C.1750, 13 3/4 In ............................... *Illus* 400.00
Chinese Export, Charger, Famille Rose, Figures, Ornithological, 1820s, 16 In. ..................... 170.00
Chinese Export, Charger, Famille Rose, Peonies, C.1750, 12 1/4 In. ................................. 175.00
Chinese Export, Coffeepot, Lighthouse, Blue & White, Continuous Scene, 1790s ................... 450.00
Chinese Export, Coffeepot, Lighthouse, Eagle Design, C.1780, 10 In. High ......................... 4000.00
Chinese Export, Compote, Blue On White, Bat Border, 2 Scholars, Goose ........................... 95.00
Chinese Export, Creamer, Helmet Shape, American Eagle, C.1850 ................................... 425.00
Chinese Export, Creamer, Helmet Shape, Falconer, Diaper Ground, C.1780 ......................... 175.00
Chinese Export, Creamer, Helmet Shape, Famille Rose ............................................. 75.00
Chinese Export, Cup & Saucer, Armorial, C.1765 ............................... *Illus* 600.00
Chinese Export, Cup & Saucer, Armorial, Famille Rose Enamels, C.1750 ........................... 250.00
Chinese Export, Cup & Saucer, Breakfast, Fitzhugh, Green, C.1820, Pair ........................... 300.00
Chinese Export, Cup & Saucer, Gold Dragon On Iron Red, White Inside ............................. 25.00
Chinese Export, Cuspidor, Famille Rose, Scenic, C.1820 ............................... *Illus* 375.00
Chinese Export, Dish & Stand, Hot Water, Covered, Fitzhugh, Green, Oval, 1820s ............... 2000.00
Chinese Export, Dish, Hot Water, Blue Enamel Bands, Gilt Trelliswork, 1790s ....................... 140.00
Chinese Export, Dish, Hot Water, Blue Enamel, C.1790 ............................... *Illus* 200.00
Chinese Export, Dish, Kidney Shape, Blue & White Fitzhugh, Unicorn, C.1790 ..................... 295.00
Chinese Export, Dish, Lotus, Oriental Fruits & Flowers, C.1740, 5 1/2 In. ......................... 200.00
Chinese Export, Dish, Meat, Blue & White, Chien-Lung, C.1790, 13 X 10 In. ....................... 250.00
Chinese Export, Dish, Shell, Famille Rose, C.1810, Pair ............................... *Illus* 500.00
Chinese Export, Dish, Soup, Octagonal, Roses & Blossom, C.1790, 9 In. ........................... 80.00
Chinese Export, Ecuelle, Covered, Gilt Filigree Ground, 6 In.Wide, Pair ........................... 250.00
Chinese Export, Figurine, Chinese Family Group, Lemon Peel Base, Pair ........................... 125.00
Chinese Export, Figurine, Chinese Man, Bisque Type Face & Hands, 9 1/2 In. ....................... 15.00
Chinese Export, Figurine, Foo Dog, Yellow, Green Mane & Back ..................................... 95.00
Chinese Export, Figurine, Sitting Cat, Yellow & Brown, Orchid Ribbon ............................. 75.00
Chinese Export, Garden Seat, 19th Century, 19 3/4 In. ............................... *Illus* 325.00
Chinese Export, Garniture Set, En Grisaille, Baluster Vases, C.1760, 3 Piece ................... 1500.00
Chinese Export, Group, Hotei & Five Children, God Of Fertility, 10 In. ............................. 145.00
Chinese Export, Hat & Wig Stand, Blue & White, Vase Shape, 25 In., Pair ......................... 248.00
Chinese Export, Jar, Covered, Blue & White, Figures, 3 1/2 In. ..................................... 12.00
Chinese Export, Jar, Ginger, Blue & White, Lid, 9 In.High ......................................... 95.00
Chinese Export, Jar, Ginger, Covered, Puce & Green Figures, Teak Stand ........................... 45.00
Chinese Export, Jar, Ginger, Flat Lid, Blue On White, C.1850, 9 In., Pair ......................... 175.00
Chinese Export, Jar, Hawthorn, Kang H'si, 11 In. ................................................... 175.00
Chinese Export, Jar, Temple, Covered, Underglaze Blue, Kang H'si, Pair ......................... 2000.00
Chinese Export, Jardiniere, Blue, Green, & Rose On Yellow, C'hien Lung ........................... 195.00
Chinese Export, Jug, Covered, Pear Shape, Overlapping Petals, C.1850 ............................. 450.00
Chinese Export, Jug, Hot Water, Covered, Pear Shape, Flowers, 5 3/8 In. ........................... 150.00
Chinese Export, Jug, Hot Water, Covered, Pyriform, Famille Rose, C.1750 ......................... 325.00
Chinese Export, Jug, Milk, Armorial, Pear Shape, Loop Handle, C.1750, 4 In. ..................... 150.00
Chinese Export, Jug, Milk, Covered, Pyriform, Famille Rose, Figures, C.1750 ....................... 90.00
Chinese Export, Jug, Milk, Covered, Pyriform, Mandarin Palette, C.1780 ........................... 120.00
Chinese Export, Jug, Milk, Covered, Shepherd Medallion, C.1770, 5 5/8 In. ......................... 250.00
Chinese Export, Jug, Milk, Jesuit, En Grisaille, Couple Drinking, C.1760 ........................... 500.00
Chinese Export, Jug, Milk, Mythological Decoration, Pyriform, C.1760, 5 In. ....................... 125.00
Chinese Export, Mug, Armorial, Red Scale Ground, C.1770, 4 7/8 In.High ........................... 1200.00

Chinese Export, Garden Seat, 19th Century, 19 3/4 In.
*(See Page 96)*

Chinese Export, Dish, Shell, Famille Rose, C.1810, Pair
*(See Page 96)*

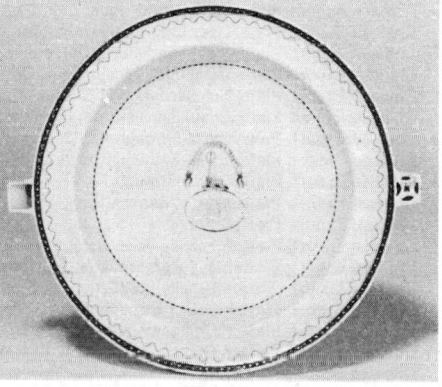

Chinese Export, Cuspidor, Famille Rose,
Scenic, C.1820
*(See Page 96)*

Chinese Export, Dish, Hot Water, Blue Enamel, C.1790
*(See Page 96)*

Chinese Export, Plate, Famille Rose,
C.1750, 8 3/4 In.
*(See Page 98)*

Chinese Export, Plate, Judgment Of Paris,
C.1740, 9 In.
*(See Page 98)*

| | |
|---|---|
| Chinese Export, Mug, Bacchus, Grape & Leaf Wreath, Loop Handle, C.1785, 5 In. | 600.00 |
| Chinese Export, Mug, Cylindrical, Flowering Peonies & Mums, C.1750, 5 In. | 300.00 |
| Chinese Export, Mug, Cylindrical, Shield, Blue & Gold Star Rims, C.1790 | 250.00 |
| Chinese Export, Mug, Famille Rose, Oriental Figures Panel, C.1780 | 425.00 |
| Chinese Export, Mug, Famille Rose, Twisted Handle, 4 1/2 In.High | 165.00 |
| Chinese Export, Mug, Famille Rose, Twisted Handle, 5 3/4 In.High | 225.00 |
| Chinese Export, Mug, Nanking Border, Twisted Strap Handles, 5 In.Wide | 395.00 |
| Chinese Export, Pitcher, Armorial, Barrel Shaped, Stag's Head Crest, 11 In. | 375.00 |
| Chinese Export, Pitcher, Helmet, French Style Decoration, 5 1/2 In.High | 148.00 |
| Chinese Export, Pitcher, Milk, Famille Rose, Blue & Green Dragons, C.1825 | 195.00 |
| Chinese Export, Plate, Armorial, Jesuit Ware, Men & Women, C.1740, 9 In. | 700.00 |
| Chinese Export, Plate, Dessert, Famille Rose, Peonies, Bird, Butterfly, 1820s | 21.00 |
| Chinese Export, Plate, Dinner, Armorial, Gilt Monogram Below Shell, 1750 | 250.00 |
| Chinese Export, Plate, Dinner, Famille Rose, Peonies, Bird, & Butterfly, 1820s | 31.00 |
| Chinese Export, Plate, Famille Rose, C.1750, 8 3/4 In. _Illus_ | 225.00 |
| Chinese Export, Plate, Famille Rose, Figures Medallion, C.1770, 6 5/8 In. | 40.00 |
| Chinese Export, Plate, Famille Rose, Figures, Birds, C.1820, 7 5/8 In. | 18.00 |
| Chinese Export, Plate, Famille Verte, Birds & People, C.1850, 9 In. | 30.00 |
| Chinese Export, Plate, Fitzhugh, Green, Eagle, Puce Ribbon, C.1790, 9 7/8 In. | 200.00 |
| Chinese Export, Plate, Gold Spray On Gray, 5 Part Gold Rim, C.1765, 10 In. | 90.00 |
| Chinese Export, Plate, Imari Palette, Stag, Birds, Garden, C.1740, 9 1/8 In. | 65.00 |
| Chinese Export, Plate, Judgment Of Paris, C.1740, 9 In. _Illus_ | 1100.00 |
| Chinese Export, Plate, Lime Green, Willow Pattern, C.1810, 8 5/8 In., Pair | 250.00 |
| Chinese Export, Plate, Mandarin Palette, Octagonal, C.1760, 6 1/2 In., Pair | 140.00 |
| Chinese Export, Plate, Octagonal, Famille Rose, Duck On Leaf, C.1730, 10 In. | 175.00 |
| Chinese Export, Plate, Scholar Sits With Dishes, Plum Blossoms, 9 In. | 39.50 |
| Chinese Export, Plate, Soup, Famille Rose, Peonies, Bird, & Butterfly, C.1820 | 31.00 |
| Chinese Export, Plate, Soup, Fitzhugh, Green, C.1820, 9 7/8 In. | 112.50 |
| Chinese Export, Plate, Soup, Fitzhugh, Green, C.1820, 9 7/8 In., Pair | 450.00 |
| Chinese Export, Plate, Soup, Fitzhugh, Green, Emerald Tone, C.1820, 9 3/4 In. | 425.00 |
| Chinese Export, Plate, Wan Li Karrack Style, Blue & White, C.1750, 8 In. | 175.00 |
| Chinese Export, Platter, Armorial, Floral Vignettes, C.1750, 10 1/4 In.Long | 325.00 |
| Chinese Export, Platter, Famille Rose, Octagonal, C.1780, 20 In.Long | 250.00 |
| Chinese Export, Platter, Famille Rose, Oval, Flowers, C.1765, 11 In., Pair | 325.00 |
| Chinese Export, Platter, Famille Rose, Peonies, Blue Rockwork, C.1750, Pair | 500.00 |
| Chinese Export, Platter, Green Fitzhugh, Central Medallion, C.1820, 15 In. | 500.00 |
| Chinese Export, Platter, Octagonal, Shield, Blue & Iron Rim, C.1790, 18 In. | 200.00 |
| Chinese Export, Platter, Orange Peel Bottom, Clipped Corners, C.1750 | 168.00 |
| Chinese Export, Platter, Oval, Blue & White, Roses, Floral, C.1790, 15 1/8 In. | 160.00 |
| Chinese Export, Platter, Oval, Floral Basket Center, Bouquets On Rim, C.1780 | 150.00 |
| Chinese Export, Platter, Oval, Gilt Floral, Blue Bands, C.1790, 17 1/2 In. | 200.00 |
| Chinese Export, Platter, Puce & Lavender Bouquets, Oval, C.1750, 15 1/4 In. | 90.00 |
| Chinese Export, Platter, Tang Style, San-Sai, 3 Color, C.1850, 12 In. | 140.00 |
| Chinese Export, Platter, Thousand Butterflies, 14 In. | 275.00 |
| Chinese Export, Platter, Well & Tree, Fitzhugh, Green, C.1820, 19 1/8 In. | 800.00 |
| Chinese Export, Pot De Creme, Blue Fitzhugh, Berry Finial | 75.00 |
| Chinese Export, Pot, Chocolate, Cylindrical, Blue & White, Scene, C.1790 | 350.00 |
| Chinese Export, Pot, Punch, Globular, Oriental Figures Medallions, C.1760 | 200.00 |
| Chinese Export, Potpourri, White Hawthorn Flowers On Blue, Pair | 75.00 |
| Chinese Export, Rose Bowl, Millefleur, Wood Platform, 6 In. High | 165.00 |
| Chinese Export, Salt, Decorated, 5 Footed, Signed, 2 1/2 In. | 18.00 |
| Chinese Export, Salt, Trencher, Blue & White, C.1750 _Illus_ | 190.00 |
| Chinese Export, Sauceboat, Double Lipped, White, Double Twig Handles, 1850s | 85.00 |
| Chinese Export, Saucer, Classical Figure With Dog, C.1740, 4 3/4 In. | 200.00 |
| Chinese Export, Saucer, Fitzhugh, Green, C.1820 | 83.35 |
| Chinese Export, Saucer, Sepia Eagle, Gilt Floral, C.1790 | 450.00 |
| Chinese Export, Stand, Oval, Reticulated, Pierced Basketwork Rim, C.1780 | 250.00 |
| Chinese Export, Stand, Teapot, Fluted, Eagle Design, 5 7/8 In.Diameter | 750.00 |
| Chinese Export, Stand, Tureen, Armorial, Floral Bouquets, C.1760, 14 In. | 350.00 |
| Chinese Export, Sugar, Covered, Medallion, Blue & Gold Star Rims, C.1790 | 140.00 |
| Chinese Export, Taperstick, Figural, Court Maiden, C.1850, 11 1/2 In., Pair | 1900.00 |
| Chinese Export, Tea Caddy, Jesuit, Ovoid, En Grisaille Painted, C.1760 | 250.00 |
| Chinese Export, Tea Caddy, Shield & Crest, Blue Dentil Band, C.1790 | 225.00 |
| Chinese Export, Teabowl & Saucer, Armorial, C.1740 _Illus_ | 275.00 |
| Chinese Export, Teabowl & Saucer, Boy Riding Elephant, C.1770, Pair | 600.00 |
| Chinese Export, Teabowl, Dutch Market, Baroque Palmettes, C.1725, 3 In. | 200.00 |

Chinese Export, Teapot Stand,
Famille Rose, Miniature
*(See Page 100)*

Chinese Export, Teapot Stand,
Famille Rose, C.1760
*(See Page 100)*

Chinese Export, Tray, Spoon,
En Grisaille, C.1780
*(See Page 100)*

Chinese Export, Teapot Stand,
Hunting Scene, C.1760
*(See Page 100)*

Chinese Export, Teapot Stand, Pink & Coral, C.1770
*(See Page 100)*

Chinese Export, Teapot, Batavia,
Famille Rose, C.1760
*(See Page 100)*

Chinese Export, Salt, Trencher,
Blue & White, C.1750
*(See Page 98)*

Chinese Export, Teapot,
Cadogan, C.1850, 6 1/8 In.
*(See Page 100)*

| | |
|---|---:|
| Chinese Export, Teabowl, Jesuit, En Grisaille Painting Of Lovers, C.1760 | 90.00 |
| Chinese Export, Teacup & Saucer, Fitzhugh, Green, C.1820, Pair | 290.00 |
| Chinese Export, Teapot Stand, Famille Rose, C.1760 *Illus* | 150.00 |
| Chinese Export, Teapot Stand, Famille Rose, Miniature *Illus* | 110.00 |
| Chinese Export, Teapot Stand, Hunting Scene, C.1760 *Illus* | 325.00 |
| Chinese Export, Teapot Stand, Pink & Coral, C.1770 *Illus* | 140.00 |
| Chinese Export, Teapot, Armorial, Silver Shape, Scroll Handle, 5 1/4 In. | 225.00 |
| Chinese Export, Teapot, Batavia, Famille Rose, C.1760 *Illus* | 450.00 |
| Chinese Export, Teapot, Cadogan, C.1850, 6 1/8 In. *Illus* | 325.00 |
| Chinese Export, Teapot, Clobbered, Globular, Landscapes, Black Scrolls, 1760s | 200.00 |
| Chinese Export, Teapot, Covered, Loop Handle, Flowers, C.1750, 4 1/8 In.High | 225.00 |
| Chinese Export, Teapot, Cylindrical, Blue & White, Willow Variation, C.1790 | 275.00 |
| Chinese Export, Teapot, Cylindrical, Green Monochrome, Urns, C.1790, 5 In. | 175.00 |
| Chinese Export, Teapot, Cylindrical, Mandarin Palette, Figures, C.1780 | 200.00 |
| Chinese Export, Teapot, Cylindrical, Sepia Eagle, Gilt Floral, C.1790 | 950.00 |
| Chinese Export, Teapot, Cylindrical, Shield, Entwined Strap Handle, C.1790 | 250.00 |
| Chinese Export, Teapot, Double Ogee Shape, Famille Rose, Medallions, C.1770 | 300.00 |
| Chinese Export, Teapot, Entwined Serpent Forms Handle, Blue Underglaze | 395.00 |
| Chinese Export, Teapot, Famille Jeune, Miniature | 45.00 |
| Chinese Export, Teapot, Lighthouse, C.1790, 9 3/4 In. *Illus* | 375.00 |
| Chinese Export, Teapot, Melon Shape, Mandarin Palette, 2 Ladies, C.1780 | 225.00 |
| Chinese Export, Teapot, Melon Shape, Peonies & Floral On Pink, C.1750 | 170.00 |
| Chinese Export, Teapot, Melon Shaped, Mandarin Figures, Peach Knop, 6 In. | 150.00 |
| Chinese Export, Teapot, Miniature, Rockwork, Floral Sprigs, 2 3/4 In. | 200.00 |
| Chinese Export, Teapot, Oriental Figures, Padded Wicker Case | 75.00 |
| Chinese Export, Teapot, Pear Shape, Floral Encrusted, Pierced Work, C.1850 | 350.00 |
| Chinese Export, Teapot, Pomegranate Shape, Pale Pink, C.1850 | 275.00 |
| Chinese Export, Teapot, Roses On White, C.1850 | 100.00 |
| Chinese Export, Teapot, Strap Handle, Fruit & Ribbon Finial, Floral, C.1780 | 200.00 |
| Chinese Export, Tray, Famille Rose, C.1820, 10 7/8 In. *Illus* | 250.00 |
| Chinese Export, Tray, Spoon, En Grisaille, C.1780 *Illus* | 130.00 |
| Chinese Export, Tray, Spoon, Octagonal, Famille Rose, C.1780, 4 5/8 In.Long | 125.00 |
| Chinese Export, Tureen & Stand, Sauce, Covered, Oval, Floral Vases, C.1790 | 375.00 |
| Chinese Export, Tureen, Covered, Meissen Style, Oval, Crown Knop, C.1760 | 1200.00 |
| Chinese Export, Tureen, Covered, Oval, Fitzhugh, Blue, Strap Handles, C.1780 | 1150.00 |
| Chinese Export, Tureen, Oriental Scenes, Ormolu Border, C.1770, 24 In.High | 750.00 |
| Chinese Export, Vase, Famille Noire, Birds, Reds, & Blues On Black, 18 In. | 250.00 |
| Chinese Export, Vase, Famille Rose, C.1820, Pair *Illus* | 200.00 |
| Chinese Export, Vase, Famille Rose, Lady & Floral, Square, C.1850, 10 In. | 50.00 |
| Chinese Export, Vase, Gourd Shape, Miniature, C.1820, 2 1/2 In.High | 20.00 |
| Chinese Export, Vase, Hexagonal Baluster, Scenic, C.1850, 16 3/4 In., Pair | 2000.00 |
| Chinese Export, Vase, Kaga, Floral & Bird Decoration, C.1870, 6 In. | 35.00 |
| Chinese Export, Vase, Openwork Ear Handles, Garden Tea Party, 23 In., Pair | 850.00 |
| Chinese Export, Vase, Scenic, Blue & White, 6 Sided, C.1880, 12 In. | 100.00 |
| Chinese Export, Vase, Six Color Floral & Orbs On Yellow, C.1860, 8 In. | 140.00 |
| Chinese Export, Vase, Trees, Flowers, & Birds On Green, Signed, 10 In.High | 150.00 |

Chinese Export, Teapot, Lighthouse, C.1790, 9 3/4 In.

Chinese Export,
Vase, Famille Rose,
C.1820, Pair

Chinese Export,
Tray, Famille Rose,
C.1820, 10 7/8 In.

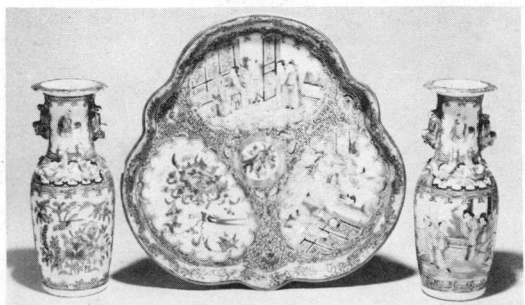

Chinese Export, Vase, Yellow Ground, Hexagonal, Oriental Figures, 21 In. ........................ 1200.00
Chinese Export, Washstand Set, Famille Rose, 18 3/4 In.Basin, 2 Piece ...................... 1350.00

*Chocolate glass, sometimes mistakenly called caramel slag, was made by the
Indiana Tumbler and Goblet Company of Greentown, Indiana, from 1900
to 1903.*

Chocolate Glass, Berry Set, Palm Leaf, 7 Piece ........................ 235.00
Chocolate Glass, Bowl, Cut Glass Pattern, 6 1/8 In. Diameter ........................ 175.00
Chocolate Glass, Bowl, Dewey, Covered, Small Size ........................ 40.00
Chocolate Glass, Bowl, Leaf Bracket, 8 1/8 In. Diameter ........................ 50.00
Chocolate Glass, Butter, Austrian, Covered ........................ 90.00
Chocolate Glass, Butter, Cactus, Covered, High Standard ........................ 275.00
Chocolate Glass, Butter, Cactus, Covered, Low ........................ 85.00
Chocolate Glass, Butter, Daisy, Covered, Greentown ........................ 100.00
Chocolate Glass, Butter, Leaf Bracket, Covered, Low ........................ 60.00
Chocolate Glass, Butter, Palm Leaf ........................ 115.00
Chocolate Glass, Compote, Cactus, Greentown, 5 1/2 In. High ........................ 135.00
Chocolate Glass, Compote, Cactus, 5 1/4 In. Diameter ........................ 55.00
Chocolate Glass, Compote, Chrysanthemum Leaf, 4 1/2 In. Diameter ........................ 130.00
Chocolate Glass, Compote, Jelly, Cactus, Greentown, 5 In High ........................ 59.00
Chocolate Glass, Compote, Melorse, Dark Base Shading To Light, 6 In. ........................ 70.00
Chocolate Glass, Creamer, Cactus, Footed, Greentown ........................ 58.00
Chocolate Glass, Cruet, Cactus ........................ 100.00
Chocolate Glass, Cruet, Cactus, Greentown ........................ 85.00
Chocolate Glass, Cruet, Cactus, Stopper ........................ 90.00
Chocolate Glass, Cruet, Leaf Bracket, Greentown ........................ 150.00
Chocolate Glass, Cruet, Wild Rose With Bowknot, Stopper ........................ 250.00
Chocolate Glass, Cup, Punch, Shuttle, Deep Color ........................ 40.00
Chocolate Glass, Dish, Cat Cover, Hamper Base, Square, Greentown ........................ 225.00
Chocolate Glass, Dish, Dolphin With Fish Cover, Greentown ........................ 100.00 To 135.00
Chocolate Glass, Hatpin Holder, Orange Tree ........................ 170.00
Chocolate Glass, Jar, Cracker, Cactus ........................ 25.00 To 130.00
Chocolate Glass, Mug, Cactus, Greentown ........................ 50.00
Chocolate Glass, Mug, Drinking Men & Castle Scene, 4 1/2 In. ........................ 50.00 To 80.00
Chocolate Glass, Mug, Herringbone Buttress ........................ 50.00
Chocolate Glass, Mug, Stein Shape, Troubador Scenes, 1/2 Pint ........................ 55.00
Chocolate Glass, Nappy, Leaf Bracket, Triangular ........................ 30.00
Chocolate Glass, Nappy, Masonic, Triangular ........................ 70.00
Chocolate Glass, Nappy, Shell, Triangular ........................ 18.00
Chocolate Glass, Nappy, Shuttle, Dark Color ........................ 50.00
Chocolate Glass, Parfait, Scalloped Flange ........................ 25.00
Chocolate Glass, Pitcher, Water, Ruffled Eye, 8 In. High ........................ 300.00
Chocolate Glass, Pitcher, Water, Running Deer, 8 7/8 In. High ........................ 225.00
Chocolate Glass, Pitcher, Water, Squirrel, 8 1/2 In. High ........................ 200.00
Chocolate Glass, Pitcher, Water, Wild Rose With Bowknot, 8 In. High ........................ 250.00
Chocolate Glass, Plate, Cactus, 7 1/2 In. ........................ 45.00 To 50.00
Chocolate Glass, Plate, Serenade, 6 3/8 In. ........................ 130.00
Chocolate Glass, Plate, Serenade, 8 3/8 In. ........................ 100.00 To 125.00
Chocolate Glass, Relish, Cut Glass, Pattern, 10 1/4 X 5 1/4 In. ........................ 175.00
Chocolate Glass, Relish, Leaf Bracket, Oval, 7 1/4 In. Long ........................ 30.00
Chocolate Glass, Rose Bowl, Chrysanthemum Leaf ........................ 150.00
Chocolate Glass, Salt & Pepper, Cactus, Greentown ........................ 59.00
Chocolate Glass, Saltshaker, Cactus, Pewter Top, Greentown ........................ 20.00 To 40.00
Chocolate Glass, Saltshaker, Leaf Bracket, Aluminum Top ........................ 25.00
Chocolate Glass, Sauce, Cactus, Footed, Round, Greentown, 5 In. ........................ 20.00 To 35.00
Chocolate Glass, Sauce, Cactus, Greentown ........................ 35.00 To 40.00
Chocolate Glass, Sauce, Leaf Bracket ........................ 37.00
Chocolate Glass, Sauce, Leaf Bracket, Footed ........................ 15.00
Chocolate Glass, Sauce, Leaf Bracket, Footed, Red Agate Coloring, 4 5/8 In. ........................ 50.00
Chocolate Glass, Sauce, Scroll Edge, Deep Red Chocolate Color ........................ 110.00
Chocolate Glass, Spooner, Cactus ........................ 60.00
Chocolate Glass, Spooner, Dewey ........................ 20.00 To 50.00
Chocolate Glass, Sugar, Cat In Hamper, Covered ........................ 170.00
Chocolate Glass, Sugar, Cactus ........................ 15.00
Chocolate Glass, Sugar, Cactus, Covered ........................ 95.00
Chocolate Glass, Sugar, Daisy, Red Agate Cover, Greentown ........................ 60.00

| | |
|---|---|
| Chocolate Glass, Sugar, Geneva, Covered | 100.00 |
| Chocolate Glass, Sugar, Wild Rose With Bowknot, Covered | 150.00 |
| Chocolate Glass, Syrup, Cactus, Dewey Cover | 35.00 |
| Chocolate Glass, Syrup, Cactus, Dewey Top, Greentown | 59.00 |
| Chocolate Glass, Syrup, Cord Drapery, Nickel Plated Brass Lid | 75.00 |
| Chocolate Glass, Syrup, Shuttle | 50.00 |
| Chocolate Glass, Syrup, Strigil | 75.00 |
| Chocolate Glass, Toothpick, Cactus | 50.00 |
| Chocolate Glass, Toothpick, Cactus, Greentown | 32.00 |
| Chocolate Glass, Toothpick, Inverted Fan & Feather | 65.00 |
| Chocolate Glass, Toothpick, Wild Rose | 40.00 |
| Chocolate Glass, Tray, Leaf Bracket, 5 1/2 X 11 In. | 72.00 |
| Chocolate Glass, Tumbler, Acanthus Leaf, 4 In. | 40.00 |
| Chocolate Glass, Tumbler, Cactus, 5 In. | 38.00 To 50.00 |
| Chocolate Glass, Tumbler, Cattail & Water Lily | 245.00 |
| Chocolate Glass, Tumbler, Fleur-De-Lis | 145.00 |
| Chocolate Glass, Tumbler, Leaf Bracket | 27.00 To 55.00 |
| Chocolate Glass, Tumbler, Lemonade, Cactus | 40.00 |
| Chocolate Glass, Vase, Molded Chrysanthemum Design, 7 In. High | 150.00 |
| Christmas Light, Edison, Mazda | 5.00 |
| Christmas Plate, see Collector, Plate | |
| Christmas Tree Ornament, Angel Holding Trumpet, Candleholder, Metal | 7.50 |
| Christmas Tree Ornament, Lantern, Tin, Glass On 3 Sides, Marked Depose | 20.00 |
| Christmas Tree Ornament, Light Bulb, Bell With Santa Face, Milk Glass | 3.50 |
| Christmas Tree Ornament, Light Bulb, Cat, Milk Glass | 5.00 |
| Christmas Tree Ornament, Light Bulb, Clown | 18.00 |
| Christmas Tree Ornament, Light Bulb, Cobalt Blue | 8.00 |
| Christmas Tree Ornament, Light Bulb, Dog In Basket | 18.00 |
| Christmas Tree Ornament, Light Bulb, Elephant, Milk Glass | 5.00 |
| Christmas Tree Ornament, Light Bulb, Japanese Lantern | 18.00 |
| Christmas Tree Ornament, Light Bulb, Lion, Ringmaster's Dress, Milk Glass | 6.00 |
| Christmas Tree Ornament, Light Bulb, Santa's Head, Milk Glass | 5.00 |
| Christmas Tree Ornament, Light Bulb, Snowman, Milk Glass | 5.00 |
| Cigar Cutter, see Brass, Cigar Cutter, Iron, Cigar Cutter, | |
| Silver, Sterling, Cigar Cutter, Store, Cigar Cutter | |
| Cigar Store Indian, see Wooden, Cigar Store Indian | |

*Cinnabar is a vermilion or red lacquer. Some pieces are made with hundreds of thicknesses of the lacquer that is later carved.*

| | |
|---|---|
| Cinnabar, Box, Covered, 3 3/4 X 5 1/2 X 2 In. | 50.00 |
| Cinnabar, Box, Hinged, Dragon, Phoenix Bird, Enamel Lined | 65.00 |
| Cinnabar, Box, 2 Color Chinese Lacquer On Red Herringbone, C.1750 | 55.00 |
| Cinnabar, Brush Holder, Black, Mums & Foliage, Oriental, 2 Section | 95.00 |
| Cinnabar, Brush Holder, Chrysanthemums & Characters On Black, 2 Section | 95.00 |

*Civil War mementos are important collectors' items. Most of the pieces are military items used from 1861 to 1865.*

| | |
|---|---|
| Civil War, Beaker, Medical, Glass, Clear, Spout, 6 In.High, Tin Lined Case | 29.50 |
| Civil War, Box, Cartridge, .58 Caliber | 48.50 |
| Civil War, Broadside, Camp Followers, Hustlers, & Venereal Disease, 1864 | 79.50 |
| Civil War, Broadside, Drafting, Taunton, Mass., Nov.30, 1863 | 54.50 |
| Civil War, Broadside, To The People Of Maryland, Jan.3, 1861 | 395.00 |
| Civil War, Buckle, Belt, U.S., Oval, Lead Back | 16.50 |
| Civil War, Candleholder, Officer's, Wooden, Cups Screw In, Pair | 89.50 |
| Civil War, Candleholder, Wooden, Turned Cups Screw Into Position, Pair | 89.50 |
| Civil War, Candlestick, Officer's, Brass, 2 Piece Doughnut Shape Cups, Pair | 84.50 |
| Civil War, Canteen, Bull's-Eye | 17.50 |
| Civil War, Canteen, Confederate, Wooden, Iron Hoops & Crosspiece, 'G.Mock' | 195.00 |
| Civil War, Dentist's Instruments, Marked Durroch-London, 9 Pieces | 84.50 |
| Civil War, Dog Tag, Soldier's | 18.50 |
| Civil War, Field Glasses, Navy Officer's, Brass Housing, French Maker | 39.50 |
| Civil War, Flag, Fort Beauregard, Nov.7, 1861, Homespun Linen | 97.50 |
| Civil War, Flag, Handmade, 36 Stars, Adopted In 1864, 42 X 44 In. | 97.50 |
| Civil War, Hardtack, From Camp In Maryland | 64.50 |
| Civil War, Jacket, Shell, Mounted Artilleryman's, Blue Wool, Brass Buttons | 125.00 |
| Civil War, Knapsack, Wooden Frame, Black Canvas, Leather Straps, 'J.Floyd' | 175.00 |
| Civil War, Knife & Tablespoon, Folding, Camillus | 20.00 |

Civil War, Mess Gear, Iron, Walnut Handle, Brass Ferrule, 2 Piece Set ............................ 39.50
Civil War, Poster, A Proclamation For A Day Of Thanksgiving, Mass., 1863 ............... 84.50
Civil War, Poster, Recruiting, Amesbury, Mass., June 7, 1864, 16 X 17 In. ................. 195.00
Civil War, Poster, Thanksgiving, Massachusetts, 1863 ........................................... 84.50
Civil War, Pouch, Bullet, Leather, Loops ...................................................................... 23.00
Civil War, Pouch, Cartridge, Cavalry, Black Leather, For 20 Cartridges ..................... 27.50
Civil War, Pouch, Cartridge, Infantryman's, Black Leather, Brass Plate ...................... 64.50
Civil War, Razor, Sailor's, Wade & Butcher, Sheffield, Etched Sailing Vessel ............. 67.50
Civil War, Saddle, Cavalry, McClellan, Brass Trim, Owner N.Atwood ......................... 750.00
Civil War, Saddle, Officer's Nameplate ........................................................................ 225.00
Civil War, Saw, Surgeon's, Nickel Finish, Marked Pilling-Phila. .................................. 39.50
Civil War, Surgeon's Field Kit, Marked Snowden-Phila., 8 Tools, Case ...................... 650.00
Civil War, Tin, Meat, Combination Cooking & Eating, Iron Handle, C.1870 ................ 34.50
Civil War, Trephine, Surgeon's, To Bore Holes In Skull, Arnold, London ..................... 37.50

*Clambroth glass, popular in the Victorian era, is a grayish color and is*
*semiopaque like the soup.*
Clambroth, Bowl, Swirling Water Cover, Fish Finial, Basket Weave Base, Oval ............ 52.50
Clambroth, Candlestick, Dolphin, Pair ......................................................................... 525.00
Clambroth, Cornucopia, Scalloped Top, 6 In.Long ....................................................... 13.00
Clambroth, Mug, Birds, Miniature ................................................................................ 30.00
Clambroth, Mug, Child's, Washington & Lafayette, Blue ............................................. 24.00
Clambroth, Plate, Grape, Ruffled ................................................................................. 15.00
Clambroth, Salt, Opaque, New England ....................................................................... 105.00
Clambroth, Toothpick, Lacy Medallion ......................................................................... 15.00
Clambroth, Tumbler, Pink Flower, Green Leaves, Souvenir, Rochester, N.Y. .............. 15.00
Clewell, Mug, Riveted Copper Exterior ........................................................................ 50.00
Clewell, Vase, Copper On Pottery, 8 1/4 In. ................................................................ 35.00

*Clews pottery was made by George Clews & Co.of Brownhill Pottery,*
*Tunstall, England, from 1906 to 1961.*
Clews, see also Flow Blue
Clews, Bowl, Rebecca At The Well, Blue, 5 3/4 In.Diameter ....................................... 110.00
Clews, Bowl, Vegetable, Far East Scene, Deep Blue, 8 1/2 X 6 1/4 In. ....................... 88.00
Clews, Bowl, Water Girl, Dark Blue, 5 3/4 In. .............................................................. 105.00
Clews, Cup Plate, Floral, Light Blue, 3 7/8 In. ............................................................. 15.00
Clews, Cup Plate, Ivy Bridge, Blue, 4 1/2 In. .............................................................. 185.00
Clews, Cup Plate, Worcester Cathedral, Dark Blue, 3 3/4 In. ...................................... 55.00
Clews, Plate, Coronation, Blue & White, 10 In. ........................................................... 90.00
Clews, Plate, Dr.Syntax Disputing The Bill, 1900, 10 1/2 In. ...................................... 88.00
Clews, Plate, Dr.Syntax Reading His Tour, Dark Blue, 8 3/4 In. .................................. 85.00
Clews, Plate, Dr.Syntax Reading His Tour, Dark Blue, 9 In. ........................................ 105.00
Clews, Plate, Dr.Syntax Reading His Tour, Dark Blue, 10 1/2 In. ................................ 110.00
Clews, Plate, Dr.Syntax Takes Possession Of His Living, Dark Blue, 10 In. ................. 70.00
Clews, Plate, Hudson River, Black & White, C.1830, 8 1/2 In. .................................... 45.00
Clews, Plate, Hudson River, Fishkill, Brown, 10 1/2 In. ............................................... 75.00
Clews, Plate, Hudson River, Purple, 9 In. .................................................................... 58.00
Clews, Plate, Landing Of Lafayette At Castle Garden, Dark Blue, 8 7/8 In. ................. 95.00
Clews, Plate, Landing Of Lafayette At Castle Garden, 1824, Blue, 9 In. ...................... 130.00
Clews, Plate, Landing Of Lafayette, Blue Transfer, 10 In. ........................................... 165.00
Clews, Plate, Near Fishkill, Hudson River, Purple, 10 1/2 In. ...................................... 68.00
Clews, Plate, Near Fishkill, Hudson River, Sepia, 10 1/2 In. ....................................... 75.00
Clews, Plate, Peace & Plenty, Blue, 10 1/4 In. ............................................................ 175.00
Clews, Plate, Playing At Draughts, Wilkie, Dark Blue, 6 3/4 In. ................................... 90.00
Clews, Plate, Safari Hunting Scene, Medium Blue, C.1830, 10 In. ............................... 35.00
Clews, Plate, Scene Near Hudson, Hudson River, Black & White, 9 In. ........................ 55.00
Clews, Plate, Soup, Windsor Castle, Deep Blue, 9 3/4 In. ....................................*Illus* 40.00
Clews, Plate, States, Deep Blue, 10 1/2 In. ................................................................. 240.00
Clews, Plate, The Valentine, Blue, Wilkie Series, 10 In. .............................................. 125.00
Clews, Plate, The Valentine, Dark Blue, 10 In. ............................................................ 80.00
Clews, Plate, The Valentine, Deep Blue, Wilkie, 10 1/4 In. ......................................... 115.00
Clews, Plate, Troy From Mt.Ida, N.Y., Purple, 10 1/4 In. ............................................ 75.00
Clews, Plate, Tuscan Rose, Light Blue, 10 3/8 In. ....................................................... 18.00
Clews, Platter, Landing Of Lafayette, Deep Blue, Octagonal, 15 3/8 In. ..................... 550.00
Clews, Platter, London Zoo, Pink, 15 1/2 In. ............................................................... 78.00
Clews, Platter, Newburgh, Hudson River, Black & White, 15 1/2 In. ........................... 95.00
Clews, Platter, Windsor Castle, Deep Blue, Octagonal ........................................*Illus* 160.00

Clews, Platter, Windsor Castle,
Deep Blue, Octagonal
(See Page 103)

Clews, Plate, Soup,
Windsor Castle,
Deep Blue, 9 3/4 In.
(See Page 103)

Clock, Brille A Paris,
Ormolu Mounted, C.1775, 12 In.
(See Page 105)

Clock, Bracket, Delaistre A Paris,
C.1725, 41 In.High
(See Page 105)

Clock, Benjamin Morris, Pa.,
C.1775, Walnut, Tall Case
(See Page 105)

Clock, Atkins & Downs, Bristol, Conn.,
C.1835, Mahogany
(See Page 105)

Clock, Banjo, Simon Willard,
C.1805, Mahogany
(See Page 105)

Clock, Aaron Willard,
Dish Dial, C.1805
(See Page 105)

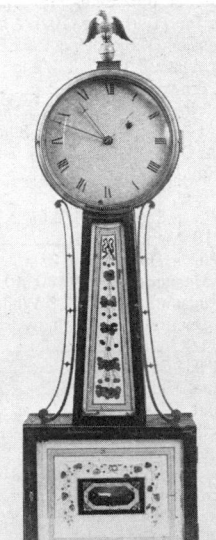

Clews, Tea Set, Mt.Vernon, English Town, Water Girl, Blue, 3 Piece .............. 550.00
Clifton, Vase, Artist-Signed, Dated 1906, 7 1/2 In.High ........................ 36.00
Clock, A.E.Hotchkiss Patent, Meriden, Conn., 1876, Vaseline Glass, Canary ...... 110.00
Clock, A.Hopkins, Litchfield, Grandfather, Wooden Works, 30 Hour ............... 650.00
Clock, A-Week On Bottom Glass, Short Drop, Miniature, 19 In. ................... 95.00
Clock, Aaron Willard, Banjo, Mahogany & Parcel Gilt, Eglomise Panel, C.1815 .... 1900.00
Clock, Aaron Willard, Dish Dial, C.1805 .................................. *Illus* 7500.00
Clock, Advertising, American Mould, Wall, Glass, 7 In.Dial .................... 87.50
Clock, Advertising, American, Carved Wooden Dial, 2 Monks Drinking ............ 165.00
Clock, Advertising, American, Lever Movement, Disc Moves Counterclockwise ..... 95.00
Clock, Advertising, Calvert Whiskeys, Electric, Plexiglass & Tin .............. 10.00
Clock, Alarm, Big Ben Type .................................................... 14.00
Clock, Alarm, Travel, French, Brass Case, Dated 1878, Makers Mark ............. 125.00
Clock, American, Square Pressed Glass Columns, 15 1/2 In.High ................. 90.00
Clock, Ansonia On Bottom Glass, Long Drop, Miniature .......................... 115.00
Clock, Ansonia, Calendar, Rosewood Case, 24 In. .............................. 150.00
Clock, Ansonia, Carriage Shape, Victorian Metal Case, 30 Hour ................. 55.00
Clock, Ansonia, Carriage, White Metal Case, Winged Lady's Head On Corners ..... 125.00
Clock, Ansonia, Fisherman Swinging Arm ....................................... 650.00
Clock, Ansonia, French Carriage Style, Brass & Glass, 15 1/2 In.High .......... 225.00
Clock, Ansonia, Japanned Case, 4 3/4 In. Dial ................................ 175.00
Clock, Ansonia, Kitchen, Hanging, Oak, 26 In. ................................ 95.00
Clock, Ansonia, Lever Movement, Rosewood Case, 7 In.Dial ..................... 67.50
Clock, Ansonia, Mantel, Oak Case, Brass Double Dial .......................... 185.00
Clock, Ansonia, Mantel, Oak Case, Porcelain Dial ............................. 165.00
Clock, Ansonia, Muse, Ball Swinger ........................................... 750.00
Clock, Ansonia, Ormolu, Painted Panel, Porcelain Dial ........................ 165.00
Clock, Ansonia, School, Oak Case, Long Drop .................................. 275.00
Clock, Ansonia, School, Rosewood Case, 7 In. Dial ............................ 165.00
Clock, Ansonia, School, Walnut Case, Long Drop ............................... 275.00
Clock, Ansonia, Standard Time In Bottom Glass, 30 In. ........................ 145.00
Clock, Ansonia, Weight, 30 Hour .............................................. 65.00
Clock, Art Deco, Silver Gilt & Enamel, Geneva Watch Co., C.1930, 4 1/2 In. .... 700.00
Clock, Art Nouveau, Cherub With Floral Garlands, Paper Face .................. 45.00
Clock, Atkins & Downs, Bristol, Conn., C.1835, Mahogany .................. *Illus* 375.00
Clock, Atkins Clock Co., Bristol, Conn., Walnut Shelf, 8 Day, Door Bottom ..... 165.00
Clock, Banjo, Alarm .......................................................... 1800.00
Clock, Banjo, D.Williams, A Frame, Dead Beat ................................. 2500.00
Clock, Banjo, Howard Type, Size No.5 ......................................... 500.00
Clock, Banjo, Mahogany & Parcel Gilded, E.H.Nutter, C.1825, 39 In.Long ....... 2800.00
Clock, Banjo, Mahogany & Parcel Gilded, New England, C.1825, 33 In.High ...... 1400.00
Clock, Banjo, New Haven, Bride's, 30 Day .................................... 375.00
Clock, Banjo, New Haven, Pendulum Type ....................................... 120.00
Clock, Banjo, Riggs & Bros., Octagonal Base, Narrow Throat ................... 775.00
Clock, Banjo, Simon Willard, C.1805, Mahogany ........................... *Illus* 7000.00
Clock, Banjo, Stennis, Crossbanded Case ...................................... 495.00
Clock, Banjo, Willards Patent, Rope Front, Gold Gilt, Presentation ........... 1250.00
Clock, Battery, Oval Glass Dome, 5 In.High ................................... 195.00
Clock, Beating Heart, Alabaster & Brass Frame, Hanging Stand ................. 85.00
Clock, Beehive, Rosewood, Connecticut Clock Co. .............................. 90.00
Clock, Benjamin Morris, Pa., C.1775, Walnut, Tall Case .................. *Illus* 3800.00
Clock, Bisque, Pastel Colors, 16 1/2 In.High ................................. 92.00
Clock, Black, Starr, & Frost, Mantel, Bronze & Marble, 26 X 14 X 6 In. ....... 1500.00
Clock, Black, Starr, & Frost, Mantel, Dore Bronze, Marble, Classic Figures ... 2250.00
Clock, Boardman & Wells, Wooden Works ........................................ 85.00
Clock, Boudoir, Cut Glass, Sinclaire, Copper Wheel Engraved Floral ........... 175.00
Clock, Boulle, Battery, Glass Dome, 11 In.High ............................... 135.00
Clock, Boulle, Battery, Glass Dome, 15 In.High ............................... 215.00
Clock, Bracket, Delaistre A Paris, C.1725, 41 In.High ................... *Illus* 1600.00
Clock, Bracket, Ebonized, Brass Moldings, Dwerrihouse, C.1775, 13 In.High .... 2100.00
Clock, Brass, Porcelain, Face, Alarm, Marked 1904, 3 X 3 In. ................. 40.00
Clock, Brassac Les Mines, Portall, Wall, Black Lacquer, Brass Dial, 8 Day .... 155.00
Clock, Brewster & Son, Gothic Steeple, 8 Day ................................. 525.00
Clock, Brille A Paris, Ormolu Mounted, C.1775, 12 In. ................... *Illus* 2300.00
Clock, Bronze & Onyx, Elephants Supporting Clock, 14 1/2 In.High ............. 190.00
Clock, Budweiser, Bar Room, Revolving, Pocket Watch Shape .................... 65.00

| | |
|---|---|
| Clock, C.W.Simms, Ironbridge, English School, Time & Strike | 148.50 |
| Clock, Calendar, French, Wooden Case, Black Face, Gold Numerals, 8 Day | 245.00 |
| Clock, Camel Form, Viennese, Silver Gilt & Enamel, C.1880, 7 3/4 In.High | 1500.00 |
| Clock, Carriage, A.Stowell & Co., Boston, Zinc Case, Gold Plate, Faces | 175.00 |
| Clock, Carriage, Brass, Alarm, Glass Panel, Key, 3 3/4 In.High | 375.00 |
| Clock, Carriage, French, Burnished Brass, Porcelain Face | 137.50 |
| Clock, Carriage, French, Repeater, Beveled Glass On 2 Sides, Brass Case | 285.00 |
| Clock, Carriage, French, Repeater, Brass Case, Beveled Glass, 5 1/4 In.High | 265.00 |
| Clock, Carriage, New Haven Clock Co., Beveled Glass, Brass Case, Miniature | 95.00 |
| Clock, Cartel, Mother-Of-Pearl Inlay, Bisque Dial | 225.00 |
| Clock, Cartier, Traveling, Art Deco, 14K 2 Color Gold, 17 Jewel, C.1930 | 750.00 |
| Clock, Cartier, Traveling, Nephrite, Gold & Champleve Enamel, Rubies, C.1930 | 800.00 |
| Clock, Cartier, Traveling, Rock Crystal, Gold, & Enamel Chinoiserie, C.1930 | 2700.00 |
| Clock, Case, Hand-Carved Mahogany, Oil Of The Christ, Artist Carver | 200.00 |
| Clock, Cast Iron, Statue, Looks Like Brass | 30.00 |
| Clock, Charles X, Ormolu, Cherubs, Naked Male Figure, C.1890, 20 1/2 In. | 400.00 |
| Clock, China, Floral On White, Blue Border, Key Wind, 7 1/4 In.High | 75.00 |
| Clock, Chiparus, Gilt Bronze, Ovoid Face, Flower Filled Urns, Marble Base | 425.00 |
| Clock, Chronometer, Arnold, London, Mahogany Case, C.1800 | 295.00 |
| Clock, Commemorative, Soldier & Sailor, 8 Day | 60.00 |
| Clock, Dickensware, Sam Weller, Pickwick Papers, Tan Ground, 8 In.High | 85.00 |
| Clock, Durnstein, Zappler, Pendulum, Oval Glass Dome, Embossed Front | 395.00 |
| Clock, E.N.Welch Co., Forrestville, Black Iron | 40.00 |
| Clock, E.N.Welch, School, Rosewood Case, 7 In.Dial | 165.00 |
| Clock, Elgin, Cadillac, Gold Filled Case, Black Numerals | 85.00 |
| Clock, Empire, Gilt Metal, Rose Sprays, Bun Feet, Flower Heads, C.1820, 8 In. | 260.00 |
| Clock, English, Post Office, Fusee Movement, 16 In.Diameter | 65.00 |
| Clock, Festeau, Le Jeune, Louis XVI Style, Gilt Metal & Gros Bleu China | 1600.00 |
| Clock, Figural, George Washington, Metal, 24 In.High | 200.00 |
| Clock, Floor, Regulator, Cherry Case, Jeweled Movement, Double Weight | 2500.00 |
| Clock, Fr.Baumann Hofahrmacher, Mantel, Louis XV Style, Boulle, C.1850 | 875.00 |
| Clock, French, Crystal, Mercury Pendulum, Decorated Porcelain Dial | 165.00 |
| Clock, French, Mantel, Beveled Crystal Pendulum, Strikes Hour & 1/2 Hour | 115.00 |
| Clock, French, Porcelain Dial, Girl Playing Violin, Dog, Dated 1846 | 250.00 |
| Clock, G.Becker, Wall, German, Walnut, Westminster Chimes | 350.00 |
| Clock, G.E.Cake Top Refrigerator, Electric | 15.00 |
| Clock, Gale, Calendar, Double Dial | 625.00 |
| Clock, German, China, Hand-Painted White & Red Roses, & Lilacs, Openwork | 150.00 |
| Clock, German, Grandfather, Oak Case, Open Well | 1250.00 |
| Clock, German, Kitchen, Wall, China, Pendulum, 8-Day | 15.00 |
| Clock, German, School, Octagonal Maple Case, Short Drop | 195.00 |
| Clock, German, Shelf, Brass Case, 11 In. High | 65.00 |
| Clock, German, Walnut Case, 4 Tube Westminster Chime | 2500.00 |
| Clock, Gilbert, Calendar, Marinville, 34 In. | 425.00 |
| Clock, Gilbert, Kitchen, Oak Case | 52.00 |
| Clock, Gilbert, Mantel, Pendulum, Windup, 8 Day | 30.00 |
| Clock, Gilbert, Tornado, Alarm, Nickel, Bell On Top, Patent 1904 | 12.00 |
| Clock, Gilbert, Winsted, Conn., Walnut Case, Brass Works, Painted Dial, 13 In. | 100.00 |
| Clock, Gingerbread, Strikes, 25 In.High | 64.00 |
| Clock, Girandole, Federal Style, Parcel Gilded, Eagle On Top, 49 1/2 In. | 3000.00 |
| Clock, Gold Filled, Cherry Case, 9 Chime Tubes, 2 Tunes, Moon Phases | 1500.00 |
| Clock, Grandfather, German, Brass Weights, Face, & Pendulum, Oak Case | 495.00 |
| Clock, Grandfather, Mahogany, 12 Tune Regina Music Box Plays On Hour | 2750.00 |
| Clock, Grandfather, Signed A.Hopkins Litchfield, Painted Face, 30 Hour | 650.00 |
| Clock, Gray & Black Marble, Women Reading Songbook On Top, 8 Day | 125.00 |
| Clock, Herschede, Grandfather, Mahogany, Carved, Moon Dial, Dated 1903 | 4400.00 |
| Clock, Ingersoll, Big Bad Wolf, Alarm | 200.00 |
| Clock, Ingraham, Banjo, Treasure Isle | 250.00 |
| Clock, Ingraham, Banjo, 39 In.High | 250.00 |
| Clock, Ingraham, Calendar, Gingerbread, Oak | 125.00 |
| Clock, Ingraham, Calendar, Regulator, Box | 185.00 |
| Clock, Ingraham, Calendar, Schoolhouse, Oak, Embossed Case, Long Drop | 200.00 |
| Clock, Ingraham, Doric, Strikes, Alarm, 7-Day | 65.00 |
| Clock, Ingraham, Figure 8, Double Dial, Lewis Calendar | 795.00 |
| Clock, Ingraham, Ionic, Strikes | 225.00 |
| Clock, Ingraham, Treasure Isle Banjo, 40 In. High | 265.00 |

| | |
|---|---|
| Clock, Ingram, Kitchen, Mayflower, Bristol, Conn., Alarm, 24 In.High | 92.00 |
| Clock, International Time Recorder, Pendulum, 10 In.Dial | 55.00 |
| Clock, Iron Front Case With Lower Bezel, Figures, Ornate | 20.00 |
| Clock, Ithaca, Calendar, Poney, 17 In. | 345.00 |
| Clock, Ithaca, Index In Gold Leaf On Door, Walnut Case, 28 In. | 675.00 |
| Clock, J.Cope, Mahogany Case, Moon Dial, Calendar, Gold Filled | 1150.00 |
| Clock, Jade, Dark Green, Ormolu Mounts, Phoenix Birds, 20 1/2 In.High | 8250.00 |
| Clock, Japanese, Pine Cased Figure 8, American Movement | 265.00 |
| Clock, Jerome & Co., New Haven, Wall, Ogee, Gold Border, Painting On Glass | 125.00 |
| Clock, Jerome, Cottage, Alarm, 11 1/2 In.High | 45.00 |
| Clock, Junghans, Musical, Glass Sides, Carriage Type, 6 In. High | 110.00 |
| Clock, Junghans, Spring Wind, Vienna Regulator | 165.00 To 195.00 |
| Clock, Junghans, Vienna, Walnut Case, 2 Weights, 34 In. | 275.00 |
| Clock, Kitchen, Carved Case, Mirrors On Sides | 95.00 |
| Clock, Kitchen, Ingraham, Oak, 8 Day, Time & Strike, Alarm | 85.00 |
| Clock, Kitchen, Oak, Gilbert, 8 Day | 55.00 |
| Clock, Kitchen, Steeple, Waterbury, Oak | 55.00 |
| Clock, Kitchen, Waterbury, Walnut Case, 8 Day, Time & Strike, Alarm | 85.00 |
| Clock, Lapis Lazuli, Silver Gilt, Enamel, Jewels, 1800s, 9 1/4 In. | 4300.00 |
| Clock, Le Roy A Paris, Ormolu, C.1800, 18 In.High *Illus* | 1200.00 |
| Clock, Le Roy & Fils, Carriage, Gilt Metal, Repeating, Alarm, C.1880, 5 In. | 400.00 |
| Clock, Lepine, Mantel, Cupids & Nude, Ormolu Mounted, 19 1/2 In.High | 2600.00 |
| Clock, Liberty & Co., Tudric Pewter & Enamel, C.1900, 8 In. High | 750.00 |
| Clock, Louis XVI Style, Boulle Bracket, Ormolu, Bronze Father Time, 1890s | 850.00 |
| Clock, Lyre, Carved Mahogany, Simon Willard & Son, C.1825, Landscape | 3100.00 |
| Clock, Mantel, Art Nouveau, Gilt Metal, New Haven, C.1900, 11 In.High | 70.00 |
| Clock, Mantel, Black, Columns & Lions' Heads | 65.00 |
| Clock, Mantel, Brass, French, Angels, Putti, & Dolphin, 52 X 16 In. | 525.00 |
| Clock, Mantel, Gilt Metal & Hardstone, Quadrangular Case, C.1900, 11 In. | 800.00 |
| Clock, Mantel, Gilt Metal, Scrolling Foliage, Spanish Market, C.1850, 8 In. | 425.00 |
| Clock, Mantel, Golden Oak, Curved Hood, Brass & Silver Dial | 55.00 |
| Clock, Mantel, Josef Hoffman, C.1920, Silver, 9 In.High *Illus* | 3100.00 |
| Clock, Mantel, Miniature, Art Deco, Gold & Enamel, Mauboussin, C.1930 | 1600.00 |
| Clock, Mantel, Pressed Glass, Daisy & Button, Vaseline, 13 1/2 In.Long | 135.00 |
| Clock, Mantel, Sessions, 8 Day | 55.00 |
| Clock, Meriden, Conn., Canary Glass, Dated 1876-1882 | 105.00 |
| Clock, Movado Factories, Gilt Metal & Enamel, Red Face, Smoky Glass | 190.00 |
| Clock, Movado, Chrome & Bakelite, Rectangular Frame, Nailhead Numerals | 160.00 |
| Clock, Muehlebach Beer, Back Bar, Electric | 12.50 |
| Clock, New Haven, Banjo, Reverse Painting, Strikes, 37 In. | 175.00 |
| Clock, New Haven, Banjo, Reverse Painting, 30-Day, 42 In. | 350.00 |
| Clock, New Haven, Beehive Type, Reverse Painting On Glass, 15 1/4 In.High | 100.00 |
| Clock, New Haven, Calendar, Regulator, Box | 185.00 |
| Clock, New Haven, Calendar, Rosewood Case, 23 In. | 135.00 |
| Clock, New Haven, Cut Glass, 8 Day, 8 In. High | 195.00 |
| Clock, New Haven, Grocery Store, Regulator, 11 In.Dial | 115.00 |

Clock, Le Roy A Paris,
Ormolu, C.1800,
18 In.High

Clock, Mantel,
Josef Hoffman, C.1920,
Silver, 9 In.High

| | |
|---|---:|
| Clock, New Haven, Mantel, Art Nouveau, Gilt Metal, Girl Figure, C.1895 | 300.00 |
| Clock, New Haven, Mantel, Victorian, "Blackie" | 35.00 |
| Clock, New Haven, Pairpoint Cut Crystal | 100.00 |
| Clock, New Haven, Regulator, Walnut & Oak Case, Weight Bank Model | 400.00 |
| Clock, New Haven, School, Drop, Rosewood Case | 125.00 |
| Clock, New Haven, School, German Walnut Case, Long Drop | 265.00 |
| Clock, New Haven, School, Rosewood Case, Short Drop, Calendar | 275.00 |
| Clock, New Haven, Schoolhouse, Embossed Case, Long Drop | 175.00 |
| Clock, New Haven, Schoolhouse, Walnut, Round Head, Long Drop | 200.00 |
| Clock, New Haven, Schoolhouse, 7 1/4 X 11 1/2 In. | 100.00 |
| Clock, New Haven, Table, Benedict Adam Bronze Case | 25.00 |
| Clock, New Haven, Wall, Oak Case, 44 X 16 In. | 35.00 |
| Clock, Niagara, Wall, Battery | 100.00 |
| Clock, Novotny, World, 1884, Fusee Movement, Porcelain Dial | 1850.00 |
| Clock, Oak Case, Round Drop, 7 In.Dial | 90.00 |
| Clock, Open Pendulum, Brass Face, 8 Day, Strikes Hour & 1/2 Hour | 260.00 |
| Clock, Ormolu & Lapis Lazuli, Omega Watch Co., C.1900, 6 In.High | 275.00 |
| Clock, Plymouth, Mantel, Windup, Strikes 15 Minutes & Hour | 85.00 |
| Clock, Poole, Battery, Glass Dome | 125.00 |
| Clock, Porcelain, German, White & Pink, 6 In. High | 35.00 |
| Clock, Regulator A On Bottom Glass, Long Drop, Miniature, 7 In.Dial | 95.00 |
| Clock, Regulator, A On Bottom, Glass, Short Drop, 9 In.Dial | 110.00 |
| Clock, Rosewood Case, Short Drop, 9 In.Dial | 90.00 |
| Clock, Royal Doulton, Nankin Pattern, Florals On Cobalt Blue, 5 X 6 In. | 180.00 |
| Clock, Sambo, Blinking Eye | 495.00 |
| Clock, School, Advertising, Hard Security On Bottom Glass, 7 In.Dial | 95.00 |
| Clock, School, American, Rosewood Case, Drop | 95.00 |
| Clock, School, Drop, 4 3/4 In.Dial | 125.00 |
| Clock, Schultz, Konigsberg, Table, Gilt Metal, Hexagonal, Engraved, C.1680 | 4000.00 |
| Clock, Sedan Chair, Regency, Hardwood Case, C.1825, 6 In.Diameter | 150.00 |
| Clock, Sessions, Banjo, Pendulum, 8-Day | 125.00 |
| Clock, Sessions, Kitchen, Oak Case, Alarm | 55.00 |
| Clock, Sessions, Mantel, Humpback | 75.00 |
| Clock, Sessions, Wall, Oak, Mission, Strikes | 60.00 |
| Clock, Seth Thomas No.2, Office, Weight Regulator | 325.00 |
| Clock, Seth Thomas, Barbershop, Maple | 195.00 |
| Clock, Seth Thomas, Brass & Glass, 8 Day, Beveled Glass Sides, Time & Strike | 125.00 |
| Clock, Seth Thomas, Brass Bezel On Bakelite Case, 8 Day, Double Mainsprings | 85.00 |
| Clock, Seth Thomas, Brass, Beveled Glass, Brass Columns, 11 In.High | 225.00 |
| Clock, Seth Thomas, Calendar, Big Bell Fashion No.4 | 850.00 |
| Clock, Seth Thomas, Calendar, Rosewood Case, Weight, 43 In. | 525.00 |
| Clock, Seth Thomas, Calendar, Wall, Weight, Rosewood Case, 42 In. | 650.00 |
| Clock, Seth Thomas, Candlestand, Porcelain Dial | 350.00 |
| Clock, Seth Thomas, Double Dial, Perpetual Calendar | 495.00 |
| Clock, Seth Thomas, Gothic Mahogany Case, Chimes | 120.00 |
| Clock, Seth Thomas, Long Case, Silvered Steel Dial, Moon Dial, C.1900 | 700.00 |
| Clock, Seth Thomas, Perpetual Calendar, Walnut Case, Double Dial | 450.00 |
| Clock, Seth Thomas, Schoolhouse, Oak | 165.00 |
| Clock, Seth Thomas, Schoolhouse, Walnut | 175.00 |
| Clock, Seth Thomas, Ship's, Brass, Lutside Bell | 250.00 |
| Clock, Seth Thomas, Ship's, Brass, 14 Day, 7 In. Diameter | 145.00 |
| Clock, Seth Thomas, Ship's, Silver Plate Case, Wood Base, Striking | 250.00 |
| Clock, Seth Thomas, Sonora, Marquetry, Chimes On Hour & 1/4 Hour | 195.00 |
| Clock, Seth Thomas, Wall, Double Dial | 650.00 |
| Clock, Seth Thomas, Wall, Rosewood, C.1850, 24 In.High | 130.00 |
| Clock, Sevres, Mantel, Celeste Blue, 3 Piece | 350.00 |
| Clock, Shelf, French, Solid Brass, Beveled Glass, Dated 1881, Porcelain Face | 85.00 |
| Clock, Shelf, Gilbert, Inlaid Rosewood, Arched Case, Panel Decoration | 80.00 |
| Clock, Shelf, Inlaid Mahogany, Elisha Hotchkiss, C.1820, 31 1/4 In.High | 125.00 |
| Clock, Shelf, Munger, Eagle Pendulum | 1000.00 |
| Clock, Shelf, New Hampshire, Mirror, Collins, Time & Strike | 1600.00 |
| Clock, Shelf, Pillar & Scroll, Mahogany, Ephraim Downs, C.1825, 29 In. High | 950.00 |
| Clock, Shelf, Seth Thomas, Painted, Inlaid Rosewood, C.1866, 32 In.High | 225.00 |
| Clock, Shelf, Seth Thomas, Satin Wood Case, Scenic Panel | 65.00 |
| Clock, Ship, Chelsea, U.S.Maritime Commission, Silver Dial, Bakelite Case | 95.00 |
| Clock, Ship's, Chelsea, Engine Room, Bronze Case | 80.00 |

Clock, Table, Repeating, Alarm, Gilt Metal, C.1725

Clock, Tall Case, Pine, New England, C.1825

Clock, Tall Case, Walnut, John Jones, C.1773, 7 Ft.High

| | |
|---|---:|
| Clock, Ship's, Metal, Mounted On Ship's Wheel, 23 In.Diameter | 135.00 |
| Clock, Ship's, Seth Thomas, Exposed Ball | 225.00 |
| Clock, Shreve, Crump, & Low Co., Tall Case, Corinthian Columns, C.1850 | 1500.00 |
| Clock, Skeleton, Cathedral, Brass, English, C.1850, 19 In.High | 950.00 |
| Clock, Skeleton, English, Fusee, Dome, White Marble Base, 16 In. | 385.00 |
| Clock, Skeleton, French, Glass Dom, 8 Day, Pendulum, 8 In.High | 325.00 |
| Clock, Staffordshire, Two Girl Figurines Each Side, 6 1/2 In. | 37.50 |
| Clock, Standard Electric Time Co., Wall, Round Copper Case, 12 In. | 30.00 |
| Clock, Star Brand Shoes, Metal | 14.00 |
| Clock, Store, Duquesne Beer, Electric, Lights Up, 15 In.Square | 20.00 |
| Clock, Store, Mincemeat, Squash, Pumpkin, Etc., Tin, Easel Back, 9 1/2 In. | 65.00 |
| Clock, Sundial, Bronze, Octagonal, Pierced Gnomon, Dated 1693, 4 In.Diameter | 195.00 |
| Clock, Sundial, Brass, Rectangular, Jas.Green, New York, C.1800 15 X 13 In. | 400.00 |
| Clock, Table, Ivory, Revolving Top, Pointer Tells Time, American | 12.00 |
| Clock, Table, Repeating, Alarm, Gilt Metal, C.1725 .......... Illus | 3400.00 |
| Clock, Table, Silver & Enamel, Form Of A Parasol, Swiss, C.1900 | 250.00 |
| Clock, Tall Case, Federal, Inlaid Mahogany, Aaron Willard, C.1810 | 5750.00 |
| Clock, Tall Case, Inlaid Mahogany, Massachusetts, C.1800 | 2600.00 |
| Clock, Tall Case, Pine, New England, C.1825 .......... Illus | 325.00 |
| Clock, Tall Case, Regency, Mahogany, Brass Inlaid, C.1825, 6 Ft.5 In.High | 1200.00 |
| Clock, Tall Case, Walnut, John Jones, C.1773, 7 Ft.High .......... Illus | 3000.00 |
| Clock, Thomas Parker, Phila., Shelf, Mahogany, Brass Bail Handle, C.1785 .......... Illus | 5000.00 |
| Clock, Tiffany, see Tiffany, Clock | |
| Clock, Timepiece, Wall, Japanese, Mahogany & Brass, Vase Of Flowers, C.1800 | 1700.00 |
| Clock, United Electric Clock Co., N.Y., F.D.R. At Helm Of Ship's Wheel | 100.00 |
| Clock, Venworth Transition, Paw Feet | 335.00 |
| Clock, Vienna, Gustav Becker, Mahogany Case, 3 Weights | 500.00 |
| Clock, Vienna, J.W.Benson, London, Rosewood Case, 2 Weights | 295.00 |
| Clock, Viennese, Gilt Metal & Enamel, Verge, C.1890 .......... Illus | 1300.00 |
| Clock, Viennese, Gilt Metal, Enamel, C.1890, 9 3/4 In. .......... Illus | 1000.00 |
| Clock, Viennese, Silver, Champleve Enamel, C.1890 .......... Illus | 2800.00 |
| Clock, Wall, Brass Buttons, Round Bottom Door, 7 In.Dial | 85.00 To 92.50 |
| Clock, Wall, French, Wormy Rosewood, Carved Roses, Pendulum, Chimes | 235.00 |
| Clock, Wall, Inlaid Mahogany, Elisha Manross, Conn., C.1850, 26 In.High | 250.00 |
| Clock, Wall, Regulator Oak Case, 38 X 18 In. | 35.00 |

Clock, Viennese,
Gilt Metal & Enamel,
Verge, C.1890
*(See Page 109)*

Clock, Viennese, Silver,
Champleve Enamel, C.1890
*(See Page 109)*

Clock, Viennese,
Gilt Metal, Enamel,
C.1890, 9 3/4 In.
*(See Page 109)*

| | |
|---|---:|
| **Clock, Wall,** 11 In.Dial, 35 In.High | 120.00 |
| **Clock, Waltham,** Desk, Brass Case, Double Dial, 8-Day | 65.00 |
| **Clock, Waltham,** Desk, 2 Faces | 50.00 |
| **Clock, Waltham,** Floor, Regulator, Carved Mahogany Case, Silvered Dial | 3500.00 |
| **Clock, Waterbury No.18,** Oak Case, 2 Weights | 600.00 |
| **Clock, Waterbury,** Calendar, Shelf, Walnut Case, Double Dial | 550.00 |
| **Clock, Waterbury,** Carriage, Beveled Glass, Porcelain Face, 3 1/2 In.High | 175.00 |
| **Clock, Waterbury,** Figurine, Man In Big Hat, Bronze Finish, Porcelain Face | 85.00 |
| **Clock, Waterbury,** Kitchen, Oak Case, Calendar | 195.00 |
| **Clock, Waterbury,** Mantel, Cast Iron | 40.00 |
| **Clock, Waterbury,** Mantel, Iron & Brass, 8-Day | 75.00 |
| **Clock, Waterbury,** Porcelain, Decorated, 6 1/2 In.High | 42.00 |
| **Clock, Waterbury,** School, Carved Oak Case, 24 In.High | 110.00 |
| **Clock, Waterbury,** Schoolhouse, Oak, Embossed Case | 160.00 |
| **Clock, Waterbury,** Strikes, 30-Hour | 65.00 |
| **Clock, Waterbury,** Wall, Regulator, Walnut | 225.00 |
| **Clock, Waterbury,** Weight, Brass Works, Walnut Case, Ship On Glass, 30 Hour | 135.00 |
| **Clock, Waterbury,** Weight, 30 Hour | 65.00 |
| **Clock, Wendell,** Albany, N.Y., Mantel, Black Slate, Outside Escapement | 50.00 |
| **Clock, Westclox,** Big Ben | 7.50 |
| **Clock, Western Union,** Gallery, Self Winding Clock Co., Round, C.1925 | 65.00 |
| **Clock, Western Union,** Oak Case, Self Winding, 18 X 28 In. | 175.00 |
| **Clock, Windmill,** Barometer, Brass Gallery, 2 Keys, 16 1/2 In.High | 250.00 |

*Cloisonne enamel was developed during the nineteenth century. A glass
enamel was applied between small ribbonlike pieces of metal on a metal base.
Most Cloisonne is Japanese.*

| | |
|---|---:|
| **Cloisonne, Bottle,** Snuff, Blue & Pink Floral On Beige | 60.00 |
| **Cloisonne, Bottle,** Snuff, Metal With Coral Top, C.1850 | 90.00 |
| **Cloisonne, Bowl,** Covered, Dragon On Black, 3 Legs, 1 3/4 In. | 22.00 |
| **Cloisonne, Bowl,** Covered, Goldstone, Brown, Green, Red, Blue, & White | 48.00 |
| **Cloisonne, Bowl,** Floral & Chinese Characters Inside & Out, 10 In. | 135.00 |
| **Cloisonne, Bowl,** Multicolor On Blue, Decorated Inside, 6 1/2 In. | 65.00 |
| **Cloisonne, Bowl,** White Flowers On Red, 4 1/2 In.Wide | 12.00 |
| **Cloisonne, Bowl,** Yellow Dragons On Black Ground, 10 In.Diameter, 3 In.High | 160.00 |
| **Cloisonne, Box,** Birds & Floral On Blue, 2 1/2 In. Long | 95.00 |
| **Cloisonne, Box,** Black Fish Scale, Yellow & Green Design, 3 X 3 In. | 45.00 |
| **Cloisonne, Box,** Cigarette, White Jade Decoration On Lid, Red Scrolls, Floral | 35.00 |
| **Cloisonne, Box,** Covered, Round, Blue, 3 In.High | 25.00 |
| **Cloisonne, Box,** Foo Dog Finial, Cobalt Florals On Lemon, 5 In.Diameter | 30.00 |
| **Cloisonne, Box,** Heart Shape, Green Stone Top, Flowers, 2 1/4 In. | 55.00 |
| **Cloisonne, Box,** Hinged, Chinese Red, Blue Enamel Lined, 4 Sections | 65.00 |

| | |
|---|---:|
| Cloisonne, Box, Hinged, Fish Scale On Cobalt, 3 X 2 In. | 22.00 |
| Cloisonne, Box, Ring At Lid Lock, Silver, Chinese, Oval, 3 Parts, 2 In.High | 185.00 |
| Cloisonne, Box, White Floral On Light Blue, Spiral Cloisons, 3 In. Diameter | 18.00 |
| Cloisonne, Buckle, Belt, 3 1/2 X 5 In. | 65.00 |
| Cloisonne, Buckle, Butterflies, Flowers, & Gold, 3 1/4 In. | 45.00 |
| Cloisonne, Candlestick, Ormolu Trim, Barbedienne, 13 3/4 In.High, Pair | 325.00 |
| Cloisonne, Charger, Birds & Flowers, Scalloped, 14 1/2 In. | 250.00 |
| Cloisonne, Charger, Cranes & Flowers, Scalloped, 18 In. | 350.00 |
| Cloisonne, Charger, Phoenix Birds & Floral On Black, C.1780, 12 1/2 In.High | 475.00 |
| Cloisonne, Figurine, Swan, Seated, 5 X 5 In., Pair | 950.00 |
| Cloisonne, Humidor, Floral On Black | 88.75 |
| Cloisonne, Jar, Covered, White Apple Blossoms & Green Leaves On Rust, 4 In. | 48.00 |
| Cloisonne, Jar, Ginger, Covered, Blue Ground, Pair | 125.00 |
| Cloisonne, Jar, Ginger, Covered, Pink & White Peonies & Green On Black | 35.00 |
| Cloisonne, Jar, Ginger, Multicolor On Black, 8 1/2 In.High | 165.00 |
| Cloisonne, Jar, Man Feeding Chickens On Porcelain Cover | 75.00 |
| Cloisonne, Lamp Base, Brass Base Marked C P, Multicolored Floral, Pair | 185.00 |
| Cloisonne, Lamp, Mahogany Base, Pigeon Blood On White, 20 In.High | 60.00 |
| Cloisonne, Lamp, Table, Bronze Base | 340.00 |
| Cloisonne, Plaque, Florals & Birds On Blue, 12 In.Diameter | 115.00 |
| Cloisonne, Plaque, Flowers, Birds, & Butterfly, Gold Braided Frame | 85.00 |
| Cloisonne, Plate, Dragonflies & Leaves On Black, C.1850, 12 In., Pair | 325.00 |
| Cloisonne, Plate, Flying Bird & Bird On Leaf On Blue, 9 1/2 In. | 65.00 |
| Cloisonne, Plate, Pair Of Pheasants, Floral, & Trees On Blue, C.1870, 12 In. | 260.00 |
| Cloisonne, Salt, Individual | 13.00 |
| Cloisonne, Saltshaker, Dragons On White, Brass Top & Base, 1 1/2 In.High | 16.00 |
| Cloisonne, Teapot, Birds & Butterflies, Goldstone | 165.00 |
| Cloisonne, Teapot, Blue, Mauve, & Pink Floral & Butterflies On Green, Brass | 78.00 |
| Cloisonne, Teapot, Butterflies & Flowers On Black & Brown, Pedestal | 88.75 |
| Cloisonne, Teapot, Goldstone & Butterfly, Miniature, Japanese | 80.00 |
| Cloisonne, Tray, Pin, Multicolor On Black, 3 1/2 In. | 12.00 |
| Cloisonne, Vase, Birds, Floral, & Flowering Branches On Blue, 16 In.High | 220.00 |
| Cloisonne, Vase, Bluebirds On Flowering Tree On Green, Silver Rim, 7 In. | 50.00 |
| Cloisonne, Vase, Butterflies & Flowers On Blue To Green At Base, 7 1/4 In. | 125.00 |
| Cloisonne, Vase, Covered, Dragon & Birds, 2 Handles, 7 1/4 In.High | 225.00 |
| Cloisonne, Vase, Crane & Foliage On Red, 7 1/2 In.High | 90.00 |
| Cloisonne, Vase, Dragon Decoration On Black, 10 In.High | 135.00 |
| Cloisonne, Vase, Dragon Vignettes, Light Blue, 7 1/2 X 4 In., Pair | 135.00 |
| Cloisonne, Vase, Dragon With 5 Claws, 4 In.High | 85.00 |
| Cloisonne, Vase, Dragon, Blue, Red, & Purple On Turquoise, 5 In.High | 75.00 |
| Cloisonne, Vase, Floral Sprays & Burnt Orange Bands On Dark Blue, 5 In. | 45.00 |
| Cloisonne, Vase, Flying Cranes & Bamboo Shoots On Dark Blue, Pair | 175.00 |
| Cloisonne, Vase, French, Flowers & Butterfly On Light Blue, 6 In. | 75.00 |
| Cloisonne, Vase, French, Flowers & Butterfly, 6 1/2 In.High | 70.00 |
| Cloisonne, Vase, Green & Blue Macaw On Cherry Blossom Branch On Blue | 145.00 |
| Cloisonne, Vase, Green, Red, & Black Flowers On Dark, 8 In.High | 45.00 |
| Cloisonne, Vase, Honeycomb, Floral On Blue, 2 Circular Handles, 7 In. | 45.00 |
| Cloisonne, Vase, Hydrangea, Wild Flowers, & Insect, Imperial, 11 In.High | 185.00 |
| Cloisonne, Vase, Japanese Fish Scale, Storks, Pale Blue Ground, 3 3/4 In. | 175.00 |
| Cloisonne, Vase, Japanese Pigeon Blood, Birds In Bamboo Tree, 15 In.High | 225.00 |
| Cloisonne, Vase, Japanese, Red Enamel Over Bird & Bamboo Motif, 7 1/2 In. | 125.00 |
| Cloisonne, Vase, Lotus, Dahlias, Plum Blossoms, & Chrysanthemums, 6 1/2 In. | 110.00 |
| Cloisonne, Vase, Multicolor Floral In Lavender Panels On Blue, 8 1/2 In. | 125.00 |
| Cloisonne, Vase, Pear Shape, Floral Spray On White, 5 In. | 35.00 |
| Cloisonne, Vase, Pigeon Blood On Silver, 7 1/2 In. | 40.00 |
| Cloisonne, Vase, Pink & White Hydrangeas On Black, 12 1/2 In. | 195.00 |
| Cloisonne, Vase, Prunus Branches, Flowers, Birds, Green, Brass Top, 8 In.High | 155.00 |
| Cloisonne, Vase, Red, Roses & Foliage, 7 In., Pair | 70.00 |
| Cloisonne, Vase, Roses On Red, 7 1/2 In.High, Pair | 75.00 |
| Cloisonne, Vase, Wood Pigeons & Floral On Royal Blue, C.1850, 54 1/4 In. | 900.00 |

*Cluthra glass is a two-layered glass with small air pockets that form white spots. The Steuben Glass Works of Corning, New York, made it after 1903. Kimball Glass Company of Vineland, New Jersey, made Cluthra from about 1925.*

**Cluthra, see also Steuben**

| | |
|---|---:|
| Cluthra, Bowl, Apricot Color, Spider Web Effect, Flared Sides, 14 1/2 In. | 190.00 |

| | |
|---|---|
| Cluthra, Chandelier, Noveroy, Iron Mounts, Yellow To Blue Green, 14 In. | 190.00 |
| Cluthra, Lamp, Table, Noveroy, Bronzed Metal Base, Mottled Gray, 12 1/4 In. | 70.00 |
| Cluthra, Vase, Blue & White Shaded, Signed, 8 1/2 In.High | 310.00 |
| Cluthra, Vase, Bulbous, Ruby, Bubbles, Blue At Top, C.1888, 10 1/4 In. High | 150.00 |
| Cluthra, Vase, Clear Sides, Burst Bubbles, C.1930, Daum Nancy, 4 3/8 In. | 75.00 |
| Cluthra, Vase, Emerald Green, Bubbles, Flared Top, Applied Floral, 7 3/4 In. | 90.00 |
| Cluthra, Vase, Flared Top, Bulbous, Applied Green Florals & Bow, C.1888 | 89.50 |
| Cluthra, Vase, Green Jade, Flared, 6 In.High | 50.00 |
| Cluthra, Vase, Kimball, Blue 6 1/2 In.High | 200.00 |
| Cluthra, Vase, Kimball, Ovoid, White, Flared Top, Signed, 6 1/2 In. | 115.00 |
| Cluthra, Vase, Kimball, Oyster White, 6 In.High | 175.00 |
| Cluthra, Vase, Kimball, Pearl Opalescent, Trapped Air Bubbles, 4 In. | 95.00 |
| Cluthra, Vase, Kimball, Yellow & White, Signed & Dated, 9 In.High | 235.00 |

*Coalbrookdale was made by the Coalport porcelain factory of England during the Victorian period. The pieces are heavily decorated with floral encrustations.*

| | |
|---|---|
| Coalbrookdale, Basket, Flower Encrusted, Apple Green, C.1820, 12 In.Long | 200.00 |
| Coalbrookdale, Basket, Flower Filled, Oval, Green, Scroll Handles, C.1820 | 300.00 |
| Coalbrookdale, Ewer, Flower Encrusted, Apple Green, C.1820, 6 In.High | 100.00 |
| Coalbrookdale, Inkstand, Flower Encrusted, Diamond Shape, 2 Pots, C.1830 | 700.00 |
| Coalbrookdale, Jar, Insects On Cover, Flower Encrusted, Twig Handle, C.1820 | 150.00 |
| Coalbrookdale, Pot, Bough, D Shape, Leaf Handles, Pierced Lid, C.1851, Pair | 625.00 |
| Coalbrookdale, Pot, Cover & Stand, Floral Bouquets, C.1820, 5 1/2 In.High | 200.00 |
| Coalbrookdale, Vase, Pear Shape, Flower Encrusted, Handled, C.1830, Pair | 100.00 |

*Coalport ware has been made by the Coalport Porcelain Works of England from 1795 to the present time.*

| | |
|---|---|
| Coalport, Bowl, Rectangular, Farm & 2 Travellers, Scrolls, C.1820, 10 3/4 In. | 40.00 |
| Coalport, Box & Stand, Cabbage, Overlapping Leaves Form Stand, C.1830 | 80.00 |
| Coalport, Cup & Saucer, Bouillon, Double Handled, Cobalt, Gold, Roses | 11.75 |
| Coalport, Cup & Saucer, Demitasse, Wine Color, Gold, Jewels, Gold Lined | 42.00 |
| Coalport, Cup & Saucer, Multicolor Floral On White, C.1881, Large Size | 28.00 |
| Coalport, Cup, Loving, Gold Handles & Lining, Encrusted Gold On Cobalt | 375.00 |
| Coalport, Dish, Sunflower Growing From Green Stalk, C.1825, Pair | 125.00 |
| Coalport, Inkwell, Shell Shape, Tulips & Roses, C.1835, 7 1/2 In.Long | 90.00 |
| Coalport, Jug, Baluster, White Leaf Spout, Floral On Gros Bleu, C.1830 | 80.00 |
| Coalport, Jug, Roses & Bouquets, Baluster Shape, C.1825, 6 1/4 In. | 40.00 |
| Coalport, Perfume, Floral Stopper, Flower Encrusted, Gilt, C.1815, Pair | 110.00 |
| Coalport, Perfume, Jeweled, 3 1/4 In.High | 175.00 |
| Coalport, Plate, Castle Center, Apple Green & Gold Border, C.1825 | 25.00 |
| Coalport, Plate, Dinner, Astor, Blue & White | 12.00 |
| Coalport, Plate, Gold Border, Made For Tiffany & Co., 5 1/2 In | 6.65 |
| Coalport, Plate, Orange & Gold Floral On White, Gold Trim, C.1820, 9 In. | 15.00 |
| Coalport, Plate, Tree Of Life, 7 In. | 7.50 |
| Coalport, Sugar & Creamer, Flowers & Pagodas, Silver Plate Holder, 1790 | 45.00 |
| Coalport, Tea Set, Flower Groups & Gold On White, Green Crown Mark, 3 Piece | 95.00 |
| Coalport, Vase, Flask Shaped, Yellow With Gold Neck Band, 5 1/4 In.High | 45.00 |
| Coalport, Vase, Jeweled, Gold Beading On Aqua, Signed, 3 1/2 In.High | 85.00 |

*Cobalt blue glass was made using oxide of cobalt. The characteristic bright dark blue identifies it for the collector. Most cobalt glass found today was made after the Civil War.*

**Cobalt Blue, see also Shirley Temple**

| | |
|---|---|
| Cobalt Blue, Bobeche, Ruffled, Gold Edge, 3 In., Pair | 7.00 |
| Cobalt Blue, Bottle, Dutch, 9 In.High | 3.00 |
| Cobalt Blue, Bottle, Oil, Clock | 1.50 |
| Cobalt Blue, Bowl & Underplate, Finger, Blown | 18.50 To 35.00 |
| Cobalt Blue, Box, Enamel Geometric Floral On Hinged Lid, 2 In. Diameter | 45.00 |
| Cobalt Blue, Box, Hinged Cover, 3 X 3 1/2 In. | 21.00 |
| Cobalt Blue, Box, Patch, Hinged Brass Snap Cover, Yellow Enamel Stars, Round | 22.00 |
| Cobalt Blue, Box, Trinket, Enamel Decoration, 1 In.High | 25.00 |
| Cobalt Blue, Candleholder, 5 In.Base, 9 1/2 In.High, Pair | 42.50 |
| Cobalt Blue, Candlestick, Hexagonal Base & Top | 42.00 |
| Cobalt Blue, Christmas Light, Diamond-Quilted | 10.00 |
| Cobalt Blue, Christmas Light, Pressed Glass, Allover Diamond Pattern | 12.00 |
| Cobalt Blue, Compote, Applied Opaque Rim, Round Foot, 4 1/2 In.High | 70.00 |
| Cobalt Blue, Cruet, Swirled Rib, Clear Stopper & Handle | 28.00 |

*Ticonderoga* and the Colchester Reef Lighthouse, Shelburne, Vermont.

Horseshow barn made from nine old barns.

Bandbox with paddle-wheel-steamboat designed paper, 1835.

Bandbox with log cabin and hard cider commemorating the presidential campaign of William Henry Harrison, c. 1840.

Bandbox with paper decorated with "Peep at the Moon," 18 by 14 inches, c. 1840.

Man's hatbox shaped like a high hat, 12 by 15 inches, third quarter 19th century.

Hatbox room, Shelburne Museum.

Doll's tea set marked "Made in Japan," 20th century.

Toy mechanical velocipede with doll rider, patent No. 103957, 1870.

Crewelwork embroidery, English, 28½ by 23 inches.

Quilt with "boxes" pattern, New England, 19th century.

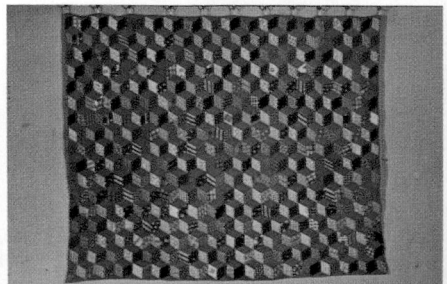

Jack plane, with curved cutting edge on blade. Marked Earson Wright, 13½ inches long.

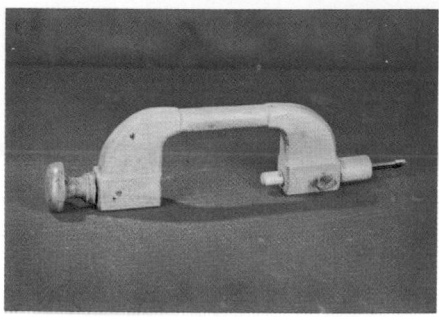

Carpenter's brace made by Richard Smith, c. 1800.

Frame saw with a wide serrated steel blade, made by Richard Smith.

Wooden butter worker, 19th century.

An apple parer made of iron and wood, mid-19th century.

Scandinavian mangle board of painted wood, 22¼ inches long.

Hooked rug depicting Christmas, 37 by 42 inches.

Mid-19th-century quilt, 88 by 85 inches. The 1876 Centennial center was added later.

Geometrical rug with shell motifs, canvas backing, 31 by 41 inches.

Cravena type yarn was used to make this spaniel dog rug, 46 by 31 inches.

Two double-woven Jacquard coverlets of the second quarter of the 19th century.

Floral rug with burlap backing and twill linen crash lining, 61 by 34½ inches.

Drop leaf, painted table made in Connecticut c. 1810–1820. Height 28¼ inches.

Hutch chair-table, 23½ inches high, originally painted black, late 18th century.

Twentieth-century toys made from tin and celluoid.

Painted chest of drawers probably made in Connecticut, c. 1680–1710. Highchair, 18th century.

American oak and pine four-drawer chest from Dedham, Massachusetts, c. 1690, 34½ inches high.

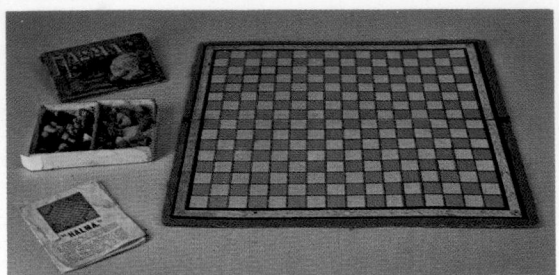

"Halma," a game published by E. I. Horsman, New York, 1885.

Folk art figure of the Goddess of Liberty made from copper and brass pipe tube, 41 inches high, 19th century.

Toy fire patrol wagon made of iron.

Quaker lady doll, glass eyes, wooden body, cotton arms and legs, 8½ inches high.

China-headed doll with a horsehair-filled cloth body and kid arms, 22½ inches high.

Caleche, c. 1890, used in a parade to honor Admiral Dewey.

Swan and mate decoys made in Maryland, 1814.

Doll and fan from the 19th century.

Dollhouse vignette of the 19th century.

Dollhouse kitchen, English Gothic period.

Locomotive weather vane made from zinc, brass, and iron, c. 1840, 34 inches long.

Piebald horse weather vane of cast iron with a tin tail, mid-19th century.

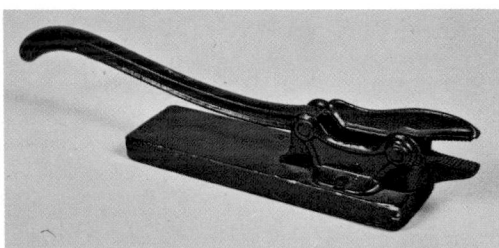

Cork press made of iron with a wooden base, patented May 17, 1850, R. Frisbie, Middletown, Connecticut.

Rooster weather vane of wood covered with gold leaf c. 1820.

Five wooden butter prints, 19th century.

| | |
|---|---:|
| Cobalt Blue, Cruet, Vinegar, Gold Design | 10.00 |
| Cobalt Blue, Dresser Set, Gold Trim, 7 Piece | 65.00 |
| Cobalt Blue, Eyecup, John Bull, Dated 1917, Stemmed | 12.00 |
| Cobalt Blue, Eyecup, Optrix, Made In Argentine | 16.00 |
| Cobalt Blue, Eyecup, Wyeth, Pedestal | 7.00 |
| Cobalt Blue, Hat, High, Ring Bottom, Ribbon Neck Brim, 2 1/4 X 2 1/4 In. | 15.00 |
| Cobalt Blue, Jar, Pickle Castor, Yellow Floral Enamel, 4 5/8 In.High | 45.00 |
| Cobalt Blue, Jug, Water, 7 In.High | 12.00 |
| Cobalt Blue, Mayonnaise, Attached Liner, Lid And Spoon | 7.00 |
| Cobalt Blue, Mug, Applied Handle, 4 In. | 10.00 |
| Cobalt Blue, Pitcher, Squat, Applied Handle, Blown, 3 In.High | 200.00 |
| Cobalt Blue, Pitcher, Water, Clear Applied Reeded Handle, 9 In.High | 45.00 |
| Cobalt Blue, Punch Set, Miniature, Nursery Tales, 5 Piece | 175.00 |
| Cobalt Blue, Rolling Pin, C.1850 | 26.00 |
| Cobalt Blue, Salt, Silver Holder | 15.00 |
| Cobalt Blue, Salt, Swan, 5 In. | 8.00 |
| Cobalt Blue, Salt, Swirl, Free-Blown, Flower Form, Rough Pontil | 3.35 |
| Cobalt Blue, Shot Glass, Design On Top & Bottom, Pontil Marked, 2 1/2 In. | 35.00 |
| Cobalt Blue, Spooner | 5.95 |
| Cobalt Blue, Sugar & Creamer, Rectangular | 5.00 |
| Cobalt Blue, Swan, Free Blown, Square Pressed Base, Midwestern, Pair | 200.00 |
| Cobalt Blue, Swan, L.E.Smith Glass Co., 8 In. Long | 37.50 |
| Cobalt Blue, Toothpick, Boot Shape | 4.50 |
| Cobalt Blue, Toothpick, Top Hat | 6.00 |
| Cobalt Blue, Tumbler, Honeycomb Base, 4 Ozs. | 6.00 |
| Cobalt Blue, Tumbler, Honeycomb Base, 8 Ozs. | 8.00 |
| Cobalt Blue, Vase, Bud, Tapered, 3 Footed Silver Base, Benedict, 1894-1909 | 37.00 |
| Cobalt Blue, Vase, Bulbous Body, Scalloped Top, Melon Ribbed, 7 In.High | 7.50 |
| Cobalt Blue, Vase, Cut To Clear, Thumbprint & Panel, 12 In.High | 125.00 |
| Cobalt Blue, Vase, Gleaners, Gold Decoration, Marked Germany, 9 In.High | 48.00 |
| Cobalt Blue, Vase, Hyacinth, Free-Blown, Footed, Folded Lip, 3 3/4 In.High | 70.00 |
| Cobalt Blue, Vase, Silver Overlay, Swans, 4 1/2 In.High | 5.00 |
| Cobalt Blue, Vase, 2 Clear Reeded Handles, 9 1/2 In.High | 37.50 |
| Cobalt Blue, Wine Set, Gold Trim, 7 Piece | 35.00 |
| Cobalt Blue, Wine, Clear Knob Stem & Base, 4 3/4 In. | 9.00 |
| Cobalt Blue, Witch's Ball, 1800, 6 In.Diameter | 42.50 |

*Coca-Cola advertising items have become a special field for collectors.*

| | |
|---|---:|
| Coca-Cola, Knife, Dated 1933 | 4.95 |
| Coca-Cola, Ad, 1906, Adds A Refreshing Relish To Every Form Of Exercise | 10.00 |
| Coca-Cola, Ad, 1919, After The Walk Your First & Best Thought Is Coca-Cola | 10.00 |
| Coca-Cola, Bag, Overnight | 12.50 |
| Coca-Cola, Booklet, 1923, Facts | 7.00 |
| Coca-Cola, Bottle Opener, "Drink Coca-Cola, " Cast Iron | 1.00 |
| Coca-Cola, Bottle Opener, Embossed | 2.50 |
| Coca-Cola, Bottle Opener, Iron, Stationary, The Starr X | 6.00 |
| Coca-Cola, Bottle Opener, Solid Metal Handle, "Coca-Cola, 5 Cents" | 3.00 |
| Coca-Cola, Bottle Opener, Wall, Metal, "Drink Coca-Cola" | 1.00 |
| Coca-Cola, Bottle, King Size, White Script, Mexico, 20 In.High | 20.00 |
| Coca-Cola, Bottle, Plastic, 24 In., Red Plastic Case, 1 5/8 In. | 5.00 |
| Coca-Cola, Bottle, Script, Straight Sided, Green | 2.95 |
| Coca-Cola, Bottle, Soda Water, Square | 2.00 |
| Coca-Cola, Bottle, Straight Sided, Aqua | 7.50 |
| Coca-Cola, Bottle, To Promote King Size Coke In Mexico, 20 In.High | 20.00 |
| Coca-Cola, Bus, Metal | 5.00 |
| Coca-Cola, Calendar, 1951 | 8.00 |
| Coca-Cola, Cards, Playing, "It's The Real Thing" | 4.00 |
| Coca-Cola, Carrier, 6 Bottle, Wooden | 20.00 |
| Coca-Cola, Case, Shipping, Wooden, 48 Bottle | 95.00 |
| Coca-Cola, Clock, Tin | 17.50 |
| Coca-Cola, Doorstop, Bottle Shape | 25.00 |
| Coca-Cola, Hangar, Airplane, 1943, 20 World War II Cardboard Planes | 105.00 |
| Coca-Cola, Holder, Grocery Cart | 5.00 |
| Coca-Cola, Ice Pick | 4.00 |
| Coca-Cola, Kerchief, Couple Dancing, Couple Drinking Coke, 29 X 33 In. | 15.00 |
| Coca-Cola, Knife, Dated 1933 | 3.95 |
| Coca-Cola, Knife, Pocket, Gold Coke Glass, Nail File & Money Clip | 18.00 |

| | |
|---|---:|
| Coca-Cola, Knife, Pocket, Zippo, Gold Coke Bottle, 2 Blades | 18.00 |
| Coca-Cola, Knife, Single Blade, Brass Liner, Pearl, Spring Action | 2.00 |
| Coca-Cola, Letter Opener, Solid Metal Handle, "Coca-Cola, 5 Cents" | 2.50 |
| Coca-Cola, Lighter, Cigarette, Bottle Shape, 2 1/2 In. | 2.50 |
| Coca-Cola, Mirror, Pocket, 1909, Girl, 2 X 3 In. | 99.00 |
| Coca-Cola, Notebook, 1920s, Leather, Picture Of Home Office, Atlanta | 3.00 |
| Coca-Cola, Notebook, 1930, Lined Paper, Girl Drinking Coke, 8 X 10 In. | 14.00 |
| Coca-Cola, Opener, Bottle, 1920s, "Drink Coca-Cola" | 3.50 |
| Coca-Cola, Pen, Ball-Point, Drink Coca-Cola, Red, White, & Blue | 1.00 |
| Coca-Cola, Pen, Ball-Point, Red & White, Telephone Dialer On End | 2.00 |
| Coca-Cola, Pen, Ink, Wooden, Drink Coca-Cola In Script, 1930s | 1.50 |
| Coca-Cola, Pencil, Mechanical, 1938, "Drink Coca-Cola" | 12.50 |
| Coca-Cola, Poster, 1911, 9 X 13 In. | 18.95 |
| Coca-Cola, Pump Top | 20.00 |
| Coca-Cola, Radio, Bottle Shape, Red Bakelite, 24 In.High | 150.00 |
| Coca-Cola, Razor, Straight, Trans Pan, 1915 | 30.00 |
| Coca-Cola, Ruler, Wooden, 12 In. | 3.50 |
| Coca-Cola, Sign, Restaurant, 1950s, Space For Menus, 20 X 28 In. | 15.00 |
| Coca-Cola, Sign, Thermometer, Hanging | 15.00 |
| Coca-Cola, Sign, 1943, World War II A36 Attack Bomber, Cardboard | 13.50 |
| Coca-Cola, Sign, 1943, World War II Corvair F4U Fighter, Cardboard | 13.50 |
| Coca-Cola, Sign, 1943, World War II Curtis Helldiver, Cardboard | 13.50 |
| Coca-Cola, Sign, 1943, World War II P38 Pursuit, Cardboard | 13.50 |
| Coca-Cola, Sign, 1943, World War II P39 Pursuit, Cardboard | 13.50 |
| Coca-Cola, Sign, 1943, World War II Wildcat F4f Fighter, Cardboard | 13.50 |
| Coca-Cola, Sign, 1943, YR4 Helicopter, Cardboard | 13.50 |
| Coca-Cola, Sign, 1947, Tin, 40 In.Long | 3.95 |
| Coca-Cola, Sign, 1954, Fall & Winter Seasonal Scenes, 19 1/2 X 28 In. | 25.00 |
| Coca-Cola, Spoon, Mixing, Fountain, Bottle Opener Handle, 8 In.Long | 16.00 |
| Coca-Cola, Thermometer, Bottle Shape, Tin, 1923 | 19.00 |
| Coca-Cola, Token & Chain, 50th Anniversary, Brass Bottle | 4.00 |
| Coca-Cola, Tray, Change, Mexican Street Scene Of 1860s, Tin | 1.00 |
| Coca-Cola, Tray, Change, 1904, World's Fair | 55.00 |
| Coca-Cola, Tray, Change, 1909, Girl, Oval | 90.00 |
| Coca-Cola, Tray, Change, 1912, World's Fair | 65.00 |
| Coca-Cola, Tray, Change, 1914, Betty | 50.00 |
| Coca-Cola, Tray, Change, 1917, World's Fair | 55.00 |
| Coca-Cola, Tray, Coke Bottle, Tin, 13 In.Diameter | 2.00 |
| Coca-Cola, Tray, Girl With Coke In Hand | 17.50 |
| Coca-Cola, Tray, Girl With Menu | 8.00 |
| Coca-Cola, Tray, Hand Pouring Bottle | 8.00 |
| Coca-Cola, Tray, Pushcart Design | 5.00 |
| Coca-Cola, Tray, 1909, Hamilton King Girl's Picture, 10 3/4 X 14 3/4 In. | 150.00 |
| Coca-Cola, Tray, 1914, Betty, Oval | 110.00 To 125.00 |
| Coca-Cola, Tray, 1917, Elaine | 49.00 To 55.00 |
| Coca-Cola, Tray, 1920, Garden Girl, Oval | 85.00 |
| Coca-Cola, Tray, 1921, Summer Girl | 98.00 |
| Coca-Cola, Tray, 1923, Flapper Girl | 25.00 To 50.00 |
| Coca-Cola, Tray, 1925, Girl At Party· | 38.00 To 42.00 |
| Coca-Cola, Tray, 1927, Curb Service | 39.00 |
| Coca-Cola, Tray, 1927, Fountain Clerk | 38.00 |
| Coca-Cola, Tray, 1929, Girl In Swimsuit Holding Glass | 42.50 |
| Coca-Cola, Tray, 1930, Bathing Beauty | 32.50 |
| Coca-Cola, Tray, 1931, Farm Boy With Dog | 47.50 |
| Coca-Cola, Tray, 1932, Girl In Swimsuit Holding Bottle | 25.00 |
| Coca-Cola, Tray, 1933, Francis Dee | 45.00 |
| Coca-Cola, Tray, 1934, Johnny Weissmuller | 145.00 |
| Coca-Cola, Tray, 1935, Madge Evans | 22.50 To 45.00 |
| Coca-Cola, Tray, 1936, Hostess | 10.00 To 25.00 |
| Coca-Cola, Tray, 1937, Girl In Bathing Suit | 38.00 |
| Coca-Cola, Tray, 1938, Girl In Yellow Hat & Dress | 20.00 |
| Coca-Cola, Tray, 1939, Bathing Beauty | 20.00 To 24.00 |
| Coca-Cola, Tray, 1940, Sailor Girl | 20.00 |
| Coca-Cola, Tray, 1941, Girl Ice Skater | 23.00 |
| Coca-Cola, Tray, 1942, Two Girls At Car | 23.00 |
| Coca-Cola, Tray, 1943, Girl With Wind In Her Hair | 13.00 |

Coca-Cola, Tray, 1950, Girl With Menu ................................................................................ 16.00
Coca-Cola, Tray, 1959, Pansies & Lady's Hand ................................................................ 4.25
Coca-Cola, Truck, Matchbox, C.1962 ................................................................................ 10.00
Coca-Cola, Tumbler, Embossed Base, 6 In. ...................................................................... 2.50
Coca-Cola, Wallet, Advertising, Leather ............................................................................ 6.00

*Coffee grinders, home size, were first made about 1894. They lost favor by*
*the 1930s.*

Coffee Grinder, American Duplex, 21 X 29 In., Weighs 70 Lbs. ...................................... 260.00
Coffee Grinder, Arcade, Cast Iron, Wall Type, Glass Jar Top ........................................ 28.00
Coffee Grinder, Cast Iron, 1 Wheel, Drawer, 9 In.High .................................................. 35.00
Coffee Grinder, Coles Mfg.Co., Phila., Red Paint, 9 1/2 In.Wheels ............................ 100.00
Coffee Grinder, Coles, Philadelphia, Cast Iron, Drawer, Crank, Red Paint ................ 85.00
Coffee Grinder, Crown, Landers, Frary, & Clark, Iron, Clamp On Table, Painted ........ 30.00
Coffee Grinder, Dovetailed, Brass Top ............................................................................ 24.50
Coffee Grinder, Enterprise Mfg.Co., Penna., Pat.July 12, Cast Iron, Wooden ............ 140.00
Coffee Grinder, Enterprise, Clamp On Table Model, Stenciled ...................................... 20.00
Coffee Grinder, Enterprise, Double Wheels, Stenciling, Flowers .................................. 215.00
Coffee Grinder, Enterprise, Tin Coffee Catcher, 22 In. .................................................. 120.00
Coffee Grinder, Fluted Tin, Wooden Top & Bottom, Porcelain Liner, Civil War ............ 30.00
Coffee Grinder, German, Wooden, Drawer ...................................................................... 12.00
Coffee Grinder, Iron, 15 1/2 In Wheel .............................................................................. 14.50
Coffee Grinder, J.M.F., Cast Iron, Painted Wooden Drawer, 1 Wheel .......................... 66.00
Coffee Grinder, Porcelain, Glass Container, Hand-Painted, 'Kafee' .............................. 45.00
Coffee Grinder, R.Z., Wall Type, Cast Iron, Square White Glass Top .......................... 32.00
Coffee Grinder, Tin, Cast Iron Top Handle, Raised Concentrics, C.1850 ...................... 22.00
Coffee Grinder, Universal, Tin, Black, Copyright 1905 .................................................. 20.00
Coffee Grinder, Wall Type, Ceramic ................................................................................ 20.00
Coffee Grinder, Wall, Arcade, Glass Top ........................................................................ 22.00
Coffee Grinder, Wooden, Dovetailed, Brass Top & Drawer ............................................ 38.00
Coffee Grinder, Wooden, 6 X 5 In. .................................................................................. 34.00
Coffee Mill, Wall, Porcelain .............................................................................................. 16.00

*Christmas plates were made by several firms. The most famous were made by*
*the Bing & Grondahl Factory of Denmark, after 1895, and the Royal*
*Copenhagen Factory, after 1908. Each of these plates has a blue-and-white*
*glaze with a scene in the center, the date, and the word Jule.*

Collector, Bell, Berta Hummel, Christmas, 1973, Nativity .............................................. 15.00
Collector, Bell, Noritake, Christmas, 1972 ...................................................................... 12.50
Collector, Candleholder, Frankoma, 1971, Oral Roberts ................................................ 3.00
Collector, Cup, Noritake, Father's Day, 1972, 1st Issue ................................................ 15.00
Collector, Egg, Noritake, Easter, 1971, 1st Issue .......................................................... 47.00
Collector, Egg, Noritake, Easter, 1972 ............................................................................ 18.00
Collector, Egg, Noritake, Easter, 1973 ............................................................................ 15.00
Collector, Mug, Hans Christian Andersen, Christmas, 1969 .......................................... 8.50
Collector, Mug, Hans Christian Andersen, Christmas, 1970 .......................................... 8.00
Collector, Mug, Hummel, Child's Day, 1973 .................................................................... 9.50
Collector, Mug, Wedgwood, Christmas, 1972 .................................................................. 20.00
Collector, Plate, Bareuther, Christmas, 1967 .................................................................. 55.00
Collector, Plate, Bareuther, Christmas, 1968 .................................................................. 20.00
Collector, Plate, Bareuther, Christmas, 1969 .................................................................. 7.00
Collector, Plate, Bareuther, Christmas, 1970 .................................................................. 10.00
Collector, Plate, Bareuther, Father's Day, 1969 ............................................................ 28.00
Collector, Plate, Bareuther, Father's Day, 1970 ............................................................ 7.00
Collector, Plate, Bareuther, Mother's Day, 1969 ............................................................ 28.00
Collector, Plate, Bareuther, Mother's Day, 1970 ............................................................ 7.00
Collector, Plate, Belleek, Christmas, 1971 ...................................................................... 35.00
Collector, Plate, Belleek, Christmas, 1972 ...................................................................... 32.00
Collector, Plate, Berlin, Mother's Day, 1971 .................................................. 12.50 To 20.00
Collector, Plate, Berlin, Mother's Day, 1972 .................................................................. 16.00
Collector, Plate, Berlin, Mother's Day, 1973 .................................................................. 20.00
Collector, Plate, Berta Hummel, Mother's Day, 1973 .................................................... 12.50
Collector, Plate, Bing & Grondahl, Christmas, 1895 ............................ 2000.00 To 2800.00
Collector, Plate, Bing & Grondahl, Christmas, 1896 .............................. 975.00 To 1300.00
Collector, Plate, Bing & Grondahl, Christmas, 1897 ................................ 625.00 To 780.00
Collector, Plate, Bing & Grondahl, Christmas, 1898 ................................ 350.00 To 480.00
Collector, Plate, Bing & Grondahl, Christmas, 1899 ................................ 600.00 To 795.00
Collector, Plate, Bing & Grondahl, Christmas, 1900 ................................ 400.00 To 600.00

Collector, Plate, Bing & Grondahl, Christmas, 1901 .................................................. 218.00 To 250.00
Collector, Plate, Bing & Grondahl, Christmas, 1902 .................................................. 135.00 To 165.00
Collector, Plate, Bing & Grondahl, Christmas, 1903 .................................................. 125.00 To 160.00
Collector, Plate, Bing & Grondahl, Christmas, 1904 .................................................. 70.00 To 90.00
Collector, Plate, Bing & Grondahl, Christmas, 1905 .................................................. 50.00 To 90.00
Collector, Plate, Bing & Grondahl, Christmas, 1906 .................................................. 51.00 To 65.00
Collector, Plate, Bing & Grondahl, Christmas, 1907 .................................................. 80.00 To 100.00
Collector, Plate, Bing & Grondahl, Christmas, 1908 .................................................. 39.00 To 57.50
Collector, Plate, Bing & Grondahl, Christmas, 1909 .................................................. 52.00 To 75.00
Collector, Plate, Bing & Grondahl, Christmas, 1910 .................................................. 48.00 To 65.00
Collector, Plate, Bing & Grondahl, Christmas, 1911 .................................................. 48.00 To 60.00
Collector, Plate, Bing & Grondahl, Christmas, 1912 .................................................. 48.00 To 65.00
Collector, Plate, Bing & Grondahl, Christmas, 1913 .................................................. 48.00 To 65.00
Collector, Plate, Bing & Grondahl, Christmas, 1914 .................................................. 37.00 To 52.50
Collector, Plate, Bing & Grondahl, Christmas, 1915 .................................................. 66.00 To 90.00
Collector, Plate, Bing & Grondahl, Christmas, 1916 .................................................. 39.00 To 60.00
Collector, Plate, Bing & Grondahl, Christmas, 1917 .................................................. 39.00 To 60.00
Collector, Plate, Bing & Grondahl, Christmas, 1918 .................................................. 39.00 To 55.00
Collector, Plate, Bing & Grondahl, Christmas, 1919 .................................................. 39.00 To 65.00
Collector, Plate, Bing & Grondahl, Christmas, 1920 .................................................. 36.00 To 52.00
Collector, Plate, Bing & Grondahl, Christmas, 1921 .................................................. 36.00 To 52.00
Collector, Plate, Bing & Grondahl, Christmas, 1922 .................................................. 35.00 To 50.00
Collector, Plate, Bing & Grondahl, Christmas, 1923 .................................................. 36.00 To 50.00
Collector, Plate, Bing & Grondahl, Christmas, 1924 .................................................. 36.00 To 52.00
Collector, Plate, Bing & Grondahl, Christmas, 1925 .................................................. 36.00 To 52.00
Collector, Plate, Bing & Grondahl, Christmas, 1926 .................................................. 36.00 To 52.00
Collector, Plate, Bing & Grondahl, Christmas, 1927 .................................................. 44.00 To 65.00
Collector, Plate, Bing & Grondahl, Christmas, 1928 .................................................. 36.00 To 52.00
Collector, Plate, Bing & Grondahl, Christmas, 1929 .................................................. 44.00 To 60.00
Collector, Plate, Bing & Grondahl, Christmas, 1930 .................................................. 51.00 To 70.00
Collector, Plate, Bing & Grondahl, Christmas, 1931 .................................................. 41.00 To 60.00
Collector, Plate, Bing & Grondahl, Christmas, 1932 .................................................. 40.00 To 65.00
Collector, Plate, Bing & Grondahl, Christmas, 1933 .................................................. 36.00 To 52.00
Collector, Plate, Bing & Grondahl, Christmas, 1934 .................................................. 36.00 To 52.00
Collector, Plate, Bing & Grondahl, Christmas, 1935 .................................................. 36.00 To 52.00
Collector, Plate, Bing & Grondahl, Christmas, 1936 .................................................. 43.00 To 52.00
Collector, Plate, Bing & Grondahl, Christmas, 1937 .................................................. 44.00 To 68.00
Collector, Plate, Bing & Grondahl, Christmas, 1938 .................................................. 65.00 To 90.00
Collector, Plate, Bing & Grondahl, Christmas, 1939 .................................................. 85.00 To 125.00
Collector, Plate, Bing & Grondahl, Christmas, 1940 .................................................. 95.00 To 125.00
Collector, Plate, Bing & Grondahl, Christmas, 1941 .................................................. 175.00 To 240.00
Collector, Plate, Bing & Grondahl, Christmas, 1942 .................................................. 95.00 To 135.00
Collector, Plate, Bing & Grondahl, Christmas, 1943 .................................................. 77.50 To 135.00
Collector, Plate, Bing & Grondahl, Christmas, 1944 .................................................. 65.00 To 120.00
Collector, Plate, Bing & Grondahl, Christmas, 1945 .................................................. 65.00 To 120.00
Collector, Plate, Bing & Grondahl, Christmas, 1946 .................................................. 38.00 To 53.00
Collector, Plate, Bing & Grondahl, Christmas, 1947 .................................................. 47.00 To 80.00
Collector, Plate, Bing & Grondahl, Christmas, 1948 .................................................. 36.50 To 62.00
Collector, Plate, Bing & Grondahl, Christmas, 1949 .................................................. 36.00 To 52.00
Collector, Plate, Bing & Grondahl, Christmas, 1950 .................................................. 49.00 To 68.00
Collector, Plate, Bing & Grondahl, Christmas, 1951 .................................................. 39.00 To 55.00
Collector, Plate, Bing & Grondahl, Christmas, 1952 .................................................. 39.00 To 55.00
Collector, Plate, Bing & Grondahl, Christmas, 1953 .................................................. 36.00 To 60.00
Collector, Plate, Bing & Grondahl, Christmas, 1954 .................................................. 57.00 To 60.00
Collector, Plate, Bing & Grondahl, Christmas, 1955 .................................................. 48.00 To 65.00
Collector, Plate, Bing & Grondahl, Christmas, 1956 .................................................. 65.00 To 115.00
Collector, Plate, Bing & Grondahl, Christmas, 1957 .................................................. 65.00 To 115.00
Collector, Plate, Bing & Grondahl, Christmas, 1958 .................................................. 58.00 To 83.00
Collector, Plate, Bing & Grondahl, Christmas, 1959 .................................................. 85.00 To 110.00
Collector, Plate, Bing & Grondahl, Christmas, 1960 .................................................. 80.00 To 125.00
Collector, Plate, Bing & Grondahl, Christmas, 1961 .................................................. 60.00 To 85.00
Collector, Plate, Bing & Grondahl, Christmas, 1962 .................................................. 32.50 To 45.00
Collector, Plate, Bing & Grondahl, Christmas, 1963 .................................................. 66.00 To 95.00
Collector, Plate, Bing & Grondahl, Christmas, 1964 .................................................. 25.00 To 40.00
Collector, Plate, Bing & Grondahl, Christmas, 1965 .................................................. 25.00 To 40.00
Collector, Plate, Bing & Grondahl, Christmas, 1966 .................................................. 20.00 To 33.00

Collector, Plate, Bing & Grondahl, Christmas, 1967 .......................................................... 15.00 To 30.00
Collector, Plate, Bing & Grondahl, Christmas, 1968 .......................................................... 16.00 To 25.00
Collector, Plate, Bing & Grondahl, Christmas, 1969 .......................................................... 13.00 To 22.00
Collector, Plate, Bing & Grondahl, Christmas, 1970 ............................................................ 9.00 To 20.00
Collector, Plate, Bing & Grondahl, Christmas, 1971 ............................................................ 8.00 To 17.00
Collector, Plate, Bing & Grondahl, Christmas, 1972 ............................................................ 7.00 To 16.00
Collector, Plate, Bing & Grondahl, Christmas, 1973 .......................................................... 11.00 To 20.00
Collector, Plate, Bing & Grondahl, Easter, 1910 ................................................................................ 40.00
Collector, Plate, Bing & Grondahl, Easter, 1914 ................................................................................ 40.00
Collector, Plate, Bing & Grondahl, Easter, 1920 ................................................................................ 40.00
Collector, Plate, Bing & Grondahl, Easter, 1924 ................................................................................ 40.00
Collector, Plate, Bing & Grondahl, Easter, 1928 ................................................................................ 50.00
Collector, Plate, Bing & Grondahl, Easter, 1930 .............................................................................. 100.00
Collector, Plate, Bing & Grondahl, Easter, 1932 .............................................................................. 100.00
Collector, Plate, Bing & Grondahl, Easter, 1934 .............................................................................. 300.00
Collector, Plate, Bing & Grondahl, Easter, 1935 .............................................................................. 500.00
Collector, Plate, Bing & Grondahl, Jubilee, 1915 ............................................................................... 90.00
Collector, Plate, Bing & Grondahl, Jubilee, 1920 ............................................................................... 80.00
Collector, Plate, Bing & Grondahl, Jubilee, 1925 .............................................................................. 100.00
Collector, Plate, Bing & Grondahl, Jubilee, 1930 .............................................................................. 175.00
Collector, Plate, Bing & Grondahl, Jubilee, 1935 .............................................................................. 550.00
Collector, Plate, Bing & Grondahl, Jubilee, 1940 ............................................................................ 1100.00
Collector, Plate, Bing & Grondahl, Jubilee, 1945 .............................................................................. 250.00
Collector, Plate, Bing & Grondahl, Jubilee, 1950 .............................................................................. 140.00
Collector, Plate, Bing & Grondahl, Jubilee, 1955 .............................................................................. 130.00
Collector, Plate, Bing & Grondahl, Jubilee, 1960 .............................................................................. 100.00
Collector, Plate, Bing & Grondahl, Jubilee, 1965 .............................................................................. 100.00
Collector, Plate, Bing & Grondahl, Jubilee, 1970 ............................................................................... 25.00
Collector, Plate, Bing & Grondahl, Mother's Day, 1969 ................................................. 150.00 To 250.00
Collector, Plate, Bing & Grondahl, Mother's Day, 1970 ................................................... 12.50 To 30.00
Collector, Plate, Bing & Grondahl, Mother's Day, 1971 ..................................................... 5.00 To 12.00
Collector, Plate, Bing & Grondahl, Mother's Day, 1972 ..................................................... 7.50 To 13.00
Collector, Plate, Bing & Grondahl, Mother's Day, 1973 ..................................................... 7.50 To 13.00
Collector, Plate, Capo-Di-Monte, Christmas, 1972 ............................................................................ 75.00
Collector, Plate, Capo-Di-Monte, Mother's Day, 1973 ........................................................................ 55.00
Collector, Plate, Castleton, U.S.Air Force, 1972, Blue & White, 9 In. ............................................ 10.00
Collector, Plate, Castleton, U.S.Army, 1972, A Soldier's Soldier, Blue, White ........................... 10.00
Collector, Plate, Delft, Father's Day, 1970 ......................................................................................... 11.00
Collector, Plate, Delft, Mother's Day, 1970 ........................................................................................ 11.00
Collector, Plate, Dresden, Christmas, 1971, 1st Issue ...................................................................... 40.00
Collector, Plate, Dresden, Christmas, 1972 ........................................................................................ 15.00
Collector, Plate, Dresden, Christmas, 1973 ........................................................................................ 16.00
Collector, Plate, Dresden, Mother's Day, 1972, 1st Issue ................................................................ 20.00
Collector, Plate, Dresden, Mother's Day, 1973 .................................................................................. 16.00
Collector, Plate, Dresden, Mother's Day, 1974 .................................................................................. 20.00
Collector, Plate, Franklin Mint, Mother's Day, 1972 .................................................... 125.00 To 145.00
Collector, Plate, Frankoma, Christmas, 1967 ...................................................................................... 30.00
Collector, Plate, Frankoma, Easter, 1972 .............................................................................................. 5.00
Collector, Plate, Fuerstenberg, Christmas, 1971, 1st Issue .............................................................. 15.00
Collector, Plate, Fuerstenberg, Christmas, 1972 ................................................................................ 15.00
Collector, Plate, Fuerstenberg, Christmas, 1973 ................................................................................ 15.00
Collector, Plate, Fuerstenberg, Easter, 1971 ...................................................................................... 40.00
Collector, Plate, Fuerstenberg, Easter, 1972 ...................................................................................... 15.00
Collector, Plate, Fuerstenberg, Easter, 1973 ...................................................................................... 20.00
Collector, Plate, Fuerstenberg, Mother's Day, 1972 ......................................................................... 32.00
Collector, Plate, Fuerstenberg, Mother's Day, 1973 ......................................................................... 32.00
Collector, Plate, Fuerstenberg, Mother's Day, 1974 ......................................................................... 20.00
Collector, Plate, Galway, Christmas, 1972, Cut Glass ...................................................................... 50.00
Collector, Plate, Georg Jensen, Christmas, 1972, 1st Issue ............................................................ 15.00
Collector, Plate, Granget, Christmas, 1972 ......................................................................................... 85.00
Collector, Plate, Granget, Christmas, 1973 ......................................................................................... 75.00
Collector, Plate, Hans Christian Andersen, Christmas, 1969 ............................................................ 8.50
Collector, Plate, Hans Christian Andersen, Christmas, 1970 ............................................................ 8.00
Collector, Plate, Haviland Parlon, Christmas, 1972 .......................................................................... 50.00
Collector, Plate, Haviland, Christmas, 1970, 1st Issue ..................................................................... 90.00
Collector, Plate, Haviland, Christmas, 1972 ....................................................................................... 30.00

Collector, Plate, Haviland, Christmas, 1973 ............................................................. 28.50
Collector, Plate, Haviland, Mother's Day, 1973, 1st Issue ........................ 30.00
Collector, Plate, Haviland, Mother's Day, 1974 ...................................... 29.50
Collector, Plate, Hummel, Berta, Christmas, 1971 ................................ 22.00
Collector, Plate, Hummel, Berta, Christmas, 1972 ................................ 14.00
Collector, Plate, Hummel, Berta, Christmas, 1973 ................................ 14.00
Collector, Plate, Hummel, Goebel, Christmas, 1971 .............................. 125.00
Collector, Plate, Jean Paul Loup, Christmas, 1971 ................................ 350.00
Collector, Plate, Kaiser, Christmas, 1970 ............................................ 30.00
Collector, Plate, Kaiser, Christmas, 1971 ............................................ 16.00
Collector, Plate, Kaiser, Christmas, 1972 ............................................ 15.00
Collector, Plate, Kaiser, Christmas, 1973 ............................................ 18.00
Collector, Plate, Kaiser, Mother's Day, 1971 ...................................... 31.00
Collector, Plate, Kaiser, Mother's Day, 1972 ...................................... 31.00
Collector, Plate, Kaiser, Mother's Day, 1973 ...................................... 17.00
Collector, Plate, Kaiser, Mother's Day, 1974 ...................................... 20.00
Collector, Plate, Kate Greenaway, Mother's Day, 1971, Meakin .............. 24.95
Collector, Plate, Kate Greenaway, Mother's Day, 1972, Meakin .............. 19.95
Collector, Plate, Kate Greenaway, Mother's Day, 1973, Meakin .............. 16.95
Collector, Plate, Lenox, Boehm Bird, 1972, 3rd Issue .......................... 68.00
Collector, Plate, Lincoln Mint, Easter, 1972, Silver ............................ 150.00
Collector, Plate, Lladro, Mother's Day, 1971, 1st Issue ........................ 70.00
Collector, Plate, Lladro, Mother's Day, 1972 ...................................... 20.00
Collector, Plate, Moser, Christmas, 1970, 1st Issue ............................ 300.00
Collector, Plate, Moser, Christmas, 1971 ............................................ 75.00
Collector, Plate, Moser, Mother's Day, 1971, 1st Issue ........................ 200.00
Collector, Plate, Moser, Mother's Day, 1972 ...................................... 75.00
Collector, Plate, Porsgrund, Christmas, 1968, 1st Issue ...................... 75.00
Collector, Plate, Porsgrund, Christmas, 1969 .................................... 7.00
Collector, Plate, Porsgrund, Christmas, 1970 .................................... 7.00
Collector, Plate, Porsgrund, Christmas, 1971 .................................... 7.00
Collector, Plate, Porsgrund, Mother's Day, 1971 ................................ 5.00
Collector, Plate, Rorstrand, Christmas, 1970 .................................... 8.00
Collector, Plate, Rorstrand, Father's Day, 1971 ................................ 8.00
Collector, Plate, Rorstrand, Mother's Day, 1971 ................................ 8.00
Collector, Plate, Rorstrand, Mother's Day, 1972 ................................ 8.00
Collector, Plate, Royal Copenhagen, Christmas, 1908 ............. 850.00 To 1000.00
Collector, Plate, Royal Copenhagen, Christmas, 1909 ............... 65.00 To 100.00
Collector, Plate, Royal Copenhagen, Christmas, 1910 ............... 60.00 To 95.00
Collector, Plate, Royal Copenhagen, Christmas, 1911 ............... 65.00 To 110.00
Collector, Plate, Royal Copenhagen, Christmas, 1911, Small .............. 2000.00
Collector, Plate, Royal Copenhagen, Christmas, 1912 ............... 81.00 To 100.00
Collector, Plate, Royal Copenhagen, Christmas, 1913 ............... 80.00 To 105.00
Collector, Plate, Royal Copenhagen, Christmas, 1914 ............... 73.00 To 90.00
Collector, Plate, Royal Copenhagen, Christmas, 1915 ............... 63.00 To 90.00
Collector, Plate, Royal Copenhagen, Christmas, 1916 ............... 48.00 To 65.00
Collector, Plate, Royal Copenhagen, Christmas, 1917 ............... 48.00 To 65.00
Collector, Plate, Royal Copenhagen, Christmas, 1918 ............... 48.00 To 65.00
Collector, Plate, Royal Copenhagen, Christmas, 1919 ............... 48.00 To 65.00
Collector, Plate, Royal Copenhagen, Christmas, 1920 ............... 40.00 To 60.00
Collector, Plate, Royal Copenhagen, Christmas, 1921 ............... 36.50 To 52.50
Collector, Plate, Royal Copenhagen, Christmas, 1922 ............... 36.50 To 52.50
Collector, Plate, Royal Copenhagen, Christmas, 1923 ............... 50.00 To 65.00
Collector, Plate, Royal Copenhagen, Christmas, 1924 ............... 50.00 To 60.00
Collector, Plate, Royal Copenhagen, Christmas, 1925 ............... 50.00 To 60.00
Collector, Plate, Royal Copenhagen, Christmas, 1926 ............... 50.00 To 60.00
Collector, Plate, Royal Copenhagen, Christmas, 1927 ............... 65.00 To 80.00
Collector, Plate, Royal Copenhagen, Christmas, 1928 ............... 45.00 To 65.00
Collector, Plate, Royal Copenhagen, Christmas, 1929 ............... 45.00 To 60.00
Collector, Plate, Royal Copenhagen, Christmas, 1930 ............... 45.00 To 60.00
Collector, Plate, Royal Copenhagen, Christmas, 1931 ............... 47.50 To 60.00
Collector, Plate, Royal Copenhagen, Christmas, 1932 ............... 47.00 To 65.00
Collector, Plate, Royal Copenhagen, Christmas, 1933 ............... 65.00 To 80.00
Collector, Plate, Royal Copenhagen, Christmas, 1934 ............... 65.00 To 80.00
Collector, Plate, Royal Copenhagen, Christmas, 1935 ............... 75.00 To 87.00
Collector, Plate, Royal Copenhagen, Christmas, 1936 ............... 77.00 To 100.00

| Item | Price |
|---|---|
| Collector, Plate, Royal Copenhagen, Christmas, 1937 | 85.00 To 100.00 |
| Collector, Plate, Royal Copenhagen, Christmas, 1938 | 150.00 To 215.00 |
| Collector, Plate, Royal Copenhagen, Christmas, 1939 | 150.00 To 215.00 |
| Collector, Plate, Royal Copenhagen, Christmas, 1940 | 250.00 To 300.00 |
| Collector, Plate, Royal Copenhagen, Christmas, 1941 | 175.00 To 275.00 |
| Collector, Plate, Royal Copenhagen, Christmas, 1942 | 225.00 To 300.00 |
| Collector, Plate, Royal Copenhagen, Christmas, 1943 | 300.00 To 450.00 |
| Collector, Plate, Royal Copenhagen, Christmas, 1944 | 90.00 To 125.00 |
| Collector, Plate, Royal Copenhagen, Christmas, 1945 | 225.00 To 325.00 |
| Collector, Plate, Royal Copenhagen, Christmas, 1946 | 90.00 To 120.00 |
| Collector, Plate, Royal Copenhagen, Christmas, 1947 | 100.00 To 150.00 |
| Collector, Plate, Royal Copenhagen, Christmas, 1948 | 65.00 To 95.00 |
| Collector, Plate, Royal Copenhagen, Christmas, 1949 | 75.00 To 115.00 |
| Collector, Plate, Royal Copenhagen, Christmas, 1950 | 70.00 To 110.00 |
| Collector, Plate, Royal Copenhagen, Christmas, 1951 | 175.00 To 220.00 |
| Collector, Plate, Royal Copenhagen, Christmas, 1952 | 50.00 To 70.00 |
| Collector, Plate, Royal Copenhagen, Christmas, 1953 | 50.00 To 70.00 |
| Collector, Plate, Royal Copenhagen, Christmas, 1954 | 75.00 To 105.00 |
| Collector, Plate, Royal Copenhagen, Christmas, 1955 | 100.00 To 195.00 |
| Collector, Plate, Royal Copenhagen, Christmas, 1956 | 65.00 To 105.00 |
| Collector, Plate, Royal Copenhagen, Christmas, 1957 | 60.00 To 75.00 |
| Collector, Plate, Royal Copenhagen, Christmas, 1958 | 65.00 To 80.00 |
| Collector, Plate, Royal Copenhagen, Christmas, 1959 | 75.00 To 100.00 |
| Collector, Plate, Royal Copenhagen, Christmas, 1960 | 75.00 To 100.00 |
| Collector, Plate, Royal Copenhagen, Christmas, 1961 | 80.00 To 100.00 |
| Collector, Plate, Royal Copenhagen, Christmas, 1962 | 120.00 To 130.00 |
| Collector, Plate, Royal Copenhagen, Christmas, 1963 | 37.50 To 50.00 |
| Collector, Plate, Royal Copenhagen, Christmas, 1964 | 35.00 To 40.00 |
| Collector, Plate, Royal Copenhagen, Christmas, 1965 | 35.00 To 45.00 |
| Collector, Plate, Royal Copenhagen, Christmas, 1966 | 30.00 To 36.00 |
| Collector, Plate, Royal Copenhagen, Christmas, 1967 | 22.00 To 29.00 |
| Collector, Plate, Royal Copenhagen, Christmas, 1968 | 20.00 To 25.00 |
| Collector, Plate, Royal Copenhagen, Christmas, 1969 | 15.00 To 20.00 |
| Collector, Plate, Royal Copenhagen, Christmas, 1970 | 12.50 To 18.50 |
| Collector, Plate, Royal Copenhagen, Christmas, 1971 | 10.00 To 16.00 |
| Collector, Plate, Royal Copenhagen, Christmas, 1972 | 10.00 To 16.00 |
| Collector, Plate, Royal Copenhagen, Christmas, 1973 | 15.00 To 22.00 |
| Collector, Plate, Royal Copenhagen, Mother's Day, 1971 | 45.00 To 55.00 |
| Collector, Plate, Royal Copenhagen, Mother's Day, 1972 | 10.00 To 16.00 |
| Collector, Plate, Royal Copenhagen, Mother's Day, 1973 | 9.00 To 16.00 |
| Collector, Plate, Royal Copenhagen, Olympiade, 1972 | 25.00 |
| Collector, Plate, Royal Delft, Mother's Day, 1971, 1st Issue | 35.00 |
| Collector, Plate, Royal Doulton, Mother's Day, 1973, 1st Issue | 35.00 |
| Collector, Plate, Royal Doulton, Mother's Day, 1974 | 40.00 |
| Collector, Plate, Royale, Christmas, 1970 | 10.00 |
| Collector, Plate, Royale, Christmas, 1971 | 10.00 |
| Collector, Plate, Royale, Father's Day, 1970 | 15.00 |
| Collector, Plate, Royale, Father's Day, 1971 | 10.00 |
| Collector, Plate, Royale, Mother's Day, 1970 | 15.00 To 28.00 |
| Collector, Plate, Royale, Mother's Day, 1971 | 10.00 |
| Collector, Plate, Spode, Christmas, 1971 | 16.00 |
| Collector, Plate, Spode, Persian Commemorative, 1972 | 110.00 |
| Collector, Plate, Stumar, Christmas, 1970 | 6.00 |
| Collector, Plate, Svend Jensen, Mother's Day, 1970 | 8.00 |
| Collector, Plate, Svend Jensen, Mother's Day, 1971 | 8.00 |
| Collector, Plate, Svend Jensen, Mother's Day, 1972 | 8.00 |
| Collector, Plate, Veneto Flair, Christmas, 1971 | 125.00 |
| Collector, Plate, Veneto Flair, Christmas, 1972 | 65.00 |
| Collector, Plate, Veneto Flair, Christmas, 1973 | 55.00 |
| Collector, Plate, Veneto Flair, Easter, 1973, 1st Issue | 75.00 |
| Collector, Plate, Veneto Flair, Mother's Day, 1972 | 75.00 |
| Collector, Plate, Veneto Flair, Mother's Day, 1973 | 55.00 |
| Collector, Plate, Wedgwood, Christmas, 1969 | 125.00 |
| Collector, Plate, Wedgwood, Christmas, 1970 | 125.00 |
| Collector, Plate, Wedgwood, Christmas, 1972 | 22.00 |
| Collector, Plate, Wedgwood, Christmas, 1973 | 30.00 |

Collector, Plate, Wedgwood, Mother's Day, 1971 ................................................................. 25.00
Collector, Plate, Wedgwood, Mother's Day, 1972 ................................................................. 20.00
Collector, Plate, Wedgwood, Mother's Day, 1973 ................................................................. 20.00
Collector, Plate, Wedgwood, Mother's Day, 1974 ................................................................. 20.00
Collector, Plate, Wellings Mint, Christmas, 1971, 1st Issue ............................................. 100.00
Collector, Spoon, Michelsen, Christmas, 1910 ............................................... 75.00 To 110.00
Collector, Spoon, Michelsen, Christmas, 1911 ............................................... 75.00 To 110.00
Collector, Spoon, Michelsen, Christmas, 1912 ............................................... 75.00 To 110.00
Collector, Spoon, Michelsen, Christmas, 1913 ............................................... 75.00 To 110.00
Collector, Spoon, Michelsen, Christmas, 1914 ............................................... 75.00 To 110.00
Collector, Spoon, Michelsen, Christmas, 1915 ............................................... 75.00 To 110.00
Collector, Spoon, Michelsen, Christmas, 1916 ............................................... 75.00 To 110.00
Collector, Spoon, Michelsen, Christmas, 1917 ............................................... 75.00 To 110.00
Collector, Spoon, Michelsen, Christmas, 1918 ............................................... 75.00 To 110.00
Collector, Spoon, Michelsen, Christmas, 1919 ............................................... 75.00 To 110.00
Collector, Spoon, Michelsen, Christmas, 1920 ................................................. 36.00 To 52.00
Collector, Spoon, Michelsen, Christmas, 1921 ................................................. 36.00 To 52.00
Collector, Spoon, Michelsen, Christmas, 1922 ................................................. 36.00 To 52.00
Collector, Spoon, Michelsen, Christmas, 1923 ................................................. 36.00 To 52.00
Collector, Spoon, Michelsen, Christmas, 1924 ................................................. 36.00 To 52.00
Collector, Spoon, Michelsen, Christmas, 1925 ................................................. 36.00 To 52.00
Collector, Spoon, Michelsen, Christmas, 1926 ................................................. 36.00 To 52.00
Collector, Spoon, Michelsen, Christmas, 1927 ................................................. 36.00 To 52.00
Collector, Spoon, Michelsen, Christmas, 1928 ................................................. 36.00 To 52.00
Collector, Spoon, Michelsen, Christmas, 1929 ................................................. 36.00 To 52.00
Collector, Spoon, Michelsen, Christmas, 1930 ................................................. 36.00 To 46.00
Collector, Spoon, Michelsen, Christmas, 1931 ................................................. 36.00 To 46.00
Collector, Spoon, Michelsen, Christmas, 1932 ................................................. 36.00 To 46.00
Collector, Spoon, Michelsen, Christmas, 1933 ................................................. 36.00 To 46.00
Collector, Spoon, Michelsen, Christmas, 1934 ................................................. 36.00 To 46.00
Collector, Spoon, Michelsen, Christmas, 1935 ................................................. 36.00 To 46.00
Collector, Spoon, Michelsen, Christmas, 1936 ................................................. 36.00 To 46.00
Collector, Spoon, Michelsen, Christmas, 1937 ................................................. 36.00 To 46.00
Collector, Spoon, Michelsen, Christmas, 1938 ................................................. 36.00 To 46.00
Collector, Spoon, Michelsen, Christmas, 1939 ................................................. 36.00 To 46.00
Collector, Spoon, Michelsen, Christmas, 1940 ................................................. 33.00 To 38.00
Collector, Spoon, Michelsen, Christmas, 1941 ................................................. 33.00 To 38.00
Collector, Spoon, Michelsen, Christmas, 1942 ................................................. 33.00 To 38.00
Collector, Spoon, Michelsen, Christmas, 1943 ................................................. 33.00 To 38.00
Collector, Spoon, Michelsen, Christmas, 1944 ................................................. 33.00 To 38.00
Collector, Spoon, Michelsen, Christmas, 1945 ................................................. 33.00 To 38.00
Collector, Spoon, Michelsen, Christmas, 1946 ................................................. 33.00 To 38.00
Collector, Spoon, Michelsen, Christmas, 1947 ................................................. 33.00 To 38.00
Collector, Spoon, Michelsen, Christmas, 1948 ................................................. 33.00 To 38.00
Collector, Spoon, Michelsen, Christmas, 1949 ................................................. 33.00 To 38.00
Collector, Spoon, Michelsen, Christmas, 1950 ................................................. 30.00 To 32.00
Collector, Spoon, Michelsen, Christmas, 1951 ................................................. 30.00 To 32.00
Collector, Spoon, Michelsen, Christmas, 1952 ................................................. 30.00 To 32.00
Collector, Spoon, Michelsen, Christmas, 1953 ................................................. 30.00 To 32.00
Collector, Spoon, Michelsen, Christmas, 1954 ................................................. 30.00 To 32.00
Collector, Spoon, Michelsen, Christmas, 1955 ................................................. 30.00 To 32.00
Collector, Spoon, Michelsen, Christmas, 1956 ................................................. 30.00 To 32.00
Collector, Spoon, Michelsen, Christmas, 1957 ................................................. 30.00 To 32.00
Collector, Spoon, Michelsen, Christmas, 1958 ................................................. 30.00 To 32.00
Collector, Spoon, Michelsen, Christmas, 1959 ................................................. 30.00 To 32.00
Collector, Spoon, Michelsen, Christmas, 1960 ................................................. 28.50 To 30.00
Collector, Spoon, Michelsen, Christmas, 1961 ................................................. 28.50 To 30.00
Collector, Spoon, Michelsen, Christmas, 1962 ................................................. 28.50 To 30.00
Collector, Spoon, Michelsen, Christmas, 1963 ................................................. 28.50 To 30.00
Collector, Spoon, Michelsen, Christmas, 1964 ................................................. 28.50 To 30.00
Collector, Spoon, Michelsen, Christmas, 1965 ................................................. 28.50 To 30.00
Collector, Spoon, Michelsen, Christmas, 1966 ................................................. 28.50 To 30.00
Collector, Spoon, Michelsen, Christmas, 1967 ................................................. 28.50 To 30.00
Collector, Spoon, Michelsen, Christmas, 1968 ................................................. 28.50 To 30.00
Collector, Spoon, Michelsen, Christmas, 1969 ................................................. 28.50 To 30.00
Collector, Spoon, Michelsen, Christmas, 1970 ................................................. 28.50 To 30.00

| | |
|---|---|
| Collector, Spoon, Michelsen, Christmas, 1971 | 27.00 |
| Collector, Spoon, Michelsen, Christmas, 1972 | 27.00 |
| Collector, Spoon, Michelsen, Christmas, 1973 | 36.00 |

*Commemoration items have been made to honor members of royalty and those of great national fame. World's fairs and important historical events are also remembered with commemoration pieces.*

Commemoration, see also Coronation

| | |
|---|---|
| Commemoration, Beaker, George V, Doulton | 18.00 |
| Commemoration, Beaker, 25th Anniversary Juliana & Bernhard, Dutch, 4 In. | 12.00 |
| Commemoration, Bowl, Boer War, "Bravery Of Irish Soldiers, 1900, " China | 17.50 |
| Commemoration, Box, George VI, Round, Tin, 6 In. | 7.00 |
| Commemoration, Cup, Boston, Marked Austria | 10.00 |
| Commemoration, Cup, Lewis & Clark, 1805-1905, Engraved, Silver, 1 1/2 In.High | 9.00 |
| Commemoration, Cup, Loving, Edward VII, Doulton | 60.00 |
| Commemoration, Jug, Alexandra & Prince Of Wales Wedding, 1863, 4.& M.Bell | 115.00 |
| Commemoration, Jug, Queen Victoria Diamond Jubilee, Blue, Doulton, Lambeth | 200.00 |
| Commemoration, Mug, King Edward VIII Coronation, 1937 | 7.95 |
| Commemoration, Pitcher, Shakespeare, Hayne S.Bennet Co., 7 1/2 In.High | 55.00 |
| Commemoration, Pitcher, Victoria & Albert, Leopold & Victoria On Back | 115.00 |
| Commemoration, Pitcher, Water, Clear Glass, Battleship Olympia | 75.00 |
| Commemoration, Plate, Albert Edward, Prince Of Wales, Nov.9, 1841, 6 1/4 In. | 45.00 |
| Commemoration, Plate, George V Coronation, C.1911, Royal Doulton | 27.60 |
| Commemoration, Plate, Queen Victoria 1887 Jubilee, Pressed, Beaded, 10 In. | 20.00 |
| Commemoration, Plate, Robert E.Lee, Lee On Horse, Flags, 10 3/4 In. | 15.00 |
| Commemoration, Plate, Views Of Woonsocket, R.I., Blue & White, England, 9 In. | 10.00 |
| Commemoration, Plate, Wilhelmina, 1898-1923, Blue, Sailing Ship, 9 In. | 35.00 |
| Commemoration, Plate, 25th National Convention Of Port Authorities, 1914 | 24.00 |
| Commemoration, Stand, Teapot, Round Tile, Edward VII Portrait, Minton | 22.00 |
| Commemoration, Tray, Pin, Elizabeth II, 4 In. | 6.00 |
| Commemoration, Vase, George VI & Elizabeth, 1937, 2 Handles, Royal Doulton | 295.00 |
| Compass, Johannes Martin, Silver & Gilt Metal, Hinged, Engraved, C.1690 | 1300.00 |
| Compass, Officer's, Pocket, Bleuler-London, Silver Case, Black Enamel Face | 175.00 |
| Compass, Singer's Patent, Night, Brass, Round, Black & White Dial | 54.50 |

*W.I.Copeland & Sons, Ltd., ran the Spode Works in Staffordshire, England, from 1847 to the present. Copeland & Garrett was the firm name from 1833 to 1847.*

Copeland, see also Spode

| | |
|---|---|
| Copeland Spode, Bowl & Underplate, Soup, Peacock | 15.00 |
| Copeland Spode, Bowl, Italian, Blue & White, Floral Border | 22.50 |
| Copeland Spode, Bowl, Tower, Dark Blue, 8 X 10 In. | 30.00 |
| Copeland Spode, Cup & Saucer, Chinese Rose, Green Enamel Band | 14.50 |
| Copeland Spode, Cup & Saucer, Coffee, Wickerlane | 7.00 |
| Copeland Spode, Feeder, Child's, Blue Transfer, Country Scene, C.1840 | 50.00 |
| Copeland Spode, Jug, Classical Cameo Figures On Blue, Registry 1884, 3 In. | 45.00 |
| Copeland Spode, Pitcher, Tower, Royal Blue & White, 8 1/2 In.High | 85.00 |
| Copeland Spode, Pitcher, White Embossed Figures On Dark Blue, 7 In. | 35.00 |
| Copeland Spode, Plate, Floral & Fruit, Sculptured Daisies Rim, 9 In. | 10.00 |
| Copeland Spode, Plate, Imari Pattern, Gold Trim, C.1810, 7 In. | 58.00 |
| Copeland Spode, Plate, Peacock, Enameled, 8 1/2 In. | 18.00 |
| Copeland Spode, Plate, Shanghai, 9 In. | 8.00 |
| Copeland Spode, Platter, Bird On Branch, Floral Border, 10 X 14 In. | 10.00 |
| Copeland Spode, Ramekin, Delft, English Countryside Scene, Maroon & Pink | 10.00 |
| Copeland, Basket, Parian, Basket Weave, 14 X 7 X 6 In. | 75.00 |
| Copeland, Bowl, Italian Pattern, Blue & White, Spode, 5 3/4 In. | 8.00 |
| Copeland, Coffeepot, Jasperware, Blue, Hunting Scene | 58.00 |
| Copeland, Creamer, The Mall, Boston Common, 6 In. | 12.00 |
| Copeland, Cup & Saucer, Pink Willow, England | 18.00 |
| Copeland, Cup, Demitasse, Chintz, Signed | 15.00 |
| Copeland, Dish, Sweetmeat, Covered, Royal Crown Derby Type Decoration | 45.00 |
| Copeland, Figurine, Maidenhood, Parian, 22 In.High | 245.00 |
| Copeland, Mug, Hunting Scene On Gray, England, 1894-1900 | 35.00 |
| Copeland, Pitcher, Blue & White Transfer, Bridge, Fort, & Country, C.1840 | 28.50 |
| Copeland, Pitcher, Squirrels & Bees With Leaves, Parian, Marked | 44.00 |
| Copeland, Plaque, Loch Lomond, Artist D.Yale, Sepia, C.1850, 12 In. | 75.00 |
| Copeland, Plate, Christmas Tree, Maroon Border, 10 In. | 15.00 |

| | |
|---|---|
| Copeland, Plate, Colossus Of Rhodes, Blue & White | 22.00 |
| Copeland, Plate, Faneuil Hall, Green Blue, 9 In. | 4.75 |
| Copeland, Plate, Imari Pattern, Gold Trim, C.1847, 7 1/4 In.Square | 58.00 |
| Copeland, Plate, Public Garden, Boston, Green Blue, 9 In. | 4.75 |
| Copeland, Plate, Pyramids Of Egypt, Blue & White | 22.00 |
| Copeland, Plate, Why Don't You Speak For Yourself, John, Blue & White, 9 In. | 15.00 |
| Copeland, Sugar & Creamer, Jasperware, Blue, Hunting Scene | 38.00 |
| Copeland, Teapot, Jasperware, Blue, Hunting Scene | 58.00 |
| Copeland, Teapot, Raised Floral On White, Green Vines At Spout, Cadogan | 150.00 |
| Copeland, Vase, Bulbous, Enameled Flowers On Gray, C.1847, 10 1/2 In.High | 75.00 |
| Copeland, Vase, Colored Birds, Pair | 100.00 |
| Copeland, Vase, Urn Shape, Gold & Pink Enamel, Turquoise Jewels, 5 1/2 In. | 115.00 |
| Copeland, Water Set, White Cameo Type Decoration On Deep Blue, 7 Piece | 170.00 |
| Copper Luster, see Luster, Copper | |
| Copper, Ashtray, 10 Gallon Hat | 3.00 |
| Copper, Belt Plate, British Officer's, Oval, Cross, Silver Finish, C.1803 | 74.50 |
| Copper, Bowl, Mixing, Brass Ring Handle, Dated 1846, 12 In.Diameter | 55.00 |
| Copper, Box, Jewel, Hinged, Brass Mounts, Art Nouveau Courting Scenes | 65.00 |
| Copper, Box, Sterling Silver Decoration, 3 1/2 X 4 1/2 X 2 In. | 10.00 |
| Copper, Bucket, Ale, Raised Figures On Front, Spout, 20 In. | 45.00 |
| Copper, Can, Oil, Swing Spout | 35.00 |
| Copper, Coffeepot Urn, Brass Stand, Burner, Handles, Universal, 1906 | 40.00 |
| Copper, Coffeepot, Glass Top, Alcohol Burner | 40.00 |
| Copper, Coffeepot, Pewter Spout & Handle, Raised Art Nouveau Concentrics | 65.00 |
| Copper, Container, Round, 2 Copper Handles, 12 X 13 In. | 24.50 |
| Copper, Cup, Tin Lined, 3 In.Diameter | 10.00 |
| Copper, Dish, Chafing, Figural Finial, 3 High Bowfront Legs, 1898 | 35.00 |
| Copper, Ewer, China, Engraved, 7 1/2 In.Base, 5 In.High | 12.00 |
| Copper, Font, Holy Water, Nickel Plated, Designs, C.1800 | 8.00 |
| Copper, Funnel, Burnished, Gallon | 16.00 |
| Copper, Inkwell, Hammered, Square, Crest On Top, 3 X 3 X 2 In. | 22.00 |
| Copper, Kettle, Apple Butter, Handles, 18 In.Diameter | 98.00 |
| Copper, Kettle, Bird Spout | 22.50 |
| Copper, Mask, Lion, Molded, Open Mouth, C.1850, 16 X 16 In., Pair | 275.00 |
| Copper, Match Holder, Art Nouveau Girl Holding Shirt With Pockets | 27.00 |
| Copper, Measure, Pint, Pour Lip | 18.00 |
| Copper, Mug, Applied Brass Heart & Handle | 14.00 |
| Copper, Pan, Sauce, Duparquet, N.Y., Iron Handle, Tin Lined, 10 In. | 85.00 |
| Copper, Plate, Printer's, Steam Engine, On Wooden Block | 15.00 |
| Copper, Poker Chip Holder, Barroom, 5 Troughs, 8 1/2 X 9 In. | 15.00 |
| Copper, Pot, Bean, 10 In. | 22.00 |
| Copper, Potlid, Handmade, Hammered, Pull Handle, 10 1/4 In.Diameter | 15.00 |
| Copper, Scoop, Hook For Hanging, 28 In.Long | 35.00 |
| Copper, Spittoon, Hand Hammered | 20.00 |
| Copper, Stamp, Printer's, Eagle | 12.50 |
| Copper, Sugar & Creamer, Pedestal Bases | 15.00 |
| Copper, Teakettle, American, 1/2 Gallon | 110.00 |
| Copper, Teakettle, Beehive, Pewter Bird | 19.50 |
| Copper, Teakettle, Gooseneck Spout, Copper Handle, 4 Quart | 42.50 |
| Copper, Teakettle, Hammered, Hinged Spout Cover, 12 In. | 45.00 |
| Copper, Teakettle, Hand Rolled & Dovetailed, C.1800, 2 Quart | 58.00 |
| Copper, Teakettle, P.Blada On Handle, American Made, Dovetailed, Gooseneck | 250.00 |
| Copper, Teakettle, Sternau & Co., N.Y., 4 Legged Stand | 18.00 |
| Copper, Teakettle, Wrought Iron Stand & Burner, Patented 1892 | 45.00 |
| Copper, Teapot On Stand, Brass Spout, Wood Handle, Bowman, 1904 | 48.00 |
| Copper, Teapot, Pewter Handle & Spout, Brass Hinge & Finial, Miniature | 18.00 |
| Copper, Teapot, Swedish, Dated 1891 | 25.00 |
| Copper, Tinderbox, Pocket, Oval, American, C.1830 | 65.00 |
| Copper, Token, Indian Trade, Indian On Face, Pre-Civil War | 12.50 |
| Copper, Toothpick, Marked China, Oval, Fluted, Blue Enamel Lined | 12.00 |
| Copper, Tray, Gold Plated, Oval, Relief Of St.George & Dragon Center | 35.00 |
| Copper, Tray, Hammered, Fluted Turned-Up Rim, Embossed Ivy, 24 3/4 In. Long | 30.00 |
| Copper, Tray, Pewter Rim, Eagle Mark, Manning-Bowman, 14 1/2 In.Diameter | 32.00 |
| Copper, Tray, Russian, Hand Hammered, Side Handles, 13 1/2 In.Diameter | 14.75 |
| Copper, Umbrella Stand, Ornate, 20 In.High | 40.00 |
| Copper, Vase, Enamel Cupids In Garden, Brass 4 Footed Base, 5 1/2 In. | 195.00 |

| | |
|---|---|
| Copper, Vase, Enameled, Artist Signed Vallet, 7 3/4 In.High | 245.00 |
| Copper, Warmer, Bed, Iron Handle | 39.50 |
| Copper, Warmer, Bed, Pan, Hand Hammered, Incised, C.1850 | 60.00 |
| Copper, Warmer, Bed, Pan, Hand Hammered, Incised, Wooden Handle, Date 1700 | 68.00 |
| Copper, Wash Boiler, Covered, Maple Handles | 49.00 |

*Coralene glass was made by firing many small colored beads on the outside of glassware. It was made in many patterns in the United States and Europe in the 1880s. Reproductions are made today.*

| | |
|---|---|
| Coralene, Bowl, Pink Seaweed On Blue, Footed, Signed, Patent, 5 In. | 215.00 |
| Coralene, Ewer, Roses & Gold On Light Blue, Cobalt Handle, Patent 1909 | 120.00 |
| Coralene, Perfume, Multicolored Beads In Random Pattern On Blue, 6 In. | 155.00 |
| Coralene, Perfume, Transparent Blue, Random Beads, 6 In.High | 155.00 |
| Coralene, Toothpick, Yellow Seaweed & Beads On Pale To Deep Blue | 150.00 |
| Coralene, Tumbler, Butterscotch, Mother-Of-Pearl, Blue Coralene Seaweed | 235.00 |
| Coralene, Tumbler, Horned Beetle, Gold & White Enamel | 42.00 |
| Coralene, Tumbler, White Beading In Seaweed Pattern, Enamel Floral, Clear | 120.00 |
| Coralene, Vase, Blue & Pink, 10 1/2 In.High | 225.00 |
| Coralene, Vase, Cranberry, Multicolor Peacock On Front, Enameling On Back | 650.00 |
| Coralene, Vase, Japanese, Gold Decorated Handles, Signed, 10 1/2 X 6 1/2 In. | 225.00 |
| Coralene, Vase, Japanese, Scenic, Lavender, Blue, Orange, & Green | 95.00 |
| Coralene, Vase, Japanese, 8 In. High | 195.00 |
| Coralene, Vase, Melon Shape, Applied Yellow Beading, Pink To White, 9 In. | 282.00 |
| Coralene, Vase, Orange Seaweed On Frosted To Yellow, 7 1/2 In.High | 250.00 |
| Coralene, Vase, Seaweed, Raised Orange Beading On Frosted, Clear & Yellow | 280.00 |

*Coronation cups have been made since the 1800s. Pieces of pottery or glass with a picture of the monarch and the date have been made as souvenirs for many coronations.*

**Coronation, see also Commemoration**

| | |
|---|---|
| Coronation, Beaker, Edward VII, 1902, Royal Doulton | 21.50 |
| Coronation, Beaker, George VI, 1937, 4 In.High | 11.00 |
| Coronation, Beaker, George V, 1911, Sepia Coloring, Royal Doulton | 20.00 |
| Coronation, Beer Glass, Edward, 1937, Etched Portrait, 5 In. | 18.00 |
| Coronation, Book, Coloring, 1953 | 4.00 |
| Coronation, Book, George V, Color Plates | 30.00 |
| Coronation, Bowl, Edward VII & Alexandra, 1902, Glass, 8 1/2 In. | 28.00 |
| Coronation, Bowl, Edward VIII, Fluted Edge, Gold, Meakin | 15.00 |
| Coronation, Bowl, Edward VIII, May 12, 1937 | 15.00 |
| Coronation, Bowl, Elizabeth II, 1953, Bone China, 6 In. | 4.95 |
| Coronation, Bowl, Queen Louise, Lavender, Floral Rim, 10 In. | 48.00 |
| Coronation, Bowl, Victoria, 1897, Stoneware, Square, 2 1/2 In.High | 11.00 |
| Coronation, Box, Edward VIII, Hinged Cover, Tin, 8 Sided, 5 3/4 In.Long | 6.95 |
| Coronation, Cloth, George V & Mary, June, 1911, 25 X 28 In. | 25.00 |
| Coronation, Container, Elizabeth II & Philip, 1953, Tin, Oval, 11 1/2 In. | 4.95 |
| Coronation, Container, Elizabeth II, 1953, Tin, 5 In.Diameter | 2.95 |
| Coronation, Cup & Saucer, Victoria & Albert, Portraits, Purple Transfer | 65.00 |
| Coronation, Cup, Edward VIII, Coronation That Never Happened, 3 In. | 12.00 |
| Coronation, Cup, George VI & Elizabeth, Meakin | 12.00 |
| Coronation, Cup, Loving, Edward VIII, Lion Handles, Paragon China, 3 In. | 50.00 |
| Coronation, Dish, Edward VII, 1902, Heart Shape, Glass | 24.00 |
| Coronation, Jar, Covered, Elizabeth II, 1953, 5 In.High | 18.00 |
| Coronation, Match Safe, Edward VII, Pocket, Gutta-Percha | 24.00 |
| Coronation, Mug, Edward VIII, Portrait & Royal Arms, Meakin | 10.00 |
| Coronation, Mug, Edward VIII, The King Who Never Was | 30.00 |
| Coronation, Mug, Edward VIII, 1937, 3 1/2 In.High | 15.00 |
| Coronation, Mug, Elizabeth II | 9.00 |
| Coronation, Mug, Elizabeth II, 1953, 2 Handled, Doulton, Noke | 155.00 |
| Coronation, Mug, George V, 1911, Kettering | 12.00 |
| Coronation, Plate, Edward VII, 1902, Porcelain, 8 In. | 16.00 |
| Coronation, Plate, Elizabeth II, England, 8 3/4 In. | 8.00 |
| Coronation, Plate, Elizabeth II, Hand-Engraved, Maddock & Son, 8 1/2 In. | 17.50 |
| Coronation, Plate, Elizabeth II, 1953, 6 1/2 In. | 4.95 |
| Coronation, Plate, Elizabeth II, 1953, 7 5/8 In. | 3.95 |
| Coronation, Plate, Elizabeth II, 1953, 9 In. | 7.50 |
| Coronation, Plate, Elizabeth II, 6 In. | 5.00 |
| Coronation, Plate, Elizabeth, 1953, Gold Beaded Edge, White, Castleton, 10 In. | 18.00 |

| | |
|---|---|
| Coronation, Plate, George VI & Elizabeth, May 12, 1937, Portrait, 8 1/2 In. | 15.00 |
| Coronation, Plate, George VI, May 12, 1937, Scalloped Rim, Gold, 10 In. | 15.00 |
| Coronation, Plate, George VI, 1937, Princess Elizabeth Picture, 7 In. | 10.00 |
| Coronation, Plate, George V, 1911, 10 In. | 12.00 |
| Coronation, Scrapbook, Elizabeth, 1953 | 7.50 |
| Coronation, Spoon, George & Wife, 1937, Ornate Handle, Sterling Silver | 6.00 |
| Coronation, Sugar, Mary & George V | 32.00 |
| Coronation, Teapot, Elizabeth II, 1953, Chrome Finish Aluminum, Crown | 5.95 |
| Coronation, Teapot, Victoria, 1897, 6 In.High | 45.00 |
| Coronation, Tin, Edward VII, 1902 | 10.00 |
| Coronation, Tin, Elizabeth II, 1953, Covered, 5 In.Diameter | 3.75 |
| Coronation, Tin, Elizabeth II, 1953, Royal Couple & Windsor Castle | 10.00 |
| Coronation, Tin, Elizabeth II, 1953, 5 In. Diameter | 2.95 |
| Coronation, Tin, Queen Elizabeth, Round | 6.00 |
| Coronation, Tray, King Ferdinand & Louise, Tin | 3.50 |
| Coronation, Tumbler, Edward VII, 1902, Porcelain, 3 1/2 In.High | 25.00 |
| Coronation, Tumbler, Edward VIII, White Relief Bust On Pink | 15.00 |
| Coronation, Westminster Abbey Cathedral, 1953, Metal, 1 3/4 In.High | 12.50 |

*Cosmos pattern glass is a pattern of pressed milk glass with colored flowers.*

| | |
|---|---|
| Cosmos, Butter, Covered | 165.00 To 173.00 |
| Cosmos, Compote, Starred, Open Ruffled Edge, 8 X 6 In. | 18.50 |
| Cosmos, Condiment Set, Blue & Yellow, 4 Piece | 52.00 |
| Cosmos, Creamer | 100.00 |
| Cosmos, Creamer, Pink Band | 95.00 |
| Cosmos, Creamer, Starred, Gold Trim | 10.50 |
| Cosmos, Cruet, Cone Shape, 9 1/2 In. | 20.00 |
| Cosmos, Dish, Honey, Covered, Starred, 4 Legs, 5 1/4 In. Square | 27.50 |
| Cosmos, Lamp Base, Pink Band With Pink, Yellow, & Blue Embossed Flowers | 65.00 |
| Cosmos, Lamp, Pink Rims, Miniature | 190.00 |
| Cosmos, Lamp, Pink, Blue, & Yellow Flowers, Beaded Edge Chimney, 18 In. | 42.50 |
| Cosmos, Lamp, Yellow & Pink Paint, 7 In. High | 40.00 |
| Cosmos, Salt & Pepper | 38.00 |
| Cosmos, Sugar, Covered | 145.00 |
| Cosmos, Syrup | 100.00 |
| Cosmos, Syrup, 7 In.High | 85.00 |
| Cosmos, Tumbler, Banded, Gold Trim | 9.00 |
| Cosmos, Tumbler, Pink Band | 43.00 |
| Cosmos, Tumbler, Pink Band With Yellow, Pink, & Green Flowers | 32.50 |

Country Store, see Store

*Cowan pottery was made in Cleveland, Ohio, from 1913 to 1920. Most pieces of the art pottery were marked with the name of the firm in various ways.*

| | |
|---|---|
| Cowan, Ashtray, Shell, Pink To Blue, 3 3/4 In.Long, Marked | 7.00 |
| Cowan, Candlestick, Pale Yellow, High Embossed Leaves, 4 1/2 In., Pair | 14.00 |
| Cowan, Dish, Soap, Pedestal, Seahorse, Ivory, Pink Interior, 5 5/8 In.Long | 25.00 |
| Cowan, Figurine, Beaver, Matte Green | 95.00 |
| Cowan, Figurine, Nude, White, Flower Holder At Base, 15 1/2 In.High | 75.00 |
| Cowan, Flower Holder, Art Nouveau, Lady, White, 6 1/2 In.High | 26.50 |
| Cowan, Penholder, Cream, 9 In. High    *Illus* | 35.00 |
| Cowan, Urn, Covered, Ivory With Ram's Head Design In Gold, 13 1/4 In.High | 15.00 |
| Cowan, Vase, Turquoise, Six-Sided, 6 In.High, Marked | 15.00 |
| Cowan, Wall Pocket, Metallic Blue, 8 1/2 In.High, Marked | 15.00 |

*Crackle glass was originally made by the Venetians, but most of the ware found today dates from the 1800s. The glass was heated, cooled, and refired so that many small lines appeared inside the glass. It was made in many factories in the United States and Europe.*

Crackle Glass, see also Fry

| | |
|---|---|
| Crackle Glass, Cruet, Amber | 4.00 |
| Crackle Glass, Goblet, Beehive Type, Amber, Round | 5.00 |
| Crackle Glass, Goblet, Cranberry Serpent Around Stem, Gold Trim, C.1860 | 55.00 |
| Crackle Glass, Jug, Clear, 6 Applied Berry Prunts & Handle, 7 In. | 15.00 |
| Crackle Glass, Pitcher, Green, Applied Handle | 17.50 |
| Crackle Glass, Tumbler, Royal Ivy | 50.00 |

*Cranberry glass is an almost transparent yellow red glass. It resembles the color of cranberry juice.*

Cranberry Glass, see also Rubena Verde, etc.

Cowan, Penholder, Cream, 9 In. High
(See Page 124)

| | |
|---|---:|
| Cranberry Glass, Basket, White Cased Exterior, Crystal Feet & Handle | 45.00 |
| Cranberry Glass, Bell, Cut To Clear, Hobstar & Fan, 4 1/2 In.High | 40.00 |
| Cranberry Glass, Boat, Banana, Delaware | 45.00 |
| Cranberry Glass, Bonbon, Crystal Ball Finial, Crystal Stem, Enameled Gold | 65.00 |
| Cranberry Glass, Bottle, Castor, Inverted Thumbprint | 6.50 |
| Cranberry Glass, Bottle, Scent, Straight Sides, Silver Hinge, 2 3/4 In.High | 50.00 |
| Cranberry Glass, Bowl & Underplate, Finger, Opalescent Swirl, Gold Trim | 55.00 |
| Cranberry Glass, Bowl, Bride's, Opalescent, 9 In. | 45.00 |
| Cranberry Glass, Bowl, Clear Rigaree, Footed & Handled Silver Plate Holder | 45.00 |
| Cranberry Glass, Bowl, Convex Then Turns In & Flares Out At Top, 2 1/2 In. | 24.50 |
| Cranberry Glass, Bowl, Cut To Clear, Fan & Oval Punty, 3 In.Diameter, Pair | 200.00 |
| Cranberry Glass, Bowl, Cut To Clear, Strawberry Diamond & Fan, 36 Star Base | 200.00 |
| Cranberry Glass, Bowl, Finger, Cartouche-Shaped, 3 In.High | 38.00 |
| Cranberry Glass, Bowl, Finger, Cut To Clear, Strawberry Diamond & Fan | 75.00 |
| Cranberry Glass, Bowl, Finger, Inverted Thumbprint, 4 3/4 In.Diameter | 18.00 |
| Cranberry Glass, Bowl, Finger, Polished Pontil, 4 In. | 32.00 |
| Cranberry Glass, Bowl, Finger, Swirled, Shaded | 29.50 |
| Cranberry Glass, Bowl, Flared, Eight Thumbprint Feet, Applied Handle | 70.00 |
| Cranberry Glass, Bowl, Footed Base, 5 1/4 In.Diameter, 2 3/4 In.Deep | 34.50 |
| Cranberry Glass, Bowl, Opalescent To Crimped Ruffled Rim, 6 1/4 In. | 30.00 |
| Cranberry Glass, Bowl, Powder, Covered, Clear Feet, Applied Knob, 4 In.Diam. | 75.00 |
| Cranberry Glass, Bowl, Ribbed, Applied Clear Feet, Oval, French | 165.00 |
| Cranberry Glass, Bowl, Ruffled, Overshot, Metal Base | 58.00 |
| Cranberry Glass, Bowl, Slanted Sides, 4 3/4 In.Diameter Top, 3 1/4 In.Base | 55.00 |
| Cranberry Glass, Bowl, Star Cut Pontil, Gold Leaf Garlands, St.Louis | 189.00 |
| Cranberry Glass, Box, Candy, Finial, White Enamel Floral, Bottom, Round | 85.00 |
| Cranberry Glass, Box, Enamel Wild Flowers On Hinged Lid, 1 7/8 In. | 35.00 |
| Cranberry Glass, Box, Hinged, French Enamel & Gilt, Ormolu Mounting | 220.00 |
| Cranberry Glass, Box, Hinged, Gilt Strawberries, White Woman & Lyre, Round | 115.00 |
| Cranberry Glass, Box, Hinged, Round, Floral Enamel, Gold Tracery, Brass Base | 70.00 |
| Cranberry Glass, Box, Powder, White Enamel Cherub On Hinged Top, Swirled | 87.50 |
| Cranberry Glass, Box, White Enamel Buildings On Hinged Lid, 1 3/4 In. High | 60.00 |
| Cranberry Glass, Bride's Basket, Bull's-Eye, Fluted Ruffles, Holder | 145.00 |
| Cranberry Glass, Bride's Bowl, Ruffled Edge, Metal Pedestal | 84.00 |
| Cranberry Glass, Butter, Covered, Round, Opalescent, Resist | 65.00 |
| Cranberry Glass, Butter, Crystal Ball Finial, Crystal Ribbon Edge | 105.00 |
| Cranberry Glass, Carafe, Water, Blown, C.1870, 6 1/2 In. | 65.00 |
| Cranberry Glass, Castor, Pickle, Inverted Thumbprint, Silver Holder | 145.00 |
| Cranberry Glass, Celery, Inverted Thumbprint, Enameled Daisies | 135.00 |
| Cranberry Glass, Celery, Overlay, Pedestal Base, Enamel Decoration | 125.00 |
| Cranberry Glass, Claret, Crystal Stem | 12.00 |
| Cranberry Glass, Compote, Candy, Covered, Diamond Point, 12 In.High | 18.00 |
| Cranberry Glass, Compote, Clear Ball Stem, Flint, 5 1/4 In.High | 45.00 |
| Cranberry Glass, Condiment Set, Barrel Shape, Silver Footed Holder, 3 Piece | 95.00 |
| Cranberry Glass, Cornucopia, Mounted In Brass Hand, C.1840 | 150.00 |
| Cranberry Glass, Creamer, Blown, Applied Clear Handle, Gold Trim, Enamel | 55.00 |

| | |
|---|---|
| Cranberry Glass, Creamer, Blown, Scalloped Top, Clear Handle, 6 1/2 In. | 35.00 |
| Cranberry Glass, Creamer, Corset Shape, Stretched, Clear Handle & Rigaree | 48.00 |
| Cranberry Glass, Creamer, Emil Larson, Cranberry & White | 195.00 |
| Cranberry Glass, Creamer, Ruffled Top, 6 In.High | 50.00 |
| Cranberry Glass, Cruet Set, Teardrop Stoppers, Silver Frame, 2 Piece | 165.00 |
| Cranberry Glass, Cruet, Bulbous, Inverted Thumbprint, Stopper | 150.00 |
| Cranberry Glass, Cruet, Diamond-Quilted, Applied Clear Handle, Stopper | 95.00 |
| Cranberry Glass, Cruet, Diamond-Quilted, 3 Lip, Applied Clear Handle & Base | 60.00 |
| Cranberry Glass, Cruet, Diamond, Clear Handle & Stopper, Rough Pontil, 8 In. | 97.50 |
| Cranberry Glass, Cruet, Inverted Thumbprint, Bulbous, Stopper | 125.00 |
| Cranberry Glass, Cruet, Milk Glass Swirl | 18.50 |
| Cranberry Glass, Cruet, Opalescent Dot | 40.00 |
| Cranberry Glass, Cruet, Open Swirl | 40.00 |
| Cranberry Glass, Cruet, Ovoid Body, Blown, Applied Crystal Handle, 7 In. | 50.00 |
| Cranberry Glass, Cruet, Pointed Hobnail, Clear Applied Handle, Stopper | 75.00 |
| Cranberry Glass, Cruet, Quilted | 15.00 |
| Cranberry Glass, Cruet, Swirl Pattern, Crystal Handle, Cut Stopper, Blown | 125.00 |
| Cranberry Glass, Cup & Saucer, Cut To Clear, White Enameling, Clover Shape | 55.00 |
| Cranberry Glass, Decanter, Clear Applied Handle, Applied Silver Rye | 42.00 |
| Cranberry Glass, Decanter, Cologne, Steeple Stopper, Pair | 70.00 |
| Cranberry Glass, Decanter, Cut Stopper, Gold Color, Filigree Case | 35.00 |
| Cranberry Glass, Decanter, Thumbprint, Applied Clear Reeded Handle | 65.00 |
| Cranberry Glass, Decanter, Wine, Enameled Flowers, Polished Pontil | 75.00 |
| Cranberry Glass, Dish, Heart Shape, Clear Handle & Petal Feet, 5 In.Long | 35.00 |
| Cranberry Glass, Epergne, Single, Opalescent Edge & Stripe, Fluted Base | 90.00 |
| Cranberry Glass, Epergne, 10 In.Bowl, 3 Vases, 2 Scrolls | 150.00 |
| Cranberry Glass, Ewer, Ovoid Body, Crystal Handle, 7 In.High | 50.00 |
| Cranberry Glass, Goblet, Ribbed, Clear Stem & Foot, 8 In.High | 10.00 |
| Cranberry Glass, Hat, Swirled, 6 1/2 In.High | 125.00 |
| Cranberry Glass, Hat, Threaded, Flint, 3 In.High | 30.00 |
| Cranberry Glass, Inkwell, Drapery Pattern, Brass Lid, Clear Well, 5 In. | 45.00 |
| Cranberry Glass, Jar, Biscuit, Silver Plate Cover, Twisted Finial & Bail | 75.00 |
| Cranberry Glass, Jar, Sweetmeat, Clear Thorn Finial, 7 X 4 In. | 75.00 |
| Cranberry Glass, Jug, Cranberry To Light Pink, Enameled Flowers | 42.00 |
| Cranberry Glass, Lampshade, Hanging, Swirl, 14 In. | 325.00 |
| Cranberry Glass, Muffineer, Beveled Panels, Cutout Silver Top | 48.00 |
| Cranberry Glass, Muffineer, Blown, Paneled, Silver Plate, Dome Cover | 35.00 |
| Cranberry Glass, Muffineer, Brass Top, Clear Paneled, 5 In.High | 45.00 |
| Cranberry Glass, Muffineer, Bulbous Shape, 6 1/2 In.High | 50.00 |
| Cranberry Glass, Muffineer, Candy Stripe, Opalescent, 4 1/2 In.High | 70.00 |
| Cranberry Glass, Muffineer, Inverted Thumbprint | 74.00 |
| Cranberry Glass, Muffineer, Opalescent Coin Spot, Cranberry To Clear | 75.00 |
| Cranberry Glass, Muffineer, Opalescent Diamond-Quilted, Ribbed, 4 1/2 In. | 50.00 |
| Cranberry Glass, Muffineer, Paneled, Pierced Sterling Top, 5 1/2 In.High | 48.50 |
| Cranberry Glass, Muffineer, Paneled, 10 Sided Base, Cutout Silver Top | 48.00 |
| Cranberry Glass, Muffineer, Quilted, Metal Top | 52.00 |
| Cranberry Glass, Muffineer, Royal Ivy, Cranberry To Frosted | 65.00 |
| Cranberry Glass, Muffineer, Threaded, Cranberry To Clear | 85.00 |
| Cranberry Glass, Muffineer, Thumbprint | 50.00 |
| Cranberry Glass, Mug, Applied Clear Handle, 7 1/4 In.High | 90.00 |
| Cranberry Glass, Perfume, Bulbous, Cut To Clear, Gold Lined Oval Cuttings | 65.00 |
| Cranberry Glass, Perfume, Cut Glass, Ornate, 2 3/4 X 1 7/8 In. | 36.50 |
| Cranberry Glass, Perfume, Pyramid Shape, Horizontal Gilt Stripes, Pair | 44.50 |
| Cranberry Glass, Pitcher, Applied Clear Handle, Ground Pontil, 6 1/2 In. | 35.00 |
| Cranberry Glass, Pitcher, Applied Clear Reeded Handle, Ruffled, Floral, Gold | 98.50 |
| Cranberry Glass, Pitcher, Blown, Paneled, Bulbous, Clear Reeded Handle | 78.00 |
| Cranberry Glass, Pitcher, Bulbous, Opalescent Stripes, Cranberry To Clear | 84.00 |
| Cranberry Glass, Pitcher, Coin Spot, Applied Clear Handle, Ruffled Top | 45.00 |
| Cranberry Glass, Pitcher, Diamond-Quilted, Applied Clear Handle, 3 1/2 In. | 15.00 |
| Cranberry Glass, Pitcher, Gilt Decoration, Flared Top, 6 1/2 In. | 58.00 |
| Cranberry Glass, Pitcher, Inverted Panel, Applied Clear Ribbed Handle | 75.00 |
| Cranberry Glass, Pitcher, Inverted Thumbprint, Applied Clear Reeded Handle | 85.00 |
| Cranberry Glass, Pitcher, Melon Shape, Inside Ribs, Applied Clear Handle | 85.00 |
| Cranberry Glass, Pitcher, Milk, Applied White Threading & Crystal Handle | 55.00 |
| Cranberry Glass, Pitcher, Panel & Drape, Enameled Floral, Clear Handle | 65.00 |
| Cranberry Glass, Pitcher, Ribbed, Opalescent Daisies, Applied Clear Handle | 125.00 |

| Cranberry Glass, Pitcher, Sandwich Overshot, Applied Clear Reeded Handle | 125.00 |
|---|---|
| Cranberry Glass, Pitcher, Thumbprint, Clear Reeded Handle, Enamel Florals | 95.00 |
| Cranberry Glass, Pitcher, Water, Applied Reeded Chartreuse Handle, Silver | 125.00 |
| Cranberry Glass, Pitcher, Water, Inverted Thumbprint, Clear Handle, 7 In. | 65.00 |
| Cranberry Glass, Pitcher, Water, Opalescent Coin Spot | 85.00 |
| Cranberry Glass, Pitcher, Water, Straight Sides, Applied Handle, 8 1/2 In. | 120.00 |
| Cranberry Glass, Pitcher, Water, White Overlay, Clear Applied Handle | 195.00 |
| Cranberry Glass, Plate, Blown, Rough Pontil, 7 In. | 45.00 |
| Cranberry Glass, Plate, Diamond Pattern Border, 6 In. | 8.50 |
| Cranberry Glass, Rose Bowl, Drape, Applied Clear Feet, Flared Rim, 5 In. | 68.00 |
| Cranberry Glass, Rose Bowl, Opalescent Swirl, Crimped Top, 4 1/2 In.High | 48.00 |
| Cranberry Glass, Rose Bowl, Opaline Swirl, Crimped Top | 45.00 |
| Cranberry Glass, Salt & Pepper, Baby Thumbprint, Cut To Clear | 68.00 |
| Cranberry Glass, Salt, Master, English, Clear Rigaree, Silver Plate Holder | 37.50 |
| Cranberry Glass, Salt, Oval, Silver Filigree Holder | 15.00 |
| Cranberry Glass, Saltshaker, Opaque White & Clear, Marbleized | 7.00 |
| Cranberry Glass, Saltshaker, Ribbed, Crisscross, Opalescent | 20.00 |
| Cranberry Glass, Sherbet, Ribbed, Clear Knob Stem, 5 1/2 In.High | 10.00 |
| Cranberry Glass, Stein, Pewter Top & Base, Faces On Base, Fancywork Top | 285.00 |
| Cranberry Glass, Tankard, Milk, Clear Reeded Handle, Polished Pontil | 55.00 |
| Cranberry Glass, Tankard, Water, Big Daisy, 13 In. | 127.00 |
| Cranberry Glass, Toothpick, Inverted Coin Dot | 30.00 |
| Cranberry Glass, Toothpick, Ribbed, Bulbous | 35.00 |
| Cranberry Glass, Tumbler, Blown, Enameled Flowers & Gold Leaves, 4 In. | 37.50 |
| Cranberry Glass, Tumbler, Coin Spot | 20.00 |
| Cranberry Glass, Tumbler, Cut To Clear, Notched & Fan | 55.00 |
| Cranberry Glass, Tumbler, Diamond-Quilted | 25.00 |
| Cranberry Glass, Tumbler, French, Gold Trim, 5 1/2 In.High | 20.00 |
| Cranberry Glass, Tumbler, Gold & White Enamel | 15.00 |
| Cranberry Glass, Tumbler, Inverted Baby Thumbprint, Blown | 30.00 |
| Cranberry Glass, Tumbler, Inverted Crisscross | 25.00 |
| Cranberry Glass, Tumbler, Inverted Thumbprint | 37.00 |
| Cranberry Glass, Tumbler, Juice, C.1860, 4 In. | 18.00 |
| Cranberry Glass, Tumbler, Opalescent Coin Spot, 3 3/4 In.High | 38.00 |
| Cranberry Glass, Tumbler, Opalescent Swirl, 4 In. | 25.00 |
| Cranberry Glass, Tumbler, Paneled, Paperweight Base, Gold Decoration | 55.00 |
| Cranberry Glass, Vanity Set, 3 Piece | 35.00 |
| Cranberry Glass, Vase, Applied Crystal Thorns & Petal Feet, 11 In.High | 55.00 |
| Cranberry Glass, Vase, Bulbous Bottom, Enameled Chrysanthemums, C.1888 | 37.00 |
| Cranberry Glass, Vase, Bulbous, Ruffled Top, Rough Pontil, 3 1/4 In., Pair | 32.00 |
| Cranberry Glass, Vase, Clear Base & Top Ruffle, 8 In.High | 95.00 |
| Cranberry Glass, Vase, Clear Bulbous Bottom, Enameled Mums, 8 In.High | 45.00 |
| Cranberry Glass, Vase, Enameled Floral, Gold Trim, 6 Sided Top, 11 In.High | 75.00 |
| Cranberry Glass, Vase, End-Of-Day, Pale Blue Swirls, 10 1/2 In.High, Pair | 20.00 |
| Cranberry Glass, Vase, Engraved Gray Flowers & Ferns, Gold Band, 7 In. | 125.00 |
| Cranberry Glass, Vase, Flower & Leaf Enameling, 7 1/2 In.High | 47.50 |
| Cranberry Glass, Vase, Hand Holding Torch, 6 In.High | 35.00 |
| Cranberry Glass, Vase, Inverted Thumbprint, Ruffled Top, Opalescent, 9 In. | 75.00 |
| Cranberry Glass, Vase, Iridescent, Metal Fittings, 9 1/4 In. | 95.00 |
| Cranberry Glass, Vase, Round Base, Slender Neck, 4 1/2 In.High | 45.00 |
| Cranberry Glass, Vase, Silver Overlay, 6 In.High | 95.00 |
| Cranberry Glass, Vase, Swirled, Ruffled, Opalescent Edge, 3 3/4 In.High | 20.00 |
| Cranberry Glass, Vase, Thumbprint, Pinched Sides, 7 In. High | 50.00 |
| Cranberry Glass, Vase, Trumpet, Opaline Cased, Vaseline Lip, Bronze Base | 65.00 |
| Cranberry Glass, Vase, White Enameled Lily Of The Valley, Paneled, 9 In. | 45.00 |
| Cranberry Glass, Washstand Set, Swirled, Applied Crystal Handle, 2 Piece | 95.00 |
| Cranberry Glass, Water Set, Opalescent Hobnail, Reed Handle, 5 Piece | 165.00 |
| Cranberry Glass, Wine, Clear Oval Thumbprints & Stem, 4 In. | 12.50 |
| Cranberry Glass, Wine, Clear Stem & Foot | 11.00 |

*Creamware, or queensware, was developed by Josiah Wedgwood about 1765. It
is a cream-colored earthenware that has been copied by many factories.*

| Creamware, Bowl, Brown Bands, Staffordshire, C.1820 .................... *Illus* | 100.00 |
|---|---|
| Creamware, Bowl, Iron Roses & Blue Floral Inside & Out, C.1800, 9 1/2 In. | 200.00 |
| Creamware, Cachepot, Applied Charcoal Gray Sand Decoration, Rolled Edge | 90.00 |
| Creamware, Cachepot, Olive, Blue, & Gold Geometrics, Scalloped Edge | 135.00 |
| Creamware, Candlestick, Corinthian, 8 1/4 In.High, Pair | 27.50 |

Creamware, Bowl, Brown Bands,
Staffordshire, C.1820
*(See Page 127)*

**Creamware, Cup & Saucer,** Luster Floral, Spur Handle, C.1820 ........................................................ 25.00

*Croesus glass is a special pattern of pressed glass made about 1897. It was made in clear glass, emerald green, or amethyst. Each piece was decorated with gold.*

**Croesus, Green,** Berry Set, 5 Piece ................................................................................... 225.00
**Croesus, Green,** Butter, Gold Edging .................................................................................. 75.00
**Croesus, Green,** Pitcher, Water .......................................................................................... 125.00
**Croesus, Green,** Pitcher, 10 1/2 In.High ........................................................................... 190.00
**Croesus, Green,** Sauce, Gold, 4 In. ..................................................................................... 30.00
**Croesus, Green,** Spooner .................................................................................................... 55.00
**Croesus, Green,** Sugar, Covered, Gold Trim ....................................................... 40.00 To 65.00
**Croesus, Green,** Table Set, Gold Trim, 4 Piece .................................................................. 300.00
**Croesus, Green,** Tankard ................................................................................................... 135.00
**Croesus, Green,** Toothpick, Gold ......................................................................................... 50.00
**Croesus, Green,** Tumbler .................................................................................................... 26.00
**Croesus, Green,** Tumbler, Water, Set Of 4 ......................................................................... 75.00
**Croesus, Green,** Water Set, Footed Pitcher, 4 Piece .......................................................... 199.50
**Croesus, Purple,** Bowl, Berry, 6 1/2 In. .............................................................................. 135.00
**Croesus, Purple,** Butter, Domed ......................................................................................... 150.00
**Croesus, Purple,** Salt & Pepper, Gilt Trim ........................................................................... 72.50
**Croesus, Purple,** Sauce ....................................................................................................... 55.00
**Croesus, Purple,** Spooner, Gold Trim ................................................................... 95.00 To 135.00
**Croesus, Purple,** Sugar, Covered, Gold Trim ...................................................... 135.00 To 165.00
**Croesus, Purple,** Table Set, Gold Trim, 4 Piece .................................................................. 350.00
**Croesus, Purple,** Toothpick, Gold ........................................................................................ 75.00
**Croesus, Purple,** Tray, Pickle, Gold .................................................................................... 85.00
**Croesus, Purple,** Tumbler, Gold Trim .................................................................................. 67.00
**Croesus, Purple,** Water Set, 7 Piece ................................................................................... 625.00

*Crown Derby is the nickname given to the works of the Royal Crown Derby Factory wich began working in England in 1859. An earlier and more famous English Derby factory existed from 1750 to 1848. The two factories were not related. Most of the porcelain found today with the Derby mark is the work of the later Derby factory.*
**Crown Derby, see also Royal Crown Derby**
**Crown Derby, Bowl,** Serving, Covered, Imari Pattern, Handled, 8 1/2 In. ............................ 78.00
**Crown Derby, Candlestick,** Gold Decoration & Floral Panels On Blue, Pair ....................... 425.00
**Crown Derby, Plate,** Imari Pattern, 10 1/4 In. ...................................................................... 34.00
**Crown Derby, Teapot,** Miniature, Cobalt Blue, Gold, & Red, 2 In.High ................................ 45.00
**Crown Derby, Vase,** Bulbous, Yellow, Encrusted Gold Flowers, 7 1/2 In.High .................... 175.00
**Crown Derby, Vase,** Imari Design, Cobalt & Orange, Round, C.1890 .................................... 85.00
**Crown Derby, Vase,** Parrots & Flowers, Gilded, C.1880, 13 3/8 In.High ............................. 225.00
**Crown Ducal, Box,** Covered, Square, Oriental Motif ............................................................... 5.50
**Crown Ducal, Hatpin Holder,** Rose Color ............................................................................. 14.00
**Crown Ducal, Plate,** Marriage Of Pocahontas, Blue & White, 10 1/2 In. ............................... 9.00
**Crown Ducal, Plate,** Washington Bicentenary, 1732-1932, Pink ......................................... 10.00
**Crown Ducal, Potty,** Gold Rim, Floral & Scroll On Ivory Glaze, 9 In. ................................... 20.00
**Crown Ducal, Tea Set,** Beige, Birds Of Paradise, Tile, Pot, & Pitcher ................................. 32.00

*Crown Milano glass was made by Frederick Shirley about 1890. It had a plain biscuit color with a satin finish. It was decorated with flowers, and often had large gold scrolls.*

| | |
|---|---|
| Crown Milano, Basket, Bride's, Floral, Silver Plate Holder, 7 1/4 In.Long | 1500.00 |
| Crown Milano, Bowl, Triangular, Enameled Flowers, Biscuit Finish | 395.00 |
| Crown Milano, Candlestick, Blue & Gold Floral, Pairpoint Silver Base, Pair | 650.00 |
| Crown Milano, Creamer, Floral Bouquets, Applied Reeded Handle, 5 In.High | 1050.00 |
| Crown Milano, Dish, Sweetmeat, Covered, Melon Ribbed, White, Roses & Leaves | 500.00 |
| Crown Milano, Dish, Sweetmeat, Embossed Gold Floral & Scroll On Ribbed | 250.00 |
| Crown Milano, Jar, Biscuit, Hobnail, Yellow Flowers, Gold Scrolls, Silver Lid | 600.00 |
| Crown Milano, Jar, Cookie, Covered, Gold & Pansies On Cream, Signed | 525.00 |
| Crown Milano, Jar, Sweetmeat, Pink To Cream, Multicolor Pansies, Gold Trim | 340.00 |
| Crown Milano, Jardiniere, Pansy Design, Signed, 7 In.High | 975.00 |
| Crown Milano, Lamp Base, Pansies And Gold Rings | 275.00 |
| Crown Milano, Muffineer, Egg Shape, Decorated With Flowers | 325.00 |
| Crown Milano, Pitcher, Floral Bouquet, Applied Reeded Handle, 8 1/4 In. | 1800.00 |
| Crown Milano, Salt & Pepper, Tomato, Mt.Washington | 60.00 |
| Crown Milano, Tray, Card, Scalloped, Folded Over Edges, Pansies On White | 175.00 |
| Crown Milano, Tumbler, Raised Gold Bows & Flower Chains, Red Wreath Signed | 325.00 |
| Crown Milano, Tumbler, Shiny, Signed Red Enamel Wreath, Crown, & Number | 325.00 |
| Crown Milano, Vase, Applied Reeded Handles, Raised Floral, Gold, 5 1/2 In. | 995.00 |
| Crown Milano, Vase, Biscuit Color, 2 Handled, Signed, 8 In.High | 695.00 |
| Crown Milano, Vase, Handled, Orchidlike Gold Outlined Floral On Ivory | 700.00 |
| Crown Milano, Vase, Multicolor Floral On Pink, Mottled Biscuit Base, 9 In. | 695.00 |
| Crown Milano, Vase, Stick, Gold Accented Multicolor Floral On Biscuit | 850.00 |
| Crown Tuscan, see Cambridge | |

*Cruets of glass or porcelain were made to hold vinegar or oil. They were especially popular during Victorian times.*

Cruet, see also, Amber Glass, Pressed Glass, and other glass sections

| | |
|---|---|
| Cruet Set, 2 Paneled Bottles, Open Salt, Silver Plate Heart-Handled Frame | 20.00 |
| Cruet Set, 4 Cruets, Pewter & Milk Glass Handle & Base | 40.00 |
| Cruet, Blown Glass, Applied Handle, 9 1/2 In.High | 15.00 |
| Cruet, Blue Opaque, Forget-Me-Not | 95.00 |
| Cruet, Blue, Applied Clear Handle, Cut Stopper, Flat Sides, 6 1/2 In. | 65.00 |
| Cruet, Bulbous, Beaded Swirl, Red & White, Clear Disc Band, Faceted Stopper | 30.00 |
| Cruet, Emerald Green, Enameled Flowers, 8 1/2 In. | 65.00 |
| Cruet, Fern Leaf, Sapphire Blue, Blue Stopper | 85.00 |
| Cruet, Green, Enameled Decoration Of Flowers & Leaves, Applied Handle | 25.00 |
| Cruet, Royal Crystal, 3 1/2 In. | 22.00 |

*Cup plates are small glass or china plates that held the cup, while a gentleman of the mid-nineteenth century drank his coffee or tea from the saucer. The most famous cup plates were made of glass at the Boston and Sandwich Factory located in Massachusetts. The L numbers refer to the book "American Glass Cup Plates" by Lee and Rose.*

Cup Plate, see also other glass & porcelain categories

| | |
|---|---|
| Cup Plate, "Gladstone For The Millions," glass | 85.00 |
| Cup Plate, Amethyst, L-321c | 85.00 |
| Cup Plate, Armitage Park, Enoch Wood, Porcelain, 4 1/2 In. | 44.00 |
| Cup Plate, Bunker Hill, L-642 | 14.00 |
| Cup Plate, Cadmus, L-610c | 14.00 |
| Cup Plate, Clear L-678 | 45.00 |
| Cup Plate, Clear, Dated 1831, L-659 | 29.00 |
| Cup Plate, Dark Blue, Stubbs Kent Longport Shell Design, Porcelain, 4 In. | 50.00 |
| Cup Plate, Eagle, Dated 1831, L-661 | 14.00 |
| Cup Plate, Garfield, Frosted Bust In Base | 30.00 |
| Cup Plate, Harrison, L-568 | 20.00 |
| Cup Plate, Heart, Opalescent | 48.00 |
| Cup Plate, Henry Clay, Lacy, Facing Right | 200.00 |
| Cup Plate, Henry Clay, Peacock Blue | 95.00 |
| Cup Plate, Lacy, Clear, Fort Pitt Glass Works | 50.00 |
| Cup Plate, Lacy, Clear, Midwestern | 50.00 |
| Cup Plate, Light Olive, L-502 | 60.00 |
| Cup Plate, Mayflower, Scroll, 3 1/2 In. | 12.50 |
| Cup Plate, Midwestern, Gray Blue | 125.00 |

| | |
|---|---:|
| Cup Plate, Milky Opal, L-522 | 20.00 |
| Cup Plate, Olive Green, L-374 | 60.00 |
| Cup Plate, Opalescent, L-465j | 50.00 |
| Cup Plate, Sheaf Of Wheat Border, L-28 | 17.00 |
| Cup Plate, Shell Border, L-245 | 14.00 |
| Cup Plate, Victoria, Lacy | 45.00 |
| Cup Plate, Washington, Star Rim, 3 1/2 In. | 12.50 |

*Currier & Ives made the famous American lithographs marked with their name from 1857 to 1907.*

| | |
|---|---:|
| Currier & Ives, A Midnight Race On The Mississippi, 1860 | 800.00 |
| Currier & Ives, American Speckled Brook Trout, 1864 | 450.00 |
| Currier & Ives, Bombardment & Seizure Of Cape Hatteras | 75.00 |
| Currier & Ives, Burial Of The Bird, Walnut Crisscross Frame | 20.00 |
| Currier & Ives, Cottage Life, Summer, 19 X 14 1/2 In. | 35.00 |
| Currier & Ives, Darktown Wedding, Send Off | 65.00 |
| Currier & Ives, Death Of President Lincoln, Black & White | 38.00 |
| Currier & Ives, Fast Trotters On Harlem Lane, N.Y., 1870 | 650.00 |
| Currier & Ives, Fruits Of The Seasons, 15 X 12 In. | 25.00 |
| Currier & Ives, Funeral Of President Lincoln, Black & White, Walnut Frame | 40.00 |
| Currier & Ives, Just My Style | 35.00 |
| Currier & Ives, Lake George, Framed, 11 1/2 X 13 1/2 In. | 65.00 |
| Currier & Ives, Landing Of The Pilgrims At Plymouth, Color, Framed | 70.00 |
| Currier & Ives, Little Caroline, Framed | 28.00 |
| Currier & Ives, National Game Of Baseball, Hoboken, N.J., 1866 | 7000.00 |
| Currier & Ives, New England Winter Scene, 1861 | 2800.00 |
| Currier & Ives, New York Bay, From Bay Ridge, L.I., 1860, Lithograph, Color | 300.00 |
| Currier & Ives, Pope Pius IX | 25.00 |
| Currier & Ives, Pope Pius Lying In State | 25.00 |
| Currier & Ives, Print, Little Brothers, Gold Frame | 35.00 |
| Currier & Ives, Staten Island & Narrows, From Fort Hamilton, 1861, Color | 300.00 |
| Currier & Ives, Stonewall Jackson In Uniform, Black & White, 12 X 16 In. | 55.00 |
| Currier & Ives, Summer, 1871 | 32.00 |
| Currier & Ives, The Celebrated Clipper Ship Bark "Grapeshot" | 95.00 |
| Currier & Ives, The Express Train, 1870 | 650.00 |
| Currier & Ives, The Home Of Washington, Mount Vernon, 16 1/4 X 21 1/4 | 150.00 |
| Currier & Ives, The Mill Stream, Color, Lithograph, Framed, 15 1/2 X 19 In. | 135.00 |
| Currier & Ives, The Old Farm Gate, Large Folio | 150.00 |
| Currier & Ives, The Old Farm House, 1872 | 325.00 |
| Currier & Ives, The Playful Family | 42.00 |
| Currier & Ives, The Queen Of Beauty | 28.00 |
| Currier & Ives, The Roadside Mill, 1870, Lithograph, Color, Small Folio | 25.00 |
| Currier & Ives, The Sacred Tomb Of The Blessed Virgin, Frame, 10 X 14 In. | 18.50 |
| Currier & Ives, The Soldier's Home, The Vision, Color, Small Folio, Frame | 56.00 |
| Currier & Ives, The Valley Of The Susquehanna | 300.00 |
| Currier & Ives, The Wedding Day | 35.00 |
| Currier & Ives, View Of Park Fountain & City Hall, N.Y., Small Folio | 125.00 |
| Currier & Ives, Winter Morning, 1861, Fannie F.Palmer, Small Folio | 58.00 |
| Currier & Ives, Winter Scene, Framed, 9 1/2 X 13 In. | 20.00 |
| Currier & Ives, Yosemite Falls, California | 75.00 |
| Currier, American Country Life, May Morning, 1855 | 325.00 |
| Currier, American Country Life, Summer's Evening, 1855 | 275.00 |
| Currier, Hainey At Dragoon Fight At Medelin, March 25, 1847, Color, Frame | 55.00 |
| Currier, James K.Polk, Mahogany Frame | 55.00 |
| Currier, Jas.Meyers, N.Y.C., Store Front, 1839, Lithograph, Billhead | 35.00 |
| Currier, Our Saviour, Lithograph, Color, Framed, 10 X 14 In. | 10.00 |
| Currier, President Zachary Taylor, Framed | 55.00 |
| Currier, Search The Scriptures | 25.00 |
| Currier, The Destruction Of Tea At Boston Harbor, Color, Lithograph | 300.00 |
| Currier, The Young Cavalier | 43.00 |
| Currier, The Young Cavalier, Framed | 45.00 |
| Currier, View Of Baltimore, Small Folio, Framed | 125.00 |
| Currier, Washington's Reception By The Ladies At Trenton, April, 1789 | 125.00 |
| Currier, William Penn's Treaty With The Indians, 1842 | 170.00 |

*Custard glass is an opaque glass sometimes known as buttermilk glass. It was first made after 1886 at the La Belle Glass Works, Bridgeport, Ohio.*

Custard Glass, Banana Boat, Argonaut Shell, Opalescent, Turned Up Sides .................................. 36.00
Custard Glass, Banana Boat, Autumn, Green ......................................................................................... 52.50
Custard Glass, Banana Boat, Chrysanthemum Sprig, Signed Northwood ........................................ 150.00
Custard Glass, Banana Boat, Grape & Cable, Blue ............................................................................. 325.00
Custard Glass, Banana Boat, Louis XV, Gold Trim, Footed ............................................ 110.00 To 190.00
Custard Glass, Basket, Cherries, Amber Handle, 6 In.High ................................................................ 175.00
Custard Glass, Basket, Handled, Cambridge, 11 In. ........................................................................... 115.00
Custard Glass, Berry Set, Cherry & Scales, 7 Piece .......................................................................... 425.00
Custard Glass, Berry Set, Ring & Band, 7 Piece ................................................................................ 450.00
Custard Glass, Bowl, Basket Weave, Three Fruits Inside, Marked N, 8 In. ....................................... 38.50
Custard Glass, Bowl, Berry, Chrysanthemum Sprig, Northwood In Script ........................................ 50.00
Custard Glass, Bowl, Berry, Inverted Fan & Feather, Small Size ....................................................... 40.00
Custard Glass, Bowl, Berry, Master, Fluted Scrolls, Gold Flower Band, Footed .............................. 95.00
Custard Glass, Bowl, Chrysanthemum Sprig, Colored Flower Band, Marked N ............................... 185.00
Custard Glass, Bowl, Grape & Cable, Marked N, 7 In. ....................................................... 50.00 To 60.00
Custard Glass, Bowl, Grape & Cable, Pedestal, 4 3/7 In.Diameter .................................................... 38.00
Custard Glass, Bowl, Ribbed, Opalescent, Green, Footed, 5 1/2 In. ................................................. 25.00
Custard Glass, Bowl, Scrolls With Flowers, Footed, Fluted, Scalloped Top ..................................... 95.00
Custard Glass, Bowl, Swan Handle, Marked Sowerby, C.1888 .......................................................... 25.00
Custard Glass, Box, Puff, Buckhorn ...................................................................................................... 60.00
Custard Glass, Butter, Argonaut Shell, Script Signed ........................................................................ 160.00
Custard Glass, Butter, Ivorna Verde ..................................................................................................... 120.00
Custard Glass, Butter, Louis XV, Gold Trim, Covered, Northwood ............................... 96.00 To 225.00
Custard Glass, Butter, Winged Scroll .................................................................................................... 90.00
Custard Glass, Compote, Bakewell Pears, Opalescent, 10 Petal Edge, Footed ............................... 90.00
Custard Glass, Compote, Berry, Intaglio, Blue Trim, Large Size ....................................................... 135.00
Custard Glass, Compote, Intaglio, Green Scroll, Gold Flowers, 9 In. ................................................ 165.00
Custard Glass, Compote, Jelly, Argonaut Shell, Signed Northwood In Script ................................... 85.00
Custard Glass, Compote, Jelly, Chrysanthemum Sprig ..................................................... 35.00 To 80.00
Custard Glass, Creamer & Spooner, Winged Scroll, Gold Feet & Trim ............................................. 125.00
Custard Glass, Creamer, Argonaut Shell, Script Signed ..................................................................... 100.00
Custard Glass, Creamer, Chrysanthemum Sprig, Gold Legs .............................................................. 45.00
Custard Glass, Creamer, Diamond Peg, Drum Shape, Roses, Miniature ............................................ 32.00
Custard Glass, Creamer, Edgar Nebraska High School, 4 3/4 In. High ............................................. 35.00
Custard Glass, Creamer, Louis XV, 4 1/2 In.High ............................................................. 55.00 To 95.00
Custard Glass, Creamer, Raspberry Design Band, Pedestal, McKee ................................................. 15.00
Custard Glass, Creamer, Rose Decoration, H.Lanesboro, 2 1/2 In.High ........................................... 28.00
Custard Glass, Cruet, Chrysanthemum Sprig, Painted Gold ............................................. 65.00 To 85.00
Custard Glass, Cruet, Inverted Fan & Feather ..................................................................................... 500.00
Custard Glass, Cruet, Louis XV, Stopper .............................................................................................. 200.00
Custard Glass, Cup, Chocolate, Diamond Peg, Roses ........................................................................ 22.00
Custard Glass, Cup, Diamond Peg, Copper Luster Rim, Miniature ..................................................... 30.00
Custard Glass, Goblet, Rose, "Girard, Kansas" .................................................................................... 47.00
Custard Glass, Hat, Fedora, White, Blue Trim ..................................................................................... 25.00
Custard Glass, Inkwell, 2 Pieces ........................................................................................................... 35.00
Custard Glass, Lamp Base, Green .......................................................................................................... 98.00
Custard Glass, Lamp, Art Nouveau Style, Green & Yellow, 9 1/8 In.High ....................................... 35.00
Custard Glass, Muffineer, Barrel ............................................................................................................ 58.00
Custard Glass, Muffineer, Maize, Green Leaves, Cylindrical, Libbey ................................................ 185.00
Custard Glass, Muffineer, Melon, Blue .................................................................................................. 85.00
Custard Glass, Mug, Band Of Alternating Stars & Punties At Base, 3 1/4 In. .................................. 22.50
Custard Glass, Mug, Beaded Band At Base, Souvenir, Grand Rapids, Mich. .................................... 25.00
Custard Glass, Mug, Beer, Troubadour Scene ...................................................................................... 50.00
Custard Glass, Mug, Diamond Peg, Krystol, Roses, Beloit, Kansas .................................................. 35.00
Custard Glass, Mug, New Duluth, Minn., 2 3/8 In.High ...................................................................... 25.00
Custard Glass, Mug, Tom & Jerry, McKee ............................................................................................ 3.00
Custard Glass, Pitcher, Chrysanthemum Sprig, 4 Gold Legs, 5 In.High ........................................... 55.00
Custard Glass, Pitcher, Diamond Peg, Copper Luster Rim, 4 1/2 In. ................................................. 32.00
Custard Glass, Pitcher, Measuring, Green, McKee, Pink ..................................................................... 8.00
Custard Glass, Pitcher, Water, Blue Floral With Red Centers, Green Leaves .................................... 175.00
Custard Glass, Pitcher, Water, Louis XV, Gold Trim, Northwood .................................. 125.00 To 155.00
Custard Glass, Plate, Grape & Cable, Basket Weave Reverse ............................................................ 30.00
Custard Glass, Plate, Grape With Nutmeg, Basket Weave Underside, N, 8 In. ................................ 35.00
Custard Glass, Plate, Holly, Green, McKee ........................................................................................... 5.00
Custard Glass, Rose Bowl, Beaded Cable, Ruffled Edge, Footed, Signed N .................................... 85.00
Custard Glass, Rose Bowl, Finecut & Roses, 3 Footed, 4 1/2 In.High .............................................. 87.50

Custard Glass, Rose Bowl, Persian Medallion, Green Shading At Top, 4 In. .......... 65.00
Custard Glass, Salt & Pepper, Gold Intaglio & Relief Florals, Pewter Tops .......... 88.00
Custard Glass, Saltshaker, Geneva .......... 35.00
Custard Glass, Sauce, Argonaut Shell, Gold Trim, Northwood .......... 32.50 To 45.00
Custard Glass, Sauce, Beaded Swag, Souvenir .......... 27.00
Custard Glass, Sauce, Chrysanthemum Sprig, Northwood In Script .......... 65.00
Custard Glass, Sauce, Grape Band, Opaque, Footed, 4 1/2 In. .......... 35.00
Custard Glass, Sauceboat, Chrysanthemum Sprig, Gold Trim, Northwood .......... 60.00
Custard Glass, Shade, Gas, Opalescent, Flint .......... 11.00
Custard Glass, Spooner, Chrysanthemum Sprig, Flower Band .......... 67.00 To 88.00
Custard Glass, Spooner, Diamond Peg, Roses .......... 32.00
Custard Glass, Spooner, Fluted Scrolls, Gold Flower Band, Footed, Northwood .......... 55.00
Custard Glass, Spooner, Louis XV, Gold Trim, Northwood .......... 40.00 To 95.00
Custard Glass, Spooner, Winged Scroll .......... 45.00
Custard Glass, Sugar & Creamer, Breakfast, Little Gem .......... 80.00
Custard Glass, Sugar & Creamer, Cover, Ring Band, Wild Rose Decoration, Gold .......... 135.00
Custard Glass, Sugar & Creamer, Louis XV, Gold Trim, Footed, Northwood .......... 130.00
Custard Glass, Sugar, Argonaut Shell, Script Signed .......... 70.00
Custard Glass, Sugar, Little Gem .......... 50.00
Custard Glass, Sugar, Louis XV .......... 95.00 To 110.00
Custard Glass, Sugar, Maple Leaf .......... 40.00
Custard Glass, Syrup, Geneva, Red & Green Decoration .......... 210.00
Custard Glass, Table Set, Argonaut Shell, Gold, Cover, Northwood, 3 Piece .......... 325.00
Custard Glass, Table Set, Chrysanthemum Sprig, Gold Trim, 3 Piece .......... 210.00
Custard Glass, Table Set, Intaglio, Blue Trim, 4 Piece .......... 365.00
Custard Glass, Table Set, Maple Leaf, 4 Piece .......... 565.00
Custard Glass, Table Set, Memphis, Green, Gold Trim, 4 Piece .......... 225.00
Custard Glass, Table Set, Northwood Fan, Diamond Co., 4 Piece .......... 475.00
Custard Glass, Toothpick, Charles City, Iowa .......... 27.50
Custard Glass, Toothpick, Harvard, Souvenir Marengo, Ill. .......... 25.00
Custard Glass, Toothpick, Little Gem, Gold Beading, 4 Gem Feet, Iowa .......... 25.00
Custard Glass, Toothpick, Putney Band .......... 40.00
Custard Glass, Toothpick, Shelbina, Mo. .......... 30.00
Custard Glass, Toothpick, Tuscola Public Library, Ill. .......... 24.50
Custard Glass, Tray, Card, Argonaut Shell, Opalescent White To Yellow, N .......... 25.00
Custard Glass, Tumbler, Argonaut Shell, Gold .......... 55.00
Custard Glass, Tumbler, Diamond Peg, Krystol .......... 35.00
Custard Glass, Tumbler, Diamond Peg, Roses .......... 30.00
Custard Glass, Tumbler, Geneva, Green Shells & Gilt .......... 30.00 To 45.00
Custard Glass, Tumbler, Grape & Arches .......... 40.00
Custard Glass, Tumbler, Green Opaque, McKee .......... 12.00
Custard Glass, Tumbler, Intaglio, Green Trim .......... 35.00 To 50.00
Custard Glass, Tumbler, Ivory, McKee .......... 12.00
Custard Glass, Tumbler, Louis XV, Gold Trim .......... 28.50 To 56.00
Custard Glass, Tumbler, Maple Leaf, Gold Trim .......... 45.00
Custard Glass, Tumbler, Maple Leaf, Green, Gold Trim .......... 50.00
Custard Glass, Tumbler, Tarentum's Victoria, Gold .......... 30.00
Custard Glass, Tumbler, Whiskey, Diamond Peg .......... 40.00
Custard Glass, Tumbler, Winged Scroll .......... 45.00
Custard Glass, Vase, Diamond Peg, Roses, Copper Luster Rim, 6 In. .......... 25.00
Custard Glass, Vase, Drape, Nutmeg Stain, Northwood, 9 In. .......... 45.00
Custard Glass, Vase, Fluted, Cripple Creek, Colorado, 6 In. .......... 12.00
Custard Glass, Vase, Hand Holding Torch, 8 In.High .......... 45.00
Custard Glass, Vase, Hat, Berry Design On Brim .......... 25.00
Custard Glass, Vase, Pulpit Top With Clear Edge, Swirled, Bulbous .......... 25.00
Custard Glass, Vase, Rose, Souvenir Skeedee, Okla., 6 In.High .......... 45.00
Custard Glass, Water Set, Intaglio, Blue Trim, 6 Piece .......... 365.00

*Cut glass has been made since ancient times, but the large majority of the
pieces now for sale date from the brilliant period of glass design, 1880 to
1905. These pieces had elaborate geometric designs with a deep miter cut.*

Cut Glass, Atomizer, Fan & Comet, Heavy Brilliant, 5 In.High .......... 32.00
Cut Glass, Atomizer, Paperweight, Marked Tuthill, 10 In. .......... 135.00
Cut Glass, Atomizer, Perfume, Cobalt To Clear, Maltese Cross, Czechoslovakia .......... 45.00
Cut Glass, Banana Boat, Hobnail, Starred Diamond Point Buttons, 11 1/2 In. .......... 110.00
Cut Glass, Basket, Double Thumbprint Handle, Intaglio & Crosshatching .......... 250.00
Cut Glass, Basket, Fan, Hobstar, Notch, Diamond, & Flute, Crimped, Hawkes .......... 185.00

| | |
|---|---|
| Cut Glass, Basket, Flattened Body, Cut Handle, Step Cut Base, C.B.Monogram | 300.00 |
| Cut Glass, Basket, Harvard, Horizontal Steps, Double Handle, 14 1/2 In. | 375.00 |
| Cut Glass, Basket, Hobstar, Fan, & Bull's-Eye, Floral In Handle, 6 In. | 70.00 |
| Cut Glass, Basket, Intaglio Floral & Leaf, Intaglio Leaf Handle, Libbey | 95.00 |
| Cut Glass, Basket, Intaglio Flower, Bull's-Eye & Notched Prism Handle | 300.00 |
| Cut Glass, Basket, Twisted Rope Handle, Hobstar, Pinwheel, Prism, & Fan | 165.00 |
| Cut Glass, Bell, C.1850, 5 In.High | 27.50 |
| Cut Glass, Bobeche, Diamond Bull's-Eye, 3 1/2 In., Pair | 7.00 |
| Cut Glass, Bobeche, 10 Scallops With Prisms, 4 In., Pair | 15.00 |
| Cut Glass, Book, Diamonds, Hobstars On Back, Monogram K.P., 4 In.High | 150.00 |
| Cut Glass, Bottle, Bitters, Tiffany Sterling Top, Diamond & Prism, St.Louis | 150.00 |
| Cut Glass, Bottle, Cane, Ornate Silver Top, 4 3/4 In.High | 65.00 |
| Cut Glass, Bottle, Cologne, Cosmos & Foliage, 4 1/2 In.High | 34.50 |
| Cut Glass, Bottle, Cologne, Diamond Cut Stopper, Croesus Pattern, 5 1/2 In. | 135.00 |
| Cut Glass, Bottle, Dresser, Hobstar, Crosshatching, & Fan, Hollow Stopper | 35.00 |
| Cut Glass, Bottle, Oil & Vinegar, Etched, Mushroom Stopper, Signed Hawkes | 32.00 |
| Cut Glass, Bottle, Oil & Vinegar, Hawkes | 45.00 |
| Cut Glass, Bottle, Pepper Sauce, Hobstar, Zipper, & Strawberry Diamond | 125.00 |
| Cut Glass, Bottle, Smelling Salts, Cane, Tiffany Sterling Screw Cap, 7 In. | 37.50 |
| Cut Glass, Bottle, Smelling Salts, Russian & Clear Button, Sterling Cover | 75.00 |
| Cut Glass, Bottle, Water, Diamond & Fan, 8 In.High, Pair | 150.00 |
| Cut Glass, Bowl & Base, Punch, Buzz Star, Crosscut, & Diamond, 10 In. Wide | 425.00 |
| Cut Glass, Bowl & Pitcher, Hobstar, Split, Star, & Panel, Scalloped Edges | 500.00 |
| Cut Glass, Bowl & Underplate, Bouillon, Handled, Engraved Floral, Hawkes | 15.00 |
| Cut Glass, Bowl & Underplate, Mayonnaise, Allover Cut, 6 1/4 In.Bowl | 95.00 |
| Cut Glass, Bowl & Underplate, Mayonnaise, Harvard & Floral, American | 45.00 |
| Cut Glass, Bowl & Underplate, Punch, Pinwheel, Cane, & Hobstar, 10 In. | 210.00 |
| Cut Glass, Bowl, Acid Cut, Scalloped Edge, 7 1/2 X 3 In. | 85.00 |
| Cut Glass, Bowl, Allover Cuttings, Low, 9 In.Diameter | 100.00 |
| Cut Glass, Bowl, Allover Cuttings, Serrated Rim, 8 In. | 48.00 |
| Cut Glass, Bowl, Banana, Harvard, 5 Intaglio Flowers On Sides, 11 1/2 In. | 125.00 |
| Cut Glass, Bowl, Berry, Pinwheel & Fan, Sawtooth Edge, 8 In.Diameter | 35.00 |
| Cut Glass, Bowl, Berry, Single Stars, Miters, & 3 Hobstars, Hawkes, 8 In. | 110.00 |
| Cut Glass, Bowl, Buzz & Star, 8 In.Diameter | 65.00 |
| Cut Glass, Bowl, Cactus, Libbey, 6 X 1 1/2 In. | 55.00 |
| Cut Glass, Bowl, Canoe Shape, Hobstar & Starred Button, Floral, 12 1/2 In. | 150.00 |
| Cut Glass, Bowl, Center, Allover Cutting, 3 Footed, 7 1/2 In.Wide | 75.00 |
| Cut Glass, Bowl, Center, Allover Cuttings, 9 In.Wide | 150.00 |
| Cut Glass, Bowl, Console, Almond Cut Top, Round & Oval Thumbprints, Hawkes | 150.00 |
| Cut Glass, Bowl, Deep Allover Cuttings, 8 X 3 3/4 In. | 55.00 |
| Cut Glass, Bowl, Dessert, Cluster Variant, American, 6 In. | 50.00 |
| Cut Glass, Bowl, Dessert, Copper Wheel Engraved Holly & Berries, Libbey | 58.35 |
| Cut Glass, Bowl, Dessert, Persian, Hawkes, Monogram Blank | 60.00 |
| Cut Glass, Bowl, Diamond Point & Fan, 8 In. | 65.00 |
| Cut Glass, Bowl, Double Handles, Hobstar, Cane, Strawberry Diamond, & Fan | 65.00 |
| Cut Glass, Bowl, Etched Holly Berry & Leaf, Blaze Edge, Libbey, 7 In. | 43.00 |
| Cut Glass, Bowl, Etched Orchid, 12 In.Square Top | 18.00 |
| Cut Glass, Bowl, Fan & Hobstar, 2 Strawberry Diamonds, 8 In. | 65.00 |
| Cut Glass, Bowl, Fan & Hobstar, 6 In.Wide | 20.00 |
| Cut Glass, Bowl, Fan, Diamond, & Crosscutting, 6 In. | 20.00 |
| Cut Glass, Bowl, Finger, Band Of Strawberry Diamond At Top | 7.00 |
| Cut Glass, Bowl, Finger, Diamonds, Copper Wheel Fleur-De-Lis, Star Base | 4.50 |
| Cut Glass, Bowl, Finger, Mum, Gravic, Signed Hawkes | 75.00 |
| Cut Glass, Bowl, Finger, Punty With Flute | 15.00 |
| Cut Glass, Bowl, Finger, Scallops From Base To 5/8 In. From Top, Libbey | 7.50 |
| Cut Glass, Bowl, Florene, 6 Sided, Corning, Hoare, 7 In.Diameter | 65.00 |
| Cut Glass, Bowl, Fruit, Serrated Rim, Allover Deep Cuttings, 8 In. | 55.00 |
| Cut Glass, Bowl, Grape & Leaf, Cut To Clear, Red Flashed, 13 1/2 In. | 79.00 |
| Cut Glass, Bowl, Gravic Gray Chrysanthemums & Leaves, 3 Footed, Hawkes | 250.00 |
| Cut Glass, Bowl, Greek Key, Signed Hawkes, 7 1/4 X 3 1/4 In. | 125.00 |
| Cut Glass, Bowl, Handle, Scalloped Edge, 6 In.Wide | 22.00 |
| Cut Glass, Bowl, Harvard, Low, 8 In. | 110.00 |
| Cut Glass, Bowl, Hinsberger, Patent 5/19/08, American, 5 1/2 X 2 3/4 In. | 60.00 |
| Cut Glass, Bowl, Hobstar & Crosscut Diamond, Libbey, 9 In.Diameter | 225.00 |
| Cut Glass, Bowl, Hobstar & Crosshatching, Star Base, 7 In. | 35.00 |
| Cut Glass, Bowl, Hobstar & Fan, American, 8 X 3 1/2 In. | 55.00 |

Cut Glass, Bowl, Hobstar, Fan, & Crosshatching, Star Base, 4 1/2 In.Diameter ............................. 18.00
Cut Glass, Bowl, Hobstar, Prism, Fan, & Strawberry Diamond, Maple City ............................ 65.00
Cut Glass, Bowl, Hobstars, Hawkes, 7 1/2 In.Diameter ............................................ 65.00
Cut Glass, Bowl, Hobstars, 8 In. .................................................................. 95.00
Cut Glass, Bowl, Hobstars, 9 1/2 In. ............................................................. 95.00
Cut Glass, Bowl, Hunt's Royal, American, 8 In.Diameter ......................................... 185.00
Cut Glass, Bowl, Hunt's Royal, Low, American, 8 In. ............................................ 195.00
Cut Glass, Bowl, Intaglio Flower, Leaf, & Butterfly, 5 3/4 In.Diameter ........................ 35.00
Cut Glass, Bowl, Maple Leaf & Orchid Panel, Scalloped Top, Signed, 9 In. .................... 95.00
Cut Glass, Bowl, Oblong, Etched Floral & Butterflies, Scale, Pa., 19 In. ...................... 20.00
Cut Glass, Bowl, Oblong, Shell Shape Sides, 10 In. .............................................. 45.00
Cut Glass, Bowl, Openwork Sterling Rim, Fluted, Frosted Geometrics, 11 In. ................. 75.00
Cut Glass, Bowl, Orange, Hobstar, Nailhead, & Blaze, 10 1/2 In.Long .......................... 130.00
Cut Glass, Bowl, Oval, Butterfly & Rose, Sawtooth Edge, 8 X 11 1/4 In. ....................... 89.00
Cut Glass, Bowl, Oval, Silver Edge, 9 1/4 In. .................................................... 37.00
Cut Glass, Bowl, Panels Of Hobstar & Fan, Signed Taylor & Co., 9 In. ........................ 110.00
Cut Glass, Bowl, Pedestal, Diamond Point, Crosshatching, & Floral, 9 1/4 In. ............... 135.00
Cut Glass, Bowl, Pinwheel, Fan, & Palm Leaf, 8 In. .............................................. 40.00
Cut Glass, Bowl, Pinwheel, Hobstar, & Strawberry Diamond, Clarke, 8 In. .................... 115.00
Cut Glass, Bowl, Punch, Hobstars, American, 12 1/2 In. .......................................... 225.00
Cut Glass, Bowl, Punch, Inverted Derby Shape, Butterflies, Pairpoint ......................... 375.00
Cut Glass, Bowl, Punch, J.Hoare & Co., Corning, 1853, 14 In.Diameter ....................... 500.00
Cut Glass, Bowl, Punch, Pinwheel, Fan, & Hobstar, 2 Piece .................................... 350.00
Cut Glass, Bowl, Punch, Standard, Hobstar, Cane, & Star, Scalloped Rims ................... 325.00
Cut Glass, Bowl, Punch, 2 Piece, Hobstar, Strawberry Diamond, & Fan, Hawkes ............ 1200.00
Cut Glass, Bowl, Round, Scalloped Edge, 7 1/4 In.Diameter .................................... 47.00
Cut Glass, Bowl, Salad, Russian, Ambassador Button, 32-Point Star Base, 9 In. ............. 275.00
Cut Glass, Bowl, Scalloped Edge, Hawkes, 7 In. Diameter ...................................... 40.00
Cut Glass, Bowl, Scalloped Edges, Shallow, Corning, J.Hoare & Co., 8 In. ................... 45.00
Cut Glass, Bowl, Scalloped Edges, Shallow, Libbey, 8 In. ...................................... 90.00
Cut Glass, Bowl, Scalloped Top, Signed Elite In Maple Leaf, 6 In.Diameter ................. 45.00
Cut Glass, Bowl, Scalloped, Hobstar In Diamond, Rayed Base, Libbey, 8 In. ................. 65.00
Cut Glass, Bowl, Scalloped, Libbey, 7 In.Diameter .............................................. 75.00
Cut Glass, Bowl, Serving, Diamond Points, Star Base, Stuart, 11 X 9 In. .................... 40.00
Cut Glass, Bowl, Shallow, Deep Cuttings, 8 3/4 In. .............................................. 58.50
Cut Glass, Bowl, Signed Sinclaire, Blue, Disc Base, 5 1/4 In. ................................. 30.00
Cut Glass, Bowl, Sinclaire, 5 1/2 In.Wide, 1 In.High ............................................ 25.00
Cut Glass, Bowl, Square, Allover Cut, Hawkes, 8 In.Across .................................... 175.00
Cut Glass, Bowl, Square, Flashing Hobs, Miter Cuts, Scalloped Top ........................... 48.00
Cut Glass, Bowl, Star Cut Bottom, 5 1/4 In.Diameter ........................................... 6.50
Cut Glass, Bowl, Star With Fan Rays, Hobstar & Flashed Rim, 8 In. .......................... 87.00
Cut Glass, Bowl, Sterling Rim, Sinclaire Type, 7 In.Diameter .................................. 80.00
Cut Glass, Bowl, Straus's Drape, 9 In.Diameter ................................................. 175.00
Cut Glass, Bowl, Strawberry Diamond & Fan, Shallow, 8 In. ................................... 85.00
Cut Glass, Bowl, Strawberry Diamond, 8 In. ..................................................... 175.00
Cut Glass, Bowl, Strawberry, American, 9 In.Diameter .......................................... 95.00
Cut Glass, Bowl, Trilobed, Allover Cut, Libbey, 7 1/2 In.Diameter ........................... 85.00
Cut Glass, Box, Butterfly In Net, Hinged, Sinclaire, 3 In.High, 5 In.Across ................. 110.00
Cut Glass, Box, Collar & Cuff, Hinged Silver Collar, 6 Sided, Cane Vesicas ................. 450.00
Cut Glass, Box, Covered, Intaglio Pear & Leaves, Diamond & Star, 7 1/4 In. ............... 110.00
Cut Glass, Box, Glove, Hinged Silver Collar, 6 Sided, Cane Vesicas .......................... 325.00
Cut Glass, Box, Handkerchief, Hinged Silver Collar, Square, Cane Vesicas .................. 295.00
Cut Glass, Box, Hinged Silver Plate Top, Engraved Butterfly, Sinclaire ...................... 110.00
Cut Glass, Box, Hinged, Arcadia, Star Base, Oval, American, 5 1/2 X 4 X 3 In. ............. 175.00
Cut Glass, Box, Hinged, Oval, Sunburst Pattern, 5 In.Long ................................... 250.00
Cut Glass, Box, Hobstar On Cover, Hobstar & Prism, American, 5 In.Diameter .............. 65.00
Cut Glass, Box, Jewel, Hinged Cover, 5 1/4 In. Diameter ...................................... 85.00
Cut Glass, Box, Powder, Hinged, Intaglio Daisy, Thumbprint Edge, Silver Rim ............. 75.00
Cut Glass, Box, Russian Top & Bottom, Diamond Buttons, 5 1/2 In.Diameter ............... 325.00
Cut Glass, Box, Sterling Knob, Diamonds, Hawkes, 4 3/8 In.Long ............................ 175.00
Cut Glass, Bucket, Ice, Allover Cut, Tab Handles ............................................... 95.00
Cut Glass, Bucket, Ice, Harvard & Hobstar, Harvard Tabs, American .......................... 150.00
Cut Glass, Bucket, Ice, Hobstar, Fan, & Crosshatching, Stars On Tabs ....................... 85.00
Cut Glass, Bucket, Ice, Hobstar, Strawberry Diamond, & Fan, Hobstar Base .................. 85.00
Cut Glass, Bucket, Ice, Hobstar, Strawberry Diamond, Hobnail, & Cane, American ......... 95.00
Cut Glass, Bucket, Ice, Silver Rim & Handle, Strawberry Diamond & Fan ..................... 85.00

Cut Glass, Bucket, Ice, Silver Trim, Hawkes, 6 In. High ............................................................ 17.50
Cut Glass, Bucket, Ice, Triple Notched Handles, Curved Miter & Cane Panels ................. 95.00
Cut Glass, Butter Pat, Hobstar Center, Crosshatching, Diamond, & Fan ........................... 12.00
Cut Glass, Butter Pat, Serrated Edges, Hawkes, 2 1/2 In.Diameter ................................... 45.00
Cut Glass, Butter Pat, Signed Hawkes, Allover Cut ............................................................. 35.00
Cut Glass, Butter Pat, Strawberry Diamond & Fan, Handled, 4 In. ...................................... 9.50
Cut Glass, Butter Pat, Strawberry Diamond, Scalloped Edge, 3 In. .................................... 17.50
Cut Glass, Butter, Fan, Strawberry Diamond, & Hobstar, Round ....................................... 245.00
Cut Glass, Butter, Faceted Knob On Dome, Scalloped Base, 8 In.Diameter ................... 155.00
Cut Glass, Butter, Geometric Bands, Rosette Flowers, Underplate .................................... 65.00
Cut Glass, Butter, Harvard & Floral, American ................................................................... 115.00
Cut Glass, Butter, Harvard, Criss Cross, Fern, & Floral, Faceted Knob ........................... 195.00
Cut Glass, Butter, Hobstar, Strawberry Diamond, & Hobnail, Dome Top ......................... 225.00
Cut Glass, Butter, Monarch, Covered, American ............................................................... 225.00
Cut Glass, Butter, Star & Diamond Dome, Notched Finial, Rayed & Notched ................. 135.00
Cut Glass, Candlestick, Air Twist Stem, Signed Libbey, 8 In.High ..................................... 65.00
Cut Glass, Candlestick, Allover Russian, Teardrop Center, American ............................... 250.00
Cut Glass, Candlestick, Double Teardrop, Pair ................................................................. 425.00
Cut Glass, Candlestick, English Cut, Folded Top & Base, Hawkes, 10 In., Pair ............... 650.00
Cut Glass, Candlestick, Faceted Knob Stem With Bubble, 5 In.High .................................. 65.00
Cut Glass, Candlestick, Flute Socket, Faceted & Knob Stem, 7 3/4 In., Pair ................... 110.00
Cut Glass, Candlestick, Hollow Body, Roundel & Hobstar, Hawkes, Pair ........................ 175.00
Cut Glass, Candlestick, Leafage, Circular Foot, 7 In.High, C.1888, Pair ........................... 40.00
Cut Glass, Candlestick, Paneled Teardrop Stem, Star Base, American, Pair ................... 235.00
Cut Glass, Candlestick, Paneled, Teardrop Stem, Rayed Base, 6 1/4 In., Pair ................. 85.00
Cut Glass, Candlestick, Paneled, Teardrop Stem, Star Base, Hawkes, 6 In., Pair ............ 75.00
Cut Glass, Candlestick, Russian, Teardrop Center, 8 1/4 In.High ..................................... 250.00
Cut Glass, Candlestick, Step Top, Teardrop In Base, Cane & Floral, Pair ....................... 375.00
Cut Glass, Candlestick, Teardrop Knobbed Stem, 10 In.High, Pair ................................... 135.00
Cut Glass, Candlestick, Teardrop Stem, Cornflower, Leaf, & Swirl, Pair ........................... 185.00
Cut Glass, Canoe, Harvard & Floral, 8 1/2 In. ................................................................... 35.00
Cut Glass, Canoe, Harvard, 24 Point Hobstar Base, 11 1/2 In. Long .............................. 125.00
Cut Glass, Canoe, Harvard, 8 In. ........................................................... 112.00 To 150.00
Cut Glass, Carafe, Buzz & Fan ........................................................................................... 60.00
Cut Glass, Carafe, Drape, Straus ...................................................................................... 75.00
Cut Glass, Carafe, Hobstars, Fans, & Diamonds, Signed Shreve .................................. 125.00
Cut Glass, Carafe, Lotus, Egginton .................................................................................. 125.00
Cut Glass, Carafe, Mushroom Shape, Hobstar Band, Strawberry Diamond, & Fan ........ 55.00
Cut Glass, Carafe, Notched Panels Neck, Diamond Band Shoulder, Star Base ............... 50.00
Cut Glass, Carafe, Pinwheel & Other Cuttings ................................................................... 45.00
Cut Glass, Carafe, Water, Cobalt To Clear, Bull's-Eye, Split, Fan, & Rose ...................... 30.00
Cut Glass, Carafe, Water, Florence .................................................................................... 48.00
Cut Glass, Carafe, Water, Fluted Neck, Buzz Star & Crosscutting .................................... 32.00
Cut Glass, Carafe, Water, Gravic, Carnation, Hawkes .................................................... 140.00
Cut Glass, Carafe, Water, Hobstar & Fan, Hawkes, 7 3/4 In. ........................................... 68.00
Cut Glass, Carafe, Water, Pinwheel & Fan, 24 Point Star Base ...................................... 57.50
Cut Glass, Card Holders, Pyramid Shaped, Set Of 12 ...................................................... 24.00
Cut Glass, Celery, Clarke, 11 1/2 In. Long ........................................................................ 87.00
Cut Glass, Celery, Crosscut & Checkered Diamond, Hobstar, & Fan, American .............. 60.00
Cut Glass, Celery, Fan & English Diamond Block, C.1820, 8 1/2 In. High ........................ 80.00
Cut Glass, Celery, Hobstar, Cane, Crosshatching, & Fan, 11 1/2 In. ............................... 50.00
Cut Glass, Celery, Hobstar, Diamond, & Fan, Hawkes, 5 X 11 In. .................................... 70.00
Cut Glass, Celery, Hobstar, Strawberry Diamond, & Hobnail, American ........................... 35.00
Cut Glass, Celery, Hunt's Royal, American ...................................................................... 150.00
Cut Glass, Celery, Lee, Flint, Pair ...................................................................................... 95.00
Cut Glass, Celery, Oval, Fan Center, Crosshatching, Hobstar, & Pinwheel ..................... 35.00
Cut Glass, Celery, Strawberry Diamond, Hobstar, & Medallions ...................................... 38.50
Cut Glass, Centerpiece, Cane & Thumbprint, Silver Bronze Stem & Base ..................... 325.00
Cut Glass, Centerpiece, Console, Vesica, Hobstar, & Strawberry Diamond ................... 225.00
Cut Glass, Champagne, Engraved Border, Cut Prisms, 5 1/4 In.High ............................... 16.00
Cut Glass, Champagne, Greek Key & Laurel, Sinclaire ...................................................... 25.00
Cut Glass, Champagne, Hobstar Diamond & Fan, Knob Stem With Bubble ....................... 37.50
Cut Glass, Champagne, Hollow Stem, Copper Wheel Engraved Band & Garlands .......... 12.00
Cut Glass, Champagne, Hollow Stem, Hoare, 5 In.High ................................................... 90.00
Cut Glass, Champagne, Hollow Stem, Prisms, Floral Garlands, Wheat, Ferns ................ 22.80
Cut Glass, Champagne, Kalana Lily, Dorflinger, 1905 ........................................ 45.00 To 60.00

| | |
|---|---|
| Cut Glass, Champagne, Knob Stemmed, Signed Hawkes | 8.00 |
| Cut Glass, Champagne, Paneled, Double Facet Cut Knob Stem, C.1800 | 15.00 |
| Cut Glass, Champagne, Silhouette, Opalescent Squirrel Stem, Libbey | 125.00 |
| Cut Glass, Champagne, Webb | 12.00 |
| Cut Glass, Chocolate Pot On Stand, Silver Plate, Collar, Cover, & Handle | 95.00 |
| Cut Glass, Claret, Louis XIV, Monogrammed, Hawkes, 6 3/4 In.High | 75.00 |
| Cut Glass, Cologne, Engraved Bird & Floral Medallions, Signed Hawkes | 75.00 |
| Cut Glass, Cologne, Geometrics, 6 In. | 25.00 |
| Cut Glass, Cologne, Hobstar, Fan, & Crosshatching, Hobstar Base, 6 1/2 In. | 65.00 |
| Cut Glass, Cologne, Lay Down, Harvard, 16 In. | 45.00 |
| Cut Glass, Compote, Diamond & Horizontal Step, C.1800, 7 X 4 In. | 55.00 |
| Cut Glass, Compote, Engraved Leaves, Hollow Stem, Turned Rim, C.1800, 9 In. | 50.00 |
| Cut Glass, Compote, Fan, Star, & Hobstar, Notched Stem, Folded Edge, 9 In. | 90.00 |
| Cut Glass, Compote, Feathered Fan, Hobstar, & Crosshatching, 7 X 6 In. | 70.00 |
| Cut Glass, Compote, Footed, Octagon Diamonds, Large Stars, 8 X 5 1/2 In. | 165.00 |
| Cut Glass, Compote, Gravic Blackberry, Flaring, Pedestal, Hawkes, 6 In.High | 400.00 |
| Cut Glass, Compote, Hobstar & Fan, Skirted Notched Base, 5 1/2 In., Pair | 125.00 |
| Cut Glass, Compote, Hobstar & Fan, Triple Diamond Center, Star Base | 95.00 |
| Cut Glass, Compote, Hobstar & Vesica, Step Cut Base, 5 In.High | 55.00 |
| Cut Glass, Compote, Hobstar, Cane, Fan, & Checkering, 10 In. High | 120.00 |
| Cut Glass, Compote, Hobstar, Diamond Point, & Vesica, Step Cut Stem, 6 In. | 110.00 |
| Cut Glass, Compote, Hobstars, Paperweight Standard, 5 1/2 In.High | 350.00 |
| Cut Glass, Compote, Leaf & Hobstar, Topaz Stem, 8 In. | 250.00 |
| Cut Glass, Compote, Miniature, Double Teardrop Stem, Dutch, C.1820 | 85.00 |
| Cut Glass, Compote, Old Colony, Dorflinger, 7 3/4 X 8 1/2 In. | 175.00 |
| Cut Glass, Compote, Paneled, Cut Stem, Step Base, Blown, C.1800, 11 1/2 In. | 75.00 |
| Cut Glass, Compote, Scalloped Base, American, 9 In.High | 87.50 |
| Cut Glass, Compote, Serrated Edge, Tuthill, 6 X 4 1/2 In. | 98.00 |
| Cut Glass, Compote, Swag, Star, & Geometric, Star Base, Plain Stem, 5 In. | 38.00 |
| Cut Glass, Compote, Teardrop, Hobstar, Star, & Strawberry, 7 1/2 In.High, Pair | 175.00 |
| Cut Glass, Compote, 2 Gilt Metal Grotesque Winged Serpents Support, 10 In. | 170.00 |
| Cut Glass, Condiment Set, Paneled, Silver Plate Holder, 3 Piece | 20.00 |
| Cut Glass, Console Set, Cobalt Blue, Square Base Bowl, 3 Piece | 450.00 |
| Cut Glass, Cooler, 2 Florence Hobstars, Hobstar & Crosshatching, 7 In. | 60.00 |
| Cut Glass, Cordial, Blown, Engraved, Amelung Type, Square Stepped Base, 1750 | 18.00 |
| Cut Glass, Cordial, Cut Stem & Bowl, Engraved, C.1800, 3 1/2 In. | 9.00 |
| Cut Glass, Cordial, Hobstar, Cane, Fan, & Star, Tulip Shape Top, Ball Stem | 21.75 |
| Cut Glass, Cordial, Paneled, Engraved, C.1800 | 9.00 |
| Cut Glass, Cordial, Tulip Shape Top, Hobstar, Can, Fan, & Star, Ball Stem | 21.45 |
| Cut Glass, Creamer, Engraved Frosted Ribbon, Pedestal, Hawkes | 15.00 |
| Cut Glass, Creamer, Hobstar, Strawberry Diamond, & Cane, American, 3 In. | 32.00 |
| Cut Glass, Creamer, Strawberry Diamond & Fan, Miniature | 12.00 |
| Cut Glass, Creamer, Swag & Panel, Gold Top, C.1800 | 20.00 |
| Cut Glass, Cruet, American, Tankard Shape, Intaglio Leaf & Frosted Floral | 30.00 |
| Cut Glass, Cruet, Checkered Diamond & Fan, Faceted Stopper | 27.50 |
| Cut Glass, Cruet, Floral, Conical, Three Pouring Lips | 20.00 |
| Cut Glass, Cruet, Hobstars, Notched Handle, Bubbles In Stopper, Hawkes | 65.00 |
| Cut Glass, Cruet, Mushroom Shape, Electric, American | 40.00 |
| Cut Glass, Cruet, Notched Handle, Hobstar & Flashed Fan, Facet Stopper | 50.00 |
| Cut Glass, Cruet, Oil & Vinegar, Double Lip, Dated, Hawkes | 40.00 |
| Cut Glass, Cruet, Old Colony, Pairpoint, 7 1/2 X 3 In. | 45.00 |
| Cut Glass, Cruet, Pressed Stopper, Pinwheel, Panel, Notch, & Fan, 3 Lips | 28.00 |
| Cut Glass, Cruet, Prisms, Applied Clear Handle, Facet Cut Stopper, Star Base | 28.00 |
| Cut Glass, Cruet, Russian, Clear Buttons, Faceted Stopper, Notched Handle | 95.00 |
| Cut Glass, Cruet, Russian, Clear Buttons, Flat Sided, Lapidary Stopper | 80.00 |
| Cut Glass, Cruet, Strawberry Diamond, Fan, Hobstar, & Pinwheel, English | 37.50 |
| Cut Glass, Cruet, Tankard Shape, Faceted Stopper, American, 7 1/2 In. | 38.00 |
| Cut Glass, Cruet, Vinegar, Diamond & Fan, 5 In.High | 45.00 |
| Cut Glass, Cruet, Waterford Type, Sheffield Silver Hinged Cover, C.1750 | 32.00 |
| Cut Glass, Cruet, Zipper, Rayed Base, Stopper | 18.00 |
| Cut Glass, Cup, Loving, Sterling Rim, Small Flowers, Dated 1897, 9 In.High | 250.00 |
| Cut Glass, Cup, Loving, Sterling Top, Embossed Floral, Dated 1907 | 395.00 |
| Cut Glass, Cup, Punch, Alternation Hobstar & Strawberry Diamond, & Fan | 15.00 |
| Cut Glass, Cup, Punch, American, Hobstar, Diamond, & Vesica, Star Base | 14.00 |
| Cut Glass, Cup, Punch, Hobstar & Fan, Egginton | 18.00 |
| Cut Glass, Cup, Punch, Hobstar & Fan, Hobstar Bottom, 2 Handled | 20.00 |

Cut Glass, Cup, Punch, Old Colony, Flared Top, Star Base, Footed, American .............................. 19.00
Cut Glass, Cup, Punch, Star Cut Designs, Applied Handle ............................................. 2.50
Cut Glass, Cup, Sherbet, Signed Hawkes, Engraved Flower Festoons, Pedestal ................... 25.00
Cut Glass, Decanter, Alternate Bands Of Crosscut & Strawberry Diamond ..................... 200.00
Cut Glass, Decanter, Brandy, Diamond Pattern Bowl, Ground Stopper, Pair .................... 30.00
Cut Glass, Decanter, Brandy, Diamonds, Ground Stopper .......................................... 30.00
Cut Glass, Decanter, Canes .............................................................................. 55.00
Cut Glass, Decanter, Captain's, Gorham Ball Stopper, Hobstar, Cane, & Fan ................. 450.00
Cut Glass, Decanter, Captain's, Teardrop Stopper, Strawberry Diamond & Fan ............... 175.00
Cut Glass, Decanter, Cranberry To Clear ........................................................... 100.00
Cut Glass, Decanter, Deep Cutting, 3 Ring Neck, 12 In.High ...................................... 85.00
Cut Glass, Decanter, Diamond Point At Center, Paneled Base, Cut Stopper .................... 32.00
Cut Glass, Decanter, Faceted Ball Stopper, Double Lozenge, 12 In. ............................. 135.00
Cut Glass, Decanter, Flaring Neck, Pestle Form, C.1850, 13 1/2 In.High, Pair ............... 50.00
Cut Glass, Decanter, Flute, Applied Neck Rings, Mushroom Stopper, C.1800 ................... 30.00
Cut Glass, Decanter, Geometrics, Cut Stopper, C.1800, 14 In.High, Pair ...................... 275.00
Cut Glass, Decanter, Handle, Strawberry Diamond & Fan, Bulbous, American ................. 55.00
Cut Glass, Decanter, Handled, Hobstar, Crosscut Diamond, & Fan, Star Base ................. 110.00
Cut Glass, Decanter, Hobstar, Cane, Crosshatch Panel, & Split, Handle, Pair ................ 400.00
Cut Glass, Decanter, Hobstar, Crosshatching, & Pinwheel, Cut Stopper, Pair ............... 450.00
Cut Glass, Decanter, Honeycomb & Punty, Hollow Stopper, Pint ............................... 65.00
Cut Glass, Decanter, Nailhead Cut, American, Stopper, 13 3/4 In.High ...................... 100.00
Cut Glass, Decanter, Ruby, Gold Wash Leaf Decoration, Signed ............................. 350.00
Cut Glass, Decanter, Square, Geometrics, 16 Point Star Base, 8 1/2 In. ..................... 70.00
Cut Glass, Decanter, St.Louis, Step Cut Shoulder, Stopper, 11 1/2 In.High ................. 165.00
Cut Glass, Decanter, Sulfide Bust Of A Man, Cut Stopper, 11 In. ............................ 200.00
Cut Glass, Decanter, Wine, Miniature, Stopper, 2 In.High ...................................... 10.00
Cut Glass, Decanter, Wine, Square, Cut Stopper ............................................... 75.00
Cut Glass, Dessert Set, Kalana Lily, Dorflinger, 1905, 2 Piece ............................. 135.00
Cut Glass, Dish & Underplate, Cheese, Covered, American, Harvard & Fan ................. 250.00
Cut Glass, Dish & Underplate, Cheese, Covered, Diamonds, C.1800 ......................... 75.00
Cut Glass, Dish, Candy, Crosshatching, Copper Wheel Engraved, Libbey .................... 95.00
Cut Glass, Dish, Candy, Floral & Leaves, Scalloped Edge, American ......................... 20.00
Cut Glass, Dish, Candy, Greek Key & Laurel, Green, Stemmed, Sinclaire ................... 90.00
Cut Glass, Dish, Candy, Hobstar & Fan, Scalloped, American ................................. 56.00
Cut Glass, Dish, Candy, Hobstars, On Standard, American ................................... 55.00
Cut Glass, Dish, Candy, Rectangular, Hobstar, Strawberry Diamond, & Fan ............... 65.00
Cut Glass, Dish, Candy, Round, Maple Leaf, Scalloped, Signed, 5 In.Diameter ............ 45.00
Cut Glass, Dish, Candy, Round, Russian Pattern, 6 In.Diameter ............................ 75.00
Cut Glass, Dish, Candy, Six Sided, Hobstars & Baby Cane .................................. 35.00
Cut Glass, Dish, Candy, Square, Russian, Rayed Bottom, American, 5 3/4 In. ............ 95.00
Cut Glass, Dish, Candy, Star, Cane, & Floral, Sterling Rim ................................ 95.00
Cut Glass, Dish, Candy, 4 Sections, 2 Cut Loop Handles, American ........................ 67.00
Cut Glass, Dish, Cheese, Covered, Flowers & Fans, 8 1/2 X 8 1/2 In. ..................... 125.00
Cut Glass, Dish, Cheese, Covered, Harvard & Floral, Blank, American .................... 300.00
Cut Glass, Dish, Cocktail, Stemmed, Insert, Star In Foot, American ...................... 79.50
Cut Glass, Dish, Dessert, Intaglio Holly & Berry, Ruffled Edge, Libbey .................. 54.15
Cut Glass, Dish, Expanding Star, 6 In.Diameter ........................................... 65.00
Cut Glass, Dish, Heart Shape, Brilliant Cut, 7 In. Diameter ............................. 95.00
Cut Glass, Dish, Heart Shape, Covered, Cane & Hobstar, 2 In.High ...................... 75.00
Cut Glass, Dish, Jelly, Round, 6 Point Star Base, 6 1/8 In. ............................. 42.50
Cut Glass, Dish, Olive, Crosshatching, Hobstar, & Strawberry Diamond ................. 28.00
Cut Glass, Dish, Olive, Daisy Design, Signed Clark, 8 In.Diameter ...................... 48.00
Cut Glass, Dish, Pickle, Allover Cuttings, 3 1/2 In.Diameter ........................... 38.00
Cut Glass, Dish, Pickle, Harvard, 7 X 5 In. ............................................. 55.00
Cut Glass, Dish, Pickle, Venetian, Hawkes, 7 X 3 3/4 In. ............................... 95.00
Cut Glass, Dish, Pinwheel, Strawberry Diamond, & Star, Compartment, 2 Handles ....... 75.00
Cut Glass, Dish, Pinwheels, Double Thumbprint Handles, 4 Compartments ............... 150.00
Cut Glass, Dish, Powder, Harvard, Overlapping Cover .................................... 65.00
Cut Glass, Epergne, Four Embellished Cosmos Flowers, Sterling Holder .................. 85.00
Cut Glass, Fernery, Harvard, 3 Legs, 4 In.High ......................................... 135.00
Cut Glass, Fernery, Pinwheel & Fan, 3 Applied Peg Feet, 7 3/4 In. ..................... 65.00
Cut Glass, Fernery, Pinwheel & Fern, Footed, 4 1/2 In.High ............................ 45.00
Cut Glass, Flower Center, Clarke, 7 1/4 In.Diameter .................................... 150.00
Cut Glass, Flower Center, Florence, Prism Step Cut Neck, 24 Point Star Base .......... 325.00
Cut Glass, Flower Center, Hobstar, Strawberry Diamond, & Prism, Clarke ............... 225.00

Cut Glass, **Flower Center**, Hobstars, 6 In.Diameter .................................................... 125.00
Cut Glass, **Frame**, Picture, Triple Row Of Strawberry Diamonds, Hawkes ................ 100.00
Cut Glass, **Goblet**, Band Of Fine Diamond Over Flute, Engraved, C.1800 ................. 18.00
Cut Glass, **Goblet**, Double Lozenge, American, 6 In.High .......................................... 62.50
Cut Glass, **Goblet**, Engraved Feather Spray, Floral, & Drapery, Hawkes .................. 16.00
Cut Glass, **Goblet**, Engraved Winged Serpent-Drawn Chariot, C.1800 ..................... 18.00
Cut Glass, **Goblet**, Flute Band & Checkered Diamond, Green Inside, Sinclaire ......... 125.00
Cut Glass, **Goblet**, Green To Clear, Diamond Thumbprint, Engraved Grapes ............. 37.50
Cut Glass, **Goblet**, Intaglio Deers, Trees, & Dogs, Sapphire Blue ............................ 45.00
Cut Glass, **Goblet**, Kalana Lily, Dorflinger, 1905 ..................................................... 65.00
Cut Glass, **Goblet**, Pineapple, 16-Point Stars, Pair ................................................. 78.00
Cut Glass, **Goblet**, Pinwheels, Knob Stem ............................................................. 15.50
Cut Glass, **Goblet**, Ruby Flashed, Etched Panel Of Flowers & Lyre ......................... 50.00
Cut Glass, **Goblet**, Smoky Bowl, Melon Ribbed Stem, Libbey ................................. 8.50
Cut Glass, **Goblet**, St.Louis Diamond, Hexagonal Stem, Notched Prisms, Star ......... 30.00
Cut Glass, **Goblet**, Stylized Flower, Teardrop Stem ................................................ 17.00
Cut Glass, **Goblet**, Swags & Panels On Dome Foot, C.1800, 6 1/2 In. ..................... 25.00
Cut Glass, **Hair Receiver & Powder Jar**, Cover, Crosshatching, Hobstar, & Fan ....... 160.00
Cut Glass, **Hair Receiver**, Covered, Buzz Cuttings, 5 1/2 In. Wide .......................... 50.00
Cut Glass, **Hair Receiver**, Floral & Spray, 4 In.High ............................................... 22.50
Cut Glass, **Hair Receiver**, Harvard & Floral, American .......................................... 35.00
Cut Glass, **Humidor**, Greek Key, 5 1/2 In.High ...................................................... 50.00
Cut Glass, **Humidor**, Tobacco, Hobstar Cover, Strawberry Diamond & Fan, 5 In. ...... 225.00
Cut Glass, **Inkwell**, Pyramid Shape, Pewter Rim, Hinged, 3 1/2 In.High ................. 55.00
Cut Glass, **Inkwell**, Stevens & Williams, Water Lily, Domed Sterling Cover .............. 95.00
Cut Glass, **Jar & Underplate**, Mustard, Covered, Vertical Notching, Prism Top ......... 69.00
Cut Glass, **Jar & Underplate**, Mustard, Prisms ..................................................... 35.00
Cut Glass, **Jar**, Candy, Covered, Intaglio Wild Roses & Leaves, Amber To Clear ....... 40.00
Cut Glass, **Jar**, Cookie, Art Nouveau Gorham Lid, Hobstar, Fan, & Star .................. 225.00
Cut Glass, **Jar**, Cracker, Square, Silver Lid & Bail ................................................ 68.50
Cut Glass, **Jar**, Dresser, Relief Floral, Sterling Top, Signed Unger Bros. .................. 40.00
Cut Glass, **Jar**, Marmalade, Ball Finial, Hobstar, Fan, & Diamond, Hawkes ............. 175.00
Cut Glass, **Jar**, Mucilage, Oval & Strawberry Diamond, Sterling Holder Top ............ 60.00
Cut Glass, **Jar**, Mucilage, Notched Vesicas, Repousse Sterling Cover, 3 In. ............. 35.00
Cut Glass, **Jar**, Mustard, Cover, Hobstars & Prism, 4 1/4 In.High .......................... 20.00
Cut Glass, **Jar**, Mustard, Vertical Line & Dragonfly, Sterling Top & Spoon .............. 20.00
Cut Glass, **Jar**, Pomade, Overlay, Blue To White To Clear, Silver Top ..................... 30.00
Cut Glass, **Jar**, Pomade, Paneled, Sterling Art Nouveau Lid, Dated 1918 ................ 16.00
Cut Glass, **Jar**, Powder, Art Nouveau Turtle On Cover, Zipper, Rayed Base ............. 15.00
Cut Glass, **Jar**, Powder, Engraved Sterling Lid, Notched Ray, Fan, & Star ............... 25.00
Cut Glass, **Jar**, Powder, Five Petal Flowers & Leaf Spray ...................................... 50.00
Cut Glass, **Jar**, Powder, Ornate Sterling Lid, 4 In.Wide ........................................ 25.00
Cut Glass, **Jar**, Powder, Sterling Lid, Copper Wheel Engraved Floral & Birds .......... 50.00
Cut Glass, **Jar**, Powder, Sterling Top, Star & Fan, Star Base, Round, 2 3/4 In. ......... 48.50
Cut Glass, **Jar**, Sachet, Gold Washed Ivory Inlaid Sterling Top, Diamonds .............. 85.00
Cut Glass, **Jar**, Sachet, Star Cut Lid, 5 In. ......................................................... 95.00
Cut Glass, **Jar**, Sweetmeat, Mushroom Finial, Diamond & Horizontal Step, 1800s ... 100.00
Cut Glass, **Jar**, Tobacco, Buzz, Hobstar, Fan, & Diamond Point, 5 1/2 In. ............... 120.00
Cut Glass, **Jardiniere**, Allover Cut, 5 In.High ...................................................... 180.00
Cut Glass, **Jardiniere**, Hobstar, Cane, & Star, 5 In.High ....................................... 150.00
Cut Glass, **Jug**, Whiskey, Triple Cut Handle, Notched Prisms, Flat Sided ................ 175.00
Cut Glass, **Knife Rest**, Diamond & Fan Ball Ends, 3 3/4 In. ................................... 11.00
Cut Glass, **Knife Rest**, Divan Shape, Green ......................................................... 16.00
Cut Glass, **Knife Rest**, Dumbbell Ends, Notched Shank, American, 4 In. .................. 23.00
Cut Glass, **Knife Rest**, Dumbbell Type, Faceted Ends, 4 In.Long ............................ 15.00
Cut Glass, **Knife Rest**, Faceted Knobs, Cross-Hatching, 8-Sided, Pair ..................... 27.50
Cut Glass, **Knife Rest**, Hobstars, Diamond Point, & Fans, 5 3/4 In.Long ................. 28.00
Cut Glass, **Knife Rest**, Inverted Pointed Thumbprint, Serrated Center ..................... 25.00
Cut Glass, **Knife Rest**, Lapidary Ball Ends, 3 7/8 In. ............................................ 10.00
Cut Glass, **Knife Rest**, Lapidary Ball Ends, 5 In. ................................................. 18.00
Cut Glass, **Knife Rest**, Lapidary Ball Ends, 5 1/2 In. ............................................ 20.00
Cut Glass, **Knife Rest**, Prism Cut, 4 3/4 In.Long ................................................. 18.00
Cut Glass, **Knife Rest**, Ruby Ball Ends, Lapidary Cut, 5 In. ................................... 70.00
Cut Glass, **Knife Rest**, Serrated & Inverted, Pointed Thumbprint, Star Ends ............ 28.00
Cut Glass, **Knife Rest**, Star Ends, 5 In. .............................................................. 14.00
Cut Glass, **Knife Rest**, Vaseline Color ................................................................ 16.00

**Cut Glass, Ladle,** Punch, Gorham Double Lip, Hobstar & Strawberry Diamond .............................. 400.00
**Cut Glass, Lamp,** Heavy Cut Base & Shade, 17 In.High ................................................................. 350.00
**Cut Glass, Lampshade,** Mushroom, Hobstar & Pinwheel, 6 3/4 In.Wide ............................. 65.00
**Cut Glass, Liqueur,** Vesica & Thumbprint, Long Stem, Hawkes .......................................... 14.35
**Cut Glass, Match Holder,** Flared Sides, 2 1/2 In.High ......................................................... 15.00
**Cut Glass, Muffineer,** Beveled Panels, Cranberry ................................................................ 48.00
**Cut Glass, Muffineer,** Ornate Wilcox Sterling Silver Lid, 4 1/2 In. ................................. 95.00
**Cut Glass, Napkin Holder,** Harvard Cutting, 2 1/4 In.Wide ............................................... 65.00
**Cut Glass, Nappy,** American, Handled, 6 In.Diameter ......................................................... 24.00
**Cut Glass, Nappy,** Flower Design, 6 In. Diameter ............................................................... 25.00
**Cut Glass, Nappy,** Gravic, Carnation, Hawkes, 7 X 7 X 2 1/4 In. ..................................... 30.00
**Cut Glass, Nappy,** Harvard, Hobstar, & Daisy, Lacy, Loop Handle, Signed Hoare .............. 35.00
**Cut Glass, Nappy,** Heavy Cuttings, Unger, 5 In.Diameter ................................................... 22.00
**Cut Glass, Nappy,** Hobstar & Crosscut Diamond, Handled, 6 In.Diameter ..................... 45.00
**Cut Glass, Nappy,** Hobstars, Lacy, Facet Cut Top, Loop Handle, American ..................... 27.00
**Cut Glass, Nappy,** Hobstars, Triple Thumbprint Side Handle ........................................... 55.00
**Cut Glass, Nappy,** Hunt's Royal Pattern, Handled, 6 In. ................................................... 95.00
**Cut Glass, Nappy,** Loop Handle, Hobstar & Harvard Within Design, 7 1/4 In. ................. 35.00
**Cut Glass, Nappy,** Pineapple & Fan, Signed Hawkes ......................................................... 25.00
**Cut Glass, Nappy,** Rose Pattern, Cut Bottom, 6 In. ........................................................... 25.00
**Cut Glass, Nappy,** Signed Hawkes, 1890, 6 In.Diameter ................................................... 55.00
**Cut Glass, Nappy,** Strawberry Diamond & Fan, 6 In. ........................................................ 17.00
**Cut Glass, Nappy,** Strawberry Diamond, Crosshatching, & Pinwheel, 6 1/2 In. .............. 35.00
**Cut Glass, Nappy,** Strawberry Diamond, Crosshatching, & Pinwheel, 7 1/2 In. .............. 45.00
**Cut Glass, Parfait,** Primrose, Intaglio, Pedestal, 6 In. ...................................................... 35.00
**Cut Glass, Perfume,** Bevel Cut Geometrics, Gilded Plunger Top, Blue ............................ 25.00
**Cut Glass, Perfume,** Etched Flowers & Leaves, Stopper, Signed Hawkes, 8 In. ............... 95.00
**Cut Glass, Perfume,** French Ormolu Top With Paris Scene, Ruby, 3 1/4 In. .................... 75.00
**Cut Glass, Perfume,** Hallmarked Sterling Cap, 3 In.High ................................................... 12.50
**Cut Glass, Perfume,** Harvard, Hinged Sterling Cap, Repousse, Unger Bros. ..................... 35.00
**Cut Glass, Perfume,** Lay Down, Cane Pattern ..................................................................... 10.00
**Cut Glass, Perfume,** Octagonal Diamond, Sterling Screw Cap, 5 1/4 In. ......................... 72.50
**Cut Glass, Perfume,** Russian, Repousse Sterling Silver Top, 3 1/2 In.High ..................... 60.00
**Cut Glass, Perfume,** Russian, Strawberry Diamond, & Button, American ......................... 90.00
**Cut Glass, Perfumer,** Purse Size, Sterling Cap, 2 1/2 In. ................................................... 15.00
**Cut Glass, Pitcher,** Allover Cut, Thumbprint Handle, 9 In.High ........................................ 135.00
**Cut Glass, Pitcher,** Cider, Hobstar, Fan, Nailhead, & Diamond, Hoare, 6 3/4 In. ............ 87.00
**Cut Glass, Pitcher,** Columns Of Notched Prisms, Sterling Collar, 6 3/4 In. .................... 65.00
**Cut Glass, Pitcher,** Green To Clear, Cane Pattern, Gold Trim, 8 In.High .......................... 80.00
**Cut Glass, Pitcher,** Hobstar, Cane, & Diamond, Double Cut Handle, 10 In. ..................... 375.00
**Cut Glass, Pitcher,** Intaglio Floral, 5 In. ........................................................................... 10.00
**Cut Glass, Pitcher,** Lemonade, Base Cut, Silver Handle, 10 1/2 In.High .......................... 50.00
**Cut Glass, Pitcher,** Lemonade, Silver Collar, Handle, Spout, & Lid, Geometrics ............. 50.00
**Cut Glass, Pitcher,** Martini, Sterling Top, 11 3/4 In.High ................................................. 175.00
**Cut Glass, Pitcher,** Milk, Ball Shape, Hawkes, 6 In. .......................................................... 95.00
**Cut Glass, Pitcher,** Ornate Sterling Top Rim, Prisms, 9 1/2 In.High ................................ 75.00
**Cut Glass, Pitcher,** Pinwheel, Crosshatching, & Crosscut Diamond, Scalloped .............. 160.00
**Cut Glass, Pitcher,** Ruby Flashed, Panels & Stars, 8 1/2 In. .............................................. 75.00
**Cut Glass, Pitcher,** Strawberry, Notched Handle, 10 1/2 In.High ..................................... 165.00
**Cut Glass, Pitcher,** Swags, Sterling Thumb Lift Cover, Hawkes, 2 In.High ..................... 50.00
**Cut Glass, Pitcher,** Triple Square, Signed Clarke, 10 1/2 In.High ..................................... 150.00
**Cut Glass, Pitcher,** Triple Squares, Right Angle Cut Top, Clarke, 10 1/2 In. .................... 150.00
**Cut Glass, Pitcher,** Water, Allover Cut, American, 10 In.High ............................................ 265.00
**Cut Glass, Pitcher,** Water, Deep Cut, Cut Handle, 12 In.High ............................................ 65.00
**Cut Glass, Pitcher,** Water, Harvard Bottom, Floral Top, American .................................... 45.00
**Cut Glass, Pitcher,** Water, Harvard From Base, Panels At Top ........................................... 55.00
**Cut Glass, Pitcher,** Water, Hobstar, Cane, Crosshatching, Hobnail Vesica, & Fan .......... 145.00
**Cut Glass, Pitcher,** Water, Pinwheels, 7 1/2 In.High .......................................................... 50.00
**Cut Glass, Pitcher,** Water, Prism & Strawberry, Signed Hoare, 8 1/4 In.High ................. 85.00
**Cut Glass, Pitcher,** Water, Sunburst, Double Thumbprint Handle ..................................... 275.00
**Cut Glass, Plate,** Allover Cuttings, Libbey, Saber Mark, 7 In. ............................................ 85.00
**Cut Glass, Plate,** Allover Cut, American, 7 In. ................................................................... 55.00
**Cut Glass, Plate,** Allover Cut, 7 In. .................................................................................. 55.00
**Cut Glass, Plate,** Allover Cuttings, Libbey, Saber Mark, 7 In. ............................................ 85.00
**Cut Glass, Plate,** Bread, Allover Cut, Pinwheels In Corners, 5 X 12 In. ............................ 115.00
**Cut Glass, Plate,** Bread, Hobstar, Strawberry Diamond, & Fan, Turned-Up Ends ............ 250.00

Cut Glass, Plate, Bread, Pinwheels In Corners, Allover Balance Cut, American ............... 115.00
Cut Glass, Plate, Cake, Harvard, Intaglio Center, 3 Footed, Tuthill, 9 In. ...................... 225.00
Cut Glass, Plate, Cake, Hobstar, Fan, & Prism, Turned Up Sawtooth Edge, 10 In. ........... 48.00
Cut Glass, Plate, Cake, Paperweight Bottom, Bergen, 8 In. ...................................... 95.00
Cut Glass, Plate, Cornflowers, 16-Point Star Base, 5 1/4 In. .................................... 8.00
Cut Glass, Plate, Flower Center, Thistle & Leaves Border, Tuthill, 9 In. ...................... 45.00
Cut Glass, Plate, Hobstar, Crosshatching, Zipper, Star, & Fan, American, 9 In. .............. 65.00
Cut Glass, Plate, Hobstar, Diamond, & Fan, Hawkes, 6 1/2 In. ................................. 30.00
Cut Glass, Plate, Hobstar, Strawberry Diamond, & Fan, Libbey, 7 In. ........................ 85.00
Cut Glass, Plate, Intaglio, Cut Melon, Leaves, & Vines, 7 In. ................................... 59.00
Cut Glass, Plate, Leaf Shape, Raised Starred Buttons & Hobstars, 7 In. ...................... 69.00
Cut Glass, Plate, Parisian, Dorflinger, 7 In. ..................................................... 55.00
Cut Glass, Plate, Pie, Garland & Butterfly On Gallery, Pairpoint, 10 In. ...................... 125.00
Cut Glass, Plate, Stars & Stripes, Hawkes, 10 In. ............................................... 165.00
Cut Glass, Plate, Strawberry & Fan, 7 In. ........................................................ 21.00
Cut Glass, Plate, Strawberry Diamond, Hobstar, Fan, & Flashed Star, 7 In. .................. 49.00
Cut Glass, Plate, 4 Row Band Of Diamonds, 24-Point Star Base, 7 In. ........................ 8.00
Cut Glass, Platter, Ice Cream, Strawberry & Fan .............................................. 195.00
Cut Glass, Prism, Hanging Lamp, Faceted, Victorian, 5 In., Set Of 18 ........................ 17.00
Cut Glass, Punch Set, Miniature, Strawberry Diamond & Fan, 7 Piece ........................ 58.00
Cut Glass, Relish, Floral & Awlwork, Tuthill, 6 X 4 1/2 In. ..................................... 65.00
Cut Glass, Relish, Oval, Maple Leaf, Signed Elite ............................................. 36.00
Cut Glass, Relish, Rectangular, Scalloped & Serrated, Hobstars, American ................... 27.00
Cut Glass, Rose Bowl, Allover Cut With Vesicas ............................................... 150.00
Cut Glass, Rose Bowl, Allover Cuttings, Libbey, Saber Mark ................................. 295.00
Cut Glass, Rose Bowl, American, Buzz, Star, Fan, & Vesica, Notched Top, Rayed ........... 49.00
Cut Glass, Rose Bowl, Bank Of Hobstars Surrounded By Pinwheels, 6 In. .................... 85.00
Cut Glass, Rose Bowl, Diamonds, Pedestal, 17 In. ............................................. 95.00
Cut Glass, Rose Bowl, Floral & Leaf, Sharp Uneven Edge, 17 In. .............................. 65.00
Cut Glass, Rose Bowl, Hobstar & Diamond, 4 In. ............................................. 45.00
Cut Glass, Rose Bowl, Hobstar & 3 Clear Vesicas Surrounded By Fine Cutting ............... 175.00
Cut Glass, Rose Bowl, Hobstar Rosette & Notched Prism, Star Base, American ............... 45.00
Cut Glass, Rose Bowl, Hobstar, Notched Prism, & Crosshatched Diamond, Rayed ........... 40.00
Cut Glass, Rose Bowl, Hobstars, 11 In. ......................................................... 35.00
Cut Glass, Rose Bowl, Pedestal, Hobstar On Base ............................................. 125.00
Cut Glass, Rose Bowl, Strawberry Diamond & Fan, Notched Edge, 6 In.High .................. 110.00
Cut Glass, Rose Bowl, Strawberry Diamond & Fan, 6 In.High, 6 1/2 In.Diam. ................ 110.00
Cut Glass, Rose Bowl, Strawberry Diamond & Star, American, 7 In. Diameter ............... 165.00
Cut Glass, Rose Bowl, Wheeler, American, 4 3/4 In.High ...................................... 65.00
Cut Glass, Salt & Pepper, Engraved, Sterling Tops, Libbey .................................... 25.00
Cut Glass, Salt & Pepper, Hobstar & Fan, 3 In.High ........................................... 18.00
Cut Glass, Salt & Pepper, Notched Prisms, Sterling Tops ..................................... 10.00
Cut Glass, Salt & Pepper, Prism & Hobstar Chain At Base ..................................... 35.00
Cut Glass, Salt & Pepper, Sterling Top, 4 In. .................................................. 7.50
Cut Glass, Salt & Pepper, Vertical Zipper, Green Cut Screw-On Bottoms ...................... 30.00
Cut Glass, Salt, Allover Cuttings, Hawkes ..................................................... 28.00
Cut Glass, Salt, Apple Green, Faceted, Star Base .............................................. 8.50
Cut Glass, Salt, Cut & Engraved, Elevated Base, Hawkes, Set Of 6 ............................ 65.00
Cut Glass, Salt, Footed, 3 In. Diameter ........................................................ 165.00
Cut Glass, Salt, Harvard, 1 3/4 In.Square ...................................................... 10.00
Cut Glass, Salt, Individual, 2 1/4 In.Diameter, Pair ............................................ 12.50
Cut Glass, Salt, Open Rose, Hawkes ........................................................... 8.25
Cut Glass, Salt, Oval, Squared Ends, Upright Tabs, Diamond Points, Star Base ............... 22.00
Cut Glass, Salt, Paneled, Prisms, Square ...................................................... 5.50
Cut Glass, Salt, Prisms, Square, 1 1/2 In. ...................................................... 5.50
Cut Glass, Salt, Strawberry Diamond & Fan, American, 1 1/4 In.Diameter .................... 12.50
Cut Glass, Server Set, Salad, Hollow Handles, Twist Stems, Silver, 2 Piece ................... 90.00
Cut Glass, Sherbet, Gravic, Carnations, Hawkes .............................................. 73.75
Cut Glass, Sherbet, Kalana Lily, Dorflinger, 1905 ............................................. 60.00
Cut Glass, Sherbet, Ribbon, Drapery, & Floral, Engraved Base, Hawkes ...................... 6.00
Cut Glass, Sherry, Half Star & Fan, Cut Bottom ............................................... 10.00
Cut Glass, Shot Glass, Russian & Hobstar Button .............................................. 50.00
Cut Glass, Shot Glass, Strawberry ............................................................. 12.50
Cut Glass, Spooner, Hobstar & Crosshatching, 4 3/4 In. High ................................. 55.00
Cut Glass, Spooner, Hobstar, Star, & Strawberry Diamond, Star Base, American ............ 75.00
Cut Glass, Sugar & Creamer, Aladdin Lamp Shape, Pedestal, Flower & Leaf ................. 125.00

| | |
|---|---|
| Cut Glass, Sugar & Creamer, Ball Shape Creamer, Square Sugar, Hobstars | 125.00 |
| Cut Glass, Sugar & Creamer, Cane, Hobstar, Diamond Point, & Miter | 150.00 |
| Cut Glass, Sugar & Creamer, Finecut | 65.00 |
| Cut Glass, Sugar & Creamer, Flying Bird, Double Thumbprint Handles | 88.00 |
| Cut Glass, Sugar & Creamer, Footed, Intaglio, Daisies & Leaves, 3 Bands Cane | 90.00 |
| Cut Glass, Sugar & Creamer, Harvard & Floral, American | 60.00 |
| Cut Glass, Sugar & Creamer, Heart, American | 85.00 |
| Cut Glass, Sugar & Creamer, Hobstar & Fan, Star Bases, Notched Handles | 50.00 |
| Cut Glass, Sugar & Creamer, Hobstar & Sunburst | 75.00 To 80.00 |
| Cut Glass, Sugar & Creamer, Hobstar & Swirl | 265.00 |
| Cut Glass, Sugar & Creamer, Hobstar, Fan, & Cane, Scalloped Rims | 90.00 |
| Cut Glass, Sugar & Creamer, Hobstars, Libbey | 150.00 |
| Cut Glass, Sugar & Creamer, Joan, Straus | 150.00 |
| Cut Glass, Sugar & Creamer, Oval Shape, Floral & Concentric, Notched, Flint | 80.00 |
| Cut Glass, Sugar & Creamer, Pedestal, Corning | 295.00 |
| Cut Glass, Sugar & Creamor, Rose Design | 65.00 |
| Cut Glass, Sugar & Creamer, Russion Button, Cane, & Diamond, Rayed Bases | 75.00 |
| Cut Glass, Sugar & Creamer, Scalloped Edges, Triple Notched Handles | 135.00 |
| Cut Glass, Sugar & Creamer, Strawberry Diamonds, Signed Clarke | 95.00 |
| Cut Glass, Sugar & Creamer, Sunburst, Scalloped Serrated Tops | 32.50 |
| Cut Glass, Sugar & Creamer, Zippered Panel, Sunburst, & Geometric, Hawkes | 100.00 |
| Cut Glass, Sugar & Creamer, 3 In.High ......... *Illus* | 40.00 |

Cut Glass, Sugar & Creamer, 3 In.High

| | |
|---|---|
| Cut Glass, Sugar, French Cut, Sterling Pedestal Base, Hawkes | 32.00 |
| Cut Glass, Sugar, Hobstars, 2 Handled, 4 In.Diameter | 15.00 |
| Cut Glass, Syrup, Ball Shape, Silver Plated Lid, 4 1/2 In. | 85.00 |
| Cut Glass, Syrup, Bulbous, Silver Plated Helmet Shaped Top | 50.00 |
| Cut Glass, Syrup, Pineapple & Fan, 4 1/4 In.High | 45.00 |
| Cut Glass, Syrup, Silver Handle, Collar, & Lift Top, Ribbed Edges, American | 41.00 |
| Cut Glass, Syrup, Strawberry & Fan, Silver Plate Collar, Handle, & Spout | 39.00 |
| Cut Glass, Tankard, Allover Harvard, Double Cut Handle, American | 250.00 |
| Cut Glass, Tankard, Alternating Star & Strawberry Diamond Bands | 95.00 |
| Cut Glass, Tankard, Harvard, 8 1/4 In.High | 250.00 |
| Cut Glass, Tankard, Hobstar & Pinwheel, Prismatic Underspout, American | 77.00 |
| Cut Glass, Tankard, Water, Notched Edge, Double Faceted Handle, Star & Fan | 125.00 |
| Cut Glass, Toothpick, Flat Hobnail & Sawtooth Band | 24.00 |
| Cut Glass, Toothpick, Harvard | 13.50 |
| Cut Glass, Toothpick, Intaglio, Marked Sterling Base, 3 1/2 In.High | 20.00 |
| Cut Glass, Toothpick, Notched Prism & Almond Thumbprint, American | 22.00 |
| Cut Glass, Tray, Harvard Buttons, American, 8 X 5 1/2 In. | 135.00 |
| Cut Glass, Tray, Heart Shape, Gallery, 10 In.Diameter At Widest Point | 125.00 |
| Cut Glass, Tray, Hobstar Extending To Fan Edge, Dorflinger, Round, 12 In. | 220.00 |
| Cut Glass, Tray, Hobstar, Crosscut Diamond, & Cane, 12 In. Diameter | 350.00 |
| Cut Glass, Tray, Ice Cream, Bands Of Cane With Floral, 11 1/2 In. | 125.00 |
| Cut Glass, Tray, Ice Cream, Boat Shape, Allover Cut, 14 In. | 95.00 |
| Cut Glass, Tray, Ice Cream, Crosscut Diamond & Fan, Rayed Center, Scalloped | 145.00 |
| Cut Glass, Tray, Ice Cream, Crosscut Diamond & Fan, Scalloped Edge | 135.00 |
| Cut Glass, Tray, Ice Cream, Floral In Squares Separated By Cane Bands | 65.00 |
| Cut Glass, Tray, Ice Cream, Strawberry Fan | 145.00 |
| Cut Glass, Tray, Oval, Hobstar, Miter, & Fan, Intaglio Floral, Tuthill | 135.00 |
| Cut Glass, Tub, Ice, Cut Tabs, Pinwheel Bottom | 75.00 |
| Cut Glass, Tub, Ice, Pinwheel Bottom, Star Cut Tabs, 5 In.High | 115.00 |

| | |
|---|---|
| Cut Glass, Tub, Mayonnaise, Russian, Floral & Flower Leaves, 5 1/4 X 3 In. | 40.00 |
| Cut Glass, Tumble-Up, Cobalt Cut To Clear | 75.00 |
| Cut Glass, Tumble-Up, Ruby Cased, Engraved Daisies, Bull's-Eye, & Punty | 43.00 |
| Cut Glass, Tumbler, Alternate Hobstar, Pinwheel, & Fan | 20.00 |
| Cut Glass, Tumbler, Carolyn, Signed J.Hoare | 25.00 |
| Cut Glass, Tumbler, Cobalt To Clear, Bull's-Eye, Split, Fan, & Rose | 20.00 |
| Cut Glass, Tumbler, Daisies & Leaves, American, 3 1/2 In.High | 5.00 |
| Cut Glass, Tumbler, Daisies & Leaves, American, 4 In. | 5.00 |
| Cut Glass, Tumbler, Engraved Floral Panels & 2 24 Point Hobstars, Hawkes | 50.00 |
| Cut Glass, Tumbler, Gravic Iris, Sinclaire, 3 3/4 In.High, Pair | 80.00 |
| Cut Glass, Tumbler, Harvard & Fan, 3 7/8 In.High | 11.00 |
| Cut Glass, Tumbler, Hobstar & Fan | 20.50 |
| Cut Glass, Tumbler, Hobstar & Fan, Hawkes | 28.00 |
| Cut Glass, Tumbler, Iced Tea, Heavy Cutting & Blanks, Egginton, 5 In.High | 30.00 |
| Cut Glass, Tumbler, Leaves, American | 15.00 |
| Cut Glass, Tumbler, Middlesex Variation With Bull's-Eyes, American | 47.25 |
| Cut Glass, Tumbler, Middlesex, Signed Hawkes | 26.25 |
| Cut Glass, Tumbler, Punty & Miter, American | 16.00 |
| Cut Glass, Tumbler, Queen's Pattern, Hawkes | 35.00 |
| Cut Glass, Tumbler, Signed Hawkes, Roman Key, White Satin Rim, Wide Panels | 35.00 |
| Cut Glass, Tumbler, Star & Fan, Star Base | 12.50 |
| Cut Glass, Tumbler, Star & Wheat, Libbey With Sword | 45.00 |
| Cut Glass, Tumbler, Whiskey, Hobstar & Fan, Hawkes, 2 3/4 In.High | 18.75 |
| Cut Glass, Tumbler, 13 Vertical Bars Of Engraved Frosted Ribbon, Hawkes | 6.00 |
| Cut Glass, Vase, Brilliant Cut, Hawkes, 15 X 5 In. | 225.00 |
| Cut Glass, Vase, Brunswick, Hawkes, 14 In.High | 175.00 |
| Cut Glass, Vase, Bud, Chalice Shape, Signed Tuthill, 8 In.High | 175.00 |
| Cut Glass, Vase, Bud, Cranberry To Clear, Diamond & Fan, St.Louis, 7 In. | 38.00 |
| Cut Glass, Vase, Cane & Notch, Silver Trim, Birmingham, 1902, 6 In., Pair | 60.00 |
| Cut Glass, Vase, Checkerboard Panels, Allover Etchings, Hawkes, 8 In. | 28.50 |
| Cut Glass, Vase, Corning, J.Hoare & Co., 10 1/4 In. | 25.00 |
| Cut Glass, Vase, Corset Shape, Hobstars, American, 11 In. High | 45.00 |
| Cut Glass, Vase, Emerald Green, Cut To Clear, Flint, 7 In. | 70.00 |
| Cut Glass, Vase, Engraved Flamingo & Foliage, Libbey, C.1910, 18 In. | 1950.00 |
| Cut Glass, Vase, Etched Kalana Pansy Sweet Pea, Dorflinger, 5 1/2 In. | 105.00 |
| Cut Glass, Vase, Fan & Diamond, Harbridal, 5 1/2 In.High | 14.00 |
| Cut Glass, Vase, Fan, Etched Floral, Green Base, Hawkes, 7 1/2 In. | 55.00 |
| Cut Glass, Vase, Fern, Intaglio Floral, & Stylized Butterfly, 10 In.High | 35.00 |
| Cut Glass, Vase, Flared Scalloped & Serrated Top, American, 6 1/2 In.High | 33.00 |
| Cut Glass, Vase, Floral, Leaf, & Foliage, Tuthill, 13 In.High | 350.00 |
| Cut Glass, Vase, Florals, 8 In. | 22.50 |
| Cut Glass, Vase, Flower And Leaf Cutting, 12 In.High, 5 In.Diameter | 65.00 |
| Cut Glass, Vase, Flower, Signed Webb Corbett, 10 In.High | 55.00 |
| Cut Glass, Vase, Green Cut To Clear, Leaded Crystal | 170.00 |
| Cut Glass, Vase, Green, Diamond-Quilted, Floral & Leaf, Cut Ball Insert Stem | 185.00 |
| Cut Glass, Vase, Harvard, Acid Cut Flowers, Leaves, & Stems, 10 In. | 75.00 |
| Cut Glass, Vase, Harvard, Floral Detail, 13 In.High | 110.00 |
| Cut Glass, Vase, Hobstar & Cane, American, 18 In. High | 395.00 |
| Cut Glass, Vase, Hobstar Top, Zipper Bottom, 10 In.High | 60.00 |
| Cut Glass, Vase, Hobstar, Miter, & Diamond, Rayed Base, 12 In.High | 47.50 |
| Cut Glass, Vase, Intaglio & Strawberry Diamond, American, 12 In.High | 60.00 |
| Cut Glass, Vase, Intaglio Bird, Hawkes, 8 1/2 In.High | 56.00 |
| Cut Glass, Vase, Intaglio Floral, Hawkes, 10 In. | 75.00 |
| Cut Glass, Vase, Inverted Cone Shape, Deep Cut, Signed Hawkes, 12 In. | 95.00 |
| Cut Glass, Vase, Irving, Honesdale, Pa., Paper Label | 60.00 |
| Cut Glass, Vase, Paperweight, Cut & Frosted Morning Glories, 8 1/2 In. | 47.50 |
| Cut Glass, Vase, Pinwheel, Bull's-Eye, & Star, Hobstar Bottom, 14 In.High | 65.00 |
| Cut Glass, Vase, Queen, Pedestal Foot, Hawkes, 12 In.High | 375.00 |
| Cut Glass, Vase, Queen's, Hawkes, 10 In.High | 48.00 |
| Cut Glass, Vase, Ruby To Clear, Geometric Squares & 4 Petal Splits, 12 In. | 250.00 |
| Cut Glass, Vase, Ruffled, 4 In.High | 45.00 |
| Cut Glass, Vase, Signed Hawkes, Cone Shape, Waffle, Notched Rim, 7 1/2 In. | 75.00 |
| Cut Glass, Vase, Stick, Etched Scene Of Leaping Deer, 8 In. | 30.00 |
| Cut Glass, Vase, Straight Sided, Floral, American, 14 In.High | 35.00 |
| Cut Glass, Vase, Thistles, Silver Plate Stand, 4 1/2 In.High | 9.00 |
| Cut Glass, Vase, Tiffany Sterling Band, Engraved Thistles, Star Base, 11 In. | 125.00 |

| | |
|---|---|
| Cut Glass, Vase, Trumpet, Flat Diamond & Drape, Clear Blown Blank, 12 In. | 35.00 |
| Cut Glass, Water Set, Brunswick, Hawkes, 2 Piece | 395.00 |
| Cut Glass, Water Set, Flower, Butterfly, Star, & Strawberry Diamond, 6 Piece | 135.00 |
| Cut Glass, Water Set, Hobstars, Star Bottom, 7 Piece | 200.00 |
| Cut Glass, Water Set, Pineapple & Fan, 5 Piece | 125.00 |
| Cut Glass, Water Set, Sunburst Flower & Leaf, Corning, 5 Piece | 175.00 |
| Cut Glass, Whiskey Set, Hobstar, Strawberry Diamond, & Fan, Clarke, 7 Piece | 325.00 |
| Cut Glass, Whiskey Set, Orchids In Panels, Signed Elite, 4 Piece | 95.00 |
| Cut Glass, Wine Rinser, Amber, Honeycomb, Double Lip, C.1850 | 45.00 |
| Cut Glass, Wine Set, Amber, 7 Piece | 168.00 |
| Cut Glass, Wine, Cranberry Bowl, Clear Notched Stem, Germany, 7 1/2 In.High | 45.00 |
| Cut Glass, Wine, Cranberry Panels, Yellow Enamel, Gilt Trim | 25.00 |
| Cut Glass, Wine, Cut & Engraved, C.1800 | 20.00 |
| Cut Glass, Wine, Engraved Forest Scene, Intaglio Birds, Green To Clear | 125.00 |
| Cut Glass, Wine, Etched Open Bud & Moth, Faceted Stem, Jacobite, C.1765 | 75.00 |
| Cut Glass, Wine, Etched Open Bud & Moth, Ovoid Bowl, Jacobite, C.1765 | 75.00 |
| Cut Glass, Wine, Fan & Strawberry, 4 In. | 9.00 |
| Cut Glass, Wine, Fans, Star Base | 30.00 |
| Cut Glass, Wine, Fine Diamond & Panel, Engraved, C.1800 | 9.00 |
| Cut Glass, Wine, Fine Groove Cutting, Engraved, St.Louis, C.1800, 6 3/4 In. | 20.00 |
| Cut Glass, Wine, Flute, Double Knob Stem, Engraved, C.1800 | 9.00 |
| Cut Glass, Wine, Green Bowl, Clear Notched Stem, Germany, 7 1/2 In., High | 45.00 |
| Cut Glass, Wine, Hobnail, Teardrop Stem, Overlay, Orange To Clear, Hawkes | 55.00 |
| Cut Glass, Wine, Louis XIV, Monogrammed, Hawkes, 4 1/2 In.High | 65.00 |
| Cut Glass, Wine, Overlay, Orange To Clear Hobnail, Teardrop Stem, Hawkes | 55.00 |
| Cut Glass, Wine, Paneled Bowl, Engraved, Double Knob Stem, C.1800 | 15.00 |
| Cut Glass, Wine, Paneled, Blown Flint, 4 1/2 In. High | 10.00 |
| Cut Glass, Wine, Paneled, Engraved, C.1800, 4 1/4 In. | 8.00 |
| Cut Glass, Wine, Signed Webb, England | 12.00 |
| Cut Glass, Wine, Star & Strawberry Diamond, Notched Stem, Bulbous | 15.00 |
| Cut Glass, Wine, Stemmed, Alternate Pinwheel & Thistle, Star Foot, 5 In. | 25.00 |
| Cut Glass, Wine, Stemmed, Argus, C.1820, 5 In.High | 25.00 |
| Cut Glass, Wine, Strawberry & Fan, Cut & Open Teardrop Stem | 28.00 |
| Cut Glass, Wine, Strawberry Diamond & Fan, Hollow Cut Baluster Stem, Hawkes | 50.00 |
| Cut Glass, Wine, Thumbprint, Engraved, C.1800 | 9.00 |
| Cut Glass, Wine, Waterford, 6 In. | 16.50 |

*Cut velvet is a special type of art glass made with two layers of blown glass, which shows a raised pattern. It usually had an acid finish or velvetlike texture. It was made by many glass factories during the late Victorian years.*

| | |
|---|---|
| Cut Velvet, Bowl, Basket Weave, Satin, Red To Pink, Crimped Rim, Cream Lined | 250.00 |
| Cut Velvet, Creamer, Butterscotch, White Lining, Reeded Handle, Bulbous | 135.00 |
| Cut Velvet, Pitcher, Pink, White Lining, 6 In. | 250.00 |
| Cut Velvet, Rose Bowl, Butterscotch & Yellow Stripes, Ruffled, 5 In.High | 165.00 |
| Cut Velvet, Tumbler, Deep Pink | 55.00 |
| Cut Velvet, Vase, Bulbous, Blue, White Casing, 5 In.High | 125.00 |
| Cut Velvet, Vase, Vertical Ribbing, Square Top, Blue, 7 In. | 60.00 |
| Cut Velvet, Water Set, Diamond-Quilted, Butterscotch, 7 Piece | 595.00 |

Daguerreotype, see Photography, Daguerreotype
D'Albret, Paperweight, see Paperweight, D'Albret
Danish Christmas Plate, see Collector, Plate
Dant, see Bottle, Dant

*D'Argental was a French cameo glassmaker of the late Victorian period.*

| | |
|---|---|
| D'Argental, Bowl, Acid Cut, Tiger Lilies, Lavenders, 5 In.High | 115.00 |
| D'Argental, Bowl, Blue Cut Thistles On Lemon Satin, Signed, 3 1/2 In. | 195.00 |
| D'Argental, Vase, Brown On Ocher, Mums & Leaves, Rolled Neck, C.1900, 14 In. | 325.00 |
| D'Argental, Vase, Brown Trumpet Floral On Orange, 12 In.High | 265.00 |
| D'Argental, Vase, Cabinet, Cherries On Gray White & Red Frosted, 4 In. | 160.00 |
| D'Argental, Vase, Deep Red To Dark Brown, Cherries & Leaves, 4 In.High | 295.00 |
| D'Argental, Vase, Egyptian Scenic, Purple & White, 2 Acid Cuts, 7 In. | 450.00 |
| D'Argental, Vase, Polished, Signed, Cameo, 11 1/2 X 5 In. | 495.00 |
| D'Argental, Vase, Purple & Lavender Berries & Leaves On Blue, 7 In. | 350.00 |
| D'Argental, Vase, Scenic, Brown, Russet, & Gold, 18 In. High | 895.00 |
| D'Argental, Vase, Sweet Pea Design, Cameo Cut, Signed, 9 1/2 In. | 260.00 |
| D'Argental, Vase, 4 Petal Flowers, Signed, 6 In.High | 250.00 |

Date Nail, see Railroad, Date Nail

*Daum Nancy is the mark used by Auguste and Antonin Daum on pieces of French cameo glass made after 1875.*

| | |
|---|---:|
| Daum Nancy, Bottle, Berries & Leaves, Green, Enamel, C.1900, 3 In. | 100.00 |
| Daum Nancy, Bottle, Blue, Berries & Leaves, Gold Enamel, C.1900, 3 In. | 150.00 |
| Daum Nancy, Bowl, Acid Etched & Enamel Floral & Fern On Yellow, 5 1/2 In. | 160.00 |
| Daum Nancy, Bowl, Blueberries & Leafage In Blue & White, C.1900, 5 3/4 In. | 175.00 |
| Daum Nancy, Bowl, Grape Pattern, 5 3/4 In.Diameter | 195.00 |
| Daum Nancy, Bowl, Mottled Purple, Maroon, Signed, 7 In. | 100.00 |
| Daum Nancy, Bowl, Rectangular, Violets On Chipped Frosted, 4 1/2 In.High | 125.00 |
| Daum Nancy, Bowl, Silveria, Gold Foil Spatter In Orange Glass, Signed | 55.00 |
| Daum Nancy, Bowl, Squatty, Satin Glass, Bluish Green, Orange Tint, 7 In. | 73.00 |
| Daum Nancy, Bowl, Sweet Peas On Mottled White To Yellow To Orange, Signed | 275.00 |
| Daum Nancy, Bowl, White Enamel Berries & Cut Green & Gold Floral On Green | 125.00 |
| Daum Nancy, Box, Lift-Off Lid, Square, Purple Spatter On Frosted, Violets | 335.00 |
| Daum Nancy, Cruet, Bleeding Hearts & Butterflies, Signed | 225.00 |
| Daum Nancy, Jar, Ovoid Dome Lid, 16 Butterflies On Blue, 9 In.High | 450.00 |
| Daum Nancy, Lamp Base, Light Inside, Acid-Cut-Back Oriental Poppies, Signed | 475.00 |
| Daum Nancy, Lamp, Art Nouveau Style, 4 Colors, 19 In.High | 675.00 |
| Daum Nancy, Lamp, Fruit On Peach & Green To Yellow, 12 In.High | 950.00 |
| Daum Nancy, Lamp, Table, Yellow Conical Shade, Graduated Circles, 8 1/2 In. | 300.00 |
| Daum Nancy, Lamp, Trees & Water Scenes, Pale Green, 13 1/2 In.High | 650.00 |
| Daum Nancy, Liqueur Set, Enameled Gold Berries On Crystal, 7 Piece | 250.00 |
| Daum Nancy, Night-Light, Brown & Black Cameo Boats On Yellow | 295.00 |
| Daum Nancy, Pitcher, Milk, Gold Decorated Floral & Butterflies On Frosted | 145.00 |
| Daum Nancy, Plate, Collar Base, Smoky Amber, Stippled, Signed, 8 1/2 In. | 135.00 |
| Daum Nancy, Rose Bowl, Cameo & Gilt Prunus On Cranberry, Sterling Pedestal | 250.00 |
| Daum Nancy, Rose Bowl, Enameled Winter Scene, Crimped Top, Signed, 7 In.High | 135.00 |
| Daum Nancy, Salt, Scenic, Black Trees Over Frosty Ground, Signed | 110.00 |
| Daum Nancy, Salt, Tub Shape, Signed, Cameo | 85.00 |
| Daum Nancy, Shot Glass, Cut Pansies & Green Leaves On Frosted Acid Cut | 75.00 |
| Daum Nancy, Tumbler, Cut White Berries & Gold Leaves On Frosted Cranberry | 125.00 |
| Daum Nancy, Tumbler, Cut White Berries & Gold Leaves On Frosted Green | 125.00 |
| Daum Nancy, Tumbler, Mottled Orange To Yellow, Signed | 75.00 |
| Daum Nancy, Tumbler, White To Yellow, Fuchsias, C.1900, 5 In.High | 200.00 |
| Daum Nancy, Vase, Acid Cut Red & Yellow Vine Flowers On Red & Gold, Signed | 225.00 |
| Daum Nancy, Vase, Applied & Carved Bleeding Hearts, 9 In. | 190.00 |
| Daum Nancy, Vase, Autumn Color Scenes, 3 Layers, Flaring Top, 8 In.High | 495.00 |
| Daum Nancy, Vase, Baluster, Yellow, Red, & Green, Seascape, C.1900, 7 1/2 In. | 325.00 |
| Daum Nancy, Vase, Brown & Red On Orange, River Landscape, C.1900, 4 3/4 In. | 150.00 |
| Daum Nancy, Vase, Brown On Green, C.1900, 12 1/2 In. *Illus* | 475.00 |
| Daum Nancy, Vase, Bulbous, Metallic Inclusions On Amber, Gray Handles, 7 In. | 250.00 |
| Daum Nancy, Vase, Caramel Mottling, Acid Finish, Signed, 7 X 4 3/4 In. | 125.00 |
| Daum Nancy, Vase, Carved Long Leaves & Orange Floral On Orange & Yellow | 205.00 |
| Daum Nancy, Vase, Crackle, Enameled, Cameo Cut, Signed, 14 In. | 300.00 |
| Daum Nancy, Vase, Crystal, Etched, Applied Clear Rigaree, 6 1/2 In. | 35.00 |
| Daum Nancy, Vase, Enameled Gooseberries & Raised Branches On Matte, 10 In. | 295.00 |
| Daum Nancy, Vase, Enameled Violet Flowers On Pernod To White Mica, 5 In. | 175.00 |
| Daum Nancy, Vase, Footed, Fall Scene With Sailboats On Brown To Yellow | 246.00 |
| Daum Nancy, Vase, Four Bug Cabochons In Spider Web, Russet & Browns | 950.00 |
| Daum Nancy, Vase, Green Foliage Cut To Frosted, Applied Orange Flowers | 175.00 |
| Daum Nancy, Vase, Green, Signed, Cameo, 9 X 3 In. | 95.00 |
| Daum Nancy, Vase, Lobed, Green & Orange, Chestnuts & Leafage, 8 In. | 700.00 |
| Daum Nancy, Vase, Lozenge, Yellow, Green, Purple, & Orange, C.1900, 4 1/2 In. | 200.00 |
| Daum Nancy, Vase, Majorelle, Iron Mounted, Amber, Stylized Flowers, 9 1/4 In. | 425.00 |
| Daum Nancy, Vase, Mottled Reds, 13 1/2 In.High | 65.00 |
| Daum Nancy, Vase, Oriental Motif, Signed Cross Of Lorraine, 8 In. | 298.00 |
| Daum Nancy, Vase, Oval, Autumn Leaves, Signed, 7 X 8 1/2 In. | 250.00 |
| Daum Nancy, Vase, Ovoid, Birch Trees, Cameo, Miniature, Signed, 1 3/4 In.High | 185.00 |
| Daum Nancy, Vase, Ovoid, Sailboats, Cameo, Miniature, Signed, 1 3/4 In.High | 185.00 |
| Daum Nancy, Vase, Padded & Wheel Carved Orange Poppies, Slender, 12 In. | 450.00 |
| Daum Nancy, Vase, Pale & Deep Magenta, Poppies, Footed, C.1900, 13 1/2 In. | 250.00 |
| Daum Nancy, Vase, Pate De Verre, Red & Purple, 4 1/2 In.High | 100.00 |
| Daum Nancy, Vase, Persimmons On Pale Orange To Green, 13 3/4 In. | 495.00 |
| Daum Nancy, Vase, Pink, Green, & Brown, 14 3/4 In.High *Illus* | 375.00 |
| Daum Nancy, Vase, Poinsettias, Maroon & Green On Frosted Hammered, 11 In. | 395.00 |
| Daum Nancy, Vase, Purple On Yellow & Blue, River Scene, C.1900, 13 3/4 In. | 375.00 |

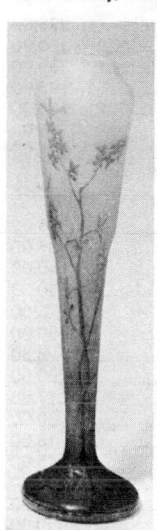

Daum Nancy, Vase, Pink, Green, & Brown, 14 3/4 In.High
*(See Page 144)*

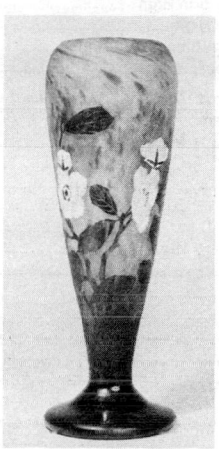

Daum Nancy, Vase,
Brown On Green,
C.1900, 12 1/2 In.
*(See Page 144)*

Daum Nancy, Vase,
Yellow & Purple,
C.1900, 8 In.High

| | |
|---|---:|
| Daum Nancy, Vase, Pyriform, Etched Ovals & Arcs, Aquamarine, Bubbles, 11 In. | 300.00 |
| Daum Nancy, Vase, Round, Red & Gold Background, Green & Yellow Leaves, 4 In. | 225.00 |
| Daum Nancy, Vase, Sailboats & Lake, Pedestal, Cameo, 6 In.Diameter | 395.00 |
| Daum Nancy, Vase, Square, Enameled Floral On Frosted Amber To White, Cased | 175.00 |
| Daum Nancy, Vase, Square, Scenic, Gold, Brown, & Rusty Red, 5 In.High | 225.00 |
| Daum Nancy, Vase, Violets On Fine Stems On Violet To Green, Gold Top, 3 In. | 315.00 |
| Daum Nancy, Vase, Water Lilies, 3 Colors, Bulbous Bottom, Tapered, 11 In. | 325.00 |
| Daum Nancy, Vase, Yellow & Purple, C.1900, 8 In.High .............................*Illus* | 300.00 |
| Daum Nancy, Vase, 2 Black Birds Flying Toward Sun On Frosted White | 275.00 |

*Davenport pottery and porcelain were made at the Davenport Factory in
Longport, Staffordshire, England, from 1793 to 1887. Earthenwares,
creamwares, porcelains, ironstone wares, and other products were made. Most of
the pieces are marked with a form of the word Davenport.*

| | |
|---|---:|
| Davenport, Bowl, Blue Transfer, Marked Friburg Ironstone, 6 In. | 6.00 |
| Davenport, Bowl, British Scenery, Lavender, C.1856, 13 In. | 50.00 |
| Davenport, Bowl, Vegetable, Covered, Corn Finial & Handles, C.1861 | 42.00 |
| Davenport, Cup Plate, Vines & Berries Border, C.1852 | 7.50 |
| Davenport, Pitcher, Franklin, Flying Kite Near Philadelphia, Sepia | 110.00 |
| Davenport, Plate, Bird & Floral, Blue, 8 In. | 7.00 |
| Davenport, Plate, Cyprus, Mulberry, Impressed Anchor, 10 1/2 In. | 22.50 |
| Davenport, Plate, Decorated To Look Like Marble, 7 3/8 In. | 17.50 |
| Davenport, Plate, Gaudy Ironstone, 10 In. | 38.00 |
| Davenport, Plate, Hunting Scene, Burleigh, England, 9 In. | 6.00 |
| Davenport, Plate, Light Blue, Friburg Ironstone, C.1835, 9 In. | 18.00 |
| Davenport, Plate, Underglaze Blue Anchor Mark, Pat.No.24, C.1805, 8 In. | 28.00 |
| Davenport, Plate, Underglaze Blue Anchor Mark, Pat.No.24, C.1805, 9 In. | 31.00 |
| Davenport, Platter, Blue & White, 21 X 16 In. | 125.00 |
| Davenport, Platter, Oriental Scene, Dark Blue, C.1810, 10 1/4 X 9 1/4 In. | 45.00 |
| Davy Crockett, Bowl, Cereal, Milk Glass, Blue Design, 5 In. | 5.00 |
| Davy Crockett, Bowl, Cereal, Milk Glass, Red Design, 5 In. | 5.00 |
| Davy Crockett, Hat, Coonskin | 4.25 |
| De Gue, Vase, Red Shading To Purple On Yellow, Signed, 11 1/2 In.High | 150.00 |
| De Gue, Vase, Green & Orange, Cameo, 14 In.High | 200.00 |

*De Vez is a name found on special pieces of French cameo glass made by
the Cristallerie de Pantin about 1890. Monsieur de Varreux was the art
director of the glassworks and he signed pieces 'De Vez'.*

| | |
|---|---:|
| De Vez, Atomizer, Cut Brown Florals On Yellow Satin, Signed, 7 1/2 In.High | 150.00 |
| De Vez, Rose Bowl, Green & Pink Mountain & Forest Scene On Citron, 4 In. | 325.00 |
| De Vez, Rose Bowl, Scalloped Top, Clear Floral On Pomona Type, 11 In. | 250.00 |

De Vez, Vase, Cameo, Pink To Yellow, Blue River Scene, 6 3/4 In.High ....................... 375.00
De Vez, Vase, Elk Crossing Stream, Castle, Snow, Blues, 8 In. ................................ 380.00
De Vez, Vase, Elliptical, Blue Tropical Jungle Scene On Yellow, 8 1/2 In. ................. 350.00
De Vez, Vase, Lake, Birds, & Trees Scene, Cameo, Signed, 5 In.High .................... 195.00
De Vez, Vase, Scenic, Yellow To Coral To Purple, 5 1/4 In.High ......................... 238.00
De Vez, Vase, Trees, Mountains, Water, & Floral Scenes On Blue, 10 In.High ............ 495.00
De Vez, Vase, Water Scene, Frosted, Fuchsia, Carved Crescents Top, 6 1/4 In. ......... 235.00

*Decoys are carved or turned wooden copies of birds. The decoy was placed in the water to lure flying birds to the pond for hunters.*

Decoy, Black Duck, Hollow, Hand-Carved, White Cedar, Cape May, N.J., 1920 ......... 45.00
Decoy, Black Duck, Ira Hudson, Oversize ............................................... 85.00
Decoy, Brant Duck, Original Paint .................................................... 40.00
Decoy, Canada Goose, Hollow, 1800s, 11 X 25 In. ...................................... 650.00
Decoy, Canada Goose, Ken Harris, Woodville, N.Y., 21 X 10 In. ........................ 125.00
Decoy, Canvasback, Drake, Mike Pavolic, Monroe, Michigan, 1945, Painted ............. 60.00
Decoy, Coot, Hand-Carved, Wooden ...................................................... 6.50
Decoy, Dowitcher, Carved Eyes ......................................................... 200.00
Decoy, Duck, Carved, Painted, Glass Eyes, 16 In. Long ................................ 17.50
Decoy, Duck, 16 In. Long .............................................................. 30.00
Decoy, Goose, Balsa, Painted .......................................................... 15.00
Decoy, Goose, Hand-Carved, Glass Eye, Painted, 19 In. ................................ 45.00
Decoy, Goose, Signed Beddle, Painted .................................................. 35.00
Decoy, Goose, Wooden, Painted, 22 In. ................................................. 45.00
Decoy, Great Blue Heron, A.Elmer Crowell, Wooden ..................................... 8000.00
Decoy, Hudsonian Curlew, South Jersey, Carved Eyes, Pronounced Wishbone ............. 185.00
Decoy, Plover, Tin, Decorated ......................................................... 69.00
Decoy, Sandpiper, Jethro Midgett, Branch Head, Ocracoke, N.C. ........................ 200.00
Decoy, Shorebird, White & Plack Paint ................................................. 55.00
Decoy, Widgeon Drake, Joe Lincoln, Accord, Mass. ..................................... 375.00
Decoy, Yellow Legs, Homer Lawrence ................................................... 750.00

*The Dedham Pottery Company of Dedham, Massachusetts, started making pottery in 1866. It was reorganized as the Chelsea Pottery Company in 1891, and became the Dedham Pottery Company in 1895. The factory was famous for its crackleware dishes, which picture blue outlines of animals, flowers, and other natural motifs.*

Dedham, Ashtray, Rabbit, 6 1/2 In. ................................................... 75.00
Dedham, Bowl, Rabbit, Round, 6 In. ................................................... 70.00
Dedham, Bowl, Rabbit, 4 3/8 X 1 3/4 In. .............................................. 47.00
Dedham, Bowl, Rabbit, 9 In.Diameter .................................................. 250.00
Dedham, Creamer, Rabbit, 2 3/4 In. ........................................ 50.00 To 70.00
Dedham, Pitcher, Night & Day ......................................................... 275.00
Dedham, Plate, Azalea, 6 In. ......................................................... 36.00
Dedham, Plate, Azalea, 7 1/2 In. ..................................................... 45.00
Dedham, Plate, Duck, 8 In. ........................................................... 58.00
Dedham, Plate, Grape, 6 In. .......................................................... 36.00
Dedham, Plate, Grape, 8 In. .......................................................... 50.00
Dedham, Plate, Grape, 10 In. .............................................. 65.00 To 75.00
Dedham, Plate, Horse Chestnut Border, 8 In. .......................................... 45.00
Dedham, Plate, Magnolia & Pond Lily, 6 In. ........................................... 35.00
Dedham, Plate, Magnolia, 6 In. ....................................................... 36.00
Dedham, Plate, Magnolia, 8 1/2 In. ................................................... 45.00
Dedham, Plate, Pond Lilies, 6 In. .................................................... 36.00
Dedham, Plate, Pond Lilies, 8 1/4 In. ................................................ 37.50
Dedham, Plate, Rabbit, Dark Blue, H.F.G.Co., 11/3/15, 6 In. .......................... 34.00
Dedham, Plate, Rabbit, 7 1/4 In. ..................................................... 58.00
Dedham, Plate, Rabbit, 9 1/4 In. ..................................................... 45.00
Dedham, Plate, Raised Rabbit Border, 8 1/2 In. ....................................... 55.00
Dedham, Plate, Raised Single-Eared Rabbit, 8 1/2 In. ................................. 50.00
Dedham, Plate, Snowtree, 6 In. ....................................................... 36.00
Dedham, Plate, Thistle, Rabbit Signature, 8 1/2 In. .................................. 65.00
Dedham, Salt & Pepper, Rabbits ....................................................... 125.00
Dedham, Sugar, Covered, Rabbit ....................................................... 68.50
Dedham, Tile, Jello Advertisement, Roaring Lion, Roberston Hallmark .................. 25.00

*Delatte glass is a French cameo glass made by Andre Delatte. It was*

Delft, Figurine, Cow, Iron,
Yellow, & Green, C.1780, Pair

*first made in Nancy, France, in 1921. Lighting fixtures and opaque*
*glassware in imitation of Bohemian opaline were made.*

| | |
|---|---:|
| Delatte Nancy, Bottle, Enamel Flowers On Orange, Art Deco, Signed | 85.00 |
| Delatte Nancy, Lamp, Cameo, Butterflies On Yellow, Foliage On Base | 975.00 |
| Delatte Nancy, Tray, Pin, Enamel Flowers On Orange, Art Deco, Signed | 45.00 |
| Delatte, Bowl, Green Aventurine, Metal Cage | 110.00 |
| Delatte, Vase, Fused Glass, Andrea Delatte, Signed Nancy, France, 7 In. | 50.00 |
| Delatte, Vase, Mottled Orange & Blue, 20 In. High | 165.00 |

**Delaware. see Pressed Glass**

**Deldare. see Buffalo Pottery, Deldare**

*Delft is a tin-glazed pottery that has been made since the seventeenth*
*century. It is decorated with blue on white or with colored decorations.*
*Most of the pieces sold today were made after 1891, and the name Holland*
*appears with the Delft factory marks.*

| | |
|---|---:|
| Delft, Ashtray, Shoe, Hand-Painted, Blue Windmill, Marked, 5 1/2 In. | 4.00 |
| Delft, Bowl, Inscribed Success To Trade, English, C.1750, 8 7/8 In.Diameter | 175.00 |
| Delft, Bowl, Peacock & Flowering Shrubbery, C.1750, 14 In. | 115.00 |
| Delft, Bowl, Polychrome, Iron, Yellow, & Green Floral, C.1750, 10 In. | 150.00 |
| Delft, Box, Covered, Marine Scene, Cameo, Crossed Pipes Mark, 3 In. Diameter | 28.00 |
| Delft, Box, Grape, Covered, Leaf Feet, Deep Purple, C.1760, 5 1/2 In.Long | 800.00 |
| Delft, Charger, Basket Of Flowers, Scrolls, C.1720, 13 1/4 In. | 175.00 |
| Delft, Creamer, Cow, Sailboat Design, Germany | 12.50 |
| Delft, Dish, Candy, Windmill Scene, Scalloped, Royal Bonn Delft | 29.00 |
| Delft, Dish, Cheese, Handled Cover, Rectangular, Blue & White Windmill Scene | 20.00 |
| Delft, Dish, Leaf Shape, Marine Scene With Church, Scalloped, Crossed Pipes | 16.50 |
| Delft, Figurine, Cat & Dog, Seated, Decorated, C.1720, 6 3/4 In., Pair | 2000.00 |
| Delft, Figurine, Cow, Iron, Yellow, & Green, C.1780, Pair .....................*Illus* | 1700.00 |
| Delft, Garniture, Three Piece, Blue & White, C.1764 | 200.00 |
| Delft, Inkwell, Faience, Marked Dex, 1759 | 50.00 |
| Delft, Jug, Blue & White, Dutch Mill, Erven Lucas Bols | 60.00 |
| Delft, Jug, Decoration Similar To Peter Cooper's Steam Engine, Blue Mark | 45.00 |
| Delft, Mug, Child's, Seascape, Lithophane Of Child In Bottom, Marked | 45.00 |
| Delft, Pitcher, Bulbous, Dutch Figures, 8 1/2 In. | 35.00 |
| Delft, Plaque, Windmills & Boats, Signed Naar Apol, Shield Shape, Pair | 375.00 |
| Delft, Plate, Hanging, River Front Scene, 16 In. | 28.00 |
| Delft, Plate, Judgment Of Christ, C.1730, 8 7/8 In. | 150.00 |
| Delft, Plate, Peacock, C.1740, 9 1/4 In., Pair | 250.00 |
| Delft, Plate, Peacock, C.1744, 10 1/2 In. | 100.00 |
| Delft, Plate, Signed Boch Freres, Belgium, 11 In. | 35.00 |
| Delft, Pocket, Wall, Rococo Style, Shape, & Decoration, C.1750 | 175.00 |
| Delft, Rack, Letter, Windmill Scene, Scalloped Edge, Raised Foot, 1 Tier | 38.00 |
| Delft, Tile, Blue Windmill On White, Marked Utrecht, Holland, 5 In.Square | 5.00 |
| Delft, Tile, Oriental Figures, Pair | 12.00 |
| Delft, Toothpick, Marine Scene, Crossed Pipes Mark | 18.00 |

*Depression glass was an inexpensive glass manufactured in large quantities*
*during the 1920s and early 1930s. It was made in many colors and patterns by*
*dozens of factories in the United States. The name depression glass is a*
*modern one.*

| | |
|---|---:|
| Depression Glass, Ashtray, Adam, Green | 4.00 |
| Depression Glass, Ashtray, Adam, Pink | 5.75 |
| Depression Glass, Ashtray, Florentine No.2, Yellow | 3.50 |
| Depression Glass, Ashtray, Sunflower, Green | 2.50 |

| | |
|---|---|
| Depression Glass, Ashtray, Waffle | 1.00 |
| Depression Glass, Basket, Grapes & Leaves, Apple Green, 9 1/2 In. High | 20.00 |
| Depression Glass, Berry Set, Newport, Blue, 7 Piece | 20.00 |
| Depression Glass, Boat, Windsor, Green | 7.00 |
| Depression Glass, Bonbon, Lace Edge, Pink, Covered | 20.00 |
| Depression Glass, Bottle, Vinegar, Cameo, Green | 8.00 |
| Depression Glass, Bowl, Adam, Green, 7 3/4 In. | 5.00 |
| Depression Glass, Bowl, Adam, Pink, 8 In. | 4.50 |
| Depression Glass, Bowl, American Sweetheart, Monax, 6 In. | 7.50 |
| Depression Glass, Bowl, American Sweetheart, Monax, 9 In. | 25.00 |
| Depression Glass, Bowl, American Sweetheart, Pink, Oval, 10 In. | 3.50 |
| Depression Glass, Bowl, American Sweetheart, Pink, 5 3/4 In. | 2.75 |
| Depression Glass, Bowl, American Sweetheart, Pink, 6 In. | 2.00 |
| Depression Glass, Bowl, American Sweetheart, Pink, 8 1/2 In. | 4.00 |
| Depression Glass, Bowl, American Sweetheart, Pink, 9 In. | 5.50 |
| Depression Glass, Bowl, Berry, Adam, Pink, Small Size | 3.00 |
| Depression Glass, Bowl, Berry, American Sweetheart, Pink, 3 3/4 In. | 3.50 |
| Depression Glass, Bowl, Berry, Block, Green, 4 3/8 In. | .35 |
| Depression Glass, Bowl, Berry, Cherry Blossom, Green, 8 1/2 In. | 6.50 |
| Depression Glass, Bowl, Berry, Cherry Blossom, Pink, 4 3/4 In. | 2.50 |
| Depression Glass, Bowl, Berry, Master, Cameo, Green, 8 1/4 In. | 5.00 |
| Depression Glass, Bowl, Berry, Royal Lace, Blue, Large Size | 18.00 |
| Depression Glass, Bowl, Berry, Sierra, Green, 8 1/2 In. | 5.50 |
| Depression Glass, Bowl, Block Optic, Green, 4 1/2 In. | 1.00 |
| Depression Glass, Bowl, Bowknot, Green, 4 1/2 In. | 1.00 |
| Depression Glass, Bowl, Bubble, Blue, 4 1/2 In. | .75 |
| Depression Glass, Bowl, Bubble, Blue, 8 In. | 3.50 |
| Depression Glass, Bowl, Bubble, Pink, Shallow, 8 In. | 2.50 |
| Depression Glass, Bowl, Cameo, Green, 5 1/2 In. | 3.00 |
| Depression Glass, Bowl, Cameo, Green, 8 1/4 In. | 5.00 |
| Depression Glass, Bowl, Cereal, American Sweetheart, Monax | 5.00 |
| Depression Glass, Bowl, Cereal, American Sweetheart, Pink, 6 In. | 2.00 To 2.50 |
| Depression Glass, Bowl, Cereal, Cherry Blossom, Pink, 5 3/4 In. | 2.50 |
| Depression Glass, Bowl, Cereal, Cherry, Pink | 2.50 |
| Depression Glass, Bowl, Cereal, Dogwood, Pink, 5 1/2 In. | 3.00 To 3.50 |
| Depression Glass, Bowl, Cereal, Lace Edge, Pink | 1.75 |
| Depression Glass, Bowl, Cereal, Madrid, Amber, 7 In. | 2.50 |
| Depression Glass, Bowl, Cereal, Miss America, Clear | 3.00 |
| Depression Glass, Bowl, Cereal, Miss America, Green | 4.00 |
| Depression Glass, Bowl, Cereal, Miss America, 6 1/4 In. | 2.00 |
| Depression Glass, Bowl, Cereal, No.612, Yellow | 4.00 |
| Depression Glass, Bowl, Cereal, Sandwich, Green, Hocking | 1.00 |
| Depression Glass, Bowl, Cereal, Sierra, Green, 5 1/2 In. | 2.50 |
| Depression Glass, Bowl, Cereal, Spoke, Amber | 1.25 |
| Depression Glass, Bowl, Cherry Blossom, Green, Handled, 9 In. | 7.00 |
| Depression Glass, Bowl, Cherry Blossom, Pink, Handled, 9 In. | 6.00 To 7.50 |
| Depression Glass, Bowl, Cherry Blossom, Pink, 4 3/4 In. | 2.75 |
| Depression Glass, Bowl, Cherry, Blue, Delphite, 2 Handles, 9 In. | 9.00 |
| Depression Glass, Bowl, Cherry, Pink, Handled, 9 In. | 5.00 |
| Depression Glass, Bowl, Cherry, Pink, 3 Legs, 10 1/2 In. | 10.00 |
| Depression Glass, Bowl, Cherry, Pink, 8 In. | 5.00 |
| Depression Glass, Bowl, Clover, Green, Round, 8 In. | 5.00 |
| Depression Glass, Bowl, Console, American Sweetheart, Monax, 18 In. | 175.00 |
| Depression Glass, Bowl, Console, Cameo, Pink | 15.00 |
| Depression Glass, Bowl, Console, Cherry, Green | 20.00 |
| Depression Glass, Bowl, Console, Cherry, Pink | 10.00 |
| Depression Glass, Bowl, Console, Cherry, Pink, Footed | 12.00 |
| Depression Glass, Bowl, Console, Gold Encrusted, Pink, Rolled Edge | 6.00 |
| Depression Glass, Bowl, Console, Madrid, Amber | 6.75 |
| Depression Glass, Bowl, Console, Madrid, Amber, Flared | 8.00 |
| Depression Glass, Bowl, Console, Royal Lace, Pink, Ruffled, Footed | 10.00 |
| Depression Glass, Bowl, Console, Swirl, Ultramarine, Footed, Handled | 9.00 |
| Depression Glass, Bowl, Crackle Rose, Green | 4.00 |
| Depression Glass, Bowl, Cream Soup, American Sweetheart, Monax | 20.00 |
| Depression Glass, Bowl, Cream Soup, American Sweetheart, Pink | 6.50 To 7.00 |
| Depression Glass, Bowl, Cream Soup, Cameo, Green | 25.00 |

Depression Glass, Bowl, Cream Soup, Daisy, Amber ........................................................ 1.75
Depression Glass, Bowl, Cream Soup, Diamond-Quilted, Pink ..................................... 3.00
Depression Glass, Bowl, Cream Soup, Diana, Crystal .................................................. 3.00
Depression Glass, Bowl, Cream Soup, Florentine No.2, Green ..................................... 3.00
Depression Glass, Bowl, Cream Soup, Florentine, Green, 4 3/4 In. ............................. 2.50
Depression Glass, Bowl, Cream Soup, Florentine, Pink, 4 3/4 In. ............................... 3.50
Depression Glass, Bowl, Cream Soup, Madrid, Amber ................................................. 2.75
Depression Glass, Bowl, Cream Soup, Mayfair, Pink ............................... 5.00 To 10.00
Depression Glass, Bowl, Cream Soup, Moderntone, Cobalt ..................... 2.50 To 3.00
Depression Glass, Bowl, Cream Soup, Newport, Blue ................................................. 3.00
Depression Glass, Bowl, Cream Soup, Patrician, Amber ............................................. 3.00
Depression Glass, Bowl, Cream Soup, Rosemary, Amber ........................................... 3.00
Depression Glass, Bowl, Cream Soup, Royal Lace, Crystal ........................................ 4.00
Depression Glass, Bowl, Cream Soup, Royal Lace, Green ........................................... 8.50
Depression Glass, Bowl, Cream Soup, Royal Lace, Pink, Handled ................ 3.00 To 4.00
Depression Glass, Bowl, Cream Soup, Sharon, Pink, 5 In. ......................................... 3.50
Depression Glass, Bowl, Cream Soup, Spoke, Amber ................................................. 2.50
Depression Glass, Bowl, Cubist, Crystal, 6 1/2 In. .................................................... 3.00
Depression Glass, Bowl, Cubist, Green, 7 1/2 In. ...................................................... 3.50
Depression Glass, Bowl, Cubist, Pink, 6 1/2 In. ....................................................... 3.00
Depression Glass, Bowl, Daisy, Amber, 10 In. .......................................................... 4.75
Depression Glass, Bowl, Dessert, Sandwich, Dark Green, 4 1/2 In. ............................ 1.25
Depression Glass, Bowl, Diana, Pink, 5 In. ............................................................... 1.00
Depression Glass, Bowl, Dogwood, Green, 5 1/2 In. ................................................... 3.00
Depression Glass, Bowl, Dogwood, Pink, 5 1/2 In. ..................................................... 2.50
Depression Glass, Bowl, Dogwood, Pink, 8 In. ........................................................... 8.50
Depression Glass, Bowl, Dogwood, Pink, 8 1/2 In. ..................................................... 8.00
Depression Glass, Bowl, Doric, Green, 4 1/2 In. ........................................................ 1.60
Depression Glass, Bowl, Doric, Pink, Handled, 9 In. ................................................. 4.50
Depression Glass, Bowl, Doric, Pink, 4 1/2 In. .......................................................... 1.75
Depression Glass, Bowl, Floral, Green, Oval, 9 In. .................................................... 4.50
Depression Glass, Bowl, Floral, Pink, Deep, 7 1/2 In. ................................................ 4.00
Depression Glass, Bowl, Floral, Pink, 4 In. ............................................................... 1.50
Depression Glass, Bowl, Floral, Pink, 7 In. ............................................................... 4.00
Depression Glass, Bowl, Floral, Pink, 7 1/2 In. ............................................ 3.00 To 4.50
Depression Glass, Bowl, Florentine No.2, Yellow, 8 In. .............................................. 5.00
Depression Glass, Bowl, Florentine, Pink, Handled, 5 1/2 In. ..................................... 3.00
Depression Glass, Bowl, Florentine, Yellow, 6 In. ...................................................... 3.00
Depression Glass, Bowl, Florentine, Yellow, 8 In. ...................................................... 8.00
Depression Glass, Bowl, Flower, Lace Edge, Pink, Crystal Frog ................................. 4.50
Depression Glass, Bowl, Fruit, Cherry Blossom, Green, 19 1/2 In. ............................. 15.00
Depression Glass, Bowl, Fruit, Cherry Blossom, Pink, 3 Footed, 10 1/2 In. ................. 15.00
Depression Glass, Bowl, Fruit, Heritage, Crystal, 10 1/2 In. ...................................... 4.00
Depression Glass, Bowl, Fruit, Iris & Herringbone, Marigold, Ruffled, 11 In. ............... 4.00
Depression Glass, Bowl, Fruit, Mayfair, Green, Flared, Large Size ............................. 15.00
Depression Glass, Bowl, Fruit, Miss America, Crystal, 8 1/4 In. ................................. 3.00
Depression Glass, Bowl, Fruit, Queen Mary, Pink, 6 In. ............................................. 3.00
Depression Glass, Bowl, Fruit, Sharon, Amber, 10 1/2 In. .......................................... 4.50
Depression Glass, Bowl, Fruit, Windsor, Pink, Boat Shape ........................................ 12.00
Depression Glass, Bowl, Georgian, Green, 4 1/2 In. ................................................... 1.75
Depression Glass, Bowl, Georgian, Green, 7 1/2 In. ................................................... 4.00
Depression Glass, Bowl, Heritage, Clear, 5 In. ......................................................... 1.75
Depression Glass, Bowl, Heritage, Clear, 10 1/2 In. .................................................. 4.00
Depression Glass, Bowl, Ice, Sailboat, Cobalt, Tongs & Chromium Stand, 9 In. .......... 10.00
Depression Glass, Bowl, Iris, Carnival, 9 In. ............................................................ 4.00
Depression Glass, Bowl, Lace Edge, Pink, Ribbed, 9 1/2 In. .......................... 3.75 To 4.25
Depression Glass, Bowl, Lace Edge, Pink, 6 1/2 In. ................................................... 2.00
Depression Glass, Bowl, Laurel 'McK,' Jade Green, 5 In. ........................................... 6.00
Depression Glass, Bowl, Lydia Ray, Green, 4 1/2 In. .................................................. 3.00
Depression Glass, Bowl, Madrid, Amber, 5 In. .......................................................... 2.00
Depression Glass, Bowl, Madrid, Amber, 7 In. .......................................................... 3.00
Depression Glass, Bowl, Madrid, Amber, 8 1/4 In. ..................................................... 5.00
Depression Glass, Bowl, Madrid, Amber, 9 In. .......................................................... 6.00
Depression Glass, Bowl, Madrid, Amber, 9 1/2 In. ..................................................... 10.00
Depression Glass, Bowl, Mayfair, Blue, Flat, 11 3/4 In. ............................................. 25.00
Depression Glass, Bowl, Mayfair, Blue, Oval, 9 1/2 In. .............................................. 20.00

| | |
|---|---:|
| Depression Glass, Bowl, Mayfair, Blue, 10 In. | 10.00 |
| Depression Glass, Bowl, Mayfair, Pink, Flared, 12 In. | 8.50 To 10.00 |
| Depression Glass, Bowl, Mayfair, Pink, Handled, 10 In. | 5.00 |
| Depression Glass, Bowl, Mayfair. Pink, 7 In. | 4.50 |
| Depression Glass, Bowl, Mayfair, Pink, 10 In. | 3.50 |
| Depression Glass, Bowl, McK, Poudre Blue, 9 In. | 6.00 |
| Depression Glass, Bowl, Miss America, Clear, Curved At Top, 8 In. | 12.00 |
| Depression Glass, Bowl, Miss America, Clear, Divided, 12 In. | 10.00 |
| Depression Glass, Bowl, Miss America, Curved In, 8 In. | 10.00 |
| Depression Glass, Bowl, Miss America, Moonstone, Flat, 7 3/4 In. | 3.00 |
| Depression Glass, Bowl, Miss America, Moonstone, 9 1/2 In. | 7.00 |
| Depression Glass, Bowl, Moderntone, Blue, 5 In. | 3.00 |
| Depression Glass, Bowl, Moderntone, Blue, 9 In. | 5.50 |
| Depression Glass, Bowl, Moderntone, Cobalt, 4 In. | 2.00 |
| Depression Glass, Bowl, No.612, 7 3/8 In. | 4.00 |
| Depression Glass, Bowl, No.612, 9 3/8 In. | 7.50 |
| Depression Glass, Bowl, Normandie, Sunburst, 5 In. | 1.50 |
| Depression Glass, Bowl, Normandie, Sunburst, 6 1/2 In. | 3.50 |
| Depression Glass, Bowl, Normandie, Sunburst, 8 1/2 In. | 8.00 |
| Depression Glass, Bowl, Oatmeal, Princess, Green, 5 1/2 In. | 3.75 |
| Depression Glass, Bowl, Old Florentine, Pink, 6 In. | 3.00 |
| Depression Glass, Bowl, Open Lace, Pink, 9 1/2 In. | 2.25 |
| Depression Glass, Bowl, Oyster & Pearl, Pink, 10 In. | 6.50 |
| Depression Glass, Bowl, Parrot, Green, Oval, 10 In. | 10.00 |
| Depression Glass, Bowl, Patrician, Amber, Oval, 10 1/2 In. | 6.00 |
| Depression Glass, Bowl, Patrician, Amber, 5 In. | 1.50 |
| Depression Glass, Bowl, Patrician, Amber, 8 1/2 In. | 6.00 |
| Depression Glass, Bowl, Petalware, Clear, 5 3/4 In. | .50 |
| Depression Glass, Bowl, Petalware, Pink, 8 In. | 2.00 |
| Depression Glass, Bowl, Princess, Green, Hat Shape, 9 1/2 In. | 4.00 To 6.00 |
| Depression Glass, Bowl, Princess, Green, Miniature | 4.50 |
| Depression Glass, Bowl, Princess, Pink, 4 1/2 In. | 1.75 |
| Depression Glass, Bowl, Queen Mary, Clear, 7 In. | 1.50 |
| Depression Glass, Bowl, Queen Mary, Pink, Handled, 4 In. | 1.00 |
| Depression Glass, Bowl, Queen Mary, Pink, Handled, 8 In. | 3.50 |
| Depression Glass, Bowl, Royal Lace, Pink, Ruffled, 6 Legs, 10 In. | 8.00 To 12.00 |
| Depression Glass, Bowl, Royal Lace, Pink, 5 In. | 2.50 |
| Depression Glass, Bowl, Royal Lace, Pink, 10 In. | 5.00 To 9.00 |
| Depression Glass, Bowl, Royal Ruby, Handled, 6 1/2 In. | 3.00 |
| Depression Glass, Bowl, Royal Ruby, 8 1/2 In. | 3.50 |
| Depression Glass, Bowl, Salad, Avocado Pear, Green, 9 In. | 9.50 |
| Depression Glass, Bowl, Salad, Madrid, Amber, 9 1/2 In. | 10.00 |
| Depression Glass, Bowl, Salad, Princess, Green, 9 In. | 5.00 |
| Depression Glass, Bowl, Salad, Princess, Pink, Octagonal | 6.00 |
| Depression Glass, Bowl, Salad, Royal Ruby, 11 1/2 In. | 10.00 |
| Depression Glass, Bowl, Sandwich, Amber, Hocking, 4 3/4 In. | 2.00 |
| Depression Glass, Bowl, Sandwich, Amber, Hocking, 9 1/4 In. | 10.00 |
| Depression Glass, Bowl, Sandwich, Pink, Hocking, 8 1/2 In. | 8.50 |
| Depression Glass, Bowl, Sandwich, Red, Hocking, 8 1/2 In. | 18.50 |
| Depression Glass, Bowl, Serving, American Sweetheart, Pink, 8 1/2 In. | 4.00 |
| Depression Glass, Bowl, Serving, Royal Ruby, 8 In. | 12.50 |
| Depression Glass, Bowl, Sharon, Amber, 5 In. | 2.50 |
| Depression Glass, Bowl, Sharon, Amber, 6 In. | 2.00 |
| Depression Glass, Bowl, Sharon, Amber, 8 1/2 In. | 2.00 |
| Depression Glass, Bowl, Sharon, Amber, 10 In. | 4.75 |
| Depression Glass, Bowl, Sharon, Pink, 6 In. | 3.00 |
| Depression Glass, Bowl, Sharon, Pink, 8 In. | 2.00 |
| Depression Glass, Bowl, Sharon, Pink, 10 In. | 5.50 |
| Depression Glass, Bowl, Sierra, Green, 8 1/2 In. | 3.00 |
| Depression Glass, Bowl, Soup, American Sweetheart, Flat, 9 1/2 In. | 4.50 |
| Depression Glass, Bowl, Soup, American Sweetheart, Monax, Rim, 10 In. | 20.00 |
| Depression Glass, Bowl, Soup, Bubble, Blue, 7 3/4 In. | 1.75 |
| Depression Glass, Bowl, Soup, Cameo, Green, Flanged, 9 In. | 7.00 To 9.00 |
| Depression Glass, Bowl, Soup, Cherry Blossom, Pink, Rim, 7 3/4 In. | 10.00 To 15.00 |
| Depression Glass, Bowl, Soup, Holiday, Pink, 7 3/4 In. | 5.00 |
| Depression Glass, Bowl, Soup, Madrid, Green, 7 In. | 4.50 |

| Depression Glass, Bowl, Strawberry, Green, 7 1/2 In. | 5.00 |
|---|---|
| Depression Glass, Bowl, Swirl, Delphite, 9 In. | 9.00 |
| Depression Glass, Bowl, Swirl, Ultramarine, Footed, 10 1/2 In. | 9.50 |
| Depression Glass, Bowl, Vegetable, Adam, Green, 9 In. | 8.00 |
| Depression Glass, Bowl, Vegetable, American Sweetheart, Pink, Oval, 11 In. | 6.00 |
| Depression Glass, Bowl, Vegetable, Ballerina, Green, Oval, 10 In. | 3.25 |
| Depression Glass, Bowl, Vegetable, Cameo, Green, Oval, 10 In. | 4.00 |
| Depression Glass, Bowl, Vegetable, Cherry Blossom, Green, Oval, 9 In. | 6.00 |
| Depression Glass, Bowl, Vegetable, Floral, Pink, Oval, 9 In. | 3.00 To 4.00 |
| Depression Glass, Bowl, Vegetable, Madrid, Amber, Oval, 10 In. | 3.50 To 4.25 |
| Depression Glass, Bowl, Vegetable, Miss America, Pink, Oval, 10 In. | 6.50 |
| Depression Glass, Bowl, Vegetable, Princess, Green, Oval, 10 In. | 4.00 |
| Depression Glass, Bowl, Windsor Diamond, Pink, Oval, 9 1/2 In. | 7.00 |
| Depression Glass, Bowl, Windsor Diamond, Pink, 8 1/2 In. | 7.00 |
| Depression Glass, Bowl, Yvonne, Yellow, Handled, 8 In. | 4.00 |
| Depression Glass, Bridge Set, Sierra, Pink, Roshf Bros., Iowa, 14 Piece | 30.00 |
| Depression Glass, Bucket, Ice, Block, Green | 2.50 |
| Depression Glass, Bucket, Ice, Block, Pink | 7.50 |
| Depression Glass, Bucket, Ice, Etched, Green | 6.00 |
| Depression Glass, Bucket, Ice, Ribbed, Green, Ground Bottom | 8.00 |
| Depression Glass, Bucket, Ice, Ribbed, Ruby | 10.00 |
| Depression Glass, Bucket, Ice, Ribbed, Yellow, Ground Bottom | 8.00 |
| Depression Glass, Bucket, Ice, Stippled, Clear Band | 6.75 |
| Depression Glass, Butter, Adam, Pink | 37.50 |
| Depression Glass, Butter, Anniversary, Pink | 15.00 |
| Depression Glass, Butter, Block, Green, Covered, 3 X 5 In. | 9.00 To 15.00 |
| Depression Glass, Butter, Buttons & Bows, Pink | 16.00 |
| Depression Glass, Butter, Cherry Blossom, Green, Covered | 25.00 To 60.00 |
| Depression Glass, Butter, Cherry Blossom, Pink, Covered | 35.00 To 46.00 |
| Depression Glass, Butter, Cherry, Pink | 45.00 |
| Depression Glass, Butter, Colonial Block, Clear | 18.50 |
| Depression Glass, Butter, Colonial Block, Green | 18.50 |
| Depression Glass, Butter, Colonial Block, Pink | 18.50 |
| Depression Glass, Butter, Colonial, Clear | 18.00 |
| Depression Glass, Butter, Colonial, Green, Covered | 25.00 |
| Depression Glass, Butter, Columbia, Clear, Covered, Round | 10.50 To 12.50 |
| Depression Glass, Butter, Columbia, Green | 10.00 |
| Depression Glass, Butter, Cubist, Green | 35.00 |
| Depression Glass, Butter, Cubist, Pink | 30.00 |
| Depression Glass, Butter, Doric, Pink | 45.00 |
| Depression Glass, Butter, Floragold, Iridescent, Oblong | 6.00 |
| Depression Glass, Butter, Floragold, Round | 15.00 |
| Depression Glass, Butter, Floral, Green | 55.00 |
| Depression Glass, Butter, Floral, Pink, Covered | 35.00 To 52.50 |
| Depression Glass, Butter, Florentine No.2, Yellow | 40.00 To 65.00 |
| Depression Glass, Butter, Georgian, Green | 28.00 To 35.00 |
| Depression Glass, Butter, Holiday, Pink | 15.00 |
| Depression Glass, Butter, Homespun, Pink | 35.00 |
| Depression Glass, Butter, Indiana, Custard, Covered | 48.00 |
| Depression Glass, Butter, Lace Edge, Pink, Covered | 15.00 To 20.00 |
| Depression Glass, Butter, Lovebird, Green, Covered | 30.00 |
| Depression Glass, Butter, Madrid, Amber | 35.00 To 47.50 |
| Depression Glass, Butter, Madrid, Green | 45.00 To 55.00 |
| Depression Glass, Butter, Mayfair, Pink | 30.00 |
| Depression Glass, Butter, Oatmeal | 20.00 |
| Depression Glass, Butter, Open Lace, Pink | 18.00 |
| Depression Glass, Butter, Patrician, Amber | 40.00 To 42.50 |
| Depression Glass, Butter, Patrician, Pink | 47.50 |
| Depression Glass, Butter, Princess, Green | 35.00 To 47.50 |
| Depression Glass, Butter, Princess, Pink | 37.50 |
| Depression Glass, Butter, Royal Lace, Clear, Covered | 25.00 To 29.50 |
| Depression Glass, Butter, Royal Lace, Green | 200.00 |
| Depression Glass, Butter, Sandwich, Clear | 18.00 |
| Depression Glass, Butter, Sandwich, Clear, Anchor Hocking | 10.00 |
| Depression Glass, Butter, Sharon, Amber | 37.50 |
| Depression Glass, Butter, Sharon, Amber, Covered | 28.00 To 35.00 |

| | |
|---|---:|
| Depression Glass, **Butter**, Sharon, Green | 75.00 |
| Depression Glass, **Butter**, Sharon, Green, Covered | 48.00 |
| Depression Glass, **Butter**, Sharon, Pink | 20.00 To 23.00 |
| Depression Glass, **Butter**, Sharon, Pink, Covered | 28.00 To 30.00 |
| Depression Glass, **Butter**, Sierra, Pink | 25.00 |
| Depression Glass, **Butter**, Waterford, Crystal, Covered | 10.00 |
| Depression Glass, **Butter**, Windsor Diamond, Pink | 30.00 |
| Depression Glass, **Butter**, Windsor, Green | 16.00 |
| Depression Glass, **Butter**, Windsor, Pink, Covered | 15.00 To 18.00 |
| Depression Glass, **Cake Stand**, Cubist, Clear, 10 In. | 10.00 |
| Depression Glass, **Candleholder**, Adam, Pink, Pair | 16.00 |
| Depression Glass, **Candleholder**, Cameo, Green | 10.00 |
| Depression Glass, **Candleholder**, Florentine No.2, Green, Pair | 10.00 |
| Depression Glass, **Candleholder**, Indiana Sandwich, Crystal, Low, Pair | 5.00 |
| Depression Glass, **Candleholder**, Iris, Crystal, Pair | 5.00 |
| Depression Glass, **Candleholder**, Lace Edge, Pink, Hand-Painted Floral, Pair | 18.00 |
| Depression Glass, **Candleholder**, Madrid, Amber, Low, Pair | 10.00 |
| Depression Glass, **Candleholder**, Madrid, Amber, Pair | 8.75 |
| Depression Glass, **Candleholder**, Miss America, Moonstone, Pair | 6.50 |
| Depression Glass, **Candleholder**, Royal Lace, Pink, Rolled Edge, Pair | 12.00 |
| Depression Glass, **Candleholder**, Royal Lace, Pink, Ruffled | 6.00 |
| Depression Glass, **Candleholder**, Swirl, Ultramarine, Pair | 15.00 |
| Depression Glass, **Candleholder**, Twisted Swirl, Pink, Pair | 6.50 |
| Depression Glass, **Candlestick**, Adam, Pink | 6.00 To 15.00 |
| Depression Glass, **Candlestick**, Adam, Pink, Pair | 15.00 To 18.50 |
| Depression Glass, **Candlestick**, Cameo, Green, Pair | 30.00 |
| Depression Glass, **Candlestick**, Diamond-Quilted, Green, Pair | 5.50 |
| Depression Glass, **Candlestick**, Florentine, Green, Pair | 14.00 |
| Depression Glass, **Candlestick**, Florentine, Yellow, Pair | 14.00 To 15.00 |
| Depression Glass, **Candlestick**, Iris, Clear, Pair | 8.00 |
| Depression Glass, **Candlestick**, Madrid, Amber, Pair | 9.00 |
| Depression Glass, **Candlestick**, Madrid, Amber, 2 In. | 4.50 |
| Depression Glass, **Candlestick**, Madrid, Pink | 9.00 |
| Depression Glass, **Candlestick**, Opalescent Hobnail, Moonstone, Low, Pair | 7.00 |
| Depression Glass, **Candlestick**, Oyster & Pearl, Ruby, Pair | 10.00 |
| Depression Glass, **Candlestick**, Royal Lace, Pink | 7.50 |
| Depression Glass, **Casserole**, Adam, Pink | 7.50 |
| Depression Glass, **Celery**, Mayfair, Pink | 6.00 |
| Depression Glass, **Celery**, Miss America, Clear | 2.50 To 4.50 |
| Depression Glass, **Celery**, Miss America, Pink | 4.50 To 5.00 |
| Depression Glass, **Child's Set**, Cherry, Delfite, 14 Piece | 175.00 |
| Depression Glass, **Coaster**, Adam, Pink, 3 7/8 In. | 3.50 |
| Depression Glass, **Coaster**, Cherry Blossom, Pink | 5.00 |
| Depression Glass, **Coaster**, Cubist, Green | 2.00 To 3.00 |
| Depression Glass, **Coaster**, Cubist, Pink | 2.00 |
| Depression Glass, **Coaster**, Doric, Pink | 3.00 |
| Depression Glass, **Coaster**, Floral, Green | 2.00 To 2.50 |
| Depression Glass, **Coaster**, Floral, Pink | 1.75 To 2.50 |
| Depression Glass, **Coaster**, Florentine No.2, Green | 1.25 To 2.25 |
| Depression Glass, **Coaster**, Florentine No.2, Yellow | 1.50 |
| Depression Glass, **Coaster**, Florentine, Green | 2.50 |
| Depression Glass, **Coaster**, Florentine, Pink | 2.50 |
| Depression Glass, **Coaster**, Twisted Optic, Pink | 4.00 |
| Depression Glass, **Coaster**, Waterford, Crystal | 1.50 |
| Depression Glass, **Cocktail Shaker**, Angelfish, Cobalt, Sportsman Series | 10.00 |
| Depression Glass, **Cocktail Shaker**, Windmill, Cobalt | 10.00 To 12.50 |
| Depression Glass, **Compote**, Block Optic, Green | 4.50 |
| Depression Glass, **Compote**, Floral & Diamond Band, Green | 6.50 |
| Depression Glass, **Compote**, Florentine, Pink, Ruffled, 3 1/2 In. | 4.00 |
| Depression Glass, **Compote**, Lace Edge, Pink, Footed | 3.00 |
| Depression Glass, **Compote**, Miss America, Clear, 5 In. | 3.00 To 5.00 |
| Depression Glass, **Compote**, Miss America, Pink | 4.50 To 9.00 |
| Depression Glass, **Console Set**, Oyster & Pearls, Pink & White, Opaque | 7.50 |
| Depression Glass, **Creamer**, Adam, Pink | 3.50 |
| Depression Glass, **Creamer**, American Sweetheart, Monax | 4.00 To 4.50 |
| Depression Glass, **Creamer**, American Sweetheart, Pink | 2.50 To 4.00 |

Depression Glass, Creamer, Bubble, Blue ..................................................... 3.00
Depression Glass, Creamer, Cameo, Green, Cone Shape ......................... 2.50
Depression Glass, Creamer, Cameo, Green, 3 In. ................................... 2.50
Depression Glass, Creamer, Cameo, Green, 3 1/4 In. ............................. 2.50
Depression Glass, Creamer, Cameo, Green, 4 In. ................................... 3.00
Depression Glass, Creamer, Cameo, Yellow ........................................... 3.50
Depression Glass, Creamer, Cherry Blossom, Delfite .............................. 15.00
Depression Glass, Creamer, Cherry Blossom, Green ............................... 4.50
Depression Glass, Creamer, Cherry Blossom, Pink ............... 3.00 To 3.50
Depression Glass, Creamer, Cherry, Pink ........................... 2.50 To 4.00
Depression Glass, Creamer, Child's, Cherry, Delfite ............................... 30.00
Depression Glass, Creamer, Child's, Cherry, Pink ................................... 25.00
Depression Glass, Creamer, Cloverleaf, Green ....................................... 2.50
Depression Glass, Creamer, Colonial, Clear ........................................... 3.00
Depression Glass, Creamer, Cubist, Clear, 2 In. .................................... 1.50
Depression Glass, Creamer, Cubist, Green, 3 In. ................................... 3.00
Depression Glass, Creamer, Cubist, Pink, 2 In. ..................................... 1.50
Depression Glass, Creamer, Cubist, Pink, 3 In. ..................................... 3.00
Depression Glass, Creamer, Double Shield, Cobalt ................................ 4.50
Depression Glass, Creamer, Floragold, Iridescent ................................. 2.50
Depression Glass, Creamer, Floral, Pink ............................................... 2.00
Depression Glass, Creamer, Florentine No.2, Green ............. 2.50 To 3.50
Depression Glass, Creamer, Florentine, Yellow ...................................... 3.00
Depression Glass, Creamer, Georgian, Green ......................................... 2.00
Depression Glass, Creamer, Georgian, Green, 4 In. ............................... 3.00
Depression Glass, Creamer, Holiday, Pink .......................... 2.00 To 2.25
Depression Glass, Creamer, Iris, Crystal ............................................... 2.50
Depression Glass, Creamer, Lace Edge, Pink ........................................ 4.25
Depression Glass, Creamer, Madrid, Amber ........................ 1.50 To 2.75
Depression Glass, Creamer, Miss America, Pink ................... 4.25 To 5.00
Depression Glass, Creamer, Moderntone, Amethyst ............................... 3.00
Depression Glass, Creamer, Moderntone, Blue ...................................... 2.25
Depression Glass, Creamer, Moderntone, Burgundy ............................... 2.50
Depression Glass, Creamer, Moderntone, Cobalt .................. 2.25 To 2.50
Depression Glass, Creamer, Oatmeal Lace, Clear .................................. 2.00
Depression Glass, Creamer, Parrot, Green ............................................. 6.00
Depression Glass, Creamer, Patrician, Amber ...................... 2.50 To 3.00
Depression Glass, Creamer, Princess, Green .......................................... 3.00
Depression Glass, Creamer, Royal Lace, Cobalt .................................... 10.50
Depression Glass, Creamer, Royal Lace, Pink ....................................... 3.75
Depression Glass, Creamer, Royal Lace, Ritz Blue ................................ 12.00
Depression Glass, Creamer, S Pattern, Clear ........................................ 2.50
Depression Glass, Creamer, Sharon, Pink ............................ 2.00 To 3.50
Depression Glass, Creamer, Sierra, Green ............................................. 3.00
Depression Glass, Creamer, Strawberry, Pink, Large Size ...................... 6.00
Depression Glass, Creamer, Sunflower, Green ....................................... 3.00
Depression Glass, Creamer, Sunflower, Pink .......................................... 4.50
Depression Glass, Creamer, Swirl, Ultramarine .................... 2.50 To 2.75
Depression Glass, Creamer, Tearoom, Green, Large Size ....................... 4.00
Depression Glass, Creamer, Wedding Band, Cobalt Blue ....................... 2.00
Depression Glass, Cup & Saucer, Adam, Pink ...................... 3.50 To 5.50
Depression Glass, Cup & Saucer, American Sweetheart, Monax ... 6.50 To 7.00
Depression Glass, Cup & Saucer, American Sweetheart, Pink ... 3.50 To 5.50
Depression Glass, Cup & Saucer, American Sweetheart, Red .................. 125.00
Depression Glass, Cup & Saucer, Block Optic, Green, Round .................. 3.00
Depression Glass, Cup & Saucer, Bubble, Blue ..................... 1.00 To 1.75
Depression Glass, Cup & Saucer, Cameo, Green .................................... 4.50
Depression Glass, Cup & Saucer, Cherry Blossom, Green ....................... 7.50
Depression Glass, Cup & Saucer, Cherry Blossom, Pink .......... 5.75 To 6.00
Depression Glass, Cup & Saucer, Cherry, Green ..................................... 7.50
Depression Glass, Cup & Saucer, Cherry, Pink ....................................... 6.00
Depression Glass, Cup & Saucer, Child's, Cherry, Delfite ........................ 30.00
Depression Glass, Cup & Saucer, Child's, Cherry, Pink ........................... 18.00
Depression Glass, Cup & Saucer, Child's, Doric & Pansy, Ultramarine ..... 20.00
Depression Glass, Cup & Saucer, Clover, Green ..................................... 2.50
Depression Glass, Cup & Saucer, Cloverleaf, Clear ................................ 2.50

Depression Glass, Cup & Saucer, Columbia, Clear ........................................ 2.50
Depression Glass, Cup & Saucer, Daisy, Amber ........................... 2.00 To 3.00
Depression Glass, Cup & Saucer, Daisy, Dark Amber ............................ 4.00
Depression Glass, Cup & Saucer, Dogwood, Green ............................... 6.50
Depression Glass, Cup & Saucer, Dogwood, Pink ................... 3.00 To 4.50
Depression Glass, Cup & Saucer, English Hobnail, Pink ..................... 4.00
Depression Glass, Cup & Saucer, Floral, Green .................... 4.00 To 6.00
Depression Glass, Cup & Saucer, Floral, Pink ..................... 4.00 To 5.50
Depression Glass, Cup & Saucer, Fruits, Green ............................. 2.50
Depression Glass, Cup & Saucer, Georgian, Green ............................ 2.75
Depression Glass, Cup & Saucer, Heritage, Clear ............................. 1.75
Depression Glass, Cup & Saucer, Holiday, Pink ............................... 4.00
Depression Glass, Cup & Saucer, Iris, Crystal ................................. 5.00
Depression Glass, Cup & Saucer, Lace Edge, Pink ........................... 5.00
Depression Glass, Cup & Saucer, Laurel 'McK, ' Jade Green ................. 8.00
Depression Glass, Cup & Saucer, Lovebirds, Green ........................... 4.00
Depression Glass, Cup & Saucer, Madrid, Amber ................. 2.75 To 5.50
Depression Glass, Cup & Saucer, Mayfair, Pink ............................ 10.00
Depression Glass, Cup & Saucer, Miss America, Clear ..................... 5.00
Depression Glass, Cup & Saucer, Miss America, Pink ...................... 7.50
Depression Glass, Cup & Saucer, Moderntone, Blue ................. 3.25 To 3.50
Depression Glass, Cup & Saucer, Moderntone, Cobalt ..................... 3.00
Depression Glass, Cup & Saucer, Moroccan, Amethyst ..................... 2.50
Depression Glass, Cup & Saucer, No.612, Green ................ 3.00 To 6.00
Depression Glass, Cup & Saucer, Normandie, Amber ....................... 3.00
Depression Glass, Cup & Saucer, Normandie, Carnival ..................... 4.25
Depression Glass, Cup & Saucer, Normandie, Pink ......................... 3.00
Depression Glass, Cup & Saucer, Old Florentine, Pink ..................... 3.75
Depression Glass, Cup & Saucer, Patrician, Amber ............... 4.00 To 5.00
Depression Glass, Cup & Saucer, Patrician, Clear ......................... 3.00
Depression Glass, Cup & Saucer, Patrician, Green ......................... 4.00
Depression Glass, Cup & Saucer, Petalware, Cremax ...................... 3.25
Depression Glass, Cup & Saucer, Princess, Green .......................... 2.25
Depression Glass, Cup & Saucer, Princess, Yellow ......................... 2.75
Depression Glass, Cup & Saucer, Queen Mary, Pink ....................... 3.50
Depression Glass, Cup & Saucer, Royal Lace, Blue ....................... 12.50
Depression Glass, Cup & Saucer, Royal Lace, Clear ....................... 3.50
Depression Glass, Cup & Saucer, Royal Lace, Cobalt ..................... 10.00
Depression Glass, Cup & Saucer, Royal Lace, Green ............ 9.50 To 10.00
Depression Glass, Cup & Saucer, Royal Lace, Pink ............... 5.00 To 6.00
Depression Glass, Cup & Saucer, Royal Ruby ................... 2.25 To 6.50
Depression Glass, Cup & Saucer, S Pattern, Clear ......................... 3.00
Depression Glass, Cup & Saucer, Sandwich, Amber, Hocking ............. 5.00
Depression Glass, Cup & Saucer, Sandwich, Green, Hocking ............. 8.50
Depression Glass, Cup & Saucer, Sharon, Amber ........................... 3.50
Depression Glass, Cup & Saucer, Sharon, Pink ................... 3.00 To 4.00
Depression Glass, Cup & Saucer, Sierra, Green ............................. 4.50
Depression Glass, Cup & Saucer, Swirl, Green ............................. 3.50
Depression Glass, Cup & Saucer, Swirl, Ultramarine ..................... 3.75
Depression Glass, Cup & Saucer, Victory, Pink ............................. 7.75
Depression Glass, Cup, Adam, Green ...................................... 4.00
Depression Glass, Cup, Adam, Pink ........................................ 4.00
Depression Glass, Cup, American Sweetheart, Monax ..................... 5.75
Depression Glass, Cup, American Sweetheart, Pink ....................... 3.00
Depression Glass, Cup, Anniversary, Pink ................................. 2.00
Depression Glass, Cup, Block Optic, Green ................................ 2.00
Depression Glass, Cup, Bowknot, Green ................................... 2.00
Depression Glass, Cup, Bubble, Blue ...................... 1.00 To 1.50
Depression Glass, Cup, Cameo, Green ..................................... 3.00
Depression Glass, Cup, Cameo, Yellow ................... 2.25 To 2.85
Depression Glass, Cup, Cherry Blossom, Green ........................... 3.50
Depression Glass, Cup, Cherry, Delfite .................................... 8.00
Depression Glass, Cup, Cloverleaf, Green ................................. 1.75
Depression Glass, Cup, Cloverleaf, Pink ................................... 2.50
Depression Glass, Cup, Colonial, Pink ..................................... 2.00
Depression Glass, Cup, Custard, Cherry, Crystal ......................... 13.00

| | |
|---|---|
| Depression Glass, Cup, Custard, Sandwich, Green, Hocking | 1.00 |
| Depression Glass, Cup, Floragold, Iridescent | 1.50 |
| Depression Glass, Cup, Floral, Green | 2.25 To 3.50 |
| Depression Glass, Cup, Floral, Pink | 2.25 |
| Depression Glass, Cup, Florentine No.2, Green | 1.75 |
| Depression Glass, Cup, Florentine No.2, Yellow | 2.50 |
| Depression Glass, Cup, Florentine, Clear | 2.00 |
| Depression Glass, Cup, Florentine, Yellow | 2.00 |
| Depression Glass, Cup, Fruits, Green | 1.50 |
| Depression Glass, Cup, Georgian, Green | 2.25 |
| Depression Glass, Cup, Holiday, Pink | 1.50 |
| Depression Glass, Cup, Horseshoe, Green | 2.25 |
| Depression Glass, Cup, Iris, Clear | 2.75 |
| Depression Glass, Cup, Jello, Moderntone, Cobalt | 2.00 To 2.50 |
| Depression Glass, Cup, Lace Edge, Pink | 4.00 |
| Depression Glass, Cup, Laurel, Blue | 5.00 |
| Depression Glass, Cup, Lorain, Yellow | 2.50 |
| Depression Glass, Cup, Madrid, Amber | 2.00 To 2.50 |
| Depression Glass, Cup, Madrid, Pink | 3.00 |
| Depression Glass, Cup, Manhattan, Clear | 1.00 |
| Depression Glass, Cup, Mayfair, Pink | 3.50 |
| Depression Glass, Cup, Measuring, HMW No.300, Green | 5.00 |
| Depression Glass, Cup, Miss America, Pink | 3.00 To 6.00 |
| Depression Glass, Cup, Moderntone, Amethyst | 2.50 |
| Depression Glass, Cup, Moderntone, Burgundy | 2.50 |
| Depression Glass, Cup, Moderntone, Cobalt | 2.50 |
| Depression Glass, Cup, No.612, Green | 2.50 |
| Depression Glass, Cup, Normandie, Pink | 2.50 |
| Depression Glass, Cup, Normandie, Sunburst | 3.00 |
| Depression Glass, Cup, Nut, English Hobnail, Pedestal, Card Holder | 5.00 |
| Depression Glass, Cup, Old Cafe, Pink | 3.00 |
| Depression Glass, Cup, Optic Block, Green | 1.75 |
| Depression Glass, Cup, Patrician, Crystal | 2.50 |
| Depression Glass, Cup, Petalware, Monax, Orange Green Trim | 2.50 |
| Depression Glass, Cup, Princess, Green | 1.75 To 3.00 |
| Depression Glass, Cup, Princess, Pink | 1.75 To 3.00 |
| Depression Glass, Cup, Princess, Topaz | 2.50 |
| Depression Glass, Cup, Punch, Royal Ruby | 1.00 |
| Depression Glass, Cup, Queen Mary, Clear | 1.00 |
| Depression Glass, Cup, Queen Mary, Pink | 1.50 To 2.75 |
| Depression Glass, Cup, Roulette, Green | 1.50 To 2.50 |
| Depression Glass, Cup, Royal Lace, Blue | 8.50 To 10.00 |
| Depression Glass, Cup, Royal Lace, Cobalt | 7.50 |
| Depression Glass, Cup, Royal Lace, Pink | 2.00 To 2.50 |
| Depression Glass, Cup, Royal Lace, Ritz Blue | 10.00 |
| Depression Glass, Cup, Royal Ruby | 2.50 |
| Depression Glass, Cup, Sandwich Hocking, Golden Amber | 2.00 |
| Depression Glass, Cup, Sharon, Amber | 2.00 |
| Depression Glass, Cup, Spiral, Green | 2.50 |
| Depression Glass, Cup, Sunflower, Green | 2.50 |
| Depression Glass, Cup, Sunflower, Pink | 3.50 |
| Depression Glass, Cup, Swirl, Ultramarine | 2.75 |
| Depression Glass, Decanter, Mayfair, Pink | 40.00 To 45.00 |
| Depression Glass, Decanter, Sandwich, Clear | 25.00 |
| Depression Glass, Dish, Candy, Adam, Pink | 15.00 |
| Depression Glass, Dish, Candy, Adam, Pink, Covered | 18.00 |
| Depression Glass, Dish, Candy, Adam, Pink, Low | 15.00 |
| Depression Glass, Dish, Candy, Anniversary, Pink, Covered | 10.00 |
| Depression Glass, Dish, Candy, Block Optic, Yellow, Covered, Flat | 8.50 |
| Depression Glass, Dish, Candy, Cameo, Green, Covered | 10.00 To 60.00 |
| Depression Glass, Dish, Candy, Cameo, Green, Covered, 4 In. | 9.00 To 16.50 |
| Depression Glass, Dish, Candy, Cameo, Green, 4 In. | 7.75 |
| Depression Glass, Dish, Candy, Cubist, Green, Covered | 9.00 |
| Depression Glass, Dish, Candy, Diana, Pink, Covered | 6.50 |
| Depression Glass, Dish, Candy, Doric, Pink, Covered | 10.00 |
| Depression Glass, Dish, Candy, Floral, Pink, Covered | 9.00 |

Depression Glass, Dish, Candy, Florentine, Crystal, Covered, 6 In. .................................................. 20.00
Depression Glass, Dish, Candy, Iris, Clear ........................................................................................ 3.00
Depression Glass, Dish, Candy, Lace Edge, Pink ............................................................................ 6.00
Depression Glass, Dish, Candy, Mayfair, Pink ................................................................ 6.00 To 12.00
Depression Glass, Dish, Candy, Mayfair, Pink, Covered .............................................................. 42.00
Depression Glass, Dish, Candy, Miss America, Clear, Metal Lid .................................................. 18.00
Depression Glass, Dish, Candy, Miss America, Pink, Covered ...................................................... 55.00
Depression Glass, Dish, Candy, Old Cafe, Pink .............................................................................. 4.50
Depression Glass, Dish, Candy, Princess, Green, Covered .......................................................... 10.00
Depression Glass, Dish, Candy, Sharon, Amber, Covered ............................................................ 12.50
Depression Glass, Dish, Candy, Sharon, Pink, Covered ................................................................ 12.50
Depression Glass, Dish, Candy, Spiral, Green ................................................................................ 6.50
Depression Glass, Dish, Candy, Swirl, Ultramarine, 3 Legs, 5 1/2 In. ............................................ 5.00
Depression Glass, Dish, Cheese, Kraft, Blue .................................................................................. 9.00
Depression Glass, Dish, Fruit, Sharon, Pink, 5 In. .......................................................................... 3.00
Depression Glass, Dish, Jam, Madrid, Amber, 7 In. ........................................................................ 4.50
Depression Glass, Dish, Jam, Patrician, Amber .............................................................................. 7.50
Depression Glass, Dish, Jello, Madrid, Amber ................................................................................ 3.35
Depression Glass, Dish, Jelly, English Hobnail, Amber, Footed .................................................... 6.00
Depression Glass, Dish, Jelly, Ribbed, Marigold, Footed .............................................................. 9.00
Depression Glass, Dish, Miss America, Moonstone, Cloverleaf Shape ........................................ 3.50
Depression Glass, Dish, Nut, Florentine No.2, Green, Handled .................................................... 2.00
Depression Glass, Dish, Nut, Moderntone, Blue, Ruffled .............................................................. 2.50
Depression Glass, Dish, Olive, Avocado Pear, Pink, 2 Handles .................................................... 6.00
Depression Glass, Dish, Pickle, Ballerina, Green, Divided ............................................................ 3.00
Depression Glass, Dish, Pickle, Queen Mary, Pink, Oval .............................................................. 3.75
Depression Glass, Doll's Set, Cherry, Pink, 14 Piece .................................................................. 145.00
Depression Glass, Eggcup, McK, Jade Green, Footed, No.258 ...................................................... 3.50
Depression Glass, Goblet, Block Optic, Green, Gold Trim, 6 In. .................................................... 6.50
Depression Glass, Goblet, Block Optic, Pink, 4 1/2 In. .................................................................. 3.00
Depression Glass, Goblet, Cocktail, Block, Green, 4 In. ................................................................ 4.50
Depression Glass, Goblet, Cocktail, Mayfair, Pink, 4 In. ............................................ 30.00 To 32.00
Depression Glass, Goblet, Colonial, Clear, 3 Ozs., 4 In. ................................................................ 5.00
Depression Glass, Goblet, Etched, Clear ........................................................................................ 2.50
Depression Glass, Goblet, Etched, Green ........................................................................................ 3.00
Depression Glass, Goblet, Etched, Pink .................................................................... 2.50 To 3.00
Depression Glass, Goblet, Iris, Clear, 4 In. .................................................................................... 4.00
Depression Glass, Goblet, Iris, Clear, 4 1/2 In. ........................................................ 4.00 To 5.00
Depression Glass, Goblet, Iris, Clear, 4 Ozs., 5 3/4 In. ............................................ 5.00 To 6.00
Depression Glass, Goblet, Loraine, Green, Footed ........................................................................ 6.00
Depression Glass, Goblet, Mayfair, Blue, 7 1/4 In. ........................................................................ 45.00
Depression Glass, Goblet, Mayfair, Pink, 5 3/4 In. ........................................................................ 18.00
Depression Glass, Goblet, Mayfair, Pink, 7 1/2 In. ........................................................................ 45.00
Depression Glass, Goblet, Miss America, Clear, Footed, 10 Ozs. ............................ 7.00 To 9.00
Depression Glass, Goblet, Miss America, Moonstone .................................................................... 5.25
Depression Glass, Goblet, Royal Ruby, Knob Stem ........................................................................ 3.50
Depression Glass, Goblet, Swirl, Buttermilk .................................................................................. 16.50
Depression Glass, Goblet, Swirled Top, Green Stem ...................................................................... 2.75
Depression Glass, Goblet, Yellow Block, Long Stem, 7 1/4 In. ...................................................... 4.00
Depression Glass, Jar, American Pioneer, Green, Covered, Low, 3 1/2 In. .................................. 10.00
Depression Glass, Jar, Candy, Adam, Pink .................................................................................... 18.00
Depression Glass, Jar, Candy, Adam, Pink, Covered .................................................................... 16.50
Depression Glass, Jar, Candy, Cubist, Green, Covered ................................................................ 10.00
Depression Glass, Jar, Candy, Cubist, Pink, 7 1/2 In. .................................................................... 6.00
Depression Glass, Jar, Candy, Floral, Green .................................................................................. 9.00
Depression Glass, Jar, Candy, Mayfair, Pink, Covered, Footed .................................................... 12.00
Depression Glass, Jar, Candy, Miss America, Clear, Covered ...................................................... 55.00
Depression Glass, Jar, Candy, Miss America, Pink, Covered ........................................................ 42.50
Depression Glass, Jar, Candy, Princess, Green ........................................................ 4.50 To 10.00
Depression Glass, Jar, Candy, Sharon, Amber .............................................................................. 10.00
Depression Glass, Jar, Candy, Twisted Optic, Green ...................................................................... 3.00
Depression Glass, Jar, Cookie, Amber ............................................................................................ 11.00
Depression Glass, Jar, Cookie, Cameo, Green .......................................................... 8.00 To 12.50
Depression Glass, Jar, Cookie, Cameo, Green, Covered .............................................................. 10.00
Depression Glass, Jar, Cookie, Lace Edge, Pink .......................................................................... 15.00
Depression Glass, Jar, Cookie, Madrid, Amber .............................................................................. 12.00

| | |
|---|---:|
| Depression Glass, Jar, Cookie, Madrid, Pink | 13.00 |
| Depression Glass, Jar, Cookie, Mayfair, Pink | 12.00 |
| Depression Glass, Jar, Cookie, Mayfair, Pink, Covered | 12.00 To 12.50 |
| Depression Glass, Jar, Cookie, Patrician, Amber, Covered | 16.00 |
| Depression Glass, Jar, Cookie, Patrician, Pink, Covered | 16.00 |
| Depression Glass, Jar, Cookie, Princess, Green | 7.00 |
| Depression Glass, Jar, Cookie, Princess, Green, Covered | 7.00 To 10.00 |
| Depression Glass, Jar, Cookie, Princess, Pink | 5.00 |
| Depression Glass, Jar, Cookie, Royal Lace, Green | 15.00 To 24.50 |
| Depression Glass, Jar, Cookie, Royal Lace, Green, Covered | 25.00 To 30.00 |
| Depression Glass, Jar, Cookie, Royal Lace, Pink | 10.00 To 15.00 |
| Depression Glass, Jar, Cookie, Royal Lace, Pink, Covered | 12.75 |
| Depression Glass, Jar, Cookie, Sandwich, Amber | 20.00 |
| Depression Glass, Jar, Cookie, Sandwich, Gold, Hocking | 25.00 |
| Depression Glass, Jar, Cracker, Cameo, Green, Covered | 16.00 |
| Depression Glass, Jar, Cracker, Madrid, Amber | 10.00 |
| Depression Glass, Jar, Cracker, Madrid, Amber, Covered | 10.00 To 15.00 |
| Depression Glass, Jar, Cracker, Mayfair, Pink, Covered | 7.50 |
| Depression Glass, Jar, Cracker, Royal Lace, Green | 20.00 |
| Depression Glass, Jar, Cracker, Royal Lace, Green, Covered | 25.00 |
| Depression Glass, Jar, Cracker, Royal Lace, Pink, Covered | 17.50 |
| Depression Glass, Jar, Mustard, Waterford, Crystal, Covered | 3.00 |
| Depression Glass, Jar, Powder, Cubist, Green, Covered | 8.00 |
| Depression Glass, Jar, Powder, Cubist, Pink, Covered | 5.00 To 8.00 |
| Depression Glass, Jar, Tobacco, Royal Lace, Burgundy, Metal Holder & Lid | 50.00 |
| Depression Glass, Jug, Juice, Mayfair, Blue, 37 Ozs. | 35.00 |
| Depression Glass, Jug, Milk, Windsor, Crystal, 16 1/2 Ozs. | 8.50 |
| Depression Glass, Jug, Patrician, Amber, 60 Ozs. | 20.00 |
| Depression Glass, Juice Set, Fine Rib, Cobalt, 7 Piece | 22.00 |
| Depression Glass, Juice Set, Plain, Forest Green, 9 Piece | 15.00 |
| Depression Glass, Juice Set, Royal Lace, Pink, 7 Piece | 25.00 |
| Depression Glass, Juice Set, Ruby Red, 5 Piece | 15.00 |
| Depression Glass, Juicer, Sunkist, Green | 4.00 |
| Depression Glass, Juicer, Sunkist, White, Opaque | 3.00 |
| Depression Glass, Luncheon Set, S Pattern, Monax, 22 Piece | 55.00 |
| Depression Glass, Mold, Jello, Madrid, Amber | 3.00 To 3.50 |
| Depression Glass, Muffineer, McK, Jade Green | 3.00 |
| Depression Glass, Nappy, Bubble, Blue, 4 1/2 In. | .60 To 1.00 |
| Depression Glass, Nappy, Bubble, Blue, 8 In. | 1.25 |
| Depression Glass, Nappy, Cameo, Green, 7 In. | 4.00 |
| Depression Glass, Nappy, Cherry Blossom, Green, 5 3/4 In. | 5.00 |
| Depression Glass, Nappy, Cherry Blossom, Green, 8 1/2 In. | 6.00 |
| Depression Glass, Nappy, Cherry Blossom, Pink, 4 3/4 In. | 1.75 |
| Depression Glass, Nappy, Cubist, Pink, 6 1/2 In. | 1.75 |
| Depression Glass, Nappy, English Hobnail, Green, Flared | 6.50 |
| Depression Glass, Nappy, Floral, Pink, 4 In. | 2.00 |
| Depression Glass, Nappy, Florentine No.2, Green, 8 In. | 5.25 To 6.00 |
| Depression Glass, Nappy, Georgian, Green, 5 3/4 In. | 2.25 |
| Depression Glass, Nappy, Iris, Carnival, 5 In. | 2.00 |
| Depression Glass, Nappy, Iris, Clear, Ruffled, 5 In. | 1.25 |
| Depression Glass, Nappy, Lace Edge, Pink, 9 1/2 In. | 3.60 |
| Depression Glass, Nappy, Madrid, Amber, 5 In. | 1.50 |
| Depression Glass, Nappy, Miss America, Clear, 6 1/4 In. | 3.00 |
| Depression Glass, Nappy, Optic Block, Green, 4 1/2 In. | .75 |
| Depression Glass, Nappy, Optic Block, Green, 5 1/4 In. | 1.00 |
| Depression Glass, Nappy, Patrician, Crystal | 1.75 |
| Depression Glass, Nappy, Royal Lace, Pink, 10 In. | 3.50 |
| Depression Glass, Nappy, Royal Ruby, 4 1/2 In. | 1.50 |
| Depression Glass, Nappy, Sharon, Amber, 5 In. | 1.25 |
| Depression Glass, Nappy, Sharon, Pink, 5 In. | 1.25 |
| Depression Glass, Nappy, Sierra, Green, 5 1/2 In. | 2.25 |
| Depression Glass, Parfait, Florentine No.2, Yellow | 20.00 |
| Depression Glass, Parfait, Florentine, Green, 6 In. | 10.00 |
| Depression Glass, Perfume, Hobnail, Moonstone | 6.00 |
| Depression Glass, Perfume, Miss America, Moonstone | 4.50 |
| Depression Glass, Pitcher, Adam, Pink | 10.00 |

Depression Glass, Pitcher, Adam, Pink, Cone ..................................................................... 10.00
Depression Glass, Pitcher, Adam, Pink, Square Base, 8 In. .............................................. 14.00
Depression Glass, Pitcher, Adam, Pink, 8 In. .................................. 8.50 To 11.00
Depression Glass, Pitcher, American Sweetheart, Pink, Ice Lip ....................................... 150.00
Depression Glass, Pitcher, American Sweetheart, Pink, 7 1/2 In. .................................... 135.00
Depression Glass, Pitcher, Block Optic, Green, 8 In. .......................................................... 10.00
Depression Glass, Pitcher, Block Optic, Green, 8 1/4 In. ................................................... 8.50
Depression Glass, Pitcher, Block, Clear, Rope Edge, 54 Ozs., 8 In. ............................... 8.50
Depression Glass, Pitcher, Block, Green, Rope Edge, 54 Oz., 8 In. ............................... 10.00
Depression Glass, Pitcher, Cameo, Green, 8 In. ................................................................ 15.00
Depression Glass, Pitcher, Cameo, Green, 8 1/2 In. ........................................................ 18.00
Depression Glass, Pitcher, Cherry Blossom, Green, Cone Shape, Footed ...................... 18.00
Depression Glass, Pitcher, Cherry Blossom, Green, Straight Sides ................................ 18.00
Depression Glass, Pitcher, Cherry, Green ........................................................................... 30.00
Depression Glass, Pitcher, Cherry, Pink, 42 Ozs. .............................................................. 18.00
Depression Glass, Pitcher, Colonial, Clear, Ice Lip, 7 1/2 In. .......................................... 15.00
Depression Glass, Pitcher, Crisscross, Green, 8 1/2 In. ................................................... 8.00
Depression Glass, Pitcher, Diamond Line, Crystal .............................................................. 7.50
Depression Glass, Pitcher, Dogwood, Pink, Decorated ...................................................... 65.00
Depression Glass, Pitcher, Doric, Pink, 36 Ozs. ................................................................ 18.00
Depression Glass, Pitcher, Floragold .................................................................................. 12.00
Depression Glass, Pitcher, Floragold, Iridescent ................................................................ 10.00
Depression Glass, Pitcher, Floral & Diamond Band, Green .............................................. 28.00
Depression Glass, Pitcher, Floral, Green, Conical .............................................................. 8.00
Depression Glass, Pitcher, Floral, Green, 32 Ozs., 8 In. ............................... 9.50 To 10.00
Depression Glass, Pitcher, Floral, Pink, Conical ................................................................ 8.00
Depression Glass, Pitcher, Floral, Pink, 8 In. .................................................................... 9.50
Depression Glass, Pitcher, Floral, Yellow, Conical, Pedestal, 7 1/4 In. ......................... 6.00
Depression Glass, Pitcher, Florentine No.1, Green, Straight Sided, 54 Ozs. ................. 30.00
Depression Glass, Pitcher, Florentine No.1, Green, 6 1/2 In. .......................................... 19.50
Depression Glass, Pitcher, Florentine No.2, Amber ........................................................... 13.00
Depression Glass, Pitcher, Florentine No.2, Yellow, Conical ............................................ 8.00
Depression Glass, Pitcher, Florentine, Green, Straight Sided .......................................... 20.00
Depression Glass, Pitcher, Florentine, Yellow .................................................................... 29.50
Depression Glass, Pitcher, Florentine, Yellow, Cone Shape ............................................. 14.50
Depression Glass, Pitcher, Hobnail, Ruby .......................................................................... 38.00
Depression Glass, Pitcher, Holiday, Pink, 16 Ozs. ............................................................ 8.00
Depression Glass, Pitcher, Holiday, Pink, 7 In. ................................................................ 7.00
Depression Glass, Pitcher, Honeycomb, Green ................................................................... 8.00
Depression Glass, Pitcher, Iris, Clear ................................................................................. 7.00
Depression Glass, Pitcher, Iris, Clear, 9 1/2 In. ............................................................... 8.00
Depression Glass, Pitcher, Juice, Cameo, Green, Rope Rim, 6 In. ................................. 13.50
Depression Glass, Pitcher, Juice, Cherry Blossom, Pink ................................................. 16.00
Depression Glass, Pitcher, Juice, Madrid, Amber ............................................................. 9.00
Depression Glass, Pitcher, Juice, Princess, Green ............................................ 8.50 To 9.00
Depression Glass, Pitcher, Juice, Princess, Pink .............................................................. 8.75
Depression Glass, Pitcher, Madrid, Amber ......................................................................... 35.00
Depression Glass, Pitcher, Madrid, Amber, Ice Lip ........................................................... 35.00
Depression Glass, Pitcher, Madrid, Amber, Ice Lip, 8 1/2 In. ......................................... 19.00
Depression Glass, Pitcher, Madrid, Amber, Square, 8 In. ........................... 15.00 To 25.00
Depression Glass, Pitcher, Madrid, Amber, 8 1/2 In. ........................................................ 30.00
Depression Glass, Pitcher, Mayfair, Pink, 8 In. ................................................................. 13.50
Depression Glass, Pitcher, Mayfair, Pink, 60 Ozs. ............................................................ 12.50
Depression Glass, Pitcher, Mayfair, Pink, 80 Ozs. ............................................................ 17.50
Depression Glass, Pitcher, Milk, Cameo, Green ................................................................ 150.00
Depression Glass, Pitcher, Miss America, Pink, 65 Ozs. ................................................. 37.50
Depression Glass, Pitcher, Normandie, Pink ...................................................................... 30.00
Depression Glass, Pitcher, Old Florentine, Green, 6 1/2 In. ............................................ 17.50
Depression Glass, Pitcher, Parrot, Green ........................................................................... 275.00
Depression Glass, Pitcher, Patrician, Amber, 8 In. ........................................................... 28.00
Depression Glass, Pitcher, Patrician, Pink, Flat ................................................................ 18.50
Depression Glass, Pitcher, Poppy, Yellow, 32 Ozs., 7 1/2 In. ..................... 9.00 To 9.75
Depression Glass, Pitcher, Princess, Green, 6 In. ............................................................ 10.00
Depression Glass, Pitcher, Princess, Green, 60 Ozs., 8 In. ......................... 12.00 To 16.00
Depression Glass, Pitcher, Princess, Pink, 5 In. ........................................... 9.00 To 9.50
Depression Glass, Pitcher, Princess, Pink, 60 Ozs., 8 In. ........................... 18.00 To 19.00

Depression Glass, Pitcher, Ring, Red, Black, Yellow, 8 1/2 In. ............................................. 8.00
Depression Glass, Pitcher, Royal Lace, Clear, 8 1/2 In. ....................................................... 20.00
Depression Glass, Pitcher, Royal Lace, Pink, 8 In. ............................................................. 25.00
Depression Glass, Pitcher, Royal Lace, Pink, 68 Ozs. ......................................................... 17.50
Depression Glass, Pitcher, Sailboat, Cobalt, Sailboat Series, 9 In. ...................................... 12.00
Depression Glass, Pitcher, Sharon, Pink ........................................................................... 25.00
Depression Glass, Pitcher, Sharon, Pink, Ice Lip ............................................................... 25.00
Depression Glass, Pitcher, Spoke, Amber .......................................................................... 28.00
Depression Glass, Pitcher, Water, Adam, Pink, Cone ......................................................... 14.00
Depression Glass, Pitcher, Water, Cameo, Green ................................................. 12.00 To 24.00
Depression Glass, Pitcher, Water, Colony, Green, 6 1/2 In. ................................................ 5.00
Depression Glass, Pitcher, Water, Floragold ....................................................... 12.00 To 14.00
Depression Glass, Pitcher, Water, Floral, Green, Footed .................................................... 5.00
Depression Glass, Pitcher, Water, Florentine, Yellow, Cone Shape .................................... 10.00
Depression Glass, Pitcher, Water, Florentine, Yellow, Footed ............................................ 12.00
Depression Glass, Pitcher, Water, Holliday, Pink ............................................................... 11.00
Depression Glass, Pitcher, Water, Iris, Clear ....................................................... 9.00 To 10.00
Depression Glass, Pitcher, Water, Madrid, Amber .............................................................. 18.00
Depression Glass, Pitcher, Water, Mayfair, Blue, 80 Oz.8 1/2 In.High .............................. 75.00
Depression Glass, Pitcher, Water, Mayfair, Pink, Large Size ............................................. 16.50
Depression Glass, Pitcher, Water, Normandie, Amber ........................................................ 22.50
Depression Glass, Pitcher, Water, Pillar Optic, Pink ........................................................... 8.50
Depression Glass, Pitcher, Water, Poinsettia, Green .......................................................... 15.00
Depression Glass, Pitcher, Water, Sierra, Pink ................................................................... 15.00
Depression Glass, Pitcher, Water, Windsor Diamond, Pink, 6 3/4 In. .................................. 14.00
Depression Glass, Pitcher, Water, Windsor, Pink ............................................................... 11.00
Depression Glass, Pitcher, Windsor Diamond, Pink ............................................................ 17.50
Depression Glass, Pitcher, Windsor, Pink, 6 1/2 In. ........................................................... 10.00
Depression Glass, Plate, Adam, Green, 6 In. ..................................................................... 1.75
Depression Glass, Plate, Adam, Green, 7 In. ..................................................................... 2.25
Depression Glass, Plate, Adam, Green, 9 In. ..................................................................... 3.50
Depression Glass, Plate, Adam, Pink, Divided ................................................................... 4.00
Depression Glass, Plate, Adam, Pink, 6 In. ........................................................... 1.25 To 1.75
Depression Glass, Plate, Adam, Pink, 9 In. ....................................................................... 3.00
Depression Glass, Plate, American Sweetheart, Monax, 6 In. ............................................. 2.50
Depression Glass, Plate, American Sweetheart, Monax, 8 In. ............................... 2.50 To 4.00
Depression Glass, Plate, American Sweetheart, Monax, 9 In. ............................... 4.00 To 5.00
Depression Glass, Plate, American Sweetheart, Opalescent, 8 In. ...................................... 4.50
Depression Glass, Plate, American Sweetheart, Pink, 6 In. ................................... 1.25 To 3.00
Depression Glass, Plate, American Sweetheart, Pink, 6 1/2 In. .......................................... 1.50
Depression Glass, Plate, American Sweetheart, Pink, 8 In. ................................................ 1.50
Depression Glass, Plate, American Sweetheart, Pink, 9 5/8 In. .......................................... 2.00
Depression Glass, Plate, American Sweetheart, Pink, 10 In. .............................................. 3.00
Depression Glass, Plate, American Sweetheart, Pink, 12 In. .............................................. 4.00
Depression Glass, Plate, American Sweetheart, Red, 8 In. ................................................. 75.00
Depression Glass, Plate, Avocado Pear, Pink, 6 In. ........................................................... 3.75
Depression Glass, Plate, Ballerina, Green, Divided ............................................................ 3.00
Depression Glass, Plate, Ballerina, Green, 8 In. ................................................................ 2.50
Depression Glass, Plate, Beaded Panels, Clear, 6 In. ........................................................ 1.50
Depression Glass, Plate, Block Optic, Green, 8 In. ............................................................ 1.50
Depression Glass, Plate, Block Optic, Green, 9 In. ................................................ .75 To 2.00
Depression Glass, Plate, Block Optic, Green, 10 In. ........................................................... 2.50
Depression Glass, Plate, Block, Pink, 6 In. ........................................................................ .75
Depression Glass, Plate, Block, Pink, 8 In. ........................................................................ 1.00
Depression Glass, Plate, Block, Yellow, 6 In. ..................................................................... .75
Depression Glass, Plate, Bowknot, Green, 7 In. ................................................................. 1.50
Depression Glass, Plate, Bread & Butter, American Sweetheart, Pink ................................ 1.25
Depression Glass, Plate, Bread & Butter, Bubble, Blue .......................................... .65 To .75
Depression Glass, Plate, Bread & Butter, Holliday, Pink .................................................... 1.00
Depression Glass, Plate, Bread & Butter, Sharon, Amber ................................................... 1.25
Depression Glass, Plate, Bread & Butter, Sharon, Pink .......................................... 1.00 To 1.25
Depression Glass, Plate, Bubble, Blue, 6 3/4 In. .................................................... .50 To .75
Depression Glass, Plate, Bubble, Blue, 10 In. .................................................................... 1.50
Depression Glass, Plate, Cabbage Rose, Amber, 9 In. ....................................................... 2.50
Depression Glass, Plate, Cake, Adam, Green, Footed ........................................................ 6.00
Depression Glass, Plate, Cake, Adam, Pink, Footed, 10 In. ............................................... 5.00

Depression Glass, Plate, Cake, Cameo, Green, Footed ............................................ 3.75 To 4.50
Depression Glass, Plate, Cake, Cameo, Green, Footed, 10 In. .................................... 4.50
Depression Glass, Plate, Cake, Cameo, Green, 10 In. ............................................... 7.50
Depression Glass, Plate, Cake, Cherry Blossom, Green ............................................ 4.00
Depression Glass, Plate, Cake, Cherry Blossom, Pink ............................................ 3.50 To 4.00
Depression Glass, Plate, Cake, Cherry Blossom, Pink, Footed, 10 1/4 In. ..................... 8.00
Depression Glass, Plate, Cake, Cherry Blossom, Pink, 2 Handled ............................... 6.00
Depression Glass, Plate, Cake, Cherry, Pink ....................................................... 4.50 To 5.00
Depression Glass, Plate, Cake, Daisy, Green, 11 1/2 In. ........................................... 2.75
Depression Glass, Plate, Cake, Doric, Pink ........................................................... 7.00
Depression Glass, Plate, Cake, Madrid, Amber, 11 1/2 In. ......................................... 6.00
Depression Glass, Plate, Cake, Mayfair, Blue ........................................................ 28.00
Depression Glass, Plate, Cake, Mayfair, Blue, Open Handles, 12 In.Wide ...................... 15.00
Depression Glass, Plate, Cake, Mayfair, Blue, 12 In. ............................................... 19.50
Depression Glass, Plate, Cake, Mayfair, Pink ........................................................ 3.50 To 6.75
Depression Glass, Plate, Cake, Miss America, Clear ............................................... 8.50 To 10.00
Depression Glass, Plate, Cake, Miss America, Clear, Footed ...................................... 9.00
Depression Glass, Plate, Cake, Miss America, Pink .................................................. 10.00
Depression Glass, Plate, Cake, Miss America, Pink, Footed ....................................... 16.50
Depression Glass, Plate, Cake, Moderntone, Blue .................................................. 3.25
Depression Glass, Plate, Cake, Princess, Green, Footed, 10 In. .................................. 11.00
Depression Glass, Plate, Cake, S Pattern, Amber .................................................... 20.00
Depression Glass, Plate, Cake, Sharon Rose, Amber, 11 1/2 In. .................................. 8.00
Depression Glass, Plate, Cake, Sharon, Pink, Footed, 11 1/2 In. ................................. 9.00
Depression Glass, Plate, Cake, Sunflower, Green .................................................... 4.00
Depression Glass, Plate, Cake, Thistle, Green ........................................................ 20.00
Depression Glass, Plate, Cake, Windsor Diamond, Pink ............................................ 11.00
Depression Glass, Plate, Cameo, Green, Handled, 10 1/2 In. ...................................... 3.00
Depression Glass, Plate, Cameo, Green, 6 In. ........................................................ 1.50
Depression Glass, Plate, Cameo, Green, 8 In. ........................................................ 1.50 To 2.00
Depression Glass, Plate, Cameo, Green, 8 1/4 In. .................................................... 1.75
Depression Glass, Plate, Cameo, Green, 9 1/4 In. .................................................... 2.50
Depression Glass, Plate, Cameo, Green, 9 1/2 In. .................................................... 3.90 To 4.00
Depression Glass, Plate, Cameo, Rose, 7 In. ......................................................... 1.25
Depression Glass, Plate, Cameo, Yellow, 6 In. ....................................................... 1.50 To 2.75
Depression Glass, Plate, Cameo, Yellow, 8 In. ....................................................... 2.75
Depression Glass, Plate, Cameo, Yellow, 9 In. ....................................................... 2.75
Depression Glass, Plate, Cherry Blossom, Green, 7 In. ............................................. 3.50
Depression Glass, Plate, Cherry Blossom, Green, 9 In. ............................................. 4.50
Depression Glass, Plate, Cherry Blossom, Pink, 9 In. ............................................... 2.50 To 3.50
Depression Glass, Plate, Cherry, Green, 6 In. ........................................................ 1.75
Depression Glass, Plate, Cherry, Green, 7 In. ........................................................ 4.00
Depression Glass, Plate, Cherry, Green, 9 In. ........................................................ 5.00
Depression Glass, Plate, Cherry, Pink, 7 In. .......................................................... 3.25
Depression Glass, Plate, Child's, Cherry Blossom, Delfite .......................................... 9.50
Depression Glass, Plate, Child's, Cherry, Delfite .................................................... 9.00
Depression Glass, Plate, Child's, Cherry, Pink ....................................................... 6.00
Depression Glass, Plate, Chop, American Sweetheart, Monax, 11 In ............................. 5.50 To 6.00
Depression Glass, Plate, Clover, Green, 8 In. ......................................................... 1.50
Depression Glass, Plate, Colonial, Pink, 6 1/2 In. .................................................... 1.50
Depression Glass, Plate, Colonial, Pink, 8 1/2 In. .................................................... 2.50
Depression Glass, Plate, Columbia, Crystal, 11 3/4 In. ............................................. 3.00
Depression Glass, Plate, Coronation, Pink, 6 In. ..................................................... 1.00
Depression Glass, Plate, Crackle, Crystal, 10 In. .................................................... 1.00
Depression Glass, Plate, Cremax Petalware, Gold Band ............................................ 2.50
Depression Glass, Plate, Cubist, Green, 8 In. ......................................................... 3.00
Depression Glass, Plate, Cubist, Pink, 6 In. .......................................................... .75
Depression Glass, Plate, Cubist, Pink, 8 In. .......................................................... 3.00
Depression Glass, Plate, Daisy, Amber, 6 In. ......................................................... 1.00 To 1.25
Depression Glass, Plate, Daisy, Amber, 7 In. ......................................................... 1.50
Depression Glass, Plate, Daisy, Amber, 7 3/8 In. ..................................................... 1.75
Depression Glass, Plate, Daisy, Amber, 8 3/8 In. ..................................................... 2.00
Depression Glass, Plate, Daisy, Amber, 9 3/8 In. ..................................................... 2.90
Depression Glass, Plate, Daisy, Amber, 11 1/2 In. .................................................... 4.00
Depression Glass, Plate, Daisy, Dark Amber, 7 1/2 In. .............................................. 1.75
Depression Glass, Plate, Daisy, Dark Amber, 9 In. ................................................... 2.25

Depression Glass, Plate, Daisy, Green, 7 In. .................................................................. 1.00
Depression Glass, Plate, Daisy, Green, 9 In. .................................................................. 2.00
Depression Glass, Plate, Diamond-Quilted, Green, 6 In. ................................................ 1.00
Depression Glass, Plate, Diana, Clear, 9 1/2 In. ........................................................... 1.50
Depression Glass, Plate, Diana, Pink, 6 In. ............................................................ .75 To 1.00
Depression Glass, Plate, Dinner, Adam, Green ....................................................... 3.00 To 3.50
Depression Glass, Plate, Dinner, Adam, Pink ................................................................ 3.50
Depression Glass, Plate, Dinner, American Sweetheart, Monax, 9 3/4 In. ..................... 5.00
Depression Glass, Plate, Dinner, American Sweetheart, Monax, 10 In. ......................... 5.00
Depression Glass, Plate, Dinner, American Sweetheart, Pink ....................................... 3.00
Depression Glass, Plate, Dinner, Bubble, Blue .................................................... 1.00 To 1.10
Depression Glass, Plate, Dinner, Bubble, Blue, 9 3/8 In. .............................................. 1.50
Depression Glass, Plate, Dinner, Cabbage Rose, Amber ......................................... 2.75 To 4.50
Depression Glass, Plate, Dinner, Cameo, Green .......................................................... 4.00
Depression Glass, Plate, Dinner, Cameo, Green, Divided .............................................. 2.00
Depression Glass, Plate, Dinner, Cameo, Green, 9 1/4 In. ............................................ 3.50
Depression Glass, Plate, Dinner, Cameo, Green, 9 1/2 In. ............................................ 3.00
Depression Glass, Plate, Dinner, Cherry Blossom, Green, 9 In. ..................................... 4.50
Depression Glass, Plate, Dinner, Cherry Blossom, Pink, 9 In. ....................................... 3.00
Depression Glass, Plate, Dinner, Cherry, Green ........................................................... 5.50
Depression Glass, Plate, Dinner, Cherry, Pink ............................................................. 3.00
Depression Glass, Plate, Dinner, Child's, Cherry, Pink .................................................. 6.00
Depression Glass, Plate, Dinner, Daisy, Amber, 9 3/8 In. ............................................. 2.00
Depression Glass, Plate, Dinner, Dogwood, Pink .................................................. 3.25 To 6.00
Depression Glass, Plate, Dinner, Dogwood, Pink, 9 In. ................................................ 4.00
Depression Glass, Plate, Dinner, Doric, Green ............................................................. 3.00
Depression Glass, Plate, Dinner, Doric, Pink ............................................................... 2.50
Depression Glass, Plate, Dinner, Doric, Pink, 9 In. ...................................................... 2.00
Depression Glass, Plate, Dinner, Floral, Green ............................................................ 3.00
Depression Glass, Plate, Dinner, Floral, Pink ............................................................... 2.50
Depression Glass, Plate, Dinner, Florentine, Clear ....................................................... 1.90
Depression Glass, Plate, Dinner, Forest, Green, Anchor Hocking, Square ...................... 1.75
Depression Glass, Plate, Dinner, Georgian, Green ........................................................ 2.50
Depression Glass, Plate, Dinner, Iris, Clear ................................................................. 3.50
Depression Glass, Plate, Dinner, Lace Edge, Pink ........................................................ 3.50
Depression Glass, Plate, Dinner, Lace Edge, Pink, Divided .......................................... 4.00
Depression Glass, Plate, Dinner, Madrid, Amber .................................................. 2.50 To 8.00
Depression Glass, Plate, Dinner, Madrid, Blue, 10 1/2 In. ............................................ 10.00
Depression Glass, Plate, Dinner, Madrid, Green ........................................................... 4.00
Depression Glass, Plate, Dinner, Madrid, Green, 10 1/2 In. .......................................... 5.75
Depression Glass, Plate, Dinner, Manhattan, Clear ...................................................... 1.70
Depression Glass, Plate, Dinner, Mayfair, Pink ............................................................ 4.15
Depression Glass, Plate, Dinner, Mayfair, Pink, 9 1/2 In. ............................................. 6.00
Depression Glass, Plate, Dinner, Miss America, Clear .................................................. 3.00
Depression Glass, Plate, Dinner, Miss America, Clear, Divided ..................................... 4.00
Depression Glass, Plate, Dinner, Miss America, Pink .................................................... 5.50
Depression Glass, Plate, Dinner, Moderntone, Blue ...................................................... 1.75
Depression Glass, Plate, Dinner, Moderntone, Cobalt ............................................ 1.75 To 2.00
Depression Glass, Plate, Dinner, Moroccan, Amethyst .................................................. 2.50
Depression Glass, Plate, Dinner, Patrician, Amber ................................................ 1.00 To 2.50
Depression Glass, Plate, Dinner, Patrician, Amber, Divided .......................................... 2.00
Depression Glass, Plate, Dinner, Petalware, Pink, 9 1/4 In. .......................................... 2.50
Depression Glass, Plate, Dinner, Princess, Green, Divided, Handled .............................. 2.50
Depression Glass, Plate, Dinner, Princess, Green, 9 1/2 In. .......................................... 1.75
Depression Glass, Plate, Dinner, Princess, Pink ........................................................... 3.50
Depression Glass, Plate, Dinner, Princess, Pink, 9 1/2 In. ............................................ 1.75
Depression Glass, Plate, Dinner, Royal Lace, Clear ...................................................... 2.70
Depression Glass, Plate, Dinner, Royal Lace, Cobalt .................................................... 6.50
Depression Glass, Plate, Dinner, Royal Ruby ............................................................... 2.00
Depression Glass, Plate, Dinner, Sailboat, Cobalt, Sailboat Series ................................ 3.00
Depression Glass, Plate, Dinner, Sharon, Amber .................................................. 2.25 To 10.00
Depression Glass, Plate, Dinner, Sharon, Pink ............................................................ 2.00
Depression Glass, Plate, Dinner, Sierra, Green ............................................................ 3.00
Depression Glass, Plate, Dinner, Sunflower, Green ....................................................... 2.50
Depression Glass, Plate, Dinner, Swirl, Green .............................................................. 2.50
Depression Glass, Plate, Dinner, Swirl, Ultramarine ..................................................... 2.50

Depression Glass, Plate, Dinner, Wedding Band, Cobalt Blue ............................................ 2.00
Depression Glass, Plate, Dogwood, Green, 6 In. ............................................................ 2.00
Depression Glass, Plate, Dogwood, Green, 8 In. ............................................................ 2.50
Depression Glass, Plate, Dogwood, Pink, Handled, 8 In. .................................................. 10.00
Depression Glass, Plate, Dogwood, Pink, 6 In. .............................................................. 1.25
Depression Glass, Plate, Dogwood, Pink, 7 3/4 In. ........................................................ 2.25
Depression Glass, Plate, Dogwood, Pink, 8 In. ................................................ 1.00 To 3.50
Depression Glass, Plate, Dogwood, Pink, 9 1/4 In. ........................................................ 4.50
Depression Glass, Plate, Doric, Green, 6 In. ...................................................... 1.00 To 1.50
Depression Glass, Plate, Doric, Pink, 9 In. ................................................................. 3.42
Depression Glass, Plate, Floragold, Iridescent, 8 1/2 In. ................................................ 4.00
Depression Glass, Plate, Floral, Green, 6 In. ............................................................... 1.50
Depression Glass, Plate, Floral, Green, 9 In. ............................................................... 3.00
Depression Glass, Plate, Floral, Pink, 6 In. ................................................................. 1.00
Depression Glass, Plate, Floral, Pink, 8 In. ..................................................... 2.00 To 2.50
Depression Glass, Plate, Floral, Pink, 9 In. ................................................................. 2.50
Depression Glass, Plate, Florentine No.1, Green, 8 In. ................................................... 1.50
Depression Glass, Plate, Florentine No.2, Green, 8 1/4 In. .............................................. 1.50
Depression Glass, Plate, Florentine No.2, Green, 9 In. ................................................... 3.50
Depression Glass, Plate, Florentine No.2, Green, 10 In. .................................................. 3.00
Depression Glass, Plate, Florentine No.2, Yellow, 8 1/2 In. ............................................. 1.65
Depression Glass, Plate, Florentine, Clear, 10 In. ......................................................... 2.75
Depression Glass, Plate, Florentine, Green, 8 1/2 In. ..................................................... 2.00
Depression Glass, Plate, Florentine, Yellow, 6 In. ............................................. 1.25 To 3.00
Depression Glass, Plate, Florentine, Yellow, 8 1/2 In. ........................................ 1.75 To 2.00
Depression Glass, Plate, Florentine, Yellow, 10 In. ...................................................... 3.00
Depression Glass, Plate, Fruit Center, Azure Blue, 12 In. ............................................... 6.50
Depression Glass, Plate, Fruits, Green, 8 In. ............................................................... 1.75
Depression Glass, Plate, Georgian, Green, 6 In. ................................................ 1.00 To 1.50
Depression Glass, Plate, Georgian, Green, 8 In. ................................................ 1.50 To 2.00
Depression Glass, Plate, Georgian, Green, 9 1/2 In. ...................................................... 3.00
Depression Glass, Plate, Grill, Adam, Green ................................................................ 2.25
Depression Glass, Plate, Grill, Adam, Green, 9 In. ........................................................ 2.50
Depression Glass, Plate, Grill, Cameo, Green .................................................... 2.25 To 2.50
Depression Glass, Plate, Grill, Cameo, Green, 10 In. ...................................................... 2.50
Depression Glass, Plate, Grill, Cameo, Green, 10 1/4 In. ................................................. 3.00
Depression Glass, Plate, Grill, Cameo, Yellow .................................................. 1.75 To 2.00
Depression Glass, Plate, Grill, Daisy, Green ................................................................ 1.75
Depression Glass, Plate, Grill, Doric, Green ................................................................ 2.75
Depression Glass, Plate, Grill, Doric, Pink ................................................................. 1.75
Depression Glass, Plate, Grill, Florentine No.2, Green, 10 1/2 In. ..................................... 1.75
Depression Glass, Plate, Grill, Florentine, Clear .......................................................... 1.75
Depression Glass, Plate, Grill, Lace Edge, Pink ............................................................ 1.60
Depression Glass, Plate, Grill, Madrid, Amber, 10 1/2 In. ............................................... 4.00
Depression Glass, Plate, Grill, Mayfair, Blue ............................................................... 12.00
Depression Glass, Plate, Grill, Miss America, Pink ............................................ 4.00 To 4.50
Depression Glass, Plate, Grill, Normandie, Sunburst, 10 1/4 In. ...................................... 3.50
Depression Glass, Plate, Grill, Patrician, Amber ........................................................... 1.00
Depression Glass, Plate, Grill, Patrician, Clear ............................................................ 1.60
Depression Glass, Plate, Grill, Patrician, Green, 10 1/2 In. ............................................ 2.35
Depression Glass, Plate, Grill, Princess, Green ............................................................ 3.50
Depression Glass, Plate, Grill, Princess, Pink, Handled .................................................. 1.50
Depression Glass, Plate, Grill, Princess, Yellow ........................................................... 1.75
Depression Glass, Plate, Grill, Royal Lace, Clear .......................................................... 2.25
Depression Glass, Plate, Grill, Royal Lace, Pink ........................................................... 2.50
Depression Glass, Plate, Grill, W No.202, Cobalt Blue, 7 In. ........................................... 2.50
Depression Glass, Plate, Heritage, Clear, 12 In. ............................................... 2.50 To 4.00
Depression Glass, Plate, Hobnail, Pink, 8 1/2 In. ......................................................... 1.50
Depression Glass, Plate, Holiday, Pink, 9 In. .............................................................. 2.00
Depression Glass, Plate, Iris, Clear, 5 1/2 In. ............................................................. 1.25
Depression Glass, Plate, Lace Edge, Clear, 8 1/2 In. ..................................................... 1.95
Depression Glass, Plate, Lace Edge, Pink, Solid Lace, 13 In. ........................................... 4.50
Depression Glass, Plate, Lace Edge, Pink, 7 1/4 In. ...................................................... 1.50
Depression Glass, Plate, Lace Edge, Pink, 8 1/2 In. ...................................................... 2.50
Depression Glass, Plate, Lace Edge, Pink, 10 1/2 In. ..................................................... 4.00
Depression Glass, Plate, Lorain, Green, 9 In. .............................................................. 2.50

| | |
|---|---|
| Depression Glass, Plate, Lovebirds, Green, 6 In. | 1.00 |
| Depression Glass, Plate, Lovebirds, Green, 8 In. | 2.00 |
| Depression Glass, Plate, Luncheon, Cameo, Green, 8 In. | 2.50 |
| Depression Glass, Plate, Luncheon, Cathedral, Pink | 2.35 |
| Depression Glass, Plate, Luncheon, Columbia, Crystal, 9 1/2 In. | 1.50 |
| Depression Glass, Plate, Luncheon, Diamond-Quilted, Pink, 8 In. | 1.50 |
| Depression Glass, Plate, Luncheon, Dogwood, Green | 1.65 To 3.00 |
| Depression Glass, Plate, Luncheon, Dogwood, Pink | 11.00 |
| Depression Glass, Plate, Luncheon, English Hobnail, Crystal, Square | 3.50 |
| Depression Glass, Plate, Luncheon, Florentine No.2, Green | 1.75 |
| Depression Glass, Plate, Luncheon, Florentine No.2, Yellow | 2.00 |
| Depression Glass, Plate, Luncheon, Madrid, Amber | 5.00 |
| Depression Glass, Plate, Luncheon, Mayfair, Pink | 3.25 |
| Depression Glass, Plate, Luncheon, Mayfair, Pink, 8 1/2 In. | 3.00 |
| Depression Glass, Plate, Luncheon, Moderntone, Cobalt | 1.75 |
| Depression Glass, Plate, Luncheon, Moderntone, Cobalt, 7 3/4 In. | 1.50 |
| Depression Glass, Plate, Luncheon, No.161 Vernon, Crystal, 8 In. | 3.00 |
| Depression Glass, Plate, Luncheon, Parrot, Green, 7 1/2 In. | 6.50 |
| Depression Glass, Plate, Luncheon, Patrician, Amber | 1.75 |
| Depression Glass, Plate, Luncheon, Roulette, Green | 1.75 |
| Depression Glass, Plate, Luncheon, Royal Ruby | 1.50 |
| Depression Glass, Plate, Luncheon, Wedding Band, Cobalt Blue | 2.00 |
| Depression Glass, Plate, Lydia Ray, Green, 8 1/2 In. | 2.00 |
| Depression Glass, Plate, Madrid, Amber, 6 In. | 1.75 |
| Depression Glass, Plate, Madrid, Amber, 7 1/2 In. | 1.25 To 2.00 |
| Depression Glass, Plate, Madrid, Amber, 8 In. | 1.75 |
| Depression Glass, Plate, Madrid, Amber, 9 In. | 1.25 To 2.50 |
| Depression Glass, Plate, Madrid, Pink, 6 In. | 1.25 |
| Depression Glass, Plate, Mayfair, Blue, Off Center Indentation, 6 1/2 In. | 8.50 |
| Depression Glass, Plate, Mayfair, Blue, 9 1/2 In. | 14.00 |
| Depression Glass, Plate, Mayfair, Pink, Square, 6 In. | 4.00 |
| Depression Glass, Plate, Mayfair, Pink, 8 1/2 In. | 3.00 |
| Depression Glass, Plate, Miss America, Clear, 5 3/4 In. | 1.50 |
| Depression Glass, Plate, Miss America, Clear, 10 In. | 3.00 |
| Depression Glass, Plate, Miss America, Green, 6 In. | 4.00 |
| Depression Glass, Plate, Miss America, Pink, 6 In. | 1.75 To 2.25 |
| Depression Glass, Plate, Miss America, Pink, 8 1/2 In. | 3.25 |
| Depression Glass, Plate, Miss America, Pink, 10 1/4 In. | 6.25 |
| Depression Glass, Plate, Miss America, Pink, 10 1/2 In. | 6.00 |
| Depression Glass, Plate, Moderntone, Amethyst, 6 In. | 1.25 |
| Depression Glass, Plate, Moderntone, Blue, 6 In. | 1.25 |
| Depression Glass, Plate, Moderntone, Blue, 7 In. | 1.00 To 2.25 |
| Depression Glass, Plate, Moderntone, Blue, 8 In. | 1.10 To 2.50 |
| Depression Glass, Plate, Moderntone, Blue, 10 1/2 In. | 8.00 |
| Depression Glass, Plate, Moderntone, Blue, 10 3/4 In. | 5.50 |
| Depression Glass, Plate, Moderntone, Burgundy, 6 In. | 1.25 |
| Depression Glass, Plate, Moderntone, Burgundy, 8 In. | 2.00 |
| Depression Glass, Plate, Moderntone, Cobalt, 6 In. | 1.25 |
| Depression Glass, Plate, Moderntone, Cobalt, 8 In. | 2.00 |
| Depression Glass, Plate, Moderntone, Cobalt, 9 In. | 2.50 |
| Depression Glass, Plate, No.612, Green, 6 In. | 2.25 |
| Depression Glass, Plate, No.612, Green, 8 1/2 In. | 2.00 |
| Depression Glass, Plate, No.612, Green, 9 1/2 In. | 3.00 |
| Depression Glass, Plate, No.612, Yellow, 6 In. | 2.00 |
| Depression Glass, Plate, No.612, Yellow, 8 In. | 2.50 |
| Depression Glass, Plate, Normandie, Pink, 6 In. | .75 |
| Depression Glass, Plate, Normandie, Pink, 8 In. | 1.75 |
| Depression Glass, Plate, Normandie, Sunburst, 6 In. | 1.75 |
| Depression Glass, Plate, Normandie, Sunburst, 10 1/2 In. | 4.00 |
| Depression Glass, Plate, Old Florentine, Green, 9 3/4 In. | 2.50 |
| Depression Glass, Plate, Old Florentine, Pink, 6 In. | 1.09 |
| Depression Glass, Plate, Old Florentine, Pink, 9 3/4 In. | 3.00 |
| Depression Glass, Plate, Opalescent Hobnail, Moonstone, 6 In. | 2.00 |
| Depression Glass, Plate, Oyster & Pearl, Ruby, 15 1/2 In. | 10.00 |
| Depression Glass, Plate, Patrician, Amber, 7 1/2 In. | 1.50 |
| Depression Glass, Plate, Patrician, Amber, 10 1/2 In. | 1.50 To 1.75 |

Depression Glass, Plate, Patrician, Clear, 8 In. ............................................................ 1.60
Depression Glass, Plate, Patrician, Clear, 9 In. ............................................................ 1.60
Depression Glass, Plate, Petalware, Clear, 8 In. .......................................................... 1.00
Depression Glass, Plate, Petalware, Clear, 11 In. ......................................................... 2.00
Depression Glass, Plate, Petalware, Cremax, 6 In. ........................................................ .90
Depression Glass, Plate, Petalware, Monax, Gold Trim, 8 In. ....................................... 2.00
Depression Glass, Plate, Petalware, Monax, 6 In. ......................................................... 1.25
Depression Glass, Plate, Petalware, Monax, 6 1/4 In. .................................................. 1.50
Depression Glass, Plate, Petalware, Pink, 8 In. ............................................................ 1.00
Depression Glass, Plate, Petalware, Pink, 11 In. .......................................................... 2.50
Depression Glass, Plate, Pie, Cameo, Yellow ............................................................... 1.00
Depression Glass, Plate, Princess, Green, Handled, 11 In. .......................................... 3.00
Depression Glass, Plate, Princess, Green, 8 In. .................................... 1.50 To 2.75
Depression Glass, Plate, Princess, Green, 8 1/2 In. ..................................................... 1.50
Depression Glass, Plate, Princess, Green, 9 In. ........................................................... 3.50
Depression Glass, Plate, Princess, Green, 9 1/2 In. ..................................................... 2.50
Depression Glass, Plate, Princess, Pink, 9 1/2 In. ....................................................... 2.50
Depression Glass, Plate, Princess, Yellow, 6 In. .......................................................... 1.00
Depression Glass, Plate, Queen Mary, Clear, 6 In. ....................................................... .50
Depression Glass, Plate, Queen Mary, Clear, 8 1/2 In. ....................................... .75 To 1.50
Depression Glass, Plate, Queen Mary, Pink, 6 In. ........................................................ 1.00
Depression Glass, Plate, Queen Mary, Pink, 10 In. ...................................................... 2.90
Depression Glass, Plate, Ring, Clear, Platinum Trim, 8 In. ........................................... 1.00
Depression Glass, Plate, Rosemary, Amber, 9 1/2 In. .................................................. 2.50
Depression Glass, Plate, Roulette, Green, 6 In. ............................................................ .75
Depression Glass, Plate, Round Robin, Green, 6 In. ..................................................... .75
Depression Glass, Plate, Royal Lace, Clear, 8 1/2 In. ................................................... 2.50
Depression Glass, Plate, Royal Lace, Clear, 10 In. ....................................................... 3.00
Depression Glass, Plate, Royal Lace, Cobalt, 8 In. ...................................................... 9.50
Depression Glass, Plate, Royal Lace, Green, 10 In. ...................................................... 6.00
Depression Glass, Plate, Royal Lace, Pink, 6 In. .......................................................... 1.50
Depression Glass, Plate, Royal Lace, Pink, 8 In. .......................................................... 2.25
Depression Glass, Plate, Royal Lace, Pink, 8 1/2 In. .................................................... 3.50
Depression Glass, Plate, Royal Lace, Pink, 10 In. ........................................................ 4.50
Depression Glass, Plate, Royal Lace, Ritz Blue, 6 In. ................................................... 3.00
Depression Glass, Plate, Royal Ruby, 6 In. .................................................................. 1.75
Depression Glass, Plate, Royal Ruby, 8 In. .................................................................. 2.00
Depression Glass, Plate, Royal Ruby, 9 In. .................................................................. 2.50
Depression Glass, Plate, S Pattern, Clear, 8 In. ........................................................... 2.00
Depression Glass, Plate, S Pattern, Monax, 6 In. ......................................................... 19.50
Depression Glass, Plate, S Pattern, Yellow, 8 In. ......................................................... 1.25
Depression Glass, Plate, Salad, Adam, Green .................................... 2.00 To 2.25
Depression Glass, Plate, Salad, American Sweetheart, Monax ................................... 3.00
Depression Glass, Plate, Salad, Avocado Pear, Green, 8 In. ....................................... 4.50
Depression Glass, Plate, Salad, Cameo, Green, Square ............................................... 12.00
Depression Glass, Plate, Salad, Cherry Blossom, Pink, 7 In. ...................................... 4.00
Depression Glass, Plate, Salad, Cherry, Green ............................................................ 4.00
Depression Glass, Plate, Salad, Cloverleaf, Green ...................................................... 1.35
Depression Glass, Plate, Salad, Double Shield, Cobalt, 8 In. ...................................... 3.00
Depression Glass, Plate, Salad, Floral, Green .............................................................. 2.00
Depression Glass, Plate, Salad, Lace Edge, Pink ........................................................ 2.25
Depression Glass, Plate, Salad, Laurel 'McK, ' Jade Green, 7 1/4 In. .......................... 5.00
Depression Glass, Plate, Salad, Madrid, Blue .............................................................. 6.00
Depression Glass, Plate, Salad, Miss America, Clear .......................... 1.75 To 2.75
Depression Glass, Plate, Salad, Miss America, Clear, 7 1/2 In. ................................... 2.75
Depression Glass, Plate, Salad, Moderntone, Cobalt ................................................... 1.50
Depression Glass, Plate, Salad, Petalware, Cremax, 8 In. ........................................... 2.00
Depression Glass, Plate, Salad, Princess, Green ......................................................... 2.00
Depression Glass, Plate, Salad, Princess, Pink ........................................................... 1.75
Depression Glass, Plate, Salad, Wedding Band, Cobalt ............................................... 1.25
Depression Glass, Plate, Sandwich, Amber, Hocking, 9 In. ......................................... 3.25
Depression Glass, Plate, Sandwich, Clear, 7 In. .......................................................... 1.00
Depression Glass, Plate, Sandwich, Dark Green, Miniature ......................................... 1.00
Depression Glass, Plate, Sandwich, Green, Hocking, Miniature ................................... .50
Depression Glass, Plate, Scroll, Green, 6 In. ............................................................... 1.50
Depression Glass, Plate, Serving, American Sweetheart, Monax, 13 In. ...................... 10.00

| | |
|---|---|
| Depression Glass, Plate, Serving, Lace Edge, Pink, Divided | 6.00 |
| Depression Glass, Plate, Serving, Madrid, Amber, 12 In. | 7.00 |
| Depression Glass, Plate, Sharon, Amber, 9 1/4 In. | 3.50 |
| Depression Glass, Plate, Sharon, Pink, 6 In. | 2.50 |
| Depression Glass, Plate, Sharon, Pink, 9 1/4 In. | 3.50 |
| Depression Glass, Plate, Sherbet, Cameo, Green | 1.25 |
| Depression Glass, Plate, Sherbet, Cameo, Green, 6 In. | 1.50 |
| Depression Glass, Plate, Sherbet, Cameo, Yellow | 1.20 |
| Depression Glass, Plate, Sherbet, Cherry, Pink | 1.50 To 2.00 |
| Depression Glass, Plate, Sherbet, Diamond-Quilted, Pink | .75 |
| Depression Glass, Plate, Sherbet, Floral, Pink | 1.00 To 1.25 |
| Depression Glass, Plate, Sherbet, Florentine No.2, Yellow | 1.00 To 1.50 |
| Depression Glass, Plate, Sherbet, Georgian, Green | 1.25 |
| Depression Glass, Plate, Sherbet, Mayfair, Pink | 3.00 |
| Depression Glass, Plate, Sherbet, Mayfair, Pink, Off Center, 6 1/2 In. | 5.50 |
| Depression Glass, Plate, Sherbet, Miss America, Moonstone | 1.25 |
| Depression Glass, Plate, Sherbet, Moderntone, Cobalt | 1.25 |
| Depression Glass, Plate, Sherbet, No.612, Green | 1.50 |
| Depression Glass, Plate, Sherbet, Petalware, Cremax | 1.20 |
| Depression Glass, Plate, Sherbet, Royal Lace, Cobalt | 3.00 |
| Depression Glass, Plate, Sherbet, Swirl, Ultramarine | 1.25 |
| Depression Glass, Plate, Soup, Cherry, Green, Flat | 10.00 |
| Depression Glass, Plate, Spiral, Green, 8 In. | 1.50 |
| Depression Glass, Plate, Spoke, Amber, 11 In. | 2.25 |
| Depression Glass, Plate, Starlight, Crystal, 8 1/2 In. | 1.00 |
| Depression Glass, Plate, Strawberry, Pink, 6 In. | 1.25 |
| Depression Glass, Plate, Swirl, Green, 6 In. | 1.50 |
| Depression Glass, Plate, Tree Of Life, Amber, 8 In. | 2.50 |
| Depression Glass, Plate, Twisted Optic, Amber, 8 In. | 1.50 |
| Depression Glass, Plate, Twisted Optic, Pink, 8 In. | 1.50 |
| Depression Glass, Plate, Twisted Swirl, Pink, 8 In. | 1.50 |
| Depression Glass, Plate, Victory, Pink, 8 In. | 2.00 |
| Depression Glass, Plate, Waterford, Pink, 13 1/2 In. | 3.75 |
| Depression Glass, Plate, Windsor, Pink, 9 In. | 2.25 |
| Depression Glass, Platter, Adam, Green | 4.50 |
| Depression Glass, Platter, Adam, Green, 12 In. | 5.75 |
| Depression Glass, Platter, Adam, Pink | 4.00 To 6.50 |
| Depression Glass, Platter, Adam, Pink, 12 In. | 3.75 To 6.50 |
| Depression Glass, Platter, American Sweetheart, Monax, 13 In. | 13.00 |
| Depression Glass, Platter, American Sweetheart, Pink | 5.00 |
| Depression Glass, Platter, American Sweetheart, Pink, Oval | 8.00 |
| Depression Glass, Platter, American Sweetheart, Pink, Oval, 13 In. | 5.00 |
| Depression Glass, Platter, American Sweetheart, Pink, 13 In. | 6.00 |
| Depression Glass, Platter, Ballerina, Green, 12 In. | 3.75 |
| Depression Glass, Platter, Bouquet & Lattice, Marigold, Oval | 3.50 |
| Depression Glass, Platter, Bubble, Blue | 1.75 |
| Depression Glass, Platter, Bubble, Blue, 12 In. | 3.00 |
| Depression Glass, Platter, Cabbage Rose, Pink | 6.00 |
| Depression Glass, Platter, Cameo, Green | 3.00 To 4.00 |
| Depression Glass, Platter, Cameo, Green, Closed Handles, 12 In. | 4.00 |
| Depression Glass, Platter, Cameo, Green, 10 1/4 In. | 5.00 |
| Depression Glass, Platter, Cherry Blossom, Green, 11 In. | 7.00 |
| Depression Glass, Platter, Cherry Blossom, Green, 13 In. | 13.00 |
| Depression Glass, Platter, Cherry Blossom, Pink, Divided, 13 In. | 8.00 To 12.50 |
| Depression Glass, Platter, Cherry Blossom, Pink, 11 In. | 5.50 |
| Depression Glass, Platter, Cherry Blossom, Pink, 13 In. | 12.00 |
| Depression Glass, Platter, Daisy, Amber, 10 1/4 In. | 4.50 |
| Depression Glass, Platter, Floral, Green, Oval | 3.50 |
| Depression Glass, Platter, Floral, Green, 10 3/4 In. | 4.50 |
| Depression Glass, Platter, Floral, Pink | 2.50 To 4.00 |
| Depression Glass, Platter, Floral, Pink, 10 3/4 In. | 4.00 |
| Depression Glass, Platter, Florentine, Clear, 11 In. | 5.00 |
| Depression Glass, Platter, Florentine, Yellow, 11 In. | 5.00 |
| Depression Glass, Platter, Georgian, Green, Oval | 5.00 |
| Depression Glass, Platter, Homespun, Pink, Oval | 5.00 |
| Depression Glass, Platter, Lace Edge, Pink | 4.00 |

Depression Glass, Platter, Lace Edge, Pink, 5 Sections .......................................................... 4.00
Depression Glass, Platter, Madrid, Amber ................................................................. 3.50 To 4.00
Depression Glass, Platter, Madrid, Amber, 11 1/2 In. ............................................................ 4.00
Depression Glass, Platter, Madrid, Blue .................................................................. 9.00 To 10.00
Depression Glass, Platter, Mayfair, Pink .................................................................... 3.00 To 4.00
Depression Glass, Platter, Miss America, Clear ................................................................... 4.75
Depression Glass, Platter, Miss America, Clear, 12 In. ........................................................ 4.00
Depression Glass, Platter, Miss America, Pink ............................................................ 5.25 To 7.00
Depression Glass, Platter, Miss America, Pink, Large Size ................................................ 11.00
Depression Glass, Platter, Miss America, Pink, Oval, 12 In. ................................................ 5.00
Depression Glass, Platter, Moderntone, Amethyst, 12 In. ...................................................... 6.00
Depression Glass, Platter, Moderntone, Blue, Oval, 9 In. ...................................................... 3.50
Depression Glass, Platter, No.612, Green .............................................................................. 5.00
Depression Glass, Platter, Normandie, Sunburst, 12 In. ....................................................... 6.00
Depression Glass, Platter, Old Florentine, Green, 11 1/2 In. ................................................ 5.00
Depression Glass, Platter, Open Lace, Pink ........................................................................... 2.25
Depression Glass, Platter, Open Rose, Pink, Oval .................................................................. 6.00
Depression Glass, Platter, Parrot, Green, 11 In. ..................................................................... 9.75
Depression Glass, Platter, Patrician, Amber .............................................................. 4.50 To 5.90
Depression Glass, Platter, Patrician, Amber, 11 1/2 In. ......................................................... 5.00
Depression Glass, Platter, Patrician, Clear .............................................................................. 5.00
Depression Glass, Platter, Petalware, Pink .............................................................................. 3.00
Depression Glass, Platter, Poinsettia, Pink, Oval, 10 In. ....................................................... 5.00
Depression Glass, Platter, Princess, Green ............................................................................. 3.50
Depression Glass, Platter, Princess, Green, Oval .................................................................... 5.00
Depression Glass, Platter, Princess, Green, Oval, 12 In. ..................................................... 24.00
Depression Glass, Platter, Rosemary, Amber, Oval, 8 1/2 X 12 In. ..................................... 4.50
Depression Glass, Platter, Royal Lace, Blue ......................................................................... 15.00
Depression Glass, Platter, Royal Lace, Green ....................................................................... 15.00
Depression Glass, Platter, Royal Lace, Green, 13 In. .......................................................... 15.00
Depression Glass, Platter, Royal Lace, Pink ........................................................................... 4.00
Depression Glass, Platter, Royal Lace, Pink, 13 In. ............................................................... 4.00
Depression Glass, Platter, Sharon, Amber .............................................................................. 3.00
Depression Glass, Platter, Sharon, Amber, 12 1/2 In. ........................................................... 4.50
Depression Glass, Platter, Sharon, Green ............................................................... 4.00 To 4.50
Depression Glass, Platter, Sharon, Pink .................................................................................. 2.75
Depression Glass, Platter, Sharon, Pink, 12 1/2 In. ............................................... 3.50 To 4.50
Depression Glass, Punch Set, Moderntone, Blue, 11 Piece ............................................... 40.00
Depression Glass, Punch Set, Sandwich, Milk, Gold Trim, 14 Piece ................................. 20.00
Depression Glass, Relish Set, Old Cafe, Ruby & Crystal, 7 Piece ..................................... 25.00
Depression Glass, Relish, Adam, Green .................................................................................. 3.75
Depression Glass, Relish, Adam, Green, 2 Part ..................................................................... 4.50
Depression Glass, Relish, Cameo, Green, Footed, Divided .................................................. 3.00
Depression Glass, Relish, Cameo, Green, 3 Part ................................................................... 4.50
Depression Glass, Relish, Cameo, Green, 3 Part, 3 Legs ..................................................... 5.00
Depression Glass, Relish, Cameo, Green, 3 Part, 7 1/2 In. .................................................. 5.00
Depression Glass, Relish, Floral, Green, 2 Part ..................................................................... 4.00
Depression Glass, Relish, Floral, Pink ..................................................................................... 3.00
Depression Glass, Relish, Floral, Pink, 2 Compartments, 5 X 6 1/2 In. ............................. 4.00
Depression Glass, Relish, Floral, Pink, 2 Part ....................................................... 3.00 To 4.00
Depression Glass, Relish, Florentine, Yellow, 10 In. ............................................................. 5.00
Depression Glass, Relish, Gold Encrusted, Pink, 3 Part ....................................................... 8.00
Depression Glass, Relish, Lace Edge, Pink, Divided ............................................................. 2.75
Depression Glass, Relish, Lace Edge, Pink, 3 Part, Round .................................................. 4.00
Depression Glass, Relish, Lace Edge, Pink, 3 Part ............................................... 3.75 To 4.00
Depression Glass, Relish, Lace Edge, Pink, 3 Part, 7 1/2 In. .............................................. 4.25
Depression Glass, Relish, Lace Edge, Pink, 4 Part ............................................................... 2.50
Depression Glass, Relish, Lorain, Yellow, Divided ................................................................ 4.50
Depression Glass, Relish, Lorain, Green, Divided, Original Label ....................................... 4.50
Depression Glass, Relish, Madrid, Amber, 10 In. .................................................................. 4.00
Depression Glass, Relish, Mayfair, Blue, Oval, 11 X 6 In. ................................................. 26.00
Depression Glass, Relish, Mayfair, Blue, 2 Part ................................................................. 13.50
Depression Glass, Relish, Mayfair, Pink, 4 Compartments ................................................. 5.00
Depression Glass, Relish, Miss America, Clear, Divided .................................................... 10.00
Depression Glass, Relish, Miss America, Clear, Oval ........................................................... 2.00
Depression Glass, Relish, Miss America, Moonstone, Divided ............................................ 3.75

Depression Glass, Relish, Miss America, Pink, 4 Part ............................................................. 3.50 To 7.00
Depression Glass, Relish, No.173, Moonstone, Divided ............................................................. 4.50
Depression Glass, Relish, No.612, Green, Divided ............................................... 4.00 To 4.50
Depression Glass, Relish, Princess, Green, Scalloped Edge, 8 1/2 In. ................................. 18.00
Depression Glass, Relish, Princess, Pink, 4 Part ............................................................. 3.75
Depression Glass, Salt & Pepper, Adam, Green ............................................................. 50.00
Depression Glass, Salt & Pepper, Adam, Pink ............................................... 15.00 To 17.50
Depression Glass, Salt & Pepper, Cameo, Green ............................................... 20.00 To 21.00
Depression Glass, Salt & Pepper, Cloverleaf, Green ............................................................. 12.00
Depression Glass, Salt & Pepper, Cubist, Green ............................................................. 10.00
Depression Glass, Salt & Pepper, Cubist, Pink ............................................................. 8.00
Depression Glass, Salt & Pepper, Diana, Pink ............................................................. 25.00
Depression Glass, Salt & Pepper, Doric, Pink ............................................................. 18.00
Depression Glass, Salt & Pepper, Floral Motif In Relief, Red, 3 3/4 In.High ......................... 18.00
Depression Glass, Salt & Pepper, Floral, Green ............................................... 10.00 To 18.00
Depression Glass, Salt & Pepper, Floral, Pink ............................................... 10.50 To 15.00
Depression Glass, Salt & Pepper, Floral, Pink, Footed ............................................................. 10.00
Depression Glass, Salt & Pepper, Floral, Pink, Short ............................................................. 15.00
Depression Glass, Salt & Pepper, Floral, Pink, Tall ............................................................. 18.00
Depression Glass, Salt & Pepper, Floral, Pink, 4 In. ............................................................. 10.00
Depression Glass, Salt & Pepper, Florentine, Yellow ............................................................. 15.00
Depression Glass, Salt & Pepper, Honeycomb, Green ............................................................. 8.00
Depression Glass, Salt & Pepper, Madrid, Amber ............................................... 14.50 To 15.00
Depression Glass, Salt & Pepper, Madrid, Amber, Flat ............................................................. 15.00
Depression Glass, Salt & Pepper, Madrid, Amber, Straight Sides ............................................. 18.50
Depression Glass, Salt & Pepper, Mayfair, Pink ............................................................. 20.00
Depression Glass, Salt & Pepper, Miss America, Pink ............................................................. 24.00
Depression Glass, Salt & Pepper, Moderntone, Blue ............................................... 7.00 To 8.50
Depression Glass, Salt & Pepper, Moderntone, Cobalt ............................................... 7.00 To 10.00
Depression Glass, Salt & Pepper, Patrician, Amber ............................................................. 50.00
Depression Glass, Salt & Pepper, Poppy, Green ............................................................. 14.00
Depression Glass, Salt & Pepper, Princess, Green, Short ............................................................. 15.00
Depression Glass, Salt & Pepper, Princess, Green, Tall ............................................................. 18.00
Depression Glass, Salt & Pepper, Princess, Green, 5 1/2 In. ............................................................. 12.00
Depression Glass, Salt & Pepper, Royal Lace, Blue ............................................................. 100.00
Depression Glass, Salt & Pepper, Royal Lace, Green ............................................................. 75.00
Depression Glass, Salt & Pepper, Sharon, Amber ............................................... 12.50 To 18.00
Depression Glass, Salt & Pepper, Sharon, Amber, Short ............................................................. 15.00
Depression Glass, Salt & Pepper, Sharon, Green, NH Mark Under Lid ................................. 34.00
Depression Glass, Salt & Pepper, Sharon, Pink ............................................... 12.00 To 18.00
Depression Glass, Salt & Pepper, Spoke, Crystal ............................................................. 17.50
Depression Glass, Salt & Pepper, Starlight, Clear ............................................................. 15.00
Depression Glass, Salt & Pepper, Tearoom, Green ............................................................. 22.50
Depression Glass, Salt & Pepper, Windsor, Clear ............................................................. 8.00
Depression Glass, Salt Dip, Amber ............................................................. 3.00
Depression Glass, Salt Dip, Hobnail, Green ............................................................. 3.00
Depression Glass, Saltshaker, Cubist, Green ............................................................. 5.00
Depression Glass, Saltshaker, Cubist, Pink ............................................................. 5.00
Depression Glass, Saltshaker, Diana, Clear ............................................................. 5.00
Depression Glass, Saltshaker, Floral, Pink, 4 In. ............................................................. 5.00
Depression Glass, Salver, American Sweetheart, Monax, 12 In. ............................................. 5.75
Depression Glass, Salver, American Sweetheart, Pink, 12 In. ............................................... 2.50 To 4.50
Depression Glass, Salver, American Sweetheart, Red, 12 In. ............................................................. 115.00
Depression Glass, Salver, Petalware, Monax, 11 In. ............................................... 2.50 To 4.00
Depression Glass, Sauce, Holiday, Pink, 5 In. ............................................................. 1.00
Depression Glass, Sauce, Madrid, Amber ............................................................. .75
Depression Glass, Sauce, Windsor, Green ............................................................. 1.25
Depression Glass, Saucer, Adam, Green ............................................................. 1.75
Depression Glass, Saucer, American Sweetheart, Monax ............................................... 1.50 To 2.50
Depression Glass, Saucer, American Sweetheart, Pink ............................................... 1.25 To 1.50
Depression Glass, Saucer, Ballerina, Green ............................................................. 2.00
Depression Glass, Saucer, Ballerina, Yellow ............................................................. 2.00
Depression Glass, Saucer, Bubble, Blue ............................................................. .65 To .75
Depression Glass, Saucer, Cameo, Green ............................................................. 1.00
Depression Glass, Saucer, Cameo, Green, 5 In. ............................................................. 2.50
Depression Glass, Saucer, Cherry Blossom, Pink ............................................................. 1.50

| | |
|---|---|
| Depression Glass, Saucer, Cherry, Pink | 1.50 |
| Depression Glass, Saucer, Cubist, Green | 2.00 |
| Depression Glass, Saucer, Daisy, Dark Amber | 1.75 |
| Depression Glass, Saucer, Dogwood, Pink | 1.25 |
| Depression Glass, Saucer, Floragold, Iridescent | 1.00 |
| Depression Glass, Saucer, Floral, Green | 1.00 To 2.00 |
| Depression Glass, Saucer, Floral, Pink | 1.25 To 1.50 |
| Depression Glass, Saucer, Florentine No.2, Green | 1.00 To 1.25 |
| Depression Glass, Saucer, Florentine No.2, Yellow | 1.25 |
| Depression Glass, Saucer, Florentine, Clear | 1.10 |
| Depression Glass, Saucer, Florentine, Yellow | 1.50 |
| Depression Glass, Saucer, Georgian, Green | 1.00 To 1.50 |
| Depression Glass, Saucer, Holiday, Pink | 1.00 |
| Depression Glass, Saucer, Lace Edge, Pink | 1.65 |
| Depression Glass, Saucer, Madrid, Amber | .75 To 1.50 |
| Depression Glass, Saucer, Mayfair, Pink, Hocking, Cup Ring | 5.75 |
| Depression Glass, Saucer, Mayfair, Pink, Ring | 4.50 |
| Depression Glass, Saucer, Miss America, Pink | 1.75 |
| Depression Glass, Saucer, Moderntone, Burgundy | 1.50 |
| Depression Glass, Saucer, Moderntone, Cobalt | 1.25 To 1.50 |
| Depression Glass, Saucer, No.612, Green | 1.25 |
| Depression Glass, Saucer, Normandie, Pink | 1.00 To 1.25 |
| Depression Glass, Saucer, Normandie, Sunburst | 2.50 |
| Depression Glass, Saucer, Patrician, Clear | 1.00 To 1.25 |
| Depression Glass, Saucer, Petalware, Cremax | .75 |
| Depression Glass, Saucer, Petalware, Monax | 1.50 |
| Depression Glass, Saucer, Princess, Green | 1.25 To 2.00 |
| Depression Glass, Saucer, Princess, Yellow | 2.00 |
| Depression Glass, Saucer, Roulette, Green | 1.00 To 1.50 |
| Depression Glass, Saucer, Royal Lace, Pink | 1.25 |
| Depression Glass, Saucer, Royal Lace, Ritz Blue | 3.00 |
| Depression Glass, Saucer, S Pattern, Yellow | 1.00 |
| Depression Glass, Saucer, Sandwich Hocking, Golden Amber | 1.00 |
| Depression Glass, Saucer, Sharon, Amber | 1.25 |
| Depression Glass, Saucer, Sharon, Pink | 1.00 |
| Depression Glass, Saucer, Sunflower, Green | 1.50 |
| Depression Glass, Saucer, Sunflower, Pink | 2.50 |
| Depression Glass, Saucer, Swirl, Ultramarine | 1.00 |
| Depression Glass, Saucer, Vitrock, White | .50 |
| Depression Glass, Saucer, Wedding Band, Cobalt Blue | 1.00 |
| Depression Glass, Server, Mayfair, Blue, Center Handle | 24.00 |
| Depression Glass, Server, Mayfair, Green, Center Handle | 15.00 |
| Depression Glass, Server, Mayfair, Pink, Center Handle | 6.00 To 6.90 |
| Depression Glass, Sherbet, Adam, Green, Footed | 3.25 |
| Depression Glass, Sherbet, American Sweetheart, Clear, Holder | 1.50 To 4.00 |
| Depression Glass, Sherbet, American Sweetheart, Monax | 8.00 |
| Depression Glass, Sherbet, American Sweetheart, Monax, Footed | 6.00 |
| Depression Glass, Sherbet, American Sweetheart, Monax, Low Footed, 4 1/2 In. | 4.00 |
| Depression Glass, Sherbet, American Sweetheart, Pink, Footed | 2.50 |
| Depression Glass, Sherbet, American Sweetheart, Pink, Footed, Low | 2.25 |
| Depression Glass, Sherbet, American Sweetheart, Pink, 6 In. | 1.50 |
| Depression Glass, Sherbet, Block Optic, Green | 1.00 |
| Depression Glass, Sherbet, Block Optic, Green, Gold Trim, 5 In. | 4.00 |
| Depression Glass, Sherbet, Bouquet & Lattice, Marigold, Footed | 1.50 |
| Depression Glass, Sherbet, Bouquet & Lattice, Pink | 2.00 |
| Depression Glass, Sherbet, Cameo, Green | 1.50 To 8.00 |
| Depression Glass, Sherbet, Cameo, Green, High Stem | 5.00 |
| Depression Glass, Sherbet, Cameo, Green, Stemmed, 5 In. | 8.00 |
| Depression Glass, Sherbet, Cameo, Green, 3 In. | 2.50 To 3.50 |
| Depression Glass, Sherbet, Cameo, Green, 4 3/4 In. | 8.00 |
| Depression Glass, Sherbet, Cherry Blossom, Delfite | 10.00 |
| Depression Glass, Sherbet, Cherry Blossom, Pink | 2.00 To 3.50 |
| Depression Glass, Sherbet, Cherry, Green | 4.00 To 4.50 |
| Depression Glass, Sherbet, Cherry, Green, Footed | 3.00 |
| Depression Glass, Sherbet, Cherry, Pink | 2.75 To 3.00 |
| Depression Glass, Sherbet, Clover, Pink | 1.50 |

Depression Glass, Sherbet, Cloverleaf, Green ............................................................... 1.75
Depression Glass, Sherbet, Cloverleaf, Yellow ............................................................... 3.00
Depression Glass, Sherbet, Colonial, Green ................................................................. 2.00
Depression Glass, Sherbet, Crackle, Clear ................................................................... 1.00
Depression Glass, Sherbet, Daisy, Amber ....................................................... 1.50 To 2.50
Depression Glass, Sherbet, Diamond-Quilted, Pink ...................................................... 1.50
Depression Glass, Sherbet, Dogwood, Pink .................................................... 3.25 To 3.50
Depression Glass, Sherbet, Doric, Delfite Blue ............................................................ 3.00
Depression Glass, Sherbet, Etched, Clear .................................................................... 2.50
Depression Glass, Sherbet, Etched, Green .................................................................... 2.50
Depression Glass, Sherbet, Floral & Diamond Band, Green ........................................... 1.92
Depression Glass, Sherbet, Floral, Green ..................................................................... 2.50
Depression Glass, Sherbet, Floral, Pink .......................................................... 1.50 To 2.00
Depression Glass, Sherbet, Floral, Pink, Footed ......................................................... 2.00
Depression Glass, Sherbet, Florentine No.1, Green ...................................................... 1.50
Depression Glass, Sherbet, Florentine No.1, Pink ........................................................ 2.75
Depression Glass, Sherbet, Florentine No.2, Green ...................................................... 2.50
Depression Glass, Sherbet, Georgian, Green ................................................... 1.50 To 2.00
Depression Glass, Sherbet, Holiday, Pink ........................................................ 1.25 To 2.00
Depression Glass, Sherbet, Honeycomb, Ruby ............................................................ 6.00
Depression Glass, Sherbet, Iris & Herringbone, Marigold, Footed ................................. 2.00
Depression Glass, Sherbet, Iris, Clear, 3 1/2 In. ........................................................... 2.25
Depression Glass, Sherbet, Madrid, Amber ..................................................... 1.00 To 1.50
Depression Glass, Sherbet, Madrid, Amber, Conical ........................................ 1.50 To 2.25
Depression Glass, Sherbet, Many Windows, Green ...................................................... 2.00
Depression Glass, Sherbet, Mayfair, Pink .................................................................... 3.00
Depression Glass, Sherbet, Mayfair, Pink, Footed ....................................................... 2.50
Depression Glass, Sherbet, Mayfair, Pink, 3 1/4 In. ...................................................... 3.00
Depression Glass, Sherbet, Mayfair, Pink, 4 3/4 In. ...................................................... 13.00
Depression Glass, Sherbet, Miss America, Clear .......................................................... 2.00
Depression Glass, Sherbet, Miss America, Pink ............................................... 3.25 To 4.50
Depression Glass, Sherbet, Moderntone, Blue ................................................. 2.00 To 2.25
Depression Glass, Sherbet, Moderntone, Cobalt .............................................. 2.00 To 2.50
Depression Glass, Sherbet, Moderntone, Cobalt, Footed .............................................. 2.00
Depression Glass, Sherbet, Moderntone, Platonite ...................................................... 2.00
Depression Glass, Sherbet, No.612, Green ....................................................... 3.00 To 3.25
Depression Glass, Sherbet, No.612, Yellow ................................................................. 2.50
Depression Glass, Sherbet, Normandie, Pink ............................................................... 2.00
Depression Glass, Sherbet, Normandie, Sunburst ........................................................ 3.00
Depression Glass, Sherbet, Old Florentine, Pink .......................................................... 3.00
Depression Glass, Sherbet, Opalescent Hobnail, Moonstone ....................................... 3.00
Depression Glass, Sherbet, Optic Block, Green, Cone ................................................. 1.25
Depression Glass, Sherbet, Panel Optic, Green, Cone .................................................. 1.00
Depression Glass, Sherbet, Parrot, Green .................................................................... 5.75
Depression Glass, Sherbet, Patrician, Amber ................................................... 2.00 To 2.35
Depression Glass, Sherbet, Patrician, Amber, Footed .................................................. 2.25
Depression Glass, Sherbet, Patrician, Clear ................................................................. 2.00
Depression Glass, Sherbet, Princess, Green, Footed ................................................... 3.00
Depression Glass, Sherbet, Princess, Pink ...................................................... 1.50 To 2.25
Depression Glass, Sherbet, Princess, Yellow ............................................................... 5.00
Depression Glass, Sherbet, Ribbon, Green ................................................................. 1.50
Depression Glass, Sherbet, Roulette, Green ..................................................... 1.50 To 1.75
Depression Glass, Sherbet, Royal Lace, Blue ............................................................. 8.00
Depression Glass, Sherbet, Royal Lace, Green ................................................ 6.00 To 7.90
Depression Glass, Sherbet, Royal Lace, Pink .................................................. 2.50 To 3.00
Depression Glass, Sherbet, Royal Ruby ...................................................................... 1.50
Depression Glass, Sherbet, Royal Ruby, Knob Stem .................................................... 2.50
Depression Glass, Sherbet, Sandwich, Dark Green, Low ............................................. 1.25
Depression Glass, Sherbet, Sharon, Pink, Footed ....................................................... 2.00
Depression Glass, Sherbet, Spiral, Green ......................................................... 1.00 To 2.00
Depression Glass, Sherbet, Spoke, Amber ....................................................... 1.75 To 2.00
Depression Glass, Sherbet, Strawberry, Green ............................................................ 2.00
Depression Glass, Sherbet, Strawberry, Pink ............................................................. 2.50
Depression Glass, Sherbet, Sylvan Parrot, Green, 2 3/4 In. ......................................... 4.00
Depression Glass, Sherbet, Twisted Optic, Pink, Footed ............................................. 2.00
Depression Glass, Sherbet, Waterford, Crystal ........................................................... 1.45

**Depression Glass, Sherbet,** Wedding Band, Cobalt Blue, Footed ............................ 2.00
**Depression Glass, Sherbet,** Wedding Band, White, Milk Glass, Footed ................ .70
**Depression Glass, Sugar & Creamer,** Adam, Green, Cover ................................ 16.00
**Depression Glass, Sugar & Creamer,** Adam, Pink, Cover ................ 9.50 To 15.00
**Depression Glass, Sugar & Creamer,** American Sweetheart, Monax ................ 8.00
**Depression Glass, Sugar & Creamer,** American Sweetheart, Pink ................ 6.00
**Depression Glass, Sugar & Creamer,** American Sweetheart, Red ................ 190.00
**Depression Glass, Sugar & Creamer,** Avocado Pear, Pink ................ 15.00
**Depression Glass, Sugar & Creamer,** Bubble, Blue ................ 7.50
**Depression Glass, Sugar & Creamer,** Cabbage Rose, Amber ................ 6.50
**Depression Glass, Sugar & Creamer,** Cameo, Green, Round ................ 8.00
**Depression Glass, Sugar & Creamer,** Cameo, Green, Slender, 4 In. ................ 22.00
**Depression Glass, Sugar & Creamer,** Cameo, Green, Tall ................ 7.00
**Depression Glass, Sugar & Creamer,** Cameo, Yellow ................ 6.50 To 8.00
**Depression Glass, Sugar & Creamer,** Cherry Blossom, Green ................ 8.00
**Depression Glass, Sugar & Creamer,** Cherry Blossom, Pink, Cover ................ 8.75
**Depression Glass, Sugar & Creamer,** Cherry, Delfite ................ 20.00
**Depression Glass, Sugar & Creamer,** Cherry, Green ................ 10.00 To 12.50
**Depression Glass, Sugar & Creamer,** Cherry, Green, Cover ................ 12.00
**Depression Glass, Sugar & Creamer,** Child's, Cherry, Pink ................ 35.00
**Depression Glass, Sugar & Creamer,** Christmas Candy, Crystal ................ 6.00
**Depression Glass, Sugar & Creamer,** Cloverleaf, Green ................ 5.00
**Depression Glass, Sugar & Creamer,** Colonial Fluted Rope, Green, Cover ................ 7.50
**Depression Glass, Sugar & Creamer,** Colonial, Green, Fluted ................ 4.00
**Depression Glass, Sugar & Creamer,** Crackle, Clear ................ 4.50
**Depression Glass, Sugar & Creamer,** Cubist, Clear ................ 4.50
**Depression Glass, Sugar & Creamer,** Cubist, Green, Cover ................ 10.00
**Depression Glass, Sugar & Creamer,** Cubist, Green, 3 In. ................ 7.50
**Depression Glass, Sugar & Creamer,** Cubist, Milk Glass ................ 3.00 To 5.75
**Depression Glass, Sugar & Creamer,** Cubist, Pink, Cover ................ 5.00 To 8.00
**Depression Glass, Sugar & Creamer,** Daisy, Amber ................ 6.50
**Depression Glass, Sugar & Creamer,** Diana, Amber ................ 6.00
**Depression Glass, Sugar & Creamer,** Dogwood, Green ................ 15.00
**Depression Glass, Sugar & Creamer,** Dogwood, Pink ................ 5.25
**Depression Glass, Sugar & Creamer,** Dogwood, Pink, Thick ................ 6.50
**Depression Glass, Sugar & Creamer,** Dogwood, Pink, Thin ................ 6.50
**Depression Glass, Sugar & Creamer,** Doric, Green ................ 5.00
**Depression Glass, Sugar & Creamer,** Doric, Green, Cover ................ 14.00
**Depression Glass, Sugar & Creamer,** Doric, Pink, Cover ................ 8.50
**Depression Glass, Sugar & Creamer,** English Hobnail, Pink ................ 8.00
**Depression Glass, Sugar & Creamer,** Floral, Green, Cover ................ 7.50 To 9.50
**Depression Glass, Sugar & Creamer,** Floral, Pink ................ 6.50
**Depression Glass, Sugar & Creamer,** Floral, Pink, Cover ................ 7.00 To 10.50
**Depression Glass, Sugar & Creamer,** Flowered Rim, Milk Glass ................ 6.00
**Depression Glass, Sugar & Creamer,** Georgian, Green ................ 2.75
**Depression Glass, Sugar & Creamer,** Georgian, Green, 4 In. ................ 6.00
**Depression Glass, Sugar & Creamer,** Holiday, Pink, Cover ................ 5.00 To 6.50
**Depression Glass, Sugar & Creamer,** Horizontal Rib, Pink ................ 6.00
**Depression Glass, Sugar & Creamer,** Indiana, Custard ................ 10.00
**Depression Glass, Sugar & Creamer,** Iris, Clear, Cover ................ 6.00 To 6.50
**Depression Glass, Sugar & Creamer,** Lovebird, Green ................ 5.00
**Depression Glass, Sugar & Creamer,** Madrid, Amber ................ 3.50 To 6.00
**Depression Glass, Sugar & Creamer,** Madrid, Amber, Cover ................ 11.50
**Depression Glass, Sugar & Creamer,** Madrid, Green, Cover ................ 20.00
**Depression Glass, Sugar & Creamer,** Manhattan, Clear ................ 2.00
**Depression Glass, Sugar & Creamer,** Mayfair, Pink ................ 6.00
**Depression Glass, Sugar & Creamer,** Miss America, Clear ................ 10.00
**Depression Glass, Sugar & Creamer,** Miss America, Pink ................ 10.00
**Depression Glass, Sugar & Creamer,** Moderntone, Blue ................ 6.00
**Depression Glass, Sugar & Creamer,** Newport, Amethyst ................ 9.00
**Depression Glass, Sugar & Creamer,** Newport, Burgundy ................ 7.50
**Depression Glass, Sugar & Creamer,** Newport, Ritz Blue ................ 7.50
**Depression Glass, Sugar & Creamer,** No.173, Moonstone ................ 5.00
**Depression Glass, Sugar & Creamer,** No.2390, Opaque White ................ 18.00
**Depression Glass, Sugar & Creamer,** No.612, Green ................ 6.00 To 8.00
**Depression Glass, Sugar & Creamer,** Old Florentine, Green, Cover ................ 8.00

| | |
|---|---|
| Depression Glass, Sugar & Creamer, Old Florentine, Pink | 8.00 |
| Depression Glass, Sugar & Creamer, Old Florentine, Yellow | 10.00 |
| Depression Glass, Sugar & Creamer, Opalescent Hobnail, Moonstone | 6.00 |
| Depression Glass, Sugar & Creamer, Optic Block, Pink | 2.25 |
| Depression Glass, Sugar & Creamer, Optic Ribbed, Iridescent | 6.50 |
| Depression Glass, Sugar & Creamer, Paneled, Green | 5.00 |
| Depression Glass, Sugar & Creamer, Patrician, Green | 7.50 |
| Depression Glass, Sugar & Creamer, Princess, Green | 6.00 |
| Depression Glass, Sugar & Creamer, Princess, Topaz, Cover | 8.00 |
| Depression Glass, Sugar & Creamer, Queen Mary, Pink | 6.00 |
| Depression Glass, Sugar & Creamer, Ribbed, Ruby Red, Miniature | 10.00 |
| Depression Glass, Sugar & Creamer, Royal Lace, Blue | 25.00 |
| Depression Glass, Sugar & Creamer, Royal Lace, Clear | 7.00 To 8.00 |
| Depression Glass, Sugar & Creamer, Royal Lace, Cobalt | 25.00 |
| Depression Glass, Sugar & Creamer, Royal Lace, Green | 12.00 |
| Depression Glass, Sugar & Creamer, Royal Lace, Pink | 9.00 |
| Depression Glass, Sugar & Creamer, Royal Lace, Pink, Cover | 15.00 |
| Depression Glass, Sugar & Creamer, Royal Ruby | 4.00 |
| Depression Glass, Sugar & Creamer, Sandwich, Green, Hocking | 18.00 |
| Depression Glass, Sugar & Creamer, Sharon, Amber | 5.50 |
| Depression Glass, Sugar & Creamer, Sharon, Amber, Cover | 12.00 |
| Depression Glass, Sugar & Creamer, Sharon, Green, Cover | 16.00 |
| Depression Glass, Sugar & Creamer, Sharon, Pink | 4.50 |
| Depression Glass, Sugar & Creamer, Sharon, Pink, Cover | 8.75 |
| Depression Glass, Sugar & Creamer, Swirl, Green | 4.00 |
| Depression Glass, Sugar & Creamer, Swirl, Ultramarine | 7.50 |
| Depression Glass, Sugar & Creamer, Tearoom, Pink, Small Size | 7.00 |
| Depression Glass, Sugar & Creamer, Victory, Pink | 8.00 |
| Depression Glass, Sugar & Creamer, W No.202, Cobalt Blue, 3 In. | 5.00 |
| Depression Glass, Sugar & Creamer, Waterford, Clear, Cover | 4.50 To 6.00 |
| Depression Glass, Sugar & Creamer, Windsor, Green | 4.00 |
| Depression Glass, Sugar & Creamer, Windsor, Pink, Cover | 6.00 |
| Depression Glass, Sugar, Adam, Green, Covered | 4.50 |
| Depression Glass, Sugar, Adam, Pink, Covered | 4.00 |
| Depression Glass, Sugar, American Sweetheart, Monax | 3.00 To 4.75 |
| Depression Glass, Sugar, American Sweetheart, Pink | 2.50 To 3.00 |
| Depression Glass, Sugar, Block Optic, Yellow | 1.75 |
| Depression Glass, Sugar, Bubble, Blue | 3.50 |
| Depression Glass, Sugar, Cameo, Green | 2.50 |
| Depression Glass, Sugar, Cameo, Green, Short | 2.50 |
| Depression Glass, Sugar, Cameo, Green, 3 In. | 2.50 |
| Depression Glass, Sugar, Cameo, Green, 3 1/4 In. | 2.50 |
| Depression Glass, Sugar, Cherry Blossom, Green, Covered | 6.00 |
| Depression Glass, Sugar, Cherry Blossom, Pink, Covered | 4.00 |
| Depression Glass, Sugar, Cherry, Delfite | 10.00 |
| Depression Glass, Sugar, Cherry, Pink, Covered | 4.00 To 5.00 |
| Depression Glass, Sugar, Child's, Cherry, Delfite | 30.00 |
| Depression Glass, Sugar, Child's, Cherry, Pink | 25.00 |
| Depression Glass, Sugar, Cloverleaf, Black | 6.00 |
| Depression Glass, Sugar, Cloverleaf, Green | 2.50 |
| Depression Glass, Sugar, Cubist, Clear, 2 In. | 1.50 |
| Depression Glass, Sugar, Cubist, Green, Covered | 4.00 To 5.00 |
| Depression Glass, Sugar, Cubist, Green, Covered, 3 In. | 4.00 |
| Depression Glass, Sugar, Cubist, Pink, 2 In. | 1.50 |
| Depression Glass, Sugar, Cubist, Pink, 3 In. | 3.00 |
| Depression Glass, Sugar, Floragold, Iridescent, Covered | 3.00 |
| Depression Glass, Sugar, Floral, Pink, Covered | 3.00 To 6.50 |
| Depression Glass, Sugar, Florentine No.1, Green | 2.00 |
| Depression Glass, Sugar, Florentine No.2, Green | 2.50 |
| Depression Glass, Sugar, Florentine No.2, Yellow | 2.00 To 2.75 |
| Depression Glass, Sugar, Florentine, Clear | 3.00 |
| Depression Glass, Sugar, Florentine, Yellow | 3.00 |
| Depression Glass, Sugar, Georgian, Green | 1.50 To 2.00 |
| Depression Glass, Sugar, Georgian, Green, 4 In. | 3.00 |
| Depression Glass, Sugar, Heritage, Clear | 1.75 |
| Depression Glass, Sugar, Holiday, Pink | 2.75 |

| | |
|---|---|
| Depression Glass, Sugar, Iris, Clear | 20.00 |
| Depression Glass, Sugar, Iris, Clear, Covered | 3.50 |
| Depression Glass, Sugar, Lace Edge, Pink | 3.50 To 4.50 |
| Depression Glass, Sugar, Lorain, Green | 3.50 |
| Depression Glass, Sugar, Lorain, Yellow | 3.00 |
| Depression Glass, Sugar, Madrid, Amber | 2.25 To 3.00 |
| Depression Glass, Sugar, Madrid, Amber, Covered | 5.00 To 10.00 |
| Depression Glass, Sugar, Mayfair, Pink | 3.00 To 4.00 |
| Depression Glass, Sugar, Miss America, Clear | 4.00 |
| Depression Glass, Sugar, Miss America, Moonstone | 2.50 |
| Depression Glass, Sugar, Moderntone, Amethyst | 3.00 |
| Depression Glass, Sugar, Moderntone, Blue | 2.25 |
| Depression Glass, Sugar, Moderntone, Burgundy | 2.50 |
| Depression Glass, Sugar, Moderntone, Cobalt | 2.25 To 2.50 |
| Depression Glass, Sugar, No.612, Green | 2.50 |
| Depression Glass, Sugar, No.612, Yellow | 3.00 |
| Depression Glass, Sugar, Patrician, Amber | 2.00 To 3.00 |
| Depression Glass, Sugar, Patrician, Pink | 8.00 |
| Depression Glass, Sugar, Petalware, Monax | 2.00 |
| Depression Glass, Sugar, Princess, Green | 3.50 |
| Depression Glass, Sugar, Princess, Green, Covered | 4.25 To 4.50 |
| Depression Glass, Sugar, Pyramid, Pink | 4.00 |
| Depression Glass, Sugar, Quadruped, Clear | 2.00 |
| Depression Glass, Sugar, Queen Mary, Clear | 2.50 |
| Depression Glass, Sugar, Royal Lace, Blue | 15.00 |
| Depression Glass, Sugar, Royal Lace, Cobalt | 10.50 |
| Depression Glass, Sugar, Royal Lace, Green | 7.00 |
| Depression Glass, Sugar, Royal Lace, Pink | 4.00 |
| Depression Glass, Sugar, Royal Lace, Pink, Covered | 5.00 To 8.50 |
| Depression Glass, Sugar, Royal Lace, Ritz Blue | 15.00 |
| Depression Glass, Sugar, S Pattern, Clear | 2.50 |
| Depression Glass, Sugar, Sandwich, Green, Hocking | 2.00 |
| Depression Glass, Sugar, Sharon, Pink | 3.50 |
| Depression Glass, Sugar, Sharon, Pink, Covered | 5.00 To 6.50 |
| Depression Glass, Sugar, Sierra, Green | 5.00 |
| Depression Glass, Sugar, Sunflower, Green | 3.00 |
| Depression Glass, Sugar, Sunflower, Pink | 4.50 |
| Depression Glass, Sugar, Swirl, Ultramarine | 2.50 |
| Depression Glass, Sugar, Tearoom, Green | 3.00 |
| Depression Glass, Tea Set, Child's, Homespun, Pink, 8 Piece | 50.00 |
| Depression Glass, Tray, American Sweetheart, Pink, Chrome, Indented Center | 10.00 |
| Depression Glass, Tray, Cherry Blossom, Pink, Handled | 4.25 |
| Depression Glass, Tray, Cherry Blossom, Pink, Handled, 10 1/2 In. | 4.00 |
| Depression Glass, Tray, Cherry Blossom, Pink, 10 1/2 In. | 5.00 |
| Depression Glass, Tray, Cherry, Pink, Handled | 4.00 |
| Depression Glass, Tray, Cherry, Pink, 10 1/2 In. | 4.50 |
| Depression Glass, Tray, Domino, Cameo, Green | 32.50 To 35.00 |
| Depression Glass, Tray, Doric, Green, Square, 7 In. | 3.00 |
| Depression Glass, Tray, Doric, Pink, Square, 8 In. | 4.00 To 5.00 |
| Depression Glass, Tray, Double Shield, Cobalt, Handled, 8 1/2 In. | 4.75 |
| Depression Glass, Tray, Etched, Pink, Handles, 10 In. | 5.00 |
| Depression Glass, Tray, Floragold, 13 In. | 6.00 |
| Depression Glass, Tray, Hobnail, Moonstone, 2 X 3 X 5 In. | 5.00 |
| Depression Glass, Tray, Holiday, Pink, Round, 10 1/2 In. | 5.75 |
| Depression Glass, Tray, Sandwich, Cherry, Blue, Delphite, 10 1/2 In. | 15.00 |
| Depression Glass, Tray, Sandwich, Cherry, Green, Handled | 8.00 |
| Depression Glass, Tray, Sandwich, Cherry, Pink, Handled | 6.00 |
| Depression Glass, Tray, Sandwich, Doric, Green, 10 In. | 4.75 |
| Depression Glass, Tray, Sandwich, Mayfair, Pink, Handled | 10.00 |
| Depression Glass, Tray, Sandwich, No.612, Green | 5.00 |
| Depression Glass, Tray, Serving, Sierra, Green, Handled, 10 1/2 In. | 5.00 |
| Depression Glass, Tray, Serving, Waffle, Green, Clear Inserts, 13 In. | 8.00 |
| Depression Glass, Tub, Ice, Cameo, Green | 75.00 |
| Depression Glass, Tumble-Up, Block, Green, 3 Pieces | 7.50 |
| Depression Glass, Tumbler, Adam, Green, Cone Shape, 5 1/2 In. | 9.50 |
| Depression Glass, Tumbler, Adam, Green, 5 1/2 In. | 7.00 |

| | |
|---|---:|
| Depression Glass, Tumbler, Adam, Pink, 5 1/2 In. | 10.00 |
| Depression Glass, Tumbler, American Sweetheart, Pink, 4 1/2 In. | 12.00 |
| Depression Glass, Tumbler, Block, Green, Flat, 5 1/2 In. | 2.25 |
| Depression Glass, Tumbler, Bowknot, Green, Footed, 5 In. | 3.50 |
| Depression Glass, Tumbler, Bubble, Clear, Flat, 4 1/4 In. | 3.00 |
| Depression Glass, Tumbler, Bubble, Clear, Footed, 7 In. | 5.00 |
| Depression Glass, Tumbler, Cameo, Green, Cone, 4 3/4 In. | 9.50 |
| Depression Glass, Tumbler, Cameo, Green, Flat, 4 In. | 5.00 |
| Depression Glass, Tumbler, Cameo, Green, Footed, 5 In. | 7.50 |
| Depression Glass, Tumbler, Cameo, Green, Footed, 5 3/4 In. | 10.00 |
| Depression Glass, Tumbler, Cameo, Green, Footed, 6 In. | 8.00 |
| Depression Glass, Tumbler, Cameo, Green, 5 In. | 7.75 |
| Depression Glass, Tumbler, Cameo, Rose, 5 In. | 2.75 |
| Depression Glass, Tumbler, Candle, Royal Ruby, 2 In. | 1.00 |
| Depression Glass, Tumbler, Cherry Blossom, Green, Footed, 3 1/2 In. | 6.50 |
| Depression Glass, Tumbler, Cherry Blossom, Green, 4 1/4 In. | 5.00 |
| Depression Glass, Tumbler, Cherry Blossom, Pink, Flat, 4 In. | 5.50 |
| Depression Glass, Tumbler, Cherry Blossom, Pink, 4 In. | 3.00 To 7.50 |
| Depression Glass, Tumbler, Cherry Blossom, Pink, 4 1/2 In. | 9.75 |
| Depression Glass, Tumbler, Cherry Blossom, Pink, 5 In. | 9.50 |
| Depression Glass, Tumbler, Cherry, Delfite, Footed, 9 Ozs. | 9.00 |
| Depression Glass, Tumbler, Cherry, Green, 9 Ozs. | 5.00 |
| Depression Glass, Tumbler, Clover, Green, Footed, 6 In. | 4.00 |
| Depression Glass, Tumbler, Cloverleaf, Green, Footed, 10 In. | 6.00 |
| Depression Glass, Tumbler, Cloverleaf, Green, 4 In. | 3.50 |
| Depression Glass, Tumbler, Crisscross, Green, 3 3/4 In. | 1.50 |
| Depression Glass, Tumbler, Cubist, Clear, 9 Ozs. | 5.00 |
| Depression Glass, Tumbler, Diana, Clear, 9 Ozs., 4 1/8 In. | 4.00 |
| Depression Glass, Tumbler, Dogwood, Pink, Decorated, 5 In. | 12.00 |
| Depression Glass, Tumbler, Fish, Cobalt, Sportsman Series, 4 1/2 In. | 3.00 |
| Depression Glass, Tumbler, Floragold, Footed, 5 In. | 4.00 |
| Depression Glass, Tumbler, Floragold, Iridescent, 10 Oz. | 2.50 |
| Depression Glass, Tumbler, Floral, Green, 4 3/4 In. | 4.50 To 5.75 |
| Depression Glass, Tumbler, Floral, Pink, Footed, 7 Ozs. | 4.00 |
| Depression Glass, Tumbler, Floral, Pink, 4 In. | 3.00 To 4.50 |
| Depression Glass, Tumbler, Floral, Pink, 4 5/8 In. | 5.50 |
| Depression Glass, Tumbler, Floral, Pink, 4 3/4 In. | 4.75 |
| Depression Glass, Tumbler, Florentine No.2, Green, Footed, 5 In. | 6.00 |
| Depression Glass, Tumbler, Florentine No.2, Yellow, Footed | 4.00 |
| Depression Glass, Tumbler, Florentine No.2, Yellow, 5 In. | 5.50 |
| Depression Glass, Tumbler, Florentine, Green, Flat, 4 1/4 In. | 4.75 |
| Depression Glass, Tumbler, Florentine, Green, Footed, 4 In. | 3.50 |
| Depression Glass, Tumbler, Florentine, Green, Footed, 5 In. | 4.50 |
| Depression Glass, Tumbler, Florentine, Green, 5 Ozs. | 4.00 |
| Depression Glass, Tumbler, Florentine, Green, 9 Ozs. | 5.00 |
| Depression Glass, Tumbler, Florentine, Green, 12 Ozs. | 6.00 |
| Depression Glass, Tumbler, Florentine, Pink, 4 In. | 5.00 |
| Depression Glass, Tumbler, Florentine, Yellow, Footed, 5 In. | 5.75 |
| Depression Glass, Tumbler, Florentine, Yellow, 3 1/2 In. | 4.75 |
| Depression Glass, Tumbler, Georgian, Green, 9 Oz., 4 In. | 8.00 |
| Depression Glass, Tumbler, Holiday, Pink, Footed, 4 In. | 8.00 |
| Depression Glass, Tumbler, Holiday, Pink, 4 In. | 5.00 To 5.50 |
| Depression Glass, Tumbler, Iced Tea, Lovebirds, Green, 12 Ozs. | 9.00 |
| Depression Glass, Tumbler, Iced Tea, Madrid, Amber | 8.00 |
| Depression Glass, Tumbler, Iced Tea, Madrid, Amber, 5 1/2 In. | 5.25 |
| Depression Glass, Tumbler, Iced Tea, Madrid, Blue, 5 1/2 In. | 16.00 |
| Depression Glass, Tumbler, Iris, Carnival, Footed, 6 In. | 3.75 |
| Depression Glass, Tumbler, Iris, Clear, Footed, 6 In. | 3.50 To 5.00 |
| Depression Glass, Tumbler, Iris, Clear, Footed, 7 In. | 4.00 To 5.00 |
| Depression Glass, Tumbler, Juice, American Sweetheart, Pink | 13.00 To 15.00 |
| Depression Glass, Tumbler, Juice, Cameo, Green, Flat | 8.00 |
| Depression Glass, Tumbler, Juice, Cameo, Green, 3 In. | 7.50 To 8.00 |
| Depression Glass, Tumbler, Juice, Cameo, Green, 3 1/2 In. | 7.00 |
| Depression Glass, Tumbler, Juice, Cherry Blossom, Pink, Footed | 5.00 To 6.00 |
| Depression Glass, Tumbler, Juice, Cherry, Pink, Footed | 4.50 |
| Depression Glass, Tumbler, Juice, Cherry, Pink, Footed, 3 1/4 In. | 4.00 |

Depression Glass, Tumbler, Juice, Florentine No.2, Yellow, Footed .................................. 5.00
Depression Glass, Tumbler, Juice, Florentine, Pink, 3 1/2 In. ..................................... 5.00
Depression Glass, Tumbler, Juice, Homespun, Pink, Footed ........................................ 2.75
Depression Glass, Tumbler, Juice, Madrid, Amber, Footed ......................................... 9.00
Depression Glass, Tumbler, Juice, Madrid, Amber, 3 3/4 In. ...................................... 8.00
Depression Glass, Tumbler, Juice, Miss America, Clear, Footed ................................... 9.00
Depression Glass, Tumbler, Juice, Queen Mary, Pink ............................................. 2.50
Depression Glass, Tumbler, Juice, Royal Lace, Blue ............................................. 18.00
Depression Glass, Tumbler, Juice, Royal Lace, Pink, 3 In. ....................................... 5.00
Depression Glass, Tumbler, Juice, Sailboat, Cobalt, Sailboat Series ............................. 2.50
Depression Glass, Tumbler, Juice, W No.202, Cobalt Blue, 4 In. .................................. 2.50
Depression Glass, Tumbler, Lydia Ray, Amethyst, 3 1/2 In. ...................................... 4.50
Depression Glass, Tumbler, Lydia Ray, Green, 4 In. ............................................. 4.00
Depression Glass, Tumbler, Madrid, Amber, Flat, 5 1/2 In. ...................................... 7.00
Depression Glass, Tumbler, Madrid, Amber, Footed, 4 In. ........................................ 8.00
Depression Glass, Tumbler, Madrid, Amber, Footed, 10 Ozs. ......................... 9.00 To 9.50
Depression Glass, Tumbler, Madrid, Amber, 4 In. ............................................... 6.00
Depression Glass, Tumbler, Madrid, Amber, 4 1/2 In. .............................. 4.50 To 6.50
Depression Glass, Tumbler, Madrid, Amber, 5 1/2 In. ........................................... 6.00
Depression Glass, Tumbler, Madrid, Pink, 9 Ozs. ............................................... 3.75
Depression Glass, Tumbler, Manhattan, Clear .................................................. 1.50
Depression Glass, Tumbler, Mayfair, Amber .................................................... 15.00
Depression Glass, Tumbler, Mayfair, Pink, Cone, 6 3/4 In. ...................................... 12.50
Depression Glass, Tumbler, Mayfair, Pink, Footed, 5 1/2 In. .................................... 6.00
Depression Glass, Tumbler, Miss America, Clear ................................................ 9.00
Depression Glass, Tumbler, Miss America, Clear, 4 1/2 In. ...................................... 6.50
Depression Glass, Tumbler, Miss America, Clear, 6 In. ............................... 8.00 To 9.00
Depression Glass, Tumbler, Miss America, Green ................................................ 6.00
Depression Glass, Tumbler, Miss America, Pink ................................................. 7.00
Depression Glass, Tumbler, Moderntone, Blue .................................................. 3.75
Depression Glass, Tumbler, Moderntone, Blue, 4 In. ............................................ 5.00
Depression Glass, Tumbler, No.358, Pink ...................................................... 4.50
Depression Glass, Tumbler, Old Cafe, Pink, 5 In. .............................................. 2.25
Depression Glass, Tumbler, Old Florentine, Green, Footed, 5 In. ................................ 7.50
Depression Glass, Tumbler, Patrician, Pink, 4 In. ............................................. 7.80
Depression Glass, Tumbler, Pink Block, 5 In. .................................................. 3.00
Depression Glass, Tumbler, Poinsettia, Pink, 4 3/4 In. ........................................ 4.50
Depression Glass, Tumbler, Princess, Green, Footed, 10 Ozs. .................................... 6.00
Depression Glass, Tumbler, Princess, Green, Footed, 5 1/4 In. .................................. 5.00
Depression Glass, Tumbler, Princess, Green, 5 1/4 In. ......................................... 5.00
Depression Glass, Tumbler, Princess, Pink, Footed, 5 1/4 In. ....................... 5.90 To 7.00
Depression Glass, Tumbler, Princess, Topaz, Footed, 5 1/4 In. .................................. 5.00
Depression Glass, Tumbler, Princess, Yellow, Footed, 6 1/2 In. ................................. 4.50
Depression Glass, Tumbler, Queen Anne, Clear, Footed, 6 1/2 In. ............................... 4.50
Depression Glass, Tumbler, Queen Mary, Pink, 3 In. ........................................... 1.50
Depression Glass, Tumbler, Queen Mary, Pink, 4 In. ........................................... 2.00
Depression Glass, Tumbler, Quilted Optic, Green, 4 In. ........................................ 1.65
Depression Glass, Tumbler, Roly-Poly, Sailboat, Cobalt, Sailboat Series ........................ 3.00
Depression Glass, Tumbler, Royal Lace, Blue, 4 1/2 In. ........................................ 12.00
Depression Glass, Tumbler, Royal Lace, Cobalt, Flat, 4 In. ..................................... 12.00
Depression Glass, Tumbler, Royal Lace, Cobalt, 3 1/2 In. ...................................... 10.00
Depression Glass, Tumbler, Royal Lace, Cobalt, 9 Ozs. ......................................... 12.00
Depression Glass, Tumbler, Royal Lace, Cobalt, 10 Ozs. ........................................ 13.50
Depression Glass, Tumbler, Royal Lace, Green, 5 1/4 In. ....................................... 16.50
Depression Glass, Tumbler, Royal Lace, Pink, 4 In. ........................................... 4.00
Depression Glass, Tumbler, Royal Lace, Pink, 4 1/4 In. ........................................ 7.50
Depression Glass, Tumbler, Royal Lace, Pink, 5 In. ........................................... 8.50
Depression Glass, Tumbler, Royal Lace, Pink, 9 Ozs. ........................................... 5.00
Depression Glass, Tumbler, Royal Ruby, Footed, 5 In. .......................................... 4.00
Depression Glass, Tumbler, Royal Ruby, 3 3/8 In. ............................................. 2.25
Depression Glass, Tumbler, Royal Ruby, 5 Ozs. ................................................ 2.50
Depression Glass, Tumbler, Royal Ruby, 9 Ozs. ................................................ 3.50
Depression Glass, Tumbler, Royal Ruby, 10 Ozs. ............................................... 2.50
Depression Glass, Tumbler, Ruby, Red, Footed, 5 In. ........................................... 5.00
Depression Glass, Tumbler, Ruby, Red, White Sailboats, 4 3/4 In. ............................... 7.00
Depression Glass, Tumbler, S Pattern, Clear, 12 Ozs., 5 In. ......................... 3.75 To 4.50

Depression Glass, Tumbler, Sailboat, Cobalt, Sailboat Series, 3 3/4 In. .................................... 2.75
Depression Glass, Tumbler, Sailboat, Cobalt, Sailboat Series, 4 1/2 In. .................................... 3.00
Depression Glass, Tumbler, Sandwich, Dark Green, 5 Ozs. ........................................................ 1.25
Depression Glass, Tumbler, Sandwich, Dark Green, 9 Ozs. ........................................................ 1.50
Depression Glass, Tumbler, Sandwich, Forest, Hocking, 9 Ozs. ................................................ 2.50
Depression Glass, Tumbler, Sandwich, Green, Hocking, 3 1/2 In. ............................................ 1.25
Depression Glass, Tumbler, Sandwich, Green, Hocking, 4 In. .................................................. 2.00
Depression Glass, Tumbler, Sharon, Pink, Flat, Thick, 4 In. ...................................................... 5.75
Depression Glass, Tumbler, Sharon, Pink, Flat, 5 1/4 In. .......................................................... 7.50
Depression Glass, Tumbler, Sharon, Pink, Footed ...................................................... 10.00 To 10.50
Depression Glass, Tumbler, Sharon, Pink, Footed, 6 1/2 In. ...................................... 8.75 To 9.00
Depression Glass, Tumbler, Sharon, Pink, 4 In. ........................................................................ 4.50
Depression Glass, Tumbler, Sharon, Pink, 5 1/4 In. .................................................................. 8.00
Depression Glass, Tumbler, Strawberry, Pink, 3 1/2 In. ............................................................ 8.00
Depression Glass, Tumbler, Sunflower, Pink, 5 In. .................................................................... 6.50
Depression Glass, Tumbler, Swirl, Ruby .................................................................................... 2.25
Depression Glass, Tumbler, Swirl, Ultramarine, Footed, 9 Oz. .................................................. 8.50
Depression Glass, Tumbler, Thumbprint, Green, 4 In. .............................................................. 1.65
Depression Glass, Tumbler, Whiskey, Colonial, Pink ................................................................ 4.50
Depression Glass, Tumbler, Whiskey, Roulette, Pink, 1 1/2 Ozs. .............................................. 3.50
Depression Glass, Tumbler, Windsor Diamond, Pink ................................................................ 3.50
Depression Glass, Tumbler, Windsor, Clear, Footed, 5 In. ........................................................ 3.50
Depression Glass, Tumbler, Windsor, Pink, 3 In. ...................................................................... 3.00
Depression Glass, Vase, Anniversary, Pink, 6 1/2 In. ................................................................ 3.50
Depression Glass, Vase, Cameo, Green, 8 In. ............................................................... 4.50 To 8.00
Depression Glass, Vase, Cameo, Green, 8 1/2 In. .................................................................... 9.00
Depression Glass, Vase, Princess, Green, 8 In. ............................................................ 4.00 To 4.50
Depression Glass, Vase, Royal Ruby, 6 1/2 In. ........................................................................ 4.00
Depression Glass, Vase, Sweet Pea, Mayfair, Blue, Flared, 8 1/2 X 5 1/2 In. ........................ 26.00
Depression Glass, Vase, Swirl, Ultramarine, 8 1/2 In. .............................................................. 7.00
Depression Glass, Vase, Twisted Optic, Green, With Frog, 4 In. .............................................. 5.00
Depression Glass, Water Set, Floral, Green, 5 Piece ................................................................ 42.00
Depression Glass, Water Set, White Sailboat, Cobalt, 7 Piece ................................................ 32.00
Depression Glass, Wine, Homespun, Pink, Footed, 4 In. .......................................................... 2.50
Depression Glass, Wine, Iris, Clear .......................................................................................... 5.00
Depression Glass, Wine, Knife & Fork ...................................................................................... 2.00
Depression Glass, Wine, Knife & Fork, Footed .......................................................................... 4.00
Depression Glass, Wine, Mayfair, Pink, 4 1/2 In. .................................................................... 30.00
Depression Glass, Wine, Miss America, Pink, 3 1/2 In .......................................................... 20.00
Depression Glass, Wine, Paneled, Green .................................................................................. 2.00
Depression Glass, Wine, Royal Ruby, Footed, 2 1/2 Oz. .......................................................... 4.00
Depression Glass, Wine, Royal Ruby, Stemmed ...................................................................... 4.50

*Derby porcelain was made in Derby, England, from 1756 to the present. The factory changed names and marks several times. Chelsea Derby (1770-1784), Crown Derby (1784-1811), and the modern Royal Crown Derby are some of the most famous periods of the factory.*

Derby, see also Crown Derby, Royal Crown Derby, Chelsea

Derby, Basket, Basket Weave, Rope Handle, Turquoise Florettes, C.1755 .......................... 200.00
Derby, Bowl, Fish, Rainbow Trout, C.1880, 9 1/4 In.Diameter .......................................... 100.00
Derby, Butter Boat, Leaf Molded, English Floral Bouquets, C.1760 .................................. 100.00
Derby, Candlestick, Bocage, Central Tree, Flowers, Spaniel, C.1770, 8 3/4 In. ................ 425.00
Derby, Candlestick, Bocage, Seated Boy & Girl, C.1780, 6 3/4 In., Pair ............................ 750.00
Derby, Coffee Can, Marked, 2 1/2 In.High .......................................................................... 35.00
Derby, Comport, Openwork Bowl, Stevenson & Hancock, C.1890, 9 1/4 In., Pair ............ 375.00
Derby, Compote & Underplate, Japan Pattern, C.1880, 9 1/2 In.Plate .............................. 225.00
Derby, Cup & Saucer, Gilt Spiral Bands, Bouquets, C.1790 ................................................ 60.00
Derby, Cup & Saucer, Japan Pattern, Blue, Green, Red, & Gold, C.1905 ............................ 50.00
Derby, Cup & Saucer, Japan Pattern, Red, Blue, Green, & Gold, C.1914 ............................ 50.00
Derby, Dish, Shell Shape, Scroll Handles, Ruin & Waterfall, C.1820, Pair ........................ 225.00
Derby, Figurine, Boy & Garland, Girl & Basket Of Fruit, C.1800, Pair .............................. 225.00
Derby, Figurine, Cow, Recumbent, Brown Spotted, Tree, C.1770, Pair .............................. 275.00
Derby, Figurine, Harvester, Standing, Holding Grape Cluster, C.1780, 5 In. ...................... 200.00
Derby, Figurine, Mansion House Dwarfs, C.1785, 7 In. ...................................... *Illus* 2200.00
Derby, Figurine, Musician, Horn & Drum, Triangle, Standing, C.1775, Pair ...................... 400.00
Derby, Figurine, Putto, White Flowers On Arm, C.1770, 4 1/4 In.High .............................. 85.00
Derby, Figurine, Shepherd & Companion, Fruit & Dog, C.1805, 8 1/2 In., Pair .................. 275.00

Derby, Figurine, Mansion House Dwarfs, C.1785, 7 In.
*(See Page 175)*

Derby, Group, Tithe Pig,
C.1750, 6 1/2 In. High

| | |
|---|---|
| Derby, Figurine, Squirrel, Holding Nut In Paws, C.1770, 2 7/8 In. | 475.00 |
| Derby, Figurine, Squirrel, Red, Gold Collar, Nut In Paws, C.1750, 3 3/8 In. | 400.00 |
| Derby, Figurine, Squirrel, Seated, Holding Nut, C.1770, 3 3/8 In.High | 300.00 |
| Derby, Group, Hairdresser & Shoeshiner, 7 1/4 In.High, Pair | 400.00 |
| Derby, Group, The Welsh Tailor And His Wife, On Goat, Baby, C.1765 | 450.00 |
| Derby, Group, Tithe Pig, C.1750, 6 1/2 In. High *Illus* | 450.00 |
| Derby, Group, Virgins Awakening Cupid, C.1750, 12 In. | 300.00 |
| Derby, Mug, Bell Shape, Scroll Handle, Flower Bouquet, C.1755, 4 In. | 350.00 |
| Derby, Mug, Jupiter, Loop Handle, C.1780, 3 3/4 In.High | 300.00 |
| Derby, Plaque, Cluster Of Grapes, Other Fruit, On Brown, C.1825, 4 3/4 In. | 400.00 |
| Derby, Plate, Luncheon, Imari Style, 1888 | 32.50 |
| Derby, Pot, Toilet, Two Men & Dog, C.1820, 5 3/8 In.Diameter | 250.00 |
| Derby, Potted Plant, Flowering, Gold & White 4 Footed Vase, C.1800 | 220.00 |
| Derby, Stirrup Cup, Red Fox's Mask, Inscribed Tallyho In Gold, C.1780 | 375.00 |
| Derby, Tureen, Cover & Stand, Paw Feet, Blue Enamel, C.1825, 8 3/8 In.Long | 175.00 |
| Derby, Vase, Tulip, Puce, Green Stem, Tree Trunk Support, C.1825, 6 In. | 475.00 |
| Derby, Vase, Tulip, Yellow & Purple, Brown Base, C.1825, 6 1/8 In. | 125.00 |
| DeVilbiss, Atomizer, Black Dragonflies On Lavender, Footed, 6 1/2 In. | 22.00 |
| DeVilbiss, Atomizer, Cut Glass Stemmed Body, Gold Trim, 7 In.High | 10.00 |
| DeVilbiss, Atomizer, Gold On Pink Glass, Signed | 16.00 |
| DeVilbiss, Atomizer, Gold Wiggly Lines On Frosted Glass, 4 1/2 In. | 18.00 |
| DeVilbiss, Atomizer, Silver On Black, 6 1/2 In.High, Signed | 25.00 |
| Dick Tracy, Badge, Crime Stopper | 13.00 |
| Dick Tracy, Badge, Detective Club, Brass | 5.25 |
| Dick Tracy, Radio, Wrist, Remco | 7.00 |
| Dionne Quintuplet, Book, Growing Up | 6.00 |
| Dionne Quintuplet, Book, Soon We'll Be 3 | 8.50 |
| Dionne Quintuplet, Book, Story Of The Dionne Quintuplets | 8.50 |
| Dionne Quintuplet, Book, We're Two Years Old | 13.50 |
| Dionne Quintuplet, Calendar, 1936 | 6.00 |
| Dionne Quintuplet, Dish, Baby's, Names, Chrome | 7.50 |
| Dionne Quintuplet, Doll, Cecile, Toddler, Alexander, Dressed, 7 1/4 In. | 60.00 |
| Dionne Quintuplet, Doll, Emilie, Toddler, Alexander, Dressed, 15 In. | 60.00 |
| Dionne Quintuplet, Doll, Yvonne, Toddler, Alexander, Dressed, 7 1/2 In. | 60.00 |
| Disney, see Walt Disney | |
| Doctor, Bleeder, Brass, 3 Sliding Blades | 65.00 |
| Doctor, Field Set, Surgeon's, Presentation, Mr.Kirkland, Mahogany Box, Brass | 425.00 |
| Doctor, Forceps, Tooth, Dental, Iron, In Box With Lock Handles | 30.00 |
| Doctor, Instrument, Nickel Plated, Leather Case, Chicago Firm, Set Of 14 | 20.00 |
| Doctor, Kit, Dissecting, Bausch & Lomb Co., Folding Case, Imitation Leather | 16.00 |
| Doctor, Saw, Surgeon's, Civil War, Bronze | 32.00 |
| Doctor, Stomach Pump, Brass, Ivory Handle, Mahogany Case | 79.50 |
| Doctor, Tool, Bleeder, Brass | 35.00 |
| Doctor, Tool, Blood Letter, Metal, Rounded Top Box | 40.00 |
| Doctor, Tube, Blood Transfusion, Needle On Both Ends | 3.50 |

| | |
|---|---|
| Doll, A L & Co., Limoges, Cherie 10, A.Lauternier & Co.Voice Box, 24 In.Tall | 210.00 |
| Doll, A 3m Made In Germany 390, Bisque Head, Ball Jointed, 19 In.Tall | 90.00 |
| Doll, A 6 1/2 M 390 Drgm 246/1, Bisque Head, Ball Jointed, 21 In.Tall | 100.00 |
| **Doll, A.M., see also Doll, Armand Marseille** | |
| Doll, A.M., Baby, 5 Piece Composition Body, Intaglio Eyes, 7 In. Tall | 145.00 |
| Doll, A.M., Bisque Head, Nun's Habit, Jointed Composition Body, 24 In. Tall | 145.00 |
| Doll, A.M., Bisque Socket Head, Ball Jointed Composition Body, Wig, 21 In. | 135.00 |
| Doll, A.M., Blonde Wig, Blue Sleep Eyes, Dressed, 20 In.Tall | 97.00 |
| Doll, A.M., Dream Baby, Cloth Body, Blue Sleep Eyes, 11 1/2 In.Tall | 135.00 |
| Doll, A.M., Dream Baby, Colored, Marked | 310.00 |
| Doll, A.M., Dream Baby, Composition Body, Open Mouth, Blue Eyes, 11 In.Tall | 135.00 |
| Doll, A.M., Dream Baby, Crying, Cloth Body, Blue Sleep Eyes, 10 1/2 In.Tall | 275.00 |
| Doll, A.M., Dream Baby, Crying, Cloth Body, Brown Sleep Eyes, 10 1/2 In.Tall | 275.00 |
| Doll, A.M., Floradora, Kid Body, Blue Sleep Eyes, Open Mouth, 14 In. | 70.00 |
| Doll, A.M., Germany, Dream Baby, Sleep Eyes, Celluloid Hands, 12 In.Tall | 85.00 |
| Doll, A.M., No.323, Goo-Goo, 5 Piece Composition Body, Blue Eyes, 7 In.Tall | 285.00 |
| Doll, A.M., No.323, Goo-Goo, 5 Piece Composition Body, Brown Eyes, 7 In.Tall | 285.00 |
| Doll, A.M., No.390 12/0X, Bisque Head, Dutch Girl Dress, Jointed, 9 In. | 55.00 |
| Doll, A.M., No.390, Ball Jointed Body, 18 In. Tall | 50.00 |
| Doll, A.M., No.390, Ball Jointed Body, 23 In. Tall | 80.00 |
| Doll, A.M., No.390, Composition Body, Brown Mohair Wig, 7 In. Tall | 50.00 |
| Doll, A.M., No.500, Character Baby, Composition Body, Intaglio Eyes, 8 In. | 135.00 |
| Doll, A.M., No.990, Baby, Character Face, Open Mouth, 13 In. 105.00 To | 150.00 |
| Doll, A.M., Oriental Girl, Open Mouth, 9 In.Tall | 200.00 |
| Doll, A.M., Rock-A-Bye Baby, Bisque Head, Composition Body, 16 1/2 In.Tall | 175.00 |
| Doll, A.M., Rock-A-Bye Baby, Bisque Head, Jointed Composition Body, 25 In. | 245.00 |
| Doll, A.M., Scowling Indian, 5 Piece Composition Body, 15 In. | 250.00 |
| Doll, A W., Bisque, 21 In.Tall | 50.00 |
| Doll, ABG 1362 Made In Germany, Jointed Composition Body, 25 In. | 150.00 |
| Doll, ABG, Character, Toddler Torso, Molded Shoes, 8 In.Tall | 175.00 |
| Doll, Alexanderkin, Brown Wig, Dressed, 7 In.Tall | 8.00 |
| Doll, Alma, Kid Body, 22 In.Tall | 175.00 |
| Doll, American Schoolboy, Kid Body, Brown Glass Eyes, 17 1/2 In.Tall | 350.00 |
| Doll, American Schoolboy, Virginia, Cloth Body, Dressed, 14 In. | 350.00 |
| Doll, Amosandra, Negro, Baby, Jointed, Sun Rubber Co., 10 In. Tall | 28.50 |
| Doll, Amosandra, 10 In.Tall | 10.00 |
| Doll, Andy & Raggedy Ann, Gruelle, Pair | 32.50 |
| Doll, Angel, Christmas, Composition Head, Celluloid Arms, 1930s | 4.00 |
| Doll, Annie Oakley, Embossed On Dress, 17 In.Tall | 45.00 |
| Doll, Apple Head, William Tell, Treutler, 13 In.Tall | 25.00 |
| **Doll, Armand Marseille, see also Doll, A.M.** | |
| Doll, Armand Marseille, Bisque Head, Arms, & Legs, Mabel, Kid Body, 18 In. | 115.00 |
| Doll, Armand Marseille, Bisque Head, Ball Jointed Body, 29 In. Tall | 150.00 |
| Doll, Armand Marseille, Bisque Head, Composition Body, Brown Hair, 22 In. | 119.00 |
| Doll, Armand Marseille, Bisque Head, Human Hair Wig, Floradora, 16 In.Tall | 125.00 |
| Doll, Armand Marseille, 370 Am-3-Dep, Bisque Shoulder Head, Kid Body, 21 In. | 85.00 |
| Doll, Armand Marseille, 370, Bisque Head, Composition Body, Wig, 29 In. | 255.00 |
| Doll, Armand Marseille, 390 D.R.G.M.240/1, Bisque Head, Composition Body | 95.00 |
| Doll, Armand Marseille, 390 DRGM 246/1 A6M, Bisque Head, 23 1/2 In. | 158.00 |
| Doll, Armand Marseille, 390N, D.R.G.M., Bisque Head, Composition, 16 In. | 75.00 |
| Doll, Armand Marseille, 390-01/2M, Germany, Bisque Head, Jointed, 16 In. | 65.00 |
| Doll, Armand Marseille, 560-A5M-DRMR 232/1, Baby, Bent Leg, 17 In. Tall | 110.00 |
| Doll, Baby Bud, Bisque, 7 In. Tall 200.00 To | 225.00 |
| Doll, Baby Joan Palooka, In Blanket, 1952 Birth Certificate | 7.00 |
| Doll, Baby Sue, American, Cloth Body, Blonde, 15 In. Tall | 14.50 |
| Doll, Baby Sue, American, Fur Wig, 20 In. Tall | 18.00 |
| Doll, Baby Trix, Uneeda, Carrying Case, 15 In.Tall | 17.00 |
| Doll, Baby, Enigma, Brown Glass Eyes, C.1840, 6 1/2 In. | 125.00 |
| Doll, Baby, Enigma, Brown Glass Eyes, C.1840, 7 3/4 In. | 125.00 |
| Doll, Baby, Germany 50, Papier-Mache Body, 2 Teeth, Brown Sleep Eyes, 23 In. | 175.00 |
| Doll, Baby, Incised Hans, Open Mouth, 12 In.Tall | 150.00 |
| Doll, Baby, Marked 152/2, 11 In.Tall | 185.00 |
| Doll, Bahr & Proschild, Boy Toddler, Wig, Dressed, 18 In. Tall | 240.00 |
| Doll, Bahr & Proschild, Blue Sleep Eyes, Open & Close Mouth, 11 In.Tall | 250.00 |
| Doll, Bahr & Proschild, 585, 10 In. Tall | 120.00 |
| Doll, Ball Jointed, 34 In.Tall | 275.00 |

Doll, Ball Jointed, 35 In.Tall .......................................................................... 300.00
Doll, Bam Bam, Flintstone's, Dressed, 1964, 12 In. Tall ....................... 9.25 To 25.00
Doll, Barbara Eden, I Dream Of Jeannie, Harem Outfit, 20 In. ......... 17.50 To 19.20
Doll, Bavaria, Baby, Gray Eyes, Open Mouth, 11 In.Tall ............................ 110.00
Doll, Belton, Beauty, 26 In. ........................................................................... 675.00
Doll, Belton, Bisque Head, Jointed Composition Body, Gray Eyes, 16 In. Tall .............. 475.00
Doll, Belton, Blue Paperweight Eyes, Closed Mouth, 23 In.Tall .................... 650.00
Doll, Betsy McCall, Summer Dress, 7 1/2 In.Tall ........................................ 17.50
Doll, Betsy McCall, Sunsuit, 7 1/2 In.Tall .................................................. 17.50
Doll, Betsy-Wetsy, Curly Mohair Wig, Plastic, Suitcase, 13 In. Tall ............. 16.50
Doll, Betsy-Wetsy, Ideal, Composition Head, Patent No.225207 ................... 35.00
Doll, Betty Bows, Sun Rubber Co., 12 In. Tall .......................................... 17.00
Doll, Biedermeier, China Arms & Legs, 14 In.Tall ...................................... 375.00
Doll, Bisque Bonnet Head, Arms, & Legs, Am, La Motte-60, Cloth Body, 14 In. ........ 65.00
Doll, Bisque Bonnet Head, Bisque Arms & Feet, Cloth Body, 8 1/2 In. .......... 85.00
Doll, Bisque Head & Hands, German, Lady, Composition Body, Teeth, 25 In.Tall ...... 135.00
Doll, Bisque Head & Hands, Kid Body, Solid Dome, Closed Mouth, 16 In.Tall .......... 285.00
Doll, Bisque Head & Limbs, Dollhouse, Maid, Cloth Body, 4 3/4 In.Tall ......... 36.00
Doll, Bisque Head Marked 985 A 3/om, Composition Body, 16 In.Tall ............ 325.00
Doll, Bisque Head, Alma, Germany, Kid Body, Brown Eyes, Open Mouth, 16 In. ...... 65.00
Doll, Bisque Head, Arms, & Legs, Marked 16/0 Germany, Cloth Body, 9 1/2 In. ...... 62.00
Doll, Bisque Head, Arms, & Legs, Nippon, Cloth Body, 6 In. ......................... 16.00
Doll, Bisque Head, Arms, & Shoulder Head, Solid Dome, Kid Body, 12 In.Tall ...... 85.00
Doll, Bisque Head, Baby, Jointed Composition Body, 2 Teeth, 18 1/2 In. ........ 350.00
Doll, Bisque Head, Bavaria, Composition Body, Alpine Dress, 9 In., Twins, Pair .... 75.00
Doll, Bisque Head, Bavaria, P.M. Baby, Gray Stationary Eyes, 11 In. ............. 135.00
Doll, Bisque Head, Candy Box, Crepe Paper Dress Conceals Box, 6 In.Tall ...... 50.00
Doll, Bisque Head, Christmas Star, Composition Body, Blue Eyes, 23 In. ........ 135.00
Doll, Bisque Head, Composition Body, Brown Mohair Wig, 4 3/4 In.Tall .......... 45.00
Doll, Bisque Head, Composition Body, Painted Eyes, Peasant Dress, 5 In.Tall ...... 35.00
Doll, Bisque Head, Composition Body, Painted Eyes, 5 In.Tall ...................... 30.00
Doll, Bisque Head, Dream Baby, Open Mouth, 2 Lower Teeth, Dressed ............ 325.00
Doll, Bisque Head, F.Y., Leather Body, Composition Hands, 2 Teeth, 15 In. ...... 55.00
Doll, Bisque Head, French, Closed Mouth, Dressed, 20 In.Tall ..................... 400.00
Doll, Bisque Head, French, Jointed Composition Body, Glass Eyes, 14 In.Tall .... 380.00
Doll, Bisque Head, French, Toddler, Papier-Mache Body, Open Mouth, 15 1/2 In. .... 85.00
Doll, Bisque Head, German, Ball Jointed Body, Dressed, 22 In.Tall ................ 77.00
Doll, Bisque Head, Germany 390 A 8 M, Jointed Composition Body, 24 In. ....... 75.00
Doll, Bisque Head, Germany, B.J.Body, 23 In.Tall ....................................... 75.00
Doll, Bisque Head, Impressed Dep, Composition Body, Brown Eyes, 6 1/2 In. ...... 62.00
Doll, Bisque Head, Impressed G.B.10, Baby, Jointed Composition Body, 18 In. ...... 150.00
Doll, Bisque Head, Impressed 1909 Dep R 15/0 A, Composition Body, 7 In. ....... 35.00
Doll, Bisque Head, Japanese, Eyes Close, Squeeze Box Voice, C.1936, 5 In.Tall ...... 20.00
Doll, Bisque Head, Kaiser Baby Type, Marked 11, Composition Body, 15 In.Tall ...... 395.00
Doll, Bisque Head, Kid Body, Brown Stationary Eyes, Open Mouth, Teeth, 18 In. ...... 65.00
Doll, Bisque Head, Kid Body, Fur Eyebrows, 22 In.Tall ............................... 125.00
Doll, Bisque Head, Kid Body, Open Mouth, Teeth, Blue Eyes, 16 1/2 In. ......... 55.00
Doll, Bisque Head, Leather Body, Blue Paperweight Eyes, Blonde Wig, 19 In. ...... 55.00
Doll, Bisque Head, Lily, Leather Body, Open Mouth, Teeth, Blue Eyes, 16 In. ...... 65.00
Doll, Bisque Head, M.H.Ger., Indian Girl, Composition Body, Glass Eyes, 7 In. .... 105.00
Doll, Bisque Head, Marked Ab 1362 Made In Germany, Composition Body, 25 In. .... 150.00
Doll, Bisque Head, Marked M H 20/0, Indian, Jointed At Shoulder & Hip, 7 In. ...... 65.00
Doll, Bisque Head, Marked Mo.2-16 A, B, 1362, Made In Germany, Composition ...... 75.00
Doll, Bisque Head, Marked Moa Ger 200 0/0, Stick Body, 15 1/2 In.Tall .......... 69.00
Doll, Bisque Head, S * PB & H, Negro, Hanna, Composition Body, 7 1/2 In. ...... 125.00
Doll, Bisque Head, S * PB & H, Negro, Toddler, Sleep Eyes, 9 In. Tall ........... 165.00
Doll, Bisque Head, Sunburst, Brown Stationary Eyes, 9 In.Tall .................... 65.00
Doll, Bisque Head, 14 In.Circumference, Bye-Lo Body, Painted Features ......... 125.00
Doll, Bisque Head, 19 W 13, German, Jointed Composition Body, 25 In. Tall ...... 150.00
Doll, Bisque Head, 26-139 H, Kid Body, Composition Arms & Legs, 22 In.Tall ...... 85.00
Doll, Bisque Head, 390 DRGM 246 A 6-1/2 M, Jointed Composition Body ......... 145.00
Doll, Bisque Head, 6970, Germany, Sailor Boy, Composition Body, 11 In. Tall .... 235.00
Doll, Bisque Shoulder Head & Arms, Boy, Character, Kid Body, 12 1/2 In.Tall .... 270.00
Doll, Bisque Shoulder Head & Arms, German Fashion, Kid Body, 18 In.Tall ...... 315.00
Doll, Bisque Shoulder Head & Arms, German, Kid Body, Blonde Hair, 14 In.Tall ...... 60.00
Doll, Bisque Shoulder Head & Arms, Kid Body, Bulging Eyes, 13 1/2 In. .......... 85.00

Doll, Bisque Shoulder Head & Arms, Kid Body, Composition Legs, 12 In. ............. 68.50
Doll, Bisque Shoulder Head & Arms, Marked 32, Character, Boy, Kid, 17 In.Tall ............. 185.00
Doll, Bisque Shoulder Head & Arms, 991 Ger. Kiddiejoy A8M, 25 1/2 In. ............. 235.00
Doll, Bisque Shoulder Head & Limbs, Dollhouse Lady, Cloth Body, 6 In.Tall ............. 45.00
Doll, Bisque Shoulder Head & Limbs, Marked 354 8/9, Lady, Cloth Body, 7 In. ............. 50.00
Doll, Bisque Shoulder Head, Boy, Chopped Bangs, Molded Shirt, 9 In.Tall ............. 185.00
Doll, Bisque Shoulder Head, Dollhouse Lady, Cloth Body, 7 1/4 In.Tall ............. 50.00
Doll, Bisque Shoulder Head, Germany, Jointed Kid Body, Brown Eyes, 23 In. ............. 235.00
Doll, Bisque Shoulder Head, Girl, Blonde, French Dress, 8 In.Tall ............. 65.00
Doll, Bisque Shoulder Head, Impressed Germany-Mabel, Kid Body, 24 In.Tall ............. 100.00
Doll, Bisque Shoulder Head, Kid Body & Arms, Cloth Legs, Marked Alma ............. 55.00
Doll, Bisque Shoulder Head, Marked 1, Kid Body, Brown Eyes, 18 In. ............. 250.00
Doll, Bisque Socket Head, 29 Queen Louise 100 Germany, Wolf & Co., 24 In. ............. 150.00
Doll, Bisque Socket Head, 390 Germany A 3 1/2 M, Composition Body, 20 In. ............. 135.00
Doll, Bisque Swivel Head, 133-12, Girl, Jointed Body, Glass Eyes, 8 1/2 In. ............. 295.00
Doll, Bisque, A&q7-Dep, Princess, F O C, Sleep Eyes, Open Mouth, 19 In.Tall ............. 80.00
Doll, Bisque, Baby Boy, Organically Correct, 19 In.Tall ............. 40.00
Doll, Bisque, Baby, Bent Limb, Jointed Body, Painted Eyes, 4 1/2 In. ............. 58.00
Doll, Bisque, Baby, Blonde, 3 3/4 In.Tall ............. 35.00
Doll, Bisque, Baby, Jointed, Swivel Neck, Painted Eyes & Hair, 10 In. ............. 475.00
Doll, Bisque, Baby, Molded Blonde Hair, Blue Intaglio Eyes, 4 In.Tall ............. 32.50
Doll, Bisque, Baby, Pastel, Diaper, 3 1/2 In.Tall ............. 49.00
Doll, Bisque, Baby, Swivel Head, Painted Eyes & Hair, 6 In. ............. 100.00
Doll, Bisque, Baby, 3 Faced, Reproduction, 14 In.Tall ............. 35.00
Doll, Bisque, Ball Head, Turned To Side, Paperweight Eyes, 17 In.Tall ............. 195.00
Doll, Bisque, Bathing Beauty, Diving Pose, Blue Suit, C.1915, 18 In.Tall ............. 150.00
Doll, Bisque, Bathtub Baby, Molded Hair, Painted Features, 1 3/4 In.Tall ............. 18.50
Doll, Bisque, Blonde, 2 1/2 In.Tall ............. 8.50
Doll, Bisque, Boy, German, Jointed, Dressed, 4 1/2 In.Tall ............. 15.00
Doll, Bisque, Boy, Painted Eyes, Jointed At Shoulders, 5 1/2 In.Tall ............. 65.00
Doll, Bisque, Cowboy, Movable Arms, Painted Features, 5 In.Tall ............. 5.50
Doll, Bisque, Cowgirl, Movable Arms, Painted Features, 5 In.Tall ............. 5.50
Doll, Bisque, Cupid, 5 Piece Body, Side Glancing Eyes, Clown Suit, 5 3/4 In. ............. 75.00
Doll, Bisque, Emma, Bonnet Head, Pink, 15 In. ............. 140.00
Doll, Bisque, Flapper, Black Painted Hair, Dressed, 3 In.Head ............. 22.00
Doll, Bisque, French Type, 7 In.Tall ............. 225.00
Doll, Bisque, French, Painted Features, 13 In.Tall ............. 13.00
Doll, Bisque, French, 8093-0 1/2, Jointed Arms, Dressed, 4 In.Tall ............. 47.50
Doll, Bisque, German, Baby, Painted Features, Movable Arms & Legs, 4 In. ............. 20.00
Doll, Bisque, German, Boy, Jointed Body, Molded Blonde Hair, 4 1/2 In.Tall ............. 85.00
Doll, Bisque, German, Boy, Jointed Body, Molded Hair, 3 In.Tall ............. 35.00
Doll, Bisque, German, Boy, 4 1/2 In.Tall ............. 15.00
Doll, Bisque, German, Character, Baby, Molded Teeth, Sleep Eyes, 5 In.Tall ............. 200.00
Doll, Bisque, German, Jointed Body, Brown Stationary Eyes, 3 1/2 In.Tall ............. 50.00
Doll, Bisque, German, Jointed Body, Intaglio Eyes, Blonde Wig, 5 In.Tall ............. 40.00
Doll, Bisque, German, Jointed Body, Painted Eyes, Brown Wig, 3 In.Tall ............. 28.00
Doll, Bisque, German, Jointed Body, Painted Eyes, Molded Hair, 3 In.Tall ............. 20.00
Doll, Bisque, German, Kid Body, Blue Sleep Eyes, Open Mouth, 15 In.Tall ............. 65.00
Doll, Bisque, German, Sleep Eyes, Dressed, 6 In.Tall ............. 150.00
Doll, Bisque, German, Tinted, Jointed Body, Painted Eyes, Brown Wig, 5 In.Tall ............. 30.00
Doll, Bisque, Germany, Boy, Colored, Movable Hands & Feet ............. 15.00
Doll, Bisque, Germany, Bride & Groom, Dressed, Jointed, 3 1/2 In., Pair ............. 62.50
Doll, Bisque, Germany, Dollhouse, Blonde Hair, C.1930, 4 1/2 In. ............. 20.00
Doll, Bisque, Germany, Girl, Molded Hair, Painted Eyes, 4 1/2 In.Tall ............. 40.00
Doll, Bisque, Germany, Molded Buster Brown Haircut, Dressed, 5 In. ............. 42.00
Doll, Bisque, Germany, Molded Hair, Painted Eyes, 5 3/4 In.Tall ............. 65.00
Doll, Bisque, Germany, Pink & Blue Dresses, Twins, Pair ............. 30.00
Doll, Bisque, Germany, Toddler, Molded Blonde Hair, Jointed, 4 In.Tall ............. 40.00
Doll, Bisque, Girl, German, Marked W.& C., Kid Body, Open Mouth, 23 In.Tall ............. 75.00
Doll, Bisque, Girl, German, Open Mouth, Jointed Body, Blue Eyes, 21 In.Tall ............. 75.00
Doll, Bisque, Girl, Molded Hair With Blue Bows, Blue Eyes, 6 In.Tall ............. 85.00
Doll, Bisque, Girl, Molded Hair With Blue Ribbon, Blue Eyes, 6 In.Tall ............. 75.00
Doll, Bisque, Girl, Movable Limbs, Long Brown Hair, Dressed, 5 1/2 In.Tall ............. 32.50
Doll, Bisque, Glass Eyes, Wig, Dressed, 16 In.Tall ............. 25.00
Doll, Bisque, H 17/1, Germany, Cloverleaf, Girl, Blue Eyes, 3 3/4 In. Tall ............. 27.50
Doll, Bisque, Impressed Japan, Molded Red Tam On Brown Hair, 5 In.Tall ............. 10.00

Doll, Bisque, Japan, Betty Boop Type, Molded Hair, 7 1/2 In. ........................................ 9.00 To 9.50
Doll, Bisque, Japan, Black Baby, Movable Arms & Legs, 4 In.Tall ........................................ 12.00
Doll, Bisque, Japan, Girl, Painted, Jointed Arms, 5 1/2 In.Tall ........................................ 13.50
Doll, Bisque, Japanese, Yellow Molded Curly Hair, 5 In.Tall ........................................ 7.00
Doll, Bisque, Jointed At Shoulders, Painted Side Turned Eyes, 6 In.Tall ........................................ 95.00
Doll, Bisque, Jointed Hips & Shoulders, Brown Eyes, Blonde Wig, 6 In.Tall ........................................ 50.00
Doll, Bisque, Jointed Hips & Shoulders, Molded Blonde Hair, 3 1/2 In.Tall ........................................ 37.50
Doll, Bisque, Jointed, Blonde, Dressed, 4 1/4 In.Tall ........................................ 37.00
Doll, Bisque, Lilly, German, Blue Sleep Eyes, Human Hair Wig, 20 In. Tall ........................................ 85.00
Doll, Bisque, Mabel, 12 In.Tall ........................................ 37.00
Doll, Bisque, Movable Arms, Blonde Hair, Knee Length Hose, 9 In.Tall ........................................ 10.00
Doll, Bisque, Movable Head, Carrying Bouquet Of Flowers, 3 1/4 In.Tall ........................................ 25.00
Doll, Bisque, Negro, Baby, Jointed, 2 1/2 In. ........................................ 4.25
Doll, Bisque, Negro, Jointed, Diaper, Twins In Basket, 2 1/2 In.Tall, Pair ........................................ 8.25
Doll, Bisque, Nergo, Jointed, Painted Features, 2 1/2 In.Tall ........................................ 4.25
Doll, Bisque, Nippon, Bonnet, 4 3/4 In.Tall ........................................ 18.00
Doll, Bisque, Nippon, Boy, Jointed Body, Molded Swimsuit, 5 In.Tall ........................................ 55.00
Doll, Bisque, Occupied Japan, Jointed At Shoulders, 3 In.Tall ........................................ 2.50
Doll, Bisque, Occupied Japan, Molded Blonde Hair, Dressed, 4 1/2 In.Tall ........................................ 15.00
Doll, Bisque, Occupied Japan, Molded Blonde Hair, Jointed, 4 3/4 In.Tall ........................................ 15.00
Doll, Bisque, Occupied Japan, Movable Arms, Red Molded Hair, 7 In.Tall ........................................ 15.00
Doll, Bisque, Occupied Japan, Strung Arms, 3 In.Tall ........................................ 6.00
Doll, Bisque, Open Mouth, Molded Shoes & Socks, 6 In.Tall ........................................ 65.00
Doll, Bisque, P607/0 Ger, Jointed Body, Gray Sleep Eyes, 6 1/2 In. Tall ........................................ 85.00
Doll, Bisque, Painted Blue Eyes, Jointed Hips & Shoulders, 5 1/4 In.Tall ........................................ 35.00
Doll, Bisque, Painted Eyes Looking To Side, 4 1/2 In. ........................................ 25.00
Doll, Bisque, Painted Eyes, Braided Hair Wig, Molded Socks & Shoes, 5 In. ........................................ 30.00
Doll, Bisque, S.W.& C., Wig, Dressed, 4 1/2 In.Tall ........................................ 25.00
Doll, Bisque, Sitting, Clapping Hands, Nude, 2 3/4 In. ........................................ 10.00
Doll, Bisque, Snow White & 7 Dwarfs, Japan, 3 1/2 & 2 1/2 In., Set Of 8 ........................................ 50.00
Doll, Bisque, U.S.A., Molded Buster Brown Haircut, Movable Limbs, 5 1/2 In. ........................................ 29.00
Doll, Bisque, Uncle Walt, Comic Nodder, 4 In. ........................................ 32.00
Doll, Bisque, Wide Awake Type, Movable Arms, Molded Shoes & Socks, 4 1/2 In. ........................................ 65.00
Doll, Bisque, Wide Awake Type, Movable Arms, Molded Shoes & Socks, 6 1/2 In. ........................................ 85.00
Doll, Bisque, World War I Army Medic, Dressed, 4 In.Tall ........................................ 35.00
Doll, Bisque, 3 Piece Body, Molded Orange Rompers, 5 1/2 In.Tall ........................................ 65.00
Doll, Bisque, 5 10/1 Ger., Girl, 3 3/4 In. Tall ........................................ 65.00
Doll, Bisque, 203 Ger., Baby, Closed Mouth, Wig, 4 1/2 In. Tall ........................................ 85.00
Doll, Bisque, 280 5/0 1/2, Movable Limbs, Painted Features, 2 In.Tall ........................................ 12.00
Doll, Bisque, 620-3, Girl, Painted Eyes, Jointed Body, Closed Mouth, 5 In. ........................................ 55.00
Doll, Bisque, 682/9 1/2 Germany, Baby, Jointed, Molded Hair, 4 In.Tall ........................................ 65.00
Doll, Bisque, 809501/2 J, Jointed Body, Closed Mouth, 4 In. Tall ........................................ 65.00
Doll, Black Topsy Baby, Composition Body ........................................ 18.00
Doll, Boudoir, Satin Outfit, 1920 ........................................ 35.00
Doll, Boy, Character, Marked BSW In Heart, Brown Sleep Eyes, 29 In.Tall ........................................ 450.00
Doll, Boy, Dutch, Grace Drayton Type, 8 In.Tall ........................................ 37.00
Doll, Bru, Pull String, Says Mama, Throws A Kiss, Teeth, 21 In. Tall ........................................ 1200.00
Doll, Bru, 2/11, Cloth Body, Human Hair Wig, Brown Eyes, 16 In.Tall ........................................ 200.00
Doll, Bru, 8, Italian Coloring, French Ball Jointed Body, 16 1/2 In. Tall ........................................ 250.00
Doll, Bruno Schmidt, Baby, Brown Glass Eyes, Blonde Wig, 14 In.Head ........................................ 185.00
Doll, Bruno Schmidt, Character, Brown Eyes, 12 In. Tall ........................................ 125.00
Doll, Bubbles, Dressed, Chain & Locket, 18 In.Tall ........................................ 50.00
Doll, Bubbles, 20 In.Tall ........................................ 20.00
Doll, Buddy Lee, Dressed ........................................ 150.00
Doll, Bye-Lo, Baby, Celluloid Hands, 12 1/2 In.Head ........................................ 310.00
Doll, Bye-Lo, Baby, Cloth Body, Celluloid Hands, Blue Sleep Eyes, 13 In.Tall ........................................ 200.00
Doll, Bye-Lo, Bisque, Brown Eyes, Dressed, Wicker Basket, Bottle ........................................ 225.00
Doll, Bye-Lo, Blue Eyes, Dressed, 11 In.Head Circumference ........................................ 295.00
Doll, Bye-Lo, Blue Sleep Eyes, Long Organdy Dress, 13 In.Tall ........................................ 285.00
Doll, Bye-Lo, Celluloid Head, Blue Sleep Eyes, Dressed, 10 In.Head ........................................ 165.00
Doll, Bye-Lo, Grace S.Putnam, Bisque Head, Cloth Body, 12 In. ........................................ 175.00 To 275.00
Doll, Bye-Lo, Signed Torso, 14 In.Circumference Head, 16 In.Tall ........................................ 395.00
Doll, C.M. E.D., French Girl, 16 In. ........................................ 555.00
    Doll, C.M.Bergmann, see also Doll, S.&H., Doll, Simon & Halbig
Doll, C.M.Bergmann, Simon & Halbig, Bisque Head, Composition Body, 29 In. ........................................ 195.00
Doll, C.M.Bergmann, Simon & Halbig, Taffeta & Lace Dress, 25 In. Tall ........................................ 125.00

| | |
|---|---|
| Doll, C.M.Bergmann, Waltershausen 1916-6, Jointed Composition Body, 25 In. | 150.00 |
| Doll, C.Nook, Baby, Wax Over Clay, Squalling, 13 In.Head | 80.00 |
| Doll, Cameo, Miss Peep, 18 In.Tall | 13.00 |
| Doll, Campbell Kid, Can't Break-Em Type | 38.00 |
| Doll, Celluloid Head, Arms, & Legs, Germany, Kid Body, Boy, Blue Glass Eyes | 75.00 |
| Doll, Celluloid Head, Arms, & Legs, J.D.K., Jointed Leather Body, Wig | 95.00 |
| Doll, Celluloid Head, Baseball Player, Stuffed Body, Painted Features, 4 In. | 2.50 |
| Doll, Celluloid Head, Football Player, Stuffed Body, 8 In. Tall | 4.00 To 10.00 |
| Doll, Celluloid Head, Kid Body, Bisque Arms, Human Hair, 13 In.Tall | 48.00 |
| Doll, Celluloid Head, Mechanical, French, Swimming, Bathing Suit, 16 1/2 In. | 400.00 |
| Doll, Celluloid Head, Sailor, Stuffed Body, Hand-Painted Features, 4 In. | 2.50 |
| Doll, Celluloid Shoulder Head, Kid Body, Bisque Hands, Cloth Feet | 20.00 |
| Doll, Celluloid, Baby Boy, 10 In.Tall | 10.00 |
| Doll, Celluloid, Baby, Crocheted Dress, 12 In.Tall | 30.00 |
| Doll, Celluloid, Boy, Jointed Body, Painted Shoes, Sleep Eyes, 4 In.Tall | 6.50 |
| Doll, Celluloid, Carmen Miranda Type, Small Size | 6.50 |
| Doll, Celluloid, France, Baby, Glass Sleep Eyes, Molded Black Hair, 11 In. | 45.00 |
| Doll, Celluloid, Hula Girls, Hand-Painted Faces & Hair, Pair | 7.50 |
| Doll, Celluloid, Indian Boy, 6 In. | 3.00 |
| Doll, Celluloid, Jackie Coogan As The Kid, 5 In.Tall | 28.00 |
| Doll, Celluloid, Kewpie, Gold Painted Hair, Colored Feathers, 7 In | 3.50 |
| Doll, Celluloid, Muffie, Jointed, Flirty Eyes, Ponytail, Dressed, 7 3/4 In. | 14.00 |
| Doll, Celluloid, Negro Boy, Dressed As Sultan, French, 8 In.Tall | 45.00 |
| Doll, Celluloid, Occupied Japan, Squaw, 10 In. | 8.00 |
| Doll, Celluloid, Occupied Japan, Toddling Baby, Windup | 5.00 |
| Doll, Celluloid, Scotch, Turtle Mark, 8 1/2 In.Tall | 45.00 |
| Doll, Celluloid, Sunburst Mark, Jointed At Shoulders, 7 3/4 In.Tall | 25.00 |
| Doll, Celluloid, Toddler Girl, Glass Eyes, Squeaker, Turtle Mark, 20 In.Tall | 50.00 |
| Doll, Celluloid, Wind-Up, Tin Body, 6 1/2 In.Tall | 17.00 |
| Doll, Chad Valley, Glass Eyes, 16 In.Tall | 32.00 |
| Doll, Chalk, Kewpie Type, Wings, Chubby, 12 In.Tall | 10.00 |
| Doll, Charlie Chaplin, Little Tramp Outfit, 1972, 19 In. | 20.00 |
| Doll, Charmin Chatty, Glasses | 12.00 |
| Doll, Chase, Stockinette Baby, Paper Label & Stamp, 12 1/2 In. | 350.00 |
| Doll, Chase, Stockinette Baby, 21 In | 125.00 |
| Doll, Chase, Stockinette, Dressed, 31 In.Tall | 95.00 |
| Doll, Chase, Stockinette, Jointed, Blue Eyes, Blonde Hair, 24 In.Tall | 150.00 |
| Doll, Chase, Stockinette, Oil Painted Cloth, Sewn Fingers & Toes, 11 3/4 In. | 120.00 |
| Doll, Chatty Baby, Voice Box, Dressed, 14 In.Tall | 8.00 |
| Doll, Chatty Cathy, Long Blonde Hair, Dressed, Voice Box, 20 In. Tall | 10.00 |
| Doll, Chatty Cathy, 10 In.Tall | 12.00 |
| Doll, Chin Chin, Bisque, German, 4 1/2 In. Tall | 65.00 |
| Doll, China Head & Hands, Man, Cloth Body, Apple Cheeks, Blue Eyes, 20 In. | 650.00 |
| Doll, China Head, Arms, & Legs, Black Hair, Painted Boots, Dressed, 15 In. | 65.00 |
| Doll, China Head, Arms, & Legs, Currier & Ives Type, Long Hair, 18 In. | 440.00 |
| Doll, China Head, Arms, & Legs, Flat Face, Apple Cheeks, Cloth Body, 15 In. | 85.00 |
| Doll, China Head, Bisque Hands, Shoes, & Socks, Cloth Body, Blonde, 5 1/4 In. | 22.00 |
| Doll, China Head, Black Molded Hair, Wig, Dressed, 15 In.Tall | 95.00 |
| Doll, China Head, Black, Blue Eyes, Cloth Body, Handmade Wooden Arms & Legs | 85.00 |
| Doll, China Head, Cloth Body, Wasp Waist, Painted Blue Eyes, 32 In.Tall | 175.00 |
| Doll, China Head, Feet, & Arms, Cloth Body, Flat Hairdo, Dressed, 13 In.Tall | 150.00 |
| Doll, China Head, Flat Top, 2863, 20 1/2 In.Tall | 150.00 |
| Doll, China Head, Hands, & Legs, Man, Cloth Body, Georgian Gentleman, 20 In. | 550.00 |
| Doll, China Head, Jenny Lind, Cloth Body, Leather Arms & Feet, 26 In. | 425.00 |
| Doll, China Head, Kid Arms & Hands, Dressed, 22 In.Tall | 290.00 |
| Doll, China Head, Man, Black Mustache, 9 1/2 In.Tall | 35.00 |
| Doll, China Head, Marked 9 Germany, Black Hair, Dressed, 5 1/2 In.Tall | 65.00 |
| Doll, China Head, Vertical Curls | 45.00 |
| Doll, China Shoulder Head, Black Hair, Blue Eyes, 1 1/4 In.Tall | 15.00 |
| Doll, China Shoulder Head, Germany 3, Cloth Body, Painted Eyes, 11 1/2 In. | 75.00 |
| Doll, China Shoulder Head, Hands, & Feet, Germany, Dressed, 7 In. | 45.00 |
| Doll, China Shoulder Head, Pink Luster, Blue Eyes, Brown Hair, 4 In. | 250.00 |
| Doll, China, Agnes, Black Hair, 15 In. | 125.00 |
| Doll, China, Bangs, Blue Eyes, Molded Lip With Red Lines, 30 In.Tall | 225.00 |
| Doll, China, Bertha, Blonde Hair, 27 In. | 200.00 |
| Doll, China, Black Hair, 11 Sausage Curls, Blue Eyes, 10 1/2 In.Tall | 195.00 |
| Doll, China, Claramaid, 19 In.Tall | 55.00 |

| | |
|---|---|
| Doll, China, Cloth Body, Luster Shoes, Black Hair, 24 In. | 65.00 |
| Doll, China, Ethel, 14 In.Tall | 45.00 |
| Doll, China, Farmer, Marked, 21 In.Tall | 18.00 |
| Doll, China, Lady, Puff & Bun Hairdo, Bisque Arms & Legs, 4 In.Tall | 38.00 |
| Doll, China, Mabel, Blonde Hair, 29 In. | 200.00 |
| Doll, China, Man, Bisque Arms & Legs, Feather Marks, 4 1/4 In.Tall | 45.00 |
| Doll, China, Pauline, Black Hair, 24 In. | 175.00 |
| Doll, China, Pink Luster, Blue Eyes, Black Hair Drawn Into Bun, 14 In.Tall | 350.00 |
| Doll, China, Pink Luster, C.1850, 10 1/2 In. | 310.00 |
| Doll, China, Pink Luster, Kid & Cloth Body, Blue Eyes, Black Hair, 26 In.Tall | 300.00 |
| Doll, Cindy Lee, Ruth Newton, Sun Rubber Co., 14 In. Tall | 14.00 To 21.50 |
| Doll, Clear, 1943, Bisque Shoulder Head, Arms & Legs, Glass Eyes, 20 In.Tall | 75.00 |
| Doll, Closed Mouth, Blue Stationary Eyes, 8 1/2 In.Tall | 120.00 |
| Doll, Closed Mouth, Turned Face, Blue Stationary Eyes, 24 In.Tall | 275.00 |
| Doll, Cloth, Allied Van Lines, Stuffed, 17 1/2 In.Tall | 10.00 |
| Doll, Cloth, Buster Brown, Human Hair Wig, Painted Features, 30 In.Tall | 85.00 |
| Doll, Cloth, Campbell Kid, Boy, Stuffed, Lithographed, 15 In.Tall | 9.50 |
| Doll, Cloth, Campbell Kid, Girl, Stuffed, Lithographed, 15 In.Tall | 9.50 |
| Doll, Cloth, Dolly Dimples, Stuffed, 19 In. Tall | 27.50 |
| Doll, Cloth, Jack Frost, Stuffed, Advertising, 19 In.Tall | 8.25 |
| Doll, Cloth, Miss Korn Krisp, C.1910, 26 In. Tall | 35.00 |
| Doll, Cloth, Negro, Lithographed, Dated, 8 In.Tall | 16.00 |
| Doll, Cloth, Negro, Mammy, Stuffed, Dressed, Made In U.S.A., 8 In.Tall | 7.50 |
| Doll, Cloth, Negro, Rastus, Cream Of Wheat, 18 In. Tall | 24.00 |
| Doll, Cloth, Swiss Musicbox Inside, 19 In.Tall | 15.00 |
| Doll, Clown, Circus, Schoenhut | 50.00 |
| Doll, Clown, Emmett Kelly, Dressed, 16 In. | 40.00 |
| Doll, Clown, Emmett Kelly, 15 In. | 28.00 |
| Doll, Composition Head & Arms Marked Elektra, Inc.N.Y., Cloth Body, 30 In. | 119.00 |
| Doll, Composition Head & Arms, Negro Boy, Stuffed Body, 23 In.Tall | 100.00 |
| Doll, Composition Head & Limbs, Madame Hendron, Cry Box, 17 In.Tall | 60.00 |
| Doll, Composition Head, Arms, & Legs, Chinese Boy, Cloth Body, 16 In. | 50.00 |
| Doll, Composition Head, Arms, & Legs, Chuckles, Cloth Body, American | 35.00 |
| Doll, Composition Head, Arms, & Legs, Sleep Eyes, Molded Hair, 19 In.Tall | 30.00 |
| Doll, Composition Head, Cloth Body, Googly Eyes, 19 In. Tall | 42.00 |
| Doll, Composition Head, Dutch Girl, Cloth Body, Painted Eyes, 23 In.Tall | 35.00 |
| Doll, Composition Head, Indian, Seated, Straw Stuffed Body, 8 In. | 9.75 |
| Doll, Composition Head, Mad Magazine Cover Boy, Stuffed Body, 14 In. | 55.00 |
| Doll, Composition Head, Samy, Stuffed Body, Painted Features, 17 In.Tall | 20.00 |
| Doll, Composition Head, Stuffed Body, Googly Eyes, Closed Mouth, 14 In.Tall | 50.00 |
| Doll, Composition Head, Stuffed Body, Sleep Eyes, Mohair Wig, 20 In. | 19.75 |
| Doll, Composition Head, Tiny Tears, 11 1/2 In.Tall | 10.00 |
| Doll, Composition Head, Tiny Tears, 14 In.Tall | 15.00 |
| Doll, Composition Head, Trollydoll No. 923, Germany, Smoking Pipe, 11 In. | 6.75 |
| Doll, Composition Shoulder Head, Girl, Glass Eyes, Blonde Hair, 27 In.Tall | 265.00 |
| Doll, Composition, Alexander, Bride, 14 1/2 In.Tall | 55.00 |
| Doll, Composition, Alice In Wonderland, Vogue, 1930, 6 In.Tall | 30.00 |
| Doll, Composition, Anne Shirley, Closed Mouth, Brown Eyes, 15 In. | 85.00 |
| Doll, Composition, Anne Shirley, 22 In.Tall | 120.00 |
| Doll, Composition, Baby, Dressed, 20 In.Tall | 10.00 |
| Doll, Composition, Buttercup, 10 1/2 In.Circumference Head, Dressed | 35.00 |
| Doll, Composition, Chinese Boy, Dressed, Indian Reed Cradle, 9 In.Tall | 37.50 |
| Doll, Composition, Chinese, 7 1/2 In., Pair | 15.00 |
| Doll, Composition, Colored, Black Pupilless Eyes, 6 In. | 150.00 |
| Doll, Composition, Fisherman, Chinese, 10 1/2 In. | 45.00 |
| Doll, Composition, French, Kid Body, Bamboo Teeth, Glass Eyes, 29 In. | 300.00 |
| Doll, Composition, Jointed Baby Body, Painted Eyes, Closed Mouth, 14 In.Tall | 95.00 |
| Doll, Composition, Jointed, Painted Blue Eyes, Blonde Wig, 15 In.Tall | 40.00 |
| Doll, Composition, Marked Nancy, Dressed, 16 In. | 40.00 |
| Doll, Composition, Marked 1911, Cloth Body, Baby Clothes, 23 In.Tall | 52.50 |
| Doll, Composition, Negro Baby, 8 In. | 10.00 |
| Doll, Composition, Negro Baby, 9 In. | 15.00 |
| Doll, Composition, Negro, Mohair Wig, Dressed, 19 In. | 20.00 |
| Doll, Composition, Negro, Smiling | 15.00 |
| Doll, Composition, Puppet, Danny O'Day, Head & Hands | 5.00 |
| Doll, Composition, Santa Claus | 25.00 |

Doll, Composition, Sleep Eyes, Open Mouth, 22 In.Tall .................................................... 22.00
Doll, Composition, Tin Eyes, Molded Hair, 16 In.Tall .................................................... 14.00
Doll, Composition, Toddler, Mobile Tongue, Movable Blue Eyes, 20 In.Tall ........................ 65.00
Doll, Composition, Twins, Boy & Girl, Blue Glass Eyes, 12 In.Tall, Pair ........................ 165.00
Doll, Coquette, Original Box, 15 In.Tall .................................................................... 12.00
Doll, Cricket, Hair Grows, American, 9 1/2 In.Tall .................................................... 6.00
Doll, Cuno & Otto Dressel, Bisque, Germany, 1912, 22 In. Tall .................................... 77.50
Doll, Cuno & Otto Dressel, Flirty Eyes, Human Hair Wig, Dressed, 27 In. Tall ................ 165.00
Doll, Cutout, Stuffed, Underwear, 24 In.Tall .............................................................. 16.00
Doll, Davy, Monkees, Rock & Roll Group, Movable Head & Arms, 5 In. ............................ 3.00
Doll, Deanna Durbin, 20 In.Tall ............................................ 65.00 To 85.00
Doll, Dennis The Menace ................................................................................ 3.00
Doll, Dick Tracy, Composition, Movable Mouth, Pull String, Dressed, 1930s ..................... 30.00
Doll, Dimples, Composition, Marked 1929, 20 In. Tall ................................................ 40.00
Doll, Dionne Quintuplet, Toddler, Marked, 7 1/2 In.Tall ............................................. 23.00
Doll, Dionne Quintuplet, Wig, 10 1/2 In.Tall ............................................................. 55.00
Doll, Doctor's, Lady, Carved Ivory, Teakwood Base, 9 In.Tall ....................................... 78.00
Doll, Dollhouse, Bride & Groom, Blue Glass Eyes, 6 1/2 In., Pair ................................ 250.00
Doll, Dolly Dingle, Blue Boy & Pink Lady, Metal, Dressed, 3 In., Pair ........................... 12.50
Doll, Dome Head, Y-G, German, Blue Paperweight Eyes, C.1880, 21 In. ........................... 385.00
Doll, Dopey, Hand Puppet, Dwarf, Composition ........................................................ 12.00
Doll, Double Ended, Blue Eyed Blonde & Negro, Kid Body, 9 1/2 In. .............................. 25.00
Doll, Dream Baby, Jointed Torso, 12 In. .................................................................. 150.00
Doll, Dream Baby, Open Mouth, Rock-A-Bye ............................................................. 165.00
Doll, Dream Baby, Puppet, 8 1/2 In. Head ................................................................ 135.00
Doll, Dream Baby, 12 In.Head Circumference ............................................................ 170.00
Doll, Dream Baby, 17 In.Tall ................................................................................ 145.00
Doll, E & S, Bisque Shoulder Head, Kid Body, Composition Legs & Arms, 12 In. ............... 68.50
Doll, E.D., French, Blue Paperweight Eyes, Open Mouth, 21 In. ..................................... 395.00
Doll, E.D., French, Blue Paperweight Eyes, Open Mouth, 24 In.Tall ............................... 500.00
Doll, E.D., French, Blue Paperweight Eyes, Open Mouth, 25 In.Tall ............................... 595.00
Doll, Eegee, Susan Stroller, Walker, Plastic, 22 In. Tall ............................................. 26.50
Doll, Effanbee, Anne Shirley, Composition, Heart Mole On Face, Dressed ......................... 65.00
Doll, Effanbee, Baby Grumpy, C.1917 ..................................................................... 38.00
Doll, Effanbee, Bubbles, Dressed, 18 In.Tall ............................................................ 35.00
Doll, Effanbee, Bubbles, Dressed, 22 In.Tall ............................................................ 40.00
Doll, Effanbee, Bydee, Lamb's Wool Hair, Applied Ears, 16 In.Tall ............................... 17.00
Doll, Effanbee, Composition Head, Arms, & Legs, Cloth Body, Twins, 16 In., Pair ............. 170.00
Doll, Effanbee, Ginyette ...................................................................................... 26.00
Doll, Effanbee, Negro, Emily Anne, V.Austin, Composition, 13 In. ................ 175.00 To 225.00
Doll, Effanbee, Patsy Ann, Fur Coat, 19 In.Tall ....................................................... 60.00
Doll, Effanbee, Patsy Joan, Composition, 15 1/2 In. Tall ............................................ 48.50
Doll, Effanbee, Suzane .......................................................................................... 15.00
Doll, Emma Clews, Bonnet, Dated '40 ..................................................................... 150.00
Doll, Eskimo, Dressed, 8 In.Tall ............................................................................ 20.00
Doll, F.G. On Shoulder Plate, Kid Body, Blue Glass Eyes, Blonde Wig, 15 In. .................. 410.00
Doll, F.G., Body Marked Bebee Gesland S.G.D.G. 5 Rue Paris, 26 In.Tall ....................... 495.00
Doll, F.G., Fisherman, Terra-Cotta Hands, 13 1/2 In. Tall .......................................... 325.00
Doll, F.G., French, Closed Mouth, Brown Eyes, 25 In.Tall .......................................... 625.00
Doll, F.G., Signed Gesland Cloth Torso, Closed Mouth, 23 In. ..................................... 650.00
Doll, F/o Germany, Bisque Head, Ball Jointed, Kid Body, 20 In.Tall ............................. 75.00
Doll, Famlee, Three Heads, Cloth Body, Composition Hands & Legs ................................ 55.00
Doll, Fanny Brice, Composition Head, Hands, Feet, Legs, & Arms, 12 In.Tall ................... 65.00
Doll, Fashion, Cloth Body, Bisque Hands, Blown Glass Eyes, 20 In.Tall ......................... 225.00
Doll, Fashion, French, Dressed, 13 In.Tall ............................................................... 450.00
Doll, Fashion, French, Kid Body, Stiff Neck, Cobalt Paperweight Eyes, 12 In. .................. 450.00
Doll, Fashion, French, Swivel Chest, Brown Eyes, 15 1/2 In.Tall .................................. 25.00
Doll, Fashion, Solid Dome, Kid Body, Closed Mouth, 17 In.Tall .................................... 295.00
Doll, Fashion, Swivel Neck, Cloth Body, Red Hair, Brown Eyes, 13 In.Tall ...................... 150.00
Doll, Finland, Dressed, 11 In.Tall .......................................................................... 28.00
Doll, Finland, Man, Dressed, 12 In.Tall ................................................................... 35.00
Doll, Flapper Era, Man, Molded Top Hat, Dressed, 3 1/2 In.Tall ................................... 22.00
Doll, Flapper, Black Hair, Painted Shoes & Socks, Dressed, 3 In. ................................. 22.00
Doll, Flapper, Blue Molded Hat, Red Strap Shoes, 3 1/4 In.Tall .................................... 19.00
Doll, Flora McFlimsey, Composition, 15 In. Tall ....................................................... 55.00
Doll, Floradora, A 6/OM, Germany, Jointed Kid Body, Brown Eyes, 14 In.Tall ................... 78.50

| | |
|---|---|
| Doll, Floradora, A.M., Made In Germany, Bisque Head, Kid Body, 24 In. Tall | 85.00 |
| Doll, Floradora, Bisque Head, Composition Body, 16 1/2 In.Long, Marseille | 110.00 |
| Doll, Floradora, Bisque Head, Papier-Mache Body, Open Mouth, 22 In. Tall | 85.00 |
| Doll, Floradora, Blond Wig, 17 In.Tall | 105.00 |
| Doll, Flossie Flirt, Composition, Flirty Eyes, Dated 1927, 21 In.Tall | 25.00 |
| Doll, Flying Nun, Portrait Of Sally Fields, 1965 | 28.00 |
| Doll, Franz Schmidt, Baby, Large Size | 375.00 |
| Doll, French Artist, Dressed, Parasol In Her White Gloved-Hand, Dated 1888 | 195.00 |
| Doll, French Face & Body, Human Hair Wig, Open Mouth, Dressed, 18 In. | 275.00 |
| Doll, French Fashion, Bisque Head, Closed Mouth, Kid Arms, Cloth Body, 14 In. | 375.00 |
| Doll, French Fashion, Bisque, Kid Body, Swivel Neck, Blue Glass Eyes, 17 In. | 295.00 |
| Doll, French Fashion, Girl, Jumeau Body | 450.00 |
| Doll, French Fashion, Mona Lisa, 16 In.Tall | 475.00 |
| Doll, French Fashion, Simone, Kid Arms & Body, Blue Glass Eyes, 17 In.Tall | 500.00 |
| Doll, French Fashion, Swivel Neck, Pierced Ears, Brown Eyes, 16 In.Tall | 225.00 |
| Doll, French Girl, Signed Paris, Cries Mama, Blue Paperweight Eyes, 17 In. | 600.00 |
| Doll, French, Character, Girl, Auburn Human Hair Wig, Closed Mouth, 21 In. | 325.00 |
| Doll, French, Girl, Blonde, Open Mouth, 5 Piece Body, Wig, 24 In.Tall | 300.00 |
| Doll, French, Marked C14 Depose, Open Mouth, Blue Eyes, 28 In.Tall | 450.00 |
| Doll, French, Toddler, 27 In.Tall | 295.00 |
| Doll, Frozen Charlotte, Bisque, German, No.665B, Movable Arms, 6 In.Tall | 40.00 |
| Doll, Frozen Charlotte, Bisque, Impressed 340 7, Brown Hair, Blue Eyes, 3 In. | 18.00 |
| Doll, Frozen Charlotte, Black Hair, 1 In.Tall | 10.00 |
| Doll, Frozen Charlotte, Blonde, 14 In.Tall | 350.00 |
| Doll, Frozen Charlotte, Boy, Purple Luster Body, Blonde Hair, 11 In.Tall | 390.00 |
| Doll, Frozen Charlotte, China, Black Hair, 5 In.Tall | 50.00 |
| Doll, Frozen Charlotte, Pink Luster Face, Blonde, 14 In.Tall | 325.00 |
| Doll, Frozen Charlotte, Pink Luster Face, Painted Hair, 16 In. Tall | 495.00 |
| Doll, Fulper, Baby | 125.00 |
| Doll, G.Heubach, Character Toddler, Blue Sleep Eyes, Blonde Hair, 16 1/2 In. | 185.00 |
| Doll, G-K, 390 A120xm, Boy & Girl, Bisque Head, Dressed, 8 & 9 In., Pair | 139.00 |
| Doll, General Douglas MacArthur, Composition, Molded Hat, 18 In.Tall | 80.00 |
| Doll, Georgene Averill, Baby, Composition, 17 In. Tall | 65.00 |
| Doll, Georgene Averill, Cloth Body, Composition Hands & Feet, 19 In. Tall | 625.00 |
| Doll, Georgene Averill, Dressed, 21 In.Tall | 475.00 |
| Doll, Gerber Baby, Jointed, Painted Eyes, Molded Hair, 1972, 14 In.Tall | 10.00 |
| Doll, German Porcelain, Doll's House Family, Set Of 6 | 450.00 |
| Doll, German, Brown Stationary Eyes, Closed Mouth, 19 In.Tall | 295.00 |
| Doll, German, Composition Body, Blue Paperweight Eyes, Open Mouth, 18 In. | 135.00 |
| Doll, German, Walker, 8 In.Tall | 68.00 |
| Doll, Germany & Clover, Bisque, Baby, Jointed, Blonde Molded Hair, 5 In. | 35.00 |
| Doll, Germany 182, Ball Jointed Body, 4 Teeth, Blue Sleep Eyes, 26 In.Tall | 225.00 |
| Doll, Giggles, Ideal, 1966, 18 In.Tall | 5.00 |
| Doll, Ginnette, Sleep Eyes | 8.00 |
| Doll, Ginny Walker, Vogue, Red Wig, Dressed, 7 In. Tall | 8.00 To 16.00 |
| Doll, Ginny, Dressed, White Metal Trunk Of 1950s, 8 In. Tall | 35.00 |
| Doll, Girl, French, Head Marked Paris, Jointed Composition Body, 10 1/2 In. | 350.00 |
| Doll, Girl, Head Marked 32 29, Blue Eyes, Black Human Hair Wig, 17 In.Tall | 325.00 |
| Doll, Gladdie Boy, 19 In. | 450.00 |
| Doll, Godey, China Head, Black Hair, China Hands & Feet, Dressed, 11 1/2 In. | 30.00 |
| Doll, Greiner-58 Patent, Leather Arms, Dressed, 24 In.Tall | 285.00 |
| Doll, Happi-Time, Girl, Walker, Plastic, Blonde Mohair Wig, 17 In.Tall | 15.00 |
| Doll, Harriet Hubbard Ayer, 14 In.Tall | 18.50 |
| Doll, Head, Bisque Shoulder, Brown Eyes, 3 In. | 22.00 |
| Doll, Head, Bisque, Germany, Size 20 | 70.00 |
| Doll, Head, Bisque, Limoges, Painted Eyes, 4 In.Circumference | 15.00 |
| Doll, Head, China, Black Hair, 3 In. | 30.00 |
| Doll, Head, China, Blonde Hair, Blue Eyes, 5 In. | 75.00 |
| Doll, Head, China, Marked S In Circle, Black Molded Hair, Blue Painted Eyes | 57.50 |
| Doll, Hebee Shebee, Bisque, Made In Japan, 6 1/4 In.Tall | 125.00 |
| Doll, Hebee Shebee, Wooden, Jointed, 12 In.Tall | 125.00 |
| Doll, Hedda Get Bedda, Hospital Bed, Original Box | 30.00 |
| Doll, Heinrich Handwerck, Priscilla, Bisque Head, Composition Body, 23 In. | 175.00 |
| Doll, Heinrich Handwerck, Simon & Halbig, Bisque Head, Ball Jointed, 30 In. | 180.00 |
| Doll, Heinrich Handwerck, Simon & Halbig, Greasy Bisque Head, 32 In. Tall | 250.00 |
| Doll, Heinrich Handwerck, Simon & Halbig, Jointed Composition Body, 26 In. | 150.00 |

Doll, Heinrich Handwerck, Simon & Halbig, 24 In. ............................................ 135.00
Doll, Helen, China Head, Arms, & Legs, Black Hair, Blue Eyes, 20 In.Tall ............ 100.00
Doll, Herm Steiner, Composition Body, Open Mouth, Sleep Eyes, 9 In. .................. 95.00
Doll, Heubach Kopplesdorf 250-16/0 Ger, Bisque Head, Composition Body ............ 65.00
Doll, Heubach Kopplesdorf 320-12/0 Ger, Toddler, Breather, 10 In.Tall ................ 150.00
Doll, Heubach Kopplesdorf 320-1210, Toddler, Composition Body, 10 In. ............ 150.00
Doll, Heubach Kopplesdorf 320-4, Toddler, Jointed, Blue Sleep Eyes, 19 In. ........ 225.00
Doll, Heubach Kopplesdorf 3208, Baby, Breather, Composition Body, 24 In. ........ 285.00
Doll, Heubach Kopplesdorf, Baby, Breather, 10 In.Head ...................................... 95.00
Doll, Heubach Kopplesdorf, Baby, Jointed Composition Baby Body, 18 In.Tall ........ 240.00
Doll, Heubach Kopplesdorf, Blue Sleep Eyes, Open Mouth, Blonde Wig, 8 In. ........ 60.00
Doll, Heubach Kopplesdorf, Composition, Bent Limbs, 15 In.Tall .......................... 85.00
Doll, Heubach Kopplesdorf, Negro Baby, Marked No.399-6/0 D.R.G.M., 12 In. ........ 285.00
Doll, Heubach Kopplesdorf, Negro Baby, Bisque Head, Composition Body ............ 235.00
Doll, Heubach Kopplesdorf, 3027, Bisque Head, Ball Jointed, 28 In. Tall .............. 255.00
Doll, Heubach, Baby, Boy, Papier-Mache Body, Intaglio Eyes, 9 1/4 In.Tall ........ 185.00
Doll, Heubach, Baby, Composition Body, Intaglio Eyes, 7 1/2 In. Tall .................. 150.00
Doll, Heubach, Baby, Signed Dome Head, Open & Closed Mouth, 8 1/2 In. ............ 200.00
Doll, Heubach, Baby, Sunburst Mark, Intaglio Eyes, Molded Hair, 9 In.Tall .......... 185.00
Doll, Heubach, Bisque Head, Pouty Boy, Glass Eyes, 33 In.Tall, 13 7246 .............. 975.00
Doll, Heubach, Bisque Head, Stationary Brown Eyes, Jointed, 22 1/2 In. .............. 140.00
Doll, Heubach, Blue Intaglio Eyes, Open & Close Mouth, 2 Teeth, 17 1/2 In. ........ 350.00
Doll, Heubach, Boy, Intaglio Eyes, 2 Teeth, Molded Hiar, 13 In. ........................ 225.00
Doll, Heubach, Boy, Kid Body, Intaglio Eyes, Teeth, 11 In. Tall ........................ 250.00
Doll, Heubach, Cloth Body, Bisque Hands, Blue Intaglio Eyes, 13 In. .................. 225.00
Doll, Heubach, Flapper, Intaglio Eyes Look To Side, Smiling, 16 In.Tall .............. 400.00
Doll, Heubach, Kid Body, Blue Intaglio Eyes, 2 Lower Teeth, 17 1/4 In. .............. 350.00
Doll, Heubach, L, 6894, Germany, Ball Jointed Body, Blue Intaglio Eyes, 16 In. .... 275.00
Doll, Heubach, Laughing Boy, 2 Bottom Teeth, Intaglio Eyes, 11 In. Tall .............. 50.00
Doll, Heubach, Sailor Boy, Sunburst Mark, Dressed, 11 In.Tall .......................... 195.00
Doll, Heubach, Shoulder Head, Kid Body, Bisque Hands, Intaglio Eyes, 16 In. ...... 250.00
Doll, Heubach, Sunburst Mark, Ball Jointed Body, Intaglio Eyes, 11 1/2 In. .......... 225.00
Doll, Honey Moon, Daughter Of Moon Maid & Son Of Dick Tracy, 1965 ................ 28.00
Doll, Horseman, Blonde, 14 In.Tall ................................................................ 28.00
Doll, Hotten Top, 11 In.Tall .......................................................................... 4.00
Doll, Hummel, Baby, Blue Checked Dress & Bonnet, 12 In. .............................. 19.25
Doll, Hummel, Dwarf, Rubber, Beard, 9 1/2 In. Tall .......................................... 25.00
Doll, Hummel, Vagabond, Goose Girl, Vinyl, 10 In.Tall .................................... 12.00
Doll, Hummel, Vagabond, Radish Boy, Vinyl, 10 In.Tall .................................... 12.00
Doll, Hungary, Dressed, 9 1/2 In.Tall ............................................................ 25.00
Doll, Ideal, Boy, Celluloid, 11 In. Tall ............................................................ 8.00
Doll, Ideal, Kissy, 1961 ................................................................................ 20.00
Doll, Ideal, P-90, Vinyl, Dressed, 14 In. Tall .................................................. 25.00
Doll, Ideal, Real Live Lucy, Blonde, Baby, Shakes Head, 21 In. ........................ 13.50
Doll, Ideal, Toni, 15 In.Tall .......................................................................... 17.50
   Doll, Indian, see Indian, Doll
Doll, Indian, Movable Arms & Legs, 7 In.Tall .................................................. 5.00
Doll, Italian, Furga, 18 In.Tall ...................................................................... 15.00
   Doll, J.D.K., see also Doll, Kestner
Doll, J.D.K., Baby, 30 In. Tall ...................................................................... 475.00
Doll, J.D.K., Blue Sleep Eyes, Open Mouth, 2 Upper Teeth, 12 In.Tall ................ 150.00
Doll, J.D.K., Germany, Baby, Jointed Composition Body, Blue Eyes, 17 In.Tall ...... 250.00
Doll, J.D.K., Hilda, Ges.Gesh., Open Mouth, Blue Sleep Eyes, 2 Teeth, 11 In. ...... 175.00
Doll, J.D.K., Hilda, Open Crown, Plaster Of Paris Pate, Dressed, 22 In.Tall .......... 650.00
Doll, J.D.K., Open & Close Mouth, Blue Sleep Eyes, Molded Hair, 11 In.Tall ........ 125.00
Doll, J.D.K., Toddler, 23 In.Tall .................................................................... 275.00
Doll, J.D.K., 211, Baby Body, Sleep Eyes, Open Mouth, 16 1/2 In. Tall .............. 250.00
Doll, J.D.K., 211, Open & Close Mouth, Blue Sleep Eyes, 11 In.Tall .................. 175.00
Doll, J.D.K., 245, Hilda, Brown Eyes, 14 In. Tall ............................................ 650.00
Doll, J.D.K., 247, Baby, Blue Sleep Eyes, 9 1/4 In. Head ................................ 125.00
Doll, J.D.K., 257, Baby, Sleep Eyes, 17 In. Tall ............................................ 195.00
Doll, J.D.K., 257, Composition Body, Blonde Hair, 14 1/2 In. Tall ...................... 172.00
Doll, J.Steiner S.G.D.G. Paris A7 Le Parisien, Paperweight Eyes, 14 In. ............ 650.00
Doll, Jackie Kennedy, 20 In.Tall .................................................................. 65.00
Doll, Japanese, Bisque, Girl, Painted Pink, Jointed Arms, C.1920, 5 In.Tall ........ 12.00
Doll, Japanese, Teacher's, Wig, 4 1/2 In.Tall, Pair .......................................... 9.00

Doll, Jerry Lee, Marked, 15 In. Tall ..................................................... 22.00 To 25.00
Doll, Julian, French, 29 In.Tall ............................................................................ 395.00
Doll, Julian, Jointed Composition Body, Brown Stationary Eyes, 14 In.Tall ............. 300.00
Doll, Jumeau, Bisque Head & Arms, Mechanical, Music Box, 20 In. ......................... 1500.00
Doll, Jumeau, Bisque Head, E 7 J Depose, Girl, Pierced Ears, 16 1/2 In. ................ 795.00
Doll, Jumeau, Bisque Head, Marked Unis France 301, Composition Body, 20 In. ....... 185.00
Doll, Jumeau, Blue Paperweight Eyes, Pierced Ears, Closed Mouth, 32 In.Tall ......... 1200.00
Doll, Jumeau, Brown Paperweight Eyes, Human Hair Wig, Dressed, 27 In.Tall ......... 785.00
Doll, Jumeau, Closed Mouth, Human Hair, Dressed, 24 In.Tall .............................. 695.00
Doll, Jumeau, Closed Mouth, 35 In.Tall ............................................................ 1200.00
Doll, Jumeau, Fashion, Bisque Head, Kid Body, Medaille D'Or Paris, 19 In. ............ 825.00
Doll, Jumeau, Head Marked E 10 J, Closed Mouth, Pierced Ears, 22 1/2 In.Tall ...... 675.00
Doll, Jumeau, Incised 5, Portrait, Signed Torso, Closed Mouth, 14 In. Tall ............. 695.00
Doll, Jumeau, Marked Head & Body, Brown Paperweight Eyes, Blonde, 25 1/2 In. .... 350.00
Doll, Jumeau, Marked J.Brown Human Hair, Blue Eyes, Open Mouth, 17 In.Tall ....... 175.00
Doll, Jumeau, Marked S.F.B.J., B.J.Body, Blue Sleep Eyes, Dressed, 18 In.Tall ...... 235.00
Doll, Jumeau, Open Mouth, Hair Wig, 24 In.Tall .............................................. 315.00
Doll, Jumeau, Open Mouth, Pierced Ears, Blue Sleep Eyes, Brown Wig, 21 In. ....... 225.00
Doll, Jumeau, Signed 1907, Open Mouth, Blue Eyes, 16 In.Tall ............................ 325.00
Doll, Jumeau, 107, Blue Paperweight Eyes, 22 In. Tall ...................................... 395.00
Doll, Jumeau, 1907/15, 33 In.Tall .................................................................. 550.00
Doll, Junior Miss Ballerina, Hasbro, No.1526x300, Zipper Case ............................ 15.00
Doll, K * R, Baby, Blue Flirty Eyes, Dressed, 15 In. Head .................................. 250.00
Doll, K * R, Composition Body, Open Mouth, Blue Eyes, 28 In.Tall ...................... 235.00
Doll, K * R, Halbig, Blue Sleep Eyes, Pierced Ears, Blonde Wig, 19 In. Tall .......... 95.00
Doll, K * R, Kaiser Baby, Bisque Head, Jointed Composition Body, 15 In. Tall ........ 395.00
Doll, K * R, Kaiser Baby, No.100, 13 In.Tall ................................................... 395.00
Doll, K * R, R/S&H128, Baby, 30 In.Tall ....................................................... 425.00
Doll, K * R, S.& H., 121, Brown Sleep Eyes, Open Mouth, 2 Teeth, 11 In. Tall ...... 150.00
Doll, K * R, Simon & Halbig 126, Baby, Composition Body, 22 In. ........................ 220.00
Doll, K * R, Simon Halbig 62, Ball Jointed, 25 In. ........................................... 145.00
Doll, K * R, Simon & Halbig, Bisque Head, Ball Jointed Body, 29 In. Tall .............. 200.00
Doll, K * R, 101, Pouty, 16 In. Tall .............................................................. 750.00
Doll, K * R, 116 A, Character, Open & Closed Mouth, Dressed, 12 In.Tall ............. 575.00
Doll, K * R, 121, Baby, Linen Dress ............................................................. 200.00
Doll, K * R, 126, Baby, White Baby Clothes, 17 In. Tall .................................... 165.00
Doll, K * R, 121, Character, Flirty Eyes, 18 In. Tall ......................................... 175.00
Doll, K * R, 126, Character Baby, Flirty Eyes, Says Mama, 17 In. Tall .................. 225.00
Doll, K * R, 126, Character Baby, 11 In. Tall .................................................. 150.00
Doll, K * R, 126, Character, Composition Baby Body, Sleep Eyes, 11 In. Tall ......... 150.00
Doll, K.& H., Germany, Bisque Head, Baby, Composition Body, Open Mouth, 19 In. .. 150.00
Doll, K.& H., 525, Baby, Open & Closed Mouth, 9 In. Tall .................................. 250.00
Doll, Kaiser, Baby, 15 In.Tall ...................................................................... 350.00
Doll, Kathe Kruse, Boy, 17 In.Tall ............................................................... 100.00
Doll, Kathe Kruse, Brown Human Hair Wig, Brown Eyes, Dressed, 20 In. Tall ........ 155.00
Doll, Kayser, Baby, Bisque, Dressed, 11 In.Head Circumference ......................... 300.00
Doll, Kelloggs Pop ..................................................................................... 8.00
Doll, Kerr & Hinz, Baby, Bisque, Bunting, Maple Cradle, 1940s, 4 1/2 In. Tall ....... 6.50
Doll, Kerr & Hinz, Baby, Bisque, Highchair, 1940s, 4 1/2 In. Tall ........................ 7.50
Doll, Kerr & Hinz, Baby, Bisque, Movable Arms & Legs, 1940s, 4 1/2 In.Tall ......... 3.50
Doll, Kerr & Hinz, Baby, Peg O' My Heart, Bisque, Movable Arms, 1940s, 7 In. ..... 6.50
    Doll, Kestner, see also Doll, J.D.K.
Doll, Kestner, Ball Jointed, 26 In. Tall ................................................. 175.00 To 230.00
Doll, Kestner, Bisque Head & Arms, Kid Body, Brown Sleep Eyes, 17 1/2 In. ......... 125.00
Doll, Kestner, Bisque Head Marked 199 40, Character Baby, Composition Body ....... 95.00
Doll, Kestner, Bisque Head, 7 1/2 In. ......................................................Illus 150.00
Doll, Kestner, Blue Sleep Eyes, 32 In.Tall ..................................................... 275.00
Doll, Kestner, Character, Boy, Open & Closed Mouth, 14 In.Tall ......................... 265.00
Doll, Kestner, Fur Eyebrows, Composition Hands, Dressed, 17 In.Tall .................. 85.00
Doll, Kestner, Jointed Composition Body, Blue Stationary Eyes, 31 In.Tall ............ 495.00
Doll, Kestner, M 1/2 Germany 16 1/2, 34 In.Tall ............................................. 325.00
Doll, Kestner, Marked JDK, Character Baby, Dome Head, Blue Glass Eyes ............. 175.00
Doll, Kestner, Molded Eyebrows, Pigtails, 21 In.Tall ........................................ 210.00
Doll, Kestner, Toddler, Maroon Velvet Outfit, 15 In.Head .................................. 325.00
Doll, Kestner, 131, Baby, 11 In. Head .......................................................... 175.00
Doll, Kestner, 142 0, Blue Intaglio Eyes, Molded Hair, Curved Limbs, 10 In. ......... 175.00

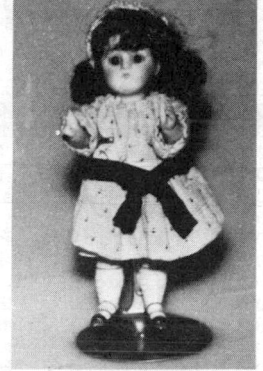

Doll, Kestner, Bisque Head, 7 1/2 In.
*(See Page 186)*

| | |
|---|---:|
| Doll, Kestner, 150/13, Bisque Head, Character Baby, Composition Body, 24 In. | 275.00 |
| Doll, Kestner, 152, Toddler, Character, Molded Tongue, 2 Teeth, 10 In. Tall | 95.00 |
| Doll, Kestner, 154, Bisque Arms, Kid Body, Brown Sleep Eyes, 16 In. Tall | 95.00 |
| Doll, Kestner, 154, Kid Body, 14 In. Tall | 100.00 |
| Doll, Kestner, 154, 15 In. Tall | 70.00 |
| Doll, Kestner, 154, 30 In. Tall | 185.00 |
| Doll, Kestner, 164, Bisque Head, Composition Body, Mohair Wig, 32 In. Tall | 275.00 |
| Doll, Kestner, 168, Ball Jointed Body, Brown Sleep Eyes, Open Mouth, 20 In. | 135.00 |
| Doll, Kestner, 171, Ball Jointed Body, Brown Sleep Eyes, Open Mouth, 24 In. | 195.00 |
| Doll, Kewpie, see Kewpie, Doll | |
| Doll, Kewty, Toddler, Composition, Molded Hair, Swivel Head, 12 In. Tall | 50.00 |
| Doll, Kiddie Pal, Dressed, 25 In. Tall | 23.00 |
| Doll, Kiddiejog A8m, 991 Germany, Character, Shoulder Head, Kid Body, 26 In. | 225.00 |
| Doll, Kidnapped Baby, Cameo, Stationary Eyes, White Bunting, 18 In. | 35.00 |
| Doll, Klay & Hahn, Baby, Open Mouth, Glass Eyes, 11 In. Head | 155.00 |
| Doll, Klay & Hahn, 282 Walkure 5-1/2 Ger., Jointed Composition Body, 28 In. | 250.00 |
| Doll, Lady, French, Swivel Head, Pierced Ears, Blue Glass Eyes, 18 In. Tall | 525.00 |
| Doll, Laurie Joan, The Teenage Darling, Active Doll, Corp., No.14r, 20 In. | 35.00 |
| Doll, Lenci Type, Marked Farnell's Alpha Toys, England, Felt, Cloth Body | 85.00 |
| Doll, Lenci, Coquette, Felt Clothes, 36 In. Tall | 125.00 |
| Doll, Lenci, Dutch Costume, Paper Tag On Skirt, 18 In. Tall | 100.00 |
| Doll, Lenci, Scandinavian Costume, Brown Eyes & Hair, 11 In. Tall | 50.00 |
| Doll, Lenci, Scandinavian Costume, Brown Hair, Black Eyes, 14 In. Tall | 65.00 |
| Doll, Lenci, Scottish Clad, 12 In. Tall | 40.00 |
| Doll, Lenci, Spanish, 31 In. Tall | 76.00 |
| Doll, Lily, Germany, Bisque Arms, Kid Body, Brown Stationary Eyes, 14 In. | 79.00 |
| Doll, Limoges, Ball Jointed Body, Stationary Brown Eyes, Open Mouth, 23 In. | 265.00 |
| Doll, Limoges, Bebe Jumeau Body, Molded Teeth, Paperweight Eyes, 25 In. | 225.00 |
| Doll, Limoges, Blue Sleep Eyes, Pierced Ears, Porcelain Teeth, 24 In. Tall | 235.00 |
| Doll, Limoges, Brown Paperweight Eyes, Teeth, Blonde Wig, 22 In. Tall | 225.00 |
| Doll, Limoges, Character, French, 12 In. Tall | 95.00 |
| Doll, Limoges, Favorite, Character, Blue Paperweight Eyes, H.H.Torso, 32 In. | 425.00 |
| Doll, Limoges, Toddler, Brown Stationary Eyes, 13 1/2 In. | 225.00 |
| Doll, Linda Williams, Dressed, 14 In. Tall | 7.00 |
| Doll, Lissy, 11 In. Tall | 25.00 |
| Doll, Little Lulu, Stuffed Body, Red Yarn Hair, Dressed, 18 In. | 8.50 |
| Doll, Little Orphan Annie & Sandy, Cadeaux, Pair | 25.00 |
| Doll, Little Orphan Annie, Rag, Remco | 22.50 |
| Doll, Little Orphan Annie, 1972, 18 In. | 12.50 |
| Doll, Louis Satchmo Armstrong | 50.00 |
| Doll, Lovums-Effanbee, Composition Swivel Head, Arms, & Legs, Cloth Body | 45.00 |
| Doll, Lyndon B.Johnson, Rubber & Plastic, 6 1/2 In. Tall | 8.00 |
| Doll, M.B.Japan, Baby, Jointed Composition Body, 9 In. Tall | 75.00 |
| Doll, M.B.Japan, Baby, 2 Upper Teeth, Gray Eyes, 12 1/2 In. Tall | 90.00 |
| Doll, M.B., Girl, Dressed, 19 In. Tall | 115.00 |
| Doll, M.H.20/0, Indian, Frowning Face, Jointed Body, Wig, Dressed, 7 1/2 In. | 85.00 |
| Doll, Mabel, Bisque Shoulder Head, Kid Body, 11 1/2 In. Tall | 70.00 |

| | |
|---|---|
| Doll, Mabel, Kid Body, Blue Sleep Eyes, 16 In.Tall | 52.00 |
| Doll, Madalaine, Composition, 15 In. Tall | 55.00 |
| Doll, Madame Alexander, Ballet Dancer, Dressed, 14 In. Tall | 45.00 |
| Doll, Madame Alexander, Bennie, Walker, Composition, 14 In. Tall | 20.00 |
| Doll, Madame Alexander, Bennie, Walker, 26 In. Tall | 65.00 |
| Doll, Madame Alexander, Bride, Composition, 22 In. Tall | 45.00 |
| Doll, Madame Alexander, Cissy, Dressed, 20 In.Tall | 20.00 |
| Doll, Madame Alexander, Cissy, 15 In.Tall | 15.00 |
| Doll, Madame Alexander, Cissy, 17 In.Tall | 17.00 |
| Doll, Madame Alexander, Debutante, Jointed, Sleep Eyes, 21 In. Tall | 30.00 |
| Doll, Madame Alexander, Dionne Quintuplet, Molded Head, 16 In. Tall | 50.00 |
| Doll, Madame Alexander, Dressed As Bride, C.1940, 21 In. Tall | 49.00 |
| Doll, Madame Alexander, Elizabeth II, Coronation Robe, 18 In.Tall | 75.00 |
| Doll, Madame Alexander, Girl, Flirty Eyes, 15 In.Tall | 17.00 |
| Doll, Madame Alexander, Little Genius, Dressed | 35.00 |
| Doll, Madame Alexander, Marionette, Marked Tony Sarg, Negro & White, Pair | 25.00 |
| Doll, Madame Alexander, Marme, Kelly Green Dress, 8 In.Tall | 23.00 |
| Doll, Madame Alexander, Mary Ellen, Jointed, 14 In. Tall | 30.00 |
| Doll, Madame Alexander, Miss Curity, Composition, 21 In. Tall | 35.00 |
| Doll, Madame Alexander, Nina, The Ballerina, 1940s, 17 1/2 In. Tall | 22.00 |
| Doll, Madame Alexander, Princess Elizabeth, Composition, Wig, 13 In.Tall | 55.00 |
| Doll, Madame Alexander, Scarlett O'Hara, Composition, 14 1/2 In.Tall | 65.00 |
| Doll, Madame Alexander, Scarlett O'Hara, Dressed, 17 In.Tall | 95.00 |
| Doll, Madame Alexander, So Big, Dressed, 24 In. Tall | 30.00 |
| Doll, Madame Alexander, Sonja Henie, Composition, 19 In. Tall | 65.00 |
| Doll, Madame Alexander, Snow White, Composition, 13 In. Tall | 55.00 |
| Doll, Madame Alexander, Wave Uniform Of World War II, Sleep Eyes, 12 In. | 45.00 |
| Doll, Madame Alexander, Wendy Ann, Jointed, Sleep Eyes, 21 In. Tall | 30.00 |
| Doll, Madame Hendren, Tagged, 15 In.Tall | 22.00 |
| Doll, Maggie, Ballerina, Plastic, 14 In. Tall | 20.00 |
| Doll, Magic Skin, Baby, Composition Head | 18.00 |
| Doll, Magic Skin, Bridesmaid, Box | 18.00 |
| Doll, Magic Skin, Sleepy Baby, Box | 18.00 |
| Doll, Magic Skin, Sparkle Plenty, 14 In. Tall | 30.00 |
| Doll, Margot, Ballerina, Plastic, 14 In. Tall | 20.00 |
| Doll, Marionette, Hand-Carved, 1920, 26 In.Tall | 42.00 |
| Doll, Marionette, Rootie Kazootie, 12 In.Tall | 9.00 |
| Doll, Marks Bros., Boy, Celluloid Head, Kid Body, Painted Eyes, 22 In.Tall | 95.00 |
| Doll, Mary & Joseph, Neapolitan, Terra-Cotta Head, Papier-Mache, C.1810, Pair | 350.00 |
| Doll, Mary Ann, Composition Head, Incised, C.1917 | 35.00 |
| Doll, Mary Martin, 17 In.Tall | 60.00 |
| Doll, Mary Poppins, Dressed, Carrying Case, 1964, 11 In.Tall | 11.00 |
| Doll, Mascotte, No.11, Wooden Arms & Legs, Blue Paperweight Eyes, 18 In.Tall | 595.00 |
| Doll, Max Handwerck, Bisque Head, Ball Jointed, Dressed, 26 In.Tall | 140.00 |
| Doll, Max Handwerck, Marked 30hk3, Plumed Hat, Blue Satin Dress, 24 In.Tall | 125.00 |
| Doll, McDonald's, Advertising Hamburger, Cape, 17 1/4 In.Tall | 3.00 |
| Doll, Mechanical, Hawaiian Dancer, Zarden, Composition, Original Box, C.1918 | 25.00 |
| Doll, Mickey, Monkees, Rock & Roll Group, Movable Head & Arms, 5 In. | 3.00 |
| Doll, Mignonette, Bisque Girl, Marked Germany, No.513, Blue Sleep Eyes, 5 In. | 65.00 |
| Doll, Mike, Monkees, Rock & Roll Group, Movable Head & Arms, 5 In. | 3.00 |
| Doll, Milliner's Model, Center Part Black Hair, Braided Bun, 15 In.Tall | 225.00 |
| Doll, Minerva, Girl, Tin, 17 In.Tall | 37.00 |
| Doll, Minnie Mouse, Vinyl Face, Cloth Body, Red Polka Dot Dress, 25 In. Tall | 25.00 |
| Doll, Miss Curity, Story Book Boy, 6 In. | 5.00 |
| Doll, Miss Curity, Uniform | 8.00 |
| Doll, Miss Peep, Snowsuit, 18 In.Tall | 22.50 |
| Doll, Morimura Bros., Bisque Head Marked 22 Mb Japan, Baby, 10 In.Tall | 150.00 |
| Doll, Morimura Brothers, Baby, 18 In.Tall | 150.00 |
| Doll, Mrs.Beasley, 9 In. Tall | 7.00 |
| Doll, My Sweetheart, Brown Sleep Eyes, Dressed, 24 In. | 155.00 |
| Doll, Neapolitan Creche, Wood Hands & Feet, Gesso, Straw Body, C.1811 | 378.00 |
| Doll, Negro Baby, Plaster Type Body, Pigtails All Over Head | 15.00 |
| Doll, Negro, Hand-Painted, Black Wig, Brown Sleep Eyes, 13 1/2 In.Tall | 10.00 |
| Doll, Negro, Hand-Painted, Black Wig, Brown Sleep Eyes, 20 1/2 In.Tall | 15.00 |
| Doll, Negro, Papier-Mache Head, Cloth Body, C.1890, 13 1/2 In. Tall | 125.00 |
| Doll, Negro, Rubber Head, Composition Body | 10.00 |

Doll, Nellie Bly, China Head, Arms & Legs, Cloth Body, Dressed, 22 In.Tall ............... 100.00
Doll, Nippon, A985M/8, Baby, Blue Sleep Eyes, Painted Teeth, 11 In.Tall ............... 135.00
Doll, Nippon, Baby, Bent Limbs, Blue Sleep Eyes, 15 In.Tall .............................. 85.00
Doll, Nippon, Jointed Composition Body, Blue Sleep Eyes, 19 In. ..................... 110.00
Doll, Norah Wellings, Italian Girl, Dressed, Marked, 8 In.Tall .......................... 7.00
Doll, O.M., A10, Googlie, Marked G253b, Brown Sleep Eyes, Dressed, 7 1/2 In. ... 200.00
Doll, Old Lady, Seated, Hand-Painted Cloth Face, 17 In.Tall ......................... 50.00
Doll, Olive Oyle, Rubber ................................................................. 8.00
Doll, Oriental Baby, Cryer, Glass Eyes, Fat, 10 In.Tall ............................... 37.50
Doll, Oriental Baby, 7 In.Tall ........................................................ 16.00
Doll, Oriental Girl, 8 In.Tall ......................................................... 16.00
Doll, Orphan Annie ..................................................................... 10.00
Doll, Our Pet, Germany, Bisque Head, Composition Body, Jointed, 12 In.Tall ..... 35.00
Doll, Our Pet, Registered, Ger.10/0, 4 Piece Composition Body, 8 In.Tall ......... 85.00
Doll, Pansey, III Germany, Ball Jointed Body, Brown Sleep Eyes, 23 In.Tall ....... 90.00
Doll, Paper, Babour's Irish Flax, Stand Up .......................................... 5.00
Doll, Paper, Barbara Britten, Boxed ................................................. 6.50
Doll, Paper, Child, Standing, Worcester Salt Lithograph, Pair ..................... 6.50
Doll, Paper, George Washington, Boston Globe Supplement, Uncut ................. 5.00
Doll, Paper, Judy Holliday, Uncut .................................................... 5.25
Doll, Paper, Lucille Ball, Dated 1945, Uncut ........................................ 7.25
Doll, Paper, Marilyn Monroe, Uncut .................................................. 10.50
Doll, Paper, Petunia & Boy Patches, Betty Bell Rea, 1937, Uncut ................. 25.00
Doll, Paper, Primrose Peanut Butter .................................................. 2.50
Doll, Paper, Rhonda Fleming, Boxed .................................................. 6.50
Doll, Paper, Sandra Dee, Uncut ....................................................... 4.75
Doll, Paper, Signed Tuck, Valentine, Plumed Hat, Verse On Muff, 6 3/4 In.Tall ... 12.00
Doll, Paper, Signed Tuck, 4 3/4 In.Tall, Set Of 5 ................................... 35.00
Doll, Paper, Terri Lee, Clothes ...................................................... 15.00
Doll, Paper, Tuck, Dressed, Hats, 4 3/4 In.Tall, Set Of 5 .......................... 35.00
Doll, Papier-Mache Dipped In Wax Head, Western Man, Straw Stuffed Body ....... 90.00
Doll, Papier-Mache Shoulder Head, Greiner Type, Black Glass Eyes, 24 In. ..... 285.00
Doll, Papier-Mache, Boy & Girl, English, C.1900, Pair .............................. 25.00
Doll, Papier-Mache, Brown Wig, Glass Eyes, Dressed, 17 In.Tall ................... 95.00
Doll, Papier-Mache, Child, Mohair Wig, C.1920 ..................................... 35.00
Doll, Papier-Mache, Child, Molded Braid, C.1930 ................................... 55.00
Doll, Papier-Mache, Child, Straw Stuffed Body, Blonde Wig ........................ 35.00
Doll, Papier-Mache, Chinese Ceremonial, Brocade Dressed, 10 1/2 In., Pair ..... 80.00
Doll, Papier-Mache, Germany, Girl, Jointed Arms, Painted, 1930, 4 3/4 In. ..... 10.00
Doll, Papier-Mache, Girl, Blonde, Dressed, 26 In.Tall .............................. 275.00
Doll, Papier-Mache, Milliner's Model, 8 1/2 In.Tall ................................. 265.00
Doll, Papier-Mache, Oriental, Male & Female, C.1874, Pair ........................ 135.00
Doll, Papier-Mache, Waxed, Molded Hat, Yellow Plume Glass Eyes, 15 In. Tall ... 220.00
Doll, Parian Head, Arms, & Feet, Child, Cloth Body, Blue Glass Eyes, 20 In. .... 900.00
Doll, Parian Head, Arms, & Legs, Boy, Straw Filled Body, Molded Hair, 8 In. .... 42.00
Doll, Parian Head, Cloth Body, Marked No.22, Blue Intaglio Eyes, 19 In. ........ 200.00
Doll, Parian Head, Hands, & Feet, Empress Eugenie, Cloth Body, 12 In. ......... 425.00
Doll, Parian Shoulder Head, Blue Painted Eyes, Pierced Ears, 4 1/2 In. ......... 225.00
Doll, Parian, Baby Jesus, Molded Swaddling Clothes ............................... 85.00
Doll, Parian, Bathing Baby, Molded Clothes, 2 1/2 In.Tall ......................... 35.00
Doll, Parian, Bisque Arms, Cloth Body, Blonde Curls, 15 In.Tall .................. 265.00
Doll, Parian, Blonde, Bow In Hair, Blue Eyes, 4 In.Tall ............................ 50.00
Doll, Parian, Closed Mouth, Glass Eyes, Pierced Ears, Dressed, 22 In.Tall ...... 325.00
Doll, Parian, Cloth Body, Cobalt Blue Glass Eyes, Solid Dome, 20 1/2 In. ....... 250.00
Doll, Parian, Cloth Body, Pink & Green Luster Trim, 12 In.Tall .................... 450.00
Doll, Parian, Highland Mary, Kid Body, Bisque Hands, 20 In.Tall .................. 195.00
Doll, Parian, Lady, Molded Gold Beads On Hair, 16 In.Tall ......................... 465.00
Doll, Parian, Molded Blouse & Blonde Hair, Gold Bead Trim, 7 1/2 In.Tall ....... 95.00
Doll, Parian, Molded Blouse & Blonde Hair, Pink Bows, 7 1/2 In.Tall ............. 85.00
Doll, Pat-A-Cake, Horsemen, C.1918 ................................................. 65.00
Doll, Patsy, Babyette, 8 In. Tall ...................................................... 25.00
Doll, Patsy, Composition, 20 In. Tall ................................................. 80.00
Doll, Patta-Burp, 13 In. ............................................................... 4.00
Doll, Pebbles, Flintstones, 1964 ..................................................... 25.00
Doll, Peggy Nisbet, Elizabeth II, State Robes ...................................... 27.50
Doll, Peggy Nisbet, Prince Charles .................................................. 22.00

Doll, Pincushion, 3 1/2 In.High

| | |
|---|---:|
| Doll, **Peggy Nisbet**, Prince Philip | 22.00 |
| Doll, **Penny Brite**, Red & White Dress, Carrying Case, 8 In. | 6.50 |
| Doll, **Penny**, Captain Kangaroo | 35.00 |
| Doll, **Phoenix**, French, Girl, Blue Paperweight Eyes, 21 In.Tall | 50.00 |
| Doll, **Pickwick Character**, Kimport, 1940s | 20.00 |
| Doll, **Pincushion**, Bisque, Boy, Painted Tailor Suit, 3 1/2 In.Tall | 10.00 |
| Doll, **Pincushion**, Green Hat, 3 1/2 In. Tall | 10.00 |
| Doll, **Pincushion**, Porcelain, Germany, Ornate Hairdo, 6 In. | 15.00 |
| Doll, **Pincushion**, 3 1/2 In.High ............................................... *Illus* | 12.50 |
| Doll, **Pink Luster Flat Top Head**, Arms, & Legs, Blue Eyes, 21 In. | 195.00 |
| Doll, **Pinky Lee**, 1940 ................................................ 45.00 To 55.00 | |
| Doll, **Pinocchio**, Composition Head, Wooden Body, Movable Parts, Ideal Toy Co. | 18.00 |
| Doll, **Pinocchio**, Lenci | 22.00 |
| Doll, **Pinocchio**, Stuffed Green & Gold Plush Body, 1940s, 8 1/2 In.Tall | 7.50 |
| Doll, **Plaster Type Body**, 1930s, 12 In.Tall | 15.00 |
| Doll, **Plastic**, Brown Sleep Eyes, Blonde Hair, 18 In.Tall | 16.00 |
| Doll, **Plastic**, Dutch Boy, 5 In. | 6.25 |
| Doll, **Plastic**, Dutch Girl, 5 In. | 6.25 |
| Doll, **Plastic**, Marked R & B, Bride's Outfit, 12 In.Tall | 25.00 |
| Doll, **Plastic**, R.& B., Bride, Walker, 18 In.Tall | 14.50 |
| Doll, **Poland**, Dressed, 14 In.Tall | 35.00 |
| Doll, **Poor Pitiful Pearl** | 25.00 |
| Doll, **Poor Pitiful Pearl**, Wardrobe, Original Box | 75.00 |
| Doll, **Poppin Fresh**, Dough Boy | 3.50 |
| Doll, **Porzellan Fabrik No.169**, Baby, 11 1/2 In.Head | 95.00 |
| Doll, **Princess Elizabeth**, 19 In.Tall | 27.00 |
| Doll, **Priscilla & John Alden**, C.1935, Pair | 32.00 |
| Doll, **Puppet**, Indonesian Kulit, Leather, 28 In.Tall | 34.50 |
| Doll, **Puppet**, Wimpy, Cloth Body, Vinyl Arms & Legs, 12 In. | 4.75 |
| Doll, **Puppet**, Wooden, Complete Cast Of Punch & Judy, C.1850, Set Of 8 | 425.00 |
| Doll, **Queen Louise**, Composition Body, Blonde Hair, 22 In.Tall | 150.00 |
| Doll, **Queen Louise**, Ger.1, By A.M. For Louis Wolf & Co., 15 In. Tall | 150.00 |
| Doll, **Queen Louise**, Germany, Auburn Mohair Wig & Lashes, Crown, 22 In. | 250.00 |
| Doll, **Queen Louise**, Human Hair Eyebrows, 23 In.Tall | 95.00 |
| Doll, **Queen Louise**, Wig, 34 In.Tall | 245.00 |
| Doll, **Queen Louise**, 100 Germany, Bisque Head, Composition Body, 25 In.Tall | 135.00 |
| Doll, **R & B**, Hard Plastic, Dressed, 21 In.Tall | 30.00 |
| Doll, **R.& A.**, Character Boy, Closed Mouth, 7 1/2 In. | 115.00 |
| Doll, **R.A.**, 5 1/2 In.Circumference Head, Papier-Mache Body, 7 In.Tall | 70.00 |
| Doll, **R.A.By T.Recknagel**, Jointed Body, 15 In.Tall | 115.00 |
| Doll, **R.D.**, French, Blue Paperweight Eyes, 19 1/2 In. | 650.00 |
| Doll, **Raggedy Ann & Andy**, Black, Handmade, 20 In.Tall, Pair | 18.50 |
| Doll, **Raleigh**, Composition, 10 3/4 In.Tall | 50.00 |
| Doll, **Ravca**, Empress Eugenie, 5 In.Tall | 22.00 |
| Doll, **Ravca**, Fan Dancer, 8 In. Tall | 30.00 |
| Doll, **Ravca**, French, Old Man & Woman, Stockinette Body, 10 In., Pair | 150.00 |
| Doll, **Ravca**, Scottish Man & Lady, 7 In., Pair | 50.00 |
| Doll, **Red Ragsy**, Cloth, O'Neill, 17 In.Tall | 50.00 |
| Doll, **Revlon**, 18 In.Tall | 19.50 |
| Doll, **Ricky**, Jr., American, 16 In.Tall | 23.50 |

Doll, Rock-A-Bye Baby, A.M., 351, Brown Eyes, Dressed, 13 In. Tall .......... 150.00
Doll, Rock-A-Bye Baby, Bald Head, Cloth Body, Composition Hands, 7 In. Tall .......... 150.00
Doll, Rock-A-Bye Baby, Cloth Body, Molded Hair, Sleep Eyes, 7 In.Tall .......... 185.00
Doll, Rubber, Boy, Peasant, White Tunic, Blue Vest, 7 1/2 In.Tall .......... 10.00
Doll, Rubber, Negro, Molded Hair & Clothes, 5 In.Tall .......... 4.00
Doll, Rubber, Negro, Squeeze, Molded Hair & Clothes, 5 In.Tall .......... 5.00
    Doll S & H, see also Doll, C.M.Bergmann, Doll, Simon & Halbig
Doll, S & H, Ball Jointed Body, Brown Sleep Eyes, Brown Hair, 20 In. Tall .......... 187.50
Doll, S & H, Bisque Face, Poupard, Musical, Twirling, Dressed .......... 204.00
Doll, S & H, Blue Sleep Eyes, 9 1/2 In. Tall .......... 65.00
Doll, S & H, Oriental, Glass Eyes, Dressed, 11 In.Tall .......... 525.00
Doll, S & H, 5 Piece Composition Body, Blue Glass Eyes, 7 In. Tall .......... 45.00
Doll, S & H, 550, 25 In.Tall .......... 175.00
Doll, S & H, 1923 SP 53/4 Germany, Composition Body, 22 In. Tall .......... 150.00
Doll, S.F.B.J., Bisque Socket Head, Ball Jointed Composition Body, 11 In. .......... 125.00
Doll, S.F.B.J., Character Child, 2 Teeth, Blue Sleep Eyes, 12 1/2 In. .......... 375.00
Doll, S.F.B.J., French, Walker, Bisque Head, Wood & Composition Body, 21 In. .......... 245.00
Doll, S.F.B.J., Girl, French, Hazel Paperweight Eyes, Open Mouth, 27 In.Tall .......... 285.00
Doll, S.F.B.J., Laughing Boy, French Toddler Body, 22 In.Tall .......... 725.00
Doll, S.F.B.J., Paris, Human Hair, 25 In.Tall .......... 175.00
Doll, S.F.B.J., 60 Paris, Bisque Head, Jointed Composition Body, 20 In.Tall .......... 145.00
Doll, S.F.B.J., 60 Paris, Blue Sleep Eyes, Blue Velvet Dress, 17 In. Tall .......... 110.00
Doll, S.F.B.J., 60 Paris, Jointed Composition Body, Paperweight Eyes, 15 In. .......... 195.00
Doll, S.F.B.J., 60 Paris, 21 In. Tall .......... 250.00
Doll, S.F.B.J., 60, Composition Body, Blue Eyes, Human Hair Wig, 20 In. Tall .......... 325.00
Doll, S.F.B.J., 60, Composition Body, Open Mouth, Sleep Eyes, 17 In. Tall .......... 170.00
Doll, S.F.B.J., 60, Girl, Open Mouth, Blue Paperweight Eyes, 22 In. Tall .......... 235.00
Doll, S.F.B.J., 60, Open Mouth, Blue Eyes, 16 In. Tall .......... 185.00
Doll, S.F.B.J., 60, Red Hair, Blue Eyes, 11 In. Tall .......... 110.00
Doll, S.F.B.J., 236 Paris, Character, Toddler, Human Hair, 24 In. Tall .......... 495.00
Doll, S.F.B.J., 236 Paris, Toddler, Jointed Composition Body, 28 In. Tall .......... 550.00
Doll, S.F.B.J., 236 Paris 6, Child, Laughing, Composition Baby Body, 14 In. .......... 425.00
Doll, S.F.B.J., 236, Baby, 10 In. Tall .......... 225.00
Doll, S.F.B.J., 236, Baby, 18 In. Tall .......... 475.00
Doll, S.F.B.J., 236, Boy, 13 In. Tall .......... 425.00
Doll, S.F.B.J., 236, French, Character Baby, Sleep Eyes, 27 In. Tall .......... 650.00
Doll, S.F.B.J., 239 Paris, Poulbot, 13 1/2 In. Tall .......... 2500.00
Doll, S.F.B.J., 251, French, Character Baby, Vaseline Skin, 18 1/2 In. Tall .......... 425.00
Doll, S.F.B.J., 251, Girl, Toddler, 19 In. Tall .......... 600.00
Doll, S.F.B.J., 301 Paris 2/0, Jointed Body, Human Hair Wig, 10 In. Tall .......... 210.00
Doll, S.F.B.J., 301 Paris, Clown, Blue Paperweight Eyes, 19 In. Tall .......... 375.00
Doll, S.F.B.J., 301, Jumeau On Torso, Blue Lashed Sleep Eyes, 15 In. Tall .......... 225.00
Doll, Saucy Walker, Colored .......... 20.00
Doll, Schmitt, Bisque Head & Hands, Mechanical, On Music Box, 13 1/2 In. .......... 495.00
Doll, Schoenhut, Baby, Dated .......... 165.00
Doll, Schoenhut, Boy, Bald Head, Sailor Suit, 11 In.Tall .......... 150.00
Doll, Schoenhut, Boy, Bald Head, 11 1/2 In.Tall .......... 190.00
Doll, Schoenhut, Boy, Dressed, 11 3/4 In.Tall .......... 250.00
Doll, Schoenhut, Boy, Molded Teeth, 17 In.Tall .......... 120.00
Doll, Schoenhut, Boy, Molded Teeth, 19 In.Tall .......... 120.00
Doll, Schoenhut, Girl, Bobbed Wig, Painted Brown Eyes, 4 Teeth, 16 In. Tall .......... 182.00
Doll, Schoenhut, Girl, Carved Hair, Molded Blue Ribbon, 15 In.Tall .......... 325.00
Doll, Schoenhut, Girl, Incised Mark, Brown Intaglio Eyes, 21 In. .......... 260.00
Doll, Schoenhut, Girl, Long Wig, Painted Blue Eyes, 4 Teeth, 21 In. Tall .......... 200.00
Doll, Schoenhut, Girl, Molded Teeth, Brown Eyes, Wig, Dressed, 16 In.Tall .......... 165.00
Doll, Schoenhut, Girl, Molded Teeth, 17 In.Tall .......... 175.00
Doll, Schoenhut, Girl, Wig, 14 In.Tall .......... 165.00
Doll, Schoenhut, Toddler, Elastic Strung, 14 In.Tall .......... 165.00
Doll, Schoenhut, Toddler, Girl, Brown Sleep Eyes, Brown Wig, 14 In.Tall .......... 350.00
Doll, Schoenhut, Walkable, 16 In.Tall .......... 375.00
Doll, Schoenhut, Walking Legs, 14 In.Tall .......... 175.00
Doll, Schoenhut, Wooden, Spring Hinged, 15 In.Tall .......... 145.00
Doll, Scottles, Composition, Dress & Bonnet, 16 In. Tall .......... 135.00
Doll, Shoen & Hoffmeister, Human Hair Wig, Dressed, 25 In.Tall .......... 170.00
    Doll, Simon & Halbig, see also Doll, C.M.Bergmann, Doll, S.&H.
Doll, Simon & Halbig, Bisque Head, Jointed Composition Body, 30 In.Tall .......... 325.00

Doll, Simon & Halbig, Cloth Body, Swivel Neck Shoulder Plate, 12 In.Tall ................... 150.00
Doll, Simon & Halbig, Fashion, Dressed, 12 In.Tall ................................................. 295.00
Doll, Simon & Halbig, Flirty Eyes, Jointed Body, 10 In. .......................................... 250.00
Doll, Simon & Halbig, K*r, Red Riding Hood, Bisque Body, Arms, & Feet, 8 In. ........... 125.00
Doll, Simon & Halbig, 939, Closed Mouth, 19 1/2 In. Tall ....................................... 395.00
Doll, Simon & Halbig, 1009 Dep.S.T., Swivel Head, Cloth Body, 4 Teeth, 17 In. ......... 175.00
Doll, Simon & Halbig, 1039, Walker, Jointed, Voice Box, Flirty Eyes, 22 In. ............... 300.00
Doll, Simon & Halbig, 1079 DEP, Kid Body, Human Hair Wig, 19 In. Tall ................... 80.00
Doll, Simon & Halbig, 1160-2, Kid Body, Brown Eyes, Closed Mouth, 13 1/2 In. ......... 265.00
Doll, Simon & Halbig, 1249, Santa, Blue Sleep Eyes, 20 In. Tall ............................. 265.00
Doll, Singing Chatty, Sings ................................................................................. 15.00
Doll, Skookum, Indian, Girl, Red Blanket, 6 1/2 In. Tall .......................................... 10.00
Doll, Skookum, Indian, Male, Fierce, Compotype Face, Straw Stuffed, 11 1/2 In. ........ 10.00
Doll, Snow White & Seven Dwarfs, Stuffed, 13 1/2 In. & 4 1/2 In.Tall ..................... 21.00
Doll, Snow White, Papier-Mache, French, Signed, 1920 ........................................... 28.00
Doll, Snow White, Walt Disney, Composition, 12 1/2 In. Tall ................................... 45.00
Doll, Snow White, 4 1/4 In.Tall ........................................................................... 10.00
Doll, Sonja Henie, RD, Plastic, 18 In. Tall ............................................................ 30.00
Doll, Sonja Henie, 14 In. Tall ............................................................................. 40.00
Doll, Sonja Henie, 21 In. .................................................................................... 60.00
Doll, Soupy Sales, 5 In.Tall ................................................................................ 5.25
Doll, Steiff, Clown, "Clownie, " 8 In. .................................................................... 8.75
Doll, Steiner, Bisque Head, Girl, Mechanical, Key Wind, 6 Teeth, 17 In. ................... 595.00
Doll, Steiner, Closed Mouth, 30 In.Tall ............................................................... 1000.00
Doll, Steiner, French, Marked Head & Body, 15 In.Tall ........................................... 525.00
Doll, Stewart Baby Type, Cloth Body, Bisque Hands & Feet, 8 1/2 In.Tall ................. 85.00
Doll, Story Book, Baby, Composition, 3 1/2 In. Tall ................................................ 5.00
Doll, Story Book, Bisque, Movable Arms, Painted Eyes, 6 1/2 In.Tall ....................... 10.00
Doll, Sur, Signed, Ball Jointed Body, Blue Sleep Eyes, Dressed, 30 In. ..................... 140.00
Doll, Susan Stroller, Walker, Plastic, 22 In. Tall .................................................... 18.50
Doll, Sweet Alice, American, 21 In.Tall ................................................................ 22.00
Doll, Sweet Girl, 24 In.Tall ................................................................................. 95.00
Doll, Sweet Sue, American, 15 In.Tall .................................................................. 13.75
Doll, Sweet Sue, Walker, 14 In. Tall .................................................................... 25.00
Doll, Swiss Child, Turtle Mark, 7 In.Tall, Pair ....................................................... 10.00
Doll, Swiss, Dressed, 12 In.Tall .......................................................................... 30.00
Doll, Talking, Schilling, Tags .............................................................................. 45.00
Doll, Terra-Cotta Head, Legs, & Hands, Angel, Neapolitan, Papier-Mache, 1811 ......... 125.00
Doll, Terri Lee, Blonde, Dressed, 16 In.Tall .......................................................... 30.00
Doll, Terri Lee, Blonde, 10 In.Tall ....................................................................... 25.00
Doll, Terri Lee, Marked, 15 In.Tall ...................................................................... 25.00
Doll, Terri Lee, Marked, 17 In.Tall ...................................................................... 40.00
Doll, Tete Jumeau B Te S.G. D.G., Depose, Jointed Composition Body, 16 In. ........... 595.00
Doll, Tete Jumeau, Ball Jointed Body, Brown Paperweight Eyes, 25 In.Tall ............... 375.00
Doll, Tete Jumeau, Blue Eyes, Closed Mouth, 16 In.Tall ........................................ 675.00
Doll, Tete Jumeau, Blue Paperweight Eyes, Closed Mouth, Dressed, 15 In.Tall .......... 535.00
Doll, Tete Jumeau, Blue Sleep Eyes, Pull String, Says Mama, Papa, 20 In. ............... 450.00
Doll, Tete Jumeau, Closed Mouth, Jointless Wrists, Blue Eyes, 19 In. ...................... 750.00
Doll, Tete Jumeau, Closed Mouth, Jointless Wrists, Brown Eyes, 16 In. .................... 695.00
Doll, Tete Jumeau, Closed Mouth, 21 1/2 In.Tall ................................................. 650.00
Doll, Tete Jumeau, Depose, Jointed Composition Body, Blue Eyes, 26 In.Tall ............ 450.00
Doll, Tete Jumeau, Depose, Walker, Jointed Composition Body, 21 In.Tall ................ 675.00
Doll, Tete Jumeau, Jointed Composition Body, Blue Paperweight Eyes, 26 In. ............ 450.00
Doll, Tete Jumeau, Jointed Composition Body, Brown Paperweight Eyes, 18 In. ......... 325.00
Doll, Tete Jumeau, Jointed Composition Body, Brown Paperweight Eyes, 24 In. ......... 375.00
Doll, Tete Jumeau, Jointed Composition Body, Brown Paperweight Eyes, 29 In. ......... 485.00
Doll, Tete Jumeau, Jointed Composition Body, Paperweight Eyes, 12 In.Tall ............. 495.00
Doll, Tete Jumeau, S.F.B.J., Blue Sleep Eyes, Open Mouth, 21 In. .......................... 395.00
Doll, Tete Jumeau, 1907, Jointed Composition Body, Paperweight Eyes, 25 In. .......... 375.00
Doll, Three Headed, Little Red Riding Hood, Grandma, & The Wolf, Handmade ........... 5.00
Doll, Tillie Tinker, Wooden, Dancing, Dated 1917, Original Box ............................... 13.00
Doll, Tin Head, Boy, Dressed, 17 In.Tall .............................................................. 40.00
Doll, Tin Head, Leather Body, Jointed Hips & Knees .............................................. 50.00
Doll, Tintair, F.& B., Walker, Plastic, 16 In. Tall .................................................... 17.50
Doll, Tiny Tears, American, Clothes, 13 In. Tall ..................................... 9.00 To 14.75
Doll, Tiny Tears, Hard Head, American Character, 15 In.Tall ..................... 6.00 To 12.00

Doll, Tiny Tears, Rocking Crib, Clothes, 16 In.Tall ............................................. 21.50
Doll, Tiny Tears, Rubber Body, Woolly Wig, 18 In.Tall ...................................... 21.50
Doll, Tiny Tears, 10 In.Tall ................................................................................. 8.00
Doll, Tiny Tears, 12 In.Tall ................................................................................. 8.00
Doll, Tod-L-Dee, Twins, Sun Rubber Co., Carrying Case, 10 In., Pair ................ 12.00
Doll, Toni, Walker, Blonde, Dressed ................................................................... 15.00
Doll, Toni, 14 In.Tall .......................................................................................... 18.00
Doll, Toni, 15 In.Tall .......................................................................................... 18.00
Doll, Toodles, American, Blonde, Dressed, 21 In.Tall .......................................... 21.50
Doll, Trudy, Dream Baby, Composition, Three Face, 21 In.Tall ............................ 75.00
Doll, Turkey, Dressed, 8 1/2 In.Tall ................................................................... 18.00
Doll, Turned Face, Bisque Hands, Kid Torso, Teeth, Brown Eyes, 26 In.Tall ........ 225.00
Doll, Turned Shoulder Head, 370 AM O DEP, Kid Body, Brown Eyes, 18 In. ........ 110.00
Doll, Turned Shoulder Head, 370 AM 8 DEP, Kid & Composition, 25 1/2 In. ........ 185.00
Doll, Tyrol, 22 In.Tall ........................................................................................ 165.00
Doll, Unis, France, Child, Dressed, 11 In. Tall ................................................... 190.00
Doll, Unis, France, Lady, 27 In.Tall .................................................................... 320.00
Doll, Unis, France, Lashed Blue Eyes, Dressed, 20 In. Tall ................................ 175.00
Doll, Unis, France, Signed Head, Blue Sleep Eyes, Blonde Wig, Jointed, 14 In. .... 110.00
Doll, Unis, France, 71-147 301 E R T, Composition Body, Hair Wig, 17 In. Tall .... 195.00
Doll, Unis, France, 251, Character, Boy, 24 In. Tall ........................................... 380.00
Doll, Unis, France, 301 DRT, Blue Sleep Eyes, Lashes, 23 In.Tall ..................... 125.00
Doll, Unis, France, 301, Boy, Bisque Head, Dressed, 6 In. Tall ........................... 65.00
Doll, Unis, France, 301, Girl, Bisque Head, Dressed, 6 1/2 In. Tall .................... 230.00
Doll, Unis, France, 301, Girl, Wig, Dressed, 24 In. Tall ..................................... 235.00
Doll, Unis, France, 301, Jointed Body, Human Hair Wig, 6 1/2 In. Tall .............. 150.00
Doll, Vanessa, Armand Marseille, Bisque Head, Composition Body, 23 1/2 In. ...... 150.00
Doll, Vanta, Baby, Composition, 16 In.Tall ....................................................... 10.00
Doll, Vanta, Baby, Composition, 17 In.Tall ....................................................... 20.00
Doll, Verlingue, French, Girl, Open Mouth, 5 Piece Body, 16 In.Tall ................... 140.00
Doll, Virga, Hand-Painted, Angel Costume, 5 1/2 In.Tall .................................. 8.00
Doll, Vogue, Ginnette's Layette, Painted Eyes, Clothes, Baby Bottle ................... 12.00
Doll, Voice Box Head, A.M. 580, Toddler, Closed Mouth, 13 In. ........................ 450.00
Doll, W.P.A., Cloth, Made In Milwaukee, 21 1/2 In.Tall .................................... 65.00
Doll, Walkure, Blue Sleep Eyes, Pierced Ears, Dressed, 24 In.Tall .................... 100.00
Doll, Waltershausen, Lady, 19 In.Tall ............................................................... 70.00
Doll, Wax Over Clay, Squalling Baby, Mrs.C.Nook, 1939, 21 In.Tall ................. 80.00
Doll, Wax Over Composition Head, Cloth Body, Wooden Limbs, 14 In.Tall .......... 230.00
Doll, Wax Over Papier-Mache, Baby ................................................................. 120.00
Doll, Wax Over Papier-Mache, French, Bulgy Glass Eyes ................................. 120.00
Doll, Wax, Closed Mouth, 21 In.Tall ................................................................. 225.00
Doll, Wax, Holt Masse, Sausage Curls, Center Part, 20 In. ............................... 150.00
Doll, Wax, Louis Sorenson, Lady Peddler, Glass Eyes ....................................... 125.00
Doll, Willie The Clown, Original Box ......................................................... 35.00 To 45.00
Doll, Wolf & Co., 301, Bisque Head, Composition Body, Brown Eyes, 22 In. Tall .. 135.00
Doll, Wooden, Lady, Carved Curls, Black Painted Hair, C.1786, 6 3/4 In. .......... 100.00
Doll, Wooden, Margie, Molded Hair, Painted Blue Eyes, Mouth, & Teeth ........... 15.00
Doll, Wooden, Marionette, Ballet Dancer, Hand-Carved, Painted ....................... 45.00
Doll, Wooden, Queen Anne Type, Peg Jointed, Painted Features, 8 1/2 In. ........ 500.00
Doll, X Pansy VV, For Sears Roebuck, 1914, Human Hair Wig, 23 In.Tall ........... 185.00
Doll, Young Man, Neapolitan, Papier-Mache, Terra-Cotta Head, C.1810 ............. 125.00
Doll, Zaiden, Baby, Wooden, 18 In.Head .......................................................... 160.00
    Donald Duck, see Walt Disney
    Doorstop, see Iron, Doorstop
Dorchester, Bowl, Pinecone, 5 3/4 In. ............................................................. 24.00
Dorchester, Bowl, Swirled, Round, 5 3/4 In. .................................................... 24.00
Dorchester, Casserole, Blueberry, Round, 7 In. ............................................... 65.00
Dorchester, Chamberstick, Blueberry ............................................................... 35.00
Dorchester, Chamberstick, Pinecone ................................................................ 35.00
Dorchester, Coffeepot, Blueberry, 4 3/4 In.High .............................................. 50.00
Dorchester, Coffeepot, Pinecone, 5 In.High ..................................................... 50.00
Dorchester, Coffeepot, Swirled, 5 3/4 In.High .................................................. 50.00
Dorchester, Cup & Saucer, Pinecone ............................................................... 45.00
Dorchester, Cup & Saucer, Swirled .................................................................. 45.00
Dorchester, Mug, Blueberry, 2 3/4 In.High ...................................................... 17.00
Dorchester, Mug, Pinecone .............................................................................. 17.00

| | |
|---|---|
| Dorchester, Mug, Swirled, 2 3/4 In.High | 17.00 |
| Dorchester, Plate, Shaded Blue, 6 1/2 In. | 17.00 |
| Dorchester, Toby Mug, Brown Glaze, Unsigned | 225.00 |
| Dorchester, Trivet, Coffeepot, Blue | 17.00 |

*Doulton pottery and porcelain were made by Doulton and Co.of Burslem, England, after 1882. The name Royal Doulton appeared on thier wares after 1902.*

Doulton, see also Royal Doulton

| | |
|---|---|
| Doulton, Barrel, Biscuit, Fish & Seaweed On Cream, Silver Lid & Handle, 1882 | 115.00 |
| Doulton, Barrel, Biscuit, Slater's Floral Decoration, Silver Lid | 49.00 |
| Doulton, Basket, Melon Shape, Bambora Castle Scene, Artist Signed, 4 In. | 48.00 |
| Doulton, Beaker, Lambeth, Tavern Decoration, Brown Ground, 4 1/2 In.High | 25.00 |
| Doulton, Beaker, Simulated Leather, Sterling Rim, C.1890, 4·1/4 In. High | 45.00 |
| Doulton, Bowl, Punch, Blue On White Hunting Scenes, Gold Bands, C.1900 | 85.00 |
| Doulton, Candlestick, Sterling Trim, Blue, Arthur Barlow, 1873, Lambeth | 115.00 |
| Doulton, Cup & Saucer, Floral & Gilt, Matte Finish, Burslem | 18.00 |
| Doulton, Cup, Loving, 3 Handled, Applied Blue Willow China On Brown, Lambeth | 65.00 |
| Doulton, Decanter, "Scotch, " Brown & Blue, Relief Floral, C.1891, Lambeth | 110.00 |
| Doulton, Ewer, Beige Tapestry Body, Mottled Blue Top & Bottom, 9 In.High | 48.00 |
| Doulton, Ewer, Handled, Pedestal, Gold Florals P Band On Cream, Burslem, 1872 | 75.00 |
| Doulton, Ewer, Red Floral On Beige Mosaic, Lambeth, 7 In. | 45.00 |
| Doulton, Jar, 'Ye Olde Cheshire Cheese, 1667, ' Brown Stoneware, Lambeth | 5.00 |
| Doulton, Jar, Biscuit, Art Nouveau Designs, Silver Plate Lid & Bail, Burslem | 52.00 |
| Doulton, Jar, Mustard, Silver Plate Lid, Pate Sur Pate Birds, F.Barlow, 1884 | 135.00 |
| Doulton, Jar, Tobacco, Covered, Brown & Tan, Embossed Figures, Lambeth | 35.00 |
| Doulton, Jar, Tobacco, Lid, White Figures On Browns, Lambeth, C.1891 | 45.00 |
| Doulton, Jardiniere, Cobalt & Beige, Heavy Beading, Medallions, 11 1/2 In. | 85.00 |
| Doulton, Jigger, Sterling Rim, Blue On Brown, Lambeth, 2 In. | 8.00 |
| Doulton, Jug, Brown & Tan, Figures, Lambeth, 7 In. | 50.00 |
| Doulton, Jug, Browns & Blues, Lambeth, Dated 1875, 6 In.High | 107.50 |
| Doulton, Jug, Browns & Blues, Lambeth, Dated 1877, 5 1/4 In.High | 99.50 |
| Doulton, Jug, Buff With Brown, "Old Sarum Kettle, " Lambeth, C.1881 | 58.50 |
| Doulton, Jug, Dewar's Whisky, Green & Brown, Embossed Scene, Lambeth | 45.00 |
| Doulton, Jug, Egyptian, Tan & White On Brown, Lambeth, C.1891, 5 1/2 In. | 65.00 |
| Doulton, Jug, Egyptian, Tan & White On Brown, Lambeth, C.1891, 6 1/2 In. | 90.00 |
| Doulton, Jug, Egyptian, Tan & White On Brown, Lambeth, C.1891, 7 1/2 In. | 110.00 |
| Doulton, Jug, Handled, Silver Rim, Incised Decoration, Lambeth, 7 In.High | 350.00 |
| Doulton, Jug, Herons In Water, Bulrushes, Barlow, 1874, Lambeth, 7 1/2 In. | 375.00 |
| Doulton, Jug, Initials EB Incised, Handled, Doulton & Slater, 3 1/2 In. | 24.00 |
| Doulton, Jug, Lambeth, Victoria Diamond Jubilee, 7 In.High, 1897 | 55.00 |
| Doulton, Jug, Puzzle, Stoneware, 5 Spouts, 2 Brown Bands At Base, Lambeth | 145.00 |
| Doulton, Jug, Silver Rim, Sheep On Buff, Handled, Hannah Barlow, 1875, Lambeth | 350.00 |
| Doulton, Jug, Stoneware, Brown Salt Glaze, Raised Hunting Scenes, Lambeth | 65.00 |
| Doulton, Mug, Loving, 3 Handled, Stoneware, Relief Design On Blue | 62.50 |
| Doulton, Pitcher, Brown Cats On Yellow, Proverb On Reverse Side, 6 1/2 In. | 85.00 |
| Doulton, Pitcher, Commemorative, General Gordon, 1884, 7 1/2 In.High | 65.00 |
| Doulton, Pitcher, English Hunting Scenes Applied, Lambeth, 5 1/2 In. | 37.00 |
| Doulton, Pitcher, Floral, Blue With Cream, Burslem, 8 1/2 In. | 60.00 |
| Doulton, Pitcher, Hunt & Drinking Scenes, Brown & Tan, Lambeth, 6 1/2 In. | 25.00 |
| Doulton, Pitcher, Hunt & Drinking Scene, Brown & Tan, Lambeth, 9 In. | 60.00 |
| Doulton, Pitcher, Lord Nelson & 6 Sailing Vessels, Sunset, Punched Spout | 135.00 |
| Doulton, Pitcher, Oliver Asks For More, Rectangular | 100.00 |
| Doulton, Pitcher, Raised White Limbs & Floral On Brown, Blue Bands, Lambeth | 58.00 |
| Doulton, Pitcher, Stoneware, Brown & Tan, "Let Not A Man be Seen," Lambeth | 45.00 |
| Doulton, Pitcher, Stoneware, Cobalt, Brown Floral Band, Birds, Vines, Lambeth | 35.00 |
| Doulton, Pitcher, Three Women On Beach, 2 1/2 In. | 20.00 |
| Doulton, Pitcher, Water, Blue & White, Scenic, Bulbous Shape | 38.00 |
| Doulton, Plate, Admiral | 9.50 |
| Doulton, Plate, Hudson Fulton Celebration, Transfers, Blue, 10 1/2 In. | 24.00 |
| Doulton, Plate, International Steamship Co., Blue, Gold, Burslem, 9 1/2 In. | 30.00 |
| Doulton, Plate, Jester | 9.50 |
| Doulton, Plate, Madras, 10 In. | 22.00 |
| Doulton, Plate, Pink & Yellow Floral, Scalloped Rim, Burslem, C.1891, 9 In. | 12.00 |
| Doulton, Plate, Watteau, 7 5/8 In. | 11.00 |
| Doulton, Platter, Mandarin, 13 X 16 In. | 38.00 |
| Doulton, Salt, Master, Cream, Silver Overlay, 4 Footed, Burslem | 18.00 |

Doulton, Saltshaker, Old England Scenes, Brown & Tan ......................................... 28.00
Doulton, Sewer Pipe Coupling, Stoneware, Salesman's Sample, C.1885, Lambeth .............. 50.00
Doulton, Toby Mug, Napoleon, Signed Doulton & Wotts, 6 In. ..................................... 155.00
Doulton, Toby Mug, Seated Man Holding Glass & Jug, Blue Coat, Lambeth .................. 125.00
Doulton, Vase, Blue & White Floral, Signed J.Walker, Corolianware, Burslem .............. 115.00
Doulton, Vase, Faience, Pink Wild Roses, Agnes Baigent, 1902, Lambeth, 13 In. .......... 135.00
Doulton, Vase, Incised Donkeys, Brown & Blue Border, Hannah Barlow, 18 In. ............. 300.00
Doulton, Vase, Pate Sur Pate Dog's Head Medallion, Dunn, 1883, Lambeth, 6 In. ......... 195.00
Doulton, Vase, Silicon, Applied Decoration, Blue Floral, White Stoneware ................... 75.00
Doulton, Vase, Slip Cast, Winged Beasts On Green, Pope, Lambeth, C.1910, Pair ......... 182.50
Doulton, Vase, Tapestry With Daisylike Floral, Doulton Chine, C.1886, Pair ................ 165.00
Doulton, Vase, White Floral On Brown, Elisa Simmance, C.1905, 11 In. High .............. 200.00
Doulton, Vase, Windsor Castle, Fountain, Shaded Brown, 8 1/2 In.High, Pair ................ 85.00
Doulton, Vase, Woodcut Farm Scene, Brown With Black, Burslem, 6 1/2 In. ................ 70.00
Doulton, Vase, Zigzags, 3 Leaves, Blues & Greens, London, 1883, Lambeth .............. 95.00
Doulton, Wine Cooler, White Grape Garlands & Doves On Blue, 1883, Lambeth ........... 200.00
Dr.Syntax, see Adams, Staffordshire

*Dresden china is any china made in the town of Dresden, Germany. The*
*most famous factory in Dresden is the Meissen factory.*
Dresden, see also Meissen
Dresden, Bowl, Hand Painted Flowers Inside & Out, Gold Trim, Square, C.1895 ............ 58.00
Dresden, Cake Stand, White & Pink Roses, Lacy Edge, 8 In.Diameter ...................... 12.00
Dresden, Compote, Openwork Border & Base, Florals, 6 3/8 In.Diameter .................. 45.00
Dresden, Compote, 4 Floral Medallions On Gold Lattice Edge, 9 In. ........................ 150.00
Dresden, Figurine, Full-Skirted Lady Holding Pug Dog, Dog At Feet ...................... 225.00
Dresden, Figurine, Macaw, Red Porcelain, Green, Blue, Yellow Feathering, Pair ......... 450.00
Dresden, Figurine, Monkey, White, Flowers At Base, Green Apple In Hand ............... 300.00
Dresden, Handle, Cane, Bust Of Fashionable Lady, Green Cap, C.1850, 12 Cm. .......... 225.00
Dresden, Jar & Underplate, Honey, Floral Bouquets On White ........................... 40.00
Dresden, Jar, Cracker, Multicolored Floral, 2 Handled ................................. 35.00
Dresden, Jar, Toilet Water, Floral, Marriage Stopper, Square, 5 In.High ................. 10.00
Dresden, Lamp, Colonial Man & Woman, Handmade Lace Shade, 9 3/4 In., Pair .......... 35.00
Dresden, Planter, 18th Century Figures, 2 Sections, H.Wolfson, C.1845, 8 In. ........... 175.00
Dresden, Plate, Cake, Floral, Scalloped & Pierced Rim, Gilt Trim, C.1850 ................ 32.00
Dresden, Plate, Dessert, Potschappel, Reticulated, Pierced, Floral, C.1890 .............. 37.50
Dresden, Plate, Floral Decoration, 8 1/2 In. ........................................... 15.00
Dresden, Plate, Floral, Openwork Scalloped Border, 8 3/8 In. ........................... 30.00
Dresden, Plate, Medallion, Gold Outlined Pierced Rim, 9 In. ............................ 15.00
Dresden, Plate, R.S.Prussia Melon Boy Scene, American, Scrolled Border ................ 38.00
Dresden, Platter, Hand-Painted Floral, 18 1/2 X 14 1/4 In. ............................. 88.00
Dresden, Platter, Maroon & Turquoise Enamels, Signed, 18 In.Diameter .................. 45.00
Dresden, Platter, Raised Enameled Floral In Burgundy & Turquoise ...................... 39.00
Dresden, Sugar, Covered, Floral, Signed, 4 1/2 In. ..................................... 38.50
Dresden, Sugar, Covered, Floral, Signed, 5 In. ......................................... 36.50
Dresden, Tea Set, Gold Decoration, 3 Piece ............................................ 195.00
Dresden, Tea Set, Villeroy & Boch, 17 Piece ........................................... 95.00
Dresden, Urn, Covered, Helene Wolfsohn Artist, Miniature, C.1860, Pair ................ 120.00
Dresden, Vase, Globular, Applied Flowering Vines, Insect, Serpent, C.1850 .............. 175.00
Dresden, Vase, Three Scenic Panels, 3 Handled, 6 1/2 In.High .......................... 250.00
Duncan & Miller, Butter Pat, No.42, Star Shape ....................................... 9.00
Duncan & Miller, Carafe, Water, No.42 ............................................... 18.00
Duncan & Miller, Tumbler, Juice, No.42, 4 In. ........................................ 12.00
Duncan & Miller, Vase, Opalescent With Pink, 3 Flute Top, 5 In.High .................. 25.00

*Durand glass was made by Victor Durand from 1879 to 1935 at several*
*factories. Most of the iridescent Durand glass was made by Victor*
*Durand, Jr., from 1912 to 1924 at the Durand Art Glass Works in*
*Vineland, New Jersey.*
Durand, Bowl & Underplate, Finger, Cranberry, Swirled Bowl ........................... 65.00
Durand, Bowl, Ovoid, Blue Iridescent, Applied Silver Threading, 6 3/4 In. ............... 250.00
Durand, Compote, Blue, Pulled Blue Vine & Hearts, Amber Stand, 6 1/2 In. .............. 415.00
Durand, Console Set, Pink & White Feather On Cranberry, Amber Base, 3 Piece .......... 725.00
Durand, Cruet, Captain's, Gold Iridescent ............................................. 450.00
Durand, Cup & Saucer, Gold Luster, Pink Highlights ................................... 210.00
Durand, Lamp Base, Iridescent Blue, Threaded, 12 In.High .............................. 200.00
Durand, Lamp Base, Iridescent White Ground, Leafy Vines, 7 X 4 In. .................... 149.00

| | |
|---|---|
| Durand, Lamp Base, King Tut, Green, Gold, & Purple On Orange, Pair | 200.00 |
| Durand, Lamp, Fairy, Pulled & Looped, Green, Pink, White | 295.00 |
| Durand, Lamp, Gold, Threaded, Metal Fittings | 165.00 |
| Durand, Parfait, Feather, Applied Spanish Yellow Foot, Ruby Top & Cut Band | 175.00 |
| Durand, Peacock Blue, White Decorated, Signed, 8 1/2 In.High | 675.00 |
| Durand, Rose Bowl, Blue, Gold Foot, Signed | 425.00 |
| Durand, Rose Bowl, Gold Base, Blue Aurene Colored Top, Footed | 295.00 |
| Durand, Rose Bowl, Green Luster King Tut On Yellow, 4 In.High | 425.00 |
| Durand, Sherbet, Orange Iridescent, Pulled-Up Green Loopings | 210.00 |
| Durand, Teacup & Saucer, Iridescent Orange, Blue, Gold, & Pink Highlights | 300.00 |
| Durand, Vase, Acid-Cut-Back Vines On Matte Blue, 8 3/4 In.High | 825.00 |
| Durand, Vase, Amethyst, Ribbed, Signed Durand In A V, 14 In. | 150.00 |
| Durand, Vase, Apple Green, King Tut, Gold Luster, Flared Rim, 6 In. | 600.00 |
| Durand, Vase, Aurene Blue, Opalescent Coiled Pattern, 4 1/2 In. | 340.00 |
| Durand, Vase, Beehive, Blue, 6 1/2 In.High | 675.00 |
| Durand, Vase, Blue & Gold, C.1900-1925, 12 In.High ............. *Illus* | 1250.00 |
| Durand, Vase, Blue Green Leaf & Vine On Orange Iridescent, 6 3/4 In. | 275.00 |
| Durand, Vase, Blue Iridescent, Coiled Pattern, 5 In.High | 425.00 |
| Durand, Vase, Blue Iridescent, King Tut, 6 1/2 In.High | 575.00 |
| Durand, Vase, Blue, Amber Circular Foot, 7 1/2 In.High | 300.00 |
| Durand, Vase, Crackle, Silver On Green, 7 In. | 485.00 |
| Durand, Vase, Cranberry, White & Pink Feather Design, 10 In.High | 275.00 |
| Durand, Vase, Gold Iridescent, Signed, 5 In.High | 265.00 |
| Durand, Vase, Gold Iridescent, Threaded, Signed, 8 In.High | 450.00 |
| Durand, Vase, Gold Threaded, 6 In.Tall | 200.00 |
| Durand, Vase, Iridescent Amber, C.1900, 8 1/2 In. .......... *Illus* | 350.00 |
| Durand, Vase, Iridescent Butterscotch, Pinched Sides, 8 In. High | 150.00 |
| Durand, Vase, Iridescent, Wide Mouth, Signed, 8 In.High | 395.00 |
| Durand, Vase, Overlay, Ruby Red To Crystal, Floral Decoration, 10 1/2 In. | 150.00 |
| Durand, Vase, White Heart & Clinging Vine On Blue Iridescent, 8 3/4 In. | 550.00 |
| Enamel, Beaker, Russian, Copper, Coronation Of Nicholas II In 1896 | 150.00 |
| Enamel, Beaker, Russian, Gilded Silver, Floral, Kuzmitchev, C.1890, 4 7/8 In. | 1200.00 |
| Enamel, Bowl, Russian, Silver, Plique A Jour, Floral, Artel, C.1900, 5 In. | 6500.00 |
| Enamel, Bowl, Scalloped, Floral On Yellow, Chinese, 3 In.Diameter | 12.50 |
| Enamel, Bowl, Stylized Flowers, Green, Gray, & Black, Faure, C.1925, 10 In. | 350.00 |
| Enamel, Box, Russian, Gold Wash, Artist Signed, Marked 88, 2 3/4 In.Diameter | 775.00 |
| Enamel, Compact, Hand-Painted, Engraved Silver | 65.00 |
| Enamel, Egg, Easter, Gilded Silver, Opens At Center, Floral, Chlebnikov, 1900s | 4200.00 |
| Enamel, Egg, Easter, Russian, Gilded Silver, Opens At Center, Saltykov, C.1900 | 4000.00 |
| Enamel, Eggcup, Russian, Silver, Champleve, Gratchev, C.1890, Set Of 12 | 1300.00 |
| Enamel, Flask, Perfume, Russian, Gilded Silver, Cathedrals, C.1900, 2 3/4 In. | 1100.00 |
| Enamel, Fork & Spoon, Salad, Russian, Wooden, Gilded Silver, C.1850 | 225.00 |
| Enamel, French, Binoculars | 120.00 |
| Enamel, Gorham, Vase, Silver, Blue Floral Banding, Cylindrical, 1931, 10 In. | 425.00 |
| Enamel, Holder, Cigarette, Russian, Ivory Mouthpiece, Silver Gilt | 75.00 |
| Enamel, Kovsh, Russian, Gilded Silver, Champleve, Plique A Jour, Chlebnikov | 1600.00 |

Durand, Vase, Blue & Gold,
C.1900-1925, 12 In.High

Durand, Vase, Iridescent Amber, C.1900, 8 1/2 In.

Enamel, Vase,
Limoges, Faure,
Art Deco, C.1925, 7 In.

Enamel, Vase,
Limoges, Faure, Salmon,
White, Black, C.1925

| | |
|---|---|
| Enamel, Kovsh, Russian, Gilded Silver, Floral & Beads, R Handle, C.1900 | 1000.00 |
| Enamel, Liqueur, Russian, Gilded Silver, Pansies, C.1900, 1 7/8 In. High | 850.00 |
| Enamel, Oriental, Vase, Red, Mother-Of-Pearl Bird Of Paradise, Brass Inside | 37.50 |
| Enamel, Perfume, Viennese, 2 1/2 In. High | 175.00 |
| Enamel, Pillbox, French, Hinged, Art Deco Style, Mirror Insert, Bronze Base | 40.00 |
| Enamel, Plaque, Christ Before Pontius Pilate, French, C.1890, 8 3/4 In. Wide | 250.00 |
| Enamel, Plaque, English, Palladian Buildings, Harbor View, C.1790, 5 1/2 In. | 300.00 |
| Enamel, Salt Dip, French, On Brass, 3 Ball Feet, 2 In. Diameter | 16.00 |
| Enamel, Sofa, Viennese, Miniature, 3 In. Long | 235.00 |
| Enamel, Spoon, Demitasse, Russian, Gilded Silver, Chlebnikov, 1900s, Set Of 12 | 800.00 |
| Enamel, Spoon, Demitasse, Russian, Gilded Silver, Nikolaev, C.1900, Set Of 12 | 1200.00 |
| Enamel, Spoon, Lady's Portrait On Handle, Truier St., Matthiaskirche Bowl | 12.50 |
| Enamel, Spoon, Medicine, Blue & White Dots Around Border | 75.00 |
| Enamel, Spoon, Russian, Gilded Silver, Crane In Pool, Zverev, C.1900 | 750.00 |
| Enamel, Spoon, Russian, Green Over White & Turquoise, Floral, Silver Gilt | 115.00 |
| Enamel, Spoon, Serving, Russian, Gilded Silver, Champleve, Kuzmitchev, C.1890 | 200.00 |
| Enamel, Spoon, Serving, Russian, Gilded Silver, Floral, Birds, Kuzmitchev, 1888 | 475.00 |
| Enamel, Spoon, Serving, Russian, Gilded Silver, Twisted Handle, Artel, C.1900 | 750.00 |
| Enamel, Strainer, Tea, Russian, Gilded Silver, Floral, Scrolls, Artel, C.1900 | 450.00 |
| Enamel, Strainer, Tea, Russian, Gilded Silver, Klingert, C.1900, Pair | 800.00 |
| Enamel, Tea Caddy, Gilded Silver, Champleve, Kuzmitchev, 1886, 6 In. High | 2000.00 |
| Enamel, Tea Caddy, Russian, Gilded Silver, Floral, Scrolls, Kuzmitchev, 1888 | 2900.00 |
| Enamel, Tea Set, Russian, Gilded Silver, Floral, Semenova, C.1900, 3 Piece | 9500.00 |
| Enamel, Tea Set, Yellow Decoration, 14 Piece | 15.00 |
| Enamel, Tray, Russian, Gilded Silver, Handled, Kuzmitchev, C.1890, 8 1/8 In. | 2500.00 |
| Enamel, Tray, Russian, Gilded Silver, Round, Floral, Saltykov, 1895, 8 3/8 In. | 2500.00 |
| Enamel, Vase, F Bienvenu, On Copper, Squat, Red Nude Females, 6 In. | 100.00 |
| Enamel, Vase, Face Of Young Woman, Red Holly Berries, Green Leaves, 4 In. | 165.00 |
| Enamel, Vase, Limoges, Faure, Architectural Pattern, Bulging, C.1925, 6 In. | 1000.00 |
| Enamel, Vase, Limoges, Faure, Art Deco, C.1925, 7 In.      *Illus* | 1300.00 |
| Enamel, Vase, Limoges, Faure, Art Deco, Geometrics, Burgundy, White, & Black | 650.00 |
| Enamel, Vase, Limoges, Faure, Salmon, White, Black, C.1925      *Illus* | 1200.00 |
| Enamel, Vase, Limoges, Sarlandi, Wooded Landscape, 5 Deer, & Gothic Castle | 385.00 |

*End-of-day glass is now an out-of-fashion name for spattered glass. The glass was made of many bits and pieces of colored glass. Traditionally, the glass was made by workmen from the odds and ends left from the glass used during the day. Actually it was a deliberately manufactured product popular about 1880 to 1900, and some of it is still being made.*

| | |
|---|---|
| End-Of-Day, Lampshade, 10 In. Diameter Opening | 125.00 |
| End-Of-Day, Pitcher, White & Blood Red On Blue, 8 1/2 In. High | 50.00 |
| End-Of-Day, Pitcher, Yellow & White, Gold Trim, 5 1/2 In.High | 22.00 |
| End-Of-Day, Vase, Cased, Applied Clear Foot, 6 1/4 In. High | 68.00 |
| End-Of-Day, Vase, Cased, Applied Clear Glass Handles, 12 In. High, Pair | 125.00 |
| End-Of-Day, Vase, Cased, Applied Clear Handle, 12 3/4 In. High, Pair | 125.00 |
| End-Of-Day, Vase, Cased, Yellow, Pink, Green, White, Bulbous Base, 7 1/2 In. | 25.00 |
| End-Of-Day, Vase, Yellow, Red, & Green Streaks On Dark Blue, 8 In.High | 55.00 |

| | |
|---|---:|
| ES Germany, Plate, 11 In. ........................................................ *Illus* | 62.50 |
| ES Germany, Sugar & Creamer, Covered, Portrait, Red, Green, & Gold ................ | 60.00 |
| ES Germany, Sugar & Creamer, Swags Of Pastel Florals, Gold Trim, Hanging .......... | 30.00 |

Etruscan Majolica, see Majolica
Ezra Brooks, see Bottle, Ezra Brooks

*Faberge, Carl Gustavovich, was a goldsmith and jeweler to the Russian
Imperial Court from about 1870 to 1914.*

| | |
|---|---:|
| Faberge, Beaker, Parcel Gilt Silver, Geometrics & Swags, Moscow, 1896 .............. | 450.00 |
| Faberge, Bowl & Ladle, Punch, Silver, To R.J.Barret By Nicholas II, 1909 ........... | 4500.00 |
| Faberge, Bowl, Cut Stellar, Diamond, & Fan, Silver Mounted, C.1900, 8 1/2 In. ...... | 450.00 |
| Faberge, Box, Cigarette, Gold Mounted Gilded Silver, Enamel, Wigstrom, C.1900 ...... | 2100.00 |
| Faberge, Box, Powder, Cut Diamond & Fan, Hinged Silver Lid, C.1900, 5 3/8 In. ...... | 750.00 |
| Faberge, Case, Cigarette, German Silver, Gold, Miniature On Ivory, Zehngraf ........ | 1200.00 |
| Faberge, Case, Cigarette, Gilded Silver, Cobalt Enamel, Afanassiev, C.1900 ......... | 1500.00 |
| Faberge, Case, Cigarette, Gilded Silver, Enamel, Diamond Chips, Wigstrom, 1900 ..... | 1900.00 |
| Faberge, Case, Cigarette, Silver, Repousse Courting Scene, Signed .................. | 850.00 |
| Faberge, Cuff Link, Gold, Monogrammed, Signed Agathon Faberge, Pair ................ | 475.00 |
| Faberge, Cup, Trophy, Silver, Imperial Racing Society Of Moscow, 1909 .............. | 8000.00 |
| Faberge, Figurine, Pig, Agate, C.1900, 1 1/8 In. High ........................ *Illus* | 2100.00 |
| Faberge, Fish Service, Silver, Scallop Ends, C.1900, For 12 ........................ | 1100.00 |
| Faberge, Frame, Picture, Gilded Silver, Green Enamel, Gustav, C.1900 ............... | 3200.00 |
| Faberge, Handle, Cane, Silver, Signed, 4 In. Long ................................. | 500.00 |
| Faberge, Knife, Paper, Nephrite & Red Enamel, Guilloche Ground, C.1900 ............. | 550.00 |
| Faberge, Kovsh, Glazed Pottery, Silver Mounted, Sapphire Inset, Perchin, 1900 ...... | 1800.00 |
| Faberge, Kovsh, Silver, Imperial Eagle, Chased, Ball Feet, Moscow, C.1900 .......... | 4100.00 |
| Faberge, Pad, Desk, Leather, Silver Mounted, Floral Draped Torcheres, C.1900 ....... | 800.00 |
| Faberge, Spoon, Demitasse, Gilded Silver, Enamel, Ruckert ..................... *Illus* | 100.00 |
| Faberge, Spoon, Gilded Silver, Enamel, C.1900 ................................. *Illus* | 1200.00 |
| Faberge, Spoon, Gilded Silver, Enamel, Ruckert, 1900 .......................... *Illus* | 1450.00 |
| Faberge, Spoon, 5 1/4 In.Long ..................................................... | 400.00 |
| Faberge, Tea Caddy, Parcel Gilt Silver, Chinoiserie, Screw On Top, 1893 ............ | 750.00 |
| Faberge, Tray, Silver, Leaf Tips, Beads, 4 Ball Feet, Wakeva, C.1900, 5 5/8 In. .... | 325.00 |
| Faience, Beaker, Alcora, Church, Ruin & Gnarled Trees, C.1740, 3 3/4 In. ........... | 175.00 |
| Faience, Bowl, Barber's, Fauchier Factory, Dancers, Cockerel, C.1750, 15 In. ....... | 1200.00 |
| Faience, Bowl, Barber's, Rouen, Iron & Blue Floral Basket, C.1790, 15 In. .......... | 850.00 |
| Faience, Bowl, French, L'arbre D'amour, Dated 1734, 14 1/4 In. ..................... | 900.00 |
| Faience, Centerpiece, Continental, Basket, 3 Partially Clad Figures, C.1850 ........ | 75.00 |
| Faience, Ewer, Fauchier Factory, Pear Shape, Lovers Scene, C.1750, 8 In. ........... | 1600.00 |
| Faience, Inkstand, Talavera, Recumbent Lion, 2 Apertures, C.1690, 7 7/8 In. ........ | 325.00 |
| Faience, Jug, German, Pewter Mountings, Floral On Yellow, C.1750, 9 1/2 In. ........ | 350.00 |
| Faience, Jug, German, Unicorn & Tree, Pear Shape, C.1750, 7 7/8 In. ................ | 925.00 |
| Faience, Plaque, Castelli, Lady On Horse In Farm Scene, C.1720, 9 3/8 In. .......... | 550.00 |
| Faience, Plate, Castelli, Lady, Cherub, Cartouches, C.1720, 7 In. .................. | 650.00 |
| Faience, Plate, Continental, Fruit Encrusted, 9 1/4 In., Pair ..................... | 275.00 |
| Faience, Plate, French, Scalloped, Yellow Orange Floral, C.1770, 9 In. ............. | 50.00 |
| Faience, Plate, Nove, Fruits & Vegetables, C.1750, 9 1/4 In., Pair ................. | 425.00 |
| Faience, Spice Cellar, Triangular, Yellow Lion Masks, C.1650, 6 In.Long ............ | 125.00 |
| Faience, Tub, Flower, Nevers, Blue & White, Rope Handles, Ship Scene, C.1690 ....... | 325.00 |
| Faience, Tureen, Duck, German, C.1760, 7 In.Long ............................... *Illus* | 7000.00 |
| Faience, Tureen, French, Melon Shape, Twig Handle & Finial, C.1750 ................. | 650.00 |
| Faience, Vase, Milano, Pear Knop, Inverted Pear Shape, Birds, Farm, Pair ........... | 250.00 |

*Fairings are small souvenir china boxes sold at country fairs during the
nineteenth century.*

| | |
|---|---:|
| Fairing, Figurine, White Lamb Lying Down, Staffordshire, 3 1/2 In. ................. | 32.50 |
| Fairing, Pot, Group, "Shall We Sleep First Or What, "c.1850 ........................ | 125.00 |
| Fairing, Turtle Shape Bisque Covered Box With Lady's Head & Extremities ............ | 25.00 |

Famille Rose, see Chinese Export

| | |
|---|---:|
| Fan, Beige Lace, Mother-Of-Pearl Sticks, Gold & Black Carvings .................... | 80.00 |
| Fan, Black Lace, Sequins, Black Lacquered Gold Decorated Sticks .................... | 15.00 |
| Fan, Black Silk Lace, Hand-Painted Roses, Gold, 14 Ebony Sticks .................... | 25.00 |
| Fan, Carved Ivory, Lace, 9 In.Long ................................................ | 28.00 |
| Fan, Carved Ivory, 28 Sticks ...................................................... | 20.00 |
| Fan, Colonial Scene Of Boy Musician, Satin, 16 Ribs ............................... | 35.00 |
| Fan, Ivory Lace, Mother-Of-Pearl Sticks, Openwork, Silk Lined ..................... | 80.00 |
| Fan, Japanese, Lacquer, Color Scenes On Paper ..................................... | 5.00 |

Faberge, Spoon, Gilded Silver,
Enamel, Ruckert, 1900
*(See Page 198)*

Faberge, Spoon,
Demitasse,
Gilded Silver,
Enamel, Ruckert
*(See Page 198)*

Faberge, Spoon,
Gilded Silver, Enamel, C.1900
*(See Page 198)*

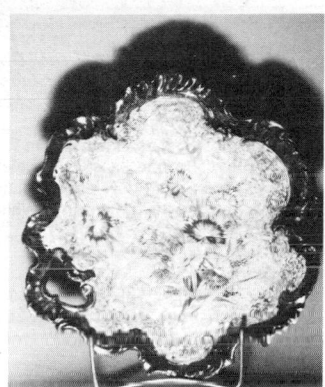

ES  Germany, Plate, 11 In.
*(See Page 198)*

Faberge, Figurine, Pig, Agate, C.1900, 1 1/8 In. High
*(See Page 198)*

Faience, Tureen, Duck, German, C.1760, 7 In.Long
*(See Page 198)*

| | |
|---|---|
| Fan, Lace, Needlepoint, Tortoiseshell Sticks, Doves, Butterflies, & Floral | 65.00 |
| Fan, Philadelphia, 1841 Chestnut Street, Dated 1865, Muslin & Wood | 15.00 |
| Fan, Silk & Mother-Of-Pearl, Hand-Painted Ducks On Water, Duvelleroy, Paris | 47.00 |
| Fan, Twelvetrees, 3 Children Playing Doctor, Product 666 | 6.50 |
| Fan, Wedding, Lace, Mother-Of-Pearl Sticks, Satin Backed, 10 1/2 In.Long | 28.00 |
| Fan, White Ostrich Feather, Folding | 12.00 |

*Fenton Art Glass Company, founded in Martins Ferry, Ohio, by
Frank L.Fenton, is now located in Williamstown, West Virginia. It
is noted for early carnival glass produced between 1907 and 1920. Many other
types of glass were also made.*

| | |
|---|---|
| Fenton, Bowl, Wild Daisy & Lotus, 3 Feet, 9 1/2 In. | 38.00 |
| Fenton, Jar, Candy, Covered, Blue Stretch, 6 Recessed Panels, 10 1/2 In. | 32.00 |
| Fenton, Jar, Candy, Covered, Jade Green, 6 Recessed Panels, 10 1/2 In. | 22.00 |
| Fenton, Vase, Fan Shaped, Mosaic, Yellow, Orange, & Blue, 8 In.High | 125.00 |
| Fenton, Vase, Fan, Mosaic, Yellow, Orange & Blue, White Lining, 8 In.High | 125.00 |
| Fenton, Vase, Fan, White, 4 1/4 In.High | 4.50 |
| Fenton, Vase, Mosaic, Iridescent, 7 In.High | 125.00 |

| | |
|---|---:|
| Fenton, Vase, Ribbed, Blue, Dark Blue Base, 11 In.High, Pair | 25.00 |
| Fiesta Ware, Coffeepot, Aqua | 8.00 |
| Fiesta Ware, Candleholder, Cobalt, Round | 3.00 |
| Fiesta Ware, Tumbler, Cobalt | 4.00 |
| Fiesta Ware, Vase, Bud, Cobalt | 3.00 |
| Fiesta Ware, Vase, Green, Square Bottom, Round Ball Top, 4 In. High | 3.00 |

*Findlay, or onyx, glass was made using three layers of glass. It was manufactured by the Dalzell Gilmore Leighton Company about 1889 in Findlay, Ohio. The silver, ruby, or black pattern was molded into the glass. The glass came in several colors, but was usually white or ruby.*

| | |
|---|---:|
| Findlay Onyx, Muffineer | 250.00 |
| Findlay Onyx, Spooner, Platinum On White, 4 1/4 In. High | 375.00 |
| Findlay Onyx, Spooner, Raspberry Color, 4 In.High | 450.00 |
| Findlay Onyx, Sugar, Covered, Platinum Decoration On White, 5 3/4 In.High | 450.00 |
| Findlay Onyx, Sugar, Platinum On White, 4 3/4 In.High | 475.00 |
| Findlay Onyx, Tumbler, Gothic | 8.50 |
| Fire, Alarm Box, Glass, Chain | 12.50 |
| Fire, Alarm, Faraday | 15.00 |
| Fire, Andiron, Brass, American, Ball Top, Ball Finial, C.1810, Pair, 15 In.High | 275.00 |
| Fire, Andiron, Brass, American, C.1825, Pair *Illus* | 375.00 |
| Fire, Andiron, Brass, Urn Top, Valanced Skirt, Penny Feet, 23 In.High, Pair | 375.00 |
| Fire, Andiron, Brass, 17 In., Pair | 98.00 |
| Fire, Andiron, Cast Iron, Male Bust With Mustache, Dated 1880, Pair | 75.00 |
| Fire, Badge, Fireman's, Captain, West View, Pennsylvania | 15.00 |
| Fire, Bell, Alarm, Double | 7.00 |
| Fire, Bellows, Wooden, Hand-Carved Domed Building | 17.00 |
| Fire, Bellows, Wooden, 18 In. | 12.00 |
| Fire, Bin, Log, Covered, Brass, England, Cast Paw Feet, C.1840, 19 1/2 In.High | 450.00 |
| Fire, Box, Bronze, Ornate | 28.00 |
| Fire, Box, Coal, Iron, Covered | 22.50 |
| Fire, Bucket, Coal, Black Painted Tole, Lion's Paw Feet, C.1825, 19 In.High | 150.00 |
| Fire, Bucket, Coal, Brass, American, Helmet Shape, 18 In. | 148.00 |
| Fire, Bucket, Leather, 'G.W., H.H., ' C.1820 | 85.00 |
| Fire, Bucket, Leather, Painted, Salem, Mass., C.1800, Pair *Illus* | 1000.00 |
| Fire, Bucket, Parmelee No.1, New England, 1800s, Leather | 150.00 |
| Fire, Chenet, Ormolu, C.1775, 15 1/4 In.High, Pair *Illus* | 1200.00 |
| Fire, Chenet, Two Cupids Flanking Column, Ormolu, 1800s, 14 In.High, Pair | 275.00 |
| Fire, Crane, Fireplace, Wrought Iron, 37 X 17 In. | 20.00 |
| Fire, Extinguisher, American Chemical, Lebanon, Pa., Dry Powder, Red | 25.00 |
| Fire, Fender, Brass, English, 44 X 15 In. | 135.00 |
| Fire, Fender, Brass, English, 57 X 12 In. | 135.00 |
| Fire, Fender, Fireplace, Brass, Pierced, Paw Feet, Spark Pan, C.1750, 40 In. | 125.00 |
| Fire, Firedog, Brass, Urn Top, Squared Base, For Basket Or Grate, C.1850, Pair | 65.00 |
| Fire, Furnace, Salesman's Sample | 110.00 |

Fire, Andiron, Brass, American, C.1825, Pair

Fire, Bucket, Leather, Painted,
Salem, Mass., C.1800, Pair

Fire, Chenet, Ormolu, C.1775, 15 1/4 In.High, Pair
*(See Page 200)*

Fire, Horn, Fireman's, Silver,
Chased. C.1850, 20 3/4 In.

| | |
|---|---:|
| Fire, Grate, Cast Iron, 15 X 12 X 21 3/4 In. | 35.00 |
| Fire, Hat, Chief, Red Muslin Type Cloth, Large Size | 2.00 |
| Fire, Hatchet, Nazi German Fireman's, Engraved Ladder, Men, & Helmets | 165.00 |
| Fire, Helmet, Fireman's, Assistant Chief, Red, Leather Shield | 50.00 |
| Fire, Hod, Coal, Brass, Ball Feet, Ring Handles, Floral In Relief, Liner | 75.00 |
| Fire, Hod, Coal, Bug Shape, Decorated, Insert | 125.00 |
| Fire, Hod, Coal, Copper, Covered, Brass Handles & 3 Feet, Round, 16 In.High | 60.00 |
| Fire, Hod, Coal, Covered, Iron, White Enamel, Picture Of Deer | 37.50 |
| Fire, Hod, Coal, English, Walnut, Double Doors, Bottom Drawer With Brass Tray | 170.00 |
| Fire, Holder, Tool, Brass, Pair | 29.50 |
| Fire, Horn, Fireman's, Silver, Chased, C.1850, 20 3/4 In. ......... *Illus* | 500.00 |
| Fire, Lighter, Fireplace, Brass, Cape Cod | 10.00 |
| Fire, Mantel, Fireplace, Inlaid Ash, English, C.1895 | 275.00 |
| Fire, Mantel, Fireplace, Slate, Made To Resemble Marble | 100.00 |
| Fire, Medallion, Fire Insurance, Eagle, INA & 1792, Gold Paint, 11 In. | 75.00 |
| Fire, Nozzle, Brass, United Brass, N.Y., 12 In. Long | 12.00 |
| Fire, Nozzle, Hose, Brass, 12 In.Long | 8.00 |
| Fire, Pike, Fireman's, Hand-Forged | 15.00 |
| Fire, Plate, Stove, Tree, Floral & Hex Sign, Initialed T.M., Pa., 1747 | 750.00 |
| Fire, Pot, Fireplace, Lighter, Brass, 3 Legs, 4 1/2 X 5 In. | 14.00 |
| Fire, Screen, Brass, Fan Shape, 27 X 38 In. | 80.00 |
| Fire, Screen, Brass, Sailing Ship, 15 X 24 In. | 35.00 |
| Fire, Screen, Fireplace, Leather, Mahogany Feet & Frame, Decorated, C.1840 | 89.00 |
| Fire, Screen, Grospoint, Brass Stand, Mahogany Feet, English, C.1850 | 95.00 |
| Fire, Shovel, Fireplace, Brass, Ornamental, 13 In.Long | 46.00 |
| Fire, Shovel, Iron | 1.50 |
| Fire, Stand, Tool, Brass, Flemish, C.1600s | 225.00 |
| Fire, Stove, Box, Ranson & Co., Albany, Patent 1851, Cast Iron, 25 In. Long | 75.00 |
| Fire, Stove, Child's, Embossed Blue Bird, Cast Iron | 8.00 |
| Fire, Stove, Child's, Embossed Queen, Cast Iron | 4.00 |
| Fire, Stove, Franklin, Cast Iron & Brass, Foliage Design, American, C.1825 | 250.00 |
| Fire, Stove, King Heater, Tin, Salesman's Sample, 12 X 10 1/2 X 7 1/2 In. | 40.00 |
| Fire, Stove, Parlor, Cast Iron, Scroll Decoration, Curving Legs, 45 In.High | 160.00 |
| Fire, Tongs & Shovel, Fireplace, Brass Ball Tops, C.1750, 20 In.Long | 20.00 |
| Fire, Tongs, Ember, Brass | 15.00 |
| Fire, Trammel, Fireplace, Wrought Iron, Adjustable, 40 X 68 In. | 28.00 |
| Fire, Trammel, Fireplace, Wrought Iron, 36 In. | 20.00 |
| Fire, Trivet, Fireplace, Shoe Shape Brass Top, Black Iron, & Padded Feet | 55.00 |
| Fire, Trivet, Fireplate, Brass, Pierced Design, Weighted Base, 10 In.High | 48.50 |

*Fireglow glass resembles English Bristol glass. But a reddish-brown
color can be seen when the piece is held to the light. It is a form of art
glass made by the Boston and Sandwich Glass Co.of Massachusetts, and
other companies.*

Fireglow, Ewer, Jack-In-The-Pulpit Top, Applied Shell Handle, Pink Base ............... 85.00
Fireglow, Vase, Blue Flowers & Green Leaves On Tan, Gold, Signed P K .................. 125.00
Fireplace Tools, see Fire, Tongs, etc.

*Fischer porcelain was made in Herend, Hungary. The factory was founded in 1839, and has continued working into the twentieth century. The wares are sometimes referred to as Herend porcelain.*

Fischer, Bowl, Blue & White Reticulated Handles, Enameled Floral, Signed ............... 70.00
Fischer, Bowl, Swirl Shape, Pierced, Budapest .......................................... 55.00
Fischer, Box, Heart Shape, Embossed Rose On Top, Herend ............................... 23.00
Fischer, Can, Sprinkling, Signed Twice ................................................. 145.00
Fischer, Dish, Viking Boat Shape, Pierced .............................................. 45.00
Fischer, Jardiniere, Sprays Of Flowers, C.1880, 13 3/8 In. High, Pair .................. 325.00
Fischer, Urn, Blue & Gold, White Trim, Footed, Marked Herend, 1839-1939, 4 In. ........ 20.00
Fischer, Vase, Pitcher Type, Budapest, 9 In. High ...................................... 125.00
Flash Gordon, Book, Coloring, Whitman, 1952 ........................................... 10.00
Flash Gordon, Necktie, Purple With 3 1/2 In.Picture Of Flash, 1930s ................... 25.00

*Flow blue, or flo blue, was made in England about 1830 to 1900. The plates were printed with designs using a cobalt blue coloring. The color flowed from the design to the white plate so the finished plate had a smeared blue design. The plates were usually made of ironstone china.*

Flow Blue, Biscuit Barrel, Art Nouveau Design, Gold Edging, 8 In.High ................. 65.00
Flow Blue, Bowl, Ayr, W.E.Corn, 8 1/4 In. ............................................. 20.00
Flow Blue, Bowl, Blossom, 10 In. ...................................................... 26.00
Flow Blue, Bowl, Centerpiece, Scinde, Openwork Border & Handles, Alcock, 1840 ......... 175.00
Flow Blue, Bowl, Cereal, Iowa, Royal Staffordshire, 6 1/4 In. ......................... 8.50
Flow Blue, Bowl, Cereal, Marie ........................................................ 9.00
Flow Blue, Bowl, Cereal, Mongolia, Johnson, 6 1/4 In. ................................. 7.50
Flow Blue, Bowl, Cereal, Touraine, Stanley, 6 1/4 In. ................................. 17.50
Flow Blue, Bowl, Cereal, Watteau, Flange Edge, Doulton, 7 1/2 In. ..................... 15.00
Flow Blue, Bowl, Cream Soup, Wentworth ................................................ 22.00
Flow Blue, Bowl, Excelsior, Flanged Edge, Thos.Fell, C.1850, 10 1/2 In. ............... 45.00
Flow Blue, Bowl, Fruit, Celtic, Footed, 12 X 8 1/4 In. ................................ 85.00
Flow Blue, Bowl, Fruit, Melbourne, 11 In. ............................................. 80.00
Flow Blue, Bowl, Grace, 8 1/2 In. ..................................................... 15.00
Flow Blue, Bowl, Hong Kong, Flanged Edge, Chas.Meigh, C.1845, 10 1/4 In. .............. 45.00
Flow Blue, Bowl, Jenny Lind, 7 1/2 In. ................................................ 45.00
Flow Blue, Bowl, Lois, Embossed, Scalloped Rim, New Wharf, 8 In. Diameter ............. 15.00
Flow Blue, Bowl, Lois, Embossed, Scalloped Rim, New Wharf, 9 1/4 In.Diameter .......... 20.00
Flow Blue, Bowl, Meissen, 9 1/2 In. ................................................... 14.50
Flow Blue, Bowl, Serving, Albany, Round, Johnson, 9 1/4 In. ........................... 20.00
Flow Blue, Bowl, Serving, Amoy, Davenport, C.1844, 10 1/2 X 7 3/4 In. ................. 75.00
Flow Blue, Bowl, Serving, Argyle, Grindley, 10 1/4 In. ................................ 30.00
Flow Blue, Bowl, Serving, Bisley, Oval, Grindley, 10 In. .............................. 15.00
Flow Blue, Bowl, Serving, Celtic, 9 1/4 In. Diameter .................................. 22.50
Flow Blue, Bowl, Serving, Celtic, 10 1/2 In.Diameter .................................. 30.00
Flow Blue, Bowl, Serving, Celtic, 11 1/4 X 8 In. ...................................... 25.00
Flow Blue, Bowl, Serving, Conway, Round, New Wharf Pottery, 7 1/4 In. ................. 17.50
Flow Blue, Bowl, Serving, Conway, Round, New Wharf Pottery, 8 1/4 In. ................. 20.00
Flow Blue, Bowl, Serving, Covered, Celtic, 10 In. ..................................... 85.00
Flow Blue, Bowl, Serving, Covered, Celtic, 11 1/2 X 7 3/4 In. ......................... 85.00
Flow Blue, Bowl, Serving, Covered, Clarence, Footed, 10 1/2 In.Diameter ............... 85.00
Flow Blue, Bowl, Serving, Covered, Floral, Meakin, 11 1/2 X 7 1/2 In. ................. 25.00
Flow Blue, Bowl, Serving, Covered, Holland, Johnson, 11 X 8 In. ....................... 75.00
Flow Blue, Bowl, Serving, Covered, Le Pavot, Scalloped Base & Rim ..................... 55.00
Flow Blue, Bowl, Serving, Covered, Lorne, Grindley, 12 X 7 1/2 In. .................... 75.00
Flow Blue, Bowl, Serving, Covered, Melbourne, 10 In.Diameter .......................... 75.00
Flow Blue, Bowl, Serving, Covered, Paris, Stanley, 12 1/2 X 7 3/4 In. ................. 60.00
Flow Blue, Bowl, Serving, Delph, Wood, 10 1/2 In. ..................................... 25.00
Flow Blue, Bowl, Serving, Floral, Round, 10 In. ....................................... 15.00
Flow Blue, Bowl, Serving, Gainsborough, Ridgway, 9 X 6 3/4 In. ........................ 22.50
Flow Blue, Bowl, Serving, Geisha, Upper Hanley, 9 3/4 In. ............................. 30.00
Flow Blue, Bowl, Serving, Iris, Oblong, Royal Staffordshire, 10 1/2 In.Long ........... 20.00
Flow Blue, Bowl, Serving, Lorne, Oblong, 10 X 7 1/2 In. ............................... 17.50
Flow Blue, Bowl, Serving, Melbourne, Handled, 9 In. ................................... 25.00

Flow Blue, Bowl, Serving, Mongolia, Round, Johnson, 8 1/2 In. .................................................. 25.00
Flow Blue, Bowl, Serving, Oregon, Johnson, 9 3/4 In. ............................................................... 30.00
Flow Blue, Bowl, Serving, Osborne, Grindley, 9 In. ................................................................. 30.00
Flow Blue, Bowl, Serving, Pekin, Royal Staffordshire, 9 1/2 In. .............................................. 40.00
Flow Blue, Bowl, Serving, Savoy, Johnson, 9 3/4 X 7 3/4 In. ................................................... 17.00
Flow Blue, Bowl, Serving, Touraine, Oblong, Alcock, 9 X 6 1/4 In. ......................................... 30.00
Flow Blue, Bowl, Serving, Touraine, Oblong, Stanley, 9 X 6 1/4 In. ........................................ 30.00
Flow Blue, Bowl, Serving, Touraine, Oblong, Stanley, 10 X 7 1/4 In. ...................................... 35.00
Flow Blue, Bowl, Serving, Touraine, Stanley, 9 1/4 In. ............................................................ 35.00
Flow Blue, Bowl, Serving, Touraine, 10 In. ............................................................................. 35.00
Flow Blue, Bowl, Soup, Amoy, Flanged Edge, Davenport, C.1844, 8 1/2 In. ............................ 25.00
Flow Blue, Bowl, Soup, Anemone, Flange Edge, 10 1/2 In. ..................................................... 18.50
Flow Blue, Bowl, Soup, Argyle, Flange Edge, Grindley, 9 In. .................................................. 10.00
Flow Blue, Bowl, Soup, Argyle, Grindley, 7 1/2 In. .................................................................. 15.00
Flow Blue, Bowl, Soup, Bexley, Flange Edge, Bisto, 10 1/4 In. ............................................... 15.00
Flow Blue, Bowl, Soup, Cambridge, Flange Edge, New Wharf Pottery, 9 In. ............................ 17.50
Flow Blue, Bowl, Soup, Candia, Cauldon, 8 3/4 In. ................................................................. 10.00
Flow Blue, Bowl, Soup, Celtic, Grindley, 8 In. ........................................................................ 15.00
Flow Blue, Bowl, Soup, Cheswick, Booth, 10 1/2 In. ............................................................... 15.00
Flow Blue, Bowl, Soup, Clarence, Grindley, 8 In. .................................................................... 15.00
Flow Blue, Bowl, Soup, Conway, Flange Edge, New Wharf Pottery, 9 In. ................................ 17.50
Flow Blue, Bowl, Soup, Delamere, Alcock, 7 3/4 In. ............................................................... 10.00
Flow Blue, Bowl, Soup, Glenmore, Grindley, 8 In. .................................................................. 7.00
Flow Blue, Bowl, Soup, Gothic, Flange Edge, Jacob Furnival, C.1850, 9 1/4 In. ..................... 35.00
Flow Blue, Bowl, Soup, Holland, Johnson, 7 1/2 In. ............................................... 5.00 To 15.00
Flow Blue, Bowl, Soup, Hong Kong, 9 1/4 In. .......................................................................... 61.11
Flow Blue, Bowl, Soup, Kyber, 8 In. ....................................................................................... 15.00
Flow Blue, Bowl, Soup, Leicester, Flange Edge, Burgess & Leigh, 10 In. ............................... 15.00
Flow Blue, Bowl, Soup, Lorne, New Wharf Pottery, 7 3/4 In. .................................................. 15.00
Flow Blue, Bowl, Soup, Marguerite, Flange Edge, Grindley, 9 In. ........................................... 10.50
Flow Blue, Bowl, Soup, Montana, Flange Edge, Johnson, 9 In. ............................................... 10.00
Flow Blue, Bowl, Soup, Poppy, Flange Edge, Johnson, 9 In. ................................................... 10.00
Flow Blue, Bowl, Soup, Roseville, Hughes, 9 In. .................................................................... 10.00
Flow Blue, Bowl, Soup, Touraine, Alcock, 7 3/4 In. ................................................................ 16.00
Flow Blue, Bowl, Soup, Touraine, Flange Edge, Alcock, 9 In. ................................................. 16.50
Flow Blue, Bowl, Soup, Touraine, Stanley, 7 3/4 In. ............................................................... 16.00
Flow Blue, Bowl, Soup, Vermont, Flange, Burgess & Leigh, 10 1/2 In. ................................... 12.50
Flow Blue, Bowl, Soup, Watteau, Flange Edge, Doulton, 9 1/2 In. .......................................... 25.00
Flow Blue, Bowl, Vegetable, Argyle, Oval, 9 In. ...................................................................... 19.00
Flow Blue, Bowl, Vegetable, Covered, Chatsworth, Handled, 12 In. ........................................ 32.00
Flow Blue, Bowl, Vegetable, Covered, Clarence, 12 1/2 X 8 In. .............................................. 85.00
Flow Blue, Bowl, Vegetable, Covered, Scinde, 13 In.Long ..................................................... 325.00
Flow Blue, Bowl, Victoria, Wood & Son, 10 In.Diameter ......................................................... 36.00
Flow Blue, Bowl, Waldorf, New Wharf Pottery, 0 In. ............................................................... 00.00
Flow Blue, Bowl, Waste, Conway, New Wharf, 5 1/4 In. .......................................................... 25.00
Flow Blue, Bowl, Watteau, Doulton, 10 X 3 In. ........................................................................ 27.50
Flow Blue, Butter Pat, Avondo, Meakin ................................................................................... 12.00
Flow Blue, Butter Pat, Brooklyn, Johnson Bros. ..................................................................... 10.00
Flow Blue, Butter Pat, Haviland .............................................................................................. 7.50
Flow Blue, Butter Pat, Japan .................................................................................................. 9.00
Flow Blue, Butter Pat, Regalia ............................................................................................... 8.75
Flow Blue, Butter Pat, Touraine, Gold Trim ............................................................................. 15.00
Flow Blue, Butter Pat, Watteau, Doulton ............................................................... 8.50 To 12.50
Flow Blue, Butter Pat, Waverly ............................................................................................... 8.50
Flow Blue, Butter, Covered, Brooklyn, Johnson Bros. ............................................................. 50.00
Flow Blue, Butter, Covered, Celtic, 3 Pieces .......................................................................... 30.00
Flow Blue, Butter, Covered, Clarence, Grindley ...................................................................... 75.00
Flow Blue, Butter, Covered, Devon, Round, Meakin, 10 1/2 In. ............................................... 85.00
Flow Blue, Cake Stand, Cauldon, Octagonal, 9 In. ................................................................. 24.00
Flow Blue, Celery, Argyle, 8 1/2 In. ....................................................................................... 16.00
Flow Blue, Celery, Celtic, 9 X 5 In. ........................................................................................ 17.50
Flow Blue, Celery, Clarence, 8 3/4 X 5 1/4 In. ....................................................................... 12.50
Flow Blue, Celery, Iris, 8 1/2 X 5 In. ...................................................................................... 17.50
Flow Blue, Celery, La Belle, 13 In. Long, 2 In. Deep .............................................................. 65.00
Flow Blue, Compote, Balmoral, Footed, J.& C.Meakin, 4 1/2 In.High ...................................... 47.50
Flow Blue, Creamer, Celtic .................................................................................................... 75.00

Flow Blue, Creamer, Dahlia, 8 Sided ............................................................ 75.00
Flow Blue, Creamer, Dyber, Mulberry, 5 In.High ............................................. 38.00
Flow Blue, Creamer, Idris, Grindley .............................................................. 25.00
Flow Blue, Creamer, Iris, Royal Staffordshire ............................................... 65.00
Flow Blue, Creamer, LePavot, Grindley .......................................................... 25.00
Flow Blue, Creamer, Lorne ............................................................................. 75.00
Flow Blue, Creamer, Lugano, Ridgway ........................................................... 50.00
Flow Blue, Creamer, Melbourne, Grindley ...................................................... 75.00
Flow Blue, Creamer, Portman, Grindley, 4 1/2 In. .......................................... 75.00
Flow Blue, Creamer, Touraine ....................................................................... 50.00
Flow Blue, Creamer, Turin, Gold Trim, Johnson ............................................. 25.00
Flow Blue, Creamer, Waldorf, New Wharf Pottery .......................................... 75.00
Flow Blue, Cup & Saucer, Amoy, Handleless Cup, Davenport, C.1844 ............ 60.00
Flow Blue, Cup & Saucer, Ashburton ............................................................. 22.50
Flow Blue, Cup & Saucer, Brooklyn, Johnson Bros. ....................................... 25.00
Flow Blue, Cup & Saucer, Clarence, Grindley ................................................ 25.00
Flow Blue, Cup & Saucer, Demitasse, Floral, Footed Cup .............................. 25.00
Flow Blue, Cup & Saucer, Demitasse, Watteau, Doulton ................................ 20.00
Flow Blue, Cup & Saucer, Florida, Johnson ................................................... 25.00
Flow Blue, Cup & Saucer, Haddon, Grindley .................................................. 25.00
Flow Blue, Cup & Saucer, Handleless, Rust & Green Enamels On Copper Luster ...... 48.00
Flow Blue, Cup & Saucer, Handleless, Sprays Of Fernlike Leaves .................. 47.50
Flow Blue, Cup & Saucer, Hindustan, Handleless, Maddocks, C.1855 ........ 35.00 To 50.00
Flow Blue, Cup & Saucer, Iris, Royal Staffordshire ....................................... 27.50
Flow Blue, Cup & Saucer, Lancaster, New Wharf .......................................... 25.00
Flow Blue, Cup & Saucer, Lorne, Grindley ..................................................... 25.00
Flow Blue, Cup & Saucer, Luneville, K.G.France ........................................... 35.00
Flow Blue, Cup & Saucer, Manilla, Handleless ............................................... 22.00
Flow Blue, Cup & Saucer, Navy, Till & Son .................................................... 20.00
Flow Blue, Cup & Saucer, Nelson .................................................................. 25.00
Flow Blue, Cup & Saucer, Oregon, Johnson ................................................... 25.00
Flow Blue, Cup & Saucer, Palermo, Handleless Cup, Clementson, C.1840 ...... 35.00
Flow Blue, Cup & Saucer, Roseville, Hughes ................................................. 25.00
Flow Blue, Cup & Saucer, Scinde, Alcock ...................................................... 53.00
Flow Blue, Cup & Saucer, Touraine, Alcock & Stanley ................................... 30.00
Flow Blue, Cup & Saucer, Touraine, Stanley .................................................. 30.00
Flow Blue, Cup Plate, Amoy ........................................................................... 38.00
Flow Blue, Cup Plate, Oriental Castle & Garden Scene, Scalloped, Embossed ...... 20.00
Flow Blue, Cup, Celtic .................................................................................... 20.00
Flow Blue, Cup, Oregon .................................................................................. 7.50
Flow Blue, Dish, Bone, Crescent ................................................................... 17.00
Flow Blue, Dish, Bone, Globe Mark, England ................................................ 10.00
Flow Blue, Dish, Bone, Nonpareil ................................................................... 9.50
Flow Blue, Dish, Bone, Regal ........................................................................ 18.75
Flow Blue, Dish, Bone, Touraine, Gold Trim ................................................. 17.50
Flow Blue, Dish, Honey, California, Wedgwood, C.1849 ................................ 17.50
Flow Blue, Dish, Honey, Nonpareil, Burgess & Leigh .................................... 12.00
Flow Blue, Dish, Honey, Troy, Charles Meigh, C.1840 .................................. 17.50
Flow Blue, Gravy Boat & Underplate, Brooklyn, Johnson Bros. ..................... 50.00
Flow Blue, Gravy Boat & Underplate, Crumlin, Footed .................................. 42.50
Flow Blue, Gravy Boat & Underplate, Lily, Adams ......................................... 38.00
Flow Blue, Gravy Boat & Underplate, Scinde, Alcock, 1840 .......................... 75.00
Flow Blue, Gravy Boat & Underplate, Tokyo, Johnson ................................... 25.00
Flow Blue, Gravy Boat, Celtic ........................................................................ 20.00
Flow Blue, Gravy Boat, Drip Dish, Gironde .................................................... 45.00
Flow Blue, Gravy Boat, Iris, Royal Staffordshire ........................................... 25.00
Flow Blue, Gravy Boat, Kelvin, Meakin .......................................................... 20.00
Flow Blue, Gravy Boat, Kenworth, Johnson Bros. .......................................... 45.00
Flow Blue, Gravy Boat, Lorne ............................................................. 17.00 To 30.00
Flow Blue, Gravy Boat, Melbourne ...................................................... 22.50 To 25.00
Flow Blue, Gravy Boat, Nonpareil ....................................................... 17.00 To 45.00
Flow Blue, Gravy Boat, Paris, Stanley ............................................................ 17.50
Flow Blue, Gravy Boat, Portman, Grindley ..................................................... 15.00
Flow Blue, Gravy Boat, Roseville, Hughes ..................................................... 25.00
Flow Blue, Jardiniere, Floral, Gold Trim, 9 X 10 In. ...................................... 35.00
Flow Blue, Mug, Singa, Large Size ................................................................. 52.00

| | |
|---|---|
| Flow Blue, Pitcher, Milk, Celtic, 6 3/4 In.High | 85.00 |
| Flow Blue, Pitcher, Milk, Geisha, Upper Hanley, 6 3/4 In.High | 75.00 |
| Flow Blue, Pitcher, Milk, Hindustan, Maddocks, C.1855, 5 1/2 In. | 85.00 |
| Flow Blue, Pitcher, Milk, Jewel, Johnson, 5 3/4 In.High | 75.00 |
| Flow Blue, Pitcher, Milk, Manhattan, Alcock, 6 1/4 In.High | 75.00 |
| Flow Blue, Pitcher, Milk, Portman, Grindley, 5 1/4 In. | 85.00 |
| Flow Blue, Pitcher, Milk, Shell, E.Challinor, C.1860, 6 3/4 In. | 100.00 |
| Flow Blue, Pitcher, Milk, Touraine, 1/2 Gallon | 150.00 |
| Flow Blue, Pitcher, Milk, Touraine, 6 In. | 85.00 |
| Flow Blue, Pitcher, Removable Pewter Lid, Porcelain Knob, Sylva F.& Sons | 75.00 |
| Flow Blue, Pitcher, Scinde, Bulbous, 6 Sided, 2 1/2 Quart | 125.00 |
| Flow Blue, Pitcher, Vinranka, Applied Handle, A.A.A.Gefle, Sweden | 75.00 |
| Flow Blue, Pitcher, Water, Touraine, Scalloped Rim & Base, Fluted, 2 Quart | 75.00 |
| Flow Blue, Plaque, Babes In The Woods, Will-Of-The-Wisp, Oval, Doulton | 125.00 |
| Flow Blue, Plate, Albany, 9 In. | 19.50 |
| Flow Blue, Plate, Amoy, Davenport, C.1844, 7 1/2 In. | 20.00 |
| Flow Blue, Plate, Amoy, Davenport, C.1844, 8 1/2 In. | 30.00 |
| Flow Blue, Plate, Amoy, Davenport, Incised 1844, 10 5/8 In. | 50.00 |
| Flow Blue, Plate, Arabesque, T.J.& J.Mayer, C.1855, 9 3/4 In. | 40.00 |
| Flow Blue, Plate, Argyle, Ford & Sons, 9 3/4 In. | 10.00 |
| Flow Blue, Plate, Argyle, Grindley, 8 3/4 In. | 17.50 |
| Flow Blue, Plate, Argyle, Johnson, 8 3/4 In. | 15.00 |
| Flow Blue, Plate, Asiatic Pheasants, Hughes, 8 3/4 In. | 17.50 |
| Flow Blue, Plate, Avondo, Meakin, 7 In. | 10.00 |
| Flow Blue, Plate, Avondo, Meakin, 8 In. | 10.00 |
| Flow Blue, Plate, Avondo, Meakin, 9 In. | 15.00 |
| Flow Blue, Plate, Beaufort, Grindley, 6 3/4 In. | 7.50 |
| Flow Blue, Plate, Beaufort, Grindley, 8 3/4 In. | 12.00 |
| Flow Blue, Plate, Beauties Of China, Mellor Venables, C.1845, 7 1/2 In. | 20.00 |
| Flow Blue, Plate, Beauties Of China, Mellor Venables, C.1845, 8 1/2 In. | 30.00 |
| Flow Blue, Plate, Bentick, Cauldon, 10 In. | 15.00 To 25.00 |
| Flow Blue, Plate, Blossom, 10 1/2 In. | 25.00 |
| Flow Blue, Plate, Blue Danube, 9 In. | 20.00 |
| Flow Blue, Plate, Blue Danube, 10 In. | 25.00 |
| Flow Blue, Plate, Brooklyn, Johnson Bros., 7 In. | 10.00 |
| Flow Blue, Plate, Brooklyn, Johnson Bros., 9 In. | 15.00 |
| Flow Blue, Plate, Brooklyn, 9 In. | 18.00 |
| Flow Blue, Plate, Cake, Touraine, 9 In. | 35.00 |
| Flow Blue, Plate, California, Wedgwood, Dated 1849, 8 In. | 20.00 |
| Flow Blue, Plate, Cambridge, New Wharf Pottery, 8 3/4 In. | 15.00 |
| Flow Blue, Plate, Canterbury, 10 1/4 In. | 12.00 |
| Flow Blue, Plate, Carolina, Mulberry, Hall, 6 In. | 20.00 |
| Flow Blue, Plate, Cecil, Teal & Sons, 9 In. | 25.00 |
| Flow Blue, Plate, Celtic, Grindley, 8 In. | 10.00 |
| Flow Blue, Plate, Celtic, Grindley, 9 3/4 In. | 17.50 |
| Flow Blue, Plate, Chapoo, Wedgwood, C.1850, 7 1/2 In. | 20.00 |
| Flow Blue, Plate, Chapoo, Wedgwood, Ironstone, 10 1/2 In. | 45.00 |
| Flow Blue, Plate, Chatsworth, 10 1/4 In. | 18.00 |
| Flow Blue, Plate, Chen Si, John Meir, C.1835, 7 1/2 In. | 20.00 |
| Flow Blue, Plate, Chen Si, Maddock, C.1855, 10 3/4 In. | 45.00 |
| Flow Blue, Plate, Chinese, T.Dimmock, R.C., 6 3/4 In. | 12.00 |
| Flow Blue, Plate, Chinese, 7 1/8 In. | 16.00 |
| Flow Blue, Plate, Chusan, Thos.Fell, C.1850, 8 1/2 In. | 30.00 |
| Flow Blue, Plate, Chusan, Wedgwood, Incised 1882, 10 1/2 In. | 40.00 |
| Flow Blue, Plate, Clarence, Grindley, 8 In. | 12.00 |
| Flow Blue, Plate, Clarence, Grindley, 8 3/4 In. | 15.00 |
| Flow Blue, Plate, Colonial, 10 In. | 25.00 |
| Flow Blue, Plate, Conway, New Wharf Pottery, 9 3/4 In. | 20.00 |
| Flow Blue, Plate, Conway, 9 In. | 27.50 |
| Flow Blue, Plate, Crumlin, 9 In. | 15.00 |
| Flow Blue, Plate, Crystal Palace, Rural Scene Border, T.Goodwin, 10 1/2 In. | 40.00 |
| Flow Blue, Plate, Cyprus, Davenport, Dated 1848, 7 1/4 In. | 20.00 |
| Flow Blue, Plate, Delft, 8 3/4 In. | 22.00 |
| Flow Blue, Plate, Duchess, 8 In. | 7.00 |
| Flow Blue, Plate, Ebor, Ridgway, 8 3/4 In. | 12.50 |
| Flow Blue, Plate, Fairy Villas, 9 In. | 25.00 |

Flow Blue, Plate, Fifteen States, Martha Washington, 6 In. ....................................................................... 8.00
Flow Blue, Plate, Floral Center, Beaded, Gold Tracery Of Floral, 5 1/2 In. .................................. 12.00
Flow Blue, Plate, Florida, Johnson, 8 3/4 In. ............................................................................ 15.00
Flow Blue, Plate, Formosa, Bourne & Son, C.1845, 10 1/4 In. ..................................................... 45.00
Flow Blue, Plate, Formosa, 7 1/2 In. .......................................................................................... 30.00
Flow Blue, Plate, Gothic, Jacob Furnival, C.1850, 10 1/2 In. ...................................................... 45.00
Flow Blue, Plate, Haddon, Grindley, 8 3/4 In. ........................................................................ 12.00
Flow Blue, Plate, Haddon, Johnson, 8 In. ................................................................................ 11.00
Flow Blue, Plate, Haddon, 9 In. ................................................................................................ 20.00
Flow Blue, Plate, Haddon, 10 In. .............................................................................................. 25.00
Flow Blue, Plate, Harwood, 9 In. .............................................................................................. 18.00
Flow Blue, Plate, Hindustan, Maddock, C.1855, 9 3/4 In. ........................................................... 40.00
Flow Blue, Plate, Holland, Johnson, 9 3/4 In. ........................................................................... 20.00
Flow Blue, Plate, Hong Kong, 14 Sided, Chas.Meigh, 10 1/2 In. ............................................... 45.00
Flow Blue, Plate, Hunter, Dogs, & Fallen Deer, Royal Doulton, 10 1/2 In. ............................... 32.25
Flow Blue, Plate, Indian Jar, Furnival, C.1843, 8 1/2 In. ........................................................... 30.00
Flow Blue, Plate, Indian, F.& R.Pratt, C.1840, 9 1/2 In. ............................................................ 40.00
Flow Blue, Plate, Indian, F.& R.Pratt, C.1840, 10 3/4 In. ........................................................... 45.00
Flow Blue, Plate, Iris, Royal Staffordshire, 7 In. ...................................................................... 12.00
Flow Blue, Plate, Iris, Royal Staffordshire, 8 In. ...................................................................... 13.00
Flow Blue, Plate, Iris, Royal Staffordshire, 9 3/4 In. ................................................................ 17.50
Flow Blue, Plate, Italia, W In Diamond Mark, 8 1/2 In. ............................................................. 18.00
Flow Blue, Plate, Italian Scenery, Gold Border, 9 1/2 In. ......................................................... 24.50
Flow Blue, Plate, Japan, Incised, Thomas Fell & Co., C.1860, 9 1/4 In. ................................... 40.00
Flow Blue, Plate, Japan, 9 In. .................................................................................................. 37.00
Flow Blue, Plate, Jewel, Johnson, 6 1/2 In. .............................................................................. 7.50
Flow Blue, Plate, Jewel, Johnson, 8 3/4 In. .............................................................................. 15.00
Flow Blue, Plate, Kaolin, Podmore & Walker, C.1845, 7 3/4 In. ................................................ 20.00
Flow Blue, Plate, Kaolin, Podmore & Walker, C.1845, 9 3/4 In. ................................................ 40.00
Flow Blue, Plate, Kelvin, Meakin, 8 3/4 In. .............................................................................. 15.00
Flow Blue, Plate, Kyber, 6 1/4 In. ............................................................................................. 19.00
Flow Blue, Plate, Kyber, 9 In. .................................................................................................. 29.00
Flow Blue, Plate, Kyber, 10 In. .................................................................... 18.00 To 22.00
Flow Blue, Plate, Ladas, 9 In. .................................................................................................. 20.00
Flow Blue, Plate, Lancaster, New Wharf Pottery, 8 3/4 In. ....................................................... 15.00
Flow Blue, Plate, Le Pavot, 8 In. .............................................................................................. 9.00
Flow Blue, Plate, Le Pavot, 9 In. .............................................................................................. 15.00
Flow Blue, Plate, Leicester, Burgess & Leigh, 8 3/4 In. ........................................................... 12.00
Flow Blue, Plate, Leicester, Maddox, 9 3/4 In. ......................................................................... 15.00
Flow Blue, Plate, Lois, 8 In. ..................................................................................................... 10.00
Flow Blue, Plate, Lonsdale, 10 In. ............................................................................................ 25.00
Flow Blue, Plate, Loretta, Mulberry, Sam Alcock, Hill Pottery, 7 In. ....................................... 10.00
Flow Blue, Plate, Lorne, Grindley, 8 3/4 In. ............................................................................. 15.00
Flow Blue, Plate, Lorne, Grindley, 9 3/4 In. ............................................................................. 17.50
Flow Blue, Plate, Lorne, New Wharf Pottery, 6 1/2 In. ............................................................. 10.00
Flow Blue, Plate, Lorne, New Wharf Pottery, 8 In. ................................................................... 12.00
Flow Blue, Plate, Madras, Doulton, 7 1/2 In. ........................................................................... 15.00
Flow Blue, Plate, Madras, Doulton, 7 3/4 In. ........................................................................... 18.00
Flow Blue, Plate, Madras, Doulton, 9 3/4 In. ........................................................................... 25.00
Flow Blue, Plate, Madras, Impressed Circle Mark, Doulton, C.1891, 9 1/2 In. ........................ 19.50
Flow Blue, Plate, Manilla, Podmore & Walker, C.1845, 9 3/4 In. ............................................. 40.00
Flow Blue, Plate, Marguerite, 10 In. ......................................................................................... 12.50
Flow Blue, Plate, Marie, Grindley, 8 In. ................................................................................... 11.00
Flow Blue, Plate, Martha Washington ...................................................................................... 18.00
Flow Blue, Plate, Martha Washington States, Advertising On Back ......................................... 45.00
Flow Blue, Plate, Melbourne, Grindley, 8 In. ........................................................................... 16.00
Flow Blue, Plate, Melbourne, Grindley, 8 3/4 In. ..................................................................... 17.50
Flow Blue, Plate, Melbourne, Grindley, 9 3/4 In. ..................................................................... 25.00
Flow Blue, Plate, Melbourne, 8 In. ........................................................................................... 10.00
Flow Blue, Plate, Melrose, 9 1/4 In. .......................................................................................... 15.00
Flow Blue, Plate, Mongolia, 9 In. ............................................................................................. 20.00
Flow Blue, Plate, Mongolia, 10 In. ............................................................................................ 25.00
Flow Blue, Plate, Montana, Johnson, 8 In. ............................................................................... 10.00
Flow Blue, Plate, Montana, Johnson Bros., 9 3/4 In. ................................................................ 12.50
Flow Blue, Plate, Moorish Palace, 9 1/2 In. .............................................................................. 24.00
Flow Blue, Plate, Nelson, 9 In. ................................................................................................. 22.00

Flow Blue, Plate, Ning Po, R.Hall, C.1845, 7 1/2 In. ......................................... 20.00
Flow Blue, Plate, Nonpareil, Burgess & Leigh, 10 In. ........................................ 22.50
Flow Blue, Plate, Nonpareil, Burleigh & Leigh, 7 1/2 In. .................................... 15.00
Flow Blue, Plate, Normandy, Johnson, 8 3/4 In. .............................................. 15.00
Flow Blue, Plate, Oregon, Johnson, 8 3/4 In. ........................................ 6.00 To 12.50
Flow Blue, Plate, Oregon, T.J.& J.Mayer, C.1845, 9 3/4 In. .............................. 40.00
Flow Blue, Plate, Ormonde, Meakin, 9 3/4 In. ................................................ 15.00
Flow Blue, Plate, Ormonde, 9 In. ................................................................... 20.00
Flow Blue, Plate, Osborne, Brindley, 8 3/4 In. ............................................... 15.00
Flow Blue, Plate, Osborne, Ridgway, 8 In. ..................................................... 11.00
Flow Blue, Plate, Osborne, Ridgway, 9 5/8 In. ............................................... 13.50
Flow Blue, Plate, Palermo, Clementson, C.1840, 7 1/2 In. ............................... 12.50
Flow Blue, Plate, Palermo, Clementson, C.1840, 8 1/2 In. ............................... 20.00
Flow Blue, Plate, Palermo, Clementson, C.1840, 9 3/4 In. ............................... 30.00
Flow Blue, Plate, Paris, New Wharf Pottery, 8 3/4 In. ....................................... 5.00
Flow Blue, Plate, Peach Royal, Johnson Bros., 7 In. ....................................... 10.00
Flow Blue, Plate, Peach Royal, Johnson Bros., 8 1/2 In. ................................. 12.50
Flow Blue, Plate, Peach Royal, Johnson Bros., 10 In. ..................................... 16.00
Flow Blue, Plate, Pekin, 9 In. ...................................................................... 20.00
Flow Blue, Plate, Pelew, E.Challinor, C.1840, 9 3/4 In. ................................... 40.00
Flow Blue, Plate, Persian, 9 In. ................................................................... 20.00
Flow Blue, Plate, Poppy, Grindley, 8 In. ........................................................ 8.00
Flow Blue, Plate, Portman, Grindley, 8 3/4 In. ............................................... 15.00
Flow Blue, Plate, Progress, 8 In. .................................................................. 10.00
Flow Blue, Plate, Progress, 9 In. .................................................................. 24.00
Flow Blue, Plate, Raleigh, 10 In. .................................................................. 18.00
Flow Blue, Plate, Rhone, Mulberry, T.J.& J.Mayer, 8 3/4 In. ............................ 10.00
Flow Blue, Plate, Rock, Challinor, C.1850, 9 3/4 In. ....................................... 40.00
Flow Blue, Plate, Roseville, Hughes, 8 3/4 In. ............................................... 10.00
Flow Blue, Plate, Roseville, Hughes, 9 3/4 In. ............................................... 12.50
Flow Blue, Plate, Roseville, 9 In. .................................................................. 20.00
Flow Blue, Plate, Savoy, Johnson Bros., 8 2/3 In. .......................................... 20.00
Flow Blue, Plate, Scinde, Alcock, C.1840, 8 1/2 In. ....................................... 30.00
Flow Blue, Plate, Scinde, Alcock, C.1840, 9 1/4 In. ....................................... 40.00
Flow Blue, Plate, Scinde, J.& G.Alcock, C.1840, 10 1/4 In. ............................. 50.00
Flow Blue, Plate, Scinde, 6 1/2 In. ............................................................... 48.00
Flow Blue, Plate, Scinde, 7 1/2 In. ............................................................... 30.00
Flow Blue, Plate, Scinde, 9 1/2 In. ............................................................... 18.00
Flow Blue, Plate, Shanghai, J.Furnival & Co., C.1860, 7 1/4 In. ....................... 20.00
Flow Blue, Plate, Shanghai, 7 In. ................................................................. 15.00
Flow Blue, Plate, Shanghai, 10 In. ............................................................... 18.75
Flow Blue, Plate, Shell, E.Challinor, C.1860, 9 1/2 In. .................................... 40.00
Flow Blue, Plate, Soup, Cashmere, Morley & Co., 9 3/8 In. ............................. 30.00
Flow Blue, Plate, Soup, Delmar, Grindley, 9 In. ............................................. 10.60
Flow Blue, Plate, Soup, Florentine Villas, Light Blue ....................................... 7.50
Flow Blue, Plate, Soup, Kyber ..................................................................... 20.00
Flow Blue, Plate, Soup, Madras, Doulton, Burslem, 8 1/2 In. .......................... 18.50
Flow Blue, Plate, Soup, Marguerite .............................................................. 14.00
Flow Blue, Plate, Soup, Marie ..................................................................... 12.00
Flow Blue, Plate, Soup, Melrose, Doulton ..................................................... 15.00
Flow Blue, Plate, Soup, Touraine, Alcock ...................................................... 15.00
Flow Blue, Plate, Soup, Watteau, 9 In. .......................................................... 14.00
Flow Blue, Plate, Souvenir Of Niagara Falls, Rolled Edge, R.& M., 9 3/4 In. ..... 25.00
Flow Blue, Plate, Spinach, Prussian, 10 In. ................................................... 35.00
Flow Blue, Plate, Summertime, 8 3/4 In. ....................................................... 9.00
Flow Blue, Plate, Sutherland Border, Charles Meigh, C.1851, 9 1/4 In. ............. 20.00
Flow Blue, Plate, Sutherland Border, Charles Meigh, C.1851, 10 1/2 In. ........... 30.00
Flow Blue, Plate, Temple, Pearlstone Ware, Podmore & Walker, 9 3/4 In. ......... 40.00
Flow Blue, Plate, Temple, Podmore Walker & Co., C.1850, 8 In. ...................... 20.00
Flow Blue, Plate, Toga, F.Winkle, 9 3/4 In. .................................................... 26.00
Flow Blue, Plate, Togo, 8 3/4 In. .................................................................. 16.50
Flow Blue, Plate, Togo, 9 3/4 In. .................................................................. 19.00
Flow Blue, Plate, Tonquin, J.H., 8 1/2 In. ...................................................... 35.00
Flow Blue, Plate, Tonquin, W.Adams & Sons, C.1845, 9 3/4 In. ....................... 40.00
Flow Blue, Plate, Touraine, Alcock, 8 3/4 In. .................................................. 17.50
Flow Blue, Plate, Touraine, Alcock, 9 3/4 In. .................................................. 27.50

Flow Blue, Plate, Touraine, Gold Trim, 7 3/4 In. ........................ 16.00
Flow Blue, Plate, Touraine, Gold Trim, 10 In. ........................ 22.00
Flow Blue, Plate, Touraine, Stanley, 8 3/4 In. ........................ 17.50
Flow Blue, Plate, Touraine, Stanley, 9 3/4 In. ........................ 27.50
Flow Blue, Plate, Touraine, 8 1/4 In. ........................ 11.00
Flow Blue, Plate, Tulip, Copeland, C.1850, 10 1/2 In. ........................ 35.00
Flow Blue, Plate, Tulip, 9 3/4 In. ........................ 18.00
Flow Blue, Plate, Turkey, Ridgway, 9 3/4 In. ........................ 30.00
Flow Blue, Plate, Vermont, Burgess & Leigh, 8 In. ........................ 8.00
Flow Blue, Plate, Vermont, New Wharf Pottery, 9 3/4 In. ........................ 15.00
Flow Blue, Plate, Vermont, 10 In. ........................ 20.00
Flow Blue, Plate, Waldorf, New Wharf Pottery, 9 3/4 In. ........................ 27.50
Flow Blue, Plate, Waldorf, 9 In. ........................ 16.50
Flow Blue, Plate, Watteau, 5 1/2 In. ........................ 12.00
Flow Blue, Plate, Waverly, John Maddock & Sons, England, 1896, 8 In. ........................ 12.00
Flow Blue, Plate, Waverly, John Maddock & Sons, 1896, 8 In. ........................ 10.00
Flow Blue, Plate, Windmill Scene, Gold Scalloped Seashell Edge, 9 In. ........................ 27.50
Flow Blue, Plate, 2 Couples On A Picnic, Royal Doulton, 10 1/2 In. ........................ 32.25
Flow Blue, Platter, Alaska, Grindley, 16 1/4 X 11 3/4 In. ........................ 30.00
Flow Blue, Platter, Amoy, Davenport, Incised 1844, 18 X 14 In. ........................ 150.00
Flow Blue, Platter, Anemone, 14 1/2 X 10 1/2 In. ........................ 17.00
Flow Blue, Platter, Argyle, 8 1/2 X 12 1/2 In. ........................ 45.00
Flow Blue, Platter, Argyle, 13 X 17 1/2 In. ........................ 30.00
Flow Blue, Platter, Astoria, 11 X 14 In. ........................ 45.00
Flow Blue, Platter, Ayr, 10 1/2 In. ........................ 24.00
Flow Blue, Platter, Bamboo, 15 1/4 In.Long ........................ 100.00
Flow Blue, Platter, Berkly, 13 3/4 X 10 1/2 In. ........................ 24.50
Flow Blue, Platter, Brooklyn, Johnson Bros., 14 1/3 X 10 In. ........................ 45.00
Flow Blue, Platter, Brooklyn, 14 3/4 X 9 3/4 In. ........................ 60.00
Flow Blue, Platter, Cake, Le Pavot, Self Handled ........................ 20.00
Flow Blue, Platter, Cashmere, 15 In.Long ........................ 135.00
Flow Blue, Platter, Celtic, Grindley, 10 3/4 X 15 1/2 In. ........................ 30.00
Flow Blue, Platter, Chatsworth, Oval, 16 X 12 3/4 In. ........................ 38.00
Flow Blue, Platter, Chatsworth, Oval, 18 X 14 1/2 In. ........................ 48.00
Flow Blue, Platter, Conway, 8 X 10 1/2 In. ........................ 25.00
Flow Blue, Platter, Duchess, Grindley, 16 X 11 1/4 In. ........................ 27.50
Flow Blue, Platter, Fish, La Francais, Trout, 15 3/4 In. ........................ 55.00
Flow Blue, Platter, Grace, 12 1/2 In. ........................ 25.00
Flow Blue, Platter, Haddon, 10 X 14 In. ........................ 50.00
Flow Blue, Platter, Historical, Ironstone, 20 1/2 X 16 In. ........................ 108.00
Flow Blue, Platter, Indian, F.& R.Pratt, C.1840, 15 1/2 X 11 3/4 In. ........................ 100.00
Flow Blue, Platter, Iris, Royal Staffordshire, 12 3/4 X 9 In. ........................ 27.50
Flow Blue, Platter, Iris, Royal Staffordshire, 16 3/8 X 1.1 3/4 In. ........................ 50.00
Flow Blue, Platter, Janeite, 15 In.Long ........................ 55.00
Flow Blue, Platter, Kelvin, Meakin, 18 1/4 X 12 1/2 In. ........................ 45.00
Flow Blue, Platter, Keswick, Deep, Wood & Son, 12 X 9 In. ........................ 16.50
Flow Blue, Platter, Kyber, Adams, 15 X 11 1/4 In. ........................ 85.00
Flow Blue, Platter, Kyber, 10 X 7 In. ........................ 30.00
Flow Blue, Platter, Lodos, Floral Border, 19 1/2 X 14 1/2 In. ........................ 65.00
Flow Blue, Platter, Lonsdale, 14 X 18 In. ........................ 60.00
Flow Blue, Platter, Lorne, Grindley, 10 X 7 1/2 In. ........................ 20.00
Flow Blue, Platter, Lorne, Grindley, 12 X 8 1/2 In. ........................ 25.00
Flow Blue, Platter, Lorne, Grindley, 14 1/4 X 10 1/4 In. ........................ 30.00
Flow Blue, Platter, Lorne, Oval, 10 In. ........................ 20.00
Flow Blue, Platter, Marechal Niel, 11 1/2 X 16 In. ........................ 45.00
Flow Blue, Platter, Marguerite, Grindley, 16 1/4 X 11 1/4 In. ........................ 30.00
Flow Blue, Platter, Marie, Grindley, 17 1/2 X 12 1/2 In. ........................ 45.00
Flow Blue, Platter, Marie, 11 1/4 X 8 In. ........................ 22.00
Flow Blue, Platter, Melbourne, 14 X 10 In. ........................ 40.00
Flow Blue, Platter, Messian, Cauldon, 13 X 16 In. ........................ 45.00
Flow Blue, Platter, Mikado, Wilkinson, 10 In. ........................ 20.00
Flow Blue, Platter, Montana, Johnson, 12 1/2 X 9 1/2 In. ........................ 16.00
Flow Blue, Platter, Montana, Johnson, 16 1/4 X 12 1/2 In. ........................ 25.00
Flow Blue, Platter, Nonpareil, 12 In. ........................ 38.00
Flow Blue, Platter, Normandy, 13 1/2 In. ........................ 28.00
Flow Blue, Platter, Paris, Stanley, 14 1/4 X 10 1/4 In. ........................ 30.00

| | |
|---|---:|
| **Flow Blue, Platter,** Portman, Grindley, 10 1/4 X 7 1/2 In. | 20.00 |
| **Flow Blue, Platter,** Rochester Castle, Staffordshire, 13 X 17 In. | 135.00 |
| **Flow Blue, Platter,** Roseville, Deep, Hughes, 14 3/4 X 9 1/4 In. | 35.00 |
| **Flow Blue, Platter,** Scinde, Alcock, C.1840, 15 1/2 X 11 3/4 In. | 100.00 |
| **Flow Blue, Platter,** Shanghai, 14 In. | 48.00 |
| **Flow Blue, Platter,** Sterling, 9 X 12 In. | 35.00 |
| **Flow Blue, Platter,** Summerset, 12 X 16 In. | 55.00 |
| **Flow Blue, Platter,** Togo, 16 In. | 35.00 |
| **Flow Blue, Platter,** Tonquin, W.Adams & Sons, C.1845, 11 1/4 X 8 1/2 In. | 55.00 |
| **Flow Blue, Platter,** Touraine, Stanley, 15 X 10 1/2 In. | 50.00 |
| **Flow Blue, Platter,** Touraine, Stanley, 17 1/4 X 12 In. | 60.00 |
| **Flow Blue, Platter,** Triood, Blenheim, 16 1/2 X 13 1/4 In. | 25.00 |
| **Flow Blue, Platter,** Victoria, 12 X 16 1/4 In. | 35.00 |
| **Flow Blue, Platter,** W.A.A. & Co., England, 16 X 13 In. | 26.00 |
| **Flow Blue, Platter,** Waldorf, Deep, New Wharf Pottery, 10 1/2 X 7 1/4 In. | 25.00 |
| **Flow Blue, Platter,** Waldorf, New Wharf Pottery, 10 1/2 X 7 3/4 In. | 25.00 |
| **Flow Blue, Platter,** Waldorf, New Wharf Pottery, 10 3/4 X 9 In. | 27.50 |
| **Flow Blue, Platter,** Waldorf, New Wharf Pottery, 14 1/4 X 10 1/4 In. | 40.00 |
| **Flow Blue, Platter,** Waldorf, 10 X 7 In. | 30.00 |
| **Flow Blue, Platter,** Watteau, Doulton, 10 3/4 X 13 1/2 In. | 35.00 |
| **Flow Blue, Relish,** Oregon, Shell Shape, T.J.& J.Mayer, C.1845, 9 1/4 In.Long | 40.00 |
| **Flow Blue, Salt,** Touraine | 18.00 |
| **Flow Blue, Sauce Set,** Linnea, Grimwades, Gold Trim, C.1886, 3 Piece | 45.00 |
| **Flow Blue, Sauce,** Argyle, Grindley | 7.50 |
| **Flow Blue, Sauce,** Ashburton | 9.00 |
| **Flow Blue, Sauce,** Avondo, Meakin, 5 In. | 10.00 |
| **Flow Blue, Sauce,** Brooklyn, Johnson Bros., 5 In. | 8.00 |
| **Flow Blue, Sauce,** Celtic | 5.00 |
| **Flow Blue, Sauce,** Celtic, Grindley | 7.50 |
| **Flow Blue, Sauce,** Clarence | 4.00 |
| **Flow Blue, Sauce,** Clarence, Grindley | 7.50 |
| **Flow Blue, Sauce,** Devon, Meakin | 4.00 To 7.50 |
| **Flow Blue, Sauce,** Fairy Villas | 9.00 |
| **Flow Blue, Sauce,** Florida, Grindley | 5.00 To 7.50 |
| **Flow Blue, Sauce,** Greyville, Till & Sons | 7.50 |
| **Flow Blue, Sauce,** Holland, Johnson | 7.50 |
| **Flow Blue, Sauce,** Johnson | 7.50 |
| **Flow Blue, Sauce,** Le Pavot | 7.00 |
| **Flow Blue, Sauce,** Lorne, New Wharf Pottery | 7.50 |
| **Flow Blue, Sauce,** Marie, Grindley | 7.50 |
| **Flow Blue, Sauce,** Melbourne, Grindley | 10.00 |
| **Flow Blue, Sauce,** Melrose, Doulton | 7.50 |
| **Flow Blue, Sauce,** Mongolia, Johnson | 7.50 |
| **Flow Blue, Sauce,** Montana | 2.00 |
| **Flow Blue, Sauce,** Montana, Johnson | 7.50 |
| **Flow Blue, Sauce,** Oregon, Johnson | 3.00 |
| **Flow Blue, Sauce,** Ovando, Meakin | 7.50 |
| **Flow Blue, Sauce,** Paris | 5.00 |
| **Flow Blue, Sauce,** Paris, Johnson | 7.50 |
| **Flow Blue, Sauce,** Poppy | 4.00 |
| **Flow Blue, Sauce,** Poppy, Johnson | 7.50 |
| **Flow Blue, Sauce,** Richmond, Meakin | 7.50 |
| **Flow Blue, Sauce,** Spinach | 12.00 |
| **Flow Blue, Sauce,** Touraine, Gold Trim, 5 1/4 In. | 15.00 |
| **Flow Blue, Sauce,** Waldorf, New Wharf Pottery | 5.00 |
| **Flow Blue, Sauceboat,** Candia, Floral, 4 1/2 In.Long | 25.00 |
| **Flow Blue, Saucer,** Amoy, Davenport, Dated 1844 | 17.50 |
| **Flow Blue, Saucer,** Grecian Scroll, T.J.& J.Mayer, C.1845 | 10.00 |
| **Flow Blue, Saucer,** Hong Kong, C.Meigh, C.1845 | 17.50 |
| **Flow Blue, Saucer,** Oregon, T.J.& J.Mayer, C.1845 | 17.50 |
| **Flow Blue, Saucer,** Oriental, Ridgeway | 5.00 |
| **Flow Blue, Saucer,** Shell, Challinor, C.1860 | 17.50 |
| **Flow Blue, Saucer,** Tonquin, Wm.Adams & Son, C.1845 | 17.50 |
| **Flow Blue, Saucer,** Touraine, Stanley | 5.00 |
| **Flow Blue, Spooner,** Celtic, Grindley | 150.00 |
| **Flow Blue, Spooner,** Melbourne, Grindley | 150.00 |

| | |
|---|---|
| Flow Blue, Spooner, Portman, Grindley | 150.00 |
| Flow Blue, Sugar, Covered, Brooklyn, Johnson Bros. | 50.00 |
| Flow Blue, Sugar, Covered, Celtic | 75.00 |
| Flow Blue, Sugar, Covered, Dahlia, 8 Sided | 75.00 |
| Flow Blue, Sugar, Hong Kong, Meigh, C.1845 | 40.00 |
| Flow Blue, Sugar, Lorne | 75.00 |
| Flow Blue, Sugar, Melbourne | 25.00 |
| Flow Blue, Sugar, Nonpareil | 18.00 |
| Flow Blue, Sugar, Scinde, Alcock | 67.00 |
| Flow Blue, Sugar, Shell, Challinor | 98.00 |
| Flow Blue, Teacup & Saucer, Celtic, Grindley | 25.00 |
| Flow Blue, Teapot, Manhattan | 65.00 |
| Flow Blue, Teapot, Nonpareil, Flower Finial, 10 3/4 In.High | 130.00 |
| Flow Blue, Teapot, Touraine | 135.00 |
| Flow Blue, Toothpick, Scenic, Coal Hod | 30.00 |
| Flow Blue, Toy Dinner Service, Forget-Me-Not, 35 Pieces | 750.00 |
| Flow Blue, Tray, Gravy Boat, Warwick | 10.00 |
| Flow Blue, Tureen & Attached Underplate, Covered, Victoria, Handled, 5 In. | 28.00 |
| Flow Blue, Tureen & Ladle, Soup, Oval | 100.00 |
| Flow Blue, Tureen & Underplate, Raleigh, Burgess & Leigh | 35.00 |
| Flow Blue, Tureen & Underplate, Soup, Acorn Finial, Madras, Handled | 185.00 |
| Flow Blue, Tureen & Underplate, Soup, Madras | 165.00 |
| Flow Blue, Tureen, Covered, Brooklyn, Johnson Bros., 11 X 8 In. | 50.00 |
| Flow Blue, Tureen, Covered, Lily, Double Handled, Footed, Adams | 52.00 |
| Flow Blue, Tureen, Covered, Nonpareil, Burgess & Leigh | 95.00 |
| Flow Blue, Tureen, Covered, Scenic, Burgess & Leigh, 8 3/4 In. | 85.00 |
| Flow Blue, Tureen, Covered, Touraine, Oval, 11 X 6 1/2 In. | 90.00 |
| Flow Blue, Tureen, Covered, Touraine, Oval, 12 X 7 1/2 In. | 100.00 |
| Flow Blue, Tureen, Messina, Cauldon, Handled, Flared Top Rim, 8 In.High | 57.50 |
| Flow Blue, Tureen, Underplate, & Ladle, Covered, Chatsworth, 8 1/2 In. | 38.00 |
| Flow Blue, Tureen, Vegetable, Covered, Rosetta, Burgess & Leigh, C.1890 | 35.00 |
| Flow Blue, Tureen, Vegetable, Scinde, 13 In.Long, 8 In.High | 250.00 |
| Flow Blue, Tureen, Vegetable, Touraine, 11 In.Long | 125.00 |
| Flow Blue, Tureen, Watteau, Embossed Leaves Finial & Handles, Doulton, 6 In. | 80.00 |
| Flow Blue, Tureen, Watteau, Embossed Leaves Finial & Handles, Doulton, 7 In. | 95.00 |
| Flow Blue, Turkey Set, Turkey Center, Ridgway, 7 Piece | 225.00 |
| Flow Blue, Vase, Babes In The Woods, Gold Trim, Royal Doulton, 9 1/2 In. | 85.00 |
| Flow Blue, Vase, Sitting Girl, 6 1/2 In.High | 75.00 |
| Flow Blue, Washstand Set, Warwick, Doulton, 6 Piece | 250.00 |

*Foo dogs are mythical Chinese figures, part dog and part lion. They were made of pottery, porcelain, carved stone, and wood.*

| | |
|---|---|
| Foo Dog, Ceramic, Japanese, Green & Olive Gray, C.1850, 7 In., Pair | 300.00 |

# FOSTORIA

*Fostoria glass was made in Fostoria, Ohio, from 1887 to 1891. The factory was moved to Moundsville, West Virginia, and most of the glass seen in shops today is a twentieth-century product.*

| | |
|---|---|
| Fostoria, Bonbon, Etched, Turned-Up Sides, 2 Handled | 7.00 |
| Fostoria, Bookend, Horse, Pair | 28.00 |
| Fostoria, Bookend, Rearing Horse, Pair | 18.00 |
| Fostoria, Bowl, Fruit, Pedestal, 12 1/2 In.Diameter | 45.00 |
| Fostoria, Bucket, Ice, Glacier Pattern, Chrome Handle, 4 1/2 In.High | 8.00 |
| Fostoria, Candlestick, Baroque, Pair | 10.00 |
| Fostoria, Candlestick, Hexagonal, No.1204, Pair | 35.00 |
| Fostoria, Candlestick, Navarre, Crystal, Pair | 16.50 |
| Fostoria, Cocktail & Underplate, Shrimp, American | 4.00 |
| Fostoria, Cocktail Glass, Etched Meadow Rose, Signed, Paper Label | 17.00 |
| Fostoria, Compote, Etched Grape, Green, 6 In.High | 17.00 |
| Fostoria, Creamer, American, 4 1/4 In.High | 6.00 |
| Fostoria, Cup & Saucer, American | 3.50 |
| Fostoria, Decanter, American | 20.00 |
| Fostoria, Dish, Candy, American, Heart Shaped | 4.50 |
| Fostoria, Dish, Candy, Covered, Baroque, Topaz, 3 Compartments | 10.00 |
| Fostoria, Dish, Candy, Trojan, Yellow | 9.00 |
| Fostoria, Figurine, Sitting Horse, On Base | 15.00 |
| Fostoria, Goblet, American, Tall | 4.00 |
| Fostoria, Goblet, Chapel Bells | 3.00 |

Fostoria, Goblet, June, Topaz ............................................................................................................ 18.10
Fostoria, Jar, Biscuit, Silver Plate Cover, Brazilian ....................................................................... 35.00
Fostoria, Mayonnaise Set, American, 3 Piece ................................................................................ 10.00
Fostoria, Pitcher, Glacier Pattern, 2 Quart, 7 1/2 In.High ........................................................... 8.00
Fostoria, Pitcher, Water, Louise ........................................................................................................ 22.50
Fostoria, Plate, Dinner, American ...................................................................................................... 3.00
Fostoria, Plate, Salad, American ....................................................................................................... 2.00
Fostoria, Plate, Serving, Octagonal, Center Handle, Grape Brocade Etching ........................... 22.50
Fostoria, Plate, Victoria, 6 In. ........................................................................................................... 6.50
Fostoria, Rose Bowl, Iridescent Gold, Etched N.E.L.A., 1901-1911 ......................................... 140.00
Fostoria, Salt & Pepper, American, Blown, Rough Pontils ............................................................ 10.00
Fostoria, Saltshaker, Edgewood, Sterling Silver Top ..................................................................... 10.00
Fostoria, Sherbet, American ............................................................................................................... 2.50
Fostoria, Sherbet, Drape Bowl, Paneled Stem, Iridescent, Touchmark ..................................... 16.00
Fostoria, Sherbet, June, Topaz .......................................................................................................... 8.00
Fostoria, Sherbet, Virginia, Cone Shape ......................................................................................... 2.50
Fostoria, Sugar & Creamer, Individual, American ......................................................................... 8.00
Fostoria, Sugar, Etched Wild Rose ................................................................................................... 6.00
Fostoria, Syrup, Wedding Bells, Pink Flashed, Spring Lid ............................................................ 58.00
Fostoria, Tumbler, Virginia, Cone Shape ......................................................................................... 3.35
Fostoria, Vase, Fan, Acorn & Leaf With Cameo Appearance, Pink, 8 1/2 In. .......................... 20.00
Fostoria, Vase, Globe, Oak, Pink Tapestry, 3 1/2 In. .................................................................. 9.00
Fostoria, Vase, Heavy Drape, No.1300, 12 In. ............................................................................... 21.50
Fostoria, Water Set, Green Base, Cane Shape, Swirl Cover, 7 Piece ......................................... 62.00
Fostoria, Wine, Alexis ......................................................................................................................... 8.00
    Foval, see Fry Foval
    Frame, see Furniture, Frame, Goofus Glass, Frame, Faberge, Frame

    *Francisware is an amber hobnail glassware.*
Francisware, Berry Set, Amber Swirl, 6 Piece ................................................................................ 65.00
Francisware, Berry Set, Frosted Hobs, Amber Rims, Square Bowls, 5 Piece ........................... 135.00
Francisware, Bowl, Berry ..................................................................................................................... 55.00
Francisware, Bowl, Frosted Hobnail .................................................................................................. 33.00
Francisware, Bowl, Small Size ........................................................................................................... 45.00
Francisware, Box, Covered, Round, C.1880, 6 In.High .................................................................. 75.00
Francisware, Creamer ........................................................................................................................... 50.00
Francisware, Dish, Candy, Amber Finial, Frosted Hobs With Amber, 5 1/2 In. ...................... 57.00
Francisware, Pitcher, Water ................................................................................................................ 110.00
Francisware, Relish, 5 1/2 X 7 1/2 In. ........................................................................................... 34.00
Francisware, Sauce, Polished Pontil .................................................................................................. 16.00
Francisware, Sugar ............................................................................................................................... 45.00
Francisware, Sugar, Covered ............................................................................................................... 49.00
Francisware, Toothpick, Amber Rim .................................................................................................. 45.00
Francisware, Toothpick, Ruffled Top ................................................................................................. 30.00
Francisware, Toothpick, 3 In.High ..................................................................................................... 35.00
Francisware, Tumbler ........................................................................................................................... 22.00
Frankenthal, Cup & Saucer, Travelers Near A Ruin, C.1770 ..................................................... 80.00
Frankenthal, Group, Allegorical, Spring, 1771, 6 1/4 In. ............................................. *Illus* 800.00

Frankenthal, Group, Allegorical, Spring,
1771, 6 1/4 In.

| | |
|---|---|
| Frankenthal, Group, Shepherd & Shepherdess, C.1770, 4 3/4 In. High | 750.00 |
| Frankenthal, Plate, Pierced Rim, Bouquet In Center, 1780, 9 1/8 In. | 175.00 |
| Frankenthal, Tea Caddy, Puce Camaieu Rural Views Cartouches, C.1755 | 800.00 |

*Fry glass was made by the famous H.C.Fry Glass Company of
Rochester, Pennsylvania. It includes cut glass, but the famous Fry glass
today is the foval, or pearl, art glass. This is an opal ware decorated with
colored trim. It was made from 1922 to 1933.*

**Fry, see also Cut Glass**

| | |
|---|---|
| Fry Foval, Compote, Blue, Green Edge, 8 In. | 85.00 |
| Fry Foval, Compote, Jade Green Rims, Footed | 85.00 |
| Fry Foval, Cup & Saucer, Pearl Ware | 53.00 |
| Fry Foval, Goblet, Pink Cone Top, Opalescent Base & Stem | 38.00 |
| Fry Foval, Jug, Cobalt Trim | 160.00 |
| Fry Foval, Lemonade Set, Blue Handles, 7 Pieces | 550.00 |
| Fry Foval, Perfume, Engraved Flowers, Cobalt Stopper | 50.00 |
| Fry Foval, Pitcher, Water, Bulbous, Applied Blue Handle, Creamy Opalescent | 87.50 |
| Fry Foval, Plate, Divided, Marked | 10.00 |
| Fry Foval, Reamer, Large Size | 15.00 |
| Fry Foval, Sherbet, Green | 50.00 |
| Fry Foval, Sherbet, Jack-In-The-Pulpit, Etched Rose Rim | 20.00 |
| Fry Foval, Tea Set, White Opalescent, Green Handles, 3 Piece | 65.00 |
| Fry Foval, Teacup & Saucer | 45.00 |
| Fry Foval, Vase, Flared Top, Jade Foot, 9 1/4 In.High | 125.00 |
| Fry Foval, Vase, Jack-In-The-Pulpit, Violet Border | 75.00 |
| Fry Foval, Vase, Jade Green, 7 In. High | 50.00 |
| Fry Foval, Vase, Opalescent Stripes On Green, Crimped To Form 6 Point Star | 65.00 |
| Fry Foval, Vase, Trumpet, Cobalt Base, 10 In.High, Pair | 225.00 |
| Fry Foval, Water Set, Opalescent Stripes, 5 Piece | 145.00 |
| Fry, Basket, Cut, Easter Type, Signed, 10 1/2 X 6 1/2 X 8 In. | 215.00 |
| Fry, Bowl, Cut Glass, Hobstars, Signed, 8 1/2 In. | 80.00 |
| Fry, Casserole, Baking, Covered | 10.00 To 12.00 |
| Fry, Cup & Saucer, Pink | 6.00 |
| Fry, Cup, Custard, Baking, Marked | 3.00 To 5.00 |
| Fry, Lemon Squeezer | 15.00 |
| Fry, Lemonade Set, Crackle, Green Handle & Knob On Cover, 3 Piece | 60.00 |
| Fry, Lemonade Set, Handled Mugs, 7 Piece | 550.00 |
| Fry, Lemonade Set, Radio Glass, Canary, Cobalt Handles & Coasters, 13 Piece | 325.00 |
| Fry, Lemonade Set, Vertical Stripes, Applied Blue Handles, 7 Piece | 425.00 |
| Fry, Liqueur, Trumpet Shape, Footed, Fans & Single Stars, Signed, 4 1/4 In. | 25.00 |
| Fry, Mug, Crackle, Amber, 5 In. | 12.00 |
| Fry, Perfume, Etched On Shaded Blue Opalescent | 50.00 |
| Fry, Pitcher, Crackle, Blown, Transparent Lime Green Handle, 9 1/2 In.High | 75.00 |
| Fry, Pitcher, Opalescent Stripes On Vaseline, Cobalt Handle | 75.00 |
| Fry, Pitcher, Water, Crackle Glass, Inverted Thumbprint, Green, Amber Handle | 58.00 |
| Fry, Pitcher, Water, Crackle Glass, Transparent Lime Green Handle | 65.00 |
| Fry, Plate, Pie | 6.00 |
| Fry, Plate, Pie, Baking, Marked | 5.00 |
| Fry, Trivet, Ovenware, 3 Footed, Signed, 8 In. | 18.50 |
| Fry, Vase, Crackle Glass, Applied Green Leaves, 8 X 4 In. | 95.00 |
| Fry, Vase, Crackle Glass, Blue Applied Leaves, 12 In.High | 50.00 |
| Fry, Vase, Crackle, Applied Green Leaves, 7 X 5 In. | 75.00 |
| Fry, Vase, Crackle, Blue Pedestal & 4 Applied Rings, 9 1/2 In.High | 35.00 |
| Fry, Vase, Crackle, Urn Shape, Amber Pedestal | 35.00 |
| Fry, Vase, Horizontal Optics, Crystal Ball At Base, Light Blue, Pair | 145.00 |
| Fulham, Jug & Filter, Brown Glaze, 7 In.High | 5.00 |

*Fulper is the mark used by the American Pottery Company of
Flemington, New Jersey. The art pottery was made from 1910 to 1929.
The firm had been making bottles, jugs, and housewares from 1805. Doll heads
were made about 1928. The firm became Stangl Pottery in 1929.*

| | |
|---|---|
| Fulper, Bowl, Beige & Pale Green, Signed, 5 7/8 In.Diameter, 1 3/4 In.High | 14.00 |
| Fulper, Bowl, Green, Black & Rust, Iridescent Glaze, 11 In.Wide | 20.00 |
| Fulper, Bowl, Green, 6 1/2 In.High, 11 In.Wide | 10.00 |
| Fulper, Box, Dresser, Lady On Top, Signed | 60.00 |
| Fulper, Candleholder, Relief Fruits, 1 1/2 X 5 In., Pair | 14.00 |
| Fulper, Humidor, Tobacco, Dark Brown Glaze | 25.00 |

| | |
|---|---|
| Fulper, Jar, Powder, Multicolored, Girl, Artist Signed, 6 1/2 In. | 40.00 |
| Fulper, Lamp, Stained Glass Shade, C.1915, 16 1/2 In. *Illus* | 325.00 |
| Fulper, Perfume Base, Lamp-Shape, Purple, 1 1/2 In.High | 20.00 |
| Fulper, Stein, Green Glaze, Pewter Lid, 5 In. | 40.00 |
| Fulper, Vase, Blue, 10 In.High | 10.00 |
| Fulper, Vase, Brown, Blue Ringed Trim, 2 Handles | 15.00 |
| Fulper, Vase, Brown, Tan Drip, 2 Handled, 4 3/4 X 6 In. | 20.00 |
| Fulper, Vase, Bulbous, Blue & Green Shaded, Serpent Around Neck, 8 In.High | 38.00 |
| Fulper, Vase, Bulbous, Persian Rose, 2 Handled | 18.00 |
| Fulper, Vase, Cat's-Eye, Cobalt, Gray, & Yellowish Flambe, 4 In.High | 38.00 |
| Fulper, Vase, Flambe Glaze, Blue To Rose, 8 X 7 1/2 In. | 20.00 |
| Fulper, Vase, Green To Rose, Handled, 7 1/2 In. | 20.00 |
| Fulper, Vase, Hexagonal, Bulbous, Blue & Lavender, Matte, Signed, 11 In.High | 35.00 |
| Fulper, Vase, Mottled Blue, 9 In. | 26.00 |
| Fulper, Vase, Thin Neck, Brown To Clear Glaze At Top, Blue Bottom, 8 In.High | 26.00 |
| Fulper, Vase, Urn Shape, Gray Blue Glaze, C.1900, 10 In.High | 70.00 |
| Furniture, Armchair, Bugatti, Ebonized Walnut, Inlaid Metal, C.1900 | 1300.00 |
| Furniture, Armchair, Caned, Scrolls & Foliage, C.1750, Pair | 1200.00 |
| Furniture, Armchair, Carved Mahogany, Ogival Wings, N.E., C.1790 | 500.00 |
| Furniture, Armchair, Carved Mahogany, Wing, Scrolled Arms, Conn., C.1815 | 475.00 |
| Furniture, Armchair, Cherry, Turned, Banister Back, New England, C.1720 | 475.00 |
| Furniture, Armchair, Child's, Chippendale Style, Mahogany, Ball & Claw Feet | 125.00 |
| Furniture, Armchair, Child's, Maple, Turned, Splint Seat *Illus* | 950.00 |
| Furniture, Armchair, Chippendale, Mahogany, Wing, Massachusetts, C.1760 | 1700.00 |
| Furniture, Armchair, Chippendale, Serpentine Cresting, Mass., C.1780 | 900.00 |
| Furniture, Armchair, Federal, Mahogany, Barrel Back, Wing, C.1800 | 1900.00 |
| Furniture, Armchair, Flemish, Walnut, Turned Legs, Pair | 675.00 |
| Furniture, Armchair, George II. Mahogany, Pair *Illus* | 1900.00 |
| Furniture, Armchair, George II, Walnut, Rectangular Backrest | 550.00 |
| Furniture, Armchair, Inlaid Mahogany, Barrel Back, Seymour School, C.1800 | 8000.00 |
| Furniture, Armchair, Ladder Back, Miniature, Green, C.1800, 15 In. High | 425.00 |
| Furniture, Armchair, Mahogany, Balloon Back, C.1850 | 237.50 |
| Furniture, Armchair, Mahogany, C.1775, Pair *Illus* | 2600.00 |
| Furniture, Armchair, Mahogany, Shield Back, New York, C.1790, Pair | 2000.00 |
| Furniture, Armchair, Queen Anne, Cherry, Slat Back, Ball Finials, Rush Seat | 550.00 |
| Furniture, Armchair, Rosewood, C.1850 *Illus* | 250.00 |
| Furniture, Armchair, Russian, Carved Ebonized Wood, Horseshoe Back, C.1850 | 600.00 |
| Furniture, Armchair, Victorian, Wicker, 1st National Bank, Ft.Worth, Texas | 45.00 |
| Furniture, Armchair, Windsor, Bamboo Turned, New England, C.1800 | 250.00 |
| Furniture, Armchair, Windsor, Comb Back, Cupid's-Bow Crest, N.E., C.1780 | 1300.00 |
| Furniture, Armchair, Windsor, Comb Back, New England, C.1800 | 575.00 |
| Furniture, Armchair, Windsor, Delaware River, C.1800 *Illus* | 550.00 |
| Furniture, Armchair, Windsor, Sack Back, Pennsylvania, C.1800 | 500.00 |
| Furniture, Armoire, Victorian, Pine, 82 In.High, 46 In.Wide | 160.00 |
| Furniture, Bathtub, Claw Footed, 5 Ft. | 100.00 |
| Furniture, Bed, Cannonball, Rope, Vinegar Painting, 52 X 76 In. | 900.00 |
| Furniture, Bed, Curly Maple, Urn Finials, Bird's-Eye Head, Rope, 55 X 79 In. | 250.00 |
| Furniture, Bed, High Post, Carved Mahogany, Acanthus, American, C.1780 | 1300.00 |
| Furniture, Bed, Hospital, Iron, Salesman's Sample | 85.00 |
| Furniture, Bed, Iron & Brass, Victorian, Romantic Landscapes, C.1875 | 175.00 |
| Furniture, Bed, Iron, Acanthus & Rosette, 7 Spindles, 54 X 72 In. | 65.00 |
| Furniture, Bed, Low Post, Cherry, Ball Finials, New England, C.1835 | 225.00 |
| Furniture, Bed, Mahogany, Carved, Mushroom Finials, New York, C.1820 | 850.00 |
| Furniture, Bed, Pencil Post, Painted, Turned Maple, C.1750 | 3750.00 |
| Furniture, Bed, Pencil Post, Turned Maple, New England, C.1750 | 1200.00 |
| Furniture, Bed, Trundle, Pine, Turned Posts, Ball Finials, Pa., C.1820 | 375.00 |
| Furniture, Bed, Trundle, Rope, Turned Posts, Wooden Roller Feet, 43 X 68 In. | 100.00 |
| Furniture, Bed, Walnut, Turned Posts, Shaped Head & Foot, Rope, 24 In. Long | 70.00 |
| Furniture, Bedroom Suite, Victorian, Walnut, White Marble, 4 Piece | 2100.00 |
| Furniture, Bench, Butcher, Pennsylvania Dutch, Oak Top, Hickory Legs | 100.00 |
| Furniture, Bench, Cobbler's, Wooden | 125.00 |
| Furniture, Bench, Garden, Iron, Black | 95.00 |
| Furniture, Bench, Wagon, Maple & Cherry, Double Rush Seat, N.E., C.1800 | 375.00 |
| Furniture, Bench, Water, C.1750 | 59.00 |
| Furniture, Bonheur Du Jour, Louis Philippe, Black Lacquer & Boulle | 900.00 |
| Furniture, Bonheur Du Jour, Louis Philippe, Marquetry & Parquetry, C.1850 | 1200.00 |

Fulper, Lamp, Stained Glass Shade,
C.1915, 16 1/2 In.
(See Page 213)

Furniture, Armchair, Mahogany, C.1775, Pair
(See Page 213)

Furniture, Armchair, Windsor,
Delaware River, C.1800
(See Page 213)

Furniture, Armchair, Child's, Maple,
Turned, Splint Seat
(See Page 213)

Furniture, Armchair,
George II, Mahogany, Pair
(See Page 213)

Furniture, Cabinet On Stand,
German, Parcel Gilt, C.1850
(See Page 216)

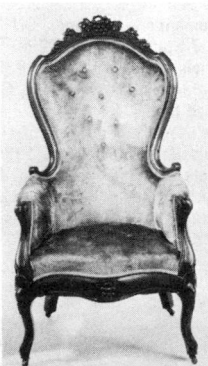

Furniture, Armchair,
Rosewood, C.1850
(See Page 213)

Furniture, Candlestand,
Oak & Curly Maple,
N.E., C.1735
*(See Page 216)*

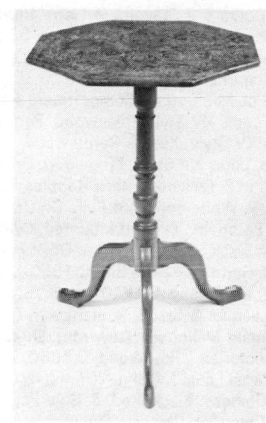

Furniture, Chair, Corner, Turned Maple,
N.E., C.1750
*(See Page 216)*

Furniture, Candlestand,
Mahogany & Walnut,
N.E., C.1760
*(See Page 216)*

Furniture, Cabinet, Side, Oak, C.1650
*(See Page 216)*

Furniture, Chair, Corner,
Walnut, N.Y., C.1740
*(See Page 216)*

Furniture, Chair, Corner,
Cherry & Maple, C.1745
*(See Page 216)*

Furniture, Chair, Hall, Mahogany, C.1750, Set Of 5
*(See Page 217)*

Furniture, Bonheur Du Jour, Napoleon III, King & Rosewood, Parquetry ......................... 800.00
Furniture, Bookcase Cabinet, Walnut, Floral Marquetry, 2 Doors, C.1890 ...................... 750.00
Furniture, Bookcase, Bureau, Mahogany, C.1775 ....................... 2500.00
Furniture, Bookcase, George III, Satinwood, Painted, Bow Front ....................... 2600.00
Furniture, Bookcase, Inlaid Mahogany & Maple, New York, C.1815, Gothic Door ............ 1700.00
Furniture, Bookcase, Library, Victorian, Walnut ....................... 325.00
Furniture, Bookcase, Oak, 2 Doors & 2 Drawers, 4 Lions' Heads, 4 X 5 Feet .................. 375.00
Furniture, Bookcase, Victorian, Painted, Gilded Palmettes, 33 In. High .................. 650.00
Furniture, Bookshelf, Carved Fruitwood, Inlaid Pictures, 17 X 6 1/2 In. ...................... 75.00
Furniture, Bookstand, Sheraton, Mahogany, Revolving ....................... 428.00
Furniture, Box, Knife, Wall, Wooden, Bottom Compartment For Soap .................. 30.00
Furniture, Bureau De Dame, Louis XV Style, Rosewood, Parquetry, C.1890 .................. 400.00
Furniture, Bureau Plat, Louis XV Style, King & Purplewood, Ormolu Mounted ................. 3000.00
Furniture, Bureau Plat, Petite, Louis XV Style, Kingwood, Ormolu, C.1850 .................. 1700.00
Furniture, Bureau, Black Walnut & Fruitwood, Iron Handles, Beading ...................... 85.00
Furniture, Bureau, Child's, Play, White Porcelain Pulls On Drawers .................. 55.00
Furniture, Bureau, Victorian, Parquetry, Ormolu Mounted, Cylinder Top, C.1850 .......... 1000.00
Furniture, Cabinet On Stand, Black Lacquer, Mother-Of-Pearl, C.1850 ...................... 550.00
Furniture, Cabinet On Stand, German, Parcel Gilt, C.1850 ....................... Illus 900.00
Furniture, Cabinet, Bookcase, Mahogany, C.1850 ....................... 700.00
Furniture, Cabinet, Chinese Lacquer & Stone, Rectangular, Gold On Black .................. 175.00
Furniture, Cabinet, Display, Inlaid Mahogany, Bowfront, English, C.1855 .................. 475.00
Furniture, Cabinet, Display, Victorian, , Rosewood, C.1850, 7 Ft.5 In.High .................. 375.00
Furniture, Cabinet, F.Linke, Paris, Louis XV Style, Ormolu Mounted, 1850s .................. 5800.00
Furniture, Cabinet, Jewelry, Chinese, Black, Red, & Gold Pagodas & Mountains ............ 35.00
Furniture, Cabinet, Lacquer, Cinnabar, Chinese, Oriental Designs ...................... 250.00
Furniture, Cabinet, Oak, 30 Drawer, 15 Drawers High, For Law Forms .................. 189.00
Furniture, Cabinet, On Chest, Victorian, Oak, Arched Door, 7 Ft.High .................. 1500.00
Furniture, Cabinet, Printer's, Pine, 18 Drawer, 58 X 28 In. ....................... 250.00
Furniture, Cabinet, Side, Charles X, Satinwood, Marble Top, C.1890, Pair .................. 150.00
Furniture, Cabinet, Side, Oak, C.1650 ....................... Illus 1700.00
Furniture, Cabinet, Side, Painted, Gray Marble Top, C.1825 ...................... 600.00
Furniture, Cabinet, Side, Victorian, Mahogany, Carved, 6 Doors, 32 In. High .................. 225.00
Furniture, Cabinet, Smoker's, English, Oak, Glass Door, Pipe Rack, Drawer .................. 79.00
Furniture, Cabinet, Spice, Oak, White Porcelain Pulls, 8 Drawer ...................... 65.00
Furniture, Cabinet, Spice, Pine, 1 Drawer, White Porcelain Knobs & Labels .................. 50.00
Furniture, Cabinet, Spice, Wall, Handmade, Painted White, 13 X 16 In. .................. 14.50
Furniture, Cabinet, Spice, Wall, 8 Drawer, 17 In.High ....................... 95.00
Furniture, Cabinet, Spice, 3 Drawer, Porcelain Knobs ....................... 95.00
Furniture, Cabinet, Spice, 3 Drawer, Wooden Knobs ....................... 95.00
Furniture, Cabinet, Spool, 2 Drawer, 8 In.High, 21 In.Wide ....................... 49.50
Furniture, Cabinet, Vitrine, Louis Philippe, Purplewood, Quatrefoil Top ...................... 325.00
Furniture, Candlestand, Chippendale, Walnut, Philadelphia, C.1760, 25 In.High .......... 1800.00
Furniture, Candlestand, Dutch, Marquetry, 5 Ft.High, C.1680 ...................... 400.00
Furniture, Candlestand, Federal, Octagonal Top, Cherry, New England, C.1810 .......... 250.00
Furniture, Candlestand, Hardwood, Carved Bird's Heads On Legs, Grooved Top .......... 38.00
Furniture, Candlestand, Mahogany & Walnut, N.E., C.1760 ....................... Illus 1500.00
Furniture, Candlestand, Oak & Curly Maple, N.E., C.1735 ....................... Illus 1400.00
Furniture, Candlestand, Pilgrim Century, Turned Maple, New England, C.1720 .......... 450.00
Furniture, Candlestand, Serpentine Top, Mahogany, Philadelphia, C.1800 .................. 400.00
Furniture, Candlestand, Tilt Top, Inlaid Mahogany & Maple, New England .................. 350.00
Furniture, Candlestand, William & Mary, Maple, Turned, Octagonal Top .................. 200.00
Furniture, Cellaret, Dutch, Mahogany, Coat Of Arms, C.1850, 19 In.High .................. 130.00
Furniture, Cellaret, Federal, Mahogany, Octagonal Brassbound Lid, C.1800 .................. 900.00
Furniture, Chair, Arrow Back, Painted & Decorated, New England, C.1840, Pair .......... 275.00
Furniture, Chair, Arrow Back, Plank Bottom ....................... 30.00
Furniture, Chair, Black Paint, Stenciled, Cane Seat, N.E., C.1825 ...................... 27.25
Furniture, Chair, Child's, Oak, Ladder Back, Cowhide Seat ....................... 27.50
Furniture, Chair, Child's, Walnut, Caned Seat, C.1675 ....................... 225.00
Furniture, Chair, Corner, Cherry & Maple, C.1745 ....................... Illus 850.00
Furniture, Chair, Corner, Turned Cherry & Maple, New England, C.1740 .................. 850.00
Furniture, Chair, Corner, Turned Maple, N.E., C.1750 ....................... Illus 1000.00
Furniture, Chair, Corner, Walnut, N.Y., C.1740 ....................... Illus 4300.00
Furniture, Chair, Dining, Mahogany, Cabriole Legs, 19th Century, Set Of 12 .................. 4250.00
Furniture, Chair, Eastlake, Carved ....................... 120.00

**Furniture, Chair,** Easy, Inlaid Mahogany, Barrel Back, Green Leather, C.1790 ................................ 800.00
**Furniture, Chair,** Four Slat Back, Rush Seat, C.1750 .................................................................... 150.00
**Furniture, Chair,** Gentleman's, Victorian ...................................................................................... 265.00
**Furniture, Chair,** Hall, Mahogany, C.1750, Set Of 5 ......................................................... *Illus* 2100.00
**Furniture, Chair,** Hall, Oak, Carved With Rose, Tudor ................................................................. 350.00
**Furniture, Chair,** Hepplewhite Country Style, Shield Back, Green Leather ................................. 540.00
**Furniture, Chair,** Hitchcock Type, Yellow Paint, Deer On Top Slat, Cane Seat .......................... 33.00
**Furniture, Chair,** Hitchcock, Conn., C.1835 ................................................................... *Illus* 137.50
**Furniture, Chair,** Hitchcock, Rush Seat, C.1810 ......................................................................... 75.00
**Furniture, Chair,** Ice Cream, Bull's-Eye & Heart, Pair ................................................................ 35.00
**Furniture, Chair,** Ice Cream, Loop Back ...................................................................................... 25.00
**Furniture, Chair,** Italian, Sagabello, Carved & Pierced Back, 47 In.High ................................. 125.00
**Furniture, Chair,** Ladder Back, Chippendale, Cherry, Three Slats, C.1780 .............................. 175.00
**Furniture, Chair,** Ladder Back, Mahogany, Federal Style, 3 Slats, Set Of 8 ........................... 1400.00
**Furniture, Chair,** Lady's, Victorian, Walnut, Carved Roses & Daisies ..................................... 275.00
**Furniture, Chair,** Library, Mahogany, C.1825 ................................................................... *Illus* 750.00
**Furniture, Chair,** Lolling, Martha Washington, Mahogany, Mass., C.1790, Pair ...................... 5500.00
**Furniture, Chair,** Louis XV, Miniature, Silver & Dore, Back Is Watch Holder ......................... 50.00
**Furniture, Chair,** Mahogany & Monel Metal, French ......................................................... *Illus* 112.50
**Furniture, Chair,** Martha Washington, Lolling, Federal, Mahogany, Curved Back ...................... 2600.00
**Furniture, Chair,** New York, C.1835, Set Of 6 ................................................................. *Illus* 450.00
**Furniture, Chair,** Ohio, Balloon Back, Dark Graining, Stenciling, Signed S. .......................... 135.00
**Furniture, Chair,** Oriental, Hand Carved, Dragons ..................................................................... 350.00

Furniture, Chair, Library,
Mahogany, C.1825

Furniture, Chair, Mahogany & Monel Metal, French

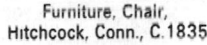

Furniture, Chair,
Hitchcock, Conn., C.1835

Furniture, Chair, New York, C.1835, Set Of 6

Furniture, Chair, Ormolu Mounted, C.1725, Pair .......... *Illus* 3300.00
Furniture, Chair, Parlor, Victorian, Mahogany, C.1850 .......... 110.00
Furniture, Chair, Pilgrim, Maple, New England, C.1700 .......... *Illus* 225.00
Furniture, Chair, Plank Bottom, Stenciled, Bird, Morning Glories, Leaves .......... 50.00
Furniture, Chair, Potty, Child's, Walnut, Graniteware Pot, Lift Hinged Cover .......... 75.00
Furniture, Chair, Prie-Dieu, English, C.1860 .......... 110.00
Furniture, Chair, Queen Anne, Country .......... 215.00
Furniture, Chair, Scroll Back, Duncan Phyfe, Mahogany, New York, C.1805, 8 .......... 2000.00
Furniture, Chair, Sheraton, Decorated .......... 75.00
Furniture, Chair, Side, Balloon Seat, Walnut, New England, C.1740 .......... 1500.00
Furniture, Chair, Side, Birch, Ladder Back, Upholstered Seat, Mass., C.1780 .......... 275.00
Furniture, Chair, Side, Black Lacquer, Mother-Of-Pearl, Balloon Splat, 1890s .......... 75.00
Furniture, Chair, Side, Burr Walnut, Waved Backrest, Pad Feet, C.1725, Pair .......... 6000.00
Furniture, Chair, Side, Carved Mahogany, Pierced Foliate Splat, Phila., 1870s .......... 2000.00
Furniture, Chair, Side, Carved Mahogany, Prince Of Wales Plumes, N.Y., 1800s .......... 275.00
Furniture, Chair, Side, Chinese Chippendale Style, Ribbonback, Rush Seat .......... 275.00
Furniture, Chair, Side, Chippendale, Carved Walnut, Philadelphia, C.1760, Pair .......... 5250.00
Furniture, Chair, Side, Chippendale, Ladder Back, Red, Hand-Camphored .......... 89.00
Furniture, Chair, Side, Chippendale, Mahogany, Carved, Massachusetts, C.1770 .......... 700.00
Furniture, Chair, Side, Federal, Carved, Mahogany, C.1800, Pair .......... 1050.00
Furniture, Chair, Side, Federal, Mahogany, C.1800, Set Of 6 .......... 1900.00
Furniture, Chair, Side, Inlaid Mahogany, Art Nouveau, Crest Rail, Saddle Seat .......... 225.00
Furniture, Chair, Side, Italian, Ebonized Ivory, Mother-Of-Pearl, C.1850, Pair .......... 425.00
Furniture, Chair, Side, Louis Philippe, Boulle, Brass, Tortoiseshell Inserts .......... 175.00
Furniture, Chair, Side, Lyre Back, Mahogany, New York, C.1815 .......... 175.00
Furniture, Chair, Side, Mahogany & Walnut, C.1830, Set Of 4 .......... 265.00
Furniture, Chair, Side, Mahogany, Balloon Back, C.1850 .......... *Illus* 62.50
Furniture, Chair, Side, Mahogany, C.1750, Pair .......... *Illus* 2100.00
Furniture, Chair, Side, Mahogany, Serpentine Top Rail, Needlework, C.1775 .......... 250.00
Furniture, Chair, Side, Maple, Pa., C.1735 .......... *Illus* 1100.00
Furniture, Chair, Side, Maple, Pierced Vasiform Splat, Conn., C.1760 .......... 366.65
Furniture, Chair, Side, Maple, Rush Seat, Savery, Phila., C.1745 .......... 1700.00
Furniture, Chair, Side, Maple, Spooned Vasiform Splat, Rush Seat, N.E., C.1720 .......... 1200.00
Furniture, Chair, Side, Napoleon III, Painted, Stuffed Seat, C.1890 .......... 25.00
Furniture, Chair, Side, Oak, Jacobean Carved, Cane Seat & Back, Set Of 6 .......... 450.00
Furniture, Chair, Side, Oak, Turned Spindles, Heart Handles, Set Of 4 .......... 99.00
Furniture, Chair, Side, Queen Anne, Maple, Rush Seat, C.1740 .......... 900.00
Furniture, Chair, Side, Queen Anne, Walnut, New York, C.1740, Pair .......... 7000.00
Furniture, Chair, Side, Sheraton, Gilt Stenciling, Yellow Stripes, Rush Seat .......... 80.00
Furniture, Chair, Side, Slat Back, Curly Maple, Pennsylvania, C.1720, 5 Slats .......... 1100.00
Furniture, Chair, Side, Victorian, Walnut, Eastlake .......... 49.00
Furniture, Chair, Side, Victorian, Walnut, Little Arms, Set Of 4 .......... 115.00
Furniture, Chair, Side, Victorian, Walnut, Pair .......... 89.00
Furniture, Chair, Windsor, Bow Back .......... 560.00
Furniture, Chair, Windsor, Butterfly, J.Chestnut, Wilmington, 1760-1780 .......... 225.00
Furniture, Chair, Windsor, Chicken Coop, Bamboo Turnings, Green Paint .......... 200.00
Furniture, Chair, Windsor, Comb Back, Saddle Seat, C.1800 .......... 300.00
Furniture, Chair, Windsor, Hoop Back, J.C.Tuttle, Mass., C.1800, Pair .......... 900.00
Furniture, Chair, Windsor, Step Down, Black Paint, Gilt Trim .......... 95.00
Furniture, Chair, Windsor, Step Down, Original Stenciling .......... 185.00
Furniture, Chair, Windsor, Writing Arm, Saddle Seat, New England, C.1830 .......... 250.00
Furniture, Chair, Windsor, Writing, New England, C.1830 .......... *Illus* 550.00
Furniture, Chair, Windsor, Yew And Elmwood, C.1775 .......... *Illus* 1900.00
Furniture, Chest Of Drawers, Pine, 3 Drawer, N.H., C.1800, Miniature .......... 325.00
Furniture, Chest On Frame, Oyster Burl, William & Mary, 1690 .......... 4950.00
Furniture, Chest, Apothecary, Pine, 20 Drawer, Floor Standing .......... 395.00
Furniture, Chest, Blanket, Hinged Lid, Legs, 45 1/2 In.Long .......... 80.00
Furniture, Chest, Blanket, Miniature, Painted & Decorated, C.1820, 10 In.High .......... 325.00
Furniture, Chest, Blanket, New England, C.1830 .......... *Illus* 200.00
Furniture, Chest, Blanket, New England, Grained Decoration, Lift Top .......... 265.00
Furniture, Chest, Blanket, New England, Lift Top, Red, 2 Drawer .......... 285.00
Furniture, Chest, Blanket, Pa., 1849, Miniature .......... 1600.00
Furniture, Chest, Blanket, Pa., 1849, 10 3/8 X 6 1/4 In. .......... *Illus* 1350.00
Furniture, Chest, Blanket, Painted & Decorated, New England, C.1800 .......... 500.00
Furniture, Chest, Blanket, Pennsylvania Dutch, Pine, 24 X 14 X 16 In. .......... 100.00
Furniture, Chest, Blanket, Pilgrim, Carved Oak, Massachusetts, C.1680 .......... 3500.00

Furniture, Chair, Side,
Maple, Pa., C.1735
*(See Page 210)*

Furniture, Chair, Side,
Mahogany, C.1750, Pair
*(See Page 218)*

Furniture, Chair, Windsor,
Yew And Elmwood, C.1775
*(See Page 218)*

Furniture, Chair, Ormolu Mounted,
C.1725, Pair
*(See Page 218)*

Furniture, Chair, Side,
Mahogany, Balloon Back,
C.1850
*(See Page 218)*

Furniture, Chair, Pilgrim,
Maple, New England, C.1700
*(See Page 218)*

Furniture, Chair, Windsor,
Writing, New England, C.1830
*(See Page 218)*

Furniture, Chest, Blanket, Pa., 1849, 10 3/8 X 6 1/4 In.
*(See Page 218)*

Furniture, Chest, Chippendale,
Maple, New England, C.1790

Furniture, Chest, Cherry, New England, C.1790

Furniture, Chest, Blanket,
New England, C.1830
*(See Page 218)*

| | |
|---|---|
| **Furniture, Chest,** Blanket, Pine & Poplar, Design On Lid, C.1850 | 150.00 |
| **Furniture, Chest,** Blanket, Pine, Dovetailed, Footed, 37 In.Long | 65.00 |
| **Furniture, Chest,** Blanket, Pine, New England, C.1800 | 250.00 |
| **Furniture, Chest,** Blanket, Pine, 30 X 15 X 19 In. | 60.00 |
| **Furniture, Chest,** Blanket, Pine, 6 Boards, Board Feet, Vinegar Painting | 160.00 |
| **Furniture, Chest,** Blanket, Poplar, Red & Black Graining, Bracket Feet | 425.00 |
| **Furniture, Chest,** Blanket, Queen Anne, Pine | 595.00 |
| **Furniture, Chest,** Blanket, Walnut, 2 Bottom Drawers, Ogee Feet, Pa., C.1760 | 800.00 |
| **Furniture, Chest,** Block Front, Chippendale, Mahogany, Massachusetts, C.1760 | 6000.00 |
| **Furniture, Chest,** Bow Front, Chippendale, Mahogany, Massachusetts, C.1760 | 3000.00 |
| **Furniture, Chest,** Bow Front, Mahogany, Massachusetts, C.1815, 4 Drawers | 500.00 |
| **Furniture, Chest,** Cherry & Curly Maple, New England, C.1800 | 325.00 |
| **Furniture, Chest,** Cherry & Curly Maple, 4 Drawer, Bracket Feet, N.E., C.1780 | 550.00 |
| **Furniture, Chest,** Cherry, New England, C.1790 *Illus* | 650.00 |
| **Furniture, Chest,** Child's, Walnut, Salesman's, White Porcelain Pulls | 60.00 |
| **Furniture, Chest,** Chippendale, Inlaid Cherry, Connecticut, C.1790 | 1800.00 |
| **Furniture, Chest,** Chippendale, Maple, New England, C.1790 *Illus* | 950.00 |
| **Furniture, Chest,** Chippendale, Serpentine Front, Walnut, Mass., C.1760 | 3600.00 |
| **Furniture, Chest,** Country Sheraton, Curly Maple, Pine, & Walnut, 4 Drawer | 275.00 |
| **Furniture, Chest,** Dower, Oak, C.1650, 40 X 21 1/2 X 24 In. | 398.00 |
| **Furniture, Chest,** Dower, Pennsylvania Dutch, 1810-1820 | 1375.00 |
| **Furniture, Chest,** Federal, Mahogany, Three Drawers, C.1775 | 500.00 |

Furniture, Chest, High, Chippendale, Walnut, Pennsylvania, C.1760 .............................................. 1600.00
Furniture, Chest, High, Mahogany, Stenciled, New York, C.1830 ................................................. 375.00
Furniture, Chest, Inlaid Birch & Bird's-Eye Maple, 4 Drawer, N.E., C.1810 .................................. 425.00
Furniture, Chest, Inlaid Burl Walnut, French, C.1920 ................................................ *Illus* 800.00
Furniture, Chest, Inlaid Mahogany & Pine, Serpentine, 2 Drawer, 10 1/2 In. ............................ 160.00
Furniture, Chest, Inlaid Mahogany, Birch, Four Drawer, C.1800 ............................................. 900.00
Furniture, Chest, Inlaid Mahogany, Mass., C.1800 ......................................... *Illus* 2500.00
Furniture, Chest, Inlaid Mahogany, 6 Drawer, Brasses, French Feet, N.Y., 1800s ..................... 600.00
Furniture, Chest, Lawn Tennis, Lithograph Inside Lid, Horsman, C.1880 ................................ 35.00
Furniture, Chest, Mahogany & Maple, Mass., C.1810 ..................................... *Illus* 1200.00
Furniture, Chest, Mahogany On Pine, French Feet, 4 Drawer, 22 In. High ............................. 250.00
Furniture, Chest, Mahogany, Painted, MacIntire, C.1810 ............................. *Illus* 2500.00
Furniture, Chest, Mahogany, Salem, Mass., C.1820 .................................... *Illus* 900.00
Furniture, Chest, Mahogany, 4 Drawer, Curved Front, Turned Legs, N.E., C.1820 ................. 250.00
Furniture, Chest, Miniature, Mahogany, C.1775, 20 In.High ............................................. 400.00
Furniture, Chest, Ocher & Reddish Brown Grain, 4 Drawer, 19 1/2 In. High ..................... 175.00
Furniture, Chest, Oxboy, Chippendale, Inlaid Cherry, 4 Drawers, C.1790 ......................... 4500.00
Furniture, Chest, Pine, Carved, Wooden Hinges, C.1700, 10 1/2 In.High ........................... 190.00
Furniture, Chest, Sewing, Teak, Sandalwood, & Ivory, Mosaic, Carved, 1854 ..................... 145.00
Furniture, Chest, Sheraton, Mahogany & Satinwood, Bowfront, N.H., 4 Drawer ................... 1150.00
Furniture, Chest, Spice, Oak, C.1895, 16 In. High ................................. *Illus* 350.00
Furniture, Chest, Spice, Pine, Cornice Top, Red. Brass Pulls, 7 Drawer, C.1860 ................ 80.00
Furniture, Chest, Veneered Pine, 11 X 12 X 5 1/2 In. ...................................................... 40.00
Furniture, Chifforobe, Oak, Beveled Mirror, Brass Knobs, 30 X 17 In. .................................. 65.00
Furniture, Coffer, Oak, English, C.1749 ................................................................. 425.00
Furniture, Commode, Louis XV Style, Green Lacquer, Serpentine, C.1850, Pair ................... 2100.00
Furniture, Commode, Painted, 1 Drawer, 2 Doors Below .................................................. 80.00
Furniture, Commode, Pine, Lift Top ............................................................................... 59.00
Furniture, Commode, Portuguese, Walnut, Three Drawers, C.1750 ................................... 3750.00
Furniture, Commode, Spool Legs ................................................................................. 40.00
Furniture, Cradle, Baby's, Stenciled ............................................................................ 79.00
Furniture, Cupboard, Corner, Cherry & Tulip Poplar, C.1825, Coved Cornice ................... 1700.00
Furniture, Cupboard, Corner, Cherry, N.E., C.1810 ............................................ *Illus* 1200.00
Furniture, Cupboard, Corner, Pine, Coved Cornice, 3 Butterfly Shelves ............................ 1500.00
Furniture, Cupboard, Corner, Pine, 2 Piece, Candle Drawer, Mustard On Red ..................... 650.00
Furniture, Cupboard, Corner, Tulip Poplar, Two Part, Pennsylvania, C.1825 ..................... 650.00
Furniture, Cupboard, Grained, Painted Birds, Ferns, & Floral, 1 Door, 30 In. ................. 150.00
Furniture, Cupboard, Hanging, Painted, Drawer, 2 Shelf, Brass Knob, 7 X 9 In. ............... 85.00
Furniture, Cupboard, Pewter, Pine, C.1830 ................................................. *Illus* 850.00
Furniture, Cupboard, Pewter, Pine, New England, 1800s, Valanced Cornice ..................... 250.00
Furniture, Cupboard, Pine, Painted, Molded Cornice, New England, C.1720 ..................... 350.00
Furniture, Cupboard, Wall, Cherry, Brass Rosettes, New England, C.1815 ..................... 650.00
Furniture, Cupboard, Wall, Cherry, 2 Piece, Pie Shelf, Scrolled Apron, 88 In. .............. 675.00
Furniture, Cupboard, Wall, Corner, Oak, Mirror In Door, 3 Shelves ............................... 55.00
Furniture, Desk & Drawing Board, Child's, The Chatauqua, Dated 1895 ........................ 35.00
Furniture, Desk On Stand, Inlaid Walnut, C.1690 ....................................... *Illus* 650.00
Furniture, Desk, Block Front, Chippendale, Mahogany, Massachusetts 1760 ................. 7260.00
Furniture, Desk, Buried Wood, Drop Writing Ledge, Pigeonholes, 4 In. High ................... 14.50
Furniture, Desk, Cherry & Walnut, Phila., C.1710 ................................... *Illus* 7000.00
Furniture, Desk, Child's, Rolltop ............................................................................. 85.00
Furniture, Desk, Countinghouse, Pine & Maple, New England, C.1800 ......................... 375.00
Furniture, Desk, Davenport, Mahogany, 5 Drawer, Green Leather, C.1890 ................... 350.00
Furniture, Desk, Davenport, Rosewood, Leather Lined, C.1850 .................................. 1200.00
Furniture, Desk, Lady's, Inlaid Mahogany, 3 Parts, Seymour School, C.1790 ............... 1500.00
Furniture, Desk, Lady's, Pennsylvania Dutch, Black Walnut ................................... 145.00
Furniture, Desk, Lady's, Victorian, Walnut, Cylinder, Paine's Label, 1887 ................ 550.00
Furniture, Desk, Lap, Marquetry, Mother-Of-Pearl, English ..................... 55.00 To 65.00
Furniture, Desk, Lap, Oak ........................................................................................ 45.00
Furniture, Desk, Lap, Victorian, Walnut, Black & Bronze, 9 X 13 X 4 1/4 In. ................ 25.00
Furniture, Desk, Lap, Walnut, Inlaid Brass Plaque On Lid, 8 1/2 X 11 3/4 In. .............. 50.00
Furniture, Desk, Mahogany, Haines Connelly, C.1810 ............................... *Illus* 3750.00
Furniture, Desk, Mahogany, Mass., C.1770 ............................................ *Illus* 7000.00
Furniture, Desk, Mahogany, Pedestal, Red Leather Rectangular Top, C.1890 ............... 275.00
Furniture, Desk, New England, 1 Drawer, Red ......................................................... 285.00
Furniture, Desk, Oak, S-Roll Top, 66 X 37 X 51 In. ............................................... 800.00
Furniture, Desk, Painted, Black, Red, Gold, & Blue, C.1890 ..................... *Illus* 650.00

Furniture, Chest, Inlaid Burl Walnut, French, C.1920
(See Page 221)

Furniture, Chest, Inlaid Mahogany, Mass., C.1800
(See Page 221)

Furniture, Chest, Mahogany,
Painted, MacIntire, C.1810
(See Page 221)

Furniture, Chest, Spice,
Oak, C.1895, 16 In. High
(See Page 221)

Furniture, Chest,
Mahogany & Maple, Mass., C.1810
(See Page 221)

Furniture, Chest, Mahogany, Salem, Mass., C.1820
(See Page 221)

Furniture, Desk, Painted, Black, Red, Gold, & Blue, C.1890
*(See Page 221)*

Furniture, Cupboard, Corner, Cherry, N.E., C.1810
*(See Page 221)*

Furniture, Cupboard, Pewter, Pine, C.1830
*(See Page 221)*

Furniture, Desk, Mahogany, Mass., C.1770
*(See Page 221)*

Furniture,
Desk On Stand,
Inlaid Walnut,
C.1690
*(See Page 221)*

Furniture, Desk, Cherry & Walnut,
Phila., C.1710
*(See Page 221)*

Furniture, Desk, Mahogany, Haines Connelly, C.1810
*(See Page 221)*

Furniture, Desk, School, Slant-Front,
Maple & Cherry

| | | |
|---|---|---|
| **Furniture, Desk,** Partners', Georgian | | 2175.00 |
| **Furniture, Desk,** School, Slant-Front, Maple & Cherry | *Illus* | 200.00 |
| **Furniture, Desk,** Ship Captain's, Portable, Burled Walnut, Brassbound, C.1840 | | 225.00 |
| **Furniture, Desk,** Slant Front, Chippendale, Curly Maple, C.1760 | | 1400.00 |
| **Furniture, Desk,** Slant Front, Chippendale, Maple, C.1770 | *Illus* | 2400.00 |
| **Furniture, Desk,** Slant Front, Chippendale, 4 Drawers, New England, C.1760 | | 1800.00 |
| **Furniture, Desk,** Slant Front, Queen Anne, Walnut, C.1720 | | 3000.00 |
| **Furniture, Desk,** Traveling, Mahogany, Ganes, C.1825 | | 350.00 |
| **Furniture, Desk,** Walnut, Mass., C.1760, 44 1/2 In. High | *Illus* | 3100.00 |
| **Furniture, Desk,** Wooten Patent, C.1880, 4 Ft.7 In. High | *Illus* | 1300.00 |
| **Furniture, Door,** Walnut, Double, Etched Glass Panels, C.1870, 2 Pair | | 500.00 |
| **Furniture, Dresser,** English Oak, Cabriole Legs, C.1740, 87 X 20 X 35 In. | | 4100.00 |
| **Furniture, Dresser,** Victorian, Walnut, 3 Drawer, Paneled Ends | | 110.00 |
| **Furniture, Dry Sink,** Pennsylvania Dutch, Brown Stippled, Drawer, 2 Doors | | 160.00 |
| **Furniture, Dry Sink,** Pine, Brown Graining, 20 1/2 X 24 X 8 3/4 In. | | 115.00 |
| **Furniture, Dry Sink,** Pine, Double Lift Lid, Cutout Base | | 165.00 |
| **Furniture, Dry Sink,** Plank Ends, Bracket Base, 2 Drawer, 2 Doors | | 175.00 |
| **Furniture, Etagere,** Mahogany, Massachusetts, C.1825 | | 650.00 |
| **Furniture, Fauteuil,** Italian, C.1775 | *Illus* | 500.00 |
| **Furniture, Fauteuil,** Italian, Carved, Painted, Cartouche Back, C.1850 | | 400.00 |
| **Furniture, Footstool,** Round, Beaded Design On Top, 3 Short Feet, 10 1/2 In. | | 48.50 |
| **Furniture, Fountain,** Parlor, Cast Iron, Cloverleaf Bowls, Cupid, Patent 1879 | | 175.00 |
| **Furniture, Frame,** Crisscross, Gold Liner, Leaves, 6 X 4 3/4 In. | | 15.00 |
| **Furniture, Frame,** Hand-Carved Wood, Black, Cupid On Top, C.1840 | | 35.00 |
| **Furniture, Frame,** Picture, Art Nouveau, Marquetry, Berries & Leaves, 5 In. | | 65.00 |
| **Furniture, Frame,** Picture, Double Gold Leaf Liner, 10 X 12 In. | | 7.50 |
| **Furniture, Frame,** Picture, Dull Gold, Raised Grapes & Leaves, 10 X 20 In. | | 7.50 |
| **Furniture, Frame,** Picture, Gilt, Embossed, 13 X 15 In. | | 15.00 |
| **Furniture, Frame,** Picture, Gold, Oval, Concave Glass, 14 X 20 In. | | 17.50 |
| **Furniture, Frame,** Picture, Gold, Oval, Raised Scrolls, 14 X 17 In. | | 12.50 |
| **Furniture, Frame,** Picture, Gold, Oval, U.S.A. Top, Flags Bottom, 14 X 20 In. | | 14.50 |
| **Furniture, Frame,** Picture, Gold, Raised Acorns & Oak Leaves, 10 X 14 In. | | 9.00 |
| **Furniture, Frame,** Picture, Gold, Round, Glass, 21 1/2 In., Pair | | 52.50 |
| **Furniture, Frame,** Picture, Hand Carved, Leaf Corners, 10 X 14 In. | | 4.75 |
| **Furniture, Frame,** Picture, Mahogany Grain, Gold Leaf Liner, 13 X 19 In. | | 12.50 |
| **Furniture, Frame,** Picture, Oak, Gold Leaf Liner, 16 X 20 In. | | 5.00 |
| **Furniture, Frame,** Picture, Pine, Handmade, Inlaid Hearts, 21 X 16 In. | | 18.00 |
| **Furniture, Frame,** Picture, Pine, Mahogany Finish, Oval, 16 X 20 In. | | 9.00 |
| **Furniture, Frame,** Picture, Pine, Raised Corners, 14 X 18 1/2 In. | | 5.75 |
| **Furniture, Frame,** Picture, Pine, Walnut Finish, Gold Leaf Liner, 10 X 12 In. | | 6.00 |
| **Furniture, Frame,** Picture, Pine, Walnut Finish, Oval, 8 X 10 In., Pair | | 12.50 |
| **Furniture, Frame,** Picture, Plaster On Pine, 9 1/2 X 11 In. | | 4.50 |

| | |
|---|---|
| **Furniture, Frame,** Picture, Plaster Over Pine, 15 X 20 In. | 6.00 |
| **Furniture, Frame,** Picture, Plaster Over Pine, 16 X 20 In. | 5.00 |
| **Furniture, Frame,** Picture, Shadow Box, Oak, 25 X 30 In. | 24.50 |
| **Furniture, Frame,** Picture, Tramp Art, Carved Wood, 6 1/2 X 8 In. | 10.00 |
| **Furniture, Frame,** Picture, Tramp Art, 10 X 12 In. | 45.00 |
| **Furniture, Frame,** Picture, Walnut, Carved Crabs On Corners, 9 X 11 In. | 6.00 |
| **Furniture, Frame,** Picture, Walnut, Carved, Glass, 8 X 5 In. | 25.00 |
| **Furniture, Frame,** Picture, Walnut, Crisscross With Leaf Corners, 8 X 10 In. | 4.75 |
| **Furniture, Frame,** Picture, Walnut, Gold Leaf Liner, 10 X 14 In. | 5.75 |
| **Furniture, Frame,** Picture, Walnut, Gold Leaf Liner, 12 X 16 In. | 7.50 |
| **Furniture, Frame,** Picture, Walnut, Gold Leaf Liner, 14 X 18 In. | 9.00 |
| **Furniture, Frame,** Picture, Walnut, Gold Leaf Liner, 15 X 18 In. | 7.50 |
| **Furniture, Frame,** Picture, Walnut, Gold Leaf Liner, 16 X 20 In. | 9.00 |
| **Furniture, Frame,** Picture, Walnut, Hand-Carved, Gold Leaf Liner, 10 X 12 In. | 6.75 |
| **Furniture, Frame,** Picture, Walnut, Hand-Carved, Gold Leaf Liner, 10 X 14 In. | 5.75 |
| **Furniture, Frame,** Picture, Walnut, Hand-Carved, Gold Liner, 9 X 11 1/2 In. | 5.75 |
| **Furniture, Frame,** Picture, Walnut, Hand-Carved, 14 X 20 In. | 5.75 |
| **Furniture, Frame,** Picture, Walnut, Hand-Carved, 15 X 19 In. | 9.00 |
| **Furniture, Frame,** Picture, Walnut, Painted, Leaf Corners, 8 X 10 In. | 6.00 |
| **Furniture, Frame,** Picture, Walnut, 12 X 16 In. | 4.50 |
| **Furniture, Frame,** Picture, Walnut, 9 1/2 X 11 1/2 In. | 4.50 |
| **Furniture, Hall Tree,** Oak | 100.00 |

Furniture, Desk, Wooten Patent,
C.1880, 4 Ft.7 In. High
*(See Page 224)*

Furniture, Desk, Slant Front,
Chippendale, Maple, C.1770
*(See Page 224)*

Furniture, Fauteuil, Italian, C.1775
*(See Page 224)*

Furniture, Desk, Walnut, Mass.,
C.1760, 44 1/2 In. High
*(See Page 224)*

Furniture, **Hall Tree,** Victorian, Walnut, White Marble, Canes, Boston ............... 395.00
Furniture, **Highboy,** Cherry & Maple, R.I., C.1740 ............................... *Illus* 4500.00
Furniture, **Highboy,** Cherry, Bonnet Top, C.1785 ................................. *Illus* 8000.00
Furniture, **Highboy,** Chippendale Style, Mahogany, Carved, Bonnet Top ............ 2800.00
Furniture, **Highboy,** Chippendale, Bonnet Top, Cherry, Conn., C.1760 .............. 2400.00
Furniture, **Highboy,** Queen Anne, Cherry, Connecticut, C.1750 ..................... 850.00
Furniture, **Highboy,** Queen Anne, Flat Top, Cherry, Connecticut, C.1750 ........... 4000.00
Furniture, **Highboy,** Queen Anne, Flat Top, Walnut, C.1750 ........................ 1200.00
Furniture, **Highboy,** William & Mary, Inlaid Walnut, Two Parts, Turnip Feet ....... 1200.00
Furniture, **Highchair & Stroller Combination,** Carved, Germany ................... 85.00
Furniture, **Highchair,** Maple, New England, C.1775 ....................... *Illus* 250.00
Furniture, **Ice Cream Set,** Child's, Twisted Steel, Wooden Seats, 5 Piece ......... 39.50
Furniture, **Ice Cream Set,** Wire & Wood, 5 Piece ............................... 125.00
Furniture, **Jardiniere,** Italian, Painted, Gilt Metal Edge, Masks, C.1850 ......... 300.00
Furniture, **Linen Press,** English, 17th Century ............................... 1750.00
Furniture, **Lit De Repos,** Charles X, Rolled Over Wood Head & Foot .............. 425.00
Furniture, **Love Seat,** Victorian, Walnut, Mirror Frame Back, Carved Leaves ...... 189.00
Furniture, **Lowboy,** Chippendale, Mahogany, Salem, Massachusetts, C.1760 ....... 9500.00
Furniture, **Lowboy,** Queen Anne, Carved Walnut, Fan Carved Drawer, C.1740 ...... 7500.00
Furniture, **Lowboy,** Queen Anne, Cherry, Arcaded Apron, Oblong Top ............. 1200.00
Furniture, **Lowboy,** Queen Anne, Curly Maple, Cabriole Legs, Pad Feet ........... 2000.00
Furniture, **Lowboy,** Queen Anne, Mahogany, American ......................... 2950.00
Furniture, **Lowboy,** Queen Anne, Maple & Curly Maple, Fan Carved Drawer ....... 1000.00
Furniture, **Lowboy,** William & Mary, Cherry & Maple, New York, Dated 1737 ...... 8500.00
Furniture, **Lowboy,** William & Mary, Inlaid Walnut, Ball Feet ................... 1100.00
Furniture, **Mirror,** Art Deco Type, Folding, 3 Section .......................... 7.00
Furniture, **Mirror,** Beveled, Oak Frame, 20 In.Square ......................... 12.00
Furniture, **Mirror,** Bridal, Brass, Easel Back, Reticulated Frame, Cupids ......... 110.00
Furniture, **Mirror,** Bridal, French, Champleve, Footed Marble Base, Scalloped .... 225.00
Furniture, **Mirror,** Carved Ivory, Cartouche Shape, French, C.1890, 33 In., Pair .. 375.00
Furniture, **Mirror,** Cheval, Empire Style, Double Legs, Ormolu Mount, 60 In. ..... 250.00
Furniture, **Mirror,** Chippendale Style, Curly Maple .................... *Illus* 200.00
Furniture, **Mirror,** Chippendale, Mahogany & Parcel Gilded, C.1760, 37 In. ...... 1300.00
Furniture, **Mirror,** Chippendale, Mahogany & Parcel Gilded, C.1770, 41 In. ...... 1400.00
Furniture, **Mirror,** Courting, Embossed Brass On Pine, 20 X 10 1/2 In. .......... 155.00
Furniture, **Mirror,** Dressing Glass, Inlaid Mahogany, Bowfront, C.1800 .......... 300.00
Furniture, **Mirror,** Gilt Wood, Carved, C.1775, 4 Ft.2 In.High ................. 3700.00
Furniture, **Mirror,** Girandole, Federal, Gilt Wood & Gesso, 1800s, 42 In. ....... 450.00
Furniture, **Mirror,** Hired Man's, Pine, Triangular, Glass Inset, 3 3/4 X 11 In. ... 85.00
Furniture, **Mirror,** Inlaid Mahogany, New England, C.1825 ............... *Illus* 250.00
Furniture, **Mirror,** Italian, Carved Gilt Wood, Scrolling Acanthus, C.1890 ....... 275.00
Furniture, **Mirror,** Mantel, Antique Gold, 3 Ft.X 18 In. ....................... 49.00
Furniture, **Mirror,** Mantel, Oak, 3 Mirrors, Galleries ......................... 90.00
Furniture, **Mirror,** Oak, Rococo Frame, C.1750, 36 In.High .................... 200.00
Furniture, **Mirror,** Pier, Silver Plate, Floral & Leaf, C.1890, 37 In. ............ 325.00
Furniture, **Mirror,** Plateau, Flat, 17 In. .................................... 35.00
Furniture, **Mirror,** Queen Anne, Fretwork With Inlay, New England ............. 395.00
Furniture, **Mirror,** Queen Anne, Mahogany & Parcel Gilded, C.1740, 36 In. ...... 1700.00
Furniture, **Mirror,** Silver Mounted, George III, Wood Base, Boulton, 1806 ....... 1100.00
Furniture, **Mirror,** Silver Plate, Repousse, Medallions, C.1890, 41 1/2 In. ...... 200.00
Furniture, **Mirror,** Teakwood, Carved, Foliage, 25 X 26 In. ................... 150.00
Furniture, **Mirror,** Venetian Glass, Blue Mirror Border, Scrolls, C.1850, 5 Ft. ... 180.00
Furniture, **Mirror,** Victorian, Carved Oak, Pierced, Scrolls, 29 1/2 In. .......... 50.00
Furniture, **Mirror,** Victorian, Carved Walnut, Oval Plate, Pierced Frame ......... 75.00
Furniture, **Mirror,** Wall, Carved Mahogany & Gilt Wood, Scroll Crest, C.1760 .... 1600.00
Furniture, **Mirror,** Wall, Chippendale Style, Mahogany & Parcel Gilt, 25 In. ..... 100.00
Furniture, **Mirror,** Wall, Chippendale, Mahogany, C.1800, 20 In.High ........... 300.00
Furniture, **Mirror,** Wall, Chippendale, Walnut & Parcel Gilded, C.1760 .......... 1000.00
Furniture, **Mirror,** Wall, Gilt Wood, Eglomise Panel, N.E., C.1810, 19 1/4 In. ... 375.00
Furniture, **Mirror,** Wall, Mahogany, Carved, Scroll Crest, Gilded Slip, C.1760 ... 450.00
Furniture, **Mirror,** Wall, Queen Anne, Walnut, C.1720, 52 In.High ............. 1500.00
Furniture, **Mirror,** Wall, Walnut & Gilt Wood, Eglomise Panel, C.1720, 4 Ft. .... 1100.00
Furniture, **Nest Of Tables,** Mahogany, Turned Legs, Reeded Edge, 4 ........... 125.00
Furniture, **Nightstand,** Country, Walnut, Splay Legs, 1 Drawer, 27 1/2 In. ...... 90.00
Furniture, **Ornament,** Wicker, For Incense, Pink & Green Jade Beads, China ..... 35.00
Furniture, **Parlor Set,** Victorian, Mahogany, Flame Ornament, 3 Piece .......... 300.00

Furniture, Highboy,
Cherry & Maple,
R.I., C.1740
*(See Page 226)*

Furniture, Highboy, Cherry,
Bonnet Top, C.1785
*(See Page 226)*

Furniture, Highchair, Maple,
New England, C.1775
*(See Page 226)*

Furniture, Mirror,
Chippendale Style,
Curly Maple
*(See Page 226)*

Furniture,
Mirror, Inlaid Mahogany,
New England, C.1825
*(See Page 226)*

| | |
|---|---:|
| **Furniture, Parlor Suite,** Victorian, Walnut, 5 Piece | 695.00 |
| **Furniture, Pedestal,** Teakwood, Chinese, Pink & White Marble Slab, 35 In.High | 175.00 |
| **Furniture, Pen,** Play, Child's, 21 X 23 X 25 In. | 22.50 |
| **Furniture, Pianoforte,** Rosewood, Inlaid Mahogany, Daniel Thomas, C.1825 | 200.00 |
| **Furniture, Pie Safe,** Pine, Yellow Stain, Punched Tin Panels, 55 1/2 In. High | 185.00 |
| **Furniture, Pie Safe,** Tin Panels, Tulip On Each Side, 2 Door, Drawer | 210.00 |
| **Furniture, Press,** Linen, Miniature, Island Mahogany, Mirror In Cupboard | 175.00 |
| **Furniture, Rack,** Coat, Oak, Art Nouveau Style, Brass Hardware, Marquetry | 475.00 |
| **Furniture, Rack,** Hall, Victorian, Folding, Porcelain Knobs | 10.00 |
| **Furniture, Rack,** Letter, Wall, Carved Walnut, Animal In Center | 20.00 |
| **Furniture, Rack,** Towel, Victorian, Spool Type, 4 Bar, Stands On Floor | 25.00 |
| **Furniture, Rocker,** Arms, Ladder Back, Rush Seat, Black Paint, Gilt Trim | 65.00 |
| **Furniture, Rocker,** Arms, Ladder Back, Woven Split Seat, Red Paint | 85.00 |
| **Furniture, Rocker,** Beacon's Bench, Maple, Double | 40.00 |
| **Furniture, Rocker,** Birch & Maple, Arms, Pierced Vasiform Splat, N.E., C.1760 | 425.00 |
| **Furniture, Rocker,** Child's, Arms, Slat Back, Woven Cane Seat, Red Paint | 25.00 |
| **Furniture, Rocker,** Child's, Mission Oak, Brass, Stickley Bros. Label | 35.00 |
| **Furniture, Rocker,** Child's, Wicker, White | 45.00 |
| **Furniture, Rocker,** Ladder Back, Covered Seat | 35.00 |
| **Furniture, Rocker,** Mahogany, Carved Grape & Floral Crest, Padded Arms, 1850s | 175.00 |
| **Furniture, Rocker,** Pilgrim, Sausage Turnings, C.1690 | 395.00 |
| **Furniture, Rocker,** Steel, S-Shape Frame, Leather & Suede Padding | 325.00 |

| | |
|---|---:|
| **Furniture, Rocker,** Victorian, Ebony, Platform, Carved, Signed | 365.00 |
| **Furniture, Rocker,** Victorian, Wicker, Platform | 59.00 |
| **Furniture, Screen,** Carved Walnut, 1900s, 5 Ft.7 1/4 In.High | 1600.00 |
| **Furniture, Screen,** Fire, Walnut, Needlework Panel, 4 Ft.5 In.High | 250.00 |
| **Furniture, Screen,** French Enamel, Ormolu Frame, 2 Panels | 275.00 |
| **Furniture, Screen,** Louis XV Style, Carved, Gilt Wood, Tapestry, Fourfold | 1000.00 |
| **Furniture, Screen,** Silk, Threefold, Hand-Painted Scenes, 14 X 18 In. | 25.00 |
| **Furniture, Screen,** Table, Chinese, Gold Leaf On Green Jade, C.1850, Pair | 275.00 |
| **Furniture, Screen,** Table, Oriental, Carved Stone, Dark Base, 12 In. | 145.00 |
| **Furniture, Screen,** Threefold, Arched Top, Rape Of Europa, 4 Ft.8 In. | 400.00 |
| **Furniture, Screen,** Twelvefold, Chinese Lacquer, C.1720, 9 Ft.High | 6500.00 |
| **Furniture, Screen,** Victorian, Decoupage, Black, Fourfold, 5 Ft.5 In. High | 400.00 |
| **Furniture, Seat,** Window, Italian, Walnut, C.1755 | 160.00 |
| **Furniture, Secretaire Bookcase,** Oak & Burr Walnut, Roll Top, C.1890 | 650.00 |
| **Furniture, Secretary Bookcase,** Inlaid Mahogany, Mass. ............................*Illus* | 2000.00 |
| **Furniture, Secretary Bookcase,** Mahogany, Meeks, C.1835 ....................*Illus* | 1600.00 |
| **Furniture, Secretary-Bookcase,** Chippendale, Mahogany, Connecticut, C.1760 | 2900.00 |
| **Furniture, Secretary,** Mahogany, Sandwich Knobs, Claw Feet, C.1830 | 595.00 |
| **Furniture, Settee,** Bugatti, Inlaid Walnut, Ebonized Wood, C.1900 | 1000.00 |
| **Furniture, Settee,** Carved, Gilt Wood, C.1775 | 275.00 |
| **Furniture, Settee,** Chippendale, Carved, Claw & Ball Feet, C.1750 | 950.00 |
| **Furniture, Settee,** Federal Style, Inlaid Mahogany, Canted Back, Damask | 2000.00 |
| **Furniture, Settee,** Federal, Oblong Back, Mahogany, C.1800, 5 Ft.8 In.Long | 1800.00 |
| **Furniture, Settee,** Mahogany & Ormolu, Griffin, Empire Style | 300.00 |
| **Furniture, Settee,** Mahogany, Serpentine Crest, Grapes, Upholstered, C.1850 | 225.00 |
| **Furniture, Settee,** Victorian, Griffins & Urn, Upholstered, 5 Ft.Long | 150.00 |
| **Furniture, Settee,** Victorian, Mahogany, Serpentine, C.1850 | 200.00 |
| **Furniture, Settee,** Walnut, Art Nouveau, Upholstered, Carved Flowers | 700.00 |
| **Furniture, Settee,** Windsor, Bamboo Turned, N.E., C.1800 ....................*Illus* | 2400.00 |
| **Furniture, Settee,** Windsor, C.1800, 6 Ft.8 In.Long ............................*Illus* | 1900.00 |
| **Furniture, Settle,** Serpentine Cresting, Walnut, Box Base, Plank Seat | 300.00 |
| **Furniture, Shadow Box,** Round, Mahogany, Gold Liner, 16 X 3 1/4 In. | 55.00 |
| **Furniture, Shadow Box,** Square, Walnut Frame, 13 1/2 X 15 1/2 In. | 15.00 |
| **Furniture, Shadow Box,** Walnut, 2 Gold Liners, Round, 16 In. | 45.00 |
| **Furniture, Shelf,** Clock, Corner, Hand-Carved, Deer's Head In Center | 45.00 |
| **Furniture, Shelf,** Wall, Hand-Carved, Hinged Sides, 4 X 12 X 10 In. | 9.75 |
| **Furniture, Shelf,** Whatnot, Wall, Hand-Painted Gold, 3 Shelves, 2 Drawers | 15.00 |
| **Furniture, Sideboard,** Block Front, Inlaid Walnut, North Carolina, C.1800 | 2000.00 |
| **Furniture, Sideboard,** Curly Maple, 4 Doors & Drawers, Tennessee, C.1810 | 3500.00 |
| **Furniture, Sideboard,** Empire, Inlaid Mahogany, New England, C.1830 | 200.00 |
| **Furniture, Sideboard,** Inlaid Mahogany, Bowfront, Reeded Legs, Phila., C.1810 | 850.00 |
| **Furniture, Sideboard,** Inlaid Mahogany, Marble, C.1810 ......................*Illus* | 1600.00 |
| **Furniture, Sideboard,** Inlaid Mahogany, Serpentine, Tapered Legs, C.1790 | 3000.00 |
| **Furniture, Sideboard,** Mahogany, C.1825 ......................................*Illus* | 1500.00 |
| **Furniture, Sideboard,** Mahogany, Kneehole Front, Cellaret Drawer, C.1775 | 1700.00 |
| **Furniture, Sideboard,** Monel Metal Outlines, French ............................*Illus* | 500.00 |
| **Furniture, Sideboard,** Oak, Beveled Mirror, Brass Drop Handles, 3 Drawer | 85.00 |
| **Furniture, Sideboard,** Serpentine, Inlaid Mahogany, Federal, 5 Ft.4 In.Long | 1200.00 |
| **Furniture, Sofa,** Camelback, Chippendale, Carved Walnut, 9 Ft.2 In.Long | 1200.00 |
| **Furniture, Sofa,** Camelback, Chippendale, Mahogany, Scrolled Arms | 1400.00 |
| **Furniture, Sofa,** Duncan Phyfe, Mahogany, Federal Period, 6 Ft.8 In.Long | 900.00 |
| **Furniture, Sofa,** Duncan Phyfe, Mahogany, New York, C.1810, 6 Ft.6 In.Long | 6000.00 |
| **Furniture, Sofa,** Empire Style, Mahogany Frame, Claw Feet, Picture Frame Back | 350.00 |
| **Furniture, Sofa,** Louis XV, Miniature, Silver & Dore, Red Damask Upholstery | 65.00 |
| **Furniture, Sofa,** Mahogany, Cabriole, Canted Back, Upholstered, C.1850 | 1500.00 |
| **Furniture, Sofa,** New England, C.1810 | 1200.00 |
| **Furniture, Sofa,** Victorian, Upholstered, 6 Cabriole Legs, C.1890, 7 Ft.3 In. | 500.00 |
| **Furniture, Stand,** Basin, Queen Anne, Walnut, Snake Feet, 31 In.High | 600.00 |
| **Furniture, Stand,** Cherry, Green Stencil, Twined Legs, 2 Drawer | 125.00 |
| **Furniture, Stand,** Cherry, Square Tapered Legs, 1 Drawer, C.1790 | 175.00 |
| **Furniture, Stand,** Cutlery, Mahogany, Divided Well, Raised Molding | 180.00 |
| **Furniture, Stand,** Kettle, Chippendale, Carved Mahogany, C.1760, 28 In.High | 750.00 |
| **Furniture, Stand,** Music, Four Slatted Shelves, Brass Trim, C.1880 | 200.00 |
| **Furniture, Stand,** Pine, Yellow Decorated, 1 Drawer, C.1810 | 165.00 |
| **Furniture, Stand,** Plant, Inlaid Mahogany, English, C.1880 | 90.00 |
| **Furniture, Stand,** Shaving, Inlaid Mahogany, 1 Drawer | 95.00 |

Furniture, Secretary Bookcase,
Inlaid Mahogany, Mass.
*(See Page 228)*

Furniture, Secretary Bookcase,
Mahogany, Meeks, C.1835
*(See Page 228)*

Furniture, Settee, Windsor, C.1800, 6 Ft.8 In.Long
*(See Page 228)*

Furniture, Settee, Windsor, Bamboo Turned, N.E., C.1800
*(See Page 228)*

Furniture, Sideboard, Mahogany, C.1825
(See Page 228)

Furniture, Sideboard, Inlaid Mahogany, Marble, C.1810
(See Page 228)

Furniture, Table, Bedside,
Cherry & Maple, N.E., C.1825
(See Page 232)

Furniture, Table, Book, Parquetry, C.1775
(See Page 232)

Furniture, Sideboard, Monel Metal Outlines, French
(See Page 228)

Furniture, Table, Console,
Mahogany, C.1850
*(See Page 232)*

Furniture, Table, Console,
Pine, C.1775
*(See Page 232)*

Furniture, Table, Card,
Mahogany & Satinwood, N.E., 1790s
*(See Page 232)*

Furniture, Table, Chippendale,
Maple, Pa., C.1770
*(See Page 232)*

Furniture, **Steps,** Library, Mahogany, C.1800, 47 In.High ............................................ 375.00
Furniture, **Stool,** Federal, Mahogany, New York, C.1800 ............................................ 450.00
Furniture, **Stool,** Ice Cream, Wire, Wooden Top, Counter Size ............................................ 18.00
Furniture, **Stool,** Milking, Rosewood, 14 In.High, Tripod Legs ............................................ 130.00
Furniture, **Stool,** Organ, Oak, High Back, Glass Ball & Claw Feet ............................................ 69.00
Furniture, **Stool,** Piano, Oak, High Back, Glass Ball Feet ............................................ 69.00
Furniture, **Stool,** Victorian, Rectangular Seat, Scrolls & Urns On Black ............................................ 250.00
Furniture, **Table & Music Box,** Game, Hepplewhite, Inlaid, 8 Tunes ............................................ 400.00
Furniture, **Table Stool,** Turned Maple, Molded Oblong Top, Mass., C.1720 ............................................ 1300.00
Furniture, **Table,** Bedside, Cherry & Maple, N.E., C.1825 ............................................ *Illus* 275.00
Furniture, **Table,** Bedside, Federal, Cherry & Mahogany, New England, C.1810 ............................................ 275.00
Furniture, **Table,** Book, Parquetry, C.1775 ............................................ *Illus* 2200.00
Furniture, **Table,** Breakfast, Carved Cherry, 2 D Shape Leaves, Mass., C.1820 ............................................ 150.00
Furniture, **Table,** Breakfast, Cherry & Maple, Drop Leaf, Oval, Conn.C, .1740 ............................................ 825.00
Furniture, **Table,** Breakfast, Inlaid Cherry, New England, C.1800 ............................................ 600.00
Furniture, **Table,** Bugatti, Ebonized Walnut & Metal Inlaid, C.1900 ............................................ 2600.00
Furniture, **Table,** Burl Walnut, Eastlake ............................................ 165.00
Furniture, **Table,** Card, Burr Walnut, D-Shaped Top, C.1675 ............................................ 3500.00
Furniture, **Table,** Card, Carved Mahogany, Hinged Oblong Top, C.1760 ............................................ 2200.00
Furniture, **Table,** Card, Chinese Chippendale, Mahogany, Swing Leg ............................................ 350.00
Furniture, **Table,** Card, Five Legs, Michael Allison, New York, C.1800 ............................................ 3100.00
Furniture, **Table,** Card, Inlaid Mahogany & Birch, Serpentine, Mass., C.1790 ............................................ 800.00
Furniture, **Table,** Card, Inlaid Mahogany, Hinged Oblong Top, Mass., C.1810 ............................................ 1200.00
Furniture, **Table,** Card, Mahogany & Satinwood, N.E., 1790s ............................................ *Illus* 2100.00
Furniture, **Table,** Card, Mahogany, Leather Top, C.1820 ............................................ 85.00
Furniture, **Table,** Card, Mahogany, Rounded Corners, New England, C.1820 ............................................ 350.00
Furniture, **Table,** Card, Rosewood, English, C.1820 ............................................ 325.00
Furniture, **Table,** Card, Serpentine Front, Inlaid Mahogany, Mass., C.1800 ............................................ 1000.00
Furniture, **Table,** Card, Serpentine, Inlaid Mahogany, Massachusetts, C.1800 ............................................ 1200.00
Furniture, **Table,** Card, Sheraton, Inlaid, New England ............................................ 600.00
Furniture, **Table,** Card, Spiral Turned Legs, Mahogany, New York, C.1815 ............................................ 275.00
Furniture, **Table,** Center, Drop Leaf, Oval, English, C.1860 ............................................ 375.00
Furniture, **Table,** Cherry, Tilt Top, 3 Legs ............................................ 225.00
Furniture, **Table,** Chess, Octagonal, Ivory Inlaid, 2 Drawers With Men ............................................ 200.00
Furniture, **Table,** Chessboard, Italian, Marquetry, 3 Splayed Legs, 28 In. High ............................................ 150.00
Furniture, **Table,** Chippendale, Maple, Pa., C.1770 ............................................ *Illus* 250.00
Furniture, **Table,** Console, Mahogany, C.1850 ............................................ *Illus* 1900.00
Furniture, **Table,** Console, Pine, C.1775 ............................................ *Illus* 2700.00
Furniture, **Table,** Corner, Walnut, Breadboard Edge, 17 X 30 In. ............................................ 95.00
Furniture, **Table,** Dining, Cherry, 6 Leg, N.E., C.1800 ............................................ *Illus* 350.00
Furniture, **Table,** Dining, French, Art Deco, Monel Metal Outlines, 30 In. High ............................................ 500.00
Furniture, **Table,** Dining, Mahogany, Swing Leg, C.1820 ............................................ 595.00
Furniture, **Table,** Dining, Mahogany, 3 Part, Square Tapered Legs, Va., C.1800 ............................................ 4000.00
Furniture, **Table,** Dining, Maple, Drop Leaf, N.E., C.1750 ............................................ *Illus* 2100.00
Furniture, **Table,** Dining, Oak, Round ............................................ 85.00
Furniture, **Table,** Dressing, New England, C.1830 ............................................ *Illus* 250.00

Furniture, Table, Dining, Cherry, 6 Leg,
N.E., C.1800

Furniture, Table, Game, Mahogany, C.1725

Furniture, Table,
Library, Stairs, Mahogany, C.1850
(See Page 234)

Furniture, Table, Dining, Maple, Drop Leaf, N.E., C.1750
(See Page 232)

Furniture, Table, Dressing, New England, C.1830
(See Page 232)

| | |
|---|---|
| **Furniture, Table**, Dressing, Painted & Decorated, New England, C.1835 | 425.00 |
| **Furniture, Table**, Dressing, Queen Anne, Maple & Cherry, Valanced Apron | 375.00 |
| **Furniture, Table**, Drop Leaf, Chippendale, Pennsylvania, C.1760 | 1000.00 |
| **Furniture, Table**, Drop Leaf, Mahogany, Benjamin Frothingham, Mass., C.1760 | 1900.00 |
| **Furniture, Table**, Drop Leaf, Mahogany, Fretwork Gallery, C.1725 | 750.00 |
| **Furniture, Table**, Drop Leaf, Queen Anne, Walnut, Philadelphia, C.1740 | 1800.00 |
| **Furniture, Table**, Drop Leaf, Valanced Skirt, C.1760, 29 In.High | 750.00 |
| **Furniture, Table**, End, Mahogany, Marquetry Top | 65.00 |
| **Furniture, Table**, Galle, Marquetry, Nightshade Blossoms, 2 Tier, 28 3/4 In. | 500.00 |
| **Furniture, Table**, Game, Burr Walnut, Green Baize Surface, C.1725 | 1400.00 |
| **Furniture, Table**, Game, Checkerboard Top, Mahogany, C.1775 | 1200.00 |
| **Furniture, Table**, Game, Hepplewhite, Inlaid Wood, 8 Tune Music Box | 400.00 |
| **Furniture, Table**, Game, Italian, Marquetry, Burr Walnut, Carved, C.1890 | 1600.00 |
| **Furniture, Table**, Game, Mahogany, C.1725 ............ *Illus* | 1100.00 |
| **Furniture, Table**, Game, Oak, Heroic Carved, 4 Griffins Form Base, Round | 450.00 |
| **Furniture, Table**, Game, Rosewood, Lyre Base, C.1825 | 450.00 |
| **Furniture, Table**, Game, Scrimshaw Whalebone & Carved Wood, C.1850 | 275.00 |
| **Furniture, Table**, Game, William IV, 1 Drawer In Frieze, Reeded Legs, 29 In. | 200.00 |
| **Furniture, Table**, Gateleg, Cherry & Maple, Turned, New England, C.1700 | 1600.00 |

Furniture, Table, Gateleg, William & Mary, Walnut, New England, C.1700 ..................................... 775.00
Furniture, Table, Hutch, Pennsylvania, Green ........................................................................ 385.00
Furniture, Table, Inlaid Mahogany, Art Nouveau, 2 Drawer, 30 In. High ............................... 700.00
Furniture, Table, Library, Mahogany, Rectangular Top, Leather, C.1825 ............................... 1100.00
Furniture, Table, Library, Mahogany, 2 Drawers, 36 X 60 X 31 In. ....................................... 75.00
Furniture, Table, Library, Stairs, Mahogany, C.1850 ................................................. Illus 1100.00
Furniture, Table, Mahogany, Cabriole Legs, Ball & Claw Feet, 12 In. Diameter ................... 25.00
Furniture, Table, Mahogany, Drop Leaf, Pad Feet, English, C.1750 ...................................... 475.00
Furniture, Table, Mahogany, New York, C.1830 ................................................. Illus 575.00
Furniture, Table, Mahogany, Tilt Top, Miniature, 10 In.Diameter, 6 In.High ......................... 75.00
Furniture, Table, Maple, Pennsylvania, Half Round ........................................................ 99.00
Furniture, Table, Marble Top, Square ........................................................................ 195.00
Furniture, Table, Marquetry, Dutch, C.1850 ................................................. Illus 1200.00

Furniture, Table, Mahogany,
New York, C.1830

Furniture, Table,
Marquetry, Dutch, C.1850

Furniture, Table, Nancy, France, Mahogany & Fruitwood, Birds, 2 Tier, 32 In. ............................ 475.00
Furniture, Table, Napoleon III, Painted, Tripod, Round, 27 1/4 In. High ........................... 200.00
Furniture, Table, Occasional, Galle, Marquetry Flowers & Foliage, C.1900 ........................ 450.00
Furniture, Table, Occasional, Maple, Painted, C.1775 ........................................... 550.00
Furniture, Table, Occasional, Turned Cherry, Plain Skirt, New England, C.1830 ............... 110.00
Furniture, Table, Occasional, Victorian, Mother-Of-Pearl, Papier-Mache, Round ............... 175.00
Furniture, Table, Occasional, Victorian, Painted, Yellow On Black, 28 In. ...................... 190.00
Furniture, Table, Occasional, Victorian, Papier-Mache, Mother-Of-Pearl, Oval ............... 180.00
Furniture, Table, Occasional, William IV, Painted, Rectangular, 28 In. High ................... 150.00
Furniture, Table, Papier-Mache, Black & Gold Top, Mother-Of-Pearl Floral ..................... 175.00
Furniture, Table, Parlor, Turned Legs, 24 In.Diameter ....................................... 75.00
Furniture, Table, Pembroke, Chippendale, Mahogany, Square Legs, C.1760 ................... 750.00
Furniture, Table, Pembroke, Hepplewhite, Mahogany, 1 Drawer, Inlaid ....................... 425.00
Furniture, Table, Pembroke, Mahogany, Cutout Leaves, C.1790 ............................... 295.00
Furniture, Table, Pembroke, Mahogany, New England, C.1810 ............................... 325.00
Furniture, Table, Pembroke, Mahogany, Serpentine Drop Leaf, C.1775 ..................... 1000.00
Furniture, Table, Pembroke, Mahogany, 1 Drawer, Shaped Leaves, 28 1/2 In. ............... 300.00
Furniture, Table, Pool, Brunswick, Inlaid, C.1875 ........................................... 5000.00

Furniture, Table, Tavern,
Maple & Curly Maple, C.1730

Furniture, Table, Tea, Cherry,
Tilt Top, Conn., C.1770

| | |
|---|---:|
| **Furniture, Table,** Rectangular, Marble Top, Swan's Head Post, Rockland, Me. | 365.00 |
| **Furniture, Table,** Refectory, Oak, C.1650, 28 X 60 X 28 In. | 898.00 |
| **Furniture, Table,** Rosewood, Tilt Top, Round, England, C.1830 | 2500.00 |
| **Furniture, Table,** Round, Oak, Pedestal Base, Claw Foot | 200.00 |
| **Furniture, Table,** Sawbuck, Scrub Top, Gray Base, 5 Ft. Long | 350.00 |
| **Furniture, Table,** Serving, Inlaid Mahogany, English, C.1866 | 275.00 |
| **Furniture, Table,** Serving, Oak, English, C.1830 | 600.00 |
| **Furniture, Table,** Serving, Oak, Oval, 2 Tiered, English, C.1900 | 225.00 |
| **Furniture, Table,** Sewing, Black Lacquer & Mother-Of-Pearl, Hinged Top, 1850s | 150.00 |
| **Furniture, Table,** Side, Galle, Marquetry Blossoms, C.1900 | 900.00 |
| **Furniture, Table,** Side, Oak, Cabriole Legs, C.1725 | 250.00 |
| **Furniture, Table,** Tavern, Maple & Curly Maple, N.E., C.1730 ............ *Illus* | 1300.00 |
| **Furniture, Table,** Tavern, Maple & Pine, N.E., C.1710 ............ *Illus* | 800.00 |
| **Furniture, Table,** Tavern, Maple & Pine, N.E., C.1720 ............ *Illus* | 500.00 |
| **Furniture, Table,** Tavern, Oak, C.1650, 29 X 34 X 24 In. | 498.00 |
| **Furniture, Table,** Tavern, Turned Maple & Pine, New England, C.1720 | 200.00 |
| **Furniture, Table,** Tavern, Turned Maple, Button Feet, Pennsylvania, C.1750 | 750.00 |
| **Furniture, Table,** Tavern, Turned Maple, Frieze Drawer, Oblong, Mass., C.1720 | 900.00 |
| **Furniture, Table,** Tavern, Turned Walnut, Pennsylvania, C.1750 | 375.00 |
| **Furniture, Table,** Tavern, Walnut, Turned, Oblong Top, 2 Drawer, Pa., C.1740 | 850.00 |
| **Furniture, Table,** Tavern, Windsor, Oblong, Breadboard Ends, N.E., C.1750 | 325.00 |
| **Furniture, Table,** Tea, Cherry, Tilt Top, Conn., C.1770 ............ *Illus* | 815.00 |
| **Furniture, Table,** Tea, Queen Anne, Maple & Cherry, Valanced Skirt, Oval | 700.00 |
| **Furniture, Table,** Tea, Queen Anne, Maple, Valanced Skirt, Pad Feet | 475.00 |
| **Furniture, Table,** Tea, Walnut, Tilt Top, Pa., C.1770 ............ *Illus* | 1200.00 |

Furniture, Table, Tavern, Maple & Pine, N.E., C.1720          Furniture, Table, Tavern, Maple & Pine, N.E., C.1710

Furniture, Table, Tea, Walnut,
Tilt Top, Pa., C.1770
*(See Page 235)*

Furniture, Table, Work,
Inlaid Mahogany, Boston, C.1800

Furniture, Table, Work,
Mahogany & Maple, American, 1800s

Furniture, Table, Work,
Mahogany, Mass., C.1800

| | |
|---|---|
| **Furniture, Table,** Tilt Top, Cherry, Oval, Cutout Corners, 3 Legs | 200.00 |
| **Furniture, Table,** Tilt Top, Chippendale, Mahogany, Pennsylvania, C.1760 | 1100.00 |
| **Furniture, Table,** Trestle, Pine, Two Board Top, X-Braces, 45 In.Long | 200.00 |
| **Furniture, Table,** Tripod, Mahogany, Piecrust Edge, C.1750 | 425.00 |
| **Furniture, Table,** Two Tier, Majorelle, Marquetry, Floral Branches, C.1900 | 450.00 |
| **Furniture, Table,** Victorian, Metal, Mother-Of-Pearl, Marquetry, Ormolu, 29 In. | 400.00 |
| **Furniture, Table,** Walnut Base, Oval Marble Top, Brass Casters, 30 In.High | 100.00 |
| **Furniture, Table,** Work, American, Mahogany, C.1825, Bun Feet | 100.00 |
| **Furniture, Table,** Work, Federal, Cherry & Maple, New England, C.1810 | 250.00 |
| **Furniture, Table,** Work, Federal, Mahogany, C.1810 | 450.00 |
| **Furniture, Table,** Work, Inlaid Mahogany, Astragal Ends, Hinged, Phila., C.1800 | 750.00 |
| **Furniture, Table,** Work, Inlaid Mahogany, Boston, C.1800 *Illus* | 950.00 |
| **Furniture, Table,** Work, Mahogany & Figured Birch, Brasses, Mass., C.1800 | 2500.00 |
| **Furniture, Table,** Work, Mahogany & Maple, American, 1800s *Illus* | 400.00 |
| **Furniture, Table,** Work, Mahogany, Mass., C.1800 *Illus* | 375.00 |
| **Furniture, Table,** Work, Pine, Scrubbed Top, Mortised Construction, 29 In. | 85.00 |
| **Furniture, Tea Caddy,** Mahogany Veneer, 2 Hinged Tins & Waterford Bowl, 1890 | 125.00 |
| **Furniture, Tea Caddy,** Mahogany, Bristol Bowl, Ivory Escutcheon, C.1750 | 188.00 |
| **Furniture, Tea Caddy,** Mahogany, Double Hinged Compartments, Bun Feet, 1850 | 125.00 |
| **Furniture, Tea Caddy,** Rosewood, Crystal Bowl, C.1845 | 165.00 |
| **Furniture, Tray,** Butler's, Mahogany, Stand, C.1775 | 325.00 |

| | |
|---|---|
| Furniture, **Washstand**, C.1890 | 85.00 |
| Furniture, **Washstand**, Duncan Phyfe, Mahogany, New York, C.1810 | 2300.00 |
| Furniture, **Washstand**, Mahogany, Single Drawer, C.1810 | 130.00 |
| Furniture, **Whatnot**, Mahogany, Three Shelves, C.1800 | 150.00 |
| Furniture, **Whatnot**, Victorian, Walnut, Flat, 4 Shelves | 65.00 |
| Furstenberg, **Coffeepot**, Floral Bouquets, Garlands, C.1790, 8 5/8 In. | 150.00 |
| Furstenberg, **Cup & Saucer**, Coffee, Battle Scenes, Gilt Scrolls, C.1770 | 450.00 |
| Furstenberg, **Jug**, Hot Water, Covered, Inverted Pear Shape, Bouquets, C.1775 | 230.00 |
| Furstenberg, **Plate**, Bouquet Center, Birds In Cartouches, C.1765, 9 1/8 In. | 175.00 |
| Furstenberg, **Sauceboat**, Silver Shape, Travelers In Landscapes, C.1775 | 170.00 |
| Furstenberg, **Teacup & Saucer**, Peasant Woman, Gallant & Lady, C.1770 | 170.00 |

*Galle glass was made by the Galle factory founded by Emile Galle of France. The firm made cameo glass, furniture, and other Art Nouveau items from 1879 to 1905.*

| | | |
|---|---|---|
| Galle, **Atomizer**, Acid Cut Back Lavender Flowers, Signed | | 245.00 |
| Galle, **Atomizer**, Ovoid, Flaring Foot, Red Poppies, Metal Mounts, 8 3/4 In. | | 130.00 |
| Galle, **Bottle**, Scent, Mushroom Stopper, Purple On Yellow, Lily Pads, C.1900 | | 275.00 |
| Galle, **Bottle**, Scent, Teardrop Stopper, Red On Yellow, Clematis, C.1900, 4 In. | | 250.00 |
| Galle, **Bowl**, Boat Shape, Lake & Trees Scene, Pink, Green, & Brown, 12 In.Wide | | 395.00 |
| Galle, **Bowl**, Enamel Dragonflies & Water Lilies On Amber, Oval, 9 1/2 In. | | 475.00 |
| Galle, **Bowl**, Hexagonal Opening, Floral On Moss Green & Mauve, 5 In. | | 250.00 |
| Galle, **Bowl**, Water Lilies Floating On Water, 3 Cornered, 5 1/4 In. | | 400.00 |
| Galle, **Box**, Covered, Floral On Pale Yellow To Red, 3 1/2 In.Wide | | 250.00 |
| Galle, **Cachepot**, Yellow To Green Base, Lily Pads & Grasses, C.1900 | | 325.00 |
| Galle, **Chandelier**, Conical Shade, Green Nasturtiums On Olive Green, 15 In. | | 375.00 |
| Galle, **Compote**, Blue & White Edge, Galle Crest, St.Clement Faience, Signed | | 145.00 |
| Galle, **Decanter Set**, Enameled Glass, 7 Piece | *Illus* | 750.00 |
| Galle, **Decanter**, Green Dill & Sea Leaves On Clear To Opalescent, Stopper | | 750.00 |
| Galle, **Decanter**, Swirl Ribbed, Enameled Butterflies, Amber, 10 1/2 In.High | | 750.00 |
| Galle, **Dish**, Sweetmeat, Triangular, Signed, 5 X 1 1/2 In. | | 129.00 |
| Galle, **Figurine**, Cat, Faience, Seated, Black, Green Eyes, C.1900, 13 1/2 In. | | 300.00 |
| Galle, **Jardiniere**, Pottery, Pierced, Insects, Sepia, Black, Gilt, 1900, 10 In. | | 350.00 |
| Galle, **Jug**, Raised Floral Enamel On Dark, Art Nouveau Free-Form Shape | | 235.00 |
| Galle, **Lamp**, Carved Butterfly On Shade, Brass Base, 7 In.High | | 295.00 |
| Galle, **Lamp**, Float, Silver, Opalescent, Pink, C.1890, 14 In | *Illus* | 1150.00 |
| Galle, **Night-Light**, Carved Butterflies On Top, Bronze Base, Miniature | | 225.00 |
| Galle, **Perfume**, Enameled & Outlined Cut Clover Flowers On Topaz, Signed | | 275.00 |
| Galle, **Perfume**, Orange Overlay On Robin's Egg Blue, "Etude, " 6 1/2 In. | | 275.00 |
| Galle, **Scent Burner**, Metal Top, Dark & Medium Blue Cut Floral On Light | | 395.00 |
| Galle, **Shot Glass**, Polished Green Ferns On Acid Cut Cameo, 2 1/2 In.High | | 85.00 |
| Galle, **Shot Glass**, Shaded Green Ferns On Green & Camphor Glass, Signed | | 85.00 |

Galle, Lamp, Float,
Silver, Opalescent,
Pink, C.1890, 14 In

Galle, Decanter Set, Enameled Glass, 7 Piece

Galle, Toothpick, Polished Amber Florals On Green & Vaseline, Signed .......................................... 155.00
Galle, Tray, Wooden, Inlaid Butterfly & Leaves, Honey To Brown, 11 3/4 In. ............................... 150.00
Galle, Tray, Wooden, Inlaid, Marquetry Cat, Signed, 22 X 14 In. ........................................... 295.00
Galle, Tumbler, Polished Pink Floral On Frosty Acid, Signed, 3 1/2 In.High ............................... 135.00
Galle, Vase, Acid Cut Back Leaves, Apple Green, Raspberry, & White, 4 In. .............................. 185.00
Galle, Vase, Amber Pinecones & Needles On Acid, 9 1/2 In. ................................................ 275.00
Galle, Vase, Apricot On White, Poppies, Fire Polished, C.1900, 18 In. ..................................... 425.00
Galle, Vase, Baluster, Lemon Yellow, Blue Overlay, Clematis, C.1900, 9 In. ............................. 275.00
Galle, Vase, Banjo Shape, Brown, Yellow, & Orange, 4 1/2 In.High ....................................... 225.00
Galle, Vase, Blown-Out, Blue & Purple Floral On Gold, 8 In.High .......................................... 950.00
Galle, Vase, Boat Shape, Scenic, 3 Colors, 6 X 4 In. ...................................................... 325.00
Galle, Vase, Brown & Buff, C.1905, 13 1/4 In.High ................................................ *Illus* 300.00
Galle, Vase, Brown Foliage On Yellow To Brown, 3 1/4 In. ................................................. 350.00
Galle, Vase, Bud, Pink & Yellow Enamel Floral On Clear, Cylindrical, 8 In. ............................... 250.00
Galle, Vase, Bud, Wine Bleeding Heart Buds On Yellow, 5 1/4 In.High ................................... 175.00
Galle, Vase, Bulging, Waisted Neck, Gray & Yellow, Lilacs, 16 1/4 In. ................................... 650.00
Galle, Vase, Burnt Sienna On Orange, Oak Leaves & Acorns, C.1900, 13 5/8 In. ....................... 400.00
Galle, Vase, C.1905, 13 1/4 In.High .............................................................. *Illus* 300.00
Galle, Vase, Cabinet, Green Ferns & Grass On White Frosted, 4 In.High .................................. 145.00
Galle, Vase, Cabinet, Purple Berries On Shaded Lavender, Signed, 3 In.High .............................. 145.00
Galle, Vase, Cabinet, Three Color, Reds & Browns, 5 In.High .............................................. 180.00
Galle, Vase, Carved Bed Of Nasturtiums On White Matte, 8 In. ........................................... 295.00
Galle, Vase, Carved Chartreuse On Frosted & Pink, Uneven Texture, 15 In. ............................... 425.00
Galle, Vase, Covered, 2 Layers Each Of Yellow & Orange, 4 1/2 In.High .................................. 375.00
Galle, Vase, Cylindrical Neck, White Mustard, & Olive On Clear, 1900s, 15 In. ....................... 1150.00
Galle, Vase, Cylindrical, Brownish Pink Wisteria On Yellow & Tan, 11 In. ................................ 300.00
Galle, Vase, Deep Pink On Lemon Yellow Ground, Vine & Leaf, 3 1/2 In. .................................. 210.00
Galle, Vase, Double Gourd, Carnelian Floral On White & Carnelian, 9 3/8 In. ............................ 248.00
Galle, Vase, Double Overlay, Blue Flowers & Green On Flame, 14 In.High ................................. 395.00
Galle, Vase, Floral, 2 Colors, Top Flares Out, 5 In.High .................................................. 165.00
Galle, Vase, Floral, 3 Colors, Bulbous Bottom, Slender Neck, 23 In.High ................................. 425.00
Galle, Vase, Floral, 4 Colors, Bulbous Bottom, Slender Neck, 17 In.High ................................. 425.00
Galle, Vase, Gold, Green, & White Enamels On Mauve Glass, 17 1/4 In.High .............................. 650.00
Galle, Vase, Gourd Shape, Green On White & Orange, Maple Leaves, 1900s, 3 In. ....................... 150.00
Galle, Vase, Grapes & Leaves, Tapering, 3 Colors, 11 3/4 In.High ....................................... 395.00
Galle, Vase, Green On Red, Maple Leaves & Buds, C.1900, 11 1/2 In. .................................... 175.00
Galle, Vase, Inverted Pyriform, Lilac On Opalescent, Berries, C.1900, 9 In. ............................. 225.00
Galle, Vase, Lake & Woods, Greens & Browns On White, 6 1/2 In. ....................................... 390.00
Galle, Vase, Lavender Leaves & Flowers On Camphor, 6 In.High ........................................... 195.00
Galle, Vase, Leaf And Berries, Mint Green On White, 3 In.High, Signed .................................. 200.00
Galle, Vase, Light Green Flower & Foliage Cut To Pink, Signed, 8 1/4 In. ............................... 175.00
Galle, Vase, Lime Flowers & Ferns On Green To Tangerine, 15 In.High ................................... 375.00

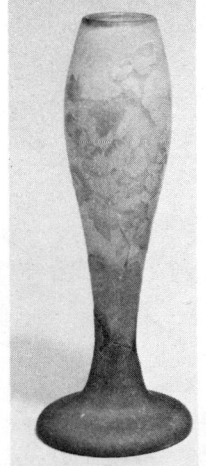

Galle, Vase, C.1905, 13 1/4 In.High

Galle, Vase, Brown & Buff,
C.1905, 13 1/4 In.High

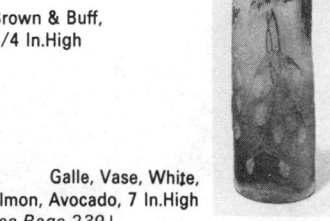

Galle, Vase, White,
Salmon, Avocado, 7 In.High
*(See Page 239)*

Galle, Vase, Rhododendrons, 10 1/2 In.High

| | |
|---|---|
| Galle, Vase, Lozenge Shape, Silver Mounts, Emerald, Enamel, C.1890, 8 In. | 275.00 |
| Galle, Vase, Maroon & Green Ferns On Pink & White, 18 In. High | 475.00 |
| Galle, Vase, Orchids & Poppies On Frosted Green Pebbled, Handle, 10 In. | 450.00 |
| Galle, Vase, Pastel Cut Blossoms, Signed, 10 1/2 X 4 In. | 395.00 |
| Galle, Vase, Pastel, Apricot & Avocado, Blossoms, Cameo, 14 1/2 X 7 In. | 495.00 |
| Galle, Vase, Pastel, 4 Colors, Cut Poppies, Cameo, 11 X 4 In. | 435.00 |
| Galle, Vase, Pear Shape, Window Technique Carving, 3 Color, 8 In. High | 350.00 |
| Galle, Vase, Pestle Shape, Orange & Yellow Clematis, 13 3/8 In.High | 450.00 |
| Galle, Vase, Portrait Of Old Beggar, Pottery, Signed Galle, Nancy, 12 In. | 225.00 |
| Galle, Vase, Pottery, Raised Roses & Buds, 9 1/2 In.High | 75.00 |
| Galle, Vase, Pussy Willows & Cattails In Marsh, Signed, 7 In.High | 165.00 |
| Galle, Vase, Rhododendrons, 10 1/2 In.High ............................ *Illus* | 1600.00 |
| Galle, Vase, Scenic, 3 Colors, 15 3/4 In.High | 425.00 |
| Galle, Vase, Scenic, 4 Colors, 12 1/2 In.High | 395.00 |
| Galle, Vase, Shiny Green On White, Orange Floral, 3 In. | 175.00 |
| Galle, Vase, Squat Body, Long Neck, Pendant Fuchsias In Red & Black, 14 In. | 120.00 |
| Galle, Vase, Sun Colors Through Cattails & Pussywillows, 7 3/4 In. | 185.00 |
| Galle, Vase, Tapered Cylinder, Yellow & Orange Flowering Vine, 4 In. | 165.00 |
| Galle, Vase, Teardrop Shape, Cranberry On White, Irises, C.1900, 10 3/4 In. | 300.00 |
| Galle, Vase, Trees, Birds, & Water, Brown & Greens, Flared Top, 6 1/2 In. | 185.00 |
| Galle, Vase, Triangular, Orange On Camphor Coloring, Signed, 6 In.High | 185.00 |
| Galle, Vase, Wheel Cut Blue & Purple Floral On Iridescent Gold, 8 In. | 695.00 |
| Galle, Vase, Wheel Cut Blue, Purple & Green Floral On Frosted, 10 In. | 850.00 |
| Galle, Vase, White, Salmon, Avocado, 7 In.High ............................ *Illus* | 200.00 |
| Galle, Vase, Yellow, Brick Overlay, Bleeding Hearts, C.1900, 9 3/4 In. | 300.00 |
| Galle, Vase, Yellow, Deep Lavender, Signed, 9 1/2 In.High | 250.00 |
| Galle, Water Set, Enameled Pink & Lavender Floral On Amber, 6 Piece | 1250.00 |
| Galle, Wine Set, Enameled Decoration On Deep Amber, 7 Piece | 950.00 |
| Galle, Wine, Enameled Thistles & Cross Of Lorraine On Amber, 3 In.High | 105.00 |
| Game Plate, Pheasant, Mother Teaching Babies, Victoria, Austria, 12 1/2 In. | 27.50 |
| Game Plate, Prairie Chicken Running, Uneven Edge, Marked France, 8 1/2 In. | 27.50 |
| Game Plate, Rabbit, Vegetables, & Rifle Center, Crown Victoria, 9 3/4 In. | 15.00 |
| Game Plate, Snipe In Rushes, Scalloped, Uneven Gold Border, 7 1/2 In. | 22.00 |
| Game, Authors, Parker Bros. | 6.00 |
| Game, Backgammon, Ebony Veneer & Marquetry Case, Ivory Dice, C.1890 | 180.00 |
| Game, Backgammon, Ivory, Natural & Tinted, Chinese, C.1850 | 250.00 |
| Game, Bang Bird Target, 2 Celluloid Birds, Cork Gun, Net, Dated 1924 | 15.00 |
| Game, Baseball, Poosh-M-Up, Wooden Frame, Bagatelle | 6.50 |
| Game, Ben Casey, Md., Vince Edwards, Boxed | 4.50 |
| Game, Billiard Match, Mechanical, Original Box | 100.00 |
| Game, Blondie's Comic Construction Set, 1934 | 8.00 |
| Game, Board, Chess, Lacquered Wood, Hinged, Chinese, C.1850, 19 3/8 In. | 80.00 |
| Game, Buck Rogers, 25th Century, Boxed Board | 8.75 |
| Game, Card, Disneyland Characters, 1964 | 5.00 |
| Game, Card, Howdy Doody | 3.00 |
| Game, Card, Reg'lar Fellers, Gene Byrnes, Cartoon, 1926 | 18.00 |
| Game, Checkers, Sanitary, Dated 1921 | 5.00 |
|     Game, Chess Set, see also Wedgwood, Chess Set | |
| Game, Chess Set, Bone, Natural & Tinted, French, C.1820, 33 Piece | 350.00 |

Game, **Chess Set,** Bone, Natural, French, Baluster Shape, C.1790, 32 Piece .............. 850.00
Game, **Chess Set,** Bone, White & Red, English, 19th Century ........................ 150.00
Game, **Chess Set,** Cast Iron, Black & Gray, Zimmerman, C.1850, 32 Piece .............. 500.00
Game, **Chess Set,** Cast Iron, Gilt & Coppered, German, C.1890, 32 Piece .............. 700.00
Game, **Chess Set,** Cast Metal, Silvered & Coppered, Russian, C.1850, 32 Piece .............. 650.00
Game, **Chess Set,** China, Capitalists Vs. Communists, Russian, 1925, 32 Piece .............. 2300.00
Game, **Chess Set,** Faience, St.George's, French, C.1890, 32 Piece .............. 1600.00
Game, **Chess Set,** Iron, German, E.G.Zimmermann, C.1850 ........................ 700.00
Game, **Chess Set,** Ivory, Carved, All Pawns Different, 4 In.High ........................ 225.00
Game, **Chess Set,** Ivory, India, C.1775 ........................................ *Illus* 2500.00
Game, **Chess Set,** Ivory, Indian, Natural & Brown, C.1820, 33 Piece .............. 1300.00
Game, **Chess Set,** Ivory, Indians Versus Mongols, Natural, C.1820, 32 Piece .............. 2300.00
Game, **Chess Set,** Ivory, Lacquered, Indian, Green, Black, & Red, C.1820, 32 Piece .............. 2900.00
Game, **Chess Set,** Ivory, Natural & Black, French, C.1850, 32 Piece .............. 950.00
Game, **Chess Set,** Ivory, Natural & Brown, Japanese, C.1890, 33 Piece .............. 400.00
Game, **Chess Set,** Ivory, Natural & Red, Cantonese, C.1850, 33 Piece .............. 950.00
Game, **Chess Set,** Ivory, Natural & Red, Chinese, C.1890, 32 Piece .............. 150.00
Game, **Chess Set,** Ivory, Natural & Red, English, C.1850, 33 Piece .............. 250.00
Game, **Chess Set,** Ivory, Natural & Red, French, C.1850, 32 Piece .............. 1000.00
Game, **Chess Set,** Ivory, Natural 3 Ivory, Chinese, Macao, C.1850, 32 Piece .............. 800.00
Game, **Chess Set,** Mother-Of-Pearl, Black & Light, C.1920, 34 Piece .............. 250.00
Game, **Chess Set,** Painted Wood, Burmese, 1700s, 32 Pieces ........................ 700.00
Game, **Chess Set,** Silver & Silver Gilt, German, C.1890, 32 Piece .............. 2000.00
Game, **Chess Set,** Silver Gilt, Lapis Lazuli, Malachite, Hungarian, C.1815 .............. 7500.00
Game, **Chess Set,** Walrus Ivory, Russian, C.1750, 32 Pieces .............. 1500.00
Game, **Chess Set,** Wood & Bone, French, C.1800, 32 Piece .............. 400.00
Game, **Chess Set,** Wooden, Green & Black, Burmese, 32 Piece .............. 250.00
Game, **Chess Set,** Wooden, Natural & Black, Jaques, London, C.1890, 33 Piece .............. 550.00

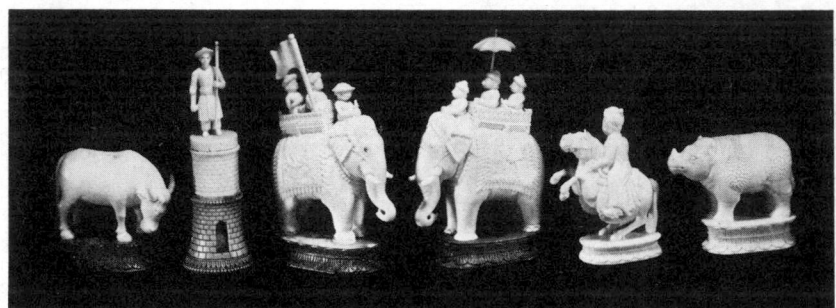

Game, Chess Set, Ivory, India, C.1775

Game, **Chess,** Black & Natural, Lacquered, Hand-Carved ........................ 25.00
Game, **Chinese Checkers,** Hopalong Cassidy, Dated 1950 ........................ 8.75
Game, **Chinese Sticks,** Ivory, Carved, Tube With Screw Top, 6 X 3/4 In. .............. 250.00
Game, **Court,** Cards, West & Lee Game Co., Mass., 1874 ........................ 5.00
Game, **Cribbage,** Inlaid Ivory On Wooden Board, Leatherette Case ........................ 15.00
Game, **Crokinole,** Pool Type Game, J.Ottman, N.Y., Boxed ........................ 5.00
Game, **Davy Crockett,** Alamo, Boxed ........................................ 4.00
Game, **Dick Tracy,** Crime Stopper, Battery Operated, Boxed ........................ 5.00
Game, **Domino Set,** Wooden ........................................ 2.00
Game, **Dominoes,** "American Eagle, " Wooden, Boxed ........................ 5.00
Game, **Dominoes,** Ivory & Dark Wood, Wooden Box, Sliding Cover, Dovetailed .............. 30.00
Game, **Dominoes,** Ivory & Rosewood, Box, Set Of 28 ........................ 30.00
Game, **Dominoes,** Metal Pinned Ebony & Bone ........................ 29.00
Game, **Dominoes,** Musical, Wooden, Wooden Box, Dated 1893 ........................ 12.00
Game, **Dominoes,** Whalebone, Rosewood Bottoms, Carved, 28 Pieces .............. 54.50
Game, **Dominos,** Chinese, Black & White Milk Glass Markers, Tin Box .............. 25.00
Game, **Eddie Cantor,** Boxed ........................................ 5.25
Game, **Fibber McGee & Molly,** The Wistful Vista ........................ 4.75
Game, **Football,** Tournament Of Roses, 1928 ........................ 11.00
Game, **Hit Me Hard,** Clay Marbles, Klee, Fuerth, Bavaria, Boxed .............. 10.00

Gardner, Figurine, Cossack Woman,
C.1850, 6 3/4 In.

Gardner, Figurine, Coachman,
C.1850, 7 1/2 In.

| | |
|---|---|
| Game, Hook-Em, Cardboard, Lithographed, Milton Bradley, Dated 1947 | 4.75 |
| Game, King Kong, 1966, R.K.O., Boxed | 2.25 |
| Game, Little Bopeep, Parker Bros., Cardboard Box | 12.50 |
| Game, Little Wooden Negro Boys, 3 Balls To Toss, C.1910, Box | 45.00 |
| Game, Lotto, Bingo Type, McLaughlin Bros., N.Y., Glass & Wooden | 8.00 |
| Game, Mah-Jongg, Ivory & Bamboo Tiles, Ivory Money, C.1923, Wooden Case | 34.00 |
| Game, Mah-Jongg, Ivory, 173 Piece | 25.00 |
| Game, Mah-Jongg, Simulated Leather Case | 58.00 |
| Game, Mah-Jongg, Wooden Holders, Leatherette Covered Wooden Case | 10.00 |
| Game, Marble Pin Game, Lindstrom Toy Co., 15 X 23 In. | 10.00 |
| Game, Marble Shooting, Sunny Andy, Tin, Wolverine, 13 In.Long | 6.75 |
| Game, Peg Board Game, Wooden | 18.00 |
| Game, Peter Coddle & His Trip To New York, Reading Game, J.H.Singer Co. | 5.00 |
| Game, Photographic Card, Old Masters, Soule, Boston, 25 Piece | 25.00 |
| Game, Poosh-M-Up Marble, Steel Marbles, Dated 8-29-33 | 20.00 |
| Game, Puzzle, see also Store, Game, Puzzle | |
| Game, Puzzle, Animal Sections, 5 Animals, 5 1/2 X 7 1/2 X 1 In. | 5.00 |
| Game, Puzzle, Dutch Families By Sea, Wooden, Parker, C.1910 | 4.50 |
| Game, Puzzle, Fire Department, Sectional, Milton Bradley, Boxed | 7.00 |
| Game, Puzzle, Jigsaw, Kidnapped, Milton Bradley Co., Wooden | 5.00 |
| Game, Puzzle, Jigsaw, Sweet Memories, Ullman's Society, 1902 | 5.95 |
| Game, Puzzle, Train, Screened Color, 10 1/2 X 20 In. | 5.00 |
| Game, Puzzle, United States, Uncle Sam & Flags, Cardboard, 21 X 14 In. | 10.00 |
| Game, Raggedy Anne, Gruelle, 1956, Boxed | 2.25 |
| Game, Robbing The Miller, McLoughlin Bros., N.Y., 1888, Boxed | 12.00 |
| Game, Rook, Parker Bros. | 6.00 |
| Game, Round The World Joe, Reading Game, Parker Bros., Boxed | 5.00 |
| Game, Set, Ivory, Chess, Backgammon, Cards, Checkers, & Cribbage, English, 1850s | 400.00 |
| Game, Teddy Bear, Linen, 1906, 24 X 15 In. | 18.00 |
| Game, The Adams Family, Board, Photographs, 1964, Boxed | 2.25 |
| Game, The Bughouse Puzzle | 3.00 |
| Game, The House That Jack Built, Parker Bros., Boxed | 5.00 |
| Game, The Lost Battalion, Patent Pending | 2.50 |
| Game, Twiggy, Box, Photographs, 1967, Boxed | 2.25 |
| Game, Underdog, Cartoon, 1964, Boxed | 2.25 |
| Game, West Point Cadet, Parker Bros., C.1895, Boxed | 15.00 |
| Game, Which, What Or Where, Geographical Game, Milton Bradley, 1903, Boxed | 7.00 |
| Gardner, Figurine, Cat, Gray & White Striped, C.1850, 4 1/2 In. Long | 300.00 |
| Gardner, Figurine, Coachman, C.1850, 7 1/2 In. _Illus_ | 300.00 |
| Gardner, Figurine, Constable, Bisque, C.1890, 3 3/4 In. | 325.00 |
| Gardner, Figurine, Cossack Woman, C.1850, 6 3/4 In. _Illus_ | 175.00 |
| Gardner, Figurine, Dog, Mastiff, Bisque, C.1855, 4 3/4 In.High | 375.00 |
| Gardner, Figurine, Glazier, Bisque, C.1850, 7 5/8 In. | 250.00 |
| Gardner, Figurine, Kitchen Maid, Seated, Bisque, C.1890, 5 3/4 In. | 150.00 |
| Gardner, Figurine, Man Sitting Drinking From Stein, C.1880, 6 3/4 In.High | 300.00 |
| Gardner, Figurine, Man, Bisque, Mustache, Fur Hat, C.1890, 10 1/4 In. | 175.00 |

| | |
|---|---|
| Gardner, Figurine, Peasant Woman, C.1850, 5 3/8 In. | 140.00 |
| Gardner, Pitcher, Birch Tree Trunk Shape, Lid, Woodpecker Handle, C.1890 | 350.00 |
| Gardner, Plate, Italianate Scenes On White, C.1850, 8 1/4 In., Pair | 120.00 |

> Gaudy Dutch pottery was made in England for America from about 1810 to
> 1820. It is a white earthenware with Imari style decorations of red, blue,
> green, yellow, and black. Only sixteen patterns of Gaudy Dutch were made:
> Butterfly, Carnation, Dahlia, Double Rose, Dove, Grape, Leaf,
> Oyster, Primrose, Single Rose, Strawflower, Sunflower, Urn,
> War Bonnet, Zinnia, and No Name. Other similar wares are called
> Soft Paste, Gaudy Ironstone, or Gaudy Welsh.

| | |
|---|---|
| Gaudy Dutch, Bowl, Single Rose, 5 1/2 In.Diameter | 500.00 |
| Gaudy Dutch, Cup & Saucer, Double Rose | 500.00 |
| Gaudy Dutch, Cup & Saucer, Single Rose | 500.00 |
| Gaudy Dutch, Pitcher, Oyster, 5 In. | 66.50 |
| Gaudy Dutch, Plate, Butterfly, 8 1/4 In. | 600.00 |
| Gaudy Dutch, Plate, Carnation, 8 1/4 In. | 600.00 |
| Gaudy Dutch, Plate, Carnation, 9 1/8 In. | 650.00 |
| Gaudy Dutch, Plate, Single Rose, 6 3/4 In. | 500.00 |
| Gaudy Ironstone, Compote, Imari Pattern, Footed, 7 1/4 X 13 In. | 68.00 |
| Gaudy Ironstone, Cup & Saucer, Strawberry | 25.00 |
| Gaudy Ironstone, Pitcher, Blue Serpent Handle, Puce Mark, Mason's, 11 In. | 75.00 |
| Gaudy Ironstone, Pitcher, Green Serpent Handle, Puce Mark, Mason's, 11 In. | 89.00 |
| Gaudy Ironstone, Pitcher, Mason's, 5 1/2 In. | 80.00 |
| Gaudy Ironstone, Plate, Cleopatra, 9 In. | 36.00 |
| Gaudy Ironstone, Plate, Dessert, Strawberry, Copper Luster On Flow Blue | 66.50 |
| Gaudy Ironstone, Plate, Dinner, Blackberry Pattern, Walley, Paris, 9 5/8 In. | 50.00 |
| Gaudy Ironstone, Plate, Imari Pattern, 9 In. | 14.00 |
| Gaudy Ironstone, Plate, Impressed Ashworth, 9 1/2 In. | 17.60 |
| Gaudy Ironstone, Plate, Impressed Mark, Mason's, 10 In. | 41.00 |
| Gaudy Ironstone, Plate, Strawberry, Copper Luster On Flow Blue | 87.50 |
| Gaudy Ironstone, Platter, Budge, Ridgway, 15 X 11 In. | 35.00 |
| Gaudy Ironstone, Platter, Mason's, 17 X 13 3/4 In. | 188.00 |
| Gaudy Ironstone, Platter, Orange & Cobalt On White, Westbourne S.H.& S. | 145.00 |
| Gaudy Ironstone, Platter, Oriental Decoration, Lobed Rim, Ashworth Bros. | 47.00 |
| Gaudy Ironstone, Platter, Oriental Pattern, Mason's, 17 X 13 3/4 In. | 94.00 |
| Gaudy Ironstone, Teapot, 7 1/2 In. | 58.00 |
| Gaudy Ironstone, Tureen, Covered, 4 Footed, Minton, Nov.11, 1846 | 198.00 |

> Gaudy Welsh is an Imari decorated earthenware with red, blue, green, and
> gold decorations. It was made after 1820.

| | |
|---|---|
| Gaudy Welsh, Bowl, Footed, 7 In. | 68.00 |
| Gaudy Welsh, Bowl, Rust & Blue With Gold Floral, Dec.4, 1845 | 65.00 |
| Gaudy Welsh, Creamer, Oyster, 3 3/4 In.High | 45.00 |
| Gaudy Welsh, Creamer, Oyster, 4 3/4 In.High | 50.00 |
| Gaudy Welsh, Cup & Saucer | 48.00 |
| Gaudy Welsh, Cup & Saucer, Handleless, Primrose Color | 100.00 |
| Gaudy Welsh, Cup & Saucer, Oyster | 98.00 |
| Gaudy Welsh, Cup & Saucer, Tulip | 22.00 |
| Gaudy Welsh, Cup & Saucer, Tulip | 48.00 |
| Gaudy Welsh, Cup & Saucer, Wagon Wheel | 32.50 |
| Gaudy Welsh, Jar, Cracker, Etched Floral Silver Cover & Bail | 50.00 |
| Gaudy Welsh, Mug, Handled, Oyster Pattern | 68.00 |
| Gaudy Welsh, Mug, Oyster, Allerton's, 1831, 3 3/8 In.High | 50.00 |
| Gaudy Welsh, Mug, Oyster, 3 In.High | 48.00 |
| Gaudy Welsh, Mug, 3 Handles | 75.00 |
| Gaudy Welsh, Pitcher, Allerton, 4 3/4 In.High | 40.00 |
| Gaudy Welsh, Pitcher, Buttermilk, Morning Glory, 9 1/2 In.High | 195.00 |
| Gaudy Welsh, Pitcher, Milk, 6 3/4 In. | 50.00 |
| Gaudy Welsh, Pitcher, Oyster, 3 3/4 In. | 40.00 To 45.00 |
| Gaudy Welsh, Pitcher, Oyster, 4 3/4 In. | 55.00 |
| Gaudy Welsh, Pitcher, Oyster, 5 In.High | 55.00 |
| Gaudy Welsh, Pitcher, Serpent Handle, 6 In. | 65.00 |
| Gaudy Welsh, Pitcher, 3 In.High | 25.00 |
| Gaudy Welsh, Plate, Dinner, Oyster, Allerton's, 1831, 9 In. | 45.00 |
| Gaudy Welsh, Plate, Dinner, Wagon Wheel, Earthenware, C.1850, 10 In. | 45.00 |
| Gaudy Welsh, Plate, Luncheon, Oyster, Allerton's, 1831, 8 In. | 18.75 |
| Gaudy Welsh, Plate, Oyster Pattern, 6 3/4 In. | 22.00 |

Gaudy Welsh, Plate, Oyster, Alberton, 9 In. ............................................................................. 18.00
Gaudy Welsh, Plate, Square, 9 In. ........................................................................................... 58.00
Gaudy Welsh, Plate, 6 In. ......................................................................................................... 12.50
Gaudy Welsh, Saucer, Oyster, Allerton's, 1831, 5 3/4 In. ................................................... 12.50
Gaudy Welsh, Sugar, Covered .................................................................................................. 88.00
Gaudy Welsh, Tea Set, Child's, Octagon Shapes, 7 Piece .................................................. 195.00
Gaudy Welsh, Teapot, Blue & Rusts ....................................................................................... 85.00
Gaudy Welsh, Teapot, Deep Blue & Rust On Cream .......................................................... 90.00
Gaudy Welsh, Teapot, 6 In. ...................................................................................................... 68.00
Gene Autry, Book, Coloring, Dated 1950 ............................................................................... 4.00
Gene Autry, Book, Gene Autry, 1944, Better Little Books .................................................. 5.00

*Gibson Girl plates were made in the early 1900s by the Royal Doulton Pottery at Lambeth, England. There are twenty-four different plates featuring a picture of the Gibson Girl by the artist Charles Dana Gibson.*

Gibson Girl, Fan, Picnic, Car, Paper, Lithograph, Advertising .......................................... 12.50
Gibson Girl, Plate, Day After Journey's End ........................................................................ 55.00
Gibson Girl, Plate, Failing To Find Rest & Quiet In The Country .................................... 48.00
Gibson Girl, Plate, Heads, Royal Doulton, 9 In. ................................................................. 42.00
Gibson Girl, Plate, Outside World .......................................................................................... 55.00
Gibson Girl, Plate, Profile Facing Left, Royal Doulton, 1900, 9 1/4 In. ......................... 39.50
Gibson Girl, Plate, Profile Facing Right, Royal Doulton, 1899, 9 1/4 In. ....................... 39.50
Gibson Girl, Plate, She Goes Into Retirement ...................................................................... 48.50
Gibson Girl, Plate, She Goes To The Fancy Dress Ball As Juliet, 10 In. ........................ 55.00
Gibson Girl, Plate, She Is The Subject Of More Hostile Criticism ................................... 48.00
Gibson Girl, Plate, She Looks For Relief Among Old Ones, 10 1/2 In. ............................ 47.50
Gibson Girl, Plate, Some Think She Remained In Retirement Too Long .......... 50.00 To 52.00
Gibson Girl, Plate, They All Go Skating, Royal Doulton, 10 1/2 In. ................................ 55.00
Gibson Girl, Plate, They Take A Morning Run, 10 In. ........................................................ 55.00

GILLINDER    *Gillinder pressed glass was first made by William T.Gillinder of Philadelphia in 1863. Many pressed glass items were made for the Centennial.*

Gillinder, Buddha, Red, Marked ............................................................................................. 35.00
Gillinder, Celery, Deer & Dog, Pointed Top, Etched Signature ......................................... 67.50
Gillinder, Figurine, Buddha, Opaque, Signed, 6 In.High ................................................... 65.00
Gillinder, Figurine, Chicken, Frosted, Philadelphia Centennial, "Just Out" ................... 50.00
Gillinder, Paperweight, Buddha, Amber, 6 In. ...................................................................... 50.00
Gillinder, Plate, Liberty Bell, Side Handles, 1776 1876, 6 In.Diameter .......................... 35.00
Gillinder, Slipper, Centennial, Clear, Marked ...................................................................... 22.00
Gillinder, Slipper, Centennial, Frosted, Marked ................................................................... 25.00
Gillinder, Slipper, Clear, Signed ............................................................................................. 19.00
Gillinder, Slipper, Frosted, Signed ......................................................................................... 24.00
Gillinder, Vase, Hand, Centennial, Satin Finish, Signed, 7 In., Pair ............................... 17.50
Girandole, Brass Peasant Man & Girl Dancing, Etched Prisms, Pair ............................. 275.00
Girandole, India, Gilt, Marble Base, 5 Arm, 50 Long Prisms .......................................... 395.00
Girandole, Boy & Girl, Prisms, Pair ....................................................................................... 100.00
Glasses, Brass, Handmade, Oval Lens, Signed Heltner, Sliding Temples, C.1825 ......... 17.50
Glasses, Case, Dated 1856 ...................................................................................................... 15.00
Glasses, Granny, Brass Frames, Green Glass, Bows Extend, Leather Case ...................... 10.00
Glasses, Granny, Gold Filled .................................................................................................... 3.75
Glasses, Granny, Gold Rims .................................................................................................... 5.00
Glasses, Granny, Silver Rims .................................................................................................. 5.00
Glasses, Granny, Wire Frames ................................................................................................ 1.50
Glasses, Nose, Cobalt Blue, Gold Hairpin And Chain ....................................................... 27.50
Glasses, Pince-Nez, Gold Frames & Chain, Raised Motif ................................................... 25.00
     Glove Stretcher, see Ivory, Glove Stretcher, Silver Plate,
     Glove Stretcher, Silver, Sterling, Glove Stretcher, Store,
     Glove Stretcher
Gold, Bag, Mesh, Sapphire, Thumbpiece, 4 3/4 In.Long .................................................... 300.00
Gold, Box, Cigarette, Oval Plaque, 14 K, C.1930, 4 1/2 In.Long ..................................... 250.00
Gold, Box, Patch, Empire, Slip On Cover, Italian Mosaic Of Spaniel, C.1810 ............... 450.00
Gold, Case, Cigarette, Cartier, Black Enamel, 6 Rose Diamonds, 3 In. ........................... 550.00
Gold, Case, Cigarette, 2 Color, Enamel, Leather Envelope, 3 1/8 In. ............................. 300.00
Gold, Compact, Stripes & Hobnails, 18 K, Cartier, 3 1/4 In.Long ................................... 625.00

| | |
|---|---|
| Gold, Compact, Two Color, Louis XVI Style, Cartier, 4 1/4 In.Long | 1600.00 |
| Gold, Crucifix, Continental, Engraved, Figure Of Christ, C.1690, 3 In. | 500.00 |
| Gold, Cup, Covered, Yard Inc., Pedestal Foot, 18 K, 12 3/4 In.High | 3000.00 |
| Gold, Figurine, Nude Woman By Tree Trunk, 3 3/4 In.High | 950.00 |
| Gold, Snuffbox, Directoire, Vachette, Gouache Under Glass On Lid, C.1790 | 4250.00 |
| Gold, Snuffbox, Louis XV, Enamel, Ceres, Venus, & Cupid, Hardvilliers, 1744 | 4500.00 |
| Gold, Snuffbox, Louis XVI, 3 Color, Marguerite, Oval, Chases, 1783, 3 In. Long | 3000.00 |
| Gold, Tazza, Fluted, Central Flowerhead, Tiffany & Co., C.1910, 5 In.Diameter | 2000.00 |
| Gold, Toilet Service, Cartier, C.1910, 14 Pieces .................................... Illus | 2600.00 |
| Gold, Vase, Cartier, Trumpet Shape, Flowers, Molded Foot, 14 K, 11 In.High | 850.00 |

*Goofus glass was made from about 1900 to 1920 by many American factories.
It was orginally painted gold, red, green, bronze, pink, purple, and other bright
colors.*

| | |
|---|---|
| Goofus Glass, Berry Set, Master & 6 Carnations, 7 Piece | 18.00 |
| Goofus Glass, Berry Set, Rose Pattern, 7 Piece | 26.00 |
| Goofus Glass, Bowl, Deep, 7 In.Diameter | 9.50 |
| Goofus Glass, Frame, Picture, Hanging Chain, Round Picture, 5 In. Square | 6.50 |
| Goofus Glass, Jar, Pickle, Grapes & Leaves, Red & Gold Paint | 12.00 |
| Goofus Glass, Plate, Carnations, 11 In. | 8.00 |
| Goofus Glass, Plate, Grape Design | 10.00 |
| Goofus Glass, Plate, Red Grapes & Leaves On Gold, Beaded Edge, 10 1/2 In. | 11.00 |
| Goofus Glass, Vase, Clear Grapes, 7 In. | 10.00 |
| Goofus Glass, Vase, Grapes, Browns & Reds, 9 1/2 In. | 10.00 |
| Goofus Glass, Vase, Grapes, 7 In.High | 7.95 |

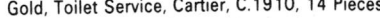

*Goss china has been made since 1858. English potter William Henry
Goss first made it at the Falcon Pottery in Stoke-on-Trent. In 1934
the factory name was changed to Goss China Company when it was taken over
by Cauldon Potteries. Goss china resembles Irish Belleek in both body
and glaze. The company also made popular souvenir china.*

**W.H.COSS**

| | |
|---|---|
| Goss, Creamer, Arms Of Chagford, 2 In. | 15.00 |
| Goss, Cup & Saucer, Arms Of Crediton | 20.00 |
| Goss, Cup & Saucer, Gold Rims, Crests, Signed W.H.Goss | 9.00 |
| Goss, Figurine, Christchurch | 6.00 |
| Goss, Jug, City Of Liverpool Crest, Handled, Falcon Mark | 8.00 |
| Goss, Kettle, Hastings, Miniature | 6.00 |
| Goss, Teapot, Broadstairs Crest, 1 1/2 Cup Size, Signed W.H.Goss | 15.00 |

*Gouda is a district in Holland famous for tin-glazed pottery and tiles.
Gouda pottery has been made by many factories in the district since the
seventeenth century and is still being made. Most of the pieces found today
are from the nineteenth and twentieth centuries.*

| | |
|---|---|
| Gouda, Ashtray, Sun & House Design, Red, Blue, Gold & Pearl, Marked | 35.00 |
| Gouda, Bell, Dutch Girl Handle, Marked | 25.00 |
| Gouda, Bowl, Covered, Mosaic Type Design, Orange, Blue, Green, 3 1/4 In. | 15.00 |

Gold, Toilet Service, Cartier, C.1910, 14 Pieces

Gouda, Bowl, Crocus, 6 X 2 1/2 In. ............................................................................. 55.00
Gouda, Bowl, Floral, 10 1/2 In. ................................................................................. 48.00
Gouda, Bowl, Matte Finish, Marked Rhodian, Artist Signed, 5 In.Diameter ................ 35.00
Gouda, Bowl, Shallow, Handles, Signed Sulet, 9 In.Diameter ................................... 75.00
Gouda, Butter Pat, Tobris, Black Interior, Colorful Stylized Flowers ........................ 16.00
Gouda, Candlestick, Clareth, 10 In. .......................................................................... 95.00
Gouda, Candlestick, Yellow, Orange, & Black, Marked Regina, 4 1/4 In., Pair ............ 25.00
Gouda, Chamberstick, Holland Green, Handled, Initials P.C., 14 In. .......................... 110.00
Gouda, Charger, Florals & Geometric Pattern, Varied Colors, 14 In.Diameter ............ 95.00
Gouda, Compote, Brown Yellow Floral On Turquoise, Artist Signed, 7 1/2 In. ............ 65.00
Gouda, Compote, Fancy Pattern On Turquoise, Low, 5 In.Wide .............................. 24.00
Gouda, Compote, Matte Turquoise, Yellow Floral Rim, Kaba Royal, 7 1/2 In. ............ 65.00
Gouda, Dish, Candy, Flowers, Signed, 5 5/8 In.Diameter ....................................... 15.00
Gouda, Humidor, Tobacco, Man, Windmill, & Boats, Marked Royal Goedewaagen ...... 40.00
Gouda, Jar, Acorn Finial, Ovoid, Orange & Yellow On Blue, 14 3/4 In., Pair ............ 200.00
Gouda, Jar, Covered, Ovoid, Black With Poppies, C.1900, 11 In.High ...................... 80.00
Gouda, Jug, Oriental Pattern, 7 1/2 In.High ............................................................ 75.00
Gouda, Jug, Zenith, Stopper, 10 1/4 In.High ........................................................... 95.00
Gouda, Pitcher, Blue Tulips, Rust Cherries, Aqua Ground, Black Handle, 5 In. .......... 67.00
Gouda, Pitcher, Bulbous, Art Deco, Rim, Spout, & Handle Edged In Gold, 5 In. ........ 62.00
Gouda, Pitcher, Cream, W.B., 4 1/2 In. ................................................................... 38.00
Gouda, Pitcher, Linsar, Black Rim, Lavender Ground, Stylized Floral, 8 In. .............. 65.00
Gouda, Pitcher, Miniature, Irene, Beige Ground, White Flowers, 3 In.High ................ 42.00
Gouda, Planter, Indian Pattern ................................................................................ 75.00
Gouda, Plate, 'Gouda Ware, Unique Styles & Artistic Decorations, ' Gold .................. 75.00
Gouda, Pot, Bean, Footed, 2 Handled, Plazuid, Holland, 3 In. ................................ 35.00
Gouda, Shoe, Princess Ivora, Allover Pattern, H.I.Gouda, Holland, 8 In. ................... 90.00
Gouda, Tile, After Cornelis Springer, C.1890 ........................................................... 800.00
Gouda, Tile, Boy & Girl, Holland Boat Scene, Square, 3 1/2 In., Pair ........................ 24.00
Gouda, Tray, Black Background, Colorful Geometric Pattern, 12 In.Diameter ............ 65.00
Gouda, Urn, Zenith, 2 Handled, Fantasie, Initials G.S., 11 1/2 In., Pair .................... 185.00
Gouda, Vase, Bulbous, Hand-Painted Art Nouveau Design, 6 1/2 In.High .................. 65.00
Gouda, Vase, Cylindrical, White Sides, Pendant Decoration, Amphora, 16 In. ............ 60.00
Gouda, Vase, Dark Brown, Stylized Florals, Signed IbsPalu, 5 5/8 In.High ................ 65.00
Gouda, Vase, Flowers On Blue, 5 In. ........................................................................ 80.00
Gouda, Vase, Ivora, High Glaze, B.B.Gouda, Holland, 6 In.High ............................... 90.00
Gouda, Vase, Miniature, 2 1/2 In.High ..................................................................... 25.00
Gouda, Vase, Nadka, Rust & Brown Decoration, Artist Signed, 13 In.High ................ 95.00
Gouda, Vase, Orange, Red, Blue, & Yellow Decoration, Marked Candia, 10 In. .......... 35.00
Gouda, Vase, Rust & Yellow Lions On Beige & Tan, 8 In. ......................................... 85.00
Gouda, Vase, Signed C-Erla, 5 In ............................................................................ 37.50
Gouda, Vase, Varicolored Triangles On Cobalt, 3 In.High ........................................ 28.00

*Graniteware is an enameled tinware that has been used in the kitchen from the
late nineteenth century to the present. Earlier graniteware was green or
turquoise blue, with white spatters. The later ware was gray with white
spatters. Reproductions are being made in all colors.*

Graniteware, Bedpan, Covered, Gray, Bulbous ...................................................... 25.00
Graniteware, Bowl, Soup, Flanged, 8 In. ................................................................ 1.20
Graniteware, Coffeepot, Cowboy, White, 11 In. ...................................................... 8.00
Graniteware, Coffeepot, Gray, Tin Dome Lid, Curved Spout, 8 1/2 In. ...................... 12.00
Graniteware, Collander, Blue, Gray, & White, High Foot, Deep, 11 In. ...................... 12.00
Graniteware, Collander, Dark Gray, 2 Handled, Deep, 11 In. ................................... 10.00
Graniteware, Kettle, Blue & Gray, Wooden Bail, Straight Sided, 3 1/2 Quarts ............ 12.00
Graniteware, Ladle, Blue, Holes ............................................................................. 4.50
Graniteware, Pan, Muffin, Dark Blue & White, 14 X 7 In. ......................................... 7.00
Graniteware, Pan, Oven, Mottled Gray, Handled, 15 1/2 X 9 In. ............................... 3.50
Graniteware, Pitcher, Blue & White, Sponge Type, 5 1/2 Quarts .............................. 14.00
Graniteware, Potty, Cobalt & White ......................................................................... 6.00
Graniteware, Spoon, Gray, 15 In.Long ..................................................................... 3.00
Graniteware, Washbasin, Blue ................................................................................ 6.00

*Greentown glass was made by the Indiana Tumbler and Goblet Company of
Greentown, Indiana, from 1894 to 1903. In 1899, the factory name was changed
to National Glass Company. A variety of pressed, milk, and chocolate
glass was made.*
**Greentown, see also Pressed Glass, Slag, Caramel**

Grueby, Vase, Green Glaze, Yellow, C.1891, 12 1/4 In.

| | |
|---|---|
| Greentown, Bowl, Mitted Hand | 25.00 |
| Greentown, Butter, Covered, Canary | 165.00 |
| Greentown, Carafe, Water, Masonic | 45.00 |
| Greentown, Creamer, Brickwork | 12.00 |
| Greentown, Creamer, Daisy, Opaque White | 37.50 |
| Greentown, Cruet, Austrian | 30.00 |
| Greentown, Iced Tea, No.11 | 7.50 |
| Greentown, Match Holder, Picture Frame, Amber | 87.50 |
| Greentown, Mug, Elf Scene, Teal Blue Opaque, 5 In. | 78.00 |
| Greentown, Mug, Serenade, Opaque Blue | 37.00 |
| Greentown, Mug, Troubadour, Blue, 5 In. | 30.00 |
| Greentown, Relish, 10 3/4 In.Long | 12.50 |
| Greentown, Saltshaker, Austrian | 22.50 |
| Greentown, Sauce, Teardrop & Tassel | 8.50 |
| Greentown, Stein, Dark Milk & Blue, Troubadour Scene | 38.00 |
| Greentown, Sugar, Covered, Dewey, Canary | 25.00 |
| Greentown, Toothpick, No.11 | 12.00 |
| Greentown, Tumbler, Frosted Wild Rose With Bowknot | 18.50 |
| Greentown, Tumbler, Lemonade, No.11 | 7.50 |
| Greentown, Vase, Ruffled & Scalloped, 4 3/4 In.High | 12.50 |
| Greentown, Wheelbarrow, Nile Green | 65.00 |
| Greentown, Wine, Shuttle | 16.50 |

*Grueby Faience Company of Boston, Massachusetts, was incorporated in 1897 by William H. Grueby. Garden statuary, art pottery, and architectural tiles were made until 1920.*

| | |
|---|---|
| Grueby, Tile, Faience Co., Boston, Green, 6 In. Square | 55.00 |
| Grueby, Tile, Pirate Ship, Signed, 4 In.Square | 147.50 |
| Grueby, Vase, Green Glaze, Yellow, C.1891, 12 1/4 In. .........*Illus* | 900.00 |
| Gun, see Weapon, Gun | |

*Gunderson glass was made at the Gunderson Pairpoint Works of New Bedford, Massachusetts, from 1952 to 1957. Gunderson Peachblow is especially famous.*

| | |
|---|---|
| Gunderson, Burmese, Dish, Sweetmeat, Pink To Yellow, Footed Silver Holder | 215.00 |
| Gunderson, Burmese, Rose Bowl, 3 1/4 In.Wide, 2 3/4 In.High | 65.00 |
| Gunderson, Compote, Light Blue, Swirled Knob Stem, Clear Glass Foot | 40.00 |
| Gunderson, Compote, Shallow, Medium Blue Bowl, Clear Foot, 6 1/2 X 7 1/2 In. | 40.00 |
| Gunderson, Peachblow, Bowl, 3 Applied Triangular Leaf Feet, 7 In. | 195.00 |
| Gunderson, Peachblow, Creamer, Footed, Applied Reeded Handle, Pink To Blue | 225.00 |
| Gunderson, Peachblow, Vase, Bulbous, White Casing, 9 In.High | 350.00 |
| Gunderson, Peachblow, Vase, Pear Shape, Bulbous, 9 In. | 285.00 |
| Gutta-Percha, see also Album, Photography | |
| Gutta-Percha, Looking Glass, Raised Grapes & Leaves, Patent 1868, 9 1/2 In. | 16.75 |
| Hampshire, Bowl, Tulip, Green, Raised White Florals, Robertson Mark | 35.00 |
| Hampshire, Chamberstick, Mottled Green, Matte Glaze, Round Base, 5 In.High | 28.00 |
| Hampshire, Lamp, Stained Glass Shade, 20 In. High | 275.00 |

| | |
|---|---:|
| Hampshire, Plate, Cream & Gold, Marked, 8 In. | 17.00 |
| Hampshire, Vase, Dark & Light Blue Matte Finish, 7 1/2 In. | 35.00 |
| Hampshire, Vase, Green, Squatty, 4 In. | 18.00 |
| Hampshire, Vase, Matte Blue Drip Glaze, 7 In.High, Early | 38.00 |

*Philip Handel worked in Meriden, Connecticut, about 1885 and in New York City from about 1900 to the 1930s. His firm made art glass and other types of lamps.*

| | |
|---|---:|
| Handel, Humidor, Cigar, Horse's Head, Green & Brown Marbleized Ground | 165.00 |
| Handel, Lamp Base, Yellow Slag, 4 Part Shade, Metal Berries & Leaves | 200.00 |
| Handel, Lamp, Autumn Leaves On Crackle Glass, Signed, 22 In.High | 395.00 |
| Handel, Lamp, Boudoir, Arabs On Horses, Desert Scenery, Signed | 275.00 |
| Handel, Lamp, Boudoir, Butterflies On Tree Trunk Base, Square Shade | 235.00 |
| Handel, Lamp, Dogwood Blossoms On Leaded Shade, Uneven Border, 16 In. | 1300.00 |
| Handel, Lamp, Floor, Harp, Signed Handel Brown 606, 54 In. High | 140.00 |
| Handel, Lamp, Lily Pad, Green & White, Signed | 2200.00 |
| Handel, Lamp, Matte Green Shade, Bronze, Base, 14 In.Diameter | 450.00 |
| Handel, Lamp, Pond Lily, Two Branch, Pink & Ocher Shade, 21 In.High | 125.00 |
| Handel, Lamp, Red Cattails & Green Leaf Base, Bronze Lamp, 23 In.High | 1050.00 |
| Handel, Lamp, Scenic, Painted Inside & Out, Artist Signed, 18 In.High | 675.00 |
| Handel, Lamp, Student, Pine Trees On Purple To Green, Signed, 19 In.High | 250.00 |
| Handel, Lamp, Table, 8 Tortoiseshell Panels, Red Rocos & Green Leaves Skirt | 235.00 |
| Handel, Lamp, 14 In.Maroon Shade, Marked | 275.00 |
| Handel, Night-Light, Egg Shape Frosted Crackle Floral Shade, Metal Base | 200.00 |
| Handel, Toby Mug, Old Man In Hat, Gold Accents On White, 6 In.High | 85.00 |
| Handel, Vase, Desert Scene Decoration, Enameled, 9 In.High | 135.00 |
| Handel, Vase, Floral Sprays On Cream, Beaded Metal Rim, Ribbed, 12 In.High | 110.00 |
| Hatpin Holder, see also Porcelain and various porcelain categories | |
| Hatpin Holder & Attached Underplate, Red Roses On Green | 25.00 |
| Hatpin Holder, Deep Purple Violets, Gold Trim | 17.50 |
| Hatpin Holder, Floradora, Green, Gold, Footed | 25.00 |
| Hatpin Holder, Geisha Girl, Red, Gold, Signed | 10.00 |
| Hatpin Holder, Hand-Painted Flowers, Gold Trim, Signed, 4 1/2 In.High | 12.00 |
| Hatpin Holder, Pink & Red Roses, Gold Decoration | 16.00 |
| Hatpin Holder, Roses On Beige, Gold, Marked G.U.M.Germany | 32.00 |
| Hatpin Holder, Scene Of The Gleaners, Silver Top | 35.00 |
| Hatpin, Blue Enameled Swastika Top | 2.95 |
| Hatpin, Blue Glass, Pearlized Effect | 4.00 |
| Hatpin, Blue Oval Glass Set With Rhinestones | 8.50 |
| Hatpin, Blue Stone In Gilt Mount | 7.50 |
| Hatpin, Blue, Yellow, & Jeweled, Pair | 8.00 |
| Hatpin, Carved Jet, Hearts & Design | 10.00 |
| Hatpin, Clear Cut Glass Ball | 3.75 |
| Hatpin, Fan Shape, Mosaic Inlay | 11.00 |
| Hatpin, Glass Ball With Circus Glass Applications, Pair | 10.00 |
| Hatpin, Gold Top With 3 Turquoise Insets | 5.85 |
| Hatpin, Gold Twisted Knot | 3.50 |
| Hatpin, Jet Ball, Cut | 3.75 |
| Hatpin, Jet, Elongated Top | 3.75 |
| Hatpin, Metal Fleur-De-Lis | 3.50 |
| Hatpin, Mother-Of-Pearl Button | 3.90 |
| Hatpin, Papier-Mache, Multicolor, Pair | 8.00 |
| Hatpin, Pearl Top | 5.00 |
| Hatpin, Pink & Green Enamel On Sterling Silver | 6.00 |
| Hatpin, Pink Swirled Glass Ball | 4.75 |
| Hatpin, Purple & White Enamel | 6.50 |
| Hatpin, Purple Enamel | 4.75 |
| Hatpin, Red Stone Surrounded By Rhinestones | 6.50 |
| Hatpin, Rhinestone, Gay Nineties | 28.50 |
| Hatpin, Sea Blue Glass, Pearlized Effect | 4.00 |
| Hatpin, Silver Feather, Pair | 7.00 |
| Hatpin, Silver Flying Griffin, Pair | 11.00 |
| Hatpin, Silver Lace, Round | 5.00 |
| Hatpin, Spatter Glass, Black, Gold, & Silver | 4.00 |
| Hatpin, Sterling Silver Boy & Dolphin | 6.00 |
| Hatpin, Tortoiseshell-Like Button Top Inlaid With Rhinestones | 5.00 |
| Hatpin, 1890 Dime With Initials | 10.00 |

*Haviland china has been made in Limoges, France, since 1846. The factory was started by the Haviland Brothers of New York City. Other factories worked in the town of Limoges making a similar chinaware.*

| | |
|---|---|
| Haviland, Bowl, Berry, No.540 | 3.50 |
| Haviland, Bowl, Fruit, Apple Blossom | 3.00 |
| Haviland, Bowl, Fruit, Delaware | 4.00 |
| Haviland, Bowl, Fruit, Rosalinde | 3.00 |
| Haviland, Bowl, No.98c | 16.00 |
| Haviland, Bowl, Punch, Fruit & Foliage, Signed Seidel, 12 In.Diameter | 285.00 |
| Haviland, Bowl, Salad, No.57B, 9 1/2 In. | 25.00 |
| Haviland, Bowl, Soup, Flat, No.94, Black Outlined Yellow Design | 4.00 |
| Haviland, Bowl, Soup, No.248A | 4.00 |
| Haviland, Bowl, Soup, No.472C | 7.50 |
| Haviland, Bowl, Soup, No.57W, 8 1/2 In. | 4.00 |
| Haviland, Bowl, Vegetable, Covered, Oval, No.248A | 16.00 |
| Haviland, Bowl, Vegetable, Covered, Oval, No.472C | 27.50 |
| Haviland, Bowl, Vegetable, Covered, Oval, No.57W | 16.00 |
| Haviland, Bowl, Vegetable, Covered, Oval, No.94, Black Outlined Yellow Design | 22.00 |
| Haviland, Bowl, Vegetable, Covered, Oval, Ranson Blank, No.52 | 28.00 |
| Haviland, Bowl, Vegetable, Covered, Round, No.540 | 22.50 |
| Haviland, Bowl, Vegetable, Covered, 2 Handles, Blue Daisies, Chas.Field | 16.50 |
| Haviland, Bowl, Vegetable, Delaware, Oval | 10.00 |
| Haviland, Bowl, Vegetable, No.472C | 17.50 |
| Haviland, Bowl, Vegetable, Oval, No.94, Black Outlined Yellow Design | 18.00 |
| Haviland, Bowl, Waste, No.540 | 14.00 |
| Haviland, Butter Pat, No.31A | 3.00 |
| Haviland, Butter Pat, No.540 | 3.50 |
| Haviland, Butter Pat, Ranson, No.1 | 4.00 |
| Haviland, Butter Pat, Red Clover Decoration, Gold Trim | 2.50 |
| Haviland, Butter Pat, Smooth Blank, No.242F | 3.00 |
| Haviland, Butter, Countess, Liner | 24.00 |
| Haviland, Butter, Covered, No.146N | 30.00 |
| Haviland, Cake Set, Pink Roses On Blue Ground, Hand-Painted, 7 Piece | 42.50 |
| Haviland, Celery, Pink & Green Trailing Flowers, Haviland & Co. | 16.00 |
| Haviland, Chamberstick, Saucer Type, Gold Handle, Pink Roses, Limoges | 29.00 |
| Haviland, Chocolate Pot, White & Gold | 35.00 |
| Haviland, Compote, Spray Of Roses, Green & Gold Leaves | 32.40 |
| Haviland, Creamer, Delaware | 8.00 |
| Haviland, Cup & Saucer, Bouillon, Apple-Blossom | 9.00 |
| Haviland, Cup & Saucer, Bouillon, Princess | 9.50 |
| Haviland, Cup & Saucer, Bouillon, Roses, Limoges | 4.50 |
| Haviland, Cup & Saucer, Butterflies, Butterfly Handle, Blue Mark | 60.00 |
| Haviland, Cup & Saucer, Clover | 16.50 |
| Haviland, Cup & Saucer, Cloverleaf, No.98 | 18.00 |
| Haviland, Cup & Saucer, No.29A | 12.00 |
| Haviland, Cup & Saucer, No.94, Black Outlined Yellow Design | 15.00 |
| Haviland, Cup & Saucer, No.146N | 15.00 |
| Haviland, Cup & Saucer, No.149F, Signed T.Haviland | 9.00 |
| Haviland, Cup & Saucer, No.540 | 13.50 |
| Haviland, Cup & Saucer, Pink Flowers, Green Leaves, Blue Scrolls | 14.00 |
| Haviland, Cup & Saucer, Ranson Blank, No.52 | 16.00 |
| Haviland, Cup & Saucer, Ranson, No.1 | 18.00 |
| Haviland, Cup & Saucer, Rosalinde | 8.00 |
| Haviland, Cup & Saucer, Rosemary | 10.00 |
| Haviland, Cup & Saucer, Silver Anniversary, No.19 | 20.00 |
| Haviland, Cup & Saucer, Star, White | 12.50 |
| Haviland, Cup, Delaware | 6.00 |
| Haviland, Cup, Demitasse, St.Regis | 5.00 |
| Haviland, Cup, Friendship, 3 Handled, Blue & Gold On White, 6 In. | 95.00 |
| Haviland, Cup, Loving, Three Handled, Drapery & Blue Bellflowers On White | 110.00 |
| Haviland, Dish, Acorn, 2 Sailboats, Charles Field | 8.00 |
| Haviland, Dish, Bone, Princess | 13.35 |
| Haviland, Dish, Candy, Scallop Forms Handle, Floral, Gold Bowknot & Beading | 13.00 |
| Haviland, Dish, Compote, Scrolls & Rose Garland, Charles Field | 4.00 |
| Haviland, Dish, Pancake, Covered, Apple Blossoms, Limoges | 25.00 |
| Haviland, Dish, Pancake, Covered, No.146 | 50.00 |

H&C°
DEPOSE

| | |
|---|---|
| Haviland, **Dish**, Vegetable, Lafayette, Gold On Handles | 25.00 |
| Haviland, **Eggcup**, Double, Roses, Gold, Blue Flowers, Marked Haviland & Co. | 9.50 |
| Haviland, **Gravy Boat & Attached Underplate**, No.29 | 25.00 |
| Haviland, **Gravy Boat**, Arcadia | 9.00 |
| Haviland, **Matchbox**, Striker Under Lid, Pink Roses, Limoges | 28.00 |
| Haviland, **Nappy**, No.472C | 14.00 |
| Haviland, **Pitcher**, Tankard Type, Grapes & Leaves, Gold Handle, G.D.A., 10 In. | 69.50 |
| Haviland, **Pitcher**, Water, Gold Trim, No.53, 8 In. | 45.00 |
| Haviland, **Pitcher**, Water, No.87J | 67.50 |
| Haviland, **Planter**, Miniature Rose Garlands, Pink, Blue, Pointed End | 10.00 |
| Haviland, **Plate**, Blackberries & White Blossoms, Scalloped, 8 1/2 In. | 10.00 |
| Haviland, **Plate**, Bread & Butter, Antoinette | 5.00 |
| Haviland, **Plate**, Bread & Butter, Delaware | 5.00 |
| Haviland, **Plate**, Bread & Butter, Lilac, Regent Park | 5.00 |
| Haviland, **Plate**, Bread & Butter, No.94, Black Outlined Yellow Design | 5.00 |
| Haviland, **Plate**, Bread & Butter, No.232A, Trailing Arbutus | 4.00 |
| Haviland, **Plate**, Bread & Butter, No.242F | 4.00 |
| Haviland, **Plate**, Bread & Butter, No.497A | 5.00 |
| Haviland, **Plate**, Bread & Butter, No.510 | 4.00 |
| Haviland, **Plate**, Cake, Baltimore Rose | 20.00 |
| Haviland, **Plate**, Cake, Blue Lauria, Open Handled | 10.00 |
| Haviland, **Plate**, Cake, Hand-Painted Pink & White Roses, Gold Handles | 32.00 |
| Haviland, **Plate**, Chop, Ranson | 28.00 |
| Haviland, **Plate**, Christmas, 1917 | 23.00 |
| Haviland, **Plate**, Dessert, Scrolls & Rose Garland, Charles Field | 4.00 |
| Haviland, **Plate**, Dinner, Delaware | 8.00 |
| Haviland, **Plate**, Dinner, Embassy | 8.00 |
| Haviland, **Plate**, Dinner, Harrison Rose, No.150 | 8.75 |
| Haviland, **Plate**, Dinner, Marie, No.161A | 6.00 |
| Haviland, **Plate**, Dinner, No.57W | 6.00 |
| Haviland, **Plate**, Dinner, No.94, Black Outlined Yellow Design | 6.00 |
| Haviland, **Plate**, Dinner, No.124 | 7.00 |
| Haviland, **Plate**, Dinner, No.294 | 4.00 |
| Haviland, **Plate**, Dinner, No.540 | 7.50 |
| Haviland, **Plate**, Dinner, Pink Band, Gold | 6.25 |
| Haviland, **Plate**, Dinner, Ranson, No.1 | 6.50 |
| Haviland, **Plate**, Dinner, Rosalinde | 8.00 |
| Haviland, **Plate**, Dinner, Scrolls & Rose Garland, Charles Field | 8.00 |
| Haviland, **Plate**, Dinner, Silver Anniversary, No.19 | 8.00 |
| Haviland, **Plate**, Dinner, Spray Of Roses, Green & Gold Leaves | 8.50 |
| Haviland, **Plate**, Dinner, Springtime | 7.50 |
| Haviland, **Plate**, Dinner, Trailing Arbutus, No.232A | 7.00 |
| Haviland, **Plate**, Drop Rose, 6 In. | 15.00 |
| Haviland, **Plate**, Ferrand | 7.00 |
| Haviland, **Plate**, Floral, Scalloped Pink Border, Limoges, 9 1/2 In. | 9.00 |
| Haviland, **Plate**, Hand-Painted Birds Center, 24K Gold Band On Green | 18.50 |
| Haviland, **Plate**, Luncheon, Harrison Rose, No.150 | 8.75 |
| Haviland, **Plate**, Luncheon, No.57W | 5.00 |
| Haviland, **Plate**, Luncheon, No.94, Black Outlined Yellow Design | 5.00 |
| Haviland, **Plate**, Luncheon, No.540 | 7.00 |
| Haviland, **Plate**, Luncheon, Ranson, No.1 | 6.00 |
| Haviland, **Plate**, Luncheon, Silver Anniversary, No.19 | 7.00 |
| Haviland, **Plate**, Luncheon, Trailing Arbutus, No.232A | 4.00 |
| Haviland, **Plate**, No.29G, Blank, 8 1/2 In. | 6.00 |
| Haviland, **Plate**, No.124, 8 In. | 6.00 |
| Haviland, **Plate**, No.152, 6 1/2 In. | 4.00 |
| Haviland, **Plate**, No.152, 7 1/2 In. | 6.00 |
| Haviland, **Plate**, No.416, 8 3/4 In. | 5.00 |
| Haviland, **Plate**, Oyster, Blue To Gray, Gold Oyster Shells, Limoges, 7 3/4 In. | 25.00 |
| Haviland, **Plate**, Oyster, Gold Trim | 22.50 |
| Haviland, **Plate**, Oyster, Medallions, Floral, & Gold, Green Border | 18.00 |
| Haviland, **Plate**, Oyster, Norma | 35.00 |
| Haviland, **Plate**, Oyster, Rutherford B.Hayes, Dated 1880 | 310.00 |
| Haviland, **Plate**, Red Clover, 6 In. | 7.00 |
| Haviland, **Plate**, Red Clover, 7 1/2 In. | 9.00 |
| Haviland, **Plate**, Salad, Camellia | 6.00 |

Haviland, Plate, Salad, Delaware ............................................................................................... 6.00
Haviland, Plate, Salad, No.94, Black Outlined Yellow Design ......................................... 5.00
Haviland, Plate, Salad, Ranson, No.1 ...................................................................................... 5.50
Haviland, Plate, Salad, Scrolls & Rose Garland, Charles Field ...................................... 5.00
Haviland, Plate, Strawberries & Leaves On Yellow & Pink, 7 1/2 In. ......................... 16.00
Haviland, Plate, Swags Of Pink Roses & Green Leaves, 6 In. ........................................ 4.00
Haviland, Plate, White, Blue Scrolls, Pink Rosebuds, Gold, Limoges, 7 1/2 In. ........ 2.50
Haviland, Platter, Meat, Delaware, Well, Oval, Medium Size ......................................... 12.00
Haviland, Platter, No.57W, 12 In. ............................................................................................ 12.00
Haviland, Platter, No.540, Medium Size ................................................................................ 17.50
Haviland, Platter, Oval, France, 11 X 8 In. ............................................................................ 10.00
Haviland, Platter, Ranson Blank, No.52, 14 In. .................................................................... 18.00
Haviland, Platter, Ranson Blank, No.52, 16 In. .................................................................... 20.00
Haviland, Platter, Silver Anniversary, No.19, Large Size ................................................. 25.00
Haviland, Platter, Turkey, No.472C ......................................................................................... 35.00
Haviland, Platter, Turkey, Two Wells, No.98 ...................................................................... 37.50
Haviland, Platter, Wedding Ring, 13 1/2 X 10 In. .............................................................. 16.50
Haviland, Platter, Well & Tree, No.57W, 18 1/2 In. .......................................................... 19.00
Haviland, Pot, Jam, Ribbon Finial & Handles, Pink Sweet Peas, Limoges, 4 In. ...... 22.00
Haviland, Relish, Round, No.6 ................................................................................................. 8.00
Haviland, Relish, Silver Anniversary, No.19 ........................................................................ 11.00
Haviland, Sauce, No.57A, 6 1/8 In. ......................................................................................... 5.00
Haviland, Sauce, No.94, Black Outlined Yellow Design .................................................... 3.50
Haviland, Sauce, Ranson, No.1 ............................................................................................... 3.50
Haviland, Sauce, Silver Anniversary, No.19 ........................................................................ 5.00
Haviland, Saucer, Delaware ...................................................................................................... 2.00
Haviland, Saucer, Fruit, No.291 ............................................................................................... .50
Haviland, Saucer, No.57W ........................................................................................................ .50
Haviland, Strawberry Set, Scalloped, Pink Roses, Limoges, 7 Piece ............................ 32.50
Haviland, Sugar & Creamer, No.63B ..................................................................................... 37.50
Haviland, Sugar & Creamer, No.94, Black Outlined Yellow Design .............................. 22.00
Haviland, Sugar & Creamer, Rosalinde ................................................................................ 25.00
Haviland, Sugar, Covered, Delaware ...................................................................................... 8.00
Haviland, Sugar, Lambelle, Bowknot Finial ......................................................................... 32.50
Haviland, Sugar, No.528A ......................................................................................................... 8.00
Haviland, Tea Set, No.486C, 28 Piece ................................................................................... 175.00
Haviland, Teacup & Saucer, Laurelton, Made In America ............................................... 8.50
Haviland, Teacup & Saucer, No.39X ...................................................................................... 12.00
Haviland, Tray, Dresser, Oval, Scalloped, 2 Handles, Wreath Of Pink Roses ............ 25.00
Haviland, Tray, Dresser, Oval, 2 Handles, Scalloped Edge, Pink Roses Wreath ........ 25.00
Haviland, Tureen & Attached Tray, Sauce, Covered, Twist Handles, Gold, Floral ...... 20.00
Haviland, Tureen & Attached Underplate, Gravy, Brown & Yellow, Limoges ............. 25.00
Haviland, Tureen, Covered, Scrolls & Rose Garland, Charles Field, Oval ................... 22.00
Haviland, Tureen, Gold Finial & Handles, Hand-Painted Designs ................................. 65.00
Haviland, Tureen, Rope Handles On Lid & Sides, Gold Band, 12 1/2 In.Long ........... 65.00
Haviland, Tureen, Soup, Gold & Yellow Floral, Gray Leaves On White, C.1885 ........ 37.50
Haviland, Vase, Centennial, Bronze & Pottery, 1876, 29 In .................................... *Illus* 700.00

Haviland, Vase, Centennial, Bronze & Pottery, 1876, 29 In

Haviland, Vase, Pottery, 2 Mallards, Artist Signed, 16 In.High ................................................ 375.00

  *T.G.Hawkes & Company of Corning, New York, was founded in 1880.*
*The firm cut glass made at other firms until 1962. Many pieces are marked*
*with the trademark, a trefoil ring enclosing a fleur-de-lis and two hawks.*

Hawkes, see also Cut Glass
Hawkes, Atomizer, Blue Crystal, Gold Band, Signed, Paper Label ......................................... 35.00
Hawkes, Bottle, Oil & Vinegar, Copper Wheel Engraving, Sterling Stopper ....................... 35.00
Hawkes, Cruet, Oil & Vinegar & Floral Engraving, Sterling & Glass Stopper ................... 32.50
Hawkes, Cup, Sherbet, Stemmed, Engraved Floral Festoons, Signed ................................. 15.00
Hawkes, Jar, Candy, Pagoda Shape Lid, Gold Bands On Clear, Pedestal ........................... 28.00
Hawkes, Relish, Frosted Ribbon Stripe Of 10 Threads Each, 5 Compartment .................. 20.00
Hawkes, Vase, Apple Green, Engraved Design, Gold Decoration, Flat Rim, 8 In. ............. 55.00

**H**       *Heisey glass was made from 1895 to 1958 in Newark, Ohio, by A.H.*
*Heisey and Co., Inc.*

Heisey, Ashtray Set, Sun Purpled, Signed, 4 Piece ............................................................. 25.00
Heisey, Ashtray, Dolly Madison, Cut, Paper Label ................................................................ 9.50
Heisey, Ashtray, Sahara, Crystolite, Signed, 3 1/4 In.Square ............................................ 25.00
Heisey, Ashtray, Zircon, Crystolite, Signed, 3 1/4 In.Diameter .......................................... 29.00
Heisey, Basket, Etched Butterflies & Flowers, No.459, Marked, 7 In. ............................... 70.00
Heisey, Basket, Etched Flowers & Leaves, Marked, 8 X 11 In. ........................................... 45.00
Heisey, Basket, Fruit, Cut & Pressed, Handled, Marked ..................................................... 68.50
Heisey, Basket, Hexagonal, Intaglio Floral & Leaf, 24 Point Star Base ............................ 55.00
Heisey, Basket, Intaglio Daisy, Round, Handle, Signed, 7 1/4 In. ...................................... 35.00
Heisey, Basket, Moongleam, Octagonal, Signed ................................................................. 55.00
Heisey, Basket, No.465, Marked, 8 In. .................................................................................. 46.00
Heisey, Basket, Sahara, Clear Paneled, Etched Narcissus ................................................. 95.00
Heisey, Berry Set, Fluted, Oval, Signed, 8 Piece ................................................................. 48.00
Heisey, Bonbon, Individual, Twist, Flamingo Handle, Signed ............................................ 9.50
Heisey, Bonbon, Minuet, 3 Dolphin Feet, 5 1/4 In.Diameter .............................................. 27.50
Heisey, Bonbon, Ridgeleigh, Handled, Signed, 6 3/4 In. .................................................... 14.00
Heisey, Bottle, Bar, Hunter & Dog In Silver Deposit, Etched .............................................. 75.00
Heisey, Bottle, Toilet Water, Signed ..................................................................................... 2.50
Heisey, Bottle, Water, Fancy Loop, 9 1/2 In.High ................................................................ 35.00
Heisey, Bowl & Stand, Punch, Beaded Panel & Sunburst, Marked ................................... 55.00
Heisey, Bowl, Berry, Master, Opalescent, Floral Painted Scene ........................................ 78.00
Heisey, Bowl, Berry, Master, Prince Of Wales Plumes, Signed ......................................... 55.00
Heisey, Bowl, Boat Shape, Sawtooth Edge, 11 In.Long ..................................................... 12.50
Heisey, Bowl, Center, Moonglass, Signed, 11 In. ............................................................... 20.00
Heisey, Bowl, Centerpiece, Swan ......................................................................................... 26.50
Heisey, Bowl, Cereal, Dawn, Signed ................................................................................... 13.00
Heisey, Bowl, Covered, Sahara, Queen Anne, 6 1/2 In.Long ............................................ 45.00
Heisey, Bowl, Dawn, Lodestar, Marked, 13 In. .................................................................. 42.00
Heisey, Bowl, Diamond Swag, Flat, 9 1/2 In. ...................................................................... 35.00
Heisey, Bowl, Double Handles, Signed, 5 1/2 In.Diameter ................................................ 7.00
Heisey, Bowl, Embossed, Patent Date 1913, 8 1/2 In. ....................................................... 27.50
Heisey, Bowl, Emerald Green, Winged Scroll, 8 In. ........................................................... 38.00
Heisey, Bowl, Empress, Sahara, Signed, 6 X 6 7/8 In. ....................................................... 9.50
Heisey, Bowl, Etched Orchid, Footed, 5 1/2 In.Diameter ................................................... 12.00
Heisey, Bowl, Etched, Cut Floral Diamond, H Mark, 8 In. ................................................. 15.00
Heisey, Bowl, Fancy Loop, Footed, 8 In. ............................................................................ 65.00
Heisey, Bowl, Finger, Diamond Optic, Alexandrite ........................................................... 30.00
Heisey, Bowl, Flaring Paneled Sides, Rayed Bottom, Signed, 5 1/2 In.Diameter ........... 7.50
Heisey, Bowl, Flower Shape, Oblong, Curled Over Sides, 12 X 5 1/2 In. ......................... 17.50
Heisey, Bowl, Gondola Shape, Marked, 11 X 5 X 4 In. ...................................................... 25.00
Heisey, Bowl, Greek Key, Signed, 8 In. .............................................................................. 25.00
Heisey, Bowl, Icicle, Scalloped, 10 1/2 In. ......................................................................... 19.50
Heisey, Bowl, Narrow Flute, Flared, Dated, 8 In. ............................................................... 12.50
Heisey, Bowl, Oceanic, Flamingo, Oval, Signed, 7 In. ...................................................... 10.00
Heisey, Bowl, Orchid, Etched, Triangular Base, 6 In. Top Diameter ................................ 12.50
Heisey, Bowl, Paneled, Scalloped Edge, Rayed Base, Signed, 6 1/4 In. .......................... 6.00
Heisey, Bowl, Peerless, 6 3/4 In. ......................................................................................... 25.00
Heisey, Bowl, Pineapple And Fan, Clear, 8 1/2 In. ............................................................ 18.00
Heisey, Bowl, Prism, Oval, Marked, 8 In. ........................................................................... 15.00
Heisey, Bowl, Punch, Fancy Loop, 10 3/4 X 5 1/4 In. ....................................................... 100.00

| | |
|---|---|
| Heisey, Bowl, Ridgeleigh, Blue, 8 In. | 14.00 |
| Heisey, Bowl, Ridgeleigh, Round, 10 In. | 16.00 |
| Heisey, Bowl, Sahara, Swirled, 2 Handled, 6 3/4 In. | 20.00 |
| Heisey, Bowl, Swirled, Green, Signed, 9 1/4 In. | 25.00 |
| Heisey, Bowl, Victorian, Divided, 8 In.Diameter | 18.00 |
| Heisey, Bowl, Wide Rib, Marked, 8 1/2 In. | 18.00 |
| Heisey, Box, Cigarette, Covered, Ridgeleigh, 3 3/4 X 2 5/8 In. | 10.50 |
| Heisey, Box, Cigarette, Horse's Head, Ruby Flashed, 6 X 4 In. | 30.00 |
| Heisey, Box, Covered With Horse Head, 6 In. | 45.00 |
| Heisey, Box, Powder, Covered, Allover Silver Overlay Flowers, 2 1/2 In.High | 25.00 |
| Heisey, Box, Powder, Cut Glass Design, Silver Plated Lid, Large | 32.00 |
| Heisey, Butter Pat, Clear, Marked, Pair | 5.00 |
| Heisey, Butter Pat, Cobalt, Signed | 22.50 |
| Heisey, Butter Pat, Diamond Point, Signed | 4.00 |
| Heisey, Butter Pat, Etched Flower Center, Sandwich | 8.00 |
| Heisey, Butter Pat, Square, Cobalt Blue, Signed | 22.50 |
| Heisey, Butter, Covered, Sunburst | 19.50 |
| Heisey, Butter, No.1255, Clear, Gold Trim | 26.00 |
| Heisey, Butter, Pony Finial, Square | 45.00 |
| Heisey, Cake Stand, Prince Of Wales, Marked, 9 In. | 75.00 |
| Heisey, Candelabra, Colonial, Triple, Patent On Rim, Miniature, Pair | 25.00 |
| Heisey, Candelabra, Colonial, 2 Light | 22.00 |
| Heisey, Candleholder, Colonial, Miniature, Pair | 12.00 |
| Heisey, Candleholder, Cornucopia, Warwick, 2 1/4 In.High, Pair | 35.00 |
| Heisey, Candleholder, Etched Orchid | 14.00 |
| Heisey, Candleholder, Lariat, Double, Pair | 15.00 |
| Heisey, Candlestick, Cherub, Flamingo, Pair | 75.00 |
| Heisey, Candlestick, Cornucopia, 2-Light, Pair | 35.00 |
| Heisey, Candlestick, Orchids On Base, 2-Light, Pair | 30.00 |
| Heisey, Candlestick, Ridgeleigh, Bobeche & Prisms | 25.00 |
| Heisey, Candlestick, Rose Etched, 2-Light | 22.00 |
| Heisey, Candlestick, Zodiac, Two Light, Pair | 75.00 |
| Heisey, Carafe, Water, Colonial, Blown Pontil | 27.00 |
| Heisey, Celery, Adonis | 18.50 |
| Heisey, Celery, Colonial, Clear, 11 3/4 In. | 15.00 |
| Heisey, Celery, Etched Border, Star Base, Gold, Signed, 12 In.Long | 15.00 |
| Heisey, Celery, Flamingo, Pink, Star Base, 2 Self Handles, 12 In. | 15.00 |
| Heisey, Celery, Kalonyal, Marked | 35.00 |
| Heisey, Celery, Leaf Shape, Green, Signed | 20.00 |
| Heisey, Celery, Paneled, Scalloped Edge, Signed, 11 3/4 In. | 11.00 |
| Heisey, Chamberstick, Colonial, Ring Handle, 2 In.High | 7.00 |
| Heisey, Champagne, Colonial, Signed, 5 Ozs. | 11.00 |
| Heisey, Champagne, Sheffield | 8.00 |
| Heisey, Coaster, Signed, Set Of 6 | 16.50 |
| Heisey, Cocktail Shaker, Ridgeleigh | 40.00 |
| Heisey, Cocktail, Oyster, Puritan, Footed, Signed, 6 Ozs. | 8.50 |
| Heisey, Cologne, Blue Satin, Gold Trim, Footed, Orange Enamel Dots, Signed | 24.50 |
| Heisey, Cologne, Cut Flowers & Leaf, Sterling & Pink Enamel Stopper, 1 Oz. | 26.00 |
| Heisey, Compote, Candy, Covered, Pink, Yellow, & Blue Enameled Flowers, Gold | 25.00 |
| Heisey, Compote, Covered, Paneled, Ribbed, Blue & Red Floral Enamel, Gold | 32.00 |
| Heisey, Compote, Crystal, Queen Anne, Signed | 22.00 |
| Heisey, Compote, Diamond Optic, Green, Signed, 4 In.High | 15.00 |
| Heisey, Compote, Enameled, 6 1/2 In.High, Pair | 65.00 |
| Heisey, Compote, Kalonyal, Crimped Edge, Marked, 10 In. | 75.00 |
| Heisey, Compote, Locket On Chain, 7 1/2 In.High, 8 1/2 In.Diameter | 65.00 |
| Heisey, Compote, Orchid, Crystal, Stemmed, 5 1/2 In. | 20.00 |
| Heisey, Compote, Plantation, 5 X 7 1/2 In. | 45.00 |
| Heisey, Condiment Set, Victorian, 5 Piece | 25.00 |
| Heisey, Console Set, Etched Design, Ribbed Panels, Octagonal Bowl, 3 Piece | 35.00 |
| Heisey, Console Set, Grape Cluster | 125.00 |
| Heisey, Console Set, Ridgeleigh, Oval, 10 In.Candlesticks, 3 Piece | 64.00 |
| Heisey, Cordial, Narrow Flute, Hand Decorated, Gold Trim, Signed | 22.00 |
| Heisey, Cornucopia, Signed, 9 In. | 15.00 |
| Heisey, Cornucopia, 7 1/2 In.High, Pair | 15.00 |
| Heisey, Creamer, Dawn | 25.00 |
| Heisey, Creamer, Etched Orchid | 15.00 |

| | |
|---|---|
| Heisey, **Creamer**, Fluted, Applied Handle, Signed | 19.00 |
| Heisey, **Creamer**, No.1255, Clear, Gold Trim | 22.00 |
| Heisey, **Cruet**, Banded Flute, Pair | 30.00 |
| Heisey, **Cruet**, No.1255, Clear, Gold Trim | 20.00 |
| Heisey, **Cruet**, Paneled, Stopper, Marked | 28.00 |
| Heisey, **Cruet**, Pleat & Panel, Flamingo | 27.50 |
| Heisey, **Cruet**, Twist | 20.00 |
| Heisey, **Cruet**, Wagon Wheel | 18.00 |
| Heisey, **Cup Plate**, Greek Key, Marked, 4 In. | 5.00 |
| Heisey, **Cup Plate**, Pink, 4 1/2 In. | 2.50 |
| Heisey, **Cup**, Almond, Individual, Narrow Flute, Footed, Signed | 5.00 |
| Heisey, **Cup**, Bouillon, Vaseline, Signed | 75.00 |
| Heisey, **Cup**, Custard, Fancy Loop, Stemmed, 4 1/4 In. High | 27.00 |
| Heisey, **Cup**, Dessert, Queen Anne, 2 Handled, Liner, C.1929 | 12.00 |
| Heisey, **Cup**, Punch, Colonial, Signed | 3.00 |
| Heisey, **Cup**, Punch, Old Williamsburg, Set Of 8 | 28.00 |
| Heisey, **Cup**, Punch, Peerless, Signed | 8.50 |
| Heisey, **Cup**, Punch, Punty & Diamond Point | 7.50 |
| Heisey, **Cup**, Punch, Victorian | 5.00 |
| Heisey, **Cup**, Punch, Williamsburg | 4.65 |
| Heisey, **Cup**, Queen Anne, Sahara | 7.50 |
| Heisey, **Decanter Set**, Pied Piper, 16 Ozs., 5 Piece | 125.00 |
| Heisey, **Decanter**, Liquor, Black Amethyst, Golfer | 135.00 |
| Heisey, **Dish & Saucer**, Dessert, Flamingo, Signed | 15.00 |
| Heisey, **Dish**, Candy, Clear, Sides Roll Up At Handles, Pair | 16.00 |
| Heisey, **Dish**, Candy, Covered, Etched, Gold Band, 10 1/2 In.High | 45.00 |
| Heisey, **Dish**, Candy, Covered, Etched, 6 X 5 1/2 In. | 50.00 |
| Heisey, **Dish**, Candy, Covered, Gold Band | 30.00 |
| Heisey, **Dish**, Candy, Metal Lid, Flower Handle, Crystolite, 3 Compartments | 18.00 |
| Heisey, **Dish**, Candy, Paneled, 7 In.Diameter | 16.00 |
| Heisey, **Dish**, Candy, Silver Overlay Finial On Lid, Silver Rim, Star Base | 50.00 |
| Heisey, **Dish**, Jelly, Cut Rib & Flower, Octagonal, Handled, 5 1/2 In.Diameter | 9.00 |
| Heisey, **Dish**, Jelly, Diamond Point, 3 1/4 In. | 4.50 |
| Heisey, **Dish**, Jelly, Narrow Flute, Handled, Marked | 11.00 |
| Heisey, **Dish**, Mint, Paneled, Clear, 2 Handles | 6.50 |
| Heisey, **Dish**, Nut, Pink, Flared Bottom, Patent 6/12/21 | 8.00 |
| Heisey, **Dish**, Olive, Colonial | 7.50 |
| Heisey, **Eggcup**, Continental, Marked | 14.00 |
| Heisey, **Figurine**, Duck, Mallard, Wings Up | 45.00 |
| Heisey, **Figurine**, Gazelle, Marked, 10 7/8 In.High | 850.00 |
| Heisey, **Figurine**, Giraffe, Erect, Signed | 135.00 |
| Heisey, **Figurine**, Goose, Wings Halfway Down | 30.00 |
| Heisey, **Figurine**, Goose, Wings Halfway Up | 40.00 To 55.00 |
| Heisey, **Figurine**, Goose, Wings Up | 45.00 |
| Heisey, **Figurine**, Gosling, Head Turned Right | 60.00 |
| Heisey, **Figurine**, Mallard Duck, Wings Half Up | 125.00 |
| Heisey, **Figurine**, Pheasant, Asiatic, Hand Decorated, Pair | 125.00 |
| Heisey, **Figurine**, Piglet, Signed | 60.00 |
| Heisey, **Figurine**, Plug Horse, Signed | 90.00 To 125.00 |
| Heisey, **Figurine**, Pony, Kicking | 97.00 |
| Heisey, **Figurine**, Pony, Standing | 40.00 To 65.00 |
| Heisey, **French Dressing Boat & Underplate**, Diamond Optic, Flamingo | 22.00 |
| Heisey, **French Dressing Boat & Underplate**, Narrow Flute, Footed, Signed | 22.50 |
| Heisey, **Fruit Set**, Ring Band, Custard, 7 Piece | 225.00 |
| Heisey, **Goblet**, Alexandrite, 5 In.High | 35.00 |
| Heisey, **Goblet**, Cobalt, Clear Base, Park Lane, 8 Ozs. | 10.00 |
| Heisey, **Goblet**, Colonial, Signed | 8.50 To 10.50 |
| Heisey, **Goblet**, Continental, Signed | 6.40 |
| Heisey, **Goblet**, Diamond Optic, Flamingo | 9.00 |
| Heisey, **Goblet**, Moonglow, Cut, Signed Max Seidel | 13.50 |
| Heisey, **Goblet**, New Era | 4.00 |
| Heisey, **Goblet**, Orchid | 14.25 |
| Heisey, **Goblet**, Pleat & Panel, Signed | 8.50 |
| Heisey, **Goblet**, Shawl Dancer, Flamingo | 18.00 |
| Heisey, **Goblet**, Sheffield | 8.00 |
| Heisey, **Goblet**, Tangerine | 225.00 |

| | |
|---|---:|
| Heisey, Goblet, Victorian, Marked | 10.00 |
| Heisey, Goblet, Wedding Band, Marked | 10.00 |
| Heisey, Hair Receiver & Powder Box, Covered, Etched, Star Bottoms | 60.00 |
| Heisey, Jar, Candy, Covered, Ribbed, Signed, 13 In.High | 22.00 |
| Heisey, Jar, Dresser, Silver Plate Art Nouveau Floral Top, Marked | 24.00 |
| Heisey, Jar, Mustard, Etched Flowers | 22.00 |
| Heisey, Jar, Pickle, Metal Lid, Fork, & Holder, Scenes On Land & Sea | 75.00 |
| Heisey, Jar, Powder, Colonial, Crystal, Celluloid Lid, Signed | 8.00 |
| Heisey, Jug, Greek Key, 1/2 Gallon | 45.00 |
| Heisey, Knife Rest, Flat Panel, Signed, 4 3/4 In.Long | 55.00 |
| Heisey, Mayonnaise Set, Alexandrite, 2 Piece | 95.00 |
| Heisey, Mug, Punty Band, Ruby Flashed | 40.00 |
| Heisey, Mustard Set, Williamsburg, Signed, 2 Piece | 12.00 |
| Heisey, Nappy, Narrow Flute, Plain Rim, Dated 4/15/13, Signed | 5.50 |
| Heisey, Nappy, Peerless, Signed, 4 In.Diameter | 5.00 |
| Heisey, Nappy, Starburst Bottom | 14.00 |
| Heisey, Perfume, Drip Stopper, Cut Design, Petalled Flowers, Ferns | 22.50 |
| Heisey, Perfume, Flashed Amber, Gold Embossed Stopper, Signed | 38.00 |
| Heisey, Pitcher, Colonial, Signed | 11.00 |
| Heisey, Pitcher, Enameled On Paneled Design, Dated 6/25/12, 6 1/2 In.High | 95.00 |
| Heisey, Pitcher, Etched On Upper Edge Of Panel, 6 1/2 In. | 75.00 |
| Heisey, Pitcher, Milk, Melon Ribbed, Applied Handle, Signed | 19.00 |
| Heisey, Pitcher, Milk, Ribbed, Signed, 5 In. | 8.00 |
| Heisey, Pitcher, Pattern 300, 4 In.High | 22.50 |
| Heisey, Pitcher, Puritan, Signed, 2 Quart | 36.00 |
| Heisey, Pitcher, Ribbed, Signed | 38.00 |
| Heisey, Pitcher, Silver Openwork Top, Marked | 225.00 |
| Heisey, Pitcher, Water, Colonial, Bulbous, Marked | 35.00 |
| Heisey, Pitcher, Water, Colonial, Squatty, Marked | 25.00 |
| Heisey, Pitcher, Water, Groove And Slash, Half Gallon | 39.50 |
| Heisey, Pitcher, Water, Ipswich | 68.00 |
| Heisey, Pitcher, Water, Pleat & Panel | 27.00 |
| Heisey, Pitcher, Water, Sahara, Old Sandwich | 48.50 |
| Heisey, Pitcher, Water, Sunburst | 85.00 |
| Heisey, Plate, Beehive, Amethyst Flashed & Crystal, 4 In. | 15.00 |
| Heisey, Plate, Cake, Rib & Panel, Signed, 7 In. | 4.00 |
| Heisey, Plate, Clear With Blue & Gold, 5 1/2 In. | 2.00 |
| Heisey, Plate, Colonial, Flat, Marked, 12 In. | 12.50 |
| Heisey, Plate, Dessert, Marked, 7 1/4 In. | 15.00 |
| Heisey, Plate, Fancy Loop, 8 In. | 25.00 |
| Heisey, Plate, Flamingo, Augusta, Diamond Optic, 1916, 8 In. | 2.40 |
| Heisey, Plate, Flamingo, Triple Octagon, 7 1/4 In. | 3.75 |
| Heisey, Plate, Greek Key, Marked, 5 In. | 4.00 |
| Heisey, Plate, Marigold, Twist, Marked, 8 In. | 12.50 |
| Heisey, Plate, Minuet, 7 1/2 In. | 17.50 |
| Heisey, Plate, Narrow Panel, 7 3/8 In. | 3.25 |
| Heisey, Plate, Old Williamsburg, Signed, 8 3/8 In. | 6.65 |
| Heisey, Plate, Paneled Clear Edge, 4 3/4 In. | 3.50 |
| Heisey, Plate, Party, Orchid, 14 In. | 35.00 |
| Heisey, Plate, Pattern 1401, Signed, 6 1/8 In. | 3.50 |
| Heisey, Plate, Pattern 1401, 7 1/2 In. | 4.00 |
| Heisey, Plate, Pleated Effect, Star Base, Marked, 7 1/4 In. | 14.00 |
| Heisey, Plate, Queen Anne, Tangerine, Marked, 8 1/2 In. | 150.00 |
| Heisey, Plate, Ribbed, Pink, 7 1/2 In. | 3.00 |
| Heisey, Plate, Sahara, Queen Anne, Marked, 6 In. | 4.65 |
| Heisey, Plate, Star Base, Etched Design, Gold Rim, Signed, 7 1/4 In. | 10.00 |
| Heisey, Plate, Sunburst Center, Clear, 5 1/2 In. | 2.50 |
| Heisey, Plate, Sunburst Center, Pink, 37 Ribs, 8 In. | 3.75 |
| Heisey, Plate, Swirl Ribbed, Fluted Edge, Green, 7 1/4 In. | 4.15 |
| Heisey, Platter, Amber, Paneled Edge, Star Center | 38.50 |
| Heisey, Punch Set, Greek Key, 12 Cups, 2 Piece Bowl & Pedestal | 250.00 |
| Heisey, Relish, Pillows, Rolled-In Rim, Marked, 9 1/2 X 5 In. | 22.50 |
| Heisey, Relish, Pink, Three Compartments, Marked | 14.00 |
| Heisey, Relish, Pointed Leaf Shape, Green, Signed | 22.00 |
| Heisey, Relish, Ribbed Panel, Oval, Marked | 7.00 |
| Heisey, Relish, Scalloped, Star Base, Signed, 7 In. | 9.00 |

| | |
|---|---|
| **Heisey, Salt & Pepper,** Moongleam, Signed | 37.50 |
| **Heisey, Salt & Pepper,** No.1255, Clear, Gold Trim, 3 In.High, Pair | 15.00 |
| **Heisey, Salt & Pepper,** Victorian | 15.00 |
| **Heisey, Salt,** Diamond Point, Signed | 4.00 |
| **Heisey, Salt,** Fancy Loop | 9.00 |
| **Heisey, Salt,** Flared, Flamingo, Dated 1916, 3 1/2 In. | 8.50 |
| **Heisey, Salt,** Ridgeleigh, Square, Marked | 6.00 |
| **Heisey, Salt,** Sandwich, Scalloped Rim, Signed | 10.50 |
| **Heisey, Saltshaker,** Pineapple & Fan | 12.00 |
| **Heisey, Sauce,** Burg, Scalloped, 5 1/2 In. | 3.00 |
| **Heisey, Sauce,** Colonial, Clear, Marked | 4.50 |
| **Heisey, Sauce,** Ispwich, Footed, Signed | 8.75 |
| **Heisey, Sauce,** Punty & Diamond Point, Flat, 4 3/4 In. | 4.50 |
| **Heisey, Saucer,** Loops On Edge | 3.00 |
| **Heisey, Saucer,** Rose Pattern | 3.00 |
| **Heisey, Server,** Etched Crystal, Center Handle, Signed | 24.50 |
| **Heisey, Sherbet,** Colonial, Crystal, Hexagonal Base, Stemmed, 4 1/2 In. | 7.50 |
| **Heisey, Sherbet,** Crystolite | 4.50 |
| **Heisey, Sherbet,** Etched Orchid | 10.00 |
| **Heisey, Sherbet,** Flamingo, Augusta, Diamond Optic, Low Foot, 1916, 5 Ozs. | 3.35 |
| **Heisey, Sherbet,** Greek Key | 8.00 |
| **Heisey, Sherbet,** Green, Yeoman, Signed | 8.50 |
| **Heisey, Sherbet,** Narrow Flute, Flared, Signed | 7.50 |
| **Heisey, Sherbet,** Orchid | 14.25 |
| **Heisey, Sherbet,** Ridgeleigh, Footed, Marked | 6.00 |
| **Heisey, Sherbet,** Wedding Band, Clear, Tall Stem, Diamond H Mark | 6.00 |
| **Heisey, Shot Glass,** Sandwich | 9.00 |
| **Heisey, Soda Glass,** Saturn, 12 Oz., Set Of 6 | 30.00 |
| **Heisey, Spooner,** Diamond Swag | 5.00 |
| **Heisey, Spooner,** Prince Of Wales Plumes, Signed | 45.00 |
| **Heisey, Sugar & Creamer On Oval Tray,** Miniature | 20.00 |
| **Heisey, Sugar & Creamer,** Child's, Flute | 20.00 |
| **Heisey, Sugar & Creamer,** Child's, Ribbed Pattern | 12.50 |
| **Heisey, Sugar & Creamer,** Colonial, Miniature | 29.00 |
| **Heisey, Sugar & Creamer,** Crystal, Greek Key, Signed | 30.00 |
| **Heisey, Sugar & Creamer,** Crystolite | 9.00 |
| **Heisey, Sugar & Creamer,** Cut-Flower, Signed | 48.00 |
| **Heisey, Sugar & Creamer,** Flamingo, Footed | 15.00 |
| **Heisey, Sugar & Creamer,** Green, Art Deco Form | 25.00 |
| **Heisey, Sugar & Creamer,** Individual, Green, Narrow Flute, Signed | 12.00 |
| **Heisey, Sugar & Creamer,** Pink, Rectangular | 16.00 |
| **Heisey, Sugar & Creamer,** Quator Hotel, Dated 9/9/12, Signed | 28.50 |
| **Heisey, Sugar & Creamer,** Ribbed, Clear, Oval, Bulbous, Marked | 14.00 |
| **Heisey, Sugar & Creamer,** Ridgeleigh, Miniature | 18.00 |
| **Heisey, Sugar & Creamer,** Ruby Flashed, Colonial, Miniature | 35.00 |
| **Heisey, Sugar & Creamer,** Toy, Flute, Marked | 35.00 |
| **Heisey, Sugar & Creamer,** Waffle, Signed | 25.00 |
| **Heisey, Sugar,** Clear, Fluted | 7.50 |
| **Heisey, Sugar,** Covered, Beaded Panel & Sunburst | 36.00 |
| **Heisey, Sugar,** Covered, Wedding Band | 27.00 |
| **Heisey, Sugar,** Flute | 6.50 |
| **Heisey, Sugar,** No.1255, Clear, Gold Trim | 12.00 |
| **Heisey, Sugar,** Paneled, Handled, Miniature, Signed, 2 1/4 In. | 7.50 |
| **Heisey, Sugar,** Silver Overlay Border, 6 Panels, 2 1/2 In.High | 5.00 |
| **Heisey, Sugar,** Victorian, Marked | 8.00 |
| **Heisey, Syrup,** Crystal, Cut Floral, Sterling Lid, Bailey, Banks, & Biddle | 68.00 |
| **Heisey, Syrup,** Cut & Etched, Applied Handle, Metal Top, Marked | 20.00 |
| **Heisey, Syrup,** Cut Rose Design, Pewter Top, Marked | 28.00 |
| **Heisey, Syrup,** Tin Lid, Coarse Ribbed, Patent Dates | 6.00 |
| **Heisey, Tankard,** Prince Of Wales Plumes, Signed | 85.00 |
| **Heisey, Toothpick,** Beaded Swag, Ruby Flashed | 45.00 |
| **Heisey, Toothpick,** Colonial | 12.00 |
| **Heisey, Toothpick,** Colonial, Silver Overlay, Fluted Edge | 45.00 |
| **Heisey, Toothpick,** Crystolite, Pedestal, 3 3/4 In.High | 18.50 |
| **Heisey, Toothpick,** Fandango | 45.00 |
| **Heisey, Toothpick,** Ivorina Verde, Gold Decoration | 68.00 |

| | |
|---|---|
| Heisey, Toothpick, Paneled Cane, Marked | 22.00 |
| Heisey, Toothpick, Peerless, 2 1/4 In.High | 20.00 |
| Heisey, Toothpick, Pink, Oceanic, Signed | 32.00 |
| Heisey, Toothpick, Punty Band, Custard Glass, Souvenir | 50.00 |
| Heisey, Toothpick, Stars, Marked | 15.00 |
| Heisey, Toothpick, Victorian | 15.00 |
| Heisey, Tray, Old Williamsburg, 1902-1910, 12 1/4 X 8 In. | 35.00 |
| Heisey, Tray, Pickle, Fandango, 6 In. | 12.50 |
| Heisey, Tray, Spoon, Colonial, 7 In.Long, Signed | 9.50 |
| Heisey, Tub & Underplate, Ice, Puritan, Tab Handles, Signed | 47.00 |
| Heisey, Tub, Butter, Narrow Panel, 4 In.High | 25.00 |
| Heisey, Tub, Ice, Greek Key, Hotel | 65.00 |
| Heisey, Tumbler, Block | 8.00 |
| Heisey, Tumbler, Colonial, Marked | 7.50 |
| Heisey, Tumbler, Fancy Loop | 18.50 |
| Heisey, Tumbler, Juice, Wedding Band, Marked | 8.00 |
| Heisey, Tumbler, Old Fashion, Sahara, Paneled Halfway Up | 14.50 |
| Heisey, Tumbler, Peerless, Star Base, Flared, 6 Ozs. | 14.00 |
| Heisey, Tumbler, Peerless, 2 3/4 In.High | 10.00 |
| Heisey, Tumbler, Red, Provincial, Footed, 5 1/2 In.High | 85.00 |
| Heisey, Tumbler, Sahara, Sandwich | 15.00 |
| Heisey, Vase, Bud, Pineapple & Fan, 6 In.High | 6.00 |
| Heisey, Vase, Cornucopia, Signed, 9 In. | 25.00 |
| Heisey, Vase, Fan, Etched Orchids, Lariat Handles, Signed, 7 1/2 In.High | 25.00 |
| Heisey, Vase, Heavy Panel, Silver Overlay, 8 3/4 In.High, 5 In.Diameter | 70.00 |
| Heisey, Vase, Horn Of Plenty, Warwick, Signed, 5 1/2 In.High | 12.75 |
| Heisey, Vase, Light Green, 4 1/2 In. | 18.00 |
| Heisey, Vase, Paperweight Bottom, Flared Top, Clear, Signed, 7 3/4 In. | 16.00 |
| Heisey, Vase, Punty P Diamond Point, Scalloped Top, 10 1/4 In.High | 55.00 |
| Heisey, Vase, Ribbed, Signed, 9 In. | 32.50 |
| Heisey, Vase, Rose, Signed, 6 5/8 In.High | 35.00 |
| Heisey, Vase, Trumpet, Scalloped Rim, 18 1/2 In. | 75.00 |
| Heisey, Wine, Colonial, Stemmed | 6.50 |
| Heisey, Wine, Fancy Loop Variant | 35.00 |
| Heisey, Wine, Flamingo Habitat | 19.50 |
| Heisey, Wine, Flute | 5.00 |
| Heisey, Wine, Pied Piper, Stemmed, Signed | 15.00 |
| Heisey, Wine, Wedding Band, Marked | 10.00 |
| Herend, see Fischer | |
| Heubach, Vase, Pate Sur Pate Oval Cameo On Royal Blue, Gold Double Handles | 225.00 |

*Higbee glass was made by the J.B.Higbee Company of Bridgeville, Pennsylvania, about 1900.*   **HIG**

Higbee, see also Amberina

| | |
|---|---|
| Higbee, Bowl, Berry, Hawaiian Lei, Bee Mark, Large Size | 15.00 |
| Higbee, Bowl, Paneled Thistle, Deep, 6 3/4 In. | 14.00 |
| Higbee, Bowl, Paneled Thistle, Footed, Bee Mark, 9 In.Diameter | 22.00 |
| Higbee, Bowl, Paneled Thistle, Oval, Bee Mark, 7 1/4 X 5 1/2 X 2 In. | 18.00 |
| Higbee, Bowl, Paneled Thistle, Shallow, Top Curves In, 9 In. | 18.00 |
| Higbee, Bowl, Paneled Thistle, Shallow, 9 1/2 In. | 18.00 |
| Higbee, Bowl, Paneled Thistle, 6 1/2 In. | 12.00 |
| Higbee, Butter, Covered, Hawaiian Lei, Bee Mark, Miniature | 28.00 |
| Higbee, Butter, Covered, Paneled Thistle, Bee Signature | 45.00 |
| Higbee, Cake Stand, Child's, Flute, 6 1/2 X 3 1/2 In. | 15.00 |
| Higbee, Cake Stand, Paneled Thistle, 9 1/2 In. | 19.00 |
| Higbee, Celery, Hawaiian Lei, Bee Mark | 16.00 |
| Higbee, Celery, Paneled Thistle, 2 Handled | 20.00 |
| Higbee, Compote, Paneled Thistle, Bee Mark, 8 In. | 20.00 |
| Higbee, Compote, Paneled Thistle, 8 1/2 In.Diameter | 20.00 |
| Higbee, Creamer, Paneled Thistle, Bee Signature | 35.00 |
| Higbee, Creamer, Paneled, Rosette Base, Bee Mark | 4.75 |
| Higbee, Dish, Honey, Covered, Paneled Thistle, Square, 5 1/2 In. | 35.00 To 46.50 |
| Higbee, Nappy, Hawaiian Lei, Footed, B Mark, 4 1/4 In. Diameter | 9.50 To 16.00 |
| Higbee, Nappy, Paneled Thistle, 5 1/2 In. | 12.00 |
| Higbee, Pitcher, Milk, Paneled Thistle, Bee Mark | 40.00 |
| Higbee, Plate, Paneled Thistle, 7 1/2 In. | 16.00 |

| | |
|---|---:|
| Higbee, Plate, Paneled Thistle, 9 In. | 18.00 |
| Higbee, Plate, Paneled Thistle, 10 1/2 In. | 20.00 |
| Higbee, Plate, Paneled Thistle, 10 3/4 In. | 25.00 |
| Higbee, Plate, Serving, Hawaiian Lei, Scalloped Rim, Marked, 10 1/2 In. | 25.00 |
| Higbee, Relish, Cane Spray, Bee In Base | 16.00 |
| Higbee, Relish, Hawaiian Lei, Oval, Scalloped Rim, 11 1/2 X 4 3/4 In. | 10.00 |
| Higbee, Rose Bowl, Hawaiian Lei, Scalloped Rim, 4 In. High | 21.00 |
| Higbee, Sauce, Paneled Thistle, Flat | 8.50 |
| Higbee, Sauce, Paneled Thistle, Knob Feet | 8.50 |
| Higbee, Sauce, Perkins, Footed, Signed | 4.75 |
| Higbee, Sugar, Covered, Paneled Thistle, Bee Signature | 35.00 |
| Higbee, Sugar, Scalloped, 2 Handled, Signed | 22.00 |
| Higbee, Toothpick, Paneled Thistle, Signed With Bee & H.I.G. | 45.00 |
| Higbee, Tray, Candy, Store, Finecut, Signed, 7 In., Pair | 14.00 |
| Higbee, Vase, Harvard, Bee Mark, 5 In.High | 11.00 |
| Higbee, Vase, Hawaiian Lei, Flared, 5 1/4 In. High | 19.50 |
| Higbee, Vase, Paneled Thistle, 6 In.High | 14.00 |
| Higbee, Wine, Colonial, Signed With Bee | 12.00 |

**Historic Blue, see Adams, Clews, Staffordshire**

*Hobnail glass is a pattern of pressed glass with bumps in an allover pattern. Dozens of hobnail patterns and variants have been made. Reproductions of many types of hobnail glass can be found.*

**Hobnail, see also Francisware**

| | |
|---|---:|
| Hobnail, Bottle, Dresser, Amber | 14.00 |
| Hobnail, Bowl, Blue, Opalescent, Handled, Flared, Rounded Foot, 6 In. | 12.00 |
| Hobnail, Bowl, Blue, Scalloped Base, 8 In. | 35.00 |
| Hobnail, Bowl, Fan Top, Blue, 8 X 5 In. | 24.00 |
| Hobnail, Bowl, Finger, Opalescent White To Clear, Ruffled Top | 22.50 |
| Hobnail, Bowl, Finger, Opalescent, Ruffled Top, 4 1/2 In. Diameter | 28.00 |
| Hobnail, Bowl, Satin Finish, Yellow, Ruffled Top, 1 1/2 X 4 1/2 In. | 42.00 |
| Hobnail, Box, Dresser, Covered, Round, Amber | 12.00 |
| Hobnail, Candlestick, Blue Opalescent, Pair | 24.00 |
| Hobnail, Condiment Set, English, Rectangular Tray, 4 Piece | 40.00 |
| Hobnail, Cornucopia, White Opalescent, 3 1/2 In.High, Pair | 12.00 |
| Hobnail, Creamer, Blue Opalescent, 3 In. | 20.00 |
| Hobnail, Cruet, English, Bulbous, Stopper, Miniature | 14.00 |
| Hobnail, Cruet, Pointed Hobs, 9 In.High | 25.00 |
| Hobnail, Cup, Ornamented Band | 8.00 |
| Hobnail, Cup, Punch, Child's, Set Of 6 | 12.00 |
| Hobnail, Decanter, Wine, Pointed Hobs, 11 In.High | 38.00 |
| Hobnail, Epergne, Blue Opalescent, Ruffled Bowl, 3 Center Lilies | 65.00 |
| Hobnail, Ice Cream Set, Fiery Opalescent, 8 3/4 X 13 3/4 In.Tray, 11 Piece | 145.00 |
| Hobnail, Mug, Blue, 3 In.High | 12.50 |
| Hobnail, Mug, Deep Blue, Ruffled Handle | 14.00 |
| Hobnail, Pitcher, Clear Opalescent, Applied Handle, White Ribbon Edge, 8 In. | 42.50 |
| Hobnail, Plate, Toddy, Paneled, Amber, Footed Wire Frame, 4 1/2 In. | 14.50 |
| Hobnail, Rose Bowl, Green To Opalescent, 6 In. | 35.00 |
| Hobnail, Salt & Pepper, Blue | 25.00 |
| Hobnail, Spooner, Honey Amber | 25.00 |
| Hobnail, Sugar & Creamer, Blue To Opalescent, Miniature | 24.00 |
| Hobnail, Sugar & Creamer, English, Buckle | 28.00 |
| Hobnail, Toothpick, Opalescent, 3 Scalloped Feet | 23.50 |
| Hobnail, Tray, Condiment Set, English, 3 X 4 In. | 2.00 |
| Hobnail, Tray, Pen & Pencil, 2 X 10 In. | 3.00 |
| Hobnail, Tumbler, Clear Tipped Hobs | 11.00 |
| Hobnail, Tumbler, Nine Rows Of Pointed Hobs, Green To Cranberry Base | 27.50 |
| Hobnail, Tumbler, Pointed, Blue | 20.00 |
| Hobnail, Tumbler, 10 Rows, Sapphire Blue, Polished Pontil | 75.00 |
| Hobnail, Tumbler, 8 Rows Of Hobs, Blue, Opalescent | 34.00 |
| Hobnail, Vase, Fan, High Hobs, Canary, Opalescent, 6 In. | 12.00 |
| Hobnail, Vase, Fluted Top, Opalescent Pink, 4 1/2 In.High | 14.00 |
| Hobnail, Vase, Handkerchief, Blue Opalescent, Fluted Top, 8 In.High | 18.50 |

*Hochst, or Hoechst, porcelain was made in Germany from 1746 to 1796. It was marked with a six-spoke wheel.*

| | |
|---|---:|
| Hochst, Cup & Saucer, Chocolate, Trembleuse, Ruins, Floral, Gilt, C.1775 | 225.00 |

Hochst, Figurine,
Print Seller, C.1775,
7 1/4 In.High

Hochst, Figurine,
Trinket Seller, C.1775,
7 1/2 In.High

| | |
|---|---:|
| **Hochst, Cup & Saucer,** Coffee, Sheep On Grassy Plateau, Gilt Scrolls, C.1770 | 400.00 |
| **Hochst, Figurine,** Print Seller, C.1775, 7 1/4 In.High ................................. *Illus* | 2600.00 |
| **Hochst, Figurine,** Sultan & Sultana, C.1770, 7 In.High, Pair | 3200.00 |
| **Hochst, Figurine,** Trinket Seller, C.1775, 7 1/2 In.High ................................. *Illus* | 2600.00 |
| **Hochst, Jug,** Cream, Pear Shape, Sheep & River, C.1750, 3 1/2 In.High | 250.00 |
| **Hochst, Pot,** Bough, Covered, Harbor Scene, D Shape, 4 Columnar Feet | 100.00 |
| **Hochst, Saucer,** Cockerel On Scrollwork, Fruit, Scroll Rim, C.1755 | 200.00 |
| **Hochst, Saucer,** Puce Camaieu Farm Building, Insects, Gilt, C.1765 | 110.00 |
| **Hochst, Teapot,** Bullet Shape, Serpent Spout, Galland & Lady, C.1765 | 1050.00 |

*Holly amber, or golden agate, glass was made by the Indiana Tumbler and
Goblet Company from January 1, 1903, to June 13, 1903. It is a pressed
glass pattern featuring holly leaves in the amber shaded glass.*

| | |
|---|---:|
| **Holly Amber, Bowl,** Oval, Deep, 7 1/2 X 4 1/2 X 1 3/4 In. | 275.00 |
| **Holly Amber, Butter,** Covered, Beaded, 7 1/4 In.Diameter | 550.00 |
| **Holly Amber, Compote,** Jelly, 4 1/2 In.High | 550.00 |
| **Holly Amber, Creamer,** Mold Roughness On Spout, 4 1/2 In.High | 490.00 |
| **Holly Amber, Cruet,** Stopper | 1150.00 |
| **Holly Amber, Mug** | 350.00 |
| **Holly Amber, Plate,** 7 1/2 In. | 550.00 |
| **Holly Amber, Sauce,** Flat | 175.00 |
| **Holly Amber, Toothpick** | **175.00 To 295.00** |
| **Holly Amber, Tumbler,** 3 3/4 In. High | 205.00 To 395.00 |
| **Hopalong Cassidy, Banner,** Black Felt, Picture Of Hopalong & Topper, IO In. | 3.50 |
| **Hopalong Cassidy, Barbell & Exercise Set,** Hard Rubber, 5 Piece | 8.50 |
| **Hopalong Cassidy, Book,** Coloring | 5.50 |
| **Hopalong Cassidy, Book,** Hoppy & Danny, Color, Hard Cover | 1.50 |
| **Hopalong Cassidy, Book,** Hoppy Lends A Helping Hand, Color, Hard Cover | 1.50 |
| **Hopalong Cassidy, Exercise Set,** Rubber Barbell, 5 Piece | 7.75 |
| **Hopalong Cassidy, Lunch Bucket,** Thermos, Picture On Each, Metal | 16.00 |
| **Hopalong Cassidy, Mug** | 2.50 |
| **Hopalong Cassidy, Ring & Badge** | 5.00 |
| **Hopalong Cassidy, Ring,** Nickel Plated Brass, Picture Of Hopalong | 5.00 |
| **Hopalong Cassidy, Seal,** Bread | .50 |
| **Hopalong Cassidy, Tumbler,** Milk Glass | 10.00 |
| **Horn, Candlesnuffer,** Cone Shape | 3.00 |
| **Horn, Handle,** Umbrella, Silver Trim | 4.50 |
| **Horn, Ladle,** Carved, Sterling Mounts | 8.50 |
| **Horn, Letter Opener,** Crocodile's Head | 7.50 |
| **Howdy Doody, Book,** 1951 | 2.00 |
| **Howdy Doody, Card Game** | 3.00 |
| **Howdy Doody, Hat,** Sailor, White Cotton | 3.75 |
| **Howdy Doody, Paint Set,** Boxed | 5.75 |
| **Howdy Doody, Puppet** | 14.00 |
| **Howdy Doody, Ring,** Club, 1953 | .50 |

*Hull pottery is made in Crooksville, Ohio. The factory started in 1903
as the Acme Pottery Company. Art pottery was first made in 1917.*

| | |
|---|---|
| Hull, Basket, 9 In. | 12.00 |
| Hull, Bowl, Light To Dark Green, 10 1/2 In.Diameter | 4.00 |
| Hull, Candlestick, Pipe Shape, Beige, 2 1/2 In.High, Pair | 7.00 |
| Hull, Cookie Jar, Duck, White, 12 In.High | 35.00 |
| Hull, Cornucopia, Glazed Beige, Brown Wheat, 8 In.High, Pair | 15.00 |
| Hull, Creamer, Pink, Yellow, & Blue Floral, Marked | 10.00 |
| Hull, Figurine, Parrot Pulling Cart, Red & Green, 6 1/2 In.High | 12.00 |
| Hull, Pitcher, Pink Floral On Yellow, 4 In. | 6.50 |
| Hull, Planter, Clover Shape, Green On Wine, 4 1/2 In. | 6.50 |
| Hull, Planter, Green To Yellow, Pink Flowers, Twig Handles, 4 X 10 In. | 15.00 |
| Hull, Planter, Spade Shape, Green On Wine, 4 1/2 In. | 6.50 |
| Hull, Planter, Swan | 8.95 |
| Hull, Vase, Blue & White Ground, Blue, Green, Yellow Flowers, 9 In.High | 7.00 |
| Hull, Vase, Blue To White, Pink Floral Design, 8 In.High | 7.00 |
| Hull, Vase, Camellia, Pink & Aqua, 10 In.High | 15.00 |
| Hull, Vase, Floral On Blue Base, Pink Top, Handled, 10 In. | 10.00 |
| Hull, Vase, Floral, Yellow, Handled, 9 In. | 11.00 |
| Hull, Vase, Glazed Pink With White Dogwood, 6 X 2 1/2 In. | 10.00 |
| Hull, Vase, Green To Pink, Leaf Design On Rim, 6 In.High | 5.00 |
| Hull, Vase, Large Bird In Flight, 9 1/2 In.High | 9.00 |
| Hull, Vase, Pink To Blue, Yellow Floral Design, 5 In.High | 6.00 |
| Hull, Vase, Pitcher Shape, White, Pink, & Yellow Flower On Blue, 13 1/2 In. | 20.00 |
| Hull, Vase, Pitcher, Blue, White, Pink, Yellow Flower, 13 1/2 In.High | 20.00 |
| Hull, Vase, Shell Design, Blue, 7 In.High, 4 In.Wide | 6.00 |
| Hull, Vase, Urn Type, Green Decorated With Gold, Gold Lions Heads, 9 In. | 15.00 |
| Hull, Vase, White Matte Glaze, Egg & Dart Molding, 4 In.High | 4.00 |

*Hummel figurines, based on the drawings of Berta Hummel, are made by the W.Goebel Porzellanfabrik of Oeslau, Germany. They were first made in 1934.*

| | |
|---|---|
| Hummel, Candleholder, Angel Playing Mandolin, Kneeling Child | 65.00 |
| Hummel, Figurine, Adoration, 6 1/4 In. | 55.00 |
| Hummel, Figurine, Adventure Bound | 625.00 |
| Hummel, Figurine, Angel In Cloud Font, Blue Bee In V Mark | 35.00 |
| Hummel, Figurine, Angel Serenade, 3 In. | 18.00 |
| Hummel, Figurine, Angel Set, 3 Pieces | 37.50 |
| Hummel, Figurine, Apple Tree Boy, Prewar Mark, 6 In. | 55.00 |
| Hummel, Figurine, Apple Tree Boy, 10 1/2 In. | 225.00 |
| Hummel, Figurine, Apple Tree Girl, Prewar Mark, 6 In. | 55.00 |
| Hummel, Figurine, Apple Tree Girl, 6 In. | 43.00 |
| Hummel, Figurine, Apple Tree Girl, 10 1/2 In. | 225.00 |
| Hummel, Figurine, Auf Wiedersehen, 5 1/4 In. | 39.50 |
| Hummel, Figurine, Bandleader, 5 1/4 In. | 35.00 |
| Hummel, Figurine, Barnyard Hero, 4 In. | 29.50 |
| Hummel, Figurine, Barnyard Hero, 5 1/2 In. | 45.50 |
| Hummel, Figurine, Be Patient, 4 1/4 In. | 32.00 |
| Hummel, Figurine, Blessed Event, 5 1/2 In. | 63.00 |
| Hummel, Figurine, Bookworm, 4 In. | 40.00 |
| Hummel, Figurine, Boy Leading Orchestra, Black Mark & Blue Bee Mark | 55.00 |
| Hummel, Figurine, Boy With 2 Lambs, 7 In. | 65.00 |
| Hummel, Figurine, Carnival, 6 In. | 35.00 |
| Hummel, Figurine, Chick Girl, 3 1/2 In. | 23.00 |
| Hummel, Figurine, Cinderella, 4 1/4 In. | 45.00 |
| Hummel, Figurine, Close Harmony, 5 1/2 In. | 46.00 |
| Hummel, Figurine, Confidentially, 5 1/4 In. | 39.50 |
| Hummel, Figurine, Doctor, 4 3/4 In. | 25.00 To 33.00 |
| Hummel, Figurine, Doll Bath, 5 1/4 In. | 36.00 |
| Hummel, Figurine, Doll Mother, 4 3/4 In. | 45.00 |
| Hummel, Figurine, Duet, 5 1/4 In. | 35.00 To 43.00 |
| Hummel, Figurine, Easter Time, 4 In. | 45.00 |
| Hummel, Figurine, Eventide, 4 3/4 In. | 55.00 |
| Hummel, Figurine, Farm Boy, 5 1/4 In. | 27.00 To 36.00 |
| Hummel, Figurine, For Father, 5 1/2 In. | 35.00 |
| Hummel, Figurine, For Mother, 5 1/4 In. | 29.50 |
| Hummel, Figurine, Friends, 5 In. | 37.50 |
| Hummel, Figurine, Girl & Basket, Boy & Pipe, Goebel, 6 1/2 In., Pair | 45.00 |

| | |
|---|---:|
| Hummel, Figurine, Globetrotter, 5 1/4 In. | 35.00 |
| Hummel, Figurine, Going To Grandma's, 4 3/4 In. | 40.00 |
| Hummel, Figurine, Good Friends, 4 In. | 25.00 To 30.00 |
| Hummel, Figurine, Good Hunting, 5 1/4 In. | 30.00 To 40.00 |
| Hummel, Figurine, Goosegirl, 4 In. | 33.00 |
| Hummel, Figurine, Goosegirl, 4 3/4 In. | 25.00 To 38.00 |
| Hummel, Figurine, Happiness, 4 3/4 In. | 28.00 |
| Hummel, Figurine, Happy Birthday, 5 1/2 In. | 30.00 |
| Hummel, Figurine, Happy Days, 4 1/4 In. | 37.00 |
| Hummel, Figurine, Hear Ye Hear Ye, 5 1/4 In. | 38.00 |
| Hummel, Figurine, Heavenly Angel, 4 1/4 In. | 29.00 |
| Hummel, Figurine, Heavenly Angel, 6 In. | 38.00 |
| Hummel, Figurine, Hello, 6 1/4 In. | 30.00 |
| Hummel, Figurine, Home From Market, 4 3/4 In. | 35.00 |
| Hummel, Figurine, Home From Market, 5 1/2 In. | 35.00 |
| Hummel, Figurine, Just Resting, 4 In. | 25.50 |
| Hummel, Figurine, Just Resting, 5 1/2 In. | 37.00 |
| Hummel, Figurine, Kiss Me, 6 In. | 39.50 |
| Hummel, Figurine, Knitting Lesson, 7 1/2 In. | 75.00 |
| Hummel, Figurine, Latest News, 5 1/4 In. | 36.00 |
| Hummel, Figurine, Little Bookkeeper, 4 3/4 In. | 35.00 |
| Hummel, Figurine, Little Cellist, 6 In. | 38.00 |
| Hummel, Figurine, Little Fiddler, 4 3/4 In. | 31.50 |
| Hummel, Figurine, Little Pharmacist, 6 In. | 42.00 |
| Hummel, Figurine, Lost Sheep, 4 1/2 In. | 25.00 |
| Hummel, Figurine, Madonna & Child, Blue Mark, 9 In. | 13.50 |
| Hummel, Figurine, Madonna, 12 In.High, Blue Bee In V Signature | 120.00 |
| Hummel, Figurine, March Winds, 5 In. | 28.00 |
| Hummel, Figurine, Meditation, 5 1/4 In. | 34.50 |
| Hummel, Figurine, Merry Wanderer, Large | 280.00 |
| Hummel, Figurine, Merry Wanderer, 4 1/2 In. | 26.00 |
| Hummel, Figurine, Mother's Darling, 5 1/2 In. | 38.00 |
| Hummel, Figurine, Mother's Helper, 5 In. | 38.50 |
| Hummel, Figurine, Not For You, 6 In. | 42.00 |
| Hummel, Figurine, On Secret Path, 5 1/4 In. | 43.00 |
| Hummel, Figurine, Postman, 5 1/4 In. | 36.00 |
| Hummel, Figurine, Retreat To Safety, 4 In. | 32.00 |
| Hummel, Figurine, Sacred Heart Of Jesus, Blue Mark, 10 In. | 13.50 |
| Hummel, Figurine, Schoolboy, 4 In. | 25.00 |
| Hummel, Figurine, Schoolboy, 7 1/2 In. | 165.00 |
| Hummel, Figurine, Schoolboys, 9 1/2 In. | 525.00 |
| Hummel, Figurine, Schoolgirl, 4 In. | 25.00 |
| Hummel, Figurine, Schoolgirl, 5 1/4 In. | 32.50 |
| Hummel, Figurine, Schoolgirl, 7 1/2 In. | 165.00 |
| Hummel, Figurine, Schoolgirls, 9 1/2 In. | 525.00 |
| Hummel, Figurine, Sensitive Hunter, 4 3/4 In. | 28.00 |
| Hummel, Figurine, Sensitive Hunter, 5 1/2 In. | 37.00 |
| Hummel, Figurine, Signs Of Spring, 5 In. | 39.50 |
| Hummel, Figurine, Sister, 4 3/4 In. | 26.00 |
| Hummel, Figurine, Skier, Goebel, 5 1/4 In. | 34.00 |
| Hummel, Figurine, Smart Little Sister, 4 3/4 In. | 41.50 |
| Hummel, Figurine, Stargazer, 4 3/4 In. | 38.00 |
| Hummel, Figurine, Stormy Weather, 6 1/4 In. | 79.50 |
| Hummel, Figurine, The Builder, 5 1/2 In. | 41.50 |
| Hummel, Figurine, The Photographer, 4 3/4 In. | 47.50 |
| Hummel, Figurine, The Tooter | 12.00 |
| Hummel, Figurine, Umbrella Boy, 4 3/4 In. | 98.00 |
| Hummel, Figurine, Umbrella Boy, 8 In. | 325.00 |
| Hummel, Figurine, Umbrella Girl, 4 3/4 In. | 98.00 |
| Hummel, Figurine, Umbrella Girl, 8 In. | 325.00 |
| Hummel, Figurine, Virgin Mary, Blue Mark, 9 In. | 13.50 |
| Hummel, Figurine, Volunteers, 5 1/4 In. | 35.00 |
| Hummel, Figurine, Waiter, 6 In. | 35.00 |
| Hummel, Figurine, Wayside Harmony, 3 3/4 In. | 18.00 |
| Hummel, Figurine, Wayside Harmony, 4 In. | 25.50 |
| Hummel, Group, Boy With Girl, Holding Basket With Bottle & Flowers, Signed | 69.00 |

Hummel, Group, Surprise, Boy & Girl With Basket, 5 1/2 In.High ........................ 20.00
Hummel, Group, Wayside Devotion, Bee & Goebel Mark ................................ 45.00
Hutchenreuther, Tray, Octagonal, Country Landscape, C.1860, 9 X 13 In. ............ 70.00
Hyten, Saltshaker, Eagle & U.S.Red & Blue Shield, Benton, Arkansas, 1882 ........ 25.00
Icon, Russian, Birth Of The Virgin, C.1720, Silvered Metal, 12 X 10 1/8 In. ........ 800.00
Icon, Russian, Christ, Pantocrator, C.1820, Repousse Silvered Metal ................ 225.00
Icon, Russian, Complete Resurrection, C.1820, Repousse Gilt Metal ................ 250.00
Icon, Russian, Extended Diesis, C.1650, 7 X 18 1/4 In. ............................ 2100.00
Icon, Russian, John The Baptist, C.1820, 20 1/2 X 16 1/4 In. ...................... 225.00
Icon, Russian, Madonna & Child, Pierced Cross Above, Brass, Enameled ............ 68.00
Icon, Russian, Old Testament Trinity, C.1890, 14 X 12 1/4 In. ...................... 450.00
Icon, Russian, Our Lady Iverskaya, C.1820, Gilt Metal, 12 1/4 X 13 1/2 In. ........ 150.00
Icon, Russian, Our Lady Iverskaya, C.1850, Repousse Gilt Metal .................... 150.00
Icon, Russian, Our Lady Of The Sign, C.1890, 12 1/4 X 10 1/2 In. .................. 150.00
Icon, Russian, Our Lady Pecheraskaya, C.1890, Repousse Gilt Metal ................ 300.00
Icon, Russian, Our Lady Tchinaya, C.1820, 13 3/8 X 11 1/2 In. .................... 200.00
Icon, Russian, St.Alexander, C.1890, 8 3/4 X 6 3/4 In. ............................ 300.00
Icon, Russian, St.Nicholas, The Miracleworker, C.1850, Silvered Metal ............ 80.00
Icon, Russian, St.Sophia, C.1890, Parcel Gilt Silver, 4 5/8 X 3 5/8 In. ............ 200.00
Icon, Russian, Sts.Sergei & German, Silver, C.1850, 2 1/2 X 2 In. .................. 175.00
Icon, Russian, The Vernicle, C.1820, Repousse Gilded Silver, 16 X 13 1/2 In. ...... 175.00
Icon, Russian, Veronica's Veil, Silver, Dated 1848, 2 1/4 X 2 In. .................. 165.00
Icon, Russian, Virgin & Child, Silver, C.1850, 2 1/2 X 2 In. ........................ 165.00
Icon, Russian, Virgin Enthroned, Silver, Dated 1826, 4 1/2 X 3 1/2 In. ............ 250.00

*Imari patterns are named for the Japanese ware decorated with orange and
blue stylized flowers. The design on the Japanese ware became so
characteristic that the name Imari has come to mean any pattern of this type.
It was copied by the European factories of the eighteenth and early
nineteenth centuries.*

Imari, Bowl, Bird In Garden Scene, 7 In. .......................................... 50.00
Imari, Bowl, Blue Scene, C.1850, 5 1/2 In. ........................................ 18.75
Imari, Bowl, Cobalt Floral Exterior, Bird Panel Interior, 8 In. .................... 26.00
Imari, Bowl, Covered, 5 In.Diameter .............................................. 125.00
Imari, Bowl, Rice, Covered, Orange, Circular Design On Blue, 3 1/2 In High ...... 38.50
Imari, Bowl, Scenic, Blue, C.1850 ................................................ 20.00
Imari, Bowl, Shallow, Three Panels, Trees, Birds, Orange, Blue, 13 1/2 In. ........ 95.00
Imari, Bowl, 6 Sided, Scalloped, Cobalt & Iron Red Decoration, 9 1/2 In. .......... 150.00
Imari, Bowl, 8 Panels With Chinese Junk In Center, 5 In.Diameter ................ 20.00
Imari, Charger, Black & White, Signed, 19 1/2 In. ................................ 158.00
Imari, Charger, C.1860, 16 In. .................................................... 128.00
Imari, Charger, 15 3/4 In. ........................................................ 128.00
Imari, Charger, 16 In. ............................................................ 118.00
Imari, Cup & Saucer, Handleless, Red & Blue Floral With Gilt ...................... 62.00
Imari, Cup & Saucer, Miniature, Handleless, Red & Blue Floral With Gilt .......... 40.00
Imari, Cup, Flared, Blue & White Geometrics With Flowers, 2 1/2 In. .............. 10.00
Imari, Cup, Saki, Blue, C.1820 .................................................... 16.75
Imari, Dish, Sweetmeat, Raised Sides, Blue & White Floral, Brown Rim, 5 In. ...... 18.50
Imari, Jar, Ginger, Covered, Colored Block Pattern ................................ 50.00
Imari, Plaque, Scenic, Blue & Gold, 18 In., Pair .................................. 900.00
Imari, Plate, Basket Of Flowers Center, Blue, Green, & Red, 8 1/2 In. ............ 20.00
Imari, Plate, Butterflies & Flowers, Blue, Orange, Red, & Gold, 9 1/2 In. .......... 27.50
Imari, Plate, Fan, Blue, White, & Red, C.1840 .................................... 70.00
Imari, Plate, Fish & Foliage, Blue & White, 7 3/4 In. .............................. 48.00
Imari, Plate, Flying Crane, Blue, Rust, Green, 14 3/4 In.Diameter ................ 90.00
Imari, Plate, Orange & Cobalt, 8 In. .............................................. 65.00
Imari, Plate, Oriental Trees & Pavilions, C.1725, 8 5/8 In. ........................ 150.00
Imari, Plate, Prunus Tree, Open Scroll, C.1750, 8 3/4 In. .................. *Illus* 120.00
Imari, Plate, Scalloped, Landscapes, Mums, Prunus, Japanese, C.1890, 18 In. ...... 150.00
Imari, Plate, Vase With Flowers, Underglaze Blue, C.1720, 8 3/4 In. .............. 175.00
Imari, Salt, Floral Enamel Inside & Out, 2 In.Across .............................. 20.00
Imari, Tea Caddy, C.1850, 4 In.High .............................................. 95.00
Imari, Teapot, 5 In.High .......................................................... 225.00
Imari, Vase, Double Gourd, Red & Blue, 6 1/2 In. ................................ 34.00

*Imperial Glass Corporation was founded in Bellaire, Ohio, in 1902.
Stretch glass and art glass are two of the many kinds of glass made.*

Imperial Glass, Bowl, Console, Stretch, Blue .................................... 20.00

Imari, Plate, Prunus Tree,
Open Scroll, C.1750, 8 3/4 In.
*(See Page 261)*

| | |
|---|---:|
| Imperial Glass, Compote, Jewels, Stretch Glass | 65.00 |
| Imperial Glass, Compote, Stretch, Blue Iridescent, 5 In. | 19.00 |
| Imperial Glass, Sherbet, Stretch, Green | 5.00 |
| Imperial Glass, Vase, White Calcite Leaf & Vine On Cobalt, Orange Throat | 150.00 |
| Imperial Glass, Vase, White Hearts On Frosted Ground, Blue Border, 9 In. | 125.00 |
| Imperial Vase, Cobalt Drag Loop On Orange, Acid Etched Signature, 10 In. | 195.00 |
| Imperial, Bowl, Jewel, Green, 10 In.Diameter | 22.50 |
| Imperial, Nappy, Beaded Band & Panel, Handled, Cross Mark, 5 In. | 12.00 |
| Imperial, Sugar, Pink, 2 Handled, Cross Mark | 14.00 |
| Imperial, Tumbler, Grape, M Mark | 22.00 |
| Imperial, Vase, Blue Abstract On Orange Ground, Freehand, 6 In.High | 95.00 |
| Imperial, Vase, Free Form, Metallic Iridescence, Blue, Handles & Foot, 6 In. | 190.00 |
| Imperial, Vase, Rubigold Luster Cut To Clear, 9 1/8 In.High | 80.00 |
| Imperial, Water Set, Frosted Windmill Medallion, Orange, 7 Piece | 45.00 |

*Indian Tree is a china pattern that was popular during the last half of the
nineteenth century. It was copied from earlier patterns of English china
that were very similar. The pattern includes the crooked branch of a tree and
a partial landscape with exotic flowers and leaves. It is colored green, blue,
pink, and orange. King's Rose pattern of soft paste Staffordshire was made
in England from about 1820 to 1830. It was decorated in pink, red, yellow, and
green. The pattern featured a large roselike flower.*

| | |
|---|---:|
| Indian Tree, Bowl, Vegetable, Covered, Gold Rim, Maddock, 8 1/2 In.Diameter | 9.00 |
| Indian Tree, Creamer, Copeland Spode | 10.00 |
| Indian Tree, Cup & Saucer, Coalport | 12.50 |
| Indian Tree, Plate, Blue & Red, Adams, 9 In.Diameter | 10.00 |
| Indian Tree, Plate, Chop, Round, D.Mason & Sons, 14 In. | 35.00 |
| Indian Tree, Plate, Coalport, 7 1/2 In. | 8.00 |
| Indian Tree, Plate, Meakin, 10 In. | 16.00 |
| Indian Tree, Platter, John Maddock, England, 14 1/2 X 11 In. | 14.00 |

*Indian art from North America has attracted the collector for many years.
Each tribe has its own distinctive designs and techniques. Baskets, jewelry,
and leatherwork are of greatest collector interest.*

| | |
|---|---:|
| Indian, Arrowhead, Buffalo, Flint | 3.00 |
| Indian, Arrowhead, Fish Hook, Flint | 3.00 |
| Indian, Arrowhead, Folsom | 5.00 To 10.00 |
| Indian, Arrowhead, Thunderbird, Flint | 3.00 |
| Indian, Arrowhead, Turtle, Flint | 3.00 |
| Indian, Bag, Pipe, Sioux, Beaded | 90.00 |
| Indian, Basket, Maine, Stenciled Dye, Handled, 12 1/2 In. Diameter | 25.00 |
| Indian, Basket, Papago, 5 1/2 X 8 1/2 In. | 25.00 |
| Indian, Basket, Storage, Mariposa | 25.00 |
| Indian, Basket, Trinket, Papago, Woven Bear Grass, Round, 3 1/2 In. | 30.00 |
| Indian, Basket, Yaqui, Coil, 3 1/2 In.Diameter | 25.00 |
| Indian, Basket, Yaqui, Coil, 4 1/2 In.Across Top | 40.00 |
| Indian, Beaded Bag, Floral, Multicolor, 2 Flaps, Ribbon Rope | 35.00 |
| Indian, Beads, Crematory, Early California, 62 In.Long | 35.00 |
| Indian, Beads, Hudson's Bay Trade, From California, Red, White, & Black, 1860 | 35.00 |

| | |
|---|---|
| Indian, Beads, Trade, Blue Glass, Double Strand, C.1850 | 18.50 |
| Indian, Bell, Dance, River Crows, Montana, Buckskin Ties, 1911, 6 On Strap | 75.00 |
| Indian, Belt, Concha, Hand Hammered Silver Conchas, Lady's | 495.00 |
| Indian, Belt, Concha, Sandcast Silver, Turquoise, 12 Conchas | 595.00 |
| Indian, Belt, Concha, Sterling Silver Hand Hammered Buckle, Turquoise Stone | 595.00 |
| Indian, Blanket, Navajo, Red, Black & White Greek Key On Gray Border | 185.00 |
| Indian, Bola Tie, Man's, Navajo, 6 Turquoise Stones, Silver Buffalo Skull | 195.00 |
| Indian, Bow & Arrow, Hand-Carved, Feather & Flint Tied With Rattlesnake | 35.00 |
| Indian, Bowl, San Ildefonso, Black On Black, 1940s, 3 1/2 In. | 35.00 |
| Indian, Bracelet, Arrowhead Center, Light Turquoise, Crossed Arrows | 23.00 |
| Indian, Bracelet, Crow, Bison Horn, Diamond Back Rattlesnake, 1890 | 25.00 |
| Indian, Bracelet, Hopi, Lady's, 2 Turquoises & 1 Oxblood Coral In Silver | 125.00 |
| Indian, Bracelet, Navajo, Five Coral Stones, Sterling | 155.00 |
| Indian, Bracelet, Navajo, Green Turquoise With Orange Matrix, Sterling | 59.50 |
| Indian, Bracelet, Navajo, Lady's, Turquoises, Silver Settings | 250.00 |
| Indian, Bracelet, Navajo, Large Stone, Ornate Silver | 250.00 |
| Indian, Bracelet, Navajo, Man's, Bisbee Turquoise In Shadow Boxes, Silver | 275.00 |
| Indian, Bracelet, Navajo, Oxblood Coral, Silver Settings, 1930s | 150.00 |
| Indian, Bracelet, Navajo, Sand Cast, Cross, Inlaid Turquoise | 75.00 |
| Indian, Bracelet, Navajo, Silver, Sand Cast, Turquoise Stones, Gray Matrix | 89.50 |
| Indian, Bracelet, Navajo, Silver, 3 Stones In Round Shadow Box | 50.00 |
| Indian, Bracelet, Navajo, Turquoise, Sterling Silver, Oval | 185.00 |
| Indian, Bracelet, Navajo, Two Blue Stones, Sterling Silver | 195.00 |
| Indian, Bracelet, Navajo, 3 Turquoises In Silver | 250.00 |
| Indian, Bracelet, Zuni, Man's, 87 Blue Gem Stones, Sterling Silver | 425.00 |
| Indian, Bracelet, Zuni, Petit Point, Blue Turquoise, Sterling Silver | 244.00 |
| Indian, Buckle, Belt, Man's, Zuni, Silver, Turquoises, Signed Effie C. | 195.00 |
| Indian, Buckle, Belt, Navajo, Man's, Pawn, Hand Hammered Sterling, Turquoise | 95.00 |
| Indian, Buffalo Horn, Billings, Montana, Colored Beads & Buckskin Top | 20.00 |
| Indian, Button, Navajo, Silver Dollar, 1890 | 22.50 |
| Indian, Button, Navajo, Silver Dollar, 1896 | 22.50 |
| Indian, Button, Navajo, Silver Dollar, 1921 | 22.50 |
| Indian, Choker, Zuni, Coral, Jet, Mother-Of-Pearl, & Turquoise | 325.00 |
| Indian, Cradle, Shoshoni | 75.00 |
| Indian, Cross With Chain, Navajo, Turquoise, Sterling Silver | 40.00 |
| Indian, Doll, Kachina, Hopi, Dancing Maiden, 8 1/2 In.Tall | 55.00 |
| Indian, Doll, Kachina, Hopi, Hand-Carved, Dressed, 8 1/2 In.Tall | 55.00 |
| Indian, Doll, Man, Buckskin, Beadwork, C.1850, 12 1/2 In.Tall | 50.00 |
| Indian, Doll, Navajo Woman, Beadwork, Tin Concho Belt, 1920s, 9 In.Tall | 15.00 |
| Indian, Doll, Shoshoni, Leather Face & Cradle | 250.00 |
| Indian, Dress, Squaw, Nez Perce, Deerskin, Red & Blue Beads, Fringe, 1900 | 300.00 |
| Indian, Earring, Zuni, Pierced, 2 Hoops, 3 Triangles Of Turquoise | 38.00 |
| Indian, Earrings, Navajo, Turquoise & Melon & Shell Beads, 5 In.Long | 149.95 |
| Indian, Earrings, Zuni, Pierced, Diamond Shape Silver, Round Turquoise | 45.00 |
| Indian, Earrings, Zuni, Pierced, Floral, 7 Pieces Of Turquoise | 25.00 |
| Indian, Earrings, Zuni, Pierced, 4 Diamond Shaped Turquoises, 1 Coral | 35.00 |
| Indian, Earrings, Zuni, Pierced, 5 Teardrop Turquoises In Silver | 55.00 |
| Indian, Earrings, Zuni, Pierced, 7 Pieces In Turquoise In Solid Teardrop | 35.00 |
| Indian, Earrings, Zuni, Silver, 13 Petit Point Turquoises, 4 Bangles | 65.00 |
| Indian, Epaulet, Beadwork, Scout's, C.1870, Pair | 15.00 |
| Indian, Fetish, Bird, Zuni, Turquoise, Mother-Of-Pearl, Shell Heische | 600.00 |
| Indian, Glove, Shoshoni, Gauntlet, Beaded, Pair | 30.00 |
| Indian, Image, Southern Illinois, Stone, Brown, Human Face On Front | 75.00 |
| Indian, Jug, Water, Navajo, Woven Reeds, Pinon Pine Pitch Sealed, 12 In. | 60.00 |
| Indian, Mask, Ceremonial, Tarascan, Wooden | 75.00 |
| Indian, Mask, Norhtwest Coast, Red Cedar, Painted Red, Black, & Blue | 140.00 |
| Indian, Mask, Northwest Coast, Red, Black, & Blue Paint, 1940 | 150.00 |
| Indian, Medallion, Shoshoni, Filigree Type, Turquoise Nuggets Inlaid | 150.00 |
| Indian, Moccasin, Shoshoni, Beaded, Pair | 25.00 |
| Indian, Necklace & Earrings, Navajo, Blue Turquoise, Coral, Sterling Silver | 100.00 |
| Indian, Necklace & Earrings, Navajo, Sandcast Squash Blossom, Naja, Set | 450.00 |
| Indian, Necklace & Earrings, Navajo, Squash Blossom, Turquoises, Sterling | 1500.00 |
| Indian, Necklace, Heishe, Blue Turquoises Separated By Shells, 25 In. | 125.00 |
| Indian, Necklace, Heishe, Orange Shell, Jet, & Turquoises & Shell | 110.00 |
| Indian, Necklace, Heishe, Oyster, 41 Turquoise Nuggets, 30 In.Long | 225.00 |
| Indian, Necklace, Hopi, Shadow Box, Blue Turquoise, Sterling Silver | 600.00 |

| | |
|---|---|
| Indian, Necklace, Navajo, Blue Diamond Squash Blossom, Sterling Silver | 8.25 |
| Indian, Necklace, Navajo, Blue Turquoise Nuggets, Shell Heishe | 200.00 |
| Indian, Necklace, Navajo, Choker, Naja, 66 Sterling Beads, 15 In.Long | 75.00 |
| Indian, Necklace, Navajo, Graduated Silver Beads | 55.00 |
| Indian, Necklace, Navajo, Green Turquoise Nuggets, Shell Heishe | 200.00 |
| Indian, Necklace, Navajo, Heishe & Turquoise Nuggets, 15 In. | 95.00 |
| Indian, Necklace, Navajo, Morenci Turquoise Squash Blossom, 190 Carats | 750.00 |
| Indian, Necklace, Navajo, Morenci Turquoise, 2 Squash Blossoms, Sterling | 8.75 |
| Indian, Necklace, Navajo, Squash Blossom, Blue Turquoise, 34 In.Long | 675.00 |
| Indian, Necklace, Navajo, Squash Blossom, Graduated Beads, 36 In.Long | 1150.00 |
| Indian, Necklace, Navajo, Squash Blossom, Handmade Beads | 750.00 |
| Indian, Necklace, Navajo, Squash Blossom, Morenci Turquoise | 1150.00 |
| Indian, Necklace, Navajo, Squash Blossom, Pawn, Turquoise, Sterling Silver | 850.00 |
| Indian, Necklace, Navajo, Squash Blossom, Shadow Box, Turquoise, Silver, C.1900 | 995.00 |
| Indian, Necklace, Navajo, Squash Blossom, Silver Beads, Turquoises, C.1910 | 1495.00 |
| Indian, Necklace, Navajo, Squash Blossom, Turquoise In Naja, Silver | 200.00 |
| Indian, Necklace, Navajo, Squash Blossom, 12 Blossoms, Naja With Stone | 495.00 |
| Indian, Necklace, Navajo, Turquoise & Red Coral, 500 Heishe Shell Beads | 295.00 |
| Indian, Necklace, Navajo, Turquoise Nuggets, Silver Beads, 14 In. | 85.00 |
| Indian, Necklace, Pueblo, Turquoise Separated By Wampum & Silver Beads | 80.00 |
| Indian, Necklace, Sioux, 3 Large Millefiori Beads | 30.00 |
| Indian, Necklace, Squash Blossom, Turquoise, Spider Web, Sterling Silver | 1250.00 |
| Indian, Necklace, Zuni, Beads, Hairpipes & Cowrie Shells | 20.00 |
| Indian, Necklace, Zuni, Bird Fetish, Turquoise & Mother-Of-Pearl | 375.00 |
| Indian, Necklace, Zuni, Fetish, Mary Tsikewa, 3 Strands Of Birds | 950.00 |
| Indian, Necklace, Zuni, Owl, 5 On Each Side, 2 In Naja | 800.00 |
| Indian, Necklace, Zuni, Squash Blossom, Sunburst, Silver Beads, Sterling | 1600.00 |
| Indian, Necklace, Zuni, Squash Blossom, Turquoise, Sterling Silver | 800.00 |
| Indian, Painting, Navajo, Sand On Board, 7 1/2 X 13 In., Pair | 35.00 |
| Indian, Painting, Sand, 2 Figures, Arms Up, Irene Begay, 12 In.Square | 30.00 |
| Indian, Pendant, Navajo, Blue Turquoise, Signed | 250.00 |
| Indian, Pin, Zuni, Inlaid Owl | 45.00 |
| Indian, Pipe Tomahawk, Iron Head, Vertical Center Flutings, C.1840 | 275.00 |
| Indian, Pipe, Sioux, Owl Effigy, Beaded | 55.00 |
| Indian, Pipe, Trade, Effigy Face | 3.00 |
| Indian, Pot, Maricopa, Effigy, 2 Headed | 25.00 |
| Indian, Pot, Marie & Julian, Red Clay Color, Tan Matte Design At Top | 350.00 |
| Indian, Pot, San Ildefonso, Black On Black, 3 In.High | 35.00 |
| Indian, Rattle, Northwest Coast, Albatross Carrying Man On Back | 175.00 |
| Indian, Ring, Lady's, Navajo, Silver Snake, Turquoise | 95.00 |
| Indian, Ring, Lady's, Zuni, Silver Snake, Turquoise | 95.00 |
| Indian, Ring, Man's, Navajo, Silver Snake, Turquoise | 95.00 |
| Indian, Ring, Man's, Navajo, Turquoise & Red Coral, Sand Cast Sterling | 30.00 |
| Indian, Ring, Man's, Zuni, Silver Snake, Turquoise | 95.00 |
| Indian, Ring, Navajo, Lady's, Blue Turquoise, Sterling Silver, C.1900 | 60.00 |
| Indian, Ring, Navajo, Lady's, 30K Turquoise, Leaf Design, Silver | 100.00 |
| Indian, Ring, Navajo, Man's, Blue Diamond Turquoise, Sterling Silver | 70.00 |
| Indian, Ring, Navajo, Man's, Leaf Design, 1 Coral & 1 Turquoise, Silver | 100.00 |
| Indian, Ring, Navajo, Morenci Turquoise, Looped Silverwork | 69.00 |
| Indian, Ring, Navajo, Silver Chain Around Turquoise | 90.00 |
| Indian, Ring, Woman's, Navajo, Spider Web Type Turquoise, Silver Filigree | 29.50 |
| Indian, Ring, Woman's, Navajo, 2 Turquoise Stones, Oval Shadow Box Setting | 29.50 |
| Indian, Ring, Woman's, Navajo, 2 Turquoise Stones, Rope & Leaf Design | 27.95 |
| Indian, Ring, Zuni, Man's, Silver Snake Encircles Blue Nugget | 120.00 |
| Indian, Ring, Zuni, Pawn, Blue Turquoise, 32 Stones, Sterling Silver | 55.00 |
| Indian, Rug, Buffalo Fur, 5 X 6 Ft. | 79.50 |
| Indian, Rug, Chimayo, Gray, Red, Blue, & White, C.1920, 17 X 58 In. | 45.00 |
| Indian, Rug, Chimayo, Red, White, Gray, Blue, & Black, C.1920, 17 X 58 In. | 45.00 |
| Indian, Rug, Ganado, Red, Black, & Tan, 5 Ft.8 In.X 3 Ft.10 In. | 300.00 |
| Indian, Rug, Navajo, Birds On Tree Of Life, 23 X 32 In. | 995.00 |
| Indian, Rug, Navajo, Black & White Geometrics On Gray, 46 X 76 In. | 195.00 |
| Indian, Rug, Navajo, Brown, Light Brown, & White, C.1920, 18 X 19 In. | 15.00 |
| Indian, Rug, Navajo, Gray, Black, White, & Red, C.1920, 26 X 33 In. | 35.00 |
| Indian, Rug, Navajo, Klagetoh, Red, Black, Gray, & White, 33 X 40 In. | 400.00 |
| Indian, Rug, Navajo, Mother Earth, Blue Figure, 31 X 37 In. | 350.00 |
| Indian, Rug, Navajo, Orange Wool On Cotton, Black Flying Geese, 21 X 47 In. | 115.00 |

Indian, Rug, Navajo, Orange, Black, Brown, Tin, Red, & White, C.1920, 17 X 35 In. .................. 35.00
Indian, Rug, Navajo, Red, Gold, Orange, Black, & Gray, C.1910, 5 Ft.4 In.X 3 Ft. ............ 250.00
Indian, Rug, Navajo, Red, White, Black, & Gray, C.1920, 18 X 35 In. ............................... 35.00
Indian, Rug, Navajo, Reverse Swastika, 9 X 12 Ft. .................................................... 1500.00
Indian, Rug, Navajo, Roses, Red, Pink, Green, Black, & Yellow, C.1920, 6 X 8 Ft. ......... 250.00
Indian, Rug, Navajo, White, Red, Gray, & Black, C.1920, 20 X 41 In. ........................... 40.00
Indian, Rug, Navajo, Woolen, Black, Gold, Gray, & White, 28 X 58 In. .......................... 45.00
Indian, Rug, Navajo, Woolen, Storm Pattern, 32 X 60 In. ........................................... 295.00
Indian, Rug, Navajo, Woolen, Two Gray Hills, 28 X 40 In. ........................................... 240.00
Indian, Rug, Navajo, Yei, Gold, Black, & Gray, Vegetable Dyed, 22 X 32 In. ............... 190.00
Indian, Rug, Two Gray Hills, Black, Tan, & White, 5 Ft.X 3 Ft.6 In. ............................. 350.00
Indian, Rug, Yei, Wool, Seven Bright Colors On White, C.1958, 60 X 29 1/2 In. ......... 115.00
Indian, Sash, Navajo, Red Wool, Fringe, Handwoven, 54 In.Long ................................. 25.00
Indian, Shield, Ceremony, Hopi, Kachina Dancer, Leather, Painted, 15 1/2 In. ............. 65.00
Indian, Shield, Shawnee, War, Buffalo Face ............................................................... 75.00
Indian, Toy, Navajo, Loom Weaver & Baby ............................................................... 25.00
Indian, Tray, Serving, Papago ................................................................................... 25.00
Indian, Vase, San Ildefonso, Black On Black, Signed Desideria, 5 In.High .................. 60.00
Indian, Vase, Santa Clara, Black On Black, Signed Petra, 5 In. .................................. 85.00
Inkstand, French Champleve Enamel, Sevres Insert, Cupids, C.1750, 12 X 5 In. ......... 395.00
Inkstand, Porcelain Mounted, Victorian, Medallion & Scrolls, C.1880 .......................... 160.00
   Inkwell, see also Brass, Inkwell, Pewter, Inkwell, Porcelain, Inkwell,
     various porcelain categories
Inkwell & Pen Rack, Iron, Bronze, & Glass, Horseshoe Shape, Patent 1877 .............. 14.95
Inkwell & Quill Holder, Black, Round, Glass Insert, 2 1/2 In.Diameter ......................... 20.00
Inkwell, Agate, Oriental, Gilt Metal Mounts, Birds On Foliage, Jade Finial .................. 125.00
Inkwell, Blown & Pressed Glass, Green, Tree Trunk, Patented 1871 ........................... 50.00
Inkwell, Blown, Three Mold, Coventry, Dark Amber ................................................... 80.00
Inkwell, Bradley & Hubbard, Brass, Square Base, Glass Well ...................................... 9.00
Inkwell, Brass, Dutch Boy, Beveled Glass Hinged Well, 6 X 4 1/2 In. ....................... 23.50
Inkwell, Brass, Pewter Liner, Hinged Rolling Top, C.1860 ......................................... 32.50
Inkwell, Cobalt Blue Turtle, Blown Glass .................................................................. 100.00
Inkwell, Copper, Sterling Design, Chest Shaped, Glass Insert, 3 1/2 X 4 In. .............. 75.00
Inkwell, Covered, Miniature, Clear Baccarat Swirl, Relief Bar Around Body ............... 18.00
Inkwell, Desk, School, Black Bakelite Top ................................................................. 2.50
Inkwell, Double, Clear Cut Inserts, Brass Hinged Tops, Pen Groove, 4 Feet .............. 150.00
Inkwell, Double, Mason's Ironstone, Gondola Shaped, Imari Colors ............................ 175.00
Inkwell, English, Swirled Glass, Sterling Collar & Hinged Domed Lid .......................... 19.00
Inkwell, Fox's Head, Lift Up Cap, Round Wood Base, 5 In.High ................................. 40.00
Inkwell, Glass, Bronze Flower Petal Lift Off Cover, Square, 2 1/2 In. ......................... 4.95
Inkwell, Glass, Ribbed, Hinged Brass Lid, Variegated Colors Inside ............................ 16.00
Inkwell, Green Patterned Iridescent Glass, Hinged Brass Lid, 3 In. Square ................. 30.00
Inkwell, Hand-Blown, Southern Mexico, Cobalt, 1 3/4 In.High ................................... 1.50
Inkwell, Hand-Carved Wood, Tyrolean Hat Shape, Hinged Top, Clear Insert ............... 12.75
Inkwell, Hinged Brass Art Nouveau Lid, Brass Tray, Clear Square Well ....................... 45.00
Inkwell, Hinged Brass Lid, Hexagonal, Double Stepped Base, Clear Well .................... 50.00
Inkwell, Hinged Embossed Brass Lid, Grooved Glass Well ......................................... 14.00
Inkwell, Iron, Lion's Head, Open Mouth, Insert ........................................................ 35.00
Inkwell, Kaiser Helmet, World War I ......................................................................... 25.00
Inkwell, Lion, Metal, Glass Well In Jaws, Fang Teeth ................................................ 24.50
Inkwell, Loetz, 2 X 2 X 2 3/4 In. ..................................................................Illus 65.00
Inkwell, Manzanita Root, 3 1/2 In.Long .................................................................... 10.00
Inkwell, Metal Bear By Barrel, Hinged Lid, Porcelain Insert, C.1890 .......................... 42.00
Inkwell, Metal, Coppertone Finish, Glass Insert ........................................................ 5.00
Inkwell, Paperweight, Red Lily In Top, Multicolor Lilies, Teardrops Base ..................... 40.00
Inkwell, Porcelain, Hinged, White, Hand-Painted House & Mission Church ................... 55.00
Inkwell, Porcelain, Oriental, Edward I.Farmer, Mauve Glaze, 5 In.High ...................... 200.00
Inkwell, Porcelain, Scene On Beveled Square Hinged Cover & Body ........................... 55.00
Inkwell, Porcelain, Square, Hinged Lid, Floral On Rust ............................................. 21.00
Inkwell, Red Stone, Black Glaze, Primitive, 1 3/4 In.High ......................................... 14.00
Inkwell, Roman's Helmeted Head, Lifts Up, Round Wood Base, 6 In.High ................... 50.00
Inkwell, Round, Flat, Clear, Solid Glass Bird Stopper ................................................ 25.00
Inkwell, Sedan, 2 Door, Chrome Plated, Porcelain Insert, 5 In.Long .......................... 38.00
Inkwell, Sterling On Bronze, Hinged, Square, Signed, Dated 1912, 2 1/2 In. ............. 75.00
   Inkwell, Tiffany, see Tiffany, Inkwell
Inkwell, Traveling, Maroon Leather, Signed Hannover, Roller Blotter & Brush ............. 37.50

Inkwell, Loetz, 2 X 2 X 2 3/4 In.
*(See Page 265)*

*Insulators of glass or pottery have been made for use on telegraph or telephone poles since 1844.*

| | |
|---|---|
| Insulator, **A.T.& T.Co.**, Embosses On Side Of Crown, Light Aqua | 7.00 |
| Insulator, **Agee,** Purple | 12.00 |
| Insulator, **American Telephone Co.,** CD 121-1P, Toll, Aqua | 21.50 |
| Insulator, **Armstrong,** No.10, CD 214, Clear | 4.00 |
| Insulator, **Armstrong,** No.511A, CD 272, Root Beer Amber | 4.00 |
| Insulator, **Armstrong,** No.512U, CD 216, Root Beer Amber | 4.00 |
| Insulator, **Armstrong,** No.512U, CD 216, Clear | 4.00 |
| Insulator, **Brookfield,** CD 126, Light Aqua | 4.00 |
| Insulator, **Brookfield,** CD 133, 45 Cliff St., N.Y., Light Aqua | 4.00 |
| Insulator, **Brookfield,** CD 145, Dark Lime Green | 4.00 |
| Insulator, **Brookfield,** CD 145, N.Y., Patent 1883, Aqua | 4.00 |
| Insulator, **Brookfield,** CD 145, 45 Cliff St., N.Y., Light Aqua | 4.00 |
| Insulator, **Brookfield,** CD 151, New York, Light Aqua | 4.00 |
| Insulator, **Brookfield,** CD 152, Drip Points, Aqua | 4.00 |
| Insulator, **Brookfield,** CD 164, New York, Lime Green | 4.00 |
| Insulator, **Brookfield,** No.36, CD 162, Aqua | 4.00 |
| Insulator, **C.D.& P.Tel.Co.,** CD 121, Light Aqua | 4.00 |
| Insulator, **Cable,** CD 259, Inner Skirt Threads, Dark Aqua | 15.00 |
| Insulator, **Cable,** No.4, VNM | 135.00 |
| Insulator, **California,** CD 260, Narrow Groove, Aqua | 100.00 |
| Insulator, **California,** CD 260, Sage | 45.00 |
| Insulator, **Canada,** CD 121, Light Aqua | 4.00 |
| Insulator, **Canadian Pacific Railroad Co.,** CD 143, Light Blue | 4.00 |
| Insulator, **Canadian Pacific Railroad Co.,** CD 143, Light Green | 4.00 |
| Insulator, **Canadian Pacific Railroad,** Beehive, Aqua | 7.50 |
| Insulator, **Candaian,** CD 143, Unembossed, Sea Mist Green | 4.00 |
| Insulator, **CD 211,** No Leak D With Insert | 500.00 |
| Insulator, **Duquesne Keg,** Blue | 125.00 |
| Insulator, **ESS,** 401 | 90.00 |
| Insulator, **F.M. Locke,** Victor, N.Y., CD 287, B-N015, Smooth Base, Aqua | 6.50 |
| Insulator, **Hard Rubber** | 3.00 |
| Insulator, **Hemingray,** CD 147, Spiral Groove, Patent 1907, Aqua | 4.00 |
| Insulator, **Hemingray,** CD 464, Drip Point, Clear | 4.00 |
| Insulator, **Hemingray,** D-990, Deep Greenish Blue | 4.50 |
| Insulator, **Hemingray,** D-990, Ice Blue | 4.50 |
| Insulator, **Hemingray,** No.D-510, CD 168, Clear | 4.00 |
| Insulator, **Hemingray,** No.D-510, CD 168, Ice Blue Tint | 4.00 |
| Insulator, **Hemingray,** No.D-510, CD 168, Ice Green Tint | 4.00 |
| Insulator, **Hemingray,** No.11, Aqua | 5.00 |
| Insulator, **Hemingray,** No.17, CD 122, Straw | 4.00 |
| Insulator, **Hemingray,** No.19, CD 163, Stubby Type, Straw | 4.00 |
| Insulator, **Hemingray,** No.40, CD 152, Sharp Drips, Emerald Green | 4.00 |
| Insulator, **Hemingray,** No.42-04, Cobalt Blue, 4 1/4 In. | 25.00 |
| Insulator, **Hemingray,** No.43, CD 214, Aqua | 4.00 |
| Insulator, **Hemingray,** No.43, CD 214, Clear | 4.00 |
| Insulator, **Hemingray,** No.55, CD 205, Aqua | 4.00 |
| Insulator, **Hemingray,** No.62, CD 252, Clear | 4.00 |
| Insulator, **Hemingray,** No.660, CD 219, Clear | 4.00 |
| Insulator, **Kimble,** No.820, CD 231, Clear | 4.00 |

| | |
|---|---:|
| Insulator, Kimble, No.820, CD 231, Flat Top, Clear | 4.00 |
| Insulator, Kimble, No.820, CD 231, Flat Top, Straw | 4.00 |
| Insulator, Kimble, No.820, CD 231, Pink | 4.00 |
| Insulator, Kimble, No.820, CD 231, Straw | 4.00 |
| Insulator, Kimble, No.820, CD 531, Flat Top, Clear | 4.00 |
| Insulator, Kimble, No.820, CD 531, Flat Top, Straw | 4.00 |
| Insulator, LAC P & W, NM | 75.00 |
| Insulator, Locke, No.15 | 4.00 |
| Insulator, Locke, VNMporcelain & Glass, 11 1/2 In. | 95.00 |
| Insulator, Lynchburg, CD 251 | 30.00 |
| Insulator, Lynchburg, 181, VVNM | 150.00 |
| Insulator, Maydwell, No.16, CD 122, Clear With Green Tint | 4.00 |
| Insulator, Maydwell, CD 252, Golden Straw Color | 30.00 |
| Insulator, McLaughlin, No.19, Dark Emerald Green | 15.00 |
| Insulator, McMicking, Threadless Hat, Aqua | 10.00 |
| Insulator, Mulford & Biddle, Threadless Hat, Dark Blue | 10.00 |
| Insulator, N.E.G.M., CD 145, Aqua | 4.00 |
| Insulator, N.M., Canadian | 14.00 |
| Insulator, O.V.G.Co., No.11, Aqua | 5.00 |
| Insulator, Pennsylvania Railroad, CD 462, Aqua | 4.00 |
| Insulator, Pennsylvania Railroad, CD 462, B On Skirt, Aqua | 4.00 |
| Insulator, Pin, Wooden | 1.00 |
| Insulator, Pony, Double Groove, CD 112, Stars, Shades Of Aqua | 3.50 |
| Insulator, Porcelain, Imperial | 35.00 |
| Insulator, Porcelain, Keg Style | 3.00 |
| Insulator, Porcelain, Lima | 45.00 |
| Insulator, Porcelain, Signal, Brown | 1.00 |
| Insulator, Porcelain, Signal, Cobalt Blue | 4.00 |
| Insulator, Porcelain, Signal, White | 1.50 |
| Insulator, Porcelain, Victor, Cobalt Blue | 4.00 |
| Insulator, Postal, CD 210, Aqua | 4.00 |
| Insulator, Pyrex, Carnival Glass | 20.00 |
| Insulator, Star, CD 162, Lime Green | 4.00 |
| Insulator, T.S., Carnival | 4.50 |
| Insulator, TH, 9200 | 115.00 |
| Insulator, Telephone, Boyes To Alzada Line, 1920s | 3.00 |
| Insulator, Transformer, Derby Hat, Rough Pontil, Green, 3 1/4 In.High | 12.50 |
| Insulator, V.N.M., Canadian | 18.50 |
| Insulator, Whitall Tatum, No.3, CD 115, Light Aqua | 4.00 |
| Insulator, Whitall Tatum, No.5, CD 164, Straw | 4.00 |
| Insulator, Whitall Tatum, No.10, CD 214, Clear | 4.00 |
| Insulator, Whitall Tatum, No.511A, CD 272, Dark Amber | 4.00 |
| Insulator, Whitall Tatum, No.511A, CD 272, Root Beer Amber | 4.00 |
| Insulator, Whitall Tatum, No.512U, CD 216, Root Beer Amber | 4.00 |
| Insulator, U.S.Tel.Co., Threadless Hat, Green | 10.00 |
| Iron, see also Kitchen, Tool, Store | |
| Iron, Apple Peeler & Corer | 8.00 |
| Iron, Apple Peeler, Turn Table, Lockey & Howland, Patent June & Dec., 1856 | 18.00 |
| Iron, Bit, Horse, U.S. No.3, Yale & Towne, Chain Top, 7 In. | 15.00 |
| Iron, Bit, Horse, U.S. No.3, Yale & Towne, Rings At Each End, 11 3/4 In. | 5.00 |
| Iron, Bit, Horse's, Rings At Each End, 12 In. | 5.00 |
| Iron, Bit, Horse's, Twisted | 1.50 |
| Iron, Boiler, Wash, Oval | 12.00 |
| Iron, Bookend & Candlestick, Nude Woman With Pair Of Greyhounds, Pair | 35.00 |
| Iron, Bookend, Fox Terrier Shape, Painted, 4 1/2 In.High, Pair | 12.75 |
| Iron, Bookend, Homer & Dante, Pair | 5.00 |
| Iron, Bookend, Indian On Horse, "The End Of The Trail, " Bronze Finish, Pair | 5.95 |
| Iron, Bookend, Liberty Bell, Bronzed, Pair | 5.00 |
| Iron, Bookend, Nude Lady With Flowing Drape, Gray & Flesh Paint, Pair | 12.00 |
| Iron, Bookend, Punch & Judy, Pair | 5.00 |
| Iron, Bookend, Raised Design Of Kettle Hanging In Fireplace, Pair | 4.75 |
| Iron, Bookend, Roaring Lion, Nickel Plated, 6 In.Long, Pair | 11.75 |
| Iron, Boot Pull, Lady's, Design On Handle, 7 In. | 15.00 |
| Iron, Bootjack, Beetle, Painted | 25.00 |
| Iron, Bootjack, Beetle, 9 In. | 2.50 |
| Iron, Bootjack, Cricket | 22.00 |

| | |
|---|---:|
| Iron, Bootjack, Design & Circle On End To Hang Up, 12 In.Long | 20.00 |
| Iron, Bootjack, Folding, Slide Down Prongs, 8 In. Long | 25.00 |
| Iron, Bootjack, Foot Shape Top, Single Jaws, Wooden Bottom, 1859, 15 In. | 15.00 |
| Iron, Bootjack, Heart Tip Towards Prongs, Single End, 13 In.Long | 35.00 |
| Iron, Bootjack, Lyre Type, Hole In End, 3 Ribs | 9.00 |
| Iron, Bootjack, Lyre Type, Hole In End, 4 Straight Lines, 11 In. | 25.00 |
| Iron, Bootjack, Lyre Type, 4 Straight Lines, End Hole To Hand Up, 10 1/2 In. | 25.00 |
| Iron, Bootjack, Naughty Nellie, 9 1/2 In.Long | 32.00 |
| Iron, Bootjack, Naughty Nellie, 11 In. Long | 40.00 |
| Iron, Bootjack, Nude Lady, 10 In. | 27.50 |
| Iron, Bootjack, Pistol Shape | 35.00 |
| Iron, Bootjack, Tree, 2 Limbs, Heart & Fan Tail | 20.00 |
| Iron, Bootjack, Triangles, Double End, 2 X 2 In. | 25.00 |
| Iron, Bootjack, Try Me | 30.00 |
| Iron, Bootjack, Vine | 20.00 |
| Iron, Bootjack, 2 Legs, 3 Ribs Around Top To Hang Up, 14 1/2 In. | 20.00 |
| Iron, Bracket, Shelf, Lacy, 7 X 5 In., Pair | 3.98 |
| Iron, Bracket, Shelf, Lacy, 8 X 6 In., Pair | 4.95 |
| Iron, Bracket, Shelf, Lacy, 9 X 6 3/4 In., Pair | 4.95 |
| Iron, Branding Iron, Bent Arrow | 8.00 |
| Iron, Branding Iron, Hand-Forged, Socket End Type Handle | 4.50 |
| Iron, Branding Iron, Handwrought, Letters C.W., 17 In.Long | 14.95 |
| Iron, Branding Iron, Letter E | 7.00 |
| Iron, Branding Iron, Number 5 | 6.00 |
| Iron, Calf Weaner | 12.50 |
| Iron, Can Opener, Plain, 5 In.Long | 3.25 |
| Iron, Candleholder, Christmas, Holly Sprig, Green & Red, Patent 1921, Pair | 8.00 |
| Iron, Candleholder, Circular Spiral | 98.00 |
| Iron, Candleholder, Miner's, Spike | 85.00 |
| Iron, Candleholder, Round Base, 16 1/4 In. | 85.00 |
| Iron, Candleholder, Spiral, Adjustable | 110.00 |
| Iron, Candleholder, Sticking Tommy, Gloucester Fishing Boat | 14.75 |
| Iron, Candleholder, Swirl, Wooden Base, 8 In. | 105.00 |
| Iron, Candlesnuffer, Hand-Forged, American, C.1750 | 25.00 |
| Iron, Candlesnuffer, Scissors Shape, Wick Trimmer, Dated Dec.27, 1864 | 39.50 |
| Iron, Candlestand, Floor, Wrought, Rushlight Holder, Tripod Base, 35 In. | 350.00 |
| Iron, Candlestick, Alpine, C.1750, 13 In. | 165.00 |
| Iron, Candlestick, Cast, 9 In.High, Pair | 40.00 |
| Iron, Candlestick, Hog Scraper, Wedding Band | 90.00 |
| Iron, Candlestick, Spiral, Turned Wooden Base, Wrought, 7 1/2 In.High | 120.00 |
| Iron, Candlestick, Sticking Tommy, Hand-Forged, 7 1/2 In. | 65.00 |
| Iron, Canister Set, 3 3-Mold Bottles, Red Paint, Stenciled | 75.00 |
| Iron, Clip, Bill, Wall, Marked Auto File, Patent 1889 & Dec.22, 1899 | 5.95 |
| Iron, Clip, Bill, Wall, Shape Of Indian In Full Headdress, Painted | 11.75 |
|     Iron, Coffee Grinder, see Coffee Grinder | |
| Iron, Compote, Openwork Design Of Gods & Goddesses, 3 1/2 In.High | 8.75 |
| Iron, Container, Match, Hinged Cover, Bronze Finish, Bradley & Hubbard, Conn. | 9.95 |
| Iron, Container, Match, Wall, Hinged Cover, Striker Bottom, Patent 1864 | 14.75 |
| Iron, Curling Iron, France | 7.50 |
| Iron, Door Knocker, Dog's Head Holding Master's Stick, Black Paint, C.1860 | 31.00 |
| Iron, Door Knocker, Ship's Anchor With Iron Rope Knocker | 14.00 |
| Iron, Door Knocker, Spread Winged Eagle | 14.00 |
| Iron, Door Knocker, Woman's Hand Holding Ball, Ruffled Sleeve, 7 In.Long | 39.00 |
| Iron, Door, Chimney, Cast, Girl Emerging From A Flower, 8 X 11 In. | 20.00 |

*Iron doorstops have been made in all types of designs. The vast majority of the doorstops sold today are cast iron and were made from about 1890 to 1930. Most of them are shaped like people, animals, flowers, or ships.*

| | |
|---|---:|
| Iron, Doorstop, Basket Of Flowers, High Handle, 6 In. | 7.00 |
| Iron, Doorstop, Basket Of Flowers, 8 3/4 In. | 7.75 |
| Iron, Doorstop, Basket Of Pansies, Painted, 6 1/4 In.High | 9.00 |
| Iron, Doorstop, Boston Terrier, Sitting, 9 In. Long | 14.75 To 23.00 |
| Iron, Doorstop, Bulldog, 10 In. High | 15.00 To 32.00 |
| Iron, Doorstop, Cat With Bow Around Neck, 8 In.High | 12.75 |
| Iron, Doorstop, Cat, Black, Pink Ribbon | 22.00 |
| Iron, Doorstop, Colonial Lady, Full Figure | 16.00 |
| Iron, Doorstop, Cottage, 5 3/5 In.High | 6.95 |

| | |
|---|---|
| Iron, Doorstop, Dwarf | 22.00 |
| Iron, Doorstop, Elephant At Coconut Palm Tree, 13 In.High | 12.75 |
| Iron, Doorstop, Flowers | 3.75 |
| Iron, Doorstop, Frog Shape, 3 1/2 In.Long | 9.75 |
| Iron, Doorstop, Frog, B Cast Under Bottom | 8.00 |
| Iron, Doorstop, Frog, Dark Green Top, White Belly | 18.00 |
| Iron, Doorstop, German Shepherd, Signed Davison | 22.00 |
| Iron, Doorstop, Girl In Old-Fashioned Dress Carrying Hat & Flowers | 12.75 |
| Iron, Doorstop, Gloucester Fisherman, Painted | 18.00 |
| Iron, Doorstop, Horse, Standing, 12 In. Long | 40.00 |
| Iron, Doorstop, House Of Seven Gables, 8 In.Long, 5 In.High | 16.00 |
| Iron, Doorstop, Old-Fashioned Girl In Hoopskirt & Bonnet, 5 3/4 In.High | 12.75 |
| Iron, Doorstop, Parrot In Loop | 20.00 |
| Iron, Doorstop, Parrot On Perch, 8 In. | 25.00 |
| Iron, Doorstop, Parrot, 7 3/4 In.High | 16.00 |
| Iron, Doorstop, Pointer Dog, 14 In. Long | 25.00 |
| Iron, Doorstop, Ram, White, Black, & Green Paint, 6 1/4 In. High | 75.00 |
| Iron, Doorstop, Scottie Dog, Double | 13.00 |
| Iron, Doorstop, Scottie Dog, Sitting | 10.00 |
| Iron, Doorstop, Scottie Dog, Standing, 10 In. Long, 5 In. High | 23.00 |
| Iron, Doorstop, Spanish Galleon In Full Sail, 11 In.High | 12.75 |
| Iron, Doorstop, The Marchioness From Old Curiosity Shop, 13 In. | 20.00 |
| Iron, Doorstop, The Patrol, Old Fisherman With Lantern | 16.00 |
| Iron, Doorstop, Two Sitting Scotties | 20.00 |
| Iron, Doorstop, Victorian Girl, Painted, 4 1/2 In.High | 17.00 |
| Iron, Doorstop, Wirehaired Fox Terrier | 22.00 |
| Iron, Dryer, Corn | 4.00 |
| Iron, Eagle, American, Wings Spread, Initials N., R., & A., Green Paint, 24 In. | 65.00 |
| Iron, Figurine, Amish Man & Woman, 4 1/2 In.High, Pair | 65.00 |
| Iron, Figurine, Boston Bulldog, Brown & White, 9 In.High | 15.00 |
| Iron, Figurine, Bulldog & 3 Puppies, Painted, 3 In.High, Set Of 4 | 15.00 |
| Iron, Figurine, Elephant, Trunk Up, 3 1/2 In.High | 9.95 |
| Iron, Figurine, Elephant, Trunk Up, 6 In.Long | 9.95 |
| Iron, Figurine, Indian On Horseback, 4 In. | 60.00 |
| Iron, Figurine, The Thinker, 2 1/2 In High | 3.75 |
| Iron, Figurine, World War I German Soldier, Bronzed Finish, 13 In.Tall | 145.00 |
| Iron, Flower Stand, Stork, Diamond Shape Base, 15 In.High | 10.00 |
| Iron, Footscraper, Ram's Horn Curled Top, Handwrought | 30.00 |
| Iron, Fork & Spatula, Primitive, 15 X 18 In. | 22.00 |
| Iron, Fork, Handwrought, 2 Tines, C.1750 | 28.00 |
| Iron, Fork, X Decoration, 13 In. | 35.00 |
| Iron, Frame, Easel, Ornate, Open Scrollwork Border, Gold Finish, 12 In. High | 13.75 |
| Iron, Frame, Picture, Base Is Head Of Moose, Gold Finish, Standing | 16.75 |
| Iron, Gate, Art Deco, Medieval Figures, Trelliswork, 5 Ft.9 In., Pair | 300.00 |
| Iron, Grating, Window, Lacy, Hearts & Stars, 21 X 11 In., Pair | 28.00 |
| Iron, Griddle, Pancake, Oval Shape, Open Handles | 20.00 |
| Iron, Hatchet Head, Broad, Miniature | 4.00 |
| Iron, Hinge, Barn Door, Pennsylvania German, Pair | 20.00 |
| Iron, Hinge, Strap, 22 In.Long, Pair | 12.00 |
| Iron, Hinge, Strap, 24 In.Long, Pair | 12.00 |
| Iron, Hinge, Strap, 26 In.Long, Pair | 12.00 |
| Iron, Hinge, Strap, 27 In.Long, Pair | 12.00 |
| Iron, Hitching Post, Horse's Head, White & Black Paint, 10 3/4 In. High | 35.00 |
| Iron, Hitching Post, Seated Poodle, Tapering Octagonal Post, 57 1/2 In. | 275.00 |
| Iron, Holder, Flagpole, 4 Ball & Claw Feet, Dated 1888 | 6.00 |
| Iron, Holder, Lamp, Wall Bracket, Pair | 3.75 |
| Iron, Holder, Spool, Finial At Top Screws On To Hold Spool | 4.95 |
| Iron, Hook, Bail, Wooden Handle, 9 1/2 In. | 3.00 |
| Iron, Hook, Ceiling, Ornate, Screw In Type, 11 In.Long | 2.95 |
| Iron, Hook, Wall, Bracket, Screw In Type, Extends 7 1/2 In.From Wall | 2.75 |
| Iron, Hook, Wall Bracket, Screw In Type, Extends 11 1/2 In. From Wall | 3.95 |
| Iron, Horseshoe, Good Luck In Raised Lettering, P B & R On Top, 10 In. | 12.75 |
| Iron, Kettle, Bail Handle & Ring On Side, 11 In. | 10.00 |
| Iron, Kettle, Bundt, Footed, Bail, 10 In. | 85.00 |
| Iron, Kettle, Long Handle, 9 X 7 In. | 12.50 |
| Iron, Kettle, Over Handle, 9 In.Wide | 12.00 |

Iron, Kettle, Round, Rounded Sides, 11 In. ............ 6.00
Iron, Kettle, Round, Straight Sides, 10 In. ............ 6.00
Iron, Kettle, 11 X 6 In. ............ 8.50
Iron, Kettle, 11 X 8 In. ............ 9.75
Iron, Kettle, 3 2 In.Triangular Feet, 9 In. ............ 16.00
Iron, Key, Door, 4 In. ............ 1.00
Iron, Key, Door, 4 1/2 In. ............ 1.25
Iron, Key, Door, 5 In. ............ 1.50
Iron, Key, Italian Cabinet, C.1750, 5 1/4 In.Long ............ 10.50
Iron, Key, Italian Chest, C.1650, 5 In. ............ 17.50
Iron, Key, Italian Chest, C.1750, 4 1/2 In. ............ 15.75
Iron, Key, Italian Chest, Dated 1790, 3 3/4 In.Long ............ 7.00
Iron, Key, Italian Chest, Dated 1820, 4 3/4 In.Long ............ 8.00
Iron, Key, Italian Palace Door, C.1550, 7 1/2 In. ............ 26.25
Iron, Key, Italian, Palace Gate, C.1650, 10 1/8 In.Long ............ 35.00
Iron, Ladle Strainer, Decoration On Handle, 18 In. ............ 33.00
Iron, Ladle, For Pouring Lead Into Bullet Mold, Hand-Forged, C.1750 ............ 37.50
Iron, Letter Holder, Brass Plated, Bradley & Hubbard, Footed, 2 Figures ............ 14.50
Iron, Lock, Door, Box, Corbin, Patent 1871 ............ 10.00
Iron, Match Container, Square Base, Marked Strike On The Box, 3 1/8 In. ............ 9.95
Iron, Match Container, Standing, Basket Shape, Brass Handle & Lift Up Cover ............ 9.75
Iron, Match Container, Standing, Scrolls On Hinged Cover, Striker Bottom ............ 11.75
Iron, Match Container, Wall, Hinged Cover, Patent Jan.21, 1862, Striker ............ 19.75
Iron, Match Container, Wall, Openwork Back, Scrolls & Leaves ............ 9.95
Iron, Match Container, Wall, Openwork Scroll Back, 2 Pockets ............ 11.75
Iron, Match Container, Wall, Raised Design On Hinged Cover, Striker Bottom ............ 9.95
Iron, Match Container, Wall, Single Pocket, Openwork Back, 4 In.Long ............ 9.95
   Iron, Match Holder, see also Match Holder
Iron, Match Holder, Art Nouveau Woman's & Man's Head, 3 1/2 In.High ............ 11.75
Iron, Match Holder, Double Boots & Bootjack On Base, Striker On Jack ............ 30.00
Iron, Match Holder, Hanging, Colored Grapes & Leaves, 5 In.High ............ 7.00
Iron, Match Holder, Hanging, Openwork Scroll Back, 2 Compartments, 7 In. ............ 11.75
Iron, Match Holder, Hanging, 2 Pocket, Lacy Back, 6 1/4 In.High ............ 9.50
Iron, Match Holder, Lady's High Buttoned Shoe, Striker, Green, 5 1/4 In.High ............ 12.75
Iron, Match Holder, Openwork Back Of Grapes, Single Pocket ............ 9.75
Iron, Match Holder, Rectangular Basket Shape, Brass Handle, Lift Up Cover ............ 9.75
Iron, Match Holder, Standing, Lift Lid, Dog At Top, 3 X 3 5/8 X 3 In. ............ 14.75
Iron, Match Holder, Wall, Bronze Color, Smiling Monk's Head ............ 15.00
Iron, Match Holder, Wall, Double, Rabbit & Quail ............ 27.50
Iron, Match Holder, Wall, Hinged Cover, D.M.& Co., New Haven, Patent 1864 ............ 14.75
Iron, Match Safe, Acorn Shape, Patent Jan.21, 1862, 4 In.High ............ 22.00
Iron, Mirror, Wrought, Leaf Scroll, C.1925, 44 In.High ............ 500.00
Iron, Mold, Springerle, 5 X 9 In. ............ 85.00
Iron, Mortar & Pestle, Pedestal Base, 3 1/2 In.Diameter, 4 In.High ............ 15.00
Iron, Mortar & Pestle, 5 In. High ............ 25.00
Iron, Nutcracker, Dog, 12 In.Long ............ 22.00
Iron, Nutcracker, Home, Clamp On Table Type ............ 7.75
Iron, Nutcracker, Jaw Type, On Board ............ 5.00
Iron, Nutcracker, Squirrel, Brown, Cast ............ 11.00
Iron, Nutcracker, St.Bernard Dog ............ 22.00
Iron, Opener, Bottle, Sitting Donkey, Open Mouth Is Opener, 3 3/4 In.High ............ 10.00
Iron, Padlock, 'U.S.Mail-1852, ''Jones Patent 1852' ............ 32.50
Iron, Padlock, Military Issue, War Of 1812, Bronze Swivel Over Keyhole ............ 39.50
Iron, Paperweight, Abraham Lincoln, Sitting, Kraeuter & Co., N.J., C.1890 ............ 65.00
Iron, Pencil Sharpener, Patent Date 1895 ............ 45.00
Iron, Pestle, 9 In. Long ............ 6.00
Iron, Pipe Rack, Hanging, Scene Of Dog Chasing Fox ............ 40.00
Iron, Plaque, Lincoln, Round, 10 In. ............ 22.00
Iron, Pot, Glue, Painted Black, 2 Piece ............ 10.00
Iron, Ring, Stovepipe, Inside, 6 In. ............ 3.75
Iron, Ring, Stovepipe, Outside, 15 In. ............ 3.75
Iron, Rush Holder, Wrought, Spring Loaded Jaws, Ram's Head Thumbpress ............ 185.00
Iron, Rush Holder, Wrought, 3 Legs, 3 Toed Feet, 7 In.High ............ 135.00
Iron, Rushlight Holder, Clamp To Hold Rush, Tripod Feet, 27 In. ............ 55.00
Iron, Rushlight, Hourglass Shape Spring Holds Rush, Tripod Base, 19 1/2 In. ............ 85.00
Iron, Rushlight, Twisted Wrought Stem, Wooden Base, C.1750, 13 In. ............ 145.00

| | |
|---|---|
| Iron, Sconce, Candle, Scroll With 2 Birds On Top, C.1850, 15 In., Pair | 142.00 |
| Iron, Scraper, Foot, Rolled Arms, Set In Masonry Block, 15 1/2 In.Long | 165.00 |
| Iron, Seal, Colorado Silver Mine, Similar To Notary Type | 20.00 |
| Iron, Seat, Buckeye, Akron, O. | 30.00 |
| Iron, Seat, Evans Type | 45.00 |
| Iron, Seat, Hoosier | 30.00 |
| Iron, Seat, Moline Type | 30.00 |
| Iron, Shoe Last, Child's Size | 1.25 |
| Iron, Shoe Last, Stand | 3.00 |
| Iron, Skewer, Handwrought, C.1750, 23 In.Long | 48.00 |
| Iron, Snow Eagle, Pennsylvania, Dated 1893, 5 X 6 1/2 In. | 12.00 |
| Iron, Spatula, Signed Cook, 18 In. | 20.00 |
| Iron, Spike, Candle, Miner's | 85.00 |
| Iron, Spittoon, Porcelain Covering | 25.00 |
| Iron, Spurs, Spanish, 3 In. Rowels | 2.25 |
| Iron, Stand, Flag, Grand Army Of The Republic, 1883 | 7.50 |
| Iron, Stand, Whiskey Bottle, Tripod Legs, C.1930, 13 In.High | 4.00 |
| Iron, Stove Plate, Pennsylvania, C.1750, 20 X 22 In. ............ Illus | 800.00 |
| Iron, String Holder, Beehive, Dated | 18.50 |
| Iron, Taper Jack, Handle, 3 Legs | 425.00 |
| Iron, Teakettle, Marked Use Erie Ware, The Best, Miniature | 12.00 |
| Iron, Teakettle, Painted Black, Swivel Lid | 12.00 |
| Iron, Tether, Horse, Hand-Forged, Pointed Rod, Swivel & Ring | 10.00 |
| Iron, Tieback, Enameled, Pair | 8.50 |
| Iron, Tongs, Blacksmith's, 19 In.Long | 6.00 |
| Iron, Tongs, Blacksmith's, 22 In.Long | 6.00 |
| Iron, Tongs, Ice, 13 In.Long | 5.00 |
| Iron, Trammel, Lighting, For Big Candle, 36 In.Long | 125.00 |
| Iron, Trammel, Sawtooth, Ring On 1 End For Hanging Kettles, 30 In.Long | 35.00 |
| Iron, Turner, Pancake, 18 In.Long | 10.00 |
| Iron, Urn & Pedestal, C.1890 | 49.00 |
| Iron, Weight, Windmill, Horse, Cast Iron Base, C.1850, 17 1/4 In. High | 130.00 |
| Iron, Wick Trimmer | 12.50 |

*Ironstone china was first made in 1813. It gained its greatest popularity during the mid-nineteenth century. The heavy, durable, off-white pottery was made in white or was colored with any of hundreds of patterns. Much flow blue pottery was made of ironstone. Some of the pieces had raised decorations.*

**Ironstone, see also Chelsea Grape, Gaudy Ironstone**

| | |
|---|---|
| Ironstone, Bowl, Vegetable, Wheatlike Pattern, Oblong, Anthony Shaw, 12 In. | 25.00 |
| Ironstone, Bowl, Vegetable, White, Paneled, Kiln Marks, 7 In. | 16.50 |
| Ironstone, Butter Pat, Dark Blue, Chain Border, 3 1/2 In. | 2.00 |
| Ironstone, Butter Pat, Portrait, Bust Of Lady In Plumed Hat, Grindley | 18.00 |
| Ironstone, Butter Pat, White, Feather Edge, Meakin | 3.00 |
| Ironstone, Cake Stand, White, Pedestal, Signed S.C.Richard, Dated 1899 | 22.00 |
| Ironstone, Canister, Oriental Floral In & Out, C.1825 ............ Illus | 110.00 |
| Ironstone, Coffeepot, Wheat Pattern, Marked J & G Meakin | 40.00 |

Iron, Stove Plate, Pennsylvania,
C.1750, 20 X 22 In.

Ironstone, Canister,
Oriental Floral In & Out, C.1825

Ironstone, **Coffeepot,** Wheatlike Pattern, Anthony Shaw, 10 3/4 In.High ............... 62.50
Ironstone, **Compote,** Tonquin, 6 X 8 X 10 1/2 In. ............... 250.00
Ironstone, **Cup & Saucer,** Swan, Dark Pink, Woods ............... 38.00
Ironstone, **Cup Plate,** White, C.1858 ............... 4.50
Ironstone, **Cup,** Handleless, Leaf & Berry ............... 5.00
Ironstone, **Dish,** Leaf, Derby Coloring, Gold Trim, Mason's, 7 1/8 X 11 In. ............... 110.00
Ironstone, **Dish,** Soap, White ............... 5.00
Ironstone, **Dish,** Vegetable, Covered, Japan, 1800s, 12 1/4 In.Long ............... 160.00
Ironstone, **Dishes,** Child's, Stag Pattern, Mulberry & White, 21 Pieces ............... 75.00
Ironstone, **Eggcup,** Gold Rim ............... 5.00
Ironstone, **Ewer,** Pewter Mounted, Hexagonal, Japan Pattern, Mason, C.1850, 8 In ............... 80.00
Ironstone, **Gravy Boat & Ladle,** Covered, Leaf Twist Handles, Blue & White ............... 18.00
Ironstone, **Gravy Boat,** Astoria, Blue & White, Stoke-On-Trent, England ............... 12.00
Ironstone, **Gravy Boat,** Purple Grapes, Leaves, James Edwards, C.1840 ............... 12.00
Ironstone, **Inkwell,** Double, Imari Colors, Handle, 4 Quill Holes, Mason's ............... 175.00
Ironstone, **Jardiniere,** Covered, Imari Type Pattern & Colors, C.1830 ............... 92.50
Ironstone, **Jardiniere,** Covered, Oriental Pattern, Cobalt, Gold, C.1830 ............... 110.00
Ironstone, **Jardiniere,** Gold Foo Dog On Top, Cobalt, Gold, Wilbur, C.1830 ............... 99.00
Ironstone, **Jug,** Oriental Scene On White, Snake Handle, 8 Sided, C.1820 ............... 48.00
Ironstone, **Ladle,** Blue Design On Handle, Blue English Scene In Bowl, 12 In. ............... 20.00
Ironstone, **Ladle,** Gravy, Blue Transfer ............... 7.50
Ironstone, **Pitcher,** Allover Decoration, Mason's, 7 X 5 1/2 In. ............... 49.50
Ironstone, **Pitcher,** Blue & Rust On White, Serpent Handle, Mason's ............... 38.50
Ironstone, **Pitcher,** Cobalt, Red, & Green Floral, Flight, Barr & Barr, C.1813 ............... 55.00
Ironstone, **Pitcher,** Damascus, Blue & White, W.Adams & Son, 11 In.High ............... 85.00
Ironstone, **Pitcher,** Dragon Handle, Black & White Birds & Floral, Mason's ............... 28.00
Ironstone, **Pitcher,** Embossed Grapes & Leaves At Handle, Anthony Shaw ............... 25.00
Ironstone, **Pitcher,** Rose Decoration, Johnson Bros., 5 In. High ............... 7.00
Ironstone, **Pitcher,** Sculptured Owl, Yellow & Brown Feathers, Gold, 8 In. ............... 45.00
Ironstone, **Pitcher,** Sheaf Of Wheat, Johnson Bros., 6 In. ............... 12.00
Ironstone, **Pitcher,** White, Marked Verbanum Stone, Laveno, Eagle, 12 In.High ............... 32.00
Ironstone, **Pitcher,** Windermere, Alfred Meakin, 7 In. ............... 10.50
Ironstone, **Plate,** American Marine Scenes, Medium Blue, Signed, Mason's ............... 24.00
Ironstone, **Plate,** Athens, Blue & White, W.Adams & Sons, 9 1/4 In. ............... 12.00
Ironstone, **Plate,** Blue Transfer Country Scene, Pearlized, 7 1/2 In. ............... 17.50
Ironstone, **Plate,** Brown Leaf & Flower Spray On Rim, J.& G.Meakin.10 In. ............... 7.50
Ironstone, **Plate,** Brown Sprays Of Flowers, 9 1/2 In. ............... 6.00
Ironstone, **Plate,** Chinoiserie, Bamboo, Flower, Scrolls, Basket Center, Mason's ............... 25.00
Ironstone, **Plate,** Corean, Mulberry, P.W.& Co., 10 In. ............... 32.50
Ironstone, **Plate,** Dinner, Blue Exotic Bird Transfer, Orange Border, C.1840 ............... 60.00
Ironstone, **Plate,** Fountain, Deep Pink, E.Woods & Sons, 8 1/2 In. ............... 29.50
Ironstone, **Plate,** Hand-Painted Design, 9 In. ............... 7.80
Ironstone, **Plate,** Hot Water, Green Garlands On White, Handled, Metal Holder ............... 8.00
Ironstone, **Plate,** Minerva, John Edwards, England, 9 3/4 In. ............... 12.00
Ironstone, **Plate,** Panama, Mulberry, 7 In. ............... 13.00
Ironstone, **Plate,** Pelew, Mulberry, E.Challinor, 10 In. ............... 32.50
Ironstone, **Plate,** Rome Scenery, Mulberry, Coburg, 10 1/2 In. ............... 16.50
Ironstone, **Plate,** Soup, Wheat, White, Shallow, 8 In. ............... 6.50
Ironstone, **Plate,** White, T.& R.Booth Royal Patent Ironstone, 9 3/4 In. ............... 2.95
Ironstone, **Platter,** Beaver Falls, Pa., White, J.& B.Mayer, 1i In. ............... 40.00
Ironstone, **Platter,** Export Design, Multicolor, Mason's, C.1810, 10 1/2 In. ............... 95.00
Ironstone, **Platter,** Hand-Painted, Mulberry, E.Challinor, C.1840 ............... 40.00
Ironstone, **Platter,** Hudson, Homer Laughlin, 6 1/4 In. ............... 3.00
Ironstone, **Platter,** Warranted, Crest, 14 In.Long ............... 65.00
Ironstone, **Platter,** Well & Tree, Maltese, Cobalt, Rust, & Gold, Grove & Stark ............... 95.00
Ironstone, **Platter,** White, 14 X 9 1/2 In. ............... 4.98
Ironstone, **Pot,** Chamber, Blue Flowers On White, England ............... 10.00
Ironstone, **Pot,** Chamber, White, Marked S.C.Richard, C.1890 ............... 16.50
Ironstone, **Relish,** Leaf ............... 5.00
Ironstone, **Relish,** Melbourne, Grindley, 9 X 5 In. ............... 12.50
Ironstone, **Saucer,** Dark Blue Floral Border, Medway, Meakin ............... 2.00
Ironstone, **Saucer,** Hiasina, Light Blue, Burslem ............... 4.00
Ironstone, **Spittoon,** Red & Black Swirl Pattern Outside, C.1900, 8 In. ............... 45.00
Ironstone, **Sugar & Creamer,** Floating Leaf, Gray On Cream, Johnson Bros. ............... 4.50
Ironstone, **Sugar & Creamer,** Raised Wheat, W.& E.Corn, England ............... 49.50
Ironstone, **Sugar,** Covered, Morning Glory ............... 15.00

Ironstone, Sugar, Covered, Wheatlike Pattern, Anthony Shaw, Burslem ............... 50.00
Ironstone, Syrup, Pewter Top, 4 1/2 In.High ................................................... 21.00
Ironstone, Tea Leaf, Bowl, Soup, Meakin .......................................................... 6.00
Ironstone, Tea Leaf, Bowl, Soup, Portland Grape, Elsmore & Forster, Tunstall ........ 18.00
Ironstone, Tea Leaf, Bowl, Square, A.Meakin, 7 In. ........................................... 30.00
Ironstone, Tea Leaf, Bowl, Vegetable, Covered, Meakin, 10 1/2 In. ....................... 37.50
Ironstone, Tea Leaf, Butter Pat, Alfred Meakin ................................................ 9.50
Ironstone, Tea Leaf, Butter Pat, Powell Bishop, Gold ......................................... 5.00
Ironstone, Tea Leaf, Butter Pat, Square .......................................................... 6.00
Ironstone, Tea Leaf, Cup Plate, Gold Luster Leaf, 4 In. ......................... 7.50 To 18.00
Ironstone, Tea Leaf, Dish, Bond, Shaw ........................................................... 13.50
Ironstone, Tea Leaf, Dish, Soap, Covered, Insert, Square Handle, Meakin .............. 20.00
Ironstone, Tea Leaf, Gravy Boat, Meakin ........................................................ 24.50
Ironstone, Tea Leaf, Pitcher, Water, Alfred Meakin ........................................... 62.50
Ironstone, Tea Leaf, Plate, A.Meakin, 8 In. ..................................................... 7.50
Ironstone, Tea Leaf, Plate, Clementson, With Berries, 10 In. ............................... 10.00
Ironstone, Tea Leaf, Plate, Meakin, 6 1/2 In. ................................................... 7.00
Ironstone, Tea Leaf, Plate, Meakin, 8 In. ......................................................... 8.00
Ironstone, Tea Leaf, Plate, Meakin, 8 1/2 In. ................................................... 5.00
Ironstone, Tea Leaf, Plate, Meakin, 9 In. ......................................................... 9.00
Ironstone, Tea Leaf, Plate, Meakin, 10 In. ....................................................... 15.00
Ironstone, Tea Leaf, Plate, Mellor, 9 In. .......................................................... 8.00
Ironstone, Tea Leaf, Plate, Pie, A.Meakin, 6 5/8 In. ......................................... 7.50
Ironstone, Tea Leaf, Plate, Royalstone China, Wedgwood & Co., England .............. 12.00
Ironstone, Tea Leaf, Plate, Shaw, 9 In. ........................................................... 7.00
Ironstone, Tea Leaf, Plate, Soup .................................................................... 14.00
Ironstone, Tea Leaf, Plate, 9 In. ..................................................................... 5.25
Ironstone, Tea Leaf, Platter, Eight Sided, Meakin, 14 X 10 In ............................. 25.00
Ironstone, Tea Leaf, Platter, Meakin, 19 X 15 In. ............................................. 35.00
Ironstone, Tea Leaf, Platter, Mellor & Taylor, 16 X 13 In. ................................. 25.00
Ironstone, Tea Leaf, Platter, Oblong, Wedgwood & Co., 10 X 14 In. ..................... 38.00
Ironstone, Tea Leaf, Platter, Open Handles, Oval, Anthony Shaw, 11 5/8 In. ......... 18.00
Ironstone, Tea Leaf, Platter, S.W.Deane-Edge Malkin, Burslem, 12 X 16 In. .......... 30.00
Ironstone, Tea Leaf, Sauce, Round .................................................................. 6.00
Ironstone, Tea Leaf, Saucer, Meakin ............................................................... 5.00
Ironstone, Tea Leaf, Saucer, Mellor ................................................................ 3.00
Ironstone, Tea Leaf, Sugar, Covered, Meakin ........................................ 28.00 To 45.00
Ironstone, Tea Leaf, Sugar, Two Hand Applied Handles ..................................... 35.00
Ironstone, Tea Leaf, Teapot, Meakin ............................................................... 65.00
Ironstone, Tea Leaf, Tea Set, English, 13 Piece ............................................... 110.00
Ironstone, Tea Leaf, Tureen, Copper Luster, Wedgwood Mark, 8 In. Square ........... 48.00
Ironstone, Tea Leaf, Washstand Set, Copper Luster, Johnson Bros., 2 Piece .......... 150.00
Ironstone, Tea Set, Child's, White, Signed, 9 Piece ........................................... 25.00
Ironstone, Tea Set, Trailing Flower & Leaf, Johnson Bros.3 Piece ........................ 45.00
Ironstone, Teapot, Basket Weave Base, Pink & Turquoise Floral, Shaw & Son ........ 42.50
Ironstone, Teapot, Brunswick, Reds, Mulberry, & Blue Floral, 10 In.High .............. 45.00
Ironstone, Teapot, Burmak, Birds & Butterflies, Brown On Cream, Grindley ........... 48.00
Ironstone, Toothbrush Holder, Brown & White, T.& R.Boote, Dated 1879 .............. 10.00
Ironstone, Toothbrush Holder, Covered, Burslem, Cornucopia, No. 54654 .............. 10.00
Ironstone, Tureen & Underplate, Covered, Blue & White Oriental, Mason, 1820 ...... 105.00
Ironstone, Tureen, Covered, Blue & White, Handled, Marked Belmont With Crown ... 15.00
Ironstone, Tureen, Gravy, Covered, Footed, James Edward & Son ........................ 22.00
Ironstone, Tureen, Underplate, & Ladle, Grape Finial, White, Embossed Grapes ...... 15.00
Ironstone, Tureen, Underplate, & Ladle, Soup, Covered, Redcliff, C.1800, 16 In. .... 75.00
Ironstone, Tureen, Underplate, & Ladle, White, Johnson Brothers, 10 In.High ......... 75.00
Ironstone, Tureen, White, Gold Handles, Grindley, 10 In. ................................... 30.00
Ironstone, Urn, Covered, Imari Pattern, Mask Handles, C.1840, 11 1/2 In., Pair ..... 150.00
Ironstone, Urn, Covered, Imari Pattern, Mask Handles, C.1840, 13 In. .................. 110.00
Ironstone, Vase, Blue Dragon On White, 8 Sided, Mason's, 5 1/2 In. .................... 17.50
Ironstone, Vase, Foo Dog Finial, Cobalt & Gold, Mason's, 18 In., Pair ................. 575.00
Ironstone, Washstand Set, White, Bulbous Pitcher, 2 Piece ................................ 24.50
Ivory, see also Bottle, Snuff, Netsuke
Ivory, Ball, Billiard, Carved, C.1860 .............................................................. 28.00
Ivory, Bottle, Snuff, Carved On Both Sides, Signed .......................................... 60.00
Ivory, Box, Carved Floral On Top .................................................................. 22.00
Ivory, Box, Covered, Round, Allover Carved Flowers, 2 3/4 In.High ..................... 85.00

| | |
|---|---:|
| Ivory, Box, Hinged, Carved Birds & Flowers, 3 1/2 X 6 X 1 1/2 In. | 75.00 |
| Ivory, Box, Jewel, Dieppe, Carved, Hinged, Applied Leafage, 10 In. High | 350.00 |
| Ivory, Box, Ring, Mother-Of-Pearl Insects, Carved Insects, 1 1/4 In. | 25.00 |
| Ivory, Brushpot, Carved Panoramic Scene, C.1750 | 275.00 |
| Ivory, Bust, Davy Crockett, 6 In. High | 155.00 |
| Ivory, Buttonhook | 5.00 |
| Ivory, Candlestick, Carved, Polar Bear On Rectangular Base, 7 1/2 In., Pair | 165.00 |
| Ivory, Carving, Calla Lilies In Flowerpot, 6 In.High | 35.00 |
| Ivory, Carving, Camel, Red Eyes | 22.50 |
| Ivory, Carving, Elephant Bridge, 7 Elephants Graduating In Size, 17 In. | 140.00 |
| Ivory, Carving, Kuan Yin, Mother-Of-Pearl Inlay In Forehead | 150.00 |
| Ivory, Carving, Tulips In Flowerpot, 6 In.High | 35.00 |
| Ivory, Case, Calling Card, Book Form, Sterling Floral Applied, Satin Lined | 19.00 |
| Ivory, Chessman, Queen, Turkish, Baluster Form, C.1750, 6 7/8 In. High | 225.00 |
| Ivory, Container, Smelling Salts, Shape Of Owl, Brass Base, Austrian | 35.00 |
| Ivory, Cylinder, Satyr & Nymph Carving, C.1880, 6 3/4 In.Long | 250.00 |
| Ivory, Dresser Set, Dupont, Paris, Cut Glass Inserts, 15 Piece | 22.50 |
| Ivory, Eggcup, Peep View Of "Inselburg 41" In Stem, 3 1/4 In. High | 25.00 |
| Ivory, Fan, Carved, Orange Feathers, Pre-World War I, Original Box | 8.50 |
| Ivory, Fan, French, Floral Frame, 7 1/2 X 12 In. | 35.00 |
| Ivory, Figurine, Austrian Goose Boy, Carved, C.1750, 9 1/2 In.High | 325.00 |
| Ivory, Figurine, Beautiful Woman Holding Basket Of Flowers, 7 In.High | 100.00 |
| Ivory, Figurine, Boy, Standing On 1 Foot, Frog On Head, Holding Flower | 120.00 |
| Ivory, Figurine, Chinese Boy With Satchel & Ball, Teakwood Base, 5 1/2 In. | 50.00 |
| Ivory, Figurine, Foo Dog, Male & Female, Carved, 6 In.High, Pair | 395.00 |
| Ivory, Figurine, God Of Contentment, Carved From Tip Of Tusk, C.1821 | 110.00 |
| Ivory, Figurine, Snake Charmer, Seated, Oriental, Wooden Base, 2 1/2 In.High | 40.00 |
| Ivory, Group, Putti Riding A Goat, Another Crawling, Fruit, Dieppe, C.1890 | 225.00 |
| Ivory, Group, Seven Immortals On Stand, C.1750, Carved | 550.00 |
| Ivory, Holder, Cigar, Tiger | 10.00 |
| Ivory, Holder, Cigarette, Carved Dragon | 15.00 |
| Ivory, Holder, Cigarette, Incised Elephant, 5 In. | 9.00 |
| Ivory, Knife, Dinner, Pewter Inlaid, Steel Blade, Russell, Green River, 5 | 20.00 |
| Ivory, Letter Opener, Carved, Elephant Handle | 12.00 |
| Ivory, Letter Opener, Pen In Hollow Handle | 12.00 |
| Ivory, Manicure Set, 4 Piece | 15.00 |
| Ivory, Scorer, Game | 7.50 |
| Ivory, Shoehorn, Seashell Design On Handle, 5 1/2 In.Long | 10.00 |
| Ivory, Stretcher, Glove | 10.00 |
| Ivory, Tankard, Carved, Putti, Satyr, Winged Standard-Bearers, Dieppe, 1850s | 625.00 |
| Ivory, Toothbrush Set, Mr.& Mrs., Art Nouveau Silver Handles, 2 Piece | 30.00 |
| Ivory, Toothpick, Carved | 2.00 |
| Ivory, Tusk, Battle Scene Carvings, German, 42 In.Long, C.1900 | 1400.00 |
| Ivory, Umbrella Handle, Carved Dog's Head | 18.00 |
| Ivory, Umbrella Handle, Hand Holding Ball | 12.00 |
| Ivory, Watch Holder, Miniature Easel, C.1840, 4 In.High | 40.00 |

*Jack-In-The-Pulpit vases were named for their odd trumpetlike shape
that resembles the wild plant called jack-in-the-pulpit. The design orginated
in the late Victorian years.*

| | |
|---|---:|
| Jack-In-The-Pulpit, Vase, Clear To Amethyst, Blown In The Mold, 7 3/8 In. | 58.00 |
| Jack-In-The-Pulpit, Vase, Cranberry Flare To Curled Clear Stem, Pair | 125.00 |
| Jack-In-The-Pulpit, Vase, Cream To Deep Mahogany, 7 In. | 35.00 |
| Jack-In-The-Pulpit, Vase, Opalescent Cranberry Ruffled Top, Green Tint | 45.00 |
| Jack-In-The-Pulpit, Vase, Opalescent, 6 In.High, Pair | 38.50 |
| Jack-In-The-Pulpit, Vase, Pale Green Overlay On Opalescent, 5 Clear Feet | 63.00 |
| Jack-In-The-Pulpit, Vase, Pink Ribbed, Applied Amber & White Floral & Top | 50.00 |
| Jack-In-The-Pulpit, Vase, Ruffled Rim, Opalescent, Blown, Blue, 4 3/4 In. | 45.00 |

*Jackfield ware was orginally a black glazed pottery made in Jackfield,
England, since 1630. A yellow glazed ware has also been called Jackfield
ware. Most of the pieces referred to as Jackfield are black pieces made
during the Victorian era.*

| | |
|---|---:|
| Jackfield, Creamer, Covered, Cow, Floral On Black | 40.00 |
| Jackfield, Creamer, Eagle Handle, C.1850, 3 In. | 40.00 |
| Jackfield, Dog, Staffordshire Type, Gold Chain, C.1860, 10 In. | 48.00 |
| Jackfield, Figurine, Cat, Black & White, Red & Green Base, 7 1/4 In., Pair | 150.00 |
| Jackfield, Figurine, Cat, Glass Eyes, 12 In.High, Pair | 85.00 |

Jackfield, Pitcher, Milk, Golden Barred Handle, Pink Roses On Black ............................. 36.00
Jackfield, Pitcher, Water, Gold Trim, C.1870 .................................................................... 55.00
Jackfield, Teapot, Black, 6 1/2 In.High ............................................................................. 65.00
Jacob Petit, Box, Asparagus, Covered, Blue Ribbon, Bow Forms Handle, C.1830 ............ 300.00
Jacob Petit, Group, First Haircut, Cat At Feet Of Barber, Pinks, Green .......................... 85.00
Jacob Petit, Perfume, Figural, Man & Woman, 6 In. High, Pair ...................................... 110.00
Jade, Bowl, Petal Scalloped Edge, 1920s, 9 In. ............................................................... 12.50
Jade, Carving, Cluster Of 20 Grapes & 5 Leaves, Green ................................................. 100.00
Jade, Casket, Gilt Metal Mounts, Chinese Design, Edward Farmer, 6 3/4 In. ............... 1600.00
Jade, Casket, Oriental Style, Silver, Edward I.Farmer, 4 3/4 In.Long ............................ 950.00
Jade, Figurine, Squirrel, Bushy Tail, 3 In.High ................................................................ 80.00

> Jasperware is a fine-grained pottery developed by Josiah Wedgwood in
> 1755. The jasper was made in many colors including the most famous, a light
> blue. It is still being made.

Jasperware, see also Wedgwood

Jasperware, Ashtray, Indian With Ax, German, Signed Elsie Maxson ............................. 25.00
Jasperware, Bowl, Oval, Green & White, Lion's Heads At Base Form Feet ...................... 46.50
Jasperware, Candleholder, Blue, Heart Shape, White Ring Handle, Scalloped .............. 38.00
Jasperware, Candleholder, Saucer Base, Egyptian's Head Handle, 5 In. ...................... 35.00
Jasperware, Cup, Loving, Green & White, 3 Handled, Miniature, Children, Floral ........... 16.00
Jasperware, Dish, Cheese, Sunburst & Rope Finial, Blue, Cows, Sheep, & Goats ......... 325.00
Jasperware, Hair Receiver, Blue, Heart Shape, Girl In Grecian Dress, Cupid ................ 40.00
Jasperware, Hatpin Holder, White Scrolled Cupid Medallion On Green, 5 In. ................ 65.00
Jasperware, Muffineer, Raised Classical Figures On Dark Green ................................... 32.00
Jasperware, Pitcher, White Bird & Foliage On Blue, Marked Paxton .............................. 75.00
Jasperware, Plaque, Greek Girl Kissing Angel On Green, Leaf & Flower Edge ............... 30.00
Jasperware, Plaque, Greek Girl Pouring Wine On Green, Grape Leaves Edge ............... 25.00
Jasperware, Plaque, Indian Smoking Pipe, Green, 4 1/2 In.Diameter ........................... 38.00
Jasperware, Plaque, Lovers, Blue & White, French .......................................................... 65.00
Jasperware, Plaque, Old Gristmill Scene On Green, Pierced For Hanging ....................... 20.00
Jasperware, Pot, Mustard, Hinged Silver Plate Top, Mythical Figures On Blue .............. 15.00
Jasperware, Salt, Mythical Figures On Blue, Silver Plate Rim ........................................ 12.50
Jasperware, Sugar & Creamer, Seaweed On Brown, Impressed Mark .............................. 45.00
Jasperware, Teapot, Royal Blue, White Swallow, Butterflies & Floral, S.S.Co. ............... 125.00
Jasperware, Tray, Pin, Art Nouveau Lady's Hair Forms Rim, Butterfly ............................ 32.00
Jasperware, Vase, Blue, Cylindrical, White Classical Figures, 4 In. ................................ 75.00
Jasperware, Vase, German, 2 Women, 3 1/2 In.High ....................................................... 12.00

Jewelry, see also Coronation

Jewelry, Bangle, Gold, Pearl, & Diamond, Three Flower Heads, C.1870 ........................ 525.00
Jewelry, Bracelet & Chain Attached Ring, Pinchbeck, Sardonyx, C.1700 ..................... 250.00
Jewelry, Bracelet, Diamonds, Emeralds, Rubies, 8 1/2 In. ........................... *Illus* 6200.00
Jewelry, Bracelet, Georg Jensen, Silver, Flexible, Green Cabachon Onyx ..................... 75.00
Jewelry, Bracelet, Gold & Enamel, C.1875, 16 1/2 In. ............................... *Illus* 3100.00

Jewelry, Bracelet, Gold & Enamel, C.1875, 16 1/2 In.

Jewelry, Bracelet, Diamonds, Emeralds, Rubies, 8 1/2 In.

Jewelry, Bracelet, Gold, Citrine Quartz, & Enamel, France, C.1930 ............... 450.00
Jewelry, Bracelet, Gold, Engraved Scene, Marked 18K, Patent '84 ............... 38.00
Jewelry, Bracelet, Napoleon III, 15K Gold, Pearl ............... 195.00
Jewelry, Bracelet, Platinum On White Gold Filigree, 8 .70K Diamonds ............... 225.00
Jewelry, Bracelet, Rectangular 14K Gold Links & Alternate Oval Rings ............... 52.00
Jewelry, Bracelet, Victorian, Gold Filled, Small Size ............... 18.00
Jewelry, Bracelet, White Gold Filigree, 2 15K Diamonds ............... 100.00
Jewelry, Bracelet, 6 Gold Mounted Carved Lava Medallions, 6 Color, C.1850 ............... 125.00
Jewelry, Brooch, Art Deco, Platinum, Diamond & Enamel, Octagonal ............... 325.00
Jewelry, Brooch, Art Nouveau, Lady With Flowing Hair, Bird On Shoulder ............... 12.00
Jewelry, Brooch, Black, Starr, & Frost, Gold, Crescent, Pearls & Diamonds ............... 400.00
Jewelry, Brooch, Cameo, Carnelian Shell, Carved Diana's Hunting, C.1850 ............... 350.00
Jewelry, Brooch, Cameo, Profile Of A Bacchante, Gold Mounted, C.1890 ............... 300.00
Jewelry, Brooch, French, Tremblant Diamond Floral Spray, C.1850, 9.5 Cm. ............... 1500.00
Jewelry, Brooch, Platinum On White Gold, 3 .45K Diamonds ............... 125.00
Jewelry, Brooch, Portrait Enamel Of Queen Louise, Artist Signed ............... 58.00
Jewelry, Brooch, Scottish, Highland Dress, Silver, Victorian Era, Motto ............... 79.50
Jewelry, Brooch, Star Shaped, Gold, Diamonds & Pearls ............... *Illus* 450.00
Jewelry, Brooch, Victorian, Florentine Mosaic, Ovoid Bar, 1 1/2 In.Long ............... 40.00
Jewelry, Brooch, Victorian, Gold, Amethyst, & Pearl, Gold Acorns ............... 150.00
Jewelry, Brooch, Victorian, Gold, Enamel & Agate, C.1870, Circular ............... 375.00
Jewelry, Brooch, Victorian, Scottish, Silver, Thistle, For Tartan Cape ............... 79.50
Jewelry, Brooch, Victorian, Tremblant Diamond Spray, Flower Heads, 11.5 Cm. ............... 600.00
Jewelry, Brooch, Victorian, 1750s Lad Painted On Oval Porcelain, Gold Frame ............... 50.00
Jewelry, Cameo, Sardonyx, Gold Mounted, 17th Century Woman, 1 1/8 In. ............... 700.00
Jewelry, Chain & Slide, Watch, Lady's, Gold Filled, Snake Type, Opal Mount ............... 30.00
Jewelry, Chatelaine, Victorian, Horseshoe, 3 Chains, Sterling Silver ............... 15.00
Jewelry, Clip, Dress, Turquoise & Lapis Lazuli, A.Marchak, Paris, C.1924 ............... 225.00
Jewelry, Clip, Skirt, Embossed Rose, Dated 1870 ............... 22.00
Jewelry, Clip, Watch, Gold & Sapphire, Charlton, C.1930 ............... 40.00
Jewelry, Comb, Mantilla, Imitation Ivory, Egyptian Enamel Designs, 1912 ............... 35.00
Jewelry, Comb, Spanish, Blue Glass Stones, 7 In.Long ............... 40.00
Jewelry, Cross, Gold, Emeralds, C.1820, Chain ............... 2100.00
Jewelry, Cuff & Stud Set, Italian, Gold, Mosaics Picture, C.1850, 5 Piece ............... 98.00
Jewelry, Cuff Links, Art Nouveau, Sterling Silver, 4 Oval Relief Discs ............... 35.00
Jewelry, Cuff Links, Etruscan Style, Gold & Coral, Cameo Heads, Dated 1876 ............... 250.00
Jewelry, Cuff Links, Mother-Of-Pearl, C.1901 ............... 1.00
Jewelry, Cuff Links, Watch Chain, & Fob, Intaglio Onyx, Dec.1883 ............... 50.00
Jewelry, Earrings, Diamond, Long Drops, C.1820 ............... 875.00
Jewelry, Earrings, Gold, Etruscan Style, Oval Rings, C.1890 ............... 150.00
Jewelry, Earrings, Pearl, Diamond, Openwork Foliate Scrolls, C.1890 ............... 275.00
Jewelry, Earrings, Ship Form, Gold, Cloisonne, Eastern Mediterranean, C.1850 ......... 475.00 To 600.00
Jewelry, Indian, see Indian
Jewelry, Locket Set, Heart Shaped, Gold & Enamel, Diamonds, C.1875 ............... 325.00
Jewelry, Locket, Daguerrean, Gold Filled, Engraved L.To S., 3/4 In. ............... 30.00
Jewelry, Locket, Daguerrean, Gold, Oval, 3/4 In. ............... 50.00
Jewelry, Locket, Intaglio Carving Of God Mercury ............... 30.00
Jewelry, Locket, Picture, Gutta-Percha, Oval, Relief Eagle On Cover ............... 33.00
Jewelry, Locket, Picture, Round, 14K Gold, 5/8 In.Diameter ............... 15.00
Jewelry, Locket, Silver, 3 Color Gold Trim, Award, Speaking Contest, 1883 ............... 50.00
Jewelry, Locket, Victorian, Gold Filled, Etruscan Around A Cameo ............... 35.00
Jewelry, Locket, Victorian, Gold Filled, Oval, 4 Turquoises, 2 Garnets, Pearls ............... 35.00
Jewelry, Locket, Victorian, Gold, Set With Jewels, C.1880 ............... 1150.00
Jewelry, Lorgnette, Art Deco, Gold Filled ............... 35.00
Jewelry, Necklace, Diamond Paste, Bowknot Center With Drop, France, 1840 ............... 125.00
Jewelry, Necklace, Georg Jensen, Leaf Motif, Silver, Cabochon Carnelians ............... 150.00
Jewelry, Necklace, Gold, Enamel, Maltese Cross, Eastern Mediterranean, 1850s ............... 130.00
Jewelry, Necklace, Green Jadeite, Chinese, 41 Balls, Gold Clasp ............... 250.00
Jewelry, Necklace, Green Jadeite, 63 Balls, 65 14K Gold Beads & Clasp ............... 150.00
Jewelry, Necklace, Lapis Lazuli, 66 Large Balls, Gold Clasp ............... 460.00
Jewelry, Necklace, Simulated Tourmaline, Silver, Flower Heads, C.1890 ............... 90.00
Jewelry, Necklace, Sterling Silver, Carved Flat Circlets & Rose, C.1890 ............... 75.00
Jewelry, Necklace, 10K Gold Beads, Choker Length ............... 75.00
Jewelry, Necklace, 9 Oval Carnelians In 14K Yellow Gold, Filigree, C.1860 ............... 150.00
Jewelry, Pen & Pendant, Gold, Blue & White Enamel, Diamond, C.1920 ............... 210.00

**Jewelry, Pendant, see also Pate de Verre, Pendant**

| | |
|---|---:|
| **Jewelry, Pendant,** Art Nouveau, Gold, Enamel, Pearl, Leaves, C.1900 | 125.00 |
| **Jewelry, Pendant,** Black Gutta-Percha, Carved Flowers, 3 In.Diameter | 22.00 |
| **Jewelry, Pendant,** Cameo, Pink Coral, Gold Frame, Gold Chain | 38.00 |
| **Jewelry, Pendant,** Cameo, White On Blush White, 1 In., Gold Setting | 35.00 |
| **Jewelry, Pendant,** Devotional, Gold Mounted, Christ & Virgin, 1700s | 475.00 |
| **Jewelry, Pendant,** Gold, Amethyst, & Pearl, C.1875 *Illus* | 275.00 |
| **Jewelry, Pendant,** Gold, Enamel & Pearl, Art Nouveau Style | 125.00 |
| **Jewelry, Pendant,** Gold, Enamel, & Pearl, Sunburst Shape, Christ, C.1800 | 700.00 |
| **Jewelry, Pendant,** Ship Form, Gold, Cloisonne, Eastern Mediterranean, C.1850 | 400.00 |
| **Jewelry, Pendant,** Victorian, Diamond Shape, 300 Seed Pearls, Mother-Of-Pearl | 50.00 |
| **Jewelry, Pin Set,** Art Nouveau, Pearl, Quartz, & Diamond, C.1900 | 125.00 |
| **Jewelry, Pin,** Applied Black Jet Flower, 14K Gold | 33.00 |
| **Jewelry, Pin,** Art Deco, Diamond, Carnelian, Enamel, C.1925 *Illus* | 350.00 |
| **Jewelry, Pin,** Bar, Victorian, Emerald & 6 Diamonds, Gold, S Shape | 350.00 |
| **Jewelry, Pin,** Bar, Victorian, Gold Prong Mounted Garnet At One End | 25.00 |
| **Jewelry, Pin,** Bar, Victorian, Gold, Filigree Hearts, Pearls, 2 1/8 In.Long | 35.00 |
| **Jewelry, Pin,** Bar, 14K Gold, Openwork Filigree In Row Of Hearts, Pearls | 32.00 |
| **Jewelry, Pin,** Bird & Leaf, Silver, Georg Jensen, 2 In. | 25.00 |
| **Jewelry, Pin,** Cameo, Gold, 1 1/2 In.Diameter | 22.50 |
| **Jewelry, Pin,** Danish, Silver, Round, Openwork, Cutout Fish | 65.00 |
| **Jewelry, Pin,** Mother Of Pearl, 'Mother' | 3.00 |
| **Jewelry, Pin,** Persian, Enameled Silver, 1 3/4 In.Long | 15.00 |
| **Jewelry, Pin,** Sunburst, Gold, Pearls, Garnet Center, Victorian | 95.00 |
| **Jewelry, Pin,** Victorian, Diamond & Pearl, 14K Gold | 65.00 |
| **Jewelry, Ring,** Amethyst, Clear Sapphires On Side, Gold | 55.00 |
| **Jewelry, Ring,** Apple Green Jade In Openwork Gold Setting, 2 Diamonds | 200.00 |
| **Jewelry, Ring,** Australian Opal, Victorian Mount | 36.00 |
| **Jewelry, Ring,** Black Enamel & Diamond *Illus* | 700.00 |
| **Jewelry, Ring,** Cut Diamond In Victorian Mount | 50.00 |
| **Jewelry, Ring,** Diamond In Tiffany Type Mount, Victorian | 35.00 |

Jewelry, Pendant, Gold,
Amethyst, & Pearl, C.1875

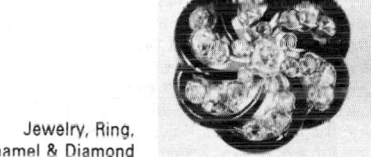

Jewelry, Ring,
Black Enamel & Diamond

Jewelry, Brooch, Star Shaped,
Gold, Diamonds & Pearls
*(See Page 276)*

Jewelry, Ring, Garnet,
Victorian, Flower Head Design
*(See Page 278)*

Jewelry, Pin, Art Deco, Diamond,
Carnelian, Enamel, C.1925
*(See Page 277)*

Jewelry, Set, Gold & Enamel,
Rose Diamonds, C.1840

| | |
|---|---:|
| **Jewelry, Ring,** Dinner, White Gold, Openwork, Round Ruby | 35.00 |
| **Jewelry, Ring,** Double Amethyst In Fancy Mount, Victorian | 45.00 |
| **Jewelry, Ring,** Double Garnet In Fancy Mount, Victorian | 40.00 |
| **Jewelry, Ring,** Garnet & 2 Oriental Pearls, Fancy Shank, Victorian | 35.00 |
| **Jewelry, Ring,** Garnet Cluster In Silver Gilt Mount, Victorian | 20.00 |
| **Jewelry, Ring,** Garnet, Victorian, Flower Head Design ................................ *Illus* | 275.00 |
| **Jewelry, Ring,** George Washington Mourning, Gold, Fevret De St.Memin, C.1800 | 1400.00 |
| **Jewelry, Ring,** Green Garnet & Diamonds, Gold Mounted, Pierced, Chased, C.1900 | 200.00 |
| **Jewelry, Ring,** Green Jadeite, Gold Filigree, Gold Washed Silver, C.1930 | 65.00 |
| **Jewelry, Ring,** Lady's, Gold, 3 Green Emeralds | 95.00 |
| **Jewelry, Ring,** Lady's, 16.89K Black Opal, 8 9-Point Diamonds, 14K Gold | 1350.00 |
| **Jewelry, Ring,** Man's, 10K Gold, World War I | 27.50 |
| **Jewelry, Ring,** Platinum, 1 9mm. Star Sapphire & 12 Diamonds | 350.00 |
| **Jewelry, Ring,** Turquoise With Pearls, Victorian | 30.00 |
| **Jewelry, Ring,** Victorian, Peridot, Gold & Oval Faceted, Prong Mounted | 95.00 |
| **Jewelry, Ring,** Watch, Schulz, Gold Bezel, C.1920 | 250.00 |
| **Jewelry, Ring,** Wedding Band, 14K Gold, Dated 1959, Size 5 | 27.50 |
| **Jewelry, Ring,** White Gold Mounted 2 Carat Peridot, 10 Rose Diamonds, 1870 | 95.00 |
| **Jewelry, Ring,** 8 Pearls On Fancy Shank, Victorian Mount, Amethysts | 25.00 |
| **Jewelry, Rosary,** Carnelian, Copper Cross, Brass Christ, 16 In.Long | 45.00 |
| **Jewelry, Set,** Gold & Enamel, Rose Diamonds, C.1840 ............................ *Illus* | 9000.00 |
| **Jewelry, Stickpin,** Art Nouveau Head Of Girl With Flowing Hair, Sterling | 2.95 |
| **Jewelry, Stickpin,** Blown-Out 1902 Liberty Head Dime | 18.00 |
| **Jewelry, Stickpin,** Brockton, Ma., Fair, 1917, Marching Soldier With Rifle | 4.75 |
| **Jewelry, Stickpin,** California Gold Piece With Indian's Head, Date 1849 | 3.95 |
| **Jewelry, Stickpin,** Camel Shape | 2.95 |
| **Jewelry, Stickpin,** Diamond Shaped Garnet, With 4 Small Garnets | 18.00 |
| **Jewelry, Stickpin,** Fox Head, Red Glass Eyes | 3.50 |
| **Jewelry, Stickpin,** Gold, Lover's Knot Around Recessed Square With Garnet | 22.00 |
| **Jewelry, Stickpin,** Gold, Pearl, Ruby, & Sapphire Flower | 35.00 |
| **Jewelry, Stickpin,** Oval, Blue Stone | 2.50 |
| **Jewelry, Stickpin,** Snake Frame, Oval Pearl | 4.00 |
| **Jewelry, Stickpin,** Turquoise Encircled By 8 Clear Stones | 2.50 |

Jewelry, Stickpin, 14 K Gold Wishbone, Pearl Center ........................................................ 9.75
Jewelry, Stickpin, 15K Gold Loveknot, Diamond ............................................................. 22.50
Jewelry, Tiara, Gold & Enamel, Jewels, C.1840 ............................................................. 1250.00
Jewelry, Watch Rope, Lady's, Victorian, Gold Filled, Opals, Pearls, Slide ................. 47.00
   Jewelry, Watch, see Watch
Jewelry, Wedding Band, Lady's, Platinum, Inscribed 1919 .......................................... 48.00

   *John Rogers statues were made from 1859 to 1892. The originals were*
   *bronze, but the thousands of copies made by Rogers factory were of painted*
   *plaster. Eighty different figures were made.*
John Rogers, Group, Coming To The Parson, Signed ...................................................... 325.00
John Rogers, Group, Council Of War, Signed ................................................................ 850.00
John Rogers, Group, Favored Scholar, Signed .............................................................. 350.00
John Rogers, Group, Fugitive's Story, Signed ............................................................... 700.00
John Rogers, Group, Going For The Cows ..................................................................... 450.00
John Rogers, Group, Playing Doctor ............................................................................. 775.00
John Rogers, Group, Taking The Oath .......................................................................... 400.00
John Rogers, Group, Why Don't You Speak For Yourself, John, Signed ......................... 425.00
Jugtown Ware, Bowl, Floral, Brown Glaze, 14 In.Wide, 2 In.High ................................. 10.00
Jugtown, Bowl, Blue & Gray, Marked, 3 1/4 X 4 1/2 In. ............................................. 45.00
Jugtown, Bowl, Floral, Brown Glaze, 14 In.Diameter, 2 In.High .................................... 10.00
Jugtown, Plate, Orange With Mottled Green, Marked, 1930s, 6 3/4 In. ........................ 12.00

   *Kate Greenaway, who was a famous illustrator of children's books, drew*
   *pictures of children in high-waisted Empire dresses. She lived from about*
   *1846 to 1901. Her designs appear on china, glass, and other pieces.*
Kate Greenaway, Almanac, 1882, Signed .................................................................... 20.00
Kate Greenaway, Book, Birthday, Color Picture On Cover .............................................. 22.00
Kate Greenaway, Book, Language Of Flowers, French .................................................. 15.00
Kate Greenaway, Book, Little Ann ............................................................................... 50.00
Kate Greenaway, Book, Mother Goose, Warne Publisher .............................................. 25.00
Kate Greenaway, Book, Mother Goose, 4 1/4 X 5 1/4 In. ........................................... 75.00
Kate Greenaway, Book, The Queen Of The Pirate Isle, 1st American Edition ................. 27.00
Kate Greenaway, Book, The Queen Of The Pirate Isle, 1st English Edition .................... 37.00
Kate Greenaway, Book, Under The Window, Drawn On Stone, Wemple & Co. ................. 75.00
Kate Greenaway, Book, Under The Window, Routledge, 1st Edition ............................... 35.00
Kate Greenaway, Bowl, Girl From Under The Window .................................................. 15.00
Kate Greenaway, Box, Powder, Cream Bristol, Boy & Girl On Hinged Lid, Round ........... 75.00
Kate Greenaway, Calendar, Calendar Of The Seasons, 1881, Marcus Ward & Co. .......... 33.00
Kate Greenaway, Figurine, Girl On Swing Holding White Dog ....................................... 75.00
Kate Greenaway, Figurine, Victorian Girl, Seated, Highback Chair, Bisque ................... 15.00
Kate Greenaway, Knife & Fork, Child's, Girl & Boy, Marked Sterling 1882 .................... 28.00
Kate Greenaway, Marigold Garden, Routledge, 1st Edition ........................................... 40.00
Kate Greenaway, Pencil Drawing, Framed, 3 X 4 In. .................................................... 75.00
Kate Greenaway, Pin, Seesaw From Mother Goose, Jasperware .................................... 12.00
Kate Greenaway, Plate, Cup & Saucer, Child's, Groups Of Children, Porcelain .............. 68.50
Kate Greenaway, Salt & Pepper, Figural, Boy & Girl, Porcelain, 4 1/4 In. ..................... 65.00
Kate Greenaway, Salt & Pepper, Little Boy & Girl In Peroid Clothing, 3 In. ................... 40.00
Kate Greenaway, Salt, Girl In Pale Blue Coat, White Fur Trim & Hat ............................ 32.00
Kate Greenaway, Salt, Girl In Yellowish Coat, Brown Fur, Black Hat ............................ 32.00
Kate Greenaway, Saltshaker, Blonde Girl In Long Coat & Hat ...................................... 25.00
Kate Greenaway, Saltshaker, Girl In Roped Basket ...................................................... 15.00
Kate Greenaway, Toothpick, Bisque, Girl In Pink Hat, Mauve Dress, 7 In. .................... 18.00
Kate Greenaway, Tray, Calling Card, Silver, Butterflies, Birds, & Flowers .................... 37.00
Kate Greenaway, Tureen, Child's, Covered, Handled, Gold Trim ................................... 20.00
Kate Greenaway, Vase, Blue Opaline Glass, 6 In.High .......................................... *Illus*  75.00
Kate Greenaway, Vase, Five Little Sisters, 6 1/2 In.High ............................................. 28.00
Kate Greenaway, Vase, Little Sisters & My House Is Red, Bristol, 9 In., Pair ............... 140.00
Kate Greenaway, Vase, Painted Scenes From Under The Window ................................. 75.00
Kate Greenaway, Vase, Scenes From The Birthday Book, Porcelain, Square .................. 88.00
Kate Greenaway, Whistle, Porcelain ............................................................................ 6.00

   *Kauffmann refers to the type of work done by Angelica Kauffmann, a painter*
   *and decorative artist for Adam Brothers in England between 1766 and 1781.*
   *She designed small-scale pictorial subjects in the neoclassic manner. Most*
   *porcelains signed Kauffmann were made in the nineteenth century.*
Kauffmann, Bowl, Orchid Luster, Sleeping Maiden & Cupid, Gold, 13 In. ...................... 35.00
Kauffmann, Box, Trinket, Hinged, Brass Mounts, Floral, Scene, 3 In. Diameter ............. 35.00

Kate Greenaway, Vase,
Blue Opaline Glass, 6 In.High
*(See Page 279)*

Kauffmann, Plate, 6 1/2 In.

| | |
|---|---:|
| **Kauffmann, Box,** Trinket, Hinged, Brass Mounts, Pastoral Scene, Angelica, Round | 45.00 |
| **Kauffmann, Chocolate Pot,** Medallion Of Girl & Sleeping Youth, Blue Beehive | 50.00 |
| **Kauffmann, Chocolate Pot,** Women & Angel, Cobalt & Gold, 9 In. | 36.00 |
| **Kauffmann, Cup & Saucer,** Allegorical Scene, Gold Leafing, Signed | 15.00 |
| **Kauffmann, Cup & Saucer,** Classical Scene, Signed | 38.00 |
| **Kauffmann, Jar,** Cracker, Beehive | 75.00 |
| **Kauffmann, Jar,** Cracker, Signed Angelica Kaufmann, 7 In.High | 50.00 |
| **Kauffmann, Plate,** Blue Border, No.184 | 50.00 |
| **Kauffmann, Plate,** Classic, Beehive Mark, 11 In. | 35.00 |
| **Kauffmann, Plate,** Dark Green Border, 4 Women In Center, Signed, Austrian | 25.00 |
| **Kauffmann, Plate,** Etched Border, Signed, 6 In. | 24.00 |
| **Kauffmann, Plate,** Figures Scene, 1700s Gold Designs, 9 In. | 88.00 |
| **Kauffmann, Plate,** Scenic Figures, 8 In.Diameter, Signed | 58.00 |
| **Kauffmann, Plate,** 6 1/2 In. ...................................................................................... *Illus* | 28.50 |
| **Kauffmann, Sugar & Creamer,** Draped Figures, Gold, Eleanora, Germany | 22.50 |
| **Kauffmann, Tray,** Square, Scene With 3 Ladies, Signed | 45.00 |

*Kaziun glass has been made by Charles Kaziun since 1942. His
paperweights have been gaining fame steadily. Most of his glass and all of
the paperweights are signed with A K designed cane worked into the design.
He makes buttons, earrings, perfume bottles, and paperweights.*
**Kaziun, see also Paperweight**

| | |
|---|---:|
| **Kaziun, Cologne,** Yellow Rose Stopper, Square Pedestal, Signed, 9 1/2 In. | 485.00 |

**KELVA** *Kelva glassware was made by the C.F.Monroe Company of Meriden,
Connecticut, about 1904. It is a pale pastel painted glass decorated with
flowers, designs, or scenes.*

| | |
|---|---:|
| **Kelva, Blotter,** Octagonal, Glossy Mottled Black & Green, White Beading | 150.00 |
| **Kelva, Bowl,** Pink Frilly Flowers On Mottled Green, Scalloped Ribbing | 140.00 |
| **Kelva, Box,** Covered, Pink & White Floral On Mottled Blue & White, Round | 475.00 |
| **Kelva, Box,** Hinged, Reticulated Brass Bottom & 4 Feet, 4 1/2 In. | 195.00 |
| **Kelva, Box,** Hinged, Silver Repousse Rim, Daisies On Pink, 8 In.Diameter | 275.00 |
| **Kelva, Box,** Jewel, Hinged, Hexagonal, Wild Roses On Green, 4 1/2 In. | 188.00 |
| **Kelva, Box,** Jewel, Hinged, Irregular Edges, Pink & Blue Floral, Green | 295.00 |
| **Kelva, Box,** Jewel, Hinged, Ormolu Mounts, Primroses, Square, 4 In. | 285.00 |
| **Kelva, Box,** Jewel, Hinged, Signed, 4 1/2 In.Wide | 250.00 |
| **Kelva, Box,** Jewel, Roses, Relief Enamels, 4 1/4 In.Diameter | 250.00 |
| **Kelva, Vase,** Brass Footed Base, 6 Sided, Pink Blossoms On Green, 14 In. | 295.00 |
| **Kelva, Vase,** Silver Rim, Hand-Painted Orange Carnations On Peach, 7 In. | 175.00 |
| **Kelva, Vase,** 6 Panel, Sponge Olive Green, Bronze Feet | 275.00 |

*Kew Blas is the name used by the Union Glass Company of Somerville,
Massachusetts. The name refers to an iridescent golden glass made from the
1890s to 1924.*

| | |
|---|---:|
| **Kew Blas, Base,** Green & Gold Iridescent Leafage On White, 5 1/2 In.High | 250.00 |
| **Kew Blas, Bowl & Underplate,** Gold Color, Pink & Blue Highlights, Signed | 285.00 |
| **Kew Blas, Bowl & Underplate,** Gold Luster, Fluted, Signed | 335.00 |

| | |
|---|---|
| **Kew Blas, Tumbler,** Gold Iridescent | 225.00 |
| **Kew Blas, Vase,** Floriform, Amber Iridescent, 14 3/4 In.High | 400.00 |
| **Kew Blas, Vase,** Ruffled, Caramel Color, 4 In.High | 235.00 |

*Kewpies were first pictured in the 'Ladies' Home Journal' by Rose O'Neill. The pixielike figures became an immediate success, and Kewpie dolls started appearing in 1911. Kewpie pictures and other items soon followed.*

| | |
|---|---|
| **Kewpie, Bank,** Ceramic, Wears Glasses | 10.00 |
| **Kewpie, Book,** Jello & The Kewpies, Color | 18.00 |
| **Kewpie, Bowl,** Signed Rose O'Neill, A.B.C., 6 Kewpies On White, 7 In. | 95.00 |
| **Kewpie, Bowl,** 5 Kewpies On Side, 2 Center, Z.S. & Co., Bavaria, 10 In. | 75.00 |
| **Kewpie, Box,** Candy, 2 Action Kewpies, Tin, Black | 13.50 |
| **Kewpie, Button,** Rose O'Neill, Bisque, Bisque Kewpie On Pearl, 4 5/8 In. | 51.00 |
| **Kewpie, Camera,** In Original Box, 5 X 7 In. | 65.00 |
| **Kewpie, Candy Container,** Standing Next To Barrel, Painted | 30.00 |
| **Kewpie, Card,** Christmas, Signed Rose O'Neill, Envelope, 2 1/2 X 3 1/2 In. | 6.00 |
| **Kewpie, Card,** Greeting, Valentine | 3.00 |
| **Kewpie, Charm,** Bell, Silver | 35.00 |
| **Kewpie, Charm,** Doll, Pearlized Over Sterling, Attached Loop, 1 In. | 45.00 |
| **Kewpie, Creamer,** Seven Action Kewpies, Green Jasperware, Butterflies, Floral | 105.00 |
| **Kewpie, Cup & Saucer,** Signed Mrs.Rose O'Neill Wilson, 2 Action Kewpies | 75.00 |
| **Kewpie, Cup & Saucer,** Signed O'Neill, 4 Kewpies On Green & Cream | 75.00 |
| **Kewpie, Dish,** Feeding, Signed O'Neill, Pale Blue, Royal Rudolstadt | 110.00 |
| **Kewpie, Doll,** Baby, Snowsuit, 18 In.Tall | 30.00 |
| **Kewpie, Doll,** Beanbag | 5.00 |
| **Kewpie, Doll,** Bisque, Action | 4.50 |
| **Kewpie, Doll,** Bisque, Frozen Charlotte Type Arms | 6.00 |
| **Kewpie, Doll,** Bisque, Huggies, Bride's Dress | 100.00 |
| **Kewpie, Doll,** Bisque, Huggies, Groom's Suit | 75.00 |
| **Kewpie, Doll,** Bisque, Jointed Arms, Signed On Foot, 4 1/2 In.Tall | 62.50 |
| **Kewpie, Doll,** Bisque, Movable Arms | 6.00 |
| **Kewpie, Doll,** Bisque, Red Cap & Sword, Holding Rifle, 3 3/4 In. | 95.00 |
| **Kewpie, Doll,** Bisque, Red Heart, Pair | 7.50 |
| **Kewpie, Doll,** Bisque, Red Heart, Pair Kissing | 7.50 |
| **Kewpie, Doll,** Bisque, Signed, 4 1/2 In. Tall | 38.00 |
| **Kewpie, Doll,** Bisque, The Thinker | 5.00 |
| **Kewpie, Doll,** Bisque, Winking | 6.00 |
| **Kewpie, Doll,** Bisque, Yellow Hair Bow | 4.50 |
| **Kewpie, Doll,** Bisque, 4 3/8 In., Signed | 45.00 |
| **Kewpie, Doll,** Carnival, Mechanical, Composition, 1920, 13 In. | 48.00 |
| **Kewpie, Doll,** Carnival, Movable Arms & Legs, Dangles From Cone, 7 In. | 5.00 |
| **Kewpie, Doll,** Carnival, Red Hair, Hula Skirt | 65.00 |
| **Kewpie, Doll,** Celluloid, Dressed As Charlie Chaplin With Cane, 3 In. | 18.00 |
| **Kewpie, Doll,** Celluloid, Farmer, Rake & Shovel, Baby Chick, 3 In. | 35.00 |
| **Kewpie, Doll,** Celluloid, Fireman, Holding Ax, On Wooden Base, 3 In. | 22.00 |
| **Kewpie, Doll,** Celluloid, Hawaiian Girl, 3 In. | 25.00 |
| **Kewpie, Doll,** Celluloid, Movable Arms, Marked Pan Am, C.1900, 3 In.Tall | 14.00 |
| **Kewpie, Doll,** Celluloid, Oriental, Long Queue, On Piece Of Ivory, 3 In. | 25.00 |
| **Kewpie, Doll,** Celluloid, Student, Painted Gray Suit, On Paperweight, 3 In. | 22.00 |
| **Kewpie, Doll,** Celluloid, Wedding Party, Gold Frame Shadowbox, Set Of 3 | 60.00 |
| **Kewpie, Doll,** Chalk, Blonde Hair | 9.50 |
| **Kewpie, Doll,** Composition, 12 In.Tall | 55.00 |
| **Kewpie, Doll,** Composition, 12 1/2 In.Tall | 35.00 |
| **Kewpie, Doll,** Composition, 14 In.Tall | 35.00 |
| **Kewpie, Doll,** Crystal, Painted Features | 10.00 |
| **Kewpie, Doll,** Floppy Hat & Pantaloons | 5.00 |
| **Kewpie, Doll,** Huggers, Bisque, 3 3/4 In.Tall | 75.00 |
| **Kewpie, Doll,** Kuddly | 5.00 |
| **Kewpie, Doll,** Lapel, 2 In.Molded Stud In Back, Label | 68.00 |
| **Kewpie, Doll,** Little Eve, 7 In.Tall | 3.50 |
| **Kewpie, Doll,** Negro Hot 'n Tot, 11 In.Tall | 8.50 |
| **Kewpie, Doll,** O'Neill, Bisque, 5 1/2 In.Tall | 80.00 |
| **Kewpie, Doll,** Paper, Signed Rose O'Neill, Dress, Doodle Dog, Set Of 3 | 10.00 |
| **Kewpie, Doll,** Ragsy | 2.50 To 5.00 |
| **Kewpie, Doll,** Rubber, Cameo, 10 In. Tall | 10.00 |

Kewpie, Doll, Rubber, Cameo, Red, Squeaks, 8 In. .......................................................... 12.00
Kewpie, Doll, Stuffed, Red, Wings ................................................................................. 12.00
Kewpie, Doll, Sunbonnet ................................................................................................. 8.50
Kewpie, Doll, Vinyl, Sitting, 3 1/2 In.High, Marked Rose O'Neill .................................... 7.50
Kewpie, Doll, Wax ........................................................................................................... 5.00
Kewpie, Doll, With Baby Bottle ...................................................................................... 4.50
Kewpie, Figurine, Bisque, Traveler, Signed O'Neill ........................................................ 125.00
Kewpie, Figurine, Seated Beside Washtub, Bisque, 2 In.High ....................................... 20.00
Kewpie, Figurine, Sitting Next To Dog, Bundled In Coats, Bisque, 3 1/4 In. .................. 75.00
Kewpie, Flannel, Cherry Picker ...................................................................................... 12.50
Kewpie, Flannel, Signed Rose O'Neill, Leapfrog, 1914 .................................................. 10.00
Kewpie, Flannel, Signed Rose O'Neill, Riding A Fish, 1914 .......................................... 10.00
Kewpie, Hair Receiver, Signed Rose O'Neill, 10 Kewpies, Jasper, Germany .................. 110.00
Kewpie, Mold, Chocolate, Tin, 1930s, 3 X 2 In. ........................................................... 12.00
Kewpie, Painting, Signed Rose O'Neill ........................................................................... 500.00
Kewpie, Paperweight ...................................................................................................... 20.00
Kewpie, Pendant, Signed Rose O'Neill, Carved Ivory Kewpie On Gold Chain ............... 45.00
Kewpie, Pillow Kit, Pillow Top With 4 Kewpies, Instructions, 1913 ............................... 35.00
Kewpie, Pillowcase, Baby's, Four Kewpies .................................................................... 77.00
Kewpie, Pin, Lapel, Celluloid, Figural Kewpie ............................................................... 14.00
Kewpie, Pincushion, Celluloid, Marked Nippon On Base ............................................... 16.00
Kewpie, Plate, Signed O'Neill & Rudolstadt, 5 Action Kewpies, 6 1/4 In. ...................... 45.00
Kewpie, Plate, Signed Rose O'Neill, Action Kewpies, Pink Luster Trim, 5 In. ............... 40.00
Kewpie, Plate, Signed Rose O'neill, Army, Carpenter, Etc., Royal Rudolstadt ............... 65.00
Kewpie, Plate, Signed Rose O'Neill, Seven Kewpies, 7 In. ........................................... 55.00
Kewpie, Plate, Signed Rose O'Neill, 2 Kewpies, Gold Edge, Royal Rudolstadt ............. 48.00
Kewpie, Plate, Signed Rose O'Neill, 3 Kewpies, 6 In. ................................................... 48.00
Kewpie, Plate, 6 Action Kewpies, 6 1/2 In. .................................................................. 45.00
Kewpie, Plate, 8 Kewpies, Royal Rudolstadt, 8 1/2 In. ................................................. 125.00
Kewpie, Postcard, Signed O'Neill, Easter ...................................................................... 4.50
Kewpie, Postcard, Signed O'Neill, 3 Kewpies & Chick In Egg ...................................... 10.00
Kewpie, Poster, Kewpie Baseball Team, Eating Pink Ice Cream, 14 In. High ................ 15.00
Kewpie, Poster, Signed Rose O'Neill, Kewpie With Books & Test Tube ........................ 35.00
Kewpie, Print, Kewpie With Glasses & Instruments, Ice Cream Company ...................... 25.00
Kewpie, Print, Signed O'Neill, Pastel Color, Framed, 6 1/2 X 7 1/2 In. ......................... 15.00
Kewpie, Shaker, Powder, Rose O'Neill, Kewpie Design, Patent 43280, 1913, 6 In. ...... 65.00
Kewpie, Spoon, Rose O'Neill At Bonnie Brook, 1874-1944, Silver, 5 In. ...................... 100.00
Kewpie, Sugar & Creamer, Seven Action Kewpies, Pearlized ........................................ 125.00
Kewpie, Sugar & Creamer, Signed Rose O'Neill ........................................................... 135.00
Kewpie, Tea Set, Signed Rose O'Neill, Kewpies, Pink Luster, 3 Piece ......................... 200.00
Kewpie, Tin, Chocolate, 1930s ...................................................................................... 8.00
Kewpie, Toothpick, Glass ............................................................................................... 8.50
Kewpie, Toothpick, Signed Rose O'Neill, Clear Glass ................................................... 45.00
Kewpie, Toy, Santa Express, Reindeer Pulling Santa, Kewpie On Sack, Windup ......... 20.00
Kewpie, Tray, Signed O'Neill, 12 Kewpies & Blackberries ............................................ 150.00
Kewpie, Tray, Tin, Serving, Keeley's Ice Cream ........................................................... 48.00
Kewpie, Wedding Party, Celluloid, 2 1/2 In.High, 4 Pieces .......................................... 25.00
    Kimball, see also Cluthra
Kimball, Vase, Cluthra, Yellow, 2 Handled, Numbered On Base, 7 In.High .................... 90.00
Kimball, Vase, Pearl Opalescence, Air Trapped Bubbles, 4 In. High ............................. 95.00
Kimball, Vase, White, Signed, 8 In., Pair ...................................................................... 150.00
    King's Rose, see Soft Paste
    Kitchen, see also Iron, Store, Tool, Wooden
Kitchen, Apple Peeler, Cast Iron, Wooden Base, 13 X 3 1/2 In.Base ........................... 50.00
Kitchen, Apple Peeler, Iron, Clamp On Type, Signed, Dated ........................................ 20.00
Kitchen, Apple Peeler, Reading Hardware, Patent 1872 ............................................... 14.00
Kitchen, Apple Peeler, Sinclair Scott Co., 8 Gears ...................................................... 25.00
Kitchen, Apple Peeler, Wooden ..................................................................................... 65.00
Kitchen, Asparagus Cutter & Buncher ........................................................................... 30.00
Kitchen, Basket, Boiling, Wire, 6 1/2 In.High ............................................................... 42.00
Kitchen, Basket, Rye Straw, Handle, 13 1/2 In. Diameter ............................................. 35.00
Kitchen, Board, Chopping, Wooden, Round, 11 In. ....................................................... 13.00
Kitchen, Board, Cookie, Carved Wood, 13 X 11 In. ...................................................... 15.00
Kitchen, Board, Cookie, Horse Carving, 6 X 6 1/2 In. .................................................. 8.00
Kitchen, Board, Cookie, Sheep Carving, 6 X 6 1/2 In. .................................................. 8.00
Kitchen, Board, Smoothing, Chip Carved Wood, Star, Horse Handle, 1765 .................. 165.00

Kitchen, **Board,** Wooden Peg, Black Mammy, "Reckon Ah Needs, " Lists Foods ............................. 15.00
Kitchen, **Boiler,** Pudding, The Queens, Challis, No.14, China & Tin ............................................... 9.75
Kitchen, **Bowl,** Burl, Round, 16 In.Diameter ............................................... 165.00
Kitchen, **Bowl,** Burl, 10 In.Diameter, 5 1/2 In.High ............................................... 70.00
Kitchen, **Bowl,** Butter, 13 1/2 X 14 1/2 In. ............................................... 7.00
Kitchen, **Box,** Knife, Pine, Compartmented, Center Handle, Hand-Painted Leaves ............ 12.00
Kitchen, **Box,** Salt, Hanging, Pine, Black Paint, "Potatismjol Hventemjol" ............ 45.00
Kitchen, **Box,** Salt, Hanging, Pine, Round, Cutout Heart Splat, 9 3/4 In. High ............ 75.00
Kitchen, **Box,** Salt, Oak, Hinged ............................................... 11.00
Kitchen, **Box,** Salt, Wooden, Double, Swivel Cover, Handle, 12 X 3 In. ............ 35.00
Kitchen, **Box,** Spice, Pine, Handle ............................................... 12.00
Kitchen, **Breadboard,** Carved Bread & Sheaf, Round, 11 In. ............ 25.00
Kitchen, **Breadboard,** Walnut, 13 1/2 X 20 X 1 In. ............ 10.00
Kitchen, **Broiler,** Fireplace, Wrought Iron, Straight Legs, 12 X 22 In. ............ 50.00
Kitchen, **Broiler,** Wrought Iron, Revolving, Tripod Base, Handle, 20 In. ............ 45.00
Kitchen, **Bucket,** Ice Cream, Wooden, 15 In.Diameter, 19 In.High ............ 15.00
Kitchen, **Butter Maker,** Wooden, Metal Handled Roller, Hinged Legs, Triangular ............ 125.00
Kitchen, **Butter Stamp,** Fern Frond With 3 Concentric Rings ............ 18.00
Kitchen, **Cabinet,** Spice, Hanging, Tin, Porcelain Knobs, 6 Drawer, 19 In. High ............ 55.00
Kitchen, **Can Opener & Fruit Jar Opener,** Metal ............ 6.00
Kitchen, **Canister Set,** Raised Floral, Japan, 1920s, 12 Piece ............ 42.00
Kitchen, **Carving Set,** Bone Handles, Bridgeport Knife Co. ............ 10.00
Kitchen, **Cherry Pitter,** Blue, Iron, Patent 8-7-'17 ............ 7.50
Kitchen, **Chopper,** Food, Bell, Metal, 6 Blades, C.1850 ............ 15.00
Kitchen, **Chopper,** Food, Iron, Clamp On Table ............ 3.50
Kitchen, **Chopper,** Food, Iron, Double Bladed ............ 2.00
Kitchen, **Chopper,** Food, Iron, Single Blade ............ 1.50
Kitchen, **Chopper,** Food, Tin, Handmade ............ 3.50
Kitchen, **Churn,** Butter, Dazey, 14 In. High ............ 20.00
Kitchen, **Churn,** Butter, Dazey, Wooden Paddle, Dazey Strainer Lid ............ 18.50
Kitchen, **Churn,** Butter, Saylor Of St.Louis, Glass, Gallon ............ 10.00
Kitchen, **Churn,** Butter, White Cedar, Cylinder Type, 3 Gallon ............ 32.00
Kitchen, **Churn,** Dazey, Glass, 1/2 Gallon ............ 10.00
Kitchen, **Cleaning Outfit,** For Steel Knives, Brick Slides Into Compartment ............ 25.00
    Kitchen, **Coffee Grinder, see Coffee Grinder**
Kitchen, **Colander,** Tin, Soldered On Strap Handles, Collared Base ............ 6.00
Kitchen, **Cookie Cutter,** Bird, Tin, Pennsylvania Dutch ............ 9.00
Kitchen, **Cookie Cutter,** Deer, Tin, Pennsylvania Dutch, 5 1/2 X 6 In. ............ 40.00
Kitchen, **Cookie Cutter,** Dog, Tin, Pennsylvania Dutch ............ 6.00
Kitchen, **Cookie Cutter,** Fish, Tin, Pennsylvania Dutch ............ 7.00
Kitchen, **Cookie Cutter,** Heart, Tin, Pennsylvania Dutch ............ 5.00
Kitchen, **Cookie Cutter,** Rabbit, Tin, Pennsylvania Dutch ............ 6.00
Kitchen, **Cookie Cutter,** Rooster, Tin, Pennsylvania Dutch ............ 7.00
Kitchen, **Cookie Cutter,** Scalloped Circle, Tin, Pennsylvania Dutch ............ 2.50
Kitchen, **Cookie Sheet,** Ladyfinger, Tin ............ 1.50
Kitchen, **Cover,** Food, Dome Top, Tin & Wire Mesh, "Keep The Flys Off" ............ 15.00
Kitchen, **Cup,** Measuring, Marked Kellogg's, Pink Tinted Glass ............ 2.75
Kitchen, **Cutter,** Cabbage, Disston & Morse, Walnut, Knife Blade, 17 1/2 In. ............ 3.00
Kitchen, **Cutter,** Cabbage, Wooden, Arched Top With Cutout Heart ............ 36.00
Kitchen, **Cutter,** Cookie, Amish Lady, Tin ............ 22.50
Kitchen, **Cutter,** Cookie, Butterfly, Tin, Handle ............ 12.50
Kitchen, **Cutter,** Cookie, Deer, Tin, Pennsylvania Dutch, 5 1/2 X 6 In. ............ 40.00
Kitchen, **Cutter,** Cookie, Horse, Tin ............ 27.50
Kitchen, **Dipper,** Glass, Wooden Handle ............ 11.00
Kitchen, **Dish,** Soap, Wire, Woven, Hangs On Wall, 6 1/2 X 4 1/4 X 6 In. ............ 5.50
Kitchen, **Dough Scraper,** Iron ............ 7.00
Kitchen, **Drainer,** Cheese, Pierced Tin, 2 Handles ............ 30.00
Kitchen, **Drainer,** Utensil, Enamelware, White ............ 1.50
Kitchen, **Dutch Oven,** Savery, New York, C.1830, Iron, Round, Ear Handles ............ 70.00
Kitchen, **Egg Poacher,** Copper, Long Handle, 12 In.Diameter ............ 20.00
Kitchen, **Egg Timer,** Brass, Running Sand ............ 12.00
Kitchen, **Eggbeater,** Patent Applied For, Lyon ............................ *Illus* 10.00
Kitchen, **Eggbeater,** Patent Date 1908, Hand-Turned ............ 5.00
Kitchen, **Eggbeater,** Taplans, Iron ............ 7.00
Kitchen, **Fish Broiler,** Heart, Wrought Iron, Footed, American, 18 In.Long ............ 200.00
Kitchen, **Flatiron,** Iron, Twisted Handle, 9 3/4 In. Long ............ 17.00

| | |
|---|---|
| Kitchen, Flatiron, Marked 5W, Twisted Handle | 8.00 |
| Kitchen, Fluter, Table, "Penn, " Patent 1875-77-80, Table Clamp | 24.00 |
| Kitchen, Fluter, Table, Mrs.Susan R.Knox, Dated 1866, Brass Rollers | 30.00 |
| Kitchen, Food Chopper, Double Blade | 10.00 |
| Kitchen, Food Chopper, Triangular Opening, Wrought Iron, 11 In.Long | 18.00 |
| Kitchen, Food Warmer, Camphene Oil Lamp, Stenciled Decoration | 65.00 |
| Kitchen, Fork, Table, Wooden, Hand-Hewn, 3 Tine, 10 In.Long | 15.00 |
| Kitchen, Frypan, Round, Iron, Hand-Forged Ring Handle, 14 In. Diameter | 35.00 |
| Kitchen, Frypan, Wrought Iron, Signed Whitfield | 30.00 |
| Kitchen, Funnel, Fruit Jar Filler, Measure Dipper, Tin | 3.00 |
| Kitchen, Grater, Almond, Table Model | 5.25 |
| Kitchen, Grater, Crumb, Table Model, Daisy, Germany | 8.50 |
| Kitchen, Grater, Nutmeg, Acorn, Rosewood & Ivory | 90.00 |
| Kitchen, Grater, Nutmeg, Marked The Edgar, Patent 1890, Wooden Handle, Metal | 8.50 |
| Kitchen, Grater, Nutmeg, Tin, Hanging, Hinged Flap Top, Pair | 4.50 |
| Kitchen, Grater, Nutmeg, Wooden Barrel Top | 38.00 |
| Kitchen, Grater, Pierced Brass, C.1750, 13 In. | 50.00 |
| Kitchen, Grater, Pierced Tin Bottom, Wooden Sides, Round, 14 In. | 65.00 |
| Kitchen, Grater, Vegetable, Schroeter, Tin, Iron, & Wood | 5.00 |
| Kitchen, Griddle, Pancake, Iron, 10 X 21 In. | 3.50 |
| Kitchen, Grinder, Meat, Rollman No.11, Mt.Joy, Cast Iron, 7 In. | 10.00 |
| Kitchen, Grinder, Meat, Russell & Erwin, New Britain, Conn., Cast Iron | 10.00 |
| Kitchen, Grinder, Meat, Russwin, 1901, Cast Iron, 10 In. | 10.00 |
| Kitchen, Grinder, Sausage, Enterprise, Iron | 12.00 |
| Kitchen, Grinder, Sausage, Wooden | 27.50 |
| Kitchen, Heater, Soup, Tin & Cast Iron, Whale Oil Burner, Cover, Handle, 9 In. | 50.00 |
| Kitchen, Ice Cream Maker, 15 In.High, 13 In.Diameter | 25.00 |
| Kitchen, Iron, British, Adjustable Fender Trivet | 15.00 |
| Kitchen, Iron, Charcoal, Mexico | 4.50 |
| Kitchen, Iron, Child's, Porcelain, Wooden Handle | 8.00 |
| Kitchen, Iron, Child's, Trivet, Cutwork | 4.00 |
| Kitchen, Iron, Fluting, Geneva, Marked Heat This On Base, Patent 1866 | 21.00 |
| Kitchen, Iron, Gasoline, Diamond, Self-Pump | 8.50 |
| Kitchen, Iron, Waffle, Cast Iron, 4 Geometric Designs, Handle, 26 In. Long | 25.00 |
| Kitchen, Iron, Waffle, In Stand That Fits Over Stove Lid | 10.00 |
| Kitchen, Iron, Waffle, Jr.Stover, 5 In. | 16.00 |
| Kitchen, Iron, Waffle, 1910 | 4.00 |
| Kitchen, Ironing Board, Child's, Wooden, 33 In.Long | 10.00 |
| Kitchen, Jar, Batter, 2 Tin Caps | 75.00 |
| Kitchen, Jar, Measuring, Rochester Tumbler Co., Patent 1880, Clear, Quart | 4.95 |
| Kitchen, Juicer, Orange, Sunkist, White Milk Glass | 12.00 |
| Kitchen, Juicer, Universal, Table Model, Aluminum, L.F.C.Co., Conn., 1920 | 28.00 |
| Kitchen, Kettle Lifter, Twisted Shaft, Hand Wrought, Flat Hook, 4 X 6 In. | 25.00 |
| Kitchen, Knife, Kraut, Double Bladed | 3.00 |
| Kitchen, Lard Squeezer, Wooden | 3.00 |
| Kitchen, Lemon Squeezer, Cast Iron | 15.00 |

Kitchen, Mold, Candle, 12 Tube,
Pewter, Pine, U.S., C.1850
*(See Page 285)*

Kitchen, Eggbeater, Patent Applied For, Lyon
*(See Page 283)*

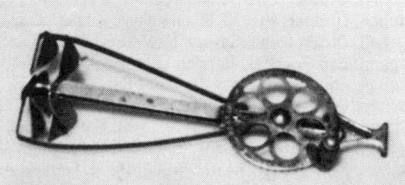

| | |
|---|---:|
| Kitchen, Lemon Squeezer, Clear Glass | 2.50 |
| Kitchen, Lemon Squeezer, Pearl, Iron & Walnut | 22.50 |
| Kitchen, Lemon Squeezer, Sunkist, White | 10.00 |
| Kitchen, Lemon Squeezer, Wooden, 12 In. | 20.00 |
| Kitchen, Masher, Potato, Tiger Maple, 12 In. | 35.00 |
| Kitchen, Match Holder, Shape Of Man's Pipe, Blue Glass | 9.00 |
| Kitchen, Meat Juicer, Iron | 19.00 |
| Kitchen, Meat Tenderizer, Wooden | 3.00 |
| Kitchen, Mold, Butter, Beaver, Wooden, Round, 1/2 Pound | 95.00 |
| Kitchen, Mold, Butter, Central Flower & Leaves, Round, 3 1/2 In. | 17.50 |
| Kitchen, Mold, Butter, Clover Pattern, Round, 1/2 Pound | 22.00 |
| Kitchen, Mold, Butter, Concentric Circles, Round | 32.00 |
| Kitchen, Mold, Butter, Double Sheaf Of Wheat, Rectangular, 3 Part | 32.50 |
| Kitchen, Mold, Butter, Fish & Leaves, Wooden, 3 In. Diameter | 85.00 |
| Kitchen, Mold, Butter, Flower, Border Design, Cased Wood, 3 1/4 In. Diameter | 20.00 |
| Kitchen, Mold, Butter, Flower, Buds, & Leaves | 30.00 |
| Kitchen, Mold, Butter, Flower, Miniature | 15.00 |
| Kitchen, Mold, Butter, Foliage, Round, 3 1/2 In. | 15.00 |
| Kitchen, Mold, Butter, Four Flower Design, Square, Brass Hooks | 28.00 |
| Kitchen, Mold, Butter, Geometric Star, Chip Carved, 3 1/2 In. Diameter | 45.00 |
| Kitchen, Mold, Butter, Geometric Star, Round, 3 1/4 In. | 20.00 |
| Kitchen, Mold, Butter, Heart & Leaves, Wooden, 3 3/4 In. Diameter | 25.00 |
| Kitchen, Mold, Butter, Pineapple With Shield, Wooden, Square | 50.00 |
| Kitchen, Mold, Butter, Pineapple, Round, 4 1/2 In. | 25.00 To 30.00 |
| Kitchen, Mold, Butter, Pineapple, Wooden, Square | 50.00 |
| Kitchen, Mold, Butter, Rosette, 3 In.Diameter | 7.50 |
| Kitchen, Mold, Butter, Sheaf Of Wheat & Leaves, Wooden, 4 1/4 In. Diameter | 25.00 |
| Kitchen, Mold, Butter, Sheaf Of Wheat, Wooden, 4 In.Diameter | 30.00 |
| Kitchen, Mold, Butter, Sheep, Wooden, 2 3/4 In. Diameter | 115.00 |
| Kitchen, Mold, Butter, Star Print, Wooden, C.1850, 5 In. Diameter | 39.50 |
| Kitchen, Mold, Butter, Star Shaped Flower & Leaves, Cased Wood, 3 1/2 In. | 25.00 |
| Kitchen, Mold, Butter, Strawberry & Leaf, Cased Wooden, 4 1/2 In. Diameter | 30.00 |
| Kitchen, Mold, Butter, Stylized Flower & Foliage, Round, 3 7/8 In. | 20.00 |
| Kitchen, Mold, Butter, Stylized Foliage, Round, 3 3/4 In. | 27.50 |
| Kitchen, Mold, Butter, Stylized Tulips, Rectangular, 3 3/8 X 4 7/8 In. | 75.00 |
| Kitchen, Mold, Butter, Swimming Swan, Carved Border, Wooden, 3 1/2 In. | 25.00 |
| Kitchen, Mold, Butter, Swimming Swan, Wooden, 2 5/8 In. Diameter | 30.00 |
| Kitchen, Mold, Butter, Tulip & Flowers, P.S. On Handle, 4 1/2 In. Diameter | 100.00 |
| Kitchen, Mold, Butter, Wheat, Round, Plunger Type, Pound | 22.00 |
| Kitchen, Mold, Butter, 2 Stars, Rectangular, 1 Lb. | 12.00 |
| Kitchen, Mold, Butter, 3 1/4 In. Diameter | 30.00 |
| Kitchen, Mold, Butter, 8 5-Pointed Stars In Squares, Hand-Carved, 2 Pounds | 49.50 |
| Kitchen, Mold, Candle, see also Tin, Mold, Candle | |
| Kitchen, Mold, Candle, 1 Tube, Cathedral, Handle, Round Top, 18 In. | 150.00 |
| Kitchen, Mold, Candle, 6 Tube | 14.00 |
| Kitchen, Mold, Candle, 12 Tube, Pewter, Pine, U.S., C.1850 .......... Illus | 600.00 |
| Kitchen, Mold, Candle, 48 Tube, Tin | 200.00 |
| Kitchen, Mold, Jelly, Glass, Tin Cover | 3.50 |
| Kitchen, Mold, Pudding, Coffeepot In Relief, Copper, 8 In.Diameter | 65.00 |
| Kitchen, Mold, Pudding, Grape & Leaf, Arch Border, White, Flat Base | 25.00 |
| Kitchen, Mold, Pudding, Ribbed, Fluted, Bundt Type, Tin | 5.00 |
| Kitchen, Mold, Pudding, Rose In Base, Fluted, White, 4 1/2 X 5 3/4 In. | 15.50 |
| Kitchen, Mortar & Pestle, Bronze Mortar, Brass Pestle, C.1680 | 75.00 |
| Kitchen, Mortar & Pestle, Bronze Mortar, Brass Pestle, C.1860 | 130.00 |
| Kitchen, Mortar & Pestle, Clear Glass, Marked U.S.A., 1 Oz. | 7.50 |
| Kitchen, Mortar & Pestle, Earthenware, White, Signed | 23.00 |
| Kitchen, Mortar & Pestle, Gallon Size | 48.00 |
| Kitchen, Muffin Cutter, Tin | 2.00 |
| Kitchen, Nutcracker, Clown's Head | 75.00 |
| Kitchen, Oven Peel With Pie Board, Wooden, Tapered End, Arched Handle | 49.00 |
| Kitchen, Oven, Dutch, Wagner Ware, Iron, Embossed Drip Drop Roaster On Lid | 10.00 |
| Kitchen, Oven, Warming, Iron, Ornate | 15.00 |
| Kitchen, Paddle, Butter, Maple | 7.50 |
| Kitchen, Paddle, Butter, Wooden, Handmade, Hook Type Handle | 9.00 |
| Kitchen, Paddle, Lard, Wooden, Flat, Rounded | 10.00 |
| Kitchen, Pan, Breadstick, 11 Sections | 7.00 |

Kitchen, Posnet, Bell Metal,
New England, C.1775

Kitchen, Sadiron, 5 1/2 In.
(See Page 287)

| | |
|---|---|
| Kitchen, Pan, Chafing, Brass & Copper, Stand | 10.00 |
| Kitchen, Pan, Corn Muffin, 12 Compartments, Cast Iron | 5.00 |
| Kitchen, Pan, Cornpone, Corn Pattern, Cast Iron, Patent 1920 | 7.00 |
| Kitchen, Pan, Dough Rising, Covered, Tin, 15 In. Diameter | 16.00 |
| Kitchen, Pan, Milk, Tin, Round, 2 1/2 X 10 1/2 In. | 2.65 |
| Kitchen, Pan, Milk, Tin, Round, 3 1/2 X 15 In. | 9.50 |
| Kitchen, Pan, Muffin, Iron, Oblong | 3.50 |
| Kitchen, Peel, Pie, Tin, 20 In. | 18.00 |
| Kitchen, Peeler, Apple, Goodell Co., Dated 1898, Iron | 20.00 |
| Kitchen, Peeler, Apple, White Mountain, Spiral Shape | 12.00 |
| Kitchen, Peeler, Apple, Wrought Iron & Wood | 37.50 |
| Kitchen, Peeler, Potato, Nu-Way Automatic, Cast Iron | 25.00 |
| Kitchen, Pie Crimper, Brass Wheel | 14.00 |
| Kitchen, Pie Safe, Folding, Glass Doors, Completely Collapsible | 185.00 |
| Kitchen, Pie Safe, Wooden, Pierced Tin, 5 Point Stars, Circle Corners, 50 In. | 210.00 |
| Kitchen, Pitcher, Measuring, With Green Reamer, Depression Glass, 2 Cup Size | 9.00 |
| Kitchen, Posnet, Bell Metal, New England, C.1775 .................................... Illus | 275.00 |
| Kitchen, Pot, Cooking, Cast Iron, Marietta, Pennsylvania, Long Handle, 3 Quart | 30.00 |
| Kitchen, Pot, Cooking, Cast Iron, Oval, Footed, Handle | 30.00 |
| Kitchen, Pot, Cooking, Copper, Brass Ring On Lid, Iron Handle, C.1700 | 60.00 |
| Kitchen, Potato Masher, Wooden | 4.50 |
| Kitchen, Potholder, Iron, Acorn, For Back Of Cookstove, Pair | 4.50 |
| Kitchen, Press, Butter, Nut Design, Wooden, 3 In.High | 14.00 |
| Kitchen, Press, Cheese, Pine, Two Plungers | 30.00 |
| Kitchen, Press, Cottage Cheese, 2 Plungers, 2 Wooden Lids, 2 Shelves | 30.00 |
| Kitchen, Rack, Broiler, Wrought Iron, Adjustable, Penny Feet, 28 In. High | 135.00 |
| Kitchen, Rack, Clothes, Pine & Iron, Empire Clothes Dryer, R.I., Expandable | 15.00 |
| Kitchen, Rack, Meat, Scalloped, 7 Hooks | 30.00 |
| Kitchen, Raisin Seeder, Cast Iron, Wet The Raisins | 9.00 |
| Kitchen, Reamer, Juice, Sunkist, Green Opaque Glass | 4.50 |
| Kitchen, Reamer, Lemon, Light Blue To Opalescent Glass | 8.75 |
| Kitchen, Reamer, Orange Juice, Marked Easley's Patent 1900, Clear | 3.75 |
| Kitchen, Rolling Pin, Blown Glass, Blue | 30.00 |
| Kitchen, Rolling Pin, Blown Glass, Hand-Painted | 12.00 |
| Kitchen, Rolling Pin, Burl Maple, 12 In.Long | 10.00 |
| Kitchen, Rolling Pin, Cobalt Blue, Glass, 14 1/4 In.Long | 50.00 |
| Kitchen, Rolling Pin, Glass, Clear, Hollow, 1 Piece, 15 In.Long | 18.00 |
| Kitchen, Rolling Pin, Glass, Cobalt Blue | 32.00 |
| Kitchen, Rolling Pin, Maple, 1 Piece | 12.00 |
| Kitchen, Rolling Pin, Pine, 1 Piece | 15.00 |
| Kitchen, Rolling Pin, Porcelain, Hand-Painted Esteem The Giver | 45.00 |
| Kitchen, Rolling Pin, Porcelain, Wooden Handles, Blue Forget-Me-Nots, Gold | 20.00 |
| Kitchen, Rolling Pin, Wooden, Solid | 5.00 |
| Kitchen, Rug Beater, Interwoven Wire Loop, 31 In. | 5.00 |

Kitchen, **Sadiron & Trivet,** Child's, Iron, 3 In.Trivet ............................................................ 8.50
Kitchen, **Sadiron,** Bless & Drake, Newark, N.J., Patent 1871, Double Pointed ............ 4.75
Kitchen, **Sadiron,** Child's, Double Pointed, Nickel Plate On Iron, 4 1/4 In. ................... 4.95
Kitchen, **Sadiron,** Double Pointed, Bless & Drake, N.J., Patent 1871, Handle ............ 4.75
Kitchen, **Sadiron,** Double Pointed, Detachable Handle, Bless & Drake, 1871 ............ 4.75
Kitchen, **Sadiron,** Double Pointed, Removable Handle, Enterprise Mfg.Co. ............... 3.75
Kitchen, **Sadiron,** Keystone, Triangular Shape, 5 In. .............................................. 3.95
Kitchen, **Sadiron,** Mahony, Troy, N.Y., Waffled Base ............................................ 8.50
Kitchen, **Sadiron,** Miniature, 2 1/2 In. ............................................................... 10.00
Kitchen, **Sadiron,** Polishing, Diamond Shape, Stubby, Indentations On Bottom ......... 5.95
Kitchen, **Sadiron,** Sensible, No.3 ..................................................................... 8.50
Kitchen, **Sadiron,** Sensible, No.5 ..................................................................... 8.00
Kitchen, **Sadiron,** Twist Handle, No.16 .............................................................. 12.50
Kitchen, **Sadiron,** 5 1/2 In. ........................................................................*Illus* 8.00
Kitchen, **Safe,** Cake, Tin, Black, Stenciled, Round, 16 X 11 X 10 In. ....................... 35.00
Kitchen, **Saltshaker,** Melon Shape, Melon Ribbed, Peach Forget-Me-Not ................. 12.50
Kitchen, **Sausage Gun,** Tole, Turned Wooden Plunger, 16 In. ................................. 15.00
Kitchen, **Scoop,** Apple Butter, Hand-Hewn, Rectangular, Long Handle, 1 Piece ......... 65.00
Kitchen, **Scoop,** Melon Ball, Steel Scoop, Brass Ferrule, 6 1/2 In. .......................... 5.00
Kitchen, **Scoop,** Soft Soap, Wooden, 1 Piece, Hole In Handle For Hanging ............... 36.00
Kitchen, **Scoop,** Sugar, Grain Scoop Type, Wooden, 1 Piece, 9 In. .......................... 35.00
Kitchen, **Skewer,** Forged Iron, 24 In. ................................................................. 10.00
Kitchen, **Skillet,** Cast Iron, Large Size ............................................................... 2.00
Kitchen, **Skillet,** Wrought Iron, Long Handle ....................................................... 32.50
Kitchen, **Skimmer,** Brass, Hand-Forged, Iron With Ring Handle, American, 21 In. ...... 39.00
Kitchen, **Slicer & Egg Scale,** Harras, Iron .......................................................... 4.75
Kitchen, **Slitter & Scraper,** Corn, Silver Color, Handled, Dated 1911 ....................... 4.50
Kitchen, **Spatula,** Forged Iron, 8 In. .................................................................. 8.00
Kitchen, **Spatula,** Forged Iron, 15 In. ................................................................ 10.00
Kitchen, **Spatula,** Wrought Iron, Twisted Handle, 8 In. ......................................... 24.00
     Kitchen, **Spinning Wheel, see Tool, Spinning Wheel**
Kitchen, **Spit,** Bird, For Open Hearth ................................................................. 145.00
Kitchen, **Spoon,** Horn, Handmade, 6 In. ............................................................. 3.00
Kitchen, **Spoon,** Iron, 15 In. ........................................................................... 7.00
Kitchen, **Spoon,** Measuring, Metal, Wooden Handle, 1/2 Teaspoon ......................... 4.00
Kitchen, **Spoon,** Tasting, Iron, 7 In. .................................................................. 8.00
Kitchen, **Strainer,** Food, Brass, 8 X 2 In. ........................................................... 9.00
Kitchen, **String Holder,** China, Wall Type, Three Ladies ........................................ 6.50
Kitchen, **Stuffer,** Sausage, Iron, Painted ........................................................... 10.00
Kitchen, **Tea Ball,** Chain, Silver, Round ............................................................. 4.75
Kitchen, **Tea Warmer,** 4 Scenic Lithophanes In Footed Nickel Plate Stand ............... 95.00
Kitchen, **Teakettle,** Cast Iron & Brass ............................................................... 35.00
Kitchen, **Tongs,** Baked Potato, Iron, Flat Round Ends, 14 In.Long .......................... 12.00
Kitchen, **Tool,** Multipurpose, Tin ...................................................................... 10.00
Kitchen, **Towel Holder,** Roller, Wooden .............................................................. 14.00
Kitchen, **Tray,** Baking, Corn Muffin, Iron, 12 Muffins, Openwork ............................ 18.00
Kitchen, **Tray,** Carved, Hand Painted, 14 In.Diameter ........................................... 5.00
Kitchen, **Tray,** Knife, Walnut, Dovetailed, Arched Carrying Handle, 2 Section ........... 36.00
Kitchen, **Tray,** Wicker, 20 X 12 1/2 X 2 3/4 In. .................................................. 8.00
Kitchen, **Trivet,** Cast Iron, Best On Earth, 7 1/2 In.Long ...................................... 8.00
Kitchen, **Turner,** Pancake, Brass, Cast Iron Handle, Hook End, 17 In.Long ............... 35.00
Kitchen, **Utensil,** Cooking, Copper, Iron Handle, Brass Ring On Lid, C.1700 ............. 65.00
Kitchen, **Waffle Iron & Stand,** Cast Iron, Dated 1877 .......................................... 6.50
Kitchen, **Washtub,** Child's, Curved Top, Wooden ................................................. 20.00
Kitchen, **Washtub,** Crystal, Miniature ............................................................... 5.00
Kitchen, **Washboard,** National Washboard Co., Top Notch, Glass & Wood ................ 7.50
Kitchen, **Washboard,** Wooden, Brass Scrubber .................................................... 3.00
Kitchen, **Washboard,** Wooden, Glass Scrubber ................................................... 3.50
Kitchen, **Washing Machine,** Horseshoe Brand, Patent Feb.12, 1907, Michigan .......... 195.00
Kitchen, **Washing Machine,** Patented, C.1850 .................................................... 15.00
Kitchen, **Washing Machine,** Tempest, Patent 1892, Tin, Brass, Wooden Plunger ....... 12.00
Kitchen, **Washing Machine,** Wooden, Patented, 2 Rollers, 11 X 20 In. ..................... 12.00
Kitchen, **Washtub & Washboard,** Wooden, Miniature ............................................ 25.00
Kitchen, **Whipper,** Potato, Diamond Shape, Metal End, Wooden Handle ................... 8.00
Kitchen, **Wringer,** American Wringer Co., Wooden, Pan American, 1901 ................... 30.00
Kitchen, **Wringer,** Clothes, Household, A.M.Wringer Co., New York, U.S.A. ............... 12.50

Kitchen, Wringer, Wooden, Floor Standing .................................................................... 17.50
    Knowles, Taylor & Knowles, see Lotus Ware, KTK
Koch, Bowl, Fruit, Apple, J.& C.Louise Bavaria, 10 In. ................................................... 22.00
Koch, Bowl, Fruit, Grapes, J.& C.Louise, Bavaria, 10 In. ............................................... 22.00
Koch, Plate, Apple, J.& C.Louise, Bavaria, 6 1/4 In. ..................................................... 8.50
Koch, Plate, Apple, J.& C.Louise, Bavaria, 7 3/4 In. ..................................................... 13.00
Koch, Plate, Grape, J.& C.Louise, Bavaria, 6 In. .......................................................... 8.50
Koch, Plate, Grape, J.& C.Louise, Bavaria, 6 1/4 In. ..................................................... 8.50
Koch, Plate, Grapes, Irregular Edge, Louis, Bavaria, 8 3/4 In. ....................................... 37.50
Koch, Plate, Grapes, Irregular Edge, Signed, 7 In. ....................................................... 29.00
Koch, Plate, Grapes, Irregular Edge, Signed, 9 In. ....................................................... 45.00
Koch, Plate, Grapes, Louise, Bavaria, Signed, 8 1/2 In. ............................................... 37.50
Koch, Plate, Grapes, 2 Colors, Green To Yellow, Gold Trim, 8 1/2 In. ........................... 27.00
Koch, Plate, Vintage Grapes, Scalloped Gold Edge, Louise Bavaria Mark ....................... 37.50
Koch, Plate, Yellow Orange Pears On Salmon, Signed Obert, 8 3/4 In. .......................... 22.50
Koch, Sauce, Grape, Tinted, Signed .......................................................................... 14.50
Korean, Bowl, Flower, Monkey In White & Blue Robe On Red, 5 In. ................................ 60.00
Korean, Mug, Red, Raised Figure ....................................................................... *Illus* 75.00
Korean, Vase, Child In Blue & White Robe, Black & Brown, 5 In. ................................... 45.00

Korean, Mug, Red, Raised Figure

*K. P. M*

*KPM is part of one of the marks used about 1723 by the Meissen factory Konigliche Porzellan Manufaktur. Other firms using the letters include the Royal Manufactory of Berlin, Germany, that worked from 1832 to 1847. A factory in Scheibe, Germany, used the mark in 1928. The mark was also used in Waldenburg, Germany, and other German cities during the twentieth century.*

KPM, Bowl, Oval, Scalloped Gold Edge, Open Handled, Floral Center, 13 In. .................. 27.50
KPM, Bowl, Swan Shape, White, Neck Forms Handle, C.1840, 12 In.Long ...................... 225.00
KPM, Cake Set, Green Leaves On White, Gold Rim, Open Handles, 7 Piece .................... 85.00
KPM, Cup & Saucer, Hand-Painted Wild Roses ........................................................... 10.00
KPM, Cup & Saucer, Pink Shaded Dresden Roses ....................................................... 15.00
KPM, Cup & Saucer, Roses & Blackberries, Luster Lining, Gold Handle .......................... 8.00
KPM, Cup & Saucer, White, Pink, & Gold .................................................................. 10.00
KPM, Dish Rest, Transfer Of Boston Church, Pink, Gold Bands, 7 In.Diameter ................. 15.00
KPM, Feeding Set, Child's, Children At Play, Toys, Numbered, 3 Piece ........................... 35.00
KPM, Figurine, Seminude With Lion, Signed, 6 X 8 In. ................................................ 550.00
KPM, Lithophane, Pewter Frame, Hanging Chain ......................................................... 85.00
KPM, Mustache Cup, Pink Carnations, Gold Trim ........................................................ 25.00
KPM, Painting On Porcelain, Portrait Of Girl, 6 X 8 In. ............................................... 625.00
KPM, Painting, On Porcelain, Man, Artist-Signed, Gold Leaf Frame ................................ 350.00
KPM, Pitcher, White, 10 In.High ............................................................................... 50.00
KPM, Plaque, Profile Of Fair Skinned Maiden, Oval, C.1890, 10 5/8 In. ......................... 600.00
KPM, Plaque, Young Woman, Seventeenth Century Dress, C.1890, 9 X 7 In. .................. 1100.00
KPM, Plate, Child's, Pioneer Flour Mills, 1929, Children, Floral, Toys Rim ..................... 24.00
KPM, Plate, Fruit Decoration, Blue Mark, 6 In. ........................................................... 15.00
KPM, Plate, Multicolored Floral Center, 7 1/2 In. ........................................................ 6.00

KPM, Plate, Pink Floral Center, Cream & Gold Border, C.1832, 8 1/4 In. ....................... 25.00
KPM, Teapot, White, Gold & Blue Trim, C.1847, 8 1/2 In.High ........................... 60.00

KTK are the initials of the Knowles, Taylor and Knowles Company of
East Liverpool, Ohio, founded by Isaac W.Knowles in 1853. The
company is still working. They made Lotus Ware.
KTK, Dish, Leaf, White Lotus Ware, 4 In.Diameter ........................... 100.00
    KTK Lotus Ware, see Lotus Ware
KTK, Plate, Chickens, 6 1/2 In. ........................... 16.00
KTK, Syrup, Pink, Gold Trim, Ironstone, Dated Top ........................... 37.50
KTK, Washstand Set, Yellow Floral & Gold On White, Scalloped, 4 Piece ........................... 125.00
Ku Klux Klan, Dollar, 1922 ........................... 30.00
Ku Klux Klan, Medallion, 1928, Brass ........................... 15.00
Ku Klux Klan, Stickpin ........................... 22.00

Kutani ware is a Japanese porcelain made after the mid-seventeenth century.
Most of the pieces found today are nineteenth century.
Kutani, Bowl, Ming Style, Tokugawa Period ........................... 500.00
Kutani, Cup & Saucer, Demitasse, Japanese ........................... 8.00
Kutani, Cup & Saucer, Orange People, Birds & Trees, White Ground ........................... 15.00
Kutani, Dessert Set, Birds, Waterfowl, Butterflies, & Floral, 12 Piece ........................... 185.00
Kutani, Figurine, Buddha, Signed, 3 In.High ........................... 12.00
Kutani, Goblet, Orange Stem, Figures Inside & Out, 7 1/2 In.High ........................... 60.00
Kutani, Jar, Ginger, Covered, Round, Footed, 5 3/4 X 4 1/8 In. ........................... 98.00
Kutani, Plate, Foo Dog Surrounded By 1, 000 Faces & Figures, 9 1/2 In. ........................... 95.00
Kutani, Sugar & Creamer, Gold Decoration, Footed ........................... 52.50
Kutani, Tea Set, Handleless Cups, Peonies, Green Leaves, Gold, 7 Piece ........................... 175.00
Kutani, Teapot, Flowers & Birds Scenes, 6 1/2 In. ........................... 45.00
Lacquer, Bowl, Black, Gold Floral, Gold Lion Inside, 4 In. ........................... 25.00
Lacquer, Bowl, Black, Gold Floral, Gold Water Buffalo Inside, 4 In. ........................... 25.00
Lacquer, Bowl, Black, Oriental Figures On Gold, Gold Horse Inside, 4 In. ........................... 30.00
Lacquer, Japanese, Tray, Black, Man Cheats At Games, Humorous, 10 X 4 3/4 In. ........................... 16.00

Lalique glass was made by Rene Lalique's factory in Paris, France, from
1860 to 1945. The glass was molded, pressed, and engraved. Many of the most
familiar designs were clear or with a bluish-tinged glass molded into birds,
animals, or foliage.
Lalique, Ashtray, Frosted Fish, Tail Extends To Rim To Form Groove ........................... 55.00
Lalique, Bowl, Allover Ferns, Marked R.Lalique, No.3213, 9 In. ........................... 120.00
Lalique, Bowl, Covered, Opalescent, 6 In.Diameter ........................... 225.00
Lalique, Bowl, Etched, 4 Feet Come Out Of Lily Center, Signed, 9 In. ........................... 137.00
Lalique, Bowl, Fish Decoration, Signed R.Lalique, 11 In. ........................... 185.00
Lalique, Bowl, Fish On Frosted Base, Clear Top, Signed, 3 In. ........................... 35.00
Lalique, Bowl, Frosted Leaf 2 In, Rim, 9 In.Diameter ........................... 55.00
Lalique, Bowl, Frosted With Clear Bull's-Eye, Scalloped, 4 1/4 In.Diameter ........................... 47.50
Lalique, Bowl, Leafage & Loops, Tinted Yellow, Deep, 8 1/4 In. ........................... 110.00
Lalique, Bowl, Opalescent, Sirens, 8 In.Diameter ........................... 90.00
Lalique, Bowl, Shallow, Swirls Of Bubbles, Signed, 10 In. ........................... 75.00
Lalique, Bowl, Sirens, 6 Mermaids In Spray, Opalescent, 8 1/4 In. ........................... 130.00
Lalique, Box, Covered, Birds Of Paradise, 3 1/2 In.Diameter, Signed ........................... 120.00
Lalique, Box, Covered, Children, Floral, Frosted, 4 1/4 In.Diameter ........................... 120.00
Lalique, Box, Jewelry, Dragonfly, 8 In.Diameter ........................... 95.00
Lalique, Box, Molded Petal Cover, Round, Frosted, Black Enamel, 6 In. ........................... 55.00
Lalique, Butter Pat, Engraved, Double Border, Script Signature, 3 In. ........................... 14.00
Lalique, Cologne, Bulbous, Intaglio Floral, Lavender On Frosted ........................... 98.00
Lalique, Cologne, Mauve To Clear, 4 1/4 In.High ........................... 80.00
Lalique, Cologne, Raised Lacy Spiral On Clear, Signed, 5 1/2 In.High, Pair ........................... 70.00
Lalique, Decanter, Wine, Beaded Rings On Frosted, Cut Crystal Stopper ........................... 110.00
Lalique, Figurine, Fish On Pedestal, Molded, Label, 6 1/2 In. ........................... 50.00
Lalique, Figurine, Owl, Clear & Frosted, Signed, 3 1/2 In. ........................... 20.00
Lalique, Figurine, Perch, Clear & Frosted, Signed, 6 1/2 In. ........................... 26.00
Lalique, Figurine, Rooster, Frosted, 7 1/4 In. High ........................... 60.00
Lalique, Figurine, Sitting Sparrow On Underplate, Clear Yellow ........................... 185.00
Lalique, Figurine, Sitting Wolf On Underplate, Green Opalescent ........................... 185.00
Lalique, Flower Frog, Lady, Ice Blue, 2 Piece, Signed, 7 1/2 In. ........................... 125.00
Lalique, Globe, Swirled, Opalescent, 7 X 7 1/2 In. ........................... 250.00
Lalique, Goblet, Frosted Stem, Grapes, 4 1/2 In.High ........................... 32.00
Lalique, Jar, Powder, Embossed Beige Flowers On Lid, Signed R.Lalique ........................... 68.00

| | |
|---|---|
| Lalique, Knife Rest, Crystal, Camphor Satin Babies' Heads At Ends | 25.00 |
| Lalique, Lampshade, 2 Rows Of Veins Folded Back From Edge, 4 In., Pair | 57.50 |
| Lalique, Mirror, Hand, Peacock Design | 130.00 |
| Lalique, Ornament, Hood, Crouching Cock, 8 In.High | 175.00 |
| Lalique, Ornament, Hood, Freestanding Fish On Circular Base, 4 In.High | 150.00 |
| Lalique, Ornament, Hood, Pierce Arrow, Archer Design, Patent No.309301 | 375.00 |
| Lalique, Perfume, Beehive Shape, Signed | 45.00 |
| Lalique, Perfume, Disc Shape, Spirals Of Beading, 5 3/4 In.High | 62.00 |
| Lalique, Perfume, Flat Swelling Shape, "Martial Armand, " Woman's Head | 130.00 |
| Lalique, Perfume, Spray, 4 Art Nouveau Seminude Figures, Signed | 50.00 |
| Lalique, Pin, Bar, Berries & Leaves On Blue Glass | 290.00 |
| Lalique, Pin, Bar, Frosted Glass & Gilt Metal, Berries & Leaves, C.1925 | 120.00 |
| Lalique, Plate, Grape Design Accented With Brownish Stain, 9 In. | 90.00 |
| Lalique, Sauce, Cherubs, Flower Border, Signed | 30.00 |
| Lalique, Tray, Ring, Opalescent, Bird | 75.00 |
| Lalique, Tray, Ring, Opalescent, Mouse | 75.00 |
| Lalique, Tumbler, Border Of Leaping Fish, Footed, Signed, 6 In. | 35.00 |
| Lalique, Tumbler, Honey Color, Elongated Arches, Serrated, Frosted | 55.00 |
| Lalique, Vase, Amazons Shooting Bows At Cranes, Smoke Color, 10 In.High | 575.00 |
| Lalique, Vase, Ball Shape, Acanthus Leaves On Frosted, 4 1/2 In.Diameter | 47.50 |
| Lalique, Vase, Bulbous, 3 Panels Of Reindeer, 8 1/4 In. | 395.00 |
| Lalique, Vase, Carved Leaves & Flowers, Frosted & Clear, Signed, 6 In. | 120.00 |
| Lalique, Vase, Clear & Frosted Decoration, Signed, 5 In.High | 37.50 |
| Lalique, Vase, Frosted, Relief Thistles & Leaves, C.1925, 8 3/4 In.High | 170.00 |
| Lalique, Vase, Frosted, Spiral Ribs, Flattened Short Neck, C.1930, 8 1/4 In. | 75.00 |
| Lalique, Vase, Frosted, 7 1/8 In.                                          *Illus* | 225.00 |
| Lalique, Vase, Goldfish On Opalescent, Signed R.Lalique, 6 3/4 In. | 250.00 |
| Lalique, Vase, Indented Strips With Ladder Decoration, 6 In.High | 125.00 |
| Lalique, Vase, Inverted Pyriform, Branches & Leafage, Copper Tint, 6 1/4 In. | 160.00 |
| Lalique, Vase, Leaves In High Relief, 5 In.High | 38.50 |
| Lalique, Vase, Opalescent, Green Tinge, Relief Thistles, C.1930, 8 3/4 In. | 200.00 |
| Lalique, Vase, Ovoid, Lovebirds On Leafy Branches, Aqua & Clear, 10 1/2 In. | 225.00 |
| Lalique, Vase, Ovoid, Thistles & Foliage, Smoky, 9 In. | 160.00 |
| Lalique, Vase, Tapering Sides, Thistles & Leafage, Emerald Green, 8 3/4 In. | 550.00 |
| Lalique, Vase, Waisted Neck, Molded Ferns, 14 1/2 In.High | 200.00 |
| Lalique, Vase, 3 Relief Nudes Around Body, Different Poses, 8 1/2 In.High | 125.00 |
| Lalique, Vase, 5 Tiers Of Frosted Floral, Signed, 6 1/2 In. | 125.00 |
| Lalique, Wine Set, Overlapping Stylized Shells, Black Enamel, 10 Piece | 350.00 |
| Lalique, Wine, Cutout Dancing Figures & Flowers Stem | 38.00 |
| Lalique, Wine, Cutout Rooster Stem | 45.00 |
| Lalique, Wine, Nude Female Bacchanalian Figural Stem, Dancing On Grapes | 45.00 |
| Lalique, Wine, Nude Male Bacchanalian Figural Stem, Dancing On Grapes | 45.00 |
| Lamp, Akro, Pale Green With Caramel, 13 1/2 In.High | 18.00 |
| Lamp, Aladdin, Alacite, Bracket | 45.00 |
| Lamp, Aladdin, Alacite, Lincoln Drape | 45.00 |
| Lamp, Aladdin, Alacite, Spiral, Electric, 15 In.High, Pair | 20.00 |
| Lamp, Aladdin, Alacite, Wall, Pair | 27.50 |
| Lamp, Aladdin, Brass Fount, Model 188 | 60.00 |
| Lamp, Aladdin, Caboose, Shade, Mantle, Chimney, & Wick Trim | 42.00 |
| Lamp, Aladdin, Caramel Luster, Garland of Daisies | 16.00 |
| Lamp, Aladdin, Drape, Pink, 10 1/2 In. | 40.00 |
| Lamp, Aladdin, Green, White Shade | 135.00 |
| Lamp, Aladdin, Kerosene, Floor, Wip-O-Lipe Shade | 67.00 |
| Lamp, Aladdin, Kerosene, Green Glass | 42.50 |
| Lamp, Aladdin, Lemon Colored, Ribbed | 125.00 |
| Lamp, Aladdin, Model B, Style 104, Clear Hobnail, 1933 | 25.00 |
| Lamp, Aladdin, Model B53 | 20.00 |
| Lamp, Aladdin, Model B54 | 38.50 |
| Lamp, Aladdin, Model B81 | 45.00 |
| Lamp, Aladdin, Model B82 | 60.00 |
| Lamp, Aladdin, Model B106 | 45.00 |
| Lamp, Aladdin, Model B111 | 85.00 |
| Lamp, Aladdin, Model B112 | 110.00 |
| Lamp, Aladdin, Model B115 | 65.00 |
| Lamp, Aladdin, Model B116 | 80.00 |
| Lamp, Aladdin, Model B124 | 85.00 |

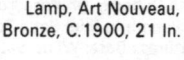

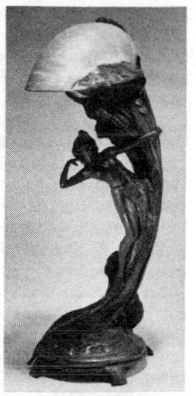

Lamp, Astral, Brass,
Glass, Electric, C.1850,
18 1/2 In.

Lalique, Vase, Frosted, 7 1/8 In.
*(See Page 290)*

| | |
|---|---:|
| Lamp, Aladdin, Model 012, Desk, Bronze Finish, Green & White Shade, Inkwells | 85.00 |
| Lamp, Aladdin, Model 5, Nickel, Table | 40.00 |
| Lamp, Aladdin, Model 11 | 25.00 |
| Lamp, Aladdin, Model 12 | 25.00 |
| Lamp, Aladdin, Model 100 | 35.00 |
| Lamp, Aladdin, Model 106 | 60.00 |
| Lamp, Aladdin, Model 716, Hanging, White Satin Shade, No.3 Extension Fixture | 135.00 |
| Lamp, Aladdin, Pink & White, Electric, 16 1/2 In.High | 25.00 |
| Lamp, Aladdin, Pink One Piece Glass Shade, Embossed Roses, Metal, 1930s, Pair | 385.00 |
| Lamp, Aladdin, Pink, White Trim, Electrified, 16 1/2 In.High | 60.00 |
| Lamp, Aladdin, Table, Brass Base, Frosted & Painted Mushroom Shade | 37.50 |
| Lamp, Aladdin, 1214-N, Hanging, No.3 Extension Fixture | 185.00 |
| Lamp, Alcohol, Embossed Porter On Sides, Amber Glass, 2 1/4 In. | 10.00 |
| Lamp, All Night, Nickel Plated, Reflector | 50.00 |
| Lamp, Amber Glass, Embossed Design Base, Burner & Chimney | 23.00 |
| Lamp, Amethyst Glass, Embossed Pattern On Square Base | 110.00 |
| Lamp, Amethyst Glass, White Enamel, Gilt | 137.50 |
| Lamp, Angle, Brass, Frosted Fonts, Blue Opalescent Chimneys | 150.00 |
| Lamp, Angle, Brass, The Angle Lamp Co., N.Y. | 150.00 |
| Lamp, Arabian Night, Cast Metal | 47.50 |
| Lamp, Art Deco, Light Fits In Jarlike Container On Green Alabaster Base | 55.00 |
| Lamp, Art Deco, Marked Frankart, Silhouette, Frosted Glass, Bronze Finish | 45.00 |
| Lamp, Art Nouveau, Bronze, C.1900, 21 In. ............................................. *Illus* | 1200.00 |
| Lamp, Art Nouveau, Draped Nude, Sunflowers, Bronzed, Spatter Glass Shade | 78.00 |
| Lamp, Art Nouveau, Helmet Shaped Shade, With Amber Jewels, Marble Base | 275.00 |
| Lamp, Art Nouveau, Metal Lady, Carved Marble, Wooden Base, 16 1/2 In.High | 90.00 |
| Lamp, Art Nouveau, Paneled Bent Glass Shade, Embossed Base, FL Cleveland | 245.00 |
| Lamp, Art Nouveau, Signed L.Beck, Bronzed, Nude With One Leg Bent, Art Glass | 125.00 |
| Lamp, Artichoke, P.& A.Mfg.Co. Burner, Miniature | 55.00 |
| Lamp, Astral, Brass, Embossed Font, 4 Camphene Burners, 8 In.High | 37.00 |
| Lamp, Astral, Brass, Glass, Electric, C.1850, 18 1/2 In. ................... *Illus* | 279.00 |
| Lamp, Astral, Cut Tulip Shape, Pair Clear Hexagonal Sandwich Candlesticks | 45.00 |
| Lamp, Astral, 8 Cut Prisms, Cut & Frosted Shade, Gold Leaf & Brass Base | 325.00 |
| Lamp, Atterbury, Black Jenny Lind Base, White On Green Font, Sept.29, 1868 | 245.00 |
| Lamp, Banquet, Brass Base Signed P.& A., Hand-Decorated Pansies, 17 1/2 In. | 150.00 |
| Lamp, Banquet, Brass, Blue House On Ribbed Milk Glass Shade, Miniature | 130.00 |
| Lamp, Banquet, Brass, Custard Glass Pieces In Stem, Floral Milk Glass Shade | 250.00 |
| Lamp, Banquet, Brass, Electric, 28 In.High | 98.00 |
| Lamp, Banquet, Cranberry Shade, Design On Brass Base, 28 In.High | 130.00 |
| Lamp, Banquet, Embossed Slip In Font, Marble Stem, Hand-Painted Globe, 1890s | 149.00 |

| | |
|---|---|
| Lamp, Banquet, Enameled Daffodils On Rose To Yellow, 11 1/2 In. | 140.00 |
| Lamp, Banquet, Feather Pattern In Blue Satin Font | 55.00 |
| Lamp, Banquet, Green & Brass Base, White Satin Globe | 250.00 |
| Lamp, Banquet, Hand-Painted Pink Roses, Open Fretwork On Font, 32 In.High | 195.00 |
| Lamp, Banquet, Marble Center Post, Britannia Base & Font, Cupids, 34 In.High | 85.00 |
| Lamp, Banquet, Oil Font, Marble Center Post, Britannia Metal Base, 2 Branch | 85.00 |
| Lamp, Banquet, Rubena Verde Ribbed Font, Brass Base, Green Onyx Stem, 19 In. | 105.00 |
| Lamp, Base, Aladdin, Hanging, White Moonstone | 40.00 |
| Lamp, Base, Blue Milk Glass Font, Mercury Glass Base, 12 In.High | 40.00 |
| Lamp, Base, Blue Opalescent Hobnail, 7 In.High | 45.00 |
| Lamp, Base, Blue, Opalescent Stripe, 9 In.High | 50.00 |
| Lamp, Base, Chamber, Pressed, Artichoke, Brass Ferrule | 40.00 |
| Lamp, Base, Columbian Exposition, Landing Of Columbus, 1492-1892 | 75.00 |
| Lamp, Base, Cosmos, Brass, Harp For Shade | 65.00 |
| Lamp, Base, Fairy, Press Cut Harvard, Receptacle Prism Underside, Pedestal | 19.00 |
| Lamp, Base, Kerosene, Double Burner, Custard Glass, Metal Base | 59.00 |
| Lamp, Base, Kerosene, Ovoid Footed Brass Base & Font, Pink Floral & Insect | 45.00 |
| Lamp, Base, Kerosene, Yellow Milk Glass, Sailboats & Windmills In Frames | 28.00 |
| Lamp, Base, Milk Glass, Burner & Wick, 10 In.High | 65.00 |
| Lamp, Base, Miniature, Bull's-Eye, Clear | 22.50 |
| Lamp, Base, Oil, Guard, Handled, Dated Sept.20, 1870, 4 1/4 In.High | 15.00 |
| Lamp, Base, Oil, Guard, Handled, Dated Sept.20, 1870, 6 In.High | 18.00 |
| Lamp, Base, Opaline, Green, Miniature | 55.00 |
| Lamp, Base, Pressed Glass, Currier & Ives, Bellaire Goblet Co., 9 In. | 35.00 |
| Lamp, Base, Satin Glass, Moire Yellow, Mother-Of-Pearl Cased, Square, 7 In. | 100.00 |
| Lamp, Base, Satin Glass, Red, Square | 30.00 |
| Lamp, Base, Wedgwood, Jasperware, Light Green, Raised White Figures | 85.00 |
| Lamp, Base, Whale Oil, Petal, Pair | 195.00 |
| Lamp, Beaded Glass, Flower Basket Shape, Glass Fruit, 9 In.High | 98.50 |
| Lamp, Beauty, Comet Type, Brass, White Beehive Shade, Lion's Head At Base | 37.50 |
| Lamp, Beauty, Embossed Comet, Brass, White Shade | 20.00 |
| Lamp, Betty, Hanging, Tin, Name Incised On Cover, 1824 | 50.00 |
| Lamp, Betty, Ipswich | 125.00 |
| Lamp, Betty, Ipswich, Tall | 275.00 |
| Lamp, Betty, Iron, Double | 12.00 |
| Lamp, Betty, Lard, Double, Iron | 12.50 |
| Lamp, Betty, Tin, Affixed To Pedestal And Saucer Base, Handle | 175.00 |
| Lamp, Betty, Tin, American, 3 X 5 X 5 In. | 125.00 |
| Lamp, Betty, Tin, Stand, Hanger, & Pick, 11 In. | 200.00 |
| Lamp, Betty, Wrought Iron, On Trammel, 28 In. | 175.00 |
| Lamp, Bisque Type, 2 Swan Handles, Clear Chimney, 6 1/2 In.High | 29.00 |
| Lamp, Blown Glass, Blue, Woman's Hand Base, Mushroom Shade | 135.00 |
| Lamp, Blown, Cranberry, Optic, Applied Clear Crimped Feet, Miniature | 30.00 |
| Lamp, Blue Daisy & Button Font, Pottery Stem, Iron Base | 47.50 |
| Lamp, Blue Glass, Daisy & Cube, Miniature | 75.00 |
| Lamp, Blue Glass, Embossed Pattern On Square Base | 110.00 |
| Lamp, Blue Milk Glass, Fired On Decoration Of Angels & Flowers | 140.00 |
| Lamp, Blue Milk Glass, Pressed Base, White Globe, 7 1/4 In. | 40.00 |
| Lamp, Blue Porcelain, Ornate Metal Base | 3.50 |
| Lamp, Blue Satin Glass, Embossed Vine & Flowers | 400.00 |
| Lamp, Boudoir, Aurene, Stick, Blue, Silver Roycroft Base | 175.00 |
| Lamp, Boudoir, Blue Jasperware Signed Adams, 7 In.High, Pair | 165.00 |
| Lamp, Bracket, Blue Milk Glass, Reflector | 60.00 |
| Lamp, Bracket, Mercury Reflector | 30.00 |
| Lamp, Bracket, Stained Glass & Bronze, Acanthus Leafage, 15 In.High | 60.00 |
| Lamp, Bracket, Tin, Handled, Reflector, Red Paint | 35.00 |
| Lamp, Bracket, W VG Co., Waterbury, Conn., Brass, Tin Reflector, 7 1/2 In. | 20.00 |
| Lamp, Bradley & Hubbard Reverse Painted Shade, Art Nouveau, Bronze Base | 200.00 |
| Lamp, Brass Base, Cranberry Font & Shade, 21 In.High | 150.00 |
| Lamp, Brass Saucer Base, Tinned, Burner & Chimney | 20.00 |
| Lamp, Brass, Double Spout, 11 1/2 In.High | 36.00 |
| Lamp, Brass, Handled, Burner & Chimney, 7 1/2 In.High | 10.00 |
| Lamp, Brass, Patent, Handled, Flat Wick, 4 1/2 X 5 In. | 10.00 |
| Lamp, Brass, The Rochester, Pewter Handles, Country Stream Scene Shade | 105.00 |
| Lamp, Bristol, Autumn Colored Flowers, Miniature | 85.00 |
| Lamp, Bristol, Gray, Blue Enameled Flowers, 4 In. | 40.00 |

| | |
|---|---|
| Lamp, Bristol, Pale Blue, Florals & Cherub, 4 1/2 In.High | 42.50 |
| Lamp, Bristol, Pale Blue, Round Base, Raised Design, 4 1/4 In. | 37.50 |
| Lamp, Bristol, White Globed Shade, Amethyst Base, Miniature | 75.00 |
| Lamp, Bristol, White, Hand-Painted Floral, Pink Lined, Miniature | 105.00 |
| Lamp, Bronze Base, Leaded Shade, Green With Pink Flowers, Yellow Centers | 325.00 |
| Lamp, Bronze, Dragon At Neck Holds Crystal Ball In Claw, Harp Finial | 125.00 |
| Lamp, Bronze, Reptile Standard, Holding Triple Chain & Green Lamp | 120.00 |
| Lamp, Buggy, Kerosene, 3 Glass Sides, Pair | 50.00 |
| Lamp, Buttercup, Cobalt Blue, Miniature | 39.50 |
| Lamp, Butterscotch Shade, Roman Key Border, Brass & Iron Base, 19 In.High | 105.00 |
| Lamp, Cameo Glass, Bronze Base, Roaring Lion, Arsall, 22 In.High | 600.00 |
| Lamp, Camphene, American Pewter, Marked Capen Molineux, N.Y., 4 In. | 125.00 |
| Lamp, Camphene, Clear Glass, Diamond Shape Base, June 26, 1883 | 22.75 |
| Lamp, Candelabra, French, Grapes, 2-Light, Amethyst, Lavender, Amber, Pair | 175.00 |
| Lamp, Candle, Art Nouveau, Brass Reliefs & Openwork, Acid Finish Shade, Pair | 85.00 |
| Lamp, Candle, Brass, Fancy Collar, Frosted Shade, 14 In. | 15.00 |
| Lamp, Candle, Carriage, Candle, 2 Red Glasses On Side, Clear Glass Front | 35.00 |
| Lamp, Candle, Ceramic Base, Cafe Scenes, Flint Shade, Hoyrup, Denmark | 20.00 |
| Lamp, Candle, Double, Painted Tin, Pierced Gallery On Shade, C.1800, 23 In. | 375.00 |
| Lamp, Candle, Filigree Shade, Beaded Fringe, 14 In. | 17.50 |
| Lamp, Candle, Hurricane, Nickel On Brass, Pink Shade, 14 In., Pair | 24.50 |
| Lamp, Candle, Sconce, Amethyst Glass, Brass, C.1850, Pair | 475.00 |
| Lamp, Candle, Spring Loaded, Brass, Frosted Shade | 85.00 |
| Lamp, Caramel Slag, Wild Rose With Bowknot, 8 1/2 In.High | 350.00 |
| Lamp, Carbide, Victorian High Wheel Bicycle | 75.00 |
| Lamp, Cased Glass, Pink, Basket Weave, Miniature | 40.00 |
| Lamp, Ceiling Fixture, Bronze, Art Deco, 5-Light | 35.00 |
| Lamp, Ceiling Fixture, White Painted Brass, Double, Glass Shades | 22.50 |
| Lamp, Ceiling, Blue Satin Shade, Enameled Floral, Brass Attachment | 37.00 |
| Lamp, Chamber, Pressed Glass, Shaped Chimney, 10 1/2 In. | 25.00 |
| Lamp, Chamber, Tin Base, "Eavinson, Snuff Me Often, For Best Light, " 6 In. | 25.00 |
| Lamp, Chamber, Tin, American, Pewter Wick Cover, 4 In. | 65.00 |
| Lamp, Chandelier, see also Steuben, Chandelier, Tiffany, Chandelier | |
| Lamp, Chandelier, Brass, Queen Anne Style, Six Arms, 15 In.Diameter | 375.00 |
| Lamp, Chandelier, Brass, Six Arms, C.1600, 50 In.Diameter | 1700.00 |
| Lamp, Chandelier, Empire Style, Gilt Metal & Cut Glass, 8-Arm, C.1890, 29 In. | 600.00 |
| Lamp, Chandelier, French, Gilt Metal, Acanthus Leaves, 6-Arm, C.1890, 37 In. | 800.00 |
| Lamp, Chandelier, Gilt Metal & Cut Glass, French, 16-Arm, C.1890, 44 1/2 In. | 500.00 |
| Lamp, Chandelier, Louis XV Style, Acanthus In Rococo Styling, Brass | 350.00 |
| Lamp, Chandelier, Napoleon III, Gilt Metal, Painted, Etched, 8-Arm, 38 In. | 650.00 |
| Lamp, Chandelier, Ormolu, Louis Philippe, C.1850, Swans, Trumpet Head, 25 In. | 325.00 |
| Lamp, Chandelier, Silver, 36 X 24 In., 4 Matching Sconces | 2500.00 |
| Lamp, Chandelier, Spherical, Beaded, Crystal, Draped Prisms, 4 Ft Around | 365.00 |
| Lamp, Chandelier, Turned Wood Center, Red Paint, 8-Arm, C.1850, 24 In. | 250.00 |
| Lamp, Chandelier, Victorian, Overlay Glass, 5-Arm, White On Emerald, 28 In. | 50.00 |
| Lamp, Chandelier, White Glass Held By 3 Iron Chains To Brass Canopy | 85.00 |
| Lamp, Chandelier, Wooden, 3 Wrought Iron Brackets, Blue Gray Paint, 12 In. | 195.00 |
| Lamp, Chandelier, Wrought Iron & Copper, Italian, 1800s, 6 Ft.3 In.Long | 210.00 |
| Lamp, Chandelier, 3-Arm, Crystal, Brass, Painted White, C.1800 | 1500.00 |
| Lamp, Chinese Export, Hand-Painted Floral On White, 9 1/2 In.High | 35.00 |
| Lamp, Clear Glass, Embossed Flowers | 40.00 |
| Lamp, Clear Pressed Glass Font, Milk Glass Base, Jeweled Shade, 12 1/4 In. | 45.00 |
| Lamp, Climax Burner, Opaline Glass Footed Base, Embossed Lilies, 11 In. | 42.00 |
| Lamp, Coach, Beveled Glass, Pair | 410.00 |
| Lamp, Coal Miner's, Brass, 8 1/2 In. | 45.00 |
| Lamp, Colza, Gilt Metal, Etched Opaque Glass Shades, Tripod, C.1850, 24 In. | 150.00 |
| Lamp, Cranberry Glass, Hornet Burner, 8 1/4 In. | 160.00 |
| Lamp, Cranberry Glass, Swirled Shade, Applied Handle | 17.50 |
| Lamp, Cranberry Stain Pattern Glass, Sawtooth & Block, Silk Shade, 23 In. | 45.00 |
| Lamp, Crusie, Holder | 48.00 |
| Lamp, Cupid, 4 Panel Slag Shade, Miniature | 30.00 |
| Lamp, Custard Glass, Embossed Diamond Point | 90.00 |
| Lamp, Cut Glass & Bronze, Rams Heads, Medallion Handles, 16 In.High | 135.00 |
| Lamp, Cut Glass, Mushroom Shade, Cornflowers, Buttons, Prisms, 12 In.High | 145.00 |
| Lamp, Cut Glass, Pinwheel & Hobstar, 1 Light, 32 Prisms, 10 In.Dome | 750.00 |
| Lamp, Cut Glass, Prisms, Harvard, Floral, Diamond, Fan, & Cane, 22 1/2 In. | 950.00 |

| | |
|---|---|
| Lamp, **Cut Glass,** Prisms, Matching Shade, 13 In.High | 145.00 |
| Lamp, **Cut Glass,** Russian, Button, Intaglio Floral, & Leaf, Pointed Shade | 1200.00 |
| Lamp, **Cut Glass,** Silver & Epergne Base, Prisms | 695.00 |
| Lamp, **Czechoslovakian Porcelain,** Beaded Fruit Basket | 89.00 |
| Lamp, **Degue,** Cameo, Red Art Deco Motif On Black, Signed, 17 In.High | 550.00 |
| Lamp, **Depression Glass,** Dolphin, Green | 35.00 |
| Lamp, **Depression Glass,** Dolphin, Pink | 35.00 |
| Lamp, **Depression Glass,** English Hobnail, Clear, Brass Burner, 9 In. | 40.00 |
| Lamp, **Depression Glass,** English Hobnail, Pink, 6 1/4 In. | 75.00 |
| Lamp, **Desk,** Emerald, Green Overlay Shade, Brass, Signed | 85.00 |
| Lamp, **Desk,** Handle, Chipped Ice Shade, Flower Band Border | 195.00 |
| Lamp, **Desk,** Multicolored Floral On Blue Glass Shade, Blue Enameled Bronze | 50.00 |
| Lamp, **Dome,** Signed G.Ve Croismore, Opalescent & Pink Ash Tone, 14 In. | 125.00 |
| Lamp, **Double Bull's-Eye,** Tin, Brass Burner, 9 1/4 In. | 300.00 |
| Lamp, **Dresden Base,** Cherubs On Brown, Quilted Yellow Satin Shade, 13 In. | 325.00 |
| Lamp, **Dresser,** Depression Glass, Colonial Lady, Pink, Pair | 40.00 |
| Lamp, **Duffner & Kimberly Style,** Gilt Bronze, Ocher & Green, C.1915, 24 In. | 600.00 |
| Lamp, **Emerald Green Honeycomb Base,** Chimney | 35.00 |
| Lamp, **Empire Style,** Bronze, Gilt Metal, Acanthus Wreath Base, C.1890, 32 In. | 90.00 |
| Lamp, **End-Of-Day,** Beaded, Ribbed, Brown & Cream, Red Splashes | 100.00 |
| Lamp, **Excelsior With Maltese Cross,** Marble Base | 60.00 |
| Lamp, **Fairy, Burmese, see Burmese , Lamp, Fairy** | |
| Lamp, **Fairy,** Artichoke Shape, Pale Frosted Green, Scalloped Top, 4 1/2 In. | 25.00 |
| Lamp, **Fairy,** Bisque Cat's, Dog's, & Owl's Heads, Glass Eyes, Lid, Triangular | 105.00 |
| Lamp, **Fairy,** Bisque Owl, Glass Eyes, Violet Painted Base | 50.00 |
| Lamp, **Fairy,** Bisque, Shaggy Dog, Open Head With Inner Candle, 3 In.High | 95.00 |
| Lamp, **Fairy,** Brass, Candleholder, Inner Candle, Jeweled Filigree Shade | 85.00 |
| Lamp, **Fairy,** Clarke Base, Amber Glass, Applied White Spiral Threading | 85.00 |
| Lamp, **Fairy,** Clarke Base, Blue Crown Top, Queen Alexandra's Coronation | 55.00 |
| Lamp, **Fairy,** Clarke Base, Cased Spatter Glass, White Lined | 85.00 |
| Lamp, **Fairy,** Clarke Base, Cranberry Glass, Applied White Spiral Threading | 85.00 |
| Lamp, **Fairy,** Clarke Base, Cranberry Glass, White Nailsea Loopings, 4 1/2 In. | 75.00 |
| Lamp, **Fairy,** Clarke Base, Monk's Head, Smiling Face, Camphor Satin Glass | 85.00 |
| Lamp, **Fairy,** Clarke Base, Monk's Head, Smiling Face, Green Satin Glass | 95.00 |
| Lamp, **Fairy,** Clarke Base, Red Satin Glass, 2 Faced Owl Shade | 70.00 |
| Lamp, **Fairy,** Clarke Base, Sapphire Blue Glass, White Nailsea Loopings | 75.00 |
| Lamp, **Fairy,** Clarke Base, Webb Burmese, 3 3/4 In.High | 135.00 |
| Lamp, **Fairy,** Clarke Base, Webb Burmese, 5 In.High | 195.00 |
| Lamp, **Fairy,** Clarke Base, White Nailsea Loopings, Cranberry, 3 1/2 In.High | 75.00 |
| Lamp, **Fairy,** Clarke Base, White Nailsea Loopings, Cranberry, 4 1/2 In.High | 85.00 |
| Lamp, **Fairy,** Clarke Base, White Spiral Threaded Cranberry Shade, 3 1/2 In. | 65.00 |
| Lamp, **Fairy,** Clarke Base, White Spiral Threaded Cranberry Shade, 5 In. | 75.00 |
| Lamp, **Fairy,** Clarke Base, Yellow Mother-Of-Pearl Satin, 4 In.High | 185.00 |
| Lamp, **Fairy,** Clarke, Amber Top, Clear Base, 5 In. | 95.00 |
| Lamp, **Fairy,** Clarke, Blue Diamond-Quilted Mother-Of-Pearl, Clear Base | 35.00 |
| Lamp, **Fairy,** Colored Jewels In Cobweb Shade, Brass Filigree Base, Handle | 57.00 |
| Lamp, **Fairy,** Cricklite, Clear Shade, Pressed Diamond Base, Clarke, Brass | 39.00 |
| Lamp, **Fairy,** English Cameo, White Overlay On Yellow To Strawberry | 2800.00 |
| Lamp, **Fairy,** Filigree Brass Shade, Jewel Inlay, Brass Cup, 4 1/2 In.High | 85.00 |
| Lamp, **Fairy,** Frosted Rigaree On Pink Satin Top, Green Leaves Feet, 5 In. | 145.00 |
| Lamp, **Fairy,** Metal, 2 Part, Jeweled Inserts | 95.00 |
| Lamp, **Fairy,** Nailsea In Cranberry & White Satin Glass, Clear Base, 6 In. | 150.00 |
| Lamp, **Fairy,** Nailsea, Blue, Ruffled Rim, Clarke Base, 6 3/4 In.High | 325.00 |
| Lamp, **Fairy,** Pyramid, Diamond Point, Shade, Amber, Clear Base, Clarke | 25.00 |
| Lamp, **Fairy,** Red Diamond Point Top, Clear Base, Signed Clarke | 35.00 |
| Lamp, **Fairy,** Ruby Glass, Clarke Base | 25.00 |
| Lamp, **Fairy,** Teapot Shape, Porcelain, Floral & Ivy | 100.00 |
| Lamp, **Fairy,** Yellow To White Frosted Glass, 3 Pieces, 9 1/4 In. High | 195.00 |
| Lamp, **Famos 120 C.P. Foreign,** Copper Base, Flowered Shade, 19 In. | 29.50 |
| Lamp, **Fat,** Phoebe, Double Pan, Hook | 30.00 |
| Lamp, **Figural Metal,** 2 Kneeling Amazons, Fayral, France, C.1920, 20 In. | 275.00 |
| Lamp, **Figural Milk Glass Stem,** Iron Base, Engraved Font & Shade, 21 In. | 30.00 |
| Lamp, **Figural Stem,** Marble Base, Engraved Glass Font & Shade, Wired, 21 In. | 32.00 |
| Lamp, **Figural,** Santa Claus, 9 3/8 In. | 700.00 |
| Lamp, **Figural,** Victory Column, Revolution Of July 1830, French Crystal | 45.00 |
| Lamp, **Findlay,** Clark Pattern Stem, 10 In.High | 39.00 |

Lamp, Finger, Beehive, Blown In The Mold, Brass Collar, Applied Handle, Flint ............ 32.00
Lamp, Finger, Miniature, Miller, Nickel Over Brass, Green Shade, Dated 1898 .............. 65.00
Lamp, Finger, Miniature, White Shade, Ornate Brass, Chimney, Dated 1897, 6 In. ......... 85.00
Lamp, Finger, Pressed Glass, 101 .............................................................................. 22.00
Lamp, Float, Double, Iron Base, Raised Insects, Glass Cups, 11 In.High ..................... 36.00
Lamp, Floor, Brass, Double Wick, Scenic & Floral Globe, 5 Ft.High ........................... 375.00
Lamp, Floor, Walnut, Wicker Shade ........................................................................... 37.50
Lamp, Fluid, Flint, Bull's-Eye & Fleur-De-Lis, Scalloped Base, 8 3/4 In. ................... 120.00
Lamp, Fluid, Milk Glass Base, Vaseline Font, Brass Collar, 11 In.High ....................... 70.00
Lamp, Fluid, Pattern Glass, Cut Glass Font, C.1850, 10 1/8 In.High, Pair ................... 60.00
Lamp, Fluid, Pressed Glass, Blue, D.C.Ripley & Co., 1840 .............................. *Illus* 175.00
Lamp, Fluid, Sandwich, Bull's-Eye & Fleur-De-Lis Font, Marble Base, Brass ............ 110.00
Lamp, Fluid, Sandwich, Bull's-Eye & Fleur-De-Lis, Opaque White & Blue ................ 850.00
Lamp, Fluid, Sandwich, Opalescent Green Loopings On Clear, Brass Collar ............. 175.00
Lamp, Fluid, Victorian, Clear Vertical Ribbed Font, Black Amethyst Base ................. 35.00
Lamp, Fluid, Victorian, Cranberry Ribbed Font, Free-Blown Opaline Base ................ 65.00
Lamp, Font, Hanging, Amber Hobnail ........................................................................ 37.50
Lamp, Font, Hanging, Diamond-Quilted Cranberry Glass ........................................... 95.00
Lamp, French, Male & Female Figures, Marble Base, Silk Shade, 30 In., Pair ........... 125.00
Lamp, Gas, Sunshine Company ................................................................................. 10.00
Lamp, Gilded Cupid, 1 Part Yellow Slag Shade ......................................................... 40.00
Lamp, Gilt Metal Base, Iridescent Glass, Scrolling & Green Feather, 13 In. ............... 85.00
Lamp, Gimbel, Brass, 5 1/2 In. .................................................................................. 17.50
Lamp, Glass Stem With Match Holder, Marked Patent Pending, 7 1/2 In. .................. 42.00
Lamp, Glass, Human Head, Atterbury, Dated 1868 .................................................... 22.00
Lamp, Globe, Engraved Warrior On Horse, Clear, 5 1/2 In. ......................................... 7.50
Lamp, Gone With The Wind, Blown Out Floral, Cherries, 19 1/2 In.High .................... 250.00
Lamp, Gone With The Wind, Blue & Red Poppies On Shade, 24 In.High ..................... 265.00
Lamp, Gone With The Wind, Indian On Top & Bottom ............................................... 350.00
Lamp, Gone With The Wind, Kerosene, Floral On Lavender & Pink, Dated 1893 ........ 210.00
Lamp, Gone With The Wind, Melon Ribbed Cranberry Shade, Flaring Brass Base ...... 225.00
Lamp, Gone With The Wind, Milk Glass, Embossed & Painted Irises, 1890 ............... 180.00
Lamp, Gone With The Wind, Milk Glass, Morning Glories, Brass Feet, Iron Base ....... 520.00
Lamp, Gone With The Wind, Ornate Brass Base, Deep Pink Roses, 24 In.High ......... 85.00
Lamp, Gone With The Wind, Pear Shape Base On Square Foot, Cranberry Shade ...... 225.00
Lamp, Gone With The Wind, Pink Floral Sprays On Yellow & Russet, 21 In. .............. 165.00
Lamp, Gone With The Wind, Pink, Blue, & Green ...................................................... 190.00
Lamp, Gone With The Wind, Red & Yellow Roses, Metal Base Signed Phoenix ......... 150.00
Lamp, Gone With The Wind, Red Satin Glass ............................................................ 395.00
Lamp, Gone With The Wind, Red Satin, Grape Pattern .............................................. 400.00
Lamp, Grease, Colored Glass ................................................................................... 55.00
Lamp, Grease, Dore Bronze, Hanging, Coiled Reptile Standard ................................. 125.00
Lamp, Grease, Iron, 4 Cornered, Stand, Crown Base ................................................ 72.00
Lamp, Green & White Overlay, 18 In.High ................................................................ 200.00
Lamp, Green Milk Glass Swan, Shade ...................................................................... 675.00
Lamp, Greensburg Glass Co., Dewdrop In Points, Dated 8/12/87 ............................. 35.00
Lamp, Gurschner Bronze Wave Base, Shell Shade, Girl Terminal, 20 1/2 In. ............. 3100.00

Lamp, Fluid, Pressed Glass, Blue, D.C.Ripley & Co., 1840

| | |
|---|---|
| Lamp, Hall, Cranberry, Inverted Thumbprint | 109.00 |
| Lamp, Hall, Green Satin Finish, Band Of Wild Geese Around Center | 109.00 |
| Lamp, Hall, Green, Frosted Band Of Dragons Around Center | 109.00 |
| Lamp, Hand, Benedict & Burnham, Brass, Handle, Chimney, Dated 1867, 10 In. | 45.00 |
| Lamp, Hand, Brass, Ring Handle, Chimney, Miniature | 12.75 |
| Lamp, Hand, Coolidge Drape, Clear, Pair | 70.00 |
| Lamp, Hand, Embossed Crow's-Foot Pattern | 22.00 |
| Lamp, Hand, Flint, Bell Shape, Applied Handle, Tooled | 23.00 |
| Lamp, Hand, Greek Key Border Around Bowl, Pedestal, High Handle | 23.00 |
| Lamp, Hand, Green Spirea Band | 50.00 |
| Lamp, Hand, Pressed Glass, Bull's-Eye & Fan, Green | 60.00 |
| Lamp, Hand, Pressed Glass, Green Spirea Band | 50.00 |
| Lamp, Hand, Pressed Glass, Heart Pattern | 20.00 |
| Lamp, Hand, Pressed Glass, Hearts | 21.00 |
| Lamp, Hand, Raised Greek Key On Round Base, Amethyst, 2 1/2 In. | 37.50 |
| Lamp, Hand, Smoke Shade, Carrying Handle On Ratchet, 8 3/4 In. | 40.00 |
| Lamp, Hand, Tole, Petticoat, Single Burner, 4 In. High | 35.00 |
| Lamp, Hand, Zipper Center, Applied Handle, Patent On Bottom | 20.00 |
| Lamp, Handel, see Handel, Lamp | |
| Lamp, Hanging Dome, Tiffany Type, Red, Green, & Amber Leaded Glass | 650.00 |
| Lamp, Hanging, Bent Glass, Gold & Green, Brass Trim | 275.00 |
| Lamp, Hanging, Blown, Smoke Bell | 110.00 |
| Lamp, Hanging, Brass Font, White Shade, 32 In. | 97.50 |
| Lamp, Hanging, Brass, Cutout Shade, 14 In. | 135.00 |
| Lamp, Hanging, Cast Iron, Clear Peg Font, Dated 1875, Milk Glass Smoke Bell | 127.50 |
| Lamp, Hanging, French, Inverted, Le Gras Type, Enameled Decoration | 290.00 |
| Lamp, Hanging, Hexagonal, Copper Frame, 6 Etched, Frosted & Clear Panels | 35.00 |
| Lamp, Hanging, Iron, 4 Color Blown Discs, Openwork Scrolls, Lantern Shape | 175.00 |
| Lamp, Hanging, Milk Glass, Font, Bristol Shade, Iron Frame & Chains, 36 In. | 74.50 |
| Lamp, Hanging, Mission, 8 Panel, Metal Basket & Grapes, Amber Art Glass | 200.00 |
| Lamp, Hanging, Ornate Frame, Matching Font & Shade, 14 In. | 325.00 |
| Lamp, Hanging, Swirled Cranberry Shade, Smoke Bell, Brass, 1889, 21 In. | 190.00 |
| Lamp, Hanging, White To Rose Shiny Peachblow Shade, Prisms | 1000.00 |
| Lamp, Heisey, Electro Portable, 1900 | 75.00 |
| Lamp, Heisey, Table, Cranberry Flashed Cut To Clear, 26 In.High | 150.00 |
| Lamp, Hobnail Font & Chimney Shade, Ribbed Bottom, 7 In. | 12.00 |
| Lamp, Hobnail On Clear Font & Shade, Pedestal Base, Miniature | 55.00 |
| Lamp, Hurricane, Clear, "soft As Silk Flour, " Pair | 10.00 |
| Lamp, Hurricane, Cranberry Cut To Clear Shade, 8 Teardrop Prisms, Pair | 63.00 |
| Lamp, Hurricane, Cranberry, Etched & Cut To Clear, Bobeches & Prisms, Pair | 100.00 |
| Lamp, Hurricane, Crystal Base, Cranberry Shade, 14 In.High | 10.00 |
| Lamp, Hurricane, Etched, Prisms, Clear, Pair | 30.00 |
| Lamp, Hurricane, Hobnail Base, Paneled Red Glass, Trumpet Shade, 16 In., Pair | 35.00 |
| Lamp, Icon, Hanging, Frosted Cranberry 6 In. Globe | 35.00 |
| Lamp, Iron Base, 14 In.To Top Of Burner | 24.50 |
| Lamp, Iron Bracket, Glass Font, Mercury Reflector | 55.00 |
| Lamp, Jefferson, Table, Red Poppies On Linenfold Type Yellow | 350.00 |
| Lamp, Jeweler's, Cobalt, Brass Holder, Patent Sept.14, 1880 | 17.50 |
| Lamp, Juno, Brass, Protruding Lady's Head, White Opalescent Shades | 140.00 |
| Lamp, Kerosene, Banquet, Amber Optic Globe, Brass Legs, Marble Stem, C.1890 | 175.00 |
| Lamp, Kerosene, Banquet, Pewter Base, Dragon's Head On Sides, Ruby Shade | 300.00 |
| Lamp, Kerosene, Beaded Swirl, Miniature, C.1890 | 59.00 |
| Lamp, Kerosene, Brass Relfector, Miniature, C.1890 | 39.00 |
| Lamp, Kerosene, Brass, Cone Shape, 4 In.High | 6.00 |
| Lamp, Kerosene, Bubble Glass, Pink, Miniature | 12.50 |
| Lamp, Kerosene, Clear Diamond Lattice, Iron Base, Flowered Design, 9 1/2 In. | 25.00 |
| Lamp, Kerosene, Clear Glass, 3 Mold, Miniature, C.1890 | 79.00 |
| Lamp, Kerosene, End Of Day, Red, Yellow, Orange, 5 In.High | 50.00 |
| Lamp, Kerosene, Flint, Hamilton With Leaf, Scalloped Foot | 55.00 |
| Lamp, Kerosene, Fluted Blue To Clear Thumbprint Shade, Iron Base, C.1890 | 69.00 |
| Lamp, Kerosene, Frosted Etched Font, Lady's Head, Chimney | 36.00 |
| Lamp, Kerosene, Hanging, Embossed Kosmos, Clear Base, Brass Burner | 65.00 |
| Lamp, Kerosene, Marked Acorn Mfg.Co., Miniature | 8.50 |
| Lamp, Kerosene, Pewter Lady, Head To Waist, Glass Font, Brass & Onyx Base | 88.00 |
| Lamp, Kerosene, Pink Satin Font, Art Nouveau Copper, Tulip Shade, C.1870 | 249.00 |
| Lamp, Kerosene, Pressed Glass, Two Panel, Amber | 32.00 |

| | |
|---|---|
| Lamp, Kerosene, Pressed Glass, Zippered Loop | 34.00 |
| Lamp, Kerosene, Pressed, Columbian Coin, Skirtlike Camphor Shade | 115.00 |
| Lamp, Kerosene, Sandwich Star Bowl, White Satin Ball In Brass Stem | 88.00 |
| Lamp, Kerosene, Square Iron Base, Metal Girl & Dog Column, Frosted Font | 20.00 |
| Lamp, Kerosene, Stein, Satin Fleur-De-Lis Globe, Brass Font, C.1890, 13 In. | 159.00 |
| Lamp, Kerosene, Table, Brass, Ruby Thumbprint Shade, 19 In. | 55.00 |
| Lamp, Kerosene, Teardrops & Eyewinker, Findlay | 35.00 |
| Lamp, Kerosene, Wedding Ring Pattern, Brass Standard, Marble Base | 85.00 |
| Lamp, Kosmos Burner, Portrait Base, Cranberry Shade, Beaded Fringe, 15 In. | 165.00 |
| Lamp, Lacemaker's Type, Masks & Flowers On Square Base, Lacy, Clear | 275.00 |
| Lamp, Lacemaker's, Free-Blown, Globe Type Reservoir, C.1750, 8 3/4 In. | 125.00 |
| Lamp, Lard Oil, Kinnear Patent, Tin | 90.00 |
| Lamp, Leaded Geometric Shade, Caramel, Green, Ruby, & Butterscotch, 21 In. | 210.00 |
| Lamp, Lithophane, Woman Base, 3 Panels & 3 Caramel Glass Panels | 325.00 |
| Lamp, Little Buttercup, Amethyst, Miniature | 50.00 |
| Lamp, Loom Light, Adjustable, Hanging, Candle & Rush | 310.00 |
| Lamp, Lucerna, Miniature, 8 1/2 In. | 2.00 |
| Lamp, Manilla, Patent, Brass Plated Base & Handle, Cobalt, Miniature | 30.00 |
| Lamp, Marked Glo, Milk Glass Shade, Clear Base | 50.00 |
| Lamp, Marriage, Match Holder Between Fonts, Milk Glass Stem, Blue & White | 225.00 |
| Lamp, Marriage, Signed Ripley, Twin Font, Clambroth Dome Base & Shaft, 1870 | 475.00 |
| Lamp, Match Holder, Sapphire Blue Glass, Ribbed Font, Basket Weave Holder | 65.00 |
| Lamp, Melon Ribbed Base & Shade, Roses & Pansies, White & Green, 16 In.High | 95.00 |
| Lamp, Milk Glass Font, Repousse Tole Sconce | 45.00 |
| Lamp, Milk Glass Owl, Fired On Green Paint | 260.00 |
| Lamp, Milk Glass, Basket Weave Base, Brown Paint On Pineapple Globe | 65.00 |
| Lamp, Milk Glass, Block, Miniature | 50.00 |
| Lamp, Milk Glass, Blue, Square Base, Raised Design, 4 X 3 In. | 37.50 |
| Lamp, Milk Glass, Embossed Basket Of Flowers, Cream Paint, Gilt Embossing | 85.00 |
| Lamp, Milk Glass, Fire On Flowers On Base, Plain Shade, Miniature | 35.00 |
| Lamp, Milk Glass, Glass Shade, Miniature | 45.00 |
| Lamp, Milk Glass, Match Holder, Ribbed Font, Basket Weave Holder | 95.00 |
| Lamp, Milk Glass, Melon Ribbed, Fancy Bordered, Miniature | 25.00 |
| Lamp, Milk Glass, Pear Shape Font, Harp Finial, Ribbed Square Fluted Base | 85.00 |
| Lamp, Milk Glass, Windmill In Blue, Miniature | 60.00 |
| Lamp, Milk Glass, Yellow & Gilt Maltese Cross Pattern | 95.00 |
| Lamp, Millefiori, Urn Shape, Art Nouveau, C.1915, 15 In.High | 145.00 |
| Lamp, Miller, Tin, Handled, Sunray, 8 X 3 1/4 In. | 8.00 |
| Lamp, Miller, 6 Acid Etched Palm Trees Panels, 14 1/2 In.High | 95.00 |
| Lamp, Miner's, Auto Lite, Brass, 3 1/2 In. | 10.00 |
| Lamp, Miner's, Brass, 4 In. | 12.00 |
| Lamp, Miner's, Cap, Tin & Brass | 15.00 |
| Lamp, Miner's, Carbide, Brass | 9.75 |
| Lamp, Miner's, Gimble, Iron | 58.00 |
| Lamp, Miner's, Monongahela, Pa., Washinton Co., Patent July 12, 1904 | 12.00 |
| Lamp, Miniature, Blue Milk Glass, Enamel Floral Decoration, Pair | 160.00 |
| Lamp, Miniature, Brass Burner Marked P.L.S.Mfg.Co., Acorn, 8 In.High | 22.50 |
| Lamp, Miniature, Bull's-Eye | 25.00 |
| Lamp, Miniature, Butterscotch Blown-Out Plumes | 195.00 |
| Lamp, Miniature, Clean Pressed Glass, Chimney, 7 In.High | 18.00 |
| Lamp, Miniature, Clear Beaded Swirl, Pair | 57.00 |
| Lamp, Miniature, Clear Glass, Swirled Design, Metal Handle, 6 In. | 20.00 |
| Lamp, Miniature, Clear, Swirled Yellow Frosted Base & Round Top | 22.50 |
| Lamp, Miniature, Cobalt Blue, Marked Handy | 28.75 |
| Lamp, Miniature, Cobalt, Nutmeg, Brass Band & Handle, Chimney | 25.00 |
| Lamp, Miniature, Coin Spot, Sapphire Blue | 85.00 |
| Lamp, Miniature, Cosmos, Milk Glass, Pink Border On Base & Shade | 132.00 |
| Lamp, Miniature, Crystal, Footed Ball Base & Cone, Ribbed Clear & Red Top | 13.00 |
| Lamp, Miniature, Crystal, Raised Flowers, Painted, Gold, Red, & Black | 43.00 |
| Lamp, Miniature, Flute & Hobnail | 20.00 |
| Lamp, Miniature, Gray Elephant With Lavender Basket, Peachblow Type Shade | 250.00 |
| Lamp, Miniature, Greek Key, Clear, Floral Painted Chimney | 32.00 |
| Lamp, Miniature, Hand-Painted Bird On Rose Base, Chimney | 80.00 |
| Lamp, Miniature, Lincoln Drape, Clear Font, Frosted Half Shade | 45.00 |
| Lamp, Miniature, Little Buttercup, Amethyst, Burner & Chimney | 45.00 |
| Lamp, Miniature, Milk Glass, Vine Decoration, Chimney, 9 1/2 In.High | 39.00 |

Lamp, **Miniature**, Nutmeg Burner, Embossed Brass Reflector ............... 39.00
Lamp, **Miniature**, Octagonal Shape, Opaque White ........................ 70.00
Lamp, **Miniature**, Red Bull's-Eye, Burner & Chimney ..................... 27.50
Lamp, **Miniature**, Rochester, Nickel Plate ............................. 45.00
Lamp, **Miniature**, Royal Key, Clear, Chimney, 6 In.High ................ 15.00
Lamp, **Miniature**, Satin Glass, Red, 5 In.High ......................... 60.00
Lamp, **Miniature**, Swirl, Squeeze Base, Chimney ........................ 15.00
   Lamp, **Mt.Washington, see Mt.Washington, Lamp**
Lamp, **Nailsea**, Red & White, Clear Handle, Miniature .................. 85.00
Lamp, **Narcissus**, Green & White, Handled, Signed ...................... 450.00
Lamp, **Nelly Bly**, Miniature .......................................... 65.00
Lamp, **New England Glass Co.**, House, Water, & Boat Scene, C.1880, 19 In. ... 165.00
Lamp, **Night-Light**, Pressed Glass, Stars & Stripes, Advertising ....... 30.00
Lamp, **Night-Light**, Stars & Stripes, Clear ........................... 25.00
Lamp, **Night-Light**, Stars & Stripes, Dark Green ...................... 30.00
Lamp, **Night-Light**, Stars & Stripes, Emerald Green ................... 30.00
Lamp, **Night-Light**, Tea Warmer, Frosted Insert, Footed Frame, Bail Handle ... 35.00
Lamp, **Night-Light**, Tiffany Style, Iridescent, Optic, Bronze, C.1910, Pair ... 125.00
Lamp, **Nursing**, Pap, Tin ............................................. 55.00
Lamp, **Nutmeg Burner**, Pressed Bar & Diasy, Miniature ................. 28.50
Lamp, **Nutmeg**, Cobalt Base, Brass Band & Handle, Milk Glass Globe Shade ... 58.00
Lamp, **Oil**, Aqua, Ball Shape, Bubbly, Tavern Scene, Brass Fittings, Mexico ... 12.00
Lamp, **Oil**, Ball Shaped Ribbed Mercury Base, Umbrella Shade, Miniature ... 15.00
Lamp, **Oil**, Brass Cap & Hanger, 3 1/2 In. ........................... 25.00
Lamp, **Oil**, Brass Font, Scenic Mushroom Shade, Cottages, Mountains, 18 In. ... 189.00
Lamp, **Oil**, Bristol, Blue, Blown & Molded, Hand Base, Mushroom Shade, 24 In. ... 150.00
Lamp, **Oil**, Columbian Coin Glass, Burner & Chimney ................... 55.00
Lamp, **Oil**, Coolidge Drape Font, Stem, & Base, Burner & Chimney, 5 In.Diameter ... 27.00
Lamp, **Oil**, Coolidge Drape Font, Stem, & Base, Burner & Chimney, 7 In.Diameter ... 29.00
Lamp, **Oil**, Cranberry Glass Font, Fluted Baccarat Shade, Brass Base, Florals ... 265.00
Lamp, **Oil**, Enameled Cameo, Cosmos Burner, Iron Base, Bronze Chestnuts, Enamel ... 125.00
Lamp, **Oil**, Flint, Clambroth, 15 In.High ............................. 110.00
Lamp, **Oil**, Flint, Fine Rib, Applied Handle, 13 In. .................. 24.00
Lamp, **Oil**, Flint, Handled, Marked Oil Guard, 1870, 13 In. ........... 23.00
Lamp, **Oil**, Glass, 8 Sided, Block, Patent 1878, Chimney & Burner ..... 30.00
Lamp, **Oil**, Green Glass, 12 Sided, Raised Panels, Wired .............. 20.00
Lamp, **Oil**, Hand, Oil Guard Type, Fluted Base, Dated Sept.20, 1870 ... 20.00
Lamp, **Oil**, Hanging, Prisms, Apple Blossoms On Aqua, Cutout Frame .... 295.00
Lamp, **Oil**, Hanging, Prisms, Cutout Butterflies, Apple Blossoms On Aqua ... 295.00
Lamp, **Oil**, Milk Glass, Painted Morning Glories, Miniature ........... 60.00
Lamp, **Oil**, Milk Glass, Paneled Pansy, Embossed, Beads & Scrolls ..... 75.00
Lamp, **Oil**, Milk Glass, Urn Shape, Embossed Leaves & Shells, 6 1/2 In. ... 55.00
Lamp, **Oil**, Miniature, Milk Glass, Hobnail & Spiral Band Base, 8 In.High ... 22.00
Lamp, **Oil**, Napoleon III, Brass, Repousse Acanthus, C.1890, 20 In. ... 50.00
Lamp, **Oil**, Noxall, Milk Glass, 3 Embossed Feathers .................. 15.00
Lamp, **Oil**, Nutmeg, Cobalt Blue, Brass Band & Handle ................. 15.00
Lamp, **Oil**, Paneled Wheat On Round Font, Stem, & Base, Burner & Chimney ... 28.00
Lamp, **Oil**, Peanut, Clear, Brass, Pottery, & Iron Stem & Base, Goat Painting ... 60.00
Lamp, **Oil**, Peanut, Handled, 6 1/4 In. ............................... 18.00
Lamp, **Oil**, Pressed Glass, Beaded Rim & Base, Rope Handle, 13 In. .... 16.00
Lamp, **Oil**, Pressed Glass, Coolidge Drape, Handled, 13 In. ........... 23.00
Lamp, **Oil**, Pressed Glass, Embossed Rosettes & Fans, Handled, 13 In. ... 21.00
Lamp, **Oil**, Pressed Glass, Hearts, Handled, Footed, 13 In. ........... 20.00
Lamp, **Oil**, Pressed Glass, Reversed Teardrops, Handled, 13 In. ....... 18.00
Lamp, **Oil**, Pressed Glass, Ribbed & Veined Leaves, Handled, 13 In. ... 22.00
Lamp, **Oil**, Pressed Glass, Star Bottom, Applied Handle, 13 In. ....... 16.00
Lamp, **Oil**, Ripley, Double Handled, 1868, 13 In. .................... 25.00
Lamp, **Oil**, Russian, Brass, Glass Shade, C.1890, 21 In., Pair ........ 100.00
Lamp, **Oil**, Sandwich, Clambroth Base, Stars On Font, C.1873, 9 In.High ... 65.00
Lamp, **Oil**, Sandwich, Flint, Clear Ribbed Swag Font, Opalescent Base ... 26.00
Lamp, **Oil**, Sandwich, Thumbprint Font, Brass Stem, Marble Base, Patent 1870 ... 52.00
Lamp, **Oil**, Shasta Daisies On Yellow To Burnt Orange, Double Burner ... 125.00
Lamp, **Oil**, Slate Base, Sandwich Font, Brass Fittings, Blue Overlay Stem ... 98.00
Lamp, **Oil**, Star Impressions In Base, Dome Stem, Glass Font, Burner, Chimney ... 16.00
Lamp, **Oil**, Table, Milk Glass Base, Brass Connector, Clear Font ...... 45.00
Lamp, **Oil**, Tin, Brass Burner & Nameplate, New England Gas Light Co., 3 In. ... 30.00

| | |
|---|---:|
| Lamp, Oil, Tin, Ring Handle, Dated 1867 | 8.50 |
| Lamp, Oil, Torch & Wreath, 16 In. | 27.50 |
| Lamp, Oil, Triple Overlay, Rose, White, & Clear, 14 In., Pair | 1800.00 |
| Lamp, Oil, Victorian Cherub Design, Shade, Electrified | 145.00 |
| Lamp, Oil, White Flint Base, Blackberry Design, Blown Font, 10 1/2 In.High | 37.50 |
| Lamp, Oil, Yellow Goofus Glass | 80.00 |
| Lamp, Ormolu, Louis XVI Style, Acanthus Leaves, Interlacing Ribbons, 24 In | 175.00 |
| Lamp, P & A Mfg.Co., Ruby, 8 1/2 In. | 20.00 |
| Lamp, P.& A.Mfg. Burner, Acanthus Leaf, Pink Globe, White & Gold Base, 8 In. | 65.00 |
| Lamp, Pairpoint, see Pairpoint, Lamp | |
| Lamp, Pan-American Exposition, Blue Fired On Ground | 250.00 |
| Lamp, Pan, Wick Trough, Brass, Open | 65.00 |
| Lamp, Parade, Tin, Swinging, Handle, 5 In.High | 19.00 |
| Lamp, Pedestal, Swinging Font, Signed Frowo, German Made, 7 3/4 In. | 15.00 |
| Lamp, Peg, Blue Bubbly Glass, Melon Ribbed, Brass Candlestick, Pair | 195.00 |
| Lamp, Peg, Clarke's Cricklite, Burmese, 5 In. | 165.00 |
| Lamp, Peg, Free-Blown, Ruby Glass, For Use In Candlesticks, Pair | 180.00 |
| Lamp, Peg, Green Art Glass Font, Gold Enamel, Satin Finish | 85.00 |
| Lamp, Peg, Overlay, Light Blue & Clear | 350.00 |
| Lamp, Peg, White Satin Glass, Hand-Painted Gold Ribbons & Flowers, Pair | 235.00 |
| Lamp, Pewter, see Pewter, Lamp | |
| Lamp, Pewter Base, Angles & Flowers, Opalescent Swirl Shade, 19 In.High | 95.00 |
| Lamp, Phoebe, Double, Wrought Iron, Ram's Horn, American, 7 1/2 In. | 115.00 |
| Lamp, Pig, Tin, Food Warmer, Brass Snuffers, 8 In. | 300.00 |
| Lamp, Pink & Frosted Bristol Vase, Ruffled Top, Gold & Enamel, 31 In.High | 75.00 |
| Lamp, Pink Cased Glass, Embossed Acanthus, Umbrella Shade, 8 1/2 In. | 130.00 |
| Lamp, Porcelain Elephant Base, Green Tiffany Type Shade | 90.00 |
| Lamp, Porcelain Mother Cat & Umbrella, Blue Milk Glass Shade, Glass Eyes | 110.00 |
| Lamp, Porcelain Owl, Glass Eyes, Pale Green Overlay Shade & Base, 7 In. | 95.00 |
| Lamp, Pressed Glass, Bellflower, Single Vine, Scalloped Base, Flint | 95.00 |
| Lamp, Pressed Glass, Buckle Pattern, Milk Glass Base | 60.00 |
| Lamp, Pressed Glass, Buckle, Clambroth Base | 70.00 |
| Lamp, Pressed Glass, Bull's-Eye & Fleur-De-Lis, Marble Base | 64.00 |
| Lamp, Pressed Glass, Columbian Coin | 77.50 |
| Lamp, Pressed Glass, Currier & Ives, 8 In.High | 32.50 |
| Lamp, Pressed Glass, Fine Rib, 6 1/2 In.High | 34.00 |
| Lamp, Pressed Glass, Flint, Bull's-Eye & Fleur-De-Lis, Marble Base, C.1850 | 85.00 |
| Lamp, Pressed Glass, Lincoln Drape, Miniature | 47.50 |
| Lamp, Pressed Glass, Moon, Star, & Punty | 125.00 |
| Lamp, Pressed Glass, Peacock Feather, Wired, 10 In. | 39.50 |
| Lamp, Pressed Glass, Sparking, Crimped Handle | 24.50 |
| Lamp, Pressed Glass, Torpedo, Patent On Base & Bowl, 8 In. | 40.00 |
| Lamp, Pressed, Daisy, Burner & Chimney | 34.00 |
| Lamp, Pressed, Maltese Cross With Maltese Cross, Marble Base | 60.00 |
| Lamp, Pressed, Fleur-De-Lis & Drape, Collared Base, Handled, 4 In. | 25.00 |
| Lamp, Pressed, Fleur-De-Lis & Drape, Collared Base, Handled, 4 3/4 In | 30.00 |
| Lamp, Pressed, Greek Key Base, Burner & Chimney | 19.00 |
| Lamp, Pressed, Peanut, Electrified, Shade | 42.00 |
| Lamp, Priest's, Brass, Engraved Decoration & Initials, Dutch, C.1750 | 125.00 |
| Lamp, Rayo Type, "The Jr.Rochester Pat.1896, " Ruby Mushroom Shade, 12 In. | 55.00 |
| Lamp, Rayo Type, Fruit Painted On Inside Of Satin Glass Shade, 11 In. | 75.00 |
| Lamp, Rayo, Brass, Cream Shade, Cap Marked B & H, 9 1/2 In. | 25.00 |
| Lamp, Rayo, Brass, Victorian, Quilted, Amber Petticoat Shade, Dated 1882 | 100.00 |
| Lamp, Red Satin Glass, Beaded Drape | 165.00 |
| Lamp, Red Satin Glass, Miniature | 80.00 |
| Lamp, Rembrandt, Hammered Brass, 2-Light, Electric | 47.50 |
| Lamp, Rushlight & Candleholder, Pyramid, Wooden Bottom | 160.00 |
| Lamp, Rushlight With Holder, Dated 1721, 8 In. | 235.00 |
| Lamp, Rushlight, Wrought Iron, Wood Base, 30 In. | 65.00 |
| Lamp, Sanctuary, Brass, Cranberry Font, 38 In. | 97.50 |
| Lamp, Sandwich Glass, Beehive, Horizontal Ribbing, Elliptical Font | 45.00 |
| Lamp, Sandwich Glass, Heart Pattern | 50.00 |
| Lamp, Sandwich Glass, Honeycomb Font, Brass Stem, Marble Base, Pair | 155.00 |
| Lamp, Sandwich Glass, Opalescent Font & Base, Brass Fixtures, 9 In.High | 45.00 |
| Lamp, Sandwich Glass, Opalescent, Brass Fixtures, Marble Base, 9 1/2 In. | 65.00 |
| Lamp, Sandwich Glass, Sweetheart, Snuffer | 250.00 |

Lamp, Sandwich, Blue Overlay In Mirror Pattern, Brass Stem, Marble, Pair ............... 550.00
Lamp, Sandwich, Flint, Opal Baroque Base, Blue Marbleized Font, 17 1/2 In. ........ 38.00
Lamp, Sandwich, Flint, Square Stepped Base, Etched & Cut Font, Brass Collar ........... 90.00
Lamp, Sandwich, Green Overlay Mirror Pattern, Pear Shape Font, Brass Collar ............. 300.00
Lamp, Sandwich, Smocking ....................................................... 95.00
    Lamp, Satin Glass, see Satin Glass, Lamp
Lamp, Sconce, Rock Crystal & Cut Glass, Ormolu, Five Light, Pair ................ 1400.00
Lamp, Sconce, Wall, Charles X, Ormolu, 4-Light, C.1890, 25 1/2 In., Pair ........... 850.00
Lamp, Shade, Carnival Glass, Marigold, Signed Nuart ........................... 20.00
Lamp, Ship's, Alcohol, Horn Handle Tipped In Sterling Silver, Miniature ............... 52.50
Lamp, Signed Moe Bridges, Painted Scene ....................................... 450.00
Lamp, Skater's, Brass, Chain & Ring, Dated Dec.24, 1867 ......................... 45.00
Lamp, Skater's, Signed U.S., Brass, Tubular, 12 In. ............................... 65.00
Lamp, Slag, Chocolate, Wild Rose & Bowknot, Greentown ...................... 480.00
Lamp, Slag, Green, 1910 Wiring, Pair .......................................... 49.00
Lamp, Sleigh, Brass, October 28th, '79, Persimmon Fired On Shade ............... 210.00
Lamp, Solar Carbide, Red & Green Bull's-Eyes, 7 In.High, Pair ..................... 30.00
Lamp, Sparking, Glass Bell Shape, Burner ...................................... 46.00
Lamp, Sparking, Pewter, Saucer Base, Handle ................................... 125.00
Lamp, Sparking, Sun Colored Purple Glass, 4 In. ................................ 45.00
Lamp, Sperm Oil, Tin, Blue Paint ............................................. 45.00
Lamp, Stained Glass & Bronze, Dome Shade Of Green Tiles, 26 In.High ............. 650.00
Lamp, Stained Glass & Bronze, Dragonflies In Red, Bigelow & Kennard, 24 In. ....... 750.00
Lamp, Stained Glass & Bronze, Ocher Tile Shade, Anemones, 24 In.High ........... 475.00
Lamp, Student, Brass, American ............................................. 185.00
Lamp, Student, Brass, Green Shade, Patent Dates 1870-1888, Electrified ............ 155.00
Lamp, Student, Brass, Milk Glass Shade, Wired ................................. 210.00
Lamp, Student, Brass, Single, White Shade, Dated ............................... 125.00
Lamp, Student, Brass, White Bristol Shade, Adjustable Screw, 15 In.High ............ 195.00
Lamp, Student, Single, Brass, R.Douglas & Co., N.Y. ............................ 185.00
Lamp, Student, Single, Green Ribbed Shade, Manhattan Brass Co., May '97 ......... 175.00
Lamp, Student's, Single, Shade, Wired, C.1930 ................................. 75.00
Lamp, Sweetheart Pattern, Green, 10 In.High ................................... 85.00
Lamp, Swirled Font & Chimney, 7 In. .......................................... 5.00
Lamp, Table, Art Nouveau, Signed Rainaud, 2-Light, Bent Glass Panels, 1944 ........ 37.50
Lamp, Table, Bradley & Hubbard, Enamel Base, Handel Shade, Green With Roses ....... 275.00
Lamp, Table, Indian Warrior, Brass, Frosted Handel Shade, Woodland Scene .......... 350.00
    Lamp, Tiffany, see Tiffany, Lamp
Lamp, Tiffany Type, Caramel Slag Shade, 8 Panels, 13 In.Diameter ................ 165.00
Lamp, Tiffany Type, Desk, Plain Brass Base, Green Dome Shade, 15 In. High ......... 75.00
Lamp, Tiffany Type, Green & White Paneled Red Squares, Brass Base ............... 350.00
Lamp, Tiffany Type, Metal Base, Dome Shade, Marble Glass, Tan & Brown, 20 In. ..... 180.00
Lamp, Time, Clear, Milk Glass Beehive Shape ................................... 105.00
Lamp, Tin, Handled, Brass Tube Burner, 4 1/2 X 5 In. ............................ 10.00
Lamp, Tin, Patented 1858, 7 In. .......................................... *Illus* 10.00
Lamp, Tree Trunk Base, Decorated & Threaded Shade, 7 In.Diameter ............... 295.00
Lamp, Ufford Patent, 1851 .................................................. 195.00
Lamp, Vapo-Cresolene, Milk Glass Chimney, Patent 1881 & 1895 ...... 11.75 To 25.00
Lamp, Vapolene, Pressed Glass ............................................... 25.00
Lamp, Vigil Light, Free-Blown Clear, Expanded Diamond, Folded Rim, 3 1/4 In. ...... 22.00
Lamp, Wall Bracket, Mercury Reflector, Dated ................................. 31.00
Lamp, Wall Fixture, Brass, Gold Lined Calcite Shade ............................ 42.00
Lamp, Wall Light, Louis XV Style, Ormolu, 3-Arm, C.1850, 23 In., Pair ............. 450.00
Lamp, Wall, Tin, Round, Reflector ............................................ 27.00
Lamp, Walt Disney, Figural, Dopey, Snow White & Dwarfs Shade, 1930s ............ 35.00
Lamp, Whale Oil, Bellflower, Pressed Glass .................................... 115.00
Lamp, Whale Oil, Blown & Pressed, Sandwich, Flint ............................. 70.00
Lamp, Whale Oil, Blown Font, Pressed Pedestal, Pewter Collar, Brass, C.1830 ....... 67.50
Lamp, Whale Oil, Blown Font, Stepped Pressed Glass Turtle Base, 4 3/4 In. ......... 45.00
Lamp, Whale Oil, Blown Tumbler With Pierced Cone Top, Drop ................... 160.00
Lamp, Whale Oil, Brass, C.1825, 10 In., Pair .......................... *Illus* 200.00
Lamp, Whale Oil, Brass, Handled, 3 1/4 In.High Base ........................... 10.00
Lamp, Whale Oil, Brass, Lemon Top, Burner, 8 1/4 In. High, Pair ................. 80.00
Lamp, Whale Oil, Brass, 1 Burner, 7 In.High ................................... 90.00
Lamp, Whale Oil, Brass, 2 Burner, 7 1/2 In.High ................................ 86.00
Lamp, Whale Oil, Brown & Pressed, Double Wafer Connection .................... 65.00

Lamp, Tin, Patented 1858, 7 In.
(See Page 300)

Lamp, Whale Oil, Brass,
C.1825, 10 In., Pair
(See Page 300)

| | |
|---|---:|
| Lamp, Whale Oil, Burner On Candlesticks, Japanned Saucer Base | 75.00 |
| Lamp, Whale Oil, Cast Brass, Slender Stem, Conical Cover, Saucer Base, 7 In. | 48.00 |
| Lamp, Whale Oil, Clear Blown Font, Paneled Pressed Glass Base, 7 In. High | 15.00 |
| Lamp, Whale Oil, Copper, Oblong, Handle, Signed | 72.00 |
| Lamp, Whale Oil, Elliptical Font, Flange Feet, Flint, 5 3/4 In., Pair | 55.00 |
| Lamp, Whole Oil, Engraved Glass, Applied Handle, 4 1/2 In. High | 85.00 |
| Lamp, Whale Oil, Flint Glass, Brass Column, Marble Base, 9 1/2 In. | 115.00 |
| Lamp, Whale Oil, Flint, Blown Font, 3 Step Molded Base | 31.00 |
| Lamp, Whale Oil, Flint, Bull's-Eye, Brass Collar, Wafer Connection, 8 In. | 70.00 |
| Lamp, Whale Oil, Flint, Excelsior With Maltese Cross, 2 Prong Burner, Pair | 195.00 |
| Lamp, Whale Oil, Flint, Giant Sawtooth, Brass Collar, 6 Sided Base, 10 In. | 90.00 |
| Lamp, Whale Oil, Flint, Gothic Font, Hexagonal Stem & Base | 31.00 |
| Lamp, Whale Oil, Flint, Prism Font, 6 Sided, Threaded Pewter Top, 10 1/2 In. | 50.00 |
| Lamp, Whale Oil, Flint, Ribbed 4 Sided Font, 8 Sided Stem, Square Base | 37.00 |
| Lamp, Whale Oil, Flint, Star Font, Hexagonal Stem & Base | 31.00 |
| Lamp, Whale Oil, Flint, Waffle & Thumbprint On Font & Base | 38.00 |
| Lamp, Whale Oil, Giant Sawtooth, Flint, Wafer Connection, Brass Collar | 85.00 |
| Lamp, Whale Oil, Giant Sawtooth, Marble Base, Pair | 150.00 |
| Lamp, Whale Oil, Hand, American Shield | 50.00 |
| Lamp, Whale Oil, McKearin 194, No.1, Sandwich, Acanthus Leaf, White Font | 400.00 |
| Lamp, Whale Oil, Miner's, Betty, Iron | 78.00 |
| Lamp, Whale Oil, Miner's, To Hook On Cap | 20.00 |
| Lamp, Whale Oil, Miniature, Clear, Round Scalloped Step Down Base | 65.00 |
| Lamp, Whale Oil, Oven, 2 Burner | 85.00 |
| Lamp, Whale Oil, Petticoat, Double Burner, Tin, Handle & Peg, 5 In.High | 50.00 |
| Lamp, Whale Oil, Petticoat, Tin, 1 Burner | 78.00 |
| Lamp, Whale Oil, Pewter, Attributed To Dunham, 8 In. | 295.00 |
| Lamp, Whale Oil, Pewter, Marked Lampe Perfection Etain Fin Garanti, No.3 | 110.00 |
| Lamp, Whale Oil, Pewter, Rufus Dunham, Westbrook, Me., C.1840, 6 In., Pair | 650.00 |
| Lamp, Whale Oil, Pressed Glass, Flattened Sawtooth | 50.00 |
| Lamp, Whale Oil, Pressed Glass, Moon & Star | 38.50 |
| Lamp, Whale Oil, Pressed Glass, 2 Wick Burner, 7 1/2 In. | 42.50 |
| Lamp, Whale Oil, Sandwich Glass, Acanthus Leaf, White Font, McKearin 383 | 395.00 |
| Lamp, Whale Oil, Sandwich, Flint, Heart, 2 Prong Burner, 11 1/2 In., Pair | 185.00 |
| Lamp, Whale Oil, Sandwich, Pear Shape Font, Pewter Collar & Burner | 50.00 |
| Lamp, Whale Oil, Saucer Type, Handle, 2 Round Burners, Dark Brown, 6 In. | 115.00 |
| Lamp, Whale Oil, Tin, Bucket Font, Saucer Base | 60.00 |
| Lamp, Whale Oil, Tin, Cone Top Snuffer | 175.00 |
| Lamp, Whale Oil, Tin, Conical Foot Supports Tank | 85.00 |
| Lamp, Whale Oil, Tin, Hinged Wind Cover, Mica Window, Blue Paint | 65.00 |
| Lamp, Whale Oil, Tin, Pewter & Brass Burner, Pewter Snuffs, 4 1/2 In. | 65.00 |
| Lamp, Whale Oil, Tin, Saucer Base, Tin & Brass Burner & Hinged Cup, 4 In. | 50.00 |
| Lamp, Whale Oil, Tortoiseshell, Blown, 7 In.High | 90.00 |

| | |
|---|---|
| Lamp, Whale Oil, Tumbler, C.1874 | 135.00 |
| Lamp, Whale Oil, Witch's Hat, Blue Paint | 80.00 |
| Lamp, Whale Oil, Wooden, Pewter Lining | 165.00 |
| Lamp, White Milk Glass, Enameled Roses, Bulbous Base, 3 1/2 In.High | 34.00 |
| Lamp, White To Rose Satin Glass, Embossed Shell & Acanthus, 10 1/4 In. | 45.00 |
| Lamp, Wicker, 22 1/2 In.High | 65.00 |
| Lamp, Wiener Werkstatte Pottery, Goblet Shape, Circles, C.1935, 10 In. | 225.00 |
| Lamp, Wood, Mushroom Type Shade, Golden Amber, Brown Eyes, 11 1/2 In. | 28.00 |
| Lamp, Wrought Iron, Frosted Glass Dome, Red & Yellow Mums, 14 In. | 79.50 |
| Lamp, Wrought Iron, Grapes & Leaves, Frosted Dome, 3 Glass Shades For Sides | 79.50 |
| Lampshade, Brass, Embossed Design, Beaded Fringe | 12.00 |
| Lampshade, McKinley Portrait Medallion, Ball Shape, Gold Dollar Signs | 22.00 |
| Lampshade, Pressed Glass, Diamond Ridge, Flared Base, 8 In. | 12.00 |
| Lampshade, Tiffany Type, Leaded, Jewel Grape, 24 In. Diameter | 450.00 |
| Lantern, see also Railroad, Lantern, Silver, Sheffield, Lantern | |
| Lantern, Barn, Red Globe | 15.50 |
| Lantern, Buggy, Deitz, Embossed, Dashboard Clamp | 24.00 |
| Lantern, Candle, Revere, Pierced Tin, Cylindrical | 85.00 |
| Lantern, Candle, Revere, Pierced Tin, Swirl Design | 65.00 |
| Lantern, Candle, Revere, Tin, Door, Cone Top, Solid Base | 70.00 |
| Lantern, Candle, Tin, Bull's-Eye Lens, 7 1/4 In. | 40.00 |
| Lantern, Candle, Tin, Semicircular, Cone Shape Top, Ring Handle, 17 In. | 65.00 |
| Lantern, Carriage, Candle Burning, Tin, Beveled Glass, Red Reflector To Rear | 45.00 |
| Lantern, Coal Oil, S.Sargeant, Dated 1861, Perforated Tin, Brass Cap | 80.00 |
| Lantern, Dietz Type, Battery, Silver Color, Bail Handle, 11 In.High | 4.00 |
| Lantern, Dietz Type, Kerosene, Red, Bail Handle, 11 In.High | 4.00 |
| Lantern, Dietz, Down Draft, Signed, 7 1/2 In. | 17.50 |
| Lantern, Dietz, Scout, Tin, Patent 1908, 8 In.High | 15.00 |
| Lantern, Junker, Brass, Curved Glass, Carrying Handle | 55.00 |
| Lantern, Kerosene, Shapleigh Hardware | 5.00 |
| Lantern, Lanthorne, Horn Panels, C.1750, 14 In. | 235.00 |
| Lantern, Medicine Man, Tin, Pair | 25.00 |
| Lantern, Pireced Tin, Hanging, Electirfied | 75.00 |
| Lantern, Policeman's, Liquid Fuel, Hand Operated, Tin, Bull's-Eye Lens | 35.00 |
| Lantern, Railroad, see, Railroad, Lantern | |
| Lantern, Reliable, U.S.In Raised Letters On Clear Globe, World War I | 25.00 |
| Lantern, Ship's, Proctor's Patent 1876, Green Globe, Tin, 13 In. | 40.00 |
| Lantern, Skater's, Tin, Clear Lens, Bail Handle, 7 In.High | 28.00 |
| Lantern, Tin, Black Paint, Red Glass Front, Wooden Knob Regulator | 15.00 |
| Lantern, Tin, Cylindrical Glass Globe Holds Taper, Folding Doors, 7 In. | 150.00 |
| Lantern, Tin, Isinglass Panels, 15 1/2 In. | 140.00 |
| Lantern, Tin, Rectangular, Colored Glass, 4 In.High | 25.00 |
| Lantern, Travel, Chinese, Tin & Glass, Collapsible, Floral On Glass, C.1890 | 48.00 |
| Lantern, Whale Oil, Buggy, Dietz | 32.00 |
| Lantern, Whale Oil, Folding, Glass Sides | 35.00 |
| Lantern, Whale Oil, Tin, Ring Handle, Flint Globe, 18 In.High | 95.00 |
| Lantern, Whale Oil, Watchman's, Marked Police, Tin | 34.00 |
| Lapis Lazuli, Necklace, Afghanistan, 66 12 Mm.Lapis, 14K Gold Clasp | 395.00 |
| Lapis Lazuli, Tree, Bosanji, Weeping, Jade Pot, 8 1/2 X 11 In. | 225.00 |

*Le Gras glass was made by August J.F.Le Gras in Saint-Denis,*
*France, between 1864 and 1914. Cameo, acid cut, and enameled glass were made.*

| | |
|---|---|
| Le Gras, Box, Covered, Round, Shepherd Scene, 5 In. Diameter | 225.00 |
| Le Gras, Jar, Cracker, Brass Lid & Bail, Burgundy Leaves On Camphor | 350.00 |
| Le Gras, Lamp, Bronze, Cameo, Pink Gray, C.1900, 15 In. *Illus* | 600.00 |
| Le Gras, Lamp, Enameled Swag, Black Tree Scene, Orange Carnival Type Glass | 165.00 |
| Le Gras, Planter, Enameled Winter Scene, Signed | 100.00 |
| Le Gras, Rose Bowl, Crimped Top, Enameled Winter Scene, 7 In.High | 135.00 |
| Le Gras, Rose Bowl, Winter Scene, Enameled, Signed, 3 3/4 In.High | 65.00 |
| Le Gras, Vase, Brown & Green Seashell & Weeds On Salmon, C.1900, 13 In. | 200.00 |
| Le Gras, Vase, Canoe Shape, Brown, Green, & Orange, River & Sailboats, 11 In. | 425.00 |
| Le Gras, Vase, Cluthra, Red & Brown, Etched Flying Sparrows, 9 In. | 275.00 |
| Le Gras, Vase, Enameled Autumn Scene, Not Cameo, Signed, 8 In. | 65.00 |
| Le Gras, Vase, Enameled, Coral & Yellow River Scene, 11 In.High | 100.00 |
| Le Gras, Vase, Enameled, Not Cameo, Signed, 8 In. | 65.00 |
| Le Gras, Vase, Flowers On Pale Orchid, Signed, 8 1/2 In.High | 195.00 |
| Le Gras, Vase, Long Expanding Teardrop Form, Cranberry Frosted, 8 In. | 195.00 |

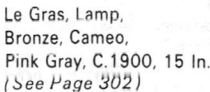

Le Gras, Lamp,
Bronze, Cameo,
Pink Gray, C.1900, 15 In.
(See Page 302)

Leeds, Plate, Yellow & Black, 9 In.
(See Page 304)

| | |
|---|---|
| Le Gras, Vase, Mottled Aquamarine & White, Swirls, Geometrics, 7 In. | 80.00 |
| Le Gras, Vase, Ovoid, Yellow & Orange In Clear, Deer, Landscape, 9 1/2 In. | 200.00 |
| Le Gras, Vase, Purple Art Deco On Frosted Lavender, Signed, 15 1/2 In.High | 225.00 |
| Le Gras, Vase, Riverscape, Orange, White, Green, & Brown, 8 3/4 In. High | 225.00 |
| Le Gras, Vase, Riverscape, Salmon, Green, & Brown, C.1900, 6 In. High | 140.00 |
| Le Gras, Vase, Sailboats On Lake, Banana Shape, Brown, Tan, & Green, 5 1/2 In. | 285.00 |
| Le Gras, Vase, Winter Trees Scene, Orange & Brown, 4 1/2 In. High | 225.00 |
| Le Gras, Vase, Wooded Winter Scene, Oval Top, Signed, 4 In. High | 185.00 |

*Le Verre Francais cameo glass was made in Paris during the late
nineteenth and early twentieth centuries. The glass is mottled and usually
decorated with floral designs.*

| | |
|---|---|
| Le Verre Francais, Bowl, Mottled Purple Base, Cut Floral On Yellow, 7 In. | 165.00 |
| Le Verre Francais, Lamp, Cameo, Purples & Orange, 14 In.High | 525.00 |
| Le Verre Francais, Vase, Acid Cut Beetle, Cameo, 12 In.High | 179.00 |
| Le Verre Francais, Vase, Brown To Orange Flowers, Signed Charder, 14 In. | 325.00 |
| Le Verre Francais, Vase, Cameo, Lemon Background, Brown Leaves, 3 1/2 In. | 135.00 |
| Le Verre Francais, Vase, Carved Tortoiseshell Leaves On Yellow, 12 In. | 250.00 |
| Le Verre Francais, Vase, Cat Motif, Brown, Signed, 11 1/2 In.High | 235.00 |
| Le Verre Francais, Vase, Dark Green & Red, 19 In.High | 400.00 |
| Le Verre Francais, Vase, Gourd Shape, Yellow, Red Berries, C.1910, 3 1/2 In. | 130.00 |
| Le Verre Francais, Vase, Green, Cinnamon Overlay, Floral, C.1925, 10 In. | 150.00 |
| Le Verre Francais, Vase, Pink Mottled Ground, Roses, 7 1/2 In.High | 185.00 |
| Le Verre Francais, Vase, Purple To Pink, 19 In. High | 160.00 |
| Le Verre Francais, Vase, Tortoiseshell Floral, Red Base, 18 In.High | 200.00 |
| Le Verre Francais, Wine, Cut Flower Petals In Yellow & Beige, Crystal Stem | 105.00 |
| Leather, Belt, Saber, U.S.Dragoon, White Buff, Buckle, C.1850 | 150.00 |
| Leather, Handbag, Armadillo, Cloth Lined, 1920s | 25.00 |
| Leather, Holder, Playing Cards, Double, Venetian, Gold Tooled Decoration | 15.00 |
| Leather, Holster, Shoulder, Colt Single Action, A.Furstnow, C.1870 | 225.00 |
| Leather, Neck Stock, U.S.Officer's, Black, Marked B.L.Warden, C.1850 | 59.50 |
| Leather, Neck Stock, U.S.Officer's, Maker B.L.Warden, C.1890 | 59.50 |
| Leather, Pouch, Flares For Signal Gun, U.S.L.S.S., Watervliet Arsenal | 97.50 |
| Leather, Purse, Change, Art Nouveau Silver Woman's Head On Top | 13.00 |
| Leather, Sabretache, British Officer's Dress, Black, Gold Bullion, C.1850 | 125.00 |
| Leather, Sabretache, Royal Artillery British Officer's, Black, C.1850 | 125.00 |
| Leather, Shoe, Baby's, Hightop, Buttons, Pair | 5.00 |
| Leather, Wallet, American Officer's, Eagle & Shield, Russet, C.1820 | 54.50 |
| Leather, Wallet, U.S.Officer's, Russet, Embossed, C.1820 | 54.50 |

*Leeds pottery was made at Leeds, Yorkshire, England, from 1774 to 1878.
Most Leeds ware was not marked. Early Leeds pieces had distinctive
twisted handles with a greenish glaze on part of the creamy ware. Later ware
often had blue borders on the creamy pottery.*

| | |
|---|---|
| Leeds, Bowl, Creamware, Oval, Pierced Border, Blue Rim, 9 In. | 39.50 |

| | |
|---|---|
| Leeds, Bowl, Diamond Shape, Melon Ribbed, Queen Shells In Corners, C.1750 | 285.00 |
| Leeds, Charger, Molded Edge, Blue Decoration, 14 1/2 In. | 50.00 |
| Leeds, Creamer, Green Blanket Stitch | 15.00 |
| Leeds, Gravy Boat, Green Edge | 45.00 |
| Leeds, Jar, Sugar, Covered, Black, Red, & Green Decoration | 55.00 |
| Leeds, Ladle, Gravy, Blue Border, Curved Handle | 55.00 |
| Leeds, Mold, Cheese, Creamware, Pierced | 75.00 |
| Leeds, Muffineer, Green | 95.00 |
| Leeds, Plate, Creamware, Yellow Garlands, Feather Edge, C.1750, 9 1/2 In. | 85.00 |
| Leeds, Plate, Gaudy Blue, Molded Feather Edge, 8 In. | 130.00 |
| Leeds, Plate, Yellow & Black, 9 In. _Illus_ | 30.00 |
| Leeds, Platter, Blue Combed Edge, Adams Mark With Eagle, 15 X 12 In. | 30.00 |
| Leeds, Platter, Creamware, Pierced Basket Loop 1 1/2 In.Border, 9 3/4 In. | 30.00 |
| Leeds, Teabowl, Floral Garlands & Sprigs, Creamware, C.1775, Set Of 6 | 225.00 |
| Leeds, Teapot, Urn Decorated Flower Knop, Twisted Handle, Iron & Green, 1750 | 375.00 |

*Lenox china was made in Trenton, New Jersey, after 1906. The firm also makes a porcelain similar to Belleek.*

| | |
|---|---|
| Lenox, Ashtray, Brown Line Drawing Of Schooner Columbia, Artist Holmes | 35.00 |
| Lenox, Barrel, Ivory, Marked G.A.C.In Wreath, 3 1/2 In.High | 45.00 |
| Lenox, Bowl, Cream Soup, Gold Trim, Cream, 2 Handled Sterling Holder | 14.50 |
| Lenox, Bowl, Ice, Tab Handles, Hexagonal, Sterling Overlay | 44.00 |
| Lenox, Bowl, Oval, Pink, Fluted Sides, Green Wreath Mark, 12 X 6 In. | 25.00 |
| Lenox, Bowl, Soup, Cream, Sterling Silver Holder | 10.00 |
| Lenox, Box, Covered, World's Fair, 1939, White, 3 1/2 X 5 In. | 17.50 |
| Lenox, Box, Puff, Hattie Carnegie Embossed On Side | 38.00 |
| Lenox, Butter Pat, Scallop Shape, Cream Tone, 3 1/2 X 3 1/8 In. | 3.50 |
| Lenox, Cachepot, Melon Shape, Gold Trim, Green Mark, 6 In. | 24.00 |
| Lenox, Chocolate Set, Cream Color, Footed, 3 Piece | 45.00 |
| Lenox, Coffee Set, Ivory & Gold, Green Wreath Mark, 3 Piece | 75.00 |
| Lenox, Console Set, Red & Blue Coat Of Arms, Gold Trim, Belleek, 3 Piece | 35.00 |
| Lenox, Cup & Saucer, Bouillon, Ming, 2 Handled | 8.00 |
| Lenox, Cup & Saucer, Demitasse, Art Deco, Silver Bands, Green Wreath Mark | 15.00 |
| Lenox, Cup & Saucer, Demitasse, Fountain, Enameled Floral, Black L Mark | 25.00 |
| Lenox, Cup & Saucer, Demitasse, Hexagonal, White, Silver Overlay, Palette | 42.00 |
| Lenox, Cup & Saucer, Demitasse, White, Square Handle, Green Wreath Mark | 12.00 |
| Lenox, Cup & Saucer, Ming, Green Wreath Mark | 21.00 |
| Lenox, Cup, Bouillon, Floral Garlands, Pierced 2 Handled Gorham Holder | 65.00 |
| Lenox, Cup, Bouillon, Gold Bands, Sterling 2 Handled Holder | 17.50 |
| Lenox, Cup, Demitasse, Gold Bands, Sterling Silver Holder | 18.50 |
| Lenox, Cup, Nut, Pedestal, Gold Trim, Green Wreath Mark, 1 3/4 In. High | 12.50 |
| Lenox, Dessert Set, Coral, Fluted White Rims, Green Wreath Mark, 24 Piece | 155.00 |
| Lenox, Dish, Candy, Embossed Shell Type Design, Scalloped, Fluted, Round | 8.00 |
| Lenox, Dish, Heart Shape, White, Gold Decorated, Embossed, 1940s, 4 In. | 35.00 |
| Lenox, Dish, Shell, Cream, Green Mark | 7.50 |
| Lenox, Dish, Swan, Pink, Blue Wreath | 17.50 |
| Lenox, Figurine, Angel, Green Mark, 4 1/2 In.High | 11.00 |
| Lenox, Figurine, Birds, Pink, Green Mark, 3 1/2 In.High, Pair | 25.00 |
| Lenox, Figurine, Dog, Art Deco | 25.00 |
| Lenox, Jug, William Penn, Blue Handle | 65.00 |
| Lenox, Lamp Base, 2 White Ladies On Gray, 11 1/2 In.High | 35.00 |
| Lenox, Mug, Barrel Shape, Pasture, Pond, & 6 Deer, "to You From Me, " Palette | 40.00 |
| Lenox, Mug, Battle Monument, Baltimore, Minga P.Patchin, Green Wreath | 37.50 |
| Lenox, Mug, Jolly Monk In Front Of Keg Of Beer, Green & White, Gold | 55.00 |
| Lenox, Mug, King Neptune Scenes, Gold Decoration, 3 1/2 In.High | 30.00 |
| Lenox, Pitcher, Green, Cream Lining & Handle, Gold Wreath, 7 1/2 In. | 22.00 |
| Lenox, Pitcher, Mask Face, Hammered Finish, White, Green Wreath Mark, 7 In. | 70.00 |
| Lenox, Pitcher, Water, Floral & Gold On Ivory, Artist Signed | 70.00 |
| Lenox, Place Setting, Nydia, C.1920, 5 Piece | 37.50 |
| Lenox, Place Setting, Orleans, Gold Trim | 25.00 |
| Lenox, Plate, Art Deco Shape, Cream, Green Wreath Mark | 18.00 |
| Lenox, Plate, Bread & Butter, Kingsley | 6.00 |
| Lenox, Plate, Breakfast, Olympia | 6.00 |
| Lenox, Plate, Dessert, Romance, 6 In. | 2.25 |
| Lenox, Plate, Gold Trim, Cream, Embossed Border, 7 1/2 In. | 7.00 |
| Lenox, Plate, Jeweled, Marked Trent, 5 3/4 In. | 4.15 |

| | |
|---|---|
| Lenox, Plate, Salad, Kingsley | 6.00 |
| Lenox, Plate, Soup, Engraved Gold Bands On White, 9 1/4 In. | 7.00 |
| Lenox, Salt Dip, Individual, Covered, Gold, Ruffled Edge, Belleek | 10.00 |
| Lenox, Slat Dip, Rosebuds & Green Leaves, Belleek | 9.50 |
| Lenox, Salt, Pedestal, Factory Gold | 8.50 |
| Lenox, Salt, Swan, Belleek | 10.00 |
| Lenox, Salt, White, Sterling Overlay, 2 1/4 In.Diameter | 12.50 |
| Lenox, Spooner, Miniature | 14.00 |
| Lenox, Sugar & Creamer, Floral, Gold Trim, Pedestal Base, Palette Mark | 60.00 |
| Lenox, Sugar, Covered, Silver Overlay On Cobalt, Green Wreath Mark | 55.00 |
| Lenox, Sugar, White, Silver Overlay, Green Wreath L Mark | 55.00 |
| Lenox, Swan, Pink, 4 In. | 19.00 |
| Lenox, Swan, Pink, 4 1/2 In. | 11.00 |
| Lenox, Swan, White, Green Wreath, 4 In.High | 22.50 |
| Lenox, Tea Set, Silver Overlay On Brown, Belleek, 3 Piece | 165.00 |
| Lenox, Tea Set, Sterling Overlay On Cream, Green Wreath Mark, 3 Piece | 110.00 |
| Lenox, Teacup & Saucer, Embossed Gold Bands On White, Green Mark | 9.50 |
| Lenox, Teapot, Sterling Overlay On Brown | 52.00 |
| Lenox, Toby Mug, William Penn, Pink, White Handle | 175.00 |
| Lenox, Urn, Swan Handles, Lenox Rose, Ivory Background, 11 In.High | 50.00 |
| Lenox, Vase, Blue Handle, Green Wreath Mark, 5 In.High | 20.00 |
| Lenox, Vase, Bud, Cream Ground, Raised Decoration | 10.00 |
| Lenox, Vase, Bud, Cream, Green Wreath Mark | 15.00 |
| Lenox, Vase, Butterflies With Woman's Extremities, Purple, Belleek, 10 In. | 130.00 |
| Lenox, Vase, Cornucopia, Rose, Gold Trim, 5 In.High | 18.00 |
| Lenox, Vase, Cylindrical, Black Bands On Cream, 9 1/2 In. High | 25.00 |
| Lenox, Vase, Cylindrical, Sky Blue, Green Mark, 11 In.High | 34.00 |
| Lenox, Vase, Five Peacocks On Limb, Black On Ivory, 27 1/2 In Diameter | 90.00 |
| Lenox, Vase, Silver Overlay On Ivory, Green Wreath Mark, 10 In.High | 85.00 |
| Lenox, Vase, White Coral Handles & Base, Ruffled Top, Green Wreath Mark | 28.00 |
| Lenox, Vase, White Dogwood On Green, Artist Signed, Green Wreath Mark | 80.00 |
| Libbey, Bowl, Bulbous, Applied Peridot Lily Pads, 9 X 10 In. | 125.00 |
| Libbey, Champagne, Flute, Teardrop Stem, C.1909 | 35.00 |
| Libbey, Cup, Punch, Flute, Footed, C.1909 | 32.00 |
| Libbey, Goblet, Flute, Teardrop Stem, C.1909 | 35.00 |
| Libbey, Goblet, Opalescent, Cat Stem, Signed | 85.00 |
| Libbey, Silhouette Glass, Kangaroo, Signed | 155.00 |
| Libbey, Silhouette Glass. Monkey, Signed | 145.00 |
| Lighting Devices, see Candloholder, Candlestick, Lamp, etc. | |
| Lightning Rod, Arrow, Milk Glass Ball | 18.50 |

*Lightning rod balls are collected for their variety of shape and color.
These glass balls were at the center of the rod that was attached to the
roof of a house or barn to avoid lightning damage*

| | |
|---|---|
| Lightning Rod, Ball, Amber Glass, Allover Pattern | 18.00 |
| Lightning Rod, Ball, Moon & Star, Milk Glass | 9.25 |
| Lightning Rod, Ball, Moon & Star, Milk Glass, Blue | 9.25 |
| Lightning Rod, Ball, Moon & Star, Sun Colored Amethyst | 10.00 |
| Lightning Rod, Ball, Quilted, Amber | 25.00 |
| Lightning Rod, Ball, Ribbed Grape, Milk Glass | 6.50 |
| Lightning Rod, Ball, W.C.Shinn Co., Milk Glass | 16.00 |
| Lightning Rod, Double Fleur-De-Lis Tail, Ruby | 27.00 |
| Lightning Rod, Gilt Brass & Copper, Scrolls & Trefoils, C.1875, 6 Ft.4 In. | 400.00 |

*Limoges porcelain has been made in Limoges, France, since the
mid-nineteenth century. Fine porcelains were made by many factories,
including Haviland, Ahrenfeldt, Guerin, Pouyat, Elite, and others.*

Limoges, see also Haviland

| | |
|---|---|
| Limoges, Atomizer, Iridescent Blue, Gold Trim, 2 1/2 In.High | 8.00 |
| Limoges, Basket, Candy, Forget-Me-Nots, Coin Gold Reverse S Handle, Signed | 22.00 |
| Limoges, Bell, Dinner, Hand-Painted Floral, Butterfly Handle, Haviland | 40.00 |
| Limoges, Berry Set, Flow Blue Trim, Purple Grapes, Set Of 7 | 67.50 |
| Limoges, Bowl & Underplate, Soup, Floral Band, C.Ahrenfeldt, 1918 | 6.25 |
| Limoges, Bowl, Berry, Hand-Painted Strawberries | 25.00 |
| Limoges, Bowl, Free-Form Shell, Dragon Climbing Over Rim, Gold & Green | 150.00 |
| Limoges, Bowl, Green Luster, 6 In.Diameter | 5.50 |
| Limoges, Bowl, Hand-Painted Flowers, Gold, Scalloped, Artist J.Tuca | 15.00 |

| | |
|---|---|
| Limoges, Bowl, Mucha Type Woman On Cover, Pearlized, 7 1/2 In. | 85.00 |
| Limoges, Bowl, Punch, Footed, Grapes In & Out, Green, Brown, & Yellow, 14 In. | 150.00 |
| Limoges, Bowl, Soup, Abbey, 8 In. | 2.50 |
| Limoges, Bowl, Transfer Quails In Reserve Inside & Out, 5 3/8 In. | 15.00 |
| Limoges, Bowl, Vegetable, Round, Hand-Painted Brown & Green Floral, C.1885 | 22.00 |
| Limoges, Box, Covered, Round, Art Deco Floral On Blue, T.& V. | 13.50 |
| Limoges, Box, Heart Shape, Couple In Garden Scene, Blue & Gold | 12.00 |
| Limoges, Box, Jewel, Covered, Oval, Dresden Style Decoration, 4 Gold Legs | 24.00 |
| Limoges, Box, Patch, Floral, Gold, France | 10.00 |
| Limoges, Box, Pink Roses On Lid, Molded Scrolls, Blue, 1904, 4 1/2 In. | 48.00 |
| Limoges, Box, Powder, Tea Roses On Cream, Gold Edge & 3 Feet, 3 1/4 In. | 12.00 |
| Limoges, Butter Pat, Fluted Rim, Square, 2 1/2 In. | 2.50 |
| Limoges, Butter Pat, Hand-Painted Floral, Irregular Gold Edge | 2.50 |
| Limoges, Butter Pat, Lacy Poppy On Ivory, Signed Crown Pairpoint, 3 In. | 10.00 |
| Limoges, Butter Pat, Marked France, C.A.Depose Limoges Patented, 12 | 45.00 |
| Limoges, Butter Pat, White, Gold Scalloped Edge, Red & Gold Floral | 2.00 |
| Limoges, Butter Pat, White, Green & Gold Decoration, Gold Edge | 2.00 |
| Limoges, Butter Pat, White, Haviland | 2.50 |
| Limoges, Cake Set, Flowers, Gold, William Guerin, 7 Piece | 65.00 |
| Limoges, Cameo, Ceramic, White On Blue | 18.00 |
| Limoges, Candlestick, Blue Flowers, 5 1/4 In., Pair | 49.00 |
| Limoges, Candlestick, Yellow Roses On Shaded Ground, 5 In.High, Pair | 7.50 |
| Limoges, Chocolate Pot, Pink Roses, Gold Decoration | 47.50 |
| Limoges, Chocolate Pot, White, Gold Handle, 11 In. | 27.50 |
| Limoges, Chocolate Set, Signed, 17 Piece | 265.00 |
| Limoges, Chop Set, Pheasant Decoration, 12 In.Platter, 6 Piece | 235.00 |
| Limoges, Coffeepot, Holly, Gold Handles & Rim, T.& V., 9 1/2 In.High | 115.00 |
| Limoges, Crepe-Suzette Set, Scalloped Gold Edge, Floral, Gold, 2 Piece | 100.00 |
| Limoges, Cup & Saucer, Beauvais, Haviland, France | 5.75 |
| Limoges, Cup & Saucer, Beige, White, & Gold, Oversized | 16.50 |
| Limoges, Cup & Saucer, Bouillon, Pink & Blue Floral In & Out, 2 Handled | 8.00 |
| Limoges, Cup & Saucer, Bouillon, Pink Flowers, Gold Trim | 10.50 |
| Limoges, Cup & Saucer, Coffee, White, Ivory, & Gold, C.A.France | 16.50 |
| Limoges, Cup & Saucer, Demitasse, Blue Flowers & Bands, Gold Handle | 2.50 |
| Limoges, Cup & Saucer, Demitasse, Fabrique A Limoges, F.A.France | 8.00 |
| Limoges, Cup & Saucer, Demitasse, Gold Leaf Sprays On Blue To White | 18.00 |
| Limoges, Cup & Saucer, Demitasse, Magenta Border, Gold Scroll & Leaf | 6.35 |
| Limoges, Cup & Saucer, Demitasse, Pale Blue, White Border Edged In Gold | 14.00 |
| Limoges, Cup & Saucer, Demitasse, Pink Roses, Gold Handle & Trim | 14.50 |
| Limoges, Cup & Saucer, Demitasse, Roses, Gold Border, Haviland | 11.50 |
| Limoges, Cup & Saucer, Hand-Painted Birds On Peach | 12.00 |
| Limoges, Cup & Saucer, Hand-Painted Floral & Cupids, Rose & Gilt, 2 Handled | 30.00 |
| Limoges, Cup & Saucer, Lacy Poppy On Ivory, Signed Crown Pairpoint | 90.00 |
| Limoges, Cup & Saucer, Roses & Forget-Me-Nots | 6.50 |
| Limoges, Cup, Chocolate, Pink Decoration, Flaring Top, Floral, Gilt Handle | 8.75 |
| Limoges, Dish, Bone, Floral | 7.50 |
| Limoges, Dish, Candy, Ruffled, Elite | 15.00 |
| Limoges, Dish, Candy, Violets On Blue, Gold Handle & Edge, T. & V. | 29.00 |
| Limoges, Dish, Pickle, Pink Roses, Elite, 7 1/2 In. | 6.50 |
| Limoges, Doorknob, Blue Flower Decoration, Signed Singer | 14.00 |
| Limoges, Dresser Set, Pink Tea Roses, Blue & Cream, Gold Trim, 3 Piece | 55.00 |
| Limoges, Eggcup, Mother-Of-Pearl & Gold | 9.00 |
| Limoges, Fish Set, Gold Border, Irregular Edge, Signed Reix, 7 Piece | 250.00 |
| Limoges, Fish Set, Signed Duvay, Coronet, 9 Piece | 265.00 |
| Limoges, Frame, Picture, Double, Rainbow-Colored Pansies, Gold, 12 1/4 In. | 52.00 |
| Limoges, Hair Receiver & Powder Jar, Cobalt & Gold | 25.00 |
| Limoges, Hair Receiver, Floral, Artist Signed | 25.00 |
| Limoges, Hair Receiver, Tan With Lavendar Flowers, Signed Vignaud | 17.00 |
| Limoges, Hair Receiver, Wreaths Of Roses | 18.50 |
| Limoges, Hatpin Holder, Blue Forget-Me-Nots | 13.00 |
| Limoges, Holder, Card, Flowers, Gold Trim, Marked T.& V., France | 22.00 |
| Limoges, Ice Cream Set, Violets, Platter With 8 Dishes | 135.00 |
| Limoges, Inkwell, Lidded, Saucer Base, Pink To Cerise Floral, Ahrenfeldt | 39.00 |
| Limoges, Inkwell, 2 On Attached Tray & Penholder, Floral, Gold, Elite | 35.00 |
| Limoges, Jar & Underplate, Jam, Covered, Gold Handles & Beading, Blue | 30.00 |
| Limoges, Jar, Pink & Yellow Roses, Gold Tracery, Green Leaves, J.P.L., 7 In. | 35.00 |

| | |
|---|---|
| **Limoges, Jar,** Powder, Covered, Florals On Cream, Gold Edges, Marked T.& V. | 18.00 |
| **Limoges, Jar,** Powder, Gold & Roses, 5 In.Diameter | 18.00 |
| **Limoges, Milk Holder,** Can, Green & Gold Floral, 2 Piece | 20.00 |
| **Limoges, Mug,** Autumn Leaves, 5 1/2 In. | 45.00 |
| **Limoges, Mug,** Gold Filigree Handle, Purple Grapes & Leaves On Vine, 6 In. | 62.00 |
| **Limoges, Mug,** Grape And Corn Decoration, Signed J.P.L., 6 In.High | 25.00 |
| **Limoges, Mug,** Hand-Painted Autumn Leaves, 5 1/2 In. | 45.00 |
| **Limoges, Pendant,** Courting Scene, Oval | 15.00 |
| **Limoges, Perfume,** Pedestal Shape, Enamel With Silver Gilt, 4 In.High | 650.00 |
| **Limoges, Pitcher,** Cider, Art Nouveau, Floral On Multicolor Ground, 6 In. | 75.00 |
| **Limoges, Pitcher,** Deer Scene, Signed, 7 3/4 In.High | 45.00 |
| **Limoges, Pitcher,** Lemonade, Floral On Cream Ground, Gold Trim, 9 In.High | 60.00 |
| **Limoges, Plaque,** Enamel, Elegant Lady, Signed L.Dubois, 6 In.Square | 195.00 |
| **Limoges, Plaque,** Grape Clusters, Signed Worrell, 16 In. | 300.00 |
| **Limoges, Plaque,** Les Joyeux Buveurs, Signed Armand, C.1878, 11 1/2 X 15 In. | 1300.00 |
| **Limoges, Plaque,** Pope, Ornate Brass Frame, Signed | 22.50 |
| **Limoges, Plaque,** Raised White Boy & Lamb On Blue, Gold Frame, Round | 35.00 |
| **Limoges, Plaque,** Retour De Fete, Signed Armand, C.1878, 11 1/2 X 15 In. | 1250.00 |
| **Limoges, Plate,** A.Kauffmann Center, Maroon, Cream, & Cobalt Border, 9 1/2 In. | 32.00 |
| **Limoges, Plate,** Admiral Dewey Portrait, Gold Fern Garland, 8 1/2 In. | 22.50 |
| **Limoges, Plate,** Amstel, 6 1/4 In. | 4.50 |
| **Limoges, Plate,** Bread & Butter, Ivory Border, Gold Bands, Gold Leaf | 6.00 |
| **Limoges, Plate,** Bread & Butter, Roses, 2 Seashells Merged As One, T. & V. | 6.50 |
| **Limoges, Plate,** Bread, Open Handles, Red, Pink, & White Roses, T.& V., France | 20.00 |
| **Limoges, Plate,** Cake, Grapes & Other Fruit, Gold Rococo Border, Flambeau | 50.00 |
| **Limoges, Plate,** Cake, Open Gold Handles, 4 Chrysanthemums, 12 In. | 27.00 |
| **Limoges, Plate,** Dessert, Hand-Painted Floral, Scalloped, Gilt Edge | 13.75 |
| **Limoges, Plate,** Dessert, Mums, Beaded Gold Border, 8 1/2 In. | 5.95 |
| **Limoges, Plate,** Dinner, Gold Band | 9.50 |
| **Limoges, Plate,** Fish In Water, Aquatic Plants, M.Redon, 9 In. | 9.00 |
| **Limoges, Plate,** Fish, Embossed Gold Border, Artist Signed, 9 1/2 In. | 32.50 |
| **Limoges, Plate,** Fish, Green Border With Gold, Haviland, 9 In. | 18.00 |
| **Limoges, Plate,** Fish, Hand-Painted, Signed, Heavy Gold Border, Pair | 120.00 |
| **Limoges, Plate,** Fish, Octagonal, Artist Signed, 9 1/2 In. | 25.00 |
| **Limoges, Plate,** Fish, Perch, Water Lilies, Signed Roche, 9 1/4 In. | 25.00 |
| **Limoges, Plate,** Fish, Swimming, Autumn Colors, Gold Border, 11 1/2 In. | 75.00 |
| **Limoges, Plate,** Fish, 2 Fish Swimming Under Water | 14.00 |
| **Limoges, Plate,** Fish, 8 1/2 In. | 17.50 |
| **Limoges, Plate,** Four-Leaf Clover & Flower Border, Gold Edge, 8 In. | 4.50 |
| **Limoges, Plate,** Fruit & Copper Kettle On Green, A Broussillon, 13 In. | 185.00 |
| **Limoges, Plate,** Fruit, Berries, Signed Love, 7 In. | 7.50 |
| **Limoges, Plate,** Fruit, Strawberries, Signed Love, 7 In. | 7.50 |
| **Limoges, Plate,** Fuchsias, Green, Gold, & Yellow, J.P.L., 9 In. | 21.00 |
| **Limoges, Plate,** Game Bird, Flying Pheasant, Gold Edge, 10 3/8 In. | 45.00 |
| **Limoges, Plate,** Game Bird, Turkey, Signed L.Coudert, Gold Edge, 10 In. | 69.00 |
| **Limoges, Plate,** Game, Flying Bird, Artist Rene, Gold Rococo Border, 9 1/2 In. | 49.00 |
| **Limoges, Plate,** Game, Flying Bird, Gold Rococo Border, Artist Meville, 10 In. | 85.00 |
| **Limoges, Plate,** Game, Grouse In Flight, Signed Valenim, Gold Border, 10 In. | 75.00 |
| **Limoges, Plate,** Game, Pheasant, Gold Edge, Flambeau | 37.50 |
| **Limoges, Plate,** Game, Quail, Irregular Gold Edge, 10 1/2 In. | 125.00 |
| **Limoges, Plate,** Game, Rabbits, Artist Signed, Coronet, 10 In. | 58.00 |
| **Limoges, Plate,** Green & Blue Garlands With Pink Rosebuds, Gold Edge, 6 In. | 4.50 |
| **Limoges, Plate,** Green & Gold, Scalloped Rim, 8 In. | 3.50 |
| **Limoges, Plate,** Hand-Painted Floral, Gold Trim, 7 3/4 In. | 12.00 |
| **Limoges, Plate,** Hand-Painted Flowers, Gold Edge, Artist B.Bohm, 6 1/2 In. | 12.00 |
| **Limoges, Plate,** Horseback Rider Waving To Women In Boat, 7 1/2 In. | 28.00 |
| **Limoges, Plate,** Lacy Poppy On Ivory, Signed Crown Pairpoint, 7 1/2 In. | 30.00 |
| **Limoges, Plate,** Luncheon, Ivory Border, Gold Bands, Gold Leaf, 8 3/4 In. | 7.90 |
| **Limoges, Plate,** Monk, Artist Signed, Coronet, 10 In. | 40.00 |
| **Limoges, Plate,** Multicolor Sprigs, 7 In. | 3.00 |
| **Limoges, Plate,** Multicolor Sprigs, 10 In. | 4.50 |
| **Limoges, Plate,** Orange & Red Poppies, Black & Gold, Artist Signed, 8 1/4 In. | 35.00 |
| **Limoges, Plate,** Oyster, Greens & Russets, 5 Depressions, Haviland, 1885 | 48.00 |
| **Limoges, Plate,** Oyster, Pink & Gold | 15.00 |
| **Limoges, Plate,** Oyster, Pink Flowers, Scalloped Edge | 18.50 |
| **Limoges, Plate,** Pansies, Gold Border, French, 9 In. | 27.00 |

| | |
|---|---|
| Limoges, Plate, Pink Floral, Green, Red Outline, White, Haviland, 6 1/8 In. | 5.50 |
| Limoges, Plate, Pink Roses & Blue Forget-Me-Nots, Gold, 8 In. | 2.00 |
| Limoges, Plate, Portrait, Marie Antoinette, Cobalt & Gold, Signed | 29.00 |
| Limoges, Plate, Portrait, Monk, Brown, Signed LePic, 10 In. | 50.00 |
| Limoges, Plate, Red Iceland Poppy & Buds, Gold, Signed Lamour, Coronet, 9 In. | 18.00 |
| Limoges, Plate, Roses & Blue Border, Signed Terrell, 1906, 6 In. | 6.50 |
| Limoges, Plate, Roses & Vines, Gold Edge, 8 In. | 20.00 |
| Limoges, Plate, Service, Floral & Net Decoration, Gold Border, Ahrenfeldt | 8.50 |
| Limoges, Plate, Sweet Peas On Ivory, Scalloped Scrolled Gold Edge, 13 In. | 65.00 |
| Limoges, Plate, Violets & Leaves, Burnished Gold, Elite, Artist-Signed, 8 In. | 18.00 |
| Limoges, Plate, Wall, Bird & Scenery, Scalloped, Artist M.A.X., 10 In. | 135.00 |
| Limoges, Plate, Wall, Bull In Water, Gold Border, Artist Signed, 10 In. | 48.00 |
| Limoges, Plate, Yellow Shaded Roses, Pansies, Gold Rim, T.& V., 7 1/2 In. | 7.50 |
| Limoges, Platter, Clusters Of Pink & White Roses, Rose Center, Gold Trim | 17.50 |
| Limoges, Platter, Fish, Gold Border & Open Handles, Fish, Lobster, & Fruit | 75.00 |
| Limoges, Platter, Fish, Scalloped, Oval, Signed Worrell, 24 1/4 In.Long | 300.00 |
| Limoges, Platter, Game Bird, Flowers & Gold Trim, Flambeau, 17 In.Long | 45.00 |
| Limoges, Platter, Game Bird, Quails & Fruit, Gold Scalloped Border | 95.00 |
| Limoges, Platter, Rose Garlands Around Rim, Gold Border, Elite, Round | 28.00 |
| Limoges, Platter, Round, Hand-Painted Pansies, Gold, 12 In. | 25.00 |
| Limoges, Ramekin, White, Sterling Holder | 12.50 |
| Limoges, Relish, Floral On White, Gold Decoration, J.P., France, 9 3/4 In. | 14.00 |
| Limoges, Relish, Turned Up Scalloped & Fluted Rim Forms Handle, Coronet | 45.00 |
| Limoges, Ring Tree, White, Gold Edged, 'For Nellie, Christmas, '94' | 14.50 |
| Limoges, Salt Dip, Blue, Gold Lined, 3 Footed Base, 2 1/2 In. | 8.50 |
| Limoges, Sauceboat, Ornate, Artist Signed, Dated 1896 | 37.50 |
| Limoges, Saucer, Ramekin, White, Heavy Gold | 12.50 |
| Limoges, Server & Underplate, Pudding, Orange Poppies, Gold, Signed Kelly | 22.50 |
| Limoges, Server, Vegetable, Covered, Gold Handles, Decorated Border, Marked | 15.00 |
| Limoges, Snack Set, Oriental Motif, Pale Blue, Artist Signed, 11 Piece | 90.00 |
| Limoges, Soup Set, Blue Cornflowers, Gold Trim, 6 Piece | 45.00 |
| Limoges, Sugar & Creamer, Hand-Painted Violets, Medium Size | 18.00 |
| Limoges, Sugar, Bee Pattern, 3 In. | 5.75 |
| Limoges, Syrup, Autumn Leaf Trim On White, Gold Floral Finial & Handle | 22.00 |
| Limoges, Tea Set, Hand-Painted Roses, Gold, Lanternier, 3 Piece | 60.00 |
| Limoges, Tea Set, Plum & Gold Vines On White, Gold Twisted Handles, 3 Piece | 45.00 |
| Limoges, Tea Set, Raised Gold Floral On Beige, Gold Handles, 25 Piece | 225.00 |
| Limoges, Tea Set, Roses, Gold Trim, Miniature, 7 Piece | 10.50 |
| Limoges, Teacup & Saucer, Orchid Iris & Yellow Flowers On Ivory, Gold Trim | 25.00 |
| Limoges, Teacup & Saucer, Violets, Gold Edges, A.Delinieres & Co. | 14.00 |
| Limoges, Teapot, Bamboo, Gold Floral, Peacock, Octagon, Haviland, France | 35.00 |
| Limoges, Tile, Verse Titled Good Night, Pink & White Roses, Frames | 55.00 |
| Limoges, Toothpick, Hand-Painted Ship Scenes, J.P.L., 3 In. | 12.00 |
| Limoges, Tray, Dresser, Pink Roses, Irregular Rim, Gold, 1893, 12 X 8 In. | 35.00 |
| Limoges, Tray, Forget-Me-Nots, Hand-Painted, 9 X 7 In. | 32.00 |
| Limoges, Tray, Ice Cream, Rectangular, Floral, Duck, Turkey, & Pig, Pink Band | 22.50 |
| Limoges, Tray, Lavender Floral On White, Gold Edge, M.Redon, 17 X 11 In. | 37.50 |
| Limoges, Tray, Palette Shape, Violets & Greenery, Irregular Gold Edge | 45.00 |
| Limoges, Tray, Pin, Floral, Marked | 15.00 |
| Limoges, Tray, Red, Blue, & Pink On Black, Medallion Border, Elite, 12 In. | 25.00 |
| Limoges, Tureen & Underplate, Covered, 2 Handles, Roses, Jules Etienne | 35.00 |
| Limoges, Tureen, Hand-Painted Brown & Green Floral, C.1885 | 30.00 |
| Limoges, Tureen, Handles, Gold Trim, Pink Roses, Pouyat, 11 1/2 In. | 22.00 |
| Limoges, Vase, Gourd Shape, Fluted, Pink Asters, Gold Trim, Artist Signed | 30.00 |
| Limoges, Vase, Hand-Painted Roses, Signed B.& C.Limoges, France, 10 In. | 55.00 |
| Limoges, Vase, Pitcher Type, Grape Clusters, 13 3/4 In. High | 125.00 |
| Lindbergh, Pinback, Picture, 1 1/4 In. | 5.00 |
| Lindbergh, Plate, 1927, Plane, Eiffel Tower, Statue Of Liberty, 8 1/2 In. | 15.00 |

*Lithophanes are porcelain pictures made by casting clay in layers of various
thicknesses. When a piece is held to the light, a picture of light and shadow
is seen through it. Most lithophanes date from the 1825 to 1875 period. A
few are still being made.*

| | |
|---|---|
| Lithophane, Castle Scene, Marked P.P.M., 5 1/2 In.Bottom | 38.00 |
| Lithophane, Martin Luther & Family Sitting Around Christmas Tree, 6 In. | 48.00 |
| Lithophane, Mug, Green Floral, Austria | 68.00 |
| Lithophane, Plaque, French, People & Forest Scene, Brass Hanger | 45.00 |

Liverpool, Jug, Transfer Printed,
J.H.Almabury, 1795

Liverpool, Pitcher,
Washington Memorial, C.1800

| | |
|---|---|
| **Lithophane, Plaque,** Scenic, People, Woodlands, French Sickle Mark | 45.00 |
| **Lithophane, Tea Warmer,** Nite Lite, Brass Legs & Burner, 4 Scenes | 77.00 |
| **Lithophane, Tea Warmer,** 4 Scenic Panels, Oil Burner, 4 X 5 In. | 95.00 |
| **Lithophane, View From West Point,** 3 1/4 X 2 1/4 In. | 25.00 |
| **Lithophane, Young Lovers On River,** Hills & Church, KPM, 11 X 9 In. | 185.00 |
| **Lithyalin, Vase,** Dark Green, Cut Panels, 14 In., Pair | 160.00 |
| **Little Orphan Annie, Book,** Little Orphan Annie & Sandy, Big Little Book | 9.50 |
| **Little Orphan Annie, Book,** Little Orphan Annie, 1944, Harold Gray | 5.50 |
| **Little Orphan Annie, Mug,** Signed Harold Gray | 15.00 |
| **Little Orphan Annie, Stove,** Large Size | 7.00 |

*Liverpool, England, has been the site of several pottery and porcelain
factories from 1716 to 1785. Some earthenware was made with transfer
decorations. Sadler and Green made print-decorated wares from 1756. Many
of the pieces were made for the American market and featured patriotic
emblems such as eagles, flags, and other special-interest motifs.*

| | |
|---|---|
| **Liverpool, Bowl,** Washington, "Long Live The President" | 450.00 |
| **Liverpool, Cup & Saucer,** Handleless, Black Transfer Design | 20.00 |
| **Liverpool, Cup & Saucer,** London Shape, Printed House Decoration | 39.00 |
| **Liverpool, Jug,** Transfer Printed, J.H.Almabury, 1795   *Illus* | 250.00 |
| **Liverpool, Mug,** George Washington, Long Live The President | 450.00 |
| **Liverpool, Pitcher,** James Madison | 450.00 |
| **Liverpool, Pitcher,** John Adams | 700.00 |
| **Liverpool, Pitcher,** Mischievous | 99.00 |
| **Liverpool, Pitcher,** Thomas Jefferson, Portrait | 700.00 |
| **Liverpool, Pitcher,** Washington Memorial, C.1800   *Illus* | 400.00 |
| **Liverpool, Plate,** Polychrome Delft, Fazackerly Colors, C.1760, 9 In. | 125.00 |

*Loetz glass was made in Austria in the late nineteenth century. Many
pieces are signed Loetz, Loetz-Austria, or Austria, and a pair of crossed
arrows in a circle. Some unsigned pieces are confused with Tiffany glass.*

| | |
|---|---|
| **Loetz Type, Basket,** Berry Prunts, Red To Iridescent Gold, Applied Handle | 125.00 |
| **Loetz Type, Vase,** Iridescent, Drapery Folds, Green & Amber, 10 1/2 In.High | 325.00 |
| **Loetz, Bowl,** Blown-Out, Metal Rim, Iridescent, Signed, 9 In. | 150.00 |
| **Loetz, Compote,** Gold Luster, Blue Spattering, 6 In.High, Signed | 325.00 |
| **Loetz, Inkwell,** Insert, Red | 195.00 |
| **Loetz, Inkwell,** Iridescent, Swirl Design In Gold Green & Blue, 2 1/2 In. | 95.00 |
| **Loetz, Jar,** Cracker, Green Iridescent, Silver Bail & Lid, Unsigned | 148.00 |
| **Loetz, Jug,** Claret, Dark Green On Light Green, 5 3/4 In. | 75.00 |
| **Loetz, Perfume,** Enameled Flowers, Blue Iridescent | 55.00 |
| **Loetz, Tumbler,** Green, Veined | 75.00 |
| **Loetz, Vase,** Bottle, Gourd Shaped, Multicolor Iridescence, 6 1/2 In.High | 145.00 |
| **Loetz, Vase,** Bowl Shape, Amethyst, Iridescent Threading, 6 In. | 135.00 |
| **Loetz, Vase,** Bublous, Thin Flared Neck, Green Iridescent, Signed, 10 In.High | 155.00 |
| **Loetz, Vase,** Conical, Carved Wild Rosebush On Yellow, 3 Layer, 7 1/4 In. | 450.00 |

Loetz, Vase, Enamel Decoration On Green, Signed, 6 In.High ............ 75.00
Loetz, Vase, Footed, Ruffled Rim, Gold Luster, Blue Highlights, 6 In.High ............ 215.00
Loetz, Vase, Gold Iridescent, Dimpled Sides, 4 1/4 In.High ............ 75.00
Loetz, Vase, Gold Iridescent, Pinched In Sides, Signed, 6 In.High ............ 135.00
Loetz, Vase, Gold Pulled Design On Smoky Blue, 4 In.High ............ 395.00
Loetz, Vase, Gold, Green Iridescence, Signed, 6 In.High ............ 150.00
Loetz, Vase, Gourd Shape, Iridescent Yellow, Silver Overlay, 1890s, 6 1/4 In. ............ 225.00
Loetz, Vase, Gourd, Iridescent Blue & Green, 9 1/4.In High ............ 225.00
Loetz, Vase, Green Iridescent, Oval, 12 In.Wide ............ 145.00
Loetz, Vase, Green Iridescent, Signed Austria, 4 In.High ............ 75.00
Loetz, Vase, Iridescent Blue On Coral Ground, 8 In.High ............ 125.00
Loetz, Vase, Iridescent Blue, Applied Teardrops, C.1900, 5 3/8 In.High ............ 450.00
Loetz, Vase, Peacock's Tail Colors On Purple, Art Nouveau Metal Holder ............ 62.00
Loetz, Vase, Pinched, Oil Spots On Green Iridescent, 9 3/4 In. High ............ 100.00
Loetz, Vase, Pink To Burgundy, White Cased Inside, Signed Austria, Pair ............ 175.00
Loetz, Vase, Silverized & Iridized, 5 In. ............ 85.00
Loetz, Vase, Tiffany Type, 13 In. ............ 150.00
Loetz, Vase, Tulip, Iridescent Blue Base, Iridescent Pink Top, 9 1/2 In.High ............ 475.00
Loetz, Vase, Two Colors Of Green, Signed, 5 In. ............ 140.00
Loetz, Vase, White, Gold, & Pink Pulled Loops On Yellow, 9 1/2 In.High ............ 65.00
Lone Ranger, Flashlight, Signal, Siren, Boxed ............ 40.00
Lone Ranger, Flashlight, Signal, Siren, Lithographed, Tin, 6 In. ............ 9.25
Lone Ranger, Flashlight, Signal, Siren, Silver Bullet Code, C.1949 ............ 10.00
Lone Ranger, Game, Pressman, 1966, Boxed ............ 6.50
Lone Ranger, Game, Target, Lithographed, Metal, Marx, 1938 ............ 24.50
Lone Ranger, Guitar, Lone Ranger & Tonto On Front ............ 10.00
Lone Ranger, Hat, Felt, White ............ 7.00
Lone Ranger, Knife, Picture Of Lone Ranger, Silver Bullet ............ 11.00
Lone Ranger, Knife, 1940s ............ 35.00
Lone Ranger, Pistol, Tin, Clicker, Dated 1938, 9 In.Long ............ 16.00
Longton Hall, Bottle, Perfume, Stopper, Rococo Vase Shape, C.1754, Pair, 7 In. ............ 200.00
Longton Hall, Dish, Cos Lettuce Leaf, Puce Veins, Twig Handle, C.1755 ............ 500.00
Longton Hall, Dish, Strawberry Leaf, Oval, C.1754, 10 3/4 In.Long ............ 300.00

*Lonhuda Pottery Company of Steubenville, Ohio, was organized in 1892 by
William Long, W. H. Hunter and Alfred Day. Brown underglaze
slip decorated pottery was made. The firm closed in 1896.*

Lonhuda, Bowl, Two Fish, 3 Footed ............ 365.00
Lonhuda, Bowl, Two Handles, Floral Decoration, Brown Glaze, 6 1/2 In.Diam. ............ 75.00
Lonhuda, Rose Bowl, Yellow Floral, Artist Signed, 3 Footed ............ 135.00

*Lotus ware was made by the Knowles, Taylor & Knowles Company of East
Liverpool, Ohio, from 1890 to 1900.*

Lotus Ware, Bowl, Gold Decoration, Knowles, Taylor, & Knowles ............ 300.00
Lotus Ware, Bowl, Transfer Of French Children, Gold On Twig Handle, 14 In. ............ 250.00
Lotus Ware, Creamer, Hand-Painted Multicolor Floral, 4 1/2 In. ............ 125.00
Lotus Ware, Cup & Saucer, Demitasse, Hand-Painted Geometric Floral ............ 95.00
Lotus Ware, Dish, Quatrefoil, White, Twig Feet, 6 1/2 In. ............ 70.00
Lotus Ware, Jug, Gilt Handle & Rum, Enamel Flowers, K.T.K., 7 1/4 In. ............ 70.00
Lotus Ware, Pitcher, Embossed Veined Leaves, Twisted Rope Handle, 5 1/4 In. ............ 150.00
Lotus Ware, Pitcher, Leaves & Berries, Gilt Handle, I.T.McNutt '96, 5 In. ............ 200.00
Lotus Ware, Pitcher, Milk, Decorated ............ 285.00
Lotus Ware, Pitcher, Milk, Gold Outlined Magenta Floral On White, K.T.K. ............ 175.00
Lotus Ware, Rose Bowl, Embossed Designs, Orange & Gilt Dots, 3 3/4 In. ............ 65.00
Lotus Ware, Rose Bowl, Fish Scale, Gold Floral, K.T.K., Artist Signed ............ 500.00
Lotus Ware, Rose Bowl, 22K Gold Fish Scale Complexities, K.T.K., 1895 ............ 500.00
Lotus Ware, Strainer, Tea, Encrusted Gold On Light Blue ............ 185.00
Lotus Ware, Sugar & Creamer, Cover, White Fishnet ............ 350.00
Lotus Ware, Tray, Shell Shape, White, K.T.K., 5 1/4 In.Long ............ 160.00
Lotus Ware, Vase, Applied Green Foliage On White, 7 In. ............ 375.00
Lotus Ware, Vase, Applied White Foliage On Green, 7 1/2 In. ............ 375.00
Lotus Ware, Vase, Bulbous, Scalloped Top, Gold & Red Roses & Floral, Handles ............ 280.00
Lotus Ware, Vase, Cremonium Pattern, Gold Handles & Band, 6 In. ............ 110.00
Lotus Ware, Vase, Lotus Design, K.T.K., 8 1/2 In. ............ 475.00
Lotus Ware, Vase, Twisted Handle, Hand-Painted, Pontil Flower, 7 In. ............ 200.00
Lotus Ware, Vase, White, 2 Handled, 7 1/2 In. ............ 125.00

Low, Tile, Old Man, Signed Arthur Osborne

*Low art tiles were made by the J. and J.G. Low Art Tile Works of Chelsea, Massachusetts, from 1877 to 1902. A variety of art and other tiles were made.*

| | |
|---|---|
| Low, Tile, Blue, Embossed Woman's Head, Marked, 4 3/8 In. Square | 25.00 |
| Low, Tile, Old Man, Signed Arthur Osborne ............................................. *Illus* | 50.00 |
| **Lowestoft, see also Chinese Export** | |
| Lowestoft, Bowl, Shallow, Pink & Green Floral & Ribbon On White, 5 1/2 In. | 48.00 |
| Lowestoft, Creamboat, Blue & White, Wishbone Handle, C.1775, 4 In.Long | 80.00 |
| Ludwigsburg, Basket, Floral Bouquet, Oval, C.1765, 6 7/8 In.Long | 300.00 |
| Ludwigsburg, Figurine, Recumbent Hound, White & Rust, C.1765, 3 1/2 In. | 600.00 |
| Ludwigsburg, Plate, Basketwork Rim, Floral Bouquet, C.1770, 10 In. | 120.00 |
| Ludwigsburg, Plate, Puce Rose, Scrollwork & Feathering, C.1765, 9 3/8 In. | 160.00 |

*Luneville, a French faience factory, was established in 1731 by Jacques Chambrette. It is best known for its fine biscuit figures and groups and for large faience dogs and lions. The early pieces were unmarked. The Terre de Lorraine of T.D.L.impression was used after 1766.*

| | |
|---|---|
| Luneville, Group, Boy Fishermen, Biscuit, C.1770, 6 In.High | 325.00 |
| Luneville, Smoking Set, Yellow & White Daisies On Black & Green, 4 Piece | 72.00 |

*Lusterware was meant to resemble copper, silver, or gold. It has been used since the sixteenth century. Most of the luster found today was made during the nineteenth century.*

| | |
|---|---|
| Luster, Black, Washstand Set, Peaches, English, C.1920, 6 Piece | 75.00 |
| Luster, Copper, Bowl, Blue Band, Red Flowers, Green Leaves, Footed, 4 1/4 In | 37.50 |
| Luster, Copper, Bowl, Tan Band, Copper Flowers, Footed, 4 1/2 In.Diameter | 37.50 |
| Luster, Copper, Chocolate Pot, Gold Floral, Marked Germany, 9 In.High | 15.00 |
| Luster, Copper, Creamer, Blue Neck Band, 3 Rows Beading, 5 In. | 47.50 |
| Luster, Copper, Creamer, Blue Trim, Grapes, 6 In. | 125.00 |
| Luster, Copper, Creamer, Helmet Spout, Light Blue Band, Raised Cosmos, Green | 45.00 |
| Luster, Copper, Creamer, Raised Polychrome Decoration On Blue Band | 20.00 |
| Luster, Copper, Creamer, Yellow, Green, & Lavender Floral, 4 In.High | 29.50 |
| Luster, Copper, Cup & Saucer, Blue Band With Copper Flowers | 35.00 |
| Luster, Copper, Eggcup, Blue Band, Floral, Ribbed Bottom, Footed, 4 In.High | 55.00 |
| Luster, Copper, Goblet, Yellow Band, Pink & Copper Decoration, 4 1/2 In.High | 65.00 |
| Luster, Copper, Jug, Cherubs, Goats & Other Animals On 3 In.Blue Band, 1825 | 125.00 |
| Luster, Copper, Jug, Marked Carter Poole, 14 1/2 In.High | 150.00 |
| Luster, Copper, Jug, Pink Luster Bands, Foliate, Scroll Handles, C.1820, Pair | 110.00 |
| Luster, Copper, Mug, Blue & Yellow Bands, 2 3/4 In.High | 22.00 |
| Luster, Copper, Mug, Child's, Green Decorated Band, 2 1/2 In. High | 30.00 |
| Luster, Copper, Mug, Cream Band With Multicolored Decoration | 37.50 |
| Luster, Copper, Mug, Pink Luster Band Inside, 3 In.High | 30.00 |
| Luster, Copper, Mug, Sand Colored Band, Blue Flowers, White Lining | 37.50 |
| Luster, Copper, Mug, Shaving, Raised Enamel Flowers, 3 1/2 In.Diameter | 55.00 |
| Luster, Copper, Pepper Pot, Embossed Pink Enameled Roses, C.1845, 4 1/2 In. | 45.00 |
| Luster, Copper, Pitcher, Blue & Tan Bands, 3 1/2 In. | 35.00 |
| Luster, Copper, Pitcher, Blue Band, Allerton's, Longton, England, 4 In.High | 22.00 |

| | |
|---|---|
| Luster, Copper, Pitcher, Blue Band, Raised Figures, Quart | 75.00 |
| Luster, Copper, Pitcher, Blue Band, 7 In. | 50.00 |
| Luster, Copper, Pitcher, Blue Dancing Girls, 6 3/4 In.High | 45.00 |
| Luster, Copper, Pitcher, Blue Floral Band, 2 1/2 In. | 18.00 |
| Luster, Copper, Pitcher, Blue Scroll, 2 Men Playing Cards & Drinking | 150.00 |
| Luster, Copper, Pitcher, Blue Trim, Dancing Figures, 7 In.High | 55.00 |
| Luster, Copper, Pitcher, Cobalt, Canary & White Decoration, Duck Head Handle | 90.00 |
| Luster, Copper, Pitcher, Colored Embossed Floral On Blue Band, Face Spout | 48.00 |
| Luster, Copper, Pitcher, Decorated, 6 1/2 In. | 33.00 |
| Luster, Copper, Pitcher, Duck's Head & Serpent Handle, Cobalt, Canary, White | 90.00 |
| Luster, Copper, Pitcher, Green Band With Decorations, 2 1/2 In. | 45.00 |
| Luster, Copper, Pitcher, Jug Type, Girl & Lamb Painting On Sides, 5 In. | 55.00 |
| Luster, Copper, Pitcher, Leafy Design On Dark Blue Band, 2 1/2 In.High | 22.00 |
| Luster, Copper, Pitcher, Milk, Blue Figures, 8 In. | 48.50 |
| Luster, Copper, Pitcher, Milk, Embossed, Fluted, Footed, 9 1/4 In. | 48.00 |
| Luster, Copper, Pitcher, Multicolor Floral, 6 In. | 35.00 |
| Luster, Copper, Pitcher, Pink Flower, Green & Yellow Leaves, 7 In.High | 55.00 |
| Luster, Copper, Pitcher, Pink Luster Trim, Sanded Band, 2 In.High | 12.00 |
| Luster, Copper, Pitcher, Sanded, 5 In.High | 55.00 |
| Luster, Copper, Pitcher, Scenic, Old-Fashioned Ladies & Children, 8 1/2 In. | 110.00 |
| Luster, Copper, Pitcher, Urn Form, Canary Body, Fruit, 9 1/8 In.High, C.1850 | 175.00 |
| Luster, Copper, Pitcher, William Harrison | 250.00 |
| Luster, Copper, Pitcher, Yellow Band, Floral, Pint | 38.50 |
| Luster, Copper, Pitcher, 2 Blue Bands With Yellow & Luster Enamel, 3 In. | 35.00 |
| Luster, Copper, Plate, Embossed Flowers, Ironstone, 8 1/2 In. | 8.00 |
| Luster, Copper, Pot, Pepper, Blue Band, Embossed Pink & Luster Floral, 4 In. | 45.00 |
| Luster, Copper, Salt, Sanded Band, Footed | 25.00 |
| Luster, Copper, Salt, Trencher, Blue Band, 3 In. | 45.00 |
| Luster, Copper, Saucer, Blue, Rust, Floral, Deep | 10.00 |
| Luster, Copper, Syrup, Hinged Pewter Lid & Rim, Raised Leaf Thumb Rest | 125.00 |
| Luster, Copper, Tea Leaf, see Ironstone, Tea Leaf | |
| Luster, Copper, Teacup & Saucer, Blue Band With Copper Scrolls | 45.00 |
| Luster, Copper, Toothpick, Blue & Tan Bands, Beading, White Lining, C.1850 | 18.50 |
| Luster, Copper, Toothpick, Sanded Band | 35.00 |
| Luster, Fairyland, see also Wedgwood | |
| Luster, Fairyland, Bowl, Footed, Midnight Decoration, 2 1/4 In.High | 375.00 |
| Luster, Green, Shoe, Forget-Me-Nots On Toes, Germany, Joined Pair | 8.00 |
| Luster, Lavender, Mug, Child's, Gold Flowers, Letter P Handle, R.I. | 17.00 |
| Luster, Pink, Bowl, Lobster, Gold Trim, J.S.Germany | 45.00 |
| Luster, Pink, Creamer, 5 1/2 In. | 35.00 |
| Luster, Pink, Cup & Saucer, Allerton, England | 38.00 |
| Luster, Pink, Cup & Saucer, Applied Handles, Flower & Leaf, Paneled | 12.00 |
| Luster, Pink, Cup & Saucer, English | 12.00 |
| Luster, Pink, Cup & Saucer, Floral & Fruit | 20.00 |
| Luster, Pink, Cup & Saucer, Handleless, Staffordshire | 14.65 |
| Luster, Pink, Cup & Saucer, House Pattern | 45.00 |
| Luster, Pink, Cup & Saucer, Pink & Blue Floral, Deep Saucer, Staffordshire | 6.00 |
| Luster, Pink, Cup & Saucer, Splashy Floral Decoration, No Handle | 35.00 |
| Luster, Pink, Cup & Saucer, Twig Handle, Transfer Girl & Dog, C.1820 | 32.50 |
| Luster, Pink, Cup & Saucer, Wedding, Wishbone Handle, Black Transfer, 1820 | 20.00 |
| Luster, Pink, Jug, Orange Association & William III Medallions, C.1820 | 425.00 |
| Luster, Pink, Mug, Child's, Child's Swimming Party On White | 10.00 |
| Luster, Pink, Mug, Schoolhouses, 2 1/2 In.High | 45.00 |
| Luster, Pink, Pitcher, Full-Rigged Ship Under Spout, Verses, C.1850 | 195.00 |
| Luster, Pink, Plate, Deep, 7 1/4 In. | 15.00 |
| Luster, Pink, Plate, Pink Band, Rose Decoration, 7 1/2 In. | 17.00 |
| Luster, Pink, Saucer, House | 13.00 |
| Luster, Pink, Slipper, German | 9.00 |
| Luster, Pink, Sugar & Creamer, Hunting Scene | 55.00 |
| Luster, Pink, Teacup & Saucer, House, Deep Drinking Saucer | 40.00 |
| Luster, Pink, Teapot, Strainer, 4 In. High To Finial | 68.00 |
| Luster, Silver, Chalice, From Platinum, 2 Handled, Copper Luster Lined, 1820 | 65.00 |
| Luster, Silver, Creamer, C.1850 | 55.00 |
| Luster, Silver, Pitcher, Resist Flowering Vines, Paneled Shape, C.1810 | 125.00 |
| Luster, Silver, Tea Set, Rudolstadt, 16 Piece | 100.00 |
| Luster, Silver, Teapot, Basket Weave & Flower | 75.00 |

| | |
|---|---|
| Luster, White, Plate, Red & Pink Carnations, 8 In. | 15.00 |
| Luster, White, Plate, Wild Roses, Yellow Butterfly, 7 1/2 In. | 14.00 |
| Luster, Yellow, Boot, Floral Decoration, Porcelain | 20.00 |

*Lustre Art Glass Company was founded in Long Island, New York, in 1920 by Conrad Vahlsing and Paul Frank. The company made lampshades and globes that are almost indistinguishable from those made by Quezal.*

| | |
|---|---|
| Lustre Art, Lamp, Hanging, Brass, 2 Gold & Green Threaded Shades, 14 In.Wide | 100.00 |
| Lustre Art, Lamp, Perfume, Eygptian Lady Holds Up Fishnet Shade, Pair | 450.00 |
| Lustre Art, Shade, Gold Calcite, Signed, 5 3/4 In.High | 40.00 |
| Lustre, Opalescent Caramel, 10 1/4 In.High, Pair | 98.00 |

*Lustres are mantel decorations, or pedestal vases, with many hanging glass prisms. The name really refers to the prisms, and it is proper to refer to a single glass prism as a lustre. Either spelling, luster or lustre, is correct.*

| | |
|---|---|
| Lustres, Candle, Gold On Crystal, Hand-Painted Portraits In Scallops, Pair | 375.00 |
| Lustres, Cranberry Enameled, Enameled Daisies, Long Cut Prisms, Pair | 165.00 |
| Lustres, Double Row Of Spearhead Prisms, Green Enamel, Gold, 14 In., Pair | 250.00 |
| Lustres, Etched Deer & Trees On Faceted Amber Stems, Pair | 175.00 |
| Lustres, Georgian, 12 Prisms, C.1800, 9 In. High | 75.00 |
| Lustres, Ruby Overlay, Rough Pontil, 9 In.High, Pair | 195.00 |
| Lustres, Ruby, Double Row Of Drops, Gilt, 14 In.High, Pair | 325.00 |
| Lustres, Ruby, Gold Decoration, Double Rows Of Drops, Pair | 250.00 |
| Lustres, Triple Overlay, Gold Trim, Notched Prisms, C.1860, 12 In., Pair | 425.00 |
| Lustres, Water Crystal, Double Rows Of Prisms, Paneled Middle, Pair | 450.00 |
| Lustres, White Overlay On Emerald Green, Pastel Flowers, Cut Crystals, Pair | 195.00 |

*Lutz glass was made in the 1870s by Nicholas Lutz at the Boston and Sandwich Company. He made a delicate and intricate threaded glass of several colors. Other similar wares are referred to as Lutz.*

| | |
|---|---|
| Lutz Type, Bowl, Finger, Rose On Clear, Threaded | 35.00 |
| Lutz, Cruet, Blown Stopper, White & Gold Latticinio Threading, 7 In., Pair | 197.00 |
| Lutz, Dish, Candy, Latticinio Stripe & Goldstone, 8 1/2 In.Diameter | 75.00 |
| Lutz, Dish, Candy, White Latticinio, Squarish, 4 1/2 In.Diameter | 69.00 |
| Lutz, Paperweight, 5 Pears, Green Leaves, Latticinio, Bubbles, N.E. | 400.00 |
| Lutz, Perfume, Latticinio, Lay Down, 4 In. | 35.00 |
| Lutz, Perfume, Turquoise & White, Cap | 40.00 |
| Lutz, Plate, Whirlings Over Mustard Gold, Mica, Ruffled, 7 In. | 11.00 |
| Lutz, Salt, Footed, Latticinio | 45.00 |
| Lutz, Toothpick, Latticinio Swirl, White Webbing, Scalloped Top | 75.00 |
| Lutz, Vase, Flared Top, Bulbous Bottom, Blue, Iridescent, 9 In. High, Pair | 195.00 |
| Maastricht, Plate, Abbey, Cobalt Blue & White, 9 1/4 In. | 5.50 |
| Maastricht, Plate, Abbey, Luster Border, 6 1/2 In. | 2.50 |
| Maastricht, Plate, Fruit, 9 In. | 9.00 |
| Maastricht, Plate, Timor, P.Regout & Co., 8 1/4 In. | 9.00 |
| Maastricht, Plate, Timor, 8 1/4 In. | 15.00 |
| Maastricht, Rice Set, Timor Pattern, 7 Piece | 69.00 |

*Maize glass, sold by the W.L.Libbey & Son Company of Toledo, Ohio, was made by Joseph Locke in 1889. It is pressed glass formed like an ear of corn. Most pieces were made for household use.*

| | |
|---|---|
| Maize, Muffineer, Pewter Top, 5 1/2 In. | 50.00 |
| Maize, Tumbler, Decorated | 95.00 |

*Majolica is any pottery glazed with a tin enamel. Most of the majolica found today is decorated with leaves, shells, branches, and other natural shapes and in natural colors. It was a popular nineteenth-century product.*

**Majolica, see also Wedgwood, Minton**

| | |
|---|---|
| Majolica Type, Pitcher, Basket Weave, Raised Flowers, Green, Yellow, & Pink | 20.00 |
| Majolica, Ashtray & Match Holder, Frog Sitting Beside Tray Playing Uke | 30.00 |
| Majolica, Bowl, Basket Shape, Berry Sprays On Basket Weave, 5 1/4 In. | 24.50 |
| Majolica, Bowl, Center, Castle Hedingham, Bingham, England, C.1890, 10 1/2 In. | 110.00 |
| Majolica, Bowl, Etruscan, Shell & Seaweed, 5 1/4 In.Diameter | 21.00 |
| Majolica, Bowl, Germany, Basket Weave, Pink Carnations On Blue, 9 1/2 In. | 45.00 |
| Majolica, Bowl, Green Maple Leaves On Cream, 10 X 2 In. | 18.00 |
| Majolica, Bowl, Green, Raised Fruit Center, 8 1/2 In. | 20.00 |
| Majolica, Bowl, Landscape, Females, & Sheep, 12 3/8 In. | 70.00 |
| Majolica, Bowl, Mythological Figures In Landscape, C.1950, 11 1/4 In. | 40.00 |

Majolica, Bowl, Oval, Honey Caramel Glaze Over Floral, 12 In.Wide ............................... 65.00
Majolica, Bowl, Punch, Footed, Yellow Flowers, 10 In.Diameter ................................... 58.00
Majolica, Bowl, Shell & Seaweed, Etruscan, 8 1/2 X 3 1/2 In. .................................. 45.00
Majolica, Box, Sardine, Sardine On Lid, Basket Weave, 6 X 3 In. ............................... 35.00
Majolica, Box, Sugar, Cauliflower Shape ......................................................... 18.00
Majolica, Butter Chip, Geranium Leaves .......................................................... 4.00
Majolica, Cake Set, Green & Gold Border, Mottled Center, Wedgwood, 7 Piece ............... 250.00
Majolica, Cake Stand, Etruscan, Maple Leaves On Top, Tree Base, 5 X 9 In. ................. 50.00
Majolica, Cake Stand, Green Ivy Decoration, Signed GHS ...................................... 27.00
Majolica, Compote, Etruscan, Sunflower, Marked GHS, 5 In. High .............................. 45.00
Majolica, Creamer, Etruscan, Bamboo, Marked, 4 1/2 In.High .................................. 35.00
Majolica, Creamer, Fans, Flowers, & Birds On Cream, 2 1/2 In. High .......................... 8.75
Majolica, Cup & Saucer, Etruscan, Cauliflower .................................................. 20.00
Majolica, Dish, Etruscan, Leaf Shape, 6 1/2 X 9 In. ........................................... 22.00
Majolica, Dish, Leaf, Etruscan, Rose, Yellow, & Green, Signed ................................ 45.00
Majolica, Dish, Pickle, Green Leaf With Stem, Fruit Decoration, 11 1/2 In. ................. 22.00
Majolica, Dish, Sardine, Fish On Cover, Green, Yellow, & Brown, Wedgwood ................. 55.00
Majolica, Dish, Soap, Covered, Leaf Shape ...................................................... 8.50
Majolica, Ewer, Brown, Green, & Ivory, Signed, 15 In.High, Pair .............................. 80.00
Majolica, Jar, Biscuit, White, Tan, Red Floral Design, Brass Cover ........................... 40.00
Majolica, Jar, Tobacco, Crying Baby With Pink Hat, Blue Jacket, 5 In. ....................... 48.50
Majolica, Jar, Tobacco, Raised Cap & Pipe On Cover, Pink Floral, 4 Footed .................. 32.00
Majolica, Jardiniere, Raised Blue Floral With Yellow Centers, Green Lined .................. 35.00
Majolica, Jardiniere, Red & Green, Cherub Angels .............................................. 38.00
Majolica, Pitcher, Blue, Yellow, & Pink, 7 1/2 In. ...................................... *Illus* 67.50
Majolica, Pitcher, Etruscan, Shell & Seaweed, Green, Brown, & Cream ...................... 135.00
Majolica, Pitcher, French, Art Nouveau, Moss Green, Rose Floral & Lining ................... 26.50
Majolica, Pitcher, French, Barrel Shape, Birds, Bees, & Flowers On Tin Glaze .............. 15.00
Majolica, Pitcher, GHS, Flying Dragons & Woman's Head On Cobalt, 11 In. ................... 42.00
Majolica, Pitcher, Parrot ........................................................................ 75.00
Majolica, Pitcher, Pink Rose & Green Leaves On Brown & Cream, Pink Lined .................. 15.00
Majolica, Pitcher, Red Floral & Blue Gilt Veined Leaves On Cream, 6 In. .................... 10.00
Majolica, Plate, Begonia Leaf, Etruscan, 9 In. ................................................ 18.00
Majolica, Plate, Bird & Cherry, 8 In. ........................................................... 16.00
Majolica, Plate, Branch Handles, Oval, Beige Leaf, Brown Edge, 11 X 9 In. ................. 17.00
Majolica, Plate, Bread, Oval, Raised Ferns On Medium Green, Brown, White .................. 25.00
Majolica, Plate, Cauliflower, 8 In. .............................................................. 20.00
Majolica, Plate, Dog & Deer, 11 In. ............................................................ 22.00
Majolica, Plate, Etruscan, Basket Weave, Berries, 9 In. ...................................... 16.00
Majolica, Plate, Etruscan, Grape, 6 In. ........................................................ 25.00
Majolica, Plate, Etruscan, Green Leaf On Tan Basket Weave, 8 3/4 In. ....................... 20.00
Majolica, Plate, Fish, 11 In. .................................................................... 30.00
Majolica, Plate, Fish, 12 In. .................................................................... 35.00
Majolica, Plate, Fisher Ware, 4 Heart Shape Sections, Openwork, 15 In. .................... 100.00
Majolica, Plate, French Rabbits Eating Lettuce & Cabbage, Green, 8 1/2 In. ................ 28.00
Majolica, Plate, Germany, Basket Weave, Grape & Gooseberry, 9 1/4 In. .................... 8.00
Majolica, Plate, Green Leaf On Basket Weave, 9 In. .......................................... 18.00
Majolica, Plate, Leaf, Yellow, Green, & Brown, Ruffled Edge, 7 X 9 1/2 In. ................ 12.00
Majolica, Plate, Mustard, Art Nouveau Bluebells, 9 In. ....................................... 7.50
Majolica, Plate, Oval, Pink Dogwood Flowers, Ivory Ground, 11 1/2 In. ..................... 19.75
Majolica, Plate, Oyster, Place For 6 Oysters & Sauces, 9 3/4 In. ........................... 22.00
Majolica, Plate, Purple Grapes & Green Leaves On Cream, 8 1/4 In. ......................... 15.00
Majolica, Plate, Shell & Seaweed, Etruscan, 6 In. ........................................... 15.00
Majolica, Plate, Shell & Seaweed, Etruscan, 9 In. ........................................... 25.00
Majolica, Plate, Shell, Coral, 7 3/8 In. ........................................................ 9.00
Majolica, Plate, Zell, Gold Water Lily Pad With Pink Lily, 9 In. ............................. 7.00
Majolica, Platter, Blackberry, Marked Cliftonware ............................................. 25.00
Majolica, Platter, Brown & Red Grapes, Green Leaves, 12 1/2 X 9 1/2 In. .................. 15.00
Majolica, Platter, Brown Bows & Green Strawberries On Yellow Basket Weave ............... 25.00
Majolica, Platter, Green Leaves, Bamboo Edges, Tortoiseshell Back ......................... 12.00
Majolica, Platter, Yellows, Browns, Green, & Rose Flower Wreath Center .................... 25.00
Majolica, Saltshaker, Relief Seashells & Seaweeds, 2 Part Pewter Cover .................... 25.00
Majolica, Sugar & Creamer, Cover, Basket Weave Ground ..................................... 38.50
Majolica, Sugar & Creamer, Lavender Blackberries On Turquoise, Tan Trim .................. 25.00
Majolica, Sugar, Covered, Fans, Flowers, & Birds On Cream, 3 1/2 In.High .................. 8.75
Majolica, Sugar, Etruscan, Cauliflower ......................................................... 25.00

| | |
|---|---:|
| Majolica, Sugar, Pineapple | 20.00 |
| Majolica, Syrup, Blackberries On Cream, Metal Top, Bennet's Patent, 1873 | 27.00 |
| Majolica, Syrup, Etruscan, Sunflower | 52.00 |
| Majolica, Teapot, Blue Floral On Green, Gold Bamboo Trim, English, 7 1/2 In. | 55.00 |
| Majolica, Teapot, Ears Of Corn Decoration, Bamboo | 16.00 |
| Majolica, Teapot, Etruscan, Cauliflower | 35.00 |
| Majolica, Teapot, Pineapple | 22.00 |
| Majolica, Teapot, Raised Blackberries & Leaves On Yellow, Pink Inside | 15.00 |
| Majolica, Teapot, Shell & Seaweed, Porcelain Strainer, 4 1/2 In.High | 75.00 |
| Majolica, Teapot, Yellows, Browns, Green, & Rose Flower Wreath | 25.00 |
| Majolica, Toby Mug, Smiling Clown's Face, 7 In.High | 46.00 |
| Majolica, Tray, Czechoslovakia, Oval, Asparagus In Relief, 13 X 8 1/4 In. | 18.00 |
| Majolica, Tray, Round, Yellow Basket Weave Border, Pink & Lavender Center | 29.75 |
| Majolica, Vase, Figural, Girl At Well, 11 In.High | 100.00 |
| Map, see Print, Map | |
| Marble Carving, Bust, Charles Sumner, White, Civil War Era, 12 1/2 In. High | 135.00 |
| Marble Carving, Bust, George Washington, Toga On Shoulder, 25 In. High | 450.00 |
| Marble Carving, Bust, Lady, Head To Left, Neoclassical, Rome, 1868, 24 In. | 875.00 |
| Marble Carving, Female, White Draped, 24 In. High | 275.00 |
| Marble Carving, Nymphs, C.1875, 33 1/2 In., Pair ......................... Illus | 800.00 |

Majolica, Pitcher, Blue, Yellow, & Pink, 7 1/2 In.
(See Page 314)

Marble Carving, Nymphs,
C.1875, 33 1/2 In., Pair

*Marbles of glass were made during the nineteenth century. Venetian swirl,*
*clear glass, sulfides, and marbles with frosted white animal figures embedded in*
*the glass were popular. Handmade clay marbles were made in many places, but*
*most of them came from the pottery factories of Ohio and Pennsylvania.*
*Occasionally, real stone marbles of onyx, carnelian, or jasper can be found.*

| | |
|---|---:|
| Marble, Bennington, Blue, 1 1/4 In. | 6.50 |
| Marble, Bennington, Brown, 1 1/4 In. | 6.50 |
| Marble, Blown, Multicolor Twist, Pontil Scar, Mexico | .15 |
| Marble, Bust, Bohemian Lady | 325.00 |
| Marble, Cat's-Eye, Shooter | .25 |
| Marble, Clay, 1/2 In. | 2.00 |
| Marble, End-Of-Day, 8 In. | 35.00 |
| Marble, Mica, Amber, 1 In.Diameter, C.1890 | 22.00 |
| Marble, Mica, Deep Blue, 1 In.Diameter, C.1890 | 22.00 |
| Marble, Mica, White, C.1890, 1 In. | 22.00 |
| Marble, Pedestal, Circular Platform, Octagonal Base, 41 1/2 In.High | 100.00 |
| Marble, Pedestal, Square Platform, Molded Column, 39 In.High, Pair | 325.00 |
| Marble, Sandwich Swirl, 3/4 In. | 8.00 |
| Marble, Sandwich, Red & White Swirls Over Latticinio, 1 1/2 In.Wide | 17.50 |
| Marble, Shooter, Cat's-Eye | .25 To 1.50 |
| Marble, Sulfide, Bear, 1 1/8 In. | 45.00 |
| Marble, Sulfide, Dog, Bubbles | 55.00 |

Marble, Sulfide, Elephant, Standing, 2 In.Diameter ........................................................ 140.00
Marble, Sulfide, Goat, 6 1/2 In. ....................................................................................... 45.00
Marble, Sulfide, Pheasant, Standing, 2 In.Diameter ....................................................... 140.00
Marble, Sulfide, Pig, Large Size ...................................................................................... 37.50
Marble, Sulfide, Rooster, 2 1/4 In. .................................................................................. 42.00
Marble, Sulfide, Sitting Cat, Large Size .......................................................................... 40.00
Marble, Sulfide, Sitting Dog, 1 3/4 In. ............................................................................. 55.00
Marble, Sulfide, Sitting Dog, 5 In. ................................................................................... 60.00
Marble, Sulfide, Sitting Rabbit, Medium Size .................................................................. 35.00
Marble, Sulfide, Squirrel Insert, 2 In.Diameter ............................................................... 38.00
Marble, Sulfide, Standing Bear, Medium Size ................................................................. 35.00
Marble, Sulfide, Standing Bear, Sandwich, 1 1/2 In. ...................................................... 30.00
Marble, Sulfide, Standing Spread-Winged Eagle, 1 1/2 In. ............................................ 50.00
Marble, Swirl, Large Size ................................................................................................. 22.00
Marble, Swirl, 2 1/4 In.Diameter ..................................................................................... 60.00
Marble, Swirled, Colored, 1 1/2 In.Diameter ................................................................... 30.00
Marble, Swirled, Colored, 1 3/4 In.Diameter ................................................................... 30.00
Marble, Swirled, Colored, 2 In.Diameter ......................................................................... 30.00
Marble, Swirled, Polychrome, 3 In. .................................................................................. 27.00
Marble, Swirled, Polychrome, 4 In. .................................................................................. 26.00
Marble, Swirled, Polychrome, 4 1/2 In. ........................................................................... 32.00
Marble, Swirled, Polychrome, 4 3/4 In. ........................................................................... 29.50
Marble, Swirled, Polychrome, 4 3/8 In. ........................................................................... 28.75
Marble, Swirled, Polychrome, 5 1/4 In. ........................................................................... 38.00
Marble, Swirled, Polychrome, 6 In. .................................................................................. 40.00
Mariaga, Vase, Blue, Green, Red, & Yellow On Pink, 5 In. High ................................... 65.00

> Martinware is a salt-glazed stoneware made by the Martin Brothers of
> Middlesex, England, between 1873 and 1915. Many figural jugs and vases were
> made.

Martinware, Figurine, Bird, Quizzical, Blue & Green, 1884, 19 1/4 In. .......................... 1300.00
Martinware, Jug, Flask Shape, Dragons & Snakes, Brown & Gunmetal, 1897 ............... 375.00
Martinware, Jug, Gothic, Signed R.W.Martin, 1881, 8 1/2 In. ....................................... 350.00
Martinware, Jug, Handled, Brown Dragons & Snakes On Gray, Dated 1897 ................. 3500.00
Martinware, Vase, Sgraffito White Flowers & Dark Leaves, 6 1/4 In.High ..................... 80.00

> Mary Gregory glass is identified by a characteristic white figure painted
> on dark glass. It was made from 1870 to 1910. The name refers to any glass
> decorated with a white silhouette figure and not just the Sandwich glass
> originally painted by Miss Mary Gregory.

Mary Gregory, Ale Glass, Amber, White Girl & Foliage, 6 1/4 In. ................................. 58.00
Mary Gregory, Ale Glass, Blue, Girl, Footed, 8 1/2 In. High ......................................... 50.00
Mary Gregory, Ale Glass, Honey Amber, White Enamel Boy, 7 1/2 In. ......................... 35.00
Mary Gregory, Ale Glass, Olive Green, Boy, Tinted Face, 6 1/2 In.High ....................... 35.00
Mary Gregory, Bottle, Wine, Crystal, Girl, Tinted Face, Teardrop Stopper ................... 50.00
Mary Gregory, Box, Blue, Boy With Bow & Arrow, Hinged, 3 1/2 In. ........................... 73.50
Mary Gregory, Box, Camphor Satin, Girl & Basket Of Flowers, Covered, Paneled ....... 70.00
Mary Gregory, Box, Cranberry, Enamel Girl On Hinged Lid, 1 3/4 In. Diameter .......... 80.00
Mary Gregory, Box, Hinged, Amber, Ormolu Heads On Base, Round, 6 In. .................. 175.00
Mary Gregory, Box, Powder, Boy, Foliage, & Beading On Blue ..................................... 100.00
Mary Gregory, Box, Powder, White Girl, Apple Green, Brass Rim & Catch, Round ....... 135.00
Mary Gregory, Carafe, Cranberry, Girl With Flower, Inverted Thumbprint ..................... 250.00
Mary Gregory, Cup, Miniature, Amber, Blue Handle ....................................................... 85.00
Mary Gregory, Decanter, Blue, Boy Holding Bird In Air, Girl Watching, 15 In. ............. 195.00
Mary Gregory, Decanter, Blue, White Enameled Girl With Ball, Cut Stopper ................ 75.00
Mary Gregory, Decanter, Light Green, Boy Figure .......................................................... 60.00
Mary Gregory, Jar, Biscuit, Green, Cherub, Brass Cover, 6 1/2 In.High ....................... 95.00
Mary Gregory, Lamp, Black Amethyst, Girl At Easel, Camphor Satin Shade ................ 175.00
Mary Gregory, Lamp, Black Amethyst, Girl, Kerosene .................................................... 250.00
Mary Gregory, Lamp, Hanging, Red ................................................................................. 250.00
Mary Gregory, Lamp, Kerosene, Tan Bristol Shade, White Boy, Tree, & Flowers ........ 225.00
Mary Gregory, Napkin Holder, Cranberry, White Enameled Boy ................................... 75.00
Mary Gregory, Napkin Holder, Sapphire Blue, White Enameled Girl ............................. 75.00
Mary Gregory, Patch Box, Blue, Hinged .......................................................................... 105.00
Mary Gregory, Pitcher, Amber, Bulbous, 5 In.High ........................................................ 120.00
Mary Gregory, Pitcher, Blue Green, Girl With Basket, 6 In.High ................................... 75.00
Mary Gregory, Pitcher, Bulbous, Amber, 5 In.High ........................................................ 120.00

| | |
|---|---|
| Mary Gregory, Pitcher, Clear, Man & Foliage, Blown, Ruffled Edge, 9 1/2 In. | 140.00 |
| Mary Gregory, Pitcher, Cobalt Blue, Ruffled Top, 9 In. | 130.00 |
| Mary Gregory, Pitcher, Cranberry, Boy Playing, Ground Pontil, 6 1/4 In. | 325.00 |
| Mary Gregory, Pitcher, Cranberry, Boy, Applied Crystal Handle, 8 1/2 In.High | 165.00 |
| Mary Gregory, Pitcher, Green, White Little Girl, 6 1/2 In.High | 62.50 |
| Mary Gregory, Pitcher, Melon Panels, Boy & Girl, Clear, 8 1/2 In.High | 150.00 |
| Mary Gregory, Pitcher, Milk, Cobalt Green, White Stag, Clear Ribbed Handle | 62.00 |
| Mary Gregory, Pitcher, Olive Amber, Boy, Inverted Thumbprint, Blue Handle | 175.00 |
| Mary Gregory, Pitcher, Olive Green, White Enameled Man, Applied Handle | 135.00 |
| Mary Gregory, Pitcher, Water, Blue, White Figures, Tinted Faces, Blown, 12 In. | 185.00 |
| Mary Gregory, Pitcher, Water, Green, White Girl & Foliage, Blown, 12 In.High | 195.00 |
| Mary Gregory, Tankard, Crystal, Boy & Florals, Pewter Hinged Lid, Handle | 145.00 |
| Mary Gregory, Tea Warmer, Cranberry, Children & Animals, Silver Holder | 150.00 |
| Mary Gregory, Tea Warmer, Pink Inset, Boy Catching Butterflies | 145.00 |
| Mary Gregory, Tumble-Up Bottle & Tumbler, Cranberry, White Enameled Girl | 145.00 |
| Mary Gregory, Tumble-Up, Green, Paneled, Boy & Girl | 105.00 |
| Mary Gregory, Tumbler, Amber, Girl On Branch, Tinted Blossoms, Gold Trim | 50.00 |
| Mary Gregory, Tumbler, Cranberry, Boy, 5 In.High | 45.00 |
| Mary Gregory, Tumbler, Cranberry, Girl, 5 In.High | 45.00 |
| Mary Gregory, Tumbler, Cranberry, White Enamel Boy, 4 1/2 In. | 17.50 |
| Mary Gregory, Tumbler, Crystal, Boy & Florals, 5 1/2 In.High | 27.00 |
| Mary Gregory, Tumbler, Green, Figure Of Boy | 37.50 |
| Mary Gregory, Tumbler, Olive Amber, Boy, Paneled, Footed, Flint, 6 In.High | 50.00 |
| Mary Gregory, Tumbler, Olive Green, White Enameled Man Blowing Horn | 32.00 |
| Mary Gregory, Tumbler, Turquoise, Boy Blowing Bubbles | 30.00 |
| Mary Gregory, Vase, Amber, Little Girl, 6 In.High | 50.00 |
| Mary Gregory, Vase, Apple Green, Boy & Foliage, 6 In.High | 42.50 |
| Mary Gregory, Vase, Black Amethyst, Full Figure, 10 1/2 In.High | 130.00 |
| Mary Gregory, Vase, Black Amethyst, Girl, Frilly Dress, 10 In.High | 95.00 |
| Mary Gregory, Vase, Black Amethyst, Girl, Gold Sawtooth Top, 15 In.High | 145.00 |
| Mary Gregory, Vase, Blue, Fluted Top, 10 In.High | 79.50 |
| Mary Gregory, Vase, Cranberry, Girl With Bird, Boy With Horn, 5 In., Pair | 300.00 |
| Mary Gregory, Vase, Emerald Green, Girl, Rippled Top, 8 1/2 In.High | 55.00 |
| Mary Gregory, Vase, Green, Boy & Girl, Tinted Faces, 7 1/4 In., Pair | 85.00 |
| Mary Gregory, Vase, Satin Glass, White Beading Top & Bottom, 9 In., Pair | 260.00 |

*Masonic Shrine glassware was made from 1893 to 1917. It is occasionally*
*called Syrian Temple Shrine glassware. Most pieces are dated.*

| | |
|---|---|
| Masonic, Ashtray, Bronze, 5 In. | 12.00 |
| Masonic, Billfold, Black, Calf, Pocket Secretary, Dated 6/29/46 | 7.50 |
| Masonic, Bottle, El Kahir Temple Cedar Rapids, Iowa, Ear Of Corn, 6 1/2 In. | 35.00 |
| Masonic, Box, Gutta-Percha Lid, Wooden, Square, 4 3/4 In. | 90.00 |
| Masonic, Button, Lapel, Copper, 3/4 In. | 6.50 |
| Masonic, Button, Shank, Gold, Gold Emblem On Blue Enamel | 5.50 |
| Masonic, Chalice, Rochester, N.Y., 1911, Syria Shrine | 52.00 |
| Masonic, Champagne, Louisville, Kentucky, 1909, Syria Shrine, Tobacco Leaf | 45.00 |
| Masonic, Champagne, Rochester, N.Y., 1911, Syria Shrine | 25.00 To 45.00 |
| Masonic, Champagne, Syria Shrine, 1900 | 60.00 |
| Masonic, Champagne, Syria Shrine, 1902 | 60.00 |
| Masonic, Champagne, Syria Shrine, 1909 | 40.00 |
| Masonic, Champagne, Syria Shrine, 1911 | 48.00 |
| Masonic, Creamer, Applied Handle | 20.00 |
| Masonic, Cup & Saucer, Los Angeles, 1906, Syria Shrine | 50.00 To 60.00 |
| Masonic, Cup & Saucer, Syria Shrine, 1906 | 50.00 |
| Masonic, Cup, Loving, Syria Shrine, 1905, 3 Handles, Porcelain Inserts | 55.00 |
| Masonic, Easel, Brass, Emblem Photograph Frame, 11 In.High | 50.00 |
| Masonic, Figurine, Shriner, Metal | 12.00 |
| Masonic, Goblet, Los Angeles, 1907, Syria Shrine, Etched | 55.00 |
| Masonic, Hat, Islam, Original Container | 15.00 |
| Masonic, Hat, Syria, Original Container | 15.00 |
| Masonic, Insignia, Car, Metal, 1923 | 10.00 |
| Masonic, Medallion, Key, Masonic Casualty Co., Boston, "I Am A Mason" | 2.50 |
| Masonic, Mug, Atlantic City, 1904, Syria Shrine, Fish Handle | 48.00 |
| Masonic, Mug, Indian, 1903, Syria Shrine | 50.00 |
| Masonic, Mug, Louisville, 1909, Tobacco Leaf Stem, Shriner's | 40.00 To 45.00 |
| Masonic, Mug, Pittsburgh, 1904, 3 1/2 In. | *Illus* 65.00 |
| Masonic, Mug, San Francisco, 1902, Syria Shrine | 60.00 |

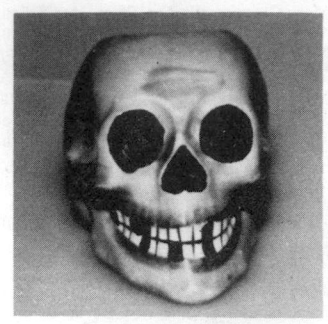

Masonic, Mug, Pittsburgh, 1904, 3 1/2 In.
*(See Page 317)*

Match Holder, Skull,
Carlsbad, 2 1/2 In.High

| | |
|---|---:|
| Masonic, Mug, Saratoga, 1903, Syria Temple, Indian | 50.00 |
| Masonic, Mug, Washington, D.C., 1900, Syria Shrine | 60.00 |
| Masonic, Paperweight, Bronze, 5 In. | 10.00 |
| Masonic, Paperweight, Shrine, Gentile | 7.50 |
| Masonic, Perfume, Polar Star & 1913 In Silver Overlay On Green Glass | 65.00 |
| Masonic, Pin, Eastern Star, 50 Year | 27.00 |
| Masonic, Pin, Mother-Of-Pearl & Ruby | 15.00 |
| Masonic, Pitcher, Ensigns Of State That Feed Our Pride, Pink Luster Trim | 65.00 |
| Masonic, Plate, Amicable Lodge, No.25, Baltimore, 1797-1947, 10 5/8 In. | 42.50 |
| Masonic, Plate, Knight Templar, 1907, Pittsburgh, Joan Of Arc, 8 In. | 36.00 |
| Masonic, Plate, Philadelphia Meeting, 1907, 9 3/4 In. | 13.00 |
| Masonic, Plate, Vaux Lodge, No.393, June 28, 1904, 10 In. | 19.00 |
| Masonic, Ring, Past Potentate, Shriner's, 5/8 Carat Diamond | 325.00 |
| Masonic, Ring, 14th Degree, 14K Gold | 35.00 |
| Masonic, Ring, 33rd Degree, Gold, Mecca Temple, N.Y., 1870, Walter Fleming | 85.00 |
| Masonic, Spoon, Chicago, Temple In Bowl, Sterling Silver | 13.50 |
| Masonic, Spoon, Order Of Eastern Star, Silver Plate | 3.75 |
| Masonic, Stein, A.A.O.N.M.S., Germany | 5.00 |
| Masonic, Sword, Templar, Dress, Ivory Handle, Etched Blade & Sheath | 95.00 |
| Masonic, Tumbler, Palestine, Providence, R.I., A.A.O.N.M.S., 1886-1906 | 12.75 |
| Masonic, Vase, Cut Glass, Elblem, Zenobia, Toledo, Diamond & Roundel, Libbey | 75.00 |
| Masonic, Watch Fob, Emblem, Pearl Skull, Red Set Eyes, Book Open, Chain | 35.00 |
| Masonic, Watch Fob, Flat Link Vest Chain | 13.00 |
| Masonic, Watch Fob, 32nd Degree, Hinged, Gold Double Chain, T Bar | 295.00 |
| Masonic, Wine, Syria Temple, June, 1899 | 60.00 |
| Match Holder, see also Iron, Match Holder, Staffordshire, Match Holder, Store, Match Holder | |
| Match Holder, Figural, Mortar, Glass | 17.00 |
| Match Holder, Girl's Head, Brown Hair, Yellow Hat, Porcelain | 43.50 |
| Match Holder, Iron, Lift-Up Cover, Striker On Base, 2 In.High | 10.00 |
| Match Holder, Monk's Head | 10.00 |
| Match Holder, Mortar Figural, Clear | 16.00 |
| Match Holder, Scenic Riders With Hounds, Porcelain, Diamond Shape | 46.00 |
| Match Holder, Skull, Carlsbad, 2 1/2 In.High ................................ *Illus* | 60.00 |
| Match Safe, see also Silver Plate, Match Safe, Silver, Sterling, Match Safe | |
| Match Safe, Centennial, Pocket, George Washington, 1776-1876, Tin | 25.00 |
| Match Safe, Figural, Barrel On Goat Drawn Cart, Robed Girl, White Metal | 45.00 |
| Match Safe, Figural, Silver Clam Shell | 65.00 |
| Match Safe, Silver, Art Nouveau, Raised Crawling Lizard On Side | 12.50 |
| Matchbox, Hinged Top, Hallmarked Silver, Engraved, Initial Blank | 25.00 |

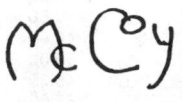

*McCoy pottery is made in Roseville, Ohio. The J.W.McCoy
Pottery was founded in 1899. It became the Brush McCoy Pottery
Company in 1911. The name changed to the Brush Pottery in 1925. The
Nelson McCoy Sanitary and Stoneware Company was founded in
Roseville, Ohio, in 1910. This firm made art pottery after 1926. In 1933
it became the Nelson McCoy Pottery. Pieces marked McCoy were made
by the Nelson McCoy Company.*

McCoy, Basket, Green Leaf & Red Berry, 9 1/2 In. ........................................ 9.50
McCoy, Bowl, Flower, Lavender, 5 In.High, 5 1/2 In.Diameter ........................ 50.00
McCoy, Bowl, Rust Red, 8 In. ............................................................................. 4.50
McCoy, Compote, White, Stemmed, Signed ..................................................... 2.25
McCoy, Creamer, 14K Gold Overlay .................................................................. 4.50
McCoy, Ewer, Antique Rose, White With Red Rose, Gold Trim, 6 In.High ....... 12.00
McCoy, Figurine, Baby Shoe, High White Glaze, Old Mark .............................. 4.50
McCoy, Jar, Cookie, Apple ................................................................................. 15.00
McCoy, Jar, Cookie, Black, Kookie Kettle, 8 In. High ..................................... 15.00
McCoy, Jar, Cookie, Bronze, 9 In. High ........................................................... 15.00
McCoy, Jar, Cookie, Clown ................................................................................ 17.50
McCoy, Jar, Cookie, Coffee Grinder Shape ..................................................... 10.00
McCoy, Jar, Cookie, Covered Wagon ............................................................... 25.00
McCoy, Jar, Cookie, Covered, Drum Shape, Signed ....................................... 8.75
McCoy, Jar, Cookie, Drum .................................................................................. 9.00
McCoy, Jar, Cookie, Duck .......................................................... 6.50 To 8.00
McCoy, Jar, Cookie, Duck, Lid .......................................................................... 8.00
McCoy, Jar, Cookie, Indian ............................................................................... 10.00
McCoy, Jar, Cookie, Log Cabin, 7 In. High ..................................................... 15.00
McCoy, Jar, Cookie, Pinecones & Owls, Greens & Browns .............................. 14.50
McCoy, Jar, Cookie, Wagon ............................................................................... 18.00
McCoy, Jar, Cookie, Wishing Well, "Wish I Had A Cookie" .............................. 17.50
McCoy, Jar, Cookie, World Globe ...................................................................... 10.00
McCoy, Jardiniere, Green Berries & Leaves, Brown Ground ........................... 7.00
McCoy, Jardiniere, Green Ribbed, Leaves, 7 1/2 X 8 1/2 In. .......................... 15.00
McCoy, Lamp Base, Dark Blue, Thistles, 2 Handled, Bulbous, 8 In.High ....... 18.75
McCoy, Planter, Green Bathtub, Footed .......................................................... 2.00
McCoy, Planter, Pelican ..................................................................................... 4.00
McCoy, Planter, Quail ......................................................................................... 5.50
McCoy, Planter, Roses, 6 In. High .................................................................... 16.00
McCoy, Planter, Spinning Wheel ....................................................................... 4.00
McCoy, Planter, Turtle ........................................................................................ 5.00
McCoy, Planter, Wild Rose, Blue With Pink Roses, 4 In High .......................... 10.00
McCoy, Planter, Wishing Well, Signed ................................................ 6.50 To 10.00
McCoy, Planter, Yellow Wagon, Matte Finish ................................................... 3.50
McCoy, Shoe, Blue, Rose On Top ...................................................................... 7.50
McCoy, Sugar & Creamer, All Gold, Marked 24K Gold .................................... 15.00
McCoy, Sugar & Creamer, Floral Decoration ................................................... 5.00
McCoy, Tea Set, Elongated Shape, Green To Cream Shading, 3 Piece .......... 17.00
McCoy, Tea Set, Ivy, 3 Piece ............................................................................. 20.00
McCoy, Tea Set, Pine Cone, Green, 3 Piece .................................................... 18.00
McCoy, Tea Set, Pinecone, 3 Piece .................................................................. 17.50
McCoy, Teapot, Brown Glaze, 4 1/2 In.High .................................................... 4.00
McCoy, Teapot, Green Branch Handle & Finial ................................................ 9.50
McCoy, Vase, Art Deco, Blue, Matte Finish, 1 3/4 In. Opening, 12 1/2 In. ..... 6.75
McCoy, Vase, Blossomtime, Yellow, 8 In.High ................................................. 10.00
McCoy, Vase, Blue, Square, Flower Decoration, 4 In.High .............................. 2.50
McCoy, Vase, Green, Signed, 6 In.High ............................................................ 5.75
McCoy, Vase, Molded Grapes, 9 1/2 In.High .................................................... 4.00
McCoy, Vase, Pearlized, 7 In.High .................................................................... 60.00
McCoy, Vase, Pink Glazed, Mum Decoration, 7 In.High .................................. 6.00
McCoy, Vase, Rose Matte, Green Berries & Leaves At Top, 6 In.High ............. 10.50
McCoy, Vase, Square, Red Bird Inside Hole, 9 In. High ................................... 10.00
McCoy, Vase, 3 Mums, 5 In.High ...................................................................... 9.00
McCoy, Wishing Well, Green & Gray .................................................................. 5.00
McKee, Bowl, Serrated, Scalloped Edge, 8 1/2 In. .......................................... 10.00
McKee, Carafe, Aztec, 7 In.High ....................................................................... 15.00
McKee, Compote, Amber, Allover Embossing, Footed ..................................... 7.00
McKee, Creamer, Toltec ..................................................................................... 2.00
McKee, Cup, Punch, Aztec ................................................................................. 2.00
McKee, Cup, Yutec .............................................................................................. 2.00
McKee, Dish, Candy, Puritan, Handled .............................................................. 8.00
McKee, Sugar & Creamer, Aztec, 6 In.High ..................................................... 20.00
McKee, Tumbler, Nortec, 4 In.High ................................................................... 5.00
McKee, Tumbler, Toltec ...................................................................................... 2.00

Mechanical Bank, see Bank, Mechanical
*Meerschaum pipes and other carved pieces of Meerschaum date from the*
*nineteenth century to the present time.*
Meerschaum, Cigar Holder, Carved Horse & Dog, Case ............................................... 38.00
Meerschaum, Cigar Holder, Hunter ....................................................................... 15.00
Meerschaum, Pipe, Bearded Man's Face, Lined Leather Case .................................. 12.50
Meerschaum, Pipe, Carved Dog On Front, Brown Coloring, Dated 1817 .................. 95.00
Meerschaum, Pipe, Hand Holding Skull .............................................................. 195.00
Meerschaum, Pipe, Running Horse At Top, L Shape, Case, 4 In.Long ...................... 32.00
*Meissen is a town in Germany where porcelain has been made since 1710.*
*Any china made in that town can be called Meissen, although the famous*
*Meissen factory made the finest porcelains of the area.*
Meissen, see also Dresden, Onion
Meissen, Basket, Openwork, Stalk Handles Ending In Feet, C.1890, 15 In. ............... 200.00
Meissen, Beaker & Saucer, Chinaman & Tea Table, Horoldt Style, C.1723 ............. 700.00
Meissen, Beaker, Chinoiserie Decoration, Floral Festoons, C.1725, 3 1/8 In. ........... 180.00
Meissen, Bowl, Alt Osier, Quatrefoil, C.1755, 7 In. Long .................................... 160.00
Meissen, Bowl, Birds & Plants On Gold, C.1725, 6 5/8 In. .................................. 110.00
Meissen, Bowl, Covered, Lovers In Gardens, C.1750, 5 1/2 In.High ....................... 150.00
Meissen, Bowl, Kakiemon, Quatrefoil, Flying Fox, C.1730, 4 1/2 In. Wide ............. 750.00
Meissen, Bowl, Kakiemon, Tiger & Floral Sprays, C.1740, 11 3/8 In. ................... 2000.00
Meissen, Bowl, Oriental Scenery, Red Mark, Bottger Ware, C.1700, 8 3/4 In. ......... 200.00
Meissen, Bowl, Serving, Free-Drawn Roses & Forget-Me-Nots, 11 X 8 1/2 In. ......... 35.00
Meissen, Bowl, Vegetable, Covered, Handled, 10 1/2 In.Diameter ......................... 198.00
Meissen, Box, Asparagus, Pale Brown Ribbon, Marcolini Period, 9 In. .................. 1400.00
Meissen, Box, Covered, Round, Florals & Insects, Crossed Swords Mark ............... 75.00
Meissen, Box, Lemon, Flower Encrusted, C.1830, 6 In., Pair ............................... 400.00
Meissen, Box, Melon, Twig Handle, Green & Brown, Marcolini Period, 7 In. ......... 1000.00
Meissen, Box, Pear, Flower Encrusted, C.1830, 7 In. Long .................................. 200.00
Meissen, Bust, Bacchus, 5 In.High ....................................................................... 260.00
Meissen, Cabaret Set, Blue Panels, Figures, Covered Cups, C.1750, 8 Piece ......... 600.00
Meissen, Cachepot, Ogee Shape, Neu Osier, Double Shell Handles, Dot Period ....... 70.00
Meissen, Candelabra, Figural, Tree Form, Girl & Boy, Gardener, C.1750 ............... 2500.00
Meissen, Centerpiece, 2 Partially Draped Women & Putti, C.1755 ....................... 450.00
Meissen, Charger, Kakiemon, Yellow Tiger, C.1740, 13 1/4 In. ......................... 2000.00
Meissen, Chessman, Knight, Horse's Head, C.1740, 2 3/4 In. ............................. 450.00
Meissen, Chocolate Pot, Gold Mounted, Yellow Ground, C.1740, 6 In. High ......... 5750.00
Meissen, Clock, Arms Of Poland, Scrollwork Case, C.1850, 23 1/2 In.High ......... 1400.00
Meissen, Coffee Service, Garland Pattern, Roses & Cobalt Blue, For 6 ............... 480.00
Meissen, Coffee Service, Single Rose, Gold Edge, Crossed Swords, For 10 ......... 700.00
Meissen, Coffeepot, Branch Handle, White, Relief Grapevines, C.1735 ............... 275.00
Meissen, Coffeepot, Equestrian Figure & Harbor View, C.1735, 8 1/2 In. ......... 2700.00
Meissen, Coffeepot, Floral Decoration On Yellow, C.1740, 7 1/4 In. ............... 275.00
Meissen, Coffeepot, Pear Shape, Three Figures & Harbor View, C.1740 ........... 550.00
Meissen, Coffeepot, Silver Gilt Mounted Lid, Applied Flowers, C.1735 ........... 1600.00
Meissen, Creamer, Floral & Gold, Footed, Crossed Swords Mark, 4 1/2 In.High ... 33.00
Meissen, Cup & Saucer, Coffee, Kakiemon, Floral, Bamboo, C.1725 ............... 175.00
Meissen, Cup & Saucer, Coffee, White, Relief Flowers, C.1740 ..................... 200.00
Meissen, Cup & Saucer, French Romantic Scene Cup, Tools Saucer ............... 7.50
Meissen, Cup & Saucer, Green Ivy, Crossed Swords ................................... 32.00
Meissen, Cup & Saucer, Octagonal, Red Vignettes & Florettes, C.1730 ......... 2600.00
Meissen, Cup & Saucer, Orchids & Forget-Me-Nots On White, Crossed Swords ... 12.00
Meissen, Cup & Saucer, Pastoral Scene On Purple, Crossed Swords ............... 125.00
Meissen, Cup & Saucer, Raised Swans ................................................... 75.00
Meissen, Cup & Saucer, Small Green Leaves ........................................... 29.00
Meissen, Cup & Saucer, Turquoise Ground, Floral Decoration, C.1745 ........... 400.00
Meissen, Cup, Double Handle, Watteau, Floral, Gold, Marked AR ................. 12.50
Meissen, Dish, Leaf, Pink Indian, Applied Handles, Crossed Swords, Pair ....... 100.00
Meissen, Dish, Lozenge Shape, Kakiemon, Flying Fox, C.1735, 9 1/4 In. ......... 400.00
Meissen, Dish, Muffin, Lemon Knop, Pink Scalework, Gilt Scrolls, Marcolini ..... 70.00
Meissen, Dish, Nut, Leaf Shape, Hand-Painted Floral, Crossed Swords ........... 22.00
Meissen, Dish, Sweetmeat, Male & Female Figures, C.1870, Crossed Swords, Pair ... 1150.00
Meissen, Figurine, Aktaeon, Myers, 6 1/2 In.High ................................... 235.00
Meissen, Figurine, Archer, Negro Warrior, Lavender Turban, C.1740, 5 1/4 In. ... 625.00
Meissen, Figurine, Bluetit, C.1740, 5 1/4 In.High .................................. 1700.00
Meissen, Figurine, Boy Dressed At Evening, Owl, Crossed Swords, 7 1/2 In. ..... 200.00

| | |
|---|---:|
| Meissen, Figurine, Children, C.1880, 5 In.High, Pair | 550.00 |
| Meissen, Figurine, Drinking Peasant, Sitting Cross-Legged, C.1736, 7 In.High | 3000.00 |
| Meissen, Figurine, Elephant, Standing, Trunk Up, C.1740, 5 1/4 In.High | 4000.00 |
| Meissen, Figurine, Farm Girl With Geese, Pastel Colors, C.1850, 9 1/2 In. | 325.00 |
| Meissen, Figurine, Female Gardener, Dot Period, 4 1/2 In. | 200.00 |
| Meissen, Figurine, Fruit Seller, C.1745, 7 In.High | 650.00 |
| Meissen, Figurine, Gallant With Dog, Kaendler, C.1745, 4 3/4 In. | 1550.00 |
| Meissen, Figurine, Gardener, Tree Stump, C.1740, 5 1/2 In.High | 500.00 |
| Meissen, Figurine, Guinea Hen, Black & White Plumage, C.1750, 2 In. | 325.00 |
| Meissen, Figurine, Hare, Crouching, Brown & Black, C.1740, 4 In. Long | 1800.00 |
| Meissen, Figurine, Hound, Seated, White & Black, C.1740, 1 3/4 In. | 175.00 |
| Meissen, Figurine, Lady Playing Cards, Standing, C.1850, 6 1/4 In. | 350.00 |
| Meissen, Figurine, Man & Woman, Period Costumes, Gold Trim, Marked, Pair | 165.00 |
| Meissen, Figurine, Monkey Plays Harp, Signed O.Pilz, 10 1/2 In. | 150.00 |
| Meissen, Figurine, Monkey, Musical, Leader & 9 Band Members, Set Of 10 | 1825.00 |
| Meissen, Figurine, Pheasant, Hen, C.1750, 1 3/4 In. | 475.00 |
| Meissen, Figurine, Putto, Tambourine To Ear, C.1740, 3 3/8 In.High | 175.00 |
| Meissen, Figurine, Recumbent Goat, C.1740, 2 1/2 In.Long | 600.00 |
| Meissen, Figurine, Recumbent Pug, Black & White, C.1740, 2 3/4 In.Long | 1300.00 |
| Meissen, Figurine, Seated Bear, C.1743, 3 3/4 In.High | 9000.00 |
| Meissen, Figurine, Seated Man In Colonial Costume Holding Gold Coin | 210.00 |
| Meissen, Figurine, Seated Monkey, Arms Around Tree, C.1740, 7 1/4 In.High | 2000.00 |
| Meissen, Figurine, Seated Turk, C.1745, 6 1/2 In.High | 250.00 |
| Meissen, Figurine, Squirrel, White & Brown, C.1750, 1 3/4 In. | 425.00 |
| Meissen, Figurine, The Violinist, Kandler Period | 1500.00 |
| Meissen, Figurine, Young Boy Holding Grapes & Basket On Stick, C.1850 | 150.00 |
| Meissen, Group, Apotheosis, Kaendler & Eberlein, C.1740, 9 In. | 800.00 |
| Meissen, Group, Crinoline, Lady & Moorish Child, Scheurich, C.1925, Pair | 600.00 |
| Meissen, Group, Musicians, Peasant Girl, Yount, C.1850, 6 1/4 In. | 200.00 |
| Meissen, Group, Rooster With Hen In Mating Position, 2 1/4 In.High | 135.00 |
| Meissen, Inkwell, Hand-Painted, Two Covered Wells, Signed Lue | 135.00 |
| Meissen, Jar, Biscuit, Garden Flowers On White Reserve, Crossed Swords | 85.00 |
| Meissen, Jug, Hot Water, Gilt Mask Spout, Travelers, Herold Style, C.1730 | 350.00 |
| Meissen, Matchbox, Bird Of Paradise & Floral, Striker Under Cover | 48.00 |
| Meissen, Plaque, Gellert, White, Crossed Swords, C.1750 | 95.00 |
| Meissen, Plate, Blue Flowers & Butterfly On White, Basket Weave Edge, 8 In. | 13.75 |
| Meissen, Plate, Bread & Butter, Green Ivy, Crossed Swords | 17.50 |
| Meissen, Plate, Cake, Green Ivy, Crossed Swords | 20.00 |
| Meissen, Plate, Cake, Pattern Similar To Onion, Blue & White, 10 1/4 In. | 28.00 |
| Meissen, Plate, Dessert, White, Rose Spray Center, Rosebud Border, C.1860 | 13.75 |
| Meissen, Plate, Dinner, Green Ivy, Crossed Swords | 25.00 |
| Meissen, Plate, Dragons & Fantastic Birds, White & Blue, Gold, 10 In. | 25.00 |
| Meissen, Plate, Gold Morning Glories On White, 11 1/4 In.Across | 120.00 |
| Meissen, Plate, Gros Bleu, Scalloped Borders, Classic Figures, C.1850, 13 In. | 200.00 |
| Meissen, Plate, Imari Pattern, Blue, C.1738, 8 3/4 In., Pair | 850.00 |
| Meissen, Plate, Kakiemon, Heron, Winged Kylin, Insects, C.1735, 9 1/8 In. | 400.00 |
| Meissen, Plate, Pierced Rim, Bouquet, Basketwork, Dot Period, 9 1/8 In. | 125.00 |
| Meissen, Plate, Single Rose, Openwork, 9 1/2 In. | 32.50 |
| Meissen, Plate, Soup, Floral Garlands, Yellow Border, Gold, 9 1/2 In. | 15.00 |
| Meissen, Plate, Soup, Floral, Scalloped Border, 8 3/8 In. | 20.00 |
| Meissen, Plate, Soup, Green Ivy, Crossed Swords | 25.00 |
| Meissen, Rack, Toast, 4 Slice | 45.00 |
| Meissen, Salt, Triangular, Footed, Floral, Marcolini Period | 50.00 |
| Meissen, Saltshaker, Leaf, Green Ivy, Crossed Swords | 20.00 |
| Meissen, Saucer, Chinoiserie, J.G.Horoldt Style, C.1725 | 375.00 |
| Meissen, Saucer, Hausmaler, Sailing Scene Medallion, C.1720 | 450.00 |
| Meissen, Saucer, Landscape Medallion On Puce, C.1730 | 225.00 |
| Meissen, Sucrier, Covered, Puce Scalework, Gilt Scrolls, Cherubs, C.1755 | 250.00 |
| Meissen, Sucrier, Open Bud Knop, Harbor & Quay Scenes, Augustus Rex | 275.00 |
| Meissen, Tea Caddy, Covered, Turquoise, Harbor View & Landscape, C.1730 | 2200.00 |
| Meissen, Tea Caddy, Puce Floral Knob, Travelers Cartouches, Floral, C.1755 | 425.00 |
| Meissen, Tea Kettle, Ormolu Mount, Stand, 15 1/2 In. ... Illus | 1200.00 |
| Meissen, Teabowl & Saucer, Italian Armorial, Herold Style, C.1730 | 2000.00 |
| Meissen, Teabowl & Saucer, Scenic Quatrefoil Panels On Yellow, C.1740 | 525.00 |
| Meissen, Teabowl & Saucer, Travelers, Ruins, River, Churches, C.1740 | 500.00 |
| Meissen, Teacup & Saucer, Battlemalerei, Puce Camaieu, C.1745 | 300.00 |

Meissen, Tea Kettle,
Ormolu Mount,
Stand, 15 1/2 In.
(See Page 321)

Meissen, Tureen,
Pineapple, Red, Yellow,
Marcolini Period

| | |
|---|---|
| Meissen, Teacup & Saucer, Gallant & Lady, Pansies, C.1745 | 100.00 |
| Meissen, Teacup & Saucer, Puce Scalework Border, Gilt Scrolls, C.1750, Pair | 200.00 |
| Meissen, Teacup & Saucer, Scenic Medallion On Coral, C.1750 | 1500.00 |
| Meissen, Teacup & Saucer, Yellow Tiger, Kakiemon, C.1740 | 1500.00 |
| Meissen, Teapot, Bullet Shape, Neu Osier, Twig Handle, C.1740 | 110.00 |
| Meissen, Teapot, Form Of Monkey, C.1735, 7 In.High | 3700.00 |
| Meissen, Teapot, Inverted Pear Shape, Puce Floral Knop, Floral, Dot Period | 250.00 |
| Meissen, Teapot, Kakiemon, Bullet Shape, Serpent Spout, Bamboo, Floral, 1700s | 1900.00 |
| Meissen, Tureen, Covered, Circular, Flowers & Tiger, C.1740, 7 3/4 In. | 2500.00 |
| Meissen, Tureen, Pineapple, Red, Yellow, Marcolini Period ...............................Illus | 600.00 |
| Meissen, Urn, Diana Hunting Scene, Handled, Medusa Heads, C.1850, 39 1/8 In. | 5000.00 |
| Meissen, Vase, Augustus Rex, Covered, Yellow Ground, C.1735, 13 In.High | 7000.00 |
| Meissen, Vase, Pate-Sur-Pate Panel, White On Blue, 12 3/8 In.High | 800.00 |

*Mercury, or silvered, glass was first made in the 1850s. It lost favor for a*
*while but became popular again about 1910. It looks like a piece of silver.*

| | |
|---|---|
| Mercury Glass, Ball, Christmas Tree, Light Green, 3 1/2 In.Diameter | 10.00 |
| Mercury Glass, Ball, Christmas Tree, Light Green, 4 In.Diameter | 10.00 |
| Mercury Glass, Ball, Christmas Tree, Light Green, 4 1/2 In.Diameter | 10.00 |
| Mercury Glass, Candlestick, Etched Flowers & Leaves, Pair | 10.00 |
| Mercury Glass, Candlestick, Hand-Painted, Red Tips, 10 In.High, Pair | 7.00 |
| Mercury Glass, Creamer, Pinched Spout, Applied Handle | 48.50 |
| Mercury Glass, Ornament, Christmas, Grape Cluster, Brass Cap & Ring, Gold | 18.00 |
| Mercury Glass, Ornament, Christmas, Grape Cluster, Brass Cap & Ring, Green | 18.00 |
| Mercury Glass, Reflector, 7 1/2 In. | 6.50 |
| Mercury Glass, Salt, Master, Silver | 18.75 |
| Mercury Glass, Sugar, Covered | 27.50 |
| Mercury Glass, Sugar, Covered, Frosted Birds & Leaves, Amber Lining | 68.00 |
| Mercury Glass, Tieback, Etched Grapes & Leaves, Pair | 22.50 |
| Mercury Glass, Tieback, Flower Shape, Pair | 25.00 |
| Mercury Glass, Tieback, Pewter Base, Pair | 15.00 |
| Mercury Glass, Vase, Bud, 3 In.High | 3.50 |
| Mercury Glass, Vase, Floral & Wild Geese In Flight, 12 1/2 In.High, Pair | 45.00 |
| Mercury Glass, Vase, 4 In. | 5.00 |

*Mettlach, Germany, is a city where the Villeroy and Boch factories*
*worked. Steins from the firm are known as Mettlach steins. They date from*
*about 1842.*

| | |
|---|---|
| Mettlach, Beaker, No.1094 | 45.00 |
| Mettlach, Beaker, No.2206, 3 Liter, Etched | 600.00 |
| Mettlach, Beaker, No.2327/1023, Mercury Mark | 48.50 |
| Mettlach, Beaker, No.2327/1200, Stadt Berlin, Castle Mark | 48.50 |
| Mettlach, Beaker, No.2327/1290B, Mercury Mark | 48.50 |
| Mettlach, Bowl, Art Nouveau, Hexagonal, Engraved Design, Cream, Beige, & Blue | 150.00 |
| Mettlach, Bowl, Pate Sur Pate, Classic Figures, Blue Green Body | 160.00 |

| | |
|---|---:|
| Mettlach, Chalice, No.2171 | 210.00 |
| Mettlach, Coaster, Dwarf Motif, Set Of 6 | 360.00 |
| Mettlach, Dish, Cheese, No.3362, Handles, Cover, Engraved Stoneware, 9 In. | 65.00 |
| Mettlach, Ewer, No.1284 | 110.00 |
| Mettlach, Ewer, No.2433, Art Nouveau Iris On Terra-Cotta, Castle Mark, 9 In. | 120.00 |
| Mettlach, Flowerpot, No.2965, Etched, Castle Mark, 9 In.High | 200.00 |
| Mettlach, Mug, Elks, Minneapolis, Minn., 1897 | 60.00 |
| Mettlach, Mug, Hires' Root Beer, Baby Transfer, C.1914, 4 1/4 In.High | 40.00 |
| Mettlach, Pitcher, No.1492, Pedestal, Floral, Castle Mark, 15 In.High | 250.00 |
| Mettlach, Pitcher, No.2258, Marked Geschutz, Castle Mark, 6 1/2 In. High | 98.00 |
| Mettlach, Pitcher, No.2947, Beige, Blue, & Ivory, Castle Mark, 8 In.High | 95.00 |
| Mettlach, Pitcher, No.2947, Blue, White, & Gold, Castle Mark, 6 1/2 X 7 In. | 95.00 |
| Mettlach, Plaque, Jason & Argonauts, Pate Sur Pate, Stahl, 1903, 18 3/8 In. | 800.00 |
| Mettlach, Plaque, No.831, Oval, Cocoa Underside, Embossed, V.& B., 12 X 10 In. | 95.00 |
| Mettlach, Plaque, No.2187 | 1150.00 |
| Mettlach, Plaque, No.2188 | 1150.00 |
| Mettlach, Plaque, No.2534, The Ruined Castle, Gold Border, 17 1/2 In. | 595.00 |
| Mettlach, Plaque, No.2698 | 650.00 |
| Mettlach, Plaque, No.3112, Cameo | 550.00 |
| Mettlach, Plaque, Nos.3272 & 3273, Cameo, Pair | 395.00 |
| Mettlach, Plate, No.1044, Grapes & Strawberries, Villeroy & Boch, 8 In. | 28.00 |
| Mettlach, Plate, No.2960, Beige, Blue, & Ivory, Castle Mark, 15 In. | 95.00 |
| Mettlach, Plate, No.3096, 8 In. | 45.00 |
| Mettlach, Plate, Octagonal, Art Nouveau, Engraved Design, 7 In., Pair | 150.00 |
| Mettlach, Stein Set, Nos.1737 & 1745, 1 3 Liter & 6 1/4 Liter, 7 Piece | 925.00 |
| Mettlach, Stein, No.74, 1/2 Liter | 295.00 |
| Mettlach, Stein, No.171, 1/4 Liter, White Wine Makers On Blue | 175.00 |
| Mettlach, Stein, No.171, 1/2 Liter, 5 White Relief Figures On Blue | 210.00 |
| Mettlach, Stein, No.468, Pewter Handle & Rim Lid, Radish On Top, V.& B. | 98.50 |
| Mettlach, Stein, No.568/1526, Pug, Music Scroll | 60.00 |
| Mettlach, Stein, No.606, Pug, Mercury Mark | 125.00 |
| Mettlach, Stein, No.1028, 1/2 Liter, Cream Relief On Brown | 165.00 |
| Mettlach, Stein, No.1132, 1/2 Liter, Castle Mark | 300.00 |
| Mettlach, Stein, No.1154, 1 Liter | 450.00 |
| Mettlach, Stein, No.1266, 1/4 Liter, Insert Lid | 120.00 |
| Mettlach, Stein, No.1396, 1/2 Liter | 275.00 |
| Mettlach, Stein, No.1479, 1/2 Liter, Etched | 275.00 |
| Mettlach, Stein, No.1480, 1/2 Liter, Castle Mark | 275.00 |
| Mettlach, Stein, No.1526, 1 Liter, Brown Pug | 85.00 |
| Mettlach, Stein, No.1526, 4/10 Liter, Seattle Brewing & Malting Co. | 85.00 |
| Mettlach, Stein, No.1527, 1/2 Liter, Etched Men Sitting Around Table | 240.00 |
| Mettlach, Stein, No.1530, 1/2 Liter, Fraternity Student | 265.00 |
| Mettlach, Stein, No.1675, 1/2 Liter, Inlaid Lid, City Of Heidelberg | 335.00 |
| Mettlach, Stein, No.1725, 1/4 Liter | 90.00 |
| Mettlach, Stein, No.1786, St.Florian | 400.00 |
| Mettlach, Stein, No.1795, 1/2 Liter | 260.00 |
| Mettlach, Stein, No.1863, 1/2 Liter | 325.00 |
| Mettlach, Stein, No.1909/727, 1/2 Liter, Pug, Signed Schlitt | 140.00 |
| Mettlach, Stein, No.1909/980, 1/2 Liter, King, Mine Shaft, Dwarfs | 180.00 |
| Mettlach, Stein, No.1947, Etched | 165.00 |
| Mettlach, Stein, No.1947, 1/2 Liter, Castle Mark | 300.00 |
| Mettlach, Stein, No.1977, 1/4 Liter, Pewter Lid, Dated 1892, Castle Mark | 255.00 |
| Mettlach, Stein, No.1995, 1/2 Liter, Etched | 290.00 To 325.00 |
| Mettlach, Stein, No.1995, 1/2 Liter, Gnome On Thumblift | 300.00 |
| Mettlach, Stein, No.1997, 1/2 Liter, Castle Mark | 275.00 |
| Mettlach, Stein, No.2002, 1/2 Liter | 275.00 |
| Mettlach, Stein, No.2028, 1/2 Liter, Etched, Pewter Lid | 250.00 |
| Mettlach, Stein, No.2043, 1/2 Liter | 350.00 |
| Mettlach, Stein, No.2052, 1/4 Liter, Figure Holding 2 Steins | 165.00 |
| Mettlach, Stein, No.2057, 3/10 Liter, Dancing Figures | 185.00 |
| Mettlach, Stein, No.2057, 1/2 Liter, Dancers With Steins On Terra-Cotta | 325.00 |
| Mettlach, Stein, No.2077, 3/10 Liter, Pewter & Ceramic Lid, Mercury Mark | 155.00 |
| Mettlach, Stein, No.2090, 3/10 Liter, Etched, Castle Mark | 220.00 |
| Mettlach, Stein, No.2099, 3/10 Liter, Etched, Inlaid Lid, Mercury Mark | 245.00 |
| Mettlach, Stein, No.2104, 2 Liter, Etched | 450.00 |
| Mettlach, Stein, No.2181, 1/2 Liter, Castle Mark | 110.00 |

Mettlach, Stein, No.2182, 1/2 Liter, Bowler In Relief On Blue .................................................. 265.00
Mettlach, Stein, No.2182, 1/2 Liter, Cream Bowlers On Terra-Cotta ........................................ 245.00
Mettlach, Stein, No.2211, 3/10 Liter, Bowling Scene In Relief, Inlaid, Blue ........................... 125.00
Mettlach, Stein, No.2271, 1/2 Liter ....................................................................................... 225.00
Mettlach, Stein, No.2286, 3 Liter, Castle Mark .................................................................... 600.00
Mettlach, Stein, No.2327, Gibson Girl Smoking ..................................................................... 35.00
Mettlach, Stein, No.2388, 1/2 Liter, Pretzel ......................................................................... 335.00
Mettlach, Stein, No.2580, 1/2 Liter ....................................................................................... 450.00
Mettlach, Stein, No.2889, 1/2 Liter, Castle Mark ................................................................. 365.00
Mettlach, Stein, No.2959, 1/2 Liter ....................................................................................... 325.00
Mettlach, Teapot, No.2946, Etched, Art Nouveau, Ocher, Blue, Cream, Castle Mark .............. 165.00
Mettlach, Tile, Hand-Painted Floral Bouquet, Signed T.Tessier, 1852, Square ........................ 65.00
Mettlach, Urn, Coral Color, Jewel Tone Enameling, 2 Handled, 15 In.High ........................... 450.00
Mettlach, Urn, Turquoise Enamel Jewels On Terra-Cotta, 15 X 8 In. ..................................... 385.00
Mettlach, Vase, No.1255, Ornate, Blue, White, Rust, Cream .................................................. 750.00
Mettlach, Vase, No.1336, Glazed Jewel Colors, Castle Mark, 11 1/2 In.High ........................ 165.00
Mettlach, Vase, No.1591, Paneled, Children, Flowers, Leaves, 12 1/2 In.High ..................... 200.00
Mettlach, Vase, No.1596, Bulbous, Jeweled Decoration On Red, Castle Mark ...................... 165.00
Mettlach, Vase, No.2851, Elephant Head & Trunk Handles ................................................... 325.00
Mettlach, Vase, Silver Luster On Gray, Scrolls & Cherubs, C.1880, 12 In. ........................... 285.00
Mickey Mouse, Acrobat, Wooden, Squeeze Toy ........................................................................ 8.00
Mickey Mouse, Badge, Mickey Mouse Club, 3 1/2 In. ............................................................. 2.50
Mickey Mouse, Bag, School, Pictures, 14 X 10 In. ................................................................... 8.00
Mickey Mouse, Ball, Rubber, 5 In. ......................................................................................... 20.00
Mickey Mouse, Book, Big Little Book ....................................................................................... 8.00
Mickey Mouse, Book, Cartoon, Philadelphia, 1934 ................................................................ 29.00
Mickey Mouse, Book, Here They Are, Walt Disney, 1940, Color .............................................. 5.00
Mickey Mouse, Book, Mickey Mouse Has A Party, School Reader, Whitman, 1938 ................ 25.00
Mickey Mouse, Book, Mickey Sees The U.S.A., 1944 ................................................ 2.50 To 8.00
Mickey Mouse, Book, Pluto, 1957 ........................................................................................... 2.00
Mickey Mouse, Book, School Days In Disneyville, 1939 ........................................................... 8.00
Mickey Mouse, Book, Story, Copyright 1931 ......................................................................... 15.00
Mickey Mouse, Bottle, Hot Water, Mickey Mouse Shape, 12 In. .............................................. 6.75
Mickey Mouse, Bowl, Cereal, Plastic, Walt Disney Enterprises ................................................ 7.50
Mickey Mouse, Box, Pencil, Cardboard, Walt Disney Enterprises .......................................... 18.00
Mickey Mouse, Brush, Decal ................................................................................................... 5.00
Mickey Mouse, Camera .......................................................................................................... 6.50
Mickey Mouse, Cards, Playing, Canasta Set, Dated 1950, Boxed ............................................ 3.75
Mickey Mouse, Charm, Silver, Circle C On Head, 3/4 In. ...................................................... 12.50
Mickey Mouse, Dish, Soap, Donald Duck Floating, Sun Rubber Co. ........................................ 8.00
Mickey Mouse, Doll, Bisque, Japanese, 3 1/4 In. .................................................................. 12.00
Mickey Mouse, Doll, Bisque, Marked Walt E.Disney, Japan, 3 1/2 In.Tall ............................. 18.00
Mickey Mouse, Doll, Donald Duck, Celluloid, 3 In. ................................................................. 3.00
Mickey Mouse, Doll, Dopey, Bisque, 3 In. .............................................................................. 7.00
Mickey Mouse, Doll, Dopey, Hard Rubber, 6 In. ...................................................................... 8.00
Mickey Mouse, Doll, Mickey Mouse, Soft Rubber, Squeeze Toy ............................................... 6.50
Mickey Mouse, Doll, Rubber, Whistle In Bottom .................................................................... 12.00
Mickey Mouse, Doll, Rubber, Whistle, Red Felt Cape, Marked C, 9 1/2 In.Tall ..................... 17.00
Mickey Mouse, Doll, Sun Rubber Co. ..................................................................................... 28.00
Mickey Mouse, Erector Set, Metal ......................................................................................... 20.00
Mickey Mouse, Figurine, Mickey On Rock, Bisque, 2 In.High ................................................. 20.00
Mickey Mouse, Figurine, Miniature, With Umbrella, Plinth Base, 2 In. ..................................... 6.00
Mickey Mouse, Figurine, Rubber, Holding Daisy Behind Back, 8 In.High ............................... 14.00
Mickey Mouse, Film, Mickey's Bad Break, 1932, 16 Mm. ...................................................... 10.00
Mickey Mouse, Fire Engine, Hard Rubber, Walt Disney Enterprises ....................................... 15.00
Mickey Mouse, Game, Tic Tac Toe, Tin, Walt Disney Productions ......................................... 10.00
Mickey Mouse, Gong Bell, Talking Telephone, Metal, Picture On Dial .................................... 14.25
Mickey Mouse, Head, Porcelain, 1 3/4 In.High ..................................................................... 18.50
Mickey Mouse, Lunch Box, Bus .............................................................................................. 6.75
Mickey Mouse, Lunch Box, Club, Thermos, Tin ...................................................................... 10.00
Mickey Mouse, Magazine, August, 1936, Vol.1, No.11 .......................................................... 12.50
Mickey Mouse, Mickey Drummer, Pull, Wooden, Metal Drum ................................................ 12.25
Mickey Mouse, Mickey In Car, Windup, Marx ........................................................................ 35.00
Mickey Mouse, Mouskemovers Van, Lithographed, Tin, 12 In. ................................................. 8.00
Mickey Mouse, Mug, Root Beer, Minnie Mouse Decal, Walt Disney ......................................... 5.00
Mickey Mouse, Napkin Ring, Lucitelike Material ................................................................... 11.00

| | |
|---|---:|
| Mickey Mouse, Planter, Mickey & Minnie | 8.00 |
| Mickey Mouse, Projector, 3 Films, Original Box | 65.00 |
| Mickey Mouse, Puppet, Finger, Face, Sponge Rubber | 5.00 |
| Mickey Mouse, Puppet, Hand, Minnie Mouse, Walt Disney | 6.00 |
| Mickey Mouse, Puppet, Hand, Plastic Head, Cloth Body | 3.50 |
| Mickey Mouse, Puppet, Hand, Soft Rubber, Cloth Body | 3.50 |
| Mickey Mouse, Racing Set, Mickey & Donald Speedway, Lithographed, Tin | 12.75 |
| Mickey Mouse, Ring, Club, 1955 | .50 |
| Mickey Mouse, Rubber Mold & Coloring Set, Mickey & Gang, Walt Disney | 12.25 |
| Mickey Mouse, Salt & Pepper, Mickey & Minnie, Walt Disney Marked | 25.00 |
| Mickey Mouse, Spoon, Silver Plate | 4.00 To 5.50 |
| Mickey Mouse, Tea Set, Child's, Blue Luster, 10 Piece | 10.00 |
| Mickey Mouse, Tea Set, Marked Disney, Box, 20 Piece | 65.00 |
| Mickey Mouse, Thermometer, Mickey's Mechanical Hand Points | 75.00 |
| Mickey Mouse, Toy, Drummer, Pull Toy | 15.00 |
| Mickey Mouse, Toy, Mickey Playing Drum, Pull Toy | 22.50 |
| Mickey Mouse, Toy, Ride On Bus, Gong Bell Toy Co., 20 In. | 25.00 |
| Mickey Mouse, Tractor, Rubber | 20.00 |
| Mickey Mouse, Tray, Tin, 7 1/2 X 5 1/2 In. | 6.50 |
| Mickey Mouse, Truck, Fire, Rubber, Mickey Driving, Donald Duck On Back | 20.00 |
| Mickey Mouse, Watch, Ingersoll, Round, 1930s | 75.00 |
| Mickey Mouse, Watch, Wrist, Ingersoll, Gold Expansion Band | 110.00 |
| Mickey Mouse, Watch, Wrist, Ingersoll, Red Leather Strap | 75.00 |
| Mickey Mouse, Watch, Wrist, Round Dial, Metal Band, 1st Model | 90.00 |
| Mickey Mouse, Weather House | 12.50 |
| Mickey Mouse, Yo-Yo | 10.00 |

*Milk glass was named for its milky white color. It was first made in England during the 1700s. The height of its popularity in the United States was from 1870 to 1880. It is now correct to refer to some colored glass as blue milk glass, black milk glass, etc. The numbers B-xx refer to the book "Milk Glass" by E.Belknap.*

### Milk Glass, see also Cosmos

| | |
|---|---:|
| Milk Glass, Ashtray, Blue, Stetson Hat Shaped | 6.50 |
| Milk Glass, Basket, Black, Shopping Bag Shape, 5 In. | 12.00 |
| Milk Glass, Basket, Blue, Basket Weave, Pinched In At Handle, 3 1/4 In. | 20.00 |
| Milk Glass, Basket, Blue, Embossed Beads, Scrolls & Rope Rim, 5 X 3 In. | 24.50 |
| Milk Glass, Basket, Fish Scale, Rope Handle, Patent 1874 | 38.50 |
| Milk Glass, Boot, Black, Spur | 30.00 |
| Milk Glass, Boot, Black, Wrinkles In Ankle, 5 In.High | 10.00 |
| Milk Glass, Boot, Painted Decoration, 3 In.High | 18.50 |
| Milk Glass, Bottle, Dresser, Leaf Pattern, Stopper | 22.00 |
| Milk Glass, Bottle, Dresser, Mushroom Stopper, Leaf & Vine, 10 In. | 25.00 |
| Milk Glass, Bottle, Figural, Senorita | 20.00 |
| Milk Glass, Bottle, World's Fair, 1939 | 18.00 |
| Milk Glass, Bowl, Beaded Rib, Open Edge, 9 3/4 In.Diameter, B-150-138b | 47.50 |
| Milk Glass, Bowl, Blue, Paneled Daisy & Button, Oval, 9 X 7 X 4 1/2 In. | 15.00 |
| Milk Glass, Bowl, Centerpiece, Blue, Hobnail, Fluted Edge, 10 In. Diameter | 50.00 |
| Milk Glass, Bowl, Cereal, Davy Crockett | 5.50 |
| Milk Glass, Bowl, Closed Lattice Edge, Wild Rose Painting, 8 In. | 29.00 |
| Milk Glass, Bowl, Cut Flowers & Leaves, Sawtooth Edge, 8 In.Long | 35.00 |
| Milk Glass, Bowl, Green, Atterbury Arch Border, 7 In. | 45.00 |
| Milk Glass, Bowl, Lace Edge, Round, 3 X 8 In. | 50.00 |
| Milk Glass, Bowl, Lacy Crimped Edge, 7 X 10 In. | 18.00 |
| Milk Glass, Bowl, Lacy Edge, 8 In. | 17.00 |
| Milk Glass, Bowl, Lacy, Fluted Edge, 8 1/2 In.Diameter | 35.00 |
| Milk Glass, Bowl, Open Lattice Edge, 9 In.Diameter | 42.50 |
| Milk Glass, Bowl, Shell, Footed, 6 X 10 In. | 21.00 |
| Milk Glass, Bowl, Shell, Patent Oct.1872, 5 1/4 In., Pair | 15.00 |
| Milk Glass, Bowl, 9 3/4 In.Long, B-114 | 18.00 |
| Milk Glass, Box, Covered, Needlepoint, Round | 20.00 |
| Milk Glass, Box, Covered, Round, 3 1/4 In.Diameter, 2 1/2 In.High | 10.00 |
| Milk Glass, Box, Glove, 10 In. | 47.50 |
| Milk Glass, Box, Heart Shape, Plume Pattern, Painted | 7.00 |
| Milk Glass, Box, Pin, Lift-Off Cover, Raised Scroll Design | 10.50 |
| Milk Glass, Box, Stamp, White, Lift Lid, Irregular Edge, Painted, Reliefs | 18.00 |
| Milk Glass, Box, Trinket, Covered, Heart Shape | 10.00 To 15.00 |

Milk Glass, Box, Trinket, Painted Decoration ............................................. 12.00
Milk Glass, Bust, Nicholas II & Alexandra, C.1920, 12 3/4 In., Pair ............ 110.00
Milk Glass, Butter, Blackberry ................................................................. 56.50
Milk Glass, Butter, Child's, Covered, Liner, Flat Diamond & Sunburst ......... 55.00
Milk Glass, Butter, Child's, Dome Top, 3 1/2 In. ..................................... 6.00
Milk Glass, Butter, Covered, Cabbage ....................................................... 58.00
Milk Glass, Butter, Covered, Melon With Fern, Patent Date ........................ 45.00
Milk Glass, Butter, Covered, Panel & Flower ............................................ 35.00
Milk Glass, Butter, Covered, Roman Cross ............................................... 37.50
Milk Glass, Butter, Covered, Tree Of Life, Challinor ................................. 37.50
Milk Glass, Butter, Covered, Versailles, Pink & Gold Roses, 6 Sided Base ... 69.50
Milk Glass, Butter, Lacy Dewdrop ............................................................ 22.50
Milk Glass, Cake Stand, Mixed Flowers, 9 In. .......................................... 20.00
Milk Glass, Cake Stand, Open Handled, Pedestal, 11 Point Star On Top, B-138 ... 85.00
Milk Glass, Cake Stand, Trumpet Vine, 9 In. ........................................... 20.00
Milk Glass, Candleholder, Circle & Fan, Embossed Grapes, Pair ................. 45.00
Milk Glass, Candleholder, Crucifix, Pair ................................................... 18.00
Milk Glass, Candlestick, French, 3 1/2 In.High, Pair ................................. 15.00
Milk Glass, Candlestick, Swirled, Fiery, 3 1/4 In.High, Pair ....................... 18.00
Milk Glass, Candy Container, Suitcase, Clear & Decal Victorian Scene ......... 40.00
Milk Glass, Celery, Jewel ........................................................................ 40.00
Milk Glass, Christmas Light, Embossed Decoration, American Flag, On Chain ... 12.50
Milk Glass, Cologne, Floral, 9 1/2 In.High ............................................... 25.00
Milk Glass, Compote, Blue, Lattice Edge, Basket Weave Stem, 9 In.High ..... 100.00
Milk Glass, Compote, Blue, Wicket Top & Base, 8 3/4 In.High, B-261 ......... 45.00
Milk Glass, Compote, Closed Lattice Edge, Wild Rose Painted, 7 X 9 In. ..... 35.00
Milk Glass, Compote, Covered, Lacy Dewdrop, 12 X 8 1/2 In. ................... 35.00
Milk Glass, Compote, Crossed Ferns, Scalloped Edge, 7 In. ....................... 13.50
Milk Glass, Compote, Diamond Block With Fans, 8 X 8 In. ......................... 18.00
Milk Glass, Compote, Floral Decoration, 7 1/4 In.High ............................. 40.00
Milk Glass, Compote, Lattice Edge, 7 1/2 In.High ..................................... 50.00
Milk Glass, Compote, Lattice, Flared, Hand-Painted Apple Blossoms, 8 1/2 In. ... 45.00
Milk Glass, Compote, Looped Edge, 8 X 4 1/4 In. ................................... 15.00
Milk Glass, Compote, Open Lattice Edge, Pedestal Base, 9 In. .................... 65.00
Milk Glass, Compote, Scrolled, Knob Stem, Flint, 8 In.High ....................... 75.00
Milk Glass, Compote, 5 In.Diameter, 2 1/2 In.High .................................. 15.00
Milk Glass, Creamer, Apple Blossom, Blue Collar ..................................... 54.00
Milk Glass, Creamer, Blackberry .............................................................. 42.00
Milk Glass, Creamer, Diamond Sunburst, Miniature ................................... 11.00
Milk Glass, Creamer, Dolphin Cover ........................................................ 55.00
Milk Glass, Creamer, Grape .................................................................... 25.00
Milk Glass, Creamer, Grape With Overlapping Foliage, Dated ..................... 18.50
Milk Glass, Creamer, Paneled Wheat, 5 7/8 In. High ................................ 25.00
Milk Glass, Creamer, Royal Oak, Enameled .............................................. 30.00
Milk Glass, Creamer, Versailles, Pink Decoration ...................................... 25.00
Milk Glass, Cruet, S Repeat ................................................................... 20.00
Milk Glass, Cruet, Tree Of Life ............................................................... 68.50
Milk Glass, Cup & Saucer, Candlewick ..................................................... 8.75
Milk Glass, Decanter, Blue Ship Scene, Embossed Dutch Mill ..................... 10.00
Milk Glass, Dish, American Hen Cover ..................................................... 50.00
Milk Glass, Dish, Battleship Cover, Boat Base .......................................... 55.00
Milk Glass, Dish, Battleship Cover, Marked Dewey, B-184-A ....................... 60.00
Milk Glass, Dish, Battleship Cover, Marked Dewey, Tile Base ............ 35.00 To 48.00
Milk Glass, Dish, Battleship Cover, Marked Maine ..................................... 35.00
Milk Glass, Dish, Beehive Cover, C.1920 ................................................. 15.00
Milk Glass, Dish, Boat Cover, Wheeling .................................................... 45.00
Milk Glass, Dish, Camel Cover ................................................................ 75.00
Milk Glass, Dish, Cannon On Drum Cover ........................................ 70.00 To 97.50
Milk Glass, Dish, Cat Cover .................................................................... 20.00
Milk Glass, Dish, Cat Cover, Blue, Drum Base, Signed Portieux .................. 50.00
Milk Glass, Dish, Cat Cover, Drum Base, Signed Portieux ........................... 50.00
Milk Glass, Dish, Cat Cover, Eyes, Lacy Edge, Atterbury ........................... 115.00
Milk Glass, Dish, Cat Cover, Ribbed Base ................................................ 40.00
Milk Glass, Dish, Cat Cover, Split Ribbed Base, McKee .............................. 70.00
Milk Glass, Dish, Chick & Eggs Cover, Atterbury, Dated, B-141 ....... 100.00 To 145.00
Milk Glass, Dish, Chick & Eggs Cover, Lacy Edge Base, High Base, Atterbury ... 250.00

**Milk Glass, Dish,** Chick Cover, Sleigh Base, Paint .............................................................. 27.00 To 37.50
**Milk Glass, Dish,** Chick Emerging From Egg Cover, Sleigh Base ....................................... 50.00
**Milk Glass, Dish,** Chicks Cover, Round Basket Base, B-142B ............................................ 65.00
**Milk Glass, Dish,** Chicks Cover, Square Basket Base ......................................................... 145.00
**Milk Glass, Dish,** Cow Cover, Oval Base, Vallerystahl ........................................................ 65.00
**Milk Glass, Dish,** Dog Cover, Bed Base ............................................................................... 50.00
**Milk Glass, Dish,** Dog Cover, Blue & White, Oval Picket Fence Base ................................ 35.00
**Milk Glass, Dish,** Dog Cover, Dogwood Base, Signed Vallerystahl .................................... 18.50
**Milk Glass, Dish,** Dog Cover, Ribbed Base .......................................................................... 24.50
**Milk Glass, Dish,** Dove Cover, Basket Weave Base, Round, Greenish Tint ....................... 250.00
**Milk Glass, Dish,** Duck Cover, Atterbury, Dated ....................................................... 150.00 To 185.00
**Milk Glass, Dish,** Duck Cover, Clear Amethyst Head, Atterbury, C.1930 ........................... 55.00
**Milk Glass, Dish,** Duck Cover, Brass Base .............................................................. 55.00 To 65.00
**Milk Glass, Dish,** Duck Cover, Ribbed Base, Eyes ............................................................. 75.00
**Milk Glass, Dish,** Duck Cover, Wavy Base, 11 In. ................................................... 65.00 To 87.50
**Milk Glass, Dish,** Entwined Fish Cover, B-163a ...................................................... 85.00 To 160.00
**Milk Glass, Dish,** Fox Cover, Ribbed Base, Dated, Atterbury ............................................ 145.00
**Milk Glass, Dish,** Hand & Dove Cover, Atterbury, B-163b ..................................... 72.50 To 85.00
**Milk Glass, Dish,** Hand Holding Bird Cover, Lacy, Dated 1880 .......................................... 40.00
**Milk Glass, Dish,** Hen Cover, Basket Weave Base, Glass Eyes ......................................... 145.00
**Milk Glass, Dish,** Hen Cover, Basket Weave Base, Marked Kempel, 7 In. ........................ 38.00
**Milk Glass, Dish,** Hen Cover, Blue & White ......................................................................... 35.00
**Milk Glass, Dish,** Hen Cover, Blue Base, White Hen, Blue Head, 4 1/4 In.High ............... 30.00
**Milk Glass, Dish,** Hen Cover, Blue Head ............................................................................. 27.00
**Milk Glass, Dish,** Hen Cover, Blue Marbleized, Lacy Base, Atterbury, B-144 .................. 145.00
**Milk Glass, Dish,** Hen Cover, Blue Opaque, Molded Eyes, 6 X 8 In. ................................ 250.00
**Milk Glass, Dish,** Hen Cover, Blue, Handled Basket Base .................................................. 50.00
**Milk Glass, Dish,** Hen Cover, Chick Base, Flaccus .............................................................. 146.00
**Milk Glass, Dish,** Hen Cover, Lacy Base, 7 In. ..................................................................... 27.50
**Milk Glass, Dish,** Hen Cover, Nest Base, Red Glass Eyes, 7 In. ......................................... 35.00
**Milk Glass, Dish,** Hen Cover, Ribbed Base, Gilt Comb, L In Base, 4 1/2 In. ...................... 32.50
**Milk Glass, Dish,** Hen Cover, Sleigh Base ........................................................................... 67.50
**Milk Glass, Dish,** Hen Cover, Straight Head ......................................................................... 65.00
**Milk Glass, Dish,** Hen Cover, The American Hen, "Pat.Appl'd For" .................................... 45.00
**Milk Glass, Dish,** Hen Cover, Vallerystahl, 8 3/4 In. ............................................................ 66.00
**Milk Glass, Dish,** Hen, Chicks, & Eggs Cover, Blue Basket Base, Gold Chicks ................ 35.00
**Milk Glass, Dish,** Horse Cover ............................................................................................. 150.00
**Milk Glass, Dish,** Horse Cover, Split Ribbed Base, McKee ................................................. 70.00
**Milk Glass, Dish,** Lion Cover, Lacy Base, Atterbury, Dated, B-168 .................................... 60.00
**Milk Glass, Dish,** Lion Cover, McKee .................................................................................... 75.00
**Milk Glass, Dish,** Lion Cover, White, Fluted Base, Atterbury, 1889, B-181 ........................ 85.00
**Milk Glass, Dish,** Moses In Bullrushes Cover ...................................................................... 120.00
**Milk Glass, Dish,** Mule-Eared Rabbit Cover, 5 1/4 X 3 1/2 In. ............................................. 45.00
**Milk Glass, Dish,** Owl Cover, Glass Eyes, 7 In.High ........................................................... 110.00
**Milk Glass, Dish,** Pickle, Fish, Atterbury, Dated June 4, 1872 ............................................. 22.00
**Milk Glass, Dish,** Pintail Duck Cover, Basket Weave Base, Painted Decoration ................ 32.50
**Milk Glass, Dish,** Quail Cover, B-193 ................................................................................... 27.50
**Milk Glass, Dish,** Rabbit Cover, Blue, Dated March 9th, 1886 ............................... 75.00 To 350.00
**Milk Glass, Dish,** Robin Cover, Flat Round Base, Signed Vallerystahl ............................... 80.00
**Milk Glass, Dish,** Robin Cover, Flowered Pedestal Base, Eyes, Greentown ...................... 80.00
**Milk Glass, Dish,** Robin Cover, Nest Base .......................................................................... 145.00
**Milk Glass, Dish,** Scottie Dog Cover ................................................................................... 32.00
**Milk Glass, Dish,** Setter Dog Cover, Blue, Carpet Base, Vallerystahl, Signed ................... 49.00
**Milk Glass, Dish,** Setter Dog Cover, Blue, Gold Decoration .............................................. 150.00
**Milk Glass, Dish,** Setter Dog Cover, Vallerysthal, B-159 .................................................... 115.00
**Milk Glass, Dish,** Swan Cover, Blue, Vallerystahl ............................................................... 65.00
**Milk Glass, Dish,** Swan Cover, Nest Base, McKee ............................................................. 37.50
**Milk Glass, Dish,** Swan Cover, Square Block, Atterbury, 8 In. ........................................... 150.00
**Milk Glass, Dish,** Swan On Water Cover, Basket Weave Base, Atterbury .......................... 145.00
**Milk Glass, Dish,** Turtle Cover ............................................................................................. 69.00
**Milk Glass, Dish,** Uncle Sam Battleship Cover, 4 1/2 In.High, B-199 ................................ 105.00
**Milk Glass, Dish,** Uncle Sam Cover, Battleship Base ......................................................... 60.00
**Milk Glass, Dish,** Wooly Lamb Cover, Hexagonal Base ..................................................... 55.00
**Milk Glass, Doorstop,** Puppy ............................................................................................... 65.00
**Milk Glass, Egg,** Chick Breaking Through Shell, "Easter, " Painted, 3 In. ........................... 23.00
**Milk Glass, Egg,** Chick Breaking Through Shell, "Easter, " Painted, 4 5/8 In. ..................... 29.00

| | |
|---|---|
| **Milk Glass, Egg,** Easter, Blown, Horseshoe Design, 11 In. | 21.00 |
| **Milk Glass, Egg,** Nesting, Blown | 2.50 |
| **Milk Glass, Egg,** Painted, 13 In.Circumference | 13.00 |
| **Milk Glass, Egg,** Raised Basket Of Flowers & Easter In Gold | 15.00 |
| **Milk Glass, Eggcup,** Apple Blossom, Double | 6.75 |
| **Milk Glass, Eggcup,** Basket Weave, Atterbury, Set Of 4 | 15.00 |
| **Milk Glass, Eggcup,** Beaded Swirl | 12.00 |
| **Milk Glass, Eggcup,** Chicken Figural, 3 1/2 In. | 5.00 |
| **Milk Glass, Eggcup,** Swirl | 9.00 |
| **Milk Glass, Eggnog Set,** Flower In Bottom Of Bowl, 7 Piece | 15.00 |
| **Milk Glass, Feeding Set,** Child's, Painted Flowers, 3 Piece | 25.00 |
| **Milk Glass, Figurine,** Duck, White, Glass Eyes, 11 In. | 135.00 |
| **Milk Glass, Figurine,** Rabbit, White, Atterbury, 9 3/4 In.Long, B-177 | 175.00 |
| **Milk Glass, Goblet,** Blackberry | 30.00 |
| **Milk Glass, Goblet,** Lacy Dewdrop | 12.50 |
| **Milk Glass, Goblet,** Plain | 19.50 |
| **Milk Glass, Goblet,** Stars & Bars | 12.00 |
| **Milk Glass, Hat,** Straw | 25.00 |
| **Milk Glass, Hat,** Top, Black, Dobbs On Brim, 2 In.High | 15.00 |
| **Milk Glass, Hat,** Uncle Sam | 20.00 To 26.00 |
| **Milk Glass, Hat,** Uncle Sam, Painted | 17.50 To 32.00 |
| **Milk Glass, Ice Tea Set,** Embossed Grape, 9 Piece | 26.00 |
| **Milk Glass, Jar,** Cold Cream, 1906 | 2.50 |
| **Milk Glass, Jar,** Covered, Basket Weave, Handled, Vallerystahl | 15.00 |
| **Milk Glass, Jar,** Covered, Monkey's Face | 7.50 |
| **Milk Glass, Jar,** Covered, Queen Victoria | 50.00 To 65.00 |
| **Milk Glass, Jar,** Cow Cover, Painted, Fiery Opalescent | 60.00 |
| **Milk Glass, Jar,** Cracker, Cream, Hand-Painted Moss Rose & Floral, Silver Lid | 65.00 |
| **Milk Glass, Jar,** Dresser, Covered, Gold Paint, B-196b | 6.00 |
| **Milk Glass, Jar,** Eagle, B-178a | 95.00 |
| **Milk Glass, Jar,** Horseradish, Custard Shade, 2 Horse's Heads Form Handles | 16.00 |
| **Milk Glass, Jar,** Metal Lid, Dated 1880, 2 1/2 In.High | 12.00 |
| **Milk Glass, Jar,** Ointment, Covered, Octagonal, 4 In. | 12.00 |
| **Milk Glass, Jar,** Owl, Atterbury, B-182 | 145.00 |
| **Milk Glass, Jar,** Powder, Covered, Melon Shape, Vallerystahl | 28.00 |
| **Milk Glass, Juicer,** Sunkist, Cambridge | 5.00 |
| **Milk Glass, Knife Rest** | 10.00 |
| **Milk Glass, Lamp Base,** Carnations On Shade, Brass Foot | 20.00 |
| **Milk Glass, Lamp Base,** Decorated, 6 1/2 In. High | 35.00 To 45.00 |
| **Milk Glass, Lamp, see Lamp, Milk Glass** | |
| **Milk Glass, Match Holder,** Bark | 10.00 |
| **Milk Glass, Match Holder,** Bulldog's Head, Striker | 26.00 |
| **Milk Glass, Match Holder,** Cherub | 27.50 |
| **Milk Glass, Match Holder,** Columbus, Hanging | 22.00 |
| **Milk Glass, Match Holder,** Hand Holding Fan, 4 In.High | 25.00 |
| **Milk Glass, Match Holder,** Hanging, Kettle Shape, Embossed Grapes, Painted | 32.50 |
| **Milk Glass, Match Holder,** Indian's Head, Standing | 40.00 |
| **Milk Glass, Muffineer,** Blue, Cone, Miniature | 55.00 |
| **Milk Glass, Muffineer,** Blue, Paneled, Narrow Tapered Neck, 6 In.High | 24.00 |
| **Milk Glass, Muffineer,** Blue, Ribbed Swirl | 35.00 |
| **Milk Glass, Muffineer,** Blue, Waffle | 55.00 |
| **Milk Glass, Muffineer,** Embossed Grapes | 15.00 |
| **Milk Glass, Muffineer,** Enameled Pink Forget-Me-Nots | 43.00 |
| **Milk Glass, Muffineer,** Floral | 20.00 |
| **Milk Glass, Muffineer,** Green, Cone, Miniature | 55.00 |
| **Milk Glass, Muffineer,** Hand-Painted Flowers, 5 In. | 16.00 |
| **Milk Glass, Muffineer,** Hand-Painted Stork & Cattails, Pewter Top | 30.00 |
| **Milk Glass, Muffineer,** Royal Oak, Pink & Green Leaves | 53.00 |
| **Milk Glass, Muffineer,** Royal Oak, Waffle Ground, Gold Leaves | 52.00 |
| **Milk Glass, Mug,** Beer, Embossed Scenes, 5 In. | 17.00 |
| **Milk Glass, Mug,** Child's, Bleeding Hearts | 9.00 |
| **Milk Glass, Mug,** Child's, Swan, Head & Neck Form Handle, Pedestal | 22.00 |
| **Milk Glass, Mug,** Child's, 2 Swans, Ring Handle, Pedestal | 21.00 |
| **Milk Glass, Mug,** St.Louis World's Fair, Greentown | 38.00 |
| **Milk Glass, Mug,** Washington, Lafayette | 30.00 |
| **Milk Glass, Nappy,** Blue, Hobnail, Square, Ruffled | 36.00 |

| | |
|---|---|
| Milk Glass, Pitcher, Water, Blue, Beaded Circle Variant | 75.00 |
| Milk Glass, Pitcher, Water, Fostoria | 150.00 |
| Milk Glass, Pitcher, Water, Owl, Eyes, Atterbury | 100.00 |
| Milk Glass, Pitcher, Water, 1, 000-Eye, Pink Casing, Applied Handle, Ruffled | 125.00 |
| Milk Glass, Plate, Alphabet, Letters, Beaded Edge, Gilt, 7 In., B-12 | 18.00 |
| Milk Glass, Plate, Angel's Head, 9 In. | 17.00 |
| Milk Glass, Plate, Apple Blossom Center, Lattice Edge, 10 1/4 In. | 55.00 |
| Milk Glass, Plate, Balky Mule, 7 In. | 28.00 |
| Milk Glass, Plate, Battleship Maine, Shell & Club Rim, 7 In. | 12.00 |
| Milk Glass, Plate, Battleship Maine, 7 1/4 In. | 19.50 |
| Milk Glass, Plate, Black, Gothic Edge, Canton Glass Co., 11 1/2 In. | 22.50 |
| Milk Glass, Plate, Black, Gothic, 9 In. | 14.00 |
| Milk Glass, Plate, Blue, Gothic, 7 1/2 In. | 29.50 |
| Milk Glass, Plate, Blue, Latticework & Basket Weave, 8 1/4 In. | 20.00 |
| Milk Glass, Plate, Bread, Basket Weave, Dated | 40.00 To 45.00 |
| Milk Glass, Plate, Bread, Columbus | 25.00 |
| Milk Glass, Plate, Bread, Diamond Grill | 34.00 To 45.00 |
| Milk Glass, Plate, Bread, Retriever | 65.00 |
| Milk Glass, Plate, Cake, Black, Scalloped, Open Handles, 9 In. | 9.00 |
| Milk Glass, Plate, Cake, Chain & Petal Rim, Collared Base, Floral, 10 1/2 In. | 27.50 |
| Milk Glass, Plate, Club & Shell Waffle Center, 9 1/2 In. | 10.00 |
| Milk Glass, Plate, Columbus, Dated 1892, 9 1/2 In. | 45.00 |
| Milk Glass, Plate, Daisy & Cattail Decoration, Open Lattice, 10 1/2 In. | 45.00 |
| Milk Glass, Plate, Eagle & Fleur-De-Lis Border, Dated 1903, 7 1/2 In. | 26.00 |
| Milk Glass, Plate, G.A.R., 33rd, Phila., 1899, Diamond Peg Border, 8 1/4 In. | 32.00 |
| Milk Glass, Plate, Gothic Border, 9 In. | 18.00 |
| Milk Glass, Plate, Indian's Head, 7 1/4 In. | 24.00 |
| Milk Glass, Plate, Lattice Edge, 10 In. | 15.00 |
| Milk Glass, Plate, No Easter Without Us, Painted, 6 1/4 In. | 32.00 |
| Milk Glass, Plate, Owl Lovers, Gilt Decoration, 7 1/2 In., B-11 | 21.00 |
| Milk Glass, Plate, Scroll & Eye, Hand-Painted Apple Blossoms, 10 1/4 In. | 42.50 |
| Milk Glass, Plate, Scroll & Eye, 8 In. | 12.00 |
| Milk Glass, Plate, Serenade, 6 1/2 In. | 35.00 |
| Milk Glass, Plate, Souvenir Lachine Rapids, Openwork Border, 7 In. | 7.00 |
| Milk Glass, Plate, Three Kittens, 7 In. .........Illus | 18.00 |

Milk Glass, Plate, Three Kittens, 7 In.

| | |
|---|---|
| Milk Glass, Plate, Triple Forget-Me-Not, Canton Glass Co., 8 1/4 In. | 12.00 |
| Milk Glass, Plate, Trumpet Vine, Lattice Edge, 10 In., B-29 | 35.00 |
| Milk Glass, Plate, Wicket, 7 1/2 In. | 6.00 |
| Milk Glass, Plate, Wicket, 9 In. | 8.00 |
| Milk Glass, Platter, Actress, 11 1/2 In. | 80.00 |
| Milk Glass, Platter, Bisons' Heads, 7 X 12 In. | 16.00 |
| Milk Glass, Platter, John Hancock, Liberty Bell, 13 1/2 X 9 1/2 In. | 175.00 |
| Milk Glass, Platter, Retriever | 60.00 To 100.00 |
| Milk Glass, Platter, Wheat & Barley | 40.00 |
| Milk Glass, Salt & Pepper On Tray, Raised Enamel Flowers | 22.50 |
| Milk Glass, Salt & Pepper, Beaded Vertical, 3 In.High | 19.50 |

| | |
|---|---|
| Milk Glass, Salt & Pepper, Black | 17.50 |
| Milk Glass, Salt & Pepper, Dice | 9.50 |
| Milk Glass, Salt & Pepper, G.E.Refrigerator, Original Labels | 15.00 |
| Milk Glass, Salt & Pepper, Green | 1.00 |
| Milk Glass, Salt & Pepper, Hand-Painted, Pewter Top, 3 3/4 In.High | 15.00 |
| Milk Glass, Salt & Pepper, Paneled, Palmette, Scrolls, Blue Salt, Pink Pepper | 18.00 |
| Milk Glass, Salt & Pepper, Pink, Ribbed, Tomato Shape, Forget-Me-Nots | 17.50 |
| Milk Glass, Salt & Pepper, Ribbed Collar & Base, Hand-Painted Floral | 18.00 |
| Milk Glass, Salt & Pepper, Scrolls, Brass Tops | 15.00 |
| Milk Glass, Salt, Blackberry, Footed | 18.00 |
| Milk Glass, Salt, Blue, Duck | 25.00 |
| Milk Glass, Salt, Double, Basket Shape, Applied Twisted Handle | 14.00 |
| Milk Glass, Salt, English Hobnail, Round, Serrated Edge | 8.50 |
| Milk Glass, Salt, Master, Birch Leaf, Pedestal Base, Flint, 2 3/4 In. | 18.00 |
| Milk Glass, Salt, Master, Blackberry, 2 1/2 In. | 45.00 |
| Milk Glass, Salt, Master, Rose Leaf, Footed | 22.50 |
| Milk Glass, Saltshaker, Basket | 5.00 |
| Milk Glass, Saltshaker, Basket Weave | 17.50 To 18.00 |
| Milk Glass, Saltshaker, Blue, Melon Shape, Challinor's No.20 | 12.50 |
| Milk Glass, Saltshaker, Blue, Ribbon Band, Tin Top, 3 1/2 In. | 12.50 |
| Milk Glass, Saltshaker, Blue, Rose Relievo | 15.00 |
| Milk Glass, Saltshaker, Blue, Sunset | 22.00 |
| Milk Glass, Saltshaker, Bunch Of Grapes On Pedestal, 4 In. | 8.00 |
| Milk Glass, Saltshaker, Bunker Hill | 12.50 |
| Milk Glass, Saltshaker, Butterfly | 7.50 |
| Milk Glass, Saltshaker, Diamond Base | 6.00 |
| Milk Glass, Saltshaker, Double Fan Band | 5.00 |
| Milk Glass, Saltshaker, Embossed Rabbits | 35.00 |
| Milk Glass, Saltshaker, Flower Bouquet | 10.00 |
| Milk Glass, Saltshaker, Green, Cactus | 15.00 |
| Milk Glass, Saltshaker, Green, Overlapping Shell | 15.00 |
| Milk Glass, Saltshaker, Hat Plume, Silver Cover | 18.00 |
| Milk Glass, Saltshaker, Icebox | 4.50 |
| Milk Glass, Saltshaker, Large Rose | 5.00 |
| Milk Glass, Saltshaker, Plume | 17.50 |
| Milk Glass, Saltshaker, Rose Color, Melon Shape, Challinor's No.20 | 12.50 |
| Milk Glass, Saltshaker, Stained Apple Blossoms, Silver Top | 22.00 |
| Milk Glass, Saltshaker, Sunset | 12.00 |
| Milk Glass, Saltshaker, Waist Cord | 6.00 |
| Milk Glass, Sauce, Blackberry, 4 In. | 7.00 |
| Milk Glass, Shade, Leaded, 19 In.Diameter | 75.00 |
| Milk Glass, Shoe, Child's, Shabby | 22.00 |
| Milk Glass, Slipper, Daisy & Button, Cat's Head | 15.00 |
| Milk Glass, Slipper, Lady's, Blue, Kitten, 5 3/4 In. | 10.00 |
| Milk Glass, Spittoon, 7 1/4 In.Diameter, 5 3/8 In.High | 25.00 |
| Milk Glass, Spooner, Black | 6.00 |
| Milk Glass, Spooner, Blackberry | 18.00 To 27.50 |
| Milk Glass, Spooner, Coreopsis, Pale Green Band | 25.00 |
| Milk Glass, Spooner, Gooseberry | 28.00 |
| Milk Glass, Spooner, Grape, Marked Pat. Feb., 1870 | 15.00 |
| Milk Glass, Spooner, Royal Oak, Pink & Green Leaves | 35.00 |
| Milk Glass, Stein, Blue, Troubador | 18.00 |
| Milk Glass, Stein, Covered, Troubadour, Greentown | 24.00 |
| Milk Glass, Sugar & Creamer, Blackberry | 85.00 |
| Milk Glass, Sugar & Creamer, Cover, Scalloped Top, Painted | 38.00 |
| Milk Glass, Sugar & Creamer, Crown Covered | 35.00 |
| Milk Glass, Sugar & Creamer, Flute & Crown, Footed, Westmoreland, 1896 | 27.50 |
| Milk Glass, Sugar & Creamer, Swan | 32.00 |
| Milk Glass, Sugar, Blackberry | 26.00 |
| Milk Glass, Sugar, Blue, Turret Top Cover, Scrolled, Square | 27.50 |
| Milk Glass, Sugar, Covered, Bears | 38.00 |
| Milk Glass, Sugar, Covered, Blackberry | 40.00 |
| Milk Glass, Sugar, Covered, Double Loop | 82.50 |
| Milk Glass, Sugar, Covered, Lacy Edge | 35.00 |
| Milk Glass, Sugar, Covered, Roman Cross | 37.50 |
| Milk Glass, Sugar, Covered, Royal Oak, Pink & Green Leaves | 45.00 |

| | |
|---|---:|
| Milk Glass, Sugar, Covered, Tree Of Life | 23.00 To 25.00 |
| Milk Glass, Swan, Black, Detailed Feathers, Scalloped Top, 8 3/4 In. | 34.00 |
| Milk Glass, Syrup, Alba, Enamel Trim | 25.00 |
| Milk Glass, Syrup, Apple Blossom, Silver Plated Hinged Top, Dated 1881-82 | 42.00 |
| Milk Glass, Syrup, Applied Handle, Enameled Blud Daisies, Pewter Top, 1884 | 30.00 |
| Milk Glass, Syrup, Bulbous, Applied Handle, Floral Decoration | 24.50 |
| Milk Glass, Syrup, Collared Base, Flip Off Top | 29.50 |
| Milk Glass, Syrup, Floral, Yellow Moon | 33.00 |
| Milk Glass, Syrup, Raised Pansies | 52.00 |
| Milk Glass, Syrup, Tree Of Life | 40.00 |
| Milk Glass, Table Set, Blackberry, Blackberry Finials, 4 Piece | 159.00 |
| Milk Glass, Tankard, Water, White, Beaded Circle Variant, Applied Handle | 45.00 |
| Milk Glass, Teacup & Saucer, Pink Roses & Green & Yellow Leaves Top, 1800s | 50.00 |
| Milk Glass, Toothpick, Auto Shape | 25.00 |
| Milk Glass, Toothpick, Basket Weave | 7.00 |
| Milk Glass, Toothpick, Beaded Belt, Silver Rim | 6.50 |
| Milk Glass, Toothpick, Blue, Enameled Decoration | 15.00 |
| Milk Glass, Toothpick, Hand Holding Torch, 4 In. | 20.00 |
| Milk Glass, Toothpick, Hand-Painted Craig Castle, Meriden, Conn. | 9.00 |
| Milk Glass, Toothpick, Ribbed Base, Hand-Painted Roses | 9.00 |
| Milk Glass, Toothpick, Scrolled Shell | 12.00 |
| Milk Glass, Toothpick, Violets, 2 1/2 In.High | 18.00 |
| Milk Glass, Toothpick, White, Flesh Color Figural Hand, Decorated | 15.00 |
| Milk Glass, Toothpick, Yellow Decoration | 14.00 |
| Milk Glass, Toothpick, Yellow, Blue Violets | 16.00 |
| Milk Glass, Toothpick, 101 | 10.00 |
| Milk Glass, Tray, Actress, Oval | 35.00 |
| Milk Glass, Tray, Blue, Raised Roses Center, Scalloped, Gold, 6 In. | 8.50 |
| Milk Glass, Tray, Dresser, Beaded Edge, Paint, 8 1/2 X 4 1/2 In. | 5.00 |
| Milk Glass, Tray, Dresser, Blue, Hand-Painted Landscape, Pink Border | 40.00 |
| Milk Glass, Tray, Dresser, Butterfly Shape, Gilt Paint, 4 X 5 In. | 8.00 |
| Milk Glass, Tray, Dresser, Heart Shape, Gilt Paint, 4 X 5 In. | 8.00 |
| Milk Glass, Tray, Lady & Fan | 24.00 |
| Milk Glass, Tray, Powder Box, & Pin Box, White, Gold Trim, Violets | 60.00 |
| Milk Glass, Tray, White, Irregular Edge, Painted, Reliefs, Opalescent Edge | 16.00 |
| Milk Glass, Tumbler, Acme, Cover & Dose Indicator, "Take Next Dose," 1896 | 7.95 |
| Milk Glass, Tumbler, Actress, 4 1/2 In. | 16.00 |
| Milk Glass, Tumbler, Boston, Multicolor Ground, Gold Trim | 9.50 |
| Milk Glass, Tumbler, Guttate | 15.00 |
| Milk Glass, Tumbler, Louisiana Purchase Exposition, 5 In. | 18.00 To 23.50 |
| Milk Glass, Tumbler, Opaque Scroll | 18.00 |
| Milk Glass, Tumbler, Rose & Fan | 15.00 |
| Milk Glass, Vase, Blue & White, Hand-Painted Flying Birds, 5 In. | 10.00 |
| Milk Glass, Vase, Blue, Ruffled Top, 6 1/4 In.High, Pair | 40.00 |
| Milk Glass, Vase, Hand-Painted Arab Bust In Browns, Fostoria, 4 1/4 In. | 20.00 |
| Milk Glass, Vase, Hand-Painted Indian Maiden In Browns, Fostoria, 7 In. | 25.00 |
| Milk Glass, Vase, Hand-Painted Indian Portrait, 8 1/2 In.High | 18.00 |
| Milk Glass, Vase, Roses, 7 In. | 20.00 |
| Milk Glass, Vase, Sculptured Floral, 6 1/2 In. | 15.00 |

*Millefiori means many flowers. It is a type of glasswork popular in paperweights. Many small flowerlike pieces of glass are grouped together to form a design.*

**Millefiori, see also Paperweight**

| | |
|---|---:|
| Millefiori, Cruet | 30.00 |
| Millefiori, Figurine, Turtle, 6 X 3 In. | 57.00 |
| Millefiori, Muffineer, 5 In.High | 65.00 |
| Millefiori, Pitcher, Flared Top, Applied Candy Cane Handle, 4 1/2 In. | 55.00 |
| Millefiori, Pitcher, 4 3/4 In.High | 55.00 |
| Millefiori, Plate, Yellow & Maroon Coloring, 7 In. | 28.00 |
| Millefiori, Shoe, Applied Clear Heel | 36.00 |
| Millefiori, Slipper, Camphor Glass, High Heel | 85.00 |
| Millefiori, Syrup, Vase Shape, Camphor Handle, Copper Lid | 78.00 |
| Millefiori, Toothpick, Top Hat, 2 1/4 In. | 35.00 |
| Millefiori, Tumbler, 3 1/2 In. | 15.00 |
| Millefiori, Vase, Applied Cane Handle, Beaded Colors, Slim Neck, 4 1/2 In. | 43.00 |

| | |
|---|---:|
| Millefiori, Vase, Bowl Shaped, Scalloped, Light Colors, 5 1/2 X 3 3/8 In. | 65.00 |
| Millefiori, Vase, Browns & Reds, 3 In.High | 65.00 |
| Millefiori, Vase, Cabinet, Applied Camphor At Bottom, 3 In. | 35.00 |
| Millefiori, Vase, Miniature, Blue & Brown Canes On Ivorine, 2 1/2 In.High | 35.00 |
| Millefiori, Vase, Multicolor, Sharp Canes, 4 1/2 In.High | 85.00 |
| Miniature, Bowl, Punch, Pressed Glass, Footed, 3 1/2 In.High | 15.00 |
| Miniature, Bowl, Vegetable, Oval, Lacy, Scalloped Rim, Central Medallion | 75.00 |
| Miniature, Cruet, Pressed Glass, 2 1/4 In.High | 8.50 |
| Miniature, Cup, 'love The Giver, ' 1 3/4 In. | 5.00 |
| Miniature, Knocker, Door, Lion's Head, Ring In Mouth, Dated 1880, 2 1/2 In. | 17.50 |
| Miniature, Mug, Blue Glass, Amber Glass Handle, 1 1/2 In.High | 10.50 |
| Miniature, Rose Bowl, Clear Glass, Turned In Top, 2 In.High | 10.50 |
| Miniature, Rose Bowl, Pressed Glass, Crimped Top, 2 1/2 In.Diameter | 16.50 |
| Miniature, Table Set, Fan & Diamond, Turning Amethyst, 4 Piece | 45.00 |
| Miniature, Table, Work, Mahogany, American, C.1825, 8 1/2 In.High | 425.00 |

*Minton china has been made in England from 1793 to the present time.*

| | |
|---|---:|
| Minton, Bowl, Covered, Potpourri, Twig Handles, Flowers, 1867, 9 In.Wide | 175.00 |
| Minton, Bowl, Vegetable, Covered, 4 Classic Figures, Brown, Blue, Pinks | 25.00 |
| Minton, Box, Spitz Dog On Lid, Heart Shape, Artist-Signed, 2 1/4 In.Long | 110.00 |
| Minton, Breakfast Set, Marlow, 9 Piece | 45.00 |
| Minton, Candlestick, Boy & Girl Seated On Stumps, C.1830, 6 3/8 In., Pair | 200.00 |
| Minton, Candlestick, Tripod Base, Elephant Head Handles, Pair, C.1872 | 300.00 |
| Minton, Casserole, Covered, Round, Decorated Inside & Out | 65.00 |
| Minton, Chocolate Set, Hand-Painted Pink Floral, C.1900, 13 Piece | 135.00 |
| Minton, Cup & Saucer, Bittersweet & Gilt On Cobalt, Marks For 1851 | 35.00 |
| Minton, Cup & Saucer, Flower Pot Shape, Turquoise Flowers, Gold | 18.00 |
| Minton, Cup & Saucer, Imari Pattern, Bittersweet, Cobalt & Gold, C.1851 | 40.00 |
| Minton, Cup & Stand, Custard, Tulip Form, Purple, Butterfly Handle, C.1830 | 85.00 |
| Minton, Dish, Fish Shape, Blue & Brown Decoration On Green Gray, Dated | 18.00 |
| Minton, Drain, Dish, Oval, Scrolls, Floral, Red, Gold, Patent Dated 1878 | 20.00 |
| Minton, Inkwell, Double, Flower Encrusted, Leaf Form, Bumblebee Knops, 1830s | 475.00 |
| Minton, Jug, Molded Stoneware, Salt Glaze, Fox Handle, Animals, C.1830 | 150.00 |
| Minton, Pitcher, Ivory & Gold, Tiffany & Co., 5 X 5 In. | 29.00 |
| Minton, Pitcher, Parian, W Handle, Round Foot, Raised Ivy Vine, Dated 1855 | 45.00 |
| Minton, Plate, Aqueduct, Middlesex Canal, Shawsheen River, Mass., 10 In. | 15.00 |
| Minton, Plate, Asparagus, Cream Glaze, Elevated Sauce Holder Center | 12.00 |
| Minton, Plate, Chop, Marlow, 12 1/2 In. | 19.00 |
| Minton, Plate, Dessert, Central Floral Spray, Puce & Gilt Rim, C.1850 | 22.50 |
| Minton, Plate, Dinner, Montrose | 10.00 |
| Minton, Plate, Flower Encrusted, Insects, C.1830, 8 1/4 In. | 250.00 |
| Minton, Plate, Gaudy Ironstone, 7 1/4 In. | 12.00 |
| Minton, Plate, Girard College, Blue, 10 In. | 22.00 |
| Minton, Plate, Gold Butterflies & Flowers On Blue, C.1875, 9 In. | 44.00 |
| Minton, Plate, Hand-Painted Floral Garlands, Blue Border, 10 In. | 8.00 |
| Minton, Plate, Oyster, Majolica, 8 7/8 X 7 1/2 In. | 28.00 |
| Minton, Plate, Salad, White, Gold Bands, C.1911, 7 3/4 In. | 8.00 |
| Minton, Platter, Cake, Gold & Roses On Cream, Fluted Corners, 9 In.Square | 19.50 |
| Minton, Platter, Red, Blue, & Orange Decoration, 21 1/2 X 17 In. | 95.00 |
| Minton, Pot, Match, Dresden, Flaring Foot, Floral, Rectangular, C.1830 | 100.00 |
| Minton, Sauceboat & Underplate, White, Translucent, 8 1/4 In. Long | 32.50 |
| Minton, Seat, Garden, Blue & White, 6 Sided, 13 1/2 In.Diameter | 225.00 |
| Minton, Sugar, Covered, Green Fleur-De-Lis, Miniature | 7.50 |
| Minton, Sugar, Imari Pattern, Bittersweet, Cobalt & Gold, C.1851 | 60.00 |
| Minton, Tazza, Green Panels, Floral Groupings, Bird Center, Footed | 16.00 |
| Minton, Teapot, Squat, Floral On Lilac, Green Handle & Spout, C.1830, 4 In. | 275.00 |
| Minton, Tile, Acanthus, Brown, 6 In. | 17.00 |
| Minton, Tile, Birthplace Of Oliver Wendell Holmes, Browns, 6 In.Square | 20.00 |
| Minton, Tile, Dyer, Brown On White, 6 In.Square | 12.00 |
| Minton, Tile, Evening, White Figures On Brown, 8 In. Square | 14.00 |
| Minton, Tile, Fox & Duck In Marsh Grass, Turquoise, 8 In.Square | 22.50 |
| Minton, Tile, Magnolialike Flowers On Cobalt & Gold, Framed | 16.00 |
| Minton, Tile, Mason, Brown On White, 6 In.Square | 12.00 |
| Minton, Tile, Night, White Figures On Brown, Stoke-On-Trent, 8 In. Square | 14.00 |
| Minton, Tile, Noon, White Figures On Brown, Stoke-On-Trent, 8 In. Square | 14.00 |
| Minton, Tile, Old Hancock House, Beacon Street, Boston, 1739-1863 | 20.00 |

Minton, Vase, Earthenware, Aqua,
Avocado, 1900s, 11 1/2 In

Minton, Vase,
Earthenware,
Cream, Green,
1900s, 9 3/4 In.

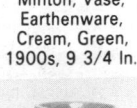

Minton, Vase, Earthenware,
White, Red, Avocado, 1900s, 9 In

| | |
|---|---|
| **Minton, Tile,** The Antiovary, Sir Arthur & Dovsterswivel, 8 In.Square | 32.00 |
| **Minton, Tile,** Views Of Old Holmes' House, Cambridge, Brown, 6 In. | 21.00 |
| **Minton, Tile,** Weaver, Brown On White, 6 In.Square | 12.00 |
| **Minton, Trinket Holder,** Majolica, Shape Of 3 Eggcups, Handle, 4 In. | 45.00 |
| **Minton, Tureen,** Covered, Oriental Design, Footed, Nov.11, 1846, 10 1/2 In. | 188.00 |
| **Minton, Urn,** Majolica, Covered, Louis XVI Style, Dionysus, 1870, 25 1/2 In. | 150.00 |
| **Minton, Vase,** Art Nouveau, Red Salmon & Brown Glaze, Silver Luster, 10 In. | 59.00 |
| **Minton, Vase,** Earthenware, Aqua, Avocado, 1900s, 11 1/2 In ............*Illus* | 75.00 |
| **Minton, Vase,** Earthenware, Cream, Green, 1900s, 9 3/4 In. ............*Illus* | 100.00 |
| **Minton, Vase,** Earthenware, D-Scroll Handles, Medallions, C.1900, 12 In. | 125.00 |
| **Minton, Vase,** Earthenware, Green Outlined Dogwoods, C.1900, 14 1/2 In. | 175.00 |
| **Minton, Vase,** Earthenware, White, Red, Avocado, 1900s, 9 In ............*Illus* | 100.00 |
| **Minton, Vase,** Salt Glaze, Tulip, Reclining Cupid On Round Base, 7 In. | 20.00 |

**Mirror, see Furniture, Mirror**

*Mocha ware is an English-made product that was sold in America during the
early 1800s. It is a heavy pottery with pale coffee and cream coloring.
Designs of blue, brown, green, orange, or black or white were added to the
pottery.*

| | |
|---|---|
| **Mocha, Bowl,** Black Seaweed On Yellow, 6 In.High | 90.00 |
| **Mocha, Bowl,** Blue & Black Bands On White, Pearlware, C.1840, 5 1/2 In. | 45.00 |
| **Mocha, Bowl,** White Band & Blue Seaweed On Yellow, Thin Walled, C.1855, 6 In. | 55.00 |
| **Mocha, Chamber Pot,** Seaweed, 9 1/2 In. Diameter ............ 45.00 To | 50.00 |
| **Mocha, Jug,** Banded Creamware, Blue & White, Applied Leaf Handle, C.1850 | 55.00 |
| **Mocha, Mug,** Seaweed, Blue Band, Marked V.R.I. Imperial, C.1850, 5 In. | 95.00 |
| **Mocha, Mug,** Seaweed, 5 1/4 In. | 110.00 |
| **Mocha, Mug,** Yellow, Red Seaweed Handle, 4 White Bands Top & Bottom | 25.00 |
| **Mocha, Pepperpot,** Chocolate & Rust Stripes, 4 1/2 In. | 55.00 |

**Mold, Bullet, see Weapon, Mold, Bullet**
**Mold, Candle, see Kitchen, Mold, Candle, Tin, Mold, Candle**
**Mold, Ice Cream, see Pewter, Mold, Ice Cream**

| | |
|---|---|
| **Monart, Vase,** Brown Mica, Green, 4 In. | 12.00 |
| **Monart, Vase,** Cobalt To Pale Blue, Gold Flecks, Label, 10 1/2 In. | 95.00 |
| **Monart, Vase,** Reds, Golds, & Topaz, Weighs 5 Pounds, 7 1/4 In.High | 90.00 |

**Mont Joye, see Mt.Joye**

| | |
|---|---|
| **Montereau, Plate,** Black & Yellow, C.1830, 8 1/4 In., 4 ............*Illus* | 300.00 |

*Moorcroft Pottery was founded in Burslem, England, in 1914 by William
Moorcroft. The earlier wares are similar to those made today, but color and
marking will help indicate the age.*

| | |
|---|---|
| **Moorcroft, Bowl,** Bouquet Of Wheat On Green Tan, Matte, Signed W.M.8 1/2 In. | 80.00 |

| | |
|---|---|
| Moorcroft, Bowl, Covered, Cobalt To Green, Floral & Leaf, 5 1/2 In. | 44.50 |
| Moorcroft, Bowl, Orange Floral On Green, 5 3/4 In.Diameter | 15.00 |
| Moorcroft, Box, Covered, Footed, Yellow, Blue, & Red Flowers, 5 1/2 In. | 45.00 |
| Moorcroft, Box, Covered, Oval, Cobalt, 5 In. | 25.00 |
| Moorcroft, Candleholder, Floral, Berries, & Leaves On Green Blue, W.M. | 56.00 |
| Moorcroft, Compote, High Glaze, Deep Colors, 6 X 8 In. | 79.00 |
| Moorcroft, Dish, Candy, Covered, Floral Decoration On Green | 40.00 |
| Moorcroft, Jar, Ginger, Covered, Purple & Yellow Fruit On Blue, Signed | 110.00 |
| Moorcroft, Jardiniere, Blue Ground, Leaves, 4 1/4 In.Diameter, 4 1/4 In.High | 38.00 |
| Moorcroft, Plate, Cake, Cobalt Blue Fruit Decoration, Silver Plate Pedestal | 40.00 |
| Moorcroft, Pot, Jam, Green, Silver Plate Rim And Lid, Bale, Spoon | 30.00 |
| Moorcroft, Teapot, Signed, 7 X 7 In. | 95.00 |
| Moorcroft, Vase, Bulbous, Green Irish Decoration, Marked WM In Blue, 6 In. | 48.00 |
| Moorcroft, Vase, Bulbous, Orchid & Flower On White, 3 In. | 18.00 |
| Moorcroft, Vase, Cobalt With Orchids, Signed W.M., 6 1/2 In.High | 45.00 |
| Moorcroft, Vase, Fruit On Cobalt, Green Script Signature, 8 In. | 45.00 |
| Moorcroft, Vase, Grape & Leaves, 9 1/4 In. | 95.00 |
| Moorcroft, Vase, Green Ground, Orchid Decoration, 4 In.High | 25.00 |
| Moorcroft, Vase, Incised Cobalt With Fruit Decoration, 4 3/4 In.High | 34.50 |
| Moorcroft, Vase, Miniature, Floral Decoration, 1 3/4 In.High | 12.00 |
| Moorcroft, Vase, Orange Luster Glaze, 9 1/2 In.High | 50.00 |
| Moorcroft, Vase, Pink & Purple Floral On Green, England, 5 1/2 In. | 40.00 |
| Moorcroft, Vase, Pomegranates On Blue, Script-Signed, 8 In. | 45.00 |
| Moorcroft, Vase, Pomegranates On Cobalt, Green Script Signed, 5 In.High | 38.00 |
| Moorcroft, Vase, Red, Orange, & Purple Plums On Dark Blue, C.1925, 10 In. | 165.00 |
| Moorcroft, Vase, Shaded Green Ground, Pink Poppies, 5 1/4 In.High | 50.00 |
| Moorcroft, Vase, Trumpet, Green, Blue With Fruits, Signed, 8 1/2 In. | 60.00 |
| Moriaga, Ashtray, White Beading, Pink Roses On Blue, Footed, Scalloped | 45.00 |
| Moriaga, Bonbon, Floral & Beading, 3 Handled, 6 In. Diameter | 35.00 |
| Moriaga, Cup & Saucer, Floral, Translucent | 30.00 |
| Moriaga, Salt & Pepper, Raised Enameling | 10.00 |
| Moriaga, Tankard, Red Orchids, Buds, & Green Leaves, 10 1/2 In. High | 110.00 |
| Moriaga, Vase, Blue, Green, Red, & Yellow On Pink, 5 In. High | 65.00 |
| Moriaga, Vase, Ovals Of Roses, Beaded, 5 In. High, 5 3/4 In. Diameter | 42.00 |

*Mosaic Tile Company of Zanesville, Ohio, was started by Karl Langenbeck and Herman Mueller in 1894. Many types of plain and ornamental tiles were made until 1959. The company closed in 1967.*

| | |
|---|---|
| Mosaic Tile Company, Tile, Incised Cat, Hand-Painted, 4 X 4 In. | 15.00 |
| Mosaic Tile Company, Tile, Lincoln, Jasperware, Blue *Illus* | 20.00 |
| Mosaic Tile Company, Tile, Round, Sesquicentennial, Zanesville, Ohio, 1947 | 3.00 |

*Moser glass was made by Kolomon Moser in the early 1900s. The Art Nouveau type glassware had detailed exotic enamel designs.*

| | |
|---|---|
| Moser, Bottle, Amber Enamel, Applied Alligator & Turtle, Cut Crystal Stopper | 75.00 |
| Moser, Bottle, Yellow, Globe Shape, Signed, 5 3/4 In. | 50.00 |
| Moser, Bowl & Underplate, Finger, Amethyst To Clear, Intaglio Clematis | 150.00 |
| Moser, Bowl, Berry, Cranberry, Gold Enamel & Feet, Pink & Blue Floral | 135.00 |
| Moser, Bowl, Clambroth, Jeweled Acorns, Amber Applied Handle, 2 1/4 In.High | 265.00 |
| Moser, Bowl, Covered, Cut Intaglio Floral, Signed Moser, Karlsbad, 4 In. | 40.00 |
| Moser, Bowl, Finger, Amethyst, Etched Male Figure In Orchid Color, Signed | 200.00 |
| Moser, Bowl, Finger, Amethyst, Mary Gregory Figure, Signed | 225.00 |
| Moser, Bowl, Finger, Cranberry, Gold & Floral Decoration, Signed, 5 In. | 105.00 |
| Moser, Bowl, Multicolor Enameling, 4 1/2 X 3 In. | 60.00 |
| Moser, Bowl, Ruby, Gold Design On Pansies, 3 X 5 1/2 In. | 22.00 |
| Moser, Box, Covered, Deep Green, Gold & Enamel, 3 1/2 In.High | 37.50 |
| Moser, Box, Jewel, Blue, Gold Floral Enamel, 5 In.High | 190.00 |
| Moser, Candlestick, Incised Gold Band, Spartan Warriors, Paneled, Pair | 95.00 |
| Moser, Cologne, Bulbous, Floral On Pale Lavender, 6 1/4 In.High | 95.00 |
| Moser, Compote, Amber, Classical Warriors & Maidens In Gilt, C.1930, 8 In. | 130.00 |
| Moser, Cordial, Clear, Signed | 9.00 |
| Moser, Cup & Saucer, Amberina, Gold & Silver Decoration | 125.00 |
| Moser, Cup & Saucer, Amethyst, Gold Enamel, Glass Jewels | 150.00 |
| Moser, Cup & Saucer, Colored Enamel & Applied Acorns On Transparent Blue | 245.00 |
| Moser, Cup & Saucer, Demitasse, Green To Clear, Gold Trim, Signed | 125.00 |
| Moser, Cup, Cordial, Cranberry, Decorated | 32.50 |

| | |
|---|---|
| Moser, Decanter, Clear, Gold Trim, Signed | 65.00 |
| Moser, Ewer, Miniature, Cranberry, Gold Enameling, Flowers, 4 In.High | 55.00 |
| Moser, Rose Bowl, Amethyst To Clear, Carved Intaglio Poppies, 2 In.High | 80.00 |
| Moser, Rose Bowl, Clear To Cranberry, Gold Decoration, 3 Legs | 95.00 |
| Moser, Rose Bowl, Rubena Verde, Green To Cranberry, Enameled Floral & Bird | 125.00 |
| Moser, Salt, Rose & Leaf, Clear & Frosted Amethyst, Pedestal, Pair | 130.00 |
| Moser, Sherbet, Alexandrite, Signed, 3 1/2 In.High | 175.00 |
| Moser, Shot Glass, Cranberry & Clear Overlay, Applied Flower, Pedestal, Gold | 50.00 |
| Moser, Teapot, Gold Floral On Emerald Green, Signed, 6 In.High | 165.00 |
| Moser, Tumbler, Amber, Enameled Floral, Ladybugs, & Dragonflies, Signed | 90.00 |
| Moser, Tumbler, Cranberry To Clear, Enamel Grapes & Leaves | 98.00 |
| Moser, Tumbler, Cranberry, 2 Enameled Flying Birds & Flowers, 4 1/2 In. | 95.00 |
| Moser, Tumbler, Juice, Amethyst, Gold Enamel, Glass Jewels | 195.00 |
| Moser, Vase, Acid Cut, Etched Deer & Forest On Topaz Glass, 8 In.High | 375.00 |
| Moser, Vase, Alexandrite, Peacock Eye, 9 1/2 In.High | 230.00 |
| Moser, Vase, Amber, Warrior Band, Signed, 9 In.High | 175.00 |
| Moser, Vase, Amethyst, Enameled Floral, 8 Applied Bees, Signed, 10 In.High | 195.00 |
| Moser, Vase, Amethyst, Gold, Signed, 14 1/2 In.High | 150.00 |
| Moser, Vase, Amethyst, Incised Gold Band, Spartan Warriors, Paneled, 9 3/4 In | 110.00 |
| Moser, Vase, Covered, Clear To Green Bud Top, Raised Gold & Floral, 8 In. | 130.00 |
| Moser, Vase, Cranberry, Enamel & Gold Decoration, Signed, 6 In. | 85.00 |
| Moser, Vase, Cranberry, Enamel & Gold Decoration, Signed, 6 1/2 In. | 65.00 |
| Moser, Vase, Cranberry, Gold Enamel, Ovoid, Metal Feet, Signed, 4 In. | 70.00 |
| Moser, Vase, Cranberry, Long Neck, Ovoid Body, Ormolu Feet, Gold Enamel, 4 In. | 65.00 |
| Moser, Vase, Emerald To Clear, Cut Iris & Lilies On Sides, 5 In. | 195.00 |
| Moser, Vase, Enameled Decoration & Applied Bees On Blue, Signed, 11 In.High | 165.00 |

Montereau, Plate,
Black & Yellow, C.1830,
8 1/4 In., 4
(See Page 333)

Mosaic Tile Company, Tile,
Lincoln, Jasperware, Blue
(See Page 334)

Moss Rose, Teapot & Creamer, 6 In.
(See Page 336)

Moser, Vase, Fluted, Clear To Cranberry, Gold Trim & Floral, 3 1/4 In.High ................................. 85.00
Moser, Vase, Green, Applied Gold Metal Bees, 13 1/2 In. High ................................. 295.00
Moser, Vase, Green, Floral Enameling, Signed, 10 In.High ................................. 135.00
Moser, Vase, Paperweight, Emerald Green Crystal, 6 In.High ................................. 28.00
Moser, Vase, Pink To Cranberry Fluted Top, Enameled Chrysanthemums, 10 In. ................................. 175.00
Moser, Vase, Rectangular Block, Gold, Clear To Amethyst Top, 5 In. ................................. 65.00
Moser, Vase, Seven Panels, Amber, Marked, 8 In. ................................. 70.00
Moser, Vase, Trumpet, Cranberry, Gold Enamel, Paperweight Bottom, 13 In. ................................. 110.00
Moser, Vase, Yellow, Amber, & Clear, Intaglio, Trefoil Lip, 11 In. ................................. 750.00
Moser, Wine, Melon Shape Green Bowl, Engraved, Enameled, Gold Wash, Signed ..................... 50.00

*Moss Rose china was made by many firms from 1808 to 1900. It refers to any*
*china decorated with the moss rose flower.*
Moss Rose, Coffeepot, 9 In. ................................. 38.00
Moss Rose, Compote, Lattice Sides, Bolt Type, Gold Trim, 9 In. ................................. 30.00
Moss Rose, Dish, Soap, Covered, Insert ................................. 20.00
Moss Rose, Jug, Water, Furnival Ironstone, 11 In.High ................................. 25.00
Moss Rose, Mug, 4 In.High ................................. 8.50
Moss Rose, Pitcher, Milk, White Ground, Knowles, Taylor, & Knowles, C.1900 ..................... 40.00
Moss Rose, Pitcher, 8 In.High ................................. 10.00
Moss Rose, Plate, Gaudy Ironstone, C.1850, 7 1/2 In. ................................. 35.00
Moss Rose, Plate, 8 1/4 In. ................................. 5.00
Moss Rose, Saucer, Gold Edge, Leonard, Vienna, Austria & M ................................. 3.00
Moss Rose, Spooner ................................. 12.50
Moss Rose, Syrup, White, Black Handle, Vertical Ribbing, Dated Top ................................. 37.50
Moss Rose, Tea Set, Ironstone, Signed Powell & Bishop, 44 Piece ................................. 225.00
Moss Rose, Teapot & Creamer, 6 In. ................................. *Illus* 20.00
Moss Rose, Tureen, Covered, For Ladle, Gold Trim, Limoges ................................. 95.00
Moss Rose, Vase, 5 In.High ................................. 5.00

*Mother-of-pearl glass, or pearl satin glass, was first made in the 1850s in*
*England and in Massachusetts. It was a special type of mold-blown satin*
*glass with air bubbles in the glass, giving it a pearlized color.*
Mother-of-Pearl, see Pearl
Mother-Of-Pearl Glass, Basket, Raspberry To White Base, Diamond-Quilted ..................... 225.00
Mother-Of-Pearl Glass, Bowl & Underplate, Finger, Ribbon, Blue & Green ..................... 335.00
Mother-Of-Pearl Glass, Jar, Cracker, Satin Moire, Rose, White Lining ..................... 245.00
Mother-Of-Pearl Glass, Pitcher, Water, Diamond-Quilted, Blue, Thorn Handle ..................... 375.00
Mother-Of-Pearl Glass, Rose Bowl, Blue, Herringbone, Crimped Rim, 5 In. ................................. 100.00
Mother-Of-Pearl Glass, Tumbler, Yellow To White, Diamond-Quilted, Floral ..................... 295.00
Mother-Of-Pearl Glass, Vase, Apricot, Diamond-Quilted, 12 In. High ................................. 200.00
Mother-Of-Pearl Glass, Vase, Blue To Bittersweet, Herringbone, 10 1/2 In. ..................... 60.00
Mother-Of-Pearl Glass, Vase, Blue, Diamond-Quilted, Coralene Trim, 8 In. ..................... 895.00
Mother-Of-Pearl Glass, Vase, Blue, Diamond-Quilted, Footed, 4 1/2 In. High ..................... 175.00
Mother-Of-Pearl Glass, Vase, Diamond-Quilted, American Beauty Red, 8 In. ..................... 95.00
Mother-Of-Pearl Glass, Vase, Diamond-Quilted, Tan To Chocolate, 7 In.High ..................... 180.00
Mother-Of-Pearl Glass, Vase, Quilted, Raspberry, Gourd Shape, 10 In. ................................. 150.00
Mother-Of-Pearl Glass, Vase, White, Hobnail, Blue Quadrifold Top, 5 In. ..................... 550.00
Mother-of-Pearl, Satin Glass, see also Satin Glass, Smith
Brothers, Tiffany, etc.
Moustache Cup, see Mustache Cup

*Mt. Joye is an enameled cameo glass made in the late nineteenth and*
*twentieth centuries by Saint-Hilaire Touvior de Varraux and Co.of*
*Pantin, France. This same company produced De Vez glass.*
Mt.Joye, Jar, Covered, Multicolor Floral, Gold, Polished Pontil, 7 1/2 In. ..................... 65.00
Mt.Joye, Vase, Enameled Dogwood On Green Chipped, Square, 5 1/2 In.High ..................... 65.00
Mt.Joye, Vase, Gold Cameo Cut Flowers, Round Body, 11 In. High ................................. 150.00
Mt.Joye, Vase, White, Yellow, & Green Gold Floral On Lavender, 18 In., Pair ..................... 125.00

*Mt.Washington Glass was made at the Mt.Washington Glass Co.*
*located in New Bedford, Massachusetts. Many types of art glass were made*
*there from 1850 to the 1890s.*
Mt.Washington, see also Burmese, Crown Milano
Mt.Washington, Box, Covered, Scrolls & Enamel Floral On Aqua, Bail Handle ..................... 275.00
Mt.Washington, Box, Domed Lid, Brass Collar, Heart Shape, Floral, Gold ..................... 65.00

| | |
|---|---|
| Mt.Washington, Box, Hinged, Ivory Satin, Angel Blowing Horn & Floral, Round | 75.00 |
| Mt.Washington, Bride's Basket, Acid Cut Back Blue To White, Medallions | 300.00 |
| Mt.Washington, Bride's Basket, Beaded Enamel, Tuft's Silver Frame | 350.00 |
| Mt.Washington, Celery, Diamond-Quilted, Square, Scalloped Top, 4 3/4 In.High | 175.00 |
| Mt.Washington, Cruet, Enamel Decoration, Metal Collar & Handle | 210.00 |
| Mt.Washington, Dish, Sweetmeat, Fig Shape, Silver Lid & Handle, Aqua & White | 165.00 |
| Mt.Washington, Egg, Easter, 'a Happy Easter, ' Robin On Flower Twig | 37.50 |
| Mt.Washington, Ewer, Yellow, Orange, & Green Enamel On Pale Green, 10 In. | 70.00 |
| Mt.Washington, Jar, Cracker, Melon Ribbed, Blue, Pink, & Green Floral | 140.00 |
| Mt.Washington, Jar, Cracker, Melon Shape, Blue On White, Blossoms, Silver Lid | 165.00 |
| Mt.Washington, Jar, Cracker, Silver Lid & Bail, Melon Ribbed Peach Satin | 275.00 |
| Mt.Washington, Jar, Powder, 6 Flower Panels, Numbered, 4 1/2 In.Across | 175.00 |
| Mt.Washington, Jug, Verona, Applied Reeded Crystal Handle, Gold Floral | 95.00 |
| Mt.Washington, Lamp, Egg Shape Base, Floral On Apricot, 3 3/4 In. | 110.00 |
| Mt.Washington, Muffineer, Cream, Melon Ribbed, Apple Blossoms, Repousse Top | 145.00 |
| Mt.Washington, Muffineer, Egg Shape, Apple Blossoms On Blue To Biscuit | 165.00 |
| Mt.Washington, Muffineer, Egg Shape, Maidenhair Fern On Lusterless White | 150.00 |
| Mt.Washington, Muffineer, Egg Shape, Pale Yellow, Pansies, Pewter Top | 145.00 |
| Mt.Washington, Muffineer, Egg Shape, Tan To Dull Orange, Enameled Daisies | 135.00 |
| Mt.Washington, Muffineer, Fig, Lava, Blue Floral On Lemon, Steffin, 1893 | 375.00 |
| Mt.Washington, Muffineer, Pansies | 110.00 |
| Mt.Washington, Muffineer, Tomato Shape, Blue To White, Repousse Top | 105.00 |
| Mt.Washington, Pepper Shaker, Egg Shape, White, Floral, Pewter Top, 2 1/2 In. | 35.00 |
| Mt.Washington, Perfume, Green Satin, Silver & Gold Floral, 7 1/2 In. | 95.00 |
| Mt.Washington, Pitcher, Water, Cranberry, Thumbprint, Crystal Handle, 1880s | 95.00 |
| Mt.Washington, Plate, Enameled Green & Orchid Lilacs On White, 10 In. | 20.00 |
| Mt.Washington, Plate, Hand-Painted Posies, Lusterless White, 8 In. | 15.00 |
| Mt.Washington, Plate, Hand-Painted Red Roses, 9 3/4 In. | 12.50 |
| Mt.Washington, Plate, Pink Satin, Yellow Flowers, 12 In.Diameter | 12.00 |
| Mt.Washington, Pot, Glue, Fig Shape, Green, Decorated | 145.00 |
| Mt.Washington, Pot, Glue, Figural, Peach Sectioned, Pink & White Flowers | 280.00 |
| Mt.Washington, Potpourri, Prunt On Cover, Inner Lid, Lusterless White | 75.00 |
| Mt.Washington, Rose Bowl, Blue, Ribbed, Crimped Top, 3 1/2 In.High | 58.00 |
| Mt.Washington, Rose Bowl, Decorated, 5 In.High | 190.00 |
| Mt.Washington, Rose Bowl, Pink To Deep Rose, Satin, 14 In.Diameter | 85.00 |
| Mt.Washington, Rose Bowl, White, Rose Decoration, Crimped Polished Pontil | 23.00 |
| Mt.Washington, Salt & Pepper, Egg Shape, Blue, Floral, Pewter Tops, 1889 | 80.00 |
| Mt.Washington, Salt & Pepper, Egg Shape, Decorated, White, Silver Holder | 75.00 |
| Mt.Washington, Salt & Pepper, Egg Shape, Floral On Lusterless White | 165.00 |
| Mt.Washington, Salt & Pepper, Figs, One Yellow, One Rose, Enamel Decoration | 195.00 |
| Mt.Washington, Salt & Pepper, Floral Decoration | 75.00 |
| Mt.Washington, Salt Dip, Individual, Melon Ribbed, Pansies On Yellow | 35.00 |
| Mt.Washington, Salt Dip, Melon Ribbed, Beaded Top Edge, Red Floral, White | 50.00 |
| Mt.Washington, Salt Set, Multicolor Floral Enamel, Holder, 4 Piece | 125.00 |
| Mt.Washington, Salt, Beaded Dot Florals On Ribbed | 75.00 |
| Mt.Washington, Salt, Yellow & Orange Bark, Raised White Flowers | 95.00 |
| Mt.Washington, Saltshaker, Columbian Exposition | 60.00 |
| Mt.Washington, Saltshaker, Egg, Blue Floral On Yellow To White, Pair | 85.00 |
| Mt.Washington, Saltshaker, Egg, Lusterless White, Rosebuds, Green Leaves | 55.00 |
| Mt.Washington, Saltshaker, Egg, Satin, Violets, Pansies, Carnations, & Daisies | 30.00 |
| Mt.Washington, Saltshaker, Fig Shape | 95.00 |
| Mt.Washington, Saltshaker, Fig, Yellow Daisies On Shaded Beige | 55.00 |
| Mt.Washington, Saltshaker, Melon Ribbed, Marked Pat.May 18, 1883 | 40.00 |
| Mt.Washington, Saltshaker, Melon Ribbed, Satin, White, Berries | 27.50 |
| Mt.Washington, Saltshaker, Pale Blue Flowers, 5 Puffed Panels | 25.00 |
| Mt.Washington, Saltshaker, Tomato, Burmese Color, Floral, Blue & White Dots | 50.00 |
| Mt.Washington, Saltshaker, Raised Gold Lilies & "Easter" | 40.00 |
| Mt.Washington, Saltshaker, Ribbed, Raised Blue Dots, Enameled Floral | 45.00 |
| Mt.Washington, Saltshaker, Tomato, White Ground, Flowers | 25.00 To 95.00 |
| Mt.Washington, Saltshaker, White, Melon Ribbed, Blue Dots, Enamel Floral | 45.00 |
| Mt.Washington, Sugar & Creamer, Cover, Opaline, Hand-Painted | 195.00 |
| Mt.Washington, Sugar & Creamer, Pink, Shell, Enameled Floral, Silver Tops | 275.00 |
| Mt.Washington, Syrup, Hand-Painted Asters, Silver Lid & Handle | 245.00 |
| Mt.Washington, Syrup, Opalescent, Blue Floral On White | 40.00 |
| Mt.Washington, Toothpick, Hat Shape, White, 2 1/2 In.High | 37.00 |
| Mt.Washington, Toothpick, Tricorner Top | 210.00 |

| | |
|---|---|
| Mt.Washington, Vase, Olive To Amberina, Inverted Thumbprint, 9 1/2 In. | 80.00 |
| Mt.Washington, Vase, Pink Cameo, Flowers, Leaves, & Hummingbird, 5 3/4 In. | 450.00 |
| Mt.Washington, Vase, Pink Floral Decoration, 2 1/2 In.High | 70.00 |
| Mt.Washington, Vase, Pink, Cameo, 8 In.High | 850.00 |
| Mt.Washington, Vase, Verona, Magenta & Purple Violets, Coin Gold, 4 1/2 In. | 75.00 |
| Mt.Washington, Vase, Yellow To White, Flower & Leaf, Gold Beading, 6 3/4 In. | 150.00 |
| Muffineer, Apple Green, 2 Groups Of Horizontal Rings, 8 Inverted Panels | 45.00 |
| Muffineer, Blue Phlox | 65.00 |
| Muffineer, Bulbous, Frosted With Clear Reliefs, Hazelnuts & Flowers | 48.00 |
| Muffineer, Ceramic, Light Blue, White Band Of Small Flowers | 16.50 |
| Muffineer, Clear, Ribbed Base | 7.00 |
| Muffineer, Cone, Pink Cased Glass | 60.00 |
| Muffineer, Embossed Daffodils, Color Decoration | 18.00 |
| Muffineer, Emerald Green Glass, Quilted Phlox | 75.00 |
| Muffineer, English Block Crystal, E.P.N.S.Top | 22.00 |
| Muffineer, Green Glass, Silver Top, 6 1/2 In.High | 35.00 |
| Muffineer, Hand-Painted Pastel Daisies | 18.50 |
| Muffineer, Pink Acorn, Gold Decoration | 95.00 |
| Muffineer, Vaseline, Opalescent Swirl, Reverse Swirl Glass Ribs | 58.00 |

*Muller Freres, French for Muller Brothers, made cameo and other art glass from the early 1900s to the late 1930s. Their factory was first located in Luneville and later moved to Croismaire, France.*

| | |
|---|---|
| Muller Freres, Chandelier, Pate De Verre, Gilt Metal, Floral Bowls | 225.00 |
| Muller Freres, Lamp, Cameo, Orange, Brown, & Black, Dog Eyeing Pheasant | 1095.00 |
| Muller Freres, Rose Bowl, Blue & Orange With Silver, Luneville, 4 1/2 In. | 110.00 |
| Muller Freres, Rose Bowl, Mottled Blue, Orange, & Silver, Luneville, 5 In. | 75.00 |
| Muller Freres, Vase, Cameo, Light Blue Mottled Ground, Irises, 9 In.High | 175.00 |
| Muller Freres, Vase, Cameo, Mustard, Brown, Dutch River Scene, 13 1/4 In.High | 350.00 |
| Muller Freres, Vase, Footed, Luneville, Signed, 13 X 4 In. | 395.00 |
| Muller Freres, Vase, Forest Scene On Blue, 4 Cuttings, 6 In.High | 210.00 |
| Muller Freres, Vase, Red & Peach On Blue & Yellow, Berries, 1900s, 5 1/2 In. | 270.00 |
| Muller Freres, Vase, Shepherdess, Autumn, Ocher, Purple, & Opalescent, 12 In. | 475.00 |
| Muller Freres, Vase, Stick, Pate De Verre, Black, Orange, 9 In. | 165.00 |
| Muller Freres, Vase, Yellow To Red, Pewter Overlay, Leaves & Acorns, 9 In. | 125.00 |
| Music, Album, Little Mischief Bubble Book, Columbia Graphophone Co. | 25.00 |
| Music, Album, Phonograph, Dick Tracy, Dated 1947, 2 Records | 6.25 |
| Music, Album, Record, Rendezvous With Destiny, F.D.R.Speeches | 25.00 |
| Music, Album, Tippy Toe Bubble Book, Columbia Graphophone Co., 3 Records | 25.00 |
| Music, Amberola, Edison, Cylinder | 150.00 |
| Music, Automaton, Monkey, 3 Movements, Glass Case, Fur, 11 X 10 In. | 450.00 |
| Music, Bagpipes, Scottish, Military | 150.00 |
| Music, Banjo Mandolin, Vega, 8 String | 225.00 |
| Music, Banjo, Encore, Tuning Instruction Book | 8000.00 |
| Music, Banjo, 5 String, Mother-Of-Pearl Inlay, Rosewood Handle, Nickel Plate | 40.00 |
| Music, Bazouki, Greek, Mother-Of-Pearl Inlaid, Stringed, 4 Ft.Long | 100.00 |
| Music, Bell, Orchestra, Deagan, Model 1832, Oak Folding Case, Patent 1908 | 90.00 |
| Music, Book, Boy Scout Song, Dated 1920 | 5.00 |
| Music, Box, Automatic Changer, Oak Case, 12 Tune, 64 X 34 X 24 In. | 3500.00 |
| Music, Box, Birdcage, Brass Ornate Cage, Bluebird, 10 1/2 In. High | 338.00 |
| Music, Box, Canary In Cage, Clock Center, 7 1/2 In.High | 37.50 |
| Music, Box, Couple Dancing Under Dome, Dance, Ballerina, Dance | 25.00 |
| Music, Box, Criterion, Carved Mahogany Case, 16 Tune, 22 X 20 X 12 In. | 1250.00 |
| Music, Box, Dancing Girl, Red & Gold Leather, Mirror In Lid, La Paloma | 22.50 |
| Music, Box, French, 2 Tunes, Wooden, Crank Handle, Boy In Sailor Suit On Top | 30.00 |
| Music, Box, Mira, Mahogany Case, 20 Tune, 17 X 15 X 10 In. | 875.00 |
| Music, Box, Nickole Freres, Inlaid Case, 8 Tune, 20 In.Long | 675.00 |
| Music, Box, Nickole Freres, Piano Forte, 6 Tune, 24 In.Long | 775.00 |
| Music, Box, Polyphone, Inlaid Carved Case, 12 Tune, 24 X 22 X 14 In. | 1250.00 |
| Music, Box, Polyphone, Upright, Walnut Case, Coin-Operated, 12 Tune, 38 In. | 1750.00 |
| Music, Box, Red Bird In Gold Cage, 7 1/2 In.High | 25.00 |
| Music, Box, Regina, Eight 8 In.Discs, 12 In.Square | 385.00 |
| Music, Box, Regina, Oak Case, 8 8 In.Discs | 395.00 |
| Music, Box, Regina, Orchestral, Mahogany Case, 12 27 In. Discs, 79 In.Long | 2850.00 |
| Music, Box, Regina, Table Model, Mahogany Case, 12 Tune, 16 X 15 X 10 In. | 875.00 |
| Music, Box, Regina, Table Model, Oak Case, 12 Tune, 20 X 22 X 13 In. | 975.00 |

| | |
|---|---|
| Music, Box, Regina, Table Model, Walnut Case, 6 Tune, Storage In Case, 15 In. | 475.00 |
| Music, Box, Regina, Walnut Case, Mandrel Type, 6 Tune, 9 X 8 X 7 In. | 275.00 |
| Music, Box, Reginaphone, Combination Music Box & Gramophone | 1150.00 |
| Music, Box, Singing Canary In Cage, Gold, 7 1/2 In.High | 25.00 |
| Music, Box, Sterling Silver & Petit Point, 4 1/2 X 6 X 1 1/2 In. | 75.00 |
| Music, Box, Swiss Movement, Thoren, Hurdy-Gurdy, Enamel On Metal | 90.00 |
| Music, Box, Swiss Movement, Thoren, Olivewood Baby Grand Piano | 42.50 |
| Music, Box, Swiss Movement, Thoren, Silver Metal Horse & Carriage | 42.50 |
| Music, Box, Swiss, Butterfly Strikers, 3 Bells, 10 Tune, 20 In.Long | 375.00 |
| Music, Box, Swiss, Cylinder, Glass Inner Lid, 8 Tune | 285.00 |
| Music, Box, Swiss, Cylinder, Inlaid, 12 Tune | 675.00 |
| Music, Box, Swiss, Cylinder, Rosewood Case, Floral Marquetry, 8 Tune, C.1890 | 200.00 |
| Music, Box, Swiss, Cylinder, Toymaker's Dream & Parade Of Wooden Soldiers | 35.00 |
| Music, Box, Swiss, Fancy Decoration, Blue Danube, Old Folks At Home | 25.00 |
| Music, Box, Swiss, Inlaid Burl Walnut, 3 Tunes, 5 1/2 X 3 In. | 39.00 |
| Music, Box, Swiss, Inlaid Case, Large Cylinder, 6 Tune, 35 In.Long | 1200.00 |
| Music, Box, Swiss, Inlaid Top, 12 Tune, 31 X 13 X 8 1/2 In. | 1100.00 |
| Music, Box, Swiss, Inlaid Walnut, 3 Tunes, 6 1/4 X 3 3/4 In. | 39.00 |
| Music, Box, Swiss, 12 Tune, 20 In.Long | 375.00 |
| Music, Box, Symphonion, Black Case, 6 Tune, 12 1/2 X 12 1/2 X 7 In. | 525.00 |
| Music, Box, Symphonion, Upright, Walnut Case, 12 Tune, 36 X 25 X 14 In. | 1750.00 |
| Music, Box, Symphonion, Walnut Case, 12 Tune, 18 X 15 X 10 In. | 750.00 |
| Music, Box, Troubador, Walnut Case, 8 Tune, 11 X 11 X 7 In. | 475.00 |
| Music, Bugle, Copper, 12 X 6 1/2 In. | 15.00 |
| Music, Bugle, Rexcratt, Official Boy Scout Of America, Mahogany, Metronome | 12.00 |
| Music, Bugle, U.S.Regulation | 15.00 |
| Music, Calliope, Walnut Case, 10 Tune, 18 X 16 X 10 In. | 775.00 |
| Music, Calliope, Walnut Case, 16 Tune, 24 X 18 X 10 In. | 875.00 |
| Music, Calliope, 43 Whistle, Mounted On Truck | 7000.00 |
| Music, Disc, Break The News To Mother, Regina, 15 1/2 In. | 5.00 |
| Music, Disc, Calliope, 13 1/4 In. | 5.00 |
| Music, Disc, Goodby, Mignonette, Polyphone, 19 3/4 In. | 5.00 |
| Music, Disc, I Love Thee, I Adore Thee, Stella, 17 3/8 In. | 5.75 |
| Music, Disc, La Rein Des Fats, Polyphone, 19 3/4 In. | 5.00 |
| Music, Disc, March From Tannhauser, Calliope, 9 1/4 In. | 2.50 |
| Music, Disc, Mikado Waltz, Symphonion, Metal, 7 1/2 In. | 2.50 |
| Music, Disc, Prayer From William Tell, Symphonion, 13 5/8 In. | 3.00 |
| Music, Disc, Santay Cherrie Soge Man, Polyphone, 19 3/4 In. | 5.00 |
| Music, Disc, There's A Green Hill Far Away, Polyphone, 19 3/4 In. | 5.00 |
| Music, Disc, Wer Kann Dafur Walzar, Llzenpflichtig, Zinc, 6 1/2 In. | 2.50 |
| Music, Flute, Reddish Black Wood, Silver Fittings & Keys, Marked E.V.N. | 22.00 |
| Music, Gramophone, Reliance, Birmingham, England, C.1920 | 50.00 |
| Music, Guitar, Roy Rogers, Wood & Pressboard, Lithographed Roy & Dale | 13.50 |
| Music, Harmonica, Lone Ranger, Gold Colored, Etched Lone Ranger Picture | 10.50 |
| Music, Harmonica, Regla Fellers | 6.00 |
| Music, Harmonica, The Brass Band, 40 Reeds | 10.00 |
| Music, Harmonium, C.1850, 14 In.High | *Illus* 475.00 |
| Music, Harp, Sebastian Erards, C.1825, 5 Ft.8 In.High | *Illus* 950.00 |
| Music, Harpsichord, Andrew Phochead, Scotland, 19th Century | 850.00 |
| Music, Horn, Blowing, Carved Horn, "Taylor Furgerson, " C.1850 | 225.00 |
| Music, Horn, Germany, Tin, 8 Note | 8.50 |
| Music, Hurdy-Gurdy, Colson, Amirecourt, France, Lute Shape, 6 String | 1500.00 |
| Music, Hurdy-Gurdy, Street Grinder's, Barrel Piano, 10 Tune, 40 In. High | 1200.00 |
| Music, Hurdy-Gurdy, Street Grinder's, Monkey Organ, Wood & Pewter Pipes | 2000.00 |
| Music, Instrument, Flex-A-Tone, Instructions, 1920s Pictures On Box | 5.00 |
| Music, Juke Box, Wurlitzer, 5, 10, & 25 Cent Slots, 24 78 R.P.M. Selections | 1000.00 |
| Music, Mandolin, Italian, Wood Case, Mother-Of-Pearl, Ivory, C.1880 | 95.00 |
| Music, Mouth Organ, Rolomonica, Bakelite, Patent 1925 | 22.50 |
| Music, Needle, Phonograph, His Master's Voice, Brass Box, 200 | 10.00 |
| Music, Organ, Barrel, Clemerio & Comn.Y, London, Mahogany, George II Style | 500.00 |
| Music, Organ, Player, Gem, 1906, 4 Rolls | 150.00 |
| Music, Organ, Reed, Estey, Manual Pedal With Blower | 50.00 |

*The phonograph, invented by Thomas Edison in the 1880s, has been made by many firms.*

| | |
|---|---|
| Music, Phonograph, Edison Gem, Cylinder | 325.00 |
| Music, Phonograph, Edison Home, H Reproducer, Large Horn | 175.00 |

Music, Harp,
Sebastian Erards,
C.1825, 5 Ft.8 In.High
*(See Page 339)*

Music, Harmonium,
C.1850, 14 In.High
*(See Page 339)*

| | |
|---|---:|
| **Music, Phonograph,** Edison Triumph, C Reproducer, Brass Horn | 275.00 |
| **Music, Phonograph,** Edison, Amberole, Cylinder, 10 Records | 145.00 |
| **Music, Phonograph,** Edison, Fireside | 250.00 |
| **Music, Phonograph,** Edison, Home, Cylinder, 4 Records | 250.00 |
| **Music, Phonograph,** Edison, Home, Suitcase | 225.00 |
| **Music, Phonograph,** Edison, Model R, Reproducer | 75.00 |
| **Music, Phonograph,** Edison, Standard, Morning Glory Horn | 350.00 |
| **Music, Phonograph,** Edison, Suitcase, Home | 225.00 |
| **Music, Phonograph,** Elite, Mahogany Cabinet, Large Horn | 175.00 |
| **Music, Phonograph,** Polyphone, Walnut Cabinet, Crank Type, Disc Type | 295.00 |
| **Music, Phonograph,** Reproducer, Model R | 75.00 |
| **Music, Phonograph,** Standard, Model A, Disc | 200.00 |
| **Music, Phonograph,** Standard, Model X, Morning Glory Horn, Front Mount | 250.00 |
| **Music, Phonograph,** The Yankee Prince, Table Model, Morning Glory Horn | 127.50 |
| **Music, Phonograph,** Victor II, Original Black Horn And Reproducer | 225.00 |
| **Music, Phonograph,** Victor V, Original Horn, Brass Bell | 275.00 |
| **Music, Phonograph,** Victor, Brass Bell Horn, Back Mount | 250.00 |
| **Music, Phonograph,** Victor, Outside Horn | 150.00 |
| **Music, Phonograph,** Victor, Table Model | 85.00 |
| **Music, Phonograph,** Zonophone, Red Morning Glory Horn, Disc Model | 325.00 |
| **Music, Piano-Neola,** Brevete S.G.D.G., Paris, Napoleon III, Rosewood | 325.00 |
| **Music, Piano,** Acoustigrande, Lowrey Organo Attachment, Chickering Bros. | 1200.00 |
| **Music, Piano,** Grand, Knabe Ampico, Player Mechanism, 5 Ft.8 In. | 1500.00 |
| **Music, Piano,** Player, Weber 5-8 Grand, Walnut Case, Square Legs, Duart Action | 1500.00 |
| **Music, Piano,** Schoenhut, Upright, Colored Lithograph, 17 Keys, 17 1/2 In.Long | 48.00 |
| **Music, Piano,** Steinway & Sons, Baby Grand, Black Lacquer, 1869, 5 Ft.10 In. | 2900.00 |
| **Music, Record Duster,** Celluloid Picture Of Bing Crosby | 4.00 |
| **Music, Record,** And The Parrot Said, Cylinder, Edison, Blue Amberole | 1.25 |
| **Music, Record,** Belle Of Kentucky, Cylinder, Edison, Blue Amberole | 1.25 |
| **Music, Record,** Buddy Boy, Collins, Cylinder, Edison, Blue Amberole | 1.25 |
| **Music, Record,** Casey On The Telephone, Nov.4, 1895 | 35.00 |
| **Music, Record,** Daddy Long Legs, Columbia Graphophone Co. | 6.00 |
| **Music, Record,** Dancing On The House Tops, Cylinder, Edison, Blue Amberole | 1.25 |
| **Music, Record,** Dixie, W.D.Connors, Oct.14, 1896 | 35.00 |
| **Music, Record,** Floppy Fly & Spider & The Fly, Columbia Graphophone Co. | 6.00 |
| **Music, Record,** Herman & Minnie, Cylinder, Edison, Blue Amberole | 1.25 |
| **Music, Record,** Honeybee's Honeymoon, Cylinder, Edison, Blue Amberole | 1.25 |
| **Music, Record,** How I Need You, Cylinder, Edison, Blue Amberole | 1.25 |
| **Music, Record,** Hymns of The Old Church Choir, Cylinder, Edison, Blue Amberole | 1.25 |
| **Music, Record,** I'm Getting Ready For My Mother-In-Law, Cylinder, Edison | 1.25 |
| **Music, Record,** Instantaneous, German Silver, 24K Gold Plate, 1917 | 11.95 |
| **Music, Record,** La Donna E Mobile, F.A.Giannini, Jan.21, 1896 | 400.00 |
| **Music, Record,** Little Flatterer Band, Cylinder, Edison, Blue Amberole | 1.25 |
| **Music, Record,** Little Girl You'll Do, Cylinder, Edison, Blue Amberole | 1.25 |
| **Music, Record,** Lorena, Cylinder, Edison, Blue Amberole | 1.25 |
| **Music, Record,** Mary's Lamb, David C.Bangs, Nov.23, 1895 | 35.00 |
| **Music, Record,** Memories Of Mother, Cylinder, Edison, Blue Amberole | 1.25 |

| | |
|---|---:|
| Music, Record, Nearer My God To Thee, Cylinder, Edison, Blue Amberole | 1.25 |
| Music, Record, Nearer My God To Thee, E.R.Johnson, Victor, White Label | 75.00 |
| Music, Record, Old Black Joe, The Band At Ross's | 35.00 |
| Music, Record, Reel Solo From The Magic Flute, Cylinder, Edison | 1.25 |
| Music, Record, Santa Claus, Playtime Series, C.1920, 2 Sides | 5.00 |
| Music, Record, Silver Star, Cylinder, Edison, Blue Amberole | 1.25 |
| Music, Record, Story Of The Gramophone, David C.Bangs, Feb.15, 1896 | 150.00 |
| Music, Record, Tell Mother I'll Be There, Cylinder, Edison, Blue Amberole | 1.25 |
| Music, Record, The Lord's Prayer & 23rd Psalm, Talmage, April 8, 1898 | 150.00 |
| Music, Record, Throw Out The Life Line, Cylinder, Edison, Blue Amberole | 1.25 |
| Music, Record, Victor, Drink To Me Only With Thine Eyes, John McCormack | 10.00 |
| Music, Record, Victor, Roamin In The Gloamin, Harry Lauder | 10.00 |
| Music, Record, Victrola, Carmen, Habanera, Emma Calve | 10.00 |
| Music, Record, Victrola, Old Folks At Home | 10.00 |
| Music, Record, Victrola, St.Paul, But The Lord Is Mindful | 10.00 |
| Music, Record, Victrola, Tannhauser & O Du Mein Holder | 10.00 |
| Music, Record, Vitrola, Tannhauser, Dich Theure Halle, Johanna Gadski | 10.00 |
| Music, Record, Whistling Pete, Cylinder, Edison, Blue Amberole | 1.25 |
| Music, Record, Will He Answer "Goo Goo", Cylinder, Edison, Blue Amberole | 1.25 |
| Music, Sheet, A Requiem In Memory Of Lt.Ellsworth, 1861 | 25.00 |
| Music, Sheet, Alabama Coon Jigger | 4.00 |
| Music, Sheet, Barney Google, Barney & Spark Plug Cover, 1923 | 5.00 |
| Music, Sheet, Boys Who Wore Southern Gray, Columbia, Tenn. | 4.00 |
| Music, Sheet, Coon Smiles, 1913 | 3.00 |
| Music, Sheet, Coontown Patrol, March, 1904 | 3.00 |
| Music, Sheet, Dixie Doodle, Louisiana, Dated 1862 | 54.50 |
| Music, Sheet, Gone Again Corrigan, Corrigan & Planer, 1938 | 4.00 |
| Music, Sheet, Gregorian Chant, Pigskin Parchment, Dated 1710 | 27.00 |
| Music, Sheet, Home Delights, Ordway's-Wood's Minstrels, 1854 | 4.00 |
| Music, Sheet, Jeff In Petticoats, 1865 | 25.00 |
| Music, Sheet, Mary Pickford, The Darling Of Them All, Autographed | 15.00 |
| Music, Sheet, Massa's In The Cold, Cold Ground, Foster, Ticknor, 1889 | 5.00 |
| Music, Sheet, My Bamboo Queen, 1909 | 2.50 |
| Music, Sheet, My Pony Boy, 1909 | 2.50 |
| Music, Sheet, Nelly Wants To Marry, Christy Minstrels, 1852 | 5.00 |
| Music, Sheet, Old Jessy, Charlie Converse, 1852 | 5.00 |
| Music, Sheet, Pigskin Parchment, Polyphonic, Movable Treble Clef, 1707 | 25.00 |
| Music, Sheet, Poor Old Slave, 1851 | 4.00 |
| Music, Sheet, Sam The Old Accordion Man, 1927, Color Lithograph Of Negro | 3.00 |
| Music, Sheet, Sipping Cider Thru A Straw, 1919, Picture Of Fatty Arbuckle | 2.00 |
| Music, Sheet, Uncle Joe's Hail Columbia, Henry Work, 1862 | 10.00 |
| Music, Sheet, Wake Dinah, Ordway's-Wood's & Christy Minstrels, 1854 | 6.00 |
| Music, Sheet, You Flew Over, Lindbergh & Spirit Of St.Louis, 1927 | 5.00 |
| Music, Sheet, 10 Nights In A Bar Room, Illustrated, Woodcuts | 8.50 |
| Music, Symphonion, 25 Disc, Coin Operated | 1200.00 |
| Music, Talking Machine, United, Oak, Morning Glory Horn, 20 Records | 650.00 |
| Music, Victorola, 1907 Model, Enclosed Horn, Serial No.1881 | 525.00 |
| Music, Violano-Virtuoso, Single Violin, Oak Case, Feeder Motor | 1950.00 |
| Music, Violin, Base, Hand-Carved, H.F.Yarbrough, Wooden Case, 10 In.Long | 350.00 |
| Music, Violin, Hawaiian Art | 45.00 |

*Mustache cups were popular from 1850 to 1900. A ledge of china or silver held the hair out of the liquid in the cup.*

| | |
|---|---:|
| Mustache Cup & Saucer, Belleek, Tridacna, Green Trim, Black Mark | 110.00 |
| Mustache Cup & Saucer, Belleek, Tridacna, Pink Trim, 2nd Black Mark | 145.00 |
| Mustache Cup & Saucer, Blue, White, & Gold | 45.00 |
| Mustache Cup & Saucer, English Coat Of Arms On Both Pieces | 29.50 |
| Mustache Cup & Saucer, Floral | 25.00 |
| Mustache Cup & Saucer, German Verse, Ornate | 39.00 |
| Mustache Cup & Saucer, Gold On White | 32.00 |
| Mustache Cup & Saucer, Meissen, Fluted Sides, Gold Trim, Crossed Swords | 45.00 |
| Mustache Cup & Saucer, Multifloral Decoration, Scalloped, Gold Handle | 32.50 |
| Mustache Cup & Saucer, Nippon, Gold Floral & Beading On Beige, Green Leaf | 38.00 |
| Mustache Cup & Saucer, Ornate, "Papa" | 36.00 |
| Mustache Cup & Saucer, Pink Flowers, Large Size | 22.00 |
| Mustache Cup & Saucer, Pink, Blue Flowers, Gold | 22.00 |
| Mustache Cup & Saucer, Pumpkin Shape & Color, Pedestal Base, Gold Handle | 42.50 |

| | |
|---|---|
| Mustache Cup & Saucer, Quadruple Plate, Stevens Mfg.Co., Portland | 49.00 |
| Mustache Cup & Saucer, R.S.Prussia, Red Mark, White Floral On Green, Footed | 125.00 |
| Mustache Cup & Saucer, Raised Flowers, German, 3 1/2 In ...........*Illus* | 35.00 |
| Mustache Cup & Saucer, Raised Flowers, "Think Of Me" | 9.50 |
| Mustache Cup & Saucer, Red Strawberries, Foliage, & Gold, Altwasser | 25.00 |
| Mustache Cup & Saucer, Silver Plate, Mom & Dad, Pair | 75.00 |
| Mustache Cup & Saucer, Victorian Child In Blue Dress, Large Size | 50.00 |
| Mustache Cup & Saucer, White & Pink Roses On White, Gold Trim, Germany | 24.75 |
| Mustache Cup, Nippon, Boating Scene, Lima Mark 25 | 28.00 |
| Mustache Cup, White, Embossed, 4 Corners | 22.50 |
| Mustache Cup, With Saucer, White With Pink & Purple Violets, Gold Trim | 25.00 |
| MZ Austria, Bouillon Set, Rosebud Pattern, Marked, 15 Piece | 45.00 |
| MZ Austria, Box, Pin, Covered, Hand-Painted Blue & Gold Design, 3 1/2 In. | 4.00 |
| MZ Austria, Plate, Pink & Yellow Roses On Blue, 10 Sided, 8 1/2 In. | 13.00 |
| MZ Austria, Ring Tree, White | 12.00 |

*Nailsea glass was made in the Bristol District in England from 1788 to
1873. Many pieces were made with loopings of colored glass as decorations.*

| | |
|---|---|
| Nailsea, Basket, Applied Clear Thorn Handle, Clear Cased, Gold, 11 1/4 In. | 112.50 |
| Nailsea, Bowl & Underplate, Finger, Yellow & White Satin, Crimped | 150.00 |
| Nailsea, Flask, Double, Light Blue & Opalescent, 8 In. | 90.00 |
| Nailsea, Flask, White Loopings In Cranberry, Rough Pontil, 6 In.High | 125.00 |
| Nailsea, Lamp, Fairy, Cranberry & White, Clarke Candleholder, Frosted Feet | 395.00 |
| Nailsea, Pipe, Cranberry & White Loopings, White Threading On Bowl | 125.00 |
| Nailsea, Pitcher, White Stripe On Blue, Applied Clear Handle & Base, 8 In. | 100.00 |

*Nakara is a trade name for a white glassware made around 1900 that was
decorated in pastel colors. It was made by the C.F.Monroe Company of
Meriden, Connecticut.*

| | |
|---|---|
| Nakara, Box, Dresser, Covered, Art Nouveau Portrait Of Lady, Olive Green | 155.00 |
| Nakara, Box, Floral On Olive Green, 4 Brass Feet | 225.00 |
| Nakara, Box, Hinged, Dusty Pink, Signed, 3 3/4 In. Diameter | 189.00 |
| Nakara, Box, Hinged, Floral On Cover, Robin's Egg Blue, 4 1/2 In. | 150.00 |
| Nakara, Box, Hinged, Hand-Painted Orchids On Olive Green, 4 1/2 In. | 195.00 |
| Nakara, Box, Jewel, Hinged, Relief Blue Orchids On Lavender Blue, 4 In. | 175.00 |
| Nakara, Box, Jewel, Pink & White Tulips On Cover, Blue To Tan, Signed | 250.00 |
| Nakara, Box, Jewel, Portrait Of A Lady, White Beading, 6 1/2 X 4 1/2 In. | 295.00 |
| Nakara, Box, Powder, Hinged, Square, Enameled Flowers, Signed, 4 In. | 125.00 |
| Nakara, Box, Swivel Mirror, Signed | 275.00 |
| Nakara, Box, Trinket, Round, Light Green, Iris Beaded Scroll | 180.00 |
| Nakara, Humidor, Indian Portrait, Signed | 300.00 |
| Nakara, Humidor, Pipe & Bulldog, "The Old Sport, " Brass Lid | 250.00 |
| Nakara, Planter, Beaded Scroll, Irises, Green, Round, Signed, 7 1/2 In. | 179.00 |

*Nanking china is a blue-and white porcelain made in China for export during
the eighteenth century.*

| | |
|---|---|
| Nanking, Plate, Blue & White, Fitzhugh Border, Man On Bridge, C.1820, 8 In. | 30.00 |
| Nanking, Vase, Garden Scene, Cobalt Blue, 10 Character Reign Mark | 125.00 |
| Nantgarw, Plate, Teal In Water Weeds, Gilt Border, C.1817, 9 1/4 In. | 1200.00 |

*Napkin rings were popular from 1869 to about 1900.*

| | |
|---|---|
| Napkin Ring, Amber Glass, English | 5.00 |
| Napkin Ring, Brass, 2 Soldiers On Sides, Yellow Band | 25.00 |
| Napkin Ring, Carved Bone | 10.00 |
| Napkin Ring, Celluloid, Ivory | 3.00 |
| Napkin Ring, Ceramic, Hand-Painted Yellow Roses | 6.50 |
| Napkin Ring, Child's, Embossed Animals, Silver | 5.00 |
| Napkin Ring, Child's, Figural, Bird, Thick Pyrolin Type Material | 4.00 |
| Napkin Ring, Child's, Goosey Goosey Gander, 'Aug.12, '09, ' Initial | 17.50 |
| Napkin Ring, China, Colored Ground, 8 3/8 In.Diameter | 9.75 |
| Napkin Ring, Cobalt Blue Glass, English | 5.00 |
| Napkin Ring, Coin Silver, Grapes & Leaves, A.Wetherell, Dec.16, 1864 | 12.75 |
| Napkin Ring, Condiment Set, Bird Center, Taunton Silver Co. | 165.00 |
| Napkin Ring, Copper, Views Of Washington, D.C. | 4.50 |
| Napkin Ring, Cut Glass, Cut & Etched Thistle Decoration | 18.00 |
| Napkin Ring, Emblem Of Canada, Glass With Silver Deposit | 11.00 |
| Napkin Ring, English Silver, Engraved | 10.00 |
| Napkin Ring, Engraved A.T.Quint, C.1850, Coin | 4.95 |

Mustache Cup & Saucer, Raised Flowers,
German, 3 1/2 In
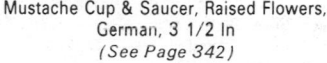
*(See Page 342)*

Napkin Ring, Figural, Bird, Derby Silver Co.

| | |
|---|---|
| Napkin Ring, Figural, Action Kewpie, Sterling Silver | 75.00 |
| Napkin Ring, Figural, Alligator On Base, Silver | 65.00 To 72.50 |
| Napkin Ring, Figural, Baby Girl & Boy Hold Ring, Dresden Type Porcelain | 37.50 |
| Napkin Ring, Figural, Begging Dog, Ornate Stand, Knickerbocker Silver Plate | 87.50 |
| Napkin Ring, Figural, Bird Of Prey, Lion & Eucalyptus, Australian, Embossed | 15.00 |
| Napkin Ring, Figural, Bird On Handle, Wavy Leaf Base | 52.50 |
| Napkin Ring, Figural, Bird On Top, White Pottery | 15.00 |
| Napkin Ring, Figural, Bird Salt & Pepper On Each Side Of Ring, Clear Glass | 55.00 |
| Napkin Ring, Figural, Bird With Spread Wings Watching Nest | 65.00 |
| Napkin Ring, Figural, Bird, Derby Silver Co. *Illus* | 150.00 |
| Napkin Ring, Figural, Bird, Wings Outstretched, Leaf Base, Toronto Silver | 65.00 |
| Napkin Ring, Figural, Boy Holding Ring On Round Base, Meriden, Silver Plate | 64.00 |
| Napkin Ring, Figural, Boy On High Bicycle, Tufts, 2649 | 195.00 |
| Napkin Ring, Figural, Boy Playing Soldier, Gun, Silver Plate | 58.00 |
| Napkin Ring, Figural, Boy Pushing Barrel, Meriden | 45.00 |
| Napkin Ring, Figural, Broken Egg On Crossed Wishbones, "Best Wishes" | 26.00 |
| Napkin Ring, Figural, Bulldog Alongside Beaded Ring, Silver Plate | 67.50 |
| Napkin Ring, Figural, Butterfly On Base, Fan On Sides, Rogers Silver Plate | 65.00 |
| Napkin Ring, Figural, Cat On Base, Knickerbocker | 74.00 |
| Napkin Ring, Figural, Cherub & Dog, Silver | 135.00 |
| Napkin Ring, Figural, Cherub & Wishbone, Claw Foot, Engraved, Wilcox Silver | 57.00 |
| Napkin Ring, Figural, Cherub At Each Side Of Barrel, Silver Plate | 38.00 |
| Napkin Ring, Figural, Cherub Holds Artist's Palette, Silver Plate | 52.50 |
| Napkin Ring, Figural, Cherub On Platform Base, Silver Plate | 25.00 |
| Napkin Ring, Figural, Chicken On Wishbone, Engraved Wildflowers, Silver | 48.00 |
| Napkin Ring, Figural, Child Coaxing Dog, Silver Plate | 75.00 |
| Napkin Ring, Figural, Crawling Baby | 110.00 |
| Napkin Ring, Figural, Crowing Rooster On Shovel, Meriden Silver Co. | 90.00 |
| Napkin Ring, Figural, Cupid Holding Ring On His Back, Square Base, Meriden | 125.00 |
| Napkin Ring, Figural, Cupid Holding Tassels On Sled, Meriden | 125.00 |
| Napkin Ring, Figural, Cupid, Boy, Barking Dog, 2 Hearts, Rogers | 150.00 |
| Napkin Ring, Figural, Cupids Holding Ring | 63.00 |
| Napkin Ring, Figural, Curly Haired Dog, Ornate Rectangular Base, Chain | 85.00 |
| Napkin Ring, Figural, Deer, Ears Up, Behind Fence, Meriden | 75.00 |
| Napkin Ring, Figural, Deer, Ring On Back | 135.00 |
| Napkin Ring, Figural, Dog Drinking From Bottle, Monarch Silver Co., Plated | 75.00 |
| Napkin Ring, Figural, Dog, Ring At Side | 50.00 |
| Napkin Ring, Figural, Dove Each Side Of Ring, Homan Mfg.Co., No.1481, Silver | 65.00 |
| Napkin Ring, Figural, Dove On Each Side, Engraved, Meriden & Co.146 | 65.00 |
| Napkin Ring, Figural, Eagle Each Side Of Ring, Meriden Plate | 41.50 |
| Napkin Ring, Figural, Eagle On Top Of Ring, Silver Plate | 64.50 |
| Napkin Ring, Figural, Elephant, "Coolidge Boyhood Home, " Silver | 55.00 |
| Napkin Ring, Figural, Eskimo Holding Pole, Meriden Plate | 60.00 |
| Napkin Ring, Figural, Floral Stand On Lily Pad, Silver Plate, 3 1/2 In.High | 35.00 |
| Napkin Ring, Figural, Flying Cupid On Round Ring, Silver Plate | 32.00 |
| Napkin Ring, Figural, Frog On Lily Pad On Each Side Of Ring, Meriden | 70.00 |

Napkin Ring, Figural, Geese In Flight, Silver Plate, 2 In. Ring .................................................. 3.00
Napkin Ring, Figural, Goose Hanging On Skirt Of Little Girl Climbing Ring ................................ 78.00
Napkin Ring, Figural, Griffins Each Side Of Oval, Sterling ........................ 35.00 To 75.00
Napkin Ring, Figural, Handled Fan, Ring On Ball, Pairpoint Silver ................................ 35.00
Napkin Ring, Figural, Handled Suitcase, Signed Pairpoint ........................................ 46.00
Napkin Ring, Figural, Horseshoe Attached To Engraved Ring ................................ 30.00
Napkin Ring, Figural, Horseshoe On Front Of Ring, Silver, Floral ................................ 30.00
Napkin Ring, Figural, Kangaroo With Babies In Pouch, Sterling ................................ 58.00
Napkin Ring, Figural, Kangaroo, Emu, Boomerang ........................................ 50.00
Napkin Ring, Figural, Kate Greenaway Boy Kneeling With Bird, Nest, Meriden ................ 100.00
Napkin Ring, Figural, Kate Greenaway Boy Pushing Ring ................................ 75.00
Napkin Ring, Figural, Kate Greenaway Girl With Dog, Rogers ................................ 60.00
Napkin Ring, Figural, Kate Greenaway Victorian Lady, J.W.Tufts, No.18 ................ 110.00
Napkin Ring, Figural, Lily Bud On Leaf, Silver ........................................ 40.00
Napkin Ring, Figural, Lily Pad ........................................................ 30.00
Napkin Ring, Figural, Lily Pad, Twisted Stem & Bud, Silver ................................ 32.00
Napkin Ring, Figural, Lion With Ring On His Back, Rogers ................................ 71.50
Napkin Ring, Figural, Long Basset Hound Has Ring On Back, Silver Plate ................ 68.00
Napkin Ring, Figural, Mama Owl At Base, 2 Baby Owls On Branch, Footed ................ 85.00
Napkin Ring, Figural, Mouse On Top, James Tufts Quadruple Plate ................ 35.00
Napkin Ring, Figural, Old Fashioned Sleigh, Toronto Silver Plate Co. ................ 55.00
Napkin Ring, Figural, Ostrich & Kangaroo, Australian .................... 35.00 To 69.00
Napkin Ring, Figural, Ostrich, Kangaroo, & Boomerang, Australia, Sterling ................ 95.00
Napkin Ring, Figural, Prairie Falcon, Engraved Leaf Base, Silver Plate ................ 75.00
Napkin Ring, Figural, Ring On Leaf, Bird On Stem, Rogers Bros. Silver Plate ................ 45.00
Napkin Ring, Figural, Ring On Wishbone, "best Wishes, " Middletown Plate ................ 22.50
Napkin Ring, Figural, Robin, Chain Looped Around Neck, Meriden ................ 95.00
Napkin Ring, Figural, Scroll Holder, On Platform, Silver Plate ................ 45.00
Napkin Ring, Figural, Sled With Ring On Top ........................................ 55.00
Napkin Ring, Figural, Sphinx On Each Side Of Base, Silver Plate ................ 73.00
Napkin Ring, Figural, Sphinx With Ring On His Base, Meriden ................ 90.00
Napkin Ring, Figural, Squirrel Eating Nut On Top, Applied Acorns & Leaves ................ 52.00
Napkin Ring, Figural, Squirrel Eating Nut On Twiglike Base ................ 85.00
Napkin Ring, Figural, Squirrel On Tree Branch ........................................ 75.00
Napkin Ring, Figural, Squirrel Pulling Ring On Sledlike Base ................ 85.00
Napkin Ring, Figural, Squirrel With Chain Pulling Ring ................ 65.00
Napkin Ring, Figural, Stork With Ring On His Back ................ 98.00
Napkin Ring, Figural, Turtle ........................................................ 65.00
Napkin Ring, Figural, Two Boys Kicking, Balancing Ring, Meriden, No.333 ................ 80.00
Napkin Ring, Figural, Two Butterflies On Base, Meriden ................ 49.50
Napkin Ring, Figural, Two Cockatoos On Each Side Of Pedestal, Meriden, 271 ................ 65.00
Napkin Ring, Figural, Two Doves On Base, Meriden ................ 40.00
Napkin Ring, Figural, Two Eagles, Engraved, Monogrammed, Meriden ................ 39.00 To 50.00
Napkin Ring, Figural, Two Foxes, Crouching, Acme Silver Plate, No.703 ................ 75.00
Napkin Ring, Figural, Two Schoolboys With Hats, Middletown, No.87 ................ 95.00
Napkin Ring, Figural, Warriors On Each Side, Rectangular Base, Silver Plate ................ 65.00
Napkin Ring, Figural, Wheelbarrow, James Tufts, Boston ................ 57.00
Napkin Ring, Figural, Winged Egyptian Woman, Fanback Base, Silver ................ 58.00
Napkin Ring, Flowers & Scrolls, Silver Plate ........................................ 3.75
Napkin Ring, Ivory, Hand-Carved, Incised Design Of Men & Trees ................ 7.95
Napkin Ring, Ivory, Hand-Turned, Ridged Border, 3/4 In.Wide ................ 5.50
Napkin Ring, Nippon, Blue, Gold Beads & Roses ................ 22.00
Napkin Ring, Nippon, Scalloped Edges, Oval, Floral, Gold Beading ................ 35.00
Napkin Ring, Nippon, Scenic Bisque Blue Leaf ................ 45.00
Napkin Ring, Noritake, Birds & Roses On Pink ................ 20.00
Napkin Ring, Noritake, Hand-Painted ........................................ 12.00
Napkin Ring, Noritake, Opera Buff In Flowing Cape ................ 12.00
Napkin Ring, Noritake, Pink Ground, Birds & Roses ................ 20.00
Napkin Ring, Octagonal, Birds & Jewels, Amethyst, Initial E ................ 35.00
Napkin Ring, Open Salt On One Side, Pepper On Other ................ 25.00
Napkin Ring, Oriental Lacquer ........................................................ 3.50
Napkin Ring, Russian Silver, Bright Cut Designs ................ 48.00
Napkin Ring, Russian Silver, Gold Washed, Bright Cut, Pair ................ 98.00
Napkin Ring, Russian Silver, Triangular, Floral, Boysev, C.1850 ................ 130.00
Napkin Ring, Satsuma, Triangular, Gold, 2 Scenes ................ 7.00
Napkin Ring, Sterling Silver, Beaded Edges, "Charlotte" ................ 6.00

| | |
|---|---:|
| Napkin Ring, Sterling Silver, Blue French Enamel, Engraved Christiana | 12.50 |
| Napkin Ring, Sterling Silver, Bopeep & Her Sheep, Embossed | 30.00 |
| Napkin Ring, Sterling Silver, Engraved, English | 10.00 |
| Napkin Ring, Sterling Silver, Initials N.R.M. | 4.95 |
| Napkin Ring, Sterling Silver, Jack & Jill, Embossed | 30.00 |
| Napkin Ring, Sterling Silver, Plain 1/2 In.Band | 5.50 |
| Napkin Ring, Sterling Silver, Squarish Design, Engraved | 5.00 |
| Napkin Ring, Sterling Silver, Victorian, "G.S.B. 1876, " 1 1/2 In.Wide | 12.50 |
| Napkin Ring, Sterling Silver, 4 Cherubs' Heads In High Relief | 25.00 |
| Napkin Ring, Tiffany, Repousse, Parade Of Children | 95.00 |
| Napkin Ring, Vaseline Glass, English | 5.00 |
| Napkin Ring, Wedgwood, Floral, Portland Vase Mark | 6.50 |
| Napkin Ring, Wedgwood, Hathaway Rose | 2.50 |
| Napkin Ring, Wooden, Round | 6.00 |
| Napoli, Cup, Punch, Decorated With Palmer Cox Brownies, Signed | 950.00 |

*Nash glass was made in Corona, New York, by Arthur Nash and his sons
after 1919. He worked at the Webb factory in England and for the
Tiffany Glassworks in the United States.*

| | |
|---|---:|
| Nash, Bowl, Pontil, Signed, 2 X 4 In. | 135.00 |
| Nash, Candlestick, Green Chintz Top, Clear To Blue, 8 Prisms, Pair | 225.00 |
| Nash, Candlestick, Iridescent Gold, Gold & Blue Highlights, Pair | 325.00 |
| Nash, Champagne, Flute, Teardrop Stem, Libbey, 1909 | 35.00 |
| Nash, Champagne, Malmaison, Libbey, 1933 | 24.00 |
| Nash, Champagne, Monticello, Libbey, 7 In. | 65.00 |
| Nash, Champagne, Ruby Threaded, Twisted Stem, Libbey | 41.65 |
| Nash, Cocktail, Malmaison, Libbey, 1933 | 20.00 |
| Nash, Cocktail, Trylon, Pale Citron To Rose, Signed, 6 In.High | 75.00 |
| Nash, Cup, Punch, Flute, Footed, Libbey, 1909 | 32.00 |
| Nash, Glass, Pilsner, Malmaison, Libbey, 1933 | 28.00 |
| Nash, Goblet, Flute, Teardrop Stem, Libbey, 1909 | 35.00 |
| Nash, Perfume, Green & Blue Chintz On Aquamarine, Signed, 5 1/4 In. | 250.00 |
| Nash, Plate, Chintz Pattern, Mint Green & Blue, 8 1/2 In.Diameter, Unsigned | 85.00 |
| Nash, Plate, Chintz, Orange Iridescent, 8 1/2 In. | 110.00 |
| Nash, Plate, Malmaison, Libbey, 1933, 7 1/2 In. | 10.00 |
| Nash, Plate, Red, Ribbed, Turned Up & Scalloped Rim, 5 1/2 In. | 175.00 |
| Nash, Tumbler, Champagne, Flute, Libbey, 1909 | 25.00 |
| Nash, Tumbler, Footed, Chintz Pattern, 6 1/2 In.High, Bright Blue & Green | 110.00 |
| Nash, Vase, Engraved Looped Circles & Fern, Libbey, 1040, 7 1/2 In.High | 40.00 |
| Nash, Vase, Gold Iridescent, 4 1/2 In.High, Signed | 160.00 |
| Nash, Vase, Iridescent, Amber, Tapering Body, 9 1/2 In.High | 225.00 |

**Needlework, see Textile, Picture, Textile, Sampler**

*Netsuke are small ivory, wood, metal, or porcelain pieces used as the button on
the end of a cord holding a Japanese money pouch. The earliest date from
the sixteenth century.*

| | |
|---|---:|
| Netsuke, Actor, Seated With Soles Of Feet Pressed Together, Hogetsu | 200.00 |
| Netsuke, Animals & People, Ivory, Polychrome Finish, Signed | 18.50 |
| Netsuke, Boar, Wood, Sleeping On Bed Of Leaves, Jugyoku | 1400.00 |
| Netsuke, Chick In Egg, Elephant Ivory | 20.00 |
| Netsuke, Comical Badger, 19th Century    *Illus* | 1000.00 |
| Netsuke, Dragon, Ivory, Attached To Embossed Leather Purse | 55.00 |
| Netsuke, Dwarf, Pottery, Woman With Black Hair | 125.00 |
| Netsuke, Frog On Leaf, Ivory | 55.00 |
| Netsuke, Gourd, Boxwood, Clinging Leaf, 19th Century, Large | 200.00 |
| Netsuke, Kabuki Dancer, Revolving Face | 55.00 |
| Netsuke, Lotus Pod, Partially Lacquered, Gilt Frog On Outside, 1800s | 125.00 |
| Netsuke, Monkey, Kaigyokusai    *Illus* | 3500.00 |
| Netsuke, Monkeys, Kaigyokusai    *Illus* | 1200.00 |
| Netsuke, Mortar, Ivory Pestle, 19th Century | 1000.00 |
| Netsuke, No Mask, Boxwood, Laughing Man With Open Mouth, Kakihan | 375.00 |
| Netsuke, Old Man, With Bag, Carved Ivory | 20.00 |
| Netsuke, Peony, Homin School    *Illus* | 850.00 |
| Netsuke, Quail, Ivory, Head Turned Backward, Anraku | 300.00 |
| Netsuke, Rabbit, Fat Small Seated Rabbit, Horn Eyes, C.1900 | 150.00 |
| Netsuke, Rat, Ebony, Seated Rat Gnawing Nut, Ivory Teeth, Tomokazu | 1300.00 |
| Netsuke, Sashi Fish, Wood, Unsigned | 125.00 |
| Netsuke, Tiger, Seated With Head Down, Wood, Tomokazu School | 1500.00 |

Netsuke, Comical Badger,
19th Century
*(See Page 345)*

Netsuke, Monkeys, Kaigyokusai
*(See Page 345)*

Netsuke, Monkey, Kaigyokusai
*(See Page 345)*

Netsuke, Peony, Homin School
*(See Page 345)*

| | |
|---|---|
| **Netsuke, Tiger,** Seated, Ivory Eyes, Ichiyu | 150.00 |
| **Netsuke, Toad,** Bumpy Skit, Squatting On Sandal, Masanao | 200.00 |
| **New Hampshire, Bowl,** Green, 3 In. | 45.00 |
| **New Hampshire, Lamp,** Oil, Green, Globe | 250.00 |
| **Newcastle, Pitcher,** Red & Yellow Floral On Blue & White, Maling Ware | 35.00 |
| **Newcastle, Teapot,** Red & Yellow Floral On Blue & White, Maling Ware | 52.50 |

Ⓝ *Newcomb Pottery was founded by Ellsworth and William Woodward at Sophie Newcomb College, New Orleans, Louisiana, in 1896. The work continued through the 1940s. Pieces of this art pottery are marked with the letter N inside the letter C.*

| | |
|---|---|
| **Newcomb, Vase,** Blue Gray, Floral At Top, Artists C.L. & J.M., 3 In. | 95.00 |
| **Newcomb, Vase,** Blue Gray, Morning Glories, Harriet Baily, 8 1/4 In. | 150.00 |
| **Newcomb, Vase,** Clematis On Shoulder, Nicholson & Meyer, C.1920, 8 1/2 In. | 150.00 |
| **Newcomb, Vase,** Dark Blue, White Flower Border, Blue Drippings, 3 1/2 In.High | 95.00 |
| **Newcomb, Vase,** Fuchsias On Blue Matte, Lavender At Base, Signed, 1896 | 135.00 |
| **Newcomb, Vase,** Pink Floral & Green Leaves On Blue, 9 1/2 X 7 In. | 105.00 |
| **Newcomb, Vase,** Scenic, Cypress Trees In Blue & Green, Artist-Signed, 4 In. | 110.00 |

*Newhall Porcelain Manufactory was started at Newhall, Shelton, Staffordshire, England, in 1782. Simple decorated wares were made. Between 1810 and 1825, the factory made a glassy bone porcelain marked with the factory name.*

| | |
|---|---|
| **Newhall, Can,** Coffee, Blue Band, Coral & Yellow Floral, C.1820, 2 1/2 In.High | 39.00 |
| **Newhall, Cup & Saucer,** Blue Transfer Chinoiserie Polychrome, C.1810 | 32.00 |
| **Newhall, Cup & Saucer,** Hard Paste, C.1750 | 65.00 |
| **Newhall, Plate,** Transfer Fruit Filled Basket, C.1825, 8 1/8 In., Pair | 30.00 |
| **Newhall, Teabowl & Saucer,** Hand-Painted Enamel Floral & Ribbon, C.1790 | 62.50 |

Newhall, Teabowl, Oriental Decoration, C.1820 ........................................................... 20.00

Niloak Pottery (Kaolin spelled backwards) was made at the Hyten
Brothers Pottery in Bremen, Arkansas, between 1909 and 1946. Although
the factory did make cast and molded wares, collectors are most interested in
the marbleized art pottery line.

Niloak, Bowl, Signed, 4 3/4 In.Diameter, 2 1/2 In.High ....................................... 12.00
Niloak, Dish, Swan, Blue, 5 In.High ...................................................................... 7.50
Niloak, Jar, Strawberry .......................................................................................... 4.00
Niloak, Planter, Green ............................................................................................ 2.50
Niloak, Planter, Polar Bear .................................................................................... 16.00
Niloak, Planter, Squirrel ........................................................................................ 12.00
Niloak, Planter, Swan, Blue ................................................................................... 12.00
Niloak, Shoe, Dutch ............................................................................................... 9.00
Niloak, Vase, Blue, 3 1/2 In. ................................................................................. 8.00
Niloak, Vase, Bulbous, Marbleized, Tapers To 3 In.Opening, 5 3/4 In.High ........... 15.00
Niloak, Vase, Inside Glaze, 5 1/2 In.High .............................................................. 65.00
Niloak, Vase, Marbleized Blue, Brown, & Cream, 10 1/2 In.High ........................... 15.00
Niloak, Vase, Pitcher Shape, Pink Gray, Posy, 3 In. ............................................. 9.00
Niloak, Vase, Swirled Colors, 3 1/4 In. .................................................................. 4.50
Niloak, Vase, 4 1/2 In.High .................................................................................... 15.00

Nippon-marked porcelain was made in Japan after 1891.

Nippon, Ashtray & Matchbox Holder, Red On Yellow, Applied Flowers .................. 45.00
Nippon, Ashtray, Painted Lion's Head Inside, Beaded, Handled ............................. 45.00
Nippon, Ashtray, Scenic, EOH ............................................................................... 30.00
Nippon, Ashtray, Stylized Birds, Beige & Brown Beaded Bands, 4 5/8 In.Long ...... 25.00
Nippon, Ashtray, Triangular, Scenic, Beaded Enamel, Art Nouveau Decoration ...... 32.00
Nippon, Basket, Band Of Yellow & Green Leaves On White, Gold Handle ............... 30.00
Nippon, Basket, Center Picture, Capitol, Washington, D.C., Roses, Gold Beading .... 35.00
Nippon, Berry Set, Blue Flowers, Gold Trim, 7 Piece ............................................ 35.00
Nippon, Berry Set, Geishas In Flower Garden, Cobalt & Gold, 6 Piece .................. 29.00
Nippon, Berry Set, Scenic, Jeweled, Gold Trim, 6 Piece ........................................ 79.00
Nippon, Berry Set, 6 Medallions Of Landscapes & Ladies, 7 Piece ....................... 85.00
Nippon, Bonbon, Gold Decoration, 6 Sided, 3 Tall Gold Legs ................................ 17.00
Nippon, Bottle, Pink Roses, Signed Oriental China, Nippon & Symbol .................... 40.00
Nippon, Bowl & Attached Underplate, Dip, Covered, Blue Forget-Me-Nots, Gold ..... 24.00
Nippon, Bowl & Ladle, Cracker & Jelly, Floral, Gold & Black Borders ................... 16.00
Nippon, Bowl & Underplate, Jam, Rose Swage, Gold Trim, 3 1/4 In.High .............. 24.00
Nippon, Bowl, Berry, Black & Gold With Fruit, Hand-Painted .................................. 5.00
Nippon, Bowl, Browns & Gold, Inside Painted, 3 Footed, Green Wreath, 5 In. ......... 5.00
Nippon, Bowl, Center Transfer Of Reclining Women, Iridescent Border, 10 In. ........ 40.00
Nippon, Bowl, Cereal, Child's Head, 5 3/4 In.Diameter ......................................... 55.00
Nippon, Bowl, Crimped, Green Leaves & Raised Almonds, 6 In. ............................. 38.00
Nippon, Bowl, Double Handled, Pink & Yellow Roses On Brown, 4 1/2 In. .............. 27.50
Nippon, Bowl, Footed, Hand-Painted Scene, 5 In. .................................................. 8.00
Nippon, Bowl, Footed, 2 Handled, Jeweled, Rowboat Scene, 6 In. ......................... 35.00
Nippon, Bowl, Gold Flowers Over Blue Band, 2 Handled, 6 In. Diameter .............. 20.00
Nippon, Bowl, Gold Rim, Raised Scrolls, Lattice, Black Stars, Roses, 10 In. ......... 25.00
Nippon, Bowl, Indian In Canoe Shooting Elk, 7 In.Diameter ................................... 115.00
Nippon, Bowl, Large Acorns, Burrs, Trees, Matte Finish, 8 1/2 In.Diameter ........... 34.00
Nippon, Bowl, Pierced Handles, Leaves & Nuts On Dark Satin, 9 In. ..................... 65.00
Nippon, Bowl, Pink Roses & Gold Design On White, 4 1/4 In. ............................... 4.75
Nippon, Bowl, Poppies On Shaded, Gold Edge, M In Wreath Mark, 8 In.Long ........ 14.50
Nippon, Bowl, Raised Gold Design On White, 10 In. .............................................. 25.00
Nippon, Bowl, Scenic, Cobalt & Gold Top Border, Footed, 6 In. ............................ 32.00
Nippon, Bowl, Scenic, Footed, 5 In. ...................................................................... 9.00
Nippon, Bowl, Serving, Pedestal, 2 Tiered, Raised Gold, 8 3/4 In. Lower Plate ...... 30.00
Nippon, Bowl, Serving, Pickard Style Floral, Gold Handle, Black Outlines ............. 25.00
Nippon, Box, Button, Blossoms & Leaves, Pedestal Feet ....................................... 12.00
Nippon, Box, Collar Button, Floral, Beading, Pedestal, Green Wreath Mark ........... 15.00
Nippon, Box, Covered, Floral Medallion, Gold Trim & Beading, Green M Mark ....... 55.00
Nippon, Box, Covered, Light Blue, Navy Trim, Floral Medallion ............................. 38.00
Nippon, Box, Covered, National Capitol, Floral Border .......................................... 11.00
Nippon, Box, Covered, Round, Gold Branches & Green Bands, 3 Footed, 4 1/4 In. ... 18.00
Nippon, Box, Covered, Serpentine, Gold, Pink Roses, Gilt Feet, 2 In.High .............. 25.00

| | |
|---|---:|
| Nippon, Box, Heart Shape, White & Green Flowers | 14.00 |
| Nippon, Box, Powder & Pin, Covered, Round, Man & Camel, Signed, Pair | 15.00 |
| Nippon, Box, Powder, Gold Beading, Floral, Green M Mark, 3 3/4 In. Diameter | 10.00 |
| Nippon, Box, Powder, Pink & Gold Floral, 3 Legs, Green Wreath Mark | 17.00 |
| Nippon, Box, Powder, Purple Flowers, Green Bands, Gold | 10.00 |
| Nippon, Box, Powder, Scenic Lid, Cobalt & Gold Overlay, 3 Cobalt Feet, Round | 55.00 |
| Nippon, Box, Pumpkin, Hand-Painted Floral | 18.00 |
| Nippon, Box, Sardine, Fish Shape Finial | 49.00 |
| Nippon, Box, Trinket, Covered, Pink & Blue Florets, Gold Edges, 2 In.Square | 6.00 |
| Nippon, Box, Trinket, Orange Azalea & Green Leaves, Gold Edges, Round | 7.00 |
| Nippon, Butter, Covered, Floral & Geometrics, Gold Beading & Trim | 22.00 |
| Nippon, Butter, Covered, Lima 162, Marked 5 | 25.00 |
| Nippon, Butter, Rural Scene, Bisque | 48.00 |
| Nippon, Cake Set, Scenic, Jeweled, 7 Piece | 95.00 To 125.00 |
| Nippon, Cake Set, Yellow Border, Raised Gilt Scrolls, Open Handles, 6 Piece | 13.75 |
| Nippon, Candleholder, Chamber, Floral & Gold, Handled | 29.00 |
| Nippon, Candleholder, Opalescent, Green, & Gold, 7 In.High, Pair | 25.00 |
| Nippon, Candlestick, Desert Scene, Flower Trim, Beading, Bisque, 7 1/2 In. | 42.00 |
| Nippon, Candlestick, Gold Outlined Flowers & Buds On Gray, 8 1/4 In.High | 45.00 |
| Nippon, Candlestick, Heavy Gold Flowers, Beading, 5 1/4 In.High | 22.00 |
| Nippon, Celery Set, Bluebirds, Long Handled Tray, 7 Piece | 45.00 |
| Nippon, Celery Set, Gold Leaves & Outlined Floral On White, 7 Piece | 18.50 |
| Nippon, Celery Set, Hand-Painted Floral, Marked, 6 Piece | 13.00 |
| Nippon, Celery Set, Purple Violets, Leaves, Banded, Cream & Gold, 7 Piece | 35.00 |
| Nippon, Celery Set, Scenic, Satin Finish, 7 Piece | 40.00 |
| Nippon, Celery Set, White & Yellow Roses, Blues, 7 Piece | 55.00 |
| Nippon, Celery, Canoe Shape, Open Handled, 6 Gold Outlined Swans On Blue | 20.00 |
| Nippon, Celery, Floral & Medallions, Yellow Figures, Gold, Blue Mark | 24.00 |
| Nippon, Celery, Incised Handles, Wreaths Of Roses & Green Leaves, Gold Trim | 12.00 |
| Nippon, Celery, Pink & Yellow Roses, Gold Trim | 16.00 |
| Nippon, Celery, Raised Yellow Over Magenta, Pink Floral | 15.00 |
| Nippon, Celery, Rose Garlands, Gold Beading, Blue Mark | 15.00 |
| Nippon, Celery, Swags Of Pink Roses, Green Leaves, Gold, 2 Handles, 12 In. | 12.00 |
| Nippon, Chocolate Pot, Allover Floral Decoration, Gold Trim | 47.50 |
| Nippon, Chocolate Pot, Gold Handle, Finial, & Curlicues, Pink & Blue Floral | 22.50 |
| Nippon, Chocolate Pot, Peaches On Green, Gold Handle & Trim, Blue Mark | 65.00 |
| Nippon, Chocolate Pot, Pink Flowers, Gold Beading, Marked M, 9 In.High | 30.00 |
| Nippon, Chocolate Pot, Prunus Tree, Gold Bands & Handle, Green Wreath Mark | 22.00 |
| Nippon, Chocolate Set, Banded Flowers, Green Mark, 11 Piece | 62.50 |
| Nippon, Chocolate Set, Floral Decoration, Magenta Mark, 6 Piece | 40.00 |
| Nippon, Chocolate Set, Flowers, Gold Trim, 5 Piece | 20.00 |
| Nippon, Chocolate Set, Gold Flowers & Leaves, Signed, 12 Piece | 62.00 |
| Nippon, Chocolate Set, Gold Storks, Signed, 11 Piece | 58.00 |
| Nippon, Chocolate Set, Green Wreath, 7 Piece | 100.00 |
| Nippon, Chocolate Set, Lavender Violets, Gold Enamel & Handles, 9 Piece | 95.00 |
| Nippon, Chocolate Set, Multicolor Floral, Gold Trim, 7 Piece | 125.00 |
| Nippon, Chocolate Set, Oriental Figures, Rust Red Trim, 9 Piece | 75.00 |
| Nippon, Chocolate Set, Pink Roses, Cobalt & Gold, Rising Sun Mark, 12 Piece | 75.00 |
| Nippon, Chocolate Set, Wild Rose Decoration, 11 Piece | 50.00 |
| Nippon, Coaster Set, Floral, Yellow Gold Trim, Rising Sun Mark, 6 Piece | 15.00 |
| Nippon, Coaster, Flowers, Gold Band, 3 1/2 In.Diameter | 9.00 |
| Nippon, Coffee Set, Demitasse, Giesha Scene, Gold On Red, 3 Piece | 58.00 |
| Nippon, Coffee Set, Demitasse, Pink & White Floral, Gold Beading, 12 Piece | 78.00 |
| Nippon, Cologne, Pink Flowers On White & Yellow Ground, Gold Bands | 25.00 |
| Nippon, Cologne, Scenic, Pastel Coloring, Green M Mark | 45.00 |
| Nippon, Condiment Set, Figural, See No Evil, Monkeys, 3 Piece On Tray | 72.00 |
| Nippon, Condiment Set, On Round Handled Tray, Raised Gold, 3 Piece | 22.00 |
| Nippon, Condiment Set, White Decoration, Gold Encrusted, 6 Piece | 35.00 |
| Nippon, Creamer & Underplate, Green Wreath Mark | 18.00 |
| Nippon, Creamer, Gold Band At Bottom, Gold Embossed Top, Pink Roses | 7.50 |
| Nippon, Creamer, Pink Roses | 6.00 |
| Nippon, Creamer, Red Roses, Gold Trim, Marked No.6 | 15.00 |
| Nippon, Creamer, Roses, Enamel & Beading | 15.00 |
| Nippon, Cup & Saucer, American Beauty & Pink Roses, Gold, Rose Inside | 7.50 |
| Nippon, Cup & Saucer, Azalea | 6.50 |
| Nippon, Cup & Saucer, Blue & Pink Floral On White, Gold Trim | 30.00 |

Nippon, Cup & Saucer, Bluebirds On Blossom Branch, Marked ............................ 10.00
Nippon, Cup & Saucer, Chocolate, Gold Trim, Signed 23 ................................ 8.50
Nippon, Cup & Saucer, Demitasse, Raised Gold Dragons, Black Trim ..................... 4.75
Nippon, Cup & Saucer, Demitasse, Roses ............................................... 4.25
Nippon, Cup & Saucer, Floral & Gold, Gold Top & Handle ............................... 5.50
Nippon, Cup & Saucer, Footed Cup, Roses, Beaded Enamel, Gold ......................... 20.00
Nippon, Cup & Underplate, Bouillon, Gold Flowers, Tinted Ground, Beading ............. 17.00
Nippon, Cup, Demitasse, Hand-Painted Pink Roses, Gold, Maple Leaf Mark ............... 5.50
Nippon, Cup, Nut, Acorns With Raised Caps, Enamel Beading, 3 Footed .................. 5.00
Nippon, Dish, Candy, Blown-Out, Acorns & Leaves ..................................... 20.00
Nippon, Dish, Candy, Bowl Type, Floral, 6 Corners, 6 1/2 In.Diameter ................. 10.00
Nippon, Dish, Candy, Open Handles, Autumn Scene, M In Green Wreath ................... 9.00
Nippon, Dish, Candy, Square, Scalloped, Red & Yellow Roses, Green Base ............... 12.00
Nippon, Dish, Cheese & Cracker, Tiered, Gold Outlined Floral On Green ................ 28.00
Nippon, Dish, Cheese & Cracker, White Hydrangeas On Green, 9 1/2 In. ................. 40.00
Nippon, Dish, Cheese, Covered, Slanted, Rising Sun Mark .............................. 30.00
Nippon, Dish, Cheese, Rising Sun, Gold Handles, Pink Flowers, Two Piece .............. 35.00
Nippon, Dish, Cheese, White, Gold Trim .............................................. 22.50
Nippon, Dish, Divided, Handled, Blue Forget-Me-Nots, Green Mark, 9 1/4 In. ........... 22.00
Nippon, Dish, Divided, 4 Sections, Violets, Artist G.Nadiska ........................ 37.00
Nippon, Dish, Nut, Embossed Walnuts In Bottom, Browns, Greens, Branches .............. 25.00
Nippon, Dish, Nut, Heart Shape, Handled, Hand-Painted ............................... 8.50
Nippon, Dish, Nut, Octagonal, Scenic, Sailboats, Gold Handles, 7 In.Diameter ........ 12.00
Nippon, Dish, Pancake, Covered, Blue & White, Scenic, Royal Sometuke ................. 24.00
Nippon, Dish, Pancake, Covered, Jeweled ............................................. 88.00
Nippon, Dish, Pickle, Pale Blue Flowers, Gold Beading ............................... 10.00
Nippon, Dresser Set, Allover Painted Background, 2 Piece ............................. 20.00
Nippon, Dresser Set, Oval Tray, Water, Beach, Boat, & Birds, Gold Trim, 5 Piece ...... 85.00
Nippon, Dresser Set, Pink Roses, Much Gold, 5 Piece ................................. 60.00
Nippon, Fernery, Blown Out, Grapes & Leaves Outlined In Gold, Gold Trim .............. 87.00
Nippon, Fernery, Footed, Scenic, Jeweled, Satin Finish, 7 1/4 In.High ............... 58.00
Nippon, Fernery, Footed, Woods & Water Scene, Enameled, Jeweled, 2 Handles ........... 69.00
Nippon, Gravy Boat & Underplate, Floral & Gold ...................................... 22.00
Nippon, Gravy Boat & Underplate, Oval, Lotus Design On White, M Mark ................. 35.00
Nippon, Hair Receiver & Powder Jar, Gold, Gilded Roses, 3 Legs ...................... 20.00
Nippon, Hair Receiver, Cartouche, Washington Souvenir, Footed, Roses, Gold .......... 25.00
Nippon, Hair Receiver, Florals, Red & Gold Borders .................................. 12.00
Nippon, Hair Receiver, Hand-Painted Floral & Gold ................................... 15.00
Nippon, Hair Receiver, Heavy Gold Decoration, Plain ................................. 9.50
Nippon, Hair Receiver, Pink Roses, Apple Green & Gold, 3 Scroll Feet, 3 In. ......... 15.00
Nippon, Hair Receiver, Roses & Gold On Lid, Lima Mark, No.20, 3 1/2 In.High .......... 14.00
Nippon, Hair Receiver, Violets ...................................................... 23.00
Nippon, Hatpin Holder & Attached Tray, Floral, Gold Beading ......................... 35.00
Nippon, Hatpin Holder, Country Scene On Satin Finish ................................ 18.00
Nippon, Hatpin Holder, Cylinder Shape, Floral Decoration ............................ 11.00
Nippon, Hatpin Holder, Floral Decoration, Blue Maple Leaf Mark, 4 3/4 In. ........... 18.00
Nippon, Hatpin Holder, Green & Gold Decoration ...................................... 22.00
Nippon, Hatpin Holder, Scalloped Top, Apricot Floral Decoration, Gold Trim .......... 38.00
Nippon, Hatpin Holder, Washington D.C., Gold Outlined Floral On White ............... 12.00
Nippon, Holder, Stickpin, Scalloped Top & Bottom, Magenta Roses, Gold Top ........... 26.50
Nippon, Hostess Set, Applied Flowers, Lavender, Papier-Mache Box, 6 Piece ........... 55.00
Nippon, Humidor, Covered, Palm Trees On Orange, Jeweled, 3 Footed ................... 85.00
Nippon, Humidor, Covered, River Scenes In Oval Reserves, 4 Sided .................... 49.00
Nippon, Humidor, Egyptian Figures, Jeweled, Miniature, Signed ....................... 80.00
Nippon, Humidor, Gold Beads & Pinecones, 3 Handled .................................. 95.00
Nippon, Humidor, Golf Bag & Clubs, Enamel Beading, Green Wreath ..................... 85.00
Nippon, Humidor, Match Stick & Pipe On Cover, Cards On Body, Jeweled ................ 110.00
Nippon, Humidor, Scenes On 3 Sides On Marbleized Beige, Green Mark .................. 75.00
Nippon, Incense Burner, Heavily Embossed Design, 3 1/2 In.High ...................... 35.00
Nippon, Inkwell, Covered, Apple Green, Insert ....................................... 39.00
Nippon, Jam Set, Covered, Scenic, Green M Wreath Mark, 2 Piece ...................... 25.00
Nippon, Jar & Attached Underplate, Mustard, Hand-Painted, Signed .................... 15.00
Nippon, Jar & Underplate, Jam, Covered, Gold Handles & Beading On White ............. 30.00
Nippon, Jar & Underplate, Jam, Covered, Gold Handles, Pink Apple Blossoms ........... 18.00
Nippon, Jar & Underplate, Jam, Covered, Pink Roses & Blue Bands On White ............ 22.50
Nippon, Jar & Underplate, Jam, Hand-Painted Flowers, Gold ........................... 15.00

Nippon, Jar, Cookie, Green Enamel Beads On Lid & Base, Melon Ribbed, 3 Feet ......................... 50.00
Nippon, Jar, Cracker, Footed, Paneled, Rose Garlands, Gold Trim, Bulbous ...................... 75.00
Nippon, Jar, Cracker, Gold Finial, Cobalt & Gold On White & Pink .................... 27.00
Nippon, Jar, Cracker, Marsh Scene, 2 Swans, Green M Mark ............................ 85.00
Nippon, Jar, Cracker, Red Poppies & Butterfly, Gold Handles & Trim ....................... 32.00
Nippon, Jar, Cricket, Landscape & Water Scene, 5 3/4 In.High ...................... 45.00
Nippon, Jar, Ginger, Pine Needles & Gold Pinecones On Green, Blue Mark ............... 48.00
Nippon, Jar, Powder, Covered, White, Green, & Gold ........................ 12.00
Nippon, Jar, Powder, Marked 5, 184 ...................................... 35.00
Nippon, Jar, Powder, Orange & Green Flowers On White ........................ 12.00
Nippon, Jar, Powder, Poppies, Gold Beading, Leaf Mark .................... 25.00
Nippon, Jar, Rose Petal, Covered, Pink Roses, Gilt & Cream, 4 In., Pair .................. 50.00
Nippon, Jar, Tobacco, Pink Flowers, Gold Trim ............................ 55.00
Nippon, Ladle, Mayonnaise, Gold ...................................... 4.00
Nippon, Lemonade Set, Large Red Poppies, Foliage, 5 Piece ................... 68.00
Nippon, Lemonade Set, Lavender, Gray, Green, & White Flowers, 6 Piece .............. 110.00
Nippon, Lemonade Set, Pink Roses, Bisque Finish, 6 Piece ..................... 50.00
Nippon, Match Holder & Attached Heart Shape Underplate, Red Roses, Gold ............... 33.00
Nippon, Match Holder, Hanging, Bisque Finish, Water Scene, Green Wreath ............... 28.00
Nippon, Matchbox Holder & Attached Tray, Multicolored Floral Garland ............... 32.00
Nippon, Mayonnaise Set, Hand-Painted, Rising Sun Mark, 3 Piece ................ 10.50
Nippon, Mayonnaise Set, Large Pink Flowers, Gold Trim, 3 Piece ................. 22.00
Nippon, Mayonnaise Set, Roses, Rising Sun Mark, 3 Piece .................... 8.50
Nippon, Mocha Set, Rising Sun Mark, 9 Piece ..................... 75.00
Nippon, Muffineer, Floral & Gold, Fancy Handle, Signed ................. 32.00
Nippon, Muffineer, Hexagonal Handle, Marked 3 ..................... 22.00
Nippon, Muffineer, Raspberries, Floral Panels, Gold Beading, Handle ................ 35.00
Nippon, Mug, Lemonade, Blue & White, Flying Turkey, Royal Sometsuke ............... 6.00
Nippon, Mustard Set, Pink Flowers, White Decoration, Gold, Handled, 2 Piece ............ 10.00
Nippon, Mustard Set, Pink Roses, White Swirls, Gold, Handled, 2 Piece ............. 12.00
Nippon, Napkin Ring, Scenic, Hand-Painted ...................... 12.00
Nippon, Nappy, Pink Roses, Gold Trim, Square, Rising Sun Mark ................ 10.00
Nippon, Nappy, Pink Roses, Green Leaves, Gold, Cobalt Ruffled Edge, 6 1/2 In. ............ 20.00
Nippon, Nappy, Roses, Gold, Square, Open Handle, Marked .................... 9.00
Nippon, Nut Set, Ball Feet, Gold Rims, Raised Gold, Blue Mark, 7 Piece ................ 28.00
Nippon, Nut Set, Footed, Signed, 5 Piece ..................... 18.50
Nippon, Nut Set, Lavender Floral Spray, Gold Encrusted, 5 Piece ............... 32.00
Nippon, Nut Set, Peanut Shape, Blown-Out, Tan, Brown, Peach, & Orange, 6 Piece ......... 75.00
Nippon, Nut Set, Pink Roses & Blue Floral, Footed, Scalloped, Gold, 6 Piece ........... 65.00
Nippon, Nut Set, Yellow Flowers, Gold, Footed Dishes, 4 Piece ............... 27.00
Nippon, Pitcher & Underplate, Condensed Milk, Covered, Gold Handled, Floral ........... 58.00
Nippon, Pitcher, Milk, Covered, Arabian Scene, Beaded & Jeweled, 6 In.High ........... 115.00
Nippon, Pitcher, Milk, Covered, Flowers, Raised Gold Trim, 4 3/4 In.High ........... 35.00
Nippon, Pitcher, Milk, Wide Gold Band, Pink & Red Roses, 5 1/8 In. High ........... 25.00
Nippon, Pitcher, Tapestry, Marked Patent ...................... 85.00
Nippon, Planter, Pedestal Foot, Royal Blue Bands, Lake Scene, 2 Holes ............. 48.00
Nippon, Planter, Pink Flowers, Gold Borders, Four Pedestaled Feet .............. 35.00
Nippon, Planter, Pink Poppies, Gold Stamen, Heavy Gold Trim, 4 5/8 In.High ........... 24.00
Nippon, Planter, Round, Half Pillars On Sides, Greek Key Band, 5 1/2 In. ............ 29.00
Nippon, Planter, Square, Gold & White Pillars, Scenic, Gold, Green Wreath ............ 45.00
Nippon, Plaque, Applied Yellow & Red Flowers On Brown & Pink, 9 1/2 In. ............ 48.00
Nippon, Plaque, Art Deco, Wooded Landscape, Burnt Oranges, 10 1/4 In. ............. 55.00
Nippon, Plaque, Cow Scenic, Green M Wreath Mark, 10 1/4 In. ............... 70.00
Nippon, Plaque, Egyptian Scenic, Arab, Mosque, Green M Wreath Mark, 7 1/2 In. ......... 22.00
Nippon, Plaque, Fall Scenic, Green M Wreath Mark, 9 In. ................ 55.00
Nippon, Plaque, Fishing Boat On Shore, Flying Birds On Bisque, Green M ............. 40.00
Nippon, Plaque, Indian In Full Headdress, 10 In.Diameter ................ 125.00
Nippon, Plaque, Indian With Full Headdress, 8 In. ................ 65.00
Nippon, Plaque, Limoges Type Painting, Gold Trim, 10 In. .................. 65.00
Nippon, Plaque, Parrot On Cherry Blossom Bough, 10 In.Diameter .............. 85.00
Nippon, Plate, Bread, Pierced Handles, Roses, Gold Scalloped Edge, Cobalt ........... 38.50
Nippon, Plate, Cake, Pink Roses, Light Blue Border, 9 1/2 In. ............... 13.00
Nippon, Plate, Cake, Raised Gold Beading On White Floral, 6 In. .............. 6.00
Nippon, Plate, Cake, White & Gold Daisies Outlined In Gold, Incised Handles ........... 17.50
Nippon, Plate, Child's, Blown-Out Eyes, Nose, Lips, Hands, & Bowtie, Signed .......... 35.00
Nippon, Plate, Floral & Leaves On White To Yellow Aqua, Gold, 11 In. ............ 24.00

Nippon, Plate, Flying Geese On Green, Gold, Red & Blue Jewels, 10 In. ........................ 18.00
Nippon, Plate, Flying White Geese, Jeweled Edge, Gold Trim, Green, 10 In. ................. 15.00
Nippon, Plate, Gold Bands, Green Medallions, Pastel Floral, 10 1/4 In. ...................... 19.00
Nippon, Plate, Gold Borders, Incised Handles, Pink Roses, 6 In. .............................. 3.50
Nippon, Plate, Luncheon, Nagoya ........................................................................ 2.00
Nippon, Plate, Old Mill & Wheel, Jeweled, Satin Finish, 8 1/2 In. ........................... 18.50
Nippon, Plate, Pink Roses, Butterfly, Turned-Up Rim, Gold Border, 6 In. .................. 8.00
Nippon, Plate, Portrait, Queen Louise, Jeweled, Gold Beading, 8 3/4 In. .................. 110.00
Nippon, Plate, Roses & Interweaving Vine, Rising Sun Mark, 6 1/2 In. ..................... 1.75
Nippon, Plate, Scenic, Oval, Gold Figures Border, 9 1/2 In. .................................. 19.00
Nippon, Plate, Serving, Raised Gold, Flowers, Beading, 2 Handles, Red M Mark .......... 10.00
Nippon, Plate, Violets, 6 In. .............................................................................. 3.50
Nippon, Plate, Wall Hanging, Windmill Scene, Blues & Purples, Beading, 9 In. ........... 55.00
Nippon, Platter, Phoenix Bird, Blue & White, Blue Leaf Mark, 11 3/4 X 17 In. ........... 35.00
Nippon, Pot, Cobalt Blue, Gold Encrusted, 10 1/2 In. .......................................... 56.00
Nippon, Pot, Mustard, Handled, Art Nouveau Shape, Gold Beading & Floral ............. 11.00
Nippon, Powder Set, Pink Flowers With Stems, Leaves, 3 Piece ............................ 16.00
Nippon, Punch Set, Gold Grapes & Leaves, Signed, 7 Piece ................................. 70.00
Nippon, Ramekin Set, Flowers, Blue & Gold Trim, 8 Piece .................................... 25.00
Nippon, Ramekin, Hand-Painted, Pink & Yellow Flowers, Gold Branches ................. 20.00
Nippon, Relish, Double Handles, Hand-Painted Roses, M Mark, 6 3/8 In. ................. 37.50
Nippon, Relish, Peacock & Butterfly Design, Gold Trim, 8 1/2 X 5 In. ..................... 32.50
Nippon, Relish, Pink & Green Flowers On White, Gold Border, Marked ................... 30.00
Nippon, Salt & Pepper, Floral & Beading On Light Green ..................................... 6.50
Nippon, Salt & Pepper, Ivory & White, Floral .................................................... 4.00
Nippon, Salt & Pepper, Pink & Blue Floral, 6 Sided, 2 1/2 In. ............................... 8.00
Nippon, Salt & Pepper, Roses On Blue Band, 3 In.High ....................................... 9.00
Nippon, Salt Dip, Gold Decoration, 3 In. Diameter .............................................. 10.00
Nippon, Salt Set, Pierced Handles, Floral, Gold Trim, 5 Piece ............................... 36.00
Nippon, Salt Set, Rose Medallions, Garlands, Set Of 7 ........................................ 22.00
Nippon, Salt, Oval, Hand-Painted, Gold, Pink Roses ........................................... 2.45
Nippon, Salt, Pepper, & Tray, Scenic, Pink & Blue Jewels, Green Wreath Mark .......... 20.00
Nippon, Salt, Scrollled Feet, Pink Flowers, Gold & Green, 3 1/4 In. ........................ 6.50
Nippon, Saltshaker, Imperial Nippon, 3 1/2 In., Pair .................................... Illus   8.00

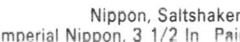

Nippon, Saltshaker,
Imperial Nippon, 3 1/2 In  Pair

Nippon, Saltshaker, Paintings Of People ........................................................... 4.00
Nippon, Sauce, Hand-Painted Floral, 5 In. ........................................................ 1.75
Nippon, Server, Blue, Gold, & Pink Border, 2 Raised Gold Handles, 7 In. ................. 8.50
Nippon, Server, Cheese & Cracker, 2 Tier, Pink Floral, Raised Gold, Blue Mark .......... 30.00
Nippon, Server, Pancake, Covered, Strap Handle, Gold Trim, 9 In.Diameter .............. 35.00
Nippon, Server, Vegetable, Roses, Raised Gold, Marked, 11 1/4 In.High .................. 11.00
Nippon, Smoking Set, Sailboat In Oval Panel, Brown Bands, 3 Piece ...................... 56.75
Nippon, Sugar & Creamer, Cover, Blue Iris, Gold Beading, M In Wreath ................. 24.00
Nippon, Sugar & Creamer, Cover, Melon Ribbed, 3 Footed, Gold, Turquoise Jewel ...... 30.00
Nippon, Sugar & Creamer, Cover, Raised Gold Floral, Blue Mark ........................... 18.00
Nippon, Sugar & Creamer, Cover, Royal Moriye, Hand-Painted ............................ 125.00
Nippon, Sugar & Creamer, Gold Decoration On Cobalt ....................................... 30.00
Nippon, Sugar & Creamer, Heavy Gold Detail, Pedestal Bases, Hand-Painted .......... 38.00
Nippon, Sugar & Creamer, Pink Flowers, Lacy Gold, Green Leaves, Blue Lining ........ 12.50

Nippon, Sugar & Creamer, Rust Phoenix Type Birds, Gold Trim ............................ 38.00
Nippon, Sugar & Creamer, Scenic Trees, Octagon Shape, Gold Trim ...................... 30.00
Nippon, Sugar & Creamer, Scenic, Shaded Brown, Jeweled Handles ...................... 38.00
Nippon, Sugar & Creamer, Trees & House ........................................................ 22.00
Nippon, Sugar & Creamer, Yellow Band, Rose Flowers, Gold Trim ...................... 15.00
Nippon, Sugar, Covered, Hand-Painted Rising Sun Mark ................................... 6.50
Nippon, Sugar, Cube Holder, Lake & Swan Scene, Jeweled, Handled ................... 25.00
Nippon, Sugar, For Cubes, Scenic, Handled .................................................... 40.00
Nippon, Syrup & Underplate, Green & Black Geometrics, Gold Floral & Beads ........ 20.00
Nippon, Syrup, Floral & Gold ..................................................................... 15.00
Nippon, Syrup, Green Floral & Raised Gold Vines On White, 4 In.High ................ 35.00
Nippon, Tankard, Cherries & Grapes On Lavender To Yellow, Jeweled, 12 In. ........ 150.00
Nippon, Tankard, Flowers ......................................................................... 75.00
Nippon, Tea Set, Blue Floral, Gold Trim, R.C. Mark, 3 Piece ............................. 48.00
Nippon, Tea Set, Females In Kimonoes, Gold, Royal Koga, 11 Piece ................... 59.50
Nippon, Tea Set, Gold Handles & Beading, Pink Floral On White, 13 Piece ........... 40.00
Nippon, Tea Set, Gray Blue Flowers On Glossy Yellow, 18 Piece ........................ 15.00
Nippon, Tea Set, Hand-Painted, Gold Jewels, 9 Piece ...................................... 42.00
Nippon, Tea Set, Pink & Green Floral, Gold Drape Beading, 11 Piece ................... 40.00
Nippon, Tea Set, Pink Floral On White, Cobalt Edges & Handles, Gold, 3 Piece ..... 27.50
Nippon, Tea Set, Raised Dragons On Gray, 11 Piece ....................................... 60.00
Nippon, Tea Set, Two Color Gold Brocade & Beading, Blue Bands, 7 Piece ........... 50.00
Nippon, Tea Set, White Medallions With Roses On Blue, Tan Beads, 3 Piece ......... 85.00
Nippon, Tea Strainer & Holder, Marked 1 ...................................................... 32.00
Nippon, Tea Strainer, Floral & Gold Decoration .............................................. 29.00
Nippon, Tea Strainer, Flowers, Gold, Green Wreath Mark .................................. 20.00
Nippon, Tea Strainer, Pastel Florals, Gold Bands, 2 Piece, Red Wreath Mark ........ 28.00
Nippon, Teapot, Green & Ivory Country Scene, Black Beading Around Lid ............. 40.00
Nippon, Teapot, Square, Orange Shaded Bisque, Jeweled Rim, Floral .................. 16.50
Nippon, Tile, Tea, Octagonal, Blue & Orange, 6 1/2 In.Diameter ........................ 9.00
Nippon, Tile, Tea, Scenic, Octagonal ........................................................... 21.00
Nippon, Toothpick, Blue Delft Sailboats & Windmill On White, 2 Handles ............. 14.00
Nippon, Toothpick, Floral Decoration, Scalloped Feet, 2 Handles ........................ 12.00
Nippon, Toothpick, Gold & Floral, Gold Handles & 3 Feet, Imperial Nippon ........... 22.00
Nippon, Toothpick, Gold Handles, Feet, & Beading, Medallions, Tea Roses ........... 15.00
Nippon, Toothpick, Green & Gold, Paneled, 3 Gold Handles, Hisaiki ................... 22.00
Nippon, Toothpick, Pink Floral, Blue Band Top, Embossed Medallions, Gold .......... 10.00
Nippon, Tray, Dresser, Butterflies On Cream, Gold, & White, Open Handled .......... 16.50
Nippon, Tray, Dresser, Violets, Blue & White, 10 1/2 X 7 1/2 In. ....................... 12.00
Nippon, Tray, Ice Cream, Purple Violets, Gold Trim, Set Of 6 ............................ 30.00
Nippon, Tray, Pierced Handles, Cobalt Glaze, Gold Beading, Medallion Center ....... 32.00
Nippon, Tray, Red & Blue Jewels, Barnyard Scene, 10 In. ................................ 55.00
Nippon, Tray, Violets, 9 1/2 X 6 1/2 In. ...................................................... 12.00
Nippon, Urn, Covered, Handled, Footed, Gold & Dot Enamel On Green & White ..... 85.00
Nippon, Urn, Double Handled, Cover, Turquoise Flowers, Gold Medallions ............ 125.00
Nippon, Urn, Flowers & Gold On White, M In Wreath Mark, 10 7/8 In. ................ 35.00
Nippon, Urn, Gilded Bows, Crowns, & Cornucopias, Pedestal, Green Mark, 11 In. .. 75.00
Nippon, Urn, Jewel Trim, Swirled Handles & Base, Scenic, 5 1/2 In.High ............. 55.00
Nippon, Urn, Scenic, Green & Gold, Handled, Pedestal, 7 In. ............................ 20.00
Nippon, Vase, Applied Tree Branches, Acorns, & Leaves, Gold Beading, 6 In. ........ 49.00
Nippon, Vase, Arab Desert Scene, 6 Sided, Cobalt & Gold Trim, 9 1/4 In. ............ 80.00
Nippon, Vase, Black & Gold Butterfly On Neck, Roses, 2 Handled, 9 1/2 In. .......... 47.50
Nippon, Vase, Black, Gold, & Red Roses Medallions, Gold Beading, 3 1/2 In. ........ 90.00
Nippon, Vase, Blue Flowers On 4 Yellow Panels, Lavender Trim, 6 1/2 In.High ...... 18.00
Nippon, Vase, Bluebird, 4 In.High ............................................................... 8.00
Nippon, Vase, Boat Scene, Gold Handles & Trim, 9 1/4 In.High .......................... 45.00
Nippon, Vase, Bulbous, Gold Beading & Red & Yellow Roses On Pink, 6 In. .......... 18.00
Nippon, Vase, Continuous Farm Scene, Jeweled Handle, Neck, & Band, 7 1/2 In. ... 60.00
Nippon, Vase, Coralene, Buff & Brown Floral, Signed R.S.Nippon, 7 In. ............... 120.00
Nippon, Vase, Coralene, Cobalt Ground, 2 Handled, 7 1/4 In.High ...................... 195.00
Nippon, Vase, Coralene, 2 Handles, 7 1/4 In.High .......................................... 225.00
Nippon, Vase, Cottage Scene, Hills, Red & Green Flowers, 12 In.High ................. 65.00
Nippon, Vase, Country Scene, Gold Decoration & Handles, 7 1/2 In.High .............. 33.00
Nippon, Vase, Covered, 2 Handled, Red & Pink Roses On Green, 14 In.High .......... 65.00
Nippon, Vase, Cowboy, Enameled At Neck, Imperial Mark, 7 1/4 In.High .............. 35.00
Nippon, Vase, Double Handled, Boat Scene, Floral, Signed M, 8 In. ..................... 50.00

Nippon, Vase, Elephants' Heads Handles, Mum Medallions, 10 In.High .............. 45.00
Nippon, Vase, Embossed Palm Tree, Hand-Painted, 12 1/2 In. ....................... 145.00
Nippon, Vase, Farm Scene, Beaded, 2 Handled, 7 1/2 In.High ...................... 85.00
Nippon, Vase, Flowers On Tan Ground, Scenic Lake, Sky & Swan, 5 1/2 In. ...... 22.00
Nippon, Vase, Gold Elephant Handles, Raised Leaves, Orchids, Blue Mark, 9 In. ... 30.00
Nippon, Vase, Gold Outlined Anemones, Lake & Mountain Scene, 9 1/2 In. ......... 33.00
Nippon, Vase, Gold Outlined Flowers, 11 In.High, 7 In.Diameter ................... 38.00
Nippon, Vase, Gold Outlined Red, Pink, & Yellow Flowers, 12 In.High ............. 58.00
Nippon, Vase, Gourd Shaped, Hand-Painted, 5 3/4 In.High ........................ 40.00
Nippon, Vase, Handled, Red Floral On Blue Green, Gold Trim, 9 In. .............. 18.00
Nippon, Vase, Indian In Canoe Shooting At A Deer, Superior Mark, 7 In. ......... 115.00
Nippon, Vase, Iris, Matte Finish, Gold Trim, 12 In.High ......................... 75.00
Nippon, Vase, Large Pink Flowers & Leaves, Gold Trim, 6-Sided, 9 In.High ...... 32.00
Nippon, Vase, Lavender Flower Decoration, 2 Handled, 8 In.High ................. 14.00
Nippon, Vase, Lighthouse Scene, 13 In.High, Pair ............................... 80.00
Nippon, Vase, Orange & Light Blue Poppies, Satin Finish, 9 In.High ............. 45.00
Nippon, Vase, Ovoid, Double Handled, Gilded, Cabbage Roses, Scene, 8 1/4 In. ... 65.00
Nippon, Vase, Pastoral Scene, Gold Handled & Embossed Collar, 12 In.High ...... 65.00
Nippon, Vase, Pink & Yellow Roses, Ornate Handles, 10 1/4 In.High ............. 45.00
Nippon, Vase, Pink Flowers & Gold On Beige, 11 1/2 In.High, Pair .............. 110.00
Nippon, Vase, Pink Roses & White, Green, & Blue Jewels On Black, 10 1/2 In. .... 95.00
Nippon, Vase, Pitcher Type, Roses & Foliage, Cobalt Ground, 9 1/2 In.High ...... 130.00
Nippon, Vase, Portrait, Cobalt, Gold Overlay, 7 In.High ........................ 125.00
Nippon, Vase, Raised Flying Birds & Blue Ocean, 2 Handled, 10 In. ............. 125.00
Nippon, Vase, Raised Ribbon Type Decorations, Violets, 8 In.High .............. 28.00
Nippon, Vase, Red & Pink Flowers, Leaves, Tinted Ground, 5 In.High ........... 14.00
Nippon, Vase, Roses On Beige, Gold Cable Rope & Pink Jewels, 8 1/2 In. ....... 85.00
Nippon, Vase, Roses, Gold Handles, Satin Finish, 6 In.High .................... 28.00
Nippon, Vase, Scenery Bands, Jeweled, 12 In.High, Pair ........................ 165.00
Nippon, Vase, Scenic, Brown Floral On Beige, Gold, 9 1/2 In.High .............. 60.00
Nippon, Vase, Scenic, Floral, Gold Trim, 8 In. ................................ 29.00
Nippon, Vase, Scenic, House, Water, Double Handled, 3 Footed, 5 1/2 In.High ... 39.00
Nippon, Vase, Sea Serpent On Side, Black, 6 In.High ........................... 35.00
Nippon, Vase, Trees & Stream, Gold, 2 Handled, Green Mark, 12 1/2 In.High ..... 45.00
Nippon, Vase, Wall, Blue Ground, Flowers & Birds, 6 In.Long ................... 25.00
Nippon, Vase, Yellow Ground, Mauve, Cerise, & Pink Flowers, Gold, 14 1/2 In. ... 93.00

*Nodders or nodding figures, or pagods, are porcelain figures with heads and hands that are attached to wires. Any slight movement causes the parts to move up and down. They were made in many countries during the eighteenth and nineteenth centuries.*

Nodder, Andy Gump's Min, Bisque, German ................................... 14.50
Nodder, Black Faced, Siamese Costumes, Pair ............................... 85.00
Nodder, Boy Wearing Glasses In Blue & White Old Fashioned Clothing ...... 55.00
Nodder, Boy, String, Bisque, Marked Germany, Painted, 5 In.High .......... 18.50
Nodder, Candelabra, 2 Arm, Seesaw, Children At Each End, Porcelain, White ... 95.00
Nodder, Drinking Man & Frau Holding Mugs On High, Bisque, 6 In.Pair ..... 125.00
Nodder, Girl With Dog, White, Light Blue Dress, 6 1/2 In. ................. 69.75
Nodder, Girl With Market Basket, 6 1/2 In. ............................... 68.75
Nodder, Happy Doll's Head, Hands Move, Dresden, 10 In.High .............. 295.00
Nodder, Man & Woman, Spectacles, German, Bisque, 5 1/2 In.High ......... 50.00
Nodder, Monkey, Papier-Mache, Glass Eyes, Moving Tongue ................ 53.00
Nodder, Negro Child Holding Red Polkadot Undies, Bisque, Japan .......... 39.00
Nodder, Oriental Couple, Bisque, Raised Gold Design, 6 1/2 In.High, Pair ... 345.00
Nodder, Salt & Pepper, Japanese, Spring Mounted, Pair .................... 5.00
Nodder, Salt & Pepper, Man & Woman Shape ............................... 28.00
Nodder, Skeezix & Brownie Playing Accordion, German Bisque, Pair ........ 30.00
Nodder, Woman, Head Nods, Holds Dog, Blue & White, Gold Trim, Porcelain ... 55.00

*Noritake-marked porcelain was made in Japan after 1904 by Nippon Toki Kaisha.*

Noritake, Bowl, Gilt Edge, Festoons Of Roses, Green M Mark, 5 1/4 In. ...... .75
Noritake, Bowl, Handled, Bird & Flowers On Limb On Pearlized, 9 In. ....... 10.00
Noritake, Bowl, Oval, Pierced Handles, Water Scene, House, 10 1/4 In. ...... 9.00
Noritake, Bowl, Scenic Decoration, Applied Handles, Gold Floral, 7 1/2 In. ... 12.00
Noritake, Bowl, Soup, Gilt Edge, Festoons Of Roses, Green M Mark, 7 1/4 In. ... 2.00
Noritake, Cake Set, Blue Horn Of Plenty With Fruit, Gold Trim, 5 Piece ...... 17.50

| | |
|---|---|
| Noritake, Celery Set, Blue Luster Rims, Floral Centers, 6 Piece | 10.00 |
| Noritake, Celery Set, Celery Stalks & Radishes On Lavender, Gold, 7 Piece | 45.00 |
| Noritake, Chocolate Set, Blue Luster, Art Nouveau Floral, 9 Piece | 26.00 |
| Noritake, Creamer, Hand-Painted Trees, Lake, Boat, 6 In. | 8.00 |
| Noritake, Cup & Saucer, Azalea | 5.00 |
| Noritake, Cup & Saucer, Bouillon, Malvern, Gold Handles & Trim | 3.60 |
| Noritake, Cup & Saucer, Bouillon, The Pagoda | 6.00 |
| Noritake, Cup & Saucer, Pink Blossoms, Green M In Wreath Mark | 6.00 |
| Noritake, Cup & Saucer, Rosedale | 18.00 |
| Noritake, Dish & Attached Underplate, Nut, Azalea, Footed | 15.00 |
| Noritake, Eggcup, Pink Roses | 4.00 |
| Noritake, Figurine, Hen, Laying, Nippon Tohi Kaisha, 6 In. | 12.00 |
| Noritake, Gravy Boat & Attached Underplate, Pink Roses On Green Band | 10.00 |
| Noritake, Hatpin Holder, Raised Gold Bridge & Birds On Coral | 22.00 |
| Noritake, Inkwell, Gold Owl, 3 1/2 In.High | 24.00 |
| Noritake, Jar & Underplate, Jam, Covered, Pink, Blue, & Lavender Roses, Gold | 22.50 |
| Noritake, Lunch Set, Blue, Gold, & Orange Border, 6 Piece | 15.00 |
| Noritake, Mayonnaise Set, Azalea, 3 Piece | 10.00 |
| Noritake, Muffineer, Blue Luster, Art Deco Design On Gold Band | 10.00 |
| Noritake, Muffineer, Scenic, Gold Trim, Dome Top, Marked M, 3 1/2 In.High | 15.00 |
| Noritake, Plate, Azalea, 7 3/4 In. | 7.00 |
| Noritake, Plate, Black Handles, 3 Floral Groupings, 7 In. | 8.50 |
| Noritake, Plate, Bread & Butter, Brunswick | 1.25 |
| Noritake, Plate, Bread & Butter, Gilt Edge, Festoons Of Roses, Green M Mark | 1.00 |
| Noritake, Plate, Cake, Gilt Edge, Festoons Of Roses, Green M Mark, 8 In. | 1.50 |
| Noritake, Plate, Diamond Shape, Girl In Hoop Skirt, Art Deco, 4 3/4 In. | 24.00 |
| Noritake, Plate, Dinner, Gilt Edge, Festoons Of Roses, Green M Mark | 2.50 |
| Noritake, Plate, Dinner, Hartford Pattern | 4.00 |
| Noritake, Plate, Gold Decoration, 7 In. | 4.50 |
| Noritake, Plate, Hand-Painted Violets, Gold Banded, 7 1/2 In. | 6.50 |
| Noritake, Plate, House, Water, & Sunset, Green Wreath Mark, 6 1/4 In. | 3.00 |
| Noritake, Plate, Open Handles, Chestnut Blossoms, 7 In. | 10.50 |
| Noritake, Platter, Fleurgold, 14 1/2 In. Long | 15.00 |
| Noritake, Platter, Gilt Edge, Festoons Of Roses, Oval, Green M Mark, 12 In. | 4.00 |
| Noritake, Platter, Monnette, 13 1/2 In. | 3.50 |
| Noritake, Relish, Gilt Edge, Festoons Of Roses, Oval, Green M Mark, 8 1/4 In. | 2.50 |
| Noritake, Relish, Oval, Azalea | 6.50 |
| Noritake, Salt & Pepper, Gold Floral, 3 1/2 In.High | 4.75 |
| Noritake, Sauce Set, Bird & Floral, Black & Orange, M In Wreath, 3 Piece | 12.00 |
| Noritake, Sauce, Azalea | 4.00 |
| Noritake, Saucer, Azalea | 3.00 |
| Noritake, Saucer, Colored Band On White, Green Wreath Mark | 1.50 |
| Noritake, Saucer, Pandora, Green Wreath Mark | 1.50 |
| Noritake, Sugar & Creamer, Cover, Gilt Edge, Festoons Of Roses, Green M Mark | 12.00 |
| Noritake, Sugar & Creamer, Cover, Rosedale | 15.00 |
| Noritake, Sugar & Creamer, White, Blue, Gold, C.1910 | 15.00 |
| Noritake, Sugar, Covered, Azalea | 10.00 |
| Noritake, Tea Set, Azalea, 3 Piece | 25.00 |
| Noritake, Tea Set, Girl In Bouffant Skirt, Purple, Green, & Orange, 8 Piece | 57.50 |
| Noritake, Tea Set, Ivory Bands On White, Gold Floral & Scrolls, 17 Piece | 65.00 |
| Noritake, Tea Set, White, Gold Decoration, 7 Piece | 40.00 |
| Noritake, Tile, Tea, Gold Design On White, 5 1/2 In. Diameter | 8.50 |
| Noritake, Tray, Pin, Little Roses, Green Wreath Mark | 4.00 |
| Noritake, Vase, Gold Floral On Oyster White, Green Mark, 13 In.High | 55.00 |
| Noritake, Vase, Sunset Lake Scene, 2 Handled, 5 3/4 X 3 1/2 X 2 3/4 In. | 15.00 |

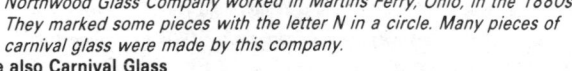

*Northwood Glass Company worked in Martins Ferry, Ohio, in the 1880s. They marked some pieces with the letter N in a circle. Many pieces of carnival glass were made by this company.*

**Northwood, see also Carnival Glass**

| | |
|---|---|
| Northwood, Banana Boat, Green, Rambler Rose, Gold Trim | 35.00 |
| Northwood, Berry Set, Near Cut, Gold Trim, 7 Piece | 55.00 |
| Northwood, Bowl, Atlas, 9 In. | 15.00 |
| Northwood, Bowl, Berry, Green, Peach, Gold Trim, Signed, 9 In. | 35.00 |
| Northwood, Bowl, Berry, Pearl Yellow Opalescent, Alaska | 24.00 |
| Northwood, Bowl, Blue Opalescent, Argonaut Shell, Dome Footed, 6 X 8 In. | 35.00 |

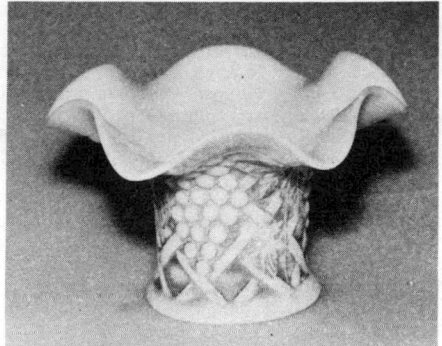

Northwood, Bowl, Custard Glass, Grape & Cable

| | |
|---|---:|
| Northwood, Bowl, Blue Opalescent, Fluted Scrolls, Footed, 7 In. | 28.50 |
| Northwood, Bowl, Blue Opalescent, Fluted Scrolls, Footed, 8 In. | 38.00 |
| Northwood, Bowl, Blue Opalescent, Vintage, Footed, 8 In. | 30.00 |
| Northwood, Bowl, Blue To Opalescent, Fluted, Wide Prisms, Flat, 7 In. | 18.50 |
| Northwood, Bowl, Cherry Thumbprint With Cable, 8 In. | 25.00 |
| Northwood, Bowl, Clear To Opalescent, Leaf & Beads, Footed, Fluted, 8 In. | 22.00 |
| Northwood, Bowl, Crushed Fruit, Covered, Singing Birds, Signed | 50.00 |
| Northwood, Bowl, Crystal, Pears & Peaches, Scalloped Rim, 10 In. | 36.00 |
| Northwood, Bowl, Custard Glass, Grape & Cable .......................... Illus | 65.00 |
| Northwood, Bowl, Fruit, Green Opalescent, Tokyo, 8 1/4 In. | 30.00 |
| Northwood, Bowl, Green, Netted Roses, Fluted, Marked, 8 In. | 25.00 |
| Northwood, Bowl, Near Cut, Turned-Up Sides, Signed, 8 1/2 In. | 20.00 |
| Northwood, Bowl, Opalescent Green, Ruffled, 6 1/2 In.Diameter | 32.00 |
| Northwood, Bowl, Opalescent To Clear, Leaf & Beads, Gold & Ruby Paint, 9 In. | 29.75 |
| Northwood, Bowl, Opalescent, Argonaut Shell, Dome Footed, Signed, 6 X 8 In. | 35.00 |
| Northwood, Butter, Covered, Green, Memphis, Gold Trim | 75.00 |
| Northwood, Candlestick, Green, Grape & Cable, N, 5 1/2 In., Pair | 38.00 To 58.00 |
| Northwood, Carafe, Crystal Queen Pattern, Rippled Lip | 14.50 |
| Northwood, Compote, Green, Tri-Flower, 5 1/2 In. | 10.00 |
| Northwood, Compote, Jelly, Blue Opalescent, Intaglio, Pedestal | 38.00 |
| Northwood, Compote, Jelly, Green Opalescent, Scroll With Acanthus | 28.50 |
| Northwood, Compote, Jelly, Vaseline Opalescent, Intaglio | 36.00 |
| Northwood, Compote, Jelly, White Opalescent, Intaglio | 16.50 |
| Northwood, Creamer, Blue Opalescent, Intaglio | 38.75 |
| Northwood, Creamer, Cranberry To Clear, Royal Oak | 95.00 |
| Northwood, Creamer, Vaseline Opalescent, Argonaut Shell, Signed | 45.00 |
| Northwood, Cruet, Crystal Queen, Clear, Blown | 30.00 |
| Northwood, Goblet, Strawberry & Cable | 28.50 |
| Northwood, Muffineer, Clear & Frosted, Royal Oak | 50.00 |
| Northwood, Muffineer, Cranberry To Clear, Royal Ivy | 95.00 |
| Northwood, Muffineer, Cranberry, Leaf Umbrella | 125.00 |
| Northwood, Muffineer, Lemon Color, Leaf Umbrella, White Cased | 135.00 |
| Northwood, Mug, Bluebird, Singing Bird & Flowers, Blue, Opalescent | 35.00 |
| Northwood, Nappy, Memphis, Clear, "Cash Rotherts Furniture, Carpets, Altoona" | 37.00 |
| Northwood, Nut Set, Flute, Vaseline, Pedestal Dish, Marked N, 5 Piece | 89.00 |
| Northwood, Pitcher, Cherry Thumbprint, Signed | 35.00 |
| Northwood, Pitcher, Water, Cherry Cable | 65.00 |
| Northwood, Pitcher, Water, Cherry Thumbprint, Red, Gold Trim | 60.00 |
| Northwood, Pitcher, Water, Red Flashing, Gold, Signed With Circle | 70.00 |
| Northwood, Plate, Ribbon Star & Bows, Cobalt, Gold Trim, Experimental, 9 In. | 75.00 |
| Northwood, Plate, Sweets, Goofus Paint, Green, Signed, 7 In. | 12.00 |
| Northwood, Salt & Pepper, Royal Ivy, Cranberry & Clear | 58.00 |
| Northwood, Salt & Pepper, Royal Oak, Cranberry & Clear | 58.00 |
| Northwood, Sauce, Alaska, White Opalescent | 9.00 |
| Northwood, Sauce, Cherry & Cable, Red Cherries, Gold Cable, Marked N | 10.80 |
| Northwood, Sauce, Cherry With Thumbprint | 17.00 |
| Northwood, Sauce, Emerald, Peach, 5 In. | 20.00 |
| Northwood, Sauce, Jeweled Heart, White Opalescent | 9.00 |

| | |
|---|---|
| Northwood, Sauce, Northwood Peach, Green, Gold Trim, Marked N | 14.50 |
| Northwood, Sauce, Singing Birds, Clear, 5 In. | 12.50 |
| Northwood, Spooner, Alaska, Emerald Green | 22.00 |
| Northwood, Spooner, Dewdrop, Opalescent | 18.00 |
| Northwood, Sugar & Creamer, Frosted Water Lilies & Cattails | 55.00 |
| Northwood, Sugar, Covered, Cherry With Thumbprint, Signed N | 27.50 To 38.00 |
| Northwood, Sugar, Covered, Paneled Cherry & Grape, Signed | 25.00 |
| Northwood, Sugar, Covered, Royal Oak, Cranberry To Clear | 120.00 |
| Northwood, Sugar, Drapery, Blue Opalescent, Covered, Gold Trim, Signed N | 48.00 |
| Northwood, Table Set, Cherry Thumbprint, Gold Trim, Signed N, 4 Piece | 195.00 |
| Northwood, Table Set, White Opalescent, Drapery, Gold Trim, 6 Piece | 225.00 |
| Northwood, Tankard, Green, Enameled Flowers & Leaves, Gold Trim | 47.50 |
| Northwood, Toothpick, Leaf Umbrella, Raspberry | 75.00 |
| Northwood, Toothpick, Royal Ivy, Cranberry & Clear | 58.00 |
| Northwood, Toothpick, Shell, Green, Opalescent | 28.00 |
| Northwood, Town Pump, Blue Opalescent, Signed | 89.00 |
| Northwood, Tumbler, Block, Gold Trim, Signed | 10.00 |
| Northwood, Tumbler, Cherry & Cable, Red, Gold Trim | 17.50 |
| Northwood, Tumbler, Memphis, Green, Gold Trim | 15.00 |
| Northwood, Tumbler, Paneled Holly | 20.00 |
| Northwood, Tumbler, Peach, Emerald, Gold Trim | 15.00 To 30.00 |
| Northwood, Tumbler, Poppy, Green | 6.00 |
| Northwood, Tumbler, Royal Oak, White Opaque, Pink & Green Decoration | 18.00 |
| Northwood, Vase, Clear Opalescent, Coin Spot, 7 In. | 13.00 |
| Northwood, Vase, Diamond Point, Opalescent Blue, 11 In.High | 30.00 |
| Northwood, Vase, Tree Trunk, Blue Opalescent, 12 In.High, Marked | 35.00 |
| Northwood, Water Set, Atlas, Clear, Signed, 7 Piece | 60.00 |
| Northwood, Water Set, Enameled Flowers, 5 Piece | 45.00 |
| Northwood, Water Set, Lattice Cherry, Paint & Gold Trim, 9 Piece | 250.00 |
| Northwood, Water Set, Peach, Green, Gold Trim, Signed N, 7 Piece | 235.00 |
| Northwood, Water Set, Pullup, Tumble-Up Tumbler, Ruby Feathers, Gold, 2 Piece | 125.00 |
| Nuart, Vase, Cobalt With Green Highlights, Signed, 8 In. | 55.00 |

*Nymphenburg, a German porcelain factory, was established at Neudeck-ob-der-Au in 1753 and moved to Nymphenburg in 1761. The company is still in existence. Modern marks include a shield superceded by a star or crown, and a crowned CT with a checkered shield.*

| | |
|---|---|
| Nymphenburg, Candlestick, Roman Column, White, Pair | 200.00 |
| Nymphenburg, Cup & Saucer, Coffee, Chintz, C.1790 | 80.00 |
| Nymphenburg, Cup & Saucer, Girl In Red Skirt On Donkey, C.1760 | 120.00 |
| Nymphenberg, Figurine, Mouse, Standing, Gray, 2 3/4 In. | 40.00 |
| Nymphenburg, Figurine, Shepherd & Shepherdess, White, C.1763, Pair | 450.00 |
| Nymphenburg, Figurine, Terrier, Begging Position, Artist-Signed, 10 In. | 165.00 |
| Nymphenburg, Plate, Bouquets, Basket Work Rim, Gilt, C.1765, 9 1/4 In. | 150.00 |
| Nymphenburg, Plate, Fruit Center, Insects Rim, C.1760, 9 3/8 In., Pair | 175.00 |
| Nymphenburg, Plate, Shipwreck, Black & Gilt Rim, C.1755, 8 3/4 In. | 450.00 |
| Nymphenburg, Teacup & Saucer, Floral, Spiral Ribbed | 15.00 |
| Nymphenburg, Teacup & Saucer, Neoclassical, Portrait Medallions, C.1775 | 100.00 |

*Occupied Japan is the mark used on pieces of pottery and porcelain made during the American occupation of Japan after World War II. Collectors are now buying these pieces. The items were made for export to the United States.*

| | |
|---|---|
| Occupied Japan, Bowl, Green, Opalescent, Low, Tokyo, 8 1/2 In. | 30.00 |
| Occupied Japan, Bowl, Ladies & Child, Wisteria, Marked, 8 1/2 X 3 In. | 6.50 |
| Occupied Japan, Chair, Miniature | 4.50 |
| Occupied Japan, Chocolate Set, Floral, 13 Piece | 37.50 |
| Occupied Japan, Christmas Ornament, Santa On Sleigh | 3.00 |
| Occupied Japan, Coaster Set, Papier-Mache, Floral Designs, 8 Piece | 10.00 |
| Occupied Japan, Cup & Saucer, Blue Willow | 4.00 |
| Occupied Japan, Cup & Saucer, Child's, Blue Willow | 3.50 |
| Occupied Japan, Cup & Saucer, Child's, Maroon Fruit On White, 8 Sided | 5.00 |
| Occupied Japan, Cup & Saucer, Gold Decoration & Handle On Pink | 6.50 |
| Occupied Japan, Cup & Saucer, Hand-Painted, 3 Ladies | 6.50 |
| Occupied Japan, Cup & Saucer, Large Rose On Black | 6.00 |
| Occupied Japan, Cup & Saucer, Tan Luster, Raised Enamel Decoration | 5.00 |

| | |
|---|---|
| Occupied Japan, Cup & Saucer, Trimont ........................................................ | 10.00 |
| Occupied Japan, Dish, Candy, Apple & Fruit, 6 In. ...................................... | 8.50 |
| Occupied Japan, Doll, Bisque, Moveable Parts, 3 In.Tall ............................. | 7.00 |
| Occupied Japan, Fan, Aqua Silk, Bamboo, Mother-Of-Pearl Appliques, Roses ......... | 10.00 |
| Occupied Japan, Fan, Mother-Of-Pearl Panels On Bamboo Ribs, Aqua Silk ......... | 10.00 |
| Occupied Japan, Figurine, Boy Carrying Golf Clubs .................................... | 4.00 |
| Occupied Japan, Figurine, Boy With Dog, 2 1/2 In. .................................... | 2.25 |
| Occupied Japan, Figurine, Colonial Gentleman, 3 5/8 In. ............................. | 3.00 |
| Occupied Japan, Figurine, Dancing Girl, 6 In.High, Pair .............................. | 7.50 |
| Occupied Japan, Figurine, Dancing Lady, 5 1/2 In.High ............................... | 5.00 |
| Occupied Japan, Figurine, Dog, Floppy Ears, 2 1/2 In. ............................... | 2.00 |
| Occupied Japan, Figurine, Hen, Bisque .................................................... | 3.95 |
| Occupied Japan, Figurine, Lady & Gentleman, 7 1/2 In.High, Pair ................... | 15.00 |
| Occupied Japan, Figurine, Lady, Art Deco Type, 3 In. ................................. | 2.25 |
| Occupied Japan, Figurine, Oriental Man With Beard, Blue Robe ...................... | 5.00 |
| Occupied Japan, Figurine, Turbanned Boy & Pig, 3 7/8 In. ........................... | 3.00 |
| Occupied Japan, Group, Colonial Couple, 3 In. .......................................... | 2.25 |
| Occupied Japan, Group, French Dandy Man & Woman, 3 X 3 1/2 In. ................. | 7.50 |
| Occupied Japan, Group, Man & Seated Woman, Colonial Costumes, Miniature ...... | 3.00 |
| Occupied Japan, Group, 3 Ivory Colored Elephants On Carved Wooden Base ...... | 3.75 |
| Occupied Japan, Jardiniere, Negro Boy Eating Watermelon, 4 1/2 In ............... | 4.00 |
| Occupied Japan, Lamp, Porcelain, Victorian Man & Lady, 14 In.High ............... | 30.00 |
| Occupied Japan, Lighter, Cigarette, Camera On Tripod, Metal, 4 In. ............... | 8.00 |
| Occupied Japan, Match Holder, Wall Plaque, Bisque, Colonial Couple .............. | 18.50 |
| Occupied Japan, Mug, Beer, Miniature ..................................................... | 3.00 |
| Occupied Japan, Piano, Chair, Miniature .................................................. | 4.50 |
| Occupied Japan, Pitcher, Colonial Gentleman, 2 In. ................................... | 3.00 |
| Occupied Japan, Pitcher, Colonial Lady, 2 In ............................................ | 3.00 |
| Occupied Japan, Pitcher, Hand-Painted Roses, 3 1/2 In.High ........................ | 6.00 |
| Occupied Japan, Planter, Wall, Man & Woman Under Tree, Marked Paimux, Pair ...... | 25.00 |
| Occupied Japan, Plaque, Wall, Girl In Relief ............................................. | 7.50 |
| Occupied Japan, Plate, Cobalt & Rust Open Handles On White, Square, Amherst ...... | 30.00 |
| Occupied Japan, Plate, Palette Shape, Open Handled, White Mums, Butterflies ...... | 15.00 |
| Occupied Japan, Salt & Pepper, Dutch Boy & Girl ....................................... | 5.00 |
| Occupied Japan, Salt & Pepper, Floral & Gold On White, Handled, On Tray ........ | 8.00 |
| Occupied Japan, Salt & Pepper, Pigs Playing Violins ................................... | 5.00 |
| Occupied Japan, Saltshaker, Teapot, 2 In. ............................................... | 2.25 |
| Occupied Japan, Slipper, Blue Angel On Toe, 7 In. ..................................... | 10.00 |
| Occupied Japan, Tea Set, Child's, Flower Design, 8 Piece ............................ | 20.00 |
| Occupied Japan, Tea Set, Doll's, Vases & Urns, 10 Piece ............................. | 20.00 |
| Occupied Japan, Tea Set, Green & Tan Pearl Ground, Pink Flowers, 8 Piece ...... | 10.00 |
| Occupied Japan, Tea Set, Miniature, Floral On White, 9 Piece ....................... | 12.00 |
| Occupied Japan, Tea Set, Red & Green Floral, Blue Trim, Miniature, 7 Piece ...... | 10.50 |
| Occupied Japan, Toby Mug, General MacArthur, 3 1/2 In. ............................ | 7.00 |
| Occupied Japan, Toothbrush Holder, Dwarf, Doc, Metal, 4 1/2 In.High ............. | 5.00 |
| Occupied Japan, Vase, Lacquer, Gold Phoenix On Red, 8 In.High .................... | 20.00 |

| | | |
|---|---|---|
| **G. E. OHR, BILOXI.** | *Ohr pottery was made by George E.Ohr in Biloxi, Mississippi, between 1883 and 1918. The pieces were made of very thin clay and were twisted, folded and dented into odd, graceful shapes.* | |
| Ohr, Mug, Puzzle, Black, C.1895 ............................................................ | | 65.00 |
| Ohr, Mug, Puzzle, Brown, C.1895 ........................................................... | | 65.00 |
| Ohr, Mug, Puzzle, Mottled Decoration, Signed .......................................... | | 55.00 |
| Ohr, Vase, Yellow & Brown, 4 In. High ................................................ *Illus* | | 50.00 |

| | |
|---|---|
| *Old ivory china was made in Silesia, Germany, at the end of the nineteenth century. It is often marked with a crown and the word Silesia. The pattern numbers appear on the base of each piece.* | |
| Old Ivory, Berry Set, Lavender Floral, Green, Gold Trim, 5 Piece ................... | 70.00 |
| Old Ivory, Berry Set, No.32, Marked Ohme, Silesia, 7 Piece ......................... | 125.00 |
| Old Ivory, Bowl, Berry, No.25, Silesia ..................................................... | 55.00 |
| Old Ivory, Bowl, Berry, No.82 ............................................................... | 10.00 |
| Old Ivory, Bowl, Berry, No.84 ............................................................... | 29.00 |
| Old Ivory, Bowl, No.16, Signed Silesia, 6 1/4 In. Diameter ........................... | 32.00 |
| Old Ivory, Bowl, No.16, 9 1/2 In. Diameter .............................................. | 55.00 |
| Old Ivory, Bowl, No.27, 9 1/2 In. Diameter .............................................. | 48.00 |

Ohr, Vase, Yellow & Brown, 4 In. High
*(See Page 357)*

| | |
|---|---:|
| Old Ivory, **Bowl,** No.84, Ivory & Beige Tea Roses & Gold Scrolls On Cream | 35.00 |
| Old Ivory, **Celery,** Purple Thistle, Silesia, 9 1/2 X 4 1/2 In. | 9.50 |
| Old Ivory, **Chocolate Set,** Brown Roses, Marked Silesia, 13 Piece | 375.00 |
| Old Ivory, **Chocolate Set,** Ornate Handle & Finial, C.T.Chantilly, 9 Piece | 110.00 |
| Old Ivory, **Creamer,** No.16, Roses, Marked Silesia, Clairon | 38.00 |
| Old Ivory, **Cup & Saucer,** Roses, Silesia | 20.00 |
| Old Ivory, **Dish,** Pickle, No.30, Oval, Apricots & Roses, Silesia | 32.50 |
| Old Ivory, **Fernery,** Liner, White Roses, Pink Centers, Royal Bayreuth | 165.00 |
| Old Ivory, **Nappy,** No.84, Handled, Ohme, Silesia, 6 3/8 In. | 28.00 |
| Old Ivory, **Pitcher,** No.84 | 25.00 |
| Old Ivory, **Plate,** Azaleas, Marked No.IV Elysee, 7 3/4 In. | 15.00 |
| Old Ivory, **Plate,** Bread & Butter, Brown Roses, Marked Silesia | 20.00 |
| Old Ivory, **Plate,** Cake, No.22, Holly, Open Handles | 65.00 |
| Old Ivory, **Plate,** Cake, No.84, Open Handles, 10 In. | 30.00 |
| Old Ivory, **Plate,** Cake, Open Handles, Thistle, Gold Trim, 10 In. | 25.00 |
| Old Ivory, **Plate,** Chop, No.16, 13 1/2 In. | 85.00 |
| Old Ivory, **Plate,** Floral & Scrolls, Scalloped, St.P.M.Trianon, 8 1/4 In. | 22.00 |
| Old Ivory, **Plate,** No.16, 6 1/2 In. | 18.00 |
| Old Ivory, **Plate,** No.16, 7 1/2 In. | 16.50 |
| Old Ivory, **Plate,** No.73, 6 1/2 In. | 18.00 |
| Old Ivory, **Plate,** No.82, 9 In. | 20.00 |
| Old Ivory, **Plate,** No.84, 6 In. | 7.00 |
| Old Ivory, **Plate,** Thistle, Open Handles, 10 In. | 25.00 |
| Old Ivory, **Plate,** V.Corona, New Rochelle, N.Y., K.T.& K., 10 In. | 5.00 |
| Old Ivory, **Plate,** XVII, Open Handles, Holly & Berries, Silesia, 10 In. | 45.00 |
| Old Ivory, **Platter,** No.94-E, Oval, Syracuse, 7 X 5 In. | 1.00 |
| Old Ivory, **Pot,** Mustard, No.84 | 35.00 |
| Old Ivory, **Relish,** No.84 | 12.00 |
| Old Ivory, **Relish,** No.84, Ivory & Beige Tea Roses & Gold Scrolls On Cream | 19.00 |
| Old Ivory, **Sauce,** Hand-Painted, Royal Bayreuth, Blue Mark, 5 3/4 In. | 27.50 |
| Old Ivory, **Saucer,** Syracuse | 1.00 |
| Old Ivory, **Sugar & Creamer,** Silesia | 65.00 |
| Old Ivory, **Toothpick,** No.84 | 32.00 To 75.00 |
| Old Paris, **Tea Set,** Gold Rose Bud Finials & Banding, White Ground, 15 Piece | 175.00 |

*Onion, originally named 'Bulb Pattern, ' is a white ware decorated with
cobalt blue. Although it is commonly associated with Meissen, other
companies made the pattern in the latter part of the nineteenth century.*

| | |
|---|---:|
| Onion, **Bowl,** Meissen, 5 3/4 In. | 8.00 |
| Onion, **Bowl,** Pierced Floral On 2 1/2 In. Border, Meissen, 8 1/2 In. | 50.00 |
| Onion, **Bowl,** Scalloped, Square, Meissen, 4 1/8 In.High | 250.00 |
| Onion, **Bowl,** Soup, Marked Meissen, 9 In. | 20.00 |
| Onion, **Bowl,** Square, Irregular Edge, Meissen, Crossed Swords, 10 In. | 115.00 |
| Onion, **Cup & Saucer,** Demitasse, Meissen | 19.25 |
| Onion, **Feeder,** Pap, Flower | 8.50 |
| Onion, **Gravy Boat & Attached Tray,** Meissen | 30.00 |
| Onion, **Infant Feeder,** Tettau, German Mark | 15.00 |

| | |
|---|---:|
| Onion, Invalid Feeder, Made In Germany, 2 In.High, 7 In.Across | 12.00 |
| Onion, Knife & Fork, Meissen, Set Of 12 | 150.00 |
| Onion, Mustard Set, Blue, Marked T With Unicorn, 2 Piece | 14.00 |
| Onion, Plate, Bread & Butter | 3.00 |
| Onion, Plate, Cake, Dresden, Dated Dec.24, 1875, 10 In. | 20.00 |
| Onion, Plate, Dinner, Shanango Pottery | 6.00 |
| Onion, Plate, Meissen, Crossed Swords Front & Back, 10 In. | 20.00 |
| Onion, Plate, Scalloped Rim, Meissen, Crossed Swords, 10 In. | 20.00 |
| Onion, Plate, Staffordshire, Marked Rd.576812, 10 In. | 25.00 |
| Onion, Platter, Meissen In Circle, 15 In. | 35.00 |
| Onion, Salt, Meissen, C.1860, 1 X 1 1/2 X 1 1/2 In. | 14.00 |
| Onion, Spoon Rest, Parmelee-Dohrman Co., L.A., Greenwood China, Trenton.N.J. | 12.00 |
| Onion, Sugar, Rosebud Finial On Cover, Blue & White, Meissen | 32.00 |
| Onion, Teacup & Saucer, Meissen, Crossed Swords | 18.00 |
| Onion, Teapot, Rosebud Finial, Blue & White, Meissen | 65.00 |
| Onion, Tureen & Attached Underplate, Gravy, Meissen, Crossed Swords | 60.00 |
| Onyx, Box, Jewel, Pink, Gold, Metal Bound | 19.50 |
| Onyx, Jar, Powder, Domed Lid On Brass Ring, White, Round, 7 In. | 25.00 |

*Opalescent glass is translucent glass that has the bluish-white tones of the opal gemstone. It is often found in pressed glassware made in Victorian times. Some dealers use the terms opaline and opalescent for any of the bluish-white translucent wares.*

| | |
|---|---:|
| Opalescent, Base, Blue, Ribbed, 8 In.High, Pair | 30.00 |
| Opalescent, Base, Blue, 7 In.High | 25.00 |
| Opalescent, Bonbon, Swan | 16.00 |
| Opalescent, Bowl, Argonaut Shell, Turned Up Sides, Footed, 7 In. | 30.00 |
| Opalescent, Bowl, Berry, Blue, Lion's Leg | 45.00 |
| Opalescent, Bowl, Blue, Basket Weave, Openwork Border, 9 In. | 18.00 |
| Opalescent, Bowl, Blue, Fluted & Beaded Edges, 8 1/2 X 2 In. | 25.00 |
| Opalescent, Bowl, Blue, Fluted Rim, Scalloped Loop Variant, 8 1/2 In. | 27.50 |
| Opalescent, Bowl, Blue, Hobnail, Crimped Ruffled Rim, 2 In. Deep | 30.00 |
| Opalescent, Bowl, Blue, Hobnail, Crimped & Ruffled, 11 In. | 20.00 |
| Opalescent, Bowl, Blue, Jefferson's Wheel, 3 Footed, 6 In. | 42.50 |
| Opalescent, Bowl, Blue, Meander, Ruffled, Footed, 8 In. | 30.00 |
| Opalescent, Bowl, Blue, Rim Ruffled, 8 1/2 In. | 26.50 |
| Opalescent, Bowl, Blue, Scalloped Loop Variant, Fluted, 8 1/2 In.Diameter | 27.50 |
| Opalescent, Bowl, Canary, Astrol, Footed, Flared, 8 1/4 In. | 25.00 |
| Opalescent, Bowl, Canary, Inverted Fan & Feather, 4 Footed. 7 In | 48.00 |
| Opalescent, Bowl, Canary, Shadow, Footed, 7 1/2 In. | 16.00 |
| Opalescent, Bowl, Diamond-Quilted, Square, Crimped Edges, 7 In. | 20.00 |
| Opalescent, Bowl, Green, Astrol, Fluted, 8 In. | 16.50 |
| Opalescent, Bowl, Green, Fleur-De-Lis, 9 1/2 In. | 18.00 |
| Opalescent, Bowl, Green, Many Loops, Fluted, 8 1/2 In. | 32.50 |
| Opalescent, Bowl, Inverted Fan & Feather, 4 Footed, 7 In. | 35.00 |
| Opalescent, Bowl, Many Loops, Opalescent Trim, Ruffled Top, 6 1/2 In. | 20.00 |
| Opalescent, Bowl, Peach, Single Flower, 9 In. | 24.00 |
| Opalescent, Bowl, Ruffles & Rings, Footed, 8 In. | 30.00 |
| Opalescent, Cake Stand, Canary, Leaves & English Hobnail Diamonds, 7 In. | 44.00 |
| Opalescent, Celery, Hobnail, Clambroth Base, Ruffled Scalloped Top | 20.00 |
| Opalescent, Compote, Blue, Paneled, Beaded, Footed, 4 X 8 In. | 18.00 |
| Opalescent, Compote, Canary, Dolphin, 5 1/2 In. | 35.00 |
| Opalescent, Compote, Dolphin, Petticoat, McKearin 196-5, Pair | 135.00 |
| Opalescent, Compote, Jelly, Blue, Argonaut Shell | 28.00 |
| Opalescent, Compote, Jelly, White, Iris Meander | 15.00 |
| Opalescent, Creamer, Blue, Jeweled Heart | 40.00 |
| Opalescent, Cruet, Daisy & Fern, Floral Shape, Cut Stopper | 48.00 |
| Opalescent, Dish, Candy, Green, Many Loops, Fluted & Ruffled Rim, 8 In. | 22.00 |
| Opalescent, Epergne, Blue, Hobnail, Diamond Pattern, 3 White Horns | 135.00 |
| Opalescent, Epergne, One Lily, Fluted Cranberry Edge, Flared Bowl | 60.00 |
| Opalescent, Hat, Coin Spot, 3 3/4 In.High | 38.00 |
| Opalescent, Hat, Vertical Stripes, Rolled Down Rim, 3 3/4 In.High | 12.50 |
| Opalescent, Jar, Powder, Covered, Blue, Fluted Scrolls, Footed | 35.00 |
| Opalescent, Knob, Drawer | 10.00 |
| Opalescent, Muffineer, Bulbous, Feather Design | 35.00 |
| Opalescent, Muffineer, Coinspot | 39.00 |
| Opalescent, Mug, Gold Wreath Decorated, Remember Me In Gold Script | 25.00 |

| | |
|---|---|
| Opalescent, Pitcher, Green To Vaseline, Coin Spot, Ruffled Top, 9 In. | 70.00 |
| Opalescent, Pitcher, Water, Sky Blue | 84.00 |
| Opalescent, Pitcher, Water, Swirl, Frilly Rim | 65.00 |
| Opalescent, Pitcher, Water, Swirled, Applied Clear Ribbed Handle | 50.00 |
| Opalescent, Plate, Pastel Yellow, Swirls, 8 1/2 In. | 35.00 |
| Opalescent, Rose Bowl, Blue, Scalloped Top, 5 1/2 In.High | 25.00 |
| Opalescent, Rose Bowl, Green, Palm & Scroll | 28.00 |
| Opalescent, Rose Bowl, White, Devils' Heads | 30.00 |
| Opalescent, Rose Bowl, Wreath And Shell | 21.50 |
| Opalescent, Salt, Blue, Bird With Seed | 40.00 |
| Opalescent, Salt, Blue, Swan, Gold Trim, 5 In. Long | 25.00 |
| Opalescent, Saltshaker, Blue, Swirl, 2 1/2 In. High | 16.00 |
| Opalescent, Saltshaker, Egg Shape, Columbian, 1893 Embossed In Red & Blue | 45.00 |
| Opalescent, Saltshaker, Pink, Panel Leaf, Footed | 25.00 |
| Opalescent, Saltshaker, Polka Dot, Opalescent Blue Dots | 17.50 |
| Opalescent, Sauce, Beatty's Rib | 7.50 |
| Opalescent, Sauce, Canary, Shell & Wreath | 15.00 |
| Opalescent, Sauce, Scroll With Acanthus, Footed, 5 In.Diameter | 12.00 |
| Opalescent, Sherbet, 1, 000-Eye, Set Of 6 | 75.00 |
| Opalescent, Spooner, Blue, Daisy | 37.00 |
| Opalescent, Spooner, Blue, Drapery | 25.00 |
| Opalescent, Spooner, Hobnail In Squares, Standard | 29.50 |
| Opalescent, Spooner, White Swirl | 20.00 |
| Opalescent, Sugar & Creamer, Pale Yellow, Pink Flowers, Metal Tops | 90.00 |
| Opalescent, Sugar, Covered, Blue, Palm Beach | 45.00 |
| Opalescent, Sugar, Covered, Swirled Clear To Opalescent Ribs | 32.50 |
| Opalescent, Sugar, White, Intaglio | 14.50 |
| Opalescent, Syrup, Blue, Coin Spot, Nine Panels | 68.00 |
| Opalescent, Syrup, White, Coin Spot, Patent Date 1881 On Silver Lid | 40.00 |
| Opalescent, Tieback, Morning Glories, Pewter Stem, 4 1/2 In.Diameter | 30.00 |
| Opalescent, Toothpick, White, Overall Hobnail, Footed | 10.00 |
| Opalescent, Tumbler, Hobnail, 1, 000-Eye, 6 In. | 15.00 |
| Opalescent, Vase, Canary, Trumpet, Flaring Fluted Top, 7 In. | 26.00 |
| Opalescent, Vase, Green, Basket Weave, Openwork Top, Footed, 5 In. | 10.00 |
| Opalescent, Vase, Green, Tree Bark, 9 In.High | 15.00 |
| Opalescent, Vase, Ice Blue, Drape & Beaded Medallion, 12 In. | 30.00 |
| Opalescent, Vase, Iridescent Pastel Pink, White Stripes, 5 In. | 550.00 |
| Opalescent, Water Set, Blue, Opalescent Stripes, 7 Piece | 100.00 |

*Opaline glass, or opal glass, was made in white, apple green, and other colors. The glass had a matte surface and a lack of transparency. It was often gilded or painted. It was a popular mid-nineteenth-century European glassware.*

| | |
|---|---|
| Opaline, Bowl, Deep Blue, Hat, Fluted, White Enamel, 3 1/2 In. | 27.50 To 32.50 |
| Opaline, Bowl, Light Blue, Fluted, 3 1/2 In. High | 17.50 To 22.50 |
| Opaline, Box, Dresser, Covered, Round, Pink Blossoms On Green, 4 In. | 32.50 |
| Opaline, Carafe & Tumbler, Tumble-Up, Green, French, C.1830, 7 In.High | 110.00 |
| Opaline, Compote, Candy, Yellow, White Footed Base, Crystal & Gold Trim | 45.00 |
| Opaline, Cruet, Pink | 18.50 |
| Opaline, Goblet, White, Green Snakes Around Stem, Gilt Trim, Pair | 30.00 |
| Opaline, Jar, Lift Off Domed Lid, Green, Gold Decoration, 2 1/2 In. | 22.00 |
| Opaline, Newel Post Top, French, Melon Ribbed, Emerald, Pair | 75.00 |
| Opaline, Pitcher, Cherubs' Heads, Signed Ahne, C.1873, 7 In. High | 250.00 |
| Opaline, Ring Tree, Green & White, Gold Decoration, Ground Pontil, 5 In. | 75.00 |
| Opaline, Ring Tree, Green, Footed | 28.00 |
| Opaline, Tray, White, Gilt Trim, 12 1/2 In. Diameter | 15.00 |
| Opaline, Vase, Baluster-Shaped, Roses On White, 6 1/4 In.High | 20.00 |
| Opaline, Vase, Deep Blue, Fluted Top, White Flowers Inside, 6 1/2 In. | 25.00 |
| Opaline, Vase, Trumpet, French, Blue To Clear To Aqua, Fluted Edge, 15 In. | 90.00 |
| Opaline, Vase, White Floriform, Blue Foot & Stem, French, C.1825, 8 In. | 85.00 |
| Opaline, Water Set, Hobnail, Blue, 7 Piece | 69.00 |
| Opaline, Wine, French, Pink, Gold & Silver Trim, C.1889 | 40.00 |
| Opera Glasses, Balland, Paris, Mother-Of-Pearl, Brass Frames | 38.00 |
| Opera Glasses, Brass & Leather | 7.00 |
| Opera Glasses, French, Bronze & Pearl | 18.00 |
| Opera Glasses, L.B.& Co., Paris, Mother-Of-Pearl, Engraved John Robert | 35.00 |
| Opera Glasses, Le Maire, France, Pink Mother-Of-Pearl, Case | 20.00 |

| | |
|---|---|
| Opera Glasses, Le Maire, Ft., Paris, Gold Finish, Suede Drawstring Holder | 27.50 |
| Opera Glasses, Le Maire, Paris, Gold Finished Metal, Suede Holder | 35.00 |
| Opera Glasses, Marked Chevalier, Paris, Mother-Of-Pearl, Brass, Leather Case | 11.75 |
| Opera Glasses, Wollensak Biascope | 14.00 |
|     Organ, see Music, Organ | |
| Ormolu, Wax Jack, Leaf Design | 185.00 |

*Orrefors Glassworks, located in the Swedish province of Smaland, was*
*established in 1916.*

| | |
|---|---|
| Orrefors, Vase, Cobalt Crystal, 5 1/4 In.High, Pair | 75.00 |
| Orrefors, Vase, Oval, Etched Ship Decoration, 3 1/2 In.High | 18.50 |
| Orrefors, Vase, Paperweight, Fish Design On Interior | 295.00 |
| Ott & Brewer, Cup & Saucer, Demitasse, Gold Twig Handle | 75.00 |
| Ouachita, Vase, Ship Decoration On Green Matte Glaze, Artist Initials | 55.00 |

**OWENS**
**UTOPIAN**

*Owens Pottery was made in Zanesville, Ohio, from 1891 to 1928. The*
*first art pottery was made after 1896. Utopian Ware, Cyrano, Navarre,*
*Feroza, and Henri Deux were made. Pieces were usually marked with a form*
*of the name Owens. About 1907 the firm began to make tile and gave up the*
*art pottery wares.*

| | |
|---|---|
| Owens, Candlestick, Lessell Ware, Red Trees, Water & Mountains, Pair | 150.00 |
| Owens, Jardiniere, Majolica, Marked | 25.00 |
| Owens, Jug, Utopian, Golden Poppies, 7 1/4 In.High | 75.00 |
| Owens, Lamp Base, Similar To Utopian, Orange Floral On Brown, 11 In.High | 45.00 |
| Owens, Mug, Floral, 5 In. High | 75.00 |
| Owens, Mug, Molded Trees, Matte Green | 45.00 |
| Owens, Mug, Utopian, Leaves & Berries On High Glaze, 4 1/2 In. | 75.00 |
| Owens, Mug, Utopian, Mistletoe Design On Glaze, Artist-Signed | 80.00 |
| Owens, Mug, Utopian, 5 1/4 In. | 45.00 |
| Owens, Planter, Wall, Green Acorn, Owensart, 7 1/8 In.High | 25.00 |
| Owens, Tankard, Utopian, 12 In. | 125.00 |
| Owens, Vase, Brown Glaze, Blue Flowers, 6 1/2 In.High, Unmarked | 50.00 |
| Owens, Vase, Bud, Utopian, Floral, Signed, 4 1/2 In. | 58.00 |
| Owens, Vase, Floral On Brown, 4 Sided, Initials F.F., 6 1/4 In. | 55.00 |
| Owens, Vase, Hand-Painted Leaves & Cattails On Brown Glaze, 10 1/2 In. | 60.00 |
| Owens, Vase, Light Ground, Pink Rose, Artist-Signed, 12 1/2 In. High | 95.00 |
| Owens, Vase, Navarre, Art Nouveau Style, Black, White Figure Of Girl, 9 In. | 225.00 |
| Owens, Vase, Squatty, Berries & Leaves On Brown, Handled, Utopian, 5 In. | 45.00 |
| Owens, Vase, Utopian, Brown Ground, Red & Yellow Flowers, 8 1/2 In.High | 65.00 |
| Owens, Vase, Utopian, Brown, Rust & Green Floral Decoration, 7 In.High | 80.00 |
| Owens, Vase, Utopian, Floral On Brown, Artist Initials, 7 In. | 65.00 |
| Owens, Vase, Utopian, Orange Floral On Shaded Brown, 8 In. High | 67.50 |
| Owens, Vase, Utopian, Russet Floral & Green Leaves On Brown, 5 In. | 40.00 |
| Owens, Vase, Utopian, Rust & Green Floral On Brown, 7 In.High | 80.00 |
| Owens, Vase, Utopian, Rust, Orange, & Yellow Leaves On Brown, 4 In.High | 35.00 |
| Owens, Vase, Utopian, Signed Delores Harvey, 11 In. _Illus_ | 125.00 |
| Owens, Vase, Water Lily, Signed, 10 In.High | 180.00 |
| Oyster Plate, Clear Glass, Shell & Tassel, 9 1/2 In. | 57.00 |

Owens, Vase, Utopian, Signed Delores Harvey, 11 In.

Painting, Fraktur, Taufschein, 1805, 8 X 12 1/2 In.

Painting, Fraktur, Dated 1839, 15 X 12 In.

| | |
|---|---|
| **Oyster Plate, Green & Red Floral,** Gold, Hand-Painted, Set Of 6 | 85.00 |
| **Oyster Plate, Oyster Shell Shape,** Pink Luster, Shelllike Indentations | 19.00 |
| **Oyster Plate, Shell Shape & Decoration,** Marked UPW, Jan.4, 1881, 8 1/2 In. | 28.00 |
| **Painting, Fraktur,** Birth Record Of David Raub, 1811, Pa., 8 X 13 In. | 700.00 |
| **Painting, Fraktur,** Birth Record Of Earl Hagebuck, 1811, Pa., 8 X 13 In. | 300.00 |
| **Painting, Fraktur,** Birth Record Of Geoug Herter, 1807, Martin Brechall, Pa. | 1050.00 |
| **Painting, Fraktur,** Birth Record Of Johannes Weirich, 1768, Pa., 8 X 12 In. | 2125.00 |
| **Painting, Fraktur,** Birth Record Of Johathan Beijfelmann, 1813, Pa. | 550.00 |
| **Painting, Fraktur,** Birth Record Of Leah Schirt, July 1828, Mount Pleasant | 490.00 |
| **Painting, Fraktur,** Birth Record Of Maria Minnig, 1832, 9 1/4 X 7 1/4 In. | 45.00 |
| **Painting, Fraktur,** Birth Record Of Peter Weidman, Mount Pleasant | 400.00 |
| **Painting, Fraktur,** Birth Record Of Salome Herschberger, 1821, Mt.Pleasant | 450.00 |
| **Painting, Fraktur,** Bookplate, Foliage, Star Shape Flowers, 1832, 4 X 5 In. | 200.00 |
| **Painting, Fraktur,** Bookplate, Vase Of Tulips, Pennsylvania, C.1810, 7 X 8 In. | 400.00 |
| **Painting, Fraktur,** Certificate, Heart, Indians, Soft Colors, 9 3/4 X 14 In. | 325.00 |
| **Painting, Fraktur,** Dated 1817, Bright Colors, Sponge Trimmed Gilt Frame | 200.00 |
| **Painting, Fraktur,** Dated 1839, 15 X 12 In. *Illus* | 1300.00 |
| **Painting, Fraktur,** Marriage Certificate, Ephrata, J.Bauman, 17 X 20 In. | 300.00 |
| **Painting, Fraktur,** Peacocks & Floral, Certificates, 1790-1837, 13 X 15 In. | 600.00 |
| **Painting, Fraktur,** Schwenkfelder Design, C.1835, 9 1/2 X 14 1/4 In. | 2000.00 |
| **Painting, Fraktur,** Taufschein, Hearts, Pious Sayings, Pennsylvania, 1800 | 550.00 |
| **Painting, Fraktur,** Taufschein, 1805, 8 X 12 1/2 In. *Illus* | 500.00 |

Painting, **Fraktur,** Tulips & Flowers In Vase, Birds & Fish, 9 In. .................................. 300.00
Painting, **Fraktur,** Washington Commemorative, Goodwin, Mass., 1842, 7 X 11 In. ............... 425.00
Painting, **Fraktur,** Woman, Man, & Heart, Anna Weift, 1788, 8 1/2 X 11 In. ........................ 350.00
Painting, **Miniature On Ivory,** Emperor Francis, 1792-1835, Oval, Ivory Frame ............... 300.00
Painting, **Miniature On Ivory,** Katherine The Great, Signed Benner, 1760 ........................ 110.00
Painting, **Miniature On Ivory,** Mozart & Bride, Signed, Pair ......................................... 50.00
Painting, **Miniature On Ivory,** Napoleon, Signed ........................................................ 65.00
Painting, **Miniature,** Dr.Robert French, Amberian, Oval, Gold Frame, 3 In. .................. 1400.00
Painting, **Miniature,** Fox Terrier, Signed M.Arnud, 1907, Oval, Frame ......................... 45.00
Painting, **Miniature,** Gentleman, Sinister, Black Coat, American, Oval ......................... 70.00
Painting, **Miniature,** Gentlemen, George Place, C.1790, Oval, 2 3/4 In.High .................. 425.00
Painting, **Miniature,** Lady With Plumed Hat, Borny, French, 1 7/8 In.Diameter ............... 250.00
Painting, **Miniature,** Lieutenant Oliver Tod, American, Rectangular .............................. 190.00
Painting, **Miniature,** Oil On Ivory, Sea Captain, C.1810 ............................................. 375.00
Painting, **Miniature,** On Porcelain, Young Girl, Brass Frame, 2 In. ............................... 90.00
Painting, **Oil On Barrel Lid,** Horse's Head, Red Ground, 13 In. Diameter ..................... 65.00
Painting, **Oil On Board,** Peaches & Basket, Gilt Frame, 20 1/2 X 26 In. ........................ 190.00
Painting, **Oil On Board,** Whaling Scene, C.1890, 22 X 27 In. ...................................... 425.00
Painting, **Oil On Canvas,** British Naval Officer, Napoleonic Era, C.1810 ....................... 650.00
Painting, **Oil On Canvas,** Clipper Cavalier, Square Rigged, C.1840 .............................. 795.00
Painting, **Oil On Canvas,** Maine Coastal Scene, Carved Wooden Frame ......................... 60.00
Painting, **Oil On Canvas,** Middle-Aged Man & Woman, American Gothic, C.1800 ............ 225.00
Painting, **Oil On Canvas,** Square Rigged Clipper Cavalier, C.1840 ............................... 795.00
Painting, **On Ivory,** Boy In Period Costume, 2 1/2 X 1 3/4 In. ..................................... 50.00
Painting, **On Ivory,** Lady, Square Frame, Gold Liner, 1 3/8 In.Diameter ........................ 60.00
Painting, **On Ivory,** Oval, Beautiful Girl, Signed Kuva, 3 X 3 1/2 In. ............................. 110.00
Painting, **On Ivory,** Oval, Girl With Doe In Lap, Signed Reymon, 2 X 2 1/2 In. ............... 125.00
Painting, **On Porcelain,** Alexis, Son Of Czar Nicholas, K.P.M., 6 1/2 In.High ................ 750.00
Painting, **On Porcelain,** Gypsy Girl, Head & Shoulders, Oval, 7 1/2 In. ........................ 350.00
Painting, **On Porcelain,** Lady & Little Child Walking, K.P.M., 7 X 8 In. ......................... 950.00
Painting, **On Porcelain,** Marie Louise Of France, 9 1/2 In.High ................................... 325.00
Painting, **On Porcelain,** Queen Louise, Oval, Carved Wooden Frame, 2 In.High ............... 40.00
Painting, **On Porcelain,** Young Girl, Framed, 5 X 7 In. ............................................. 395.00
Painting, **On Silk,** Bunch Of Flowers, Dated 1880, 14 X 8 In. .................................... 27.00
Painting, **On Silk,** Ship, 14 X 8 In. ....................................................................... 25.00
Painting, **On Wood Panel,** Heron Standing On One Foot, Water Lilies, Cattails ............... 15.00
Painting, **On Woven Bark,** Man Fishing, Houses, Mountain, Japanese, Framed ............... 30.00
Painting, **Reverse On Glass,** Clipper Ship, Bird's-Eye Veneer Frame, 28 In. .................. 175.00
Painting, **Reverse On Glass,** Night Scene, House, Fish, Curved Oval, 23 In. .................. 20.00
Painting, **Reverse On Glass,** Oriental Scene, Framed, Mother-Of-Pearl Inlays ............... 68.00
Painting, **Reverse On Glass,** Pair Of Doves, Floral Wreath, Gilt Frame ........................ 185.00
Painting, **Reverse On Glass,** Royal Figures, 1800s, 24 X 33 In., Pair ........................ 1200.00
Painting, **Reverse On Glass,** Scene In Venice, Framed, 18 X 28 In. ............................. 36.00
Painting, **Reverse On Glass,** Sinking Of The Titanic, April 15, 1912 ............................. 125.00
Painting, **Reverse On Glass,** Statue Of Liberty, Dated 1917, Oval ............................... 22.50
Painting, **Reverse On Glass,** White House, D.C., Mother Of Pearl Windows ................... 37.50
Painting, **Reverse On Glass,** 17th Century Courting Scene, 10 X 12 In. ........................ 24.00
Painting, **Theorem,** On Velvet, Bird, Blues & Browns, 7 1/2 X 9 1/2 In. ....................... 125.00
Painting, **Watercolor,** Angel Gabriel, Primitive, Patriotic, C.1850 ............................... 195.00
Painting, **Watercolor,** Child & Hobbyhorse & Whip, 7 X 8 1/4 In. ............................... 300.00
Painting, **Watercolor,** House, Dated 1724, 4 X 5 1/2 In. .......................................... 105.00
Painting, **Watercolor,** House, Pine Frame, 11 1/2 X 13 1/2 In. ................................... 750.00
Painting, **Watercolor,** Portraits Of Lady & Gentleman, Gilt Frames, Pair ....................... 120.00
Painting, **Watercolor,** Reindeer Pulling Angels In Sleigh, W.Granville Smith .................. 45.00
Painting, **Watercolor,** Small Girl Picking Fruit, Oval, 6 1/2 X 8 1/4 In. ......................... 375.00
Painting, **Watercolor,** Theorem On Paper, Basket Of Flowers, Gilt Frame ...................... 300.00
Painting, **Watercolor,** Woman With Book, C.1850, Maple Frame, 6 X 7 In. ..................... 75.00

*Pairpoint Corporation was a silver and glass firm founded in New
Bedford, Massachusetts, in 1880.*

**Pairpoint, Bowl,** Blue & Rose Poppies On Tan Ground, Gold Trim, 9 In. ........................ 75.00
**Pairpoint, Bowl,** Cut Glass, Urn With Flame, 8 In.Diameter, 2 In.Deep ......................... 125.00
**Pairpoint, Box,** Collar, Dresden Decoration, Blown Out Leaves, 6 X 4 In. ...................... 395.00
**Pairpoint, Box,** Trinket, Ivory Body, Raised Gold Floral Decoration, Signed .................. 275.00
**Pairpoint, Candleholder,** Canary, Vintage Engraving, 12 In. High, Pair ........................ 145.00

| | |
|---|---:|
| Pairpoint, Candlestick, Amber, Crystal Bubble Ball, Pair, 10 3/4 In.High | 110.00 |
| Pairpoint, Candlestick, Blue Flowers On White, Metal Base, 12 In.High, Pair | 150.00 |
| Pairpoint, Candlestick, Canary, Etched Leaves, Intaglio Grapes, 16 In. | 95.00 |
| Pairpoint, Candlestick, Clear, 16 In., Pair | 350.00 |
| Pairpoint, Candlestick, Silver Plated Socket & Base, Signed, 10 In., Pair | 200.00 |
| Pairpoint, Centerpiece, Floral & Leaf, Hobstar Bottom, Albert Steffin | 120.00 |
| Pairpoint, Cologne, Ruby, Intaglio Carved Gold Floral & Leaf, Stopper | 100.00 |
| Pairpoint, Compote, Amber, Fine Cutting, 7 1/4 In.High | 75.00 |
| Pairpoint, Compote, Cobalt, Clear Paperweight Connector, 8 In.Diameter | 55.00 |
| Pairpoint, Compote, Green Crystal, Bubble Ball Stem, 8 X 5 In. | 45.00 |
| Pairpoint, Compote, Silver Top, Clear Glass Base, Signed, 12 3/8 In.Diameter | 65.00 |
| Pairpoint, Flower Holder, Frosted Green, Pierced Brass Stand, Ball Feet | 43.00 |
| Pairpoint, Jar, Biscuit, Silver Top & Footed Bottom Rim, Floral On Cherry | 245.00 |
| Pairpoint, Jar, Cracker, Flute, Embossed Top & Bottom Scrolls, Silver Cover | 129.50 |
| Pairpoint, Jar, Tobacco, Bear Finial On Cover, Embossed Metal Collar | 69.00 |
| Pairpoint, Lamp Base, Brass, Ceramic Push-Up, Pair | 70.00 |
| Pairpoint, Lamp, Art Nouveau, Reverse Painted Shade, Castle Scene, 24 In. | 325.00 |
| Pairpoint, Lamp, Bedroom, Puffy Roses, Silver Base | 465.00 |
| Pairpoint, Lamp, Boudoir, Green Shade, Water Lilies & Dragonflies, 14 In. | 475.00 |
| Pairpoint, Lamp, Boudoir, Purple Flowers, Green Leaves, 15 In.High, Signed | 325.00 |
| Pairpoint, Lamp, Clear Paperweight Base & Knop, Cranberry Font, 11 In. | 70.00 |
| Pairpoint, Lamp, Desert Scene Shade, Signed W.Macy, 22 In.High | 350.00 |
| Pairpoint, Lamp, Painting Of Seasons Under Glass | 500.00 |
| Pairpoint, Lamp, Paneled, Bronze Base, Enameled, Ribbed Outside, 24 In. | 300.00 |
| Pairpoint, Lamp, Pink, Orange, & Floral On Frosted White & Black, Signed | 650.00 |
| Pairpoint, Lamp, Puffed Out, Grapes, Bananas, & Apples, 4 Footed Base, 15 In. | 200.00 |
| Pairpoint, Lamp, Reverse Floral Painting On Green, Frosted Crackle, Footed | 435.00 |
| Pairpoint, Lamp, Ship Scene, Shade Signed Durand, 18 In.Diameter | 475.00 |
| Pairpoint, Lamp, White Satin Shade, Signed Base | 48.00 |
| Pairpoint, Lamp, 3 Dolphin Base | 92.00 |
| Pairpoint, Muffineer, Delft, Paneled, Dutch Scenes, Green, Silver Shell Top | 225.00 |
| Pairpoint, Paperweight, Pear, Ruby Stem | 46.00 |
| Pairpoint, Paperweight, Red Rose & 4 Green Leaves On Ultramarine, Signed | 200.00 |
| Pairpoint, Perfume, Cornucopia, Cobalt & Cyrstal Paperweight Body, Footed | 50.00 |
| Pairpoint, Perfume, Paperweight Type, Pear-Shaped Stopper, 6 1/2 In.High | 75.00 |
| Pairpoint, Plate, Ruffled Edges, Graduated Bubbles, Applied Grapes, 8 In. | 45.00 |
| Pairpoint, Saltshaker, Amethyst, Sterling Top, 2 1/4 In.High | 20.00 |
| Pairpoint, Sugar & Creamer, Stippled, Engraved Band | 17.50 |
| Pairpoint, Syrup, Strawberry Diamond & Fan, Silver Plate Top, 5 1/4 In.High | 150.00 |
| Pairpoint, Tazza, Canary, Bubbles In Clear Knop Stem, 7 In. | 50.00 |
| Pairpoint, Tea Caddy, Repousse Design, 5 In. | 55.00 |
| Pairpoint, Tea Set, Art Nouveau, Silver On Copper Tray, 5 Piece | 225.00 |
| Pairpoint, Vase, Brass, Green Glass Liner, Signed, 9 3/4 In.High | 27.50 |
| Pairpoint, Vase, Bulbous, Deep Cobalt, 8 3/4 In.High | 25.00 |
| Pairpoint, Vase, Delft, Windmill, Sailing Ships, & Gulls, Melon Ribbed, 4 In. | 150.00 |
| Pairpoint, Vase, Gravic Grapes, Amethyst, Clear Bubbly Ball Stem, 12 In. | 75.00 |
| Pairpoint, Vase, Green, Crystal Bubble Ball Stem, Scalloped, 12 In.High | 55.00 |
| Pairpoint, Vase, Miniature, Delft, Windmill, Melon Ribbed, 4 In.High | 150.00 |
| Pairpoint, Vase, Paperweight, Amethyst, Blown, Bubbles, 9 1/2 In. | 35.00 |
| Pairpoint, Vase, Trumpet, Bubble Ball At Footed Base, 22 In. | 95.00 |
| Palmer Cox Brownies, Plate, Porcelain, Spider On Back, 6 1/4 In. | 18.00 |
| Palmer Cox, Book, Primer, The First Trousers, 1897, Color | 10.00 |
| Palmer Cox, Dish, Child's, 19 Brownies, Engraved Polar Bear, Forbes Silver | 48.00 |
| Paper, Almanac, Ayers American, 1915 | 2.50 |
| Paper, Almanac, Dr.D.Jayne's, 1918 | 2.50 |
| Paper, Almanac, Dr.D.Jayne's, 1919 | 5.00 |
| Paper, Almanac, Dr.D.Jayne's, 1928 | 2.50 |
| Paper, Almanac, Dr.Miles, 1924-1927, Each | 2.50 |
| Paper, Almanac, Dr.Miles, 1929 | 2.50 |
| Paper, Almanac, Goodrich, 1939 | 1.00 |
| Paper, Almanac, Hostetter's Bitters, 1880 | 2.50 |
| Paper, Almanac, Hostetter's Bitters, 1890 | 2.00 |
| Paper, Almanac, Household, 1916 | 1.00 |
| Paper, Almanac, International Harvester, 1918 | 1.00 To 2.50 |
| Paper, Almanac, McDonald's, 1920 | 2.50 |
| Paper, Almanac, Rawleigh's, 1912 | 2.50 |

| | |
|---|---:|
| Paper, Almanac, Swamp Root, Dream Book, 1939 | 3.00 |
| Paper, Almanac, The Lady's Birthday, 1910 | 1.00 |
| Paper, Almanac, The Nyal Family, 1910-1913, Each | 2.50 |
| Paper, Almanac, The Peruna, 1904 | 2.50 |
| Paper, Almanac, The Practical Farmer's, 1899 | 4.50 |
| Paper, Almanac, Watkins, 1918 | 1.00 |
| Paper, Book, Coloring, Smilin' Jack, Dated 1946 | 5.00 |
| Paper, Book, The Animated Peter Rabbit, Marion Merrill, Dated 1945 | 2.75 |
| Paper, Catalogue, A.J.Fisher, Cap Pistols, 1877 | 20.00 |
| Paper, Catalogue, Aisenstein & Woronock, N.Y., Watch & Clock, 1911 | 20.00 |
| Paper, Catalogue, Alamo Gas Engines, 1904 | 12.50 |
| Paper, Catalogue, Baltimore Price Reducer, 1928, Toys, Games | 40.00 |
| Paper, Catalogue, Barnum Iron & Wire Works, Detroit, Jail Cells, Vaults, 1926 | 7.50 |
| Paper, Catalogue, Bicycle & Baby Carriages, E.C.Meacham & Sons, 1892 | 10.00 |
| Paper, Catalogue, Boyington Chiffonier Folding Beds, Chicago, 1885 | 6.00 |
| Paper, Catalogue, Blatz Malt Syrup, 1929 | 10.00 |
| Paper, Catalogue, Brown & Sharpe Small Tools, 1935 | 3.00 |
| Paper, Catalogue, Butler Bros., 1889, Toys | 15.00 |
| Paper, Catalogue, Butler Bros., 1891, Banks, Toys | 25.00 |
| Paper, Catalogue, Butler Bros., 1930, Banks, Toys | 20.00 |
| Paper, Catalogue, Crescent Bicycles, 1902 | 10.00 |
| Paper, Catalogue, Dunham, Buckley & Co., New York, Toys, 1805 | 30.00 |
| Paper, Catalogue, E-B Farm Tractor, Emerson Brantingham Imp.Co., Ill., 1920 | 7.50 |
| Paper, Catalogue, Edison, Amberola, 1909 | 17.50 |
| Paper, Catalogue, Edison, Embassy Phonograph, 1923 | 12.50 |
| Paper, Catalogue, Ehrich Bros., New York, Banks, Toys, & Dolls, 1892 | 30.00 |
| Paper, Catalogue, Firefighting Equipment, 1927 | 4.00 |
| Paper, Catalogue, Hartman Furniture & Carpet Co., Chicago, 1914 | 5.00 |
| Paper, Catalogue, Henry Moss Co., Phila., Badges, Celluloid, & Ribbon, 1929 | 3.00 |
| Paper, Catalogue, J.E.Stevens Co., 1906, Toys & Banks | 35.00 |
| Paper, Catalogue, Kenton Hardware Co., 1934 | 135.00 |
| Paper, Catalogue, King & Co., Harness Makers, Owego, N.Y., 1895 | 15.00 |
| Paper, Catalogue, Lyon & Healy Band Instruments & Uniforms, 1913 | 8.00 |
| Paper, Catalogue, Macy's, Fall & Winter, 1909-1910 | 30.00 |
| Paper, Catalogue, Macy's, Spring & Summer, 1907 | 30.00 |
| Paper, Catalogue, McCadden & Bros., Phila., Toys & Banks, 1890 | 60.00 |
| Paper, Catalogue, McCormick Deering, 1924 | 4.50 |
| Paper, Catalogue, Mead Bicycles & Sporting Goods, 1911 | 5.00 To 17.50 |
| Paper, Catalogue, Montgomery Ward, Summer, 1930 | 10.00 |
| Paper, Catalogue, Montgomery Ward, 1932, Full | 12.00 |
| Paper, Catalogue, Pantasote Covered Furniture, 1906 | 6.00 |
| Paper, Catalogue, Paye & Baker Silversmiths, R.I., 1902 | 6.95 |
| Paper, Catalogue, Plymouth, DeLuxe, 1936 | 9.50 |
| Paper, Catalogue, Queen Quality Shoes, 1914 | 6.00 |
| Paper, Catalogue, Sears Roebuck & Co., Summer, 1928 | 12.00 |
| Paper, Catalogue, Sears Roebuck, 1947 | 3.50 |
| Paper, Catalogue, Sears Roebuck, 1949 | 3.50 |
| Paper, Catalogue, Selchow & Righter, Games & Toys, 1894-95 | 130.00 |
| Paper, Catalogue, Singer, Sewing Machine, 1897 | 6.00 |
| Paper, Catalogue, Smith & Davis Co., Brass & Iron Beds, 1904 | 22.00 |
| Paper, Catalogue, Spiegel, May, Stern, Co., Fall, 1910 | 25.00 |
| Paper, Catalogue, Stern Bros., Fall & Winter, 1882-1883 | 14.00 |
| Paper, Catalogue, Thompson Submachine Guns & Semi-Automatic Carbine, 1922 | 7.00 |
| Paper, Catalogue, Tohrsen & Caddady, Guns, 1894 | 25.00 |
| Paper, Catalogue, Victor Records, 1920 | 5.75 |
| Paper, Catalogue, Victor Records, 1922 | 5.75 |
| Paper, Catalogue, Victor Records, 1930 | 5.00 |
| Paper, Catalogue, Victor, Red Seal Records, 1923 | 7.50 |
| Paper, Catalogue, Ward, Spring & Summer, 1933 | 10.00 |
| Paper, Catalogue, Winton Bicycles, Cleveland, 1896 | 12.50 |
| Paper, Catalogue, Wood Mowing & Reaping Machine Company, 1884 | 10.00 |
| Paper, Catalogue, Wurlitzer Musical Instruments, 1926 | 8.00 |
| Paper, Doll, see Doll, Paper | |
| Paper, Egg, Easter, Cardboard, Rabbits On Sides, Blue Necktie | 14.00 |
| Paper, Magazine, Playboy, January, 1955 | 6.00 |
| Paper, Magazine, Post, Norman Rockwell Cover, 1916-1930, Each | 5.00 |

| | |
|---|---:|
| Paper, Magazine, Post, Norman Rockwell Cover, 1930s, Each | 4.00 |
| Paper, Map, Carte De La Louisiane, Et Pays Voisins, Bellin, Paris, 1757 | 150.00 |
| Paper, Map, City Of New York, C.1850, Koch & Co. | 20.00 |
| Paper, Map, Eastern Hemisphere, 1910, Rand McNally, School, Roll Down | 7.00 |
| Paper, Map, Pennsylvania, 1928, Thayer's Industrial, School, Roll Down | 12.00 |
| Paper, Map, Western Hemisphere, 1918, School, Roll Down | 10.00 |
| Paper, Scrapbook, Victorian, Circus Cutouts & Trade Cards | 16.00 |
| Paper, Scrapbook, Victorian, Embossed Child On Cover, 42 Pages | 45.00 |
| Paper, Scrapbook, Victorian, Gold Dust Twins Trade Cards & Others | 28.00 |
| Paper, Scrapbook, Victorian, Trade Cards, Cutouts, 46 Pages | 35.00 |
| **Paperweight, see also Baccarat, Paperweight, Store, Paperweight** | |
| Paperweight, Advertising, Brass, Nude Woman | 7.00 |
| Paperweight, Aluminum Beer Barrels, Benson Mfg.Co., Picture Of Beer Barrel | 10.00 |
| Paperweight, Anvil Shape, Copper, 2 1/4 In.High | 10.00 |
| **Paperweight, Baccarat, see Baccarat, Paperweight** | |
| Paperweight, Bacchus, Concentric Millefiori, 3 1/8 In. | 550.00 |
| Paperweight, Bacchus, Double Overlay, Encased, Cobalt & Mauve, 2 3/4 In. | 800.00 |
| Paperweight, Bandstand, Revere Beach, Mass., Glass, Rectangular | 4.95 |
| Paperweight, Battleship U.S.S. Brooklyn, C.1898, Glass, Rectangular | 5.95 |
| Paperweight, Bell Telephone, "Southwest Bell Telephone, " Cobalt | 55.00 |
| Paperweight, Bell Telephone, Blue | 26.00 |
| Paperweight, Bell Telephone, Blue Glass, Western Electric Co. | 35.00 |
| Paperweight, Bisque Dutch Girl In Snow, Glass Ball, Atlas Crystal Works | 18.00 |
| Paperweight, Block House, 1764, Pittsburgh, Pa., Rayed Sunburst | 29.50 |
| Paperweight, Bohemian, Scattered Millefiori, Four Running Hare Canes | 165.00 |
| Paperweight, Boston Safe Deposit & Trust Co., Glass, Oval, Milk White | 5.75 |
| Paperweight, Burlington Buggy Co., Iowa, Interior Beaded Border | 65.00 |
| Paperweight, Capitol, Albany, N.Y., Glass, Rectangular, 4 1/8 X 2 3/4 In. | 3.95 |
| Paperweight, Chinese, Blue Flower On Stem On White Latticinio, Faceted | 125.00 |
| Paperweight, Chinese, Nosegay & Multicolored Canes On White Latticinio | 125.00 |
| Paperweight, Clear Glass Horseshoe, Center Medallion For Picture | 20.00 |
| Paperweight, Clear Glass, Controlled Bubbles | 27.50 |
| Paperweight, Clichy, Chequer, Crimson Florette, 2 7/8 In. | 300.00 |
| Paperweight, Clichy, Concentric Millefiori, 2 9/16 In. *Illus* | 1200.00 |
| Paperweight, Clichy, Double Overlay, Pink, 2 5/8 In. *Illus* | 4600.00 |
| Paperweight, Clichy, Double Overlay, Turquoise, 3 In. *Illus* | 2900.00 |
| Paperweight, Clichy, Flat Bouquet, 3 Canes, 4 Leaves, Rose, 2 1/4 In. | 350.00 |
| Paperweight, Clichy, Green & Pink Circlets, White Cane, Faceted, 2 1/2 In. | 300.00 |
| Paperweight, Clichy, Queen Victoria & Prince Albert, Sulfide, 2 5/8 In. | 275.00 |
| Paperweight, Clichy, Scattered Millefiori, Pink & Green Rose, 2 3/16 In. | 250.00 |
| Paperweight, Clichy, Three Roses Of 18 Canes, White Latticinio Swirls | 700.00 |
| Paperweight, Crystal, Faceted, Sand Holder | 25.00 |
| Paperweight, Cut Glass, Book Shape, Hobnail & Crosscutting, Pen Grooves | 45.00 |
| Paperweight, Cut Glass, Round, 24 Point Hobstar On Flat Top, American | 65.00 |
| Paperweight, D'Albret, Albert Schweitzer, Overlay | 110.00 To 160.00 |
| Paperweight, D'Albret, Albert Schweitzer, Sulfide | 62.00 |
| Paperweight, D'Albret, Ernest Hemingway, Overlay | 160.00 |
| Paperweight, D'Albret, Ernest Hemingway, Sulfide | 62.00 |
| Paperweight, D'Albret, F.D.Roosevelt, Overlay | 160.00 |
| Paperweight, D'Albret, F.D.Roosevelt, Sulfide | 62.00 |
| Paperweight, D'Albret, General Douglas MacArthur, Overlay | 160.00 |
| Paperweight, D'Albret, General Douglas MacArthur, Sulfide | 62.00 |
| Paperweight, D'Albret, Jenny Lind, 1974, Overlay | 170.00 |
| Paperweight, D'Albret, Jenny Lind, 1974, Sulfide | 68.00 |
| Paperweight, D'Albret, John & Jacqueline Kennedy, Faceted, 3 In. | 45.00 |
| Paperweight, D'Albret, John J.Audubon, Sulfide | 68.00 |
| Paperweight, D'Albret, John Paul Jones, 1974 | 68.00 |
| Paperweight, D'Albret, John Paul Jones, 1974, Overlay | 170.00 |
| Paperweight, D'Albret, King Adolph VI Of Sweden, Overlay | 160.00 |
| Paperweight, D'Albret, King Adolph VI Of Sweden, Sulfide | 62.00 |
| Paperweight, D'Albret, Leonardo Da Vinci, Overlay | 160.00 |
| Paperweight, D'Albret, Leonardo Da Vinci, Sulfide | 62.00 |
| Paperweight, D'Albret, Mark Twain, Overlay | 160.00 |
| Paperweight, D'Albret, Mark Twain, Sulfide | 62.00 |
| Paperweight, D'Albret, Paul Revere, Overlay | 160.00 |
| Paperweight, D'Albret, Paul Revere, Sulfide | 62.00 |

Paperweight, Clichy, Double Overlay, Pink, 2 5/8 In.
(See Page 366)

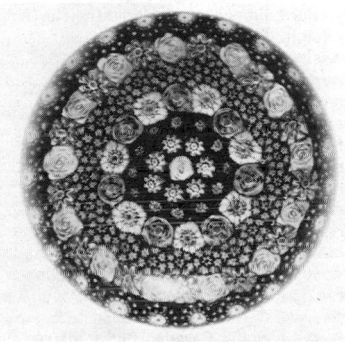

Paperweight, Clichy,
Concentric Millefiori, 2 9/16 In.
(See Page 366)

Paperweight, Clichy, Double Overlay, Turquoise, 3 In.
(See Page 366)

Paperweight, Pinchbeck, Couples In Garden, Pewter Base
(See Page 368)

Paperweight, Pinchbeck,
Man Toasting Boy, 3 1/4 In.
(See Page 368)

Paperweight, Pinchbeck,
Campers Around Fire, 3 1/8 In.
(See Page 368)

| | |
|---|---|
| Paperweight, D'Albret, Prince Charles, Overlay | 160.00 |
| Paperweight, D'Albret, Prince Charles, Sulfide | 62.00 |
| Paperweight, Dog, Cast Iron | 6.75 |
| Paperweight, Dummy Fuse & Warhead For 105 Shell | 8.00 |
| Paperweight, Egg, Swedish Crystal, Etched Feathers, Signed | 22.50 |
| Paperweight, Everette Glass Co., Ltd., Pa., Crystal, Color & White Printing | 50.00 |
| Paperweight, Ferris Wheel At Columbian Exposition, 1893, Glass | 25.00 |
| Paperweight, Floral Design, Faceted, Signed Lew Kaines | 85.00 |
| Paperweight, French, Multicolored Double Tiered Flower, Dated 1899 | 75.00 |
| Paperweight, Gentile, Butterfly | 7.50 |
| Paperweight, Gentile, Christmas, 1971 | 10.00 |
| Paperweight, Gentile, Easter, 1972 | 10.00 |
| Paperweight, Gentile, Kiwanis | 7.50 |
| Paperweight, Gentile, Lincoln, 1963 | 20.00 |
| Paperweight, Gentile, Moose | 7.50 |
| Paperweight, Gentile, Mother's Day, 1972 | 10.00 |
| Paperweight, Gentile, Mushroom, 1971 | 10.00 |
| Paperweight, Gentile, Pearl Harbor, 1971 | 10.00 |
| Paperweight, Glass, Bristol, Clear Cone, Flame Colors, Pedestal, C.1850 | 110.00 |
| Paperweight, Glass, Marley Advertising | 5.00 |
| Paperweight, Glass, Masonic Emblem In Center | 12.50 |
| Paperweight, Globe, Time | 3.50 |
| Paperweight, God Bless This House | 8.50 |
| Paperweight, Golfer Carrying Clubs, Marked B.W., 2 1/4 In. | 30.00 |
| Paperweight, Hardstone, Apple Shape | 12.00 |
| Paperweight, Home Sweet Home, Glass | 25.00 |
| Paperweight, J.Smith In White On Dome, Trumpet Flower, Blue Petals | 85.00 |
| Paperweight, John F.Kennedy, Sulfide Head, Clear Glass | 45.00 |
| Paperweight, John F.Kennedy, Sulfide Head, Waffle Pattern, Ruby, Gold | 35.00 |
| Paperweight, Kaziun, Orange Red Flower On Goldstone, Miniature, Signed | 185.00 |
| Paperweight, Kaziun, Snake | 515.00 |
| Paperweight, Kosta, Etched Egg With Feather, No.92279, V.Lindstrand | 22.50 |
| Paperweight, Laboratory & Fish Hatching House, Mass., Glass, Rectangular | 4.95 |
| Paperweight, Lincoln, Glass, Rectangular, Frosted Underside, 1 In.High | 95.00 |
| Paperweight, Lion, Metal, 4 In.Long | 5.00 |
| Paperweight, Marked China, Orange & Yellow Flower | 6.00 |
| Paperweight, Martha Washington Portrait On Multicolor | 45.00 |
| Paperweight, McPhail Gold Medal Pianoforte, Boston, Glass, Rectangular | 5.95 |
| Paperweight, Millville, Mushroom, 3 1/2 In. | 60.00 |
| Paperweight, Murano, Apollo II, Sulfide, Magnum | 35.00 |
| Paperweight, Natural Arch Bridge, Rectangular | 9.50 |
| Paperweight, New England, Swirl, Pink & White Florette, 2 3/8 In. | 180.00 |
| Paperweight, Obelisk, Thermometer, Clear Cut Glass, 5 In.High | 22.50 |
| Paperweight, Ohio Valley, Pink & Green Spatter, Airtraps Form Blue Flower | 47.00 |
| Paperweight, Pairpoint, see Pairpoint, Paperweight | |
| Paperweight, Peacock, Millefiori | 5.00 |
| Paperweight, Pershing, Pressed Glass | 15.00 |
| Paperweight, Perthshire, Mistletoe On Red | 100.00 |
| Paperweight, Photograph Of Phillips Exeter Academy In Base, Glass | 3.95 |
| Paperweight, Pinchbeck, Campers Around Fire, 3 1/8 In. .........Illus | 275.00 |
| Paperweight, Pinchbeck, Couples In Garden, Pewter Base .........Illus | 250.00 |
| Paperweight, Pinchbeck, Man Toasting Boy, 3 1/4 In. .........Illus | 275.00 |
| Paperweight, Pink Mica Flakes, 6 Bubbles, 5 In.High | 20.00 |
| Paperweight, Plaque, Black Carrara Marble, Mosaic Butterflies, C.1850 | 85.00 |
| Paperweight, Plaque, White Carrara Marble, Mosaic Baroque Plant, Oval | 85.00 |
| Paperweight, Plymouth Rock, Glass, Marked Providence Inkstand Co. | 28.00 |
| Paperweight, Post Office, Taunton, Mass., Glass, Rectangular, 4 X 2 1/2 In. | 4.95 |
| Paperweight, President Cleveland | 35.00 |
| Paperweight, Purdee Anvil | 7.50 |
| Paperweight, Ray Banford, Snake Raising Head Over Red Rose, Yellow Border | 60.00 |
| Paperweight, Red & Yellow Floral, Pontil, Aqua, C.1860 | 42.00 |
| Paperweight, Roses, Name, & Date 1884, 3 3/4 In. | 45.00 |
| Paperweight, Salamander, Green, Flower, Signed | 150.00 |
| Paperweight, Sand Dunes, Encased | 23.00 |
| Paperweight, Sandwich, Double Clematis, Pink, 2 3/4 In. | 200.00 |
| Paperweight, Sandwich, Fruit, Pears & Cherries, 2 1/2 In. | 175.00 |

| | |
|---|---|
| Paperweight, Sandwich, Weedflower, Red, Blue, & White, 2 5/8 In. | 260.00 |
| Paperweight, Seven-Point Star, Gold Flower Decoration, Raised Dome | 10.00 |
| Paperweight, Snow, House, Trees | 8.00 |
| Paperweight, St.Louis, Carpet Ground | 170.00 |
| Paperweight, St.Louis, Closed Concentric, 3 Rows Coral, Blue, White Canes | 125.00 |
| Paperweight, St.Louis, Concentric Millefiori, Miniature, 1 7/8 In. | 300.00 |
| Paperweight, St.Louis, Concentric Millefiori, 3 1/8 In. | 1550.00 |
| Paperweight, St.Louis, Crown, Dog Cane Center, 3 1/8 In. | 950.00 |
| Paperweight, St.Louis, Doily, 5 Rosettes, Pink & White Canes On Blue, 1972 | 170.00 |
| Paperweight, St.Louis, Faceted Jasper Ground, Red & White, 2 In. | 70.00 |
| Paperweight, St.Louis, Flat Bouquet, 3 In. | 300.00 |
| Paperweight, St.Louis, Marbrie, Magnum | 200.00 |
| Paperweight, St.Louis, Millefiori Canes & 6 Twisted Lace Bars, 1972-73 | 190.00 |
| Paperweight, St.Louis, Millefiori On Blood Red Underlay, 1973-74 Series | 210.00 |
| Paperweight, St.Louis, Millefiori With Lace | 190.00 |
| Paperweight, St.Louis, Mushroom, White Overlay | 210.00 |
| Paperweight, St.Louis, Patterned Millefiori, White & Blue Canes, 1972-73 | 130.00 |
| Paperweight, St.Louis, Pinwheel Swirl, Blue & White | 140.00 |
| Paperweight, St.Louis, Pinwheel Swirl, Five Colors | 140.00 |
| Paperweight, St.Louis, Pistachio Dahlia, 1970, Faceted, 3 1/4 In. | 95.00 |
| Paperweight, St.Louis, Pompon, Pink, 2 3/8 In. | 1300.00 |
| Paperweight, St.Louis, Red Dahlia, 1970, Faceted, 3 In. | 120.00 |
| Paperweight, St.Louis, Red Flower, Faceted | 140.00 |
| Paperweight, St.Louis, Three Poinsettias On Snow White, Limited | 140.00 |
| Paperweight, St.Louis, White Flower On Opaque Orange Underlay, 1973-74 | 190.00 |
| Paperweight, St.Louis, White Latticinio & Multicolor Canes, 1972 | 110.00 |
| Paperweight, St.Louis, Yellow Flower, Faceted | 140.00 |
| Paperweight, Sulfide, Rooster | 15.00 |
| Paperweight, Taunton, Mass., Post Office, Glass, Rectangular | 4.75 |
| Paperweight, The Capitol, Washington, D.C., Glass, Rectangular, 4 X 2 3/4 In. | 4.95 |
| Paperweight, The Crawford Shoe, Phila., 1882, High Shoe Shape, Glass | 9.95 |
| Paperweight, The Judd Mfg.Co., Iron, Ornate, 4 3/4 In.Long | 7.95 |
| Paperweight, Thermometer, Victorian, Colored Sand, 4 In. | 13.50 |
| Paperweight, Timken, Oval, Glass | 6.00 |
| Paperweight, U.S.Glass Co., Pittsburgh, Pa., Glass, Oval | 12.75 |
| Paperweight, Victor Phonograph, Glass, His Master's Voice | 28.00 |
| Paperweight, Washington Mansion, Mt.Vernon, Va., Glass, Rectangular | 4.95 |
| Paperweight, Water, Snow, Girl, Red Hat, Blue Coat | 12.00 |
| Paperweight, Water, Snow, Lighthouse | 12.00 |
| Paperweight, Weave Room No.11, Amosbeag, Manchester, N.H., Glass, Oblong | 4.50 |
| Paperweight, Whimsey, Pig, Millefiori | 85.00 |
| Paperweight, White Anchor Encircled By 2 Rings, 8 White Dots, 3 3/8 In. | 40.00 |
| Paperweight, White Bear In Snow, Brown Pottery Base, 4 In.High | 15.00 |
| Paperweight, Whittemore, Bleeding Heart, Emerald Ground | 350.00 |
| Paperweight, Whittemore, Christmas Stocking, 1972 | 350.00 |
| Paperweight, Whittemore, Holly & Partridge In A Pear Tree | 300.00 |
| Paperweight, Whittemore, Hummingbird, Wine Red Ground | 350.00 |
| Paperweight, Whittemore, Lavender Three Flower Violet, Dome | 300.00 |
| Paperweight, Whittemore, Minnesota Showy Lady Slipper | 350.00 |
| Paperweight, Whittemore, Pink Open Rose & Bud, Dome | 300.00 |
| Paperweight, Whittemore, Upright Blue Rose, Pedestal, 2 1/2 In. | 165.00 |
| Paperweight, Whittemore, Upright White Rose, Pedestal, 2 1/2 In. | 135.00 |
| Paperweight, Wholesale Lumber Co., Omaha, Nebraska, Metal Lion | 9.50 |
| Paperweight, Winchester, Repeating Arms Co., 1910, White Glass | 225.00 |
| Paperweight, Ysart, Colored Butterfly On Twisted Latticinio | 190.00 |
| Paperweight, Ysart, Dragonfly, Blue & White Jasper Ground | 180.00 |
| Paperweight, Ysart, Fish Swimming Over Sand | 280.00 |
| Paperweight, Ysart, Floral Bouquet On Twisted Latticinio, Ribbon | 190.00 |
| Paperweight, Ysart, Flower In Basket | 190.00 |
| Paperweight, Ysart, Large Flower With Leaves | 190.00 |
| Paperweight, Ysart, Lavender Flower On Latticinio | 190.00 |
| Paperweight, Ysart, Lavender Flower, Green & White Latticinio, 2 5/8 In. | 112.50 |
| Paperweight, Ysart, Millefiori On Green Muslin | 130.00 |
| Paperweight, Ysart, Millefiori On Yellow Muslin | 130.00 |
| Paperweight, Ysart, Orange Red Butterfly On Latticinio | 190.00 |
| Paperweight, Ysart, Red & Yellow Flower, Cut Windows, 2 3/4 In. | 65.00 |

| | |
|---|---|
| **Paperweight, Ysart,** Red Flower On Latticinio | 190.00 |
| **Paperweight, Ysart,** Snake | 450.00 |

*Papier-mache is a decorative form made from paper mixed with glue, chalk, and other ingredients, then molded and baked. It becomes very hard and can be decorated. Boxes, trays, and furniture were made of papier-mache. Some of the early nineteenth-century pieces were decorated with mother-of-pearl.*

**Papier-Mache, see also Doll, Furniture**

| | |
|---|---|
| **Papier-Mache, Box,** Courting Scene, Gold Cartouche, Square, 7 1/2 In. | 22.00 |
| **Papier-Mache, Box,** Knife, Handle, 2 Compartments, Stenciled, 12 In.Long | 10.00 |
| **Papier-Mache, Box,** Painting Of Sheik Under Glass On Lid, Black, Oval | 24.00 |
| **Papier-Mache, Box,** Sewing, Victorian, Lacquered, Gold Motifs, 6 1/2 In. High | 100.00 |
| **Papier-Mache, Box,** Victorian, Mother-Of-Pearl Medallion, Hinged, C.1850 | 70.00 |
| **Papier-Mache, Case,** Glasses, Black, Hinged, Mother-Of-Pearl, Inlaid Silver | 14.00 |
| **Papier-Mache, Casket,** Jewel, Victorian, Hinged, Mother-Of-Pearl, 12 In. High | 160.00 |
| **Papier-Mache, Casket,** Mother-Of-Pearl Inlaid, Bombe Shape, C.1850 | 125.00 |
| **Papier-Mache, Figurine,** Cow With Horns, Standing, Glass Eyes, 6 3/4 In.High | 18.00 |
| **Papier-Mache, Inkwell,** Double, Mother-Of-Pearl Inlaid, London | 85.00 |
| **Papier-Mache, Inkwell,** English, 2 Glass Wells, Stamp Box, Mother-Of-Pearl | 48.00 |
| **Papier-Mache, Monkey,** Windup, Glass Eyes | 25.00 |
| **Papier-Mache, Shoe,** Pump, Gilt, 2 In. | 4.00 |
| **Papier-Mache, Snuffbox,** Hinged, Black, Inlaid Silver & Mother-Of-Pearl | 14.00 |
| **Papier-Mache, Snuffbox,** Hinged, Inlaid Pewter Wire & Mother-Of-Pearl | 22.00 |
| **Papier-Mache, Tray Set,** Black, Mother-Of-Pearl, Gold Leaf, Oval, 3 Piece | 230.00 |
| **Papier-Mache, Tray,** Oval, Mother-Of-Pearl Decoration, 24 X 19 In. | 75.00 |
| **Papier-Mache, Tray,** Oval, 29 X 14 In. | 178.00 |

*Parian is a fine-grained, hard-paste porcelain named for the marble it resembles. It was first made in England in 1846 and gained in favor in the United States about 1860. Figures, tea sets, vases, and other items were made of Parian at many English and American factories.*

| | |
|---|---|
| **Parian, Box,** Powder, Basket Of Flowers Shape | 15.00 |
| **Parian, Box,** Trinket, Parian Hand On Top | 25.00 |
| **Parian, Bust,** Adelina Patti, Marked Robinson & Leadbeater, Victorian Gown | 125.00 |
| **Parian, Bust,** Josephine, 7 1/2 In. | 30.00 |
| **Parian, Bust,** Lady, Grecian Hairdo, Off The Shoulder Dress, Footed, 5 In. | 19.00 |
| **Parian, Bust,** Lord Kitchner, City Of London Crest | 22.00 |
| **Parian, Bust,** Moliere, 5 In.High | 12.50 |
| **Parian, Bust,** Queen Victoria, W.H.Goss, Dated 1881, 6 In. | 70.00 |
| **Parian, Bust,** Robert Burns, Marked R & L, 7 1/2 In.High | 65.00 |
| **Parian, Bust,** Sir Walter Scott, Robinson & Leadbeater, C.1870, 7 In. | 35.00 |
| **Parian, Bust,** Thorwaldsen, Danish Sculptor, White, 9 3/4 In.High | 55.00 |
| **Parian, Bust,** Venus, 6 In. | 22.00 |
| **Parian, Bust,** Young Woman, Titled Music, Signed L.A.Malempre, Copeland | 125.00 |
| **Parian, Compote,** Hand Holding Shell, Bennington Type, 8 1/2 In. | 30.00 |
| **Parian, Creamer,** Dolphin, 3 In.High | 10.00 |
| **Parian, Dish,** Hen Cover, 4 In. | 37.75 |
| **Parian, Figurine,** Boy & Dog, 11 X 8 In. | 110.00 |
| **Parian, Figurine,** Cat, Sitting, 6 In.High | 27.50 |
| **Parian, Figurine,** Child Reading Book, German Mark For Hertwig & Co. | 130.00 |
| **Parian, Figurine,** Classical Nude, 22 In.High | 190.00 |
| **Parian, Figurine,** Colin Minton Campbell, Signed Mintons, 19 1/2 In.High | 175.00 |
| **Parian, Figurine,** Nude, Incised E 2282, 22 X 7 In. | 185.00 |
| **Parian, Figurine,** Nude, 22 In.High | 250.00 |
| **Parian, Figurine,** Ruth, White, Oval Base, 13 In.High | 65.00 |
| **Parian, Figurine,** Venus De Milo, Marked Germany, 6 1/2 In. | 35.00 |
| **Parian, Figurine,** Young Boy Holding Wheat, W.H.Goss, 7 In. High | 40.00 |
| **Parian, Pitcher,** Battle Scene In White Relief, Alcock & Co., C.1850 | 50.00 |
| **Parian, Pitcher,** Gypsy, Signed Jones & Walley, Cobridge, C.1842 | 90.00 |
| **Parian, Pitcher,** Hound Handle, 9 In.High | 195.00 |
| **Parian, Pitcher,** Raised Grapes & Leaves, 4 1/4 In. | 48.00 |
| **Parian, Pitcher,** Twisted Handle, Children At Play, 8 1/2 In.High | 87.50 |
| **Parian, Pitcher,** Water, White, Embossed Nude Girl & Cupid, 8 1/4 In. | 75.00 |
| **Parian, Pitcher,** White, Relief Boy With Bow & Arrow & Eagle, 9 1/2 In. | 125.00 |
| **Parian, Plaque,** George Washington, Oval, Blue & White | 29.50 |
| **Parian, Plaque,** The Selling Of Babies, 11 X 7 In. | 75.00 |
| **Parian, Ring Tree,** Leaves | 12.50 |
| **Parian, Syrup,** Pewter Hinged Lid, Embossed Design | 58.00 |

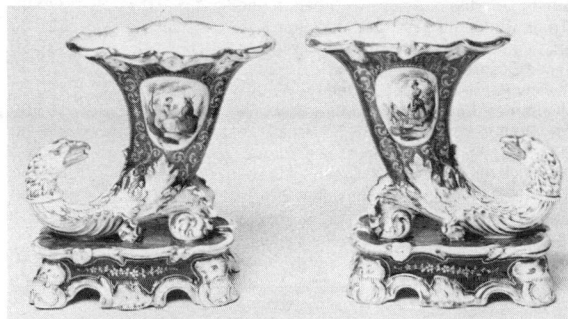

Paris, Cornucopia, Crimson,
Gilding, C.1890, 9 In., Pair

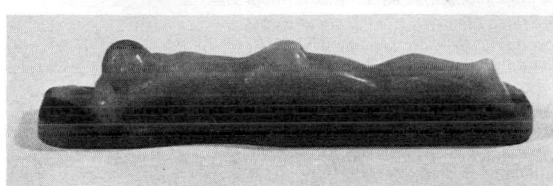

Pate De Verre, Figurine, Female, A.Walter Nancy

Pate De Verre, Vase, Yellow Green,
Walter Nancy, C.1920
(See Page 372)

| | |
|---|---|
| **Parian, Vase,** Prince Albert's Portrait, Grapes & Leaves, C.1847, 8 1/2 In. | 130.00 |
| **Paris, Cachepot,** Shell Handles, Floral Medallions, 4 1/8 In., Pair | 325.00 |
| **Paris, Cornucopia,** Crimson, Gilding, C.1890, 9 In., Pair *Illus* | 250.00 |
| **Paris, Cup & Saucer,** Empire, Serpent Handle, Flower Filled Basket, C.1815 | 125.00 |
| **Paris, Flowerpot,** Covered, 4 Gilt Claw Feet, Landscapes, C.1815, Pair | 225.00 |
| **Paris, Matchbox,** Asparagus Form, Covered, Blue Bow, Red Ribbon, Striker, 1850 | 90.00 |
| **Paris, Pitcher,** Milk, Oval, Hand-Painted Multicolor Floral, Gold, C.1850 | 65.00 |
| **Paris, Plaque,** Derby Style Floral Bouquet, C.1890, 17 3/4 In. | 1200.00 |
| **Paris, Plate,** Three Travelers, Mountains, Green Border, C.1790, 9 1/8 In. | 100.00 |
| **Paris, Tea Set,** Gold Bands, Leaves Edged In Gold, 5 Piece | 95.00 |
| **Paris, Tea Set,** Inverted Pear Shape, Gold Medallions, Turquoise, 21 Piece | 155.00 |
| **Paris, Urn,** Campana Shape, Cavalier & Lady Reserves On Gold, C.1890, Pair | 200.00 |
| **Paris, Urn,** Ovoid, Sphinx Shape Handles, Scenic, C.1850, 26 In., Pair | 450.00 |
| **Paris, Vase,** Blue Trim, Hand-Painted Bird & Floral, 17 In.High, Pair | 195.00 |
| **Paris, Vase,** Empire, Double Cherub Handles, Classical Figures, C.1820, Pair | 400.00 |
| **Paris, Vase,** Hunters Outside Villa, Gilt Scrollwork, C.1800s, 7 1/4 In.High | 60.00 |
| **Paris, Vase,** Open Blossom Shape, Reserve Panel, C.1890, 12 1/2 In., Pair | 75.00 |
| **Paris, Vase,** Portrait, Dark Haired Woman, Green, 11 In.High, Pair | 175.00 |
| **Paris, Vase,** Winged Figure Handles, Chactas & Atala, C.1890, 11 1/2 In., Pair | 300.00 |
| **Paris, Veilleuse,** Teapot, White, Gold Gilt Decoration, 5 Pieces | 115.00 |

> *Pate De Verre is an ancient technique in which glass is made by blending and refining powdered glass of different colors into molds. The process was revived by French glassmakers, especially Galle, around the end of the nineteenth century.*

| | |
|---|---|
| **Pate De Verre, Ashtray,** Rectangular, Handles, Green, 8 3/4 In. Long | 700.00 |
| **Pate De Verre, Bowl,** A.Walter Nancy, Yellow Green, Fish On End, 8 3/4 In. | 850.00 |
| **Pate De Verre, Bowl,** Blue, Stylized Leafage, 4 1/2 In. | 800.00 |
| **Pate De Verre, Coupe,** Yellow, Orange, & Purple Decoration, G.Argy-Rousseau | 300.00 |
| **Pate De Verre, Dish,** Chameleon Cover, Clear, Traces Of Lavender, 5 In. | 375.00 |
| **Pate De Verre, Dish,** Lemon To Orange, Salamander On End, Walter Nancy, 1920s | 1100.00 |
| **Pate De Verre, Dish,** Ocher & Yellow, Cockroach At Center, Walter Nancy, 1925 | 900.00 |
| **Pate De Verre, Figurine,** Bird, Signed A.Walter Nancy | 950.00 |
| **Pate De Verre, Figurine,** Female, A.Walter Nancy *Illus* | 425.00 |

Pate De Verre, Figurine, Monkey, Sitting On Stump, Amber To Green, Signed ............................ 375.00
Pate De Verre, Inkwell Disc, Tree Trunk On Round Base, Bee, A.Walter & Berg ........................ 525.00
Pate De Verre, Liqueur, Blue Flowers, Signed G.Argy-Rousseau, 2 In.High ............................... 36.50
Pate De Verre, Mask, Napoleon, Signed Despret, White .......................................................... 295.00
Pate De Verre, Pendant, Purple & Yellow Pansy On Green, Signed A.W. .................................. 150.00
Pate De Verre, Pendant, S.A.R., Holly Berries, Rousseau ....................................................... 165.00
Pate De Verre, Vase, Classical Shape, Orange Poppies, G.Argy-Rousseau .............................. 375.00
Pate De Verre, Vase, Fuchsia Floral On Gray Blue, G.Argy-Rousseau ..................................... 360.00
Pate De Verre, Vase, G.Argy-Rousseau, Cylindrical, Mauve & Green In Gray ........................... 475.00
Pate De Verre, Vase, Green, Brown & Yellow, Raised Keystones, 3 1/2 In. ............................. 500.00
Pate De Verre, Vase, Hexagonal, Integral Geometric Handles, Purple, 9 In. ............................ 850.00
Pate De Verre, Vase, Red Shell At Base, Purple Mottled, G.Argy-Rousseau ............................ 450.00
Pate De Verre, Vase, Red, Yellow, Brown, & Black Geometrics, G.Argy-Rousseau .................... 525.00
Pate De Verre, Vase, Yellow Green, Walter Nancy, C.1920 ................................... *Illus*   800.00
> *Pate-Sur-Pate means paste on paste. The design was made by painting layers*
> *of slip(which see) on the piece until a relief decoration was formed. The*
> *method was developed at the Sevres factory in France about 1850. It*
> *became even more famous at the English Minton factory about 1870.*
Pate-Sur-Pate, Box, Puff, Covered, Winged Cherubs, Floral, & Bird, Pink ................................ 47.00
Pate-Sur-Pate, Plaque, Five Nude Women & Swan In Woodland, 12 X 9 In. .............................. 175.00
Pate-Sur-Pate, Plaque, 2 Hunting Dogs, Foliage, & Brace Of Birds, Green ............................... 155.00
Patent Model, Shoe, No.26939 & 31673, L.Warden, G.Mitchell, March 1861 ............................ 64.50
Patent Model, Shoe, No.30034, J.Allen, Boot & Shoe, Sept.18, 1860, Leather ......................... 47.50
Paul Revere, Bowl, Band Of Reclining Rabbits & Blue Sky Over Gray ..................................... 75.00
Paul Revere, Plate, Blue Gray Flowers, Signed S.E.G. ......................................................... 25.00
Paul Revere, Plate, Pinecones, S.E.G., 6 1/2 In. ............................................................... 36.00
Pauline Pottery, Bowl, Poppy Decoration, Shaded Yellow Glaze, 9 1/2 In.Diam. ...................... 115.00
> *Peachblow glass originated about 1883 at Hobbs, Brockunier and Company of*
> *Wheeling, West Virginia. It is a glass that shades from yellow to peach.*
> *It was lined in white. New England Peachblow is a one-layer glass with a*
> *lining shading from red to white. Mt.Washington Peachblow shades from pink*
> *to blue. Reproductions of Peachblow have been made, but they are of a poor*
> *quality and can be detected.*
Peachblow, see also Webb, Peachblow
Peachblow, Bowl, Finger, Wheeling ................................................................................. 295.00
Peachblow, Bowl, Gunderson, Deep To Cream Base, 3 Leaflike Feet, Round ............................ 175.00
Peachblow, Bowl, New Martinsville, Sunburst, Ruffled, Ribbed, Burmese Inside ...................... 245.00
Peachblow, Bowl, Ruffled Top, Shades To Deep Rose, 5 1/4 In. ........................................... 300.00
Peachblow, Bowl, Wheeling, 4 In. ................................................................................... 75.00
Peachblow, Bride's Basket, New Martinsville, Silver Plated Holder ........................................ 185.00
Peachblow, Compote, Pairpoint, Bryden, 6 In.Diameter ....................................................... 35.00
Peachblow, Compote, Sweetmeat, Pairpoint ...................................................................... 35.00
Peachblow, Creamer, Wheeling, Applied Amber Handle, Mahogany To Yellow Base ................... 695.00
Peachblow, Creamer, Wheeling, Mustard Base To Mahogany Top, 4 1/2 In.High ....................... 750.00
Peachblow, Cruet, Moss Rose Decoration .......................................................................... 25.00
Peachblow, Cruet, Wheeling, Applied Amber Reeded Handle, Amber Stopper ......................... 1050.00
Peachblow, Cruet, Wheeling, Flattened Ovoid, Rope Handle, Amber Stopper ........................... 975.00
Peachblow, Cruet, Wheeling, Yellow To Mahogany Shading .................................................. 695.00
Peachblow, Cup, Punch, Libbey, Applied White Handle, "World's Fair, 1893" ........................... 300.00
Peachblow, Cup, Punch, Wheeling .................................................................................. 235.00
Peachblow, Decanter, Wheeling, Flattened Ovoid, Rope Handle, Amber Stopper ...................... 1295.00
Peachblow, Dish, Candy, Pairpoint, Bryden, Decorated, Fluted, Signed .................................. 45.00
Peachblow, Gunderson, see Gunderson, Peachblow
Peachblow, Jar, Powder, New England, Decorated, White Lining, 3 1/2 In. ............................. 400.00
Peachblow, Lamp, Pedestal, Fittings, Chimney .................................................................. 200.00
Peachblow, Pear, New England, Stem, 5 In.High, 3 In.Diameter ........................................... 135.00
Peachblow, Pear, Wheeling, Stem ................................................................................... 85.00
Peachblow, Pitcher, Wheeling, Acid Finish, Applied Lemon Handle, 6 1/2 In. .......................... 200.00
Peachblow, Rose Bowl, Libbey, Fluted Top, 3 In.High ......................................................... 175.00
Peachblow, Rose Bowl, New England, World's Fair, 1893 ..................................................... 350.00
Peachblow, Salt, Original Top ........................................................................................ 125.00
Peachblow, Shade, Sandwich, Ruffled, Scalloped, Hobnail, Opalescent, 5 In. .......................... 55.00
Peachblow, Toothpick, New England, Glossy ..................................................................... 325.00
Peachblow, Toothpick, New England, Square Top, 2 1/4 In.High .......................................... 225.00
Peachblow, Toothpick, Wheeling, Bulbous Center .............................................................. 350.00
Peachblow, Tumbler, New England, Glossy, Coloring Halfway Down ...................................... 275.00

| | |
|---|---|
| Peachblow, Tumbler, Shades To Deep Rose, 3 1/2 In. | 170.00 |
| Peachblow, Vase, Gunderson, Bulbous, 9 In. | 350.00 |
| Peachblow, Vase, Lily, Yellow To Burgundy At Top, 6 In. | 275.00 |
| Peachblow, Vase, New England, Gourd Shape, Enameled Lydia, World's Fair, 1893 | 275.00 |
| Peachblow, Vase, New England, Jack-In-The-Pulpit, Raspberry To White Base | 400.00 |
| Peachblow, Vase, New England, 3 Petal Lily, Acid Finish, 7 3/4 In.High | 475.00 |
| Peachblow, Vase, Sandwich, Piecrust Jack-In-The-Pulpit Top, 4 In., Pair | 195.00 |
| Peachblow, Vase, Urn Shape, Webb Type, Applied Clear Handles, C.1895, 6 In. | 75.00 |
| Peachblow, Vase, Wheeling, Double Gourd, To Deep Mahogany, 7 1/2 In. | 240.00 |
| Peachblow, Vase, Wheeling, Stick Top, Bulbous Bottom, Acid Finish | 695.00 |
| Peachblow, Vase, Wheeling, 6 In.High | 350.00 |
| Pearl, Carving Set, Sheffield Ferrules, Leather Case, 3 Piece | 65.00 |
| Pearl, Carving Set, Sterling Ferrules, Universal Blade & Tines, 2 Piece | 14.50 |
| Pearl, Counter, Game, Chinese, Fish Shape, Engraved Scenes | 2.00 |
| Pearl, Fish Set, Engraved Blades, Sterling Ferrules, 10 Piece | 78.00 |
| Pearl, Fork, Serving, Wide Silver Tines, 8 1/4 In.Long | 10.00 |
| Pearl, Fork, Serving, 8 1/2 In. | 9.50 |
| Pearl, Fork, 3 Tines, 5 1/2 In.Long | 4.00 |
| Pearl, Fruit Set, Beaded Knives & Forks, Set Of 4 | 59.00 |
| Pearl, Knife & Fork, Sterling Ferrule & Cap, Set Of 12 In Wooden Box | 195.00 |
| Pearl, Knife & Fork, Sterling Ferrules, Mother Of Pearl, Landers, Frary, Clark | 12.85 |
| Pearl, Knife, Butter, Bamboo Design | 9.00 |
| Pearl, Knife, Butter, Plain Handle | 8.00 |
| Pearl, Knife, Carving, Embossed Silver Ferrule, 11 1/2 In.Long | 11.00 |
| Pearl, Knife, Dinner, Cut Florals On Handle, Sheffield Blade | 14.50 |
| Pearl, Knife, Dinner, Sterling Fittings, English Hallmarked, C.1905 | 7.50 |
| Pearl, Knife, Luncheon, Plated Blade, Sterling Ferrules, Set Of 6 | 35.00 |
| Pearl, Knife, Luncheon, Silver Plated Blade, Landers, Frary, & Clark | 5.85 |
| Pearl, Knife, Luncheon, Sterling Ferule, Silver Plate Blade | 5.75 |
| Pearl, Knife, Sterling Band, Landers, Frary, & Clard, 7 In. | 5.00 |
| Pearl, Knife, Sterling Ferule, Lambert, Frary, & Clark, Set Of 12 | 58.00 |
| Pearl, Knife, Sterling Ferules, 8 In. Long, Set Of 12 | 42.00 |
| Pearl, Server, Cheese, Decorated Blade | 16.00 |
| Pearl, Server, Vegetable, Cutout Oblong Bowl, 8 1/4 In. | 9.50 |
| Pearl, Shell, Carved, Chinese Scenes | 20.00 |
| Pearl, Spoon, Serving, Ladlelike Bowl, Silver, 8 1/2 In. | 10.00 |
| Pearl, Spreader, Butter, Silver, 7 1/2 In.Long | 8.50 |
| Pearl, Snuffbox, Gold Mounts, Chinoiserie, 2 3/4 In. Long | 2000.00 |
| Pearl, Snuffbox, Silver Mounts, Cartouche Shape, C.1850 | 300.00 |

*Peking glass is a Chinese cameo glass of the eighteenth and nineteenth centuries.*

| | |
|---|---|
| Peking, Beads, Trade, Hudson Bay, Hen's Eggs, Black & Blue, 49 On Strand | 59.50 |
| Peking, Beads, Trade, Jade Green, 30 In.Long String | 10.00 |
| Peking, Bottle, Snuff, Blue Floral Overlay, Bronze Forms | 65.00 |
| Peking, Bottle, Snuff, Red & Green Floral Overlay On Yellow | 240.00 |
| Peking, Bowl, Amethyst, Deep, 2 1/4 In.High, Pair | 75.00 |
| Peking, Bowl, Mandarin Yellow, Carved Floral & Leaf, 7 In. | 210.00 |
| Peking, Box, Rose, Yellow, & Green On Blue, Floral & Fruit, C.1750 | 195.00 |
| Peking, Matchbox, Silver, Enameled, Gold & Cobalt On Light Blue, 2 In.High | 75.00 |
| Peking, Teapot, Figural Painting On Pink & Green, Bale Handle | 165.00 |
| Peking, Toothpick, Blue, 1 7/8 In.High | 15.00 |
| Peking, Toothpick, Peachblow | 25.00 |
| Peking, Toothpick, Spinach Green | 25.00 |
| Peking, Vase, Blue Cameo Floral On White, 3 1/2 In.High | 95.00 |
| Peking, Vase, Bulbous, Long Neck, Scarlet Cut To Yellow, Cameo, 5 3/4 In. | 345.00 |
| Peking, Vase, Red Overlay Blossoms On Tree Bough On White, C.1950, Pair | 225.00 |

*Peloton glass is European glass with small threads of colored glass rolled onto the surface of clear or colored glass. It is sometimes called spaghetti or shredded coconut glass.*

| | |
|---|---|
| Peloton, Jar, Biscuit, Purple, Colored Filaments, Pewter Cover | 95.00 |
| Peloton, Pitcher, Cranberry, Polychrome Shredded Coconut, Clear Handle | 145.00 |
| Peloton, Pitcher, Pink, White, Yellow, & Blue Spaghetti On Light Blue, 6 In. | 125.00 |
| Peloton, Pitcher, Vermiculated Decoration, Pink Floral On Blue, 6 In. | 150.00 |
| Peloton, Pitcher, Water, Bulbous, White, Enameled Floral, Applied Handle | 185.00 |

Peloton, Plate, Rose Spaghetti On Clear, Enameled, 5 1/2 In. .................................... 55.00
Peloton, Syrup, Ribbed Purple Iridescent, Self Threading, Hinged Pewter Lid ........................ 55.00
    Pen, see Store, Pen
    Pencil, see Store, Pencil
Peoria, Jar, Cookie, Marked ......................................................................... 20.00
Peoria, Jug, Gallon ................................................................................ 30.00

> *Peters and Reed Pottery Company of Zanesville, Ohio, was founded by*
> *John D. Peters and Adam Reed in 1897. Chromal, Landswn, Montene,*
> *Pereco, and Persian are some of the art lines that were made until the*
> *company closed in 1920.*

Peters & Reed, Vase, Chromal, 5 1/2 In.High ..................................................... 20.00

> *Pewter is a metal alloy of tin and lead. Some of the pewter made after*
> *about 1840 has a slightly different composition and is called Britannia*
> *metal.*

Pewter, Ashtray, Selangor, Malaysia, Singapore, Round, 5 In. ...................................... 22.50
Pewter, Basin, American, 8 In. ..................................................................... 65.00
Pewter, Basin, American, 8 In. Diameter ........................................................... 100.00
Pewter, Basin, Curtis & Co., Boy & Dolphin Touchmark, 10 In. ..................................... 225.00
Pewter, Basin, Double Porringer Type Side Lip Handles, 12 X 9 X 5 In. ............................ 135.00
Pewter, Basin, Marked K.T.R. & Kel-Rie No.1043, Side Handles, 12 In. .............................. 20.00
Pewter, Basin, Touchmark, 6 5/8 In. ............................................................... 85.00
Pewter, Basin, 8 In.Diameter, 2 In.Deep ........................................................... 75.00
Pewter, Basket, Standard, R.H.May Co., 6 1/2 In. .................................................. 12.00
Pewter, Beaker, American, 3 In. High .............................................................. 45.00
Pewter, Beaker, Kayzerzinn, Embossed Grapes & Leaves, 'Ergo Bibamus' .............................. 45.00
Pewter, Beaker, Samuel Danforth, Molded Foot, Flaring Rim, C.1775, 5 1/4 In. ...................... 375.00
Pewter, Bedpan, 11 1/2 In.Diameter ................................................................ 35.00
Pewter, Bowl, Boardman & Co., N.Y., C.1825, 9 5/8 In. .................................... *Illus* 175.00
Pewter, Bowl, Continental, Deep, C.1850, 9 1/4 In. Diameter ....................................... 45.00
Pewter, Bowl, Crescent, Footed, 8 1/4 In.Diameter ................................................. 11.00
Pewter, Bowl, English, Hammered, 4 1/4 In.Diameter ................................................ 4.25
Pewter, Bowl, Kayzerzinn, Tulip, Leaves, 11 X 2 In. ............................................... 25.00
Pewter, Bowl, Serving, Continental, 2 Handles, 8 1/2 X 15 In. ..................................... 35.00
Pewter, Bowl, Soup, Incised W.P. In Rim, Deep, 11 1/2 In. ........................................ 200.00
Pewter, Box, Pen, Monogrammed J.W., Footed, 7 1/4 X 5 In. ......................................... 75.00
Pewter, Bust, Young Woman In Bonnet, German, Signed Schreiner, 11 1/2 In. ........................ 350.00
Pewter, Can, Nathaniel Austin, Domed Foot, Strap Handle, C.1763, 6 1/4 In. ...................... 1600.00
Pewter, Can, Peter Young, Cylindrical, Scroll Handle, Molded Base, C.1775 ....................... 1000.00
Pewter, Can, Samuel Hamlin, R.I., Cylindrical, Scroll Handle, C.1771, 6 In. ..................... 1100.00
Pewter, Candelabra, K.S.Co., Marked P402, Pair .................................................... 50.00
Pewter, Candleholder, B.L.Co., 4 In.High, Pair .................................................... 65.00
Pewter, Candleholder, Marked B, 4 In. High, Pair .................................................. 50.00
Pewter, Candlesnuffer, Lily Shape, Twisted Brass Handle, Jade & Amber, China ...................... 27.00

Pewter, Bowl, Boardman & Co.,
N.Y., C.1825, 9 5/8 In.

Pewter, Coffeepot, Allen Porter, Maine, C.1830, 12 In.
*(See Page 375)*

Pewter, Inkstand, C.1800, 3 X 9 In.
*(See Page 376)*

Pewter, Flagon, Boardman & Co.,
N.Y., C.1826, 12 1/2 In.

| | |
|---|---:|
| Pewter, Candlestick, C.1850, 8 3/4 In.High | 50.00 |
| Pewter, Candlestick, English, 10 In.High, Pair | 125.00 |
| Pewter, Candlestick, Queen Anne, 8 In.High, Pair | 105.00 |
| Pewter, Candlestick, Taunton Britannia, Ring Turned, Vasiform, C.1830, Pair | 400.00 |
| Pewter, Candlestick, Vase Shape Center Post, 7 1/2 In.High, Pair | 50.00 |
| Pewter, Candlestick, 10 In., Pair | 145.00 |
| Pewter, Canteen, Drum Shape, Spout, 6 In.Diameter, C.1800 | 97.50 |
| Pewter, Castor Frame, 5 Hole | 9.75 |
| Pewter, Castor Stand, For Four Bottles, Plain Pattern | 12.00 |
| Pewter, Centerpiece, Tudric, England, Squat, 3 Applied Bilobed Handles, 9 In. | 275.00 |
| Pewter, Chalice, R.Strickland, Albany, N.Y., 7 1/8 In., Pair | 400.00 |
| Pewter, Chalice, William Calder, 6 In. | 245.00 |
| Pewter, Charger, American, 13 In. | 410.00 |
| Pewter, Charger, American, 16 In., Pair | 550.00 |
| Pewter, Charger, Edgar Co., Smooth Brim, 18 In. | 165.00 |
| Pewter, Charger, English, 16 In. | 175.00 |
| Pewter, Charger, Erasmus Dole, 13 3/4 In. | 325.00 |
| Pewter, Charger, London Hallmarks, Engraved Armorial Bearing, C.1765, 17 In. | 195.00 |
| Pewter, Charger, Samuel Ellis, 16 In. | 150.00 |
| Pewter, Charger, Touchmark, 13 1/2 In. | 145.00 |
| Pewter, Charger, Touchmark, 15 In. | 95.00 |
| Pewter, Charger, 12 In. | 100.00 |
| Pewter, Charger, 13 In. | 120.00 |
| Pewter, Coat Of Arms, French, 10 3/4 In.Square | 128.00 |
| Pewter, Coffeepot, Allen Porter, Maine, C.1830, 12 In. *Illus* | 400.00 |
| Pewter, Coffeepot, Atkin Brothers, Wooden Handle, 10 In. | 36.00 |
| Pewter, Coffeepot, Boardman & Co., N.Y., No Lid, 9 In.High | 100.00 |
| Pewter, Coffeepot, Boardman, Lion Touchmark, 11 In. | 280.00 |
| Pewter, Coffeepot, Chelsea Type, Early 19th Century | 125.00 |
| Pewter, Coffeepot, F.Porter, Westbrook, Me., C.1840, 11 3/4 In. | 465.00 |
| Pewter, Coffeepot, Morey & Ober | 225.00 |
| Pewter, Coffeepot, Rockford Co., 10 1/2 In.High | 75.00 |
| Pewter, Coffeepot, Sheets Co., 9 In.High | 50.00 |
| Pewter, Coffeepot, Unmarked, C.1870, 11 In.High | 75.00 |
| Pewter, Coffeepot, Vickers, 12 In. | 78.00 |
| Pewter, Console Set, Mayflower, WB Mfg. Co., Russian Wolfhounds, 3 Piece | 125.00 |
| Pewter, Cruet Stand, 5 Glass Cruets | 68.00 |
| Pewter, Cup, Beer, German Military Motif, Relief Decoration, 5 1/2 In.High | 110.00 |
| Pewter, Cup, Chalice, Kaiserzinn, Art Nouveau Style, 6 1/2 In.High | 45.00 |
| Pewter, Cup, Collapsible, Tin Case | 5.95 |
| Pewter, Dish, Chinese, Leaf Form, White Jade Stem Handle, Brass Rim | 22.00 |
| Pewter, Dish, Nut, Old George Inn, London, Victorian Period | 32.00 |
| Pewter, Flagon, Boardman & Co., N.Y., C.1826, 12 1/2 In. *Illus* | 900.00 |
| Pewter, Flagon, Boardman & Co., N.Y., Domed Top, Double Scroll Handle, C.1825 | 1000.00 |
| Pewter, Flagon, Civil War Era, 12 1/2 In.High | 900.00 |
| Pewter, Flagon, Thomas & Sherman Boardman, Double Scroll Handle, C.1810 | 1300.00 |

| | |
|---|---:|
| Pewter, Flagon, William Will, Phila., Domed Top, Scroll Handle, C.1764, 14 In. | 7000.00 |
| Pewter, Flagon, 11 1/2 In. | 155.00 |
| Pewter, Flask, British Officer's Field, Oval, Initials R.A.E., 1858-1860 | 125.00 |
| Pewter, Frame, Easel, Engraved, George Washington Picture, Copyright 1893 | 35.00 |
| Pewter, Frame, Photograph, Filigree, Oval Inside, 6 X 8 In. | 13.50 |
| Pewter, Funnel, C.1840 | 45.00 |
| Pewter, Funnel, Georgian, Large Size | 65.00 |
| Pewter, Humidor, Inset Enamel Plaque Of Landscape, Liberty & Co., 8 In. | 60.00 |
| Pewter, Inkstand, Badger, 2 Ring Turned Inks On Oblong Footed Tray, C.1750 | 200.00 |
| Pewter, Inkstand, C.1800, 3 X 9 In. *Illus* | 250.00 |
| Pewter, Inkstand, Cobalt Liner, 6 Quill Holes | 98.00 |
| Pewter, Inkwell, Capstan, Hinged Cover, 4 Hole | 38.00 |
| Pewter, Inkwell, Round, Dome Roll Top, 5 In.Base | 65.00 |
| Pewter, Inkwell, School Desk | 45.00 |
| Pewter, Jar, Tobacco, 5 1/2 In.High To Top Of Cover | 24.00 |
| Pewter, Ladle, John Yates, 12 In. | 45.00 |
| Pewter, Ladle, John Yates, 14 In. | 60.00 |
| Pewter, Ladle, Wooden Handle, 14 In.Long | 45.00 |
| Pewter, Lamp, Brass Burner, 3 3/4 In. | 115.00 |
| Pewter, Lamp, American, Urn Font, Tall Pedestal, 12 In. | 75.00 |
| Pewter, Lamp, American, Bell Shape | 50.00 |
| Pewter, Lamp, Nursing, Putnam, Mass., Saucer Base, Loop Handle, C.1830 | 100.00 |
| Pewter, Match Safe, Pocket, Marked Puritan Pewter, Engraved Swinging Golfer | 18.00 |
| Pewter, Measure, Gill, Irish, Noggin | 65.00 |
| Pewter, Measure, Grain, Gill, American | 24.00 |
| Pewter, Measure, Grain, Pint, American, Double C Scroll Handle, Baluster | 50.00 |
| Pewter, Measure, Grain, Pint, American, Glass Bottom | 45.00 |
| Pewter, Measure, Grain, Quart, Yates & Birch, Baluster | 60.00 |
| Pewter, Measure, Grain, 1/4 Gill, Mason | 21.00 |
| Pewter, Measure, Grain, 1/2 Gill, Mason | 22.00 |
| Pewter, Measure, Grain, 1/2 Pint, American | 20.00 |
| Pewter, Measure, Pint, Baluster, Scrolled Handle | 60.00 |
| Pewter, Measure, Spirit, Cylindrical, Loop Handles, C.1800, 2 1/8 In. High | 37.00 |
| Pewter, Measure, Spirit, Cylindrical, Loop Handles, C.1800, 2 5/8 In. High | 40.00 |
| Pewter, Measure, 1/2 Gill, English, C.1840 | 45.00 |
| Pewter, Measuring Set, Baluster, S Handles, Pint To 1/4 Gill, 5 Piece | 135.00 |
| Pewter, Measuring Set, Liter To 2 Centiliters, Alphabet Rims, Set Of 7 | 110.00 |
| Pewter, Medallion, Princess Victoria, Age 18, Dated May 24, 1837, 2 In. | 19.00 |
| Pewter, Mold, Candle, 18 Tube, Pine Frame, W.Webb, N.Y., C.1810, 18 In.High | 525.00 |
| Pewter, Mold, Chocolate, Bell And Top, Dutch | 20.00 |
| Pewter, Mold, Chocolate, Upright Rabbit, 6 1/2 In.High | 14.00 |
| Pewter, Mold, Dessert, Santa Claus, Hinged, 5 In.High | 18.50 |
| Pewter, Mold, Double Lamb, Marked Weygandt, N.Y., 6629 | 16.00 |
| Pewter, Mold, For Chalk Horse, Marked C.C., 3 Sections, 9 1/2 In. | 65.00 |
| Pewter, Mold, For Chalk Kissing Doves, Marked C.C., 3 Sections, 11 1/2 In. | 30.00 |
| Pewter, Mold, Ice Cream, American Beauty Rose | 10.00 |
| Pewter, Mold, Ice Cream, Baby On Chick | 11.50 |
| Pewter, Mold, Ice Cream, Baby's Basinette | 9.00 |
| Pewter, Mold, Ice Cream, Basket, Oval | 10.00 |
| Pewter, Mold, Ice Cream, Bell With Cupid | 12.00 |
| Pewter, Mold, Ice Cream, Book, Open, Marked DES COP RD 1882 | 10.00 |
| Pewter, Mold, Ice Cream, Carnation | 10.00 |
| Pewter, Mold, Ice Cream, Christmas Wreath | 18.00 |
| Pewter, Mold, Ice Cream, Chrysanthemum | 12.00 |
| Pewter, Mold, Ice Cream, Cluster Of Cherries | 9.00 |
| Pewter, Mold, Ice Cream, Corn With Husk | 13.00 |
| Pewter, Mold, Ice Cream, Cupid, Sitting | 10.00 |
| Pewter, Mold, Ice Cream, Cupid, Standing | 12.00 |
| Pewter, Mold, Ice Cream, Daisy | 11.50 |
| Pewter, Mold, Ice Cream, Engagement Ring Diamond With Flowers | 10.00 |
| Pewter, Mold, Ice Cream, George Washington's Hatchet With G.W. | 13.00 |
| Pewter, Mold, Ice Cream, Lily, Calla | 10.00 |
| Pewter, Mold, Ice Cream, Lily, Easter | 10.00 |
| Pewter, Mold, Ice Cream, Mars Star | 14.00 |
| Pewter, Mold, Ice Cream, Masonic Square & Compass, Hinged, 2 Part | 17.75 |
| Pewter, Mold, Ice Cream, Rabbit, Sitting | 11.00 |

Pewter, Mold, Ice Cream, Rosebud ................................................................. 10.00
Pewter, Mold, Ice Cream, Santa Claus, Hinged, 5 In. ................................... 24.00
Pewter, Mold, Ice Cream, Slipper ........................................ 4.50 To 10.00
Pewter, Mold, Ice Cream, Snowball, Flower ................................................. 10.00
Pewter, Mold, Ice Cream, Star Medallion ..................................................... 12.00
Pewter, Mold, Ice Cream, Top Hat .................................................................. 18.00
Pewter, Mold, Ice Cream, Tulip ....................................................................... 12.00
Pewter, Mold, Ice Cream, Turkey, Roasted ................................................... 9.00
Pewter, Mold, Ice Cream, Turkey, Standing .................................................. 12.00
Pewter, Mold, Ice Cream, Two Cooing Doves ............................................... 12.00
Pewter, Mold, Ice Cream, Valentine Heart ..................................................... 10.00
Pewter, Mold, Ice Cream, Wedding Ring With Fancy Flowers ..................... 10.00
Pewter, Mold, Question Mark, Hinged, Marked S.& Co., 288 ..................... 16.50
Pewter, Mold, Sailing Ship, T.Mills & Bros., Phila., 1865, 2 Piece ............ 35.00
Pewter, Mold, Spoon, For Brass Tablespoons, C.1750 ............................. 240.00
Pewter, Mortar, Double Handled, Apothecary Display Piece, 14 X 8 In. ..... 248.00
Pewter, Mug, Chinese, Glass Bottom, Raised Dragon Motif, C.1850, 4 In.High .... 22.50
Pewter, Mug, Chinese, Raised Dragon Decoration, Glass Bottom, 4 In.High ...... 22.50
Pewter, Mug, Drinking, Chinese Markings, Glass Bottom, 5 1/2 In. ............ 22.50
Pewter, Mug, Footed, Fishtail Handle, C.1830, 1/2 Pint, Set Of 4 ............. 168.00
Pewter, Mug, Handleless, 1/2 Pint, Set Of 6 .............................................. 168.00
Pewter, Mug, James Yates, Double C Scroll Handle, Tapered, Pint ............ 50.00
Pewter, Mug, James Yates, Fishtail Handle & Side Spout, Footed, C.1890, Pint ...... 98.00
Pewter, Mug, Joseph Sicart, Feinn-Zinn, 5 In. .............................................. 42.00
Pewter, Mug, Marked Nunn Hertford, Straight Sides, C.1840, Quart .......... 45.00
Pewter, Opener, Letter, Nazi, Screaming Eagle At Top ................................ 14.00
Pewter, Pitcher, Boardman, Hartford, C.1860, Hinged Lid, 10 In. .............. 595.00
Pewter, Pitcher, Freeman Porter, Maine, C.1835, 6 3/4 In. ............... Illus  300.00
Pewter, Pitcher, Homan & Co., Cincinnati, Covered, 7 1/2 In. ................... 165.00
Pewter, Pitcher, Signed, 7 1/4 In.High ............................................................ 22.00
Pewter, Pitcher, Water, Boardman & Hart, N.Y., 8 In. ................................ 280.00
Pewter, Pitcher, Water, Kayserzinn, Mephistopheles, Art Nouveau, 12 1/2 In. ...... 130.00
Pewter, Pitcher, Water, Reed & Barton, 8 3/8 In.High .................................. 20.00
Pewter, Plate, B.Barnes, Phila., Eagle Touchmark With B.B., 8 In. ........... 155.00
Pewter, Plate, B.Barns, Phila., C.1815, 7 7/8 In. ...................... 250.00 To 275.00
Pewter, Plate, Benjamin & Joseph Harbeson, Molded Rim, C.1793, 5 7/8 In. ...... 350.00
Pewter, Plate, Boardman & Co., Conn., Deep, C.1825, 9 3/8 In. ............... 325.00
Pewter, Plate, Bronstrom, Lovebird's Mark, Molded Rim, Phila., C.1781, 6 In. .... 500.00
Pewter, Plate, Colonel John Carnes, Boston, Molded Rim, C.1723, 7 1/2 In. ...... 800.00
Pewter, Plate, D.Mellvile, Newport, 8 In. ...................................................... 270.00
Pewter, Plate, David Melville, R.I., C.1780, 8 1/4 In. ................................... 305.00
Pewter, Plate, English, Applied Square Rigged Warship Medallion, 1709, 7 In. .... 150.00
Pewter, Plate, English, Touchmark, C.1750, 8 In. ......................................... 45.00
Pewter, Plate, English, Touchmark, C.1750, 9 In. ......................................... 45.00
Pewter, Plate, Hot Water, Calder, Scalloped Handles, 9 In. ...................... 195.00
Pewter, Plate, Hot Water, Calder, 2 Scroll Handles, 9 In. ......................... 146.00
Pewter, Plate, I.B.Finck, 8 1/4 In. ................................................................... 40.00
Pewter, Plate, Love, Phila., C.1800, 8 In. .................................................... 295.00
Pewter, Plate, Love, Phila., 7 3/4 In. ............................................................ 250.00
Pewter, Plate, Marked Schroeder Feinzinn, Deer, 9 In. ............................... 50.00
Pewter, Plate, Nathaniel Austin, Mass., C.1770, 8 3/8 In. ......................... 395.00
Pewter, Plate, S.Kilburn & Eagle Touchmark, 7 3/4 In. .............................. 310.00
Pewter, Plate, Samuel Danforth, Eagle Touchmark & Hartford, 8 In. ........ 200.00
Pewter, Plate, Samuel Ellis, Hammered Booge, C.1750, 7 3/4 In. .............. 45.00
Pewter, Plate, Schroeder, Feinzinn Justice, Sword & Scales, Deer, 8 3/4 In. ...... 40.00
Pewter, Plate, Thomas Badger, Boston, C.1790, 8 1/2 In. ........................ 325.00
Pewter, Plate, Thomas Badger, Eagle & Badge Touchmark, 8 3/8 In. ....... 195.00
Pewter, Plate, Thomas Danforth III, Philadelphia, 7 3/4 In. ....................... 210.00
Pewter, Plate, Thomas Danforth, Molded Rim, C.1790, 6 1/8 In. .............. 475.00
Pewter, Plate, W.Ballantyne, Glasgow, 1760, 9 In. ....................................... 48.00
Pewter, Platter, Kayserzinn, Embossed Design, Oval, 21 In.Long ............... 35.00
Pewter, Platter, Kayzerzinn, Embossed Pheasant, Vegetables On Border ...... 50.00
Pewter, Platter, Pilgrim, J.F., 15 3/4 X 11 1/2 In. ........................................ 50.00
Pewter, Porringer, American, Basin Shape, C.1825, 3 3/4 In.Wide ........... 225.00
Pewter, Porringer, American, Basin Shape, English Style Handle, C.1825, 4 In. ...... 195.00
Pewter, Porringer, Child's, Germany, Dog Chasing Rabbit, Lion Feet, 5 In. ...... 45.00

Pewter, Pitcher, Freeman Porter,
Maine, C.1835, 6 3/4 In.
*(See Page 377)*

Pewter, Porringer, Rhode Island,
C.1775, 5 In.

| | |
|---|---|
| **Pewter, Porringer,** David & Thomas Melville, R.I., Trefoil Handle, C.1793 | 1700.00 |
| **Pewter, Porringer,** Double Handled, C.1750, Set Of 4 | 798.00 |
| **Pewter, Porringer,** Elisha Kirk, Pa., Pierced Hole In Tab Handle, C.1785 | 2600.00 |
| **Pewter, Porringer,** Flowered Handle, Frederick Bassett, Conn., C.1761, 5 In. | 175.00 |
| **Pewter, Porringer,** France, Coat Of Arms, Shell Handle | 5.00 |
| **Pewter, Porringer,** Hamlin & Eagle Touchmark, Flowered Handle, 5 1/2 In. | 405.00 |
| **Pewter, Porringer,** Impressed Horsehead & Stede, 6 In. | 10.00 |
| **Pewter, Porringer,** Pennock, Pa., Pierced Hole In Tab Handle, C.1785 | 1800.00 |
| **Pewter, Porringer,** Rhode Island, C.1775, 5 In. *Illus* | 200.00 |
| **Pewter, Porringer,** S.G., Crown Handle, 5 1/2 In. | 185.00 |
| **Pewter, Porringer,** Samuel Hamlin, Flower Handle, 5 In. | 465.00 |
| **Pewter, Pot,** Chamber, S Handle | 125.00 |
| **Pewter, Pot,** Pouring, Legs, Handle, 11 In.Across | 54.00 |
| **Pewter, Pot,** Sugar, England, Rose & Leaf Finial On Lid, 3 3/4 In. | 27.50 |
| **Pewter, Powder Horn,** Fluted, Brass Trim | 29.00 |
| **Pewter, Salt & Pepper,** Marked Mayflower, W.B.Mfg.Co., 3234, 2 1/4 In.High | 3.00 |
| **Pewter, Salt & Pepper,** Marked Peerless, Side Handles, 4 3/4 In.High | 4.75 |
| **Pewter, Salt,** Master, 3 Legs, C.1855, Pair | 30.00 |
| **Pewter, Snuffbox,** Hinged Lid, 1 1/4 X 3 In. | 20.00 |
| **Pewter, Spoon,** Angle Mark, Initialed, 9 In., Pair | 60.00 |
| **Pewter, Spoon,** Child's, 4 In. | 10.00 |
| **Pewter, Spoon,** Dutch, Ornate Molded Cherub | 7.00 |
| **Pewter, Spoon,** Luther Boardman, Chester, Conn., C.1830 | 50.00 |
| **Pewter, Spoon,** Rattail, Round Bowl | 12.50 |
| **Pewter, Spoon,** Shellback, 8 In. | 15.00 |
| **Pewter, Spoon,** White House, 5 In. | 16.00 |
| **Pewter, Stein,** City Scene, Figural Half Nude Girl Thumb Lift, 1/2 Liter | 195.00 |
| **Pewter, Stein,** Serving, Kayserzinn, Engraved, Presentation, 16 3/4 In. | 228.00 |
| **Pewter, Sugar & Creamer,** Brewster, C.1800 | 95.00 |
| **Pewter, Tablespoon,** Shellback, American, 8 In. | 6.00 |
| **Pewter, Tablespoon,** Shellback, Newmarket, Va. | 10.00 |
| **Pewter, Tankard,** Colonel William Will, Phila., C.1764 *Illus* | 5600.00 |
| **Pewter, Tankard,** Commemorative, George V, 1910-1935, Glass Bottom, 4 3/4 In. | 95.00 |
| **Pewter, Tankard,** German, Claw & Ball Feet, Domed Cover, C.1780, 9 3/4 In.High | 300.00 |
| **Pewter, Tankard,** Parks Boyd, Phila., C.1795, 7 1/2 In. *Illus* | 2900.00 |
| **Pewter, Tankard,** Peter Young, C.1775, 6 3/4 In. *Illus* | 5600.00 |
| **Pewter, Tankard,** Victorian, Glass Bottom | 27.50 To 37.50 |
| **Pewter, Tea & Coffee Set,** Hammered, Rosewood Handles, C.1920, 5 Piece | 140.00 |
| **Pewter, Tea Caddy,** Crown, London, & X, Regency Style, 4 Claw Feet, Hinged | 125.00 |
| **Pewter, Tea Set,** Homan, C.1830, 3 Piece | 165.00 |
| **Pewter, Tea Set,** Japanned Handles, James Dixon & Sons, 1836, 3 Piece | 120.00 |
| **Pewter, Teapot,** A.Porter | 250.00 |
| **Pewter, Teapot,** Ashbil Griswold, Meriden, Conn., C.1830, 6 1/2 In. | 295.00 |
| **Pewter, Teapot,** Britannia Metal, Pear Shape, Wooden Handle, 11 In. High | 55.00 |

| | |
|---|---|
| Pewter, Teapot, E.Stacey, Ivory Finial, Footed, 5 1/2 In. | 58.00 |
| Pewter, Teapot, E.W.& J., Crossed Arrows, 7 In.High | 45.00 |
| Pewter, Teapot, James Dixon & Son, Puff Shape, Wooden Handle & Finial | 125.00 |
| Pewter, Teapot, M.Simmons, Copper Bottom, 11 In.High | 62.00 |
| Pewter, Teapot, Manning, Copper Bottom, 9 In. | 55.00 |
| Pewter, Teapot, Marked Morey & Over, Boston, Wooden Finial, Tapering | 65.00 |
| Pewter, Teapot, Marked Savage, 7 In. | 195.00 |
| Pewter, Teapot, Reed & Barton, Classical Shape | 65.00 |
| Pewter, Teapot, Reed & Barton, Octagonal Sides, Acorn Shape, Ebony Handle | 45.00 |
| Pewter, Teapot, Reed & Barton, Pear Shape, Flower Finial, Melon Ribbed, 1850 | 42.00 |
| Pewter, Teapot, Squat, Engraved '1821, H.L., ' Ball Feet, Wooden Handle | 65.00 |
| Pewter, Teapot, Wood Finial, Morey, Smith & Over, C.1850 | 65.00 |
| Pewter, Token, Communion, English | 4.00 |
| Pewter, Urn, Coffee, Dutch, Turned Wood Finial, Pyriform, Scroll Legs, C.1850 | 200.00 |
| Pewter, Vase, Bullet Shape, Stylized Flowers, Liberty & Co., Pair, 7 In.High | 50.00 |
| Pewter, Vase, Cherub Holding Trumpet, 8 In.High | 12.50 |
| Pewter, Vase, Signed H, Trumpet, Reclining Cherub At Base, 9 In. | 14.50 |
| Pewter, Vase, Trumpet Type, 9 1/2 In.High | 70.00 |
| Pewter, Whistle, Hole At Top, 2 1/2 In. | 5.00 |
| Pewter, Whistle, Police | 6.95 |

*Phoenix Glass Company was founded in 1880 in Pennsylvania. The firm
made commercial products such as lampshades, bottles, glassware. Collectors
today are interested in the sculptured glassware made by the company from the
1930s until the mid-1950s.*

| | |
|---|---|
| Phoenix, Base, Fan-Shaped, Raised Bird Of Paradise & Flowers, 7 In.High | 30.00 |
| Phoenix, Candlestick, Double, Pale Blue, Frosted Yellow Daffodils, Pair | 30.00 |
| Phoenix, Console Set, Deep Amethyst, Fish & Water Lilies, 3 Piece | 166.00 |
| Phoenix, Lamp Base, Bittersweet & Foxglove On White, 11 In. High | 50.00 |
| Phoenix, Lamp, Blue & White, 12 In.High | 85.00 |
| Phoenix, Lamp, Bluebirds & Pink Fruit In White, Ribbed, 13 In. | 90.00 |
| Phoenix, Lamp, Red Berries & Green Leaves On White, Metal Mounting | 56.00 |
| Phoenix, Pitcher, Water, Green Bubbly, Applied Handle, 8 1/4 In. | 62.50 |
| Phoenix, Plate, Beige Tone, Sculptured Dancing Nudes, 8 1/2 In. | 36.00 |
| Phoenix, Plate, Green Bubble, 8 In. | 15.00 |
| Phoenix, Plate, Green Bubbly, Circular Pattern, 8 1/4 In. | 22.00 |
| Phoenix, Rose Bowl, Sculptured Roses, Ice Blue | 40.00 |
| Phoenix, Shade, Gas, Stalacite, Custard Color, Pointed | 18.50 |
| Phoenix, Shade, Opalescent, Flint, Ruffled Rim | 16.00 |
| Phoenix, Vase, Blue Hummingbirds On White Satin, 7 In. | 32.00 |
| Phoenix, Vase, Blue Satin, Sculptured Flying Geese, 10 In. | 75.00 |
| Phoenix, Vase, Blueberries, Leaves, & Vines On White, 9 1/2 In.High | 40.00 |
| Phoenix, Vase, Brown Chrysanthemum Type Flowers On Cream, 9 1/4 In. High | 62.50 |
| Phoenix, Vase, Bulbous, Brown Pinecones On Cream, 7 In.High | 62.50 |

| | | |
|---|---|---|
| | Pewter, Tankard, | |
| Pewter, Tankard, Peter Young, | Colonel William Will, | Pewter, Tankard, Parks Boyd, |
| C.1775, 6 3/4 In. | Phila., C.1764 | Phila., C.1795, 7 1/2 In. |
| *(See Page 378)* | *(See Page 378)* | *(See Page 378)* |

Phoenix, Vase, Cattails & Dragonflies, 6 In. ........................................................ 35.00
Phoenix, Vase, Fan, Praying Mantis, Clear On Frosted, 8 3/4 In. High ...................... 45.00
Phoenix, Vase, Flared, Grasshoppers, 8 1/2 X 8 In. ............................................... 75.00
Phoenix, Vase, Flower & Vine, Fiery Opalescent, 7 In.High, Pair .............................. 75.00
Phoenix, Vase, Madonna, Cameo White On Cocoa, 10 In. ....................................... 45.00
Phoenix, Vase, Madonna, Iridescent, 10 In.High .................................................... 35.00
Phoenix, Vase, Owl, Deep Amethyst, 6 X 5 In. ...................................................... 65.00
Phoenix, Vase, Praying Mantis, Lip, White On White, 7 X 8 In. ............................... 45.00
Phoenix, Vase, Relief Hummingbirds & Flowering Branches On Green, 5 In. ............... 45.00
Phoenix, Vase, Translucent Leaf Decoration, 8 In. ................................................. 50.00
Phoenix, Vase, Triangular, Green Opaque, 3 Nudes, 8 1/2 In.High ........................... 45.00
Phoenix, Vase, Yellow Flowers, Green Stems, 6 1/2 In.High .................................... 30.00
    Phonograph, see Music, Phonograph
Photograph, Album, Victorian, Velvet Covered ....................................................... 26.00
Photography, Album, Boston Police Department, 1880, Mug Shots ........................... 150.00
Photography, Album, Carte De Visite, Purple Velvet, Brass Edge & Clasps ................. 18.00
Photography, Album, Celluloid Covered .................................................................. 4.00
Photography, Album, Embossed Leather, Gold Edges, 8 1/2 X 7 X 2 In. .................... 40.00
Photography, Album, Grecian Scene Cover, Mirror, Velvet & Ormolu Stand ................ 95.00
Photography, Album, History Of Brockton, Mass., 1898, By W.H.Caldwell ................. 45.00
Photography, Album, House Of Representatives, Massachusetts, 1876, Brown ........... 70.00
Photography, Album, Iowa City College, Class 1890, 6 X 9 In.Photographs ............... 45.00
Photography, Album, Leather, Robert Wilson McLAUGHRY, NOV.23, 1888 ................ 85.00
Photography, Album, Miniature, Red Leather, Gold Trim, 3 1/4 X 2 In. ..................... 10.00
Photography, Album, Ornate, Stand-Up Type, Brass Frame, Brass On Leather ........... 55.00
Photography, Album, Pennsylvania, By Lamer Of Harrisburg, 1889, Oblong ............... 65.00
Photography, Album, Senate Of Massachusetts, 1873, Carte De Visite, Brown .......... 50.00
Photography, Album, Shell Shape, Brocade Velvet, Braid, Victorian, 11 In. ............... 85.00
Photography, Album, Souvenir, Boston Police Department, 1894, Oblong ................... 95.00
Photography, Album, Souvenir, California, 1919 ..................................................... 7.50
Photography, Album, Tintype, Pocket, Red, Gold Designs, Brass Lock Clip ............... 35.00
Photography, Album, Tintypes, Porcelain Rests, 4 X 4 X 5 In. ................................ 14.00
Photography, Album, Travel, U.S., Canada, & Hawaii, C.1880, Oblong ..................... 100.00
Photography, Ambrotype Case, Angel With Trumpet, Ninth Plate, Union, Brown ........ 32.00
Photography, Ambrotype Case, Birds On Fountain, Ninth Plate, Union ...................... 24.00
Photography, Ambrotype Case, Gutta-Percha, Littlefield, Parsons & Co., Union ......... 30.00
Photography, Ambrotype Case, Jardiniere Of Flowers, Sixth Plate, Union .................. 30.00
Photography, Ambrotype Case, Linked Scrolls, Sixty Plate, Union ............................ 35.00
Photography, Ambrotype Case, Moorish Design, Ninth Plate, Union, Black ................ 22.00
Photography, Ambrotype Case, Octagonal, Sixth Plate, Union, Scrolls ...................... 45.00
Photography, Ambrotype Case, Ribbon Motif, Ninth Plate, Union, Black .................... 24.00
Photography, Ambrotype, Civil War Father & Son, Gilt Frame, Leather Box ............... 47.50
Photography, Ambrotype, Civil War Infantryman, Teenager, Gilt Frame ..................... 34.50
Photography, Ambrotype, Father & Son Union Infantrymen, Gilt Frame ..................... 47.50
Photography, Ambrotype, Fish Hanging From Stick, Sixth Plate ............................... 22.00
Photography, Ambrotype, Four-Year-Old Girl & Doll, C.1850, Gilt Frame .................. 22.50
Photography, Ambrotype, Man & Accordion, Sixth Plate, Leather Case ..................... 35.00
Photography, Ambrotype, Niagara Falls, Whole Plate .............................................. 170.00
Photography, Ambrotype, Ninth Plate, Civil War Soldier .......................................... 18.00
Photography, Ambrotype, Ninth Plate, Mother Holding Baby Twins, Framed ............. 25.00
Photography, Ambrotype, Nude Woman On Couch, Stereo, C.1880 .......................... 150.00
Photography, Ambrotype, Painting Of Woman, Quaker Type Bonnet, Sixth Plate ....... 15.00
Photography, Ambrotype, Pair Young Ladies, C.1865, Paper Covered Case ............... 11.00
Photography, Ambrotype, Pennsylvania German Couple, C.1875, Paper Case ............ 11.00
Photography, Ambrotype, Post-Mortem Little Girl, Sixth Plate, Leather Case ............. 15.00
Photography, Ambrotype, Seated Civil War Soldier, Sixth Plate, Leather Case ........... 30.00
Photography, Ambrotype, Street Scene With People, 1/4 Plate ................................ 110.00
Photography, Ambrotype, Union Soldier, Kepi & Frock Coat, Gilt Frame ................... 29.50
Photography, Ambrotype, Woman Knitting, Sixth Plate, Leather Case ....................... 10.00
Photography, Ambrotype, Young Man, Miniature, Paper Covered Case ...................... 9.50
Photography, Ambrotype, 2 Military Men, Quarter Plate, Leather Case ..................... 65.00
Photography, Camera, Adlake Special, Adams & Westlake Co., C.1900 ..................... 60.00
Photography, Camera, Ansco, No.2-A, Box ............................................................ 6.50
Photography, Camera, Brownie, Box, No.2 ............................................................. 6.00
Photography, Camera, Brownie, Englaring, For 4 X 5 In.To 8 X 10 In., 1915 ............ 25.00
Photography, Camera, Brownie, Model D, Box, RollFilm, 120, Patent 1916 ............... 12.00

| | |
|---|---|
| Photography, Camera, Brownie, Model No.2-A | 5.50 |
| Photography, Camera, Brownie, Model 6-16, Junior | 5.50 |
| Photography, Camera, Brownie, No.3a, Model A, Horizontal Format | 25.00 |
| Photography, Camera, Brownie, 2A, Folding, Automatic, Patent 1913 | 8.50 |
| Photography, Camera, Cadet, Model D-6 | 4.50 |
| Photography, Camera, Certo Dollina, 35mm., Speeds To 1/100 | 20.00 |
| Photography, Camera, Chicago View, Montgomery Ward & Co., Folding, 1906 | 65.00 |
| Photography, Camera, Cyclone, Rochester Optical Co., Magazine, C.1902 | 65.00 |
| Photography, Camera, Eastman Kodak, Hawkeye, Vest Pocket, No.3832, C.1917 | 10.00 |
| Photography, Camera, Eastman Plate, No.5, Series D, Folding, C.1895 | 145.00 |
| Photography, Camera, Eastman, Foldout, Dated 1917, Military Case | 12.00 |
| Photography, Camera, English, Magazine, Vertical Format, Wood Interior, 1910 | 100.00 |
| Photography, Camera, Ensign, Houghtons, Ltd., London, Box, Roll Film | 20.00 |
| Photography, Camera, Goerz Anschutz, Folding, Focal Plane Shutter, C.1910 | 100.00 |
| Photography, Camera, Ica, Dresden, Germany, Vest Pocket, Ivory Finder | 15.00 |
| Photography, Camera, Kodak, Autographic Brownie, No.2, Folding | 10.95 |
| Photography, Camera, Kodak, Autographic, 1920s, Booklet | 12.00 |
| Photography, Camera, Kodak, Autographic, 3-A, Stylus | 12.00 |
| Photography, Camera, Kodak, Box, Detective Style, Dates 1890 & 1892 | 350.00 |
| Photography, Camera, Kodak, Brownie, No.0, Model A, Cardboard, Patent 1903 | 15.00 |
| Photography, Camera, Kodak, Bull's-Eye, Model Of 1898, Leather Covering | 40.00 |
| Photography, Camera, Kodak, Bullet, Brown Bakelite, C.1940 | 15.00 |
| Photography, Camera, Kodak, Cartridge, No.4, Model E, Folding, Dated 1898 | 60.00 |
| Photography, Camera, Kodak, Duoflex IV, Twin Lens, For 127 Film | 15.00 |
| Photography, Camera, Kodak, Eastman, Vest Pocket, Portrait Lens | 15.00 |
| Photography, Camera, Kodak, Enlarging, For Vpk Negatives, Vest Pocket, 1916 | 20.00 |
| Photography, Camera, Kodak, Enlarging, 16mm., For Enlarging To 620 Size | 35.00 |
| Photography, Camera, Kodak, Flexo, No.2, Box, 3 Sides Fall Away, C.1890 | 35.00 |
| Photography, Camera, Kodak, Junior, 620 Series II, Folding, Leather Case | 25.00 |
| Photography, Camera, Kodak, Model C, Folding, Patent Dec.1, 1890, Case | 40.00 |
| Photography, Camera, Kodak, Model C, 1921, Case | 18.00 |
| Photography, Camera, Kodak, No.1a, Pocket, Folding, Dated 1898 | 30.00 |
| Photography, Camera, Kodak, Pocket, 1st Model, Intregal Shutter, 1895 | 60.00 |
| Photography, Camera, Kodak, Premonette, Film Pack, Red Bellows, Patent 1903 | 18.00 |
| Photography, Camera, Kodak, Studio, Century, 9a, Wooden, Double Bellows, 1915 | 100.00 |
| Photography, Camera, Kodak, Vest Pocket, Model Vpk, Pull Out Front, C.1913 | 60.00 |
| Photography, Camera, Pathex, Cine-Camera, Hand Crank, 9.5 M., Leather Cover | 30.00 |
| Photography, Camera, Pilot Super Reflex, German, Pilotar Lens, C.1937 | 45.00 |
| Photography, Camera, Polaroid, 95a, Pull Up Sportsfinder, Series 40 Film | 25.00 |
| Photography, Camera, Pony Premo, No.2, Rochester Optical Co., Folding Plate | 60.00 |
| Photography, Camera, Ray, No.4, Folding, Polished Wood, C.1899 | 45.00 |
| Photography, Camera, Recomar, 18, German Made Kodak, Anastigmat Lens, C.1933 | 50.00 |
| Photography, Camera, Rochester Optical Co., Single View Lens, C.1892 | 125.00 |
| Photography, Camera, Rolleicord, Twin Lens, For 120 Roll Film, C.1935 | 50.00 |
| Photography, Camera, Seneca, Box, Plate, Sealskin Leatherette Covering | 15.00 |
| Photography, Camera, Seneca, No.1, Folding, Roll Film, Tbi Uno Shutter | 15.00 |
| Photography, Camera, Seneca, 6a, Folding Plate, Leather Cover, C.1910 | 25.00 |
| Photography, Camera, Seroco, Folding Plate, Wooden, Brass, & Leather | 85.00 |
| Photography, Camera, Target Six, Brownie, Model 16 | 5.50 |
| Photography, Camera, Universal Corp., Cine-Master II, Model G-8, 8 Mm. | 40.00 |
| Photography, Camera, Univex Iris, Universal Corp., Cast Metal Construction | 15.00 |
| Photography, Camera, Zeiss Maximar 207/3, Folding, Double Bellows | 40.00 |
| Photography, Candle Lamp, Kodak, Fold Up Red Paper Safelight, Metal Rims | 15.00 |
| Photography, Carte De Visite Lithograph, Jeb Stuart | 4.00 |
| Photography, Carte De Visite Lithograph, Stonewall Jackson | 4.00 |
| Photography, Carte De Visite, General John Pope, 1885 | 3.50 |
| Photography, Case, Union & Constitution, Sixth Plate, Case | 45.00 |
| Photography, Daguerreotype Case, Cobalt & Gold Scrolls, Husband & Wife | 12.00 |
| Photography, Daguerreotype Case, Fruited Bough, Ninth Plate, Union, Oval | 30.00 |
| Photography, Daguerreotype Case, Gutta-Percha, Acorn Motif, Cameo | 29.00 |
| Photography, Daguerreotype Case, Gutta-Percha, Angel Scattering Roses | 50.00 |
| Photography, Daguerreotype Case, Gutta-Percha, Angel With Harp, Cameo | 39.00 |
| Photography, Daguerreotype Case, Gutta-Percha, Apple Picker | 40.00 |
| Photography, Daguerreotype Case, Gutta-Percha, Beehive, Grain Border | 30.00 |
| Photography, Daguerreotype Case, Gutta-Percha, Bobby Shafto | 75.00 |
| Photography, Daguerreotype Case, Gutta-Percha, Chess Players | 40.00 |

| | |
|---|---|
| **Photography, Daguerreotype Case,** Gutta-Percha, Children & Lambs, Seiler | 150.00 |
| **Photography, Daguerreotype Case,** Gutta-Percha, Children, Butterflies, C.1850 | 50.00 |
| **Photography, Daguerreotype Case,** Gutta-Percha, Children, Fence, Lamb, Oval | 80.00 |
| **Photography, Daguerreotype Case,** Gutta-Percha, Civil War, Shield & Flags | 90.00 |
| **Photography, Daguerreotype Case,** Gutta-Percha, Colonial Lady At Spinet | 45.00 |
| **Photography, Daguerreotype Case,** Gutta-Percha, Egyptian Lady, Oval | 85.00 |
| **Photography, Daguerreotype Case,** Gutta-Percha, Embossed Sailboat, Leather | 35.00 |
| **Photography, Daguerreotype Case,** Gutta-Percha, Fruited Bough, Oval | 35.00 |
| **Photography, Daguerreotype Case,** Gutta-Percha, Geometric | 30.00 |
| **Photography, Daguerreotype Case,** Gutta-Percha, Geometric Block | 25.00 |
| **Photography, Daguerreotype Case,** Gutta-Percha, Geometric, Civil War Soldier | 45.00 |
| **Photography, Daguerreotype Case,** Gutta-Percha, Gypsy Fortune Teller | 75.00 |
| **Photography, Daguerreotype Case,** Gutta-Percha, Helmet, Crossed Flags, Shield | 80.00 |
| **Photography, Daguerreotype Case,** Gutta-Percha, Huntress & Falcon, 2 Picture | 65.00 |
| **Photography, Daguerreotype Case,** Gutta-Percha, Mary & Her Lamb | 65.00 |
| **Photography, Daguerreotype Case,** Gutta-Percha, Mary & Lamb, Octagonal, Brown | 35.00 |
| **Photography, Daguerreotype Case,** Gutta-Percha, Monitor & Fort | 55.00 |
| **Photography, Daguerreotype Case,** Gutta-Percha, Mother-Of-Pearl Inlay | 25.00 |
| **Photography, Daguerreotype Case,** Gutta-Percha, Mother-Of-Pearl, Bijou | 65.00 |
| **Photography, Daguerreotype Case,** Gutta-Percha, Ninth Plate, Ribbon Motif | 35.00 |
| **Photography, Daguerreotype Case,** Gutta-Percha, Ninth Plate, Scrolls | 22.00 |
| **Photography, Daguerreotype Case,** Gutta-Percha, Oval, Children & Lamb | 37.50 |
| **Photography, Daguerreotype Case,** Gutta-Percha, Rosette & Scrolls, 2 Picture | 35.00 |
| **Photography, Daguerreotype Case,** Gutta-Percha, Sheaf Of Wheat & Sickle | 30.00 |
| **Photography, Daguerreotype Case,** Gutta-Percha, Sir Roger De Coverly | 48.00 |
| **Photography, Daguerreotype Case,** Gutta-Percha, Soldier | 35.00 |
| **Photography, Daguerreotype Case,** Gutta-Percha, The Blind Beggar | 40.00 |
| **Photography, Daguerreotype Case,** Gutta-Percha, The Faithful Hound | 90.00 |
| **Photography, Daguerreotype Case,** Gutta-Percha, The Flower Bier | 100.00 |
| **Photography, Daguerreotype Case,** Gutta-Percha, The Proud Elk, Signed | 70.00 |
| **Photography, Daguerreotype Case,** Gutta-Percha, The Wheat Sheaves, Brown | 42.00 |
| **Photography, Daguerreotype Case,** Gutta-Percha, Union, Banners, Shield, Stars | 50.00 |
| **Photography, Daguerreotype Case,** Gutta-Percha, Woman Holding Child | 70.00 |
| **Photography, Daguerreotype Case,** Gutta-Percha, 2 Toddlers, Floral | 25.00 |
| **Photography, Daguerreotype Case,** Gutta-Percha, 3 Ladies, Wall Hanging | 22.00 |
| **Photography, Daguerreotype Case,** Leather, Scrolled, Red Satin, Man | 10.00 |
| **Photography, Daguerreotype Case,** Monitor & Merrimac, 3 1/4 X 3 3/4 In. | 170.00 |
| **Photography, Daguerreotype Case,** Scroll & Grapes, Ninth Plate, Union | 20.00 |
| **Photography, Daguerreotype Case,** Scrolled, Hook, Lady In Checkered Dress | 12.50 |
| **Photography, Daguerreotype Case,** Strawberry Motif, Ninth Plate, Union | 25.00 |
| **Photography, Daguerreotype,** Anthony Gould, 1801-1858, Whole Plate | 300.00 |
| **Photography, Daguerreotype,** Bearded Gent, Meade Brothers, N.Y., Sixth Plate | 25.00 |
| **Photography, Daguerreotype,** Bearded Gentleman, Hinged Leather Case | 15.00 |
| **Photography, Daguerreotype,** Bearded Man, European, Passe Partout Mount | 85.00 |
| **Photography, Daguerreotype,** Blind Man With Cane, Sixth Plate, Leather Case | 15.00 |
| **Photography, Daguerreotype,** Boy With Toy, Sixth Plate, Leather Case | 20.00 |
| **Photography, Daguerreotype,** Concertinaist, Sixth Plate, Leather Case | 35.00 |
| **Photography, Daguerreotype,** Elderly Man, Anson, Rufus, N.Y., Sixth Plate | 22.00 |
| **Photography, Daguerreotype,** Engraving Of Daniel Webster, Ninth Plate, Case | 100.00 |
| **Photography, Daguerreotype,** Gentleman Portrait, Half Plate, Leather Case | 50.00 |
| **Photography, Daguerreotype,** Girl, Tinted, Gutta-Percha Case | 20.00 |
| **Photography, Daguerreotype,** House With Chimneys, Captain's Walk, & Flag | 150.00 |
| **Photography, Daguerreotype,** Lady With Gold Jewelry, Tompkins, Sixth Plate | 25.00 |
| **Photography, Daguerreotype,** Man In Buggy, Sixth Plate | 200.00 |
| **Photography, Daguerreotype,** Man In Top Hat, Quarter Plate, Case | 25.00 |
| **Photography, Daguerreotype,** Man With Dog, Quarter Plate, Split Leather Case | 60.00 |
| **Photography, Daguerreotype,** Man With Goatee, Quarter Plate | 20.00 |
| **Photography, Daguerreotype,** Man With Pen In Hand, Sixth Plate, Leather Case | 10.00 |
| **Photography, Daguerreotype,** Man With Violin, Ninth Plate, Leather Case | 60.00 |
| **Photography, Daguerreotype,** Man, Papier-Mache Case | 8.50 |
| **Photography, Daguerreotype,** Nude Statue, French Artist, Double Sixth Plate | 150.00 |
| **Photography, Daguerreotype,** Old Lady In Lace, Quarter Plate, Half Case | 20.00 |
| **Photography, Daguerreotype,** Painting Of Judge, Sixth Plate, Leather Case | 25.00 |
| **Photography, Daguerreotype,** Post-Mortem, Small Girl, Sixth Plate, Case | 35.00 |
| **Photography, Daguerreotype,** Woman With Rose, Sixth Plate, Leather Case | 12.00 |
| **Photography, Daguerreotype,** Young Couple, Holmes, N.Y., Sixth Plate | 30.00 |

Photography, Daguerreotype, Young Girl, Flowers & Scrolls On Case ............................ 15.00
Photography, Daguerreotype, Young Mother & Baby, Hinged Case ............................ 25.00
Photography, Daguerreotype, 3 Solemn People, Crapo, Lockport, Quarter Plate ............................ 35.00
Photography, Daguerreotype, 3 Young Ladies, Brady's Gallery, Quarter Plate ............................ 125.00
Photography, Desk, Retouching, G.Gennert, N.Y., Portable, Ground Mirror, 1890 ............................ 25.00
Photography, Edison At Schenctady, By W.H.Butler, 1892 ............................ 25.00
Photography, Engraving, Meade's Daguerreotype Gallery, N.Y., C.1850, Tinted ............................ 20.00
Photography, Gutta-Percha Case, Oval Design, Flowers ............................ 25.00
Photography, Hydrometer, Eastman, C.1918 ............................ 4.00
Photography, Kodak, Movie, Model B, 16mm., C.1925 ............................ 30.00
Photography, Magic Lantern, Kerosene Lamp Inside, C.1866, 22 Slides ............................ 116.00
Photography, Magic Lantern, Kerosene Lamp, Celluloid Films, C.1890 ............................ 95.00
Photography, Magic Lantern, Mechanical Industries, Keystone, C.1910, 17 ............................ 15.00
Photography, Magic Lantern, Oil Lamp Inside, Made In Germany ............................ 55.00
Photography, Magic Lantern, Slide, American Views, C.1900, 31 ............................ 15.00
Photography, Magic Lantern, Slide, Architectural Series, C.1900, 21 ............................ 12.00
Photography, Magic Lantern, Slide, Automobiles, C.1910, 2 ............................ 2.00
Photography, Magic Lantern, Slide, Beaches, C.1910, 9 ............................ 10.00
Photography, Magic Lantern, Slide, Children With Toys, C.1910, 4 ............................ 4.00
Photography, Magic Lantern, Slide, Children's Scenes, Toys, Circus, Glass, 6 ............................ 6.00
Photography, Magic Lantern, Slide, England, C.1900, 8 ............................ 5.00
Photography, Magic Lantern, Slide, Florida Scenery, Amateur, 16 ............................ 8.00
Photography, Magic Lantern, Slide, France, C.1900, 20 ............................ 10.00
Photography, Magic Lantern, Slide, Harness Racing, C.1910, 4 ............................ 7.00
Photography, Magic Lantern, Slide, Italy, Amateur, 40 ............................ 20.00
Photography, Magic Lantern, Slide, Italy, C.1910, 10 ............................ 6.00
Photography, Magic Lantern, Slide, Massachusetts, C.1900, 7 ............................ 5.00
Photography, Magic Lantern, Slide, Mechanical Industries, Keystone, 21 ............................ 20.00
Photography, Magic Lantern, Slide, New York City, 1903, 7 ............................ 7.00
Photography, Magic Lantern, Slide, Policemen, Erl Co., Boston, C.1910, 4 ............................ 5.00
Photography, Magic Lantern, Slide, Sculpture & Painting, C.1900, 28 ............................ 15.00
Photography, Magic Lantern, Slide, Ships & Boats, C.1910, 49 ............................ 30.00
Photography, Magic Lantern, Slide, Washington, D.C., C.1870, 6 ............................ 10.00
Photography, Magic Lantern, Slide, Washington, D.C., C.1900, 18 ............................ 13.00
Photography, Magic Lantern, Slide, World War I, 50 ............................ 50.00
Photography, Mask, Printing, Manning, For 5 X 7 In.Negatives, C.1910, 23 ............................ 3.00
Photography, Movie, Airplane Trip To Atlanta, 1934, 16 Mm., Home ............................ 7.00
Photography, Movie, Asbury Park, N.J., Morro Castle Shipwreck, 16 Mm. ............................ 10.00
Photography, Movie, Calendar Girl, Sound, 16 Mm. ............................ 45.00
Photography, Movie, Chateau-Thierry Battle, World War I, U.S., 16 Mm. ............................ 10.00
Photography, Movie, Lindbergh's First Flight, 16 Mm. ............................ 15.00
Photography, Movie, Postmark For Danger, Sound, 16 Mm. ............................ 45.00
Photography, Movie, Stan Laurel, 8mm. ............................ 16.00
Photography, Mutoscope, On Stand, Charlie Chaplin Reel ............................ 450.00
Photography, Negative, Glass, Dry Plate, Baby In Carriage, C.1910 ............................ 3.00
Photography, Negative, Glass, Dry Plate, Boy With Bicycle, C.1910 ............................ 11.00
Photography, Negative, Glass, Dry Plate, Boy With Toy, C.1910 ............................ 3.00
Photography, Negative, Glass, Dry Plate, Boy With Wagon, C.1910 ............................ 3.00
Photography, Negative, Glass, Dry Plate, Bride, C.1910, 8 X 10 In. ............................ 2.50
Photography, Negative, Glass, Dry Plate, Charles Earley, Ford Dealer, C.1910 ............................ 6.60
Photography, Negative, Glass, Dry Plate, Lady At Spinning Wheel, C.1910 ............................ 5.50
Photography, Negative, Glass, Dry Plate, Lady In Flowered Hat, C.1910 ............................ 5.00
Photography, Negative, Glass, Dry Plate, Lady Violinist, C.1910 ............................ 3.00
Photography, Negative, Glass, Dry Plate, Lady With Bicycle, C.1910 ............................ 8.80
Photography, Negative, Glass, Dry Plate, Mansfield Basketball Team, 1903 ............................ 8.80
Photography, Negative, Glass, Dry Plate, Mansfield Basketball Team, 1904 ............................ 8.80
Photography, Negative, Glass, Dry Plate, Mansfield Football Team, 1897 ............................ 8.80
Photography, Negative, Glass, Dry Plate, Mansfield Football Team, 1909 ............................ 8.80
Photography, Negative, Glass, Dry Plate, Musical Group, C.1910, 10 X 12 In. ............................ 22.00
Photography, Negative, Glass, Dry Plate, Musician With Clarinet, C.1910 ............................ 6.60
Photography, Negative, Glass, Dry Plate, Policeman, C.1910, 8 X 10 In. ............................ 8.80
Photography, Negative, Glass, Dry Plate, Railroad Station, Mansfield, 1910 ............................ 11.00
Photography, Negative, Glass, Dry Plate, Small Boy In Striped Knickers ............................ 5.00
Photography, Negative, Glass, Dry Plate, Theatrical, Buffalo Bill Show, 1910 ............................ 11.00
Photography, Negative, Glass, Dry Plate, Two Fife & Drum Lads ............................ 6.00
Photography, Negative, Glass, Wet Plate, Family Portrait, C.1870, 10 X 12 In. ............................ 16.50

| | |
|---|---:|
| Photography, Negative, Glass, Wet Plate, Small Boy In Fringed Chair | 7.70 |
| Photography, Negative, Glass, Wet Plate, Three Women, Period Costumes | 6.60 |
| Photography, Negative, Glass, Wet Plate, Young Girl In Bustled Dress | 4.00 |
| Photography, Negative, Glass, Wet Plate, Young Lad | 12.00 |
| Photography, Negative, Glass, Wet Plate, Young Lady | 6.60 |
| Photography, Oil Colors, Probus-Mandeville Photo, Metal Cans, C.1910, 14 | 10.00 |
| Photography, Photograph, Across The Royal Gorge, Denver, William Jackson | 10.00 |
| Photography, Photograph, Albumen, Bethlehem, Bonfils, C.1870 | 17.00 |
| Photography, Photograph, Albumen, Confederate Camp Scene, By J.D.Edwards | 125.00 |
| Photography, Photograph, Albumen, Deck Of U.S.Ship Vermont, By H.P.Moore | 32.50 |
| Photography, Photograph, Albumen, Egyptian Hieroglyphics, Beato, C.1860 | 20.00 |
| Photography, Photograph, Albumen, Encampment Of Clayton Guards, By Edwards | 97.50 |
| Photography, Photograph, Albumen, Encampment Of Perote Guards, Civil War | 125.00 |
| Photography, Photograph, Albumen, Fishing Boats In Harbor, Beato, C.1860 | 20.00 |
| Photography, Photograph, Albumen, Gateway Of The Garden Of The Gods, Colo. | 40.00 |
| Photography, Photograph, Albumen, Lighthouse, Tybee Island, Ga., By H.P.Moore | 24.50 |
| Photography, Photograph, Albumen, Louisiana Tigers, New Orleans, 1861 | 125.00 |
| Photography, Photograph, Albumen, Martello Tower, Georgia, By H.P.Moore | 29.50 |
| Photography, Photograph, Albumen, Mortar, U.S.Schooner, C.P.Williams, N.H. | 34.50 |
| Photography, Photograph, Albumen, Rear Of Fort Barrancas, By J.D.Edwards | 94.50 |
| Photography, Photograph, Albumen, Roches Moutonnies, Jackson | 40.00 |
| Photography, Photograph, Albumen, Union Soldier, Winter Gear, Dated 1862 | 59.50 |
| Photography, Photograph, Albumen, Water Buffalo Working, Beato, C.1860 | 35.00 |
| Photography, Photograph, Captain H.B.Foster, Civil War, Washington, D.C. | 5.00 |
| Photography, Photograph, Civil War Soldier, Jacobs, New Orleans | 4.00 |
| Photography, Photograph, Civil War Soldier, Miller, Charlestown | 4.00 |
| Photography, Photograph, Civil War Soldiers On Cleanup Detail | 35.00 |
| Photography, Photograph, Cowboys Of The Dolores, E.H.Allen, C.1870 | 44.50 |
| Photography, Photograph, Deadwood, Dakota Territory, Grabill, C.1890 | 20.00 |
| Photography, Photograph, Dizzy Dean Carried Off Field, St.Louis & Detroit | 30.00 |
| Photography, Photograph, Dr.E.H.R.Revere In Uniform, Whipple, Boston | 4.00 |
| Photography, Photograph, Encampment Of Clayton Guards, Civil War | 97.50 |
| Photography, Photograph, Engraved Plate On Wood Block, Man, C.1880 | 10.00 |
| Photography, Photograph, Family Of 5, R.Williams, Photographer, Arizona, 1870 | 14.50 |
| Photography, Photograph, Grave Of H.H. On Cheyenne Mountaine, Jackson | 10.00 |
| Photography, Photograph, Great Flood In Denver, May 19, 1864 | 4.50 |
| Photography, Photograph, Grizzly, Giant Redwood, & Man, Taber | 10.00 |
| Photography, Photograph, H.R.Dalton, Surgeon, Kirk, N.J. | 4.00 |
| Photography, Photograph, Hanging Rock, Clear Creek, William H.Jackson | 10.00 |
| Photography, Photograph, Indian In War Paint & Bonnet, Shooting Rifle | 70.00 |
| Photography, Photograph, Indians At San Diego, E.A.Bonine, A.J.Joslin, Yuma | 32.50 |
| Photography, Photograph, Iron Springs Hotel, Manitou, Colo., Mellon, C.1880 | 6.00 |
| Photography, Photograph, Labeled Cowboys Of The Dolores, C.1870, Denver | 44.50 |
| Photography, Photograph, Labeled Indians At San Diego, A.J.Joslin, Yuma | 32.50 |
| Photography, Photograph, Lighthouse, Tybee Island, Ga., Civil War | 24.50 |
| Photography, Photograph, Lindbergh's Welcome Home By Coolidge, 39 X 10 In. | 40.00 |
| Photography, Photograph, Louisiana Tigers, New Orleans, 1861, Zouave Dress | 125.00 |
| Photography, Photograph, Marilyn Monroe, 1944, 5 X 7 In. | 1.50 |
| Photography, Photograph, Martello Tower, Tybee Island, Ga., Civil War | 29.50 |
| Photography, Photograph, Michigan Soldiers' & Sailors' Monument, 1867 | 4.00 |
| Photography, Photograph, Mongomery Ave., Independence, Colo., C.1885 | 10.00 |
| Photography, Photograph, Mother Grundy, Clear Creek, Jackson | 10.00 |
| Photography, Photograph, People's Dry Dock, Shewan & Palmer, N.Y., C.1890 | 69.50 |
| Photography, Photograph, Prince Of Wales Inspecting Enterprises, 1933 | 15.00 |
| Photography, Photograph, Rear Of Fort Barrancas, Civil War | 94.50 |
| Photography, Photograph, Seated Soldier, Hand Inside Coat, No.25 On Cap | 3.00 |
| Photography, Photograph, Sgt.H.B.George, Sterlin, Vt., Tax Stamp | 5.00 |
| Photography, Photograph, Shewan & Palmer, Shipwrights, N.Y., C.1890 | 69.50 |
| Photography, Photograph, Siamese Twins, Adolph & Rudolph, Wendt Of Boston | 7.00 |
| Photography, Photograph, Soldier & Wife, Borse, Tennessee | 4.00 |
| Photography, Photograph, Soldier, Gihou & Rizou, Philadelphia | 3.00 |
| Photography, Photograph, Sour Dope Bull Hill, Colo., C.1890 | 10.00 |
| Photography, Photograph, Sunrise, Pike's Peak, Jackson | 10.00 |
| Photography, Photograph, Tom Thumb & Bride | 45.00 |
| Photography, Photograph, Tom Thumb Wedding Party | 20.00 |
| Photography, Photograph, Union Soldier In Winter Dress, Black, Boston | 4.00 |

Photography, Photograph, Union Soldier, Beniczky, N.Y. ....................................... 5.00
Photography, Photograph, Union Soldier, Black & Batchelder, Boston ....................................... 3.00
Photography, Photograph, Union Soldier, Hat On Chair, Holding Sword ....................................... 4.00
Photography, Photograph, Union Soldier, Vignetted, Lord, N.Y., Tax Stamp ....................................... 3.00
Photography, Photograph, Union Soldier, Whipple, Boston ....................................... 4.00
Photography, Photograph, William J.Bryan, Harris & Ewing, 6 X 9 In. ....................................... 50.00
Photography, Photograph, Winchester Arms Factory, C.1880, Framed, 19 In. ....................................... 48.00
Photography, Photograph, Yosemite Falls, Taber, Tinted, 5 X 8 In. ....................................... 7.00
Photography, Photograph, Yours In Haste, Cartoon, Military, Ward, Boston ....................................... 4.00
Photography, Photograph, 19 Farm Hands & Steam Tractor, 4.Hamlin, Dakota ....................................... 22.50
Photography, Photograph, 4 Hunters In Open Touring Model T Ford, C.1915 ....................................... 12.50
Photography, Projector, Movie Slide, Bausch & Lomb, Case ....................................... 95.00
Photography, Projector, Movie, Keystone, Moviegraph, Model 281w, Hand Crank ....................................... 30.00
Photography, Projector, Movie, Keystone, 16mm., 1930s ....................................... 25.00
Photography, Splicing Outfit, Kodakscope, C.1915 ....................................... 3.00
 Photography, Stereo, see Stereo
Photography, Tintype, Blacksmith Shop, Indoor ....................................... 30.00
Photography, Tintype, Blacksmith Shop, Outdoor ....................................... 21.00
Photography, Tintype, Buckboard & Horse, Outdoor ....................................... 6.00
Photography, Tintype, Civil War Caralryman, Kepi & Shell Jacket, Gilt Frame ....................................... 44.50
Photography, Tintype, Civil War Cavalryman & Son, Leather Case, Pair ....................................... 47.50
Photography, Tintype, Civil War Cavalryman, Holding Sword, Gilt Frame ....................................... 44.50
Photography, Tintype, Civil War Infantry Corporal, Bearded, Gilt Frame ....................................... 27.50
Photography, Tintype, Civil War Private Of 2nd U.S.Dragoons, Gilt Frame ....................................... 44.50
Photography, Tintype, Civil War Soldier, Cavalry Blouse, Tinted, Gilt Frame ....................................... 24.50
Photography, Tintype, Civil War Soldier, Kepi & Civilian Coat, Gilt Frame ....................................... 27.50
Photography, Tintype, Civil War Soldier, Kepi & Frock Coat, Gilt Frame ....................................... 34.50
Photography, Tintype, Civil War Soldier, Teenage Boy, Kepi, Gilt Frame ....................................... 32.50
Photography, Tintype, Man With Pistol, Indoor ....................................... 9.00
Photography, Tintype, Ninth Plate, Boy Candy Hawker, Framed ....................................... 28.00
Photography, Tintype, Pre-Civil War Private, 2nd U.S.Dragoons, Gilt Frame ....................................... 44.50
Photography, Tintype, Sailor With Binoculars & Pistol, Indoor ....................................... 20.00
Photography, Tintype, Union Army Corporal, Frock Coat, Musket, Gilt Frame ....................................... 39.50
Photography, Tintype, Union Officer, Bearded, Tinted, M1850 Sword ....................................... 54.50
Photography, Tintype, Union Soldier, Kepi & Bowtie, Gilt Frame, Book Type ....................................... 29.50
Photography, Tintype, 2 Soldiers With Springfields & Bayonets ....................................... 35.00
Photography, Tintype, 3 Union Soldiers, Gutta-Percha Case ....................................... 39.50
Photography, Trimming Board, Eastman Kodak Co., No.2 ....................................... 12.75
Photography, Tripod, Studio, Nickel Plated Tubing, Tilt Top, Polished Wood ....................................... 45.00
Photography, Viewer, Box Type, Magnifying Glass, 84 Cards, Not Stereo ....................................... 22.75
Photography, Viewer, Magnifying, Mahogany Box, Black Rimmed Lens In Lid ....................................... 15.00
Photography, Woman, On Milk Glass, Sixth Plate, Half Leather Case ....................................... 15.00
Piano Baby, Bisque, Crying Eyes ....................................... 25.00
Piano Baby, Bisque, Large Size ....................................... 8.50
Piano Baby, Bisque, Marked Heubach, 6 In.Tall, Pair ....................................... 100.00
Piano Baby, Boy, Germany ....................................... 8.50
Piano Baby, Girl, Germany ....................................... 8.50
Piano Baby, Kestner, Sitting, Smiling, Tooth, Tousled Hair, 12 In. ....................................... 360.00
Piano Baby, Seated, Signed Heubach, 8 In. ....................................... 75.00 To 95.00
 Piano, see Music, Piano

 *Pickard china was started in 1898 by Wilder Pickard. Hand-painted china*
 *was a featured product. The firm is still working in Antioch, Illinois.*
Pickard, Bowl & Underplate, Dutch Girl, Signed ....................................... 75.00
Pickard, Bowl & Underplate, Jelly, Lavender Floral, Gold Borders ....................................... 46.00
Pickard, Bowl, Center, Embossed Floral On Gold, 2 Handled, 9 In.Diameter ....................................... 39.00
Pickard, Bowl, Footed, Swag Bouquets, Handles, Signed Challinor, 9 In.Diam. ....................................... 72.00
Pickard, Bowl, Gold Edge, Pink & Green Floral, Artist Marked, 7 In. ....................................... 37.50
Pickard, Bowl, Grapes & Foliage, Gold Trim, Signed Acoufall, 14 3/4 In. ....................................... 350.00
Pickard, Bowl, Purple Iris, Gold Trim, Limoges Blank, 2 Handles, 1905 ....................................... 48.75
Pickard, Box, Floral, Pink Borders, High Legged, Artist Signed ....................................... 40.00
Pickard, Chocolate Pot, Square, Gold Etched Floral On Blue Luster ....................................... 65.00
Pickard, Compote, Footed, Handled, Etched, Gold & Blue Decoration ....................................... 75.00
Pickard, Creamer, Bulbous, Orange Red Poppies & Gold On Cream, L.O.H., 1912 ....................................... 35.00
Pickard, Cup & Saucer, Aura Argenta Linear, Signed Vobor, 1908 ....................................... 75.00
Pickard, Cup & Saucer, Iris, Gold Decoration ....................................... 35.00

Pickard, Dish, Candy, Gold Etched Border, Peacock, Artist Signed ................................. 28.00
Pickard, Dish, Cheese & Cracker, Pink Roses, Gold Trim, Pedestal, 1925, 7 In. ............. 18.00
Pickard, Humidor, Orange Poppies, Maroon Shading, Signed R.G., 5 In.High .............. 150.00
Pickard, Jar, Candy, Covered, Signed .................................................................. 20.00
Pickard, Muffineer, Floral & Gold ....................................................................... 19.00
Pickard, Mug, Purple Grapes, Gold, Signed O.Goess, 6 In. High ............... 125.00 To 150.00
Pickard, Nappy, Purple Floral & Leaves, Gold Bands, Signed ................................. 28.00
Pickard, Pitcher, Shattering Oaks By Challinor, 12 In. ........................................... 235.00
Pickard, Plate, Art Nouveau Floral, Gilt Edged Bavarian Blank, 8 1/2 In. ................. 55.00
Pickard, Plate, Basket, Flowers, Gold Etching, Artist Signed, 8 In.Diameter .............. 18.50
Pickard, Plate, Blue, Pink, & Yellow Ground, Yellow Flowers, Scalloped Border .......... 32.00
Pickard, Plate, Cake, Open Handles, Green Shamrocks, Gold Border ....................... 15.00
Pickard, Plate, Cookie, Hand-Painted Violets .................................................... 22.00
Pickard, Plate, Easter Lilies On Gold & Maroon, Signed Yeschek, 9 In. .................... 50.00
Pickard, Plate, Flowers On Stone Column, Handled, Yeschek, 8 1/2 In. .................... 95.00
Pickard, Plate, Hand-Painted Yellow Flowers, Signed Wight ................................. 32.00
Pickard, Plate, Lake & Ruins In Moonlight, Handled, Marker, 8 1/2 In. ...................... 95.00
Pickard, Plate, Mother-Of-Pearl Ground, Leaves, Hops, & Wheat, 12 In. .................. 25.00
Pickard, Plate, Mountain & Lake, Marker, 8 1/2 In. .............................................. 95.00
Pickard, Plate, Open Handle, Golden Pheasant By Marker, 10 In. ........................... 145.00
Pickard, Plate, Painted Tulips Around Edge, Signed, 8 1/2 In. ................................ 32.50
Pickard, Plate, Purple Plums, Gold Edge, Signed Leroy, 6 1/4 In. ........................... 27.00
Pickard, Plate, Scene By E.Challinor, 8 In. ......................................................... 95.00
Pickard, Plate, Scene By Marker, 9 In. ............................................................... 110.00
Pickard, Plate, Windmill, Floral & Apples, Artist Signed, 8 3/4 In. ........................... 35.00
Pickard, Plate, Yellow Floral On Blue, Pink, & Yellow, Gold, Signed Wight ................. 32.00
Pickard, Relish, Bird On Branch, Flowers, Butterflies, White Ground ....................... 31.50
Pickard, Salt & Pepper, Allover Gold, Signed P Numbered, 3 1/2 In.High ................. 12.00
Pickard, Salt & Pepper, 3 1/2 In. ....................................................................... 10.00
Pickard, Sauce, Strawberries, Gold, Artist Yeschek, 1898-1904 Mark ...................... 17.50
Pickard, Sugar & Creamer, Basket Shape, Gold Decorated ................................... 30.00
Pickard, Sugar & Creamer, Cover, Forest Scene, Artist Signed, 1915 ...................... 85.00
Pickard, Sugar & Creamer, Fish, Purple Violets, Gold Trim ................................... 60.00
Pickard, Sugar & Creamer, Gold Handles & Pedestals, Purple Pansies, Lemke ........ 95.00
Pickard, Sugar & Creamer, Roses On Maize Blue Stems, Black Border, Signed ......... 35.00
Pickard, Sugar & Creamer, Violets, 1905, Signed E.Gib., Gold Trim ........................ 58.00
Pickard, Swan, Gold Inside & Out, Signed, 3 In.Long ............................................ 10.00
Pickard, Tea Set, Gold, Gold Florals Inside Creamer, 3 Piece ................................. 75.00
Pickard, Vase, Double Gold Handles, Orange Poppies, Gold Trim, 6 1/2 In. .............. 55.00
Pickard, Vase, Peacock By Marker, 10 In.High ................................................... 195.00
Pickard, Vase, Pink Roses On Trellis, Challinor, 9 In. ........................................... 95.00
   Picture, see also Painting, Print
   Picture Frame, see Furniture, Frame
Picture, Bird, Real Feathers, 6 X 14 In. ............................................................. 8.50
Picture, Chalk, General Andrew Jackson, Polychromed, Under Glass, 4 X 5 In. .......... 450.00
Picture, Charcoal, Landscape With Mountain Lake, American School, C.1850 ........... 160.00
Picture, Crewel On Linen, The Youth's Request, Margaret Fell, 1777 ....................... 80.00
Picture, Cutout, Tulips & Hearts, Silvered Frame, 12 1/2 In. Diameter ...................... 65.00
Picture, Embroidery & Watercolor, Mourning, Lady Kneeling, June 22, 1804 ............ 225.00
Picture, Embroidery On Silk, Lady, Face & Hands In Watercolor, C.1850 .................. 175.00
Picture, Embroidery, Full Rigged Ship, American Flag, C.1850, 17 X 23 In. ................ 150.00
Picture, Embroidery, Ship, American & Other Flags, 11 X 15 In., Framed ................... 80.00
Picture, Foil, Victorian Girl, Frames, 7 X 11 In. ................................................... 10.00
Picture, Hair, Shadowbox Frame, Oval, 14 1/4 X 12 In. ......................................... 35.00
Picture, India Ink With Gold & Ink Wash, Silhouette, Gilt Frame ............................ 105.00
Picture, Ink Drawing, Fraktur Type, Sabina Ann Asper, 1822, 7 1/2 X 8 In. ............... 225.00
Picture, Ink Drawing, Horse On Lined Paper, 4 1/4 X 7 1/4 In. ............................... 40.00
Picture, Mourning, Elizabeth & Richard Salter, Velvet, 21 X 16 In. .......................... 400.00
Picture, Mourning, John Adams, Watercolor, 18 X 15 In. ...................................... 450.00
Picture, Mourning, Maine Widow, Painting On Velvet, 1830, 14 X 21 In. ................... 350.00
Picture, Mourning, Martha Davis Foster, Painting On Glass, C.1817, 13 X 11 ............ 250.00
Picture, Mourning, McFarlan Family, Embroidery On Silk, C.1813, 19 X 24 In ............ 300.00
Picture, Mourning, Thomas & Elizabeth Knowlton, Velvet, 19 X 23 In., C.1833 ........... 350.00
Picture, Mourning, Watercolor, C.1810, 13 X 17 In. ............................................. 250.00
Picture, Mourning, Willard & Andrew Peters, Watercolor, 14 X 16 In. ....................... 500.00
Picture, Penmanship Engraving, Jenny Lind, 23 X 19 In. ...................................... 225.00

| | |
|---|---:|
| Picture, Pin Prick, Floral Wreath, Framed, C.1850, 14 3/4 X 16 3/4 In. | 40.00 |
| Picture, Silhouette, Boston Gentleman & His Mother, Julius White, 1881, Pair | 45.00 |
| Picture, Silhouette, Bust Of Young Man, Eglomise, C.1815, 5 1/2 In.Square | 75.00 |
| Picture, Silhouette, Full Figure Of Lady In Bonnet, C.1850, Mahogany Frame | 60.00 |
| Picture, Silhouette, Full Length Man, By Edouart | 85.00 |
| Picture, Silhouette, Lady & Gentleman, Hand-Painted, Signed S.E.B., Pair | 15.00 |
| Picture, Silhouette, Lady & Gentleman, Signed Martin, Pine Frames, Pair | 50.00 |
| Picture, Silhouette, Portrait Of Woman & Man, Bird's-Eye Maple Frame | 85.00 |
| Picture, Silk & Chenille Embroidery, In Memoriam, Maryann Hines, 1828 | 275.00 |
| Picture, Silk Embroidery, American Eagle On Shield, Flags, Chinese, C.1850 | 500.00 |
| Picture, Silk Embroidery, Eagle On Shield, Wings Spread, Chinese, Framed | 125.00 |
| Picture, Sulphite, Bust Of Washington, Dated 1799 .................................... *Illus* | 300.00 |
| Picture, Three Birds On Branch, Real Feathers, 7 X 15 In. | 9.50 |
| Picture, Tinsel, Floral Garland, Gilt Frame, 22 3/4 X 29 1/2 In. | 225.00 |
| Picture, Tinsel, Flowers In Vase On Black, 12 X 14 In. | 50.00 |
| Picture, Wax, Berries & Leaves, Walnut Finished Pine Shadowbox Frame | 19.50 |
| Picture, Wax, Bust Of Benjamin Franklin, S.Brown, 1806 .................... *Illus* | 425.00 |
| Picture, Wax, Bust Of Henry I, Red Satin Ground, Black Wood Frame | 55.00 |
| Picture, Wax, Bust Of Josephine, Red Satin Ground, Black Wood Frame | 55.00 |
|     Pigeon Blood, see Cranberry Glass, Ruby Glass | |
| Pilkington, Vase, Double Gourd Shape, Sunstone Glaze, Dated 1907, 4 1/2 In. | 85.00 |
|     Pink Slag, see Slag, Pink | |
| Pipe, Briar Stem, China Bowl, German Country Scene, 9 In.Long | 65.00 |
| Pipe, Clay Bowl, Wooden Stem, 6 In.Long | 10.00 |
| Pipe, Dunhill, Marbleized Bit | 25.00 |
| Pipe, German, Wooden, Silver Lid, Family Crest On Front Of Bowl In Silver | 125.00 |
| Pipe, Horn Stem, Carved Old Man's Face, China Bowl, German Scene | 65.00 |
| Pipe, Josef Rugor Wier, Carlsbad, Man, Horn, Dog, Case | 25.00 |
|     Pipe, Meerschaum, see Meerschaum, Pipe | |
| Pipe, Pistol Shape, Wooden Bowl | 6.50 |
| Pipe, Pottery, Carved Frog On Top, 8 In.Long | 10.00 |
| Pipe, Rest, Clear Glass, Byron Thompson, Jacksonville | 4.75 |
| Pirkenhammer, Chocolate Set, Scenes On Turquoise, Gilt Trim, C.1815, 4 Piece | 225.00 |
| Pirkenhammer, Plate, Hand-Painted Blueberries, Signed, 6 3/4 In. | 10.00 |

*Pisgah pottery pieces that are marked Pisgah Forest Pottery were made from 1926 until the present. Vases, teapots, jugs, candlesticks, and many other items were made.*

| | |
|---|---:|
| Pisgah Forest, Bowl, Plum Color, 1915, 7 In. | 20.00 |
| Pisgah Forest, Bowl, Plum Color, 1939, 5 In. | 20.00 |
| Pisgah Forest, Vase, Blue-Green Exterior, Pink Interior, 1941, 4 1/2 In.High | 8.00 |
| Pisgah Forest, Vase, Signed Stephen, Turquoise Crackle Glaze, 7 In. | 58.00 |
|     Plate, see under special types such as ABC, Calendar, Christmas | |
| Plated Amberina, Creamer | 4200.00 |
| Plated Amberina, Pitcher, Bulbous, Firing Check In Applied Amber Handle | 2250.00 |
| Plated Amberina, Sugar | 4700.00 |
| Plated Amberina, Tumbler, Lemonade, Firing Check In Applied Amber Handle | 1200.00 |
|     Plated Silver, see Silver Plate | |

Picture, Sulphite,
Bust Of Washington,
Dated 1799

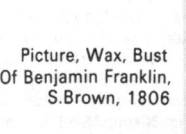

Picture, Wax, Bust
Of Benjamin Franklin,
S.Brown, 1806

Plique A Jour, Kovsh,
Scandinavian, Silver, 6 In.Long

*Plique a jour is an enameling process. The enamel was laid between thin
raised metal lines and heated. The finished piece has transparent enamel held
between the thin metal wires.*

| | |
|---|---:|
| **Plique A Jour, Bowl,** Fantail Gold Fish, Green Ground, 5 In.Diameter | 200.00 |
| **Plique A Jour, Bowl,** Mums & Dahlias On Green Shading, 5 1/2 In. | 225.00 |
| **Plique A Jour, Kovsh,** Scandinavian, Silver, 6 In.Long *Illus* | 1500.00 |
| **Plique A Jour, Spoon,** Floral Design, Pair | 100.00 |
| **Plique A Jour, Vase,** Multicolored Mums & Dahlias On Pastel Green, 6 In. | 220.00 |
| **Plique A Jour, Vase,** Ovoid, Siamese Fighting Fish & 2 Angel Fish, Seaweed | 245.00 |
| **Political Campaign, Autograph,** Richard Nixon As Vice President | 35.00 |
| **Political Campaign, Badge,** Democratic National Convention, 1944, Alternate | 12.00 |
| **Political Campaign, Ballot,** Sample, National Democratic, 1896 | 10.00 |
| **Political Campaign, Ballot,** Sample, Prohibition, 1896, Presidential | 10.00 |
| **Political Campaign, Ballot,** Sample, Prohibition, 1982, Presidential | 10.00 |
| **Political Campaign, Bank,** Wallace, 1968, Bell, Iron, "stand Up For America" | 18.00 |
| **Political Campaign, Book,** Song, Garfield & Arthur, 1880 | 25.00 |
| **Political Campaign, Booklet,** General William Henry Harrison, 1840 | 37.50 |
| **Political Campaign, Booklet,** This Is Ike, 1952, Pictures | 3.00 |
| **Political Campaign, Bowl,** Wm.H.Taft Band, Heart Shape, Glass, 5 1/2 In. | 8.00 |
| **Political Campaign, Bumper Sticker,** McGovern & Eagleton | .50 |
| **Political Campaign, Bust,** John F.Kennedy, 1964, Cardboard | 4.00 |
| **Political Campaign, Button,** Adlai Stevenson, 1956, Picture, Flasher | 1.00 |
| **Political Campaign, Button,** Dewey | 2.00 |
| **Political Campaign, Button,** Dewey & Bricker | 3.00 |
| **Political Campaign, Button,** Dewey & Warren | 3.00 |
| **Political Campaign, Button,** Flasher, All The Way With Adlai, 2 1/2 In. | 1.25 |
| **Political Campaign, Button,** Flasher, Mamie Start Packing | 3.00 |
| **Political Campaign, Button,** I Like Ike, Flasher, 2 1/2 In. | 1.00 |
| **Political Campaign, Button,** I Like Ike, 1956, Picture, Flasher | 1.00 |
| **Political Campaign, Button,** John F.Kennedy, Flasher, 2 1/2 In. | 1.00 To 3.00 |
| **Political Campaign, Button,** L.B.J., Flasher, 2 1/2 In. | 1.00 |
| **Political Campaign, Button,** McGovern & Eagleton, Flasher, 2 1/2 In. | 1.00 |
| **Political Campaign, Button,** Nixon & Agnew, Round, 6 In. | 3.00 |
| **Political Campaign, Button,** Nixon & Agnew, 1968, Picture, Flasher | 1.00 |
| **Political Campaign, Button,** Robert Kennedy, Flasher, 2 1/2 In. | 1.00 |
| **Political Campaign, Button,** Warren & Coolidge | 5.00 |
| **Political Campaign, Button,** Willkie & McNary | 5.00 |
| **Political Campaign, Button,** Wm.McKinley, Ribbon | 10.00 |
| **Political Campaign, Button,** Wm.McKinley, Small | 10.00 |
| **Political Campaign, Card,** Inaugural Ball, Cleveland & Hendricks, Mar.4, 1885 | 25.00 |
| **Political Campaign, Card,** Song, J.F.Kennedy, Marchin' To Washington, 1960 | 3.95 |
| **Political Campaign, Certificate,** Dollar, Dewey, 1948 | 3.00 |
| **Political Campaign, Certificate,** Dollar, Willkie & McNary | 1.50 To 3.00 |
| **Political Campaign, Cigar,** Bubble Gum, Humphrey, 1968, Carton | 7.50 |
| **Political Campaign, Cigar,** Bubble Gum, Nixon, 1968, Carton | 7.50 |
| **Political Campaign, Cigar,** Bubble Gum, Wallace, 1968, Carton | 15.00 |

| | |
|---|---:|
| Political Campaign, Compact, Dewey For President, Picture, 2 3/4 In. | 20.00 |
| Political Campaign, Dollar, Democrat, 1940 | 2.50 |
| Political Campaign, Handbill, Urging Citizenry To Vote, 1940s | 6.50 |
| Political Campaign, Inaugural Invitation, Nixon & Agnew, 1973 | 4.00 |
| Political Campaign, Jug, Herbert Hoover, Syracuse China | 60.00 |
| Political Campaign, Jugate, Goldwater & Miller, 3 1/2 In. | 1.50 |
| Political Campaign, Jugate, Johnson & Humphrey, 1 In. | 10.00 |
| Political Campaign, Jugate, Lincoln & Johnson, 1864, Penny Size | 48.00 |
| Political Campaign, Jugate, McGovern & Eagleton, 3 In. | 1.25 |
| Political Campaign, Jugate, Nixon & Agnew, 1968, 3 In. | 1.50 |
| Political Campaign, Jugate, Taft | 20.00 |
| Political Campaign, Jugate, Taft & Jacobson, Black & White | 15.00 |
| Political Campaign, Lapel Stud, Cox, 1920, Rooster | 20.00 |
| Political Campaign, Light Bulb, Republican Elephant Inside | 14.50 |
| Political Campaign, Matches, Nixon | .50 |
| Political Campaign, Medal, Woodrow Wilson | 5.25 |
| Political Campaign, Mug, Bobby For President, Red, White, & Blue, Picture | 4.50 |
| Political Campaign, Mug, Dawson Of Springfield, Illinois, Picture | 13.50 |
| Political Campaign, Mug, F.D.R., Picture, The New Deal | 9.00 |
| Political Campaign, Mug, President Taft, Figural, German Porcelain | 65.00 |
| Political Campaign, Pennant, Dewey For President, Picture | 8.00 |
| Political Campaign, Pin, Gerald R.Ford, Appointed Vice President, Picture | .50 |
| Political Campaign, Pin, Gerald R.Ford, Picture, 2 1/8 In. | .50 |
| Political Campaign, Pin, Gop, 1940, Elephant's Head, Brass, High Relief | 12.00 |
| Political Campaign, Pin, Harry Truman, Picture, Memorial, 2 1/8 In. | .50 |
| Political Campaign, Pin, Hoover, Bronze, Picture | 6.00 |
| Political Campaign, Pin, John W.Davis, Picture | 42.00 |
| Political Campaign, Pin, La Follette & Wheeler, 3rd Party, Bronze | 35.00 |
| Political Campaign, Pin, McGovern & Eagleton, 1972, 1 1/4 In. | 1.00 |
| Political Campaign, Pin, Robert F.Kennedy, Photograph, 1 3/4 In. | 12.00 |
| Political Campaign, Pin, Socialist, May Day, 1930 | 6.00 |
| Political Campaign, Pinback, B.F.Carroll, For Governor, 2nd Time | 2.50 |
| Political Campaign, Pinback, Benjamin Harrison, Pabst Beer | 5.00 |
| Political Campaign, Pinback, Bryan | 6.00 |
| Political Campaign, Pinback, Douglas MacArthur, Man Of The Hour | 4.50 |
| Political Campaign, Pinback, Eugene V.Debs For President, Picture | 50.00 |
| Political Campaign, Pinback, Harding | 5.00 |
| Political Campaign, Pinback, Harding For Governor, 1/2 In. | 2.50 |
| Political Campaign, Pinback, Hoover & Curtis, Elephant On Keystone | 6.00 |
| Political Campaign, Pinback, John D.Davis | 80.00 |
| Political Campaign, Pinback, La Follette & Wheeler, Bronze, Signed Gerber | 19.00 |
| Political Campaign, Pinback, McKinley, Picture, God's Will, Not Ours | 4.00 |
| Political Campaign, Pinback, Oscar S.Straus For Governor | 2.50 |
| Political Campaign, Pinback, Otto Bremer For Mayor | 2.50 |
| Political Campaign, Pinback, Wm.B.Allison, Our Choice For Senator | 2.50 |
| Political Campaign, Pinback, Woodrow Wilson | 8.00 |
| Political Campaign, Plate, Blaine & Logan, Ivy Border | 50.00 |
| Political Campaign, Plate, McKinley, 1896, Portrait, White Pressed Glass | 39.50 |
| Political Campaign, Postcard, Bryan & Kern | 4.50 |
| Political Campaign, Postcard, Taft & Bryan, 1908, "i'm For Bill" | 30.00 |
| Political Campaign, Poster, Dick Gregory For President | 5.95 |
| Political Campaign, Program, Inaugural Ball, Cleveland & Hendricks, 1885 | 25.00 |
| Political Campaign, Ribbon, Fremont & Daton, 1856, Pictures, Silk | 200.00 |
| Political Campaign, Ribbon, Win With Willkie, Paper, 2 1/2 X 10 In. | 4.00 |
| Political Campaign, Statuette, McKinley, Opaque | 130.00 |
| Political Campaign, Sticker, Roosevelt, 1934, Red, White, & Blue, 12 In. | 2.00 |
| Political Campaign, Stickpin, Benjamin Harrison, Picture | 20.00 |
| Political Campaign, Thimble, Landon & Knox, Metal | 3.00 |
| Political Campaign, Toby Mug, Herbert Hoover, Patriotic Products, 6 3/4 In. | 35.00 |
| Political Campaign, Token, Bryan For President, Picture, Silver Dollar Size | 37.00 |
| Political Campaign, Tray, Blaine & Logan, 1884, Frosted Center Portraits | 150.00 |
| Political Campaign, Tray, Change, Taft & Sherman, 1908, G.O.P. | 40.00 |

*Pomona glass is clear with a soft amber border decorated with pale blue or rose-colored flowers and leaves. The colors are very, very pale. The background of the glass is covered with a network of fine lines. It was made from 1885 to 1888 by the New England Glass Company.*

Pomona, Bowl, Berry, Cornflowers, Amber Fluted Rim, 1st Grind, 9 In. ............................ 274.00
Pomona, Bowl, Conical, Cornflower, Applied 10 Toed Foot, Scalloped, 1st Grind ............ 225.00
Pomona, Bowl, Finger, Hexagonal Rim, 2nd Grind ....................................................... 95.00
Pomona, Bowl, Finger, Midwest, Diamond-Quilted ....................................................... 35.00
Pomona, Bowl, Finger, Ruffled Border, 2nd Grind ....................................................... 45.00
Pomona, Bowl, Finger, Thumbprint ........................................................................... 65.00
Pomona, Bowl, Scalloped Top, Ground Off Base, 1st Grind, 5 1/2 X 2 1/2 In. .............. 62.00
Pomona, Bowl, Scalloped Top, Ground Off Base, 2nd Grind, 5 1/2 X 2 1/2 In. ............. 48.00
Pomona, Candlestick, Low, Green, Signed, Pair ......................................................... 100.00
Pomona, Castor, Pickle, Blue Cornflower, Inverted Thumbprint, Meriden Holder ............ 325.00
Pomona, Celery, Cornflower Decoration, First Grind ................................................... 200.00
Pomona, Celery, Inverted Thumbprint, Fluted Rim & Base, 1st Grind ........................... 150.00
Pomona, Cup, Punch, New England, Diamond-Quilted, 1st Grind .................. 55.00 To 95.00
Pomona, Pitcher, Blue Cornflowers, 2nd Grind, 6 3/4 In. ............................................ 140.00
Pomona, Pitcher, Water, Amber Top ........................................................................ 185.00
Pomona, Pitcher, Water, Inverted Thumbprint, Enameled Flowers, 7 1/2 In. ................. 150.00
Pomona, Pitcher, Water, Thumbprint ....................................................................... 185.00
Pomona, Rose Bowl, Midwestern, 3 Amber Feet, Enameled Bird & Floral ..................... 85.00
Pomona, Tankard, New England, Diamond-Quilted, 1st Grind ...................................... 170.00
Pomona, Tankard, Water, Cornflower Decoration ....................................................... 250.00
Pomona, Tumbler, Butterfly & Pansy ....................................................................... 225.00
Pomona, Tumbler, Diamond Thumbprint, New England, 1st Grind ................................ 78.00
Pomona, Tumbler, Diamond-Quilted, Acanthus Leaf, New England, 1st Grind ............... 135.00
Pomona, Tumbler, Diamond-Quilted, Cornflower, New England, 2nd Grind .................... 115.00
Pomona, Tumbler, Diamond-Quilted, Pansy & Butterfly, New England, 2nd Grind .......... 175.00
Pomona, Tumbler, Inverted Thumbprint, 2nd Grind, 3 1/2 In. ..................... 49.00 To 55.00
Pomona, Tumbler, Lemonade, 1st Grind ................................................................... 85.00
Pomona, Tumbler, Oak Leaf & Acorn, Gold Trim, Blown, 1st Grind .............................. 98.00
Pomona, Vase, Inverted Thumbprint, Scalloped Amber Band Rim, 2nd Grind ................. 55.00
      Pontypool, see Tole
Popeye, Book, Popeye's Ghost Ship To Treasure Island, Big Little Book ........................ 12.50
Popeye, Doll, 21 In.Tall ........................................................................................ 14.00
Popeye, Game, The Juggler, Tin & Glass, Painted, Dated 1929, 5 X 3 1/2 In. ............... 12.00
Popeye, Harmonica, 1929 ...................................................................................... 8.00
Popeye, Spoon & Fork ........................................................................................... 6.00
      Porcelain, see also Copeland, Nippon, R.S.Prussia, etc.
Porcelain, Ashtray & Cigarette Holder, Japanese, 3 Negro Children ............................ 4.00
Porcelain, Barrel, Biscuit, S.F.& Co., Elm, Floral, Silver Plate Lid & Bail ..................... 25.00
Porcelain, Basket, Czechoslovakia, Red, Black Handle ............................................... 26.00
Porcelain, Berry Set, MW Co., Germany, Roses, Scalloped, 7 Piece .............................. 30.00
Porcelain, Berry Set, Russian, Shell Shape, Roses, Gold, 3 Piece ................................. 45.00
Porcelain, Berry Set, Weimar, Germany, Roses On Dark, Gold Trim, 7 Piece .................. 32.50
Porcelain, Bonbon, Czechoslovakia, Handle, Divided, Floral, 8 In. ................................ 9.25
Porcelain, Bottle, Scent, Russian, Popov, Raised Floral, C.1830 ................................... 95.00
Porcelain, Bottle, Toilet Water, Pink Floral, Beading, 5 1/2 In.High .............................. 8.00
Porcelain, Bow, Jewel, France, Portrait Of Man & Lady, Blue & Gold ........................... 175.00
Porcelain, Bowl & Underplate, Mayonnaise, Austria, Pink Roses, Handle ..................... 17.50
Porcelain, Bowl Set, Ascoha, Germany, Eggshell, 3 Piece ........................................... 9.00
Porcelain, Bowl Set, M.Z.Austria, Eggshell, 4 Piece .................................................. 12.00
Porcelain, Bowl, C T Germany, Shell Shape, Gold Edge, Lilacs & Floral ........................ 27.50
Porcelain, Bowl, Punch, German, White, Gold Band & 'tom & Jerry' ............................. 32.00
Porcelain, Bowl, Royal In Gold Wreath Mark, Yellow Roses, 10 1/2 In. ........................ 25.00
Porcelain, Bowl, Serving, Japanese, 3 Section, Floral Lacquer Box, 8 In. ...................... 15.00
Porcelain, Box, Dresser, Covered, Pink Wild Roses, Gold Edges, A.K.France .................. 60.00
Porcelain, Box, English, Fat Boy In Relief Looks Like Toby, 5 In. ................................. 18.00
Porcelain, Box, French, Domed Lid, Brass Rope Collar, Gold Scrolls, Scene ................... 70.00
Porcelain, Box, Germany, Covered, Applied Pink Flowers, 3 In. .................................... 9.00
Porcelain, Box, Jewel, De La Courtille, Paris, Hinged, Footed, Scene, 1773 .................. 68.00
Porcelain, Box, Jewel, France, Cobalt Blue, Gold Trim, Courting Scene ......................... 145.00
Porcelain, Box, Patch, French, Enamel Floral On Lid, Brass Hinges, White, 1850 ........... 48.00
Porcelain, Box, Trinket, Japanese, Hinged, Scenic, Gilt Trim, Round ............................ 25.00
Porcelain, Bridge Set, L.D.B.Co., Germany, Playing Card Decoration, 10 Piece ............... 42.00
Porcelain, Bust, George Washington, 3 1/2 In.High ................................................... 38.00
Porcelain, Butter Pat, Cloverleaf & Austria, Hand-Painted, Gold, Set Of 7 ..................... 8.50
Porcelain, Butter Pat, Heubach, Hand-Painted Ships & Castles, Set Of 12 ..................... 200.00
Porcelain, Butter, Czechoslovakia, Baskets Of Flowers, Gold ....................................... 20.00

Porcelain, **Cake Set,** Japan, Open Handles, Gilt Scrolls, Yellow, 6 Piece .............................. 12.50
Porcelain, **Can,** Coffee, Paris, Blue & Pink Floral, Gold, C.1790, 2 1/2 In. .......................... 37.00
Porcelain, **Can,** Coffee, Paris, Bourbon Sprig, C.1790, 2 1/2 In.High ................................ 37.00
Porcelain, **Can,** Coffee, Paris, Intertwined Roses & Gold, C.1790, 2 1/2 In. ...................... 37.00
Porcelain, **Canister Set,** Mikoriware, Blue Florals, Pull Tops, 4 Piece ........................... 12.50
Porcelain, **Celery Set,** Leuckenburg, Germany, Lavender Flowers, 7 Piece ..................... 50.00
Porcelain, **Celery,** Germany, Hand-Painted Roses, Pierced Handles, 12 In. ..................... 8.50
Porcelain, **Chamberstick,** Pink Roses, Gilt, Drip Pan, C.1800, 3 3/4 In.Wide ................ 85.00
Porcelain, **Charger,** Hanging, White Roses, Green Foliage, 12 1/2 In.Diameter .............. 13.00
Porcelain, **Chocolate Pot,** Austria, Flower Clusters, Scrolls, Gold Trim ........................ 28.00
Porcelain, **Chocolate Pot,** Austrian, Floral On White, Branch Handle ............................ 13.00
Porcelain, **Chocolate Pot,** Gold Top Rim, Blue Floral On White ................................... 15.00
Porcelain, **Chocolate Pot,** J.& E.Mayer, Scattered Pink Roses, 8 1/2 In. ....................... 17.00
Porcelain, **Chocolate Set,** C.T. Altwasser, Pansies In Bands, 7 Piece ........................... 135.00
Porcelain, **Chocolate Set,** C.T.Germany, Pink & White Roses, Gilt, 3 Piece .................. 45.00
Porcelain, **Chocolate Set,** Child's, Children Playing, Multicolor, 13 Piece ..................... 80.00
Porcelain, **Chocolate Set,** Japan, Blue & Orange, 9 Piece ......................................... 30.00
Porcelain, **Chopstick,** Gotham, Austria, Hand-Painted Flowers, Gold Feet, Pair ............ 32.00
Porcelain, **Clock & Vase Set,** Germany, Deep Blue & White, 3 Piece ........................... 110.00
Porcelain, **Coffeepot,** Altwasser, Germany, Black & Gold Designs. 11 In. High ............. 40.00
Porcelain, **Coffeepot,** Marked Burroughs, Mountford, Thistles, Gold, C.1880 ................ 35.00
Porcelain, **Coffeepot,** Russian, Animal's Head Spout, Italianate Scenes, 1850s ............. 70.00
Porcelain, **Compote,** German, Chinoiserie, Hide & Seek .......................................... 475.00
Porcelain, **Compote,** Pink Floral, Gilt, Davenport Longport, 9 In.Diameter ................... 50.00
Porcelain, **Creamer,** Althrohla, Austria, Court Gentleman Medallion, 4 3/4 In. ............. 25.00
Porcelain, **Creamer,** Austria, Moose, Ovoid Base, 5 In.High ...................................... 18.50
Porcelain, **Creamer,** Cow, Czechoslovakia, 4 In.High ............................................... 6.50
Porcelain, **Creamer,** Crown & Star Marked, German, Woman With Basket On Back ........ 40.00
Porcelain, **Creamer,** Czechoslovakia, Cow's Head, 4 1/2 In.High ............................... 18.50
Porcelain, **Creamer,** Czechoslovakia, Tropical Bird Shape, Multicolored ...................... 4.75
Porcelain, **Creamer,** German, Ribbon Handle, Pink Sprays, Green Panels ..................... 8.50
Porcelain, **Creamer,** Germany, Figural, Cow, 5 In.High ............................................ 29.00
Porcelain, **Creamer,** Germany, Figural, Robin, 5 In. ............................................... 10.00
Porcelain, **Creamer,** Germany, Hen & Roosters On White, 3 1/4 In.High ...................... 6.75
Porcelain, **Creamer,** Japan, Hand-Painted Violets ................................................. 8.00
Porcelain, **Creamer,** Marked Erphila, Germany, Cat Shape, Removable Head ................ 22.50
Porcelain, **Creamer,** Parrot, Czechoslovakia, 4 5/8 In.High ...................................... 4.95
Porcelain, **Creamer,** Pelican, Colorful, German, 3 3/4 In.High .................................. 7.50
Porcelain, **Cruet,** Two Birds Intertwined Form Body, Marked V & O ........................... 35.00
Porcelain, **Cup & Saucer,** Chocolate, German, Pink Roses On Rust, Gold Trim .............. 3.50
Porcelain, **Cup & Saucer,** Cloverleaf, Austria, Hand-Painted Floral, Gold Edge ............ 15.00
Porcelain, **Cup & Saucer,** Crown Allerton, White & Green Chinese Designs .................. 10.00
Porcelain, **Cup & Saucer,** Cuthbertson House, England, Christmas Decoration .............. 6.50
Porcelain, **Cup & Saucer,** Demitasse, French, Gold Ivy & Vine, Fleur-De-Lis ............... 10.00
Porcelain, **Cup & Saucer,** Demitasse, German, Pink Luster Bands, White ...................... 6.00
Porcelain, **Cup & Saucer,** Demitasse, Laughlin, Bluebird .......................................... 3.00
Porcelain, **Cup & Saucer,** Demitasse, Victoria, Austria, Pink Flowers .......................... 7.00
Porcelain, **Cup & Saucer,** Demitasse, Victoria, Nude Lady Lithophane Bottom ............... 12.00
Porcelain, **Cup & Saucer,** English, R.M., Yellow On White, Pedestal Cup, C.1868 ......... 12.00
Porcelain, **Cup & Saucer,** German, Gold Trim & Ball Feet, Applied Floral .................... 16.50
Porcelain, **Cup & Saucer,** German, Hand-Painted House Scenes, Gold, Enamel ............. 15.00
Porcelain, **Cup & Saucer,** Imperial Crown Austria, Holly & Berries, Coach ................... 18.00
Porcelain, **Cup & Saucer,** Kornilow Bros., St.Petersburg, Art Nouveau, C.1900 ........... 42.00
Porcelain, **Cup & Saucer,** Marked Germany, White, Green Edges, Yellow Roses ........... 17.50
Porcelain, **Cup & Saucer,** Rosebuds, Green Trim, Marked Foley, Miniature ................... 5.00
Porcelain, **Cup & Saucer,** Royal Austria, Rose Pompadour, Artist Signed ...................... 25.00
Porcelain, **Cup & Saucer,** Signed M.Skoozenikev, Gold Luster, Floral Inside ................. 55.00
Porcelain, **Cup & Saucer,** Victoria, Czechoslovakia, Pink Rose Groups ......................... 6.00
Porcelain, **Cup,** Berlin, Friendship, Coat-Of-Arms Decoration .................................... 35.00
Porcelain, **Cup,** German, "be Always Happy, " 3 In. ............................................... 10.00
Porcelain, **Cup,** J.P.L., France, Three Handled, Artist Signed Views, Gold Trim ............. 70.00
Porcelain, **Cup,** New Hapsburg, Austria, Blue Band, Gold ........................................ 5.00
Porcelain, **Dish,** Baby's, Feeding, DF Czechoslovakia, Transfer Scene, Gold ................ 20.00
Porcelain, **Dish,** Candy, Dante, Palais Royal, Covered, Basket, Ormolu Handle ............. 40.00
Porcelain, **Dish,** Candy, Royal Berlin, Handled, Flowers, Gold, Blue, Scepter Mark ........ 14.00
Porcelain, **Dish,** Candy, Royale Saxe, Germany, Florals, Gold Trim, Round ................... 10.50

Porcelain, Figurine,
Woman Reading,
Russian, C.1850

Porcelain, Figurine,
Man With Barrel,
Russian, C.1850

Porcelain, Figurine,
Dancing Woman, Popov, C.1820

| | |
|---|---|
| Porcelain, Dish, Candy, Signed E.Ten Eyck, 1909, Hand-Painted Blackberries | 8.50 |
| Porcelain, Dish, Candy, Thomas, Germany, B Mark, Gold Finial, Gold & Blue | 17.00 |
| Porcelain, Dish, Cheese, Covered, Flowers, Loop Stem, Mylott, 9 In.Diameter | 22.00 |
| Porcelain, Dish, Cheese, German Mark, Orange & Purple Pansies On Green | 40.00 |
| Porcelain, Dish, Duck Cover, Marked Russian | 95.00 |
| Porcelain, Dish, Feeding, Child's, Germany, Old Fashioned Auto | 12.50 |
| Porcelain, Dish, Feeding, English, Cat Toying With Biwing Airplane, Signed | 28.50 |
| Porcelain, Dish, Lobster Cover, Czechoslovakia, Red, 3 1/2 In. | 5.00 |
| Porcelain, Dish, Nut, M.Z.Austria, Hand-Painted Acorn & Leaf Design | 8.50 |
| Porcelain, Dish, Powder, French Marks, Covered, Tan, Lions' Heads On Sides | 10.00 |
| Porcelain, Dish, Russian, Melon Form, Khrapunov-Novyi Decorated, C.1890 | 150.00 |
| Porcelain, Dish, Sardine, Victoria, Austria, Covered, Sardine Handle, Floral | 35.00 |
| Porcelain, Dresser Set, Victoria, Austria, Roses, Gold Rope Trim, 6 Piece | 55.00 |
| Porcelain, Egg, Easter, Russian, Cyrillic Letters XB, Navy Blue, C.1850 | 90.00 |
| Porcelain, Egg, Easter, Russian, Violets On Pink, C.1890, 4 1/2 In. | 200.00 |
| Porcelain, Ewer, Austria, Hand-Painted Roses, 6 In. | 12.00 |
| Porcelain, Ewer, Austrian, Handled, Portrait Of Busty Woman, Squatty, 4 In. | 19.00 |
| Porcelain, Ewer, Italian, Melon Ribbed, Midnight Blue, Gold Trim, Floral | 40.00 |
| Porcelain, Feeding Set, Germany, Witch Decoration, 3 Piece | 35.00 |
| Porcelain, Figurine, Bathing Beauty, German, Lavender Suit | 15.00 To 21.50 |
| Porcelain, Figurine, Bird, German, 6 1/2 In. High | 20.00 |
| Porcelain, Figurine, Cat, Sleeping, Japanese, White, Gold Trim, 5 1/2 In. | 16.00 |
| Porcelain, Figurine, Cockatoo, Hornberg, C.1850, 8 1/4 In.High | 75.00 |
| Porcelain, Figurine, Dancing Woman, Popov, C.1820 *Illus* | 150.00 |
| Porcelain, Figurine, Dancing Woman, Russian, C.1850, 7 1/2 In. | 80.00 |
| Porcelain, Figurine, Girl & Man In Court Costumes, Marked Suhl, Pair | 195.00 |
| Porcelain, Figurine, Girl, German, Green Dress, 9 In.High | 16.50 |
| Porcelain, Figurine, Man & Woman With Lute, Japanese, 6 3/4 In.High, Pair | 40.00 |
| Porcelain, Figurine, Man With Barrel, Russian, C.1850 *Illus* | 225.00 |
| Porcelain, Figurine, Monkey Drummer, German | 85.00 |
| Porcelain, Figurine, Monkey Oboeist, German | 85.00 |
| Porcelain, Figurine, Sailor Boy, German, Cobalt, Light Blue, & Gold | 18.00 |
| Porcelain, Figurine, Scottish Lassie, Stewart Royal, 7 In. | 16.00 |
| Porcelain, Figurine, Seminude, Holding Thread Of Life, 3 1/2 X 5 1/2 In. | 150.00 |
| Porcelain, Figurine, Setter, Long Haired, Vienna, Sitting, White, Tan Spots | 37.00 |
| Porcelain, Figurine, Shepherd Carrying Sheep, Russian, C.1750, 6 In.High | 175.00 |
| Porcelain, Figurine, Whippet, Vienna, White & Gray, Paws Outstretched | 58.00 |
| Porcelain, Figurine, Woman Reading, Russian, C.1850 *Illus* | 80.00 |
| Porcelain, Fish Set, Austria, 13 Piece | 185.00 |
| Porcelain, Fish Set, German, 7 In.Plates, 14 Piece | 125.00 |
| Porcelain, Flower Holder, Nude With Scarf, 6 1/4 In.High | 8.00 |
| Porcelain, Gravy Boat, John Haddock & Sons, Floral On White, Gilt Trim | 8.50 |
| Porcelain, Hair Receiver, Cameo Lady's Head On Dark Green Ground, German | 22.00 |
| Porcelain, Hair Receiver, Germany, Green & Gold, Rose Sprays | 12.50 |
| Porcelain, Hair Receiver, Sky Blue, Forget-Me-Nots, Bavaria | 22.00 |
| Porcelain, Hair Receiver, White, Gold Border, Blue Twisted Rope, German | 7.50 |
| Porcelain, Hatpin Holder, Austria, White, Blue Flowers, 4 1/2 In. | 14.50 |
| Porcelain, Hatpin Holder, French, 3 Eagles' Heads Support Perforated Part | 35.00 |

| | |
|---|---:|
| Porcelain, Hatpin Holder, Germany, Pink & White Roses On White To Beige | 16.00 |
| Porcelain, Holder, Card, German, Dog Shape, 2 3/4 In.High | 6.00 |
| Porcelain, Holder, Playing Cards, English, Card Suits, Pencil Holder | 12.00 |
| Porcelain, Holder, Toothbrush, English, Dark Blue & Gold Decoration | 8.00 |
| Porcelain, Humidor, Covered, Pheasant Decoration, Gray's Pottery, 5 In. | 22.50 |
| Porcelain, Inkwell, Japanese, Ball Lid, Figures, Paris Exposition, 1889 | 100.00 |
| Porcelain, Invalid Feeder, German, Raised Flowers On White | 5.00 |
| Porcelain, Invalid Feeder, Oriental, White, 4 People In Outdoor Scene | 30.00 |
| Porcelain, Jar, Cookie, Windsor, Floral On Cream, Silver Plate Handle | 27.50 |
| Porcelain, Jar, Cracker, English, Stag & Doe, Silver Lid & Bail | 32.00 |
| Porcelain, Jar, Ginger, Leuchenburg, Germany, Roses On Pastel, Gold | 47.50 |
| Porcelain, Jar, Mustard, Covered, Three Crown Germany, Pink Floral On White | 10.00 |
| Porcelain, Jar, Roses, Gold Trim, Gold Finial, French, Amoge, 8 1/2 In.High | 17.00 |
| Porcelain, Jar, Tobacco, Austria, Man With Derby Hat, Pipe In Mouth, 6 In. | 40.00 |
| Porcelain, Jar, Tobacco, French, Marbleized, Footed, Bronze & Ebony, 5 1/2 In. | 47.50 |
| Porcelain, Jardiniere On Stand, English, Gilt, Enamel, C.1890, 5 1/4 In., Pair | 200.00 |
| Porcelain, Jardiniere, English, Pastoral Scene, Claw Feet, C.1800, 4 1/8 In. | 60.00 |
| Porcelain, Jelly Set, German, Open Handled Tray, Fruit & Berries, 7 Piece | 22.00 |
| Porcelain, Knife & Fork, French, Hand-Painted Flowers, Gold Colored Metal | 8.50 |
| Porcelain, Ladle, Flora K & Co., Blue Flowers, Gold | 16.00 |
| Porcelain, Letter Holder, German, Cobalt Blue Glaze, Gold, Graduated | 28.00 |
| Porcelain, Luncheon Set, Austrian, Apple Blossoms On White, Gold, 41 Piece | 195.00 |
| Porcelain, Mortar & Pestle, Marked Germany, White, 3 In.Across | 18.00 |
| Porcelain, Muffineer, Gold Pheasant On Beige, Silver Top, Locke, England | 45.00 |
| Porcelain, Muffineer, Three Crown China, Brown Roses On Cream | 25.00 |
| Porcelain, Muffineer, Victoria, Owl & Crest, Iridescent | 20.00 |
| Porcelain, Mug & Saucer, Child's, Germany, A Close Finish, Boys, Toy Horse | 35.00 |
| Porcelain, Mug & Saucer, Child's, Germany, The Regatta, Children, Dogs, Cats | 35.00 |
| Porcelain, Mug, German Luster, Pink Drapes, Raised Gold Trim, 4 Gold Feet | 6.50 |
| Porcelain, Mug, German, Hand-Painted Cherries & Peaches | 10.00 |
| Porcelain, Mug, Germany, Kate Greenaway Type, Luster Band At Top | 9.00 |
| Porcelain, Mug, Little Pig, Walt Disney Entertainers, Pale Yellow | 5.00 |
| Porcelain, Mug, Three Crown, Germany, Wolf In Red Riding Hood's Clothes | 15.00 |
| Porcelain, Mug, Vitrock, Little Bopeep, Opaque White | 6.00 |
| Porcelain, Mustard Set, German, Figural, Sailor, 4 In.Jar, 2 Piece | 12.00 |
|     Porcelain, Napkin Ring, see Napkin Ring | |
|     Porcelain, Oyster Plate, see Oyster Plate | |
| Porcelain, Perfume, French, Octagonal, Mushroom Top, White & Blue, 5 1/2 In. | 27.00 |
| Porcelain, Perfume, Marked Royal Sitzendorf, Floral & Gilt, Crown Stopper | 20.00 |
| Porcelain, Pitcher, American China Co., Gypsy Girl On Brown, C.1900, 12 In. | 70.00 |
| Porcelain, Pitcher, Austria, Moose's Head, 4 1/2 In. | 8.00 |
| Porcelain, Pitcher, Czechoslovakia, Blue & White, 4 In. | 4.00 |
| Porcelain, Pitcher, Czechoslovakia, Figural Eagle | 14.00 |
| Porcelain, Pitcher, German, Railroad Ave., Sylvan Beach, N.Y., 2 1/4 In. | 8.00 |
| Porcelain, Planter, M.Z. Austria, Clay Liner, Handled, Pink & White Floral | 22.00 |
| Porcelain, Plaque, English, Shaded Roses On White, J.Simpson, C.1890, 12 In. | 275.00 |
| Porcelain, Plaque, Wagner, Obese Elderly Monk At Table, C.1890, 6 X 4 In. | 225.00 |
| Porcelain, Plate & Mug, Child's, Germany, Newly Hatched Yellow Chicks | 30.00 |
| Porcelain, Plate, Altenburg, Germany, Pink & Red Roses, Gold Edge, 9 1/2 In. | 22.00 |
| Porcelain, Plate, Bread & Butter, Saxe, ES Germany, Roses On Cream, Gold | 4.95 |
| Porcelain, Plate, Bread, French, Open Handles, Hand-Painted Roses, Signed | 22.50 |
| Porcelain, Plate, Bust Of Lady In Big Hat, Cobalt Rim, Old Ivory Syracuse | 28.00 |
| Porcelain, Plate, C.D. R.N.922770, Butterflies, Gold Leaf Band, 8 1/2 In. | 25.00 |
| Porcelain, Plate, Carlsbad, Violets, Double Open Handles | 6.00 |
| Porcelain, Plate, Cheese & Cracker, M.Z.Austria, Center Pedestal, Floral | 15.00 |
| Porcelain, Plate, Chinese Decoration, Blue & White, Allertons, 9 In. | 9.00 |
| Porcelain, Plate, Christmas, Plummer, N.Y., Tree & Toys, 1930s, 8 1/4 In. | 5.00 |
| Porcelain, Plate, Czechoslovakia, Dutch Figures, Windmill, Deep, 6 1/2 In. | 7.00 |
| Porcelain, Plate, Dessert, Altwasser, Germany, Black & Gold Designs, 7 In. | 4.45 |
| Porcelain, Plate, Dessert, Leutchenberg, Germany, Signed | 15.00 |
| Porcelain, Plate, Doe & Buck, Forest Scene, Signed, 8 1/4 In. | 18.00 |
| Porcelain, Plate, E.Proctor, Pansy Spray On Blue, Gold Edge, 8 In. | 12.00 |
| Porcelain, Plate, English, Primrose Center, Gold Decoration, 9 In. | 7.50 |
| Porcelain, Plate, French, Cupid Center, Gold Decorated Edge, 7 7/8 In. | 5.00 |
| Porcelain, Plate, French, Cupid Center, Gold Scalloped Edge, 11 1/2 In. | 15.00 |
| Porcelain, Plate, French, Terre De Fer, Musical Series, Comical | 25.00 |

Porcelain, Plate, Fruit On Cream, Signed T.Shibota, 10 1/4 In. ............................ 6.00
Porcelain, Plate, Fruit, Peaches & Foliage, Clement, France, 8 3/8 In. ....................... 7.00
Porcelain, Plate, German, Children & Rabbits, 5 In. ........................................ 6.00
Porcelain, Plate, Germany, Fruit Center, Pink Luster Border, 7 In. ......................... 7.00
Porcelain, Plate, Germany, Hydrangea, Open Handles, 9 1/4 In. ............................ 14.00
Porcelain, Plate, Germany, Open Handle, Red Roses, White Blossoms, 9 1/2 In. .......... 15.00
Porcelain, Plate, Germany, Open Handles, Orchids, Gold Trim, 10 3/4 In. .................. 39.50
Porcelain, Plate, Germany, Pink & White Floral, Blue Green Edge, 7 1/2 In. ............... 6.00
Porcelain, Plate, Germany, White Roses On Pink, Mauve & Cream Rim, 8 1/4 In. ......... 12.50
Porcelain, Plate, Green, "nell Finds Schoolmaster Reading, "8 In. ......................... 24.00
Porcelain, Plate, Hand-Painted Pink Roses, 9 In.Signed .................................... 30.00
Porcelain, Plate, Hot, Carlsbad, Austria, Blue Flowers, Gold Trim, Round .................. 7.50
Porcelain, Plate, Imperial Austria, Spaniel Pointing At Flying Bird, 9 In. ................. 32.00
Porcelain, Plate, J.S.Germany, Peaches, Blackberries, Blossoms, 8 In. ..................... 10.00
Porcelain, Plate, Japanese, 6 Figures & Floral, Gold Trim .................................. 25.00
Porcelain, Plate, Leuchtenberg, Germany, Water Lilies, 6 1/4 In. .......................... 8.00
Porcelain, Plate, M.Z.Austria, Pink Roses On White, Gold Edge, 10 In. .................... 30.00
Porcelain, Plate, M.Z.Austria, Pink Roses, Gold Border, 7 1/2 In. .......................... 7.50
Porcelain, Plate, Marked G.D.A.France, Tea Roses, Gold, Open Handles, 8 In. ............. 5.75
Porcelain, Plate, Napkin, English, White Napkin on Blue Basket Weave, Pansies ........... 32.00
Porcelain, Plate, Marked Saxe & Crown, Hand-Painted Floral, Lattice Border ............... 45.00
Porcelain, Plate, Oyster, Austrian, Floral Sprigs On White, 8 In. .......................... 12.00
Porcelain, Plate, Oyster, J.S. With Eagle, White With Pink & Gold, 8 1/2 In. ............... 15.00
Porcelain, Plate, Queen Louise Bust, Gold Scalloped Rim, 7 1/2 In. ........................ 20.00
Porcelain, Plate, Royal Munich, Elk In Forest, Irregular Edge, 11 1/2 In. .................. 42.50
Porcelain, Plate, Saxe, White Floral & Gold Leaf On Green, 10 1/2 In. ..................... 39.00
Porcelain, Plate, Signed Larsen, 2 Women By Lake, 10 1/2 In. ............................. 28.00
Porcelain, Plate, Stag And Young Deer, Scenic Background, 12 In. ......................... 17.50
Porcelain, Plate, T.Crown, Germany, Pink Pansies, Gold Band, 8 1/2 In. ................... 25.00
Porcelain, Plate, Tea, German, Openwork Border, Romantic Scenes, Set Of 8 ............... 32.00
Porcelain, Plate, Thomas, Red & Pink Roses, Signed, 10 In. ................................ 36.00
Porcelain, Pot, Mustard, Lid, Arabs On Camels In Desert Scene ............................ 7.50
Porcelain, Ramekin, French, White Fluted Sides, Vegetables ................................ 2.00
Porcelain, Relish, M.Z.Austria, Yellow Roses On Cream, Gold Scalloped Edge .............. 10.00
Porcelain, Saki Set, Japanese, Blue & White, 6 Piece ...................................... 35.00
Porcelain, Salt & Pepper, Arita, Figural, Mask Of Devil & Woman ......................... 20.00
Porcelain, Salt & Pepper, Victoria, Austria, Silver Plate Tops & Holder .................... 20.00
Porcelain, Salt, French, Double, Flambe Red, 4 In. ........................................ 9.50
Porcelain, Samovar, Kuznetsov Factory, Gilded, C.1750, 7 In.High ......................... 70.00
Porcelain, Sauce, Schwartzburg, Forget-Me-Nots, Gold Edge, 5 In. ......................... 5.35
Porcelain, Saxe, ES Germany, Roses On Front, Iridescent, 4 1/2 In.High ................... 23.00
Porcelain, Shaker, Talcum Powder, Vienna, Austria, Yellow Roses On Blue, Gold ........... 18.00
Porcelain, Shoe, German, Green Luster, Flower On Front, 3 1/4 In. ......................... 10.00
Porcelain, Stud, Shirt, Signed WLC, Gold Border, Carnation, Pair .......................... 6.00
Porcelain, Sugar & Creamer, Cover, M.Z.Austria, Pink Tulips On White ..................... 55.00
Porcelain, Sugar & Creamer, German, Scalloped Tops, Ribbon Handles, Roses .............. 13.50
Porcelain, Sugar & Creamer, Germany, White, Playing Card Suits, Black Edges ............. 16.00
Porcelain, Sugar & Creamer, Japan, Ribbed, Pink Floral On Blue & White ................... 20.00
Porcelain, Sugar & Creamer, P.V.Germany, Vessra, Hand-Painted Pink Poppies .............. 25.00
Porcelain, Sugar, Covered, Germany, Hand-Painted ........................................ 8.50
Porcelain, Sugar, Creamer, & Tray, Austrian, Cover, Gold Handles & Floral ................. 38.50
Porcelain, Tea & Dessert Set, Child's, Japanese, Scenic, Oranges, 20 Piece ................ 23.50
Porcelain, Tea Set, Child's, English, King Edward VII, 6 Piece ............................. 40.00
Porcelain, Tea Set, Child's, German, Hand-Painted, Raised Floral, 17 Piece ................ 50.00
Porcelain, Tea Set, Child's, Japan, Pink Kittens, 20 Piece ................................. 38.00
Porcelain, Tea Set, Child's, Japanese, Dog & Bear, Yellow, 11 Piece ....................... 11.00
Porcelain, Tea Set, Czechoslovakia, Marked Phoenix, Roses, 3 Piece ....................... 30.00
Porcelain, Tea Set, Japan, Black & Orange, 18 Piece ....................................... 25.00
Porcelain, Tea Set, Japan, Hand-Painted Scenes, 3 Piece ................................... 25.00
Porcelain, Tea Set, Japanese, Floral On White, Oranges & Blues, 17 Piece .................. 25.00
Porcelain, Tea Set, Japanese, Geisha Girl, Gold Trim, 9 Piece .............................. 35.00
Porcelain, Tea Set, Japanese, Oriental Figures, Green Scalloped, 15 Piece ................. 55.00
Porcelain, Tea Set, Oriental, Butterflies, Floral, & Scenes, Footed, 13 Piece .............. 100.00
Porcelain, Teacup & Saucer, M.Z.Austria, Pink Roses, Gold Band ........................... 8.25
Porcelain, Teacup & Saucer, Russian, Soviet Constructivist Designs, 1923 ................. 70.00
Porcelain, Teacup, Russian, Soviet Constructivist Designs, 1923 ........................... 30.00

| | |
|---|---:|
| Porcelain, Thermometer, Danish, Crown Mark, Seated Fox Front, Centigrade | 73.00 |
| Porcelain, Tieback, Czechoslovakia, Floral, Shafts, Pair | 12.50 |
| Porcelain, Tile, Tea, R & M, The Mayflower, Blue, Round | 15.00 |
| Porcelain, Toothpick, German, Kewpie Type, Baby Kneeling Next To Pumpkin | 40.00 |
| Porcelain, Toothpick, Weimar, Germany, Purple Orchids & Berries On White | 10.00 |
| Porcelain, Tray, Cake, C.T.Altwasser, Triangular, Sectional, Floral, C.1890 | 25.00 |
| Porcelain, Tray, Pin, FBS France, Oval, Crest Center, Pink & Blue Floral | 8.00 |
| Porcelain, Tray, Pin, Germany, Amour Scene, 4 X 5 1/4 In. | 8.50 |
| Porcelain, Tray, Pin, Hanley, England, Ye Olden Days Scene, 5 X 3 1/2 In. | 8.00 |
| Porcelain, Tureen & Attached Tray, Gravy, Cloverleaf & Austria, Flowers | 13.00 |
| Porcelain, Tureen & Underplate, Fisher's P&7, Covered, Children Fishing | 26.50 |
| Porcelain, Tureen & Underplate, Soup, Leonard, Vienna, Orchids, Handled | 85.00 |
| Porcelain, Tureen & Underplate, Soup, Marked Russian | 500.00 |
| Porcelain, Vase, Arcadian, "United We Stand, " 1914, 2 In.High | 3.00 |
| Porcelain, Vase, Austria, Cylinder, Hand-Painted Poppies, 15 In.High | 65.00 |
| Porcelain, Vase, Austrian, Signed Lulu Mumper, Asters, 2 Gold Handles | 25.00 |
| Porcelain, Vase, England, Urn Shape, Etruscan Decoration, Plum Red, C.1860 | 75.00 |
| Porcelain, Vase, English, Horse & Colt On Shaded Blue, 7 In. | 37.50 |
| Porcelain, Vase, English, Windsor & Durham Castles, Royal Crests, 1884, Pair | 300.00 |
| Porcelain, Vase, German, Orchid, Raised Jewels, Gold Edges, 4 In. High | 32.00 |
| Porcelain, Vase, Japanese, Blue Designs, 1880s, 12 In. High | 85.00 |
| Porcelain, Vase, Japanese, Signed Inouye, Birds & Flowers, 2 1/2 In.High | 7.50 |
| Porcelain, Vase, Patriot Girl, Boy With Banner, 8 In.High, 2 Handles, German | 15.00 |
| Porcelain, Vase, Portrait, Cream, Classical Couple In Garden, 8 In.High | 28.00 |
| Porcelain, Vase, Russian, Alexander Column In Palace Square, C.1820, 16 In. | 225.00 |
| Porcelain, Vase, Russian, Fruit Cornucopiae, C.1850, 12 3/4 In. | 225.00 |
| Porcelain, Veilleuse, Pratt Type Decoration, Hand-Painted, 3 Piece | 245.00 |
| Portobello, Jug, 4 3/4 In High | 85.00 |
| Portrait, Plate, Gypsy Girl, Head To Waist, 9 In. | 35.00 |
| Portrait, Plate, Lovers In Garden, Signed Bauer, 7 1/4 In. | 22.00 |
| Portrait, Plate, Pope Leo XIII, 1878-1903, East Liverpool Potteries Co. | 12.00 |
| Portrait, Plate, Two Little Girls, 7 In. | 15.00 |
| Portrait, Plate, Young Lady, Gold Rim, 9 5/8 In. | 25.00 |
| Portrait, Vase, Girl In White On Green & Gold, Marked Gesetzlich | 75.00 |

*Postcards were first legally permitted in Austria on October 1, 1869.*
*The United States passed postal regulations allowing the card in 1873.*
*Most of the picture postcards collected today date from 1910.*

Postcard, see also Album, Postcard

| | |
|---|---:|
| Postcard, Austen, Busy Bears, No.436 | 2.75 |
| Postcard, Birchbark, 1905 | 2.00 |
| Postcard, Buster Brown & Tige, Halloween | 5.00 |
| Postcard, Campbell Soup Kids | 5.00 |
| Postcard, Child, Flag, & Wreath, Clap | 3.00 |
| Postcard, Children, Christmas Wreaths, Munk | 6.00 |
| Postcard, Embossed We Fell Right Into Things Here With A Splash | 1.00 |
| Postcard, Ethel, Ad For Quaker Oats Co. | 1.50 |
| Postcard, Halloween, Girls, Winsch | 3.00 |
| Postcard, Halloween, Negro, Whitney | 4.00 |
| Postcard, Halloween, Set Of 8 | 4.00 |
| Postcard, Harrison Fisher, Girl, Color | 3.00 |
| Postcard, Hold-To-Light, Illuminated Art | 6.50 |
| Postcard, Holiday, 12 | 2.00 |
| Postcard, I Greet Thee, Valentine | 1.00 |
| Postcard, January Birthday, Garnet & Snowdrops | 1.00 |
| Postcard, Kitten, Meow When Squeezed | .40 |
| Postcard, Leather, C.1900 | 2.00 |
| Postcard, Lincoln, Bein | 4.00 |
| Postcard, Lincoln, Chapman | 4.00 |
| Postcard, Lincoln, Nash, No.1 | 3.60 |
| Postcard, Lincoln, Tuck | 4.00 |
| Postcard, Lord's Prayer, Philadelphia Postcard Co., Set Of 8 | 15.00 |
| Postcard, Making Up, B.C.Pease | 4.00 |
| Postcard, Military In London, Tuck, Set Of 6 | 12.00 |
| Postcard, Old Auto Filled With Holly | 1.00 |
| Postcard, Patriot, Clap, No.2443 | 2.50 |

| | |
|---|---|
| Postcard, Patriotic, Twelvetrees | 3.00 |
| Postcard, Pekinese In A Basket, Munk | 6.00 |
| Postcard, Robert E.Lee, Attached Golden Eagle, Tuck | 7.00 |
| Postcard, Roosevelt, Bears | 4.50 |
| Postcard, Santa, Clap | 3.50 |
| Postcard, Santa, Green & Blue | 28.00 |
| Postcard, Santa, In A Balloon | 3.00 |
| Postcard, Santa, In Airplane | 10.00 |
| Postcard, Santa, On Bicycle | 4.00 |
| Postcard, Santa, On Ice Skates | 3.00 |
| Postcard, Santa, On Showshoes | 3.00 |
| Postcard, Santa, Snowman, & Tots | 3.00 |
| Postcard, Santa, Three Santas | 3.00 |
| Postcard, Ten Commandments, Set Of 10 | 35.00 |
| Postcard, Thanksgiving, Tots, Brundage | 4.00 |
| Postcard, The Meeting, Cupid & Girl Friend | 1.00 |
| Postcard, The Merry Widow Hat | 1.00 |
| Postcard, The Virginian, Miss Fluffy Scene | 1.00 |
| Postcard, Tot Sewing Flag, Clap | 4.00 |
| Postcard, Tots, M.L.Atwell | 4.00 |
| Postcard, Tots, Munk, S.P.Pearse | 6.00 |
| Postcard, Tuck, Jamestown A.& V.Co., Exposition, No.107 | 10.00 |
| Postcard, Tuck, Pastel | 1.95 |
| Postcard, Valentine, Set Of 6 | 2.50 |
| Postcard, Walker Baker Chocolate, La Belle Lady | 3.50 |
| Postcard, Washington, Clap, No.16209 | 4.00 |
| Postcard, Washington, F.L., No.255/1 | 3.00 |
| Postcard, Washington, No.51646 | 4.00 |
| Postcard, What's In The Glass, Saxe Roping | 1.00 |
| Postcard, Winsch, Girl | 1.00 |
| Postcard, Woodwards Candy, Photograph | 3.00 |
| Postcard, World's Columbian Exposition | 3.00 |
| Postcard, Young Girl, P.F.B. | 2.15 |
| Postcard, Your Fortune, Set Of 12 | 5.00 |
|     Poster, see Political Campaign, Poster, Store, Poster, | |
|     World War I, Poster, World War II, Poster | |
|     Potlid, see Pratt | |
|     Pottery, see also Buffalo Pottery, Staffordshire, Wedgwood, etc. | |
| Pottery, Bowl, Blue & Tan Sponge, 'werner's Market, ' 8 1/2 In. | 8.00 |
| Pottery, Bowl, Blue & White, Scrolls Around Rim, Shallow, 13 In. | 17.00 |
| Pottery, Bowl, Mixing, Brown & White Stripes On Buff, 6 1/2 In. | 4.00 |
| Pottery, Bowl, Pudding, Brown Earthworm Pattern On Buff Inside & Out | 8.00 |
| Pottery, Bowl, Pudding, Cream Outside, Brown Glaze Inside | 3.00 |
| Pottery, Butter, Covered, Blue & White, Floral Decoration | 22.00 |
| Pottery, Butter, Covered, Blue & White, Indian Good Luck Sign, Bail | 25.00 |
| Pottery, Candelabra, Moss Green, 3-Branch, Artist Signed, 11 In.High | 20.00 |
| Pottery, Candlestick, Double, 2 Orange Birds On Green Base, Arklow, Ireland | 12.50 |
| Pottery, Churn, Hart Sherburne, N.Y., Gray Flowers, Wooden Legs, 3 Gallon | 70.00 |
| Pottery, Container, Wine, Spout At Base, Marked N.P., 1864, 20 In.High | 250.00 |
| Pottery, Crock, Finger-Painted, 2 Handles, 7 X 9 In. | 17.50 |
| Pottery, Crock, Finger-Painted, 2 Handles, 9 X 12 In. | 27.60 |
| Pottery, Crock, Squatty, Finger-Painted, Wooden Cover, 7 1/2 X 9 1/2 In. | 18.00 |
| Pottery, Dish, Baby's Feeding, Dog & Ducks In Clothes, Metal Encased, 1920s | 3.50 |
| Pottery, Dish, Candy, Covered, Italian, Artichoke Shape, Bird On Top, 6 In. | 27.50 |
| Pottery, Dish, Sweetmeat, Stoke-On-Trent, Green Shells, Maroon Poppies, Gilt | 30.00 |
| Pottery, Figurine, Dog, Seated, White, Dark Brown Glaze, 7 1/2 In. | 30.00 |
| Pottery, Figurine, Duck, Chinese, On Stand, 2 1/2 X 2 1/4 In. | 3.00 |
| Pottery, Group, Stag, New Jersey, C.1860, 10 7/8 In.High    *Illus* | 950.00 |
| Pottery, Jar, Fountain, 7 X 8 In. | 3.00 |
| Pottery, Jar, Mustard, Metal Top, Blue, English | 15.00 |
| Pottery, Jar, Snuff, Brown, Large Size | 3.50 |
| Pottery, Jardiniere, White Fruit Filled Band On Black | 17.50 |
| Pottery, Jug, Brown Glaze, 2 Handled, 10 1/2 In.High | 32.50 |
| Pottery, Jug, Green Glaze, Paper Transfer Of Ladies In Costume | 10.00 |
| Pottery, Jug, Ovoid, Blue Floral, 3 Gallon, 15 1/2 In. High | 50.00 |
| Pottery, Jug, Ram's Head Handle, White, Brown, & Blue, France, 3/4 Liter | 25.00 |

Pottery, Group, Stag, New Jersey,
C.1860, 10 7/8 In.High
*(See Page 396)*

Pottery, Pitcher, Hound Handle,
A.Harker, C.1850, 10 In.

Pottery, Pitcher, Toby,
American Pottery Co., C.1840

| | |
|---|---:|
| **Pottery, Match Holder,** Tapered Barrel Shape, Blue & White, Grooved | 12.00 |
| **Pottery, Mold,** Pudding, Ear Of Corn, Oblong, Tan, 5 In.Long | 11.75 |
| **Pottery, Mold,** Pudding, Thumbprint & Swirl, Round, Tan, 4 1/2 In. | 11.75 |
| **Pottery, Mug,** Tea, Cover & Strainer, Western Germany, Multicolor Floral | 5.00 |
| **Pottery, Pitcher,** Art Nouveau, Slender, Peacock Under Brown Glaze, 11 In. | 75.00 |
| **Pottery, Pitcher,** Barrel Shape, Simulated Wood Grain, Staves, Green, 9 In. | 12.00 |
| **Pottery, Pitcher,** Blue & White, Scrolls, 11 1/2 In. | 30.00 |
| **Pottery, Pitcher,** Finger-Painted, "Tiroler Stuben, Annast," 7 In. | 14.50 |
| **Pottery, Pitcher,** Hound Handle, A.Harker, C.1850, 10 In. *Illus* | 275.00 |
| **Pottery, Pitcher,** Milk, Embossed Basket Weave & Floral On Green, 8 3/4 In. | 12.00 |
| **Pottery, Pitcher,** Milk, Santa's Head, 5 3/4 In. | 4.00 |
| **Pottery, Pitcher,** Toby, American Pottery Co., C.1840 *Illus* | 325.00 |
| **Pottery, Plate,** Bread, Persian Ware, Germany, Blue, 6 In. | 5.25 |
| **Pottery, Plate,** New York World's Fair, 1939, Blue, 7 In. | 6.00 |
| **Pottery, Plate,** Quail, Signed Edwin Megaree, 'irricana Supply Store, ' 1900 | 4.00 |
| **Pottery, Plate,** Red Riding Hood & The Wolf, Embossed Border, 7 1/4 In. | 25.00 |
| **Pottery, Plate,** The American Potter, Blue, 7 In. | 6.00 |
| **Pottery, Pot,** Posset, 2 Handled, Burnt Orange, Pointed Spout, C.1750 | 45.00 |
| **Pottery, Salt & Pepper,** Figural, Wrestlers, 4 In. | 4.00 |
| **Pottery, Saltbox,** Hanging, Blue & White, Grapes Decoration | 20.00 |
| **Pottery, Spittoon,** Caramel Glaze | 6.00 |
| **Pottery, Spittoon,** Dark Brown, Earthenware | 6.00 |
| **Pottery, Spittoon,** Green, Raised Grapes & Leaves | 7.50 |
| **Pottery, Tankard,** Picture Of Ebling Brewing Co., N.Y., Dated 1800s | 7.75 |
| **Pottery, Teapot,** Rebecca At The Well, Ohio Brownware, 9 In.High | 68.00 |
| **Pottery, Toothbrush Holder,** Blue & White, Floral | 16.00 |
| **Pottery, Urn,** Gold, Orange & Green Poppies, 2 Handles, B.& K.Ltd., Pair | 35.00 |
| **Pottery, Vase,** Brown & Green, Glazed Repousse Roses Front, 12 In. | 25.00 |
| **Pottery, Vase,** German, Maroon, Black Bands Inlaid With White Porcelain, Pair | 15.00 |
| **Pottery, Vase,** Grotesque Oriental Heads In Relief, 14 In. | 85.00 |
| **Pottery, Vase,** Oriental Gargoyle Type Faces In Relief, 14 In.High | 95.00 |

**Powder Horn, see Weapon, Powder Horn**

PRATT
FENTON

*Pratt ware means two different things. It was an early Staffordshire pottery, cream-colored with colored decorations, made by Felix Pratt during the late eighteenth century. There was also Pratt ware made with transfer designs during the mid-nineteenth century.*

| | |
|---|---|
| Pratt, Box, Covered, Charing Cross, 4 In.Diameter | 45.00 |
| Pratt, Creamer, Old Creek, Black & White, Gold Trim, 3 3/4 In.High | 42.00 |
| Pratt, Cup, Blind Man's Bluff | 35.00 |
| Pratt, Jar, Black & Yellow Transfer Hunting Scene On Wedgwood Blue, Pair | 100.00 |
| Pratt, Jar, Meat, The Fox Hunt, Gold On Blue, Dated Jan.19, 1856, 4 In. High | 36.00 |
| Pratt, Jar, Pomade, Dock Fishing Scene, Pratt Potlid Coloring, 3 In.High | 32.75 |
| Pratt, Jar, Snuff, Blue, Gold, & Black, Marked 1856 | 18.00 |
| Pratt, Jar, Snuff, Tan & Black Transfer Of Men & Animals On Blue, 4 In.High | 18.00 |
| Pratt, Mug, Blue, Hunters Registry Mark For March 1856 | 45.00 |
| Pratt, Plate, Robinson Crusoe, 7 1/2 In. | 48.00 |
| Pratt, Plate, Skewbald Horse, 7 1/4 In. | 45.00 |
| Pratt, Plate, The Village Wedding, 7 In. | 45.00 |
| Pratt, Plate, The Young Florist, June 14, 1847, 7 1/2 In. | 24.00 |
| Pratt, Potlid, Dr.Johnson | 65.00 |
| Pratt, Potlid, Hamlet Sees His Father's Ghost, Ebony Frame, 6 In. | 85.00 |
| Pratt, Potlid, Shakespeare's Home, Framed In Wooden Ring For Hanging | 57.50 |
| Pratt, Potlid, Shepherd Boy | 27.50 |
| Pratt, Potlid, Shepherd Girl | 27.50 |
| Pratt, Potlid, The Game Bag | 75.00 |
| Pratt, Potlid, The Shrimpers, Framed | 35.00 |
| Pratt, Potlid, Uncle Toby, Ebony Frame | 48.50 |
| Pratt, Potlid, Village Wedding | 65.00 |
| Presidential China, Bowl, Vegetable, Andrew Jackson, Cauliflower Finial | 1700.00 |
| Presidential China, Cup & Saucer, Millard Fillmore, Gilt Rims & Handles | 425.00 |
| Presidential China, Pitcher, Chester A.Arthur, U.S.Seal *Illus* | 350.00 |
| Presidential China, Plate, Benjamin Harrison, Limoges, 1892, 8 1/2 In. | 700.00 |
| Presidential China, Plate, Dessert, James K.Polk | 100.00 |
| Presidential China, Plate, Dessert, Lincoln, Haviland *Illus* | 1600.00 |
| Presidential China, Plate, Dinner, Grant, Haviland, 4 *Illus* | 3700.00 |
| Presidential China, Plate, Dinner, Ulysses S.Grant, Haviland & Co. | 600.00 |
| Presidential China, Plate, Ice Cream, Rutherford B.Hayes, Haviland & Co. | 950.00 |
| Presidential China, Plate, Oyster, Rutherford B.Hayes, Haviland & Co. | 385.00 |
| Presidential China, Plate, Soup, Rutherford B.Hayes, Haviland & Co. | 850.00 |
| Presidential Glass, Carafe & Stand, Water, U.S.Grant, Scrolls, Strapwork | 250.00 |
| Presidential Glass, Goblet, Abraham Lincoln, Dorflinger, C.1860 | 1500.00 |
| Presidential Glass, Wine Rinser, Abraham Lincoln, Eagle & Shield | 650.00 |

*Pressed glass was first made in the United States in the 1820s after the invention of pressed-glass machines. Hundreds of patterns of pressed glass were made in complete table settings. Although the Boston and Sandwich Works was the most famous of the pressed glass factories, there were about sixteen other factories making pressed glass from 1830 to 1850, and still more from 1850 to 1900, when pressed glass reached its greatest popularity. It is now being widely reproduced.*

Pressed Glass, see also Cosmos, Croesus, etc.

| | |
|---|---|
| Pressed Glass, Ale Glass, Argus, Footed, Flint, 5 1/2 In.High | 40.00 |
| Pressed Glass, Ale Glass, Mephistopheles, Flint | 35.00 |
| Pressed Glass, Ale Glass, Mephistopheles, Frosted & Clear, Flint | 24.00 |
| Pressed Glass, Ale Glass, New York Honeycomb, Flint | 18.50 |
| Pressed Glass, Ale Glass, Pillar, Flint, 6 In.High | 15.00 |
| Pressed Glass, Ale Glass, Pillar, 8 7/8 In.High | 22.50 |
| Pressed Glass, Banana Boat, Delaware, Green, Gold Trim | 32.00 To 34.00 |
| Pressed Glass, Banana Boat, Reverse Torpedo, High Standard, 9 In.High | 70.00 |
| Pressed Glass, Banana Boat, Sawtooth | 65.00 |
| Pressed Glass, Banana Stand, Fleur-De-Lis | 23.50 |
| Pressed Glass, Banana Stand, Hand, Crystal | 18.00 |
| Pressed Glass, Banana Stand, Palm Leaf Fan, 7 3/8 In. | 26.50 |
| Pressed Glass, Banana Stand, Reversed Torpedo | 85.00 |
| Pressed Glass, Banana Stand, Rexford | 27.50 |
| Pressed Glass, Banana Stand, Twin Teardrops | 23.00 |
| Pressed Glass, Bar Set, Lined Long Panels, 5 Piece | 125.00 |
| Pressed Glass, Basket, Ashman, Silver Handle, Stemmed | 36.00 |
| Pressed Glass, Basket, Cube, Handled, 7 In. | 22.00 |

Presidential China, Plate, Dinner, Grant, Haviland, 4
*(See Page 398)*

Presidential China, Plate,
Dessert, James K. Polk
*(See Page 398)*

Presidential China, Pitcher,
Chester A. Arthur, U.S. Seal
*(See Page 398)*

Presidential China, Plate,
Dessert, Lincoln, Haviland
*(See Page 398)*

| | |
|---|---:|
| **Pressed Glass, Basket,** Fluted Ribs, 8 1/2 In. High | 8.50 |
| **Pressed Glass, Basket,** Paneled, Clear | 15.00 |
| **Pressed Glass, Berry Set,** Ashland, Portland, 13 Piece | 40.00 |
| **Pressed Glass, Berry Set,** Banded Portland, Gold Trim, 7 Piece | 65.00 |
| **Pressed Glass, Berry Set,** Button, 6 Piece | 45.00 |
| **Pressed Glass, Berry Set,** Candlewick, 7 Piece | 40.00 |
| **Pressed Glass, Berry Set,** Child's, Lacy Daisy, 7 Piece | 27.50 To 65.00 |
| **Pressed Glass, Berry Set,** Colorado, Beaded Top Rims, Footed, 7 Piece | 125.00 |
| **Pressed Glass, Berry Set,** Cord Drapery, 7 Piece | 60.00 |

Pressed Glass, Berry Set, Dahlia & Lens, Green, 7 Piece ................................... 55.00
Pressed Glass, Berry Set, Daisy And Button, Panel, 5 Piece ........................... 40.00
Pressed Glass, Berry Set, Delaware, Green, Gold Trim, 7 Piece .................... 100.00
Pressed Glass, Berry Set, Delaware, Rose, 5 Piece ......................................... 125.00
Pressed Glass, Berry Set, Esther, 7 Piece .......................................................... 67.00
Pressed Glass, Berry Set, Garden, Pink, 5 Piece .............................................. 3.00
Pressed Glass, Berry Set, Jeweled Heart, White Opalescent, 7 Piece ............. 110.00
Pressed Glass, Berry Set, Kokomo, 6 Piece ..................................................... 42.00
Pressed Glass, Berry Set, Loop & Jewel, 7 Piece ............................................. 35.00
Pressed Glass, Berry Set, Ribbed Opal, 7 Piece ............................................... 90.00
Pressed Glass, Berry Set, Roman Key, 5 Piece ................................................. 60.00
Pressed Glass, Berry Set, Shell & Jewel, 9 Piece ............................................. 55.00
Pressed Glass, Berry Set, Swag With Bracket, Green & Opalescent, 5 Piece ...... 78.00
Pressed Glass, Berry Set, Swag With Bracket, Green, Footed, 6 Piece .............. 135.00
Pressed Glass, Boat, Currier & Ives, 5 In. .......................................................... 22.00
Pressed Glass, Boat, Currier & Ives, 10 In. ........................................................ 29.00
Pressed Glass, Boat, Shell & Tassel .................................................................. 25.00
Pressed Glass, Bonbon, Water Lily & Cattail, Green, Opalescent, 2 Handled ...... 28.00
Pressed Glass, Bookend, Frosted Child's Head, Clear Eyes, Pair ..................... 30.00
Pressed Glass, Boot, Cane, Purple, Scroll Base, Bouquet Holder, Patent ......... 36.00
Pressed Glass, Boot, Daisy & Button, Amethyst, 2 1/2 In.High ........................ 7.50
Pressed Glass, Boot, Finecut, Blue, 4 In.High .................................................. 32.00
Pressed Glass, Boot, Sequoia, Green, Buttoned ............................................... 15.00
Pressed Glass, Bootee, Daisy & Button, Blue, Pair .......................................... 40.00
Pressed Glass, Bottle, Bar, Ashburton, Bar Lip ................................................ 38.00
Pressed Glass, Bottle, Bar, Diamond Point ............................... 35.00 To 55.00
Pressed Glass, Bottle, Bar, Flute, Pair .............................................................. 40.00
Pressed Glass, Bottle, Bar, Lattice & Oval Panels, Pint, Flint .......................... 22.00
Pressed Glass, Bottle, Bar, Paneled Lattice & Ovals, Flint ............................... 25.00
Pressed Glass, Bottle, Bar, Pillar, Small Size ................................................... 33.50
Pressed Glass, Bottle, Bitters, Pillar, Flint ........................................................ 28.00
Pressed Glass, Bottle, Bitters, Pillar, 6 1/2 In.High ......................................... 24.50
Pressed Glass, Bottle, Castor, Bellflower, Double Lip ....................................... 32.50
Pressed Glass, Bottle, Castor, Etched Grape & Fern Band .............................. 4.50
Pressed Glass, Bottle, Diamond Point, Globe Shape, Stopper, 5 X 4 In. ......... 22.50
Pressed Glass, Bottle, Dresser, Actress, Large Size, Pair ............................... 87.50
Pressed Glass, Bottle, Water, Smocking, Flint .................................................. 35.00
Pressed Glass, Bouquet Holder, Teardrop & Fan ............................................. 9.00
Pressed Glass, Bowl & Base, Punch, Duncan & Miller No.42 ........................... 65.00
Pressed Glass, Bowl, Actress, Oblong, Large Size .......................................... 50.00
Pressed Glass, Bowl, Alaska, Blue, Opalescent, Footed, 7 1/2 In. .................. 19.50
Pressed Glass, Bowl, Albany Ribbed Spiral, Opalescent & Clear, Collared ...... 29.50
Pressed Glass, Bowl, Amazon, Covered, Oval, Lion's Head Knob & Handles .... 25.00
Pressed Glass, Bowl, Amberette, 8 3/4 In. ....................................................... 55.00
Pressed Glass, Bowl, Anthemion, Square, Flat, 7 1/4 In. ................................. 15.00
Pressed Glass, Bowl, Art, Footed Base, Flared Rim, 6 3/4 In. ......................... 15.00
Pressed Glass, Bowl, Artichoke, Nickel Plated Foot, 9 In. ............................... 7.50
Pressed Glass, Bowl, Balder, Gold Trim, Flat, 8 1/4 In. ................................... 22.50
Pressed Glass, Bowl, Baltimore Pear, 8 1/2 In.Diameter ................................. 8.00
Pressed Glass, Bowl, Banana, Delaware, Rose, Light Lavender Flashing Top ...... 35.00
Pressed Glass, Bowl, Banded Portland, Maiden's Blush, Raised Ends, 8 1/2 In. ...... 27.00
Pressed Glass, Bowl, Barberry, Oval, 7 1/4 In.Long ........................................ 10.00
Pressed Glass, Bowl, Bead & Scroll, 8 In. ........................................................ 8.50
Pressed Glass, Bowl, Beaded Grape, Emerald Green, Rectangular, 11 In.Long ...... 25.00
Pressed Glass, Bowl, Beaded Grape, Green, Square, 7 1/4 In. ....................... 24.00
Pressed Glass, Bowl, Beaded Oval & Scroll ..................................................... 5.00
Pressed Glass, Bowl, Berry, Alaska, Emerald Green, Large Size ..................... 55.00
Pressed Glass, Bowl, Berry, Ashland, 7 3/4 In. ................................................ 8.50
Pressed Glass, Bowl, Berry, Beatty Rib, Blue Opalescent ............................... 22.00
Pressed Glass, Bowl, Berry, Button Arches, Scalloped Top, 7 1/4 In. ............. 9.50
Pressed Glass, Bowl, Berry, Child's, Flattened Diamond & Fan ...................... 6.00
Pressed Glass, Bowl, Berry, Classic, Hexagonal, 6 Legs, 8 In. ....................... 85.00
Pressed Glass, Bowl, Berry, Colorado, Green, Gold Trim, Ruffled, 8 1/2 In. .... 28.50
Pressed Glass, Bowl, Berry, Czarina ................................................................. 12.50
Pressed Glass, Bowl, Berry, Daisy In Oval Panel, Round, Gold Trim, 8 1/2 In. ...... 12.50
Pressed Glass, Bowl, Berry, Delaware, Green, Gold Trim, 8 In. ...................... 30.00

Pressed Glass, Bowl, Berry, Delaware, Rose, Round ............... 45.00
Pressed Glass, Bowl, Berry, Duncan Miller No.42, Ruby Stained Top, 8 In. ............... 35.00
Pressed Glass, Bowl, Berry, Everglades, Blue Opalescent, Gold Trim, Large ............... 120.00
Pressed Glass, Bowl, Berry, Faggot, Frosted & Clear ............... 18.50
Pressed Glass, Bowl, Berry, Festoon, Rectangular, 7 X 4 1/2 In. ............... 19.50
Pressed Glass, Bowl, Berry, Festoon, Rectangular, 9 In. ............... 15.00
Pressed Glass, Bowl, Berry, Festoon, Round, 7 In. ............... 14.50
Pressed Glass, Bowl, Berry, Finecut & Tulip, Miniature ............... 5.00
Pressed Glass, Bowl, Berry, Fishscale, 8 In. ............... 12.50
Pressed Glass, Bowl, Berry, Fleur-De-Lis & Drape, 8 1/4 In. ............... 16.50
Pressed Glass, Bowl, Berry, Flower & Pleat, Frosted & Color, 8 1/2 In. ............... 24.00
Pressed Glass, Bowl, Berry, Frosted Blocked Arches ............... 24.50
Pressed Glass, Bowl, Berry, Frosted Circle, 8 1/2 In.Deep ............... 19.50
Pressed Glass, Bowl, Berry, Grasshopper, No Insect ............... 35.00
Pressed Glass, Bowl, Berry, Hartley, Blue, Footed, 8 1/4 In. ............... 35.00
Pressed Glass, Bowl, Berry, Hartley, Footed, 8 1/4 In. ............... 21.50
Pressed Glass, Bowl, Berry, Hexagon Block, Ruby Stained, Scalloped Top ............... 25.00
Pressed Glass, Bowl, Berry, Intaglio, Clear & Opalescent, Square, Footed ............... 15.00
Pressed Glass, Bowl, Berry, Inverted Thistle, Green, Scalloped, Near Cut ............... 12.50
Pressed Glass, Bowl, Berry, Iris With Meander, Sapphire Blue, Gold, 4 1/4 In. ............... 18.00
Pressed Glass, Bowl, Berry, King's 500, Dark Blue, Gilt Trim, 8 In. ............... 26.50
Pressed Glass, Bowl, Berry, Lacy Daisy, 9 In. ............... 10.00
Pressed Glass, Bowl, Berry, Lion's Leg, Green ............... 32.00
Pressed Glass, Bowl, Berry, Manhattan, Gold Rim ............... 14.50
Pressed Glass, Bowl, Berry, Manhattan, 8 1/4 In. ............... 14.50
Pressed Glass, Bowl, Berry, Maryland, 8 1/4 In. ............... 22.50
Pressed Glass, Bowl, Berry, Moon & Star, 9 In. ............... 25.00
Pressed Glass, Bowl, Berry, Nailhead, Scalloped Edge, Round, 8 In. ............... 9.50
Pressed Glass, Bowl, Berry, New Hampshire, Gold Trim, 8 1/2 In. ............... 8.00
Pressed Glass, Bowl, Berry, Paneled Forget-Me-Not ............... 12.50
Pressed Glass, Bowl, Berry, Paneled Hobnail, Footed, 8 In. ............... 18.00
Pressed Glass, Bowl, Berry, Pillow & Dot, Beaded Rim, 4 In. ............... 3.00
Pressed Glass, Bowl, Berry, Pressed Diamond, Blue, Square, 8 In. ............... 27.50
Pressed Glass, Bowl, Berry, Priscilla, Ruby Flashed On Moons, 8 In. ............... 27.50
Pressed Glass, Bowl, Berry, Ribbed, Opalescent, 9 In. ............... 20.00
Pressed Glass, Bowl, Berry, Rose Sprig, Footed, 8 In. ............... 21.50
Pressed Glass, Bowl, Berry, Royal Oak, Frosted & Clear, 7 1/2 In. ............... 25.00
Pressed Glass, Bowl, Berry, Shield ............... 18.50
Pressed Glass, Bowl, Berry, Six Panel Finecut, Amber Panels, Footed, Findlay ............... 20.00
Pressed Glass, Bowl, Berry, Thistle, Scalloped Top ............... 20.00
Pressed Glass, Bowl, Berry, Tokyo, Blue Opalescent, Large Size ............... 60.00
Pressed Glass, Bowl, Berry, Tokyo, Green Opalescent, Large Size ............... 50.00
Pressed Glass, Bowl, Berry, Water Lily & Cattail, Amethyst, Opalescent Edge ............... 35.00
Pressed Glass, Bowl, Berry, Wild Bouquet, Blue Opalescent, Large Size ............... 95.00
Pressed Glass, Bowl, Birch Leaf ............... 7.50
Pressed Glass, Bowl, Bird & Strawberry, Footed, 10 In. ............... 35.50
Pressed Glass, Bowl, Bird & Strawberry, Oval, Footed, 9 1/2 X 6 In. ............... 37.00
Pressed Glass, Bowl, Bird & Strawberry, 7 1/2 In. Diameter ............... 18.00
Pressed Glass, Bowl, Block & Fan, Footed, 8 In. ............... 11.50 To 12.50
Pressed Glass, Bowl, Blueberry, Teardrop & Tassel ............... 40.00
Pressed Glass, Bowl, Budded Ivy, Oval, 7 1/4 In.Long ............... 3.75
Pressed Glass, Bowl, Button Arches, Flat, 8 1/4 In. ............... 42.50
Pressed Glass, Bowl, Cameo ............... 16.00
Pressed Glass, Bowl, Cameo, Footed, 7 1/2 In. ............... 17.50
Pressed Glass, Bowl, Center, Amberette, 11 In.Diameter ............... 48.50
Pressed Glass, Bowl, Center, Strawberry, 8 In. ............... 25.00 To 32.00
Pressed Glass, Bowl, Centerpiece, Horseshoe, 7 1/2 In.Diameter ............... 38.00
Pressed Glass, Bowl, Circle, Flat, 8 1/4 In. ............... 14.00
Pressed Glass, Bowl, Classic, 6 In. ............... 16.00
Pressed Glass, Bowl, Colorado, Beaded Gold Edge, Footed, 4 1/2 In.Diameter ............... 15.00
Pressed Glass, Bowl, Colorado, Blue, Triangular, Applied Handle, Footed ............... 35.00
Pressed Glass, Bowl, Colorado, Footed, Round, 7 In. ............... 13.00
Pressed Glass, Bowl, Colorado, Green, Clear Crimped Edge, Footed, 6 In. ............... 6.00
Pressed Glass, Bowl, Colorado, Green, Gold Trim ............... 65.00
Pressed Glass, Bowl, Colorado, Green, Gold Trim, Crimped Edge, Footed, 9 In. ............... 27.00
Pressed Glass, Bowl, Colorado, Green, Large Size ............... 50.00

Pressed Glass, Bowl, Colorado, Green, Triangular, Applied Handle, Footed ................... 28.00
Pressed Glass, Bowl, Colorado, Square, 6 In. ................... 7.50
Pressed Glass, Bowl, Colorado, Triangular, Open Feet, 6 In. ................... 10.00
Pressed Glass, Bowl, Colorado, Tricorner, Handled ................... 8.00
Pressed Glass, Bowl, Cornell, Emerald Green, Squared, 5 1/2 In. ................... 18.00
Pressed Glass, Bowl, Cornell, 8 1/2 In. ................... 12.00
Pressed Glass, Bowl, Cottage, Findlay, 9 1/4 X 6 1/2 X 2 1/2 In. ................... 12.00
Pressed Glass, Bowl, Cracker, Three Panel, Blue, 10 In. ................... 48.75
Pressed Glass, Bowl, Crystal Wedding, 7 In. ................... 36.00
Pressed Glass, Bowl, Cupid & Venus, Footed, 8 In. ................... 29.50 To 39.95
Pressed Glass, Bowl, Currier & Ives, Little Husking Partridge, Covered ................... 35.00
Pressed Glass, Bowl, Currier & Ives, Oval, Flat, Collared Base, 10 In. ................... 25.00
Pressed Glass, Bowl, Currier & Ives, Oval, 9 3/4 X 5 3/4 X 4 1/2 In. ................... 14.50
Pressed Glass, Bowl, Daisy & Button With Amber Panels, Flat, 8 In. ................... 49.50
Pressed Glass, Bowl, Daisy & Button With Crossbar, Dark Amber, Pedestal ................... 22.50
Pressed Glass, Bowl, Daisy & Button With V Ornament, Flat, 8 In. ................... 16.00
Pressed Glass, Bowl, Daisy & Button, Amber Buttons, Amber & Clear Daisies ................... 47.50
Pressed Glass, Bowl, Daisy & Button, Apple Green, 4 X 10 In. ................... 52.00
Pressed Glass, Bowl, Daisy & Button, Apple Green, 4 3/4 X 2 1/2 In. ................... 18.00
Pressed Glass, Bowl, Daisy In Oval Panels, Flat, 8 1/4 In. ................... 11.50
Pressed Glass, Bowl, Delaware, Cranberry To Clear, Silver Plate Frame ................... 85.00
Pressed Glass, Bowl, Delaware, Green, Boat Shape ................... 18.00
Pressed Glass, Bowl, Delaware, Green, Gilt Trim, 8 In.Diameter ................... 42.00
Pressed Glass, Bowl, Delaware, Oval ................... 22.00
Pressed Glass, Bowl, Delaware, Rose, Gilt Trim, 8 In. ................... 37.00
Pressed Glass, Bowl, Dessert, Atlanta, Green, Ruffled Edge ................... 7.10
Pressed Glass, Bowl, Dessert, Banded Portland, Gold Trim, Small Size ................... 9.00
Pressed Glass, Bowl, Dessert, Good Luck, Small Size ................... 12.00
Pressed Glass, Bowl, Dessert, Lion, Footed, Small Size ................... 12.00
Pressed Glass, Bowl, Dessert, Nail, Small Size ................... 9.00
Pressed Glass, Bowl, Dessert, Paneled Daisy & Button, Small Size ................... 12.00
Pressed Glass, Bowl, Dessert, Paneled Daisy, Small Size ................... 8.00
Pressed Glass, Bowl, Dessert, Paneled Grape, Small Size ................... 9.00
Pressed Glass, Bowl, Dessert, Ribbon, Small Size ................... 10.00
Pressed Glass, Bowl, Dessert, Shrine, Small Size ................... 9.00
Pressed Glass, Bowl, Dew & Raindrop, Flat, 8 In. ................... 15.00
Pressed Glass, Bowl, Dewdrop & Star, 6 1/4 In. ................... 10.00
Pressed Glass, Bowl, Dewdrop In Points, Oval, 9 In.Long ................... 7.50
Pressed Glass, Bowl, Dewey, Amber, Footed ................... 6.50
Pressed Glass, Bowl, Diamond & Buckle, Scalloped Top, 9 In. ................... 15.00
Pressed Glass, Bowl, Diamond Medallion, Oval, 2 X 9 X 6 1/4 In. ................... 10.00
Pressed Glass, Bowl, Diamond Thumbprint, Footed, Flint, 8 X 3 In. ................... 45.00
Pressed Glass, Bowl, Diamond-Quilted, Amethyst, 7 1/2 In. ................... 25.00
Pressed Glass, Bowl, Diamond-Quilted, Bull's-Eye Border, Flint, 4 In. ................... 6.50
Pressed Glass, Bowl, Double Beetle Band, Dark Amber, Scalloped Rim ................... 36.00
Pressed Glass, Bowl, Duncan & Miller No.42, Scalloped, Pedestal ................... 15.00
Pressed Glass, Bowl, Duncan & Miller No.42, Square ................... 12.00
Pressed Glass, Bowl, Etched Apollo, Shallow, 9 1/2 In.Square ................... 14.50
Pressed Glass, Bowl, Excelsior, Footed, Scalloped Rim, Flint, 4 1/2 In.High ................... 37.50
Pressed Glass, Bowl, Excelsior, Scalloped Rim, Flint ................... 35.00
Pressed Glass, Bowl, Feather, Footed, 7 1/4 In.Diameter ................... 10.00
Pressed Glass, Bowl, Feather, Footed, 8 1/2 In.Diameter ................... 10.00
Pressed Glass, Bowl, Feather, Oval, 8 3/8 In.Long ................... 10.00
Pressed Glass, Bowl, Feather, Oval, 9 1/2 In. ................... 8.50 To 15.00
Pressed Glass, Bowl, Festoon ................... 12.00
Pressed Glass, Bowl, Festoon, Flat, 9 1/4 In. ................... 16.50
Pressed Glass, Bowl, Festoon, Rectangular, 5 1/2 X 9 In. ................... 10.00
Pressed Glass, Bowl, Festoon, Round, 9 1/2 In.Diameter ................... 15.00
Pressed Glass, Bowl, Festoon, 7 In. ................... 14.00
Pressed Glass, Bowl, Festoon, 9 In. ................... 15.00 To 20.00
Pressed Glass, Bowl, Fine Rib, Footed ................... 26.00
Pressed Glass, Bowl, Fine Rib, Footed, Flint ................... 27.50
Pressed Glass, Bowl, Finecut & Block, Amber Blocks, Handled, 9 In. ................... 34.00
Pressed Glass, Bowl, Finecut & Block, Footed, 6 1/2 X 3 1/4 In. ................... 8.50
Pressed Glass, Bowl, Finger, Daisy & Button With Crossbar, Blue ................... 27.50
Pressed Glass, Bowl, Finger, Daisy & Button With Panel ................... 6.00

| | |
|---|---|
| Pressed Glass, Bowl, Finger, Duncan & Miller No.42 | 10.00 |
| Pressed Glass, Bowl, Finger, Inverted Thumbprint, Blue | 22.00 |
| Pressed Glass, Bowl, Finger, Pointed Hobnail, Honey Amber, Flat Bottom | 22.50 |
| Pressed Glass, Bowl, Fishscale, Square, 8 1/2 In. | 7.50 |
| Pressed Glass, Bowl, Flaming Sword, Sapphire Blue, 10 In.Long | 75.00 |
| Pressed Glass, Bowl, Flat Panel, Ruby Flashed, 8 In. | 23.00 |
| Pressed Glass, Bowl, Fleur-De-Lis & Drape, Footed, 6 1/4 In. | 10.00 |
| Pressed Glass, Bowl, Fleur-De-Lis & Drape, Green, Rectangular, 8 1/4 In. | 22.50 |
| Pressed Glass, Bowl, Fleur-De-Lis & Drape, Rectangular, 8 1/4 X 5 1/4 In. | 15.00 |
| Pressed Glass, Bowl, Fleur-De-Lis, Footed, 10 In. | 12.50 |
| Pressed Glass, Bowl, Floral & Palm, Opalescent, 8 1/2 In. | 12.50 |
| Pressed Glass, Bowl, Fluted Scrolls, Blue, Opalescent, Footed, 7 1/4 In. | 16.50 |
| Pressed Glass, Bowl, Fluted Scrolls, Blue, Opalescent, Turned Up Edges | 16.00 |
| Pressed Glass, Bowl, Frosted & Clear Dogwood, Duncan & Miller, 11 In. | 12.00 |
| Pressed Glass, Bowl, Frosted Artichoke, 9 In. | 40.00 |
| Pressed Glass, Bowl, Fruit, Daisy & Button With Amber Panels, 8 In. | 65.00 |
| Pressed Glass, Bowl, Fruit, Manhattan, Maiden's Blush, 9 1/2 In. | 30.00 |
| Pressed Glass, Bowl, Fruit, Moon & Star, 10 1/2 X 2 In. | 17.00 |
| Pressed Glass, Bowl, Fruit, Paneled Daisy & Button, Amber, Double Scalloped | 10.00 |
| Pressed Glass, Bowl, Fruit, Paneled Ivy, Shallow, 10 In. | 20.00 |
| Pressed Glass, Bowl, Fruit, Pinwheel, Pres Cut, Large Size | 14.00 |
| Pressed Glass, Bowl, Fruit, Sheaf Of Wheat, Rayed Bottom, Scalloped Top | 15.00 |
| Pressed Glass, Bowl, Fruit, Stag & Holly, Pink | 17.50 |
| Pressed Glass, Bowl, Galloway, Gold Trim, 5 1/2 In. | 9.50 |
| Pressed Glass, Bowl, Grape & Festoon With Shield, Oblong | 6.00 |
| Pressed Glass, Bowl, Grape, 8 In. | 12.00 |
| Pressed Glass, Bowl, Grasshopper, Covered, Footed | 32.00 |
| Pressed Glass, Bowl, Grasshopper, No Insect, Open Feet, 8 3/4 In. | 8.50 |
| Pressed Glass, Bowl, Haley's Comet, Oblong | 8.50 To 12.00 |
| Pressed Glass, Bowl, Hanover, Flat, 10 1/2 In. | 32.50 |
| Pressed Glass, Bowl, Hartley, Blue, Footed, 8 1/4 In. | 35.00 |
| Pressed Glass, Bowl, Hartley, Footed, 8 1/4 In. | 16.50 |
| Pressed Glass, Bowl, Hartley, Petticoat Base, 8 In. | 10.00 |
| Pressed Glass, Bowl, Heart & Thumbprint, Fluted, Round | 14.00 |
| Pressed Glass, Bowl, Heart & Thumbprint, Gold Trim, 9 In. | 19.50 |
| Pressed Glass, Bowl, Heart & Thumbprint, 10 In. | 24.00 |
| Pressed Glass, Bowl, Hobnail With Fan, 10 X 7 1/4 In. | 22.50 |
| Pressed Glass, Bowl, Hobnail, Opalescent, Fluted, 8 1/2 In | 30.00 |
| Pressed Glass, Bowl, Horseshoe, Footed, 7 In.Diameter | 22.50 |
| Pressed Glass, Bowl, Horseshoe, Oblong, 6 X 9 In. | 19.50 |
| Pressed Glass, Bowl, Ice, Frosted Polar Bear | 75.00 |
| Pressed Glass, Bowl, Inverted Feather & Fan, Canary, Opalescent, Footed | 28.00 |
| Pressed Glass, Bowl, Inverted Feather & Fan, Opalescent, Footed | 20.00 |
| Pressed Glass, Bowl, Inverted Hearts, Shallow, Mt.Washington, Flint, 6 In. | 21.50 |
| Pressed Glass, Bowl, Inverted Hearts, Shallow, Mt.Washington, Flint, 8 In. | 27.50 |
| Pressed Glass, Bowl, Jacob's Ladder, 7 In. | 5.00 |
| Pressed Glass, Bowl, Jewel & Dewdrop, Clear, Metal Band Top, Signed S.W. | 10.00 |
| Pressed Glass, Bowl, Leaf & Berry, Green Opalescent, Pedestal Base | 19.00 |
| Pressed Glass, Bowl, Leaf & Dart, Oval, 8 1/4 In.Long | 7.50 |
| Pressed Glass, Bowl, Leaf Bracket | 15.00 |
| Pressed Glass, Bowl, Loop With Leaf, Oval, 5 X 7 In. | 35.00 |
| Pressed Glass, Bowl, Manhattan, 8 In. | 12.00 |
| Pressed Glass, Bowl, Many Loops, Blue, Flint, 6 In.Diameter | 35.00 |
| Pressed Glass, Bowl, Many Loops, Green, Opalescent, 8 1/4 In. | 15.00 |
| Pressed Glass, Bowl, Many Loops, Green, 8 1/2 In. | 16.50 |
| Pressed Glass, Bowl, Maple Leaf, Amber, Footed, Oval, 7 1/2 X 12 In. | 32.50 |
| Pressed Glass, Bowl, Maple Leaf, Emerald Green, Oval, Footed, 10 In. | 49.50 |
| Pressed Glass, Bowl, Maple Leaf, Oval, Footed, 11 In. | 23.00 |
| Pressed Glass, Bowl, Maryland, Flat, 8 1/4 In. | 13.50 |
| Pressed Glass, Bowl, Meander, Blue, Opalescent, 3 Feet, 8 3/4 In. | 22.00 |
| Pressed Glass, Bowl, Meander, Blue, Opalescent, 3 Spatula Feet, 9 In. | 24.00 |
| Pressed Glass, Bowl, Meander, Blue, Opalescent, 8 3/4 In. | 22.00 |
| Pressed Glass, Bowl, Meander, Green, Opalescent, 8 3/4 In. | 22.00 |
| Pressed Glass, Bowl, Mitted Hand | 32.00 |
| Pressed Glass, Bowl, Moon & Star, Flat, 7 In. | 17.50 |
| Pressed Glass, Bowl, Moon & Star, 7 In. | 13.50 |

| | |
|---|---|
| **Pressed Glass, Bowl,** Moon & Star, 7 1/4 In. | 15.00 |
| **Pressed Glass, Bowl,** Moon & Star, 8 In. | 17.50 |
| **Pressed Glass, Bowl,** New Jersey, Flat, 9 In. | 16.50 |
| **Pressed Glass, Bowl,** New Jersey, 8 In. | 10.00 |
| **Pressed Glass, Bowl,** Nortec, Amber, 4 1/2 X 6 In. | 9.00 |
| **Pressed Glass, Bowl,** Orange Peel, Oval, 7 In.Long | 3.75 |
| **Pressed Glass, Bowl,** Palm Leaf, Clear & Opalescent, Square Base, 8 In. | 14.00 |
| **Pressed Glass, Bowl,** Paneled Forget-Me-Not, Covered, 6 1/4 In.Diameter | 25.00 |
| **Pressed Glass, Bowl,** Paneled Oak, Flat, 9 1/4 In. | 10.50 |
| **Pressed Glass, Bowl,** Paneled Thistle, Knob Feet, 4 In.High | 20.00 |
| **Pressed Glass, Bowl,** Paneled Thistle, 3 In.High | 23.50 |
| **Pressed Glass, Bowl,** Paneled Thistle, 8 Footed, 7 In. | 15.00 |
| **Pressed Glass, Bowl,** Paneled Thistle, 9 In. | 12.00 |
| **Pressed Glass, Bowl,** Paneled, Round, 8 X 3 3/4 In. | 5.98 |
| **Pressed Glass, Bowl,** Peacock Feather, Flat, 8 1/2 In. | 15.00 |
| **Pressed Glass, Bowl,** Peacock Feather, 6 In. | 11.50 |
| **Pressed Glass, Bowl,** Peacock Feather, 8 In. | 12.00 |
| **Pressed Glass, Bowl,** Pennsylvania, Covered, 2 In.High | 50.00 |
| **Pressed Glass, Bowl,** Pillar, Flat, Findlay, 9 In. | 19.50 |
| **Pressed Glass, Bowl,** Pittsburgh, Deep Blue, C.1840, Flint, 7 X 1 1/2 In. | 80.00 |
| **Pressed Glass, Bowl,** Porridge, Good Luck, 5 In.Diameter | 10.00 |
| **Pressed Glass, Bowl,** Portland Rose Band, Flat, 7 1/4 In. | 15.00 |
| **Pressed Glass, Bowl,** Portland, 9 In.Diameter, 4 In.Deep | 16.50 To 18.50 |
| **Pressed Glass, Bowl,** Pres Cut, Handled, 6 In. | 7.00 |
| **Pressed Glass, Bowl,** Pressed Leaf, Oval, 8 In.Long | 10.00 |
| **Pressed Glass, Bowl,** Primrose, Amber, 8 In. | 23.50 |
| **Pressed Glass, Bowl,** Primrose, 7 In. | 15.00 |
| **Pressed Glass, Bowl,** Primrose, 8 In. | 17.50 |
| **Pressed Glass, Bowl,** Princess Feather | 26.50 |
| **Pressed Glass, Bowl,** Priscilla, Findlay, 8 X 3 In. | 25.00 |
| **Pressed Glass, Bowl,** Priscilla, Round, Scalloped Edge, Findlay | 22.50 |
| **Pressed Glass, Bowl,** Priscilla, Shallow, 10 3/4 In.Diameter | 20.00 |
| **Pressed Glass, Bowl,** Prism & Sawtooth, Collared, Flint, 7 1/4 In. | 28.50 |
| **Pressed Glass, Bowl,** Punch, Child's, Feather & Arches | 17.00 |
| **Pressed Glass, Bowl,** Punch, Elegance, Miniature | 15.00 |
| **Pressed Glass, Bowl,** Punch, Feather & Arches, Miniature | 10.00 |
| **Pressed Glass, Bowl,** Punch, Hickman, 16 In.Diameter | 45.00 |
| **Pressed Glass, Bowl,** Punch, Miniature, Tulip & Honeycomb | 20.00 |
| **Pressed Glass, Bowl,** Punch, Pineapple & Fan, 12 In.Diameter | 35.00 |
| **Pressed Glass, Bowl,** Punch, Star Arches, Miniature | 12.50 |
| **Pressed Glass, Bowl,** Quaker Lady, 6 1/4 In.Diameter | 20.00 |
| **Pressed Glass, Bowl,** Ribbed & Beaded, Ruby Flashed, 3 X 4 X 2 In. | 7.00 |
| **Pressed Glass, Bowl,** Ribbed Spiral, Opalescent, Footed, 7 1/4 In. | 23.50 |
| **Pressed Glass, Bowl,** Rose In Snow, Oval, 8 1/4 In.Long | 20.00 |
| **Pressed Glass, Bowl,** Rose Sprig, Amber, 8 In. | 28.50 |
| **Pressed Glass, Bowl,** Rose Sprig, Blue, 8 In. | 28.50 |
| **Pressed Glass, Bowl,** Rose Sprig, Footed, 8 In. | 17.50 |
| **Pressed Glass, Bowl,** Rosette, Covered, 7 1/4 In. | 29.50 |
| **Pressed Glass, Bowl,** Royal Crystal, Covered, 4 In. | 20.00 |
| **Pressed Glass, Bowl,** Ruffled Top, 2 1/4 In.High | 11.50 |
| **Pressed Glass, Bowl,** Salad, Teardrop, Crystal, Shallow, 12 In.Diameter | 10.00 |
| **Pressed Glass, Bowl,** Serving, Cattails & Water Lily, Blue Opalescent | 25.00 |
| **Pressed Glass, Bowl,** Shrine, 6 In. | 14.50 |
| **Pressed Glass, Bowl,** Shrine, 8 In. | 18.50 |
| **Pressed Glass, Bowl,** Skilton, Ruby & Clear, Flat, 8 In. | 25.00 |
| **Pressed Glass, Bowl,** Snail, Oval, 8 In.Long | 7.50 |
| **Pressed Glass, Bowl,** Spirea Band, Amber, Oval, 8 In.Long | 10.00 |
| **Pressed Glass, Bowl,** Stag & Holly, 11 In. | 115.00 |
| **Pressed Glass, Bowl,** Stippled Daisy, Rectangular, 9 X 5 3/4 In. | 8.50 |
| **Pressed Glass, Bowl,** Stippled Forget-Me-Not, Oval, 7 In.Long | 10.00 |
| **Pressed Glass, Bowl,** Sunk Daisy, 7 In. | 6.00 |
| **Pressed Glass, Bowl,** Three Panel, Amber, Footed, 8 1/2 In. | 34.00 |
| **Pressed Glass, Bowl,** Three Panel, Amber, 10 In. | 35.00 |
| **Pressed Glass, Bowl,** Thumbprint, Low Stand, Flint | 25.00 |
| **Pressed Glass, Bowl,** Torpedo, 8 In. | 14.00 To 15.00 |
| **Pressed Glass, Bowl,** Tulip, Flaring Sides, Flint, 7 In. | 22.00 |

Pressed Glass, Bowl, Two Panel, Oval, Footed, 10 1/2 In. ........................................ 35.00
Pressed Glass, Bowl, Vegetable, Cord & Drapery, 9 1/2 X 6 In. ............................ 10.00
Pressed Glass, Bowl, Vegetable, Feather, Oval .......................................................... 15.00
Pressed Glass, Bowl, Vegetable, Frosted Bird, Clear, Bird Finial On Lid, Pair .............. 150.00
Pressed Glass, Bowl, Vegetable, Good Luck, 5 X 8 In. ............................................ 20.00
Pressed Glass, Bowl, Vegetable, Jacob's Ladder, 5 X 7 In. .................................... 15.00
Pressed Glass, Bowl, Vera, 8 3/4 In. .......................................................................... 18.50
Pressed Glass, Bowl, Victoria, 9 In. ............................................................................ 12.00
Pressed Glass, Bowl, Virginia, 7 In. ............................................................................ 18.50
Pressed Glass, Bowl, Waste, Barred Hobnail ............................................................ 12.50
Pressed Glass, Bowl, Waste, Block & Fan .................................................................. 28.00
Pressed Glass, Bowl, Waste, Etched Nail .................................................................. 23.75
Pressed Glass, Bowl, Waste, Etched Torpdeo .......................................................... 35.00
Pressed Glass, Bowl, Waste, Fan Band ...................................................................... 8.00
Pressed Glass, Bowl, Waste, Frosted Ribbon ........................................ 23.75 To 35.00
Pressed Glass, Bowl, Waste, Good Luck, 4 X 2 1/2 In. .......................................... 35.00
Pressed Glass, Bowl, Waste, Horseshoe .................................................................. 24.50
Pressed Glass, Bowl, Waste, Inverted Thumbprint, Blue ........................................ 12.50
Pressed Glass, Bowl, Waste, Polar Bear .................................................................... 75.00
Pressed Glass, Bowl, Waste, Pressed Diamond ........................................................ 3.75
Pressed Glass, Bowl, Waste, Sunburst ...................................................................... 10.00
Pressed Glass, Bowl, Waste, Tree Of Life .................................................................. 10.00
Pressed Glass, Bowl, Waste, Tree Of Life, Medium Blue ........................................ 35.00
Pressed Glass, Bowl, Wildflower, Flat Base, 5 3/4 In. Square ................................ 15.00
Pressed Glass, Bowl, Wildflower, Flat Base, 7 3/4 In. Square ................................ 15.00
Pressed Glass, Bowl, Wildflower, Square, 5 3/4 In. .................................................. 12.00
Pressed Glass, Bowl, Wildflower, Square, 6 In. ........................................................ 9.00
Pressed Glass, Bowl, Willow Oak, Covered, 7 In. .................................................... 29.50
Pressed Glass, Bowl, Willow Oak, 7 1/4 In. .............................................................. 17.50
Pressed Glass, Box, Powder, Duncan & Miller, Duck .............................................. 16.00
Pressed Glass, Box, Star, Diamond, & Fan, Round, Footed, 3 1/4 In. High .............. 30.00
Pressed Glass, Box, Zipper, Tin Lid, 2 In. .................................................................. 1.25
Pressed Glass, Bride's Basket, Diamond Point, Flint, Meriden Frame .................... 75.00
Pressed Glass, Bucket, Ice, Block & Fan .................................................................. 24.00
Pressed Glass, Bust, Dewey, Amber .......................................................................... 65.00
Pressed Glass, Butter Pat, Daisy & Button With V Ornament, Round ...................... 5.00
Pressed Glass, Butter Pat, Daisy & Button, Round .................................................. 3.00
Pressed Glass, Butter Pat, Daisy & Button, Square .................................................. 6.00
Pressed Glass, Butter Pat, Duncan & Miller No.42 .................................................. 7.50
Pressed Glass, Butter Pat, Finecut, Plain Rim, Round, Flat .................................... 4.00
Pressed Glass, Butter Pat, Hidalgo ............................................................................ 6.00
Pressed Glass, Butter Pat, Open Plaid ...................................................................... 3.50
Pressed Glass, Butter Pat, Pleat & Panel .................................................................. 22.50
Pressed Glass, Butter Pat, Tree Of Life, Shell Shape .............................................. 3.00
Pressed Glass, Butter, Acorn & Stippled Oak Leaf Base, Squirrel Finial ................ 95.50
Pressed Glass, Butter, Acorn Medallion .................................................................... 42.50
Pressed Glass, Butter, Actress, Covered .................................................................... 85.00
Pressed Glass, Butter, Alabama, Covered .................................................................. 35.00
Pressed Glass, Butter, Alaska, Green, Covered ........................................................ 70.00
Pressed Glass, Butter, Aztec, Blue, Covered ............................................................ 39.50
Pressed Glass, Butter, Baby Thumbprint & Swirl, Cobalt Blue ................................ 55.00
Pressed Glass, Butter, Balder, Covered, Flared Type Base .................................... 35.00
Pressed Glass, Butter, Baltimore Pear, Covered ...................................................... 50.00
Pressed Glass, Butter, Banner, Blue .......................................................................... 86.50
Pressed Glass, Butter, Banner, Covered .................................................................... 45.00
Pressed Glass, Butter, Barley, Covered ...................................................................... 25.00
Pressed Glass, Butter, Beaded Acorn Medallion, Covered ...................................... 25.00
Pressed Glass, Butter, Beaded Band .......................................................................... 19.00
Pressed Glass, Butter, Beaded Grape Medallion, Covered ........................ 35.00 To 45.00
Pressed Glass, Butter, Beaded Oval With Scroll, Covered ...................................... 18.50
Pressed Glass, Butter, Bellflower, Covered, Flint ...................................... 65.00 To 80.00
Pressed Glass, Butter, Bellflower, Flint ...................................................................... 85.00
Pressed Glass, Butter, Bird & Strawberry, Covered .................................. 16.00 To 65.00
Pressed Glass, Butter, Block & Fan, Covered ............................................ 35.00 To 36.00
Pressed Glass, Butter, Bull's-Eye & Daisy, Covered, Cranberry Eyes .................... 35.00
Pressed Glass, Butter, Bullet & Emblem, Covered .................................................... 240.00

| | |
|---|---|
| Pressed Glass, Butter, Butterfly Handles | 30.00 |
| Pressed Glass, Butter, Cabbage Rose, Covered | 30.00 |
| Pressed Glass, Butter, Cable, Covered, Flint | 80.00 |
| Pressed Glass, Butter, Carmen, Covered | 28.00 |
| Pressed Glass, Butter, Checkerboard | 20.00 |
| Pressed Glass, Butter, Chestnut Band, Covered | 22.50 |
| Pressed Glass, Butter, Child's, Oval Star, Covered | 18.00 |
| Pressed Glass, Butter, Cord Drapery | 35.00 |
| Pressed Glass, Butter, Cosmos | 45.00 |
| Pressed Glass, Butter, Cut Log, Covered | 39.50 |
| Pressed Glass, Butter, Czarina, Covered | 22.50 |
| Pressed Glass, Butter, Dahlia, Covered, Footed | 32.50 |
| Pressed Glass, Butter, Dakota | 28.50 |
| Pressed Glass, Butter, Dakota, Covered | 24.00 |
| Pressed Glass, Butter, Delaware, Green, Covered, Gold | 70.00 |
| Pressed Glass, Butter, Delaware, Pink With Clear Stipple, Gold Trim | 55.00 |
| Pressed Glass, Butter, Delaware, Rose | 90.00 |
| Pressed Glass, Butter, Dewdrop, Covered | 40.00 |
| Pressed Glass, Butter, Diamond Medallion | 18.50 |
| Pressed Glass, Butter, Diamond Point Discs, Covered | 35.00 |
| Pressed Glass, Butter, Diamond Point Loops, Amber | 18.50 |
| Pressed Glass, Butter, Egyptian, Covered | 45.00 |
| Pressed Glass, Butter, Empress, Emerald, Gold Trim | 60.00 |
| Pressed Glass, Butter, Esther | 16.00 |
| Pressed Glass, Butter, Etched Dakota, Covered | 26.00 |
| Pressed Glass, Butter, Etched Dakota, Covered, Fern & Berry | 34.00 |
| Pressed Glass, Butter, Etched Fern Leaf, Frosted Old Abe Eagle Finial, Foot | 50.00 |
| Pressed Glass, Butter, Etched Grasshopper, Covered | 45.00 |
| Pressed Glass, Butter, Etched Mascotte, Covered | 35.00 |
| Pressed Glass, Butter, Eyewinker, Covered, 6 X 6 In. | 85.00 |
| Pressed Glass, Butter, Famous | 22.50 |
| Pressed Glass, Butter, Fancy Diamond, Covered | 26.00 |
| Pressed Glass, Butter, Feather | 23.00 |
| Pressed Glass, Butter, Feather, Covered | 20.00 To 38.00 |
| Pressed Glass, Butter, Fishscale, Covered | 24.00 To 24.50 |
| Pressed Glass, Butter, Flat Iron, Vaseline | 45.00 |
| Pressed Glass, Butter, Flattened Diamond With Sunburst, Covered, Miniature | 15.00 |
| Pressed Glass, Butter, Flower Flange, Green, Covered | 25.00 |
| Pressed Glass, Butter, Frosted Artichoke, Covered | 30.00 |
| Pressed Glass, Butter, Frosted Lion With Etched Fern, Covered | 48.00 |
| Pressed Glass, Butter, Frosted Star, Covered, Round | 25.00 |
| Pressed Glass, Butter, Galloway | 15.00 |
| Pressed Glass, Butter, Grand, Covered | 18.50 |
| Pressed Glass, Butter, Grape & Festoon With Stippled Leaf, Acorn Finial | 28.00 |
| Pressed Glass, Butter, Grape & Vine, Covered | 23.00 |
| Pressed Glass, Butter, Hamilton With Frosted Leaf, Covered | 75.00 |
| Pressed Glass, Butter, Horn Of Plenty, Covered, Flint | 68.50 To 95.00 |
| Pressed Glass, Butter, Horseshoe | 62.50 |
| Pressed Glass, Butter, Icicle | 19.50 |
| Pressed Glass, Butter, Inverted Fern, Covered | 50.00 |
| Pressed Glass, Butter, Iris & Herringbone, Covered | 7.50 |
| Pressed Glass, Butter, Iron, Amber | 45.00 |
| Pressed Glass, Butter, Jersey Swirl, Covered | 37.50 |
| Pressed Glass, Butter, Jewel & Dewdrop, Covered | 40.00 |
| Pressed Glass, Butter, Lacy Daisy | 32.50 |
| Pressed Glass, Butter, Liberty Bell                                                 *Illus* | 55.00 |
| Pressed Glass, Butter, Liberty Bell, Bell Finial | 35.00 |
| Pressed Glass, Butter, Liberty Bell, Covered | 70.00 To 72.50 |
| Pressed Glass, Butter, Loop & Jewel | 22.00 |
| Pressed Glass, Butter, Lorne, Covered, Oval | 27.50 |
| Pressed Glass, Butter, Marsh, Pink, Covered, Square | 25.00 |
| Pressed Glass, Butter, Minerva, Covered | 55.00 |
| Pressed Glass, Butter, Mitered Prism | 22.00 |
| Pressed Glass, Butter, Nursery Tales | 55.00 |
| Pressed Glass, Butter, Palmette, Covered | 27.50 |
| Pressed Glass, Butter, Paneled Forget-Me-Not | 35.00 |

Pressed Glass, Butter, Royal

Pressed Glass, Butter, Liberty Bell
*(See Page 406)*

Pressed Glass, Butter, Paneled Forget-Me-Not, Covered ................................................ 22.00 To 32.50
Pressed Glass, Butter, Paneled Grape, Covered ................................................ 35.00
Pressed Glass, Butter, Paneled Thistle, Covered ................................................ 29.50
Pressed Glass, Butter, Peacock Feather ................................................ 24.00
Pressed Glass, Butter, Pear, Covered ................................................ 27.00 To 35.00
Pressed Glass, Butter, Portland ................................................ 26.00
Pressed Glass, Butter, Pressed Diamond ................................................ 22.50
Pressed Glass, Butter, Red Block, Covered ................................................ 67.50
Pressed Glass, Butter, Ribbed Acorn, Covered, Flint ................................................ 80.00
Pressed Glass, Butter, Ribbon, Covered ................................................ 45.00
Pressed Glass, Butter, Rose In Snow, Covered, Round ................................................ 18.00 To 34.00
Pressed Glass, Butter, Rose In Snow, Square ................................................ 45.00
Pressed Glass, Butter, Royal ................................................ *Illus* 35.00
Pressed Glass, Butter, Sawtooth, Covered, Flint ................................................ 38.00 To 70.00
Pressed Glass, Butter, Scroll, Covered ................................................ 21.50
Pressed Glass, Butter, Smocking, Covered, Flint ................................................ 65.00
Pressed Glass, Butter, Sprig, Covered ................................................ 30.00 To 55.00
Pressed Glass, Butter, Stippled Cabbage Leaf, Bunnies On Cover ................................................ 65.00
Pressed Glass, Butter, Strawberry, Covered ................................................ 28.00
Pressed Glass, Butter, Swirl ................................................ 15.00
Pressed Glass, Butter, Swirl, Covered, Miniature ................................................ 17.00 To 18.00
Pressed Glass, Butter, Tacoma, Ruby-Stained ................................................ 78.00
Pressed Glass, Butter, Tennessee ................................................ 26.50
Pressed Glass, Butter, The States, Covered ................................................ 24.00
Pressed Glass, Butter, Three Shields ................................................ 32.00
Pressed Glass, Butter, Twin Snowshoes, Covered ................................................ 22.00
Pressed Glass, Butter, Valencia Waffle, Apple Green ................................................ 45.00
Pressed Glass, Butter, Viking, Covered ................................................ 45.00
Pressed Glass, Butter, Viking, Frosted Finial, Collared Base ................................................ 39.50
Pressed Glass, Butter, Waffle ................................................ 47.50 To 65.00
Pressed Glass, Butter, Westward Ho, Covered, Pedestal ................................................ 125.00
Pressed Glass, Butter, Wheat & Barley ................................................ 25.50
Pressed Glass, Butter, Wheat & Barley, Covered ................................................ 28.50
Pressed Glass, Butter, Whirling Star, Covered, Toy ................................................ 15.50
Pressed Glass, Butter, Wildflower, Covered ................................................ 26.00
Pressed Glass, Butter, Wildflower, Covered, Round ................................................ 35.00
Pressed Glass, Butter, Willow Oak, Amber, Covered ................................................ 45.00
Pressed Glass, Butter, Willow Oak, Covered, Square, Flange Type ................................................ 29.50
Pressed Glass, Cake Stand, Adonis, Cobalt Blue, 9 3/4 In. ................................................ 28.50
Pressed Glass, Cake Stand, Amazon, 9 1/4 In. ................................................ 29.50
Pressed Glass, Cake Stand, Arrowhead In Oval, Miniature ................................................ 20.00
Pressed Glass, Cake Stand, Barley, 9 In. ................................................ 13.00
Pressed Glass, Cake Stand, Barley, 9 1/4 In. ................................................ 18.00
Pressed Glass, Cake Stand, Barley, 9 1/2 In. ................................................ 20.00
Pressed Glass, Cake Stand, Barley, 9 5/8 In. ................................................ 25.00
Pressed Glass, Cake Stand, Barred Forget-Me-Not ................................................ 25.00
Pressed Glass, Cake Stand, Beaded Band, 9 In. ................................................ 18.00

Pressed Glass, Cake Stand, Beaded Grape, Pedestal .......... 35.00
Pressed Glass, Cake Stand, Beaded Loop, 9 1/2 In. .......... 15.00
Pressed Glass, Cake Stand, Beautiful Lady, 8 1/2 In. .......... 15.00
Pressed Glass, Cake Stand, Beveled Mirror, Eureka Silver Rim & Feet, 12 In. .......... 125.00
Pressed Glass, Cake Stand, Block & Fan, 10 In. .......... 35.00
Pressed Glass, Cake Stand, Buckle, 10 In. .......... 15.00
Pressed Glass, Cake Stand, Bull's-Eye & Fan, 9 1/4 In. .......... 16.00
Pressed Glass, Cake Stand, Cabbage Rose, 9 1/2 In. .......... 30.00
Pressed Glass, Cake Stand, Child's, Cane & Flowers, Scalloped Edge, 6 In. .......... 18.50
Pressed Glass, Cake Stand, Child's, Hawaiian Lei .......... 18.50
Pressed Glass, Cake Stand, Child's, Louisiana .......... 18.00
Pressed Glass, Cake Stand, Child's, Open Cryptic .......... 16.00
Pressed Glass, Cake Stand, Clear Panels With Cord Band, 11 In. .......... 18.00
Pressed Glass, Cake Stand, Clear Ribbon, 8 1/2 In. .......... 21.50
Pressed Glass, Cake Stand, Cord & Tassel, 10 In. .......... 25.00
Pressed Glass, Cake Stand, Cottage, 9 In. .......... 14.00 To 17.50
Pressed Glass, Cake Stand, Cut Log, 10 In. .......... 20.50 To 47.50
Pressed Glass, Cake Stand, Dakota, 9 1/4 In. .......... 18.00
Pressed Glass, Cake Stand, Dakota, 9 1/2 In. .......... 14.00
Pressed Glass, Cake Stand, Deer & Pine Tree, 9 In. .......... 45.00
Pressed Glass, Cake Stand, Dewdrop & Star, 9 1/4 In. .......... 18.50
Pressed Glass, Cake Stand, Dewdrop, 9 1/2 In. .......... 30.00
Pressed Glass, Cake Stand, Diamond Medallion, Footed .......... 10.00
Pressed Glass, Cake Stand, Diamond Medallion, 4 1/2 In. High .......... 22.50
Pressed Glass, Cake Stand, Diamond Medallion, 8 1/2 In. .......... 16.00
Pressed Glass, Cake Stand, Diamond Medallion, 9 In. .......... 9.50 To 13.00
Pressed Glass, Cake Stand, Diamond Medallion, 10 1/4 In. .......... 22.00
Pressed Glass, Cake Stand, Etched Button Band, 9 1/2 In. .......... 37.50
Pressed Glass, Cake Stand, Etched, Salesman's Sample, Miniature, 3 In.High .......... 22.50
Pressed Glass, Cake Stand, Eyewinker, 10 In. .......... 36.00 To 37.50
Pressed Glass, Cake Stand, Feather, 8 In. .......... 19.00
Pressed Glass, Cake Stand, Feather, 8 1/4 In. .......... 15.00
Pressed Glass, Cake Stand, Feather, 8 1/2 In. .......... 16.00 To 27.50
Pressed Glass, Cake Stand, Feather, 9 1/2 In. .......... 19.50
Pressed Glass, Cake Stand, Feather, 10 In. .......... 16.00
Pressed Glass, Cake Stand, Festoon, Tall, 10 In. .......... 16.00
Pressed Glass, Cake Stand, Festoon, 9 In. .......... 17.00 To 23.50
Pressed Glass, Cake Stand, Festoon, 10 In. .......... 25.00 To 35.00
Pressed Glass, Cake Stand, Festoon, 10 1/4 In. .......... 29.50
Pressed Glass, Cake Stand, Finecut & Fan, 6 In. .......... 13.00
Pressed Glass, Cake Stand, Fishscale, 8 In. .......... 22.50
Pressed Glass, Cake Stand, Fishscale, 9 In. .......... 19.00 To 24.50
Pressed Glass, Cake Stand, Fishscale, 10 1/2 In. .......... 21.00
Pressed Glass, Cake Stand, Fleur-De-Lis, 9 1/2 In. .......... 18.50
Pressed Glass, Cake Stand, Florida Palm, 9 In. .......... 12.00 To 18.50
Pressed Glass, Cake Stand, Florida Palm, 10 3/8 In. .......... 25.00
Pressed Glass, Cake Stand, Florida Palm, 10 1/2 In. .......... 16.50
Pressed Glass, Cake Stand, Frosted Circle, 9 In. .......... 20.00
Pressed Glass, Cake Stand, Gaelic, 10 1/2 In. .......... 27.00
Pressed Glass, Cake Stand, Galloway .......... 30.00
Pressed Glass, Cake Stand, Garden, Pink, 9 1/2 In. .......... 18.00
Pressed Glass, Cake Stand, Garfield Drape .......... 37.50
Pressed Glass, Cake Stand, Good Luck .......... 22.50
Pressed Glass, Cake Stand, Grand, Fan Edge, 8 1/4 In. .......... 19.50
Pressed Glass, Cake Stand, Grand, 8 1/4 In. .......... 14.00
Pressed Glass, Cake Stand, Grand, 8 3/4 In. .......... 21.50
Pressed Glass, Cake Stand, Grand, 10 In. .......... 23.50
Pressed Glass, Cake Stand, Grand, 10 1/4 In. .......... 16.00 To 26.00
Pressed Glass, Cake Stand, Hanover, Amber, 10 1/2 In. .......... 42.50
Pressed Glass, Cake Stand, Hanover, 10 In. .......... 19.00
Pressed Glass, Cake Stand, Hanover, 10 1/4 In. .......... 29.50
Pressed Glass, Cake Stand, Herringbone, Emerald Green, 9 In. .......... 35.00
Pressed Glass, Cake Stand, Hexagonal Bull's-Eye, Findlay, 9 In. .......... 21.50
Pressed Glass, Cake Stand, Horseshoe, 9 In. .......... 22.50
Pressed Glass, Cake Stand, Horseshoe, 10 In. .......... 19.00
Pressed Glass, Cake Stand, Horseshoe, 12 In.Diameter .......... 70.00

| | |
|---|---|
| Pressed Glass, Cake Stand, Huckle, 8 1/2 In. | 16.50 To 18.50 |
| Pressed Glass, Cake Stand, Ivy In Snow, 10 In. | 21.00 |
| Pressed Glass, Cake Stand, Jasper, 10 1/4 In. | 16.50 |
| Pressed Glass, Cake Stand, Jeweled Moon & Star, 10 1/2 In. | 29.50 |
| Pressed Glass, Cake Stand, Lacy Spiral, 9 1/4 In. | 20.00 |
| Pressed Glass, Cake Stand, Lattice, 12 1/2 In. | 45.00 |
| Pressed Glass, Cake Stand, Louisiana, 9 1/4 In. | 19.50 To 27.00 |
| Pressed Glass, Cake Stand, Maine, 8 3/4 In. | 25.00 |
| Pressed Glass, Cake Stand, Medallion, Blue | 39.50 |
| Pressed Glass, Cake Stand, Minerva, 7 1/2 In.High, 10 In.Diameter | 42.50 |
| Pressed Glass, Cake Stand, Minerva, 9 In. | 60.00 |
| Pressed Glass, Cake Stand, Moon & Star, 6 In.Diameter | 42.50 |
| Pressed Glass, Cake Stand, Nailhead, 8 3/4 In. | 11.50 |
| Pressed Glass, Cake Stand, Nailhead, 12 In. | 32.00 |
| Pressed Glass, Cake Stand, Palm & Scroll, Pedestal Base, 9 In. | 22.50 |
| Pressed Glass, Cake Stand, Paneled Cable, 9 1/2 In. | 10.00 |
| Pressed Glass, Cake Stand, Paneled Forget-Me-Not, 10 In. | 22.00 To 23.00 |
| Pressed Glass, Cake Stand, Paneled Herringbone, Clear, 9 1/4 In. | 16.50 |
| Pressed Glass, Cake Stand, Paneled Thistle, 5 In.High | 23.50 |
| Pressed Glass, Cake Stand, Paneled Thistle, 10 In. | 15.00 |
| Pressed Glass, Cake Stand, Pittsburgh With Frosted Hand, 9 In.Diameter | 35.00 |
| Pressed Glass, Cake Stand, Pleat & Panel, 10 In. | 27.50 |
| Pressed Glass, Cake Stand, Primrose, Clear, 5 In.High | 18.50 |
| Pressed Glass, Cake Stand, Priscilla, C.1890, 9 1/2 In. Diameter | 28.50 |
| Pressed Glass, Cake Stand, Queen, Blue, 8 1/2 In. | 45.00 |
| Pressed Glass, Cake Stand, Rexford, 11 In. | 20.00 |
| Pressed Glass, Cake Stand, Ribbed Ellipse, 9 In. | 24.95 |
| Pressed Glass, Cake Stand, Ribbon Candy, 8 In. | 18.50 |
| Pressed Glass, Cake Stand, Ribbon Candy, 8 1/4 In. | 17.00 |
| Pressed Glass, Cake Stand, Ribbon Candy, 9 1/2 In. | 17.50 |
| Pressed Glass, Cake Stand, Rose In Snow, Extended Handles, 9 1/2 In. | 18.00 |
| Pressed Glass, Cake Stand, Rose Sprig, Octagonal, 9 In. High | 18.50 |
| Pressed Glass, Cake Stand, Rose Sprig, 9 1/4 In. | 25.00 To 29.50 |
| Pressed Glass, Cake Stand, Rose Sprig, 9 1/4 In. Square | 29.50 |
| Pressed Glass, Cake Stand, Rose Sprig, 10 In. | 35.00 |
| Pressed Glass, Cake Stand, Rose Sprig, 10 In.Square | 35.00 |
| Pressed Glass, Cake Stand, Rosette With Palm, 9 1/2 In. | 16.00 To 25.00 |
| Pressed Glass, Cake Stand, Rosette With Palm, 10 In. | 25.00 To 28.50 |
| Pressed Glass, Cake Stand, Rosette With Palm, 11 In. | 18.50 |
| Pressed Glass, Cake Stand, Sawtooth Top, 10 In. | 15.00 |
| Pressed Glass, Cake Stand, Scroll With Star, Miniature | 10.50 |
| Pressed Glass, Cake Stand, Sheaf & Diamonds, 9 1/4 In. | 11.50 |
| Pressed Glass, Cake Stand, Shell & Tassel, 12 In. | 40.00 |
| Pressed Glass, Cake Stand, Sheraton, Amber, 10 1/4 In. | 35.00 |
| Pressed Glass, Cake Stand, Starred Block, Skirted, 9 In.Diameter | 37.50 |
| Pressed Glass, Cake Stand, Stippled Chain, 10 1/2 In. | 35.00 |
| Pressed Glass, Cake Stand, Stippled Forget-Me-Not, Findlay, 8 In.Diameter | 35.00 |
| Pressed Glass, Cake Stand, Stippled Forget-Me-Not, 9 In. | 25.00 |
| Pressed Glass, Cake Stand, U.S.Coin, 10 X 6 1/2 In. | 385.00 |
| Pressed Glass, Cake Stand, Utah, 8 1/2 In. | 23.50 |
| Pressed Glass, Cake Stand, Valencia Waffle, 10 In.Square | 29.50 |
| Pressed Glass, Cake Stand, Virginia, 9 1/2 In. | 25.00 |
| Pressed Glass, Cake Stand, Washington Centennial, 8 1/2 In. | 27.50 |
| Pressed Glass, Cake Stand, Wheat & Barley, Blue, 8 In.Diameter | 38.50 |
| Pressed Glass, Cake Stand, Wildflower, 10 1/2 In. | 25.00 |
| Pressed Glass, Cake Stand, Willow Oak, Amber, 10 In. | 40.00 |
| Pressed Glass, Cake Stand, Willow Oak, 8 1/4 In. | 25.00 |
| Pressed Glass, Candlestick, Clear Swirl, Miniature | 10.00 |
| Pressed Glass, Candlestick, Dolphin, McKearin 196-6, Pair | 135.00 |
| Pressed Glass, Candlestick, Excelsior, Pewter Inset, 9 1/4 In. High | 70.00 |
| Pressed Glass, Candlestick, Petal & Loop, Canary, Pair | 450.00 |
| Pressed Glass, Candlestick, Pittsburgh, 3 3/4 In.High, Pair | 23.00 |
| Pressed Glass, Canoe, Daisy & Button, Amber, 8 In. | 25.00 |
| Pressed Glass, Canoe, Daisy & Button, Amber, 12 In. | 45.00 |
| Pressed Glass, Canoe, Valencia Waffle, 9 1/2 In. | 25.00 |
| Pressed Glass, Cap, Military, Amber | 35.00 |

| | |
|---|---|
| **Pressed Glass, Carafe,** Barred Ovals | 16.00 |
| **Pressed Glass, Carafe,** Imperial | 11.00 |
| **Pressed Glass, Carafe,** Water, Albany Ribbed Swirl, Clear & Opalescent | 49.00 |
| **Pressed Glass, Carafe,** Water, Balder | 35.00 |
| **Pressed Glass, Carafe,** Water, Barred Ovals | 30.00 |
| **Pressed Glass, Carafe,** Water, Block & Fan | 35.00 |
| **Pressed Glass, Carafe,** Water, Jeweled Moon & Star | 32.50 |
| **Pressed Glass, Celery,** Almond Thumbprint | 13.00 To 22.50 |
| **Pressed Glass, Celery,** Alternating Holly & Floral Panels, Braid Rim | 28.50 |
| **Pressed Glass, Celery,** Amberette | 55.00 |
| **Pressed Glass, Celery,** Amberette, Petticoat Base, 6 3/4 In. High | 75.00 |
| **Pressed Glass, Celery,** Ashburton | 40.00 To 60.00 |
| **Pressed Glass, Celery,** Ashburton, Flint | 58.00 |
| **Pressed Glass, Celery,** Ashman | 14.00 |
| **Pressed Glass, Celery,** Banded Portland | 9.00 To 12.00 |
| **Pressed Glass, Celery,** Barberry | *Illus* 12.00 |

Pressed Glass,
Celery, Barberry

Pressed Glass,
Celery, Holly Band
*(See Page 411)*

| | |
|---|---|
| **Pressed Glass, Celery,** Barberry, Oval Berries | 15.00 |
| **Pressed Glass, Celery,** Beaded Grape, Green, 5 X 11 In. | 40.00 |
| **Pressed Glass, Celery,** Beveled Diamond & Star | 11.00 To 16.50 |
| **Pressed Glass, Celery,** Block & Fan | 11.25 To 18.00 |
| **Pressed Glass, Celery,** Block & Fan, 12 In. | 11.00 |
| **Pressed Glass, Celery,** Block & Thumbprint | 33.50 |
| **Pressed Glass, Celery,** Block & Thumbprint, Flint | 35.00 |
| **Pressed Glass, Celery,** Blockade | 21.50 |
| **Pressed Glass, Celery,** Blocked Arches | 12.50 |
| **Pressed Glass, Celery,** Broken Column | 27.00 |
| **Pressed Glass, Celery,** Bull's-Eye & Diamond Point | 125.00 |
| **Pressed Glass, Celery,** Bull's-Eye & Diamond Point, Flint | 125.00 |
| **Pressed Glass, Celery,** Bull's-Eye & Fleur-De-Lis, Flint | 75.00 |
| **Pressed Glass, Celery,** Bull's-Eye & Fleur-De-Lis, Scalloped Foot, Flint | 85.00 |
| **Pressed Glass, Celery,** Bull's-Eye, Flared & Scalloped Top, Knob Stem, Flint | 40.00 |
| **Pressed Glass, Celery,** Cable | 95.00 |
| **Pressed Glass, Celery,** Cable, Flint | 75.00 To 95.00 |
| **Pressed Glass, Celery,** Carmen, Flat, Oblong, 9 X 6 In. | 9.00 |
| **Pressed Glass, Celery,** Chandelier | 18.50 To 21.50 |
| **Pressed Glass, Celery,** Checkerboard | 15.00 |
| **Pressed Glass, Celery,** Checkerboard, Footed | 16.00 |
| **Pressed Glass, Celery,** Classic | 65.00 To 117.00 |
| **Pressed Glass, Celery,** Cord & Tassel, Scalloped Top | 25.00 |
| **Pressed Glass, Celery,** Cottage, Bellaire Goblet Co. | 21.00 |
| **Pressed Glass, Celery,** Cottage, Footed | 17.00 |
| **Pressed Glass, Celery,** Cottage, Pittsburgh, C.1870 | 15.00 |
| **Pressed Glass, Celery,** Crystal Wedding | 58.00 |
| **Pressed Glass, Celery,** Cube | 6.00 |
| **Pressed Glass, Celery,** Cupid & Venus | 35.00 |
| **Pressed Glass, Celery,** Curtain | 16.50 |
| **Pressed Glass, Celery,** Cut Log, 6 1/2 In. | 14.50 |

Pressed Glass, Celery, Daisy & Button With Amber Panels, Boat Shape, 9 In. ....................... 23.00
Pressed Glass, Celery, Daisy & Button With Crossbar, Amber ................. 22.00 To 32.00
Pressed Glass, Celery, Daisy & Button With V Ornament ................. 12.50 To 13.50
Pressed Glass, Celery, Daisy & Button With V Ornament, Amber ................................ 27.00
Pressed Glass, Celery, Daisy & Button, Apple Green, Yacht, 9 3/4 In. ...................... 27.50
Pressed Glass, Celery, Daisy & Button, Triangular ........................ 21.50
Pressed Glass, Celery, Daisy, Button, & Crossbar, Blue ......................... 36.00
Pressed Glass, Celery, Dakota ............................... 16.50 To 24.00
Pressed Glass, Celery, Dakota With Etched Leaf & Berry ........................ 24.00
Pressed Glass, Celery, Dewdrop With Star ........................ 37.50
Pressed Glass, Celery, Diagonal Band ........................ 17.50
Pressed Glass, Celery, Diamond Block With Fan, Clear, Footed .................. 16.00
Pressed Glass, Celery, Diamond Block, 8 In. ........................ 6.00
Pressed Glass, Celery, Diamond Point ........................ 45.00
Pressed Glass, Celery, Diamond Point With Panels, Scalloped, Pedestal, Flint ................ 55.00
Pressed Glass, Celery, Diamond Point, Flared Rim, Flint ........................ 55.00
Pressed Glass, Celery, Diamond Point, Knob Stem, Flint ........................ 50.00
Pressed Glass, Celery, Diamond Thumbprint, Flint ........................ 100.00
Pressed Glass, Celery, Diamond Quilted, Sapphire Blue ........................ 17.00
Pressed Glass, Celery, Double Daisy ........................ 22.50
Pressed Glass, Celery, Egyptian ........................ 30.00
Pressed Glass, Celery, Etched Band, Scalloped Rim, 8 1/2 In. ........................ 14.50
Pressed Glass, Celery, Etched Fern ........................ 12.00
Pressed Glass, Celery, Etched Pavonia ........................ 32.50
Pressed Glass, Celery, Etched Pavonia, Bird, Flat, 3 In. ........................ 27.00
Pressed Glass, Celery, Etched Tropical Villas ........................ 22.00
Pressed Glass, Celery, Etched York Herringbone ........................ 12.00
Pressed Glass, Celery, Fan & Diamond ........................ 18.00
Pressed Glass, Celery, Feather ........................ 20.00 To 32.00
Pressed Glass, Celery, Fickle Block ........................ 8.00
Pressed Glass, Celery, Fine Rib, Flint ........................ 52.50
Pressed Glass, Celery, Fishscale ........................ 20.00
Pressed Glass, Celery, Flamingo Habitat ........................ 32.00
Pressed Glass, Celery, Fleur-De-Lis ........................ 9.50 To 25.00
Pressed Glass, Celery, Fleur-De-Lis & Drape ........................ 17.50
Pressed Glass, Celery, Frosted Blocked Arches ........................ 22.50
Pressed Glass, Celery, Frosted Eagle ........................ 22.50
Pressed Glass, Celery, Frosted Flower & Pleat, Amber Stained Flowers ........................ 30.00
Pressed Glass, Celery, Frosted Hidalgo ........................ 15.00 To 17.50
Pressed Glass, Celery, Frosted Lion ........................ 50.00 To 55.00
Pressed Glass, Celery, Frosted Ribbon ........................ 37.00
Pressed Glass, Celery, Frosted Ribbon, Footed ........................ 32.00
Pressed Glass, Celery, Frosted Roman Key ........................ 35.00
Pressed Glass, Celery, Frosted Roman Key, Flint ........................ 64.50 To 70.00
Pressed Glass, Celery, Galloway ........................ 15.00 To 17.00
Pressed Glass, Celery, Garfield Drape ........................ 27.50
Pressed Glass, Celery, Garfield Drape, Pedestal ........................ 25.00
Pressed Glass, Celery, Giant Prism With Thumbprint, Flint ........................ 125.00
Pressed Glass, Celery, Gothic ........................ 165.00
Pressed Glass, Celery, Gothic Arches, Flint ........................ 65.00
Pressed Glass, Celery, Gothic, Flint ........................ 55.00 To 150.00
Pressed Glass, Celery, Grand, Fan Edge ........................ 16.00
Pressed Glass, Celery, Grasshopper, Purplish Tinge, 3 Grasshoppers ........................ 28.00
Pressed Glass, Celery, Grasshopper, With Insect ........................ 23.00
Pressed Glass, Celery, Hand ........................ 28.00
Pressed Glass, Celery, Hand, 9 In.High ........................ 23.00
Pressed Glass, Celery, Hanover ........................ 12.00
Pressed Glass, Celery, Hartley ........................ 11.00
Pressed Glass, Celery, Hawaiian Lei, Handled ........................ 17.50
Pressed Glass, Celery, Heart Stem, Amber ........................ 35.00
Pressed Glass, Celery, Hero ........................ 11.00
Pressed Glass, Celery, Hidalgo ........................ 12.50
Pressed Glass, Celery, Hidalgo, Frosted & Clear, Boat Shape ........................ 25.00
Pressed Glass, Celery, Hobnail, Canary, 4 Footed ........................ 37.00
Pressed Glass, Celery, Hobnail, Fan Top, Findlay ........................ 18.50
Pressed Glass, Celery, Holly Band ........................ Illus  20.00

Pressed Glass, Celery, Honeycomb, Scalloped, Pedestal, Flint, 8 1/2 In. ............................. 35.00
Pressed Glass, Celery, Honeycomb, Stemmed ........................................................... 16.50
Pressed Glass, Celery, Horn Of Plenty ..................................................................... 125.00
Pressed Glass, Celery, Horses' Heads Medallion, Portland ........................................ 30.00
Pressed Glass, Celery, Horseshoe, Pedestal ............................................................ 25.00
Pressed Glass, Celery, Hummingbird ............................................................. 30.00 To 48.50
Pressed Glass, Celery, Ivy In Snow ........................................................................ 20.00
Pressed Glass, Celery, Jacob's Ladder ............................................................ 18.00 To 30.00
Pressed Glass, Celery, Jeweled Moon & Star ................................................. 15.50 To 24.50
Pressed Glass, Celery, Kokoma ............................................................................. 20.00
Pressed Glass, Celery, Lattice ........................................................................ 13.00 To 18.50
Pressed Glass, Celery, Lightning .......................................................................... 10.00
Pressed Glass, Celery, Lily Of The Valley .............................................................. 38.50
Pressed Glass, Celery, Lion ................................................................................. 35.00
Pressed Glass, Celery, Little River ........................................................................ 44.00
Pressed Glass, Celery, Loop & Dart ...................................................................... 18.50
Pressed Glass, Celery, Loop & Dart With Diamond Ornament ......................... 15.00 To 22.50
Pressed Glass, Celery, Loop, Scalloped, Flint, 9 1/2 In.High, Pair ........................... 60.00
Pressed Glass, Celery, Marquisette, Tall ................................................................ 15.00
Pressed Glass, Celery, Mascotte ........................................................................... 24.00
Pressed Glass, Celery, Mikado Fan ....................................................................... 9.00
Pressed Glass, Celery, Mitered Diamonds .............................................................. 20.00
Pressed Glass, Celery, Mitered Frieze, Findlay ....................................................... 25.00
Pressed Glass, Celery, Mitered Prism .................................................................... 25.00
Pressed Glass, Celery, Mitered Prism, Findlay ....................................................... 17.50
Pressed Glass, Celery, Mitered Prism, Handled ...................................................... 22.50
Pressed Glass, Celery, Moon & Star .............................................................. 22.00 To 26.00
Pressed Glass, Celery, Nail, Ruby Flashed, Etched Ferns ........................................ 29.50
Pressed Glass, Celery, Nailhead ........................................................................... 18.00
Pressed Glass, Celery, New Era ............................................................................ 9.00
Pressed Glass, Celery, New York Honeycomb, Flint ................................................ 20.00
Pressed Glass, Celery, Palmette .................................................................... 17.00 To 25.00
Pressed Glass, Celery, Paneled Acorn Band ........................................................... 32.00
Pressed Glass, Celery, Paneled Daisy, Findlay ....................................................... 21.00
Pressed Glass, Celery, Paneled Forget-Me-Not .............................................. 16.00 To 24.50
Pressed Glass, Celery, Paneled Thistle With Bee .................................................... 19.50
Pressed Glass, Celery, Pavonia ............................................................................ 14.50
Pressed Glass, Celery, Pigmy ............................................................................... 15.00
Pressed Glass, Celery, Pioneer's Victoria .............................................................. 14.50
Pressed Glass, Celery, Pitcairn ............................................................................. 13.50
Pressed Glass, Celery, Pittsburgh Drape, Hollow Stem, Flint ................................... 45.00
Pressed Glass, Celery, Plume ............................................................................... 24.50
Pressed Glass, Celery, Portland .................................................................... 14.50 To 15.00
Pressed Glass, Celery, Portland, Pewter Frame ...................................................... 48.00
Pressed Glass, Celery, Pressed Diamond ............................................................... 11.00
Pressed Glass, Celery, Prism Arc .................................................................. 15.00 To 19.00
Pressed Glass, Celery, Prism Block, C.1880, 9 1/2 In.High ..................................... 20.00
Pressed Glass, Celery, Psyche & Cupid ................................................................. 24.00
Pressed Glass, Celery, Quartered Block No.2 ......................................................... 10.00
Pressed Glass, Celery, Ray, Flint .......................................................................... 32.00
Pressed Glass, Celery, Ribbed Palm, Flint ............................................................. 49.50
Pressed Glass, Celery, Ribbon .............................................................................. 18.00
Pressed Glass, Celery, Ribbon, Clear Panels ......................................................... 10.00
Pressed Glass, Celery, Roman Key, Flint ............................................................... 62.50
Pressed Glass, Celery, Rose Sprig ........................................................................ 16.00
Pressed Glass, Celery, Rose Sprig, Blue, Pedestal ................................................. 47.50
Pressed Glass, Celery, Rosette With Palm ..................................................... 12.00 To 22.50
Pressed Glass, Celery, Sawtooth, Flint .................................................................. 28.00
Pressed Glass, Celery, Sawtooth, Flint, 9 1/8 In.High ............................................. 35.00
Pressed Glass, Celery, Sawtooth, Knob Stem ......................................................... 18.00
Pressed Glass, Celery, Scalloped Tape, Footed ...................................................... 16.00
Pressed Glass, Celery, Seneca Loop, Scalloped Top, Footed ................................... 42.50
Pressed Glass, Celery, Seneca Loop, 7 In. ............................................................ 24.00
Pressed Glass, Celery, Sheaf & Block .................................................................... 8.00
Pressed Glass, Celery, Shell & Tassel, Round ........................................................ 30.00
Pressed Glass, Celery, Snail ........................................................................ 20.00 To 25.00

Pressed Glass, Celery, Star & Oval With Etching ............................................................ 15.00
Pressed Glass, Celery, Star & Oval, Collared Base ........................................................ 12.50
Pressed Glass, Celery, Star & Oval, Frosted Center ...................................................... 11.00
Pressed Glass, Celery, Star & Pillar .............................................................................. 15.00
Pressed Glass, Celery, Stippled Grape & Festoon .......................................... 15.00 To 20.00
Pressed Glass, Celery, Stippled Grape & Festoon With Clear Leaf ................................ 19.50
Pressed Glass, Celery, Stippled Star .............................................................................. 25.00
Pressed Glass, Celery, Strawberry & Currant, Stemmed Rose & Celery Stalk ............... 23.00
Pressed Glass, Celery, Strigel ........................................................................................ 17.50
Pressed Glass, Celery, Sunk Daisy ................................................................................ 10.00
Pressed Glass, Celery, Sunk Daisy, Boat Shape, 10 1/2 In. ........................................... 13.00
Pressed Glass, Celery, Three Faces ............................................................................... 45.00
Pressed Glass, Celery, Thumbprint, Block, Findlay, 6 1/2 In. ........................................ 20.00
Pressed Glass, Celery, Thumbprint, Flint, 10 In.High .................................................... 95.00
Pressed Glass, Celery, Thumbprint, Ruby Flashed ........................................................ 29.00
Pressed Glass, Celery, Thumbprint, Scalloped Top, Round Base, Flint .......................... 60.00
Pressed Glass, Celery, Tiny Long Star, C.1860, Flint ..................................................... 22.50
Pressed Glass, Celery, Torpedo ..................................................................................... 15.00
Pressed Glass, Celery, Triangular Prism, Flint ............................................................... 23.50
Pressed Glass, Celery, Tropical Villa, Etched ................................................................ 20.00
Pressed Glass, Celery, Tulip ................................................................... 21.50 To 37.50
Pressed Glass, Celery, Tulip Shape, Flint, Pair .............................................................. 45.00
Pressed Glass, Celery, Tulip With Sawtooth .................................................................. 25.00
Pressed Glass, Celery, Two Panel ................................................................................. 14.50
Pressed Glass, Celery, Two Panel, Blue ........................................................................ 35.00
Pressed Glass, Celery, Valencia Waffle .......................................................................... 25.00
Pressed Glass, Celery, Valencia Waffle, Amber ............................................................. 37.50
Pressed Glass, Celery, Vintage, Engraved, Paneled Sides ............................................ 13.00
Pressed Glass, Celery, Virginia ..................................................................................... 24.50
Pressed Glass, Celery, Waffle & Spearpoints, Turning Amethyst, Pedestal .................... 22.50
Pressed Glass, Celery, Waffle, Faceted Knop Stem, Flint, 9 1/2 In. High ...................... 48.00
Pressed Glass, Celery, Waffle, Flint ........................................................ 33.00 To 75.00
Pressed Glass, Celery, Waffle, Flint, 10 In.High ............................................................ 35.00
Pressed Glass, Celery, Washington Centennial .............................................................. 27.50
Pressed Glass, Celery, Westmoreland ........................................................................... 10.00
Pressed Glass, Celery, Westward Ho ............................................................................ 125.00
Pressed Glass, Celery, Whirling Star ............................................................................. 12.50
Pressed Glass, Celery, Willow Oak, Pedestal ................................................................ 35.00
Pressed Glass, Celery, Windflower, Apple Green ........................................................... 37.50
Pressed Glass, Celery, Zipper ....................................................................................... 12.00
Pressed Glass, Celery, Zipper Slash .............................................................................. 12.00
Pressed Glass, Celery, 1, 000-Eye ................................................................................. 18.00
Pressed Glass, Celery, 1, 000-Eye, Apple Green ........................................................... 32.00
Pressed Glass, Celery, 1, 000-Eye, Opalescent ............................................................. 47.50
Pressed Glass, Celery, 1, 000-Eye, 3 Knob Stem ................................... 18.50 To 21.50
Pressed Glass, Celery, 1, 000-Eye, 7 1/2 In.High .......................................................... 26.00
Pressed Glass, Celery, 101 ..................................................................... 16.00 To 28.00
Pressed Glass, Champagne, Almond Thumbprint, Flint .................................................. 28.50
Pressed Glass, Champagne, Argus, Flint .............................................. 34.50 To 47.50
Pressed Glass, Champagne, Ashburton, Flint ................................................................ 30.00
Pressed Glass, Champagne, Banded Vernon Honeycomb, Flint ..................................... 30.00
Pressed Glass, Champagne, Blaze, Flint ........................................................................ 25.00
Pressed Glass, Champagne, Colonial, Flint .................................................................... 55.00
Pressed Glass, Champagne, Cut Argus, Flint ................................................................. 17.50
Pressed Glass, Champagne, Dahlia ....................................................... 30.00 To 45.00
Pressed Glass, Champagne, Dewberry, Gold ................................................................... 9.50
Pressed Glass, Champagne, Diamond Point ........................................... 35.00 To 55.00
Pressed Glass, Champagne, Diamond-Quilted, Amethyst ............................................... 32.50
Pressed Glass, Champagne, Diamond-Quilted, 6 In. ...................................................... 18.50
Pressed Glass, Champagne, Double Beetle Band ........................................................... 15.00
Pressed Glass, Champagne, Eureka ..................................................... 20.00 To 22.50
Pressed Glass, Champagne, Fine Rib, Flint .................................................................... 47.50
Pressed Glass, Champagne, Fine Rib, Flint, 5 1/4 In.High ............................................. 32.50
Pressed Glass, Champagne, Frosted Roman Key, Flint ................................................... 30.00
Pressed Glass, Champagne, Hercules' Pillar .................................................................. 20.00
Pressed Glass, Champagne, Hercules' Pillar, 5 1/2 In.High ........................................... 18.75

| | |
|---|---|
| Pressed Glass, Champagne, Horn Of Plenty, Flint | 90.00 |
| Pressed Glass, Champagne, King's Crown, Green Eyes, Gold Trim | 12.50 |
| Pressed Glass, Champagne, Laminated Petals, Flint | 32.00 |
| Pressed Glass, Champagne, Peerless | 25.00 |
| Pressed Glass, Champagne, Pressed Leaf, Flint | 24.00 |
| Pressed Glass, Champagne, Ripple | 14.00 |
| Pressed Glass, Champagne, Roman Key, Clear | 45.00 |
| Pressed Glass, Champagne, Stedman, Flint | 25.00 |
| Pressed Glass, Champagne, Three Faces, Deep Bowl | 35.00 |
| Pressed Glass, Champagne, Waffle & Thumbprint, Polished Pontil, Flint | 32.50 |
| Pressed Glass, Champagne, Waffle, Flint | 40.00 |
| Pressed Glass, Champagne, Wildflower, Amber | 40.00 |
| Pressed Glass, Champagne, Wildflower, Clear | 24.00 |
| Pressed Glass, Cheese Keeper, Etched Mascotte | 40.00 |
| Pressed Glass, Christmas Light, 1, 000-Eye, Blue | 24.50 |
| Pressed Glass, Claret, Ashburton, Flint | 32.50 To 40.00 |
| Pressed Glass, Claret, Ashburton, 5 3/4 In.High | 40.00 |
| Pressed Glass, Claret, Honeycomb | 48.00 |
| Pressed Glass, Claret, Lattice & Oval Panel, Flint | 65.00 |
| Pressed Glass, Claret, Lattice & Oval Panel, Flower Etched, Flint | 60.00 |
| Pressed Glass, Coal Hod, Green | 10.00 |
| Pressed Glass, Cologne, Block & Panel, Stopper, 7 In.High | 8.00 |
| Pressed Glass, Cologne, Block, Cut Faceted Stopper, Findlay | 15.00 |
| Pressed Glass, Cologne, Daisy & Button, Square Sided, Stopper, 7 In. | 25.00 |
| Pressed Glass, Cologne, Nailhead, Amber, Made In Italy, 10 In.High, Pair | 20.00 |
| Pressed Glass, Comb Rack, Daisy & Button, Sapphire Blue, Hanging | 110.00 |
| Pressed Glass, Compote, Actress, Fannie Davenport & Maggie Mitchell, 8 In. | 38.00 |
| Pressed Glass, Compote, Actress, Low, 7 In. | 30.00 |
| Pressed Glass, Compote, Amazon, Crystal, Scalloped, 10 In. | 55.00 |
| Pressed Glass, Compote, Arched Fleur-De-Lis, 8 In. | 18.00 |
| Pressed Glass, Compote, Arched Ovals, Covered, 8 3/4 In.High | 25.00 |
| Pressed Glass, Compote, Art, 8 In. | 25.00 |
| Pressed Glass, Compote, Art, 10 In. | 37.50 |
| Pressed Glass, Compote, Ashman, Covered, 6 1/2 In. | 39.50 |
| Pressed Glass, Compote, Atlanta, Lion's Head, 8 In. | 42.00 |
| Pressed Glass, Compote, Bakewell Pears, Ivory Opalescent, 12 In. | 125.00 |
| Pressed Glass, Compote, Banded Portland, Short Stem, 7 1/4 In. | 18.00 |
| Pressed Glass, Compote, Beaded Dewdrop, High Standard, 7 1/4 In. | 19.00 |
| Pressed Glass, Compote, Beaded Oval Loop With Sunburst, 6 In.High | 22.00 |
| Pressed Glass, Compote, Beautiful Lady, 8 In. | 14.00 |
| Pressed Glass, Compote, Bellflower, Flint, 8 In. | 42.00 |
| Pressed Glass, Compote, Bellflower, Low Foot, Flint, 8 1/2 X 5 In. | 75.00 |
| Pressed Glass, Compote, Bellflower, Scalloped Rim, 5 In.High | 45.00 |
| Pressed Glass, Compote, Bellflower, Scalloped Rim, 5 1/4 In. | 55.00 |
| Pressed Glass, Compote, Bellflower, Scalloped Top, Flint, 8 In.Diameter | 45.00 |
| Pressed Glass, Compote, Bellflower, Single Vine, Coarse Rib, Flint, 8 1/2 In. | 55.00 |
| Pressed Glass, Compote, Bellflower, Single Vine, Scalloped Top, 7 3/4 In. | 50.00 |
| Pressed Glass, Compote, Bellflower, Single Vine, 6 3/4 In.Diameter | 80.00 |
| Pressed Glass, Compote, Bellflower, Single Vine, 8 In.Diameter | 65.00 |
| Pressed Glass, Compote, Bellflower, 5 X 8 1/2 In. | 50.00 |
| Pressed Glass, Compote, Beveled Diamond & Star, 8 In. | 12.00 |
| Pressed Glass, Compote, Bigler, Knob Stem, Flint, 5 3/4 In.High | 45.00 |
| Pressed Glass, Compote, Bird & Strawberry, 7 3/4 In. Diameter | 40.00 |
| Pressed Glass, Compote, Broad Flute, Footed, Flint, 3 In.High, Pair | 44.00 |
| Pressed Glass, Compote, Broad Flute, 6 1/4 In.Diameter | 18.75 |
| Pressed Glass, Compote, Broken Column, High Standard, 7 In. | 27.50 |
| Pressed Glass, Compote, Broken Column, High Standard, 9 In. | 52.50 |
| Pressed Glass, Compote, Broken Column, 5 3/4 In.High, Pair | 52.00 |
| Pressed Glass, Compote, Bryce, High Standard, 8 In. | 16.00 |
| Pressed Glass, Compote, Buckle And Star, 8 In.Diameter | 20.00 |
| Pressed Glass, Compote, Cable, Low Standard, Flint, 9 In. | 35.00 |
| Pressed Glass, Compote, Cameo, Footed, 4 X 7 1/2 In. | 18.50 |
| Pressed Glass, Compote, Canadian, Footed, 6 In. | 20.00 |
| Pressed Glass, Compote, Canadian, Low, 6 In. | 20.00 |
| Pressed Glass, Compote, Carmen, 8 X 5 1/2 In. | 14.00 |
| Pressed Glass, Compote, Cathedral, Amber, Fluted, 9 1/2 X 6 1/2 In. | 45.00 |

| | | |
|---|---|---|
| Pressed Glass, Compote, Classic | *Illus* | 38.00 |
| Pressed Glass, Compote, Clear Circle, High Standard, 6 3/4 In. | | 15.00 |
| Pressed Glass, Compote, Clear Circle, High Standard, 8 1/4 In. | | 25.00 |
| Pressed Glass, Compote, Corrigan, Covered, 7 1/2 In.High | | 30.00 |
| Pressed Glass, Compote, Crystal Wedding, Frosted, 7 In. | | 45.00 |
| Pressed Glass, Compote, Cupid & Venus, 8 1/2 In. Diameter | | 30.00 |
| Pressed Glass, Compote, Cupid's Hunt, Covered, 8 X 10 1/2 In. | | 65.00 |
| Pressed Glass, Compote, Cupid's Hunt, Findlay, 6 X 5 3/4 In. | | 19.00 |
| Pressed Glass, Compote, Currier & Ives, Tall Standard, 9 3/4 In.High | | 22.00 |
| Pressed Glass, Compote, Cut Log, High Standard, 6 In. | | 20.00 |
| Pressed Glass, Compote, Cut Log, Low Standard, 9 1/2 In.High | | 30.00 |
| Pressed Glass, Compote, Cut Log, 5 In.High | | 15.00 |
| Pressed Glass, Compote, Cut Log, 6 In.Diameter | | 24.00 |
| Pressed Glass, Compote, Cut Log, 6 X 6 In. | | 18.00 |
| Pressed Glass, Compote, Cut Log, 8 1/2 In.High | | 45.00 |
| Pressed Glass, Compote, Dahlia, 9 In. | | 23.00 |
| Pressed Glass, Compote, Daisy & Button With Crossbar, Amber, 8 In. | | 27.00 |
| Pressed Glass, Compote, Daisy & Button With Crossbar, Low, 8 In. | | 22.00 |
| Pressed Glass, Compote, Daisy With Clear Stripe, High Standard, 7 1/2 In. | | 25.00 |
| Pressed Glass, Compote, Daonis, McKee, 4 1/2 In. | | 9.50 |
| Pressed Glass, Compote, Deer & Dog, Frosted Dog Finial, 6 In. | | 48.00 |
| Pressed Glass, Compote, Diagonal Band & Fan, High Standard, 8 3/4 In. | | 13.50 |
| Pressed Glass, Compote, Diagonal Band & Fan, Low Standard, 8 In. | | 9.00 |
| Pressed Glass, Compote, Diamond Thumbprint, Flint, 7 1/2 X 4 In. | | 52.00 |
| Pressed Glass, Compote, Diamond Thumbprint, Low, Flint, 7 In.Diameter | | 45.00 |
| Pressed Glass, Compote, Diamond Thumbprint, Scalloped Rim, Flint, 3 1/2 In. | | 45.00 |
| Pressed Glass, Compote, Diamond Thumbprint, Scalloped Rim, Flint, 4 1/2 In. | | 60.00 |
| Pressed Glass, Compote, Diamond Thumbprint, Scalloped Rim, Flint, 6 In.High | | 75.00 |
| Pressed Glass, Compote, Dolphin, Clear, Shell, Bakewell Pears, 7 In.High | | 69.50 |
| Pressed Glass, Compote, Dolphin, Frosted, Shell, Bakewell Pears, 9 1/4 In. | | 89.50 |
| Pressed Glass, Compote, Dolphin, Pittsburgh, 8 In. | *Illus* | 95.00 |
| Pressed Glass, Compote, Double Eye Hobnail, High Standard, 9 3/4 In. | | 45.00 |
| Pressed Glass, Compote, Duncan & Miller No.42, High Standard, 8 3/4 In. | | 32.50 |
| Pressed Glass, Compote, Duncan & Miller No.24, Square Bowl, 8 In. | | 22.50 |
| Pressed Glass, Compote, Egyptian, 7 1/2 In. | *Illus* | 75.00 |
| Pressed Glass, Compote, Elk Medallion, High Standard, 8 In. | | 25.00 |
| Pressed Glass, Compote, English, Registry Mark, Jan.1855, Flint, 5 1/2 In. | | 28.00 |
| Pressed Glass, Compote, Etched Applied Bands, 9 1/2 In. | | 20.00 |
| Pressed Glass, Compote, Etched Atlanta, 7 In. | | 62.00 |
| Pressed Glass, Compote, Etched Dakota, High Standard, 5 In. | | 29.00 |
| Pressed Glass, Compote, Etched Fern, Covered, 8 In. | | 18.00 |
| Pressed Glass, Compote, Everglades, Blue Opalescent, Gold Trim, 5 In.High | | 28.00 |
| Pressed Glass, Compote, Eyewinker, Covered, 8 X 12 1/2 In. | | 135.00 |
| Pressed Glass, Compote, Fan, Covered, 7 1/2 In. | | 26.00 |
| Pressed Glass, Compote, Feather, 6 In.High | | 10.00 |
| Pressed Glass, Compote, Feather, 8 In. | | 28.00 |

Pressed Glass, Compote, Dolphin, Pittsburgh, 8 In.

Pressed Glass, Compote, Classic

Pressed Glass, Compote, Egyptian, 7 1/2 In.
(See Page 415)

Pressed Glass, Compote,
Lincoln Drape, 8 1/2 In.
(See Page 417)

| | |
|---|---:|
| Pressed Glass, Compote, Fishscale, High Standard, 9 1/4 In. | 24.00 |
| Pressed Glass, Compote, Flamingo Habitat, 5 1/2 X 6 In. | 19.50 |
| Pressed Glass, Compote, Flower & Quill, Covered, Square, 11 In.High | 45.00 |
| Pressed Glass, Compote, Frosted Circle, Covered, 7 In. | 67.50 |
| Pressed Glass, Compote, Frosted Circle, High Standard, 8 1/2 In. | 20.00 |
| Pressed Glass, Compote, Frosted Circle, 10 1/2 In.Wide | 45.00 |
| Pressed Glass, Compote, Frosted Dog & Deer, Covered, 7 1/2 X 6 In. | 65.00 |
| Pressed Glass, Compote, Frosted Dolphin, 8 1/2 In.Diameter | 55.00 |
| Pressed Glass, Compote, Frosted Eagle, Covered, 8 In. | 195.00 |
| Pressed Glass, Compote, Frosted Eagle, High Standard, 7 In. | 20.00 |
| Pressed Glass, Compote, Frosted Greek Key, 5 1/2 In.High | 30.00 |
| Pressed Glass, Compote, Frosted Hand, Etching Around Top, 7 In.High | 35.00 |
| Pressed Glass, Compote, Frosted Lion, Covered, Oval, 7 3/8 X 4 1/2 In. | 49.50 |
| Pressed Glass, Compote, Frosted Lion, Covered, Standard, 7 1/2 In. High | 40.00 |
| Pressed Glass, Compote, Frosted Lion, Covered, 4 1/2 X 9 In. | 55.00 |
| Pressed Glass, Compote, Frosted Lion, Covered, 5 1/2 X 9 In. | 60.00 |
| Pressed Glass, Compote, Frosted Lion, Covered, 8 In.High | 135.00 |
| Pressed Glass, Compote, Frosted Lion, Frosted Head Finial, 6 X 7 1/2 In. | 75.00 |
| Pressed Glass, Compote, Frosted Lion, Rampant Lion Cover, 11 1/2 In.High | 75.00 |
| Pressed Glass, Compote, Frosted Lion, Rampant Lion Finial, 7 X 6 In. | 75.00 |
| Pressed Glass, Compote, Frosted Ribbon, Covered, 9 1/2 In.High | 40.00 |
| Pressed Glass, Compote, Frosted Ribbon, Frosted Dolphin Stem, 7 In. High | 135.00 |
| Pressed Glass, Compote, Frosted Ribbon, Silver Plated Stand, 7 1/2 In.High | 25.00 |
| Pressed Glass, Compote, Frosted Ribbon, 8 In. | 18.50 |
| Pressed Glass, Compote, Frosted Vera, 9 In. | 29.50 |
| Pressed Glass, Compote, Gaelic, 7 In.High | 18.00 |
| Pressed Glass, Compote, Garden, Pink, 5 X 4 3/4 In. | 12.00 |
| Pressed Glass, Compote, Giant Sawtooth, Air Bubbles, Flint, 7 1/2 X 5 In. | 25.00 |
| Pressed Glass, Compote, Good Luck, 7 In. | 25.00 |
| Pressed Glass, Compote, Grand, High Standard, 7 1/2 In. | 17.50 |
| Pressed Glass, Compote, Grape & Festoon With Shield, Covered, 13 In.High | 50.00 |
| Pressed Glass, Compote, Hamilton, Flint, 5 1/2 In.High | 60.00 |
| Pressed Glass, Compote, Hamilton, 5 1/4 X 8 In. | 40.00 |
| Pressed Glass, Compote, Hand, 8 In. | 20.00 |
| Pressed Glass, Compote, Hanover, High Standard, 8 1/2 In. | 23.00 |
| Pressed Glass, Compote, Hickman, High Standard, 7 1/4 In. | 17.00 |
| Pressed Glass, Compote, Honeycomb, Covered, Flint, 6 1/2 X 8 1/2 In. | 95.00 |
| Pressed Glass, Compote, Honeycomb, Flint, 8 X 5 1/4 In. | 35.00 |
| Pressed Glass, Compote, Honeycomb, Scalloped Edge, Flint, 7 1/4 In. | 35.00 |
| Pressed Glass, Compote, Horn Of Plenty, Flint, 8 In.High | 92.00 |
| Pressed Glass, Compote, Horn Of Plenty, Flint, 10 In. High | 85.00 |
| Pressed Glass, Compote, Horn Of Plenty, High Standard, 7 In. | 82.50 |
| Pressed Glass, Compote, Horn Of Plenty, Scalloped Top, Flint, 7 1/2 In. | 45.00 |
| Pressed Glass, Compote, Horn Of Plenty, 7 1/2 In.High | 70.00 |

Pressed Glass, Compote, Horn Of Plenty, 8 In. .................................................................. 90.00 To 92.00
Pressed Glass, Compote, Horseshoe, Covered, Low Standard, 8 In. .................................... 46.00
Pressed Glass, Compote, Horseshoe, Covered, 8 In.High ...................................................... 55.00
Pressed Glass, Compote, Horseshoe, 7 1/2 In. ..................................................................... 28.50
Pressed Glass, Compote, Huber, Washington Base, Flint, N.E., 9 1/2 In. ........................... 50.00
Pressed Glass, Compote, Jacob's Ladder, 7 In. Diameter ..................................................... 24.50
Pressed Glass, Compote, Jacob's Ladder, 7 1/2 In. ............................................... 25.00 To 36.00
Pressed Glass, Compote, Jelly, Amazon ................................................................................ 15.00
Pressed Glass, Compote, Jelly, Candy Ribbon, 5 3/4 In.Diameter ...................................... 14.00
Pressed Glass, Compote, Jelly, Circle .................................................................................... 16.00
Pressed Glass, Compote, Jelly, Circled Scroll, Clear Opalescent ........................................ 37.50
Pressed Glass, Compote, Jelly, Cottage, Emerald ............................................................... 15.00
Pressed Glass, Compote, Jelly, Crystal Wedding, Covered .................................................. 10.00
Pressed Glass, Compote, Jelly, Duncan & Miller No.42, Scalloped Edge, 5 In .................... 24.00
Pressed Glass, Compote, Jelly, Esther .................................................................................. 18.50
Pressed Glass, Compote, Jelly, Etched Bead & Scroll, 5 In. ................................................ 16.00
Pressed Glass, Compote, Jelly, Eyewinker ............................................................. 18.00 To 35.00
Pressed Glass, Compote, Jelly, Eyewinker, 4 X 5 In. ............................................................ 37.50
Pressed Glass, Compote, Jelly, Feather ................................................................. 15.00 To 18.00
Pressed Glass, Compote, Jelly, Feather & Indiana Swirl, 4 1/2 In.High ............................... 12.50
Pressed Glass, Compote, Jelly, Feather Swirl, 6 In. ............................................................. 12.00
Pressed Glass, Compote, Jelly, Feather, 4 1/2 In.High ........................................................ 14.50
Pressed Glass, Compote, Jelly, Fishscale ............................................................... 9.00 To 15.00
Pressed Glass, Compote, Jelly, Fishscale, 4 1/2 In. ............................................................. 11.00
Pressed Glass, Compote, Jelly, Fleur-De-Lis & Drape, Green, 5 1/4 In. .............................. 21.50
Pressed Glass, Compote, Jelly, Frosted Circle ...................................................................... 14.00
Pressed Glass, Compote, Jelly, Huckle .................................................................................. 12.50
Pressed Glass, Compote, Jelly, Ivy In Snow .......................................................................... 20.00
Pressed Glass, Compote, Jelly, Maryland .............................................................................. 15.00
Pressed Glass, Compote, Jelly, Pleat & Panel ...................................................................... 17.50
Pressed Glass, Compote, Jelly, Pogo Stick, 6 In. ................................................................. 9.00
Pressed Glass, Compote, Jelly, Quartered Block, No.2, 4 1/2 In. ......................................... 9.00
Pressed Glass, Compote, Jelly, Rose In Snow ...................................................................... 20.00
Pressed Glass, Compote, Jelly, Rosette ................................................................... 9.50 To 12.50
Pressed Glass, Compote, Jelly, Scroll With Acanthus, Opalescent Rim ............................. 13.00
Pressed Glass, Compote, Jelly, Tokyo, Green Opalescent ................................................... 22.00
Pressed Glass, Compote, Jelly, Wheat & Barley .................................................... 13.50 To 14.00
Pressed Glass, Compote, Jelly, Wheat & Barley, Amber ..................................................... 24.00
Pressed Glass, Compote, Jelly, Wheat & Barley, Blue ......................................................... 24.50
Pressed Glass, Compote, Jelly, Wheat & Barley, Stemmed, 4 1/2 In. ................................. 8.75
Pressed Glass, Compote, Jeweled Moon & Star, Scalloped Top, 9 1/2 In. .......................... 18.50
Pressed Glass, Compote, Kentucky, Square Bowl, 5 3/4 In.High ....................................... 12.00
Pressed Glass, Compote, King's Crown, Ruffled Edge, 9 In. High ...................................... 75.00
Pressed Glass, Compote, Kokomo, Covered, Low, 8 In .................................................... 25.00
Pressed Glass, Compote, Lacy Spiral, Scalloped Rim, 7 3/4 In. ......................................... 18.00
Pressed Glass, Compote, Laverne, 9 1/2 In. ........................................................................ 23.00
Pressed Glass, Compote, Leaf, Green, Pedestal, 3 Twig Shape Stem, 5 In. ....................... 22.00
Pressed Glass, Compote, Lincoln Drape, Flint, 3 1/2 In.High .............................................. 37.50
Pressed Glass, Compote, Lincoln Drape, Flint, 8 1/4 In. ..................................................... 40.00
Pressed Glass, Compote, Lincoln Drape, High Standard, Flint, 8 1/4 In. ............................ 45.00
Pressed Glass, Compote, Lincoln Drape, Rayed Base, 6 In.High ....................................... 55.00
Pressed Glass, Compote, Lincoln Drape, 8 1/2 In. ............................................... *Illus*    65.00
Pressed Glass, Compote, Lion, Covered, 13 In.Diameter .................................................... 75.00
Pressed Glass, Compote, Loop, Covered, Pedestal, Flint, 8 1/4 In.High ............................. 75.00
Pressed Glass, Compote, Marquisette, 7 3/4 In.High .......................................................... 30.00
Pressed Glass, Compote, Marsh Fern, Covered, 10 1/2 In.High ......................................... 28.00
Pressed Glass, Compote, Maryland, 7 In. ............................................................................. 13.00
Pressed Glass, Compote, Medallion Sunburst, Covered, 10 1/2 In.High ............................ 32.50
Pressed Glass, Compote, Medallion Sunburst, High Standard, 8 In. ................................... 12.50
Pressed Glass, Compote, Mirror, Flint, 8 In.High ................................................................. 60.00
Pressed Glass, Compote, Mitered Diamonds, Low Standard, 7 1/2 In. ............................... 10.00
Pressed Glass, Compote, Mitered Ovals, Covered, Flint, 5 1/2 In.High .............................. 48.00
Pressed Glass, Compote, Mitered Prism, 6 In. ..................................................................... 16.00
Pressed Glass, Compote, Mitered Prism, 7 In. ..................................................................... 18.00
Pressed Glass, Compote, Moon & Star, Collared Base, 11 In.High ..................................... 65.00
Pressed Glass, Compote, Moon & Star, Covered, High Standard, 8 In.High ....................... 55.00

Pressed Glass, Compote, Moon & Star, Covered, 10 In. High .......... 35.00 To 275.00
Pressed Glass, Compote, Moon & Star, High Standard, 7 1/4 In.Diameter .......... 27.00
Pressed Glass, Compote, Moon & Star, Scalloped Rim, High Standard, 8 In. .......... 32.50
Pressed Glass, Compote, Moon & Star, Scalloped Rim, 8 1/4 In. .......... 40.00
Pressed Glass, Compote, Moon & Star, Stemmed, 9 In. .......... 25.00
Pressed Glass, Compote, Moon & Star, Stemmed, 10 In. .......... 35.00
Pressed Glass, Compote, Moon & Star, 6 In. .......... 18.50
Pressed Glass, Compote, Moon & Star, 7 1/2 In.High .......... 25.00
Pressed Glass, Compote, Moon & Star, 8 In. .......... 35.00
Pressed Glass, Compote, Nailhead, 8 1/2 In. .......... 10.00
Pressed Glass, Compote, New England Pineapple, Flint, 5 In.High .......... 65.00
Pressed Glass, Compote, New England Pineapple, 5 X 8 1/4 In. .......... 58.00
Pressed Glass, Compote, New England Pineapple, 7 In.Diameter .......... 80.00
Pressed Glass, Compote, Opposing Pryamids, Low Standard, 7 In. .......... 10.00
Pressed Glass, Compote, Paneled Daisy, Covered, 5 In. .......... 45.00
Pressed Glass, Compote, Paneled Forget-Me-Not, Covered, 7 X 7 In. .......... 35.00
Pressed Glass, Compote, Paneled Forget-Me-Not, Ruffled Rim, 6 1/2 In. .......... 18.00
Pressed Glass, Compote, Paneled Forget-Me-Not, Ruffled Rim, 8 1/2 In. .......... 20.00
Pressed Glass, Compote, Paneled Forget-Me-Not, 7 In.High .......... 28.00
Pressed Glass, Compote, Paneled Forget-Me-Not, 8 1/2 In.Diameter .......... 20.00
Pressed Glass, Compote, Paneled Ivy, Turned Amethyst, 4 1/2 In.High .......... 15.00
Pressed Glass, Compote, Paneled Thistle, Footed, 7 1/2 In. .......... 26.00
Pressed Glass, Compote, Paneled Thistle, Scalloped Rim, Curled Inward .......... 36.00
Pressed Glass, Compote, Paneled Thistle, 4 3/4 In.High .......... 25.00
Pressed Glass, Compote, Paneled Thistle, 7 In.High .......... 24.50
Pressed Glass, Compote, Paneled, Flint, 7 In. .......... 18.00
Pressed Glass, Compote, Pequot, Covered, 8 1/4 In.Diameter .......... 100.00
Pressed Glass, Compote, Picket Fence, Square Bowl, 5 1/2 In.High .......... 18.50
Pressed Glass, Compote, Picket, Covered, 7 X 10 1/2 In. .......... 48.50
Pressed Glass, Compote, Picket, High Standard, 8 In. .......... 25.00
Pressed Glass, Compote, Picket, 7 In. Square .......... 30.00
Pressed Glass, Compote, Pittsburgh Tree Of Life, Clear Hand Stem, 7 In. .......... 36.00
Pressed Glass, Compote, Pleat & Panel, Covered, High Standard, 8 In. .......... 40.00
Pressed Glass, Compote, Plume, Covered, 6 3/4 In.High .......... 22.00
Pressed Glass, Compote, Plutec, 7 In. .......... 15.00
Pressed Glass, Compote, Portland, Covered, 7 In.High .......... 25.00
Pressed Glass, Compote, Post, Covered, 10 In.High, 5 In.Square .......... 35.00
Pressed Glass, Compote, Pressed Block, Baluster Stem, Flint, 6 1/2 In. .......... 42.00
Pressed Glass, Compote, Pressed Diamond, Amber, 6 In.High .......... 35.00
Pressed Glass, Compote, Pressed Diamond, Yellow, 7 1/2 In.Diameter .......... 32.00
Pressed Glass, Compote, Princess Feather, Bakewell Pears Co., 8 In.Diameter .......... 20.00
Pressed Glass, Compote, Prism & Flute, Footed, 9 In. .......... 27.50
Pressed Glass, Compote, Prism & Sawtooth, Low Standard, Flint, 7 1/2 In. .......... 30.00
Pressed Glass, Compote, Prism, Covered, Flint, 7 X 8 1/2 In. .......... 48.00
Pressed Glass, Compote, Psyche & Cupid, 4 3/4 X 7 In. .......... 25.00
Pressed Glass, Compote, Queen's Necklace, 8 1/2 X 8 In. .......... 45.00
Pressed Glass, Compote, Reverse Torpedo, Fluted Top, 10 In. .......... 48.00
Pressed Glass, Compote, Reverse Torpedo, Ruffled, 10 1/2 X 8 X 8 1/2 In. .......... 65.00
Pressed Glass, Compote, Ribbed Grape, High Standard, Flint, 7 1/4 In. .......... 35.00
Pressed Glass, Compote, Ribbed Ivy, Bell Shape Bowl, Flint, 9 In. .......... 195.00
Pressed Glass, Compote, Ribbed Ivy, Scalloped Edge, Flint, 8 In. .......... 55.00
Pressed Glass, Compote, Ribbon, Covered, Low Standard, 6 1/4 In. .......... 27.50
Pressed Glass, Compote, Roman Rosette, Covered, 8 1/2 X 12 1/2 In. .......... 85.00
Pressed Glass, Compote, Rose In Snow, 4 3/4 In.High .......... 50.00
Pressed Glass, Compote, Rose In Snow, 5 1/2 In. .......... 17.00 To 17.50
Pressed Glass, Compote, Rose Sprig, Low Standard, 9 In. .......... 15.00
Pressed Glass, Compote, Ruby Thumbprint, 5 1/2 In. .......... 25.00
Pressed Glass, Compote, Sawtooth, Covered, Flint, 12 In. .......... 125.00
Pressed Glass, Compote, Sawtooth, High Standard, Flint, 9 In. .......... 37.50
Pressed Glass, Compote, Sawtooth, Pagoda Cover, 12 In.High .......... 95.00
Pressed Glass, Compote, Sawtooth, 7 In. .......... 30.00
Pressed Glass, Compote, Scalloped Diamond Point, Covered, 8 In.High .......... 20.00
Pressed Glass, Compote, Scalloped Lines, Covered, 7 1/2 In. .......... 20.00
Pressed Glass, Compote, Scroll With Acorn, , Covered, 7 In.High .......... 35.00
Pressed Glass, Compote, Scroll With Flowers, 8 In. .......... 22.50
Pressed Glass, Compote, Seneca Loop, Footed, 6 X 8 1/2 In. .......... 22.50

Pressed Glass, Compote, Seneca Loop, Scalloped, 12 In. ......................................... 45.00
Pressed Glass, Compote, Sheaf & Diamonds, High Standard, 9 1/4 In. ...................... 17.50
Pressed Glass, Compote, Shell & Tassel, 6 1/2 In. ......................................... *Illus* 25.00
Pressed Glass, Compote, Shell & Tassel, Square, 7 1/2 In.High ............................... 32.50
Pressed Glass, Compote, Smocking, Scalloped Foot, Flint, 3 In.High .......................... 35.00
Pressed Glass, Compote, Snail, Covered, 7 1/2 In.High ...................................... 30.00
Pressed Glass, Compote, Spirea Band, 7 1/4 In.Diameter .................................... 17.00
Pressed Glass, Compote, Sprig, Covered, 6 1/2 In.High ...................................... 18.00
Pressed Glass, Compote, Sprig, 8 In. ...................................................... 20.00
Pressed Glass, Compote, Sprig, 10 In. ..................................................... 20.00
Pressed Glass, Compote, Star Galaxy, High Standard ........................................ 85.00
Pressed Glass, Compote, Stedman, Low Standard, Flint, 7 In. ............................... 28.00
Pressed Glass, Compote, Stippled Forget-Me-Not, 6 In. ..................................... 18.00
Pressed Glass, Compote, Strawberry, Covered, 3 Mold, 9 1/2 In. ........................... 39.00
Pressed Glass, Compote, Strawberry, Covered, 9 In. ........................................ 15.00
Pressed Glass, Compote, Sunburst & Diamond, 6 In.High ..................................... 12.00
Pressed Glass, Compote, Sweetmeat, Almond Thumbprint, Covered, Flint ...................... 50.00
Pressed Glass, Compote, Swirl, Right Swirl, 5 In.High ....................................... 9.00
Pressed Glass, Compote, Three Faces, Covered, 4 1/2 X 8 In. ............................... 75.00
Pressed Glass, Compote, Three Faces, 6 In. ................................................ 35.00
Pressed Glass, Compote, Three Faces, 7 In. ................................................ 45.00
Pressed Glass, Compote, Three Panel, Amber, Low Footed, 8 1/2 In. ......................... 45.00
Pressed Glass, Compote, Three Panel, Amber, 7 In. ......................................... 25.00
Pressed Glass, Compote, Three Panel, Blue, 10 In. ......................................... 47.00
Pressed Glass, Compote, Three Panel, Footed, 7 In.Diameter ................................ 15.00
Pressed Glass, Compote, Thumbprint, Covered, Flint, 7 1/4 In. ............................. 95.00
Pressed Glass, Compote, Thumbprint, Covered, 9 In.High .................................... 28.50
Pressed Glass, Compote, Thumbprint, Flint, 8 In.Diameter .................................. 38.00
Pressed Glass, Compote, Thumbprint, Flint, 8 X 4 In. ...................................... 52.00
Pressed Glass, Compote, Thumbprint, Flint, 9 In.Diameter .................................. 38.00
Pressed Glass, Compote, Thumbprint, Knob Stem, Flint, 7 In. ............................... 34.00
Pressed Glass, Compote, Thumbprint, 5 In. Diameter ........................................ 42.50
Pressed Glass, Compote, Tree Of Life, Hand Column, 10 1/2 In. ............................. 55.00
Pressed Glass, Compote, Tree Of Life, Hand Stem, Portland, 8 1/2 In High .................. 60.00
Pressed Glass, Compote, Tree Of Life, 8 X 9 3/4 In. ....................................... 65.00
Pressed Glass, Compote, Tree Of Life, 9 In. ............................................. *Illus* 68.00
Pressed Glass, Compote, Tulip & Sawtooth, Flint, 5 1/4 In. High ........................... 32.50
Pressed Glass, Compote, Tulip & Sawtooth, Flint, 9 3/4 In. High ........................... 35.00
Pressed Glass, Compote, Two Panel, Apple Green, 8 1/4 In.High ............................. 35.00
Pressed Glass, Compote, Two Panel, Green, Oval, 8 X 7 1/2 X 8 1/4 In. ..................... 35.00
Pressed Glass, Compote, Two Panel, Oval, 6 1/2 X 8 X 7 In. ................................ 18.00
Pressed Glass, Compote, Valencia Waffle, Blue, Covered, 12 1/2 In.High .................... 80.00
Pressed Glass, Compote, Vernon Honeycomb, Flint, 6 1/4 In.High ............................ 75.00
Pressed Glass, Compote, Vernon Honeycomb, 8 In. .......................................... 20.00
Pressed Glass, Compote, Vernon Honeycomb, 11 In ......................................... 75.00
Pressed Glass, Compote, Victoria, C.1850, 6 In. .......................................... 38.00
Pressed Glass, Compote, Victoria, Covered, 10 X 14 1/2 In. ............................... 145.00
Pressed Glass, Compote, Victoria, Flint, 9 In.High ....................................... 100.00
Pressed Glass, Compote, Virginia, 10 In. .................................................. 25.00

Pressed Glass, Compote, Tree Of Life, 9 In.

Pressed Glass, Compote,
Shell & Tassel, 6 1/2 In.

Pressed Glass, Compote, Washington Centennial, High Standard, 8 In. ........................ 23.00
Pressed Glass, Compote, Washington Centennial, High Standard, 8 1/4 In. .................... 25.00
Pressed Glass, Compote, Washington Centennial, High Standard, 10 In. ...................... 32.00
Pressed Glass, Compote, Washington Centennial, 7 1/2 In. ...................................... 18.00
Pressed Glass, Compote, Westward Ho, Covered, Oval, 7 3/4 X 4 3/4 In. .................... 140.00
Pressed Glass, Compote, Westward Ho, Covered, Oval, 10 In.High ............................ 125.00
Pressed Glass, Compote, Westward Ho, Covered, Oval, 12 In.High ............................ 165.00
Pressed Glass, Compote, Westward Ho, Covered, 7 X 4 In. ...................................... 70.00
Pressed Glass, Compote, Westward Ho, Covered, 8 In. ........................ 115.00 To 150.00
Pressed Glass, Compote, Westward Ho, Covered, 12 1/2 In. High .............................. 185.00
Pressed Glass, Compote, Westward Ho, High Standard, 6 In.Diameter ........................ 85.00
Pressed Glass, Compote, Westward Ho, Low Standard, 4 1/2 In. High ........................ 25.00
Pressed Glass, Compote, Westward Ho, Round, 9 In.High ........................................ 75.00
Pressed Glass, Compote, Westward Ho, 7 In.Diameter ............................................ 40.00
Pressed Glass, Compote, Westward Ho, 9 X 9 In. .................................................. 60.00
Pressed Glass, Compote, Wildflower, Apple Green, Low Foot, 7 In.Diameter ................ 28.00
Pressed Glass, Compote, Wildflower, Covered, 6 In. .............................................. 22.00
Pressed Glass, Compote, Wildflower, Covered, 8 In. .............................................. 22.00
Pressed Glass, Compote, Wildflower, Covered, 12 In. ............................................ 35.00
Pressed Glass, Compote, Wildflower, Low, 7 In. .................................................. 10.00
Pressed Glass, Compote, Willow Oak, Amber, High Standard, 6 In.High ...................... 22.50
Pressed Glass, Compote, Willow Oak, Covered, High Standard, 6 1/4 In. .................... 37.50
Pressed Glass, Compote, Willow Oak, High Standard, 7 1/2 In. ................................ 17.50
Pressed Glass, Compote, Wisconsin, 3 1/2 In.High .............................................. 12.50
Pressed Glass, Compote, Wyoming, High Standard, 7 1/2 In. .................................. 23.00
Pressed Glass, Compote, Yuma Loop, Flint, 8 X 6 In. ............................................ 65.00
Pressed Glass, Compote, 1, 000-Eye, Apple Green, Square, 6 1/2 In. High .................. 52.50
Pressed Glass, Compote, 1, 000-Eye, Blue, 3 Knob Stem, 8 3/4 In. ............................ 48.50
Pressed Glass, Compote, 1, 000-Eye, Honey Amber, 3 Knob Stem, 6 In. ...................... 25.00
Pressed Glass, Compote, 1, 000-Eye, Squared & Flared S Knob Type, 8 In. .................. 35.00
Pressed Glass, Compote, 1, 000-Eye, 8 X 4 1/2 In. .............................................. 18.00
Pressed Glass, Condiment Set, Child's, English Hobnail, 4 Piece .............................. 25.00
Pressed Glass, Cookie Stand, Good Luck, 8 In. .................................................. 25.00
Pressed Glass, Cordial Set, Daisy & Button With Narcissus, Pink, 4 Piece .................. 65.00
Pressed Glass, Cordial, Bellflower, Single Vine, Flint .............................. 35.00 To 60.00
Pressed Glass, Cordial, Bulging Bars, Findlay, 3 In. .............................................. 16.50
Pressed Glass, Cordial, Cupid & Venus ................................................ 50.00 To 55.00
Pressed Glass, Cordial, Dew & Raindrop ............................................................ 11.50
Pressed Glass, Cordial, Duncan & Miller No.42 .................................................. 24.00
Pressed Glass, Cordial, Fine Rib, Flint .............................................................. 24.00
Pressed Glass, Cordial, Flute, 8 Flutes, Applied Base, Flint ...................................... 7.00
Pressed Glass, Cordial, Hand ........................................................................ 35.00
Pressed Glass, Cordial, Heart & Thumbprint, 3 In. .............................................. 39.50
Pressed Glass, Cordial, Honeycomb, Flint .......................................................... 15.00
Pressed Glass, Cordial, Knife & Fork, Green ...................................................... 12.00
Pressed Glass, Cordial, Magnet & Grape With Frosted Leaf, Flint ............................ 70.00
Pressed Glass, Cordial, Paneled Dewdrop .......................................................... 20.00
Pressed Glass, Cordial, Paneled Finecut, Amber .................................................. 20.00
Pressed Glass, Cordial, Ribbon Candy .............................................................. 21.00
        Pressed Glass, Creamer & Sugar, see Pressed Glass, Sugar & Creamer
Pressed Glass, Creamer, Acorn Variant ............................................................ 25.00
Pressed Glass, Creamer, Actress .................................................................... 36.00
Pressed Glass, Creamer, Alaska, Blue .............................................................. 42.50
Pressed Glass, Creamer, Alaska, Blue, Opalescent .............................. 39.50 To 42.50
Pressed Glass, Creamer, Anthemion .............................................................. 16.50
Pressed Glass, Creamer, Apollo .................................................................... 15.00
Pressed Glass, Creamer, Apollo, Applied Handle, Pedestal Base .............................. 15.00
Pressed Glass, Creamer, Ashburton, Flint, 6 In.High ............................................ 78.50
Pressed Glass, Creamer, Austrian, Greentown .................................... 14.00 To 17.50
Pressed Glass, Creamer, Austrian, Large Size .................................................... 40.00
Pressed Glass, Creamer, Baby Lion ................................................................ 45.00
Pressed Glass, Creamer, Balder, Gold Trim ...................................................... 15.00
Pressed Glass, Creamer, Ball & Swirl ................................................ 9.50 To 20.00
Pressed Glass, Creamer, Ball & Swirl, Footed .................................................... 18.00
Pressed Glass, Creamer, Ball & Swirl, 6 1/2 In.High .............................................. 9.50
Pressed Glass, Creamer, Banded Portland ........................................................ 17.50

Pressed Glass, Creamer, Banded Raindrop ............................................................... 21.00
Pressed Glass, Creamer, Banded Star .................................................................... 20.00
Pressed Glass, Creamer, Barberry ........................................................................ 42.50
Pressed Glass, Creamer, Barberry, Oval Berries .................................................. 21.50
Pressed Glass, Creamer, Barley ........................................................................... 20.00
Pressed Glass, Creamer, Basket Weave, Canary ................................................. 20.00
Pressed Glass, Creamer, Beaded Ellipse .............................................................. 17.00
Pressed Glass, Creamer, Beaded Fan ................................................................... 10.00
Pressed Glass, Creamer, Beaded Finecut ........................................... 12.00 To 15.00
Pressed Glass, Creamer, Beaded Grape, Green .................................................. 27.00
Pressed Glass, Creamer, Beaded Loop ................................................................ 24.00
Pressed Glass, Creamer, Beaded Medallion, 5 1/2 In.High ................................. 16.00
Pressed Glass, Creamer, Beaded Oval & Scroll ................................................. 18.00
Pressed Glass, Creamer, Beaded Swirl Loop ...................................................... 11.50
Pressed Glass, Creamer, Bearded Man ............................................................... 13.50
Pressed Glass, Creamer, Berry Cluster ............................................................... 16.00
Pressed Glass, Creamer, Bethlehem Star ........................................................... 1.00
Pressed Glass, Creamer, Bird & Berry, Ball Feet .............................................. 30.00
Pressed Glass, Creamer, Bird & Strawberry ....................................... 11.50 To 28.00
Pressed Glass, Creamer, Blackberry .................................................................... 35.00
Pressed Glass, Creamer, Bleeding Heart, 4 1/2 In.High ..................................... 45.00
Pressed Glass, Creamer, Bleeding Hearts, Applied Handle ................................ 32.00
Pressed Glass, Creamer, Block & Fan ................................................................. 18.00
Pressed Glass, Creamer, Bouquet ....................................................................... 15.00
Pressed Glass, Creamer, British Cane ................................................................. 10.00
Pressed Glass, Creamer, Broken Column ............................................................ 35.00
Pressed Glass, Creamer, Bryce ............................................................................ 16.50
Pressed Glass, Creamer, Buckle With Star ......................................... 12.00 To 25.00
Pressed Glass, Creamer, Bull's-Eye & Diamond Panel ...................................... 35.00
Pressed Glass, Creamer, Bull's-Eye & Drape ..................................................... 22.50
Pressed Glass, Creamer, Buttressed Sunburst .................................................... 24.00
Pressed Glass, Creamer, Cameo .......................................................................... 15.00
Pressed Glass, Creamer, Canadian ...................................................................... 30.00
Pressed Glass, Creamer, Candlewick .................................................. 10.00 To 24.00
Pressed Glass, Creamer, Cane & Rosette, 6 In.High .......................................... 22.50
Pressed Glass, Creamer, Cane Spray ................................................................... 16.00
Pressed Glass, Creamer, Cardinal Bird ............................................... 30.00 To 34.50
Pressed Glass, Creamer, Cathedral ...................................................... 22.50 To 38.00
Pressed Glass, Creamer, Chain ............................................................................ 14.00
Pressed Glass, Creamer, Chain & Star ................................................................ 18.00
Pressed Glass, Creamer, Chain With Shield ....................................... 10.50 To 13.50
Pressed Glass, Creamer, Chain With Shield Band .............................................. 17.00
Pressed Glass, Creamer, Chandelier .................................................... 18.50 To 24.50
Pressed Glass, Creamer, Checkerboard, Large Size .......................................... 12.00
Pressed Glass, Creamer, Cherry, Applied Handle ............................... 35.00 To 36.00
Pressed Glass, Creamer, Child's, Austrian ......................................................... 38.00
Pressed Glass, Creamer, Child's, Daisy & Button .............................................. 8.00
Pressed Glass, Creamer, Child's, Diamond Flute ............................................... 14.50
Pressed Glass, Creamer, Child's, Hobnail, Opalescent ...................................... 15.00
Pressed Glass, Creamer, Child's, Snowflake ...................................................... 12.00
Pressed Glass, Creamer, Child's, Tappan, Amber ............................................. 12.00
Pressed Glass, Creamer, Circled Scrolls, Opalescent ........................................ 19.50
Pressed Glass, Creamer, Classic Medallion ........................................ 10.00 To 12.00
Pressed Glass, Creamer, Clear Diagonal Band ................................................... 14.00
Pressed Glass, Creamer, Clover, 3 1/2 In. ............................................... *Illus* 12.00
Pressed Glass, Creamer, Colorado, Green, Gold Trim, Souvenir ...... 18.50 To 29.00
Pressed Glass, Creamer, Colorado, Green, Gold Trim, Name & Date ............... 23.00
Pressed Glass, Creamer, Colorado, Green, Gold, Large Size ............................. 37.50
Pressed Glass, Creamer, Colorado, Green, Souvenir ......................................... 29.00
Pressed Glass, Creamer, Cord & Tassel .............................................................. 35.00
Pressed Glass, Creamer, Cornucopia ................................................................... 17.50
Pressed Glass, Creamer, Cornucopia, Molded Handle ........................................ 10.00
Pressed Glass, Creamer, Cottage ......................................................... 15.00 To 18.50
Pressed Glass, Creamer, Cottage, Hand & Bar Handle, Bellaire Goblet Co. ..... 19.50
Pressed Glass, Creamer, Cottage, 5 1/2 In. ........................................................ 18.00
Pressed Glass, Creamer, Cradled Prisms ............................................................ 13.50

Pressed Glass, Creamer, Clover, 3 1/2 In.
(See Page 421)

Pressed Glass, Creamer, Diagonal Band

| | |
|---|---|
| Pressed Glass, Creamer, Crow's Foot | 35.00 |
| Pressed Glass, Creamer, Crystal Wedding | 22.00 |
| Pressed Glass, Creamer, Cupid & Psyche | 35.00 |
| Pressed Glass, Creamer, Cupid & Venus | 27.50 To 28.50 |
| Pressed Glass, Creamer, Currier & Ives | 15.00 To 19.00 |
| Pressed Glass, Creamer, Curtain | 14.50 To 15.00 |
| Pressed Glass, Creamer, Cut Log | 14.50 To 15.00 |
| Pressed Glass, Creamer, Cut Log, Small Size | 15.50 |
| Pressed Glass, Creamer, Cut Log, 2 7/8 In. | 12.00 |
| Pressed Glass, Creamer, Cut Log, 5 In. | 15.00 |
| Pressed Glass, Creamer, Cyclone | 22.00 |
| Pressed Glass, Creamer, Dahlia | 15.00 To 35.00 |
| Pressed Glass, Creamer, Daisy & Button With Crossbar | 34.00 |
| Pressed Glass, Creamer, Daisy & Button With Crossbar, Amber | 28.50 |
| Pressed Glass, Creamer, Daisy & Button With Crossbar, Amber, Footed | 30.00 |
| Pressed Glass, Creamer, Daisy & Button With Crossbar, Amber, Small Size | 20.00 |
| Pressed Glass, Creamer, Daisy & Button With Crossbar, Amber, 6 1/2 In.High | 20.50 |
| Pressed Glass, Creamer, Daisy & Button With V Ornament | 19.50 |
| Pressed Glass, Creamer, Daisy & Button With V Ornament, Dark Amber, 5 In. | 25.00 |
| Pressed Glass, Creamer, Daisy & Button, Cane On Sides | 12.00 |
| Pressed Glass, Creamer, Daisy Medallion | 13.50 |
| Pressed Glass, Creamer, Dakota, Etched Fern & Berry | 42.50 |
| Pressed Glass, Creamer, Dakota, Footed | 27.50 |
| Pressed Glass, Creamer, Dart, Footed | 14.50 |
| Pressed Glass, Creamer, Dart, High Stem | 23.50 |
| Pressed Glass, Creamer, Delaware, Gold | 10.00 |
| Pressed Glass, Creamer, Delaware, Green, Gold | 45.00 |
| Pressed Glass, Creamer, Dewdrop & Flower | 20.00 |
| Pressed Glass, Creamer, Dewdrop In Points | 20.50 |
| Pressed Glass, Creamer, Dewdrop In Points, Molded Handle | 12.00 |
| Pressed Glass, Creamer, Dewey, Amber, Large Size | 37.50 |
| Pressed Glass, Creamer, Diagonal Band *Illus* | 15.00 |
| Pressed Glass, Creamer, Diagonal Band & Fan, Footed | 15.00 |
| Pressed Glass, Creamer, Diamond & Cross, 4 1/2 In.High | 50.00 |
| Pressed Glass, Creamer, Diamond & Fan | 12.50 |
| Pressed Glass, Creamer, Diamond & Sunburst | 9.00 |
| Pressed Glass, Creamer, Diamond Band | 8.75 |
| Pressed Glass, Creamer, Diamond Band & Fan, Footed | 27.50 |
| Pressed Glass, Creamer, Diamond Block & Fan | 20.00 |
| Pressed Glass, Creamer, Diamond Mirror | 15.00 |
| Pressed Glass, Creamer, Diamond Point Loop With Etching, Blue | 40.00 |
| Pressed Glass, Creamer, Diamond Point Loop, Light Amber | 22.50 |
| Pressed Glass, Creamer, Diamond Point With Ribs, Flint | 125.00 |
| Pressed Glass, Creamer, Diamond, Amber | 25.00 |
| Pressed Glass, Creamer, Divided Block & Sunburst | 14.95 |
| Pressed Glass, Creamer, Double Arches, Green, Gold Trim, 4 1/4 In.High | 30.00 |

Pressed Glass, Creamer, Double Frosted Ribbon ............................................... 22.00
Pressed Glass, Creamer, Double Spear, Molded Handle ...................................... 9.00
Pressed Glass, Creamer, Drapery ......................................................................... 18.00
Pressed Glass, Creamer, Drapery, Applied Crimped Handle ............................... 30.00
Pressed Glass, Creamer, Drapery, Applied Handle ............................... 30.00 To 30.50
Pressed Glass, Creamer, Ear Of Corn, Miniature ............................................... 22.50
Pressed Glass, Creamer, Egg In Sand ................................................................ 15.00
Pressed Glass, Creamer, Egg In Sand, Blue ........................................ 27.50 To 37.50
Pressed Glass, Creamer, Egyptian ....................................................................... 27.00
Pressed Glass, Creamer, Egyptian, 6 In.High ..................................................... 22.50
Pressed Glass, Creamer, Esther, Green, Gold Decoration ................................... 65.00
Pressed Glass, Creamer, Etched Apollo ............................................................... 27.00
Pressed Glass, Creamer, Etched Baby Lion ......................................................... 45.00
Pressed Glass, Creamer, Etched Floral, 3 1/2 In. ................................................. 4.50
Pressed Glass, Creamer, Etched Garden Fruit, C.1860 ........................................ 18.00
Pressed Glass, Creamer, Etched Marsh Fern ....................................................... 25.00
Pressed Glass, Creamer, Etched Marsh Fern, Tankard Shape .............................. 26.50
Pressed Glass, Creamer, Etched Mascotte ........................................................... 21.50
Pressed Glass, Creamer, Fan & Diamond ............................................................ 18.00
Pressed Glass, Creamer, Fan Band ......................................................... 8.00 To 10.00
Pressed Glass, Creamer, Fashion ......................................................................... 11.50
Pressed Glass, Creamer, Feather ............................................................ 10.50 To 32.00
Pressed Glass, Creamer, Feather Duster .............................................................. 12.50
Pressed Glass, Creamer, Feather, Green .............................................................. 40.00
Pressed Glass, Creamer, Fernland ....................................................................... 12.00
Pressed Glass, Creamer, Festoon ............................................................ 16.50 To 20.00
Pressed Glass, Creamer, Fickle Block .................................................................. 11.50
Pressed Glass, Creamer, Fine Rib, Applied Handle, Flint ..................................... 75.00
Pressed Glass, Creamer, Finecut & Panel .............................................. 12.00 To 12.50
Pressed Glass, Creamer, Finecut, Amber ............................................................. 35.00
Pressed Glass, Creamer, Fishscale .......................................................... 18.00 To 20.00
Pressed Glass, Creamer, Flamingo Habitat .......................................................... 22.50
Pressed Glass, Creamer, Fleur-De-Lis & Drape, Green .......................... 22.50 To 30.00
Pressed Glass, Creamer, Flora, Blue, Opalescent, Beaumont Glass Co. ............... 37.75
Pressed Glass, Creamer, Florida Palm ..................................................... 9.50 To 17.50
Pressed Glass, Creamer, Flower Flange, Amber .................................................. 35.00
Pressed Glass, Creamer, Flower With Cane, Gold .................................. 7.50 To 16.50
Pressed Glass, Creamer, Flowerpot ......................................................... 19.50 To 35.00
Pressed Glass, Creamer, Fluted Scrolls, Blue, Opalescent ................................... 38.00
Pressed Glass, Creamer, Frosted Blocked Arches ................................................ 18.00
Pressed Glass, Creamer, Frosted Circle ............................................................... 30.00
Pressed Glass, Creamer, Frosted Crystal ............................................................. 18.00
Pressed Glass, Creamer, Frosted Divided Squares, Amber Rim ........................... 17.50
Pressed Glass, Creamer, Frosted Dolphin ............................................................ 67.50
Pressed Glass, Creamer, Frosted Dolphin, Frosted Base ...................................... 100.00
Pressed Glass, Creamer, Frosted Eagle .................................................. 30.00 To 47.50
Pressed Glass, Creamer, Frosted Flower Band ..................................................... 65.00
Pressed Glass, Creamer, Frosted Flower Band, Molded Handle ........................... 30.00
Pressed Glass, Creamer, Frosted Lion .................................................... 30.00 To 52.00
Pressed Glass, Creamer, Frosted Ribbon ................................................ 30.00 To 45.00
Pressed Glass, Creamer, Fuchsia, Square ........................................................... 25.00
Pressed Glass, Creamer, Galloway ...................................................................... 12.50
Pressed Glass, Creamer, Garden, Pink ................................................................ 13.00
Pressed Glass, Creamer, Garfield Drape ................................................. 18.00 To 35.00
Pressed Glass, Creamer, Garfield Drape, Molded Handle .................................... 20.00
Pressed Glass, Creamer, Girl's Face .................................................................... 16.50
Pressed Glass, Creamer, Globe & Star ................................................................ 19.00
Pressed Glass, Creamer, Good Luck, 6 In. .............................................. 18.00 To 27.50
Pressed Glass, Creamer, Gooseberry ...................................................... 19.50 To 25.00
Pressed Glass, Creamer, Gothic, Applied Handle, Flint ....................................... 67.50
Pressed Glass, Creamer, Grace ............................................................................ 16.50
Pressed Glass, Creamer, Grand ........................................................................... 16.50
Pressed Glass, Creamer, Grape & Berry .............................................................. 45.00
Pressed Glass, Creamer, Grapevine With Ovals, Blue, Miniature ......................... 22.00
Pressed Glass, Creamer, Grasshopper, No Insect ................................... 16.00 To 30.00
Pressed Glass, Creamer, Grille ................................................................ 8.75 To 10.50

Pressed Glass, Creamer, Hamilton, Pressed Handle, Flint ................................... 22.50 To 25.00
Pressed Glass, Creamer, Hand ................................... 24.00 To 38.00
Pressed Glass, Creamer, Hartley ................................... 15.00
Pressed Glass, Creamer, Heart ................................... 55.00
Pressed Glass, Creamer, Heart & Snakeskin, 4 In. ................................... 10.50
Pressed Glass, Creamer, Heart & Thumbprint ................................... 35.00
Pressed Glass, Creamer, Heart Band, Gold Trim, 4 In. ................................... 15.00
Pressed Glass, Creamer, Henrietta ................................... 15.00
Pressed Glass, Creamer, Herringbone ................................... 12.50 To 32.00
Pressed Glass, Creamer, High Hob ................................... 9.50
Pressed Glass, Creamer, Hobnail & Bar ................................... 25.00
Pressed Glass, Creamer, Holland ................................... 10.00
Pressed Glass, Creamer, Honeycomb, Applied Handle ................................... 45.00
Pressed Glass, Creamer, Horn Of Plenty, Flint ................................... 135.00
Pressed Glass, Creamer, Horsemint ................................... 12.50
Pressed Glass, Creamer, Horseshoe ................................... 18.00 To 35.00
Pressed Glass, Creamer, Huckle ................................... 12.50
Pressed Glass, Creamer, Hummingbird ................................... 20.00 To 32.00
Pressed Glass, Creamer, Illinois ................................... 8.00 To 12.50
Pressed Glass, Creamer, Individual, Banded Portland, Gilt Trim ................................... 6.50
Pressed Glass, Creamer, Individual, Banded Portland, Yellow Flashing ................................... 16.00
Pressed Glass, Creamer, Individual, Block ................................... 5.00
Pressed Glass, Creamer, Individual, Cut Log ................................... 7.00
Pressed Glass, Creamer, Individual, Daisy & Button With Crossbar, Amber ................................... 20.00
Pressed Glass, Creamer, Individual, Galloway ................................... 15.00
Pressed Glass, Creamer, Individual, Portland, Gold Trim ................................... 7.00
Pressed Glass, Creamer, Individual, Ruby Flashed Band ................................... 5.00
Pressed Glass, Creamer, Individual, Ruby Thumbprint ................................... 18.50
Pressed Glass, Creamer, Individual, Smocking, Emerald, Applied Handle, Flint ................................... 125.00
Pressed Glass, Creamer, Individual, Sunburst ................................... 8.75
Pressed Glass, Creamer, Individual, Texas ................................... 6.50
Pressed Glass, Creamer, Individual, Virginia ................................... 6.50
Pressed Glass, Creamer, Inomanata ................................... 9.50
Pressed Glass, Creamer, Intaglio Sunflower ................................... 12.50
Pressed Glass, Creamer, Intaglio, Clear & Opalescent ................................... 24.50
Pressed Glass, Creamer, Intaglio, Opalescent ................................... 27.50
Pressed Glass, Creamer, Inverted Fern, 6 In. ................................... *Illus* ................................... 55.00
Pressed Glass, Creamer, Inverted Thumbprint, Amber, Applied Reeded Handle ................................... 40.00
Pressed Glass, Creamer, Iris & Herringbone, Gold Trim ................................... 3.00

Pressed Glass, Creamer, Inverted Fern, 6 In.

Pressed Glass, Creamer, Jacob's Ladder ................................... 18.00 To 27.50
Pressed Glass, Creamer, Jacob's Ladder, Pedestal Base ................................... 21.00 To 22.50
Pressed Glass, Creamer, Jardiniere ................................... 15.00
Pressed Glass, Creamer, Jefferson 271, Gold Trim ................................... 13.00
Pressed Glass, Creamer, Jefferson, Footed ................................... 7.00
Pressed Glass, Creamer, Jersey ................................... 15.00
Pressed Glass, Creamer, Jeweled Heart, Green ................................... 13.00
Pressed Glass, Creamer, King's Crown, Applied Handle ................................... 35.00
Pressed Glass, Creamer, King's Crown, Ruby Flashed ................................... 25.00

Pressed Glass, Creamer, Knobby Bull's-Eye, Amethyst, Gold ............................................ 14.50
Pressed Glass, Creamer, Lacy Daisy ....................................... 12.50 To 27.00
Pressed Glass, Creamer, Leaf & Dart, Applied Handle ............................................ 30.00
Pressed Glass, Creamer, Leaf & Dart, Applied Handle, Bulbous ............................ 28.50
Pressed Glass, Creamer, Leaf & Flowers, Amber Flowers ...................................... 29.50
Pressed Glass, Creamer, Leaf Medallion, Amethyst .............................................. 28.50
Pressed Glass, Creamer, Leaf Medallion, Green, Gold .......................................... 32.50
Pressed Glass, Creamer, Leaflets .......................................................................... 5.00
Pressed Glass, Creamer, Liberty Bell, Applied Handle .......................................... 89.50
Pressed Glass, Creamer, Lily Of The Valley, Applied Handle ................................. 42.50
Pressed Glass, Creamer, Lily Of The Valley, 3 Footed ................. 30.00 To 55.00
Pressed Glass, Creamer, Lion .............................................................................. 47.50
Pressed Glass, Creamer, Loop & Dart ............................................. 34.00 To 42.00
Pressed Glass, Creamer, Loop & Dart With Diamond Ornament .......................... 28.00
Pressed Glass, Creamer, Loop & Dewdrop ...................................... 17.50 To 22.50
Pressed Glass, Creamer, Maiden's Blush, Small Size .......................................... 35.00
Pressed Glass, Creamer, Manhattan .................................................. 4.50 To 9.50
Pressed Glass, Creamer, Marsh, Pink .................................................................. 16.00
Pressed Glass, Creamer, Melrose, Tankard Style ................................................ 15.00
Pressed Glass, Creamer, Michigan, Ruby ............................................................ 29.00
Pressed Glass, Creamer, Minerva ................................................... 28.50 To 47.50
Pressed Glass, Creamer, Missouri ........................................................................ 15.00
Pressed Glass, Creamer, Moon & Star ............................................ 36.50 To 45.00
Pressed Glass, Creamer, Nailhead ...................................................................... 22.50
Pressed Glass, Creamer, New Hampshire ...................................... 10.50 To 14.50
Pressed Glass, Creamer, New Jersey .................................................................. 12.50
Pressed Glass, Creamer, Oaken Bucket ............................................................... 15.00
Pressed Glass, Creamer, Oaken Bucket, Miniature .............................................. 28.00
Pressed Glass, Creamer, Ohio ............................................................................. 5.00
Pressed Glass, Creamer, Opalescent Crossbar, Blue, Beatty Co., 3 In. ............... 18.50
Pressed Glass, Creamer, Opalescent Swirl, Beatty Co., 5 In. .............................. 32.50
Pressed Glass, Creamer, Opalescent Swirl, Blue, Beatty Co., 5 In. ..................... 37.50
Pressed Glass, Creamer, Oval Medallion, Blue .................................................... 25.00
Pressed Glass, Creamer, Oval Thumbprint .......................................................... 40.00
Pressed Glass, Creamer, Palm & Diamond Point ................................................ 10.00
Pressed Glass, Creamer, Palmette ...................................................................... 35.00
Pressed Glass, Creamer, Palmette, Applied Handle ....................... 22.50 To 30.00
Pressed Glass, Creamer, Pamper Flower ............................................................. 12.00
Pressed Glass, Creamer, Paneled Anthemion ................................. 10.00 To 12.50
Pressed Glass, Creamer, Paneled Cane ............................................................... 13.50
Pressed Glass, Creamer, Paneled Dewdrop, Pattern On Base ............................. 22.50
Pressed Glass, Creamer, Paneled Fine Cut .......................................................... 10.00
Pressed Glass, Creamer, Paneled Forget-Me-Not .......................... 15.00 To 25.00
Pressed Glass, Creamer, Paneled Heather ........................................................... 13.50
Pressed Glass, Creamer, Paneled Thistle ....................................... 22.50 To 25.00
Pressed Glass, Creamer, Paneled Wild Daisy ...................................................... 12.00
Pressed Glass, Creamer, Parthenon, 6 In.High .................................................... 22.50
Pressed Glass, Creamer, Peace & Plenty, Fruits ................................................. 21.50
Pressed Glass, Creamer, Peacock Feather ........................................................... 18.50
Pressed Glass, Creamer, Pillow & Sunburst, Covered .......................................... 10.00
Pressed Glass, Creamer, Pineapple & Fan, Applied Handle, Small Size ............... 12.50
Pressed Glass, Creamer, Pleat & Panel .......................................... 16.50 To 20.00
Pressed Glass, Creamer, Pleat & Tuck ................................................................ 22.50
Pressed Glass, Creamer, Pointed Jewel ............................................................... 9.75
Pressed Glass, Creamer, Popcorn ....................................................................... 34.00
Pressed Glass, Creamer, Popcorn With Raised Ears ........................................... 22.50
Pressed Glass, Creamer, Portland, Small Size ...................................................... 5.50
Pressed Glass, Creamer, Pres Cut, Sawtooth Edge ............................................. 10.00
Pressed Glass, Creamer, Pressed Leaf ................................................................ 22.50
Pressed Glass, Creamer, Pressed Leaf, 6 1/2 In.High .......................................... 16.00
Pressed Glass, Creamer, Primrose ....................................................................... 15.00
Pressed Glass, Creamer, Princess Feather .......................................................... 30.00
Pressed Glass, Creamer, Princess Feather, Applied Handle ................................. 25.00
Pressed Glass, Creamer, Prism Arc ...................................................................... 8.50
Pressed Glass, Creamer, Queen Anne .................................................................. 30.00
Pressed Glass, Creamer, Quixote, Green ............................................................. 12.00

Pressed Glass, Creamer, Radiant .................................................. 15.00
Pressed Glass, Creamer, Raspberry & Grape ........................................ 26.00
Pressed Glass, Creamer, Ribbed Grape ............................................. 95.00
Pressed Glass, Creamer, Ribbed Opal .............................................. 24.50
Pressed Glass, Creamer, Ribbed Palm, Flint ...................... 55.00 To 64.50
Pressed Glass, Creamer, Ribbed Sawtooth .......................................... 19.50
Pressed Glass, Creamer, Ribbed, Blue, Opalescent ................................. 28.75
Pressed Glass, Creamer, Ribbed, Blue, Opalescent, Davidson, English, 4 In. ...... 16.75
Pressed Glass, Creamer, Ribbed, Green, Gold Trim .................................. 8.00
Pressed Glass, Creamer, Ribbon Candy ............................................. 17.00
Pressed Glass, Creamer, Roman Rosette ....................... 12.50 To 13.75
Pressed Glass, Creamer, Roman Rosette, Footed .................................... 16.50
Pressed Glass, Creamer, Romeo .................................................... 10.00
Pressed Glass, Creamer, Rose In Snow ............................... *Illus* 20.00
Pressed Glass, Creamer, Rose In Snow, Round .................. 24.00 To 28.50
Pressed Glass, Creamer, Rose In Snow, Square ................. 35.00 To 38.50
Pressed Glass, Creamer, Rosette ................................................... 8.75
Pressed Glass, Creamer, Rosette Medallion, Applied Handle ........................ 12.00
Pressed Glass, Creamer, Rosette With Pinwheel .................................... 16.50
Pressed Glass, Creamer, Royal .................................................... 15.00
Pressed Glass, Creamer, Ruby Thumbprint, Bulbous ................................. 48.00
Pressed Glass, Creamer, Sawtooth, Applied Handle ................................. 15.00
Pressed Glass, Creamer, Sawtooth, Flint .......................................... 60.00
Pressed Glass, Creamer, Scalloped Diamond Point, Footed .......................... 18.00
Pressed Glass, Creamer, Scalloped Tape ........................................... 15.00
Pressed Glass, Creamer, Scroll & Daisy, Measuring Cup ............................ 12.00
Pressed Glass, Creamer, Scroll With Flowers ...................................... 10.00
Pressed Glass, Creamer, Sedan, Molded Handle ...................................... 9.00
Pressed Glass, Creamer, Shell & Tassel, Round .................................... 19.50
Pressed Glass, Creamer, Shell & Tassel, Square ............... 25.00 To 42.00
Pressed Glass, Creamer, Sheraton ................................................. 12.00
Pressed Glass, Creamer, Sheraton, Amber .......................................... 22.50
Pressed Glass, Creamer, Short Swirl, Tall ........................................ 12.00
Pressed Glass, Creamer, Smocking, Flint .......................................... 125.00
Pressed Glass, Creamer, Smocking, Small Size ..................................... 125.00
Pressed Glass, Creamer, Snowshoe ................................................. 14.00
Pressed Glass, Creamer, Spearhead ................................................ 17.00
Pressed Glass, Creamer, Spirea Band, Blue ........................................ 25.00
Pressed Glass, Creamer, Stars & Stripes ........................ 7.50 To 11.50
Pressed Glass, Creamer, Stippled Grape & Festoon, Applied Handle ................. 27.50
Pressed Glass, Creamer, Stippled Grape Festoon ................................... 38.00
Pressed Glass, Creamer, Stippled Oak Leaf, Amber ................................. 22.00
Pressed Glass, Creamer, Stork .................................................... 18.50
Pressed Glass, Creamer, Strawberry, 5 1/2 In. ...................... *Illus* 50.00
Pressed Glass, Creamer, Sunken Teardrop .......................................... 15.00
Pressed Glass, Creamer, Swan .................................. 42.00 To 45.00
Pressed Glass, Creamer, Swan, Clambroth .......................................... 45.00

Pressed Glass, Creamer, Rose In Snow

Pressed Glass, Creamer, Strawberry, 5 1/2 In.

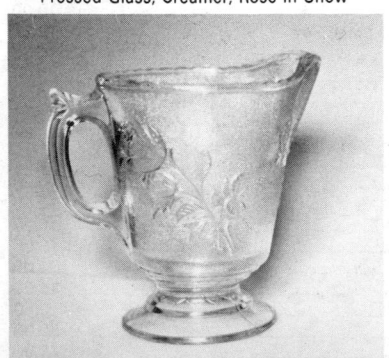

| | |
|---|---:|
| Pressed Glass, Creamer, Sweetheart, Miniature | 14.50 |
| Pressed Glass, Creamer, Teardrop & Tassel | 14.00 |
| Pressed Glass, Creamer, Teardrop & Thumbprint, Blue | 37.00 |
| Pressed Glass, Creamer, Teardrop, Cobalt | 24.50 |
| Pressed Glass, Creamer, Texas, Gold Luster Top | 10.00 |
| Pressed Glass, Creamer, Thistle, Applied Handle | 25.00 |
| Pressed Glass, Creamer, Threading | 15.00 |
| Pressed Glass, Creamer, Three Flowers | 10.00 |
| Pressed Glass, Creamer, Three Panel | 16.50 |
| Pressed Glass, Creamer, Three Panel, Amber | 22.50 To 43.00 |
| Pressed Glass, Creamer, Three Panel, Canary | 43.00 To 45.00 |
| Pressed Glass, Creamer, Three Panel, Light Amber | 32.50 To 43.00 |
| Pressed Glass, Creamer, Three Panel, Vaseline | 37.50 |
| Pressed Glass, Creamer, Torpedo | 37.50 |
| Pressed Glass, Creamer, Transverse Ribs | 13.50 |
| Pressed Glass, Creamer, Tree Of Life, Hand In Handle, Pittsburgh | 39.00 |
| Pressed Glass, Creamer, Tree Of Life, Portland | 45.00 |
| Pressed Glass, Creamer, Triple Triangle, Ruby Flashed | 25.00 |
| Pressed Glass, Creamer, Twin Snowshoes, Miniature | 12.00 |
| Pressed Glass, Creamer, U.S.Rib, Green | 9.50 |
| Pressed Glass, Creamer, Victoria Jubilee, 5 In. | 35.00 |
| Pressed Glass, Creamer, Victoria, Green, Gold Trim, Tarentum | 25.00 |
| Pressed Glass, Creamer, Viking | 23.00 To 35.00 |
| Pressed Glass, Creamer, Vine & Flower, Amber, Wheeling | 46.00 |
| Pressed Glass, Creamer, Waffle, Applied Crimped Handle, Flint | 95.00 |
| Pressed Glass, Creamer, Waffle, Opalescent, Beatty | 27.50 |
| Pressed Glass, Creamer, Westward Ho | 63.00 To 65.00 |
| Pressed Glass, Creamer, Westward Ho, Large Size | 60.00 |
| Pressed Glass, Creamer, Westward Ho, Pedestal | 78.00 |
| Pressed Glass, Creamer, Wheat & Barley | 14.00 To 18.50 |
| Pressed Glass, Creamer, Whirling Star | 12.00 |
| Pressed Glass, Creamer, Whirling Star, Toy | 13.00 |
| Pressed Glass, Creamer, Wild Bouquet, Blue Opalescent | 50.00 |
| Pressed Glass, Creamer, Wildflower | 10.00 To 18.50 |
| Pressed Glass, Creamer, Wildflower, Blue | 22.50 To 23.00 |
| Pressed Glass, Creamer, Willow Oak | 16.50 To 28.00 |
| Pressed Glass, Creamer, Willow Oak, Amber | 30.00 To 43.00 |
| Pressed Glass, Creamer, Willow Oak, Blue, Pedestal | 35.00 |
| Pressed Glass, Creamer, Willow Oak, Canary | 35.00 |
| Pressed Glass, Creamer, Windflower | 16.50 To 18.50 |
| Pressed Glass, Creamer, 1, 000-Eye | 40.00 |
| Pressed Glass, Creamer, 1, 000 Eye, Opalescent Trim | 45.00 |
| Pressed Glass, Creamer, 1, 000-Eye, 3 Knob | 27.50 |
| Pressed Glass, Creamer, 101 | 13.00 |
| Pressed Glass, Creamer, 101, Souvenir, Iowa City | 37.50 |
| Pressed Glass, Cruet, see also Cruet | |
| Pressed Glass, Cruet Set, Basket Weave, Amber, 3 Piece | 110.00 |
| Pressed Glass, Cruet, Alabama | 17.50 |
| Pressed Glass, Cruet, Austrian, Faceted Stopper | 25.00 |
| Pressed Glass, Cruet, Beaded Circle | 25.00 |
| Pressed Glass, Cruet, Beaded Panels, Stopper, C.1880 | 12.00 |
| Pressed Glass, Cruet, Beaded Swirl | 15.00 |
| Pressed Glass, Cruet, Beveled Block & Fan, Findlay | 15.00 |
| Pressed Glass, Cruet, Block & Fan | 12.00 To 22.00 |
| Pressed Glass, Cruet, Block & Thumbprint, 6 In. | 20.00 |
| Pressed Glass, Cruet, Bull's-Eye & Spearhead | 23.00 |
| Pressed Glass, Cruet, Buttons & Bars | 10.00 |
| Pressed Glass, Cruet, Cape Cod | 8.50 |
| Pressed Glass, Cruet, Castor, Bellflower, Flint | 22.00 |
| Pressed Glass, Cruet, Checkerboard | 16.00 To 20.00 |
| Pressed Glass, Cruet, Checkerboard, Bulbous | 15.00 |
| Pressed Glass, Cruet, Coral Gables | 17.50 |
| Pressed Glass, Cruet, Currier & Ives, Blown Stopper | 5.00 |
| Pressed Glass, Cruet, Cut Log, 6 3/4 In. | 26.50 |
| Pressed Glass, Cruet, Daisy & Button | 16.00 |
| Pressed Glass, Cruet, Daisy & Cube, Amber | 50.00 |

Pressed Glass, Cruet, Daisy & Cube, Stopper ........................................... 13.50
Pressed Glass, Cruet, Daisy With Fern, Opalescent ................................... 54.50
Pressed Glass, Cruet, Diamond Ridge ...................................................... 25.00
Pressed Glass, Cruet, Etched Dakota, Blown Stopper ............................... 35.00
Pressed Glass, Cruet, Etched Dakota, Matching Stopper ........................... 65.00
Pressed Glass, Cruet, Feather Swirl ......................................................... 16.50
Pressed Glass, Cruet, Fringed Drape, Clear, Stopper, 7 In.High ............... 15.00
Pressed Glass, Cruet, Herringbone, Emerald Green, Clear Stopper ........... 25.00
Pressed Glass, Cruet, Hinoto, Applied Handle ......................................... 32.00
Pressed Glass, Cruet, Honeycomb, Blown Stopper ................................... 5.00
Pressed Glass, Cruet, Horseshoe, Amber, Stopper ................................... 32.00
Pressed Glass, Cruet, Horseshoe, Green .................................................. 32.00
Pressed Glass, Cruet, Inverted Thumbprint, Amber, Stopper ..................... 125.00
Pressed Glass, Cruet, Kentucky ............................................................... 28.00
Pressed Glass, Cruet, Loop & Dart .......................................................... 18.50
Pressed Glass, Cruet, Maple Leaf, Albany ............................................... 22.50
Pressed Glass, Cruet, Michigan ............................................................... 38.00
Pressed Glass, Cruet, Moon & Star .......................................................... 10.00
Pressed Glass, Cruet, New Jersey ............................................................ 17.50
Pressed Glass, Cruet, Opalescent Dot, Blue ............................................. 35.00
Pressed Glass, Cruet, Paneled Daisy & Button, Blown Stopper ................. 12.50
Pressed Glass, Cruet, Paneled Daisy & Button, Cut Stopper ..................... 32.00
Pressed Glass, Cruet, Paneled Grape, Bark Handle, Blown Pontil ............ 22.50
Pressed Glass, Cruet, Paneled Thistle, Bell & Ball Shape ......................... 22.75
Pressed Glass, Cruet, Peacock Feather ......................................... 16.50 To 19.50
Pressed Glass, Cruet, Peacock Feather, Pontil ......................................... 20.00
Pressed Glass, Cruet, Petticoat, 6 1/2 In.High ......................................... 22.00
Pressed Glass, Cruet, Pigmy .................................................................... 20.00
Pressed Glass, Cruet, Pineapple, 6 1/2 In.High ....................................... 12.00
Pressed Glass, Cruet, Pogo Stick ............................................................. 11.00
Pressed Glass, Cruet, Portland ................................................................ 25.00
Pressed Glass, Cruet, Quihote ....................................................... 16.50 To 17.50
Pressed Glass, Cruet, Rose Point Band, 7 In. ........................................... 14.00
Pressed Glass, Cruet, Royal Crystal ......................................................... 18.00
Pressed Glass, Cruet, Royal Crystal, Small Size ....................................... 18.50
Pressed Glass, Cruet, S Repeat ............................................................... 18.50
Pressed Glass, Cruet, Shoshone .................................................... 16.50 To 35.00
Pressed Glass, Cruet, Six Sides, Teardrop In Stopper, 7 1/2 In. ............... 25.00
Pressed Glass, Cruet, Star In Bull's-Eye, Stopper ................................... 26.50
Pressed Glass, Cruet, Stars & Bars, Amber, Stopper, Findlay ................... 58.00
Pressed Glass, Cruet, Stars & Bars, Amber, Stopper, Indiana ................... 46.50
Pressed Glass, Cruet, Stars & Stripes, McKee .......................................... 17.50
Pressed Glass, Cruet, Swirl, Blue, Opalescent ......................................... 35.00
Pressed Glass, Cruet, Swirl, Miniature ..................................................... 19.00
Pressed Glass, Cruet, Torpedo ................................................................ 35.00
Pressed Glass, Cruet, Twin Sunburst ....................................................... 9.50
Pressed Glass, Cruet, U.S.Coin, Quarters Around Bottom, Dimes Stopper ... 450.00
Pressed Glass, Cruet, Williamsburg ......................................................... 8.50
Pressed Glass, Cruet, Wine, Thumbprint, Green ...................................... 40.00
Pressed Glass, Cruet, 1, 000-Eye, Amber, 3 Knob Stopper ...................... 48.50
Pressed Glass, Cup & Saucer, Basket Weave ........................................... 24.00
Pressed Glass, Cup & Saucer, Basket Weave, Amber ..................... 15.00 To 24.00
Pressed Glass, Cup & Saucer, Candlewick ............................................... 12.50
Pressed Glass, Cup & Saucer, Child's, Cat & Dog ................................... 18.00
Pressed Glass, Cup & Saucer, Child's, Lion's Head ................................. 20.00
Pressed Glass, Cup & Saucer, Ivy Leaves, Findlay ................................... 17.50
Pressed Glass, Cup & Saucer, Lion, Miniature ......................................... 30.00
Pressed Glass, Cup & Saucer, Many Windows, Green ............................... 4.00
Pressed Glass, Cup & Saucer, Ruby Thumbprint ...................................... 30.00
Pressed Glass, Cup & Saucer, Sandwich Loop & Petal ............................. 100.00
Pressed Glass, Cup & Saucer, Sandwich Loop & Petal, Canary ............... 220.00
Pressed Glass, Cup Plate, Bunker Hill .............................................. 7.50 To 16.50
Pressed Glass, Cup Plate, Butterfly ......................................................... 7.50
Pressed Glass, Cup Plate, Hearts ............................................................ 17.50
Pressed Glass, Cup Plate, Primrose, Amber ............................................. 7.00
Pressed Glass, Cup Plate, Snakeskin & Dot ............................................ 5.00

| | |
|---|---|
| **Pressed Glass, Cup Plate,** Valentine | 7.50 |
| **Pressed Glass, Cup,** Basket Weave, Blue | 12.00 |
| **Pressed Glass, Cup,** Boy's & Girl's, Faces, Blue | 27.50 |
| **Pressed Glass, Cup,** Child's, Leaf & Grape | 10.00 |
| **Pressed Glass, Cup,** Colorado, Green, Iona State Fair '09 | 16.50 |
| **Pressed Glass, Cup,** Currier & Ives | 7.50 |
| **Pressed Glass, Cup,** Currier & Ives, Findlay | 12.00 |
| **Pressed Glass, Cup,** Daisies In Oval Panel, Gold Trim, 3 1/4 In. | 9.50 |
| **Pressed Glass, Cup,** Grape & Festoon *Illus* | 18.00 |

Pressed Glass, Cup, Grape & Festoon

| | |
|---|---|
| **Pressed Glass, Cup,** Jewel & Dewdrop | 10.50 |
| **Pressed Glass, Cup,** Lion, Miniature | 15.00 |
| **Pressed Glass, Cup,** Paisley, Cranberry Eyes, Gold Top | 7.50 |
| **Pressed Glass, Cup,** Punch, Arched Oval, Cranberry Stain | 8.50 |
| **Pressed Glass, Cup,** Punch, Beaded Dewdrop | 16.25 |
| **Pressed Glass, Cup,** Punch, Beaded Swag | 7.50 |
| **Pressed Glass, Cup,** Punch, Buckle | 3.00 |
| **Pressed Glass, Cup,** Punch, Bull's-Eye & Star, Gold Trim, Purple Eyes | 6.00 |
| **Pressed Glass, Cup,** Punch, Button Arches, Ruby | 13.75 |
| **Pressed Glass, Cup,** Punch, Cane & Fan | 3.50 |
| **Pressed Glass, Cup,** Punch, Dew & Raindrop | 3.00 To 7.50 |
| **Pressed Glass, Cup,** Punch, Diamond Ridge | 4.75 |
| **Pressed Glass, Cup,** Punch, Duncan & Miller No.42 | 5.00 |
| **Pressed Glass, Cup,** Punch, Empress | 6.50 |
| **Pressed Glass, Cup,** Punch, Flattened Diamond & Sunburst, Miniature | 6.50 |
| **Pressed Glass, Cup,** Punch, Galloway | 4.00 To 4.25 |
| **Pressed Glass, Cup,** Punch, Loop & Pyramid | 2.50 |
| **Pressed Glass, Cup,** Punch, Majestic | 2.50 |
| **Pressed Glass, Cup,** Punch, Nursery Rhyme, Miniature | 12.00 |
| **Pressed Glass, Cup,** Punch, Paneled Grape | 9.50 |
| **Pressed Glass, Cup,** Punch, Pennsylvania | 5.00 |
| **Pressed Glass, Cup,** Punch, Roman Cross | 2.50 |
| **Pressed Glass, Cup,** Punch, Shuttle | 5.00 |
| **Pressed Glass, Cup,** Punch, Star Arches, Miniature | 6.50 |
| **Pressed Glass, Cup,** Punch, Sunk Daisy, Portland | 5.00 |
| **Pressed Glass, Cup,** Tycoon, Findlay, 2 3/4 In.Diameter | 6.50 |
| **Pressed Glass, Cup,** Wm.Jennings Bryan, Picture, Covered | 45.00 |
| **Pressed Glass, Decanter,** Ashburton, Bar Lip, Quart, Flint | 32.00 |
| **Pressed Glass, Decanter,** Ashburton, Blob Top, Flint | 40.00 |
| **Pressed Glass, Decanter,** Ashburton, Pint, Flint | 125.00 |
| **Pressed Glass, Decanter,** Bar, Pillar & Bird's-Eye, Collared Lip, Quart, Flint | 30.00 |
| **Pressed Glass, Decanter,** Bellflower, Double Vine, Quart | 90.00 |
| **Pressed Glass, Decanter,** Bull's-Eye & Diamond Point, Bar Lip | 95.00 |
| **Pressed Glass, Decanter,** Cable, Pint, Flint | 90.00 |
| **Pressed Glass, Decanter,** Cleat, Bar Lip | 95.00 |
| **Pressed Glass, Decanter,** Diamond Thumbprint, Bar Lip, Pint, Flint | 95.00 |
| **Pressed Glass, Decanter,** Diamond Thumbprint, Pewter Cork, Flint, Quart | 125.00 |
| **Pressed Glass, Decanter,** Fairy, Applied Bar Lip, Flint, 10 1/4 In.High | 95.00 |
| **Pressed Glass, Decanter,** New England, Stopper, Pint | 150.00 |

| | |
|---|---|
| Pressed Glass, Decanter, Paneled Flattened Sawtooth, Flint | 45.00 |
| Pressed Glass, Decanter, Thumbprint, Bar Lip, Flint, 12 In. | 70.00 |
| Pressed Glass, Decanter, Waffle & Thumbprint, Flint | 72.50 |
| Pressed Glass, Decanter, Wine, Thumbprint, 11 In.High | 17.00 |
| Pressed Glass, Dessert Set, Cape Cod, Cranberry Band, 16 Piece | 70.00 |
| Pressed Glass, Dish, Banana, Jeweled Moon & Star | 25.00 |
| Pressed Glass, Dish, Battleship Maine Cover, 4 In.High | 18.00 |
| Pressed Glass, Dish, Bird & Leaves, Heart Shape, Pedestal Base | 10.00 |
| Pressed Glass, Dish, Bone, Cane | 5.85 To 6.50 |
| Pressed Glass, Dish, Butter, see Pressed Glass, Butter | |
| Pressed Glass, Dish, Candy, Diamonds With Double Fan, 8 X 5 In. | 7.50 |
| Pressed Glass, Dish, Candy, Rose In Snow, Covered | 40.00 |
| Pressed Glass, Dish, Candy, Sea Spray, Green, Opalescent, Handled, Triangular | 18.50 |
| Pressed Glass, Dish, Cheese, Checkerboard, Dome Top | 35.00 |
| Pressed Glass, Dish, Cheese, Colorado, Covered | 26.00 |
| Pressed Glass, Dish, Cheese, Dewdrop & Star, Dome Cover, 11 In.Diameter | 95.00 |
| Pressed Glass, Dish, Cheese, Flamingo Habitat, Covered | 50.00 |
| Pressed Glass, Dish, Cheese, Owl & Pussy Cat, Frosted, Covered | 195.00 |
| Pressed Glass, Dish, Chick Cover, Basket Base, Painted | 75.00 |
| Pressed Glass, Dish, Covered Wagon Cover | 125.00 |
| Pressed Glass, Dish, Daisy & Button, Amber, Fan Shape, 10 1/2 In. Wide | 25.00 |
| Pressed Glass, Dish, Daisy & Button, Fan Shape, 10 1/2 In. Wide | 15.00 |
| Pressed Glass, Dish, Dewdrop, Heart Shape, Divided, Low, 7 Balls On Top | 8.00 |
| Pressed Glass, Dish, Dewey Cover, Greentown | 125.00 |
| Pressed Glass, Dish, Duck Cover, Frosted | 100.00 |
| Pressed Glass, Dish, Duck Cover, Frosted, Naturalistic Base | 60.00 |
| Pressed Glass, Dish, Fish Cover, Frosted | 50.00 |
| Pressed Glass, Dish, Florida, Tricornered, 5 In. | 4.50 |
| Pressed Glass, Dish, Frosted Pheasant Cover, 101 Border On Base | 60.00 |
| Pressed Glass, Dish, Hen Cover, Dark Blue, Nest Base, 2 1/2 In. Long | 15.00 |
| Pressed Glass, Dish, Hen Cover, Frosted Pink, Nest Base, 2 1/2 In. Long | 15.00 |
| Pressed Glass, Dish, Hen Cover, Light Blue, Nest Base, 2 1/2 In. Long | 15.00 |
| Pressed Glass, Dish, Hen Cover, Opalescent, Glass Eyes, Painted, Flint | 54.00 |
| Pressed Glass, Dish, Honey, Acorn | 7.00 |
| Pressed Glass, Dish, Honey, Ashburton, 3 1/2 In.Diameter | 5.00 |
| Pressed Glass, Dish, Honey, Ballflower, Concentric Ring Base, Flint | 10.00 |
| Pressed Glass, Dish, Honey, Bee & Beehive, Amber | 10.80 |
| Pressed Glass, Dish, Honey, Bellflower, Flint | 10.00 |
| Pressed Glass, Dish, Honey, Bellflower, Rayed Base, Flint, 3 1/2 In. | 10.00 |
| Pressed Glass, Dish, Honey, Bellflower, Single Vine | 12.00 |
| Pressed Glass, Dish, Honey, Bellflower, Single Vine, Flint | 12.00 To 18.00 |
| Pressed Glass, Dish, Honey, Bleeding Heart | 12.50 |
| Pressed Glass, Dish, Honey, Bull's-Eye With Diamond Point, 3 1/2 In. | 10.00 |
| Pressed Glass, Dish, Honey, Cable | 6.50 |
| Pressed Glass, Dish, Honey, Diamond Thumbprint | 10.00 |
| Pressed Glass, Dish, Honey, Diamond Thumbprint, Flint, 3 1/2 In. | 10.00 |
| Pressed Glass, Dish, Honey, Feather | 10.00 |
| Pressed Glass, Dish, Honey, Fleur-De-Lis & Drape, 3 1/2 In. | 5.00 |
| Pressed Glass, Dish, Honey, Horn Of Plenty | 10.00 |
| Pressed Glass, Dish, Honey, Horn Of Plenty, Flint | 12.00 |
| Pressed Glass, Dish, Honey, Inverted Fern | 9.50 To 12.00 |
| Pressed Glass, Dish, Honey, Loop & Dart | 13.75 |
| Pressed Glass, Dish, Honey, New England Pineapple, Flint, 3 1/2 In. | 13.00 |
| Pressed Glass, Dish, Honey, Pampas Flower, Footed | 2.50 |
| Pressed Glass, Dish, Honey, Paneled Thistle, Covered, Round, 5 1/4 In. | 35.75 |
| Pressed Glass, Dish, Honey, Roman Rosette, 4 In. | 18.50 |
| Pressed Glass, Dish, Honey, Stars & Bars, Footed, 1 1/2 In.High | 5.00 |
| Pressed Glass, Dish, Honey, Thumbprint, Flint, 3 1/3 In.Diameter | 9.50 |
| Pressed Glass, Dish, Ice Cream, Daisy & Button, Amber, Clover Shape | 20.00 |
| Pressed Glass, Dish, Jelly, Actress, Oblong | 18.00 |
| Pressed Glass, Dish, Jelly, Fishscale, Stemmed | 18.00 |
| Pressed Glass, Dish, Jelly, Flute, High Handle, Marked BC | 6.00 |
| Pressed Glass, Dish, Jelly, Westward Ho, Covered, 4 In. | 75.00 |
| Pressed Glass, Dish, Locomotive Cover | 50.00 |
| Pressed Glass, Dish, Marmalade, Frosted Lion, Crouched Lion Finial On Cover | 48.00 |
| Pressed Glass, Dish, Mint, Hickman, Green | 12.50 |

| | |
|---|---|
| Pressed Glass, Dish, Olive, Illinois | 4.50 |
| Pressed Glass, Dish, Pickle, Banded Portland, 8 1/2 X 4 In. | 10.00 |
| Pressed Glass, Dish, Pickle, Beaded Loop | 8.00 |
| Pressed Glass, Dish, Pickle, Birds In The Nest | 12.00 |
| Pressed Glass, Dish, Pickle, Buckle | 5.00 |
| Pressed Glass, Dish, Pickle, Chair Bottom, Signed Nu Cut | 5.00 |
| Pressed Glass, Dish, Pickle, Cord Drapery | 12.00 |
| Pressed Glass, Dish, Pickle, Double Fan | 7.50 |
| Pressed Glass, Dish, Pickle, Egyptian | 9.00 |
| Pressed Glass, Dish, Pickle, Emblem, Eagle Handles | 22.00 |
| Pressed Glass, Dish, Pickle, Frosted Lion, Lion Handles | 25.00 |
| Pressed Glass, Dish, Pickle, Herringbone, Emerald Green | 18.50 |
| Pressed Glass, Dish, Pickle, Horsemint, Oval, 8 In. | 6.50 |
| Pressed Glass, Dish, Pickle, Horseshoe | 10.00 |
| Pressed Glass, Dish, Pickle, Jacob's Ladder | 7.00 To 15.00 |
| Pressed Glass, Dish, Pickle, Jacob's Ladder, Maltese Cross Handles | 9.00 |
| Pressed Glass, Dish, Pickle, King's 500, Dark Blue, Handled | 12.00 |
| Pressed Glass, Dish, Pickle, Lattice | 6.00 |
| Pressed Glass, Dish, Pickle, Lily Of The Valley | 10.00 |
| Pressed Glass, Dish, Pickle, Lily Of The Valley, 8 In., Pair | 15.00 |
| Pressed Glass, Dish, Pickle, Lion | 12.50 |
| Pressed Glass, Dish, Pickle, Lotus | 12.50 |
| Pressed Glass, Dish, Pickle, Manhattan | 6.00 |
| Pressed Glass, Dish, Pickle, Moon & Star | 12.00 |
| Pressed Glass, Dish, Pickle, New Jersey | 7.00 |
| Pressed Glass, Dish, Pickle, Pleat & Panel | 6.00 |
| Pressed Glass, Dish, Pickle, Portland, Green Flashed | 12.50 |
| Pressed Glass, Dish, Pickle, Primrose | 8.00 |
| Pressed Glass, Dish, Pickle, Rose In Snow | 12.50 |
| Pressed Glass, Dish, Pickle, Rose In Snow, Oval | 10.00 |
| Pressed Glass, Dish, Pickle, Rose In Snow, 7 In.Diameter | 52.50 |
| Pressed Glass, Dish, Pickle, Royal Crystal, Handled | 7.50 |
| Pressed Glass, Dish, Pickle, Star Rosette | 5.00 To 6.00 |
| Pressed Glass, Dish, Pickle, Washington Centennial, Bears' Paws Handles | 30.00 |
| Pressed Glass, Dish, Pickle, Wildflower | 9.50 |
| Pressed Glass, Dish, Pickle, Wildflower, Blue | 16.00 |
| Pressed Glass, Dish, Rose Sprig, Amber, Boat Shape, 8 In. | 18.00 |
| Pressed Glass, Dish, Rose Sprig, Boat Shape, 8 In. | 19.50 |
| Pressed Glass, Dish, Santa Cover, Sleigh Base | 60.00 |
| Pressed Glass, Dish, Soap, Double Beaded Band | 5.00 |
| Pressed Glass, Dish, Sunk Daisy, 7 1/2 X 1 1/2 In.High | 7.00 |
| Pressed Glass, Dish, Sweetmeat, Oval Miter, Covered, Oval, Flint, 6 In. | 52.50 |
| Pressed Glass, Dish, Sweetmeat, Ribbed Acorn, Covered, Flint, 6 In.Diameter | 67.50 |
| Pressed Glass, Dish, Sweetmeat, Westward Ho, Covered, 8 1/2 In.High | 137.00 |
| Pressed Glass, Dish, Tree Of Life, Leaf Shape, Portland, 5 X 6 3/4 In., Pair | 15.00 |
| Pressed Glass, Dish, Tree Of Life, Leaf Shape, Portland, 7 X 4 1/2 In. | 8.00 |
| Pressed Glass, Dish, Turkey Cover, 7 1/2 In. | 35.00 |
| Pressed Glass, Doughnut Stand, Baby Thumbprint | 13.00 |
| Pressed Glass, Doughnut Stand, Eyewinker, 8 1/4 In. | 40.00 |
| Pressed Glass, Doughnut Stand, Good Luck, 8 In.Diameter | 32.50 |
| Pressed Glass, Doughnut Stand, Hand Stem | 40.00 |
| Pressed Glass, Doughnut Stand, Paneled Thistle | 22.50 |
| Pressed Glass, Doughnut Stand, Ribbon Candy, Emerald Green, 6 In. | 14.50 |
| Pressed Glass, Doughnut Stand, Shrine | 22.50 |
| Pressed Glass, Dresser Set, Star & Thumbprint, 9 In.Candlesticks, 6 Piece | 15.00 |
| Pressed Glass, Eggcup, Argus | 13.00 To 32.00 |
| Pressed Glass, Eggcup, Argus, Flint | 14.00 To 19.50 |
| Pressed Glass, Eggcup, Ashburton | 15.50 To 35.00 |
| Pressed Glass, Eggcup, Ashburton, Flint | 17.00 To 22.50 |
| Pressed Glass, Eggcup, Banded Beaded Grape Medallion | 15.00 |
| Pressed Glass, Eggcup, Banded Buckle | 16.00 |
| Pressed Glass, Eggcup, Banded Buckle, Flint | 22.50 To 23.50 |
| Pressed Glass, Eggcup, Barberry | 15.00 To 16.50 |
| Pressed Glass, Eggcup, Barberry, Footed | 16.00 |
| Pressed Glass, Eggcup, Basket Weave, Dated | 10.00 |
| Pressed Glass, Eggcup, Basket Weave, Milk White, Double | 20.00 |

Pressed Glass, Eggcup, Beaded Circle, Flint ............................................................ 20.00
Pressed Glass, Eggcup, Beaded Grape Medallion ...................................................... 24.00
Pressed Glass, Eggcup, Bellflower ...................................................... 22.50 To 32.00
Pressed Glass, Eggcup, Bellflower & Fine Rib, Single Vine ........................................ 35.00
Pressed Glass, Eggcup, Bellflower, Flared Rim .......................................................... 23.50
Pressed Glass, Eggcup, Bellflower, Flint ........................................... 22.50 To 30.00
Pressed Glass, Eggcup, Bellflower, Single Vine .......................................................... 35.00
Pressed Glass, Eggcup, Bellflower, Single Vine, Flared .............................................. 35.00
Pressed Glass, Eggcup, Bellflower, Single Vine, Flint .......................... 25.00 To 32.00
Pressed Glass, Eggcup, Belted Worcester, Flared Top ................................................ 12.50
Pressed Glass, Eggcup, Belted Worcester, Flared Top, Flint ........................................ 9.00
Pressed Glass, Eggcup, Belted Worcester, Flint ........................................................ 18.00
Pressed Glass, Eggcup, Bessimer Flute, Flint ............................................................ 18.00
Pressed Glass, Eggcup, Birch Leaf, Flint .................................................................... 18.00
Pressed Glass, Eggcup, Blackberry, Milk White, Double ............................................ 60.00
Pressed Glass, Eggcup, Bleeding Heart ........................................... 22.00 To 32.50
Pressed Glass, Eggcup, Buckle ................................................................................ 22.00
Pressed Glass, Eggcup, Buckle, Flint ........................................................................ 18.00
Pressed Glass, Eggcup, Bull's-Eye & Bar .................................................................. 75.00
Pressed Glass, Eggcup, Bull's-Eye, Flint ........................................... 25.00 To 38.50
Pressed Glass, Eggcup, Cable ........................................................... 28.00 To 35.00
Pressed Glass, Eggcup, Cable, Flint ................................................. 27.50 To 34.00
Pressed Glass, Eggcup, Centennial ............................................................................ 45.00
Pressed Glass, Eggcup, Colonial ................................................................................ 5.00
Pressed Glass, Eggcup, Currant ......................................................... 6.50 To 18.00
Pressed Glass, Eggcup, Dahlia, Double ...................................................................... 18.00
Pressed Glass, Eggcup, Diamond Ornament .............................................................. 16.00
Pressed Glass, Eggcup, Double Spear ................................................ 7.50 To 14.95
Pressed Glass, Eggcup, Duncan & Miller, No.30, 3 3/4 In.High .................................. 9.50
Pressed Glass, Eggcup, Duncan Block ...................................................................... 12.00
Pressed Glass, Eggcup, Excelsior .............................................................................. 25.00
Pressed Glass, Eggcup, Excelsior, Double Ring Stem ................................................ 15.00
Pressed Glass, Eggcup, Excelsior, Double Ring Stem, Flint ........................................ 10.00
Pressed Glass, Eggcup, Excelsior, Flint .................................................................... 27.00
Pressed Glass, Eggcup, Fine Diamond Point, Flint .................................................... 18.00
Pressed Glass, Eggcup, Fine Prism, Flint .................................................................. 19.00
Pressed Glass, Eggcup, Fine Rib ...................................................... 30.00 To 32.50
Pressed Glass, Eggcup, Fine Rib, Flint ...................................................................... 27.50
Pressed Glass, Eggcup, Finecut & Block .................................................................... 19.50
Pressed Glass, Eggcup, Finecut & Block, Double ...................................................... 19.50
Pressed Glass, Eggcup, Finecut & Block, Yellow ...................................................... 26.00
Pressed Glass, Eggcup, Flat Diamond & Panel, Flint .................................................. 22.00
Pressed Glass, Eggcup, Flute, Covered, Flint ............................................................ 30.00
Pressed Glass, Eggcup, Flute, Double ...................................................................... 12.50
Pressed Glass, Eggcup, Flute, Flint .................................................. 15.00 To 18.00
Pressed Glass, Eggcup, Flute, Hexagonal Knob Stem, Flint ...................................... 18.00
Pressed Glass, Eggcup, Framed Circle Variant, Flint .................................................. 28.00
Pressed Glass, Eggcup, Framed Circle, Flint .............................................................. 26.00
Pressed Glass, Eggcup, Gothic ......................................................... 27.50 To 28.00
Pressed Glass, Eggcup, Gothic, Flint ................................................ 22.00 To 29.00
Pressed Glass, Eggcup, Grape .................................................................................. 6.50
Pressed Glass, Eggcup, Grape & Festoon .................................................................. 9.00
Pressed Glass, Eggcup, Hairpin, Flint ........................................................................ 15.00
Pressed Glass, Eggcup, Hamilton .............................................................................. 24.50
Pressed Glass, Eggcup, Hamilton, Flint ...................................................................... 25.00
Pressed Glass, Eggcup, Heron, Fish Base .................................................................. 45.00
Pressed Glass, Eggcup, Honeycomb .................................................. 12.00 To 14.00
Pressed Glass, Eggcup, Honeycomb With Diamond .................................................. 6.50
Pressed Glass, Eggcup, Honeycomb, 'success Raises The Dough' ............................ 25.00
Pressed Glass, Eggcup, Honeycomb, Flint .......................................... 9.00 To 18.50
Pressed Glass, Eggcup, Honeycomb, Four Rows ........................................................ 9.00
Pressed Glass, Eggcup, Horn Of Plenty .............................................. 28.00 To 45.00
Pressed Glass, Eggcup, Horn Of Plenty, Flint .................................... 28.00 To 35.00
Pressed Glass, Eggcup, Huber .................................................................................. 7.50
Pressed Glass, Eggcup, Huber, Flint .......................................................................... 12.00
Pressed Glass, Eggcup, Inverted Fern ................................................ 19.50 To 28.50

Pressed Glass, Eggcup, Inverted Fern, Flint .................................................... 23.00 To 26.00
Pressed Glass, Eggcup, Jeweled Band .................................................................................. 12.00
Pressed Glass, Eggcup, Lincoln Drape ................................................................................. 35.00
Pressed Glass, Eggcup, Lincoln Drape, Flint ..................................................... 9.75 To 37.50
Pressed Glass, Eggcup, Loop & Dart ..................................................................................... 16.00
Pressed Glass, Eggcup, Loop & Dart With Diamond Ornament ...................................... 13.50
Pressed Glass, Eggcup, Loop & Dart, Footed ...................................................................... 9.00
Pressed Glass, Eggcup, Magnet & Grape ............................................................................. 13.50
Pressed Glass, Eggcup, Moose-Eye & Loop With Star, Flint ........................................... 45.00
Pressed Glass, Eggcup, New England Pineapple .............................................. 30.00 To 32.00
Pressed Glass, Eggcup, Open Rose .................................................................... 12.50 To 16.00
Pressed Glass, Eggcup, Palmette ........................................................................................... 18.00
Pressed Glass, Eggcup, Paneled Fern, Blue, Double ........................................................ 18.00
Pressed Glass, Eggcup, Paneled Ovals, Flint ..................................................................... 38.00
Pressed Glass, Eggcup, Peerless ........................................................................................... 22.00
Pressed Glass, Eggcup, Peerless, Saucer Base ................................................ 20.00 To 22.00
Pressed Glass, Eggcup, Powder & Shot, Flint ..................................................................... 42.50
Pressed Glass, Eggcup, Pressed Leaf, Flint ....................................................... 16.00 To 20.00
Pressed Glass, Eggcup, Princess Feather ............................................................................ 22.00
Pressed Glass, Eggcup, Princess Feather, Flint .................................................................. 18.00
Pressed Glass, Eggcup, Prism .................................................................................................. 32.00
Pressed Glass, Eggcup, Prism With Diamond Point, Flint ............................................... 25.00
Pressed Glass, Eggcup, Prism, Rayed Base .......................................................................... 28.50
Pressed Glass, Eggcup, Raindrop, Amber, Double .............................................................. 20.00
Pressed Glass, Eggcup, Ribbed Ivy ...................................................................... 20.00 To 22.50
Pressed Glass, Eggcup, Ribbed Ivy, Flint .............................................................................. 25.00
Pressed Glass, Eggcup, Ribbed Palm ..................................................................................... 16.50
Pressed Glass, Eggcup, Ribbed Palm, Flint ........................................................ 15.00 To 25.00
Pressed Glass, Eggcup, Ripple ................................................................................................. 7.50
Pressed Glass, Eggcup, Roman Key, Flint .............................................................................. 20.00
Pressed Glass, Eggcup, Sandwich Loop, Flint ...................................................................... 24.50
Pressed Glass, Eggcup, Sawtooth, Flint ................................................................................. 25.00
Pressed Glass, Eggcup, Scalloped .......................................................................................... 6.50
Pressed Glass, Eggcup, Scroll ................................................................................................. 12.00
Pressed Glass, Eggcup, Selby .................................................................................................. 12.00
Pressed Glass, Eggcup, Smocking, Flint ................................................................................ 45.00
Pressed Glass, Eggcup, Stedman ............................................................................................ 22.00
Pressed Glass, Eggcup, Stippled Medallion ......................................................................... 15.00
Pressed Glass, Eggcup, Sunburst ......................................................................... 10.00 To 11.00
Pressed Glass, Eggcup, Thistle ................................................................................................ 20.00
Pressed Glass, Eggcup, Thumbprint, Standard, 3 In.High ................................................ 10.00
Pressed Glass, Eggcup, Tulip & Sawtooth, Flint .................................................................. 45.00
Pressed Glass, Eggcup, Tulip With Ribs ................................................................................. 25.00
Pressed Glass, Eggcup, Umbilicated Sawtooth ................................................................... 22.00
Pressed Glass, Eggcup, Umbilicated Sawtooth, Flint ....................................... 15.00 To 25.00
Pressed Glass, Eggcup, Waffle & Thumbprint .................................................... 23.00 To 26.00
Pressed Glass, Eggcup, Waffle & Thumbprint, Flared, Flint ............................................. 27.00
Pressed Glass, Eggcup, Waffle & Thumbprint, Flint ........................................................... 25.00
Pressed Glass, Eggcup, Waffle, Flint ...................................................................................... 26.50
Pressed Glass, Eggcup, Washington, Flint ............................................................................ 65.00
Pressed Glass, Eggcup, Westmoreland Block ...................................................................... 10.00
Pressed Glass, Eggcup, 1, 000-Eye, 3 Knob Stem .............................................................. 25.00
Pressed Glass, Figurine, Harrison, Frosted Top .................................................................. 375.00
Pressed Glass, Frappe, Delaware, Rose ................................................................................ 40.00
Pressed Glass, Glass, Sugar, Dragon, Buttermilk, Goblet Type ....................................... 35.00
Pressed Glass, Goblet, Acorn Medallion ............................................................................... 17.00
Pressed Glass, Goblet, Actress ............................................................................ 40.00 To 65.00
Pressed Glass, Goblet, Actress, Flint ..................................................................................... 68.00
Pressed Glass, Goblet, Almond Thumbprint ...................................................... 8.00 To 12.00
Pressed Glass, Goblet, Almond Thumbprint, Flint ............................................................. 20.00
Pressed Glass, Goblet, Amboy, Gold ...................................................................................... 6.75
Pressed Glass, Goblet, Arched Grape ....................................................................... Illus   13.50
Pressed Glass, Goblet, Argosy, Flint ...................................................................................... 19.50
Pressed Glass, Goblet, Argus ................................................................................ 11.00 To 50.00
Pressed Glass, Goblet, Argus, Barrel, Flint .......................................................................... 37.50
Pressed Glass, Goblet, Argus, Five Rows, Flint .................................................................... 54.00

Pressed Glass, Goblet, Balder

Pressed Glass, Goblet, Broken Column
*(See Page 435)*

Pressed Glass, Goblet, Bellflower
*(See Page 435)*

Pressed Glass, Goblet, Arched Grape
*(See Page 433)*

| | |
|---|---|
| **Pressed Glass, Goblet,** Argus, Flared, Flint | 30.00 |
| **Pressed Glass, Goblet,** Argus, Flint | 22.00 To 45.00 |
| **Pressed Glass, Goblet,** Art | 36.00 |
| **Pressed Glass, Goblet,** Ashburton | 20.00 To 55.00 |
| **Pressed Glass, Goblet,** Ashburton, Barrel, Flint | 30.00 |
| **Pressed Glass, Goblet,** Ashburton, Flared Top | 30.00 |
| **Pressed Glass, Goblet,** Ashburton, Flint | 21.50 To 45.00 |
| **Pressed Glass, Goblet,** Ashburton, Knob Stem | 30.00 |
| **Pressed Glass, Goblet,** Ashburton, Semisquare | 22.00 |
| **Pressed Glass, Goblet,** Ashburton, Squared, Flint | 23.50 |
| **Pressed Glass, Goblet,** Ashman | 20.00 |
| **Pressed Glass, Goblet,** Atlanta | 10.50 To 20.00 |
| **Pressed Glass, Goblet,** Aurora | 16.50 |
| **Pressed Glass, Goblet,** Austrian | 26.00 |
| **Pressed Glass, Goblet,** Aztec, Gold Trim | 15.00 |
| **Pressed Glass, Goblet,** Baby Thumbprint, Wide Band | 7.50 |
| **Pressed Glass, Goblet,** Balder | *Illus* 10.00 |
| **Pressed Glass, Goblet,** Balder, Gold Trim | 10.00 To 19.00 |
| **Pressed Glass, Goblet,** Ball & Swirl | 10.00 To 15.00 |
| **Pressed Glass, Goblet,** Ball & Swirl, Plain Stem | 12.50 |
| **Pressed Glass, Goblet,** Banded Flute, Flint | 13.00 |
| **Pressed Glass, Goblet,** Banded Knife & Fork | 7.50 |
| **Pressed Glass, Goblet,** Banded Panel, Stippled Bowl | 7.50 |
| **Pressed Glass, Goblet,** Bar, 12 Fluted, Ground Pontil | 10.00 |
| **Pressed Glass, Goblet,** Barberry | 13.50 To 19.50 |
| **Pressed Glass, Goblet,** Barberry, Oval Berries | 18.50 To 27.50 |
| **Pressed Glass, Goblet,** Barberry, Round Berries | 18.00 |
| **Pressed Glass, Goblet,** Barley | 13.50 To 15.00 |
| **Pressed Glass, Goblet,** Barred Argus, Flint | 37.50 |
| **Pressed Glass, Goblet,** Barred Forget-Me-Not | 14.75 To 19.00 |
| **Pressed Glass, Goblet,** Barrel Argus, Flint | 50.00 |
| **Pressed Glass, Goblet,** Barrel Honeycomb, Flint | 10.00 |
| **Pressed Glass, Goblet,** Barrel Huber, Flint | 18.00 |
| **Pressed Glass, Goblet,** Basket Weave, Amber | 15.00 To 20.00 |

Pressed Glass, Goblet, Basket Weave, Blue ............................................................................. 18.00
Pressed Glass, Goblet, Basket Weave, Canary ........................................................................ 18.00
Pressed Glass, Goblet, Beaded Band ..................................................................... 12.00 To 14.50
Pressed Glass, Goblet, Beaded Chain ..................................................................... 12.00 To 13.50
Pressed Glass, Goblet, Beaded Dart Band ............................................................................. 12.00
Pressed Glass, Goblet, Beaded Finecut & Panel, Findlay ....................................................... 24.50
Pressed Glass, Goblet, Beaded Grape Medallion ..................................................... 12.00 To 30.00
Pressed Glass, Goblet, Beaded Grape Medallion, Design On Foot .......................................... 13.00
Pressed Glass, Goblet, Beaded Grape Medallion, Lady .......................................................... 15.00
Pressed Glass, Goblet, Beaded Mirror ................................................................................. 18.50
Pressed Glass, Goblet, Beaded Mirror, Flint ........................................................... 16.00 To 22.00
Pressed Glass, Goblet, Beaded Rosette ................................................................................ 19.00
Pressed Glass, Goblet, Beaded Rosette, Findlay ................................................................... 16.50
Pressed Glass, Goblet, Beaded Tulip ..................................................................... 11.00 To 21.00
Pressed Glass, Goblet, Belcher Loop .................................................................................... 10.00
Pressed Glass, Goblet, Bellflower ............................................................................. Illus 27.50
Pressed Glass, Goblet, Bellflower, Barrel Shape ................................................................... 23.00
Pressed Glass, Goblet, Bellflower, Barrel Shape, Flint ............................................ 23.00 To 27.50
Pressed Glass, Goblet, Bellflower, Coarse Rib, Flint ............................................... 21.00 To 27.00
Pressed Glass, Goblet, Bellflower, Flint ................................................................. 18.50 To 45.00
Pressed Glass, Goblet, Bellflower, Knob Stem, Flint ............................................................. 26.00
Pressed Glass, Goblet, Bellflower, Knob Stem, Rayed Base, Flint ......................................... 20.00
Pressed Glass, Goblet, Bellflower, Rayed Base, Flint .............................................. 18.00 To 22.50
Pressed Glass, Goblet, Bellflower, Single Vine ..................................................................... 30.00
Pressed Glass, Goblet, Bellflower, Single Vine, Flint .............................................. 20.00 To 48.00
Pressed Glass, Goblet, Bellflower, Single Vine, Knob Stem, Flint .......................................... 38.00
Pressed Glass, Goblet, Bellflower, Straight, Flint ................................................................. 22.50
Pressed Glass, Goblet, Belted Worcester, Flared Top, Flint ................................................... 21.00
Pressed Glass, Goblet, Bent Buckle ..................................................................................... 9.50
Pressed Glass, Goblet, Bent Buckle, Gold Top ....................................................................... 9.50
Pressed Glass, Goblet, Bessemer Flute, Flint .......................................................... 15.00 To 16.00
Pressed Glass, Goblet, Bigler .................................................................................. 22.00 To 28.00
Pressed Glass, Goblet, Bigler, Flaring Groove ...................................................................... 28.00
Pressed Glass, Goblet, Bigler, Flaring Groove, Flint ............................................... 29.00 To 29.50
Pressed Glass, Goblet, Bigler, Flint ........................................................................ 19.00 To 32.50
Pressed Glass, Goblet, Birch Leaf ....................................................................................... 12.00
Pressed Glass, Goblet, Birds At Fountain ................................................................ 17.50 To 24.50
Pressed Glass, Goblet, Blackberry ........................................................................... 11.50 To 19.00
Pressed Glass, Goblet, Bleeding Heart ..................................................................... 12.00 To 27.50
Pressed Glass, Goblet, Bleeding Heart, Base Rocks .............................................................. 12.50
Pressed Glass, Goblet, Bleeding Heart, Knob Stem ............................................................... 29.50
Pressed Glass, Goblet, Block On Stilts ..................................................................... 10.00 To 12.50
Pressed Glass, Goblet, Block With Stars ............................................................................... 16.00
Pressed Glass, Goblet, Block, Amber ................................................................................... 28.50
Pressed Glass, Goblet, Bogatah ............................................................................................ 5.50
Pressed Glass, Goblet, Bosworth ............................................................................... 8.50 To 9.50
Pressed Glass, Goblet, Bouquet .......................................................................................... 10.00
Pressed Glass, Goblet, Bradford Blackberry, Flint ................................................................ 55.00
Pressed Glass, Goblet, Brilliant, Flint .................................................................................. 25.00
Pressed Glass, Goblet, Broken Column ...................................................................... Illus 16.00
Pressed Glass, Goblet, Brooch Band, Flint ............................................................................. 9.00
Pressed Glass, Goblet, Brooklyn Flute, Flint ........................................................................ 14.00
Pressed Glass, Goblet, Buckle .................................................................................. Illus 22.00
Pressed Glass, Goblet, Buckle & Diagonal Band ................................................................... 10.00
Pressed Glass, Goblet, Buckle With Star .................................................................. 16.50 To 22.50
Pressed Glass, Goblet, Buckle, Flint ....................................................................... 15.00 To 30.00
Pressed Glass, Goblet, Buckle, Rayed Bowl .......................................................................... 14.50
Pressed Glass, Goblet, Budded Ivy .......................................................................... 11.00 To 17.00
Pressed Glass, Goblet, Bull's-Eye & Daisy, Gold Top, Rose Eyes .......................................... 14.50
Pressed Glass, Goblet, Bull's-Eye & Diamond Point, Flint ...................................... 65.00 To 95.00
Pressed Glass, Goblet, Bull's-Eye & Fleur-De-Lis .................................................. 45.00 To 58.00
Pressed Glass, Goblet, Bull's-Eye & Fleur-De-Lis, Flint ......................................... 50.00 To 60.00
Pressed Glass, Goblet, Bull's-Eye, Flint .................................................................. 42.00 To 45.00
Pressed Glass, Goblet, Bull's-Eye, Knob Near Base, Flint ....................................... 22.50 To 24.00
Pressed Glass, Goblet, Butterfly & Fan .................................................................... 13.00 To 20.00
Pressed Glass, Goblet, Button Arches, Clambroth ................................................................. 32.50

Pressed Glass, Goblet, Button Arches, Clambroth, Gold Stripes .......................................... 25.00 To 26.50
Pressed Glass, Goblet, Cable ....................................................................................................... 60.00
Pressed Glass, Goblet, Cable, Flint ........................................................................ 42.00 To 45.00
Pressed Glass, Goblet, Canadian ............................................................................ 20.00 To 35.00
Pressed Glass, Goblet, Cane ...................................................................................................... 13.00
Pressed Glass, Goblet, Cane, Amber ...................................................................................... 25.00
Pressed Glass, Goblet, Cane, Green ......................................................................................... 22.00
Pressed Glass, Goblet, Cannonball ......................................................................... 10.00 To 21.50
Pressed Glass, Goblet, Cantilever Band ................................................................................. 10.00
Pressed Glass, Goblet, Cape Cod ............................................................................................. 28.50
Pressed Glass, Goblet, Capitol Building .............................................................. 25.00 To 30.00
Pressed Glass, Goblet, Cardinal Bird ................................................................... 18.00 To 32.50
Pressed Glass, Goblet, Cardinal Bird, Flint ......................................................................... 32.00
Pressed Glass, Goblet, Carolina .............................................................................................. 14.50
Pressed Glass, Goblet, Casco, Portland Glass Co. ............................................................ 13.75
Pressed Glass, Goblet, Cathedral, Amber .............................................................................. 27.00
Pressed Glass, Goblet, Cattail & Fern ................................................................. 15.00 To 22.00
Pressed Glass, Goblet, Centennial, 1876 ........................................................... 25.00 To 30.00
Pressed Glass, Goblet, Chain ................................................................................. 10.00 To 18.00
Pressed Glass, Goblet, Chain With Shield ............................................................................. 20.00
Pressed Glass, Goblet, Chain With Star ............................................................... 11.00 To 18.00
Pressed Glass, Goblet, Challinor Thumbprint ...................................................................... 12.00
Pressed Glass, Goblet, Chandelier ........................................................................................... 35.00
Pressed Glass, Goblet, Cherry ............................................................................... 17.00 To 18.50
Pressed Glass, Goblet, Chestnut Band .................................................................................. 10.00
Pressed Glass, Goblet, Chicken, Medium Turquoise To Pale Turquoise ....................... 14.50
Pressed Glass, Goblet, Classic ................................................................................................. 135.00
Pressed Glass, Goblet, Clear Ribbon ...................................................................................... 20.00
Pressed Glass, Goblet, Clematis .............................................................................................. 18.00
Pressed Glass, Goblet, Coachman's Cape ............................................................................ 10.00
Pressed Glass, Goblet, Colonial Lady, Flint ......................................................................... 21.00
Pressed Glass, Goblet, Colonial, Jefferson ...........................................................*Illus* 13.00
Pressed Glass, Goblet, Colonial, Knob Stem, Flint ........................................................... 38.00
Pressed Glass, Goblet, Colossus .............................................................................................. 12.50
Pressed Glass, Goblet, Colombian Coin ................................................................................ 35.00

Pressed Glass, Goblet, Buckle
*(See Page 435)*

Pressed Glass, Goblet, Colonial, Jefferson

Pressed Glass, Goblet, Daisies In Oval
*(See Page 437)*

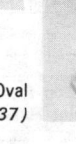

Pressed Glass, Goblet, Daisy & Button With Crossbar
*(See Page 437)*

Pressed Glass, Goblet, Columbian Coin, Gold Trim ........................................................ 50.00
Pressed Glass, Goblet, Columbian Exposition ...................................... 10.00 To 28.50
Pressed Glass, Goblet, Columbian Exposition, Flint ...................................... 13.00
Pressed Glass, Goblet, Columbian Exposition, Ring Stem ...................................... 19.00
Pressed Glass, Goblet, Colossus ...................................................................... 11.00
Pressed Glass, Goblet, Comet ............................................................ 48.00 To 55.00
Pressed Glass, Goblet, Comet, Flint .................................................. 55.00 To 70.00
Pressed Glass, Goblet, Connecticut Flute, Flint .................................................. 13.00
Pressed Glass, Goblet, Connecticut Flute, Knob Stem, Flint .................................................. 13.00
Pressed Glass, Goblet, Corcoran ...................................................................... 11.00
Pressed Glass, Goblet, Cord & Tassel ........................................... 15.00 To 18.00
Pressed Glass, Goblet, Cord Rosettes ............................................................ 18.50
Pressed Glass, Goblet, Cottage .................................................... 10.00 To 18.50
Pressed Glass, Goblet, Cottage, Bellaire Goblet Co. .................................................. 16.50
Pressed Glass, Goblet, Crochet Band .................................................. 9.00
Pressed Glass, Goblet, Crow's-Foot .................................................. 24.50 To 28.00
Pressed Glass, Goblet, Crystal ........................................................ 12.00 To 21.00
Pressed Glass, Goblet, Crystal, Flint .................................................. 13.00
Pressed Glass, Goblet, Cube .......................................................... 8.75
Pressed Glass, Goblet, Cube, Purple Hue, Square Stem .................................................. 21.00
Pressed Glass, Goblet, Cube, Square Stem .................................... 9.50 To 15.00
Pressed Glass, Goblet, Cupid & Venus .......................................... 40.00 To 55.00
Pressed Glass, Goblet, Curled Leaf .................................................. 12.50
Pressed Glass, Goblet, Currant ...................................................... 12.00 To 20.00
Pressed Glass, Goblet, Currier & Ives .......................................... 13.75 To 17.50
Pressed Glass, Goblet, Currier & Ives, Findlay .......................... 15.00 To 20.00
Pressed Glass, Goblet, Currier & Ives, Knob Stem .................................................. 16.50
Pressed Glass, Goblet, Curtain ...................................................... 12.50 To 18.00
Pressed Glass, Goblet, Curtain Tieback ........................................ 10.00 To 17.00
Pressed Glass, Goblet, Cut Log ...................................................... 22.50 To 30.00
Pressed Glass, Goblet, Cyclone ...................................................................... 5.00
Pressed Glass, Goblet, Dahlia ...................................................................... 20.00
Pressed Glass, Goblet, Daisies In Oval ............................................... Illus 9.00
Pressed Glass, Goblet, Daisy & Button With Crossbar ............................... Illus 12.00
Pressed Glass, Goblet, Daisy & Button With Crossbar, Amber .......................... 20.00 To 35.00
Pressed Glass, Goblet, Daisy & Button With Narcissus .................................................. 12.50
Pressed Glass, Goblet, Daisy & Button With Rimmed Ovals .................................................. 10.00
Pressed Glass, Goblet, Daisy & Button With Thumbprint ............................... Illus 14.00
Pressed Glass, Goblet, Daisy & Button, Amber .................................................. 35.00
Pressed Glass, Goblet, Daisy & Button, Amber, Plain Top .................................................. 21.00
Pressed Glass, Goblet, Daisy & Button, Blue .................................................. 27.50
Pressed Glass, Goblet, Daisy & Button, Flat Stem .................................................. 20.00
Pressed Glass, Goblet, Daisy Whorl With Diamond Band ............................... Illus 11.50
Pressed Glass, Goblet, Dakota ........................................................ 13.50 To 21.00
Pressed Glass, Goblet, Dakota, Etched Fern & Berry .................................................. 22.00
Pressed Glass, Goblet, Dart ...................................................................... 4.00
Pressed Glass, Goblet, Deer & Doe With Lily Of The Valley .................................................. 25.00
Pressed Glass, Goblet, Deer & Dog ............................................... Illus 50.00
Pressed Glass, Goblet, Deer & Elk .................................................. 25.00
Pressed Glass, Goblet, Deer & Pine Tree ...................................... 30.00 To 38.50
Pressed Glass, Goblet, Dew & Raindrop ........................................ 12.50 To 19.50
Pressed Glass, Goblet, Dewdrop .................................................................. 12.00
Pressed Glass, Goblet, Dewdrop & Star ........................................ 8.50 To 10.00
Pressed Glass, Goblet, Dewdrop Band ........................................... 7.00 To 14.00
Pressed Glass, Goblet, Dewdrop With Small Star .................................................. 8.00
Pressed Glass, Goblet, Diagonal Band ........................................... Illus 12.50
Pressed Glass, Goblet, Diagonal Band & Fan .................................. 12.00 To 28.00
Pressed Glass, Goblet, Diamond & Horseshoe .................................................. 8.50
Pressed Glass, Goblet, Diamond Band ........................................... 9.00 To 20.00
Pressed Glass, Goblet, Diamond Band, Amber .................................................. 15.00
Pressed Glass, Goblet, Diamond Block With Fan, 6 1/4 In.High .................................................. 14.00
Pressed Glass, Goblet, Diamond Cut With Leaf .................................................. 15.00
Pressed Glass, Goblet, Diamond In Diamond .................................................. 8.00
Pressed Glass, Goblet, Diamond Medallion ...................................... 11.50 To 16.50
Pressed Glass, Goblet, Diamond Medallion, Ring Stem .................................................. 12.50
Pressed Glass, Goblet, Diamond Point .......................................... 12.50 To 32.00

Pressed Glass, Goblet,
Daisy & Button With Thumbprint
*(See Page 437)*

Pressed Glass, Goblet, Egyptian
*(See Page 439)*

Pressed Glass, Goblet,
Diagonal Band
*(See Page 437)*

Pressed Glass,
Goblet, Deer & Dog
*(See Page 437)*

Pressed Glass, Goblet,
Daisy Whorl With Diamond Band
*(See Page 437)*

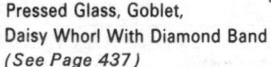

| | |
|---|---:|
| **Pressed Glass, Goblet,** Diamond Point With Panels, Flint | 25.00 To 26.00 |
| **Pressed Glass, Goblet,** Diamond Point, Flint | 20.00 To 37.50 |
| **Pressed Glass, Goblet,** Diamond Point, Ground Foot, Flint | 18.00 |
| **Pressed Glass, Goblet,** Diamond Point, Knob At Center Of Stem, Flint | 35.00 |
| **Pressed Glass, Goblet,** Diamond Point, Knob At Top Of Stem, Flint | 39.00 |
| **Pressed Glass, Goblet,** Diamond Point, Knob Stem | 29.00 |
| **Pressed Glass, Goblet,** Diamond Point, Knob Stem, Flint | 32.00 To 35.00 |
| **Pressed Glass, Goblet,** Diamond Splendor, Gold Band | 12.00 |
| **Pressed Glass, Goblet,** Diamond With Double Fans, Ruby Top | 14.00 |
| **Pressed Glass, Goblet,** Diamond-Quilted, Amethyst | 55.00 |
| **Pressed Glass, Goblet,** Diamond-Quilted, Blue | 19.50 To 28.75 |
| **Pressed Glass, Goblet,** Diamond-Quilted, Canary | 17.50 |
| **Pressed Glass, Goblet,** Diamond-Quilted, Light Amber | 25.75 |
| **Pressed Glass, Goblet,** Diamond, Flint | 15.00 |
| **Pressed Glass, Goblet,** Dickenson | 17.50 |
| **Pressed Glass, Goblet,** Diedre | 9.75 |
| **Pressed Glass, Goblet,** Double Beetle Band, Findlay | 13.50 |
| **Pressed Glass, Goblet,** Double Leaf & Dart | 18.00 |
| **Pressed Glass, Goblet,** Double Loop & Dart | 9.00 To 12.50 |
| **Pressed Glass, Goblet,** Double Ribbon | 16.50 To 17.50 |
| **Pressed Glass, Goblet,** Double Vine, Clear, Flint, C.1840, 6 1/4 In. | 250.00 |
| **Pressed Glass, Goblet,** Double Wedding Ring | 15.00 |
| **Pressed Glass, Goblet,** Double Wedding Ring, Flint | 28.00 |
| **Pressed Glass, Goblet,** Doyle's Shell | 12.50 |
| **Pressed Glass, Goblet,** Drapery | 13.00 To 16.00 |
| **Pressed Glass, Goblet,** Drapery Band With Stars | 10.50 |
| **Pressed Glass, Goblet,** Drapery With Star Band | 8.50 |
| **Pressed Glass, Goblet,** Duke | 9.50 To 15.00 |
| **Pressed Glass, Goblet,** Duncan Block, Ruby Flashed | 22.00 |
| **Pressed Glass, Goblet,** Duquesene | 18.00 |
| **Pressed Glass, Goblet,** Eastern Chestnut Band | 10.00 |

| | |
|---|---|
| Pressed Glass, Goblet, Edgerton | 9.00 |
| Pressed Glass, Goblet, Effulgent Star | 32.50 |
| Pressed Glass, Goblet, Egg In Sand | 15.00 To 26.00 |
| Pressed Glass, Goblet, Egg In Sand, Amber | 27.50 To 35.00 |
| Pressed Glass, Goblet, Egyptian | *Illus* 25.00 |
| Pressed Glass, Goblet, Elk Medallion | 45.00 |
| Pressed Glass, Goblet, Elongated Barberry | 19.00 |
| Pressed Glass, Goblet, Enamel Floral, Flint | 7.50 |
| Pressed Glass, Goblet, Engraved Chicken | 16.00 |
| Pressed Glass, Goblet, Engraved Dakota | 28.00 |
| Pressed Glass, Goblet, Engraved Fern & Cattails | 18.00 |
| Pressed Glass, Goblet, Engraved Fern, Riverside's | 12.50 |
| Pressed Glass, Goblet, Esther, Amber Band, Enameled Flowers, Riverside, 1896 | 18.50 |
| Pressed Glass, Goblet, Etched Amazon | 18.00 To 22.50 |
| Pressed Glass, Goblet, Etched Apollo | 16.00 To 18.50 |
| Pressed Glass, Goblet, Etched Chandelier | 35.00 |
| Pressed Glass, Goblet, Etched Dahlia | 13.50 To 16.00 |
| Pressed Glass, Goblet, Etched Dahlia, C.1860 | 12.50 |
| Pressed Glass, Goblet, Etched Dakota | 12.00 To 25.00 |
| Pressed Glass, Goblet, Etched Dakota, Fern, & Berry | 27.50 |
| Pressed Glass, Goblet, Etched Dakota, Flower Etching | 22.00 |
| Pressed Glass, Goblet, Etched Dog With Rabbit In Mouth | 35.00 |
| Pressed Glass, Goblet, Etched Elmino, 3 Lions Around Top | 8.50 |
| Pressed Glass, Goblet, Etched Fern | 5.00 |
| Pressed Glass, Goblet, Etched Flamingo Habitat | 55.00 |
| Pressed Glass, Goblet, Etched Hidalgo | 11.00 To 15.00 |
| Pressed Glass, Goblet, Etched Honeycomb, Flint | 20.00 |
| Pressed Glass, Goblet, Etched Horseshoe Wreath, Words Good Luck In Center | 19.50 |
| Pressed Glass, Goblet, Etched Ibex | 55.00 |
| Pressed Glass, Goblet, Etched Lily Of The Valley | 12.00 To 18.00 |
| Pressed Glass, Goblet, Etched Lily Of The Valley, Bulb Stem | 12.00 |
| Pressed Glass, Goblet, Etched Lily Of The Valley, C.1860 | 12.50 |
| Pressed Glass, Goblet, Etched Lily Of The Valley, Slight Knob Stem | 13.50 |
| Pressed Glass, Goblet, Etched Maple Leaf | 12.50 To 18.00 |
| Pressed Glass, Goblet, Etched Marsh Fern | 10.00 |
| Pressed Glass, Goblet, Etched Melrose | 12.50 To 17.50 |
| Pressed Glass, Goblet, Etched Nicotiana | 16.00 To 20.00 |
| Pressed Glass, Goblet, Etched Nicotiana, Etched Morning Glory Stem | 16.50 |
| Pressed Glass, Goblet, Etched Pavonia | 18.50 To 21.00 |
| Pressed Glass, Goblet, Etched Post | 25.00 |
| Pressed Glass, Goblet, Etched Square Panes With Post | 25.00 |
| Pressed Glass, Goblet, Etched Stag | 55.00 |
| Pressed Glass, Goblet, Etched Stork Eating | 60.00 |
| Pressed Glass, Goblet, Etched Swan | 49.50 |
| Pressed Glass, Goblet, Etched Teardrop | 15.00 |
| Pressed Glass, Goblet, Etched Three Faces | 65.00 |
| Pressed Glass, Goblet, Etched Torpedo | 30.00 |
| Pressed Glass, Goblet, Etched Yoke Band | 9.75 |
| Pressed Glass, Goblet, Eugenie, Flint | 42.50 |
| Pressed Glass, Goblet, Eureka | 15.00 To 25.00 |
| Pressed Glass, Goblet, Eureka, Flint | 12.50 To 25.00 |
| Pressed Glass, Goblet, Excelsior With Maltese Cross | 29.00 |
| Pressed Glass, Goblet, Excelsior With Maltese Cross, Flint | 32.00 |
| Pressed Glass, Goblet, Excelsior, Barrel, Flint | 26.00 |
| Pressed Glass, Goblet, Excelsior, Flint | 25.00 To 32.50 |
| Pressed Glass, Goblet, Fan & Girl | 22.50 |
| Pressed Glass, Goblet, Fan With Diamond | 8.50 To 12.00 |
| Pressed Glass, Goblet, Feather | 30.00 |
| Pressed Glass, Goblet, Feeding Swan | 25.00 |
| Pressed Glass, Goblet, Fern Burst | *Illus* 7.50 |
| Pressed Glass, Goblet, Fine Rib With Cut Ovals, 3 Rows, Flint | 195.00 |
| Pressed Glass, Goblet, Fine Ribbed Ivy, Flint | 32.50 |
| Pressed Glass, Goblet, Finecut & Block | 14.00 To 30.00 |
| Pressed Glass, Goblet, Finecut & Block, Amber | 20.00 To 32.50 |
| Pressed Glass, Goblet, Finecut & Panel | 15.00 To 27.50 |
| Pressed Glass, Goblet, Fishscale | 18.50 To 20.00 |

Pressed Glass, Goblet, Fern Burst
*(See Page 439)*

Pressed Glass, Goblet,
Frosted Ribbon, Double Bands

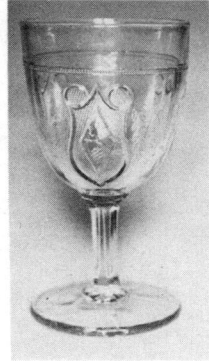

Pressed Glass, Goblet,
Grape & Festoon
With Shield
*(See Page 441)*

Pressed Glass, Goblet,
Hairpin With Rayed Base
*(See Page 441)*

Pressed Glass, Goblet,
Heavy Paneled, Fine cut
*(See Page 441)*

| | |
|---|---|
| **Pressed Glass, Goblet,** Flat Diamond | 25.00 |
| **Pressed Glass, Goblet,** Fleur-De-Lis | 20.00 |
| **Pressed Glass, Goblet,** Florida Palm | 8.50 To 15.00 |
| **Pressed Glass, Goblet,** Flute, Flint | 17.00 |
| **Pressed Glass, Goblet,** Flute, 10 Flutes, Applied Stem & Foot, Flint | 20.00 |
| **Pressed Glass, Goblet,** Flying Stork | 35.00 |
| **Pressed Glass, Goblet,** Forget-Me-Not | 18.00 |
| **Pressed Glass, Goblet,** Forget-Me-Not In Scroll | 10.50 |
| **Pressed Glass, Goblet,** Frog & Spider | 73.00 |
| **Pressed Glass, Goblet,** Frosted Apollo | 18.50 |
| **Pressed Glass, Goblet,** Frosted Artichoke | 24.50 |
| **Pressed Glass, Goblet,** Frosted Flower Band | 37.00 |
| **Pressed Glass, Goblet,** Frosted Hidalgo | 13.50 |
| **Pressed Glass, Goblet,** Frosted Leaf | 65.00 |
| **Pressed Glass, Goblet,** Frosted Leaf, Flint | 75.00 |
| **Pressed Glass, Goblet,** Frosted Lion | 45.00 To 50.00 |
| **Pressed Glass, Goblet,** Frosted Lion With Etched Fern | 38.50 |
| **Pressed Glass, Goblet,** Frosted Magnet & Grape | 35.00 To 45.00 |
| **Pressed Glass, Goblet,** Frosted Magnet & Grape, Flint | 49.00 |
| **Pressed Glass, Goblet,** Frosted Polar Bear | 48.00 |
| **Pressed Glass, Goblet,** Frosted Ribbon | 12.50 To 25.00 |
| **Pressed Glass, Goblet,** Frosted Ribbon, Double Bands | *Illus*   17.50 |
| **Pressed Glass, Goblet,** Frosted Roman Key | 40.00 |
| **Pressed Glass, Goblet,** Frosted Roman Key With Ribs, Flint | 35.00 |
| **Pressed Glass, Goblet,** Frosted Roman Key, Flint | 22.50 To 36.00 |
| **Pressed Glass, Goblet,** Frosted, 2 Clear Etched Panels, 1 Frosted | 24.00 |
| **Pressed Glass, Goblet,** Fuchsia | 20.00 |
| **Pressed Glass, Goblet,** G.A.R. | 30.00 |
| **Pressed Glass, Goblet,** Galloway, Gold Top | 16.50 |
| **Pressed Glass, Goblet,** Garfield Drape, 5 5/8 In. High | 20.00 To 25.00 |
| **Pressed Glass, Goblet,** Garfield Drape, 6 1/4 In. | 24.50 |
| **Pressed Glass, Goblet,** Giant Bull's-Eye, Marked Half Pint On One Eye, Flint | 18.00 |

Pressed Glass, Goblet, Giant Prism, Flint ........................................................... 45.00
Pressed Glass, Goblet, Giant Sawtooth ............................................................... 65.00
Pressed Glass, Goblet, Giant Sawtooth, Flint ..................................................... 65.00
Pressed Glass, Goblet, Girl With Fan ................................................................... 22.50
Pressed Glass, Goblet, Girl With Fan, Flint .......................................................... 32.00
Pressed Glass, Goblet, Good Luck ....................................................................... 25.00
Pressed Glass, Goblet, Good Luck, Knob Stem .................................................. 18.00
Pressed Glass, Goblet, Gothic, Flint ................................................... 38.00 To 55.00
Pressed Glass, Goblet, Graduated Diamonds ..................................................... 13.00
Pressed Glass, Goblet, Grand ............................................................................... 18.50
Pressed Glass, Goblet, Grand Army Of The Republic ........................................ 30.00
Pressed Glass, Goblet, Grand, Ring Stem ........................................................... 12.50
Pressed Glass, Goblet, Grand, 3 Ring Stem ........................................................ 21.50
Pressed Glass, Goblet, Grape & Festoon ............................................. 10.00 To 22.50
Pressed Glass, Goblet, Grape & Festoon With Shield ................................ Illus 28.00
Pressed Glass, Goblet, Grape & Festoon With Stippled Leaf .............. 9.50 To 15.00
Pressed Glass, Goblet, Grape Band ...................................................... 10.00 To 15.00
Pressed Glass, Goblet, Grape Festoon ................................................................ 18.50
Pressed Glass, Goblet, Grape Medallion ............................................................. 13.50
Pressed Glass, Goblet, Gypsy ............................................................................... 12.00
Pressed Glass, Goblet, Hairpin ............................................................................. 15.00
Pressed Glass, Goblet, Hairpin & Thumbprint, Flint .......................... 20.00 To 25.00
Pressed Glass, Goblet, Hairpin With Rayed Base ...................................... Illus 10.00
Pressed Glass, Goblet, Hairpin, Flint ................................................................... 28.00
Pressed Glass, Goblet, Halley's Comet ................................................ 12.50 To 20.00
Pressed Glass, Goblet, Hamilton ........................................................... 22.00 To 35.00
Pressed Glass, Goblet, Hamilton With Leaf ........................................................ 45.00
Pressed Glass, Goblet, Hamilton With Leaf, Flint .............................................. 28.00
Pressed Glass, Goblet, Hamilton, Flint ................................................. 25.00 To 48.00
Pressed Glass, Goblet, Hand ................................................................. 25.00 To 30.00
Pressed Glass, Goblet, Hanover .............................................................. 8.75 To 13.50
Pressed Glass, Goblet, Hartley ............................................................. 14.50 To 17.50
Pressed Glass, Goblet, Hartley, Blue ................................................................... 20.00
Pressed Glass, Goblet, Hartley, Canary ............................................................... 20.00
Pressed Glass, Goblet, Hawaiian Pineapple, Flint ............................................. 55.00
Pressed Glass, Goblet, Heart ................................................................ 22.50 To 25.00
Pressed Glass, Goblet, Heart & Thumbprint ........................................ 22.50 To 25.00
Pressed Glass, Goblet, Heart & Thumbprint, Emerald, Gold Trim ...................... 35.00
Pressed Glass, Goblet, Heart & Thumbprint, Gold Trim ..................................... 25.00
Pressed Glass, Goblet, Heavy Paneled, Fine Cut ....................................... Illus 7.00
Pressed Glass, Goblet, Herringbone ..................................................... 10.00 To 11.00
Pressed Glass, Goblet, Herringbone Band ........................................................... 10.00
Pressed Glass, Goblet, Herringbone, Emerald .................................................... 35.00
Pressed Glass, Goblet, Herringbone, Green ........................................................ 35.00
Pressed Glass, Goblet, Hickman, Gold Trim ....................................................... 12.00
Pressed Glass, Goblet, Hickman, Green, Gold On Rim ....................................... 21.00
Pressed Glass, Goblet, Hidalgo .............................................................. 7.50 To 13.00
Pressed Glass, Goblet, Hidalgo, Frosted Top ..................................................... 12.50
Pressed Glass, Goblet, Hobnail, Double Eye ...................................................... 18.00
Pressed Glass, Goblet, Hobstar .............................................................................. 8.50
Pressed Glass, Goblet, Honeycomb ........................................................ 7.35 To 48.00
Pressed Glass, Goblet, Honeycomb & Diamond, Plain Base ............................... 6.50
Pressed Glass, Goblet, Honeycomb, Amber ........................................................ 17.50
Pressed Glass, Goblet, Honeycomb, Flint ................................................... Illus 15.00
Pressed Glass, Goblet, Honeycomb, Knob Stem, Flint ....................................... 24.00
Pressed Glass, Goblet, Honeycomb, Purple Hue ................................................ 15.00
Pressed Glass, Goblet, Hooks & Eyes .................................................... 6.00 To 12.50
Pressed Glass, Goblet, Hops Band ...................................................................... 12.50
Pressed Glass, Goblet, Hops Band, Flint ............................................................. 14.00
Pressed Glass, Goblet, Horizontal Oval Frames, Flint ....................................... 40.00
Pressed Glass, Goblet, Horn Of Plenty, Flint ...................................... 36.00 To 65.00
Pressed Glass, Goblet, Horn Of Plenty, Ground Pontil, Flint ............................. 45.00
Pressed Glass, Goblet, Horn Of Plenty, Knob Stem, Flint .................................. 45.00
Pressed Glass, Goblet, Horsemint, Gold Trim ...................................................... 9.50
Pressed Glass, Goblet, Horseshoe ........................................................ 17.00 To 25.00
Pressed Glass, Goblet, Horseshoe, Plain Stem ................................... 20.00 To 25.00

Pressed Glass, Goblet, Huber .......................................................................... 22.00
Pressed Glass, Goblet, Huber, Flint ........................................... 8.00 To 24.00
Pressed Glass, Goblet, Huber, Purple Hue ................................................. 26.00
Pressed Glass, Goblet, Hummingbird ................................... 20.00 To 34.00
Pressed Glass, Goblet, Icicle, Star Base, Flint ....................................... 35.00
Pressed Glass, Goblet, Iconoclast .......................................... *Illus* 25.00
Pressed Glass, Goblet, Inverted Fern ..................................... 19.00 To 28.00
Pressed Glass, Goblet, Inverted Fern, Flint ......................... 20.00 To 30.00
Pressed Glass, Goblet, Inverted Thumbprint With Daisy Band, Green, Gold ............. 37.50
Pressed Glass, Goblet, Inverted Thumbprint, Amber, Acme ........................ 20.00
Pressed Glass, Goblet, Inverted Thumbprint, Amber, Ferguson ................... 14.00
Pressed Glass, Goblet, Inverted Thumbprint, Amber, Oval Prints ................. 20.00
Pressed Glass, Goblet, Inverted Thumbprint, Blue, Oval Prints ................. 22.50
Pressed Glass, Goblet, Inverted Thumbprint, Tegman .............................. 10.00
Pressed Glass, Goblet, Iowa City ............................................................ 50.00
Pressed Glass, Goblet, Isis ...................................................................... 9.00
Pressed Glass, Goblet, Janssen ............................................................. 13.75
Pressed Glass, Goblet, Jersey Swirl, Buttermilk ................................... 18.50
Pressed Glass, Goblet, Jewel & Dewdrop .............................................. 26.50
Pressed Glass, Goblet, Jewel Band ....................................................... 12.00
Pressed Glass, Goblet, Jeweled Drapery ................................................ 9.00
Pressed Glass, Goblet, Jeweled Moon & Star ........................................ 30.00
Pressed Glass, Goblet, Job's Tears ....................................................... 12.50
Pressed Glass, Goblet, Kalbach ............................................................ 12.00
Pressed Glass, Goblet, King's Crown ..................................................... 11.00
Pressed Glass, Goblet, King's Crown With Green Thumbprint ................. 15.00
Pressed Glass, Goblet, King's Crown, Amethyst Thumbprints ................. 17.50
Pressed Glass, Goblet, King's Crown, Gold Band ................................... 12.00
Pressed Glass, Goblet, King's Crown, Green & Clear .............................. 16.00
Pressed Glass, Goblet, Knife & Fork ..................................................... 10.75
Pressed Glass, Goblet, Knife & Fork, Flint ............................. 22.00 To 30.00
Pressed Glass, Goblet, Knobby Bull's-Eye, Gold Trim ............................. 8.50
Pressed Glass, Goblet, Kokomo ............................................. 15.00 To 16.50
Pressed Glass, Goblet, Lace ................................................................. 15.00
Pressed Glass, Goblet, Lady's, Beaded Grape Medallion ........................ 17.50
Pressed Glass, Goblet, Lady's, Broken Column ..................................... 32.50
Pressed Glass, Goblet, Lady's, Cable, Flint ........................................... 60.00
Pressed Glass, Goblet, Lady's, Frosted Leaf, Flint ................................. 65.00
Pressed Glass, Goblet, Lady's, New England Pineapple, Flint .... 30.00 To 55.00
Pressed Glass, Goblet, Laredo Honeycomb ............................. 6.00 To 9.00
Pressed Glass, Goblet, Lattice .............................................. 12.00 To 16.00
Pressed Glass, Goblet, Laverne ............................................................ 16.50
Pressed Glass, Goblet, Leaf & Dart ....................................... *Illus* 15.00
Pressed Glass, Goblet, Liberty Bell ........................................ *Illus* 65.00
Pressed Glass, Goblet, Lily Of The Valley .............................................. 27.50
Pressed Glass, Goblet, Lincoln Drape, Flint ............................ 40.00 To 65.00
Pressed Glass, Goblet, Lined Smocking, Flint ....................................... 45.00
Pressed Glass, Goblet, Little Bullet Band, Findlay ................................. 12.00
Pressed Glass, Goblet, Log & Star ........................................................ 19.00
Pressed Glass, Goblet, Loop & Dart ....................................... 9.50 To 16.50
Pressed Glass, Goblet, Loop & Dart With Diamond Ornament ................. 13.75
Pressed Glass, Goblet, Loop & Dart With Round Ornament ....... 10.00 To 16.50
Pressed Glass, Goblet, Loop & Honeycomb ............................ 13.00 To 14.50
Pressed Glass, Goblet, Loop & Moose-Eye ............................................ 30.00
Pressed Glass, Goblet, Loop & Moose-Eye, Flint ................................... 20.00
Pressed Glass, Goblet, Loop & Oval, Flint ............................................. 18.00
Pressed Glass, Goblet, Loop With Crystal .............................................. 22.50
Pressed Glass, Goblet, Loop With Fisheye .............................. *Illus* 12.50
Pressed Glass, Goblet, Loop With Fisheye, Flint ................................... 16.50
Pressed Glass, Goblet, Lotus ............................................................... 22.00
Pressed Glass, Goblet, Louisiana .......................................................... 13.00
Pressed Glass, Goblet, Magnet & Grape ................................. 11.00 To 16.00
Pressed Glass, Goblet, Magnet & Grape With Frosted Leaf, Flint .. 42.50 To 65.00
Pressed Glass, Goblet, Magnet & Grape, Knob Stem, Design In Base, Flint ....... 65.00
Pressed Glass, Goblet, Magnet & Grape, Stippled Leaf ............ *Illus* 15.00
Pressed Glass, Goblet, Maiden's Blush ................................................. 45.00

Pressed Glass, Goblet, Honeycomb, Flint
*(See Page 441)*

Pressed Glass, Goblet, Iconoclast
*(See Page 442)*

Pressed Glass, Goblet,
Leaf & Dart
*(See Page 442)*

Pressed Glass, Goblet,
Loop With Fisheye
*(See Page 442)*

Pressed Glass, Goblet,
Magnet & Grape, Stippled Leaf
*(See Page 442)*

Pressed Glass,
Goblet, Liberty Bell
*(See Page 442)*

| | |
|---|---|
| Pressed Glass, Goblet, Majestic, Ruby & Clear | 32.50 |
| Pressed Glass, Goblet, Manhattan | 6.00 |
| Pressed Glass, Goblet, Maple Leaf | 65.00 To 85.00 |
| Pressed Glass, Goblet, Marquisette | 12.50 To 18.00 |
| Pressed Glass, Goblet, Master, Argus, Bulbous Stem, Flint | 52.50 |
| Pressed Glass, Goblet, Medallion | 15.00 To 16.50 |
| Pressed Glass, Goblet, Medallion, Amber | 30.00 |
| Pressed Glass, Goblet, Medallion, Apple Green | 32.50 |
| Pressed Glass, Goblet, Melrose | 16.50 |
| Pressed Glass, Goblet, Melton | 10.00 |
| Pressed Glass, Goblet, Michigan, Gold Trim | 17.00 |
| Pressed Glass, Goblet, Milton | 12.50 |
| Pressed Glass, Goblet, Milton, Findlay | 15.50 To 16.00 |
| Pressed Glass, Goblet, Minnesota | 16.00 To 16.50 |
| Pressed Glass, Goblet, Minnesota, Gold Trim | 13.50 |
| Pressed Glass, Goblet, Mirror, Flint | 25.00 |
| Pressed Glass, Goblet, Mirror, Knob Stem, Flint | 25.00 |
| Pressed Glass, Goblet, Mirror, Stocky, Flint | 45.00 |
| Pressed Glass, Goblet, Mitered Bars | 8.50 To 10.00 |
| Pressed Glass, Goblet, Mitered Diamond | *Illus* 10.00 |
| Pressed Glass, Goblet, Mitered Ovals, Flint | 18.00 To 25.00 |

**Pressed Glass, Goblet,** Mitered Prisms ................................................... 11.00 To 15.00
**Pressed Glass, Goblet,** Mitered Prisms, Findlay ............................................ 11.50
**Pressed Glass, Goblet,** Mitered Thumbprint .................................................. 8.50
**Pressed Glass, Goblet,** Moon & Star ................................................ 16.00 To 35.00
**Pressed Glass, Goblet,** Moon & Stork ...................................................... *Illus*   75.00
**Pressed Glass, Goblet,** Moon & Stork, Straw Mark In Making ........................... 50.00
**Pressed Glass, Goblet,** Moose-Eye In Sand ................................................. 13.50
**Pressed Glass, Goblet,** Morning Glory, Flint .............................................. 200.00
**Pressed Glass, Goblet,** Mountain Laurel .................................................... 12.50
**Pressed Glass, Goblet,** My Lady's Workbox .................................. 8.50 To 15.00
**Pressed Glass, Goblet,** Nailhead ........................................... 12.50 To 20.00
**Pressed Glass, Goblet,** Naturalistic Blackberry ............................................ 16.00
**Pressed Glass, Goblet,** Nebraska Star .................................................... 17.50
**Pressed Glass, Goblet,** Nestlings ........................................................ 32.50
**Pressed Glass, Goblet,** Netted Arches & Prisms ........................................... 10.00
**Pressed Glass, Goblet,** New England ..................................................... 16.00
**Pressed Glass, Goblet,** New England Flute, Flint ........................... 13.00 To 18.00
**Pressed Glass, Goblet,** New England Pineapple ............................ 28.00 To 48.00
**Pressed Glass, Goblet,** New England Pineapple, Flint ...................... 29.00 To 48.00
**Pressed Glass, Goblet,** New Hampshire, Amethyst Band At Top ...................... 18.00
**Pressed Glass, Goblet,** New Hampshire, Gold Trim ................................... 14.00
**Pressed Glass, Goblet,** New Jersey, Gold Trim ........................... 17.00 To 24.00
**Pressed Glass, Goblet,** New York Honeycomb, Flint ....................... 13.00 To 16.00
**Pressed Glass, Goblet,** Nokomis Swirl, Canary ......................................... 16.50
**Pressed Glass, Goblet,** Oak Leaf Band .................................... 11.50 To 12.50
**Pressed Glass, Goblet,** Odd Fellows ...................................... 22.50 To 25.00
**Pressed Glass, Goblet,** Open Plaid ........................................ 8.50 To 14.00
**Pressed Glass, Goblet,** Open Rose ...................................................... *Illus*   21.50
**Pressed Glass, Goblet,** Orange Peel .................................................... *Illus*   9.50

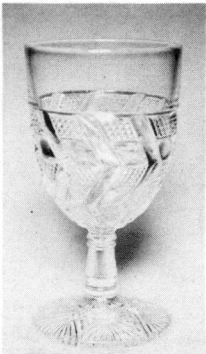

Pressed Glass, Goblet, Mitered Diamond
*(See Page 443)*

Pressed Glass, Goblet, Moon & Stork

Pressed Glass, Goblet,
Open Rose

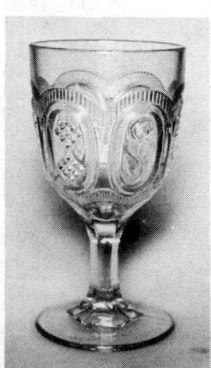

Pressed Glass, Goblet, Orange Peel

Pressed Glass, Goblet,
Paneled Diamond & Flowers
*(See Page 445)*

| | |
|---|---|
| Pressed Glass, Goblet, Oriental Fan | 25.00 |
| Pressed Glass, Goblet, Ornate Star, Gilt Rim | 8.00 |
| Pressed Glass, Goblet, Ostrich Looking At Moon | 60.00 |
| Pressed Glass, Goblet, Oswego Waffle | 10.00 |
| Pressed Glass, Goblet, Oval Medallion, Amber | 16.00 |
| Pressed Glass, Goblet, Oval Miter | 8.00 |
| Pressed Glass, Goblet, Oval Miter, Flint | 18.00 To 22.00 |
| Pressed Glass, Goblet, Oval Panels, Blue | 17.50 |
| Pressed Glass, Goblet, Owl & Possum | 35.00 |
| Pressed Glass, Goblet, Owl In Horseshoe | 20.00 To 40.00 |
| Pressed Glass, Goblet, Paisley, Clear Eyes | 15.00 |
| Pressed Glass, Goblet, Palm Leaf & Fan | 8.00 |
| Pressed Glass, Goblet, Palm Stub | 12.50 |
| Pressed Glass, Goblet, Palmette | 14.50 To 20.00 |
| Pressed Glass, Goblet, Palmette, Findlay | 17.00 |
| Pressed Glass, Goblet, Paneled Acorn Band | 15.00 To 20.00 |
| Pressed Glass, Goblet, Paneled Apple Blossoms | 15.00 |
| Pressed Glass, Goblet, Paneled Bull's-Eye & Diamond, Purple Hue | 24.00 |
| Pressed Glass, Goblet, Paneled Cane | 9.00 To 18.00 |
| Pressed Glass, Goblet, Paneled Daisy | 17.50 To 25.00 |
| Pressed Glass, Goblet, Paneled Daisy & Button, Amber | 21.00 |
| Pressed Glass, Goblet, Paneled Dewdrop | 19.00 |
| Pressed Glass, Goblet, Paneled Dewdrop, Pattern On Base | 22.50 |
| Pressed Glass, Goblet, Paneled Diamond | 6.50 To 12.50 |
| Pressed Glass, Goblet, Paneled Diamond & Flowers | Illus 12.00 |
| Pressed Glass, Goblet, Paneled Diamond Cut & Fan | 10.00 |
| Pressed Glass, Goblet, Paneled Fern | 21.50 To 23.50 |
| Pressed Glass, Goblet, Paneled Fine Diamond Cut | 11.00 |
| Pressed Glass, Goblet, Paneled Finecut | 9.00 To 10.00 |
| Pressed Glass, Goblet, Paneled Flowers | 13.50 To 16.00 |
| Pressed Glass, Goblet, Paneled Flowers & Diamonds | 14.00 |
| Pressed Glass, Goblet, Paneled Forget-Me-Not | 20.00 To 26.00 |
| Pressed Glass, Goblet, Paneled Grape | 12.00 To 20.00 |
| Pressed Glass, Goblet, Paneled Grape Band, 5 In. | 14.50 To 16.50 |
| Pressed Glass, Goblet, Paneled Herringbone, Dark Green | 25.00 |
| Pressed Glass, Goblet, Paneled Jewels | 11.00 To 12.50 |
| Pressed Glass, Goblet, Paneled Jewels, Amber | 27.50 |
| Pressed Glass, Goblet, Paneled Julep | 12.75 |
| Pressed Glass, Goblet, Paneled Long Jewel | 15.00 |
| Pressed Glass, Goblet, Paneled Nightshade | 16.50 To 20.00 |
| Pressed Glass, Goblet, Paneled Ovals, Flint | 30.00 |
| Pressed Glass, Goblet, Paneled Sage | 35.00 To 50.00 |
| Pressed Glass, Goblet, Paneled Stars | 17.00 |
| Pressed Glass, Goblet, Paneled Sunflower | 12.00 To 35.00 |
| Pressed Glass, Goblet, Paneled Thistle | 26.50 To 33.00 |
| Pressed Glass, Goblet, Parrot | 18.50 To 26.00 |
| Pressed Glass, Goblet, Parrot & Fan | 20.00 |
| Pressed Glass, Goblet, Pavonia | 15.00 To 24.00 |
| Pressed Glass, Goblet, Pear | 15.00 To 20.00 |
| Pressed Glass, Goblet, Peerless | 16.00 |
| Pressed Glass, Goblet, Pequot | 15.00 To 16.50 |
| Pressed Glass, Goblet, Philadelphia Centennial | 29.50 To 38.50 |
| Pressed Glass, Goblet, Picket | 20.00 |
| Pressed Glass, Goblet, Picket Band | 11.50 |
| Pressed Glass, Goblet, Pioneer's Victoria | 12.00 To 24.00 |
| Pressed Glass, Goblet, Pitcairn | 11.00 |
| Pressed Glass, Goblet, Pittman | 5.00 |
| Pressed Glass, Goblet, Plaid | 9.00 |
| Pressed Glass, Goblet, Pleat & Panel | 14.00 To 16.00 |
| Pressed Glass, Goblet, Plume | 16.00 To 27.00 |
| Pressed Glass, Goblet, Pointed Jewels | 18.00 To 18.50 |
| Pressed Glass, Goblet, Polar Bear | 75.00 |
| Pressed Glass, Goblet, Polar Bear, Clear & Frosted | 50.00 |
| Pressed Glass, Goblet, Popcorn | 23.00 |
| Pressed Glass, Goblet, Portland | 16.00 To 18.00 |
| Pressed Glass, Goblet, Portland, Gold | 14.00 |

| | |
|---|---|
| Pressed Glass, Goblet, Powder & Shot | 35.00 To 38.00 |
| Pressed Glass, Goblet, Powder & Shot, Etching On Band, Flint | 30.00 |
| Pressed Glass, Goblet, Powder & Shot, Flint | 32.00 To 45.00 |
| Pressed Glass, Goblet, Pressed Leaf | 9.00 To 15.00 |
| Pressed Glass, Goblet, Pressed Leaf, Flint | 22.00 |
| Pressed Glass, Goblet, Primrose | 12.00 |
| Pressed Glass, Goblet, Princess Feather | 17.00 To 22.50 |
| Pressed Glass, Goblet, Prism & Broken Column | 14.50 |
| Pressed Glass, Goblet, Prism & Daisy Band, Amber | 21.50 |
| Pressed Glass, Goblet, Prism & Daisy Bar | 5.00 |
| Pressed Glass, Goblet, Prism & Daisy Bar, Amber | 20.00 |
| Pressed Glass, Goblet, Prism & Flute, Flint | 22.50 To 27.50 |
| Pressed Glass, Goblet, Prism & Globules | 15.00 |
| Pressed Glass, Goblet, Prism & Latticed Sawtooth | 45.00 |
| Pressed Glass, Goblet, Prism & Loop | 9.50 |
| Pressed Glass, Goblet, Prism & Loop, Purple Hue | 15.00 |
| Pressed Glass, Goblet, Prism Arc | 11.00 |
| Pressed Glass, Goblet, Prism, Rayed Base | 32.50 To 42.50 |
| Pressed Glass, Goblet, Psyche & Cupid | 20.00 To 29.50 |
| Pressed Glass, Goblet, Pyramid Flute | 22.00 |
| Pressed Glass, Goblet, Queen, Blue | 28.50 |
| Pressed Glass, Goblet, Radiant | 15.00 |
| Pressed Glass, Goblet, Rail Fence Band | 10.00 To 11.00 |
| Pressed Glass, Goblet, Rayed Flower | 16.00 |
| Pressed Glass, Goblet, Rayed Pineapple | 16.00 |
| Pressed Glass, Goblet, Recessed Ovals | 9.50 To 19.00 |
| Pressed Glass, Goblet, Red Block | 24.00 |
| Pressed Glass, Goblet, Rexford | *Illus* 9.50 |
| Pressed Glass, Goblet, Ribbed Bellflower | 25.00 |
| Pressed Glass, Goblet, Ribbed Grape | 27.00 To 30.00 |
| Pressed Glass, Goblet, Ribbed Grape, Flint | 20.00 To 35.00 |
| Pressed Glass, Goblet, Ribbed Ivy | 25.00 |
| Pressed Glass, Goblet, Ribbed Ivy, Flint | 20.00 To 29.50 |
| Pressed Glass, Goblet, Ribbed Palm | 28.00 To 33.00 |
| Pressed Glass, Goblet, Ribbed Palm, Flint | 15.00 To 27.50 |
| Pressed Glass, Goblet, Ribbon | 18.00 To 22.00 |
| Pressed Glass, Goblet, Ripple | 6.25 |
| Pressed Glass, Goblet, Rising Sun, Gold Eyes | 14.50 |
| Pressed Glass, Goblet, Roanoke Star | 12.50 |
| Pressed Glass, Goblet, Roman Cross | *Illus* 9.50 |
| Pressed Glass, Goblet, Roman Key, Flint | 15.00 To 16.00 |
| Pressed Glass, Goblet, Roman Rosette | 18.00 To 25.00 |
| Pressed Glass, Goblet, Romeo | 12.50 To 14.50 |
| Pressed Glass, Goblet, Rope Band | 7.50 To 22.50 |
| Pressed Glass, Goblet, Rose In Snow | 19.00 To 35.00 |
| Pressed Glass, Goblet, Rose In Snow, Amber | 26.50 |
| Pressed Glass, Goblet, Rose In Snow, Canary, Gold Band | 45.00 |
| Pressed Glass, Goblet, Rose In Snow, Clear & Stippled | 29.00 |
| Pressed Glass, Goblet, Rose Leaf | 9.00 To 13.25 |
| Pressed Glass, Goblet, Rose Leaf, Flint | 14.50 To 16.50 |
| Pressed Glass, Goblet, Rose Leaf, Purple Hue | 18.00 |
| Pressed Glass, Goblet, Rose Of Sharon | 12.00 |
| Pressed Glass, Goblet, Rose Sprig | *Illus* 28.00 |
| Pressed Glass, Goblet, Rose Sprig, Amber | 27.50 |
| Pressed Glass, Goblet, Rosette & Palms | 14.00 |
| Pressed Glass, Goblet, Rosette Band | 100.00 |
| Pressed Glass, Goblet, Ruby Thumbprint, Souvenir | 15.00 |
| Pressed Glass, Goblet, Sandwich Loop | 28.00 |
| Pressed Glass, Goblet, Sawtooth | 18.00 |
| Pressed Glass, Goblet, Sawtooth, Knob Stem | 15.00 To 30.00 |
| Pressed Glass, Goblet, Sawtooth, Knob Stem, Flint | 18.00 |
| Pressed Glass, Goblet, Sawtooth, Plain Stem | 9.00 |
| Pressed Glass, Goblet, Sawtooth, Sharp Teeth, 6 1/4 In.High | 15.00 |
| Pressed Glass, Goblet, Sawtooth, 3 Mold | 8.00 |
| Pressed Glass, Goblet, Saxton Flute, Flint | 13.00 |
| Pressed Glass, Goblet, Scalloped Daisy & Fan, Emerald | 35.00 |

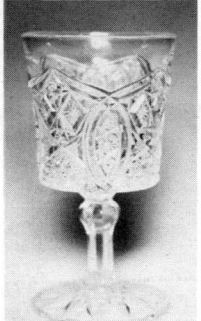

Pressed Glass, Goblet, Rexford
*(See Page 446)*

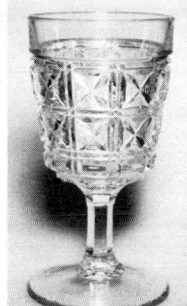

Pressed Glass, Goblet, Roman Cross
*(See Page 446)*

Pressed Glass, Goblet,
Rose Sprig
*(See Page 446)*

Pressed Glass, Goblet,
Tandem Diamonds
With Thumbprint
*(See Page 448)*

Pressed Glass,
Goblet,
Scroll With Flowers

| | |
|---|---|
| Pressed Glass, Goblet, Scalloped Tape | 14.50 |
| Pressed Glass, Goblet, Scarab, Flint | 75.00 |
| Pressed Glass, Goblet, Scottish Rites | 15.00 |
| Pressed Glass, Goblet, Scroll | 8.00 To 13.50 |
| Pressed Glass, Goblet, Scroll With Flowers | *Illus* 14.00 |
| Pressed Glass, Goblet, Seashell | 12.50 |
| Pressed Glass, Goblet, Sedan | 9.50 To 12.50 |
| Pressed Glass, Goblet, Selby | 7.00 |
| Pressed Glass, Goblet, Seneca Loop | 10.00 To 28.00 |
| Pressed Glass, Goblet, Seneca Loop, Flint | 25.00 To 32.00 |
| Pressed Glass, Goblet, Sexton, Flint | 15.00 |
| Pressed Glass, Goblet, Sheaf & Diamond | 12.50 To 13.50 |
| Pressed Glass, Goblet, Sheaf Of Wheat | 15.00 |
| Pressed Glass, Goblet, Sheraton | 16.00 |
| Pressed Glass, Goblet, Shields | 18.00 |
| Pressed Glass, Goblet, Shovel | 8.00 To 14.00 |
| Pressed Glass, Goblet, Six Panel | 13.50 |
| Pressed Glass, Goblet, Snail | 10.00 |
| Pressed Glass, Goblet, Snake Drape | 12.50 To 18.00 |
| Pressed Glass, Goblet, Snakeskin & Dot | 14.00 To 16.50 |
| Pressed Glass, Goblet, Snakeskin & Dot Band | 18.50 |
| Pressed Glass, Goblet, Spearhead | 9.00 |
| Pressed Glass, Goblet, Spirea Band | 8.00 |
| Pressed Glass, Goblet, Spirea Band, Amber | 15.00 To 20.00 |
| Pressed Glass, Goblet, Sprig | 20.00 |
| Pressed Glass, Goblet, Star & Palm | 6.50 |
| Pressed Glass, Goblet, Star Band | 10.00 |
| Pressed Glass, Goblet, Star In Bull's-Eye | 13.00 |
| Pressed Glass, Goblet, Star Of David | 12.50 To 15.00 |
| Pressed Glass, Goblet, Star Rosette | 14.50 To 18.00 |
| Pressed Glass, Goblet, Star Whorl | 13.00 |

Pressed Glass, Goblet, Starred Block .................................................... 27.50
Pressed Glass, Goblet, Stars & Bars .................................................... 15.00
Pressed Glass, Goblet, States .................................................... 22.50
Pressed Glass, Goblet, Stedman, Flint .................................................... 15.00
Pressed Glass, Goblet, Stippled Band .................................................... 12.00
Pressed Glass, Goblet, Stippled Bowl, Flint .................................................... 12.00
Pressed Glass, Goblet, Stippled Double Loop .................................................... 8.50
Pressed Glass, Goblet, Stippled Fleur-De-Lis, Green .................................................... 32.50
Pressed Glass, Goblet, Stippled Flower .................................................... 12.00
Pressed Glass, Goblet, Stippled Forget-Me-Not .................................................... 18.00
Pressed Glass, Goblet, Stippled Fuchsia .................................................... 18.00
Pressed Glass, Goblet, Stippled Ivy .................................................... 11.00 To 17.00
Pressed Glass, Goblet, Stippled Maidenhair Fern .................................................... 12.00 To 13.00
Pressed Glass, Goblet, Stippled Medallion, Flint .................................................... 22.50
Pressed Glass, Goblet, Stippled Peppers .................................................... 15.00
Pressed Glass, Goblet, Stippled Scroll .................................................... 12.50
Pressed Glass, Goblet, Stippled Starflower .................................................... 6.00 To 17.00
Pressed Glass, Goblet, Stork .................................................... 35.00
Pressed Glass, Goblet, Stourbridge, Flint, C.1860, 6 In.High .................................................... 55.00
Pressed Glass, Goblet, Straight Banded Worcester, Flint .................................................... 25.00
Pressed Glass, Goblet, Strawberry .................................................... 9.00 To 22.50
Pressed Glass, Goblet, Strawberry & Currant .................................................... 17.00 To 20.00
Pressed Glass, Goblet, Strawberry, Fairfax .................................................... 22.00
Pressed Glass, Goblet, Sunburst .................................................... 4.00
Pressed Glass, Goblet, Sunburst Medallion .................................................... 13.50
Pressed Glass, Goblet, Sunk Daisy .................................................... 12.00
Pressed Glass, Goblet, Swan, Amber .................................................... 65.00
Pressed Glass, Goblet, Swirl, Short .................................................... 15.00
Pressed Glass, Goblet, Swirled Star Base .................................................... 19.50
Pressed Glass, Goblet, Tackleblock, Flint .................................................... 40.00
Pressed Glass, Goblet, Tailored .................................................... 8.75
Pressed Glass, Goblet, Tandem Bicycle .................................................... 12.00 To 20.00
Pressed Glass, Goblet, Tandem Diamonds With Thumbprint .................................................... *Illus* 10.00
Pressed Glass, Goblet, Tape Measure, Flint .................................................... 15.00
Pressed Glass, Goblet, Teardrop Stem, Flint .................................................... 25.00
Pressed Glass, Goblet, Teasel, 6 In. .................................................... 15.00
Pressed Glass, Goblet, Texas Bull's-Eye .................................................... 12.50 To 15.00
Pressed Glass, Goblet, Texas Centennial, Flags & Dates 1836-1936 .................................................... 28.50
Pressed Glass, Goblet, Thistle .................................................... 35.00
Pressed Glass, Goblet, Threaded .................................................... 7.50
Pressed Glass, Goblet, Three Faces .................................................... 25.00 To 62.50
Pressed Glass, Goblet, Three Faces With Etched Fern .................................................... 48.50
Pressed Glass, Goblet, Three Faces, Engraved .................................................... 65.00
Pressed Glass, Goblet, Three Panel, Dark Amber .................................................... 35.00
Pressed Glass, Goblet, Three Stories .................................................... 8.75
Pressed Glass, Goblet, Thumbprint .................................................... 25.00
Pressed Glass, Goblet, Thumbprint & Diamond, Flint .................................................... 8.00
Pressed Glass, Goblet, Thumbprint, Flint .................................................... 19.25
Pressed Glass, Goblet, Thumbprint, Hotel .................................................... 16.00
Pressed Glass, Goblet, Thumbprint, Plain Stem .................................................... 26.00
Pressed Glass, Goblet, Thumbprint, Purple Hue .................................................... 18.00
Pressed Glass, Goblet, Thumbprint, 3 Rows .................................................... 16.00
Pressed Glass, Goblet, Tidy .................................................... 12.00
Pressed Glass, Goblet, Tidy, Short .................................................... 8.00 To 9.00
Pressed Glass, Goblet, Torpedo .................................................... 30.00
Pressed Glass, Goblet, Tree Of Life, Flint .................................................... 40.00
Pressed Glass, Goblet, Tree Of Life, Green Tinge, Flint .................................................... 20.00
Pressed Glass, Goblet, Tree Of Life, Portland .................................................... 25.00
Pressed Glass, Goblet, Tulip & Sawtooth .................................................... 17.50 To 19.00
Pressed Glass, Goblet, Tulip, Flint .................................................... 32.00
Pressed Glass, Goblet, Two Panel .................................................... 15.00
Pressed Glass, Goblet, Two Panel, Amber .................................................... 15.00 To 32.00
Pressed Glass, Goblet, Two Panel, Apple Green .................................................... 22.50 To 28.00
Pressed Glass, Goblet, Two Panel, Blue .................................................... 17.50
Pressed Glass, Goblet, Two Panel, Canary .................................................... 30.00
Pressed Glass, Goblet, Two Panel, Green .................................................... 29.50 To 31.50

| | |
|---|---|
| Pressed Glass, Goblet, Valencia Waffle | 15.50 |
| Pressed Glass, Goblet, Valencia Waffle, Amber | 28.50 |
| Pressed Glass, Goblet, Valencia Waffle, Round Base | 16.50 |
| Pressed Glass, Goblet, Valencia Waffle, Square Base | 14.50 |
| Pressed Glass, Goblet, Valentine | 25.00 |
| Pressed Glass, Goblet, Vernon Honeycomb | 30.00 |
| Pressed Glass, Goblet, Waffle & Thumbprint | 39.00 |
| Pressed Glass, Goblet, Waffle & Thumbprint, Flint | 42.00 |
| Pressed Glass, Goblet, Wahoo, Flint | 14.00 |
| Pressed Glass, Goblet, Washington Centennial | 25.00 |
| Pressed Glass, Goblet, Way's Currant | 12.00 |
| Pressed Glass, Goblet, Wedding Band | 12.50 |
| Pressed Glass, Goblet, Wedding Ring, Flint | 33.00 |
| Pressed Glass, Goblet, Westward Ho | 50.00 To 75.00 |
| Pressed Glass, Goblet, Wheat & Barley | 16.00 |
| Pressed Glass, Goblet, Wheat & Barley, Amber | 20.00 To 25.00 |
| Pressed Glass, Goblet, Wide Band Baby Thumbprint | 7.50 |
| Pressed Glass, Goblet, Wild Fruits | 13.75 |
| Pressed Glass, Goblet, Wildflower | 16.00 |
| Pressed Glass, Goblet, Wildflower, Amber | 16.00 To 27.50 |
| Pressed Glass, Goblet, Wildflower, Blue | 30.00 To 35.00 |
| Pressed Glass, Goblet, Wildflower, Canary | 28.00 |
| Pressed Glass, Goblet, Willow Oak | 17.00 To 25.00 |
| Pressed Glass, Goblet, Willow Oak, Amber | 28.50 |
| Pressed Glass, Goblet, Windflower | 16.50 To 18.00 |
| Pressed Glass, Goblet, Yellow Frosted Vintage | 8.00 |
| Pressed Glass, Goblet, Yoked Loop | 20.00 |
| Pressed Glass, Goblet, Yoked Loop, Flint | 16.00 To 20.00 |
| Pressed Glass, Goblet, Yuma Loop | 9.75 To 13.00 |
| Pressed Glass, Goblet, Zipper | 11.00 To 12.00 |
| Pressed Glass, Goblet, 101 | 12.50 To 20.00 |
| Pressed Glass, Goblet, 1, 000-Eye | 20.00 |
| Pressed Glass, Goblet, 1, 000-Eye, Amber | 30.00 |
| Pressed Glass, Goblet, 1, 000-Eye, Apple Green | 27.00 To 32.50 |
| Pressed Glass, Goblet, 1, 000-Eye, Ice Blue | 35.00 |
| Pressed Glass, Gum Stand, Teaberry | 12.00 |
| Pressed Glass, Hairpin, Flat, Flint, 4 In. | 6.50 |
| Pressed Glass, Hat, Coin Spot, Opalescent, 5 3/4 X 4 1/4 In. | 32.50 |
| Pressed Glass, Hat, Cube | 7.50 To 10.00 |
| Pressed Glass, Hat, Cube, Blue | 22.00 |
| Pressed Glass, Hat, Daisy & Button, Amber | 10.00 |
| Pressed Glass, Hat, Daisy & Button, Opalescent Rim, 5 1/2 In. | 12.50 |
| Pressed Glass, Hat, Finecut | 10.00 |
| Pressed Glass, Hat, Horizontal Ribs, Green | 18.00 |
| Pressed Glass, Hat, Ribbed | 9.50 |
| Pressed Glass, Hat, Ribbed, Green | 12.50 |
| Pressed Glass, Hat, Top, Intaglio Strawberries, Dark Amber, Near Cut | 13.00 |
| Pressed Glass, Hat, 1, 000-Eye | 28.00 |
| Pressed Glass, Hatchet, Washington, St.Louis, 1904 | 28.00 |
| Pressed Glass, Inkwell, Twisted, Hinged Top | 20.00 |
| Pressed Glass, Jar, Biscuit, Cordova | 27.50 |
| Pressed Glass, Jar, Candy, Vintage, Iridescent Blue, Covered, 2 Mold | 38.00 |
| Pressed Glass, Jar, Candy, Wedding Bells, Rose & Clear, Covered, Footed | 45.00 |
| Pressed Glass, Jar, Cookie, Beveled Diamond With Star | 10.00 |
| Pressed Glass, Jar, Cookie, Finecut, Silver Rim, Lid, & Handle, Nearcut | 45.00 |
| Pressed Glass, Jar, Cracker, Crescent & Fan, Covered | 28.50 To 33.00 |
| Pressed Glass, Jar, Cracker, Diamond & Notched Panel Variant, 8 X 5 In. | 27.50 |
| Pressed Glass, Jar, Cracker, Three In One, Covered | 22.50 |
| Pressed Glass, Jar, Drug, Viking | 35.00 |
| Pressed Glass, Jar, Etched Greek Key, Hinged Silver & Glass Top, Miniature | 15.00 |
| Pressed Glass, Jar, Jam, Canadian, Covered | 30.00 |
| Pressed Glass, Jar, Jam, Cupid & Venus, Covered | 35.00 |
| Pressed Glass, Jar, Jam, Deer & Oak Tree | 24.50 |
| Pressed Glass, Jar, Jam, Finecut Medallion, Covered | 12.50 |
| Pressed Glass, Jar, Jam, Frosted Deer | 95.00 |
| Pressed Glass, Jar, Jam, Frosted Lion | 35.00 |

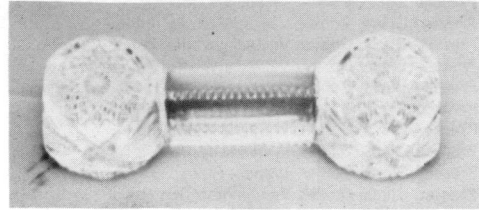

Pressed Glass, Knife Rest, 4 3/4 In.

Pressed Glass, Jar, Marmalade, Jumbo

| | |
|---|---:|
| **Pressed Glass, Jar,** Jam, Grace | 35.00 |
| **Pressed Glass, Jar,** Jam, Horseshoe, Covered | 45.00 |
| **Pressed Glass, Jar,** Jam, King's Crown | 18.75 |
| **Pressed Glass, Jar,** Jam, Marsh, Pink | 20.00 |
| **Pressed Glass, Jar,** Jam, Ribbon | 20.00 |
| **Pressed Glass, Jar,** Jam, Ribbon, 2 Piece | 7.50 |
| **Pressed Glass, Jar,** Marmalade, Cupid & Venus | 45.00 |
| **Pressed Glass, Jar,** Marmalade, Frosted Lion, Covered | 50.00 To 55.00 |
| **Pressed Glass, Jar,** Marmalade, Frosted Lion, Rampant Lion Finial | 85.00 |
| **Pressed Glass, Jar,** Marmalade, Horseshoe | 65.00 |
| **Pressed Glass, Jar,** Marmalade, Jumbo *Illus* | 290.00 |
| **Pressed Glass, Jar,** Marmalade, Little River, Covered | 35.00 |
| **Pressed Glass, Jar,** Marmalade, Westward Ho | 165.00 |
| **Pressed Glass, Jar,** Mustard, Castor, Gothic, Pewter Top, Flint | 15.00 |
| **Pressed Glass, Jar,** Mustard, Elongated Honeycomb, Footed, Flint, 3 X 3 In. | 15.00 |
| **Pressed Glass, Jar,** Mustard, Sawtooth, Silver Plate Cover, 2 1/2 X 3 1/2 In. | 13.00 |
| **Pressed Glass, Jar,** Powder, Cane & Fan, Art Nouveau Silver Plate Lid | 20.00 |
| **Pressed Glass, Jar,** Powder, Duncan & Miller No.42, Sterling Top | 25.00 |
| **Pressed Glass, Jar,** Powder, Honeycomb, Blue, Covered, 2 X 3 In. | 20.00 |
| **Pressed Glass, Jar,** Powder, Three Scotties, Covered | 9.00 |
| **Pressed Glass, Jar,** Relish, Heart With Thumbprint, Handle, Tin Plated Lid | 24.00 |
| **Pressed Glass, Jar,** Sawtooth, Covered, Pumpkin Handle | 12.00 |
| **Pressed Glass, Jar,** Trinket, Paneled, Green, Open Rose Top, Gold Trim | 18.00 |
| **Pressed Glass, Jug,** Spirits, Model Peerless, Stopper, Indiana, 8 1/2 In.High | 29.50 |
| **Pressed Glass, Jug,** Water, Grape, Covered | 30.00 |
| **Pressed Glass, Jug,** Whiskey, King's 500, Key | 75.00 |
| **Pressed Glass, Kettle,** Gypsy, Cane, Amber, Bail | 15.00 |
| **Pressed Glass, Kettle,** Gypsy, Cane, Blue, Bail | 16.00 |
| **Pressed Glass, Knife Rest,** Dumbbell Ends | 11.00 |
| **Pressed Glass, Knife Rest,** 4 3/4 In. *Illus* | 10.00 |
| **Pressed Glass, Lamp Base,** Arched Fan, 9 1/2 In.High | 30.00 |
| **Pressed Glass, Lamp Base,** Flattened Sawtooth, Amber, Brass Top, Pair | 65.00 |
| **Pressed Glass, Lamp Base,** Sweetheart, Findlay, 8 In.High | 45.00 |
| **Pressed Glass, Lamp,** Miniature, Lincoln Drape, Frosted Amber, 6 3/4 In. | 92.00 |
| **Pressed Glass, Lampshade,** Frosted Beaded Rib & Melon Rib, Ball, Opalescent | 45.00 |
| **Pressed Glass, Light,** Christmas, Checkered Sawtooth, Blue | 4.00 |
| **Pressed Glass, Light,** Christmas, Diamond Points, Amber | 12.00 |
| **Pressed Glass, Light,** Christmas, Diamond Points, Blue | 12.00 |
| **Pressed Glass, Light,** Christmas, 1, 000-Eye, Blue | 25.00 |
| **Pressed Glass, Loving Cup,** Reverse Four, 2 Handles, 11 X 4 In. | 85.00 |
| **Pressed Glass, Match Holder,** Daisy & Button, Amber, Half Canoe, 8 1/2 In. | 22.00 |
| **Pressed Glass, Match Holder,** Daisy & Button, Slipper Shape, Hanging | 37.50 |
| **Pressed Glass, Match Holder,** Michigan | 12.00 |
| **Pressed Glass, Match Holder,** Oaken Bucket, Amber, Wire Bail | 7.00 |
| **Pressed Glass, Match Holder,** Oaken Bucket, Blue, Wire Handle | 12.00 |
| **Pressed Glass, Match Holder,** Oaken Bucket, Wire Bail | 6.00 |

| | |
|---|---|
| Pressed Glass, **Match Holder**, Shield Back, Heart Shape, Hanging, 4 In.Long | 20.00 |
| Pressed Glass, **Match Holder**, Three Dolphins, Amber | 36.00 |
| Pressed Glass, **Match Safe**, Mt.Holyoke, Mt.Tom Railroad, Colored Picture | 15.00 |
| Pressed Glass, **Muffineer**, Banded Portland | 18.00 |
| Pressed Glass, **Muffineer**, Block & Fan | 19.50 |
| Pressed Glass, **Muffineer**, Cone | 54.00 |
| Pressed Glass, **Muffineer**, Feather | 50.00 |
| Pressed Glass, **Muffineer**, Flower & Pleat, Brass Top, 5 1/2 In.High | 35.00 |
| Pressed Glass, **Muffineer**, Gargoyle | 68.00 |
| Pressed Glass, **Muffineer**, Hidalgo | 22.00 |
| Pressed Glass, **Muffineer**, Horseshoe, Amber | 39.00 |
| Pressed Glass, **Muffineer**, Leaf Base, Painted Decoration, Pair | 12.50 |
| Pressed Glass, **Muffineer**, Opalescent Crossbar, Beatty Co., 3 1/2 In.High | 45.00 |
| Pressed Glass, **Muffineer**, Phlox, Green | 58.00 |
| Pressed Glass, **Muffineer**, Quilted Phlox, Emerald Green, Transparent | 75.00 |
| Pressed Glass, **Muffineer**, Teepee | 15.00 |
| Pressed Glass, **Mug**, Angel's Head, Wings, & Flowers | 18.00 |
| Pressed Glass, **Mug**, Austrian, Large Size | 18.00 |
| Pressed Glass, **Mug**, Austrian, Small Size | 14.00 |
| Pressed Glass, **Mug**, Baby Thumbprint, Amber, Pale Blue Handle | 15.00 |
| Pressed Glass, **Mug**, Baby Thumbprint, Amber, White Enamel Florals, 1 3/4 In. | 8.00 |
| Pressed Glass, **Mug**, Barred Hobnail, Blue | 13.00 |
| Pressed Glass, **Mug**, Beaded Arch Panels | 9.75 |
| Pressed Glass, **Mug**, Beaded Scroll, 2 In. High | 3.50 |
| Pressed Glass, **Mug**, Beaded Swirl | 8.50 |
| Pressed Glass, **Mug**, Beer, Etched Leaves & Berries | 15.00 |
| Pressed Glass, **Mug**, Bent Buckle | 10.00 |
| Pressed Glass, **Mug**, Bird & Harp | 21.50 |
| Pressed Glass, **Mug**, Bird On Nest | 18.00 |
| Pressed Glass, **Mug**, Birds On Rose Branches | 18.00 |
| Pressed Glass, **Mug**, Bordered Ellipse, Ruby, 3 In.High | 18.00 |
| Pressed Glass, **Mug**, Butterflies, Sapphire Blue, 3 1/4 In. | 22.00 |
| Pressed Glass, **Mug**, Butterfly With Spray | 16.00 |
| Pressed Glass, **Mug**, Cameo, Blue | 13.00 |
| Pressed Glass, **Mug**, Cat & Dog | 28.00 |
| Pressed Glass, **Mug**, Ceres | 22.00 |
| Pressed Glass, **Mug**, Child's, Birds & Owl, Blue, Chandelier Co. | 26.00 |
| Pressed Glass, **Mug**, Child's, Birds On Branches, Green | 25.00 |
| Pressed Glass, **Mug**, Child's, Cut Log | 12.00 |
| Pressed Glass, **Mug**, Child's, Dahlia | 25.00 |
| Pressed Glass, **Mug**, Child's, Deer & Pine Tree, Olive Green, Gilt Trim | 28.00 |
| Pressed Glass, **Mug**, Child's, Deer Feeding | 18.00 |
| Pressed Glass, **Mug**, Child's, Dogs & Chicks, Canary, Petticoat Base, 2 In. | 37.00 |
| Pressed Glass, **Mug**, Child's, Drum, Gold On Eagle | 16.00 |
| Pressed Glass, **Mug**, Child's, English Hobnail | 10.00 |
| Pressed Glass, **Mug**, Child's, Fighting Cats | 12.00 |
| Pressed Glass, **Mug**, Child's, Humpty-Dumpty & Tom The Piper's Son | 19.50 |
| Pressed Glass, **Mug**, Child's, Medallion Sunburst | 6.00 |
| Pressed Glass, **Mug**, Child's, Owl & Bird In Branches, Clear, Teardrop Handle | 25.00 |
| Pressed Glass, **Mug**, Child's, Rabbit | 10.00 |
| Pressed Glass, **Mug**, Child's, Roman Rosette | 12.00 |
| Pressed Glass, **Mug**, Child's, Squirrel | 17.50 |
| Pressed Glass, **Mug**, Child's, Squirrel On Branch | 14.00 |
| Pressed Glass, **Mug**, Child's, Swan | 17.00 |
| Pressed Glass, **Mug**, Child's, Swirl | 10.00 |
| Pressed Glass, **Mug**, Child's, Windmill & Lighthouse | 18.00 |
| Pressed Glass, **Mug**, Child's, Windmill Scene | 19.50 |
| Pressed Glass, **Mug**, Child's, 1, 000-Eye, Hobnail | 10.00 |
| Pressed Glass, **Mug**, Comet, Flint | 50.00 |
| Pressed Glass, **Mug**, Cord Drapery | 18.00 |
| Pressed Glass, **Mug**, Crossed Cords & Prism, Miniature | 10.00 |
| Pressed Glass, **Mug**, Cupid & Venus, 3 1/2 In. High | 15.00 To 18.50 |
| Pressed Glass, **Mug**, Cut Log, 3 1/2 In. | 7.00 To 12.50 |
| Pressed Glass, **Mug**, Dahlia | 21.50 |
| Pressed Glass, **Mug**, Daisy & Button With Crossbar | 12.50 |
| Pressed Glass, **Mug**, Daisy & Button With V Ornament | 12.50 |

| | |
|---|---|
| **Pressed Glass, Mug,** Dewdrop | 15.00 |
| **Pressed Glass, Mug,** Dewey, Green, Greentown | 45.00 |
| **Pressed Glass, Mug,** Dot In Square With Ornament Band | 7.50 |
| **Pressed Glass, Mug,** Drum, Large Size | 15.00 |
| **Pressed Glass, Mug,** Enameled Flowers, Blue, 2 X 3 1/2 In. | 11.00 |
| **Pressed Glass, Mug,** Engraved Saratoga 1890 | 7.00 |
| **Pressed Glass, Mug,** Etched Ball & Swirl, Applied Handle | 10.00 |
| **Pressed Glass, Mug,** Fan With Acanthus Leaf | 7.50 |
| **Pressed Glass, Mug,** Flute, 7 Flutes, Applied Handle, Sheared Top, Flint | 20.00 |
| **Pressed Glass, Mug,** Galloway, "Lansburg Dept. Store, Wash., D.C." | 18.00 |
| **Pressed Glass, Mug,** Garfield Memorial | 42.00 |
| **Pressed Glass, Mug,** Gooseberry, Large Size | 25.00 |
| **Pressed Glass, Mug,** Grape Festoon With Shield | 16.00 |
| **Pressed Glass, Mug,** Hanging Grapes | 12.50 |
| **Pressed Glass, Mug,** Hanover | 15.00 |
| **Pressed Glass, Mug,** Heart Band, Ruby Top, McKee, 3 1/2 In. | 12.50 |
| **Pressed Glass, Mug,** Heron & Peacock, Blue | 20.00 |
| **Pressed Glass, Mug,** Heron & Peacock, Handled | 20.00 |
| **Pressed Glass, Mug,** Hobnail, 3 In. | 3.50 |
| **Pressed Glass, Mug,** Humpty-Dumpty | 23.50 To 32.00 |
| **Pressed Glass, Mug,** Inverted Hobnail Arches, Findlay | 21.50 |
| **Pressed Glass, Mug,** Jeweled Dewdrop, Blue | 22.50 |
| **Pressed Glass, Mug,** Kansas, Canary | 12.00 |
| **Pressed Glass, Mug,** Kansas, Large Size | 28.00 |
| **Pressed Glass, Mug,** Knights Of Labor | 18.00 To 24.00 |
| **Pressed Glass, Mug,** Lacy Medallion, Green, Gold Trim, "Lydia 1909" | 12.00 |
| **Pressed Glass, Mug,** Lacy Medallion, Green, Gold Trim, Dated 1901 | 12.50 |
| **Pressed Glass, Mug,** Lacy Medallion, Green, Gold, 'mother 1914' | 14.50 |
| **Pressed Glass, Mug,** Lacy Medallion, Green, Wykoff, Minn., Gold Trim, 3 1/2 In. | 13.00 |
| **Pressed Glass, Mug,** Liberty Bell, Miniature | 68.00 |
| **Pressed Glass, Mug,** Log & Star, Miniature, Handled, Bellaire Goblet Co. | 12.00 |
| **Pressed Glass, Mug,** Lotus & Serpent | 32.00 |
| **Pressed Glass, Mug,** Martyr's, Lincoln, Garfield | 40.00 |
| **Pressed Glass, Mug,** Massachusetts, Large Size | 18.00 |
| **Pressed Glass, Mug,** Massachusetts, Small Size | 16.00 |
| **Pressed Glass, Mug,** McKinley Campaign | 19.00 |
| **Pressed Glass, Mug,** McKinley, Covered | 40.00 |
| **Pressed Glass, Mug,** Medallion Sunburst, 3 In.High | 8.00 |
| **Pressed Glass, Mug,** Milton, Amber, Findlay, 2 5/8 In.High | 12.50 |
| **Pressed Glass, Mug,** Minnesota | 7.50 |
| **Pressed Glass, Mug,** Minnesota, Gold | 10.50 |
| **Pressed Glass, Mug,** Monkey | 35.00 |
| **Pressed Glass, Mug,** New Hampshire | 7.50 |
| **Pressed Glass, Mug,** Paneled Palm | 8.00 |
| **Pressed Glass, Mug,** Paneled Palm, Gold | 7.50 |
| **Pressed Glass, Mug,** Pavonia | 18.50 |
| **Pressed Glass, Mug,** Pointed Hobnail | 10.00 |
| **Pressed Glass, Mug,** Prism Arc | 7.50 |
| **Pressed Glass, Mug,** Red Block | 20.00 |
| **Pressed Glass, Mug,** Ribbed Forget-Me-Not | 16.50 |
| **Pressed Glass, Mug,** Ribbed Leaves | 10.00 To 16.00 |
| **Pressed Glass, Mug,** Robin, Blue | *Illus* 18.50 |
| **Pressed Glass, Mug,** Rose In Snow, "In Remembrance" | 17.50 |
| **Pressed Glass, Mug,** Rosette | 9.00 |
| **Pressed Glass, Mug,** Sedan | 7.50 |
| **Pressed Glass, Mug,** Sheaf And Diamond | 6.00 |
| **Pressed Glass, Mug,** Singing Birds, Purple | 40.50 |
| **Pressed Glass, Mug,** Stippled Forget-Me-Not | 15.00 |
| **Pressed Glass, Mug,** Tennessee | 17.50 To 22.00 |
| **Pressed Glass, Mug,** Thumbprint, Cobalt, Ground Bottom | 25.00 |
| **Pressed Glass, Mug,** Tree Of Life, Cobalt Blue, Portland, 2 3/4 In. | 38.50 |
| **Pressed Glass, Mug,** Troubadour, Nile Green, Greentown | 22.50 |
| **Pressed Glass, Mug,** Wellsburg, Handle, Findlay | 12.50 |
| **Pressed Glass, Mug,** Whiskey, Cut Argus, Applied Handle, Flint | 60.00 |
| **Pressed Glass, Mug,** William McKinley | 17.00 |
| **Pressed Glass, Mug,** 1, 000-Eye, Amber, 3 1/2 In. High | 13.00 To 16.50 |

Pressed Glass, Pitcher, Actress

Pressed Glass, Mug, Robin, Blue
*(See Page 452)*

| | |
|---|---|
| Pressed Glass, Mug, 1,000-Eye, Blue | 20.00 |
| Pressed Glass, Nappy, Colorado, Triangular, Footed | 8.00 |
| Pressed Glass, Nappy, Heart & Thumbprint, Gold | 13.50 |
| Pressed Glass, Nappy, Heart & Thumbprint, Triangular | 12.00 |
| Pressed Glass, Nappy, Lotus With Fig, Handled, Portland, 6 1/4 In. | 10.00 |
| Pressed Glass, Nappy, Priscilla, Handled | 14.00 |
| Pressed Glass, Nappy, Stippled Ivy, Handled | 13.00 |
| Pressed Glass, Nappy, Tree Of Life, Leaf Shape | 8.75 |
| Pressed Glass, Nappy, Wildflower, 5 3/4 In. | 9.00 |
| Pressed Glass, Nappy, Windflower, Marigold, Tricorner, Handle, 7 X 6 In. | 30.00 |
| Pressed Glass, Perfume, Diamond Point With Panels, Hollow Stopper, Flint | 42.00 |
| Pressed Glass, Perfume, Star & Punty, Flint | 68.00 |
| Pressed Glass, Pickle, Castor, Optic Panel, Blue Corset Shaped Inset | 88.00 |
| Pressed Glass, Pitcher, Actress ................................................. *Illus* | 45.00 |
| Pressed Glass, Pitcher, Admiral Dewey | 37.50 |
| Pressed Glass, Pitcher, Admiral Dewey, Gridley | 67.00 |
| Pressed Glass, Pitcher, Barberry, Oval Berries | 45.00 |
| Pressed Glass, Pitcher, Bell & Fan With Yellow Crossbar, 9 In. | 27.50 |
| Pressed Glass, Pitcher, Bellflower, 8 3/4 In. | 250.00 |
| Pressed Glass, Pitcher, Chain & Shell ................................................. *Illus* | 16.00 |
| Pressed Glass, Pitcher, Cherry & Fig, 7 1/2 In.High | 22.50 |
| Pressed Glass, Pitcher, Columbian Coin, Dollars, 10 In.High | 130.00 |
| Pressed Glass, Pitcher, Crystal, Attached Handle | 25.00 |
| Pressed Glass, Pitcher, Cupid & Venus, 7 1/2 In. | 42.50 |
| Pressed Glass, Pitcher, Daisy & Button With Crossbar | 35.00 |
| Pressed Glass, Pitcher, Daisy & Button, Blue, 4 In. | 35.00 |
| Pressed Glass, Pitcher, Deer & Oak Tree | 60.00 |
| Pressed Glass, Pitcher, Delaware, Rose Color, 9 1/2 In. ................................................. *Illus* | 58.50 |
| Pressed Glass, Pitcher, Diagonal Band With Fan | 25.00 |
| Pressed Glass, Pitcher, Etched Deer & Dog, Applied Ribbed Handle | 65.00 |
| Pressed Glass, Pitcher, Etched Loop | 21.00 |
| Pressed Glass, Pitcher, Etched Pavonia, 9 1/2 In. | 42.00 |
| Pressed Glass, Pitcher, Excelsior, McKee, 7 1/2 In. | 135.00 |
| Pressed Glass, Pitcher, Fishscale, 7 1/2 In.High | 19.00 |
| Pressed Glass, Pitcher, Fishscale, 8 In.High | 18.00 |
| Pressed Glass, Pitcher, Flowerpot, Large Size | 35.00 |
| Pressed Glass, Pitcher, Flying Mallard | 25.00 |
| Pressed Glass, Pitcher, Frosted Double Ribbon | 33.00 |
| Pressed Glass, Pitcher, Gridley | 65.00 |
| Pressed Glass, Pitcher, Inverted Strawberry | 24.00 |
| Pressed Glass, Pitcher, Jacob's Ladder ................................................. 28.00 To 50.00 |  |
| Pressed Glass, Pitcher, Jersey, 7 In.High | 11.00 |
| Pressed Glass, Pitcher, Jeweled Band | 18.00 |
| Pressed Glass, Pitcher, Lemonade, Encircled Pillow, Applied Handle, Findlay | 37.50 |
| Pressed Glass, Pitcher, Lily Of The Valley, Applied Handle, Bulbous | 65.00 |

Pressed Glass, Pitcher, Chain & Shell
*(See Page 453)*

Pressed Glass, Pitcher, Delaware,
Rose Color, 9 1/2 In.
*(See Page 453)*

Pressed Glass, Pitcher, Primrose, 7 In.
*(See Page 455)*

| | |
|---|---:|
| Pressed Glass, Pitcher, Lotus & Serpent | 55.00 |
| Pressed Glass, Pitcher, Medallion, Blue | 40.00 |
| Pressed Glass, Pitcher, Milk, Basket Weave, Blue, 7 In.High | 38.50 |
| Pressed Glass, Pitcher, Milk, Beaded Loop | 18.50 |
| Pressed Glass, Pitcher, Milk, Beaded Tulip | 65.00 |
| Pressed Glass, Pitcher, Milk, Bryce | 35.00 |
| Pressed Glass, Pitcher, Milk, Cameo | 12.50 |
| Pressed Glass, Pitcher, Milk, Canadian | 42.50 To 59.50 |
| Pressed Glass, Pitcher, Milk, Cherry & Fig | 28.00 |
| Pressed Glass, Pitcher, Milk, Classic, Log Feet, 9 In. | 225.00 |
| Pressed Glass, Pitcher, Milk, Cordova | 27.50 |
| Pressed Glass, Pitcher, Milk, Cupid & Venus | 45.00 |
| Pressed Glass, Pitcher, Milk, Currier & Ives | 32.00 |
| Pressed Glass, Pitcher, Milk, Currier & Ives, Bellaire Goblet Co. | 24.00 |
| Pressed Glass, Pitcher, Milk, Currier & Ives, 5 1/2 In.High | 25.00 |
| Pressed Glass, Pitcher, Milk, Dahlia | 17.00 To 29.50 |
| Pressed Glass, Pitcher, Milk, Daisy & Button With Almond Band | 26.50 |
| Pressed Glass, Pitcher, Milk, Daisy & Button With Crossbar | 35.00 |
| Pressed Glass, Pitcher, Milk, Daisy & Button With Crossbar, Amber | 35.00 |
| Pressed Glass, Pitcher, Milk, Deer & Pine Tree | 85.00 |
| Pressed Glass, Pitcher, Milk, Egg In Sand | 19.50 |
| Pressed Glass, Pitcher, Milk, Eyewinker | 58.00 |
| Pressed Glass, Pitcher, Milk, Fishscale, 8 In. High | 17.00 To 25.00 |
| Pressed Glass, Pitcher, Milk, Fleur-De-Lis & Drape, Green | 36.50 |
| Pressed Glass, Pitcher, Milk, Frosted Ribbon, Footed, 6 1/2 In.High | 18.50 |
| Pressed Glass, Pitcher, Milk, Garfield Drape, Applied Handle, Bulbous | 42.50 |
| Pressed Glass, Pitcher, Milk, Hartley | 13.50 |
| Pressed Glass, Pitcher, Milk, Hearts & Fleur-De-Lis, Green, Gold Trim | 12.50 |
| Pressed Glass, Pitcher, Milk, Herringbone, Clear & Emerald Green | 25.00 |
| Pressed Glass, Pitcher, Milk, Hobnail, Ruby & Clear, 3 In.Ruby Top Band | 42.50 |
| Pressed Glass, Pitcher, Milk, Horn Of Plenty, Flint, 8 1/2 In.High | 295.00 |
| Pressed Glass, Pitcher, Milk, Horseshoe | 75.00 |
| Pressed Glass, Pitcher, Milk, Hummingbird, Amber | 35.00 |
| Pressed Glass, Pitcher, Milk, Lattice | 29.50 |
| Pressed Glass, Pitcher, Milk, Long Buttress | 15.00 |
| Pressed Glass, Pitcher, Milk, Loop & Fans | 24.50 |
| Pressed Glass, Pitcher, Milk, Maryland | 23.50 To 25.00 |
| Pressed Glass, Pitcher, Milk, Paneled Forget-Me-Not | 16.50 |
| Pressed Glass, Pitcher, Milk, Paneled Thistle | 38.50 |

| | |
|---|---:|
| Pressed Glass, Pitcher, Milk, Pleat & Panel | 30.00 |
| Pressed Glass, Pitcher, Milk, Primrose | 29.50 |
| Pressed Glass, Pitcher, Milk, Prism Arc | 23.50 |
| Pressed Glass, Pitcher, Milk, Rosette | 26.00 |
| Pressed Glass, Pitcher, Milk, Royal Oak, Frosted To Clear | 30.00 |
| Pressed Glass, Pitcher, Milk, Seneca Loop, Applied Handle | 32.50 |
| Pressed Glass, Pitcher, Milk, Sheraton | 25.00 |
| Pressed Glass, Pitcher, Milk, U.S.Coin, 1/2 Dollars Around Base, 8 1/2 In. | 450.00 |
| Pressed Glass, Pitcher, Milk, Willow Oak | 30.00 |
| Pressed Glass, Pitcher, Milk, Willow Oak, Amber | 45.00 |
| Pressed Glass, Pitcher, Milk, Zipper, Blue | 55.00 |
| Pressed Glass, Pitcher, Milk, 1, 000-Eye | 35.00 |
| Pressed Glass, Pitcher, Paneled, Moss Green, Clear Rigaree Handle, England | 45.00 |
| Pressed Glass, Pitcher, Portland | 8.50 |
| Pressed Glass, Pitcher, Pressed Leaf | 55.00 |
| Pressed Glass, Pitcher, Primrose, 7 In. *Illus* | 22.00 |
| Pressed Glass, Pitcher, Psyche & Cupid | 48.00 |
| Pressed Glass, Pitcher, Red Block, 8 In. | 65.00 |
| Pressed Glass, Pitcher, Reeding Bands | 25.00 |
| Pressed Glass, Pitcher, Rope Band | 18.00 |
| Pressed Glass, Pitcher, Shell & Jewel, 8 1/2 In.High | 18.50 |
| Pressed Glass, Pitcher, Sheraton | 15.00 |
| Pressed Glass, Pitcher, Shimmering Star | 30.00 |
| Pressed Glass, Pitcher, Stippled Forget-Me-Not, 8 1/4 In. | 37.50 |
| Pressed Glass, Pitcher, Sunk Diamond & Lattice | 25.00 |
| Pressed Glass, Pitcher, Thumbprint, Blue, Amber Handle, Bulbous, 5 1/2 In. | 45.00 |
| Pressed Glass, Pitcher, Thumbprint, Ruby Flashed, 8 In. | 52.00 |
| Pressed Glass, Pitcher, Washington Centennial, 8 In. | 57.75 |
| Pressed Glass, Pitcher, Water, Admiral Dewey | 50.00 To 52.00 |
| Pressed Glass, Pitcher, Water, Aegis, Applied Handle, Bulbous | 50.00 |
| Pressed Glass, Pitcher, Water, Alert Deer | 85.00 |
| Pressed Glass, Pitcher, Water, Anthemion | 27.50 |
| Pressed Glass, Pitcher, Water, Aquarium | 75.00 |
| Pressed Glass, Pitcher, Water, Aquarium, 6 Fish In High Relief | 65.00 |
| Pressed Glass, Pitcher, Water, Baltimore Pear | 45.00 |
| Pressed Glass, Pitcher, Water, Banded Icicle | 20.00 |
| Pressed Glass, Pitcher, Water, Barley | 28.50 |
| Pressed Glass, Pitcher, Water, Barred Forget-Me-Not | 28.00 |
| Pressed Glass, Pitcher, Water, Basket Weave, Green | 30.00 |
| Pressed Glass, Pitcher, Water, Beaded Band | 23.00 To 30.00 |
| Pressed Glass, Pitcher, Water, Beaded Tulip | 37.50 To 45.00 |
| Pressed Glass, Pitcher, Water, Bearded Head | 32.50 |
| Pressed Glass, Pitcher, Water, Bellflower, Double Vine, Flint | 250.00 |
| Pressed Glass, Pitcher, Water, Blocked Arches | 35.00 |
| Pressed Glass, Pitcher, Water, Bracket & Swag, Green, Opalescent | 75.00 |
| Pressed Glass, Pitcher, Water, Branched Tree, Findlay | 65.00 |
| Pressed Glass, Pitcher, Water, Buckle | 58.00 |
| Pressed Glass, Pitcher, Water, Buckle, Applied Star Handle | 32.00 |
| Pressed Glass, Pitcher, Water, Bull's-Eye With Fleur-De-Lis, Flint | 350.00 |
| Pressed Glass, Pitcher, Water, Button Arches, Quart | 15.00 |
| Pressed Glass, Pitcher, Water, Cane | 20.00 To 23.00 |
| Pressed Glass, Pitcher, Water, Cane, Amber | 29.50 |
| Pressed Glass, Pitcher, Water, Cane, Blue | 32.50 |
| Pressed Glass, Pitcher, Water, Chain With Shield | 19.50 |
| Pressed Glass, Pitcher, Water, Classic, Collared Base | 165.00 |
| Pressed Glass, Pitcher, Water, Classic, Log Feet, 10 In. | 175.00 |
| Pressed Glass, Pitcher, Water, Clear Ribbon | 28.50 |
| Pressed Glass, Pitcher, Water, Cleat | 145.00 To 150.00 |
| Pressed Glass, Pitcher, Water, Cleat, Flint | 175.00 |
| Pressed Glass, Pitcher, Water, Coin Spot, Green, Urn Shape, 11 In. | 58.00 |
| Pressed Glass, Pitcher, Water, Colorado, Green, Large Size | 95.00 |
| Pressed Glass, Pitcher, Water, Cordova | 20.00 To 23.00 |
| Pressed Glass, Pitcher, Water, Cottage | 27.00 |
| Pressed Glass, Pitcher, Water, Cottage, Hand & Bar Handle, Bellaire | 27.50 |
| Pressed Glass, Pitcher, Water, Cupid & Venus | 30.00 To 80.00 |
| Pressed Glass, Pitcher, Water, Currier & Ives | 27.50 |

Pressed Glass, Pitcher, Water, Dahlia .................................................................. 16.00 To 29.50
Pressed Glass, Pitcher, Water, Daisy & Button With Crossbar ........................... 25.00 To 38.00
Pressed Glass, Pitcher, Water, Daisy & Button With Crossbar, Amber ............................. 30.00
Pressed Glass, Pitcher, Water, Daisy & Button With Finecut Panels ................................ 27.50
Pressed Glass, Pitcher, Water, Daisy & Button With V Ornament ..................................... 25.00
Pressed Glass, Pitcher, Water, Daisy & Button, Amber ................................................... 35.00
Pressed Glass, Pitcher, Water, Daisy & Diamond ........................................................... 28.50
Pressed Glass, Pitcher, Water, Daisy In Oval Panels, Gilt Trim ....................................... 27.50
Pressed Glass, Pitcher, Water, Dakota, Tankard Type, 9 3/4 In.High ............................... 39.00
Pressed Glass, Pitcher, Water, Deer & Dog, Ribbed Handle ........................................... 75.00
Pressed Glass, Pitcher, Water, Dewdrop In Points ......................................................... 29.50
Pressed Glass, Pitcher, Water, Dewey .......................................................... 38.00 To 42.00
Pressed Glass, Pitcher, Water, Diagonal Band, Footed, 9 In. .......................................... 18.00
Pressed Glass, Pitcher, Water, Diamond In Diamond, Applied Handle, Bulbous ................ 28.50
Pressed Glass, Pitcher, Water, Diamond Medallion ........................................................ 29.50
Pressed Glass, Pitcher, Water, Diamond, Blue, 9 In.High ............................................... 35.00
Pressed Glass, Pitcher, Water, Double Arch .................................................................. 35.00
Pressed Glass, Pitcher, Water, Egg In Sand ................................................... 28.00 To 30.00
Pressed Glass, Pitcher, Water, Enigma ......................................................................... 29.50
Pressed Glass, Pitcher, Water, Etched Ball & Swirl ....................................................... 35.00
Pressed Glass, Pitcher, Water, Etched Hidalgo .............................................................. 23.50
Pressed Glass, Pitcher, Water, Etched Nail .................................................................... 37.00
Pressed Glass, Pitcher, Water, Etched Picture Window ................................................... 22.50
Pressed Glass, Pitcher, Water, Etched Regal Block ....................................................... 20.00
Pressed Glass, Pitcher, Water, Fashion ......................................................................... 45.00
Pressed Glass, Pitcher, Water, Feather .......................................................... 19.00 To 30.00
Pressed Glass, Pitcher, Water, Feather Duster, Green .................................................... 28.00
Pressed Glass, Pitcher, Water, Festoon ......................................................................... 29.50
Pressed Glass, Pitcher, Water, Finecut & Block, Amber ................................................ 150.00
Pressed Glass, Pitcher, Water, Finecut & Rib ................................................................ 28.00
Pressed Glass, Pitcher, Water, Finecut, Blue ................................................................. 45.00
Pressed Glass, Pitcher, Water, Fleur-De-Lis & Drape, Green .......................................... 45.00
Pressed Glass, Pitcher, Water, Flora, Green, Gold Decoration, 1890s ............................. 78.00
Pressed Glass, Pitcher, Water, Flower & Pleat ............................................................... 65.00
Pressed Glass, Pitcher, Water, Fluted Scrolls With Flower Band, Blue ............................ 49.50
Pressed Glass, Pitcher, Water, Fluted Scrolls, Blue Opalescent ...................................... 95.00
Pressed Glass, Pitcher, Water, Frosted Dolphin, 10 In.High ........................................... 95.00
Pressed Glass, Pitcher, Water, Frosted Double Ribbon ................................................... 40.00
Pressed Glass, Pitcher, Water, Frosted Lion, Small Size, 8 1/2 In. ................................ 170.00
Pressed Glass, Pitcher, Water, Frosted Ribbon .............................................................. 65.00
Pressed Glass, Pitcher, Water, Galloway ........................................................ 18.00 To 22.00
Pressed Glass, Pitcher, Water, Garfield Drape ................................................. 42.50 To 48.00
Pressed Glass, Pitcher, Water, Garfield Drape, Applied Handle ......................... 39.00 To 45.00
Pressed Glass, Pitcher, Water, Good Luck ..................................................................... 48.00
Pressed Glass, Pitcher, Water, Grand ........................................................................... 29.50
Pressed Glass, Pitcher, Water, Grasshopper, Without Insect ............................. 28.50 To 32.00
Pressed Glass, Pitcher, Water, Gridley ............................................................ 65.00 To 75.00
Pressed Glass, Pitcher, Water, Hanging Basket ............................................................. 60.00
Pressed Glass, Pitcher, Water, Heron ........................................................................... 55.00
Pressed Glass, Pitcher, Water, Holly Band ...................................................... 50.00 To 55.00
Pressed Glass, Pitcher, Water, Honeycomb ................................................................... 62.50
Pressed Glass, Pitcher, Water, Honeycomb, Applied Handle, Etched Grapes ................... 42.50
Pressed Glass, Pitcher, Water, Honeycomb, McKearin No.206-7 ..................................... 65.00
Pressed Glass, Pitcher, Water, Horn Of Plenty ............................................................. 220.00
Pressed Glass, Pitcher, Water, Horseshoe ....................................................... 45.00 To 62.50
Pressed Glass, Pitcher, Water, Huckle, Green ............................................................... 42.50
Pressed Glass, Pitcher, Water, Hummingbird, Dark Amber .............................................. 42.00
Pressed Glass, Pitcher, Water, Inverted Thumbprint, Applied Clear Handle ...................... 50.00
Pressed Glass, Pitcher, Water, Inverted Thumbprint, Blue, Bulbous ................................. 85.00
Pressed Glass, Pitcher, Water, Iris, Blue, Opalescent ..................................................... 80.00
Pressed Glass, Pitcher, Water, Ivy In Snow, Gold Trim ................................................... 35.00
Pressed Glass, Pitcher, Water, Jacob's Ladder, 11 In.High .............................................. 18.00
Pressed Glass, Pitcher, Water, Jewel & Dewdrop ............................................. 16.00 To 25.00
Pressed Glass, Pitcher, Water, Jeweled Heart, Green ....................................... 24.00 To 27.00
Pressed Glass, Pitcher, Water, Jeweled Moon & Star ..................................................... 37.50
Pressed Glass, Pitcher, Water, Jubilee .......................................................................... 18.00

| | |
|---|---|
| Pressed Glass, Pitcher, Water, Knife & Fork | 7.00 |
| Pressed Glass, Pitcher, Water, La Verne, Applied Handle, Bulbous | 25.00 |
| Pressed Glass, Pitcher, Water, Lattice | 15.00 To 35.00 |
| Pressed Glass, Pitcher, Water, Laverne | 35.00 |
| Pressed Glass, Pitcher, Water, Lion | 25.00 |
| Pressed Glass, Pitcher, Water, Loop, Applied Handle | 55.00 |
| Pressed Glass, Pitcher, Water, Lotus With Serpent | 85.00 |
| Pressed Glass, Pitcher, Water, Marsh, Pink | 24.00 To 27.00 |
| Pressed Glass, Pitcher, Water, Maryland | 22.50 To 32.50 |
| Pressed Glass, Pitcher, Water, Maypole, Silver Sheen | 22.50 |
| Pressed Glass, Pitcher, Water, Medallion, Blue | 45.00 |
| Pressed Glass, Pitcher, Water, Michigan | 25.00 To 29.00 |
| Pressed Glass, Pitcher, Water, Nailhead | 16.50 |
| Pressed Glass, Pitcher, Water, Nailhead, 2 In.Band At Top, Rayed Base | 27.50 |
| Pressed Glass, Pitcher, Water, New Jersey, Gold Trim | 32.00 |
| Pressed Glass, Pitcher, Water, Palmette | 55.00 |
| Pressed Glass, Pitcher, Water, Palmette, Applied Handle | 42.00 To 49.50 |
| Pressed Glass, Pitcher, Water, Panel, Rib, & Shell | 50.00 |
| Pressed Glass, Pitcher, Water, Paneled Herringbone, Emerald Green, 9 1/2 In. | 55.00 |
| Pressed Glass, Pitcher, Water, Paneled Primula | 14.00 |
| Pressed Glass, Pitcher, Water, Paneled Thistle | 50.00 |
| Pressed Glass, Pitcher, Water, Paneled Wee Blossoms | 20.00 |
| Pressed Glass, Pitcher, Water, Panelled Forget-Me-Not | 35.00 |
| Pressed Glass, Pitcher, Water, Pavonia | 20.00 |
| Pressed Glass, Pitcher, Water, Pea Pods | 34.50 |
| Pressed Glass, Pitcher, Water, Picket | 32.00 To 47.50 |
| Pressed Glass, Pitcher, Water, Pleat & Panel | 35.00 To 37.50 |
| Pressed Glass, Pitcher, Water, Pressed Leaf | 47.50 |
| Pressed Glass, Pitcher, Water, Pressed Leaf, Applied Handle, Bulbous, Flint | 50.00 |
| Pressed Glass, Pitcher, Water, Primrose | 22.00 To 35.00 |
| Pressed Glass, Pitcher, Water, Prince Albert | 35.00 |
| Pressed Glass, Pitcher, Water, Princess Feather, Bulbous | 47.00 |
| Pressed Glass, Pitcher, Water, Queen | 38.50 |
| Pressed Glass, Pitcher, Water, Ramsey Grape | 25.00 |
| Pressed Glass, Pitcher, Water, Red Block | 55.00 |
| Pressed Glass, Pitcher, Water, Ribbed Palm, Applied Handle | 50.00 |
| Pressed Glass, Pitcher, Water, Ribbed Swirl, Blue, 9 In. | 48.00 |
| Pressed Glass, Pitcher, Water, Rose In Snow | 45.00 |
| Pressed Glass, Pitcher, Water, Rose Sprig | 23.00 To 39.50 |
| Pressed Glass, Pitcher, Water, Rosette, 9 1/4 In.High | 18.50 |
| Pressed Glass, Pitcher, Water, S Repeat, Blue, Gold Trim | 65.00 |
| Pressed Glass, Pitcher, Water, Sedan | 16.50 |
| Pressed Glass, Pitcher, Water Shell & Jewel | 16.00 To 25.00 |
| Pressed Glass, Pitcher, Water, Shell & Jewel, 8 In.High | 15.00 |
| Pressed Glass, Pitcher, Water, Shell & Jewel, 8 1/2 In.High | 29.50 |
| Pressed Glass, Pitcher, Water, Shimmering Star | 25.00 |
| Pressed Glass, Pitcher, Water, Shrine | 22.00 To 38.00 |
| Pressed Glass, Pitcher, Water, Single Rose, 10 In.High | 35.00 |
| Pressed Glass, Pitcher, Water, Six Panel Finecut, Findlay | 17.00 |
| Pressed Glass, Pitcher, Water, Snakeskin & Dot | 22.50 |
| Pressed Glass, Pitcher, Water, Sprig | 32.50 |
| Pressed Glass, Pitcher, Water, Squirrel | 95.00 |
| Pressed Glass, Pitcher, Water, Squirrel, Greentown | 75.00 To 95.00 |
| Pressed Glass, Pitcher, Water, Star Whorl | 17.50 |
| Pressed Glass, Pitcher, Water, Stars | 16.00 |
| Pressed Glass, Pitcher, Water, States | 38.00 |
| Pressed Glass, Pitcher, Water, Stippled Cherry | 25.00 |
| Pressed Glass, Pitcher, Water, Stippled Grape & Festoon | 55.00 To 56.00 |
| Pressed Glass, Pitcher, Water, Stippled Grape & Festoon With Clear Leaf | 45.00 |
| Pressed Glass, Pitcher, Water, Stippled Shell & Jewel | 25.00 |
| Pressed Glass, Pitcher, Water, Strawberry, Applied Handle | 30.00 |
| Pressed Glass, Pitcher, Water, Sunk Diamond & Lattice | 18.50 |
| Pressed Glass, Pitcher, Water, Swan | 43.00 To 65.00 |
| Pressed Glass, Pitcher, Water, Swirled Star | 18.00 |
| Pressed Glass, Pitcher, Water, Teardrop & Tassel, Blue | 95.00 |
| Pressed Glass, Pitcher, Water, Tidy, Applied Handle | 25.00 |

| | |
|---|---|
| Pressed Glass, Pitcher, Water, Two Panel | 40.00 |
| Pressed Glass, Pitcher, Water, Two Panel, Amber | 35.00 To 47.50 |
| Pressed Glass, Pitcher, Water, Two Panel, Blue, 9 In.High | 52.50 |
| Pressed Glass, Pitcher, Water, Utah | 19.00 |
| Pressed Glass, Pitcher, Water, Viking | 65.00 |
| Pressed Glass, Pitcher, Water, Wedding Bells, Gold Bulb Base, Applied Handle | 37.50 |
| Pressed Glass, Pitcher, Water, Westward Ho | 135.00 To 145.00 |
| Pressed Glass, Pitcher, Water, Wheat, Footed | 32.00 |
| Pressed Glass, Pitcher, Water, Wildflower | 18.00 |
| Pressed Glass, Pitcher, Water, Wildflower, Blue | 65.00 |
| Pressed Glass, Pitcher, Water, Willow Oak | 39.50 |
| Pressed Glass, Pitcher, Water, Wilson's Block | 11.50 |
| Pressed Glass, Pitcher, Water, Wyoming | 29.00 |
| Pressed Glass, Pitcher, Wedding Ring | 22.50 |
| Pressed Glass, Pitcher, Wildflower | 24.00 |
| Pressed Glass, Pitcher, Willow Oak, Quart | 25.00 |
| Pressed Glass, Pitcher, Willow Oak, 8 In.High | 25.00 |
| Pressed Glass, Pitcher, Wyoming | 29.50 |
| Pressed Glass, Plate, "Presents For Good Children, " 6 1/4 In. | 17.50 |
| Pressed Glass, Plate, Admiral Dewey | 22.00 |
| Pressed Glass, Plate, Admiral Dewey, Blue, 10 In. | 40.00 |
| Pressed Glass, Plate, Admiral George Dewey, 6 In. | 20.00 |
| Pressed Glass, Plate, Anthemion, 10 In. | 18.00 |
| Pressed Glass, Plate, Anthemion, 10 1/4 In. | 19.50 |
| Pressed Glass, Plate, Arched Fleur-De-Lis, 10 In. | 10.00 |
| Pressed Glass, Plate, Arched Leaf, 7 In. | 22.50 |
| Pressed Glass, Plate, Arched Leaf, 10 In. | 15.00 |
| Pressed Glass, Plate, Baltimore Pear, 9 In. | 20.00 |
| Pressed Glass, Plate, Barberry, Oval Berry, 6 In. | 8.25 |
| Pressed Glass, Plate, Barred Forget-Me-Not, Amber, 2 Handled, 9 In. | 20.00 |
| Pressed Glass, Plate, Beaded Chain, 6 1/4 In. | 8.50 |
| Pressed Glass, Plate, Beaded Dewdrop, Green, Advertising | 35.00 |
| Pressed Glass, Plate, Beaded Grape, 8 In.Square | 20.00 |
| Pressed Glass, Plate, Beaded Swirl Loop, 10 1/4 In. | 12.50 |
| Pressed Glass, Plate, Beautiful Lady, Square, 7 1/4 In. | 10.50 |
| Pressed Glass, Plate, Beautiful Lady, 11 In. | 10.00 |
| Pressed Glass, Plate, Bigler, 6 In. | 15.00 |
| Pressed Glass, Plate, Blackberry, 3 Compartments, 8 1/2 In. | 5.00 |
| Pressed Glass, Plate, Block & Fan, 6 1/4 In. | 20.00 |
| Pressed Glass, Plate, Block & Fan, 10 In. | 28.50 |
| Pressed Glass, Plate, Bread, Actress | 47.50 To 75.00 |
| Pressed Glass, Plate, Bread, Actress, "Give Us This Day-" | 60.00 |
| Pressed Glass, Plate, Bread, Actress, Pinafore | 46.00 |
| Pressed Glass, Plate, Bread, Admiral George Dewey | 20.00 |
| Pressed Glass, Plate, Bread, American Eagle, 8 1/2 In. | 22.00 |
| Pressed Glass, Plate, Bread, Arched Leaf | 12.00 |
| Pressed Glass, Plate, Bread, Barley | 18.50 |
| Pressed Glass, Plate, Bread, Barred Forget-Me-Not | 21.00 |
| Pressed Glass, Plate, Bread, Barry, Frosted Center | 68.00 |
| Pressed Glass, Plate, Bread, Basket Weave, Round, 8 1/2 In. | 14.00 |
| Pressed Glass, Plate, Bread, Be Industrious, Frosted 101 Border, Ohio City | 45.00 |
| Pressed Glass, Plate, Bread, Beaded Grape | 30.00 |
| Pressed Glass, Plate, Bread, Beaded Loop | 18.00 |
| Pressed Glass, Plate, Bread, Beaded Ovals | 11.00 |
| Pressed Glass, Plate, Bread, Beehive, 'Be Industrious, ' Egg & Dart Border | 60.00 |
| Pressed Glass, Plate, Bread, Bible | 34.00 To 35.00 |
| Pressed Glass, Plate, Bread, Birds | 25.00 |
| Pressed Glass, Plate, Bread, Blue Wildflower | 40.00 |
| Pressed Glass, Plate, Bread, Butterfly & Fan | 21.00 |
| Pressed Glass, Plate, Bread, Centennial, Dated 1875, 13 In. | 125.00 |
| Pressed Glass, Plate, Bread, Centennial, Eagle | 45.00 |
| Pressed Glass, Plate, Bread, Chain & Shield | 15.00 To 35.00 |
| Pressed Glass, Plate, Bread, Chain, Amber | 20.00 |
| Pressed Glass, Plate, Bread, Columbus | 30.00 |
| Pressed Glass, Plate, Bread, Constitution | 40.00 |
| Pressed Glass, Plate, Bread, Constitution, Eagle Center | 49.00 To 50.00 |

Pressed Glass, Plate, Bread, Continental Hall ............................................................ 48.00 To 59.00
Pressed Glass, Plate, Bread, Cupid & Venus ................................................................ 19.00 To 37.00
Pressed Glass, Plate, Bread, Cupid & Venus, Round ..................................................... 25.00
Pressed Glass, Plate, Bread, Cupid's Hunt .................................................................. 25.00 To 48.00
Pressed Glass, Plate, Bread, Currier & Ives, Frosted Center, Rural Scene ..................... 100.00
Pressed Glass, Plate, Bread, Daisy & Button With Crossbar ......................................... 12.00
Pressed Glass, Plate, Bread, Daisy & Button With Diamond Point ................................ 38.00
Pressed Glass, Plate, Bread, Daisy & Button, Amber, 10 In. ........................................ 22.00 To 38.00
Pressed Glass, Plate, Bread, Daisy & Button, Deep Blue, Open Handles ....................... 55.00
Pressed Glass, Plate, Bread, Daisy, Amber ................................................................ 45.00
Pressed Glass, Plate, Bread, Daisy, Amber, 'Give Us This Day, ' 9 1/2 In. ................... 19.50
Pressed Glass, Plate, Bread, Deer & Pine Tree ........................................................... 32.50
Pressed Glass, Plate, Bread, Deer & Pine Tree, Apple Green ....................................... 42.50
Pressed Glass, Plate, Bread, Deer & Pine Tree, 8 X 13 In. ......................................... 20.00 To 27.50
Pressed Glass, Plate, Bread, Dewdrop & Points, Vine Border ...................................... 16.50
Pressed Glass, Plate, Bread, Dewdrop With Sheaf Of Wheat ....................................... 22.00 To 45.00
Pressed Glass, Plate, Bread, Dewdrop With Star ......................................................... 48.00
Pressed Glass, Plate, Bread, Diamond Grill ................................................................ 40.00
Pressed Glass, Plate, Bread, Diana, Cupids In Each Corner, Chased, Oblong ................ 16.50
Pressed Glass, Plate, Bread, Dog Chasing Rabbit Pulling Children In Cart ..................... 45.00
Pressed Glass, Plate, Bread, Doric, 10 In ................................................................... 22.00
Pressed Glass, Plate, Bread, Egg In Sand .................................................................. 12.00 To 15.00
Pressed Glass, Plate, Bread, Egyptian ....................................................................... 42.50
Pressed Glass, Plate, Bread, Egyptian, Cleopatra Center ............................................ 35.00
Pressed Glass, Plate, Bread, Egyptian, Seated Figure ................................................. 38.00
Pressed Glass, Plate, Bread, Egyptian, 10 In., Handled .............................................. 19.00
Pressed Glass, Plate, Bread, Elaine ........................................................................... 50.00
Pressed Glass, Plate, Bread, Elaine, Frosted, 101 Border ........................................... 40.00
Pressed Glass, Plate, Bread, Eureka .......................................................................... 22.00 To 35.00
Pressed Glass, Plate, Bread, Faith, Hope, & Charity ................................................... 39.00 To 49.00
Pressed Glass, Plate, Bread, Finecut With Panels ....................................................... 15.00
Pressed Glass, Plate, Bread, Finecut, Amber ............................................................. 25.00
Pressed Glass, Plate, Bread, Fitzhugh Lee ................................................................. 20.00
Pressed Glass, Plate, Bread, Flowerpot ..................................................................... 38.00
Pressed Glass, Plate, Bread, Four Petal ..................................................................... 15.00
Pressed Glass, Plate, Bread, Frosted Double Ribbon .................................................. 19.00
Pressed Glass, Plate, Bread, Frosted Elaine, 101 Border, Ohio City ............................. 35.00
Pressed Glass, Plate, Bread, Frosted Garfield, 6 In. ................................................... 14.00
Pressed Glass, Plate, Bread, Frosted Lion .................................................................. 28.00 To 60.00
Pressed Glass, Plate, Bread, Frosted Lion, Lion Handles, Oval .................................... 65.00
Pressed Glass, Plate, Bread, Frosted Lion, Oblong ..................................................... 45.00
Pressed Glass, Plate, Bread, Frosted Lion, Tree Of Life Border, Round ........................ 65.00
Pressed Glass, Plate, Bread, Frosted Stork ................................................................ 45.00 To 60.00
Pressed Glass, Plate, Bread, Frosted Teddy Roosevelt ............................................... 60.00 To 75.00
Pressed Glass, Plate, Bread, Garden Of Eden ............................................................ 19.00 To 24.00
Pressed Glass, Plate, Bread, Garfield Drape ............................................................... 36.00
Pressed Glass, Plate, Bread, Garfield Memorial .......................................................... 22.00 To 32.00
Pressed Glass, Plate, Bread, Garfield Star ................................................................. 20.00 To 25.00
Pressed Glass, Plate, Bread, Gladstone For The Millions ............................................ 18.00
Pressed Glass, Plate, Bread, Glascow Exhibition ........................................................ 35.00
Pressed Glass, Plate, Bread, Golden Rule .................................................................. 32.50
Pressed Glass, Plate, Bread, Grant's Peace, "Let Us Have Peace" ............................... 34.00 To 38.00
Pressed Glass, Plate, Bread, Grape ........................................................................... 22.50
Pressed Glass, Plate, Bread, Grape, "It Is Pleasant To Labor" ..................................... 20.00 To 35.00
Pressed Glass, Plate, Bread, Grape Vintage ............................................................... 27.50
Pressed Glass, Plate, Bread, Halley's Comet, Rectangular .......................................... 18.00
Pressed Glass, Plate, Bread, Hand, Oval ................................................................... 12.50
Pressed Glass, Plate, Bread, Harrison & Morton ........................................................ 175.00 To 225.00
Pressed Glass, Plate, Bread, Herringbone, Emerald Green .......................................... 35.00
Pressed Glass, Plate, Bread, Horseshoe .................................................................... 19.00 To 45.00
Pressed Glass, Plate, Bread, Horseshoe, Double Handled ........................................... 38.00
Pressed Glass, Plate, Bread, Huckle .......................................................................... 23.50
Pressed Glass, Plate, Bread, Independence Hall ......................................................... 75.00 To 90.00
Pressed Glass, Plate, Bread, Jefferson Davis .............................................................. 30.00
Pressed Glass, Plate, Bread, John Mitchell ................................................................. 125.00
Pressed Glass, Plate, Bread, Lady & The Lions ........................................................... 45.00 To 49.00

Pressed Glass, Plate, Bread, Last Supper, Yellow To Red ............................................... 10.80
Pressed Glass, Plate, Bread, Liberty Bell, Signers ........................................................ 60.00
Pressed Glass, Plate, Bread, Liberty Bell, 13 States Border ...................................... 75.00
Pressed Glass, Plate, Bread, Little Red Riding Hood, Egg & Dart Border, Iowa ............... 50.00
Pressed Glass, Plate, Bread, Maltese Cross In Circles ............................................. 18.00
Pressed Glass, Plate, Bread, Maryland .......................................................................... 12.50
Pressed Glass, Plate, Bread, McKinley Memorial .................................... 22.00 To 45.00
Pressed Glass, Plate, Bread, McKinley Memorial, Laurel Border ............................... 22.50
Pressed Glass, Plate, Bread, Medallion, Open Rim .................................................... 15.00
Pressed Glass, Plate, Bread, Minerva ...................................................... 55.00 To 60.00
Pressed Glass, Plate, Bread, Minerva, Round, 10 In. ................................................... 45.00
Pressed Glass, Plate, Bread, Mitered Diamond, Amber, 8 X 11 In. .............................. 30.00
Pressed Glass, Plate, Bread, Nailhead, 9 In. ............................................................... 12.00
Pressed Glass, Plate, Bread, Old Statehouse, Large Size .......................................... 59.00
Pressed Glass, Plate, Bread, Paneled Dewdrop, Motto ............................................... 22.00
Pressed Glass, Plate, Bread, Paneled Forget-Me-Not .................................................. 21.50
Pressed Glass, Plate, Bread, Paneled Forget-Me-Not, Oblong ..................................... 23.00
Pressed Glass, Plate, Bread, Paneled Oak, 11 In. ........................................................ 10.00
Pressed Glass, Plate, Bread, Pinafore ......................................................................... 55.00
Pressed Glass, Plate, Bread, Pine Tree, Blue ............................................................. 32.00
Pressed Glass, Plate, Bread, Pleat & Panel ............................................... 18.00 To 32.00
Pressed Glass, Plate, Bread, Pope Leo XIII ............................................. 18.00 To 30.00
Pressed Glass, Plate, Bread, Portland .......................................................................... 34.50
Pressed Glass, Plate, Bread, Queen Victoria, Rose Thistle Border .............................. 40.00
Pressed Glass, Plate, Bread, Queen's Jubilee, Amber .................................................. 45.00
Pressed Glass, Plate, Bread, Railroad Train ............................................. 70.00 To 75.00
Pressed Glass, Plate, Bread, Reticulated Cord, Amber ............................................... 45.00
Pressed Glass, Plate, Bread, Reticulated Cord, Round, 9 1/2 In. ................................ 28.00
Pressed Glass, Plate, Bread, Rock Of Ages .................................................................. 50.00
Pressed Glass, Plate, Bread, Rock Of Ages, Blue Center, Handled, Atterbury ............... 175.00
Pressed Glass, Plate, Bread, Rock Of Ages, Dated ..................................................... 55.00
Pressed Glass, Plate, Bread, Rock Of Ages, Milk Glass Center .................................... 95.00
Pressed Glass, Plate, Bread, Rock Of Ages, Opaque White Inlay Center ..................... 125.00
Pressed Glass, Plate, Bread, Roman Rosette ............................................................... 19.00
Pressed Glass, Plate, Bread, Rosette & Sunflower, Round, 9 In. ................................... 25.00
Pressed Glass, Plate, Bread, Rosette, Round, 9 In. ...................................................... 25.00
Pressed Glass, Plate, Bread, Sawtooth & Star, 10 In. ................................................... 20.00
Pressed Glass, Plate, Bread, Saxon .......................................................... 8.00 To 12.50
Pressed Glass, Plate, Bread, Scroll With Flowers ..................................... 11.00 To 14.00
Pressed Glass, Plate, Bread, Sedan ............................................................................. 28.00
Pressed Glass, Plate, Bread, Sequoia, Blue ................................................................. 45.00
Pressed Glass, Plate, Bread, Sheaf Of Wheat .......................................... 10.00 To 16.00
Pressed Glass, Plate, Bread, Sheaf Of Wheat, Rolled Edge ...................... 16.00 To 38.00
Pressed Glass, Plate, Bread, Sheaf Of Wheat, 12 In. .................................................. 27.50
Pressed Glass, Plate, Bread, Shell & Tassel ............................................................... 25.00
Pressed Glass, Plate, Bread, Shell & Tassel, Oval ...................................................... 35.00
Pressed Glass, Plate, Bread, Shell & Tassel, Square ................................. 35.00 To 40.00
Pressed Glass, Plate, Bread, Sheridan .......................................................................... 45.00
Pressed Glass, Plate, Bread, Spirea ............................................................................. 12.00
Pressed Glass, Plate, Bread, St.Louis World's Fair, 1904 .......................................... 18.00
Pressed Glass, Plate, Bread, Star Rosette, "Good Mother" .......................................... 40.00
Pressed Glass, Plate, Bread, Stippled Cherry, Our Daily Bread, 9 1/4 In. ..................... 14.50
Pressed Glass, Plate, Bread, Texas Centennial, Oval, Flags, Dates 1836-1936 ............. 47.50
Pressed Glass, Plate, Bread, Three Graces .................................................................. 45.00
Pressed Glass, Plate, Bread, Three Presidents .......................................... 50.00 To 58.00
Pressed Glass, Plate, Bread, Three Presidents, Frosted .............................................. 45.00
Pressed Glass, Plate, Bread, Three Presidents, Oblong ............................................... 47.50
Pressed Glass, Plate, Bread, U.S.Coin ......................................................................... 175.00
Pressed Glass, Plate, Bread, U.S.Grant, Square ........................................ 29.50 To 45.00
Pressed Glass, Plate, Bread, Virginia Dare ............................................... 25.00 To 30.00
Pressed Glass, Plate, Bread, Westward Ho, Frosted Deer Handles, Oval ..................... 95.00
Pressed Glass, Plate, Bread, Wildflower, Amber ........................................................... 38.00
Pressed Glass, Plate, Bread, Willow Oak, Amber .......................................................... 38.00
Pressed Glass, Plate, Bread, Wisconsin ....................................................................... 22.00
Pressed Glass, Plate, Cake, Arched Leaf, Handled ...................................................... 15.00
Pressed Glass, Plate, Cake, Canadian, Handled .......................................................... 45.00

| | |
|---|---|
| Pressed Glass, Plate, Cake, Chain, Handled | 35.00 |
| Pressed Glass, Plate, Cake, Dahlia, Closed Handles, 9 In. | 20.00 |
| Pressed Glass, Plate, Cake, Fishscale, 11 1/2 In. | 25.00 |
| Pressed Glass, Plate, Cake, Grand, Standard, 8 1/2 In. | 9.00 |
| Pressed Glass, Plate, Cake, New Jersey, Gold Trim, 12 In. | 18.00 |
| Pressed Glass, Plate, Cake, Paneled Thistle, 10 In. | 22.50 |
| Pressed Glass, Plate, Cake, Pineapple & Fan, 12 In. | 23.00 |
| Pressed Glass, Plate, Cake, Pleat & Panel, Standard, 8 In. | 16.50 |
| Pressed Glass, Plate, Cake, Primrose, Handled | 18.00 |
| Pressed Glass, Plate, Cake, Rose In Snow, Handled | 30.00 |
| Pressed Glass, Plate, Cake, Rose In Snow, 10 In. | 17.50 |
| Pressed Glass, Plate, Cake, Sawtooth, Knob Stem | 32.50 |
| Pressed Glass, Plate, Cake, U.S.Coin, 1892 | 435.00 |
| Pressed Glass, Plate, Cake, Wildflower, 10 In. | 12.00 |
| Pressed Glass, Plate, Cake, Willow Oak, Amber | 25.00 |
| Pressed Glass, Plate, Cake, Willow Oak, Blue, Handled | 32.00 |
| Pressed Glass, Plate, Candlewick, Handled, 7 1/2 In. | 11.00 |
| Pressed Glass, Plate, Candlewick, 6 3/4 In. | 8.75 |
| Pressed Glass, Plate, Cape Cod, Handled, 10 In. | 37.50 |
| Pressed Glass, Plate, Cavitt, 6 In. | 4.75 |
| Pressed Glass, Plate, Chain & Star, 7 3/8 In. | 12.50 |
| Pressed Glass, Plate, Chain, 7 1/4 In. | 10.00 |
| Pressed Glass, Plate, Child's, Duncan & Miller No.30, 3 5/8 In. | 4.00 |
| Pressed Glass, Plate, Chop, Feather | 25.00 |
| Pressed Glass, Plate, Chop, Priscilla | 25.00 |
| Pressed Glass, Plate, Classic Warrior, 11 1/2 In. | 90.00 |
| Pressed Glass, Plate, Cord & Drapery, Footed, 9 1/2 In. | 14.50 |
| Pressed Glass, Plate, Cottage, Amber, 9 In. | 22.50 |
| Pressed Glass, Plate, Cupid & Venus, 10 1/2 In. | 29.50 |
| Pressed Glass, Plate, Currier & Ives, Boy, Dog, & Rabbit Center, 10 In. | 28.00 |
| Pressed Glass, Plate, Currier & Ives, Dog & Rabbit, 10 In. | 22.00 |
| Pressed Glass, Plate, Curtain, 7 In. | 10.00 |
| Pressed Glass, Plate, Cut Diamond & Leaf, 7 3/8 In. | 18.00 |
| Pressed Glass, Plate, Cut Diamond & Leaf, 9 1/8 In. | 24.00 |
| Pressed Glass, Plate, Cut Flowers With 1, 000-Eye, Square, 10 In | 16.50 |
| Pressed Glass, Plate, Dahlia, Handled, 10 1/2 In. | 12.50 |
| Pressed Glass, Plate, Daisy & Button, Amber, 7 In. | 24.00 |
| Pressed Glass, Plate, Daisy & Button, Blue, Round, 7 In. | 25.00 |
| Pressed Glass, Plate, Daisy & Button, Blue, Square, 7 1/8 In. | 24.00 |
| Pressed Glass, Plate, Daisy & Button, Blue, 6 3/4 In. | 15.00 |
| Pressed Glass, Plate, Daisy & Button, Fan Shape, 10 In. | 8.00 |
| Pressed Glass, Plate, Dewdrop & Star, 11 In. | 18.75 |
| Pressed Glass, Plate, Dewdrop In Points, Handled, Vine Border, 11 1/4 In. | 12.50 |
| Pressed Glass, Plate, Dewdrop With Star, 6 In. | 8.50 |
| Pressed Glass, Plate, Dewdrop With Star, 7 1/4 In. | 7.50 To 9.50 |
| Pressed Glass, Plate, Dewdrop With Star, 8 1/4 In. | 12.50 |
| Pressed Glass, Plate, Dewey, 101 Border, 5 1/2 In. | 18.50 |
| Pressed Glass, Plate, Diagonal Band & Fan, 6 In. | 5.00 To 12.00 |
| Pressed Glass, Plate, Diagonal Band & Fan, 7 In. | 6.25 To 7.75 |
| Pressed Glass, Plate, Diagonal Band & Fan, 8 In. | 7.50 To 19.00 |
| Pressed Glass, Plate, Diamond Cut With Leaf, 7 1/4 In. | 7.50 |
| Pressed Glass, Plate, Diamond Medallion, 10 In. | 16.50 |
| Pressed Glass, Plate, Dotted Loop, 9 In. | 7.00 |
| Pressed Glass, Plate, Dotted Loop, 9 1/4 In. | 7.00 |
| Pressed Glass, Plate, Drapery, 6 In. | 8.75 To 19.00 |
| Pressed Glass, Plate, Easter Opening, Chicks, 6 3/8 In. | 15.00 |
| Pressed Glass, Plate, Elaine, Frosted Center, 9 3/4 In. | 58.00 |
| Pressed Glass, Plate, Elaine, Oval & Bar Border, 9 In. | 45.00 |
| Pressed Glass, Plate, Elaine, 101 Border, Handles, 9 In. | 65.00 |
| Pressed Glass, Plate, English Hobnail With Thumbprint, 10 1/2 In. | 12.50 |
| Pressed Glass, Plate, Esther, 10 In. | 22.00 |
| Pressed Glass, Plate, Etched Apollo, 9 1/2 In.Square | 16.00 |
| Pressed Glass, Plate, Eyewinker, 9 In. | 27.50 |
| Pressed Glass, Plate, Faith, Hope, & Charity, Handled, 10 In. | 35.00 |
| Pressed Glass, Plate, Fandango, 5 3/4 In. | 14.00 |
| Pressed Glass, Plate, Feather, 10 In. | 22.50 |

Pressed Glass, Plate, Festoon, 7 1/4 In. ............................................................................ 16.00 To 32.50
Pressed Glass, Plate, Festoon, 9 1/4 In. ............................................................................................ 14.00
Pressed Glass, Plate, Finecut & Panel, 6 1/4 In. ............................................................................... 12.00
Pressed Glass, Plate, Finecut, Umbrella Shape, 9 3/4 X 6 1/2 In. .................................................... 17.50
Pressed Glass, Plate, Finecut, 6 1/4 In. ............................................................................................. 8.00
Pressed Glass, Plate, Finecut, 7 1/4 In. ............................................................................ 13.00 To 17.00
Pressed Glass, Plate, Finecut, 10 1/2 In. .......................................................................................... 14.50
Pressed Glass, Plate, Fleur-De-Lis & Drape, 10 1/4 In. ..................................................................... 17.50
Pressed Glass, Plate, Fleur-De-Lis & Tassel, Green, 8 In. ................................................................. 24.00
Pressed Glass, Plate, Fleur-De-Lis & Tassel, 6 In. ............................................................................. 9.50
Pressed Glass, Plate, Fleur-De-Lis & Tassel, 8 In. ............................................................................. 9.00
Pressed Glass, Plate, Fleur-De-Lis & Tassel, 8 1/4 In. ....................................................................... 8.50
Pressed Glass, Plate, Fleur-De-Lis With Drape, 10 1/4 In. ................................................................ 12.00
Pressed Glass, Plate, Florida Palm, 9 1/4 In. .................................................................................... 13.50
Pressed Glass, Plate, Frosted Artichoke, 6 1/4 In. ............................................................................ 16.50
Pressed Glass, Plate, Frosted Band, Rayed Center, 6 1/4 In. ............................................................. 1.50
Pressed Glass, Plate, Frosted Band, Star Center, 7 In. ....................................................................... 1.25
Pressed Glass, Plate, Frosted Garfield, 6 In. ..................................................................................... 25.00
Pressed Glass, Plate, Garfield Drape, Star Base, 11 1/2 In. .............................................................. 20.00
Pressed Glass, Plate, Garfield Drape, "we Mourn Our Loss, " 11 1/2 In. ......................................... 28.50
Pressed Glass, Plate, Garfield Drape, 11 1/2 In. .............................................................................. 30.00
Pressed Glass, Plate, Garfield Memorial, Festoon Border, 12 In. ...................................................... 35.00
Pressed Glass, Plate, Garfield Memorial, 10 In. .............................................................. 20.00 To 28.00
Pressed Glass, Plate, Garfield, Alphabet Border, 6 In. ...................................................................... 35.00
Pressed Glass, Plate, Garfield, Frost Center, Star Border, 6 In. ....................................... 25.00 To 32.00
Pressed Glass, Plate, George Peabody, 8 In. .................................................................................... 35.00
Pressed Glass, Plate, Good Luck, 8 1/4 In. ....................................................................................... 25.00
Pressed Glass, Plate, Grand, Fan Edge, 10 In. ................................................................................. 19.00
Pressed Glass, Plate, Grant, Peace, Apple Green, Leaf Border, 10 In. ............................................. 50.00
Pressed Glass, Plate, Hamilton, Flint, 6 3/8 In. ................................................................................ 28.50
Pressed Glass, Plate, Hanover, 10 1/4 In. ........................................................................................ 12.00
Pressed Glass, Plate, Hawaiian Lei, Square, 7 3/8 In. ........................................................................ 6.25
Pressed Glass, Plate, Heart & Thumbprint, 6 1/2 In. ....................................................................... 12.50
Pressed Glass, Plate, Hobnail & Thumbprint, English, 10 1/2 In. ...................................................... 9.50
Pressed Glass, Plate, Horn Of Plenty, 6 In. ...................................................................................... 75.00
Pressed Glass, Plate, Horseshoe, 10 In. ........................................................................... 48.00 To 57.50
Pressed Glass, Plate, Iris & Meander, Blue Opalescent, 6 In. .......................................................... 22.50
Pressed Glass, Plate, Iris & Meander, Opalescent, 6 In. ..................................................................... 8.00
Pressed Glass, Plate, Iris & Meander, Opalescent, 7 1/4 In. ............................................................ 17.00
Pressed Glass, Plate, Ivanhoe, 8 In. ................................................................................................. 10.00
Pressed Glass, Plate, Ivy In Snow, 7 In. ........................................................................................... 14.00
Pressed Glass, Plate, Ivy In Snow, 10 In. ......................................................................................... 18.00
Pressed Glass, Plate, Jacob's Ladder, 6 1/4 In. ............................................................................... 22.00
Pressed Glass, Plate, Jacob's Ladder, 6 1/2 In. ............................................................................... 28.00
Pressed Glass, Plate, Jersey Swirl, Amber, 6 1/4 In. ........................................................................ 23.75
Pressed Glass, Plate, Jersey Swirl, Blue, 6 1/4 In. ........................................................................... 23.75
Pressed Glass, Plate, Jersey Swirl, 6 1/8 In. .................................................................................... 15.00
Pressed Glass, Plate, Jersey Swirl, 8 In. ........................................................................................... 12.00
Pressed Glass, Plate, Jersey Swirl, 10 In. ......................................................................................... 27.00
Pressed Glass, Plate, Lattice, 6 1/4 In. ............................................................................................... 8.75
Pressed Glass, Plate, Lattice, 10 In. ................................................................................................... 8.00
Pressed Glass, Plate, Leafy Bamboo, 6 In. ........................................................................................ 5.25
Pressed Glass, Plate, Liberty Bell, Colonies, Dated, 6 In. ................................................................. 65.00
Pressed Glass, Plate, Liberty Bell, Colonies, Dated, 8 In. ................................................................. 55.00
Pressed Glass, Plate, Liberty Bell, Dated, 6 1/4 In. .......................................................................... 55.00
Pressed Glass, Plate, Liberty Bell, Handled, 6 In. ............................................................................. 60.00
Pressed Glass, Plate, Liberty Bell, 6 In. ............................................................................ 40.00 To 45.00
Pressed Glass, Plate, Liberty Bell, 6 1/2 In. ..................................................................................... 45.00
Pressed Glass, Plate, Liberty Bell, 7 7/8 In. ..................................................................................... 55.00
Pressed Glass, Plate, Liberty Bell, 8 In. ............................................................................................ 60.00
Pressed Glass, Plate, Liberty Bell, 10 In. .......................................................................................... 60.00
Pressed Glass, Plate, Liberty Bell, 13 States, Handled, 10 In. .......................................................... 60.00
Pressed Glass, Plate, Loop & Drop, 11 In. ....................................................................................... 10.00
Pressed Glass, Plate, Loop & Pyramid, 7 In. ...................................................................................... 5.00
Pressed Glass, Plate, Lotus Leaf, Amber, 9 In. ................................................................................ 12.50
Pressed Glass, Plate, Major General Fitzhugh Lee, 6 In. .................................................................. 25.00

| | |
|---|---:|
| Pressed Glass, Plate, Maltese Cross In Circle, 7 3/4 In. | 5.00 |
| Pressed Glass, Plate, Maple Leaf, Amber, 9 In.Square | 15.00 |
| Pressed Glass, Plate, Marsh, Pink, 10 In. | 18.00 |
| Pressed Glass, Plate, Maryland, 7 In. | 9.00 |
| Pressed Glass, Plate, McKinley, "Protection & Plenty, " Gold, 9 1/4 In. | 22.50 |
| Pressed Glass, Plate, McKinley, "Protection & Plenty, " 7 1/4 In. | 25.00 |
| Pressed Glass, Plate, McKinley, 7 In. | 22.00 |
| Pressed Glass, Plate, Melrose, 6 In. | 8.75 |
| Pressed Glass, Plate, Mikado Fan, 7 1/4 In. | 5.00 |
| Pressed Glass, Plate, Minerva, General Bates, Handled, 7 1/2 In. | 65.00 |
| Pressed Glass, Plate, Nailhead, 9 In. | 11.00 |
| Pressed Glass, Plate, Nailhead, 9 1/4 In. | 12.50 |
| Pressed Glass, Plate, Palm Leaf & Fan, 9 In. | 4.00 |
| Pressed Glass, Plate, Paneled Dewdrop, 6 In. | 10.00 |
| Pressed Glass, Plate, Paneled Herringbone, Square, 7 1/2 In. | 12.50 |
| Pressed Glass, Plate, Paneled Thistle, Square, 7 1/2 In. | 14.50 |
| Pressed Glass, Plate, Pavonia, Piecrust Edge, 6 3/4 In. | 22.00 |
| Pressed Glass, Plate, Pleat & Panel, 3 1/2 In. | 23.75 |
| Pressed Glass, Plate, Pleat & Panel, 5 In. | 23.75 |
| Pressed Glass, Plate, Pleat & Panel, 6 In. | 12.00 |
| Pressed Glass, Plate, Pleat & Panel, 7 In. | 12.00 To 15.00 |
| Pressed Glass, Plate, Pope Leo XIII, 10 In. | 25.00 |
| Pressed Glass, Plate, Press Cut, 7 In. | 6.00 |
| Pressed Glass, Plate, Primrose, Amber, 4 In. | 9.00 |
| Pressed Glass, Plate, Primrose, Amber, 4 1/2 In. | 9.75 |
| Pressed Glass, Plate, Primrose, Amber, 6 In. | 12.50 To 13.50 |
| Pressed Glass, Plate, Primrose, Amber, 6 3/4 In. | 20.00 |
| Pressed Glass, Plate, Primrose, Amber, 7 In. | 14.00 To 16.50 |
| Pressed Glass, Plate, Primrose, Blue, Handled Wire Basket, 7 In. | 20.00 |
| Pressed Glass, Plate, Primrose, Blue, 6 3/4 In. | 24.00 |
| Pressed Glass, Plate, Primrose, Handled, 8 3/4 In. | 18.50 |
| Pressed Glass, Plate, Primrose, 4 1/2 In. | 6.50 To 7.00 |
| Pressed Glass, Plate, Primrose, 6 In. | 9.50 |
| Pressed Glass, Plate, Primrose, 6 7/8 In. | 18.00 |
| Pressed Glass, Plate, Priscilla, 10 In. | 22.50 |
| Pressed Glass, Plate, Priscilla, 10 1/2 In. | 18.00 |
| Pressed Glass, Plate, Prism Arc, 6 3/4 In. | 8.00 |
| Pressed Glass, Plate, Queen's Jubilee, 10 In. | 45.00 |
| Pressed Glass, Plate, Quixote, Gold, 7 3/4 In. | 7.50 |
| Pressed Glass, Plate, Rayed, Loop Border, Flint, 8 In. | 18.00 |
| Pressed Glass, Plate, Ribbed Grape, Flint, 6 In. | 42.00 |
| Pressed Glass, Plate, Ribbed Palm, 6 In. | 32.00 |
| Pressed Glass, Plate, Ripple, 5 In. | 5.00 |
| Pressed Glass, Plate, Roman Cross, 7 1/2 In. | 5.00 |
| Pressed Glass, Plate, Rose In Snow, Handled, 9 1/2 In. | 19.50 |
| Pressed Glass, Plate, Rose In Snow, 6 In. | 17.50 |
| Pressed Glass, Plate, Rose In Snow, 7 1/4 In. | 12.50 To 19.00 |
| Pressed Glass, Plate, Rose In Snow, 9 1/2 In. | 18.00 |
| Pressed Glass, Plate, Rose Sprig, Blue, 6 3/4 In. | 12.50 |
| Pressed Glass, Plate, Rose Sprig, 6 1/2 In.Square | 22.00 |
| Pressed Glass, Plate, Rosette, Tab Handles, 9 1/4 In. | 17.50 |
| Pressed Glass, Plate, Rosette, 9 In. | 10.00 |
| Pressed Glass, Plate, Sawtooth & Star, 10 In. | 14.00 |
| Pressed Glass, Plate, Scalloped Lines, 6 1/4 In. | 8.75 |
| Pressed Glass, Plate, Serving, Paneled Thistle, 7 1/2 In. | 17.00 |
| Pressed Glass, Plate, Sheraton, 5 3/4 In. | 12.50 |
| Pressed Glass, Plate, Snakeskin & Dot, Amber, 4 1/2 In. | 10.50 |
| Pressed Glass, Plate, Snakeskin & Dot, 4 1/2 In. | 5.00 To 6.50 |
| Pressed Glass, Plate, Star & Feather, Amber, 7 In. | 15.00 To 29.50 |
| Pressed Glass, Plate, Star & Feather, Green, 7 In. | 29.50 |
| Pressed Glass, Plate, Star & Feather, 7 In. | 18.00 |
| Pressed Glass, Plate, Stuart's Diamond Bar, 6 In. | 4.00 |
| Pressed Glass, Plate, Sunburst, 7 In. | 6.25 |
| Pressed Glass, Plate, Tea, Diamond-Quilted, Bull's-Eye Border, Flint, 6 In. | 23.50 |
| Pressed Glass, Plate, Texas Campaign, Blue, 8 In. | 55.00 |
| Pressed Glass, Plate, Texas Centennial, 1836-1936, 8 In. | 20.00 To 25.00 |

Pressed Glass, Plate, Three Kittens, Frosted, Pan American Exposition ............................................ 25.00
Pressed Glass, Plate, Three Owls ............................................................................................................... 27.50
Pressed Glass, Plate, Tokyo, Opalescent Edge, Footed, 8 1/2 In. ........................................... 16.50
Pressed Glass, Plate, Tokyo, Opalescent, Footed, 8 1/4 In. ...................................................... 16.50
Pressed Glass, Plate, Waffle, 6 In. ............................................................................................................ 42.50
Pressed Glass, Plate, Wheat & Barley, Amber, 7 In. .................................................................... 24.00
Pressed Glass, Plate, Wheat & Barley, 7 In. ....................................................................................... 15.00
Pressed Glass, Plate, Wildflower, Amber, 9 5/8 In. ........................................................................ 35.00
Pressed Glass, Plate, Wildflower, Blue, Square, 9 1/2 In. ........................................................... 35.00
Pressed Glass, Plate, Wildflower, Green, 10 In. ............................................................................... 20.00
Pressed Glass, Plate, Willow Oak, Blue, 9 In. .................................................................................... 40.00
Pressed Glass, Plate, Willow Oak, Handled, 9 1/4 In. .................................................................. 20.00
Pressed Glass, Plate, Yoke & Circle, 9 In. ........................................................................................... 9.00
Pressed Glass, Plate, 101, Motto & Implements, 11 In. .............................................................. 30.00
Pressed Glass, Plate, 101, 7 In. ....................................................................................... 12.00 To 16.00
Pressed Glass, Plate, 101, 8 In. ....................................................................................... 10.00 To 16.00
Pressed Glass, Plate, 808, 8 3/4 In. ............................................................................... 10.00 To 12.50
Pressed Glass, Plate, 1, 000-Eye, Amber, Folded Corners, 10 In.Square ........................... 22.50
Pressed Glass, Plate, 1, 000-Eye, Apple Green, Folded Corners, 10 In.Square ............... 24.50
Pressed Glass, Plate, 1, 000-Eye, Cut Corners, 8 In. Square .................................................. 11.00
Pressed Glass, Plate, 1, 000-Eye, Square, 8 In. .............................................................................. 9.00
Pressed Glass, Plate, 1, 000-Eye, 8 In. ................................................................................................. 12.00
Pressed Glass, Plate, 1, 000-Eye, 10 In. ..................................................................... 12.50 To 16.00
Pressed Glass, Platter, Beaded Loop ....................................................................................................... 23.50
Pressed Glass, Platter, Chain With Shield ............................................................................................ 26.50
Pressed Glass, Platter, Clear Diagonal Band ..................................................................................... 37.50
Pressed Glass, Platter, Columbus Pilot Wheel ................................................................................. 40.00
Pressed Glass, Platter, Constitution ......................................................................................................... 38.00
Pressed Glass, Platter, Currier & Ives, Round, Small Rim ......................................................... 25.00
Pressed Glass, Platter, Daisy & Button With Crossbar, Amber ............................................... 40.00
Pressed Glass, Platter, Deer & Pine Tree, Amber ........................................................................... 49.50
Pressed Glass, Platter, Diagonal Band, Amber ................................................................................. 33.50
Pressed Glass, Platter, Diagonal Band, Pale Blue, 12 In. ........................................................... 27.50
Pressed Glass, Platter, Eden ......................................................................................................................... 20.00
Pressed Glass, Platter, Egg In Sand ......................................................................................................... 25.00
Pressed Glass, Platter, Eureka ..................................................................................................................... 40.00
Pressed Glass, Platter, Faith, Hope, & Charity ................................................................................. 50.00
Pressed Glass, Platter, Fleur-De-Lis ......................................................................................................... 22.50
Pressed Glass, Platter, Frosted Double Ribbon, 9 X 13 In. ....................................................... 22.00
Pressed Glass, Platter, Frosted Stork, 101 Border .......................................................................... 45.00
Pressed Glass, Platter, G.A.R. ....................................................................................................................... 65.00
Pressed Glass, Platter, George Washington ........................................................................................ 90.00
Pressed Glass, Platter, Good Luck, 13 In.Long ................................................................................ 16.00
Pressed Glass, Platter, Harrison, Morton ........................................................................................... 225.00
Pressed Glass, Platter, Heroes Of Bunker Hill ................................................................................. 49.50
Pressed Glass, Platter, Horseshoe, Double Horseshoe Handles ......................... 24.50 To 42.50
Pressed Glass, Platter, Horseshoe, 13 In. ............................................................................................ 24.00
Pressed Glass, Platter, Huckle ..................................................................................................................... 23.50
Pressed Glass, Platter, Liberty Bell, Shells, Oval, Dated Sept.28, 1875 ........................... 105.00
Pressed Glass, Platter, Liberty Bell, Signers, 9 1/4 X 13 In. ......................... 50.00 To 65.00
Pressed Glass, Platter, Lotus & Serpent ............................................................................................... 22.00
Pressed Glass, Platter, Maine ....................................................................................................................... 25.00
Pressed Glass, Platter, Maple Leaf, Blue .............................................................................................. 45.00
Pressed Glass, Platter, Maple Leaf, Oval .............................................................................................. 15.00
Pressed Glass, Platter, McCormick Reaper ......................................................................................... 55.00
Pressed Glass, Platter, Mitered Diamonds ........................................................................................... 25.00
Pressed Glass, Platter, Niagara Falls ....................................................................................................... 85.00
Pressed Glass, Platter, Paneled Forget-Me-Not ................................................... 26.00 To 28.50
Pressed Glass, Platter, Pioneer Flour, Minneapolis ....................................................................... 69.00
Pressed Glass, Platter, Pleat & Panel, Open Handles, 8 X 11 In. .......................................... 19.50
Pressed Glass, Platter, Pope Leo XII ....................................................................................................... 25.00
Pressed Glass, Platter, Reaper ..................................................................................................................... 55.00
Pressed Glass, Platter, Rock Of Ages ..................................................................................................... 55.00
Pressed Glass, Platter, Rock Of Ages, Opaque White Center .................................................. 85.00
Pressed Glass, Platter, Roman Rosette ................................................................................................... 29.50
Pressed Glass, Platter, Rose Sprig, Handled, 11 1/2 X 6 In. ..................................................... 27.50

| | |
|---|---|
| Pressed Glass, Platter, Royal Crying Baby | 39.00 |
| Pressed Glass, Platter, Sheaf Of Wheat | 30.00 |
| Pressed Glass, Platter, Shell & Tassel | 35.00 |
| Pressed Glass, Platter, Spirea Band, Amber | 32.50 |
| Pressed Glass, Platter, Star Rosette, "Good Mother" | 40.00 |
| Pressed Glass, Platter, Teddy Roosevelt, Frosted | 65.00 |
| Pressed Glass, Platter, Texas Centennial, Alamo Center | 55.00 |
| Pressed Glass, Platter, Three Presidents | 40.00 To 75.00 |
| Pressed Glass, Platter, Two Panel | 26.50 |
| Pressed Glass, Platter, Two Panel, Amber | 37.50 |
| Pressed Glass, Platter, Virginia Dare | 30.00 |
| Pressed Glass, Platter, Westward Ho | 78.00 |
| Pressed Glass, Platter, Westward Ho, Deer Handles | 55.00 |
| Pressed Glass, Platter, Westward Ho, Oval | 55.00 |
| Pressed Glass, Platter, 1,000-Eye, Deep, 8 X 11 In. | 18.00 |
| Pressed Glass, Pot & Attached Underplate, Mustard, Paneled Herringbone | 22.50 |
| Pressed Glass, Punch Set, Chrysanthemum, 10 Piece | 48.00 |
| Pressed Glass, Punch Set, Flattened Diamond & Sunburst, Miniature, 7 Piece | 55.00 |
| Pressed Glass, Punch Set, Mardi Gras, 21 In.Underplate, 15 Piece | 52.00 |
| Pressed Glass, Punch Set, Tulip & Honeycomb, 6 Piece | 55.00 |
| Pressed Glass, Punch Set, Whirligig, 7 Piece | 60.00 |
| Pressed Glass, Relish, Actress, Love's Request | 22.50 |
| Pressed Glass, Relish, Art | 8.50 |
| Pressed Glass, Relish, Aurora | 6.50 |
| Pressed Glass, Relish, Baltimore Pear | 10.00 |
| Pressed Glass, Relish, Barberry, Oval Berries | 7.00 |
| Pressed Glass, Relish, Barred Forget-Me-Not | 10.00 |
| Pressed Glass, Relish, Beaded Cable | 8.50 |
| Pressed Glass, Relish, Beaded Grape, Green, Large Size | 18.00 |
| Pressed Glass, Relish, Beaded Tulip | 14.00 |
| Pressed Glass, Relish, Bird & Strawberry, Large Size | 23.00 |
| Pressed Glass, Relish, Bird Shape, Sapphire Blue, 2 1/4 In.High | 67.50 |
| Pressed Glass, Relish, Blackberry, White, Opaque, Flint | 18.00 |
| Pressed Glass, Relish, Bleeding Heart | 22.00 |
| Pressed Glass, Relish, Bryce | 10.00 |
| Pressed Glass, Relish, Buckle | 9.00 To 10.50 |
| Pressed Glass, Relish, Buckle With Star | 10.50 |
| Pressed Glass, Relish, Cane & Rosette | 9.00 |
| Pressed Glass, Relish, Cavitt | 7.50 |
| Pressed Glass, Relish, Chain With Star | 8.50 |
| Pressed Glass, Relish, Cord & Drapery, 5 1/2 X 9 In. | 12.00 |
| Pressed Glass, Relish, Cupid's Hunt | 22.50 |
| Pressed Glass, Relish, Cupid's Hunt, Handled, Findlay, 9 1/2 In. Long | 13.00 |
| Pressed Glass, Relish, Daisy & Button With Rimmed Ovals | 8.50 |
| Pressed Glass, Relish, Dewdrop | 8.50 |
| Pressed Glass, Relish, Double Vine, Pointed End | 9.00 |
| Pressed Glass, Relish, Egyptian, 8 1/2 In. Long | 10.00 To 14.00 |
| Pressed Glass, Relish, Feather Duster | 8.75 |
| Pressed Glass, Relish, Feather, Oval | 10.00 To 17.00 |
| Pressed Glass, Relish, Fish Shape | 14.00 |
| Pressed Glass, Relish, Flaming Sword | 27.50 |
| Pressed Glass, Relish, Florida Palm | 9.00 |
| Pressed Glass, Relish, Frosted Empress, Sterling Rim, 3 Compartments | 30.00 |
| Pressed Glass, Relish, Grape Band Scoop | 12.50 |
| Pressed Glass, Relish, Grenade, 7 3/4 X 4 1/2 In. | 10.00 |
| Pressed Glass, Relish, Horseshoe | 10.50 To 12.00 |
| Pressed Glass, Relish, Horseshoe, Oval, 8 X 5 In. | 20.00 |
| Pressed Glass, Relish, Huckle | 8.75 |
| Pressed Glass, Relish, Isis | 8.50 |
| Pressed Glass, Relish, Jacob's Ladder | 8.00 To 15.00 |
| Pressed Glass, Relish, Klondike, Frosted & Yellow, Canoe Shape | 125.00 |
| Pressed Glass, Relish, Lacy Daisy | 9.00 |
| Pressed Glass, Relish, Liberty Bell, Signers, 9 X 5 In. | 50.00 To 65.00 |
| Pressed Glass, Relish, Lily Of The Valley | 9.00 |
| Pressed Glass, Relish, Lily Of The Valley, Pointed End | 7.50 |
| Pressed Glass, Relish, Loop & Dart Scoop | 13.50 |

Pressed Glass, Relish, Loop & Dart With Diamonds ......................................... 12.00
Pressed Glass, Relish, Loops With Fans ......................................... 13.50
Pressed Glass, Relish, Maine ......................................... 10.00
Pressed Glass, Relish, Manhattan ......................................... 4.50 To 5.00
Pressed Glass, Relish, Michigan, White Enamel Forget-Me-Nots, Blue Pink Rim ......... 14.50
Pressed Glass, Relish, Moon & Star, 4 3/4 X 8 In. ......................................... 12.50
Pressed Glass, Relish, Open Rose ......................................... 12.00
Pressed Glass, Relish, Palmette ......................................... 10.00
Pressed Glass, Relish, Paneled Daisy ......................................... 12.00
Pressed Glass, Relish, Paneled Daisy, Handled ......................................... 10.00
Pressed Glass, Relish, Paneled Forget-Me-Not ......................................... 9.00 To 11.50
Pressed Glass, Relish, Paneled Forget-Me-Not, Large Size ......................................... 19.50
Pressed Glass, Relish, Paneled Forget-Me-Not, Small Size ......................................... 17.50
Pressed Glass, Relish, Paneled Thistle, Oval, 8 In.Long ......................................... 13.50
Pressed Glass, Relish, Paneled Thistle, Side Handle, Round, 5 1/4 In. ......................................... 19.50
Pressed Glass, Relish, Peacook Feather ......................................... 14.00
Pressed Glass, Relish, Primrose ......................................... 10.00 To 10.50
Pressed Glass, Relish, Prism Arc ......................................... 7.50
Pressed Glass, Relish, Rose & Fan ......................................... 7.50
Pressed Glass, Relish, Rose In Snow ......................................... 12.50
Pressed Glass, Relish, Rose Sprig, 8 X 5 In. ......................................... 12.50
Pressed Glass, Relish, Rosette, Fish Shape ......................................... 10.50
Pressed Glass, Relish, Sedan ......................................... 8.50
Pressed Glass, Relish, Sheraton, Amber, 8 1/2 In. Long ......................................... 8.00 To 12.50
Pressed Glass, Relish, Shoshone, Gold ......................................... 8.50
Pressed Glass, Relish, Star Rosette ......................................... 9.00
Pressed Glass, Relish, The States, Round, 3 Handles, 6 1/2 In.Diameter ......................................... 18.50
Pressed Glass, Relish, Thistle, Clear, Marked Near Cut, 7 1/4 In.Long ......................................... 3.75
Pressed Glass, Relish, Tidy Scoop, Flint ......................................... 10.00
Pressed Glass, Relish, Two Panel, Amber ......................................... 13.50
Pressed Glass, Relish, Vegetables ......................................... 8.50
Pressed Glass, Relish, Waffle & Finecut Fish With Upswept Tail ......................................... 16.50
Pressed Glass, Relish, Washboard, Blue, 8 1/4 In.Long ......................................... 16.00
Pressed Glass, Relish, Washington, Dated, Bear Paws ......................................... 32.00
Pressed Glass, Relish, Wildflower ......................................... 10.00
Pressed Glass, Relish, Wildflower, Amber, 10 In. ......................................... 20.00
Pressed Glass, Relish, Wisconsin ......................................... 12.50
Pressed Glass, Rose Bowl, Alaska, Blue, Opalescent, Pedestal Base ......................................... 35.00
Pressed Glass, Rose Bowl, Alaska, Blue, Opalescent, Rose Flecked Top, Footed ......................................... 31.00
Pressed Glass, Rose Bowl, Alaska, Emerald Green, Ruffled Top ......................................... 30.00
Pressed Glass, Rose Bowl, Block & Fan ......................................... 16.50 To 22.00
Pressed Glass, Rose Bowl, Block & Thumbprint, Findlay ......................................... 16.50
Pressed Glass, Rose Bowl, Block, 3 In. ......................................... 5.00
Pressed Glass, Rose Bowl, Britanic, McKee, C.1890, 5 In. ......................................... 15.00
Pressed Glass, Rose Bowl, Crescent & Fan ......................................... 11.00
Pressed Glass, Rose Bowl, Cube, 20 Point Star Base, 6 1/2 X 7 In. ......................................... 22.50
Pressed Glass, Rose Bowl, Double Snail, 3 In.High ......................................... 18.00
Pressed Glass, Rose Bowl, Flowered Scroll, Miniature, 2 1/2 In.High ......................................... 12.00
Pressed Glass, Rose Bowl, Heart With Thumbprint, Miniature, 2 1/2 In.High ......................................... 13.00
Pressed Glass, Rose Bowl, Hobnail, Fan Top, 7 1/2 In.Diameter ......................................... 25.00
Pressed Glass, Rose Bowl, Hobnail, Green To Opalescent, 6 In. ......................................... 45.00
Pressed Glass, Rose Bowl, Paneled Apple Blossom ......................................... 4.00
Pressed Glass, Rose Bowl, Paneled Thistle ......................................... 16.50 To 20.00
Pressed Glass, Rose Bowl, Priscilla ......................................... 20.00
Pressed Glass, Rose Bowl, Royal Ivy, Frosted & Clear ......................................... 38.50
Pressed Glass, Rose Bowl, Spanish Lace ......................................... 59.00
Pressed Glass, Rowboat, Daisy & Button, 14 In. ......................................... 15.00
Pressed Glass, Rummer, Grape & Festoon, 5 1/4 In. High ......................................... 10.00 To 14.50
Pressed Glass, Rummer, Thumbprint, Footed, Flint ......................................... 22.00
Pressed Glass, Salt & Pepper, Alabama ......................................... 8.75
Pressed Glass, Salt & Pepper, Beaded Grape, Purple, Square ......................................... 38.50
Pressed Glass, Salt & Pepper, Delaware, Green ......................................... *Illus* 55.00
Pressed Glass, Salt & Pepper, Diagonal Basket Weave, In Rectangular Basket ......................................... 28.00
Pressed Glass, Salt & Pepper, Iowa, Gilt Top ......................................... 16.50
Pressed Glass, Salt & Pepper, Iris & Meander, Opalescent ......................................... 45.00
Pressed Glass, Salt & Pepper, Klondike, Frosted With Amber Panel ......................................... 200.00

Pressed Glass, Salt & Pepper, Delaware, Green
*(See Page 466)*

| | |
|---|---|
| Pressed Glass, Salt & Pepper, Kokomo | 12.50 |
| Pressed Glass, Salt & Pepper, Opposing Pyramids | 15.00 |
| Pressed Glass, Salt & Poppor, Zigzag | 8.75 |
| Pressed Glass, Salt & Pepper, 1, 000-Eye | 18.00 |
| Pressed Glass, Salt Dip, Cannonball | 2.50 |
| Pressed Glass, Salt Dip, Crossed Log, Portland | 8.00 |
| Pressed Glass, Salt Dip, Fine Rib, Flint | 16.00 |
| Pressed Glass, Salt Dip, Inverted Strawberry | 10.00 |
| Pressed Glass, Salt Dip, Liberty Bell | 22.50 To 36.00 |
| Pressed Glass, Salt Dip, Polo Game, Frosted & Clear | 14.00 |
| Pressed Glass, Salt Dip, Stars & Stripes, Individual | 3.00 |
| Pressed Glass, Salt, Bellflower, Single Vine, Scalloped Rim, Footed, Flint | 25.00 |
| Pressed Glass, Salt, Crossed Log | 6.00 |
| Pressed Glass, Salt, Cube, Amber, Boat Shape | 10.00 |
| Pressed Glass, Salt, Daisy & Button, Amber, Hat, 2 In.High | 25.00 |
| Pressed Glass, Salt, Diamond Waffle, Ice Blue, Lacy, Sofa, Paw Feet | 150.00 |
| Pressed Glass, Salt, Harvard | 7.00 |
| Pressed Glass, Salt, Heavy Leaf, 3 In.Long | 43.50 |
| Pressed Glass, Salt, Hobnail, Green, Square | 8.00 |
| Pressed Glass, Salt, Horizontal Ovals, Footed, Flint | 25.00 |
| Pressed Glass, Salt, Horseshoe, Naturalistic | 17.50 |
| Pressed Glass, Salt, Individual, Loop, Scalloped Top, Footed | 3.50 |
| Pressed Glass, Salt, Individual, Picket Fence | 12.50 |
| Pressed Glass, Salt, Individual, Sawtooth | 2.50 |
| Pressed Glass, Salt, Individual, Two Panel | 4.00 |
| Pressed Glass, Salt, Individual, Two Panel, Green | 11.50 |
| Pressed Glass, Salt, Inverted Fern, Footed | 17.00 |
| Pressed Glass, Salt, Liberty Bell | 30.00 |
| Pressed Glass, Salt, Master, Arched Leaf | 15.00 |
| Pressed Glass, Salt, Master, Arched Leaf, Footed | 9.00 |
| Pressed Glass, Salt, Master, Cart | 15.00 |
| Pressed Glass, Salt, Master, Collared Bull's-Eye, Footed, Flint | 16.00 |
| Pressed Glass, Salt, Master, Cube, Footed | 4.00 |
| Pressed Glass, Salt, Master, Diamond Point With Cable, Green Opaque, Flint | 40.00 |
| Pressed Glass, Salt, Master, Diamond Thumbprint, 3 1/2 In.Diameter | 12.50 |
| Pressed Glass, Salt, Master, Eight Sided, Fancy Edge, Flint | 6.00 |
| Pressed Glass, Salt, Master, Embossed Fruit & Flowers, New England Glass | 69.00 |
| Pressed Glass, Salt, Master, Eureka, Footed, Flint | 18.00 |
| Pressed Glass, Salt, Master, Fancy Ovals, Flint | 14.00 |
| Pressed Glass, Salt, Master, Fine Prism, Footed | 9.50 |
| Pressed Glass, Salt, Master, Fine Rib | 28.50 |
| Pressed Glass, Salt, Master, Flattened Sawtooth, Flint | 12.00 |
| Pressed Glass, Salt, Master, Frosted Post | 10.00 |
| Pressed Glass, Salt, Master, Giant Sawtooth, Flint | 12.00 |
| Pressed Glass, Salt, Master, Horizontal Oval Frames, Flint | 14.00 |
| Pressed Glass, Salt, Master, Huber, Footed, Flint | 15.00 |
| Pressed Glass, Salt, Master, Jacob's Ladder | 22.00 |
| Pressed Glass, Salt, Master, Jacob's Ladder, Pointed Top | 12.50 |

Pressed Glass, Salt, Master, Loop, Flint ............................................................................. 15.00
Pressed Glass, Salt, Master, Palmette, Footed ................................................................... 16.00
Pressed Glass, Salt, Master, Paneled ................................................................................. 6.50
Pressed Glass, Salt, Master, Paneled Thistle ..................................................................... 10.00
Pressed Glass, Salt, Master, Petal & Loop, Clear .............................................................. 15.00
Pressed Glass, Salt, Master, Powder & Shot ...................................................................... 32.00
Pressed Glass, Salt, Master, Ribbed Palm, Footed, Flint ................................................... 25.00
Pressed Glass, Salt, Master, Sawtooth & Circle, Footed, Flint, Pair ................................. 30.00
Pressed Glass, Salt, Master, Sawtooth, Flint ......................................................... 9.00 To 22.50
Pressed Glass, Salt, Master, Sawtooth, 3 1/2 In. Diameter ...................................... 5.50 To 10.00
Pressed Glass, Salt, Master, Scroll With Flowers, Footed, Handled ................................... 6.00
Pressed Glass, Salt, Master, Stippled Swag, Footed .......................................................... 14.00
Pressed Glass, Salt, Master, Thumbprint Rim ..................................................................... 6.50
Pressed Glass, Salt, Master, Triangular Prism, Pedestal Foot, Flint ................................. 15.00
Pressed Glass, Salt, Master, Tulip ...................................................................................... 21.00
Pressed Glass, Salt, Master, Tulip & Sawtooth, Petal Edge ............................................... 35.00
Pressed Glass, Salt, Master, Tulip, Footed, Flint ............................................................... 18.00
Pressed Glass, Salt, Master, Valencia, Amber .................................................................... 10.00
Pressed Glass, Salt, Master, Waffle .................................................................................... 16.00
Pressed Glass, Salt, Master, Washington Centennial, Oval ................................................ 25.00
Pressed Glass, Salt, Master, Wildflower, Boat Shape, Footed, 2 In.High ............................. 9.00
Pressed Glass, Salt, New England Pineapple ...................................................................... 35.00
Pressed Glass, Salt, Panel & Ring, Flint .............................................................................. 15.00
Pressed Glass, Salt, Paneled English Hobnail With Prisms, Oval ....................................... 3.00
Pressed Glass, Salt, Picket, Rectangular, 2 In. .................................................................. 8.50
Pressed Glass, Salt, Portland .............................................................................................. 8.50
Pressed Glass, Salt, Ribbed Palm, Footed, Flint ................................................................ 15.00
Pressed Glass, Salt, Sawtooth, Covered, Footed, Flint ....................................................... 60.00
Pressed Glass, Salt, Stag Horn, Lacy, Blue Green Tint ....................................................... 35.00
Pressed Glass, Salt, Stippled Star, Footed ......................................................................... 14.50
Pressed Glass, Salt, Swan & Cart, 4 In.Long ...................................................................... 30.00
Pressed Glass, Salt, Thistle, Footed ................................................................................... 4.75
Pressed Glass, Salt, Three Face ......................................................................................... 18.50
Pressed Glass, Salt, Two Panel, Apple Green ..................................................................... 15.00
Pressed Glass, Salt, Washington, Footed, Flint ................................................................... 40.00
Pressed Glass, Saltshaker, Barrel ....................................................................................... 4.50
Pressed Glass, Saltshaker, Block & Fan ............................................................................. 6.00
Pressed Glass, Saltshaker, Cane & Cable ................................................................ 2.00 To 3.50
Pressed Glass, Saltshaker, Cane & Shield .......................................................................... 6.50
Pressed Glass, Saltshaker, Carolina, Ruby Flashed ........................................................... 8.50
Pressed Glass, Saltshaker, Cube & Diamond, Amber ......................................................... 8.50
Pressed Glass, Saltshaker, Curlicue .................................................................................... 14.00
Pressed Glass, Saltshaker, Diagonal Diamond, Amber, Pewter Top ................................... 18.00
Pressed Glass, Saltshaker, Ear Of Corn, Hand, Pewter Top .............................................. 20.00
Pressed Glass, Saltshaker, Etched Thumbprint, Ruby ........................................................ 12.75
Pressed Glass, Saltshaker, Fulton ...................................................................................... 2.25
Pressed Glass, Saltshaker, Galloway .................................................................................. 18.00
Pressed Glass, Saltshaker, Grape With Vine ...................................................................... 15.00
Pressed Glass, Saltshaker, Hobnail, Amber ........................................................................ 5.00
Pressed Glass, Saltshaker, Hobnail, Opalescent ................................................................ 7.50
Pressed Glass, Saltshaker, Inverted Honeycomb, Amber, Enameled Butterflies ................ 22.50
Pressed Glass, Saltshaker, Leaning, Blue .......................................................................... 15.00
Pressed Glass, Saltshaker, Milton, Blue, Miniature ............................................................ 12.50
Pressed Glass, Saltshaker, Mitred Bars .............................................................................. 8.00
Pressed Glass, Saltshaker, Model Peerless ........................................................................ 8.00
Pressed Glass, Saltshaker, New Hampshire .............................................................. 3.00 To 4.00
Pressed Glass, Saltshaker, Panel & Star ............................................................................ 2.00
Pressed Glass, Saltshaker, Pineapple & Fan ...................................................................... 5.00
Pressed Glass, Saltshaker, Rainbow ................................................................................... 6.50
Pressed Glass, Saltshaker, Ribbed Swirl, Blue, Opalescent Striping .................................. 15.00
Pressed Glass, Saltshaker, S Repeat, Blue ........................................................................ 18.50
Pressed Glass, Saltshaker, Shoshone, Red Flashed .......................................................... 22.50
Pressed Glass, Saltshaker, Snail, Red & Clear ................................................................... 13.00
Pressed Glass, Saltshaker, Texas Centennial, Green Metal Top, Pair ................................ 27.50
Pressed Glass, Saltshaker, Virginia ..................................................................................... 12.00
Pressed Glass, Saltshaker, World ....................................................................................... 6.50

| | |
|---|---|
| Pressed Glass, Saltshaker, Zigzag | 6.00 |
| Pressed Glass, Sauce Set, Child's, Lacy Daisy, 7 Piece | 48.50 |
| Pressed Glass, Sauce Set, Etched Nail, Footed Sauces, 7 Piece | 37.50 |
| Pressed Glass, Sauce Set, Grape, Footed, 6 Piece | 55.00 |
| Pressed Glass, Sauce Set, Paneled Daisy, 7 Piece | 35.00 |
| Pressed Glass, Sauce, Acorn, Flint, 4 In. | 5.00 |
| Pressed Glass, Sauce, Actress, Flared Base | 7.75 |
| Pressed Glass, Sauce, Actress, Footed, 4 In. | 11.00 To 14.00 |
| Pressed Glass, Sauce, Actress, Footed, 4 1/2 In. | 10.00 To 12.50 |
| Pressed Glass, Sauce, Actress, Footed, 5 In. | 12.00 |
| Pressed Glass, Sauce, Actress, Frosted, Footed, 4 1/2 In. | 10.00 To 11.00 |
| Pressed Glass, Sauce, Actress, Frosted, Footed, 5 In. | 12.00 |
| Pressed Glass, Sauce, Alaska, Opalescent Trim | 11.00 |
| Pressed Glass, Sauce, Alaska, White Opalescent | 25.00 |
| Pressed Glass, Sauce, Anderson, Flat, 4 1/4 In. | 3.00 |
| Pressed Glass, Sauce, Arabesque | 6.00 |
| Pressed Glass, Sauce, Arched Ovals | 3.50 |
| Pressed Glass, Sauce, Art Nouveau, Ruby, Flat, 4 In. | 12.50 |
| Pressed Glass, Sauce, Artichoke, Clear, 4 1/2 In. | 12.00 |
| Pressed Glass, Sauce, Atlas | 3.50 To 6.50 |
| Pressed Glass, Sauce, Atlas, Footed | 8.75 |
| Pressed Glass, Sauce, Aztec | 2.00 |
| Pressed Glass, Sauce, Balder, Gold Trim, 4 1/2 In. | 5.50 To 6.50 |
| Pressed Glass, Sauce, Banded Buckle | 7.00 |
| Pressed Glass, Sauce, Banded Grape | 3.50 |
| Pressed Glass, Sauce, Banded Portland | 3.00 |
| Pressed Glass, Sauce, Banded Portland, Gold Trim | 8.50 |
| Pressed Glass, Sauce, Banded Portland, Maiden's Blush | 9.50 |
| Pressed Glass, Sauce, Banded Portland, Ruby Flashed | 12.00 |
| Pressed Glass, Sauce, Banded Star, Clear, Footed, 4 In. | 9.00 |
| Pressed Glass, Sauce, Barberry, Flat, 4 1/2 In. | 7.50 |
| Pressed Glass, Sauce, Barley, Footed | 6.75 |
| Pressed Glass, Sauce, Barred Ovals, Ruby, Flat | 12.50 |
| Pressed Glass, Sauce, Beaded Circle, 4 Sides | 5.00 |
| Pressed Glass, Sauce, Beaded Grape Medallion, 4 In. Diameter | 6.75 |
| Pressed Glass, Sauce, Beaded Mirror, Flat, 4 In. | 5.50 |
| Pressed Glass, Sauce, Beaded Oval & Scroll | 4.50 |
| Pressed Glass, Sauce, Beautiful Lady | 4.35 |
| Pressed Glass, Sauce, Bellflower | 12.00 |
| Pressed Glass, Sauce, Bellflower, Flint | 9.50 |
| Pressed Glass, Sauce, Bellflower, Scalloped Top, Flint | 10.00 |
| Pressed Glass, Sauce, Birch Leaf | 3.75 |
| Pressed Glass, Sauce, Bird & Strawberry | 15.00 |
| Pressed Glass, Sauce, Bird & Strawberry, Footed | 9.75 To 17.50 |
| Pressed Glass, Sauce, Bird's Nest, 3 Eggs | 6.50 |
| Pressed Glass, Sauce, Block & Fan, Footed | 6.50 To 8.00 |
| Pressed Glass, Sauce, Brazen Shield, Blue, Flat, 4 1/2 In. | 4.75 |
| Pressed Glass, Sauce, Broken Column | 8.50 |
| Pressed Glass, Sauce, Buckle With Star, Footed | 4.50 To 12.95 |
| Pressed Glass, Sauce, Buckle With Star, 4 1/2 In. | 4.25 To 9.50 |
| Pressed Glass, Sauce, Buckle, Footed | 4.00 |
| Pressed Glass, Sauce, Cabbage Rose | 6.50 |
| Pressed Glass, Sauce, Cable | 11.00 |
| Pressed Glass, Sauce, Cable With Ring, Flint, 4 In. | 7.50 To 10.00 |
| Pressed Glass, Sauce, Cable, Flint | 10.00 To 12.50 |
| Pressed Glass, Sauce, Canadian | 7.50 To 10.00 |
| Pressed Glass, Sauce, Cardinal Bird, 4 In. | 8.00 |
| Pressed Glass, Sauce, Cathedral, 4 In. | 10.50 |
| Pressed Glass, Sauce, Chandelier, Flat | 7.00 |
| Pressed Glass, Sauce, Child's, Lacy Daisy | 14.00 |
| Pressed Glass, Sauce, Chrysanthemum | 15.00 |
| Pressed Glass, Sauce, Coarse Rib | 7.50 |
| Pressed Glass, Sauce, Colorado, Blue, Ruffled, Gold Trim, 5 In. | 20.00 |
| Pressed Glass, Sauce, Colombian Coin, Gold, Flat, 4 In. | 22.50 |
| Pressed Glass, Sauce, Cord Drapery, 4 1/8 In. | 5.00 To 7.50 |
| Pressed Glass, Sauce, Cord Drapery, 4 1/4 In. | 12.00 |

Pressed Glass, Sauce, Cordova, Footed ........................................................................... 5.00
Pressed Glass, Sauce, Cottage, Footed ........................................................................... 10.00
Pressed Glass, Sauce, Crossed Swords ................................................... 8.00 To 15.00
Pressed Glass, Sauce, Crow's-Foot, Footed .................................................................. 6.25
Pressed Glass, Sauce, Crow's-Foot, 4 1/4 In. .............................................................. 5.00
Pressed Glass, Sauce, Crow's-Foot, 5 1/2 In. .............................................................. 7.50
Pressed Glass, Sauce, Cupid & Venus, Footed, 3 1/2 In. ......................... 5.00 To 8.50
Pressed Glass, Sauce, Cupid & Venus, Footed, 4 1/2 In. ....................... 6.25 To 12.00
Pressed Glass, Sauce, Currier & Ives, Amber ............................................................ 15.00
Pressed Glass, Sauce, Currier & Ives, Oval, Flat, Collared Base, 5 In. ............... 16.00
Pressed Glass, Sauce, Dahlia, 4 1/2 In. ................................................... 3.50 To 6.50
Pressed Glass, Sauce, Daisy & Button With Blue Thumbprint Panel, Footed ......... 8.75
Pressed Glass, Sauce, Daisy & Button With Narcissus, Clear ................................. 5.00
Pressed Glass, Sauce, Daisy & Button With V Ornament ......................... 4.50 To 5.00
Pressed Glass, Sauce, Daisy & Button, Amber Daisy, Square, 3 3/4 In. ............... 18.00
Pressed Glass, Sauce, Daisy & Button, Amber, Square, 4 1/2 In. ......................... 16.00
Pressed Glass, Sauce, Daisy & Button, Blue, Scalloped Top, 5 In. ...................... 12.00
Pressed Glass, Sauce, Daisy & Button, Blue, Square, 4 1/2 In. ........................... 15.00
Pressed Glass, Sauce, Daisy & Button, Blue, Triangular, 4 3/4 In. ...................... 12.00
Pressed Glass, Sauce, Daisy & Button, Cloverleaf Shape ...................................... 3.75
Pressed Glass, Sauce, Daisy & Button, Scalloped, Round, 4 1/2 In. .................... 12.00
Pressed Glass, Sauce, Daisy & Button, Square, 4 1/2 In. ..................................... 12.00
Pressed Glass, Sauce, Daisy & Button, 8 Sided, Scalloped Top ........................... 6.50
Pressed Glass, Sauce, Daisy Block Edge, Clear, Clover Shape, 4 1/4 In. ............. 9.00
Pressed Glass, Sauce, Dakota, Footed ......................................................................... 8.75
Pressed Glass, Sauce, Dart, Footed ............................................................................. 3.75
Pressed Glass, Sauce, Deer & Dog, Footed ......................................... 12.50 To 15.00
Pressed Glass, Sauce, Deer & Pine Tree, Flat ......................................................... 12.50
Pressed Glass, Sauce, Deer & Pine Tree, Footed .............................. 15.00 To 18.50
Pressed Glass, Sauce, Delaware, Green, Boat Shape, Flat, Gold Trim ................. 20.00
Pressed Glass, Sauce, Delaware, Green, Round, Flat, Gold Trim ......................... 22.00
Pressed Glass, Sauce, Dew & Raindrop ...................................................................... 3.50
Pressed Glass, Sauce, Dew & Raindrop, Footed ....................................................... 5.00
Pressed Glass, Sauce, Dewdrop & Star ....................................................................... 7.50
Pressed Glass, Sauce, Dewdrop & Star, Footed, 4 In. ............................................. 4.75
Pressed Glass, Sauce, Dewey, Canary ........................................................................ 15.00
Pressed Glass, Sauce, Diagonal Band & Fan, Footed .............................................. 3.75
Pressed Glass, Sauce, Diagonal Band & Fan, 4 In. .................................................. 7.00
Pressed Glass, Sauce, Diamond Thumbprint, Flint ............................... 10.00 To 14.50
Pressed Glass, Sauce, Diamond-Quilted, Blue ........................................................... 8.00
Pressed Glass, Sauce, Diamond, Round, 4 1/4 In. ................................................... 5.00
Pressed Glass, Sauce, Double Wedding Ring ............................................................. 8.00
Pressed Glass, Sauce, Electric, Footed ........................................................................ 5.00
Pressed Glass, Sauce, Etched Dakota, 9 1/2 In. ..................................................... 27.00
Pressed Glass, Sauce, Etched Diamond Point Loop, Blue ....................................... 8.50
Pressed Glass, Sauce, Etched Garden Fruits, Footed ............................................... 3.75
Pressed Glass, Sauce, Etched Grasshopper, 4 In. ................................................... 14.00
Pressed Glass, Sauce, Etched King's Crown, Ruby & Clear, 4 1/2 In. ................. 30.00
Pressed Glass, Sauce, Eyewinker, 4 1/8 In. ......................................... 12.00 To 15.00
Pressed Glass, Sauce, Eyewinker, 5 1/8 In. ............................................................ 18.00
Pressed Glass, Sauce, Festoon, 4 1/2 In. .............................................. 4.75 To 10.00
Pressed Glass, Sauce, Finecut & Block, Blue, Footed, 4 In. ................................. 14.00
Pressed Glass, Sauce, Finecut & Block, Footed, 4 In. ......................... 6.50 To 10.00
Pressed Glass, Sauce, Fishscale, 4 1/2 In. ............................................ 3.75 To 11.00
Pressed Glass, Sauce, Fleur-De-Lis & Drape, Footed .............................................. 3.50
Pressed Glass, Sauce, Fleur-De-Lis & Drape, 4 1/2 In. ........................ 4.25 To 4.75
Pressed Glass, Sauce, Flower & Quill, Handled, Flat, Square, 3 1/2 In. .............. 7.00
Pressed Glass, Sauce, Flower Band ............................................................................. 8.50
Pressed Glass, Sauce, Flower Band, Footed .............................................................. 7.50
Pressed Glass, Sauce, Flower Flange, Emerald Green, 5 In. ................................. 15.00
Pressed Glass, Sauce, Flowerpot, Footed ................................................................... 6.25
Pressed Glass, Sauce, Fluted Scrolls, White Opalescent ....................................... 23.00
Pressed Glass, Sauce, Frosted Artichoke, Deep ...................................................... 12.50
Pressed Glass, Sauce, Frosted Artichoke, Footed, 4 1/4 In. ................................ 14.00
Pressed Glass, Sauce, Frosted Circle ..................................................... 9.00 To 9.50
Pressed Glass, Sauce, Frosted Flower & Pleat, Flat, 4 In. ................................... 12.00

Pressed Glass, Sauce, Frosted Flower Band, Footed ........................................................................ 15.00
Pressed Glass, Sauce, Frosted Lion, 4 In. ........................................................ 9.75 To 25.00
Pressed Glass, Sauce, Frosted Lion, Footed ........................................................................ 18.50
Pressed Glass, Sauce, Frosted Maple Leaf ................................................................ 3.50 To 4.00
Pressed Glass, Sauce, Frosted Stork, 4 In. .................................................... 12.50 To 14.00
Pressed Glass, Sauce, Frosted Vera, Fancy Rim, Flat, 4 3/4 In. ................................ 8.00
Pressed Glass, Sauce, Galloway ........................................................................ 5.75
Pressed Glass, Sauce, Garfield Drape, 4 In. ........................................................ 8.50
Pressed Glass, Sauce, Good Luck, Footed ........................................................ 9.00 To 9.50
Pressed Glass, Sauce, Grace, Footed ........................................................................ 5.00
Pressed Glass, Sauce, Grand, Footed, Fan Edge, 4 1/2 In. ........................................ 7.50
Pressed Glass, Sauce, Grand, 4 3/8 In. ........................................................................ 4.75
Pressed Glass, Sauce, Grape & Festoon With Clear Leaf, 4 In. ................................ 4.50
Pressed Glass, Sauce, Grape & Festoon, 4 In. ........................................................ 4.00
Pressed Glass, Sauce, Grape & Thumbprint, Footed, Marked N ................................ 25.00
Pressed Glass, Sauce, Grasshopper, Without Insect, Footed, 4 In. ................................ 8.00
Pressed Glass, Sauce, Hamilton, 4 In. ........................................................................ 12.00
Pressed Glass, Sauce, Hand, Flat, 4 1/2 In. ........................................................ 3.50
Pressed Glass, Sauce, Hartley, Amber, Footed, 4 1/8 In. ........................................ 12.50
Pressed Glass, Sauce, Hartley, Footed, 4 1/8 In. ........................................................ 7.00
Pressed Glass, Sauce, Heart & Thumbprint ........................................................ 8.50
Pressed Glass, Sauce, Herringbone, Emerald Green, 4 1/2 In. ................................ 15.00
Pressed Glass, Sauce, Herringbone, Green ........................................................ 7.00
Pressed Glass, Sauce, Hickman, Flat, Square, 4 1/4 In. ........................................ 4.50
Pressed Glass, Sauce, Hidalgo, Corner Handle, Flat, 4 1/2 In. ................................ 5.00
Pressed Glass, Sauce, Hobnail, Fan Top, Blue, Findlay, 4 3/4 In. ................................ 15.00
Pressed Glass, Sauce, Horn Of Plenty, Flint ........................................ 12.50 To 15.00
Pressed Glass, Sauce, Horn Of Plenty, Rayed Base, 4 1/2 In. ................................ 15.50
Pressed Glass, Sauce, Horseshoe, Footed, 4 In ........................................................ 8.00
Pressed Glass, Sauce, Hundred Leaved Rose, Flat, 4 1/4 In. ................................ 4.00
Pressed Glass, Sauce, Inverted Fern, Flint ........................................................ 9.00
Pressed Glass, Sauce, Inverted Heart ........................................................................ 6.00
Pressed Glass, Sauce, Inverted Thumbprint, Blue, Footed, 4 1/2 In. ................................ 15.00
Pressed Glass, Sauce, Iowa, 6 1/4 In. ........................................................................ 11.00
Pressed Glass, Sauce, Iris & Meander, Clear & Opalescent, 4 In.Diameter ................................ 10.00
Pressed Glass, Sauce, Jewel & Dewdrop, 4 1/4 In. ........................................................ 4.00
Pressed Glass, Sauce, Kentucky, Footed ........................................................ 6.00 To 6.50
Pressed Glass, Sauce, Klondike, Frosted With Amber Panel ................................ 85.00
Pressed Glass, Sauce, Lacy Floral ........................................................................ 3.00
Pressed Glass, Sauce, Lattice, Flat, 4 In. ........................................................................ 4.00
Pressed Glass, Sauce, Leaf With Amber Flowers, Flat, 4 1/2 In. ................................ 7.50
Pressed Glass, Sauce, Leaflets ........................................................................ 4.00
Pressed Glass, Sauce, Liberty Bell, Flat, Scalloped Edge ........................................ 22.00
Pressed Glass, Sauce, Liberty Bell, Footed ........................................ 22.00 To 26.00
Pressed Glass, Sauce, Liberty Bell, "proclaim Liberty, " Dates In Base ................................ 22.50
Pressed Glass, Sauce, Lily Of The Valley ........................................................................ 8.50
Pressed Glass, Sauce, Lincoln Drape, Flint ........................................................ 14.00
Pressed Glass, Sauce, Loop & Dart With Round Ornament, Flat, 3 3/4 In. ................................ 5.50
Pressed Glass, Sauce, Lotus, Footed ........................................................................ 5.00
Pressed Glass, Sauce, Lotus, Handled, Flat, 4 1/4 In. ........................................ 5.50
Pressed Glass, Sauce, Lotus, Log Handle, Flat, 5 1/4 In. ........................................ 5.50
Pressed Glass, Sauce, Magnet & Grape With Frosted Leaf, Flat, Flint ................................ 10.50
Pressed Glass, Sauce, Maiden's Blush, Gold, 4 1/2 In. ........................................ 25.00
Pressed Glass, Sauce, Maryland, Flat ........................................................................ 4.00
Pressed Glass, Sauce, Michigan ........................................................................ 6.00
Pressed Glass, Sauce, Millard, Amber Flashed, Footed ........................................ 7.50
Pressed Glass, Sauce, Minerva, Footed ........................................ 12.00 To 12.50
Pressed Glass, Sauce, Minerva, 4 In. ........................................................................ 12.00
Pressed Glass, Sauce, Mitered Diamond, Clear & Yellow, 3 1/2 In. ................................ 12.00
Pressed Glass, Sauce, Moon & Star, Footed ........................................................ 8.00
Pressed Glass, Sauce, Moon & Star, 4 1/2 In. ........................................................ 10.00
Pressed Glass, Sauce, New Hampshire, Flared, Round ........................................ 3.00
Pressed Glass, Sauce, New Hampshire, Rose, Gold Trim ........................................ 6.00
Pressed Glass, Sauce, New Hampshire, Square ........................................................ 3.75
Pressed Glass, Sauce, New Hampshire, 4 In. ........................................ 3.50 To 4.75
Pressed Glass, Sauce, New Hampshire, 4 1/8 In. ........................................................ 4.75

| | |
|---|---|
| Pressed Glass, Sauce, Opalescent Ribbed, Blue, Beatty | 11.00 |
| Pressed Glass, Sauce, Oregon | 5.50 |
| Pressed Glass, Sauce, Palmette, 4 In. | 4.00 To 5.00 |
| Pressed Glass, Sauce, Pampas Flower, Footed | 5.00 |
| Pressed Glass, Sauce, Paneled Daisy | 3.75 To 5.00 |
| Pressed Glass, Sauce, Paneled Daisy & Button, Amber Daisy | 18.00 |
| Pressed Glass, Sauce, Paneled Daisy & Button, Clover Leaf Shape, 3 Lobe | 5.85 |
| Pressed Glass, Sauce, Paneled Diamond Cross, Footed | 3.75 |
| Pressed Glass, Sauce, Paneled Forget-Me-Not | 7.50 To 12.00 |
| Pressed Glass, Sauce, Paneled Thistle | 5.00 |
| Pressed Glass, Sauce, Pavonia, Footed | 8.50 |
| Pressed Glass, Sauce, Pavonia, Ruby & Clear, Flat, Crimped, Square, 4 In. | 12.50 |
| Pressed Glass, Sauce, Peacock Feather, 4 1/4 In. | 3.75 To 7.50 |
| Pressed Glass, Sauce, Peacock Feather, 4 3/4 In. | 7.50 |
| Pressed Glass, Sauce, Peacock's-Eye | 12.00 |
| Pressed Glass, Sauce, Peacock's-Eye, Flint, 4 1/4 In. | 12.00 |
| Pressed Glass, Sauce, Pebbled Swirl | 4.00 |
| Pressed Glass, Sauce, Picket | 5.00 |
| Pressed Glass, Sauce, Picket, Footed, Large Size | 10.00 |
| Pressed Glass, Sauce, Picket, Footed, Small Size | 10.00 |
| Pressed Glass, Sauce, Pleat & Panel, Footed, 4 In. | 12.00 |
| Pressed Glass, Sauce, Pleat & Panel, Handled, 4 In. | 7.50 |
| Pressed Glass, Sauce, Portland | 2.00 To 4.50 |
| Pressed Glass, Sauce, Portland, Gold Trim, 4 1/2 In. | 4.00 To 5.50 |
| Pressed Glass, Sauce, Priscilla, 5 In. | 7.00 |
| Pressed Glass, Sauce, Prism Arc | 8.00 |
| Pressed Glass, Sauce, Reticulated Cord, 4 1/2 In. | 4.00 |
| Pressed Glass, Sauce, Ribbed Ivy, Flint | 10.00 |
| Pressed Glass, Sauce, Ribbon, Footed | 7.50 |
| Pressed Glass, Sauce, Roman Rosette, 4 1/2 In. | 4.50 To 6.00 |
| Pressed Glass, Sauce, Rose In Snow | 4.50 |
| Pressed Glass, Sauce, Rose In Snow, Footed | 8.50 |
| Pressed Glass, Sauce, Rose Sprig, Footed | 10.00 |
| Pressed Glass, Sauce, Ruby Thumbprint, Boat Shape | 16.00 |
| Pressed Glass, Sauce, Sandwich Heart, Flat, Flint, 4 1/2 In. | 12.50 |
| Pressed Glass, Sauce, Sandwich Loop, Flat, Flint, 4 In. | 6.50 |
| Pressed Glass, Sauce, Sawtooth & Star, Footed, 4 In. | 5.00 |
| Pressed Glass, Sauce, Sedan, 4 1/4 In. | 3.00 To 3.75 |
| Pressed Glass, Sauce, Shell | 2.00 |
| Pressed Glass, Sauce, Shell & Jewel | 8.00 |
| Pressed Glass, Sauce, Shell & Tassel, Footed, 4 1/2 In. | 12.00 |
| Pressed Glass, Sauce, Shell & Tassel, Handled, Square | 8.50 |
| Pressed Glass, Sauce, Shell & Tassel, Porringer Handle, 4 In. | 7.50 |
| Pressed Glass, Sauce, Shrine | 4.50 |
| Pressed Glass, Sauce, Snowdrop, Clear, Shell Shape, 4 3/4 In. | 12.00 |
| Pressed Glass, Sauce, Spiraled Triangles, Flat | 3.00 |
| Pressed Glass, Sauce, Spirea Band, Amber, Footed | 10.00 To 12.00 |
| Pressed Glass, Sauce, Spirea Band, Blue, Footed | 12.00 |
| Pressed Glass, Sauce, Sprig | 8.00 |
| Pressed Glass, Sauce, Sprig, Footed | 5.00 To 6.50 |
| Pressed Glass, Sauce, Squirrel | 9.00 To 10.50 |
| Pressed Glass, Sauce, Star Rosette | 5.00 |
| Pressed Glass, Sauce, Stippled Chain, 4 1/2 In. | 4.50 |
| Pressed Glass, Sauce, Stippled Daisy | 3.00 |
| Pressed Glass, Sauce, Stippled Grape & Festoon, 4 In. | 4.50 To 6.50 |
| Pressed Glass, Sauce, Stippled Grape Medallion | 6.50 |
| Pressed Glass, Sauce, Stippled Ivy, Flat, 5 In. | 6.50 |
| Pressed Glass, Sauce, Stippled Peppers | 4.50 |
| Pressed Glass, Sauce, Stippled Star | 6.00 |
| Pressed Glass, Sauce, Stork, Stippled & Clear, Footed, 4 1/2 In. | 7.50 |
| Pressed Glass, Sauce, Strigil, Gold Trim | 5.00 |
| Pressed Glass, Sauce, Swirl, Amber, 4 7/8 In. | 16.00 |
| Pressed Glass, Sauce, Teardrop & Tassel | 9.00 To 9.50 |
| Pressed Glass, Sauce, Teasel, Gold, Footed, 5 1/4 In. | 8.00 |
| Pressed Glass, Sauce, Texas, Scalloped Rim, 4 1/4 In. | 6.50 |
| Pressed Glass, Sauce, Texas, 4 In. | 6.00 |

| Pressed Glass, Sauce, Texas, 4 1/2 In. | 7.00 |
|---|---|
| Pressed Glass, Sauce, Texas, 4 3/4 In. | 7.00 |
| Pressed Glass, Sauce, Three Faces, Footed, 4 In. | 19.00 To 20.00 |
| Pressed Glass, Sauce, Three Faces, Footed, 4 1/4 In. | 16.00 |
| Pressed Glass, Sauce, Three Faces, Footed, 4 1/2 In. | 22.50 |
| Pressed Glass, Sauce, Three Faces, Frosted & Clear, Footed | 15.00 |
| Pressed Glass, Sauce, Three Panel, Dark Amber, Footed | 7.00 |
| Pressed Glass, Sauce, Thumbprint, Flint | 12.50 |
| Pressed Glass, Sauce, Tree Of Life | 5.00 |
| Pressed Glass, Sauce, Tree Of Life, Cranberry, Leaf Shape, Portland | 16.50 |
| Pressed Glass, Sauce, Tree Of Life, Shell Shape, Melon Ribbed, Pittsburg | 7.00 |
| Pressed Glass, Sauce, Two Panel, Apple Green, Square, 4 3/4 In. | 9.00 |
| Pressed Glass, Sauce, Two Panel, Green, Oval | 6.00 |
| Pressed Glass, Sauce, Vesta, Opalescent & Clear | 8.50 |
| Pressed Glass, Sauce, Viking, Clear, 4 1/2 In. | 12.00 |
| Pressed Glass, Sauce, Viking, Footed | 8.75 |
| Pressed Glass, Sauce, Wedding Ring, Flint | 7.00 |
| Pressed Glass, Sauce, Westward Ho, Footed, 4 In. | 24.50 |
| Pressed Glass, Sauce, Wheat & Barley, Footed | 4.50 To 8.50 |
| Pressed Glass, Sauce, Wildflower | 4.50 |
| Pressed Glass, Sauce, Wildflower, Blue, Round | 6.50 |
| Pressed Glass, Sauce, Wildflower, Blue, 4 1/0 In. | 17.00 |
| Pressed Glass, Sauce, Wildflower, Footed, Round | 7.00 |
| Pressed Glass, Sauce, Wildflower, Green | 6.00 |
| Pressed Glass, Sauce, Wildflower, Square | 4.50 To 6.50 |
| Pressed Glass, Sauce, 101, 5 In. | 12.95 |
| Pressed Glass, Sauce, 1, 000-Eye, Amber, Collared, 3 Knob Stem, 4 1/2 In. | 15.00 |
| Pressed Glass, Sauce, 1, 000-Eye, Amber, 4 1/2 In. | 10.00 |
| Pressed Glass, Sauce, 1, 000-Eye, Footed, 3 7/8 In. | 8.00 To 12.00 |
| Pressed Glass, Server, Cake, Shoshone, Green, Pedestal | 22.00 |
| Pressed Glass, Shade, Gas, Waffle, Ruffled Beaded Edge, Dated July 14, 1896 | 5.00 |
| Pressed Glass, Sherbet & Coaster, Texas Centennial, Stemmed, Flags, Dated | 18.50 |
| Pressed Glass, Sherbet, Block On Stilts, Footed | 8.00 |
| Pressed Glass, Sherbet, Flute, 2 7/8 In. | 5.80 |
| Pressed Glass, Sherbet, Paneled Heather, Footed, 3 1/2 In. Diameter | 5.00 |
| Pressed Glass, Sherbet, Westward Ho | 50.00 |
| Pressed Glass, Sherry, Duncan & Miller No.42 | 15.00 To 16.50 |
| Pressed Glass, Sherry, Knobby Bull's-Eye, Amethyst Eyes | 15.00 |
| Pressed Glass, Shoe, Bouquet Holder, Findlay | 22.50 |
| Pressed Glass, Shoe, Daisy & Button, Amber | 20.00 To 25.00 |
| Pressed Glass, Shoe, Daisy & Button, Amber, Dated Oct.19,'86 | 25.00 |
| Pressed Glass, Shoe, Daisy & Button, Amber, Dated 1888 | 24.00 |
| Pressed Glass, Shoe, Daisy & Button, Amber, 2 In. | 30.00 |
| Pressed Glass, Shoe, Daisy & Button, Amber, 6 In. | 30.00 |
| Pressed Glass, Shoe, Daisy & Button, Cobalt Blue | 34.00 |
| Pressed Glass, Shoe, Diamond Point & Ribbing, Canary, Bow On Toe | 16.00 |
| Pressed Glass, Shoe, Oxford With Bow, Canary | 40.00 |
| Pressed Glass, Shot Glass, Cornell, Gold Flashing | 4.00 |
| Pressed Glass, Sleigh, Daisy & Button, Blue, 8 In.Long | 55.00 |
| Pressed Glass, Slipper, Cane, Amber, 5 In. | 27.50 |
| Pressed Glass, Slipper, Cane, Blue | 15.00 |
| Pressed Glass, Slipper, Daisy & Button, Amber, High Heel | 16.00 |
| Pressed Glass, Slipper, Daisy & Button, Amber, 1936, 4 1/2 In. | 15.00 |
| Pressed Glass, Slipper, Daisy & Button, Amethyst, 7 1/4 In. Lon | 20.00 To 55.00 |
| Pressed Glass, Slipper, Daisy & Button, Blue, Cat's Head Top, 6 In. | 15.00 |
| Pressed Glass, Slipper, Daisy & Button, Blue, High Top | 21.00 |
| Pressed Glass, Slipper, Daisy & Button, Blue, Marked Pat'd Oct.'83 | 45.00 |
| Pressed Glass, Slipper, Daisy & Button, Golden Amber, Dated 1886 | 39.50 |
| Pressed Glass, Slipper, Daisy & Button, Ruby Flashed, Dated 1865 | 23.00 |
| Pressed Glass, Slipper, Finecut, Amber | 18.00 |
| Pressed Glass, Slipper, Puss-In-Boots, Blue, Findlay, 5 3/4 In. | 22.50 |
| Pressed Glass, Slipper, Sequoia, Amber | 18.00 |
| Pressed Glass, Spill, Arch Band, Flint | 33.50 |
| Pressed Glass, Spill, Arched Band | 33.50 |
| Pressed Glass, Spill, Argus | 35.00 |
| Pressed Glass, Spill, Argus, Flint | 30.00 |

Pressed Glass, Spill, Armorial, Flint ............................................................................................ 55.00
Pressed Glass, Spill, Baby Thumbprint .......................................................................................... 38.00
Pressed Glass, Spill, Bull's-Eye, Flint .............................................................. 28.00 To 50.00
Pressed Glass, Spill, Diamond Point, Flint ................................................................................. 25.00
Pressed Glass, Spill, Diamond Point, Knob Stem, Flint ....................................................... 20.00
Pressed Glass, Spill, Flat Sawtooth, Flint ................................................................................. 16.00
Pressed Glass, Spill, Harp ................................................................................................................ 45.00
Pressed Glass, Spill, Harp, Flint ........................................................................ 40.00 To 45.00
Pressed Glass, Spill, Horn Of Plenty ................................................................ 26.00 To 38.00
Pressed Glass, Spill, Horn Of Plenty, Flint ..................................................... 19.50 To 35.00
Pressed Glass, Spill, Loop, Flint ................................................................................................... 18.00
Pressed Glass, Spill, Lyre, Flint ..................................................................................................... 40.00
Pressed Glass, Spill, Moon & Star ............................................................................................... 33.00
Pressed Glass, Spill, New England Pineapple, Flint ............................................................... 38.50
Pressed Glass, Spill, Prism & Flattened Sawtooth, Flint ....................................................... 20.00
Pressed Glass, Spill, Ribbed Palm ............................................................................................... 17.00
Pressed Glass, Spill, Sandwich Star ............................................................................................ 25.00
Pressed Glass, Spill, Sandwich Star, Flint ........................................................ 28.00 To 35.00
Pressed Glass, Spill, Sawtooth ...................................................................................................... 30.00
Pressed Glass, Spill, Sawtooth, Flint ......................................................................................... 16.50
Pressed Glass, Spill, Star & Buckle ............................................................................................. 37.50
Pressed Glass, Spill, Star & Buckle, Flint ................................................................................ 37.50
Pressed Glass, Spill, Tulip With Short Ribs ............................................................................... 18.50
Pressed Glass, Spill, Waffle & Thumbprint, Flint .......................................... 23.00 To 38.00
Pressed Glass, Spill, Washington .................................................................................................. 35.00
Pressed Glass, Spill, Washington, Flint ...................................................................................... 45.00
Pressed Glass, Spittoon, Button Arches .................................................................................... 45.00
Pressed Glass, Spooner, Actress ................................................................................................... 32.00
Pressed Glass, Spooner, Actress, Frosted & Clear ............................................................... 45.00
Pressed Glass, Spooner, Alabama ................................................................................................ 14.00
Pressed Glass, Spooner, Arched Grape ...................................................................................... 12.50
Pressed Glass, Spooner, Arched Ovals, Gold Trim ................................................................ 8.50
Pressed Glass, Spooner, Atlas ....................................................................................................... 22.50
Pressed Glass, Spooner, Austrian, Greentown ............................................... 16.00 To 17.50
Pressed Glass, Spooner, Austrian, Greentown, Miniature .................................................. 25.00
Pressed Glass, Spooner, Banded Buckle ........................................................ 16.75 To 25.00
Pressed Glass, Spooner, Banded Buckle, Footed ................................................................. 22.00
Pressed Glass, Spooner, Banded Star ........................................................................................ 14.00
Pressed Glass, Spooner, Bar & Star Etched ........................................................................... 30.00
Pressed Glass, Spooner, Barberry ...................................................................... 15.00 To 18.00
Pressed Glass, Spooner, Barberry, Oval Berries .................................................................... 14.00
Pressed Glass, Spooner, Barberry, Scalloped Top ................................................................ 16.00
Pressed Glass, Spooner, Beaded Acorn With Leaf Band ..................................................... 16.50
Pressed Glass, Spooner, Beaded Finecut .................................................................................. 13.50
Pressed Glass, Spooner, Beaded Grape Medallion ....................................... 14.50 To 18.00
Pressed Glass, Spooner, Beaded Grape Medallion, Footed ................................................ 14.00
Pressed Glass, Spooner, Beaded Swag, Blue .......................................................................... 20.00
Pressed Glass, Spooner, Beatty Swirl, Clear To Opalescent .............................................. 19.00
Pressed Glass, Spooner, Bellflower ................................................................... 18.50 To 28.00
Pressed Glass, Spooner, Bellflower With Fine Rib, C.1830 ................................................. 45.00
Pressed Glass, Spooner, Bellflower, Double Vine .................................................................. 30.00
Pressed Glass, Spooner, Bellflower, Flint .................................................................................. 24.50
Pressed Glass, Spooner, Bellflower, Light Impression, Flint .............................................. 18.00
Pressed Glass, Spooner, Bellflower, Scalloped ....................................................................... 35.00
Pressed Glass, Spooner, Bellflower, Scalloped Top, Flint ........................... 22.00 To 35.00
Pressed Glass, Spooner, Bellflower, Single Vine .................................................................... 24.00
Pressed Glass, Spooner, Bellflower, Single Vine, Flint ........................................................ 32.50
Pressed Glass, Spooner, Bellflower, Single Vine, Scalloped Top, Flint ......................... 20.00
Pressed Glass, Spooner, Beveled Diamond With Star .......................................................... 12.50
Pressed Glass, Spooner, Beveled Star ............................................................. 15.00 To 18.00
Pressed Glass, Spooner, Blackberry ................................................................. 16.50 To 19.00
Pressed Glass, Spooner, Bleeding Heart ......................................................... 8.00 To 32.00
Pressed Glass, Spooner, Bowtie ................................................................................................... 16.00
Pressed Glass, Spooner, Broken Column ................................................................................... 16.50
Pressed Glass, Spooner, Buckle ......................................................................... 15.00 To 17.50
Pressed Glass, Spooner, Button Band .............................................................. 15.00 To 16.00

Pressed Glass, Spooner,
Cardinal Bird

Pressed Glass,
Spooner, Curtain

| | |
|---|---|
| Pressed Glass, Spooner, Cable | 25.00 |
| Pressed Glass, Spooner, Cable, Flint | 22.50 To 35.00 |
| Pressed Glass, Spooner, Cardinal Bird | Illus 12.00 |
| Pressed Glass, Spooner, Carnation, Pres Cut | 5.00 |
| Pressed Glass, Spooner, Cathedral | 12.50 To 29.95 |
| Pressed Glass, Spooner, Chain | 9.00 |
| Pressed Glass, Spooner, Chain & Star | 15.00 |
| Pressed Glass, Spooner, Chandelier | 16.50 |
| Pressed Glass, Spooner, Child's, Hobnail, Blue | 20.00 |
| Pressed Glass, Spooner, Child's, Snowflake | 12.00 |
| Pressed Glass, Spooner, Child's, Virginia | 18.00 |
| Pressed Glass, Spooner, Classic | 75.00 |
| Pressed Glass, Spooner, Classic, Open Log Feet | 75.00 |
| Pressed Glass, Spooner, Clematis | 12.00 To 16.00 |
| Pressed Glass, Spooner, Coarse Prism, Flint | 15.00 |
| Pressed Glass, Spooner, Comet, McKee | 20.00 |
| Pressed Glass, Spooner, Cottage, Bellaire Goblet Co. | 14.00 |
| Pressed Glass, Spooner, Crow's-Foot | 18.50 |
| Pressed Glass, Spooner, Crystal Wedding, Ruby Stained | 35.00 |
| Pressed Glass, Spooner, Cupid & Venus | 35.00 |
| Pressed Glass, Spooner, Currier & Ives | 15.00 |
| Pressed Glass, Spooner, Curtain | Illus 13.00 |
| Pressed Glass, Spooner, Curtain Tieback | 22.50 |
| Pressed Glass, Spooner, Cut Log | 15.00 To 22.50 |
| Pressed Glass, Spooner, Daisy & Button With Crossbar | 12.50 |
| Pressed Glass, Spooner, Daisy & Button With Pointed Panel | 16.00 |
| Pressed Glass, Spooner, Daisy & Button With V Ornament | 16.00 |
| Pressed Glass, Spooner, Daisy & Button, Sapphire Blue, 7 In. High | 15.00 |
| Pressed Glass, Spooner, Daisy In Bull's-Eye, Amethyst Eyes | 21.50 |
| Pressed Glass, Spooner, Deer & Pine Tree | 27.50 |
| Pressed Glass, Spooner, Delaware, Emerald | 38.50 |
| Pressed Glass, Spooner, Delaware, Emerald, Gold Trim | 27.00 |
| Pressed Glass, Spooner, Delaware, Rose, Gold Trim | 40.00 |
| Pressed Glass, Spooner, Dewey, Green, Greentown | 35.00 |
| Pressed Glass, Spooner, Diagonal Band & Fan | 12.50 |
| Pressed Glass, Spooner, Diamond & Sunburst, 5 3/4 In.High | 9.00 |
| Pressed Glass, Spooner, Diamond Point | 22.00 |
| Pressed Glass, Spooner, Diamond Point & Loop, Amber | 19.00 |
| Pressed Glass, Spooner, Diamond Point, Flint | 35.00 |
| Pressed Glass, Spooner, Diamond Point, Scalloped | 15.00 |
| Pressed Glass, Spooner, Diamond Rosette | 14.00 |
| Pressed Glass, Spooner, Diamond Thumbprint, Flint | 55.00 |
| Pressed Glass, Spooner, Double Paneled Diamond, Scalloped Top, Flint | 15.00 |
| Pressed Glass, Spooner, Drape | 16.00 |
| Pressed Glass, Spooner, Drapery, Footed | 24.00 |
| Pressed Glass, Spooner, Esther | 25.00 |
| Pressed Glass, Spooner, Etched Clear Ribbon | 18.50 |
| Pressed Glass, Spooner, Etched Dakota, Fern & Berry | 22.50 |

Pressed Glass, Spooner, Etched Frosted Eagle .................................................. 37.50
Pressed Glass, Spooner, Etched Mascotte ........................................................ 12.50
Pressed Glass, Spooner, Etched Star, Ruby & Clear ........................................ 32.00
Pressed Glass, Spooner, Eureka, Flint ............................................................ 20.00
Pressed Glass, Spooner, Excelsior, Flint ......................................................... 15.00
Pressed Glass, Spooner, Feather ........................................................ 7.50 To 14.00
Pressed Glass, Spooner, Feather, Scalloped Rim ............................................ 17.00
Pressed Glass, Spooner, Festoon ................................................................... 19.50
Pressed Glass, Spooner, Flattened Diamond & Sunburst, Miniature ............... 11.00
Pressed Glass, Spooner, Fleur-De-Lis & Tassel ............................................. 15.00
Pressed Glass, Spooner, Fluted Scrolls, Blue, Opalescent ............................. 25.00
Pressed Glass, Spooner, Forget-Me-Not In Scroll ........................................... 9.00
Pressed Glass, Spooner, French Flower Band ................................................. 27.50
Pressed Glass, Spooner, Frosted Circle .......................................................... 20.00
Pressed Glass, Spooner, Frosted Flower Band, 2 Handled .............................. 45.00
Pressed Glass, Spooner, Frosted Lion ................................................. 22.50 To 30.00
Pressed Glass, Spooner, Frosted Ribbon ........................................................ 13.50
Pressed Glass, Spooner, Galloway ....................................................... 9.00 To 17.00
Pressed Glass, Spooner, Garfield Drape .......................................................... 20.00
Pressed Glass, Spooner, Geddes, Pedestal Base ........................................... 20.00
Pressed Glass, Spooner, Giant Prism .............................................................. 20.00
Pressed Glass, Spooner, Giant Sawtooth ....................................................... 57.00
Pressed Glass, Spooner, Grape & Festoon ........................................... 16.00 To 19.00
Pressed Glass, Spooner, Grape & Festoon With Stippled Leaf ........................ 15.00
Pressed Glass, Spooner, Grape Scroll Medallion, Grapes Form Handles ......... 15.00
Pressed Glass, Spooner, Grasshopper, Insects .............................................. 35.00
Pressed Glass, Spooner, Hamilton ........................................................ 13.50 To 25.00
Pressed Glass, Spooner, Hamilton, Flint ............................................... 18.00 To 26.50
Pressed Glass, Spooner, Harp, Flint ............................................................... 40.00
Pressed Glass, Spooner, Hobnail, Opalescent, Fluted Top ............................. 24.50
Pressed Glass, Spooner, Honeycomb, Sawtooth Edge .................................... 8.50
Pressed Glass, Spooner, Horn Of Plenty ........................................................ 32.50
Pressed Glass, Spooner, Horn Of Plenty, Flint ............................................... 65.00
Pressed Glass, Spooner, Horseshoe ............................................................... 30.00
Pressed Glass, Spooner, Inverted Fern, Scalloped Rim, Flint ......................... 20.00
Pressed Glass, Spooner, Inverted Oval Thumbprint, Apple Green, Footed ....... 29.50
Pressed Glass, Spooner, Jersey Swirl ............................................................ 16.00
Pressed Glass, Spooner, Jeweled Moon & Star ............................................. 16.00
Pressed Glass, Spooner, King's Crown, Scalloped Top ................................... 25.00
Pressed Glass, Spooner, King's Crown, 4 In. High ................................ 7.50 To 12.00
Pressed Glass, Spooner, Lacy Daisy ..................................................... 7.50 To 12.00
Pressed Glass, Spooner, Liberty Bell ............................................................. 57.50
Pressed Glass, Spooner, Lily Of The Valley, 3 Legs ............................. 20.00 To 25.00
Pressed Glass, Spooner, Lion ............................................................... 22.50 To 24.50
Pressed Glass, Spooner, Log Cabin ............................................................... 48.00
Pressed Glass, Spooner, Loop ....................................................................... 12.00
Pressed Glass, Spooner, Loop & Dart With Round Ornament .................. 13.50 To 25.00
Pressed Glass, Spooner, Louisiana ................................................................ 10.00
Pressed Glass, Spooner, Magnet & Frosted Grape ........................................ 45.00
Pressed Glass, Spooner, Manhattan ............................................................... 10.00
Pressed Glass, Spooner, Marsh, Pink ............................................................ 12.00
Pressed Glass, Spooner, Michigan .................................................................. 15.00
Pressed Glass, Spooner, Minerva .......................................................... 15.00 To 35.00
Pressed Glass, Spooner, Missouri .................................................................. 15.00
Pressed Glass, Spooner, Mitered Bars ........................................................... 15.00
Pressed Glass, Spooner, Monkey .................................................................. 12.50
Pressed Glass, Spooner, Monkey Under Tree ................................................ 75.00
Pressed Glass, Spooner, Monkey, Opalescent ............................................... 75.00
Pressed Glass, Spooner, New England Pineapple .......................................... 26.50
Pressed Glass, Spooner, New England Pineapple, Flint .................................. 32.00
Pressed Glass, Spooner, New Hampshire .............................................. 12.00 To 15.00
Pressed Glass, Spooner, New York Honeycomb ............................................ 17.50
Pressed Glass, Spooner, Oak Wreath ............................................................ 15.00
Pressed Glass, Spooner, Old Abe ................................................................... 22.00
Pressed Glass, Spooner, Open Rose ...................................................... 15.00 To 17.00
Pressed Glass, Spooner, Oval Star, Miniature ............................................... 12.50

| | |
|---|---:|
| Pressed Glass, Spooner, Palmette | 10.00 |
| Pressed Glass, Spooner, Paneled Cane | 14.00 |
| Pressed Glass, Spooner, Paneled Daisy & Button | 24.00 |
| Pressed Glass, Spooner, Paneled Dewdrop | 12.00 |
| Pressed Glass, Spooner, Paneled Finecut | 8.00 |
| Pressed Glass, Spooner, Paneled Forget-Me-Not | 15.00 |
| Pressed Glass, Spooner, Paneled Grape Band | 11.50 |
| Pressed Glass, Spooner, Paneled Thistle | 20.00 |
| Pressed Glass, Spooner, Paneled Thistle, Handled | 13.00 To 17.50 |
| Pressed Glass, Spooner, Paneled Wheat | 15.00 |
| Pressed Glass, Spooner, Paneled Wild Daisy | 10.50 |
| Pressed Glass, Spooner, Pleat & Panel | 15.00 |
| Pressed Glass, Spooner, Pointed Jewel | 15.00 |
| Pressed Glass, Spooner, Pressed Leaf | 15.00 |
| Pressed Glass, Spooner, Primrose | 16.50 |
| Pressed Glass, Spooner, Princess Feather | 14.50 To 27.00 |
| Pressed Glass, Spooner, Priscilla, Green, Fostoria | 24.00 |
| Pressed Glass, Spooner, Prism & Diamond Band | 29.95 |
| Pressed Glass, Spooner, Prism, Flint | 15.00 |
| Pressed Glass, Spooner, Quaker Lady | 20.00 |
| Pressed Glass, Spooner, Queen, Amber | 21.00 |
| Pressed Glass, Spooner, Red Block | 29.50 |
| Pressed Glass, Spooner, Ribbed Bellflower, Fluted Top, 5 3/4 In. | 17.00 |
| Pressed Glass, Spooner, Ribbed Grape, Flint | 25.00 To 33.00 |
| Pressed Glass, Spooner, Ribbed Ivy | 25.00 |
| Pressed Glass, Spooner, Ribbed Ivy, Flint | 24.00 |
| Pressed Glass, Spooner, Ribbed Ivy, Pedestal, Flint | 30.00 |
| Pressed Glass, Spooner, Ribbed Ivy, Scalloped | 25.00 |
| Pressed Glass, Spooner, Ribbed Ivy, Scalloped Top, Flint | 22.00 |
| Pressed Glass, Spooner, Ribbed Palm | 25.00 |
| Pressed Glass, Spooner, Ribbed Palm, Flint | 22.50 To 35.00 |
| Pressed Glass, Spooner, Ribbed Palm, Footed, Flint | 24.00 |
| Pressed Glass, Spooner, Ribbon Candy | 11.00 |
| Pressed Glass, Spooner, Ribbon, Corrigan, Scalloped Foot | 12.50 |
| Pressed Glass, Spooner, Rose Band, Handled, Portland | 16.00 |
| Pressed Glass, Spooner, Rose In Snow, Square | 28.00 |
| Pressed Glass, Spooner, Rose Sprig | 24.00 |
| Pressed Glass, Spooner, Rosette With Pinwheel | 17.50 |
| Pressed Glass, Spooner, Rosette, Ruby Flashed | 13.00 |
| Pressed Glass, Spooner, Ruby Thumbprint, Etched Leaf & Grape | 35.00 |
| Pressed Glass, Spooner, Sawtooth Band | 16.00 |
| Pressed Glass, Spooner, Sawtooth, Flint | 16.00 |
| Pressed Glass, Spooner, Scalloped Diamond Point | 15.00 |
| Pressed Glass, Spooner, Scroll With Flowers | 11.00 |
| Pressed Glass, Spooner, Sedan | 9.50 |
| Pressed Glass, Spooner, Seneca Loop | 18.00 |
| Pressed Glass, Spooner, Shell & Jewel | 18.00 |
| Pressed Glass, Spooner, Shell & Tassel, Round | 30.00 |
| Pressed Glass, Spooner, Snail | 14.00 To 22.50 |
| Pressed Glass, Spooner, Spirea Band | 7.00 |
| Pressed Glass, Spooner, Stippled Band, Flint | 14.50 |
| Pressed Glass, Spooner, Stippled Chain | 11.50 To 13.50 |
| Pressed Glass, Spooner, Stippled Double Loop | 16.50 |
| Pressed Glass, Spooner, Stippled Grape & Festoon | 10.50 To 28.00 |
| Pressed Glass, Spooner, Stippled Medallion, Flint | 25.00 |
| Pressed Glass, Spooner, Stippled Scroll | 12.00 |
| Pressed Glass, Spooner, Strawberry & Raspberry | 35.00 |
| Pressed Glass, Spooner, Sweetheart, Toy | 14.00 |
| Pressed Glass, Spooner, Swirl | 16.00 |
| Pressed Glass, Spooner, Swirl, Toy | 12.50 |
| Pressed Glass, Spooner, Tape Measure, Flint | 20.00 |
| Pressed Glass, Spooner, Tappan, Miniature | 9.75 To 10.00 |
| Pressed Glass, Spooner, Teardrop & Thumbprint, Blue | 25.00 |
| Pressed Glass, Spooner, Three Panel, Dark Amber | 22.50 To 25.00 |
| Pressed Glass, Spooner, Three Panel, Light Amber | 21.50 |
| Pressed Glass, Spooner, Torpedo | 10.50 To 18.50 |

Pressed Glass, Spooner, Triple Bar With Cable ............................................................ 13.00
Pressed Glass, Spooner, Tulip & Honeycomb, Miniature ............................................. 12.00
Pressed Glass, Spooner, Tulip With Sawtooth ............................................ 14.50 To 38.00
Pressed Glass, Spooner, Tulip With Sawtooth, Petal Rim ......................................... 17.50
Pressed Glass, Spooner, Two Band ............................................................... 7.50 To 18.00
Pressed Glass, Spooner, Two Panel ................................................................................ 24.00
Pressed Glass, Spooner, U.S.Coin, Quarters ............................................................... 175.00
Pressed Glass, Spooner, Vincent Valentine, Painted Flowers ................................... 16.00
Pressed Glass, Spooner, Vine & Flower, Amber, Wheeling ........................................ 40.00
Pressed Glass, Spooner, Washington .............................................................................. 35.00
Pressed Glass, Spooner, Wedding Bells .......................................................................... 25.00
Pressed Glass, Spooner, Westward Ho ...................................................... 32.00 To 55.00
Pressed Glass, Spooner, Wheat & Barley ....................................................................... 12.00
Pressed Glass, Spooner, Whirligig, Miniature ........................................... 7.00 To 13.50
Pressed Glass, Spooner, Whirling Star, Toy ................................................................. 13.00
Pressed Glass, Spooner, Wild Bouquet, Blue Opalescent .......................................... 45.00
Pressed Glass, Spooner, Wildflower ............................................................................... 15.00
Pressed Glass, Spooner, Wildflower, Blue ..................................................................... 20.00
Pressed Glass, Spooner, Windflower ............................................................................... 8.50
Pressed Glass, Spooner, X-Ray, Gold Trim .................................................................... 20.00
Pressed Glass, Spooner, Zippered Block, Red Flashed ............................................... 18.75
Pressed Glass, Spooner, 100-Leaved Ivy ....................................................................... 10.00
Pressed Glass, Spooner, 1, 000-Eye ................................................................................ 20.00
Pressed Glass, Spooner, 1, 000-Eye, Amber, 3 Knob Feet ....................................... 28.50
Pressed Glass, Spooner, 1, 000-Eye, Apple Green ...................................................... 22.50
Pressed Glass, Spooner, 100-Leaved Ivy ....................................................................... 10.00
Pressed Glass, Stein, Maple Leaf, Miniature ............................................................... 1.75
Pressed Glass, Sugar & Creamer, Amazon & Sawtooth Band, Cover, Etched W ......... 40.00
Pressed Glass, Sugar & Creamer, Baltimore Pear ....................................................... 24.00
Pressed Glass, Sugar & Creamer, Bellflower, Double Vine, Helmet Creamer ............. 100.00
Pressed Glass, Sugar & Creamer, Bird & Strawberry, Cover, Gold Trim .................. 60.00
Pressed Glass, Sugar & Creamer, Buckle ...................................................................... 12.00
Pressed Glass, Sugar & Creamer, Button Arches, Red & Clear, Satin Band ............. 45.00
Pressed Glass, Sugar & Creamer, Cable With Ring ..................................................... 140.00
Pressed Glass, Sugar & Creamer, Cameo ...................................................................... 38.00
Pressed Glass, Sugar & Creamer, Canterbury, Crystal, Duncan ............................... 10.00
Pressed Glass, Sugar & Creamer, Child's, Arrowhead In Oval, Cover ...................... 22.00
Pressed Glass, Sugar & Creamer, Child's, Dressed Cat Leads Dog By Ribbon ........ 16.00
Pressed Glass, Sugar & Creamer, Child's, Hobnail, Opalescent ............................... 12.50
Pressed Glass, Sugar & Creamer, Cut & Pressed ........................................................ 35.00
Pressed Glass, Sugar & Creamer, Diamond Point ....................................................... 150.00
Pressed Glass, Sugar & Creamer, Etched Dakota, Cover ........................................... 35.00
Pressed Glass, Sugar & Creamer, Flat Diamond, Cover ............................................. 30.00
Pressed Glass, Sugar & Creamer, Floradora, Cranberry On Stippled, Gilt Feet ....... 75.00
Pressed Glass, Sugar & Creamer, Frosted Lion ........................................................... 57.50
Pressed Glass, Sugar & Creamer, Hobnail .................................................................... 25.00
Pressed Glass, Sugar & Creamer, Individual, Heart & Thumbprint .......................... 30.00
Pressed Glass, Sugar & Creamer, Individual, Melon Ribbed ...................................... 6.50
Pressed Glass, Sugar & Creamer, Loop & Dart ........................................................... 90.00
Pressed Glass, Sugar & Creamer, Loop & Dart, Cover ............................................... 38.00
Pressed Glass, Sugar & Creamer, Maiden's Blush, Low ............................................. 38.50
Pressed Glass, Sugar & Creamer, Memphis, Green, Gold ........................................... 50.00
Pressed Glass, Sugar & Creamer, Michigan, Pink Flashed, Cover ............................ 105.00
Pressed Glass, Sugar & Creamer, New Hampshire ...................................................... 15.50
Pressed Glass, Sugar & Creamer, Old Man In Woods ................................................. 34.00
Pressed Glass, Sugar & Creamer, Open Rose, Applied Handles ............................... 35.00
Pressed Glass, Sugar & Creamer, Paneled Palm, Scalloped Rims, Gold Trim ......... 20.00
Pressed Glass, Sugar & Creamer, Paneled 44 Green Band ........................................ 20.00
Pressed Glass, Sugar & Creamer, Rock Crystal, Pagoda Type Cover, McKee .......... 24.00
Pressed Glass, Sugar & Creamer, Roman Rosette .................................................. *Illus* 45.00
Pressed Glass, Sugar & Creamer, Rotec, Large Size ................................................... 25.00
Pressed Glass, Sugar & Creamer, Sheraton, Amethyst, Covered, Greek Key Top ...... 42.50
Pressed Glass, Sugar & Creamer, Star ........................................................................... 35.00
Pressed Glass, Sugar & Creamer, Swan ........................................................................ 75.00
Pressed Glass, Sugar & Creamer, Texas Centennial, Lone Star Finial ..................... 45.00
Pressed Glass, Sugar & Creamer, Texas, Individual, Gold ........................................ 15.00

Pressed Glass, Sugar, Arched Fleur-De-Lis

Pressed Glass, Sugar & Creamer, Roman Rosette
(See Page 478)

| | |
|---|---|
| Pressed Glass, Sugar & Creamer, Toy, Sweetheart, Cover | 28.00 |
| Pressed Glass, Sugar & Creamer, Tree Of Life, Ball & Hand Finial & Stems | 95.00 |
| Pressed Glass, Sugar, Alabama | 10.00 |
| Pressed Glass, Sugar, Alabama, Covered | 23.50 |
| Pressed Glass, Sugar, Amberette, Covered | 70.00 |
| Pressed Glass, Sugar, Anthemion, Covered | 28.50 |
| Pressed Glass, Sugar, Apollo, Covered | 38.00 |
| Pressed Glass, Sugar, Archaic Gothic, Covered | 19.50 |
| Pressed Glass, Sugar, Arched Fleur-De-Lis ............ Illus | 7.00 |
| Pressed Glass, Sugar, Argus, Covered, Flint | 75.00 |
| Pressed Glass, Sugar, Arrowhead, Covered | 15.00 |
| Pressed Glass, Sugar, Art, Covered | 27.50 To 29.00 |
| Pressed Glass, Sugar, Ashburton, Flint, 5 3/8 In. High | 30.00 To 32.00 |
| Pressed Glass, Sugar, Atlas | 17.50 |
| Pressed Glass, Sugar, Austrian | 20.00 |
| Pressed Glass, Sugar, Balder, Covered, Gold Trim, 5 In.Diameter | 16.00 |
| Pressed Glass, Sugar, Barberry, Covered | 38.00 |
| Pressed Glass, Sugar, Barley | 30.00 |
| Pressed Glass, Sugar, Beaded Acorn Medallion, Covered | 23.00 |
| Pressed Glass, Sugar, Beaded Arched Panels, Covered | 13.00 To 14.00 |
| Pressed Glass, Sugar, Beaded Band, Covered | 18.75 |
| Pressed Glass, Sugar, Beaded Banded Grape Medallion | 15.00 |
| Pressed Glass, Sugar, Beaded Chain | 15.00 |
| Pressed Glass, Sugar, Beaded Finecut, Covered | 16.00 |
| Pressed Glass, Sugar, Beaded Grape Medallion, Covered | 18.00 |
| Pressed Glass, Sugar, Beaded Medallion | 12.00 |
| Pressed Glass, Sugar, Beaded Mirror, Flint | 20.00 |
| Pressed Glass, Sugar, Bearded Man, Covered | 20.00 |
| Pressed Glass, Sugar, Bellflower, Covered, Flint | 80.00 |
| Pressed Glass, Sugar, Bellflower, Double Vine | 38.00 |
| Pressed Glass, Sugar, Bellflower, Double Vine, Coarse Rib, Flint, 5 1/2 In. | 47.50 |
| Pressed Glass, Sugar, Bellflower, Double Vine, Flint | 20.00 To 25.00 |
| Pressed Glass, Sugar, Bellflower, Flint | 35.00 To 40.00 |
| Pressed Glass, Sugar, Bellflower, Single Vine, Acorn Finial | 75.00 |
| Pressed Glass, Sugar, Bellflower, Single Vine, Flint | 25.00 |
| Pressed Glass, Sugar, Beveled Diamond, Ruby, Covered | 32.75 |
| Pressed Glass, Sugar, Bird & Strawberry | 20.00 |
| Pressed Glass, Sugar, Bird & Strawberry, Covered | 16.00 To 58.00 |
| Pressed Glass, Sugar, Blaze, Flint | 24.00 |
| Pressed Glass, Sugar, Bleeding Heart | 22.50 |
| Pressed Glass, Sugar, Broken Column, Covered | 34.50 |
| Pressed Glass, Sugar, Broken Column, Red Dot | 35.00 |
| Pressed Glass, Sugar, Bryce, Covered | 18.00 To 19.00 |
| Pressed Glass, Sugar, Buckle | 3.00 |
| Pressed Glass, Sugar, Buckle, Covered | 30.00 |
| Pressed Glass, Sugar, Buckle, Covered, Flint | 42.00 |
| Pressed Glass, Sugar, Buckle, Covered, Footed, 9 In. | 15.00 |
| Pressed Glass, Sugar, Butterfly, Covered | 13.50 To 14.50 |
| Pressed Glass, Sugar, Butterfly, 2 Handled | 7.50 |

| | |
|---|---|
| Pressed Glass, Sugar, Cabbage Rose | 24.00 |
| Pressed Glass, Sugar, Cable With Fan, Flint | 35.00 |
| Pressed Glass, Sugar, Cable With Ring, Covered | 85.00 |
| Pressed Glass, Sugar, Cable With Ring, Covered, Flint | 50.00 To 55.00 |
| Pressed Glass, Sugar, Canadian, Covered | 37.50 To 47.50 |
| Pressed Glass, Sugar, Cardinal Bird, Covered | 38.75 |
| Pressed Glass, Sugar, Cathedral | 22.50 |
| Pressed Glass, Sugar, Cathedral, Covered | 28.50 To 30.00 |
| Pressed Glass, Sugar, Chain | 9.50 |
| Pressed Glass, Sugar, Chain, Covered | 18.00 To 25.00 |
| Pressed Glass, Sugar, Child's, Hobnail, Blue | 20.00 |
| Pressed Glass, Sugar, Child's, Hobnail, Opalescent | 15.00 |
| Pressed Glass, Sugar, Child's, Oval Star, Covered | 18.00 |
| Pressed Glass, Sugar, Church Windows, Covered | 13.50 |
| Pressed Glass, Sugar, Classic | 22.50 |
| Pressed Glass, Sugar, Colonial, Covered, Flint | 54.00 |
| Pressed Glass, Sugar, Colossus, Covered | 14.00 To 22.50 |
| Pressed Glass, Sugar, Cottage, Covered, Bellaire Goblet Co. | 26.00 |
| Pressed Glass, Sugar, Crescent | 12.50 |
| Pressed Glass, Sugar, Crystal Wedding, Scalloped Edge | 20.00 |
| Pressed Glass, Sugar, Cupid & Venus | 28.00 To 28.50 |
| Pressed Glass, Sugar, Cut Log, Covered | 32.50 |
| Pressed Glass, Sugar, Dahlia, Covered | 25.00 |
| Pressed Glass, Sugar, Daisy & Button With Narcissus | 8.00 To 18.00 |
| Pressed Glass, Sugar, Daisy & Button With Ribbon | 15.00 |
| Pressed Glass, Sugar, Daisy & Button With V Ornament, Amber | 32.50 |
| Pressed Glass, Sugar, Daisy & Button, Blue, Miniature | 18.00 |
| Pressed Glass, Sugar, Daisy & Button, Urn Shape, Miniature | 5.00 |
| Pressed Glass, Sugar, Daisy In Ovals | 10.00 |
| Pressed Glass, Sugar, Daisy Medallion, Covered | 15.50 |
| Pressed Glass, Sugar, Dakota, Covered | 32.50 |
| Pressed Glass, Sugar, Deer & Pine Tree, Covered | 50.00 To 52.00 |
| Pressed Glass, Sugar, Delaware, Emerald, Gold Trim | 35.00 |
| Pressed Glass, Sugar, Dewdrop In Points | 12.50 |
| Pressed Glass, Sugar, Diagonal Band With Fan | 15.00 |
| Pressed Glass, Sugar, Diamond & Fan | 5.98 |
| Pressed Glass, Sugar, Diamond & Thumbprint, Flint | 50.00 |
| Pressed Glass, Sugar, Diamond Block With Fan, Scalloped Top | 15.00 |
| Pressed Glass, Sugar, Diamond Point Band, Covered, High Standard | 27.50 |
| Pressed Glass, Sugar, Diamond Point Loop With Etching, Blue, Covered | 45.00 |
| Pressed Glass, Sugar, Diamond Point, Covered, Flint | 50.00 |
| Pressed Glass, Sugar, Diamond Point, Flint | 28.00 |
| Pressed Glass, Sugar, Double Pear, Covered, Signed M | 20.00 |
| Pressed Glass, Sugar, Double Ribbon | 12.50 |
| Pressed Glass, Sugar, Draped Jewel, Covered, Scalloped Edge | 20.00 |
| Pressed Glass, Sugar, Drapery | 15.00 |
| Pressed Glass, Sugar, Edgerton | 10.00 |
| Pressed Glass, Sugar, Electric, Covered | 24.50 |
| Pressed Glass, Sugar, Esther, Green, Covered | 55.00 |
| Pressed Glass, Sugar, Etched Fern Leaf, Frosted Old Abe Eagle Finial | 45.00 |
| Pressed Glass, Sugar, Etched Garden Fruits, Covered | 22.00 |
| Pressed Glass, Sugar, Etched Marsh Fern, Covered | 22.00 |
| Pressed Glass, Sugar, Etched Mascotte, Covered | 23.50 |
| Pressed Glass, Sugar, Etched Plume | 17.50 |
| Pressed Glass, Sugar, Excelsior | 30.00 To 35.00 |
| Pressed Glass, Sugar, Excelsior, Thistle Finial | 95.00 |
| Pressed Glass, Sugar, Fan Band | 8.00 |
| Pressed Glass, Sugar, Fan With Diamond, Covered | 23.50 |
| Pressed Glass, Sugar, Feather | 10.00 |
| Pressed Glass, Sugar, Feather, Covered | 22.00 |
| Pressed Glass, Sugar, Fishscale | 38.00 |
| Pressed Glass, Sugar, Flame, Covered | 12.50 |
| Pressed Glass, Sugar, Flamingo | 20.00 |
| Pressed Glass, Sugar, Flattened Diamond, Covered | 12.00 |
| Pressed Glass, Sugar, Fleur-De-Lis & Drape, Covered | 26.00 |
| Pressed Glass, Sugar, Florida Palm, Covered | 15.00 |

Pressed Glass, Sugar, Flower & Cane, Covered, Gold Trim ................................ 23.50
Pressed Glass, Sugar, Flowerpot, 4 In. ................................ 18.00
Pressed Glass, Sugar, Flute, Covered, Polished Pontil, Flint, 8 3/4 In.High ................ 50.00
Pressed Glass, Sugar, Fluted Scroll, Canary ................................ 30.00
Pressed Glass, Sugar, Forget-Me-Not In Scroll ................................ 15.00
Pressed Glass, Sugar, Four Petal, Covered, Flint ................ 55.00 To 65.00
Pressed Glass, Sugar, Four Petal, Covered, Pagoda Shape, Flint ................ 82.50
Pressed Glass, Sugar, Four Petal, Covered, Round Top, Flint ................ 55.00
Pressed Glass, Sugar, Four Petal, Flint ................................ 32.00
Pressed Glass, Sugar, Frosted Circle, Covered ................................ 45.00
Pressed Glass, Sugar, Frosted Eagle, Covered ................ 67.50 To 75.00
Pressed Glass, Sugar, Frosted Lion, Covered, 8 1/2 In. High ................ 28.00 To 55.00
Pressed Glass, Sugar, Frosted Lion, Rampant Lion Finial ................ 55.00 To 85.00
Pressed Glass, Sugar, Frosted Lion, 5 In.High ................................ 35.00
Pressed Glass, Sugar, Frosted Magnolia ................................ 15.00
Pressed Glass, Sugar, Frosted Ribbon ................................ 20.00
Pressed Glass, Sugar, Frosted Ribbon, Covered ................................ 38.00
Pressed Glass, Sugar, Fuchsia ................................ 22.50
Pressed Glass, Sugar, Good Luck, Covered ................................ 33.00
Pressed Glass, Sugar, Gothic Arches, Covered ................................ 110.00
Pressed Glass, Sugar, Gothic Arches, Covered, Flint ................................ 150.00
Pressed Glass, Sugar, Gothic, Covered ................................ 125.00
Pressed Glass, Sugar, Gothic, Covered, Flint ................................ 78.50
Pressed Glass, Sugar, Gothic, Flint ................................ 32.00
Pressed Glass, Sugar, Grand, Covered ................................ 13.75
Pressed Glass, Sugar, Grape & Festoon ................................ 12.00
Pressed Glass, Sugar, Grape & Festoon With Cloverleaf ................................ 25.00
Pressed Glass, Sugar, Grape & Festoon With Stippled Leaf, Covered ................ 28.00
Pressed Glass, Sugar, Grasshopper, Covered ................ 30.00 To 35.00
Pressed Glass, Sugar, Hairpin, Covered, Flint ................................ 47.50
Pressed Glass, Sugar, Heart & Thumbprint, Emerald, Silver Rim ................................ 25.00
Pressed Glass, Sugar, Heart & Thumbprint, Small Size ................................ 13.50
Pressed Glass, Sugar, Heron ................................ 10.00
Pressed Glass, Sugar, Heron, Covered ................................ 35.00
Pressed Glass, Sugar, Hexagon Block, Ruby Flashed, Covered ................................ 42.50
Pressed Glass, Sugar, Hinoto, Covered, Flint ................................ 45.00
Pressed Glass, Sugar, Hobnail, Covered ................................ 35.00
Pressed Glass, Sugar, Holland, Covered ................................ 15.00
Pressed Glass, Sugar, Honeycomb, Green, Opalescent, Covered, Beatty ................ 37.50
Pressed Glass, Sugar, Hops Band ................................ 13.50
Pressed Glass, Sugar, Horn Of Plenty Steeple Top ................................ 75.00
Pressed Glass, Sugar, Horn Of Plenty, Covered, Flint ................ 75.00 To 90.00
Pressed Glass, Sugar, Horn Of Plenty, Flint ................ 48.00 To 50.00
Pressed Glass, Sugar, Horseshoe ................................ 4.50
Pressed Glass, Sugar, Horseshoe, Covered ................................ 45.00
Pressed Glass, Sugar, Individual, Colorado, Green, Gold Trim, Footed ................ 22.00
Pressed Glass, Sugar, Individual, Delaware, Green, Gold Trim ................ 37.75
Pressed Glass, Sugar, Individual, Delaware, Green, Man's Name On Top, Gold ................ 35.00
Pressed Glass, Sugar, Interlocking Crescent, Covered ................................ 23.50
Pressed Glass, Sugar, Inverted Fern, Covered ................................ 50.00
Pressed Glass, Sugar, Inverted Fern, Flint ................................ 25.00
Pressed Glass, Sugar, Inverted Thumbprint, Amber ................................ 14.50
Pressed Glass, Sugar, Jacob's Ladder ................................ 18.00
Pressed Glass, Sugar, Jeweled Moon & Star, Covered ................................ 38.00
Pressed Glass, Sugar, Job's Tears, Covered ................................ 19.50
Pressed Glass, Sugar, Jubilee, Covered ................................ 17.50
Pressed Glass, Sugar, King's Crown ................................ 25.00
Pressed Glass, Sugar, Klondike, Amber Bands ................................ 90.00
Pressed Glass, Sugar, Klondike, Covered, 6 3/4 In.High ................................ 75.00
Pressed Glass, Sugar, Lacy Daisy, Covered ................................ 20.00
Pressed Glass, Sugar, Laurel, French Ivory, McKee, 4 In. ................................ 9.50
Pressed Glass, Sugar, Leaf & Dart ................................ 15.00
Pressed Glass, Sugar, Leaf & Dart, Covered ................ 24.50 To 28.00
Pressed Glass, Sugar, Leaf & Dart, Footed, Drape ................................ 16.00
Pressed Glass, Sugar, Leaf Medallion, Amethyst, Covered ................................ 32.50
Pressed Glass, Sugar, Liberty Bell, Covered, Bubble On Flange ................................ 95.00

Pressed Glass, Sugar, Lily Of The Valley ............................................................. 18.00
Pressed Glass, Sugar, Lily Of The Valley, 3 Legs .............................................. 25.00
Pressed Glass, Sugar, Loop & Dart With Diamond Ornament ........................... 10.00
Pressed Glass, Sugar, Loop & Dart With Diamond Ornament, Covered ................. 29.50
Pressed Glass, Sugar, Loop & Dart, Covered ................................................... 24.50
Pressed Glass, Sugar, Loop & Dart, Diamond-Quilted, Covered ........................ 18.50
Pressed Glass, Sugar, Loop, Covered, Flint .................................................... 60.00
Pressed Glass, Sugar, Louisiana, Covered ........................................ 13.00 To 15.00
Pressed Glass, Sugar, Manhattan, Gold Scallops ............................................. 5.00
Pressed Glass, Sugar, Marsh, Pink ................................................................. 26.50
Pressed Glass, Sugar, Marsh, Pink, Covered ...................................... 25.00 To 27.00
Pressed Glass, Sugar, Mascotte, Covered, Footed ........................................... 22.50
Pressed Glass, Sugar, Michigan, Ruby, Covered .............................................. 34.50
Pressed Glass, Sugar, Minerva, Covered ............................................ 47.50 To 52.00
Pressed Glass, Sugar, Mirror, Covered ........................................................... 65.00
Pressed Glass, Sugar, Mirror, Covered, Flint .................................................. 65.00
Pressed Glass, Sugar, Modified Lee, Covered, Flat Base, Flint ........................... 45.00
Pressed Glass, Sugar, Moon & Star ............................................................... 20.00
Pressed Glass, Sugar, Nailhead ......................................................... 10.00 To 16.00
Pressed Glass, Sugar, Nailhead, Covered ....................................................... 20.00
Pressed Glass, Sugar, New England Pineapple ................................................ 85.00
Pressed Glass, Sugar, New England Pineapple, Covered, Flint ............... 65.00 To 85.00
Pressed Glass, Sugar, New Hampshire, Covered .................................. 9.50 To 17.50
Pressed Glass, Sugar, Oaken Bucket, Blue ..................................................... 22.50
Pressed Glass, Sugar, Old Abe, Covered, Etching, 2 Handled .............................. 79.50
Pressed Glass, Sugar, Open Rose ....................................................... 16.00 To 22.00
Pressed Glass, Sugar, Oval Star, Covered, Toy ................................................ 16.50
Pressed Glass, Sugar, Palmette ..................................................................... 17.50
Pressed Glass, Sugar, Panel, Green, Scalloped, 2 Handles ................................. 8.00
Pressed Glass, Sugar, Paneled Daisy, Covered ................................................ 28.00
Pressed Glass, Sugar, Paneled Forget-Me-Not, Covered .................................... 24.00
Pressed Glass, Sugar, Paneled Heather ........................................................... 6.00
Pressed Glass, Sugar, Paneled Heather, Covered, 2 Handled .............................. 15.00
Pressed Glass, Sugar, Paneled Heather, Red Flashed, Covered, Gold, Green ......... 14.00
Pressed Glass, Sugar, Paneled Thistle ............................................................ 16.00
Pressed Glass, Sugar, Paneled Thistle, Covered .................................. 25.00 To 28.50
Pressed Glass, Sugar, Paneled Wild Daisy ...................................................... 5.50
Pressed Glass, Sugar, Peacock Feather, Covered ................................ 20.00 To 29.50
Pressed Glass, Sugar, Pear, Covered .............................................................. 34.50
Pressed Glass, Sugar, Pillow & Sunburst, Covered .......................................... 10.00
Pressed Glass, Sugar, Pillow Encircled, Covered ............................................. 28.50
Pressed Glass, Sugar, Pinwheel, Covered ....................................................... 15.00
Pressed Glass, Sugar, Pleat & Panel ................................................... 16.50 To 18.00
Pressed Glass, Sugar, Pleat & Panel, Covered ................................................. 27.50
Pressed Glass, Sugar, Plutec, Covered ........................................................... 16.50
Pressed Glass, Sugar, Pointed Jewels, Covered, Findlay ................................... 32.50
Pressed Glass, Sugar, Portland, Covered ............................................ 17.50 To 20.00
Pressed Glass, Sugar, Powder & Shot, Covered, Flint ........................... 68.50 To 72.50
Pressed Glass, Sugar, Pressed Leaf, Flint ....................................................... 16.00
Pressed Glass, Sugar, Primrose, Covered ........................................... 21.00 To 22.00
Pressed Glass, Sugar, Princess Feather .............................................. 16.00 To 28.00
Pressed Glass, Sugar, Princess Feather, Covered ................................ 32.00 To 38.50
Pressed Glass, Sugar, Priscilla, Covered ......................................................... 38.00
Pressed Glass, Sugar, Prism & Clear Panel, Covered, 2 Handled ........................ 21.50
Pressed Glass, Sugar, Prism, Flint ..................................................... 10.00 To 35.00
Pressed Glass, Sugar, Punty, McKearin No.196-4 .......................................... 150.00
Pressed Glass, Sugar, Quartered Block, Covered, Gold Trim .............................. 16.00
Pressed Glass, Sugar, Ray, Covered ............................................................... 32.00
Pressed Glass, Sugar, Red Block ....................................................... 20.00 To 35.00
Pressed Glass, Sugar, Red Block, Covered ...................................................... 25.00
Pressed Glass, Sugar, Ribbed Forget-Me-Not .................................................. 12.50
Pressed Glass, Sugar, Ribbed Grape, Covered ................................................. 50.00
Pressed Glass, Sugar, Ribbed Grape, Flint ..................................................... 35.00
Pressed Glass, Sugar, Ribbed Palm, Flint ........................................... 20.00 To 28.00
Pressed Glass, Sugar, Ribbon Candy, Covered ................................................ 21.00
Pressed Glass, Sugar, Rochelle ..................................................................... 25.00

Pressed Glass, Sugar, Roman Rosette, Covered ............................................. 22.00 To 23.50
Pressed Glass, Sugar, Rose In Snow, Covered ................................................. 45.00
Pressed Glass, Sugar, Rosette With Pinwheel, Covered ................................... 18.50
Pressed Glass, Sugar, Royal Crystal, Ruby, Covered ....................................... 45.00
Pressed Glass, Sugar, Sawtooth, Covered, Flint ............................................... 75.00
Pressed Glass, Sugar, Scroll ............................................................................. 20.00
Pressed Glass, Sugar, Scroll With Flowers ...................................................... 7.50
Pressed Glass, Sugar, Sheaf & Diamond, Covered ................................. 13.00 To 13.50
Pressed Glass, Sugar, Shell & Tassel ............................................................... 12.50
Pressed Glass, Sugar, Sheraton, Amber, Covered ........................................... 24.00
Pressed Glass, Sugar, Single Rose, Green, Covered, Gold Trim ..................... 25.00
Pressed Glass, Sugar, Six Panel, Miniature, 1 1/2 In.High .............................. 5.00
Pressed Glass, Sugar, Smocking, Covered ....................................................... 50.00
Pressed Glass, Sugar, Smocking, Covered, Flint .............................................. 65.00
Pressed Glass, Sugar, Smocking, Covered, Scalloped Base, 7 1/4 In. ........... 125.00
Pressed Glass, Sugar, Snakeskin & Dot ........................................................... 7.50
Pressed Glass, Sugar, Sprig, Covered ............................................................... 32.50
Pressed Glass, Sugar, St.Bernard, Frosted Dog Finial .................................... 37.50
Pressed Glass, Sugar, Starflower, Nova Scotia ................................... *Illus*  22.00

Pressed Glass, Sugar, Starflower, Nova Scotia

Pressed Glass, Sugar, Stedman .......................................................................... 15.00
Pressed Glass, Sugar, Stippled Chain, Covered ................................... 21.50 To 22.00
Pressed Glass, Sugar, Stippled Leaf, Covered .................................................. 25.00
Pressed Glass, Sugar, Stippled Sandburr, Covered .......................................... 16.00
Pressed Glass, Sugar, Swan, Covered ............................................................... 55.00
Pressed Glass, Sugar, Swan, Swan Finial On Lid ............................................. 50.00
Pressed Glass, Sugar, Swirl, Covered, Toy ....................................................... 16.00
Pressed Glass, Sugar, Teepee, Covered ............................................................ 20.00
Pressed Glass, Sugar, Three Faces, Covered, 4 1/2 X 10 In. .......................... 45.00
Pressed Glass, Sugar, Three Panel, Blue .............................................. 18.50 To 37.50
Pressed Glass, Sugar, Three Panel, Canary, Plain Cover ................................. 44.00
Pressed Glass, Sugar, Thumbprint, Covered ..................................................... 48.00
Pressed Glass, Sugar, Thumbprint, Flint, 5 1/2 In.High ................................... 22.00
Pressed Glass, Sugar, Tong, Covered, Flint ...................................................... 50.00
Pressed Glass, Sugar, Tong, Ground Lid, Flint .................................................. 51.00
Pressed Glass, Sugar, Torpedo .......................................................................... 40.00
Pressed Glass, Sugar, Tree Of Life, Covered, Portland, Signed, P.G.Co.Patent ..... 38.00
Pressed Glass, Sugar, Triple Triangle, Ruby Flashed, 4 1/2 In.High .............. 28.50
Pressed Glass, Sugar, Two Band ....................................................................... 8.00
Pressed Glass, Sugar, Vernon Honeycomb ....................................................... 24.00
Pressed Glass, Sugar, Vesta Opal ..................................................................... 30.00
Pressed Glass, Sugar, Viking ............................................................................. 45.00
Pressed Glass, Sugar, Viking, Covered ................................................. 25.00 To 38.50
Pressed Glass, Sugar, Vine & Flower, Amber, Covered, Wheeling .................. 46.00
Pressed Glass, Sugar, Virginia ........................................................................... 18.50
Pressed Glass, Sugar, Waffle, Covered ............................................................. 125.00
Pressed Glass, Sugar, Waffle, Covered, Flint .................................................... 125.00
Pressed Glass, Sugar, Washboard ...................................................................... 12.00
Pressed Glass, Sugar, Washboard, Covered ...................................................... 13.50

| | |
|---|---|
| Pressed Glass, Sugar, Water Lily, Covered | 13.00 |
| Pressed Glass, Sugar, Westward Ho | 45.00 |
| Pressed Glass, Sugar, Wheat & Barley, Covered | 18.00 To 28.00 |
| Pressed Glass, Sugar, Wild Rose & Bowknot, Covered, French, Gold Trim | 29.00 |
| Pressed Glass, Sugar, Wildflower | 12.00 |
| Pressed Glass, Sugar, Wildflower, Covered | 24.50 |
| Pressed Glass, Sugar, Willow Oak, Covered | 28.50 |
| Pressed Glass, Sugar, Zephyr, Amber | 22.50 |
| Pressed Glass, Sugar, Zipper | 8.00 To 14.00 |
| Pressed Glass, Sugar, Zipper Slash, Covered | 19.00 |
| Pressed Glass, Sugar, Zipper, Covered | 9.50 |
| Pressed Glass, Sugar, 101, Covered | 21.50 |
| Pressed Glass, Swan, Duncan & Miller, Ruby, Original Label, 7 1/2 In. | 38.00 |
| Pressed Glass, Swan, Duncan & Miller, Ruby, Solid, 3 In. | 15.00 |
| Pressed Glass, Swan, Duncan & Miller, Ruby, Solid, 5 In. | 20.00 |
| Pressed Glass, Swan, Duncan & Miller, Ruby, 7 1/2 In. | 30.00 |
| Pressed Glass, Swan, Duncan & Miller, Ruby, 12 In. | 55.00 |
| Pressed Glass, Swan, Duncan & Miller, 7 1/4 In. | 9.50 |
| Pressed Glass, Swan, Duncan & Miller, 8 In. | 9.50 |
| Pressed Glass, Swan, Duncan & Miller, 12 In. | 12.50 |
| Pressed Glass, Syrup & Underplate, Priscilla, Metal Top, Findlay, 5 1/2 In. | 92.50 |
| Pressed Glass, Syrup, Block & Fan | 33.00 |
| Pressed Glass, Syrup, Blocked Arches | 22.50 |
| Pressed Glass, Syrup, Buckle & Star | 18.00 |
| Pressed Glass, Syrup, Coinspot, Blue | 57.00 |
| Pressed Glass, Syrup, Cornell, Patent 1872 | 18.00 To 20.00 |
| Pressed Glass, Syrup, Crystal Wedding | 125.00 |
| Pressed Glass, Syrup, Currier & Ives | 35.00 |
| Pressed Glass, Syrup, Currier & Ives, Tin Lid, Findlay | 32.00 |
| Pressed Glass, Syrup, Daisies In Ovals, Spring Lid | 28.50 |
| Pressed Glass, Syrup, Diamond Sunburst Variant, Applied Handle | 21.50 |
| Pressed Glass, Syrup, Eight Flat Panels, Snap On Flip Top | 10.00 |
| Pressed Glass, Syrup, Electric | 27.50 |
| Pressed Glass, Syrup, Electric, Applied Handle | 26.00 |
| Pressed Glass, Syrup, Galloway | 32.00 |
| Pressed Glass, Syrup, Grape Band, Applied Handle | 35.00 |
| Pressed Glass, Syrup, Inverted Thumbprint, Amber, Pewter Top, Dated 1884 | 85.00 |
| Pressed Glass, Syrup, Inverted Thumbprint, Applied Handle, Dated Top | 39.50 |
| Pressed Glass, Syrup, Inverted Thumbprint, Blue, Cover Dated 1884 | 44.50 |
| Pressed Glass, Syrup, Inverted Thumbprint, Brass Thumb Lift, "march 28, '82" | 35.00 |
| Pressed Glass, Syrup, Inverted Thumbprint, Light Amber, Inside Cover, 1884 | 55.00 |
| Pressed Glass, Syrup, Inverted Thumbprint, Tin Lid | 35.00 |
| Pressed Glass, Syrup, Inverted Tiny Thumbprint, Sapphire Blue, Spring Lid | 85.00 |
| Pressed Glass, Syrup, Lattice | 32.50 |
| Pressed Glass, Syrup, Leaf & Flower, Amber Stain | 65.00 |
| Pressed Glass, Syrup, Lincoln Drape | 60.00 |
| Pressed Glass, Syrup, Manny, Applied Handle, 7 1/2 In.High | 25.00 |
| Pressed Glass, Syrup, New Hampshire | 32.50 |
| Pressed Glass, Syrup, New Hampshire, Pewter Lid | 22.50 |
| Pressed Glass, Syrup, Paneled Cherry | 20.00 |
| Pressed Glass, Syrup, Paneled Herringbone | 27.50 |
| Pressed Glass, Syrup, Prism, Flint | 45.00 |
| Pressed Glass, Syrup, Raindrop, Paneled, Blue | 65.00 |
| Pressed Glass, Syrup, Royal Crystal | 22.00 To 27.50 |
| Pressed Glass, Syrup, Sawtooth | 24.50 |
| Pressed Glass, Syrup, Scalloped Lines | 15.00 |
| Pressed Glass, Syrup, Scalloped Lines, Applied Handle, Tin Top | 23.50 |
| Pressed Glass, Syrup, Single Rose | 25.00 |
| Pressed Glass, Syrup, Six Panel Finecut, Amber Panels, Metal Lid, Findlay | 35.00 |
| Pressed Glass, Syrup, Star & Oval | 27.50 |
| Pressed Glass, Syrup, Stippled Forget-Me-Not, Tin Top, Indiana | 35.00 |
| Pressed Glass, Syrup, Strawberry | 18.00 |
| Pressed Glass, Syrup, Sunk Daisy, Tin Top | 16.00 |
| Pressed Glass, Syrup, Torpedo | 35.00 |
| Pressed Glass, Syrup, Torpedo, Spring Lid | 30.00 |
| Pressed Glass, Syrup, Waffle, Silver Plate Top | 30.00 |

Pressed Glass, Syrup, Wedding Bells, Gold Flip Top Kissing ............ 45.00
Pressed Glass, Table Set, Beaded Banded Grape Medallion, 3 Piece ............ 110.00
Pressed Glass, Table Set, Cameo, Cover, 3 Piece ............ 40.00
Pressed Glass, Table Set, Child's, Fan & Diamond, 3 Piece ............ 9.00
Pressed Glass, Table Set, Child's, Fancy Cut, 4 Piece ............ 55.00
Pressed Glass, Table Set, Child's, Fernland, Flint, 3 Piece ............ 50.00
Pressed Glass, Table Set, Child's, Swirl, 3 Piece ............ 24.00
Pressed Glass, Table Set, Child's, Tappan, Flint, 3 Piece ............ 42.00
Pressed Glass, Table Set, Columbia, 3 Piece ............ 45.00
Pressed Glass, Table Set, Delaware, Pink, 3 Piece ............ 185.00
Pressed Glass, Table Set, Flattened Diamond & Sunburst, 4 Piece ............ 68.00
Pressed Glass, Table Set, Frosted Ribbon, 4 Piece ............ 130.00 To 140.00
Pressed Glass, Table Set, Oval Star, Miniature, 4 Piece ............ 48.00
Pressed Glass, Table Set, Paneled Strawberry With Greek Key Band, 4 Piece ............ 155.00
Pressed Glass, Table Set, Serrated Rib & Finecut, 3 Piece ............ 18.00
Pressed Glass, Table Set, Star & Bull's-Eye, Pink, Gold Trim, 3 Piece ............ 35.00
Pressed Glass, Table Set, Stippled Ivy, 3 Piece ............ 110.00
Pressed Glass, Table Set, Sweetheart, Miniature, 3 Piece ............ 59.00
Pressed Glass, Table Set, Teardrop & Tassle, Cobalt Blue, 3 Piece ............ 95.00
Pressed Glass, Table Set, Tulip & Honeycomb, 4 Piece ............ 75.00
Pressed Glass, Table Set, Two Band, 3 Piece ............ 85.00
Pressed Glass, Table Set, Wheat & Barley, Amber, 4 Piece ............ 160.00
Pressed Glass, Table Set, Wildflower, Covered Butter, 4 Piece ............ 60.00
Pressed Glass, Tankard, Daisy & Button, Amber, Applied Amber Handle, 9 In. ............ 67.50
Pressed Glass, Tankard, Etched Dakota, Oak Leaf, Large Size ............ 40.00
Pressed Glass, Tankard, Kokomo, Applied Handle, Tall ............ 35.00
Pressed Glass, Tankard, Melrose, Applied Handle ............ 15.00
Pressed Glass, Tankard, Minnesota, Tall ............ 37.50
Pressed Glass, Tankard, Pineapple & Fan, Removable Silver Plated Rim ............ 32.00
Pressed Glass, Tankard, Quaker Lady, Applied Handle, Scalloped Base ............ 30.00
Pressed Glass, Tankard, Vine & Flower, Amber, Wheeling ............ 90.00
Pressed Glass, Tankard, Water, Atlas, Tall ............ 22.50 To 24.50
Pressed Glass, Tankard, Water, Ball & Swirl, Etched Reeds & Leaves ............ 37.50
Pressed Glass, Tankard, Water, Beveled Diamond With Star ............ 22.50
Pressed Glass, Tankard, Water, Cut Log, Applied Handle, Slender, 11 3/4 In. ............ 45.00
Pressed Glass, Tankard, Water, Daisy & Button, Dark Amber ............ 40.00
Pressed Glass, Tankard, Water, Etched Dakota ............ 65.00
Pressed Glass, Tankard, Water, Kokomo ............ 23.50
Pressed Glass, Tankard, Water, Minnesota ............ 29.50
Pressed Glass, Tea Set, Baby Face, 4 Pieces ............ 300.00
Pressed Glass, Tea Set, Child's, Dewdrop, Cannonball Handles, Flint, 12 Piece ............ 25.00
Pressed Glass, Toothpick, Anvil, Blue, 4 1/2 In. ............ 24.00
Pressed Glass, Toothpick, Atlas ............ 5.00
Pressed Glass, Toothpick, Banded Portland ............ 9.50
Pressed Glass, Toothpick, Banded Portland, Gold Trim ............ 9.00
Pressed Glass, Toothpick, Banded Portland, Pink Flashed ............ 18.00
Pressed Glass, Toothpick, Basket Weave ............ 8.00
Pressed Glass, Toothpick, Beaded Drape, Red & Clear, 'Willie, 1908' ............ 18.00
Pressed Glass, Toothpick, Beaded Grape, Emerald Green ............ 26.00 To 45.00
Pressed Glass, Toothpick, Broken Egg On Chick's Back ............ 12.50
Pressed Glass, Toothpick, Button Arches, Red Top ............ 12.00
Pressed Glass, Toothpick, Button Arches, Ruby ............ 13.00
Pressed Glass, Toothpick, Colorado ............ 19.50
Pressed Glass, Toothpick, Colorado, Blue, Gold Around Top ............ 27.50
Pressed Glass, Toothpick, Colorado, Green, Gold Beaded Flared Top ............ 27.50
Pressed Glass, Toothpick, Colorado, Green, Gold Trim, Footed ............ 22.00
Pressed Glass, Toothpick, Colorado, Light Green ............ 19.00
Pressed Glass, Toothpick, Cordova ............ 7.00 To 8.50
Pressed Glass, Toothpick, Cube, Hat Shape ............ 12.00
Pressed Glass, Toothpick, Daisy & Button, Blue, Corset Shape ............ 16.00
Pressed Glass, Toothpick, Daisy & Button, Butterscotch ............ 7.50
Pressed Glass, Toothpick, Daisy & Button, Purple, Hat Shape ............ 3.50
Pressed Glass, Toothpick, Delaware, Pink With Clear Stipple, Gold Trim ............ 48.00
Pressed Glass, Toothpick, Diamond Ridge ............ 12.50
Pressed Glass, Toothpick, Dog & Top Hat, Aqua ............ 95.00
Pressed Glass, Toothpick, Finecut, Amber ............ 50.00

| | |
|---|---|
| Pressed Glass, Toothpick, Finecut, Dark Amber | 50.00 |
| Pressed Glass, Toothpick, Finecut, Hat Shape | 10.00 |
| Pressed Glass, Toothpick, Flower & Pleat | 40.00 |
| Pressed Glass, Toothpick, Galloway | 12.50 |
| Pressed Glass, Toothpick, Gold Band, 3 Handles | 15.00 |
| Pressed Glass, Toothpick, Grape With Thumbprint | 9.00 |
| Pressed Glass, Toothpick, Hobnail, Opalescent, 3 Footed | 18.50 |
| Pressed Glass, Toothpick, Illinois | 13.50 |
| Pressed Glass, Toothpick, Kansas | 30.00 |
| Pressed Glass, Toothpick, King's Crown, Ruby Top | 14.00 |
| Pressed Glass, Toothpick, Lacy Medallion, "Chicago Heights, Ill." | 15.00 |
| Pressed Glass, Toothpick, Lacy Medallion, Clear | 12.00 |
| Pressed Glass, Toothpick, Little Gem | 21.00 |
| Pressed Glass, Toothpick, Loop & Pillar, Gold Trim | 8.50 |
| Pressed Glass, Toothpick, Manhattan | 7.00 To 15.00 |
| Pressed Glass, Toothpick, Manhattan, Gold Trim | 11.00 |
| Pressed Glass, Toothpick, Michigan | 9.50 To 12.50 |
| Pressed Glass, Toothpick, Monkey | 4.95 |
| Pressed Glass, Toothpick, Monkey, Blue | 37.50 |
| Pressed Glass, Toothpick, Nevada | 10.00 |
| Pressed Glass, Toothpick, New Hampshire | 8.50 To 12.50 |
| Pressed Glass, Toothpick, Petaled Medallion, Yellow & Clear | 27.50 |
| Pressed Glass, Toothpick, Press Cut, Green, Scalloped Top | 15.00 |
| Pressed Glass, Toothpick, Prism & Diamond | 4.50 To 5.00 |
| Pressed Glass, Toothpick, Reverse 44 | 7.50 |
| Pressed Glass, Toothpick, Sawtooth | 5.00 |
| Pressed Glass, Toothpick, Soldier & Sailor On Platform, Flags & Drums | 27.50 |
| Pressed Glass, Toothpick, States, Sanitary, Horizontal | 22.00 |
| Pressed Glass, Toothpick, Sunk Daisy | 9.00 |
| Pressed Glass, Toothpick, Texas | 15.00 |
| Pressed Glass, Toothpick, The States, Gold Edge, Flat Type | 20.00 |
| Pressed Glass, Toothpick, Three Faces | 5.95 |
| Pressed Glass, Toothpick, Thumbprint, Ruby Flashed | 12.00 To 14.00 |
| Pressed Glass, Toothpick, Trench Mortar, Blue | 24.00 |
| Pressed Glass, Toothpick, U.S.Coin, Frosted Dollars, Dated 1892 | 85.00 |
| Pressed Glass, Toothpick, U.S.Coin, Square, Footed | 175.00 |
| Pressed Glass, Toothpick, Zippered Swirl & Diamond | 10.00 |
| **Pressed Glass, Tray, Bread, see Pressed Glass, Plate, Bread** | |
| Pressed Glass, Tray, Card, Fan | 24.00 |
| Pressed Glass, Tray, Card, Heart With Thumbprint, Gold Trim | 18.50 |
| Pressed Glass, Tray, Card, States, Oval, Scalloped | 14.00 |
| Pressed Glass, Tray, Chain & Shield, Oval, 12 In. | 15.00 |
| Pressed Glass, Tray, Columbia, Frosted Center | 79.50 |
| Pressed Glass, Tray, Currier & Ives, Balky Mule, 10 In. | 32.00 To 32.50 |
| Pressed Glass, Tray, Currier & Ives, Balky Mule, 12 In. | 35.00 |
| Pressed Glass, Tray, Currier & Ives, Blue, Dog & Rabbit, Series No.1, 10 In. | 46.00 |
| Pressed Glass, Tray, Daisy & Button With Thumbprint, Amber, Tab Handles | 40.00 |
| Pressed Glass, Tray, Deer & Pine Tree, Amber | 40.00 To 42.00 |
| Pressed Glass, Tray, Dresser, Delaware, Green, 5 3/4 X 11 In. | 65.00 |
| Pressed Glass, Tray, Finecut, Handled, Cut Corners, 8 X 10 In. | 10.00 |
| Pressed Glass, Tray, Hobnail With Fan, 12 X 8 In. | 17.50 |
| Pressed Glass, Tray, Ice Cream, Tree Of Life | 28.00 |
| Pressed Glass, Tray, Liberty Bell, Handled, 11 In. | 85.00 |
| Pressed Glass, Tray, Lotus, Oval, Motto | 26.00 |
| Pressed Glass, Tray, Niagara Falls, Frosted & Clear, 11 1/2 X 16 In. | 80.00 |
| Pressed Glass, Tray, Old Statehouse, "erected 1835" | 45.00 To 60.00 |
| Pressed Glass, Tray, Paneled Cane, Round | 9.50 |
| Pressed Glass, Tray, Rainbow, Round, 10 1/4 In. | 10.00 |
| Pressed Glass, Tray, Sanibel, Duncan & Miller, 13 In. | 14.00 |
| Pressed Glass, Tray, Virginia Dare | 40.00 |
| Pressed Glass, Tray, Water, Ashman, 15 In. | 35.00 |
| Pressed Glass, Tray, Water, Cane, Honey Amber, Round, 11 1/2 In. | 32.00 |
| Pressed Glass, Tray, Water, Currier & Ives, Balky Mule | 38.50 To 42.50 |
| Pressed Glass, Tray, Water, Currier & Ives, Blue, Dog & Rabbit, Basket Weave | 45.00 |
| Pressed Glass, Tray, Water, Currier & Ives, Frosted Center, Dog & Rabbit | 45.00 |
| Pressed Glass, Tray, Water, Dahlia, 11 In. | 20.00 |

| | |
|---|---|
| Pressed Glass, Tray, Water, Daisy & Button, Amber, Round Corners, Square | 42.50 |
| Pressed Glass, Tray, Water, Feather Duster, Emerald Green, 11 1/2 In. | 13.75 |
| Pressed Glass, Tray, Water, Festoon | 15.00 |
| Pressed Glass, Tray, Water, Finecut & Panel, Amber | 42.00 |
| Pressed Glass, Tray, Water, Fleur-De-Lis & Drape | 23.50 |
| Pressed Glass, Tray, Water, Frosted Polar Bear | 125.00 |
| Pressed Glass, Tray, Water, Mascotte | 24.50 |
| Pressed Glass, Tray, Water, Picket | 70.00 |
| Pressed Glass, Tray, Water, Pleat & Panel | 37.50 To 45.00 |
| Pressed Glass, Tray, Water, Primrose | 20.00 To 25.00 |
| Pressed Glass, Tray, Water, Primrose, Amber | 15.00 To 35.00 |
| Pressed Glass, Tray, Water, S Repeat, Apple Green | 35.00 |
| Pressed Glass, Tray, Water, Wildflower, 11 X 13 In. | 26.00 |
| Pressed Glass, Tray, Water, Willow Oak, 11 In. | 15.00 To 25.00 |
| Pressed Glass, Tray, Water, 1,000-Eye, Amber, Oval, 13 3/4 In. | 42.50 |
| Pressed Glass, Tray, Water, 1,000-Eye, Apple Green, Oval, 14 X 12 In. | 45.00 |
| Pressed Glass, Tray, Willow Oak, Round, 9 3/4 In. | 15.50 |
| Pressed Glass, Tray, Wine, Aurora, Ruby | 35.00 |
| Pressed Glass, Tray, Wine, Currier & Ives, Bellaire Goblet Co., 9 1/2 In. | 35.00 |
| Pressed Glass, Tray, Wine, Currier & Ives, Scenic Center, 9 In. | 30.00 |
| Pressed Glass, Tray, Wine, Daisy & Button With Narcissus, 10 In. | 18.50 |
| Pressed Glass, Tray, 1,000-Eye, Apple Green, Oval, 14 In. | 60.00 |
| Pressed Glass, Tumbler, Aberdeen, Footed | 19.50 |
| Pressed Glass, Tumbler, Acorn Band | 50.00 |
| Pressed Glass, Tumbler, Admiral Dewey | 35.00 To 40.00 |
| Pressed Glass, Tumbler, Admiral Dewey, Cannonball | 25.00 |
| Pressed Glass, Tumbler, Amber Leaves, Clear & Frosted | 15.00 |
| Pressed Glass, Tumbler, America | 11.00 |
| Pressed Glass, Tumbler, Anthemion | 10.00 |
| Pressed Glass, Tumbler, Arcadia Jenkins, No.95 | 7.50 |
| Pressed Glass, Tumbler, Arch & Forget-Me-Not Band | 7.00 |
| Pressed Glass, Tumbler, Arch & Forget-Me-Not Bands, C.1880 | 18.00 |
| Pressed Glass, Tumbler, Arched Ovals, Cranberry With Clear Ovals | 15.00 |
| Pressed Glass, Tumbler, Arched Ovals, Gold Trim | 8.50 |
| Pressed Glass, Tumbler, Ashburton | 40.00 To 60.00 |
| Pressed Glass, Tumbler, Austrian, Greentown | 12.50 To 16.00 |
| Pressed Glass, Tumbler, Balder | 11.00 To 16.00 |
| Pressed Glass, Tumbler, Banded Grape, Thumbprint Base | 24.50 |
| Pressed Glass, Tumbler, Barrel Excelsior, Footed, Polished Pontil, Flint | 30.00 |
| Pressed Glass, Tumbler, Basket Weave, Blue | 22.50 |
| Pressed Glass, Tumbler, Bay State Campaign, Patent June 25th, 1861 | 95.00 |
| Pressed Glass, Tumbler, Beaded Dewdrop | 32.00 |
| Pressed Glass, Tumbler, Beaded Grape, Apple Green | 16.00 |
| Pressed Glass, Tumbler, Beaded Grape, Emerald Green | 30.00 |
| Pressed Glass, Tumbler, Beaded Swirl, Green, Gold Beads | 14.50 |
| Pressed Glass, Tumbler, Bellflower, Single Vine, Flint | 70.00 |
| Pressed Glass, Tumbler, Bent Buckle | 15.00 |
| Pressed Glass, Tumbler, Bird & Strawberry | 18.00 |
| Pressed Glass, Tumbler, Birds & Foliage, Amber | 22.00 |
| Pressed Glass, Tumbler, Block & Lattice, Ruby | 25.00 |
| Pressed Glass, Tumbler, Broken Column, Red Dots | 32.00 |
| Pressed Glass, Tumbler, Bull's-Eye With Diamond Panel | 20.00 |
| Pressed Glass, Tumbler, Bull's-Eye, Flint | 38.00 To 42.00 |
| Pressed Glass, Tumbler, Butterfly & Fan | 7.00 To 12.00 |
| Pressed Glass, Tumbler, Button Arches | 7.50 |
| Pressed Glass, Tumbler, Button Arches, Gold Band Around Middle | 10.00 |
| Pressed Glass, Tumbler, Button Band | 16.00 |
| Pressed Glass, Tumbler, Cable, Footed, Flint | 75.00 |
| Pressed Glass, Tumbler, Cannonball | 17.50 |
| Pressed Glass, Tumbler, Cathedral, Ruby & Clear | 37.50 |
| Pressed Glass, Tumbler, Cattail & Lily, Blue, Opalescent | 18.50 |
| Pressed Glass, Tumbler, Checkerboard, 4 3/4 In.High | 7.00 |
| Pressed Glass, Tumbler, Colorado, Green, Gold Trim, Name & Date | 16.00 |
| Pressed Glass, Tumbler, Columbian Exposition | 18.00 |
| Pressed Glass, Tumbler, Cornell | 6.00 |
| Pressed Glass, Tumbler, Daisy & Button Variant, Amber, Depressed Buttons | 15.00 |

| | |
|---|---|
| Pressed Glass, Tumbler, Daisy & Button With Crossbar, Amber | 28.00 |
| Pressed Glass, Tumbler, Daisy & Button With Ribbed Oval Panels, Blue | 14.50 |
| Pressed Glass, Tumbler, Daisy & Button With Thumbprint, Amber | 16.50 |
| Pressed Glass, Tumbler, Daisy & Button, Amber | 25.00 |
| Pressed Glass, Tumbler, Daisy & Button, Amber, Etched Willie Burt, 1887 | 24.50 |
| Pressed Glass, Tumbler, Daisy & Button, Canary | 25.00 |
| Pressed Glass, Tumbler, Dakota, Ruby | 27.50 |
| Pressed Glass, Tumbler, Delaware, Green, Gold Trim | 20.00 To 21.00 |
| Pressed Glass, Tumbler, Delaware, Pink With Clear Stipple, Gold Trim | 35.00 |
| Pressed Glass, Tumbler, Dew & Raindrop | 16.50 |
| Pressed Glass, Tumbler, Dewberry, Gold Trim | 10.00 |
| Pressed Glass, Tumbler, Dewdrop, Blue | 16.50 |
| Pressed Glass, Tumbler, Dewey | 30.00 To 32.50 |
| Pressed Glass, Tumbler, Dewey, Green | 22.00 To 25.00 |
| Pressed Glass, Tumbler, Dewey, Ribbed Base, Zigzag Top, Portrait In Base | 30.00 |
| Pressed Glass, Tumbler, Diamond Point | 50.00 |
| Pressed Glass, Tumbler, Diamond Point, Flint | 40.00 |
| Pressed Glass, Tumbler, Diamond Thumbprint, Flint, 3 3/4 In. | 80.00 To 85.00 |
| Pressed Glass, Tumbler, Diamond, Amber | 25.00 |
| Pressed Glass, Tumbler, Double Swirl, Ruby | 20.00 |
| Pressed Glass, Tumbler, Duncan & Miller No.42, Gold Trim | 6.50 To 12.50 |
| Pressed Glass, Tumbler, Embossed Busts Of Napoleon III & Eugenie, Flint | 50.00 |
| Pressed Glass, Tumbler, Engraved Pittsburgh With Basket Of Flowers | 45.00 |
| Pressed Glass, Tumbler, Esther, Green, Gold Trim | 28.50 |
| Pressed Glass, Tumbler, Etched Daisy & Button | 12.00 |
| Pressed Glass, Tumbler, Etched Dewey | 10.00 To 13.50 |
| Pressed Glass, Tumbler, Etched Mascotte | 17.00 |
| Pressed Glass, Tumbler, Etched Pavonia | 16.00 |
| Pressed Glass, Tumbler, Etched Plume | 10.00 |
| Pressed Glass, Tumbler, Etched Sequoia | 7.50 To 8.75 |
| Pressed Glass, Tumbler, Etched Torpedo | 22.50 |
| Pressed Glass, Tumbler, Excelsior, Barrel, Flint | 18.50 |
| Pressed Glass, Tumbler, Feather | 20.00 |
| Pressed Glass, Tumbler, Feather Duster, Green | 13.00 |
| Pressed Glass, Tumbler, Festoon | 10.00 To 14.00 |
| Pressed Glass, Tumbler, Fine Rib | 45.00 |
| Pressed Glass, Tumbler, Flower & Leaf, Amber & Clear | 35.00 |
| Pressed Glass, Tumbler, Flower & Pleat | 20.00 |
| Pressed Glass, Tumbler, Flower With Cane | 8.50 |
| Pressed Glass, Tumbler, Flower With Cane, Green, Gold Trim | 15.00 |
| Pressed Glass, Tumbler, Flute, Flint | 9.00 To 15.00 |
| Pressed Glass, Tumbler, Flute, 8 Flutes, Footed, Polished Pontil, Flint | 30.00 |
| Pressed Glass, Tumbler, Frosted Bands | 30.00 |
| Pressed Glass, Tumbler, Frosted Fleur-De-Lis, Green | 18.00 |
| Pressed Glass, Tumbler, Galloway | 16.00 |
| Pressed Glass, Tumbler, Garfield Bust Bottom, Wreath | 17.50 |
| Pressed Glass, Tumbler, German Coin, Coin Dated 1854 In Base, 6 In.High | 175.00 |
| Pressed Glass, Tumbler, Giant Thumbprint, Flint | 27.50 |
| Pressed Glass, Tumbler, Gibson Girl | 35.00 |
| Pressed Glass, Tumbler, Grape & Festoon With Shield, Footed | 21.50 |
| Pressed Glass, Tumbler, Grenade | 6.00 |
| Pressed Glass, Tumbler, Hartford | 4.00 |
| Pressed Glass, Tumbler, Heart & Sand | 18.00 |
| Pressed Glass, Tumbler, Heart & Thumbprint | 20.00 |
| Pressed Glass, Tumbler, Herringbone, Green | 15.00 To 18.75 |
| Pressed Glass, Tumbler, Hexagonal Bull's-Eye, Findlay | 9.50 |
| Pressed Glass, Tumbler, High Hob | 8.00 |
| Pressed Glass, Tumbler, Hinoto, Footed, Flint | 24.00 To 25.00 |
| Pressed Glass, Tumbler, Hobnail | 10.00 |
| Pressed Glass, Tumbler, Hobnail, Amber, 7 Rows | 12.00 |
| Pressed Glass, Tumbler, Hops Band, Footed | 17.50 |
| Pressed Glass, Tumbler, Horn Of Plenty | 40.00 |
| Pressed Glass, Tumbler, Horn Of Plenty, Flint | 75.00 |
| Pressed Glass, Tumbler, Horseshoe | 2.50 |
| Pressed Glass, Tumbler, Huckle | 17.50 |
| Pressed Glass, Tumbler, Huckle, Green | 14.50 |

| | |
|---|---|
| Pressed Glass, Tumbler, Hummingbird, Blue | 35.00 |
| Pressed Glass, Tumbler, Inverted Coin Spot, Blue, Opalescent | 24.00 |
| Pressed Glass, Tumbler, Inverted Strawberry | 9.00 |
| Pressed Glass, Tumbler, Inverted Thumbprint, Amber | 16.50 |
| Pressed Glass, Tumbler, Inverted Thumbprint, Blue | 13.50 |
| Pressed Glass, Tumbler, Inverted Thumbprint, Light Blue | 15.00 |
| Pressed Glass, Tumbler, Inverted Thumbprint, Sapphire Blue | 16.50 |
| Pressed Glass, Tumbler, Isis | 6.75 To 8.75 |
| Pressed Glass, Tumbler, Jersey Swirl | 13.50 To 17.50 |
| Pressed Glass, Tumbler, Jewel & Flower, Blue Opalescent | 35.00 |
| Pressed Glass, Tumbler, Jeweled Heart | 10.00 To 12.50 |
| Pressed Glass, Tumbler, Jeweled Heart, Green, Opalescent | 14.00 |
| Pressed Glass, Tumbler, Jubilee, Gold Trim | 10.00 |
| Pressed Glass, Tumbler, Juice, Inverted Thumbprint, Blue | 10.00 |
| Pressed Glass, Tumbler, Juice, Pennsylvania | 5.00 |
| Pressed Glass, Tumbler, King's Crown | 19.50 To 20.00 |
| Pressed Glass, Tumbler, King's 500, Dark Blue, Gilt Trim | 16.00 |
| Pressed Glass, Tumbler, Klondike, Findlay | 120.00 |
| Pressed Glass, Tumbler, Klondike, Frosted With Amber Panel | 185.00 |
| Pressed Glass, Tumbler, Knobby Bull's-Eye, Green | 10.00 |
| Pressed Glass, Tumbler, Lacy Medallion | 15.00 |
| Pressed Glass, Tumbler, Leaf & Dart | 15.50 To 19.50 |
| Pressed Glass, Tumbler, Leaf & Dart, Footed, 6 In. | 12.75 To 18.00 |
| Pressed Glass, Tumbler, Leaf With Amber Flowers | 21.50 |
| Pressed Glass, Tumbler, Lemonade, Bull's-Eye & Fan, Handled | 12.00 |
| Pressed Glass, Tumbler, Lemonade, Checkerboard | 9.75 |
| Pressed Glass, Tumbler, Lemonade, Diamond Point | 35.00 |
| Pressed Glass, Tumbler, Lemonade, Tree Of Life, Signed, Portland | 38.50 |
| Pressed Glass, Tumbler, Loop & Crystal, Flint | 30.00 |
| Pressed Glass, Tumbler, Loop & Dart With D Ornament, Footed | 12.50 |
| Pressed Glass, Tumbler, Loop & Dart With Round Ornament, Footed | 24.50 |
| Pressed Glass, Tumbler, Loop & Moose-Eye, Flint | 45.00 |
| Pressed Glass, Tumbler, Louisiana Purchase | 15.50 |
| Pressed Glass, Tumbler, Maiden's Blush | 25.00 |
| Pressed Glass, Tumbler, Maiden's Blush & Banded Portland With Color | 32.50 |
| Pressed Glass, Tumbler, Maiden's Blush, Pink & Clear | 30.00 |
| Pressed Glass, Tumbler, Manhattan, Miniature | 8.50 |
| Pressed Glass, Tumbler, Mario, Amber & Clear | 16.00 |
| Pressed Glass, Tumbler, McKinley Memorial | 17.00 |
| Pressed Glass, Tumbler, McKinley, Bust Impressed With Name In Base | 40.00 |
| Pressed Glass, Tumbler, McKinley, Hobart Protection, Sound Currency | 35.00 |
| Pressed Glass, Tumbler, Memphis, Emerald Green | 16.00 |
| Pressed Glass, Tumbler, Memphis, Emerald Green, Gold Trim | 15.00 |
| Pressed Glass, Tumbler, Michigan | 18.00 |
| Pressed Glass, Tumbler, Michigan, Cranberry Flashed | 25.00 |
| Pressed Glass, Tumbler, Minnesota | 6.50 |
| Pressed Glass, Tumbler, Mitered Diamond, Blue | 25.00 |
| Pressed Glass, Tumbler, Moonprint, Flint | 20.00 |
| Pressed Glass, Tumbler, New England Pineapple | 55.00 To 60.00 |
| Pressed Glass, Tumbler, New Jersey, Gold Trim | 10.00 To 12.50 |
| Pressed Glass, Tumbler, Notched Ovals, Green | 14.50 |
| Pressed Glass, Tumbler, Opalescent Swirl, Blue, Beatty Co. | 27.50 |
| Pressed Glass, Tumbler, Paisley, Gold Dots | 7.50 |
| Pressed Glass, Tumbler, Paisley, Green Swirls | 10.50 |
| Pressed Glass, Tumbler, Paneled Apple Blossoms | 7.50 |
| Pressed Glass, Tumbler, Paneled Cherry | 9.50 |
| Pressed Glass, Tumbler, Paneled Daisy & Button, Amber | 24.00 |
| Pressed Glass, Tumbler, Paneled Dewdrop | 17.00 |
| Pressed Glass, Tumbler, Paneled Grape | 10.00 To 25.00 |
| Pressed Glass, Tumbler, Paneled Herringbone | 7.50 |
| Pressed Glass, Tumbler, Paneled Palm | 12.00 |
| Pressed Glass, Tumbler, Paneled Strawberry With Roman Key Band | 25.00 |
| Pressed Glass, Tumbler, Paneled Strawberry, Gilt Trim | 22.50 |
| Pressed Glass, Tumbler, Pavonia | 6.50 |
| Pressed Glass, Tumbler, Peerless, Amber | 15.00 |
| Pressed Glass, Tumbler, Pillow | 22.00 |

Pressed Glass, Tumbler, Pioneer's Victoria ................................................................ 18.00
Pressed Glass, Tumbler, Pioneer's, No.23 ................................................................... 7.00
Pressed Glass, Tumbler, Pointed Hobnail .................................................................... 9.00
Pressed Glass, Tumbler, Pointed Hobnail, Amber ....................................................... 22.50
Pressed Glass, Tumbler, Portland, Gold Trim .............................................................. 9.00
Pressed Glass, Tumbler, Prism With Ball & Button ...................................................... 6.50
Pressed Glass, Tumbler, Radiant ................................................................................ 15.00
Pressed Glass, Tumbler, Red Block ................................................... 18.00 To 22.00
Pressed Glass, Tumbler, Red Block, Square ............................................................... 15.00
Pressed Glass, Tumbler, Rexford ................................................................................ 7.00
Pressed Glass, Tumbler, Ribbed Ivy, Flint .................................................................. 75.00
Pressed Glass, Tumbler, Ribbed, Opalescent .............................................................. 30.00
Pressed Glass, Tumbler, Rising Sun, Green & Clear .................................................... 12.00
Pressed Glass, Tumbler, Rose In Snow ....................................................................... 25.00
Pressed Glass, Tumbler, Rose Spray, Handled ............................................................ 14.50
Pressed Glass, Tumbler, Ruby Thumbprint ........................................ 18.00 To 20.00
Pressed Glass, Tumbler, S Repeat, Blue ............................................ 16.50 To 22.00
Pressed Glass, Tumbler, Scroll & Cane Band, Ruby Flashed ...................................... 20.00
Pressed Glass, Tumbler, Scroll & Cane Band, Yellow Flashed .................................... 22.50
Pressed Glass, Tumbler, Scroll, Footed ...................................................................... 15.00
Pressed Glass, Tumbler, Sheaf Of Wheat, Flared Top, Marked Near Cut .................... 8.50
Pressed Glass, Tumbler, Shell & Jewel .............................................. 10.00 To 15.00
Pressed Glass, Tumbler, Shell & Jewel, Blue .................................... 22.50 To 28.00
Pressed Glass, Tumbler, Shimmering Star ................................................................... 7.50
Pressed Glass, Tumbler, Shot, Massachusetts ............................................................ 12.00
Pressed Glass, Tumbler, Skilton, Red Flashed ........................................................... 24.00
Pressed Glass, Tumbler, Spiked Argus, Flint .............................................................. 39.50
Pressed Glass, Tumbler, Star In Bull's-Eye ......................................... 6.00 To 7.00
Pressed Glass, Tumbler, Star Spangled Banner .......................................................... 11.00
Pressed Glass, Tumbler, States .................................................................................. 11.00
Pressed Glass, Tumbler, Stippled Double Loop ........................................................... 7.50
Pressed Glass, Tumbler, Stippled Fleur-De-Lis, Amber ............................................... 20.00
Pressed Glass, Tumbler, Stippled Peppers, Footed .................................................... 19.00
Pressed Glass, Tumbler, Stippled Sandburr ............................................................... 8.00
Pressed Glass, Tumbler, Stippled Shell & Jewel ........................................................ 16.00
Pressed Glass, Tumbler, Straight Banded Worcester, Footed, Flint ............................ 30.00
Pressed Glass, Tumbler, Sunbeam ..................................................... 3.00 To 3.50
Pressed Glass, Tumbler, Sunflower ............................................................................ 8.00
Pressed Glass, Tumbler, Sunk Daisy .......................................................................... 10.00
Pressed Glass, Tumbler, Teardrop & Tassel ............................................................... 15.00
Pressed Glass, Tumbler, Teardrop & Tassel, Cobalt ................................................... 35.00
Pressed Glass, Tumbler, Teardrop, Cobalt ................................................................. 12.00
Pressed Glass, Tumbler, Texas Centennial, Cobalt, Enamel Flags, Dated, Alamo ....... 22.50
Pressed Glass, Tumbler, Thistle, Footed .................................................................... 16.00
Pressed Glass, Tumbler, Thistle, Near Cut ................................................................. 10.00
Pressed Glass, Tumbler, Thumbprint, Clear ............................................................... 30.00
Pressed Glass, Tumbler, Thumbprint, Flint ................................................................. 32.00
Pressed Glass, Tumbler, Thumbprint, Footed, Flint, 4 3/8 In. ................................... 38.00
Pressed Glass, Tumbler, Thumbprint, Green, Opalescent Rim ..................................... 12.50
Pressed Glass, Tumbler, Thumbprint, Ruby Flashed ................................................... 17.00
Pressed Glass, Tumbler, Tobin ................................................................................... 5.00
Pressed Glass, Tumbler, Tree Of Life ......................................................................... 15.00
Pressed Glass, Tumbler, Tree Of Life, Footed, 6 In.High ........................................... 27.50
Pressed Glass, Tumbler, Tree Of Life, Pittsburgh ...................................................... 18.50
Pressed Glass, Tumbler, Tree, Ruby Flashed ............................................................. 15.00
Pressed Glass, Tumbler, Triple Triangle, Ruby ........................................................... 23.00
Pressed Glass, Tumbler, Truncated Cube, Ruby Flashed ............................................ 11.00
Pressed Glass, Tumbler, Truncated Square ................................................................ 10.00
Pressed Glass, Tumbler, Tulip ................................................................................... 8.50
Pressed Glass, Tumbler, Tulip & Sawtooth, Flint ....................................................... 55.00
Pressed Glass, Tumbler, U.S.Coin, Dimes Around Bottom ......................................... 175.00
Pressed Glass, Tumbler, U.S.Coin, 1879, Dollar Impressed In Bas ................ 100.00 To 135.00
Pressed Glass, Tumbler, Umbilicated Hob .................................................................. 16.00
Pressed Glass, Tumbler, Union Forever ...................................................................... 87.50
Pressed Glass, Tumbler, Utah ................................................................................... 12.50
Pressed Glass, Tumbler, Water Lily, Gold Top ........................................................... 16.00

| | |
|---|---|
| Pressed Glass, Tumbler, Whiskey, Argus, Handled | 60.00 |
| Pressed Glass, Tumbler, Whiskey, Balder | 5.00 To 9.00 |
| Pressed Glass, Tumbler, Whiskey, Bumper To The Flag | 78.50 |
| Pressed Glass, Tumbler, Whiskey, Gothic Arch, 7 Sided Base, Flint | 12.50 |
| Pressed Glass, Tumbler, Whiskey, Heart & Thumbprint | 18.00 |
| Pressed Glass, Tumbler, Whiskey, Honeycomb, Handled, Flint | 45.00 |
| Pressed Glass, Tumbler, Whiskey, Ribbed Ivy | 65.00 |
| Pressed Glass, Tumbler, Whiskey, Ribbed Ivy, Flint, 2 3/4 In. | 68.00 |
| Pressed Glass, Tumbler, Whiskey, Ribbed, Opalescent | 22.50 |
| Pressed Glass, Tumbler, Whiskey, Rose Sprig, 3 1/4 In.Across | 20.00 |
| Pressed Glass, Tumbler, Whiskey, Six Panel, Crimped Handle, Flint | 20.00 |
| Pressed Glass, Tumbler, Whiskey, Yoked Loop, Footed, Flint | 12.00 |
| Pressed Glass, Tumbler, Wild Rose & Bowknot | 16.50 |
| Pressed Glass, Tumbler, Wild Rose & Bowknot, Frosted, Enameled | 18.50 |
| Pressed Glass, Tumbler, Wildflower | 14.00 |
| Pressed Glass, Tumbler, Wildflower, Amber | 18.50 |
| Pressed Glass, Tumbler, Wildflower, Apple Green | 37.50 |
| Pressed Glass, Tumbler, Wildflower, Blue | 35.00 |
| Pressed Glass, Tumbler, Zipper Cut, Star Bottom, Flint | 15.00 |
| Pressed Glass, Tumbler, 1, 000-Eye | 17.50 |
| Pressed Glass, Tumbler, 1, 000-Eye, Amber | 16.50 |
| Pressed Glass, Tumbler, 1, 000-Eye, Amber, 8 Rows | 20.00 |
| Pressed Glass, Vase, Banded Portland, 6 In. | 12.50 |
| Pressed Glass, Vase, Banded Portland, 9 In. | 13.50 |
| Pressed Glass, Vase, Bar & Star, Findlay, 5 1/4 In. | 12.00 |
| Pressed Glass, Vase, Beaded Swirl With Disc, 6 In. | 12.50 |
| Pressed Glass, Vase, Beautiful Lady, 7 In.High | 8.00 |
| Pressed Glass, Vase, Bud, Heart & Thumbprint, 6 1/4 In. | 16.50 |
| Pressed Glass, Vase, Bud, Maiden's Blush | 24.00 |
| Pressed Glass, Vase, Bull's-Eye & Fan, 4 1/4 In. | 9.50 |
| Pressed Glass, Vase, Carnation, Scalloped Top, 17 In.High | 12.00 |
| Pressed Glass, Vase, Celery, see Pressed Glass, Celery | |
| Pressed Glass, Vase, Daisy & Button, Blue, Figural Hand, 6 In. | 21.00 |
| Pressed Glass, Vase, Dalzell 75, 8 In. | 22.00 |
| Pressed Glass, Vase, Fleur-De-Lis, 10 In. | 16.50 |
| Pressed Glass, Vase, Frosted Peacock, Painted Decoration, 10 1/2 In. | 17.00 |
| Pressed Glass, Vase, Galloway, 11 1/4 In. | 23.50 |
| Pressed Glass, Vase, Galloway, 13 1/2 In. | 23.50 |
| Pressed Glass, Vase, Heart & Thumbprint, 6 1/2 In. | 12.75 |
| Pressed Glass, Vase, Heart & Thumbprint, 10 In. | 20.00 |
| Pressed Glass, Vase, Henrietta, Findlay, 8 In. | 20.00 |
| Pressed Glass, Vase, Honeycomb, Flower Rim, 6 1/2 In. | 12.50 |
| Pressed Glass, Vase, Illinois, Green, Square, 9 1/2 In. | 39.50 |
| Pressed Glass, Vase, Klondike, Flared, 8 In. | 15.00 |
| Pressed Glass, Vase, Klondike, Trumpet, Findlay, 8 1/4 In. High | 21.00 |
| Pressed Glass, Vase, Maiden's Blush, 6 In.High | 22.50 |
| Pressed Glass, Vase, Massachusetts, Green, Flared, 9 3/4 In. Hig | 21.50 To 27.50 |
| Pressed Glass, Vase, Massachusetts, 9 3/4 In.High | 12.50 |
| Pressed Glass, Vase, Melon Ribbed, Blue, Gold & Enamel, 10 1/2 In. | 22.50 |
| Pressed Glass, Vase, Michigan, Yellow Flashed, Carnations, 8 X 4 In. | 18.00 |
| Pressed Glass, Vase, Duncan & Miller, No. 42, 10 In. | 18.50 |
| Pressed Glass, Vase, No.42, Duncan & Miller, 10 1/2 In. | 22.00 |
| Pressed Glass, Vase, Paneled Thistle, Flared Top, 5 1/2 In.High | 26.75 |
| Pressed Glass, Vase, Paneled Thistle, Tapered, 6 1/4 In.High | 20.00 |
| Pressed Glass, Vase, Paneled Thistle, Tapered, 9 In.High | 24.50 |
| Pressed Glass, Vase, Paneled Thistle, 15 In. | 19.50 |
| Pressed Glass, Vase, Paneled, Flint, 10 1/2 In. High | 15.00 |
| Pressed Glass, Vase, Portland, Scalloped, 6 In.High, Pair | 20.00 |
| Pressed Glass, Vase, Star, Millersburg, Ohio, 10 In. | 20.00 |
| Pressed Glass, Vase, Teepee, Cylindrical, 8 1/ In.High | 14.00 |
| Pressed Glass, Water Set, Admiral Dewey, 7 Piece | 150.00 |
| Pressed Glass, Water Set, Basket Weave, Amber, Scenic Tray, 7 Piece | 95.00 |
| Pressed Glass, Water Set, Basket Weave, Amber, 12 In.Tray, 8 Piece | 120.00 |
| Pressed Glass, Water Set, Child's, Virginia, Gold Trim, 7 Piece | 55.00 |
| Pressed Glass, Water Set, Currier & Ives, Balky Mule Tray, Bellaire, 7 Piece | 200.00 |
| Pressed Glass, Water Set, Currier & Ives, 2 Piece | 48.00 |
| Pressed Glass, Water Set, Currier & Ives, 4 Piece | 55.00 |

Pressed Glass, Water Set, Delaware, Rose, Gold Trim, 5 Piece ............................................. 250.00
Pressed Glass, Water Set, Floragold, 7 Piece ................................................................. 27.00
Pressed Glass, Water Set, Iris & Herringbone, Amber, 5 Piece ........................................... 35.00
Pressed Glass, Water Set, Iris & Herringbone, 5 Piece ...................................................... 25.00
Pressed Glass, Water Set, Leaf & Flower, Amber Stain, 7 Piece ......................................... 190.00
Pressed Glass, Water Set, Mephistopheles, 7 Piece ......................................................... 185.00
Pressed Glass, Water Set, Nursery Tales, 5 Piece ........................................................... 100.00
Pressed Glass, Water Set, Paneled Daisy & Button, Gold Panels, 7 Piece ........................... 95.00
Pressed Glass, Water Set, Paneled, Scalloped Edge, Flint, 7 Piece .................................... 19.00
Pressed Glass, Water Set, Portland, 3 Piece ................................................................... 30.00
Pressed Glass, Water Set, Pressed Leaf, Applied Handle, 7 Piece ..................................... 75.00
Pressed Glass, Water Set, Red Block, 7 Piece ................................................................ 250.00
Pressed Glass, Water Set, Sweet Pear, Pink, Footed Tumblers, 9 Piece .............................. 35.00
Pressed Glass, Water Set, The States, Flashed Amethyst, 7 Piece ..................................... 125.00
Pressed Glass, Water Set, Willow Oak, 7 Piece .............................................................. 100.00
Pressed Glass, Wheelbarrow, Daisy & Button ................................................................ 68.00
Pressed Glass, Whiskey Set, Ashburton, Bar Lip Quart Decanter, 2 Piece .......................... 50.00
Pressed Glass, Whiskey Taster, Lined Long Panels, Flint ................................................. 13.00
Pressed Glass, Whiskey Taster, Ribbed, Opalescent ...................................................... 25.00
Pressed Glass, Whiskey, Flute, Applied Handle, Flint ...................................................... 18.75
Pressed Glass, Wine Rinser, Frosted Greek Key Band, English, 1819, Flint ........................ 32.00
Pressed Glass, Wine Set, Iris, Crystal, 10 Piece ............................................................. 49.25
Pressed Glass, Wine, Almond Thumbprint ............................................... 11.00 To 15.00
Pressed Glass, Wine, Almond Thumbprint, Flint ............................................................ 25.00
Pressed Glass, Wine, Amazon .................................................................................... 14.50
Pressed Glass, Wine, Arched Oval, Cranberry Flashed .................................................... 16.00
Pressed Glass, Wine, Argus ............................................................... 13.00 To 25.00
Pressed Glass, Wine, Argus, Flint ............................................................................... 27.50
Pressed Glass, Wine, Ashburton ......................................................... 15.00 To 22.00
Pressed Glass, Wine, Ashburton, Disconnected Ovals ..................................................... 22.50
Pressed Glass, Wine, Ashburton, Flared Top, 4 In.High ................................................... 23.00
Pressed Glass, Wine, Ashburton, Flint ................................................... 25.00 To 40.00
Pressed Glass, Wine, Ashburton, Flint, Small Size .......................................................... 30.00
Pressed Glass, Wine, Atlas ................................................................ 18.00 To 25.00
Pressed Glass, Wine, Atlas With Etched Flower ............................................................. 18.50
Pressed Glass, Wine, Aurora ..................................................................................... 11.50
Pressed Glass, Wine, Austrian .................................................................................... 16.00
Pressed Glass, Wine, Baby Thumbprint, Yellow & Blue Enamel Trim .................................. 16.00
Pressed Glass, Wine, Balder .............................................................. 9.00 To 13.50
Pressed Glass, Wine, Banded Buckle ................................................... 18.00 To 22.00
Pressed Glass, Wine, Banded Portland ......................................................................... 19.50
Pressed Glass, Wine, Banded Portland, Gold ................................................................. 22.00
Pressed Glass, Wine, Banded Portland, Yellow Flashed ................................................... 25.00
Pressed Glass, Wine, Banded Vernon Honeycomb .......................................................... 18.00
Pressed Glass, Wine, Bar & Diamond ........................................................................... 10.00
Pressed Glass, Wine, Barberry ........................................................... 20.00 To 25.00
Pressed Glass, Wine, Barley ...................................................................................... 25.00
Pressed Glass, Wine, Basket Weave ............................................................................ 10.00
Pressed Glass, Wine, Basket Weave & Roses ................................................................ 16.00
Pressed Glass, Wine, Beaded Band ..................................................... 12.50 To 25.00
Pressed Glass, Wine, Beaded Dewdrop ........................................................................ 28.00
Pressed Glass, Wine, Beaded Oval Window, Medium Blue ............................................... 22.50
Pressed Glass, Wine, Beaded Swirl With Disc Band ........................................................ 17.00
Pressed Glass, Wine, Bellflower .................................................................................. 65.00
Pressed Glass, Wine, Bellflower, Flint .......................................................................... 95.00
Pressed Glass, Wine, Belted Worcester, Flint ................................................................ 39.00
Pressed Glass, Wine, Bent Buckle ............................................................................... 17.00
Pressed Glass, Wine, Bird & Strawberry ............................................... 25.00 To 37.00
Pressed Glass, Wine, Block & Fan ....................................................... 14.00 To 28.00
Pressed Glass, Wine, Block & Jewel ....................................................... 7.50 To 8.00
Pressed Glass, Wine, Block, Amber ...................................................... 17.00 To 25.00
Pressed Glass, Wine, Bradford Grape ........................................................................... 65.00
Pressed Glass, Wine, Bradford Grape, Flint ................................................................... 42.50
Pressed Glass, Wine, Britannic ................................................................................... 9.00
Pressed Glass, Wine, Britannic, Clear & Amber ............................................................. 15.00
Pressed Glass, Wine, Broken Column ........................................................................... 12.50

| | |
|---|---|
| Pressed Glass, Wine, Buckle | 12.00 |
| Pressed Glass, Wine, Buckle With Star | 20.00 |
| Pressed Glass, Wine, Bull's-Eye & Daisy, Red Eyes | 11.00 |
| Pressed Glass, Wine, Bull's-Eye, Flint | 35.00 To 40.00 |
| Pressed Glass, Wine, Button Arches | 10.00 To 16.00 |
| Pressed Glass, Wine, Cabbage Rose | 28.50 To 29.50 |
| Pressed Glass, Wine, Canadian | 25.00 To 30.00 |
| Pressed Glass, Wine, Carolina | 12.00 |
| Pressed Glass, Wine, Cathedral, Amber | 18.00 |
| Pressed Glass, Wine, Cathedral, Ruby & Clear | 18.00 |
| Pressed Glass, Wine, Chain | 8.00 To 14.50 |
| Pressed Glass, Wine, Checkerboard | 8.50 To 18.00 |
| Pressed Glass, Wine, Checkerboard, Flared | 13.00 |
| Pressed Glass, Wine, Co-Op Royal | 7.50 |
| Pressed Glass, Wine, Co-Op Royal, Ruby Flashed | 20.00 |
| Pressed Glass, Wine, Coachman's Cape | 15.00 |
| Pressed Glass, Wine, Colorado | 10.00 To 22.00 |
| Pressed Glass, Wine, Colorado, Green, Gold, 'linkville, Mich. | 18.50 |
| Pressed Glass, Wine, Cord & Tassel | 18.00 To 20.00 |
| Pressed Glass, Wine, Cornucopia | 12.00 |
| Pressed Glass, Wine, Cottage, 4 1/2 In.High | 15.00 |
| Pressed Glass, Wine, Crossed Ovals, Clear | 9.00 |
| Pressed Glass, Wine, Crystal | 12.00 To 12.50 |
| Pressed Glass, Wine, Crystal, Large Size | 15.00 |
| Pressed Glass, Wine, Cupid & Venus | 38.00 To 47.50 |
| Pressed Glass, Wine, Currant | 15.00 To 30.00 |
| Pressed Glass, Wine, Currier & Ives | 9.00 To 15.00 |
| Pressed Glass, Wine, Currier & Ives, Bellaire | 14.50 |
| Pressed Glass, Wine, Currier & Ives, Findlay | 12.00 |
| Pressed Glass, Wine, Currier & Ives, Knob Stem | 16.50 |
| Pressed Glass, Wine, Cut Log | 14.00 To 18.50 |
| Pressed Glass, Wine, Dahlia | 21.00 To 28.00 |
| Pressed Glass, Wine, Dahlia, Large Size | 35.00 |
| Pressed Glass, Wine, Daisy & Button With Narcissus | 12.00 To 12.50 |
| Pressed Glass, Wine, Daisy Medallion | 15.00 |
| Pressed Glass, Wine, Daisy, Gold Trim | 9.50 |
| Pressed Glass, Wine, Dakota | 14.00 To 16.50 |
| Pressed Glass, Wine, Dakota With Etched Band | 18.00 |
| Pressed Glass, Wine, Dakota, Etched Fern & Berry | 32.50 |
| Pressed Glass, Wine, Deflating Balloon | 12.50 |
| Pressed Glass, Wine, Dew & Raindrop | 5.50 To 12.50 |
| Pressed Glass, Wine, Dew & Raindrop, Patterned Stem | 12.50 |
| Pressed Glass, Wine, Diagonal Band | 10.00 |
| Pressed Glass, Wine, Diagonal Band With Fan | 24.00 |
| Pressed Glass, Wine, Diagonal Sawtooth Band | 45.00 |
| Pressed Glass, Wine, Diagonal Sawtooth Band, Flint | 27.50 To 42.00 |
| Pressed Glass, Wine, Diamond Cut With Leaf | 15.00 To 18.00 |
| Pressed Glass, Wine, Diamond Horseshoe, Red Flashed | 22.00 |
| Pressed Glass, Wine, Diamond Point Disc | 16.00 |
| Pressed Glass, Wine, Diamond Point, Flint | 65.00 |
| Pressed Glass, Wine, Diamond Prisms | 14.50 |
| Pressed Glass, Wine, Diamond-Quilted | 8.50 To 16.50 |
| Pressed Glass, Wine, Diamond-Quilted, Blue | 10.00 |
| Pressed Glass, Wine, Diamond-Quilted, C.1880 | 12.50 |
| Pressed Glass, Wine, Diamond-Quilted, Sapphire Blue | 27.50 |
| Pressed Glass, Wine, Ditto Vintage | 16.50 |
| Pressed Glass, Wine, Double Beaded Band | 13.50 |
| Pressed Glass, Wine, Double Beetle Band | 12.00 To 12.75 |
| Pressed Glass, Wine, Double Beetle Band, Blue | 25.00 |
| Pressed Glass, Wine, Double Dahlia & Lens, Green | 18.00 |
| Pressed Glass, Wine, Double Line Swirl | 15.00 |
| Pressed Glass, Wine, Double Loop, Clear | 30.00 |
| Pressed Glass, Wine, Duncan & Miller No.42 | 14.00 |
| Pressed Glass, Wine, Etched Dakota | 22.50 |
| Pressed Glass, Wine, Etched Fern | 5.00 |
| Pressed Glass, Wine, Eureka, Flint | 20.00 |

Pressed Glass, Wine, Excelsior With Maltese Cross ............ 38.00
Pressed Glass, Wine, Excelsior, Flint ............ 30.00
Pressed Glass, Wine, Feather ............ 11.00 To 22.00
Pressed Glass, Wine, Feather Duster ............ 16.50
Pressed Glass, Wine, Feather, Scalloped Top ............ 35.00
Pressed Glass, Wine, Feather, Straight Top ............ 12.00
Pressed Glass, Wine, Fern Swirl ............ 12.00
Pressed Glass, Wine, Fickle Block ............ 12.00
Pressed Glass, Wine, Fine Rib ............ 26.00
Pressed Glass, Wine, Fine Rib, Flint ............ 24.00 To 28.00
Pressed Glass, Wine, Finecut ............ 7.50
Pressed Glass, Wine, Finecut & Panel ............ 15.00
Pressed Glass, Wine, Finecut & Panel, Amber ............ 28.00
Pressed Glass, Wine, Finecut & Panel, Blue ............ 28.00 To 28.50
Pressed Glass, Wine, Finecut & Panel, Green ............ 28.00
Pressed Glass, Wine, Finecut, Small Size ............ 12.50
Pressed Glass, Wine, Floral Oval ............ 9.00
Pressed Glass, Wine, Florida Palm ............ 10.00 To 11.50
Pressed Glass, Wine, Florida Palm, Flint ............ 19.00
Pressed Glass, Wine, Flute ............ 14.00
Pressed Glass, Wine, Flute, 11 Flutes, Applied Stem & Base, Flint ............ 14.00
Pressed Glass, Wine, Forget-Me-Not ............ 24.00
Pressed Glass, Wine, Frosted Lion, Stemmed, 4 1/8 In.High ............ 160.00
Pressed Glass, Wine, Galloway ............ 13.00 To 25.00
Pressed Glass, Wine, Giant Baby Thumbprint, Flint ............ 40.00
Pressed Glass, Wine, Halley's Comet ............ 3.00 To 22.00
Pressed Glass, Wine, Hamilton With Leaf, Flint ............ 50.00
Pressed Glass, Wine, Hand ............ 25.00
Pressed Glass, Wine, Hawaiian Lei ............ 9.50
Pressed Glass, Wine, Hawaiian Lei, No Bee ............ 12.50
Pressed Glass, Wine, Heart & Thumbprint ............ 20.00 To 30.00
Pressed Glass, Wine, Hearts Of Loch Laven ............ 3.50 To 18.00
Pressed Glass, Wine, Heck ............ 15.00
Pressed Glass, Wine, Herringbone ............ 11.50
Pressed Glass, Wine, High Hob ............ 10.00
Pressed Glass, Wine, Hinoto, Flint ............ 28.00
Pressed Glass, Wine, Hobnail ............ 11.00
Pressed Glass, Wine, Honeycomb ............ 10.50 To 16.00
Pressed Glass, Wine, Honeycomb, Flint ............ 10.00 To 18.00
Pressed Glass, Wine, Honeycomb, Knob Stem, Flint ............ 25.00
Pressed Glass, Wine, Horn Of Plenty, Small Size ............ 75.00
Pressed Glass, Wine, Horsemint ............ 6.00 To 10.00
Pressed Glass, Wine, Huber, Flint ............ 16.00 To 18.00
Pressed Glass, Wine, Inverness ............ 12.00
Pressed Glass, Wine, Inverted Thumbprint ............ 6.75
Pressed Glass, Wine, Inverted Thumbprint, Amber ............ 6.50
Pressed Glass, Wine, Iowa City ............ 20.00
Pressed Glass, Wine, Ivy In Snow ............ 15.00
Pressed Glass, Wine, Jacob's Ladder ............ 20.00 To 30.00
Pressed Glass, Wine, Jewel Band ............ 12.00 To 15.00
Pressed Glass, Wine, Kansas ............ 25.00
Pressed Glass, Wine, King's Crown ............ 5.00 To 7.00
Pressed Glass, Wine, Knobby Bull's-Eye ............ 8.50
Pressed Glass, Wine, Kokomo ............ 14.50 To 15.00
Pressed Glass, Wine, La Verne ............ 12.00 To 18.00
Pressed Glass, Wine, Lacy Medallion ............ 13.50
Pressed Glass, Wine, Laredo Honeycomb, Flint ............ 10.00
Pressed Glass, Wine, Lattice ............ 10.00 To 14.50
Pressed Glass, Wine, Lattice & Oval Panels, Flint ............ 45.00 To 65.00
Pressed Glass, Wine, Leaf & Dart ............ 12.50 To 24.00
Pressed Glass, Wine, Liberty, Clear ............ 12.00
Pressed Glass, Wine, Lily Of The Valley ............ 39.50
Pressed Glass, Wine, Loop ............ 6.00 To 15.00
Pressed Glass, Wine, Loop & Block ............ 9.00
Pressed Glass, Wine, Loop & Ovals ............ 12.00
Pressed Glass, Wine, Loop With Stippled Panels ............ 18.00

| | |
|---|---|
| Pressed Glass, Wine, Loops With Fan | 15.00 |
| Pressed Glass, Wine, Maine | 15.00 |
| Pressed Glass, Wine, Majestic | 12.00 |
| Pressed Glass, Wine, Mascotte | 12.50 |
| Pressed Glass, Wine, Massachusetts | 9.50 |
| Pressed Glass, Wine, Melrose | 9.00 To 12.00 |
| Pressed Glass, Wine, Milton | 12.50 |
| Pressed Glass, Wine, Mirror | 16.00 |
| Pressed Glass, Wine, Mirror & Loop, Knob Stem, Flint | 32.00 |
| Pressed Glass, Wine, Mirror, Flint | 22.00 |
| Pressed Glass, Wine, Mitered Diamond Point | 10.00 |
| Pressed Glass, Wine, Morning Glory | 135.00 |
| Pressed Glass, Wine, Nailhead | 20.00 |
| Pressed Glass, Wine, New Hampshire | 8.50 |
| Pressed Glass, Wine, New Hampshire, Flared Top | 10.00 |
| Pressed Glass, Wine, Optic Flute | 4.00 To 4.50 |
| Pressed Glass, Wine, Oval & Shield | 10.00 |
| Pressed Glass, Wine, Palm Leaf With Fan | 9.50 |
| Pressed Glass, Wine, Paneled Dewdrop | 16.00 |
| Pressed Glass, Wine, Paneled Dewdrop, Patterned Base | 14.50 |
| Pressed Glass, Wine, Paneled Dewdrop, Plain Base | 13.50 |
| Pressed Glass, Wine, Paneled Diamond Block, Clear | 12.00 |
| Pressed Glass, Wine, Paneled English Hobnail With Prism | 8.00 |
| Pressed Glass, Wine, Paneled Fine Block | 10.00 |
| Pressed Glass, Wine, Paneled Forget-Me-Not | 35.00 To 38.00 |
| Pressed Glass, Wine, Paneled Grape | 5.85 |
| Pressed Glass, Wine, Paneled Jewels | 12.50 To 15.00 |
| Pressed Glass, Wine, Paneled Jewels, Amber | 25.00 |
| Pressed Glass, Wine, Paneled Jewels, Vaseline | 25.00 |
| Pressed Glass, Wine, Paneled Stippled Scroll, Clear | 12.00 |
| Pressed Glass, Wine, Paneled Thistle | 16.00 |
| Pressed Glass, Wine, Paneled Thistle, Flared Rim | 11.00 |
| Pressed Glass, Wine, Pecorah | 6.00 |
| Pressed Glass, Wine, Peerless | 12.00 |
| Pressed Glass, Wine, Pennsylvania | 9.00 To 14.50 |
| Pressed Glass, Wine, Pennsylvania & Knobby Bull's-Eye | 8.00 |
| Pressed Glass, Wine, Pentagon | 12.50 |
| Pressed Glass, Wine, Pinwheel & Diamond | 4.00 |
| Pressed Glass, Wine, Pioneer's Victoria | 18.00 |
| Pressed Glass, Wine, Pleat & Panel | 34.50 |
| Pressed Glass, Wine, Portland | 9.50 To 13.00 |
| Pressed Glass, Wine, Portland, Gold Trim | 9.00 To 12.00 |
| Pressed Glass, Wine, Pressed Leaf | 10.50 |
| Pressed Glass, Wine, Primrose | 15.00 |
| Pressed Glass, Wine, Priscilla, Findlay | 25.00 |
| Pressed Glass, Wine, Prism & Broken Column | 11.00 |
| Pressed Glass, Wine, Prism & Flute, Flint | 15.00 |
| Pressed Glass, Wine, Prism Buttress | 12.50 |
| Pressed Glass, Wine, Quartered Block | 12.00 |
| Pressed Glass, Wine, Queen | 13.50 To 15.00 |
| Pressed Glass, Wine, Radiant Daisy | 7.50 |
| Pressed Glass, Wine, Recessed Ovals | 12.00 |
| Pressed Glass, Wine, Red Block | 24.50 To 28.00 |
| Pressed Glass, Wine, Regal Block, Ruby Flashed | 20.00 |
| Pressed Glass, Wine, Ribbed Elipse | 8.00 |
| Pressed Glass, Wine, Ribbed Ivy, Flint | 32.50 To 65.00 |
| Pressed Glass, Wine, Ribbed Palm, Flint | 32.50 |
| Pressed Glass, Wine, Ripple | 12.00 |
| Pressed Glass, Wine, Rose Band, Portland | 18.00 |
| Pressed Glass, Wine, Rose Point | 12.00 |
| Pressed Glass, Wine, Rose Sprig | 16.50 To 25.00 |
| Pressed Glass, Wine, Rosette With Palm | 15.00 |
| Pressed Glass, Wine, Rustic Rose | 12.00 |
| Pressed Glass, Wine, S Repeat, Apple Green | 17.00 |
| Pressed Glass, Wine, Sawtooth, Flint | 28.00 |
| Pressed Glass, Wine, Scroll & Dots | 12.50 |

Pressed Glass, Wine, Scroll & Flowers ................................................................................. 14.50
Pressed Glass, Wine, Scroll & Flowers, Green ................................................................... 22.00
Pressed Glass, Wine, Sedan ..................................................................... 8.75 To 13.50
Pressed Glass, Wine, Sheaf & Diamond ..................................................... 5.50 To 9.00
Pressed Glass, Wine, Sheraton .............................................................................................. 17.50
Pressed Glass, Wine, Shoshone ............................................................................................ 17.50
Pressed Glass, Wine, Shovel .................................................................................................. 9.50
Pressed Glass, Wine, Shuttle ..................................................................... 5.50 To 13.50
Pressed Glass, Wine, Shuttle, Greentown ................................................ 12.00 To 15.00
Pressed Glass, Wine, Smocking ............................................................................................ 40.00
Pressed Glass, Wine, Snowflake ........................................................................................... 10.00
Pressed Glass, Wine, Spirea Band, Clear ........................................................................... 16.00
Pressed Glass, Wine, Star & File .......................................................................................... 7.50
Pressed Glass, Wine, Stars & Bars, Clear .......................................................................... 22.00
Pressed Glass, Wine, Stars & Stripes ...................................................... 5.50 To 10.00
Pressed Glass, Wine, Stedman, Flint .................................................................................... 30.00
Pressed Glass, Wine, Stippled Bowl ..................................................................................... 12.50
Pressed Glass, Wine, Stippled Forget-Me-Not ................................................................... 21.50
Pressed Glass, Wine, Stirgil ........................................................................ 8.00 To 15.50
Pressed Glass, Wine, Sunburst .................................................................. 10.50 To 12.00
Pressed Glass, Wine, Sunk Honeycomb, Ruby Stained .................................................... 24.50
Pressed Glass, Wine, Swirl .................................................................................................... 8.00
Pressed Glass, Wine, Swirl & Diamond, Stemmed ............................................................ 7.00
Pressed Glass, Wine, Swirled Column .................................................................................. 10.00
Pressed Glass, Wine, Teardrop ............................................................................................. 11.50
Pressed Glass, Wine, Teardrop & Thumbprint .................................................................... 12.00
Pressed Glass, Wine, Texas Bull's-Eye .................................................... 3.00 To 12.00
Pressed Glass, Wine, The States ............................................................... 13.50 To 16.00
Pressed Glass, Wine, Thistle ...................................................................... 8.75 To 15.00
Pressed Glass, Wine, Thistleblow .............................................................. 7.00 To 7.50
Pressed Glass, Wine, Three Faces ....................................................................................... 45.00
Pressed Glass, Wine, Thumbprint Band, Round, Lined, Flint, 4 In.High ....................... 13.50
Pressed Glass, Wine, Thumbprint, Flint .............................................................................. 30.00
Pressed Glass, Wine, Thumbprint, Knob Stem ................................................................... 35.00
Pressed Glass, Wine, Thumbprint, Ruby & Clear .............................................................. 30.00
Pressed Glass, Wine, Tiny Finecut ............................................................ 9.00 To 12.00
Pressed Glass, Wine, Torpedo ............................................................................................... 37.50
Pressed Glass, Wine, Tree Of Life ........................................................................................ 22.50
Pressed Glass, Wine, Triple Triangle, Red Flashed .......................................................... 22.50
Pressed Glass, Wine, Truncated Cube, Ruby & Clear ............................... 18.00 To 25.00
Pressed Glass, Wine, Tulip ..................................................................................................... 5.00
Pressed Glass, Wine, Tulip With Sawtooth ......................................................................... 18.50
Pressed Glass, Wine, Two Panel, Canary ............................................................................ 26.50
Pressed Glass, Wine, Umbilicated Sawtooth ............................................ 21.50 To 33.00
Pressed Glass, Wine, Umbilicated Sawtooth, Flint ........................................................... 25.00
Pressed Glass, Wine, Waffle ...................................................................... 6.00 To 10.00
Pressed Glass, Wine, Waffle & Star Band ........................................................................... 12.50
Pressed Glass, Wine, Waffle & Thumbprint, Flint .................................... 30.00 To 48.00
Pressed Glass, Wine, Waffle, Flint ....................................................................................... 55.00
Pressed Glass, Wine, Washington Centennial .......................................... 15.00 To 45.00
Pressed Glass, Wine, Water Lily ........................................................................................... 12.00
Pressed Glass, Wine, Westward Ho, Frosted, Knob Stem ................................................ 100.00
Pressed Glass, Wine, Westward Ho, 4 7/8 In.High ............................................................ 125.00
Pressed Glass, Wine, Wishbone ............................................................................................ 12.00
Pressed Glass, Wine, 808 ....................................................................................................... 12.50
Pressed Glass, Wine, 1, 000-Eye Band ................................................................................ 16.50
Pressed Glass, Wiskbroom, Daisy & Button With Fine Rib, Amber, Patent .................... 18.00
Print, A Sailing Galleon In Rough Seas, Edmund Dulac, Color, 7 X 9 1/2 In. .............. 8.00
Print, Abraham Lincoln, A.H.Ritchie, 13 1/2 X 9 1/2 In., Framed .................................. 150.00
Print, Abraham Lincoln, H.B.Hall, Engraving, 10 X 12 In. ............................................... 40.00
Print, Alken, Breaking Cover, Framed, 9 3/4 X 12 In. ....................................................... 75.00
Print, Alken, Full Cry, Framed, 9 3/4 X 12 In. ................................................................... 75.00
Print, Alphonse Mucha, L'Automne, 26 X 11 In. ............................................. Illus 550.00
Print, Alphonse Mucha, 'Monaco-Monte Carlo', 1897, 29 X 41 In., Signed ................. 950.00
Print, Alphonse Mucha, Rose, 1897, 40 X 16 In. ............................................................... 275.00
Print, Alphonse Mucha, 1898, Girl Lighting Cigarette Papers, 40 X 60 In. .................. 1250.00

Print, Audubon, Common Gull,
1834, Engraving, Aquatint

Print, Dutchman,
Nagasaki, Hosoban
*(See Page 498)*

Print, Alphonse Mucha,
L'Automne, 26 X 11 In.
*(See Page 496)*

| | | |
|---|---|---|
| Print, Audubon, American Scoter Duck, 1838, Engraving, Aquatint | | 500.00 |
| Print, Audubon, American Water Quezel, 1837, Engraving, Aquatint | | 300.00 |
| Print, Audubon, Arctic Yager, 1835, Engraving, Aquatint | | 650.00 |
| Print, Audubon, Black Backed Gull, 1835, Engraving, Aquatint | | 750.00 |
| Print, Audubon, Black Guillemot, 1834, Engraving, Aquatint | | 650.00 |
| Print, Audubon, Black Tern, 1835, Engraving, Aquatint | | 375.00 |
| Print, Audubon, Common Gull, 1834, Engraving, Aquatint | *Illus* | 750.00 |
| Print, Audubon, Crested Grebe, 1835, Engraving, Aquatint | | 600.00 |
| Print, Audubon, Little Auk, 1836, Engraving, Aquatint | | 425.00 |
| Print, Audubon, Rocky Mountain Plover, 1836, Engraving, Aquatint | | 325.00 |
| Print, Audubon, Ruddy Plover, 1834, Engraving, Aquatint | | 250.00 |
| Print, Audubon, Sandwich Tern, 1835, Engraving, Aquatint | | 475.00 |
| Print, Audubon, Turkey Buzzard, 1832, Engraving, Aquatint | | 700.00 |
| Print, Audubon, White-Headed Eagle, 1830, Engraving, Aquatint | | 2100.00 |
| Print, Bartlett, Baltimore Battle Monument, Black & White, 4 1/2 X 7 In. | | 6.00 |
| Print, Bartlett, Black Mountain, Lake George, C.1838, Hand-Colored | | 8.00 |
| Print, Bartlett, Caldwell, Lake George, Hudson River, C.1838, Hand-Colored | | 8.00 |
| Print, Bartlett, Centre Harbour, Black & White, 4 1/2 X 7 In. | | 6.00 |
| Print, Bartlett, Harpers Ferry, Black & White, 4 1/2 X 7 In. | | 6.00 |
| Print, Bartlett, Highlands Near Newburgh, Hudson River, C.1838, Hand-Colored | | 8.00 |

Print, Bartlett, Peekskill Landing, Hudson River, C.1838, Hand-Colored ............ 8.00
Print, Bartlett, Philadelphia Schuylkill Water Works, Black & White ............ 6.00
Print, Bartlett, Ruins Of Fort Ticonderoga, C.1838, Hand-Colored ............ 8.00
Print, Bartlett, Saratoga Lake, Hudson River, C.1838, Hand-Colored ............ 8.00
Print, Bartlett, The Park & City Hall, New York, C.1838, Hand-Colored ............ 15.00
Print, Bartlett, Trenton Falls, Black & White, 4 1/2 X 7 In. ............ 6.00
Print, Bartlett, Valley Of The Connecticut, Mt.Holyoke, C.1838, Hand-Colored ............ 8.00
Print, Bartlett, View From Hyde Park, Hudson River, C.1838, Hand-Colored ............ 8.00
Print, Bartlett, View From Mount Holyoke, Hudson, C.1838, Hand-Colored ............ 8.00
Print, Bartlett, View From Ruggle's House, Newburgh, C.1838, Hand-Colored ............ 10.00
Print, Bartlett, Village Of Sing-Sing, Hudson River, C.1838, Hand-Colored ............ 8.00
Print, Belltower & Portal, W.Fuerster, Germany, 1930, Black & White, Pair ............ 10.00
Print, Birthplace Of Benjamin Harrison, Garlick, 1889, Lithograph ............ 37.50
Print, Brig Jane & Cutter Beaufoy, Feb.20, 1823, Huggins After Duncan, 1826 ............ 110.00
Print, Bubbles, Boy Blowing Bubbles, Millais, 1886, 12 X 16 In. ............ 50.00
Print, Chicago World's Fair, 1893, Graham, Lithograph, Color, 28 X 44 In. ............ 60.00
Print, Coolidge, Dogs At Cards, C.1915, Color ............ 8.00
Print, Cupid Asleep, Parkinson, 1897, Oak Frame, Heart Shape Matte ............ 7.50
Print, Cupid Awake, Cupid Asleep, M.B.Parkinson, Copyright 1897, Framed ............ 12.50
Print, Currier & Ives, see Currier & Ives
Print, Currier, see Currier
Print, Dodge, Indian Medicine Lodge, Paris, 1887, Color, Framed, 12 X 14 In. ............ 20.00
Print, Dr.Snytax At Covent Garden, Rowlandson, 1817, 7 3/4 X 4 3/4 In. ............ 14.00
Print, Dr.Syntax At A Review, Rowlandson, 1818, 7 3/4 X 4 3/4 In. ............ 14.00
Print, Driving Her Motor Car, Harrison Fisher ............ 15.00
Print, Dutchman, Nagasaki, Hosoban ............ Illus 1100.00
Print, Eisen, Between Snow Covered Banks Of Sumida River, C.1790, Oban ............ 425.00
Print, Eisen, Sensoji Temple In Edo, C.1790, Oban ............ 850.00
Print, Eisen, Seven Gods Of Felicity, C.1790, Kakemono-E ............ 400.00
Print, Eishi, Courtesan Seated In Loose Kimono, C.1756, Oban ............ 175.00
Print, Emmy Zweybruck, Two Peasant Children, 9 1/2 X 11 In. ............ 5.00
Print, Explosion Of British Frigate Guerriere, Tanner After Barralet, 1812 ............ 400.00
Print, Fairy Figures, Edmund Dulac, Color, 7 X 9 1/2 In. ............ 8.00
Print, Flower, Blue Flower Cluster, Bessa, Paris, C.1808, Hand-Colored ............ 7.50
Print, Flower, Pink & White Cluster, Bessa, Paris, C.1808, Hand-Colored ............ 7.50
Print, Gakutei, Woman In Elaborate Gown Playing Biwa, C.1786, Surimono ............ 175.00
Print, Gallant Charge Of The 69th Regiment, Ensign, Bridgman, & Fanning ............ 40.00
Print, George Washington, Equestrian, Whitney Joclyn, 1857, Woodblock, Color ............ 15.00
Print, Germany, Royal Academy Of Science, Paris, 1795, 5 1/2 X 6 3/4 In. ............ 28.00
Print, Godey, Fashion, 1851, Framed ............ 12.00
Print, Godey, Unrivaled Colored Fashions, 1850s, Lithograph, Hand-Colored ............ 22.50
Print, Grapes, Dutch, C.1750, Pair ............ 1250.00
Print, Harrison Fisher, The Debutante, Color, 13 X 10 1/2 In. ............ 9.50
Print, Harrison Fisher, Their New Love, C.1911, Framed, 18 X 22 In. ............ 25.00
Print, Hiroshige, Asakusa Temple, 1856, Oban Tate-E ............ 150.00
Print, Hiroshige, Asakusa, C.1844, Oban Yoko-E ............ 90.00
Print, Hiroshige, Asakusa, 1857, Oban ............ 1700.00
Print, Hiroshige, Atagoshita, 1857, Oban ............ 350.00
Print, Hiroshige, Benten Temple, 1856, Oban Tate-E ............ 75.00
Print, Hiroshige, Black Grouper & Bonefish, C.1832, Oban ............ 300.00
Print, Hiroshige, Festival Of The Cock, Asakusa, 1857, Oban ............ 325.00
Print, Hiroshige, Goyu, 1855, Oban ............ 70.00
Print, Hiroshige, Harima, 1858, Oban ............ 450.00
Print, Hiroshige, Kyobashi, 1857, Oban ............ 275.00
Print, Hiroshige, Maiko, 1853, Oban ............ 290.00
Print, Hiroshige, Masaki, 1857, Oban ............ 300.00
Print, Hiroshige, Matsuchiyama, 1844, Oban Yoko-E ............ 90.00
Print, Hiroshige, Odawara, 1833, Oban ............ 475.00
Print, Hiroshige, Overhead View Of City Street, Edo, C.1844, Oban Yoko-E ............ 80.00
Print, Hiroshige, Plum Garden At Kameido, C.1844, Oban Yoko-E ............ 90.00
Print, Hiroshige, Sakuragawa, C.1835, Oban Yoko-E ............ 100.00
Print, Hiroshige, Shiba Temple, 1844, Oban ............ 120.00
Print, Hiroshige, Takanawa, 1854, Oban ............ 70.00
Print, Hiroshige, Tsukiji, C.1844, Oban Yoko-E ............ Illus 275.00
Print, Hiroshige, Tsukudajima, 1844, Oban Yoko-E ............ 90.00
Print, Hiroshige, Yorai Ferry, 1857, Oban ............ 250.00

Print, Hokusai,
Temple Of The Five Hundred Rakan,
1760s

Print, Hiroshige, Tsukiji,
C.1844, Oban Yoko-E
*(See Page 498)*

| | |
|---|---:|
| Print, Hiroshige, Yoshiwara, 1857, Oban | 225.00 |
| Print, Hokkei, Costume Of Eboshi & Other Clothing, C.1780, Surimono | 170.00 |
| Print, Hokkei, Courtesan Seated, C.1780, Surimono | 100.00 |
| Print, Hokusai, Courtesans Around Birdcage, C.1760, Surimono Yoko-E | 225.00 |
| Print, Hokusai, Eijiri In Suruga Province, C.1760, Black Outline, Oban | 325.00 |
| Print, Hokusai, Fujiwara No Yoshitaka, C.1760, Oban | 1100.00 |
| Print, Hokusai, Misaka, C.1760, Blue Outline, Oban | 1500.00 |
| Print, Hokusai, Senju In Musashino, C.1760, Blue Outline, Oban | 525.00 |
| Print, Hokusai, Sojo Henjo, C.1760, Oban | 1700.00 |
| Print, Hokusai, Suruga, Peak Of Fuji, C.1760, Oban | 750.00 |
| Print, Hokusai, Temple Of The Five Hundred Rakan, 1760s *Illus* | 550.00 |
| Print, Hokusai, Three Sparrows Above Arrowroot, C.1760, Oban Yoko-E | 300.00 |
| Print, Hokusai, Ushibori In Hitachi, C.1760, Oban | 400.00 |
| Print, Hokusai, Yamabe No Akahito, C.1760, Oban | 1600.00 |
| Print, Hokusai, 3 Sparrows Above Arrowroot, C.1760, Oban Yoko-E | 300.00 |
| Print, Icart, Apple Girl, C.1930, Color, 18 X 22 In. | 10.00 |
| Print, Icart, The Letter, C.1930, Color, 18 X 22 In. | 10.00 |
| Print, Indian Love Call, Chas.M.Russell, 1894, Snook Trading Post, Montana | 25.00 |
| Print, Indian Warrior, Peace Pipe, Markendorf, 1906, Lithograph | 7.00 |
| Print, Ishikawa Toyonobu, Segawa Kikujiro Dancing, C.1711, Hosoban | 525.00 |
| Print, Jessie Wilcox Smith, Hushaby Baby, 10 1/8 X 7 1/4 In. | 4.00 |
| Print, Kellogg & Bulkely, Southern Beauty, C.1870, Color | 20.00 |
| Print, Kellogg, Lincoln At Home, Lithograph, Color, Small Folio | 50.00 |
| Print, Kellogg, President James Polk | 38.00 |
| Print, Kiyonaga, Courtesan In Litter, Attendants, C.1742, Chuban | 700.00 |
| Print, Kiyonaga, Three Young Women Seated On Ground, C.1785, Aiban | 375.00 |
| Print, Kiyonaga, Two Girls Struggling Over Love Letter, C.1742, Chuban | 700.00 |

Print, **Knocked Out,** English Political, Tom Merry, 1886 ............................................ 10.00
Print, **Koryusai,** Courtesan, Attendant & 2 Komuro, C.1775, Chuban ................. 350.00
Print, **Kunihisa,** European Man & Wife, C.1832, Oban ......................................... 50.00
Prinit, **Kunisada,** Two Actors In Seaside Scene, C.1786, Surimono .................... 90.00
Print, **Kuniyoshi,** Lightning Thrown By Oho, C.1798, Oban ............................... 425.00
Print, **Kuniyoshi,** View Of Mt.Fuji, Tskuda Island, C.1798, Oban .................... 1900.00
Print, **Kurz & Allison,** Assault On Fort Sanders, 1891, Color ............................ 34.50
Print, **Kurz & Allison,** Battle Of Cedar Creek, 1890, Color ............................... 37.50
Print, **Kurz & Allison,** Battle Of Champion Hills, 1887, Color .......................... 34.50
Print, **Kurz & Allison,** Battle Of Corinth, 1891, Color ..................................... 37.50
Print, **Kurz & Allison,** Battle Of Franklin, 1891, Color ..................................... 37.50
Print, **Kurz & Allison,** Battle Of Opequan, Va., 1893, Color, 22 X 28 In. ......... 34.50
Print, **Kurz & Allison,** Battle Of Williamsburg, 1893, Color .............................. 37.50
Print, **Kurz & Allison,** Battle Of Wilson's Creek, 1893, Color ........................... 34.50
Print, **Kurz & Allison,** Rear Attack By General Logan, May 16, 1863, Color ...... 34.50
Print, **Kurz & Allison,** Siege Of Vicksburg, 1888, Color ................................... 32.50
Print, **Launching On The Beach At Newport,** Harrison Fisher ............................. 15.00
Print, **LeMunyan,** Sweet Enough, 1911, Framed ................................................. 19.00
Print, **Lincoln,** The Emancipation Proclamation, Ritchie, 1866, Engraving ......... 275.00
Print, **Lindbergh In Flying Togs,** Spirit Of St.Louis, F.R.Harper, Color ............. 15.00
Print, **Little Girl Sewing,** Fraeluetrees, Framed ................................................ 6.50
Print, **Lord Cornwallis,** Equestrian, W.H.Dodd, 1857, Woodblock, Color .......... 15.00
Print, **Mammoth Trees Of California,** Stillman, Chromolithograph ..................... 50.00
Print, **Map,** Canary Islands, Bellin, 1753, 9 1/8 X 7 In. ...................................... 25.00
Print, **Map,** Great Britian, Royal Academy Of Science, Paris, 1714 ..................... 28.00
Print, **Map,** Italy, Vallardi, 1880, 13 1/2 X 10 3/4 In. ......................................... 15.00
Print, **Map,** Prussia, Lippincott, 1872, 12 X 9 3/4 In. ......................................... 25.00
Print, **Map,** Spain, Academy Of Science, Paris, 1795, 5 1/2 X 6 3/4 In. ............. 28.00
Print, **Maude Humphrey,** Baby Record, 3 Page, Color ........................................ 18.00
Print, **Maude Humphrey,** Ding Dong Bell, 10 X 11 In. ......................................... 30.00
Print, **Maude Humphrey,** Little Black Girl, 1889, Color, 7 X 9 In. ....................... 25.00
Print, **Maude Humphrey,** Little Boy Blue, 1900, Color, 15 X 12 In. ...................... 22.00
Print, **Maude Humphrey,** Little Miss Muffet, 1900, Color, 15 X 12 In. ................. 22.00
Print, **Maude Humphrey,** Little White Girl, 1889, Color, 7 X 9 In. ....................... 25.00
Print, **Maude Humphrey,** Sing A Song Of Sixpence, 10 X 11 In. .......................... 30.00
Print, **Maxfield Parrish,** Circe's Palace, Collier, Gold Frame ............................. 15.00
Print, **Maxfield Parrish,** Daybreak, Framed, 12 X 19 In. .................................... 22.00
Print, **Maxfield Parrish,** Daybreak, Gold Frame, 15 X 20 In. .............................. 48.50
Print, **Maxfield Parrish,** Ecstasy, Color, Framed, 8 X 11 In. .............................. 47.50
Print, **Maxfield Parrish,** Ecstasy, Utah Power & Mazda Lamps, 1930 Calendar ... 60.00
Print, **Maxfield Parrish,** Garden Of Allah, 18 X 33 1/2 In. .................................. 55.00
Print, **Maxfield Parrish,** Knave Of Hearts, Spiral Book ..................................... 120.00
Print, **Maxfield Parrish,** Nude Adonis, Color, Frame, 12 X 20 In. ........................ 45.00
Print, **Maxfield Parrish,** Pierrot's Seranade, 1908 ............................................ 10.00
Print, **Maxfield Parrish,** Poems Of Childhood, Color .......................................... 15.00
Print, **Maxfield Parrish,** The Canyon, Handmade Frame, 13 X 16 In. .................... 31.25
Print, **Maxfield Parrish,** The Garden Of Allah, Color, Framed ............................. 12.00
Print, **Maxfield Parrish,** Wild Geese, Handmade Frame, 13 X 16 In. ..................... 31.25
Print, **Maxfield Parrish,** 2 Girls Seated By Tree Near Mountains, Framed ........... 28.00
Print, **Maxfield Parrish,** 3 Ladies Reclining By Reflecting Pool, Framed ............. 17.50
Print, **Miranda On Cliffs Overlooking The Sea,** Edmund Dulac, Color ................. 8.00
Print, **National Lancers & Reviewing Officers On Boston Common,** Lane, 1837 ... 225.00
Print, **National Temperance Society,** 'touch Not-Taste Not, ' C.1870, Color ......... 7.50
Print, **New York As Washington Knew It,** Robertson, C.1794, Engraving ............ 1400.00
Print, **New York From Weehawken Hill,** After Wall, 1823, Engraving, Aquatint ... 175.00
Print, **New York,** Mottram After J.W.Hill, 1855, Engraving & Aquatint ............... 225.00
Print, **New York,** Winter In Broadway, Girardet After Sebron, 1857, Engraving ... 450.00
Print, **Pa-She-Nine,** A Chippewa Chief, Rice & Clark, 1843, Lithograph, Color ... 60.00
Print, **Pearle Fidler,** Le Munyan, 1911, Framed ................................................ 19.00
Print, **Penitent,** Reclining Nude, Reynold H.Weidenoar, Etching, 21 X 17 In. ....... 75.00
Print, **Plain Or Ringlets,** John Leech, C.1879, Color, Steel Engraving ................ 6.50
Print, **Prang,** Battle Of Kennesaw Mountain, 1887, Lithograph, Color ................. 34.50
Print, **Prang,** Lammergeyer, 1885, Color, Bird Series, 9 X 12 In. .......................... 5.00
Print, **Prang,** Paradise Flycatcher, 1885, Color, Bird Series, 9 X 12 In. ............... 5.00
Print, **Prang,** Sheridan's Final Charge At Winchester, 1887, Lithograph, Color .... 34.50
Print, **Prang,** Six Babies, Signed Waugh, Framed .............................................. 18.00

Print, Prang, Six Seated Babies, I.Waugh, 1888, Framed, 6 1/2 X 12 In. ...................................... 30.00
Print, Prang, The American Elk, 12 X 16 In. ...................................... 40.00
Print, Prang, The Battle Of Kennesaw Mountain, 1887, Lithograph, Color ...................................... 34.50
Print, Prang, The Young Commodore, 1872, Chromolithograph, Framed ...................................... 1500.00
Print, Prang, Titmouse, 1885, Color, Bird Series, 9 X 12 In. ...................................... 5.00
Print, Prang, Weaver Birds, 1885, Color, Bird Series, 9 X 12 In. ...................................... 5.00
Print, R.E.Lee And Generals, Dated 1903, 15 X 25 Inches ...................................... 90.00
Print, Remington, Cowboys & Indians Fighting, Framed, 9 X 24 In. ...................................... 22.00
Print, Remington, Indians Attacking Covered Wagons By River, Framed ...................................... 20.00
Print, Remington, The Cattle Drive, 1904, Color, 17 X 23 1/2 In. ...................................... 22.50
Print, Roses, Lily Of The Valley, & Lilacs, T.L.Privost, Walnut Shadowbox ...................................... 18.00
Print, Sadahide, American Couple With Great Dane, C.1807, Oban ...................................... 210.00
Print, Sarony & Co., The Harbor Of Balaklava, Lithograph, Black & White ...................................... 10.00
Print, Sarony & Major, George Washington, Lithograph ...................................... 40.00
Print, Sarony & Major, President Polk, Lithograph ...................................... 35.00
Print, Sartain, The County Election, 1854, Engraving, Black & White ...................................... 175.00
Print, Shaggy Pony, A.Bartsch, Black & White, Steel Engraving ...................................... 25.00
Print, Shaker Village, Alfred Maine, Color, Walnut Frame ...................................... 300.00
Print, Ship Arrow, 117 Tons, Dutton After Taylor, 1878, Lithograph, Color ...................................... 180.00
Print, Ships Of The Plain, Sam Colman, 1872, Color, 11 X 17 1/2 In. ...................................... 18.50
Print, Shunei, Bungoro In Sumo Ring, C.1762, Oban ............................................ *Illus* 375.00
Print, Shunei, 2 Actors As Man & Woman Gathering Pine Needles, C.1762 ...................................... 800.00
Print, Shunsho, Courtesan With 2 Komuro, C.1726, Aiban ...................................... 600.00
Print, Shunsho, Ichikawa Danjuro V As Hosokawa Katsumoto, C.1726, Hosoban ...................................... 550.00
Print, Shunsho, Ichikawa Danjuro V As Sukeroku, C.1726, Hosoban ...................................... 800.00
Print, Shunsho, Matsumoto Koshiro IV In Elaborate Robes, C.1726, Hosoban ...................................... 800.00
Print, Shunsho, Monosuke As Soga No Goro, C.1726, Hosoban ...................................... 800.00
Print, Shunsho, Onoye & Ichikawa Families As Nobleman, C.1726, Chuban ...................................... 1300.00
Print, Shunsho, Onoye Matsusuke As Soma Taro, C.1726, Hosoban ...................................... 275.00
Print, Shunsho, Wrestlers, Niji-Ga-Take Somayemon & Fude-No-Umi, C.1726 ...................................... 2100.00
Print, Skating Pond, Central Park, Valentine's Manual, 1861, Lithograph ...................................... 15.00
Print, Sketch Of A Shipwreck After Romney, William Blake, 1809, Engraving ...................................... 22.00
Print, Southeast View Of New York City, Canot After Howdell, 1763, Color ...................................... 100.00
Print, Stephen A.Douglas, Elijah C.Middleton, C.1860, Chromolithograph ...................................... 275.00
Print, Succes, Gesmar Mistinguett, 1925, Lithograph, Color, Framed ...................................... 350.00
Print, Suzuki Harunobu, Man, Girl On Horse, Mt.Fuji, C.1724, Chuban ...................................... 4750.00
Print, Teague, Ambush, 32 X 22 In. ...................................... 65.00
Print, Teague, The Promised Land, 32 X 22 In. ...................................... 65.00
Print, The Apothecary, Edmund Dulac, Color, 7 X 9 1/2 In. ...................................... 8.00
Print, The Ducking Bronco, Chas.M.Russell, 1904, 10 1/2 X 14 In. ...................................... 9.00
Print, The Challenge, Deer In Arctic, Sir E.Landseer, Engraving, Framed ...................................... 24.50
Print, The Frontier Lake, Haskell & Allen, Lithograph, Hand-Colored ...................................... 65.00
Print, The Government House, Condit, 1847, Chromolithograph ...................................... 250.00
Print, The Hunt Supper, Cecil Aldin, Framed, 18 X 24 In. ...................................... 100.00
Print, The Start, Cecil Aldin, Framed, 18 X 25 In. ...................................... 150.00
Print, The War Excitement In New York, Illustrated London News, 1864 ...................................... 25.00
Print, Thomas Hart Benton, A Drink Of Water, Black & White, Lithograph ...................................... 27.50
Print, Thomas Hart Benton, In The Ozarks, Black & White, Lithograph ...................................... 27.50
Print, Timpoochee Barnard, An Uchee Warrior, Greenough, 1838, Lithograph ...................................... 100.00
Print, Tokaido, Onden, Men Climbing Up Hill To Rice Mill, C.1804 ...................................... 325.00
Print, Torii Kiyomitsu, Hikosaburo Bando As Insect Seller, C.1735, Hosoban ...................................... 1700.00
Print, Torii Kiyomitsu, Shoki, Drawn Sword, C.1735, Hosoban ...................................... 200.00
Print, Toyohiro, Man & Woman With Puppets, C.1774 ...................................... 150.00
Print, Toyokuni, Ichikawa Otara As Antoku Tenno, C.1760, Hosoban ...................................... 150.00
Print, Toyokuni, Nakamura Tomijuro-I As Nobleman, C.1769, Hosoban ...................................... 300.00
Print, Utamaro, Bust Of Courtesan & Komuro, C.1754, Oban ...................................... 275.00
Print, Utamaro, Courtesan Wearing Eboshi For Festival, C.1854, Oban ...................................... 325.00
Print, Victorian Child, Frances Brundage, Lithograph, Color ...................................... 8.50
Print, View Of Boston Harbor, Smith After Remick, 1904, Engraving, Color ...................................... 375.00
Print, View Of The Commons, Smith After Remick, 1902, Engraving ...................................... 150.00
Print, Wallace Nutting, A Bit Of Sewing, 1912, Framed, 15 1/4 X 12 1/2 In. ...................................... 29.00
Print, Wallace Nutting, A Chair For John, 1915, Frame, 7 1/4 X 9 1/4 In. ...................................... 30.00
Print, Wallace Nutting, A Checkered Road, Framed ...................................... 6.00
Print, Wallace Nutting, A Little River, Color, Framed ...................................... 18.00
Print, Wallace Nutting, A New Hampshire Bridge, Framed ...................................... 22.50
Print, Wallace Nutting, A Sip Of Tea, Signed, 11 3/4 X 9 3/4 In. ...................................... 20.00

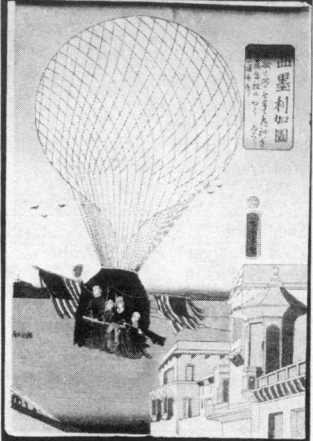

Print, Yoshitora,
Ballooning In America,
C.1830, Triptych
*(See Page 503)*

Print, Shunei,
Bungoro In Sumo Ring, C.1762, Oban
*(See Page 501)*

| | | |
|---|---|---:|
| **Print, Wallace Nutting,** An October Array, Framed, 7 3/8 X 9 3/8 In. | | 16.00 |
| **Print, Wallace Nutting,** An Old Time Romance, Framed, 11 3/4 X 9 3/4 In. | | 32.00 |
| **Print, Wallace Nutting,** Below The Arches, Gilt Frame, 10 X 13 In. | | 27.50 |
| **Print, Wallace Nutting,** Birch Bend, Gilt Frame, 10 X 13 In. | | 27.50 |
| **Print, Wallace Nutting,** Decked As A Bride, Framed, Glass, 11 1/2 X 15 In. | | 18.00 |
| **Print, Wallace Nutting,** Fireplace Scene, Signed, 9 1/2 X 7 1/2 In. | | 17.50 |
| **Print, Wallace Nutting,** Grafton Windings, Framed, 13 X 4 3/4 In. | | 24.00 |
| **Print, Wallace Nutting,** Honeymoon Windings, Framed, 11 X 18 1/2 In. | | 35.00 |
| **Print, Wallace Nutting,** Interior Of Lady In Bedroom, 5 1/2 X 7 1/2 In. | | 18.00 |
| **Print, Wallace Nutting,** Justifiable Vanity | | 35.00 |
| **Print, Wallace Nutting,** Lady At Foot Of Stairs, Signed, Matted, Copyright | | 15.00 |
| **Print, Wallace Nutting,** Lady Looking In Hall Mirror, 9 1/2 In.Framed | | 21.00 |
| **Print, Wallace Nutting,** Over The Crest, Copyright 1910, Frame | | 15.00 |
| **Print, Wallace Nutting,** Pine Landing, Gold Leaf Frame, 24 1/2 X 20 In. | | 23.50 |
| **Print, Wallace Nutting,** Ripening Tints, Framed, 7 3/8 X 9 3/4 In. | | 16.00 |
| **Print, Wallace Nutting,** River, Farmhouse, & Blossoming Trees, 4 X 3 3/8 In. | | 4.75 |
| **Print, Wallace Nutting,** Sewing By The Fire, Copyright 1909, Wooden Frame | | 20.00 |

| | |
|---|---|
| Print, Wallace Nutting, Stoney Brook Drive | 15.00 |
| Print, Wallace Nutting, Summer Wind, Framed | 15.00 |
| Print, Wallace Nutting, Tea For Two | 45.00 |
| Print, Wallace Nutting, The Bees' Paradise | 15.00 |
| Print, Wallace Nutting, The Little Hudson In The Hills, 7 1/4 X 9 1/4 In. | 25.00 |
| Print, Wallace Nutting, The Quilting Party, Framed | 26.00 |
| Print, Wallace Nutting, The Silent Shore, Framed, 18 X 15 In. | 20.00 |
| Print, Wallace Nutting, Treasure Bag | 30.00 |
| Print, Wallace Nutting, Very Satisfactory, Framed, 14 X 17 In. | 28.00 |
| Print, Weed Parsons, Hudson River Railroad Bridge, 1866, Lithograph | 4.00 |
| Print, Yoshiiku, English Couple, C.1833, Oban | 100.00 |
| Print, Yoshiiku, Englishman On Horseback, C.1833, Oban | 120.00 |
| Print, Yoshikazu, Englishwoman On Horseback, C.1840, Oban | 225.00 |
| Print, Yoshikazu, French Couple At Home, C.1840, Oban | 325.00 |
| Print, Yoshikazu, Western Woman At Sewing Machine, Family, C.1840, Oban | 70.00 |
| Print, Yoshitomi, Englishwoman Riding Sidesaddle, C.1850, Oban | 160.00 |
| Print, Yoshitora, Ballooning In America, C.1830, Oban | 425.00 |
| Print, Yoshitora, Ballooning In America, C.1830, Triptych *Illus* | 525.00 |
| Print, Yoshitora, Courtesan Gazing At Snow Covered Garden, C.1850, Uchiwa-E | 170.00 |
| Print, Yoshitora, English Couple, C.1830, Oban | 120.00 |
| Print, Yoshitora, Foreign Banquet, C.1830, Triptych | 450.00 |
| Print, Yoshitora, French Mother & Child, C.1830, Oban | 160.00 |
| Print, Yoshitora, Musicians, C.1830, Oban | 300.00 |
| Print, Yoshitora, Portraits Of Foreigners, C.1830, Oban | 100.00 |
| Print, Yoshitora, View Of London, C.1830, Triptych | 400.00 |
| Print, Young Lady, Howard Chandler Christy, Dated 1906 | 12.00 |
| Print, Yurakusai Nagahide, Kameji As Dutchman, Hosoban | 150.00 |
| Purple Slag, see Slag, Purple | |

# Quezal

*Quezal glass was made from 1901 to 1920 by Martin Bach, Sr. He made iridescent glass of the same type as Tiffany.*

| | |
|---|---|
| Quezal, Bowl, Iridescent Gold, Round, Signed, 2 1/2 In.High | 110.00 |
| Quezal, Globe, Hanging, Signed | 225.00 |
| Quezal, Lamp, Ceiling, 3 Calcite Lily Shades, Gold Aurene Interiors | 200.00 |
| Quezal, Lamp, Electric, Green, Gold, & Blue Colors, Silk Shade | 295.00 |
| Quezal, Lamp, Reticulated Globe, Bronze Webbing, Metal Base, 18 In.High | 250.00 |
| Quezal, Lamp, Tiffany Bronze Base, Amber Feathers On White Shade, 16 In. | 350.00 |
| Quezal, Lampshade, Mottled, Iridescent Pumpkin, Scalloped Purple Rim | 70.00 |
| Quezal, Lampshade, Tiffany Type Gold Iridescence, Ribbed, Corseted, Flared | 65.00 |
| Quezal, Salt, Gold Iridescent, Signed | 95.00 |
| Quezal, Shade, Art Glass, 7 In.High, 5 In.Base | 108.50 |
| Quezal, Shade, Bell Shape, Gold Calcite, Swirled, 5 In.High, Signed | 40.00 |
| Quezal, Shade, Calcite, Gold Feathers Outlined In Green, 5 In.Wide | 50.00 |
| Quezal, Shade, Gas, Aurene, Gold, Pink & Blue Highlights, Out Of 8 | 300.00 |
| Quezal, Shade, Gas, Green Feather, Signed, 5 In.High | 60.00 |
| Quezal, Shade, Gas, Green Feather, Signed, 6 In.High, Pair | 125.00 |
| Quezal, Shade, Gas, Green Feather, Unsigned, 4 3/4 In.High | 45.00 |
| Quezal, Shade, Gas, Signed, 6 In.High, 4 1/2 In.Diameter | 65.00 |
| Quezal, Shade, Gold Aurene, Red & Blue Highlights, Set Of 5 | 275.00 |
| Quezal, Shade, Gold Iridescent, Signed, 7 In.High, Pair | 65.00 |
| Quezal, Shade, Gold Spiderweb, Signed | 55.00 |
| Quezal, Shade, Iridescent Gold, Scalloped & Stretched Rim, 6 In., Set Of 6 | 500.00 |
| Quezal, Shade, Iridescent Pearl, Signed, Set Of 6 | 195.00 |
| Quezal, Shade, Ivory, Gold Lined, Signed | 45.00 |
| Quezal, Shade, Lily, Ribbed, Iridescent Gold, Signed | 185.00 |
| Quezal, Shade, Pulled Feather, White & Green, Iridescent Ground, 6 1/2 In. | 60.00 |
| Quezal, Shade, White Calcite, Signed | 30.00 |
| Quezal, Vase, Bronze, Green, Signed, 6 In.High | 85.00 |
| Quezal, Vase, Bud, Iridescent Amber, Serpents & Leaves On Bronze Base, 1910s | 300.00 |
| Quezal, Vase, Floriform, Baluster Stem, Applied Gold Luster, Domed Base | 650.00 |
| Quezal, Vase, Gold Outlined Green Waves On Calcite, 4 Platinum Feathers | 625.00 |
| Quezal, Vase, Gold, Silver Overlay, Signed, 7 In.High | 450.00 |
| Quezal, Vase, Iridescent, Pastel Highlights, Signed, 5 1/2 In.High | 225.00 |
| Quezal, Vase, Iridescent, Silver Overlay, Blue & Green, 8 1/2 In.High | 250.00 |
| Quezal, Vase, Lily, Gold Iridescent, Signed, 5 In.High | 95.00 |
| Quezal, Vase, Low, Signed | 175.00 |

Quilt, see Textile, Quilt

*Quimper pottery was made in Finistere, France, after 1900. Most of the pieces found today were made during the twentieth century. A Quimper factory has worked in France since the eighteenth century.*

| | |
|---|---:|
| Quimper, Ashtray, Shell, Peasant Design | 30.00 |
| Quimper, Bowl, Floral, 2 Handled, 4 In. | 7.00 |
| Quimper, Dish, Divided, Handle, Peasant Man & Woman On Each Side, 7 In. | 19.00 |
| Quimper, Figurine, Girl Holding Basket, Artist Chevalier Kervern | 90.00 |
| Quimper, Inkstand, Double, Peasant Man, Normandie Mark | 22.00 |
| Quimper, Inkwell, Square, Lady Figure, Insert | 35.00 |
| Quimper, Knife Rest, Gray & Blue Floral, 3 Sided | 20.00 |
| Quimper, Knife Rest, Peasant On One Side, Floral On Other, Open Ends | 24.00 |
| Quimper, Knife Rest, Woman, 3 1/4 In. | 15.00 |
| Quimper, Mug, Peasant Woman, 3 In. | 12.00 |
| Quimper, Pitcher, Figure & Foliage | 22.00 |
| Quimper, Pitcher, Milk, Rooster & Flowers, 6 1/2 In.High | 28.00 |
| Quimper, Plate, Blue Peasant Decoration On Gray, 5 1/2 In. | 10.00 |
| Quimper, Plate, Flowers, 5 1/2 In. | 6.00 |
| Quimper, Plate, Man Center, White, Yellow Rim, Blue Stripes, 8 1/4 In. | 9.00 |
| Quimper, Plate, Marked H.B.Quimper, 6 1/2 In. | 4.95 |
| Quimper, Plate, Woman Center, White, Yellow Rim, Blue Stripes, 8 1/4 In. | 9.00 |
| Quimper, Salt, Double | 12.00 |
| Quimper, Salt, Peasant Walking With Cane, Blue & White, Inner Decoration | 24.00 |
| Quimper, Salt, Swan, Signed | 17.00 |
| Quimper, Shoe, Clog, Peasant Girl Decoration, 3 1/4 In., Pair | 24.00 |
| Quimper, Vase, Blue Peasant Decoration On Gray, 5 3/4 In. | 18.50 |
| Quimper, Vase, Boy, 8 In. | 16.00 |
| Quimper, Vase, Peasant Woman, Marked Fireside, Quimper France | 32.50 |
| R.R.P.Co., Dish, Dog's, Orange, Dog | 8.50 |
| R.R.P.Co., Jardiniere, Pedestal, Cream, Brown, & Green | 25.00 |

*Radford pottery was made by Alfred Radford in Broadway, Virginia, Tiffin and Zanesville, Ohio, and Clarksburg, West Virginia, from 1891 until 1912. Jasperware, Ruko, Thera, Radera, and Velvety Art Ware were made.*

| | |
|---|---:|
| Radford, Jardiniere, Ruko, Floral Decoration, 7 1/2 In X 9 In. | 200.00 |
| Radford, Vase, Jasper, Green Ground, White Cherubs On Gray Inset, 6 In.High | 250.00 |
| Radford, Vase, Thera, Matte Glaze, Black Ground, Floral Design, 10 In.High | 225.00 |
| Radio, Atwater Kent, Receiver Set, Model 30, Dated 1924; Wooden Case, 20 In. | 45.00 |
| Radio, Brunswick, KKR | 27.50 |
| Radio, Cunningham, CX-12 | 7.50 |
| Radio, Dayton, XL-25 | 15.00 |
| Radio, Deluxe, AC/DC, C.1934 | 10.00 |
| Radio, Eagle-Picher, Battery, Demonstrator Kit | 7.50 |
| Radio, Eagle, Receiving Set, Hinged Top, Brass Pull, Dated 1923 | 90.00 |
| Radio, Eveready 2, Table Model, Speaker, Console Legs, 110 Volt | 42.50 |
| Radio, Gilfilan, Table Model Model, Speaker, Manual | 95.00 |
| Radio, Headphones, Frost 161, Original Box | 15.00 |
| Radio, Military, Utah-Chicago, 1943 | 10.00 |
| Radio, Snow White & The Seven Dwarfs | 15.00 |
| Radio, Stewart Warner 300 | 50.00 |
| Radio, Stewart Warner, Electric, Metal Case | 48.00 |
| Radio, Supreme 333, Deluxe Analyzer | 32.50 |
| Radio, Zenith 33 | 47.50 |
| Railroad, Ashtray, Chesapeake & Ohio, White With Blue, 4 In.Diameter | 25.00 |
| Railroad, Bell, Locomotive, Yoke, Small Size | 375.00 |
| Railroad, Bonbon, Mt.Tom, Mass., White, Ruffled Edge, Polychrome House Center | 5.00 |
| Railroad, Booklet, N.Y.O.& W., Summer Day Oneida Onieda Lake Homes, 1899 | 10.00 |
| Railroad, Booklet, Union Pacific, Bryce & Zion Parks, 1925 | 5.00 |
| Railroad, Bottle, Milk, Embossed Missouri Pacific Railroad, Quart | 3.00 |
| Railroad, Bottle, Milk, Embossed Missouri Pacific, 1/2 Pint | 2.00 |
| Railroad, Bowl, Cereal, The Traveler, Milwaukee Road, 1920s, China, Pink, White | 20.00 |
| Railroad, Bowl, Soup, B.& O., Lamberton | 17.50 |
| Railroad, Bowl, Soup, Baltimore & Ohio, Blue | 20.00 |
| Railroad, Box, Tool, Tin, Red Paint, Handle, 12 In.Long | 10.00 |

| | |
|---|---|
| Railroad, Button, B.& O., Brass, 1/2 In.Diameter | 1.00 |
| Railroad, Button, Conductor's, S.& P., Brass, 1/2 In. | 1.00 |
| Railroad, Button, Conductor's, S.& P., Brass, 3/4 In. | 2.00 |
| Railroad, Button, Conductor's, T.& P., Brass, 1/2 In. | 1.00 |
| Railroad, Button, Conductor's, T.& P., Brass, 3/4 In. | 2.00 |
| Railroad, Calendar, Pennsylvania R.R., 1957, Conway Yard | 10.00 |
| Railroad, Can, Oil, N.Y.O.& W., Long Snout | 15.00 |
| Railroad, Cap, L.V., Trainman, 2 Metal Buttons, Leslie Barton | 25.00 |
| Railroad, Cap, Trainman, R.& R. Buttons | 25.00 |
| Railroad, Cards, Playing, C & EI | 5.00 |
| Railroad, Cards, Playing, Southern Pacific, C.1900s | 12.00 |
| Railroad, Cart, Food, Santa Fe, Stainless Steel | 100.00 |
| Railroad, Coffeepot, New York Central, International Silver | 30.00 |
| Railroad, Creamer, Baltimore & Ohio, Thomas Viaduct, Dated 1927 | 35.00 |
| Railroad, Creamer, New York Central, International Silver | 31.00 |
| Railroad, Creamer, Philipe Thomas, 1838, Picture Of 1830 Horse-Drawn Car | 30.00 |
| Railroad, Cup & Saucer, The Traveler, Milwaukee Road, 1920s | 18.00 To 25.00 |
| Railroad, Date Nail, Copper, Round, Indented, No.24 | .50 |
| Railroad, Date Nail, Copper, Round, Indented, No.25 | .50 |
| Railroad, Date Nail, Copper, Round, Indented, No.26 | .50 |
| Railroad, Date Nail, Copper, Round, Indented, No.27 | .50 |
| Railroad, Date Nail, Copper, Round, Indented, No.28 | .50 |
| Railroad, Date Nail, Copper, Round, Indented, No.29 | .50 |
| Railroad, Date Nail, Copper, Round, Indented, No.30 | .50 |
| Railroad, Date Nail, Copper, Square, Raised, No.29 | 1.00 |
| Railroad, Date Nail, Copper, Square, Raised, No.30 | 1.00 |
| Railroad, Date Nail, Copper, Square, Raised, No.31 | 1.00 |
| Railroad, Date Nail, Copper, Square, Raised, No.32 | 1.00 |
| Railroad, Date Nail, Copper, Square, Raised, No.33 | 1.00 |
| Railroad, Date Nail, Copper, Square, Raised, No.34 | 1.00 |
| Railroad, Date Nail, Copper, Square, Raised, No.35 | 1.00 |
| Railroad, Date Nail, Copper, Square, Raised, No.36 | 1.00 |
| Railroad, Date Nail, Copper, Square, Raised, No.37 | 1.00 |
| Railroad, Date Nail, Copper, Square, Raised, No.38 | 1.00 |
| Railroad, Date Nail, Copper, Square, Raised, No.39 | 1.00 |
| Railroad, Date Nail, Copper, Square, Raised, No.40 | 1.00 |
| Railroad, Date Nail, Copper, Square, Raised, No.41 | 1.00 |
| Railroad, Date Nail, Iron, Round, Raised, No.36 | .25 |
| Railroad, Date Nail, Iron, Round, Raised, No.39 | .25 |
| Railroad, Date Nail, Iron, Round, Raised, No.40 | .25 |
| Railroad, Date Nail, Iron, Round, Raised, No.47 | .25 |
| Railroad, Date Nail, Iron, Square, Indented, No.16 | 45.00 |
| Railroad, Date Nail, Iron, Square, Indented, No.18 | 35.00 |
| Railroad, Date Nail, Iron, Square, Indented, No.19 | 35.00 |
| Railroad, Date Nail, Iron, Square, Indented, No.20 | 35.00 |
| Railroad, Date Nail, Iron, Square, Indented, No.21 | 35.00 |
| Railroad, Date Nail, Iron, Square, Indented, No.22 | 35.00 |
| Railroad, Date Nail, Iron, Square, Indented, No.23 | 35.00 |
| Railroad, Date Nail, Iron, Square, Raised, No.37 | .35 |
| Railroad, Fire Extinguisher, Chicago & N.W., Blue, Wall Brackets, Glass | 50.00 |
| Railroad, Footstool, Coach, N.Y.O.& W., Oak | 20.00 |
| Railroad, Fork, Santa Fe, Silver | 6.50 |
| Railroad, Hammer, Pein, L.V. | 10.00 |
| Railroad, Headrest, Pennsylvania | 6.00 |
| Railroad, Jug, Thermos, Pullman, Metal Silver | 40.00 |
| Railroad, Key, Baggage Car, L.V.R.R., Brass | 6.00 |
| Railroad, Key, Caboose, L.V.R.R., Brass | 6.00 |
| Railroad, Key, Coach Gaslight, Pintsch, Brass | 5.00 |
| Railroad, Key, Coach, L.V.R.R., Brass | 6.00 |
| Railroad, Key, Coach, Pacific R.R., Brass | 6.00 |
| Railroad, Key, Reading, Brass | 3.00 |
| Railroad, Key, Switch, Brass | 5.00 |
| Railroad, Kit, First Aid, P.R.R., Metal | 14.00 |
| Railroad, Kit, First Aid, P.R.R., Tin | 6.50 |
| Railroad, Knife, Santa Fe, Hollow Handle, Silver | 6.50 |
| Railroad, Lamp, Caboose, Aladdin, Hanger | 32.50 |

| | |
|---|---:|
| Railroad, Lamp, Caboose, Kerosene, Bracket | 22.50 |
| Railroad, Lamp, Head, Spanish Renfe, Copper & Iron, C.1850 | 375.00 |
| Railroad, Lamp, Station, Wall, Tin Reflector, Kerosene | 35.00 |
| Railroad, Lampshade, Depot, Enameled, Green, White Inside, 14 In. | 5.00 |
| Railroad, Lampshade, Depot, Granite, Green, White Inside, 14 In. | 5.00 |
| Railroad, Lantern, Adlake, Erie On Frame, Clear Squat Globe | 25.00 |
| Railroad, Lantern, Adlake, Erie On Frame, Red Etched Globe, Squat | 25.00 |
| Railroad, Lantern, Adlake, L.V.R.R.On Frame, Clear Marked Squat Globe | 25.00 |
| Railroad, Lantern, Arlington, Red Globe | 15.00 |
| Railroad, Lantern, Armspear Nor.& West On Frame, Clear Globe, 5 3/8 In. | 35.00 |
| Railroad, Lantern, Armspear P.R.R.On Frame, Blue Globe | 35.00 |
| Railroad, Lantern, Armspear, Erie On Frame, Red Etched Globe, Squat | 25.00 |
| Railroad, Lantern, B.& O. On Frame, Raised Letters On Clear Globe | 25.00 |
| Railroad, Lantern, B.R.& P.On Frame, Vesta, Clear Globe | 20.00 |
| Railroad, Lantern, Ball & Bonnell, Buffalo, N.Y., Bail Goes In Smoke Stack | 75.00 |
| Railroad, Lantern, Baltimore & Ohio, Adlake, Switchman's, Kerosene | 20.00 |
| Railroad, Lantern, Bell Bottom, Glass Oil Font, Whale Oil Burner | 100.00 |
| Railroad, Lantern, Brass Frame, Ring Top, & Bail, Clear Globe | 125.00 |
| Railroad, Lantern, Brass Top, Bail Goes In Smoke Stack, 9 In.High | 75.00 |
| Railroad, Lantern, C.C.C. & St.Lo. On Frame & Clear Globe, 5 3/8 In.High | 30.00 |
| Railroad, Lantern, C.R.R.Of N.J., Dressel, Etched Clear Globe | 30.00 |
| Railroad, Lantern, Cast Iron, Bell Bottom, Glass Oil Font, Clear Globe | 50.00 |
| Railroad, Lantern, Chesapeake & Ohio, Kerosene | 20.00 |
| Railroad, Lantern, Co.N.Y.C.On Frame, Keystone, Etched Clear Globe | 50.00 |
| Railroad, Lantern, Dietz Type, Bell Bottom, Glass Oil Font, Bail Handle | 100.00 |
| Railroad, Lantern, Dietz 6, N.Y.Cent.On Frame & Clear Globe, Bell Bottom | 35.00 |
| Railroad, Lantern, Dietz 39, Leh.& N.Eng., Vulcan On Frame, Red Globe | 30.00 |
| Railroad, Lantern, Dietz 39, N.Y.Cent On Red Globe, Bell Bottom | 35.00 |
| Railroad, Lantern, Dietz, Burlington Route In Red Raised Letters On Globe | 25.00 |
| Railroad, Lantern, Dietz, Empire P.& R.On Frame, Clear Marked Globe | 25.00 |
| Railroad, Lantern, Dietz, Inspector's, Clear Globe, Reflector | 35.00 |
| Railroad, Lantern, Dietz, Inspector's, N.S.R.R.On Frame | 35.00 |
| Railroad, Lantern, Dietz, N.Y.Central On Frame, Amber Globe, Reflector | 35.00 |
| Railroad, Lantern, Dietz, Red Globe, Dated 1914 | 11.00 |
| Railroad, Lantern, Dietz, Steel Clad No.39, Marked Clear Globe, 5 3/8 In. | 25.00 |
| Railroad, Lantern, Dietz, Tin, Caboose, Clear Globe, Ring At Top | 25.00 |
| Railroad, Lantern, Dietz, Vesta On Frame, N.Y.N.H.& H.On Clear Globe | 25.00 |
| Railroad, Lantern, Dietz, Vulcan L & Nash on Frame, Clear Globe, 5 3/8 In. | 35.00 |
| Railroad, Lantern, Dressel, Clear Globe | 20.00 |
| Railroad, Lantern, Erie Armspear On Frame, Clear Globe, 5 3/8 In.High | 20.00 |
| Railroad, Lantern, Erie, Adlake, 250, Red Globe | 20.00 |
| Railroad, Lantern, Erwin Patent 1862, Bell Bottom, Clear Globe, Grid Font | 50.00 |
| Railroad, Lantern, Frisco | 17.00 |
| Railroad, Lantern, German, Carbide, R.R.Emblem, Brass, Hinged Doors | 15.00 |
| Railroad, Lantern, German, Carbide, Swastika, Brass, Hinged Doors | 20.00 |
| Railroad, Lantern, Keystone Casey B.& S.On Frame, Etched Clear Globe | 35.00 |
| Railroad, Lantern, Keystone 39 P.R.R.On Frame, Clear Globe | 25.00 |
| Railroad, Lantern, L.V.On Frame, Adlake 250, Clear Globe, Squat | 20.00 |
| Railroad, Lantern, L.V.On Frame, Raised L.V. On Clear Globe | 35.00 |
| Railroad, Lantern, L.V.On Frame, Vesta, Blue Globe | 20.00 |
| Railroad, Lantern, L.V.On Frame, Vesta, Clear Red Ribbed Globe | 20.00 |
| Railroad, Lantern, L.V.On Frame, Vesta, Red Globe | 20.00 |
| Railroad, Lantern, L.V.R.R.In Raised Letters On Clear Globe | 25.00 |
| Railroad, Lantern, L.V.R.R.On Font, Clear Globe | 25.00 |
| Railroad, Lantern, Marked Midget Cold Blast | 27.50 |
| Railroad, Lantern, Miller, Meriden, Conn. On Globe, Brass Top, Galvanized | 100.00 |
| Railroad, Lantern, Missouri Pacific, Clear, 5 3/8 In.High | 20.00 |
| Railroad, Lantern, Mo.Pac.On Frame, Handlan, Clear Globe | 20.00 |
| Railroad, Lantern, N.Y. N.H. & H. R.R., Clear Marked Globe, Silver Paint | 12.75 |
| Railroad, Lantern, N.Y.C., Dietz-Signed Frame, Clear Globe | 35.00 |
| Railroad, Lantern, N.Y.C.R.R., Embossed, Red Globe | 26.00 |
| Railroad, Lantern, N.Y.O.& W.On Frame, Vesta, Clear Globe | 35.00 |
| Railroad, Lantern, Oil Burner, Tin, Ruby Globe, 10 1/4 In. High | 25.00 |
| Railroad, Lantern, P.& R., Armspear-Signed Frame, Red Globe | 35.00 |
| Railroad, Lantern, P.G.E.Co.On Frame, Clear Globe | 35.00 |
| Railroad, Lantern, P.R.R.On Frame, Clear Globe, 5 3/8 In.High | 25.00 |

| | |
|---|---:|
| Railroad, Lantern, P.R.R.On Frame, Westlake Bell Bottom, Red Globe | 40.00 |
| Railroad, Lantern, Pacific R.R., Reliable, Clear Globe, Raised Letters | 25.00 |
| Railroad, Lantern, Pittsburgh, Lake Erie On Frame, Clear Globe, 5 3/8 In. | 25.00 |
| Railroad, Lantern, Reading Transportation Dept., Vesta, Red Globe | 20.00 |
| Railroad, Lantern, Rel.P.& R. On Frame, Unmarked Globe, 6 In.High | 25.00 |
| Railroad, Lantern, Signal, L.V.On Frame & Clear Globe | 35.00 |
| Railroad, Lantern, Sou R.R., Brass, Nickel Plated, Marked XWT McKibbon | 125.00 |
| Railroad, Lantern, Switch Marker, Piper, Toronto, Brass Oil Font | 8.00 |
| Railroad, Lantern, Switchman's, C.B.& Q. | 22.00 |
| Railroad, Lantern, Switchman's, Wabash | 47.50 |
| Railroad, Lantern, Tin, Bell Bottom, Clear Globe, 13 In.High | 50.00 |
| Railroad, Lantern, Vesta, D.L.& W.On Frame, Clear Etched Globe | 25.00 |
| Railroad, Lantern, W.M.On Frame, Etched Clear Globe, 5 3/8 In.High | 40.00 |
| Railroad, Lantern, Wabash, White Globe | 15.00 |
| Railroad, Lantern, 2 Red & 2 Green Lenses, 15 X 15 X 21 In. | 45.00 |
| Railroad, Lantern, 39 R.R., Bell Bottom, Clear Globe | 25.00 |
| Railroad, Level & Grader Finder, Edward Helb R.R., Compass Marked Germany | 250.00 |
| Railroad, Light, Candle, Wall, Brass, Chimney & Wall Fixture | 30.00 |
| Railroad, Lock & Chain, Marked St.L.& H.R.R., Brass | 20.00 |
| Railroad, Lock, B.& M.R.R., Brass, Patent 1879, 3 1/2 In.Long | 4.75 |
| Railroad, Lock, L.V., Adlake, Iron, Chain, Brass Key | 25.00 |
| Railroad, Lock, L.V.R.R., Cast Iron | 15.00 |
| Railroad, Lock, Switch, Brass, Chain & Key, Bohannan, 1885 | 25.00 |
| Railroad, Lock, Switch, Chain, Erie, Corbin, Iron, Brass Key | 20.00 |
| Railroad, Lock, Switch, H.& H., Iron, Chain | 10.00 |
| Railroad, Lock, Switch, Marked Adlake & Rutland, Aluminium, Brass Key | 6.75 |
| Railroad, Lock, Switch, U.P.R.R., Brass | 10.00 |
| Railroad, Manual, Erie, Operating Rules | 5.00 |
| Railroad, Map, Southern Pacific, California, Color, C.1909, 22 X 27 In. | 20.00 |
| Railroad, Marker, Dressel, Adlake On Frame, Long Handle | 10.00 |
| Railroad, Marker, Dressel, Adlake On Frame, Short Handle | 10.00 |
| Railroad, Marker, Dressel, Yellow, Lt-P.R.R.On Frame, Red Bull's-Eye | 45.00 |
| Railroad, Marker, Light Switch, P.R.R., Shields, Oil Font | 50.00 |
| Railroad, Marker, Locomotive, Baldwin, 1943, Cast Iron, 9 1/4 In.Diameter | 60.00 |
| Railroad, Menu, Colorado Flyer Train, 1932 | 8.00 |
| Railroad, Oiler, Locomotive, Marked A.& A.R.R., Long Snout | 25.00 |
| Railroad, Pamphlet, Mt.Tamalpais, Rainier Valley | 1.75 |
| Railroad, Pick, N.Y.O.& W., Cast Iron, Hickory Handle | 10.00 |
| Railroad, Pinback, L.& N.R.R., Best Route To Louisville, Celluloid, 1896 | 22.00 |
| Railroad, Plaque, Erie, 100th Anniversary, 1851-1951, Plaster Of Paris, Wall | 15.00 |
| Railroad, Plate, B & O, Lamberton China, 10 In. | 18.00 |
| Railroad, Plate, Bread, Atlantic Coast Line, Silver, Oval | 37.50 |
| Railroad, Plate, Chesapeake & Ohio, George Washington, Gold, Buffalo China | 100.00 |
| Railroad, Plate, Soup, The Traveler, Milwaukee Road, 1920s, Pink On White | 18.00 |
| Railroad, Platter, Baltimore & Ohio, Indian Creek, Blue & White, Lamberton | 45.00 |
| Railroad, Platter, Baltimore & Ohio, Thomas Viaduct, 1855, Blue & White | 25.00 |
| Railroad, Platter, Baltimore & Ohio, Thomas Viaduct, 1927 | 27.50 |
| Railroad, Platter, The Traveler, Milwaukee Road, 1920s, Pink On White, 11 In. | 40.00 |
| Railroad, Platter, The Traveler, Milwaukee Road, 1920s, Pink On White, 8 In. | 20.00 |
| Railroad, Postcard, Rio Grande, Color | .12 |
| Railroad, Print, Rio Grande R.R., Rocky Mountain Views, Colored | 4.00 |
| Railroad, Saucer, Union Pacific, Blue & White China, Scammells, Trenton | 6.50 |
| Railroad, Shoulder Board, Police, Pair | 7.00 |
| Railroad, Spike | 2.00 |
| Railroad, Spoon, Runcible, Seaboard Mark On Handle | 10.00 |
| Railroad, Spoon, Santa Fe, Silver Plate, International Silver Co. | 4.00 |
| Railroad, Spoon, Soup, Santa Fe, Silver | 6.50 |
| Railroad, Step, Berth Ladder, Wooden, Carpet Covered, Pullman, 32 In.High | 50.00 |
| Railroad, Step, Coach, C.& O., Metal | 70.00 |
| Railroad, Step, Coach, N.Y.Central, Hudson River, Oak | 35.00 |
| Railroad, Step, Pullman, Marked, Metal | 55.00 |
| Railroad, Sugar, New York Central, International Silver | 30.00 |
| Railroad, Syrup, Illinois Central, Silver Plate, Reed & Barton, 7 Ozs. | 50.00 |
| Railroad, Tablecloth, Dining Car, Rock Island | 10.00 |
| Railroad, Tablespoon, Baltimore & Ohio | 7.00 |
| Railroad, Teapot, Illinois Central, Silver Plate, International, 12 Ozs. | 50.00 |

Railroad, Thermos, Pullman On Front, Nickel Silver, Hinged Lid ............................. 35.00
Railroad, Ticket, N.W.Va.R.R., Dated 1861 ............................................................. 15.00
Railroad, Timetable, N.Y.O.& W., 1914 ................................................................. 5.00
Railroad, Tongs, Sugar, Atlantic Coast Line, Silver ............................................. 5.50
Railroad, Torch, Engine, Brass .............................................................................. 15.00
Railroad, Torch, Engineer's, Brass, Hand-Turned, 15 1/4 In.High ...................... 55.00
Railroad, Torch, Inspection, Dated 1895, Iron, Handled, 10 In.High .................. 40.00
Railroad, Torch, Tin, Locomotive, 4 In.High ........................................................ 10.00
Railroad, Towel, Cumberland Valley, Linen, White, Red Stripe ............................ 10.00
Railroad, Towel, P.R.R.In Red, Red Band, White Linen ....................................... 3.00
Railroad, Towel, Union Pacific, Linen, White, Blue Stripe .................................. 10.00
Railroad, Tumbler, Santa Fe, 5 1/2 In.High ......................................................... 3.00
Railroad, Watch, Bunn Special, Illinois, Gold Filled Case, 21 Jewel .................. 75.00
Railroad, Whistle, Kinsley, Bridgeport, Conn., Brass, Compressed Air, 7 In. ...... 30.00
Railroad, Whistle, Steam, Locomotive, Brass, 17 In.High .................................... 100.00
Railroad, Wrench, C.R.& P., Adjustable, 17 In. .................................................. 7.00
Railroad, Wrench, Cent.Vt.R.R., Double End, 11 In.Long ................................... 4.00
Railroad, Wrench, Pipe, L.V., Stillson, 15 In.Long ............................................. 10.00
**Rainbow, see Mother-of-Pearl, Satin Glass**

*The Red Wing Pottery of Red Wing, Minnesota, was a firm started in*
*1878. It was not until the 1920s that art pottery was made. It closed in*
*1967. Rumrill pottery was made for George Rumrill by the Red Wing*
*Pottery Company and other firms. It was sold in the 1930s.*
Red Wing, Canoe, 12 In.Long ............................................................................... 20.00
Red Wing, Crock, 5 Gallon ................................................................................... 8.50
Red Wing, Jar, Cookie, Covered, Saffron Ware, 9 In.High ................................. 8.50
Red Wing, Vase, Brown, Combed Design, Yellow Inside, No.965, 9 In.High ....... 20.00
Red Wing, Vase, Classic Shape, Handles, Green, High Glaze, 9 1/2 In.High ....... 8.00
Red Wing, Vase, Cranes Standing In Water, Green & Beige, Blue Mark, 10 In. .... 35.00
Red Wing, Vase, Grecian Style, Paneled, White On Dark Teal Blue, Handled ..... 22.50

*Redware is a hard red stoneware that originated in the late 1600s and*
*continues to be made. The term is also used to describe any common clay*
*pottery that is reddish in color.*
Redware, Bedpan, Manganese Splotched ............................................................. 75.00
Redware, Bowl, Pennsylvania, Brown On Red Glaze, Tooled Edges, 5 1/2 In. .... 175.00
Redware, Bowl, Pennsylvania, Shallow, 7 In. ...................................................... 15.00
Redware, Bowl, Slip Decoration, Deep, Orange Red, Pennsylvania, 4 1/4 In. ...... 160.00
Redware, Bowl, Yellow & Black Slip Decoration, Green Glaze Spots, 8 In. ......... 170.00
Redware, Bowl, 7 1/2 X 2 In. ............................................................................... 32.00
Redware, Bundt, Swirl Pattern, Dark Brown Spatter Rim, Pennsylvania ............ 35.00
Redware, Cooler, Water, Yellow Trailings, C.1850, 15 In. ......................*Illus* 110.00
Redware, Crock, Glazed Inside, 5 In.High ............................................................ 25.00
Redware, Crock, John Bell, Inside Glaze ............................................................. 20.00
Redware, Crock, John Bell, Inside Glaze ............................................................. 75.00
Redware, Crock, Ovoid, Magnesium Glaze, 4 Gallon, 17 1/4 In. High ............... 30.00
Redware, Crock, Signed John W.Bell, 4 3/4 In.High ........................................... 125.00
Redware, Crock, Smith Womelsdorf, Pa., 5 In.High ........................................... 65.00
Redware, Flowerpot & Attached Saucer, Pennsylvania Dutch, Black Splotches .... 45.00
Redware, Flowerpot, Saucer, Light Brown, 5 1/2 In.Diameter, 4 In.High ........... 60.00
Redware, Inkwell, Shoe, Brown Glaze, 2 Hole, Penholder .................................. 70.00
Redware, Jar, Dark Green Dripping Glaze, 16 In. High ....................................... 25.00
Redware, Jar, Incised Decoration, 2 Handles, 7 3/4 In. High ............................. 45.00
Redware, Jar, Ovoid, Dark Glaze, 4 3/4 In. High ............................................... 12.50
Redware, Jar, Ovoid, Interior Glaze, 5 1/2 In. ................................................... 20.00
Redware, Jar, Snuff, Black Glazed, Wide Mouth, 8 In.High ................................ 18.00
Redware, Jar, Storage, Mottled Glaze, 10 In. High ............................................ 55.00
Redware, Jug, Puzzle, Sgraffito, 6 1/4 In.High .........................................*Illus* 350.00
Redware, Jug, Strap Handle, Miniature ............................................................... 38.00
Redware, Jug, Wine, Brown & Gray, Fills At Center, 2 Handles, 7 1/2 In. ......... 50.00
Redware, Mold, Baking, Oval, Clear & Green Glaze, 15 1/4 In. Long ................ 135.00
Redware, Mold, Baking, Turk's Head, Molded Star Design, 10 1/2 In.Diameter .... 47.50
Redware, Mold, Baking, Turk's Head, Sponge Decoration, 8 1/2 In. Diameter ..... 55.00
Redware, Mold, Pudding, Turk's Head, Medium Brown Glaze ........................... 40.00
Redware, Mold, Pudding, Turk's Head, Smooth Sides, Dark Glaze In & Out ..... 50.00
Redware, Mold, Turk's Head, Orange Green Brown Glaze, 7 In. ........................ 40.00

Redware, Jug, Puzzle,
Sgraffito, 6 1/4 In.High
*(See Page 508)*

Redware, Cooler, Water,
Yellow Trailings,
C.1850, 15 In.
*(See Page 508)*

| | |
|---|---|
| Redware, Pan, Milk, Brown Glaze Inside, 14 In. Diameter | 80.00 |
| Redware, Pan, Milk, Reddish Brown Glaze, 9 In.Diameter | 145.00 |
| Redware, Plate, Green Slip Decoration, 8 In. | 200.00 |
| Redware, Plate, Yellow Slip Crosshatched Wavy Lines, Sawtooth, 8 3/4 In. | 425.00 |
| Redware, Plate, Yellow Slip Crow's-Feet Decoration, Sawtooth Edge, 9 In. | 115.00 |
| Redware, Plate, Yellow Slip Crow's-Feet Decoration, 7 1/2 In. | 85.00 |
| Redware, Plate, Yellow Slip Decoration, 7 1/2 In. | 80.00 |
| Redware, Pot, Bean, Lid, Brown Glaze | 15.00 |
| Redware, Strainer, Holes, 3 Feet, Glazed In & Out, 5 In.Diameter Top | 50.00 |
| Redware, Teapot, Applied Green & Yellow Vine & 2 Squirrels, Twig Handle | 75.00 |
| Redware, Teapot, China Blue Slip, Paneled Body, Hexagon Rim, Gold Trim | 35.00 |
| Redware, Teapot, Oriental, Unglazed, Low Squat Shape, Green Glaze Design | 21.50 |
| Richard, Bowl, Knop Finial, Magenta On Yellow & Blue, Berries, 1900s | 275.00 |
| Richard, Vase, Acorns & Leaves, Two Color, 9 In. High | 165.00 |
| Richard, Vase, Baluster Shape, Blue Green On Yellow, Castle & River, 16 In. | 275.00 |
| Richard, Vase, Blue Black Leaves On Red, Quadrilobed Lip, Footed, 9 In. | 225.00 |
| Richard, Vase, Bulging, Red, Midnight Blue Overlay, Hibiscus, 23 1/3 In. | 325.00 |
| Richard, Vase, Cameo, Signed, 8 1/2 X 5 In. | 325.00 |
| Richard, Vase, Carved Brown Leaves & Berries On Blue Satin, 3 1/4 In.High | 190.00 |
| Richard, Vase, Carved Trees, Two Color, 7 1/2 In.High | 150.00 |
| Richard, Vase, Footed, Signed, Cameo, 14 1/2 In.High | 550.00 |
| Richard, Vase, Scenic, Long Neck, Bulbous Bottom, Signed, Cameo, 17 In.High | 475.00 |
| Richard, Vase, Scenic, Signed, Cameo, 17 X 6 In. | 375.00 |
| Richard, Vase, Scenic, Signed, Cameo, 8 In.High | 275.00 |

*Ridgway pottery has been made in the Staffordshire District in England since 1808 by a series of companies with the name Ridgway. The transfer-design dinner sets are the most widely known product. They are still being made.*

| | |
|---|---|
| Ridgway, Barrel, Biscuit, Coaching, 2 Scenes & Inscriptions, Brown, Handle | 45.00 |
| Ridgway, Basket, Fruit, Marmora, Blue, Reticulated, C.1834, 12 In. | 70.00 |
| Ridgway, Bowl, Coaching Days, A Cast Shoe, Silver Trim, 9 1/2 In. | 27.00 |
| Ridgway, Bowl, Coaching Days, Hunters & Birddogs On Gray, 9 1/2 In. | 25.00 |
| Ridgway, Bowl, Coaching Days, Silver Rim, 7 In. High | 35.00 To 68.00 |
| Ridgway, Bowl, Devonshire Dock, Bermuda, Sepia, 11 X 6 In. | 14.00 |
| Ridgway, Creamer, Coaching Days, George & Vulture & Henry VIII, 3 1/2 In. | 22.00 |
| Ridgway, Cup & Saucer, Girl & Dog In English Village, Purple, Forget-Me-Not | 38.00 |
| Ridgway, Cup & Saucer, Handleless, Medina, 12 Sided, Blue, Festoon Border | 30.00 |
| Ridgway, Dish, Mint, Coaching Days, Boat Shape, Browns | 25.00 |
| Ridgway, Mug, Beer, Luster Handle, Transfer Pattern | 22.50 |
| Ridgway, Mug, Coaching Days, Silver Band At Top & On Handle, 3 7/8 In. High | 26.00 |
| Ridgway, Mug, Coaching Days, Silver Band At Top & On Handle, 5 In. High | 35.00 |
| Ridgway, Mug, Coaching Days, White Ground, 4 1/2 In. | 17.50 |
| Ridgway, Pitcher, Coaching Days, Green, Silver Handle & Rim | 25.00 |
| Ridgway, Pitcher, Milk, Coaching Days, St.Albans On Silver Luster Rim, Roses | 21.00 |
| Ridgway, Pitcher, Molded Marsh Reeds On Gray, Dated October 1, 1835 | 65.00 |

| | |
|---|---|
| Ridgway, Plaque, The Rainbow, Royal Vistas Ware, Gold Rim, 9 1/2 In. | 20.00 |
| Ridgway, Plate, Cake, Oriental, Light Blue | 12.00 |
| Ridgway, Plate, Christ Church, Medium Blue, 10 In. | 47.00 |
| Ridgway, Plate, Coach Horse | 38.00 |
| Ridgway, Plate, Coaching Days, An Alarm By Me Guard, Brown, 10 In. | 20.00 |
| Ridgway, Plate, Delaware, Medium Blue, 3/17/1847, 9 1/4 In. | 38.00 |
| Ridgway, Plate, Italian Villas, Mulberry, 7 1/2 In. | 9.50 |
| Ridgway, Plate, Pineapple On Decoration, Blue, 10 1/4 In. | 16.00 |
| Ridgway, Plate, Pomerania, Deep Pink, 9 In. | 22.00 |
| Ridgway, Plate, Shakespeare, Hamlet, For God's Love, Caramel Luster, 8 In. | 17.00 |
| Ridgway, Plate, Sundorn Castle, Purple, 8 1/2 In. | 12.00 |
| Ridgway, Plate, Venice, Brown Luster, Royal Vistas Ware, 10 In. | 20.00 |
| Ridgway, Platter, Oriental, Blue, 10 3/4 X 12 1/4 In. | 18.75 |
| Ridgway, Platter, Oriental, Lavender, C.1850, 13 1/2 X 17 In. | 45.00 |
| Ridgway, Sugar & Creamer, Delicate Harmony, Blue Glaze | 20.00 |
| Ridgway, Sugar & Creamer, Oriental | 18.00 |
| Ridgway, Tea Set, Child's, Brown, White Paisley Pattern, 1882, 11 Piece | 95.00 |
| Ridgway, Vase, Coaching Days, 5 In. Wide Bottom | 18.50 |

*Rockingham in the United States is a brown glazed pottery with a tortoiseshell-like glaze. It was made from 1840 to 1900 by many American potteries. The mottled brown Rockingham wares were first made in England at the Rockingham factory. Other wares were also made by the English firm.*

| | |
|---|---|
| Rockingham, Bowl, Flower Encrusted, Gilt Scrolls, C.1830, 3 3/4 In., Pair | 150.00 |
| Rockingham, Bowl, Mixing, 11 In. | 20.00 |
| Rockingham, Bowl, 11 1/2 In.Across, 3 1/2 In.High | 37.50 |
| Rockingham, Box, Yellow Rose, On Green Leaves, 4 Holes In Center, C.1835 | 225.00 |
| Rockingham, Dish, Baking, Oval, Mottled Glaze, 10 1/4 X 7 3/4 In. | 60.00 |
| Rockingham, Dish, Hen Cover, Dark Chocolate, Gold Leaf Trim On Basket | 28.50 |
| Rockingham, Figurine, Dog | 135.00 |
| Rockingham, Figurine, Lion, Pair | 150.00 |
| Rockingham, Jug, Raised Decoration, 2 In.High | 12.00 |
| Rockingham, Mold, Food, 8 1/4 In. Diameter | 50.00 |
| Rockingham, Pastille Burner, Shape Of Toll House, C.1820, 3 1/2 In.High | 48.00 |
| Rockingham, Pitcher, Blackberries & Vines, 8 3/4 In. High | 55.00 |
| Rockingham, Pitcher, Octagonal Panels, 8 In. | 20.00 |
| Rockingham, Plate, Leaf, Sanded, Gold Trim, 7 1/4 In. | 15.00 |
| Rockingham, Salt, Individual, Glazed, Sterling Overlay | 15.00 |
| Rockingham, Sugar, Covered, Gold Trim | 8.00 |
| Rockingham, Tea Set, Gray & Gold Design, Crown Finial, C.1820, 13 Piece | 250.00 |
| Rockingham, Teapot, Bennington Type, Raised Ferns On Pumpkin To Brown | 55.00 |
| Rockingham, Teapot, Porcelain, Flowers & Leaves On White, English, 1843 | 165.00 |
| Rockingham, Toby Jug, Brown Glaze, C.1850 | 58.00 |
| Rockingham, Toby Mug, Man In Tricornered Hat, Brown & Yellow Mottled | 38.00 |
| Rockingham, Vase, Oval, 5 1/4 In. High | 17.50 |

*Rookwood pottery was made in Cincinnati, Ohio, from 1880 to 1960. All of this art pottery is marked, most with the famous flame mark. The R is reversed and placed back to back with the letter P. Flames surround the letters.*

| | |
|---|---|
| Rookwood, Ashtray & Box, Orange Glaze On Brown, 1931 | 18.00 |
| Rookwood, Ashtray & Cigarette Box, Rose Beige, Dragon Design, 1951 | 30.00 |
| Rookwood, Ashtray, Blue Glaze, Molded Owl In Center, 1942, 6 In.Diameter | 30.00 |
| Rookwood, Ashtray, Light Green, Rook With Extended Wings At End, 1944, 8 In. | 25.00 |
| Rookwood, Ashtray, Rook On Cream Glaze, Dated 1949, 4 In. High | 35.00 |
| Rookwood, Bookend, Dark Blue Crow, 1921 | 37.00 |
| Rookwood, Bookend, Nude Woman, Seated, Pair | 68.00 |
| Rookwood, Bookend, Seated Child, Pair | 48.00 |
| Rookwood, Bowl, Black, Jade Green Interior, Flame Mark, 1927, 7 1/4 In.High | 55.00 |
| Rookwood, Bowl, Grapes, Foliage, Apricot To Yellow-Green, 9 1/4 In., E.N.L. | 95.00 |
| Rookwood, Bowl, Olive Green, Turquoise Inside, Dated 1921, 8 In.Diameter | 12.00 |
| Rookwood, Bowl, Raised Salamander On Side, Matte Green, 1905, 8 In. | 45.00 |
| Rookwood, Bowl, Squat, Brown To Orange, Daisies, Signed M.F., 1898 | 65.00 |
| Rookwood, Bowl, Tigereye Glaze, Bookprinter, 1886    *Illus* | 125.00 |
| Rookwood, Box, Covered, Brown Glaze, Nasturtiums, E.D.F., 1890, 3 1/4 In.High | 100.00 |
| Rookwood, Box, Mosiaclike Floral, Epley, 1926, 8 1/4 In.Diameter | 135.00 |

Rookwood, Cachepot, Convex Sides, Mustard Yellow, 3 Footed, 1926, 3 1/4 In. ............... 14.50
Rookwood, Cachepot, Iris Glaze, Valentien, 1889, 5 1/2 In. .............................*Illus* 125.00
Rookwood, Creamer, Berries On Standard Glaze, Clara C.Lindeman, 1898 ............... 80.00
Rookwood, Creamer, Bisque Finish, Leaves & Stems, A.M.Bookprinter, 1886 ............... 225.00
Rookwood, Creamer, Magnolia On Brown, Artist A.B.S., 1890 ............... 175.00
Rookwood, Creamer, Yellow Flowers, Artus Van Briggle, 1889 ............... 195.00
Rookwood, Ewer, Bulbous, Pinkish Bluebells & Leaves On Brown To Moss Green ............... 110.00
Rookwood, Ewer, Floral, Signed CAS, 1898, 5 In. ............... 165.00
Rookwood, Ewer, Gorham Silver Overlay, Enamel Bittersweet, Lincoln, 1896 ............... 600.00
Rookwood, Ewer, High Glaze, Raised Flowers, Elizabeth Lincoln, 1898, 7 1/2 In ............... 200.00
Rookwood, Ewer, Pansies, Handled, Signed Sara Sax, 1898, 5 In.High ............... 170.00
Rookwood, Ewer, Yellow Jonquils Under Tan, Charles Schmidt, 1900, 6 In. ............... 150.00
Rookwood, Figurine, Bird, Blue Plumage, Signed R.H., 1946, 5 In. ............... 55.00
Rookwood, Flower Frog, Beige, 1924, 5 In.Long ............... 10.00
Rookwood, Flower Frog, Turtle Joe, Satyr Hauling Turtle, Blue Glaze, 1918 ............... 55.00
Rookwood, Humidor, Blue Matte, Hollow Knob For Sponge, Flame Mark ............... 55.00
Rookwood, Inkstand, Turquoise Glaze On Porcelain, 2 Covered Wells ............... 105.00
Rookwood, Jardiniere, Involuted, Yellow Blossoms On Green, Perkins, 1888 ............... 185.00
Rookwood, Jardiniere, Pink Matte, 4 Footed, 1921 ............... 30.00
Rookwood, Jug, Blue, Dated 1931, 5 3/4 In.High ............... 11.00
Rookwood, Jug, Swallow & Brown Foliage, Gold Flecks, Handled, ARV, 1884 ............... 235.00
Rookwood, Loving Cup, Peaches & Leaves, Signed H.E.Wilcox, 1805 ............... 375.00
Rookwood, Match Holder, 3 Floral Panels On Shaded Gray, 1921, 4 In.Diameter ............... 22.50
Rookwood, Mug, Blue Flowers, Incised Harriet E.Wilcox, 3 3/4 In. ............... 40.00
Rookwood, Mug, Woman's Portrait, Signed Bruce Horsfall, 1893, 5 In. ............... 650.00
Rookwood, Paperweight, Rook, Blue Glaze, Flame Mark, 1922 ............... 47.50
Rookwood, Pitcher, Ears Of Corn, Tan Green, Harriet Strafer, 1893, 6 In. ............... 250.00
Rookwood, Pitcher, Josephine Zettel, 1896, 4 1/8 In. ............... 95.00
Rookwood, Pitcher, Tigereye, Floral Design, Matt Daley, 1888, 8 In.High ............... 550.00
Rookwood, Plate, Pie, Birds & Foliage, Fluted Edge, Artist N.J.H., 1883 ............... 265.00
Rookwood, Plate, Shaded Green Leaf, 1950, 10 In. ............... 30.00
Rookwood, Rose Bowl, Footed, Floral On Beige Vellum, Grace Denzler, 1914 ............... 75.00
Rookwood, Rose Bowl, Green, Relief Lilies Of The Valley, Dated 1934, 5 In. ............... 35.00
Rookwood, Rose Bowl, Relief Lilies Of The Valley, Dated 1934, 4 3/4 In. ............... 45.00
Rookwood, Rose Bowl, White With Embossed Berries, 1934, 5 5/8 X 4 3/4 In. ............... 28.00
Rookwood, Tea Caddy, Covered, Yellow Floral, Butterfly Handles, M.A.D., 1888 ............... 245.00
Rookwood, Tile, Aqua Crow, 1921 Mark ............... 22.50
Rookwood, Tile, Burgundy To Gray, Large Center Rock, 5 1/2 In.Square ............... 22.00
Rookwood, Urn, Double Handled, Blue Green, 1926, 8 In.High ............... 30.00
Rookwood, Vase, Baluster, Lavender & Magenta, Gold Dusting, 1932, 7 In., Pair ............... 125.00
Rookwood, Vase, Baluster, Vellum Glaze, Blues, Landscape, Coyne, 1915, 7 In ............... 50.00
Rookwood, Vase, Berries & Leaves, Signed C.C.L., 1900, 6 In. ............... 120.00
Rookwood, Vase, Berries & Leaves, Signed C.F.B., 1901, 5 In. ............... 130.00
Rookwood, Vase, Blue & White, Dated 1923, 5 1/4 In.High ............... 11.00
Rookwood, Vase, Blue, Water Lily, 6 In. ............... 20.00
Rookwood, Vase, Brown Glaze, Autumn Leaves, Sallie Toohey, 1897 ............... 460.00
Rookwood, Vase, Brown Glaze, Chrysanthemums, A.R.V., 1885, 8 1/4 In.High ............... 275.00
Rookwood, Vase, Brown Glaze, Large Leaves, Handles, LVB, 1900, 5 1/2 In.High ............... 185.00
Rookwood, Vase, Brown Glaze, Shirayamadani, 1896, 7 In. .............................*Illus* 750.00
Rookwood, Vase, Brown Glaze, Stylized Fruit, 1921, L.N.L., 7 1/4 In.High ............... 55.00
Rookwood, Vase, Brown Glaze, Wilcox, 1890, 6 In. .............................*Illus* 150.00
Rookwood, Vase, Brown Matte, 1912, 7 In.High ............... 50.00
Rookwood, Vase, Cherries & Leaves, Signed HA., 1901, 5 In. ............... 130.00
Rookwood, Vase, Daffodils On Brown Glaze, Artist-Signed L.N.L., 6 3/4 In. ............... 185.00
Rookwood, Vase, Daffodils On Brown & Orange Tones, Artist H.F., 1898, 5 In. ............... 145.00
Rookwood, Vase, Daffodils, Caroline Steinle, C.1903, 6 1/2 In. ............... 125.00
Rookwood, Vase, Daffodils, Signed Leona Van Briggle, 1902, 7 5/8 In. ............... 85.00
Rookwood, Vase, Double Handled, Blue, Pattern No.63, 1931, 4 In.High ............... 25.00
Rookwood, Vase, Floral Decoration, Iris Glaze, Signed E.D., 1902, 6 In. ............... 155.00
Rookwood, Vase, Gold Flecked, Blue Daisies & Dragonflies, ARV, 1883, 10 In. ............... 750.00
Rookwood, Vase, Gray Red, 1924, 7 3/8 In.High ............... 27.50
Rookwood, Vase, Green & Brown, Reed, 1900, 8 1/2 In. .............................*Illus* 100.00
Rookwood, Vase, Hand Thrown, Blossoming Clover, C.S., 1900, 3 In. ............... 130.00
Rookwood, Vase, Hand-Thrown, Pink Poppies On Blue To Beige, F.R., 1931, 8 In. ............... 195.00
Rookwood, Vase, Handle, Gooseberries, Signed Kathryn Heckman, 1896, 5 In. ............... 100.00
Rookwood, Vase, Handled, Spittoon Type, 1894 ............... 350.00

Rookwood, Vase, Iris Glaze,          Rookwood, Cachepot, Iris Glaze,       Rookwood, Vase, Green & Brown,
Hurley, 1903, 8 1/2 In.                 Valentien, 1889, 5 1/2 In              Reed, 1900, 8 1/2 In.
                                        *(See Page 511)*                      *(See Page 511)*

Rookwood, Vase, Iris Glaze,          Rookwood, Bowl, Tigereye Glaze,       Rookwood, Vase, Brown Glaze,
Fechheimer, 1904, 7 In.                Bookprinter, 1886                     Wilcox, 1890, 6 In.
                                        *(See Page 510)*                      *(See Page 511)*

| | |
|---|---:|
| **Rookwood, Vase,** Hurley, Urn Shape, Flowering Branches, Vellum, 1925, 10 In. | 75.00 |
| **Rookwood, Vase,** Incised Greek Key, Rose To Gray Green, 1915, 11 X 5 1/2 In. | 40.00 |
| **Rookwood, Vase,** Inflated Cylindrical, Storks In Flight, Daly, 1899, 13 In. | 150.00 |
| **Rookwood, Vase,** Iris Glaze, Fechheimer, 1904, 7 In. ..........................*Illus* | 80.00 |
| **Rookwood, Vase,** Iris Glaze, Hurley, 1903, 8 1/2 In. ..........................*Illus* | 100.00 |
| **Rookwood, Vase,** Iris, E.D., 1902 | 200.00 |
| **Rookwood, Vase,** Iris, Gray Grapes & Green Leaves On Gray, Coyne, 1905, 7 In. | 185.00 |
| **Rookwood, Vase,** Leaves On Brown, 2 Curved Handles, L.Van Briggle, 1900 | 185.00 |
| **Rookwood, Vase,** Lemon Yellow, Melon Ribbed Base, Narrow Neck, 1924, 8 In. | 16.00 |
| **Rookwood, Vase,** Light Blue, Dated 1924, 5 In.High | 12.00 |
| **Rookwood, Vase,** Log, Flowers, Signed Harriette Rosemary Strafer, 1888, 7 In. | 135.00 |
| **Rookwood, Vase,** Long Neck, Magenta Shades, Dated 1913, 10 1/2 In.High | 58.00 |
| **Rookwood, Vase,** Marbleized Orange, Green, Brown, Sara Sax, 1925, 5 1/2 In.High | 75.00 |
| **Rookwood, Vase,** Metallic Inclusions, Grasses On Brown & Green, 1883, 8 In. | 200.00 |
| **Rookwood, Vase,** Molded Floral On Robin's Egg Blue, 1934, No.6459, 4 1/2 In. | 25.00 |
| **Rookwood, Vase,** Mottled Dark Blue Green Matte Glaze, Dated 1931, 4 In.High | 25.00 |
| **Rookwood, Vase,** Mums In Relief On Tan Matte, Gold Flecks, Laura Fry, 1887 | 185.00 |
| **Rookwood, Vase,** Nasturtium, Signed Mary Nourse, 1904, 8 1/2 In. | 95.00 |
| **Rookwood, Vase,** Oak Leaves On Brown, Loop Handles, Carl Schmidt, 1898, 5 In. | 200.00 |
| **Rookwood, Vase,** Oval, Geometrics On Red Matte, 1904, 5 3/4 In.High | 42.00 |
| **Rookwood, Vase,** Pink Matte Butterflies In Relief, 1929, 7 In.High | 18.00 |
| **Rookwood, Vase,** Pink, 1926, 5 1/2 In. High | 18.00 |

Rookwood, Vase, Brown Glaze, Shirayamadani, 1896, 7 In.
*(See Page 511)*

| | |
|---|---:|
| Rookwood, Vase, Pitcher Type, Raised Yellow Slip, Apple Blossoms, Lunt, 1896 | 145.00 |
| Rookwood, Vase, Plum, Molded Rooks Around Base, 1916, 6 In.High | 40.00 |
| Rookwood, Vase, Purple Grapes, Green & Brown Leaves On Brown & Yellow, 1902 | 95.00 |
| Rookwood, Vase, Raised Brown Pinecones, Dated 1924, 6 1/2 In.High | 20.00 |
| Rookwood, Vase, Red Clay, No.2137, 1914, 6 In. | 35.00 |
| Rookwood, Vase, Red Poppies, Mary Nourse, 1903, 9 1/2 In. | 175.00 |
| Rookwood, Vase, Red, Matte Glaze, Oval Shape, 1904, 5 3/4 In.High | 42.00 |
| Rookwood, Vase, Rose Matte, Blueberries, Artist-Signed H.M., 1923, 8 1/2 In. | 70.00 |
| Rookwood, Vase, Rose Matte, 1924, 9 In.High | 32.50 |
| Rookwood, Vase, Scenic Landscape, Edward Diers, 1915, 9 1/2 In.High | 195.00 |
| Rookwood, Vase, Scenic Vellum Of Windmills, Signed L.E., 1910, 7 In. | 175.00 |
| Rookwood, Vase, Soft Blue, Flowered Rim, McDonald, 1917, 6 In.High | 42.00 |
| Rookwood, Vase, Stippled Effect, Medium Green, 1923, 8 In.High | 48.00 |
| Rookwood, Vase, Trailing Yellow Sweetpeas & Green Vines, Rothenbusch, 1897 | 200.00 |
| Rookwood, Vase, Valentien, Green & Lilac Thistles, Crackled, 1902, 10 3/4 In. | 160.00 |
| Rookwood, Vase, Vellum, Apple Blossoms On Beige, Lorinda Epply, 1907 | 85.00 |
| Rookwood, Vase, Vellum, Art Nouveau Nasturtiums On Green, L.Asbury, 1919 | 75.00 |
| Rookwood, Vase, Vellum, Black Rook Flying Past Full Moon, Artist S.S., 1908 | 300.00 |
| Rookwood, Vase, Vellum, Ed Diers, Growing Crocus, Blue & Green On White, 1908 | 165.00 |
| Rookwood, Vase, Vellum, Landscape In Blues, F.Rothenbusch, 1919, 10 In. | 225.00 |
| Rookwood, Vase, Vellum, White Daisies On Blue, 1913, 8 In.High | 135.00 |
| Rookwood, Vase, Wall, Blue, 1925, 7 3/4 In.High | 17.00 |
| Rookwood, Vase, Yellow & Blue Iris On Brown, C.S., 1902, 7 In.High | 135.00 |
| Rookwood, Vase, Yellow & Green Decoration, Artist S.E.Coyne, 1929, 7 In. | 55.00 |
| Rookwood, Vase, Yellow Floral Decoration, Signed A.R.V., 1896, 12 1/2 In. | 325.00 |
| Rookwood, Vase, Yellow Narcissus On Green, Lenore Asbury, 1901, 7 1/2 In. | 180.00 |
| Rookwood, Vase, Yellow Tulip, Sallie Toohey, 1902, 7 In.High | 160.00 |
| Rookwood, Vase, Zettel, Blueberry Laden Branches, Crackled, 1903, 9 In. | 150.00 |
| Rookwood, Vase, 7 Fish On Green Glaze, Artist-Signed E.T.H., 1908, 6 1/2 In. | 625.00 |
| Rorstrand, Fruit Set, Willow, 17 Piece | 250.00 |
| Rorstrand, Mug, Memorial To Gustavus Vasa | 95.00 |

*Rosaline glass is a rose-colored jade glass that was made by the Steuben*
*Glass Works in Corning, New York.*

| | |
|---|---:|
| Rosaline, Compote, Alabaster Foot & Stem, Signed, 4 In.High | 150.00 |
| Rosaline, Compote, Alabaster Foot, 3 1/2 X 7 1/2 In. | 295.00 |
| Rosaline, Compote, Boat Shape, Fades To Alabaster Base, 5 In.High | 300.00 |
| Rosaline, Plate, 8 In. | 97.50 |
| Rosaline, Vase, Cluthra, Bulbous, 11 In.High | 750.00 |
| Rosaline, Vase, Trumpet, Alabaster Foot, 10 In.High | 95.00 |

*Rose bowls were popular during the 1880s. Rose petals were kept in the open*
*bowl to add fragrance to a room. The glass bowls were made with crimped tops,*
*which kept the petals inside. Many types of Victorian art glass were made*
*into rose bowls.*

**Rose Bowl, see also Porcelain, Rose Bowl, Pressed Glass, Rose**
**Bowl, special art glass categories**

| | |
|---|---:|
| Rose Bowl, Beaded, Paneled, Footed, Green, 5 1/2 In.High | 17.50 |

| | |
|---|---:|
| Rose Bowl, Egg Shape, Shaded Blue, White Lining, 7 1/2 In. | 65.00 |
| Rose Bowl, Green, Melon Ribbed, Gold Filled Grape Cuttings, 5 3/4 In. | 40.00 |
| Rose Bowl, Shadow, Opalescent Blue, Footed, 3 3/4 In. | 34.00 |
| Rose Canton, Vase, Gourd, Six Panels Of Figural Scenes, 6 In.High | 135.00 |

*Rose Medallion china was made in China during the nineteenth and twentieth centuries. It is a distinctive design picturing people, flowers, birds, and butterflies. They are colored in greens, pinks, and other colors.*

| | |
|---|---:|
| Rose Medallion, Bowl, Birds, Butterflies, & Floral Inside & Out, 8 3/4 In. | 125.00 |
| Rose Medallion, Bowl, Covered, Oval, Chinese Export, 8 3/4 X 10 1/2 In. | 165.00 |
| Rose Medallion, Bowl, Punch, C.1830, 15 3/4 In. | 298.00 |
| Rose Medallion, Bowl, Punch, 4 Cartouches Inside & Out, Floral, Birds, People | 275.00 |
| Rose Medallion, Bowl, Punch, 14 1/2 In.Diameter | 300.00 |
| Rose Medallion, Bowl, Square, Scalloped Sides, 9 In.Across | 250.00 |
| Rose Medallion, Bowl, Two Panels People & Two Floral, C.1840, 9 1/2 In. | 150.00 |
| Rose Medallion, Bowl, Vegetable, Birds, Butterflies, & Floral, 9 1/2 In. | 60.00 |
| Rose Medallion, Bowl, Vegetable, Covered, Rectangular, Birds & Butterflies | 150.00 |
| Rose Medallion, Box, Foo Dog Finial, Round, 2 Reserves On Top & Base | 90.00 |
| Rose Medallion, Butter Chip, People In Window | 18.00 |
| Rose Medallion, Candlestick, 6 In.High | 60.00 |
| Rose Medallion, Charger, Birds, Butterflies, & Floral, 14 In. | 140.00 |
| Rose Medallion, Cup & Saucer, Demitasse | 29.15 |
| Rose Medallion, Cup & Saucer, Demitasse, Tankard Style, Birds, Butterflies | 15.00 |
| Rose Medallion, Cup & Saucer, Gold, C.1830 | 67.50 |
| Rose Medallion, Cup, Saki | 10.00 |
| Rose Medallion, Dish, Leaf, 3/4 In.Rim, C.1850 | 125.00 |
| Rose Medallion, Dish, Soap, 3 Piece | 95.00 |
| Rose Medallion, Figurine, Peacock, 9 1/2 In.High, Pair | 150.00 |
| Rose Medallion, Gravy Boat, Birds, Butterflies, & Floral, 7 1/2 X 8 1/2 In. | 38.00 |
| Rose Medallion, Jardiniere, Alternating Panels Of Genre Scenes & Birds | 1250.00 |
| Rose Medallion, Mug, C.1800, 4 In.High | 137.50 |
| Rose Medallion, Mug, C.1800, 4 1/2 In.High | 162.50 |
| Rose Medallion, Plate, Bread & Butter, Birds, Butterflies, & Floral, 6 In. | 12.00 |
| Rose Medallion, Plate, Deep, Ladies, Gold Trim, 9 1/2 In. | 60.00 |
| Rose Medallion, Plate, Dessert, Birds, Butterflies, & Floral, 7 1/2 In. | 22.00 |
| Rose Medallion, Plate, Dinner, Birds, Butterflies, & Floral, 10 In. | 312.00 |
| Rose Medallion, Plate, Fluted, 6 In. | 25.00 |
| Rose Medallion, Plate, Four Panels, Gold In Hair, C.1850, 9 1/2 In. | 60.00 |
| Rose Medallion, Plate, Gold In Ladies' Hair, C.1850, 8 In. | 40.00 |
| Rose Medallion, Plate, Luncheon, Birds, Butterflies, & Floral, 8 1/2 In. | 24.00 |
| Rose Medallion, Plate, Marked Made In China In Circle, 10 In. | 15.00 |
| Rose Medallion, Plate, Medallion Scenes, Made In China, 7 1/2 In. | 32.00 |
| Rose Medallion, Plate, Reticulated, 8 1/2 In. | 44.00 |
| Rose Medallion, Plate, Soup, Birds, Butterfiles, & Floral, 8 1/2 In. | 18.00 |
| Rose Medallion, Plate, 9 1/2 In. | 42.50 |
| Rose Medallion, Plate, 9 3/4 In. | 40.00 |
| Rose Medallion, Platter, Birds, Butterflies, & Floral, 13 1/2 X 18 In. | 165.00 |
| Rose Medallion, Platter, Birds, Butterflies, & Floral, 5 1/2 X 8 3/4 In. | 22.00 |
| Rose Medallion, Platter, Birds, Butterflies, & Floral, 8 1/2 X 12 In. | 50.00 |
| Rose Medallion, Platter, Orange Peel Bottom, Deep, 16 1/2 X 14 In. | 188.00 |
| Rose Medallion, Platter, Oval, Floral, Bird, & People Decoration, 15 In. | 150.00 |
| Rose Medallion, Platter, Oval, Gold, 13 X 10 In. | 85.00 |
| Rose Medallion, Relish, Fish Shape, Birds, Butterflies, & Floral | 21.50 |
| Rose Medallion, Rose Bowl | 60.00 |
| Rose Medallion, Salt & Pepper, Pumpkin Shape, Birds, Butterflies, & Floral | 25.00 |
| Rose Medallion, Spill, Gold, C.1820, 4 1/2 In.High | 112.50 |
| Rose Medallion, Spoon, Rice | 8.00 |
| Rose Medallion, Spoon, Soup, Birds, Butterflies, & Floral | 4.00 |
| Rose Medallion, Tea Set, Birds, Butterflies, & Floral, 3 Piece | 110.00 |
| Rose Medallion, Tea Set, Handleless Cups, Basket With Brass Clasp, 3 Piece | 100.00 |
| Rose Medallion, Tea Set, Pot & 2 Cups, Wicker Basket | 115.00 |
| Rose Medallion, Teacup & Saucer, Eggshell, Birds & Butterflies, Floral | 30.00 |
| Rose Medallion, Teapot, Cylindrical, Figures, Birds, Butterflies, & Floral | 70.00 |
| Rose Medallion, Teapot, Gold, C.1830, 4 1/2 In.High | 102.00 |
| Rose Medallion, Teapot, Miniature, 3 In.High | 50.00 |
| Rose Medallion, Teapot, Wire Handles, 6 3/4 In. | 98.00 |
| Rose Medallion, Teapot, 5 In.High | 135.00 |

| | |
|---|---|
| Rose Medallion, Tray, 10 X 8 In. | 145.00 |
| Rose Medallion, Vase, Cylinder, 10 1/4 In.High | 75.00 |
| Rose Medallion, Vase, 8 In.High | 148.00 |
| Rose O'Neill, see Kewpie | |

*Rose Tapestry porcelain was made by the Royal Bayreuth Factory of Germany during the late nineteenth century. The surface of the ware feels like cloth.*

| | |
|---|---|
| Rose Tapestry, Bowl, Berry, Royal Bayreuth, Blue Mark | 275.00 |
| Rose Tapestry, Bowl, Three Color Roses, Royal Bayreuth | 100.00 |
| Rose Tapestry, Box, Covered, Brown, Orange, & Green, Royal Bayreuth, Blue Mark | 80.00 |
| Rose Tapestry, Box, Covered, Oval, Royal Bayreuth, Blue Mark | 140.00 |
| Rose Tapestry, Box, Dome Lid, Round, Pink & Yellow Roses, Royal Bayreuth | 325.00 |
| Rose Tapestry, Box, Footed, Pink Roses, Blue Mark | 125.00 |
| Rose Tapestry, Box, Powder, Dome Cover, Pink & Yellow Roses, Round, Bayreuth | 325.00 |
| Rose Tapestry, Creamer, Blue Mark, 4 In. | 185.00 |
| Rose Tapestry, Creamer, Pinched Spout, Royal Bayreuth, Blue Mark, 3 3/4 In. | 120.00 |
| Rose Tapestry, Creamer, Squatty, Royal Bayreuth, Blue Mark | 135.00 |
| Rose Tapestry, Dish, Pickle, Royal Bayreuth | 135.00 |
| Rose Tapestry, Hair Receiver, Footed, Blue Mark | 150.00 |
| Rose Tapestry, Hair Receiver, Footed, Royal Bayreuth, Blue Mark | 120.00 |
| Rose Tapestry, Hair Receiver, Pink & Green Roses, 2 Pieces, Royal Bayreuth | 115.00 |
| Rose Tapestry, Hair Receiver, 3 Colors Of Roses, Green Mark | 95.00 |
| Rose Tapestry, Hatpin Holder, Royal Bayreuth, Blue Mark, 4 1/2 In.High | 155.00 |
| Rose Tapestry, Pitcher, Royal Bayreuth, 3 1/2 In.High | 125.00 |
| Rose Tapestry, Pitcher, Three Sheep On Hillside, Royal Bayreuth, 3 1/2 In. | 118.50 |
| Rose Tapestry, Plate, Cake, Open Handled, Royal Bayreuth | 175.00 |
| Rose Tapestry, Plate, Royal Bayreuth, Blue Mark, 6 In. | 110.00 |
| Rose Tapestry, Relish, Scalloped Border, Blue Mark | 140.00 |
| Rose Tapestry, Shoe, High, Laced, Royal Bayreuth, Blue Mark | 250.00 |
| Rose Tapestry, Sugar & Creamer, Covered, Three Colors | 235.00 |
| Rose Tapestry, Sugar, Covered, Royal Bayreuth, Blue Mark | 95.00 |
| Rose Tapestry, Tray, Comb & Brush, Yellow, White, & Pink Roses, Blue Mark | 177.50 |
| Rose Tapestry, Vase, Flowers In Front Of Garden Gate, 7 In. | 105.00 |
| Rose Tapestry, Vase, Pink Flowers On Blue To White, 9 In. | 95.00 |
| Rose Tapestry, Vase, Portrait Of Lady, Hat & Muff, Royal Bayreuth, Blue Mark | 195.00 |

MARKE
Rosenthal

*Rosenthal porcelain was established in Sels, Bavaria, in 1880. The German factory still continues to make fine-quality tableware and figurines.*

| | |
|---|---|
| Rosenthal, Bowl, Leaf Shape, Lilac, Opalescent Scalloped Edge | 55.00 |
| Rosenthal, Bowl, Vegetable, Covered, Sans Souci, Handled | 20.00 |
| Rosenthal, Cake Set, Continental Ivory, Floral, 9 Piece | 15.00 |
| Rosenthal, Cup & Saucer, Aida, Marked Bahnor Selb, Germany | 8.00 |
| Rosenthal, Cup & Saucer, Bouillon, Violets, Coin Gold, 2 Handled | 12.00 |
| Rosenthal, Cup & Saucer, Demitasse, Gold Floral On Cream | 3.50 |
| Rosenthal, Figurine, Dog, Platform Base | 139.00 |
| Rosenthal, Figurine, Finch, Open Beak, Branch Base, F.Heidenreich, 6 1/4 In. | 55.00 |
| Rosenthal, Figurine, Young Moor Carrying Jug & Tray, Artist H.Meisel | 65.00 |
| Rosenthal, Jar, Cookie, Curled Leaf Finial, Floral On Scrolled White | 22.50 |
| Rosenthal, Mug, Barrel Shape, Sepia Seascape, White Rim, 6 In.High | 18.00 |
| Rosenthal, Plate, Aida, Marked Bahnor Selb, Germany, 7 1/8 In. | 6.00 |
| Rosenthal, Plate, Aida, Marked Bahnor Selb, Germany, 9 3/4 In. | 7.50 |
| Rosenthal, Plate, Art Nouveau, Stylized Trees, 11 In.Diameter, Set Of 12 | 275.00 |
| Rosenthal, Plate, Center Portrait Of Lady, Cobalt & Gold Border, 10 In. | 38.00 |
| Rosenthal, Plate, Child's, Transfer, Child Holding Candle, Cats, 7 In. | 10.00 |
| Rosenthal, Plate, Sans Souci, Cream With Gold Trim, 10 In. | 11.00 |
| Rosenthal, Plate, Serving, Aida, Marked Bahnor Selb, Germany, 11 In.Diameter | 11.00 |
| Rosenthal, Platter, Aida, Marked Bahnor Selb, Germany, 12 1/4 In.Diameter | 12.00 |
| Rosenthal, Platter, Aida, Marked Bahnor Selb, Germany, 14 1/2 In.Diameter | 14.00 |
| Rosenthal, Platter, Chop, Pink & Yellow Roses On Blue To Green, Gold, Rust | 32.00 |
| Rosenthal, Sugar & Creamer, Aida, Marked Bahnor Selb, Germany | 14.00 |
| Rosenthal, Tea Set, Pansies, Scalloped, Gold Outlines, 3 Piece | 18.50 |
| Rosenthal, Tea Set, Silver Deposit Vine & Leaf On Turquoise, 3 Piece | 40.00 |
| Rosenthal, Teacup & Saucer, Silver Deposit Vine & Leaf On Turquoise | 8.00 |
| Rosenthal, Tray, Hand-Painted Flowers, Gold Trim, 13 1/4 In. | 20.00 |
| Rosenthal, Vase, Tropical Birds & Trees, Gold Rim, 6 In. | 30.00 |

*Roseville* (handwritten)

*Roseville Pottery Company was established in 1891 in Zanesville, Ohio. Many types of pottery were made, including flower vases.*

| Item | Price |
|---|---|
| Roseville, Ashtray, Pinecone, Rust, 2 1/2 X 5 In. | 20.00 |
| Roseville, Basket, Apple Blossom, Pink, 10 In.High | 32.50 |
| Roseville, Basket, Blue & Green, Floral Decoration, 11 In.High | 20.00 |
| Roseville, Basket, Clematis, Double Handled, Blue With White Flowers | 25.00 |
| Roseville, Basket, Columbine, Blue With Yellow Flowers, 8 In.High | 25.00 |
| Roseville, Basket, Foxglove, Blue, 10 In. | 18.00 |
| Roseville, Basket, Hanging, Corinthian, 6 X 10 In. | 40.00 |
| Roseville, Basket, Hanging, Ixia, Yellow, Lavender Flowers, 5 X 7 1/2 In. | 25.00 |
| Roseville, Basket, Honeysuckle, Blue, 8 In.High | 18.00 |
| Roseville, Basket, Magnolia, Blue, 12 1/2 In.Diameter, 10 In.High | 28.00 |
| Roseville, Basket, Magnolia, Green, 13 X 6 In. | 40.00 |
| Roseville, Basket, Peony, Green, 8 X 5 In. | 25.00 |
| Roseville, Basket, Snowberry, Blue, 8 X 3 1/2 In. | 25.00 |
| Roseville, Basket, Water Lily, Green To Pink, 8 X 6 In. | 25.00 |
| Roseville, Bookend, Clematis, Green, Pair | 22.00 |
| Roseville, Bookend, White Rose Bouquet On 3 Stacked Books, Pair | 23.00 |
| Roseville, Bookend, Yellow Flower On Orange To Green, Signed, Pair | 35.00 |
| Roseville, Bowl, Apple Blossom, Blue, 6 In.Diameter, 4 1/4 In.High | 11.00 |
| Roseville, Bowl, Art Deco Motif On Pebbly Cream, Mostique, RV Mark, 7 In. | 46.00 |
| Roseville, Bowl, Center, Cosmos, Rust Color, 6 In. | 15.00 |
| Roseville, Bowl, Centerpiece, Blackberry, 2 Handles, 10 In. | 25.00 |
| Roseville, Bowl, Centerpiece, Calla Lilies, Rust & Green, 8 1/4 X 16 14 In. | 35.00 |
| Roseville, Bowl, Child's, Chicks On Green Band, Yellow Ground, 5 3/4 In. | 15.00 |
| Roseville, Bowl, Clematis, Blue, Handled, 5 X 7 1/2 In. | 18.00 |
| Roseville, Bowl, Columbine On Pink, 8 In.Diameter | 15.00 |
| Roseville, Bowl, Console, Bleeding Heart, Rose, 13 3/4 In.Diameter | 19.00 |
| Roseville, Bowl, Console, White Rose, Pink, 8 3/4 In.Diameter | 15.00 |
| Roseville, Bowl, Covered, Landscape, Windmills & Sailboats, 6 3/4 In.Wide | 100.00 |
| Roseville, Bowl, Donatello, Glossy Glaze, 6 1/2 In.Diameter | 12.50 |
| Roseville, Bowl, Donatello, Matte, 7 1/2 In.Diameter, Unmarked | 20.00 |
| Roseville, Bowl, Donatello, 2 1/2 In.High, 8 1/2 In.Diameter | 15.00 |
| Roseville, Bowl, Donatello, 5 1/4 In.Diameter | 25.00 |
| Roseville, Bowl, Florentine, Brown Matte Finish, 7 In.Diameter | 17.50 |
| Roseville, Bowl, Flower, Fuchsia Design On Rose To Orchid, 2 Handles, No.651 | 9.95 |
| Roseville, Bowl, Flower, Futura, 4 X 10 In. | 16.00 |
| Roseville, Bowl, Flower, Hanging, Blue, Apple Blossom | 15.00 |
| Roseville, Bowl, Flower, Pink, 12 In.Diameter | 25.00 |
| Roseville, Bowl, Flower, White Rose, Blue Ground, 4 In.High, 15 In.Long | 18.00 |
| Roseville, Bowl, Flower, Zephyr Lily, Green, 8 In.Diameter | 20.00 |
| Roseville, Bowl, Ixia, Green, 6 1/4 In.Diameter | 10.00 |
| Roseville, Bowl, Magnolia, Two Handles, Green Ground, Pink & White, 11 In. | 15.00 |
| Roseville, Bowl, Oval, White Flower, Orchid Tint, 12 In. | 14.00 |
| Roseville, Bowl, Persian, 6 In.High | 20.00 |
| Roseville, Bowl, Pinecone, Brown Background, 3 In.High | 8.00 |
| Roseville, Bowl, Pinecone, Green, Impressed Mark, 4 X 6 1/2 In. | 25.00 |
| Roseville, Bowl, Pinecone, Green, 3 1/4 In.High, 5 In.Diameter | 9.00 |
| Roseville, Bowl, Pinecone, Twig Handles, 8 X 2 3/4 In. | 12.50 |
| Roseville, Bowl, Poinsettia On Green, 4 1/2 In.High | 10.00 |
| Roseville, Bowl, Snowberry, Blue, Handled, Low, 12 In. | 18.00 |
| Roseville, Bowl, Snowberry, Green, Handled, Low, 8 In. | 12.50 |
| Roseville, Bowl, Water Lily, 2 Handled, Signed, 6 In. | 12.00 |
| Roseville, Bowl, Yellow, Blue & Pink Flowers, 8 In.Diameter, 3 1/2 In.High | 38.00 |
| Roseville, Box, Powder, Apple Blossom, Square, Blue | 22.50 |
| Roseville, Box, Wincraft, Square, Blue, 7 In. | 25.00 |
| Roseville, Candleholder, Heart Shape, Leaf Spray On Oxblood, 3 In.High | 5.00 |
| Roseville, Candleholder, Snowberry, Marked, 2 In.High, Pair | 8.00 |
| Roseville, Candlestick, Donatello, Pair, 6 1/2 In.High | 55.00 |
| Roseville, Candlestick, Larose, 8 In.High, Pair | 35.00 |
| Roseville, Candlestick, Peony, Yellow, 4 In.High | 8.50 |
| Roseville, Candlestick, Rust, 2 1/2 In.High, Pair | 15.00 |
| Roseville, Candlesticks, Columbine, Green To Pink, 2 1/2 In.High | 17.50 |
| Roseville, Centerpiece, Clematis, Green & Orange, 4 1/2 In.High | 12.00 |
| Roseville, Conch Shell, Pink & Green, Water Lily, 5 In. | 15.00 |
| Roseville, Console Set, Bittersweet, Vase & Candlesticks, 6 In.High | 25.00 |

| | |
|---|---|
| Roseville, Console Set, Lilies On Blue, 3 Piece | 25.00 |
| Roseville, Console Set, Magnolia, Marked | 35.00 |
| Roseville, Console Set, Moderne, 2 Center Bowls, 1 Candleholder | 45.00 |
| Roseville, Console Set, Wincraft, Green, 3 Piece | 15.00 |
| Roseville, Console Set, Yellow Tan, Ixia, Double Candleholders, 3 Piece | 35.00 |
| Roseville, Cornucopia, Apple Blossom, Rose, 9 In.Long | 14.00 |
| Roseville, Cornucopia, Bittersweet, Yellow, 8 In. | 12.50 |
| Roseville, Cornucopia, Bushberry, Blue, Attached Flower Frog, 8 In.High | 16.00 |
| Roseville, Cornucopia, Bushberry, Glazed, Brown To Light Green, 8 In. | 30.00 |
| Roseville, Cornucopia, Magnolia, Green, 6 In.Diameter | 22.50 |
| Roseville, Creamer, Child's, Rabbit On Each Side, 3 1/2 In.High | 6.00 |
| Roseville, Ewer, Clematis, Blue To Green, Squatty, 6 In.High | 35.00 |
| Roseville, Ewer, Clematis, Blue, 10 In. | 25.00 |
| Roseville, Ewer, Cremona, Blue To Pink, Green Leaves, 10 In.High | 17.50 |
| Roseville, Ewer, Gardenia On Mottled Blue, Signed, 10 In. | 25.00 |
| Roseville, Ewer, Gardenia, Gray, 10 In.High | 35.00 |
| Roseville, Ewer, Green, Squatty, 6 1/2 In.High | 15.00 |
| Roseville, Ewer, Silhouette, White With Green Insert, 10 In.High | 18.00 |
| Roseville, Ewer, Zephyr Lily, Blue, 6 1/2 In.High | 15.00 |
| Roseville, Ewer, Zephyr Lily, Rust, 10 In.High | 40.00 |
| Roseville, Fernery, Green Poinsettias, Marked & Numbered, 5 1/2 In High | 15.00 |
| Roseville, Flower Frog, Ixia, Green To Pink, 3 1/2 In.Diameter | 11.00 |
| Roseville, Flower Frog, Peony, Pink, 4 In. | 10.00 |
| Roseville, Flowerpot, Thornberry, Green, Coaster | 15.00 |
| Roseville, Jar, Cookie, Water Lilies, 10 In.High | 35.00 |
| Roseville, Jardiniere, Bleeding Heart, Pink, 6 X 8 In. | 35.00 |
| Roseville, Jardiniere, Columbine, Green To Pink, 4 X 7 In. | 20.00 |
| Roseville, Jardiniere, Corinthian | 25.00 |
| Roseville, Jardiniere, Cosmos, Blue, 5 In.Diameter | 20.00 |
| Roseville, Jardiniere, Dahlrose, 6 1/2 X 8 In. | 65.00 |
| Roseville, Jardiniere, Donatello, 5 X 6 1/2 In., Marked | 40.00 |
| Roseville, Jardiniere, Florentine, 2 Handled, RV Mark, 12 In.High | 39.00 |
| Roseville, Jardiniere, Foxglove, 6 1/2 In.High, 9 In.Diameter | 19.00 |
| Roseville, Jardiniere, Mostique, 8 1/4 In.High, 10 5/8 In.Diameter | 25.00 |
| Roseville, Jardiniere, Peony Pattern, Green & White Handles | 150.00 |
| Roseville, Jardiniere, Snowberry, Blue, 6 In. | 20.00 |
| Roseville, Jardiniere, Water Lily, Green To Pink, 10 In.High, 16 In.Diam. | 85.00 |
| Roseville, Jardiniere, White Rose, Brown, 3 X 4 1/2 In. | 10.00 |
| Roseville, Lamp, Electric, Futura | 42.50 |
| Roseville, Match Holder, Wall, Corinthian | 20.00 |
| Roseville, Match Holder, Wall, Thorn, Blue, Paper Label | 19.50 |
| Roseville, Mug, Child's, Baby Chicks, 3 1/2 In.High | 10.00 |
| Roseville, Mug, Holland, Embossed Dutch Girl & Boy, 4 1/4 In.High | 4.00 |
| Roseville, Pitcher, Blue, 8 X 8 In. | 40.00 |
| Roseville, Pitcher, Tankard, Green Freesia | 15.00 |
| Roseville, Pitcher, Water, Cream, Glaze | 40.00 |
| Roseville, Planter, Cosmos, Blue, 5 1/4 In.High, 6 In.Diameter | 10.00 |
| Roseville, Planter, Gardenia, Raised White & Green Floral On Gray, 9 In. | 15.00 |
| Roseville, Planter, Landscape, Hand-Painted, Windmills, Pastel, 4 1/2 In. | 60.00 |
| Roseville, Planter, Pinecones On Blue, Signed, 4 In.High | 10.00 |
| Roseville, Planter, Raised Pinecones, Twig Handles, 6 In.Diameter | 12.50 |
| Roseville, Plaque, Wall, Florentine | 12.50 |
| Roseville, Tea Set, Green, Zephyr Lily, 3 Piece | 45.00 |
| Roseville, Teapot, Freesia, Blue, 11 In. | 35.00 |
| Roseville, Teapot, Landscape, Blue Dutch Scene, 5 In.High | 25.00 |
| Roseville, Teardrop Shape, Orange, 6 1/4 In.High, Pair | 8.00 |
| Roseville, Umbrella Stand, Imperial | 125.00 |
| Roseville, Vase Holder, Wincraft, Double | 17.50 |
| Roseville, Vase, Apple Blossoms, 2 Brown Twig Handles, Greens, 7 1/4 In. | 10.00 |
| Roseville, Vase, Benada, Handled, 5 In. | 12.00 |
| Roseville, Vase, Bleeding Heart, Pink, 8 In.High | 18.00 |
| Roseville, Vase, Blue Barklike Texture, White Clematis, 6 1/2 In. | 14.50 |
| Roseville, Vase, Blue Magnolia, 2 Handled, 9 In.High | 23.50 |
| Roseville, Vase, Blue, Pinecone Handle, 7 1/2 In. | 10.00 |
| Roseville, Vase, Blue, Pinecone, Handle, Marked, 7 In. | 15.00 |
| Roseville, Vase, Brown To Tan Top, Raised White Floral, 2 Handles, 6 In. | 9.00 |

Roseville, Vase, Brown Tones, 2 Handled, Falline, 6 1/2 In. High .............................................. 15.00
Roseville, Vase, Bud, Donatello, Double ........................................ 24.00
Roseville, Vase, Bud, Double, Magnolia, Blue, 6 In.High ............................................ 15.00
Roseville, Vase, Bushberry, Blue, 6 In.High ................................................ 15.00
Roseville, Vase, Bushberry, Orange Over Green, 4 In.High ............................ 12.00
Roseville, Vase, Carnelian, Five Holes, Dark To Light Green, 5 1/4 In.High ................. 12.50
Roseville, Vase, Clematis, Blue With White Flowers, 7 In.High ............................... 15.00
Roseville, Vase, Corinthian, 9 In.High ........................................ 18.00
Roseville, Vase, Cosmos, Green, 6 In. ................................................ 6.50
Roseville, Vase, Cremona, Brown To Yellow, 12 In.High ................................. 30.00
Roseville, Vase, Cremona, Rust Yellow To Blue, Pair, 5 In.High ............................ 25.00
Roseville, Vase, Dahlrose, Pink & Green, 10 In. ........................................ 22.00
Roseville, Vase, Dahlrose, 10 In.High, 7 In.Diameter ....................................... 35.00
Roseville, Vase, Dogwood, 2 Handled, 8 1/2 In. ........................................ 12.00
Roseville, Vase, Donatello, 3 In.High ........................................ 20.00
Roseville, Vase, Double Handled, Water Lily, 6 1/2 In. ..................................... 15.00
Roseville, Vase, Double, Donatello, 8 X 4 1/4 In. ........................................ 25.00
Roseville, Vase, Double, Silhouette, Green, 9 In.High ...................................... 15.00
Roseville, Vase, Falline, Blue & Brown, Handled, 6 In. ..................................... 22.00
Roseville, Vase, Falline, Brown, 6 In.High ........................................ 20.00
Roseville, Vase, Florentine, Two Handles, 8 1/2 In.High .................................. 18.00
Roseville, Vase, Florentine, 6 In. ........................................ 15.00
Roseville, Vase, Florentine, 8 In.High ........................................ 35.00
Roseville, Vase, Foxglove, Deep Rose, 6 In.High ........................................ 30.00
Roseville, Vase, Foxglove, Rose, 7 1/4 In.High ........................................ 15.00
Roseville, Vase, Freesia, Blue With Yellow Flowers, 6 In.High ............................. 15.00
Roseville, Vase, Freesia, Green, Handled, 9 In. ........................................ 25.00
Roseville, Vase, Fuchsia, Blue, 6 In.High ........................................ 13.00
Roseville, Vase, Fuchsia, Round, Blue, 7 In.Diameter, 4 In.High ........................... 20.00
Roseville, Vase, Gardenia, Fluted Top, Gray, 8 In.High .................................... 13.00
Roseville, Vase, Green Iris & Leaves On Rust, 2 Handles, 5 1/2 In.High ................... 6.50
Roseville, Vase, Green To Tan, White Floral Decoration, 9 1/2 In.High ..................... 8.50
Roseville, Vase, Green Wreaths & Red Roses On Cream, 9 In.High, Pair ................. 12.50
Roseville, Vase, Iris, Blue, 4 In.High ........................................ 30.00
Roseville, Vase, Jonquil, Brown, Handled, 9 1/4 In. ........................................ 20.00
Roseville, Vase, Laurel, Orange, 6 In.High ........................................ 20.00
Roseville, Vase, Lily, 6 In. ........................................ 12.00
Roseville, Vase, Magnolia, Rust, Shaped Like Baby Carriage, 6 In.High ................... 22.50
Roseville, Vase, Magnolia, Square Chunky Base, Shaded Greens, 8 In. ................. 12.00
Roseville, Vase, Moderne, Gray, 8 In.High ........................................ 25.00
Roseville, Vase, Moss, Pink, 8 In.High ........................................ 25.00
Roseville, Vase, Moss, Pinks & Green, Signed, 9 In. ........................................ 14.00
Roseville, Vase, Orange & Green, Old Label, 7 In.High .................................... 20.00
Roseville, Vase, Peonies On Green To Rose, Double Handled, 7 In.High .................. 9.00
Roseville, Vase, Peony, Green, Handled, 7 In. ........................................ 22.00
Roseville, Vase, Peony, Signed, 12 In. ........................................ 23.50
Roseville, Vase, Pinecone, Glazed Green, 7 X 3 In. ........................................ 20.00
Roseville, Vase, Pink Ixia, Signed, 4 In. ........................................ 8.00
Roseville, Vase, Poppy, Green To Pink, Yellow Flowers, 4 X 6 In. ......................... 15.00
Roseville, Vase, Princess, Signed, 7 In.High ........................................ 15.00
Roseville, Vase, Royal Capri, Green, 8 In.High ........................................ 25.00
Roseville, Vase, Rozane, Bulbous, Thin Neck, Floral On Brown Glaze, 7 1/2 In. ......... 65.00
Roseville, Vase, Silhouette, Cornucopia Decoration, Rose, 8 In.High ...................... 13.00
Roseville, Vase, Snowberry, Blue, 6 In.Diameter, 7 In.High ............................... 15.00
Roseville, Vase, Snowberry, Double Handle, Marked, 6 1/2 In.High ...................... 9.00
Roseville, Vase, Stick, Pink, 2 Handled, Marked ........................................ 10.00
Roseville, Vase, Stippled Buff, Sgraffito Frieze, Signed E.E., C.1900, 9 In. .............. 75.00
Roseville, Vase, Sunflower, Blue & Brown, 7 In. ........................................ 22.00
Roseville, Vase, Sunflower, Paper Label, 6 In.High ........................................ 20.00
Roseville, Vase, Teasel, Light Blue, 6 In.High, 5 In.Diameter ............................... 18.00
Roseville, Vase, Thornapple, Rust, 6 In.High ........................................ 20.00
Roseville, Vase, Tourist, Touring Car & Dog, 9 1/2 In.High ............................... 45.00
Roseville, Vase, Twig Handles, Acorns On Green, Footed, 4 In.Diameter ................. 15.00
Roseville, Vase, Twig Handles, Acorns On Green, 6 In.Diameter ........................... 20.00
Roseville, Vase, Urn Shape, Yellow Flower & Green Leaves On Browns, Rozane ........ 55.00
Roseville, Vase, Vintage, Rosecraft, R.V.Mark, C.1916, 5 1/2 In. ......................... 25.00

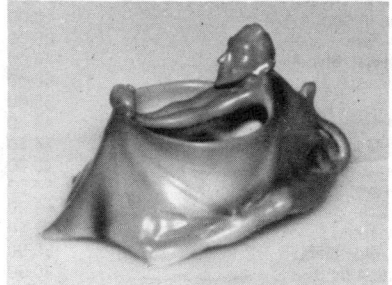 

Royal Bayreuth, Ashtray, Red Devil,
4 1/2 In.Long

Roseville, Vase, Waterlilies, 5 In.High

| | |
|---|---|
| Roseville, Vase, Wall, Gardenia, Gray, 8 In.High | 25.00 |
| Roseville, Vase, Water Lily, Blue, 6 In.High | 20.00 |
| Roseville, Vase, Waterlilies, 5 In.High .................................................. *Illus* | 14.00 |
| Roseville, Vase, White Clematis On Blue Green, Double Handled, 6 1/2 In. | 9.00 |
| Roseville, Vase, White Rose, Green To Pink, 6 In.High | 18.00 |
| Roseville, Vase, White Rose, Pale Blue, Handled, 5 X 7 In. | 22.00 |
| Roseville, Vase, Zephyr Lily, Blue, 2 Handled, Signed, 8 In. | 12.00 |
| Roseville, Vase, Zephyr Lily, Dark Blue, 6 X 7 In. | 22.00 |
| Roseville, Vase, Zephyr Lily, Green, Pink Lily, 8 In.High | 18.00 |
| Roseville, Vase, Zephyr Lily, Handled, 7 X 5 In. | 22.00 |
| Roseville, Wall Plaque, Burmese Green, Man & Woman, Pair | 35.00 |
| Roseville, Wall Pocket, Savona Pattern, Ribbed 3/4 Way Down, Grapes, Leaves | 7.50 |
| Roy Rogers, Bag, School, Pictures Of Roy, 14 X 9 In. | 9.75 |
| Roy Rogers, Bank, Roy & Trigger, Lock & Key | 12.50 |
| Roy Rogers, Binoculars, Roy & Trigger | 8.00 |
| Roy Rogers, Clock, Alarm, Rope Numerals, Animated | 35.00 |
| Roy Rogers, Crayon & Pencil Set, Graphic Box | 6.25 |
| Roy Rogers, Dishes, Porcelain, 19 Piece | 45.00 |
| Roy Rogers, Flashlight, Signal, Siren, Boxed | 4.50 |
| Roy Rogers, Flashlight, Signal, Siren, Lithographed, Tin, 6 In. | 9.25 |
| Roy Rogers, Gun & Holster, Belt, Dated 1955 | 20.00 |
| Roy Rogers, Harmonica, Metal | 5.00 |
| Roy Rogers, Lantern | 7.50 |
| Roy Rogers, Lunch Pail | 5.00 |
| Roy Rogers, Mug, Figural, Plastic | 4.00 |
| Roy Rogers, Ranch, Rodeo, Lithographed, Tin, Marx | 10.50 |
| Roy Rogers, Shooter, Cap, Repeating, Metal, Black Handle, 11 In. | 7.00 |
| Roy Rogers, Watch, Wrist, Dale Evans | 45.00 |
| Royal Austria, Hatpin Holder, White Daisies On Blue & White, Coin Gold Top | 21.00 |
| Royal Austria, Plate, Cake, Gold Roses On Shaded Green, 11 1/2 In. | 26.50 |
| Royal Austria, Plate, Cake, Gold, Roses, Green Ground, Marked H.P. | 24.00 |
| Royal Austria, Plate, White Grapes, Red & Green Leaves, Gold Border, 9 In. | 39.00 |
| Royal Austria, Salt Dip, Oval, Hand-Painted, Blue, Wreath Mark | 3.00 |

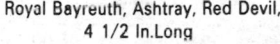

*Royal Bayreuth porcelain was made in Germany during the late nineteenth
and twentieth centuries. Many types of wares were made.*

Royal Bayreuth, see also Old Ivory, Rose Tapestry, Snow Baby,
    Sunbonnet Babies

| | |
|---|---|
| Royal Bayreuth, Ashtray, Clown, Blue Mark | 75.00 |
| Royal Bayreuth, Ashtray, Elk, 6 In. | 55.00 |
| Royal Bayreuth, Ashtray, Penguins On Yellow, Scalloped, Blue Mark | 34.00 |
| Royal Bayreuth, Ashtray, Red Devil, 4 1/2 In.Long ...................................... *Illus* | 58.00 |
| Royal Bayreuth, Bowl, Lobster, Blue Mark, 7 1/2 In.Long | 95.00 |
| Royal Bayreuth, Bowl, Openwork, Roses, Gold, Green, Blue Mark, 10 1/2 In. | 117.00 |
| Royal Bayreuth, Bowl, Poppy, Red, Green Handle, Blue Mark, 5 1/2 In. | 28.50 |
| Royal Bayreuth, Bowl, Poppy, 8 In.Across | 85.00 |
| Royal Bayreuth, Box, Powder, Covered, Yellow Roses, Blue Mark | 38.00 |
| Royal Bayreuth, Box, Powder, White, 3 Footed, Blue Mark, 3 X 3 3/4 In. | 27.50 |
| Royal Bayreuth, Candlestick, Dutch Village Scene, 4 1/4 In.High | 45.00 |

| | |
|---|---|
| Royal Bayreuth, Candlestick, House, Seagull & Woman With Basket, Blue Mark | 55.00 |
| Royal Bayreuth, Candlestick, Man On Horse Passing Man In Cart, 4 1/4 In. | 40.00 |
| Royal Bayreuth, Chocolate Pot, Little Jack Horner, Small Size | 85.00 |
| Royal Bayreuth, Chocolate Pot, Red Poppy, Slender Pedestal, Blue Mark | 175.00 |
| Royal Bayreuth, Creamer, Apple, Leaf Handle, Blue Mark | 58.00 |
| Royal Bayreuth, Creamer, Apple, No.5263F | 65.00 |
| Royal Bayreuth, Creamer, Arab On Horseback, Blue Mark | 48.00 |
| Royal Bayreuth, Creamer, Black Cat, Orange Inside, Blue Mark, 5 In.High | 74.50 |
| Royal Bayreuth, Creamer, Black Crow | 48.00 |
| Royal Bayreuth, Creamer, Conch Shell, Green, Yellow, Brown, & Blue, Blue Mark | 34.50 |
| Royal Bayreuth, Creamer, Conch Shell, Pearlized, Blue Mark | 48.00 |
| Royal Bayreuth, Creamer, Corinthian, Corset Shape, Blue Mark, 4 3/4 In. | 42.50 |
| Royal Bayreuth, Creamer, Cows & Trees, Yellow Bottom, Blue Mark, 3 1/2 In. | 50.00 |
| Royal Bayreuth, Creamer, Cows, House, Rocks, Blue Mark, 4 In. | 70.00 |
| Royal Bayreuth, Creamer, Crab, Blue Mark | 46.50 |
| Royal Bayreuth, Creamer, Crab, Red | 52.50 |
| Royal Bayreuth, Creamer, Devil & Cards, Devil Handle, Blue Mark | 45.00 To 75.00 |
| Royal Bayreuth, Creamer, Dog, 5 In. | 40.00 To 85.00 |
| Royal Bayreuth, Creamer, Donkey With Boy | 45.00 |
| Royal Bayreuth, Creamer, Duck, Blue Mark | 65.00 |
| Royal Bayreuth, Creamer, Eagle, Marked, 4 In. | 87.00 |
| Royal Bayreuth, Creamer, Elk, Blue Mark, 3 1/2 In. | 33.00 To 47.00 |
| Royal Bayreuth, Creamer, Fish, Blue Mark, 4 In.High | 65.00 |
| Royal Bayreuth, Creamer, Fisherman, Twilight, Squatty, Blue Mark | 34.00 |
| Royal Bayreuth, Creamer, Goats In Pasture | 46.00 |
| Royal Bayreuth, Creamer, Green Frog, Blue Mark | 55.00 |
| Royal Bayreuth, Creamer, Green Pepper With Vine, White & Yellow Flowers | 35.00 |
| Royal Bayreuth, Creamer, Horses With Boy | 48.00 |
| Royal Bayreuth, Creamer, Little Boy Blue | 75.00 |
| Royal Bayreuth, Creamer, Lobster On Lettuce Leaf | 20.00 To 27.00 |
| Royal Bayreuth, Creamer, Lobster, Green Handle, Blue Mark, 3 1/2 In. | 75.00 |
| Royal Bayreuth, Creamer, Lobster, Green Handle, Blue Mark, 4 In. | 55.00 |
| Royal Bayreuth, Creamer, Long Horn Cattle, Blue Mark | 58.00 |
| Royal Bayreuth, Creamer, Man In Mountain, Blue Mark | 45.00 |
| Royal Bayreuth, Creamer, Man Leading Two Horses | 35.00 |
| Royal Bayreuth, Creamer, Moose, Horns Encircle Top, Blue Mark | 36.00 |
| Royal Bayreuth, Creamer, Murex, Pearlized, Souvenir, Atlantic, Blue Mark | 26.00 |
| Royal Bayreuth, Creamer, Musicians | 28.00 |
| Royal Bayreuth, Creamer, Old Man Of The Mountain, Green Mark | 30.00 To 65.00 |
| Royal Bayreuth, Creamer, Pig, Blue Mark, 4 In. High | 95.00 To 125.00 |
| Royal Bayreuth, Creamer, Poppy, Blue Mark | 50.00 |
| Royal Bayreuth, Creamer, Red Tomato, Green Leaf Handle Spout & Base, Oval | 32.50 |
| Royal Bayreuth, Creamer, Sheep Grazing, Pinched Spout, Blue Mark, 3 1/2 In. | 45.00 |
| Royal Bayreuth, Creamer, White Cat Climbing Into Green Creamer, Blue Mark | 110.00 |
| Royal Bayreuth, Creamer, White Grecian Figures On Black, 4 1/2 In. | 35.00 |
| Royal Bayreuth, Creamer, Yawning Fish, Brown To Yellow, Pink & Orange Mouth | 35.00 |
| Royal Bayreuth, Creamer, Yawning Fish, Gray To Yellow, Pink & Orange Mouth | 69.00 |
| Royal Bayreuth, Cup & Saucer, Allover Black Leaf On Blue | 10.00 |
| Royal Bayreuth, Cup & Saucer, Allover Black Leaf On Green | 10.00 |
| Royal Bayreuth, Cup & Saucer, Allover Black Leaf On Pink | 10.00 |
| Royal Bayreuth, Cup & Saucer, Allover Black Leaf On Yellow | 10.00 |
| Royal Bayreuth, Cup & Saucer, Pink Roses, Green & White, Gold Rims & Handle | 57.50 |
| Royal Bayreuth, Cup & Saucer, Sheep Scene, Gold Rims & Handle, Blue Mark | 56.00 |
| Royal Bayreuth, Cup & Saucer, White, Heavy Gold | 17.00 |
| Royal Bayreuth, Cup, Loving, 3 Handled, Cattle Scene Band On Olive Green | 65.00 |
| Royal Bayreuth, Dish, Feeding, Little Jack Horner, Blue Mark | 63.00 |
| Royal Bayreuth, Feeding Set, Snow Babies, Blue Mark, 2 Piece | 150.00 |
| Royal Bayreuth, Figurine, Poodle, Gray, Blue Mark, 4 1/2 In. High | 115.00 |
| Royal Bayreuth, Hatpin Holder, Pink Pansy, Satinized, Blue Mark | 150.00 |
| Royal Bayreuth, Jar & Underplate, Covered, Figural, Orange, Leafy Plate | 110.00 |
| Royal Bayreuth, Jar, Dutch People, Water, 2 Handled, & Legs, Blue Mark | 40.00 |
| Royal Bayreuth, Jar, Mustard, Covered, Apple, Blue Mark | 95.00 |
| Royal Bayreuth, Jar, Mustard, Covered, Tomato, Marked | 25.00 |
| Royal Bayreuth, Lobster, Covered, Blue Mark | 23.00 |
| Royal Bayreuth, Match Holder, Clown Laying On Back, Blue Mark | 110.00 |
| Royal Bayreuth, Match Holder, Devil & Cards | 60.00 |

| | |
|---|---|
| Royal Bayreuth, Match Holder, Hanging, Hunt Scene, Blue Mark | 46.50 |
| Royal Bayreuth, Match Holder, Hanging, Shell, Iridescent, Blue Mark | 38.50 |
| Royal Bayreuth, Mustard Pot, Tomato & Lettuce, Spoon | 30.00 |
| Royal Bayreuth, Mustard Set, Covered, Tomato, Footed, 2 Piece | 28.00 |
| Royal Bayreuth, Mustard Set, Crab, Red, 2 Piece | 52.50 |
| Royal Bayreuth, Mustard Set, Tomato On Lettuce Leaf, Cover, Spoon, Blue Mark | 30.00 |
| Royal Bayreuth, Mustard Set, Tomato, Covered, Blue Mark, 3 Piece | 48.00 |
| Royal Bayreuth, Nappy, Leaves & Flowers, Side Leaf Handle, Blue Mark | 48.00 |
| Royal Bayreuth, Nappy, Pink Roses & Green Leaves On Ivory, Cutout Handle | 35.00 |
| Royal Bayreuth, Peach, Covered, Green Leaf & Finial, 3 1/2 In.High | 12.00 |
| Royal Bayreuth, Pitcher, Brittany Girls, 1 Girl, Blue Mark, 3 In.High | 29.50 |
| Royal Bayreuth, Pitcher, Brittany Maids On Green Yellow, Blue Mark, 5 In. | 65.00 |
| Royal Bayreuth, Pitcher, Cider, Elk, Blue Mark | 95.00 |
| Royal Bayreuth, Pitcher, Cider, Woman With Wicker Baskets, Birds, Blue Mark | 59.00 |
| Royal Bayreuth, Pitcher, Corset Shape, Moose Hunting Scene, Blue Mark, 4 In. | 40.00 |
| Royal Bayreuth, Pitcher, Devil & Cards, Blue Mark, 4 In. | 50.00 |
| Royal Bayreuth, Pitcher, Frog | 40.00 |
| Royal Bayreuth, Pitcher, Lobster Shape, 4 In. | 75.00 |
| Royal Bayreuth, Pitcher, Milk, Art Nouveau, Blue Mark, 6 3/4 In. | 185.00 |
| Royal Bayreuth, Pitcher, Milk, Red Poppy, Deponiert, Blue Mark, 4 1/2 In.High | 90.00 |
| Royal Bayreuth, Pitcher, Pheasants On Tomato Color, Blue Mark, 3 1/2 In. | 36.50 |
| Royal Bayreuth, Pitcher, Picture Of Lady, Tan, Pink, Yellow, & Green | 85.00 |
| Royal Bayreuth, Pitcher, Puppy, Blue Mark, 4 In. | 40.00 |
| Royal Bayreuth, Pitcher, Rose, Bulbous, Blue Mark, 6 1/2 In.High | 125.00 |
| Royal Bayreuth, Pitcher, Tapestry, Castle In Valley, Blue Mark, 4 1/4 In. | 185.00 |
| Royal Bayreuth, Pitcher, Tomato, Blue Mark, 4 1/2 In. | 35.00 |
| Royal Bayreuth, Pitcher, Tomato, Red, Green Leaf Trim, Blue Mark | 57.00 |
| Royal Bayreuth, Pitcher, Water, Shell, Blue Mark | 115.00 |
| Royal Bayreuth, Pitcher, White Grape | 50.00 |
| Royal Bayreuth, Plate, Arab With Two Horses, Blue Mark, 7 1/2 In. | 42.00 |
| Royal Bayreuth, Plate, Bouquet Of Roses & Gold Center & Border, Blue Mark | 37.50 |
| Royal Bayreuth, Plate, Brittany Girls, 2 Girls, Blue Mark, 6 1/4 In. | 29.50 |
| Royal Bayreuth, Plate, Cabbage Leaf, Tomato, & Blossoms, Blue Mark, 7 1/2 In. | 52.00 |
| Royal Bayreuth, Plate, Devil & Cards, Blue Mark, 6 In. | 125.00 |
| Royal Bayreuth, Plate, Devil & Cards, Devil Center, Bermuda In Card, 7 In. | 70.00 |
| Royal Bayreuth, Plate, Devil & Cards, Green Mark | 95.00 |
| Royal Bayreuth, Plate, Devil & Cards, 3 3/4 In. | 15.00 |
| Royal Bayreuth, Plate, Green Decoration, Snake Handle, Blue Mark, 4 In. | 17.50 |
| Royal Bayreuth, Plate, Jack & The Beanstalk, Blue Mark, 4 1/2 In. | 38.00 |
| Royal Bayreuth, Plate, Jack & The Beanstalk, 6 1/2 In. | 39.00 |
| Royal Bayreuth, Plate, Lettuce Leaf | 10.00 |
| Royal Bayreuth, Plate, Little Bo-Peep, Blue Mark | 37.50 |
| Royal Bayreuth, Plate, Little Miss Muffet, Berry & Leaf Chain, 7 1/2 In. | 55.00 |
| Royal Bayreuth, Plate, Little Miss Muffet, Verse | 72.00 |
| Royal Bayreuth, Plate, Multifloral, Blue Scroll Border, Green Mark, 6 In. | 6.00 |
| Royal Bayreuth, Plate, Pastel Rose | 18.50 |
| Royal Bayreuth, Plate, Pink Rose, Blue Flowers, Gold Leaf, 10 1/2 In. | 45.00 |
| Royal Bayreuth, Plate, Red Poppy, Blue Mark, 6 In. | 40.00 |
| Royal Bayreuth, Plate, Red Poppy, Blue Mark, 7 In. | 40.00 |
| Royal Bayreuth, Pot, Knights Drinking, Three Handles, 5 In.High | 150.00 |
| Royal Bayreuth, Pot, Mustard, Conch Shell, Pearlized, Marked Germany | 45.00 |
| Royal Bayreuth, Pot, Mustard, Covered, Tomato, Blue Mark | 19.00 To 37.50 |
| Royal Bayreuth, Ramekin & Underplate, Dresden Flowers, Blue Mark | 15.00 |
| Royal Bayreuth, Rose Bowl, Footed, Enameled Roses, Pierced Collar, Signed | 45.00 |
| Royal Bayreuth, Rose Bowl, Little Miss Muffet, Miniature, Blue Mark | 75.00 |
| Royal Bayreuth, Salt & Pepper, Conch Shell, Pearlized, Blue Mark | 70.00 |
| Royal Bayreuth, Salt & Pepper, Square, Pink Roses On Yellow & Beige, Gold | 47.50 |
| Royal Bayreuth, Saltshaker, Purple Grape, Green Leaf, Footed, Blue Mark | 25.00 |
| Royal Bayreuth, Saltshaker, Red Beet | 15.00 |
| Royal Bayreuth, Saucer, Jack In The Beanstalk | 15.00 |
| Royal Bayreuth, Shoe, Brown, Laces, 4 1/2 X 2 1/2 In., Pair | 125.00 |
| Royal Bayreuth, String Holder, Rooster, Blue Mark | 95.00 |
| Royal Bayreuth, Sugar & Creamer, Cover, Red Poppy, Blue Mark | 52.00 |
| Royal Bayreuth, Sugar & Creamer, Strawberry, Blue Mark | 67.00 |
| Royal Bayreuth, Sugar, Covered, Corinthian, Blue Mark | 29.50 |
| Royal Bayreuth, Sugar, Tomato On Footed Leaf Base, Covered, Blue Mark | 22.00 |

Royal Bayreuth, Table Set, Lobster, Covers, Blue Mark, 3 Piece ................................................ 119.00
Royal Bayreuth, Tea Set, Tomato, Footed & Handled, 3 Piece ...................... 125.00 To 185.00
Royal Bayreuth, Teapot, Figural, Orange, Green Floral Legs, Blue Mark ........................... 110.00
Royal Bayreuth, Teapot, Little Jack Horner ................................................................................ 85.00
Royal Bayreuth, Teapot, Orange Figural, Green Floral Legs, Blue Mark ......................... 110.00
Royal Bayreuth, Toby Mug, Sexton, Blue Mark, 4 1/2 In.High ......................................... 90.00
Royal Bayreuth, Tomato On Leaf, Covered, Blue Mark ......................................................... 34.00
Royal Bayreuth, Toothpick, Deer Head, Blue Mark ................................................................. 45.00
Royal Bayreuth, Toothpick, Devil & Cards, Blue Mark ........................................................... 68.00
Royal Bayreuth, Toothpick, Figural, Open Petal Rose, Gold, Blue Mark, 3 In. ................ 95.00
Royal Bayreuth, Toothpick, Moose, Blue Mark ....................................................................... 48.00
Royal Bayreuth, Tray, Card, Devil & Cards, Tricornered, Signed ....................................... 38.00
Royal Bayreuth, Tray, Perfume, Goose Girl ............................................................................. 85.00
Royal Bayreuth, Urn, Sunset Pattern, Handled, 3 In.High, Pair ......................................... 75.00
Royal Bayreuth, Vase, Hand-Painted, Blue Mark, 10 In. .................................... *Illus* 70.00

Royal Bayreuth, Vase, Hand-Painted, Blue Mark, 10 In.

Royal Bayreuth, Vase, Farm Scene, 4 1/2 In.High ................................................................. 60.00
Royal Bayreuth, Vase, Girl With Geese, 4 1/4 In. ................................................................. 57.50
Royal Bayreuth, Vase, Goats On Mountain, Blue Mark, 3 1/2 In. ...................................... 38.00
Royal Bayreuth, Vase, Gourd Shape, Man & Dog Hunting, Blue Mark, 7 1/2 In. ........... 125.00
Royal Bayreuth, Vase, Pear Shape, Cows Scene, Blue Mark, 5 In. .................................... 36.00
Royal Bayreuth, Vase, Roses, Bulbous, Handled, Blue Mark, 5 1/2 In.High ..................... 125.00
Royal Bayreuth, Vase, Sheep On Mountain, Blue Mark, 5 1/2 In. ..................................... 38.00
    Royal Berlin, see KPM

*Royal Bonn is the nineteenth century trade name for the Bonn China*
*Manufactory established in 1755 at Bonn, Germany. A general line of*
*porcelain dishes was made.*
Royal Bonn, Dish, Cheese, Covered, Oblong, Red & Yellow Mums, 8 1/2 In. ................. 17.50
Royal Bonn, Fish Set, 7 Piece ................................................................................................... 95.00
Royal Bonn, Garniture, Gold Handles, Raised Design, 3 Vases, Floral ............................... 225.00
Royal Bonn, Plate, Portrait, Van Dyke Hanging Plate, Delft, Blue & White ...................... 135.00
Royal Bonn, Vase, Art Nouveau, Multicolor, Candlestick Top, 10 In.High ........................ 150.00
Royal Bonn, Vase, Bulbous, Scenes & Floral, Cobalt, 5 1/2 In. ........................................ 18.00
Royal Bonn, Vase, Delft, Blue & White, Sailboat Medallion, 16 In.High ........................... 165.00
Royal Bonn, Vase, Gilt, Floral, & Birds On Cream, 11 In.High, Pair ................................. 48.00
Royal Bonn, Vase, Portrait, Dark Haired Girl On Pink, Gold Handles ................................. 30.00
Royal Bonn, Vase, Red, Yellow, & Green Floral, 9 3/4 In.High ......................................... 29.50
Royal Bonn, Vase, Rooster, Hens, Fence, Olive Shading, 9 3/4 In.High, Pair ................ 100.00
Royal Bonn, Vase, Signed F.Muller, 8 1/2 In. ....................................................................... 75.00

DENMARK

*Royal Copenhagen porcelain and pottery has been made in Denmark since*
*1772. It is still being made. One of their most famous wares is the*
*Christmas Plate Series.*
  Royal Copenhagen, see also Collector, Plate, Royal Copenhagen
Royal Copenhagen, Box, Shape Of Egg, Seagulls In Flight On Cover, 6 In. ..................... 75.00
Royal Copenhagen, Craquelle Set, 3 In.Diameter Bowl, 4 3/4 In.Tray, 2 Piece ............. 30.00

| | |
|---|---|
| Royal Copenhagen, Figurine, Bull, Artist Signed | 200.00 |
| Royal Copenhagen, Figurine, Elephant | 35.00 |
| Royal Copenhagen, Figurine, Peasant Girl, Signed Alex Locnir, 11 In. | 98.00 |
| Royal Copenhagen, Figurine, Polar Bear, 10 1/2 In.Long | 98.00 |
| Royal Copenhagen, Figurine, Puppy Looking At Tail, White & Gray, No.1452 | 65.00 |
| Royal Copenhagen, Figurine, Young Boy, No.1659, 12 X 10 In. | 250.00 |
| Royal Copenhagen, Group, Peasant Couple, No.1352, 17 X 11 In. | 450.00 |
| Royal Copenhagen, Mug, Footed, 3 3/8 In.High | 20.00 |
| Royal Copenhagen, Pitcher, Deep Blue Flowers, 4 In.High | 17.50 |
| Royal Copenhagen, Plaque, 2 Fish Swimming Through Sea Plants, C.1900, 6 In. | 50.00 |
| Royal Copenhagen, Plate, Commemorative, Dates 1863 & 1903, 8 In. | 250.00 |
| Royal Copenhagen, Plate, Commemorative, Dates 1869 & 1894, 7 In. | 450.00 |
| Royal Copenhagen, Salt & Pepper, Blue & White | 12.00 |
| Royal Copenhagen, Vase, Art Nouveau White Geraniums On Blue Gray, 5 In. | 65.00 |
| Royal Copenhagen, Vase, Cylindrical, Hill & Field Scenes On Blue | 52.00 |
| Royal Copenhagen, Vase, Iris And Dragonfly, 1897 Mark, Artist Signed, 8 In. | 65.00 |
| Royal Copenhagen, Vase, Seascape Scenes, 1920 Mark, 7 In.High | 68.00 |

*Royal Crown Derby Company, Ltd., was established in England in 1876.*
Royal Crown Derby, see also Crown Derby, Derby

| | |
|---|---|
| Royal Crown Derby, Cup & Saucer, Demitasse, Pink Vine | 12.00 |
| Royal Crown Derby, Jar, Jam, Covered, Strawberry & Leaves On White, Gold | 8.00 |
| Royal Crown Derby, Jar, Powder, Oriental Motif, Butterflies | 16.00 |
| Royal Crown Derby, Menu | 17.50 |
| Royal Crown Derby, Plate, Foliage & 3 Birds, Cobalt, 9 In. | 9.00 |
| Royal Crown Derby, Vase, Gold Tracery Floral On Deep Pink, Scalloped, 5 In. | 135.00 |

*Royal Doulton was the name used on pottery made after 1902. The Doulton
Factory was founded in 1815. Their wares are still being made.*
Royal Doulton, see also Doulton

| | |
|---|---|
| Royal Doulton, Base, Mother Goose, 2 3/4 In. | 18.00 |
| Royal Doulton, Beaker, Baby's, Bunnykins | 4.00 |
| Royal Doulton, Beaker, Hamlet, Shakespeare Series, 4 In.High | 22.00 |
| Royal Doulton, Beaker, Juliet, Shakespeare Series, 4 In.High | 22.00 |
| Royal Doulton, Bottle, Sherry, Zorro, Marked A | 25.00 To 47.50 |
| Royal Doulton, Bowl, Child's, Bunnykins, Artist Barbara Vernon, 7 1/2 In. | 22.50 |
| Royal Doulton, Bowl, Country Home, Open Handles, Deep, 8 Sided, 6 1/4 In. | 27.50 |
| Royal Doulton, Bowl, Dickensware, Dickens' Characters In Street Scenes | 82.50 |
| Royal Doulton, Bowl, Dickensware, Fagin, Square, 1 1/2 In.High | 29.50 |
| Royal Doulton, Bowl, Dickensware, Little Nell, 7 5/8 In. | 35.00 |
| Royal Doulton, Bowl, Dickensware, Sam Weller, Square, 1 1/2 In.High | 29.50 |
| Royal Doulton, Bowl, Punch, Dickensware, Footed, 9 In.Diameter | 175.00 |
| Royal Doulton, Bowl, Relief Daisies On Cobalt, Signed F.J., 1901, 8 In. | 65.00 |
| Royal Doulton, Bowl, Rouge Flambe, House, Trees, 10 In.Diameter | 150.00 |
| Royal Doulton, Bowl, Village Scene, Nightwatchman Making Rounds, 8 In. | 37.50 |
| Royal Doulton, Bowl, Ye Olde Cheshire Cheese, 1667, Tan Stoneware, Blue In | 5.00 |
| Royal Doulton, Box, Playing Cards, Bateman's The Revoke On Lid, Card Suits | 42.00 |
| Royal Doulton, Bust, Mr.Micawber, 2 1/2 In.High | 15.00 |
| Royal Doulton, Candlestick, Mustard Color, 6 1/2 In.High | 20.00 |
| Royal Doulton, Candlestick, Yellow Iridescent Glaze, Green Mark, Pair | 30.00 |
| Royal Doulton, Coffeepot, Reynard, The Fox | 45.00 |
| Royal Doulton, Creamer, Falstaff | 22.00 |
| Royal Doulton, Creamer, Pastoral Scene | 12.00 |
| Royal Doulton, Creamer, Reynard, The Fox | 19.50 |
| Royal Doulton, Cup & Saucer, Coaching Days | 22.00 |
| Royal Doulton, Cup & Saucer, Demitasse, Decorated, C.1850 | 30.00 |
| Royal Doulton, Cup & Saucer, Demitasse, Reynard, The Fox | 16.00 |
| Royal Doulton, Cup & Saucer, Flambe, Wreath & Scrolls | 48.00 |
| Royal Doulton, Cup & Saucer, Handleless, Child In Garden, Dated 1904 | 22.50 |
| Royal Doulton, Cup & Saucer, Old Mother Goose, Dated 1904 | 25.00 |
| Royal Doulton, Cup & Saucer, Sam Weller & Fat Boy, Mr.Pickwick & Mrs.C. | 45.00 |
| Royal Doulton, Cup & Saucer, White Cherub Handle, Floral On Brown, 1904 | 22.50 |
| Royal Doulton, Cup & Saucer, Woodman Scene, Signed Falstaff | 25.00 |
| Royal Doulton, Dish, Child's, Feeding, The Queen Of Hearts Cooking, Verse | 18.50 |
| Royal Doulton, Dish, Oval, Egyptian Scenes, 11 X 8 In. | 65.00 |
| Royal Doulton, Eggcup, Baby's, Bunnykins | 1.95 |

| | |
|---|---|
| Royal Doulton, Eggcup, Hand-Painted Florals, Pair | 17.00 |
| Royal Doulton, Feeder, Child's, Ride A Cock Horse To Banbury Cross | 32.50 |
| Royal Doulton, Figurine, A Stitch In Time, Little Old Lady Sewing | 38.00 |
| Royal Doulton, Figurine, Angela, Art Deco, 8 In. | 110.00 |
| Royal Doulton, Figurine, Autumn Breezes, 1930s, 8 In. | 45.00 |
| Royal Doulton, Figurine, Babie, 5 In.High | 18.00 |
| Royal Doulton, Figurine, Balloon Man | 39.00 |
| Royal Doulton, Figurine, Bill Sykes, Dickens' Series, 4 In.High | 12.50 |
| Royal Doulton, Figurine, Black Cat, 2 1/2 In.High | 12.00 |
| Royal Doulton, Figurine, Bulldog, Medium Size | 12.00 |
| Royal Doulton, Figurine, Bunnykin, Autumn Days | 10.00 |
| Royal Doulton, Figurine, Bunnykin, Clean Sweep | 10.00 |
| Royal Doulton, Figurine, Bunnykin, Cooling Off | 9.00 |
| Royal Doulton, Figurine, Bunnykin, Family Photograph | 12.00 |
| Royal Doulton, Figurine, Bunnykin, Helping Mother | 9.00 |
| Royal Doulton, Figurine, Bunnykin, Playtime | 12.00 |
| Royal Doulton, Figurine, Bunnykin, Sleigh Ride | 12.00 |
| Royal Doulton, Figurine, Bunnykin, Springtime | 9.00 |
| Royal Doulton, Figurine, Cairn, Miniature | 6.50 |
| Royal Doulton, Figurine, Captain Cuttle, 4 In. | 9.00 |
| Royal Doulton, Figurine, Cat, Flambe, Sitting, 5 1/2 In. | 34.00 |
| Royal Doulton, Figurine, Child So Sweet & Rare, HN 604 | 120.00 |
| Royal Doulton, Figurine, Chloe, HN 1470, Production Date 1934 | 75.00 |
| Royal Doulton, Figurine, Chow Chow | 6.50 |
| Royal Doulton, Figurine, Cissie | 26.00 |
| Royal Doulton, Figurine, Cocker Spaniel, Bandaged Paw, Miniature | 6.50 |
| Royal Doulton, Figurine, Coppelia, HN 2115 | 65.00 |
| Royal Doulton, Figurine, Dachshund | 6.50 |
| Royal Doulton, Figurine, Daffy Down Dilly | 45.00 |
| Royal Doulton, Figurine, Dalmatian, Large Size | 19.00 |
| Royal Doulton, Figurine, Day Dreams, Red | 50.00 |
| Royal Doulton, Figurine, Debutante, HN 2270 | 85.00 |
| Royal Doulton, Figurine, Delight, HN 1772 | 80.00 |
| Royal Doulton, Figurine, Denise, HN 2273 | 70.00 |
| Royal Doulton, Figurine, Diana, 1930s, 5 3/4 In. | 35.00 |
| Royal Doulton, Figurine, Dianne | 25.00 |
| Royal Doulton, Figurine, Dog, White & Brown, 2 3/4 In.High | 6.00 |
| Royal Doulton, Figurine, Drake, Miniature | 6.50 |
| Royal Doulton, Figurine, Duck, Drake, Flambe, Standing, Miniature, 3 In. | 15.00 |
| Royal Doulton, Figurine, Duck, Flambe, 1 1/2 In.High | 15.00 |
| Royal Doulton, Figurine, Easter Day, HN 2039 | 95.00 |
| Royal Doulton, Figurine, Elephant | 17.00 |
| Royal Doulton, Figurine, Ermine Coat, 7 In. | 65.00 |
| Royal Doulton, Figurine, Fagin, 4 In.High | 25.00 |
| Royal Doulton, Figurine, Falstaff | 42.00 |
| Royal Doulton, Figurine, Fox, Flambe, Laying Down, 5 In.Long | 20.00 |
| Royal Doulton, Figurine, Fox, Flambe, Sitting, 9 1/2 In.High | 115.00 |
| Royal Doulton, Figurine, German Shepherd, Miniature | 6.50 |
| Royal Doulton, Figurine, Girl As Nurse With Doll | 22.00 |
| Royal Doulton, Figurine, Goodie Two Shoes | 25.00 |
| Royal Doulton, Figurine, Grandma, HN 2052 | 70.00 |
| Royal Doulton, Figurine, Guinea Hen, Flambe, 4 In.High | 55.00 |
| Royal Doulton, Figurine, He Loves Me, Child | 38.00 |
| Royal Doulton, Figurine, Judith, 7 In. | 65.00 |
| Royal Doulton, Figurine, Kitten Licking Paws, Miniature | 6.50 |
| Royal Doulton, Figurine, Kitten Sitting, Miniature | 6.50 |
| Royal Doulton, Figurine, Kitten, Sleeping On Side With Paws Up, Miniature | 6.50 |
| Royal Doulton, Figurine, Lady Betty, Red Victorian Dress, Marked HN 1967 | 55.00 |
| Royal Doulton, Figurine, Lily, HN 1798 | 55.00 |
| Royal Doulton, Figurine, Little Nell, 4 In. | 9.00 |
| Royal Doulton, Figurine, Little Nelle Nell, 4 In. | 9.00 |
| Royal Doulton, Figurine, Lucky, Black Kitten With White Face, Miniature | 6.50 |
| Royal Doulton, Figurine, Lucy Ann, 5 1/4 In.High | 55.00 |
| Royal Doulton, Figurine, Lydia | 30.00 |
| Royal Doulton, Figurine, Marguerite, 1930s, 8 In. | 45.00 |
| Royal Doulton, Figurine, Marie Belle | 17.00 |

| | |
|---|---|
| Royal Doulton, Figurine, Marietta, Art Deco, 8 1/2 In. | 125.00 |
| Royal Doulton, Figurine, Mary Had A Little Lamb | 22.00 |
| Royal Doulton, Figurine, Maureen, 8 In. | 85.00 |
| Royal Doulton, Figurine, Melody, HN 2202 | 90.00 |
| Royal Doulton, Figurine, Mendicant, Arab Beggar, Marked HN 1365 | 75.00 |
| Royal Doulton, Figurine, Midinette, 7 In. | 65.00 |
| Royal Doulton, Figurine, Minuet, 7 In. | 65.00 |
| Royal Doulton, Figurine, Monica, 4 1/2 In. High | 40.00 |
| Royal Doulton, Figurine, Mr.Micawber, 4 In.High | 22.00 |
| Royal Doulton, Figurine, Mr.Pickwick, 4 In. | 9.00 |
| Royal Doulton, Figurine, Nanny In Rocking Chair Mending Teddy, Basket | 48.00 |
| Royal Doulton, Figurine, Old Mother Hubbard | 42.50 |
| Royal Doulton, Figurine, Oliver Twist, 4 In. | 9.00 |
| Royal Doulton, Figurine, Owl, Flambe, 12 In. | 225.00 |
| Royal Doulton, Figurine, Paisley Shawl, 7 In.High | 38.00 |
| Royal Doulton, Figurine, Peggy, HN 2038, 5 1/4 In.High | 25.00 |
| Royal Doulton, Figurine, Pekingese, Miniature | 6.50 |
| Royal Doulton, Figurine, Penelope | 62.00 |
| Royal Doulton, Figurine, Penguin, Emperor, Flambe, Standing, 6 1/2 In. | 42.00 |
| Royal Doulton, Figurine, Persian Cat, Large Size | 15.00 |
| Royal Doulton, Figurine, Poodle, White | 18.50 |
| Royal Doulton, Figurine, Pug Playing With Ball, Miniature | 9.00 |
| Royal Doulton, Figurine, Pup Playing With Slipper, Miniature | 9.00 |
| Royal Doulton, Figurine, Puppy In Basket, Miniature | 12.50 |
| Royal Doulton, Figurine, Puppy With Slipper | 9.50 |
| Royal Doulton, Figurine, Rabbit, Flambe, Laying Down, 4 In.Long | 18.00 |
| Royal Doulton, Figurine, Rabbit, Flambe, 3 In.High | 22.00 |
| Royal Doulton, Figurine, Rabbit, Miniature, Pair | 12.50 |
| Royal Doulton, Figurine, Rag Doll | 22.00 |
| Royal Doulton, Figurine, Rhapsody, HN 2267 | 75.00 |
| Royal Doulton, Figurine, Rose, Production Date 1934 | 36.00 |
| Royal Doulton, Figurine, Sairey Gamp, C.1917, 3 1/2 In.High | 38.50 |
| Royal Doulton, Figurine, Sairey Gamp, 4 In. | 9.00 |
| Royal Doulton, Figurine, Scotch Terrier, Miniature | 6.50 |
| Royal Doulton, Figurine, Sea Sprite | 35.00 |
| Royal Doulton, Figurine, She Loves Me Not, Child | 38.00 |
| Royal Doulton, Figurine, Siamese Cat, Seated, Large Size | 25.00 |
| Royal Doulton, Figurine, Sleep, Phoebe Stabler, C.1910, 8 1/4 In. | 95.00 |
| Royal Doulton, Figurine, Spaniel In Basket, Miniature | 12.50 |
| Royal Doulton, Figurine, St.Bernard | 6.50 |
| Royal Doulton, Figurine, Sweet & Twenty, 8 X 7 In. | 135.00 |
| Royal Doulton, Figurine, Sweet Anne | 70.00 |
| Royal Doulton, Figurine, Symphony, HN 2287 | 105.00 |
| Royal Doulton, Figurine, Terrier | 6.50 |
| Royal Doulton, Figurine, Terrier, Running With Ball, Miniature | 12.50 |
| Royal Doulton, Figurine, The Bather, Art Nouveau, 8 In. | 110.00 |
| Royal Doulton, Figurine, The Family Album, HN 2321 | 45.00 |
| Royal Doulton, Figurine, The Orange Lady, Brown Shawl | 42.00 |
| Royal Doulton, Figurine, Tiger, Flambe, Walking, 14 X 7 In. | 150.00 To 350.00 |
| Royal Doulton, Figurine, Tinkle Bell, 5 In.High | 18.00 |
| Royal Doulton, Figurine, Tiny Tim, 4 In. | 9.00 |
| Royal Doulton, Figurine, Tony Weller, Dickens' Series, 4 In.High | 12.50 |
| Royal Doulton, Figurine, Top O' Hill, Red | 50.00 |
| Royal Doulton, Figurine, Two Budgerigars On Stump, Signed, HN 2547 | 50.00 |
| Royal Doulton, Figurine, Valerie | 25.00 |
| Royal Doulton, Figurine, Vanity | 25.00 |
| Royal Doulton, Figurine, Veronica, 8 In.High | 75.00 |
| Royal Doulton, Figurine, Victorian Lady, HN 1452, Green Shades, 1931 | 80.00 |
| Royal Doulton, Figurine, White Poodle, Large Size | 18.50 |
| Royal Doulton, Figurine, Woman Reading To Children, 4 X 6 In. | 75.00 |
| Royal Doulton, Flagon, Micawber, The Ever Expectant, Hudson Bay Co., Brown | 65.00 |
| Royal Doulton, Flagon, Pewter Stopper, The McNab, Dewars Whisky, Brown | 75.00 |
| Royal Doulton, Flask, Dewars Whiskey, Pipe Major, Pewter Stopper | 65.00 |
| Royal Doulton, Flower Frog, Coral Color | 8.50 |
| Royal Doulton, George Washington Portrait, Blue, 10 In. | 29.00 |
| Royal Doulton, Group, Cocker Spaniels Sleeping, Miniature | 12.50 |

| | |
|---|---|
| Royal Doulton, Group, Horse & Colt, Platform Base | 149.00 |
| Royal Doulton, Group, Spaniel Pups Lying Down | 15.00 |
| Royal Doulton, Hair Receiver, Queen & Throng Decoration | 28.00 |
| Royal Doulton, Humidor, Barrel Shape, Blue Bands At Top, Beige Ground | 55.00 |
| Royal Doulton, Humidor, Blue, Viking Ships, Brown Trim | 42.00 |
| Royal Doulton, Jar, Tobacco, White Hunting Scene, Tan & Brown, Brass Lid | 45.00 |
| Royal Doulton, Jardiniere, Autumn Colors, 12 X 11 In. | 69.00 |
| Royal Doulton, Jardiniere, Blue Flowers On Tan & Brown, Rosina Brown | 75.00 |
| Royal Doulton, Jug, Athos, Miniature | 6.75 |
| Royal Doulton, Jug, Bacchus, Miniature | 6.75 |
| Royal Doulton, Jug, Dickensware, Mr.Pickwick, 2 3/4 In.High | 22.00 |
| Royal Doulton, Jug, Dickensware, Mr.Pickwick, 5 In.High | 35.00 |
| Royal Doulton, Jug, Dickensware, Tony Weller, 5 3/4 In.High | 35.00 |
| Royal Doulton, Jug, Indian Decoration, Brown Glaze, 1908 | 65.00 |
| Royal Doulton, Jug, Lawyer, Miniature | 6.75 |
| Royal Doulton, Jug, The Dickens, Signed Noke & Fenton, Limited To 1, 000 | 275.00 |
| Royal Doulton, Jug, The Gallant Fishers, Picture Of Man Fishing, 5 In.High | 30.00 |
| Royal Doulton, Jug, The Pied Piper, Signed Noke & Fenton, Limited To 600 | 300.00 |
| Royal Doulton, Jug, Whiskey, MacKinlay's Very Old Scotch, Stoneware, Blue | 55.00 |
| Royal Doulton, Jug, Whiskey, Special Highland, Norse Ship On Browns, Handle | 50.00 |
| Royal Doulton, Match & Cigarette Holder, Fagin & The Artful Dodger | 75.00 |
| Royal Doulton, Match Holder, Black Mark | 20.00 |
| Royal Doulton, Match Striker, Figural, Beehive | 35.00 |
| Royal Doulton, Mug, Baby's, Bunnykins, 2 Handled | 3.75 |
| Royal Doulton, Mug, Bunnykins On Train | 16.50 |
| Royal Doulton, Mug, Come Landlord Fill The Flowing, Tan & Brown | 30.00 |
| Royal Doulton, Mug, Stoneware, Lord Nelson, Blue & Green | 80.00 |
| Royal Doulton, Mug, Stoneware, Running Deer, Dated 1878, Hannah Barlow | 250.00 |
| Royal Doulton, Pitcher, Aubrey, Blue & White, 24 In.Base, Circumference | 85.00 |
| Royal Doulton, Pitcher, Blue Sailboats & Ocean On Cream, 7 In. | 25.00 |
| Royal Doulton, Pitcher, Brown & Green Scene, Black Mark, 5 In.High | 20.00 |
| Royal Doulton, Pitcher, Bulbous, Flowered, 4 In.High | 15.00 |
| Royal Doulton, Pitcher, Castle & Pastoral Scene, Pinched Spout, 8 In. | 65.00 |
| Royal Doulton, Pitcher, Croydon Church, 5 In.High | 35.00 |
| Royal Doulton, Pitcher, Desert Scene, 6 3/4 In.High | 28.00 |
| Royal Doulton, Pitcher, Dickensware, Fagin, Weller, & Pickwick, 7 In.High | 68.00 |
| Royal Doulton, Pitcher, Gentleman With Cane, Signed Noke, 6 3/4 In. | 45.00 |
| Royal Doulton, Pitcher, Hiawatha, 15 In. | 60.00 |
| Royal Doulton, Pitcher, Medallions & Leaves On Blue Gray, 5 In. | 50.00 |
| Royal Doulton, Pitcher, Memories Embossed In White, Strap Handle | 65.00 |
| Royal Doulton, Pitcher, Mr.Pickwick & Friend Drinking Wine, Dickensware | 75.00 |
| Royal Doulton, Pitcher, Natural Foliage On Rough Gray Blue, C.1905 | 63.00 |
| Royal Doulton, Pitcher, Ships In Full Sail, 8 In.High | 65.00 |
| Royal Doulton, Pitcher, Stagecoach Scene, 7 1/2 In. | 45.00 |
| Royal Doulton, Pitcher, That Rascally Thief, 5 1/2 In. | 26.00 |
| Royal Doulton, Pitcher, Welsh Women, 5 1/4 In.High | 22.00 |
| Royal Doulton, Plate, see also Gibson Girl, Plate | |
| Royal Doulton, Plate, Across The Moor, Signed C.Simpson, 10 3/4 In. | 18.00 |
| Royal Doulton, Plate, Across The Moor, Signed Charles Simpson, 10 1/2 In. | 25.00 |
| Royal Doulton, Plate, An Old Jarvey, 1902, 8 1/2 In. | 14.00 |
| Royal Doulton, Plate, Arundel Castle, 10 1/4 In. | 9.00 |
| Royal Doulton, Plate, Auto, "deaf" | 35.00 |
| Royal Doulton, Plate, Automobile, 2 Men Peering Under Hood, Etc., 10 1/2 In. | 65.00 |
| Royal Doulton, Plate, Baby's, Bunnykins | 6.00 |
| Royal Doulton, Plate, Battle Of Trafalgar, Blue & White, 10 In. | 22.00 |
| Royal Doulton, Plate, Black Scotty Dog, 10 1/2 In. | 28.00 |
| Royal Doulton, Plate, Blue, Eagle | 15.00 |
| Royal Doulton, Plate, Bunnykins, 1954, 7 3/4 In. | 15.00 |
| Royal Doulton, Plate, Child's, Pig Family, Bathing In The Lake | 25.00 |
| Royal Doulton, Plate, Coaching Days, 10 In. | 23.00 |
| Royal Doulton, Plate, Coaching, A Breakdown, Oval, Silver Luster Edge, 9 In. | 22.00 |
| Royal Doulton, Plate, Cobalt Enamel, Gold Scalloped Border, 8 3/4 In. | 15.00 |
| Royal Doulton, Plate, Crest, 'Ultrum Horum Mavis Accipe,' England | 10.00 |
| Royal Doulton, Plate, Desert Scenes, 10 1/4 In. | 38.00 |
| Royal Doulton, Plate, Dickens Center, Blue & White, 10 1/2 In. | 29.50 |
| Royal Doulton, Plate, Dickens, Pecksniff, 10 In. | 27.50 |

| | |
|---|---:|
| Royal Doulton, Plate, Dickensware, Alfred Jingle, 5 1/2 In. | 20.00 |
| Royal Doulton, Plate, Dickensware, Bill Sykes, 3 1/2 In. | 22.00 |
| Royal Doulton, Plate, Dickensware, Mr.Micawber, Signed Noke, 8 In. | 40.00 |
| Royal Doulton, Plate, Dickensware, Sam Weller, 6 1/2 In. | 22.00 |
| Royal Doulton, Plate, Dickensware, Sydney Carton, Signed Buzfus, 10 1/2 In. | 35.00 |
| Royal Doulton, Plate, Dickensware, Tony Weller, Signed Noke, 8 In. | 40.00 |
| Royal Doulton, Plate, Dog, 10 1/2 In. | 29.00 |
| Royal Doulton, Plate, Game Bird, Duck & Duckling, Blue Floral, 9 1/2 In. | 22.00 |
| Royal Doulton, Plate, Game Bird, Pheasant, Blue Floral Border, 9 1/2 In. | 22.00 |
| Royal Doulton, Plate, Hiawatha, Verse | 35.00 |
| Royal Doulton, Plate, Ivory, Embossed Scalloped Rim | 6.00 |
| Royal Doulton, Plate, Jackdaw Of Rewims, Off He Took, 9 1/2 In. | 38.00 |
| Royal Doulton, Plate, Kongshee & Chang Make Their Home, 9 1/2 In. | 35.00 |
| Royal Doulton, Plate, Luncheon, Cream, Gold Embossed Edge | 4.80 |
| Royal Doulton, Plate, Matsuma, 10 1/4 In. | 31.25 |
| Royal Doulton, Plate, Merry Wives Of Windsor, Black Border, 12 3/4 In. | 65.00 |
| Royal Doulton, Plate, Mounted Knights In Armor, Shield Border, 9 1/2 In. | 32.00 |
| Royal Doulton, Plate, Nursery Rhyme, Old Mother Goose | 12.00 |
| Royal Doulton, Plate, Persian, Flowers & Birds, Multicolors, 8 1/4 In. | 17.50 |
| Royal Doulton, Plate, Portia, Shakespeare Series, 6 1/2 In. | 16.00 |
| Royal Doulton, Plate, Portrait, George Washington, 10 In.Diameter | 29.00 |
| Royal Doulton, Plate, Quotes, 3 Fishermen, Isaac Walton Ware, Noke, 9 1/2 In. | 55.00 |
| Royal Doulton, Plate, Ride A Cock-Horse, 7 In. | 8.00 |
| Royal Doulton, Plate, Robert Burns, Blue, Blue Mark, Characters Around Rim | 35.00 |
| Royal Doulton, Plate, Roger Solem El Cobler, 10 1/2 In. | 20.00 |
| Royal Doulton, Plate, Romeo, Shakespeare Series, 10 In. | 23.00 |
| Royal Doulton, Plate, Rosalind, Shakespeare Series, 10 In. | 23.00 |
| Royal Doulton, Plate, Sairey Gamp | 28.50 |
| Royal Doulton, Plate, Salisbury Cathedral, 10 1/2 In. | 35.00 |
| Royal Doulton, Plate, Shakespeare, Romeo, 8 1/2 In. | 20.00 |
| Royal Doulton, Plate, Shakespeare, Sir Toby Belch, 12th Night, 10 1/4 In. | 40.00 |
| Royal Doulton, Plate, The Bear's Head Inn, Brereton, Acorn Rim, 10 1/2 In. | 38.00 |
| Royal Doulton, Plate, The Bookworm | 48.00 |
| Royal Doulton, Plate, The Coachman, 1902, 8 1/2 In. | 14.00 |
| Royal Doulton, Plate, The Doctor | 8.50 |
| Royal Doulton, Plate, The Gypsies, 10 1/2 In. | 32.50 |
| Royal Doulton, Plate, The Mayor, Rose, Black, Peack, & Yellow | 25.00 |
| Royal Doulton, Plate, The Parson, 10 1/4 In. | 22.00 To 27.50 |
| Royal Doulton, Plate, Titanian, Cockatiel, Heart, & Leaf, 8 1/2 In. | 56.00 |
| Royal Doulton, Plate, Under The Greenwood Tree, Scalloped, 10 1/2 In. | 40.00 |
| Royal Doulton, Plate, Wolsey, Shakespeare Series, 6 1/2 In. | 16.00 |
| Royal Doulton, Platter, Jackdaw Of Rheims, Bishop & Abbott & Prior, 13 In. | 50.00 |
| Royal Doulton, Potty, Child's, Tower, Signed Impressed Blue C Mark | 45.00 |
| Royal Doulton, Relish, Juliet, Shakespeare Series | 22.00 |
| Royal Doulton, Rose Bowl, Pierced Cover, Bird Finial, C.1902 | 45.00 |
| Royal Doulton, Stand, Cake, Tree Of Life, Hand-Painted, 8 3/4 In.Wide | 40.00 |
| Royal Doulton, Sugar, Covered, Black Country Scene On Gold, Handled, 5 In. | 55.00 |
| Royal Doulton, Sugar, Reynard, The Fox | 19.50 |
| Royal Doulton, Tankard, Oliver Twist, Raised Scenes, 1949 | 125.00 |
| Royal Doulton, Tankard, Orange British Lion On Black Leatherware | 75.00 |
| Royal Doulton, Tankard, Rugby Group On Brown, Double Handled, 1883, E.M. | 165.00 |
| Royal Doulton, Tankard, The Coachman | 28.50 |
| Royal Doulton, Tazza, Floral, Faience Base, Incised EB, 4 1/2 In.High | 85.00 |
| Royal Doulton, Tea Caddy, Dickensware, Mr.Pickwick, 5 1/4 In.High | 45.00 |
| Royal Doulton, Tea Caddy, Under The Greenwood Tree, Robin Hood Scenes | 35.00 |
| Royal Doulton, Tea Set, Blue & Olive Stoneware, 3 Piece | 110.00 |
| Royal Doulton, Tea Set, The Gleaners, 3 Piece | 55.00 |
| Royal Doulton, Tea Set, Zunday Zmocks, Australia, 3 Piece | 40.00 |
| Royal Doulton, Teacup & Saucer, Art Nouveau, Woodland Scene, Date 6-06 | 18.50 |
| Royal Doulton, Teapot, Dickensware, Bill Sykes, Signed Hoke | 65.00 |
| Royal Doulton, Teapot, Lord Nelson Medallion, Rope & Ships, C.1905 | 65.00 |
| Royal Doulton, Tile, Tea, Ito | 15.00 |
| Royal Doulton, Tile, Tea, So They Canonized Him By The Name Of Jim Crow | 37.50 |
| Royal Doulton, Tobacco Jar, Gray & White, Eliza Simmance, 6 1/2 In.High | 150.00 |
| Royal Doulton, Toby Mug, Apothecary | 6.50 To 9.50 |
| Royal Doulton, Toby Mug, Aramis, 4 In. | 8.00 |

Royal Doulton, Toby Mug, Aramis, 4 1/2 In. ............................................................................ 9.50
Royal Doulton, Toby Mug, Athos ............................................................................ 6.50 To 9.50
Royal Doulton, Toby Mug, Auld Mac, 2 1/4 In. ...................................................... 20.00
Royal Doulton, Toby Mug, Bacchus, Miniature ........................................................ 6.95
Royal Doulton, Toby Mug, Beefeater, 3 1/2 In. ...................................................... 19.00
Royal Doulton, Toby Mug, Blacksmith, Miniature ................................................... 6.00
Royal Doulton, Toby Mug, Bootmaker, Miniature .................................................... 6.50
Royal Doulton, Toby Mug, Captain Ahab, 7 In. ...................................................... 16.50
Royal Doulton, Toby Mug, Captain Cuttle, Small Size ............................................. 37.50
Royal Doulton, Toby Mug, Captain Henry Morgan, Miniature ................................... 6.95
Royal Doulton, Toby Mug, Cardinal, Marked A, Large Size ..................................... 60.00
Royal Doulton, Toby Mug, Cardinal, Marked A, 3 1/2 In. ....................................... 37.50
Royal Doulton, Toby Mug, Cavalier, A Mark, 3 1/2 In.High .................................... 32.00
Royal Doulton, Toby Mug, Cavalier, 6 1/2 In.High .................................................. 35.00
Royal Doulton, Toby Mug, Charley, Green 5 Mark, 2 1/2 In.High ........................... 18.00
Royal Doulton, Toby Mug, Churchill, 1940, 5 1/2 In. .............................................. 30.00
Royal Doulton, Toby Mug, Dick Turpin, Black Mark, 2 1/4 In. ............................... 22.50
Royal Doulton, Toby Mug, Dr.Johnson .................................................................... 30.00
Royal Doulton, Toby Mug, Drake, A Mark, 3 In. .................................................... 35.00
Royal Doulton, Toby Mug, Falconer, Small Size ...................................................... 9.50
Royal Doulton, Toby Mug, Falstaff, 7 In. ............................................................... 16.50
Royal Doulton, Toby Mug, Fat Boy, Full Figured .................................................... 45.00
Royal Doulton, Toby Mug, Fat Boy, Miniature ........................................................ 28.00
Royal Doulton, Toby Mug, Gardner, Miniature ....................................................... 6.75
Royal Doulton, Toby Mug, Goaler, Miniature .......................................................... 6.50
Royal Doulton, Toby Mug, Goaler, Small Size ........................................................ 9.95
Royal Doulton, Toby Mug, Gone Away, Fox Handle, 9 In. ...................................... 30.00
Royal Doulton, Toby Mug, Gone Away, Miniature ................................................... 6.75
Royal Doulton, Toby Mug, Granny, Small Size ........................................................ 9.00
Royal Doulton, Toby Mug, Gunsmith, Small Size .................................................... 9.00
Royal Doulton, Toby Mug, Honest Measure ............................................................ 11.00
Royal Doulton, Toby Mug, John Barleycorn, A Mark, 3 1/2 In. .................... 18.00 To 35.00
Royal Doulton, Toby Mug, John Barleycorn, A Mark, 6 1/4 In. ............................... 75.00
Royal Doulton, Toby Mug, John Peel, Large Size .................................................... 60.00
Royal Doulton, Toby Mug, John Peel, 3 1/4 In.High ............................................... 27.50
Royal Doulton, Toby Mug, King George, Signed Carruthers Gould ........................... 125.00
Royal Doulton, Toby Mug, Lawyer, Miniature ......................................................... 6.95
Royal Doulton, Toby Mug, Lawyer, Small Size ....................................................... 9.50
Royal Doulton, Toby Mug, Lobsterman, Small Size ................................................. 9.95
Royal Doulton, Toby Mug, Long John Silver, 6 1/4 In. ........................................... 35.00
Royal Doulton, Toby Mug, Lord Nelson .................................................................. 120.00
Royal Doulton, Toby Mug, Lumberjack, 7 In. .......................................................... 16.50
Royal Doulton, Toby Mug, Mad Hatter, Small Size ................................................. 9.50
Royal Doulton, Toby Mug, Mad Hatter, 7 In. .......................................................... 16.50
Royal Doulton, Toby Mug, Marlin, Small Size ........................................................ 9.50
Royal Doulton, Toby Mug, Mine Host, Miniature .................................................... 6.50
Royal Doulton, Toby Mug, Mine Host, 7 In. ........................................................... 16.50
Royal Doulton, Toby Mug, Monty, A Mark, 6 In.High ............................................ 60.00
Royal Doulton, Toby Mug, Monty, Large Size ......................................................... 45.00
Royal Doulton, Toby Mug, Motorist, Miniature ....................................................... 6.75
Royal Doulton, Toby Mug, Motorist, Small Size ..................................................... 9.95
Royal Doulton, Toby Mug, Mr.Micawber, Small Size .............................................. 28.50
Royal Doulton, Toby Mug, Mr.Micawber, 2 1/2 In.High ......................................... 19.00
Royal Doulton, Toby Mug, Mr.Pickwick, Small Size ............................................... 32.50
Royal Doulton, Toby Mug, Neptune, Miniature ...................................................... 6.75
Royal Doulton, Toby Mug, Night Watchman, Miniature .......................................... 6.50
Royal Doulton, Toby Mug, Night Watchman, 7 In. ................................................. 23.00
Royal Doulton, Toby Mug, North American Indian, Small Size ................................ 9.95
Royal Doulton, Toby Mug, Old Charley, Large Size ................................................ 45.00
Royal Doulton, Toby Mug, Old Charley, Marked A, 2 1/4 In. .................................. 25.00
Royal Doulton, Toby Mug, Old Charley, Small Size ................................................ 35.00
Royal Doulton, Toby Mug, Old Charley, 3 1/2 In. ................................................... 16.50
Royal Doulton, Toby Mug, Old King Cole, Small Size ............................................. 37.50
Royal Doulton, Toby Mug, Old Salt, Large Size ..................................................... 35.00
Royal Doulton, Toby Mug, Old Salt, Small Size ..................................................... 9.00
Royal Doulton, Toby Mug, Paddy, Miniature .......................................................... 25.00

| | |
|---|---:|
| Royal Doulton, Toby Mug, Paddy, 3 In. | 20.00 |
| Royal Doulton, Toby Mug, Parson Brown | 55.00 |
| Royal Doulton, Toby Mug, Parson Brown, A Mark, 4 In.High | 35.00 |
| Royal Doulton, Toby Mug, Pied Piper, Miniature | 6.75 |
| Royal Doulton, Toby Mug, Poacher, Miniature | 6.95 |
| Royal Doulton, Toby Mug, Poacher, 7 In. | 16.50 |
| Royal Doulton, Toby Mug, Porthos, Miniature | 6.50 |
| Royal Doulton, Toby Mug, Rip Van Winkle, Miniature | 37.00 |
| Royal Doulton, Toby Mug, Robin Hood, Miniature | 6.75 |
| Royal Doulton, Toby Mug, Sairey Gamp, Marked A, 3 1/4 In. | 28.00 |
| Royal Doulton, Toby Mug, Sairey Gamp, Marked A, 6 1/2 In. | 40.00 |
| Royal Doulton, Toby Mug, Sairey Gamp, Miniature | 6.50 |
| Royal Doulton, Toby Mug, Sam Weller, Date 1939, 3 1/2 In.High | 32.00 |
| Royal Doulton, Toby Mug, Simon The Cellarer, A Mark | 60.00 |
| Royal Doulton, Toby Mug, Sleuth, Miniature | 6.00 |
| Royal Doulton, Toby Mug, Smuggler, Small Size | 9.50 |
| Royal Doulton, Toby Mug, Smuggler, 4 In. | 12.00 |
| Royal Doulton, Toby Mug, Tam-O'-Shanter, Miniature | 6.75 |
| Royal Doulton, Toby Mug, Tam-O'-Shanter, Small Size | 9.95 |
| Royal Doulton, Toby Mug, Tam-O'-Shanter, 7 In. | 16.50 |
| Royal Doulton, Toby Mug, The Gardner, 7 In. | 16.50 |
| Royal Doulton, Toby Mug, The Jolly Toby, 6 In. | 13.50 |
| Royal Doulton, Toby Mug, The Motorist, 7 In. | 16.50 |
| Royal Doulton, Toby Mug, Toby Philpot, Miniature | 32.50 |
| Royal Doulton, Toby Mug, Tony Weller, Dickensware, Signed Noke, 6 3/4 In. | 85.00 |
| Royal Doulton, Toby Mug, Tony Weller, Small Size | 32.50 |
| Royal Doulton, Toby Mug, Tony Weller, 2 1/4 In.High | 25.00 |
| Royal Doulton, Toby Mug, Town Crier, Miniature | 6.50 |
| Royal Doulton, Toby Mug, Ugly Duchess, Miniature | 11.00 |
| Royal Doulton, Toby Mug, Ugly Duchess, Set Of 3 Sizes | 78.00 |
| Royal Doulton, Toby Mug, Vicar Of Bray, Large Size | 90.00 |
| Royal Doulton, Toby Mug, Viking, Miniature | 6.95 |
| Royal Doulton, Toby Mug, Winston Churchill, Large Size | 20.00 |
| Royal Doulton, Toby Mug, Winston Churchill, Medium Size | 15.00 |
| Royal Doulton, Tray, Dickensware, Barkis, 11 X 6 In. | 45.00 |
| Royal Doulton, Tray, Pin, Canterbury Pilgrims | 15.00 |
| Royal Doulton, Tray, Pin, Dickensware, Mr.Micawber | 22.00 |
| Royal Doulton, Tumbler, Bunnykins, Hobbyhorse | 16.50 |
| Royal Doulton, Tumbler, Hunt Scene, Riders Following Dogs, 3 In.High | 18.50 |
| Royal Doulton, Vase, Art Nouveau Decoration In Blue On White, 6 In. | 22.00 |
| Royal Doulton, Vase, Art Nouveau, Blue, Green, & Gray, Signed, 7 1/2 In.High | 38.00 |
| Royal Doulton, Vase, Children's, Lady And Child, 8 In.High | 80.00 |
| Royal Doulton, Vase, Colored Floral On Brown, 8 1/2 In.High | 30.00 |
| Royal Doulton, Vase, Dickensware, Alfred Jungle, Inverted Trumpet Shape | 18.50 |
| Royal Doulton, Vase, Falstaff, Anna Page, 8 In.High, Pair | 85.00 |
| Royal Doulton, Vase, Figure Of Anne Page, Handled, 11 3/4 In. | 58.00 |
| Royal Doulton, Vase, Figure Of Rosalind, Handled, 11 3/4 In. | 58.00 |
| Royal Doulton, Vase, Flambe, Sung Veined, 6 In.High | 42.00 |
| Royal Doulton, Vase, Flambe, Sung, 10 In.High | 115.00 |
| Royal Doulton, Vase, Flambe, 11 In. | 85.00 |
| Royal Doulton, Vase, Flambe, 2 In.Sterling Collar, 15 In.High | 225.00 |
| Royal Doulton, Vase, Flambe, 6 In. | 50.00 |
| Royal Doulton, Vase, Mink, Signed Noke, 9 In.High | 42.00 |
| Royal Doulton, Vase, Mother Goose, 2 1/2 In. | 18.00 |
| Royal Doulton, Vase, Stoneware, Frank Pope, 7 In.High | 65.00 |
| Royal Doulton, Vase, Three Little Girls Lost In The Woods, 13 1/2 In.High | 110.00 |
| Royal Doulton, Washstand Set, Watchman, What Of The Night, 1902, 2 Piece | 150.00 |
| Royal Doulton, Water Set, Carriage Scenes On Beige, 5 Piece | 75.00 |

*Royal Dux is a Czechoslovakian pottery made at the turn of the twentieth century. Unfortunately, reproductions are now appearing on the market.*

| | |
|---|---:|
| Royal Dux, Basket, Figure On One Side Of Handle, Signed, 8 In. High | 145.00 |
| Royal Dux, Figurine, Beetle, Blue Mark, 6 X 3 1/2 In. | 62.00 |
| Royal Dux, Figurine, Man & Woman Artists, Sitting, Decorating Pottery, Pair | 295.00 |
| Royal Dux, Figurine, Man & Woman In Mediterranean Clothes, 9 In.Pair | 350.00 |
| Royal Dux, Figurine, Stalking Lioness, Beige, Oval Gold Flecked Base | 165.00 |

| | |
|---|---|
| Royal Dux, Group, Dogs, 1 Seated, 1 Standing, 15 X 10 1/2 X 7 In. | 195.00 |
| Royal Dux, Group, Pair Of Dogs Facing Each Other, Standing & Seated, 12 In. | 250.00 |
| Royal Dux, Tray Dish, Girl Holding Boy In Her Arms, Cat, Floral, 17 In.Long | 285.00 |
| Royal Dux, Vase, Art Nouveau Lady, Floral Garlands, 15 In., Pair | 265.00 |
| Royal Dux, Vase, Art Nouveau, Yellows & Gold, 6 In. | 35.00 |
| Royal Dux, Vase, Bisque Finish, Marked, 7 In.High | 50.00 |
| Royal Dux, Vase, Green Grapes On Cream, Pink Triangle Mark, 12 In.High | 67.50 |

*Royal Flemish glass was made during the late 1880s in New Bedford, Massachusetts, by the Mt.Washington Glass Works. It is a colored satin glass decorated in dark colors with gold designs.*

| | |
|---|---|
| Royal Flemish, Box, Covered, Flying Cranes Decoration | 1050.00 |
| Royal Flemish, Cookie Jar, Coin | 1275.00 |
| Royal Flemish, Vase, Allover Flowers, Tall, Signed | 1250.00 |

*Royal Rudolstadt, a German faience factory, was established in Thuringia, Germany, in 1721. Hard paste porcelain was made by E.Bohne after 1854. Late nineteenth and early twentieth-century pieces are most commonly found today. The later mark is a shield with the letters RW inside superseded by a crown and the words Royal Rudolstadt.*
*Late nineteenth, and early twentieth-century pieces most commonly found today. The later mark is a shield with the letters RW inside superceded by a crown and the words Royal Rudolstadt.*

**Royal Rudolstadt, see also Kewpie**

| | |
|---|---|
| Royal Rudolstadt, Bowl, Handled, Blue Floral On Light Blue To White, 7 In. | 13.00 |
| Royal Rudolstadt, Chocolate Set, Gold Handle, Roses On Cream, 11 Piece | 200.00 |
| Royal Rudolstadt, Chocolate Set, White Roses & Holly, Gold Trim, 13 Piece | 125.00 |
| Royal Rudolstadt, Creamer, Floral On Biscuit Color, Vine Handle, Green Mark | 18.00 |
| Royal Rudolstadt, Dish, Candy, Clover Shape, Mauve Roses On Cream, Rodin | 12.50 |
| Royal Rudolstadt, Dish, Cheese & Cracker, Tinted Roses, 12 In.Long | 18.00 |
| Royal Rudolstadt, Jar, Sweetmeat, Covered, Handle | 95.00 |
| Royal Rudolstadt, Pitcher, Figural | 22.00 |
| Royal Rudolstadt, Plate, American Beauty Rose, Gold Scalloped Edge, 6 In. | 6.50 |
| Royal Rudolstadt, Plate, Happy Fats, 5 1/4 In. | 17.00 |
| Royal Rudolstadt, Plate, Pink Poppy On Soft Green, Signed, 8 1/2 In. | 22.50 |
| Royal Rudolstadt, Plate, Tulip, Pink To Cerise, Gold Trim, 8 1/2 In. | 18.00 |
| Royal Rudolstadt, Sugar & Creamer, Roses On Lavender & Yellow Ground | 22.00 |
| Royal Rudolstadt, Sugar, Happy Fats, Covered | 22.50 |
| Royal Rudolstadt, Toby Mug, Negro, Bulging Eyes, Long Nails, 4 1/4 In. | 95.00 |
| Royal Rudolstadt, Vase, Woman On Red Blanket Near Water On Cobalt Blue | 95.00 |

*Royal Vienna was established in Vienna by Claude Innocentius du Paquier in 1719. The factory closed in 1865. Since then, various German and Austrian factories have reproduced Royal Vienna wares, complete with the original beehive mark.*

| | |
|---|---|
| Royal Vienna, Box, Hinged, Center Figures Medallion, Brass Bound, Kauffmann | 30.00 |
| Royal Vienna, Cabaret Set, Demitasse, Pastoral, Wine Red, Gilt, 13 Piece | 350.00 |
| Royal Vienna, Cabaret Set, Gold & Pink On Blue, Kauffmann, 6 Piece | 175.00 |
| Royal Vienna, Candlestick, Classical Medallion, Gold Trim, Kauffmann, Pair | 75.00 |
| Royal Vienna, Cream Pot, Mulberry & Gold Band Tracery, Grecian Ladies | 125.00 |
| Royal Vienna, Cup & Saucer, Angelica Kauffmann Scene, Gold, Footed, C.1750 | 37.50 |
| Royal Vienna, Pitcher, Classical Figures Center Medallion, Kauffmann | 65.00 |
| Royal Vienna, Pitcher, Medallion On Pink & Blue, A.Kauffmann, 3 1/2 In. | 20.00 |
| Royal Vienna, Pitcher, Medallion On Pink & Blue, A.Kauffmann, 4 1/2 In. | 22.00 |
| Royal Vienna, Pitcher, Medallion On Pink & Blue, A.Kauffmann, 5 1/4 In. | 25.00 |
| Royal Vienna, Plate, Alhambra, 9 1/2 In. | 20.00 |
| Royal Vienna, Plate, Classical Amorous Scene, Gold, Beehive, 9 1/2 In. | 55.00 |
| Royal Vienna, Plate, Classical Dancers, Gold Scrolls, Kauffmann, 11 1/2 In. | 75.00 |
| Royal Vienna, Plate, Double Roses, Gold Beaded Edge, Scalloped, 9 3/4 In. | 88.00 |
| Royal Vienna, Plate, Drei Parzen, C.1890, 9 7/8 In. ......*Illus* | 300.00 |
| Royal Vienna, Plate, Hansel & Gretel, C.1890, 9 1/2 In. ......*Illus* | 275.00 |
| Royal Vienna, Plate, Heavy Gold Decoration, 9 1/2 In. | 28.50 |
| Royal Vienna, Plate, Kauffmann Center, Maroon Border, Roses, Gold, 12 In. | 75.00 |
| Royal Vienna, Plate, Lady & 3 Cherubs, Cobalt & Gold Border, 9 1/2 In. | 185.00 |
| Royal Vienna, Plate, Leaf Shape, Gadroons Of Roses, C.1850, Arm & Sword Mark | 35.00 |
| Royal Vienna, Plate, Meditation, C.1890, 9 5/8 In. ......*Illus* | 275.00 |
| Royal Vienna, Plate, Ornate Green & Red Border, Medallion Of Girl, 6 In. | 45.00 |
| Royal Vienna, Plate, Portrait, Amorosa, Blue Beehive Mark, 9 1/2 In. | 75.00 |

Royal Vienna, Plate,
Meditation, C.1890,
9 5/8 In.
(See Page 530)

Royal Vienna, Plate,
Hansel & Gretel,
C.1890, 9 1/2 In.
(See Page 530)

Royal Vienna, Plate,
Drei Parzen, C.1890,
9 7/8 In.
(See Page 530)

Royal Vienna, Plate,
Princess Louise,
C.1890, 9 7/8 In.

Royal Vienna, Plate,
Raucher, C.1890,
9 3/4 In.

Royal Vienna, Plate,
Ruth, C.1890, 9 7/8 In.

| | |
|---|---|
| Royal Vienna, Plate, Portrait, Angelus, Gold Tracery, Burgundy, 9 3/4 In. | 40.00 |
| Royal Vienna, Plate, Portrait, Brunette, Amorosa, Beehive, 8 3/4 In. | 65.00 |
| Royal Vienna, Plate, Princess Louise, C.1890, 9 7/8 In. _Illus_ | 300.00 |
| Royal Vienna, Plate, Raphael's Madonna Of The Chair, Beehive | 100.00 |
| Royal Vienna, Plate, Raucher, C.1890, 9 3/4 In. _Illus_ | 250.00 |
| Royal Vienna, Plate, Ruth, C.1890, 9 7/8 In. _Illus_ | 300.00 |
| Royal Vienna, Urn & Plate, Center Medallion Of Woman & Cherub, Kauffmann | 125.00 |
| Royal Vienna, Vase, Lady With Flowers In Her Hair, Gold Handles, Wagner | 135.00 |
| Royal Vienna, Vase, Turquoise Jewels On Pink Lavender & Gold, Wagner | 850.00 |
| Royal Vienna, Vase, Woman & Cupids On Maroon, Gold Neck, Signed Wagner | 175.00 |

*Royal Worcester porcelain was made in the later period of Worcester
pottery which was originally established in 1751. The Royal Worcester
trade name has been used by Worcester Royal Porcelain Company, Ltd.,
since 1862.*

**Royal Worcester, see also Worcester**

| | |
|---|---|
| Royal Worcester, Basket, Peach Basket Weave, 3 In.High | 30.00 |
| Royal Worcester, Bowl, Bird With Outstretched Wings On Pedestal, 1906 | 87.00 |
| Royal Worcester, Bowl, Magnolia, Pale Green Leaves & Buds, 2 1/2 In.High | 35.00 |
| Royal Worcester, Bowl, Multicolor Floral & Gold On Cream, 4 In.High | 55.00 |
| Royal Worcester, Bowl, Square, Gilt & Red Berries, Purple Mark, 8 In.Square | 45.00 |
| Royal Worcester, Box, Covered, Florals On Cream, 2 3/4 In. | 27.50 |
| Royal Worcester, Cake Stand, Moss Roses On Cream, Gold, Grainger, 1893 | 135.00 |
| Royal Worcester, Candlesnuffer, Cone Shape Welsh Hat, Yellow Trim, 1901 | 49.50 |
| Royal Worcester, Candlesnuffer, Monk In Brown Robe | 32.00 To 35.00 |
| Royal Worcester, Candlesnuffer, Mr.Caudel, Glazed Parian | 130.00 |
| Royal Worcester, Candlesnuffer, Standing Nun, Decorated China | 100.00 To 135.00 |
| Royal Worcester, Creamer, Bamboo Trim, No.1196 | 45.00 |
| Royal Worcester, Creamer, Bird With Foliage, 2 1/2 In. | 12.50 |
| Royal Worcester, Creamer, Floral Ewers, 4 3/4 In. | 40.00 |
| Royal Worcester, Creamer, Gold Handle & Trim, Yellow Glaze, C.1862 | 45.00 |
| Royal Worcester, Creamer, Sparrow Beak, Ribbed, Yellow Roses On White | 25.00 |

| | |
|---|---|
| Royal Worcester, Cup & Saucer, Demitasse, Bisque Medallions, Pink, Gold | 28.00 |
| Royal Worcester, Cup & Saucer, Demitasse, Pink Flowers & Green Sprigs | 10.00 |
| Royal Worcester, Cup & Saucer, Floral Ewers | 32.00 |
| Royal Worcester, Cup & Saucer, Florals On Cream | 32.00 |
| Royal Worcester, Cup & Saucer, Gold Paste Leaves & Berries On Ivory, 1886 | 42.00 |
| Royal Worcester, Egg Coddler, Blue Willow | 16.00 |
| Royal Worcester, Ewer, Floral, Gold Handle, Raised Design At Base, C.1893 | 95.00 |
| Royal Worcester, Figurine, August, Freda Doughty, Months Of Year Series | 10.00 |
| Royal Worcester, Figurine, Dutch Boy, F.Gertner, Purple Mark, 5 1/4 In.High | 49.50 |
| Royal Worcester, Figurine, Grotesque Fish, Gaping Mouth, Sabrina Ware, 1912 | 140.00 |
| Royal Worcester, Figurine, January, 1953, F.Doughty | 44.00 |
| Royal Worcester, Figurine, July, 1953, F.Doughty | 44.00 |
| Royal Worcester, Figurine, Lady In Grecian Dress, 14 In.High | 265.00 |
| Royal Worcester, Figurine, Liberty, C.1908 | 110.00 |
| Royal Worcester, Figurine, Saturday's Girl | 50.00 |
| Royal Worcester, Figurine, Seated Indian, Turban, Parnell, 1936 | 65.00 |
| Royal Worcester, Figurine, Short-Haired Gray Cat | 12.00 |
| Royal Worcester, Figurine, Sunday's Child | 50.00 |
| Royal Worcester, Figurine, Terrier Dog, White & Brown, 3 In. | 35.00 |
| Royal Worcester, Figurine, Wednesday's Child, 6 3/4 In.High | 75.00 |
| Royal Worcester, Flower Holder, Pompeiian, Double, Male & Female Heads | 200.00 |
| Royal Worcester, Jar & Underplate, Cracker, Multicolor Floral, Gold, 7 In. | 250.00 |
| Royal Worcester, Lamp, 16 In. Base, 28 In. High | 95.00 |
| Royal Worcester, Menu Holder, Beige, 4 In.High | 32.00 |
| Royal Worcester, Mug, Florals On Cream, 2 Handles, Miniature | 25.00 |
| Royal Worcester, Pitcher, Floral & Gold On Cream White, 6 1/2 In.High | 95.00 |
| Royal Worcester, Pitcher, Flowers On Cream Ground, Bulbous, Gilt Edge, 6 In. | 105.00 |
| Royal Worcester, Pitcher, Fruit Decoration, Miniature, 1 1/2 In.High | 25.00 |
| Royal Worcester, Pitcher, Gold Handle & Trim, Floral On Cream, 5 3/4 In. | 65.00 |
| Royal Worcester, Pitcher, Gold Lion's Head Spout, Claw Handle, 1888, 5 In. | 85.00 |
| Royal Worcester, Pitcher, Gold Reeded Handle, Floral On Cream, 8 In. | 85.00 |
| Royal Worcester, Pitcher, Milk, Blue Pagodas On White, Gold Twig Handle | 55.00 |
| Royal Worcester, Pitcher, Pink, Yellow, & Blue Floral & Gold On Cream, 1887 | 38.00 |
| Royal Worcester, Pitcher, Poppies, Gold & Blue, Black Mark, 10 In. High | 150.00 |
| Royal Worcester, Pitcher, Roses & Floral On Pink & Blue, 1904, 7 1/4 In. | 125.00 |
| Royal Worcester, Pitcher, White Ground, Chinese Scenes, 1883, 5 1/2 In.High | 63.50 |
| Royal Worcester, Place Setting, Lavinia, Ivory, Blackberries On Rims | 22.00 |
| Royal Worcester, Plate, Basket Of Flowers, Gold Rim, 10 1/2 In. | 45.00 |
| Royal Worcester, Plate, Bridge, Pagoda, & Figures, C.1911, 9 In. | 22.50 |
| Royal Worcester, Plate, Floral On Cream, Black & Gold Edge, 9 1/4 In. | 12.00 |
| Royal Worcester, Plate, Floral On White, Pink Border, C.1875, 8 3/4 In. | 17.50 |
| Royal Worcester, Plate, Flowers On Cream, Purple Mark, 7 In. | 29.00 |
| Royal Worcester, Plate, Flowers On Cream, Purple Mark, 8 1/2 In. | 39.00 |
| Royal Worcester, Plate, Mayor & Wife Of Worcester Portraits, Lavender, 1896 | 27.50 |
| Royal Worcester, Plate, Portrait, Worcester Mayor & Mayoress, 1896 | 27.50 |
| Royal Worcester, Plate, Royal Blue Concentric Floral, Gilt, C.1850, 10 In. | 40.00 |
| Royal Worcester, Platter, Japan, For Mortlocks, 1880 | 44.00 |
| Royal Worcester, Pot & Tray, Punch, Covered, No.1380 | 245.00 |
| Royal Worcester, Rose Bowl, Ships, Artist Signed, Purple Mark, 3 1/2 In. | 150.00 |
| Royal Worcester, Shell, Spiral, Gold Trim On Tan, Dated 1913, 5 In. Long | 55.00 |
| Royal Worcester, Sugar & Creamer, Cover, Floral On Pale Yellow, Purple Mark | 150.00 |
| Royal Worcester, Sugar, Covered, Multicolor Floral, C.1890, 4 1/2 In. | 67.50 |
| Royal Worcester, Tea Set, Child's, Oriental, 6 Piece | 32.00 |
| Royal Worcester, Teacup & Saucer, Gold & Pewter Cranes & Foliage On Blue | 50.00 |
| Royal Worcester, Teapot, Bamboo Trim, No.1196 | 85.00 |
| Royal Worcester, Teapot, Dragon Handle, Mouth Spout, Footed, Birds, 1913 | 225.00 |
| Royal Worcester, Teapot, Florals, Gold Trim, Beige Satin, 4 Cup Size | 110.00 |
| Royal Worcester, Toby Mug, Man, Tricorn Hat, Orange Vest, Blue, 3 1/2 In. | 20.00 |
| Royal Worcester, Tray, 2 Birds On Branches On Satin Beige, Gold Handles | 80.00 |
| Royal Worcester, Tureen, Soup, Chicken Finial, Blue & White, Oriental Style | 105.00 |
| Royal Worcester, Tureen, Soup, Covered, Pedestal, Tan Floral On White, C.1890 | 35.00 |
| Royal Worcester, Urn Vase, Decorated, 11 1/2 X 5 In. | 139.00 |
| Royal Worcester, Urn, Pierced Edge, Gold Handled, Church & Steeple, C.1896 | 350.00 |
| Royal Worcester, Urn, Pierced, Handled, Stratford On Avon Scene, 1896 | 350.00 |
| Royal Worcester, Vase, Ball Shape, Long Neck, Floral & Birds On Beige, 1899 | 80.50 |
| Royal Worcester, Vase, Bottle, Pierced Cover, Persian Style, 1887, 14 3/4 In. | 325.00 |

| | |
|---|---:|
| Royal Worcester, Vase, Bud, Pink & Yellow Floral On Cream, Gold, C.1894 | 65.00 |
| Royal Worcester, Vase, Bud, Spherical, Floral & Gold On Cream, 1892 | 48.00 |
| Royal Worcester, Vase, Bulbous, Hand-Painted Ferns, Peach Tones, 1891, 5 In. | 55.00 |
| Royal Worcester, Vase, Cream, 2 Gold Handles, Floral Baskets, C.1900, 9 In. | 60.00 |
| Royal Worcester, Vase, Embossed Reliefwork, Gold & Silver Floral, 1889 | 325.00 |
| Royal Worcester, Vase, Hanging, Lily Shape, Floral & Berries, 1901 | 55.00 |
| Royal Worcester, Vase, Multicolor Floral On Biscuit Color, Dated 1872 | 80.00 |
| Royal Worcester, Vase, Multicolored Flowers On Cream, Gold Trim, 11 In. | 165.00 |
| Royal Worcester, Vase, Old Ivory & Gold, Signed With Crown, 8 In.High, Pair | 100.00 |
| Royal Worcester, Vase, Open Handles, Floral Bouquets, Gold, 1902, 9 3/4 In. | 185.00 |
| Royal Worcester, Vase, Openwork Handles, Poppies & Wheat On Cream, C.1892 | 200.00 |
| Royal Worcester, Vase, Pheasants In Landscape, Footed, 1909, 4 1/2 In. | 110.00 |
| Royal Worcester, Vase, Roses On White, Gold Trim, Purple Mark, 5 In. | 75.00 |
| Royal Worcester, Vase, Violet, Hand-Painted Flowers | 39.00 |

*Roycroft products were made by the Roycrofter community of East Aurora, New York, in the late nineteenth and early twentieth centuries. The community was founded by Elbert Hubbard. The products included furniture, metalware, leatherwork, and jewelry.*

| | |
|---|---:|
| Roycroft, Blotter, Rocker, Hammered Copper, Stylized Flowers, 6 In. Long | 15.00 |
| Roycroft, Desk Set, Copper, 4 Piece | 36.00 |
| Roycroft, Jug, Brown | 14.00 |
| Roycroft, Syrup, Maple, Tag Reads Roycrofters, East Aurora, N.Y | 7.50 |
| Rozenburg, Vase, Double Gourd Shape, Pansies & Iris On Brown, 12 5/8 In. | 350.00 |
| Rozenburg, Vase, Stylized Birds In Flight, 3 In.High | 275.00 |

*RS Germany porcelain was made at the factory of Rheinhold Schlegelmilch after 1869 in Tillowitz, Germany. It was sold both decorated and undecorated.*

**RS Germany, see also RS Prussia**

| | |
|---|---:|
| RS Germany, Bowl & Underplate, Dessert, Magnolias, Green Mark | 15.00 |
| RS Germany, Bowl, Basket Type, 3 Gold Handles, 3 Compartments, Blue Floral | 26.50 |
| RS Germany, Bowl, Coral Roses, Green Mark, 10 In.Diameter | 30.00 |
| RS Germany, Bowl, Open Handled, Oval, Poppies & Roses, Magenta & Gold, 12 In. | 38.50 |
| RS Germany, Bowl, Orange Luster, Flower Design, 9 In.Diameter | 22.00 |
| RS Germany, Bowl, Pastel Floral On Matte, 10 In. | 26.50 |
| RS Germany, Bowl, Pink Sweetpeas, Gold Trim, Signed, 10 In. | 22.50 |
| RS Germany, Bowl, Salad, Tea Roses, 10 In. | 24.00 |
| RS Germany, Bowl, Salad, White Roses On Violet Shading, 9 1/2 In. | 24.00 |
| RS Germany, Bowl, Scalloped, White Azaleas, Heavy Gold, Blue Mark, 10 In. | 25.00 |
| RS Germany, Box, Powder, Lift Off Lid, Pink & Burgundy Tulips, 3 1/4 In. | 13.50 |
| RS Germany, Celery, Embossed Gold Flower, 2 Incised Handles | 24.50 |
| RS Germany, Chocolate Pot, Lavender & Gold Floral, Gold Rims & Finial | 35.00 |
| RS Germany, Chocolate Pot, Ovoid, Hand-Painted Roses & Gold | 25.00 |
| RS Germany, Chocolate Set, Pink & Peach Tulips, Gold Trim, 12 Piece | 120.00 |
| RS Germany, Chocolate Set, White Tulips On Green Ground, Signed, 7 Piece | 110.00 |
| RS Germany, Creamer, Mother Of-Pearl Luster | 6.50 |
| RS Germany, Creamer, Roses On Cream, Gold Trim | 15.00 |
| RS Germany, Cup, Roses, Marked | 7.00 |
| RS Germany, Dish, Basket Shape, Handle, Orange, Mauve, & Blue Floral, 8 In. | 25.00 |
| RS Germany, Dish, Cracker & Cheese, White Rhododendrons On Green, Marked | 22.50 |
| RS Germany, Ferner, Panels Of Roses & Foliage, Hand-Painted, 7 In.Diameter | 40.00 |
| RS Germany, Hair Receiver, Embossed Gold Cover, Gold Rim, M.Stoddard, 1914 | 24.00 |
| RS Germany, Hair Receiver, Gold Decoration On White, Scalloped | 20.00 |
| RS Germany, Hair Receiver, Gold Trim On White, Black Mark | 12.50 |
| RS Germany, Hatpin Holder, Calla Lilies, Blue Mark | 20.00 |
| RS Germany, Hatpin Holder, Floral, Pink & White | 35.00 |
| RS Germany, Hatpin Holder, Two Orange Poppies On Tan & White | 24.00 |
| RS Germany, Hatpin Holder, White Lilies, D.B.Mark, 5 In.High | 32.00 |
| RS Germany, Hatpin Holder, White Roses | 20.00 |
| RS Germany, Inkwell, Pinecone Decoration, Marked | 45.00 |
| RS Germany, Jar, Cookie, White Ground, Green Flowers, Handles, Blue Mark | 58.00 |
| RS Germany, Jar, Cracker, Orange Poppies | 65.00 |
| RS Germany, Jar, Cracker, Violets | 65.00 |
| RS Germany, Knife Rest, Hand-Painted, Artist Signed, Ram's Head Ends | 18.00 |
| RS Germany, Lamp, Owl, Glass Eyes, Takes Candle, 2 Part, White, 5 In. | 80.00 |
| RS Germany, Mug, Shaving, Pink Roses, Gold Trim, Panels, Brown Wing Mark | 35.00 |
| RS Germany, Nappy, Pastel Flowers, Gold Trim, 7 1/2 X 4 1/2 In. | 22.00 |

RS Germany, Nut Set, Oval, Open Handles, Floral, Gold Tracery, 7 Piece .................... 35.00
RS Germany, Pitcher, Embossed Orchids & Roses On Green To Cream, Red Mark .................... 85.00
RS Germany, Pitcher, Milk, Floral & Gold Trim, Blue Mark, 7 In.Diameter .................... 75.00
RS Germany, Plate, Bread & Butter, White Floral On Green Shaded, Gold .................... 5.40
RS Germany, Plate, Browns & Pinks, Flower Design, 8 In. .................... 14.00
RS Germany, Plate, Cake, Apple Blossoms On Mother-Of-Pearl Satin, Gold .................... 40.00
RS Germany, Plate, Cake, Four Pink Rosebuds, 9 1/2 In. .................... 17.50
RS Germany, Plate, Cake, Handled, Pink & Yellow Roses, Gold Trim, 11 In. .................... 18.00
RS Germany, Plate, Cheese & Cracker, Apricot & Orange Roses, Gold, 9 3/4 In. .................... 18.50
RS Germany, Plate, Dessert, White Floral Center, Green Shaded .................... 5.00
RS Germany, Plate, Green, Flower Design, 8 1/2 In. .................... 14.00
RS Germany, Plate, Pink Flowers On Shaded Green, 6 1/2 In. .................... 4.50
RS Germany, Plate, Poppy Decoration, 6 In. .................... 4.75
RS Germany, Plate, Tulip, 6 In. .................... 8.00
RS Germany, Pot, Mustard, Brown & Pink Rose Decoration, Green & Gold Trim .................... 18.50
RS Germany, Relish, Turquoise & Gold Decoration, Open Handles, Signed .................... 14.00
RS Germany, Salt, Oval, Pink Roses & Gold Floral On White, Green Mark, 3 In. .................... 2.75
RS Germany, Sauce, Rose Decoration, 5 1/2 In. .................... 8.00
RS Germany, Sugar & Creamer, White Poppies On Blue Satin, Marked .................... 22.00
RS Germany, Sugar, Covered, Roses On Blue Border, Gold Handles & Finial .................... 8.50
RS Germany, Tea Set, Yellow Floral, Green Leaves, Ruffled, Gold, 3 Piece .................... 75.00
RS Germany, Toothpick, Gold Rim, Band, & 3 Handles, Yellow Roses, Green .................... 28.50
RS Germany, Toothpick, Yellow Roses, Three Handles, Marked .................... 35.00
RS Germany, Tray, Card, Open Handles, Red Roses & Gold, D.B.Mark .................... 28.00
RS Germany, Tray, Gold Embossed Decoration, Square, 4 In. .................... 8.00
RS Germany, Tray, Open Handles, White Lilies, Gold Trim, 7 3/4 X 3 3/4 In. .................... 30.00
RS Germany, Tray, Pin, Pink & White Floral On Tan To Beige .................... 10.00
RS Germany, Vase, Hand-Painted Wild Roses, 5 1/2 In. High .................... 15.00
RS Germany, Vase, Pink & White Floral On Blue & Pink, 2 Gold Handles .................... 20.00

*RS Prussia porcelain was made at the factory of Rheinhold Schlegelmilch after 1869 in Tillowitz, Germany. The porcelain was sold decorated or undecorated.*

RS Prussia, see also RS Germany
RS Prussia, Berry Set, Melon Boy, Red Mark, 7 Piece .................... 1100.00
RS Prussia, Berry Set, Roses, Red Mark, 7 Piece .................... 115.00
RS Prussia, Berry Set, Water & Water Lilies, Red Mark, 7 Pieces .................... 225.00
RS Prussia, Bowl, Berry, Cerise Panels, Roses Center, Red Mark, 10 1/2 In. .................... 75.00
RS Prussia, Bowl, Berry, White Iris, Green & White Ground, Red Mark .................... 95.00
RS Prussia, Bowl, Blossoms Center, Pink & Gold Irregular Edge, Red Mark .................... 85.00
RS Prussia, Bowl, Cerise Panels, Roses Center, Red Mark, 5 1/2 In. .................... 15.00
RS Prussia, Bowl, Embossed Cable Edge, Raised Scrolls, Floral, 8 1/2 In. .................... 61.00
RS Prussia, Bowl, Fluted Edge, Roses On Variegated, 3 Legs, 8 In. .................... 85.00
RS Prussia, Bowl, Fruit, Scalloped Rim, Gold, Pink, Green, & Yellow Floral .................... 70.00
RS Prussia, Bowl, Ivory & Gold Wild Roses On Green, Red Mark, 10 In. .................... 65.00
RS Prussia, Bowl, Lilies, Green & Gold Trim, Red Mark, 10 1/2 In. .................... 85.00
RS Prussia, Bowl, Lilies, Green & Gold Trim, 10 1/2 In.Diameter .................... 85.00
RS Prussia, Bowl, Men Loading Sailing Ships, Scalloped, Red Mark, 10 3/4 In. .................... 185.00
RS Prussia, Bowl, Petal Shape, Panels Of Blown-Out Floral On Blue, 10 In. .................... 54.00
RS Prussia, Bowl, Pink Roses, Scalloped Edges, Red Mark, 9 1/2 X 4 In. .................... 25.00
RS Prussia, Bowl, Portrait, Blonde Lady, Rococo Rim, Gold, Floral, Red Mark .................... 285.00
RS Prussia, Bowl, Reticulated Edge, Chrysanthemums, Gold, Ring Bottom, 9 In. .................... 45.00
RS Prussia, Bowl, Roses & Daisies On Green & Gold, 11 In. .................... 68.00
RS Prussia, Bowl, Swans, Satinized, Footed, 6 In. .................... 18.00
RS Prussia, Bowl, Yellow Floral On Pink, Gold Scalloped Edge, 10 1/2 In. .................... 37.50
RS Prussia, Bowl, Yellow Roses, Green, Embossed, Red Mark, 10 In. .................... 100.00
RS Prussia, Box, Four Seasons Portrait, Fall, Red Mark .................... 225.00
RS Prussia, Box, Powder, Covered, White Floral On Green, Red Mark .................... 40.00
RS Prussia, Box, White, Gold Trim, 3 1/2 X 2 In. .................... 29.00
RS Prussia, Celery, Cutout Handles, Pink & White Roses, 9 1/2 In. .................... 45.00
RS Prussia, Celery, Gold Outlined Green & White Cutout Handles, 13 In. .................... 75.00
RS Prussia, Celery, Jeweled, Open Ends, Roses & Gold On Purple, 12 1/2 In. .................... 75.00
RS Prussia, Celery, Lilies & Fern Center, Open Handled, Red Mark, 13 In.Long .................... 42.00
RS Prussia, Celery, Open Ends, Jeweled, Pink Roses On Purple, Red Mark .................... 75.00
RS Prussia, Celery, Open Handles, White Magnolias, Gold, Green, Red Star Mark .................... 65.00
RS Prussia, Celery, Roses, Satin Finish .................... 47.50

| | |
|---|---:|
| RS Prussia, Celery, Tray, Pink & White Roses, Scalloped Edge, 9 1/2 Long | 75.00 |
| RS Prussia, Chocolate Cup & Saucer, Pink Roses On White | 20.00 |
| RS Prussia, Chocolate Pot, Pink Roses On Shaded Green, Gold, Red Mark | 185.00 |
| RS Prussia, Chocolate Pot, Red Roses, Green & Gold Trim, Red Mark, 9 In. | 90.00 |
| RS Prussia, Chocolate Pot, Rose Sprays, Powder Blue Rim, Scalloped Base | 115.00 |
| RS Prussia, Chocolate Set, Floral, Pastel, Satin Finish, Red Mark, 3 Piece | 125.00 |
| RS Prussia, Chocolate Set, White Roses & Foliage, 9 Piece | 145.00 |
| RS Prussia, Creamer, Boy, Castle, & Trees, Floriform Lip, Footed, Red Mark | 110.00 |
| RS Prussia, Creamer, Covered, Roses & Daisies With Jeweled Gold Leaves | 78.00 |
| RS Prussia, Creamer, Covered, Roses & Daisies, Gold, Satin Finish, Red Mark | 48.00 |
| RS Prussia, Creamer, Floral, Red Mark | 38.50 |
| RS Prussia, Creamer, Fruit Decoration | 25.00 |
| RS Prussia, Creamer, Swan, Gold Beading, Water & Pine Trees, Red Mark | 85.00 |
| RS Prussia, Cup & Saucer, Chocolate, Melon Ribbed, 4 Footed, Roses, Red Mark | 22.00 |
| RS Prussia, Cup & Saucer, Chocolate, Pink Roses On White | 20.00 |
| RS Prussia, Cup & Saucer, Footed Cup, Melon Ribbed, Dogwood Blossoms | 42.00 |
| RS Prussia, Cup & Saucer, Green & White Flowers | 30.00 |
| RS Prussia, Cup & Saucer, Pink & White Flowers, Red Star Mark | 40.00 |
| RS Prussia, Cup, Satin Finish, White Roses | 10.00 |
| RS Prussia, Dish, Candy, 2 Snow Birds In Winter Scene, 3 Legs, Red Mark | 175.00 |
| RS Prussia, Dish, Ice Cream, Green, Lavender, & White Floral On Pearlized | 17.50 |
| RS Prussia, Dish, Pickle, Rococo Double Border, Dogwoods, 5 In.Long | 36.00 |
| RS Prussia, Dish, 10 1/2 In. *Illus* | 28.00 |
| RS Prussia, Dresser Set, Bluebirds, Scenic, Red Mark, 4 Piece | 685.00 |
| RS Prussia, Fernery, Pink Roses, Gold Beaded Rim, Red Mark, 6 1/2 In. | 85.00 |
| RS Prussia, Hair Receiver, Covered, Rose Decoration, Signed | 35.00 |
| RS Prussia, Hair Receiver, Floral On Beige, Gold Trim, Open Handles | 75.00 |
| RS Prussia, Hair Receiver, Green, White Flowers, Footed, Red Mark | 40.00 |
| RS Prussia, Hair Receiver, Pink Roses On Green, Scalloped Base, Red Mark | 55.00 |
| RS Prussia, Hair Receiver, Rose Decoration, Red Mark | 35.00 |
| RS Prussia, Hair Receiver, White Floral On Green, Footed, Red Mark | 40.00 |
| RS Prussia, Hair Receiver, White Flowers, Green Pine Boughs, Signed | 50.00 |
| RS Prussia, Hatpin Holder, Attached Covered Box, Floral On White, Red Mark | 100.00 |
| RS Prussia, Hatpin Holder, Cream & Green, Leaf Decoration, Square Top | 35.00 |
| RS Prussia, Hatpin Holder, Pink Flowers & White Daisies On Green To White | 75.00 |
| RS Prussia, Hatpin Holder, Pink Roses On Green, Scalloped Base, Red Mark | 95.00 |
| RS Prussia, Hatpin Holder, Roses & Hydrangeas, Red Mark, 4 1/2 In. | 75.00 |
| RS Prussia, Jar, Cracker, Bulbous, Green, White, & Gold, Lid | 88.00 |
| RS Prussia, Muffineer, Paneled, Scalloped Top & Base, Floral, 4 3/4 In.High | 75.00 |
| RS Prussia, Muffineer, Pastel Roses, Red Mark, 4 3/4 In.High | 75.00 |
| RS Prussia, Muffineer, Roses, Snowballs & Floral On Cream & Lavender | 85.00 |
| RS Prussia, Muffineer, Scalloped Top, Green & White, Red Star, 5 In. | 85.00 |
| RS Prussia, Pitcher, Milk, Floral Decoration | 235.00 |
| RS Prussia, Pitcher, Pinks & Greens On Yellow, Red Mark | 250.00 |
| RS Prussia, Plate, Autumn Portrait, Girl Medallion, Open Handled, Gold | 235.00 |
| RS Prussia, Plate, Beige Floral | 49.00 |
| RS Prussia, Plate, Bread, Open Handles, Pink, Wild Flowers, Embossed Edge | 75.00 |
| RS Prussia, Plate, Cake, Lilies Of The Valley, Scalloped, Gold Tracery | 175.00 |
| RS Prussia, Plate, Cake, Open Handles, Poppies On White, Red Mark | 95.00 |

Rs Prussia, Dish, 10 1/2 In.

| | |
|---|---|
| RS Prussia, Plate, Cake, Open Handles, Scalloped, White & Pink Bouquets | 45.00 |
| RS Prussia, Plate, Cake, Poppies, Greens, Raised Silver Decoration | 95.00 |
| RS Prussia, Plate, Cake, Satin Finish, Open Handles, Signed | 95.00 |
| RS Prussia, Plate, Cake, Scalloped, Open Handle, Lilies, 10 In., Red Mark | 80.00 |
| RS Prussia, Plate, Carnations, 8 1/2 In. | 35.00 |
| RS Prussia, Plate, Cobalt & Blue Floral On White, Steeple Mark, 7 1/2 In. | 32.50 |
| RS Prussia, Plate, Fruit Center, 8 In. | 75.00 |
| RS Prussia, Plate, Gold & Cobalt Floral On White, Steeple Mark, 7 1/2 In. | 32.50 |
| RS Prussia, Plate, Gold Beading, Jeweled, Rose Bouquet, 8 1/2 In. | 55.00 |
| RS Prussia, Plate, Gold Floral Spray On Pearlized, Schlegelmilch, 7 1/2 In. | 20.00 |
| RS Prussia, Plate, Gold Open Handles, Scupltured Overlaping Flowers, 11 In. | 65.00 |
| RS Prussia, Plate, Green Floral Swags, Irregular Gold Rim, 8 1/2 In. | 15.00 |
| RS Prussia, Plate, Lily Of The Valley, Gold Scalloped Edge, 6 1/4 In. | 26.50 |
| RS Prussia, Plate, Melon Boys Counting Pennies, Lilies, Gold Rim, Marked | 300.00 |
| RS Prussia, Plate, Melon Boy, Crap Shooters, Red Mark, 8 1/2 In. | 350.00 |
| RS Prussia, Plate, Melon Boy, Red Mark, 7 In. | 150.00 |
| RS Prussia, Plate, Mill Scene, Red Mark | 185.00 |
| RS Prussia, Plate, Pheasants, Wooded Scene, Rococo Rim, Red Mark, 7 1/2 In. | 125.00 |
| RS Prussia, Plate, Pink & White Roses On Golden Shading, Red Mark, 8 In. | 45.00 |
| RS Prussia, Plate, Pink & White Roses, Scalloped Edge, Red Mark, 6 In. | 35.00 |
| RS Prussia, Plate, Pink Roses & White Daisies, Pierced Handles, 10 In. | 85.00 |
| RS Prussia, Plate, Portrait, 18th Century Courting Scene, Scalloped, 6 In. | 10.00 |
| RS Prussia, Plate, Seasons Medallions, Ship Scene, Red Mark, 8 In. | 195.00 |
| RS Prussia, Plate, Spring, Sailboat Medallions, Red Mark, 8 In. | 195.00 |
| RS Prussia, Plate, Swan Scene, Satin Finish, 8 In. | 95.00 |
| RS Prussia, Plate, Swan, Green, White Floral Rim, Red Mark, 8 1/2 In. | 85.00 |
| RS Prussia, Plate, White & Yellow Roses, Red Mark, 9 3/4 In. | 125.00 |
| RS Prussia, Plate, Winter, Birds, Snowcapped Trees, & Houses, Red Mark, 8 In. | 195.00 |
| RS Prussia, Pot, Mustard, Pink Roses & Snowballs, Greens, Red Mark | 75.00 |
| RS Prussia, Pot, Mustard, Satin Roses | 35.00 |
| RS Prussia, Relish, Purple, Magenta, Cerise, & Blue Floral, 9 1/4 In. | 24.00 |
| RS Prussia, Relish, Roses Center, Handled, Scalloped Edge, Red Mark, 10 In. | 50.00 |
| RS Prussia, Shaving Mug, Beveled Mirror Front | 100.00 |
| RS Prussia, Shaving Mug, Floral In Relief, Red Mark, 3 1/2 In. | 55.00 |
| RS Prussia, Shaving Mug, Soap Deck, Gold Tracery On Blue, Floral Panel | 55.00 |
| RS Prussia, Stein, Hinged Turret Shape Lid, Cameo Type Court Scene, 2 Liter | 298.00 |
| RS Prussia, Sugar & Creamer, Basket Shape Sugar, Signed Raised Star | 65.00 |
| RS Prussia, Sugar & Creamer, Cover, Swans & Pine Trees On Blue Green | 250.00 |
| RS Prussia, Sugar & Creamer, Floral, Footed, Large Size, Red Mark | 90.00 |
| RS Prussia, Sugar & Creamer, Fluted Base & Top, Green, Rose, Cream, & Gold | 110.00 |
| RS Prussia, Sugar & Creamer, Pink Flowers, Eggshell Thin, Red Mark | 125.00 |
| RS Prussia, Sugar & Creamer, Swans, Blue & Green Luster, Gold Trim, Red Mark | 185.00 |
| RS Prussia, Sugar, Covered, Floral, Gold Fluted Top, Red Mark | 35.00 |
| RS Prussia, Sugar, Covered, Floral, Green & Gold, 2 Handles, Red Mark | 42.00 |
| RS Prussia, Sugar, Pink Roses On Front, Back, & Cover, Red Mark | 48.00 |
| RS Prussia, Syrup & Underplate, Satin Finish, Red Mark | 49.00 |
| RS Prussia, Tankard, Daisies & Roses On Green To White, Pierced Handle | 295.00 |
| RS Prussia, Tankard, Lilies, Gray Green Shading, Gold Trim, Red Mark, 10 In. | 210.00 |
| RS Prussia, Tankard, Mill Scene, Butterscotch Base & Top, Jeweled, 9 1/2 In. | 175.00 |
| RS Prussia, Tea Set, Pedestal, Red Roses On Green, 3 Piece | 225.00 |
| RS Prussia, Tea Set, 2 Bust Portraits, Rococo, Red Mark, 3 Piece | 425.00 |
| RS Prussia, Teacup & Saucer, Melon Ribbed, Scalloped Edge, Holly & Berries | 45.00 |
| RS Prussia, Teapot, Bluebird & Blue Forget-Me-Nots, Gold Beading, Red Mark | 150.00 |
| RS Prussia, Teapot, Melon Boys, Green Ground, Legs, Red Mark | 325.00 |
| RS Prussia, Teapot, Pearl Luster, Pink Roses, Signed | 80.00 |
| RS Prussia, Toothpick, Pedestal, Pink & Blue Floral, Ruffled Top, 2 Handled | 70.00 |
| RS Prussia, Toothpick, Pink Rose On Green, 2 Handles, 6 Feet, Red Mark | 65.00 |
| RS Prussia, Toothpick, Ruffled Top, Pedestal Base, Handled, Red Mark | 69.00 |
| RS Prussia, Tray, Bun, Old Man Of The Mountains, White Swans, 13 5/8 In. | 215.00 |
| RS Prussia, Tray, Dresser, Oval, Yellow Floral, Red Mark | 32.50 |
| RS Prussia, Tray, Dresser, Pink & White Dogwood, Raised Gold Stamens | 14.00 |
| RS Prussia, Tray, Dresser, Rectangular, Rose On Green Satin | 65.00 |
| RS Prussia, Tray, Dresser, Rococo Rim, Floral On Shaded Blue, Spray Center | 65.00 |
| RS Prussia, Tray, Dresser, Satin, Lilac, Lavender, Flowers, 12 3/4 In.Long | 83.00 |
| RS Prussia, Tray, Dresser, Yellow Flowers, Oval Shape | 32.50 |
| RS Prussia, Tray, Floral, Red Mark, 11 1/2 X 7 1/4 In. | 80.00 |

| | |
|---|---|
| RS Prussia, Tray, Miniature, Decorated, Red Mark, 3 1/2 X 5 1/4 In. | 25.00 |
| RS Prussia, Tray, Miniature, Lilac & Leaves On Pearl, Gold Tracery Red Mark | 25.00 |
| RS Prussia, Tray, Peach Roses On Cream & Brown, Red Mark | 85.00 |
| RS Prussia, Tray, Perfume, Violets & Lilies Of The Valley On Pearl, Gold | 75.00 |
| RS Prussia, Tray, Pin, Roses, Red Mark, 5 1/2 X 3 1/2 In. | 30.00 |
| RS Prussia, Tray, Roses, Handled, Red Mark, 11 1/2 X 7 1/2 In. | 80.00 |
| RS Prussia, Vase, Cottage Scene, Yellow, Orange, & Green, Red Mark, 4 1/2 In. | 150.00 |
| RS Prussia, Vase, Lilies On Shades Of Green, Gold Trim, 2 Handled, Red Mark | 48.00 |
| RS Prussia, Vase, Melon Boy, Red Mark, 6 1/2 In.High | 325.00 |
| RS Prussia, Vase, Melon Boys, Eating, Dog, Basket, Red Mark, 6 1/2 In.High | 325.00 |
| RS Prussia, Vase, Spring Season, Long Neck, Handled, Yellow Satin, 10 In. | 495.00 |
| RS Prussia, Vase, Swans & Pine Trees On White, Open Handles, Red Mark | 125.00 |

*Rubena Verde is a Victorian glassware that was shaded from red to green.
It was first made by Hobbs, Brockunier and Company of Wheeling,
West Virginia, about 1890.*

| | |
|---|---|
| Rubena Verde Epergne, Center Lily, Applied Green Ring At Center | 185.00 |
| Rubena Verde, Bowl, Finger, Ruffled Rim, Round | 62.00 |
| Rubena Verde, Bowl, Squarish, Diamond-Quilted, Sides Rounded Down, 9 In. | 125.00 |
| Rubena Verde, Compote, Quilted, Ruffled & Scalloped, Handled Silver Stand | 110.00 |
| Rubena Verde, Compote, Ribbed, Scalloped, Embossed Metal Base, 9 1/2 In. | 50.00 |
| Rubena Verde, Epergne, Crimped Cranberry Top, Single Trumpet Holder, Green | 75.00 |
| Rubena Verde, Epergne, Deep Rose Lower Section, Clear Swirled Trim | 250.00 |
| Rubena Verde, Epergne, Ruffled, Repousse Sheffield 4 Footed Holder, 20 In. | 125.00 |
| Rubena Verde, Epergne, Single Center Trumpet, Crimped Base Bowl | 65.00 |
| Rubena Verde, Jar, Ball Finial On Cover, Inverted Thumbprint, Tapered | 110.00 |
| Rubena Verde, Syrup, Inverted Thumbprint | 145.00 |
| Rubena Verde, Tumbler, Enamel Decoration | 38.00 |
| Rubena Verde, Tumbler, Inverted Thumbprint, Straw Mark | 60.00 |
| Rubena Verde, Tumbler, Pointed Hobnail, Cranberry To Apple Green Top | 55.00 |
| Rubena Verde, Vase, Enameled Morning Glories, Ruby To Gold, 11 In.High | 80.00 |
| Rubena Verde, Vase, Heavy Enameled Flowers, Bulbous, Ruffled Top, 4 1/2 In. | 150.00 |

*Rubena is a glassware that shades from red to clear. It was first made by
George Duncan and Sons of Pittsburgh, Pennsylvania, about 1885.*

| | |
|---|---|
| Rubena, Bowl, Crystal, Pillar Type Ribs, 3 Shell Feet, 9 In. | 76.00 |
| Rubena, Bowl, Fruit, Cranberry To Clear, White Shasta Daisies, 7 In. | 85.00 |
| Rubena, Bowl, Opalescent, Ruffled, C.1860, 5 In.Diameter | 30.00 |
| Rubena, Box, Covered, Round, 2 3/4 X 2 1/4 In. | 30.00 |
| Rubena, Castor, Pickle, Inverted Thumbprint, Enamel Floral, Metal Lid, 7 In. | 60.00 |
| Rubena, Cup, Punch | 25.00 |
| Rubena, Cup, Punch, Overshot | 28.00 |
| Rubena, Cup, Punch, Set Of 8 | 140.00 |
| Rubena, Pitcher, Milk, Inverted Thumbprint, Hobbs, Brockunier | 130.00 |
| Rubena, Pitcher, Water, Bulbous, Clear Handle, 8 1/2 In.High | 75.00 |
| Rubena, Rose Bowl, Blown, Ribbed, Ruffled Squarish Top | 68.00 |
| Rubena, Shade, Gas, Frosted, Ruffled, Etched Lacy Design | 15.00 |
| Rubena, Tumbler, Inverted Thumbprint, Cranberry To Clear | 27.50 |
| Rubena, Tumbler, Thumbprint | 25.00 |
| Rubena, Vase, Bud, Gold Enamel Decoration, 7 In.High | 45.00 |
| Rubena, Vase, Crystal, Tall, Pair | 32.00 |
| Rubena, Vase, Cut Vine Decoration, 8 In.High | 27.00 |
| Rubena, Vase, Enameled Flowers & Other Decoration, 10 In.High | 39.50 |
| Rubena, Vase, Stretched Top, Band Of Cutting, 8 In. | 47.50 |
| Rubena, Vase, Swirled, Applied Green Verde Top | 95.00 |
| Rubena, Vase, Swirled, Enameled Pink & White Floral, Gold Trim, 10 In. | 65.00 |

*Ruby glass is a dark red color. It was a Victorian and twentieth-century
ware. The name means many different types of red glass.*

**Ruby Glass, see also Cranberry Glass**

| | |
|---|---|
| Ruby Glass, Basket, Flashed, 1923, 5 In. | 22.00 |
| Ruby Glass, Bobeche, 3 In., Pair | 5.00 |
| Ruby Glass, Bottle, Toilet, Bohemian Type, Berry With Fern, American | 60.00 |
| Ruby Glass, Bowl, Finger, 4 In.Diameter | 2.00 |
| Ruby Glass, Bowl, Fruit, Applied Clear Rim & Feet, 9 X 6 In. | 90.00 |
| Ruby Glass, Bowl, Swans, Duncan And Miller, 7 1/2 In. | 28.00 |
| Ruby Glass, Compote, Blown Venetian Diamond, Solid Stem & Base, Pair | 121.00 |

| | |
|---|---|
| Ruby Glass, Creamer, State Fair, 1921, Flashed | 21.75 |
| Ruby Glass, Creamer, Thumbprint, Small Size | 21.50 |
| Ruby Glass, Cruet, Deer & Pine | 40.00 |
| Ruby Glass, Cup & Saucer, Thumbprint | 48.00 |
| Ruby Glass, Cup, Punch, Snowflake Design, Clear Handle & Base, "Lettie 1914" | 9.00 |
| Ruby Glass, Flashed, Souvenir Of Mansfield, 4 In. _Illus_ | 12.00 |
| Ruby Glass, Goblet, Pittsburgh, Pa. | 12.50 |
| Ruby Glass, Goblet, Thumbprint | 30.00 |
| Ruby Glass, Goblet, Washington, Kansas | 22.50 |
| Ruby Glass, Hat, 4 1/2 In.High | 35.00 |
| Ruby Glass, Muffineer, Flashed | 50.00 |
| Ruby Glass, Muffineer, Paneled, Single Hole Top | 37.50 |
| Ruby Glass, Mug, Button Arches, Wildwood, N.J., 1913 | 15.00 |
| Ruby Glass, Pitcher, Applied Handle, Ruffled Top, 4 3/4 In.High | 18.50 |
| Ruby Glass, Pitcher, Milk, Button Arches, Pink Enamel Flowers, Coney Island | 45.00 |
| Ruby Glass, Salt & Pepper, Cut To Clear Fleur-De-Lis | 29.00 |
| Ruby Glass, Sauce, Boat-Shaped, Thumbprint | 29.00 |
| Ruby Glass, Spooner, Flashed | 15.00 |
| Ruby Glass, Spooner, Thumbprint, Leaf & Grape Etching | 35.00 |
| Ruby Glass, Swan, Applied Reeded Clear Glass Decoration, Pontil, 4 X 3 In. | 28.00 |
| Ruby Glass, Table Set, Royal Crystal, Sterling Band On Spooner, 4 Piece | 250.00 |
| Ruby Glass, Tankard, Water, Ruby Rosette, 13 In.High | 52.50 |
| Ruby Glass, Toothpick, Etched D.L.B., Atlantic City | 15.00 |
| Ruby Glass, Toothpick, Pedestal, Handled, Gold Trim, 3 1/2 In.High | 9.50 |
| Ruby Glass, Toothpick, Signed Mary, 1903 | 12.50 |
| Ruby Glass, Toothpick, Witch's Kettle, 'Rochester, Minn., ' Gold | 15.00 |
| Ruby Glass, Tray, Heart Shaped, Ludington, Mich., 4 1/2 In.Long | 10.00 |
| Ruby Glass, Tumbler, Flashed | 15.00 |
| Ruby Glass, Vase, Oval Top, 8 In.High | 35.00 |
| Ruby Glass, Wine, "Belle Torey, Merry Christmas, 1908, " Flashed | 12.50 |
| Ruby Glass, Wine, Clear Cut Stem, 4 In. | 6.65 |
| Ruby Glass, Wine, Cut To Clear Butterflies & Floral, Engraved Names & 1892 | 22.00 |
| Ruby Glass, Wine, Triple Triangle, Flashed | 22.50 |
| Rug, see Textile, Rug | |
| Rumrill, Candlestick, Nude Lady On Turtle Holding Cornucopia, 10 1/2 In. | 28.50 |
| Rumrill, Jug, Water, Green & Pink, Stopper | 10.00 |
| Rumrill, Vase, Green, Double Handled | 10.00 |
| Rumrill, Wishing Well, Green & Brown Coloring, 9 1/2 In.High | 11.00 |
| Sabino, Cologne, Relief Dancing Nudes, Opalescent, 6 In. | 115.00 |
| Sabino, Dish, Shell Shape, Iridescent, 7 In.Long | 40.00 |
| Sabino, Figurine, Angelfish, Molded Signature | 12.50 |
| Sabino, Figurine, Butterfly, Molded Signature | 17.50 |
| Sabino, Figurine, Owl, Opalescent, Signed, 3 1/2 In.High | 47.50 |
| Sabino, Figurine, Snail, Engraved Signature | 12.50 To 20.00 |
| Sabino, Figurine, Zebra, Signed, 5 1/2 In.High | 95.00 |
| Sabino, Knife Rest, Butterfly | 30.00 |
| Sabino, Knife Rest, Snail, Signed | 30.00 |
| Sabino, Vase, Frosted Lavender Glass, 8 1/2 In.High | 70.00 |
| Saddle, McClellan | 65.00 |

*Salopian ware was made by the Caughley Factory of England during the eighteenth century. The early pieces were in blue and white with some colored decorations. Many of the pieces called Salopian are elaborate color-transfer decorated tablewares made during the late nineteenth century.*

| | |
|---|---|
| Salopian Type, Plate, Boat Scene, Green Scalloped Edge, 9 In. | 27.50 |
| Salopian, Cup & Saucer | 175.00 |
| Salopian, Cup & Saucer, Handleless, Acorn, Leaf, & Flower Trim | 150.00 |
| Salopian, Cup & Saucer, House, Blue & White | 145.00 |
| Salt & Pepper, see Pressed Glass, Porcelain, etc. | |

*Salt glaze is a hard, shiny glaze that was developed for pottery during the eighteenth century. It is still being made.*

| | |
|---|---|
| Salt Glaze, Figurine, King & Queen, White, French, 7 1/2 In.High, Pair | 25.00 |
| Salt Glaze, Figurine, Spaniel, Curled On Fringed Pillow, Stoneware, C.1825 | 88.00 |
| Salt Glaze, Flask, Spirit, Figure Of Lady, C.1820 | 50.00 |
| Salt Glaze, Jug, Apostle, Pewter Mount, Charles Meigh, Dated 1842, 10 1/2 In. | 225.00 |
| Salt Glaze, Jug, Brown & Blue, Sterling Rim, Stoneware, Doulton-Lambeth | 35.00 |
| Salt Glaze, Jug, Relief Design, C.1858, 6 1/4 In. | 58.00 |

Ruby Glass, Flashed,
Souvenir Of Mansfield, 4 In.
*(See Page 538)*

Samson, Figurine,
Frederic The Great, C.1850, 14 In.

| | |
|---|---:|
| Salt Glaze, Mug, Bennington, Signed | 12.00 |
| Salt Glaze, Pitcher, Apostle, English, 9 1/8 In. High | 225.00 |
| Salt Glaze, Pitcher, Embossed Bust Of Napoleon & Leaves, 6 1/2 In. | 35.00 |
| Salt Glaze, Pitcher, Lavender Relief Figures On White, Alcock, C.1845 | 120.00 |
| Salt Glaze, Pitcher, Pewter Lid, White, Arabesque Design, Stoneware, C.1850 | 60.00 |
| Salt Glaze, Pitcher, Uncle Tom's Cabin, Negro Handle, Ridgeway & Abington | 165.00 |
| Salt Glaze, Pitcher, Victorian Musicians, Horns, & Scrolls On White | 18.00 |
| Salt Glaze, Pitcher, 1858, 6 1/4 In. | 58.00 |
| Salt Glaze, Plate, Basket Weave Design, Beehive Impressed Mark, 7 In. | 10.00 |
| Salt Glaze, Plate, English, Reticulated Border, 11 1/2 In. | 27.50 |
| Salt Glaze, Syrup, Vine Handle, 2 Raised Cherubs Eating Graves, Pewter Lid | 60.00 |
| Salt Glaze, Teapot, Zipper Pattern On Off White Orange Peel, Pewter Lid | 45.00 |

Sampler, see Textile, Sampler

*Samson and Company, a French firm specializing in the reproduction of collectible wares of many countries and periods, was founded in Paris in the early nineteenth century. Chelsea, Meissen, Famille Verte, and Oriental Lowestoft are some of the wares that have been reproduced by the company. The company uses a variety of marks to distinguish its reproductions. It is still in operation*

| | | |
|---|---|---:|
| Samson, Bowl, Armorial, Pink Diaperwork, Floral Panels, 7 X 3 In. | | 150.00 |
| Samson, Bowl, Armorial, Roses On White Inside & Out, 9 X 4 In. | | 175.00 |
| Samson, Figurine, Bocage, Lass & Drummer, C.1880, Pair | | 125.00 |
| Samson, Figurine, Dog, Imari, C.1880, 15 1/2 In.High | | 350.00 |
| Samson, Figurine, Frederic The Great, C.1850, 14 In. | *Illus* | 300.00 |
| Samson, Figurine, Young Man With Bagpipes, C.1850, 12 In.High | | 150.00 |

*Sandwich glass is any one of the myriad types of glass made by the Boston and Sandwich Glass Works in Sandwich, Massachusetts, between 1825 and 1888. It is often very difficult to be sure whether a piece was really made at the Sandwich factory because so many types were made there and similar pieces were made at other glass factories.*

Sandwich Glass, see also Pressed Glass, etc.

| | |
|---|---:|
| Sandwich Glass, Barrel, Biscuit, Overshot, Clear, Silver Plate Bail & Lid | 85.00 |
| Sandwich Glass, Basket, Azure Blue, Amber Handle & Applied Legs, Cased Body | 80.00 |
| Sandwich Glass, Basket, Card, Hobnail, Blue, Wire Encased, 4 1/2 In. | 22.50 |
| Sandwich Glass, Basket, Overshot, Pink, Clear Twisted Handle, Applied Blue | 65.00 |
| Sandwich Glass, Bell, Smoke, For Hanging Lamp, Stippled & Blocked, Scalloped | 35.00 |
| Sandwich Glass, Bottle, Scent, Egg Shape, Pewter Top Half, Cobalt Blue | 35.00 |
| Sandwich Glass, Bottle, Scent, Milk Glass | 30.00 |
| Sandwich Glass, Bottle, Scent, Opaque White, Pewter Screw Top, 1864 | 38.00 |
| Sandwich Glass, Bowl, Beehive, Lacy, Octagonal, Deep, Flint, 9 1/4 In. | 80.00 |
| Sandwich Glass, Bowl, Chrysanthemum Leaf, Gold Trim, Flat, 8 In. | 47.50 |
| Sandwich Glass, Bowl, Daisy, Lacy, 5 In. | 32.50 |
| Sandwich Glass, Bowl, Daisy, Lacy, 6 In. | 36.00 |
| Sandwich Glass, Bowl, Finger, Overshot, Blown | 27.50 |
| Sandwich Glass, Bowl, Finger, Threaded, Amber, Ruffled Top | 30.00 |

| | |
|---|---:|
| Sandwich Glass, Bowl, Finger, Threaded, Blue, Ruffled Top | 30.00 |
| Sandwich Glass, Bowl, Finger, Threaded, Green, Ruffled Top | 30.00 |
| Sandwich Glass, Bowl, Finger, Threaded, Pink, Ruffled Top | 30.00 |
| Sandwich Glass, Bowl, Heart Center, Heart & Sheaf Of Wheat Border, 6 In. | 45.00 |
| Sandwich Glass, Bowl, Oak Leaf, Lacy, 8 In. | 67.00 |
| Sandwich Glass, Bowl, Oblong, Lacy, Grape Border, Flint, 10 1/2 In. | 485.00 |
| Sandwich Glass, Bowl, Overshot, Silver Plate Stand, 8 In.Diameter | 125.00 |
| Sandwich Glass, Bowl, Paneled, Footed, Flint, 9 In. | 35.00 |
| Sandwich Glass, Bowl, Plume, Lacy, Amber, Flint, 6 In. | 240.00 |
| Sandwich Glass, Bowl, Princess Feather, Lacy, Clear, Open Bubble On Scallop | 60.00 |
| Sandwich Glass, Bowl, Robin's Egg Blue, Curlicue Legs, Threading, Fan Rim | 75.00 |
| Sandwich Glass, Bowl, Strawberries, Scored Daisies, Serrated Edge, Star Base | 20.00 |
| Sandwich Glass, Bowl, Tulip & Acanthus Leaf, Lacy, 9 1/4 In.Diameter | 135.00 |
| Sandwich Glass, Candleholder, Cylinder In Tauton Silver Stand, C.1835, Pair | 95.00 |
| Sandwich Glass, Candlestick, Blue Petal Top, Clambroth Bottom, 9 1/4 In. | 80.00 |
| Sandwich Glass, Candlestick, Blue Petal Top, Gilt Trim, 9 1/4 In., Pair | 425.00 |
| Sandwich Glass, Candlestick, Blue, Berries & Vines, 3 Dolphins & Shells | 25.00 |
| Sandwich Glass, Candlestick, Clambroth, Blue Semi Opaque Top, Flint | 140.00 |
| Sandwich Glass, Candlestick, Cobalt Blue, Hexagonal Base & Top | 52.00 |
| Sandwich Glass, Candlestick, Columnar, Petal Top, Double Step Base, Green | 400.00 |
| Sandwich Glass, Candlestick, Dolphin, Clear, Stepped Base, Flint, Pair | 100.00 |
| Sandwich Glass, Candlestick, Hexagonal Base, Amethyst, 7 1/2 In., Pair | 400.00 |
| Sandwich Glass, Candlestick, Hexagonal Base, Dark Opaque Blue, 8 In.High | 200.00 |
| Sandwich Glass, Candlestick, Hexagonal Base, Free-Blown Socket, 7 3/8 In. | 50.00 |
| Sandwich Glass, Candlestick, Hexagonal Base, Petal Top, Clear, Pair | 110.00 |
| Sandwich Glass, Candlestick, Hexagonal, Canary Yellow, 7 5/8 In., Pair | 150.00 |
| Sandwich Glass, Candlestick, Hexagonal, Golden Amber | 74.00 |
| Sandwich Glass, Candlestick, Lacy Socket, Melon Ribbed Stem, Stepped Base | 95.00 |
| Sandwich Glass, Candlestick, Loop & Petal, Canary, Pair | 265.00 |
| Sandwich Glass, Candlestick, Petal & Loop, Wafer Connection, Flint, Pair | 95.00 |
| Sandwich Glass, Candlestick, Petal Loop, Flint, Clear, Pair | 32.00 |
| Sandwich Glass, Candlestick, Sandy Finish, Opaque White, 8 1/4 In., Pair | 225.00 |
| Sandwich Glass, Cane, Blown, Striped, 6 In.Long | 250.00 |
| Sandwich Glass, Carafe, Etched | 35.00 |
| Sandwich Glass, Celery, Three Punty, Hexagonal Base, Scalloped Top, Flint | 45.00 |
| Sandwich Glass, Celery, Tulip Shape, Flint, 10 In. | 36.00 |
| Sandwich Glass, Celery, Waffle, Flint | 60.00 |
| Sandwich Glass, Cologne, Canary, Pair | 325.00 |
| Sandwich Glass, Cologne, Cranberry Flashed Overlay, Applied Neck Ring | 75.00 |
| Sandwich Glass, Compote, Amber, Cherub Prunts, Footed | 22.50 |
| Sandwich Glass, Compote, Horn Of Plenty, Flint, 8 In. | 87.50 |
| Sandwich Glass, Compote, Sandwich Star, Patterned Base, Flint | 75.00 |
| Sandwich Glass, Creamer, Heart | 48.00 |
| Sandwich Glass, Creamer, Ivy, Miniature | 125.00 |
| Sandwich Glass, Creamer, Lacy, 5 1/4 In. | 72.50 |
| Sandwich Glass, Creamer, New England Pineapple | 69.00 |
| Sandwich Glass, Creamer, Overshot, Light Blue, Clear Reeded Handle | 35.00 |
| Sandwich Glass, Creamer, Stippled Ivy, Miniature, 3 In.High | 65.00 |
| Sandwich Glass, Creamer, Strawberry | 50.00 |
| Sandwich Glass, Creamer, Waffle, Flint, 6 3/4 In.High | 85.00 |
| Sandwich Glass, Cup Plate, Bunker Hill | 75.00 |
| Sandwich Glass, Cup Plate, Henry Clay, Blue | 95.00 |
| Sandwich Glass, Cup Plate, Lacy, Blue | 160.00 |
| Sandwich Glass, Cup Plate, Lacy, 12 Sided | 19.00 |
| Sandwich Glass, Cup Plate, Shell, Lacy | 15.00 |
| Sandwich Glass, Cup Plate, Star Center, Fan Border | 25.00 |
| Sandwich Glass, Cup Plate, Thirteen Hearts | 15.00 |
| Sandwich Glass, Cup Plate, Trefoil & Hearts Center, Floral Border | 18.00 |
| Sandwich Glass, Cup Plate, Waffle Center | 22.00 |
| Sandwich Glass, Cup Plate, Waffle Center, Interlocking Loop Border | 20.00 |
| Sandwich Glass, Cup, Etched, Thin Walled | 8.00 |
| Sandwich Glass, Cup, Mustard, Peacock's-Eye, Lacy, Clear | 70.00 |
| Sandwich Glass, Decanter, Sandwich Star, Pair | 180.00 |
| Sandwich Glass, Dish, Honey, Roman Rosette, 3 1/2 In. | 12.50 |
| Sandwich Glass, Dish, Rabbit Cover, Opalescent | 55.00 |
| Sandwich Glass, Drawer Pull, Green | 8.00 |

| | |
|---|---|
| Sandwich Glass, Drawer Pull, Swirled, Opalescent, Nut & Bolt, Set Of 6 | 40.00 |
| Sandwich Glass, Eggcup, Hairpin, Rayed Base, Flint | 18.00 |
| Sandwich Glass, Frog, Flower, Blown | 15.00 |
| Sandwich Glass, Goblet, Baptism, Clambroth, Engraved, Dated 1856 | 120.00 |
| Sandwich Glass, Goblet, Diamond Point With Panels, Flint | 50.00 |
| Sandwich Glass, Goblet, Gothic, Flint | 37.50 |
| Sandwich Glass, Goblet, Hairpin, Flint | 17.50 |
| Sandwich Glass, Goblet, Scalloped Lines | 14.00 |
| Sandwich Glass, Goblet, Tree Of Life | 14.50 To 28.00 |
| Sandwich Glass, Inkwell, Cobalt Blue, 8 Panels, Brass Cap, 2 In. | 225.00 |
| Sandwich Glass, Inkwell, Dark Amethyst, 8 Panels, Brass Cap, 2 1/8 In. | 210.00 |
| Sandwich Glass, Jar, Biscuit, Threaded, Metal Handle & Lid, 8 1/2 In.High | 39.00 |
| Sandwich Glass, Jar, Mustard, Bear, Clear | 26.00 |
| Sandwich Glass, Jar, Pomade, Bear Shape, Black Amethyst, Flint | 195.00 |
| Sandwich Glass, Knob, Furniture, Lacy Flower Petal | 6.00 |
|     Sandwich Glass, Lamp, see Lamp | |
| Sandwich Glass, Match Holder, Light Opaque Blue, Boston & Sandwich Co. | 90.00 |
| Sandwich Glass, Paperweight, Red, Blue, White, & Green Ribbons, Canes | 75.00 |
| Sandwich Glass, Perfume, Canary, 6 In.High | 95.00 |
| Sandwich Glass, Pitcher, Milk, Paneled, Miniature, 2 3/4 In.High | 45.00 |
| Sandwich Glass, Pitcher, Overshot, Bulbous, Reeded Handle, 6 1/2 In. | 50.00 |
| Sandwich Glass, Pitcher, Threaded, Cranberry, 7 1/4 In.High | 43.00 |
| Sandwich Glass, Pitcher, Wine, Overshot, Pocket, Ropelike Handle, 9 1/2 In. | 110.00 |
| Sandwich Glass, Plate, Beehive, Octagonal | 80.00 |
| Sandwich Glass, Plate, Paneled, Blue Hobnail, 4 1/4 In. | 18.50 |
| Sandwich Glass, Plate, Plume & Diamond, Deep, 8 In. | 87.50 |
| Sandwich Glass, Plate, Rosette Variant, Lacy, 5 In. | 22.50 |
| Sandwich Glass, Plate, Toddy, Roman Rosette, Lacy, Flint, 5 In | 24.00 |
| Sandwich Glass, Pot & Underplate, Mustard, Peacock's-Eye, Lacy | 95.00 |
| Sandwich Glass, Salt, Basket Of Flowers, Clear, Boston & Sandwich Glass Co. | 40.00 |
| Sandwich Glass, Salt, Basket Of Flowers, Lacy, Clambroth, Rectangular | 65.00 |
| Sandwich Glass, Salt, Chariot, Lacy, Flint | 60.00 |
| Sandwich Glass, Salt, Christmas, Dec.25, 1877, Amethyst, Top With Agitator | 56.00 |
| Sandwich Glass, Salt, Double, Bear Climbing Log Handle, Milk White | 24.00 |
| Sandwich Glass, Salt, Footed Compote Shape, Scalloped Top, Star Bottom | 70.00 |
| Sandwich Glass, Salt, Master, Bull's-Eye, Footed, Flint | 15.00 |
| Sandwich Glass, Salt, Master, Inverted Thumbprint Ringed Base, Footed | 12.00 |
| Sandwich Glass, Salt, Master, Overshot, Reed & Barton Frame With Fox's Head | 40.00 |
| Sandwich Glass, Salt, Rectangular, Ribbed Rim, Flat Grill Base, Amber | 58.00 |
| Sandwich Glass, Salt, Scrolled Eagle, Lacy, Clear, Boston & Sandwich Glass | 100.00 |
| Sandwich Glass, Salt, Staghorn, Lacy, Flint | 45.00 |
| Sandwich Glass, Saltshaker, Christmas, Vaseline, Dana K.Alden, Dec.25, 1877 | 30.00 |
| Sandwich Glass, Sauce, Cord Drapery, Nile Green | 60.00 |
| Sandwich Glass, Sauce, Minerva, Flat | 9.00 |
| Sandwich Glass, Sauce, Oak Leat, Lacy, 4 1/2 In. | 15.00 |
| Sandwich Glass, Sauce, Peacock-Eye, Lacy, Flat, 4 1/2 In. | 16.00 |
| Sandwich Glass, Sauce, Ray With Loop Border, Flint | 7.50 |
| Sandwich Glass, Sauce, Stippled Rays, Flint | 9.00 |
| Sandwich Glass, Shoe, Flared Top Lady's Boot, Ribbed, Rosette At Front | 25.00 |
| Sandwich Glass, Shot Glass, Ribbed Sides, Ground Pontil, Cobalt Blue, 2 In. | 12.50 |
| Sandwich Glass, Spill, Grape & Vine, Opaque White | 100.00 |
| Sandwich Glass, Spill, Horn Of Plenty, Clear | 35.00 |
| Sandwich Glass, Spill, Inverted Diamond Point & Bull's-Eye, Clambroth | 85.00 |
| Sandwich Glass, Spill, Inverted Diamond Point & Bull's-Eye, Clear | 20.00 |
| Sandwich Glass, Spill, Ivy, Flint | 40.00 |
| Sandwich Glass, Spill, Paneled Four Pointed Star | 20.00 |
| Sandwich Glass, Spill, Sandwich Star, Flint | 28.00 |
| Sandwich Glass, Spill, Sawtooth | 18.00 |
| Sandwich Glass, Spooner, Beaded Circle | 22.00 |
| Sandwich Glass, Spooner, Sandwich Star, Flint, 5 In.High | 45.00 |
| Sandwich Glass, Spooner, Strawberry | 20.00 |
| Sandwich Glass, Sugar & Creamer, Loaf, Sandwich Ivy | 110.00 |
| Sandwich Glass, Sugar, Covered, Octagonal Shape | 65.00 |
| Sandwich Glass, Sugar, Ivy, Loaf, Miniature | 110.00 |
| Sandwich Glass, Sugar, Loop, Footed, Scalloped Rim, Flint | 25.00 |
| Sandwich Glass, Syrup, Star & Buckle, Applied Hollow Handle, Tin Lid, Blown | 125.00 |

| | |
|---|---|
| Sandwich Glass, Table Set, Fireglow, Tufts Silver Tray, Enameled, 3 Piece | 275.00 |
| Sandwich Glass, Tankard, Cranberry Overshot, Ribbed Crystal Shell Handle | 125.00 |
| Sandwich Glass, Tankard, Overshot, Applied Ribbed Shell Handle, Flint | 52.00 |
| Sandwich Glass, Thermometer, Monumental, Clear, 7 1/2 In. | 50.00 |
| Sandwich Glass, Tieback, Beaded Petal, Lacy, Pewter Shank, Opalescent, Pair | 25.00 |
| Sandwich Glass, Tieback, Clear Pink, 3 In. Post, Pair | 7.50 |
| Sandwich Glass, Tieback, Fire Opalescent, 2 1/4 In.Diameter, Pair | 32.00 |
| Sandwich Glass, Tieback, Fire Opalescent, 4 3/8 In.Diameter, Pair | 35.00 |
| Sandwich Glass, Tieback, Lacy, Amethyst, Pewter Screw, 3 1/8 In.Diameter | 24.50 |
| Sandwich Glass, Tieback, Lacy, Blue, Pewter Screw, 4 1/2 In.Diameter | 27.00 |
| Sandwich Glass, Tieback, Lacy, Green, Pewter Screw, 4 1/2 In.Diameter | 27.00 |
| Sandwich Glass, Tieback, Lacy, Opalescent, Pewter Screw, 2 1/2 In.Diameter | 20.00 |
| Sandwich Glass, Tieback, Opalescent, Round, Flower Center, 3 1/2 In., Pair | 45.00 |
| Sandwich Glass, Tieback, Pewter Stem, Fiery Opalescent, Pair | 28.50 |
| Sandwich Glass, Toothpick, Cat On A Pillow, Vaseline, Daisy & Button | 45.00 |
| Sandwich Glass, Tray, Lacy, Shallow, Flint, 5 1/4 X 7 3/4 In. | 55.00 |
| Sandwich Glass, Tray, Scrolled Leaf & Fleur-De-Lis, Lacy, Scalloped | 45.00 |
| Sandwich Glass, Tumbler, Loop, Footed | 16.50 |
| Sandwich Glass, Vase, Elongated Loop, Square Base, 9 In. | 75.00 |
| Sandwich Glass, Vase, Fan Shape, Pleated Ruffled Top, Cranberry, Air Bubbles | 100.00 |
| Sandwich Glass, Vase, Fireglow, Bulbous, Floral Enamel, 10 1/2 In. | 95.00 |
| Sandwich Glass, Vase, Fireglow, Handled, Mahogany Color Pedestal, 9 In. | 100.00 |
| Sandwich Glass, Vase, Pink Satin, Ruffled Top, 5 In.High | 125.00 |
| Sandwich Glass, Vase, Tulip, Clear | 60.00 |
| Sandwich Glass, Water Set, Footed Goblets, Amber, 9 Piece | 32.50 |
| Sandwich Glass, Whiskey Set, Lined, Long Panels, 5 Piece | 125.00 |
| Sandwich Glass, Whiskey Taster, Blue | 40.00 |
| Sandwich Glass, Whiskey Taster, Canary | 40.00 |
| Sandwich Glass, Whiskey Taster, Clambroth | 40.00 |
| Sandwich Glass, Whiskey Taster, Cobalt | 40.00 |
| Sandwich Glass, Whiskey Taster, Footed, Lacy, Flint, 2 1/4 In. | 25.00 |
| Sandwich Glass, Wine, Loop, Flint | 20.00 |
| Sandwich Glass, Wine, Manting | 35.00 |

*Sarreguemines pottery was first made in Lorraine, France, about 1770.*
*Most of the pieces found today date from the late nineteenth century.*

| | |
|---|---|
| Sarreguemines, Bottle, Snuff, White Porcelain, Marked, 4 In. | 9.00 |
| Sarreguemines, Bowl & Underplate, Purple Grape On Green Leaf, Cover, Handle | 25.00 |
| Sarreguemines, Dish, Grouse Cover, Nest Base | 45.00 |
| Sarreguemines, Dish, Wild Duck Cover, Nest Base, Majolica, 12 In.Across | 70.00 |
| Sarreguemines, Figurine, Gargoyle, Grotesque, Gaping, Purple, Red, & Gold | 65.00 |
| Sarreguemines, Jug, Cobalt Leaf & Brown Basket Weave On Green, 7 1/2 In. | 45.00 |
| Sarreguemines, Pitcher, Comic Man, Red Cheeks, 5 1/2 In.High | 45.00 |
| Sarreguemines, Pitcher, High Relief Decoration, Children, Eagle Mark | 35.00 |
| Sarreguemines, Plaque, Foret D'Alsace, Cobalt Border, Porcelain, 17 X 14 In. | 350.00 |
| Sarreguemines, Plate, Boy Running, "Tirerson Epingle Du Jeu, " 6 1/2 In. | 13.50 |
| Sarreguemines, Plate, Fables De La Fontaine, Gray Print, Basket Weave, 7 In. | 8.35 |
| Sarreguemines, Plate, German Weather Report, Pierced, Set Of 4 | 82.00 |
| Sarreguemines, Plate, Lohengrin | 20.00 |
| Sarreguemines, Plate, Majolica, Raised Fruit & Floral On Aqua, 8 In. | 9.35 |
| Sarreguemines, Plate, Month, Scene On Cream, January To December, Set Of 12 | 110.00 |
| Sarreguemines, Plate, Napoleonic Military, Set Of 8 | 105.00 |
| Sarreguemines, Plate, Trees, Floral, & Birds On Off White Crackle, 18 In. | 95.00 |
| Sarreguemines, Plate, Victor Hugo, 3 Scenes In French, 8 1/2 In. | 20.00 |
| Sarreguemines, Plate, Village Scene, Artist Signed, 9 1/2 In. | 11.50 |
| Sarreguemines, Plate, Wagner | 20.00 |

*Satin glass is a late nineteenth-century art glass. It has a dull finish*
*that is caused by a hydrofluoric acid vapor treatment. Satin glass was made*
*in many colors and sometimes had applied decorations.*

| | |
|---|---|
| Satin Glass, Base, Black, Sterling Overlay, 11 In. High | 65.00 |
| Satin Glass, Basket, Blue To White, Frosted Clear Handle, Embossed Leaf | 425.00 |
| Satin Glass, Basket, Bride's, Azure, Signed Webster Frame | 112.00 |
| Satin Glass, Basket, Bride's, Pink, Cased, Enameled Floral, Ruffled, Holder | 55.00 |
| Satin Glass, Basket, Rose Color, Twisted Thorn Handle, Applied Feet, Ruffled | 285.00 |
| Satin Glass, Basket, Yellow, Diamond-Quilted Mother-Of-Pearl, White Lining | 125.00 |
| Satin Glass, Bowl, Banana, Pale Green, Frosted, Clear Cane Bottom & Handles | 35.00 |
| Satin Glass, Bowl, Berry, Pink, Floral, 9 In. | 15.00 |

| | |
|---|---:|
| Satin Glass, Bowl, Blue, Gold Trim With Flowers On Bottom & Rim, 9 In. | 25.00 |
| Satin Glass, Bowl, Finger, White To Yellow, Diamond-Quilted, White Lining | 85.00 |
| Satin Glass, Bowl, Pink & White, Mother-Of-Pearl, Fluted, 4 1/2 In. | 100.00 |
| Satin Glass, Bowl, Pink To Raspberry, Raindrop, Mother-Of-Pearl, Ruffled | 85.00 |
| Satin Glass, Bowl, Purple, Boat Shape, Ribbed, White Casing, 11 In. | 40.00 |
| Satin Glass, Bowl, Red, Enameled Flowers, Silver Rim, 8 1/2 In. | 165.00 |
| Satin Glass, Box, White, Covered, Metal Fittings, Enamel Floral, Gilt, 3 In. | 225.00 |
| Satin Glass, Bride's Basket, Blue, Enameling Inside | 325.00 |
| Satin Glass, Bride's Basket, Blue, Ruffled Edge, Enameled Decoration | 295.00 |
| Satin Glass, Bride's Basket, Rose Color, Applied Feet & Handle, Ruffled | 250.00 |
| Satin Glass, Cruet, Light To Dark Pink | 18.00 |
| Satin Glass, Cup, Yellow To White, Herringbone, 2 In.High | 35.00 |
| Satin Glass, Dish, Bride's, Pigeon's Blood Red, Ruffled, Enameled Floral | 225.00 |
| Satin Glass, Dish, Green, Trefoil Shape, Ribbon Stripe Mother-Of-Pearl | 185.00 |
| Satin Glass, Epergne, Cranberry Ruffled Edge, French | 300.00 |
| Satin Glass, Ewer, Blue, Herringbone Pearl, Applied Crystal Thread & Handle | 600.00 |
| Satin Glass, Ewer, Green, Applied Flower, 10 In. High | 110.00 |
| Satin Glass, Ewer, Melon Shape | 200.00 |
| Satin Glass, Ewer, Peach To Pink Bottom, Ruffled, Camphor Handle | 150.00 |
| Satin Glass, Ewer, Pink, Enamel Decoration, Ruffled Top | 115.00 |
| Satin Glass, Ewer, Pink, White Casing, Applied Thorn Handle, Roses, Pair | 175.00 |
| Satin Glass, Ewer, White, Flowers | 35.00 |
| Satin Glass, Ewer, Wild Rose, Herringbone Mother-Of-Pearl, Thorn Handle | 185.00 |
| Satin Glass, Horn Of Plenty, Blue, Bracket, 6 In. Long | 65.00 |
| Satin Glass, Jar, Biscuit, Pink, Embossed Shells, Enamel Flower | 95.00 |
| Satin Glass, Jar, Biscuit, Pink, Puffed, Silver Plate Lid, 6 1/2 In. | 75.00 |
| Satin Glass, Jar, Cookie, Blue, Ribbed | 85.00 |
| Satin Glass, Jar, Cookie, Bulbous, Pink Roses, Enamel Trim, Silver Lid | 85.00 |
| Satin Glass, Jar, Cracker, Cream To Yellow, Enameled, Meriden Cover | 75.00 |
| Satin Glass, Jar, Cracker, Pastel Flowers, Metal Lid & Handle, 8 In. | 80.00 |
| Satin Glass, Jar, Cracker, Pink, Puffed, White Casing, Silver Bail & Lid | 100.00 |
| Satin Glass, Jar, Cracker, Pink, Quilted, Florette, Silver Plate, Lid & Bail | 195.00 |
| Satin Glass, Jar, Cracker, Rose Color, Moire, White Lining, Silver Plate Lid | 245.00 |
| Satin Glass, Jar, Red, Vertical Fluted Ribs, Enameled Floral, Silver Lid | 27.50 |
| Satin Glass, Jar, Rose, Diamond-Quilted Mother-Of-Pearl, Camphor Finial | 975.00 |
| Satin Glass, Lamp Base, Red, Grape Design | 195.00 |
| Satin Glass, Lamp, Blue, Raindrop Mother-Of-Pearl, Ribbed | 240.00 |
| Satin Glass, Lamp, Butterscotch, Miniature | 179.00 |
| Satin Glass, Lamp, Fairy, Blue, Mother-Of-Pearl, Pyramid Shape, Clarke Base | 135.00 |
| Satin Glass, Lamp, Fairy, Rose, Mother-Of-Pearl, Pyramid Shape, Clarke Base | 145.00 |
| Satin Glass, Lamp, Orange, Decorated, 24 In. High | 375.00 |
| Satin Glass, Lamp, Pink, Diagonal Ribbing, Embossed Flowers, 12 In. High | 225.00 |
| Satin Glass, Muffineer, Blue, Tiffin Type, Raised Birds, Tricornered | 15.00 |
| Satin Glass, Mug, Pink, Diamond-Quilted Mother-Of-Pearl, Camphor Handle | 295.00 |
| Satin Glass, Perfume, Pink, Leaf Motif, Cut Stopper | 25.00 |
| Satin Glass, Pitcher, Light Green, Pink Flowers & Green Leaves, 5 1/2 In. | 30.00 |
| Satin Glass, Pitcher, Pink, Applied Twisted Handle, Enameled Blue Floral | 125.00 |
| Satin Glass, Pitcher, Pink, Florette, Fostoria | 275.00 |
| Satin Glass, Pitcher, Rainbow, Mother-Of-Pearl, Coin Spot, Camphor Handle | 725.00 |
| Satin Glass, Pitcher, Water, Lemon, Hummingbird In Flight, 8 In. | 150.00 |
| Satin Glass, Pitcher, Water, Mother-Of-Pearl, Raindrop, Pink, Blue Stripes | 275.00 |
| Satin Glass, Pitcher, White To Rose, Diamond-Quilted Mother-Of-Pearl | 225.00 |
| Satin Glass, Punch Set, Blue, Enameled Flowers & Butterflies, 9 Piece | 350.00 |
| Satin Glass, Rose Bowl, Blue Shading, Cased | 125.00 |
| Satin Glass, Rose Bowl, Blue, Crimped Top, 4 1/2 In. | 56.00 |
| Satin Glass, Rose Bowl, Blue, Diamond-Quilted Mother-Of-Pearl, Scalloped | 125.00 |
| Satin Glass, Rose Bowl, Blue, White Enameled Floral | 125.00 |
| Satin Glass, Rose Bowl, Blue, White Lining, C.1850, 3 3/4 In.High | 48.00 |
| Satin Glass, Rose Bowl, Citron, White & Frosted, 2 1/2 In. | 175.00 |
| Satin Glass, Rose Bowl, Green, Enameled Flowers, Gold Ormolu Base & Collar | 48.00 |
| Satin Glass, Rose Bowl, Lemon To Pale Yellow, 3 1/2 In.High | 53.00 |
| Satin Glass, Rose Bowl, Pale To Medium Blue, White Violets, Gilt Stems | 86.50 |
| Satin Glass, Rose Bowl, Pale Yellow, Crimped Top, 3 3/4 In. | 50.00 |
| Satin Glass, Rose Bowl, Pink To Rose, Crimped Top, White Lining, 4 In. | 60.00 |
| Satin Glass, Rose Bowl, Purple To Lavender, Shells, 4 In.High | 300.00 |
| Satin Glass, Rose Bowl, Rainbow, Diamond-Quilted Mother-Of-Pearl, 3 In.High | 750.00 |

| | |
|---|---|
| Satin Glass, Rose Bowl, Robin's Egg Blue, Enamel Decoration, Crimped Edge | 55.00 |
| Satin Glass, Rose Bowl, Robin's Egg Blue, Enameled Flowers, 3 In.High | 68.00 |
| Satin Glass, Rose Bowl, Rose To Pink, Shell & Seaweed, 5 X 5 In. | 155.00 |
| Satin Glass, Rose Bowl, Rose To White, 5 In.High | 60.00 |
| Satin Glass, Rose Bowl, Yellow To White At Bottom, 4 1/2 In.High | 55.00 |
| Satin Glass, Rose Bowl, Yellow To White, Shell & Seaweed, Orange Scrolls | 175.00 |
| Satin Glass, Rose Bowl, Yellow To White, Swirl, Blown, 5 In.High | 50.00 |
| Satin Glass, Rose Bowl, Yellow To White, 8 Crimps, 4 In.Wide | 50.00 |
| Satin Glass, Rose Bowl, Yellow, Applied Pink & White Floral, Crimped Top | 95.00 |
| Satin Glass, Rose Bowl, Yellow, Blue Floral Enamel, Crimped Top, White Lined | 75.00 |
| Satin Glass, Rose Bowl, Yellow, White Lining, C.1850, 3 1/2 In.High | 48.00 |
| Satin Glass, Rose Bowl, Yellow, White, Blue, & Pink Enameled Floral, C.1880 | 75.00 |
| Satin Glass, Salt & Pepper, Pink | 75.00 |
| Satin Glass, Saltshaker, Blue, Melon Shape, Flowers | 30.00 |
| Satin Glass, Saltshaker, Egg Shape, Columbian, 1893 Embossed In Gold | 45.00 |
| Satin Glass, Saltshaker, White, Egg Shape, Flat End, Floral Decoration | 22.50 |
| Satin Glass, Shade, Fiery Opalescent, Hobnail, Ruffled, 7 In.Diameter | 56.00 |
| Satin Glass, Sugar, Chartreuse, Ribbon Mother-Of-Pearl, Tricorner, Footed | 395.00 |
| Satin Glass, Syrup, Blue, Quilted, Patent 1882 | 100.00 |
| Satin Glass, Syrup, Pink, Quilted, Puffy, Squatty | 75.00 |
| Satin Glass, Tumbler, Blue, Raindrop Mother-Of-Pearl | 55.00 |
| Satin Glass, Tumbler, Red To Cream Base, Diamond-Quilted | 95.00 |
| Satin Glass, Tumbler, Rose To Pale Pink, Herringbone, Mother-Of-Pearl | 125.00 |
| Satin Glass, Tumbler, Yellow To White, Herringbone Mother-Of-Pearl | 150.00 |
| Satin Glass, Vase, Aqua Shaded, Gourd Shape, 7 In.High | 26.00 |
| Satin Glass, Vase, Black, Sterling Overlay, 11 In.High | 65.00 |
| Satin Glass, Vase, Blue On White, Quilted, Narrow Neck, 14 1/2 In.High | 350.00 |
| Satin Glass, Vase, Blue, Decorated, 4 In.High | 65.00 |
| Satin Glass, Vase, Blue, Diamond-Quilted Mother-Of-Pearl, Brass Frame | 225.00 |
| Satin Glass, Vase, Blue, White Enamel Floral, White Casing, 7 In., Pair | 95.00 |
| Satin Glass, Vase, Blue, Yellow Flowers & Green Leaves, White Cased | 60.00 |
| Satin Glass, Vase, Brown To Butterscotch, Diamond-Quilted Mother-Of-Pearl | 850.00 |
| Satin Glass, Vase, Bulbous Base, Cased, Peachblow Coloring, 12 1/2 In.High | 160.00 |
| Satin Glass, Vase, Butterscotch, Polka Dot, Ruffled Top, 8 In.High | 135.00 |
| Satin Glass, Vase, Camphor, Pink & Blue Floral, Gold Butterfly & Leaves | 40.00 |
| Satin Glass, Vase, Caramel, Puffed Coralene Decoration, 9 In.High | 450.00 |
| Satin Glass, Vase, Cranberry To Pink, Broken Zipper, Ruffled Top, 6 1/2 In. | 29.00 |
| Satin Glass, Vase, Diamond-Quilted Mother-Of-Pearl, Bulbous, Square Top | 175.00 |
| Satin Glass, Vase, End-Of-Day, Brown Tones, Brass Flower Grid, 6 In.High | 45.00 |
| Satin Glass, Vase, Moire Yellow, White Mother-Of-Pearl Casing, 7 In.High | 100.00 |
| Satin Glass, Vase, Pale Green Frosted, Silver Holder, 9 1/2 In.High | 25.00 |
| Satin Glass, Vase, Rainbow, Diamond-Quilted Mother-Of-Pearl, Camphor Handle | 750.00 |
| Satin Glass, Vase, Raisin Brown, Hobnail Mother-Of-Pearl, Crimped & Ruffled | 350.00 |
| Satin Glass, Vase, Red & Black, Corset Shape, Cased, 7 3/4 In.High | 30.00 |
| Satin Glass, Vase, Stick, Blue, Mother-Of-Pearl, 8 In.High | 95.00 |
| Satin Glass, Vase, Vaseline, Honeycomb, Ovoid, 7 Feet, Ruffled, 1880, 8 In. | 125.00 |
| Satin Glass, Vase, White, Mama & Baby Owls On Tree Branch, 5 1/2 In.High | 30.00 |
| Satin Glass, Vase, White, Smith Brothers Type Flying Bird & Berries | 42.00 |
| Satin Glass, Vase, Yellow To White, Ruffled, 5 1/2 In.High | 50.00 |
| Satin Glass, Vase, Yellow, Footed, 4 In. High | 50.00 |
| Satin Glass, Vase, Yellow, Jack-In-The-Pulpit, Butterflies & Leaves | 110.00 |
| Satin Glass, Vase, Yellow, Jack-In-The-Pulpit, Orange Interior, 5 1/4 In. | 90.00 |
| Satin Glass, Water Set, Mother-Of-Pearl, Ruby To Pink, 7 Piece | 700.00 |
| Satin Glass, Water Set, Pink To White, Herringbone Mother-Of-Pearl, 7 Piece | 750.00 |

Satin Glass, Webb, see Webb

Satsuma is a Japanese pottery with a distinctive creamy beige crackled
glaze. Most of the pieces were decorated with blue, red, green, orange, or gold.
Almost all the Satsuma found today was made after 1860. Japanese faces
are often a part of the decorative scheme.

Satsuma, see also Button, Satsuma

| | |
|---|---|
| Satsuma, Bottle, Saki, Panels On Men On Blue, 7 1/4 In.High | 95.00 |
| Satsuma, Bowl & Underplate, Punch, 11 & 15 In.Diameter | 400.00 |
| Satsuma, Bowl, Double Open Handles, Oval, 2 Figures, Gold Trim, 6 1/2 In. | 15.00 |
| Satsuma, Bowl, Hand-Painted Country Scene In & Out, 4 3/4 In. Diameter | 15.00 |
| Satsuma, Bowl, Hand-Painted Wisteria, Black & Gold Border, 7 1/2 In. | 19.00 |
| Satsuma, Bowl, Three Figures Of Men, Gold Trim, 9 In.Diameter | 35.00 |

| | |
|---|---|
| Satsuma, Bowl, Warriors, Enameling, 6 Sided, 8 1/2 In. | 175.00 |
| Satsuma, Candlestick, Pink, Unmarked, 7 1/2 In.High | 20.00 |
| Satsuma, Cup & Saucer, Demitasse, 3 Ladies In Detailed Landscape | 66.00 |
| Satsuma, Cup & Saucer, War Lord, Raised Dragon Handle, 3 Figures In Bottom | 37.50 |
| Satsuma, Incense Burner, Warriors, Raised Enamel & Gold | 45.00 |
| Satsuma, Lamp Base, Blues, Reds, & Golds, 24 In.High | 250.00 |
| Satsuma, Pitcher, Wisteria, 3 In.High | 35.00 |
| Satsuma, Plate, Japanese Women & Children, Gold Decoration | 40.00 |
| Satsuma, Salt Dip, Individual, 6 Sided, 3 Haloed Men In Bowl, Gold | 18.00 |
| Satsuma, Sugar & Creamer, Florals, Bamboo Handles & Spout, 3 In.High | 30.00 |
| Satsuma, Sugar, Floral & Butterflies, Pink, Red, Yellow, White, & Blue, Signed | 26.00 |
| Satsuma, Tea Caddy, Urn Shape, Blue & Green, Ribbed, Gilding, Medallion | 145.00 |
| Satsuma, Tea Set, Black, Black Mark, C.1850, 3 Piece | 75.00 |
| Satsuma, Tea Set, C.1870, 15 Piece | 275.00 |
| Satsuma, Urn, Foo Dog Finial, Raised Men & Dragons On Beige, Gold, 15 In. | 95.00 |
| Satsuma, Urn, Foo Dog On Lid, Warriors, Gilded, Gold, C.1850, 19 In. | 975.00 |
| Satsuma, Urn, Green & Gold Dragon Handles, Green & Gold, Blue Bottom, 12 In. | 65.00 |
| Satsuma, Urn, Red & Blue, Four Figures In Landscape, 12 In. | 60.00 |
| Satsuma, Vase, Beige & Gold Peony On Blue Gray, Bird Handles, 10 In. | 55.00 |
| Satsuma, Vase, C.1890, 9 1/2 In.High | 50.00 |
| Satsuma, Vase, Chrysanthemum Handles, Samurai In Battle, C.1850, Pair | 600.00 |
| Satsuma, Vase, Cobalt Blue, 2 1/4 In. High | 30.00 |
| Satsuma, Vase, Crackle, Enameled Flowers, Birds, Ivory Ground, 12 In. | 110.00 |
| Satsuma, Vase, Cylindrical, Scenes Of 2 People On Sides, Gold, C.1850 | 48.00 |
| Satsuma, Vase, Floral, Gold Decoration, 9 In.High | 300.00 |
| Satsuma, Vase, Narrow Top, Gold With Reds, 5 1/2 In.High | 21.00 |
| Satsuma, Vase, Ovoid, Japanese Figures In Panels, Cobalt, Gilt, Beaded, 8 In. | 95.00 |
| Satsuma, Vase, Square, Four Scenes With Figures, Blue, Gold, 10 In. | 75.00 |
| Satsuma, Vase, Tapering, Pheasants Under Japanese Red Maple Trees, Pair | 180.00 |
| Satsuma, Vase, Tapering, Two Long-Tailed Birds, Plum Trees, Greek Key, Pair | 190.00 |
| Satsuma, Vase, Thousand Faces, Raised Gold & Beading, 6 1/2 In., Pair | 195.00 |
| Satsuma, Vase, Thousand Faces, Royal Blue & Gold, Handled, Red Mark, 5 In. | 225.00 |
| Scale, Candy Store, Standard, Balance, Brass Oval Scoop, Red Weights | 35.00 |
| Scale, Candy, Nickel Plated Scoop, Dated 1915 | 27.00 |
| Scale, Chatillon's, Spring Balance, Hanging Tray | 15.00 |
| Scale, Civil War, Brass, Shoulder, Pair | 59.50 |
| Scale, Computating, Superb Pelouze Mfg.Co., Chicago, Brass Pan, May 25, 1915 | 45.00 |
| Scale, Cotton, Hanson, Cast Iron, 160 Pound Capacity | 12.00 |
| Scale, Counter, Iron, Double Brass Bars | 24.50 |
| Scale, Country Store, Counter, Iron | 29.50 |
| Scale, Eastman Studio | 36.00 |
| Scale, Egg, Pewter | 36.00 |
| Scale, Gold Coin, Grafton's Improved Pocket Scale, Brass, Balance, C.1840 | 57.50 |
| Scale, Gold Coin, J.Allender, Brass, 5 Graduated Slots, C.1855 | 74.50 |
| Scale, Gold Dust, Reno, U.S.Assay Office, 1872-1885, Brass, Butternut Cabinet | 50.00 |
| Scale, Gold Miner's, Miner's Improved Gold Scale, Brass Trays & Chains | 110.00 |
| Scale, Gold, J.Allender, Patent, Nov.27, 1855, 6 Receptacles | 94.50 |
| Scale, Gold, Miner's, Brass Balance Chains, & Pans, Walnut Case | 59.50 |
| Scale, Gold, Miner's, Brass Pans, Chains, & Balance, Oval Tin Box | 59.50 |
| Scale, Gold, Miner's, Brass, Blue Tole Box, 'miners Improved Gold Scale | 110.00 |
| Scale, Gold, Pocket, California, Eagle On Cover | 40.00 |
| Scale, Gold, Portable, Brass Pans, Iron Balance, Cherrywood Box | 39.50 |
| Scale, Hanging, Hand-Forged Iron, 2 Pronged Hook On Each End | 75.00 |
| Scale, Hanson, Northbrook, Ill., Model No.9810, Viking, Hanging, 12 In. Long | 10.00 |
| Scale, Iceman's | 12.00 |
| Scale, Iron, Brass Scoop, Decorated | 35.00 |
| Scale, John Chalillon & Sons, N.Y., Hanging, To 50 Pounds | 5.00 |
| Scale, Measure, 100 Pounds, Brass, Landers, Spring Balance | 14.00 |
| Scale, Measure, 26 Pounds, Brass, Excelsior, Spring Balance | 7.00 |
| Scale, Purina, Feed Saver & Cow Culler | 18.00 |
| Scale, Ragpicker's, Brass Face, Hanging, 25 Lbs. | 4.00 |
| Scale, Ragpicker's, C.Forchner's Balance No.2, Hanging, July 9, 1889 | 3.95 |
| Scale, Ragpicker's, Chatillon's Improved Spring Balance, Brass, 1867 | 5.95 |
| Scale, Ragpicker's, Hanging, Brass Face, Marked P.S.& Co., 25 Lbs. | 3.95 |
| Scale, Ragpicker's, Morton & Bremmer, Hanging, Brass Face, 25 Pounds | 4.75 |
| Scale, Steelyard, Wrought Iron, Heart & Arrows, Dated 1722, 50 X 31 In. | 27.50 |

| | |
|---|---|
| Scale, Sweets, Iron & Brass, English, C.1820 | 75.00 |
| Scale, U.S.Postal, Dated 1898 | 65.00 |
| Scale, Weight, Dish Type, 2 In Bronze Container, Geometrics, C.1790 | 45.00 |
| Scale, Weights, Brass, Metric, 10 Graduated In Maple Box, Tweezers | 35.00 |
| Scale, Weights, Iron, Clover Shape, 1, 2, 3, 6, & 8, On Stand, Hook | 18.00 |

*Schneider*    Schneider Glassworks was founded in 1903 at Epinay-sur-Seine, France, by Charles and Ernest Schneider. Art glass was made between 1903 and 1930. The company still produces clear crystal glass.

| | |
|---|---|
| Schneider, Bowl, Centerpiece, Pedestal, Raspberry To Purple Base, 14 1/2 In. | 175.00 |
| Schneider, Candlestick, Tangerine Cup, Wine Color Stem, Art Deco, 3 Footed | 150.00 |
| Schneider, Chandelier, Red To Blue, Silvered Metal, 3-Arm, C.1915, 21 In. | 325.00 |
| Schneider, Compote, Mottled Blue, Purple Foot, C.1920, 14 In. Diameter | 90.00 |
| Schneider, Compote, Purple Base, Orange Center, Blue Top, Knob Stem | 165.00 |
| Schneider, Globe, Light, Acid Finish, Orange & Blue, 8 1/2 X 4 3/8 In. | 55.00 |
| Schneider, Pitcher, Mottled Purple Base To White Top, Purple Handle | 175.00 |
| Schneider, Vase, Amethyst, Signed, Umbrella Stand Size | 235.00 |
| Schneider, Vase, Art Nouveau, Red, Yellow, Green, & Violet, Metal Base, 20 In. | 125.00 |
| Schneider, Vase, Cylindrical, Footed, Mauve, Elongated Air Traps, 24 In. | 235.00 |
| Schneider, Vase, Marbleized, Amethyst, Footed, Signed, 23 1/2 In.High | 250.00 |
| Schneider, Vase, Ovoid, Mottled Blue, Iron Mounted, 5 1/2 In.High | 70.00 |
| Schneider, Vase, Trumpet, Blue Black Base, Orange Yellow Top, 12 In. | 350.00 |
| Schneider, Vase, Trumpet, Mottled Turquoise, Tortoiseshell Foot, 14 In.High | 135.00 |

Scrimshaw is bone or ivory or whale's teeth carved by sailors and others for entertainment during the sailing ship days. Some scrimshaw was carved as early as 1800.

| | |
|---|---|
| Scrimshaw, Bone, Letter Opener, Reindeer & Eskimo, 10 In. | 15.00 |
| Scrimshaw, Bone, Spoon, Tea Caddy, Signed & Dated, 5 In. | 45.00 |
| Scrimshaw, Box, Tobacco, Wood, Ivory Lid, Whale, Ship, Sextant | 70.00 |
| Scrimshaw, Gourd, British Sheild, Flags, Etc., Matthew Lipson, 1826 | 295.00 |
| Scrimshaw, Hickory, Busk, Pierced & Incised, Heart, Geometrics, Dated 1779 | 90.00 |
| Scrimshaw, Hickory, Busk, 2 Incised Hearts, C.1820, 12 X 1 3/4 In. | 40.00 |
| Scrimshaw, Ivory, Bracelet, Florals | 65.00 |
| Scrimshaw, Lavalier, Eskimo, Carving Of Bear, Artist Signed | 20.00 |
| Scrimshaw, Mother-Of-Pearl Seashell, 6 Masted Vessel, Napoleon II | 195.00 |
| Scrimshaw, Porpoise Jaw, Eagle On 1 Side, Woman On Other, 15 In. | 235.00 |
| Scrimshaw, Seashell, Mother-Of-Pearl, The Great Britain Steamship | 195.00 |
| Scrimshaw, Soup Bone, Playing Cards, French Prisoners-Of-War, C.1800, 51 | 150.00 |
| Scrimshaw, Steer's Horn, Dated 1894, Horses, Elephants, & Other Figures | 75.00 |
| Scrimshaw, Walrus Tooth, Full Rigged Ship, American Flag, American, C.1850 | 300.00 |
| Scrimshaw, Walrus Tusk, Full Rigged Vessel, American Flag, American, 1800s | 600.00 |
| Scrimshaw, Walrus Tusk, Kayak, Captured Seal, Man, Paddle, 5 3/4 In. | 60.00 |
| Scrimshaw, Walrus Tusk, Knife, Sheath, Oriental | 365.00 |
| Scrimshaw, Walrus Tusk, Polar Bear, 3 3/4 In. Long | 32.00 |
| Scrimshaw, Walrus Tusks, Ladies, Sailor, Vases, Floral, American, C.1850, Pair | 350.00 |
| Scrimshaw, Walrus's Skull With Carved Tusk, Carved Whale, Walrus, & Seal | 450.00 |
| Scrimshaw, Whale Baleen, Corset Busk, Trees, Floral, Sunburst, Human Face | 135.00 |
| Scrimshaw, Whale's Tooth, C.1850, 4 1/2 In., Pair *Illus* | 500.00 |
| Scrimshaw, Whale's Tooth, Eagle With Banner, Flags, & 3 Masted Schooner | 310.00 |
| Scrimshaw, Whale's Tooth, George Washington & American Eagle | 85.00 |
| Scrimshaw, Whale's Tooth, Maiden Praying, Mount Calvary, Cross, C.1850 | 350.00 |
| Scrimshaw, Whale's Tooth, Man Spearing Whale, 5 Men On Rowboat, Ship | 150.00 |
| Scrimshaw, Whale's Tooth, Mount Calvary & Cross, C.1850 | 350.00 |
| Scrimshaw, Whale's Tooth, Neptune On Shell, Inscribed Hedges, 1874, American | 250.00 |
| Scrimshaw, Whale's Tooth, Sperm, Young Girl In Victorian Dress | 84.50 |
| Scrimshaw, Whale's & Ivory, Swift, Barrel Shape Bottom, C.1840 | 750.00 |
| Scrimshaw, Whalebone, Cane, Brass Tip, Egg Shape Top, Tortoiseshell Inlay | 69.50 |
| Scrimshaw, Whalebone, Cane, Fluted Shell Carving At Top, C.1850 | 64.50 |
| Scrimshaw, Whalebone, Cane, Inlaid Dark Wood & Tortoiseshell, Turk's Head | 325.00 |
| Scrimshaw, Whalebone, Cane, Mother-Of-Pearl & Wood Inlay, Rope Twist | 225.00 |
| Scrimshaw, Whalebone, Cane, Octagon Handle, Rope Twist, Mother-Of-Pearl | 225.00 |
| Scrimshaw, Whalebone, Cane, Shell Carving At Top | 64.50 |
| Scrimshaw, Whalebone, Cane, Turk's Head Top, Twisted, Tortoiseshell Inlay | 325.00 |
| Scrimshaw, Whalebone, Corset Busk, British Motifs, B.Hughes To Elizabeth | 350.00 |
| Scrimshaw, Whalebone, Corset Busk, English, Dancing Sailors, Inscribed | 350.00 |
| Scrimshaw, Whalebone, Corset Busk, Hearts, Floral, Star, & Geometrics | 350.00 |

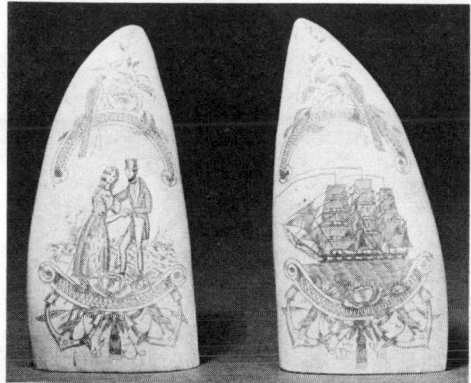

Scrimshaw, Whale's Tooth, C.1850, 4 1/2 In., Pair
*(See Page 546)*

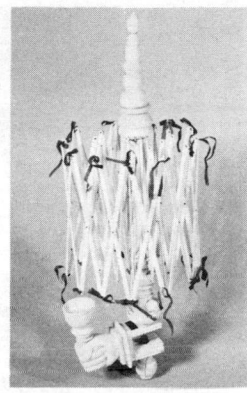

Scrimshaw, Whalebone, Swift.
C.1850, 20 1/2 In.

| | |
|---|---:|
| **Scrimshaw, Whalebone,** Corset Busk, 9 Panels Of Hearts & Flowers, C.1850 | 350.00 |
| **Scrimshaw, Whalebone,** Dominoes, Rosewood Bottoms, 28 Piece Set | 54.50 |
| **Scrimshaw, Whalebone,** Pincushion, Pedestal Base, 2 Sided | 95.00 |
| **Scrimshaw, Whalebone,** Snuff Knife, Carved Hand, 3 Blades | 80.00 |
| **Scrimshaw, Whalebone,** Swift, C.1850, 20 1/2 In. *Illus* | 600.00 |

**Scuttle Mug, see Shaving Mug, scuttle**

*Sevres porcelain has been made in Sevres, France, since 1769. Many copies of the famous ware have been made. The name originally referred to the works of the Royal Factory. The name now includes any of the wares made in the town of Sevres, France.*

| | |
|---|---:|
| **Sevres, Bowl,** Birds & Floral Panels On Pink, C.1850, 11 In. | 100.00 |
| **Sevres, Box,** Hinged, Decorated Inside & Out, 10 X 6 In. | 650.00 |
| **Sevres, Box,** Painting Of Nudes On Lid, Rectangular, Bleu Celeste, C.1820 | 325.00 |
| **Sevres, Cachepot,** Campana Shape, Double Handles, Medallions, C.1890, Pair | 650.00 |
| **Sevres, Casket,** Gilt Metal Mounts, Bleu Celeste, Medallion, C.1850 | 1100.00 |
| **Sevres, Compote,** Bisque, Figure Holding Pierced Basket, C.1870, 12 1/4 In. | 225.00 |
| **Sevres, Compote,** C.1875, A.Armand, 22 X 22 In. *Illus* | 1400.00 |
| **Sevres, Compote,** Ormolu Mounted, Medallions On Gros Bleu, C.1890, 17 In. | 1450.00 |
| **Sevres, Cup & Saucer,** Chateau De Breaux, Medallions, Gold, 1846 | 35.00 |
| **Sevres, Cup & Saucer,** Coffee, Jaune Jonquille, Gilt Bands, 1790, Pair | 325.00 |
| **Sevres, Cup & Saucer,** Jaune Jonquille, Fruiting Palms, C.1800 | 226.00 |
| **Sevres, Cup & Saucer,** Portrait Of Beefeater On Green, Gold Trim | 75.00 |
| **Sevres, Cup & Saucer,** Rose Du Barry, Double Handled, Blue Cornflowers, 1791 | 400.00 |
| **Sevres, Cup & Saucer,** Trembleuse, Covered, Blue Scrolls, Gilt Garlands, 1772 | 550.00 |
| **Sevres, Cup & Saucer,** Vincennes, Putti, Floral Sprigs, 1754 | 850.00 |
| **Sevres, Cup,** Breast, Copy Of Marie Antoinette, 2 Rams' Heads Base, 1907 | 400.00 |
| **Sevres, Ecuelle & Stand,** Yellow, 1780 *Illus* | 600.00 |
| **Sevres, Ewer,** Silver Gilt Mounted Cover, Pear Shape, Floral, Dated 1770 | 1800.00 |
| **Sevres, Group,** Putti, Parianware, C.1880, 9 1/2 In.Long | 200.00 |
| **Sevres, Incense Burner,** Art Nouveau, Brown & Green Leaves On Blue | 165.00 |
| **Sevres, Inkstand,** Louis XV Style, Ormolu Mounted, Bleu Celeste, C.1890 | 950.00 |
| **Sevres, Jar,** Biscuit, Standing Figure Of Woman Knitting, 10 In. | 95.00 |
| **Sevres, Jar,** Cracker, Daisies & Pink Floral On White, Scalloped Top | 20.00 |
| **Sevres, Monteith,** Bleu Celeste Border, Floral Vases, Oval, Handled, 1787 | 1550.00 |
| **Sevres, Plaque,** Commemorative, Edward VII & Alexandra, White On Blue | 72.00 |
| **Sevres, Plate,** Bleu Celeste, Painted Panels, Gilt Floral, C.1850, 9 1/2 In. | 33.50 |
| **Sevres, Plate,** Cherubs, Flowers, Cobalt Ground, C.1844, Signed, 9 1/2 In. | 65.00 |
| **Sevres, Plate,** Chop, Red Poinsettias, Gold Rim, Artist Ed.Heyn, 10 1/2 In. | 25.00 |
| **Sevres, Plate,** Cypher Of Louis Phillipe Center, Cupids, Cobalt, Gold, 1844 | 165.00 |
| **Sevres, Plate,** Dinner, Putti Holding Floral Garlands, Set Of 8, C.1804 | 125.00 |
| **Sevres, Plate,** Embossed, Multicolor Mums, R.S., Bavaria, 8 5/8 In. | 6.50 |
| **Sevres, Plate,** English Bulldog Center, Bold Border, Marked, 9 In. | 22.50 |
| **Sevres, Plate,** Floral Medallions, Celeste Blue, C.1844, 9 1/2 In.Diameter | 110.00 |

Sevres, Ecuelle & Stand, Yellow, 1780
*(See Page 547)*

Sevres, Compote, C.1875, A.Armand,
22 X 22 In.
*(See Page 547)*

Sevres, Vase, C.1875, 32 1/2 In.High, Pair

Sevres, Urn, 1800s, 7 1/4 In.High, Pair

| | |
|---|---|
| **Sevres, Plate,** Garden Flowers, Turquoise Ribbon Rim, 1770, 9 3/8 In. | 150.00 |
| **Sevres, Plate,** Man & Woman In Prayer In Field, Blue Border, Marked | 27.50 |
| **Sevres, Plate,** Napoleon, Gold N With Crown | 75.00 |
| **Sevres, Plate,** Portrait, Louis XV & Queen, Cobalt & Gold Border, Pair | 275.00 |
| **Sevres, Platter,** King Louis, Blue Celeste, C.1790 | 185.00 |
| **Sevres, Salt,** Garden Flowers, Blue Band, Gilt, Dated 1783, Pair | 250.00 |
| **Sevres, Tazza,** Bronze Ormolu | 375.00 |
| **Sevres, Tazza,** Porcelain, Bronze Ormolu Holder, 3 Handles & Legs, C.1835 | 359.00 |
| **Sevres, Tile,** Tea, Pink Asters, Gold & Green Border, Round | 22.50 |
| **Sevres, Tray,** Dejeuner, Square, Rose Camaieu, Floral Garlands, C.1755 | 425.00 |
| **Sevres, Tub,** Orange, Square, Corner Finials, Signed Leber, C.1850, 7 In., Pair | 200.00 |
| **Sevres, Urn,** Covered, Footed, Turquoise, Ormolu Trim, Courting Couple, Luigi | 50.00 |
| **Sevres, Urn,** Man & Woman In Outdoor Scene On Gold Filigree, C.1850 | 175.00 |
| **Sevres, Urn,** Ormolu Handles, Top, & Base, Landscape On Blue, Pair | 225.00 |
| **Sevres, Urn,** 1800s, 7 1/4 In.High, Pair *Illus* | 1500.00 |
| **Sevres, Vase,** C.1875, 32 1/2 In.High, Pair *Illus* | 2700.00 |
| **Sevres, Vase,** Covered, Louis XVI Style, Cafe Au Lait, Panels, C.1850, Pair | 850.00 |
| **Sevres, Vase,** Covered, Ormolu Mounts, Panel On Bleu Du Roi, C.1890, 23 In. | 525.00 |
| **Sevres, Vase,** Shield Shape, Panels On Bleu Celeste, C.1890, 32 In. | 1000.00 |
| **Sevres, Vase,** Urn Shape, Flolicking Couples, Bleu De Roi, C.1850, 29 In., Pair | 350.00 |

*Sewer tile figures were made by workers in the sewer tile factories in the Ohio area during the late nineteenth and early twentieth centuries.*

| | |
|---|---|
| **Sewer Tile, Cat,** Incised Eyes & Collar, Hand-Molded, Signed, 10 In. | 65.00 |
| **Sewer Tile, Dog,** Dark Red Glaze, Hand-Molded, Gray Base, 11 In. | 65.00 |
| **Sewer Tile, Dog,** Seated, Free Standing Legs, Brown Green Glaze, 9 1/2 In. | 85.00 |
| **Sewer Tile, Dog,** Seated, Gilt Ears, Clear Glaze On White, 7 In. | 45.00 |

| | |
|---|---:|
| Sewer Tile, Dog, Seated, Souvenir 1877 F.M.King Co. 1897, Red, 7 1/2 In. | 30.00 |
| Sewer Tile, Duck, Signed E.J.E., Tooled Feathers, 13 In. | 100.00 |
| Sewer Tile, Lion, Beatrice Sewer Pipe Co., Incised Work, 11 In. | 100.00 |
| Sewer Tile, Uhrichsville, O., 1955, 2 1/2 In. | 10.00 |
| Sewer Tile, Warrior's Head, Signed, 4 In. | 15.00 |
| Sewing Tool, Awl, Sterling Silver, Raised Flowers | 7.50 |
| Sewing Tool, Basket, Button, Lid, Brass Wire, Victorian, 9 In.Diameter | 45.00 |
| Sewing Tool, Basket, Needle & Pin, Multicolor, Open Top | 30.00 |
| Sewing Tool, Basket, Silver, Chain For Chatelaine With Thimble | 12.00 |
| Sewing Tool, Bird, Brass, Marked A.Geroule & Co., Pat., Needle Sharpener | 20.00 |
| Sewing Tool, Bird, Rose Velvet Cushions, Silver Wash | 55.00 |
| Sewing Tool, Bird, Wooden, Blue On White, Mirror, Iron Turnbuckle, C.1850 | 25.00 |
| Sewing Tool, Bodkin, Sterling Silver, Set Of 3 In Original Case | 9.00 |
| Sewing Tool, Bodkin, Sterling, Flowers, Silk Case | 12.00 |
| Sewing Tool, Box, Mahogany, Pincushion Top, Drawer, 6 Spool Holders | 26.50 |
| Sewing Tool, Box, Pincushion, Velvet, Bailey, Banks & Biddle Sterling | 35.00 |
| Sewing Tool, Box, Thimble, Leather | 7.50 |
| Sewing Tool, Box, Thread, Hand-Painted Robins & Floral On Hinged Cover | 10.00 |
| Sewing Tool, Box, Thread, Hinged, Compartmented, Floral Fabric, Semicircular | 4.00 |
| Sewing Tool, Box, Thread, Hinged, 9 Compartments, Robbins & Florals In Color | 10.00 |
| Sewing Tool, Box, Work, Inlaid, Multicompartment, C.1850 | 35.00 |
| Sewing Tool, Cabinet, Wooden, Pincushion Top, 1 Drawer, Spindles For Thread | 22.50 |
| Sewing Tool, Cabinet, 4 Rows For Spools, Drawer, Door In Back, 8 1/2 X 6 In. | 15.00 |
| Sewing Tool, Case, Bodkin, Repousse Silver | 10.00 |
| Sewing Tool, Case, Needle, Bell Shape, Hand-Carved Hardwood | 12.00 |
| Sewing Tool, Case, Needle, Carved Ivory | 14.00 |
| Sewing Tool, Case, Needle, Chinese Ivory, Hand-Carved, Top Portion Unscrews | 12.50 |
| Sewing Tool, Case, Needle, Egg Shape, Hand-Carved Hardwood | 12.00 |
| Sewing Tool, Case, Needle, Embossed Holly Leaves & Berries, Sterling Silver | 15.00 |
| Sewing Tool, Case, Needle, Figural Boy & Girl, Darby & Joan, Wooden, Pair | 10.00 |
| Sewing Tool, Case, Needle, Gold, 2 In.Square Floral & Pinpoint | 25.00 |
| Sewing Tool, Case, Needle, Hand-Carved Burl, Form Of Clenched Hand | 32.00 |
| Sewing Tool, Case, Needle, Hinged Metal Thimble, Gilded English Walnut | 7.50 |
| Sewing Tool, Case, Needle, Horn, American, Hat Box Shape | 25.00 |
| Sewing Tool, Case, Needle, Ivory, Allover Design | 7.50 |
| Sewing Tool, Case, Needle, Ivory, Carved | 15.00 |
| Sewing Tool, Case, Needle, Ivory, Carved, Flowers | 18.50 |
| Sewing Tool, Case, Needle, Meissen, Watteau Scenes, Silver Gilt Mounts, 1850s | 150.00 |
| Sewing Tool, Case, Needle, Sterling, Long, Flat, English | 15.00 |
| Sewing Tool, Case, Needle, Whistle, Kelsterbach, Lady's Arm, Apple, C.1765 | 450.00 |
| Sewing Tool, Case, Thimble & Spool, Marked Germany, Chased & Gilded | 12.00 |
| Sewing Tool, Case, Thimble, Sterling Silver, "eWD, " Pincushion Top | 35.00 |
| Sewing Tool, Case, Thimble, Sterling Silver, Openwork, Victorian, Round | 45.00 |
| Sewing Tool, Case, Thimble, Sterling, Openwork, Round, Loop For Chain | 45.00 |
| Sewing Tool, Case, Thread, Original Spool, Wooden, Inlaid, Cylindrical | 3.00 |
| Sewing Tool, Chest, Victorian, Wood Cased, Slant Front, Dated 1879 | 40.00 |
| Sewing Tool, Clamp, Wood & Iron | 6.00 |
| Sewing Tool, Darner, Blown In Mold, Light Green, Ribbed, Expanded, C.1850 | 36.00 |
| Sewing Tool, Darner, Glove, Ivory Top & Bottom, Mottled Ivory Center | 11.00 |
| Sewing Tool, Darner, Pottery, Sand Tone, 5 3/4 In.Long | 18.00 |
| Sewing Tool, Darner, Sock, Ebony Top, Sterling Silver Handle | 9.00 |
| Sewing Tool, Darner, Stocking, Blown Glass, Amethyst | 20.00 |
| Sewing Tool, Darner, Stocking, Blown Glass, Deep Green | 20.00 |
| Sewing Tool, Darner, Stocking, Blown Glass, Turquoise | 20.00 |
| Sewing Tool, Darner, Stocking, Maple, Mushroom Shape | 4.50 |
| Sewing Tool, Darning Egg, Black Wood, Sterling Silver Handle, Fleur-De-Lis | 9.50 |
| Sewing Tool, Darning Egg, Sterling Silver, Hollow Handle | 17.50 |
| Sewing Tool, Darning Egg, Sterling Silver, Twisted Center Bar | 11.00 |
| Sewing Tool, Darning Egg, Stocking, Wooden | 1.75 |
| Sewing Tool, Holder, Needle, Ivory, Turned, 2 1/2 In. | 15.00 |
| Sewing Tool, Holder, Needle, Ivory, Umbrella Shape, 5 1/2 In. | 20.00 |
| Sewing Tool, Holder, Scissors, Basket, Woven | 9.00 |
| Sewing Tool, Holder, Thimble, Basket With Cover | 9.00 |
| Sewing Tool, Holder, Thimble, Sterling Silver, Gold Plated, Walnut | 35.00 |
| Sewing Tool, Kit, Brass Bird & Insect Inlay On Top, Fur Velvet | 9.00 |
| Sewing Tool, Machine, Little Girl's, Singer, Dated May 16, 1910 | 22.00 |

| | |
|---|---|
| Sewing Tool, Measuring Tape, Celluloid, Ladybug Pull, Floral, Owl | 32.00 |
| Sewing Tool, Measuring Tape, Flat, Iron Handle At Back Rewinds | 18.00 |
| Sewing Tool, Measuring Tape, Metal, Cat Standing On Top | 32.00 |
| Sewing Tool, Measuring Tape, Round, Horses & Sleigh Decoration | 7.50 |
| Sewing Tool, Measuring Tape, Round, Top Wind | 6.00 |
| Sewing Tool, Needle, Net, Wooden, 11 In.Long | 4.50 |
| Sewing Tool, Needle, Thread, & Thimble Holder, Wooden | 6.50 |
| Sewing Tool, Pin Holder, Wooden Cup, Merrices Thread | 3.00 |
| Sewing Tool, Pincushion, Beautiful Lady With Baby, Advertising | 4.50 |
| Sewing Tool, Pincushion, Birch, Clover Shape, Double, Reverse Paintings | 7.00 |
| Sewing Tool, Pincushion, Birch, Clover Shape, Transfer Scene | 6.00 |
| Sewing Tool, Pincushion, Child With Pincushion | 10.00 |
|    Sewing Tool, Pincushion, Doll, see also Doll, Pincushion | |
| Sewing Tool, Pincushion, English Sterling, Camel Form | 45.00 |
| Sewing Tool, Pincushion, Figural, Swan, Metal, 3 In. | 7.50 |
| Sewing Tool, Pincushion, Flapper Doll | 7.00 |
| Sewing Tool, Pincushion, Indian, Starfish, Beads On Top | 8.00 |
| Sewing Tool, Pincushion, Indian's Head, Gold Colored Metal & Velvet Pad | 25.00 |
| Sewing Tool, Pincushion, Ivory, Barrel Shape, 4 Gold Feet, Twisted Handle | 25.00 |
| Sewing Tool, Pincushion, Lady's Shoe, Pewter Color, "Compliments, " 6 In. | 25.00 |
| Sewing Tool, Pincushion, Metal Sleigh, 4 1/2 In.Long | 7.50 |
| Sewing Tool, Pincushion, Niagara Falls, 1889, Heart Shape, Beaded | 5.50 |
| Sewing Tool, Pincushion, Red Velvet Disc, Gilt Brass Filigree Sides | 7.50 |
| Sewing Tool, Pincushion, Red Velvet On Carved Whalebone & Ivory Chain | 50.00 |
| Sewing Tool, Pincushion, Shape Of Camel, Porcelain, 1920s | 4.00 |
| Sewing Tool, Pincushion, Shape Of Lady's High Heel Shoe, Gold Finish | 3.95 |
| Sewing Tool, Pincushion, Shoe Shape, Victorian, Leather, Beading, 4 1/2 In. | 45.00 |
| Sewing Tool, Pincushion, Sterling Silver, Slipper, French Style | 18.00 |
| Sewing Tool, Pincushion, Velvet Cushion In Sterling Openwork Frame | 8.00 |
| Sewing Tool, Pincushion, Victorian, Blue Silk, Pearl Grapes | 6.50 |
| Sewing Tool, Pincushion, Victorian, Lace Top, Needlework | 5.00 |
| Sewing Tool, Pincushion, Wooden, Green Plush, Black Transfer Train | 20.00 |
| Sewing Tool, Purse, Sewing & Manicure, Plush, Instruments | 25.00 |
| Sewing Tool, Scissors, Buttonhole, Howe & Hulbert | 4.50 |
| Sewing Tool, Scissors, Buttonhole, Steel | 3.00 |
| Sewing Tool, Scissors, Embroidery, Figural, Stork, Reinhardt, Germany | 5.00 |
| Sewing Tool, Scissors, Embroidery, Germany, Butterfly | 7.00 |
| Sewing Tool, Scissors, Embroidery, Germany, Stork | 7.00 |
| Sewing Tool, Scissors, Embroidery, Sterling, Art Nouveau Lady's Head | 16.00 |
| Sewing Tool, Scissors, Gold Filled | 12.50 |
| Sewing Tool, Sewing Bird, Figured Brass | 27.50 |
| Sewing Tool, Sewing Machine, Child's, Iron, Metal Wheel, Wooden Base | 12.00 |
| Sewing Tool, Shears, Germany | 6.50 |
| Sewing Tool, Skirt Hemmer, Upright, Scaled, Tin | 5.00 |
| Sewing Tool, Spool Holder, Turned Wood, Scalloped Tiers, American, 1800s | 40.00 |
| Sewing Tool, Swift, Wooden, Clamps To Table, Telescopes, 33 In.Long | 40.00 |
| Sewing Tool, Tape Measure, Dixie Buggies, Atlanta, Ga., Lady | 16.50 |
| Sewing Tool, Tape Measure, Hand-Painted Flowers, Dated 1917 | 4.00 |
| Sewing Tool, Tatting Shuttle, Ivory | 5.00 |
| Sewing Tool, Thimble, Band Of Roses, Shield, Carnelian Top, Cutting Edge | 37.50 |
| Sewing Tool, Thimble, Birds & Forget-Me-Nots, Sterling | 25.00 |
| Sewing Tool, Thimble, Brass, Marked Her Majesty, England | 12.50 |
| Sewing Tool, Thimble, Bronzed Metal Bird Holder | 9.00 |
| Sewing Tool, Thimble, Child's, Sterling Silver, Victorian, Heavy Decoration | 10.50 |
| Sewing Tool, Thimble, English Silver | 12.50 |
| Sewing Tool, Thimble, Gold, Engraved Scene At Base, C.1850 | 75.00 |
| Sewing Tool, Thimble, Gold, Size 6 | 27.50 |
| Sewing Tool, Thimble, Heavy Gold, Large Clusters Of Grapes | 55.00 |
| Sewing Tool, Thimble, Mosaic Tip | 25.00 |
| Sewing Tool, Thimble, Persian Tailor's, Turquoise & Coral Stones | 9.00 |
| Sewing Tool, Thimble, Royal Worcester, Hand-Painted, Artist Signed | 20.00 |
| Sewing Tool, Thimble, Silver & Gold, Turquoise Stones | 35.00 |
| Sewing Tool, Thimble, Silver, Columbian Exposition, 1894 | 10.00 |
| Sewing Tool, Thimble, Silver, Egg & Dart Border | 9.00 |
| Sewing Tool, Thimble, Silver, Gold Trim, Stones, Italian, C.1890 | 35.00 |
| Sewing Tool, Thimble, Sterling Silver & Gold | 25.00 |

| | |
|---|---|
| Sewing Tool, Thimble, Sterling Silver Aesop, Wolf As Lamb, Gold Lined | 23.00 |
| Sewing Tool, Thimble, Sterling Silver, Band With Tiny Base Design | 8.00 |
| Sewing Tool, Thimble, Sterling Silver, Bridge & Buildings | 15.00 |
| Sewing Tool, Thimble, Sterling Silver, Engraved Floral Designs | 9.50 |
| Sewing Tool, Thimble, Sterling Silver, French, Enameled, Green Stone In Top | 37.50 |
| Sewing Tool, Thimble, Sterling Silver, Greek Key Design | 11.00 |
| Sewing Tool, Thimble, Sterling Silver, Jeweled, Holder | 25.00 |
| Sewing Tool, Thimble, Sterling Silver, Sunflower With Bank | 13.00 |
| Sewing Tool, Thimble, Sterling Silver, Two Birds & Flowers | 25.00 |
| Sewing Tool, Thimble, Sterling Silver, Wide Band, Paneled | 50.00 |
| Sewing Tool, Thimble, Sterling Silver, Wide Gold Decorated Band | 25.00 |
| Sewing Tool, Thimble, Sterling, Fancy Sterling Case | 12.00 |
| Sewing Tool, Thimble, Sterling, Flower Border, Anchor Mark | 13.00 |
| Sewing Tool, Thimble, Sterling, Flowers, Hallmarked | 19.00 |
| Sewing Tool, Thimble, Sterling, Red Stone In Tip | 28.00 |
| Sewing Tool, Thimble, Sterling, Scrolled Bands | 5.00 |
| Sewing Tool, Thimble, Sterling, Size 11 | 10.00 |
| Sewing Tool, Thimble, Sterling, Wide Band Of Daisies & Leaves | 13.50 |
| Sewing Tool, Thimble, Tailor's, Open End | 2.00 |
| Sewing Tool, Thimble, 12K Gold, Embossed Flowers & Scroll Band | 25.00 |
| Sewing Tool, Thimble, 14K Gold, Scrollwork At Base | 45.00 |
| Sewing Tool, Thimble, 2 Sterling In Round Case, Patent May 31, 1895 | 27.50 |
| Sewing Tool, Thread Caddy, Revolving, Mahogany, Ivory Tipped Pins, 3 Tier | 37.50 |
| Sewing Tool, Vise, Chinese Ivory, Hand-Carved, Turn Screw Fits Through Top | 15.00 |
| Sewing Tool, Winder, Thread, Ivory, Square, Concave Sides | 5.00 |
| Sewing Tool, Winder, Thread, Sterling | 10.00 |
| Shaker, Cookbook, New Favorite Recipes, 1883 | 12.00 |
| **Shaker, Furniture, see Furniture** | |
| Shaker, Mold, Basket, Oval, Laminated Pine, 24 1/2 In. Long | 125.00 |
| Shaker, Spinning Wheel | 275.00 |

*Shaving mugs were popular from 1860 to 1900. Many types were made, including occupational mugs featuring pictures of the man's job. There were scuttle mugs, silver-plated mugs, glass-lined mugs, and others.*

| | |
|---|---|
| Shaving Mug & Brush, Sterling Silver, Hallmarked | 45.00 |
| Shaving Mug, Art Nouveau, Silver, Ornate | 35.00 |
| Shaving Mug, Belleek, Gold, Yellow & Black, Dated March 31, 1894, Lenox | 145.00 |
| Shaving Mug, Blue & Red Flowers On White | 14.00 |
| Shaving Mug, Blue & Yellow Flowers On White, 'Think Of Me' | 12.00 |
| Shaving Mug, Character, Chinaman | 38.75 |
| Shaving Mug, Character, Negro | 48.75 |
| Shaving Mug, China, Says Husband | 20.00 |
| Shaving Mug, Elks Insignia, Eagle With Emblem, Name Teusaw | 37.50 |
| Shaving Mug, Embossed Floral, Thumb Rest, Rogers, Silver Plate, 1001 | 22.00 |
| Shaving Mug, Floral Decoration On White | 14.00 |
| Shaving Mug, Floral Spray, Ironstone | 10.00 |
| Shaving Mug, Floral, Rose, Blue, & Green, Divided Top | 12.00 |
| Shaving Mug, Fraternal, "T.R.Carpenter, " Gold & White, Haviland | 22.00 |
| Shaving Mug, Fraternal, Wm.Bauer, Jr., O.U.A.M. | 58.00 |
| Shaving Mug, Full Figure Of Elk Amid Scenery | 25.00 |
| Shaving Mug, Gold Trimmed Roses On Blue | 22.00 |
| Shaving Mug, Insert, Floral Decoration, Derby Silver Plate | 29.00 |
| Shaving Mug, Ironstone, Decorated With Flowers | 9.00 |
| Shaving Mug, Ironstone, Powell & Bishop, England | 10.00 |
| Shaving Mug, Limoges, Flowers, Gold, Made For Braley, Marked T. & V. | 24.00 |
| Shaving Mug, Loyal Order Moose Lodge, No.111, J.McKeone, 1924 | 20.00 |
| Shaving Mug, Man In Carriage Drawn By 2 Horses, Gold Trim | 60.00 |
| Shaving Mug, Milk Glass, Cameo | 13.50 |
| Shaving Mug, Mirror Inset On Side, Pastel Anemones, Gold Beading | 45.00 |
| Shaving Mug, Nippon, Light & Dark Pink Flowers, Green M Mark | 32.00 |
| Shaving Mug, Occupational, Bartender, S.A.McCafferty In Gold, Limoges | 110.00 |
| Shaving Mug, Occupational, Blacksmith, Anvil & Hammer, Name | 70.00 |
| Shaving Mug, Occupational, Butcher, Bull's Head, Tools On Each Side | 55.00 |
| Shaving Mug, Occupational, Butcher, Steer's Head, Knife, Cleaver, Saw | 80.00 |
| Shaving Mug, Occupational, Engineer, Black & White | 70.00 |
| Shaving Mug, Occupational, Farmer Plowing, A.L.Freed, Limoges | 97.50 |
| Shaving Mug, Occupational, Horse Trainer, E.A.Thompson, Running Horse | 65.00 |

| | |
|---|---|
| Shaving Mug, Occupational, Horse-Drawn Trolley Car | 75.00 |
| Shaving Mug, Occupational, Plowman Ploughing, 2 Horses | 85.00 |
| Shaving Mug, Occupational, Printing Press, White, T.& V.Limoges | 42.00 |
| Shaving Mug, Occupational, Senator, Pennsylvania, State Seal, Strausse & Son | 50.00 |
| Shaving Mug, Occupational, Tailor, Walter Burge, Vienna | 97.50 |
| Shaving Mug, Occupational, The Lamplighter, Sportsman's | 25.00 |
| Shaving Mug, Orange Bands, "C.Williams" | 30.00 |
| Shaving Mug, Painted Flowers, Brush Rest | 14.00 |
| Shaving Mug, Pink & Blue Flowers & Gold Scrolls, Porcelain | 9.50 |
| Shaving Mug, Pink Azaleas On Shaded Green, C.T.Altwasser, Germany | 12.50 |
| Shaving Mug, Pink Luster, Dog Picture | 40.00 |
| Shaving Mug, Purple Calla Lilies On Maize & White, Gold Trim | 18.00 |
| Shaving Mug, Raised Design, Multicolor Luster, Gold Trim, 3 1/2 In.High | 14.50 |
| Shaving Mug, Red & White Roses On Green Shading, Divided Top | 12.00 |
| Shaving Mug, Scuttle, "Tewkesbury Abbey, N.W." | 20.00 |
| Shaving Mug, Scuttle, German, Pink Blossoms | 20.00 |
| Shaving Mug, Scuttle, Germany, Sailboat Scene | 18.50 |
| Shaving Mug, Scuttle, Hand-Painted Florals | 17.00 |
| Shaving Mug, Scuttle, Hand-Painted, Reddish To Pink, 4 In.High | 16.00 |
| Shaving Mug, Scuttle, Hourglass Shape, Swirled, Melon Ribbed, Porcelain, Rose | 30.00 |
| Shaving Mug, Scuttle, Monkey Holding Shell, White, Gold Trim | 38.50 |
| Shaving Mug, Scuttle, Onion, Union Shaving Mug, Patent 1870, Copenhagen Type | 35.00 |
| Shaving Mug, Scuttle, Portrait Of Lady | 25.00 |
| Shaving Mug, Scuttle, Purple Flowers, Gold Lettering | 25.00 |
| Shaving Mug, Scuttle, Rose Shape, Pink Petals, Green Handle, Ruffled | 28.00 |
| Shaving Mug, Scuttle, Seaman's Portrait, Brown | 25.00 |
| Shaving Mug, Scuttle, Union, White & Orchid, "Pat.9/20/76" | 22.00 |
| Shaving Mug, Soap, White, Opalescent, Decorated Lower Half | 15.00 |
| Shaving Mug, Standing Horse, Name In Gold, Marked Germany | 60.00 |
| Shaving Mug, Sterling, Applied 2 1/2 In.Indian's Head, C.1880 | 50.00 |
| Shaving Mug, Three Greek Portrait Medallions on White, Marked II | 25.00 |
| Shaving Mug, Tin, Hole In Soap Compartment Feeds Lather Into Mug | 28.00 |
| Shaving Mug, Tin, Pennsylvania Dutch, Side Compartment For Brush | 35.00 |
| Shaving Mug, Transfer Printed Roses | 12.00 |
| Shaving Mug, White Ironstone, Scrolled Handle, A.J.Wilkinson, England | 10.00 |
| Shaving Mug, White Porcelain, Gold Coconut Palms, Marked Patent | 12.75 |
| Shaving Mug, White Porcelain, Soap Tray | 9.95 |
| Shaving Mug, White, Floral Decoration | 14.00 |
| Shaving Mug, Yellow & Green, Gold Divided Top | 12.00 |

*Shawnee pottery was made in Zanesville, Ohio, from 1935 until 1961.*
*Shawnee also produced pottery for George Rumrill during the late 1930s.*

| | |
|---|---|
| Shawnee, Figurine, Doe | 9.00 |
| Shawnee, Pitcher, Dolphin Handle, Beige, 8 In.High | 15.00 |
| Shawnee, Planter, Covered Wagon, Large Size | 15.00 |
| Shawnee, Salt & Pepper, Puss 'n Boots | 5.50 |
| Shawnee, Vase, Deer Design, 9 In.High | 5.00 |
| Shawnee, Vase, Planter Type, Deer Design, 6 1/2 In.High, 7 In.Wide | 5.00 |
| Sheffield, see Silver, Sheffield | |
| Shenandoah, Figurine, Lion, John Bell, Pa., C.1840, 11 In. *Illus* | 850.00 |
| Shenandoah, Salt, Cream Slip, Green & Clear Glaze, 3 1/8 In. High | 95.00 |
| Ship, Anchor & Buoy, Iron | 29.00 |
| Ship, Anchor, Wood & Stone, 1800s | 18.50 |
| Ship, Azimuth Circle, Case | 68.00 |
| Ship, Bell, see Bell, Ship's | |
| Ship, Bell & Barometer, Waterbury, Brass Cased, 4 1/2 In.Dials | 275.00 |
| Ship, Binnacle, Wood Base, Brass Head | 1000.00 |
| Ship, Binoculars, Bardou & Sons, Paris, Brown Leather Case | 55.00 |
| Ship, Bowl, Slop, Sailor's, Sheffield, Engraved, Albion Steamship Co. | 22.50 |
| Ship, Card, Asterion, For San Francisco, Coleman's California Line, C.1860 | 185.00 |
| Ship, Card, Europa, Coleman's California Line, C.1860 | 185.00 |
| Ship, Card, Golden Eagle, Coleman's California Line, C.1860 | 195.00 |
| Ship, Clock, see Clock, Ship's | |
| Ship, Compass, Brass Housing & Gimbal Mount, Maple Box, C.1850 | 84.50 |
| Ship, Compass, Brass Housing, Printed Dial, Brass Gimbal Mount, Walnut Box | 84.50 |
| Ship, Compass, Circular, N.R.Holzer, New York, C.1900, 5 In.High | 30.00 |

Ship, Figurehead, American,
19th Century, 37 In.High

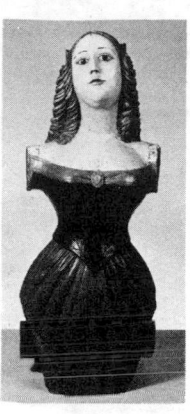

Shenandoah, Figurine, Lion,
John Bell, Pa., C.1840, 11 In.
*(See Page 552)*

| | |
|---|---:|
| Ship, Figurehead, American, 19th Century, 37 In.High *Illus* | 1600.00 |
| Ship, Figurehead, H.M.S.Hastings, 18th Century Naval Officer, Silver Finish | 84.50 |
| Ship, Hauser Ring, Wrought Iron, 14 In.Ring Base, 8 In.Diameter | 15.00 |
| Ship, Hook, Boat, Iron | 6.50 |
| Ship, Lantern, Brass, Russell & Stoll Co., New York, 17 1/2 In., Pair | 130.00 |
| Ship, Lantern, Copper, 16 In. High, Pair | 268.00 To 348.00 |
| Ship, Light, Running, Brass, Red & Green Lenses, Crisscross Pattern, Pair | 150.00 |
| Ship, Light, Running, Starboard, Brass & Copper, Removable Oil Lamp | 100.00 |
| Ship, Log, H.M.S.Nelson, Australian, 1881-1884 | 275.00 |
| Ship, Log, H.M.S.Ramillies, May 27 To Oct.25, 1778 | 750.00 |
| Ship, Model, Copper Penny, C.1825, 18 X 18 In. *Illus* | 1200.00 |
| Ship, Model, Flying Cloud, Painted, 26 X 35 In. | 200.00 |
| Ship, Model, Gloucester Fisherman, Carved & Painted Wood, Vincent, C.1890 | 275.00 |
| Ship, Model, Iron Ship, Merle, Peter Franklin, Ltd., 1851, 50 In. | 135.00 |
| Ship, Model, Italian Fishing Boat, Vincent, C.1850 *Illus* | 250.00 |
| Ship, Model, Miniature, Three Masted Clipper, American, 1800s, 7 In.High | 60.00 |
| Ship, Model, Napoleonic Prisoner Of War, Bone, C.1820, 9 1/2 In.Long | 850.00 |
| Ship, Model, Napoleonic, Bone, C.1825, 35 X 27 In. *Illus* | 4100.00 |
| Ship, Model, Schooner, Fully Rigged, Painted Black & Gold, 33 In.High | 350.00 |
| Ship, Model, Tea Clipper, Agatha, Marvin & Son, 1855, Square Rigged, 50 In. | 135.00 |
| Ship, Model, The Ern, Sailing Ship, Handmade, 30 In. Long | 125.00 |
| Ship, Pilot House Eagle, Gilt Wood, Carved, 5 Ft.8 In.Long, C.1875 | 900.00 |
| Ship, Plaque, Wooden, Hand-Carved, Anchor, Black Painted Ground, C.1750, Pair | 250.00 |
| Ship, Porthole, Brass, 16 In.Diameter, Glass | 125.00 |
| Ship, Pulley, 6 In.Long | 5.00 |
| Ship, Sextant, A.Johannsen, 149 Minories, London, Ivory Trim | 105.00 |
| Ship, Sextant, Bronze, Danish Manufactured, Brass Mounted Walnut Box, C.1900 | 146.00 |
| Ship, Stern Crown, Carved Wood, 1800s, 13 1/2 In. X 27 In.Wide | 40.00 |
| Ship, Telescope, Brass, Signed Ballard Et Paris, 23 In. Long | 75.00 |
| Ship, Telescope, Wooden Barrel, Brass Mounted, Opens To 24 In., C.1840 | 87.50 |
| Ship, Tray, U.S.Navy Officer's Mess, Silver Plate, International, C.1890 | 150.00 |
| Ship, Vase, Steamship Emblem, N.Y.K. Line, Oriental Porcelain, 3 In. | 8.00 |
| Ship, Wheel, Dutch, Turned Wood & Brass, 5 Ft.2 In.Diameter | 110.00 |
| Ship, Wheel, Inlaid Mahogany, Turned, 5 Ft.Diameter | 275.00 |
| Ship, Wheel, Pilot House, Turned Wood, Brass, 48 In.Diameter | 225.00 |
| Ship, Wheel, Turned Wood, Brass, Brass Hub, 6 Feet, 1 In.Diameter | 150.00 |
| Ship, Whistle, Bos'n's, British Naval Issue, Silver Chain Lanyard & Swivel | 59.50 |
| Ship, Whistle, Bos'n's, Silver, Marked Sterling, Braided Neck Lanyard | 84.50 |

*Shirley Temple dishes, blue glassware, and any other souvenir-type objects
with her name and picture are now collected.*

| | |
|---|---:|
| Shirley Temple, Book, Coloring, No.4584 | 10.00 |
| Shirley Temple, Book, Dimples, Saalfield, 1936, Soft Cover | 10.50 |
| Shirley Temple, Book, Fairyland, Random House, C.1958, Hard Cover | 7.50 |
| Shirley Temple, Book, Nursery Tales, Random House, C.1961, Hard Cover | 6.50 |
| Shirley Temple, Book, Screaming Specter | 5.00 |
| Shirley Temple, Book, Shirley Temple On The Movie Lot, 1936 | 1.50 |

Ship, Model, Italian Fishing Boat,
Vincent, C.1850
*(See Page 553)*

Ship, Model, Napoleonic, Bone,
C.1825, 35 X 27 In.
*(See Page 553)*

Ship, Model, Copper Penny,
C.1825, 18 X 18 In.
*(See Page 553)*

**Shirley Temple, Book,** Shirley Temple Pastime Book ............................................................. 7.50
**Shirley Temple, Book,** Shirley Temple, Little Star, 1937 ......................................................... 8.50
**Shirley Temple, Book,** Shirley Temple's Favorite Poems ........................................................ 8.50
**Shirley Temple, Book,** Song, No.2 ............................................................................................. 10.00
**Shirley Temple, Book,** Story Of Shirley Temple, Little Big Book ........................................... 7.50
**Shirley Temple, Book,** Story, Dean O.Day, Hard Cover ........................................................... 15.00
**Shirley Temple, Book,** Storybook, Random House, C.1958, Hard Cover ............................... 7.50
**Shirley Temple, Book,** Susannah Of The Mounties ................................................................. 5.00
**Shirley Temple, Book,** The Little Colonel, Big Little Book ........................................ 7.00 To 9.00
**Shirley Temple, Book,** The Littlest Rebel, 1939 ........................................................ 5.00 To 8.50
**Shirley Temple, Book,** The Real Little Girl & Her Own Honolulu Diary, 1938 .................... 10.50
**Shirley Temple, Book,** The Shirley Temple Treasury .............................................................. 6.00
**Shirley Temple, Creamer,** Blue Glass, Picture ........................................................................ 9.00
**Shirley Temple, Doll,** Brown Eyes, 21 In. ................................................................................ 110.00
**Shirley Temple, Doll,** Composition, Dressed, Signed, 16 In. Tall ........................... 65.00 To 95.00
**Shirley Temple, Doll,** Composition, Marked, 18 In. Tall ......................................... 50.00 To 60.00
**Shirley Temple, Doll,** Composition, Wig, Dressed, Ideal, 13 In.Tall ..................................... 65.00
**Shirley Temple, Doll,** Composition, 21 In.Tall ......................................................................... 85.00
**Shirley Temple, Doll,** Composition, 27 In.Tall ......................................................................... 80.00
**Shirley Temple, Doll,** Composition, 29 In.Tall ......................................................................... 150.00
**Shirley Temple, Doll,** Dressed, 1958, 12 In.Tall ..................................................................... 30.00
**Shirley Temple, Doll,** Flirty Eyes, Wig, 27 In.Tall .................................................................. 125.00
**Shirley Temple, Doll,** Ideal, Dressed, 13 1/2 In.Tall ............................................................... 20.00
**Shirley Temple, Doll,** Marked Ideal, Dressed, 14 In.Tall ........................................................ 37.50
**Shirley Temple, Doll,** Paper, Clothes ...................................................................................... 2.50
**Shirley Temple, Doll,** Vinyl, Marked, 15 In. Tall ...................................................... 15.00 To 20.00

| | |
|---|---|
| Shirley Temple, Embroidery Set, Gabriel, In 13 X 13 In. Box | 7.50 |
| Shirley Temple, Feeding Set, 3 Piece | 40.00 |
| Shirley Temple, Mirror, Picture & Signature On Back, 2 1/2 X 2 In. | 15.00 |
| Shirley Temple, Mirror, 2 1/4 In.Diameter | 12.50 |
| Shirley Temple, Mug | 9.00 |
| Shirley Temple, Photograph, 10 X 12 In. | 3.50 |
| Shirley Temple, Picture, Autographed, Sepia Tone, Cape Dress | 6.50 |
| Shirley Temple, Picture, Sepia Tone, 7 Years Old, Quaker Puffed Wheat | 10.00 |
| Shirley Temple, Pitcher, Black & White, Dated July 5, 1936, 8 X 10 In. | 6.50 |
| Shirley Temple, Pitcher, Cobalt Blue Glass, Picture, 4 1/4 In. | 9.50 To 15.00 |
| Shirley Temple, Postcard, 5 X 8 In. | 1.50 |
| Shirley Temple, Tablet, Writing, Picture On Front, Dated 1935 | 25.00 |
| Shirley Temple, Toy, Amsco T.V.Theater, Magnetic | 20.00 |
| Silesia, Berry Set, Marked, 7 Piece | 35.00 |
| Silesia, Bowl, Handle In Middle Of 2 Sections, Hand-Painted Floral, Marked | 65.00 |
| Silesia, Bowl, Pink Roses, Scalloped, 7 1/2 In. | 25.00 |
| Silesia, Bowl, White Floral, Green Leaves, Blue & Gold Border, 7 1/4 In. | 10.00 |
| Silesia, Butter, Domed, Ohme, Geneva, Custard | 11.00 |
| Silesia, Creamer, Blue Forget-Me-Nots, Signed J.Henke, R.S.Tillowitz | 18.50 |
| Silesia, Plate, Bust Of George Washington In Gold Wreath, 6 In. | 16.00 |
| Silesia, Plate, Hand-Painted Apple Blossoms & Leaves, 7 1/2 In. | 20.00 |
| Silesia, Plate, Open Handles, 10 In. | 12.00 |
| Silesia, Plate, Sprays Of Deep Pink Tulips, Marked, 9 1/2 In. | 7.50 |
| Silesia, Relish, Red Poppies, Green & White, Marked R.S.Tillowitz, 8 In. | 3.50 |
| Silesia, Vase, Self-Portrait Of Madame Le Brun & Daughter, 1845, 10 In. | 250.00 |
| Silver Deposit, Bowl, Console, Turned Down Rim, 12 In.Wide, Leaves | 14.00 |
| Silhouette, see Picture, Silhouette | |

*Silver deposit glass was made during the late nineteenth and early twentieth centuries. Solid sterling silver was applied to the glass by a chemical method so that a cutout design of silver metal appeared against a clear or colored glass.*

| | |
|---|---|
| Silver Deposit, Bowl, Ruffled Rim, Clear Drape Pattern, Butterflies, Floral | 85.00 |
| Silver Deposit, Box, 6-Sided, Vines, Flowers, Pink Glass, 4 In.Diameter | 8.00 |
| Silver Deposit, Candlestick, Turquoise, Clear Base & Stem, Blue Saucer | 17.50 |
| Silver Deposit, Compote, 5 1/4 In.High, 10 3/4 In.Wide | 23.00 |
| Silver Deposit, Console Set, Amber, Flowers, Fostoria, 3 Piece | 22.00 |
| Silver Deposit, Cordial | 5.00 |
| Silver Deposit, Cordial Set, Emerald Green, Floral & Foliage, 7 Piece | 75.00 |
| Silver Deposit, Cruet, Stopper | 30.00 |
| Silver Deposit, Decanter, Green, Stopper, Pair | 12.50 |
| Silver Deposit, Hair Receiver, Cobalt, Label F.& J.B., 4 X 2 In. | 22.00 |
| Silver Deposit, Pitcher, Blown, Molded Handle, Floral & Lines, 8 3/4 In. | 20.00 |
| Silver Deposit, Plate, Rayed Base, Marked Sterling, Alvin, 11 In. | 40.00 |
| Silver Deposit, Saltshaker | 7.50 |
| Silver Deposit, Sherbet, Silver Bands, Flowers, & Bows, 2 7/8 In.High | 3.95 |
| Silver Deposit, Sugar & Creamer, Flowers & Latticework, Applied Handles | 32.50 |
| Silver Deposit, Sugar & Creamer, Squatty, Paneled, Rayed Base, Clear | 12.75 |
| Silver Deposit, Sugar, Clear, Silver Overlay Band | 18.00 |
| Silver Deposit, Tray, Center Handle, 10 3/4 In. Diameter | 10.50 |
| Silver Deposit, Tray, Cobalt, Pierced Handles, Marked Sterling, 13 In. | 18.50 |
| Silver Deposit, Tray, Fleur-De-Lis Center, Holly Flowers, 11 In.Diameter | 14.00 |
| Silver Deposit, Vase, Acid Finish, Green To White, Silver Scrolls, 8 1/4 In. | 25.00 |
| Silver Deposit, Wine, Crystal, Banded Rim & Foot, Horizontal Bands | 2.00 |
| Silver Overlay, Bowl, Finger, Concave Sides, Figure 8 Designs, Floral, Pair | 38.50 |
| Silver Overlay, Cruet, Silver Trimmed Stopper | 35.00 |
| Silver Overlay, Cruet, Vinegar, Sterling, Openwork | 38.00 |
| Silver Overlay, Decanter, Green, 9 In.High | 17.00 |
| Silver Overlay, Plate, Clear, 5 1/2 In. | 8.00 |
| Silver Overlay, Plate, Sterling, Center Handle, Signed, 11 3/4 In. | 15.00 |
| Silver Overlay, Salt, Feather Decoration, Blue Liner | 23.00 |
| Silver Overlay, Salt, Individual | 15.00 |
| Silver Overlay, Salt, Pedestal Base | 8.00 |
| Silver Overlay, Salt, 6 Sided | 8.00 |
| Silver Overlay, Tumbler, Lemonade, Sterling, Bands, Diamond Cartouche | 7.50 |
| Silver Overlay, Vase, Bottle Shape, Engraved, Pink Iridescent, International | 150.00 |
| Silver Overlay, Vase, Persimmon, White Lining, 6 In. | 50.00 |

Silver Plate, see also Silver, Sheffield

| | |
|---|---|
| Silver Plate, Basket, Birds, Flowers, & Butterflies, Acme, Toronto, 1885-95 | 35.00 |
| Silver Plate, Basket, Bread, Scalloped, 2 Incised Handles, Pairpoint | 9.50 |
| Silver Plate, Basket, Cake, Victorian, English | 65.00 |
| Silver Plate, Basket, Cake, Victorian, Engraved Mother, Middletown Plate | 22.50 |
| Silver Plate, Basket, Cake, Victorian, Fancy Finial, Marked Meriden B.Co. | 18.00 |
| Silver Plate, Basket, Embossed Cherries, Curled Up Sides, Tufts, 5 1/2 In. | 7.50 |
| Silver Plate, Basket, Latticework, 7 In.High | 4.75 |
| Silver Plate, Basket, Oblong, Kate Greenaway Girl On Side, Reed & Barton | 150.00 |
| Silver Plate, Basket, Woven, Handled | 18.00 |
| Silver Plate, Bowl, Art Nouveau, Applied Flowers & Leaves, Scalloped, Homan | 37.50 |
| Silver Plate, Bowl, Fruit, On Copper, Handled, Raised Grapes, Engraved Inside | 37.50 |
| Silver Plate, Bowl, Nut, Pierced, Oval, Shell Footed, Ruby Liner, Meriden | 28.00 |
| Silver Plate, Bowl, Round, Forbes, 4 1/2 In.Diameter | 10.50 |
| Silver Plate, Box, Collar Button, 1894 | 12.50 |
| Silver Plate, Box, Hinged Beveled Glass Top, Footed, Openwork, 10 1/4 In. | 18.00 |
| Silver Plate, Box, Jewel, Art Nouveau Cherub On Lid, Footed, Rogers | 17.50 |
| Silver Plate, Box, Stamp, On Copper, Hinged Cover, Raised Dragon | 18.00 |
| Silver Plate, Butter & Knife, Glass Insert, Open Rim, On Copper, Rogers | 6.50 |
| Silver Plate, Butter, Domed Cover, Engraved Floral, 2 Handles, Pairpoint | 35.00 |
| Silver Plate, Butter, Footed, Liner, Meriden | 11.00 |
| Silver Plate, Cake Stand, Pivot Handle | 10.00 |
| Silver Plate, Candelabra, Rectangular Base, 3-Branch, 5 1/2 In.High, Pair | 14.00 |
| Silver Plate, Candleholder, Victorian, Blown Shade, Snuffer, English, Pair | 100.00 |
| Silver Plate, Candlestick, Art Nouveau Woman Holding Flower, 11 In., Pair | 70.00 |
| Silver Plate, Candlestick, Free-Blown Hurricane Shade, C.1850, 23 In., Pair | 125.00 |
| Silver Plate, Casket, Jewel, Cherub On Lid, Victorian, 9 1/4 In.High | 150.00 |

Silver Plate, Castor, see Castor

| | |
|---|---|
| Silver Plate, Coaster Set, Figural Golfer, 4 Coasters, Wilcox | 45.00 |
| Silver Plate, Coaster, Wine, Glass Insert | 9.00 |
| Silver Plate, Coffee Set, After Dinner, 9 Cup Pot, 3 Piece | 120.00 |
| Silver Plate, Coffeepot, Ornate, Insulated Handle, Reed & Barton, 10 In. | 75.00 |
| Silver Plate, Coffeepot, Ribbed Reed Handle, Ellis | 15.00 |
| Silver Plate, Coffeepot, Victorian, Double Lined, Ornate, Wm.Rogers, 1865-98 | 125.00 |
| Silver Plate, Compote, Globular, Ornate, Large Size | 10.00 |
| Silver Plate, Condiment Set, Center Handle, 4 Round Crystal Bottles | 37.50 |
| Silver Plate, Condiment Set, Cobalt Liners, English, E.P.N.S., 4 Piece | 18.00 |
| Silver Plate, Condiment Set, Wheelbarrow With Glass Inserts | 45.00 |
| Silver Plate, Condiment, Center Handle, 4 Round Crystal Bottles | 37.50 |
| Silver Plate, Cooler, Wine, Liner, 10 In.High | 54.00 |
| Silver Plate, Creamer, Dated '95, "Absent But Not Forgotten" | 15.00 |
| Silver Plate, Crumb Set, Art Nouveau, Flowing Iris, 2 Piece | 22.50 |
| Silver Plate, Cup & Saucer, Etched Floral, Barber Bros., Quadruple | 49.00 |
| Silver Plate, Cup, Nut, Cutout, Marked E.P.N.S., 4 In. | 3.00 |
| Silver Plate, Decanter Stand, Trefoil, Pireced, 3 Cut Glass Bottles, C.1850 | 160.00 |
| Silver Plate, Dish, Cake, Ornate, Footed, Meriden, 9 1/4 In. | 18.50 |
| Silver Plate, Dish, Candy, Leaf Shape, Quadruple, James Tufts, 7 In. | 18.00 |
| Silver Plate, Dish, Entree, Covered, Hot Water Base, Scroll Feet, C.1840, Pair | 425.00 |
| Silver Plate, Dish, Sweetmeat, Ellis, 5 1/2 In.Diameter | 5.50 |
| Silver Plate, Dish, Sweetmeat, Leaf & Flower, Sapphire Insert, J.W.T.Boston | 75.00 |
| Silver Plate, Eggcup, Hinged Top Half, Slicer Center, Engraved E.W.To C.D. | 10.00 |
| Silver Plate, Egg Set, Pierced & Footed Caddy & Cups, Spoons, 9 Piece | 48.50 |
| Silver Plate, Epergne, Black Milk Glass Vase, Openwork, Meriden, 14 In. | 135.00 |
| Silver Plate, Flask, Whiskey, Art Deco, Embossed & Engraved Golf Scene | 150.00 |
| Silver Plate, Font, Holy Water, Gothic Filigree Back, Fluted Bowl | 8.00 |
| Silver Plate, Fork, Child's, Figure Of Girl With Doll | 9.00 |
| Silver Plate, Fork, Child's, Little Red Riding Hood, Wolf In Bed, Winthrop | 10.00 |
| Silver Plate, Fork, Meat, Mother-Of-Pearl Handle | 9.00 |
| Silver Plate, Hair Receiver, Beaded Edges | 8.00 |
| Silver Plate, Hair Receiver, Raised Scrolls & Flowers | 15.00 |
| Silver Plate, Holder, Eggcup, Handled, 4 Ball Feet, For 4 Cups & Spoons | 18.00 |
| Silver Plate, Holder, Fruit Knife, Peacock Design, German Names, For 12 | 45.00 |
| Silver Plate, Inkwell, Eagle Shape, Glass Insert | 25.00 |
| Silver Plate, Jardiniere, Neptune, Lions, Sea Creatures, 18 X 34 In. | 850.00 |
| Silver Plate, Jug, Guernsey, Wicker Handle | 15.00 |
| Silver Plate, Kettle On Stand, On Copper, Burner, Paul Revere Silver Co. | 60.00 |

| | |
|---|---|
| Silver Plate, Kettle, Swinging, Queen Anne Pattern, 12 In.High | 150.00 |
| Silver Plate, Kettle, Tea, Lampstand, Victorian, Melon Finial, Pierced, 15 In. | 200.00 |
| Silver Plate, Kettle, Tea, On Lampstand, James Dixon & Sons, C.1835 | 140.00 |
| Silver Plate, Knife Rest, Fence, Closed Gate, Rocky Mound Base | 12.00 |
| Silver Plate, Knife Rest, Figural, Adam & Eve With Apple In Center | 20.00 |
| Silver Plate, Knife Rest, Greyhounds On Each End | 12.50 |
| Silver Plate, Knife Rest, Jack Ends | 6.50 |
| Silver Plate, Knife Rest, Jack Ends, Stag Center | 17.50 |
| Silver Plate, Knife Rest, Mountain Goat Ends | 12.75 To 28.50 |
| Silver Plate, Knife Rest, Prancing Horses | 27.00 |
| Silver Plate, Knife Rest, Rip Van Winkle Each End Of Bar | 26.00 |
| Silver Plate, Knife Rest, Sphinx Ends | 12.75 |
| Silver Plate, Knife Rest, Turtles | 22.00 |
| Silver Plate, Knife Rest, Two Swans On Rectangular Base | 22.00 To 31.00 |
| Silver Plate, Knife Rest, Upright Lions On Each Side | 14.00 |
| Silver Plate, Ladle, Gravy, English | 9.00 |
| Silver Plate, Ladle, Sauce, King's, English | 9.00 |
| Silver Plate, Letter Opener, Ferns & Sunflowers, 9 1/2 In.Long, Ivory Blade | 10.00 |
| Silver Plate, Match Holder, Barrel Shape, Triple Plate | 6.00 |
| Silver Plate, Match Holder, Costumed Boy In High Hat, Hartford Co. | 30.00 |
| Silver Plate, Match Holder, Kate Greenaway Holds Ring & Hound, Tufts | 30.00 |
| Silver Plate, Match Safe, Art Nouveau, Raised Figures Of Girls, Dated 1904 | 15.00 |
| Silver Plate, Match Safe, Book, Engraved Hunting Scenes | 15.50 |
| Silver Plate, Match Safe, Bottle Shape, Leather Cover | 40.50 |
| Silver Plate, Match Safe, Mother-Of-Pearl Inserts, Relief Moose & Dog | 35.00 |
| Silver Plate, Match Safe, Nickel Silver, Opens To Hold Pack Of Matches | 14.00 |
| Silver Plate, Mug, Child's, Inscribed Martha | 16.00 |
| Silver Plate, Mug, Child's, Inscribed Mary | 16.00 |
| Silver Plate, Mug, Child's, 5 Billikens With Sayings, Trade Mark Billiken | 25.00 |
| Silver Plate, Mug, Corset Shape, Repousse Floral, Pedestal, Dated 1874 | 28.00 |
| Silver Plate, Mustard Set, Hinged, Shells, Satin Liner, English, 2 Piece | 26.00 |
| Silver Plate, Nail File, Art Nouveau Lady's Profile & Floral | 5.00 |
| **Silver Plate, Napkin Ring, see Napkin Ring** | |
| Silver Plate, Pitcher, Insulated, Hinged Cover, Victorian, Meriden | 50.00 |
| Silver Plate, Pitcher, Plaque Of Church, Tacoma, Washington, Quadruple Plate | 12.50 |
| Silver Plate, Plate, Bread, Engraved Liberty Bell & Buildings, 1776-1926 | 15.00 |
| Silver Plate, Plate, Bread, Oval, England, 13 1/4 In. Long | 7.50 |
| Silver Plate, Plate, Bread, Oval, Roman Key Rim, 12 In. | 6.00 |
| Silver Plate, Plate, Dinner, Gadrooned, 9 In. | 17.50 |
| Silver Plate, Plate, Soup, Engraved Armorials, Gadrooned Rim, 10 1/2 In. | 20.50 |
| Silver Plate, Platter, Oval, Beaded Rim, 14 In. | 12.50 |
| Silver Plate, Platter, Well & Tree, Rideau, Footed, On Copper, 14 X 8 1/2 In. | 42.00 |
| Silver Plate, Platter, Well & Tree, Rogers, 11 X 16 In. | 35.00 |
| Silver Plate, Rack, Toast, Handled, Oval Pressed Center Dish, English | 22.50 |
| Silver Plate, Rack, Toast, Harby Bros., Ltd. | 10.00 |
| Silver Plate, Rattle, Baby's, Pear Shape, Rooster On Each Side, Ring At Top | 17.50 |
| Silver Plate, Rose Bowl, Relief Roses, Twisted Finial, Pairpoint, 4 In. | 27.00 |
| Silver Plate, Salt & Pepper, Three Piggies Cavorting | 7.50 |
| Silver Plate, Salt Dip, Heart Shape, Gold Washed, Footed, Spoon, Wilcox, Pair | 18.00 |
| Silver Plate, Salt, Dolphin Legs, Clear Floral Glass Top, Pairpoint, Pair | 70.00 |
| Silver Plate, Salt, Master, Footed, Blue Glass Liner, Meriden, 5 In.High | 38.00 |
| Silver Plate, Salver, Ornate Pedestal | 8.00 |
| Silver Plate, Samovar, Russian, Bone Handles, Gadrooned, Grand Prix, 1901 | 110.00 |
| Silver Plate, Scoop, Cheese, King's Pattern, English, 8 In. | 17.50 |
| Silver Plate, Server, Chased, Footed, Ornate Edge, Rogers, Patent 1883 | 18.00 |
| Silver Plate, Skewer, Bird Finial, 9 In.Long, Pair | 25.00 |
| Silver Plate, Skewer, Feather Finial, 6 1/2 In.Long, Pair | 18.00 |
| Silver Plate, Skewer, Resting Deer Finial, 9 1/2 In.Long | 25.00 |
| Silver Plate, Skewer, Sword Handle Finial, 5 In.Long | 7.00 |
| Silver Plate, Skewer, Sword Handle Finial, 9 1/2 In.Long | 10.00 |
| Silver Plate, Spoon, Baby's, Gerber | 3.50 |
| Silver Plate, Spoon, Master Salt, Plain Back, English | 5.00 |
| Silver Plate, Spoon, Serving, Stag In Bowl, "ella" | 14.00 |
| **Silver Plate, Spoon, Souvenir, see Souvenir, Spoon, Silver Plate** | |
| Silver Plate, Spoon, Soda Fountain, Twisted Handle, Coin, 4 1/2 In. | 1.50 |
| Silver Plate, Spooner, Pairpoint, Quadruple Plate, Signed | 23.00 |

| | |
|---|---:|
| Silver Plate, Sugar & Creamer, Meriden | 8.75 |
| Silver Plate, Sugar & Creamer, Signed Initials E.& J.B., Glass Inserts | 22.00 |
| Silver Plate, Sugar & Creamer, Victorian, Grape Feet, English, Hallmarked | 50.00 |
| Silver Plate, Sugar & Spoon Holder, Handled, Embossed, 12 Hooks, Middletown | 55.00 |
| Silver Plate, Sugar, Bird Finial, Spoon Rack, Open Handles, Rogers | 38.75 |
| Silver Plate, Sugar, Covered, Pedestal, Clear Tree Of Life Insert | 38.00 |
| Silver Plate, Syrup & Underplate, Brice, Hammered | 10.00 |
| Silver Plate, Tag, Decanter, Gin, Chain, Gadroon & Shell Border | 12.50 |
| Silver Plate, Tag, Decanter, Sherry, Chain, Gadroon & Shell Border | 12.50 |
| Silver Plate, Tag, Decanter, Vodka, Chain, Gadroon & Shell Border | 12.50 |
| Silver Plate, Tag, Decanter, Whiskey, English | 18.00 |
| Silver Plate, Tankard, Victorian, Repousse Foliage, Scroll Handle, 13 In. | 200.00 |
| Silver Plate, Tea & Coffee Set, E.P.N.S., England, 4 Piece | 200.00 |
| Silver Plate, Tea Ball, Shape Of Kettle | 16.00 |
| Silver Plate, Tea Set, Flower Details, Bulbous, Pairpoint, 4 Piece | 95.00 |
| Silver Plate, Tea Set, On Copper, Engraved Band, Pedestal, Wm.Rogers, 3 Piece | 34.50 |
| Silver Plate, Teakettle, Chased & Engraved, Fruit Finial, Dixon & Sons | 100.00 |
| Silver Plate, Teapot, On Stand, Swinging, Shreve, Crump, & Low, 13 In. | 45.00 |
| Silver Plate, Toast Holder, English, Alcohol Burner | 22.50 |
| Silver Plate, Toast Rack, Flat Rib, 4 Slices | 7.00 |
| Silver Plate, Toast Rack, 6 Slices, 5 1/2 In.Long | 25.00 |
| Silver Plate, Tongs, Pickle Castor, Woman's Hands Nippers | 6.95 |
| Silver Plate, Toothpick, Art Nouveau, Rabbit On Side | 25.00 |
| Silver Plate, Toothpick, Cherub Holding Ball With Holes, Quadruple | 75.00 |
| Silver Plate, Toothpick, Chick At Side | 22.00 |
| Silver Plate, Toothpick, Kate Greenaway Type Girl Beside Holder, 3 1/2 In. | 29.50 |
| Silver Plate, Toothpick, Openwork Leaf Handles, Engraved Base, Pairpoint | 15.00 |
| Silver Plate, Toothpick, Porcupine Beside Holder, Victorian, 3 In. | 28.50 |
| Silver Plate, Toothpick, Rabbit Nibbling On Leaf, Scalloped, Middletown Co. | 45.00 |
| Silver Plate, Toothpick, Squirrel | 48.00 |
| Silver Plate, Toothpick, Standing Monkey Dressed As A Man, Tufts | 22.50 |
| Silver Plate, Tray, Coffee, After Dinner, 14 1/2 In. | 45.00 |
| Silver Plate, Tray, On Copper, Handled, 13 X 18 In. | 22.00 |
| Silver Plate, Tray, Primrose, Round, On Copper, 12 In. | 18.50 |
| Silver Plate, Tray, Tea, Gadroon Rim, Armorial Center, 2 Handles, Oval | 170.00 |
| Silver Plate, Tray, Tea, Oval, Gadrooned Border & Handles, C.1850, 33 In. | 120.00 |
| Silver Plate, Tray, Tea, Oval, Grapevine Rim Handles & Feet, 35 1/2 In. | 300.00 |
| Silver Plate, Tray, Tea, Two Handles, Shell Border, Floral Decoration, 28 In. | 275.00 |
| Silver Plate, Tray, U.S.Navy Officer's Mess, Handled, Engraved, C.1890 | 150.00 |
| Silver Plate, Tureen, Cabbage Form, Pottery Liner, 12 In.High | 425.00 |
| Silver Plate, Tureen, Soup, Domed Cover, Pedestal, Beaded Rims, 14 In. | 70.00 |
| Silver Plate, Urn, Tea, Vase Shape, Engraved Scrolling Ferns, Footed, C.1870 | 180.00 |
| Silver Plate, Vase, Bud, Pierced Top Rim, 6 1/2 In.High | 6.50 |
| Silver Plate, Warmer, Spoon, Snail, English | 55.00 |
| Silver Plate, Water Set, Porcelain Lined, Polar Bears, Meriden, 4 Piece | 195.00 |
| Silver Plate, Wine, Stemmed, On Brass | 7.00 |

### Silver, American, see also Tiffany, Silver, Silver, Sterling

| | |
|---|---:|
| Silver, American, Basket, Bread, Boat Shape, Wheat Sprays, Moore, C.1850 | 325.00 |
| Silver, American, Basket, Cake, Boat Shape, Swags Of Flowers, C.1870, 15 In. | 250.00 |
| Silver, American, Basket, Cake, Swing Handle, Engraved, Kirder, Pa., C.1860 | 425.00 |
| Silver, American, Basket, Cake, Wirework, Applied Grapevine, Marquand, C.1830 | 800.00 |
| Silver, American, Basket, Flower, Grapevine Rim, Liner, Tiffany, 16 In. | 450.00 |
| Silver, American, Beaker, Cylindrical, Crest, William G.Forbes, C.1790, 4 In. | 350.00 |
| Silver, American, Beaker, Cylindrical, Hugh Wishart, C.1810, 4 In., Pair | 900.00 |
| Silver, American, Beaker, Cylindrical, John W.Forbes, C.1810, 3 1/4 In.High | 300.00 |
| Silver, American, Beaker, Fluted, William Forbes, C.1825, 3 5/8 In.High | 400.00 |
| Silver, American, Bowl & Stand, Reeded Rim, Chased, Tiffany, C.1890, 5 In. | 200.00 |
| Silver, American, Bowl, Art Nouveau Design, Tiffany, C.1910, 8 In.High | 225.00 |
| Silver, American, Bowl, Circular, Alexander Gordon, C.1790, 7 In.Diameter | 700.00 |
| Silver, American, Bowl, Circular, Reeded Rim, Peter Riker, C.1800, 6 1/4 In. | 700.00 |
| Silver, American, Bowl, Circular, Samuel Buel, Connecticut, C.1790, 6 3/4 In. | 400.00 |
| Silver, American, Bowl, Embossed Cartouches, Wood & Hughes, C.1845, 5 1/2 In. | 150.00 |
| Silver, American, Bowl, Embossed Panels & Cartouches, Gorham, C.1900, 10 In. | 150.00 |
| Silver, American, Bowl, Foliage, Pedestal Base, C.1825, 6 1/8 In.Diameter | 175.00 |
| Silver, American, Bowl, Pedestal Foot, Fletcher & Gardiner, C.1815, 6 3/4 In. | 400.00 |
| Silver, American, Bowl, Pierced, Scroll Border, Black, Starr, & Frost | 125.00 |

**Silver, American,** Bowl, Punch, Art Nouveau, Repousse Foliage, 13 5/8 In.High ......................... 375.00
**Silver, American,** Can, A.Carlile, 1790, 5 1/2 In. ................................................................................. 1200.00
**Silver, American,** Candelabra, Five Light, Tiffany, C.1900, Pair, 17 In.High ................................. 1700.00
**Silver, American,** Candlestick, Chamber, Embossed Sides, S.Kirk & Son, Pair ........................... 325.00
**Silver, American,** Candlestick, E.F.Caldwell & Co., Scrolling Foliage, Pair ................................. 450.00
**Silver, American,** Candlestick, Scrolling Foliage, Black, Starr & Frost, 4 ................................... 600.00
**Silver, American,** Candlestick, Square Base, Short, Black, Starr & Frost, 4 .............................. 300.00
**Silver, American,** Cann, Charles Oliver Bruff, C.1770 ...........................................................*Illus* 650.00
**Silver, American,** Case, Calling, Engraved, Engine Turning, Cole, C.1850, Coin .......................... 45.00
**Silver, American,** Case, Card, Silver Chain, Bright Cut, Albert Cole, C.1850 ............................... 65.00
**Silver, American,** Case, Cigar, Hinged, Bright Cut Floral & Scrolls ........................................... 19.75
**Silver, American,** Caster, Vase Shape, Reeded Borders, A.P., C.1750, 5 1/2 In. ....................... 200.00
**Silver, American,** Centerpiece, Grape Clusters, Bailey, Banks & Biddle, C.1900 ........................ 400.00
**Silver, American,** Centerpiece, Stand, Vase Form, Gorham, C.1925, 11 In High ........................ 600.00
**Silver, American,** Child's Set, Albert Cole, C.1850, Coin, 3 Piece ............................................. 27.50
**Silver, American,** Coffee & Tea Set, Kirk & Son, C.1910 .....................................................*Illus* 1600.00
**Silver, American,** Coffeepot, Howard & Co., Repousse Foliage, 1886, 9 In.High ........................ 200.00
**Silver, American,** Coffeepot, Howard & Co., Scroll Handles, 1902, 8 In.High ............................. 175.00
**Silver, American,** Comb, Hair, Ornate, Coin ..................................................................................... 18.50
**Silver, American,** Creamer, Bulbous, Strap Handle, Thomson, N.Y., C.1810 .............................. 350.00
**Silver, American,** Creamer, Double Scroll Handle, Curry & Preston, C.1830 ............................. 200.00
**Silver, American,** Creamer, Egg Shape, Leaf Capped Loop Handle, C.1790 ............................. 250.00
**Silver, American,** Creamer, Helmet Shape, Beaded Rim, Loop Handle, C.1790 ......................... 275.00
**Silver, American,** Creamer, Nathaniel Vernon, S.C., C.1815 ...............................................*Illus* 600.00

Silver, American, Cann,
Charles Oliver Bruff, C.1770

Silver, American, Creamer,
Nathaniel Vernon, S.C., C.1815

Silver, American,
Coffee & Tea Set,
Kirk & Son, C.1910

Silver, American, Creamer, Oval, Joseph Foster, C.1825, 3 3/4 In.High ............... 250.00
Silver, American, Creamer, Oval, Repousse, Harp Handle, Wood, C.1810 ............... 150.00
Silver, American, Creamer, Pear Shape, Philip Syng, Jr., C.1750, 4 3/8 In.High ............... 2000.00
Silver, American, Creamer, Wrigglework Border, Pedestal, Thomson, C.1820 ............... 200.00
Silver, American, Crumber, Engraved, J.E.Spear, 1856, Coin ............... 80.00
Silver, American, Cup & Saucer, Leaf & Stem Handle, Vanderslice & Co., Coin ............... 125.00
Silver, American, Cup, Applied Banding, Engraved, Jones, Lows & Ball, Coin ............... 165.00
Silver, American, Cup, Banding At Base, Beading At Top, Gorham, C.1863, Coin ............... 150.00
Silver, American, Cup, Engine Turned Decoration, George B.Sharp, C.1860 ............... 125.00
Silver, American, Cup, Engine Turned Decoration, Inscribed, C.1865, Coin ............... 85.00
Silver, American, Cup, Engine Turned Trim, Beading, Jaccard & Co., Coin ............... 75.00
Silver, American, Cup, Engraved Acorns & Oak Leaves, Jaccard & Co., Coin ............... 95.00
Silver, American, Cup, Leaf & Rope Banding, Repousse, Peter L.Krider, 1864 ............... 150.00
Silver, American, Cup, Repousse Floral, Beading, Wood & Hughes, Coin ............... 110.00
Silver, American, Cup, Repousse Leaves Form Cartouche, Thomas Evans & Co. ............... 115.00
Silver, American, Demitasse Set, Black, Starr & Frost, C.1915, 3 Piece ............... 275.00
Silver, American, Dish, Candy, Oval, Handled, Gold Wash Inside, 1858, Coin ............... 89.75
Silver, American, Dish, Dessert, Oval, Fruit & Game Panels, Caldwell, C.1880 ............... 140.00
Silver, American, Dish, Entree, Covered, George IV Style, Howard, 1800s, Pair ............... 700.00
Silver, American, Dish, Entree, Covered, Oval, Chased, T.B.Starr, C.1900, Pair ............... 425.00
Silver, American, Fish Server, Engraved Tines, Coin ............... 39.00
Silver, American, Fish Slice, Fiddle Thread, Albert Cole & G.Gelston, Coin ............... 125.00
Silver, American, Fork, Albert Cole, C.1850, Coin ............... 10.00
Silver, American, Fork, Dinner, Ding's, Bailey & Co., Coin ............... 9.35
Silver, American, Fork, Dinner, Fiddle & Thread, C.H.Jones & Co., N.C., 4 ............... 120.00
Silver, American, Fork, Dinner, Fiddle Thread, Salisbury, N.Y., C.1830, Coin ............... 15.00
Silver, American, Fork, Dinner, Olive Pattern, Palmer & Batchelder, C.1846 ............... 12.00
Silver, American, Fork, Engraved, Bechtel & Bro., 1810, Coin ............... 17.00
Silver, American, Fork, Engraved, N.Harding, Boston, C.1830, Coin, Set Of 6 ............... 85.00
Silver, American, Fork, Fiddle Handle, Farrington & Hunnewell, C.1840 ............... 8.50
Silver, American, Fork, Fiddle Thread, G.E.Adams, Coin ............... 18.75
Silver, American, Fork, Fiddle Thread, J.Rafel, Coin ............... 15.00
Silver, American, Fork, Fiddle Thread, Stebbins & Co., Coin ............... 17.00
Silver, American, Fork, Luncheon, Fiddle Thread, William Gale & Son, C.1835 ............... 12.40
Silver, American, Fork, Luncheon, Olive, Bigelow Bros. & Kennard, 1845, Coin ............... 12.00
Silver, American, Fork, Salad, Multifloral Decoration, S.Kirk & Son, 6 ............... 32.00
Silver, American, G.Gordon, Newburgh, N.Y., C.1835, Coin ............... 6.00
Silver, American, Goblet, Repousse Floral, Gold Washed Inside, Wm.Gale & Son ............... 135.00
Silver, American, Inkstand, Openwork, Cut Glass, Black, Starr, & Frost, 1898 ............... 225.00
Silver, American, Jug, Covered, Fluted Baluster Shape, Wm.Gale & Son, 1856 ............... 225.00
Silver, American, Jug, Hot Water, Pear Shape, Floral, Gale & Willis, C.1860 ............... 300.00
Silver, American, Kettle On Lampstand, Scroll & Shell, Hinged, Gorham, C.1890 ............... 325.00
Silver, American, Knife, Bread & Butter, Fiddle Thread, Coles Type, Coin ............... 18.00
Silver, American, Knife, Bread & Butter, Hollow Handle, H.F.In Anchor, Coin ............... 15.00
Silver, American, Knife, Bread & Butter, Olive, Engraved Blade, R.& W.Wilson ............... 18.00
Silver, American, Knife, Bread & Butter, Olive, George B.Appleton, Coin ............... 10.00
Silver, American, Knife, Bread & Butter, Oval Thread With Leaf, Coles, Coin ............... 12.50
Silver, American, Knife, Butter Serving, Engraved Blade, C.1850, Coin ............... 12.75
Silver, American, Knife, Butter Serving, Engraved Floral, Harwood Bros.Coin ............... 10.00
Silver, American, Knife, Butter Serving, Engraved, J.A.Merrill & Co., C.1850 ............... 12.75
Silver, American, Knife, Butter Serving, Olive, Farrington & Hunnewell, 1835 ............... 12.75
Silver, American, Knife, Butter Serving, Olive, J.F.Hinds, C.1850, Coin ............... 12.75
Silver, American, Knife, Butter Serving, Shell Top, Bailey & Co., C.1848, Coin ............... 12.75
Silver, American, Knife, Butter, Engraved, C.S.Ball, Jr., N.Y., C.1850, Coin ............... 11.00
Silver, American, Knife, Butter, Leaf & Scroll, Engraved Blade, Lewis, Coin ............... 17.00
Silver, American, Knife, Butter, Olive, N.Harding, Boston, C.1850, Coin ............... 18.00
Silver, American, Knife, Butter, Raised Fruit On Handle, N.Harding, 1830, Coin ............... 18.00
Silver, American, Knife, Cheese Serving, Engraved, Goddard, C.1850, Coin ............... 12.75
Silver, American, Knife, Cheese Serving, Woman's Head Medallion, C.1850, Coin ............... 11.75
Silver, American, Knife, Fiddle Thread, Albert Coles, Coin ............... 25.00
Silver, American, Knife, Fruit, Albert, Hollow Handle, Cole, C.1844, Coin ............... 16.00
Silver, American, Knife, Fruit, Lady's, Folding, Art Nouveau Handle, Coin ............... 12.00
Silver, American, Knife, Olive Pattern, Initial C., Marked Pure Coin ............... 9.00
Silver, American, Knife, Olive Pattern, Jones, Ball, & Poor, C.1840, Coin ............... 9.00
Silver, American, Knife, Olive, Albert Coles, Coin ............... 12.50
Silver, American, Knife, Olive, Pattern, Nudge & Co., N.Y., C.1848, Coin ............... 9.00

| | |
|---|---|
| Silver, American, Ladle, Beaded Edge, Alexander Coffin Ross, Ohio, Coin | 125.00 |
| Silver, American, Ladle, Beaded Oval Tip, William Gale & Son, Coin | 80.00 |
| Silver, American, Ladle, Bigelow Bros., C.1845, Coin | 35.00 |
| Silver, American, Ladle, Cream, Cut Design On Handle, Byrting, Coin | 25.00 |
| Silver, American, Ladle, Cream, Fiddle Handle, Currier & Trott, C.1835, Coin | 25.00 |
| Silver, American, Ladle, Cream, Fiddle Handle, Initials, Harding, C.1830, Coin | 22.50 |
| Silver, American, Ladle, Cream, Fiddle Handle, Inscribed, L.P.Coe, C.1819 | 45.00 |
| Silver, American, Ladle, Farrington & Hunnewell, Boston, 1830, Coin | 70.00 |
| Silver, American, Ladle, Fiddle, William Smith Pelletreau & T.Richards, Coin | 150.00 |
| Silver, American, Ladle, Gravy, Beaded Oval Tip, William Gale & Son, Coin | 22.00 |
| Silver, American, Ladle, Gravy, Bigelow Bros. & Kennard, Boston, 1845, Coin | 30.00 |
| Silver, American, Ladle, Gravy, Egg & Dart, Wood & Hughes, Coin | 22.50 |
| Silver, American, Ladle, Gravy, Fiddleback, J.Hansell, C.1825, Coin | 75.00 |
| Silver, American, Ladle, Gravy, Fiddleback, Whitney & Hoyt, C.1840, Coin | 35.00 |
| Silver, American, Ladle, Gravy, Raised Crest, C.A.W.Crosby, Boston, C.1840 | 25.00 |
| Silver, American, Ladle, Gravy, Tip On Handle, Bailey & Co., Me., C.1825, Coin | 37.50 |
| Silver, American, Ladle, Initial S, Farrington & Hunnewell, C.1835, Coin | 29.75 |
| Silver, American, Ladle, Initials J.C., E.E.Bailey, Me., C.1825, Coin | 24.75 |
| Silver, American, Ladle, Mustard, Engraved Handle, J.E.Caldwell, Phila., 1850 | 8.95 |
| Silver, American, Ladle, Mustard, Fiddle, Turned Down Handle, S.Huntington | 15.00 |
| Silver, American, Ladle, Mustard, Floral, Coin | 7.50 |
| Silver, American, Ladle, Mustard, H.L.Webster & Co., Providence, C.1831, Coin | 16.00 |
| Silver, American, Ladle, Mustard, Long Handled, Initial, E.Sutton, C.1820, Coin | 8.95 |
| Silver, American, Ladle, Olive, Shell Bowl, Gilbert, Coin | 80.00 |
| Silver, American, Ladle, Punch, Gold Washed Bowl, Coin | 85.00 |
| Silver, American, Ladle, Relish, Olive, Farrington & Hunnewell, C.1835, Coin | 16.00 |
| Silver, American, Ladle, Sauce, Applied Handle, Baldwin & Jones, C.1813, Coin | 35.00 |
| Silver, American, Ladle, Sauce, Basket Of Flowers At Handle, S.Willis, Coin | 28.00 |
| Silver, American, Ladle, Sauce, Engraved, N.Harding, Boston, C.1830, Coin | 30.00 |
| Silver, American, Ladle, Sauce, Fiddle Tip, H.Rosenberg, Coin | 35.00 |
| Silver, American, Ladle, Sauce, Fiddle Tip, Hoyt & Co., N.Y., C.1842, Coin | 18.50 |
| Silver, American, Ladle, Sauce, Fiddle Tip, Steward & Steven, Coin | 20.00 |
| Silver, American, Ladle, Sauce, Fiddle, Shell Bowl, Trask & Morse, Coin | 30.00 |
| Silver, American, Ladle, Sauce, Fiddleback, Whitney & Hoyt, C.1840, Coin | 35.00 |
| Silver, American, Ladle, Sauce, Knowles & Ladd, Providence, Coin | 15.00 |
| Silver, American, Ladle, Sauce, Monarch, Initial W, Star Mark | 15.00 |
| Silver, American, Ladle, Sauce, Shell Bowl, Harris & Stanwood, C.1835, Coin | 25.00 |
| Silver, American, Ladle, Sauce, Turned Down Handle, Emmons, C.1831, Coin | 27.50 |
| Silver, American, Ladle, Sauce, Turned Down Handle, Maker & Eagle, Coin | 37.50 |
| Silver, American, Ladle, Soup, Fiddle Thread, Wm.Gale, N.Y., C.1840 | 95.00 |
| Silver, American, Ladle, Strainer, Oval, Pierced, Palmer & Batchelder, Coin | 32.00 |
| Silver, American, Ladle, W.N.Root & Bro., Coin, 6 In. | 186.00 |
| Silver, American, Mug, Beaded Rims, Engraved, T.& W., Coin, 3 1/2 In High | 150.00 |
| Silver, American, Mug, Presentation, 1864, Coin | 81.00 |
| Silver, American, Oval End, Christian Wiltberger, Coin, Pair | 66.00 |
| Silver, American, Pap Boat, Loop Handle, John Ewan, C.1810, 5 1/4 In.Long | 1300.00 |
| Silver, American, Pendant, Beaver, Jesuit, Touchmarked U, C.1750 | 50.00 |
| Silver, American, Pitcher, Inverted Pear Shape, Repousse, Wilson, C.1840 | 275.00 |
| Silver, American, Pitcher, Milk, Engraved, J.Pitts, C.1850, 8 7/8 In., Coin | 185.00 |
| Silver, American, Pitcher, Oviform, Repousse, Ball, Black & Co., C.1860, 16 In. | 400.00 |
| Silver, American, Pitcher, Repousse Scenes, Eoff & Shepherd, 1853, Pair | 1900.00 |
| Silver, American, Pitcher, Water, Applied Grapevine Collar, Forbes, C.1820 | 950.00 |
| Silver, American, Pitcher, Water, Gorham Co., 1872 _____ Illus | 375.00 |
| Silver, American, Pitcher, Water, Rose Sprays, John Targee, C.1820, 7 In.High | 275.00 |
| Silver, American, Pitcher, Water, Simpson, Hall, & Miller, C.1850, 3 Pint | 150.00 |
| Silver, American, Pitcher, Water, Vase Shape, Key Girdle, Canfield, C.1855 | 375.00 |
| Silver, American, Plate, Gadroon Rim, Fletcher & Gardiner, C.1815, 10 In. | 450.00 |
| Silver, American, Porringer, Pierced Handle, Richardson, C.1790, 5 1/8 In. | 1200.00 |
| Silver, American, Pot, Hot Water, Octagonal, Landscape, O.Rich, C.1850, 5 In. | 170.00 |
| Silver, American, Pot, Mustard, Covered, S Scroll Handle, S.Kirk & Son, C.1846 | 85.00 |
| Silver, American, R.& W. Wilson, Phila., C.1825, Coin | 6.00 |
| Silver, American, Salt Cellar, Octagonal, Pad Feet, Gale, Wood, & Hughes, 1840 | 50.00 |
| Silver, American, Salt Dip, Wood & Hue, Coin | 2.00 |
| Silver, American, Salt Set, Gold Washed Bowl, Pedestal Base, 12 Piece | 89.75 |
| Silver, American, Salt, Master, C.1870, 3 In.Diameter | 48.00 |
| Silver, American, Salt, Master, Gold Wash Bowl, 3 Shell Feet, Wm.Gale, 1832 | 25.00 |

Silver, American, Pitcher,
Water, Gorham Co., 1872
*(See Page 561)*

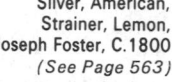

Silver, American,
Strainer, Lemon,
Joseph Foster, C.1800
*(See Page 563)*

| | |
|---|---:|
| **Silver, American,** Salt, Oval, Gadroon Rim, Gorham, C.1855, Pair | 80.00 |
| **Silver, American,** Salver, Presentation, Oak Leaf Feet, Newell Harding, 1855 | 325.00 |
| **Silver, American,** Salver, Square, Latticework Surface, S.Kirk & Son, C.1880 | 175.00 |
| **Silver, American,** Sauceboat, Amorial Cartouche, Oval, Brigden, C.1760, Pair | 8750.00 |
| **Silver, American,** Saucepan, Circular Cup, Joseph Richardson, Sr., C.1750 | 2000.00 |
| **Silver, American,** Scissors, Grape, Gorham, C.1900, 6 1/2 In.Long | 225.00 |
| **Silver, American,** Scoop, Marrow, Twisted Center, Bailey & Co., Coin | 200.00 |
| **Silver, American,** Server, Asparagus, Wm.Sumner, C.1817 | 188.00 |
| **Silver, American,** Server, Dessert, Olive, Harding & Co., Coin | 25.00 |
| **Silver, American,** Server, Pie, Farrington & Hunnewell, Coin | 45.00 |
| **Silver, American,** Shovel, Master Salt, H.L.Sawyer, Conn., Coin | 24.00 |
| **Silver, American,** Shovel, Salt, S.Higgins, Coin, 3 3/4 In.Long | 11.00 |
| **Silver, American,** Spectacles, James Belling, Hamilton, Ont., Coin | 60.00 |
| **Silver, American,** Spectacles, Marked EW, Case With Silver Mounts, Coin | 135.00 |
| **Silver, American,** Spoon, Berry, Olive Type, Fluted Bowl, J.Rudd, Coin | 14.50 |
| **Silver, American,** Spoon, Bright Cut, Pointed Turned Down Handle, W.M.B., 1750 | 25.00 |
| **Silver, American,** Spoon, Child's, Turned Down Handle, Bell, C.1837, Coin | 16.00 |
| **Silver, American,** Spoon, Child's, Turned Down Handle, James, Standard, Coin | 12.50 |
| **Silver, American,** Spoon, Coffin Handle, E.Burr, Providence, C.1800, Coin, Pair | 55.00 |
| **Silver, American,** Spoon, Demitasse, Applied Handle, Shaw, R.I., C.1802, Coin | 14.00 |
| **Silver, American,** Spoon, Demitasse, Pointed, Palmer Bachelders & Co., 1815, 8 | 38.50 |
| **Silver, American,** Spoon, Dessert, A.Skinner, Coin | 10.00 |
| **Silver, American,** Spoon, Dessert, Bigelow Bros., Kennard, Coin, Pair | 15.00 |
| **Silver, American,** Spoon, Dessert, Bright Cut, Harwood Bros., 1814, Coin | 18.00 |
| **Silver, American,** Spoon, Dessert, Chased, Engraved, Canfield Bro.& Co., 1850 | 12.00 |
| **Silver, American,** Spoon, Dessert, Fiddle Thread, Hall & Elton, Coin | 15.00 |
| **Silver, American,** Spoon, Dessert, Fiddle, Ebenezer E.Bailey, Coin | 18.00 |
| **Silver, American,** Spoon, Dessert, Fiddle, Farrington & Hunnewell, 1840, Coin | 9.50 |
| **Silver, American,** Spoon, Dessert, Fiddleback, Kitts & Werne, Ky., C.1865, Coin | 45.00 |
| **Silver, American,** Spoon, Dessert, King's Pattern, Garret Eoff, C.1835, Coin | 22.50 |
| **Silver, American,** Spoon, Dessert, N.Matson, N.Y., C.1845, Coin | 8.00 |
| **Silver, American,** Spoon, Dessert, Olive, C.F.Hanneberg, Coin | 6.00 |
| **Silver, American,** Spoon, Dessert, Pointed Handle, Titcomb, Mass., C.1816, Coin | 16.00 |
| **Silver, American,** Spoon, Dessert, S.Chapin, Coin | 10.00 |
| **Silver, American,** Spoon, Dessert, Sharp Points, Perudriaux, C.1830, Coin | 17.50 |
| **Silver, American,** Spoon, Dessert, Sheaf Of Wheat, Watson & Brown | 40.00 |
| **Silver, American,** Spoon, Dessert, T.Steele & Co., Hartford, 1805, Coin | 10.00 |
| **Silver, American,** Spoon, Dessert, Turned Down Handle, Engraved, C.1820, Coin | 16.00 |
| **Silver, American,** Spoon, Dessert, Wreath, D.Valentine, Syracuse, C.1850, Coin | 12.50 |
| **Silver, American,** Spoon, G.& L.Clawson In Script, Coin, 8 3/4 In.Long | 20.00 |
| **Silver, American,** Spoon, G.M.Dunlap In Script, N.Matson, Owego, N.Y., Coin | 17.50 |
| **Silver, American,** Spoon, Horseradish, Fiddle Thread, Bailey & Co., C.1835 | 15.00 |
| **Silver, American,** Spoon, J.Hollister, Coin, 8 3/4 In.Long | 20.00 |
| **Silver, American,** Spoon, Jelly, Twisted Stem, Engraved Top, Albert Coles, Coin | 10.00 |
| **Silver, American,** Spoon, Joel Sayre, N.Y., C.1795 | 25.00 |
| **Silver, American,** Spoon, Master Salt, Engraved Mumford, R.I., C.1813, Coin | 8.95 |
| **Silver, American,** Spoon, Master Salt, Fiddle Tip, James Ford, C.1830, Coin | 8.00 |
| **Silver, American,** Spoon, Master Salt, Initial K, Braverman & Co., 1863, Coin | 7.95 |

Silver, American, Spoon, Master Salt, Initial S, Gorham, Patent 1861, Coin ............... 7.95
Silver, American, Spoon, Master Salt, Initial, E.Sutton, C.1820, Coin ...................... 7.95
Silver, American, Spoon, Master Salt, Initials, A.S.Dygert, C.1830 ......................... 15.00
Silver, American, Spoon, Master Salt, T.Ireland, C.1840, Coin ............................. 7.95
Silver, American, Spoon, Mustard, Fiddle Tip, Edward Mead, Coin .......................... 25.00
Silver, American, Spoon, Mustard, Fiddle Tip, Palmer & Batchelder, Coin .................. 18.00
Silver, American, Spoon, Mustard, Fiddle Tip, S.P.Bailey, Coin ............................ 22.50
Silver, American, Spoon, Mustard, Fiddle, Pseudo Hallmarks, Star, Head, Anchor ........... 10.00
Silver, American, Spoon, Mustard, Initialed, Cleveland & Post, C.1815 .................... 20.00
Silver, American, Spoon, Mustard, Oval Thread, W.J.Vanderhoef, Coin ...................... 10.00
Silver, American, Spoon, Mustard, Oval Tip, Smith & Chamberlain, Coin .................... 18.00
Silver, American, Spoon, Oval Tip, Moore & Ferguson, Phila., C.1790 ...................... 25.00
Silver, American, Spoon, Potato Salad, 3 Pronged, Bright Cut, Marked Coin ................ 55.00
Silver, American, Spoon, Rattailed, C.1740, 5 In. ....................................... 60.00
Silver, American, Spoon, S.C.Frey, Coin, 6 In. .......................................... 8.00
Silver, American, Spoon, Salt, Fiddle Tip, M.K.Holt, Coin ............................... 10.00
Silver, American, Spoon, Salt, Fiddle Tip, Palmer & Batchelder, Coin, Pair ............... 25.00
Silver, American, Spoon, Salt, Fiddle, A.Stowell, Coin .................................. 10.00
Silver, American, Spoon, Salt, Fiddle, G.Green, Coin .................................... 10.00
Silver, American, Spoon, Salt, Fiddle, W.McGrew, Coin ................................... 12.00
Silver, American, Spoon, Salt, Fiddleback, Shell Bowl, Garrett, C.1825, Coin ............. 15.00
Silver, American, Spoon, Salt, Hanford, Coin ............................................ 9.00
Silver, American, Spoon, Salt, Joshua G.Davis, Boston, 1796, Coin ....................... 15.00
Silver, American, Spoon, Salt, M.& T., Coin ............................................. 7.00
Silver, American, Spoon, Salt, Pointed Tip, Oval, Richards, Phila., C.1790 ............... 37.50
Silver, American, Spoon, Salt, Shell Bowl, J.Hollister, N.Y., Coin ...................... 11.00
Silver, American, Spoon, Serving, Applied Handle, Homes, C.1750, Coin ................... 75.00
Silver, American, Spoon, Serving, Applied Handle, Hugh Wishart, C.1800, Coin ............. 60.00
Silver, American, Spoon, Serving, Applied Handle, McKeen, Phila, C.1825, Coin ............ 18.00
Silver, American, Spoon, Serving, Applied Handle, Seal, Phila., C.1810, Coin ............. 37.50
Silver, American, Spoon, Serving, Applied Handle, Shoemaker, C.1750, Coin ................ 60.00
Silver, American, Spoon, Serving, Applied Handle, Whartenby, C.1811, Coin ................ 37.50
Silver, American, Spoon, Serving, Chaudron & Co., Phila., C.1807, Coin ................... 21.50
Silver, American, Spoon, Serving, Engraved Handle & Bowl, Newell Harding ................. 35.00
Silver, American, Spoon, Serving, Engraved, Hastings, Cleveland, C.1830, Coin ............ 25.00
Silver, American, Spoon, Serving, F.& D.Kinsey, Newport, Ky., Coin ...................... 36.50
Silver, American, Spoon, Serving, F.Richmond, 1892, Coin ................................ 18.00
Silver, American, Spoon, Serving, Fiddle, Engraved, Reed & Slader, Coin .................. 35.00
Silver, American, Spoon, Serving, Medallion Handle, E.Jaccad & Co., Coin ................. 22.50
Silver, American, Spoon, Serving, Olive Type, Shell Bowl, J.E.Caldwell & Co. ............. 25.00
Silver, American, Spoon, Serving, Oval Deep Bowl, Marked Coin, 8 3/4 In ................. 24.75
Silver, American, Spoon, Serving, Pinched Fiddle, Moulton, Mass., Coin ................... 17.50
Silver, American, Spoon, Serving, Raised Tip, Bennett & Caldwell, C.1843, Coin ........... 18.00
Silver, American, Spoon, Serving, Shell Bowl, Hutchkiss & Schreuder, 1864 ................ 47.50
Silver, American, Spoon, Serving, Shell Drop, W.W.White, C.1830, Coin .................... 20.00
Silver, American, Spoon, Serving, Turned Down Applied Handle, W.Seal, C.1810 ............. 37.50
Silver, American, Spoon, Serving, Turned Down Handle, C.1806, Coin ...................... 30.00
Silver, American, Spoon, Serving, Wreath, Shell Bowl, Haddock, Lincoln & Foss ........... 35.00
Silver, American, Spoon, Sugar, Engraved, R.& W.Wilson, Phila., Coin .................... 25.00
Silver, American, Spoon, Sugar, Fiddle Tip, Shell Bowl, Starr & Goodrich, Coin ........... 22.00
Silver, American, Spoon, Sugar, Fiddle Tip, Shovel Bowl, Lewis, Pa., Coin ................ 18.50
Silver, American, Spoon, Sugar, Fiddle, Shell Bowl, Trask & Morse, Coin .................. 18.00
Silver, American, Spoon, Tea Caddy, Fiddleback, George Unite, C.1841 .................... 45.00
Silver, American, Spur, Star Shape, William Mannerback, C.1820 .......................... 425.00
Silver, American, Strainer, Lemon, Joseph Foster, C.1800 ........................ *Illus* 475.00
Silver, American, Strainer, Tea, Short Handle, B.Gorham Mfg.Co., Coin ................... 20.00
Silver, American, Sugar & Creamer, Cover, Greek Key At Top, Bailey & Co.Coin ............. 425.00
Silver, American, Sugar Shell, Bright Cut, Gold Wash Bowl, Lindsay & Co. ................. 12.75
Silver, American, Sugar Shell, Engraved, Initial A, Marked Pure Coin, C.1835 ............. 12.75
Silver, American, Sugar Shell, Fiddle Handle, Squire Bros., N.Y., C.1845, Coin ........... 11.00
Silver, American, Sugar Shell, Initial R, Farrington & Hunnell, C.1835, Coin ............. 13.75
Silver, American, Sugar Shell, Initials J.W.C., Wood & Hughes, C.1845, Coin .............. 13.75
Silver, American, Sugar Shell, Initials, George B.Appleton, C.1850, Coin ................. 13.75
Silver, American, Sugar Shell, J.W.& B.H.M.McDuffy, Coin ................................ 18.00
Silver, American, Sugar Shell, Newell Harding & Co., Boston, C.1850, Coin ................ 13.75
Silver, American, Sugar Shell, Olive Type, Fluted Bowl, J.Rudd ......................... 15.00

Silver, American, Sugar Shell, Olive, Gold Washed Shell, Cole, C.1850, Coin ............... 18.00
Silver, American, Sugar Shell, Oval Tip, C.R.Burch, Pseudo Hallmarks, Coin ............... 12.50
Silver, American, Sugar Shovel, Engraved, Speer & Cosper, Chicago, Coin ............... 25.00
Silver, American, Sugar, Baluster Finial, Scroll Handles, Lewis, C.1820 ............... 425.00
Silver, American, Sugar, Bud Finial, Scroll Handled, Eoff, N.Y., C.1830 ............... 325.00
Silver, American, Sugar, Covered, Curry & Reston, C.1830, Chased, 10 In.High ............... 200.00
Silver, American, Sugar, Covered, Rectangular, Cut Leaf Engraved, C.1820, Coin ............... 165.00
Silver, American, Tablespoon, A.Voorhees, Coin ............... 19.25
Silver, American, Tablespoon, Applied Handle, Howe & Co., N.Y., C.1837, Coin ............... 16.00
Silver, American, Tablespoon, Basket Of Flowers, Hallmarks, Head, Lion, Coin ............... 45.50
Silver, American, Tablespoon, Basket Of Flowers, Hallmarks, Leopard & Star ............... 50.00
Silver, American, Tablespoon, Basket Of Flowers, William Smith, Coin ............... 56.50
Silver, American, Tablespoon, Bolles & Childs, Hartford, 1840, Coin ............... 12.00
Silver, American, Tablespoon, Bright Cut, Wm.Gale, Jr., C.1844 ............... 35.00
Silver, American, Tablespoon, D.B.F.In Script, R.H.Bailey, Woodstock, Vt. ............... 10.00
Silver, American, Tablespoon, D.Brown, Phila., 1811, Coin ............... 15.00
Silver, American, Tablespoon, Engraved D., Marked Star, S, & Eagle, 1840s, Coin ............... 15.00
Silver, American, Tablespoon, Engraved E.A.Fay, John Polhamus, N.Y., C.1833 ............... 11.75
Silver, American, Tablespoon, Engraved E.C.Walker, Chubbuck, C.1850, Coin ............... 8.75
Silver, American, Tablespoon, Engraved Handle, J.R.Reed & Co., C.1846, Coin ............... 11.75
Silver, American, Tablespoon, Engraved Hildreth, J.Fenno, Mass., C.1825, Coin ............... 11.75
Silver, American, Tablespoon, Engraved Hildreth, Joseph Raynes, C.1835, Coin ............... 11.75
Silver, American, Tablespoon, Engraved I.A., Levenworth, Detroit, C.1840, Coin ............... 16.00
Silver, American, Tablespoon, Engraved M.P.Jenks, D.B.Warren, C.1809, Coin ............... 12.75
Silver, American, Tablespoon, Engraved MRG, D.M.Fitch, N.Y., C.1840, Coin ............... 17.50
Silver, American, Tablespoon, Engraved W.M.L., T.Schwabe, Coin ............... 15.50
Silver, American, Tablespoon, Engraved Z.D.Robinson, J.N.Gage & Co., C.1835 ............... 12.75
Silver, American, Tablespoon, Engraved, D.B.Warren, Phila., C.1835, Coin ............... 12.75
Silver, American, Tablespoon, Engraved, J.N.Gage & Co., C.1835, Coin ............... 12.75
Silver, American, Tablespoon, Engraved, Reed & Co., C.1846, Coin ............... 12.50
Silver, American, Tablespoon, F.Curtis, Coin ............... 12.00
Silver, American, Tablespoon, Feather Edge, Coin ............... 25.00
Silver, American, Tablespoon, Fiddle Thread, Bailey & Co., Coin ............... 12.50
Silver, American, Tablespoon, Fiddle Thread, Gale, Wood, & Hughes, N.Y., Coin ............... 15.00
Silver, American, Tablespoon, Fiddle Thread, Jones, Ball & Poor, Coin ............... 10.85
Silver, American, Tablespoon, Fiddle Thread, Leaf, T.Evans & Co., 1855, Coin ............... 11.00
Silver, American, Tablespoon, Fiddle, Abraham Fellows, Coin ............... 15.00
Silver, American, Tablespoon, Fiddle, Alfred L.Lockwood, Coin, Pair ............... 35.00
Silver, American, Tablespoon, Fiddle, Charles Gennet, Jr., Coin, Pair ............... 75.00
Silver, American, Tablespoon, Fiddle, Davis, Palmer, & Co., C.1841, Coin ............... 14.00
Silver, American, Tablespoon, Fiddle, E.E.Bailey, Coin ............... 35.00
Silver, American, Tablespoon, Fiddle, Erastus Cook, Coin, Pair ............... 35.00
Silver, American, Tablespoon, Fiddle, G.W.King, Hallmarks, Lion, D, Head, Coin ............... 15.00
Silver, American, Tablespoon, Fiddle, Gale & Willis, Coin, Pair ............... 25.00
Silver, American, Tablespoon, Fiddle, HL SA Maker, Coin ............... 11.10
Silver, American, Tablespoon, Fiddle, Isiah Lukens, Coin ............... 28.35
Silver, American, Tablespoon, Fiddle, J.Brock, Coin ............... 15.00
Silver, American, Tablespoon, Fiddle, Jaccard & Co., Coin ............... 15.00
Silver, American, Tablespoon, Fiddle, James M.Ford, Coin, Pair ............... 30.00
Silver, American, Tablespoon, Fiddle, John & Peter Targee, Coin ............... 55.00
Silver, American, Tablespoon, Fiddle, Joseph Ketcham, Coin ............... 18.75
Silver, American, Tablespoon, Fiddle, Joseph Shoemaker, Coin, Pair ............... 75.00
Silver, American, Tablespoon, Fiddle, Palmer & Batchelder, Coin ............... 12.50
Silver, American, Tablespoon, Fiddle, R.& W.Wilson, Coin ............... 15.00
Silver, American, Tablespoon, Fiddle, Raised Top, Engraved, I.S.Pear, Chicago ............... 17.50
Silver, American, Tablespoon, Fiddle, Raised Top, T.Levenworth, Detroit, Coin ............... 16.00
Silver, American, Tablespoon, Fiddle, Samuel Brown, Pseudo Hallmarks, Coin ............... 15.00
Silver, American, Tablespoon, Fiddle, Sherwood & Whatley, Chicago, Coin ............... 16.00
Silver, American, Tablespoon, Fiddle, Turned Down, J.T.Peabody, C.1787, Coin ............... 45.00
Silver, American, Tablespoon, Fiddle, W.Thomson, Coin ............... 10.00
Silver, American, Tablespoon, Fiddle, William Rogers, Coin ............... 15.00
Silver, American, Tablespoon, Fiddleback, C.1850, Coin ............... 15.00
Silver, American, Tablespoon, Fluted Bowl, J.Rudd, Coin ............... 15.00
Silver, American, Tablespoon, Forward Tip, Monogram Reverse, Joseph Rogers ............... 95.00
Silver, American, Tablespoon, Forward Tip, Monogram, Underhill & Vernon, Coin ............... 95.00
Silver, American, Tablespoon, G.Baker, Providence, 1825, Coin ............... 12.00

| | |
|---|---|
| **Silver, American,** Tablespoon, Hotchkiss & Schreuder, N.Y., C.1850, Coin | 13.00 |
| **Silver, American,** Tablespoon, Initial B, Currier & Trott, C.1836, Coin | 12.75 |
| **Silver, American,** Tablespoon, Initial E, Pitkin, C.1825, Coin | 12.75 |
| **Silver, American,** Tablespoon, Initials A.W., Benjamin Goddard, C.1835, Coin | 11.75 |
| **Silver, American,** Tablespoon, Initials A.W., D.W.& Co., Boston, C.1820, Coin | 11.75 |
| **Silver, American,** Tablespoon, Initials J.M.W., M & A, Utica, C.1840, Coin | 12.75 |
| **Silver, American,** Tablespoon, Initials L.C., A.W.Stearns & Co., C.1835, Coin | 8.75 |
| **Silver, American,** Tablespoon, Initials M.A.C., C.1840, Coin | 12.75 |
| **Silver, American,** Tablespoon, Initials M.A.R., A.Parker, C.1840, Coin | 8.75 |
| **Silver, American,** Tablespoon, Initials O.H., I.H.Clark & Co., C.1810, Coin | 12.75 |
| **Silver, American,** Tablespoon, Initials, Mitchell & Tyler, Va., C.1845, Coin | 14.75 |
| **Silver, American,** Tablespoon, J.G.Thompson, Coin | 15.00 |
| **Silver, American,** Tablespoon, Joseph Anthony, Jr., Coin, Pair | 95.00 |
| **Silver, American,** Tablespoon, Keystone Top, Engraved, Farrington & Hunnewell | 14.35 |
| **Silver, American,** Tablespoon, King's Pattern, P.L.Krider, C.1850, Coin, Pair | 30.00 |
| **Silver, American,** Tablespoon, Kinsey, Ky. & Cincinnati, C.1836, Coin | 37.50 |
| **Silver, American,** Tablespoon, M.A.Lewis & Co., C.1840, Coin, Pair | 14.75 |
| **Silver, American,** Tablespoon, Mulford & Wendell, C.1842, Coin | 18.00 |
| **Silver, American,** Tablespoon, Old Maryland, Engraved, A.E.Warner, Coin | 11.65 |
| **Silver, American,** Tablespoon, Oval Thread & Leaf, Albert Cole, Coin | 10.85 |
| **Silver, American,** Tablespoon, Oval Thread, Bigelow & Kennard, Coin, Pair | 25.00 |
| **Silver, American,** Tablespoon, Oval Tip, A.Sanborn, Coin | 10.00 |
| **Silver, American,** Tablespoon, Ovoid Form, Tipped Handle, Brewer & Co., C.1850 | 11.00 |
| **Silver, American,** Tablespoon, Pinched Fiddle, Kimball, Buffalo, C.1837, Coin | 15.00 |
| **Silver, American,** Tablespoon, Pointed End & Drop, John Vernon, Coin | 60.00 |
| **Silver, American,** Tablespoon, Pointed End, Raised Tip, Petersen, Coin | 16.00 |
| **Silver, American,** Tablespoon, Pointed Handle, Coin, 9 In.Long | 8.00 |
| **Silver, American,** Tablespoon, Rattail Back, C.Branda & Co., Va., C.1818, Coin | 16.75 |
| **Silver, American,** Tablespoon, Rogers & Smith, Coin | 7.50 |
| **Silver, American,** Tablespoon, Rogers, Coin | 6.00 |
| **Silver, American,** Tablespoon, Round End, Engraved, William Coffin Little | 45.00 |
| **Silver, American,** Tablespoon, Round End, J.Lynch, Coin | 45.00 |
| **Silver, American,** Tablespoon, Round End, Long Drop, John Vernon, Coin | 55.00 |
| **Silver, American,** Tablespoon, Rounded Terminal, Holland, Md., C.1800 | 50.00 |
| **Silver, American,** Tablespoon, S.C.Owen, Platt & Brother, C.1825, Coin | 12.75 |
| **Silver, American,** Tablespoon, S.K.Fish, Coin, Pair | 28.00 |
| **Silver, American,** Tablespoon, Scallop Shell Back, Bright Cut Flower, Pair | 100.00 |
| **Silver, American,** Tablespoon, Sheaf Of Wheat, Everard Benjamin & Co., Coin | 50.00 |
| **Silver, American,** Tablespoon, Tessy In Script, Leaf & Scroll, A.G. | 15.00 |
| **Silver, American,** Tablespoon, Turned Down Handle, Conrad, Phila., C.1845, Coin | 18.00 |
| **Silver, American,** Tablespoon, Turned Down Handle, Sherwood & Whatley, Coin | 12.50 |
| **Silver, American,** Tablespoon, Wrigglework Borders, Paul Revere, C.1780, Pair | 2600.00 |
| **Silver, American,** Tankard, Cylindrical, Armorials, Flat Cover, C.1750, 7 In. | 450.00 |
| **Silver, American,** Tankard, Cylindrical, Samuel Minott, C.1780, 7 3/4 In. | 2300.00 |
| **Silver, American,** Tankard, Scroll Handle, Pierced Thumbpiece, Lownes, C.1800 | 1200.00 |
| **Silver, American,** Tazza, Shallow, Wide Rims, Chased, Tiffany, C.1915, Set Of 4 | 500.00 |
| **Silver, American,** Tea & Coffee Set, Acorn Finials, Lownes, Phila., C.1830, 4 | 1500.00 |
| **Silver, American,** Tea & Coffee Set, Black, Starr & Frost, C.1925, 6 Piece | 1250.00 |
| **Silver, American,** Tea & Coffee Set, Claw Feet, Starr, C.1890, 4 Piece | 1650.00 |
| **Silver, American,** Tea & Coffee Set, Eoff & Shepherd, C.1855, 4 Piece | 750.00 |
| **Silver, American,** Tea & Coffee Set, Repousse, Chased, Kirk, C.1890, 5 Piece | 3100.00 |
| **Silver, American,** Tea Set, Hand-Chased, C.1850, 5 Piece | 1200.00 |
| **Silver, American,** Tea Set, Hearts, Ball, Tompkins & Black, C.1839, 5 Piece | 2200.00 |
| **Silver, American,** Tea Set, Key Pattern Border, Gorham, C.1890, 5 Piece | 1600.00 |
| **Silver, American,** Tea Set, William Thomson, 1831, 3 Piece    *Illus* | 1700.00 |
| **Silver, American,** Teapot, Cupids & Floral, Cupid On Rosebush Handle, Coin | 275.00 |
| **Silver, American,** Teapot, Hemispherical, Edward Lownes, C.1830, 9 3/8 In.High | 400.00 |
| **Silver, American,** Teapot, John & Peter Targee, C.1805    *Illus* | 500.00 |
| **Silver, American,** Teapot, John Jenkins, Phila., C.1785    *Illus* | 1700.00 |
| **Silver, American,** Teapot, Oval, Ball Feet, Lioness Finial, Edward Rockwell | 550.00 |
| **Silver, American,** Teapot, Oval, Melon Lobed, Engraved Floral, Robert Monteith | 850.00 |
| **Silver, American,** Teaspoon, A.Dauth, Coin | 5.85 |
| **Silver, American,** Teaspoon, A.L.Burbank, Coin | 8.50 |
| **Silver, American,** Teaspoon, A.Sanborn, Ma., C.1850, Coin | 5.95 |
| **Silver, American,** Teaspoon, Albert, Initial E, Welch, C.1850, Coin | 6.40 |
| **Silver, American,** Teaspoon, Applied Handle, Wilson, Phila., C.1830, Coin | 8.35 |

Silver, American, Teapot, John Jenkins, Phila., C.1785
*(See Page 565)*

Silver, American, Teapot,
John & Peter Targee, C.1805
*(See Page 565)*

Silver, American, Tea Set,
William Thomson, 1831,
3 Piece
*(See Page 565)*

| | |
|---|---:|
| **Silver, American,** Teaspoon, B.Goddard, Coin | 5.00 |
| **Silver, American,** Teaspoon, Basket Of Flowers, Appollos Moore, Coin | 29.25 |
| **Silver, American,** Teaspoon, Basket Of Flowers, D.B.Hempstead, Coin | 25.00 |
| **Silver, American,** Teaspoon, Basket Of Flowers, New York, Coin | 25.00 |
| **Silver, American,** Teaspoon, Basket Of Flowers, Stebbins & Howe, Coin | 27.00 |
| **Silver, American,** Teaspoon, Basket Of Flowers, William Smith, Coin, Pair | 55.00 |
| **Silver, American,** Teaspoon, Beasom & Co., N.H., C.1830, Coin | 10.00 |
| **Silver, American,** Teaspoon, Bessac In Script, C.B.Brown, Rochester, Coin | 10.00 |
| **Silver, American,** Teaspoon, Bright Cut, H.& C.Brandt, Coin, Pair | 45.00 |
| **Silver, American,** Teaspoon, Bright Cut, J.Shanck, Coin | 25.00 |
| **Silver, American,** Teaspoon, Bright Cut, Jeronimus Alstyne, Coin | 25.00 |
| **Silver, American,** Teaspoon, Bright Cut, Joseph Shoemaker, Coin | 30.00 |
| **Silver, American,** Teaspoon, Bright Cut, Timothy Bontecou, Jr., Coin | 25.00 |
| **Silver, American,** Teaspoon, Bright Cut, William Grigg, Coin | 26.50 |
| **Silver, American,** Teaspoon, Bright Cut, Z.Owen, Coin | 26.50 |
| **Silver, American,** Teaspoon, Broad Tip Handle, Reed & Sons, Pa., C.1830, Coin | 6.40 |
| **Silver, American,** Teaspoon, C.A.W. Crosby, Boston, C.1840, Coin | 6.00 |
| **Silver, American,** Teaspoon, Charles Brewer, Conn., 1880 | 10.00 |
| **Silver, American,** Teaspoon, Coffin End, Engraved, Bright Cut, Bernard Wenman | 20.00 |
| **Silver, American,** Teaspoon, Coffin End, Engraved, Bright Cut, John Boutier | 30.00 |
| **Silver, American,** Teaspoon, Coffin End, Engraved, Bright Cut, Samuel White | 30.00 |
| **Silver, American,** Teaspoon, Coffin End, Engraved, Colin V.G.Forbes, Coin | 18.00 |
| **Silver, American,** Teaspoon, Coffin End, Engraved, John Stair Blackman, Coin | 18.00 |
| **Silver, American,** Teaspoon, Coffin Handle, Baldwin, Boston, C.1813, Coin | 25.00 |
| **Silver, American,** Teaspoon, Crittendon, N.Y., C.1824, Coin | 7.00 |
| **Silver, American,** Teaspoon, E.A.Beauvals, St.Louis, C.1840, Coin, Pair | 13.00 |
| **Silver, American,** Teaspoon, E.Rouse, Jr., Coin | 7.50 |
| **Silver, American,** Teaspoon, Elongated Fiddleback, Whartenby, Phila., C.1810 | 22.50 |
| **Silver, American,** Teaspoon, Engraved D.Thomas, E.E.Bailey & Co., C.1825, Coin | 4.95 |
| **Silver, American,** Teaspoon, Engraved E.S.Samson, C.1850, Coin | 3.95 |
| **Silver, American,** Teaspoon, Engraved F.F., Gardiner, St.Louis, C.1853, Coin | 9.00 |
| **Silver, American,** Teaspoon, Engraved Handle, Reed & Co., C.1840, Coin | 4.95 |
| **Silver, American,** Teaspoon, Engraved L.M.B., Davis, Boston, C.1820, Coin | 9.00 |
| **Silver, American,** Teaspoon, Engraved McC, Webb, Baltimore, C.1840, Coin | 15.00 |
| **Silver, American,** Teaspoon, Engraved MRG, D.M.Fitch, N.Y., C.1840, Coin | 8.40 |
| **Silver, American,** Teaspoon, Engraved M.T.W., Sibley, N.Y., C.1836, Coin | 8.00 |

| | |
|---|---|
| Silver, American, Teaspoon, Engraved S, Lincoln & Foss, Boston, C.1850, Coin | 9.00 |
| Silver, American, Teaspoon, Engraved, Clark, C.1830, Coin | 10.00 |
| Silver, American, Teaspoon, Engraved, J.R.Reed & Co., C.1846, Coin | 4.95 |
| Silver, American, Teaspoon, F.Curtis, Coin | 8.00 |
| Silver, American, Teaspoon, F.S.Blackman, Danbury, 1811, Coin | 7.50 |
| Silver, American, Teaspoon, Farrington & Hunnewell, C.1840, Coin | 6.50 |
| Silver, American, Teaspoon, Fiddle Thread, Unmarked, Coin | 9.35 |
| Silver, American, Teaspoon, Fiddle Thread, William Wise, Coin | 6.50 |
| Silver, American, Teaspoon, Fiddle, A.E.Warner, Coin | 10.00 |
| Silver, American, Teaspoon, Fiddle, Brinsmaid's, Coin | 10.00 |
| Silver, American, Teaspoon, Fiddle, Colin V.G.Forbes, Coin | 5.28 |
| Silver, American, Teaspoon, Fiddle, E.Mead, Coin | 19.00 |
| Silver, American, Teaspoon, Fiddle, Engraved, Clark, N.Y.C., C.1812, Coin | 8.00 |
| Silver, American, Teaspoon, Fiddle, Engraved, William Moulton, Coin | 20.00 |
| Silver, American, Teaspoon, Fiddle, G.W.Bull, Coin | 6.00 |
| Silver, American, Teaspoon, Fiddle, H.Goodwin, Coin | 5.00 |
| Silver, American, Teaspoon, Fiddle, Hall & Hewson, Coin | 4.50 |
| Silver, American, Teaspoon, Fiddle, Harris & Wilcox, Coin | 6.00 |
| Silver, American, Teaspoon, Fiddle, J.Abbott, Coin | 10.00 |
| Silver, American, Teaspoon, Fiddle, JVD In Rectangular Cartouche, Coin | 5.00 |
| Silver, American, Teaspoon, Fiddle, James Black, Coin | 5.00 |
| Silver, American, Teaspoon, Fiddle, James Guthrie, Coin | 15.00 |
| Silver, American, Teaspoon, Fiddle, John Lynch, Coin | 11.50 |
| Silver, American, Teaspoon, Fiddle, Nicholas Hutchins, Coin | 15.00 |
| Silver, American, Teaspoon, Fiddle, No Wings, JVD In Rectangular Cartouche | 7.50 |
| Silver, American, Teaspoon, Fiddle, R.& A.Campbell, Coin | 15.00 |
| Silver, American, Teaspoon, Fiddle, Rogers & Cole, Coin | 5.00 |
| Silver, American, Teaspoon, Fiddle, S Brown, Coin, Pair | 10.00 |
| Silver, American, Teaspoon, Fiddle, Turned Down, Aiken & Coon, Ohio, Coin | 5.75 |
| Silver, American, Teaspoon, Fiddle, W.Kimball, Coin | 5.00 |
| Silver, American, Teaspoon, Fiddle, W.Mitchell, Jr., Coin | 19.00 |
| Silver, American, Teaspoon, Fiddleback, Coin | 6.00 |
| Silver, American, Teaspoon, Fiddleback, G.Loomis, Pa., C.1840, Coin | 12.00 |
| Silver, American, Teaspoon, Fiddleback, Gorham & Co., R.I., C.1840, Coin | 10.00 |
| Silver, American, Teaspoon, Fiddleback, Hart & Smith, Baltimore, C.1815, Coin | 15.00 |
| Silver, American, Teaspoon, Fiddleback, Matson, N.Y., C.1840, Coin | 12.50 |
| Silver, American, Teaspoon, Fiddleback, N.E.Crittendon, Ohio, C.1835, Coin | 15.00 |
| Silver, American, Teaspoon, Fiddleback, Ward & Cox, Phila., C.1810, Coin | 20.00 |
| Silver, American, Teaspoon, Fiddleback, Wilson, Phila., C.1830, Coin | 10.00 |
| Silver, American, Teaspoon, G.Hoyt, 1827, Coin | 8.25 |
| Silver, American, Teaspoon, Gleason & Reed, Nashua, 1830, Coin | 7.50 |
| Silver, American, Teaspoon, H.A.Coe, Coin | 5.00 |
| Silver, American, Teaspoon, H.McKeen, Phila., C.1820, Coin | 6.00 |
| Silver, American, Teaspoon, H.P.Seymour, C.1840, Marked Pure Coin | 4.95 |
| Silver, American, Teaspoon, Hollister, N.Y., C.1818, Coin | 7.00 |
| Silver, American, Teaspoon, I.Davis, Coin | 6.00 |
| Silver, American, Teaspoon, Initials D.P.P., Laconia, N.H., Coin | 5.00 |
| Silver, American, Teaspoon, Initials D.V.C., Burritt & Son, Ithaca, Coin | 10.00 |
| Silver, American, Teaspoon, Initials E.M.B., N.Matson, Coin, 6 1/8 In. | 10.50 |
| Silver, American, Teaspoon, Initials E.W., Watson & Brown, Phila., C.1820 | 4.95 |
| Silver, American, Teaspoon, Initials J.C.S., D.T.Goodhue, C.1840, Coin | 4.95 |
| Silver, American, Teaspoon, Initials M.A.C., J.Fenno, C.1825, Coin | 4.95 |
| Silver, American, Teaspoon, Initials M.I.L., C.1840, Coin | 4.95 |
| Silver, American, Teaspoon, Initials M.S., Charles C.Shaver, C.1854, Coin | 4.95 |
| Silver, American, Teaspoon, Initials M.S., T.Steele, Conn., C.1800, Coin | 4.95 |
| Silver, American, Teaspoon, Initials M.T., J.A.Inglis, C.1850, Coin, Set Of 7 | 34.75 |
| Silver, American, Teaspoon, Initials P.S.C., Phillip Huntington, C.1820, Coin | 4.95 |
| Silver, American, Teaspoon, Initials R.H.G., H.L.Webster & Co., C.1831, Coin | 4.95 |
| Silver, American, Teaspoon, Initials R.S., Pitkin & Norton, C.1825, Coin | 4.95 |
| Silver, American, Teaspoon, Initials S.K., Newell Harding, C.1820, Coin | 4.95 |
| Silver, American, Teaspoon, Initials, Gennette & Osborne, C.1830, Coin | 4.95 |
| Silver, American, Teaspoon, Initials, Storrs & Cooley, C.1831, Coin | 4.95 |
| Silver, American, Teaspoon, J.Gorham & Son, Coin | 8.50 |
| Silver, American, Teaspoon, King's Pattern, Garret Eoff, N.Y., C.1835, Coin | 16.00 |
| Silver, American, Teaspoon, L.Kimball, Coin | 8.50 |

Silver, American, Teaspoon, Livermore, Ball & Co., Coin .................................................... 6.50
Silver, American, Teaspoon, Matson, N.Y., C.1845, Coin ...................................................... 7.00
Silver, American, Teaspoon, Monogram, J.R.Benjamin, Coin .............................................. 7.00
Silver, American, Teaspoon, Monogram, W.Pitkin, Coin ....................................................... 7.00
Silver, American, Teaspoon, N.& T. Foster, Newburyport, Mass., C.1820, Coin ............ 6.00
Silver, American, Teaspoon, N.Freeborn, N.E., Coin ............................................................. 8.50
Silver, American, Teaspoon, O.Howe, Coin ............................................................................ 7.80
Silver, American, Teaspoon, O.Reed, Coin ............................................................................. 8.50
Silver, American, Teaspoon, Old English, Engraved, Hewson & Brower, Coin ............... 6.00
Silver, American, Teaspoon, Olive, Ford On Handle, Beggs & Smith, Ky., Coin ............. 10.85
Silver, American, Teaspoon, Olive, Haddock, Lincoln & Foss, Boston, C.1861 ............. 4.65
Silver, American, Teaspoon, Olive, N.Harding, Coin ............................................................. 6.25
Silver, American, Teaspoon, Oval End, Christian Wiltberger, Coin ................................. 20.00
Silver, American, Teaspoon, Oval End, J.Jackson, Coin ..................................................... 25.00
Silver, American, Teaspoon, Oval End, John Martin, Coin .................................................. 21.50
Silver, American, Teaspoon, Oval End, John Myers, Coin, Pair ......................................... 75.00
Silver, American, Teaspoon, Oval End, Philip Garrett, Coin ............................................... 22.25
Silver, American, Teaspoon, Oval End, Pricked Design On Bowl Back, Coin ................. 10.00
Silver, American, Teaspoon, Oval Thread Tipped, C.Hulse, Coin ..................................... 5.75
Silver, American, Teaspoon, Oval Thread With Leaf, Albert Cole, Coin .......................... 6.65
Silver, American, Teaspoon, Oval Thread With Leaf, Gale & Willis, Coin ....................... 5.00
Silver, American, Teaspoon, Oval Tip, Shoemaker, Phila., C.1790 .................................. 20.00
Silver, American, Teaspoon, Oval Tipped, Lowell & Senter, Coin, Pair .......................... 25.00
Silver, American, Teaspoon, Oval Top, Robt.Evans, Boston, C.1780, Pair ..................... 50.00
Silver, American, Teaspoon, Paul Revere, C.1792, 5 1/2 In ........................... *Illus* 700.00
Silver, American, Teaspoon, Picuette, Detroit, 1848, Coin ................................................ 16.00
Silver, American, Teaspoon, Platt & Bros., N.Y., C.1825, Coin ......................................... 7.00
Silver, American, Teaspoon, Pointed End, D.Osborn, Coin ................................................ 18.00
Silver, American, Teaspoon, Pointed End, Ezekiel Burr, Coin ........................................... 18.00
Silver, American, Teaspoon, Raised Tip, Bailey, Juttell & Chapman, Coin ..................... 9.10
Silver, American, Teaspoon, Rattail Base Of Handle, D.A.Kegwin, C.1820, Coin ......... 4.95
Silver, American, Teaspoon, Rogers & Smith, Coin ............................................................ 7.50
Silver, American, Teaspoon, Sanborn, Lowell, Ma., C.1850, Coin .................................. 5.80
Silver, American, Teaspoon, Sheaf Of Wheat, Benjamin B.Frobisher, Coin, Pair .......... 48.00
Silver, American, Teaspoon, Sheaf Of Wheat, Foliate Drop, B.Cleveland, Coin ........... 45.00
Silver, American, Teaspoon, Sheaf Of Wheat, Furman, Schenectady, Coin ................... 22.00
Silver, American, Teaspoon, Sheaf Of Wheat, G.Mecum, Boston, 1829, Coin .............. 40.00
Silver, American, Teaspoon, Sheaf Of Wheat, Pelletreau & Upson, Coin, Pair ............. 25.00
Silver, American, Teaspoon, Sheaf Of Wheat, William Thomson, Coin ......................... 25.00
Silver, American, Teaspoon, St.Louis, Mo., C.1823, Coin ................................................. 11.00
Silver, American, Teaspoon, Stamped Heck, Pseudo Hallmarks, C.1750, Coin ............ 25.00
Silver, American, Teaspoon, Stamson, Coin ........................................................................ 7.50
Silver, American, Teaspoon, Thomas Jackson, N.H., C.1790, Coin ................................. 22.00
Silver, American, Teaspoon, Tipped Handle, N.Matson, N.Y., Coin ................................. 5.00
Silver, American, Teaspoon, Turned Down Handle, Bolles & Childs, C.1820, Coin ...... 7.00
Silver, American, Teaspoon, Turned Down Handle, Dubois, C.1842, Coin .................... 9.00
Silver, American, Teaspoon, Turned Down Handle, Fitch, N.Y., Coin ............................. 10.00
Silver, American, Teaspoon, Turned Down Handle, Hall, Phila., C.1820, Coin ............. 13.00
Silver, American, Teaspoon, Turned Down Handle, Lescare, Phila., C.1825, Coin ...... 16.00
Silver, American, Teaspoon, Turned Down Handle, Loomis, Pa., C.1830, Coin ........... 8.00
Silver, American, Teaspoon, Turned Down Handle, Moulton, Coin ................................. 10.00
Silver, American, Teaspoon, Turned Down Handle, Polhemus, N.Y., C.1833, Coin ...... 9.00
Silver, American, Teaspoon, Turned Down Handle, Raised Tip, J.Clark, C.1810 .......... 12.00
Silver, American, Teaspoon, Twisted Stem, Engraved Oval Top, R.& W.Wilson ......... 11.65
Silver, American, Teaspoon, Urn Back, Marked JM, Bright Cut, Coin ............................ 25.00
Silver, American, Teaspoon, W.Faber & Sons, Phila., C.1825, Coin .............................. 7.00
Silver, American, Teaspoon, W.G.Bruce, Coin ................................................................... 8.65
Silver, American, Teaspoon, W.Moulton, C.1825, Coin .................................................... 12.50
Silver, American, Teaspoon, Wm.Burdick, New Haven, Conn., C.1810, Coin ............... 12.00
Silver, American, Tinderbox, President U.S.Grant From A.E.Borie, 1809-1880 ........... 900.00
Silver, American, Tongs, C.Lindley, Hartford, 1843, Coin ................................................ 40.00
Silver, American, Tongs, Joel Sayre, N.Y., C.1800 ............................................................ 60.00
Silver, American, Tongs, King's Pattern, S.Kirk, Baltimore, C.1830 .............................. 50.00
Silver, American, Tongs, Sugar, Bird's Feet Nippers, Fitch, N.Y., C.1840, Coin .......... 37.50
Silver, American, Tongs, Sugar, Bright Cut, W.Fountain, C.1825 ................................... 45.00
Silver, American, Tongs, Sugar, Fiddle, Engraved, John Targee, N.Y., C.1750 ............ 80.00

| | |
|---|---:|
| Silver, American, Tongs, Sugar, Fiddleback, Acorn Grips, Moulton, C.1820, Coin | 85.00 |
| Silver, American, Tongs, Sugar, John Targee, C.1800, Coin | 75.00 |
| Silver, American, Tongs, Sugar, Lions' Feet Nippers, R.King, C.1820, Coin | 47.00 |
| Silver, American, Tongs, Sugar, Shell Nippers, F.Rath, N.Y., C.1840, Coin | 42.00 |
| Silver, American, Tongs, Sugar, Shell Nippers, Leaf, Bailey, Jr., C.1816, Coin | 55.00 |
| Silver, American, Tongs, Tea, Bird Claw Ends, C.Bond, C.1840, Coin | 35.00 |
| Silver, American, Tongs, Tea, George C.Howe, C.1835, 6 1/2 In.Long | 38.00 |
| Silver, American, Tray, Tea, Engraved Hunter, Jones, Shreve, Brown, & Co., 1800s | 700.00 |
| Silver, American, Tray, Tea, Handled, Oval, Black, Starr & Frost, C.1915, 30 In. | 750.00 |
| Silver, American, Tray, Tea, Oval, Molded Border, New York, C.1845, 23 In. | 500.00 |
| Silver, American, Tray, Two Handles, Barnard Dupuy, C.1820, 14 In.Long | 675.00 |
| Silver, American, Tumbler, 12 Coins Dated 1842 To Civil War, Engraved, 6 Oz. | 37.50 |
| Silver, American, Urn, Sugar, Covered, Vase Shape, Richardson, C.1790, 8 In. | 1050.00 |
| Silver, American, Urn, Tea, Greek Revival Style, Sharp, Pa., C.1860, 16 In. | 750.00 |
| Silver, American, Urn, Tea, Vase Shape, Monograms, Domed Cover, C.1800, 16 In. | 750.00 |
| Silver, American, Vase, Martele, Gorham, Repousse Flowerheads, C.1899, 19 In. | 1700.00 |
| Silver, American, Vase, Martele, Gorham, 1899, 19 In.High ............... Illus | 1700.00 |
| Silver, American, Vase, Ovoid, Flowers & Foliage, Pierced Rim, C.1900, 18 In. | 250.00 |
| Silver, American, Waiter, Chased, Engraved, 3 Ball & Claw Feet, Kirk, C.1890 | 80.00 |
| Silver, American, Waiter, Circular, Christian Wiltberger, C.1790, 8 In.Diam. | 1700.00 |
| Silver, Austrian, Box, Seal, Gilt, Drum Shape, Emperor Ferdinand, 1846 | 650.00 |
| Silver, Austrian, Box, Sugar, Hinged, Leaping Deer Finial, Oval Bombe, C.1890 | 70.00 |
| Silver, Austrian, Demitasse Set, Spiral Fluting, J.Reiner, C.1900, 3 Piece | 160.00 |
| Silver, Austrian, Fork, Dinner, Hallmarked, Dated 1840 | 10.00 |
| Silver, Austrian, Pax, Gilt, Enamel, Wooden, Visit Of The Magi, C.1850 | 250.00 |
| Silver, Austrian, Snuffbox, Hinged, Book Shape, Incised Decoration, 1807 | 85.00 |
| Silver, Austrian, Tea Strainer, Irregular Border, Thumbrest, Krupp, C.1910 | 25.00 |
| Silver, Bowl, Melon Fluted, Gadroon Edge, Footed, Howard & Co., C.1896 | 300.00 |
| Silver, Brazilian, Knife & Fork | 5.00 |
| Silver, Cambodian, Tea Caddy, Cylindrical, Embossed Animals, 4 1/2 In.High | 145.00 |
| Silver, Chinese, Creamer, Baluster, Embossed, Engraved, Dragon Handle, C.1850 | 400.00 |
| Silver, Continental, Box, Hinged, Repousse, Man & Woman In Garden | 12.00 |
| Silver, Continental, Coffeepot, C.1775, 7 In.High ............... Illus | 400.00 |
| Silver, Continental, Snuffbox, Carved Ivory On Lid, Parcel Gilt, Gold Wash | 150.00 |
| Silver, Continental, Snuffbox, Hinged Lid, Square, Filigreework, C.1850 | 45.00 |
| Silver, Danish, Case, Comb, Embossed Figures, Tortoiseshell Comb | 6.50 |
| Silver, Danish, Salt Dip, Porringer Shape, Cobalt Blue Enamel Lined | 11.00 |
| Silver, Danish, Salt Dip, Porringer Shape, Green Enamel Lined | 11.00 |
| Silver, Danish, Teaspoon, Oval Tip, Bright Cut, C.1795 | 20.00 |
| Silver, Dutch, Beaker, Tapered, Engraved Putto Heads, Birds, Dordrecht, 1633 | 2250.00 |

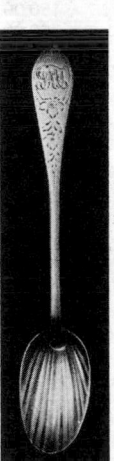

Silver, Dutch, Teapot,
I.F.Leeuwarden,
1739, 5 1/2 In.
(See Page 570)

Silver, Dutch, Teapot,
Cornelis De Haan,
The Hague, 1763
(See Page 570)

Silver, American, Vase, Martele,
Gorham, 1899, 19 In.High

Silver, American, Teaspoon,
Paul Revere, C.1792, 5 1/2 In

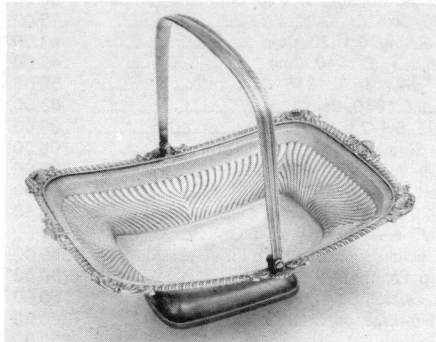

Silver, English, Basket, Cake, Burwash,
1814, 13 1/2 In.

Silver, Continental, Coffeepot,
C.1775, 7 In.High
*(See Page 569)*

| | |
|---|---:|
| Silver, Dutch, Bowl, Brandy, Chased, Pierced At Handles, Dordrecht, 1676 | 275.00 |
| Silver, Dutch, Box, Moistener With Sponge Inside, Octagonal, C.1850 | 55.00 |
| Silver, Dutch, Coffeepot On Lampstand, Wooden Finial, Pierced, Chased, 1863 | 275.00 |
| Silver, Dutch, Coffeepot, After Dinner, Wooden Side Handle, 7 3/4 In. | 225.00 |
| Silver, Dutch, Pitcher, Form Of Portly Bearded Man, Scroll Handle, 1896 | 150.00 |
| Silver, Dutch, Shoe, Allover Embossed Figures, 3 5/8 In. | 65.00 |
| Silver, Dutch, Snuffbox, Three Dimensional Design On Top & Bottom | 45.00 |
| Silver, Dutch, Spoon, Basting & Marrow Scoop, 1758 .................................... *Illus* | 900.00 |
| Silver, Dutch, Teapot, Cornelis De Haan, The Hague, 1763 ........................ *Illus* | 850.00 |
| Silver, Dutch, Teapot, I.F.Leeuwarden, 1739, 5 1/2 In. ............................... *Illus* | 1500.00 |
| Silver, Dutch, Windmill, Blades Turn, 2 In.High | 15.00 |
| Silver, English, Argyle, George III Style, Pear Shape, Harman, 1907 | 160.00 |
| Silver, English, Argyle, Vase Shape, Wood Handle, Greenway, 1794, 8 In. | 370.00 |
| Silver, English, Basket, Cake, Boat Shape, Festoons, Aldridge, 1794, 15 3/4 In. | 725.00 |
| Silver, English, Basket, Cake, Burwash, 1814, 13 1/2 In. ............................... *Illus* | 375.00 |
| Silver, English, Basket, Cake, Engraved Ribbonwork Band, W.A., 1803, 11 3/8 In | 375.00 |
| Silver, English, Basket, Cake, Oval Form, Edward Aldridge, 1762, 15 In.Long | 550.00 |
| Silver, English, Basket, Cake, Oval, Openwork, Engraved, Herbert, 1758, 14 In. | 750.00 |
| Silver, English, Basket, Cake, Oval, Pierced Lattice & Diaper, Wickes, 1737 | 1900.00 |
| Silver, English, Basket, Fruit, Oval, Pierced, Chased, Haris, C.1886, Pair | 300.00 |
| Silver, English, Basket, Sugar & Cream, Peter & Ann Bateman, 1793, Pair | 1100.00 |
| Silver, English, Basket, Sugar, Boat Shape, Peter & Ann Bateman, 1794 | 350.00 |
| Silver, English, Basket, Sugar, Boat Shape, Peter & William Bateman, 1809 | 325.00 |
| Silver, English, Basket, Sugar, George III, Boat Shape, Smith, 1788 | 150.00 |
| Silver, English, Basket, Sweetmeat, Henry Chawner, London, 1792, 5 In.Long | 250.00 |
| Silver, English, Basket, Sweetmeat, Pierced, Ball Feet, Daniel, 1774, 8 1/2 In. | 170.00 |
| Silver, English, Basket, Sweetmeat, Pierced, Pedestal, Plummer, 1774, 7 In. | 150.00 |
| Silver, English, Belt Plate, Officer's, Cross, R.Johnson, London, 1803 | 175.00 |
| Silver, English, Bonbon, Double Tier, Footed, Pierced, 8 1/2 X 12 In. | 26.00 |
| Silver, English, Bowl, Engraved Crest, Pantin, 1736, 5 1/2 In. | 550.00 |
| Silver, English, Bowl, Openwork, Repousse, Handled, Footed, 1898, 10 In. | 185.00 |
| Silver, English, Box, Patch, Round, C.1900, 1 1/2 In.Diameter | 12.00 |
| Silver, English, Box, Taper, Hinged, George III, Phipps & Robinson, C.1790 | 150.00 |
| Silver, English, Box, Tobacco, Oval, Slip On Cover, Queen Anne, Cornock, C.1710 | 225.00 |
| Silver, English, Butter Shell, George IV, Engraved Crests, Barnard, 1828 | 262.50 |
| Silver, English, Candelabra, George III Style, 4-Arm, 1894, 18 1/4 In., Pair | 850.00 |
| Silver, English, Candleholder, Detachable Snuffer, Phillip Rundell, 1819 | 275.00 |
| Silver, English, Candlesnuffer, George IV, Long Stem, T.R., 1823, 7 In, , Pair | 300.00 |
| Silver, English, Candlestick, Coker, C.1765, 14 In., Pair ............................... *Illus* | 2000.00 |
| Silver, English, Candlestick, George III, Gilt, Baluster, T.P., 1806, Pair | 2700.00 |
| Silver, English, Candlestick, Round Base, Engraved, Schofield, C.1784, Pair | 1950.00 |
| Silver, English, Candlestick, Square Base, Baluster Stem, Nelme, 1733, Pair | 1350.00 |
| Silver, English, Candlestick, Table, George III, Carter, C.1763, 12 In., Pair | 950.00 |
| Silver, English, Caster, Lighthouse Shape, Pierced Cover, Adams, 1889 | 210.00 |
| Silver, English, Caster, Pear Shape, Charles Adam, 1708, 6 In.High | 600.00 |

Silver, English, Candlestick,
Coker, C.1765, 14 In., Pair
(See Page 570)

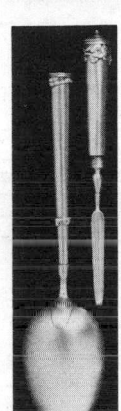

Silver, English,
Coffeepot, George II,
Cripps, 1748

Silver, Dutch, Spoon,
Basting & Marrow Scoop,
1758
(See Page 570)

Silver, English, Coaster, Wine, London, 1818, Set Of 12

| | |
|---|---|
| Silver, English, Castor, George II, Engraved, Pierced, Wickes, 1730, Pair | 3500.00 |
| Silver, English, Castor, George I, Pierced Dome Cover, Engraved, 1726 | 175.00 |
| Silver, English, Castor, Pierced Cover, Acorn Finial, Hester Bateman, 1788 | 375.00 |
| Silver, English, Castor, Queen Anne, Pierced Foliate Cap, Penstone, 1711 | 400.00 |
| Silver, English, Centerpiece, Pierced Oval Basket, Garrard, 1904, 13 In. | 825.00 |
| Silver, English, Chamberstick, Flying Scroll Handle, Emes & Barnard, 1808 | 375.00 |
| Silver, English, Chamberstick, Vase Sconce, Conical Snuffer, Cooke, 1810, Pair | 800.00 |
| Silver, English, Chocolate Pot, Beaded Borders, Leaf At Spout, Sutton, 1781 | 1000.00 |
| Silver, English, Coaster, Wine, London, 1818, Set Of 12 ............... Illus | 2500.00 |
| Silver, English, Coffee Set, Miniature, Chester, 1906, 7 Piece | 350.00 |
| Silver, English, Coffeepot, George II, Cripps, 1748 ............... Illus | 2700.00 |
| Silver, English, Coffeepot, George III, Repousse, Whiphan & Wright, 1764 | 600.00 |
| Silver, English, Coffeepot, Inverted Pear Shape, Makepeace & Carter, 1777 | 800.00 |
| Silver, English, Coffeepot, Oval, Flowers & Acorns, C.1802, 10 1/2 In.High | 900.00 |
| Silver, English, Coffeepot, Pear Shape, Wood Handle, Hester Bateman, 1782 | 2000.00 |
| Silver, English, Coffeepot, Swan Neck Spout, Footed, Godfrey, 1737 | 450.00 |
| Silver, English, Compass, Officer's, Pocket, Bleuler, London, C.1804 | 175.00 |
| Silver, English, Compote, Sweetmeat, Tripod Tea Table Shape, Pierced, C.1750 | 135.00 |
| Silver, English, Cooler, Wine, Cylindrical, Edward Wakelim, 1754, 8 3/4 In. | 2200.00 |
| Silver, English, Creamer, Beaded S-Scroll Handle, Beaded Rim, Appleton, 1782 | 130.00 |
| Silver, English, Creamer, Cow, Looped Tail Handle, Schuppe, 1766 | 2200.00 |
| Silver, English, Creamer, George III, Inverted Pear Shape, Bateman, 1780 | 275.00 |
| Silver, English, Creamer, Helmet Shape, Beaded Rim, Bateman, 1792 | 200.00 |
| Silver, English, Creamer, Helmet, Beaded Lip, Square Base, Marked Ja, C.1795 | 125.00 |
| Silver, English, Creamer, S-Scroll Handle, Reeded Rim On Circular Foot, 1738 | 150.00 |
| Silver, English, Cross, Dish, Petals Form Feet By Beading, Mills, C.1770 | 600.00 |
| Silver, English, Cruet Set, 8 Bottles, Gadrooned, T.Jenkinson, C.1827 | 450.00 |

Silver, English, Cruet, Center Handle, 2 Bottles, Wood, 1749, 9 In. High ............ 225.00
Silver, English, Cruet, Oblong, Center Handle, Footed, 4 Inserts, W.B., 1827 ............ 200.00
Silver, English, Cruet, Pierced, Center Handle, 8 Bottles, Peaston, 1774 ............ 350.00
Silver, English, Cruet, 2 Bottles, Wood, 1740, 8 3/4 In. ............................ *Illus* 900.00
Silver, English, Cruet, 4 Bottles, Boat Shape, Pierced, Hester Bateman, 1789 ............ 800.00
Silver, English, Cup, Bell Shape, Bud Finial, 2 Handled, Swift, 1756 ............ 900.00
Silver, English, Cup, Bell Shape, Pedestal, Reeded Border, W.B., 1794 ............ 225.00
Silver, English, Cup, Bell Shape, Scroll Handles, Hester Bateman, 1778 ............ 525.00
Silver, English, Cup, Bell Shape, Trumpet Foot, Engraved, Denzilow, 1801 ............ 175.00
Silver, English, Cup, Bud Finial, Campana Shape, Foliate Handles, Storr, 1809 ............ 2400.00
Silver, English, Cup, Bud Finial, Foliate Handles, Emes & Barnard, 1816 ............ 575.00
Silver, English, Cup, Caudle, Bud Finial, Charles II Style, Crichton, Pair ............ 500.00
Silver, English, Cup, Caudle, Rattail S-Scroll Handles, Locke, 1713 ............ 800.00
Silver, English, Cup, Caudle, Reeded Strap Scroll Handles, Priest, 1764 ............ 200.00
Silver, English, Cup, Caudle, S-Scroll Handles, Embossed, Chadwick, 1703 ............ 475.00
Silver, English, Cup, Caudle, Scroll Handles, Chased, Lofthouse, 1726 ............ 625.00
Silver, English, Cup, Caudle, William III, Repousse, Cartouche, Wimans, 1701 ............ 650.00
Silver, English, Cup, Child's, Pear Shape, Gold Wash Inside, Angel, 1837 ............ 85.00
Silver, English, Cup, Coconut, Sterling Hoof & Shell Applied Feet, C.1750 ............ 95.00
Silver, English, Cup, Covered, Double Scroll Handles, Chased, De Lamerie, 1719 ............ 1800.00
Silver, English, Cup, Double Scroll Handles, Bell Shape, Hester Bateman, 1782 ............ 425.00
Silver, English, Cup, George III, Bell Shape, Engraved, Hennell, 1792, Pair ............ 550.00
Silver, English, Cup, George III, Gilt, Engraved Crest, Farrell, 1814 ............ 650.00
Silver, English, Cup, George III, Trumpet Foot, Gilt Interior, Bateman, 1785 ............ 600.00
Silver, English, Cup, S-Scroll Handles, Bell Shape, Hester Bateman, 1788 ............ 375.00
Silver, English, Cup, S-Scroll Handles, Bell Shape, Hester Bateman, 1789 ............ 400.00
Silver, English, Cup, Tumbler, 3 Granulated Bands, Crests, Storr, 1836 ............ 2900.00
Silver, English, Dish & Stand, Muffin, Ring Finial, Reeded Border, 1890 ............ 600.00
Silver, English, Dish On Lampstand, Chafing, Ivory Handles, Hennell, 1841 ............ 400.00
Silver, English, Dish, Entree, Covered, George III, Crests, W.B., London, 1805 ............ 400.00
Silver, English, Dish, Entree, Covered, George III, Lamp, Sumner, 1802, Pair ............ 600.00
Silver, English, Dish, Entree, Covered, George III, W.B., London, 1815, Pair ............ 1400.00
Silver, English, Dish, Entree, Covered, George IV, Armorials, Rundell, 1820 ............ 1100.00
Silver, English, Dish, Entree, Covered, Rectangular, Paul Storr, 1816, Pair ............ 3250.00
Silver, English, Dish, Entree, Covered, Wild Game Motif, Storr, 1828, Pair ............ 7000.00
Silver, English, Dish, Entree, George III, Gadrooned Rim, G.H., 1762 ............ 125.00
Silver, English, Dish, Entree, 1804, Pair ............................ *Illus* 4250.00
Silver, English, Dish, Meat, Oval, Engraved Armorials, Greenway, 1792, 20 In. ............ 800.00
Silver, English, Dish, Meat, Oval, Gadroon Rim, Engraved, C.1810, 20 In., Pair ............ 750.00
Silver, English, Dish, Meat, Oval, Gadroon Rim, Garrard, 1814, 16 In., Pair ............ 1300.00
Silver, English, Dish, Sideboard, George IV, Feast Of The Gods, Pitts, 1820 ............ 2800.00
Silver, English, Dish, Sideboard, Gilt, Charles II Style, Crichton, 1912 ............ 250.00
Silver, English, Ewer, George III, Gilt, Scroll Handle, Smith & Sharpe, 1772 ............ 650.00
Silver, English, Fish Service, Mother-Of-Pearl Handles, Box, 2 Piece ............ 47.50
Silver, English, Flask, Whiskey, Lady's ............ 18.00
Silver, English, Fork, Dessert, Fiddle, A.B.Savory, London, 1828 ............ 21.65
Silver, English, Fork, Dinner, Fiddle, A.B.Savory, London, 1828 ............ 25.00
Silver, English, Fork, Dinner, Fiddleback, Mappin & Webb, C.1908 ............ 20.00
Silver, English, Fork, Hourglass, Paul Storr, C.1820, Set Of 6 ............ 250.00
Silver, English, Fork, Luncheon, Oval Tip, Stephen Smity, C.1867 ............ 20.00
Silver, English, Frame, Cruet, George II, Center Handle, Pierced, Wood, 1744 ............ 700.00
Silver, English, Funnel, Wine, George III, Detachable Bowl, Chawner, 1791 ............ 125.00
Silver, English, Inkstand, Footed, Taperstick, 2 Wells, Emes & Barnard, 1826 ............ 750.00
Silver, English, Inkstand, Guest & Craddock, 1808 ............................ *Illus* 650.00
Silver, English, Inkstand, Hinged, 3 Cut Glass Bottles, Pierced, Fox, C.1842 ............ 500.00
Silver, English, Inkstand, Openwork Frames, 3 Wells, Aldridge, 1759 ............ 525.00
Silver, English, Inkstand, Pierced, 2 Wells, Taperstick, Cut Glass, Fox, 1843 ............ 475.00
Silver, English, Inkstand, Taperstick, 2 Wells, Emes & Barnard, 1813 ............ 575.00
Silver, English, Jug On Lampstand, Coffee, Gilt, Eaton ............................ *Illus* 1900.00
Silver, English, Jug On Lampstand, Hot Water, Engraved, Salmon, 1801 ............ 500.00
Silver, English, Jug On Lampstand, Hot Water, George III, Storr, 1809 ............ 3700.00
Silver, English, Jug, Claret, Gilt, Cut Glass, Scrolling Foliage, C.1890, 9 In. ............ 175.00
Silver, English, Jug, Hot Water, Chased Guilloche Band, Storr, 1813 ............ 1900.00
Silver, English, Jug, Hot Water, Urn Finial, Vase Shape, Hester Bateman, 1785 ............ 1300.00
Silver, English, Jug, Hot Water, 1782, 12 1/4 In.High ............................ *Illus* 850.00
Silver, English, Kettle Stand, Triangular, Shells, Flowerheads, Dupont, 1736 ............ 1150.00

Silver, English, Inkstand, Guest & Craddock, 1808
*(See Page 572)*

Silver, English, Dish, Entree, 1804, Pair
*(See Page 572)*

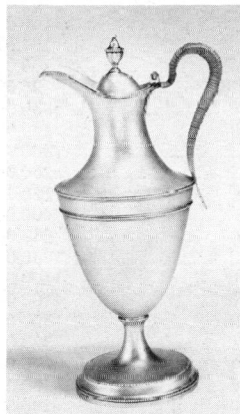

Silver, English, Jug, Hot Water,
1782, 12 1/4 In.High
*(See Page 572)*

Silver, English, Cruet, 2 Bottles,
Wood, 1/40, 8 3/4 In.
*(See Page 572)*

Silver, English, Jug On Lampstand,
Coffee, Gilt, Eaton
*(See Page 572)*

| | |
|---|---|
| Silver, English, Knife & Fork, Dinner, Pistol Handle, Wm.Alexander, C.1740 | 175.00 |
| Silver, English, Knife Rest, Bone Insert | 24.00 |
| Silver, English, Knife, Cheese, Carved Ivory Handle, Georgina Hall, 1825-26 | 20.00 |
| Silver, English, Knife, Fish, George Angell, London, 1851 | 55.00 |
| Silver, English, Knife, Table, Round Terminals, W.S., C.1780, Set Of 12 | 325.00 |
| Silver, English, Label, Bottle, Harvey Sauce, Chain, Birmingham, 1861 | 38.00 |
| Silver, English, Ladle, Brandy, Black Wood Handle, Thos.Mallison, C.1773 | 150.00 |
| Silver, English, Ladle, Sauce, Fiddle, Wallis & Hayne, London, 1819 | 37.50 |
| Silver, English, Medal, Order Of The Bath, Garrad & Co., London, 1873 | 2250.00 |
| Silver, English, Mug, Double Scroll Handle, Footed, Shaw & Priest, 1751 | 375.00 |
| Silver, English, Mug, Double Scroll Handle, Molded Foot, Fleming, 1717 | 400.00 |
| Silver, English, Mug, George I, S-Scroll Handle, Engraved, Fawdery, 1721 | 300.00 |
| Silver, English, Mug, George II, Baluster, Engraved Armorials, Cookson, 1732 | 1250.00 |
| Silver, English, Mug, George II, Double Scroll Handle, Gurney & Cooke, 1750 | 225.00 |
| Silver, English, Mug, George III, Baluster, Smith & Hayter, 1792 | 225.00 |
| Silver, English, Mull, Snuff, Scots Fusilier Grards, E.C.B., 1875 | 325.00 |
| Silver, English, Nutmeg Grater, Boat Shape, Pendant Ring, C.1720, 6 5/8 In. | 225.00 |
| Silver, English, Nutmeg Grater, Oval Form, Victorian, London, 1838 | 60.00 |
| Silver, English, Papboat, Reeded Border, Peter & Ann Bateman, 1804 | 140.00 |
| Silver, English, Pitcher, George III, Barrel Shape, Whitford, 1811, 5 In. | 550.00 |
| Silver, English, Plate, Beaded Rim, James Young, London, 1785, 9 1/2 In. | 240.00 |
| Silver, English, Plate, Dinner, Engraved Crest, Fogelberg & Gilbert, 1787 | 333.50 |
| Silver, English, Plate, Dinner, George III, Storr, 1805, 10 3/4 In. | 550.00 |
| Silver, English, Plate, Dinner, Reeded Rim, Armorial, London, 1904, 10 In. | 116.50 |
| Silver, English, Pot, Mustard, Cobalt Liner, Birmingham, 1911 | 30.00 |

| | |
|---|---|
| Silver, English, Pot, Mustard, Cobalt Liner, Wm.Eley, 1805 | 328.00 |
| Silver, English, Pot, Mustard, Drum Shape, Harp Handle, Barnard, 1829 | 200.00 |
| Silver, English, Pot, Mustard, Drum Shape, Urn Finial, Harp Handle, W.S., 1824 | 170.00 |
| Silver, English, Pot, Mustard, Footed, Cobalt Liner, Georgian, C.1811 | 248.00 |
| Silver, English, Pot, Mustard, Hinged Cover, Blue Liner, C.1884 | 35.00 |
| Silver, English, Pot, Mustard, Hinged Cover, Blue Liner, C.1901 | 27.50 |
| Silver, English, Pot, Mustard, Octagonal, Hinged, Double Scroll Handle, 1789 | 150.00 |
| Silver, English, Rack, Toast, Double Shell Feet, 8 Bars, Storr, 1815 | 675.00 |
| Silver, English, Rack, Toast, Foliate & Reeded Handle, 7 Bars, London, 1840 | 75.00 |
| Silver, English, Rack, Toast, George III, 7 Bars, Ring Handle, Whitford, 1805 | 100.00 |
| Silver, English, Rack, Toast, Openwork Frame, 9 Bars, Hester Bateman, 1788 | 250.00 |
| Silver, English, Rack, Toast, Pierced Frame, 7 Bars, Peter & Ann Bateman, 1794 | 140.00 |
| Silver, English, Rack, Toast, Victorian, Bun Feet, Ring Handle, 7 In.Long | 140.00 |
| Silver, English, Salt Cellar, Badge Of St.Andrew, Fox, 1868, Pair | 375.00 |
| Silver, English, Salt Cellar, Boat Shape, Loop Handles, Pedestal, 1799, Pair | 125.00 |
| Silver, English, Salt Cellar, Boat Shape, Rams' Masks, Hennell, 1776, Pair | 133.50 |
| Silver, English, Salt Cellar, Corded, Hoof Feet, Hester Bateman, C.1776, Pair | 162.50 |
| Silver, English, Salt Cellar, Oval, Shell & Scroll Feet, 1761, Pair | 150.00 |
| Silver, English, Salt Cellar, 3 Hoof Supports, Hester Bateman, C.1776, Pair | 162.50 |
| Silver, English, Salt, Circular, Gilt, Edward Wood, 1734, Pair | 200.00 |
| Silver, English, Salt, Master, Applied Gadroon Rim, 4 Claw Feet, London, 1806 | 95.00 |
| Silver, English, Salver, Gadroon, Shell & Scroll Rim, Sibley, 1815, 9 1/8 In. | 650.00 |
| Silver, English, Salver, Gadrooned Rim, 4 Scroll Supports, G.H., 1900, 12 In. | 150.00 |
| Silver, English, Salver, George III, Oval, Hannam & Crouch, 1804, Pair | 1900.00 |
| Silver, English, Salver, George III, Shell & Scroll Rim, Capper, 1770 | 250.00 |
| Silver, English, Salver, Shell & Foliate Rim, Footed, Sarbit, 1754, 11 In. | 220.00 |
| Silver, English, Salver, Shell & Foliate Rim, Godfrey, 1736, 12 1/4 In., Pair | 3400.00 |
| Silver, English, Salver, Shells, Scrolls, Central Crest, Robinson, 1746, 10 In. | 250.00 |
| Silver, English, Salver, Sibley, 1827, 20 1/2 In. *Illus* | 1650.00 |
| Silver, English, Salver, William IV, Shell & Scroll Rim, Reid, 1834 | 1400.00 |
| Silver, English, Sauceboat, Double Lip, Double Scroll Handle, Fraillon, 1775 | 1100.00 |
| Silver, English, Sauceboat, Double Lip, Triple Scroll Handles, Le Sage, 1728 | 1700.00 |
| Silver, English, Sauceboat, George II, Double Scroll Handle, White, 1765 | 325.00 |
| Silver, English, Sauceboat, George III, Flying Scroll Handle, London, 1770 | 175.00 |
| Silver, English, Sauceboat, Leaf Capped Double Scroll Handle, Evans, 1777 | 250.00 |
| Silver, English, Saucepan, George II, Wooden Handle, Bulbous, Swift, 1740 | 750.00 |
| Silver, English, Saucepan, Wood Handle, Reeded Base, Fleming, 1713 | 325.00 |
| Silver, English, Scoop, Cheese, Ivory Handle, Wm.Earl & Fearn, C.1801 | 95.00 |
| Silver, English, Scoop, Marrow, Double, Elizabeth Tookey, London, 1769 | 150.00 |
| Silver, English, Server, Candy, Double Tier, Pierced Design, Footed | 24.00 |
| Silver, English, Server, Caviar, Hinged Lid, Knife, Seashell Design, Glass | 35.00 |
| Silver, English, Shears, Grape, London, 1832 | 35.00 |
| Silver, English, Snuffbox, George IV, Rectangular, Bettridge, 1827 | 400.00 |
| Silver, English, Snuffbox, Samuel Pemberton, Birminhgam, C.1810, 1 X 2 In. | 85.00 |
| Silver, English, Spoon, Basting, Hanoverian, Hanet, 1732 *Illus* | 320.00 |
| Silver, English, Spoon, Basting, Hanoverian, R.P., 1754 *Illus* | 270.00 |
| Silver, English, Spoon, Basting, Hanoverian, Tattail Bowl, Petley, 1724 | 170.00 |
| Silver, English, Spoon, Basting, Queen Anne, Ladyman, 1711 *Illus* | 450.00 |
| Silver, English, Spoon, Basting, William III, Engraved Crest, Cox, 1700 | 170.00 |
| Silver, English, Spoon, Berry, Fluted Bowl, Embossed Fruit, London, 1786 | 65.00 |
| Silver, English, Spoon, Berry, Fluted Bowl, Engraved, Smith & Fearn, 1791 | 45.00 |
| Silver, English, Spoon, Berry, Hallmarked London 1804, Pair | 76.00 |
| Silver, English, Spoon, C.1770, 5 In.Long | 30.00 |
| Silver, English, Spoon, Demitasse, Bright Cut Cartouche, Hougham, 1786 | 18.00 |
| Silver, English, Spoon, Demitasse, Georgian, John Lautier, Set Of 6 | 95.00 |
| Silver, English, Spoon, Dessert, Crested, Oval Tip, Smith & Fern, C.1790 | 35.00 |
| Silver, English, Spoon, Dessert, Crowned Crest, Peter & Ann Bateman, 1794 | 36.25 |
| Silver, English, Spoon, Dessert, Crowned Crest, Sumner, London, 1809 | 25.00 |
| Silver, English, Spoon, Gravy, Pierced Divider In Bowl, Smith, C.1750 | 150.00 |
| Silver, English, Spoon, Marrow, Ivory Handle, London, 1792 | 70.00 |
| Silver, English, Spoon, Mustard, Georgian, William Bell, London, C.1819 | 15.00 |
| Silver, English, Spoon, Mustard, Round Bowl | 12.00 |
| Silver, English, Spoon, Picture Back, Fern, Cruickshank, London, 1781 | 90.00 |
| Silver, English, Spoon, Salt, Fiddleback, Crested, London, C.1828 | 15.00 |
| Silver, English, Spoon, Salt, Georgian, Thos.Stachwell, London, 1808-09 | 15.00 |
| Silver, English, Spoon, Serving, Georgian, Wm.Cafe, London, 1798 | 38.00 |

Silver, English, Spoon, Basting, Queen Anne, Ladyman, 1711
*(See Page 574)*

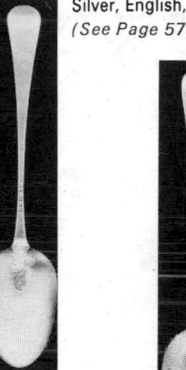

Silver, English, Spoon, Basting, Hanoverian, R.P., 1754
*(See Page 574)*

Silver, English, Spoon, Basting,
Hanoverian, Hanet, 1732
*(See Page 574)*

Silver, English, Salver,
Sibley, 1827, 20 1/2 In.
*(See Page 574)*

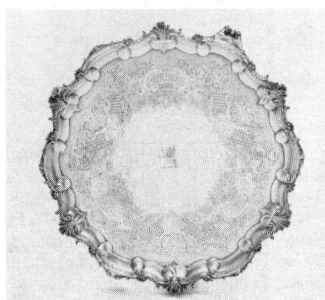

| | |
|---|---:|
| **Silver, English**, Spoon, Stuffing, Exeter, I.P. Maker, 1828 | 90.00 |
| **Silver, English**, Spoon, Stuffing, Fiddle, Thread, & Shell, WZ, London, C.1816 | 95.00 |
| **Silver, English**, Spoon, Tea Caddy, Georgian, Bright Cut, Joseph Taylor, 1795 | 65.00 |
| **Silver, English**, Spoon, Tea Caddy, Wm.Eaton, London, C.1837 | 50.00 |
| **Silver, English**, Spreader, Butter, Master, King's Pattern, Wm.Chawner, C.1832 | 35.00 |
| **Silver, English**, Spur, Officer's, Horizontal Rowels, Maker T.N., 1875, Pair | 395.00 |
| **Silver, English**, Stand, Teapot, Oval, Drapery Swags, London, 1785, 7 In.Long | 100.00 |
| **Silver, English**, Sugar & Creamer, Harp Handles, 4 Ball Feet, Burrows, 1810 | 225.00 |
| **Silver, English**, Sugar & Tongs, Fiddle & Thread, Marked SB & IB, 1818 | 35.00 |
| **Silver, English**, Sugar Set, Covered, Pierced Spoon, Cranberry Insert, 2 Piece | 55.00 |
| **Silver, English**, Sugar Tongs, Shell Nippers, Wrigglework, Preedy, C.1800 | 68.00 |
| **Silver, English**, Sugar, Crest On Domed Cover, Reeded Foot, Bentley, 1710 | 1200.00 |
| **Silver, English**, Sugar, Domed Cover, Inverted Pear Shape, Videau, 1753 | 475.00 |
| **Silver, English**, Sugar, Floral Finial, Inverted Pear Shape, Taylor, 1790 | 750.00 |
| **Silver, English**, Sugar, Gilt, Inverted Pear Shape, Scenic, Harris, 1898 | 70.00 |
| **Silver, English**, Sugar, Leaf Capped Scroll Handles, Footed, Angell, 1832 | 100.00 |
| **Silver, English**, Tablespoon, Bird & Crown Crest, George III, Hallmarked | 19.00 |
| **Silver, English**, Tablespoon, Dagger Crest, George IV, 1817-25 | 19.10 |
| **Silver, English**, Tablespoon, Initials M.F., Wm.Eaton, London, C.1844 | 22.50 |
| **Silver, English**, Tablespoon, Old English Style, Dexter, London, 1809 | 30.00 |
| **Silver, English**, Tablespoon, Old English Style, Perkins, London, 1796 | 30.00 |
| **Silver, English**, Tablespoon, Old English Style, Wintte, London, 1810 | 16.00 |
| **Silver, English**, Tablespoon, Old English, Engraved, Hester Bateman, 1744, Pair | 120.00 |
| **Silver, English**, Tablespoon, Slender Handle, Initial, John Wren, C.1785, Pair | 55.00 |
| **Silver, English**, Tag, Decanter, Brandy, Samuel Godbehere & Wm.Wigan, C.1791 | 65.00 |
| **Silver, English**, Tankard, George II, Baluster Shape, Grundy, 1749 | 3000.00 |
| **Silver, English**, Tankard, Queen Anne, S-Scroll Handle, Engraved, Green, 1712 | 1200.00 |
| **Silver, English**, Tankard, Scroll Handle, Chases, Crest, Gurney & Cook, 1739 | 425.00 |
| **Silver, English**, Tankard, Scroll Handled, Thomas Wright, London, 1768 | 875.00 |
| **Silver, English**, Tea & Coffee Set, Embossed Foliage, Hyams, 1827, 4 Piece | 1700.00 |
| **Silver, English**, Tea & Coffee Set, Gadroon Rims, Cooke, C.1800, 5 Piece | 4200.00 |
| **Silver, English**, Tea & Coffee Set, Lampstand, Birmingham, 1908, 6 Piece | 3000.00 |
| **Silver, English**, Tea Caddy, George III, Pontifex, 1796 .................................*Illus* | 1100.00 |
| **Silver, English**, Tea Caddy, Quadrangular, R.Hennell, London, 1791, 4 In.High | 500.00 |
| **Silver, English**, Tea Set, Floral Borders, Charles Fox, 1821, Armorials | 400.00 |
| **Silver, English**, Tea Set, George IV, Gadroon Rims, M.S., C.1823, 3 Piece | 350.00 |
| **Silver, English**, Tea Set, George IV, Shell & Scroll, G.H., 1827, 3 Piece | 500.00 |

Silver, English, Tureen, Sauce, G.S., 1768, Pair
*(See Page 577)*

Silver, English, Tea Caddy,
George III, Pontifex, 1796
*(See Page 575)*

| | |
|---|---:|
| Silver, English, Tea Set, Oriental Heads Handles, Angell, 1817, 3 Piece | 525.00 |
| Silver, English, Tea Set, Oval, Andrew Fogelberg, 1802, 4 Piece | 700.00 |
| Silver, English, Tea Strainer, Rests On Stand, Ball Feet | 15.00 |
| Silver, English, Tea Strainer, Hook To Fit On Cup, Preedy, 1773 | 125.00 |
| Silver, English, Teakettle On Lampstand, Inverted Pear Shape, Pierced, 1751 | 750.00 |
| Silver, English, Teakettle On Lampstand, Ivory Finial, Harris, 1878 | 250.00 |
| Silver, English, Teapot & Stand, George III, Engraved Crest, Plummer, 1783 | 325.00 |
| Silver, English, Teapot Stand, Oval, Engraved Chevron Band, Footed, W.B., 1797 | 130.00 |
| Silver, English, Teapot Stand, Oval, Engraved, Godbehere & Wigan, 1792 | 150.00 |
| Silver, English, Teapot Stand, Oval, Reeded Rim, Engraved, Emes, 1802 | 150.00 |
| Silver, English, Teapot, Chased, London, 1806, 7 In.High | 595.00 |
| Silver, English, Teapot, Drum Shaped, John Robins, 1776, 5 1/4 In.High | 300.00 |
| Silver, English, Teapot, Engraved Oval Shields, Hester Bateman, 1757 | 1100.00 |
| Silver, English, Teapot, Fluted Oval, Engraved Key & Floral, Hougham, 1807 | 275.00 |
| Silver, English, Teapot, George III, Domed Cover, Oval Shape, Emes, 1798 | 225.00 |
| Silver, English, Teapot, Oval Drum Shape, Wooden Handle & Finial, 1799 | 325.00 |
| Silver, English, Teapot, Wood Finial & Handle, Molded Girdle, Storr, 1823 | 600.00 |
| Silver, English, Teaspoon, Fiddle, Engraved AMS, Wm.Trayes, 1833 | 12.50 |
| Silver, English, Teaspoon, H.Hyman, London, 1846 | 8.00 |
| Silver, English, Telescope, British Military, Chadburn, Sheffield, 5 Sections | 195.00 |
| Silver, English, Tongs, King's Pattern, Jos.& Albert Saxony, London, C.1849 | 30.00 |
| Silver, English, Tongs, Openwork, Walter Tweedy, London, C.1770 | 60.00 |
| Silver, English, Tongs, Sugar, Ann, Peter, & Wm.Bateman, London, C.1801 | 50.00 |
| Silver, English, Tongs, Sugar, Bright Cut, Engraved, Stephen Adams, 1797 | 37.50 |
| Silver, English, Tongs, Sugar, Bright Cut, Lias, London, C.1794 | 37.00 |
| Silver, English, Tongs, Sugar, Bright Cut, Samuel Adams, 1793 | 35.00 |
| Silver, English, Tongs, Sugar, Classic Design, Hallmarked, 1868-69 | 25.00 |
| Silver, English, Tongs, Sugar, Feather Edge, Shell Nippers, Smith, C.1770 | 35.00 |
| Silver, English, Tongs, Sugar, Fiddle Thread, London, 1818 | 25.00 |
| Silver, English, Tongs, Sugar, Fiddle, Eley, Fearn, & Walker, London, 1810 | 22.00 |
| Silver, English, Tongs, Sugar, John Bridge, London, 1823, 6 In. | 23.00 |
| Silver, English, Tongs, Sugar, Spoon Nippers, R.Peppin, London, 1821 | 25.00 |
| Silver, English, Tongs, Tea, Georgian, Engraved, S.G.Over E.W., 1802 | 42.00 |
| Silver, English, Tongs, Tea, Spoon Ends, Bright Cut, S.G./e.W./i.B., 1801 | 42.00 |
| Silver, English, Tray, Rectangular, Grape Border, 22 X 16 In. | 300.00 |
| Silver, English, Tray, Snuffer, Hourglass Shape, Chased, Mortimer & Hunt, 1840 | 775.00 |
| Silver, English, Tray, Snuffer, Hourglass Shape, Hoof Feet, Handle, Gould, 1735 | 475.00 |
| Silver, English, Tray, Snuffer, Hourglass Shape, Scroll Handle, Gould, 1743 | 375.00 |
| Silver, English, Tray, Snuffer, Hourglass Shape, Scroll Handles, W.C., 1748 | 500.00 |
| Silver, English, Tray, Snuffer, Rectangular, Flying Scroll Handle, Cafe, 1761 | 500.00 |
| Silver, English, Tray, Tea, George III, Acanthus Handles, I.M., 1819, 29 In. | 2600.00 |
| Silver, English, Tray, Tea, George IV, Acanthus Handles, Bridge, 1825, 29 In. | 2750.00 |
| Silver, English, Tray, Tea, Oval, Gadroon Rim, Footed, Handles, Garrard, 1823 | 1600.00 |
| Silver, English, Tray, Tea, Oval, Handles Rising From Leaves, Crouch, 1809 | 2100.00 |
| Silver, English, Tray, Tea, Regency Style, Reeded Scroll Handles, 1901, 29 In. | 1000.00 |
| Silver, English, Tray, Tea, Scroll Rim & Handles, Elkington, 1885, 29 In. | 1100.00 |

Silver, English, Tray, Tea, Scroll Rim & Handles, Elkington, 1897, 24 3/4 In. ................................. 700.00
Silver, English, Tureen, Sauce, Ball Finial, George III, Hennell, 1788 ................................. 450.00
Silver, English, Tureen, Sauce, Covered, Armorials, Evans, 1778, Pair ................................. 1000.00
Silver, English, Tureen, Sauce, Domed Cover, Lions' Masks Handles, Storr, 1813 ...................... 1900.00
Silver, English, Tureen, Sauce, G.S., 1768, Pair ................................................. *Illus* 1000.00
Silver, English, Tureen, Sauce, Knopped Finial, Boat Shape, Pitts, 1786 ................................. 1850.00
Silver, English, Tureen, Sauce, Pod Finial, Armorial, Butty & Dumee, 1772, Pair ........................ 1000.00
Silver, English, Tureen, Sauce, Urn Finial, Boat Shape, Chawner, 1792, Pair ............................ 425.00
Silver, English, Tureen, Sauce, Urn Finial, George III, Emes & Barnard, 1816 ........................... 325.00
Silver, English, Tureen, Sauce, Urn Finial, George III, Hennell, 1794, Pair ............................ 900.00
Silver, English, Tureen, Soup, Bud Finial, Boat Shape, Wakelin & Taylor, 1788 ......................... 2200.00
Silver, English, Tureen, Soup, Urn Finial, George III, Armorial, Laver, 1786 ........................... 3100.00
Silver, English, Tureen, Soup, Wolf's Head Finial, Shell Handles, Storr, 1834 .......................... 7500.00
Silver, English, Urn, Sugar, Loop Handles, Pedestal, Peterson & Podie, 1787 ........................... 275.00
Silver, English, Urn, Tea, George III, Lions' Masks Handles, Storr, 1809 ............................... 3000.00
Silver, English, Waiter, Circular, Chased, John Carter, 1768, 6 In.Diameter ........................... 150.00
Silver, English, Waiter, Double Beaded Rim, Footed, Tweedie, 1787, 7 In. .............................. 210.00
Silver, English, Waiter, Oval, Reeded Rims, Engraved, Jay, 1791, Pair ................................. 550.00
Silver, English, Waiter, Shell & Scroll Rim, Hoof Feet, Peaston, 1755 ................................. 225.00
Silver, English, Waiter, Square, John Tuite, London, 1725, 6 1/8 In.Long .............................. 326.00
Silver, English, Wax Jack, Herbert & Co., 1761, 6 5/8 In. ....................................... *Illus* 525.00
Silver, English, Wax Jack, Herbert & Co., 1765, 5 1/4 In. ....................................... *Illus* 375.00
Silver, English, Wax Jack, I.W., London, 1758 .................................................. *Illus* 375.00
Silver, English, Whistle, Regimental, Chain, Sphinx's Head, P.F., 1882 ................................ 375.00
Silver, English, Wine Taster, St.George & Dragon Spoon, H.P., 1890, 2 Pieces ......................... 50.00
Silver, Florentine, Lorgnette, Openwork Handle, Multicolored Jewels, C.1920 .......................... 30.00
Silver, French, Basket, Dessert, Pierced, Embossed Designs, Footed .................................. 125.00
Silver, French, Beaker, Incised Floral & Leaves, C.1820, 2 3/4 In.High ............................... 45.00
Silver, French, Beaker, Louis XV, Tulip Shape, Engraved, Balduc, C.1763 .............................. 600.00
Silver, French, Beaker, Louis XV, Tulip Shape, Engraved, Hanoy, C.1765 ............................... 400.00
Silver, French, Beaker, Tulip Shape, Engraved, L.S., Orleans, C.1775, 4 In. ........................... 175.00
Silver, French, Box, Patch, Cherub & Floral Clouds On Lid, Oval, C.1800 .............................. 48.00
Silver, French, Centerpiece, Boat Shape, Female Caryatids, Putti, C.1890 ............................. 300.00
Silver, French, Centerpiece, Repousse & Chases Scroll & Shellwork, C.1890 ........................... 325.00
Silver, French, Chalice, Gilt, Chases Cherubs, Wheat, & Scrolls, C.1850 .............................. 225.00
Silver, French, Ciborium, Gilt, Champleve Enamel, Diamonds, Saints, C.1890 .......................... 425.00
Silver, French, Ciborium, Gilt, Champleve Enamel, Saints, Floral, C.1860 ............................. 450.00
Silver, French, Coffeepot, Baluster, Engraved, Wood Handle, C.1819, 6 In. ............................ 325.00
Silver, French, Condiment Set, Grapevine Handle, Gadrooned, C.1825, 5 Piece .......................... 700.00
Silver, French, Dessert Set, Ivory Handles, Marked D.L., C.1820, 24 Piece ............................ 265.00
Silver, French, Dish On Lampstand, Entree, Covered, Odiot, C.1850, Set Of 4 ......................... 6250.00
Silver, French, Dish, Cheese, Pierced, Chased, Gold Washed, Spade Shape, 1850 ...................... 27.50

Silver, English, Wax Jack,
  Herbert & Co.,
  1765, 5 1/4 In.

Silver, English, Wax Jack,
  I.W., London, 1758

Silver, English, Wax Jack,
  Herbert & Co.,
  1761, 6 5/8 In.

Silver, French, Ewer, Gilt, Pear Shaped Body, Chased, C.1900, 9 1/2 In.High ............................ 450.00
Silver, French, Fork, Fiddle, Louis XV, Ribeaucourt, 1748, Set Of 4 ........................................ 125.00
Silver, French, Frame, Easel, Color Print Of Jesus Christ, 3 1/2 In.High ............................... 10.00
Silver, French, Inkstand, Rectangular, Glass Liner, E.Hugo, C.1860, 10 In.Long ...................... 200.00
Silver, French, Jar, Preserve, On Stand, Campana, Lyres, Demi Horses, C.1809 ................... 275.00
Silver, French, Jug, Hot Water, Pear Shape, Dolphin Border, C.1900, 8 1/2 In. ..................... 275.00
Silver, French, Knife Rest, Dog, 3 1/2 In.Long ........................................................................ 15.00
Silver, French, Knife Rest, Fighting Cocks, 3 1/2 In. .............................................................. 42.00
Silver, French, Knife Rest, Fox, 3 1/2 In.Long ........................................................................ 15.00
Silver, French, Knife Rest, Pig, 3 1/2 In.Long ........................................................................ 15.00
Silver, French, Plate, Dinner, Gilt, Anthemion On Reeded, Biennais, 1800s .......................... 625.00
Silver, French, Pot, Wood Finial & Handle, Empire, Engraved, Berger, C.1798 ..................... 170.00
Silver, French, Sauceboat On Stand, Double Lip, Screw On Stand, C.1900 .......................... 125.00
Silver, French, Service, Gilt, Oertel, 1784, Set Of 36 ..................................................... *Illus* 4750.00
Silver, French, Skewer, Meat, Swimming Swan Finial, 10 In. .............................................. 40.00
Silver, French, Snuffbox, Cherubs, Goat, Scrolls, & Floral On Hinged Lid, 1750 ................ 95.00
Silver, French, Spoon & Fork, Serving, Fiddle & Thread, Crest, Paris, 1819 ..................... 65.00
Silver, French, Spoon, Serving, Pierced, Fiddle Pattern, C.1760 ........................................ 225.00
Silver, French, Taster, Wine, Louis XVI, Coiled Snake Handle, C.1780 .............................. 160.00
Silver, French, Taster, Wine, Louis XVI, Snake Ring Handle, Bedane, 1775 ....................... 550.00
Silver, French, Taster, Wine, Snake Handle, Chased, Boutheroue-Demarais, 1789 ............ 550.00
Silver, French, Tea & Coffee Set, Regence Style, Gadrooned, C.1890, 4 Piece ................. 375.00
Silver, French, Teaspoon, Fiddle Thread Handle, Crest, Initials, C.1850 ............................. 5.50
Silver, French, Toothpick, Gilt, Chinoiserie, Veyrat, C.1850, 6 In., Pair ............................ 700.00
Silver, French, Tray, Oval, Foliate Scroll Handles & Feet, C.1743, 13 1/4 In. ................... 800.00
Silver, French, Tray, Tea, Oval, Pierced Gallery, Cutout Handles, 1800s, 18 In. ................ 650.00
Silver, French, Tray, Tea, Two Handles, Chased Foliage, C.1900, 26 In.Long ................... 200.00
Silver, French, Tureen & Underplate, Bouillon, Louis XVI, Gilt, Levol, 1786 ...................... 6750.00
Silver, German, Beaker, C.1690, 3 3/8 In.High ........................................................... *Illus* 525.00
Silver, German, Beaker, Engraved Female Figurs & Fruit, C.1640, 3 1/4 In. ...................... 850.00
Silver, German, Beaker, Nuremberg, C.1690, 3 1/4 In.High ........................................ *Illus* 525.00
Silver, German, Beaker, Parcel Gilt, 3 Embossed Emperors, Straub, C.1680 .................... 1300.00
Silver, German, Canister, Parcel Gilt, Gourd Shape, Repousse, Holl, C.1690 .................... 4000.00
Silver, German, Centerpiece, Pelican Feeding Young, Lion Supports, C.1890 ................... 1400.00
Silver, German, Chalice, Covered, Presentation, Footed, Gold Washed, 1914 .................. 250.00
Silver, German, Cup, Parcel Gilt, Hansel In Cellar, Putto Stem, Ulm, C.1850 ................... 275.00
Silver, German, Cup, Parcel Gilt, Roman Warrior Stem, F.G., Danzig, C.1660 ................. 3200.00
Silver, German, Cup, Tumbler, Granulated Band, Engraved, Wagner, C.1700 .................. 525.00
Silver, German, Cup, Vase Of Flowers Finial, Stemmed, Dreghart, C.1630 ...................... 1550.00
Silver, German, Dish, Meat, Oval Form, Molded Rim, 20 1/2 In.Long, Pair ..................... 190.00
Silver, German, Dish, Sideboard, Gilt, Oval, Repousse, Scenic, C.1670, 16 In. ............... 950.00
Silver, German, Dish, Sideboard, Oval, Judgment Of Solomon, C.1670, 15 In. ................ 500.00
Silver, German, Dish, Sweetmeat, Lobed Oval Shape, Embossed Floral, C.1690 ............. 100.00
Silver, German, Figurine, Peacock, Openwork, C.1900, 13 X 18 In., Pair ....................... 800.00
Silver, German, Inkstand, Oval, Scroll Supports, Sander, Biller, C.1773 .......................... 350.00
Silver, German, Match Safe, Hinged Cover Stamp Slot, Coin Slot, Metal Pencil ............. 26.00
Silver, German, Snuffbox, Perpetual Calendar & Moon Phases On Lid, C.1790 ............... 1200.00
Silver, German, Spoon, Apostle, C.1850 ............................................................................ 35.00
Silver, German, Tankard, Gilt, Inset With Coins, Armorials, Sy & Wagner, 1880s ........... 500.00
Silver, German, Tankard, Miniature, C.1670 ............................................................. *Illus* 1000.00
Silver, German, Tankard, Renaissance Style, Putto Masks, Engraved, C.1880 ............... 300.00
Silver, German, Tray, Tea, Pierced Arch Gallery, Oval, Jungerwirth, C.1788 .................. 1800.00
Silver, Irish, Beaker, Engraved Crest, Calderwood, C.1760, Set Of 4 Graduated ........... 550.00
Silver, Irish, Castor, George II, Pierced Foliage Cover, C.1755, Pair .............................. 200.00
Silver, Irish, Coaster, Wine, John West, Dublin, C.1768, 5 3/8 In., Pair .......................... 775.00
Silver, Irish, Coffeepot, Chased Oriental Figures, Molded Foot, J.M., C.1735 ................ 2200.00
Silver, Irish, Cup, George I, 2 Harp Handles, Footed, Walker, 1719, 8 In. ...................... 550.00
Silver, Irish, Mug, Baluster, Leaf Capped S-Scroll Handle, C.1750, Pair ........................ 450.00
Silver, Irish, Salver, Applied Rim, Chased Floral, March, 1832, 16 1/4 In. ...................... 800.00
Silver, Irish, Salver, Footed, Engraved Armorials, Hamilton, C.1720, 8 3/8 In. ............... 350.00
Silver, Irish, Salver, George I, Capstan Foot, Armorials, Bell, 1717, 8 In. ...................... 350.00
Silver, Irish, Sauceboat, George II, Oval, Waved Rims, Masks, C.1750, Pair ........ *Illus* 2200.00
Silver, Irish, Spoon, Basting, Hanoverian, Dublin, 1723 ......................................... *Illus* 275.00
Silver, Irish, Spoon, Berry, Fiddle Handle, Gold Washed Bowl, M.West, 1813 .............. 65.00
Silver, Irish, Sugar, Repousse & Chased Floral, Hoof Feet, Shells, West, 1790 ............. 275.00
Silver, Irish, Teapot, Bombe Rectangular, Birds & Oriental Motif, Byrne, 1810 .............. 375.00

Silver, French, Service,
Gilt, Oertel, 1784,
Set Of 36
*(See Page 578)*

Silver, Irish, Spoon, Basting,
Hanoverian, Dublin, 1723
*(See Page 578)*

Silver, German, Tankard,
Miniature, C.1670
*(See Page 578)*

Silver, German, Beaker,
Nuremberg, C.1690,
3 1/4 In.High
*(See Page 578)*

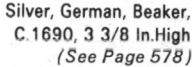

Silver, German, Beaker,
C.1690, 3 3/8 In.High
*(See Page 578)*

| | |
|---|---:|
| **Silver, Irish,** Teaspoon, Classic Design, Hallmarked, 1836, Set Of 6 | 75.00 |
| **Silver, Irish,** Tray, Snuffer, Hourglass Shape, Flying Scroll Handle, C.1750 | 400.00 |
| **Silver, Irish,** Tureen, Sauce, Bud Finial, Oval Bombe Shape, Jones, 1782, Pair | 1600.00 |
| **Silver, Italian,** Bowl, Serving, Molded Rim, Naples, 1772, 14 In. | 575.00 |
| **Silver, Italian,** Coffeepot, Pear Shape, Fluted, 3 Scroll Feet, Turin, C.1760 | 5500.00 |
| **Silver, Italian,** Font, Holy Water, Cartouche Shape Back, Chased, Pair | 210.00 |
| **Silver, Italian,** Spoon, Spiral Stem, C.1680, 7 3/8 In.Long | 325.00 |
| **Silver, Italian,** Tray, Gilt, Handled, Footed, Shells, Scrolls, Valadier, C.1790 | 8250.00 |
| **Silver, Mexican,** Goblet, Floral Pattern, Sterling, 7 3/8 In. High | 75.00 |
| **Silver, Mexican,** Pitcher, Water, Vase Shape, S-Scroll Handle, Sanborne, 11 In. | 100.00 |
| **Silver, Norwegian,** Tankard, Peg, 3 Ball & Claw Feet, Coin On Lid, Bergen, 1812 | 850.00 |
| **Silver, Persian,** Box, Oval, Hand-Painted Hunting Scene, Chased | 25.00 |
| **Silver, Plate,** Case, Coin & Makeup, Nickel Silver, Square | 15.00 |
| **Silver, Plate,** Muffineer, Wide Band Of Raised Pineapples, Pears, Etc., Tufts | 37.50 |
| **Silver, Portuguese,** Candlestick, Baluster Stem, Paw Feet, Oporto, C.1850, Pair | 225.00 |
| **Silver, Portuguese,** Chandelier, Baluster, Applied Stars, C.1850, 43 In., Pair | 2100.00 |
| **Silver, Portuguese,** Cruet, 4 Bottles, Pierced, Center Handle, Oporto, C.1790 | 175.00 |
| **Silver, Russian,** Basket, Cake, Pan-Slavic Architecturals, Chlebnikov, 1900s | 450.00 |
| **Silver, Russian,** Basket, Cake, Pan-Slavic Geometrics, Oval, Moscow, 1872 | 725.00 |
| **Silver, Russian,** Basket, Sugar, Pan-Slavic Type Roosters & Drapery, C.1900 | 70.00 |
| **Silver, Russian,** Beaker, Gilded, Niello, Medallions Of Buildings, Moscow, 1844 | 180.00 |
| **Silver, Russian,** Beaker, Wine, Incised Designs, Hallmarked, Dated 1896 | 17.50 |
| **Silver, Russian,** Belt, Niello Flowers & Geometrics, 42 Sections, C.1850 | 290.00 |
| **Silver, Russian,** Box, Cigar, Moscow, 1880, 2 1/4 X 8 In. *.....Illus* | 1600.00 |
| **Silver, Russian,** Box, Cigar, St, Petersburg, 1883, 5 1/2 In *.....Illus* | 1600.00 |
| **Silver, Russian,** Box, Sugar, Covered, Oval, Repousse, Stepan Savelev, C.1780 | 350.00 |

Silver, Russian, Box, Cigar,
Moscow, 1880, 2 1/4 X 8 In.
*(See Page 579)*

Silver, Russian, Box, Cigar,
St, Petersburg, 1883, 5 1/2 In
*(See Page 579)*

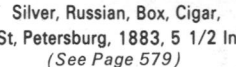

Silver, Scottish, Spoon, Basting,
Hanoverian, Ged, 1738
*(See Page 581)*

| | |
|---|---:|
| Silver, Russian, Box, Sugar, Domed Lid, Oval, Chased, Paw Feet, Moscow, C.1750 | 675.00 |
| Silver, Russian, Box, Sugar, Hinged, Ivory Finial, Handled, Moscow, 1837 | 200.00 |
| Silver, Russian, Candleholder, Chased, Baluster Stem, C.1820, 8 5/8 In., Pair | 425.00 |
| Silver, Russian, Case, Card, Niello Enamel, Initialed On Back, Dated 1891 | 150.00 |
| Silver, Russian, Case, Cigarette, Art Nouveau Engraved Design | 65.00 |
| Silver, Russian, Case, Cigarette, Basket Weave, Imperial Eagle, Moscow, 1882 | 350.00 |
| Silver, Russian, Case, Cigarette, Cushion Form, Cyrillic Name, Moscow, C.1890 | 225.00 |
| Silver, Russian, Case, Cigarette, Niello, Ship Medallion Top, B.P., C.1880 | 300.00 |
| Silver, Russian, Case, Cigarette, Repousse, Enamel Plaques, Art Nouveau, 1900s | 300.00 |
| Silver, Russian, Case, Cigarette, Samorodok, Sapphire Thumbpiece, P.J.S., 1900 | 225.00 |
| Silver, Russian, Case, Communion, Surmounted By Cross, Hinged, Moscow, 1787 | 250.00 |
| Silver, Russian, Casket, Filigree, Hinged, Pierced Scrollwork, Moscow, C.1890 | 250.00 |
| Silver, Russian, Casket, Gilded, Champleve Enamel, Kuzmitchev, 1893 | 4250.00 |
| Silver, Russian, Casket, Hinged, Gilded, Roosters & Shield, Moscow, 1874 | 1400.00 |
| Silver, Russian, Chalice, Engraved Cyrillic Prayer, Passion, Tula, 1868 | 550.00 |
| Silver, Russian, Chalice, Gilded, 4 Evengelists, Cyrillic Prayer, Moscow, 1790 | 500.00 |
| Silver, Russian, Coaster, Wine, Mahogany Base, Sazikov, 1870, Set Of 12 | 1500.00 |
| Silver, Russian, Cooler, Wine, Chased, Grape Banding, Nichols & Plinke, 1838 | 1100.00 |
| Silver, Russian, Creamer, Ovoid, Roses, Reeded Foot, Ivory Scroll Handle, 1829 | 175.00 |
| Silver, Russian, Cross, Pectoral, Carved Mother-Of-Pearl, C.1750 | 200.00 |
| Silver, Russian, Cross, Pectoral, Presentation, Czar Paul I, Dated 1797 | 675.00 |
| Silver, Russian, Cup, Vodka, Footed, Engraved Art Nouveau Design, Tapered | 25.00 |
| Silver, Russian, Cup, Wine, Incised Designs, Footed, Dated 1882, Hallmarked | 30.00 |
| Silver, Russian, Goblet, Gilded, Neillo, Floral, Berries, Moscow, 1833 | 225.00 |
| Silver, Russian, Match Safe, Initials & Coronet, 2 1/4 X 1 In. | 50.00 |
| Silver, Russian, Pin, Lapel, Coronation Nicholas II & Alexandria, 1896 | 145.00 |
| Silver, Russian, Purse, Coin, Dated Jan.26, 1900, 3 X 2 1/4 In. | 120.00 |
| Silver, Russian, Salt, Engraved Floral, 3 Ball Feet, Dated 1872 | 40.00 |
| Silver, Russian, Salt, Individual, Tula, 84 Standard | 30.00 |
| Silver, Russian, Salt, Master, Incised Designs, 3 Ball Feet, Dated 1890 | 30.00 |
| Silver, Russian, Shot Glass, Bright Cut, 84 Standard, 1 Oz. | 20.00 |
| Silver, Russian, Shot Glass, Bright Cut, 84 Standard, 3/4 Oz. | 20.00 |
| Silver, Russian, Spoon, Gold Washed, Red, White & 3 Shades Of Blue Enamel | 90.00 |
| Silver, Russian, Spoon, Salad, Karelian Birch Bowl, 8 1/4 In.Long | 75.00 |
| Silver, Russian, Spoon, Serving, Gilded, Lacquer, Peter The Great, C.1900 | 100.00 |
| Silver, Russian, Sugar, Scrolling Foliage, Franz Fagerstrom, 1853 | 175.00 |
| Silver, Russian, Tablespoon, Gilded, Lacquer, Peter The Great, C.1900 | 150.00 |
| Silver, Russian, Tankard, Gilded, Repousse, Hinged Lid, V.D., 1753, 8 In. High | 3000.00 |
| Silver, Russian, Tea Set, Scrolled, Handled, Pavel Sazikov, 1853, 3 Piece | 325.00 |
| Silver, Russian, Tea Strainer, Fiddleback, Hallmarked, Dated 1856, 7 1/2 In. | 85.00 |
| Silver, Russian, Teapot, Ivory On Handle, Mother-Of-Pearl Knob, 1837 | 400.00 |
| Silver, Russian, Teaspoon, Niello Enamel On Back, Rounded Bowl | 40.00 |
| Silver, Russian, Teaspoon, Twisted Handle, Gold Washed, Bright Cut, 1887 | 16.65 |
| Silver, Russian, Toilette Set, Nichols & Plinke, C.1850, 3 Piece | 300.00 |
| Silver, Scandinavian, Tankard, Peg, Repousse, Chased Birds, C.1690, 7 3/4 In. | 1800.00 |

Silver, Scottish, Centerpiece, Domed Center, Acorn Finial, Cunningham, 1801 ............................ 700.00
Silver, Scottish, Creamer, Leaf Capped Double Scroll Handle, Graham, C.1765 ...................... 325.00
Silver, Scottish, Ladle,"Toddy, Woman & Child Handle, Mackay & Chisholm, 1881 ................ 55.00
Silver, Scottish, Spoon, Basting, Hanoverian, Ged, 1738 .................................................... *Illus*  190.00
Silver, Scottish, Spoon, Dressing, King's Pattern, Maker W.C., 1829, 12 In. .......................... 75.00
Silver, Scottish, Spoon, Stuffing, Edinburgh, 1819, 15 In.Long ............................................ 105.00
Silver, Scottish, Striker With Wick, For Grouse Hunting, Rogart, 1925 .............................. 35.00
Silver, Scottish, Tablespoon, Dublin, 1800 .................................................................... 10.00
Silver, Scottish, Tea Set, George IV, Gadrooned Rims, G., 1823, 3 Piece .......................... 550.00
Silver, Scottish, Teapot, Chased, S-Scroll Handle, Robertson, 1767, 7 In. ........................ 400.00
   Silver, Sheffield, see also Silver Plate
Silver, Sheffield, Basket, Cake, Oval, Gadroon Rim, C.1810, 14 7/8 In. Long ...................... 175.00
Silver, Sheffield, Basket, Cake, William IV, Pierced Rim, H.& H., 1833 .............................. 350.00
Silver, Sheffield, Bowl, Boat Shape, Pedestal, Eagle's Head Handles, Repousse .............. 125.00
Silver, Sheffield, Box, Biscuit, Hinged Dome Cover, Engraved, Archer, 1865 ...................... 500.00
Silver, Sheffield, Box, Biscuit, Ivory Handles, 9 In.Long .................................................. 325.00
Silver, Sheffield, Box, John Parsons & Co., 1818, 4 1/8 X 2 5/8 X 1 5/8 In. ...................... 130.00
Silver, Sheffield, Candelabra, Removable Center Plug, C.1800, 21 In., Pair ........................ 1500.00
Silver, Sheffield, Candelabra, Rococo, Floral, Removable Bobeche, 19 In., Pair .................. 300.00
Silver, Sheffield, Candelabra, Three Light, Vase Shape, C.1820, 22 In., Pair ...................... 225.00
Silver, Sheffield, Candelabra, Vase Stem, Campana Sconce, 3-Arm, C.1820, Pair .............. 400.00
Silver, Sheffield, Candelabra, Vase Stem, 3-Arm, Settle, 1818, 20 1/2 In., Pair .................. 1500.00
Silver, Sheffield, Candlesnuffer & Tray, Hallmarked ...................................................... 42.50
Silver, Sheffield, Candlesnuffer, Scissors Type, On Tray ................................................ 55.00
Silver, Sheffield, Candlestick, George III, Corinthian, Watson, 1782, Pair .......................... 250.00
Silver, Sheffield, Candlestick, Push-Up, Removable Reflector Hood, Pair .......................... 250.00
Silver, Sheffield, Candlestick, Round Base, Bell Sconce, 1780, 11 In., Pair ........................ 750.00
Silver, Sheffield, Candlestick, Round Base, Raised Gadroon Band, C.1760, Pair .................. 55.00
Silver, Sheffield, Candlestick, Square Stepped Base, Chased, C.1765, Pair ........................ 200.00
Silver, Sheffield, Candlestick, Vase Stem, Rams' Masks, Chased, 1775, Pair ...................... 750.00
Silver, Sheffield, Candlestick, William IV, Baluster, Wilkinson, 1835, Pair ........................ 387.50
Silver, Sheffield, Coaster, Embossed Fruit Border, Pair .................................................. 90.00
Silver, Sheffield, Coaster, Hardwood Bottom, Gardooned Rim, Set Of 6 ............................ 85.00
Silver, Sheffield, Coaster, Wine, George IV, Gadrooned Rim, Creswick, 1828 ...................... 237.50
Silver, Sheffield, Coaster, Wine, Raised Border, C.1830, 6 1/2 In., Pair .............................. 95.00
Silver, Sheffield, Cooler, Wine, Campana Shape, Armorials, C.1820, Pair .......................... 550.00
Silver, Sheffield, Cooler, Wine, Campana Shape, Crests, Creswick, C.1830, Pair .............. 450.00
Silver, Sheffield, Dish, Entree, Covered, Grape & Vine, Waterhouse, C.1833 ...................... 248.00
Silver, Sheffield, Dish, Entree, Covered, Warmer, Engraved Crest, C.1820, Pair .............. 212.50
Silver, Sheffield, Dish, Meat, Foliate Ring Finial, Gadroon Rim, Boulton, 1810 .................. 450.00
Silver, Sheffield, Dish, Meat, Heraldic Finial, Warmer, P.C., C.1800, Pair .......................... 1800.00
Silver, Sheffield, Epergne, Cornucopias, Cut Glass Bowl, C.1815, 14 In.High ...................... 300.00
Silver, Sheffield, Fish Service, Engraved, Ivory Handles, Oak Case, 24 Piece ...................... 165.00
Silver, Sheffield, Fish Service, Ivory Handles, Sterling Bands, 24 Piece .......................... 180.00
Silver, Sheffield, Fish Set, Ivory Handles, Openwork, C.1913, Satin Box ............................ 45.00
Silver, Sheffield, Inkstand, Central Urn, Taperstick, 2 Wells, Roberts, 1814 ...................... 350.00
Silver, Sheffield, Knife, Cake, Ivory Blade, Embossed Handle, Sterling Ferule .................. 7.50
Silver, Sheffield, Knife, Celluloid Handle, Marked Dickinson ............................................ 1.35
Silver, Sheffield, Knife, Steak, Ornate ........................................................................ 12.50
Silver, Sheffield, Ladle, Punch, Phillip Ashbury, 1880 .................................................... 50.00
Silver, Sheffield, Plate, Pierced, 10 In. ...................................................................... 15.00
Silver, Sheffield, Salt Dip, Lion's Head & Paw At Each Of 3 Feet, Floral ............................ 15.00
Silver, Sheffield, Salt, Master, Footed, Clear Glass Liner, C.1810 ...................................... 68.00
Silver, Sheffield, Salt, Master, Footed, Cobalt Liner ...................................................... 68.00
Silver, Sheffield, Salver, Footed, Round, 11 1/2 In. ...................................................... 250.00
Silver, Sheffield, Spoon, Dressing, Maker I.W.& I.R., Georgian ........................................ 65.00
Silver, Sheffield, Spoon, Stuffing, 12 In. .................................................................... 26.50
Silver, Sheffield, Spoon, Tea Caddy, Shell Bowl, 1909 .................................................... 35.00
Silver, Sheffield, Tea & Coffee Set, Crests, Mappin & Webb, 1932, 6 Piece ........................ 2300.00
Silver, Sheffield, Tea & Coffee Set, Vase Shape, Engraved, Hall, 1868, 4 Piece .................. 925.00
Silver, Sheffield, Tea Machine, Large Urn & 2 Small Urns, C.1805 .................................... 3000.00
Silver, Sheffield, Tea Set, Bulbous Pot, Round Tray, C.1900, 4 Piece ................................ 110.00
Silver, Sheffield, Teakettle & Burner, Monogram Marx, C.1800, 12 In. High ...................... 75.00
Silver, Sheffield, Teapot, Chased & Engraved Panels, Ceramic Heat Inserts ...................... 45.00
Silver, Sheffield, Teapot, Straight Sided Oval, Beaded Borders, Younge, 1781 .................. 400.00
Silver, Sheffield, Tray, Tea, Edwardian, Engraved, Walker & Hall, 1901, 30 In. .................. 1250.00

| | |
|---|---|
| Silver, Sheffield, Tray, Tea, Foliate & Scroll Rim, Crest Center, Crown, 1825 | 375.00 |
| Silver, Sheffield, Tray, Tea, Pierced Vitruvian Scrolls Gallery, 24 In. | 225.00 |
| Silver, Sheffield, Tureen, Sauce, Covered, Oval, Paw Feet, C.1815, 8 In.Long | 100.00 |
| Silver, Sheffield, Tureen, Sauce, Domed Cover, Shell & Scroll, C.1825, Pair | 250.00 |
| Silver, Sheffield, Urn, Tea, Egyptian Woman Finial, Birds' Heads Handles | 175.00 |
| Silver, Sheffield, Urn, Tea, Lion Mask Handles, Paw Feet, C.1800, 13 In.High | 170.00 |
| Silver, Sheffield, Warmer, Covered, C.1790 | 168.00 |
| Silver, South American, Cup, Coconut, Form Of Cockerel, Ball Feet, 11 In.High | 250.00 |
| Silver, South American, Wine Set, Aztec Thumb Rest, Chased Floral, 9 Piece | 295.00 |

*Sterling silver is made with 925 parts of silver out of 1, 000 parts of metal.
The word sterling is a quality guarantee used in the United States after
about 1860.*

**Silver, Sterling, see also Silver, American**

| | |
|---|---|
| Silver, Sterling, Basket, Bonbon, Pierced Edge, Cobalt Liner | 28.00 |
| Silver, Sterling, Basket, Fruit, Art Nouveau, Openwork, Reed & Barton, 17 In. | 350.00 |
| Silver, Sterling, Basket, Greek Key Border, 11 In.Long, 9 In.Wide, Tiffany | 75.00 |
| Silver, Sterling, Basket, Pierced Sides, Oval, 4 Ball Feet, Rigid Handle | 22.00 |
| Silver, Sterling, Blotter, Rocking, Repousse | 30.00 |
| Silver, Sterling, Bonbon, Openwork, Scalloped, Floral, Monogram, 5 In. | 20.00 |
| Silver, Sterling, Bonbon, Round, Scalloped Sides, Relief Grape Clusters | 16.00 |
| Silver, Sterling, Bottle Opener, Flower Design On Handle | 6.95 |
| Silver, Sterling, Bowl, Center, Pierced, Applied Leaf Sprays, Birmingham, 1911 | 125.00 |
| Silver, Sterling, Bowl, Centerpiece, Art Nouveau Edging, Shreve & Co., 1900s | 110.00 |
| Silver, Sterling, Bowl, Chased, Pedestal, Haris, London, 1902, 9 1/4 In. | 230.00 |
| Silver, Sterling, Bowl, Finger, Towle, Patent March 26, 1929 | 15.00 |
| Silver, Sterling, Bowl, Flower, Handwrought Shirt, Pedestal Base, 3 1/4 In. | 25.00 |
| Silver, Sterling, Bowl, Heart Shape, Pierced, Repousse Scrolls, 3 Ball Feet | 110.00 |
| Silver, Sterling, Bowl, Repousse Band, 3 Raised Ornate Feet, S.Kirk & Son | 55.00 |
| Silver, Sterling, Bowl, Revere Shape, Queen Anne Style Vertical Ribbing | 85.00 |
| Silver, Sterling, Bowl, Vertical Ribbing, Reed & Barton, 9 3/4 In. | 68.00 |
| Silver, Sterling, Box, Hinged Lid, Reliefs Of Flowers, Marked | 20.00 |
| Silver, Sterling, Box, Hinged, Ball Feet, Engraved Basket Weave, Gold Wash | 225.00 |
| Silver, Sterling, Box, Hinged, Geometrics, 3 X 5 X 1 In. | 25.00 |
| Silver, Sterling, Box, Patch, Round, English, C.1900, 1 1/2 In. | 12.00 |
| Silver, Sterling, Box, Soap, Engraved, Reed & Barton, C.1875 | 11.00 |
| Silver, Sterling, Brush, Hair, Art Nouveau, Woman's Form Handle, Embossed | 85.00 |
| Silver, Sterling, Buckle, Art Nouveau, Dolphin Form, 4 1/4 In.Long | 75.00 |
| Silver, Sterling, Buckle, Belt, Lady's, Chased On Back, "MCB" | 12.00 |
| Silver, Sterling, Butter Pick, Twisted, Pointed Blade, 6 In.Long | 6.95 |
| Silver, Sterling, Buttohhook, Ornate | 10.50 |
| Silver, Sterling, Buttonhook & Nail File, Etched & Engraved Handles | 15.00 |
| Silver, Sterling, Buttonhook, Art Deco | 8.00 |
| Silver, Sterling, Buttonhook, Art Nouveau Girl On Handle, Unger Bros. | 20.00 |
| Silver, Sterling, Buttonhook, Floral Designs | 17.00 |
| Silver, Sterling, Buttonhook, Monogrammed R, English | 5.00 |
| Silver, Sterling, Buttonhook, Patent 1893, 5 5/8 In.Long | 3.95 |
| Silver, Sterling, Candelabra, Tulip Shape, 3 Arm, Gadrooned, Rogers, 1900, Pair | 69.00 |
| Silver, Sterling, Candleholder, 12 In.High, Pair | 25.00 |
| Silver, Sterling, Candleholder, 2 1/4 In.High, Pair | 15.00 |
| Silver, Sterling, Candleholder, 3 In.High, Pair | 11.00 |
| Silver, Sterling, Candlesnuffer, Cone End, Long Handled | 18.00 |
| Silver, Sterling, Candlesnuffer, Scotty Dog End, Long Handle | 22.00 |
| Silver, Sterling, Candlestick, Empire, 5 In.High, Pair | 22.00 |
| Silver, Sterling, Card Case, Oriental Lady With Fan, Gorham | 45.00 |
| Silver, Sterling, Carving Set, Horn Handles, Embossed Ribbons, 3 Piece | 17.50 |
| Silver, Sterling, Case, Cigar, Florals, Monogram, Gold Washed Inside, C.1923 | 48.00 |
| Silver, Sterling, Case, Cigar, For 3, Hammered Design, Gold Washed Inside | 25.00 |
| Silver, Sterling, Case, Cigarette, Art Nouveau, Embossed Cupids, Unger Bros. | 65.00 |
| Silver, Sterling, Case, Cigarette, Elgin, American, Initials | 12.00 |
| Silver, Sterling, Case, Cigarette, Gold Initials WB, Chester, England, 1909 | 17.50 |
| Silver, Sterling, Case, Eye Glasses, Victorian, Pince-Nez, Leaf & Scroll | 15.00 |
| Silver, Sterling, Case, Match, Striker, Four-Leaf Clovers | 32.00 |
| Silver, Sterling, Case, Playing Card, Victorian, Book Form, Openword | 28.00 |
| Silver, Sterling, Case, Stamp, Embossed, Elk's, Patent 1911, Name & City | 15.00 |
| Silver, Sterling, Clip, Money, "Money, Money, Money, Money, Money, Money" | 45. |
| Silver, Sterling, Compact, Bouchern, Sapphires, 14K Gold Decoration | 120.00 |

Silver, Sterling, Compact, Enameled, Embossed ............................................................... 85.00
Silver, Sterling, Comport, Cake, Scalloped Rim, Chippendale Style, Gorham ..................... 95.00
Silver, Sterling, Cooler, Tea, Tube Type, Blow Through, Decorated ................................... 30.00
Silver, Sterling, Creamer, Cow, Standing, Embossed, Mouth Forms Spout ....................... 150.00
Silver, Sterling, Creamer, Oriental Motif, Animal's Head Spout & Handle .......................... 50.00
Silver, Sterling, Cup & Saucer, Demitasse, Monogrammed, Lenox Liner ........................... 13.50
Silver, Sterling, Cup & Saucer, Demitasse, Wedgwood Liner, Shreve & Co. ..................... 22.50
Silver, Sterling, Cup, Child's, Rabbit On Side ................................................................... 18.00
Silver, Sterling, Cup, Coffee, Raised Flowers, Marked Edward J.Hart ............................... 25.00
Silver, Sterling, Cup, Gold Lined, Leather Case, 2 X 2 1/4 In. .......................................... 10.00
Silver, Sterling, Cup, Nut, Embossed Edge, Monogram ALW, International ........................ 5.00
Silver, Sterling, Cup, Wedding, Dutch, Repousse, 7 In. ................................................... 130.00
Silver, Sterling, Curler, Hair, Art Nouveau Design, 6 3/4 In.Long ..................................... 7.95
Silver, Sterling, Cuticle Pusher, Art Nouveau Girl On Handle, Unger Bros. ...................... 15.00
Silver, Sterling, Cutter, Cigar, Art Nouveau, Unger Brothers ............................................ 12.00
Silver, Sterling, Cutter, Cigar, Champagne Bottle & Glass ............................................... 28.00
Silver, Sterling, Cutter, Cigar, Entwined Snake ............................................................... 28.00
Silver, Sterling, Cutter, Cigar, For Watch Chain, Etched Fisherman, 1 1/2 In. ................. 10.00
Silver, Sterling, Cutter, Cigar, Long Stemmed Iris ........................................................... 28.00
Silver, Sterling, Dish, Candy, Embossed Border, Monogram, Round, 5 In. ........................ 9.00
Silver, Sterling, Dish, Candy, Round, 2 Rows Of Flower & Leaf Design ............................ 12.50
Silver, Sterling, Dish, Covered, Miniature, 2 Handles, Black, Starr, Frost ......................... 22.50
Silver, Sterling, Dish, Nut, Ornate Turned Over Rim, Signed ............................................ 5.75
Silver, Sterling, Dresser Set, Repousse, Raised Flowers, Gorham, 8 Piece ....................... 150.00
Silver, Sterling, Eraser, Blade, Long Handle, Hallmarked ................................................. 22.00
Silver, Sterling, Figurine, Elk, Long Antlers, Hallmarked, 3 Ozs. ..................................... 125.00
Silver, Sterling, Figurine, Knight, Ivory Face, Repousse, 11 In. ....................................... 450.00
Silver, Sterling, Figurine, Owl, Darn, Yellow Glass Eyes, Vermeilwork, 6 In. .................... 285.00
Silver, Sterling, Flacon, Perfume, Etched, Reserve, 2 In. ................................................. 16.00
Silver, Sterling, Flask, Whiskey, Flat Oval ...................................................................... 72.00
Silver, Sterling, Fork, Cold Meat, Patent 1907 ................................................................ 12.75
Silver, Sterling, Fork, Dinner, Chantilly, Gorham, C.1895 ................................................ 15.00
Silver, Sterling, Fork, Dinner, Olive Leaf, Bigelow Bros & Kennard, Set Of 11 .................. 65.00
Silver, Sterling, Fork, Dinner, Viola, Wood & Hughes, Victorian ....................................... 7.95
Silver, Sterling, Fork, Fiddle Thread, J.E.Caldwell ........................................................... 15.00
Silver, Sterling, Fork, Lemon, Flower Design On Handle, Patent 1892 .............................. 5.95
Silver, Sterling, Fork, Lemon, Flower On Handle, Initials M E L, Patent 1892 ................... 5.95
Silver, Sterling, Fork, Lemon, Ornate, Patent 1892 ......................................................... 5.95
Silver, Sterling, Fork, Lettuce, Frank Smith, Initials ........................................................ 10.00
Silver, Sterling, Fork, Olive, Fancy Design, Lion Touchmark ............................................ 4.95
Silver, Sterling, Fork, Oyster, Bailey Banks & Biddle Co., Set Of 12 ................................ 72.00
Silver, Sterling, Fork, Pickle, Beaded Rim ...................................................................... 5.00
Silver, Sterling, Fork, Pickle, Ornate, Initials M.L., 8 In.Long .......................................... 8.95
Silver, Sterling, Fork, Sardine, Gold Washed Tines ......................................................... 15.00
Silver, Sterling, Fork, Scrolls, 2 Tines ........................................................................... 12.00
Silver, Sterling, Fork, Strawberry, Labors Of Cupid, Dominick & Haff, 12 ........................ 85.00
Silver, Sterling, Frame, Picture, Oval, Hammered Effect, Button Feet ............................... 16.00
Silver, Sterling, Glove Stretcher, Ornate Decoration, Patented 1898 ................................ 15.00
Silver, Sterling, Glove Stretcher, Raised Florals .............................................................. 16.50
Silver, Sterling, Glovehook, Embossed ........................................................................... 7.50
Silver, Sterling, Goblet, Gadrooned Border, Monogrammed, Gorham, 6 In. High ............... 40.00
Silver, Sterling, Grape Shears, Victorian, Vines & Grapes In Relief, Pair ........................... 22.00
Silver, Sterling, Gravy Boat, Acanthus Leaves End In 3 Claw Feet, Gorham ...................... 55.00
Silver, Sterling, Hairpin, Grape Design, Chain Attached .................................................. 19.00
Silver, Sterling, Hatpin, Art Nouveau Lady's Head .......................................................... 14.00
Silver, Sterling, Hatpin, Bear On Hinge .......................................................................... 25.00
Silver, Sterling, Hatpin, Long Shaft ............................................................................... 6.00
Silver, Sterling, Holder, Baby's Bib, Rabbit Clips, Chain ................................................. 10.00
Silver, Sterling, Holder, Corncob, Ornate, 6 Pair ............................................................ 54.00
Silver, Sterling, Holder, Napkin, Victorian, Fruits, Fowl, & Angles, Gorham ...................... 13.00
Silver, Sterling, Hook, Glove, Beaded Edge With Raised Roses ........................................ 8.50
Silver, Sterling, Hook, Glove, Engraved Band, Pearl Handle ............................................. 20.00
Silver, Sterling, Inkwell, Hinged Lady's Head Lid, Cut Glass Cane Insert .......................... 30.00
Silver, Sterling, Inkwell, Hinged Top, Wooden Bottom, JD, Birmingham, 1920 ................. 20.00
Silver, Sterling, Jug, Gurnsey, Covered, England, 3 Cup Size ........................................... 85.00
Silver, Sterling, Knife & Fork, Child's, Girl Playing Croquet, Boy With Dog ....................... 28.00

Silver, Sterling, Knife & Fork, Child's, Hollow Handles, Initial M ........... 8.00
Silver, Sterling, Knife & Nail File, Pocket, Loop For Chain ................... 6.95
Silver, Sterling, Knife Rest, 4 Mice Holding Pronged Bar, Marked 800-Lemor .......... 62.50
Silver, Sterling, Knife, Butter Serving, Engraved Blade, J.Mouton, 1866 ......... 12.75
Silver, Sterling, Knife, Butter Serving, Initials A.L.B., Patent 1871 .......... 11.75
Silver, Sterling, Knife, Butter, Animal, Anchor & G Marks, Engraved 1870-95 ......... 5.25
Silver, Sterling, Knife, Butter, Beaded Edge, Jones, Shreve, & Brown, 7 In. ......... 10.00
Silver, Sterling, Knife, Fruit, Pocket, Initials A.H.P., Nutpick ............. 6.95
Silver, Sterling, Knife, Fruit, Pocket, Nut Pick Attached ................... 7.95
Silver, Sterling, Knife, Ice Cream, Peony, Wallace ....................... 15.00
Silver, Sterling, Knife, Pocket, Shape Of Reclining Hound Dog ................ 40.00
Silver, Sterling, Knife, Tea, Marie Antoinette, Dom & Haff, Set Of 6 ........ 48.00
Silver, Sterling, Ladle, Cream, Victorian, Leaves ....................... 10.75
Silver, Sterling, Ladle, Gravy, Hindustan, Victorian, Square Bowl, Gorham ...... 18.00
Silver, Sterling, Ladle, Gravy, Repousse Rose, S.Kirk & Son ............... 22.00
Silver, Sterling, Ladle, Gravy, Victorian, Easter, Whiting ............... 15.00
Silver, Sterling, Ladle, Laureate, Initials, Whiting, C.1890 ............. 50.00
Silver, Sterling, Ladle, Punch, Cut Glass Handle ....................... 250.00
Silver, Sterling, Ladle, Punch, Gold Washed Bowl, Ivory, Dated 1886 ...... 145.00
Silver, Sterling, Ladle, Sauce, Pointed Handle, S.Kirk & Son ............. 16.00
Silver, Sterling, Ladle, Sauce, Pointed Turned Down Handle, S.Kirk & Son ..... 16.00
Silver, Sterling, Ladle, Sauce, Wreath Decoration, Small Size ............. 15.00
Silver, Sterling, Letter Opener, Folding Knife, 7 In.Long ............... 5.95
Silver, Sterling, Looking Glass, Engraved Joe ....................... 18.00
Silver, Sterling, Luncheon Set, Bright Cut, Gold Wash, C.1880, 6 Piece ...... 95.00
Silver, Sterling, Manicure Set, Initial H, 4 Piece ................... 30.00
Silver, Sterling, Match Safe, Art Nouveau Full Figure Of Psyche, Embossed ..... 45.00
Silver, Sterling, Match Safe, Art Nouveau, Raised Design, Maids, Flowing Hair ..... 38.00
Silver, Sterling, Match Safe, Bird Dogs & Hunter In Relief ............... 18.00
Silver, Sterling, Match Safe, Embossed Scrolls & Flowers, Flip Top ......... 18.00
Silver, Sterling, Match Safe, Laughing Devil ......................... 28.00
Silver, Sterling, Match Safe, Ornate Scrolls ......................... 18.00
Silver, Sterling, Match Safe, Photograph Frame, Scrolling ............... 35.00
Silver, Sterling, Match Safe, Pocket, Aphrodite & Cupid In Relief ......... 52.00
Silver, Sterling, Match Safe, Pocket, Floral & Scroll, Dated 1916, Gorham ..... 11.75
Silver, Sterling, Match Safe, Pocket, Flowers ....................... 13.00
Silver, Sterling, Match Safe, Pocket, Raised Allover Leaves, Initials, 1908 ..... 20.00
Silver, Sterling, Match Safe, Shiebler ............................. 27.50
Silver, Sterling, Mirror, Art Deco, Geometrics, English Hallmarks ......... 38.00
Silver, Sterling, Mirror, Hand, Art Nouveau, Embossed Cherub & Scrolls ...... 45.00
Silver, Sterling, Mirror, Hand, Ornate, Floral & Birds, Initials M.E.S. ...... 25.00
Silver, Sterling, Mug, Embossed Design, Tiffany ....................... 48.00
Silver, Sterling, Nail Cleaner, Venus & Cupid ....................... 7.50
Silver, Sterling, Nail File, Case, Relief Design, 3 In. Long ............. 6.00
Silver, Sterling, Nail File, Lily Of The Valley ....................... 12.00
Silver, Sterling, Nail File, Monogrammed M.G., Acornlike Pattern ......... 5.00
Silver, Sterling, Nail File, Pocket, Art Nouveau, Mezzo Relief Dancing Girl ..... 12.00
Silver, Sterling, Nail File, Victorian ............................. 35.00
Silver, Sterling, Napkin Ring, see Napkin Ring
Silver, Sterling, Nutpick, Victorian, Bright Cut Engraving, 1878, Set Of 12 ..... 68.00
Silver, Sterling, Opener, Bottle, Ornate, Samuel Kirk & Son ............. 9.75
Silver, Sterling, Opener, Letter, Dagger End, German Steel Blade ......... 12.00
Silver, Sterling, Opener, Letter, Embossed Full Figure Of Art Nouveau Lady ..... 18.00
Silver, Sterling, Pen, Fountain, Incised Allover Design ............... 15.00
Silver, Sterling, Pencil, Lead, Engraved, 3 In. ....................... 6.00
Silver, Sterling, Pencil, Lead, Long Sterling Chain ................... 9.50
Silver, Sterling, Pencil, Retractible, Ornate, Loop For Chain ............. 5.75
Silver, Sterling, Pillbox, Enameled, Flowing Iris Flowers, Round ......... 100.00
Silver, Sterling, Pillbox, Enameled, Lovebirds In Flower Bed, Round ...... 100.00
Silver, Sterling, Pillbox, Oblong, Initials, Gold Washed Inside ......... 20.00
Silver, Sterling, Plate, Bread & Butter, Gadrooned Border, Caldwell ...... 15.00
Silver, Sterling, Plate, Bread, Raised Floral & Vine, Ferd. Fuchs & Bros. ..... 45.00
Silver, Sterling, Porringer, Handmade, C.1925 ....................... 45.00
Silver, Sterling, Pot, Mustard, Cutout Reveals Cranberry Glass Liner, 2 In. ..... 35.00
Silver, Sterling, Presentation, Dated 1912, Durgin ................... 35.00
Silver, Sterling, Purse, Coin, Blue Velvet, Facsimile Of Greek Coins ...... 29.50

| | |
|---|---|
| Silver, Sterling, Purse, Mesh, Ornate Frame, Jeweled Inset On Clasp | 22.00 |
| Silver, Sterling, Rattle, Baby's, Acorn Shape, Pierced Top, England, C.1903 | 35.00 |
| Silver, Sterling, Rattle, Baby's, Baby's Head, Bonnet, Mother-Of-Pearl Handle | 85.00 |
| Silver, Sterling, Rattle, Baby's, Ivory Teething Ring On End | 25.00 |
| Silver, Sterling, Rattle, Baby's, Rabbits On Sides, Mother-Of-Pearl Handle | 65.00 |
| Silver, Sterling, Razor, Straight, Victorian, Ornate | 45.00 |
| Silver, Sterling, Salad Set, Eglantine, Gold Washed, Gorham, 1870, 2 Piece | 60.00 |
| Silver, Sterling, Salad Set, Repousse, S.Kirk & Son 925-1000, 2 Piece | 65.00 |
| Silver, Sterling, Salt & Pepper, Applied Handle, Revere, 3 1/2 In.High | 15.00 |
| Silver, Sterling, Salt & Pepper, Deer, 1 1/2 In.High | 4.00 |
| Silver, Sterling, Salt & Pepper, Pumpkin Shape, Twisted Wire Stem, Repousse | 20.00 |
| Silver, Sterling, Salt & Pepper, 3 Applied Shell Feet, National, 3 3/4 In. | 15.00 |
| Silver, Sterling, Salt & Spoon, Master, Shell Shape, Footed, English Mark | 30.00 |
| Silver, Sterling, Salt, Gold Lined, Hallmarked, Pair | 25.00 |
| Silver, Sterling, Salt, Individual, Fluted Sides | 3.00 |
| Silver, Sterling, Salt, Individual, Repousse, Stieff Hallmark | 12.50 |
| Silver, Sterling, Salt, Master, Footed, Cobalt Insert, Whiting Co., C.1900 | 20.00 |
| Silver, Sterling, Salt, Ram's Head Legs, Gorham, C.1860, Pair | 90.00 |
| Silver, Sterling, Salt, Scrolls, Cobalt Blue Insert, Germany, 1 1/2 In. | 15.00 |
| Silver, Sterling, Salt, Seated Buddha, 2 1/4 In.High | 18.00 |
| Silver, Sterling, Salt, Small Horse Drawing 2 Wheeled Cart, Cobalt Insert | 22.00 |
| Silver, Sterling, Scissors, Grape, Flower Blooms, Leaves, & Scrolls In Relief | 25.00 |
| Silver, Sterling, Scissors, Grape, Victorian, Bunch Of Grapes & Vines Relief | 22.00 |
| Silver, Sterling, Scoop, Cheese, Bright Cut, Whiting Co., 7 In. | 20.00 |
| Silver, Sterling, Scoop, Cheese, Fiddle Thread, Dated 1869, 7 In. | 20.00 |
| Silver, Sterling, Server, Cake, Alexandra, Hollow Handle, Dom & Haff | 15.00 |
| Silver, Sterling, Server, Cutout Bowl, Clawed At One Side, Rattail Handle | 9.50 |
| Silver, Sterling, Server, Jelly, 6 1/4 In.Long | 6.95 |
| Silver, Sterling, Server, Pie, Cluny, Engraved Blade, Gorham | 35.00 |
| Silver, Sterling, Serving Set, Mother-Of-Pearl Handles, 3 Piece | 65.00 |
| Silver, Sterling, Shaker, Cocktail, Handled, Initial G, Gorham, 1924, 24 Oz. | 55.00 |
| Silver, Sterling, Shaving Set, Ribbon Engraving, Gorham, C.1895, 3 Piece | 60.00 |
| Silver, Sterling, Shears, Duck | 22.00 |
| Silver, Sterling, Shoehorn, Marked, 8 1/8 In. | 8.00 |
| Silver, Sterling, Shoehorn, Ornate | 8.50 |
| Silver, Sterling, Shot Glass, Thimble Form, "Only A Thimble Full," Simons | 25.00 |
| Silver, Sterling, Shovel, Serving, Weidlich | 15.00 |
| Silver, Sterling, Spoon & Fork, Salad Serving, Fluted, Black Ebony Type | 14.00 |
| Silver, Sterling, Spoon, Art Nouveau, Gorham, C.1895 | 12.00 |
| Silver, Sterling, Spoon, Baby's, Bunny In Flowerpatch | 12.50 |
| Silver, Sterling, Spoon, Baby's, Cat On Curved Handle, Scene In Bowl | 13.50 |
| Silver, Sterling, Spoon, Baby's, Curved Handle, Virgo | 6.50 |
| Silver, Sterling, Spoon, Baby's, Embossed Flowers, Engraved Irma | 6.50 |
| Silver, Sterling, Spoon, Baby's, Stork & Baby Handle | 12.50 |
| Silver, Sterling, Spoon, Berry, Lily, Marked T & E Dickinson, 1905, Whiting | 85.00 |
| Silver, Sterling, Spoon, Berry, Squirrel Handle, Ball, Black & Co., N.Y. | 58.00 |
| Silver, Sterling, Spoon, Child's, Initial B, Bridal Veil, Rogers | 5.00 |
| Silver, Sterling, Spoon, Child's, Joan Of Arc, International | 5.00 |
| Silver, Sterling, Spoon, Condiment, Green Oriental Jade Handle, 1895 | 58.00 |
| Silver, Sterling, Spoon, Demitasse, Bible, Cross, & Crown, Gold Washed Bowl | 4.00 |
| Silver, Sterling, Spoon, Demitasse, Blue Enamel, Gold Washed Bowl, Norway | 15.00 |
| Silver, Sterling, Spoon, Demitasse, Bright Cut Flowers On Handle, Initial M. | 19.95 |
| Silver, Sterling, Spoon, Demitasse, Cherub Beating Drum, Patent 1873, 8 | 43.00 |
| Silver, Sterling, Spoon, Demitasse, Chrysanthemums, Lion Hallmark, 1899 | 7.50 |
| Silver, Sterling, Spoon, Demitasse, Enamel, White Bone Knob, Birmingham, 1858 | 12.50 |
| Silver, Sterling, Spoon, Demitasse, Shreve, Crump, & Low, Boston | 3.50 |
| Silver, Sterling, Spoon, Demitasse, Vermeil, International | 8.00 |
| Silver, Sterling, Spoon, Dessert, Fiddle, Stamped WH & Crown & Lion | 16.50 |
| Silver, Sterling, Spoon, Dessert, Marquis, C.1889 | 15.00 |
| Silver, Sterling, Spoon, Dessert, Mayflower, Kirk & Son | 12.00 |
| Silver, Sterling, Spoon, Dessert, Victorian, Louis XV, Crest, Whiting | 9.25 |
| Silver, Sterling, Spoon, Folding, R.Blackinton & Co. | 10.00 |
| Silver, Sterling, Spoon, Greek God, Pan On Handle, Shell Design Bowl | 5.95 |
| Silver, Sterling, Spoon, Jelly, Relief Mosaic Hawthorns & Berries | 5.00 |
| Silver, Sterling, Spoon, Master Salt, Beaded Flange, Georg Jensen, Pair | 15.00 |
| Silver, Sterling, Spoon, Master Salt, Colonial, Gorham, C.1885, Pair | 12.50 |

Silver, Sterling, Spoon, Master Salt, Initials A.M.G., Ornate, Patent 1895 ............................ 5.95
Silver, Sterling, Spoon, Master Salt, Shell Design, Gorham, Patent 1899 .......................... 4.75
Silver, Sterling, Spoon, Mote, Twisted Handle, J.E.Caldwell, Phila., 10 In. ........................ 15.00
Silver, Sterling, Spoon, Olive, Chantilly, Gorham, Dated 1895 ........................................ 9.50
Silver, Sterling, Spoon, Olive, Pierced Bowl, 6 1/8 In.Long .......................................... 7.95
Silver, Sterling, Spoon, Olive, Rose, Pierced Bowl, Gorham ........................................ 12.00
Silver, Sterling, Spoon, Ornate, Ivory Handle ........................................................ 10.00
Silver, Sterling, Spoon, Poppy, Gorham, C.1901, 5 1/2 In. ............................................ 7.50
Silver, Sterling, Spoon, Salt, Rattail, Set Of 5 ...................................................... 45.00
Silver, Sterling, Spoon, Salt, Shaker Tip ............................................................. 6.00
Silver, Sterling, Spoon, Serving, Bright Cut, Engraved S ............................................ 20.00
Silver, Sterling, Spoon, Serving, Century, Dom & Haff, 1900 ........................................ 22.50
Silver, Sterling, Spoon, Serving, Chesterfield, Gorham, C.1911 ...................................... 10.00
Silver, Sterling, Spoon, Serving, Colonial, Scalloped Edge, Gorham, Victorian ...................... 29.00
Silver, Sterling, Spoon, Serving, Hand Monogrammed, Marked M, C.1900, Pair ........................ 26.00
Silver, Sterling, Spoon, Serving, Imperial Queen, Pear Shape Bowl, Whiting ........................ 28.00
Silver, Sterling, Spoon, Serving, Scoop Bowl, Relief Insects, Caldwell, 1880 ...................... 55.00
Silver, Sterling, Spoon, Soldier With Rifle, Dated 1895 ............................................ 27.00
    Silver, Sterling, Spoon, Souvenir, see Souvenir, Spoon, Sterling
    Silver
Silver, Sterling, Spoon, Straining, Initials ............................................................ 8.50
Silver, Sterling, Spoon, Stuffing, Gorham ............................................................. 95.00
Silver, Sterling, Spoon, Sugar Sifter, Medallion, W.K.Vanderslice, C.1890 .......................... 22.00
Silver, Sterling, Spoon, Sugar, Repousse, Scalloped Bowl, S.Kirk & Son ............................ 16.50
Silver, Sterling, Spoon, Tea Caddy, Victorian, Mt.Vernon Silver Co. ................................ 18.00
Silver, Sterling, Spoon, Wavy End, Marked HR 1788 & HR 88 ........................................ 85.00
Silver, Sterling, Spoon, Zodiac, September, Gorham .................................................. 15.00
Silver, Sterling, Spreader, Master Butter, Engraved Stone Seymour, C.1879 .......................... 15.00
Silver, Sterling, Stand, Watch, Pocket, Gold Plated, Floral Pattern, Monogram ...................... 13.00
Silver, Sterling, Sugar & Creamer, Scrolled Handles, Pedestal Bases ................................ 30.00
Silver, Sterling, Sugar & Milk Jug, Urn Shape, Reed & Barton, C.1890 .............................. 95.00
Silver, Sterling, Sugar Shell, Delft Insert In Handle, Gold Washed .................................. 16.00
Silver, Sterling, Sugar Shell, Engraved Lottie, Flowers & Leaves ..................................... 7.95
Silver, Sterling, Sugar Shell, Fluted Bowl, Floral Handle, Patent 1892 .............................. 10.95
Silver, Sterling, Sugar Shell, Gorham, Patent 1896 .................................................. 11.75
Silver, Sterling, Sugar Shell, Initial M, Gold Washed Bowl, 7 In. .................................... 9.75
Silver, Sterling, Sugar Shell, Initials A.G.M., Gold Washed Bowl .................................... 9.75
Silver, Sterling, Sugar Shell, Patent 1897 ........................................................... 11.75
Silver, Sterling, Sugar Shell, Raised Flowers, Initial W. ............................................. 7.95
Silver, Sterling, Sugar Shell, Shell Pattern, 1897 .................................................. 11.75
Silver, Sterling, Swan, Marked With Three-Leaf Clover, 2 In., Pair .................................. 30.00
Silver, Sterling, Syrup, Hourglass Shape, Fancy Handle, 3 3/4 In.High .............................. 22.50
Silver, Sterling, Tag, Decanter, Bourbon ............................................................. 10.00
Silver, Sterling, Tag, Decanter, Rye ................................................................. 10.00
Silver, Sterling, Tag, Decanter, Scotch ............................................................... 10.00
Silver, Sterling, Tag, Decanter, Sherry ............................................................... 10.00
Silver, Sterling, Tamper, Pipe, Spoon, Tamper & Pick A Hook ...................................... 15.00
Silver, Sterling, Tea & Coffee Set, Holloware, Frank W.Smith Co., 5 Piece ........................ 1000.00
Silver, Sterling, Tea Ball & Chain ................................................................... 24.00
Silver, Sterling, Tea Ball, Teapot Shape, Chain ...................................................... 25.00
Silver, Sterling, Tea Bell, Hinged, Chain & Ring, Bailey, Banks & Biddle Co. ....................... 8.00
Silver, Sterling, Tea Set, Ivory Insulators, Dominick & Haff, C.1900, 4 Piece ...................... 350.00
Silver, Sterling, Tea Set, Pear Shape, Repousse, Baltimore, C.1880, 4 Piece ........................ 1650.00
Silver, Sterling, Tea Strainer, Fits Over Cup, Beaded Rim, Raised Flowers .......................... 14.00
Silver, Sterling, Tea Strainer, Fits Over Cup, Reed & Ribbon Design, Pierced ...................... 12.50
Silver, Sterling, Teaspoon, Art Nouveau, Seminude Woman & Cupid ................................ 22.00
Silver, Sterling, Teaspoon, Bright Cut Floral, Victorian, Set Of 6 .................................. 32.00
Silver, Sterling, Teaspoon, Century, Dom & Haff, 1900 ............................................. 5.45
Silver, Sterling, Teaspoon, Flower At Top, Monogram P, Patent 1910 ............................... 5.85
Silver, Sterling, Teaspoon, Flowers & Leaves On Handle, Patent 1892 .............................. 4.95
Silver, Sterling, Teaspoon, Initial N In Laurel Wreath, Crown, Lion, 1909, 6 ....................... 65.00
Silver, Sterling, Teaspoon, Medallion Head .......................................................... 9.00
Silver, Sterling, Teaspoon, Shell & Thread, Tiffany, Set Of 1i ...................................... 84.00
Silver, Sterling, Teaspoon, Zodiac, Gemini, Watson & Co., 6 In. .................................... 16.50
Silver, Sterling, Teaspoon, Zodiac, Pisces, Watson & Co., 6 In. .................................... 16.50
    Silver, Sterling, Thimble, see Sewing Tool, Sterling Sterling

| | |
|---|---|
| Silver, Sterling, Tongs, Ice, Miniature | 12.00 |
| Silver, Sterling, Tongs, Sugar, Floral, Claw Nippers, 3 3/4 In. | 11.50 |
| Silver, Sterling, Tongs, Sugar, Floral, Claw Nippers, 4 1/2 In. | 12.50 |
| Silver, Sterling, Tongs, Sugar, Shell Ends, 4 In. | 16.00 |
| Silver, Sterling, Toothbrush, Art Nouveau | 22.00 |
| Silver, Sterling, Toothpick, Swirled All Around | 14.00 |
| Silver, Sterling, Tray, Nut, Rectangular, Fluted Design, Reed & Barton | 9.25 |
| Silver, Sterling, Tray, Pin, Art Nouveau, 5 In.Long | 35.00 |
| Silver, Sterling, Tray, Pin, Heart Shape, Etched San Francisco Bay Scene | 7.50 |
| Silver, Sterling, Tray, Scalloped Border, 5 Cherubs' Heads & Vines | 25.00 |
| Silver, Sterling, Tray, Sugar Cube, 6 In.Long | 10.00 |
| Silver, Sterling, Vase, Art Nouveau, Fleur-De-Lis Whiplash, 10 In.High | 25.00 |
| Silver, Sterling, Vase, Trumpet, Reticulated, 12 In., Pair | 89.00 |
| Silver, Sterling, Watch Holder, Heart Cutouts, Flowers, S.Kirk, C.1900 | 62.00 |
| Silver, Sterling, Wax Jack, Scissor Type Spring, Pierced, Howard & Co., 1885 | 145.00 |
| Silver, Sterling, Whiskbroom | 6.50 |
| Silver, Sterling, Wine, Scalloped Border, 4 3/8 In. High | 20.00 |
| Silver, Sugar Shell, Farrington & Hunnewell, Boston, 1830, Coin | 15.00 |
| Silver, Swedish, Basket, Cake, Boat Shape, Openwork Petals, Ryberg, 1814 | 275.00 |
| Silver, Swedish, Beaker, Trumpet Shape, Engraved, Wrigglework, Eksjo, C.1755 | 225.00 |
| Silver, Swedish, Fork, Dinner, Rounded Tip, C.1871 | 25.00 |
| Silver, Swedish, Knife Rest, Individual | 15.00 |
| Silver, Swedish, Spoon, Fig Shape Bowl, Engraved Foliage, Mattson, C.1660 | 300.00 |
| Silver, Swiss, Cup, Coconut, Parvel Gilt, Stemmed, Coins, C.1590, 8 3/4 In. | 4500.00 |
| Silver, Viennese, Comport, Hammered, Knopped Twisted Standard, Hoffman, 1920s | 800.00 |
| Silver, Viennese, Cutter, Cigar, Elk's Head, Red Jewel Eyes, Horn Handle, 1872 | 145.00 |
| Silver, Viennese, Tray, Gild, Enamel, Lapis Lazuli, Handled, C.1850, 21 In. | 5250.00 |

*Sinclaire cut glass was made by H.P.Sinclaire and Company of
Corning, New York, between 1905 and 1929. Pieces were made of crystal as
well as amber, blue, green, or ruby. Only a small percentage of Sinclaire
glass is marked.*

| | |
|---|---|
| Sinclaire, Plate, Grapes, Tendrils, & Leaves, 7 In.Diameter | 45.00 |
| Sinclaire, Vase, Black Jade, Flint Rim, Ovoid, 8 In.High | 45.00 |
| Sinclaire, Vase, Verre De Soie, Purple Intaglio Poppies, Gilt Butterflies | 145.00 |

*Slag glass is streaked with several colors. There were many types made from
about 1880. Pink slag was an American Victorian product of unknown
origin. Purple and blue slag were made in American and English factories.
Red slag is a very late Victorian product. Other colors are known, but are
of less importance to the collector.*

| | |
|---|---|
| Slag, Blue, Compote, Fruit, Basket Weave & Lattice | 65.00 |
| Slag, Blue, Mug, Troubadour Scene, Greentown, 4 3/4 In. | 68.00 |
| Slag, Caramel, see Chocolate Glass | |
| Slag, Chartreuse, Cake Stand, Atterbury, 10 In. Diameter | 150.00 |
| Slag, Green, Cachepot, Plants Decoration, 6 1/2 In.High | 70.00 |
| Slag, Green, Spooner, Marquis Of Lorne | 60.00 |
| Slag, Green, Toothpick, Urn Shape, Square Base, Beaded Top, 3 1/4 In.High | 45.00 |
| Slag, Orange, Candlestick, 8 1/2 In.High, Pair | 45.00 |
| Slag, Pink, Butter, Covered, 6 In. High | 300.00 |
| Slag, Pink, Cup, Punch, Inverted Fan & Feather | 435.00 |
| Slag, Pink, Sauce, Inverted Fan & Feather | 172.50 To 195.00 |
| Slag, Pink, Sauce, Inverted Fan & Feather, Footed | 150.00 |
| Slag, Pink, Sauce, Inverted Feather, Footed, 2 1/4 In.Diameter | 235.00 |
| Slag, Pink, Toothpick, Footed | 350.00 |
| Slag, Pink, Tumbler | 150.00 To 235.00 |
| Slag, Purple, Bowl, Dolphin Feet, English, 7 In.Diameter | 55.00 |
| Slag, Purple, Butter, Covered, Flower & Panel | 50.00 |
| Slag, Purple, Cake Stand, Dart & Bar | 90.00 |
| Slag, Purple, Celery, Flute, Challinor Taylor | 47.50 |
| Slag, Purple, Celery, Jewel | 60.00 |
| Slag, Purple, Compote, Open, Dart Bar, High Standard, 8 3/4 In.Diameter | 50.00 |
| Slag, Purple, Dish, Candy, Crimped | 38.00 |
| Slag, Purple, Dish, Soap | 38.00 To 42.50 |
| Slag, Purple, Dish, Soap, "74 Spring A.T.P.G." | 49.50 |
| Slag, Purple, Goblet | 85.00 To 110.00 |
| Slag, Purple, Jar, Mustard, Bull's Head | 50.00 |

Slag, Purple, Match Holder, Four Feet ........................................................................................ 25.00
Slag, Purple, Match Holder, Square, Four Posts ...................................................................... 20.00
Slag, Purple, Pitcher, Mosaic, Sandwich Flute, Challinor, C.1885 ........................................ 60.00
Slag, Purple, Pitcher, Water, Flower And Panel, 9 1/2 In.High ............................................... 85.00
Slag, Purple, Plate, Closed Lattice Edge, Ribbed, 10 1/4 In. .................................................. 87.50
Slag, Purple, Salt, Footed, Open Handles, Swirls, Sowerby, 1877 ......................................... 38.00
Slag, Purple, Spill, Ram's Heads & Garlands, Footed, 6 3/4 In.High ..................................... 68.00
Slag, Purple, Spill, Ribbed, Beaded Swags, 5 3/4 In.High ...................................................... 38.00
Slag, Purple, Spooner ................................................................................................................. 40.00
Slag, Purple, Toothpick, Raindrop, Embossed Just A Thimbleful ........................ 40.00 To 45.00
Slag, Purple, Tumbler, Registry Mark, 1/2 Pint ....................................................................... 50.00
Slag, Purple, Tumbler, 10 Vertical Panels, American, 4 In.High ............................................. 45.00
Slag, Purple, Vase, Footed, Rams' Heads & Garlands, American, 6 3/4 In. .......................... 75.00
Slag, Purple, Vase, Ocean Shell, Mosaic, Opalescent, Northwood ........................................ 60.00
Slag, Red, Bowl, Citizens Mutual Trust Co., Wheeling, W.Va., 1924, 9 1/2 In. .................... 48.00
Slag, Red, Bowl, 7 1/2 In.Diameter ......................................................................................... 67.50
Slag, Red, Console Set, Citizens Mutual Trust, Wheeling, 1929, 4 Piece ........................... 135.00
Slag, Red, Console Set, 3 Piece ................................................................................................ 65.00
Slag, Red, Jar, Candy, Covered, 6 Recessed Panels, Fenton, 9 1/2 In. ................................ 55.00
Slag, Red, Squeezer, Orange Juice ........................................................................................... 55.00
Slag, Red, Vase, Bud, 9 1/8 In.High .......................................................................................... 28.00
Slag, Red, Vase, Fan, Fenton, 7 X 9 In. .................................................................................... 65.00
Slag, Red, Vase, Swirled, 9 In.High ........................................................................................... 55.00
Slag, White, Candlestick, Corinthian Column & Vine, English Peacock, Pair ....................... 55.00

*Sleepy Eye pottery was made to be given away with the flour products of the*
*Sleepy Eye Milling Co., Sleepy Eye, Minnesota, from about 1893 to*
*1952. It is a heavy stoneware with blue decorations, usually the famous*
*profile of an Indian.*

Sleepy Eye, Creamer ................................................................................................................... 55.00
Sleepy Eye, Pitcher, 1/2 Gallon ................................................................................................. 80.00
Sleepy Eye, Pitcher, 7 1/2 In.High ............................................................................................ 50.00
Sleepy Eye, Vase, Flemish Blue On Gray, Indian, 8 3/4 In.High ............................................ 68.00
Sleepy Eye, Vase, 8 In.High ....................................................................................................... 75.00

*Slip is a thin mixture of clay and water, about the consistency of sour cream,*
*that is applied to the pottery for decoration. If the pottery is made with*
*red clay, the slip is mixed with yellow clay.*

Slipware, Charger, Yellow On Brick, Pa., 1820s, 15 3/4 In ..................................*Illus*  425.00
Slipware, Pitcher, Brown With Gray, 5 1/2 In. .......................................................................... 10.00
Slipware, Tureen, Reversible Cover, Swiss, Floral On Brown, 1844, 11 1/2 In. .................. 500.00

*Smith Brothers glass was made after 1878. The owners had worked for the*
*Mt.Washington Glass Company in New Bedford, Massachusetts, for*
*seven years before going into their own shop. Some of the designs were*
*similar.*

Smith Brothers, Bowl, Floral Rim, 2 Handled Silver Plate Holder, Signed ......................... 130.00
Smith Brothers, Bowl, Melon Ribbed, Flowers On Cream, 5 In.High ................................... 195.00
Smith Brothers, Box, Covered, Cream, Melon Ribbed, Daisies, 5 In.Diameter ................... 185.00
Smith Brothers, Box, Melon Ribbed Cover & Base, Violets On Old Ivory ........................... 285.00
Smith Brothers, Box, Powder, Covered, Melon Ribbed, Daisies, Signed, 4 In. .................. 150.00
Smith Brothers, Creamer, Blue To Yellow, White Roses, Green & Russet Leaves ............. 100.00
Smith Brothers, Creamer, Pink To Cream, Metal Spout & Handle, Art Nouveau ............... 165.00
Smith Brothers, Jar, Biscuit, Red Outlined Blue & Gray Pansies On Ivory ........................ 250.00
Smith Brothers, Jar, Biscuit, White, Melon Ribbed, Daisies, Silver Plate Lid ..................... 95.00
Smith Brothers, Jar, Cookie, Biscuit Color, Water Lilies, 7 In.Diameter ............................. 375.00
Smith Brothers, Jar, Cookie, Melon Ribbed, Decorated, Mt.Washington ........................... 280.00
Smith Brothers, Jar, Covered, Melon Ribbed, Pink Pansies, 5 1/2 In.High ........................ 275.00
Smith Brothers, Jar, Cracker, Gold Decoration, Silver Lid & Bail Handle ........................... 350.00
Smith Brothers, Jar, Cracker, Wisterias On Cream, Signed Rampant Lion ........................ 425.00
Smith Brothers, Jar, Sweetmeat, Cream, Pansies, Melon Ribbed, Rampant Lion .............. 275.00
Smith Brothers, Jar, White, Covered, Melon Ribbed, Enamel Pansies, 3 3/4 In. ............... 120.00
Smith Brothers, Lamp, Melon Ribbed Base, Flowers ............................................................ 125.00
Smith Brothers, Muffineer, Gold Acorns & Oak Leaves On Ivory Melon Ribbed ............... 160.00
Smith Brothers, Muffineer, Pansies On Cream Ribbed, Rampant Lion Mark ...................... 245.00
Smith Brothers, Muffineer, Rose Mums & Green Leaves On Pink To White ........................ 85.00
Smith Brothers, Plate, Santa Maria, Libbey Signature, 6 1/2 In. ......................................... 195.00

Snuffbox, Gold & Enamel,
C.1820, 2 5/8 In.

Slipware, Charger, Yellow On Brick,
Pa., 1820s, 15 3/4 In
*(See Page 588)*

| | |
|---|---:|
| Smith Brothers, Pot, Mustard, Blue Floral & Green Leaves On White | 75.00 |
| Smith Brothers, Salt, Master, Melon Shape, Gold Floral, Rampant Lion, Signed | 96.00 |
| Smith Brothers, Salt, Melon Ribbed, Golden Flowers, Acid Finish | 48.00 |
| Smith Brothers, Salt, Melon Ribbed, Multicolor Floral, Enameled Dots Top | 40.00 |
| Smith Brothers, Syrup, Melon Ribbed Base, Ivory Colored Ground, Floral | 285.00 |
| Smith Brothers, Vase, Bulbous, Trefoil Shape, Violets & Leaves, 5 In.High | 300.00 |
| Smith Brothers, Vase, Cylindrical, Hand-Painted, 6 In.High | 32.00 |
| Smith Brothers, Vase, Cylindrical, Winter Landscapes, 6 In.High, Pair | 395.00 |
| Smith Brothers, Vase, Dragonfly & Floral On Pink, Gold Embossed Rings | 65.00 |
| Smith Brothers, Vase, Flask Type, Roses, Bluetts, & Gold Clouds On White | 200.00 |
| Smith Brothers, Vase, Tricorner, Blue Asters, White Beaded Opening, 5 In. | 195.00 |
| Snow Baby, Figurine, Kris Kringle & Sleigh With Reindeer | 25.00 |
| Snow Baby, In Blue Porcelain Egg | 7.50 |
| Snow Baby, Jointed Arms & Legs, 4 In. | 78.00 |
| Snow Baby, Lying On Stomach, Black Top Hat, 1 1/2 In. | 8.50 |
| Snow Baby, On Sled, Germany, 1 1/2 In. | 20.00 |
| Snow Baby, Postcard, Clapsaddle | 10.00 |
| Snow Baby, Riding Polar Bear, Marked Germany, 3 1/4 In. | 40.00 |
| Snow Baby, Standing, On Skiis | 45.00 |
| Snow Baby, Standing, On Sled | 65.00 |
| Snuff Bottle, see Bottle, Snuff | |
| Snuffbox, Black, Mother-Of-Pearl Band, 2 1/2 X 1 1/2 In. | 12.50 |
| Snuffbox, Brass Lid & Mount, Cowrie Shell, Engraved Anchor & R.S. | 50.00 |
| Snuffbox, Bug-Eyed Man | 25.50 |
| Snuffbox, Carnelian, Gilt Mounts, Oval, C.1750 | 68.00 |
| Snuffbox, Citrine Quartz, Oval, Faceted, Gilt Metal Mounts, C.1880, 2 1/2 In. | 500.00 |
| Snuffbox, Clipper Ship Flying American Flag On Silver Lid, Horn, H.Pitt | 75.00 |
| Snuffbox, Composition, Round, Black Figure Leaning Over White Woman | 25.00 |
| Snuffbox, Gold & Enamel, C.1820, 2 5/8 In. ............................................ *Illus* | 4180.00 |
| Snuffbox, Gold, George IV, Cameo Of Man, C.1825, 3 3/4 In.Long | 1100.00 |
| Snuffbox, Hinged Lid, Agate, Brass Mounts | 65.00 |
| Snuffbox, Hinged Lid, China, Enameled, Signed | 60.00 |
| Snuffbox, Hinged Lid, Oblong, Horn & Ivory | 45.00 |
| Snuffbox, Louis XV, Three Color Gold, Paris, 1771, 3 1/2 In.Long | 8750.00 |
| Snuffbox, Louis XV, Tortoiseshell, Gold, Gouache Under Glass On Lid, 1773 | 400.00 |
| Snuffbox, Louis XVI, Gilt Metal, Oblong, Engine Turned, C.1780, 3 3/4 In. | 200.00 |
| Snuffbox, Moss Agate, Silver Mounted, C.1890, 3 1/4 In.Long | 100.00 |
| Snuffbox, Mother-Of-Pearl Center & Edges, 1 1/2 X 3 1/4 In. | 12.50 |
| Snuffbox, Papier Mache, Pewter Inlay, Scroll & Flower Design, 3 X 2 1/2 In. | 19.00 |
| Snuffbox, Papier-Mache, Round Top, Bawdy French Print, 3 1/2 In.Diameter | 85.00 |
| Snuffbox, Porcelain, Birds On Branches, Lavender Ground, C.1880, 3 1/2 In. | 225.00 |
| Snuffbox, Rectangular, Veuve Perrin Faience, Polychrome Enameling | 65.00 |
| Snuffbox, Silver, Phipps & Robinson, Octagonal, Sunray Design, 1787, 3 In. | 300.00 |
| Snuffbox, Sliding Top, Hightop Shoe Shape, Wooden, Pointed Toe, Brass Brads | 35.00 |
| Snuffbox, Sliding Top, Hightop Shoe Shape, Wooden, Square Toe, Brass Brads | 30.00 |
| Snuffbox, Swiss, Gold & Enamel, Abduction Of Amymone, C.1820, 3 3/4 In.Long | 5600.00 |
| Snuffbox, Swiss, Gold & Enamel, Bouquet Of Flowers, Cornucopias, C.1820 | 5600.00 |

**Snuffbox, Swiss,** Gold & Enamel, Children & Dog, C.1800, 3 1/2 In.Long ..................... 3400.00

*Soapstone is a mineral that was used for foot warmers or griddles because of its heat-retaining properties. Chinese soapstone carvings of the nineteenth and twentieth centuries are found in many antique shops.*

**Soapstone, Ashtray,** Leaves, 4 1/2 X 3 In. ...................................................................... 11.00
**Soapstone, Bookend,** Foo Dog At Top, Carved, 5 In., Pair .................................................. 75.00
**Soapstone, Bowl,** Double, Carvings, 4 1/2 In.Long ............................................................ 5.50
**Soapstone, Carving,** Bearded Old Man, Pale Green, Oriental, Brown Base ............................ 65.00
**Soapstone, Carving,** Chinese, Double Urn Form Pockets Separated By Fruit ......................... 25.00
**Soapstone, Carving,** Foo Dog, Black ............................................................................... 9.50
**Soapstone, Carving,** Foo Dog, Jade Color ....................................................................... 12.50
**Soapstone, Carving,** Foo Dog, Reddish Black ................................................................. 15.00
**Soapstone, Carving,** Pagoda, 11 In.High ........................................................................ 30.00
**Soapstone, Cup,** Wine, Chinese, Stepped Base, Green Gray Mottled, 2 1/4 In. .................... 10.50
**Soapstone, Dish,** Olive, Double, Carved, 4 1/2 X 2 1/2 X 1 1/2 In. .................................... 10.00
**Soapstone, Heater,** Church, Holes In Sliding Cover, Wrought Nails ...................................... 60.00
**Soapstone, Match Holder,** 3 In.High ...................................................................... *Illus* 14.00
**Soapstone, Salt,** Elephant With Bowl ............................................................................. 12.50
**Soapstone, Seal,** Red, Foo Dog Finial, Pair ...................................................................... 20.00
**Soapstone, Toothpick,** Bulbous, Flaring Sides, Spinach Color, 2 In.High .............................. 18.00
**Soapstone, Toothpick,** Oval Bowl, Large Palms & Coconut ................................................. 9.50
**Soapstone, Toothpick,** Three Carved Penguins, Marked China ............................................ 4.25
**Soapstone, Urn,** Carved, Flowers & Phoenix Birds, Off-White, 9 1/2 In., Pair .................... 200.00
**Soapstone, Vase,** Carved, Raised Flowers & Birds, Beige, 7 3/4 In. ................................... 75.00
**Soapstone, Vase,** Double, Carved Floral, 7 1/2 In.High ..................................................... 42.00
**Soapstone, Vase,** Double, Monkey Between, Carved Flowers, 4 X 9 In. ............................... 35.00
**Soapstone, Whistle,** Chinese Duck Call, Fish Shape .......................................................... 7.50
**Soft Paste, Bowl,** King's Rose, C.1820, 6 1/8 In. Diameter .............................................. 125.00
**Soft Paste, Bowl,** King's Rose, C.1820, 7 1/2 In. ............................................................ 77.25
**Soft Paste, Bowl,** King's Rose, C.1820, 8 1/4 In., Pair .................................................... 200.00
**Soft Paste, Bowl,** Willow Type Center, Butterfly Border, C.1790, 8 In. ............................... 39.00
**Soft Paste, Cup & Saucer,** Handleless, Pink Luster, Bouquet, Butterfly, C.1810 ................... 25.00
**Soft Paste, Jug,** Milk, King's Rose, Baluster Shape, C.1820, 4 1/2 In. .............................. 250.00
**Soft Paste, Mug,** Shepherd Tending Sheep, Staffordshire ................................................... 27.00
**Soft Paste, Pitcher,** Monkey, Fan & Blue Sponge Decoration, 8 3/4 In. ............................... 80.00
**Soft Paste, Plate,** Square, Raised Cameo Flowers ............................................................. 12.00
**Soft Paste, Sugar & Underplate,** Covered, King's Rose, C.1820, 5 1/4 In. High ................... 500.00
**Soft Paste, Sugar,** Queen's Rose, Shell & Ring Handle, 4 1/2 In.High ................................ 165.00
**Soft Paste, Tea Set,** Child's, Blue & White, Little May, 9 Piece ........................................... 55.00
**Soft Paste, Tea Set,** Child's, Sprig Pattern, Squat Footed Teapot, 5 Piece ........................... 95.00
**Soft Paste, Teabowl & Saucer,** King's Rose, C.1820 ........................................ 66.65 To 100.00
**Soft Paste, Teapot,** King's Rose, C.1820, 6 1/4 In. ................................................... *Illus* 425.00
**Soft Paste, Teapot,** King's Rose, C.1825, 11 In. ....................................................... *Illus* 900.00
**Soft Paste, Teapot,** Strawberry, C.1820, 5 5/8 In. .................................................... *Illus* 325.00
**Soft Paste, Teapot,** Strawberry, 6 1/2 In.High ............................................................... 475.00
**Souvenir, Arm Band,** United Confederate Reunion, Chattanooga, Oct., 1921 ..................... 34.50

Soft Paste, Teapot, King's Rose, C.1820, 6 1/4 In.

Soapstone, Match Holder, 3 In.High

Soft Paste, Teapot, Strawberry, C.1820, 5 5/8 In.
*(See Page 590)*

Soft Paste, Teapot, King's Rose, C.1825, 11 In.
*(See Page 590)*

| | |
|---|---:|
| Souvenir, **Ashtray,** California, Figural, Bear | 6.50 |
| Souvenir, **Ashtray,** Luchow's Restaurant, N.Y.C., Pottery, Blue & Ivory, German | 50.00 |
| Souvenir, **Ashtray,** World's Fair, 1939, Ford Exposition | 4.50 |
| Souvenir, **Baseball,** American League, 1950s, Signed Roger Maris | 35.00 |
| Souvenir, **Book,** A Century Of Progress, 1933 | 4.50 |
| Souvenir, **Booklet,** Pan American Exposition, 1901, Albertype | 4.00 |
| Souvenir, **Bookmark,** New Orleans Exposition, 1884, Industrial & Cotton, Silk | 10.00 |
| Souvenir, **Bottle,** Chicago Exposition, 1933, Flask Type | 4.75 |
| Souvenir, **Bowl,** Lake Almanor, California, Hand-Painted, 4 In. | 3.00 |
| Souvenir, **Bowl,** Lookout Inn, Lookout Mountain, Tenn., 5 In.Square | 2.95 |
| Souvenir, **Bowl,** Post Administration Building, Kansas, 5 1/2 In. | 3.95 |
| Souvenir, **Box,** Dresser, Caralier, N.D., Green Glass, Gold Trim, Footed | 8.00 |
| Souvenir, **Bracelet,** Columbian Exposition, 1893, Gorham, Narrow | 3.50 |
| Souvenir, **Bucket,** Coal, Monticello, Ill., Red Flashed, Wire Bail | 8.50 |
| Souvenir, **Calendar,** 1876 Centennial | 5.00 |
| Souvenir, **Card,** 1903 World Series, Boston Vs. Pittsburg | 500.00 |
| Souvenir, **Creamer,** Dominion Of Canada, Queen Victoria Picture, Porcelain | 12.00 |
| Souvenir, **Creamer,** Moline, Ill., Beaded Band, Blue | 8.50 |
| Souvenir, **Creamer,** Nantucket, Mass., Cobalt Blue, Left Handed, Germany, 4 In. | 10.00 |
| Souvenir, **Creamer,** R.A.D.Christmas, 1912, Lacy Medallion, Emerald Green | 18.00 |
| Souvenir, **Creamer,** Springfield State Fair, 1902, Colorado, Green, Gold | 35.00 |
| Souvenir, **Cup & Saucer,** Columbian Exposition, Chicago, 1893, Casino & Pier | 21.50 |
| Souvenir, **Fan,** Philadelphia Centennial, 1070, Paper, Fairmount Park | 45.00 |
| Souvenir, **Figurine,** Denver, Two Negros & Outhouse | 3.00 |
| Souvenir, **Figurine,** Lady In Canoe, Los Angeles, 1920s, Art Deco, Germany | 6.00 |
| Souvenir, **Flask,** Whiskey, A Century Of Progress, 1933, Leather Covered | 8.00 |
| Souvenir, **Fork,** Colorado Nil Sine Numine | 12.00 |
| Souvenir, **Frypan,** Panama-Pacific Exposition, 1915 | 6.00 |
| Souvenir, **Glass,** Olympic Games, Los Angeles, 1932, Etched, Slender | 18.00 |
| Souvenir, **Goblet,** Beer, Shoyer's Restaurant, Philadelphia, Diamond Embossed | 18.00 |
| Souvenir, **Goblet,** Belmont, N.H., Ditto, Pressed Glass, 4 3/4 In.High | 17.50 |
| Souvenir, **Hat,** Pepsi Cola Convention, Mexico, 1967, Sterling, Mexican Shape | 50.00 |
| Souvenir, **Hat,** Webster, Wis., Ribbed, Emerald Green, Gold Flowers, Glass | 18.00 |
| Souvenir, **Hat,** Webster, Wisconsin, Emerald Green, Gold Hand-Painted Flowers | 17.50 |
| Souvenir, **Hat,** Wilkin County Court House, Bretches Ridge, Minn., China | 9.50 |
| Souvenir, **Hatpin,** Hudson-Fulton Celebration, 1909, Bronze Top | 22.00 |
| Souvenir, **Horse Brass,** Canadian Centennial | 7.00 |
| Souvenir, **Key Holder,** Chicago World's Fair, 1893, Cutout Leaf Shape, Metal | 24.00 |
| Souvenir, **Knife,** Pocket, The Capitol, The White House, Krusius Bros., Germany | 17.50 |
| Souvenir, **Match Holder,** Loup City, Nebraska, Pipe Shape, Cobalt Blue, 6 In. | 10.00 |
| Souvenir, **Match Holder,** Merrill, Wis., Heisey, No.1200 | 32.00 |
| Souvenir, **Match Safe,** Pan American Exposition, Buffalo, Silver Plate | 22.00 |
| Souvenir, **Match Safe,** Pan American Exposition, 1901, Pocket | 3.95 |
| Souvenir, **Mirror,** Brotherhood Of American Yeomen, Pocket | 12.00 |
| Souvenir, **Mirror,** Pocket, St.Louis, 1904 | 8.00 |

| | |
|---|---|
| Souvenir, Mug, Child's, 'Centennial, 1876, ' Red Letters, Porcelain | 15.00 |
| Souvenir, Mug, Dover, N.H., Thumbprint Band, Flower, Custard Glass | 22.50 |
| Souvenir, Mug, Insignia Of I.O.O.F., Stein Type, 3 1/8 In.High | 3.95 |
| Souvenir, Mug, Niagara Falls On Raised Plaque, Quadruple Plate, 1 3/4 In. | 4.00 |
| Souvenir, Mug, World's Fair, 1893, Columbian Exposition, Embossed | 18.00 |
| Souvenir, Paperweight, Centennial Exposition, 1876, Gillinder, Frosted Lion | 65.00 |
| Souvenir, Paperweight, Huntington, West Virginia Centennial, 1871-1971 | 25.00 |
| Souvenir, Paperweight, Memorial Hall, 1876-1776, Frosted & Clear | 350.00 |
| Souvenir, Paperweight, Pan American Exposition, 1901, Temple Music, Oblong | 17.50 |
| Souvenir, Paperweight, White Mountains, Obelisk, Glass, Pair | 8.50 |
| Souvenir, Paperweight, World's Columbian Exposition, Chicago, 1893 | 70.00 |
| Souvenir, Paperweight, World's Fair, 1904, St.Louis | 5.00 |
| Souvenir, Pennant, World's Fair, 1933, Chicago | 5.00 |
| Souvenir, Perfume, Sesquicentennial, 1776-1926, Bell Shape | 18.75 |
| Souvenir, Pinback, Aviation Week, 1910, Celluloid, Color Lithograph | 25.00 |
| Souvenir, Pitcher, Newbury Port, Mass., School & Bridge, Porcelain | 6.50 |
| Souvenir, Plate, Alaska-Yukon Exposition, Porcelain, 9 In. | 24.00 |
| Souvenir, Plate, Altoona, Pa., 100th Anniversary, Bunyan Statue, 6 1/4 In. | 3.00 |
| Souvenir, Plate, Arms Of Canadian Provinces, C.1900, 8 In. | 17.50 |
| Souvenir, Plate, Avalon Bay, Catalina Island, Hand-Painted, 6 1/4 In. | 4.75 |
| Souvenir, Plate, Biddeford, Me., Imperial British Anchor, March, 1913, Blue | 15.00 |
| Souvenir, Plate, Bread, U.S.Sesquicentennial, 1776-1926, Metal, Oval | 6.50 |
| Souvenir, Plate, Bunker Hill Monument, Boston, Marked England, 7 1/2 In. | 9.00 |
| Souvenir, Plate, Canadian, Scenic, 1953, Royal Winton, 11 In. | 5.00 |
| Souvenir, Plate, Captain John Parker, Mass., Apr.19, 1775, Wedgwood | 13.75 |
| Souvenir, Plate, Fort Lauderdale Beach, Signed Germany, 6 1/4 In. | 3.00 |
| Souvenir, Plate, Gettysburg, Pa., Signed Austria, 7 1/4 In. | 3.00 |
| Souvenir, Plate, Lake Champlain, N.Y., Blue & White, 7 5/8 In. | 8.75 |
| Souvenir, Plate, Milford, Michigan, Three Bears, Milk Glass, Painted | 22.50 |
| Souvenir, Plate, Mt.Lick Observatory, Mt.Hamilton, Jasper, Hanging, Floral | 37.50 |
| Souvenir, Plate, Natural Bridge, Va., Hand-Painted, 7 In. | 4.75 |
| Souvenir, Plate, Nebraska Centennial, White, Gold, 7 In. | 5.00 |
| Souvenir, Plate, Ohio Sesquicentennial, Matthews House, Lake County, 10 In. | 15.00 |
| Souvenir, Plate, Pan American Exposition, 1901, Pewter, Art Nouveau, Buffalo | 18.50 |
| Souvenir, Plate, Pike's Peak Railroad Summit, Altitude 14, 147 Feet, 6 In. | 4.75 |
| Souvenir, Plate, Provincetown, Blair & Co., Longton, Rolled Edge | 25.00 |
| Souvenir, Plate, Republican Centennial, Profile Lincoln & Eisenhower | 30.00 |
| Souvenir, Plate, Salt Lake City, Utah, Mormon Temple, Brigham Young Monument | 5.95 |
| Souvenir, Plate, St.Louis World's Fair, 1904 | 13.00 |
| Souvenir, Plate, St.Louis, 1904, Festival Hall & Cardens, Lacy Edge | 14.00 |
| Souvenir, Plate, The Order Of The Visitation Of The Sick, 6 1/2 In. | 25.00 |
| Souvenir, Plate, Thousand Islands, 6 In. | 3.00 |
| Souvenir, Plate, Tyler, Texas, D.A.R., 1938, 10 1/2 In. | 10.00 |
| Souvenir, Plate, View Of Hudson After Fire, July 4, 1894, 8 1/4 In. | 4.75 |
| Souvenir, Plate, West Branch, Bradford, N.H., Open Handle, Gold, 10 In. | 6.00 |
| Souvenir, Plate, World's Exposition, Chicago, 1893, 7 In. | 4.75 |
| Souvenir, Plate, World's Fair, 1904, St.Louis | 10.00 |
| Souvenir, Plate, Yukon-Pacific Exposition, Orange Color, 9 1/2 In. | 35.00 |
| Souvenir, Purse, Coin, World's Fair, 1904 | 16.50 |
| Souvenir, Purse, Watkins Glen, Folding, Miniature | 4.50 |
| Souvenir, Razor, St.Louis World's Fair, 1904, Ivory Handle, 4 In. | 10.00 |
| Souvenir, Spoon, Demitasse, Sterling Silver, 'Milwaukee, Gold Washed Bowl | 6.00 |
| Souvenir, Spoon, Demitasse, Sterling Silver, 'Philadelphia, ' Gold Washed | 6.00 |
| Souvenir, Spoon, Demitasse, Sterling Silver, Alamo, 1718, Texas | 12.50 |
| Souvenir, Spoon, Demitasse, Sterling Silver, Alaska, Seal On Handle | 10.00 |
| Souvenir, Spoon, Demitasse, Sterling Silver, Atlantic City, N.J. | 15.00 |
| Souvenir, Spoon, Demitasse, Sterling Silver, Brooklyn Bridge In Bowl | 10.00 |
| Souvenir, Spoon, Demitasse, Sterling Silver, Calgary, Royal Visit, 1939 | 15.00 |
| Souvenir, Spoon, Demitasse, Sterling Silver, Chetck, Wis., Scroll Handle | 10.00 |
| Souvenir, Spoon, Demitasse, Sterling Silver, Columbian Exposition, Globe | 12.00 |
| Souvenir, Spoon, Demitasse, Sterling Silver, Denver, Colorado, Auditorium | 8.00 |
| Souvenir, Spoon, Demitasse, Sterling Silver, Eads Bridge, St.Louis, Mo. | 15.00 |
| Souvenir, Spoon, Demitasse, Sterling Silver, Edmonton, Alberta, Enameled | 12.50 |
| Souvenir, Spoon, Demitasse, Sterling Silver, Father Time, Gold Washed Bowl | 7.00 |
| Souvenir, Spoon, Demitasse, Sterling Silver, Helena, Montana, Floral Handle | 8.50 |
| Souvenir, Spoon, Demitasse, Sterling Silver, Jacksonville, Florida | 15.00 |

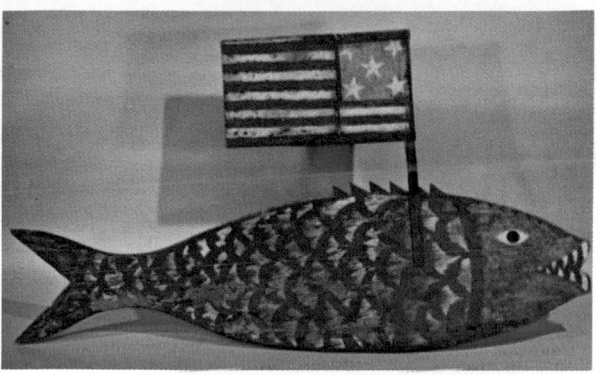

Trade sign for Stafford-
shire ware, 19½ inches
high. Two colors show
variety offered for sale.

Folk art sign of fish with flag
c. 1850–1860, 34 inches long, found
in New York State.

Chalkware figure of a girl.

Chalkware cat made from
mold c. 1860.

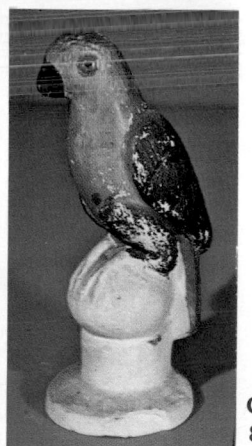

Chalkware watch holder.

Chalkware parrot, c. 1860,
8½ inches high.

Folk art eagle made of rolled iron with applied tin feathers, latter half of the 19th century.

Toy milk wagon, 20 inches long, made of painted wood.

Oil painting on canvas dated 1839, signed A. D. Fletcher.

Wooden toy Noah's ark with animals, 19th century.

Oil painting of girl with red rose in hair, 18th century.

Three covered glass chicken dishes of the late 19th century.

Milk glass covered dishes with animal covers, c. 1880.

Three different styles of pressed glass covered compotes of Westward Ho pattern.

Glass rolling pin, mid-19th century.

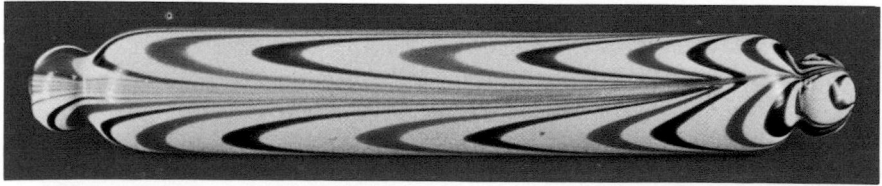

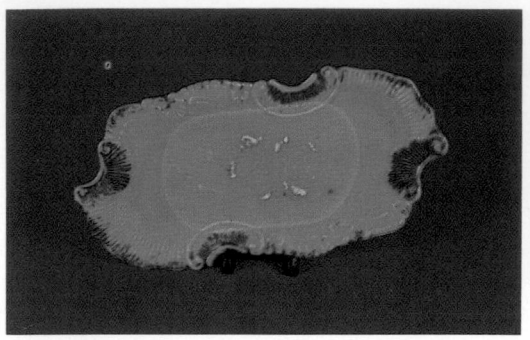

Blue milk glass plate with a scroll border c. 1880.

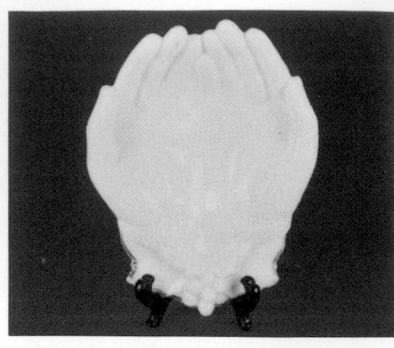

Milk glass plate of hands and grapes c. 1880.

Occupational shaving mug showing scene with blacksmith.

Flower-sprigged shaving mug of the late 19th century.

"Kate Greenaway" salt shaker of white metal c. 1890.

Life-sized wood carving of Christopher Columbus made in the 19th century.

Pierced tin lantern with an isinglass
front. The ring holder is unusual.

A pricket candlestick of brass with
a bell-shaped bottom.

A brass chamberstick with a large
circular drip pan.

Tin sconce with eight small circles
surrounding the center circle.

Tin candleholder painted black with
gold banding. The branches are adjustable for height.

Decorated comb-back Windsor rocker with a New Hampshire history.

Invalid's restraining chair made in the early 19th century.

William and Mary wing chair with flame stitch upholstery, made in England in the late 17th century.

Decorated Windsor rocking chair with a stenciled border.

A maple corner chair from Hartford, Connecticut, made about 1730–1750.

A pair of unpainted Windsor arm-
chairs made in the 18th century.

Cromwellian chair made in the last
quarter of the 17th century. It is
made of oak with Turkey carpet
upholstery. Wooden chair of the
same period.

The tags on this pair of fancy chairs
give a Boston, Massachusetts, history from the mid-19th century.

John Adams proposing Washington
for Commander in Chief of the
American Army is the transfer decoration on the 1932 plate made by
Crown Ducal, England

General Lafayette Welcome to the
Land of Liberty is the message on
this Staffordshire plate.

Upper Ferry Bridge Across the Schuylkill is the transfer decoration on this English platter.

Cup and saucer made by Enoch Wood and Sons.

Sampler of cross stitches on linen, in a maple frame. Dated 1844, 10½ by 13½ inches.

Advertising-sign oil painting for "Kendall's Spavin Cure," 27 inches by 34 inches.

Centennial Exposition wooden plaque, 2¾ by 3¾ inches.

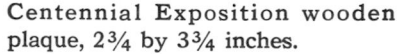

Leather hatbox with a Swedish trade card inside dated 1891.

| | |
|---|---|
| Souvenir, Spoon, Demitasse, Sterling Silver, Los Angeles, Oranges Handle | 8.00 |
| Souvenir, Spoon, Demitasse, Sterling Silver, Massachusetts State Seal | 12.50 |
| Souvenir, Spoon, Demitasse, Sterling Silver, Mt.Tacoma, Clock Handle | 15.00 |
| Souvenir, Spoon, Demitasse, Sterling Silver, Mt.Tacoma, Scroll Handle | 9.00 |
| Souvenir, Spoon, Demitasse, Sterling Silver, Niagara Falls | 8.50 |
| Souvenir, Spoon, Demitasse, Sterling Silver, Old State Home, Boston | 12.00 |
| Souvenir, Spoon, Demitasse, Sterling Silver, Plymouth, 1620, Boston, 1891 | 7.50 |
| Souvenir, Spoon, Demitasse, Sterling Silver, Portland, 1905, Gold Washed Bowl | 8.00 |
| Souvenir, Spoon, Demitasse, Sterling Silver, Royal Palms, Florida, Pierced | 12.50 |
| Souvenir, Spoon, Demitasse, Sterling Silver, San Diego, Old Mission | 10.00 |
| Souvenir, Spoon, Demitasse, Sterling Silver, San Francisco Golden Gate | 10.00 |
| Souvenir, Spoon, Demitasse, Sterling Silver, Seattle, Gold Washed Bowl | 8.50 |
| Souvenir, Spoon, Demitasse, Sterling Silver, St.Louis World's Fair, Building | 10.00 |
| Souvenir, Spoon, Demitasse, Sterling Silver, Ste.Anne, Maple Leaf Handle | 8.00 |
| Souvenir, Spoon, Demitasse, Sterling Silver, Washington & Cherry Tree | 10.00 |
| Souvenir, Spoon, Demitasse, Sterling Silver, Washington Manson, Mt.Vernon | 10.00 |
| Souvenir, Spoon, Demitasse, Sterling Silver, Washington, D.C., Buildings | 10.00 |
| Souvenir, Spoon, Demitasse, Sterling Silver, Winnipeg, Manitoba, Enameled | 12.50 |
| Souvenir, Spoon, Demitasse, Sterling Silver, World's Fair, Chicago, 1893 | 10.00 |
| Souvenir, Spoon, Demitasse, Sterling Silver, Yellowstone Park, Bear Handle | 10.00 |
| Souvenir, Spoon, Silver Plate, A Century Of Progress, 1933 | 2.50 To 5.00 |
| Souvenir, Spoon, Silver Plate, Actress, Lois Wilson | 3.75 |
| Souvenir, Spoon, Silver Plate, Actress, Norma Talmadge | 3.75 |
| Souvenir, Spoon, Silver Plate, Actress, Pola Negri | 3.75 |
| Souvenir, Spoon, Silver Plate, Betty Lou, Figure On Handle | 4.75 |
| Souvenir, Spoon, Silver Plate, Campbell Kids | 5.50 |
| Souvenir, Spoon, Silver Plate, Charlie McCarthy | 5.00 |
| Souvenir, Spoon, Silver Plate, Charlie McCarthy, Duchess | 4.00 |
| Souvenir, Spoon, Silver Plate, Chicago Exposition, 1933, Official | 3.75 |
| Souvenir, Spoon, Silver Plate, Connecticut | 2.50 |
| Souvenir, Spoon, Silver Plate, Dennis The Menace, Figural Handle | 3.00 |
| Souvenir, Spoon, Silver Plate, Dionne Quintuplet, Annette | 5.00 |
| Souvenir, Spoon, Silver Plate, Dionne Quintuplet, Cecile | 5.00 |
| Souvenir, Spoon, Silver Plate, Dionne Quintuplet, Emilie | 5.00 |
| Souvenir, Spoon, Silver Plate, Dionne Quintuplets | 5.00 |
| Souvenir, Spoon, Silver Plate, Douglas Fairbanks, Oneida Community | 6.00 |
| Souvenir, Spoon, Silver Plate, Elizabeth Opening Canadian Parliament, 1957 | 2.50 |
| Souvenir, Spoon, Silver Plate, Flagship New York, Admiral Sampson, 1898 | 2.75 |
| Souvenir, Spoon, Silver Plate, General Joffre | 2.50 |
| Souvenir, Spoon, Silver Plate, Gloria Swanson, Oneida | 4.00 |
| Souvenir, Spoon, Silver Plate, Golden Gate Exposition, 1939 | 5.00 |
| Souvenir, Spoon, Silver Plate, Great Lakes Exposition, 1937 | 2.50 |
| Souvenir, Spoon, Silver Plate, Howdy Doody | 5.00 |
| Souvenir, Spoon, Silver Plate, Huckleberry Hound | 3.00 |
| Souvenir, Spoon, Silver Plate, Illinois | 2.50 |
| Souvenir, Spoon, Silver Plate, John F.Kennedy, Friendship | 2.50 |
| Souvenir, Spoon, Silver Plate, Lois Wilson, Oneida Community | 6.00 |
| Souvenir, Spoon, Silver Plate, Louisiana | 2.50 |
| Souvenir, Spoon, Silver Plate, Mae Murray, Oneida Community | 6.00 |
| Souvenir, Spoon, Silver Plate, Maine | 2.50 |
| Souvenir, Spoon, Silver Plate, Mary Pickford, Oneida Community | 6.00 |
| Souvenir, Spoon, Silver Plate, Mexico | 2.50 |
| Souvenir, Spoon, Silver Plate, Minnesota | 2.50 |
| Souvenir, Spoon, Silver Plate, New Jersey State, Wm.Rogers | 6.00 |
| Souvenir, Spoon, Silver Plate, New York | 2.50 |
| Souvenir, Spoon, Silver Plate, New York State, Wm.Rogers | 6.00 |
| Souvenir, Spoon, Silver Plate, New York World's Fair, 1939 | 3.00 |
| Souvenir, Spoon, Silver Plate, New York World's Fair, 1939, Administration | 4.00 |
| Souvenir, Spoon, Silver Plate, New York World's Fair, 1939, Amphitheater | 4.00 |
| Souvenir, Spoon, Silver Plate, New York World's Fair, 1939, Food, Rogers | 4.00 |
| Souvenir, Spoon, Silver Plate, Norma Talmadge, Oneida Community | 6.00 |
| Souvenir, Spoon, Silver Plate, Ottawa | 2.50 |
| Souvenir, Spoon, Silver Plate, Pan American Exposition, Buffalo | 4.75 |
| Souvenir, Spoon, Silver Plate, Pennsylvania State, Wm.Rogers | 6.00 |
| Souvenir, Spoon, Silver Plate, Pennsylvania, Eagle | 7.50 |
| Souvenir, Spoon, Silver Plate, Pola Negri, Oneida Community | 6.00 |

| | |
|---|---|
| Souvenir, Spoon, Silver Plate, Ramon Novarro, Oneida Community | 6.00 |
| Souvenir, Spoon, Silver Plate, Rhode Island | 2.50 |
| Souvenir, Spoon, Silver Plate, South Carolina | 2.50 |
| Souvenir, Spoon, Silver Plate, Texas | 2.50 |
| Souvenir, Spoon, Silver Plate, Thomas Meighan, Oneida | 4.00 |
| Souvenir, Spoon, Silver Plate, Vermont | 2.50 |
| Souvenir, Spoon, Silver Plate, Virginia, Eagle | 7.50 |
| Souvenir, Spoon, Silver Plate, Warren G.Harding, Arlington, Va. | 2.50 |
| Souvenir, Spoon, Silver Plate, Washington, Eagle | 7.50 |
| Souvenir, Spoon, Sterling Silver, Atlantic City Skyline | 30.00 |
| Souvenir, Spoon, Sterling Silver, Atlantic City, Decorated Bowl & Handle | 12.50 |
| Souvenir, Spoon, Sterling Silver, Atlantic City, Gold Wash & Enamel | 24.00 |
| Souvenir, Spoon, Sterling Silver, Avalon, Santa Catalina, Tuna | 4.50 |
| Souvenir, Spoon, Sterling Silver, Baltimore, Oysters, Terrapin, Embossed | 15.00 |
| Souvenir, Spoon, Sterling Silver, Battleship U.S.S. Rhode Island, 1918 | 8.95 |
| Souvenir, Spoon, Sterling Silver, Berlin, Enameled Handle | 10.00 |
| Souvenir, Spoon, Sterling Silver, Boston, Paul Revere | 14.00 |
| Souvenir, Spoon, Sterling Silver, Bridgeport, Conn., Flower & Fern Handle | 6.50 |
| Souvenir, Spoon, Sterling Silver, Bruxelles Seal On Handle, DeVille | 7.95 |
| Souvenir, Spoon, Sterling Silver, Buffalo, N.Y. | 11.00 |
| Souvenir, Spoon, Sterling Silver, Butte, Montana, Patent 1892, Anaconda Mine | 9.50 |
| Souvenir, Spoon, Sterling Silver, California, Cutout Embossed Handle | 8.00 |
| Souvenir, Spoon, Sterling Silver, California, State Capitol | 12.00 |
| Souvenir, Spoon, Sterling Silver, Cedar Rapids | 4.50 |
| Souvenir, Spoon, Sterling Silver, Charleston | 4.00 |
| Souvenir, Spoon, Sterling Silver, Chicago, Flowered Handle | 7.50 |
| Souvenir, Spoon, Sterling Silver, Cincinnati, O., Suspension Bridge | 15.00 |
| Souvenir, Spoon, Sterling Silver, Cleveland, Garfield Memorial & Monuments | 8.50 |
| Souvenir, Spoon, Sterling Silver, Cleveland, 1893, Cutout Handle | 10.50 |
| Souvenir, Spoon, Sterling Silver, Cliff House, San Francisco, Art Nouveau | 12.50 |
| Souvenir, Spoon, Sterling Silver, Colorado Springs, Colo., Figural Miner | 7.00 |
| Souvenir, Spoon, Sterling Silver, Columbian Exposition | 18.00 |
| Souvenir, Spoon, Sterling Silver, Cutout Indian In Canoe On Handle | 24.00 |
| Souvenir, Spoon, Sterling Silver, Denver, Colorado, Etched Bowl | 13.00 |
| Souvenir, Spoon, Sterling Silver, Des Moines, Iowa, Embossed Bowl | 13.50 |
| Souvenir, Spoon, Sterling Silver, Des Moines, Iowa, State Capitol | 8.00 |
| Souvenir, Spoon, Sterling Silver, Dubuque's Grave, Dubuque, Iowa | 8.50 |
| Souvenir, Spoon, Sterling Silver, Duchess Of Windsor, Figural Bust Handle | 6.00 |
| Souvenir, Spoon, Sterling Silver, Dysart High School, Iowa | 4.50 |
| Souvenir, Spoon, Sterling Silver, East Hall Girls In Bowl, V.E.On Back | 8.50 |
| Souvenir, Spoon, Sterling Silver, Easter Scene On Handle | 5.95 |
| Souvenir, Spoon, Sterling Silver, Elkton Mine, Figure Of Prospector | 16.50 |
| Souvenir, Spoon, Sterling Silver, Ethel In Bowl, Engraved 1901 | 8.50 |
| Souvenir, Spoon, Sterling Silver, Figural Indian, 5 1/4 In.Long | 28.00 |
| Souvenir, Spoon, Sterling Silver, Florida, Cut Palm Tree Handle | 9.00 |
| Souvenir, Spoon, Sterling Silver, Fort Dearborn, Chicago, Wheat Handle | 9.00 |
| Souvenir, Spoon, Sterling Silver, Fort Dearborn, Masonic Temple | 9.95 |
| Souvenir, Spoon, Sterling Silver, Fort Pitt | 19.00 |
| Souvenir, Spoon, Sterling Silver, George Washington, Etched Bowl | 13.00 |
| Souvenir, Spoon, Sterling Silver, Gettysburg | 15.00 |
| Souvenir, Spoon, Sterling Silver, Golden Gate Exposition, 1939, Demitasse | 15.00 |
| Souvenir, Spoon, Sterling Silver, Grand Canyon, El Tovar, Cutout Handle | 5.50 |
| Souvenir, Spoon, Sterling Silver, Hartford, Conn., Embossed Charter Oak Tree | 7.50 |
| Souvenir, Spoon, Sterling Silver, Hotel Beechwood, Summit, N.J. | 6.95 |
| Souvenir, Spoon, Sterling Silver, Iowa | 6.50 |
| Souvenir, Spoon, Sterling Silver, Jacksonville, Post Office In Bowl | 15.00 |
| Souvenir, Spoon, Sterling Silver, Kansas City, Missouri | 20.00 |
| Souvenir, Spoon, Sterling Silver, Kansas, Corn Stalk Handle | 25.00 |
| Souvenir, Spoon, Sterling Silver, Kentucky | 8.50 |
| Souvenir, Spoon, Sterling Silver, L.S.Leviathan, Cutout Design On Handle | 8.95 |
| Souvenir, Spoon, Sterling Silver, Lake George, N.Y. | 12.00 |
| Souvenir, Spoon, Sterling Silver, Lancaster, Wis. | 9.00 |
| Souvenir, Spoon, Sterling Silver, Last Sacrifice Niagara | 15.00 |
| Souvenir, Spoon, Sterling Silver, Los Angeles Engraved In Bowl | 5.95 |
| Souvenir, Spoon, Sterling Silver, Los Angeles, Carmel Mission | 10.00 |
| Souvenir, Spoon, Sterling Silver, Los Angeles, Fruit In Bowl | 12.00 |

| | |
|---|---|
| Souvenir, Spoon, Sterling Silver, Maryland, Baltimore In Bowl | 12.00 |
| Souvenir, Spoon, Sterling Silver, Massena, N.Y., Ornate Handle & Bowl | 8.50 |
| Souvenir, Spoon, Sterling Silver, Menasha, Wis., Patent 1899, Lion, Anchor, & G | 5.95 |
| Souvenir, Spoon, Sterling Silver, Miner's Mule With Pack & Tools | 6.95 |
| Souvenir, Spoon, Sterling Silver, Minnehaha Falls, Raised Decorations | 6.50 |
| Souvenir, Spoon, Sterling Silver, Missouri, Gold Washed Bowl | 12.00 |
| Souvenir, Spoon, Sterling Silver, Moberly, Mo., Floral Handle | 10.00 |
| Souvenir, Spoon, Sterling Silver, Montauk Light, L.I., Ship, Fish On Handle | 5.95 |
| Souvenir, Spoon, Sterling Silver, Mormon Temple, Indian Handle | 8.00 |
| Souvenir, Spoon, Sterling Silver, Mt.Lowe, California, Cable Incline | 10.00 |
| Souvenir, Spoon, Sterling Silver, Mt.Penn Tower, Reading, Pa., 3 In. | 5.95 |
| Souvenir, Spoon, Sterling Silver, Mt.Vernon, Twisted Wire Handle | 5.95 |
| Souvenir, Spoon, Sterling Silver, Nebraska | 6.50 |
| Souvenir, Spoon, Sterling Silver, Negro, Sunny South | 24.00 |
| Souvenir, Spoon, Sterling Silver, New Orleans, Engraved The Cabildo | 12.75 |
| Souvenir, Spoon, Sterling Silver, New Orleans, Robert E.Lee In Uniform | 8.00 |
| Souvenir, Spoon, Sterling Silver, New York, Peter Stuyvesant & Henry | 15.00 |
| Souvenir, Spoon, Sterling Silver, Newburyport, 1910 In Bowl, Etched | 9.00 |
| Souvenir, Spoon, Sterling Silver, Newport, Warming Pan, Pat.Feb.10, 1891 | 8.50 |
| Souvenir, Spoon, Sterling Silver, Niagara, The White Canoe | 10.00 |
| Souvenir, Spoon, Sterling Silver, Norwegian Lutheran Church, Minnesota | 4.50 |
| Souvenir, Spoon, Sterling Silver, Oakland, California | 9.00 |
| Souvenir, Spoon, Sterling Silver, Ogden, Utah, Gold Wash Indian Handle | 18.75 |
| Souvenir, Spoon, Sterling Silver, Ogdensburg, 1901, Engraved Sailboat | 11.50 |
| Souvenir, Spoon, Sterling Silver, Old Man Of The Mountain, N.H., Mar.3, 1891 | 9.75 |
| Souvenir, Spoon, Sterling Silver, Old Point Comfort, Fort Monroe | 12.50 |
| Souvenir, Spoon, Sterling Silver, Pan American Exposition, Indian | 18.00 |
| Souvenir, Spoon, Sterling Silver, Pan American Exposition, 1901 | 15.00 |
| Souvenir, Spoon, Sterling Silver, Philadelphia, Bell | 12.00 |
| Souvenir, Spoon, Sterling Silver, Philadelphia, Benjamin Franklin | 14.00 |
| Souvenir, Spoon, Sterling Silver, Pier, Jamestown Exposition, 1907 | 8.95 |
| Souvenir, Spoon, Sterling Silver, Porterville, California | 7.00 |
| Souvenir, Spoon, Sterling Silver, Princeton | 8.00 |
| Souvenir, Spoon, Sterling Silver, Rhode Island, Gold Washed Bowl | 20.00 |
| Souvenir, Spoon, Sterling Silver, Rhode Island, Ornate Handle | 8.50 |
| Souvenir, Spoon, Sterling Silver, Rocky Mountain National Park, Cutout | 8.95 |
| Souvenir, Spoon, Sterling Silver, Sacramento, California Seal, Bear At Top | 4.75 |
| Souvenir, Spoon, Sterling Silver, Salt Lake City Temple In Bowl | 12.50 |
| Souvenir, Spoon, Sterling Silver, San Bernardino | 7.00 |
| Souvenir, Spoon, Sterling Silver, San Diego, 1916, Cutout Mission Handle | 9.00 |
| Souvenir, Spoon, Sterling Silver, San Francisco Exposition | 10.00 |
| Souvenir, Spoon, Sterling Silver, San Francisco, Bear, Miner's Boots, 1893 | 7.95 |
| Souvenir, Spoon, Sterling Silver, San Francisco, Golden Gate | 9.95 |
| Souvenir, Spoon, Sterling Silver, San Gabriel Mission, California, Cutout | 8.50 |
| Souvenir, Spoon, Sterling Silver, Santa Monica, Patent 1892 | 5.95 |
| Souvenir, Spoon, Sterling Silver, Sheridan, Wyoming, Sylvia, 1911 On Back | 8.50 |
| Souvenir, Spoon, Sterling Silver, Soo, Michigan, The Locks On Handle | 12.00 |
| Souvenir, Spoon, Sterling Silver, South Bend, Indiana | 4.50 |
| Souvenir, Spoon, Sterling Silver, Spring Valley, Minnesota | 4.50 |
| Souvenir, Spoon, Sterling Silver, St.Augustine's Church, Brooklyn, 1892 | 9.95 |
| Souvenir, Spoon, Sterling Silver, St.Catherines, Figural Bobsled At Top | 10.00 |
| Souvenir, Spoon, Sterling Silver, St.Joe, Mo. Engraved In Bowl, Patent 1900 | 5.95 |
| Souvenir, Spoon, Sterling Silver, St.Louis, Cutout Handle, Statue | 9.00 |
| Souvenir, Spoon, Sterling Silver, St.Paul, Log Cabin, Towle, Patent 1/14/08 | 12.50 |
| Souvenir, Spoon, Sterling Silver, The Alamo, Mexican Figure | 12.00 |
| Souvenir, Spoon, Sterling Silver, The Capitol, Albany, N.Y. | 3.95 |
| Souvenir, Spoon, Sterling Silver, The Hub, Boston | 5.95 |
| Souvenir, Spoon, Sterling Silver, Thompson, Iowa | 9.00 |
| Souvenir, Spoon, Sterling Silver, Toronto Exposition, 1911 | 4.50 |
| Souvenir, Spoon, Sterling Silver, Tristan Coffin, 1642, Nantucket | 8.50 |
| Souvenir, Spoon, Sterling Silver, Valley Forge, Buildings On Handle | 7.00 |
| Souvenir, Spoon, Sterling Silver, Valley Forge, Embossed Decorations | 8.00 |
| Souvenir, Spoon, Sterling Silver, Virginia, Yarmouth, Snowshoe, Maple Leaf | 12.50 |
| Souvenir, Spoon, Sterling Silver, Washington, D.C., Buildings | 9.95 |
| Souvenir, Spoon, Sterling Silver, Washington, D.C., Capitol Building | 6.95 |
| Souvenir, Spoon, Sterling Silver, Washington, D.C., Eagle, Bust, Capitol | 15.00 |

Souvenir, Spoon, Sterling Silver, Washington, D.C., Gold Washed ..................... 12.50
Souvenir, Spoon, Sterling Silver, Washington, Embossed Bust Of Washington ............... 6.00
Souvenir, Spoon, Sterling Silver, Watergap, Engraved Bowl ..................... 5.00
Souvenir, Spoon, Sterling Silver, Wilkes Barre, Pa., Woman's Profile Handle ........... 7.00
Souvenir, Spoon, Sterling Silver, William McKinley, 5 1/2 In. ..................... 10.00
Souvenir, Spoon, Sterling Silver, Windham, 1758, Frog In Bowl ..................... 12.00
Souvenir, Spoon, Sterling Silver, Wisconsin, Glass Of Beer In Bowl ............... 18.50
Souvenir, Spoon, Sterling Silver, World's Fair City ..................... 9.00
Souvenir, Spoon, Sterling Silver, Yellowstone Park, Cutout Handle ............... 11.00
Souvenir, Square, Pan American Exposition, 1901, Buffalo, Silk, 24 In. ........... 15.00
Souvenir, Sugar Shell, Panama Pacific Exposition, 1915, Horticulture Palace ......... 3.75
Souvenir, Sugar Shell, Sterling Silver, Statue Of Liberty, Cutout ............... 8.95
Souvenir, Sugar, Columbian Exposition, 1893, 4 Footed, China ............... 9.75
Souvenir, Toothpick, Fitchburg, Mass., Pig In Green Pocketbook Band ............... 15.00
Souvenir, Toothpick, Galena, Illinios, Sandwich, Stippled Yellow, Flowers ........... 25.00
Souvenir, Toothpick, Indianapolis, 1907, Pressed, Button Arches, Ruby Flashed ....... 16.50
Souvenir, Toothpick, Lewis & Clark Exposition, 1905 ..................... 8.00
Souvenir, Toothpick, Mackinac Island, 1898, Ruby Thumbprint ............... 18.00
Souvenir, Toothpick, Manchester, N.H., 2 Pigs In Front Of Egg ............... 15.00
Souvenir, Toothpick, Mitchell, Ind., Circle & Dot, Red Flashed ............... 8.50
Souvenir, Toothpick, Summit Hill, Pa., Colorado, Green, Gold ............... 25.00
Souvenir, Toothpick, Turner, 1905, Button & Arches, Red Flashed ............... 9.50
Souvenir, Toothpick, Viola, 1913, Button Arches, Clear & Red ............... 25.00
Souvenir, Toothpick, Waldorf, Minn., Gypsy Kettle, Clear Daisy & Button Rim ....... 16.00
Souvenir, Toothpick, Waldorf, Minn., Gypsy Kettle, Red, Clear Daisy & Button ....... 18.00
Souvenir, Toothpick, World's Fair, 1883, Ruby Flashed ..................... 17.00
Souvenir, Toothpick, World's Fair, 1893, Rubena, Ruby Flashed ............... 15.00
Souvenir, Tray, Change, Pan American Exposition, 1901 ..................... 9.00
Souvenir, Tray, Change, Paris ..................... 9.00
Souvenir, Tray, Grant's Monument, N.Y.C., Paperweight, Glass, Rectangular ........... 4.95
Souvenir, Tray, Pan American Exposition, 1901, Buffalo, Metal, Glass Top ........... 27.00
Souvenir, Tray, Paperweight, Grant's Monument, New York, Color View ............... 5.95
Souvenir, Tumbler, Bowman, N.Dakota, Button Arches, Clambroth ............... 16.00
Souvenir, Tumbler, Chicago World's Fair, 1893, Acid Etched Clear Glass ........... 8.75
Souvenir, Tumbler, Clare, Michigan, Lacy Medallion, Green, Gold Decoration ......... 16.00
Souvenir, Tumbler, International Exposition, Edinburgh, 1886, Picture ............... 25.00
Souvenir, Tumbler, New York World's Fair, 1939, Clear Glass ............... 2.75
Souvenir, Tumbler, Olympics, Australia, 1956, 3 In. ..................... 4.00
Souvenir, Tumbler, Pan American Exposition, 1901 ..................... 15.00
Souvenir, Tumbler, Peru, Illinois, Lacy Medallion, Green, Gold Trim ............... 13.50
Souvenir, Tumbler, Salt Lake City, Utah, Blue & White, Porcelain ............... 7.95
Souvenir, Tumbler, St.Louis Exposition, Pressed Glass, 5 In.High ............... 24.50
Souvenir, Tumbler, St.Louis Exposition, 1904, Clear ..................... 15.00
Souvenir, Tumbler, St.Louis Exposition, 1904, Green ..................... 27.50
Souvenir, Vase, Atlantic City, 2 Bisque Cats On Front, 7 In. ............... 28.00
Souvenir, Vase, Crest Of Canada, Beardmore, Sutherland Art Ware, 4 In. ........... 4.00
Souvenir, Vase, Landing & Station, Wolfeboro, N.H., Porcelain, 6 3/8 In. ........... 4.75
Souvenir, Vase, New Hotel Weirs, N.H., C.1900, White & Gold, 5 1/2 In.High ....... 7.50
Souvenir, Wine, Chagrin Falls, O., Pressed Glass, Ruby Thumbprint, 4 5/8 In. ....... 14.00
Souvenir, Wine, Jerseyville, Ill., King's Crown, Red Flashed, Stemmed ........... 13.50
Souvenir, Wine, Vernon Fair, 1908, Red Top ..................... 11.00

> Spangle glass is multicolored glass made from odds and ends of colored glass
> rods. It includes metallic flakes of mica covered with gold, silver, nickel, or
> copper. Spangle glass is usually cased with a thin layer of clear glass over
> the multicolored layer.

Spangle Glass, Creamer, Clear Overlay On Cobalt, Silver Mica Flecks ............... 175.00
Spangle Glass, Jar, Biscuit, Silver Plate Top & Handle, Melon Ribbed, Mica ........... 115.00
Spangle Glass, Toothpick, Hat Shape, Rough Pontil, 3 In.High ............... 34.00
Spangle Glass, Vase, Bud, Sapphire Blue, Silver Mica, Clear Glass Rigaree ........... 57.00
Spangle Glass, Vase, Cranberry, Gold Flecks ..................... 25.00
Spangle Glass, Vase, Victorian, Green & White, Bulbous Base, Ruffled Top ........... 38.00

> Spanish lace is a Victorian glass pattern that seems to have white lace on
> a colored background. Blue, yellow, cranberry, and clear glass was made with
> this distinctive white pattern.

Spanish Lace, Bride's Bowl, Alpine Blue, 10 1/2 In. ..................... 89.00
Spanish Lace, Celery, Fern, Vaseline ..................... 32.00

Spanish Lace, Cruet, Blue .................................................................... 38.50 To 65.00
Spanish Lace, Cruet, Cranberry ................................................................ 27.50
Spanish Lace, Cruet, Opalescent, Daisy & Fern ................................... 28.00
Spanish Lace, Muffineer, Sapphire Blue ............................................... 65.00
Spanish Lace, Pitcher, Blue, Clear Ribbed Handle, 9 In. .................... 85.00
Spanish Lace, Pitcher, Cranberry, Clear Ribbed Handle, 9 In. ............ 80.00
Spanish Lace, Rose Bowl, Clear & Opalescent, Crimped Top .............. 35.00
Spanish Lace, Rose Bowl, Clear, Ruffled Opalescent Top, 4 In.Diameter ...... 42.00
Spanish Lace, Rose Bowl, Clear, 4 In. ................................................... 40.00
Spanish Lace, Rose Bowl, Crimped Top, Clear & Opalescent, 4 In.Diameter ...... 37.50
Spanish Lace, Rose Bowl, Fluted Top, Clear, 4 In.Diameter ............... 43.00
Spanish Lace, Vase, Crystal & Opalescent, Fluted & Ruffled, 6 1/4 In., Pair ...... 65.00
Spanish Lace, Water Set, Blue Opalescent, 7 Piece ............................. 275.00

*Spatter glass is a multicolored glass made from many small pieces of different colored glass.*

Spatter Glass, Basket, Applied Cobalt Handle, Red, Yellow, & White, 4 1/2 In. ...... 48.00
Spatter Glass, Boot, Applied Clear Rigaree & Leaf ............................ 46.00
Spatter Glass, Ewer, Clear Applied Handle, Cobalt Dot Design, Lined, Pair ...... 65.00
Spatter Glass, Knife Rest, Paperweight, Blue, Green, Rose, & Black Over White ...... 60.00
Spatter Glass, Muffineer, Bulbous, Clear & Cranberry, White Spatter, Tin Top ...... 35.00
Spatter Glass, Pitcher, Cranberry & Ivory On Vaseline, Leaf Bud ...... 145.00
Spatter Glass, Pitcher, Pink & White On Clear, Applied Clear Handle ...... 65.00
Spatter Glass, Pitcher, Water, Bulbous, Square Mouth, Optics, White Swirl ...... 65.00
Spatter Glass, Pitcher, Water, Lavender & Canary, Applied Handle ...... 100.00
Spatter Glass, Pitcher, Water, Red & White, Reeded Handle, 9 In. ...... 70.00
Spatter Glass, Pitcher, Water, White Opalescent Swirl, Bulbous, Square Top ...... 65.00
Spatter Glass, Rose Bowl, Layered, Metal Grill ............................... 37.50
Spatter Glass, Toothpick, Pink & White Under Clear, Molded Melon Sections ...... 25.00
Spatter Glass, Tumbler, Cranberry & Ivory On Vaseline, Bud Leaf ...... 47.00
Spatter Glass, Vase, Cased, Applied Rigaree, Pink, Red, Yellow, & White, Pair ...... 40.00
Spatter Glass, Vase, Cased, Ribbed, Scalloped Top, Green & Rose Coloring ...... 35.00
Spatter Glass, Vase, Orange & White With Yellow Casing, 4 Clear Feet ...... 32.00
Spatter Glass, Vase, Stick, Pink & Rose Shades, Pair ...................... 17.00
Spatter Glass, Vase, Tortoise & Custard Color, Applied Handle, Swirl Casing ...... 40.00
Spatter Glass, Vase, White On Oxblood, Yellow Lined, Gold Enamel Floral ...... 38.00
Spatter Glass, Vase, Yellow & White ................................................. 34.00

*Spatterware is a creamware or soft-paste dinnerware decorated with spatter designs. The earliest pieces were made during the late eighteenth century, but most of the wares found today were made from 1800 to 1850. The spatterware dishes were made in the Staffordshire District of England for sale on the American market.*

Spatterware, Bowl, House Scene, Green & Blue, 3 1/4 In.High ......... 195.00
Spatterware, Bowl, Mauve, Red & Blue Flower, C.1850, Pair ......*Illus* 120.00
Spatterware, Bowl, Peafowl, Blue Spatter, Double Curve Form, 3 1/2 In.High ...... 135.00
Spatterware, Bowl, Vegetable, Blue, Oval, 9 In. ............................... 37.50
Spatterware, Creamer, Blue, 4 In. ....................................................... 110.00
Spatterware, Creamer, Pennsylvania Dutch, Red & Blue ................... 65.00
Spatterware, Cup & Saucer, Handleless, Red Peafowl Decoration ...... 135.00
Spatterware, Cup & Saucer, Handleless, Soft Paste, Blue & White ...... 50.00
Spatterware, Cup & Saucer, Red Roses With Green Branches, Stick Decorated ...... 50.00
Spatterware, Cup & Saucer, Ribbon Design At Middle, Geometrics On Rims ...... 22.50
Spatterware, Cup, Handleless, Yellow & Red .................................... 45.00
Spatterware, Plate, Blue, Tulip Center, 9 In. .................................... 100.00
Spatterware, Plate, Green & Red Rainbow, 8 1/4 In., Pair ............... 250.00
Spatterware, Plate, Red & Green Tulip, Green & Blue Spatter Edge, 9 In. ...... 115.00
Spatterware, Plate, Soup, Green & Floral Garland Center, Blue Rim, 9 In. ...... 85.00
Spatterware, Platter, Red, American Eagle & Shield Center, C.1850 ...... 375.00
Spatterware, Saucer, Fort, Red, Brown, & Green, Blue Border, 6 In. ...... 75.00
Spelter, Figurine, Bear, Painted Brown, 2 1/2 In. .............................. 5.00
Spelter, Figurine, Imperial German Standard Bearer, Bronze Finish, 26 In. ...... 125.00
Spelter, Figurine, La Patrie, 16 1/2 In.High ....................................... 39.50
Spelter, Figurine, Soldier With Flag, 23 In.High ............................... 69.50
Spelter, Figurine, The Good Fairy, Signed J.M.R., 1916, 12 In. High ...... 75.00
Spelter, Figurine, The Hunter, Animal Skin Attire, Tomahawk .......... 45.00
Spelter, Figurine, Woman With Basket On Arm, 17 1/2 In.High ......... 34.50
Spelter, Group, Monkeys, Back To Back, C.B.Mfg.Co., 1 3/4 In. High ...... 10.00

Spatterware, Bowl, Mauve, Red & Blue Flower, C.1850, Pair
*(See Page 597)*

St.Cloud, Figurine, White,
Damaged Neck, C.1750, 6 3/4 In
*(See Page 599)*

**Spinning Wheel, see Tool, Spinning Wheel**

*Spode pottery, porcelain, and bone china were made by the Stoke-on-Trent
Factory of England founded by Josiah Spode about 1770. The firm
became Copeland and Garrett from 1833 to 1847, then W.T.Copeland or
W.T.Copeland and Sons until the present time. The word Spode
appears on many pieces made by the Copeland Factory. Most antique dealers
include all the wares under the more familiar name of Spode.*

**Spode, see also Copeland**

| | |
|---|---:|
| **Spode, Can,** Coffee, Acorn | 35.00 |
| **Spode, Can,** Coffee, Center Orange Band, Blue Geometrics, C.1820, 2 1/2 In. | 37.00 |
| **Spode, Chamberstick,** Curled Gilt Handle, Japan, Salmon, Red, & Blue, C.1800 | 100.00 |
| **Spode, Cup & Saucer,** Blue Bowpot, Stoneware | 7.50 |
| **Spode, Dish,** Candy, White Classical Figures On Blue & Gray, 2 Handled, 6 In. | 38.50 |
| **Spode, Jar,** Tobacco, Covered, White Embossed Male Figures On Gray | 25.00 |
| **Spode, Jug,** Baluster Shape, Bacchanalian Boys, Fruiting Vines, C.1810 | 170.00 |
| **Spode, Plate,** Chop, Billingsley Rose | 22.00 |
| **Spode, Plate,** Currier & Ives, 10 3/4 In. | 22.00 |
| **Spode, Plate,** Death Of The Bear, Blue Transfer, C.1815, 10 In. | 75.00 |
| **Spode, Plate,** Hot Water, Bridge At Lucarno, Medium Blue, C.1820, 9 3/4 In. | 135.00 |
| **Spode, Plate,** Italian, Copeland, 6 1/4 In. | 8.00 |
| **Spode, Plate,** Lunch, Blue Bowpot, Stoneware | 6.00 |
| **Spode, Platter,** Blue & White Transfer, Oriental Scene, C.1835 | 35.00 |
| **Spode, Platter,** Blue & White, Transfer, Castle & Bridge, Stoke-On-Trent | 60.00 |
| **Spode, Platter,** Meat, Tree Well, Castle Pattern, Stoke-On-Trent, C.1840 | 65.00 |
| **Spode, Platter,** Spode's Tower, 17 X 13 1/2 In. | 50.00 |
| **Spode, Spill,** Drabware, Blue Relief Figures & Decoration, C.1800, 4 1/4 In. | 90.00 |
| **Spode, Teapot On Stand,** Scroll Handle & Feet, Transfer, Floral, C.1825 | 90.00 |
| **Spode, Tureen,** Soup, Flower Finial, Spode's Tower, Blue & White, Octagonal | 125.00 |
| **Spode, Vase,** Lavender & Green, Brown Tones, 8 1/2 In.High, Pair | 210.00 |
| **Spode, Vase,** Potpourri, Flower Encrusted, Tulip Shape, C.1831, 3 1/2 In. | 140.00 |
| **Spode, Vase,** White & Gold Floral On Cobalt, Gold Handles, C.1790, 6 1/2 In. | 135.00 |

*Spongeware is very similar to spatterware in appearance. The designs were
applied to the ware by daubing the color. Many dealers do not differentiate
between the two wares and use the names interchangeably.*

| | |
|---|---:|
| **Spongeware, Bowl,** Mixing, Green On White, 9 1/2 In. | 10.00 |
| **Spongeware, Bowl,** Mixing, Mottled, Blue | 29.00 |
| **Spongeware, Bowl,** Scalloped Edge, Rustic, Oatmeal | 28.00 |
| **Spongeware, Crock,** Butter, Blue, "butter, " 5 In.High | 75.00 |
| **Spongeware, Cuspidor,** Blue & White | 35.00 |
| **Spongeware, Dish,** Soap, Blue & White, 4 3/4 X 3 1/2 In. | 25.00 |
| **Spongeware, Pitcher,** Blue & White | 40.00 |
| **Spongeware, Pitcher,** Water, Bulbous, Flaring Lip, Embossed Chain Design | 65.00 |
| **Spongeware, Plate,** Cobalt Blue, C.1830, 10 In. | 55.00 |
| **Spongeware, Plate,** Cobalt Blue, 7 1/2 In. | 38.00 |

| | |
|---|---|
| Spongeware, Plate, Dark Blue, Gold Edge, 7 1/4 In. | 17.50 |
| Spongeware, Plate, Soup, Cobalt Blue, Spatterlike Center, 8 1/4 In. | 48.00 |
| Spongeware, Plate, Soup, Cobalt Blue, 8 1/2 In. | 38.00 |
| Spongeware, Plate, 8 1/8 In. | 38.00 |
| Spongeware, Spittoon, Blue & White, Pennsylvania, 5 1/4 X 7 1/2 In. | 68.00 |
| Spongeware, Tankard, Blue & White, 7 1/8 In.High | 28.00 |
| Spongeware, Tankard, Milk, Blue, 7 1/2 In. High | 35.00 |
| St.Cloud, Burner, Covered, Pastille, White, Inverted Pear Shape, Ormolu, 1750s | 2000.00 |
| St.Cloud, Figurine, White, Damaged Neck, C.1750, 6 3/4 In *Illus* | 450.00 |
| St. Louis, Nancy, Toothpick, Dark Green Flowers on Light Green Satin, Signed | 145.00 |
| St.Louis, Pitcher, Champagne, Ice Bladder, Etched, Silver Tracery, C.1890 | 300.00 |
| St.Louis, Vase, Blown, Hand-Painted Gold Flowers, 13 1/4 In.High | 95.00 |

*Staffordshire is a district in England where pottery and porcelain have
been made since the 1900s. Thousands of types of pottery and porcelain have
been made in the hundreds of factories that worked in the area. Some of the
most famous factories have been listed separately. See Royal Doulton,
Royal Worcester, Spode, Wedgwood, and others.*

### Staffordshire, see also Flow Blue

| | |
|---|---|
| Staffordshire, Basket, Blue Transfer, Castles, Cutwork Sides, C.1835 | 85.00 |
| Staffordshire, Bonbonniere, Apple Form, Enamel, Yellow & Orange, C.1780 | 425.00 |
| Staffordshire, Bonbonniere, Enamel, Dog Form, Yellow Pug, C.1790, 3 In.Long | 225.00 |
| Staffordshire, Bottle, Scent, Enamel, Green Ground, Putti, C.1780, 3 1/4 In. | 475.00 |
| Staffordshire, Bottle, Scent, Enamel, White & Yellow, Lady Walking, C.1770 | 525.00 |
| Staffordshire, Bowl, Black, Open Handles, Oval, 8 In. Deep | 19.00 |
| Staffordshire, Bowl, Blue & White Transfer, Lucano Bridge, C.1830 | 55.00 |
| Staffordshire, Bowl, Covered, Abbey Ruins, Pink, Mayer Longport | 35.00 |
| Staffordshire, Bowl, Fishing Scene, Blue, 5 In. | 30.00 |
| Staffordshire, Bowl, Flowers & Vases, Round, Marked Stone China, 6 1/2 In. | 18.00 |
| Staffordshire, Bowl, Hartford, Conn., Deep Pink, Jackson, 10 1/4 In. | 65.00 |
| Staffordshire, Bowl, Italian Buildings, R.Hall, 10 3/4 X 2 1/2 In. | 32.00 |
| Staffordshire, Bowl, Punch, Cast Iron Bridge Over River Wear, Purple, Moore | 145.00 |
| Staffordshire, Bowl, Raised Purple Scroll & Floral, Footed, Chelsea | 15.00 |
| Staffordshire, Bowl, Serving, Covered, Delhi, Mulberry, M.T.& Co., C.1840 | 100.00 |
| Staffordshire, Bowl, Soup, Rhone Scenery, Mulberry, T.J.& J.Mayer, C.1840 | 25.00 |
| Staffordshire, Bowl, Vegetable, Brown Ferns & Ivy Transfer, Handled, Dimmock | 11.00 |
| Staffordshire, Bowl, Vegetable, Covered, Washington Vase, Mulberry | 65.00 |
| Staffordshire, Bowl, Vegetable, Oriental Scene, Dark Blue, Clews | 88.00 |
| Staffordshire, Bowl, Vegetable, Oval, Deep Blue, Vegetables In Center, Floral | 32.00 |
| Staffordshire, Bowl, Vegetable, View Of Dublin, Blue, Wood, 12 1/2 In. | 120.00 |
| Staffordshire, Bowl, Vegetable, West Point, Dark Blue, 10 1/2 X 8 In | 350.00 |
| Staffordshire, Bowl, Waste, Abbey Ruins, Mulberry, Mayer Longport, 5 1/2 In. | 18.00 |
| Staffordshire, Box, Chest On Feet Shape, Lyre Shape Mirror, 3 1/4 In.High | 42.00 |
| Staffordshire, Box, Chest Shape, White, Gold Trim, Mirror Frame | 32.00 |
| Staffordshire, Box, Covered, Boy In Canoe | 27.50 |
| Staffordshire, Box, Dresser, Music On Top, Deer's Head Front, 4 Footed | 20.00 |
| Staffordshire, Box, Hairpin, Child's Head On Cover | 25.00 |
| Staffordshire, Box, Mirror & Child On Lid, Fireplace Shape, Griffons | 38.00 |
| Staffordshire, Box, Oval, Child Rowing In Round Basin, 3 1/4 In.High | 35.00 |
| Staffordshire, Box, Patch, Boy With Dog | 25.00 |
| Staffordshire, Box, Patch, Circular, Enamel, C.1770, Girl In Blue, 2 1/4 In. | 350.00 |
| Staffordshire, Box, Patch, Crown & Sceptre, Footed | 35.00 |
| Staffordshire, Box, Patch, Crown, Orb, & Scepter | 23.00 |
| Staffordshire, Box, Patch, Egg Shape, Fruit Finial, Florets | 18.00 |
| Staffordshire, Box, Patch, Faith, Hope, & Charity | 35.00 |
| Staffordshire, Box, Patch, Girl On Cover | 30.00 |
| Staffordshire, Box, Patch, Little Boy Reading Book | 55.00 |
| Staffordshire, Box, Patch, Reclining Child | 65.00 |
| Staffordshire, Box, Patch, Table With Tea Set Decoration | 32.00 |
| Staffordshire, Box, Trinket, Floral Finial, Rectangular | 16.00 |
| Staffordshire, Box, Trinket, Old Woman Spying On Girl & Man On Sofa | 28.50 |
| Staffordshire, Box, Trinket, Pug Dog Sitting On White Dresser, Mirror | 50.00 |
| Staffordshire, Box, Trinket, Round, Mirror Frame, Room Setting Scene | 45.00 |
| Staffordshire, Box, Trinket, Upright Piano Shape, Mirror On Lid, 4 In.High | 45.00 |
| Staffordshire, Box, Trinket, Watch In Center | 38.00 |
| Staffordshire, Bust, Portrait, Black Basalt, Sir Isaac Newton, 8 5/8 In. | 150.00 |
| Staffordshire, Butter, Covered, Old Foley Square, James Kent, Ltd. | 11.85 |

Staffordshire, Cottage,
Pavilion, 6 3/4 In.High

Staffordshire, Cottage,
7 1/2 In.High

Staffordshire,
Pastille Burner,
3 3/4 In.High
*(See Page 605)*

| | |
|---|---:|
| **Staffordshire, Candlestick,** Baluster, Enameled, C.1780, 9 1/4 In., Pair | 225.00 |
| **Staffordshire, Candlestick,** Cottage Shape, Greenaway Decoration, 1870, Pair | 39.00 |
| **Staffordshire, Casket,** Jewel, Footed, Framed Mirror, Crown, Orb, Scepter, 4 In. | 32.00 |
| **Staffordshire, Compote,** Gothic Castle, Dark Blue, Oval, C.1820 | 95.00 |
| **Staffordshire, Cottage,** Pavilion, 6 3/4 In.High ............................................................ *Illus* | 120.00 |
| **Staffordshire, Cottage,** 7 1/2 In.High ............................................................ *Illus* | 90.00 |
| **Staffordshire, Creamer,** Blue Transfer Print, 3 In.High | 17.50 |
| **Staffordshire, Creamer,** Boy, Cows, Ruins, Dark Blue | 40.00 |
| **Staffordshire, Creamer,** Corean, Mulberry, Podmore & Walker, C.1840 | 65.00 |
| **Staffordshire, Creamer,** Gold Outlined Acanthus Leaf, Quilted, Floral | 10.00 |
| **Staffordshire, Creamer,** Hand-Applied Red Decoration, 3 1/2 In.High | 18.50 |
| **Staffordshire, Creamer,** Italian Villas, Deep Purple, C.1835 | 28.00 |
| **Staffordshire, Creamer,** Raised Purple Scroll & Leaf, Chelsea | 20.00 |
| **Staffordshire, Creamer,** Temple, Mulberry, Podmore & Walker, C.1850 | 65.00 |
| **Staffordshire, Cup & Saucer,** Chinoiserie, Green Dots Mark | 22.00 |
| **Staffordshire, Cup & Saucer,** Coffee, For Auld Lange Syne, Blue, White, R.& M. | 22.00 |
| **Staffordshire, Cup & Saucer,** Corean, Mulberry, Handleless Cup, P.W.Co., 1840 | 37.50 |
| **Staffordshire, Cup & Saucer,** Cyprus, Mulberry, Davenport, C.1844 | 35.00 |
| **Staffordshire, Cup & Saucer,** English Lake Scene, Deep Blue | 45.00 |
| **Staffordshire, Cup & Saucer,** Floral, Mulberry, Handleless Cup, C.1845 | 25.00 |
| **Staffordshire, Cup & Saucer,** Foliage, Mulberry, Handleless Cup, C.1850 | 35.00 |
| **Staffordshire, Cup & Saucer,** Grape & Flower, Deep Blue, C.1825 | 48.00 |
| **Staffordshire, Cup & Saucer,** Dutch Vignettes, Wood & Son, C.1830 | 63.00 |
| **Staffordshire, Cup & Saucer,** Handleless, Garden Scene, Light Blue, Longport | 25.00 |
| **Staffordshire, Cup & Saucer,** Handleless, Grape & Flower, Deep Blue | 45.00 |
| **Staffordshire, Cup & Saucer,** Handleless, Homer Invoking Muses, Light Blue | 16.00 |
| **Staffordshire, Cup & Saucer,** Loretto, Mulberry, Handleless Cup | 35.00 |
| **Staffordshire, Cup & Saucer,** Montezuma, Mulberry, Handleless Cup, J.Goodwin | 35.00 |
| **Staffordshire, Cup & Saucer,** Pink Transfer Little Girl & Dog, C.1820 | 31.50 |
| **Staffordshire, Cup & Saucer,** Raised Purple Scroll & Leaf, Chelsea | 18.00 |
| **Staffordshire, Cup & Saucer,** The Cottage Girl, Purple | 38.00 |
| **Staffordshire, Cup & Saucer,** Wadsworth Tower, Blue, Shell Border, Wood | 165.00 |
| **Staffordshire, Cup & Saucer,** Wadsworth Tower, Dark Blue, Wood | 210.00 |
| **Staffordshire, Cup Plate,** Battery, N.Y., Wood, 3 1/2 In. | 150.00 |
| **Staffordshire, Cup Plate,** Corean, Mulberry, Ironstone | 17.50 |
| **Staffordshire, Cup Plate,** Country Scene, Black, 3 7/8 In. | 24.00 |

| | |
|---|---|
| Staffordshire, Cup Plate, Floral, Deep Rose, 3 7/8 In. | 12.00 |
| Staffordshire, Cup Plate, Hyena, Quadrupeds Series, Dark Blue, Hall | 40.00 |
| Staffordshire, Cup Plate, Mulberry | 25.00 |
| Staffordshire, Cup Plate, Pastoral, Light Blue, Melor Venables, 9 In. | 13.00 |
| Staffordshire, Cup Plate, Scenic, Dark Blue, 12 Sided, 4 In. | 22.00 |
| Staffordshire, Cup Plate, Scenic, Deep Blue, Pink Luster Rim, 4 In. | 20.00 |
| Staffordshire, Cup Plate, Sheltered Peasants, Dark Blue, Hall | 40.00 |
| Staffordshire, Cup, Custard, Rural Scene, Medium Blue, C.1820 | 28.00 |
| Staffordshire, Cup, Handleless, Purple Transfer, 1 3/4 In. High | 12.50 |
| Staffordshire, Cup, McDonough's Victory, Dark Blue | 145.00 |
| Staffordshire, Cup, Stirrup, Hound Dog's Head, Beige, Brown, Yellow | 45.00 |
| Staffordshire, Cup, Washington Vase, Mulberry, Handleless | 20.00 |
| Staffordshire, Dinner Set, Miniature, Shamrock, Hackwood, 1842, 38 Piece | 225.00 |
| Staffordshire, Dish, Bone, English Scenery, Blue & White, Woods | 4.75 |
| Staffordshire, Dish, Candy, Hunt Scene, Marked | 10.00 |
| Staffordshire, Dish, Cheese, Bull's Head | 110.00 |
| Staffordshire, Dish, Chicken Cover, Basket Weave Nest Base, White Chicken | 125.00 |
| Staffordshire, Dish, Hen Cover, Caramel Basket Weave Nest, White Hen, Eggs | 130.00 |
| Staffordshire, Dish, Hen Cover, Nest Base, Eggholder, C.1870, 9 In.High | 160.00 |
| Staffordshire, Dish, Hen Cover, Nest Base, Speckled Brown Feathers, 4 In. | 50.00 |
| Staffordshire, Dish, Hen Cover, Nest Base, 7 1/2 X 5 1/2 In. | 08.00 |
| Staffordshire, Dish, Hen Cover, White, Yellowish Nest Base, 7 1/2 In. | 125.00 |
| Staffordshire, Dish, Hen Cover, Yellow Basket Base, C.1850, 3 5/8 In., Pair | 190.00 |
| Staffordshire, Dish, Quatrefoil, Shannon, Blue, John Rogers, 9 In. | 50.00 |
| Staffordshire, Dish, Sweetmeat, Blue & White Transfer, Castle, C.1820 | 48.00 |
| Staffordshire, Dish, Trinket, Shell Shape, Cream & Gold | 9.00 |
| Staffordshire, Eggcup, Across The Continent, Currier & Ives, Pink & White | 25.00 |
| Staffordshire, Ewer, Tapestry Design | 125.00 |
| Staffordshire, Figurine, Bird, Bright Plumage, 12 1/2 In High, Pair | 90.00 |
| Staffordshire, Figurine, Blonde Child Sitting On A Dog | 30.00 |
| Staffordshire, Figurine, Boy & Girl With Ayrshire Cow, Pair | 175.00 |
| Staffordshire, Figurine, Boy, Blue With White, No.4534, 9 1/2 In. | 45.00 |
| Staffordshire, Figurine, Cat With Fiddle, 4 In. | 28.50 |
| Staffordshire, Figurine, Cat, Yellow, Green Cushion, 4 In.High, Pair | 24.00 |
| Staffordshire, Figurine, Child Sitting Astride Dog, Miniature | 25.00 |
| Staffordshire, Figurine, Cleopatra, Enoch Wood, C.1750, 13 In. | 450.00 |
| Staffordshire, Figurine, Dalmatian Dog, Oval Cobalt Base, C.1850, 5 1/4 In. | 38.00 |
| Staffordshire, Figurine, Dalmatian, Tan Nose, Gold Collar, Cobalt Base, Pair | 75.00 |
| Staffordshire, Figurine, Doe, Recumbent, C.1790, 6 1/8 In. | 160.00 |
| Staffordshire, Figurine, Dog On Chair, Top Lifts Off, 1 1/2 In.High | 16.00 |
| Staffordshire, Figurine, Dog, Orange & White, 9 In.High, Pair | 75.00 |
| Staffordshire, Figurine, Dog, Orange Spots, 5 1/2 In.High, Pair | 40.00 |
| Staffordshire, Figurine, Dog, White, 11 & 11 1/2 In.High, Pair | 75.00 |

Staffordshire, Figurine, Musicians, Pair
(See Page 602)

Staffordshire, Figurine,
Elephant, 7 1/2 In.High
(See Page 602)

Staffordshire, Figurine, Dogs, Reddish, Pair .......................................................................... 75.00
Staffordshire, Figurine, Elephant, 7 1/2 In.High .................................................... *Illus* 250.00
Staffordshire, Figurine, Elijah, Enoch Wood, C.1800, 9 1/2 In.High .............................. 140.00
Staffordshire, Figurine, Equestrian Hunter, C.1850, 6 5/8 In. ..................................... 425.00
Staffordshire, Figurine, Equestrian Man, Deer Over Saddle, 14 In.High ........................... 45.00
Staffordshire, Figurine, Franklin, C.1850, 14 In. High ............................... *Illus* 550.00
Staffordshire, Figurine, Franklin, Inscribed Washington ........................... *Illus* 600.00
Staffordshire, Figurine, Franklin, "Washington, " C.1850 .......................... *Illus* 475.00
Staffordshire, Figurine, Goat On Rocky Crag, 3 3/4 In.High ...................................... 20.00
Staffordshire, Figurine, Hen, Black & Gray Head, Red Wattles, Tan Base ....................... 145.00
Staffordshire, Figurine, Horse & Groom, 18th Century, 6 1/4 In.High ...................... 1900.00
Staffordshire, Figurine, Infant In Hooded Cradle, Patchwork Quilt, C.1820 ..................... 110.00
Staffordshire, Figurine, Isaac Van Amburgh, 11 1/2 In. .................................. *Illus* 130.00
Staffordshire, Figurine, Lion, C.1790, 4 3/8 In.Long ................................... *Illus* 325.00
Staffordshire, Figurine, Lion, One Foot On Ball, Pair .............................................. 150.00
Staffordshire, Figurine, Lion, Red, Pair .............................................................. 65.00
Staffordshire, Figurine, Little Boy Crying, Holding Hat At Side, 5 1/2 In. ....................... 85.00
Staffordshire, Figurine, Musician, Lady & Lute, Man & Flute, C.1790, Pair ..................... 250.00
Staffordshire, Figurine, Musicians, Pair ............................................... *Illus* 90.00
Staffordshire, Figurine, Nell & Jobson, C.1850, 6 1/2 In., Pair .................................. 200.00
Staffordshire, Figurine, Pointer, C.1830, 5 3/4 In. ................................... *Illus* 250.00
Staffordshire, Figurine, Poodle, Basket In Mouth, Oval Base, 2 3/4 In.High ..................... 15.50
Staffordshire, Figurine, Poodle, Lion Clip, Yellow Bird On Nose, C.1850, Pair .................. 210.00
Staffordshire, Figurine, Poodle, Sitting, Black Nose, Pink Luster, Pair .......................... 40.00
Staffordshire, Figurine, Poodle, White, Gold Decoration, 11 1/2 In.High, Pair ................... 50.00
Staffordshire, Figurine, Poodles On Blue Pillow, Gold Line, 2 In.High ............................ 23.00
Staffordshire, Figurine, Prince Albert, 17 1/2 In.High ............................................. 50.00
Staffordshire, Figurine, Rabbit, Recumbent, C.1850, Pair ........................................ 175.00
Staffordshire, Figurine, Ram, Creamware Body, 18th Century, 3 1/2 In.Long ..................... 110.00
Staffordshire, Figurine, Red Fox, Seated, Slain Fowl Above, 4 1/4 In.High ....................... 50.00
Staffordshire, Figurine, Robin Hood, 14 1/4 In.High ............................................... 50.00
Staffordshire, Figurine, Seated Spaniels, C.1880, Pair, 13 1/2 In.High ............................ 25.00
Staffordshire, Figurine, Shakespeare, C.1840, 18 In. ............................................. 235.00
Staffordshire, Figurine, Sheep Standing By Stump, 6 In., Pair ..................................... 48.00
Staffordshire, Figurine, Shoemaker, Browns, Yellow, & Oranges, 7 In.High ...................... 135.00
Staffordshire, Figurine, Sitting Whippet, Tan & White, 5 1/2 In.High .............................. 35.00
Staffordshire, Figurine, Spaniel Dog, Seated, White, Gold Collar, C.1850, Pair .................. 80.00
Staffordshire, Figurine, Spaniel, Seated, Orange Spots, Pair ..................................... 75.00
Staffordshire, Figurine, Spaniel, Sitting, Brown & White, 5 1/2 In.High .......................... 27.50
Staffordshire, Figurine, Spaniel, Sitting, White, 8 1/2 In.High, Pair .............................. 65.00
Staffordshire, Figurine, St.Bernard, 7 1/4 In.Long, Pair ......................................... 100.00
Staffordshire, Figurine, The Four Seasons, Wood, C.1810, 7 5/8 In., Set Of 4 .................. 400.00
Staffordshire, Figurine, The Lion Slayer, Plaid Clothing, Lion Under Foot ...................... 125.00
Staffordshire, Figurine, The Lion Slayer, Scotsman, 16 1/4 In.High .............................. 90.00
Staffordshire, Figurine, Uncle Tom & Eva, 10 3/4 In. ................................. *Illus* 150.00
Staffordshire, Figurine, Uncle Tom & Eva, 8 1/2 In.High ............................. *Illus* 140.00
Staffordshire, Figurine, Uncle Tom & Eva, 8 7/8 In.High ............................. *Illus* 150.00
Staffordshire, Figurine, Victoria & Albert, C.1841, 6 3/4 In., Pair ............................... 175.00
Staffordshire, Figurine, Whippit, Rabbit In Mouth, C.1860, 11 In. ............................... 75.00
Staffordshire, Figurine, William Wallace & Robert Bruce, C.1850, Pair .......................... 175.00
Staffordshire, Figurine, Winter, Boy In Yellow Cloak, C.1825, 6 3/4 In.High ..................... 140.00
Staffordshire, Figurine, Woman, C.1775, 4 1/8 In.High ............................... *Illus* 100.00
Staffordshire, Figurine, Young Woman, Blue Smock, Holding Ewer, C.1850, 9 In. ............... 50.00
Staffordshire, Garniture, Gold Handles, Cartouche Scenes On Pink, 3 Piece ..................... 80.00
Staffordshire, Gravy Boat, Foliage, Mulberry ................................................... 26.50
Staffordshire, Gravy Boat, Franklin's Kite, Blue & White, Miniature .............................. 60.00
Staffordshire, Gravy Boat, Wild Flowers, C.1870 ................................................ 25.00
Staffordshire, Group, Dancing Ballerina & Playing Minstrel, Bridge, Trees ...................... 39.00
Staffordshire, Group, Girl & Boy Resting On Stump, Gold & White, 4 1/2 In. .................... 50.00
Staffordshire, Group, Girl, Boy, Lamb, Dog, Watch Pocket, Black, C.1850 ...................... 55.00
Staffordshire, Group, Lovers In Bower, Dog, White, Gold, Black Hair ............................ 33.50
Staffordshire, Group, Lovers, Under An Arbor, 9 1/4 In.High ..................................... 70.00
Staffordshire, Group, Marriage, 14 1/4 In.High .................................................. 35.00
Staffordshire, Group, Pair Of Maidens, One Standing, One Seated, Garlands ..................... 30.00
Staffordshire, Group, Reclining Lambs With Rough Coats, 3 X 2 1/2 In. ......................... 65.00
Staffordshire, Group, Robin Hood, 2 Men, 3 Dogs, 14 1/2 In.High .............................. 97.50

Staffordshire, Figurine, Franklin, C.1850, 14 In. High
*(See Page 602)*

Staffordshire, Figurine, Franklin, Inscribed Washington
*(See Page 602)*

Staffordshire, Figurine,
Franklin, "Washington," C.1850
*(See Page 602)*

Staffordshire, Figurine,
Isaac Van Amburgh, 11 1/2 In.
*(See Page 602)*

Staffordshire, Figurine,
Uncle Tom & Eva,
8 7/8 In.High
*(See Page 602)*

Staffordshire, Figurine,
Uncle Tom & Eva,
10 3/4 In.
*(See Page 602)*

Staffordshire, Figurine,
Uncle Tom & Eva,
8 1/2 In.High
*(See Page 602)*

Staffordshire, Figurine, Pointer, C.1830, 5 3/4 In.
*(See Page 602)*

Staffordshire, Jug, Mask,
Canary, Potato,
C.1815, 4 1/2 In
*(See Page 605)*

Staffordshire, Jug, Mask,
Canary, Sprigs,
C.1815, 4 5/8 In
*(See Page 605)*

Staffordshire, Figurine,
Woman, C.1775,
4 1/8 In.High
*(See Page 602)*

Staffordshire, Jug, Silver Resist,
Masonic, C.1810
*(See Page 605)*

Staffordshire, Figurine, Lion, C.1790, 4 3/8 In.Long
*(See Page 602)*

Staffordshire, Jug,
Silver Resist, Chinoiserie, C.1810
*(See Page 605)*

Staffordshire, Jug,
Silver Resist, Exotic Bird, C.1810
*(See Page 605)*

Staffordshire, Group, Sheep & Lambs, Walton, C.1818, Pair ................................................ 250.00
Staffordshire, Group, The Flight Into Egypt, C.1800 ................................................ 350.00
Staffordshire, Group, The Vicar & Moses, Wood, C.1850 ................................ *Illus* 60.00
Staffordshire, Inkwell, Mother, Girl, & Boy Group On Divan, Hinged, C.1750 ................ 285.00
Staffordshire, Jar & Underplate, Jam, Strawberry Finial, Royal Crown ................................ 8.00
Staffordshire, Jar, Chemist's, Coral Tooth Paste, , Parker, Uttoxeter, White ................ 30.00
Staffordshire, Jar, Chemist's, Otto Of Rose Cold Cream, A.Parker, Uttoxeter ................ 30.00
Staffordshire, Jar, Mustard, Dog On Top, Boy On Side ................................ 15.00
Staffordshire, Jug, Black & Red Transfer On White, "george Wittle, 1846" ................ 75.00
Staffordshire, Jug, Black Transfer On Mustard ................................ 85.00
Staffordshire, Jug, Black Transfer, Canary, Platinum Banded ................................ 250.00
Staffordshire, Jug, Blue Transfer, Mill Scene With Cattle, C.1830 ................................ 135.00
Staffordshire, Jug, Canary, Silver Luster, Iron Flowering Vines, C.1810 ................ 225.00
Staffordshire, Jug, Mask, Canary, Potato, C.1815, 4 1/2 In ........................ *Illus* 400.00
Staffordshire, Jug, Mask, Canary, Sprigs, C.1815, 4 5/8 In ........................ *Illus* 325.00
Staffordshire, Jug, Milk, Lavender Transfer, 7 1/2 In.High ................................ 38.00
Staffordshire, Jug, Milk, Saltglaze, Curved Handle, Applied Leaves, C.1740 ................ 175.00
Staffordshire, Jug, Morland Hunt Scene, Blue, Platinum Resist ................................ 625.00
Staffordshire, Jug, Pearlware, Pinched Spout, Fruiting Branches, C.1780 ................ 200.00
Staffordshire, Jug, Silver Resist, Canary, Foliate Branch Panels, C.1810 ................ 425.00
Staffordshire, Jug, Silver Resist, Canary, Vertical Bamboo Sides, C.1810 ................ 225.00
Staffordshire, Jug, Silver Resist, Chinoiscrie, C.1810 ........................ *Illus* 325.00
Staffordshire, Jug, Silver Resist, Exotic Bird, C.1810 ........................ *Illus* 150.00
Staffordshire, Jug, Silver Resist, George Morland Hunters, Blue, C.1810 ................ 250.00
Staffordshire, Jug, Silver Resist, Hussars In Battle, Blue Transfer, C.1810 ................ 425.00
Staffordshire, Jug, Silver Resist, Masonic, C.1810 ........................ *Illus* 300.00
Staffordshire, Jug, Silver Resist, Panels Of Vines, Pearlware, C.1810, 6 In. ................ 250.00
Staffordshire, Jug, Silver Resist, Robin, Pearlware, C.1812, 4 1/4 In. ................ 625.00
Staffordshire, Match Holder, Boy Holding Egg, Basket Is Holder, Striker ................ 25.00
Staffordshire, Match Holder, Footed Container Between 2 Black Boots, 3 In. ................ 28.00
Staffordshire, Match Holder, Girl Sitting On Box, Puppy, Striker ................................ 38.00
Staffordshire, Match Holder, Girl, Washtub, & Puppy, Striker ................................ 38.00
Staffordshire, Match Holder, Pair Of Boots On Footed Platform, Striker ................ 20.00
Staffordshire, Match Holder, Red Riding Hood & The Wolf ................................ 15.00
Staffordshire, Match Holder, 2 Black & Orange Open Top Boots On Each Side ................ 28.00
Staffordshire, Match Safe, Galloping Horse On Cover, Footed ................................ 18.50
Staffordshire, Mug, A Friend In Need Is A Friend Indeed, Purple On White ................ 42.00
Staffordshire, Mug, Black Frog, 2 Colorful Transfer Scenes ................................ 55.00
Staffordshire, Mug, Cider, 2 Handled, Blue & White, Lucano, C.1830, Quart ................ 88.00
Staffordshire, Mug, Dr.Franklin, Maxim, Black Transfer, Verse On Sloth ................ 36.00
Staffordshire, Mug, Rugby Player Forms Handle, Silver Luster On Brown, Wood ................ 27.50
Staffordshire, Mug, 2 Handled, Blue & White, Shepherdess, C.1830, Quart ................ 85.00
Staffordshire, Mug, 2 Handled, Blue Transfer, Pagoda, C.1845, Quart ................ 80.00
Staffordshire, Ornament, Chimney, Bagpiper & Companion, C.1850, 14 In. ................ 150.00
Staffordshire, Ornament, Chimney, Clock, C.1820, Pair ................................ 200.00
Staffordshire, Ornament, Chimney, Young Man & Woman In Blue & Orange Coats ................ 55.00
Staffordshire, Pastille Burner, 3 3/4 In.High ........................ *Illus* 90.00
Staffordshire, Pitcher Set, Chung, Blue & White, Woods & Son, 3 Graduated ................ 105.00
Staffordshire, Pitcher, Classical Figures, Till & Son, Mark For 1852 ................................ 38.00
Staffordshire, Pitcher, Embossed Tulips On White, 8 1/2 In.High ................................ 20.00
Staffordshire, Pitcher, English Manor House, Medium Blue, Baluster Shape ................ 60.00
Staffordshire, Pitcher, Franklin's Tomb, Blue, Wood, 7 1/2 In. ................................ 300.00
Staffordshire, Pitcher, Milk, Lucano Bridge Near Rome, Dark Blue, C.1820 ................ 58.00
Staffordshire, Pitcher, Vintage, Blue & White, Registry Mark, 9 1/4 In.High ................ 55.00
Staffordshire, Pitcher, Water, Boston Mail, Blue Transfer, 11 1/2 In. ................ 95.00
Staffordshire, Pitcher, Water, Palestine, Black, 10 In.High ................................ 60.00
Staffordshire, Pitcher, William Harrison Transfer, 6 Sided ................................ 350.00
Staffordshire, Plate, British Scenery, Blue Transfer, C.1810, 10 In. ................ 22.50
Staffordshire, Plate, Adelaide's Bower, Green & White, 8 3/4 In. ................................ 10.50
Staffordshire, Plate, Albany, Mulberry, 8 1/4 In. ................................ 16.00
Staffordshire, Plate, Albany, Mulberry, 8 1/2 In. ................................ 48.00
Staffordshire, Plate, American Marine, Brown, G.L.A.& Bro., 7 1/2 In. ................ 25.00
Staffordshire, Plate, American Marine, Brown, 8 In. ................................ 25.00
Staffordshire, Plate, American Villa, Dark Blue, 10 In. ................................ 100.00
Staffordshire, Plate, Asbury Park, Rowland & Marcellus Co., 8 1/2 In. ................ 35.00
Staffordshire, Plate, Asiatic Beauties, Light Blue, Scalloped, 10 1/2 In. ................ 20.00

Staffordshire, Group, The Vicar & Moses, Wood, C.1850
*(See Page 605)*

| | |
|---|---|
| Staffordshire, Plate, Asiatic Pheasant, Light Blue, 10 3/4 In. | 12.00 |
| Staffordshire, Plate, Asiatic Views, Purple, Dillon, 8 3/4 In. | 24.00 |
| Staffordshire, Plate, Athens, Mulberry, W.Adams, C.1849, 8 3/4 In. | 20.00 |
| Staffordshire, Plate, Avon, Mulberry, Floral, 9 In. | 10.00 |
| Staffordshire, Plate, Baker's Falls, Hudson River, Black, 9 In. | 65.00 |
| Staffordshire, Plate, Batalha, Portugal, Dark Blue, 10 In. | 29.00 |
| Staffordshire, Plate, Battery & Co., N.Y., Sepia, 8 In. | 62.00 |
| Staffordshire, Plate, Battery Of City Of New York, Black, 8 In. | 55.00 |
| Staffordshire, Plate, Battle Of Germantown, Fruit & Flower Border, 10 In. | 42.00 |
| Staffordshire, Plate, Boccara, Mulberry, Broadhurst & Sons, C.1865, 9 1/2 In. | 12.00 |
| Staffordshire, Plate, Boston State House, Blue, Rogers, 8 3/4 In. | 75.00 |
| Staffordshire, Plate, Boston State House, Enoch Wood, 9 3/4 In. | 90.00 |
| Staffordshire, Plate, Boston State House, Medium Blue, Wood, 10 In. | 88.00 |
| Staffordshire, Plate, Boston State House, Surrey, Light Blue, Wood, 6 In. | 60.00 |
| Staffordshire, Plate, Bridge Of Lucano, Dark Blue, Enoch Wood, 10 In. | 55.00 |
| Staffordshire, Plate, British Scenery, Deep Blue, C.1810, 10 In. | 22.50 |
| Staffordshire, Plate, Caledonia, Purple, Davis, 10 1/2 In. | 20.00 |
| Staffordshire, Plate, Caledonia, Purple, 9 1/4 In. | 28.00 |
| Staffordshire, Plate, Caledonia, Red, 6 In. | 35.00 |
| Staffordshire, Plate, Canova, Blue, T.Mayer, 8 1/2 In. | 18.00 |
| Staffordshire, Plate, Cascade-Pres Chambery, Dark Blue, Wood, 7 1/2 In. | 48.00 |
| Staffordshire, Plate, Cashiobury, Hertfordshire, Deep Blue, Hall's, 7 1/2 In. | 25.00 |
| Staffordshire, Plate, Castle Of Furstenfel, Dark Blue, 8 1/2 In. | 52.00 |
| Staffordshire, Plate, Castle Of Lavenza, Dark Blue, Enoch Wood, 10 In. | 55.00 |
| Staffordshire, Plate, Catskill Mountain House, Pink, 10 1/2 In. | 70.00 |
| Staffordshire, Plate, Cave Castle, Yorkshire, Dark Blue, Wood, 8 1/4 In. | 36.00 |
| Staffordshire, Plate, Chang, Brown, Handled, Edge & Malkin, 8 In. Square | 5.00 |
| Staffordshire, Plate, Chateau Ermenonville, Wood, 10 In. | 57.50 |
| Staffordshire, Plate, Chief Justice Marshall Troy, Dark Blue, Wood, 10 In. | 195.00 |
| Staffordshire, Plate, Child's, Mr.Caterwal's Courtship, Blue, 7 In. | 25.00 |
| Staffordshire, Plate, Child's, The Kittens In The Pantry, Blue, 7 In. | 25.00 |
| Staffordshire, Plate, Circassra, Dark Blue, Alcock, 6 3/8 In. | 24.00 |
| Staffordshire, Plate, City Hall, N.Y., Dark Blue, Ridgway, 10 In. | 125.00 |
| Staffordshire, Plate, City Hotel, N.Y., Stevenson, 8 1/2 In. | 175.00 |
| Staffordshire, Plate, Corean, Mulberry, P.W.& Co., C.1850, 8 3/4 In. | 27.50 |
| Staffordshire, Plate, Corean, Mulberry, Podmore & Walker, C.1840, 9 3/4 In. | 35.00 |
| Staffordshire, Plate, Corean, Mulberry, Podmore & Walker, C.1850, 8 In. | 17.50 |
| Staffordshire, Plate, Corean, Mulberry, 7 In. | 12.00 |
| Staffordshire, Plate, Corean, Mulberry, 9 3/4 In. | 25.00 |
| Staffordshire, Plate, DeWitt Clinton Eulogy, Erie Canal, Blue, 8 1/4 In. | 175.00 |
| Staffordshire, Plate, Dinner, Arms Of New York, Deep Blue, Mayer, 10 In. | 375.00 |
| Staffordshire, Plate, Dinner, Nonpareil, Light Blue, Meyer, C.1835 | 10.00 |
| Staffordshire, Plate, Dr.Syntax Star Gazing, Raised Border, 8 1/2 In. | 95.00 |
| Staffordshire, Plate, Dreghorn House, Scotland, Blue, 6 1/2 In. | 40.00 |
| Staffordshire, Plate, European Scenery, Blue & White, Wood, 10 In. | 15.00 |
| Staffordshire, Plate, Fairmount Near Philadelphia, Dark Blue, Stubbs, 10 In. | 150.00 |
| Staffordshire, Plate, Ferry Bridge Over Schuylkill, Blue, Stubbs, 8 3/4 In. | 125.00 |
| Staffordshire, Plate, Fisherman, Woman, Child, & Dog, Blue & White, 10 In. | 70.00 |
| Staffordshire, Plate, Florentine, Blue, Mayer, 9 In. | 12.00 |

Staffordshire, Plate, Franklin's Kite, Blue & White, 2 1/2 In. ..................................... 30.00
Staffordshire, Plate, Franklin's Proverb, Embossed Wheat & Flowers, 8 In. .................... 25.00
Staffordshire, Plate, George & Martha Washington, Blue & White, 10 In. ...................... 25.00
Staffordshire, Plate, Giraffe, Light Blue, 6 In. .................................................... 35.00
Staffordshire, Plate, Girard College, Phila., Blue, Minton, 10 In.Diameter .................... 22.00
Staffordshire, Plate, Guy's Cliff, Warwickshire, Blue, 10 In. ..................... 30.00 To 48.00
Staffordshire, Plate, Hartford, Conn., Deep Pink, Jackson, 10 1/2 In. .......................... 78.00
Staffordshire, Plate, Hartford, Conn., Sepia, Jackson, 10 1/4 In. ............................... 68.00
Staffordshire, Plate, Hoboken, N.J., Dark Blue, Stubbs, 7 In. ................................... 125.00
Staffordshire, Plate, Hollywell Cottage, Blue & White, Riley, C.1800, 10 In. ................ 50.00
Staffordshire, Plate, Hospital Near Poissy, Dark Blue, 6 1/2 In. ................................. 47.00
Staffordshire, Plate, Hudson River, Baker's Falls, Purple, 9 In. ................................ 45.00
Staffordshire, Plate, Hunters & Fox, Blue, Birds & Floral Rim, 9 In. .......................... 50.00
Staffordshire, Plate, Imari Pattern, Urn & Oriental Flowers, C.1850, 10 In. ................. 29.50
Staffordshire, Plate, Iris, 8 In. ..................................................................... 12.00
Staffordshire, Plate, Italian Scenery Near Florence, Dark Blue, 8 1/2 In. ..................... 48.00
Staffordshire, Plate, Italian Scenery, Dark Blue, Enoch Wood, 10 In. ......................... 55.00
Staffordshire, Plate, Italian Villa On Coast, Deep Blue, 10 1/2 In. ............................ 25.00
Staffordshire, Plate, Ivanhoe, Blue & White, C.W.& Co., 9 3/4 In. ............................ 10.00
Staffordshire, Plate, Jackson, Hero Of New Orleans, Mulberry, 1828, 8 1/2 In. .............. 225.00
Staffordshire, Plate, Jeddo, Mulberry, Adams, C.1845, 8 1/2 In. .............................. 20.00
Staffordshire, Plate, Jenny Lind, 1795, Pink & White, 8 3/4 In .................................. 25.00
Staffordshire, Plate, Joseph Rayner Stephens, Blue Transfer, 9 1/4 In. ....................... 34.00
Staffordshire, Plate, King's Cottage, Windsor Park, Dark Blue, Riley, 7 In. ................. 22.00
Staffordshire, Plate, King's Weston, Gloucestershire, Riley, Blue, 8 3/4 In. .................. 45.00
Staffordshire, Plate, Lake Como, Italian Buildings, Blue, 10 In. ............................... 12.00
Staffordshire, Plate, Landing Of Lafayette, Blue, Clews, 9 In.Diameter ...................... 175.00
Staffordshire, Plate, Landing Of Lafayette, Dark Blue, Clews, 6 3/4 In. ...................... 125.00
Staffordshire, Plate, Landing Of Pilgrim Fathers, Light Blue, 6 In. ........................... 75.00
Staffordshire, Plate, Landing Of Pilgrim Fathers, Medium Blue, 10 In. ....................... 85.00
Staffordshire, Plate, Leopard, Dark Blue, 7 1/2 In. ............................................. 50.00
Staffordshire, Plate, Lincoln Commemorative, 1959, Blue, 10 In. ............................. 7.50
Staffordshire, Plate, Longfellow House, Blue, 10 In. ........................................... 14.00
Staffordshire, Plate, Loretta, Mulberry, Samuel Alcock, C.1840, 9 1/2 In. ................... 25.00
Staffordshire, Plate, Lovejoy, Constitution Of U.S., Blue, 7 3/4 In. .......................... 165.00
Staffordshire, Plate, Madram, Purple, Wood & Brownfield, 8 In., Pair ....................... 18.00
Staffordshire, Plate, Millennium, Sepia, 6 1/2 In. .............................................. 25.00
Staffordshire, Plate, Millennium, Sepia, 10 1/2 In. ................................ 42.00 To 50.00
Staffordshire, Plate, Montmorency, Near Quebec, Dark Blue, Wood & Son, 9 In. ............. 150.00
Staffordshire, Plate, Mount Parnell, Medium Blue, 8 1/4 In. .................................. 15.00
Staffordshire, Plate, Mue D'une Ancienne Abbaye, Dark Blue, C.1810, 9 In. ................. 60.00
Staffordshire, Plate, Napoleon, Blue & White, 9 1/2 In. ....................................... 15.00
Staffordshire, Plate, Near Conway, N.H., Pink, Adams, 9 In. .................................. 55.00
Staffordshire, Plate, Niagara Falls, 10 In. ...................................................... 16.00
Staffordshire, Plate, Nonpareil, Purple, 9 3/8 In ............................................... 18.00
Staffordshire, Plate, Old South Church, Boston, Blue & White, 10 In. ........................ 25.00
Staffordshire, Plate, Olympia, Medium Blue, P.W.& Co., 9 In. ................................. 48.00
Staffordshire, Plate, Oriental Scene, Dark Blue, Marked F & 8, 8 3/4 In. .................... 25.00
Staffordshire, Plate, Park Theatre, N.Y., Blue, Stevenson, 10 In. .................. 150.00 To 175.00
Staffordshire, Plate, Pelew, Mulberry, E.Challinor, 7 1/2 In. .................................. 16.50
Staffordshire, Plate, Peru, Mulberry, Hodgcroft & Co., 8 1/4 In. ............................. 15.00
Staffordshire, Plate, Peruvian, Mulberry, 6 In. ................................................. 10.00
Staffordshire, Plate, Race St.Bridge, Phila., Pink, Jackson, 9 1/4 In. ........................ 55.00
Staffordshire, Plate, Railroad Scenes, C.1840, 6 1/2 In. ....................................... 60.00
Staffordshire, Plate, Rhone Scenery, Mulberry, Ironstone, Coburgh, 10 1/2 In. .............. 16.50
Staffordshire, Plate, Salem Reformed Church, Allentown, Pa., Blue, 8 3/4 In. ............... 18.00
Staffordshire, Plate, Seattle, Washington, Deep Blue, C.1900, 10 In. ........................ 25.00
Staffordshire, Plate, Sebastian Gate, Appian Way, Dark Blue, C.1820, 10 In. ............... 35.00
Staffordshire, Plate, Shakespeare Scenes, Deep Blue, Rolled Edge, 10 In. .................... 22.00
Staffordshire, Plate, Shannon, Blue, Floral & Seashell Border, Rogers, 10 In. ............... 10.00
Staffordshire, Plate, Shaw's Peruvian Horse Hunt, Blue & White, 8 1/2 In. .................. 20.00
Staffordshire, Plate, Solar Rays, Brown & White, T.Green, 8 In. .............................. 12.00
Staffordshire, Plate, Soup, Canova, Brown & White, 10 1/2 In. ............................... 12.00
Staffordshire, Plate, Soup, Fairmount Near Philadelphia, Dark Blue, Stubbs .................. 145.00
Staffordshire, Plate, Soup, Hop Pickers, Dark Blue, 9 1/2 In. ................................. 58.00
Staffordshire, Plate, Soup, Hudson River, Fishkill, Brown, 10 1/2 In. ........................ 75.00

| | |
|---|---|
| Staffordshire, Plate, Soup, Klosterneuberg, Germany, Dark Blue, R.Hall's | 58.00 |
| Staffordshire, Plate, Soup, States, Dark Blue, 10 In. | 185.00 |
| Staffordshire, Plate, Soup, Yale, Light Blue, 9 1/2 In. | 30.00 |
| Staffordshire, Plate, Square, Patchwork Border, 8 3/4 In. | 12.50 |
| Staffordshire, Plate, States, Dark Blue, 10 1/2 In. | 240.00 |
| Staffordshire, Plate, Statue Of Liberty, N.Y.C., Blue, 10 In. | 14.00 |
| Staffordshire, Plate, Surrender Of Cornwallis To Washington, 6 1/4 In. | 15.00 |
| Staffordshire, Plate, Swiss Scenery, Sepia, 10 1/4 In. | 17.50 |
| Staffordshire, Plate, Swiss, Brown, R.Stevenson, C.1830, 7 1/4 In. | 24.00 |
| Staffordshire, Plate, Temple, Mulberry, Podmore, Walker, C.1850, 10 In. | 35.00 |
| Staffordshire, Plate, Texas Campaign, Pink, 10 1/2 In. | 95.00 |
| Staffordshire, Plate, Texas Campaign, Purple, 9 In. | 110.00 |
| Staffordshire, Plate, The Hospital Near Poissy, France, Blue, Hall, 6 1/2 In. | 48.00 |
| Staffordshire, Plate, The Lake, Regents' Park, Blue, Grape Border, Wood, 9 In. | 130.00 |
| Staffordshire, Plate, The Seed Is In The Ground, Mulberry, 7 1/4 In. | 18.00 |
| Staffordshire, Plate, Tivoli, Mulberry, 10 3/4 In. | 16.50 |
| Staffordshire, Plate, Toddy, Woman & Children Carrying Wheat, Mulberry, 1830 | 18.00 |
| Staffordshire, Plate, Tonquin, Brown, Scalloped, Edge & Malkin, 1883, 7 In. | 6.00 |
| Staffordshire, Plate, Union Line, Dark Blue, Shell Border, Wood, 9 In. | 210.00 |
| Staffordshire, Plate, Union Line, Dark Blue, Wood, 8 1/2 In. | 185.00 |
| Staffordshire, Plate, Venture, Mulberry, 7 1/2 In. | 15.00 |
| Staffordshire, Plate, Venus, Blue, Podmore, Walker, 10 In. | 20.00 |
| Staffordshire, Plate, Venus, Blue, Podmore, Walker, 7 1/2 In. | 15.00 |
| Staffordshire, Plate, Versailles, Furnival, 10 In. | 22.00 |
| Staffordshire, Plate, Vevay, Medium Blue, 6 3/4 In. | 550.00 |
| Staffordshire, Plate, View Of Hudson River, Blue & White, Clews, 9 In. | 75.00 |
| Staffordshire, Plate, View Of Lichfield Cathedral, Blue, Diorama, 8 1/2 In. | 30.00 |
| Staffordshire, Plate, View Of Trenton Falls, Wood, 7 1/2 In. | 175.00 |
| Staffordshire, Plate, Village Scene, Blue, Fruit & Flowers Rim, 7 1/2 In. | 35.00 |
| Staffordshire, Plate, Washington Vase, Mulberry, Podmore, Walker, 7 In. | 12.50 |
| Staffordshire, Plate, Washington Vase, Mulbery, Podmore & Walker, 8 In. | 15.00 |
| Staffordshire, Plate, Washington Vase, Mulberry, 10 In. | 14.00 |
| Staffordshire, Plate, West Point, N.Y., Black, 8 In. | 65.00 |
| Staffordshire, Plate, Whampoa, Mulberry, Mellor & Venables, C.1845, 6 1/2 In. | 15.00 |
| Staffordshire, Plate, Whampoa, Mulberry, Mellor & Venables, C.1845, 7 1/2 In. | 17.50 |
| Staffordshire, Plate, White Sulphur Springs, Ohio, Purple, Jackson, 8 In. | 250.00 |
| Staffordshire, Plate, Wm.Penn's Treaty, Red Transfer, T.Green, 9 1/4 In. | 48.00 |
| Staffordshire, Platter, American Eagle, C.1850             Illus | 450.00 |
| Staffordshire, Platter, American Marine, Brown, Ashworth, 11 X 8 1/2 In. | 75.00 |
| Staffordshire, Platter, Arms Of New Jersey, Blue, Mayer      Illus | 1500.00 |
| Staffordshire, Platter, Asiatic Pheasant, Light Blue, 11 1/4 X 13 1/2 In. | 20.00 |
| Staffordshire, Platter, Badminton, Gloucestershire, Dark Blue, Hall, 19 In. | 160.00 |
| Staffordshire, Platter, Bank Of England, Blue, Wood, 13 In. | 125.00 |
| Staffordshire, Platter, Belzoni, Carmine Transfer, C.1830, Enoch Wood & Sons | 30.00 |
| Staffordshire, Platter, Blue Transfer, Hare & Hall, Yorkshire, 14 1/4 In. | 60.00 |
| Staffordshire, Platter, Boston Mails, Saloon Scene, Blue, 14 X 18 In. | 135.00 |
| Staffordshire, Platter, Boston Mails, Saloon, Blue | 180.00 |
| Staffordshire, Platter, Boston State House, Blue, Stubbs      Illus | 350.00 |
| Staffordshire, Platter, British Views, Dark Blue, 14 3/4 X 11 3/4 In. | 128.00 |
| Staffordshire, Platter, Cape Coast Castle, Dark Blue, Wood, 16 1/2 In. | 525.00 |
| Staffordshire, Platter, Cheseapeake & Shannon Naval Battle, Blue, C.1815 | 350.00 |
| Staffordshire, Platter, Conway Castle, Hall, 15 1/2 In. | 180.00 |
| Staffordshire, Platter, Corean, Mulberry, 13 1/2 In. | 60.00 |
| Staffordshire, Platter, Corean, Mulberry, 15 3/4 X 12 In. | 48.00 |
| Staffordshire, Platter, Corean, Mulberry, 16 In. | 75.00 |
| Staffordshire, Platter, Deer Scene, Light Blue, Floral Border, 19 1/4 In. | 45.00 |
| Staffordshire, Platter, Foliage, Mulberry, 8 1/2 X 11 In. | 28.00 |
| Staffordshire, Platter, Fruit & Flower, Dark Blue, Stubb's, 16 1/4 In. | 95.00 |
| Staffordshire, Platter, Gaudy Type Design, Bunnies On Edge, Oval, 14 In. | 40.00 |
| Staffordshire, Platter, Gentleman & His Bull, Medium Blue, Oval, 22 In. | 200.00 |
| Staffordshire, Platter, Hackwood, Dark Blue, 4 1/2 In. | 35.00 |
| Staffordshire, Platter, Italian Villas, Dark Blue, Hall, 15 1/2 In. | 65.00 |
| Staffordshire, Platter, Kenilworth Castle, Pink, 12 In. | 8.00 |
| Staffordshire, Platter, La Grange, Home Of Marquis De Lafayette, Blue | 115.00 |
| Staffordshire, Platter, Lake George, Pink, Oval, 13 In. | 150.00 |
| Staffordshire, Platter, Landing Of Lafayette, Dark Blue, 9 1/2 In. | 285.00 |

Staffordshire, Platter, American Eagle, C.1850
(See Page 608)

Staffordshire, Pot, Bulb, C.1775, 8 In.High, Pair

Staffordshire, Platter, Arms Of New Jersey,
Blue, Mayer
(See Page 608)

Staffordshire, Platter, Boston State House,
Blue, Stubbs
(See Page 608)

| | |
|---|---:|
| Staffordshire, Platter, London Zoo, Pink, Clews, 15 1/2 In. | 78.00 |
| Staffordshire, Platter, Medium Blue, Impressed Bristol With Anchor, 12 In. | 168.00 |
| Staffordshire, Platter, Mendenhall Ferry, Blue, Eagle Border, Stubbs, 17 In. | 450.00 |
| Staffordshire, Platter, Mogul Scenery, Purple, T.Mayer, 12 In. | 43.00 |
| Staffordshire, Platter, Napoleon Reviewing Troops, Brown, 15 1/4 In.Long | 45.00 |
| Staffordshire, Platter, Napoleon, Blue, 12 1/4 X 15 1/2 In. | 40.00 |
| Staffordshire, Platter, Niagara Falls, Blue, Johnson Bros., 1888, 11 1/2 In. | 35.00 |
| Staffordshire, Platter, Pagoda Below Patna On Ganges, Blue, Hall, 14 1/2 In. | 65.00 |
| Staffordshire, Platter, Rhone Scenery, Mulberry, 12 X 16 In. | 45.00 |
| Staffordshire, Platter, Rome, Tiber, St.Peter's, Dark Blue, C.1815 | 58.00 |
| Staffordshire, Platter, Texas Campaign, Blue, 15 1/2 In. | 200.00 |
| Staffordshire, Platter, Texas Campaign, Brown, 18 In. | 365.00 |
| Staffordshire, Platter, Views Of Newburgh, Tan, 15 1/2 In. | 175.00 |
| Staffordshire, Platter, Washington Vase, Mulberry, Podmore & Walker, C.1845 | 75.00 |
| Staffordshire, Platter, Wilkie Series, The Valentine, 15 In. | 325.00 |
| Staffordshire, Pot, Bulb, C.1775, 8 In.High, Pair _Illus_ | 450.00 |
| Staffordshire, Saucer, Corean, Mulberry, P.W.& Co., C.1845 | 12.50 |
| Staffordshire, Saucer, Franklin's Tomb, Dark Blue, 6 In. | 75.00 |
| Staffordshire, Saucer, Pale Blue, Rust & Yellow Floral | 2.00 |
| Staffordshire, Spill, Figural, C.1850, 11 7/8 In. _Illus_ | 130.00 |
| Staffordshire, Stand, Watch, Figural, Females, Bird, 11 1/4 In.High | 70.00 |
| Staffordshire, Sugar, Corean, Mulberry, Podmore & Walker, C.1840 | 65.00 |
| Staffordshire, Sugar, Covered, Abbey Ruins, Pink, Mayer Longport | 25.00 |
| Staffordshire, Sugar, Creamer, & Bowl, Washington, Blue _Illus_ | 225.00 |
| Staffordshire, Sugar, Schuylkill Waterworks, Black | 70.00 |
| Staffordshire, Tankard, Milk, White Classical Figures On Green, Dudson, 1888 | 35.00 |
| Staffordshire, Tea Set, Child's, Castles, Lake, Mountains, 9 Piece | 45.00 |

Staffordshire, Sugar, Creamer, & Bowl, Washington, Blue
*(See Page 609)*

Staffordshire, Spill, Figural, C.1850, 11 7/8 In.
*(See Page 609)*

Staffordshire, Teapot, Pearlware,          Staffordshire, Teapot, Eagle On Shell,
Blue & White, C.1800                              Hall, C.1840

| | |
|---|---:|
| **Staffordshire, Teapot,** Black Basalt, Widow Knop, 5 1/8 In.High | 80.00 |
| **Staffordshire, Teapot,** Corean, Mulberry | 95.00 |
| **Staffordshire, Teapot,** Eagle On Shell, Hall, C.1840 .............................. *Illus* | 300.00 |
| **Staffordshire, Teapot,** Landing Of Lafayette, Dark Blue | 335.00 |
| **Staffordshire, Teapot,** Pearlware, Blue & White, C.1800 .......................... *Illus* | 110.00 |
| **Staffordshire, Toby Mug,** Blue Coat, Dotted Vest | 55.00 |
| **Staffordshire, Toby Mug,** Full Figure, Enoch Wood, Gold Anchor Mark | 95.00 |
| **Staffordshire, Toby Mug,** Guardsman, 4 1/2 In.High | 9.50 |
| **Staffordshire, Toby Mug,** Impressed J.Bull On Base, 5 In.High | 65.00 |
| **Staffordshire, Toby Mug,** Man In Tricorner Hat, Snuffbox In 1 Hand | 125.00 |
| **Staffordshire, Toby Mug,** Night Watchman, C.1825 .................................. *Illus* | 125.00 |
| **Staffordshire, Toby Mug,** Old King Cole, Full Figure, 5 1/2 In. | 30.00 |
| **Staffordshire, Toby Mug,** Parson, C.1825, 8 1/4 In. ................................. *Illus* | 400.00 |
| **Staffordshire, Toby Mug,** Sitting On Green Mound, Black Coat, Pink Vest | 75.00 |
| **Staffordshire, Toby Mug,** 4 1/2 In.High | 45.00 |
| **Staffordshire, Tray,** McDonough's Victory, Embossed Rim, Round, 7 In. | 475.00 |
| **Staffordshire, Tray,** Mt.Ida, Purple, Clews, 10 1/4 In. | 75.00 |
| **Staffordshire, Tray,** Sauce Tureen, Upper Ferry Bridge Over Schuylkill | 125.00 |
| **Staffordshire, Tureen & Stand,** Covered, Blue & White, Shepherd Scene, C.1840 | 285.00 |
| **Staffordshire, Tureen,** Lion's Head Handles & Knob, Blue & White, C.1850 | 185.00 |
| **Staffordshire, Tureen,** Sauce, Covered, English Rural Scenes, Sepia, C.1835 | 39.00 |
| **Staffordshire, Tureen,** Vegetable, Covered, Pavilion, Green, Godwin, C.1850 | 45.00 |
| **Staffordshire, Vase,** Fan, Hunter & Dog Base, Feathers Form Body, 5 1/4 In. | 35.00 |
| **Staffordshire, Vase,** Flare, Blue & Burnished Gold, 10 In.High | 125.00 |
| **Staffordshire, Vase,** Geometrics On Gray, Blue, & Brown Glaze, 10 In.High | 150.00 |
| **Staffordshire, Vase,** Mantel, Applied Flowers, Cobalt & White, Gilt, Pair | 32.00 |
| **Staffordshire, Vase,** Orange Cows With Calves, 10 In.High, Pair | 75.00 |
| **Staffordshire, Vase,** Spill, Flight Into Egypt, 9 1/4 In.High | 80.00 |

| | |
|---|---|
| Staffordshire, Vase, White Dog On Green Base, Orange Lining, Pair | 85.00 |
| Staffordshire, Washstand Set, Child's, Pink Roses On Cream, Gold, 2 Piece | 25.00 |
| Staffordshire, Washstand Set, Floral, Miniature, 2 Piece | 22.50 |
| Staffordshire, Washstand Set, Lafayette, Franklin's Tomb, Blue, Wood, 2 Piece | 475.00 |

> *Stangl pottery was organized in 1929, succeeding the*
> *Fulper Pottery Company. Stangl porcelain birds are popular*
> *collectibles.*

| | |
|---|---|
| Stangl, Bird, American Passenger Pigeon, 14 In. | 75.00 |
| Stangl, Bird, Baltimore Oriole, 3 1/4 In. | 22.00 |
| Stangl, Bird, Black, Yellow, & Red Bird On Stump, No.3402 | 18.00 |
| Stangl, Bird, Blue & Brown, On Branch With Red Flowers | 26.00 |
| Stangl, Bird, Blue & White, Artist Signed, 5 3/4 In. | 35.00 |
| Stangl, Bird, Bluebird On Branch, Signed H.G.F., 8 In. High | 65.00 |
| Stangl, Bird, Bluebird On Leaf & Berry Base, 4 1/2 In.Long | 35.00 |
| Stangl, Bird, Bluebird On Leaves, No.3456, 4 In. | 18.00 |
| Stangl, Bird, Bluebird, On Stump, Spread Wings, Signed, 10 In.High | 85.00 |
| Stangl, Bird, Bluebird, Standing, No.3589, 3 1/4 In. | 18.00 |
| Stangl, Bird, Bluejay On Stump, No.3276, 5 In. | 22.00 |
| Stangl, Bird, Brown Wren On Stump, No.3401, 5 In. | 20.00 |
| Stangl, Bird, Cardinal, Pink & Gray, 5 In. | 20.00 |
| Stangl, Bird, Cockatoo, 12 In.High | 125.00 |
| Stangl, Bird, Double Cockatoo, No.3405d, 10 In. | 45.00 |
| Stangl, Bird, Double Hummingbirds On Leaves, No.3599, 9 In.High | 75.00 |
| Stangl, Bird, Goldfinch Group On Branch, No.3635, 12 In.Long | 60.00 |
| Stangl, Bird, Green Double Parakeets, No.3582, 7 In. | 50.00 |
| Stangl, Bird, Hen, No.3446, 7 1/2 In.High | 30.00 |
| Stangl, Bird, House Wren, 4 1/2 In. | 33.50 |
| Stangl, Bird, Hummingbird, No.3634, Artist MRF | 28.00 |
| Stangl, Bird, Hummingbirds, Double, On Leaves, 9 In.High, 10 In.Long | 75.00 |
| Stangl, Bird, Kingfisher, 3 1/2 In. | 20.00 To 35.00 |
| Stangl, Bird, Multicolored Warbler, No.3593, 3 In. | 15.00 |
| Stangl, Bird, Parakeet, Green, 2 On Pedestal, 6 X 7 1/2 In. | 60.00 |
| Stangl, Bird, Parrot, 4 1/2 In.High | 22.00 |
| Stangl, Bird, Parrot, 5 In.High | 35.00 |
| Stangl, Bird, Parrot, 12 In. High | 125.00 |
| Stangl, Bird, Pheasant, No.3442, 6 In.High | 45.00 |
| Stangl, Bird, Rufus Hummingbird, 3 1/2 In. | 26.50 |
| Stangl, Bird, Two Brown Wrens On Stump, No.3401, 6 In. | 35.00 |
| Stangl, Bird, Wren, Double, Marked 3401D, Artist Signed | 40.00 |
| Stangl, Bird, Yellow & Black, No.3597, 4 In. | 25.00 |
| Stangl, Bird, Yellow Bird, Mouth Open, No.3598, 3 1/2 In. | 22.00 |
| Stangl, Bird, Yellow Bird, No.3597, 3 In. | 18.00 |
| Stangl, Bird, Yellow Head, Black Body, 5 1/2 In.Long | 26.00 |
| Stangl, Bird, Yellow, Green Wings, 3 1/2 In. | 20.00 |
| Stangl, Bird, Yellow, 3 In. | 18.00 |
| Stangl, Candlestick, Green, 3 1/2 In.High, Pair | 10.00 |
| Stangl, Plate, Cowboy With Cactus, Signed | 18.00 |
| Stangl, Plate, Terra-Cotta, Decorated, Signed G.D., 4 1/2 In. | 10.00 |

Staffordshire, Toby Mug,
Parson, C.1825, 8 1/4 In.
*(See Page 610)*

Staffordshire, Toby Mug,
Night Watchman, C.1825
*(See Page 610)*

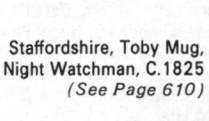

Stangl, Teapot, Tulip Design ................................................................................................ 15.00

*Steins have been used for over 500 years. They have been made of ivory, porcelain, stoneware, faience, silver, pewter, wood, or glass in sizes up to nine gallons. Although some were made by Meissen, Capo-Di-Monte, and other famous factories, most were made in Germany.*

Stein, Acorn On Handle, Pewter Lid, Liter ........................................................................... 22.50
Stein, Amber Glass, Blown, Enameled Munich Maid & German Saying, Pewter Lid ...................... 50.00
Stein, American Monk, Columbian Art Pottery, N.J., C.1880, Reading .................................... 55.00
Stein, Art Nouveau Style Lady, O'Hara Dial Co., Mass., Pewter Lid, Paris ............................. 50.00
Stein, B.T.H. Over M-Mgesceesch, Gray, Pewter Cover, 1/2 Liter ........................................ 35.00
Stein, Bowling Pin Shape, Brown Stripes & Boy On Brown, Pewter Handle ........................... 195.00
Stein, Castle Scene On Pewter Top, Child With Bible, Marked V, 4 Liter ............................. 388.00
Stein, Coblenz Rheinland, Etched, Liter .......................................................................... 135.00
Stein, Cranberry Over Clear Over White, Cut Crisscross, Pewter Lid .................................... 195.00
Stein, Elks, B.P.O., German Pottery, Man In Woods & Elk, 8 1/2 In.High ............................. 50.00
Stein, German, Crystal, Etched, Pedestal Base, Pewter Lid & Thumb Lift .............................. 37.50
Stein, German, Etched, Pewter Barmaid Lid & Thumbrest, HR Mark, 1/2 Liter ...................... 125.00
Stein, German, Man Blowing Horn, Horse, Castle, Hinged Pewter Lid ................................... 50.00
Stein, German, Naval, 1/2 Liter ...................................................................................... 47.50
Stein, German, Verse & Florals, Blue On Gray, Pewter Steeple Lid, Liter ............................. 75.00
Stein, Germany, Elk's Building, Portland Oregon, 1912, Pewter Thumb Lift .......................... 45.00
Stein, Gesetzlicht, No.1908, 1/2 Liter ............................................................................ 60.00
Stein, Glass, Floral Porcelain Insert In Lid, 1/2 Liter ........................................................ 60.00
Stein, Glass, Sapphire Blue, Pewter Lid, Glass Insert, 3 X 6 In. ........................................ 28.00
Stein, Glass, Thumbprint, Porcelain Top, Pewter Spread Eagle On Handle ............................ 85.00
Stein, Jokester Pouring Beer In Tuba, Pewter Lid, German, 1/2 Liter .................................. 28.00
Stein, Lithophane, Duck Hunt, Flower Decoration .............................................................. 95.00
Stein, Lithophane, Munich Maid, Martin Pauson, 1/2 Liter ................................................ 300.00
Stein, Lithophane, Porcelain, Country Estate Scene, 1/2 Liter ........................................... 60.00
Stein, Lithophane, Porcelain, Flowers & Writing On Side, 1/2 Liter ..................................... 60.00
Stein, Lithophane, Porcelain, Footed, "Gruls Nus Dingolfing, " 1/2 Liter ............................. 65.00
Stein, Lithophane, Porcelain, German City Scene, 1/2 Liter ............................................... 65.00
Stein, Lithophane, Porcelain, Old Man & Coat Of Arms, 1/2 Liter ...................................... 65.00
Stein, Lithophane, Successful Duck Hunt ......................................................................... 98.50
Stein, Man & Woman Drinking & Hugging, German Inscription, 1 Liter .................................. 69.00
Stein, Merkelbach Star Red Mark, White Building On Blue Oval, 1/2 Liter ............................ 50.00
    Stein, Mettlach, see Mettlach, Stein
Stein, Military, Nude Lithophane, Warrior Lid, Marked Crown Over HR ................................. 39.00
Stein, Monk, "Gaus Aus Munchen, " Pewter Top, 4 In.High ............................................... 25.00
Stein, Monk, Lithophane Bottom ................................................................................... 175.00
Stein, Munchen, Stoneware, Pewter Lid, C.1890, 3 Liter ................................................. 155.00
Stein, Munich Maid, 1/4 Liter ........................................................................................ 48.00
Stein, Musterschutz 148, Porcelain Insert In Pewter Lid, 1/2 Liter ...................................... 55.00
Stein, Musterschutz, Law, Bicycle, Lithophane ................................................................ 275.00
Stein, Musterschutz, Monkey Sleeping Holding A Stein, 1/2 Liter ....................................... 350.00
Stein, Musterschutz, Sad Turnip .................................................................................... 165.00
Stein, Musterschutz, Singing Pig, 1/2 Liter ..................................................................... 275.00
Stein, Musterschutz, Smiling Pig .................................................................................... 265.00
Stein, No.1613, Signed Gest GF Schutzt, 1/2 Liter .......................................................... 150.00
Stein, North German Lloyd Cruises Of Distinction, Pewter Lid & Thumb Rest ....................... 25.00
Stein, Pattern Glass, Pewter Top, 1/2 Liter ..................................................................... 35.00
Stein, Porcelain, Falstaff Portrait, Gold Lizard Handle, Hohenzollern, Pint ........................... 77.50
Stein, Porcelain, Silver & Green Decoration, 7 In.High ..................................................... 18.00
Stein, Pottery, Etched Boy & 2 Girls, Pewter Lid, 1/2 Liter .............................................. 115.00
Stein, Pottery, Germany, Applied Decoration, Pewter Lid, C.1895, 2 Liter .......................... 125.00
Stein, Pottery, Germany, Applied Knights, Pewter Lid, C.1895, 4 1/2 Liter ......................... 200.00
Stein, R.H. Germany, No.1191, Hand-Painted, 19 In.High ................................................. 219.00
Stein, Raised Cream Figure On Green, Pewter Top, 'Ger No.936, 15 In.High ....................... 65.00
Stein, Regimental, Guard, 1/2 Liter ............................................................................... 135.00
Stein, Regimental, Nude Lithophane Lady Bottom, Dated 1906-1909 .................................. 125.00
Stein, Regimental, Soldier On Horse, Lithophane Nude, Pewter Lid, K * R ............................ 75.00
Stein, Reinman, Munich Maid, Twin Tower Thumb Rest, 1/2 Liter ..................................... 100.00
Stein, Simon Gertz, No.1237B, 1/4 Liter, Etched Robin Hood & Lady ................................. 135.00
Stein, Simon Gertz, No.1386, Liter, Etched King Arthur & Hunter At Table .......................... 175.00
Stein, Squatty, Blue & White, 1/20 Liter ........................................................................ 22.50
Stein, Stag On Gray, Boy & Girl On Pewter Lid, Stag's Head Lift, Liter ................................. 85.00

| | |
|---|---|
| Stein, Stoneware, Blue & Gray, Raised Venus, Minerva, & Justice, C.1900 | 175.00 |
| Stein, Stoneware, Gray, Pewter Top, German, 5 1/4 In. | 35.00 |
| Stein, Stoneware, Marked No.685, Inlaid Lid, Cut Decoration, C.1890, 3 Liter | 175.00 |
| Stein, Verdi Commemorative, German, 1/2 Liter | 125.00 |
| Stein, Wanamaker Store, New York, Dark Blue Ground, 1/3 Liter | 6.75 |

*Stereo cards that were made for stereopticon viewers became popular after
1840. Two almost identical pictures were mounted on a stiff cardboard backing
so that, when viewed through a stereoscope, a three-dimensional picture could be
seen.*

| | |
|---|---|
| Stereo, Card, A Trip Through Sears, Roebuck & Co., 50 In Original Box | 15.00 |
| Stereo, Card, Anatomy, University Of Edinburgh, Imperial Co., N.Y., 324 | 300.00 |
| Stereo, Card, Blackfoot Squaw & Papoose At Home, Color | 3.00 |
| Stereo, Card, Brownville, Colorado, 1870s, New Hampshire Photographer | 14.50 |
| Stereo, Card, Chief Black Hawk With Squaw & Papoose, Color | 3.00 |
| Stereo, Card, Coal Mining In Pennsylvania, Copyright 1902 & 1905, 15 | 7.50 |
| Stereo, Card, India, Keystone, Series 1, 100 In Book Holder | 50.00 |
| Stereo, Card, Iron & Steel Industry In Pittsburgh, Copyright 1905, 19 | 9.50 |
| Stereo, Card, Keystone, Tour Of The World, 1952, 1, 200 | 500.00 |
| Stereo, Card, Lincoln Memorial, E.& H.T.Anthony | 5.00 |
| Stereo, Card, President Roosevelt Addressing Senators, Color | 5.00 |
| Stereo, Card, Silk Industry In South Manchester, Conn., Copyright 1914, 23 | 11.50 |
| Stereo, Card, Yellowstone National Park, Dated 1930, 25 | 6.25 |
| Stereo, View, Anthony, Glories Of The Yosemite, Mammoth Trees, 12 | 15.00 |
| Stereo, View, Arizona, Utah, Idaho, & Yellowstone, Savage, 4 | 8.00 |
| Stereo, View, Automobile & Hunter, 1905 | 5.00 |
| Stereo, View, Balloon Ascension, Oct.4, 1863, Yellow Mount | 10.00 |
| Stereo, View, Baltimore & Ohio Railroad, Chase, Yellow Mounts, 2 | 6.00 |
| Stereo, View, Belgium Views, C.1870, 29 | 15.00 |
| Stereo, View, Binghampton, George N.Cobb, 11 | 20.00 |
| Stereo, View, Bridge Over Mississippi At St.Paul, Carbutt | 5.00 |
| Stereo, View, Bronze Door, Senate Chamber, & House Chamber, Jarvis, 3 | 6.00 |
| Stereo, View, Buckingham Palace, Ferrier & Soulier, Glass, C.1860, 3 | 25.00 |
| Stereo, View, Buildings Of 1870s, Bell, 7 | 10.00 |
| Stereo, View, California Views, Orange Mounts, Dodge, Collier, & Perkins, 4 | 6.00 |
| Stereo, View, Cayuga Lake, Gates, Orange Mounts, 4 | 5.00 |
| Stereo, View, Centennial, 1876, Nos.1152, 698, 1267, 1122, 1458, & 1735, 6 | 17.00 |
| Stereo, View, Central Park, Moulton, Orange Mounts, 5 | 7.00 |
| Stereo, View, Charlestown, S.C., G.N.Barnard, 3 | 7.00 |
| Stereo, View, Chester Illustrated, Bedford, 1860, Yellow Mounts, 12 | 15.00 |
| Stereo, View, Chicago Fire, 1871, Lovejoy & Foster | 5.00 |
| Stereo, View, Chippewa Indians, A.W., Labeled American Scenery | 10.00 |
| Stereo, View, Clifton & Pacolet Disasters, June 6, 1903, Shuford, I | 6.00 |
| Stereo, View, Colorado Mountain Scenery, Chamberlain, 5 | 8.00 |
| Stereo, View, Dalles Of The St.Louis River & White Bear Lake, 3 | 8.00 |
| Stereo, View, Denver & Rio Grande Railroad, Nos.9155, 3150, & 3155, 3 | 12.00 |
| Stereo, View, Denver South Park & Pacific & Union Pacific Railroad, 3 | 10.00 |
| Stereo, View, Egypt, Street Scenes, 7 | 5.00 |
| Stereo, View, European Cities, Kilburn, C.1870, 6 | 6.00 |
| Stereo, View, European Cities, Sommer, C.1870, 21 | 10.00 |
| Stereo, View, Flowers, R.Y.Young, American Stereo Co., Copyright 1901, 2 | 5.00 |
| Stereo, View, Fortifications Of Quebec, Kilburn & Parks, 4 | 10.00 |
| Stereo, View, Frost Work On Mt.Washington, Bierstadt, Glass | 15.00 |
| Stereo, View, Ft.George Island, Florida, Orange Mounts, 2 | 4.00 |
| Stereo, View, Ft.Snelling & Minnehaha Falls, Illingworth & Tenney, 4 | 6.00 |
| Stereo, View, Grand Canon Of Arkansas & Manitou Series, Jackson, 4 | 13.00 |
| Stereo, View, Hayes & Wheeler Political Campaign, I.L.Rogers, 1877 | 5.00 |
| Stereo, View, Horse-Drawn Van, Three Men, & Dog, Tinted | 5.00 |
| Stereo, View, Illustrating Poem Vision Of Sir Launfal, Kilburn, 1874, 14 | 15.00 |
| Stereo, View, Indian Pueblo Of Taos, Bennett & Brown, No.78 | 13.00 |
| Stereo, View, Indian Pueblo Of Taos, Bennett & Brown, No.79 | 15.00 |
| Stereo, View, Italian Scenes, Brogi, Orange Mounts, 50 | 25.00 |
| Stereo, View, Italian Scenes, Yellow Mounts, 85 | 43.00 |
| Stereo, View, Italy, Street Scenes, Glass, 7 | 50.00 |
| Stereo, View, Keystone Cowboys, Nos.4, 10, 11, 12, 17, & 19, 6 | 10.00 |
| Stereo, View, Lake City, Colorado, Barnhouse & Wheeler, 8 | 25.00 |
| Stereo, View, Lake Superior Scenery, No.103, B.F.Childs | 8.00 |

| | |
|---|---|
| Stereo, View, Lake Tahoe, Watkins, 3 | 9.00 |
| Stereo, View, Lancaster, Waite, 12 | 14.00 |
| Stereo, View, Lincoln Memorial | 7.00 |
| Stereo, View, London Scenes, Blanchard, 1860, Yellow Mounts, 8 | 10.00 |
| Stereo, View, London Scenes, York, 1860, Yellow Mounts, 4 | 4.00 |
| Stereo, View, Lookout Mountain, Tennessee, Linn, 4 | 10.00 |
| Stereo, View, Manitou & Pike's Peak Series, Nos.307 & 368, 2 | 8.00 |
| Stereo, View, Mexico, Kilburn Bros., 1873, 5 | 6.00 |
| Stereo, View, Milan, Brogi, 32 | 16.00 |
| Stereo, View, Mill River Flood, 1874, Rollock, Alden, & Knowlton, 15 | 35.00 |
| Stereo, View, Monceniso Scenes, Brogi, 12 | 6.00 |
| Stereo, View, Mt.Washington Railroad, Kilburn, Nos.537 & 538, 2 | 5.00 |
| Stereo, View, Nantucket Whaling, J.Freeman, Tinted | 15.00 |
| Stereo, View, Nantucket, Freeman, 3 | 4.00 |
| Stereo, View, Naples, Brogi, 17 | 9.00 |
| Stereo, View, Negro Life, Kellogg, Campbell, Blessing, Ryan, & Wilson, 9 | 25.00 |
| Stereo, View, New England Lighthouses, G.W.Tirrell, 3 | 6.00 |
| Stereo, View, New York City, Horse-Drawn Street Car, Sepia | 5.00 |
| Stereo, View, Northern Pacific Series, Portland, Oregon, 6 | 15.00 |
| Stereo, View, Paris Scenes, Yellow Mounts, C.1860, 10 | 10.00 |
| Stereo, View, Paris Views, C.1878, 27 | 14.00 |
| Stereo, View, Pennsylvania Central Railroad, Purviance, Yellow Mounts, 10 | 20.00 |
| Stereo, View, Philadelphia, James Cremer, 10 | 20.00 |
| Stereo, View, Pisa, Brogi, 13 | 7.00 |
| Stereo, View, Plum Pudding Rock, Sherman & Rock Cut, Aspen, Savage, 2 | 10.00 |
| Stereo, View, Portugal, Interior & Exterior Views, Glass, 3 | 20.00 |
| Stereo, View, Pueblo Indian Girl Sweeping, Bennett & Brown, No.125 | 15.00 |
| Stereo, View, Pueblo Indian Girl, Bennett & Brown, No.126 | 15.00 |
| Stereo, View, Railroad, Houseworth, Anthony, & Kilburn, 10 | 15.00 |
| Stereo, View, Rochester, Walker, 3 | 5.00 |
| Stereo, View, Rocky Mountains, Clear Creek Series, Collier, Dated 1873, 7 | 16.00 |
| Stereo, View, Rocky Mountains, Gurnsey, Dated 1874, 2 | 5.00 |
| Stereo, View, Rocky Mountains, Snake River Series, Collier, Dated 1873, 11 | 25.00 |
| Stereo, View, Rome Views, Felici, 37 | 19.00 |
| Stereo, View, Rome Views, Felici, 40 | 20.00 |
| Stereo, View, Savannah Georgia Scenes, J.N.Wilson, 6 | 15.00 |
| Stereo, View, Spain, Interiors, Glass, 3 | 25.00 |
| Stereo, View, Spanish-American War, 18 | 35.00 |
| Stereo, View, Statues & Works Of Art, Felici, 35 | 18.00 |
| Stereo, View, Suspension Bridge Over Niagara River, Glass | 22.00 |
| Stereo, View, Switzerland, Alpine Club, William, England, Yellow Mount, 1860, 8 | 15.00 |
| Stereo, View, The Moon, Draper, Rutherford, & Bates, 3 | 8.00 |
| Stereo, View, Tour Of Sears, Roebuck & Co., 1905, Black & White, 49 | 20.00 |
| Stereo, View, Trenton Falls, John Moore, 10 | 10.00 |
| Stereo, View, Union Pacific Railroad Series, No.94, Yellow Mount | 5.00 |
| Stereo, View, Venice, Marco, Orange Mounts, 22 | 11.00 |
| Stereo, View, Versailles, Ferrier & Soulier, Glass, C.1860, 8 | 75.00 |
| Stereo, View, Washington, D.C., Bell, Anthony, & Jarvis, 13 | 20.00 |
| Stereo, View, West Point Series, Orange Mounts, 4 | 6.00 |
| Stereo, View, Westminster Abbey, Interior & Exterior, Blanchard, 3 | 5.00 |
| Stereo, View, White Mountain Scenery, Soule, Ivory Mounts, 5 | 13.00 |
| Stereo, View, Worcester, Mechanics Hall, Depot, 2 | 3.00 |
| Stereo, View, World War I, Uncle Sam's Big Fight, Lithographed, 25 | 10.00 |
| Stereo, View, World's Fair, 1893, Kilburn, Nos.7892, 8397, 8398, & 8110, 4 | 10.00 |
| Stereo, View, World's Peace Jubilee, Boston, 1872, 2 | 4.00 |
| Stereo, View, Yellowstone, Haynes, Orange & Yellow Mounts, 4 | 12.00 |
| Stereo, View, Yellowstone, Marshal, Copyright 1876, 33 | 45.00 |
| Stereo, View, Yellowstone, Marshal, Orange & Yellow Mounts, Dated 1876, 4 | 20.00 |
| Stereo, View, Yosemite, Anthony, Yellow Mounts, 3 | 9.00 |
| Stereo, View, Yosemite, Bierstadt, Orange Mounts, 6 | 15.00 |
| Stereo, View, Yosemite, C.L.Pond, Orange Mounts, 4 | 10.00 |
| Stereo, View, Yosemite, Nos.948, 952, 953, & 954, Kilburn Bros., C.1870, 4 | 7.00 |
| Stereo, View, Yosemite, Thomas Houseworth, Orange Mounts, 2 | 6.00 |
| Stereo, Viewer, A.L.Hudson, Hand Held, Wooden Handle, Cardboard Eye Hood | 25.00 |
| Stereo, Viewer, Holmes, Wooden Pedestal, Veneered Eye Hood, C.1870 | 18.00 |
| Stereo, Viewer, Stori-Viewer, Churchcraft, 20 Howdy Doody Slides, 1953 | 5.00 |

| | |
|---|---:|
| **Stereo, Viewer,** Veneered Eye Hood, Patent Dates 1863 & 1878 | 20.00 |
| **Stereo, Views,** Canadian, Parks, Vallee, & Schleyer, C.1860, 14 | 20.00 |

*Stereoscopes, or stereopticons, were used for viewing the stereo cards. The hand viewer was invented by Oliver Wendell Holmes, although more complicated table models were used before his was placed in production in 1859.*

| | |
|---|---:|
| **Stereoscope, Brass Front,** 75 German Scenes, C.1900 | 100.00 |
| **Stereoscope, Folding Type** | 17.50 |
| **Stereoscope, French,** Hardboard, 24 Glass Slides | 25.00 |
| **Stereoscope, Germany,** Brass Trim, 25 Cards | 10.00 |
| **Stereoscope, Hand Type Viewer,** Sliding Adjustment | 12.75 |
| **Stereoscope, Keystone,** Case With 35 Cards | 60.00 |
| **Stereoscope, Mahogany & White Metal,** Sun Sculpture Trademark, 44 Cards | 50.00 |
| **Stereoscope, Perfescope,** 1900 Exhibition, 15 Cards | 20.00 |
| **Stereoscope, Tiger Maple Finish,** Set Of Cards, Lined Box | 35.00 |
| **Stereoscope, Wooden,** 16 Cards | 24.00 |

**Sterling Silver, see Silver, Sterling**

*Steuben glass was made at the Steuben Glass Works of Corning, New York. The factory, founded by Frederick Carder and T.C.Hawkes, Sr., was purchased by the Corning Glass Company. They continued to make glass called Steuben. Many types of art glass were made at Steuben. The firm is still producing glass of exceptional quality.*

**Steuben, see also Aurene**

| | |
|---|---:|
| **Steuben, Atomizer,** Aurene, Blue, 6 In.High | 135.00 |
| **Steuben, Atomizer,** Perfume, Aurene, Blue, Gold Metal Fittings, Cloth Bag | 195.00 |
| **Steuben, Bottle,** Aurene, Melon Shape, Gold, Signed & Numbered, 3 1/2 In. | 125.00 |
| **Steuben, Bowl & Underplate,** Amethyst, Swirled, 6 In.Wide | 110.00 |
| **Steuben, Bowl & Underplate,** Finger, Amethyst, Optic Rib, Folded Rims | 16.25 |
| **Steuben, Bowl & Underplate,** Finger, Aurene, Gold, Signed | 195.00 |
| **Steuben, Bowl & Underplate,** Finger, Green Jade, Etched Floral Festoons, 1920 | 70.00 |
| **Steuben, Bowl & Underplate,** Verre De Soie, Signed | 55.00 |
| **Steuben, Bowl,** Aurene, Blue, Rolled Collar, Low, Signed, 12 In.Wide | 295.00 |
| **Steuben, Bowl,** Aurene, Gold, Signed & Numbered, 10 X 5 1/2 In. | 247.50 |
| **Steuben, Bowl,** Blue Aurene, Melon Ribbed, 3 In.High | 295.00 |
| **Steuben, Bowl,** Blue Aurene, Rolled Inward, Applied Feet, 6 1/4 In. | 395.00 |
| **Steuben, Bowl,** Bubbly, Clear With Amber Threads On Rim, 8 1/4 In. | 32.00 |
| **Steuben, Bowl,** Calcite, Acanthus On Cream, Carder, Brass Hardware, 18 In. | 1000.00 |
| **Steuben, Bowl,** Calcite, Gold Iridescent, Fluted, Claw Feet | 265.00 |
| **Steuben, Bowl,** Calcite, Gold, 12 X 2 1/2 In. | 110.00 |
| **Steuben, Bowl,** Calcite, 10 In. | 200.00 |
| **Steuben, Bowl,** Centerpiece, Calcite & Gold Aurene, 10 1/4 In.Diameter | 130.00 |
| **Steuben, Bowl,** Cintra, Pink & Opalescent, Flat, 9 In. | 300.00 |
| **Steuben, Bowl,** Cluthra, Crystal Domed Base, Dark Blue, 9 3/4 In.Wide | 250.00 |
| **Steuben, Bowl,** Console, Silverene, Silver Mica On Green, Air Bubbles, 12 In. | 350.00 |
| **Steuben, Bowl,** Finger, Calcite, Gold Aurene Overlay, 2 1/2 In. | 95.00 |
| **Steuben, Bowl,** Gold Aurene On Calcite, 8 In. | 125.00 |
| **Steuben, Bowl,** Green, Blue, & Amber, Bubbles, Ground Pontil, 11 X 8 1/2 In. | 350.00 |
| **Steuben, Bowl,** Green, Semiopaque, Rolled Rim, 11 In. | 175.00 |
| **Steuben, Bowl,** Grotesque, Amethyst To Clear, Signed, 7 In.Square | 165.00 |
| **Steuben, Bowl,** Grotesque, Cobalt To Clear, 11 1/2 In.Diameter | 125.00 |
| **Steuben, Bowl,** Jade & Alabaster, Handled, Signed, 12 X 8 1/2 X 5 1/2 In. | 235.00 |
| **Steuben, Bowl,** Jade, 4 Tall Clear Legs, 10 In. | 65.00 |
| **Steuben, Bowl,** Oblong, Cluthra, Amethyst, Signed Fleur-De-Lis, 4 In.High | 325.00 |
| **Steuben, Bowl,** Rosaline, Alabaster Feet, Paper Label, 12 1/2 In.Diameter | 250.00 |
| **Steuben, Bowl,** Rosaline, White Alabaster, Footed, Green Label, 4 1/2 In.High | 275.00 |
| **Steuben, Bowl,** Star Shape, Mica, Air Trap, Blue, Flared, Signed, 10 In. | 265.00 |
| **Steuben, Bowl,** Threading, Blue Color, 14 In. | 60.00 |
| **Steuben, Bowl,** Topaz, Grotesque, Signed, 12 X 6 In. | 150.00 |
| **Steuben, Bowl,** Verre De Soie, Diamond-Quilted, Ruby Threading, Handled, 9 In. | 145.00 |
| **Steuben, Bowl,** Verre De Soie, Footed, Applied Blue Rim, 12 In.Diameter | 130.00 |
| **Steuben, Bowl,** Verre De Soie, Rolled Over Edge, 12 In., Unsigned | 80.00 |
| **Steuben, Candlestick,** Cintra, Blue, Purple, & Pink Mottled, 10 In. | 550.00 |
| **Steuben, Candlestick,** Green Stem, Amber Base, 12 In.High, Pair | 225.00 |
| **Steuben, Candlestick,** Green Threading & Bubbles On Clear, 14 In., Pair | 75.00 |
| **Steuben, Candlestick,** Green, 12 In. | 28.00 |
| **Steuben, Candlestick,** Ivorene, Black Jade Base, 3-Arm, 10 In. | 225.00 |

| | |
|---|---|
| Steuben, Candlestick, Venetian Style, Celeste Blue, Ribbed, 10 In., Pair | 125.00 |
| Steuben, Champagne, Silenium Red, Tapering Bowl, Round Base, C.1920 | 37.50 |
| Steuben, Chandelier, Ivorene, Hanging, Acid Cut Back Decoration, 16 In. | 150.00 |
| Steuben, Cologne, Aurene, Engraved By Hawkes, Red & Blue Highlights | 155.00 |
| Steuben, Compote, Aurene, Blue, Applied Prunts, Swirl Standard, Carder | 500.00 |
| Steuben, Compote, Aurene, Blue, Twisted Stem, Signed, 8 In.High | 695.00 |
| Steuben, Compote, Calcite, Gold, Pink Iridescent, 11 In.Diameter | 295.00 |
| Steuben, Compote, Calcite, Gold, Stretched, Pedestal, 8 In.Diameter | 175.00 |
| Steuben, Compote, Celeste Blue, Signed, 6 In.Diameter, 4 In.High | 45.00 |
| Steuben, Compote, Cerise Ruby, Swirled, Clear Stem, 7 In.High, 7 In.Diameter | 135.00 |
| Steuben, Compote, Crystal, Open 4 Part Stem, 9 7/8 In. | 115.00 |
| Steuben, Compote, Green Jade, Signed, 5 In.High | 111.00 |
| Steuben, Compote, Green Jade, 6 In.High, Label | 55.00 |
| Steuben, Compote, Green, Marked, 3 In.High, 8 In.Diameter | 72.00 |
| Steuben, Compote, Intaglio Leaf Garlands & Ribbons On Bristol, Hawkes, Gilt | 90.00 |
| Steuben, Compote, Moss Green, Unsigned, 7 In.Diameter, 5 In.High | 16.50 |
| Steuben, Compote, Nut, Verre De Soie, 4 In.High, Pair | 45.00 |
| Steuben, Compote, Rosaline, Alabaster Stem, Signed | 115.00 To 150.00 |
| Steuben, Compote, Verre De Soie, Copper Wheel Engraving, 5 1/8 In.High | 45.00 |
| Steuben, Console Set, Ivorene, 9 In.Candlesticks, Signed, 3 Piece | 350.00 |
| Steuben, Cordial, Verre De Soie, Engraved Cup & Foot, Signed Hawkes | 70.00 |
| Steuben, Cornucopia, Crystal, On Crystal Square Block, Signed, Pair | 110.00 |
| Steuben, Cup & Saucer, Demitasse, Rosaline, Alabaster Handle | 215.00 To 300.00 |
| Steuben, Darner, Celeste Blue, Ribbed, Carder, 4 1/2 In.Long | 60.00 |
| Steuben, Dipper, Rosaline, Alabaster Handle | 95.00 |
| Steuben, Figurine, Dolphin, Standing On Tail In Curved Position, Clear | 155.00 |
| Steuben, Figurine, Gazelle, Frosted, Signed, Labels, Pair | 295.00 |
| Steuben, Figurine, Nude Female, Arms Over Head, Frosted & Clear, 13 1/2 In. | 200.00 |
| Steuben, Figurine, Penguin, Crystal, Signed, 7 In.High | 125.00 |
| Steuben, Figurine, Pheasant, Cut Glass, Signed | 550.00 |
| Steuben, Figurine, Standing Fish, Venetian Style, Rosa, Signed | 300.00 |
| Steuben, Goblet, Bright Red, Signed | 150.00 |
| Steuben, Goblet, Bristol Yellow, Signed, 5 1/4 In.High | 65.00 |
| Steuben, Goblet, Cranberry Overlay On Crystal, Engraved, 10 In.High, Signed | 175.00 |
| Steuben, Goblet, Green Jade, Etched Floral Festoons, White Stem, C.1920 | 68.50 |
| Steuben, Goblet, Jade Green Bowl, Alabaster Stem & Foot, 6 In.High | 65.00 |
| Steuben, Goblet, Lavender, Alabaster Stem & Foot, Signed, 6 In.High | 65.00 |
| Steuben, Goblet, Oriental Poppy, Green Stems & Base, Pink, F.Carder | 250.00 |
| Steuben, Goblet, Pastel Blue Bowl, Alabaster Foot & Stem, 6 In.High | 42.00 |
| Steuben, Goblet, Pastel Green Bowl, Alabaster Foot & Stem, 6 In.High | 42.00 |
| Steuben, Goblet, Pastel Lavender Bowl, Alabaster Foot & Stem, 6 In.High | 42.00 |
| Steuben, Goblet, Pastel Orange Bowl, Alabaster Foot & Stem, 6 In.High | 42.00 |
| Steuben, Goblet, Pomona Ground, Trumpet Bowl, Clear Twisted Stem, Set Of 10 | 260.00 |
| Steuben, Goblet, Selenium Red, Signed, 5 1/4 In.High | 65.00 |
| Steuben, Goblet, Verre De Soie, Bell Bowl, Baluster Stem, 6 In.High | 50.00 |
| Steuben, Goblet, Water, Bubbly, Green Threading, Signed, 9 In.High | 38.00 |
| Steuben, Jar & Underplate, Marmalade, Topaz Apple On Blue Leaf, Stem Lid | 145.00 |
| Steuben, Jar, Threaded Cover, Green Swirled Crystal, Signed, 6 1/2 In.High | 110.00 |
| Steuben, Lamp, Mandarin Yellow, Acid Cut Back | 550.00 |
| Steuben, Lamp, Table, Calcite, 5 Green Feathers On White Iridescent, 17 In. | 850.00 |
| Steuben, Lampshade, Calcite, Small Size | 29.00 |
| Steuben, Lampshade, Ivorene, White Iridescent | 60.00 |
| Steuben, Lemonade Set, Verre De Soie, Orchid Sprays, 7 Piece | 395.00 |
| Steuben, Liqueur, Amethyst Bowl, Clear Twisted Stem, Signed | 12.50 |
| Steuben, Liqueur, Blue Bowl, Clear Twisted Stem, Signed | 12.50 |
| Steuben, Liqueur, Green Bowl, Clear Twisted Stem, Signed | 12.50 |
| Steuben, Liqueur, Silenium Red, Knopped Stem, Etched Grapes, C.1920 | 37.50 |
| Steuben, Nappy, Gold Aurene, Signed No.2670 | 175.00 |
| Steuben, Paperweight, Swirl & Teardrop, Clear, Signed | 150.00 |
| Steuben, Perfume Set, Venetian Scenes On Caps, Jade & Alabaster, 4 Piece | 135.00 |
| Steuben, Perfume, Amber Teardrop Stopper, 6 1/2 In.High | 90.00 |
| Steuben, Perfume, Amber, Blue Foot, Mica Fleck & Pink Swirl Stopper, Signed | 425.00 |
| Steuben, Perfume, Aurene, Blue, Signed, 3 1/2 In.High | 575.00 |
| Steuben, Perfume, Aurene, Gold Iridescent, Signed & Numbered, 4 1/2 In.High | 275.00 |
| Steuben, Perfume, Crystal & Ruby, 7 In.High | 65.00 |
| Steuben, Perfume, Deep Amethyst, Signed, 6 3/4 In.High | 125.00 |

| | |
|---|---|
| Steuben, Perfume, Gold Aurene, Stopper, Signed & Numbered, 4 1/4 In., Pair | 450.00 |
| Steuben, Perfume, Verre De Soie, Cobalt Dipper, 3 1/2 In. | 125.00 |
| Steuben, Perfume, Verre De Soie, Florals, Sterling Cap, 4 In. | 95.00 |
| Steuben, Perfume, Verre De Soie, Melon Ribbed, Green Steeple Stopper | 125.00 |
| Steuben, Perfume, Verre De Soie, Rosaline Stopper | 125.00 |
| Steuben, Perfume, Verre De Soie, Rosaline Stopper, Carder, 8 In.High | 150.00 |
| Steuben, Plate, Amber, Fleur De Lis, 8 1/2 In.Diameter | 20.00 |
| Steuben, Plate, Crystal, Diamond-Quilted, Black Threaded Border, 8 1/2 In. | 14.00 |
| Steuben, Plate, Crystal, Rosa Applied Rim Edge, 8 1/2 In. | 14.00 |
| Steuben, Plate, Demitasse, Jade Green, 4 1/2 In. | 10.00 |
| Steuben, Plate, Dessert, Green Jade, Acid Cut Back | 50.00 |
| Steuben, Plate, Dessert, Green Rim Cut To Clear, Signed | 85.00 |
| Steuben, Plate, Jade, Blue, 8 1/2 In. | 55.00 |
| Steuben, Plate, Jade, Green, 8 1/2 In. | 33.00 |
| Steuben, Plate, Rosaline, Signed, 14 1/2 In. | 125.00 |
| Steuben, Rose Bowl, Aurene, Gold, Calcite, 7 In. Wide | 115.00 |
| Steuben, Salt, Aurene, Gold, Pedestal, Signed & Numbered | 140.00 |
| Steuben, Salt, Green Bubbly Glass, Threaded Flared Top, Pedestal, Signed | 42.00 |
| Steuben, Salt, Pedestal, Black Reeding On Bristol Yellow, Signed | 85.00 |
| Steuben, Salt, Pedestal, Bubbly Clear, Blue Trim, Signed | 75.00 |
| Steuben, Salt, Pedestal, Bubbly Clear, Green Trim, Signed | 75.00 |
| Steuben, Shade, Calcite, 12 Crimps, Signed, 3 1/4 In.Top Diameter | 58.00 |
| Steuben, Shade, Gas, Gold Aurene, Signed | 50.00 |
| Steuben, Shade, Gas, Gold Feathering, White Pearly Interior, Signed | 65.00 |
| Steuben, Shade, Gas, Gold Feathering, White To Clear Lining, Signed | 65.00 |
| Steuben, Shade, Gas, Gold Iridescent, Bell Shape, Ribbed, 5 In.High | 45.00 |
| Steuben, Shade, Gas, Ivorene, Gold Inside, Pair | 90.00 |
| Steuben, Shade, Gas, Signed, 3 In.High, 4 1/8 In.Diameter, Pair | 125.00 |
| Steuben, Shade, Gold, Ribbed, Signed | 40.00 |
| Steuben, Shade, Pulled Feathers Pattern, Signed, 5 X 3 1/4 In. | 50.00 |
| Steuben, Sherbet & Underplate, Calcite | 115.00 |
| Steuben, Sherbet & Underplate, Jade, Alabaster Stem | 85.00 |
| Steuben, Sherbet, Aurene, Twisted Stem, Signed | 125.00 |
| Steuben, Sugar & Creamer, Aurene, Gold, Reeded Handled, Signed | 650.00 |
| Steuben, Sugar & Creamer, Clear Matsu-No-Ke, Applied Coral Decoration | 275.00 |
| Steuben, Tazza, Green Jade & Alabaster, Pedestal Stem, 8 In.Diameter | 65.00 |
| Steuben, Tumbler, Blue Crystal | 11.00 |
| Steuben, Tumbler, Green Threading In Clear, Signed, 2 1/2 In. | 24.00 |
| Steuben, Tumbler, Juice, Cerise, Clear Disc Foot | 15.00 |
| Steuben, Urn, Rosaline Glass, Albaster Pedestal, Amethyst Glass Rings, Pair | 550.00 |
| Steuben, Urn, Rosaline, Alabaster Wafer & Pedestal, Amethyst Rings, Pair | 500.00 |
| Steuben, Vase, Acid Cut Back Green Birds & Foliage On Yellow, 11 In. | 875.00 |
| Steuben, Vase, Acid Cut Back Purple Mums & White On Alabaster, 16 In.High | 875.00 |
| Steuben, Vase, Apple Green, Signed, 5 In. | 40.00 |
| Steuben, Vase, Applied Green Glass Threading On Clear, 6 In.High | 30.00 |
| Steuben, Vase, Aurene, Blue Decoration, Signed & Numbered, 6 1/2 In.High | 975.00 |
| Steuben, Vase, Aurene, Blue, Signed, 6 In. | 275.00 |
| Steuben, Vase, Aurene, Blue, Signed, 7 In. | 275.00 |
| Steuben, Vase, Aurene, Gold Iridescence, 13 In.High | 750.00 |
| Steuben, Vase, Aurene, Gold Iridescent, Signed, 4 In.High | 130.00 |
| Steuben, Vase, Aurene, Gold, Ribbed, Bulbous Base, 4 5/8 In., Pair | 290.00 |
| Steuben, Vase, Aurene, Gold, Rolled Rim, Deep Amber Iridescence, 11 3/4 In.High | 130.00 |
| Steuben, Vase, Aurene, Teardrop Shape, Gold, 8 In.High, Signed | 150.00 |
| Steuben, Vase, Blue Jade, Dragon Pattern, Double Acid Cut Back, 14 1/2 In. | 2250.00 |
| Steuben, Vase, Blue, French, Carder, Signed, 7 1/2 In. | 90.00 |
| Steuben, Vase, Bud, Green Jade, Alabaster Stem, 8 1/4 In.High, Pair | 95.00 |
| Steuben, Vase, Bulbous, Ivory, 5 In. | 130.00 |
| Steuben, Vase, Classic Shape, Green Jade, Alabaster Handles, 9 3/4 In.High | 395.00 |
| Steuben, Vase, Clear Expanded Diamond, Green Threading, Flared, 3 3/4 In. | 28.00 |
| Steuben, Vase, Clear, Applied Prunts On Stem, 5 1/2 In.High, 7 In.Wide | 65.00 |
| Steuben, Vase, Cluthra, Green To Rose At Top, Boothby Pattern, 13 1/2 In. | 2500.00 |
| Steuben, Vase, Cluthra, Green To White, 7 In.High | 395.00 |
| Steuben, Vase, Cluthra, White, Black Collar, Signed, 8 In.High | 350.00 |
| Steuben, Vase, Cluthra, 3 Knobs, Green To White, Scenic, Signed, 8 1/2 In. | 425.00 |
| Steuben, Vase, Cobalt Blue, Crystal, Signed, 9 In. | 95.00 |
| Steuben, Vase, Cornucopia, Ivorene, Pink Highlights, Pair | 550.00 |

| | |
|---|---|
| Steuben, Vase, Cornucopia, Topaz Domed Base, Folded Rim, Green Ruffled | 67.00 |
| Steuben, Vase, Crystal, Flared Rim, Green Threading, 6 1/8 In.High | 48.00 |
| Steuben, Vase, Fan, Amber, Green Foot & Stem, 8 1/2 In. | 70.00 |
| Steuben, Vase, Fan, Green Foot & Stem, Amber Top, 8 In.High | 78.00 |
| Steuben, Vase, Fan, Green Jade, Alabaster Pedestal, Ribbed, Signed, 11 In. | 250.00 |
| Steuben, Vase, Fan, Jade & Alabaster, Fleur-De-Lis Signed, 9 X 11 In. | 165.00 |
| Steuben, Vase, Florentia Cinnamon Color, 12 In.High | 3000.00 |
| Steuben, Vase, French Blue, Signed, 7 1/2 In.High | 90.00 |
| Steuben, Vase, Gold Aurene, Three-Pronged Tree Stump, Carder | 275.00 |
| Steuben, Vase, Gold, Ribbed, Polished Pontil, Clear, 6 In. | 50.00 |
| Steuben, Vase, Green Crystal, Carder, Signed, 10 In.High | 150.00 |
| Steuben, Vase, Green Crystal, Diagonal Ribbing, Domed Base, 6 In.High | 47.00 |
| Steuben, Vase, Green Swirl, No.6031, 7 In. | 34.00 |
| Steuben, Vase, Green Swirl, Polished Pontil, Signed, 6 3/4 In. | 68.00 |
| Steuben, Vase, Green Swirled Crystal, Wide Shoulder, Signed, 6 1/4 In. | 49.00 |
| Steuben, Vase, Grotesque, Crystal Foot, Pale To Purple Amethyst, 9 1/4 In. | 60.00 |
| Steuben, Vase, Ivorene, Ribbed, Footed, 9 1/4 In. | 100.00 |
| Steuben, Vase, Ivory, Carder, 5 In. | 150.00 |
| Steuben, Vase, Ivory, No.913, Unsigned | 65.00 |
| Steuben, Vase, Jack-In-The-Pulpit, Ivorene | 475.00 |
| Steuben, Vase, Jade & Alabaster, Acid Cut Back, Bird Decoration, Signed | 850.00 |
| Steuben, Vase, Jade Tiger Swirl, Block Signed, 8 In.High | 175.00 |
| Steuben, Vase, Jade, 3 Applied Bands Of Rosaline Ending Up In Snake's Head | 150.00 |
| Steuben, Vase, Millefiori, 5 In.High | 550.00 |
| Steuben, Vase, Moss Agate, Browns, Yellows, Reds, & Blacks, 14 In.High | 2400.00 |
| Steuben, Vase, Pedestal, Amber With Green, 6 Sided, Swirled, 8 In.High | 110.00 |
| Steuben, Vase, Pomona, Green, 5 In. | 46.00 |
| Steuben, Vase, Ribbed, Amethyst, Pedestal Base, Flared Top, 6 In. | 87.50 |
| Steuben, Vase, Rosaline, Amphora Shape, Fades To Alabaster Base, 9 In. | 400.00 |
| Steuben, Vase, Rosaline, Matsu, Acid Cut Back, Signed, 4 1/2 In. | 850.00 |
| Steuben, Vase, Selenium Red, Swirled, Fleur-De-Lis Mark, 7 In.High | 95.00 |
| Steuben, Vase, Swirled, Blue Rim & Foot, Signed Fleur-De-Lis, 14 In.High | 70.00 |
| Steuben, Vase, Topaz Crystal, Ribbed, Signed, 6 In.High | 58.00 |
| Steuben, Vase, Topaz, Swirled, 2 Handles, Signed Fleur-De-Lis, 10 In.High | 85.00 |
| Steuben, Vase, Trumpet, Aurene, Gold, Blue Highlights, Signed, 6 In. | 375.00 |
| Steuben, Vase, Trumpet, Calcite, Stretched Aurene Interior, 6 In.High | 150.00 |
| Steuben, Vase, Urn Shape, Green Jade, M Shape Alabaster Handles, 10 1/4 In. | 450.00 |
| Steuben, Vase, Verre De Soie, Diamond-Quilted, Cobalt Threading, 8 In. | 75.00 |
| Steuben, Vase, Verre De Soie, Engraved Floral, Hawkes, 7 3/4 In. | 175.00 |
| Steuben, Vase, Verre De Soie, Floriform Braided Stem, 12 In.High | 75.00 |
| Steuben, Vase, Verre De Soie, Light Blue Rim, Footed, 5 1/2 In.High | 60.00 |
| Steuben, Wine, Aurene, Gold, Pedestal Stem, 5 3/8 In.High | 115.00 |
| Steuben, Wine, Aurene, Gold, Twisted Stem, Blue & Red Highlights, Signed | 150.00 |
| Steuben, Wine, Green Jade, Etched Floral Festoons, White Stem, C.1920 | 57.50 |
| Steuben, Wine, Oriental Jade, Opalescent Twisted Stem, Signed, 7 In.High | 225.00 |
| Steuben, Wine, Pedestal, Jade & Alabaster, 6 1/2 In.High | 45.00 |
| Steuben, Wine, Swirled Stem, Engraved Mother & Dad, Signed, Pair | 45.00 |

*Stevengraphs are woven pictures made like ribbons. They were manufactured
by Thomas Stevens of Coventry, England, and became popular in 1862.*

| | |
|---|---|
| Stevengraph, A Birthday Gift, Happy May Thy Birthday Be, T.Stevens | 35.00 |
| Stevengraph, A Merry Christmas & A Happy New Year, T.Stevens | 39.75 |
| Stevengraph, Bookmark, "A Dear Friend's Wish" | 42.00 |
| Stevengraph, Bookmark, Faith, Hope, Charity, Symbols, Blue & White | 39.00 |
| Stevengraph, Bookmark, George Washington, Signed | 195.00 |
| Stevengraph, Bookmark, Paul Bunyan, Signed, 9 In. | 45.00 |
| Stevengraph, Bookmark, Three Choir Boys On Black Ground, "We Praise Thee" | 38.75 |
| Stevengraph, Bookmark, To My Dear Sister | 42.00 |
| Stevengraph, Bookmark, To Sister, Poem Of Love, Red & Blue, Green Tassel | 22.00 |
| Stevengraph, Bookmark, We Praise Thee O God | 44.50 |
| Stevengraph, Bookmark, 1876 Centennial, George Washington | 150.00 |
| Stevengraph, Early Train, Lord Howe, Merry Christmas, Happy New Year | 57.50 |
| Stevengraph, George Washington, Green Eagle Trademark | 32.00 |
| Stevengraph, Queen Alexandra, Framed | 125.00 |
| Stevengraph, Queen Alexandria, Grant, Portrait | 125.00 |
| Stevengraph, The Angelus, Black, Gray, & White, 12 1/2 X 10 In. | 60.00 |

| | |
|---|---|
| Stevengraph, The Finish, Label | 110.00 |
| Stevengraph, The Start, Label | 110.00 |
| Stevengraph, Water Jump, Label | 110.00 |
| Stevengraph, Wellington & Blucher Meeting | 125.00 |

*Stevens & Williams of Stourbridge, England, made many types of art glass.*

| | |
|---|---|
| Stevens & Williams, Basket, Applied Branch Amber Handle & Green Leaves | 275.00 |
| Stevens & Williams, Basket, Applied Crystal Leaves On Pink, Twisted Handle | 125.00 |
| Stevens & Williams, Basket, Blue, Applied Flowers & Leaves, Footed, 8 In. | 190.00 |
| Stevens & Williams, Basket, Blue, Melon Ribbed, Crystal Thorn Handle | 95.00 |
| Stevens & Williams, Bowl Vase, Satin Glass, Pink, Mother-Of-Pearl, Swirled | 275.00 |
| Stevens & Williams, Bowl, Glossy Pink Over Pink Frosted, Gold, Signed | 450.00 |
| Stevens & Williams, Bowl, Jade, Footed, Fleur-De-Lis-Signed, 3 1/2 In.High | 115.00 |
| Stevens & Williams, Bowl, Jewel Series, Threaded Amber, Crimped Top | 65.00 |
| Stevens & Williams, Cocktail Glass, Rosaline & Alabaster, Signed | 45.00 |
| Stevens & Williams, Coralene Leaves On Green Satin, Applied Camphor Feet | 65.00 |
| Stevens & Williams, Ewer, Applied Amber Stems Form Handle, Cream Satin | 55.00 |
| Stevens & Williams, Ewer, Applique Floral On Custard, Amber Thorn Handle | 425.00 |
| Stevens & Williams, Ewer, Coralene Leaves & Enamel On Blue Satin, Handle | 90.00 |
| Stevens & Williams, Nappy, Blue, Threaded, Ruffled Top, Handle | 15.00 |
| Stevens & Williams, Nappy, Green, Threaded, Ruffled Top, Handle | 15.00 |
| Stevens & Williams, Nappy, Tangerine, Threaded, Ruffled Top, Handle | 15.00 |
| Stevens & Williams, Parfait, Green Jade, Alabaster Wafer & Pedestal | 50.00 |
| Stevens & Williams, Rose Bowl, Apricot, Moire, Air Trap, Triple Cased | 325.00 |
| Stevens & Williams, Rose Bowl, Blue, Zipper & Bull's-Eye, Ruffled Top | 45.00 |
| Stevens & Williams, Rose Bowl, Bulbous, Melon Ribbed, Rainbow, Swirled | 125.00 |
| Stevens & Williams, Rose Bowl, Clear, Jeweled, No.55693, 2 In.High | 22.00 |
| Stevens & Williams, Rose Bowl, Jewel Glass, Brown, Zipper Design, Olive | 180.00 |
| Stevens & Williams, Rose Bowl, Opaque White, Blue Lining, Acanthus Leaves | 225.00 |
| Stevens & Williams, Rose Bowl, Rainbow, Pull-Ups Cased In Clear, Crimped | 260.00 |
| Stevens & Williams, Rose Bowl, Tricorner, Sapphire Blue Floral On Cream | 250.00 |
| Stevens & Williams, Rose Bowl, Yellow Cased, Applied Roses & Leaves, Pair | 240.00 |
| Stevens & Williams, Vase, Applied Leaves & Flowers, Signed, 5 In. | 125.00 |
| Stevens & Williams, Vase, Applique, Acanthus Leaves Form Feet, Green, White | 180.00 |
| Stevens & Williams, Vase, Blue Satin, Florals, Applied Camphor Feet | 70.00 |
| Stevens & Williams, Vase, Cameo, Oak Leaves & Acorns, Green & Ocher, 6 In. | 275.00 |
| Stevens & Williams, Vase, Camphor Satin, Applied Yellow Flower, Ribbed | 55.00 |
| Stevens & Williams, Vase, Cream, 2 Applied Ferns, Rose Lined, Ruffled Rim | 72.00 |
| Stevens & Williams, Vase, Crystal, Light Green Bull's-Eyes & Applied Edge | 25.00 |
| Stevens & Williams, Vase, Diamond-Quilted Satin, Rose Color, Camphor Base | 405.00 |
| Stevens & Williams, Vase, Enameled Floral On Pink Satin, White Lined | 80.00 |
| Stevens & Williams, Vase, Fan Shape, Turned Down Amber Ribbon Edge, 6 In. | 55.00 |
| Stevens & Williams, Vase, Morning Glories, Poppies, & Dragonflies On Lemon | 34.00 |
| Stevens & Williams, Vase, Pink Satin, Lavender Pansies, Applied Leaf Feet | 95.00 |
| Stevens & Williams, Vase, Pink, Applied Flowers & Leaves, Signed, 6 In. | 125.00 |
| Stevens & Williams, Vase, Pink, Applied Overlay, 11 In. High | 375.00 |
| Stevens & Williams, Vase, Swirled Mother-Of-Pearl, Brown To Beige, Lined | 225.00 |
| Stevens & Williams, Vase, Swirled Mother-Of-Pearl, Green To Rose, 18 In. | 595.00 |
| Stevens & Williams, Vase, Swirled, Amber & Cranberry Fluted Rim, Footed | 149.00 |
| Stevens & Williams, Vase, White Pull-Ups On Frosted, Ribbed Body, 4 1/2 In. | 60.00 |
| Stiegel Type, Bottle, Case, Hexagonal, Etched Star & Flower, 8 1/4 In. | 7.50 |
| Stiegle Type, Bottle, Case, Etched Star & Flower, Half Post Neck, 6 In. | 20.00 |
| Stiegel Type, Compote, Paneled, Cobalt Blue, Blown, Round Foot, 3 In.High | 300.00 |
| Stiegel Type, Creamer, Expanded Diamond, Applied Handle, Cobalt Blue, Blown | 400.00 |
| Stiegel Type, Decanter, Whiskey, Stopper, Etched Tulips & Foliage, Pint | 30.00 |
| Stiegel Type, Flagon, Wine, Etched Vine & Flowers, Applied Handle, 12 In. | 30.00 |
| Stiegel Type, Flip, Blown, Clear, Etched Decoration Over 10 Panels | 110.00 |
| Stiegel Type, Flip, Molded Pattern, 26 Panels, Flint, 5 In. | 62.00 |
| Stiegel Type, Flip, Rough Pontil, Flint, 6 1/2 In.High | 68.00 |
| Stiegel Type, Goblet, Florals, Flint | 12.50 |
| Stiegel Type, Light, Vigil, Emerald, Molded Pattern, Diamonds, Folded Rim | 52.00 |
| Stiegel Type, Mug, Friendship, Applied Foot, Blown Hollow Handle | 75.00 |
| Stiegel Type, Salt, Diamond Molded, Petal Foot, Blown, Clear, 3 3/8 In. | 75.00 |
| Stiegel Type, Salt, Double Aqua Bowl, Clear 16 Diamond, 3 In. | 25.00 |
| Stiegel Type, Salt, Round, Footed, Cobalt Blue | 125.00 |
| Stiegel Type, Tumbler, Lime Soda, Flint, 31 Vertical Ribs, Rough Pontil | 42.00 |

Stoneware, Bank,
Blue Sprig,
C.1825, 5 3/4 In.High

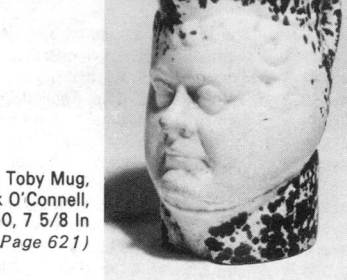

Stoneware, Toby Mug,
Patrick O'Connell,
C.1850, 7 5/8 In
*(See Page 621)*

| | | |
|---|---|---|
| **Stiegel Type, Tumbler,** Lime Soda, Molded Pattern, 31 Ribs, Flint, 3 3/4 In. | | 42.00 |
| **Stiegel Type, Wine,** Copper Wheel Swag Engraving, Round Foot, Flint | | 30.00 |
| **Stiegel Type, Wine,** Free-Blown, Open Pontil, 3 1/2 In. | | 12.50 |

*Stoneware is a coarse glazed and fired potter's ware that is used to make crocks, jugs, etc.*

| | | |
|---|---|---|
| **Stoneware, Bank,** Blue Sprig, C.1825, 5 3/4 In.High | *Illus* | 350.00 |
| **Stoneware, Bellarmine,** Fulham, C.1780, 9 1/4 In. | | 195.00 |
| **Stoneware, Bottle,** 'O.Tinkham, ' Dated 1847 | | 45.00 |
| **Stoneware, Bowl,** Apostle, Meigh, C.1842 | | 125.00 |
| **Stoneware, Bowl,** Mixing, Roman Key, Blue & White, 10 In. | | 18.00 |
| **Stoneware, Butter,** Covered, Blue & White, Basket Weave, Cosmos, Bail | | 25.00 |
| **Stoneware, Chicken Waterer,** Oak Leaf | | 3.50 |
| **Stoneware, Churn,** Syllabub, Albany, N.Y., Brown | | 160.00 |
| **Stoneware, Coller,** Gate City, Patented, Blue Basket Of Flowers, 9 Gallon | | 115.00 |
| **Stoneware, Cooler,** Parson's Generator, Ohio, Brown Pebble Glaze, 3 Gallon | | 30.00 |
| **Stoneware, Cooler,** Water, Blue Band Decoration, 5 Gallon | | 75.00 |
| **Stoneware, Cooler,** Water, Columbus Planting Flag On America, 15 In. High | | 700.00 |
| **Stoneware, Creamer,** Gray, Blue Lining | | 4.00 |
| **Stoneware, Crock,** Bird On Stump In Cabbage Patch, Fort Edward Co., 2 Gallon | | 175.00 |
| **Stoneware, Crock,** Blue, Date 1868, 1 1/2 Gallon | | 150.00 |
| **Stoneware, Crock,** Blue Hearts & Spirals, 3 Gallon | | 85.00 |
| **Stoneware, Crock,** Blue John A.Haught Shinston, W.Va. On Gray, 12 In. | | 35.00 |
| **Stoneware, Crock,** Blue Stenciled Decoration, 8 1/2 In. High | | 20.00 |
| **Stoneware, Crock,** Brady & Ryan Ellenvile, N.Y., Blue Chicken, 2 Gallon | | 190.00 |
| **Stoneware, Crock,** Bulbous, 'Hamilton & Jones, Pa., ' Cobalt Slip, 2 Gallon | | 68.00 |
| **Stoneware, Crock,** Bulbous, Cobalt Tulip Garlands, 4 Gallon | | 195.00 |
| **Stoneware, Crock,** Bulbous, Eared, 'H.Weston, Pa., ' Cobalt Scrolls, 4 Gallon | | 60.00 |
| **Stoneware, Crock,** Chicken, 2 Gallon | | 100.00 |
| **Stoneware, Crock,** Cobalt Bird, C.W.Underwood, N.Y., C.1865, 1/2 Gallon | | 65.00 |
| **Stoneware, Crock,** Cobalt Bird, J.A.& C.W.Underwood, Fort Edward, 2 Gallon | | 68.00 |
| **Stoneware, Crock,** Cobalt Decoration, S.Hart, Fulton, C.1840, 3 Gallon | | 125.00 |
| **Stoneware, Crock,** Cobalt Rooster On Hill, Fence, Whites, Utica, 2 Gallon | | 1100.00 |
| **Stoneware, Crock,** Dragonfly, 4 Gallon | | 130.00 |
| **Stoneware, Crock,** Gray, Eared, Blue Free-Hand Decoration, 7 1/2 In.High | | 8.00 |
| **Stoneware, Crock,** Gross Bros., Sterling, Pa., Blue Flower, 2 Gallon | | 35.00 |
| **Stoneware, Crock,** House & Grounds, A.O.Whittemore, Havana, N.Y., 4 Gallon | | 1000.00 |
| **Stoneware, Crock,** Impressed Eagles With Spears & Banners, 4 Gallon | | 110.00 |
| **Stoneware, Crock,** Lyre, 2 Gallon | | 110.00 |
| **Stoneware, Crock,** Nut Hatch, 2 Gallon | | 150.00 |
| **Stoneware, Crock,** Ovoid, 'Goodwin & Webster,  Cobalt Decoration, 2 Gallon | | 250.00 |
| **Stoneware, Crock,** Ovoid, Cobalt Decoration, M.Tyler, Albany, C.1834, 1 Gallon | | 50.00 |
| **Stoneware, Crock,** Ovoid, Pennsylvania, Encircling Cobalt Design, 4 Gallon | | 60.00 |
| **Stoneware, Crock,** Pink & Yellow Flowers On Sides | | 4.00 |
| **Stoneware, Crock,** Snuff, Maccaboy Snuff, Charles Sweetser & Sons, Mass. | | 78.00 |
| **Stoneware, Crock,** White, Utica, Bird, Dark Green Slip, Gallon | | 65.00 |
| **Stoneware, Crock,** 7 Point Stars, Blue Decoration, C.Crolius, 8 1/2 In.High | | 750.00 |
| **Stoneware, Decanter,** Standing Owl, Gray, Feathers Outlined In Dark Blue | | 125.00 |

Stoneware, Figurine, Napoleon, C.1820, 13 In. ........ 450.00
Stoneware, Flask, Ovoid, Gray, Brown Glaze, 7 1/2 In. ........ 55.00
Stoneware, Inkwell, English, 19th Century, 3 3/4 In. ........ 5.00
Stoneware, Inkwell, One Center Hole, 3 1/4 In.Diameter ........ 36.00
Stoneware, Jar, Butter, Lid & Bail Handle, Gray & Cobalt ........ 20.00
Stoneware, Jar, Cheese, White, Wired Lid ........ 6.50
Stoneware, Jar, Cobalt U.S.Shield & Wreath Stencil, 2 Quart ........ 100.00
Stoneware, Jar, G.A.& J.E.McCarthey, Ky., Blue Stenciled, 2 Gallon ........ 85.00
Stoneware, Jar, Round, Gray Glaze, Wooden Lid With Knob, 4 1/2 In.High ........ 10.00
Stoneware, Jar, Snuff, 6 In.High ........ 11.00
Stoneware, Jug, 'Brady & Ryan, Ellenville, ' Cobalt Bluebird, 3 Gallon ........ 60.00
Stoneware, Jug, 'N.A.White & Son, Utica, ' Cobalt Pine Tree, Gallon ........ 25.00
Stoneware, Jug, "S.Hart & Son, Fulton, "Cobalt Slip Letter S, 2 Gallon ........ 35.00
Stoneware, Jug, Batter, Dark Brown, Tin Lid & Spout Stopper, 1 1/2 Gallon ........ 35.00
Stoneware, Jug, Bird On Branch, Whites, Utica, Gray, Gallon ........ 80.00
Stoneware, Jug, Bulbous, 'G.F.Brayton, Utica, ' Cobalt Flower, 1 Gallon ........ 50.00
Stoneware, Jug, Caterpillar, 2 Gallon ........ 150.00
Stoneware, Jug, Cobalt Flower, N.Clark, Jr., Athens, N.Y., 3 Gallon ........ 58.00
Stoneware, Jug, Flower, T.G.Boone, Poughkeepsie, 2 Gallon ........ 125.00
Stoneware, Jug, Incised Cobalt Bird On Branch, I.Seymour, Troy, 2 Gallon ........ 950.00
Stoneware, Jug, Marked 2, 12 1/4 In. High ........ 15.00
Stoneware, Jug, Minster, White Relief On Blue, Meigh, 7 1/2 In ........ 95.00
Stoneware, Jug, N.White & Co., Binghamton, N.Y., Blue Sunflower, 3 Gallon ........ 75.00
Stoneware, Jug, Ovoid, 'Lyons, ' Cobalt Flower, 2 Gallon ........ 60.00
Stoneware, Jug, Ovoid, 'R.C.Remmey, Phila., ' 3 Gallon ........ 40.00
Stoneware, Jug, Ovoid, Fairfax, Va., 2 Gallon, 14 In. High ........ 85.00
Stoneware, Jug, Ovoid, Signed Charleston, 11 In. High ........ 40.00
Stoneware, Jug, Raised Blue Floral, Nichols & Boynton, Vt., C.1853, Gallon ........ 55.00
Stoneware, Jug, Reidinger & Czrie, Poughkeepsie, N.Y., Blue Floral, 2 Gallon ........ 65.00
Stoneware, Jug, Relief Blue Birds, Whites, Utica, Strap Handle, 2 Gallon ........ 125.00
Stoneware, Jug, 3 Liter, 14 In.High ........ 9.00
Stoneware, Mortar & Pestle, White, Trenton, Acid Resisting, U.S.A. ........ 12.75
Stoneware, Mortar & Pestle, White, Wooden Handle, Standard, Trenton ........ 19.75
Stoneware, Mug, Barrel, Brown ........ 1.25
Stoneware, Pitcher, Bow In Relief Near Neck, Blue & White, 9 In.High ........ 37.00
Stoneware, Pitcher, Bulbous, Cobalt Leaves & Long Stemmed Flower, 7 1/4 In. ........ 165.00
Stoneware, Pitcher, Bulbous, Tannish Green Lustre, Homer Laughlin, 6 1/2 In. ........ 9.75
Stoneware, Pitcher, Cattails & Leaves, Blue & White, 9 In. ........ 20.00
Stoneware, Pitcher, Dark Brown, Glazed Inside, 10 In.High ........ 20.00
Stoneware, Pitcher, Grapes & Leaves In Relief, Basket Weave, Blue & White ........ 40.00
Stoneware, Pitcher, Milk, White, 8 In. ........ 4.75
Stoneware, Pitcher, Milk, White, 9 In. ........ 4.75
Stoneware, Pitcher, Points Up From Bottom, Medium Blue, 8 In. ........ 20.00
Stoneware, Pitcher, White, Semi Porcelain, 8 In.High ........ 6.75
Stoneware, Plate, Yedo, Ashworth Bros., 10 1/2 In. ........ 25.00
Stoneware, Pot, Chamber, Blue Stripes On Gray, 8 In. ........ 22.00
Stoneware, Pot, Dye, Blue, Tulips, Marked Evan B.Jones, Pittston, Pa. ........ 55.00
Stoneware, Rolling Pin, Yellow, Wooden Handle ........ 35.00
Stoneware, Spittoon, Bell Shape, Cobalt Face Flowers, Slip Leaves ........ 140.00
Stoneware, Spittoon, Sponge & Stripes, Blue & White ........ 25.00
Stoneware, Teapot, Pennsylvania Dutch, Gray, Blue & Yellow Band, Green ........ 50.00
Stoneware, Toby Mug, Patrick O'Connell, C.1850, 7 5/8 In ........ *Illus* 125.00
Stoneware, Tub, Butter, Decorated With Cobalt, Imperial Stone ........ 48.00
Stoneware, Vase, Blue Foliage, Double-Headed Eagles, 14 1/2 In.High, Pair ........ 90.00
    Store, see also Card, Advertising, Coffee Grinder, Tool, Scale
Store, Abacus, Maple Frame, Painted Beads, 9 X 12 In. ........ 20.00
Store, Ad, Helmar Turkish Cigarettes, Woman, Color, Gold Leaf Frame ........ 10.00
Store, Ad, Wrigley's Gum, Negro Chased By Bulldog, 20 X 26 In. ........ 50.00
Store, Addometer, Reliable Co., Brass, 8 Wheels, 11 In.Long ........ 6.25
Store, Air Raid Clacker, Wooden, 13 In.Long ........ 6.25
Store, Ale Glass, Anheuser Busch, Raised A, 1880s ........ 18.50
Store, Ashtray, Florsheim Shoes, Brass ........ 12.50
Store, Ashtray, Goodrich Tire ........ 14.00
Store, Ashtray, Grand Prize Beer, Milk Glass ........ 8.00
Store, Ashtray, Holland Furnaces ........ 4.50
Store, Ashtray, Mr.Peanut, Metal, Dated 1906, 6 In. Diameter ........ 12.00

| | |
|---|---:|
| **Store, Ashtray,** Phillip Morris, Johnny Standing, Green Luster China | 20.00 |
| **Store, Badge,** Kellogg's Pep, Chester Gump | 2.25 |
| **Store, Badge,** Kellogg's Pep, Little King | 2.25 |
| **Store, Badge,** Kellogg's Pep, Maggie | 2.25 |
| **Store, Badge,** Kellogg's Pep, Skeezix | 2.25 |
| **Store, Badge,** Yellow Cab Company, Brass, Oval | 5.50 |
| **Store, Banner,** Drink Nehi Beverages, Gold On Purple | 2.00 |
| **Store, Banner,** Sunset Carson, Felt | 2.75 |
| **Store, Barber Pole,** Wooden, 6 In. | 200.00 |
| **Store, Barrel,** Briggs Tobacco, Wooden, "When A Feller Needs A Friend" | 15.00 |
| **Store, Basket,** Alms, Wicker, Long Handle, 42 In. | 30.00 |
| **Store, Basket,** Egg, Wire, Folding, 8 1/2 X 11 In. | 3.50 |
| **Store, Basket,** Fish, Wire, Folding, French | 2.00 |
| **Store, Basket,** Rye Straw, Made With Colored String, 16 X 10 X 4 1/2 In. | 22.00 |
| **Store, Basket,** Rye Straw, 5 1/2 In. | 22.50 |
| **Store, Basket,** Rye Straw, 11 In. | 27.50 |
| **Store, Basket,** Splint, Stenciled, Rectangular, 9 X 13 X 6 In. | 15.00 |
| **Store, Battery Charger,** Valley, Glass Top, 1920s | 48.00 |
| **Store, Beaker,** Canandaugua Pale Ale, Ye Olde Ivory, Buffalo China Co. | 17.00 |
| **Store, Bee Smoker,** Tin, Leather Bellows, C.1860 | 20.00 |
| **Store, Bee Smoker,** Tin, Wood, Leather Bellows | 5.00 |
| **Store, Beer Glass,** Bergdoll Brewing Co., 60th Anniversary, Etched Portrait | 16.00 |
| **Store, Beer Glass,** Piel Bros. Real Lager, Etched, Footed, Tapered, 7 In. | 15.00 |
| **Store, Bin,** Brenneman's Biscuits, Brass Front, Glass Insert | 22.00 |
| **Store, Bin,** Delico Sugar Wafers, Metal, Glass Front, Green & Silver | 20.00 |
| **Store, Bin,** Match, Barber's | 60.00 |
| **Store, Bin,** Tea, Japanned, Black, Gold Country Landscape | 45.00 |
| **Store, Blotter,** For Health & Happiness Drink Nehi, 1920s | 1.00 |
| **Store, Booth,** Phone, Wooden | 125.00 |
| **Store, Bootjack,** Musselman Plug Tobacco | 35.00 |
| **Store, Bottle Opener,** Metal, Crown Type | 3.00 |
| **Store, Bottle Opener,** Pepsi Cola, Bottle Shape, Lithographed, Buffalo, 1940 | 5.00 |
| **Store, Bottle Opener,** Potosi Beer, Enameled | 1.00 |
| **Store, Bottle Opener,** Universal, Giles Can Co., Chicago | 5.00 |
| **Store, Bottle Opener,** Utica Club, For Key Ring, Lady's Leg | 3.00 |
| **Store, Bottle Opener,** White Rock, Girl Figural | 3.00 |
| **Store, Bowl,** Grape Nuts, Donald Duck, ABC, Beetleware | 8.00 |
| **Store, Bowl,** Waste, Barber's, Red Glass, Gold Floral & Scroll Ribbons | 28.00 |
| **Store, Box,** Artstyle Chocolate Company Candy, Butterflies, Swans, Water | 5.50 |
| **Store, Box,** Barber's, 7 Straight Razors | 25.00 |
| **Store, Box,** Beech-Nut Tobacco, Paper | 3.50 |
| **Store, Box,** Beech-Nut Packing Co., Tin, 12 X 11 X 6 In. | 35.00 |
| **Store, Box,** Bell Brand Codfish, P.A.C.L.Co., Boston, Wooden, Dovetailed | 3.25 |
| **Store, Box,** Big Kick Tobacco, Paper | 3.50 |
| **Store, Box,** Big Nine Tobacco, Paper | 3.50 |
| **Store, Box,** Boye Curtain Fixtures, Wooden, Tin Lift Top, Square, 16 In. | 65.00 |
| **Store, Box,** Cake, Famous Tobacco | 6.00 |
| **Store, Box,** Cascarets, Hinged, Brass, Enameled Jewels, Scrolls, 2 1/4 In. | 10.00 |
| **Store, Box,** Cash Value Tobacco, Paper | 3.50 |
| **Store, Box,** Cash, Knights & Ladys Of Security, Tin | 4.00 |
| **Store, Box,** Church Collection, Handled, Walnut, Slide Hole, 6 1/2 X 13 In. | 25.00 |
| **Store, Box,** Codfish, Wooden, Stencils | 2.00 |
| **Store, Box,** Coffee Tone Cigarettes, Paper | 3.50 |
| **Store, Box,** Cracker Jacks, Metal, Brass Coated, 1930s, 6 In. | 8.50 |
| **Store, Box,** Cremo Cigars, Tin | 40.00 |
| **Store, Box,** Ding Dong Bell Savings Bank, Weeden Manufacturing Co. | 360.00 |
| **Store, Box,** Drumond's Horseshoe Tobacco, Wooden, 7 X 13 In. | 8.00 |
| **Store, Box,** Edward G.Robinson Tobacco, Paper | 3.50 |
| **Store, Box,** Five Brothers Pipe Tobacco, Wooden, Paper Label, 50 Pound Size | 20.00 |
| **Store, Box,** Five Brothers Tobacco, Paper | 3.50 |
| **Store, Box,** Fries Spice, Tin, Green, 6 Boxes Inside | 25.00 |
| **Store, Box,** Gantz Sea Foam, Best Baking Powder In The World, Tin, Oval | 3.95 |
| **Store, Box,** George Washington Tobacco, Paper | 3.50 |
| **Store, Box,** Hairpin, Ballard's Obelisk Flour, Hinged, 4 Footed, Aluminum | 3.95 |
| **Store, Box,** Havana Blossom Tobacco, Paper | 3.50 |
| **Store, Box,** Lesher & Co., Tailors, Chicago, Cast Iron Turtle, Hinged, 5 In. | 35.00 |

Store, Box, Lily White Starch, Wooden, Trunk Shape, Picture Of Little Girl ..................................... 38.00
Store, Box, Longfellow Cigars, Wooden, Hinged Lid ..................................................... 5.00
Store, Box, Lowney's Easter Candy Egg, Red Satin, Brass Plated Spoon, 6 In. ...................... 15.00
Store, Box, Lucky Strike Cigarettes, Green, Porcelain Lined, 2 Packs ................................ 22.00
Store, Box, Marvin's Golden Fruitcake, Pittsburgh, Oval, Dark Green, Gold ......................... 25.00
Store, Box, Medlar Co.Biscuits, Wooden, Paper Label, Barnyard Scene ............................ 19.00
Store, Box, Model Tobacco, Paper ................................................................. 3.50
Store, Box, Pencil, Billy Club, Wooden, Shape Of Billy Club, 6 In. ................................. 3.50
Store, Box, Pencil, Jackie Coogan, Tin, Paper Label ................................................ 7.00
Store, Box, Pencil, Pine, Swivel Cover, Shield Handle ............................................. 20.00
Store, Box, Pencil, Skippy, Signed P.L.Crosby, 1932, 11 X 6 In. ................................... 5.00
Store, Box, Poker Chip & Card, Walnut, Sterling Corners, Lift Off Top, 15 In. ..................... 250.00
Store, Box, Premier High Novelty Men's Gray Cotton Hose, Gold Lettering ......................... 2.50
Store, Box, Red Man Tobacco, Paper ............................................................. 3.50
Store, Box, Richard Hudnut, Paper Covered, C.1930, Chiffon-Clad Ladies, Trees ................... 4.00
Store, Box, Rivets, Judson Thompson Mfg., Waltham, Mass., Tin ................................... 8.00
Store, Box, Sen-Sen Gum, Book Shape, "sweet Odors, " Patent 1906 ............................. 10.00
Store, Box, Sensible Tobacco ..................................................................... 8.00
Store, Box, Spice, Painted Yellow, Set Of 4 Graduated ............................................ 25.00
Store, Box, Spice, Tin, Alphaltum Finish, 3 Boxes Inside, Stenciled Labels ....................... 25.00
Store, Box, Tiger Stripe Tobacco, Paper .......................................................... 3.50
Store, Box, Toof's Attachments, Household Sewing Machine Co., Tin ............................... 5.00
Store, Box, Union Workman Tobacco. Paper ...................................................... 3.50
Store, Box, Walking Lark, Windup ................................................................ 5.00
Store, Box, Walter Baker Chocolate, La Belle Lady Embossed, Dovetailed ......................... 6.00
Store, Box, Walter Baker Cocoa, Wooden, Dovetailed, 1/ 1/2 X 6 X 4 1/2 In. ...................... 13.75
Store, Box, Wrigley's Soap, Cardboard, 7 1/2 X 6 In. .............................................. 8.00
Store, Box, Young & Larrabee's Biscuit, Wooden, Paper Label ..................................... 19.00
Store, Branding Liquid, Kepm's, For Marking Sheep, 1929 ........................................ 2.00
Store, Broadside, Anti-Slavery Rally, Newburgh, Oct.1855, Woodcut Eagle ....................... 225.00
Store, Broadside, Buffalo Bill's Wild West, 1897, Color, 10 X 28 In. ............................... 64.50
Store, Broadside, Cole Bros., 1909, 10 X 28 In. ................................................... 6.50
Store, Broadside, Dr.Thompson's Veto, For Cure Of Thechi Libians, 1865 ......................... 4.00
Store, Broadside, Shoeing Sale, 1876 Centennial Prices, Farmington, Conn. ...................... 5.00
Store, Broadside, The Gipson Wringer, Shelby Mfg.Co., C.1860 ................................... 5.00
Store, Broadside, Uncle Tom's Cabin, 10 X 18 In. ................................................. 8.50
Store, Broadside, War Saving Stamps, Statue Of Nathan Hale, 21 X 28 In. ........................ 3.00
Store, Broadside, 100th Anniversary Of Washington's Birthday, 1832 ............................. 325.00
Store, Brush, Shaving, Dated 1905 ................................................................ 1.25
Store, Bucket, Maple Sap, Wooden Staves, Painted, 2 1/2 Gallon ................................. 4.50
Store, Bucket, Sap, Red Paint, 12 In Diameter .................................................... 6.50
Store, Bucket, Sugar, Massachusetts, Red & Gilt On Dark Green, Wire Bail ....................... 95.00
Store, Buggy Whip, Iron Handle .................................................................. 12.00
Store, Bulb, Electric, Colored Santa Claus, 3 In .................................................. 5.00
Store, Buttonhook & Shoehorn, Fashion Shoe House, Ironwood, Mich. ............................ 6.50
Store, Buttonhook, Celluloid Handle, Mother-Of-Pearl Inlay ...................................... 5.00
Store, Buttonhook, Folding ....................................................................... 3.00
Store, Buttonhook, French Ivory Shoehorn Handle ................................................ 4.00
Store, Buttonhook, Ivory Handle ............................................................ 5.00 To 7.50
Store, Buttonhook, Rall Shoes, Embossed ........................................................ 1.25
Store, Buttonhook, Steel Hook, Sterling Silver Embossed Handle, 'May' ........................... 15.00
Store, Buttonhook, Superior Spats, Chicago ...................................................... 3.25
Store, Cabinet, Carborundum, Wooden, 4 Drawer, Indian Lithograph On Lid ...................... 50.00
Store, Cabinet, Diamond Dye, Child's Face ....................................................... 165.00
Store, Cabinet, Diamond Dye, Court Jester ....................................................... 160.00
Store, Cabinet, Diamond Dye, Evolution Of Woman ............................................... 160.00
Store, Cabinet, Diamond Dye, Maypole ........................................................... 165.00
Store, Cabinet, Diamond Dyes, Tin, Children Jumping Rope, 11 X 20 In. .......................... 110.00
Store, Cabinet, Display, Putnum Dye, George Washington Escapes British, Tin .................... 45.00
Store, Cabinet, Dy-O-La Dye, Wooden, Tin Inserts ................................................ 75.00
Store, Cabinet, Electric Hair Curler Co., Tin, Girls & Car On Beach, 1921 ........................ 70.00
Store, Cabinet, Humphrey's Remedies, Wooden, Tin Inserts ...................................... 130.00
Store, Cabinet, Merrick's Spool, Mirror Front, Pull Down Type, 31 X 21 In. ...................... 215.00
Store, Cabinet, Needle, Wooden, 3 Drawer ....................................................... 30.00
Store, Cabinet, Revolving, Wooden, Plow Bolt, Octagonal ........................................ 275.00
Store, Cabinet, Service, Fairbanks Morse, Wooden, Pull Down Wall Style .......................... 45.00

| | |
|---|---:|
| Store, Cabinet, Spool, Coats Threads, 3 Drawer, Metal | 35.00 |
| Store, Cabinet, Spool, Glass Fronted Drawers, Walnut, 6 Drawers | 235.00 |
| Store, Cabinet, Spool, Royal Society, Oak, 12 Drawer | 140.00 |
| Store, Cabinet, Spoon, J.P.Coats, Walnut, 17 X 15 X 7 In. | 50.00 |
| Store, Cabinet, Wood, Bio-Pharm Cough Lozenges | 15.00 |
| Store, Calendar, Continental Insurance Co., 1885 | 5.75 |
| Store, Calendar, Maxfield Parrish, Lights Of Home, Salesman's Sample | 9.00 |
| Store, Calendar, Maxfield Parrish, Sunup, Salesman's Sample | 9.00 |
| Store, Calendar, 1888, Scott's Emulsion | 10.00 |
| Store, Calendar, 1889, Scott's Emulsion, Victorian Children | 5.00 |
| Store, Calendar, 1893, Picture Of Cat, 5 1/2 X 11 In. | 5.00 |
| Store, Calendar, 1897, Anti Kammia Tablets, Artist Signed Lithograph | 5.00 |
| Store, Calendar, 1898, Slade's Spices | 10.00 |
| Store, Calendar, 1899, Hood's, The American Girl | 15.00 |
| Store, Calendar, 1900, Mellin's Baby Food, Baby Of The Month | 6.50 |
| Store, Calendar, 1901, Scott's Emulsion, Victorian Children | 5.00 |
| Store, Calendar, 1904, Months Of Japanese Children, Tokyo | 12.00 |
| Store, Calendar, 1908, The Four Seasons, Alex.J.Rummler, 6 1/4 X 10 In. | 6.00 |
| Store, Calendar, 1908, Watchword, Scenes & Religious Verses, 6 X 4 In. | 4.00 |
| Store, Calendar, 1909, Welcome Santa Claus | 8.00 |
| Store, Calendar, 1910, Picture Of Geese, 7 3/4 X 8 3/4 In. | 3.00 |
| Store, Calendar, 1912, Art, Diamond Shape, Embossed, Diecut, Multilayer | 10.00 |
| Store, Calendar, 1914, Art, Embossed, Ladies & Florals, Multilayer | 10.00 |
| Store, Calendar, 1914, Nashville Banner, Carrier's Greeting, 3 Girls, Color | 8.50 |
| Store, Calendar, 1914, Picture Of Woman, 6 X 17 1/2 In. | 4.00 |
| Store, Calendar, 1915, Hiawatha's Wedding Journey, Brave With Bride | 8.00 |
| Store, Calendar, 1925, Colored Picture, 7 1/2 X 10 In. | .50 |
| Store, Calendar, 1930, Austin | 1.00 |
| Store, Calendar, 1930, Meierhofer Bros., Illinois, Christy Girl | 18.00 |
| Store, Can Opener, Jax Beer, Table Top, Metal | 19.00 |
| Store, Can, Alliance Coffee, Dated 1904, Cardboard, Pound | 11.00 |
| Store, Can, Argon Peanut Butter, Brass Handles, Orange & White, 15 In.High | 25.00 |
| Store, Can, Armour & Co., Star Brand Condensed Mince Meat, Bucket Shape | 3.75 |
| Store, Can, Bachman's Pretzels, Glass Insert In Lid, 14 X 12 In. | 15.00 |
| Store, Can, Beechnut Coffee, Red & White, Pound | 4.00 |
| Store, Can, Beer, Andeker | .50 |
| Store, Can, Beer, Bavarian Club | .50 |
| Store, Can, Beer, Blatz | .50 |
| Store, Can, Beer, Brown Derby | .50 |
| Store, Can, Beer, Champagne Velvet | .50 |
| Store, Can, Beer, Cooks | .50 |
| Store, Can, Beer, Country Tavern | .50 |
| Store, Can, Beer, Goetz | .50 |
| Store, Can, Beer, Hamm's Draft, 12 Ozs. | .50 |
| Store, Can, Beer, Hamm's Draft, 16 Ozs. | .50 |
| Store, Can, Beer, Heidelbrau | .50 |
| Store, Can, Beer, Huber Bock | .50 |
| Store, Can, Beer, Iron City | .50 |
| Store, Can, Beer, Katz | .50 |
| Store, Can, Beer, Metz | .50 |
| Store, Can, Beer, Near Beer | .50 |
| Store, Can, Beer, Pearl, 8 Ozs. | .50 |
| Store, Can, Beer, Pearl, 12 Ozs. | .50 |
| Store, Can, Beer, Pearl, 16 Ozs. | .50 |
| Store, Can, Beer, Pfeiffer | .50 |
| Store, Can, Beer, Pilsner Club | .50 |
| Store, Can, Beer, Potosi Brewery, Bohemian Club Beer | 1.00 |
| Store, Can, Beer, Prager | .50 |
| Store, Can, Beer, Red Cap | .50 |
| Store, Can, Beer, Red, White, & Blue | .50 |
| Store, Can, Beer, Rhinelander | .50 |
| Store, Can, Beer, Special Export | .50 |
| Store, Can, Beer, Stite | .50 |
| Store, Can, Beer, Strohs | .50 |
| Store, Can, Beer, Triumph | .50 |
| Store, Can, Beer, Tudor | .50 |

| | |
|---|---|
| Store, Can, Beer, Washington Pilsner, Picture Of An Eagle | 15.00 |
| Store, Can, Beer, Whiedemann | .50 |
| Store, Can, Beer, White Label | .50 |
| Store, Can, Beer, 9-0-5 | .50 |
| Store, Can, Bokar Coffee, Black & Gold, Pound | 4.00 |
| Store, Can, Boscul Coffee, Red & White, Pound | 7.00 |
| Store, Can, Cream, Tin, 2 Quart | 14.00 |
| Store, Can, Cream, 2 Gallon | 15.00 |
| Store, Can, Dixie Beer | .50 |
| Store, Can, DuPont Gun Powder, 1924 | 15.00 |
| Store, Can, Dust Mop, Gilmore Plunkett Chemical Co., Chicago, Tin | 12.00 |
| Store, Can, Excelsior Coffee, Orange & Brown, Pound | 5.00 |
| Store, Can, Fuel Mixing, Maytag, Tin, Pouring Spout, Handle, Measuring Cup | 15.00 |
| Store, Can, Gold Dust Scouring Cleanser, Cardboard, 5 In.High | 7.00 |
| Store, Can, Kerosene, Tin, Embossed Excelsior, Glass Insert, Screw Top | 15.00 |
| Store, Can, Measuring, Colman | 3.00 |
| Store, Can, Milk, Tin, Metal Bands, Steel Bail, Lid, 1 1/2 Gallon | 6.50 |
| Store, Can, Monarch Coffee, Ivory & Blue, Pound | 7.00 |
| Store, Can, Oil, Eagle, Embossed, Tin, Miniature | 1.50 |
| Store, Can, Old Master Coffee, Picture Of Old Man | 9.00 |
| Store, Can, Rum & Maple Pipe Mixture Tobacco, Cardboard | 4.00 |
| Store, Can, Serv-Us Coffee, Orange & Blue, Pound | 10.00 |
| Store, Canteen, Woven Straw, Round, Oval Sides, 3 Quart | 30.00 |
| Store, Cap Lifter, Potosi Beer, White Enamel | 1.00 |
| Store, Carpet Stretcher, Cast Iron, Wooden Handle, Patent 1876 | 8.00 |
| Store, Cart, Hand, Stenciling | 15.00 |
| Store, Case, Blatz, Milwaukee, Beer, Wooden | 10.00 |
| Store, Case, Boyle's Needles & Shuttles, Metal, 1906, 17 In.Diameter | 30.00 |
| Store, Case, Display, Boyce Needle Co., Oak, Beveled Glass, Patent Jan.1919 | 25.00 |
| Store, Case, Hurley Bottling Works Beer, Wooden | 10.00 |
| Store, Case, Jung Beer, Wooden | 10.00 |
| Store, Case, Needle, Lydia E.Pinkham, Metal | 8.00 |
| Store, Case, Remington Shell Display | 24.00 |
| Store, Case, Salesman's Sample, Pine, 60 Compartments, Brasses, C.1860 | 49.00 |
| Store, Case, Spectacles, Tin, Hinged Cover, Patent 1860 | 5.95 |
| Store, Case, Val Blatz Beer, Wooden | 10.00 |
| Store, Cash Register, Metal, Maskey Register, Alliance, Ohio, 1924 | 115.00 |
| Store, Cash Register, Michigan, Copper Plated, Ornate, Amount Sign At Top | 175.00 |
| Store, Cash Register, National, Model 324, Brass, C.1926 | 175.00 |
| Store, Cash Register, National, Model 349, Serial No.100847, Brass | 135.00 |
| Store, Cash Register, National, Model 356-G, Brass, Audagraphic Holder | 110.00 |
| Store, Cash Register, National, Saloon, 2 Drawer, Brass, 1880s | 500.00 |
| Store, Cash Register, National, Series 317 | 145.00 |
| Store, Chain, Surveyor's, Steel, Brass Markers & Ends | 25.00 |
| Store, Chair, Dentist's, 1919, With Equipment | 200.00 |
| Store, Chair, Doctor's, 1912 | 50.00 |
| Store, Chair, Piedmont Cigarettes, Folding, C.1900 | 60.00 |
| Store, Charm, Ideal Dog Food | 1.50 |
| Store, Chart, Eye Test, 1882 | 6.00 |
| Store, Chest, Artstyle Chocolates, Art Nouveau, Footed, Tin, 2 Pound | 20.00 |
| Store, Cigar Cutter & Knife, Pocket, Howard Bros.Mfg.Co., Mass., Gold Plated | 4.75 |
| Store, Clapper, New Year, Rudy Vallee & His Connecticut Yankees | 8.00 |
| Store, Cleaver, Meat, U.S.Cutlery | 5.00 |
| Store, Clip, Bill, Wall, Brockton Rand Co., Barbour Grooved Endless Welting | 3.95 |
| Store, Clip, Pencil, Morton's Salt | 3.00 |
| Store, Clip, Pencil, Seven-Up | 2.50 |
| Store, Coaster, Heineken Holland Beer, Round, Blotter Type, C.1948 | 1.00 |
| Store, Coffee Grinder, see Coffee Grinder | |
| Store, Comb, Mustache Trimming, Sta-Neet, Celluloid, Built In Razor Blade | 14.00 |
| Store, Compass, Jayne's Drug Store, 1 3/4 In.Circumference | 8.00 |
| Store, Container, Battery Water, Embossed Hearts, Bluish Glass, 11 In. | 12.50 |
| Store, Container, Northrup's Violet Ink Powder, Castleton, Vt., Wooden | 13.00 |
| Store, Cooler, Water, Acme, W.T. & Co., U.S.A., Tin & Glass, 6 5/8 In.High | 9.75 |
| Store, Corkscrew, Green River Whiskey | 7.50 |
| Store, Corkscrew, I.W.Harper Whiskey, Wooden Handle | 4.50 |
| Store, Corkscrew, Ivorylike Handle, 4 In.Long | 4.50 |

| | |
|---|---:|
| **Store, Corkscrew**, Police Dog, Metal, Welch's, Westfield, N.Y. | 3.00 |
| **Store, Corkscrew**, Quincy Belle, Old Seal, & Old Stand Whiskey, Metal, Wooden | 5.50 |
| **Store, Corkscrew**, Silver Handle, 5 1/2 In.Long | 5.00 |
| **Store, Corn Razor**, Like Straight Razor, 3 1/2 In.Long | 9.00 |
| **Store, Counter**, Bezique, Black Wood, Ivory Keys, Gold Enameling | 45.00 |
| **Store, Counter**, Drug, Oak, 14 Ft. | 150.00 |
| **Store, Counterfeit Coin Detector**, Berrin Co., U.S.Standard, Patent 1877 | 57.50 |
| **Store, Cow & Calf**, Guernsey, DeLaval, Tin, Envelope | 12.00 |
| **Store, Cream Skimmer**, Wooden | 50.00 |
| **Store, Crock**, Salt, Briardale Store, Lakota, Iowa, Embossed Merry Christmas | 10.00 |
| **Store, Cuff**, Butcher's, Straw, Pair | 5.00 |
| **Store, Cup**, Ranger Joe | 2.00 |
| **Store, Cup**, Van Houten's Cocoa, Dutch Boy Picture | 6.00 |
| **Store, Curling Iron**, Wooden Handle | 8.00 |
| **Store, Cutter**, Cigar, Drolls, 2 Cutting Places, 4 In. | 48.00 |
| **Store, Cutter**, Cigar, Elephant, Pot Metal, Brass Insert | 40.00 |
| **Store, Cutter**, Cigar, Naked Lady On A Pot | 75.00 |
| **Store, Cutter**, Cigar, Pocket, Clauss Cutlery | 5.25 |
| **Store, Cutter**, Cigar, Spana, Cuba, Key Wind | 20.00 |
| **Store, Cutter**, Cigar, Vest Pocket, Scissors Type, Silver Color, 2 1/4 In. | 5.00 |
| **Store, Cutter**, Tobacco, Enterprise | 30.00 |
| **Store, Cutter**, Tobacco, Penn.Hardware Co., Patent May 18, 1856 | 20.00 |
| **Store, Cutter**, Tobacco, Plug, Iron, Signed Star, Black & Gold | 20.00 |
| **Store, Cutter**, Tobacco, Queen | 30.00 |
| **Store, Cutter**, Tobacco, Spearhead | 18.50 |
| **Store, Dipper**, Cone, Tin | 12.50 |
| **Store, Dish**, Planters Peanut, New York World's Fair, 1933, Metal | 6.00 |
| **Store, Dish**, Soap, Wire | 2.00 |
| **Store, Dispenser**, Alka Seltzer | 38.00 |
| **Store, Dispenser**, Cord, Iron, Round, Pedestal | 14.00 |
| **Store, Dispenser**, Gum, One Cent, Covers To Look Like Radio | 75.00 |
| **Store, Dispenser**, Johnson & Allen, Tin | 22.50 |
| **Store, Dispenser**, Paper Cup, Glass | 2.00 |
| **Store, Dispenser**, Penny Diamond Match | 65.00 |
| **Store, Dispenser**, Soda Fountain Syrup, Chocolate, Rectangular Black Ceramic | 15.00 |
| **Store, Dispenser**, Soda Fountain Syrup, Chocolate, Round Black Ceramic | 15.00 |
| **Store, Dispenser**, Soda Fountain Syrup, Chocolate, Square Black Ceramic | 15.00 |
| **Store, Dispenser**, Soda Fountain Syrup, Orange, Rectangular Black Ceramic | 15.00 |
| **Store, Dispenser**, Soda Fountain Syrup, Orange, Round Black Ceramic | 15.00 |
| **Store, Dispenser**, Soda Fountain Syrup, Square White Ceramic | 15.00 |
| **Store, Dispenser**, Soda Fountain Syrup, Strawberry, Round Black Ceramic | 15.00 |
| **Store, Dispenser**, Soda Fountain Syrup, Strawberry, Round White Ceramic | 15.00 |
| **Store, Dispenser**, Soda Fountain Syrup, Strawberry, Square Black Ceramic | 15.00 |
| **Store, Dispenser**, Soda Fountain, Ward's Lemon Crush, Porcelain Knob | 95.00 |
| **Store, Dispenser**, Syrup, Blossom Brand, China & Glass, 13 In.High | 7.50 |
| **Store, Display Holder**, Canada Dry Soda Water, Cardboard, 3 Bottle, 1920s | 5.00 |
| **Store, Door Push**, Duke's Mixture Tobacco, Porcelain | 25.00 |
| **Store, Dose Glass**, Owl Drug | 12.50 |
| **Store, Drum**, Pepsi Cola, Metal, 17 X 15 In. | 35.00 |
| **Store, Dryer**, Corn, Iron, 4 Spines Each Side, 19 1/4 In.High | 10.00 |
| **Store, Duster**, Peacock Feather, Grained Wooden Handle, 31 In.Long | 24.00 |
| **Store, Dynamite Exploder**, DuPont | 50.00 |
| **Store, Egg Carrier**, Star, Wooden | 20.00 |
| **Store, Egg Grader**, Metal | 3.00 |
| **Store, Egg Lifter**, Handle, 6 Eggs | 6.50 |
| **Store, Engine**, Weeden, Upright, Burner Base, 8 1/2 In.High | 40.00 |
| **Store, Exterminator**, Mouse, N.J.Wigginton, Va., Patent 1918, Clear Glass | 9.50 |
| **Store, Eyecup**, Embossed Eye Design, Patent 1937 | 5.00 |
| **Store, Eyecup**, Flint Glass, Footed | 1.25 |
| **Store, Eyecup**, John Bull, Clear, Dated Aug.14, 1917 | 12.00 |
| **Store, Eyecup**, John Bull, Green | 18.00 |
| **Store, Fan**, Candee Rubber Footwear, Orange, White, & Black, Round | 6.00 |
| **Store, Fan**, Ceiling, 2 Blade | 125.00 |
| **Store, Fan**, Ceiling, 3 Speed, 4 Blades, 22 In. | 90.00 |
| **Store, Fan**, Ceiling, 4 Blade, 3 Speed | 125.00 |
| **Store, Fan**, Havana Cigar | 1.50 |

| | |
|---|---|
| Store, Fan, Moxie, Girl, Cardboard | 7.50 |
| Store, Fan, Moxie, 6 In.Round | 7.00 |
| Store, Fan, Opia Cigars, Cardboard, Color Lithograph Of Girl | 14.00 |
| Store, Fan, Putnam Fades & Dyes, General Putnam, British Dragoons, Paper | 2.00 |
| Store, Fan, Singer Sewing Machines, Folding, Paper | 11.00 |
| Store, Fan, Walter McClain, Printer, N.J., Barefoot Fisherman Print | 3.00 |
| Store, Figurine, Black Man With White Beard, "Make Mine Myers, " | 28.00 |
| Store, Figurine, Eagle, National Whiskey, Plaster | 12.00 |
| Store, Figurine, R.C.A.Victor Dog, 4 In. | 15.00 |
| Store, Figurine, Scottie Dog, Black & White Scotch, Papier-Mache, Pair | 20.00 |
| Store, Flasher Coin, Speedy Alka-Seltzer, 1956 | .50 |
| Store, Flasher Coin, Wizard Of Oz, 1959 | .50 |
| Store, Flashlight, Roy Rogers, Signal, Siren, Lithographed, Tin, 6 In. | 9.25 |
| Store, Flashlight, Tom Corbett, Signal, Siren, Boxed | 25.00 |
| Store, Flashlight, Winchester, Brass, Embossed | 7.50 |
| Store, Flashlight, 1920 | 7.00 |
| Store, Flax Carder, Wooden Box Over The Spikes | 10.00 |
| Store, Flue Cleaner, Peerless, Mechanical | 5.00 |
| Store, Fly Killer, Daisy | 3.50 |
| Store, Fly Trap, Embossed Unique Fly Trap, Glass, Conical, 3 Knob Feet | 48.00 |
| Store, Freezer, Ice Cream, Acme 5 Minute, Acmooan Co., Phila., Red Metal | 10.00 |
| Store, Freezer, Ice Cream, Top Crank | 29.50 |
| Store, Game, Domino Set, Warner's Safe Yeast & Remedies | 5.00 |
| Store, Game, Puzzle, Jigsaw, New & True Coffee | 2.00 |
| Store, Glass, Phospho-Soda, Marked Ha, Red Measures | 2.50 |
| Store, Glove Duster, Wooden, Bowl For Powder, Nozzle For Fingers Of Gloves | 6.75 |
| Store, Glove, Red Ryder, Pair | 4.00 |
| Store, Goblet, Heineken's Beer, Gold Rim, Stemmed | 2.75 |
| Store, Goblet, Moerlein's Lager Beer | 18.50 |
| Store, Goblet, Moerlein's National Beer, Cincinnati, Ohio, Stemmed | 11.00 |
| Store, Goblet, Peanut Butter, Clear | 1.50 |
| Store, Grinder, Poppy Seed, Brass & Iron, Clamp On | 35.00 |
| Store, Grinder, Spice, Brass, Removable Iron Crank, Oriental Design | 35.00 |
| Store, Gum Machine, see Store, Machine, Gum ball | |
| Store, Hame Set, U.S.Hame Co., Wooden, Iron Hardware, Brass Balls, 2 Piece | 10.00 |
| Store, Hame, Nickel Plated Brass Balls, Iron Hardware, Wooden, Leather Strap | 10.00 |
| Store, Hame, Wooden, Pair | 2.00 |
| Store, Hammer & Can Opener, Iron, Dated 1898 | 15.00 |
| Store, Handbill, "Eat Like A Horse Take Electric Bitters" | 8.50 |
| Store, Handbill, Old Reliable Virginia Negro Minstrels, 44 X 10 In. | 10.50 |
| Store, Handbill, Yankee Robinson Circus, 10 X 28 In. | 8.50 |
| Store, Hanger, Coat, Folding, Dated 1913 | 6.00 |
| Store, Hanger, Wall, Double Arm, Iron | 2.50 |
| Store, Harness Spreader, 2 Martingales, Brass Studs & Letters, Pair | 35.00 |
| Store, Hat, Henderson Motorcycles, Felt, Leather Insignia, C.1910 | 20.00 |
| Store, Heater, Curling Iron, Gas, Cast Iron, On Back Of Alligator | 22.00 |
| Store, Heater, Soapstone In Wooden Box, Sliding Cover With Holes | 60.00 |
| Store, Helmet, Miner's, Hard Boiled-Bulard Co., Lamp Holder, Dated 1925 | 22.00 |
| Store, Holder, Beer Can, Grand Prize, Blue Plastic | 4.50 |
| Store, Honing Outfit, Wadsworth Canandaigua, For Straight Razor, 4 Sides | 2.00 |
| Store, Horsecollar, Brasses, Salesman's Sample Leather, 5 1/2 X 9 1/2 In. | 50.00 |
| Store, Hosiery Clicker, Buster Brown | 10.00 |
| Store, Humidor, Cinco Tobacco, Tin | 6.00 |
| Store, Humidor, LaPalina Cigars, Lid | 9.00 |
| Store, Ice Box, Oak, 2 Glass Doors, Mirror, Brass Hardware, 5 1/2 Feet | 375.00 |
| Store, Ice Tongs, Chain Handle | 5.00 |
| Store, Jackdaw Clothes Reel, Salesman's Sample, 15 In. Arms | 25.00 |
| Store, Jar, Adams Gum | 25.00 |
| Store, Jar, Buster Brown Mustard, 2 1/2 In.High | 3.50 |
| Store, Jar, Cocanola Gum | 25.00 |
| Store, Jar, Dad's Oatmeal Cookies | 20.00 |
| Store, Jar, Dean & Sons, Licorice, New York, Embossed, Tin Top, Square | 26.00 |
| Store, Jar, Lucky Joe Mustard, Bank | 4.00 |
| Store, Jar, National Biscuit Co., Embossed | 35.00 |
| Store, Jar, Planter's Peanut, Hexagon, Mr.Peanut On Sides, Peanut Finial | 55.00 |
| Store, Jar, Planter's Peanut, Peanut Finial, 6 Sided | 72.50 |

| | |
|---|---|
| Store, Jar, Planter's Peanut, Square, Planters Embossed On Sides | 45.00 |
| Store, Jar, Planter's Peanut, Tin Lid, Slanted | 22.00 |
| Store, Jar, Tobacco, Teddy Bear, 5 In. | 22.50 |
| Store, Keg, Falstaff Beer, Aluminum, 17 Quart | 15.00 |
| Store, Keg, Powder, Grained Hardwood, 7 Wooden Lap Locked Bands, 10 In. | 32.00 |
| Store, Kit, First Aid, Official Boy Scout, Dated 1928 | 5.00 |
| Store, Knife, Barnum & Bailey Circus Engraved On Blade, Stag Handle | 5.75 |
| Store, Knife, C.F.Blanke Tea & Coffee Co., Germany, 3 Blade | 10.00 |
| Store, Knife, Ford, 1930, Key Shape, Mother-Of-Pearl Handle | 6.50 |
| Store, Knife, Ford, 1940, Folding, Case | 5.00 |
| Store, Knife, Packard Hawk, 1958 | 5.00 |
| Store, Knife, Pocket, Buckeye Beer | 6.50 |
| Store, Knife, Pocket, Miller Bros.Office | 10.00 |
| Store, Knife, Pocket, Purina | 5.00 |
| Store, Knife, Tobacco, Frary & Clark, Wooden Handle | 5.00 |
| Store, Lamp Lighter, Gas, Double Brass Tube, Wooden Handle, Wire Bound | 15.00 |
| Store, Lard Squeezer, Wooden | 10.00 |
| Store, Letter Opener, Boston Safe Deposit & Trust Co., Nickel Plated | 2.75 |
| Store, Letter Opener, Dated 1904 | 6.50 |
| Store, Letter Opener, Insure With Prudential, Brass, 7 1/2 In.Long | 2.95 |
| Store, Letter Opener, Tea & Coffee Co., Brass | 4.00 |
| Store, Letter Opener, Uneeda Biscuit Boy | 10.00 |
| Store, Lighter, Cigar, Eldred Mfg.Co., Chicago, Gasoline, 1899 | 32.50 |
| Store, Lighter, Cigarette & Cigar, Art Deco, Counter Top, Woman's Head, 1925 | 35.00 |
| Store, Lighter, Cigarette, Camel Cigarettes, Metal, Lithographed | 2.50 |
| Store, Lighter, Cigarette, Chesterfield Cigarettes, Lithographed, Metal | 2.25 |
| Store, Lighter, Cigarette, Lucky Strike Cigarettes, Metal, Lithographed | 2.50 |
| Store, Lighter, Cigarette, Salem Cigarettes, Metal, Lithographed | 2.50 |
| Store, Lighter, Cigarette, Winston Cigarettes, Metal, Lithographed | 2.50 |
| Store, Loom, Rug | 100.00 |
| Store, Lunch Box, Brotherhood Tobacco | 35.00 |
| Store, Lunch Box, Dixie Queen Tobacco, Basket Weave | 12.00 To 20.00 |
| Store, Lunch Box, Dixie Queen Tobacco, Lady | 30.00 |
| Store, Lunch Box, George Washington Tobacco | 12.50 To 19.00 |
| Store, Lunch Box, Patterson Seal Tobacco, Basket Weave | 14.00 |
| Store, Lunch Box, Sinsible Tobacco | 15.00 |
| Store, Lunch Box, Union Leader Gold Eagle Tobacco | 18.00 |
| Store, Lunch Box, Union Leader Tobacco, 1910 Stamp | 18.00 |
| Store, Lunch Pail, Dixie Queen Tobacco, Basket Weave | 10.00 |
| Store, Lunch Pail, Dixie Queen Tobacco, Lady's Picture | 28.00 |
| Store, Lunch Pail, Green Turtle Tobacco, Tin | 30.00 |
| Store, Lunch Pail, Hand Bag Tobacco, Tin | 27.50 |
| Store, Lunch Pail, J.Wright Co.'s Winner Tobacco, Tin | 18.00 |
| Store, Lunch Pail, Matthewsons's Gun Powder, Tin | 10.00 |
| Store, Lunch Pail, Patterson's Seal Tobacco, Tin | 15.00 |
| Store, Lunch Pail, Plow Boy Tobacco | 20.00 |
| Store, Lunch Pail, Redicut Tobacco, Tin | 25.00 |
| Store, Lunch Pail, Tiger Tobacco | 10.00 |
| Store, Lunch Pail, U.S.Marine Tobacco, Tin | 20.00 |
| Store, Lunch Pail, World's Navy Tobacco, Tin | 18.00 |
| Store, Machine, Adding, American Can Co., Dated Aug.27, 1912 | 20.00 |
| Store, Machine, Apple Vending, Coin-Operated, Round, 5 Cent Slot, 6 Ft.High | 250.00 |
| Store, Machine, Aspirin, 10 Cents | 20.00 |
| Store, Machine, Basketball, Long Shot | 75.00 |
| Store, Machine, Booze Barometer, Nickel | 100.00 |
| Store, Machine, Bunch, For Bunching Tobacco, Iron | 22.50 |
| Store, Machine, Butter-Kist Peanuts, Roaster | 360.00 |
| Store, Machine, Capsule, Pharmacy, Metal & Wood, Remington, Phila. | 25.00 |
| Store, Machine, Check Canceling, Banker's, Hand Operated | 22.00 |
| Store, Machine, Cigarette Slot, Penny | 100.00 |
| Store, Machine, Football, Kicker Catcher | 75.00 |
| Store, Machine, Gambling, Booster, 3 Dice In A Cup, 5 Cents | 125.00 |
| Store, Machine, Gambling, Hit Me, Blackjack, 1, 5, 10, & 25 Cents | 250.00 |
| Store, Machine, Gambling, Magic Clock, Fortune Telling Slot Type, 5 Cents | 150.00 |
| Store, Machine, Gambling, Pak-O-Cigs, 3 Dice In A Cup, 1 Cent | 130.00 |

| | |
|---|---|
| Store, Machine, Gambling, Punch-A-Ball, 2 Locks & Keys, 5 Cents | 130.00 |
| Store, Machine, Gambling, Whirl-O-Ball, 5 Balls For 1 Cent, Keeps Score | 135.00 |
| Store, Machine, Gambling, Win-A-Pack, 3 Reel Cigarette Slot, 1 Cent | 125.00 |
| Store, Machine, Garret's Improved Gold Changer, Patent, Iron, Slots, C.1850 | 175.00 |
| Store, Machine, Gum Ball, Wooden, 2 For 1 Cent Chiclets, Keys | 40.00 |
| Store, Machine, Gum Ball, 1 Cent | 75.00 |
| Store, Machine, Gum Ball, 1935, Balt Mfg.Co. | 25.00 |
| Store, Machine, Gum, Hit The Target | 85.00 |
| Store, Machine, Gum, Honey Dew | 75.00 |
| Store, Machine, Gum, Mill's Tab | 75.00 |
| Store, Machine, Gum, Moon Rocket, 5 Ft.High | 90.00 |
| Store, Machine, High Fly 5 Cents Baseball | 125.00 |
| Store, Machine, Hot Peanuts | 30.00 |
| Store, Machine, Imp Cigarettes, Slot, 3 Reel | 75.00 |
| Store, Machine, Knicker-N-Catcher | 60.00 |
| Store, Machine, Little League Baseball | 75.00 |
| Store, Machine, Marvel Cigarettes, Slot, 3 Reel | 125.00 |
| Store, Machine, Mill's Novelty Co., Chicago, 1910, Nickel Slot, 26 In.High | 300.00 |
| Store, Machine, Penny Gum, Pulver, Wall Mount | 50.00 |
| Store, Machine, Pulver Gum, Clown, Yellow, Keys | 85.00 |
| Store, Machine, Pulver Gum, Kid, Yellow, Keys | 85.00 |
| Store, Machine, Races Paces Horses | 850.00 |
| Store, Machine, Razor Blade Sharpening, Kriss Kross, Chrome Plated Brass | 4.75 |
| Store, Machine, School, Victor, Oak | 850.00 |
| Store, Machine, Slot, Five Jacks, Penny | 250.00 |
| Store, Machine, Tom Thumb Peanut, Miniature | 5.00 |
| Store, Match Holder, American Steel & Wire Co., Tin | 12.00 |
| Store, Match Holder, DeLaval Cream Separator, Wall | 20.00 To 22.50 |
| Store, Match Holder, Keene's Chop House, Striker | 10.00 |
| Store, Match Holder, McCormick Deering, Tin | 4.50 |
| Store, Match Holder, Standing, Morton Emery Wheel Co., Mass., Pyramid Shape | 2.95 |
| Store, Match Safe & Cigar Cutter, Liquor Store Ad | 5.00 |
| Store, Match Safe & Cigar Cutter, Pillsbury's Wheat Food, 1902 | 14.50 |
| Store, Match Safe, Anheuser Busch, Embossed Eagle, Letter A Trademark | 20.00 |
| Store, Match Safe, Gillette Blades, Brass | 12.50 |
| Store, Match Safe, Golden Grain Belt Beers, Minneapolis Brewing, Brass | 18.00 |
| Store, Match Safe, Hershey's Happy Home Bread, Tin, Wall, Lithograph | 32.00 |
| Store, Match Safe, Michigan Stoves Are Best, Wall, Cast Iron, 7 In. | 25.00 |
| Store, Match Safe, Pocket, Diamond Match Co., Brass On Tin | 4.95 |
| Store, Match Safe, Red Top Rye Whiskey, Celluloid, Black, Red Top | 18.00 |
| Store, Match Safe, Wadhurst Farms, Pig With Ham Under Arm, Nickel Plated | 78.00 |
| Store, Match Safe, Wall, "Michigan Stoves Are Best, " Cast Iron, 7 In. | 25.00 |
| Store, Matchbox, The John W.Stevens Co., Friction Match, Wooden, Striker | 2.95 |
| Store, Measure, Dry, Peck | 12.00 |
| Store, Measure, Dry, 1/2 Peck | 15.00 |
| Store, Measure, Dry, 2 Quart, Signed | 10.00 |
| Store, Measure, Grain, Wooden, Round, 11 In. | 13.00 |
| Store, Measure, Hat, Brass & Iron | 28.00 |
| Store, Measure, Quart, Tin, U.S.Legal | 2.50 |
| Store, Measure, Tape, Atlanta, Ga., Buggy & Lady's Head | 16.50 |
| Store, Measure, Tape, Celluloid Egg, Fly Pull | 5.00 |
| Store, Measure, Tape, Covered Wagon | 5.00 |
| Store, Measure, Tape, Davis & Furber Machinery Co., Mass. | 8.00 |
| Store, Measure, Tape, Egg Shape, Bee Pull | 6.50 |
| Store, Measure, Tape, Fab | 3.50 |
| Store, Measure, Tape, Figural, Negro | 6.00 |
| Store, Measure, Tape, Figural, 3 Feet In One Shoe | 40.00 |
| Store, Measure, Tape, Kangaroo | 5.00 |
| Store, Measure, Tape, Owl | 12.50 |
| Store, Measure, Tape, Woonsocket Napping Machinery Co., Steel | 6.00 |
| Store, Measure, Wagon Tire, Traveler | 10.00 |
| Store, Measuring Wheel, Wells Bros., Cast Iron, Wooden Handle | 10.00 |
| Store, Medicine Glass, Knopped, Trumpet Shape, Pontil, Plain Foot | 50.00 |
| Store, Mirror, Bathing Beauty | 5.00 |
| Store, Mirror, Batlin & Horowitz, Typewriters, Bronx, N.Y. | 6.00 |
| Store, Mirror, Beeman's Pepsin Gum, Picture Of Man | 16.00 |

| | |
|---|---|
| Store, Mirror, Betty Boop, Pocket, 2 1/8 In. | 1.00 |
| Store, Mirror, Bradley Shoes | 5.00 |
| Store, Mirror, Chippewa, Niagara River Line, Pocket | 7.50 |
| Store, Mirror, Clothiers, Lady, Pocket | 10.00 |
| Store, Mirror, Clover Farms Coffee, Wall, Picture Of Cans, 12 X 4 In. | 8.00 |
| Store, Mirror, D.H.Sherman Co., Sawmill Machinery, Portland, Oregon, Pocket | 18.00 |
| Store, Mirror, Dido Umbrella, Sticks & Fancy Bags For Presents, Round | 4.95 |
| Store, Mirror, Dr.O.H.Stevens, Optometry, Broken Bow, Nebraska, Pocket, Round | 12.00 |
| Store, Mirror, Duffy's Malt Whiskey, Pocket, Oval, Chemist & Book | 27.50 |
| Store, Mirror, Duflex Soles, Pocket, Round, 2 Faced Man | 30.00 |
| Store, Mirror, Enjoy Marathon Beer, Wall, 3 1/2 X 10 In. | 8.00 |
| Store, Mirror, Enna Jettick, Pocket, Rectangular, 1920s | 7.00 |
| Store, Mirror, F.C.Kidder Co., Onions, S.Deerfield, Mass. | 6.00 |
| Store, Mirror, Kyanize Varnishes, Rettig Hardware, Ohio, Pocket | 10.00 |
| Store, Mirror, Lane's Shoe Store, Pine, 9 1/4 In. Square | 27.00 |
| Store, Mirror, Laub-Zink Furniture, Pocket, Oval, 2 Faced Man | 30.00 |
| Store, Mirror, Mae Murray In Peacock Alley, Purse Size, Silver, Handle | 10.00 |
| Store, Mirror, Michelob Beer, Antique Wood Finish Frame, 16 X 24 In. | 90.00 |
| Store, Mirror, Monarch Typewriter | 8.50 |
| Store, Mirror, Naughty, French | 7.50 |
| Store, Mirror, Old Chicago Lager Beer, Antique Wood Finish, 20 X 12 In. | 75.00 |
| Store, Mirror, Olympia Beer, Antique Wood Finish Frame, 20 X 12 In. | 75.00 |
| Store, Mirror, Prudential Building, 2 In.Diameter | 12.50 |
| Store, Mirror, Quaker State, Pocket, Round | 4.50 |
| Store, Mirror, Star Brand Shoes, 3 1/2 In.Diameter | 7.00 |
| Store, Mirror, The Snow Shoe, Dog & Man Picture, Oval, 2 3/4 In. | 18.00 |
| Store, Mirror, Transill's Punch 5 Cent Cigar, Pocket | 8.50 |
| Store, Mirror, V.Linn & Son, Carriages, Brooklyn, N.Y. | 5.00 |
| Store, Mirror, Visit Krug Park, Omaha, Nebraska, Round, 4 In. | 8.00 |
| Store, Mirror, Washington Irving Steamer, Pocket | 7.50 |
| Store, Mirror, Whitehouse Coffee | 12.00 |
| Store, Mirror, Wm.F.Murphy's Sons & Co.Blank Book & Loose Leaf, Phila, 1820 | 10.00 |
| Store, Model, Milliners, 11 In.Tall | 145.00 |
| **Store, Mold, see also Tin, Mold** | |
| Store, Mold, Chocolate, Binoculars, Metal | 15.00 |
| Store, Mold, Chocolate, Rabbit, Metal, 5 In. | 5.25 |
| Store, Mold, Cigar, Double, Wooden, 8 In.Wide | 7.50 |
| Store, Mold, Cigar, Wooden, 4 1/2 In.Wide | 5.75 |
| Store, Mold, Cigar, Wooden, 22 In. Long | 8.00 |
| Store, Mold, Cigar, 11 In.Long | 15.00 |
| Store, Mold, Cigar, 22 In.Long | 20.00 |
| Store, Mold, Maple Sugar Rectangular, Cherry & Tin, 30 Sections | 45.00 |
| Store, Mold, Toy, Humpty Dumpty, Pot Metal, 2 Part | 20.00 |
| Store, Mortar & Pestle, Brass, Knob Handles, 7 1/2 In.High | 40.00 |
| Store, Mortar, Salt, Wooden, Round, Shallow, 1 Piece, 3 X 3 1/2 In. | 15.00 |
| Store, Mug, Borden Co., Picture Of Beauregard, 3 1/4 In.High | 4.00 |
| Store, Mug, Borden Co., Picture Of Beulah, 3 1/4 In.High | 4.00 |
| Store, Mug, Borden Co., Picture Of Elmer, 3 1/4 In.High | 4.00 |
| Store, Mug, Dickinson's Pine Tree Timothy Seed | 8.00 |
| Store, Mug, Elsie, The Borden Cow, Pottery | 15.00 |
| Store, Mug, Hires Root Beer, Boy Holding Mug, Villeroy & Boch | 50.00 |
| Store, Mug, Hires, Corset Shape, Crockery, Black Under Glaze, 7 In.High | 15.00 |
| Store, Mug, Jim Dandy Root Beer | 9.00 |
| Store, Mug, Lowenbrau Munich Beer, Glass | 2.50 |
| Store, Mug, Mr.Peanut | 2.00 |
| Store, Mug, O'hara Watch Co., Green China, Monk & Violin, 5 In. | 19.00 |
| Store, Mug, Pabst Beer, Elves & Barrel, White Lining, Thuemler, Pa. | 19.00 |
| Store, Mug, Rochester Root Beer, Glass | 8.50 |
| Store, Mug, Wooden, Monk On Front, Compliments Of, Etc., 5 1/2 In.High | 21.00 |
| Store, Nut Pick, Oak Box, Blue Lining, Set Of 6 | 10.00 |
| Store, Nut Set, Mr.Peanut, Planter's, Tin, Decorated, 5 Piece | 10.00 |
| Store, Nutcracker, Squirrel | 10.00 |
| Store, Oilcan, Motorol, Gas Engine Cylinders, 10 In.High | 3.50 |
| Store, Opener, Bottle, Crab Orchard Whiskey, Wooden Barrel Handle | 5.00 |
| Store, Opener, Letter, Dr.Pepper, Magnifying Glass, "Drink Dr.Pepper" | 1.75 |
| Store, Opener, Metal Beer Can, Pabst Blue Ribbon Beer | 1.00 |

| | |
|---|---|
| Store, Package, Fireside Stove Polish, H.A.Bartlett & Co. | 2.75 |
| Store, Packet, Recipe, Walter Baker Chocolate, 1904, Factory, Cardboard | 4.00 |
| Store, Paddle, Lard, Flat, Rounded, Wooden | 10.00 |
| Store, Pail, Armour Peanut Butter | 25.00 |
| Store, Pail, Butternut Coffee, Tin, Gallon | 20.00 |
| Store, Pail, Covered, Light Blue & White Mottled Enamel, 2 Quart | 8.50 |
| Store, Pail, Credo Peanut Butter | 10.00 |
| Store, Pail, Ontario Peanut Butter | 10.00 |
| Store, Pail, Oxheart Peanut Butter | 4.50 |
| Store, Pail, Rival Peanut Butter | 25.00 |
| Store, Pail, Sears & Roebuck's Tea, 5 Pounds | 30.00 |
| Store, Pail, Staple Brand Peanut Butter | 9.00 |
| Store, Pail, Sultana Peanut Butter | 10.00 |
| Store, Pail, Toyland Peanut Butter | 25.00 |
| Store, Pamphlet, Chase & Sanborn, 1889, Illustrations | 5.00 |
| Store, Pamphlet, Take No-To-Bac, Cures The Tobacco Habit, 1882 | 5.00 |
| Store, Paper Clip, Celluloid Fix | 3.00 |
| Store, Paperweight, Cummer Jones Co., Chicago, Bronze, Bell Shape | 25.00 |
| Store, Paperweight, Hornthal's Hearse, N.Y. | 15.00 |
| Store, Paperweight, Pabst Blue Ribbon Beer, Glass, 2 3/4 X 4 1/4 X 3/4 In. | 10.00 |
| Store, Paperweight, Winchester Repeating Arms Co., 1910, Glass, Red, Blue | 225.00 |
| Store, Pen & Pencil Combination, Gold Plated, Tourmaline In End Of Handle | 30.00 |
| Store, Pen, Fountain, Black, Gold Trim, 14K Gold Tip | 6.95 |
| Store, Pen, Fountain, Conklin Crescent Filler | 10.00 |
| Store, Pen, Fountain, Eversharp, Yellow Gold Filled, 14K Gold Point | 15.00 |
| Store, Pen, Fountain, Pepsi Cola, Bottle Clip, 1940s | 15.00 |
| Store, Pen, Fountain, Transo Tank Pen, Patent 1920 | 9.00 |
| Store, Pen, Mother-Of-Pearl Handle, Gold Tip | 19.50 |
| Store, Pencil Holder, Desk, Arched | 6.50 |
| Store, Pencil Sharpener, Uncle Sam, 2 In. | 4.00 |
| Store, Pencil, Dodge Brothers Motor Co., New Orleans, Metal | 9.00 |
| Store, Pencil, Gold Filled, Retractable, 3 1/2 In.Long | 4.75 |
| Store, Pencil, Mechanical, Gold Plated, Egyptian Figure Form, Enameled | 45.00 |
| Store, Pencil, Mechanical, Gold, Art Deco, Etched, Black Enamel Trojan Walls | 100.00 |
| Store, Pencil, Mechanical, Gold, Engraved Erwin Agnew, Topaz Stone | 35.00 |
| Store, Pencil, Mechanical, Silver, Cross Form, 1 5/8 In.Closed | 30.00 |
| Store, Pencil, Planter's Peanut, Mechanical | 7.50 |
| Store, Pencil, Purse, Hexagonal, Extends, Stone In End, Engraved, Decorated | 12.00 |
| Store, Pencil, Retractable, Gold Filled, 3 3/8 In.Long | 4.75 |
| Store, Penholder, Colonial Mfg.Co., N.Y., Green Polished Stone Top, Bronze | 10.00 |
| Store, Pinback, Bond Bread, Lindbergh | 4.00 |
| Store, Pinback, Pepsi Cola, Dated 1953, 2 1/2 In.Square | 4.00 |
| Store, Pinback, Sargent's Razor Suit Shavers, Patent 1896 | 2.75 |
| Store, Pinback, Starrett Tools, Dated 1891, Picture | 2.00 |
| Store, Plaiter, Young's, Board, Tin Strips, To Pleat Cloth, 10 X 15 In. | 20.00 |
| Store, Plaque, Budweiser, Plastic Horseshoe, Clydesdale Horse, Wooden | 10.50 |
| Store, Plate, Banner Baking Powder, 11 In. | 35.00 |
| Store, Plate, Falstaff Beer, Plastic | 5.00 |
| Store, Plate, Fred Krug Brewing Co., Anniversary, 1859 & 1909 Plants | 30.00 |
| Store, Plate, George Urban Milling Co., Urban Liberty Flour, N.Y., 8 In. | 5.00 |
| Store, Plate, Mathis Brewing Co., L.A., Feb.21, 1905, Tin, Portrait, 10 In. | 25.00 |
| Store, Plate, Morse Furniture Co., Boston, Tin, Girl's Picture | 22.00 |
| Store, Plate, Seagram's Whiskey, Grizzly Bear, Paul Branson, 10 In. | 10.00 |
| Store, Plate, Urban's Liberty Flour, Depression Glass, Pink, 7 3/4 In. | 15.00 |
| Store, Platter, Pioneer Flour, 90th Anniversary | 40.00 |
| Store, Poster, Andrew Downie's Circus, 1890s, Black & Green, 10 X 29 In. | 18.00 |
| Store, Poster, Christy Brothers 5 Ring Wild Animal Show, 32 In. High | 65.00 |
| Store, Poster, Hagenbeck-Wallace Circus, 41 X 25 In. | 60.00 |
| Store, Poster, Heroes Of The Regiment, Laurel & Hardy, 1934 | 25.00 |
| Store, Poster, Kar Mi Shoots A Cracker From A Man's Head, 1914 | 65.00 |
| Store, Poster, Kellogg's Toasted Corn Flakes, Box With Contents, 1917 | 12.00 |
| Store, Poster, Little Men, Kay Francis, Jack Oakie, George Bancroft, 1940 | 15.00 |
| Store, Poster, Oregon Pioneer Association, 46th Reunion, June 20, 1918 | 97.50 |
| Store, Poster, Ringling Bros. & Barnum & Bailey Combined Circus | 55.00 |
| Store, Poster, Royal Baking Powder, Miniature Can With Contents, 1923 | 16.50 |
| Store, Poster, She's In The Army, Marie Wilson, Lyle Talbot | 12.00 |

| | |
|---|---|
| Store, Poster, The Fall Of Babylon, Silent Movie, 1919, 8 X 10 In. | 7.50 |
| Store, Poster, They Meet Again, Jean Hersholt, Dorothy Lovett, 1941 | 12.00 |
| Store, Poster, U.S.Army, Uncle Sam Pointing Finger, 11 X 14 In. | 24.00 |
| Store, Poster, Undertaker's, Black, Dated 1835, 8 X 19 In. | 25.00 |
| Store, Poster, Venus Cut Tobacco, C.1860, Lithograph Nude Venus, 11 In. | 12.50 |
| Store, Pouch, George Washington Tobacco, Cloth | 3.50 |
| Store, Pouch, Oceanic Tobacco, Cloth | 3.50 |
| Store, Pouch, Union World Tobacco, Cloth | 5.50 |
| Store, Press, Lard, Lever Type, Wooden | 5.00 |
| Store, Press, Printing, Cast Iron, Wooden Box, Sliding Cover, 3 Pieces | 10.00 |
| Store, Print, Cream Of Wheat, Barefoot Boy, Fishing Pole & Fish, Scott, 1922 | 18.50 |
| Store, Print, Cream Of Wheat, Negro Chef Holding Calendar, Dated 1914 | 18.50 |
| Store, Print, Ferdinand's Blue Store, Boston, 1895, Lithograph, Color | 75.00 |
| Store, Print, Johnnie Walker Scotch & Canada Dry Ginger Ale, F.N.Davis | 3.50 |
| Store, Print, Textile, Metal & Wooden, Fits Hand, 5 X 2 X 1 In. | 25.00 |
| Store, Print, Wrigley's Spearmint Perfect Gum, Fougler Co., Lithograph | 20.00 |
| Store, Printing Block, Copper, Centennial, Main & Machinery Buildings | 75.00 |
| Store, Printing Block, Copper, 1876 Centennial, Government Building | 50.00 |
| Store, Program, Barnum & Bailey Circus, Dated 1904 | 15.00 |
| Store, Pump, Barrel, Enterprise, Records Amount | 7.50 |
| Store, Pump, Beer, Brass | 20.00 |
| Store, Pump, Beer, Nickel On Brass | 7.50 |
| Store, Puzzle, Jigsaw, Lux Soap, 1930s | 2.50 |
| Store, Puzzle, White Sewing Machine, Lady On Bicycle & U.S.Map, 1880s | 25.00 |
| Store, Rake, Nail, Hand-Forged | 3.00 |
| Store, Razor Set, Safety, Gem, Purple Lined Artificial Leather Hinged Box | 5.00 |
| Store, Razor, Gem, Brass | 2.00 |
| Store, Razor, Joseph Batta, Original Box | 3.50 |
| Store, Razor, Safety, The Star, In Tin Can Dated 1896 | 9.00 |
| Store, Razor, Straight, Beau Brummel, Amber With Brass | 6.00 |
| Store, Razor, Straight, Clover, Ivory Colored Handle, Nickel Trim | 2.75 |
| Store, Razor, Straight, Durham | 5.00 |
| Store, Razor, Straight, F.W.Engels Special, Germany | 5.00 |
| Store, Razor, Straight, Ivory Type Handle, Bossong, Providence, R.I. | 2.95 |
| Store, Razor, Straight, Ivory Type Handle, Raised Nude Girl | 4.75 |
| Store, Razor, Straight, Jet Black Handle, Wade & Butcher, Sheffield, England | 2.75 |
| Store, Razor, Straight, Marked Extra Hollow Ground, Tree Design On Handle | 2.75 |
| Store, Razor, Straight, Raised Floral & Scrolls On Black Handle | 3.95 |
| Store, Razor, Straight, Winchester, No.8535, Green Celluloid Handles | 22.00 |
| Store, Receipt, For Digging A Grave, 1 Dollar & 67 Cents, Dated 1811 | 9.00 |
| Store, Robe, Buggy, Sorrel, Horsehide, 54 X 62 In. | 75.00 |
| Store, Roller Rule, Automatic Pencil, Measuring Mathematical Instrument | 15.00 |
| Store, Rule, Folding, Wooden, Brass Trim, 12 In.Long | 4.75 |
| Store, Ruler, Black-Fraiser Motor Co., Wooden | 1.00 |
| Store, Ruler, Boy Scout Syrup | 12.00 |
| Store, Ruler, Pugh Bros. Co., R.I., 4 & 6 Cylinder Cars, Wooden | 3.95 |
| Store, Sack, White House Flour Mill, Houston, Cloth, Loaf Of Bread Picture | 3.50 |
| Store, Sack, White Satin Sugar, Cloth | 2.00 |
| Store, Safe, Gem, Salesman's Sample, Wooden, Painted, Gem Safe In Gold | 85.00 |
| Store, Safe, Wooden, Salesman's Sample | 55.00 |
| Store, Salt & Pepper, Aunt Jemima & Uncle Mose | 3.00 |
| Store, Salt & Pepper, Coors Beer, 1937 | 7.50 |
| Store, Salt & Pepper, Fort Pitt Beer, 3 & 4 In.High | 3.00 |
| Store, Salt & Pepper, R.C.A.Victor Dogs, White & Black | 8.00 |
| Store, Salt & Pepper, Westinghouse Washer & Dryer, 3 In. | 8.00 |
| Store, Saltshaker, Worcester Salt, Purest, Cleanest, Best, Aluminium, Pair | 2.75 |
| Store, Sausage Stuffer, Grained Wood, 12 In.Long | 32.00 |
| Store, Scoop, Blueberry, Spring Handle | 30.00 |
| Store, Scoop, Candy, Blue, 6 In. | 8.00 |
| Store, Scoop, Candy, Glass, 6 1/2 In. Long | 9.00 |
| Store, Scoop, Cone, Tin | 5.00 |
| Store, Scoop, Ice Cream, Cone Shape, Ring Handle | 6.00 |
| Store, Scoop, Pickle, Glass | 9.50 |
| Store, Scoop, Tin, Soldered Handle, 6 1/2 X 13 1/2 In. | 5.00 |
| Store, Screen, Huntley & Palmer, Tin, Figural, Oriental Scenes, 4 Panel | 48.00 |
| Store, Scriber, Wooden | 2.50 |

| | |
|---|---|
| Store, Seal, Wax, Initial T, Black Wooden Handle | 10.00 |
| Store, Seed Sifting Tray, Round, Splint Woven Bottom, Hickory Sides, 18 In. | 125.00 |
| Store, Sharpener, Pencil, Figural, Cowboy's Head, Painted | 7.50 |
| Store, Sharpener, Pencil, Figural, Elephant, Celluloid | 5.00 |
| Store, Sharpener, Pencil, Styewriter Shape, 1 1/2 In. | 4.00 |
| Store, Sheller, Corn, Wooden, Box Bolted To Plank, Iron Handle, 18 In. | 25.00 |
| Store, Shoe Form, Child's, Hand-Carved Wood, Metal Sole, C.1880 | 9.00 |
| Store, Shoe Last, Walnut, Mounted On Pedestal To Be Fastened To Bench | 20.00 |
| Store, Shoe Shiner, Dandy, Iron, Dated 1906 | 3.50 |
| Store, Shoe, Heineken's Beer, Wooden, Pair | 6.25 |
| Store, Shoe, Ice House Worker's, Iron Top, Wood Bottom, Leather, C.1890, Pair | 35.00 |
| Store, Shoe, Lady's Hightop, Cast Iron, Painted Green, 6 In.High | 25.00 |
| Store, Shoecase, Round Front | 58.00 |
| Store, Shot Dispenser, 8 Section | 250.00 |
| Store, Shot Glass, Albion Rye, Embossed | 5.50 |
| Store, Shot Glass, American Supply Co., St.Louis, Mo. | 6.50 |
| Store, Shot Glass, Cornhill Rye, Embossed | 5.50 |
| Store, Shot Glass, Dean & Guilfoyle Central Pharmacy, N.Y., Clear | 5.00 |
| Store, Shot Glass, Druggists For Bassetts Native Herbs, Embossed Cask | 6.00 |
| Store, Shot Glass, Hamberger Co., Chicago, Etched | 4.25 |
| Store, Shot Glass, Quincy Belle, J.H.Buher & Bro., Quincy, Illinois | 6.50 |
| Store, Shot Glass, Schenley's Whiskey, Etched | 2.75 |
| Store, Shot Glass, Seagram's 100 Pipers Scotch, 2 Ozs. | 2.00 |
| Store, Showcase, Diamond Dye, Black & White Tin, Front Rack | 20.00 |
| Store, Showcase, Wood & Glass, 6 Ft. | 150.00 |
| Store, Sign, 'Drink Cadbury's Cocoa, ' C.1880, Little Girl Serving Cocoa | 9.00 |
| Store, Sign, American Beauty, Drummond Tab.Co., C.1895, Paper, 19 X 27 In. | 65.00 |
| Store, Sign, American Optical Co., Car Wreck, Paper Under Glass, C.1920 | 30.00 |
| Store, Sign, Anheuser Busch, Doctor, House, Shadow Of Stork, Tin, 1915 | 14.75 |
| Store, Sign, Anheuser Busch, Tin, 1935, 6 X 9 In. | 8.00 |
| Store, Sign, Apothecary, 19th Century, 18 X 13 1/2 In. ............... _Illus_ | 250.00 |
| Store, Sign, Barber's, Wooden Workable Straight Razor, 20 In. | 39.00 |
| Store, Sign, Beverwyck Sub Rosa, Red & Green Ground, Tin, 9 X 24 In. | 7.50 |
| Store, Sign, Bevo Beverage, Tin, 7 X 5 In. | 8.00 |
| Store, Sign, Bickmore Gall Salves, Horse, Cardboard, 17 X 12 In. | 25.00 |
| Store, Sign, Blacksmith, Made From Horseshoes | 95.00 |
| Store, Sign, Blacksmith, Tin, 19th Century, 10 X 16 In. ............... _Illus_ | 400.00 |
| Store, Sign, Blatz, Beer, Fluorescent, 22 X 24 In. | 27.50 |
| Store, Sign, Boone Cola, "A Boone To Good Health, " C.1920, Color | 2.00 |
| Store, Sign, Borden's Klim Powdered Milk, 1920s, 20 X 32 In. | 17.50 |
| Store, Sign, Boston Pad Garter, 1912, Cardboard, 8 X 7 In. | 12.00 |
| Store, Sign, Bradley & Metcalf Shoes, Tin & Porcelain, 27 X 18 In. | 50.00 |
| Store, Sign, British Pub, Figure Of Frederick William III, C.1850 | 1250.00 |
| Store, Sign, Buckingham Rye, Reverse Under Glass, 14 X 8 In. | 65.00 |

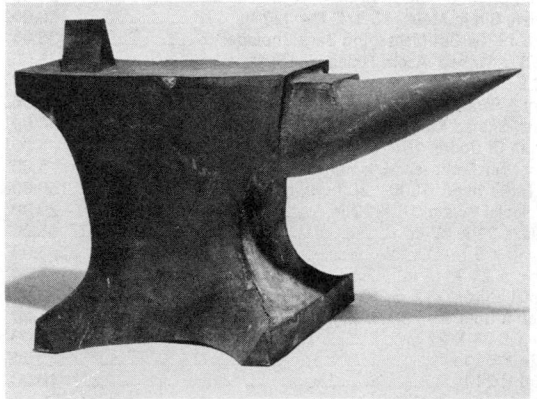

Store, Sign, Blacksmith, Tin, 19th Century, 10 X 16 In.

Store, Sign, Apothecary,
19th Century, 18 X 13 1/2 In.

Store, Sign, Bunte Candy, Rabbits & Basket Of Candy, Cardboard ............................... 5.00
Store, Sign, Butcher's, Eagle, 3 Tools, S Scrolls, Stars, Cast Iron, C.1850 ............... 325.00
Store, Sign, Canada Dry, The Original Maple Leaf Brand, Octagon, Cardboard ........... 5.00
Store, Sign, Carbonol, Heals, Cleans, Disinfects, Purifies, Metal, 33 X 50 In. ........... 50.00
Store, Sign, Carlings Brewing, Nine Pints Of The Law, Keystone Type Cops ............... 22.00
Store, Sign, Cetacolor Brightening Powder, Linen, 24 X 36 In., C.1890 ..................... 23.00
Store, Sign, Cigarette, Clown, Metal, 10 X 14 In. ................................................... 18.50
Store, Sign, Cognac Cocktails Tobacco, 1885, Paper On Canvas, 10 X 18 In. ........... 65.00
Store, Sign, Cole's Peruvian Bark & Wild Cherry Bitters, Porcelain, 16 In. ............... 65.00
Store, Sign, Continental Insurance, Metal, Locomobile Touring Car ........................... 60.00
Store, Sign, Daisy BB Gun, Tin ............................................................................ 3.50
Store, Sign, Dr.A.C.Daniel's Horse & Cattle Medicine, Wood, 29 X 12, C.1890 ....... 65.00
Store, Sign, Dr.Morse's Indian Root Pills, Cardboard, 24 In. ................................... 18.00
Store, Sign, Drink Beverwyck Sub Rosa, Tin, Red, Green, & Cream ......................... 7.50
Store, Sign, Drink Chocolate Champagne, Soda & Mineral Waters, Cardboard ........... 1.50
Store, Sign, Drink Dr.Brown's Celery Tonic, Tin, Red & Green On Yellow ................. 15.00
Store, Sign, Duffee's Laxative Tablets, Tin, 14 X 9 1/2 In. ................................... 10.00
Store, Sign, Elsie, The Borden Cow, Baked Enamel, C.1930, 15 X 22 In. ............... 18.00
Store, Sign, Embassy Cigarettes, Girl In Period Dress On Blue, Tin ......................... 50.00
Store, Sign, Falstaff Beer, Back Bar, Electric ........................................................ 10.00
Store, Sign, Fels-Naphtha, 1920s, Cardboard, Lady Smelling Soap ......................... 6.00
Store, Sign, Ferdinand's Blue Store, 1895, Color Lithograph, 23 X 33 In. ............... 75.00
Store, Sign, Fire Protection, Phoenix Rising From Flames, Copper, 9 In. ................. 85.00
Store, Sign, Fireman's Ax, Wooden, Black & Gilt Paint, 26 1/2 In. ......................... 50.00
Store, Sign, Fireman's Insurance Co., Newark, N.J., Aluminum, 25 X 19 In. ........... 35.00
Store, Sign, Fitger Beer, 1942, Cardboard, Lithographed, Calendar, Hunting ........... 16.50
Store, Sign, Flor De Berthold, Cigar, Pierced Tin, Red, Black & Yellow ................... 35.00
Store, Sign, Formetex Underwear, 1920s, Cardboard, Large Sizes, 15 X 10 In. ....... 12.00
Store, Sign, Glendora Coffee, Tin, 14 X 9 In. ...................................................... 12.00
Store, Sign, Glenwood Ranges Make Cooking Easy, Tin, 13 X 37 In. ..................... 39.50
Store, Sign, Grapette Soda, Tin, 21 X 12 In. ...................................................... 10.00
Store, Sign, Hambone 5 Cent Cigar, Cardboard, 20 X 13 In. ................................. 7.00
Store, Sign, Heine Hatters, Bethlehem, Pa., Figural Cat, 12 1/2 In. ....................... 9.00
Store, Sign, Hires Root Beer, Bottle Shape, Tin, 4 Ft.High ..................................... 60.00
Store, Sign, Hires Root Beer, Tin, 94 X 46 In. .................................................... 15.00
Store, Sign, Horner's Animal Bone Fertilizer, Tin, Yellow & Black ........................... 6.00
Store, Sign, Horse, Hollow Zinc, Iron Mounting Bracket, 38 1/2 In. Long ............... 175.00
Store, Sign, Imperial Club Cigars, Tin .................................................................. 12.00
Store, Sign, J.Palley's Hambone Cigars, Cardboard, 7 In.Diameter ......................... 7.50
Store, Sign, Livery Stable, 2 Sheet Metal Horses On Board, 32 X 11 1/2 In. ........... 150.00
Store, Sign, Longines Watch Co., Glass, Clock Face & Workings, C.1930, 8 In. ....... 28.00
Store, Sign, Luxor Cigarettes, Paper Under Glass, Lady, Art Nouveau Frame ........... 225.00
Store, Sign, Mason's Root Beer, Tin, 27 In. ........................................................ 3.95
Store, Sign, Meadville Pure Rye, Paper Under Glass, Oak Frame, Woman ............... 165.00
Store, Sign, Mecca Cigarettes, Christy Girl, 1912, Paper Under Glass, 19 In. ......... 70.00
Store, Sign, Mechanicks, Painted Wood, Man In Black Coat, C.1850, 34 In. Wide ... 350.00
Store, Sign, Miller High Life Beer, Fluorescent, 17 X 21 In. ................................... 24.00
Store, Sign, Miller High Life Beer, Tin, Girl On Moon, 36 X 45 In. ......................... 21.00
Store, Sign, Miller High Life Beer, Wooden, Girl In Moon, 13 1/2 X 4 1/2 In. ......... 10.00
Store, Sign, Mintee Massage, Cardboard, 1920s Girl Massaging Bare Shoulder ....... 25.00
Store, Sign, Mortician's Pole, Black & White Striped, Acorn Finials, C.1800 ........... 125.00
Store, Sign, Moxie, Cardboard, 37 X 30 In. ........................................................ 9.00
Store, Sign, Mrs.F.A.Woodward, Millinery & Fancy Goods, Metal ........................... 50.00
Store, Sign, Pabst Beer, Bottles & Oysters, Signed King, Paper Under Glass ........... 50.00
Store, Sign, Pepsi Cola, Cardboard, Picture Of Bottle, 16 X 8 1/4 In. ..................... 8.00
Store, Sign, Pepsi Cola, Say Pepsi, Please, Tin, Embossed Enamel ......................... 5.00
Store, Sign, Pharmacist, Carved Wood, Turk's Head, 1800s, 20 In.High ................. 150.00
Store, Sign, Pickwick Ale, Cardboard, Colonial Scene, 16 X 22 In. ......................... 20.00
Store, Sign, Piedmont Cigarettes, Porcelain, 31 X 47 In. ....................................... 65.00
Store, Sign, Potosi Beer, Metal, 3 Color, 10 X 7 In. ............................................. 3.00
Store, Sign, Potosi Beer, Porcelain, 4 Colors, 21 X 11 In. ..................................... 25.00
Store, Sign, Potosi, Wisconsin, Beer, Metal, Silver On Red, 10 X 7 In. ................... 3.00
Store, Sign, Prescriptions, Wooden, Black & Gold, Red Stenciling, 82 1/2 In. ......... 75.00
Store, Sign, R.C.A. Victor, Art Deco, Framed, 28 X 22 In. ..................................... 45.00
Store, Sign, Red White Blue Beer, Tin, 24 X 56 In. ............................................. 12.50
Store, Sign, Red White Blue Beer, Tin, 56 X 24 In. ............................................. 10.00

| | |
|---|---|
| **Store, Sign,** Ruppert Beer & Ale, On Glass, 12 1/2 X 18 In. | 15.00 |
| **Store, Sign,** Seagram's Canadian Whiskey, Paper Under Glass, Dated 1905 | 205.00 |
| **Store, Sign,** Smith Bros.Cough Drops, Tin, 28 X 11 In. | 40.00 |
| **Store, Sign,** Spark's Kidney & Liver, Mrs.Grover Cleveland, Ironstone | 300.00 |
| **Store, Sign,** Sporting Goods, Hunter & Cock Pheasant, Painted Wood, 9 Ft.High | 275.00 |
| **Store, Sign,** Stocktonia Flour, Baby In Wicker Crib, 15 X 20 In., C.1890 | 20.00 |
| **Store, Sign,** Stop For Velour Ice Cream, Tin, 20 X 28 In. | 7.50 |
| **Store, Sign,** Straight Brewed, Neuweiller Cream Ale, Tin On Cardboard, 8 In. | 10.00 |
| **Store, Sign,** The Aqua Crystal, For Sale Here, Oak Frame, 15 X 5 In. | 35.00 |
| **Store, Sign,** Tiger Tobacco, 24 X 30 In. | 300.00 |
| **Store, Sign,** Tobacconist, Iron, 19th Century _Illus_ | 800.00 |
| **Store, Sign,** Tom Palmer, World's Greatest Cigar, On Glass, C.1899 | 49.00 |
| **Store, Sign,** Trade, Dressmaker, Call Again, Wood, Gilt Letters, 9 X 21 In. | 60.00 |
| **Store, Sign,** Trade, Fish Market, Salmon, Carved & Painted Wood, 42 In.Long | 850.00 |
| **Store, Sign,** Turk's Head, Carved Wood, C.1850, 27 In.High | 895.00 |
| **Store, Sign,** Turkey Red Cigarettes, Girl With Pack, Cardboard, 16 X 20 In. | 35.00 |
| **Store, Sign,** U.S.Fidelity & Guarantee, Tin, Eagle & Shield, Framed | 15.00 |
| **Store, Sign,** Uncle John's Syrup, Cardboard, Color, 16 1/2 X 14 1/4 In. | 4.50 |
| **Store, Sign,** Universal Natural Milker, Tin, 24 X 10 In. | 10.00 |
| **Store, Sign,** Watchmaker's Shop, Pocket Watch, 19th Century, 31 In.High | 200.00 |
| **Store, Sign,** West Point, Mule, Tin, 6 In.Square | 10.00 |
| **Store, Sign,** With Every Meal Drink Double Stout, Schoidt Brewing, Cardboard | 3.00 |
| **Store, Sign,** Wrigley's Gum, Negro & Bulldog, Plasterboard, 40 X 52 In. | 50.00 |
| **Store, Sign,** Wurzburger Beer, German Soldier Blowing Foam, Cardboard | 20.00 |
| **Store, Silk,** Cigarette, Indian Chief | 1.00 |
| **Store, Sizer,** Cork, Cast Iron, Wooden Handle, 3 Slots | 15.00 |
| **Store, Snowshoe,** 42 In.Long, Pair | 60.00 |
| **Store, Soap,** Figural, Baby, Pennsylvania Soap Co., 4 1/2 In. | 20.00 |
| **Store, Spigot,** Barrel, Wooden | 2.00 |
| **Store, Spoon & Can Opener,** Metal | 4.00 |
| **Store, Spoon,** Baker's Chocolate, Figural, Lady, Silver Plate | 3.50 To 6.50 |
| **Store, Spoon,** Campbell Kids | 2.50 |
| **Store, Spoon,** Cream Top, Tin | 4.00 |
| **Store, Spoon,** Dennis The Menace | 6.50 |
| **Store, Spoon,** Log Cabin, Towle | 4.50 |
| **Store, Spoon,** Medicine, Duffy's Pure Malt, Glass | 3.00 |
| **Store, Spoon,** Old Grist, Mill Wheat Coffee | 3.75 |
| **Store, Spoon,** Planter's Peanut | 5.50 |
| **Store, Spoon,** Towle's Log Cabin Syrup, Small Size | 2.95 |
| **Store, Spoon,** Towle's Log Cabin, Log Cabin On Terminal, 4 1/2 In.Long | 9.00 |
| **Store, Stamp,** Notary Public, Iron, Patent 1854 | 13.00 |
| **Store, Stand,** Teaberry Gum, Clear Glass | 12.00 |
| **Store, Statue,** Jack Daniels, 90 Proof Whiskey, Dated 1911, 12 In. | 20.00 |
| **Store, Stereoscope, see Stereoscope** | |
| **Store, Stickpin,** Green Leaf Shape, Marked Liptons | 3.75 |
| **Store, Stirrer Holder,** Piel's Beer, Metal, Keg Shape, Drafts On It | 18.00 |
| **Store, Stirrer Holder,** Reingold Beer, Metal | 6.50 |
| **Store, Stool,** Shoeshine, Barber Shop, Wire & Wood | 48.00 |
| **Store, Straw Holder,** Soda Fountain, Glass & Metal | 20.00 |
| **Store, String Holder,** Beehive, Iron, Patent Dated 1865, 1868 | 23.00 |
| **Store, String Holder,** Ceiling, Cast Iron | 6.00 |
| **Store, String Holder,** Cone Shape, Counter Type, Iron, 3 1/4 In.High | 3.75 |
| **Store, Strop,** Razor, Kriss Kross, Boxed | 5.00 |
| **Store, Strop,** Razor, Kriss Kross, Mechanical | 15.00 |
| **Store, Sweeper,** Carpet, Air-Sweep, Wooden | 15.00 |
| **Store, Sweeper,** Vacuum, Golden Rod, Hand Operated | 37.50 |
| **Store, Syringe,** Stock, Brass, Original Box | 2.50 |
| **Store, Syrup,** Aunt Jemima & Uncle Mose | 3.00 |
| **Store, Syrup,** Rob Ross | 3.00 |
| **Store, Tablet,** School, Deanna Durbin Picture On Cover | 4.50 |
| **Store, Tap Knob,** Dobler Beer | 2.50 |
| **Store, Tap,** Beer Barrel, Old Crown, Nickel On Brass, Black Knob | 12.00 |
| **Store, Telegraph Key,** Morse Code, Wood Case, Flasher Light | 45.00 |
| **Store, Thermometer & Humidity Gauge,** Syracuse Containers, Tin Stand | 10.00 |
| **Store, Thermometer,** Bakelite Material Works, 1949, Pickaninny Peeks Out | 20.00 |
| **Store, Thermometer,** Camel, Wall, Tin | 5.00 |

Store, Sign, Tobacconist,
Iron, 19th Century
*(See Page 635)*

Store, Tin, George Washington Cut Plug,
5 X 3 1/2 In.
*(See Page 637)*

Store, Thermometer, Desk, Old Man Standing, Metal & Pottery ........................................ 8.00
Store, Thermometer, Little Black Sambo Standing, Composition, 5 In. ............................ 8.00
Store, Thermometer, Mail Pouch, Porcelain, Wood Frame, 6 Ft.Long ............................ 150.00
Store, Thermometer, Mounted On Child's Brass Sled, Hangs By Brass Rope .................. 3.95
Store, Thermometer, Negro Baby ........................................................................................ 6.00
Store, Thermometer, Royal Crown Cola, Tin, 25 1/2 In. Long ...................................... 8.00
Store, Thermometer, Taylor Candy, 1911 ........................................................................ 6.50
Store, Thermometer, W.Hilyer Bagsdale, The Candy Specialist, Copper Clips .................. 18.00
Store, Thermos, The Monkees .............................................................................................. 5.00
Store, Tin, Aleppo Tobacco, Boston, 1909, 2 X 3 In. .................................................. 15.00
Store, Tin, Angelus Marshmallows, 10 In.Diameter ........................................................ 5.00
Store, Tin, Banquet Hall Little Cigars ................................................................................ 14.00
Store, Tin, Beech-Nut Tobacco ............................................................................................ 32.50
Store, Tin, Beech-Nut, Constitution .................................................................................. 42.50
Store, Tin, Beech-Nut, Mohawk Valley .............................................................................. 42.50
Store, Tin, Beech-Nut, Mohawk Valley, 6 X 10 X 12 In. ............................................ 25.00
Store, Tin, Beech-Nut, Night Watch .................................................................................. 42.50
Store, Tin, Bohemian Plug Mixture ...................................................................................... 4.00
Store, Tin, Bond Street Tobacco, Pocket ............................................................................ 3.00
Store, Tin, Brigg's Tobacco, 1926 Stamp, Contents, Pocket ...................................... 4.00
Store, Tin, Briggs Tobacco, Pocket ...................................................................................... 6.00
Store, Tin, Buffalo Brand Peanut Butter, F.M.Hoyt & Co., Pound ............................ 4.00
Store, Tin, Bunte Marshmallows, Buster Brown Type Boy Picture, 10 In.High .......... 27.50
Store, Tin, Bunte Peanut, 10 Lbs. ...................................................................................... 20.00
Store, Tin, Campfire Marshmallows, Handle, 10 In.Diameter ...................................... 5.00
Store, Tin, Candy, Face Form .............................................................................................. 7.50
Store, Tin, Chesterfield Cigarettes, Flat ............................................................................ 4.00
Store, Tin, Climax Golden Twins Tobacco, Square, 4 In. .......................................... 7.50
Store, Tin, Climax Plug Tobacco .......................................................................................... 5.00
Store, Tin, Colgan's Violet Chips Gum, 1910, Baseball Player, Round ...................... 6.00
Store, Tin, Craven, A Virginia Cigarette, Red, Gold, & Cream .................................. 10.00
Store, Tin, Craven Tobacco, Oval ........................................................................................ 3.50
Store, Tin, D.Hough Coffee, Rockford, Ill., Round, 6 In.High .................................... 12.75
Store, Tin, Dan Patch Cut Plug ............................................................................................ 15.00
Store, Tin, Detecto Watches Your Weight, Art Deco Nudes, 1929, 4 X 3 In. .......... 3.75
Store, Tin, Diamond A Spice ................................................................................................ 1.50
Store, Tin, Dill's Best Cut Plug Tobacco ............................................................................ 2.00
Store, Tin, Dill's Best Tobacco, Pocket .............................................................................. 5.00
Store, Tin, Dixie Queen Cut Plug Tobacco ........................................................................ 21.00
Store, Tin, Dixon's Graphite .................................................................................................. 4.50
Store, Tin, Doctor Pettit's American Eye Salve ................................................................ 2.00
Store, Tin, Dr.Morse's Indian Root Pills ............................................................................ 8.00
Store, Tin, Droste's Cocoa, Hinged Lid, Dutch Children, Dated 1904, 4 In. .............. 7.00
Store, Tin, Dupont Gun Powder, Drum Type, 11 1/2 X 9 In. ...................................... 22.00

| | |
|---|---|
| Store, Tin, Dupont Gun Powder, Drum Type, 7 X 6 In. | 18.00 |
| Store, Tin, E.I.& Co., Ltd., Elizabeth & Margaret Photograph, 1930, Round | 8.75 |
| Store, Tin, Edgemont Crackers, Dated 1924 | 6.00 |
| Store, Tin, Edgeworth Pipe Tobacco | 3.00 |
| Store, Tin, Edgeworth Plug Slice Tobacco, Blue Top, C.1900 | 2.00 |
| Store, Tin, Edgeworth Ready Rubbed Tobacco | 7.00 |
| Store, Tin, Edgeworth Tobacco, Pocket | 5.00 |
| Store, Tin, Fatima Cigarettes, Flat 50 | 6.00 |
| Store, Tin, French's Chileo | 2.00 |
| Store, Tin, George Washington Cut Plug Tobacco, Round | 6.50 |
| Store, Tin, George Washington Cut Plug, 5 X 3 1/2 In. *Illus* | 14.00 |
| Store, Tin, George Washington Pipe Tobacco | 2.50 |
| Store, Tin, Gill's Best Sliced Tobacco | 3.00 |
| Store, Tin, Granger Pipe Tobacco | 3.50 |
| Store, Tin, Gumor Cleaner | 2.00 |
| Store, Tin, Half & Half Cut Plug Tobacco, Pocket | 3.00 |
| Store, Tin, Herold Sardine, Book Shape | 20.00 |
| Store, Tin, Hershey's Chocolate, 14 In.Diameter | 10.00 |
| Store, Tin, Hickok's Marshmallows, 10 In.Diameter | 5.00 |
| Store, Tin, Houdes No.1 Cut Plug Tobacco, Quebec, Trunk Shape | 25.00 |
| Store, Tin, Huntley & Palmer, Elizabeth On Horseback, Mitered Corners | 10.00 |
| Store, Tin, Huntley Palmer Biscuit, Ribbed Trunk Replica, Padlooko, Embossed | 15.00 |
| Store, Tin, Huyler's Gum, Sliding Top, Rectangular | 4.00 |
| Store, Tin, Idle Hour Cut Plug | 14.00 |
| Store, Tin, Imperial Granum, Yellow Paper Label, Square, 5 1/2 In. | 6.00 |
| Store, Tin, J.G.Dill's Best Cut Plug Tobacco, Yellow, Green, & Gold | 3.00 |
| Store, Tin, J.Goldmark's Percussion Caps, U.S.Musket, Patent 1876 | 4.95 |
| Store, Tin, Jackie Coogan Paint, Picturing The Kid | 10.00 |
| Store, Tin, Jacques' Baking Powder, Round, 1898, 5 Oz. | 5.00 |
| Store, Tin, Jean Hersholt, Country Dr.Pipe Mixture Tobacco, Paper On Tin | 5.50 |
| Store, Tin, John Sexton Co. Wholesale Tea & Coffee, Chicago, Round | 14.50 |
| Store, Tin, Johnson Gun Barrel Cleaner, Wisconsin, Screw Top, 2 Oz. | 2.00 |
| Store, Tin, Kaffe Hag, Dated 1926, Red, White, & Black, Pound | 7.00 |
| Store, Tin, Keller's Candy, Utica, N.Y., Red & Gold, Round, 5 Pound | 16.00 |
| Store, Tin, Kentucky Club Tobacco, Pocket | 4.00 |
| Store, Tin, Lily Soda, Red & White Stripes | 12.00 |
| Store, Tin, Lipton Tea, Paper Label, 4 X 5 X 4 In. | 6.50 |
| Store, Tin, Lipton's Tea, Gold & Silver Japanese Scenes, Square | 6.00 |
| Store, Tin, Loose Wiles Biscuits, Sunshine Biscuits, Basket Weave Bottom | 12.00 |
| Store, Tin, Louis Sherry, N.Y., Violets & Gold Scrolls | 5.00 |
| Store, Tin, Love's Biscuit, Hawaiian Scene, Marked 1927, 7 1/4 In. | 3.00 |
| Store, Tin, Luden's Cough Drops, Super Deluxe, 6 Compartments | 7.50 |
| Store, Tin, Martin Stove Polish | 2.00 |
| Store, Tin, Maya Tobacco, Lunch Box | 10.00 |
| Store, Tin, McCormick Banquet Tea Bags, Baltimore, 250 Bags | 22.00 |
| Store, Tin, McCormick Tea | 2.00 |
| Store, Tin, McCormick's Ginger | 1.75 |
| Store, Tin, McNess Nutmeg | 2.00 |
| Store, Tin, Mellor & Rittenhouse Licorice Lozenge, Glass Front, Green | 28.00 |
| Store, Tin, Melrose Marshmallows, 10 In.Diameter | 5.00 |
| Store, Tin, Millar's Paprika | 1.50 |
| Store, Tin, Mission Garden Tea | 2.50 |
| Store, Tin, Monarch Tea | 4.00 |
| Store, Tin, Murad, The Turkish Cigarette, 5 1/2 X 4 X 1 In. | 4.00 |
| Store, Tin, NB Biscuit, Rural Landscape On Lid, Octagonal | 10.00 |
| Store, Tin, Oceanic Cut Plug | 15.00 |
| Store, Tin, Octagon Cleanser, Full, 1940s | 1.00 |
| Store, Tin, Old Fireside Pure Tea, 1 1/2 X 2 X 1/2 In. | 5.50 |
| Store, Tin, Old London Waffles | 2.50 |
| Store, Tin, Old Mariner Tobacco | 2.00 |
| Store, Tin, Pall Mall Cigarettes, 'just Old-Fashioned Christmas Wishes' | 12.00 |
| Store, Tin, Patterson's Tuxedo Tobacco, 1910 Stamp | 12.00 |
| Store, Tin, Peak Frean's, Famous English Biscuits, 9 In.Square | 6.00 |
| Store, Tin, Pepsin Gum, Heart Form | 7.50 |
| Store, Tin, Petrine's Kake Kan Koffee, H.P.Coffee Co., St.Louis, 3 Pound | 20.00 |
| Store, Tin, Phillip Morris Cigarettes, 100s | 3.00 |

Store, Tin, Planter's Peanuts, Square ............................................................. 5.00
Store, Tin, Player's Navy Cut Cigarettes, 4 X 3 X 1 1/2 In. ....................... 6.50
Store, Tin, Prince Albert Crimp Cut Tobacco, 7 In.High ............................. 4.50
Store, Tin, Princine Baking Powder, Handle, 2 1/2 In.High ......................... 3.00
Store, Tin, Q Boid Cut Plug Tobacco ......................................................... 18.00
Store, Tin, Raleigh Tobacco, Square .......................................................... 3.00
Store, Tin, Ramon Laxative, Little Doctor On Lid, 1 In. Diameter .............. 2.00
Store, Tin, Ramseses II Egyptian Cigarettes, 100s ..................................... 9.00
Store, Tin, Ramseses II Egyptian Cigarettes, 50s ....................................... 7.00
Store, Tin, Rexall Theatrical Cold Cream ................................................... 5.00
Store, Tin, Rich's Ginger, 6 X 4 X 1 In. ..................................................... 3.50
Store, Tin, Richelieu Tea, 1/2 Pound ......................................................... 5.00
Store, Tin, Riley's Toffee, Art Deco, Mayflower Vessel, 7 3/4 In.High ........ 4.50
Store, Tin, Robin Hood Coffee ................................................................... 3.50
Store, Tin, Roly Poly, Mayo's Cut Plug Tobacco, Brownie, The Inspector ... 180.00
Store, Tin, Roly Poly, Mayo's Tobacco, Mammy ......................................... 165.00
Store, Tin, Roly Poly, Storekeeper ............................................................. 185.00
Store, Tin, Roly Poly, U.S.Marine Cut Plug, Brownie, Singing Waiter ......... 135.00
Store, Tin, Rose Scotch Snuff, Tube, Contents ........................................... 4.00
Store, Tin, Royal Marshmallows, 10 In.Diameter ....................................... 5.00
Store, Tin, Salerno Crackers, Lunch Box, Yellow Basket Weave .................. 18.00
Store, Tin, Sanka Coffee, Round, Pound .................................................... 4.00
Store, Tin, Scotch Cleaning Oil, Square ..................................................... 4.50
Store, Tin, Seal Brand Coffee, Chase & Sanborn, Round, 6 In.High ........... 5.00
Store, Tin, Southern Biscuit, Negro Butler, Children, Old Lady, 1926, Round ... 4.00
Store, Tin, Spice, Allspice, Stenciled, Square, 3 X 3 X 2 1/2 In. ................ 3.00
Store, Tin, Spice, Great American Tea Co., Green Lithographed, Set Of 4 ... 6.95
Store, Tin, Stag Tobacco, Bank, Slides Open, Embossed, Patent 1912 ....... 19.00
Store, Tin, Star Safety Razor, Patent 1899, Hinged Covers Top & Bottom ... 5.25
Store, Tin, Sterling Marshmallows, 10 In.Diameter ................................... 5.00
Store, Tin, Stevens Candy Kitchens, Apple Blossoms On Red, Round ......... 1.50
Store, Tin, Stickney & Poors Mustard ........................................................ 2.00
Store, Tin, Sunshine Biscuits, Brass Front With Glass ............................... 55.00
Store, Tin, Sweet Cuba Tobacco, Round, Large Size .................................. 45.00
Store, Tin, Tetley Tea Bags, Orange Pekoe & Pekoe, Blue, Gold, & Red ..... 4.00
Store, Tin, Triangle Club Cocoa, Montgomery Ward, C.1930, 10 In. .......... 8.00
Store, Tin, Tums, Pot-O-Gold, W.Horace Heidt On Your Radio, Thursday Night ... 5.00
Store, Tin, Tun Sol Auto Bulb, Display ....................................................... 18.00
Store, Tin, Tuxedo Tobacco, 1910 Stamp, Pocket ...................................... 5.00
Store, Tin, U.S.Marine Cut Plug Tobacco, Lunch Box ................................. 15.00
Store, Tin, Union Leader Tobacco, Eagle, Pocket ....................................... 8.00
Store, Tin, Union Leader Tobacco, Picnic Basket Type, Basket Weave Stencils ... 8.00
Store, Tin, Union Leader Tobacco, Pocket .................................................. 5.50
Store, Tin, Vantine's Ginger, 6 X 4 X 1 In. ................................................ 2.50
Store, Tin, Velvet Pipe & Cigarette Tobacco, Liggett & Meyers, 6 In.High ... 5.00
Store, Tin, Webster Cigar ........................................................................... 22.50
Store, Tin, Yellow, Sweet Burley ................................................................ 25.00
Store, Tire Gauge, Brass, 1909 ................................................................. 4.50
Store, Tobacco Cutter, Star Tobacco ......................................................... 40.00
Store, Token, Green River Whiskey, Brass, 1 1/2 In. ................................. 7.50
Store, Token, Prophylactic, Copper Clad .................................................... 8.00
Store, Token, Staffens Safe Daisy Foods, Gold Luck ................................. 6.00
Store, Toothpick, Hartman & Carpet Co., Pressed, Clear, Eureka, 3 Handled ... 18.00
Store, Toothpick, Protective Motor Service, 1922, China, Metal Insert Truck ... 30.00
Store, Top, Moxie, Celluloid, Horse & Rider, 1915 ................................... 25.00
Store, Tray, "reading The News, " Oval, Lithographed, 1910 ...................... 60.00
Store, Tray, Beatles, Autographed ............................................................. 13.00
Store, Tray, Beer, Buffalo Brewing Co., San Francisco Exposition, 1915, Girls ... 15.00
Store, Tray, Billy Baxter Ginger Ale, Red Cardinal On Black ...................... 10.00
Store, Tray, Black Horse Ale & Porter, Porcelain, Horse & Bottle Center .... 18.00
Store, Tray, Budweiser, "Say When, " C.1914, 16 In.Diameter ................... 105.00
Store, Tray, Buquesne Beer, Picture Of Prince Of Pilsner .......................... 15.00
Store, Tray, Christian Feigenspan Breweries, N.J., Tin, Girl Center ............ 5.00
Store, Tray, Christian Feigenspan Brewing Co., Tin, Round, Woman Portrait ... 16.75
Store, Tray, Clysmic Waters, Topless Woman, 10 X 13 In. ........................ 110.00
Store, Tray, Comb, Hanging, Clear Glass, Basket Weave Sides, Button Base ... 23.00

| | |
|---|---|
| Store, Tray, Consumers' Brewing Co., Oval | 75.00 |
| Store, Tray, Disneyland, Metal | 10.00 |
| Store, Tray, Dobler Brewing Co., P.O.N., Woman, Long Hair, Signed A.Asti, Tin | 12.50 |
| Store, Tray, Dr.Seuss Narragansett Beer, 1930s | 12.00 |
| Store, Tray, Dubonnet Wine, Girl Reflected In Glass | 10.00 |
| Store, Tray, Evervess Sparkling Water, Product Of Pepsi Cola Co. | 15.00 |
| Store, Tray, Falls City Ice & Beverage Co., Tin, Beer Bottle & Sandwiches | 20.00 |
| Store, Tray, Fargo, N.D. Agricultural College, Aluminum | 14.50 |
| Store, Tray, Fort Pitt Beer, Metal | 10.00 |
| Store, Tray, Grain Belt Beer, Hanging, Brass, Embossed Tavern Scene, 14 In. | 18.00 |
| Store, Tray, H.D.Beach Co., Coshocton, Ohio, Oval, Lady & Cupid, 13 3/4 In. | 15.00 |
| Store, Tray, Harvey's Imported Sherries, Grape Pickers, 12 In.Diameter | 10.00 |
| Store, Tray, Hires Root Beer, Hires Boy Holding Glass, Tin, 13 In.Diameter | 100.00 |
| Store, Tray, Iron City Beer, Metal | 10.00 |
| Store, Tray, Kist, Sailor Girl With Orange Bottle | 22.50 |
| Store, Tray, Medaglia D'oro Coffee, World's Fair, 1939 | 12.00 |
| Store, Tray, Miller's Beer, Woman On Half Moon, No.303 | 15.00 |
| Store, Tray, North Hampton Brewing Co.Lager Beer, 4 1/4 In.Diameter | 20.00 |
| Store, Tray, Nu-Grape | 8.00 |
| Store, Tray, Phoenix Komon Cream Beer, Central Consumers Co., Ky., 13 In. | 38.00 |
| Store, Tray, Pickwick Ale, Horses & Wagon | 10.00 |
| Store, Tray, Reck Beer, Metal | 10.00 |
| Store, Tray, Rheingold Beer, Metal | 10.00 |
| Store, Tray, Ruppert's Beer, Flato Characters | 10.00 |
| Store, Tray, S & H Green Stamps, Profile Of Lady, 4 1/2 In.Diameter | 20.00 |
| Store, Tray, Schaefer Beer, Metal | 10.00 |
| Store, Tray, Schlitz Beer, Metal | 10.00 |
| Store, Tray, Schmidt's Beer, Metal | 10.00 |
| Store, Tray, Silver Top Beer, Metal | 10.00 |
| Store, Tray, Stegmaier Beer, Picture Of Factory | 30.00 |
| Store, Tray, Success Manure Spreader, Horses & Wagon, 3 1/2 X 5 In. | 22.00 |
| Store, Tray, Tip, Fairy Soap | 20.00 |
| Store, Tray, Tip, Franklin Life Insurance Co. | 10.00 |
| Store, Tray, Tip, Hopski Dist., San Diego, Frog Drinking Prohibition Drink | 45.00 |
| Store, Tray, Tip, India Pale Ale | 12.00 |
| Store, Tray, Tip, J.E.Doherty Ale | 14.00 |
| Store, Tray, Tip, Kenny's Tea & Coffee, Brunette, Roses | 24.00 |
| Store, Tray, Tip, King's Pure Malt | 64.00 |
| Store, Tray, Tip, Laxol, Bottle | 20.00 |
| Store, Tray, Tip, Maltosia, Lady On Swan | 27.00 |
| Store, Tray, Tip, Marilyn Monroe | 15.00 |
| Store, Tray, Tip, Michi-Gander Brand, Brass | 8.00 |
| Store, Tray, Tip, Miller's High Life Beer | 5.00 |
| Store, Tray, Tip, Oakleaf Pin Co., Conn., Oval, Hand In Center Holding Pin | 18.00 |
| Store, Tray, Tip, Pepsi Cola, Evervess Sparkling Water, Parrot Picture | 15.00 |
| Store, Tray, Tip, Quick Meal Range | 12.50 |
| Store, Tray, Valley Forge Beer | 9.00 To 20.00 |
| Store, Tray, Welsbach Company, Scranton Gas Co., Pa., 4 1/4 In.Diameter | 15.00 |
| Store, Tray, White Top Champagne, Bottle Picture, 4 In. | 15.00 |
| Store, Tray, Zetts Bavarian Beer, Square | 40.00 |
| Store, Trumpet, Ear, Asphaltum, Straight, 21 1/2 In.Long | 75.00 |
| Store, Tube, Pencil, Bottom Twists To Give Sums, Cutout Holes, C.1900 | 15.00 |
| Store, Tumbler, Lemp Brewing Co., C.1880 | 6.00 |
| Store, Tumbler, Moxie | 8.00 To 12.00 |
| Store, Tumbler, Seven-Up, Green, 5 In. | 1.00 |
| Store, Tumbler, Virginia Dare, Clear, Picture On Glass | 3.75 |
| Store, Tumbler, Whiskey, Gold Leaf Cognac, Stemmed, 2 3/4 In. | 8.00 |
| Store, Umbrella Stand, Victorian, Bronze Colored Metal, Carvings, 17 In. | 59.00 |
| Store, Umbrella, A.E.Small, Classy Clothes, C.1910 | 50.00 |
| Store, Vibrator, Eureka Co., C.1905, Box, Instructions, & Attachments | 18.00 |
| Store, Warmer, Bed, Brass, Floral Copper Lid, Painted Wooden Handle, 44 In. | 145.00 |
| Store, Warmer, Bed, Copper & Brass, Incised Peacock In Tree, Wooden Handle | 225.00 |
| Store, Warmer, Buggy, Iron, Carpet Covered, Burns Charcoal | 7.50 |
| Store, Warmer, Foot, Buggy, 1 Drawer, Green Carpeting, Clark Heater, Handled | 12.00 |
| Store, Warmer, Foot, Carriage, Carpeted | 12.00 |
| Store, Warmer, Foot, Ceramic, White | 20.00 |

| | |
|---|---|
| Store, Warmer, Foot, Charcoal, Punched Tin, Wooden Frame, Round, 6 In. High | 85.00 |
| Store, Warmer, Foot, Metal, Carpeted, 14 X 7 In. | 22.00 |
| Store, Warmer, Foot, Pierced Tin, Wooden Frame, Coal Pan | 55.00 |
| Store, Warmer, Foot, Pierced Tin, Wooden Frame, 7 3/4 X 8 3/4 In. | 50.00 |
| Store, Warmer, Foot, Tin & Wood, Punched Diamonds, Pan, Wire Handle | 65.00 |
| Store, Warmer, Foot, Tin, Wooden Bars On Top | 48.00 |
| Store, Warmer, Foot, Wooden, Oval, Brass Handle, Cutout Hearts In Metal Top | 85.00 |
| Store, Watch, Pocket, Cracker Jacks, Toy, Tin | 8.00 |
| Store, Weaner, Calf, Iron | 5.00 |
| Store, Wheel, From Circus Wagon, Brass Hub, Wood & Iron Tire, 5 In.Diameter | 100.00 |
| Store, Wheel, Measuring, Iron | 3.00 |
| Store, Whistle, Marked Cracker Jack, Tin | 2.25 |
| Store, Whistle, Police, Round, C.1900 | 6.50 |
| Store, Whistle, Referee's, Spaulding, Wrist Strap | 7.00 |
| Store, Wick Trimmer, Patent Dec.27, 1864 | 14.00 |
| Stove, see Fire, Stove | |
| Strawberry, see Soft Paste | |
| Stretch Glass, Bowl, Black Amethyst Base & Pedestal, 7 1/2 In. | 55.00 |
| Stretch Glass, Bowl, Blue, Turned In Rim | 18.00 |
| Stretch Glass, Bowl, Celeste Blue, 1 3/4 X 6 In. | 12.00 |
| Stretch Glass, Bowl, Imperial Jewels, Ice Blue, Gold Edge, Pedestal | 18.00 |
| Stretch Glass, Bowl, Iridescent Yellow, Gold Floral Rim Band, 11 In. | 38.00 |
| Stretch Glass, Bowl, Orange, Iridescent, Pedestal | 68.00 |
| Stretch Glass, Bowl, Pink, Bulbous, 3 1/2 X 5 In. | 15.00 |
| Stretch Glass, Bowl, Serving, Pink Jewels, Center Handle, Oval, 11 In. | 18.00 |
| Stretch Glass, Bowl, Thumbprint, White, 4 3/4 In.Diameter X 2 1/2 In.High | 35.00 |
| Stretch Glass, Candleholder, Green | 10.00 |
| Stretch Glass, Candlestick, Aqua, Iridescent, 8 1/2 In.High | 12.00 |
| Stretch Glass, Compote, Imperial Jewels, Ice Blue, Pedestal, 9 In. | 24.00 |
| Stretch Glass, Compote, Marigold To Clear, 3 1/2 X 5 In. | 10.00 |
| Stretch Glass, Dish, Candy, Covered, Footed, Blue, 10 In.High | 18.00 |
| Stretch Glass, Mayonnaise Set, Pale Green, Yellow Pear Finial, 2 Piece | 25.00 |
| Stretch Glass, Plate, Imperial Jewels, Blue, 8 1/2 In. | 12.00 |
| Stretch Glass, Plate, Paneled, Iridescent | 4.15 |
| Stretch Glass, Vase, Pearl, Slender Stem, 5 1/4 In.High | 12.50 |

*Sunbonnet Babies were first introduced in 1902 in the Sunbonnet Babies Primer. The stories were by Eulalie Osgood Grover, illustrated by Bertha Corbett. The children's faces were completely hidden by the sunbonnets, and had been pictured in black and white before this time. The color pictures in the book were immediately successful. The Royal Bayreuth China Company made a full line of children's dishes decorated with the Sunbonnet Babies.*

| | |
|---|---|
| Sunbonnet Babies, Book, A.B.C., 1937 | 50.00 |
| Sunbonnet Babies, Book, In Mother Goose Land, 1939 Edition, 64 Pages | 18.00 |
| Sunbonnet Babies, Book, Overall Boys In Switzerland, 1916, Grover | 37.50 |
| Sunbonnet Babies, Book, Sunbonnet Babies In Holland, 1915, Grover | 30.00 |
| Sunbonnet Babies, Book, Sunbonnet Babies In Mother Goose Land, 1936 | 25.00 |
| Sunbonnet Babies, Book, The Sunbonnet Baby Primer, E.O.Grover | 38.00 |
| Sunbonnet Babies, Book, 1902 | 75.00 |
| Sunbonnet Babies, Candleholder, Sweeping, Handle, Royal Bayreuth, Blue Mark | 150.00 |
| Sunbonnet Babies, Candlestick, Fishing, Cape Cod Handle, Blue Mark | 185.00 |
| Sunbonnet Babies, Candlestick, Washing, Handle, Saucer Base, Blue Mark | 185.00 |
| Sunbonnet Babies, Chamberstick, Mending, Saucer Base, Ring Handle, Blue Mark | 175.00 |
| Sunbonnet Babies, Chamberstick, Sweeping, Attached Plate, Handle, Blue Mark | 150.00 |
| Sunbonnet Babies, Creamer, Mending, Royal Bayreuth | 95.00 |
| Sunbonnet Babies, Cup & Saucer, Kiss & Make Up, Girl & Overall Boy | 30.00 |
| Sunbonnet Babies, Cup, Demitasse, Beach Babies, Royal Bayreuth | 45.00 |
| Sunbonnet Babies, Dish, Feeding | 40.00 |
| Sunbonnet Babies, Doll, Rag, Handmade, 20 In.Tall | 12.00 |
| Sunbonnet Babies, Figurine, Sitting, Finger To Mouth, Satiny Bisque, 4 In. | 65.00 |
| Sunbonnet Babies, Mug, Fish, Royal Bayreuth, 3 In. | 135.00 |
| Sunbonnet Babies, Nappy, Sewing & Mending, Handled, Royal Bayreuth | 95.00 |
| Sunbonnet Babies, Pitcher, Juvenile, Roseville, RV Mark, 3 1/2 In. | 18.50 |
| Sunbonnet Babies, Pitcher, Sweeping, 4 1/2 In.High | 145.00 |
| Sunbonnet Babies, Plaque, 1910 Calendar, Hammered Brass, 8 In.High | 27.50 |

Sunbonnet Babies, Plate, Advertising, 9 In. .................................................................... 45.00
Sunbonnet Babies, Plate, Cake, Ironing Clothes, Blue Mark, 10 1/2 In. ........................ 165.00
Sunbonnet Babies, Plate, Cake, Open Handles, Royal Bayreuth .................................. 135.00
Sunbonnet Babies, Plate, Cat, Tin, 3 1/2 In. ................................................................... 9.00
Sunbonnet Babies, Plate, Cleaning, 6 In. ........................................................................ 85.00
Sunbonnet Babies, Plate, Sunbonnet Baby & Overall Boy .............................................. 28.00
Sunbonnet Babies, Plate, Washing, Royal Bayreuth, Blue Mark, 6 In. .......................... 60.00
Sunbonnet Babies, Postcard, G.E.Perry ......................................................................... 6.00
Sunbonnet Babies, Postcard, Give Us This Day ............................................................. 10.00
Sunbonnet Babies, Postcard, The Bogie Man ................................................................ 6.50
Sunbonnet Babies, Postcard, 7 Days Of The Week, Ullman, 1905, 7 .............. 60.00 To 72.00
Sunbonnet Babies, Postcard, 1913 ................................................................................ 6.00
Sunbonnet Babies, Sugar & Creamer, Sled Riding, Cover, Royal Bayreuth .................. 125.00
Sunbonnet Babies, Sugar, Turnip Shape, 2 Sand Babies, Seaside, Cleethorpes ............. 20.00
Sunbonnet Babies, Tankard, Washday, Blue Mark, 4 In. ................................................ 120.00
Sunbonnet Babies, Tray, Pin, Cleaning, Royal Bayreuth, Blue Mark .............................. 50.00
Sunbonnet Babies, Vase, Cleaning Windows & Floor, 3 Handled, Royal Bayreuth ........... 68.00
Sunbonnet Babies, Vase, Signed, 5 In.High .................................................................... 145.00
Sunbonnet Babies, Vase, Sweeping, 2 Handled, Royal Bayreuth .................................. 06.00
Sunbonnet Babies, Vase, 3 Beach Babies Playing Tag, Blue Mark, 4 1/2 In. ................. 82.50

*Sunderland luster is a name given to a characteristic pink luster made by*
*Leeds, Newcastle, and other English firms during the nineteenth century.*
*The luster glaze is metallic and glossy and sometimes appears to have bubbles*
*as a decoration.*

Sunderland, Creamer, Purple Waterlike Drops With White Marks ................................. 36.00
Sunderland, Creamer, Rose Luster Trim On Cream, Handle Higher Than Spout ............. 35.00
Sunderland, Creamer, 6 1/2 In. ....................................................................................... 69.50
Sunderland, Goblet, Mariner's ........................................................................................ 45.00
Sunderland, Jug, Pink, Pearlware, C.1810, 5 1/2 In. .................................... *Illus* 140.00
Sunderland, Pitcher, Baluster Form, The Mariner's Compass, C.1820, 7 In.High .......... 125.00
Sunderland, Pitcher, Black Masonic Transfer, 7 1/4 In. ................................................. 170.00
Sunderland, Pitcher, Shell Shape, Pink, Black Hunting Scenes ..................................... 95.00
Sunderland, Plaque, Bible Quotation, Pierced For Hanging ........................................... 35.00
Sunderland, Plaque, Old Testament Motto, Pink Luster ................................................. 98.50
Sunderland, Plaque, Prepare To Meet Thy God, Luster, 9 X 8 In. .................................. 125.00
Sunderland, Plate, Sandwich, Pink Luster Leaf, Flowers, 9 X 9 1/2 In. .......................... 23.50
Sunderland, Salt Cellar, Footed, Pair ............................................................................. 130.00
Swansea, Plate, Abram French & Co., Boston, Blue & White, 2 3/4 In. ......................... 17.00

*Teco pottery is the art pottery line made by the Terra-Cotta Tile*
*Works of Terra-Cotta, Illinois. The company was founded by William*
*D.Gates in 1881. The Teco line was first made in 1902 and continued*
*into the 1920s. It included over 500 designs, made in a variety of colors and*
*glazes.*

Sunderland, Jug, Pink, Pearlware, C.1810, 5 1/2 In.

| | |
|---|---|
| Teco, Vase, Rounded, Green, 5 In. | 40.00 |
| Teco, Vase, Fall, Green, 8 In. | 55.00 |
| Telephone, Candlestick, Burnished Brass, Oak Ringer Box | 70.00 |
| Telephone, Candlestick, Dial Type | 65.00 |
| Telephone, Candlestick, Kellogg, Brass Receiver, Patent 1908 | 40.00 |
| Telephone, Candlestick, Western Electric, Brass Receiver, Cord | 35.00 |
| Telephone, French Type, Dial | 50.00 |
| Telephone, Monophone, Automatic Electric Co., Oak | 75.00 |
| Telephone, National Cash Register Co., Department Store, Metal | 20.00 |
| Telephone, Stromberg Carlson, Desk Type, Crank | 20.00 |
| Telephone, Wall Crank, Railroad Depot, Western Electric | 75.00 |
| Telephone, Wall, Crank Type, Oak, Long Transmitter Arm | 66.00 |
| Telephone, Wall, Kellogg, Oak Case, Patent 1901 | 100.00 |
| Telephone, Wall, Maple, Large | 69.00 |
| Telephone, Wall, Oak, Carved Front | 74.00 |
| Telephone, Wall, Oak, 2 Box, S.C., 33 In. | 108.00 |
| Telephone, Wall, Oak, 22 In.High, Long Neck | 110.00 |
| Telephone, Wall, W.E. Type, Nickel Bells, Maple, 22 In. | 69.00 |
| Telephone, Western Electric, Oak, Dial Mounts On Wall Above Phone | 48.00 |
| Telescope, Brass, Pocket, Leather Covering, Opens To 14 In. | 32.50 |
| Telescope, British Officer's, German Silver, Leather, Chadburn, Sheffield | 195.00 |

*Teplitz refers to art pottery manufactured by a number of companies in the Teplitz-Turn area of Bohemia during the late nineteenth and early twentieth centuries. The Amphora Porcelain Works and the Alexandra Works were two of these companies.*

| | |
|---|---|
| Teplitz, Ashtray, Raised Cameo At Side | 18.00 |
| Teplitz, Bowl, Lion & Ball On Green, 2 In.High | 22.00 |
| Teplitz, Bowl, Lion With Ball, Green Handled, 6 In. Diameter | 18.00 |
| Teplitz, Dish, Banana Shape, Art Nouveau Women's Heads Handles, 11 In. | 70.00 |
| Teplitz, Ewer, Amphora, Lizard Handle, Raised Gold, Floral, 7 In. | 70.00 |
| Teplitz, Figurine, Camel & Rider, Amphora, Pastel, 13 1/2 X 10 1/4 In. | 265.00 |
| Teplitz, Figurine, Fish, Amphora, Lying Down, Beige, 10 In. | 70.00 |
| Teplitz, Mug, Amphora, Incised 2 Foxes Playing, 6 In. | 62.00 |
| Teplitz, Pitcher, Gold Snake At Handle, Gold Outlined Anemones On Beige | 50.00 |
| Teplitz, Urn, Art Deco, Handled, Forest Scene, Applied Mushrooms Base | 140.00 |
| Teplitz, Vase, Amphora, Handled, Brushed Gold, Woodland Colors, 6 In.High | 55.00 |
| Teplitz, Vase, Amphora, Hunter, Wolf, Raised Design, 5 1/2 In.High, Pair | 45.00 |
| Teplitz, Vase, Amphora, Iridescent Cherries, Art Nouveau Handles, 11 In. | 175.00 |
| Teplitz, Vase, Amphora, Ovoid, Dark Green, Gold & Jewels, 7 1/2 In.High | 85.00 |
| Teplitz, Vase, Applied Lily Pads On Gold, Amphora, Austria, C.1910 | 45.00 |
| Teplitz, Vase, Blue & White Orchids On Pale Green, Gold, 5 1/2 In.High | 45.00 |
| Teplitz, Vase, Figurine, Imperial Mark, 13 1/2 In.High, Amphora | 115.00 |
| Teplitz, Vase, Floral & Gilt, 4 Handles At Base, Amphora, 7 In. | 40.00 |
| Teplitz, Vase, Gold Flowers & Green Leaves, 7 In.High | 40.00 |
| Teplitz, Vase, Grotesque, Bronze Lizard, Pottery, Signed, 12 In.High | 150.00 |
| Teplitz, Vase, Man With Shield On Brown, 4 3/4 In.High, Pair | 45.00 |
| Teplitz, Vase, Pear Drops On Tan Ground, 6 1/2 In.High | 48.00 |
| Teplitz, Vase, Urn Shape, Gilt Handles, Floral, Matte Finish, 12 In., Pair | 78.00 |
| Terra-Cotta, Bust, Queen Victoria, Signed, Dated 1897, 6 In.High | 60.00 |
| Terra-Cotta, Bust, Sappho, Signed Blache, C.1850, 17 In. | 400.00 |
| Terra-Cotta, Dog's Head, 3 In.Square | 10.50 |
| Terra-Cotta, Figurine, Bearded Barefoot Man & Donkey, Signed Grasso | 57.50 |
| Terra-Cotta, Figurine, Bearded Man With Vegetable Cart, Signed Grasso | 54.50 |
| Terra-Cotta, Figurine, Boy, Brown Boots, Hat, & Basket, Signed, 27 In.High | 350.00 |
| Terra-Cotta, Figurine, Cow With Horns, Sitting, Hand-Painted, Glass Eyes | 18.00 |
| Terra-Cotta, Figurine, Man On Stump, Nanny Goat, Signed Grasso | 41.50 |
| Terra-Cotta, Group, Cupid Embracing A Female Putto, Wooden Base, 17 1/2 In. | 225.00 |
| Terra-Cotta, Muse's Head, Marked Boston Terra-Cotta Co., 2 1/2 In.Square | 12.50 |
| Terra-Cotta, Pitcher, 4 In.High | 95.00 |
| Terra-Cotta, Plaque, Art Nouveau Girl In Headdress, Polychrome, Pair | 275.00 |
| Terra-Cotta, Plaque, Scene From Carmen In Relief, Germany | 75.00 |
| Terra-Cotta, Sclupture, Head Of Man With Moustache, Wooden Base | 39.00 |
| Terra-Cotta, Whistle, Kate Greenaway Type, 2 In. High | 30.00 |

*Textile includes all types of table linens and household linens such as coverlets, quilts, fabrics, etc.*

| | |
|---|---|
| Textile, Bag, Brocade, Animals, Sterling Silver Frame | 19.00 |
| Textile, Bag, Enameled Mesh, Geometrics, Silvered Frame, Whiting & Davis Co. | 20.00 |
| Textile, Bag, Petitpoint, French, Cloisonne Frame | 15.00 |
| Textile, Bandana, Philadelphia Centennial, 1876, Gray, Red Border, 25 X 26 | 40.00 |
| Textile, Bedspread, Bleached Muslin, White Candlewick, Lace, Full Size | 85.00 |
| Textile, Bedspread, Candlewick, Abby Gallup, 2828, 3 Sections, 94 X 83 In. | 700.00 |
| Textile, Bedspread, Candlewick, Signed & Dated, Almira J.Sawyer, 1844, 90 In. | 300.00 |
| Textile, Bedspread, Cotton Voile, Lace, French Embroidery, Double Bed Size | 20.00 |
| Textile, Bedspread, Crocheted Ecru, 94 X 68 In. | 100.00 |
| Textile, Bedspread, Crocheted, White, Full Size | 65.00 |
| Textile, Bedspread, Hand Loomed, Dark Blue & Cream, C.1860 | 145.00 |
| Textile, Bedspread, Hand-Crocheted, Marguerite Pattern, Ecru, Fringe | 200.00 |
| Textile, Bedspread, Marguerite Pattern, 5 In.Fringe, Hand-Crocheted | 500.00 |
| Textile, Bedspread, Patchwork, Cotton, Triangular Pieces, Twin Size | 27.00 |
| Textile, Bedspread, Silk Satin, Dusty Rose, Silk Crewel Embroidery | 125.00 |
| Textile, Blanket, Wool, Homespun, Navy & White, 74 X 88 In. | 80.00 |
| Textile, Blouse, Fatigue, U.S.Cavalry, Blue Wool, Eagle Buttons, C.1890 | 64.50 |
| Textile, Blouse, U.S.Cavalry, Fatique, Blue Wool, Brass Buttons | 110.00 |
| Textile, Blouse, U.S.Cavalry, Indian War Issue, Blue Wool, Brass Buttons | 110.00 |
| Textile, Blouse, U.S.Marine Corps Sergeant's, 1907, Blue Wool, Red Piping | 39.50 |
| Textile, Bonnet, Lady's, Mourning, Black Wool, Norwegian | 32.50 |
| Textile, Cap, Daniel Boone, Twin Tails, Raccoon Fur, Silk Lined | 4.00 |
| Textile, Cape, Black Velvet, Beaded Trim | 25.00 |
| Textile, Cape, Lady's, Black, Floral Embroidery | 10.00 |
| Textile, Carpet, Amritzar, Oval Medallion, Ivory, 19 Ft.4 In.X 11 Ft.11 In. | 850.00 |
| Textile, Carpet, Art Deco, Geometric Designs, C.1930, 10 X 10 Ft. | 600.00 |
| Textile, Carpet, Aubusson, Directoire, Cocoa Field, 17 Ft.X 18 Ft.2 In. | 700.00 |
| Textile, Carpet, Aubusson, Flowerheads & Laurel Leaves, 21 X 13 Ft. | 1100.00 |
| Textile, Carpet, Kashan, Midnight Blue Pole Medallion, 8 Ft.10 In.X 12 Ft. | 1500.00 |
| Textile, Carpet, Kirman, Floral Medallions, Ivory, 19 Ft.7 In.X 11 Ft.9 In. | 4100.00 |
| Textile, Carpet, Kirman, Floral Pole Medallion, 12 Ft.7 In.X 8 Ft.10 In. | 2000.00 |
| Textile, Carpet, Kirman, Oval Medallion On Ivory, 19 Ft.1 In.X 9 Ft.9 In. | 750.00 |
| Textile, Carpet, Oushak, Green Medallion, Salmon, 17 Ft.4 In.X 12 Ft.4 In. | 1900.00 |
| Textile, Carpet, Sarouk, Ivory Field, Pole Medallion, 13 Ft.3 In. X 50 In. | 1800.00 |
| Textile, Carpet, Sultanabad, Cyprus Trees, 22 Ft X 10 Ft.4 In. | 950.00 |
| Textile, Carpet, Tabriz, Center Rust Medallion, 11 Ft.6 In.X 6 Ft.7 In. | 1600.00 |
| Textile, Carpet, Tabriz, Flowering Vines, 17 Ft.6 In. X 9 Ft.3 In. | 7250.00 |
| Textile, Cloth & Napkin Set, Tea, Chinese Embroidery, Openwork, 5 Piece | 30.00 |
| Textile, Cloth, Banquet, Linen, Lace Inlay, Cupid Pattern, 72 X 98 In. | 28.00 |
| Textile, Coat & Vest, Man's, Swallowtail, Black, Size 40 | 14.50 |
| Textile, Coat, Man's, Swallowtail, Striped | 10.00 |

*Linen or wool coverlets were made during the nineteenth century. Most of the coverlets date from 1800 to 1850. Four types were made, the double woven, jacquard, summer and winter, and overshot.*

| | | |
|---|---|---|
| Textile, Coverlet, American Eagles, Blue & White, 1830 | *Illus* | 750.00 |
| Textile, Coverlet, Appliqued, Pink Roses, Swag Border, Quilted, 80 X 96 In. | | 225.00 |
| Textile, Coverlet, Bird Of Paradise, Fringed, Shenandoah, Va., 72 X 81 In. | | 275.00 |
| Textile, Coverlet, Blue & White, Garnert, S.P., 1835 | *Illus* | 350.00 |
| Textile, Coverlet, Cat's Paw Design, Wool & Cotton, 76 X 92 In. | | 35.00 |
| Textile, Coverlet, Center Medallion, Grapes, Eagle, Pennsylvania, 8 Ft. | | 255.00 |
| Textile, Coverlet, Federal White On Blue, C.1860, 81 X 63, Lima, Ohio | | 185.00 |
| Textile, Coverlet, Hand-Woven, Ivory & Rust, 60 X 98 In. | | 95.00 |
| Textile, Coverlet, Jacquard, Birds, Houses, Somerset, Ohio, 1845, 78 X 85 In. | | 170.00 |
| Textile, Coverlet, Jacquard, Eagle Border, 4 Colors, M.B.Breneman, Pa., 1839 | | 275.00 |
| Textile, Coverlet, Jacquard, Village, Schooners, Blue, White, 1841, 89 X 78 In. | | 250.00 |
| Textile, Coverlet, Overshot, Blue & White, 94 X 73 In. | | 65.00 |
| Textile, Coverlet, Polychrome Embroidered Linen, Near East, 8 Ft.4 In. Long | | 300.00 |
| Textile, Coverlet, Rust & Blue, Fringes On 3 Edges, 70 X 86 In. | | 65.00 |
| Textile, Coverlet, Silk Satin, Quilted Diagonally, 72 In.Square | | 48.00 |
| Textile, Coverlet, Tobacco Premium Flanels Of Flags, Handmade, 70 X 86 In. | | 48.00 |
| Textile, Coverlet, Woven, March Co., Pa., 1841, Red, Black, Gold, & Beige, 78 In. | | 65.00 |
| Textile, Dress, Flapper, Black Lace, Black Jet Beads | | 30.00 |
| Textile, Dress, Hattie Carnegie, Black Velvet, Rhinestones & Pearls | | 20.00 |
| Textile, Dress, Lady's, White Cotton, Lace At Neck & Cuffs, C.1900 | | 12.50 |

Textile, Coverlet, American Eagles,
Blue & White, 1830
*(See Page 643)*

Textile, Coverlet, Blue & White,
Garnert, S.P., 1835
*(See Page 643)*

Textile, Quilt, Amish, Sunshine & Shadow Diamond
*(See Page 645)*

Textile, Quilt, Mariner's Compass, Calico
*(See Page 645)*

**Textile, Evening Bag,** Petitpoint, Floral, Gold & Enamel Frame, Vienna, 1900s ............................... 45.00
**Textile, Flag,** American, 36 Stars, Handmade, 3 X 6 Ft. ............................................... 74.50
**Textile, Flag,** U.S.A., 35 Stars With 11 Stars In Star Shape Center ............................... 55.00
**Textile, Flag,** U.S.A., 36 Stars, 12 X 17 In. ............................................................ 40.00
**Textile, Hand-Woven,** Rose & White, 60 X 98 In. ................................................... 95.00
**Textile, Handkerchief,** Battleship Maine Transfer On White Cotton ............................... 6.00
**Textile, Handkerchief,** Patriotic, Battle Of Manila, Dewey, 21 In.Square ....................... 25.00
**Textile, Handkerchief,** Washington Memorial, Printed Cotton, C.1800, Pair ................... 600.00
**Textile, Hanging,** Needlework, Verdure, Heron, Plants, & Trees, 7 X 4 Ft. ................... 375.00
**Textile, Hat,** Flapper, Black ................................................................................... 5.00
**Textile, Hat,** Man's, Straw, Caramel Color, 6 7/8 In. ............................................... 12.00
**Textile, Hat,** Stetson, 1940s, Tin Box ..................................................................... 4.00
**Textile, House Standard,** Scotland, Silk, Yellow, Coat Of Arms, C.1820 ...................... 165.00
**Textile, Jacket,** Mandarin, Black, Satin Band Design, M.G.M.Auction ......................... 8.00
**Textile, Lace,** From Petticoat Of Countess Of Saltown, Edinburgh, C.1894 ................. 100.00
**Textile, Napkin,** Damask Linen, Vintage Design, Fringed, Set Of 12 ............................ 42.00
**Textile, Napkin,** Linen, Damask, Silk Fringe, Set Of 6 .............................................. 8.00
**Textile, Napkin,** Luncheon, Irish Linen, Embroidered, Scalloped, Set Of 4 .................... 2.50
**Textile, Pillow Sham,** Chain Stitched, Red Peacocks, Scalloped, Pair .......................... 35.00
**Textile, Pillow Sham,** Red Embroidered Morning Glories On White, Pair ...................... 18.00
**Textile, Purse,** Minipoint, Flowers, Formal .............................................................. 19.00
**Textile, Purse,** Petitpoint, Flowers & Birds On Brown, Brass Frame ............................ 25.00

| | | |
|---|---|---|
| Textile, Quilt, Amish, Sunshine & Shadow Diamond | *Illus* | 225.00 |
| Textile, Quilt, Applique, Flowers, Red, Blue, & Tan, 76 In. Square | | 80.00 |
| Textile, Quilt, Applique, Green, Rose, & Yellow On White, 78 In.Square | | 65.00 |
| Textile, Quilt, Applique, Ivy & Geometrics, 78 X 96 1/2 In. | | 80.00 |
| Textile, Quilt, Applique, Swallows, Red & White, 75 X 76 In. | | 90.00 |
| Textile, Quilt, Applique, Tulips & Squares, Dated 1876, 81 X 77 In. | | 135.00 |
| Textile, Quilt, Center Bouquet Tied With Blue Ribbon, 76 In. X 8 Ft. | | 185.00 |
| Textile, Quilt, Cornucopia, Cotton, Prints, Blues, 1940, 58 X 86 In. | | 30.00 |
| Textile, Quilt, Cornucopia, Cotton, Prints, Greens, 1940, 58 X 86 In. | | 30.00 |
| Textile, Quilt, Crazy, Handmade, Dated 1915, 72 X 80 In. | | 25.00 |
| Textile, Quilt, Crazy, Silk & Velvet, April 16, 1890, 5 X 6 Ft. | | 85.00 |
| Textile, Quilt, Crazy, Silk & Velvet, Handmade, 64 X 78 In. | | 100.00 |
| Textile, Quilt, Crazy, Velveteen, 38 X 62 In. | | 30.00 |
| Textile, Quilt, Flower Garden, Cream Ground, Scalloped, 89 X 84 In. | | 39.50 |
| Textile, Quilt, Flower Garden, Handmade, King Size | | 75.00 |
| Textile, Quilt, Geometric Squares, Pieced, 78 X 64 In. | | 35.00 |
| Textile, Quilt, Harlequin, Patchwork, Dark Green Ground, 74 X 88 In. | | 100.00 |
| Textile, Quilt, Irish Chain, Green & White, 90 X 112 In. | | 15.00 |
| Textile, Quilt, Log Cabin Type Design, Dark Colors, Wooly, 50 X 76 In. | | 25.00 |
| Textile, Quilt, Love Apples, Red, Yellow, & Green, 76 In. X 8 Ft. | | 260.00 |
| Textile, Quilt, Mariner's Compass, Calico | *Illus* | 175.00 |
| Textile, Quilt, Patchwork, Blue On White, 69 X 85 In. | | 45.00 |
| Textile, Quilt, Patchwork, Diamond Pattern, Red, White, & Blue | | 30.00 |
| Textile, Quilt, Patchwork, Grandmother's Flower Garden, Yellow Ground | | 30.00 |
| Textile, Quilt, Patchwork, Slurred Circles, Red, White, & Blue | | 30.00 |
| Textile, Quilt, Pine Tree Type, Pink & White Calico, C.1850, 92 In.Square | | 80.00 |
| Textile, Quilt, President's Wreath | *Illus* | 375.00 |
| Textile, Quilt, Red & White Geometric Pattern, Handmade | | 37.50 |
| Textile, Quilt, Red & White Triple Irish Chain, 76 In. X 8 Ft. | | 135.00 |
| Textile, Quilt, Red & White, Rolling Pinwheel, 65 X 80 In. | | 60.00 |
| Textile, Quilt, Rising Sun, Pieced, 62 X 78 In. | | 45.00 |
| Textile, Quilt, Solomon's Puzzle, Lavender, Dated 1880, 80 X 90 In. | | 125.00 |
| Textile, Quilt, Steeplechase, Red & White, Percale, Handmade, 80 X 88 In. | | 70.00 |
| Textile, Quilt, Summer & Winter, Blue & White, 93 X 75 In. | | 125.00 |
| Textile, Quilt, Summer, Harvest Sun, White Ground, 84 In.Square | | 75.00 |
| Textile, Quilt, Triple Irish Chain Design, Pink & White On Green | | 135.00 |
| Textile, Quilt, Tulip Pattern, Green & Yellow On White, Full Size | | 150.00 |
| Textile, Quilt, Turkey Track, Handmade, King Size | | 100.00 |
| Textile, Quilt, White On Pink, 8 Point Stars, 72 X 98 In., Pair | | 250.00 |
| Textile, Quilt, Yellow Flowers In Red Pots 12 Times, 76 In. X 8 Ft. | | 145.00 |
| Textile, Ribbon, Temperance Society, Cold Water Army, C.1840, Silk, Beige | | 29.50 |
| Textile, Robe, Carriage, Scenic, 2 Deer In Forest | | 92.50 |
| Textile, Rug, Afghan, 10 Ft.3 In. X 6 Ft.6 In. | | 750.00 |
| Textile, Rug, Bidjar, Blue Medallion, Floral Meander Border, 65 X 50 In. | | 1700.00 |

Textile, Quilt, President's Wreath

Textile, Rug, Prayer, Daghestan,
6 Ft X 3 Ft.9 In.
*(See Page 646)*

| | |
|---|---|
| Textile, Rug, Black Bear, Canvas Back, Felt Fringe, 5 Ft.3 In. | 595.00 |
| Textile, Rug, Caucasian, Wine Red Field, Foliate Motifs, 12 Ft. X 41 In. | 150.00 |
| Textile, Rug, Hamadan, Long, Red Field, Cones, 8 Ft. X 4 Ft.5 In. | 130.00 |
| Textile, Rug, Hooked, American, C.1800s, 63 X 31 In. *Illus* | 400.00 |
| Textile, Rug, Hooked, Oval, Multicolor Floral, 36 X 18 3/4 In. | 20.00 |
| Textile, Rug, Kabistan, Latticework Design, 5 Ft.2 In. X 3 Ft.10 In. | 2200.00 |
| Textile, Rug, Kabistan, Stylized Flowerheads, 8 Ft.4 In. X 4 Ft.11 In. | 1100.00 |
| Textile, Rug, Kashan Vase, Blue Floral Border, 7 Ft X 4 Ft.9 In. | 1300.00 |
| Textile, Rug, Kazak, Blue Field, 3 Medallions, 5 Ft.11 In. X 4 Ft. | 350.00 |
| Textile, Rug, Kazak, 4 Conjoined Diamonds, Flowerhead Border, 3 X 6 Ft. | 275.00 |
| Textile, Rug, Kazak, 7 Ft.2 In. X 3 Ft.6 In. *Illus* | 500.00 |
| Textile, Rug, Kerman, Medallion, Cranberry, Navy, & Green, 10 Ft.6 In.X 14 Ft. | 1250.00 |
| Textile, Rug, Kilim, 5 Geometric Rectangles, 10 Ft.6 In.X 5 Ft.3 In. | 90.00 |
| Textile, Rug, Kilim, 5 Geometric Rectangles, 12 Ft.7 In.X 5 Ft.6 In. | 100.00 |
| Textile, Rug, Kirman, Central Medallion On Ivory, 12 Ft.5 In.X 9 Ft. | 900.00 |
| Textile, Rug, Kirman, Rows Of Cones, 7 Ft.10 In. X 11 Ft.8 In. | 750.00 |
| Textile, Rug, Melas, Elongated Rectangle, Meander Border, 5 Ft.3 In. X 4ft. | 475.00 |
| Textile, Rug, Oriental, Belouchi, Blue, Rust, Cream, 3 X 4 Ft. | 75.00 |
| Textile, Rug, Prayer, Daghestan, 6 Ft X 3 Ft.9 In. *Illus* | 1700.00 |
| Textile, Rug, Prayer, Kabistan, Blue Field, Floral Border, 5 Ft. X 2 Ft.8 In. | 250.00 |
| Textile, Rug, Prayer, Kazak, 3 Octagons, 6 Ft.6 In. X 4 Ft.7 In. | 800.00 |
| Textile, Rug, Prayer, Kazak, 4 Ft.8 In. X 3 Ft.8 In. *Illus* | 850.00 |
| Textile, Rug, Prayer, Makri, Blue, Spandrels, 6 Ft.7 In. X 4 Ft.2 In. | 900.00 |
| Textile, Rug, Runner, Kurdish, Geometric Devices, 11 Ft.2 In. X 3 Ft.2 In. | 475.00 |
| Textile, Rug, Sarouk, Scalloped Medallion, 7 Ft.1 In. X 4 Ft.9 In. | 2100.00 |
| Textile, Rug, Sehna, Herati Design, Floral Border, 4 Ft.3 In. X 4 Ft.8 In. | 750.00 |
| Textile, Rug, Shirvan, Octagons, 5 Ft.10 In. X 3 Ft.7 In. | 425.00 |
| Textile, Rug, Shirvan, 5 Cruciform Medallions, 3 Ft.6 In X 6 Ft.9 In. | 175.00 |
| Textile, Rug, Soumak, Cruciform Medallions, Running Dog Border, 75 X 55 In. | 600.00 |
| Textile, Rug, Tekke Turkoman Tatchli, 4 Ft. 7 In. X 3 Ft.10 In. | 1000.00 |
| Textile, Rug, Yarn, Victorian, Multicolor, Fringed, Burlap Back, 49 X 24 In. | 20.00 |
| Textile, Rug, Yuruk, Flowerhead Latticework, 3 Ft.3 In. X 5 Ft.5 In. | 425.00 |
| Textile, Runner & 4 Place Mats, Irish Linen, Cutwork Designs | 15.00 |

*Samplers were made in the United States during the early 1700s. The best examples were made from 1790 to 1840. Long narrow samplers are usually older than the square ones. Early samplers just had stitching or alphabets.*

Textile, Rug, Kazak
7 Ft.2 In. X 3 Ft.6 In.

Textile, Rug, Hooked, American,
C.1800s, 63 X 31 In.

Textile, Rug, Prayer, Kazak,
4 Ft.8 In. X 3 Ft.8 In.
*(See Page 646)*

Textile, Tapestry, Verdure, C.1890, 6 Ft.8 In. High
*(See Page 640)*

*The later examples had numerals, borders, and pictorial decorations. Those
with mottoes are mid-Victorian.*

| | |
|---|---:|
| Textile, Sampler, Adam & Eve & Serpent, Ester Brown, 1853, Homespun | 145.00 |
| Textile, Sampler, Alphabet & Number, Gertrude, 1928, Framed, 17 X 13 In. | 45.00 |
| Textile, Sampler, Alphabet & Numbers, Grapevine Border, Nancy B.Foster, 1823 | 175.00 |
| Textile, Sampler, Alphabet, Bird, Dog, Cats, Signed Ramona Coca, 22 X 14 In. | 16.00 |
| Textile, Sampler, Alphabet, Numerals, Verses, Teapot, Currier, Mass., 1866-76 | 95.00 |
| Textile, Sampler, Animals & Birds, Floral, Agnes Waddington, 1829 | 85.00 |
| Textile, Sampler, British Sailing Ships, Farm Animals, Addis, 1853 | 40.00 |
| Textile, Sampler, Easter, Victorian, Framed, 12 X 24 In. | 17.00 |
| Textile, Sampler, Floral & Birds, Lucy Liblock, 1840, Framed | 55.00 |
| Textile, Sampler, Genealogical, Husband Born May 13, 1776, Died 1822, Framed | 85.00 |
| Textile, Sampler, Little Girl Watering Flowers, Wording, Petitpoint | 25.00 |
| Textile, Sampler, Lucy Robbins, 10 Years, Alphabet, Framed, 10 X 7 In. | 30.00 |
| Textile, Sampler, Rose & Verse, Animals & Birds, Mary Young, 1828 | 165.00 |
| Textile, Sampler, Rose, Green, Blue, & Gold, Rosewood Frame, 16 X 18 In. | 120.00 |
| Textile, Sampler, The Lord's Prayer, Floral, Mary Whitty, 1758, Framed | 65.00 |
| Textile, Sampler, Verse, Alphabet, Peatowl, Floral, Perrir Clark, C.1850 | 75.00 |
| Textile, Santa Claus, Felt, Tree Hanging, C.1890, 5 1/2 In. | 10.00 |
| Textile, Scarf, Battenburg Lace, Linen, Embroidered, Handmade, 15 X 40 In. | 10.00 |
| Textile, Scarf, Battenburg Lace, Linen, Embroidered, Handmade, 32 X 04 In. | 12.00 |
| Textile, Scarf, Battenburg Lace, Linen, Embroidered, Handmade, 33 In.Diameter | 15.00 |
| Textile, Scarf, Paisley, Indian, Hand Printed, Hand Blocked, 34 1/2 X 51 In. | 17.00 |
| Textile, Scarf, Piano, White, Battenburg Lace | 8.50 |
| Textile, Shawl, Black Lace, Triangular | 15.00 |
| Textile, Shawl, China, Hand-Embroidered Net, Off-White, Macrame Fringe | 100.00 |
| Textile, Shawl, Evening, Hand-Embroidered Net, Dainty Flowers, Fringe | 100.00 |
| Textile, Shawl, Paisley, Block Center, Embroidery Woven Design, 66 X 68 In. | 35.00 |
| Textile, Shawl, Velvet, Apricot, Cut Flowers, Silk Fringe | 75.00 |
| Textile, Shawl, White Silk, Embroidered, 1887 | 22.00 |
| Textile, Silk Embroidery, 4 Mythical Female Figures, C.1750, 10 1/2 In. | 115.00 |
| Textile, Silk, Chinese Embroidery, Fish, Bridge, & Flower, 6 1/2 X 7 1/2 In. | 6.25 |
| Textile, Stocking, Child's, Black, Long, 1930s, Pair | 1.50 |
| Textile, Stocking, Child's, Brown, Long, 1930s, Pair | 1.00 |
| Textile, Tablecloth & Napkins, Linen, Crocheted Centers & Corners, Belgium | 60.00 |
| Textile, Tablecloth & 12 Napkins, Linen, Blue & White, Monogrammed | 60.00 |
| Textile, Tablecloth & 12 Napkins, White Irish Linen, Shamrocks, Banquet | 75.00 |
| Textile, Tablecloth, Battenburg Lace, 51 In.Round | 15.00 |
| Textile, Tablecloth, Crocheted, Butterfly & Flower, Ecru, 74 X 78 In. | 60.00 |
| Textile, Tablecloth, Hand-Crocheted, White, 56 X 80 In. | 35.00 |
| Textile, Tablecloth, Linen, Cream, Handmade, Cutout, Embroidery, French | 100.00 |
| Textile, Tablecloth, Linen, Damask, Poppies Border, Rosettes Center | 7.00 |
| Textile, Tablecloth, Linen, Damask, Scrolled Border, Dotted Center | 8.00 |
| Textile, Tablecloth, Linen, Red & White, Fringed, 54 X 82 In. | 36.00 |

Textile, Tam, Velvet ............................................................................................ 5.00
Textile, Tapestry, Aubusson, Floral, C.1890, 9 Ft.2 In.X 3 Ft.6 In. .................. 550.00
Textile, Tapestry, Bishop & Clergymen, French, C.1890, 3 Ft.8 In. High ............ 150.00
Textile, Tapestry, Dancing, Fiddler, Drinking, Bowling, Belgium, 18 1/2 In. .......... 75.00
Textile, Tapestry, Floral, Metal Brocade On Yellow Satin, C.1890, 6 Ft.5 In. ........ 110.00
Textile, Tapestry, Fowl & Plants, French, 19th Century, 8 X 10 Ft. .................. 3400.00
Textile, Tapestry, Game Park, Flemish Style, C.1890, 8 Ft.5 In. High .............. 2900.00
Textile, Tapestry, Nobility, Mille-Fleurs, Franco-Flemish, 1890s, 5 X 4 Ft. ........ 1700.00
Textile, Tapestry, Romance Of Procris & Cephalus, Bernardini, 1924, 11 Ft. ...... 900.00
Textile, Tapestry, Verdure, C.1890, 6 Ft.8 In. High .................................... Illus 2300.00
Textile, Tapestry, Verdure, French, Dog, Lady, Landscape, 1800s, 61 X 69 In. .... 1100.00
Textile, Towel, Linen, Border, Fringed, 1900s, Pair .......................................... 15.00
Textile, Towel, Linen, Embroidered Fleur-De-Lis, Scalloped Ends ........................ 2.50
Textile, Towel, Linen, Embroidered Pansies, Scalloped Ends ............................ 3.00
Textile, Towel, Linen, Red Border ........................................................................ 3.25
Textile, Towel, Shoe, Embroidered Tulip, Heart, & Star, Anna Meyer, 1846, Pa. .... 160.00
Textile, Towel, Show, Embroidered Floral & Anna Erhardin, 1814, Pa. ................ 55.00
Textile, Towel, Show, Embroidered Floral, Pa., 64 X 15 1/2 In. ........................ 55.00
Textile, Towel, Show, Pennsylvania, Embroidered Heart, Star, & Bird, 1844 ........ 55.00
Textile, Towel, Show, Pensylvania, Embroidered Floral, 61 In. Long .................. 65.00
Textile, Tuxedo, Swallowtail Coat, 2 Piece, Size 38 ...................................... 35.00
Textile, Uniform, World War I U.S.Captain's, Worn In France, Wool .................. 195.00
Textile, Wall Panel, Chinese, 3 Horses On Silk, Moire & Paper Mounted ............ 4.00
Tiffany Pottery, Base, Lamp, Buff With Green, Blue Drippings, 11 3/4 In.High ...... 275.00
Tiffany Pottery, Bowl, Avocado Glaze, Blossoms & Leaves, C.1904, 5 1/4 In. ...... 600.00
Tiffany Pottery, Bowl, C.1905, 5 3/4 In.High .................................... Illus 1300.00
Tiffany Pottery, Bowl, Variegated Avocado & Buff Glaze, C.1904, 6 In. .............. 125.00
Tiffany Pottery, Bowl, Yellow, Salmon, & Blue On Olive, Pitted, C.1904, 6 In. ...... 150.00
Tiffany Pottery, Ewer, Buff, C.1904, 9 1/2 In. .................................... Illus 425.00

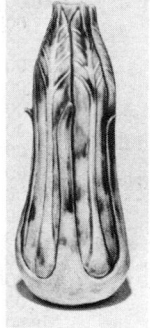

Tiffany Pottery, Vase, Ocher, C.1905, 9 1/8 In.High
(See Page 649)

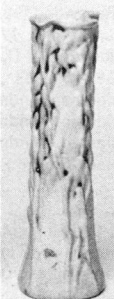

Tiffany Pottery, Vase, Green, C.1905, 10 In.High
(See Page 649)

Tiffany Pottery, Ewer, Buff,
C.1904, 9 1/2 In.

Tiffany Pottery, Vase,
Ocher, C.1904,
10 1/2 In.
(See Page 649)

Tiffany Pottery, Vase, Ocher Glaze,
C.1904, 6 1/2 In.
(See Page 649)

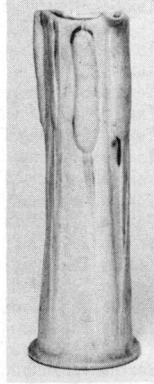

Tiffany Pottery, Ewer,
Buff, C.1904, 12 1/4 In.
(See Page 649)

Tiffany Pottery, Vase, Mint Green, C.1905, 10 In.High

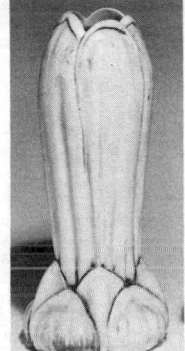

Tiffany Pottery, Vase, Artichoke, C.1905, Buff Green

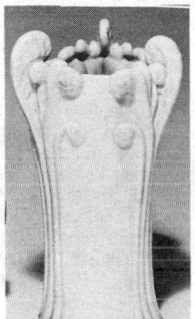

Tiffany Pottery, Vase, C.1905, 9 5/8 In.High

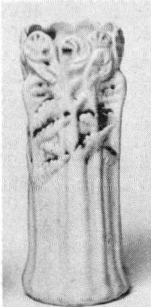

Tiffany Pottery, Vase, Buff Glaze, C.1904, 10 In.

Tiffany Pottery, Jar, Green Buff Glaze, C.1904, 9 In.

Tiffany Pottery, Bowl, C.1905, 5 3/4 In.High
(See Page 648)

| | |
|---|---|
| Tiffany Pottery, Ewer, Buff, C.1904, 12 1/4 In. ...................................................... *Illus* | 150.00 |
| Tiffany Pottery, Ewer, Cream Glaze, Avocado, Cattails, C.1905, 12 1/4 In.High ........................ | 275.00 |
| Tiffany Pottery, Jar, Covered, Buff With Avocado, Poinsettias, 8 3/4 In. ...................... | 250.00 |
| Tiffany Pottery, Jar, Green Buff Glaze, C.1904, 9 In. ..................................... *Illus* | 600.00 |
| Tiffany Pottery, Tile, Opalescent, Patent Feb.8, 1881, 3 In. Square ...................... | 20.00 |
| Tiffany Pottery, Tile, Raised Dragon, Blue, Framed, 12 In. Square ...................... | 125.00 |
| Tiffany Pottery, Tile, Turtle, Dark Green Iridescent ...................................... | 65.00 |
| Tiffany Pottery, Vase, Artichoke, C.1905, Buff Green ......................... *Illus* | 250.00 |
| Tiffany Pottery, Vase, Blue & Brown Glaze, Ocher Traces, C.1904, 7 1/4 In. ........ | 250.00 |
| Tiffany Pottery, Vase, Blue & Green, Leaves & Vines, 5 1/2 In. ...................... | 450.00 |
| Tiffany Pottery, Vase, Blue Green & Avocadd Glaze, C.1904, 8 In. ................ | 225.00 |
| Tiffany Pottery, Vase, Blue, Green, Gold, & Purple Iridescent, 4 In. ................ | 135.00 |
| Tiffany Pottery, Vase, Buff Glaze, C.1904, 10 In. ......................... *Illus* | 825.00 |
| Tiffany Pottery, Vase, Buff Glaze, Green & Blue, Pitted, C.1904, 15 In. ........ | 425.00 |
| Tiffany Pottery, Vase, Buff Green, Maple Leaves & Buds, C.1904, 7 1/2 In. ........ | 625.00 |
| Tiffany Pottery, Vase, C.1905, 9 5/8 In.High ......................... *Illus* | 450.00 |
| Tiffany Pottery, Vase, Double Gourd, Marbleized Ocher, C.1904, 4 1/2 In. ........ | 275.00 |
| Tiffany Pottery, Vase, Green, C.1905, 10 In.High ......................... *Illus* | 400.00 |
| Tiffany Pottery, Vase, Iridescent Green & Ocher, Berries, C.1904, 9 3/4 In. ........ | 350.00 |
| Tiffany Pottery, Vase, Mint Green, C.1905, 10 In.High ..................... *Illus* | 325.00 |
| Tiffany Pottery, Vase, Molded Leaf & Vine Decoration, 2 1/2 In.High ........ | 85.00 |
| Tiffany Pottery, Vase, Ocher Glaze, C.1904, 6 1/2 In. ..................... *Illus* | 650.00 |
| Tiffany Pottery, Vase, Ocher, C.1904, 10 1/2 In. ......................... *Illus* | 600.00 |
| Tiffany Pottery, Vase, Ocher, C.1905, 9 1/8 In.High ..................... *Illus* | 500.00 |

Tiffany Pottery, Vase, Ocher, Chocolate Drippings, C.1904, 9 3/4 In. ......................... 125.00
Tiffany Pottery, Vase, Ocher, Green, & Mustard Glaze, C.1904, 11 3/8 In. ................. 175.00
Tiffany Pottery, Vase, Streaked Ocher Glaze, Blue & Cream, C.1904, 10 In. ................ 275.00
Tiffany Type, Ceiling Fixture, Octagonal, Candle At Each End, Converted Gas .............. 275.00
Tiffany Type, Lamp, Daffodil Shade, Twisted Standard, 24 In. High ............................ 825.00
Tiffany Type, Vase, Swirled, Ruffled Top, Iridescent, 4 In.High, Pair .......................... 65.00

 *Tiffany glass was made by Louis Comfort Tiffany, the American glass designer who worked from about 1879 to 1933. His work included iridescent glass, art nouveau styles of design, and original contemporary styles. He was also noted for his stained glass windows, his unusual lamps, and his bronze work.*

Tiffany, Ashtray & Match Holder, Bronze, Indian Pattern, Gold Dore Finish .............. 60.00
Tiffany, Ashtray & Match Holder, Bronze, Zodiac, Signed .................................... 65.00
Tiffany, Ashtray & Match Holder, Bronze, 6 In.High ........................................... 175.00
Tiffany, Ashtray, Bronze, Double Section, Round, Raised Scallops, Gold Dore ............ 55.00
Tiffany, Ashtray, Bronze, Ribbed, Applied Handles, Gold Dore Finish ...................... 45.00
Tiffany, Ashtray, Bronze, Scalloped Edge, Gold Dore Finish ................................. 55.00
Tiffany, Ashtray, Sterling, Raised Ornate Border, 4 1/2 In.Diameter ....................... 15.00
Tiffany, Basket, Flower, Sterling Silver, Art Nouveau, Plated Liner & Holder ............. 295.00
Tiffany, Basket, Fruit, Silver Plate, Oval, Engraved, Rigid Handle .......................... 65.00
Tiffany, Beaker, Silver, Cylindrical, Beaded Border, C.1860, 3 1/2 In. ..................... 80.00
Tiffany, Blotter Corner, Desk, Brass, Embossed People, Animals, & Fish, 4 ............... 50.00
Tiffany, Blotter End, Bronze, Cutout Spider Web, 12 X 2 In., Pair .......................... 60.00
Tiffany, Blotter End, Bronze, Cutout Spider Web, 6 In., Set Of 4 .......................... 60.00
Tiffany, Blotter End, Bronze, Greenish Brown Patina, Pair .................................. 115.00
Tiffany, Blotter Ends, Greenish Metal, 12 In.Long, Pair ..................................... 65.00
Tiffany, Bonbon, Opalescent To Deep Pink At Rim, Flaring, 5 1/8 In. ...................... 200.00
Tiffany, Bottle, Crystal, Inscribed Camphor On Inside Of Cover, 3 In.High ............... 8.50
Tiffany, Bowl & Flower Holder, Centerpiece, Silvery Green, Signed, 4 In. ............... 595.00
Tiffany, Bowl & Tray, Mayonnaise, Pastel Green, 6 In.Tray, 4 3/4 In.Bowl .............. 285.00
Tiffany, Bowl & Underplate, Finger, Amber Iridescent, Prince ............................. 116.65
Tiffany, Bowl & Underplate, Finger, Gold Iridescent, Scalloped Rims .................... 190.00
Tiffany, Bowl & Underplate, Finger, Gold Iridescent, Signed .............................. 160.00
Tiffany, Bowl & Underplate, Finger, Millefiori, White Flowers, Green Vines ............. 600.00
Tiffany, Bowl & Underplate, Finger, Millefiori, 5 Petal Flowers On Brown .............. 625.00
Tiffany, Bowl, Amber Iridescent, Intaglio Grape Clusters, 3 1/2 In., Pair ............... 275.00
Tiffany, Bowl, Amber Iridescent, Spiral Ribs, Serpentine Rim, 3 1/2 In.High ........... 200.00
Tiffany, Bowl, Amber Iridescent, Spiral Ribs, Serpentine Rim, 10 In. .................... 200.00
Tiffany, Bowl, Amber Iridescent, Tooled Rim, Shallow, 6 1/4 In. ......................... 175.00
Tiffany, Bowl, Blue Iridescent, Scalloped Top, Signed, 6 1/4 In.Diameter ............... 495.00
Tiffany, Bowl, Bronze, Gold, Signed, 9 In. .................................................. 75.00
Tiffany, Bowl, Bronze, Gold, Stepped, Raised Floral, Abalone Shells, 9 In. ............. 125.00
Tiffany, Bowl, Center, Sterling, Embossed Shell & Medallion, Scalloped ................. 155.00
Tiffany, Bowl, Centerpiece, Gold Iridescent, Intaglio Carved, Holder, 10 In. ............ 595.00
Tiffany, Bowl, Dusty Rose To Clear, 4 Sided, C.1927, 10 1/2 In. ........................ 350.00
Tiffany, Bowl, Favrile, Scalloped Rim, Amber, 6 In.Diameter .............................. 90.00
Tiffany, Bowl, Finger, Double Row Of Faceted Rectangles, Arches, C.1892 ............. 100.00
Tiffany, Bowl, Finger, Gold, Blue Highlights, Signed L.C.T. ............................... 150.00
Tiffany, Bowl, Finger, Queen Pattern, Amber Iridescence ................................. 150.00
Tiffany, Bowl, Flower, Detachable Frog, Crackle Iridescent, Lily Pads, 12 In. .......... 500.00
Tiffany, Bowl, Flower, Detachable Frog, Crackled Blue, C.1919, 11 In. .................. 450.00
Tiffany, Bowl, Gold Bronze, Stepped, Raised Floral & Abalone, 9 In.Diameter .......... 175.00
Tiffany, Bowl, Gold, Pink, & Blue Coloring, Swirl Pattern, Signed, 3 X 7 In. ........... 310.00
Tiffany, Bowl, Gold, Swirled, Blue Highlights, Signed L.C.T., 7 In. ....................... 325.00
Tiffany, Bowl, Intaglio Cut Vines, Amber, 3 In.High ........................................ 250.00
Tiffany, Bowl, Iridescent Amber, Quilted, Footed, C.1892, 5 3/4 In. ..................... 150.00
Tiffany, Bowl, Iridescent Blue, Ribbed, Flared Rim, C.1892, 2 3/4 In. High ............ 375.00
Tiffany, Bowl, On Bronze Base, Marked L.C.T., 12 In. .................................... 850.00
Tiffany, Bowl, Optic Laurel Leaves On Yellow Pastel, Signed, 5 In.Diameter ........... 200.00
Tiffany, Bowl, Paneled, Serpentine Rim, Signed, 4 In.Across .............................. 185.00
Tiffany, Bowl, Pastel Turquoise, Footed, Flared, Signed, 2 1/4 X 5 In. .................. 200.00
Tiffany, Bowl, Serving, Gold Iridescent, Red Violet Highlights, 8 In. ...................... 175.00
Tiffany, Bowl, Silver, Scalloped Leaf Design, Chased Edge, 9 In.Diameter ............... 175.00
Tiffany, Bowl, Soup, Wisteria Color, Floriform, Signed .................................... 195.00
Tiffany, Bowl, Sterling Silver, Octagonal, 9 In. ............................................. 125.00
Tiffany, Bowl, Sterling Silver, Paul Revere Style, Engraved, 7 In.Diameter .............. 55.00

| | |
|---|---|
| Tiffany, Bowl, Sterling, Low Footed, Signed Tiffany 925-1000 M, 8 1/2 In. | 55.00 |
| Tiffany, Bowl, Sterling, Octagonal, 9 1/4 In.Diameter | 125.00 |
| Tiffany, Bowl, Sterling, Revere, Footed, 20 Ozs., 7 3/4 In.Diameter | 250.00 |
| Tiffany, Bowl, Sterling, Tulip Shape, 7 Petals, Signed, 7 In. | 45.00 |
| Tiffany, Box, Card, Bronze & Amber Slag, Pine Needle, 4 Ball Feet | 110.00 |
| Tiffany, Box, Cigarette, Enameled Bronze, Flowers In Blue, Red, & Yellow, 6 In | 170.00 |
| Tiffany, Box, Cigarette, Sterling, Swag Design, Initials, Wood Lined, C.1891 | 95.00 |
| Tiffany, Box, Cigarette, Vermeil, Cedar Lined, 17 Ozs., 4 5/8 In. | 195.00 |
| Tiffany, Box, Covered, Octagonal, Sterling Silver, Enameled, Pebble Design | 400.00 |
| Tiffany, Box, Enamel Design On Lid, Bronze, Gold Dore, Round, 4 1/4 In. | 200.00 |
| Tiffany, Box, Hinged Cover, Brass, Embossed People, Animals, & Fish, 5 1/4 In. | 50.00 |
| Tiffany, Box, Hinged Cover, Oval, Bronze & Enamel, Louis XVI Pattern | 65.00 |
| Tiffany, Box, Hinged, Bronze, Chinese Pattern, Cedar Lining, 3 In.High | 225.00 |
| Tiffany, Box, Jewel, Bronze, Hinged, Ball Feet, Enamel Florettes, C.1919 | 650.00 |
| Tiffany, Box, Jewel, Pine Needle Pattern, Signed | 150.00 |
| Tiffany, Box, Monogram On Lid, Sterling & Enamel, Octagonal, 5 In. | 400.00 |
| Tiffany, Box, Pincushion, Sterling, Embossed, Lined, 2 1/2 In.Diameter | 35.00 |
| Tiffany, Box, Watch, Lizard Grain Paper On Cardboard, Gray Velvet Lining | 5.00 |
| Tiffany, Brush, Sterling, Signed, Pair | 25.00 |
| Tiffany, Butter, Sterling, Trivet, Initials | 45.00 |
| Tiffany, Buttonhook, Sterling, Engraved, Monogram, Signed | 15.00 |
| Tiffany, Candelabra, Brass, 4-Arm, Signed Tiffany Studios, New York | 360.00 |
| Tiffany, Candelabra, 8-Branch, Bronze, Signed, 15 In.High | 125.00 |
| Tiffany, Candlestand, Favrile & Bronze, 7-Branch Base, Amber, 20 3/4 In. | 1000.00 |
| Tiffany, Candlestick, Amber Iridescent, Spiral Fluted, 7 In., Pair | 300.00 |
| Tiffany, Candlestick, Amber Iridescent, Spirally Fluted, 5 1/4 In., Pair | 450.00 |
| Tiffany, Candlestick, Blue To White, Footed, C.1920, 4 1/2 In. Diameter | 150.00 |
| Tiffany, Candlestick, Bronze & Favrile Glass, 16 Gold Iridescent Balls | 2500.00 |
| Tiffany, Candlestick, Bronze Bamboo Ribs, Gold Dore, 10 Prisms Top, 18 In. | 1100.00 |
| Tiffany, Candlestick, Bronze Tripod Base, Green & White Top, 1808, Pair | 1350.00 |
| Tiffany, Candlestick, Bronze, Dark Patina, Signed, 11 1/2 In.High, Pair | 475.00 |
| Tiffany, Candlestick, Bronze, Double Horseshoe, Green Glass Top, 12 1/4 In. | 475.00 |
| Tiffany, Candlestick, Bronze, Jeweled, Gold Tulip Shade, 13 In. | 1100.00 |
| Tiffany, Candlestick, Bronze, Queen Anne's Lace, Signed, 18 In. | 495.00 |
| Tiffany, Candlestick, Bronze, Urn Socket, Rod Stem, Tripod, C.1906, 13 In. | 275.00 |
| Tiffany, Candlestick, Favrile & Bronze, Amber, 13 1/4 In.High, Pair | 1200.00 |
| Tiffany, Candlestick, Green Flashed Nozzle, Opalescent Optics, 4 In., Pair | 325.00 |
| Tiffany, Candlestick, Iridescent Amber, Ribbed Baluster, C.1915, 10 In., Pair | 300.00 |
| Tiffany, Candlestick, Sterling Silver, Engraved MBL, 6 3/4 In.High, Pair | 125.00 |
| Tiffany, Candlestick, Sterling, Gold Washed, 7 In.High, Pair | 125.00 |
| Tiffany, Candlestick, Tulip Form Shade, Bronze Standard, 20 In.High | 220.00 |
| Tiffany, Case, Cigarette, 3 Color Gold, Enamel, Suede Envelope, 3 1/4 In. | 725.00 |
| Tiffany, Case, Eye Glasses, Sterling, Art Deco, Hinged, Velvet Lining | 45.00 |
| Tiffany, Centerpiece, Bronze & Enamel, 3-Arm Candelabra, 7 3/4 In.Diameter | 400.00 |
| Tiffany, Chamberstick, Silver Plate, Gadrooned Border, Footed, 3 In.High | 78.00 |
| Tiffany, Champagne, Amber Iridescent, Princess, Twisted Baluster Stem | 100.00 |
| Tiffany, Champagne, Blue Mirror Finish, Snail Pulls, Signed L.C.Tiffany | 225.00 |
| Tiffany, Champagne, Gold, Signed | 145.00 |
| Tiffany, Champagne, Wisteria Color, Floriform | 195.00 |
| Tiffany, Chandelier, Center Stalactite, 12 Lilies & Prisms, Butterscotch | 7500.00 |
| Tiffany, Clip, Paper, Green Glass, Beaded Edges | 45.00 |
| Tiffany, Clock & Candlesticks, Silver & Blue Enamel, Signed, 3 Piece | 895.00 |
| Tiffany, Clock, Carriage, French, Alarm, Beveled Glass, Brass Case | 225.00 |
| Tiffany, Clock, Desk, Zodiac, Bronze, Signed | 300.00 |
| Tiffany, Clock, French Ormolu & Cloisonne, Urn Top, Bun Feet, 14 In. | 2000.00 |
| Tiffany, Clock, Japy Freres & Co., Brass, Beveled Glass, 8 1/2 In.High | 475.00 |
| Tiffany, Clock, Mantel, Black Onyx, Ormolu Trim, Hand-Painted Porcelain | 475.00 |
| Tiffany, Clock, Mantel, Favrile Glass & Bronze, Grapevines, C.1910, 11 In. | 700.00 |
| Tiffany, Coffeepot, Silver, Vase Shape, Chased Scrolls & Floral, C.1855 | 300.00 |
| Tiffany, Cologne, Lay Down, Blue Iridescent, Purple Swirl, Silver Cap | 250.00 |
| Tiffany, Compact, Sterling Silver, Sapphires, 14K Gold Bow Over Catch | 65.00 |
| Tiffany, Compote Tazza, Stretched Bronze On Cobalt Inside, L.C.T. | 425.00 |
| Tiffany, Compote, Bronze, Enameled Etched Flowers, Gold Dore, 7 In. | 140.00 |
| Tiffany, Compote, Bronze, Gold Plated, Enamel Flowers, Signed | 1500.00 |
| Tiffany, Compote, Diamond-Quilted, Signed, 8 In.Wide | 250.00 |
| Tiffany, Compote, Footed, Bronze, 5 In.High | 75.00 |

| | |
|---|---|
| Tiffany, Compote, Gold Iridescent, Blue Inside, Signed | 210.00 |
| Tiffany, Compote, Iridescent Gold, Green Intaglio Leaves, 6 In. Diameter | 650.00 |
| Tiffany, Compote, Platinum Color, Stretched Edge, Signed, 4 1/2 In.Wide | 250.00 |
| Tiffany, Compote, Silver, Parcel Gilt, Chased, Ram's Head Handles, C.1900 | 375.00 |
| Tiffany, Container, Bath Salts, Glass, Hinged Sterling Top, 3 In.High | 47.50 |
| Tiffany, Cordial, Apricot Iridescent, Signed L.C.T. | 140.00 |
| Tiffany, Cordial, Pinched Sided, Signed | 110.00 |
| Tiffany, Cordial, Sterling, Stemmed, Signed, 2 1/4 In. | 20.00 |
| Tiffany, Creamer, Gold Iridescent, Signed, 4 In.High | 225.00 |
| Tiffany, Cup & Saucer, Gold Iridescent | 250.00 |
| Tiffany, Cup, Nut, Signed & Numbered, 3 In.Diameter | 95.00 |
| Tiffany, Cup, Punch, Green Decoration On Gold, Applied Fluted Handle, Signed | 275.00 |
| Tiffany, Cup, Sterling, 3 1/2 In.High | 65.00 |
| Tiffany, Decanter, Red, Gold Iridescent, Violet Base, Pinched Stopper | 475.00 |
| Tiffany, Desk Set, Bronze, Indian, Owls, 3 Tiered Rack, 3 Piece | 300.00 |
| Tiffany, Desk Set, Zodiac, 7 Pieces | 275.00 |
| Tiffany, Dish, Candy, Gold, Favrile, 6 In. | 220.00 |
| Tiffany, Dish, Enameled Bronze, C-Scroll Handles, Flowers, 9 3/4 In. | 80.00 |
| Tiffany, Dish, Nut, Gold Iridescent, Blue Shading, 3 In.Diameter, L.C.T. | 115.00 |
| Tiffany, Dish, Nut, Gold, Lavender Highlights, Border Of Waves, 4 1/2 In. | 230.00 |
| Tiffany, Epergne, Gold, Signed, 16 In. | 895.00 |
| Tiffany, Figurine, Reclining Woman, Harem Pants, Porcelain, Bronze Plynth | 750.00 |
| Tiffany, Flower Holder, Clear, 4 Flower Openings, C.1927, 3 1/2 In. | 60.00 |
| Tiffany, Flower Holder, Four Paw Feet, Circular Base, 7 In.High | 100.00 |
| Tiffany, Fork, Cocktail, Sterling Silver, Embossed Leaf & Vine, Set Of 12 | 90.00 |
| Tiffany, Fork, Dinner, Sterling Silver, Acanthus, C.1910 | 18.00 |
| Tiffany, Fork, Potato Salad, Sterling Silver, Gold Washed Bowl | 55.00 |
| Tiffany, Frame, Bronze, Silver Finish, Blue Enamel, Silver Emblems | 175.00 |
| Tiffany, Frame, Calendar, Paperweight, Bronze, Abalone Shell Discs, Signed | 75.00 |
| Tiffany, Frame, Calendar, Paperweight, Spider Web, Green Slag Over Bronze | 75.00 |
| Tiffany, Frame, Easel, Bronze, Chinese Pattern, 8 1/2 X 7 In. | 90.00 |
| Tiffany, Frame, Easel, Spider Web, Green Slag Over Bronze, 6 1/4 In.High | 110.00 |
| Tiffany, Frame, Picture, Abalone, Easel, Flower & Leaf, Bronze, 10 1/4 In. | 225.00 |
| Tiffany, Frame, Picture, Easel Type, Bronze, 6 X 7 1/2 In. | 90.00 |
| Tiffany, Frame, Picture, Easel, Bronze, Jeweled, 14K Gold, Etched, 7 In. | 225.00 |
| Tiffany, Frame, Picture, Sterling, Gold Washed, Oval, Reed & Leaf, 4 1/4 In. | 65.00 |
| Tiffany, Goblet, Amber, Bell Bowl, Etched Palm Fronds, Set Of 8 | 1200.00 |
| Tiffany, Goblet, Intaglio Grapes & Leafage Rim, Favrile | 120.00 |
| Tiffany, Goblet, Jade Green & Opalescent Bowl, Yellow Stem & Base | 160.00 |
| Tiffany, Goblet, Purplish Blue, Amber Stem, White Opalescence At Rim, Signed | 195.00 |
| Tiffany, Holder, Card, Bronze, Green Glass, Footed Base, Openwork | 45.00 |
| Tiffany, Holder, Card, Footed, Green Glass Around 4 Sides | 70.00 |
| Tiffany, Humidor, Cypriote, Gilt Metal, Green, 7 1/2 In.High | 1000.00 |
| Tiffany, Humidor, Gold Iridescent, Star Cut Top Knob, Signed & Numbered | 425.00 |
| Tiffany, Inkwell, Abalone, Octagon Shaped, 3 1/2 In.High, Bronze, Signed | 200.00 |
| Tiffany, Inkwell, Brass, Octagonal, Embossed Scenes, Marked Tiffany Studios | 100.00 |
| Tiffany, Inkwell, Bronze, American Indian, Gold Fore Finish, Glass Insert | 125.00 |
| Tiffany, Inkwell, Bronze, Chinese Pattern, Hinged Cover, Octagonal, Gold Dore | 185.00 |
| Tiffany, Inkwell, Bronze, Venetian, Hinged, 2 Pots, C.1906, 5 1/4 In. | 175.00 |
| Tiffany, Inkwell, Burnished Gold, Square, Tiffany Studios No.1813 | 95.00 |
| Tiffany, Inkwell, Cut Glass, Embossed Hinged Sterling Lid, 2 3/4 In.High | 55.00 |
| Tiffany, Inkwell, Double Favrile Inserts, Bronze, Butterflies | 1350.00 |
| Tiffany, Inkwell, Metal, Greenish Finish, Green Glass Insert, Square, Footed | 240.00 |
| Tiffany, Inkwell, Octagon Shape, Zodiac, Crab Sign, Bronze | 65.00 |
| Tiffany, Inkwell, Square, Bronze, Footed, Beaded Edge, Greenish Color | 175.00 |
| Tiffany, Ladle, Gravy, Sterling Silver, Acanthus, C.1910 | 45.00 |
| Tiffany, Ladle, Sterling Silver, Antique Pattern, Wave Edge, 4 In.Long | 14.00 |
| Tiffany, Ladle, Sterling, Curved Handle, Engraved Alice, 12 In. | 65.00 |
| Tiffany, Lamp Base, Iridescent Green, Baluster, Favrile, C.1892, 18 In. | 300.00 |
| Tiffany, Lamp Base, Table, Bronze, 3 Light, Signed | 450.00 |
| Tiffany, Lamp, Acorn, Green & White Shade, Bronze, C.1899, 19 In. | 1000.00 |
| Tiffany, Lamp, Arrowroot, Oil, 22 In. High _Illus_ | 7500.00 |
| Tiffany, Lamp, Boudoir, Green Shade, Stretched Iridescent Edge, Brass Base | 185.00 |
| Tiffany, Lamp, Bridge, Sapa Shell, Bronze Rod Standard, C.1899, 4 Ft.8 In. | 550.00 |
| Tiffany, Lamp, Bronze, Circular Base, Domical Bronze Geometric Band Shade | 275.00 |
| Tiffany, Lamp, Candle, Beehive Effect Shade, Gold | 550.00 |

Tiffany, Lamp,
Green On Pale Yellow,
16 In., Pair

Tiffany, Lamp,
Nautilus, Gilt Bronze,
C.1902, 13 1/2 In.

Tiffany, Lamp, Lily,
12-Light, Amber, Bronze,
20 1/2 In.

Tiffany, Lamp, Arrowroot,
Oil, 22 In. High
*(See Page 652)*

| | |
|---|---|
| Tiffany, Lamp, Candle, Kerosene, Gold Iridescent, Swirled Shade | 695.00 |
| Tiffany, Lamp, Candle, Wafer Base, Signed L.C.T., 11 In. | 300.00 |
| Tiffany, Lamp, Candlestick, Gold Iridescent, Ribbed, Twisted, Gold Shade | 425.00 |
| Tiffany, Lamp, Clematis, Purple & Green, Ribbed Base, 23 In.High | 6000.00 |
| Tiffany, Lamp, Converted Kerosene, Green, Gold, & Amber Shade, Lily Base | 2700.00 |
| Tiffany, Lamp, Desk, Double, Glass Ball Center, Green Feather Shades, Enamel | 750.00 |
| Tiffany, Lamp, Desk, Herringbone, Dark To Light Green, 23 In.High, Signed | 2000.00 |
| Tiffany, Lamp, Desk, Jeweled, Green To Blue, Bronze Platform Base, 14 In. | 1100.00 |
| Tiffany, Lamp, Desk, Liberty Bell, Gold Iridescent Swirled Bell, Bronze | 1100.00 |
| Tiffany, Lamp, Desk, Octagonal, Etched Chippendale, Bronze & Amber Slag | 950.00 |
| Tiffany, Lamp, Desk, Turtleback, Helmet Top, Jeweled Base, Dark Blue, 15 In. | 1950.00 |
| Tiffany, Lamp, Dragonfly, 6 Bronze Rods Supports, C.1899, 22 In. | 6500.00 |
| Tiffany, Lamp, Floor, Decorated Gold & White Shade, 3 Footed Base | 850.00 |
| Tiffany, Lamp, Floor, Orange & Gold Shade, 58 In.High, Signed | 2000.00 |
| Tiffany, Lamp, Floor, Radiating Green Tile Shade, Pad Feet, 6 Ft.7 In.High | 4100.00 |
| Tiffany, Lamp, Floor, Roman Helmet, Leaded, Gold Mottled, Bronze Base | 5000.00 |
| Tiffany, Lamp, Green On Pale Yellow, 16 In., Pair ............... *Illus* | 2000.00 |
| Tiffany, Lamp, Green Ruffled Shade, Harp Support, Ball Feet, 13 In.High | 375.00 |
| Tiffany, Lamp, Lily, Four Light, Amber Iridescent, 20 In.High | 1200.00 |
| Tiffany, Lamp, Lily, Three-Light, Bronze Base, 23 In.High | 500.00 |
| Tiffany, Lamp, Lily, Twelve-Light, Bronze Base, 21 1/2 In.High | 4400.00 |
| Tiffany, Lamp, Lily, 12-Light, Amber, Bronze, 20 1/2 In. ............... *Illus* | 4500.00 |
| Tiffany, Lamp, Lily, 12-Light, Iridescent Amber, Bronze, C.1899, 21 1/2 In. | 5500.00 |
| Tiffany, Lamp, Lotus Bell, Green Shades, Ribbed Bronze Base, 21 In. | 3700.00 |
| Tiffany, Lamp, Mosque, Blue Feather Design On White, Bronze Base & Cap | 850.00 |
| Tiffany, Lamp, Nautilus, Gilt Bronze, C.1902, 13 1/2 In. ............... *Illus* | 2200.00 |
| Tiffany, Lamp, Pierced Bronze & Glass Shade, Green, Bronze Base, 20 In.High | 525.00 |
| Tiffany, Lamp, Pomegranate, Bronze Urn Form Standard, C.1899, 23 In. | 800.00 |
| Tiffany, Lamp, Pomegranate, Green Tiles & Pomegranates, Chinese Base, 17 In. | 1500.00 |
| Tiffany, Lamp, Poppy, Orange, Bronze Four Virtues Base, C.1899, 26 In. | 7500.00 |

Tiffany, Lamp, Student, Amber Shade, Gilt Bronze Circular Base, 13 In.High ............................ 450.00
Tiffany, Lamp, Student, Blue Shade, Ribbed Bronze Base, 13 In. ............................ 1000.00
Tiffany, Lamp, Student, Bronze, Twelve Sided, 19 1/4 In.High ............................ 750.00
Tiffany, Lamp, Student, Desk, Blue Green Iridescent Favrile Shade, Bronze ............................ 1200.00
Tiffany, Lamp, Student, Desk, Double, Reticulated Globes, Bronze Base, 29 In. ............................ 6500.00
Tiffany, Lamp, Student, Green & Gold, Bronze Base, Signed ............................ 1950.00
Tiffany, Lamp, Student, Yellow & White Shade, Bronze, C.1904, 16 1/2 In. ............................ 800.00
Tiffany, Lamp, Table, Apple Blossom, White & Pink, Leaded, Bronze Base ............................ 3800.00
Tiffany, Lamp, Table, Black-Eyed Susan, Bronze Base, 22 In.High, Signed ............................ 3300.00
Tiffany, Lamp, Table, Fabrique, Emerald, Ruffled Borders, Bronze Base, 20 In. ............................ 2500.00
Tiffany, Lamp, Table, Fabrique, Green, Bronze Base, 1950, 26 In. ............................ 1500.00
Tiffany, Lamp, Table, Favrile Fabrique, Shade, 16 In.Diameter, Green, Signed ............................ 1900.00
Tiffany, Lamp, Table, Greek Key, Mottled, Fly Hangs On One Side, Bronze Base ............................ 3200.00
Tiffany, Lamp, Table, Green Dome Shade, Amber Loopings, Bronze, C.1904, 14 In. ............................ 600.00
Tiffany, Lamp, Table, Hanging Head Dragonfly, 22 In.Diameter, Bronze Base ............................ 9200.00
Tiffany, Lamp, Table, Helmet Shape, Green Iridescent, Pigtails, Bronze Base ............................ 2200.00
Tiffany, Lamp, Table, Lily, 18 Branch, Gold Iridescent Shades, Bronze Base ............................ 6850.00
Tiffany, Lamp, Table, Mottled Blue Leaded Shade, Urn Shape Bronze Base ............................ 2100.00
Tiffany, Lamp, Table, Pomegranate, Leaded Fly On Side, Bronze Base, 18 In. ............................ 1700.00
Tiffany, Lamp, Table, Rambling Rose, Bronze Flowerpot Base, 18 In. ............................ 7500.00
Tiffany, Lamp, Table, Red Poppy, Gold Dore Bronze Base, 22 In. ............................ 6500.00
Tiffany, Lamp, Table, Red Tulip, Dark Patina Bronze Base, 21 In. ............................ 4000.00
Tiffany, Lamp, Table, Woodbine, 16 In.Diameter, Bronze Base ............................ 4000.00
Tiffany, Lamp, Tulip Shade, 3 Branch, 16 In.High, Signed ............................ 1100.00
Tiffany, Lantern, Wall, Green Glass Tiles, Bronze Fixture, Pair ............................ 2000.00
Tiffany, Letter File, Etched Grapevines, Dore Bronze Over Caramel Slag ............................ 225.00
Tiffany, Letter Holder, Brass, Embossed People, Animals, & Fish, 2 Tier ............................ 100.00
Tiffany, Letter Opener, Zodiac, Bronze, 10 1/2 In.Long, Signed ............................ 45.00
Tiffany, Letter Rack, Bronze & Glass, Green Slag, Pine Needle Design ............................ 175.00
Tiffany, Liqueur Set, Amber Iridescence, 7 Piece ............................ 900.00
Tiffany, Magnifying Glass, Bronze Dore, Zodiac, 9 In.Long ............................ 95.00
Tiffany, Match Holder, Thistle, Dore, Caramel Glass, Signed ............................ 110.00
Tiffany, Mirror, Easel Type, Bronze, Gold Dore, Signed ............................ 75.00
Tiffany, Mirror, Hand, Ostrich Feathers ............................ 115.00
Tiffany, Mug, Sterling Silver, Handled, Engraved HML, 3 3/4 In. ............................ 75.00
Tiffany, Nappy, Heart Shape, Gold Iridescent, Handled, Pink & Blue Lights ............................ 275.00
Tiffany, Night-Light, Gold Iridescent Shade, Black Wood Base, 7 1/4 In. ............................ 350.00
Tiffany, Opener, Letter, Bronze, Chinese Pattern, Signed & Numbered ............................ 92.00
Tiffany, Paper Clip, Bronze, Chinese Pattern, 2 3/4 X 4 In.Signed ............................ 45.00
Tiffany, Paper Clip, Green Glass On Top, 1 1/2 In.High ............................ 65.00
Tiffany, Paperweight, Bronze Bulldog, Gold Dore Finish, 2 In.Long, Signed ............................ 110.00
Tiffany, Paperweight, Zodiac, Bronze, Entwined Line Pattern, Signed ............................ 60.00
Tiffany, Parfait, Aqua, Pastel, Signed L.C.Tiffany, Favrile, 6 1/2 In. ............................ 225.00
Tiffany, Pen Brush, Bronze, Zodiac Pattern, Octagonal, Geometrics, Signed ............................ 65.00
Tiffany, Pen Brush, Venetian, Band Of Ermines At Bottom ............................ 60.00
Tiffany, Pitcher, Intaglio Green Flowers & Vines, Sterling Spout & Handle ............................ 1800.00
Tiffany, Planter, Bronze, Etched Border Design, Bronze Liner, Drop Handles ............................ 200.00
Tiffany, Plate, Amber Iridescent, Scalloped Rim, Paper Label, 9 In. ............................ 160.00
Tiffany, Plate, Bread, Sterling, Reticulated Edge, Initials, 10 1/2 In.Long ............................ 70.00
Tiffany, Plate, Bronze, Gold Spatter, Intaglio Double Hearts Band, 9 In. ............................ 45.00
Tiffany, Plate, Cake, Iridescent Amber, Columnar Standard, C.1915, 5 In. ............................ 450.00
Tiffany, Plate, Favrile, Deep Blue Iridescence, 10 5/8 In.Diameter ............................ 350.00
Tiffany, Plate, Gold Iridescent, Signed L.C.T., 7 In. ............................ 125.00
Tiffany, Plate, Gold Vermeil, Raised Decoration On Rim, Signed, No.1737 ............................ 50.00
Tiffany, Plate, Green With Blue Iridescence, Signed, 8 1/2 In. ............................ 225.00
Tiffany, Plate, Pastel Mother-Of-Pearl, Green Stretched Rim, 6 1/2 In. ............................ 210.00
Tiffany, Plate, Pastel Mother-Of-Pearl, Stretched Border, 6 1/2 In. ............................ 210.00
Tiffany, Plate, Scalloped, Iridescent, Signed, 6 In. ............................ 225.00
Tiffany, Plate, Spun Bronze, Incised Rim, 9 In. ............................ 110.00
Tiffany, Plate, Wisteria, 11 In. ............................ 350.00
Tiffany, Platter, Bronze, Etched Iridescent Abalone Shells Border, 14 In. ............................ 125.00
Tiffany, Platter, Serving, Bronze, Gold Dore, 11 In.Long, 9 In.Wide, Signed ............................ 125.00
Tiffany, Pot, Jam, Iridescent Amber, Zigzag Bandings, Silver Hinged Lid, 1892 ............................ 250.00
Tiffany, Pot, Witch's, Gold, Blue Iridescence, Footed, Marked L.C.T. ............................ 130.00
Tiffany, Pot, Witch's, Gold, Swirled, Signed L.C.T., Favrile, 1988h ............................ 275.00
Tiffany, Ring Tree, Gold Iridescent, Intaglio Carved Leaves, 4 In.High ............................ 250.00

| | |
|---|---:|
| Tiffany, Rose Bowl, Purple, Thorns, Signed, Label, 2 3/4 In.High | 250.00 |
| Tiffany, Salt & Pepper, High Dome Pepper Castor, Open Salt, Pearl Spoon | 55.00 |
| Tiffany, Salt & Pepper, Sterling, Brass, & Copper, Enameled, Art Nouveau Type | 250.00 |
| Tiffany, Salt Celler, Silver, Greek Revival Style, Footed, C.1870, Pair | 100.00 |
| Tiffany, Salt Dip, Bluish, Pigtails, Signed, 2 In.Diameter | 95.00 |
| Tiffany, Salt Set, Bean Pot Shape, Gold, Rainbow, 2 Handled, 7 Piece | 1100.00 |
| Tiffany, Salt, Blue Highlights, Ruffled, Signed | 80.00 |
| Tiffany, Salt, Fluted, Gold Iridescent, Blue Highlights, L.C.T.Favrile | 110.00 |
| Tiffany, Salt, Gold Iridescent, Prunted, Signed | 110.00 |
| Tiffany, Salt, Gold, Blue Iridescence, Ruffled, Marked L.C.T., 1 In.High | 95.00 |
| Tiffany, Salt, Gold, Iridescent, Round, L.C.T. Favrile | 75.00 |
| Tiffany, Salt, Iridescent Amber, Swirled, C.1892, Set Of 6 | 500.00 |
| Tiffany, Salt, Iridescent, Pink & Blue Highlights, Ruffled Edge | 105.00 |
| Tiffany, Salt, Master, Gold Iridescent, Ruffled Edge, Blue & Pink Highlights | 140.00 |
| Tiffany, Salt, Master, Sterling Silver, Gold Washed Inside, Engraved BGF | 27.50 |
| Tiffany, Salver, Silver, Chased, Col.A.Duryee Retirement, 1859, C.1860, 10 In. | 275.00 |
| Tiffany, Salver, Silver, Oval, Applied Cast Band Floral Rim, C.1870, 15 In. | 350.00 |
| Tiffany, Sauceboat, Silver, Oval, Neo-Classical Handle, Pedestal, C.1880 | 150.00 |
| Tiffany, Scarab, Gold Iridescent | 110.00 |
| Tiffany, Scarab, Red Iridescent, 3/4 In.Long | 40.00 |
| Tiffany, Server, Cake, Sterling Silver, Acanthus, C.1910 | 90.00 |
| Tiffany, Server, Fish, Sterling, Olympian, C.1850 | 70.00 |
| Tiffany, Server, Pastry, Sterling Silver, St.Dunstan, Initials | 50.00 |
| Tiffany, Shade, Dome Shaped, Amber, Light Green, 24 In.Diameter, Signed | 4000.00 |
| Tiffany, Shade, Gas, Gourd Shape, Gold Zipper On White Reactive, 5 1/4 In. | 125.00 |
| Tiffany, Shade, Green Leaves On Yellow | 110.00 |
| Tiffany, Shade, Hanging, Dome, Emerald, Striations, Ivy Leaf, 24 In. | 400.00 |
| Tiffany, Shade, White With Gold Decoration, Signed L.C.T., Pair | 275.00 |
| Tiffany, Sherbet, Gold, Grape Border, Favrile | 185.00 |
| Tiffany, Sherbet, Gold, Purple Highlights, Favrile, L.C.Tiffany | 175.00 |
| Tiffany, Sherbet, Hollow Stem, Signed, 3 1/2 In. | 125.00 |
| Tiffany, Sherbet, Iridescent Gold, Etched Grapes & Leaves, Stemmed | 135.00 |
| Tiffany, Sherbet, Verre De Soie Pedestal & Base, Blue Stretched Edge | 225.00 |
| Tiffany, Shot Glass, Rainbow Iridescent, Dimple, Signed & Numbered | 110.00 |
| Tiffany, Smoking Set, Copper, Applied Sterling Grapes & Leaves, 6 Piece | 150.00 |
| Tiffany, Spoon, After Dinner, Gilt Sterling Silver, Twisted Handles, 6 | 75.00 |
| Tiffany, Spoon, Berry, Sterling Silver, Threaded, Gilt Bowl, C.1902 | 18.00 |
| Tiffany, Spoon, Ice Cream, Sterling Silver, Wave & Shell, Gilt Bowl, C.1884 | 9.65 |
| Tiffany, Spoon, Serving, Sterling Silver, Embossed Grapes, Scalloped Bowl | 48.00 |
| Tiffany, Spoon, Serving, Sterling, Perforated Bowl, Dainty Handle, 4 In | 22.00 |
| Tiffany, Spoon, Serving, Sterling, Ram's Head Decoration, C.1920 | 25.00 |
| Tiffany, Spoon, Soup, Sterling Silver, Acanthus, C.1910 | 18.00 |
| Tiffany, Tazza, Amber Iridescent Crackle, Serpentine Rim, 4 1/2 In. High | 200.00 |
| Tiffany, Tazza, Amber Iridescent, Ruffled Rim, Knopped Stem, 4 1/2 In | 275.00 |
| Tiffany, Tazza, Candy, Knob Stem, L.C.T., 2 3/4 In.High | 185.00 |
| Tiffany, Tazza, Diamond Quilted, Amber Iridescent, Baluster Stem, 8 In. | 200.00 |
| Tiffany, Tazza, Favrile, Ruffled Rim, Baluster Standard, Amber, 6 In.High | 225.00 |
| Tiffany, Tazza, Gold, Diamond-Quilted, Pedestal, L.C.T., 8 In. | 350.00 |
| Tiffany, Tazza, Silver Gilt, Repousse Floral, Encgrved Crest, C.1880, Pair | 450.00 |
| Tiffany, Tea Caddy, Urn Shape, 5 1/4 In. | 165.00 |
| Tiffany, Toothpick, Gold, Blue Highlights, Signed & Numbered | 175.00 |
| Tiffany, Toothpick, Gold, Blue Iridescence, Marked L.C.T., 2 In.High | 110.00 |
| Tiffany, Tray, Bronze, Bookmark Pattern, 2 Compartments, Gold Dore Finish | 55.00 |
| Tiffany, Tray, Bronze, Gold Spatter, Abalone Shells, Relief Floral, 14 In. | 110.00 |
| Tiffany, Tray, Pen & Pencil, Grape Pattern, Green, Marbleized, Signed | 65.00 |
| Tiffany, Tray, Pen, Etched Grapevines, Dore Bronze Over Caramel Slag | 85.00 |
| Tiffany, Tumbler, Blue & Gold Iridescent, Earth Form, Lily Pads, Favrile | 315.00 |
| Tiffany, Tumbler, Gold Iridescent, Round Bottom, Violet Interior, 2 In.High | 125.00 |
| Tiffany, Tumbler, Gold, Blue Iridescence, L.C.T., 4 In.High | 220.00 |
| Tiffany, Tumbler, Juice, Gold Iridescent, Lily Pad Design, L.C.T. | 150.00 |
| Tiffany, Tureen, Soup, Silver, Helmet Finial, Boat Shape, Armorials, C.1880 | 800.00 |
| Tiffany, Vase, Agate, Baluster, Olive Green, Cut & Faceted, Bull's-Eyes, 6 In. | 5500.00 |
| Tiffany, Vase, Alabaster, Gold Leaf On Base, Favrile, 20 In.High, Pair | 360.00 |
| Tiffany, Vase, Amber Iridescent, Green Zigzags, Bronze Holder, 11 1/2 In. | 450.00 |
| Tiffany, Vase, Amber Iridescent, Shouldered, Flaring Neck, 6 1/2 In. | 200.00 |
| Tiffany, Vase, Amber Iridescent, Shouldered, Straight Neck, 12 3/4 In. | 400.00 |

Tiffany, Vase, Amber On Alabaster To Apricot, 7 In.

Tiffany, Vase, Black & Cream On Green, 22 3/4 In.

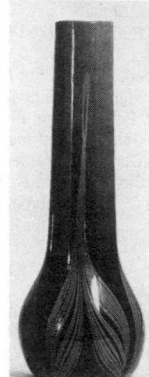

Tiffany, Vase, Laminated, Ocher,
Red, & Purple, 22 3/4 In.
(See Page 658)

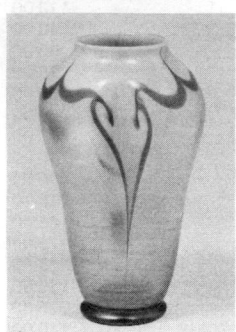

Tiffany, Vase, Favrile,
Amber, 7 In.High
(See Page 657)

Tiffany, Vase, Jack-In-The-Pulpit,
Amber, C.1906, 18 In.
(See Page 658)

| | |
|---|---|
| Tiffany, Vase, Amber On Alabaster To Apricot, 7 In. .................................................. *Illus* | 550.00 |
| Tiffany, Vase, Amber To Green Base, C.1895, 3 In. .................................................. *Illus* | 800.00 |
| Tiffany, Vase, Aurene, Gold, Ribbed, Folded Over Lip, Favrile, 8 1/2 In. ..................... | 150.00 |
| Tiffany, Vase, Baluster Shape, Amber Iridescent, Ribbed, Dome Foot, 12 In. ................. | 275.00 |
| Tiffany, Vase, Baluster, Amber Zigzags On Aqua To Deep Blue, C.1896, 21 In. ............... | 1050.00 |
| Tiffany, Vase, Black & Cream On Green, 22 3/4 In. .............................................. *Illus* | 1000.00 |
| Tiffany, Vase, Black Favrile, Ovoid, Green & Blue Decoration, 6 3/4 In.High ................ | 4250.00 |
| Tiffany, Vase, Black Iridescent, Gold Overlay, Rolled Collar, 2 1/2 In. ...................... | 2500.00 |
| Tiffany, Vase, Blue Iridescent, Ribbed, Free-Form, Dimpled, 4 1/2 In. ....................... | 475.00 |
| Tiffany, Vase, Blue-Black Iridescent, Silver Blue Swirl, 7 In.High, Signed ................... | 1300.00 |
| Tiffany, Vase, Blue, Black Decorated Collar, Tiffany Furnaces, 12 In. ......................... | 400.00 |
| Tiffany, Vase, Blue, Rainbow Highlights, Zipper Pattern, Signed, 12 In.High ................. | 750.00 |
| Tiffany, Vase, Blue, Zipper Pattern, Bulbous Bottom, Signed, 12 In.High ..................... | 650.00 |
| Tiffany, Vase, Bronze, Dragonfly On Each Side, 16 In.High .................................... | 1500.00 |
| Tiffany, Vase, Brown, Blue Iridescence, Striping & Designs, L.C.T., 10 In. ................... | 2300.00 |
| Tiffany, Vase, Bud, Bronze Base, Green Hexagonal Top, Clear Ribs, 13 In. ................... | 275.00 |
| Tiffany, Vase, Bud, Bronze Holder, Gold Iridescent, 13 1/4 In.High, Signed ................. | 275.00 |
| Tiffany, Vase, Bud, Enameled Copper Base, C.1905, 16 1/8 In., Pair .......................... | 650.00 |
| Tiffany, Vase, Bud, Iridescent Amber Feathers On Opalescent, C.1892, 18 In. ............... | 225.00 |
| Tiffany, Vase, Bud, Iridescent, Signed & Numbered, 8 In.High ................................. | 250.00 |
| Tiffany, Vase, Bud, White, Teardrop Pedestal, Yellow Leaves, Rainbow Lights .............. | 240.00 |
| Tiffany, Vase, Bulbous Top, Lemon, Green Drape, Gold, 1 1/2 In. ............................. | 525.00 |
| Tiffany, Vase, Bulbous, Amber Iridescent, Rows Of Pinched Devices, 5 1/2 In. ............. | 350.00 |
| Tiffany, Vase, Bulbous, Gold, Ribbed, Blue Highlights, Signed, 6 In.High ..................... | 200.00 |
| Tiffany, Vase, Cameo, Cut Blossoms On Crystal, Flaring Foot, C.1908, 13 In. ............... | 900.00 |
| Tiffany, Vase, Cloverleaf Shape, Pink & White Millefiori On Aqua, 4 In. ..................... | 1800.00 |
| Tiffany, Vase, Cylindrical, Amber Iridescent, Ribbed, Knop Stem, 8 1/2 In. ................. | 225.00 |
| Tiffany, Vase, Cypriote, Amber Stalagmitic Frieze On Brown Green, C.1899 ................. | 1800.00 |

Tiffany, Vase, Cypriote, Gold Ground, Violet & Pink Highlights, 7 1/2 In ........................................ 1200.00
Tiffany, Vase, Cypriote, Iridescent Amber, C.1898, 11 5/8 In. ......................................................... 700.00
Tiffany, Vase, Decorated Green Leaf, Button Pontil, Signed, 9 In. ................................................... 360.00
Tiffany, Vase, Deep Blue Satin Iridescent, Black Trim, 7 In.High ................................................... 775.00
Tiffany, Vase, Elongated Baluster Shape, Amber Iridescent, 12 1/2 In. ......................................... 225.00
Tiffany, Vase, Favrile, Amber, 7 In.High ................................................................................. Illus 575.00
Tiffany, Vase, Favrile, Bronze Standard, 14 In.High ..................................................................... 170.00
Tiffany, Vase, Floriform, Amber Iridescent Crackle, Conical Bowl, 4 3/4 In. .................................. 250.00
Tiffany, Vase, Floriform, Blue Iridescent, Footed, 3 3/4 In.High ................................................... 245.00
Tiffany, Vase, Floriform, Cameo, White & Green Petals On Clear, 13 1/8 In. ................................. 3000.00
Tiffany, Vase, Floriform, Gold Iridescent, Pulled Leaf, Green Top, 11 1/2 In. ............................... 250.00
Tiffany, Vase, Floriform, Gold, Ribbed Bottom, Signed, 10 In. ..................................................... 460.00
Tiffany, Vase, Floriform, Gold, Signed, 12 In.High ...................................................................... 390.00
Tiffany, Vase, Floriform, Green & White Striated Feathers, 13 3/4 In.High .................................... 1250.00
Tiffany, Vase, Floriform, Ruffled Rim, Amber, 16 In.High ............................................................. 725.00
Tiffany, Vase, Fluted, Gold Iridescent, 3 In.High ........................................................................ 185.00
Tiffany, Vase, Gold & White Infused Designs On Cream, 10 1/2 In. ............................................. 725.00
Tiffany, Vase, Gold Iridescent, Bulbous, Pinched Neck, Ribbed, 2 1/4 In. .................................... 250.00
Tiffany, Vase, Gold Iridescent, Crimped Sides, Signed, 3 3/4 In. ................................................. 400.00
Tiffany, Vase, Gold Iridescent, Dark Green Decoration, Signed, 9 3/4 In. .................................... 435.00
Tiffany, Vase, Gold, Blue Iridescence, Marked L.C.T., 4 In.High .................................................. 225.00
Tiffany, Vase, Gold, Cameo & Intaglio Cut Green Leaves, L.C.T., 10 In. ...................................... 1400.00
Tiffany, Vase, Gold, Green Decoration, Signed, 6 In.High ............................................................ 450.00
Tiffany, Vase, Gold, Intaglio Cut Grapes, Leaves, & Vines, 5 1/2 In.High .................................... 195.00
Tiffany, Vase, Gold, Signed & Numbered, 3 In. ........................................................................ 195.00
Tiffany, Vase, Gourd Shape, Amber Iridescent, Ribbed, 5 In. ...................................................... 225.00
Tiffany, Vase, Green & Amber, Bronze Floriform Base, C.1900, 15 In. ......................................... 900.00
Tiffany, Vase, Green & Gold, Signed, 8 In. ............................................................................... 350.00
Tiffany, Vase, Green & Gold, 5 In. ........................................................................................... 350.00
Tiffany, Vase, Green Drape On Lemon, Gold Decorated, 1 1/2 In. High ........................................ 525.00
Tiffany, Vase, Green Feathers On Mottled Brown, Signed, 5 In.High ............................................ 575.00
Tiffany, Vase, Green Iridescent, Favrile, 5 3/4 In. ................................................................. Illus 550.00
Tiffany, Vase, Green Leaves & Vines On Gold, Button Pontil, Favrile, 6 In. .................................. 475.00
Tiffany, Vase, Green Leaves On Gold, Pedestal, Signed, 13 In. ................................................... 450.00
Tiffany, Vase, Green Lily Pads On Gold, Signed & Numbered, 3 In.High ....................................... 450.00
Tiffany, Vase, Green Vines & Leaves On Blue Iridescent, C.1919, 12 1/4 In. ............................... 1450.00
Tiffany, Vase, Green, Amber Loopings, Handles, 7 3/4 In.High .................................................... 1050.00
Tiffany, Vase, Hourglass Shape, Blue Gold Iridescent, 2 1/2 In.High ............................................ 45.00
Tiffany, Vase, Inverted Pyriform, Green Tendrils On Amber, C.1915, 9 In. .................................... 525.00
Tiffany, Vase, Iridescent Amber, Bronze Floriform Base, C.1900, 13 3/4 In. ................................. 500.00
Tiffany, Vase, Iridescent Amber, Bulging, Short Neck, C.1906, 18 In ............................................ 650.00
Tiffany, Vase, Iridescent Amber, Green Feathers, C.1892, 18 In. ................................................. 400.00
Tiffany, Vase, Iridescent Amber, Slender Neck, C.1892, 16 In., Pair ............................................ 600.00
Tiffany, Vase, Iridescent Amber, Zigzag Banding, Favrile, C.1895, 7 In. ...................................... 275.00
Tiffany, Vase, Iridescent Midnight Blue, Striated Feathers, C.1895, 20 In. .................................. 1300.00
Tiffany, Vase, Iridescent, Signed & Numbered, 3 In.High ........................................................... 175.00
Tiffany, Vase, Jack-In-The-Pulpit, Amber Iridescence, 19 In.High ............................................... 3600.00

Tiffany, Vase, Amber To Green Base,
C.1895, 3 In.
(See Page 656)

Tiffany, Vase, Green Iridescent,
Favrile, 5 3/4 In.

| | |
|---|---|
| Tiffany, Vase, Jack-In-The-Pulpit, Amber, C.1906, 18 In. ........................ *Illus* | 2000.00 |
| Tiffany, Vase, Laminated, Ocher, Blue, & Purple, Amber Feathers, C.1919, 23 In. | 900.00 |
| Tiffany, Vase, Laminated, Ocher, Red, & Purple, 22 3/4 In. .................... *Illus* | 1000.00 |
| Tiffany, Vase, Laminated, Red & Green, Yellow & Silver Zipper, 8 1/2 In. ......... | 850.00 |
| Tiffany, Vase, Laminated, Red, Black Rimmed Collar, Signed & Numbered ......... | 2250.00 |
| Tiffany, Vase, Laminated, Red, Green, & Yellow, Zipper Decoration, 8 1/2 In. ...... | 850.00 |
| Tiffany, Vase, Lipstick Red, L.C.Tiffany, Favrile, 45 In. High | 1400.00 |
| Tiffany, Vase, Melon Shape, Pinched Bottom, Gold Iridescent, 1 1/2 In. .......... | 325.00 |
| Tiffany, Vase, Mottled & Streaked In Browns, Blue, & Purple, L.C.T., 5 In. ....... | 2800.00 |
| Tiffany, Vase, Onion Shape, Ribbed, Green On Amber, C.1903, 11 1/2 In. ......... | 425.00 |
| Tiffany, Vase, Optic Laurel Leaves, Pink Iridescent Interior, 14 In.High ......... | 440.00 |
| Tiffany, Vase, Ovoid, Cased, White Leafage On Salmon, Short Neck, 5 1/4 In. ..... | 2700.00 |
| Tiffany, Vase, Paperweight, Baluster Shape, Purple & Green On Clear, 9 In. ...... | 5500.00 |
| Tiffany, Vase, Paperweight, Copper Peacock's-Eye & Feathers, C.1909, 7 In. ...... | 5500.00 |
| Tiffany, Vase, Paperweight, Green Leafage On Purple To Amber, C.1892, 10 In. .... | 1700.00 |
| Tiffany, Vase, Paperweight, Marbleized Green To Lavender, 11 In.High .......... | 1100.00 |
| Tiffany, Vase, Paperweight, Reactive, Amber, White Lilies, C.1912, 9 In. ........ | 2900.00 |
| Tiffany, Vase, Paperweight, Reactive, Ovoid, Leafage On Copper, 5 In. .......... | 4100.00 |
| Tiffany, Vase, Paperweight, Rolled Foot & Lip, Orange On Deep Blue, 7 In. ....... | 5000.00 |
| Tiffany, Vase, Paperweight, White & Green Fronds On Amber, C.1903, 5 1/2 In. .... | 1800.00 |
| Tiffany, Vase, Peacock, 4 1/2 In.High | 175.00 |
| Tiffany, Vase, Pink Iridescence, White Pastel, 9 3/4 In.High .................. | 250.00 |
| Tiffany, Vase, Pyriform, Pale Yellow, Pendant Branches, 5 In.High ............. | 125.00 |
| Tiffany, Vase, Rainbow, Green, Melon, Rose, & Yellow, White Lining, 7 1/2 In. .... | 450.00 |
| Tiffany, Vase, Red, Signed L.C.T.6130 A, 11 In.High ........................ | 300.00 |
| Tiffany, Vase, Silver Overlay, Blue Green, Initials E.K.S., 1905, 3 1/2 In. ........ | 150.00 |
| Tiffany, Vase, Silver, Art Deco, Gilded Brass Flower Insert, "1906-1931" ......... | 85.00 |
| Tiffany, Vase, Squat, Blue Outlined Silver Swirls On Red, 1 1/4 In. ............. | 1100.00 |
| Tiffany, Vase, Squat, Bulbous, Blue Iridescent, Link Chain, Scroll, & Zipper ...... | 1150.00 |
| Tiffany, Vase, Sterling, Octagonal Top, 1926, 11 1/2 In.High ................. | 135.00 |
| Tiffany, Vase, Stick, Blue Insert, Signed, 15 In.High ....................... | 640.00 |
| Tiffany, Vase, Trumpet, Amber Iridescent, Ribbed, Knopped Stem, 14 1/4 In. ..... | 275.00 |
| Tiffany, Vase, Trumpet, Gold, Green Feather Design, Gold Dore Base, 15 In. ...... | 550.00 |
| Tiffany, Vase, Trumpet, Iridescent Amber, Green Feathers, C.1900, 14 1/2 In. ..... | 400.00 |
| Tiffany, Vase, Trumpet, Iridescent Amber, Intaglio Daisies, C.1916, 16 In. ....... | 600.00 |
| Tiffany, Vase, Trumpet, Iridescent White, Pink Interior, C.1892, 9 3/4 In. ....... | 275.00 |
| Tiffany, Vase, Trumpet, Vertical Devices, Yellow Interior, 1918, 7 In., Pair ....... | 350.00 |
| Tiffany, Vase, Urn Shape, Iridescent Amber, Free-Form Handles, C.1915, 3 In. .... | 175.00 |
| Tiffany, Vase, Urn Shape, Iridescent Blue, Rolled Lip, Footed, C.1919, 10 In. ..... | 575.00 |
| Tiffany, Vase, White, 2 Handles, Signed & Numbered, 3 1/2 In.High ............ | 375.00 |
| Tiffany, Wine, Clear Top, Red Heavy Base, Signed ......................... | 25.00 |
| Tiffany, Wine, Gold Favrile, Royal Pattern, Signed L.C.T. ................... | 155.00 |
| Tiffany, Wine, Gold Iridescent, Signed, 5 3/4 In.High ...................... | 125.00 |
| Tiffany, Wine, Gold, Blue Iridescence, Marked L.C.T., 5 3/4 In.High ........... | 225.00 |
| Tiffany, Wine, Gold, Cut Stem, Signed .................................. | 125.00 |
| Tiffany, Wine, Gold, Grape Border, Favrile ............................... | 165.00 |
| Tiffany, Wine, Green, Signed, 6 In.High ................................. | 150.00 |
| Tiffany, Wine, Intaglio Grapes & Leaves In Vintage, 5 3/4 In. ................ | 165.00 |
| Tiffany, Wine, Pastel Green, Signed, 6 In. ............................... | 150.00 |
| Tiffany, Wine, Pastel Iridescent, Signed, 5 In.High ........................ | 135.00 |

*Tiffin Glass Company of Tiffin, Ohio, was a subsidiary of the United States Glass Co.of Pittsburgh, Pa. Black satin glass, made by the company between 1923 and 1926, is very popular among collectors. Other types were also made.*

| | |
|---|---|
| Tiffin, Bell, Cut Crystal, Label ....................................... | 25.00 |
| Tiffin, Bowl, Black Satin, Poppy Decoration ............................. | 20.00 |
| Tiffin, Bowl, Turquoise, 9 1/2 In.Diameter .............................. | 14.00 |
| Tiffin, Chamberstick, Black, Saucer Base, 2 1/2 In.High ................... | 8.50 |
| Tiffin, Chopstick, Tomato, Satin, 8 1/2 In., Pair ......................... | 37.00 |
| Tiffin, Compote, Tomato, Stemmed, 7 In. ............................... | 48.00 |
| Tiffin, Console Set, Lemon Satin, 8 In.Candleholders, 4 Piece .............. | 50.00 |
| Tiffin, Perfume & Powder Box, Black Satin, Cover, Hand-Painted Flowers ...... | 35.00 |
| Tiffin, Pitcher, Honeycomb, Beatty, Blue Opalescent, Ohio ................. | 95.00 |
| Tiffin, Rose Bowl, Black, Embossed Poppies ............................. | 14.00 |
| Tiffin, Vase, Black Satin, Embossed Orange Poppies & Green Leaves, 8 In. ..... | 20.00 |

| | |
|---|---|
| Tiffin, Vase, Black Satin, Painted Iris, 6 1/2 In. | 14.00 |
| Tiffin, Vase, Bowl Type, Black Satin, Coralene Red Poppies, 7 In. | 30.00 |
| Tiffin, Vase, Poppy, Clear Green, 5 1/2 In. | 14.00 |
| Tiffin, Vase, Poppy, Pink Satin, 8 1/2 In. | 19.00 |
| Tiffin, Vase, Tangerine, Footed, 9 1/2 In. | 35.00 |
| Tiffin, Vase, Yellow, Blue, & Orange Poppies, 9 1/2 In. | 35.00 |
| Tile, Art, J.& J.G., Design, No.690, Brown Glaze, Low | 8.00 |
| Tile, Calendar, 1904, Jones, McDuffee, & Stratton, Constitution In Chase | 28.00 |
| Tile, Calendar, 1909, Jones, McDuffee, & Stratton, New Museum Of Fine Arts | 28.00 |
| Tile, Low Art, Chelsea, Mass., Grecian Woman's Profile, Coffee Glaze, Round | 38.00 |
| Tile, Man & Woman On Bench, Blue, 6 In.Square | 4.00 |
| Tile, Stove, Superior, 2 Cherubs Eating Grapes Beneath Arbor, 7 X 4 In. | 23.00 |
| Tile, Tea, Cottage On Water, Square, 5 In. | 5.00 |
| Tile, Tea, Sterling Silver Overlay On Clear Glass, Round, Flowers & Vines | 18.00 |
| Tile, Teddy Roosevelt, Cartlidge, 1916, J.H.Barratt & Co., 9 X 6 In. | 85.00 |
| Tile, The Half Moon, Square | 15.00 |
|  Tin, see also Store | |
| Tin, Ashtray, Cigarette Dispenser, Donkey, Painted, Mechanical, 10 In.High | 25.00 |
| Tin, Basin, 9 In. Diameter | 17.00 |
| Tin, Bathtub, Traveling, Round, C.1860 | 195.00 |
| Tin, Box, C.P.C. In Left Corner, Gold, Black, 6 X 4 In. | 7.50 |
| Tin, Box, Candle, Covered, Wall, Rounded Ends, Tole Black, 4 In.Diameter | 110.00 |
| Tin, Box, Candle, Cylindrical, 13 In. | 170.00 |
| Tin, Box, Candle, Hanging, American, Asphaltum Paint, 11 X 4 1/2 In. | 195.00 |
| Tin, Box, Candle, 13 1/2 In. | 175.00 |
| Tin, Box, Comb, Mirrored, Painted, 11 X 8 1/2 In. | 12.00 |
| Tin, Box, Covered, 10 1/2 X 5 3/4 In. | 9.00 |
| Tin, Box, Snap Lid, "Stamps, Pills, Buttons, Etc., " 1 1/2 X 1 1/2 X 1/2 In. | 5.00 |
| Tin, Box, Spice, 7 Boxes Inside, Round | 22.00 |
| Tin, Calf Weaner | 3.50 |
| Tin, Can, Milk, Steel Bail, Metal Bands Top & Bottom, 1 1/2 Gallon | 6.50 |
| Tin, Candleholder, Pennsylvania, For Windowsill, 4 In., Pair | 12.00 |
| Tin, Candleholder, Push-Up, 6 In.High | 12.00 |
| Tin, Candleholder, Saucer Base, White China Cup, A.C.Perry & Son, C.1850 | 18.00 |
| Tin, Candlestick, Hog Scraper, Push-Up, Rim Hook To Hang On Chair Back | 25.00 |
| Tin, Candlestick, Hog Scraper, 5 1/2 In.High | 15.00 |
| Tin, Candlestick, Push-Up, Painted Gold, 12 1/2 In.High | 15.00 |
| Tin, Candlestick, Saucer Base, Handle & Lift | 35.00 |
| Tin, Canister, Covered, 7 In.High, 5 In.Diameter | 4.95 |
| Tin, Case, Comb & Mirror, 2 Hairpin Holders, 8 1/2 X 7 1/4 In. | 10.00 |
| Tin, Case, Spectacle, Hinged Cover, Patent 1860, 4 3/4 In.Long | 6.95 |
| Tin, Container, Spice, Grater, Round | 20.00 |
| Tin, Cranberry Picker | 40.00 |
| Tin, Cup, Child's, "My Boy" | 8.00 |
| Tin, Cup, Child's, "My Girl" | 8.00 |
| Tin, Cup, Flared, Strap Handle, 4 1/2 In. | 1.25 |
| Tin, Cup, Nickel Plated, Civil War, Signed U.S. On Handle | 25.00 |
| Tin, Cup, Sputum, Burnitol Mfg.Co., Square, Spring Lid | 15.00 |
| Tin, Cup, 2 1/4 In.Diameter At Base Tapering To 1 7/8 In.Top | 4.75 |
| Tin, Filler, Lamp, Conical, 5 1/2 In. | 22.50 |
| Tin, Frame, Picture, Cupid Awake & Cupid Asleep, Oval, 4 X 5 In., Pair | 6.00 |
| Tin, Frame, Picture, Cupid Awake & Cupid Asleep, Oval, 9 In., Pair | 15.00 |
| Tin, Lantern, Candle, Folding, Miner's Patent 1865, Mica Sides | 35.00 |
| Tin, Match Holder, Oval, Holly Decoration | 7.50 |
| Tin, Match Holder, Wall, Lift Up Cover, Patent 1878 | 4.95 |
| Tin, Match Safe, Hanging, Curved Lid, Blue, Cylindrical | 36.00 |
| Tin, Match Safe, Standing, Cone Shape On Skirt Base, Striker, 6 In.High | 22.50 |
| Tin, Match Safe, Wall, Pressed-In Dragon Design, Cover, 2 Hanging Holes | 25.00 |
| Tin, Matchbox, Comic, The Wedding Day, 3 Weeks After, Haymes, London | 35.00 |
| Tin, Mold, Bunch Of Grapes, 3 1/2 In.Long, Set Of 4 | 2.75 |
| Tin, Mold, Candle, 1 Tube, 22 In. Long | 35.00 |
| Tin, Mold, Candle, 6 Tube | 25.00 |
| Tin, Mold, Candle, 6 Tube, Curved Risers | 54.00 |
| Tin, Mold, Candle, 6 Tube, Handle | 23.00 |
| Tin, Mold, Candle, 6 Tube, Side Handle, Square Top & Bottom, 10 1/2 In. High | 15.00 |
| Tin, Mold, Candle, 8 Tube | 30.00 |

| | |
|---|---|
| Tin, Mold, Candle, 9 Tube, Handle | 25.00 |
| Tin, Mold, Candle, 12 Tube, Handle | 75.00 |
| Tin, Mold, Candle, 12 Tube, Side Handle, Square Top & Bottom, 11 In.High | 30.00 |
| Tin, Mold, Candle, 12 Tube, 11 1/2 In.High | 39.50 |
| Tin, Mold, Candle, 24 Tube, Wooden Stand, Red Paint | 475.00 |
| Tin, Mold, Cheese, Heart Shaped, Footed, Pierced | 65.00 |
| Tin, Mold, Chocolate, Rabbit, 5 In. | 7.50 |
| Tin, Mold, Chocolate, Sitting Rabbit, 5 In.High | 9.00 |
| Tin, Mold, Chocolate, U.S.A., 6 1/2 In. | 10.50 |
| Tin, Mold, Cookie, Santa, Coat, Cap, & Mittens, Marked Made In U.S.A., No.634 | 22.00 |
| Tin, Mold, Cookie, Santa, Pack, Toys, & Bag, 6 1/4 In.High | 22.00 |
| Tin, Mold, Melon, Oval, Fluted, 2 Piece, 4 In.Diameter | 6.95 |
| Tin, Mold, Pudding, Tapered Pail Shape, Marked Hillson, 2 Piece, 5 In.High | 6.95 |
| Tin, Muffineer, Side Handle, 3 3/4 In.High | 4.75 |
| Tin, Muffineer, Side Handle, 3 5/8 In.High | 4.75 |
| Tin, Pipe, Bubble, Soap | 2.50 |
| Tin, Plate, Child's, Peter Rabbit | 5.00 |
| Tin, Plate, Girl In Rose Dress With Jug Of Flowers, C.1910, 10 In. | 10.50 |
| Tin, Plate, Grand Old Party, 1856-1908, Taft & Sherman, 1908, 9 1/2 In. | 125.00 |
| Tin, Plate, Marked Made In Belgium-Daher Ware, French People Scenes, Floral | 5.00 |
| Tin, Plate, Portrait, Brunette, Hotel Majestic On Back, 9 1/2 In. | 25.00 |
| Tin, Sander, Pounce, Desk, Octagonal, Black, Round Base & Top | 25.00 |
| Tin, Sconce, Candle, Tree Design | 85.00 |
| Tin, Sconce, Candle, 10 In., Pair | 185.00 |
| Tin, Scoop, Coffee | 6.50 |
| Tin, Scoop, For Scales, 13 In.Long | 10.00 |
| Tin, Stirrup, Sidesaddle | 3.50 |
| Tin, Strainer, Tea, Thomas Cream Of Wheat, Tried & True 50 Years | 6.00 |
| Tin, Tea Caddy, English, Lithographed Prints Of Wheatley, 7 1/2 In. High | 20.00 |
| Tin, Tea Caddy, Stenciled | 5.50 |
| Tin, Tea Set, Child's, Ohio Lithograph, Dutch Girl, 13 Pieces | 15.00 |
| Tin, Tea Set, Lithographed, Ohio Art, 9 Piece | 8.50 |
| Tin, Tinderbox, Handleless | 185.00 |
| Tin, Toothpick, Beaver Hat Shape | 20.00 |
| Tin, Tray, Apple, Oval Shape, Hand-Painted, Signed, 11 3/4 In.Long | 20.00 |
| Tin, Tray, Egyptian Design, 13 In.Diameter | 6.00 |
| Tin, Tray, Floral Designs, 13 In.Diameter | 6.00 |
| Tin, Tray, Indian Chief Black Hawk, Lithographed, Color, 11 In. | 30.00 |
| Tin, Tray, Indian Chief Joseph, Lithographed Black Bear, Lithographed, Color | 8.00 |
| Tin, Tray, Indian Chief Sitting Bull, Lithographed, Color, 11 In. | 8.00 |
| Tin, Tray, Serving, Rounded Corners, Raised Beaded Rim, Scrolls, 14 In. | 2.25 |
| Tin, Washstand Set, Enameled, Miniature, 5 Piece | 40.00 |
| Tin, Whistle, Queen Victoria Profile | 4.00 |
| Tin, Whistle, Rooster Figural | 4.00 |
| Tirschenreuth, Plate, Service, Floral Bouquet Center, Gold Border | 22.75 |

*Toby mugs have been made since the seventeenth century.*

Toby Mug, see also Royal Doulton, Toby Mug, Staffordshire, Toby Mug

| | |
|---|---|
| Toby Mug, Eisenhower, Barrington, Limited Edition, 7 In.High | 60.00 |
| Toby Mug, Full Figure, German, 3 1/2 In. | 7.00 |
| Toby Mug, George Washington, Full Figure, Patent Apr.14, 1896, 10 1/2 In. | 195.00 |
| Toby Mug, Man's Head, Johnnie Walker Red | 4.00 |
| Toby Mug, Mr.Winkle, Pickwick Series | 22.50 |
| Toby Mug, Napoleon, Full Figure, Brown, 7 In. | 55.00 |
| Toby Mug, Napoleon, Seated, Alfred B.Evans, Phila, C.1875, 9 1/2 In.High | 150.00 |
| Toby Mug, Orange Hat, Gray Hair, Crossed Arms, Half Figure, 5 In. | 40.00 |
| Toby Mug, Port Carling, 2 In. | 6.50 |
| Toby Mug, Snuff Taker, Royal Art Pottery, England, 9 In. | 25.00 |
| Toby Mug, Toby Filpot, Blue Coat, Black Tricorn, Yellow Breeches, 10 In. | 175.00 |
| Toby Mug, W.C.Fields, Kentucky Bourbon Whiskey, Tan, 8 In. | 15.00 |
| Toby Mug, Winston Churchill, Seated, Smoking Cigar, 10 In. | 54.00 |
| Tole, Birdcage, French, Gondola, 2 Tole Musicians On Top, C.1820, 20 In. | 1200.00 |
| Tole, Box, Candle, Japanned, Oval Ends, Cover | 30.00 |
| Tole, Box, Covered, Handle, Painted, 8 1/2 In.Long | 165.00 |
| Tole, Box, Document, Black Paint, Yellow & Orange Decoration, 10 X 8 1/2 In. | 70.00 |
| Tole, Box, Document, Red, White, Black, & Gold On Asphaltum Base, 5 In.High | 75.00 |

| | |
|---|---|
| Tole, Box, Document, White, Yellow, Green, & Red On Japan, 4 X 2 3/4 In. | 55.00 |
| Tole, Box, Licorice Sticks, Arched Glass Window, 7 1/2 X 5 3/4 X 3 1/2 In. | 13.50 |
| Tole, Box, Spice, Hinged, 8 Boxes Inside, Handle, Pennsylvania Dutch Type | 25.00 |
| Tole, Candlesnuffer & Tray, Gold & Black Vines & Leaves On Red | 80.00 |
| Tole, Candlestick, Saucer Type, Center Post, Push-Up, Ring Handle | 25.00 |
| Tole, Canister, Painted Red, 4 1/4 In. High | 40.00 |
| Tole, Canister, Striping & Stenciled Band On Green, 7 3/4 In. | 25.00 |
| Tole, Coffeepot, Orange & Yellow On Black, Curved Spout, 10 In. | 375.00 |
| Tole, Coffeepot, Pressed-In Sides, Patent 1865, 9 In.High | 30.00 |
| Tole, Coffeepot, Side Handle, Tapered, 9 In.High | 35.00 |
| Tole, Coffeepot, Tapered Top | 30.00 |
| Tole, Egg Poacher, Covered, Footed, Painted, American, C.1850, 10 1/2 In. | 128.00 |
| Tole, Mold, Pudding, Melon Ribbed, 2 Quart | 11.00 |
| Tole, Pitcher, Cover & Finial, Red Flowers, Green Leaves, 4 1/2 In. | 95.00 |
| Tole, Salt & Pepper, Cylindrical, Asphaltum Finish | 5.00 |
| Tole, Sconce, Candle, Tulips Decoration, 13 1/2 In., Pair | 134.00 |
| Tole, Tankard, White, Yellow, Green, Salmon, & Red On Japan, 5 3/4 In. | 250.00 |
| Tole, Torch, Campaign, Wooden Handle, Round, 40 In. | 10.00 |
| Tole, Tray, Log Cabin & American Flag Decoration, 20 X 15 In. | 230.00 |
| Tole, Tray, Naval Battle Scene, Polychrome On Black, C.1850, 24 In.Long | 130.00 |
| Tole, Tray, Oval, Gold On Black, Victorian, 20 In.Long | 40.00 |
| Tole, Urn, Covered, French, Gilt & Classical Scenes On Green, 13 In., Pair | 130.00 |
| Tom Mix, Watch Fob, Gold Ore | 35.00 |
| Tool, see also Iron, Kitchen, Store, Tin, Wooden | |
| Tool, Adze, Iron | 2.50 |
| Tool, Awl, Carpenter's, Springfield, Mass., Patent 1876 | 20.00 |
| Tool, Ax, Boy Scout, Insignia On Head & Handle | 20.00 |
| Tool, Ax, Trade, Oval Eye, Initials M.A.C., C.1850, 8 1/2 In. | 37.50 |
| Tool, Ax, Trade, Round Eye, C.1750, 10 3/4 In. | 37.50 |
| Tool, Ax, Trade, Round Eye, Initials A.J.S., C.1850, 8 1/2 In. | 37.50 |
| Tool, Bellows, Wooden, 19 1/2 In.Long | 10.00 |
| Tool, Bit Stock, Brass Socket, Signed Coulson, C.1850 | 12.00 |
| Tool, Bit Stock, Brass Socket, Signed W.Bower, Sheffield, C.1850 | 12.00 |
| Tool, Bobbing Horse's Tail, Scissor Type, Brass Mounts, Rosewood Handles | 74.50 |
| Tool, Broadax, Cast Steel, Handled, Signed D.Taft, C.1895 | 22.50 |
| Tool, Buggy Jack, 1903, Oliver Mg.Co. | 15.00 |
| Tool, Card, Wool, Wooden, Pair | 5.00 |
| Tool, Carrier, Blacksmith's, Wooden, 3 Compartments, Metal Strap At Base | 35.00 |
| Tool, Clamp, Carpenter's, Parallel, Oak & Maple | 9.50 |
| Tool, Clewing Block, Double Pulleys, Brass, 2 Pounds | 27.00 |
| Tool, Corn Cutter, Never-Fail Root-Heath Mg.Co. | 15.00 |
| Tool, Cutter, Barrel Bung | 5.00 |
| Tool, Device For Making Brooms At Home, Iron, Dated Oct.24, 1866 | 17.00 |
| Tool, Dividers With Compass, Barn Builder's, Hand-Forged Iron, 17 In. | 25.00 |
| Tool, Doctor, see Doctor | |
| Tool, Drawknife, Hollowing, J.Kolb | 15.00 |
| Tool, Drill Brace, Iron, Wooden Handle | 8.00 |
| Tool, Drill, Archimedes, Cabinetmaker's, Rosewood, Brass, 26 In. | 25.00 |
| Tool, Flail, Grain, Wooden | 14.50 |
| Tool, Flax Hatchel, Metal & Sheffield Cone Shape Vase, Engraved | 13.00 |
| Tool, For Insertion Of Metal Ring In Hog's Nose, 1872, 7 In. Long | 10.00 |
| Tool, For Removing Pot Covers In Fireplace, Cast Iron End, Metal Handle | 45.00 |
| Tool, Fork, Hay, Wooden | 22.50 |
| Tool, Frow, Splitting, Hand-Forged, 13 In.Blade, C.1750 | 25.00 |
| Tool, Gaff, English, Brass & Steel, Turned Wooden Handle, C.1850, 37 In. | 48.00 |
| Tool, Glass Cutter & Screwdriver, Brass, France | 12.50 |
| Tool, Grisette, Iron, C.1650, 13 1/2 In.Wide | 295.00 |
| Tool, Harness Riveter, Cast Iron | 2.50 |
| Tool, Hatchel, Flax, Cherry, Tin Bound, 83 Tines, Pine Cover, Pierced Edge | 23.00 |
| Tool, Hatchel, Hand Held, Brassbound Wooden Handle, Iron Tines | 18.00 |
| Tool, Hatchel, 90 4 In. Spikes, Dated 1812 | 35.00 |
| Tool, Hatchel, 90 4 In. Spikes, Dated 1845 | 35.00 |
| Tool, Hatchet, Hewing, Carpenter's, Handle | 4.00 |
| Tool, Hatchet, Iron, 2 1/2 In. | 2.00 |
| Tool, Hay Knife, C.1850 | 18.00 |
| Tool, Hoe, Grub, Iron | 2.50 |

Tool, Molding Plane, 9 X 9 In.

| | |
|---|---|
| Tool, Hog Scraper, Wooden Handle | 2.95 |
| Tool, Jack, House, Brass & Iron, Miniature | 19.00 |
| Tool, Jigsaw, New Rogers, Foot Powered, Grinder Attached | 100.00 |
| Tool, Knife, Hay, Iron | 12.50 |
| Tool, Level, Lambert Milliken & Stackpoole, Boston, Brassbound, Eagle | 33.00 |
| Tool, Level, Stanley, Cherrywood, Adjustable, 30 In. | 20.00 |
| Tool, Level, Stratton Bros. Patent 1888, Brass Trim | 20.00 |
| Tool, Lobster Trap | 25.00 |
| Tool, Loom, 4 Harness | 185.00 |
| Tool, Mallet, Burl, Round, 5 1/2 In.Diameter | 24.00 |
| Tool, Mandrel, Maple, Cone Shape, 10 Fitting Steps, 7 1/2 In.Long | 60.00 |
| Tool, Molding Plane, 9 X 9 In. _Illus_ | 25.00 |
| Tool, Muzzle, Ox, Wire, 11 In. | 9.00 |
| Tool, Nautical Measure, Walker's Patent Harpoon Yacht Log, Brass | 150.00 |
| Tool, Niddy Noddy, 17 1/2 In. | 27.50 |
| Tool, Peel, Iron, 21 In.Long | 22.00 |
| Tool, Peel, Wrought Iron, Flat Handle, Loop End, C.1750, 44 In. Long | 53.00 |
| Tool, Peel, Wrought Iron, Ram's Horn Handle, C.1750, 53 In. Long | 70.00 |
| Tool, Peel, Wrought Iron, Shovel End, 31 In.Long | 24.50 |
| Tool, Plane, Block, Black Paint, 1 In.Blade, 3 1/2 In.Long | 12.50 |
| Tool, Plane, Block, Boxwood, Moulson Bros. | 18.00 |
| Tool, Plane, Molding, D.Copeland, Round Bottom, 1 1/2 In. | 7.50 |
| Tool, Plane, Molding, Double Blade | 10.00 |
| Tool, Plane, Molding, Gardner & Murdock, Boston, Hollow On Fork Staff | 7.50 |
| Tool, Plane, Molding, Signed With 3 Names, Hollow, 2 1/8 In. | 7.50 |
| Tool, Plane, Wood, Adjustable, Rabbit, 5 Blades | 45.00 |
| Tool, Planter, Corn, Hand, Wood & Tin | 7.50 |
| Tool, Reaping Hook, C.1760, 26 In.Blade | 25.00 |
| Tool, Reel, Clock, For Winding Yarn, Wooden | 45.00 |
| Tool, Rope Server, Sailmaker's, Wooden, Hand-Carved, Mallet Shape | 37.50 |
| Tool, Rule With Level & Protractor, Lufkin, Brass & Wood, 2 Feet | 19.00 |
| Tool, Rule, Carpenter's, Wooden, Folding, Brass Fittings | 7.50 |
| Tool, Ruler, Stanley | 5.00 |
| Tool, Saw, Felloe, Frame, 23 1/2 X 22 3/4 In. | 25.00 |
| Tool, Saw, Meat, Iron | 3.50 |
| Tool, Saw, Silver, Marked E.C.Atkins & Co. Silver Saws, 1 1/2 In.Long | 6.50 |
| Tool, Saw, Table, Salesman's Sample | 55.00 |
| Tool, Scraper, Cabinet, Stanley, No.80, 2 3/4 In.Blade | 6.00 |
| Tool, Scriber, Wood | 6.50 |
| Tool, Seam Rubber, Sailmaker's, Rope Twist Design Handle, Turk's Head | 65.00 |
| Tool, Sharpener, Scissors, Steveley, New Haven, Conn., 1858, Label | 8.00 |
| Tool, Shave, Spoke, Brass Decoration, 3 In. Blade | 7.00 |
| Tool, Shave, Spoke, Iron, Cone | 3.50 |
| Tool, Shave, Spoke, Iron, 2 Blades | 2.50 |
| Tool, Shave, Spoke, No.53 | 4.50 |
| Tool, Shave, Spoke, Wooden Blade Protector | 12.50 |
| Tool, Sheep Poke, Ash, Bow Shape, Hand-Hewn, Key Shape Pin, 12 In. | 19.00 |

| | |
|---|---|
| Tool, Ship Rigging, Wooden, Paddle Shape, Top Groove For Rope, Sawteeth | 30.00 |
| Tool, Shovel, Grain, Cherry, 1 Piece | 80.00 |
| Tool, Shovel, Handwrought, 1 Piece, Salesman's Sample, 9 In. | 8.50 |
| Tool, Shovel, Snow, Child's, Wooden, 32 In.Long | 10.00 |
| Tool, Shovel, Wooden, Rounded End, 10 X 11 In. | 50.00 |
| Tool, Slick, Lumberman's, Hand-Forged, Wooden Handle, 26 In. | 25.00 |
| Tool, Spinning Wheel, Patina, C.1870, 25 In. High | 65.00 |
| Tool, Spinning Wheel, Patina, C.1870, 36 In. High | 85.00 |
| Tool, Spinning Wheel, Turned Legs, Yellow Paint, 24 In. Wheel | 60.00 |
| Tool, Spinning Wheel, 26 1/2 In. Wheel On Tripod Base, Box At One End | 45.00 |
| Tool, Steelyard, 3 Hooks, 1 Weight, 16 1/2 In. | 9.00 |
| Tool, T Bevel, Early, 9 1/4 In.Long, Brass Trim | 6.00 |
| Tool, Timberdog, Wrought Iron, Double Pronged, 17 In.Long | 9.75 |
| Tool, Tongs, Blacksmith's, Wrought Iron | 11.50 |
| Tool, Tongs, Forge, Iron | 3.00 |
| Tool, Trammel, Handwrought, Sawtooth, Adjustable, 54 To 73 In. | 57.50 |
| Tool, Trammel, Wrought Iron, C.1750, 22 To 38 In. | 45.00 |
| Tool, Trap, Animal, Victor | 1.50 |
| Tool, Trap, Bait, Copper, Brass Attachments | 20.00 |
| Tool, Trap, Bear, Oneida, No.15, Newhouse, Drag Chain, 35 In. Long | 120.00 |
| Tool, Trap, Jump, Oneida, No.3 | 5.00 |
| Tool, Trap, Mouse, Wire On Board, 1872 | 10.50 |
| Tool, Trap, Rat, Wire Cage, Torture Type | 20.00 |
| Tool, Traveler, Handwrought, 6 1/2 In. | 25.00 |
| Tool, Vise, Brown & Sharp, Horizontal Screw Type, On Base, 3 1/4 In.Long | 14.00 |
| Tool, Vise, Harness Maker's, Wooden | 7.50 |
| Tool, Vise, Salesman's Sample | 35.00 |
| Tool, Wrench, Monkey, Fordson, Embossed | 5.00 |
| Tool, Yoke, Shoulder, Hand-Carved, 7 X 31 In. | 15.00 |

*Toothpick holders are sometimes called toothpicks by collectors. The variously shaped containers made to hold the small wooden toothpicks are of glass, china, or metal. Most of the toothpicks are Victorian.*

**Toothpick, see also other categories such as Bisque, Slag, etc.**

| | |
|---|---|
| Toothpick, Acorn, Glossy Pink To White Peachblow Coloring | 75.00 |
| Toothpick, Boot, Glass | 6.00 |
| Toothpick, Canoe, Blue Glass | 6.50 |
| Toothpick, Figural, Porcupine, Silver Plate | 25.00 |
| Toothpick, Figural, Rat, Scalloped Holder, "This Is The Rat, " Silver Plate | 55.00 |
| Toothpick, Frosted, Amberina Type | 95.00 |
| Toothpick, Glass Barrel, 3 Cherubs On Sides | 25.00 |
| Toothpick, Porcelain, Violets, Gold Handles | 6.50 |
| Toothpick, Pressed Glass, Scalloped Edge, Gold Trim, Handled | 27.50 |
| Toothpick, Violets On White, Footed | 25.00 |

*Tortoiseshell glass was made during the 1800s and after by the Sandwich Glass Works of Massachusetts and some firms in Germany. Tortoiseshell glass has been reproduced.*

| | |
|---|---|
| Tortoiseshell Glass, Bowl, 5 1/4 X 2 3/4 In. | 60.00 |
| Tortoiseshell Glass, Vase, V Shape, Amber Ribbed Base, 14 In.High | 55.00 |
| Tortoiseshell, Box, For Man's Perfume Flask, Sterling Piquework, C.1780 | 135.00 |
| Tortoiseshell, Box, Powder, French, Gold Mounted, Sepia Landscape, C.1810 | 50.00 |
| Tortoiseshell, Candlestick, Silver Mounted, Guilloche Rim, 6 1/2 In., Pair | 60.00 |
| Tortoiseshell, Comb, Dragon Design | 14.00 |
| Tortoiseshell, Comb, Mantilla, Carved, 1840, 5 1/4 In. | 45.00 |
| Tortoiseshell, Comb, 4 In.High | 9.00 |
| Tortoiseshell, Snuffbox, Hinged, Curved Top & Bottom, C.1850, 1 3/4 X 3 In. | 40.00 |

**Toy, see also Card, Doll, Game, Marble**

| | |
|---|---|
| Toy, Adding Machine, Tin, Wolverine, Patent No.2243884 | 15.00 |
| Toy, Ariplane, Air Express, Cast Iron, Dent Sample, 12 In.Wingspread | 575.00 |
| Toy, Airplane, Air Force Fighter, Marked Hubley Kiddie Toy, Metal | 9.76 |
| Toy, Airplane, Loop The Loop, Tin | 40.00 |
| Toy, Airplane, Lucky Boy, Cast Iron, Dent | 10.00 |
| Toy, Airplane, Lucky Boy, Cast Iron, Dent Sample, 7 1/2 In.Wingspread | 175.00 |
| Toy, Airplane, Model, Monoplane, Motor | 15.00 |
| Toy, Airplane, Ramp, Baggage Carriers, & Jeep, Metal, Tootsietoy | 6.00 |
| Toy, Airplane, U.S.Army, Pot Metal, Hubley, 8 In.Wingspan | 10.00 |

Toy, Automobile, Clockwork, Painted, Tin, American, C.1910

| | |
|---|---|
| Toy, Airplane, World War II Bomber, Metal, Marx, 8 In. Wingspan | 7.00 |
| Toy, Airport Diner Set, Kiddy Toy, Hubley | 9.50 |
| Toy, Alabama Coon Jigger, Windup, Strauss, Patent 1910 | 75.00 |
| Toy, American Theatre, Red Riding Hood & Wolf, McCloughlin Bros., 1902 | 85.00 |
| Toy, Animal, Bobcat, Leather Covered | 20.00 |
| Toy, Animal, Camel, Leather Covered | 25.00 |
| Toy, Animal, Circus, Elephant, Schoenhut, Large Size | 55.00 |
| Toy, Animal, Circus, Elephant, Schoenhut, Small Size | 35.00 |
| Toy, Animal, Circus, Horse, Schoenhut | 50.00 |
| Toy, Animal, Circus, Rhinoceros, Cast Brass, Hubley | 25.00 |
| Toy, Animal, Circus, Tiger, Cast Brass, Hubley | 25.00 |
| Toy, Animal, Elephant, Leather Covered | 20.00 |
| Toy, Animal, Giraffe, Leather Covered | 25.00 |
| Toy, Animal, Hyena, Leather Covered | 25.00 |
| Toy, Animal, Lead, British, Hand-Painted, 7 In Box | 5.00 |
| Toy, Animal, Tiger Leather Covered | 20.00 |
| Toy, Animal, Zebra, Leather Covered | 25.00 |
| Toy, Aquaplane, Windup, Lithographed, Tin, Chein, 8 1/2 In.Long | 23.75 |
| Toy, Aquaplane, Windup, Lithographed, Tin, Chein, 9 In. | 19.50 |
| Toy, Auto Mac, The Wonder Driver, Windup, Rubber Wheels, Plastic, Marx | 11.00 |
| Toy, Auto, Cast Iron, Black Paint, Arcade, 5 In. | 45.00 |
| Toy, Automobile, Clockwork, Painted, Tin, American, C.1910 .......... Illus | 600.00 |
| Toy, Automobile, Windup, Painted, Tin, German, 5 1/2 In. Long | 35.00 |
| Toy, Ax, Iron, 3 In.Long | 2.75 |
| Toy, B.O. Plenty, Windup | 35.00 |
| Toy, Baby Tender, Ginnette's, Wooden, Vogue | 9.00 |
| Toy, Babyland Nursery, Building, Lithographed, Tin, Marx, 15 X 8 X 7 In. | 7.00 |
| Toy, Balking Mule, Tin, Lehman | 36.00 |
| Toy, Bandwagon, Eagle Design, Hubley | 575.00 |
| Toy, Barney Bear, Battery Operated, Beats Drum, Eyes Light Up | 12.50 |
| Toy, Bat, Baseball, Joe DiMaggio, Louisville Slugger, Wooden, 16 In.Long | 5.00 |
| Toy, Bath, Baby, Ginnette's, Wooden, Vogue | 9.00 |
| Toy, Bear, Grizzly, Mohair, Straw Stuffed, Metal Tag, B.W. Germany | 22.00 |
| Toy, Bear, Teddy Snow Crop, Rubber, Hanes Pajamas, Marked Irwin, 8 1/2 In. | 8.00 |
| Toy, Bear, Tiny Winnie Pooh, Marked Disney | 2.00 |
| Toy, Bed, Doll's, Metal, Spring Type Frame, Rounded Head & Footboard, 20 In. | 10.00 |
| Toy, Bed, Doll's, Wooden, C.1900, 8 X 13 In. | 10.00 |
| Toy, Bedroom Set, Dollhouse, Twin Beds & Vanity | 25.00 |
| Toy, Bell, Pull, Sheet Iron, Gilded, Victorian | 25.00 |
| Toy, Bicycle, see Bicycle | |
| Toy, Bilt E-Z Set B, The Boy Builder, C.1925 | 17.00 |
| Toy, Blocks, Alphabet, Wooden, Set Of 9 | 6.50 |
| Toy, Blocks, Child's, 63 Assorted Alphabet, Wood | 11.00 |
| Toy, Blocks, Color Lithographed, Wooden, C.1870, Set Of 48 | 85.00 |
| Toy, Blocks, Picture Learner, Wooden, Set Of 38 | 15.00 |
| Toy, Blocks, Picture, Wooden, Soldier, Sailor, & Policeman, Set Of 9 | 8.50 |
| Toy, Blushing Willie, Battery Operated, Pours Martini, Face Turns Red | 14.50 |

| | |
|---|---|
| Toy, Board, Alphabet & Tracer, Wooden Framed, 1930s | 5.00 |
| Toy, Boat, Lithographed, Crandall, C.1890, 18 X 15 In. | 85.00 |
| Toy, Boat, Tin, Penny Toy, 5 1/2 In. | 18.00 |
| Toy, Boat, Windup, Lithographed, Tin, Lindstrom, 15 In.Long | 7.25 |
| Toy, Bomb, Cap, "Say I, " Cast Iron | 35.00 To 45.00 |
| Toy, Bomb, Cap, Cast Iron, Admiral Dewey | 40.00 |
| Toy, Bookcase, Dollhouse | 10.00 |
| Toy, Bottle, Hot Water, Doll's, Sun Rubber | 1.00 |
| Toy, Bottle, Hot Water, Donald Duck Figural, 12 In. | 7.50 |
| Toy, Bow & Arrow, William Tell, Corby Collection | 525.00 |
| Toy, Boy On Handcar, Windup, Tin, German | 115.00 |
| Toy, Boy On Trapeze, Windup, Tin, Decorated, Louis Marx | 25.00 |
| Toy, Brownie Acrobats, Wooden Stick, Squeeze Toy, Volunteer | 8.00 |
| Toy, Buckboard Wagon, Nickel, 2 Seats, 12 X 3 1/2 In. | 125.00 |
| Toy, Bucking Bronco, Windup, Tin, German | 55.00 |
| Toy, Bud, Aluminum, Dent Sample, 7 1/2 In. | 50.00 |
| Toy, Buggy, Doll's, Red | 45.00 |
| Toy, Buggy, Doll's, Tin, Germany, 7 In. | 6.00 |
| Toy, Buggy, Doll's, Tin, Painted Scenes, 6 1/2 X 8 In. | 10.25 |
| Toy, Building Blocks, Architectural, Wooden, Lithographed, Schoenhut, 1927 | 18.00 |
| Toy, Bus, Cast Iron, Dent Sample, 6 1/4 In. | 70.00 |
| Toy, Bus, Cast Iron, Steel Wheels, Yellow Paint, 4 1/2 In.Long | 29.50 |
| Toy, Bus, Century Of Progress, Cast Iron, Rubber Wheels, Arcade, Blue & White | 39.00 |
| Toy, Bus, Double Decker, Driver, Solid Wheels, Cast Iron, 7 1/2 In.Long | 25.00 |
| Toy, Bus, Double Decker, Friction Motor, Advertisements On Sides, Rosko, 1950 | 6.00 |
| Toy, Bus, Double Decker, Tin, Red & Yellow Lithographed, Windup, Germany | 38.00 |
| Toy, Bus, Greyhound, Tootsietoy, 5 3/4 In.Long | 5.00 |
| Toy, Bus, Greyhound, Tootsietoy, 7 In.Long | 5.25 |
| Toy, Bus, Interstate, Autobus, Strauss | 75.00 |
| Toy, Bus, Nickel Wheels, Red, Acrade, 4 3/4 In. Long | 35.00 |
| Toy, Butterfly, Mechanical, Colored, Tin, German, 5 In.High | 30.00 |
| Toy, Caboose, Cast Iron, Harris | 4.00 |
| Toy, Caboose, Cast Iron, Hubley | 3.00 |
| Toy, Candelabra, Dollhouse, Cast Metal, 3-Arm, 2 In. | 7.50 |
| Toy, Cannon, "Young America, " Rapid Fire, Cast Iron, 15 1/2 In. | 15.00 |
| Toy, Cannon, Brass Barrel, Cast Iron, Ives | 20.00 |
| Toy, Cannon, Brass, Red Wheels, Ives, 7 In.Long | 40.00 |
| Toy, Cannon, Carbide, Iron, Wheels, 9 In.Long | 19.75 |
| Toy, Cannon, Dainty, Cast Iron, Wooden Base, 10 In. | 140.00 |
| Toy, Cannon, Iron, 3 In.Long | 5.00 |
| Toy, Cannon, Painted, Cast Iron, Patent 1894, 7 In. | 20.00 |
| Toy, Cannon, Ranger Jr., Cast Iron, 10 In. | 50.00 |
| Toy, Cannon, Shoots, Metal Wheels, Tootsie Toy | 15.00 |
| Toy, Cannon, Turned Barrel, Goat Iron, Hub Inkles, 9 1/2 In. | 15.00 |
| Toy, Car & Driver, Racing, Rubber, Blue 3 Gold, Black Wheels, Auburn Co. | 8.00 |
| Toy, Car Set, 1 Car On Loop Action, Technofix, U.S.Zone, Germany, Tin | 13.50 |
| Toy, Car, Army Squad, Windup, Flashing Light, Lithographed, Tin, Marx, 11 In. | 21.50 |
| Toy, Car, Army Staff, Windup, Siren, Tin, Marx, 11 In. | 23.50 |
| Toy, Car, F.B.I. Squad, Lithographed, Tin, Courtland | 10.00 |
| Toy, Car, Fire Chief, Friction, Japan, 12 In. | 4.00 |
| Toy, Car, Fire Chief's, Windup, Lithographed, Tin, Lupor, 7 In. | 6.00 |
| Toy, Car, G-Man, Battery Operated, Lithographed, Metal | 6.75 |
| Toy, Car, Lead, C.1928, Lead Wheels | 15.00 |
| Toy, Car, Model A Ford, Metal Wheels, Green, 1928 | 20.00 |
| Toy, Car, Model A Ford, Metal Wheels, Red, 1928 | 20.00 |
| Toy, Car, Model T Ford, Cast Iron, Arcade, 6 1/4 In. | 60.00 |
| Toy, Car, Model T Ford, Windup, Tin, Germany, 6 1/2 In. | 80.00 |
| Toy, Car, Model T, Cast Iron, 5 In.Long, Green | 35.00 |
| Toy, Car, Mystery Taxi, Rubber Wheels, Metal, Wyandotte, 13 In. | 13.50 |
| Toy, Car, Oldsmobile, 1940, Rubber, Auburn, 6 In. | 3.50 |
| Toy, Car, Passenger, Eloise, Cast Iron, Hubley | 6.00 |
| Toy, Car, Race, Driver, Black Rubber Wheels, Auburn Rubber Co., 6 In. | 4.25 |
| Toy, Car, Race, Driver, Rubber, White Rubber Wheels, Arcor Rubber Co. | 12.50 |
| Toy, Car, Race, Nickel Driver, Iron, Hubley, 5 In. | 30.00 |
| Toy, Car, Racer, Rubber, Auburn, 6 In. | 6.00 |
| Toy, Car, Racing, Driver, Painted, Tin, Germany, 5 In. Long | 60.00 |

| | |
|---|---|
| **Toy, Car,** Racing, Rubber Tires, Lead, 4 1/4 In.Long | 7.50 |
| **Toy, Car,** Racing, Windup, Driver, Wooden Wheels, Lithographed, Tin, Chein | 8.00 |
| **Toy, Car,** Racing, Windup, Lithographed, Tin, Lupor Metal Products, 7 In. | 3.50 |
| **Toy, Car,** Roadster, Electric, Japan | 12.50 |
| **Toy, Car,** Rubber, Pluto | 12.00 |
| **Toy, Car,** Sports, Open, Cast Iron, Green, Runningboard, 1 1/2 In.High | 3.00 |
| **Toy, Car,** Squad, Dick Tracy, Marx | 12.00 |
| **Toy, Car,** State Police, Siren, Lithographed, Tin, Courtland | 10.00 |
| **Toy, Car,** Station Wagon, Windup, Running Boards, Metal, 9 In. | 10.75 |
| **Toy, Car,** Taxicab, Battery Operated, Lithographed, Metal | 6.75 |
| **Toy, Car,** Touring, Amos & Andy, Marx | 12.00 |
| **Toy, Car,** Trolley, Tin, Chein, 8 In.Long | 15.00 |
| **Toy, Car,** Volkswagen, Red, Tootsietoy, 5 In. | 3.25 To 4.75 |
| **Toy, Carousel,** C.1912 | 150.00 |
| **Toy, Carousel,** Clockwork, Horse & Riders, Tin, C.1880, 9 In.High | 150.00 |
| **Toy, Carpenter,** Lead, Made In U.S.A., M In Circle Mark, 2 3/4 In.High | 3.25 |
| **Toy, Carriage,** Doll's, Metal, Folding, Fabric, Wire Wheels, 17 X 15 In. | 25.00 |
| **Toy, Carriage,** Doll's, Pewter, Victorian, Wicker Design, 3 In. | 12.00 |
| **Toy, Carriage,** Doll's, Wicker, Heart Back, Wire Wheels, Carpet Covered Seat | 150.00 |
| **Toy, Carriage,** Horse Drawn, Wilkens, Original Driver, 6 1/2 X 2 1/2 In. | 100.00 |
| **Toy, Carriage,** 2 Horses, Driver, & 2 Passengers, Metal, Landau | 70.00 |
| **Toy, Cart,** Boy Peddling, Autin, Lehmann | 115.00 |
| **Toy, Cart,** Doctor's, 2 Wheel, Figure, Painted, Ives, 10 1/4 In. | 375.00 |
| **Toy, Cart,** Goat, Painted, Cast Iron, Kenton, 7 In.Long | 115.00 |
| **Toy, Cart,** Traffic, Blue, Hubley, 5 In. | 17.00 |
| **Toy, Cat Holding Ball,** Celluloid, Turtle Mark, 2 1/4 In. | 3.00 |
| **Toy, Cat,** Celluloid, Legs Move, 5 1/2 In.Long | 8.00 |
| **Toy, Cat,** Stuffed, Patented 1899, 9 In. ............................*Illus* | 25.00 |
| **Toy, Chair,** Circus, Schoenhut | 8.00 |
| **Toy, Chair,** Doll's, Ice Cream, Spectacle Back, Iron | 40.00 |
| **Toy, Chair,** Doll's, Mahogany, Carved Back, Seat, & Arms, 5 In.High | 15.00 |
| **Toy, Chair,** Doll's, Plank Seat, Painted, Decorated, C.1750 | 75.00 |
| **Toy, Chair,** Dollhouse, Upholstered | 12.00 |
| **Toy, Chair,** 3 1/2 In.High ......................*Illus* | 10.00 |
| **Toy, Chariot,** Cast Iron, Hubley, 8 3/4 In. | 190.00 |
| **Toy, Charlie Chaplin,** Pull String, He Tips Hat, Lithographed, Tin, 4 In. | 9.00 |
| **Toy, Charlie Weaver,** Mechanical, Battery Operated, Tin | 17.00 To 23.50 |
| **Toy, Chest Of Drawers,** Cast Iron, Brown & Red Paint, 3 Drawer | 40.00 |
| **Toy, Chest Of Drawers,** Cast Iron, 3 Drawer, Brown, Red Trim, 3 1/2 In.Deep | 40.00 |
| **Toy, Chicken,** Crank, Noise, Chicken Lays Egg, Tin, 7 1/2 In.High | 15.00 |
| **Toy, Child With Hat,** Roly-Poly Type, Celluloid, 2 1/4 In. | 2.00 |
| **Toy, Chinaman,** Circus, Dressed, Schoenhut | 60.00 |
| **Toy, Churn,** Butter, Dollhouse, Wooden | 4.00 |
| **Toy, Circus Animal,** Camel, One Hump, Schoenhut | 45.00 |
| **Toy, Circus Animal,** Cow, Schoenhut | 48.00 |
| **Toy, Circus Animal,** Crocodile, Glass Eyes, Schoenhut | 48.00 |
| **Toy, Circus Animal,** Donkey, Schoenhut | 28.00 |
| **Toy, Circus Animal,** Elephant, Schoenhut | 35.00 |

Toy, Cat, Stuffed, Patented 1899, 9 In.          Toy, Chair, 3 1/2 In.High

| | |
|---|---:|
| Toy, Circus Animal, Hippopotamus, Schoenhut | 38.00 |
| Toy, Circus Animal, Mule, Schoenhut | 30.00 |
| Toy, Circus Animal, Poodle Dog, Schoenhut | 50.00 |
| Toy, Circus Animal, Rhinoceros, Glass Eyes, Schoenhut | 48.00 |
| Toy, Circus Animal, St.Bernard Dog, Schoenhut | 50.00 |
| Toy, Clock, Dollhouse, Grandfather | 8.50 |
| Toy, Clown Ringing Bell & Twirling Flag, Windup, Tin, Japanese | 45.00 |
| Toy, Clown, Circus, Dressed, Schoenhut | 28.00 |
| Toy, Clown, Walking On Hands, Windup, Chein, 5 1/2 In. | 8.00 |
| Toy, Coach, P.R.R., Cast Iron, Open Vestibules, 4 Wheels, 4 1/2 In.Long | 20.00 |
| Toy, Coach, Twin, Cast Iron, Steel Wheels, Blue Paint, 5 1/4 In.Long | 35.00 |
| Toy, Coal Cart, Donkey, Driver, Ives, 13 1/2 X 6 In. | 350.00 |
| Toy, Colored Man Grinding On Stone, Mechanical, Tin, Strauss | 35.00 |
| Toy, Combat Camouflage Set, Lithographed, Cardboard, 1942 | 11.50 |
| Toy, Coolie On Railroad, Tin, Wind-Up | 38.00 |
| Toy, Coupe, Horse, Driver, Cast Iron, Dent, 9 3/4 In. Long | 70.00 |
| Toy, Covered Wagon, Kenton, Red With 2 Black Horses | 225.00 |
| Toy, Cowboy With Pistol, Iron, 3 1/4 In.High | 2.95 |
| Toy, Cowboy With Pistol, Iron, 3 1/2 In. High | 2.95 |
| Toy, Cradle, Doll's, Folding, Rocking, Wire Bedstead, 7 X 10 X 13 In. | 22.00 |
| Toy, Cradle, Doll's, Hooded, 16 In.Long | 32.00 |
| Toy, Cradle, Doll's, Mahogany, Hooded, 12 In.Long | 25.00 |
| Toy, Cradle, Doll's, Wooden, Red, 20 In.Long | 10.00 |
| Toy, Crap Shooting Monkey, Battery Operated, Cragston | 18.50 |
| Toy, Crib, Doll's, Lithographed, Tin, Chein, 8 In.Long | 7.25 |
| Toy, Crib, Dollhouse, Iron, Yellow Paint, On Wheels, 2 1/4 In.Long | 10.00 |
| Toy, Cup & Saucer, Dollhouse, Cast Metal, Ornate | 6.00 |
| Toy, Dachshund, Begging, Celluloid, Turtle Mark, 2 1/4 In. | 3.00 |
| Toy, Dart Board, Sambo, Tin, Wyandotte | 15.00 |
| Toy, Dennis The Menace, Plays Xylophone, Battery Operated | 16.50 |
| Toy, Dilly The Dalmatian, Battery Operated, Cragstan | 9.75 |
| Toy, Dirigible, Lehmann | 115.00 |
| Toy, Dirigible, Los Angeles, Tootsietoy | 15.00 |
| Toy, Dishes, Doll's, Roses On Cream, Celluloid, 13 Piece Set | 10.00 |
| Toy, Dog, Arf Arf, Orphan Annie's | 10.00 |
| Toy, Dog, Dachshund, Stuffed, Steiff Tag, 10 In. | 12.00 |
| Toy, Dog, Mounted On Iron Wheels, 10 In.High | 28.00 |
| Toy, Dog, Plush Material On Wood, Germany, 1920s, 3 In.High | 4.00 |
| Toy, Dog, Snobby, Poodle, Button In Ear, Steiff, 13 In.Long | 12.50 |
| Toy, Dog, Windup, Celluloid, 4 In. | 12.00 |
| Toy, Dog, Windup, Tail Spins & Head Moves, Tin, Japan, 5 In.Long | 10.00 |
|     Toy, Doll, see Doll | |
| Toy, Doll In Chair, Rocks, Duck, Umbrella, Celluloid, Mechanical, Japan | 85.00 |
| Toy, Dollhouse, Colonial, 5 Rooms, Furniture, Cardboard, Uncut, 1930s | 8.50 |
| Toy, Dollhouse, Lithographed, 2 Stories, 5 Rooms, Furniture, Tin | 12.50 |
| Toy, Dollhouse, Tudor, English Country Estate, Lithographed, Foldup | 7.50 |
| Toy, Dollhouse, 2 Stories, 5 Rooms, Lithographed, Tin, 21 In.Long | 13.75 |
| Toy, Domino Set, Brass Pegged | 30.00 |
| Toy, Donkey Cart, Green & Red, Nickel Donkey, Original Man, 10 X 3 In. | 135.00 |
| Toy, Dresser, Cast Iron, 3 Drawer, 4 Hearts On Top & Drawers, 6 In.High | 50.00 |
| Toy, Drummer Boy, Windup, Lithographed, Tin, Chein, 9 In. | 23.75 |
| Toy, Drummer Boy, Windup, Marx | 22.00 To 45.00 |
| Toy, Duck, Friction, Tin, Colored, 8 In. | 25.00 |
| Toy, Duck, Roly-Poly Type, Celluloid, 2 1/4 In. | 2.00 |
| Toy, Duck, Windup, Painted, Tin, German, 5 1/2 In.High | 15.00 |
| Toy, Elephant, Rubber, Pink, Squeeze Toy, Rempel, Dated 1955 | 5.00 |
| Toy, Elephant, Standing, Celluloid, Turtle Mark, 2 1/4 In. | 3.00 |
| Toy, Elevator, Coal, Lionel | 22.50 |
| Toy, Elsie, The Borden Cow, Pull | 18.00 |
| Toy, Engine, Cast Iron, Patent Date 1888 | 7.00 |
| Toy, Engine, Fire, Windup, Tin, Japan, 1912 | 10.00 |
| Toy, Engine, Steam, Driver, 2 Horse, Cast Iron, Wilkens, 17 In. | 210.00 |
| Toy, Engine, Steam, Horizontal, G.F.N., German | 45.00 |
| Toy, Engine, Steam, Robert Fulton Line, Marvin Ind. | 6.00 |
| Toy, Engine, Windup, Tin | 12.50 |
| Toy, Erector Set, Electric, Square Girder, A.C.Gilbert Co., 1938 | 27.50 |

Toy, Fire Wagon, Iron, American, C.1850, 20 In.

| | |
|---|---|
| Toy, Erector Set, Ferris Wheel, Gilbert | 6.00 |
| Toy, Erector Set, Gilbert, Clockwork Motor, Tin Carrier, 1938 | 8.00 |
| Toy, Erector Set, Gilbert, No.7 1/2 In. | 20.00 |
| Toy, Express Wagon Pulled By Goat, Man Seated, Iron | 27.00 |
| Toy, Fan-Tel Game, Schoenhut | 8.00 |
| Toy, Farm Figure Set, Lead, Hand-Painted, England, 8 Piece | 12.00 |
| Toy, Farm Set, Lithographed, Tin, Marx, Over 100 Pieces In Box | 17.00 |
| Toy, Felix The Cat, Celluloid, Roly Poly, Colored, 4 In.High | 12.00 |
| Toy, Ferdinand, The Bull, Hard Rubber, Walt Disney Enterprises | 15.00 |
| Toy, Ferris Wheel, Hercules, Tin, Painted, Chein, 10 1/2 In.High | 50.00 |
| Toy, Figure, Western, Lead, Made In England, Set Of 6 | 5.00 |
| Toy, Filling Station, Shell, Windup, Lithographed, Tin, Technofix, Germany | 14.50 |
| Toy, Fire Patrol, Running Horse, Driver, Cast Iron, Ives | 190.00 |
| Toy, Fire Patrol, 2 Horses, Driver, 3 Figures, Cast Iron, Carpenter | 300.00 |
| Toy, Fire Wagon, Iron, American, C.1850, 20 In. ................................... Illus | 500.00 |
| Toy, Fireplace, Dollhouse, Candles On Mantel, Hanging Pot, Wooden Logs | 5.00 |
| Toy, Flatiron, Double Ended, Detachable Wooden Handle | 12.50 |
| Toy, Ford Sedan, Nickel Wheels, Cast Iron, Marked Arcade, 6 1/2 In.Long | 60.00 |
| Toy, Fred Flintstone Riding Dino, Windup, Lithographed, Tin, Mar | 9.00 To 12.00 |
| Toy, Friction Car, Red With Gold Trim, Drive, Passengers, 10 X 7 In. | 215.00 |
| Toy, Frog, Celluloid, 2 1/4 In. | 2.00 |
| Toy, Frypan, Iron, Side Handle, 3 1/2 In.Long | 2.95 |
| Toy, Frypan, Iron, 3 Footed, Side Handle, 3 1/8 In. Diameter | 2.95 |
| Toy, Furniture, Dining Room, Dollhouse, Wooden, 7 Pieces | 4.50 |
| Toy, G.I.Joe & K-9 Pups, Unique Art, N.Y.C., Tin, 8 In.High | 25.00 |
| Toy, G-Men In Car, Friction, Sparkling, Boxed | 8.00 |
| Toy, Gambling Man At Roulette Table, Battery Operated, Cragstan | 16.50 |
| Toy, Game, see Game | |
| Toy, Game Board, Wall, Little Black Sambo, Tin, Multicolor, Wyandotte | 12.00 |
| Toy, Garage Set, Metal Lithographed Trucks, Wyandotte, 4 Piece | 14.50 |
| Toy, Garage, Lithographed, Tin, Marx, 9 X 6 In. | 9.50 |
| Toy, Golden Teddy Bear Of England, 18 In.Tall | 18.50 |
| Toy, Golden Teddy Bear Of England, 24 In.Tall | 22.50 |
| Toy, Grader, Road, Cast Iron, William's, 4 1/2 In. | 35.00 |
| Toy, Graf Zeppelin, Chein, 9 In.Long | 20.00 |
| Toy, Grasshopper, Mechanical, Pull, Hubley | 325.00 |
| Toy, Grinder, Iron | 5.00 |
| Toy, Gun, Aeromatic Glider, Shoots Balsa Gliders, Metal, 9 In. | 5.00 |
| Toy, Gun, BB, Red Ryder | 25.00 |
| Toy, Gun, Colt 45, Gold Barrel, White Handles, Bullets, Hubley, 13 In. | 7.00 |
| Toy, Gun, Combat, Windup, Lithographed, Tin, Marx | 8.25 |
| Toy, Gun, Cork, Colt, Embossed, Tin | 5.00 |
| Toy, Gun, Disintegrator, Atomic Ray, Metal Hubley | 16.50 To 18.50 |
| Toy, Gun, Gene Autry, Side Loader, Revolving Barrel, Leslie Henry | 9.50 |
| Toy, Gun, Luger, Metal, Marx | 2.00 |
| Toy, Gun, Machine, Cap, Automatic, Swivel Tripod, Metal, Ben Bros., England | 6.00 |

| | |
|---|---:|
| Toy, Gun, Ray, Buck Rogers, Sonic, 1950s, Original Box | 18.00 |
| Toy, Gun, Roy Rogers, Repeater, Black Handle, Metal, Leather Holster | 12.75 |
| Toy, Gun, Roy Rogers, 2 Metal Guns In Leather Holster | 9.75 |
| Toy, Gun, The Sheriff, Repeater, Cast Iron, Stevens, 9 In. | 8.50 |
| Toy, Hammer, Sledge, Iron, 2 3/4 In.Long | 2.50 |
| Toy, Harlequin, Jolly Joy, Papier-Mache Head, Wooden & Brass Parts, C.1880 | 47.00 |
| Toy, Harold Lloyd, Comic, Windup, 1930s | 75.00 |
| Toy, Hat, Fire Chief, Child's, Red Buckram | 2.75 |
| Toy, Hen On Nest, Tin, Crank To Lay Wooden Eggs | 25.00 |
| Toy, Hen, Windup, Lays Eggs & Cackles, Tin, Baldwin, 5 In.Long | 26.00 |
| Toy, Highchair, Doll's, Wooden, Tray, 15 In. | 12.50 |
| Toy, Hitch, For Fire Engine, 3 Horse, Painted, Cast Iron, Hubley, 9 In. | 40.00 |
| Toy, Hitch, Log Wagon, 2 Oxen, Cast Iron, Hubley, 10 1/4 In. | 80.00 |
| Toy, Hitch, Log, Back, Cast Iron, Kenton | 25.00 |
| Toy, Hitch, 2 Horse, Cast Iron, Dent, 14 1/4 In. | 25.00 |
| Toy, Hitch, 2 Horse, Driver, Cast Iron, Kenton, 9 In. | 20.00 To 25.00 |
| Toy, Hobbyhorse, Wooden | 15.00 |
| Toy, Hod, Coal, Iron, 3 1/2 In.Long | 3.95 |
| Toy, Holder, Firecracker, Cast Iron, L.F.& Co., Patent Apr.1874 | 50.00 |
| Toy, Holster Set, Hopalong Cassidy, Leather | 9.75 |
| Toy, Hometown Movie Theatre, Lithographed, Tin, Marx, C.1920 | 13.75 |
| Toy, Honeymoon Express, Tin, Mechanical, Marx, 9 1/2 X 9 1/2 X 2 In. | 30.00 |
| Toy, Horse & Cowboy, Bucking Bronco, Lehmann | 115.00 |
| Toy, Horse & Rider, Walking, Mechanical, Tin, German | 35.00 |
| Toy, Horse Dray, Single, Dent, Green Body, White Horse, 15 1/2 X 5 In. | 200.00 |
| Toy, Horse Pulling Coal Cart, Wooden, S.A.Smith Co., Vermont, C.1890 | 185.00 |
| Toy, Horse Sleigh, 2 Horse, Hubley, 15 X 5 In. | 325.00 |
| Toy, Horse, Pull, Composition, Wooden Wheels, Germany, U.S.Zone | 9.50 |
| Toy, Horse, Windup, Wooden, Fisher Price, 9 X 8 In. | 19.50 |
| Toy, Hose Reeler, Men, Cast Iron, Kent | 300.00 |
| Toy, House, Doll's, Pennsylvania Folk Art | 68.00 |
| Toy, Huckleberry Hound, Vinyl Head, Hanna Barbera, Knickerbocker, 1959 | 4.00 |
| Toy, Ice Wagon, Hubley, Yellow Body, Red Wheels, White Horse, 14 X 5 In. | 295.00 |
| Toy, Ice Wagon, Nickel Plated Wagon, Team Of Horses, Black, Gold Trim, Red | 225.00 |
| Toy, Indian, Lead, Hand-Painted, England, Set Of 7 | 7.25 |
| Toy, Iron, Dover Dolly, Hood Type, Red Handle | 10.00 |
| Toy, Iron, Wooden Handle | 6.00 |
| Toy, Jantzen Beach Patrol, Hubley, 8 In.Long | 2000.00 |
| Toy, Jazzbo Jim Dancer, Mechanical, Tin, Strauss, N.Y.C., 1921, 10 In.High | 100.00 |
| Toy, Jeep, Sunbeam, Battery Operated, Rubber Wheels, Lithographed, Tin, 10 In. | 12.50 |
| Toy, Joe Penner & His Duck, Tin, Windup | 135.00 |
| Toy, Jolly Juggler | 25.00 |
| Toy, Jumpin Jeep, Windup, Tin, Marx | 45.00 |
| Toy, Junior Jazz Band, Lithographed, Tin, A & A American Metal Toy Co. | 15.00 |
| Toy, Kangaroo, Jumps, Cast Iron, 6 1/4 In. Long | 170.00 |
| Toy, Kiddie Cyclist, Windup, Lithographed, Tin, Unique Art | 35.00 |
| Toy, Kitchen Set, Campbell Kids, Tin, Wooden Handles, 6 Piece | 5.75 |
| Toy, Kitchen Set, Dollhouse, Table & 2 Chairs | 12.00 |
| Toy, Kitten, Celluloid, Tin Wheels, 1 1/2 In. | 13.00 |
| Toy, Knitting Set, Barbie, Cylindrical Container, 1962 | 3.00 |
| Toy, L'il Abner Band, Instruction Sheet | 75.00 |
| Toy, Lamb, Dy Dee, Wool Hair Ears Attached, 15 In. | 17.00 |
| Toy, Lamb, Rubber, Wheels, Hubley, Original Box | 7.00 |
| Toy, Lantern, Roy Rogers, Battery Operated, Tin, Ohio Art | 7.50 To 12.00 |
| Toy, Lighter, Cigarette, Kent Cigarettes, Metal, Lithographed | 2.50 |
| Toy, Limousine, Tin, Clockwork Chauffeur, 13 X 7 In. | 175.00 |
| Toy, Lincoln Tunnel, Mechanical, Tin, Unique Art, Boxed | 15.00 |
| Toy, Little Girl Driving Tractor, Pull, Tin Wheels, Wooden, 10 In. | 4.75 |
| Toy, Living Room Set, Dollhouse, 3 Piece | 32.00 |
| Toy, Locomotive, Clockwork, Tin, Hornby, Type 30, England, Meccano, Ltd. | 25.00 |
| Toy, Locomotive, Key Wind, Ives No.5, 7 In.Long | 25.00 |
| Toy, Lovebirds, Pip Squeak, Animated, Metal Bodies, Germany, 3 In. | 85.00 |
| Toy, Machine, Threshing, McCormick Deering, Arcade | 25.00 |
| Toy, Man In Wagon Pulled By Donkey, Windup, Tin, Marx | 45.00 |
| Toy, Man On The Flying Trapeze, Windup, Lithographed, Tin, Wyandotte, 9 In. | 21.50 |
| Toy, Man On 3 Wheel Bike, Windup, Tin, Dated 1890 | 45.00 |

| | |
|---|--:|
| Toy, **Merry-Go-Round,** Wolverine | 50.00 |
| Toy, **Mettallophone,** Schoenhut, Boxed | 11.00 |
| Toy, **Mickey Mouse, see Mickey Mouse** | |
| Toy, **Milk Wagon,** Borden, Rich Toys, Wood & Tin | 45.00 |
| Toy, **Milkman,** Lead, Made In U.S.A., M In Circle Mark, 2 3/4 In.High | 3.25 |
| Toy, **Mirror,** Hand, Snow White & The Seven Dwarfs, Lucite | 7.00 |
| Toy, **Mixer,** Concrete, Buddy L, 16 X 13 X 15 In. | 30.00 |
| Toy, **Mixer,** Rubber Wheels, Cast Iron, Jaeger | 65.00 |
| Toy, **Mold,** Cowboy On Bucking Horse, Hat In Hand, For Lead Figures | 50.00 |
| Toy, **Mold,** Cowboy Riding Horse, Shooting Rifle, For Lead Figures | 40.00 |
| Toy, **Monkey Blows Trumpet & Pushes Bee Away,** Battery Operated | 16.50 |
| Toy, **Monkey Climbing Rope,** Bruno, 1924, 10 1/2 In. | 25.00 |
| Toy, **Monkey In Clown Suit,** Mechanical, Bisque Head, Playing Violin, German | 150.00 |
| Toy, **Monkey,** Bombo, Performs On Tree, Windup, Tin | 25.00 |
| Toy, **Monkey,** Mohair Body, Velvet Hands & Feet, Glass Eyes, Atlman & Co., Eng. | 18.00 |
| Toy, **Mortimer Snerd,** Windup | 25.00 |
| Toy, **Motorcycle & Rider,** Echo, Lehmann | 155.00 |
| Toy, **Motorcycle Patrolman,** Cast Metal, Rubber Tires, Red & Blue, C.1920 | 25.00 |
| Toy, **Motorcycle Policeman,** Iron, Champion, 7 1/4 In. Long | 19.75 |
| Toy, **Motorcycle Policeman,** Siren, Key, Painted, Tin, Marx | 29.00 |
| Toy, **Motorcycle Policeman,** Windup, Metal, Marx, 8 1/2 In. | 30.00 |
| Toy, **Motorcycle With Crash Car,** Cast Iron, Red Paint, 5 In.Long | 25.00 |
| Toy, **Motorcycle,** Celluloid, Santa, Tin, Wind | 10.00 |
| Toy, **Motorcycle,** Patrol, Rubber Wheels, Cast Iron, Hubley | 17.50 |
| Toy, **Motorcycle,** Police, Champion, Iron, 7 X 5 In. | 65.00 |
| Toy, **Motorcycle,** Police, P.D.H., 4 X 2 1/2 In. | 45.00 |
| Toy, **Motorcycle,** Red, Cast Iron, Made In U.S.A., 4 In. | 6.00 |
| Toy, **Motorcycle,** 2 Rider, Cast Iron, Rubber Tires, 4 In.Long | 18.00 |
| Toy, **Mouse,** Gray, Windup, Tin, Occupied Japan | 2.50 |
| Toy, **Noah's Ark,** Gong Bell, Pull, Metal Wheels, Lithographed Animals | 7.00 |
| Toy, **Noah's Ark,** Wooden, Converse | 18.00 |
| Toy, **Ocean Liner,** Clockwork, Ives, 1912, 13 In.Long | 100.00 |
| Toy, **Oh My,** Windup | 65.00 |
| Toy, **Organ,** Battery Operated, Lithographed | 9.00 |
| Toy, **Paddy & Pig,** Mechanical, Tin, Lehmann | 150.00 |
| Toy, **Pail,** Sand, Nursery Rhymes, Lithographed, Tin, Chein | 4.75 |
| Toy, **Paint Set,** Howdy Doody, Mask, Boxed | 5.75 |
| Toy, **Paint Set,** Li'l Abner, Graphic Box, 11 X 17 In. | 5.50 |
| Toy, **Parlor Set,** Doll's House, C.1900, 6 Piece | 27.50 |
| Toy, **Pekinese Dog,** Battery Operated, Remote Control, Japan | 4.00 |
| Toy, **People & Dog,** Mechanical, Tin, Lehmann's Patent 1903 | 230.00 |
| Toy, **Piano,** Baby Grand, Wooden, Red, Japan, 7 X 5 In. | 4.00 |
| Toy, **Piano,** Schoenhut, Open & Close Keyboard, Marked | 80.00 |
| Toy, **Piano,** Schoenhut, Upright, 15 Keys, 16 In.Long | 65.00 |
| Toy, **Pickax,** Iron, 2 3/4 In.Long | 2.50 |
| Toy, **Piggy Cook,** Windup | 6.00 |
| Toy, **Piggy,** Windup, Tin, Marx | 11.00 |
| Toy, **Pile Driver,** Panama, Wolverine | 20.00 |
| Toy, **Pinocchio & Book,** Clothes, Knickerbocker Toy | 65.00 |
| Toy, **Pinocchio Playing London Bridge On Xylophone,** Battery Operated | 18.50 |
| Toy, **Pistol,** "Model, " Cast Iron, Patent 1890 | 15.00 |
| Toy, **Pistol,** "USA Liquid Pistol, Cast Iron | 10.00 |
| Toy, **Pistol,** Banner, Mechanical, Shoots Blanks, Cast Iron | 15.00 |
| Toy, **Pistol,** BB, Dated 1927 | 50.00 |
| Toy, **Pistol,** Bell, Metal, Rings, Wyandotte | 3.75 |
| Toy, **Pistol,** Buddy, Cast Iron | 20.00 |
| Toy, **Pistol,** Bull's-Eye Safety, Flared Barrel, Spring, Cast Iron | 45.00 |
| Toy, **Pistol,** Cap, Ace | 15.00 |
| Toy, **Pistol,** Cap, America, Shield, Patent 1873 | 50.00 |
| Toy, **Pistol,** Cap, American Bulldog, Cast Iron | 5.00 |
| Toy, **Pistol,** Cap, Army Automatic, Metal, Marx, 2 In. | 2.50 |
| Toy, **Pistol,** Cap, Atomic Disintegrator, Repeating, Hubley | 22.50 |
| Toy, **Pistol,** Cap, Automatic, Tin, For Roll Of Caps, Marked Yacht, 3 In.Long | 2.95 |
| Toy, **Pistol,** Cap, Automatic, Tin, Yacht, 3 In. | 2.95 |
| Toy, **Pistol,** Cap, Big Horn | 2.50 |
| Toy, **Pistol,** Cap, Big Scout | 2.50 |

Toy, Pistol, Cap, Boy's Delight, Cast Iron, Patent June 1891 ................................................ 90.00
Toy, Pistol, Cap, Brat, Cast Iron, Dent Sample .................................................................... 20.00
Toy, Pistol, Cap, Buffalo Bill, Repeater, Raised Picture, Metal, 9 In. ................................... 7.25
Toy, Pistol, Cap, Bulldog, Patent 1923, Iron, Single Shot, 6 1/4 In. ................................... 9.75
Toy, Pistol, Cap, Bulldozer, 6 Shooter, Cast Iron, July 1874 ............................................... 80.00
Toy, Pistol, Cap, Cadet ....................................................................................................... 1.65
Toy, Pistol, Cap, Cap 7 ....................................................................................................... 1.65
Toy, Pistol, Cap, Centennial, 1776-1876, Cast Iron ............................................................. 55.00
Toy, Pistol, Cap, Chinese Must Go, Mechanical ................................................................... 325.00
Toy, Pistol, Cap, Colt Six-Shooter, Metal, Marx, 2 In. ......................................................... 2.50
Toy, Pistol, Cap, Columbia, Cast Iron, Patent June 1891 ..................................................... 10.00
Toy, Pistol, Cap, Columbia, Cast Iron, 1890 ........................................................................ 20.00
Toy, Pistol, Cap, Daisy, Cast Iron, Patent Apr. 1873 ............................................................ 30.00
Toy, Pistol, Cap, Dick, Hubley 210A ................................................................................... 10.00
Toy, Pistol, Cap, Double Barrel, Cast Iron, Dated 1880 ....................................................... 35.00
Toy, Pistol, Cap, Double Barrel, Navy .................................................................................. 30.00
Toy, Pistol, Cap, Double Trigger, Cast Iron, Stephens, Patent 1873 ..................................... 60.00
Toy, Pistol, Cap, Eagle, Cast Iron, 1890 .............................................................................. 15.00
Toy, Pistol, Cap, Echo, 6-Shooter, Cast Iron, 1881 ............................................................. 55.00
Toy, Pistol, Cap, Flash, 6-Shooter, Cast Iron, Hubley .......................................................... 20.00
Toy, Pistol, Cap, Gene Autry, Repeater, Metal, Fancy Grips ................................................ 8.00
Toy, Pistol, Cap, Jumbo, Patent 1890, Iron .......................................................................... 25.00
Toy, Pistol, Cap, Kilgore .................................................................................................... 1.65
Toy, Pistol, Cap, King, Cast Iron, Patent Aug. 1879 ............................................................ 20.00
Toy, Pistol, Cap, King, Cast Iron, 1878 ............................................................................... 12.50
Toy, Pistol, Cap, Lightning Express, Mechanical ................................................................... 120.00
Toy, Pistol, Cap, Look Out, Dog's Head, Cast Iron ............................................................. 60.00
Toy, Pistol, Cap, M & L Squirt ............................................................................................ 1.65
Toy, Pistol, Cap, Magic ...................................................................................................... 80.00
Toy, Pistol, Cap, Navy, Double Barrel, Cast Iron ................................................................. 20.00
Toy, Pistol, Cap, Nigger Head, 1887 ................................................................................... 65.00
Toy, Pistol, Cap, Novelty, Cast Iron, Patent Applied For ...................................................... 60.00
Toy, Pistol, Cap, Old Ironsides, Iron, 10 3/4 In. Long ......................................................... 30.00
Toy, Pistol, Cap, Padlock, Hubley ....................................................................................... 15.00
Toy, Pistol, Cap, Pluck, Spur Trigger, Cast Iron, Patent 1887, 4 In.Long ............................. 25.00
Toy, Pistol, Cap, Punch & Judy, Animated ........................................................................... 375.00
Toy, Pistol, Cap, Ric-O-Shay, Repeater, Black Handle, Metal, Hubley, 13 In. ........................ 6.50
Toy, Pistol, Cap, Savage, Cast Iron, 7 In.Long ..................................................................... 10.00
Toy, Pistol, Cap, Senator .................................................................................................... 1.65
Toy, Pistol, Cap, Shoo Fly, Cast Iron ................................................................................... 35.00
Toy, Pistol, Cap, Smoky ...................................................................................................... 2.50
Toy, Pistol, Cap, Star .......................................................................................................... 1.65
Toy, Pistol, Cap, Star, Steer On Handle, Pot Metal .............................................................. 10.00
Toy, Pistol, Cap, Sun, Cast Iron .......................................................................................... 45.00
Toy, Pistol, Cap, Tiger ......................................................................................................... 1.65
Toy, Pistol, Cap, Volunteer, Cast Iron, Patent Apr. 1873 ..................................................... 30.00
Toy, Pistol, Cap, Yacht, Tin, Automatic, 6 In. ...................................................................... 2.95
Toy, Pistol, Cap, 25 Jr. ....................................................................................................... 1.00
Toy, Pistol, Chief, Cast Iron ................................................................................................ 10.00
Toy, Pistol, Colt, Cast Iron .................................................................................................. 7.50
Toy, Pistol, Combat, Windup, Lithographed, Tin, Marx, 1940s ............................................ 7.75
Toy, Pistol, Dig Enjun, Hammerless ..................................................................................... 40.00
Toy, Pistol, Eagle, Cast Iron ................................................................................................ 7.50
Toy, Pistol, Firecracker, 5 Barrel, Cast Iron & Brass, Painted, 1877 ..................................... 600.00
Toy, Pistol, Indian .............................................................................................................. 1.65
Toy, Pistol, Lion's Head, Cast Iron, Patent 1890 ................................................................. 50.00
Toy, Pistol, Mechanical, Royal Top ...................................................................................... 425.00
Toy, Pistol, Pal, Kilgore, Metal ............................................................................................ 3.00
Toy, Pistol, Terror, Embossed People, Cast Iron .................................................................. 70.00
Toy, Pistol, Tin, Wyandotte, 6 1/2 In. ................................................................................. 2.50
Toy, Pistol, Tin, Wyandotte, 8 1/2 In. ................................................................................. 2.50
Toy, Pistol, Victor, Cast Iron ............................................................................................... 10.00
Toy, Pistol, Water, Daisy No.71, Repeater, 3 Shot ............................................................... 4.50
Toy, Pistol, Water, Flash Gordon, 1950s ............................................................................. 17.50
Toy, Pistol, Water, Tin ......................................................................................................... 5.00
Toy, Pluto Pup, Pop-Up Kritter, Wooden ............................................................................. 25.00
Toy, Polar Bear Fishing, Battery Operated, 3 Tin Fish, Lithographed .................................... 16.50

| | |
|---|---:|
| Toy, Polar Bear With Drum, Windup, 1920, 5 1/2 In.High | 10.00 |
| Toy, Polar Bear, Painted, Cast Iron, Kenton | 5.00 |
| Toy, Polar Bear, Windup, Beats Drum & Bows, Red Hat, C.1920, 5 In.High | 22.00 |
| Toy, Police Patrol, Driver, 4 Men, 3 Horses, Dent, 21 In. | 310.00 |
| Toy, Policeman Directs Traffic In London Scenery, Windup, Technofix | 14.00 |
| Toy, Poodle, Jointed, Off-White, Steiff, 16 1/2 In. | 8.00 |
| Toy, Popeye Punching Bag, Chein | 60.00 |
| Toy, Popeye, Carrying Parrot Cages, Windup, Tin | 27.50 |
| Toy, Popeye, Pull, Popeye Surfboard, Wooden, Paper Lithographed, 12 In. | 11.50 |
| Toy, Porky Pig, Leon Schlesinger On Head, Twirling Flag, Windup, Marx, 1939 | 35.00 |
| Toy, Powerhouse, Lionel, No.435 | 12.50 |
| Toy, Preacher In The Pulpit, Mechanical, Wooden | 575.00 |
| Toy, Printing Press, Wooden | 5.00 |
| Toy, Pumper, Fire, Cast Iron, Dent Hardware Sample, 7 In. Long | 80.00 |
| Toy, Pumper, Steam, Cast-Iron Wheels, Boston, 15 1/2 In. | 2100.00 |
| Toy, Pumper, Steam, 3 Galloping Horses, Cast Iron, Wilkens | 80.00 |
| Toy, Puppet, Hand, Chimp, Plush, Steiff | 2.50 |
| Toy, Puppet, Hand, Hands & Feet, C.1900 | 3.50 |
| Toy, Puppet, Howdy Doody, Howdy & His Gang, 16 In.High, Set Of 6 | 46.00 |
| Toy, Puppet, J.Fred Muggs, Hand | 3.75 |
| Toy, Pushcart, Doll's, Red Paint, Wheels, 3 1/2 In.Long Seat | 10.00 |
| Toy, Puzzle, Flash Gordon, Board | 5.00 |
| Toy, Rabbit Pulling Basket, Chein, 1940s, 7 1/2 In. | 8.50 |
| Toy, Rabbit Pulling Cart, Lithographed, Tin, Wyandotte, 10 In. | 7.25 |
| Toy, Rabbit, Windup, Painted | 18.00 |
| Toy, Railroad Man, Businessman, Painted Metal, Barclay Type, 3 In. | 3.25 |
| Toy, Railroad Man, Mechanic, Painted Metal, Barclay Type, 3 In. | 3.25 |
| Toy, Railroad Man, Porter, Painted Metal, Barclay Type, 3 In. | 3.25 |
| Toy, Rake, Iron, 4 In.Long | 2.75 |
| Toy, Record, Alice In Wonderland, 1941 | 6.50 |
| Toy, Record, Little Black Sambo, 1941 | 6.50 |
| Toy, Record, Little Red Riding Hood, 1941 | 6.50 |
| Toy, Record, The Three Little Pigs, 1941 | 6.50 |
| Toy, Refrigerator, General Electric Sticker, Tin, Wooden Motor On Top | 10.00 |
| Toy, Rifle, Gene Autry, Cork Popping, Wooden Handle | 5.50 |
| Toy, Rifle, Official Mareslaig, Celluloid & Metal, 5 3/8 In.Long | 18.00 |
| Toy, Ring, Barbie, Official, Mattel, C.1963 | 4.00 |
| Toy, Road Grader, Cast Iron, Williams, 4 1/2 In. | 35.00 |
| Toy, Road Race Set, Lithographed, Tin, Germany, U.S.Zone, 4 Cars, Track | 13.50 |
| Toy, Rocker, Doll's, 18 In.High | 2.50 |
| Toy, Rocker, Dollhouse, Cast Iron, 2 1/2 In. | 10.00 |
| Toy, Roller Bell, Cast-Iron Wheels, 2 Half Bells Facing Each Other | 45.00 |
| Toy, Roller Skates, Buster Brown & Tige | 15.00 |
| Toy, Rolling Pin, Wooden, 6 In. | 3.00 |
| Toy, Rooster, Papier-Mache, China, Feathers, C.1895 | 7.50 |
| Toy, Rooster, Push Toy, Movable Wings, Tin, Ives, 1881 | 160.00 |
| Toy, Roulette Wheel, Colored, Tin, 2 1/4 In.Diameter | 5.00 |
| Toy, Roy Rogers Rodeo Ranch, Lithographed Building, Tin, Marx | 9.00 |
| Toy, Rug, Dollhouse, Oriental, Fringed, Printed Velvet, 9 X 13 In. | 8.50 |
| Toy, Sadiron, Double Pointed, Iron, 3 1/2 In.Long | 4.95 |
| Toy, Sadiron, Nickel Plated, 4 1/4 In.Long | 5.95 |
| Toy, Sand Scoop, Red Paint, Yellow Pails, Chain Pick Up, Tin | 60.00 |
| Toy, Sand Ship, Tin, Chein | 12.50 |
| Toy, Sand Sifter, Lithographed, Tin, Chein, 7 In.Diameter | 4.75 |
| Toy, Sand Toy, Hopper For Sand To Run Teeter-Totter, Chein | 27.00 |
| Toy, Santa Claus, Battery Operated, Beats Drum, Cragstan | 15.00 |
| Toy, Santa Claus, Sleigh & 2 Reindeer, Cast Iron, Hubley, 14 3/4 In. | 300.00 |
| Toy, Sedan, Cast Iron, Arcade, 6 1/2 In. | 65.00 |
| Toy, Sedan, Green, Lehmann | 80.00 |
| Toy, Sewing Machine, Child's, Marked Sew Master, Hand Turned, 9 X 5 1/2 In. | 5.00 |
| Toy, Sewing Machine, Child's, Singer, 1914, Box & Instructions | 12.50 |
| Toy, Sewing Machine, Metal, Germany, British Zone | 12.00 |
| Toy, Sewing Machine, Tin, Moving Parts | 10.00 |
| Toy, Sewing Set, Progressive Sewing, Dated 1941 | 5.00 |
| Toy, Ship's Model, Cruiser, Die Cut, Gray Paper, Skyline Mfg., 1940s | 5.50 |
| Toy, Shooter, Cap, 2 Dogs On Bench, William Ferguson Collection | 3000.00 |

| | |
|---|---|
| Toy, Shovel, 5 X 3 In. | 35.00 |
| Toy, Sidecar, Parcel Post, Cast Iron, Hubley | 40.00 |
| Toy, Skater Bunny, Windup, Cragstan, 8 In. | 4.25 |
| Toy, Skates, Boy's, Winchester, American Club, Black, Shoe, Size 8 | 20.00 |
| Toy, Skates, Ice, Racing, Hans | 17.50 |
| Toy, Skates, Roller, Doll's, Steel Wheels, Sherwood | 15.00 |
| Toy, Ski Boy, Windup, Lithographed, Tin, Chein | 19.75 To 23.50 |
| Toy, Slapstick, Clown, Shoots .32 Caliber Blanks, C.1880 | 39.50 |
| Toy, Sled, Doll's, Wooden, Red, Pair | 23.50 |
| Toy, Sled, Iron, Turned Up Runners, "Liberty" | 24.75 |
| Toy, Sleigh, Child's, Green, Red Interior, Gold Cord Trim, 44 In.Long | 65.00 |
| Toy, Slinky, Bucko Cat, No.300 | 7.00 |
| Toy, Smithy, Lead, Made In U.S.A., M In Circle Mark, 2 3/4 In. | 3.25 |
| Toy, Smokey Bear, Official, Ranger Badge, Knickerbocker, 14 1/2 In. | 5.00 |
| Toy, Snow White & The Seven Dwarfs, 1930s, Name On Each Label, 8 Pieces | 65.00 |
| Toy, Soldier, British, Scotch Uniform, Set Of 6 | 14.50 |
| Toy, Soldier, Elastolin, German, 4 In.High, Set Of 6 | 15.00 |
| Toy, Soldier, Lead, Hand-Painted, U.S.Soldiers, Made In England, Set Of 15 | 16.50 |
| Toy, Soldier, Wacs & Waves, Lead, England, Hand-Painted, Set Of 7 | 8.00 |
| Toy, Soldier, With Gun, Metal, Miniature | 4.50 |
| Toy, Soldier, World War I, Lead, 3 In. | .85 |
| Toy, Space Ride, Mechanical, Lithographed, Tin, Chein | 17.50 |
| Toy, Space Set, Rex Mars Space Drome, Lithographed, Tin, Marx | 9.50 |
| Toy, Space Tank, Planet Patrol, Man Pops Up, Marx | 25.00 |
| Toy, Spaceman, Dan Dare, Pilot Of The Future, Lead, England, Set Of 7 | 9.00 |
| Toy, Spaceship, Captain Video, Plastic Men, Graphic Box | 11.00 |
| Toy, Sparkle & BO Plenty, Mechanical, Tin | 30.00 |
| Toy, Speedboat, Figure, Johnson's Sea Horse, Cast Iron, 10 1/2 In. Long | 425.00 |
| Toy, Spreader, Manure, Shaft, "McCormick Deering, " Arcade | 90.00 |
| Toy, Squirrel, Windup, 6 In.Long, Early 1930s | 15.00 |
| Toy, Stand, Circus, Round, Schoenhut | 6.00 |
| Toy, Stand, Circus, Square, Schoenhut | 6.00 |
| Toy, Steam Boiler, Horizontal, Brass Tank, Marked Weeden, Cast-Iron Base | 45.00 |
| Toy, Steam Engine, Tin, Red & Black Paint, Weeden, 5 1/2 In. | 25.00 |
| Toy, Steam Engine, Weeden, Horizontal Shape, 8 In.Long | 85.00 |
| Toy, Steam Pumper, 3 Horses & Driver, Cast Iron, Colored, 18 In.Long | 150.00 |
| Toy, Steam Roller, Cast Iron, Huber, 8 In. | 10.00 |
| Toy, Steam Roller, Live Steam | 40.00 |
| Toy, Steam Roller, Painted, Cast Iron, Dent, 8 In. | 60.00 |
| Toy, Stove, Cast Iron, Royal, 7 In.High | 75.00 |
| Toy, Stove, Cook, Star, Wooden, 2 Pots | 11.95 |
| Toy, Stove, Gas Range, Royal, Green Paint, Cast Iron, 2 Burners | 18.00 |
| Toy, Stove, Hod & Pan, Royal, Cast Iron | 35.00 |
| Toy, Stove, Iron, Ideal, Bucket, Skillet, & Pot, 9 X 8 X 6 In. | 37.50 |
| Toy, Stove, Kitchen Range, Dollhouse, Cast Iron, Fancy | 5.00 |
| Toy, Stove, Kokomo, Electric, Tin, 8 X 9 1/2 In. | 16.00 |
| Toy, Stove, Little Orphan Annie, Signed Louis Marx | 36.00 |
| Toy, Stove, Orphan Annie, Electric, 3 Burner | 16.00 |
| Toy, Stove, Orphan Annie, Two Burners, 7 X 8 X 4 In. | 15.00 |
| Toy, Stove, Royal, Cast Iron, Nickel Plated, 2 Pots | 46.00 |
| Toy, Stove, Royal, Cast Iron, 2 Pans & Lifter | 35.00 |
| Toy, Stove, Tin, Colored, White Brick, Utensils, 7 In.High | 60.00 |
| Toy, Street Cleaner, Figures, Painted, Cast Iron, Hubley, 9 In. Long | 850.00 |
| Toy, Sulky, Horse Drawn, Driver, Iron, 5 In. | 30.00 |
| Toy, Superscope, Buck Rogers, 1950s | 18.00 |
| Toy, Surrey With Fringe On Top, Driver & Passenger, 2 Horse, Kenton | 60.00 |
| Toy, Surrey With Fringe On Top, 2 White Horses, Man & Woman, Iron, C.1920 | 35.00 |
| Toy, Sweeping Mammy, Windup, Lithographed, Tin, Lindstrom, 8 In. | 35.00 |
| Toy, Table & Chair, Doll's, Wooden, C.1900, 6 In.High | 10.00 |
| Toy, Table, Doll's, Ice Cream, Iron | 40.00 |
| Toy, Table, Dollhouse, 6 Legs | 14.00 |
| Toy, Talking Machine, Uncle Sam & Kaiser Bill, National Toy Co., Boxed | 45.00 |
| Toy, Talking Railroad Station, Lithographed, Pressboard, Keystone | 10.50 |
| Toy, Tank, Doughboy, Windup, Marx, 1840s | 25.00 |
| Toy, Tank, Marked U.S.Army No.3, Windup, Tin | 15.00 |
| Toy, Tank, Planet Patrol, Windup, Marx, 1940s | 25.00 |

Toy, **Tank,** Windup, Soldier Pops Up, Lithographed, Tin, Marx, 10 In. .................... 21.75
Toy, **Tank,** Wooden Wheels, Tootsietoy ...................................................................... 10.00
Toy, **Target Set,** Indian, Davy Crockett, Rifle, Figures, Keystone, 1950s ................ 8.00
Toy, **Taxi,** Amos & Andy, Original Box ...................................................................... 125.00
Toy, **Tea Set,** Alice In Wonderland, Plastic, Embossed Figures, 12 Piece ............... 6.00
Toy, **Tea Set,** Ceramic, Marked England, 12 Piece .................................................. 9.00
Toy, **Teddy Bear Playing Xylophone,** Pull Toy, Wooden, Fisher Price .................... 9.00
Toy, **Teddy Bear,** Golden, C.1920, 11 In.Tall .......................................................... 20.00
Toy, **Teddy Bear,** Holding Baby Bottle, Celluloid, Turtle Mark, 2 1/4 In. ............... 3.00
Toy, **Teddy Bear,** Movable Arms & Legs, Celluloid Eyes & Nose, 3 In.High .......... 10.00
Toy, **Teddy Bear,** Straw Stuffed, 19 In. ................................................................... 40.00
Toy, **Teddy Roosevelt,** Schoenhut ........................................................................... 45.00
Toy, **Teddy The Rhythmical Drummer,** Battery Operated, Japan, 12 In. ................ 7.00
Toy, **Telephone Set,** Wall, Dandy, 2 Piece .............................................................. 19.75
Toy, **Telephone,** Metal, Gong Bell ............................................................................ 6.50
Toy, **Telephone,** Space, Tom Corbett, 2 Way .......................................................... 7.25
Toy, **Tom-Tom Indian,** Battery Operated, Remote Control, Japan, 11 In. .............. 5.00
Toy, **Toonerville Trolley,** Tootsietoy ........................................................................ 22.50
Toy, **Top,** Mechanical, Spring Top, Colored, Tin, Drgm, Germany, Improved .......... 10.00
Toy, **Top,** Wooden, 2 1/2 In.High .............................................................................. 10.00
Toy, **Tractor Spreader,** McCormick Deering, Sheet Steel, Rubber Wheels ............. 8.00
Toy, **Tractor Trailer,** Metal, Ralstoy ......................................................................... 2.50
Toy, **Tractor,** Caterpillar, Diesel, Rubber Treads, Tootsietoy ................................... 5.50
Toy, **Tractor,** Climbing, Windup, Driver, Lithographed, Tin, Marx, 8 In. .................. 15.50
Toy, **Tractor,** Diesel Caterpillar, Tootsietoy ............................................................. 5.50
Toy, **Tractor,** Driver, Cast Metal, Wooden Wheels, C.1920 .................................... 4.00
Toy, **Tractor,** Harvester, Cast Metal, Wooden Wheels, Duct, C.1920 ...................... 3.00
Toy, **Tractor,** Rubber Wheels, Metal, Hubley, 6 In. .................................................. 6.00
Toy, **Tractor,** Windup, Driver, Lithographed, Tin, Marx, 9 In. .................................. 14.50
Toy, **Tractor,** Windup, Lithographed, Tin, Marx, 9 In. .............................................. 14.25
Toy, **Trailer,** Antiaircraft, Wooden Wheels, Tootsie Toy .......................................... 10.00
Toy, **Trailer,** Harvest, Gray Metal Wheels, Dinky Toy, No.320 ............................... 4.75
Toy, **Train Model Kit,** Wooden, Strombecker, Set Of 8 ............................................ 10.00
Toy, **Train Set,** American Flyer, No.312, 8 Piece ..................................................... 28.00
Toy, **Train Set,** American Flyer, Nos.21130, 637, & 650, 8 Piece ............................ 60.00
Toy, **Train Set,** American Flyer, Windup, 3 Cars, Track, 11 Piece ........................... 100.00
Toy, **Train Set,** Cast Iron, Engine Tender, 2 Flat Cars ............................................ 200.00
Toy, **Train Set,** Cast Iron, P.R.R.Narcissus, Hubley, 6 Piece ................................... 200.00
Toy, **Train Set,** Cast Iron, Painted, Wilkins, 3 Piece ................................................ 300.00
Toy, **Train Set,** Dent, 2 Gondolas, 2 Passengers, & 1 Caboose, 5 Piece ................ 25.00
Toy, **Train Set,** Ives, Key Wind, Cast-Iron Engine, Tin Tender, 3 Gauge Track ....... 135.00
Toy, **Train Set,** Ives, Nos. 3236, 185, 171, & 786, 4 Piece .................................... 100.00
Toy, **Train Set,** Ives, Windup, Cast-Iron Engine, 4 Tin Cars, & Track, C.1907 ........ 250.00
Toy, **Train Set,** Lionel, Model No.384, Coaches Light Up, 5 Piece ........................... 100.00
Toy, **Train Set,** Lionel, Nos 384T, 338, & 337, 3 Piece .......................................... 60.00
Toy, **Train Set,** P.R.R.Co., Cast Iron, 2 Piece ......................................................... 45.00
Toy, **Train Set,** Victor 11, Cast Iron, 3 Piece .......................................................... 15.00
Toy, **Train Set,** Windup, Lithographed, Tin, Marx, 8 Piece ...................................... 20.00
Toy, **Train Station,** Lionel, No.126 .......................................................................... 10.00
Toy, **Train,** Battery Operated, Lithographed, Tin, Cragstan .................................... 16.50
Toy, **Train,** Boxcar, No.4018, American Flyer, Standard Gauge .............................. 18.00
Toy, **Train,** Caboose, Lionel, Gauge 517 ................................................................ 25.00
Toy, **Train,** Caboose, No.4021, American Flyer, Standard Gauge ............................ 18.00
Toy, **Train,** Caboose, No.517, Lionel, Standard Gauge ........................................... 17.00
Toy, **Train,** Cast-Iron & Pressed Steel Cars, Pratt & Letchworth, 23 In.Long ......... 40.00
Toy, **Train,** Cattle Car, No.513, Lionel, Standard Gauge ......................................... 22.00
Toy, **Train,** Coach, Passenger, Cast Iron, America, 7 In. ........................................ 10.00
Toy, **Train,** Coal Car, Painted, Wilkins, 9 In. Long ................................................. 60.00
Toy, **Train,** Engine & Passenger Car, Cor-Cor-Toys, 24 In.Long ............................. 95.00
Toy, **Train,** Engine & 2 Tin Cars, 2 Switches, 16 Pieces Of Track, Marx ............... 70.00
Toy, **Train,** Flat Car, M.C.R.R., Cast Iron, 9 In. ...................................................... 7.50
Toy, **Train,** Freight Car, No.655, 4 Wheels Each Side ............................................ 8.00
Toy, **Train,** Freight Set, Lionel-Ives, Engine, Poor, Tender, & 3 Cars ..................... 50.00
Toy, **Train,** Gondola, Lionel, Gauge 512 ................................................................ 20.00
Toy, **Train,** Gondola, No.512, Lionel, Standard Gauge ........................... 10.00 To 22.00
Toy, **Train,** Honeymoon Express, Windup, Marx ..................................................... 10.00

| | |
|---|---:|
| Toy, Train, Lionel, Caboose, No.657, 8 1/2 In. | 8.00 |
| Toy, Train, Lionel, Engine, No.1684, Electric, 9 In. | 8.00 |
| Toy, Train, Lionel, Passenger, Olive, Engine, 2 Coaches, Standard No.33 | 295.00 |
| Toy, Train, Locomotive & Tender, Painted, Cast Iron, PRR, 13 In. | 30.00 |
| Toy, Train, Metal, Engine, Passenger Car, Cov-Car Toys, 24 In.Long | 195.00 |
| Toy, Train, Mono Rail, Vineta, Lehmann | 160.00 |
| Toy, Train, Passenger Car, Ives, O Gauge | 11.85 |
| Toy, Train, Passenger Car, No.35, Lionel, Standard Gauge | 15.00 |
| Toy, Train, Passenger Car, No.36, Lionel, Standard Gauge | 15.00 |
| Toy, Train, Refrigerator Car, No.514R, Lionel, Standard Gauge | 12.00 |
| Toy, Train, Santa Fe Granague, Coach, Cast Iron, Red Paint | 30.00 |
| Toy, Train, Streamline Railway, Pull, Wooden Wheels, Tin, Wyandotte, 17 In. | 12.50 |
| Toy, Train, Super Chief, Windup, Lithographed, Pressed Steel, Marx, 7 In. | 6.50 |
| Toy, Train, Tank Car, No.4010, American Flyer, Standard Gauge | 18.00 |
| Toy, Train, Tank Car, No.515, Lionel, Standard Gauge | 10.00 |
| Toy, Train, Tippy Toy, Runs On Track, Bells, Automatic, 1940s | 8.50 |
| Toy, Train, Windup, Track, Station House, U.S.Zone, Germany | 12.50 |
| Toy, Train, Zephyr 9900, Silver, Tootsie Toy, 3 3/4 In.Long | 5.00 |
| **Toy, Trapeze Girl, Schoenhut** | 48.00 |
| Toy, Trolley, Kingsbury, Orange, 14 In. | 90.00 |
| Toy, Truck, Armored, Half Track, Wooden Wheels, Tootsie Toy, 4 In. | 10.00 |
| Toy, Truck, Bell Telephone, Metal, Hubley, 8 In. | 15.00 |
| Toy, Truck, Bell Telephone, Rubber Wheels, Metal, Hubley, 12 In. | 22.50 |
| Toy, Truck, Blue, Arcade | 15.00 |
| Toy, Truck, Cast Iron, Champion, 7 1/2 In. | 35.00 |
| Toy, Truck, Cement Mixing, Black Rubber Wheels, Red Cab, Hubley, 10 In. | 15.00 |
| Toy, Truck, City, Driver, 2 Horse, Cast Iron, Wilkins | 500.00 |
| Toy, Truck, Dairy, Elsie, The Borden Cow. Wooden. Glass Bottles, Fischer, 1940 | 16.25 |
| Toy, Truck, Delivery, Nickel Plated Wheels, Red, Arcade, 6 In. | 50.00 |
| Toy, Truck, Delivery, Supermarket, Rubber Wheels, Buddy L, 13 In. | 13.50 |
| Toy, Truck, Driver, E.H.E.Co., Lehmann | 115.00 |
| Toy, Truck, Driver, Friction, May-Stern, Pittsburgh, Pa. | 100.00 |
| Toy, Truck, Dump, Cast Iron, Mack, 12 In. | 130.00 |
| Toy, Truck, Dump, Metal, C.1928 | 25.00 |
| Toy, Truck, Dump, Metal, Structo, 14 In.Long | 4.00 |
| Toy, Truck, Dump, Sand & Gravel, Lithographed, Metal, Marx, 11 In. | 6.50 |
| Toy, Truck, Dump, Tin, Blue & Red, C.1930 | 8.00 |
| Toy, Truck, Dump, Windup, Driver, Tin, Nifty, German, C.1920, 10 In. | 125.00 |
| Toy, Truck, Emergency, Search Light, Metal, Marx, 17 In. | 12.00 |
| Toy, Truck, Fire, Cast Iron, Dent Sample, 7 In. Long | 60.00 |
| Toy, Truck, Fire, Driver, Water Tank At Rear, Cast Iron, Rubber Tires, Red | 25.00 |
| Toy, Truck, Fire, Hose, Pumper, Ladder, Rubber Wheels, Metal, Germany, 1945 | 15.00 |
| Toy, Truck, Fire, Ladder & Men, Cast Iron, Dent Sample, 18 In. | 300.00 |
| Toy, Truck, Fire, Red Paint, Metal, Marked Hubley, 8 In.Long | 3.75 |
| Toy, Truck, Fire, Rubber Tires, Ladders, 2 Drivers, Aluminum, Freeport Toy | 10.50 |
| Toy, Truck, Fire, Rubber Wheels, Metal, Buddy L, 1940s | 19.50 |
| Toy, Truck, Fire, Steamer, Cast Iron, Red, Nickel Plate, Hubley, C.1920 | 20.00 |
| Toy, Truck, Fire, 2 Ladders, Lithographed, Tin, Wyandotte, 8 In. | 5.75 |
| Toy, Truck, French, Bonnet & Co. | 55.00 |
| Toy, Truck, Friction, Driver, Tin, 10 1/2 In. | 57.00 |
| Toy, Truck, Gas, Mac Cab, Cast Iron, Steel Wheels, Red Paint, 5 1/4 In.Long | 29.00 |
| Toy, Truck, Grocery, Lithographed, Metal, Marx, 15 In. | 14.75 |
| Toy, Truck, H.J.Heinz, 12 In. | 30.00 |
| Toy, Truck, Hook & Ladder, Cast Iron, Kenton, 22 In. | 60.00 |
| Toy, Truck, Hook & Ladder, 2 Horse, Figures, Cast Iron, Dent | 350.00 |
| Toy, Truck, Hook & Ladder, 3 Horse, Dent | 360.00 |
| Toy, Truck, Hose Reel, 3 Horse, Figures, Dent, 24 In. | 400.00 |
| Toy, Truck, Hose Reel, 3 Horse, Figures, Hose, Dent | 350.00 |
| Toy, Truck, Ice, Balloon Tires, Iron, Arcade, 7 In. | 65.00 |
| Toy, Truck, Ice, Canvas Tarpaulin, Ice Tongs, Buddy L, 21 In. | 18.50 |
| Toy, Truck, Ice, Tongs, Keg Of Ice, Marx, 14 In.Long | 13.50 |
| Toy, Truck, Ice, Tongs, Marx, 14 In. | 14.50 |
| Toy, Truck, Ladder, Rubber Wheels, Hubley, 5 In. | 4.00 |
| Toy, Truck, Livestock, Lithographed, Tin, Marcrest, Marx, 17 In. | 12.00 |
| Toy, Truck, Log Roller, Tootsietoy, 8 In. | 4.75 |
| Toy, Truck, Milk, White Rubber Tires, Barclay, 3 1/2 In. | 6.00 |

| | |
|---|---|
| Toy, Truck, Oil Tank, Faucet At Back, Cast Iron, Buddy L, 25 1/2 In. | 150.00 |
| Toy, Truck, Packard, Express | 80.00 |
| Toy, Truck, Sand & Gravel, Buddy L, 13 In. | 6.50 |
| Toy, Truck, Sand & Gravel, Tin Wheels, Lithographed, Metal, Marx, 16 In. | 13.50 |
| Toy, Truck, Sand Loader & Dump, Rubber Wheels, Buddy L, 22 In. | 17.25 |
| Toy, Truck, Solid Wheels, White, Tin, Structo, 18 In.Long | 30.00 |
| Toy, Truck, Stake, Mac Cab, Cast Iron, Steel Wheels, Blue Paint, 4 3/4 In.Long | 29.00 |
| Toy, Truck, Tin, Lithographed, Marked 1919, Toyland Pie Bakery | 27.00 |
| Toy, Truck, Tin, Metalcraft, St.Louis | 35.00 |
| Toy, Truck, Towing Service, Windup, Rubber Wheels, Metal, Metal Master | 8.75 |
| Toy, Truck, U.S.Mail, Mack, 2 Ft. | 49.00 |
| Toy, Truck, Winch, Steam Shovel, Tin Wheels, Marx, 20 In. | 15.00 |
| Toy, Truck, Windup, Rubber Wheels, Metal, Structo, 12 In. | 11.50 |
| Toy, Truck, Wrecker, Metal, Buddy L, 15 In.Long | 10.00 |
| Toy, Truck, 5 Wooden Barrels, Kingsbury | 85.00 |
| Toy, Trunk, see Trunk | |
| Toy, Two Coolies With Tea Chest, Peking, Nanking, & Kanton, Lehmann | 270.00 |
| Toy, Two Horse Drawn Surrey With Fringe On Top, Man & Lady, Iron, Stanley | 60.00 |
| Toy, Typewriter, Dollhouse, Moving Roller, 1 1/2 In.High | 8.50 |
| Toy, Uniform, Tom Corbett, Space Cadet | 8.50 |
| Toy, Vacuum Cleaner, Metal, Battery Operated, Super Cleaners | 7.00 |
| Toy, Van, Long Distance Moving, Metal Wheels, Lithographed, Marx, 15 In. | 9.75 |
| Toy, Vehicle, Century Cycle, 3 Wheel, Lehmann | 85.00 |
| Toy, Village, Centerville, Metal Manoil Vehicles, Skyline, Boxed | 9.25 |
| Toy, Village, Wooden Block, 5 Buildings, Lithographed, Keystone | 7.25 |
| Toy, Wagon, Cast Iron, Nickel Plated Wheels, Blue Box, 3 3/4 In.Long | 10.00 |
| Toy, Wagon, Champion Express, Red, 4 1/2 In. | 3.00 |
| Toy, Wagon, Chuck, Campbell Kids, Boxed | 12.50 |
| Toy, Wagon, Contractor's, Horses, Painted, Kenton | 75.00 |
| Toy, Wagon, Dump, 2 Horse, Lever Releases Bottom, Cast Iron, Kenton | 30.00 |
| Toy, Wagon, Express, Goat-Drawn, Driver, Iron, Red | 45.00 |
| Toy, Wagon, Farm, Driver, 2 Horse, Cast Iron, Kenton, 15 In. | 40.00 |
| Toy, Wagon, Farm, 2 Horse, Cast Iron, McCormick Deering, 12 1/2 In. | 40.00 |
| Toy, Wagon, Farm, 2 Horse, Figure, Cast Iron, Kenton, 14 1/2 In. | 45.00 |
| Toy, Wagon, Fire, Horse, Driver, Tin, Red, Windup, Orobr, Germany | 55.00 |
| Toy, Wagon, Gibbs, Lithograph, Single Horse | 65.00 |
| Toy, Wagon, Hook & Ladder, 3 Horse, Eagle & Shield On Side, Cast Iron, Hubley | 150.00 |
| Toy, Wagon, Hook & Ladder, 3 Horses, Cast Iron, Kenton, 17 In. Long | 60.00 |
| Toy, Wagon, Log, Driver, 1 Horse, Kenton, 14 1/2 In. | 110.00 |
| Toy, Wagon, Milk, Cast Iron, Kenton | 70.00 |
| Toy, Wagon, Milk, Two Dappled Gray Horses, Tin, 17 In. | 62.00 |
| Toy, Wagon, Stake, Horses, Painted, Kenton | 75.00 |
| Toy, Wagon, Stake, 2 Horse, Kenton, Original Box | 40.00 |
| Toy, Wagon, Wooden, 7 X 5 In. | 15.00 |
| Toy, Walking Egg-Laying Tin Duck, Windup, Painted | 35.00 |
| Toy, Washboard, Glass, Marked Midget-Washer, 9 X 6 In. | 20.00 |
| Toy, Washing Bear, Bubblers, Tin, Battery Operated, Rosko Steele, Inc., No.825 | 20.00 |
| Toy, Washing Machine, Sunny Suzy, Wolverine, Tin, 8 1/2 In.High | 16.00 |
| Toy, Washing Set, Iron & Wood, Little Darling, 3 Piece | 18.00 |
| Toy, Washtub & Washboard, Tin, Wood, & Metal, 6 1/2 In.Diameter | 4.50 |
| Toy, Water Pump, Sand Toy, Lithographed, Ohio Art, 10 In.High | 6.25 |
| Toy, Water Tank Truck, Buddy L, Decals | 125.00 |
| Toy, Western Figure, Lead, Made In England, Hand-Painted, Set Of 6 | 5.00 |
| Toy, Western Town, Roy Rogers, Lithographed, Tin, Marx | 22.50 |
| Toy, Western Union Telegraph Set | 15.00 |
| Toy, Wheel Hose Cart, Team Of Horses, Cast Iron, Colored, 4 Wheel, 20 In.Long | 300.00 |
| Toy, Wheelbarrow, Cast Iron, Steel Wheel, Red Paint, Kilgore, 3 3/4 In.Long | 20.00 |
| Toy, Wheelbarrow, Iron, 6 In.Long | 18.00 |
| Toy, Wheelbarrow, Iron, 6 1/2 In.Long | 11.75 |
| Toy, Whirligig, Flying Goose, Carved & Painted, 32 In.Long | 400.00 |
| Toy, Whirligig, Derby-Hatted Man, C.1850 ................................................ *Illus* | 1000.00 |
| Toy, Whirligig, 19th Century, 9 1/2 In. | 400.00 |
| Toy, Whirligig, Top-Hatted Man, C.1850, 17 1/2 In. High ................ *Illus* | 1200.00 |
| Toy, Wolverine Bowler, Andy Mill, Patent Oct.20, 1914, 20 In.High | 18.00 |
| Toy, Wonder Cyclist, Windup, Marx | 65.00 |
| Toy, Woody Woodpecker, Slides Down Metal Pole, 18 In. | 9.00 |

Toy, Whirligig, Top-Hatted Man,
C.1850, 17 1/2 In. High
(See Page 676)

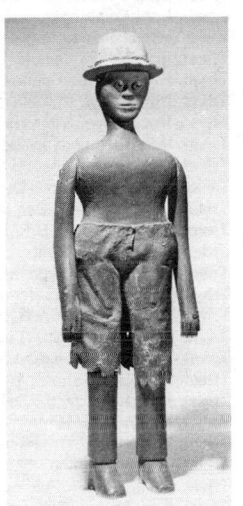

Toy, Whirligig, Derby-Hatted Man, C.1850
(See Page 676)

| | |
|---|---|
| Toy, Wrecker, Cast Iron, Steel Hauling Hook & Wheels, Green Paint, 4 3/4 In. | 22.50 |
| Toy, Wrecker, Nickel Wheels, Red, Arcade, 4 1/2 In. Long | 35.00 |
| Trampwork, Frame, Picture, Double, Cuttings, Star Trim, 14 X 9 1/4 In. | 20.00 |
| Trap, see Tool, Trap | |

*Treen are small wooden objects such as mugs, spoons, and bowls. The term is
early English but is used in the United States in many areas.*

| | |
|---|---|
| Treen, Chalice, 7 In., Pair | 40.00 |
| Treen, Needle Case, Barrel Shape, Revolving Top, German | 15.00 |
| Treen, Spoon, Serpentine Decoration, 15 In.Long | 21.00 |
| Treen, Sugar, Covered, Lathe Turned, Round Foot, 8 In.High | 85.00 |

*Trivets are now used to hold hot dishes. Most of the late nineteenth and
early twentieth century trivets were made to hold hot irons. Iron or brass
reproductions are being made of many of the old styles. The H-xx numbers
refer to the book "Trivets" by Dick Hankerson.*

| | |
|---|---|
| Trivet, Brass & Iron, Fireplace, Lyre, Adjustable | 52.00 |
| Trivet, Brass, Design, Handle, 8 1/2 In. | 20.00 |
| Trivet, Brass, Design, Handle, 9 1/2 In. | 25.00 |
| Trivet, Brass, Geometric, Handle, 9 In. | 26.00 |
| Trivet, Brass, Hearts, Lovebirds, 6 Point Star Top, Handle, 8 1/2 In. | 35.00 |
| Trivet, Brass, Inverted Hearts, Handle, 7 1/2 In. | 20.00 |
| Trivet, Brass, Marked China, Square, Burnished, Lacquered | 7.00 |
| Trivet, Brass, Oor Ain Fireside, 3 Footed, 6 In. Diameter | 18.75 |
| Trivet, Brass, Openwork Center, Flower Border, Marked China, 4 Footed, 5 In. | 4.95 |
| Trivet, Brass, Openwork Center, Flowered Border, China, 4 Footed, 5 In. | 4.95 |
| Trivet, Brass, Pierced Heart Design, 3 Footed, 6 In. Diameter | 18.00 |
| Trivet, Brass, Royal Coat Of Arms, Elizabeth II, 1953, Footed | 7.00 |
| Trivet, Brass, Schooner Design, 4 Paw Feet, 10 1/8 X 3 1/8 In. | 78.00 |
| Trivet, Brass, Turtle, Head Is Handle, Cannon, 9 In. | 15.00 |
| Trivet, Brass, Two Inverted Hearts, Handle, 7 1/2 In. | 20.00 |
| Trivet, Brass, Two Inverted Hearts, Handle, 8 1/2 In. | 20.00 |
| Trivet, Iron, B & D, H-124 | 4.75 |
| Trivet, Iron, B & D, H-134 | 4.75 |
| Trivet, Iron, Bird, Tulip Head Ends, Bird's Head, Handle, 8 In. | 15.00 |
| Trivet, Iron, Blacksmith Made, Wooden Handle, 13 In. | 45.00 |
| Trivet, Iron, Bust Of George Washington, 9 1/4 In. | 60.00 |
| Trivet, Iron, Cathedral, No.1, Handled, H-44 | 6.95 |
| Trivet, Iron, Cathedral, No.2, Handled, H-45 | 5.95 To 6.95 |

Trivet, Iron, Center Design In Scalloped Circle, Handle, 7 1/2 In. ......................... 8.00
Trivet, Iron, Child's, Cathedral, Handled, H-159 ..................................... 4.95
Trivet, Iron, Colebrookdale Crown & Maltese Cross, H-120 ......................... 4.95
Trivet, Iron, Coleman Mfg.Co. ...................................................... 10.00
Trivet, Iron, Colt, 3 Legs, 6 1/2 In. ................................. 15.00 To 20.00
Trivet, Iron, Crossed Cannons, Pryamid Cannonballs, 8 1/4 In. ..................... 20.00
Trivet, Iron, Crown & Maltese Cross, Colebrookdale, H-120 ......................... 4.95
Trivet, Iron, Crown & Maltese Cross, Royal, H-85 ................................. 6.95
Trivet, Iron, Diamonds In Center Of Hearts, H-24 ................................. 6.75
Trivet, Iron, E, Enterprise, H-114 .................................................. 4.95
Trivet, Iron, E, Openwork Center, Enterprise Mfg.Co., Phila., 3 Footed ............ 15.00
Trivet, Iron, Enterprise Bar, H-115 ................................................ 4.95
Trivet, Iron, Ferrosteel Urn, H-121 ................................................ 4.95
Trivet, Iron, Firespit Center, Mrs.Potts Crown Iron, Phila., 3 Footed ............. 15.00
Trivet, Iron, Flatiron Type, Blacksmith Made ...................................... 8.00
Trivet, Iron, Geometric, Handled, Toy, H-165 ...................................... 4.75
Trivet, Iron, H Co The W.H.Howell Co., Geneva Ill., H-124 ......................... 4.95
Trivet, Iron, Heart Shape, Bird Center, 2 Birds' Heads Handles, Tulips, Legs ...... 15.00
Trivet, Iron, H 2 H, General Specialty Co., H-63, Book 2 ................. 4.95 To 6.75
Trivet, Iron, Heart Shape, 9 1/2 In. Long ......................................... 100.00
Trivet, Iron, Heart With W, Handle, H-50 .......................................... 6.75
Trivet, Iron, Hearts, Figurative Handle, 9 1/2 In. ................................ 22.50
Trivet, Iron, Hearts, Ornamented Handle, 13 In. Long .............................. 80.00
Trivet, Iron, Horseshoe, Handle, "Good Luck To All," H-35 ......................... 9.75
Trivet, Iron, Lacy Urn, Victorian ................................................. 9.50
Trivet, Iron, Military Crossed Cannons, Pyramid Cannonballs, 8 1/4 In. ............ 20.00
Trivet, Iron, Nesco, Nickel Plated, Double Decked, Porcelain Feet ................. 15.00
Trivet, Iron, Oblong Waffle, H-75 ................................................. 4.95
Trivet, Iron, Openwork Roses & L-Pointed Star, Round, Lantz, 6 Paw Feet ........... 6.95
Trivet, Iron, Openwork, H-98 ...................................................... 4.95
Trivet, Brass, Openwork, Marked China, 4 Footed, 5 1/8 In. Diameter ............... 4.95
Trivet, Iron, Rope Border Center, Heart & Acorn Ends, Ives & Allen, Montreal ...... 15.00
Trivet, Iron, Royal W Crown & Maltese Cross, H-85 ................................. 6.95
Trivet, Iron, Spider Web, H-90 .................................................... 4.95
Trivet, Iron, Spider Web, Victorian ............................................... 6.50
Trivet, Iron, Squares, 1 3/4 In. .................................................. 6.00
Trivet, Iron, Star & Fan, The Cleveland Foundry Co., 3 Footed ..................... 15.00
Trivet, Iron, Star & Heart, Handle, 3 Legs, 4 1/2 In. ............................. 8.00
Trivet, Iron, Star & Sunburst, The Cleveland Foundry Co., H-122 ......... 4.95 To 5.95
Trivet, Iron, Star & Sunburst, Victorian .......................................... 8.50
Trivet, Iron, Star In Interlocking Circle, 7 1/2 In. Diameter ..................... 25.00
Trivet, Iron, T In Diamond, H-141 ................................................. 7.75
Trivet, Iron, T, Diamond Shape, 6 3/4 In. ......................................... 8.00
Trivet, Iron, Target, Handled, H-55 ............................................... 5.95
Trivet, Iron, Toy, Triangular, Handle ............................................. 4.75
Trivet, Iron, X In Middle, Pushed-In Sides Design, 5 X 3 1/2 In. .................. 15.00
Trivet, Iron, X Tip, 2 Hearts In Diamond Point, Handle, 3 Legs, 7 1/4 In. ......... 15.00
Trunk, Doll's, Domed Top, Wooden, Newspaper Lining, Dated 1844 .................... 14.00
Trunk, Doll's, Flat Top, Wooden, Fabric Covered, Metal & Wood Strips .............. 30.00
Trunk, Doll's, Metal Covered, Wood ................................................ 12.50
Trunk, Doll's, Metal, Brass Hinges & Corners, Pink, 12 X 7 In. .................... 6.50
Trunk, Humpback, 26 X 15 In. ...................................................... 12.00
Trunk, Wooden, Dome Top, Red Paint, 17 In. ........................................ 50.00
Trunk, Wooden, Painted, Domed, New England, C.1800 ......................... *Illus* 100.00
Typewriter, Blickensderfer No.5 ................................................... 15.00
Typewriter, Corona, Portable ...................................................... 10.00
Typewriter, Corona, Portable, Patent 1917, Leather Case ........................... 15.00
Typewriter, Oliver, No.5, Patent 1894, Inverted U Keys Upright .................... 200.00
Umbrella, Lady's Parasol, Carved Wood, Embroidered Linen, Straight ................ 30.00
Union Porcelain Works, Plate, Oyster, Irregular Shape, White, Gold Trim ........... 45.00
Union Porcelain Works, Vase, Pitcher Plant With Turtle, Signed U.P.W.-1877 ........ 350.00

*Val St Lambert*     *Val St.Lambert Cristalleries of Belgium was founded by Messieurs*
                          *Kemlin and Lelievre in 1825. The company is still in operation.*

Val St.Lambert, Bowl, Crystal, Acid Cut, Four Fruits, 6 X 1 1/4 In. ............... 18.00
Val St.Lambert, Bowl, Cut & Pressed, Clear, Decorated Metal Rim, 5 In. ............ 28.00

Trunk, Wooden, Painted, Domed,
New England, C.1800
*(See Page 678)*

| | |
|---|---:|
| Val St.Lambert, Bowl, Cut & Pressed, Crystal, Metal Rim, 5 In.Diameter | 28.00 |
| Val St.Lambert, Box, Biscuit, Cranberry Iris On Frosted, Brass Top & Bail | 315.00 |
| Val St.Lambert, Box, Bust Of Woman & Baby On Lid, Acid Etched Green, 4 In. | 58.00 |
| Val St.Lambert, Ewer, Cameo, Handle, Red On White Ground, 14 In.High | 350.00 |
| Val St.Lambert, Goblet, Cut Crystal, Signed | 45.00 |
| Val St.Lambert, Knife Rest, Amber | 23.00 |
| Val St.Lambert, Sherbet, Cranberry Cased | 25.00 |
| Val St.Lambert, Vase, Bottle Shape, Green On Frosted, Blossoms, 7 3/4 In. | 225.00 |
| Val St.Lambert, Vase, Bud, Pedestal, Cobalt Blue, 6 In.High | 95.00 |
| Val St.Lambert, Vase, Bud, Silver Rim On Narrow Neck, Clove Bulbous Bottom | 149.00 |
| Val St.Lambert, Vase, Bud, Silver Rim, Brown Mottling Over Green Opaque | 169.00 |
| Val St.Lambert, Vase, Cameo, Purple Poppies, Leaves In Relief, 8 In.High | 275.00 |
| Val St.Lambert, Vase, Carved Brown Poppies On Orange Satin, 4 1/2 In. | 180.00 |
| Val St.Lambert, Vase, Cylindrical, Lavender On Mottled, Daffodils, 10 In. | 100.00 |
| Val St.Lambert, Vase, Fleur-De-Lis In Bronze To Cobalt, Signed, 13 X 5 In. | 150.00 |
| Vallerystahl, Compote, Frosted & Clear Leaves, Footed, Signed, 6 In. High | 30.00 |
| Vallerystahl, Dish, Divided, Feather, Clambroth, Signed, 14 In. | 37.50 |
| Vallerystahl, Dish, Swan, Covered, Milk Glass, Open Neck, 6 In. | 75.00 |
| Vallerystahl, Plate, Frosted Thistled Flowers, Scalloped, Signed, 8 1/2 In. | 36.00 |
| Vallerystahl, Plate, Green Floral, 8 1/2 In. | 25.00 |

 Van Briggle Pottery was made by Artus Van Briggle in Colorado Springs, Colorado, after 1901. Mr.Van Briggle had been a decorator at the Rookwood Pottery of Cincinnati, Ohio, and he died in 1904. His wares were original and had modeled relief decorations with a soft dull glaze.

| | |
|---|---:|
| Van Briggle, Bookend, Owl, Ming Blue, Signed AA, Pair | 35.00 |
| Van Briggle, Bookend, Ship, Maroon, Pair | 16.00 |
| Van Briggle, Bowl, Conch Shape, Colorado Springs, Turquoise, 4 In.High | 25.00 |
| Van Briggle, Bowl, Plum, Pulled Leaf, Impressed Artist P, 6 In.Deep | 22.00 |
| Van Briggle, Bowl, Shaded Blues, Embossed Mushrooms | 15.00 |
| Van Briggle, Bowl, Tulip, Oblong, Frog, 8 In.Diameter | 20.00 |
| Van Briggle, Bowl, With Flower Frog, Dragonflies, Green, 8 1/2 In.Wide | 80.00 |
| Van Briggle, Candlestick, Tulips, Pair | 7.00 |
| Van Briggle, Console Set, Petal Bowl, Star Plate, Frog, Maroon, 4 Piece | 42.00 |
| Van Briggle, Console Set, Shell Bowl, Low Candlesticks, Rose Color, 3 Piece | 50.00 |
| Van Briggle, Figurine, Nude Girl Kneeling With Shell In Lap, Blue | 75.00 |
| Van Briggle, Flower Center, Brown, 3 Frogs, Dated 1910 | 45.00 |
| Van Briggle, Lamp Base, Blue-Green, Parrot On Tree Limb.9 1/2 In.High | 38.00 |
| Van Briggle, Plate, Stylized Decoration, Blue To Green, 6 In.Diameter | 25.00 |
| Van Briggle, Rose Bowl, Red, 3 In.Diameter | 10.00 |
| Van Briggle, Vase, Bud, Mulberry Color, Signed AA, Dated 1917, 8 In. | 18.50 |
| Van Briggle, Vase, Bud, Persian Rose, 8 In.High | 20.00 |
| Van Briggle, Vase, Bud, Turquoise Matte Glaze, Signed, 4 1/2 In.High | 6.00 |
| Van Briggle, Vase, Bulbous Base, Stick Top, Maroon, Flowers, 6 1/2 In.High | 12.00 |
| Van Briggle, Vase, Butterfly Design, Mountain Crag Brown, 3 3/4 In.High | 25.00 |
| Van Briggle, Vase, Dragonfly, Brown, Green, 7 In.High | 16.00 |
| Van Briggle, Vase, Four American Indians' Heads On Red Glaze | 85.00 |
| Van Briggle, Vase, Green Tulips, 6 In.High | 12.00 |
| Van Briggle, Vase, Indian, Mulberry, Signed, 11 1/4 In.High | 150.00 |
| Van Briggle, Vase, Leaf Decoration On Aqua, 4 1/2 In. | 12.00 |
| Van Briggle, Vase, Persian Rose, Stylized Butterflies.3 3/4 In.High | 22.00 |

| | |
|---|---|
| Van Briggle, Vase, Petal Shape Top, White, Hand-Decorated, 3 In. | 20.00 |
| Van Briggle, Vase, Plum, 1937, 7 1/2 In. | 9.00 |
| Van Briggle, Vase, Red Tulips, 6 In.High | 15.00 |
| Van Briggle, Vase, Seated Nude Girl Holding Shell, Blue, 7 In. | 35.00 |
| Van Briggle, Vase, Shell, Turquoise Matte Glaze, 4 In.High, 9 In.Long | 24.00 |
| Van Briggle, Vase, Stylized Decoration, Blue To Turquoise, Dated 1918, 7 In. | 45.00 |
| Van Briggle, Vase, Tan Color, Dated 1905, 13 In.High | 32.50 |
| Van Briggle, Vase, Three Molded Indians' Heads, Rose & Blue, 11 In.High | 100.00 |
| Van Briggle, Vase, Tulip Shape, Cream Color, 3 1/2 In.High | 20.00 |
| Van Briggle, Vase, Tulips, 9 1/2 In.High | 18.00 |
| Van Briggle, Vase, Turquoise, Dated 1919, 3 1/4 In.High | 35.00 |

*Vasa Murrhina is the name of a glassware made by the Vasa Murrhina
Art Glass Company of Sandwich, Massachusetts, about 1884. The
glassware was transparent and was embedded with small pieces of colored glass
and metallic flakes. Some of the pieces were cased. The same type of glass
was made in England. Collectors often confuse Vasa Murrhina glass with
aventurine, spatter, or spangle glass. There is much confusion about what
actually was made by the Vasa Murrhina Factory.*

| | |
|---|---|
| Vasa Murrhina, Bowl, Crimped & Ruffled Rim, Blue With Silver Mica, 8 In. | 87.50 |
| Vasa Murrhina, Bride's Basket, Blue, Twisted Thorn Handle | 135.00 |
| Vasa Murrhina, Candlestick, Amber, Gold Mica, Blue Threading, 8 1/2 In., Pair | 80.00 |
| Vasa Murrhina, Jar, Biscuit, Melon Ribbed, Fruit, Silver Plate Top & Handle | 115.00 |
| Vasa Murrhina, Rose Bowl, Spangle, Cased, Pink, Maroon Splotches, Gold, Lined | 95.00 |
| Vasa Murrhina, Tumbler, Gold Flecks On Salmon, Inside Cased Deep Rose | 50.00 |
| Vasa Murrhina, Vase, Blue, Silver Mica & Threading, Melon Ribbed, Handles | 85.00 |
| Vasa Murrhina, Vase, Melon Shape, Pink Cased, Mica Flecks, Ruffled, 7 In. | 42.00 |
| Vasa Murrhina, Vase, Mica On Pink & White, Applied Clear Rigaree, Pair | 65.00 |
| Vasa Murrhina, Vase, Pink Cased, Mica Flakes, Melon Ribbing, 7 In.High | 42.00 |
| Vasa Murrhina, Vase, Pink, Cased, Handled, 9 In. High | 95.00 |

*Vasart is the signature used on a late type of art glass made by the
Streathearn Glass Company of Scotland.*

| | |
|---|---|
| Vasart, Bowl & Underplate, Finger, Brown With Yellow, Signed | 35.00 |
| Vasart, Bowl, Mottled Blue Top, Yellow Bottom, 4 3/4 In.Diameter | 35.00 |
| Vasart, Hat, Top, Pink, Signed, 2 In.High | 17.00 |
| Vasart, Vase, Mottled Orange, Green Rim, 8 In.High, Signed | 75.00 |

*Vaseline glass is a greenish yellow glassware resembling petroleum jelly.
Some vaseline glass is still being made in old and new styles. Pressed
glass of the 1870s was often made of vaseline-colored glass. The old glass
was made with uranium, but the reproductions are being colored in a different
way. See Pressed Glass for more information about patterns that were also
made of vaseline-colored glass.*

**Vaseline Glass, see also Pressed Glass**

| | |
|---|---|
| Vaseline Glass, Basket, Hanging, Opalescent Trim, English, 8 1/2 In.High | 165.00 |
| Vaseline Glass, Basket, Wildflower, Oblong, 11 In.To Top Of Handle | 125.00 |
| Vaseline Glass, Berry Set, Daisy & Button With Crossbar, 5 Piece | 62.00 |
| Vaseline Glass, Boat, Daisy & Button, 12 1/2 X 4 1/4 X 2 3/4 In. | 32.00 |
| Vaseline Glass, Boat, Daisy & Button, 13 In. | 43.00 |
| Vaseline Glass, Bottle, Castor, Inverted Thumbprint | 6.50 |
| Vaseline Glass, Bowl & Underplate, Threaded | 48.00 |
| Vaseline Glass, Bowl, Berry, Daisy & Button With V Ornament | 45.00 |
| Vaseline Glass, Bowl, Berry, Daisy & Button, Four Scallops At Top, Oval | 65.00 |
| Vaseline Glass, Bowl, Diamond-Quilted, Footed, 9 In. | 29.50 |
| Vaseline Glass, Bowl, Punch, Daisy & Button, Footed | 135.00 |
| Vaseline Glass, Bowl, Punch, Daisy & Button, Paneled, Starred Buttons, 10 In. | 135.00 |
| Vaseline Glass, Bowl, Stretch, 4 Fluted Panels, Iridescent, 10 1/2 In. | 22.50 |
| Vaseline Glass, Bowl, Waste, Maple Leaf, Footed, Oval | 32.50 |
| Vaseline Glass, Brandy Set, 7 Piece | 35.00 |
| Vaseline Glass, Bride's Bowl, Tricorn Shape, Opalescent Hearts Body, 8 In. | 48.00 |
| Vaseline Glass, Butter Pat, Daisy & Button With V Ornament | 14.00 |
| Vaseline Glass, Butter, Covered, Maple Leaf, Footed | 65.00 |
| Vaseline Glass, Butter, Flatiron Shape | 45.00 |
| Vaseline Glass, Butter, Fluted Scrolls, Covered, Northwood | 50.00 |
| Vaseline Glass, Butter, Leaf Mold, Frosted, Spatter Decoration | 75.00 |

| | |
|---|---|
| Vaseline Glass, Cake Stand, Pressed Diamond, 9 3/4 In. | 39.50 |
| Vaseline Glass, Candlestick, Petal, Round, Flint, Pair | 200.00 |
| Vaseline Glass, Candlestick, Swirl Base, 3 1/2 In.High, Pair | 15.00 |
| Vaseline Glass, Candlestick, Twist Stem, 7 In.High, Pair | 40.00 |
| Vaseline Glass, Candlesticks, 3 In.High, Pair | 25.00 |
| Vaseline Glass, Celery, Daisy & Button With Crossbar | 32.00 |
| Vaseline Glass, Celery, Daisy & Button With V Ornament | 58.00 |
| Vaseline Glass, Celery, Daisy & Button With V Ornament, Scalloped Rim | 40.00 |
| Vaseline Glass, Champagne, Daisy & Button With Thumbprint Stripe | 30.00 |
| Vaseline Glass, Cologne, Diamond & Stars, Clear Stopper | 12.00 |
| Vaseline Glass, Compote, Cathedral, Fluted, 10 1/2 X 8 In. | 55.00 |
| Vaseline Glass, Compote, Covered, Daisy & Button With Thumbprint, Square | 125.00 |
| Vaseline Glass, Compote, Dolphin | 35.00 |
| Vaseline Glass, Compote, Dolphin, Opalescent | 35.00 |
| Vaseline Glass, Compote, Finecut & Panel, 10 In.Diameter, 5 3/4 In.High | 48.50 |
| Vaseline Glass, Compote, Jelly, Intaglio, Opalescent | 35.00 |
| Vaseline Glass, Compote, Three Panel, Low Standard, 7 In. | 22.00 |
| Vaseline Glass, Creamer, Cathedral | 36.00 |
| Vaseline Glass, Creamer, Child's, Austrian | 50.00 |
| Vaseline Glass, Creamer, Gold & White Enamel, Applied Handle, Biedermeier | 135.00 |
| Vaseline Glass, Creamer, Individual, Daisy & Button With Crossbar | 24.00 |
| Vaseline Glass, Creamer, Three Panel | 35.00 |
| Vaseline Glass, Cruet, Fern & Daisy, Opalescent | 50.00 |
| Vaseline Glass, Cup & Saucer, Basket Weave | 27.50 |
| Vaseline Glass, Dish, Bird Cover, Nest Base, 4 1/2 In.Diameter | 35.00 |
| Vaseline Glass, Dish, Boat Shape, Rose Sprig, 8 In. | 28.50 |
| Vaseline Glass, Dish, Bride's, Ruffled Edge, Hearts Design, 8 In.Diameter | 55.00 |
| Vaseline Glass, Dish, Daisy & Button, Boat Shape, 13 In. | 38.00 |
| Vaseline Glass, Dish, Pickle, Basket Weave, Open Handles | 27.50 |
| Vaseline Glass, Dresser Set, Swirl, 4 Piece | 35.00 |
| Vaseline Glass, Goblet, Daisy & Button With Crossbar | 22.50 |
| Vaseline Glass, Goblet, Diamond-Quilted | 25.00 |
| Vaseline Glass, Goblet, Finecut ............................................... Illus | 20.00 |
| Vaseline Glass, Goblet, Finecut & Panel | 27.50 |
| Vaseline Glass, Goblet, Inverted Thumbprint, Tegman | 23.50 |
| Vaseline Glass, Goblet, Maple Leaf | 135.00 |
| Vaseline Glass, Goblet, Maple Leaf, Open Bowl, Footed | 26.00 |
| Vaseline Glass, Goblet, Paneled Diamond Point | 27.50 |
| Vaseline Glass, Goblet, Three Panels | 25.00 |
| Vaseline Glass, Goblet, Two Panel | 27.50 |
| Vaseline Glass, Goblet, Wildflower ............................................... Illus | 22.00 |
| Vaseline Glass, Goblet, 1, 000-Eye | 30.00 |
| Vaseline Glass, Gum Stand, Teaberry | 22.50 |
| Vaseline Glass, Hat, Daisy & Button | 18.50 |
| Vaseline Glass, Hat, Daisy & Button, Spooner Size | 40.00 |
| Vaseline Glass, Hat, Daisy & Button, Toothpick Size | 18.00 |
| Vaseline Glass, Jar, Jam, Daisy & Button, Metal Cover | 55.00 |
| Vaseline Glass, Knife Rest | 19.50 |

Vaseline Glass, Goblet,
Finecut

Vaseline Glass, Goblet,
Wildflower

| | |
|---|---:|
| Vaseline Glass, Knob, Drawer | 10.00 |
| Vaseline Glass, Lemonade Set, Imitation Crackle Glass, 7 Piece | 75.00 |
| Vaseline Glass, Muffineer, Daisy & Fern, Opalescent | 58.00 |
| Vaseline Glass, Muffineer, Opalescent Swirl With Reverse Swirl Ribs | 58.00 |
| Vaseline Glass, Mug, Daisy & Button, Reeded Handle | 24.00 |
| Vaseline Glass, Mug, Inverted Thumbprint, Daisy & Button Base | 20.00 |
| Vaseline Glass, Mug, Peacock & Heron | 24.00 |
| Vaseline Glass, Perfume, Bulbous Base, 6 Sided Neck, Stopper, 7 1/2 In. | 45.00 |
| Vaseline Glass, Perfume, 2 Tiered, 6 Sided, Steeple Stopper, 5 1/2 In.High | 25.00 |
| Vaseline Glass, Pitcher, Milk, Daisy & Button With X-Bar, 6 In.High | 42.50 |
| Vaseline Glass, Pitcher, Water, Daisy & Fern, Opalescent, 10 In. | 72.50 |
| Vaseline Glass, Pitcher, Water, Finecut | 45.00 |
| Vaseline Glass, Pitcher, Water, Paneled Daisy & Button | 65.00 |
| Vaseline Glass, Pitcher, Water, Two Panel | 30.00 |
| Vaseline Glass, Pitcher, Water, Zipper, 7 1/2 In. | 33.00 |
| Vaseline Glass, Plate, Bread, Daisy & Button, Open Handles | 55.00 |
| Vaseline Glass, Plate, Bread, Daisy & Button, Oval, Handled | 45.00 |
| Vaseline Glass, Plate, Bread, Pleat & Panel, Clear Handles, 12 1/2 In.Long | 55.00 |
| Vaseline Glass, Plate, Cake, Stretched, Center Handle, 9 3/4 In. | 20.00 |
| Vaseline Glass, Plate, Finecut, 6 In. | 14.50 |
| Vaseline Glass, Plate, Finecut, 7 In. | 16.50 |
| Vaseline Glass, Plate, Grant Memorial, 10 In. | 35.00 |
| Vaseline Glass, Plate, Grant, Peace, Maple Leaf Border, 10 1/4 In. | 52.50 |
| Vaseline Glass, Plate, Memorial, Stippled Vine Border, 10 In. | 37.50 |
| Vaseline Glass, Plate, Stretch, Polished Pontil, 8 In. | 10.00 |
| Vaseline Glass, Platter, Maple Leaf, Oval, 13 In. | 32.00 |
| Vaseline Glass, Relish, Boat Shape, Rose Sprig | 28.00 |
| Vaseline Glass, Relish, Diamond-Quilted, Leaf Shape | 12.00 |
| Vaseline Glass, Relish, Finecut, Boat Shape | 25.00 |
| Vaseline Glass, Rose Bowl, Alaska, Opalescent, Northwood | 45.00 |
| Vaseline Glass, Rose Bowl, Alaska, Opalescent, Pedestal, Crimped Top | 35.00 |
| Vaseline Glass, Rose Bowl, Footed, Open Loops In Foot, 7 Jn.High | 65.00 |
| Vaseline Glass, Rose Bowl, Wreath & Shell, Opalescent, Footed, 4 1/2 In.High | 18.00 |
| Vaseline Glass, Salt Dip, Diamond-Quilted, Rectangular | 12.50 |
| Vaseline Glass, Salt, Master | 14.00 |
| Vaseline Glass, Salt, Oblong | 9.00 |
| Vaseline Glass, Saltshaker, Two Panel | 20.00 |
| Vaseline Glass, Sauce, Cathedral, Footed | 16.50 |
| Vaseline Glass, Sauce, Daisy & Button With Thumbprint, Footed | 22.00 |
| Vaseline Glass, Sauce, Daisy & Button, Square | 12.00 |
| Vaseline Glass, Sauce, Daisy & Button, Triangular | 13.50 |
| Vaseline Glass, Sauce, Daisy & Button, 4 1/2 In. | 12.00 |
| Vaseline Glass, Sauce, Iris & Meander, Opalescent | 25.00 |
| Vaseline Glass, Sauce, Mitered Diamond | 7.00 |
| Vaseline Glass, Slipper, Daisy & Button, 4 3/4 In.Long | 30.00 |
| Vaseline Glass, Spooner, Cathedral | 27.00 |
| Vaseline Glass, Spooner, Maple Leaf, Footed | 32.50 |
| Vaseline Glass, Spooner, Pressed Diamond | 27.50 |
| Vaseline Glass, Spooner, Three Panels Of Cane | 32.00 |
| Vaseline Glass, Squeezer, Lemon | 18.00 |
| Vaseline Glass, Syrup, Honeycomb, Gold Trim | 75.00 |
| Vaseline Glass, Syrup, Inverted Thumbprint, Footed | 55.00 |
| Vaseline Glass, Toothpick, Daisy & Button With V Ornament | 18.00 |
| Vaseline Glass, Toothpick, Hobnail | 16.00 |
| Vaseline Glass, Toothpick, Iris & Meander, Opalescent | 35.00 |
| Vaseline Glass, Toothpick, Ribbed Hat | 10.00 |
| Vaseline Glass, Toothpick, 1, 000-Eye | 15.00 |
| Vaseline Glass, Tray, Daisy & Button, Triangular | 45.00 |
| Vaseline Glass, Tray, Water, Daisy & Button, Triangular | 50.00 |
| Vaseline Glass, Tray, Water, Opalescent Swirl, Beatty Co. | 32.50 |
| Vaseline Glass, Tray, Water, Two Panel | 30.00 |
| Vaseline Glass, Tray, Wildflower, Oval, 11 X 13 In. | 25.00 |
| Vaseline Glass, Tumbler, Charleston Swirl, Footed | 23.50 |
| Vaseline Glass, Tumbler, Daisy & Button With 2 In.Margin | 17.50 |
| Vaseline Glass, Tumbler, Diamond-Quilted | 19.50 |
| Vaseline Glass, Tumbler, Fluted Scrolls, Gold Flower Banding, Opalescent | 21.50 |

| | |
|---|---|
| Vaseline Glass, Tumbler, Inverted Thumbprint | 14.00 |
| Vaseline Glass, Tumbler, Rose Sprig | 25.00 |
| Vaseline Glass, Vase, Fern Pattern, Opalescent | 28.00 |
| Vaseline Glass, Vase, Hobnail, Opalescent, Ruffled Top, 8 In.High | 35.00 |
| Vaseline Glass, Vase, Hobnail, Opalescent, 4 In. | 10.00 |
| Vaseline Glass, Vase, Jack-In-The-Pulpit, Opalescent Trim, 6 1/2 In.High | 59.00 |
| Vaseline Glass, Vase, Opalescent Albany Ribbed Swirl, 8 In. | 32.50 |
| Vaseline Glass, Vase, Opalescent Albany Ribbed Swirl, 9 1/2 In. | 32.50 |
| Vaseline Glass, Vase, Openwork Top, Basket Weave Bottom, 3 1/4 In. High | 18.00 |
| Vaseline Glass, Vase, Ribbed Spiral, Albany Glass, 9 1/2 In.High | 19.75 |
| Vaseline Glass, Wine, Banded Knives & Forks | 16.00 |
| Vaseline Glass, Wine, Two Panel | 22.50 To 28.50 |

*Venetian glass has been made near Venice, Italy, from the thirteenth to the twentieth century. Thin, colored glass with applied decorations is favored although many other types have been made.*

| | |
|---|---|
| Venetian Glass, Candlestick, Gold Stone & Latticinio, Applied Dragon | 115.00 |
| Venetian Glass, Decanter, Ruby & Clear, 14 In.High, Pair | 75.00 |
| Venetian Glass, Goblet, Ruby, Hand-Painted Dancers, Floral Wreaths, Gold | 55.00 |
| Venetian Glass, Pitcher, White & Blue, Encased Clear, 4 1/2 In.High | 18.00 |
| Venetian Glass, Tumbler, Opaque Net, Gold Rim | 7.50 |
| Venetian Glass, Vase, Fan, Gold Flecks On White, Camphor Edge, Pedestal | 30.00 |
| Venetian Glass, Vase, Paperweight, Millefiori & Inlaid On Mustard Color | 175.00 |
| Venetian Glass, Vase, Paperweight, Trailing Millefiore Flowers, 8 1/2 In. | 115.00 |
| Venetian Glass, Wine Set, Light Green, Gold Wash, 11 Piece | 80.00 |

*Verlys glass was made in France after 1931. Verlys was also made in the United States. The glass is either blown or molded. The American glass is signed with a diamond-point-scratched name, but the French pieces are marked with a molded signature.*

| | |
|---|---|
| Verlys, Bowl, Acorn Decoration, Footed, 6 1/2 In.Diameter, Unsigned | 18.00 |
| Verlys, Bowl, Acorn Decoration, 3 Feet, Shallow, 6 1/4 In. | 18.00 |
| Verlys, Bowl, Frosted Floral, Heisey, 8 3/4 In. | 95.00 |
| Verlys, Bowl, Lilies In Water, Pads Form Feet, Script Signed, 13 3/4 In. | 110.00 |
| Verlys, Bowl, Pineapple, Signed, 6 In. Diameter | 25.00 |
| Verlys, Bowl, Poppies, Frosted, Signed | 90.00 |
| Verlys, Bowl, Poppy, 13 1/2 In.Diameter | 75.00 |
| Verlys, Bowl, Thistle, Frosted, Signed | 50.00 |
| Verlys, Bowl, Thistle, Frosted, Unsigned | 40.00 |
| Verlys, Bowl, Thistle, Topaz, Signed | 175.00 |
| Verlys, Bowl, Water Lily Decoration, Signed, Large Size | 45.00 |
| Verlys, Bowl, Wild Ducks, Clear Satin With Blue Cast, Signed, 14 In.Diameter | 275.00 |
| Verlys, Centerpiece, Pheasant, Greenish Topaz, Signed, 18 In.Long | 400.00 |
| Verlys, Figurine, Mary & Her Lamb, Artist Signed & Dated | 2(5.00 |
| Verlys, Inkwell, Oval, Covered, Blue Opalescent Birds, Spread Wings, Signed | 180.00 |
| Verlys, Plaque, Three Raised Iridescent Swirling Fish, Signed, 9 In. | 125.00 |
| Verlys, Vase, Alpine Thistle, Signed, 9 In.High | 85.00 |
| Verlys, Vase, Dark Green Satin, Raised Apple Blossoms, 7 X 3 1/2 In. | 95.00 |
| Verlys, Vase, Frosted, Relief Female Figures Depict Autumn, 8 In. | 100.00 |
| Verlys, Vase, Lovebird, Frosted, Marked, 6 1/2 In. | 25.00 |
| Verlys, Vase, Oriental Type, Frosted Figures, Signed, 9 1/2 In.High | 105.00 |
| Verlys, Vase, Raised Chinese Motif, Signed In Script, 9 1/2 In.High | 165.00 |

*Verre de soie glass was first made by Frederick Carder at the Steuben Glass Works from about 1905 to 1930. It is an iridescent glass of soft white or very, very pale green. The name means glass of silk, and it does resemble silk. Other factories have made verre de soie, and some of the English examples were made of different colors. Verre de soie is an art glass and is not related to the iridescent pressed white carnival glass mistakenly called by its name.*

Verre De Soie, see also Steuben

| | |
|---|---|
| Verre De Soie, Perfume, Bulbous, Melon Ribbed, Green Steeple Stopper | 98.00 |
| Verre De Soie, Perfume, Engraved, Enameled Sterling Stopper, Hawkes | 48.00 |
| Verre De Soie, Perfume, White, Pink Iridescence, 4 In.High | 35.00 |
| Verre De Soie, Sherbet, Copper Wheel Engraved Floral Festoons, Hawkes | 58.00 |
| Verre De Soie, Vase, Applied Green 5 Petal Flowers At Top, 6 1/2 In. | 22.50 |

| | |
|---|---|
| Verre De Soie, Vase, Jack-In-The-Pulpit, Twisted Stem, 8 In.High, Pair | 125.00 |
| Verre De Soie, Vase, Ruffled Top, 9 Panels Of Pulled-Up Design On Sides | 75.00 |
| Verre De Soie, Water Set, Free-Blown, Iridescent, Polished Pontil, 5 Piece | 90.00 |
| Vienna Art, Plate, , Old J.B.T.Whiskey | 20.00 |
| Vienna Art, Plate, Classical Ladies & Cherubs In Garden, Tin, 1905 | 20.00 |
| Vienna Art, Plate, Classical Scene, Tin, Dated 1905 | 15.00 |
| Vienna Art, Plate, Harvard Brewing, 1907 Calendar, Girl, Poppies In Hair | 45.00 |
| Vienna Art, Plate, Jamestown, 1607-1907, John Smith & Pocahontas, 10 In. | 35.00 |
| Vienna Art, Plate, Lady With Urn, J.Pritzlaff Hardware, 1909 | 45.00 |
| Vienna, Coffeepot, Pear Shape, Scroll Handle, Bouquets, C.1790 | 125.00 |
| Vienna, Cup & Saucer, Sorgenthal, Hunter, Farm Building, Chartreuse, 1801 | 1050.00 |
| Vienna, Cup & Saucer, Sorgenthal, Moon & Sun Decoration, C.1822 | 550.00 |
| Vienna, Plate, Puce Roses & Bouquets, Basketwork Rim, C.1760, 9 1/4 In., Pair | 70.00 |
| Vienna, Pot, Hot Water, Covered, Rural Scenes, Fruit Knop, 1803, 6 3/4 In.High | 80.00 |
| Vienna, Sucrier, Pomegranate Finial, Blue & White, 1801 | 110.00 |
| Vienna, Vase, Neoclassic Figures, Blue Ground, C.1850, Pair, 24 1/2 In.High | 4000.00 |

*Villeroy & Boch Pottery of Mettlach, Germany, was founded in 1841.*
*The firm made many types of pottery, including the famous Mettlach steins.*

**Villeroy & Boch, see also Mettlach**

| | |
|---|---|
| Villeroy & Boch, Mug, Dresden, Saxony, Pair | 19.50 |
| Villeroy & Boch, Pitcher & Bowl, Pink & Blue Design, 13 1/2 In.Diameter | 85.00 |
| Villeroy & Boch, Pitcher, Gargoyle Handle & Spout, Medallion On Gray | 45.00 |
| Villeroy & Boch, Plaque, Mr.& Mrs.Rabbit On Picnic, Etched, Glazed, 12 In. | 65.00 |
| Villeroy & Boch, Plate, Fasan, Dark Blue & White, Bird & Floral, 9 1/4 In. | 20.00 |
| Villeroy & Boch, Plate, Fruit, Cherries, 7 1/2 In. | 12.50 |
| Villeroy & Boch, Plate, Fruit, Plums, 7 1/2 In. | 12.50 |
| Villeroy & Boch, Plate, Majolica, 7 3/4 In. | 10.00 |
| Villeroy & Boch, Plate, Red, Blue, Yellow, & Green Sponge Decoration, 9 In. | 18.00 |
| Villeroy & Boch, Plate, Timor, Oriental, Luster, 7 In. | 25.00 |
| Villeroy & Boch, Platter, Mettlach, Japanese Scene, 14 In. | 95.00 |
| Villeroy & Boch, Ramekin, Underplate | 12.50 |
| Villeroy & Boch, Syrup, Blue Floral, Dresden, Made In Germany, 4 In. | 35.00 |
| Villeroy & Boch, Tea Set, Black Farm Scenes On Cream, 3 Piece | 185.00 |
| Villeroy & Boch, Teapot, Gargoyle Handle & Spout, Medallion On Gray | 95.00 |
| Villeroy & Boch, Tile, Tea, Geometrics, White, Silver Plate Holder | 8.50 |
| Villeroy & Boch, Tumbler, Blue & White | 16.00 |
| Villeroy & Boch, Wash Set, Cream, Gold Trim, 3 Piece | 90.00 |
| Volkstadt, Figurine, Clown, Holding Guitar At Feet, 14 In.High | 210.00 |
| Volkstadt, Figurine, Frog, Sitting, Singing, Green | 85.00 |
| Walt Disney, Book, Donald Duck, 1956 | 2.00 |
| Walt Disney, Book, Pinocchio, 1940, Color | 5.00 |
| Walt Disney, Book, Snow White & The Seven Dwarfs, 1948 | 2.00 |
| Walt Disney, Book, Song, Dumbo, Whitman Publishing Co., 1941 | 9.00 |
| Walt Disney, Book, Uncle Remus | 2.00 |
| Walt Disney, Cup, Picture Of Three Pigs & Wolf | 10.00 |
| Walt Disney, Doll, Donald Duck, Rubber, 5 In.Tall | 6.50 |
| Walt Disney, Doll, Donald Duck, Vinyl, 8 In.Tall | 8.50 |
| Walt Disney, Doll, Dopey, Bisque, Signed Circle C, 3 In. | 10.50 |
| Walt Disney, Figurine, Ferdinand, Bisque, 3 1/2 In.High | 18.00 |
| Walt Disney, Figurine, Pluto, Ceramic | 3.50 |
| Walt Disney, Figurine, Snow White & Dwarf, Bone China, 1964, Pair | 13.00 |
| Walt Disney, Game, Donald Duck Beanbag | 15.00 |
| Walt Disney, Lunch Bucket, School Bus | 12.00 |
| Walt Disney, Mask, Pluto, Cloth | 2.00 |
| Walt Disney, Mug, Three Pigs | 12.50 |
| Walt Disney, Plate & Mug, Wolf & Three Little Pigs, Porcelain | 25.00 |
| Walt Disney, Program, Fantasia, 1940, Color | 5.00 |
| Walt Disney, Puppet, Hand, Patch, 100 Dalmatians | 6.00 |
| Walt Disney, Puzzle Frame Tray, Signed, 1956, 11 1/4 X 14 In. | 1.50 |
| Walt Disney, Tile With Thermometer, Donald Duck, Ceramic, 1939, 6 In. Square | 7.00 |
| Walt Disney, Toothbrush Holder, Figure Of Doc | 12.50 |
| Walt Disney, Toy, Ferdinand The Bull, Rubber, Marked, 3 In. High | 12.50 |
| Walt Disney, Tumbler, Donald Duck, Red Embossed Figures At Base | 7.00 |

*Warwick china was made in Wheeling, West Virginia, in a pottery factory founded in 1887.*

| | |
|---|---|
| Warwick, Bowl, Nut, Chestnuts, Green & Beige, 3 Scroll Feet | 17.00 |
| Warwick, Jar, Cracker, Multicolor Floral, Gold Trim, 2 Handles, 7 In.Diameter | 35.00 |
| Warwick, Mug, B.P.O.E., Marked | 25.00 |
| Warwick, Mug, Dickens Type Character On Brown Glaze, Marked I.O.G.A. | 35.00 |
| Warwick, Vase, Orchard, Entwined Handles, 11 1/2 In.High | 27.00 |
| Warwick, Vase, Portrait Young Woman, Bulbous, Maroon, Gold Band | 50.00 |

*Watch fobs were worn on watch chains. They were popular during Victorian times and after.*

| | |
|---|---|
| Watch Fob, Alaska-Yukon-Pacific Exposition, Seattle, 1909, 3 Coins | 15.00 |
| Watch Fob, American Legion, Cleveland Convention, 1946 | 6.00 |
| Watch Fob, Armour's Simon Pure Leaf Lard, Cook Running With Pail | 15.00 |
| Watch Fob, Baldwin, Embossed Locomotive, 1831-1950 | 12.00 |
| Watch Fob, Bucyrus Earil Oil Drilling, Heavy Equipment | 12.50 |
| Watch Fob, Caterpillar Tractor Company, Caterpillar | 12.50 |
| Watch Fob, Clabber Girl | 3.95 |
| Watch Fob, Coins, Silver | 30.00 |
| Watch Fob, Colonial Trust Co., 1910 | 12.00 |
| Watch Fob, Commercial Man's Association, Brass | 4.00 |
| Watch Fob, Compass, Gold Filled Link Vest Chain | 10.00 |
| Watch Fob, Dry Mash, The Park & Pollard Co., Rooster Carrying 2 Bags | 7.95 |
| Watch Fob, Eagle Tractor | 4.50 |
| Watch Fob, Elk's Tooth, Elk's Head, Glass Eyes, 'B.P.O.E.,' Clock | 10.00 |
| Watch Fob, Elongated Lincoln Cent, Gold Filled Vest Chain | 15.00 |
| Watch Fob, G.M.Engines | 9.50 |
| Watch Fob, Gold, Scrollwork | 25.00 |
| Watch Fob, Hercules, Associated Stover Gas Engines | 2.50 |
| Watch Fob, Hobson Caterpillar | 6.00 |
| Watch Fob, International Harvester Centennial, 1931 | 5.50 |
| Watch Fob, Kasper's Coffee | 15.00 |
| Watch Fob, Kellogg's Toasted Corn Flakes, White Metal | 8.00 |
| Watch Fob, Knox Automobile | 8.50 |
| Watch Fob, Lady's, Heart, Gold Filled Rope | 22.50 |
| Watch Fob, Lion Bonding Co. | 5.00 |
| Watch Fob, Lowe Brothers Paint Gives Best Results, Silver & Enamel | 7.95 |
| Watch Fob, Lynn Mass. Hospital, C.1917 | 6.50 |
| Watch Fob, Mack Truck | 4.95 |
| Watch Fob, Mail Pouch Tobacco | 3.95 |
| Watch Fob, Minneapolis, Case, Advance-Rumely Steamers | 2.50 |
| Watch Fob, Nude Lady | 4.25 |
| Watch Fob, OC-18 Oliver Bulldozer | 3.50 |
| Watch Fob, Oilpull, Hart-Parr, John Deere D Tractors | 25.00 |
| Watch Fob, Old Dutch Cleanser | 3.95 |
| Watch Fob, Orange Rifle Powder | 4.50 |
| Watch Fob, Panama Pacific Exposition, San Francisco, 1915 | 12.50 |
| Watch Fob, Pepsi Cola | 12.50 |
| Watch Fob, Quincy, Mass., 300th Anniversary, 1625-1925, Strap Type | 3.95 |
| Watch Fob, Schlitz Beer | 3.95 |
| Watch Fob, Seal Of Michigan, Black Ribbon, Belt | 9.00 |
| Watch Fob, Seal Supported By 8 Chain Section, 14K Gold, 5 1/4 In.Long | 85.00 |
| Watch Fob, Seal Type, Gold, Gray White Stone End, 3 Incised Symbols | 32.00 |
| Watch Fob, Syracuse Plow Co. | 5.95 |
| Watch Fob, Tigereye, Gold Filled Ornamental Link Vest Chain | 40.00 |
| Watch Fob, U.S.Seal On Front, Gold Plated On Bronze | 15.00 |
| Watch Fob, Western Pennsylvania Volunteer Fireman's 33rd Convention, 1926 | 8.00 |
| Watch, Agassiz, Chronograph, Open Face | 185.00 |
| Watch, Amir, Sandoz, & Fils, 18K Gold Case, Open Face, 13 Jewel, C.1880 | 125.00 |
| Watch, Audemars Piguet & Co., Gold Open Face, Chronograph, C.1900 | 1400.00 |
| Watch, Audemars Piguet & Co., Pocket, Gold Open Face, Repeating, C.1930 | 1100.00 |
| Watch, Automaton, Gold, C.1800    *Illus* | 2400.00 |
| Watch, Ball, B604183, Gold Filled, Open Face, 23 Jewel, C.1919 | 195.00 |
| Watch, Ball, B642601, Gold Filled, Open Face, 21 Jewel, C.1935 | 100.00 |
| Watch, Ball, Illinois, B616766, 14K Gold Filled Case, 21 Jewel | 85.00 |
| Watch, Black, Starr, & Frost, Traveling, Sterling Folding Case, 8 Day | 27.00 |
| Watch, Bothamley, Imported English Parts, Key Wind, Coin Silver Case | 130.00 |
| Watch, Brandt & Cie, Open Face, Gold & Enamel, Girl With Spaniel, C.1850 | 650.00 |

Watch, Automaton,
Gold, C.1800
*(See Page 685)*

Watch, C.H.Meylan, Pendant,
Gold, Enamel, Pin, C.1890

| | |
|---|---:|
| **Watch, British Naval Officer's Deck,** Schafer, London, Silver, Sept.1, 1881 | 1250.00 |
| **Watch, British Naval Officer's,** Silver Pair Case, Key Wind, Engraved, 1773 | 750.00 |
| **Watch, Bullingford,** Gun Metal Outer Case, Silver Inner Case, Key Wind, 1880s | 80.00 |
| **Watch, Bunn,** Special, Gold Filled Case, 1906, 21 Jewel | 95.00 |
| **Watch, Burlington,** Gold Filled Hunting Case, Patriotic Design, 21 Jewel | 65.00 |
| **Watch, C.H.Meylan,** Pendant, Gold, Enamel, Pin, C.1890 *Illus* | 500.00 |
| **Watch, Calendar,** A.V.La Crois A Paris, Verge Fusee, Silver Open Face Case | 285.00 |
| **Watch, Calendar,** Continental, Breguet Lever Escapement, 15 Jewel, Stem Wind | 135.00 |
| **Watch, Calendar,** Continental, Verge Fusee, Silver Open Face Case, Key Wind | 155.00 |
| **Watch, Calendar,** Continental, 2 Color Silver & Silver Gilt Case, 10 Jewel | 75.00 |
| **Watch, Calendar,** English, Silver Open Face Case, Stem Wind, Lever Escapement | 165.00 |
| **Watch, Calendar,** Swiss, Gunmetal & Silver Case, Stem Wind, Pin Set | 145.00 |
| **Watch, Cartier,** Gold, Enamel, Jewels, Pin *Illus* | 1000.00 |
| **Watch, Case,** Notary Public Seal, Name & Cook County, Ill. | 20.00 |
| **Watch, Chain Fusee,** Engraved Hunting Case, Name John Forest | 150.00 |
| **Watch, Cigarrillos Excelsior,** Modernista, Jump Hour, Retrograde Minute | 275.00 |
| **Watch, Colibri,** Chased Gold Case, Enamel Minerva, Stem Wind, C.1890 | 225.00 |
| **Watch, Daniel Humbert,** Gold & Enamel, C.1790 *Illus* | 1700.00 |
| **Watch, Davy Crockett** | 30.00 |
| **Watch, Delasalle,** Silver, Pair Case, Scrolling Foliage, 1785 | 225.00 |
| **Watch, Elgin,** Alaska Metal Swing Case, 7 Jewel | 20.00 |
| **Watch, Elgin,** Coin Silver Hunting Case, Name On Back, 7 Jewel, C.1879 | 70.00 |
| **Watch, Elgin,** Deck, Chronometer, 21 Jewel, Brass Mounted Mahogany Case | 325.00 |
| **Watch, Elgin,** Engraved Coin Silver Hunting Case, 15 Jewel | 75.00 |
| **Watch, Elgin,** Engraved Gold Filled Hunting Case, 11 Jewel | 55.00 |

Watch, Cartier, Gold, Enamel, Jewels, Pin

Watch, Daniel Humbert,
Gold & Enamel, C.1790

Watch, Elgin, Engraved Hunting Case, Slide & Chain, 15 Jewel ........................ 100.00
Watch, Elgin, Engraved Yellow Gold Hunting Case, 15 Jewel ........................ 110.00
Watch, Elgin, Engraved 10K Gold Case, 19 Jewel ........................ 85.00
Watch, Elgin, Engraved 25K Yellow Gold Case, Bar Type Movement, 17 Jewel ........ 85.00
Watch, Elgin, Father Time, Gold Filled Case, Lever Set, Railroad, 21 Jewel ........ 67.00
Watch, Elgin, G.M.Wheeler, Nickeloid Railroad Case, 15 Jewel ........................ 30.00
Watch, Elgin, Gold Filled Case, 17 Jewel ........................ 30.00
Watch, Elgin, Gold Filled Hunting Case, "papa To Mama, 11-18-1915" ........ 75.00
Watch, Elgin, Gold Filled Hunting Case, 17 Jewel, C.1913 ........................ 60.00
Watch, Elgin, Gold Filled Open Face Case, Porcelain Dial, 21 Jewel ........ 67.00
Watch, Elgin, Inlaid Mother-Of-Pearl Holder, 14 1/2 In.High ........................ 75.00
Watch, Elgin, Lady's, Double Engraved Case, Porcelain Face, 17 Jewel ........ 100.00
Watch, Elgin, Lady's, Engraved Gold Filled Hunting Case, Size 6 ........ 50.00
Watch, Elgin, Lady's, Gold Filled Hunting Case, Engraved, 13 Jewel ........ 70.00
Watch, Elgin, Lady's, Gold, Etched Church & Flowers, Porcelain Face ........ 125.00
Watch, Elgin, Lady's, 14K Gold Hunting Case, Diamond Chips, 7 Jewel, 1915 ........ 120.00
Watch, Elgin, Lady's, 14K Gold Hunting Case, Engraved ........................ 175.00
Watch, Elgin, Man's, Coin Silver Case, Key Wind, 17 Jewel ........................ 20.00
Watch, Elgin, Man's, Gold Filled Hunting Case, Engraved, 15 Jewel ........ 90.00
Watch, Elgin, Navigator's, Type A8, World War II, 15 Jewel, Black Case ........ 110.00
Watch, Elgin, Nickel Open Face Case, Locomotive On Back, 15 Jewel ........ 43.00
Watch, Elgin, Pocket, Crystal On Both Sides, 17 Jewel, Size 12 ........ 30.00
Watch, Elgin, Pocket, 14K Gold Hunting Case, Engraved Inside ........................ 185.00
Watch, Elgin, Raymond, Gold Filled Case, 19 Jewel ........................ 80.00
Watch, Elgin, Raymond, Montgomery, Dial Safety Burl, 17 Jewel ........ 85.00
Watch, Elgin, Raymond, Montgomery, 14K Gold Filled Case, 21 Jewel ........ 95.00
Watch, Elgin, Silverode, Open Face, Engraved Locomotive, 15 Jewel, C.1888 ........ 40.00
Watch, Elgin, Timer, Nickel Open Face Case, 15 Jewel ........................ 22.50
Watch, Elgin, Varitas, 14175347, 19 Jewel ........................ 80.00
Watch, Elgin, Veritas, Open Face Silveroid Case, 21 Jewel ........................ 60.00
Watch, Elgin, Yellow Gold Filled Case, 17 Jewel ........................ 25.00
Watch, Elgin, Yellow Gold Filled Closed Case, 15 Jewel ........................ 20.00
Watch, Elgin, 17 Jewel, Size 18 ........................ 19.00
Watch, Elgin, 18K Gold Hunting Case, Gail Borden National Watch Co., Key ........ 250.00
Watch, Elgin, 2964228, Gold Filled Hunting Case, 15 Jewel, C.1887 ........ 65.00
Watch, Elgin, 940850, Nickel Case, Open Face, Sweep Second, 16 Jewel ........ 150.00
Watch, Essex, Lady's, 14K Gold Hunting Case, Engraved, Picture Inside ........ 250.00
Watch, Farringdon C, Sterling Case, Open Face, Key Wind, Serial No.41799 ........ 75.00
Watch, Ferguson, Gold Filled Case ........................ 65.00
Watch, Football Timer, 1910 Model ........................ 90.00
Watch, French, Gold & Enamel, C.1790 ........................ *Illus* 1800.00
Watch, George Rodgers, Engraved 18K Gold Case, Key Wind, C.1840 ........ 125.00
Watch, Gold & Enamel, Breguet A Paris, C.1800 ........................ *Illus* 1500.00
Watch, H.W.Co., Brass Hunting Case, 21 Jewel ........................ 50.00
Watch, Hamilton, Burl, 20 Year Case ........................ 90.00
Watch, Hamilton, Engraved Hunting Case, Montgomery Dial, 21 Jewel ........ 110.00
Watch, Hamilton, Ferguson Dial, Gold Filled Case, 19 Jewel, Dated 1898 ........ 150.00
Watch, Hamilton, Gold Closed Case, 21 Jewel ........................ 40.00

Watch, Gold & Enamel, Breguet A Paris, C.1800

| | |
|---|---|
| Watch, Hamilton, Gold Filled Case, Lever Set, Initials, 17 Jewel | 30.00 |
| Watch, Hamilton, Porcelain Dial, 24 Hour In Center, 21 Jewel | 70.00 |
| Watch, Hamilton, Stem Set, 23 Jewel, C.1898 | 145.00 |
| Watch, Hamilton, 10K Gold Filled Case, Montgomery Dial C155294 | 120.00 |
| Watch, Hamilton, 10K Gold Filled Case, Montgomery Dial C511863 | 125.00 |
| Watch, Hamilton, 10K Gold Filled Case, Montgomery Dial 1547417 | 90.00 |
| Watch, Hamilton, 14K Gold Filled Case, Montgomery Dial 2363219 | 110.00 |
| Watch, Hamilton, 409367, Railroad, Gold Filled, Open Face, 21 Jewel, C.1898 | 65.00 |
| Watch, Hamilton, 922B, Porcelain Dial, 21 Jewel | 100.00 |
| Watch, Hamilton, 992, Gold Filled, Open Face, 21 Jewel, C.1920 | 60.00 |
| Watch, Hampden, Lady's, Engraved Gold Filled Hunting Case | 85.00 |
| Watch, Hampden, Lady's, Gold Hunting Case, Engraved, Slide & Chain | 175.00 |
| Watch, Hampden, Lady's, Yellow Gold Hunting Case, Engraved, 'ohio, '63' | 188.00 |
| Watch, Hampden, Silveroid Open Face Case, Key Wind, Size 18 | 32.50 |
| Watch, Hampden, Silveroid, Open Face, Porcelain Dial, Second Hand, 17 Jewel | 70.00 |
| Watch, Hampden, 363658, Gold Filled Hunting Case, 15 Jewel | 70.00 |
| Watch, Hampden, 70427, Coin Silver Hunting Case, Floral, Key Wind, 17 Jewel | 75.00 |
| Watch, Hass Neveux & Cie., Chased 185 Gold Case, Enamel, Pin, C.1890 | 300.00 |
| Watch, Howard, White Gold Filled Open Face, Patent '12, 17 Jewel | 55.00 |
| Watch, Howard, 14K Gold Case, Patent 1921 | 90.00 |
| Watch, Howard, 14K Gold, Open Face, 23 Jewel, Serial No.1159440 | 185.00 |
| Watch, Howell Bros., Windsor, Ont., Gold Filled Hunting Case, 16 Jewel | 35.00 |
| Watch, Hunt & Roskell, 4 Color Gold, Repeating, C.1840 ................ Illus | 850.00 |
| Watch, Hunting Case, Swiss, Minute Repeating Chronograph, C.1900 | 1400.00 |
| Watch, Hunting Case, Swiss, Minute Repeating, Gold, L.Bader, C.1900 | 1100.00 |
| Watch, Hunting Case, Swiss, Quarter Repeating Chronograph, Calender, C.1900 | 1700.00 |
| Watch, Hunting Case, Swiss, Repeating Automation, C.1900 | 1500.00 |
| Watch, Hunting Case, Waltham, Gold & Enamel, American Watch Co. | 2000.00 |
| Watch, Illinois, Bunn Special, Gold Filled, Open Face, 21 Jewel, C.1912 | 65.00 |
| Watch, Illinois, Gold Filled Case, 17 Jewel | 35.00 |
| Watch, Illinois, Gold Filled Hunting Case, Gilt Spade Hands, 11 Jewel | 60.00 |
| Watch, Illinois, 60 Hour, Bunn Special, Gold Filled, Open Face, 21 Jewel, 1928 | 125.00 |
| Watch, Ingersoll, Eclipse, Size 16 | 12.50 |
| Watch, Ingersoll, Pocket, Yankee Radiolite | 22.50 |
| Watch, Iron, Oval, Bird Head Terminals, Foliage & Fruit Case, C.1620 | 2000.00 |
| Watch, James Bond 007, Wrist, 1965 | 10.00 |
| Watch, Jules Mathey, Gold & Enamel Hunting Case, Key Wind, C.1850 | 325.00 |
| Watch, Juvenia Co., Pendant, 18K Gold, Diamonds, Stem Wind, 15 Jewel, 1910s | 250.00 |
| Watch, Le Pine, Open Face, Gold & Enamel, C.1840 | 750.00 |
| Watch, Ladies, Hunting Case, Fancy Engraving, 14K | 250.00 |
| Watch, Lady's, Engraved Gold Filled Hunting Case, Tempus Lever Set | 95.00 |
| Watch, Lady's, Gold Filled, Plated Chain, Jeweled Slide, Opal | 38.00 |
| Watch, Lady's, Gold Open Face, Enamel, Verge Movement, C.1820 | 300.00 |
| Watch, Lady's, Open Face Embossed Case, 15 Jewel | 25.00 |
| Watch, Lady's, 14K Yellow Gold Hunting Case, Engraved, Slide & Chain | 250.00 |
| Watch, Lambert, N.Y., Lady's, Bright Cut Gold Hunting Case, Chain, C.1900 | 300.00 |
| Watch, Lapel, Gold, A.Golay, Paris, C.1900 | 150.00 |
| Watch, Leroy, Open Face, Chronograph, Gold, Paris, C.1900, Plain Case | 750.00 |
| Watch, Longines, Deck, Chronometer, Brass Bound Mahogany Case | 295.00 |
| Watch, Longines, Engraved Case, Key Set, 16 Jewel, C.1880 | 100.00 |
| Watch, Longines, Yellow Gold Filled Closed Face, 15 Jewel | 30.00 |
| Watch, Louis Raymond, Lady's, Gold Hunting Case, Enamel, Key Wind, C.1850 | 400.00 |
| Watch, Louis Shibko, Chain Drive Leber, Key Wind, 1828 | 45.00 |
| Watch, Man's, Sterling Silver, Key Wind | 75.00 |
| Watch, Marcus & Co., Pendant, Gold, Pearls, Stem Wind, Pin, C.1900 | 400.00 |
| Watch, N.Y.Standard, Silveroid Swing Case, 7 Jewel | 20.00 |
| Watch, New Era, Engraved Gold Filled Open Face Case, 7 Jewel | 23.00 |
| Watch, New York Standard, Gold Filled Open Face Case, 7 Jewel | 25.00 |
| Watch, Nicolet A Lille D'Oleron, Coach, Key Wind, Silver Case, C.1800 | 165.00 |
| Watch, Open Face Case, Metal Steam Engine Base, 16 Jewel | 12.50 |
| Watch, Open Face, Gold, English, C.1900, Enamel Dial | 250.00 |
| Watch, Open Face, Platinum, Diamonds, Cartier, C.1930 | 500.00 |
| Watch, Patek Philippe & Cie., Pendant, Gold, Enamel, 1900 ........... Illus | 1700.00 |
| Watch, Patek Philippe & Co., Silver Hunting Case, Stem Wind, C.1900 | 80.00 |
| Watch, Patek Philippe, Open Face, Miniature, Gold, C.1853, Key Wind Movement | 1000.00 |
| Watch, Patek Philippe, 151551, 18K Gold Case, Open Face, 18 Jewel | 350.00 |

Watch, Swiss, Pendant, Gold,
Jewels, C.1900
*(See Page 690)*

Watch, Swiss, Gold Hunting Case,
Chronograph, C.1890
*(See Page 690)*

Watch, Pendant, Gold,
Enamel, Diamonds, Pin, C.1900
*(See Page 690)*

Watch, French,
Gold & Enamel. C. 1790
*(See Page 687)*

Watch, Swiss, Pendant,
Gold, Stem Wind,
Pin, C.1900
*(See Page 690)*

Watch, Waltham,
14K Gold Hunting Case,
Repeater, 1900s
*(See Page 690)*

Watch, Hunt & Roskell,
4 Color Gold, Repeating, C.1840
*(See Page 688)*

Watch, Patek Philippe & Cie.,
Pendant, Gold, Enamel, 1900
*(See Page 688)*

Watch, Swiss,
Gold & Enamel,
Huaud, C.1690
*(See Page 690)*

| | |
|---|---|
| Watch, Pendant, Gold, Enamel, Diamonds, Art Nouveau, Pin, C.1890 | 400.00 |
| Watch, Pendant, Gold, Enamel, Diamonds, Pin, C.1900 *Illus* | 1000.00 |
| Watch, Perrigaux, Man's, 18K Gold Hunting Case, Key Wind | 245.00 |
| Watch, Picard, Hunting Case, Minute Repeating Chronograph, Gold, C.1900 | 900.00 |
| Watch, Pocket, Enamel, Ivory, & Silver, Cartier, C.1925 | 140.00 |
| Watch, Pocket, Riverside Maximus, Hunting Case, Diamond, Jewels | 250.00 |
| Watch, Pocket, Seth Thomas, Hunting Case, Key Wind | 175.00 |
| Watch, Pocket, Timer, Auburndale | 300.00 |
| Watch, Pocket, Waltham, Maximus, Hunting Case, 23 Jewel | 225.00 |
| Watch, Pocket, Waltham, Maximus, 18K Gold | 240.00 |
| Watch, Rockford, Engraved Hunting Case, 21 Jewel | 120.00 |
| Watch, Russian, Pocket, Silver, Portrait Of Alexander II, C.1850 | 225.00 |
| Watch, Saks 5th Ave., Lady's, Lapel, 1920s | 38.00 |
| Watch, Schafer, British Naval Officer's Deck, From Prince Of Wales, 1881 | 1250.00 |
| Watch, Seth Thomas, Coin Silver Case, Open Face, Engraved, 17 Jewel, C.1890 | 80.00 |
| Watch, Silver Closed Case, Engraved, Key Wind, 8 Jewel | 20.00 |
| Watch, Silver Hunting Case, Brass Coated, Key Wind, Lancaster, Pa. | 125.00 |
| Watch, Silver, Isaac Faure A Vallen, C.1690 | 950.00 |
| Watch, Sola, Embossed Silver Case, Boar Hunt, Mild Colored Glass, 16 Jewel | 90.00 |
| Watch, South Bend, Gold Case, Gold Weights On Balance, 21 Jewel | 75.00 |
| Watch, Swiss, Alarm, Gunmetal, C.1900 | 90.00 |
| Watch, Swiss, Ben Hur Haute Precision, 14K Gold Hunting Case | 350.00 |
| Watch, Swiss, Gold & Enamel, Huaud, C.1690 *Illus* | 2900.00 |
| Watch, Swiss, Gold Hunting Case, Chronograph, C.1890 *Illus* | 1800.00 |
| Watch, Swiss, Gold Plated Case, Open Face, Month, Day, Week, Moon Phases | 175.00 |
| Watch, Swiss, Gunmetal Coated Silver, Open Face, Initials, 15 Jewel | 50.00 |
| Watch, Swiss, Lady's, Enamel Back, 10 Jewel | 20.00 |
| Watch, Swiss, Lady's, Gold Hunting Case, Enamel, Stem Wind, C.1890 | 650.00 |
| Watch, Swiss, Lady's, Lapel, Chased Gold, Rubies & Diamonds, Key Wind, C.1900 | 400.00 |
| Watch, Swiss, Lady's, Sterling Case, Open Face, Embossed Dog & Crab, 16 Jewel | 100.00 |
| Watch, Swiss, Open Face Chronograph, Patek Philippe, C.1900 | 600.00 |
| Watch, Swiss, Open Face, Gold & Enamel, Oriental Decoration, Bovet, C.1820 | 6000.00 |
| Watch, Swiss, Open Face, Gold, Patek Phillipe, C.1910 | 275.00 |
| Watch, Swiss, Pendant, Chased Gold Case, Enamel, Stem Wind, C.1900 | 425.00 |
| Watch, Swiss, Pendant, Chased 18K Gold Case, Diamonds, Stem Wind, C.1890 | 325.00 |
| Watch, Swiss, Pendant, Gold, Jewels, C.1900 *Illus* | 1500.00 |
| Watch, Swiss, Pendant, Gold, Stem Wind, Pin, C.1900 *Illus* | 800.00 |
| Watch, Swiss, Pocket, Man's, Chronometer, Gold On Enamel, Dated Feb.14, 1888 | 150.00 |
| Watch, Swiss, Repeating Chronograph, Perpetual Calendar, Gold, C.1900 | 5750.00 |
| Watch, Swiss, Silver Gilt & Enamel Case, Key Wind, Pearls, C.1850 | 275.00 |
| Watch, Swiss, Skeletonized, Stem Wind, Pin Set | 160.00 |
| Watch, Swiss, 12K Gold Closed Face, 15 Jewel | 30.00 |
| Watch, Turkish, Silver Case, Key Wind | 35.00 |
| Watch, U.S.Time Co., Cinderella | 35.00 |
| Watch, Vacherone & Constantin, 323052, 14K Gold Case, Open Face, 18 Jewel | 250.00 |
| Watch, Waltham Hillside, Coin Silver Hunting Case, Initials, Design, 7 Jewel | 70.00 |
| Watch, Waltham, Appleton Tracy, 18K Gold Closed Case, 17 Jewel | 150.00 |
| Watch, Waltham, Ball, BB262484, 19 Jewel | 89.00 |
| Watch, Waltham, Ball, Railroad Model, 19 Jewel | 90.00 |
| Watch, Waltham, Coin Silver Case, Key Wind | 32.00 |
| Watch, Waltham, Crescent Case, 14 Jewel | 30.00 |
| Watch, Waltham, Engraved 10K Gold Filled Case, 21 Jewel | 85.00 |
| Watch, Waltham, Gold Filled Hunting Case, Initials, Size O | 35.00 |
| Watch, Waltham, Gold Filled, C.1888, Size 14 | 80.00 |
| Watch, Waltham, Gold Filled, Open Face, 21 Jewel, C.1907 | 60.00 |
| Watch, Waltham, Gold Hunting Case, Engraved, 11 Jewel | 145.00 |
| Watch, Waltham, Lady's, Gold Filled Hunting Case, 15 Jewel, C.1910 | 70.00 |
| Watch, Waltham, Machine Engraved Coin Silver Opan Face, 7 Jewel | 28.00 |
| Watch, Waltham, No.24385246, Gold Plated Open Face, 21 Jewel | 70.00 |
| Watch, Waltham, Vanguard, 14K Gold Case, 23 Jewel | 140.00 |
| Watch, Waltham, 14K Gold Hunting Case, Repeater, 1900s *Illus* | 700.00 |
| Watch, Waltham, 14K Gold Open Face, Engraved, 19 Jewel | 125.00 |
| Watch, Waltham, 18K Gold Hunting Case, Engraved July 27th, 1866 | 500.00 |
| Watch, Waltham, 19057061, 21 Jewel | 95.00 |
| Watch, Waltham, 845, Gold Filled, Open Face, 21 Jewel, C.1921 | 70.00 |

| | |
|---|---|
| Watch, William Spurge, Woolwich, C.1825, Silver Pair Case, Verge Movement | 60.00 |
| Watch, Wright & Kay Co., Det. & Paris, Man's, Gold Filled Hunting Case | 75.00 |
| Watch, Wrist, Dale Evans | 30.00 |
| Watch, Wrist, Zorro | 35.00 |

*Waterford type glass glass resembles the famous glass made in the Waterford Glass Works in Ireland. It is a clear glass that was often cut for decoration. Modern glass is still being made in Waterford, Ireland.*

| | |
|---|---|
| Waterford, Compote, Large, C.1750 | 325.00 |
| Waterford, Compote, Oval, Diamond Base, 7 3/4 In.High | 125.00 |
| Waterford, Compote, Shallow, 6 Sided Base, 7 1/2 In.High | 100.00 |
| Waterford, Cruet, Set Of 5 In Robert Hennell Silver-Footed Holder, 1794 | 598.00 |
| Waterford, Jar, Sweetmeat, Sheffield Case With Hinged Lid & Ring Handles | 275.00 |
| Waterford, Pitcher, Footed, Diamond Cut | 195.00 |

**WAVE CREST WARE**

*Wavecrest glass is a white glassware manufactured by the Pairpoint Manufacturing Company of New Bedford, Massachusetts, and some French factories. It was then decorated by the C.F.Monroe Company of Meriden, Connecticut. The glass was painted pastel colors and decorated with flowers. The name Wavecrest was used after 1898.*

| | |
|---|---|
| Wavecrest, Bowl, Brass Collar, Shell Design, Yellow To White Floral | 75.00 |
| Wavecrest, Bowl, Brass Handles, Embossed & Painted Decoration, 5 3/4 In. | 62.00 |
| Wavecrest, Bowl, Enamel Floral, Pink Embossed Shells, Gold Collar, 3 1/4 In. | 35.00 |
| Wavecrest, Bowl, Hinged, Red Mark, 7 1/2 In.Diameter | 400.00 |
| Wavecrest, Bowl, Ormolu Handles & Rim, Pastel Flowers & Beading, Red Star | 175.00 |
| Wavecrest, Bowl, Ormolu Mountings, Openwork Handles, Blue Floral On White | 115.00 |
| Wavecrest, Bowl, Ormolu Rim, Open Handles, Yellow To White Swirl, Marked | 85.00 |
| Wavecrest, Bowl, Powder, Swirled, Daisies, Brass Trim | 125.00 |
| Wavecrest, Bowl, Trinket, Brass Rim, Handled, Marked, 3 1/2 In. | 75.00 |
| Wavecrest, Box, Blue & White Swirls On Cover & Base, Apple Blossoms, Beaded | 415.00 |
| Wavecrest, Box, Brass Collar & Catch, Swirl & Orange Floral On Cream | 115.00 |
| Wavecrest, Box, Brass Hinged Collar, Blue Floral, Signed, 3 In.Diameter | 125.00 |
| Wavecrest, Box, Cherubs On Hinged Top, Signed, 5 1/2 In.Diameter | 295.00 |
| Wavecrest, Box, Collars & Cuffs In Gold, Enameled Floral, 7 In.Diameter | 425.00 |
| Wavecrest, Box, Collars & Cuffs, Hinged, Puffy Egg Shape, 7 In. | 390.00 |
| Wavecrest, Box, Covered, Brass Collar, 5 In.Diameter | 225.00 |
| Wavecrest, Box, Covered, Floral Decoration, Brass Collar, 5 In.Diameter | 225.00 |
| Wavecrest, Box, Covered, Floral Swirl, 6 1/2 In | 150.00 |
| Wavecrest, Box, Covered, Gold Collar & Clasp, White Scrolls On Blue, Marked | 147.00 |
| Wavecrest, Box, Daisies On Hinged Lid, Raised Shells, Footed, 5 1/2 In. | 150.00 |
| Wavecrest, Box, Dresser, Round, Ribbed, Daisies, 4 1/2 In. | 38.00 |
| Wavecrest, Box, Dresser, Shells, Floral, Round, 3 1/2 In | 38.00 |
| Wavecrest, Box, Dresser, 2 Handled Brass Top, Round, Floral On Light Blue | 95.00 |
| Wavecrest, Box, Dresser, 2 Handled Brass Top, Round, Floral On Pale Green | 95.00 |
| Wavecrest, Box, Glove, Open Ends, Footed Ormolu Frame, Signed | 500.00 |
| Wavecrest, Box, Hinged Lid, Square, Footed, C.F.Monroe | 325.00 |
| Wavecrest, Box, Hinged Top, Swirls & Florals On White, 4 1/2 In.Diameter | 120.00 |
| Wavecrest, Box, Hinged, Cupid & Floral On Cover, 3 In. | 150.00 |
| Wavecrest, Box, Hinged, Embossed & Hand-Painted Violets, Pink Lining | 150.00 |
| Wavecrest, Box, Hinged, Embossed Shell Scrolling On Robin's-Egg Blue | 215.00 |
| Wavecrest, Box, Hinged, Floral Decoration, Red Mark, 4 In.High | 400.00 |
| Wavecrest, Box, Hinged, Hand-Painted Floral On Beige, 3 1/2 In. | 165.00 |
| Wavecrest, Box, Hinged, Lilies Of The Valley, 3 1/2 In. | 110.00 |
| Wavecrest, Box, Hinged, Oblong, Floral Panels, 6 X 4 In. | 375.00 |
| Wavecrest, Box, Hinged, Oval, Enameled Floral On White, 6 In.Diameter | 195.00 |
| Wavecrest, Box, Hinged, Oval, Signed, 5 1/2 X 3 1/2 In. | 195.00 |
| Wavecrest, Box, Hinged, Pink & Blue Swirled, White Daisies, 4 1/2 In. | 165.00 |
| Wavecrest, Box, Hinged, Pink On Blue, 3 1/2 In. | 155.00 |
| Wavecrest, Box, Hinged, Rose Colored Blossoms On Blue Green, 4 In. | 195.00 |
| Wavecrest, Box, Hinged, Rose Garlands, Blown-Out Puffs, Square, 6 In. | 250.00 |
| Wavecrest, Box, Hinged, Shell Pattern, Pink Lining, Red Banner Mark | 175.00 |
| Wavecrest, Box, Hinged, Shell Pattern, 3 1/2 In.High | 1(5.00 |
| Wavecrest, Box, Hinged, Spray Of Flowers On Top | 175.00 |
| Wavecrest, Box, Hinged, Swirl Design, Yellow & Pink Flowers | 20.00 |
| Wavecrest, Box, Hinged, Swirled On White, 3 1/2 In. | 155.00 |
| Wavecrest, Box, Hinged, Swirled, Pink Satin Lining In Cover, 3 1/2 In. | 165.00 |

Wavecrest, Box, Hinged, Swirled, 7 In. Diameter ........................................ 225.00
Wavecrest, Box, Hinged, White Daisies & Forget-Me-Nots, 4 1/2 In. ........... 165.00
Wavecrest, Box, Hinged, White, Blown-Out Puffs, Square, 4 1/2 In. ........... 180.00
Wavecrest, Box, Jewel, Brass Hinge & Collar, Apple Blossoms, Scrolls .......... 150.00
Wavecrest, Box, Jewel, Hinged Lid, Flower Sprays, Red Mark, 4 1/2 In. ....... 210.00
Wavecrest, Box, Jewel, Hinged, Decorated, 4 1/2 In.Diameter At Base .......... 110.00
Wavecrest, Box, Jewel, Hinged, Enameled Wild Flowers, 4 1/2 In. .............. 195.00
Wavecrest, Box, Jewel, Hinged, Flowers, Enameled, Signed, 4 1/2 In.Wide ...... 175.00
Wavecrest, Box, Jewel, Idyllic Scene On Cover, Embossed Scrolls On Pink ...... 225.00
Wavecrest, Box, Jewel, Ormolu Clasp, Hinge, & Mounts, Enamel Floral, 4 In. ... 195.00
Wavecrest, Box, Letter, Brass Collar, Ormolu On Corners, Puffs, Oblong ........ 250.00
Wavecrest, Box, Pin, Blue Floral Decoration, Brass Trim, Red Banner Mark ..... 45.00
Wavecrest, Box, Red Banner Mark, 3 1/2 In.Wide ................................ 42.00
Wavecrest, Box, Trinket, Brass Collar & Extended Ormolu Handle, Blue Trim .... 75.00
Wavecrest, Box, Trinket, Brass Collar, Lily Of The Valley ..................... 55.00
Wavecrest, Card Holder, Calling, Puffed Design, Floral, Ormolu Rim, Red Mark ... 135.00
Wavecrest, Card Holder, Gold Plated Collar, Raised Scroll, Pink Floral ........ 82.50
Wavecrest, Container, Cigar, Silver Collar, Lid & Bail, Lavender Luster ........ 250.00
Wavecrest, Fernery, Brass Rim & Insert, Blue Daisies, 6 In.Square ............ 145.00
Wavecrest, Fernery, Octagonal, Brass Beaded Top, Floral On Cream, 4 1/2 In. ... 220.00
Wavecrest, Hair Receiver, Blue, Red Banner Mark, 4 1/2 In. Diameter .......... 215.00
Wavecrest, Jar, Biscuit, Applied Decoration, 8 1/2 In. ....................... 75.00
Wavecrest, Jar, Biscuit, Barrel Shape, Yellow To White, Lilacs .............. 120.00
Wavecrest, Jar, Biscuit, Repousse Silver Top, Ferns On Blue White ........... 150.00
Wavecrest, Jar, Brass Collar, Blue & White Floral On Pink, 3 1/4 In. ......... 90.00
Wavecrest, Jar, Cookie, Barrel, Pansies On Ivory, Silver Plate Lid & Handle .... 125.00
Wavecrest, Jar, Cookie, Brass Collar, Square, Raised Shells, Apple Blossoms .... 160.00
Wavecrest, Jar, Cracker, Pink & White Flower With Yellow Center, Silver Lid ... 135.00
Wavecrest, Jar, Cracker, Raised Scrolls, Enamel Floral, Silver Plate Lid ...... 150.00
Wavecrest, Jar, Cracker, Square, Pastel Flowers, Metal Lid & Handle, 7 In. .... 115.00
Wavecrest, Jar, Double Pierced Handles, Floral, Blue Satin Lining ............ 90.00
Wavecrest, Jar, Floral, Metal Rim & Handles, Round, Marked, 3 X 2 In. ........ 45.00
Wavecrest, Jardiniere, Brass Rim & Insert, Embossed, Pink Floral, 8 In. ....... 225.00
Wavecrest, Muffineer, Floral, Leaf, & Ferns, White To Blue At Base .......... 165.00
Wavecrest, Muffineer, White Satin, Erie Twist, Enamel Floral, Repousse Cover ... 140.00
Wavecrest, Planter, Blue, Pink Flowers, 5 In.Square, Signed .................. 225.00
Wavecrest, Planter, Brass Inset, Embossed Scrolls On Blue, Square, 5 1/2 In. ... 250.00
Wavecrest, Planter, Brass Inset, Paneled, 7 In. ............................. 275.00
Wavecrest, Planter, Marshmallowlike Puffs & Floral Garlands, Square, 7 In. .... 225.00
Wavecrest, Planter, 6 Sided, Signed, 7 1/2 In. Diameter ..................... 225.00
Wavecrest, Sachet, Glossy Blue, Mums On White Satin Panels, 2 In.High ......... 185.00
Wavecrest, Salt & Pepper, Blue To White, Swirled, Enameled Floral ........... 45.00
Wavecrest, Salt & Pepper, Pink Enamel Florals, Scrolled 6 Sided Panels ........ 85.00
Wavecrest, Saltshaker, Apricot To White Swirls, Enamel Decorated Top ......... 28.00
Wavecrest, Saltshaker, Enamel Floral On Apricot To White, Swirled ........... 32.50
Wavecrest, Sugar & Creamer, Silver Cover & Twisted Handles, Florals, White .... 150.00
Wavecrest, Syrup, Violets .................................................. 65.00
Wavecrest, Toothbrush Holder, Grapes, Red Banner Mark ...................... 225.00
Wavecrest, Toothpick, Ormolu Feet, Pink & White Flowers, Red Banner Mark .... 175.00
Wavecrest, Tray, Pin, Brass Trim, Hand-Painted Flowers ...................... 78.00
Wavecrest, Tray, Pin, Double Handled ....................................... 42.00
Wavecrest, Tray, Pin, Enameled Floral On Blue To White, Ormolu Handles ....... 75.00
Wavecrest, Urn, Font Inset, Pair ........................................... 185.00
Wavecrest, Urn, Ormolu Collar & Handles, White Satin Medallions On Blue ....... 125.00
Wavecrest, Vase, Brass Collar, Footed Base, & Ormolu Handles, Scrolls, Pair .... 850.00
Wavecrest, Vase, Brass Ormolu Base, Collar, & Handles, Blue Floral, 5 In. ..... 159.00
Wavecrest, Vase, Bulbous Base, Pink Clovers On Blue, Gilded Top Band, 4 In. ... 32.00
Wavecrest, Vase, Bulbous, 6 In.High ........................................ 120.00
Wavecrest, Vase, Ormolu Footed, Blue Daisies On Pink, Dotted Top, 4 3/4 In. ... 75.00
Wavecrest, Vase, Ormolu Footed, Decorated, Red Banner Mark, 10 In.High ........ 215.00
Wavecrest, Vase, Pink & White, Gold Enamel, 5 X 4 In. ...................... 85.00
Weapon, Ax, Belt, Colonial American, Hand Forged From 1 Piece Of Steel ....... 97.50
Weapon, Ax, Boarding, French Navy Issue, M1833, Wooden Handle, 4 Cornered ..... 125.00
Weapon, Battleax, India, Double Headed, Iron, 7.00 Silver ................... 59.50
Weapon, Battleax, India, Iron, Crescent Blade, Inlaid Brass Decoration ........ 44.50
Weapon, Bayonet, German, Iron Scabbard .................................... 7.00

| | |
|---|---:|
| Weapon, Bayonet, Nazi Police, Scabbard, Eagle & Swastika On Grip | 15.50 |
| Weapon, Bayonet, Revolutionary War, Socket, Hand Forged, 14 1/2 In.Blade | 97.50 |
| Weapon, Bayonet, Socket, For M1835/1842 Musket, Marked U.S. | 22.50 |
| Weapon, Bayonet, Winchester, Scabbard, 13 1/2 In.Long | 33.00 |
| Weapon, Bayonet, World War I, J.Corts Sohn, Scabbard, Hallmarked | 25.00 |
| Weapon, Blunderbuss, Dag, Carved Stock, Brass Engraved Inlays | 225.00 |
| Weapon, Blunderbuss, Dag, Flared Muzzle, Silver Inlays, Brass | 225.00 |
| Weapon, Bolo, Fighting, Filipino, Horned Grips, Carved Handle, C.1890 | 75.00 |
| Weapon, Box, Cartridge, U.S., Brass, Oval, Lead Backed, Flap Buckle | 25.00 |
| Weapon, Box, Patch, Hinged, Enameled White Water Lily & Floral On Amber | 60.00 |
| Weapon, Box, Patch, Porcelain, Blue Flowers On Pink, Gold Trim | 5.00 |
| Weapon, Brass Knuckles, Aluminum, Marked P.D. | 9.50 |
| Weapon, Broadsword, Scottish Highland, Miniature, Silver, Basket Hilt, 1890 | 275.00 |
| Weapon, Broadsword, Scottish, Silver Basket Hilt & Blade, 1890, 16 In.Long | 275.00 |
| Weapon, Cannon, Bronze, English, Oak Carriage, C.1830, 19 In.Long, Pair | 1200.00 |
| Weapon, Cannon, Field, Brass, Handmade, Iron Flashpan, Spoke Wheels, Phila. | 275.00 |
| Weapon, Cannon, Japanese, Wall, Matchlock, Brass Lock, Iron Hammer, Inlaid | 350.00 |
| Weapon, Cannon, Naval, Handmade, Brass Barrel, Teakwood, 23 In.Long | 275.00 |
| Weapon, Cannon, Wall, Japanese, Matchlock, Octagonal Muzzle | 350.00 |
| Weapon, Carbine Boot, Spencer, U.S.Cavalry, Indian War, Rock Island Arsenal | 32.50 |
| Weapon, Carbine, Enfield, British, Brass Butt Plate, Iron Saddle Ring, 1868 | 150.00 |
| Weapon, Carbine, Gallager, Civil War, Percussion, Iron Patch Box | 276.00 |
| Weapon, Carbine, Sharp's New Model 1863, Percussion, Civil War | 325.00 |
| Weapon, Carbine, Sharps & Hankins, U.S.Navy, .52rF, Saddle Ring | 395.00 |
| Weapon, Carbine, Spencer, Cavalry, Repeating, 7 Shot | 225.00 |
| Weapon, Carbine, Spencer, Civil War, Repeating, .50 Caliber | 250.00 |
| Weapon, Carbine, Spencer, Civil War, 7 Shot, Repeating | 225.00 |
| Weapon, Carbine, Spencer, M1865, Cavalry, Repeating, .50 Caliber | 275.00 |
| Weapon, Carbine, Spencer, Repeating, Civil War, .50rF, 22 In.Barrel | 250.00 |
| Weapon, Carbine, U.S.Marines, M-1, Inland Division, .30 Caliber | 84.50 |
| Weapon, Carbine, Winchester, Brass Frame, Saddle Ring, .66 Caliber | 475.00 |
| Weapon, Carbine, Winchester, NRA Centennial Model No.94, .30/.30 Caliber | 97.50 |
| Weapon, Crossbow, Mid East, Hand-Carved | 35.00 |
| Weapon, Cutlass, British Naval, War Of 1812, Ribbed & Quartered Iron Grips | 97.50 |
| Weapon, Cutlass, Colonial American, Iron Guard, Bone Grips, Engraved Blade | 450.00 |
| Weapon, Cutlass, Hunting Association, Miniature, Presentation Box | 39.50 |
| Weapon, Dagger, British Commando, World War II, Joseph Rogers, Sheffield | 84.50 |
| Weapon, Dagger, French, Black Handle, Engraved Blade, C.1700, 9 In. | 65.00 |
| Weapon, Dagger, Hitler Youth, Scabbard, R Z M, 1937 On Blade | 20.00 |
| Weapon, Dagger, Leather Sheath, Deer's Foot Handle, 10 1/2 In. | 22.00 |
| Weapon, Dagger, Nazi Hunting Association, Scabbard, Miniature, 10 In. | 39.50 |
| Weapon, Dagger, Nazi S.S., Black Hilt & Scabbard, R.Z.M, 7/39 In Blade | 120.00 |
| Weapon, Dagger, Nazi Youth, Sheath, Blade Inscribed Blut Und Ehre, 1936 | 39.50 |
| Weapon, Dagger, Nazi, Silver Scabbard, Eagle Hilt, Swastika | 100.00 |
| Weapon, Dagger, Persian, Carved Agate Horse's Head Handle, C.1850 | 250.00 |
| Weapon, Derringer, American, Percussion, .41 Caliber, Engraved Silver, C.1840 | 265.00 |
| Weapon, Derringer, Brown Mfg.Co., Patent 1857, .41 Caliber, Brass, Rosewood | 750.00 |
| Weapon, Derringer, Colt, No.3, .41 Caliber, Silver On Brass, Walnut Grips | 250.00 |
| Weapon, Derringer, Colt, No.4, .22 Caliber, Pair | 59.50 |
| Weapon, Derringer, Colt, 4th Model, Silvered Frame, .22 Caliber, Walnut Grips | 37.50 |
| Weapon, Derringer, Dickinson, Brass Frame, Civil War, Ratchet Lever | 75.00 |
| Weapon, Derringer, Eclipse, Iron Frame, .25 Caliber, Bird's Head Butt | 47.50 |
| Weapon, Derringer, Nickel, Octagonal Barrel, 1870, .41 Caliber | 185.00 |
| Weapon, Derringer, Over & Under, Brass Frame, 1865, .41 Caliber | 210.00 |
| Weapon, Derringer, Percussion, .41 Caliber, Engraved German Silver | 265.00 |
| Weapon, Derringer, Remington Elliot, .32 Caliber, 4 Barrel, Ring Trigger | 125.00 |
| Weapon, Derringer, Remington, Double Barrel, .41 Caliber, Rubber Grips | 350.00 |
| Weapon, Derringer, Remington, Elliot, Nimschke Engraved, Pearl Grips | 450.00 |
| Weapon, Derringer, Remington, Over/under, Nickel Finish, .41 Caliber | 250.00 |
| Weapon, Derringer, Southerner, Brass Frame, .41 Caliber, Dated 1847 | 125.00 |
| Weapon, Dirk Set, Scottish Highland, Silver Mounted, Dated 1849, 4 Piece | 325.00 |
| Weapon, Dirk, Naval, Curved Blade, Scabbard, C.1845 | 42.50 |
| Weapon, Dirk, U.S.Naval, Silver Sheath & Hilt, Ivory Grips | 295.00 |
| Weapon, Flask, Copper, Pistol, Stag & Trees In Relief, Brass Top | 39.50 |
| Weapon, Flask, Powder, Brass, British, Octagonal, Telescopic Spout, Dated 1849 | 74.50 |
| Weapon, Flask, Powder, Brass, Pistol, Oak Leaf & Branch Designs, 4 3/4 In. | 39.50 |

Weapon, Flask, Powder, British, Brass, Presentation, Octagonal, C.1849 .................................. 74.50
Weapon, Flask, Powder, Colt Revolver, Copper, Leaf & Eagle Designs ................................. 64.50
Weapon, Flask, Powder, Copper, Colt Pistol, American, Engraved Crossed Guns ................. 64.50
Weapon, Flask, Powder, Copper, Pistol, Shell & Bush Design ............................................... 34.50
Weapon, Flask, Powder, Japanese, Matchlock Musket, C.1800, Black Leather ..................... 59.50
Weapon, Flask, Powder, Mid East, Miguelet, Oval Shape, Leather, Iron Rings .................... 39.50
Weapon, Flask, Powder, Pistol, Brass, Oak Leaf & Branch Design On Sides ....................... 39.50
Weapon, Flask, Powder, Pistol, Caucasian, Silver, Niello Floral ......................................... 225.00
Weapon, Flask, Powder, Pistol, Copper, Bag Shape, Standing Stag, Brass Top ................. 39.50
Weapon, Flask, Powder, Pistol, Copper, Shell Design On Sides ........................................... 34.50
Weapon, Flask, Powder, Rifle, Copper, Fluted Ribbed Design On Sides ............................. 34.50
Weapon, Flask, Powder, Silver Mounted, Pistol, Niello Floral & Scroll ............................. 225.00
Weapon, Flask, Powder, Wooden, African, Musket, Oval Shape, Leather Covered ............. 39.50
Weapon, Flask, Powder, Wooden, Leather Covered, Japanese, Musket, C.1800 ................. 84.50
Weapon, Flask, Powder, Zinc, Pistol, Brass Top, Wood Grouse On Tree Stump ............... 22.50
Weapon, Flask, Powder, Zinc, Pistol, Shell & Bush Design, 4 In. ....................................... 22.50
Weapon, Flask, Shot, Leather, Brass Spout & Lever, Embossed Designs ............................ 14.50
Weapon, Flask, Shot, Leather, Embossed Hunting Dogs, Brass Spout & Lever .................. 14.50
Weapon, Fowling Piece, From M1842 .69 Caliber Musket, Half Stock, C.1860 ................. 59.50
Weapon, Fowling Piece, Pennsylvania, Carved, Engraved, .75 Caliber ............................... 425.00
Weapon, Gun, Air, Poacher's, Cane Crutch, Patch Box In Silver Butt, C.1850 ................. 295.00
Weapon, Gun, Cane, Percussion ......................................................................................... 295.00
Weapon, Gun, Whale Harpoon, Cordes, Bremerhaven, Percussion, C.1850 ...................... 350.00
Weapon, Gun, Whaling, C.C.Brand, Black Painted Finish, Gold Painted Trim ................. 475.00
Weapon, Gun, Whaling, Harpoon, Percussion, Muzzle Loading, Brass Band, C.1850 ....... 350.00
Weapon, Gun, Whaling, New England, Percussion, 36 In. ................................................. 275.00
Weapon, Halberd Head, German, Cast Iron, 3 Blades, 20 1/2 In. ..................................... 25.00
Weapon, Halbred Head, Cast Iron, German, 20 In. ........................................................... 25.00
Weapon, Harpoon, Whale, Toggle Iron, Hand Forged, 7 In.Swivel Head ......................... 97.50
Weapon, Harpoon, Whale, 2 Swivel Flues With Barbs, C.1850 ......................................... 84.50
Weapon, Holster, Dragoon Colt Revolver, Brown Leather, Copper Rivets, Brass ............. 97.50
Weapon, Kinfe, Pocket, Gold, Diamond & 2 Rubies, 4 In. ................................................ 68.00
Weapon, Knife & Cigar Cutter, Pocket, Gold Finish, Loop For Chain ................................ 5.95
Weapon, Knife, Bowie, Army Issue, Dated 1917 .............................................................. 35.00
Weapon, Knife, Bowie, G.Wostenholm & Son, Washington Works, Sheffield, Eng. ......... 150.00
Weapon, Knife, Bowie, Wostenholm & Son, Sheffield, Etched Blade, Stag Grips .............. 150.00
Weapon, Knife, Boy Scout, Remington .............................................................. 19.00 To 25.00
Weapon, Knife, Bradford, 6 1/2 In. Long Open ................................................................ 75.00
Weapon, Knife, British Commando, Brass Hilt ................................................................. 18.00
Weapon, Knife, Buffalo, Wooden Box .............................................................................. 32.50
Weapon, Knife, Cattaraugus, Stag Handle, 2 Blades ........................................................ 12.50
Weapon, Knife, Deep-Sea Diver's, Siebe Gorman & Co., Brass Mounted Wood ............... 74.50
Weapon, Knife, Dirk, U.S.Naval, Silver Sheath & Hilt, 1 Piece Ivory Grips ................... 295.00
Weapon, Knife, Egyptian Officer's, Brass Scabbard, Carved Bone Handle ........................ 30.00
Weapon, Knife, Gurkha, India, Leather Sheath ................................................................. 75.00
Weapon, Knife, Kabar, Rosewood Handle ........................................................................... 8.00
Weapon, Knife, Kabar, Trapper, 2 Blades ........................................................................... 5.00
Weapon, Knife, Kodiak Bear Hunter's, Stag Handle, Scabbard ......................................... 35.00
Weapon, Knife, Lady's, Gold, Floral Designs, Marked Glaco On Blade ............................ 13.00
Weapon, Knife, Lady's, Pocket, Gold ............................................................................... 15.00
Weapon, Knife, Mother-Of-Pearl Handle, Nail File, Collar Buttonhook, Blades .............. 10.00
Weapon, Knife, Nazi Youth, Inscribed Blut Und Ehre On Blade, 1937 ........................... 75.00
Weapon, Knife, Nazi, Scabbard, Bone Handle, 15 In.Lonb ................................................ 97.50
Weapon, Knife, Pocket, Booth Bros., 7 In. ....................................................................... 15.00
Weapon, Knife, Pocket, Engraved, Fob ............................................................................. 10.00
Weapon, Knife, Pocket, Keen Kutter, 1 Blade .................................................................... 4.00
Weapon, Knife, Pocket, Lady's, Ornate, Gold Filled ........................................................... 9.00
Weapon, Knife, Pocket, Lone Ranger, Silver Bullet .......................................................... 11.00
Weapon, Knife, Pocket, Marked Nation's Allies, 11 Blades ............................................... 28.00
Weapon, Knife, Pocket, Nude Photographs On Handle ........................................................ 8.00
Weapon, Knife, Pocket, Pearl Handle, Sterling Silver Blade ............................................... 9.00
Weapon, Knife, Pocket, Putnam Barlow .............................................................................. 3.50
Weapon, Knife, Pocket, Remington, Metal Handle, 3 Blades ............................................. 23.00
Weapon, Knife, Pocket, Souvenir, The Capitol, The White House, German Made ............. 17.50
Weapon, Knife, Pocket, Ulster, 4 Blades ............................................................................. 2.50
Weapon, Knife, Pocket, Wostenholm, Steel Handle, Folding, 2 3/4 In.Long ..................... 59.50

| | |
|---|---|
| Weapon, Knife, Remington, Celluloid Handle, 2 Blades | 17.00 |
| Weapon, Knife, Remington, 2 Blade, Wood Handle | 18.00 |
| Weapon, Knife, Signed Fascine, C.1820 | 50.00 |
| Weapon, Knife, World War II Navy Pilot's Survival | 30.00 |
| Weapon, Kris, Balinese, Sheath, Brass, Inlaid Semiprecious Stones | 235.00 |
| Weapon, Lance, Confederate Cavalry, Iron Tip, Wooden Shaft, Pennant | 125.00 |
| Weapon, Lance, Whaling, 5 Ft. 4 In. | 125.00 |
| Weapon, Lance, Revolutionary Period, Brass Frame, 2 Iron Blades | 40.00 |
| Weapon, Luger, Mauser, Model 1934, Military, Nazi Insignias | 235.00 |
| Weapon, Machete, Cowhide Scabbard, Nicaragua, Garza, Brass Studs | 24.00 |
| Weapon, Machete, Silver Eagle's Head Hilt, Etched Blade, C.1900 | 24.50 |
| Weapon, Measure, Powder Shot, Brass With Collapsible Measure | 13.50 |
| Weapon, Mirror, Bayonet Periscope, Military, C.1880 | 45.00 |
| Weapon, Mold, Bullet, Brass, Gang Type, U.S.Revolutionary Period, 18 Balls | 59.50 |
| Weapon, Mold, Bullet, Brass, Scissors Type, 4 1/2 In.Long | 9.75 |
| Weapon, Mold, Bullet, Revolutionary Period, Iron, Scissor Type, .69 Caliber | 22.50 |
| Weapon, Mold, Bullet, Scissor Type, Iron, Octagonal Top, .69 Caliber, C.1750 | 37.50 |
| Weapon, Mold, Bullet, Scissor Type, Revolutionary Period, .69 Caliber, Iron | 22.50 |
| Weapon, Mold, Bullet, 2 Cavity, .36 Caliber, Brass, Unmarked | 40.00 |
| Weapon, Mortar, Civil War, Cochorn, Iron, Muzzle Loading, 'g.& G.' | 395.00 |
| Weapon, Mortar, Coohorn, Civil War, Muzzle Loading, Iron, Marked G & G | 395.00 |
| Weapon, Musket, American Colonial, 'Fish Belly, ' Club Butt, C.1750 | 595.00 |
| Weapon, Musket, Fish Belly, Club Butt, American, Octagonal Barrel, C.1750 | 595.00 |
| Weapon, Musket, Matchlock, C.1700 | 300.00 |
| Weapon, Musket, Wheel-Lock, Inlaid Bone, Ivory, & Pearl, 44 1/2 In.Long | 3000.00 |
| Weapon, Pepperbox, Allen & Thurber, Conn., Percussion, 6 Shot, .30 Caliber | 250.00 |
| Weapon, Pepperbox, Allen & Thurber, Conn., Percussion, 6 Shot, .31 Caliber | 215.00 |
| Weapon, Pepperbox, Allen & Thurber, 6 Shot, .30 Caliber, Fluted Barrels | 250.00 |
| Weapon, Pepperbox, Mosseberg, Brownie, 4 Barrel, .22 Caliber, Walnut Grips | 69.50 |
| Weapon, Pepperbox, Sharps, 4 Barrel, .22 Caliber, Rosewood Grips | 150.00 |
| Weapon, Pepperbox, Sharps, 4 Barrel, .22 Caliber, Silver On Brass | 150.00 |
| Weapon, Pepperbox, Sprague & Marston, N.Y., Percussion, 6 Shot, .31 Caliber | 235.00 |
| Weapon, Pepperbox, Sprague & Marston, N.Y., 6 Shot, .31 Caliber, Engraved | 450.00 |
| Weapon, Pepperbox, Sprague & Marston, Percussion, 6 Shot, .31 Caliber | 235.00 |
| Weapon, Pepperbox, Sprague & Marston, 6 Shot, .31 Caliber, Engraved, 1849 | 450.00 |
| Weapon, Petard, Bronze, European, Integral Flashpan & Touchhole, C.1650 | 295.00 |
| Weapon, Pike, Confederate, Iron Blade & Elliptical Cross Guard | 125.00 |
| Weapon, Pike, Confederate, Iron Blade, Brass Circular Guard & Ferrule | 110.00 |
| Weapon, Pike, Confederate, Iron Elliptical Cross Guard & Ferrule | 125.00 |
| Weapon, Pistol, Arab Chieftain's, Flintlock, Gold Inlay, Silver Butt | 475.00 |
| Weapon, Pistol, Bar, 4 Shot, .25 Caliber, Hard Rubber Grips | 175.00 |
| Weapon, Pistol, Blunt & Syms, Pocket, Double Barrel, Percussion | 395.00 |
| Weapon, Pistol, British Gentleman's Greatcoat, Stringer, Blair & Co., 1780 | 895.00 |
| Weapon, Pistol, British Greatcoat, Twigg, London, Boxlock, .56 Caliber, 1790 | 150.00 |
| Weapon, Pistol, Browning, World War II, Semiautomatic, Nazi Swastikas | 97.50 |
| Weapon, Pistol, Colt, 'National Match-Gold Cup, ' Target, .38 Caliber | 145.00 |
| Weapon, Pistol, Colt, Camp Perry Model, Target, .22 Caliber, Walnut Grips | 250.00 |
| Weapon, Pistol, Colt, Semiautomatic, .25 Caliber, Rubber Grips | 97.50 |
| Weapon, Pistol, Colt, 1860, Army, Engraving | 385.00 |
| Weapon, Pistol, Dueling, A.Wurfflein, Phila., .36 Caliber, Percussion, Pair | 1750.00 |
| Weapon, Pistol, Dueling, Robinson, Phila., Percussion, Gold Band Inlays, 1840 | 450.00 |
| Weapon, Pistol, Dueling, Twist Barrel, Le-Page A Paris | 325.00 |
| Weapon, Pistol, Dueling, William Ellis, London, .54 Caliber, C.1840, Pair | 1950.00 |
| Weapon, Pistol, Flintlock, Northern Inscription, C.1819 | 575.00 |
| Weapon, Pistol, German Officer's, Brecht-In, Weimar, .52 Caliber, C.1760 | 325.00 |
| Weapon, Pistol, Henshaw, London, Brass, 4 Barrel, Engraved, C.1790 | 1450.00 |
| Weapon, Pistol, Hero-A.S.T.Co., Brass Frame, Pocket, .36 Caliber, Walnut Grip | 79.50 |
| Weapon, Pistol, Hero, A.S.T.Co., Brass Frame, Pocket, .36 Caliber | 79.50 |
| Weapon, Pistol, Kentucky, Southern Confederate, Silver Inlay, 12 In.Long | 2150.00 |
| Weapon, Pistol, Llama, Spanish, Semiautomatic, .22 Caliber | 57.50 |
| Weapon, Pistol, Marked B.& S., N.Y., Cast Steel, Pocket, Percussion | 395.00 |
| Weapon, Pistol, Martin Patent, .455 Caliber, 4 Barrel, C.1880, Pair | 1500.00 |
| Weapon, Pistol, Mauser, Broom Handle, Military, Self Loading, M.63 Caliber | 195.00 |
| Weapon, Pistol, Olympic Trophy Model 103, Target, .22 Caliber | 84.50 |
| Weapon, Pistol, Pepperbox, English, .31 Caliber, 6 Shot | 550.00 |
| Weapon, Pistol, Pepperbox, Percussion, 1849, 4 Shot, .31 Caliber | 185.00 |

| | |
|---|---:|
| Weapon, Pistol, Sash, W.Pritchard, Birmingham, Percussion, .70 Caliber, Pair | 725.00 |
| Weapon, Pistol, Savage, M1907, Semiautomatic, .45 Caliber, Walnut Grips | 850.00 |
| Weapon, Pistol, Smith & Wesson, Model 41, Target, Semiautomatic, .22 Caliber | 110.00 |
| Weapon, Pistol, Smith & Wesson, New Model No.3, Target, .38/.44 Caliber | 950.00 |
| Weapon, Pistol, Smith & Wesson, Target, 3rd Modes, .22 Caliber, Walnut Grips | 175.00 |
| Weapon, Pistol, Spanish, Llama, Semiautomatic, .22 Caliber | 57.50 |
| Weapon, Pistol, Turkish, Flintlock, Brass Inlaid | 25.00 |
| Weapon, Pistol, W.Henshaw, London, Brass, 4 Barrel, Engraved, C.1790 | 1450.00 |
| Weapon, Pistol, W.Parker, Double Barrel, Flintlock, Engraved, London | 1475.00 |
| Weapon, Pouch, Cartridge, U.S.Army, 1830, Black Leather, James Boyd, Boston | 550.00 |
| Weapon, Pouch, Holds Flares For Signal Gun, U.S.Arsenal, Russet Leather | 97.50 |
| Weapon, Pouch, Shot, Leather, Handmade, Wooden Spout, Removable Stopper | 14.50 |
| Weapon, Pouch, Shot, Leather, Tall Brass Top, Removable Scoop Charger | 19.50 |
| Weapon, Pouch, Shot, Leather, Wooden Plug At Bottom | 10.00 |
| Weapon, Powder Flask, Copper, Concave & Convex Ribbing, Brass Measure | 35.00 |
| Weapon, Powder Flask, Horn, Brass Measure & Fittings, C.1862 | 50.00 |
| Weapon, Powder Flask, Pistol, Copper, Brass Dispenser, Leaf Decoration | 32.50 |
| Weapon, Powder Flask, Rifle, Copper, Fluted, Ribbed, Telescopic Spout | 34.50 |
| Weapon, Powder Horn, American, C.1750, Carved At Spout & Domed Wooden Base | 24.50 |
| Weapon, Powder Horn, American, Pistol, Revolutionary, Domed Wooden Base | 34.50 |
| Weapon, Powder Horn, Brass Covered Horn, Pierced, North African, C.1750 | 47.50 |
| Weapon, Powder Horn, Brass Mounted | 30.00 |
| Weapon, Powder Horn, Brass Ring At End, Rawhide Strap, 11 In.Long | 20.00 |
| Weapon, Powder Horn, Brass Spout, Carrying Rings & Cap | 75.00 |
| Weapon, Powder Horn, Brass, Man, Pheasant, Dog, & Trees In Relief, Dispenser | 48.00 |
| Weapon, Powder Horn, British Military Issue, Brown Bess Musket, C.1750 | 175.00 |
| Weapon, Powder Horn, Buildings & Coat Of Arms, C.1850, 18 In.Long | 90.00 |
| Weapon, Powder Horn, Carved, 8 In.Outside Curve, C.1863 | 135.00 |
| Weapon, Powder Horn, Civil War, Silvered Brass Mounts, American, 1862, 13 In. | 300.00 |
| Weapon, Powder Horn, Engraved John Besom, 1874, Man On Horseback, 12 In. | 375.00 |
| Weapon, Powder Horn, Horn Stopper, 6 3/4 In.     *Illus* | 650.00 |
| Weapon, Powder Horn, Horn, American, Carved Spout, Wooden Base, C.1850 | 24.50 |
| Weapon, Powder Horn, Horn, For Brown Bess, British Military, Brass Top, Wood | 175.00 |
| Weapon, Powder Horn, Horn, Military Issue, Brass Top, Wooden Base | 175.00 |
| Weapon, Powder Horn, Horn, Pistol, American Revolutionary, Wooden Base | 34.50 |
| Weapon, Powder Horn, India, Wooden, Black Leather Covered, Stubby Shape | 32.50 |
| Weapon, Powder Horn, Military Issue, American, Revolutionary, Brass Spout | 175.00 |
| Weapon, Powder Horn, Moroccan, Brass, C.1750, Piercings, 2 Brass Rings | 47.50 |
| Weapon, Powder Horn, Pouring Spout, 3 Pound Leather Bag For Lead Shot | 30.00 |
| Weapon, Powder Horn, Scottish, Etched Names Of Battles, C.1850, 16 In.Long | 150.00 |
| Weapon, Ramrod, For Gun, Threaded Wormer, Cast Iron, 38 In.Long | 10.00 |
| Weapon, Reloading Tool, Shot Shell, Cast Iron | 16.50 |
| Weapon, Revolver, Adam's Patent, Civil War, Navy, 5 Shot, .36 Caliber | 325.00 |
| Weapon, Revolver, Bacon Style, Marked Cast Steel, Semifluted Cylinder | 250.00 |
| Weapon, Revolver, Bacon, Percussion, .38 Caliber, Engraved Scenes | 135.00 |
| Weapon, Revolver, Blank, Mubis, .32 Caliber | 19.50 |
| Weapon, Revolver, Brevette, 1880, .38 Caliber, Engraved Octagonal Barrel | 75.00 |
| Weapon, Revolver, Butterfield, Civil War, Serial No.417, 5 Shot, .41 Caliber | 1250.00 |
| Weapon, Revolver, Champion, Patent March 1871, Spur Trigger, .32 Caliber | 24.50 |

Weapon, Powder Horn, Horn Stopper, 6 3/4 In.

| | |
|---|---:|
| Weapon, Revolver, Civil War, Cup Fire, Eagle, Engraved, Pearl Handle | 295.00 |
| Weapon, Revolver, Colt 44, Brass, 2 Cavity Mold | 50.00 |
| Weapon, Revolver, Colt, Dragoon, Handmade, Copper Riveted Leather Holster | 97.50 |
| Weapon, Revolver, Colt, Frontier, Lightning, .41 Caliber, Nickel Plated, 1871 | 145.00 |
| Weapon, Revolver, Colt, M1849, Percussion, .31 Caliber, Brass, Silver Finish | 325.00 |
| Weapon, Revolver, Colt, M1849, Percussion, .31 Caliber, 5 Shot, Engraved | 250.00 |
| Weapon, Revolver, Colt, M1849, Percussion, 5 Shot, .31 Caliber | 145.00 |
| Weapon, Revolver, Colt, M1849, 5 Shot, .31 Caliber, Brass Strap & Guard | 250.00 |
| Weapon, Revolver, Colt, M1853, Navy, Pocket, 5 Shot, .38 Caliber, Presentation | 895.00 |
| Weapon, Revolver, Colt, M1903, Semiautomatic, .38 Caliber, Serial No.44304 | 145.00 |
| Weapon, Revolver, Colt, M1909, U.S.Marine Corps, New Service, .45 Caliber | 350.00 |
| Weapon, Revolver, Colt, M1911, U.S.Army, 45 Caliber | 79.50 |
| Weapon, Revolver, Colt, New House, Spur Trigger, 5 Shot, .38 Caliber | 175.00 |
| Weapon, Revolver, Colt, New Line, .38 Caliber, Rosewood Grips | 325.00 |
| Weapon, Revolver, Colt, New Line, .41 Caliber, Rosewood Grips | 195.00 |
| Weapon, Revolver, Colt, New Service, M1909, U.S.Marine Corps, .45 Caliber | 350.00 |
| Weapon, Revolver, Colt, Patent Sept.19, 1871, .38 Caliber | 195.00 |
| Weapon, Revolver, Colt, S.A.A., Western Holster, Black Powder, Eagle Grips | 625.00 |
| Weapon, Revolver, Colt, U.S.Army, Engraved Scene On Cylinder, 1860 | 345.00 |
| Weapon, Revolver, Colt, U.S.Navy, Engraved Scene On Cylinder | 450.00 |
| Weapon, Revolver, Colt, 1849 Model, Percussion, Octagon Barrel, 31 Caliber | 325.00 |
| Weapon, Revolver, Colt, 1849, Pocket Model, Engraved Stagecoach Robbery | 375.00 |
| Weapon, Revolver, Colt, 1860 Model, Percussion, 8 In.Barrel, .44 Caliber | 210.00 |
| Weapon, Revolver, Confederate, Made In England, 5 Shot, .31 Caliber | 550.00 |
| Weapon, Revolver, Hi-Standard, Model B, Military, .22 Caliber, Dated 1935 | 1095.00 |
| Weapon, Revolver, Hi-Standard, Model B, Military, .22 Caliber, Semiautomatic | 225.00 |
| Weapon, Revolver, Hi-Standard, Sentinel Model, 6 Shot, .22 Caliber | 39.50 |
| Weapon, Revolver, Hopkins & Allen, XL No.4, N.Y., 5 Shot, .38 Caliber | 34.50 |
| Weapon, Revolver, Marquis Of Lorne, 5 Shot, .32 Caliber, Bird's Head Butt | 37.50 |
| Weapon, Revolver, Mass.Arms Co., Adams Patent, Civil War, Navy, .36 Caliber | 325.00 |
| Weapon, Revolver, Merwin Hulbert, Long Barrel, .44/40 Caliber, Pierced Butt | 295.00 |
| Weapon, Revolver, Merwin Hulbert, 5 Shot, .38 Caliber, Spur Trigger, Pierced | 79.50 |
| Weapon, Revolver, Pocket, F & W, 1887, Nickel Finish | 15.00 |
| Weapon, Revolver, Ranger, No.3, Hexagonal Barrel, Spur Trigger | 32.50 |
| Weapon, Revolver, Remington, New Model, Civil War, Percussion, .44 Caliber | 215.00 |
| Weapon, Revolver, Remington, Smoot, Engraved, .30 Caliber, Pearl Grips | 285.00 |
| Weapon, Revolver, Smith & Wesson, Civil War, .22 Caliber, Rosewood Grips | 57.50 |
| Weapon, Revolver, Smith & Wesson, Civil War, .32 Caliber | 59.50 |
| Weapon, Revolver, Smith & Wesson, Model 1917, Military, .45 Caliber | 97.50 |
| Weapon, Revolver, Smith & Wesson, U.S.Army, M1899, .38 Caliber, Dated 1901 | 325.00 |
| Weapon, Revolver, Smith & Wesson, 3rd Issue, .22 Caliber, Rosewood Grips | 175.00 |
| Weapon, Revolver, Whitney, Navy, Civil War, Percussion | 375.00 |
| Weapon, Revolver, Winchester, Percussion, .31 Caliber, 10 Shot, Civil War | 1250.00 |
| Weapon, Rifle, Bayard, Pieper Patent, Belgian, Boy's, .22 Caliber, Octagonal | 20.50 |
| Weapon, Rifle, Boy's, Flobert Type, 32 Caliber, Engraved At Muzzle | 57.50 |
| Weapon, Rifle, Curly Maple Stock, Engraved Silver Inlays, .41 Caliber | 600.00 |
| Weapon, Rifle, Flintlock, Roman Nose, Brass Patch Box | 625.00 |
| Weapon, Rifle, Flobert Type, Boy's, Walnut Half Stock, .32 Caliber | 57.50 |
| Weapon, Rifle, Frank Wesson, Bicycle, Brass Frame, .32 Caliber, Rosewood | 74.50 |
| Weapon, Rifle, G.Hains, Percussion, Curly Maple Stock, Patch Box | 735.00 |
| Weapon, Rifle, Griffin & Howe, Big Game, .300 Caliber Magnum, Mauser Action | 3000.00 |
| Weapon, Rifle, Hall-H.Ferry, U.S., 1838, M1819 | 850.00 |
| Weapon, Rifle, Hall-U.S.-H.Ferry-1832, M1819, Breech Loading, Percussion | 550.00 |
| Weapon, Rifle, J.A., Percussion, Maple Stock, .42 Caliber, Double Triggers | 500.00 |
| Weapon, Rifle, Jaeger, German, .62 Caliber, Walnut Stock, Patch Box, C.1740 | 750.00 |
| Weapon, Rifle, Kentucky, Boy's, Percussion, Octagonal Barrel, Brass Patch Box | 115.00 |
| Weapon, Rifle, Kentucky, Full Stock, .54 Caliber, Marked Richard Hollis, 1880 | 895.00 |
| Weapon, Rifle, Kentucky, H.E.Leman, Curly Maple, Silver Escutcheons & Insets | 495.00 |
| Weapon, Rifle, Kentucky, Patch Box, Tiger Maple Stock, Octagonal Barrel | 750.00 |
| Weapon, Rifle, Kentucky, Percussion, Gloulcher Lock Set, Patch Box | 525.00 |
| Weapon, Rifle, Kentucky, Percussion, 8-Point Silver Star, Patch Box | 650.00 |
| Weapon, Rifle, Kentucky, S.States Maker, .54 Caliber, Flintlock, C.1820 | 1450.00 |
| Weapon, Rifle, Kentucky, Tiger Maple Stock, Brass Patch Box, .40 Caliber | 650.00 |

| | |
|---|---:|
| **Weapon, Rifle,** M.L.Snyder, Percussion, Curly Maple Stock, Silver Patch Box | 325.00 |
| **Weapon, Rifle,** Marlin Ballard, .32/.40 Caliber, Single Trigger, Octagonal | 425.00 |
| **Weapon, Rifle,** Mauser Action, Engraved Designs, .30/06 Caliber, Carved Stock | 750.00 |
| **Weapon, Rifle,** Mauser-Oberndorf, Sporting, Bolt Action, .264 Caliber Magnum | 450.00 |
| **Weapon, Rifle,** Percussion, Curly Maple Stock, Brass Patch Box | 425.00 |
| **Weapon, Rifle,** Percussion, Double Barrel, Silver Inlays, Walnut, .36 Caliber | 350.00 |
| **Weapon, Rifle,** Percussion, Maple Stock, Double Triggers, .34 Caliber | 175.00 |
| **Weapon, Rifle,** Ranger, Target Barrel, World War II Marines, .22 Caliber | 150.00 |
| **Weapon, Rifle,** Remington, Boy's, Rolling Block, .25 Caliber, Octagonal | 325.00 |
| **Weapon, Rifle,** Remington, Boy's, Rolling Block, .25/20 Caliber, 'fish Belly' | 325.00 |
| **Weapon, Rifle,** Remington, Hepburn, .45 Caliber, Octagonal Barrel | 550.00 |
| **Weapon, Rifle,** Remington, Model 24, Take Down, .22 Caliber, Auto-Loading | 69.50 |
| **Weapon, Rifle,** Remington, No.4, Take Down, .32 Caliber, Octagonal Barrel | 94.50 |
| **Weapon, Rifle,** Remington, No.7, Single Shot, Target, .32 Caliber | 1750.00 |
| **Weapon, Rifle,** Remington, Take Down Action, .32 Caliber, Octagon Barrel | 94.50 |
| **Weapon, Rifle,** Rigby & Co., Dublin, .36 Caliber, Needle Fire, Octagonal | 250.00 |
| **Weapon, Rifle,** Sharp's Borchardt, Military, Old Reliable, .45 Caliber | 395.00 |
| **Weapon, Rifle,** Sporting, Custom, Mauser Action, .30/.06 Caliber, Engraved | 750.00 |
| **Weapon, Rifle,** Springfield, Cartouche On Stock, .45-.70 Caliber, C.1873 | 125.00 |
| **Weapon, Rifle,** Springfield, M1884, .45 Caliber, Bayonet | 235.00 |
| **Weapon, Rifle,** Stevens, Crack Shot, .22 Caliber | 60.00 |
| **Weapon, Rifle,** Stevens, Marksman, Boy's, .44 Caliber, Take Down Action | 79.50 |
| **Weapon, Rifle,** Stevens, New Model, Pocket, 2nd Issue, Brass Frame, .22 Caliber | 84.50 |
| **Weapon, Rifle,** 'Thone-Amsterdam,' Military, .69 Caliber, C.1850 | 1250.00 |
| **Weapon, Rifle,** U.Roos & Sohn, Stuttgart, .60 Caliber, Pin Fire, C.1860 | 225.00 |
| **Weapon, Rifle,** Warren & Steele, N.Y., Etched Plate, Brass Patch Box | 415.00 |
| **Weapon, Rifle,** Westley Richards, Bolt Action, .375 Caliber, Magnum Rimless | 1450.00 |
| **Weapon, Rifle,** Winchester, .22 Caliber, Octagonal Barrel | 84.50 |
| **Weapon, Rifle,** Winchester, Creedmoor, Hotchkiss, Long Range, .45 Caliber | 2250.00 |
| **Weapon, Rifle,** Winchester, Express, Presentation, 1876, .50 Caliber | 3750.00 |
| **Weapon, Rifle,** Winchester, Hi Wall Schuetzen Type Creedmoor, .32 Caliber | 1250.00 |
| **Weapon, Rifle,** Winchester, Hi-Wall, C45/70 Caliber, Schuetzen Type Stock | 375.00 |
| **Weapon, Rifle,** Winchester, Lo-Wall, .22 Caliber, Octagon Barrel | 84.50 |
| **Weapon, Rifle,** Winchester, Magnum, .38 Caliber, Bolt Action, Sporting | 185.00 |
| **Weapon, Rifle,** Winchester, Model 52, Target, Bolt Action, .22 Caliber | 94.50 |
| **Weapon, Rifle,** Winchester, M1873, Octagon Barrel, .22 Caliber | 550.00 |
| **Weapon, Rifle,** Winchester, M1886, Octagon Barrel, .45/70 Caliber | 1250.00 |
| **Weapon, Rifle,** Winchester, M1895, .35 Caliber, Take Down, Engraved Butt Plate | 350.00 |
| **Weapon, Rifle,** Winchester, M1906, Boy's, .22 Caliber, Pump Action | 34.50 |
| **Weapon, Rifle,** Winchester, Presentation, 1886, .45 Caliber | 2950.00 |
| **Weapon, Rifle,** Winchester, Schuetzen Type Creedmoor, .32 Caliber, 1895 | 1250.00 |
| **Weapon, Rifle,** Winchester, 1876, .50 Caliber, Presentation, Silver Inlay | 3750.00 |
| **Weapon, Rifle,** Winchester, 1886, .45 Caliber, Shotgun Butt | 1250.00 |
| **Weapon, Saber,** Civil War, U.S. & Eagle Etched, Leather Scabbard, 30 1/2 In. | 55.00 |
| **Weapon, Shot Loader,** Brass, Wooden Handle, 6 In. | 13.50 |
| **Weapon, Shotgun Over Rifle,** Stevens, Model 22, 24 In.Barrels | 47.50 |
| **Weapon, Shotgun,** A.H.Fox, Phila., S.J.Grade, Single Barrel, 12 Gauge | 450.00 |
| **Weapon, Shotgun,** Belgian Dreyse Type, Needle Fire, 12 Gauge, Double Barrel | 150.00 |
| **Weapon, Shotgun,** Belgian Type, Double Barrel, Percussion, 12 Gauge, C.1850 | 59.50 |
| **Weapon, Shotgun,** Belgian, Double Barrel, 12 Gauge, French Walnut Stock, 1850 | 135.00 |
| **Weapon, Shotgun,** C.G.Bonehill, London, Damascus Design, 12 Gauge | 235.00 |
| **Weapon, Shotgun,** Colt, Double Barrel, 12 Gauge, Outside Hammer, Engraved | 150.00 |
| **Weapon, Shotgun,** French, Double Barrel, 16 Gauge, C.1870 | 195.00 |
| **Weapon, Shotgun,** German, Hammerless, 16 Gauge, Double Barrel, Engraved | 350.00 |
| **Weapon, Shotgun,** Greener, Try, 12 Gauge, Double Barrel, Engraved | 425.00 |
| **Weapon, Shotgun,** Hermann Schneider, Zella Mehlis, 16 Gauge, Hammerless | 165.00 |
| **Weapon, Shotgun,** Ithaca Grade, Marked Krupp Fluid Steel, 12 Gauge, Boxlock | 895.00 |
| **Weapon, Shotgun,** J.Blanch & Son, London, Double Barrel, 12 Gauge, Engraved | 225.00 |
| **Weapon, Shotgun,** J.Purdey, London, Percussion, Double Barrel, 20 Gauge | 595.00 |
| **Weapon, Shotgun,** Kongl.Bayr Hofgewehrfabrik–Stiegele In Munchen, 16 Gauge | 165.00 |
| **Weapon, Shotgun,** L.C.Smith, Double Barrel, Hammerless, 12 Gauge | 550.00 |
| **Weapon, Shotgun,** L.C.Smith, Premier-Skeet, 12 Gauge, Hammerless | 475.00 |
| **Weapon, Shotgun,** L.C.Smith, 12 Gauge, Double Barrel, Hammerless, Engraved | 550.00 |
| **Weapon, Shotgun,** L.C.Smith, Premier-Skeet, 12 Gauge, Hammerless, Engraved | 475.00 |
| **Weapon, Shotgun,** Marked Kongl.Bayr Hofgewehrfabrik, Munchen, 16 Gauge | 165.00 |
| **Weapon, Shotgun,** Marked, Hermann Schneider-Zella Mehlis, 16 Gauge | 165.00 |

Weapon, Shotgun, Mauser, German Geha, Single Barrel, Bolt Action ....................... 70.00
Weapon, Shotgun, Parker Bros.DHE, Trap Grade, 12 Gauge, Engraved ................. 1250.00
Weapon, Shotgun, Parker Bros., Double Barrel, 12 Gauge, Engraved ................... 1400.00
Weapon, Shotgun, Parker Bros., Double Barrel, 12 Gauge, Hammerless ............... 1450.00
Weapon, Shotgun, Parker Bros., Meriden, Conn., Double Barrel, 12 Gauge, C.1866 ...... 250.00
Weapon, Shotgun, Parker Bros., Meriden, Conn., Double Barrel, 12 Gauge, 1875 ....... 125.00
Weapon, Shotgun, Parker, DHE Grade, 12 Gauge, Double Barrel, Engraved ........... 1400.00
Weapon, Shotgun, Parker, DHE Grade, 12 Gauge, Double Barrel ...................... 1400.00
Weapon, Shotgun, Parker, Double Barrel, 20 Gauge, Boxlock, Hammerless ........... 1295.00
Weapon, Shotgun, Parker, 12 Gauge, Hammerless, Double Barrel, Engraved .......... 1450.00
Weapon, Shotgun, Perker, Meriden, Conn., 12 Gauge, Double Barrel, 1875 ............ 125.00
Weapon, Shotgun, L.C.Smith, Pigeon Grade, 12 Gauge .............................. 525.00
Weapon, Shotgun, Stevens, Model 38-B, .410 Gauge, Bolt Action ..................... 22.50
Weapon, Shotgun, W.& C.Scott & Son, England, 10 Gauge, Percussion ............... 325.00
Weapon, Shotgun, W.W.Greener, St.Mary's Works, Birmingham, 14 Gauge ........... 295.00
Weapon, Shotgun, Westley Richards & Co., London, 12 Gauge, Double Barrel ........ 295.00
Weapon, Shotgun, Westley Richards, Double Barrel, Serial No.17472, 12 Gauge ..... 2950.00
Weapon, Shotgun, William Moore & Co., London, 12 Gauge, Muzzle Loading, Pair ..... 2250.00
Weapon, Shotgun, Winchester, Model 12, 16 Gauge, Double Barrel, Pump Action ..... 275.00
Weapon, Shoulder Stock, For Colt Buntline Special, Skeleton Type, C.1876 ........... 650.00
Weapon, Sling, Carbine, Cavalry, Black Leather, Brass Buckle, Chicopee, Mass. ..... 175.00
Weapon, Sling, Carbine, U.S.Cavalry, Black Buff Leather, Brass Buckle ............. 175.00
Weapon, Sling, Carbine, U.S.Cavalry, Black Leather, Brass Buckle, Iron Clip ........ 54.50
Weapon, Sling, Carbine, U.S.Cavalry, Spencer & Springfield, Leather, Black ......... 54.50
Weapon, Spear, Eel, Iron, American, C.1750 ..................................... 48.00
Weapon, Spontoon, British Officer's, Pre-Revolutionary, Pierced, Royal Seal ........ 350.00
Weapon, Sword, Artillery Officer's, Leather Sheath, N.P.Ames-U.S.-1844 ............ 425.00
Weapon, Sword, British Infantry Officer's, Brass Hilt, Ivory Grips, C.1810 ........... 74.50
Weapon, Sword, British Officer's, Sheath, West Indies, Brass Hilt, 1839 ............ 275.00
Weapon, Sword, Cavalry Officer's, Scabbard, M1872, Presentation, Engraved ....... 225.00
Weapon, Sword, Cavalry, N.Starr.Dated 1810 .................................... 175.00
Weapon, Sword, Ceylon, Kastane, Monster's Head Grip, Engraved, C.1750 .......... 165.00
Weapon, Sword, Civil War Field Officer's, Scabbard, Inscribed .................... 150.00
Weapon, Sword, Civil War Noncommissioned Officer's, Ames Mfg., Mass., 1864 ..... 75.00
Weapon, Sword, Civil War Officer's, Brass Handle ............................... 100.00
Weapon, Sword, Civil War Officer's, Brass Scabbard, Pearl Grips, Eagle ........... 200.00
Weapon, Sword, Civil War Officer's, Sheath, Brass Hilt, Pierced Design ............ 695.00
Weapon, Sword, Civil War, Eagle Cup, Factory Engraved, Pearl Grips .............. 285.00
Weapon, Sword, Civil War, Scabbard, Presentation, Brass Hilt & Grips ............. 850.00
Weapon, Sword, English Gentleman's, Brass Handle, 1785 ......................... 150.00
Weapon, Sword, German, Hunting, Brass Hilt, C.1840, Engraved ................... 69.50
Weapon, Sword, German, Hunting, Gold Finished Brass Hilt, Sheath, C.1850 ......... 145.00
Weapon, Sword, Imperial German Officer's, Berlin ................................. 85.00
Weapon, Sword, Imperial German Officer's, Iron Sheath, Brass Hilt, Engraved ....... 74.50
Weapon, Sword, Ivory Eagle On Handle ......................................... 69.00
Weapon, Sword, Japanese Officer's, World War II, Sheath, Copper Guard ........... 89.50
Weapon, Sword, Light Artillery, Iron Sheath, M1840, Leather Grips, U.S.1855 ....... 225.00
Weapon, Sword, M1850, Foot Officer's, Scabbard, Presentation, Etched Brass ....... 285.00
Weapon, Sword, Prussian, Lion Head Grip, Silver Over Brass, 21 In.Long ........... 65.00
Weapon, Sword, Samurai, Military .............................................. 64.00
Weapon, Sword, Spanish, Palace Guard, Scabbard, Nickel, Eagle & Cross .......... 125.00
Weapon, Sword, Springfield Armory, M1860, Leather Grips, Scabbard, Brass Trim ... 145.00
Weapon, Sword, Staff & Field, Leather Sheath & Grips, M1860, Eagle & U.S. ........ 64.50
Weapon, Sword, Staff & Field, Nickeled Sheath, G.A.R.On Brass Hilt, M1860 ........ 49.50
Weapon, Sword, Talwar, India, Disc Pommel, Iron Hilt, Gold Inlay, C.1700 .......... 125.00
Weapon, Sword, U.S.Army Musician's, Scabbard, M1840, Brass Hilt & Grips ......... 84.50
Weapon, Sword, U.S.Cavalry Officer's, Scabbard, M1872, Presentation, Engraved .... 225.00
Weapon, Sword, U.S.Foot Officer's, Revolutionary, Horn Grips, Brass Wrapping ..... 325.00
Weapon, Sword, U.S.Foot Officer's, Scabbard, M1850, Presentation, Brass Hilt ...... 285.00
Weapon, Sword, U.S.Marine Corps Musician's, Leather Sheath, Brass Hilt, 1875 ..... 325.00
Weapon, Sword, U.S.Naval Officer's, Iron Sheath, M1852, Sharkskin Grips .......... 64.50
Weapon, Sword, U.S.Naval Officer's, Leather Covered Iron Sheath, M1852 .......... 64.50
Weapon, Sword, U.S.Staff & Field Officer's, Scabbard, New Hampshire, 1850 ....... 425.00
Weapon, Sword, U.S.Staff & Field, Scabbard, M1860, G.A.R.On Brass Hilt ........... 49.50
Weapon, Sword, West Point Cadet, Nickeled Brass Mounted Sheath, C.1872 ......... 34.50
Weapon, Sword, Windsor Castle Guard's, Iron Sheath, C.1800, Bird's Head .......... 275.00

Weapon, Sword, World War II Officer's, Scabbard, Copper Guard, Iron Cap .................................. 89.50
Weather Vane, American Flag, Iron, 19th Century ....................................... *Illus* 3250.00
Weather Vane, American Indian, Sheet Iron, 19th Century ................................................. *Illus* 1000.00
Weather Vane, Cow, Copper, 19th Century ............................................... *Illus* 1700.00
Weather Vane, Cow, Gilt Copper, C.1850, 32 1/2 In. Long .......................................... 650.00
Weather Vane, Eagle, Copper, 19th Century, 20 X 15 In. ................................... *Illus* 1500.00
Weather Vane, Eagle, Spread Wings, Gold Leaf, 28 In. .................................................. 350.00
Weather Vane, Eagle, Wings Spread, On Orb, Copper, C.1850, 5 Ft.6 In. Wide .................... 650.00
Weather Vane, Horse & Jockey, Gilt Copper, C.1850, 30 1/2 In. Long ............................ 1500.00
Weather Vane, Horse & Sulky, Copper, 1800s, 30 1/4 In.High .............................. 850.00
Weather Vane, Horse & Sulky, Gilt Copper, 19th Century .................................... *Illus* 1900.00
Weather Vane, Horse, Copper, Gold Leaf, 31 In. ......................................................... 450.00
Weather Vane, Horse, Gilded, 23 In. Long ................................................................. 37.50
Weather Vane, Horse, Running, Gilt Copper, C.1850, 32 In. Long .............................. 900.00
Weather Vane, Horse, Trotting, Sheet Iron, White Paint, C.1850, 29 In. ..................... 200.00
Weather Vane, Man, Dog, & Eagle, Sheet Iron, C.1875 ............................................. *Illus* 600.00
Weather Vane, Ox, Gilt Copper, Repousse Body, C.1850, 25 In. Long .......................... 600.00
Weather Vane, Pointing Hand, C & S Scrolls, Brass, C.1850, 37 In. ............................. 350.00
Weather Vane, Ram, Copper, 19th Century ......................................................... *Illus* 1900.00
Weather Vane, Retriever Dog, Copper ............................................................... 1250.00
Weather Vane, Rooster, Cast Iron, C.1850, 36 In. Long ........................................ 1300.00
Weather Vane, Rooster, Gilt Copper, 23 X 23 In. ................................................... 500.00
Weather Vane, Rooster, Gilt Wood, 18 In. High ..................................................... 375.00
Weather Vane, Rooster, Iron, Cushing, 19th Century ........................................... *Illus* 900.00
Weather Vane, Rooster, Tin, Stylized, 19th Century, 4 Ft.7 In.High ........................... 300.00
Weather Vane, Running Horse, Gilt Copper, 19th Century, 31 In.Long ....................... 1000.00
Weather Vane, Scrolled Pointed, Letters G.M.C., Copper, Gilt, 1897, 49 In. ................. 200.00
Weather Vane, Stag, Leaping Over Fallen Tree, Gilt Copper, C.1850, 32 In. .................. 1700.00
Weather Vane, Tulip, Iron, Pennsylvania, 44 In. Long ............................................ 800.00

*Webb glass was made by Thomas Webb & Sons of Stourbridge, England.*
*Many types of art and cameo glass were made by them during the Victorian*
*era.*

Webb Burmese, Bowl, Bulbous Body, Scalloped Top, 3 1/2 In.Diameter .................... 350.00
Webb Burmese, Bowl, 3 In. ............................................................................. 380.00
Webb Burmese, Lamp, Fairy Light, Base Marked Clarke, 5 In.High ........................... 195.00
Webb Burmese, Lamp, Fairy, Clarke Candleholder, Square Base, Yellow Wafer .............. 850.00
Webb Burmese, Rose Bowl, 2 In.High ............................................................... 190.00
Webb Burmese, Salt, Master, Decorated, Signed, 2 3/4 In.Diameter .......................... 275.00
Webb Burmese, Tumbler, Juice, Ivy Vine With Shaded Green Leaves ......................... 250.00
Webb, Basket, Bride's, Rose, Pink, & White, Draped Pattern, Silver Plate Frame ............ 175.00
Webb, Bottle, Cut Glass, Covered, Cockleshells, 6 1/2 In.High .................................. 400.00
Webb, Bottle, Scent, White On Blue, C.1900, 4 1/4 In.High ...................................... *Illus* 2000.00
Webb, Bottle, White Cameo Floral On Red, Silver Top, 2 In. High .............................. 215.00
Webb, Bowl & Underplate, Finger, Ribbon Mother-Of-Pearl, Crimped .......................... 335.00
Webb, Bowl & Underplate, Iridescent Green ...................................................... 150.00
Webb, Bowl, Cameo, Miniature, Yellow To Clear, 1 1/2 In.High, 3 In.Wide ................... 280.00
Webb, Bowl, Cut Velvet, Basket Weave, Cloverleaf Top, Red To Pink, Lined .................. 265.00
Webb, Compote, Ruffled, Blue To White, Enameled Flowers, 10 1/2 In.Diameter ............ 155.00
Webb, Compote, Satin, White, Blue Inside, Camphor Ribbon Edge, Crimped, Silver .......... 95.00
Webb, Ewer Pitcher, Pink To Blue White Top, Applied Camphor Handle, Enamel ............. 70.00
Webb, Inkwell, Cameo Carved Foliage, Sterling Silver Collar & Cap ........................... 750.00
Webb, Liqueur, Cut Crystal, Miniature Diamonds, Signed ...................................... 20.00
Webb, Match Holder, Bubble Glass, Striker, Signed .............................................. 79.00
Webb, Muffineer, Cut Glass, Pierced Silver Plated Top, 6 1/2 In.High ........................ 37.50
Webb, Peachblow, Vase, Bulbous, White Cased, 9 In. High ..................................... 275.00
Webb, Peachblow, Vase, Cased, Pink To Salmon, Gold Enamel Floral, 5 In. ................... 325.00
Webb, Peachblow, Vase, Cased, Raised Enamel Flowers & Leaves, 11 In. High ............... 650.00
Webb, Peachblow, Vase, Cream Lining, Gold Decoration, 6 In. High ........................... 135.00
Webb, Peachblow, Vase, Enamel Floral & Gold On Rose To Cream, Blue Lining ............... 450.00
Webb, Peachblow, Vase, Gold & White Enamel Floral, 5 1/4 In. High .......................... 190.00
Webb, Perfume, Sterling Top, White Winged Figure & Horn On Blue, Woodall ................ 6500.00
Webb, Perfume, White On Citron, Carved, Cameo, 3 1/2 In.Long ............................. 300.00
Webb, Plaque, Apples On Branch, Cameo, C.1900, 9 3/4 In. Diameter ....................... 3300.00
Webb, Plate, Square, Blue Floral On Ivory Satin, Cut Corners, 5 In. ........................... 250.00
Webb, Ramekin & Underplate, Red Flowers & Butterfly On Crystal, Signed .................. 895.00

Weather Vane, American Flag, Iron, 19th Century
(See Page 700)

Weather Vane, Horse & Sulky,
Gilt Copper, 19th Century
(See Page 700)

Weather Vane, Ram, Copper, 19th Century
(See Page 700)

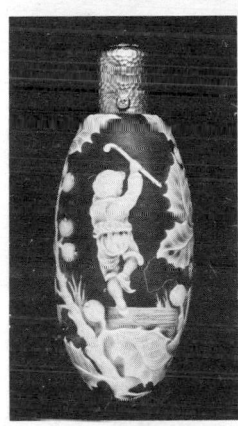

Webb, Bottle, Scent,
White On Blue, C.1900,
4 1/4 In.High
(See Page 700)

Weather Vane, Cow, Copper, 19th Century
(See Page 700)

Weather Vane, Eagle, Copper,
19th Century, 20 X 15 In.
(See Page 700)

Weather Vane, Man, Dog, & Eagle, Sheet Iron, C.1875
(See Page 700)

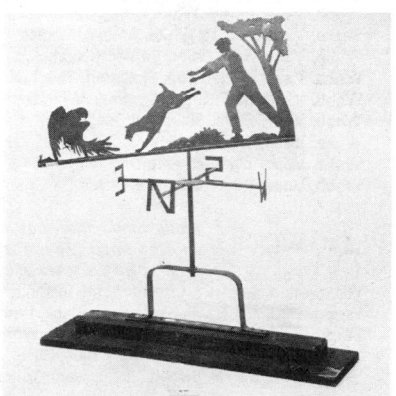

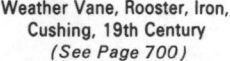

Weather Vane, Rooster, Iron,
Cushing, 19th Century
*(See Page 700)*

Weather Vane, American Indian,
Sheet Iron, 19th Century
*(See Page 700)*

| | |
|---|---|
| Webb, Rose Bowl, Alexandrite, Honeycomb, 6 Petal Rim, Blue To Amber | 725.00 |
| Webb, Rose Bowl, Diamond-Quilted Mother-Of-Pearl, Yellow Seaweed Coralene | 275.00 |
| Webb, Rose Bowl, Rose To Blue Satin, Gold Flowers & Butterfly, Miniature | 275.00 |
| Webb, Rose Bowl, Shiny Custard To Pale Green Inner Layer, Quatrefoil Top | 65.00 |
| Webb, Rose Bowl, Turquoise, Raised Gold Prunus & Butterfly, 2 1/2 In. | 235.00 |
| Webb, Salt, White Acorns & Oak Leaves On Cranberry, Gilt Band, Cameo | 475.00 |
| Webb, Tray, Pin, Branching Spray Of White 6 Petal Flowers On Cranberry | 595.00 |
| Webb, Tray, Pin, Vaseline Glass, Intaglio Polo Player & Horse | 35.00 |
| Webb, Tumbler, Coralene, Yellow Seaweed, Pink Diamond Mother-Of-Pearl | 250.00 |
| Webb, Urn, Gold Finial, Ovoid, Pedestal, Coin Gold Butterfly & Floral | 185.00 |
| Webb, Vase, Albertine, Bluebird On Tree Limb, Butterfly At Base, 11 In. | 375.00 |
| Webb, Vase, Amber Glass, Acid Cut Floral Design, Signed, 6 1/2 In.High | 58.00 |
| Webb, Vase, Blue Coralene Seaweed On Yellow To White Mother-Of-Pearl | 310.00 |
| Webb, Vase, Bronze, C.1880, 11 1/2 In.High | 70.00 |
| Webb, Vase, Butterflies & Floral On Amber, 11 In.High | 155.00 |
| Webb, Vase, Cased, Enameled Flowers & Bees On Pink, 12 In.High | 180.00 |
| Webb, Vase, Cased, Enameled Flowers & Bees On Pink, 6 In. | 145.00 |
| Webb, Vase, Cased, Gold Overlay On Pink, White Inside, 5 1/4 In.High | 65.00 |
| Webb, Vase, Copper Wheel Butterfly, Flowers, & Leaves On Clear, 10 In. | 130.00 |
| Webb, Vase, Coralene, Quilted Mother-Of-Pearl, Blue Shaded, Yellow Beading | 550.00 |
| Webb, Vase, Coralene, Quilted Mother-Of-Pearl, Pink Cased, Camphor Feet | 450.00 |
| Webb, Vase, Gourd Shape, Blue & White On Opaque, Anemones, C.1890, 6 1/4 In. | 1000.00 |
| Webb, Vase, Honeycomb, Gold Enameled Ruffled Top | 425.00 |
| Webb, Vase, Ovoid, Overlay, Intaglio Cut 10 Petal Flowers, White To Yellow | 850.00 |
| Webb, Vase, Ovoid, Silver Floral, Berries, & Leaves On White, Scrolls, 6 In. | 115.00 |
| Webb, Vase, Pink & White On Chartreuse, Miniature, Cameo, 3 In.High | 550.00 |
| Webb, Vase, Red To White, Amber Handles, 6 1/2 In.High, Pair | 225.00 |
| Webb, Vase, Rose Color, Carved Cameo | 775.00 |
| Webb, Vase, Ruffled Top, Flowered, Pink Lining, 5 In.High | 85.00 |
| Webb, Vase, Satin Glass, Caramel, Whimsey | 200.00 |
| Webb, Vase, Satin, Blue, Gold Florals & Butterfly, 8 In.High | 130.00 |
| Webb, Vase, Trumpet, Amber, 3 Rows Of Raised Ovals, Round Base, England | 125.00 |
| Webb, Vase, Trumpet, Pink On Clear, Lilies & Scrolls, C.1910, 6 1/4 In. | 250.00 |
| Webb, Vase, White Coralene Icicles On Green Satin, 13 In.High | 65.00 |

## WEDGWOOD

*Wedgwood pottery has been made at the famous Wedgwood Factory in England since 1759. A large variety of wares has been made, including the well-known jasperware, basalt, creamware, and even a limited amount of porcelain.*

| | |
|---|---|
| Wedgwood, Ashtray, Crusader Line Insignia Center, Blue & White | 10.00 |
| Wedgwood, Ashtray, Jasperware, Black, White American Eagle & Stars | 10.00 |
| Wedgwood, Barrel, Biscuit, Blue Jasper, White Classical Figures, Silver Lid | 70.00 |
| Wedgwood, Barrel, Biscuit, Dark Blue, Silver Plate Lid, 6 In.High | 95.00 |
| Wedgwood, Barrel, Biscuit, Jasperware, Yellow, Black Garlands, White Bands | 395.00 |

| | |
|---|---:|
| Wedgwood, Barrel, Biscuit, White Classical Figures On Dark Blue, Silver Lid | 65.00 |
| Wedgwood, Barrel, Biscuit, White On Mauve, Silver Plate Fittings | 325.00 |
| Wedgwood, Barrel, Jam, Green, Silver Lid | 60.00 |
| Wedgwood, Basket, Caneware, Molded Border, 5 3/4 In.Long | 175.00 |
| Wedgwood, Basket, Creamware, Green & Gold, 6 In.Long, 6 In.High | 165.00 |
| Wedgwood, Basket, Creamware, Oval, 7 1/2 X 9 In. | 30.00 |
| Wedgwood, Basket, Creamware, Ribbed Horizontal Panels, C.1780, 9 In.Long | 95.00 |
| Wedgwood, Basket, Flower, Jasperware, Blue, White Trim, 2 Piece, 4 In.High | 40.00 |
| Wedgwood, Beaker, Dragon Luster, 9 1/2 In.High, Pair ..............................*Illus* | 425.00 |
| Wedgwood, Bottle, Liqueur, Jasperware, Light Green, C.1865, Signed Wedgwood | 120.00 |
| Wedgwood, Bottle, Sherry, Sandman, Prince Of Wales, July, 1969 | 15.00 |
| Wedgwood, Bowl & Underplate, Cream Soup, Cornflower | 6.25 |
| Wedgwood, Bowl, Basalt, Black, Flaxman Figures, 2 1/2 In.Deep | 60.00 |
| Wedgwood, Bowl, Basalt, Classical Figures On Black, 7 1/2 In.Diameter | 195.00 |
| Wedgwood, Bowl, Basalt, 12 In.Diameter | 150.00 |
| Wedgwood, Bowl, Butterflies On Mother-Of-Pearl, Orange Inside, 2 3/4 In. | 110.00 |
| Wedgwood, Bowl, Creamware, Red & Gilt Floral Decoration, 1882 Mark, 9 In. | 37.00 |
| Wedgwood, Bowl, Dark Blue With White, "sacrifice To Ceres, " Footed, C.1898 | 187.50 |
| Wedgwood, Bowl, Fairyland Luster, Birds, Dark Blue, Orange Lined, 2 1/4 In. | 78.00 |
| Wedgwood, Bowl, Fairyland Luster, Blue, Mother-Of Pearl Lined, 2 3/4 In. | 95.00 |
| Wedgwood, Bowl, Fairyland Luster, Blue, Mother-Of-Pearl Lined, 4 1/2 In. | 125.00 |
| Wedgwood, Bowl, Fairyland Luster, Butterflies On Maroon, Pearl In, 3 3/4 In. | 135.00 |
| Wedgwood, Bowl, Fairyland Luster, Dragons On Blue, Orange Lined, 6 1/2 In. | 225.00 |
| Wedgwood, Bowl, Fairyland Luster, Fruit On Blue, Orange Lined, 3 7/8 In. | 120.00 |
| Wedgwood, Bowl, Fairyland Luster, Gold Dragons On Blue, Pearl In, 8 3/4 In. | 375.00 |
| Wedgwood, Bowl, Fairyland Luster, 9 3/4 In.Diameter | 1500.00 |
| Wedgwood, Bowl, Majolica, Marked 1870, 9 1/4 X 14 In. | 155.00 |
| Wedgwood, Bowl, Oval, Twig, 5 1/2 X 4 1/4 X 1 1/2 In. | 27.50 |
| Wedgwood, Bowl, Pearl Ware, Oblong, Ferrara, Brown, Lattice Edge, 9 In.Long | 330.00 |
| Wedgwood, Bowl, Salad, Silver Rim, Three Colors, 9 1/2 In.Diameter | 295.00 |
| Wedgwood, Bowl, Soup, Urn, Dark To Medium Blue, 9 In. | 7.00 To 30.00 |
| Wedgwood, Box, Candy, Jasperware, Lilac, White Vine, 3 In.Diameter | 35.00 |
| Wedgwood, Box, Covered, Heart Shape, Dark Blue, 4 In.Long | 47.00 |
| Wedgwood, Box, Covered, Jasperware, Blue, "wembley, 1924, " 3 In.Diameter | 45.00 |
| Wedgwood, Box, Covered, Jasperware, Powder Blue & White, Prince Phillip, 1953 | 85.00 |
| Wedgwood, Box, Covered, Terra-Cotta & White, Square, Reliefs, C.1958 | 97.50 |
| Wedgwood, Box, Deep Blue, Round, 2 3/4 In.Across | 25.00 |
| Wedgwood, Box, Jasperware, Cobalt Blue | 45.00 |
| Wedgwood, Box, Jasperware, Round, Classical Figures & Cupids On Royal Blue | 35.00 |
| Wedgwood, Box, Pomade, Jasperware, Round, White Classical Figures On Blue | 30.00 |
| Wedgwood, Box, Powder, Covered, Creamware, Relief Classical Figures & Leaves | 24.00 |
| Wedgwood, Box, Powder, Covered, Green & White, England | 45.00 |
| Wedgwood, Bust, Churchill, Basalt, Arnold Machin, 1940 | 100.00 |
| Wedgwood, Bust, Josiah Wedgwood, Black Basalt, Marked, 19 In.High | 475.00 |

Wedgwood, Beaker, Dragon Luster,
9 1/2 In.High, Pair

Wedgwood,
Candlestick,
Triton, 11 1/8 In.High
*(See Page 704)*

| | |
|---|---|
| Wedgwood, Bust, Shakespeare, Black Basalt, 12 1/2 In.High | 475.00 |
| Wedgwood, Bust, Shakespeare, Parianware, 13 1/2 In.High | 275.00 |
| Wedgwood, Candlestick, Basalt, Black, 11 In.High | 650.00 |
| Wedgwood, Candlestick, Classical Figures On Dark Blue, 8 In.High, Pair | 125.00 |
| Wedgwood, Candlestick, Jasperware, Deep Blue, Impressed Wedgwood, 5 In.High | 48.00 |
| Wedgwood, Candlestick, Jasperware, Green, Dated 1878, 5 In.High | 48.00 |
| Wedgwood, Candlestick, Jasperware, Light Blue, Dated 1877, 6 In.High, Pair | 120.00 |
| Wedgwood, Candlestick, Jasperware, Light Blue, 6 In.High, Pair | 125.00 |
| Wedgwood, Candlestick, Jasperware, Light Blue, 7 In.High, Pair | 145.00 |
| Wedgwood, Candlestick, Jasperware, Medium Blue, Heart Shape, Saucer Base | 32.00 |
| Wedgwood, Candlestick, Triton, 11 1/8 In.High ............*Illus* | 475.00 |
| Wedgwood, Chess Piece, Basalt, King & Queen, Pair | 40.00 |
| Wedgwood, Chess Set, Black Basalt & Blue Jasperware, Arnold Machin | 1150.00 |
| Wedgwood, Chessmen, Knights, Blue Jasperware, 3 In.High, Pair | 200.00 |
| Wedgwood, Chocolate Set, Creamware, Clovelly, 9 Piece | 85.00 |
| Wedgwood, Coffeepot, Creamware, Rouge-De-Fer & Gilt Decoration, 9 1/2 In. | 40.00 |
| Wedgwood, Coffeepot, Rockingham Glaze, Marked Wedgwood, 8 In.High | 130.00 |
| Wedgwood, Compote, Applied Cream Grape Garlands Top & Base On Cream, 9 In. | 25.00 |
| Wedgwood, Compote, Jasperware, Green | 20.00 |
| Wedgwood, Compotier, Elizabeth & Philip, Blue, 4 1/2 In., Pair | 20.22 |
| Wedgwood, Compotier, Lincoln Cathedral, Blue, 4 1/2 In. | 10.00 |
| Wedgwood, Compotier, Star Of David, Blue, 4 1/2 In. | 10.00 |
| Wedgwood, Condiment Set, Blue Jasper, 3 Piece | 125.00 |
| Wedgwood, Condiment Set, Jasperware, Dark Blue, Marked Wedgwood, 3 Piece | 125.00 |
| Wedgwood, Container, Cigarette, Jasperware, Black, White Coats Of Arms | 55.00 |
| Wedgwood, Cooler, Wine, Jasperware, Blue, Cherubs, Leaf & Chain Border, 8 In. | 275.00 |
| Wedgwood, Creamer, Basalt, Black, Raised Thistle, Harp, & Shamrock, 4 In. | 85.00 |
| Wedgwood, Creamer, Classical Figures On Dark Blue, Rope Handle, 5 1/2 In. | 32.50 |
| Wedgwood, Creamer, Cobalt, Classical Figures | 45.00 |
| Wedgwood, Creamer, Dark Blue, Grapes & Classical Figures, Rope Handle | 32.50 |
| Wedgwood, Creamer, Green With White, "domestic Employment, " C.1891 | 50.00 |
| Wedgwood, Creamer, Individual, Deep Cobalt Blue, Made In England | 28.00 |
| Wedgwood, Creamer, Salt Glaze, Berries, Leaves & Vines, 4 In.High | 75.00 |
| Wedgwood, Creamer, Stoneware, Salt Glaze, White, Molded Arabesque, C.1830 | 75.00 |
| Wedgwood, Creamer, White Classical Figures On Dark Blue, C.1942 | 35.00 |
| Wedgwood, Cup & Saucer, Basalt, C.1820 | 75.00 |
| Wedgwood, Cup & Saucer, Blue Luster Border, Gold Grapes & Handle On White | 25.00 |
| Wedgwood, Cup & Saucer, Demitasse, Portland, Robin's-Egg Blue, Gold Florals | 14.50 |
| Wedgwood, Cup & Saucer, Jasperware, Blue ............*Illus* | 325.00 |
| Wedgwood, Cup & Saucer, Majolica, Cauliflower, Etruria | 20.00 |
| Wedgwood, Cup & Saucer, Signed Ferrara, Etruria, England | 18.50 |
| Wedgwood, Cup, Jasper, White Figures On Blue | 23.50 |
| Wedgwood, Cuspidor, Basalt, Engine Turned, C.1840, 5 In. High | 295.00 |
| Wedgwood, Dish, Candy, Fairyland Luster, Stemmed, Dragons & Animals | 225.00 |
| Wedgwood, Dish, Fish Cover, Caned Effect, Marked Wedgwood | 88.00 |
| Wedgwood, Dish, Pastryware, Covered, Piecrust Rim, Fruit Knop, 8 In. | 160.00 |
| Wedgwood, Dish, Tortoiseshell, Ribbed, Scalloped, Turned Over Rim, 1866, 13 In | 115.00 |
| Wedgwood, Figurine, Elephant, Black Basalt, White Tusks, Glass Eyes, 3 1/2 In | 400.00 |
| Wedgwood, Figurine, Mother Monkey With Baby, Queensware, Skeaping, C.1927 | 250.00 |
| Wedgwood, Figurine, Polar Bear, 7 1/2 In.High, Signed Skeaping | 325.00 |
| Wedgwood, Figurine, Taurus The Bull, Queensware, Signed A.Machin, 12 In. | 235.00 |
| Wedgwood, Flowerpot, Basalt, Yellow Decoration, Basalt Holder, C.1916 | 425.00 |
| Wedgwood, Holder, Center, Majolica, Match Striker, Green, Brown, & Yellow | 48.00 |
| Wedgwood, Inkwell, Black Basalt, Drum Shaped, 3 1/2 In.Diameter | 90.00 |
| Wedgwood, Inkwell, Green Jasperware, 3 1/4 In.Diameter | 42.00 |
| Wedgwood, Ironstone, Tea Leaf, see Ironstone, Tea Leaf | |
| Wedgwood, Jar, Biscuit, Brown, Intaglio Floral & Butterfly, Silver Lid & Rim | 168.50 |
| Wedgwood, Jar, Biscuit, Dark Blue, Ladies, Cupids, & Animals, Silver Lid | 100.00 |
| Wedgwood, Jar, Biscuit, Grecian Figures On Olive Green, C.1900, 7 1/2 In. | 140.00 |
| Wedgwood, Jar, Biscuit, Grecian Ladies & Cupids On Light Blue, Silver Cover | 118.00 |
| Wedgwood, Jar, Biscuit, Jasperware, Blue, Classical Figures, 6 In. | 42.00 |
| Wedgwood, Jar, Biscuit, Jasperware, Cobalt Blue, Signed Wedgwood | 110.00 |
| Wedgwood, Jar, Biscuit, Jasperware, White Classical Figures On Blue, Silver | 125.00 |
| Wedgwood, Jar, Biscuit, Light Blue, Cupids & Greek Ladies, Silver Lid | 95.00 |
| Wedgwood, Jar, Biscuit, Silver Top, White Decoration On Green, 5 1/4 In. | 150.00 |
| Wedgwood, Jar, Canopic, Caneware, 10 1/4 In.High ............*Illus* | 1050.00 |

Wedgwood, Cup & Saucer, Jasperware, Blue
*(See Page 704)*

Wedgwood, Jar, Canopic, Caneware, 10 1/4 In.High
*(See Page 704)*

| | |
|---|---|
| Wedgwood, Jar, Cookie, Green, Silver Plate, Lid, Handle, & Footed Base | 125.00 |
| Wedgwood, Jar, Cookie, Jasperware, Blue, Silver Plate Lid & Bail | 135.00 |
| Wedgwood, Jar, Cookie, Jasperware, White Classical Figures On Dark Blue | 90.00 |
| Wedgwood, Jar, Cookie, Light Blue, Silver Plate, Top Rim, Lid, & Handle, 6 In. | 125.00 |
| Wedgwood, Jar, Cookie, Gold & Silver Floral On Cream, Ribbed, Silver Handle | 145.00 |
| Wedgwood, Jar, Covered, Classical Figures On Dark Blue, Lion's Head & Ring | 65.00 |
| Wedgwood, Jar, Cracker, Classical Figures, Urns, & Cherubs, Signed | 110.00 |
| Wedgwood, Jar, Cracker, Deep Blue, Silver Lid & Handle, C.1870 | 95.00 |
| Wedgwood, Jardiniere & Stand, Majolica, Urn Design, Swags, Cream & Blue | 750.00 |
| Wedgwood, Jardiniere, Blue, Classical Women & Lions With Wreaths, 7 In. | 155.00 |
| Wedgwood, Jardiniere, Four Muses Separated By Trees, 9 7/8 In.High | 70.00 |
| Wedgwood, Jardiniere, Friendship Consoling Affliction On Olive Green | 220.00 |
| Wedgwood, Jardiniere, Jasperware, Blue, White Classical Figures, 9 In. | 55.00 |
| Wedgwood, Jug, Ale, Cambridge, Terra-Cotta, Heraldic Emblem | 69.00 |
| Wedgwood, Jug, Basalt, Rose, Thistle, Shamrock, & Harp, 4 In.High | 90.00 |
| Wedgwood, Jug, Cambridge Ale, Red Stoneware, 5 1/2 In.High | 65.00 |
| Wedgwood, Jug, Cambridge Ale, Terra-Cotta, Date Mark For 1876, 6 1/4 In. | 95.00 |
| Wedgwood, Jug, Crimson, Signed Wedgwood, England, 5 5/8 In. | 500.00 |
| Wedgwood, Jug, Jasperware, Blue, White Classical Figures, 5 1/2 In. | 62.50 |
| Wedgwood, Jug, John Peel Commemorative, Hound Handle, 1927, 7 In. | 95.00 |
| Wedgwood, Jug, Milk, Blue, Straight Sides, 4 1/2 In.High | 20.00 |
| Wedgwood, Jug, Washington & Franklin Medallions On Dark Blue, 5 1/2 In. | 225.00 |
| Wedgwood, Jug, Water, Jasperware, Dark Blue, Rope Handle, Silver Plated Top | 75.00 |
| Wedgwood, Lipstick Holder, Blue, Cameo On Lid, Mirror | 17.50 |
| Wedgwood, Matchbox Holder, White Classical Figures On Blue, Acorn Border | 115.00 |
| Wedgwood, Matchbox, Classical Decoration On Dark Blue, Lid, Round | 42.50 |
| Wedgwood, Matchbox, Covered, Oval, White On Dark Green, Marked | 20.00 |
| Wedgwood, Medallion, Basalt, Black, Helena, 2 X 1 3/4 In. | 75.00 |
| Wedgwood, Medallion, Basalt, White Horse With Chariot & Rider, 1 In. | 37.50 |
| Wedgwood, Medallion, Beethoven, Basalt | 35.00 |
| Wedgwood, Medallion, Cupid & Psyche, Lilac & White, Framed | 127.50 |
| Wedgwood, Medallion, Earl Of Chatham, C.1775, 3 1/4 In. ............ *Illus* | 625.00 |
| Wedgwood, Medallion, Earl Of St.Vincent, Light Blue, C.1820, Brass Frame | 575.00 |
| Wedgwood, Medallion, F.D.Roosevelt, Black, No.852, 2 1/4 In. | 15.00 |
| Wedgwood, Medallion, Garrick, C.1775, 3 7/8 In. ............ *Illus* | 625.00 |
| Wedgwood, Medallion, Statesman, C.1800, 3 7/8 In. ............ *Illus* | 200.00 |
| Wedgwood, Medallion, William Pitt, C.1800, 3 3/4 In. ............ *Illus* | 225.00 |
| Wedgwood, Mold, Stocking, Child's, Queensware, 1882, 5 In.High | 55.00 |
| Wedgwood, Muffineer, White Figures On Blue, Silver Top | 85.00 |
| Wedgwood, Mug, Royal Visit To Canada, 1939, Cobalt Blue & White | 95.00 |
| Wedgwood, Paperweight, Jasperware, Black, White American Eagle | 15.00 |
| Wedgwood, Pendant, Cameo, Hercules & Nemean Lion, 4 Color, Octagon, C.1750 | 185.00 |
| Wedgwood, Pitcher, Classical Figures On Green, 8 In. | 70.00 |
| Wedgwood, Pitcher, Cobalt Blue & White, Impressed Wedgwood, 4 3/4 In. | 75.00 |
| Wedgwood, Pitcher, Cobalt Blue & White, Impressed Wedgwood, 4 5/8 In. | 55.00 |

Wedgwood, Medallion,
Statesman, C.1800,
3 7/8 In.
*(See Page 705)*

Wedgwood, Medallion,
Garrick, C.1775, 3 7/8 In.
*(See Page 705)*

Wedgwood, Medallion,
William Pitt, C.1800,
3 3/4 In.
*(See Page 705)*

Wedgwood, Medallion,
Earl Of Chatham, C.1775,
3 1/4 In.
*(See Page 705)*

| | |
|---|---:|
| Wedgwood, Pitcher, Cobalt, Marked '30, 5 1/2 In.High | 45.00 |
| Wedgwood, Pitcher, Creamware, Raised Hunting Scene On Green, Hound Handle | 38.00 |
| Wedgwood, Pitcher, Dark Blue, Classical Figures At Bottom, Grapes At Top | 58.00 |
| Wedgwood, Pitcher, Dark Blue, Classical Figures, Twisted Handle, 5 1/2 In. | 72.50 |
| Wedgwood, Pitcher, Figures & Grape Band On Dark Blue, Rope Handle, 4 In. | 32.50 |
| Wedgwood, Pitcher, Green & White, 5 In.High | 28.00 |
| Wedgwood, Pitcher, Green, England, 5 1/2 In. | 65.00 |
| Wedgwood, Pitcher, Ironstone, White, 12 In. | 15.00 |
| Wedgwood, Pitcher, Jasperware, Green, White, & Beige, 6 In.High | 97.50 |
| Wedgwood, Pitcher, Jasperware, White Classical Figures On Dark Blue | 47.50 |
| Wedgwood, Pitcher, Milk, Deep Blue, 1930, 5 1/2 In.High | 42.50 |
| Wedgwood, Pitcher, Pea Green & White, Impressed Wedgwood, England, 4 1/4 In. | 75.00 |
| Wedgwood, Pitcher, Relief White Figures On Dark Blue, C.1900, 8 1/2 In. | 95.00 |
| Wedgwood, Pitcher, Rope Twist Handle, Blue Classical Figures, 7 1/2 In. | 115.00 |
| Wedgwood, Pitcher, Terra-Cotta, Gold Tracery Pagoda, Rope Handle, 6 1/2 In. | 47.50 |
| Wedgwood, Pitcher, Terra-Cotta, Marked '57, 4 1/2 In.High | 85.00 |
| Wedgwood, Plaque, Basalt, Black, Hercules Binding Cerberus | 325.00 |
| Wedgwood, Plaque, Grecian Woman, Sage Green, Oval, 5 1/4 In. | 115.00 |
| Wedgwood, Plaque, Jasperware, Classical Figure On Green, Oval, 4 1/4 X 3 In. | 85.00 |
| Wedgwood, Plaque, Jasperware, Green, Framed, Marked Wedgwood, 3 1/2 X 2 In. | 85.00 |
| Wedgwood, Plaque, Jasperware, Green, Madame Montespan, Signed | 150.00 |
| Wedgwood, Plaque, Jasperware, Harvest On Light Blue, Signed Wedgwood | 130.00 |
| Wedgwood, Plaque, Jasperware, Mythological Figures On Green | 35.00 |
| Wedgwood, Plaque, Jasperware, Mythological Scene On Light Blue, Round, Pair | 150.00 |
| Wedgwood, Plaque, Jasperware, 4 Classical Figures On Green, Rectangular | 85.00 |
| Wedgwood, Plaque, Light Blue & White, Muses, Angels, 6 X 4 Inches, C.1880 | 300.00 |
| Wedgwood, Plaque, Lilac, 4 In. | 35.00 |
| Wedgwood, Plaque, Marriage Of Cupid & Psyche, Lilac, 3 1/2 In. | 125.00 |
| Wedgwood, Plate, Abbott Academy, Mass., 1829-1929, Blue & White, 9 3/4 In. | 12.50 |
| Wedgwood, Plate, Barometer Inset, Lilac, 9 In. | 75.00 |
| Wedgwood, Plate, Battle Of Lexington, Blue & White, 9 In. | 22.00 |

| | |
|---|---|
| Wedgwood, Plate, Beaconsfield, Green, Gold, & Gray On White, 10 1/2 In. | 7.50 |
| Wedgwood, Plate, Birds & Fans, Impressed Wedgwood, 9 In. | 25.00 |
| Wedgwood, Plate, Blue & White, Dutch Boy & Girl In Harbor Scene, 7 1/4 In. | 7.00 |
| Wedgwood, Plate, Boston Common, Blue, 9 In. | 20.00 |
| Wedgwood, Plate, Boston Post Office, 10 In. | 15.00 |
| Wedgwood, Plate, Boston Public Library, Blue & White, Rose Border, 9 In. | 22.00 |
| Wedgwood, Plate, Bread & Butter, Cornflower | 5.00 |
| Wedgwood, Plate, Captain John Parker, Green, Lexintgon, Mass., 9 In. | 17.00 |
| Wedgwood, Plate, Claude, Blue & White Transfer, C.1820, 9 1/2 In. | 45.00 |
| Wedgwood, Plate, Clipper Ship Staghound, 1938, 9 1/4 In. | 12.50 |
| Wedgwood, Plate, Clipper Ship The Anne McKim, 1938, 9 1/4 In. | 12.50 |
| Wedgwood, Plate, Creamware, Chinese Design, C.1820, 9 1/2 In. | 49.50 |
| Wedgwood, Plate, Creamware, 9 1/4 In. | 44.80 |
| Wedgwood, Plate, Dessert, Hand-Painted Foxgloves, Fluted Border, 9 In. | 7.50 |
| Wedgwood, Plate, Dinner, Cornflower | 6.00 |
| Wedgwood, Plate, Dinner, Torbay, Emerald Green On White, 10 1/4 In. | 8.75 |
| Wedgwood, Plate, Dorothy Q Mansion, 9 In. | 23.00 |
| Wedgwood, Plate, Fairbanks House, Blue & White, Rose Border, 9 In. | 22.00 |
| Wedgwood, Plate, Faneuil Hall, Blue & White, 9 In. | 15.00 To 22.00 |
| Wedgwood, Plate, Ferrara, Pink, Etruria, 8 1/4 In. | 12.00 |
| Wedgwood, Plate, Fish, Majolica, Gray Blue Fish On Turquoise, 9 1/2 In. | 17.50 |
| Wedgwood, Plate, Floral & Classic Medallions, Sterling Rim, C.1900, 12 In. | 50.00 |
| Wedgwood, Plate, Fort Ticonderoga, 1755-1955, 9 1/4 In. | 14.00 |
| Wedgwood, Plate, Guildhall, 10 In. | 12.50 |
| Wedgwood, Plate, Holy Cross College, Blue & White, 1932, 10 In. | 25.00 |
| Wedgwood, Plate, Home Of Ralph Waldo Emerson, 9 In. | 21.00 |
| Wedgwood, Plate, Home Of Washington, Blue & White, 9 In. | 18.00 |
| Wedgwood, Plate, Horticultural, Polychrome Floral Border, 1880, 10 1/2 In. | 38.00 |
| Wedgwood, Plate, Hunting Scene, 8 In. | 30.00 |
| Wedgwood, Plate, Indiana, C.1796, 9 In. | 10.00 |
| Wedgwood, Plate, Ivanhoe & Rowena, Dark Blue, 10 1/4 In. | 19.50 |
| Wedgwood, Plate, Ivanhoe Series, Blue & White, 8 In. | 12.00 |
| Wedgwood, Plate, Ivanhoe Series, Blue & White, 10 In. | 20.00 |
| Wedgwood, Plate, Ivanhoe, Front De Boeuf Exorcises Isaac, Blue, 10 1/4 In. | 18.50 |
| Wedgwood, Plate, Ivanhoe, Ivanhoe & Rowena, Blue, 10 1/4 In. | 18.50 |
| Wedgwood, Plate, Jasperware, Dark Blue, White Children, 9 In. | 115.00 |
| Wedgwood, Plate, King's Chapel, Boston, Jones, Midwest & Stratton Co | 24.00 |
| Wedgwood, Plate, Leaf Shape, Dark Green, 8 1/2 In. | 12.50 |
| Wedgwood, Plate, Leaf Shape, Green, Wedgwood & Barlaston, Etruria, 8 In. | 8.50 |
| Wedgwood, Plate, Leaf, Green Glaze, No.21, Etruria, England, 8 In. | 8.00 |
| Wedgwood, Plate, Longfellow's Home, Blue & White, 9 In. | 18.00 |
| Wedgwood, Plate, Longfellow's House, 9 In. | 17.00 |
| Wedgwood, Plate, Majolica, Shell & Seaweed, White Basket Weave, 8 3/4 In. | 20.00 |
| Wedgwood, Plate, Massachusetts Institute Of Technology, Pylon, 10 1/4 In. | 7.50 |
| Wedgwood, Plate, Old North Church, Salem St., 9 In. | 18.00 |
| Wedgwood, Plate, Old South Church, Blue & White, 9 In. | 11.00 To 22.00 |
| Wedgwood, Plate, Pearl, 9 1/4 In., Pair | 48.00 |
| Wedgwood, Plate, Pilgrim Memorial Monument, 7 In. | 14.00 |
| Wedgwood, Plate, Service, Smith College, Sepia, 10 1/4 In. | 12.00 |
| Wedgwood, Plate, Soft Paste, Chinese Man & Mandolin On Vase, Blue, 9 In. | 30.00 |
| Wedgwood, Plate, Soup, C.1850, 10 1/4 In., Pair | 48.00 |
| Wedgwood, Plate, Soup, Ivanhoe Series, Blue & White, 9 In. | 16.00 |
| Wedgwood, Plate, Soup, Soft Paste, Chinese Man & Mandolin On Vase, Blue | 30.00 |
| Wedgwood, Plate, St.James's, 10 In. | 12.50 |
| Wedgwood, Plate, St.Paul's, 10 In. | 12.50 |
| Wedgwood, Plate, Stafford Castle, Black On Cream, Etruria, 1962, 10 1/2 In. | 15.00 |
| Wedgwood, Plate, The Capitol, Blue & White, Rose Border, 9 In. | 22.00 |
| Wedgwood, Plate, The Washington Elm, 9 In. | 27.00 |
| Wedgwood, Plate, Torbay, Patrician Series, Scroll Border, 9 1/4 In. | 6.25 |
| Wedgwood, Plate, Tower Of London, 10 In. | 12.50 |
| Wedgwood, Plate, Turkey, Dark Blue, Floral Border, Marked Clytie, 9 In. | 18.00 |
| Wedgwood, Plate, University, Pa., Bicentennial, 1740-1940, 10 1/4 In. | 10.00 |
| Wedgwood, Plate, Urn, Dark To Medium Blue, 9 In. | 5.00 |
| Wedgwood, Plate, Wellesley College, Blue & White, 9 In. | 18.00 |
| Wedgwood, Plate, Whittier's Birthplace, Blue, 9 In. | 20.00 |
| Wedgwood, Plate, William Penn Bust, State Shield, 10 1/4 In. | 10.00 |

Wedgwood, Plate, Woodland, Rose Color, Hand Engraving, 9 1/2 In. ............... 18.00
Wedgwood, Plate, World War II British War Relief Society, 10 In. ............... 12.50
Wedgwood, Platter, Ivanhoe, Rowena, Blue & White, 13 In. ............... 35.00
Wedgwood, Platter, Majolica, Floral Sprays, 1880, 12 In. ............... 10.00
Wedgwood, Platter, Meat, Blue & White, Pastoral Scene ............... 57.50
Wedgwood, Platter, Queensware, Embossed Grape & Shell Rim, Oval, 12 X 16 In. ............... 20.00
Wedgwood, Platter, Vintage, Queensware, Oval, 12 X 16 In. ............... 20.00
Wedgwood, Pot, Covered, Jasperware, Blue & White, 4 1/2 In.High ............... 75.00
Wedgwood, Pot, Jam, Jasperware, Dark Blue, Silver Plate Lid ............... 45.00
Wedgwood, Pot, Jam, Jasperware, Yellow, Black Garlands, White Bands, Silver ............... 225.00
Wedgwood, Ring Tree, White Figurals, Royal Blue, Marked ............... 39.50
Wedgwood, Salad Set, Majolica, Silver Rim Bowl, C.1872, 3 Piece ............... 175.00
Wedgwood, Sauce, Ivanhoe Series, Blue & White, 4 1/2 In. ............... 6.00
Wedgwood, Spill, Basalt, Black, Arabesque Top Border, Flaxman Figures ............... 55.00
Wedgwood, Spittoon, Tall ............... 25.00
Wedgwood, Sugar & Creamer, Cover, Light Blue, Made In England, 1955 ............... 45.00
Wedgwood, Sugar & Creamer, Cover, White Classical Figures On Dark Blue ............... 87.00
Wedgwood, Sugar & Creamer, Etruria ............... 14.00
Wedgwood, Sugar & Creamer, Green, Cover, 2 Handled, England ............... 60.00
Wedgwood, Sugar, Covered, Jasperware, Light Green Figures On Dark Green ............... 45.00
Wedgwood, Sugar, Covered, White Relief Flaxman Figures On Olive Green ............... 65.00
Wedgwood, Sugar, Deep Blue, 1924, Large Size ............... 38.50
Wedgwood, Sugar, Green With White, "Sacrifice To Peace, " C.1891 ............... 55.00
Wedgwood, Sugar, Ningpo ............... 6.00
Wedgwood, Sugar, Tudor Rose, Drab, C.1800 ............... 165.00
Wedgwood, Tankard, Dark Blue, 2 Sacrificial Scenes Medallions, Sterling Rim ............... 175.00
Wedgwood, Tea Caddy, Whieldon, C.1760, 4 In.High ............... *Illus* 400.00
Wedgwood, Tea Set, Ferrara, 23 Piece ............... 240.00
Wedgwood, Tea Set, Japan Pattern, Yellow Panels, Red Flowers, 11 Piece ............... 275.00
Wedgwood, Tea Set, Jasperware, White On Dark Blue, Silver Rims, 3 Piece ............... 195.00
Wedgwood, Tea Set, White Classical Figures On Green, 4 Piece ............... 155.00
Wedgwood, Teacup & Saucer, Jasperware, Handleless, Dark Blue ............... 45.00
Wedgwood, Teapot, Bamboo Molded, Black & Green, 5 1/2 In.High ............... 2&0.00
Wedgwood, Teapot, Basalt, Black, Widow Finial, Squatty, Satin Finish ............... 105.00
Wedgwood, Teapot, Blue Jasper, Wreath Around Spout, Leaves Trim Lid ............... 75.00
Wedgwood, Teapot, Caneware, Square, Flowering Vines, 3 1/4 In.High ............... 100.00
Wedgwood, Teapot, Grecian Women, Baby, Ram, Man, & Dog On Dark Blue ............... 75.00
Wedgwood, Teapot, Jasperware, Cobalt, White Figures & Trees, C.1845, 4 In. ............... 90.00
Wedgwood, Teapot, Light Blue, England, 5 1/2 In. ............... 125.00
Wedgwood, Teapot, Rosso Antico, Squatty, Capri Enameled Flowers, 3 1/2 In. ............... 225.00
Wedgwood, Teapot, Salt Glaze, Man Of Mountain Heads, Floral, & Arabesque ............... 135.00
Wedgwood, Teapot, White Relief Flaxman Figures On Olive Green ............... 105.00
Wedgwood, Tile, Calendar, Boston Customhouse, 1915 ............... 24.00
Wedgwood, Tile, February, Etruria ............... 48.00
Wedgwood, Tile, Flowered Geometrics, Sepia, 6 In. ............... 11.00
Wedgwood, Tile, March, Blue & White, 6 In.Square ............... 50.00
Wedgwood, Tile, Midsummer Night's Dream, Cobweb, Brown & White, 8 In. ............... 50.00
Wedgwood, Tile, Midsummer Night's Dream, Demetrius, Brown & White, 8 In. ............... 50.00
Wedgwood, Tile, Midsummer Night's Dream, Lysander, Brown & White, 8 In. ............... 50.00
Wedgwood, Tile, Midsummer Night's Dream, Peaseblossom, Brown & White, 8 In. ............... 50.55
Wedgwood, Tile, November, Brown & White, 8 In.Square ............... 50.00
Wedgwood, Tile, October, Wrought Iron Bound, Footed, 6 In.Square ............... 55.00
Wedgwood, Tile, September, Russet & White, Wrought Iron Bound, Footed, 6 In. ............... 55.00
Wedgwood, Tray, Pin, Dark Green, White Cherubs On Chariot Blowing Trumpets ............... 18.00
Wedgwood, Tray, Pin, Green With White, Oval, 4 Brass Feet, 4 Figures ............... 20.00
Wedgwood, Tray, Pin, Jasperware, Powder Blue & White, Elizabeth, 1953 ............... 22.50
Wedgwood, Tray, Pin, Jasperware, Powder Blue & White, Prince Philip, 1953 ............... 22.50
Wedgwood, Tray, Pin, Round, Green Scalloped Rim, C.1960, 4 1/2 In. ............... 10.00
Wedgwood, Tray, Pin, Terra-Cotta, Square Ends, C.1945, 3 1/4 X 6 In. ............... 32.50
Wedgwood, Urn, Blue, White & Lilac, Festoons, Ram's Heads, & Medallions, 1850 ............... 950.00
Wedgwood, Urn, Classical Figures On Light Blue, Handles, England, 6 In. ............... 75.00
Wedgwood, Urn, Jasperware, Blue, White Cameo Figures, Covered, Footed, 5 In. ............... 375.00
Wedgwood, Vase, Basalt, Cylindrical, Footed, Classical Figures, 4 1/2 In. ............... 95.00
Wedgwood, Vase, Basalt, Trumpet, Panels Of Relief Vines, Strapwork, C.1830 ............... 225.00
Wedgwood, Vase, Basalt, Urn Shape, Garlands & Classical Figures, 4 1/2 In. ............... 95.00
Wedgwood, Vase, Black Basalt, C.1770, 16 1/2 In.High ............... *Illus* 1700.00

Wedgwood, Vase, Serpentine Ware,
C.1800, 6 In.High, Pair

Wedgwood, Vase,
Black Basalt, C.1770,
10 1/2 In.High
*(See Page 708)*

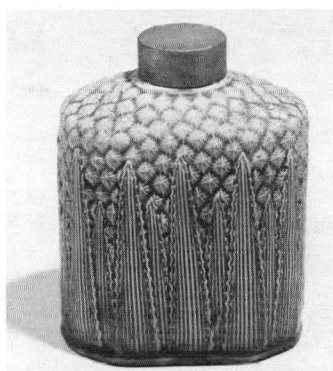

Wedgwood, Tea Caddy, Whieldon,
C.1760, 4 In High
*(See Page 708)*

Weller, Frog, Flower, Green
*(See Page 710)*

| | |
|---|---:|
| **Wedgwood, Vase,** Blue Jasper, Portland, 6 In.High, 4 1/2 In.Wide | 150.00 |
| **Wedgwood, Vase,** Bone China, Powder Ruby Color, C.1895, 10 In.High | 125.00 |
| **Wedgwood, Vase,** Classical Scenes On Blue, 5 In., Pair | 145.00 |
| **Wedgwood, Vase,** Fairyland Luster, Gold Dragon & Bees On Orange, 8 1/2 In. | 450.00 |
| **Wedgwood, Vase,** Fairyland Luster, Portland, Mother-Of-Pearl Dragons On Blue | 150.00 |
| **Wedgwood, Vase,** Fairyland Luster, Yellow Dragons On Blue, Portland Mark | 125.00 |
| **Wedgwood, Vase,** Gold Dragons On Mottled Blue Luster, Bulbous, 8 In.High | 235.00 |
| **Wedgwood, Vase,** Jar Shape, Cupids & Musical Instruments On Dark Blue, 1891 | 110.00 |
| **Wedgwood, Vase,** Portland, Cobalt Blue, C.1876, 6 1/2 In.High | 275.00 |
| **Wedgwood, Vase,** Portland, Jasperware, Blue, Pelius & Thetis, 10 1/4 In.High | 700.00 |
| **Wedgwood, Vase,** Portland, 2 Handled, 8 1/2 In.High | 600.00 |
| **Wedgwood, Vase,** Queensware, Embossed Grapes, Leaves, & Vines Band On Blue | 18.50 |
| **Wedgwood, Vase,** Redware, Black Medallions, 10 In.High | 200.00 |
| **Wedgwood, Vase,** Rosso Antico, Black Relief Decoration, C.1900, 9 1/4 In.Pair | 800.00 |
| **Wedgwood, Vase,** Serpentine Ware, C.1800, 6 In.High, Pair *Illus* | 600.00 |
| **Wedgwood, Vase,** Spill, Basalt, Floral Bas Relief, Marked Wedgwood, 4 7/8 In. | 150.00 |
| **Wedgwood, Vase,** Spill, Blue Jasper, Acanthus Leaf Relief, 5 1/2 In.High | 95.00 |
| **Wedgwood, Vase,** Stoneware, Dark Blue Relief Leaves On White, C.1810 | 195.00 |
| **Wedgwood, Vase,** Tricolor, Lilac, Green, & White, Dipping Of Achilles, 13 In. | 1100.00 |
| **Wedgwood, Vase,** White On Dark Blue, Marked Wedgwood, England, C.1890 | 95.00 |

Wedgwood, Washstand Set, Blue Design, Impressed Mark, 2 Piece ............................................. 70.00

**WELLER**  *Weller pottery was first made in 1873 in Fultonham, Ohio. The firm moved to Zanesville, Ohio, in 1882. Art wares were first made in 1893. Hundreds of lines of pottery were made including Louwelsa, Eocean, Dickens, and Sicardo before the pottery closed in 1948.*

| Item | Price |
|---|---|
| Weller, Ashtray, Dog, Brown Glaze, Marked Weller | 20.00 |
| Weller, Baby's Feeding Set, Zona, Bunnies & Birds On Cream, Marked Weller | 45.00 |
| Weller, Basket, Brown & Tan With Olive Handle, 6 X 7 Inches | 28.00 |
| Weller, Basket, Cameo, Peach, 7 1/2 X 5 In. | 18.00 |
| Weller, Basket, Forest, 9 1/2 In.High | 22.50 |
| Weller, Basket, Tutone, 8 X 9 Inches | 25.00 |
| Weller, Basket, Wild Rose, Green, 5 3/4 In.High | 15.00 |
| Weller, Basket, Wood Rose, 6 3/4 In.Diameter, 4 3/4 In.High | 21.00 |
| Weller, Bottle, Water, Ollas | 9.00 |
| Weller, Bowl, Blue, 4 Flowers On White Squares, Turned-In Rim, 10 1/2 In. | 17.00 |
| Weller, Bowl, Branch With White Blossoms, 9 1/4 In.Diameter | 14.00 |
| Weller, Bowl, Bulb, Sicardo, Free Form, Art Nouveau Style, Signed, 7 1/2 In. | 195.00 |
| Weller, Bowl, Burntwood, Ducks, 3 In.High, No Mark | 30.00 |
| Weller, Bowl, Burntwood, Fish, 2 1/4 In.High, No Mark | 30.00 |
| Weller, Bowl, Burntwood, Spider Web Decoration, No Mark, 3 1/2 In.High | 7.00 |
| Weller, Bowl, Center, White, Lavender Flowers, 12 1/2 In.Diameter | 18.00 |
| Weller, Bowl, Dickensware, Mice, Burntwood | 21.00 |
| Weller, Bowl, Flower, Boat Shape, Raised Green Leaves On Red To Yellow | 25.00 |
| Weller, Bowl, Flower, Boat Shape, Relief Red Flowers & Green Leaves On Red | 19.50 |
| Weller, Bowl, Hudson, Footed, Pastel Blossoms On Gray, 11 1/2 In. | 30.00 |
| Weller, Bowl, Knifewood, 5 1/2 In.Diameter | 15.00 |
| Weller, Bowl, Roma, Footed & Handled, 3 In.High, 7 In.Wide | 25.00 |
| Weller, Bowl, Roma, 7 3/4 In.Diameter, 3 1/2 In.High | 10.00 |
| Weller, Bowl, Shallow, Turned Rim, Marbleized, 13 3/4 In. | 45.00 |
| Weller, Bowl, Swan, Pale Green, 6 In. Long | 22.00 |
| Weller, Bowl, Water Lily Pads, Cream & Brown, 5 1/2 In.Diameter | 9.00 |
| Weller, Candelabra, 3 Branch, High Brown Glaze | 15.00 |
| Weller, Candleholder, Louwelsa, Floral, 5 1/2 In.High | 84.00 |
| Weller, Cornucopia, Ivoris, 6 1/2 In.Long | 11.00 |
| Weller, Cornucopia, Pink, 10 In.Long | 9.00 |
| Weller, Creamer, Embossed Rabbit & Bluebird, Marked | 20.00 |
| Weller, Dish, Mint, Figural Seal, 5 In. | 22.00 |
| Weller, Ewer, Louwelsa, Brown Glaze, Floral Decoration, Artist Signed, 6 In. | 80.00 |
| Weller, Ewer, Louwelsa, Brown Glaze, Yellow & White Crocus, 6 In.High | 95.00 |
| Weller, Ewer, Wild Rose, Peach, 7 In.High | 25.00 |
| Weller, Figurine, Bird, Muskota, 6 In. | 45.00 |
| Weller, Figurine, White Nude & Swan On Rock, Malta | 18.50 |
| Weller, Flower Frog, Black Embossed Stripes, 4 1/2 In.Diameter | 12.00 |
| Weller, Flower Frog, Fat Frog Sits Inside A Pond Lily | 14.00 |
| Weller, Flower Frog, Lobster Shape | 26.00 |
| Weller, Flower Frog, Nude On Rock, White | 20.00 |
| Weller, Flower Holder, Nude & Swans, Malta | 22.00 |
| Weller, Flower Holder, 3 Cornucopias On Base, Pink Floral On Green | 12.00 |
| Weller, Frog, Flower, Green *Illus* | 35.00 |
| Weller, Holder, Cigar, Florals On 9-Sided Cream Ground, 4 1/4 In.High | 14.00 |
| Weller, Holder, Letter, Roma, 4 In.High | 14.00 |
| Weller, Humidor, Florals On 9-Sided Cream Ground, 9 In.High, 6 In.Diameter | 32.00 |
| Weller, Humidor, Irishman, Artist Signed R.D. | 285.00 |
| Weller, Jardiniere & Stand, Aurelian, Grape Clusters On Browns, C.1900 | 225.00 |
| Weller, Jardiniere, Daffodils On Gold Green Brown, Louwelsa, 9 X 11 In. | 85.00 |
| Weller, Jardiniere, Dickensware, Jonquils On Mahogany Glaze | 125.00 |
| Weller, Jardiniere, Dickensware, Leaf & Berry, Brown Glaze, 11 In. | 95.00 |
| Weller, Jardiniere, Dickensware, Olive To Brown, Iris, 8 1/4 X 10 1/2 In. | 130.00 |
| Weller, Jardiniere, DuPont, Artist Signed FMR, 6 1/4 In.Diameter | 28.00 |
| Weller, Jardiniere, Etna, 3 Red Flowers On Gray, 5 X 6 1/4 In. | 55.00 |
| Weller, Jardiniere, Forest, 7 3/4 X 9 In. | 32.00 |
| Weller, Jardiniere, Ivory, Swans, 5 1/2 X 6 1/2 In. | 35.00 |
| Weller, Jardiniere, Louwelsa, Daffodils, 9 In.High, 10 In.Wide | 55.00 |
| Weller, Jardiniere, Louwelsa, Gold Crocus, 8 X 6 1/2 In. | 60.00 |
| Weller, Jardiniere, Pinecone, 5 3/4 In.High, 6 3/4 In.Diameter | 16.00 |

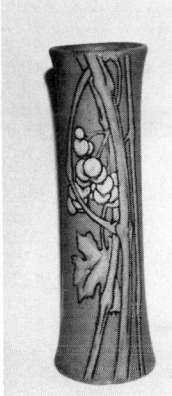

Weller, Vase,
Orange Matte, Etched,
12 1/2 In. High
*(See Page 713)*

Weller, Jug, Louwelsa,
Orange & Green
On Brown To Green

| | |
|---|---:|
| Weller, Jug, Aurelian, Floral Decoration & Handle, 3 1/4 In.High, Marked | 80.00 |
| Weller, Jug, Floral, Louwelsa, 3 In.High | 95.00 |
| Weller, Jug, Louwelsa, Orange & Green On Brown To Green ................... *Illus* | 75.00 |
| Weller, Lamp Base, Louwelsa, Cherry Decoration, Unmarked, 10 In.High | 30.00 |
| Weller, Lamp, Brown & Green Glaze, Yellow & Rust Pansies, Artist M.P. | 87.00 |
| Weller, Lamp, Electric, Roma, Currier & Ives Scenes Shade | 85.00 |
| Weller, Lamp, Gone With The Wind, Louwelsa, Floral, Brass Burner, 10 In. | 300.00 |
| Weller, Lamp, Oil, Dickensware, Pansies On Brown, 3 Footed, 12 1/2 In. | 225.00 |
| Weller, Mug, Burntwood, Unmarked | 18.00 |
| Weller, Mug, Dickensware, Lady Golfer, 9 In.High | 135.00 |
| Weller, Mug, Dickensware, Man With Pipe, Slip Decoration, 2 Handled, 6 In. | 185.00 |
| Weller, Mug, Dickensware, Second Line, Stag & Tree, 6 3/4 In.High | 175.00 |
| Weller, Mug, Etna, 5 1/4 In. | 40.00 |
| Weller, Pitcher, Art Nouveau, Figure Of Woman, Matte Glaze, 8 In.High | 75.00 |
| Weller, Pitcher, Art Nouveau, Woman's Figure, Matte Glaze, 10 1/2 In.High | 95.00 |
| Weller, Pitcher, Forest, 5 1/2 In. High | 28.00 |
| Weller, Pitcher, Green, Embossed Flowers & Leaves, Stem Handle, 5 In.High | 13.00 |
| Weller, Pitcher, Louwelsa, Floral Decoration, Green To Brown, 5 1/2 In. | 68.00 |
| Weller, Pitcher, Red & Yellow Pansies On Cream Ground, 7 In.High | 22.00 |
| Weller, Pitcher, Zona, Kingfisher, 8 1/4 In.High, No Mark | 55.00 |
| Weller, Plant Stand & Jardiniere, Sicardo, Molded Fronds On Metallic | 850.00 |
| Weller, Planter, Gray-Violet To Cream, Pink & White Pansies, 6 3/4 In. | 30.00 |
| Weller, Planter, Iris Flower On Brown Glaze, Artist-Signed, Louwelsa | 95.00 |
| Weller, Planter, Triangular, Footed, Dogwood & Berries On Green, 7 In. | 18.00 |
| Weller, Plaque, Abraham Lincoln, 4 1/2 In. | 22.00 |
| Weller, Plate, Baby, Embossed Rabbit, Bluebird, Branches, 7 In. | 18.00 |
| Weller, Plate, Zona, 7 1/4 In.Diameter | 7.00 |
| Weller, Pocket, Wall, Hudson, Hand-Painted Floral On Cream, 10 In. High | 50.00 |
| Weller, Rose Bowl, Louwelsa, Pansies, Brown, Rust, & Yellow, Footed, 4 3/4 In. | 80.00 |
| Weller, Rose Bowl, Pedestal, Nasturtiums On Umber, 2 Handles, 5 In.High | 14.00 |
| Weller, Rose Bowl, White Florals On Blue, 5 In. | 15.00 |
| Weller, Tankard, Dickensware, Jolly Monk, Second Line, Light Green Ground | 425.00 |
| Weller, Tankard, Dickensware, Second Line, Glossy, Dickens Characters | 375.00 |
| Weller, Tankard, Etna, Purple Pansies On Gray, 6 1/2 In. High | 65.00 |
| Weller, Tankard, Green Bottom, White Top, Grape Design, 11 1/2 In.High | 50.00 |
| Weller, Tea Set, Basket Weave, Lavender, 4 Piece | 45.00 |
| Weller, Teapot, Forest, High Glaze, Marked, 5 In.High | 50.00 |
| Weller, Teapot, Zona, Apple Decoration, 5 3/4 In.High | 10.00 |
| Weller, Tobacco Jar, Roma, 9-Sided, 7 In.High | 45.00 |
| Weller, Umbrella Stand, Roma | 125.00 |
| Weller, Vase, Applied Rhododendron Decoration, Blue Matte, 11 In.High | 48.00 |
| Weller, Vase, Art Nouveau, Matte Floral, Green, Pink, Yellow, 10 In.High | 40.00 |
| Weller, Vase, Art Nouveau, Raised Flowers, Brown Glaze, 5 1/2 In.High | 70.00 |
| Weller, Vase, Aurelian, Mahogany Glaze, Yellow Iris, Artist Signed, 5 In.High | 95.00 |
| Weller, Vase, Baldwin, 7 1/4 In.High | 22.00 |

Weller, Vase, Baluster, Nasturtiums On Brown, Mitchell, C.1905, 21 1/2 In. ............................ 200.00
Weller, Vase, Bird, Eggs, Nest, Water & Foliage, Glendale Ware, 6 1/2 In. ............................ 65.00
Weller, Vase, Blue & White Iris On Light Green To Rose Ground, 9 1/2 In. ............................ 85.00
Weller, Vase, Bonita, Two Handles, Floral Decoration, 5 In. High ............................ 40.00
Weller, Vase, Bouquet, Green, 12 1/2 In.High ............................ 18.00
Weller, Vase, Bradley, Lavender, 7 1/4 In.High, 10 In.Wide ............................ 16.00
Weller, Vase, Brown, Marbleized, 7 In.High ............................ 35.00
Weller, Vase, Bud, Double, Roma, 8 In.High ............................ 9.00
Weller, Vase, Bud, Jug Shape, Louwelsa, Yellow & Green Leaves, 2 3/4 In. ............................ 35.00
Weller, Vase, Bud, Louwelsa, Orange Floral On Brown, 7 In. ............................ 54.00
Weller, Vase, Bulbous, Iridescent Pink Glaze, Marked, 9 In.High ............................ 25.00
Weller, Vase, Burntwood, Daisies, 9 In. ............................ 20.00
Weller, Vase, Cabinet, Louwelsa, Yellow Flowers, Leaves, & Fronds On Brown ............................ 47.00
Weller, Vase, Chase, Tan Ground, Hunter & Dogs In White Cameo, 11 1/2 In. ............................ 175.00
Weller, Vase, Chelsea, 6 In.High, 3 1/2 In.Diameter ............................ 18.00
Weller, Vase, Chengtu, 11 In.High ............................ 55.00
Weller, Vase, Convex Sides, 3 Raised Flowers On Slate Blue, Exline, 7 In. ............................ 22.50
Weller, Vase, Coppertone, Frog With Open Flower On Lily Pad Base, 4 In. ............................ 47.00
Weller, Vase, Cornflowers On Brown Glaze, 13 1/2 In.High ............................ 50.00
Weller, Vase, Cornish, Brown With Green Leaves, 9 In.High ............................ 35.00
Weller, Vase, Crystalline, Cream Ground, Oak Leaves, 10 In.High ............................ 14.00
Weller, Vase, Delsa, White, 6 1/4 In.High ............................ 14.00
Weller, Vase, Dickensware, Dombey & Son, C.W., 9 In. ............................ 345.00
Weller, Vase, Dickensware, Etched Monk Holding Mug In Hand, Green Vines ............................ 150.00
Weller, Vase, Dickensware, Glossy Finish, Golfers, A.Dunlavy ............................ 275.00
Weller, Vase, Dickensware, Incised Indian, Artist Signed, 9 In. ............................ 275.00
Weller, Vase, Discus Shape, Triangular Opening, Yellow Pansies, 3 In.High ............................ 60.00
Weller, Vase, Double Notched Handle, Wild Rose, 8 1/2 In. ............................ 17.50
Weller, Vase, Double, Ardsley, 9 1/2 In.High ............................ 30.00
Weller, Vase, Eocean, Blue Floral Decoration, 4 1/2 In.High, Unmarked ............................ 27.50
Weller, Vase, Eocean, Dark To Light Gray, Pink Dogwood Flowers, Signed, 4 In. ............................ 67.50
Weller, Vase, Eocean, Floral Decoration, Artist Signed LJB, 7 In.High ............................ 75.00
Weller, Vase, Eocean, Pink Thistle On Shiny Glaze, Artist E.R., 10 1/2 In. ............................ 125.00
Weller, Vase, Eocean, Red Rose Decoration, 6 1/2 In.High, No Mark ............................ 35.00
Weller, Vase, Eocean, 2 Dogwood Blossoms On Gray Shading, 7 In. ............................ 67.50
Weller, Vase, Eocean, 2 Dogwood Blossoms With Yellow Centers On Gray, 4 In. ............................ 57.50
Weller, Vase, Etna, Cylindrical, Yellow Floral On Gray & White, 8 3/4 In. ............................ 60.00
Weller, Vase, Etna, 11 In.High ............................ 85.00
Weller, Vase, Fan, Multicolored Floral, 7 In.High ............................ 20.00
Weller, Vase, Floral, Artist Signed, Louwelsa, 8 In.High ............................ 50.00
Weller, Vase, Floral, Green Iridescent, Signed Sicardo, 5 1/2 In.High ............................ 175.00
Weller, Vase, Floretta, Brown Glaze, Floral Decoration, 7 In.High ............................ 75.00
Weller, Vase, Floretta, Bulbous, Grapes In Relief On Brown, 5 In. ............................ 55.00
Weller, Vase, Floretta, Relief Grapes On Brown Glaze, 11 1/2 In. ............................ 65.00
Weller, Vase, Forest, Cylindrical, Slight Flaring, 8 In. ............................ 35.00
Weller, Vase, Forest, Ovoid, 8 In. High ............................ 46.00
Weller, Vase, Forest, Ovoid, 8 1/2 In. High ............................ 35.00
Weller, Vase, Forest, 8 1/4 In. High ............................ 26.00 To 32.00
Weller, Vase, Forest, 10 1/2 In. High ............................ 35.00
Weller, Vase, Goldbrogreen, Multicolor Glaze, 7 In.High ............................ 48.00
Weller, Vase, Green Oak Leaf, 9 In. ............................ 20.00
Weller, Vase, Handled, Nasturtium Decoration, 6 1/4 In.High ............................ 35.00
Weller, Vase, Horned Shape, White Flower Decoration, 5 1/2 In.High ............................ 10.00
Weller, Vase, Hudson, Blue To Green, Pillsbury, 15 In. ............................ Illus 90.00
Weller, Vase, Hudson, Daisies On Pale Blue, Signed Pillsbury, 12 In. ............................ 70.00
Weller, Vase, Hudson, Heavy Floral Decoration, Green To Pink, 8 1/2 In. ............................ 85.00
Weller, Vase, Hudson, Vellum, Floral, 11 In., Pair ............................ 110.00
Weller, Vase, Impressed Leaves, Blossoms, Blue, Bulbous, 7 1/2 In.High ............................ 17.00
Weller, Vase, Incised Cattails & Leaves, Marvo, Middle Period, 10 In. ............................ 15.00
Weller, Vase, Ivory, 5 3/4 In.High ............................ 4.00
Weller, Vase, Jap Birdimal, Figures Of Trees, Artist Signed CMM, 7 In.High ............................ 300.00
Weller, Vase, Jap Birdimal, Teal Blue, Yellow Parrots, Signed Rhead, Faience ............................ 565.00
Weller, Vase, Knifewood, 9 In.High ............................ 65.00
Weller, Vase, L'Art Nouveau, Dark Brown To Gold, Stylized Flowers, 5 3/4 In. ............................ 60.00
Weller, Vase, Lamar, Trees & Mountains, 8 1/2 In.High ............................ 75.00

Wood Carving, Policeman,
Dated 1898, 20 In.
*(See Page 714)*

Weller, Vase, Hudson,
Blue To Green, Pillsbury, 15 In.
*(See Page 712)*

| | |
|---|---:|
| Weller, Vase, Landscape On Metallic, Lasa, 6 In. | 135.00 |
| Wollor, Vase, Lasa, Luster Glaze, Tree Decoration, 6 In.High | 100.00 |
| Weller, Vase, Louwelsa, Brown Glaze, Orange Floral Decoration, 4 1/2 In. | 66.00 |
| Weller, Vase, Louwelsa, Bust Portrait Of Hunting Dog, L.Blake, 12 3/4 In. | 175.00 |
| Weller, Vase, Louwelsa, Floral Decoration, Hester Pillsbury Artist, 7 In. | 80.00 |
| Weller, Vase, Louwelsa, Floral Decoration, Marked, Artist Signed HM, 6 In. | 67.50 |
| Weller, Vase, Louwelsa, Grapes, Leaves & Tendrils, 14 1/2 In.High, Signed | 90.00 |
| Weller, Vase, Louwelsa, Indian Squaw Profile, Signed Burgess, 12 In.High | 400.00 |
| Weller, Vase, Louwelsa, Orange Floral On Brown, 4 1/2 In. | 65.00 |
| Weller, Vase, Louwelsa, Pansy Decoration, 3 Feet & Handles, 6 1/2 In.High | 48.00 |
| Weller, Vase, Louwelsa, Red Clover & Leaves, 3 1/2 In. | 27.50 |
| Weller, Vase, Louwelsa, Vase, Brown, Yellow, & Green Ground, Flowers, 4 1/2 In. | 80.00 |
| Weller, Vase, Louwelsa, Yellow Floral Decoration, Signed, 3 1/2 In.High | 65.00 |
| Weller, Vase, Louwelsa, Yellow Floral On Brown, 6 In.Diameter | 65.00 |
| Wollor, Vase, Manhattan, Green, 8 In.High, Marked In Script | 20.00 |
| Weller, Vase, Marvo, Gray, 6 In. | 16.00 |
| Weller, Vase, Marvo, Molded Leaves On Green, 11 1/2 In. | 45.00 |
| Weller, Vase, Marvo, Relief Palm Trees, Orange & Green, 7 In. High | 22.50 |
| Weller, Vase, Modeled Matte, Frog, Gunmetal Color, 6 3/4 In.High | 40.00 |
| Weller, Vase, Orange Floral On Brown To Green, Mae Timberlake, 10 In. | 75.00 |
| Weller, Vase, Orange Matte, Etched, 12 1/2 In. High *Illus* | 55.00 |
| Wollor, Vase, Pale Green Glaze, 10 In. | 22.00 |
| Weller, Vase, Palm Trees In Relief On Orange & Green, Marvo, 7 In.High | 22.50 |
| Weller, Vase, Panella, Light & Dark Blue, 6 1/4 In.High | 14.00 |
| Weller, Vase, Pansies On Pumpkin Color, 2 Handled, 7 1/2 In. | 10.00 |
| Weller, Vase, Patricia, Bird Decoration, 6 1/2 In.High, 10 In.Long | 15.00 |
| Weller, Vase, Pearl, 6 In.High, 4 In.Diameter, Marked | 20.00 |
| Weller, Vase, Pillow, Blue Drapery, 4 1/2 In.High, 6 1/2 In.Long | 15.00 |
| Weller, Vase, Pillow, Louwelsa, Pansy Decoration, 4 1/2 In.High, Marked | 60.00 |
| Weller, Vase, Pink Cameo, 2 Handles, Signed, 5 1/2 In. | 9.00 |
| Weller, Vase, Pink Carnations On White, 13 3/4 In.High | 19.00 |
| Weller, Vase, Poinsettias, Marked 128, 7 1/2 In.High | 22.50 |
| Weller, Vase, Relief Blossom & Branch, Green Matte, 4 3/4 In.High | 14.00 |
| Weller, Vase, Relief Classical Lady Holding Grapes & Floral, 10 In. | 52.50 |
| Weller, Vase, Sicardo, Green Floral On Metallic Luster, 5 In.High | 235.00 |
| Weller, Vase, Sicardo, Thistles On Green Iridescent Glaze, 5 In. | 175.00 |
| Weller, Vase, Single Rose & Leaves, 11 In.High | 17.50 |
| Weller, Vase, Tapered, Violets, Etna, 6 In. | 52.00 |
| Weller, Vase, Tree Stump, Woodcraft, 3 Branch Handles, Applied Floral, 9 In. | 44.00 |
| Weller, Vase, Turada, Light Brown & Blue Decoration, 2 1/4 In.High | 95.00 |
| Weller, Vase, Tutone, White & Yellow Flowers, Handles, 10 In.High | 12.00 |
| Weller, Vase, Velva, Brown, 6 In.High | 11.00 |
| Weller, Vase, Wall, Red, White, & Blue Flowers On Ivory, 8 1/2 In.High | 9.00 |
| Weller, Vase, White Flowers & Foliage, 2 Twig Handles, Orange, 7 In.High | 9.00 |
| Weller, Vase, Wild Rose, Peach, 6 1/2 In.High, Marked | 10.00 |
| Weller, Vase, Wild Rose, Pink & Green, 6 3/4 In.High | 10.00 |

| | |
|---|---|
| Weller, Vase, Windmills, Land, Water & Boats, 16 In.High | 150.00 |
| Weller, Vase, Woodcraft, Browns & Greens, 10 In.High | 40.00 |
| Weller, Vase, Woodcraft, Hand-Painted Plums, 3 1/2 In.High, Marked | 30.00 |
| Weller, Vase, Woodcraft, Pink Dogwoods In Bloom, 9 1/4 In.High, Unmarked | 25.00 |
| Weller, Vase, Woodcraft, Tree Stump, 10 In.High | 32.00 |
| Wells Fargo, Coffin Tag, Metal, 'Wells Fargo Ex.Co. Human Body' | 25.00 |
| Whieldon, Figurine, Baby In Cradle, Yellow, Multicolor Quilt, C.1750, 4 In. | 125.00 |
| Whieldon, Figurine, Chair, Yellow, Ensuite Cradle, C.1750, 3 1/2 In.High | 110.00 |
| Whieldon, Muffineer, Yellow, Green, & Lavender Panels, Sponged, C.1750 | 235.00 |
| Wicker, Buggy, Baby's, Pad & Parasol, C.1890 | 200.00 |
| **Willow, see Blue Willow** | |
| Windowpane, Diamond Design, Beveled Edge Prism Leaded Glass, 56 X 16 In. | 40.00 |
| Windowpane, Diamond Light, 18 X 18 In. | 12.00 |
| Windowpane, Stained, Round Top, Jewels, 2 X 5 Ft., Pair | 500.00 |
| Wood Carving, Blacksmith, Standing At Anvil, Red & Black Paint, 11 1/4 In. | 75.00 |
| Wood Carving, Cherub's Head, Wings On Each Side, C.1850, 42 In. Long | 350.00 |
| Wood Carving, Duck, Red & Gold On Green, Marked China, 6 In.High, Pair | 42.00 |
| Wood Carving, Eagle, Brown Blown Eyes, 13 In.High | 95.00 |
| Wood Carving, Eagle, Wings Spread, Acanthus Leaf Supports, C.1825, 14 In. | 300.00 |
| Wood Carving, Face On Board, 3 Dimension, 6 X 10 In. | 100.00 |
| Wood Carving, Figure Of Negro Man, 10 1/2 In. High | 55.00 |
| Wood Carving, Fish, Painted, 10 X 20 In. | 135.00 |
| Wood Carving, Little Boy, Mute Colored Clothes, 16 In.Tall | 85.00 |
| Wood Carving, Minstrel, Kitten At Feet, 11 In.Tall | 65.00 |
| Wood Carving, Monkey Reading Book Seated On Open Book, 12 In.High | 110.00 |
| Wood Carving, Plaque, Anchors, Gilt Finish, Black Paint, C.1750, Pair | 250.00 |
| Wood Carving, Plaque, Eagle, Wings Spread, Bellamy, N.H., C.1875, 25 3/4 In. | 1400.00 |
| Wood Carving, Plaque, Eagle, Wings Spread, Shield, American Flags, C.1850 | 650.00 |
| Wood Carving, Policeman, Dated 1898, 20 In. *Illus* | 130.00 |
| Wood Carving, Rattlesnake, Painted, Open Mouth, C.1850, 34 In. Long | 375.00 |
| Wood Carving, Rooster, 5 1/2 In. High | 70.00 |
| Wood Carving, Sunfish, H.L.Boyer, 1931, Saylor's Lake, Monroe, Pa., Painted | 175.00 |
| Wood, Alligator, Stylized, Inset Bone Eyes, 1800s, 33 In.Long | 100.00 |
| Wood, Armorial, Crown Above Helmet, English, C.1800, 54 In.High | 190.00 |
| Wood, Eagle, Gilt, Carved, 1800s, Spread Wings, 18 X 31 In. | 300.00 |
| Wood, Figurine, Man Standing, Bearded, Painted & Carved, 1800s, 52 In.High | 650.00 |
| Wood, Heron, Carved & Painted, 1800s, 5ft.2 In.High | 450.00 |
| Woodall, Vase, Rock Crystal, Cut, Signed Geo.Woodall, 15 In.High | 1500.00 |
| **Wooden, see also Kitchen, Store, Tool** | |
| Wooden, Armorial, Gilt, Prince Of Wales, English, C.1900, 48 X 59 In. | 190.00 |
| Wooden, Barber Pole, Turned, Ball Finial, C.1850, 4 Ft. *Illus* | 125.00 |
| Wooden, Basket, Nantucket, Carved Bail Type Handle, 5 1/2 In.High | 125.00 |
| Wooden, Basket, Oblong, Solid Handle Long Way Of Basket, 14 In.Long | 15.00 |
| Wooden, Basket, Used For Washing, Spindle, 30 1/2 In. Long | 70.00 |
| Wooden, Blotter, Roll Type, Hand-Carved Bear | 15.00 |
| Wooden, Bootjack, Homemade | 4.00 |
| Wooden, Bootjack, Primitive | 4.00 |
| Wooden, Bootjack, Stationary Feet, Folds Long Way, Brass Hardware | 15.00 |
| Wooden, Bowl & Ladle, Hook Handle, 5 1/2 In.Diameter, 13 In.Ladle | 24.75 |
| Wooden, Bowl & Spoon, Made In Russia, Red, Black, Green, & Gold Decoration | 6.50 |
| Wooden, Bowl, Bird's-Eye Maple, Round, Thurnauer, 13 In.Diameter | 25.00 |
| Wooden, Bowl, Bird's-Eye, Burl, 9 1/2 In. | 85.00 |
| Wooden, Bowl, Burl Walnut, New Hampshire, 1840, 16 In.Diameter | 225.00 |
| Wooden, Bowl, Burl, 8 1/2 In.Diameter | 20.00 |
| Wooden, Bowl, Butter, Handmade, 10 1/2 X 11 In. | 10.00 |
| Wooden, Bowl, Chopping, Handhewn, Rectangular, Carved Table Rest, 22 1/2 In. | 52.00 |
| Wooden, Bowl, Maple, Rectangular, 20 X 11 1/2 X 5 In. | 40.00 |
| Wooden, Bowl, Oval, Sloped & Beveled Ends, 22 X 12 3/4 In. | 35.00 |
| Wooden, Bowl, Oval, 17 X 9 1/2 X 2 In. | 35.00 |
| Wooden, Bowl, Oval, 19 X 10 1/2 In. | 39.00 |
| Wooden, Bowl, Russian, Red, Black, & Gold Decoration, 15 In.Across | 58.50 |
| Wooden, Box, Candle, Pine, Slide Top, 6 X 7 X 23 In. | 65.00 |
| Wooden, Box, Covered, 8 3/4 In.Diameter | 5.95 |
| Wooden, Box, Glove, Burned Incised Design, 11 1/2 X 4 1/4 X 2 1/2 In. | 10.00 |
| Wooden, Box, Hand-Painted Floral On Black, 4 X 8 X 1 1/2 In. | 7.50 |
| Wooden, Box, Hone, Hand-Carved, Carrying Shaft, 1 Piece Construction, C.1850 | 40.00 |

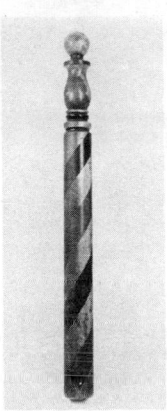

Wooden, Barber Pole, Turned, Ball Finial, C.1850, 4 Ft.
*(See Page 714)*

Wooden, Cigar Store Indian,
19th Century, 6 Ft.8 In.

Wooden, Cigar Store Indian, New York,
C.1855, 50 In.High

| | |
|---|---|
| Wooden, Box, Jewelry, Clear Glass Top, Mirror Under Lid, 2 Compartments | 10.00 |
| Wooden, Box, Knife, Center Carrying Handle, 2 Compartments | 12.75 |
| Wooden, Box, Knife, Cutout Handle, 2 Compartments | 25.00 |
| Wooden, Box, Oak, Dovetailed, 17 1/4 X 6 In. | 40.00 |
| Wooden, Box, Salt, Double, Swivel Cover, Handle, 12 X 3 In. | 35.00 |
| Wooden, Box, Tobacco, Walnut, Pipe Rack Ends | 12.00 |
| Wooden, Bucket, Grease, Conestoga Wagon, 1 Piece, 9 In.High | 50.00 |
| Wooden, Bucket, Sap, Iron Bands | 20.00 |
| Wooden, Bucket, Storage, Birch, Round, Flat Bail Held With Wooden Pins | 20.00 |
| Wooden, Bucket, Sugar, Blue Gray Paint, 12 In. | 40.00 |
| Wooden, Bucket, Well, Oak | 16.00 |
| Wooden, Bucket, Wooden Staves, 12 In. High | 22.50 |
| Wooden, Bucket, 9 X 10 In. | 3.50 |
| Wooden, Bust, Lincoln, Hand-Carved, 8 In. | 4.00 |
| Wooden, Candleholder, Bobbin, From Woolen Mills | 8.50 |
| Wooden, Candlestick, Felt Bottom, 10 1/4 In., Pair | 6.00 |
| Wooden, Candlestick, Turned, Patina, 5 1/2 In. | 25.00 |
| Wooden, Candlestick, 11 In.High, Pair | 9.50 |
| Wooden, Canteen, American, Drum Type, Hollowed Out Tree Limb | 89.50 |
| Wooden, Canteen, American, War Of 1812, Nail Fastened, Painted, Leather Strap | 59.50 |
| Wooden, Canteen, Revolutionary War, Red, Round, Buttonhole Loops | 150.00 |
| Wooden, Checkerboard, Handmade, Inlaid | 20.00 |
| Wooden, Cigar Store Indian, Headdress, Cluster Of Cigars, 49 In.High | 700.00 |
| Wooden, Cigar Store Indian, New York, C.1855, 50 In.High ............. *Illus* | 800.00 |
| Wooden, Cigar Store Indian, Skim Coat Of Gesso, 6 Ft. | 650.00 |
| Wooden, Cigar Store Indian, 19th Century, 6 Ft.8 In. ............. *Illus* | 3250.00 |
| Wooden, Clamp, Wooden Screws, 14 In. | 24.00 |
| Wooden, Comb, Hair, Arched Top, 2 1/2 X 5 In. | 35.00 |
| Wooden, Dryer, Sock, Large Size, Pair | 4.00 |
| Wooden, Dryer, Stocking, Figural Leg, 25 In.Long, Pair | 7.50 |
| Wooden, Dryer, Stocking, Figural Leg, 36 In.Long, Pair | 7.50 |
| Wooden, Eagle, Gilt Wood, Carved, Spread Winged, 19th Century, 27 In.Wide | 275.00 |
| Wooden, Eagle, John Bellamy, C.1875, 13 X 37 In. ............. *Illus* | 2750.00 |
| Wooden, Eggcup, Hand-Turned, Double Ended, Hollow Center, Pair | 7.50 |
| Wooden, Feed Bin, Walnut Slanting Top, Covered, Dovetailed, 25 In.High Back | 85.00 |
| Wooden, Figure, Blackamoors, Carved & Painted, C.1900, 42 In.High, Pair | 500.00 |
| Wooden, Figurine, Bird, Ebony, 13 In.High, Pair | 55.00 |

Wooden, Milkman & Cow, Clark Coe

Wooden, Figurine, Rooster, Schimmel,
C.1870, 7 In.High

Wooden, Figurine, Blind Justice,
19th Century, 43 In.

Wooden, Eagle, John Bellamy, C.1875, 13 X 37 In.
*(See Page 715)*

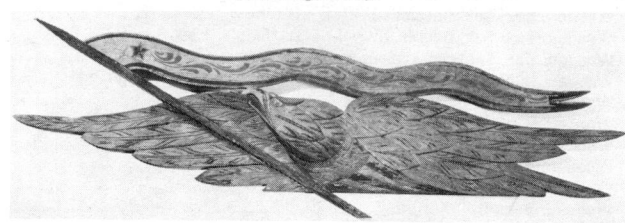

| | | |
|---|---|---|
| **Wooden, Figurine,** Blind Justice, 19th Century, 43 In. | *Illus* | 1600.00 |
| **Wooden, Figurine,** Elephant, Ebony, 10 1/2 In.High | | 72.00 |
| **Wooden, Figurine,** Mary & Joseph, Carved, 24 In.High, Pair | | 875.00 |
| **Wooden, Figurine,** Rooster, Schimmel, C.1870, 7 In.High | *Illus* | 1200.00 |
| **Wooden, Form,** Hat, Bonnet Style, 3 Piece | | 17.00 |
| **Wooden, Funnel,** One Piece, 17 1/2 In.Long | | 65.00 |
| **Wooden, Glove Stretcher,** Hand-Carved, Dog's Head Top Of Handles | | 4.75 |
| **Wooden, Horse, see Carousel Horse** | | |
| **Wooden, Humidor,** Porcelain Liner, Silver Plate, Hardware | | 28.00 |
| **Wooden, Humidor,** Rosewood, Dog On Lid, Hunting Scene, Oriental | | 60.00 |
| **Wooden, Inkstand,** Black Paint, Buffalo, N.Y. | | 30.00 |
| **Wooden, Jigger,** Whiskey, Wooden, 1 Piece, 3 In., Set Of 4 | | 60.00 |
| **Wooden, Leg,** Hand-Carved, Fits Thigh, 33 In. Long | | 23.00 |
| **Wooden, Letter Opener,** Carved As Dog Dressed In Fancy Dress | | 25.00 |
| **Wooden, Letter Opener,** Carved Man's Head On Handle, 8 1/2 In.Long | | 8.00 |
| **Wooden, Lid,** Crock, 8-Sided, 1 In.Thick | | 2.00 |
| **Wooden, Mallet,** Burl Wood, Oak Handle | | 25.00 |
| **Wooden, Match Holder,** Man's Boot, 6 1/2 In.High | | 22.00 |
| **Wooden, Match Safe,** Jacob's Ladder & Train, Mt.Washington | | 25.00 |
| **Wooden, Measure,** Dry, 2 Quart, Signed | | 12.00 |
| **Wooden, Milkman & Cow,** Clark Coe | *Illus* | 2200.00 |
| **Wooden, Mold,** Butter, Beehive Style, Geometric Design, 2 Piece | | 17.50 |
| **Wooden, Mold,** Butter, Geometrics, Round, 5 In.Diameter | | 16.75 |

Wooden, Mold, Butter, Rose & Tulip Design, 6 In.Long ....................................................... 45.00
Wooden, Mold, Butter, Star, 5 In.Diameter ........................................................................ 48.00
Wooden, Mold, Butter, Swan, Handle, 3 1/2 In.Diameter ...................................................... 35.00
Wooden, Mold, Butter, Swan, 2 Piece Plunger, Pound ......................................................... 32.00
Wooden, Mold, Butter, 6 Mold, Bird, Cherry, Flower, Snake, Fort, Pineapple, 1 Lb. ................. 14.00
Wooden, Mold, Cigar, Pittsburgh Stogies, 40 Cigar Capacity ............................................... 10.00
Wooden, Mold, Maple Sugar, Bear & Wolf, Walnut, 12 X 3 X 3/4 In. ...................................... 45.00
Wooden, Mold, Maple Sugar, Double Heart, 2 X 4 X 13 In. ................................................... 35.00
Wooden, Mold, Maple Sugar, Heart, 1 Piece, 9 X 5 X 2 In. ................................................... 45.00
Wooden, Mold, Maple Sugar, Heart, 20 X 3 X 2 In. ............................................................. 65.00
Wooden, Mold, Maple Sugar, Leaves, 2 Piece, 2 Wooden Pins ............................................. 40.00
Wooden, Mold, Maple Sugar, Shell, Walnut, 2 X 3 X 1 1/4 In. .............................................. 35.00
Wooden, Mortar & Pestle, Eggcup Shape, 4 1/2 In. ............................................................ 38.00
Wooden, Mortar & Pestle, Handmade, C.1850 ................................................................... 75.00
Wooden, Mortar & Pestle, Lignum Vitae, Turned, Natural Finish .......................................... 45.00
Wooden, Mortar, Burl, 7 In.High, 5 1/2 In.Diameter ........................................................... 95.00
Wooden, Paddle, Maple Butter, Bird's-Eye Maple, 11 In.Long ............................................... 6.50
Wooden, Pestle, 12 In.Long ........................................................................................... 7.50
Wooden, Pitcher, Milk, Fiber, 1 Piece, Lockport, N.Y., 1883, 5 In.High .................................. 20.00
Wooden, Plaque, Eagle, Carved, Gilt Wood, Spread Winged, Painted, 43 In.Long ..................... 550.00
Wooden, Plaque, Eagle, Gilt Wood, John Bellamy, C.1875, 4 Ft.3 In.Long .............................. 1050.00
Wooden, Plate, Bread, Wheat Carving, 12 In. ................................................................... 28.00
Wooden, Potty, Child's, Maple ....................................................................................... 20.00
Wooden, Pulley, Block, Hay Rope .................................................................................... 3.50
Wooden, Pulley, Rope .................................................................................................. 2.50
Wooden, Pulley, Well ................................................................................................... 4.00
Wooden, Rattle, Baby's, Hand-Hewn, Overlapping Sides, Box Type, C.1750 ........................... 25.00
Wooden, Rolling Pin, Bird's-Eye Maple ............................................................................ 8.00
Wooden, Rum Keg, American Revolutionary, Hollowed Out Tree ........................................... 84.50
Wooden, Rumlet, Bubble Shape, 3 In.High ....................................................................... 100.00
Wooden, Rumlet, Bubble Shape, 6 In.High ....................................................................... 100.00
Wooden, Rumlet, Bubble Shape, 7 In.High ....................................................................... 100.00
Wooden, Safe, Child's, Inside Drawer & Pigeon Holes, C.1880, 7 In.Square ........................... 35.00
Wooden, Salt & Pepper, Pears ........................................................................................ 1.00
Wooden, Saltbox, Covered, 7 In.High, 8 1/2 In.Diameter .................................................... 10.00
Wooden, Sander, Pounce, Desk, Turned ........................................................................... 25.00
Wooden, Scoop, Pennsylvania Dutch ............................................................................... 12.50
Wooden, Scoop, 12 In.Long ........................................................................................... 30.00
Wooden, Shoe, Ebony, Lady's, High Button & Heel, 9 1/2 In. .............................................. 85.00
Wooden, Shoe, Holland, Decorated, 9 In. Long, Pair .......................................................... 8.00
Wooden, Shoe, Man's, Hand-Carved, Raised Bunion Shape, 6 1/2 In. Long ........................... 38.00
Wooden, Shoe, Size 9, Pair ........................................................................................... 12.00
Wooden, Spoon, Carved, Whimsey Ball In Top Of Handle, 7 1/4 In.Long ............................... 30.00
Wooden, Stamp, Whale, Hand-Carved, For Stamping Ship's Log ......................................... 19.95
Wooden, Stick, Clothes Washing, Maple, Chip Carved, 2 Tines, Maine Origin ....................... 45.00
Wooden, Stopper, Heart Shape, Mica Covered Watercolor Set In, 4 1/2 In. ........................... 85.00
Wooden, Sugar & Creamer, Cover, Carved From Single Piece Of Wood ................................ 25.00
Wooden, Swift, Yarn Winding, 24 In.High ......................................................................... 65.00
   Wooden, Telephone, see Telephone
Wooden, Tray, Elongated Oval, Glass Over Inlay Design, Double Handles .............................. 14.00
Wooden, Tray, Mahogany, Brass Handles, Oval, Inlaid, Dish Top, 24 1/2 X 14 In. ................... 88.00
Wooden, Tray, Mahogany, Inlaid Horn Of Plenty, Brass Gallery & Handles ............................. 45.00
Wooden, Vase, Myrtlewood, Glass Liner, 4 In.High ............................................................ 5.00
Wooden, Whirligig, Man, Arms Extended, Painted, 21 In. High ............................................ 300.00
Wooden, Yoke, Human, Shoulder, Carved From Single Piece, C.1825 .................................... 55.00
Wooden, Yoke, Sap, Shoulder, Dark Blue ........................................................................ 35.00
Wooden, Yoke, Shoulder, Pine ....................................................................................... 16.00
   Worcester, see also Royal Worcester
Worcester, Basket, Encrusted Shells, Pink, Gilding, Chamberlain, C.1810 .............................. 120.00
Worcester, Basket, Pine Cone, Blue & White, 1st Period, 9 In.Long ...................................... 375.00
Worcester, Beaker, Scolopendrium, Green & Yellow, 1st Period, 3 1/4 In.High ....................... 450.00
Worcester, Bowl, Black Transfer, The Tea Party, No.2, 1st Period, 7 1/8 In. ........................... 150.00
Worcester, Bowl, Blue & White Transfer Scene, 1st Period, 9 1/8 In. .................................... 100.00
Worcester, Bowl, Cobalt & Gold Band Top, Fluted Sides, Dr.Wall, 6 1/2 In. ........................... 110.00
Worcester, Bowl, Flowerpot With Flowers, Bird, Gold, Scalloped, C.1820 .............................. 110.00
Worcester, Bowl, Oval, Gilt Scrolls, Pink, Barr, Flight & Barr, C.1807, Pair ............................ 60.00

Worcester, Candlesnuffer, Monk Shape, Signed .................................................................. 95.00
Worcester, Cooler, Fruit, Gilt Finial & Handles, Dragons, Chamberlain, Pair .................... 2000.00
Worcester, Cup & Saucer, Black & White Shell Transfer, Marked BFB ............................... 40.00
Worcester, Cup & Saucer, Demitasse, Biscuit Medallions ................................................... 32.00
Worcester, Cup & Saucer, Flight, C.1783 ........................................................................... 68.00
Worcester, Dish, Blind Earl, Rose Branch Handle, 1st Period, 6 1/4 In. .............................. 225.00
Worcester, Dish, Blind Earl, 1st Period, 5 3/4 In. ........................................... *Illus*   650.00
Worcester, Dish, Cabbage Leaf, Stalk Handle, 8 1/4 In.Long, 1st Period, Pair .................. 400.00
Worcester, Dish, Lozenge Shape, Scattered Floral Bouquets, C.1780, 9 3/4 In. ................ 75.00
Worcester, Dish, Muffin, Handled Dome Cover, Rosebuds On White, Chamberlain ........... 75.00
Worcester, Dish, Shell-Shaped, Blue, Green, & Red, Moths, C.1790, 7 1/2 In. ................. 275.00
Worcester, Dish, Vine Leaf, Puce Veins, Brown Stalk Handle, 1st Period .......................... 300.00
Worcester, Flowerpot, Fruit, 3 Gilt Claw Feet; Flight, Barr & Barr, C.1813 ..................... 90.00
Worcester, Flowerpot, St.Bernard's Well, Footed, Flight, Barr & Barr, C.1813 ................ 275.00
Worcester, Inkstand, Tray, Taperstick, 2 Covered Pots, Chamberlain, C.1850 ................. 250.00
Worcester, Jar, Biscuit, Leaves, Peach & Ivory, Silver Lid & Bail, Locke ......................... 85.00
Worcester, Jar, Pomade, Purple Mark .............................................................................. 12.00
Worcester, Jardiniere On Stand, Farm Scenes, Chamberlain, C.1825, Pair ...................... 250.00
Worcester, Jug, Cream, Blue & White, Pear Shape, Loop Handle, 1st Period ................... 80.00
Worcester, Jug, Mask Spout, Dr.Wall, 12 In. .................................................................. 298.00
Worcester, Jug, Milk, Black Festoons Pendant From Gilt Band, C.1776 ......................... 30.00
Worcester, Plate, Blind Earl, Fluted, Chamberlain, C.1811, 7 3/4 In. ............................. 225.00
Worcester, Plate, Blind Earl, 1st Period, 7 3/4 In., Pair ................................................. 1000.00
Worcester, Plate, Kakiemon, Exotic Birds, Oriental Sprigs, 7 3/4 In.Diameter ............... 225.00
Worcester, Plate, London Decorated, Green, Floral, 1st Period, 7 1/2 In. ........................ 75.00
Worcester, Platter, Welsh Coats Of Arms, Oval, Chamberlain, C.1811, Pair .................... 500.00
Worcester, Pot, Ink, Floral Finial, Scroll Feet, Chamberlain, C.1820, Pair ..................... 650.00
Worcester, Sauceboat, Leaf Molded, Stalk Handle, 1st Period ........................................ 375.00
Worcester, Saucer, Bengal Tiger, Famille Verte Enamels, 1st Period ............................... 150.00
Worcester, Saucer, Hop Trellis, Fluted, Gros Bleu Border, 1st Period .............................. 180.00
Worcester, Spill, Gilt Handles, Medallions On Rose, Chamberlain, C.1825, Pair .............. 300.00
Worcester, Stand, Teapot, Hexagonal, Bird Medallion On Gros Bleu, 1st Period ............. 500.00
Worcester, Sucrier, Floral Knob On Cover, Gros Bleu, Medallions, 1st Period .................. 500.00
Worcester, Sugar, Cone Finial, Apple Green, Flight, Barr & Barr, C.1813 ...................... 300.00
Worcester, Tankard, Ship Medallion, Samuel Welleton & Ceres, Chamberlain ................ 450.00
Worcester, Tea Caddy, Bengal Tiger, 1st Period ............................................. *Illus*   450.00
Worcester, Tea Caddy, Covered, Blue Fish Scale, Birds, Flowers, & Insects ................... 135.00
Worcester, Teabowl & Saucer, Bouquets On Gilt Borders, Fluted, 1st Period .................. 110.00
Worcester, Teabowl & Saucer, Dark Blue & White, Dr.Wall, C.1780 ............................. 110.00
Worcester, Teapot Stand, Jabberwocky, Fluted, Hexagonal, 1st Period ........................... 300.00
Worcester, Teapot, Man Fanning Himself, Maiden & Flute, Child, 1st Period ................. 225.00
Worcester, Tray, Spoon, Jabberwocky, Oblong, Octagonal, 1st Period, 6 1/8 In. ............ 550.00
Worcester, Tureen, Covered, Cauliflower, 1st Period ...................................................... 550.00
Worcester, Vase, Bottle Shape, Pilgrim, Floral, Gold, Green Mark, 15 1/4 In. ................ 250.00
Worcester, Vase, Floral On Beige, Footed, 4 Shoulder Handles, C.1903 ......................... 65.00
Worcester, Vase, Girl & Boy, Rustic Scene, Gold Handles, C.1800, 11 1/2 In. ............... 400.00
Worcester, Vase, Ovoid, Apple Green, Scroll Handles, Floral On Brown, C.1815 ............. 300.00
Worcester, Vase, Urn Finial, Marbleized, Barr, Flight & Barr, C.1807 ............................ 190.00
World War I, Bayonet, Scabbard, Last Ditch .................................................................. 20.00
World War I, Belt, Saber, British Officer's, Buckle, Leather, Gold Bullion ...................... 14.50
World War I, Belt, Saber, British Officer's, Buckles, Gold Embroidery ............................ 14.50
World War I, Belt, Sword, British Officer's, Buckle, Leather, C.1900 ............................. 14.50
World War I, Blouse, German Army, Gray Green Wool, Iron Buttons .............................. 39.50
World War I, Boot, American Cavalry, Pair ..................................................................... 18.00
World War I, Buckle, Brass, Gott Mitt UNS .................................................................... 6.50
World War I, Button, Italian Navy ................................................................................. 3.00
World War I, Canteen & Carrier, Cavalry ....................................................................... 12.50
World War I, Canteen, 151st Army, 1918, Script ............................................................ 7.50
World War I, Cigarette Holder, Bomb Case Replica ........................................................ 5.00
World War I, Figurine, German Soldier, Iron, Winter Overcoat, Rifle, 1914 .................... 145.00
World War I, Gas Mask, German, Lines, Screw Off Canister, Dated 1916 ...................... 49.50
World War I, Helmet, Gas Mask .................................................................................... 15.00
World War I, Knapsack, Army, 1918 .............................................................................. 5.00
World War I, Leggins, Leather ....................................................................................... 8.00
World War I, Matchbox Holder, 3 German Soldiers, 1914-18, Nickel Plate ..................... 3.95
World War I, Mess Kit & Canteen, Knife, Fork & Spoon Marked U.S. ............................. 10.00

Worcester, Dish, Blind Earl, 1st Period, 5 3/4 In.
(See Page 710)

Worcester, Tea Caddy,
Bengal Tiger, 1st Period
(See Page 718)

| | |
|---|---|
| World War I, Mug, "United We Stand, " 3 In. | 10.00 |
| World War I, Mug, Lord Kitchener, 3 In.High | 14.00 |
| World War I, Periscope, Trench, Austrian Army Issue, Iron Tube, 18 In. | 59.50 |
| World War I, Photograph, Soldier, Unfurled Flag, Emblems, Oval Frame | 22.00 |
| World War I, Plate, French, English, Russian, & Belgian Rulers, 1914, 9 In. | 15.00 |
| World War I, Poster, Be Loyal To America, J.M.Flagg, 30 X 40 In. | 90.00 |
| World War I, Poster, Berlin Or Bust | 20.50 |
| World War I, Poster, Columbia Calls, 1916, 30 X 40 In. | 55.00 |
| World War I, Poster, Duty Calls, 22 X 18 In. | 20.00 |
| World War I, Poster, Eat More Corn, Oats And Rye, L.N.Britton, 20 X 30 In. | 40.00 |
| World War I, Poster, Flag Of Freedom, 22 X 18 In. | 20.00 |
| World War I, Poster, For Every Fighter A Woman Worker, YMCA, Cardboard | 45.00 |
| World War I, Poster, Keep 'em Smiling, Help War Camps, Cardboard | 45.00 |
| World War I, Poster, Must Children Die & Mothers Plead In Vain, Bonds | 45.00 |
| World War I, Poster, Oh Boy, That's The Girl, Salvation Army Lassie | 45.00 |
| World War I, Poster, Remember Belgium, Elleworth Young, 20 X 30 In. | 25.00 |
| World War I, Poster, Victory Is A Question Of Stamina, 20 X 30 In. | 20.00 |
| World War I, Tin, Ration, Dated 1918, 7 'X 2 1/2 X 3 In. | 5.00 |
| World War I, Tumbler, Wilhelm II & Bismarck, 1914, Clear, Hand-Painted | 15.00 |
| World War I, Uniform, U.S.Army, Wool, Bronze Eagle Buttons | 39.50 |
| World War II, Armband, American 48 Star Invasion | 10.00 |
| World War II, Armband, British Invasion | 8.00 |
| World War II, Armband, Nazi Officer's, Red, Gold Emblem | 50.00 |
| World War II, Belt, Cartridge, U.S.Army, 1942 | 3.00 |
| World War II, Beret, French Sailor's | 8.00 |
| World War II, Binoculars, U.S.Navy, Bausch & Lomb, Brown Leather Case | 35.00 |
| World War II, Blouse, Nazi Storm Trooper's, Tan Cotton, Brass Buttons | 79.50 |
| World War II, Blouse, Nazi Storm Trooper's, Tan Cotton, Brass Hooks | 79.50 |
| World War II, Case, Cartridge Belt, German, Leather | 5.00 |
| World War II, Dagger, Nazi, S.S. | 70.00 |
| World War II, Goggles, Nazi Tanker's, Tinted Glass | 6.50 |
| World War II, Gun, Flare, U.S.A.F., Fires Through Cockpit | 25.00 |
| World War II, Hat, French Officer's Dress | 20.00 |
| World War II, Hat, Nazi Enlisted Man's | 15.00 |
| World War II, Helmet, Nazi | 15.00 |
| World War II, Magazine, Italian Facist | 10.00 |
| World War II, Mask, Gas, Noncombatant, Case | 5.00 |
| World War II, Mask, Gas, U.S.Army, Case | 7.00 |
| World War II, Mess Kit, Japanese Army, Oval Aluminum Box, Painted Mustard | 22.50 |
| World War II, Patch, Russian Paratrooper's | 7.00 |
| World War II, Pin, Hitler Youth, Enamel | 8.00 |
| World War II, Poster, Attack, Attack, Attack, Buy War Bonds, Color | 25.00 |
| World War II, Poster, Back The Attack, Color, 40 1/2 In. High | 25.00 |

Zanesville, Pottery, Vase, La Moro, 10 In.

World War II, Poster, Carelessness Got There First, Color, 40 1/2 In. .................................... 25.00
World War II, Poster, Save Rubber, Color, 40 1/2 In. High .................................................... 25.00
World War II, Poster, Uncle Sam As Organ Grinder, Hitler As Monkey ............................... 5.00
World War II, Spurs, Japanese Army, Pair ............................................................................. 7.50
World War II, Token, Nazi, Eagle & Swastika, Brass, Square .............................................. 3.00
World's Fair, Ashtray, 1939, Ford Car In Center, Glass ....................................................... 4.50
World's Fair, Bottle, 1939, Hemisphere, Molded, Milk Glass, 9 1/4 In.High ...................... 18.00
World's Fair, Bottle, 1939, Milk Glass, 9 In. ........................................................................ 7.00
World's Fair, Cup & Saucer, Columbian Exposition, 1893, Camphor, Libbey ..................... 37.50
World's Fair, Cup, Punch, 1893, Ruby Glass, Clear Fluted Base, "E.M.F." .......................... 9.50
World's Fair, Decanter, 1938, Milk Glass, Anchor Signed, 10 In. ........................................ 15.00
World's Fair, Doll, Miss Seattle, Case ................................................................................... 12.00
World's Fair, Egg Puzzle, Columbian World's Fair, Metal, Columbus Picture ...................... 18.00
World's Fair, Figurine, Columbus, Marked World's Fair, 1893, Frosted ............................... 60.00
World's Fair, Glass, Beer, New York, 1964, Schaffer, 6 In. .................................................. 2.75
World's Fair, Hatchet, George Washington, 1893, Clear, Libbey Glass Co. ......................... 50.00
World's Fair, Plaque, St.Louis, 1904, Palace Of Liberal Arts, 5 In. ..................................... 20.00
World's Fair, Plaque, St.Louis, 1904, Palace Of Varied Industries, 5 In. ............................ 20.00
World's Fair, Plate, Santa Maria, 1893, 7 In. ....................................................................... 135.00
World's Fair, Plate, 1904, Forget-Me-Nots, Clear, Building In Gold, 7 1/2 In. ................... 16.00
World's Fair, Tray, Chicago, 1933, Copper ........................................................................... 11.00
World's Fair, Tray, New York, 1964, Lithographed, Metal, 8 In. Diameter .......................... 6.75
World's Fair, Tumbler, Art Palace ......................................................................................... 25.00
World's Fair, Tumbler, St.Louis, Milk Glass .......................................................................... 8.00
World's Fair, Tumbler, St.Louis, Raised Scenes, 5 In. .......................................................... 20.00
Yellowware, Pan, Milk, C.1850, 11 In.Diameter ................................................................... 13.00
Yellowware, Plate, Pie, C.1850, 8 3/4 In.Diameter .............................................................. 18.00
Yellowware, Plate, Pie, 8 1/2 In. ......................................................................................... 12.00
Yellowware, Plate, Raised Leaf & Vine On Cream, Scalloped, 8 1/2 In. .............................. 65.00

> Zanesville Art Pottery was founded in 1900 by David Schmidt in
> Zanesville, Ohio. The firm made faience, umbrella stands, jardinieres, and
> pedestals. It worked until 1962.

Zanesville Pottery, Bowl, Stylized Tan Fish, Blue Swirl Ground, 6 1/2 In. ......................... 19.00
Zanesville Pottery, Tankard, Poppy Decoration, Brown Glaze, 14 3/4 In. .......................... 195.00
Zanesville, Pottery, Vase, La Moro, Floral Decoration, Brown, 6 1/4 In. ........................... 90.00
Zanesville, Pottery, Vase, La Moro, 10 In. ........................................................... Illus        40.00

> Zsolnay pottery was made in Hungary after 1855.

Zsolnay, Bowl, Iridescent, Floral Decoration, Oval, Reticulated Rim ..................................... 45.00
Zsolnay, Bowl, Oval, Reticulated Edge, Blue, Pink, & Gold Trim, 3 1/2 In. ....................... 25.00
Zsolnay, Bowl, Vultures In Trees On Blue, 3 Trunk Legs, C.1900, 15 1/8 In. .................... 100.00
Zsolnay, Ewer, Reticulated Handles & Work, Enamel Floral Bands, Signed ....................... 85.00
Zsolnay, Figurine, Bird, Sitting, Metallic Luster, 2 1/2 In. .................................................... 95.00
Zsolnay, Figurine, Cat, Art Nouveau, Iridescent Gold, 5 In. Long ....................................... 45.00
Zsolnay, Figurine, Parrot On Rock, Iridescent Parrot, 5 In.High .......................................... 185.00
Zsolnay, Jar, Covered, Red, Floral & Latticework Panels, C.1900, 4 1/4 In. ..................... 50.00
Zsolnay, Pitcher, Stylized Poodle, Mustard & Red, 15 1/4 In.High ..................................... 70.00
Zsolnay, Plate, Purple Orchids On Cobalt, 8 1/2 In. ............................................................ 35.00
Zsolnay, Vase, Ewer Shape, Handle, Rose Color Floral On Cream, Fliigree Neck ............... 45.00
Zsolnay, Vase, Mermaid On Side, Purple, Green, & Yellow, 3 1/2 X 4 1/4 In. ................... 140.00